LONDON

A-Z®

Geographers' A-Z Map Company Ltd.

www./az.co.uk

CONTENTS

ey to Map Pages	2-3
uper Scale Map Pages @ 5¾" to 1 mile	4-19
lap Pages @ approx. 3" to 1 mile	20-174
dex to Streets, Areas nd selected Places of Interest	175-446
dex to Hospitals etc.	447-453

Index to Stations	454-456
West End Theatre Maps	457
Railway Connections Map	458-459
Underground Railway Map	460-461
Congestion Charging Overview Map and Information	462

REFERENCE

Motorway	**M1**	Airport	✈
Road	A2	Car Park (selected)	🅿
Road	B408	Church or Chapel	†
ual Carriageway		Fire Station	■
ne-way Street		Hospital	🅗
raffic flow on A Roads is also indicated y a heavy line on the driver's left.		House Numbers (A & B Roads only)	51 22 19 48
oad Under Construction		Information Centre	🛈
pening dates are correct at the time of publication.		National Grid Reference	530
roposed Road		Park & Ride	Kingston upon Thames P+R
unction Name	MARBLE ARCH	Police Station	▲
estricted Access		Post Office	★
edestrianized Road		River Bus Stop	🆁

rack / Footpath	Safety Camera with Speed Limit
esidential Walkway	Fixed and long term road works cameras only. Symbols do not indicate camera direction.
ongestion Charging Zone	Fixed Speed Limit (30) Variable Speed Limit ⓥ

ow Emission Zone or information contact Transport for London ww.tfl.gov.uk/modes/driving/low-emission-zone)	Toilet:
	without facilities for the Disabled ▽
ailway	with facilities for the Disabled ▽
Tunnel / Level Crossing	Disabled use only ▽

tations:		Educational Establishment	
National Rail Network & Overground	⇄	Hospital or Healthcare Building
Docklands Light Railway	DLR	Industrial Building
Overground	Ⓔ Super Scale Map Pages Ⓔ	Leisure or Recreational Facility
Underground	● ⊖	Place of Interest
ondon Tramlink	Tunnel	Public Building
he boarding of Tramlink trams at stops may be mited to a single direction, indicated by the arrow.	Stop	Industrial Building
ostcode Boundary		Shopping Centre or Market
uilt-up Area	BANK STREET	Other Selected Buildings
lap Continuation	62 Super Scale Map Pages 12	

SCALE

Map Pages 4-19 1:11,000	Map Pages 20-174 1:22,000
⅛ ¼ Mile	¼ ½ Mile
100 200 300 400 500 Metres	0 250 500 750 Metres 1 Kilometre
5.75 inches (14.63cm) to 1 mile 9.1cm to 1 km	2.88 inches (7.31cm) to 1 mile 4.55cm to 1 km

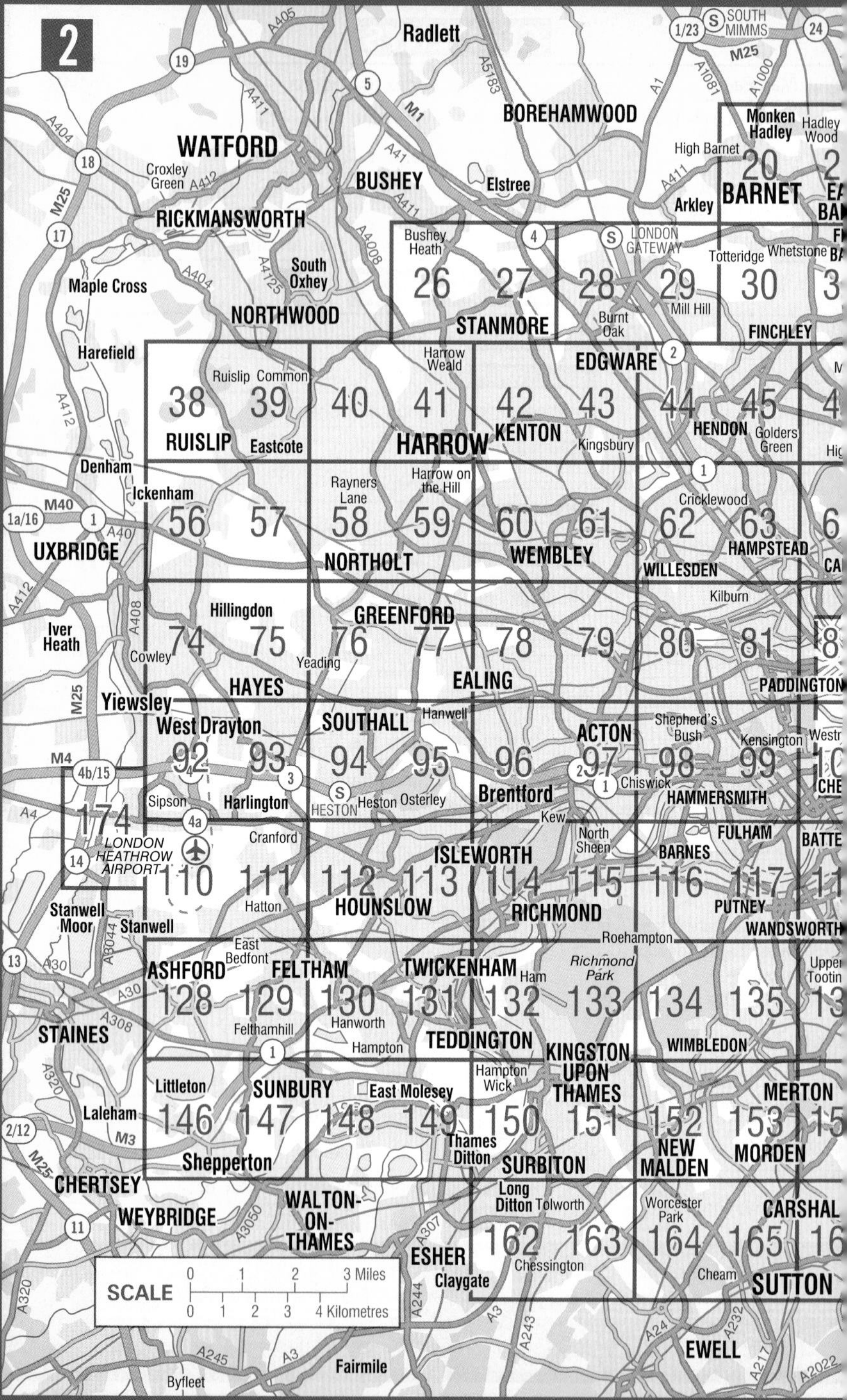
Radlett
SOUTH MIMMS
1/23
24
M25
A1000
A1081
A1
A405
19
5
A5183
M1
A411
BOREHAMWOOD
Monken Hadley
Hadley Wood
A404
18
WATFORD
Croxley Green
A412
A41
High Barnet
20
BARNET
BUSHEY
Elstree
A411
Arkley
M25
17
RICKMANSWORTH
A4008
Bushey Heath
4
LONDON GATEWAY
Totteridge
Whetstone
A404
A4125
South Oxhey
26
27
28
29
30
Maple Cross
Mill Hill
Burnt Oak
NORTHWOOD
STANMORE
FINCHLEY
Harefield
Harrow Weald
EDGWARE
2
Ruislip
Common
A412
38
39
40
41
42
43
44
45
RUISLIP
Eastcote
HARROW
KENTON
Kingsbury
HENDON
Golders Green
Denham
1
Rayners Lane
Harrow on the Hill
Cricklewood
Ickenham
M40
1a/16
1
A40
56
57
58
59
60
61
62
63
UXBRIDGE
NORTHOLT
WEMBLEY
HAMPSTEAD
WILLESDEN
Kilburn
A412
A408
Hillingdon
GREENFORD
Iver Heath
74
75
76
77
78
79
80
81
Cowley
Yeading
EALING
PADDINGTON
HAYES
M25
Yiewsley
Hanwell
Shepherd's Bush
West Drayton
SOUTHALL
ACTON
Kensington
M4
4b/15
92
93
94
95
96
97
98
99
3
2
1
Chiswick
4
HESTON
Heston
Osterley
Brentford
HAMMERSMITH
Sipson
Harlington
A4
174
4a
Kew
Cranford
North Sheen
FULHAM
LONDON HEATHROW AIRPORT
ISLEWORTH
BARNES
14
110
111
112
113
114
115
116
117
Hatton
HOUNSLOW
RICHMOND
PUTNEY
Stanwell Moor
Stanwell
A3044
WANDSWORTH
East Bedfont
Roehampton
13
A30
ASHFORD
FELTHAM
TWICKENHAM
Ham
Richmond Park
A30
128
129
130
131
132
133
134
135
A308
Hanworth
STAINES
Felthamhill
TEDDINGTON
WIMBLEDON
Hampton
1
KINGSTON UPON THAMES
A320
Hampton Wick
Littleton
SUNBURY
East Molesey
MERTON
Laleham
146
147
148
149
150
151
152
153
2/12
M3
Thames Ditton
NEW MALDEN
MORDEN
M25
Shepperton
SURBITON
MALDEN
CHERTSEY
Long Ditton
Tolworth
Worcester Park
WEYBRIDGE
WALTON-ON-THAMES
A3050
11
A307
162
163
164
165
ESHER
Chessington
SCALE
0
1
2
3 Miles
0
1
2
3
4 Kilometres
Cheam
SUTTON
Claygate
A320
A244
A3
A243
A24
A232
EWELL
A245
A3
Fairmile
A217
A2022
Byfleet

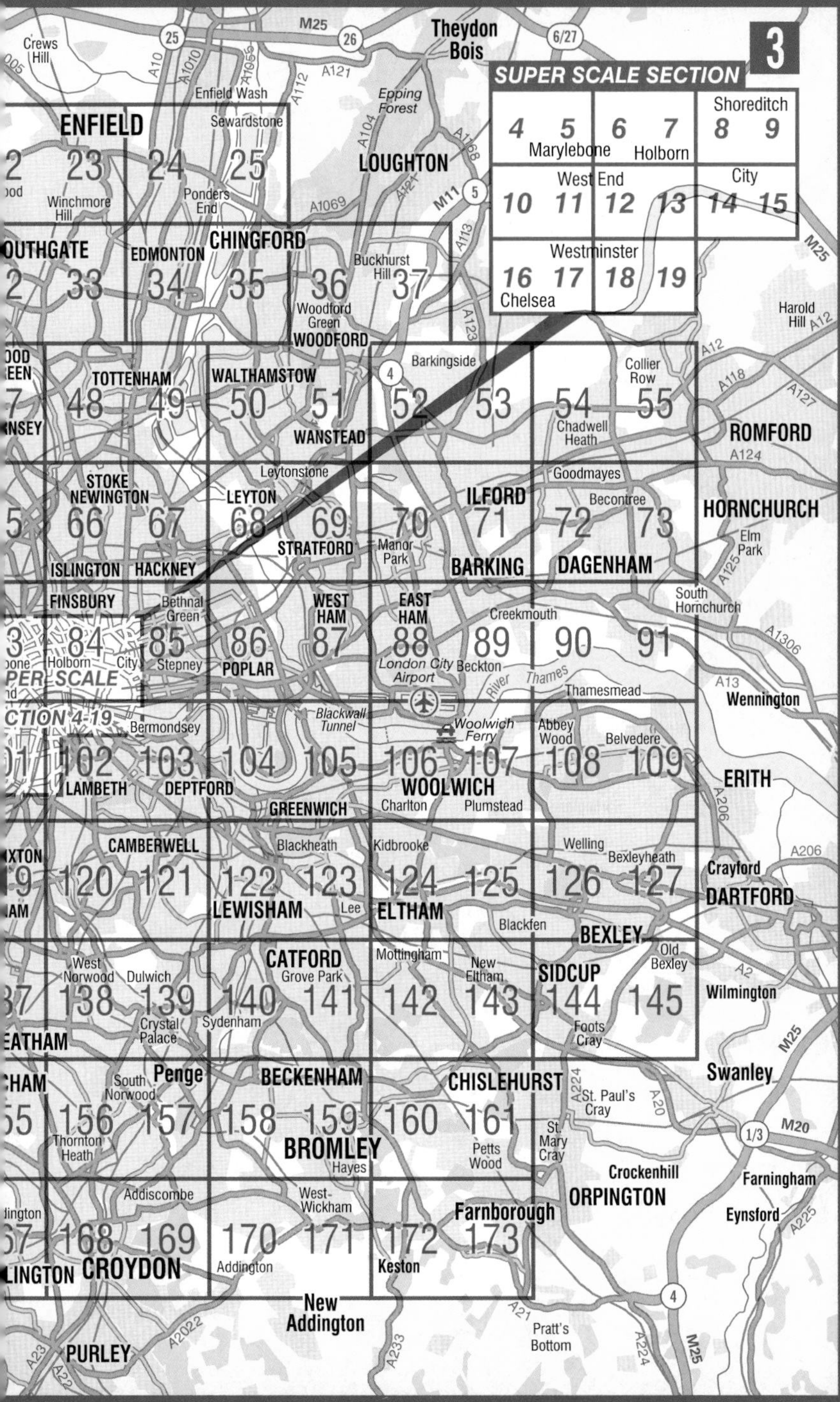

SUPER SCALE SECTION

4 5	6 7	Shoreditch
Marylebone	Holborn	8 9
West End		City
10 11	12 13	14 15
Westminster		
16 17	18 19	
Chelsea		

Crews Hill

M25 25 26 6/27

Theydon Bois

Enfield Wash

Sewardstone

Epping Forest

LOUGHTON

A121 A104 A1069 M11 A113 5

ENFIELD

2 23 24 25

Winchmore Hill

Ponders End

OUTHGATE 2 33

EDMONTON 34

CHINGFORD 35 36 37

Buckhurst Hill

Woodford Green

WOODFORD

Harold Hill A12

OOD EEN 7

TOTTENHAM 48 49

WALTHAMSTOW 50 51

Barkingside 52 53

Collier Row 54 55

ROMFORD A124

NSEY

WANSTEAD

Chadwell Heath

HORNCHURCH

Leytonstone

Goodmayes

Becontree

5

STOKE NEWINGTON 66 67

LEYTON 68 69

70

ILFORD 71 72 73

Elm Park

STRATFORD

Manor Park

ISLINGTON HACKNEY

BARKING

DAGENHAM

South Hornchurch

FINSBURY

Bethnal Green

WEST HAM 87

EAST HAM 88

Creekmouth

A1306

3 84 85 86

89 90 91

Wennington

one Holborn City Stepney

POPLAR

London City Airport

Beckton Thames

A13

PER SCALE

Thamesmead

Wennington

CTION 4-19

Bermondsey

Blackwall Tunnel

Woolwich Ferry

Abbey Wood

Belvedere

ERITH

01 102 103 104 105

106 107 108 109

A206

LAMBETH DEPTFORD

WOOLWICH

GREENWICH

Charlton Plumstead

XTON 9

CAMBERWELL 120 121

Blackheath 122 123

Kidbrooke 124 125

Welling Bexleyheath 126 127

Crayford DARTFORD

AM

LEWISHAM Lee

ELTHAM

Blackfen

BEXLEY

A206

West Norwood Dulwich

CATFORD Grove Park

Mottingham New-Eltham

Old Bexley

A2

37 138 139 140 141

142 143 144 145

Wilmington

EATHAM

Crystal Palace

Sydenham

SIDCUP

Foots Cray

M25

HAM

South Norwood

Penge

BECKENHAM

CHISLEHURST

Swanley

St. Paul's Cray

A20 M20

55 156 157 158 159 160 161

Thornton Heath

BROMLEY Hayes

Petts Wood

St. Mary Cray

1/3

Crockenhill

Farningham

Addiscombe

West-Wickham

ORPINGTON

Eynsford

ington 67 168 169 170 171 172 173

Farnborough

A225

LINGTON CROYDON

Addington

Keston

New Addington

A21

Pratt's Bottom

A224 M25

PURLEY

A2022

A233

4

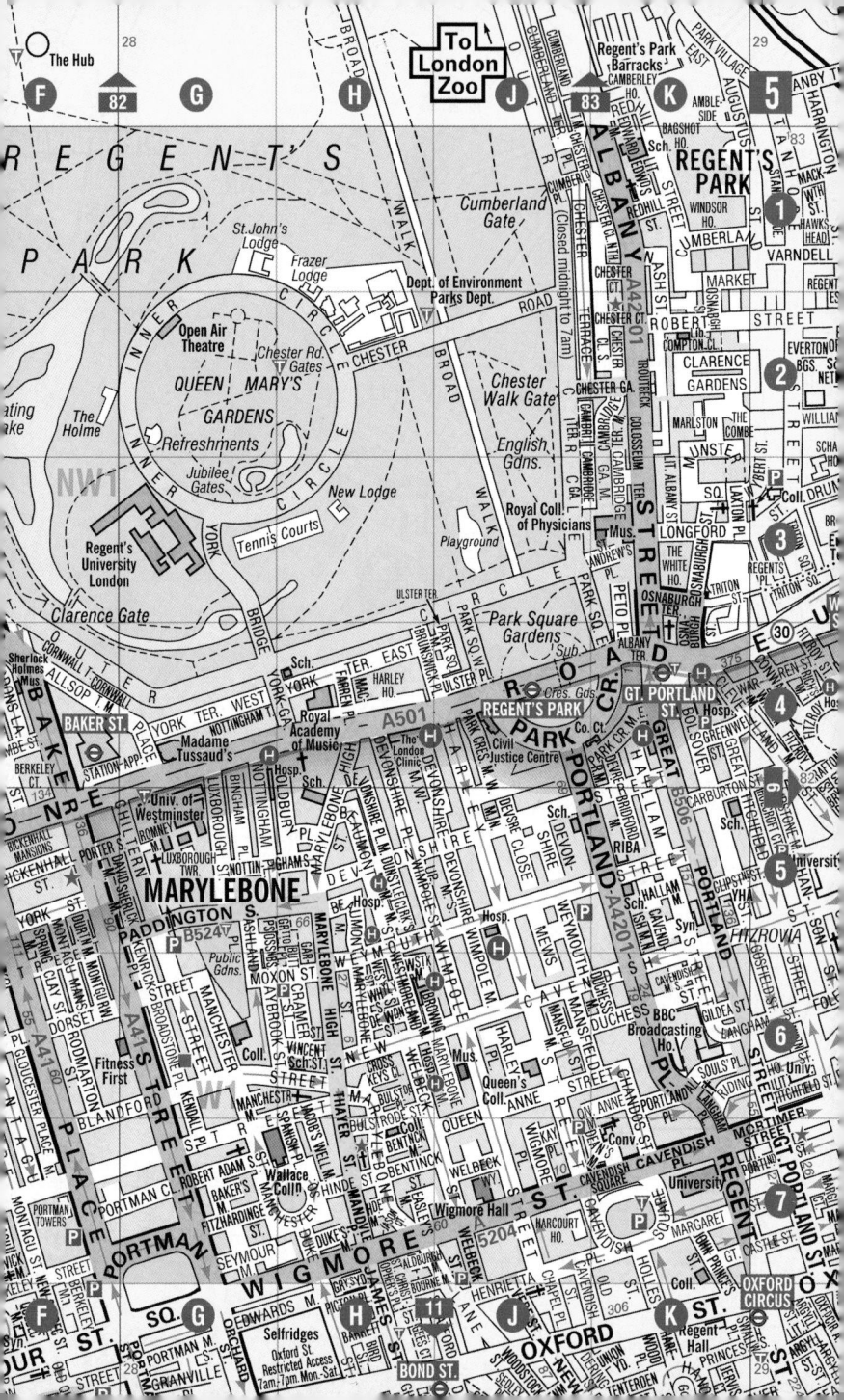

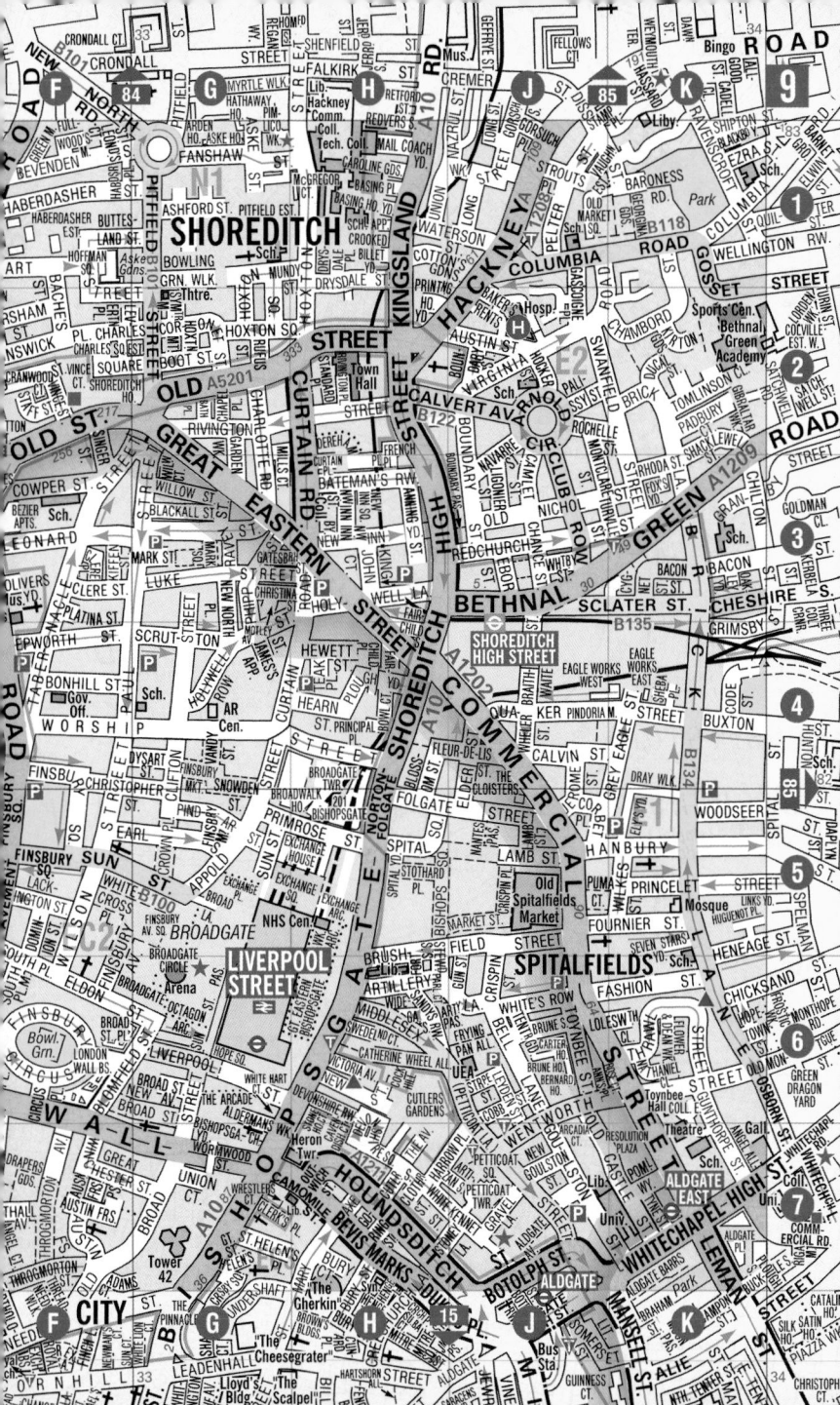

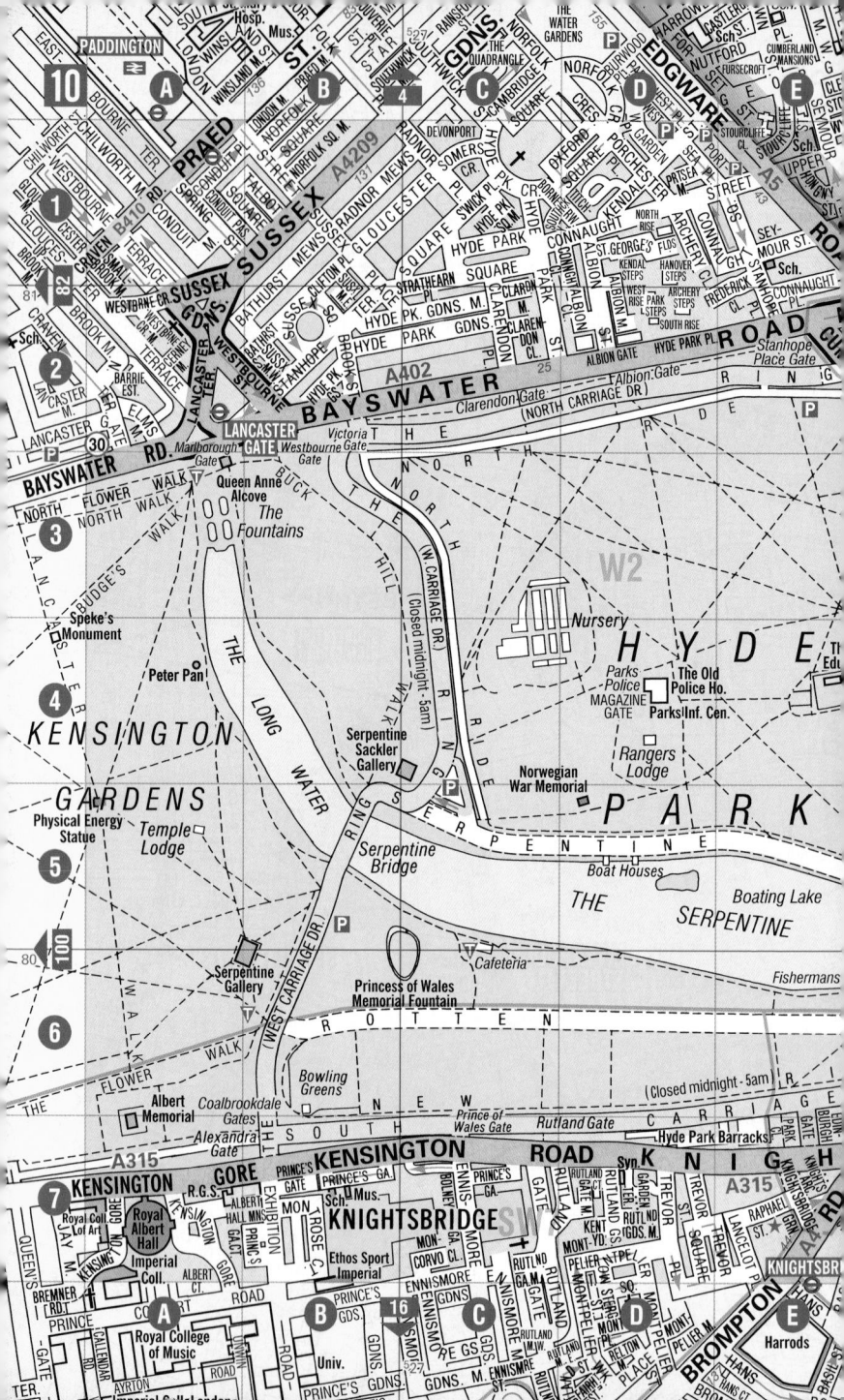

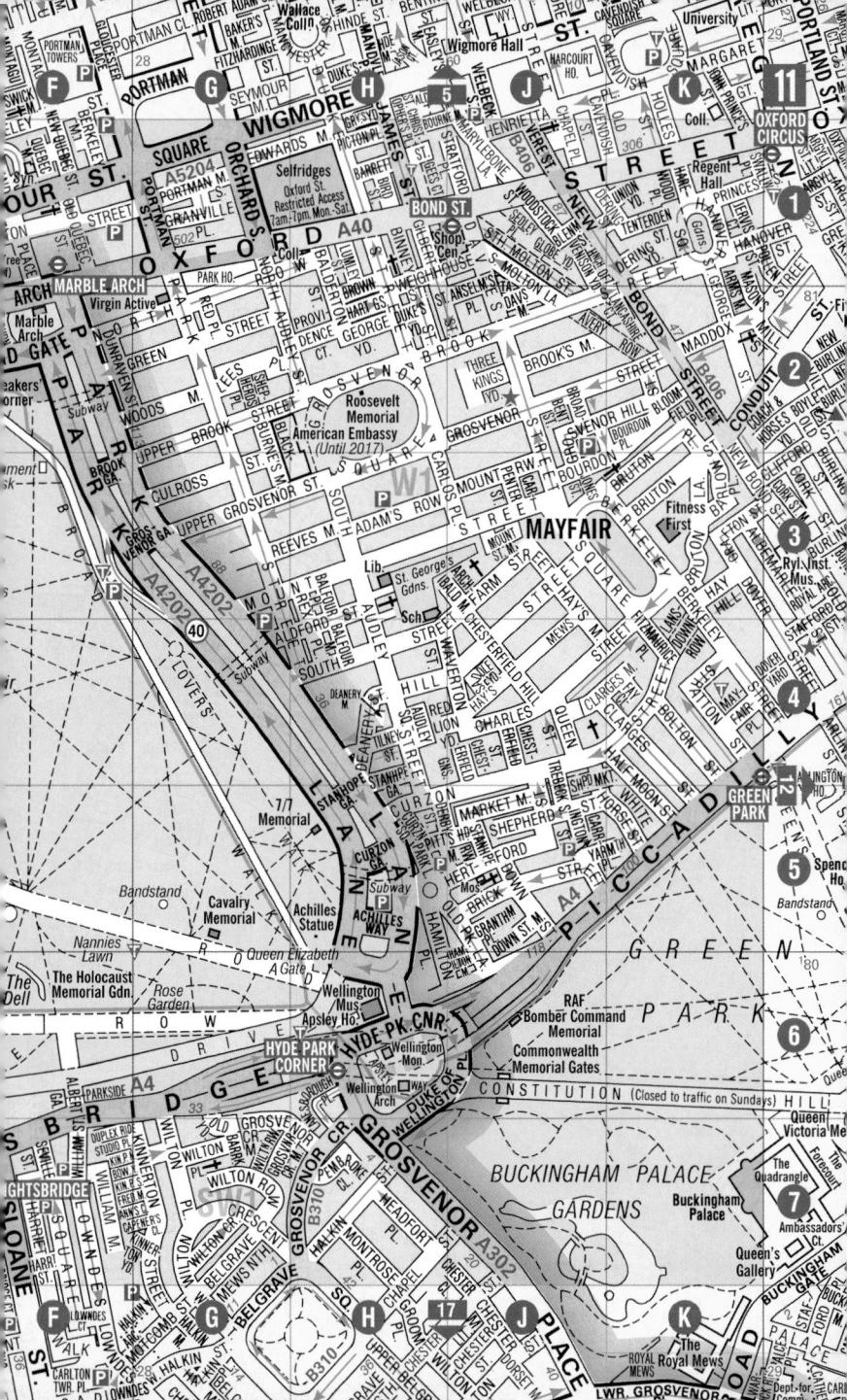

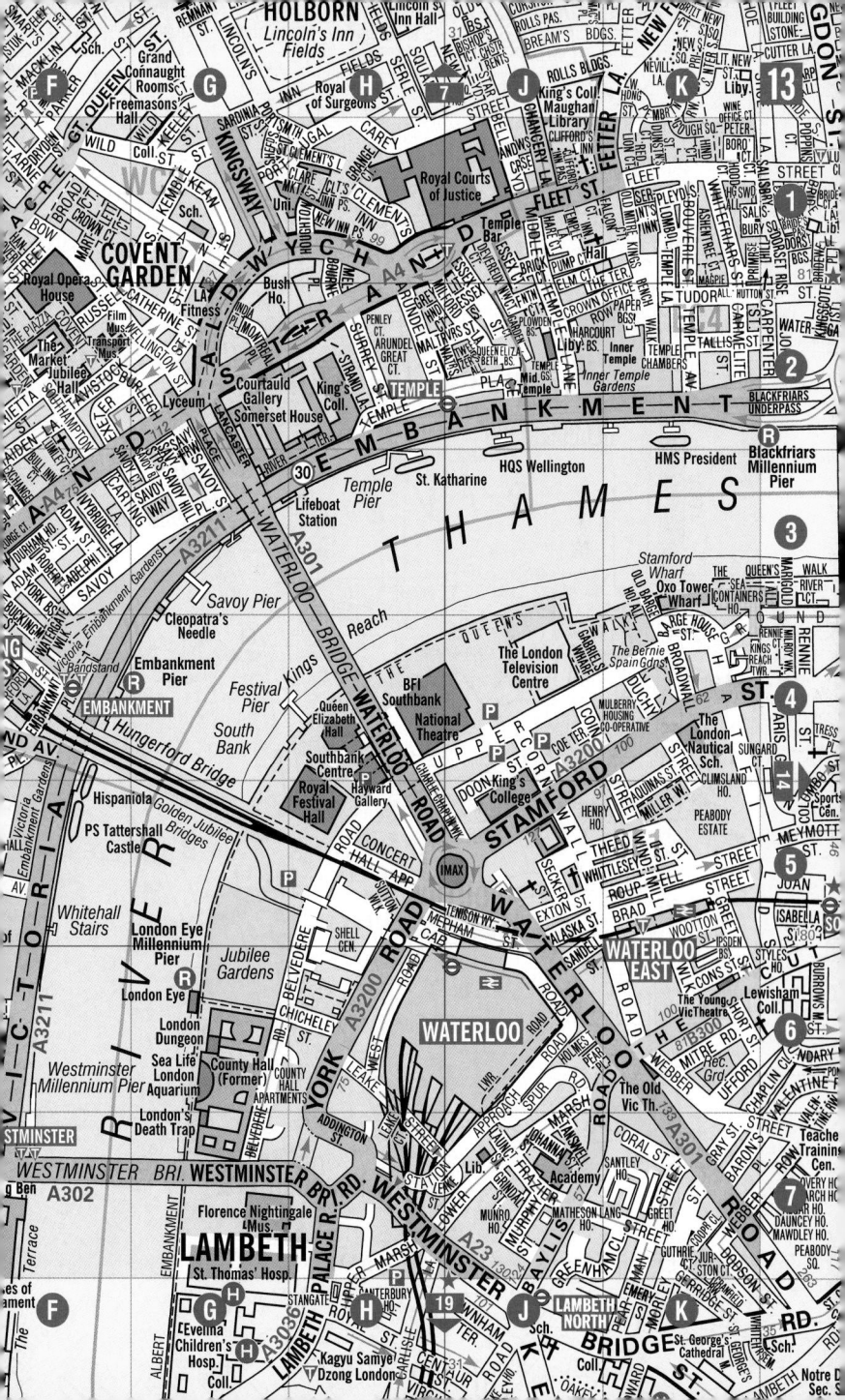

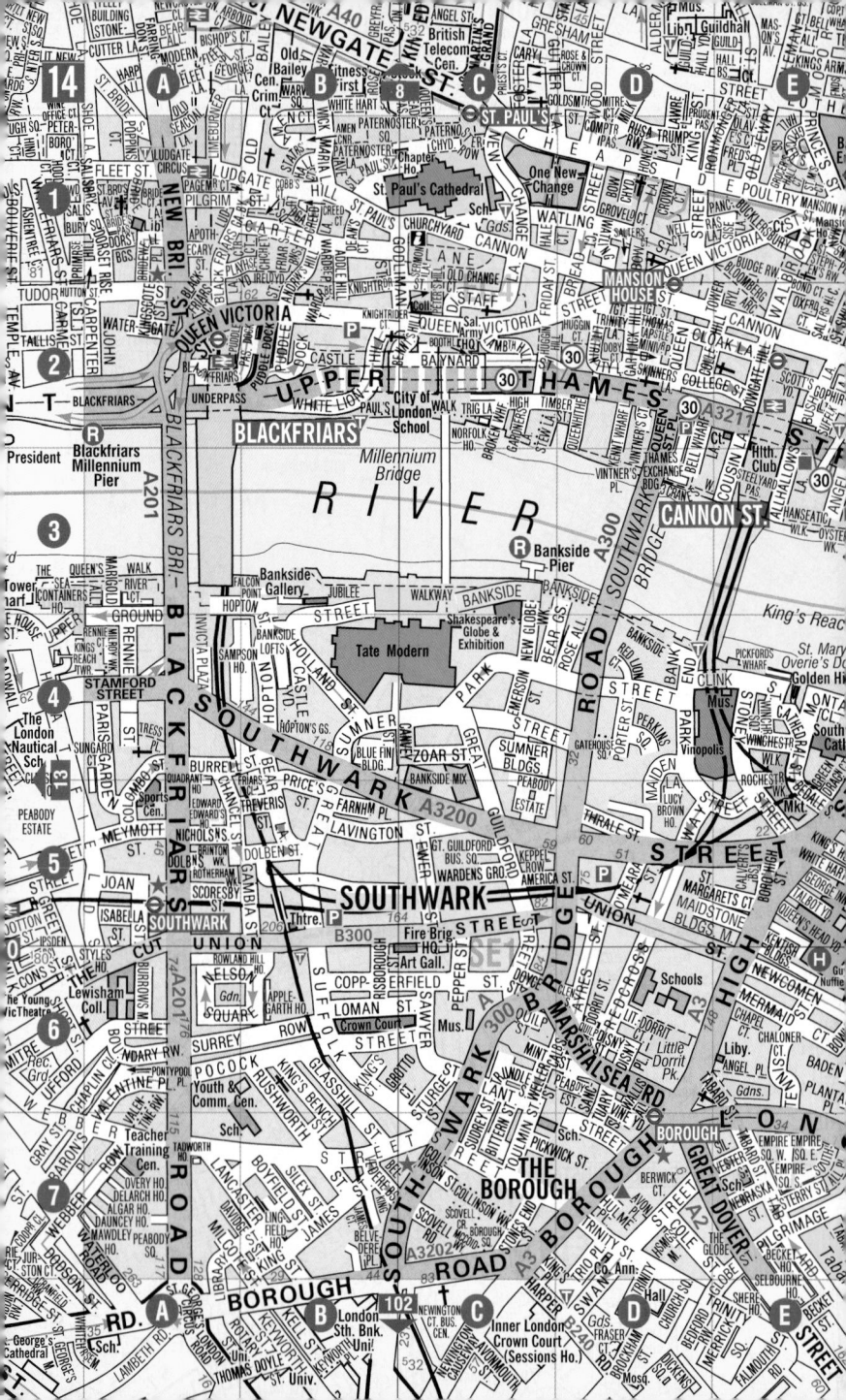

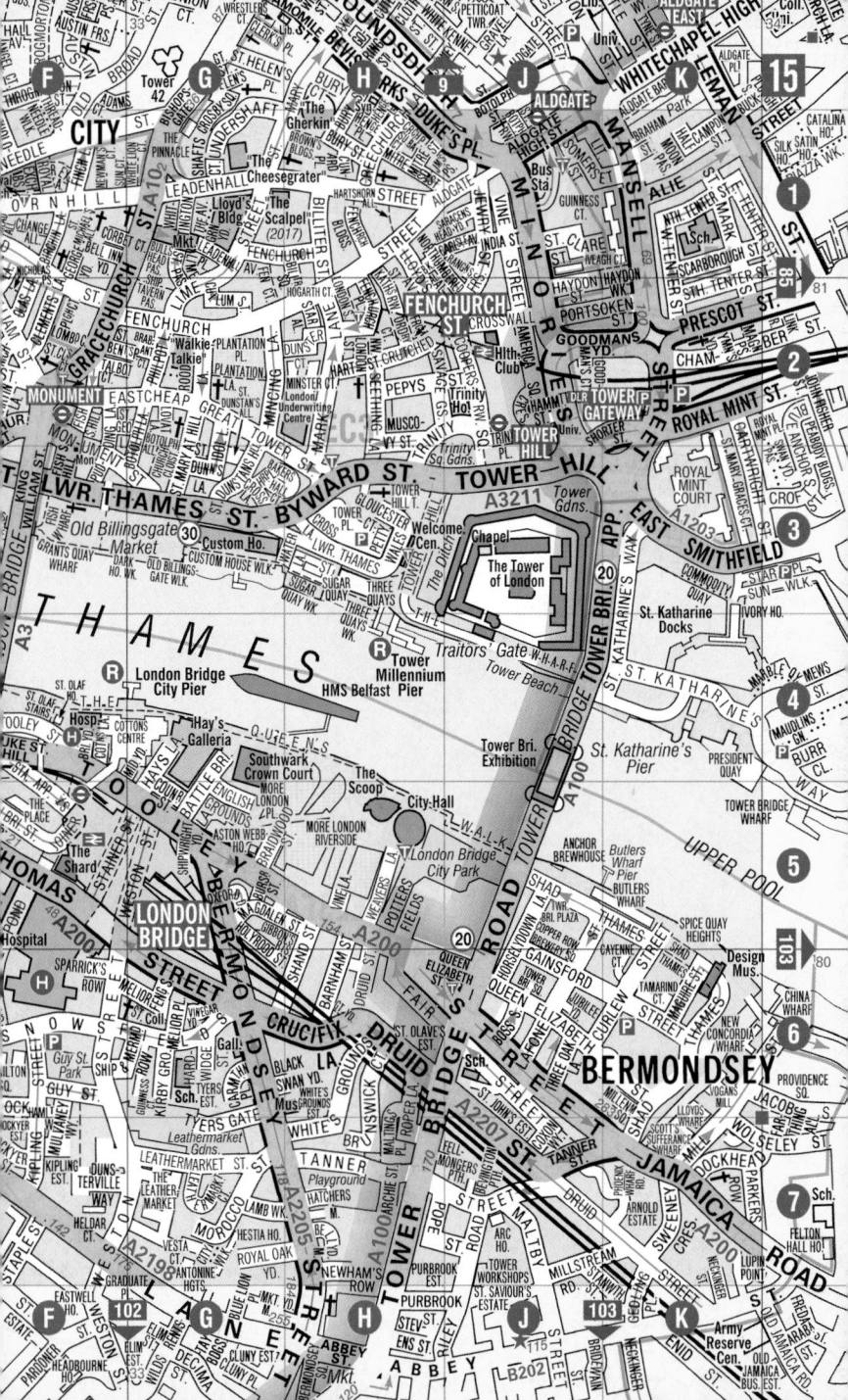

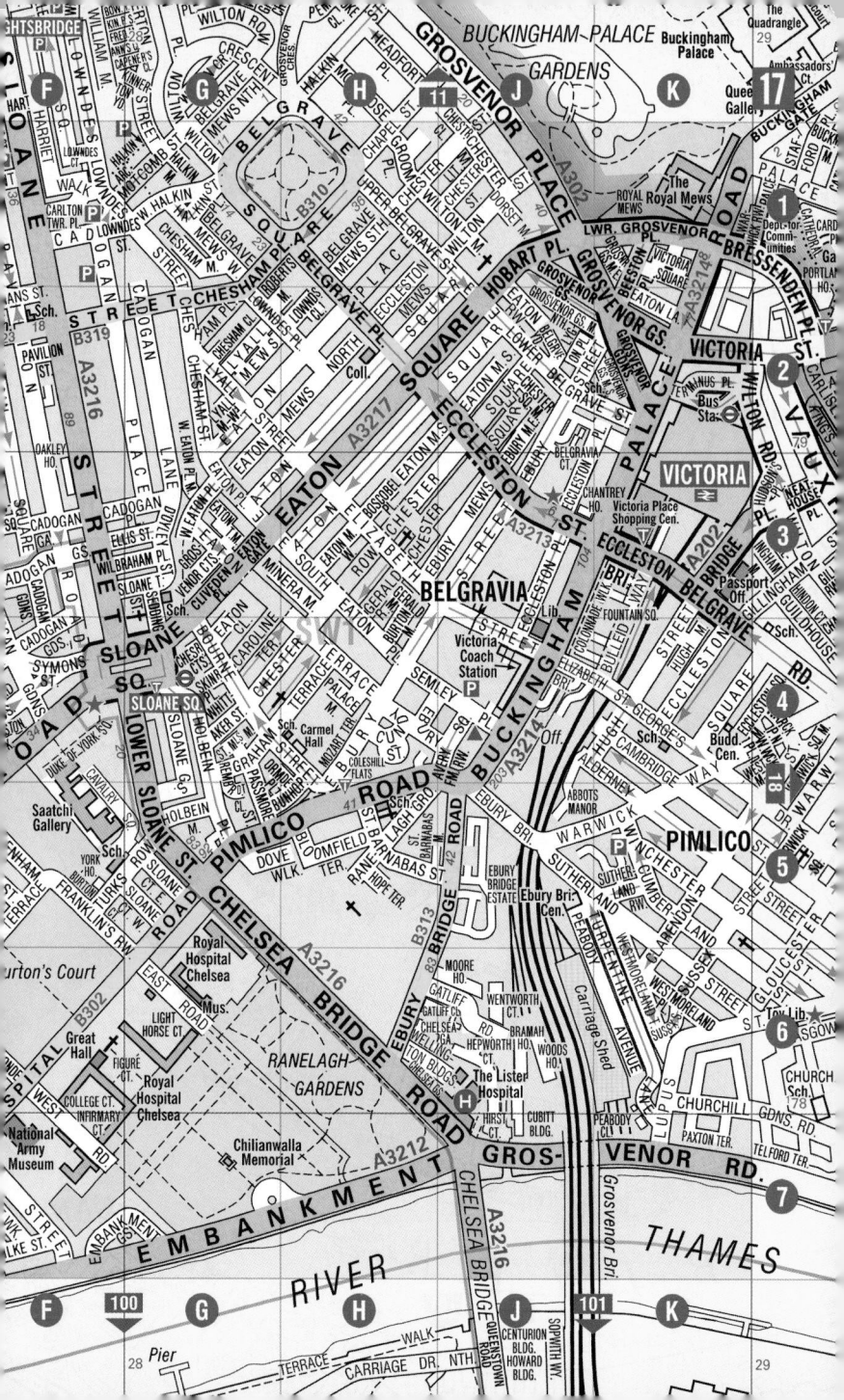

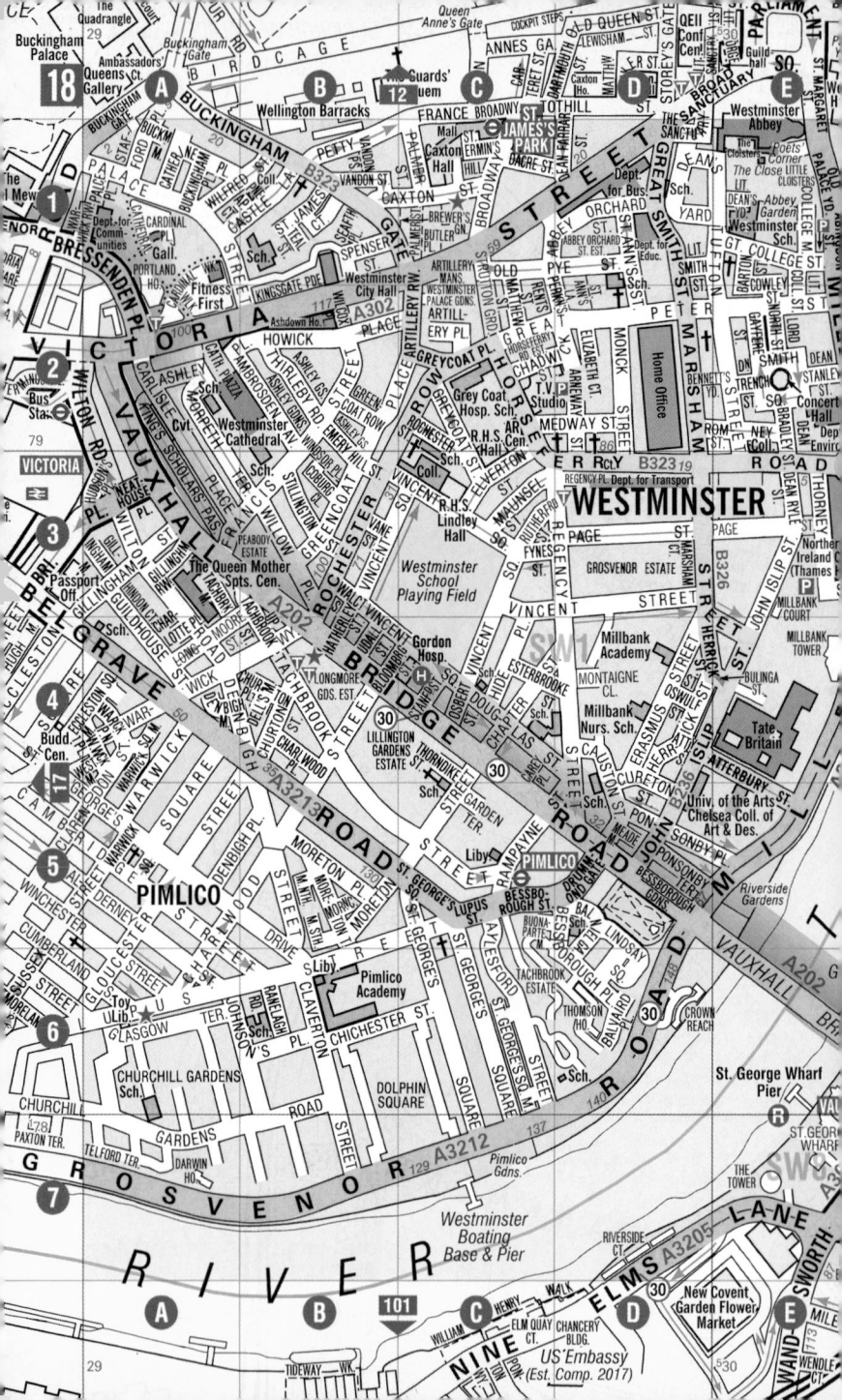

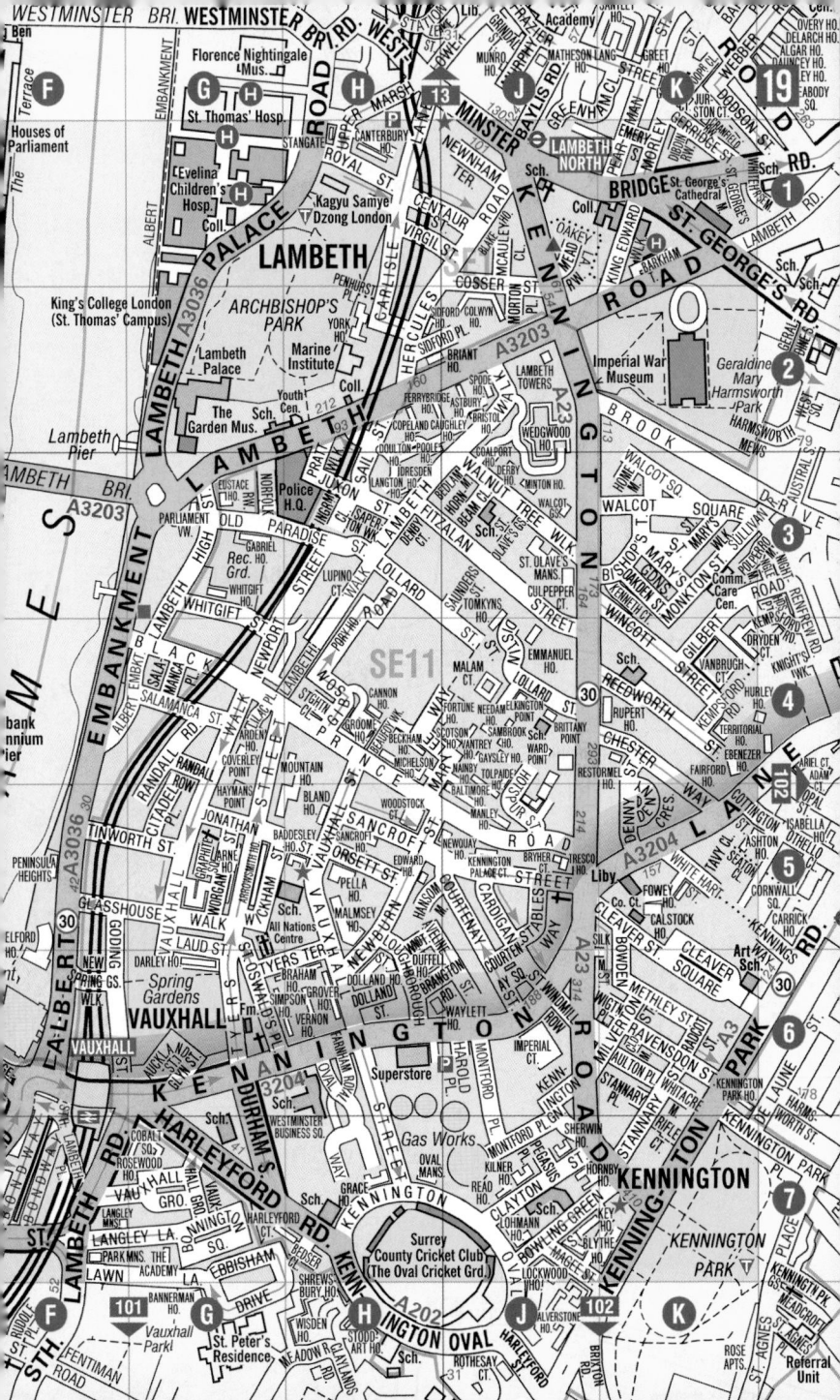

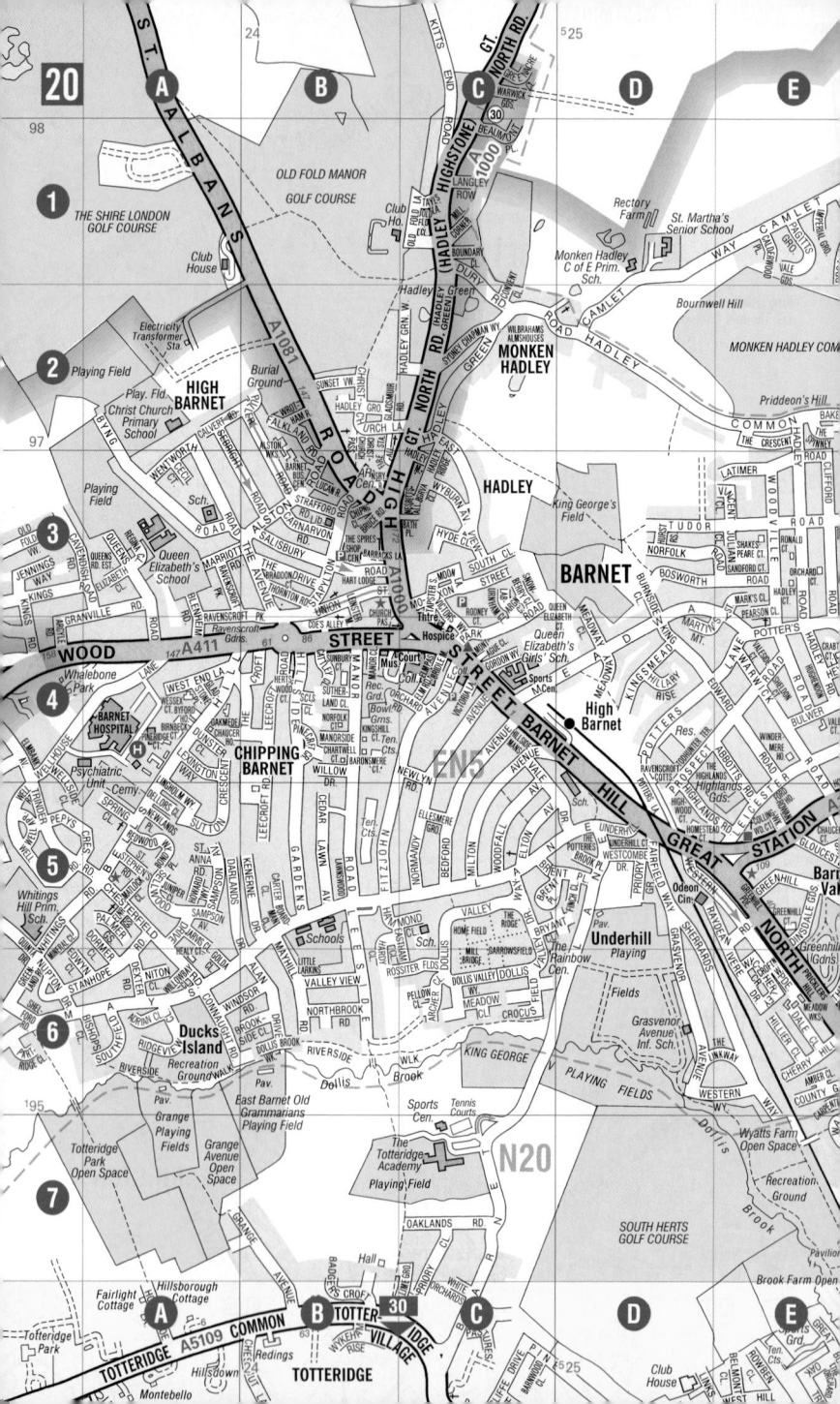

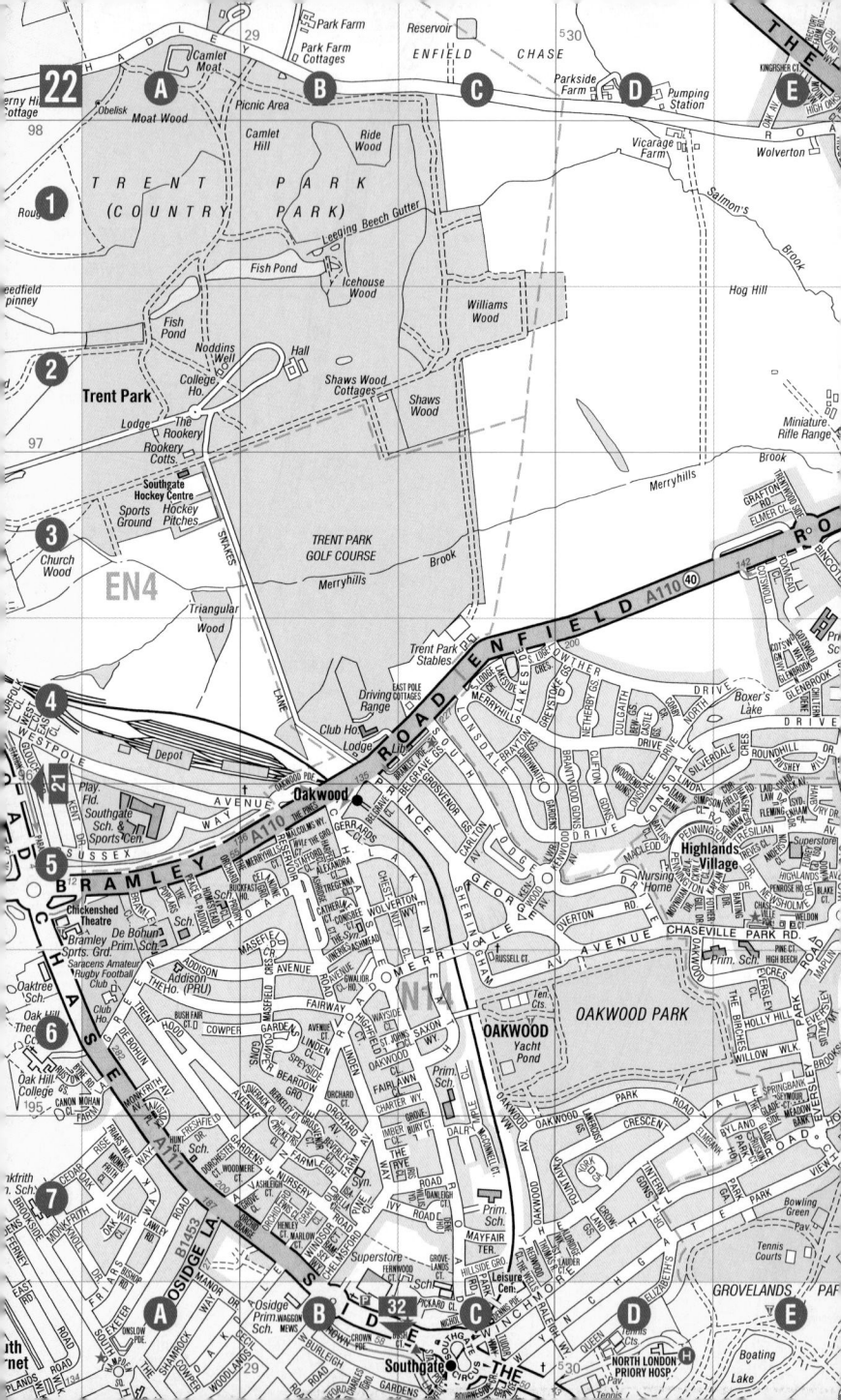

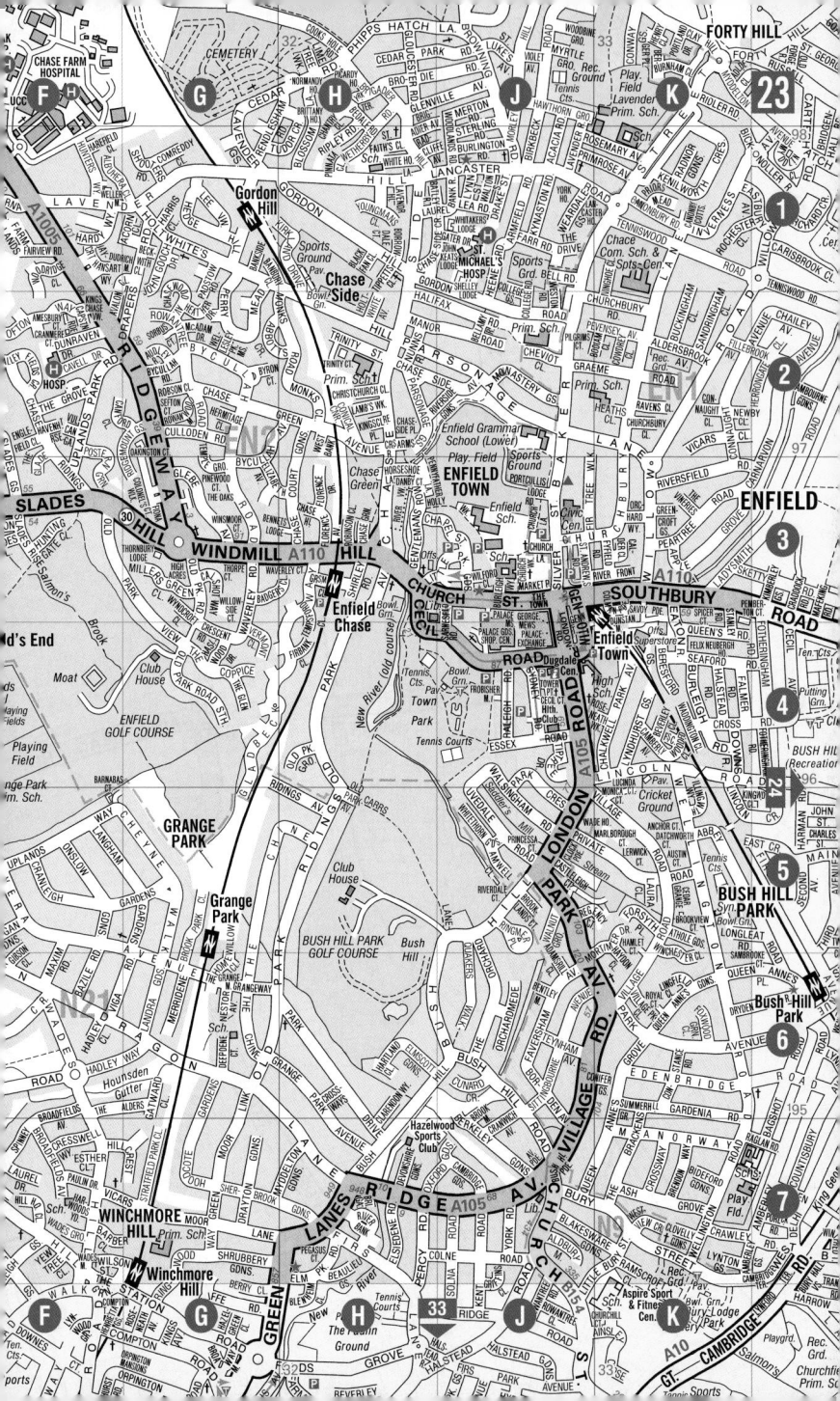

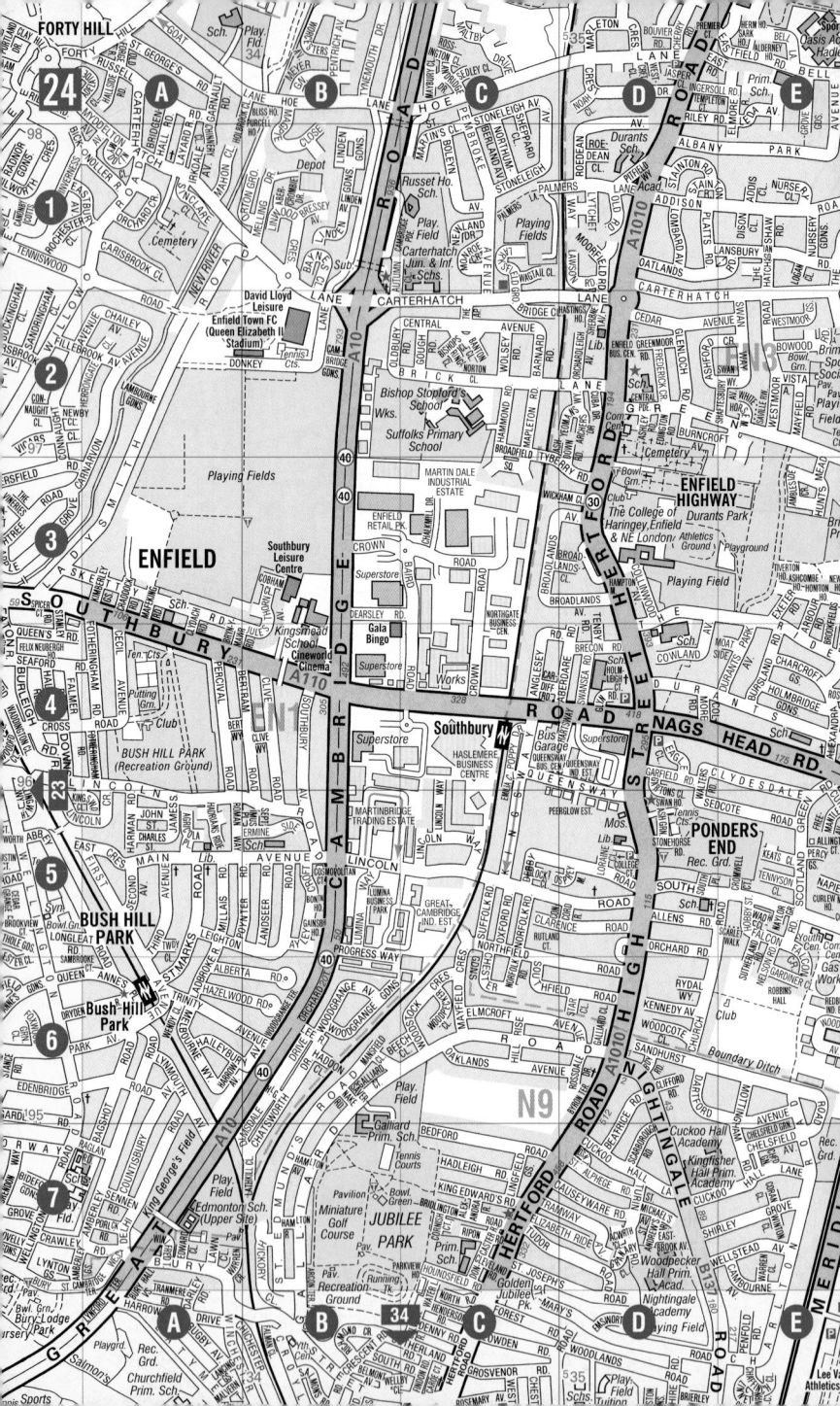

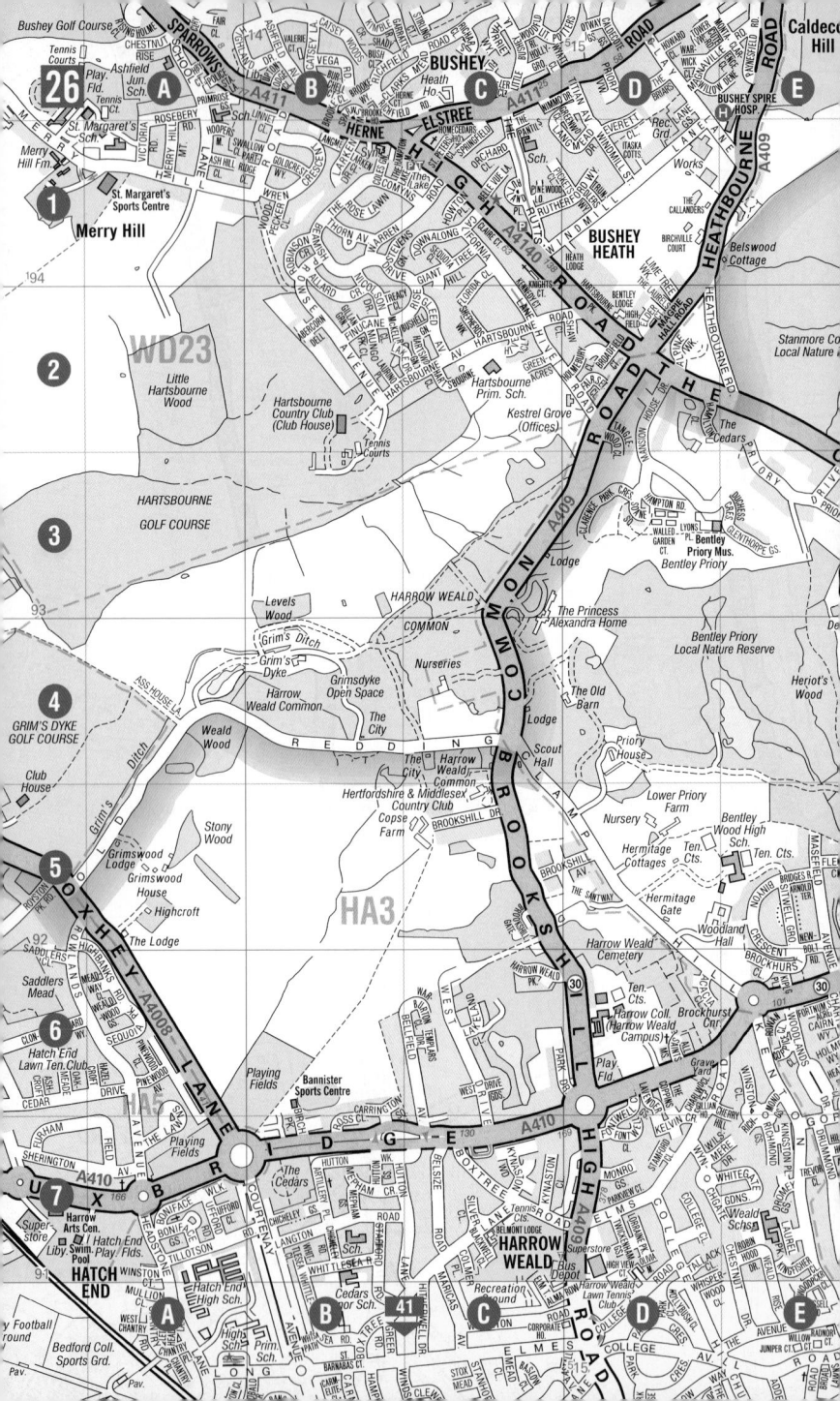

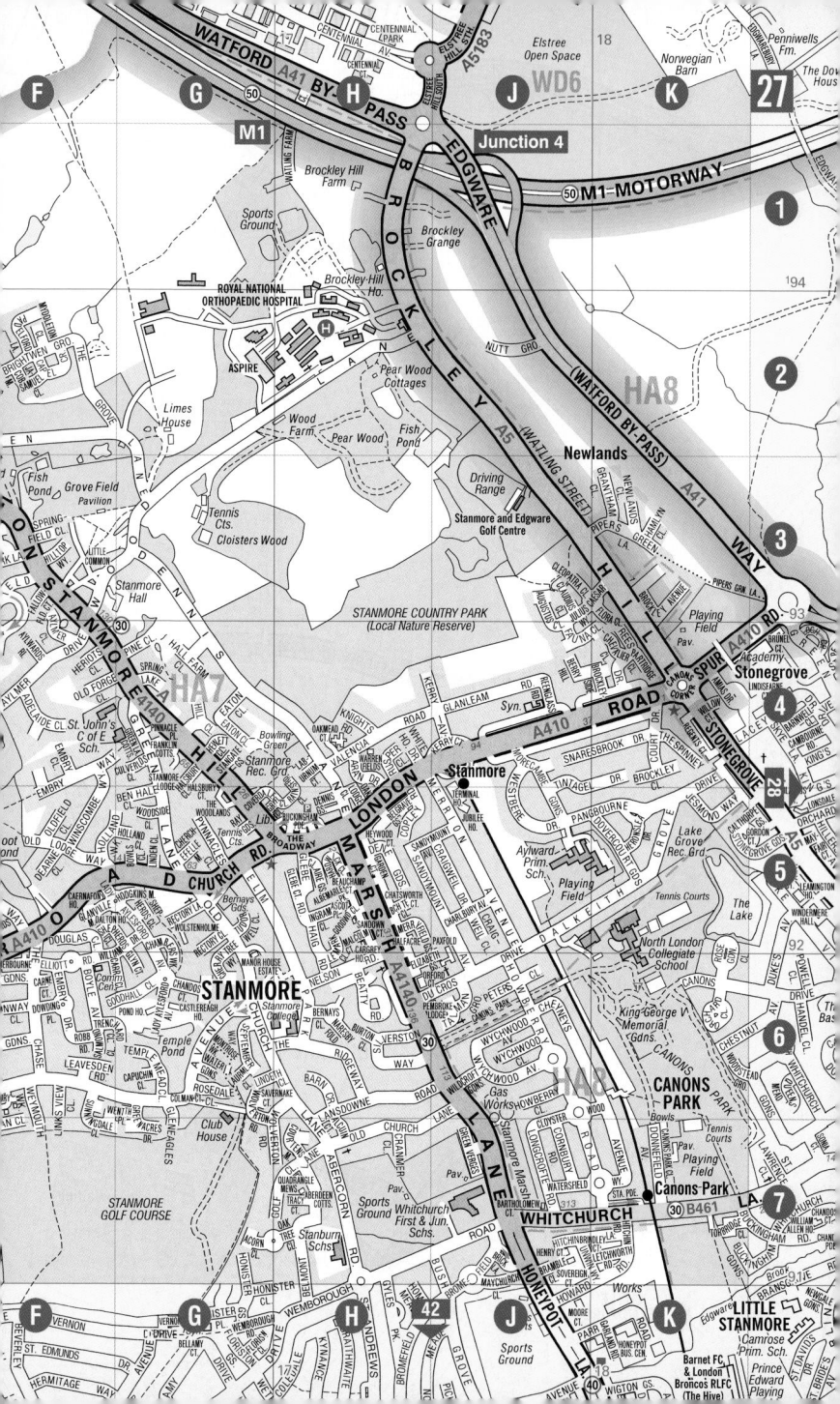

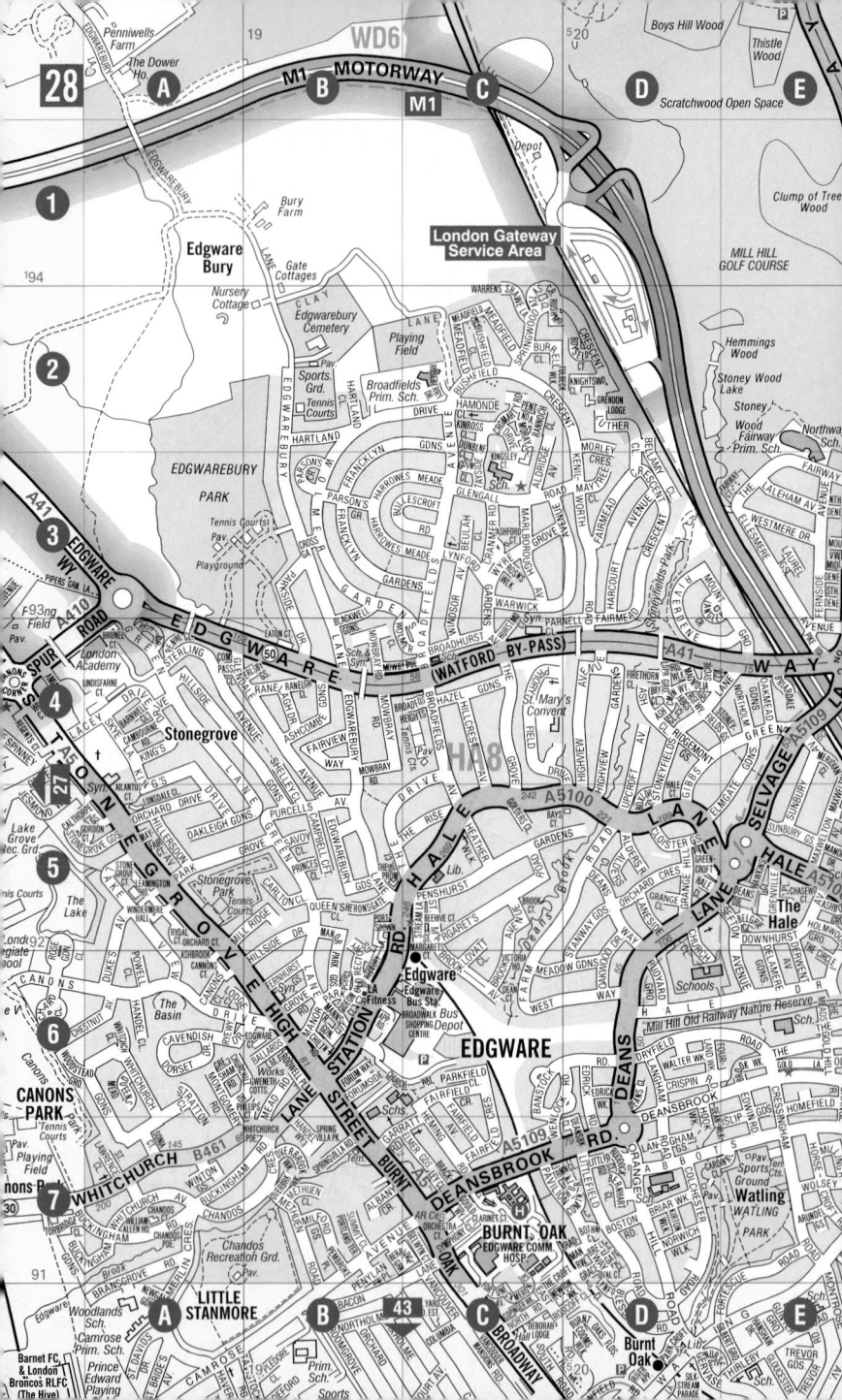

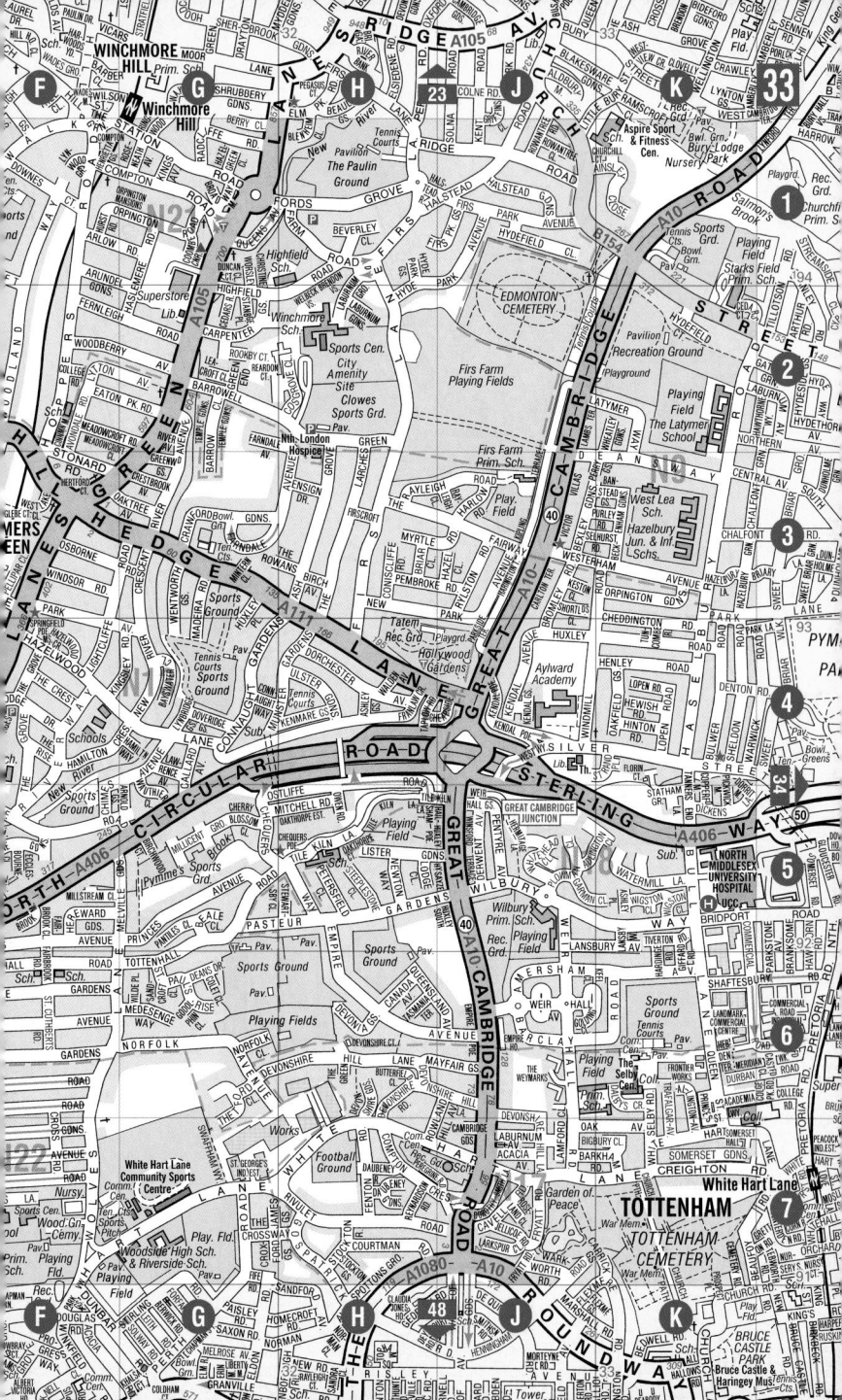

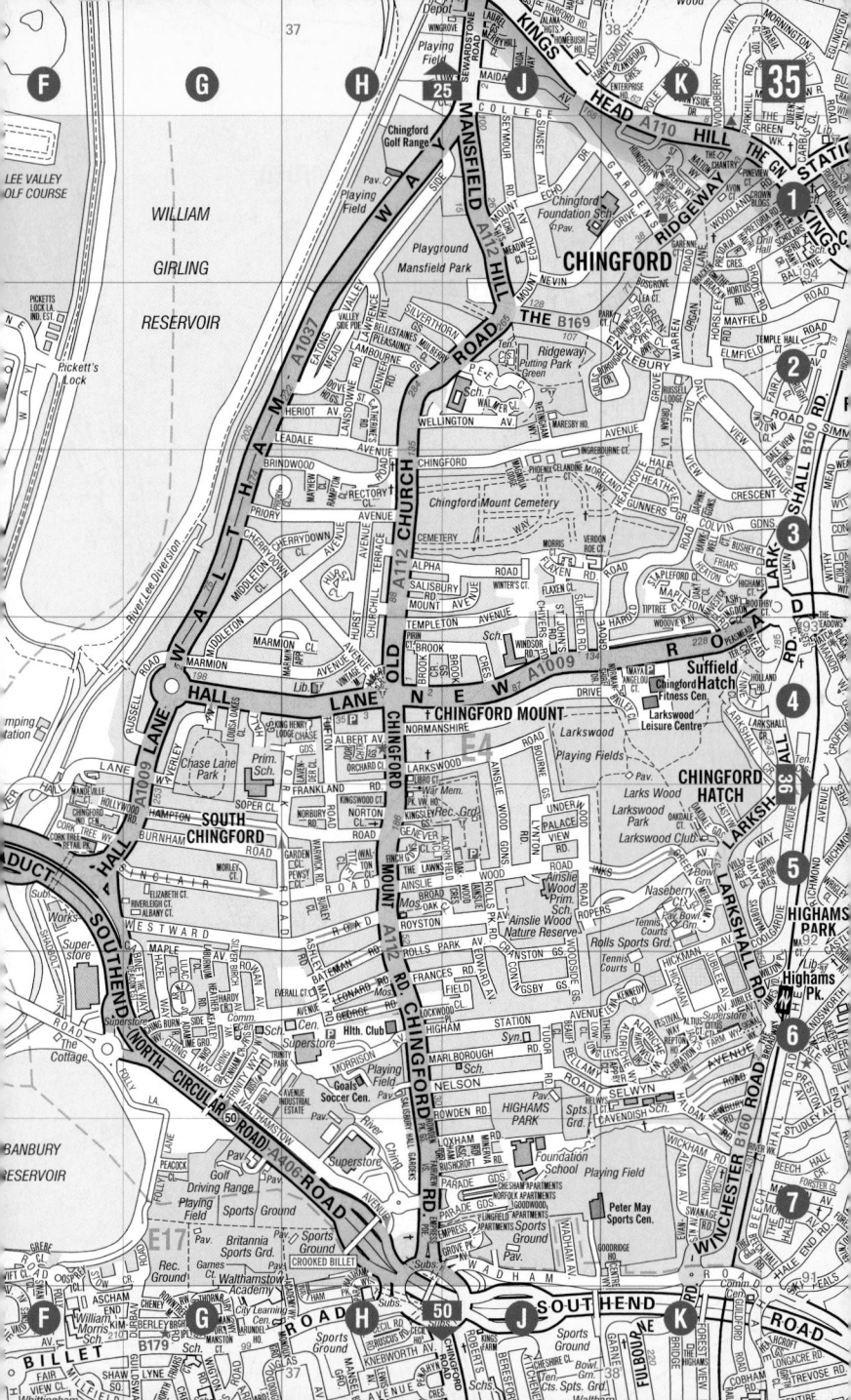

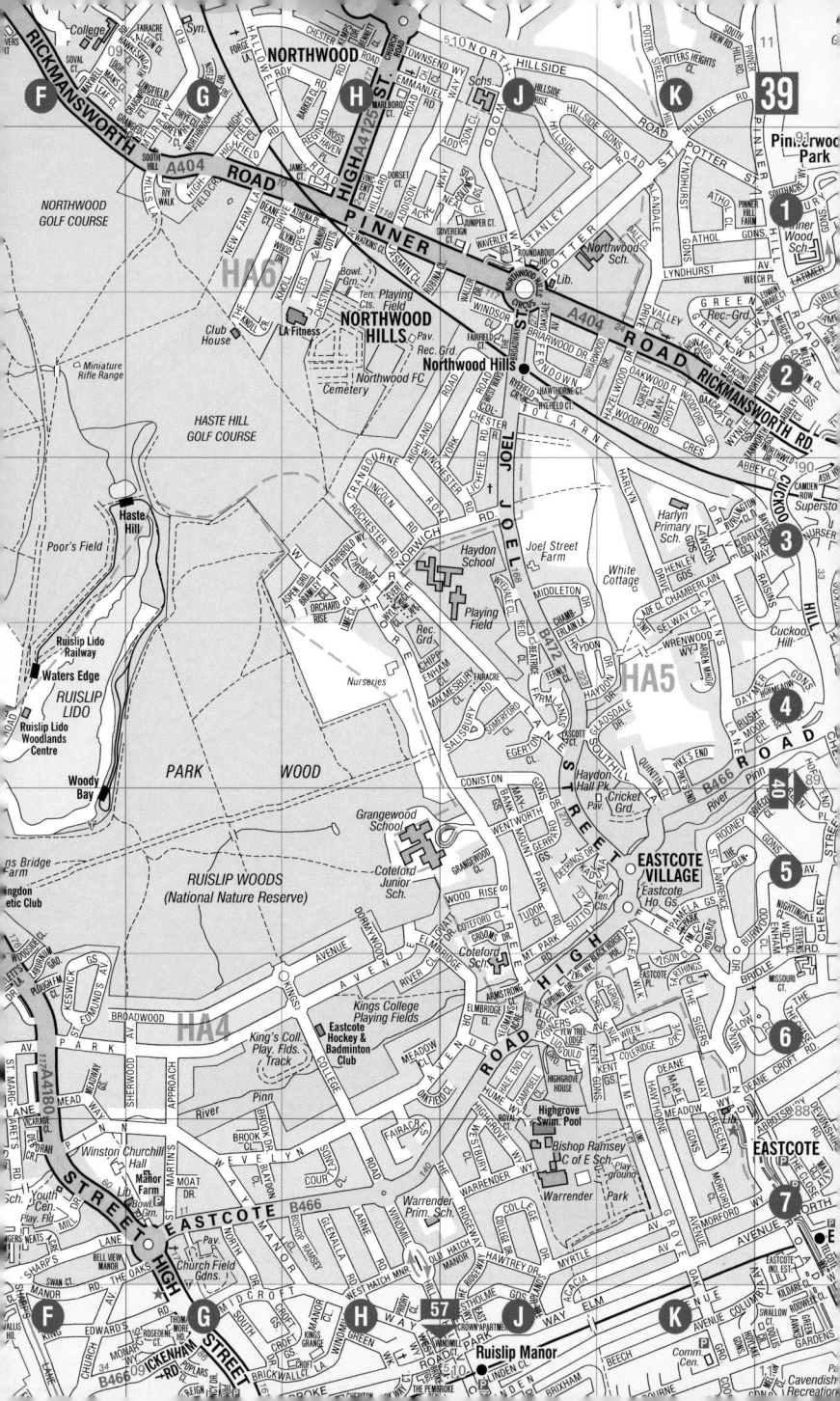

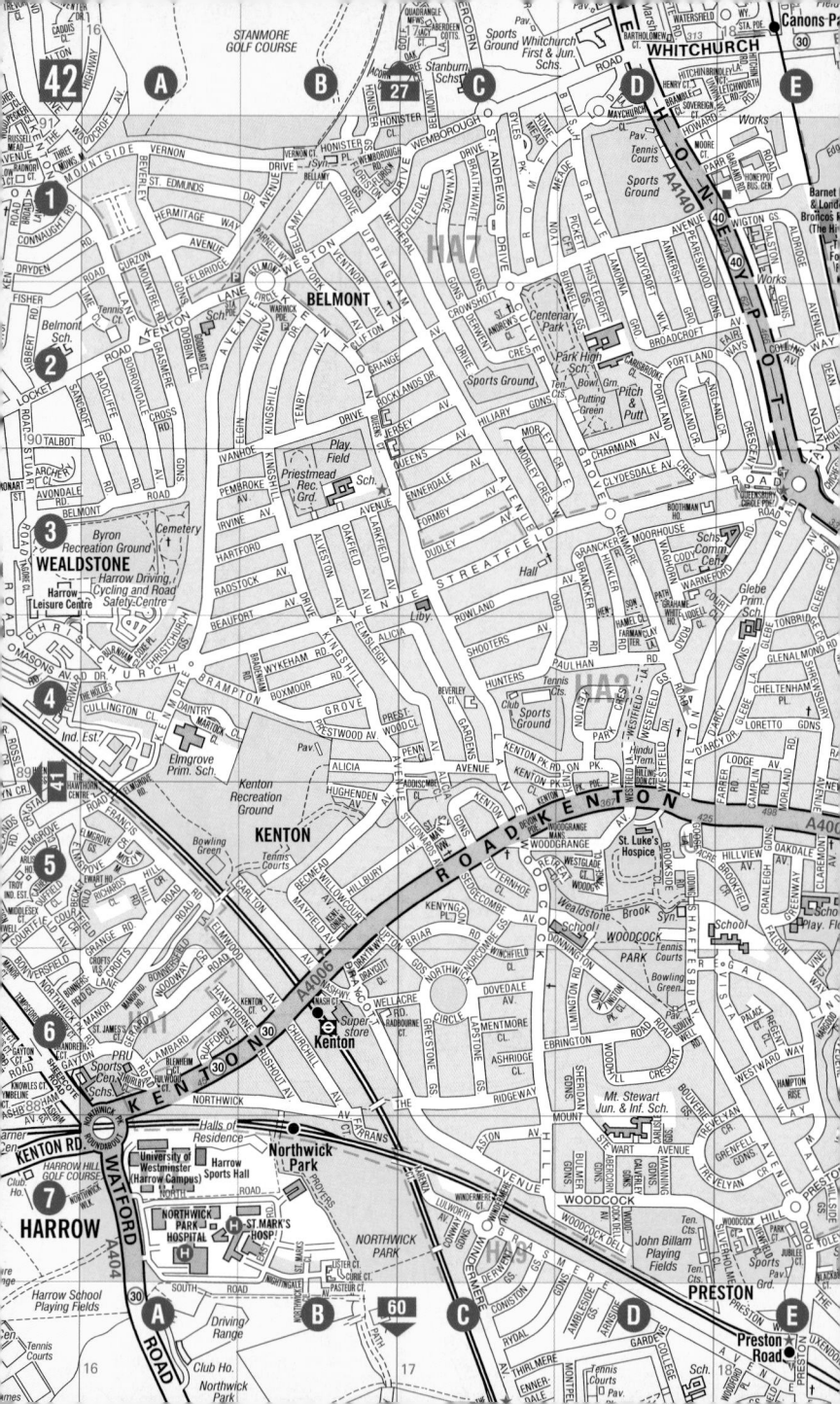

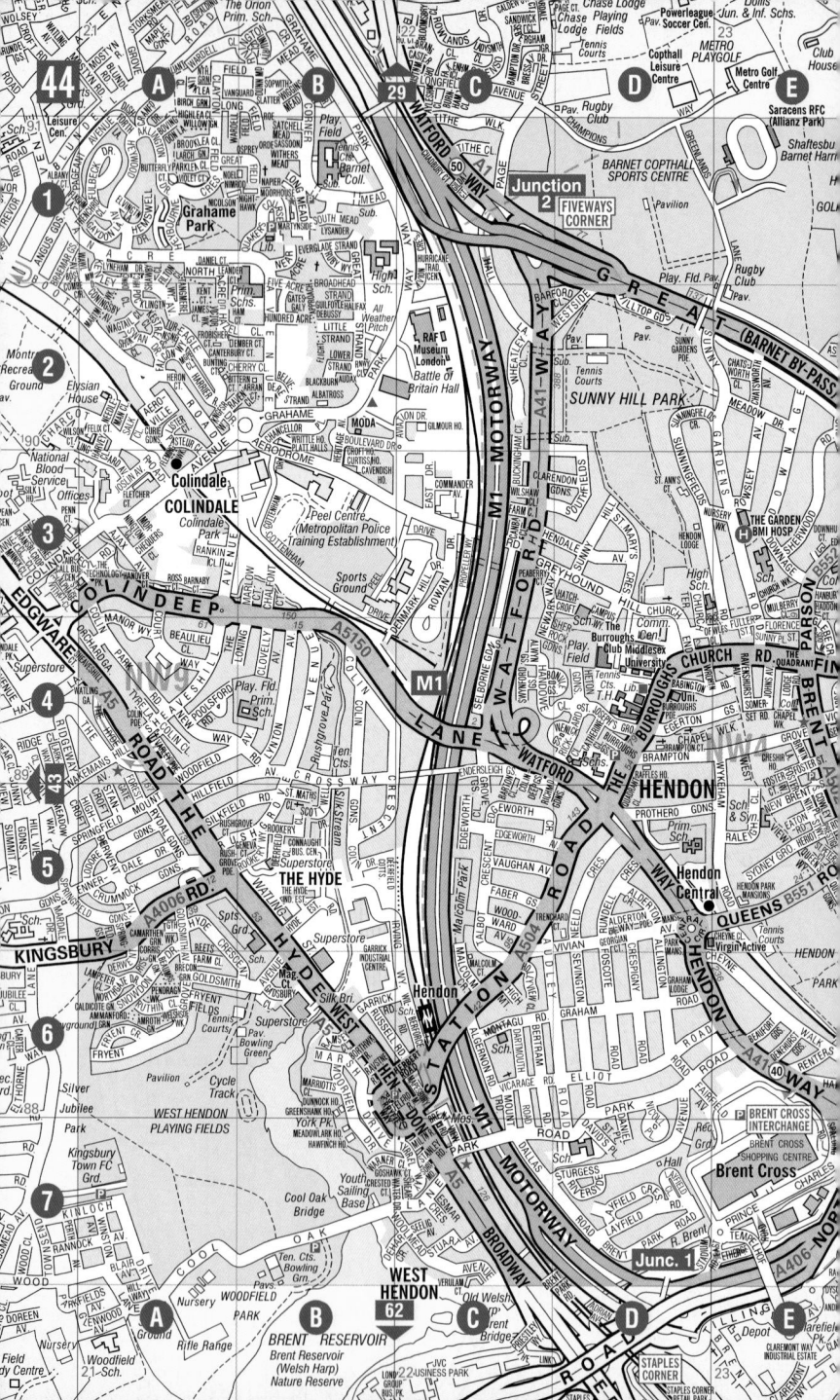

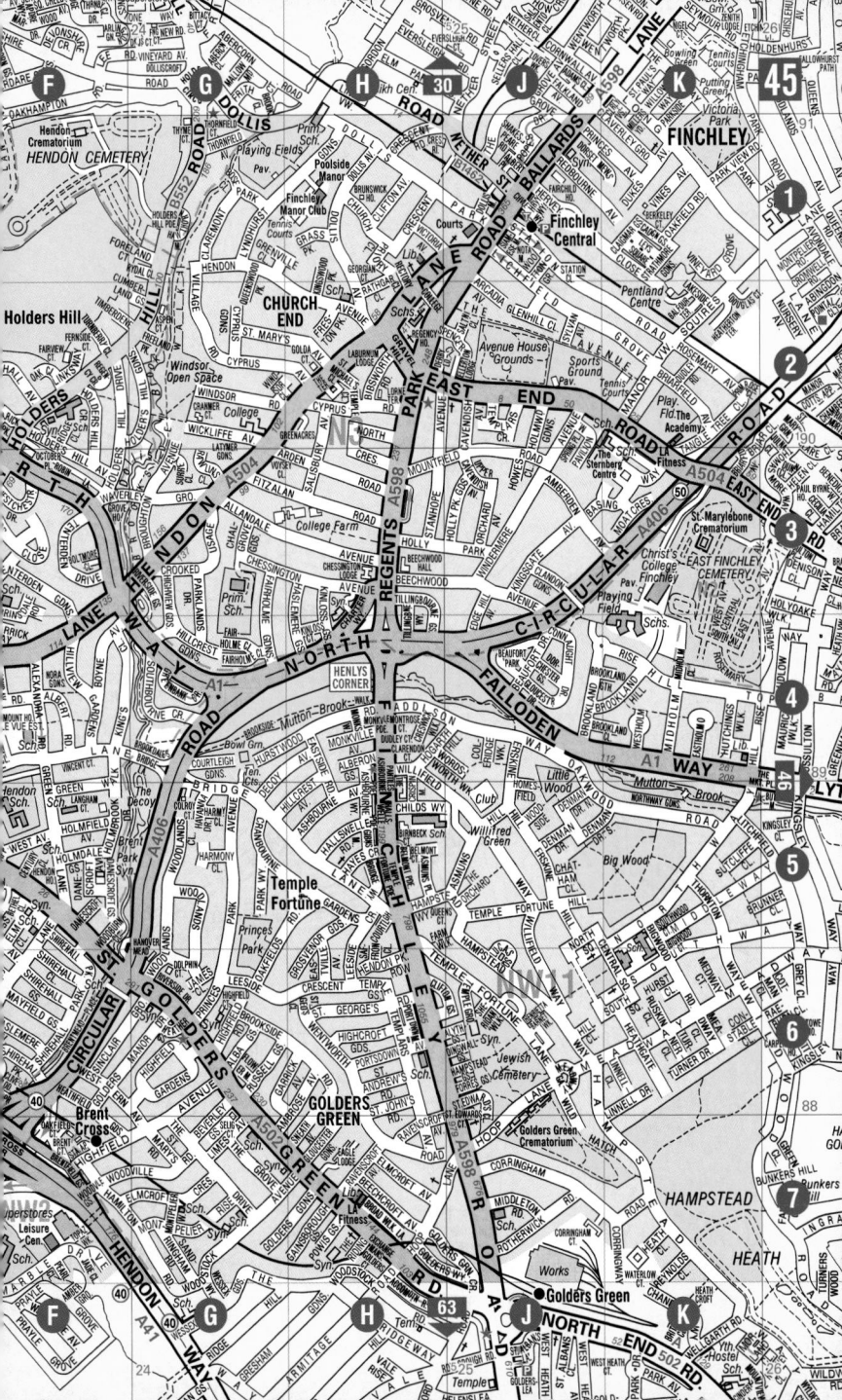

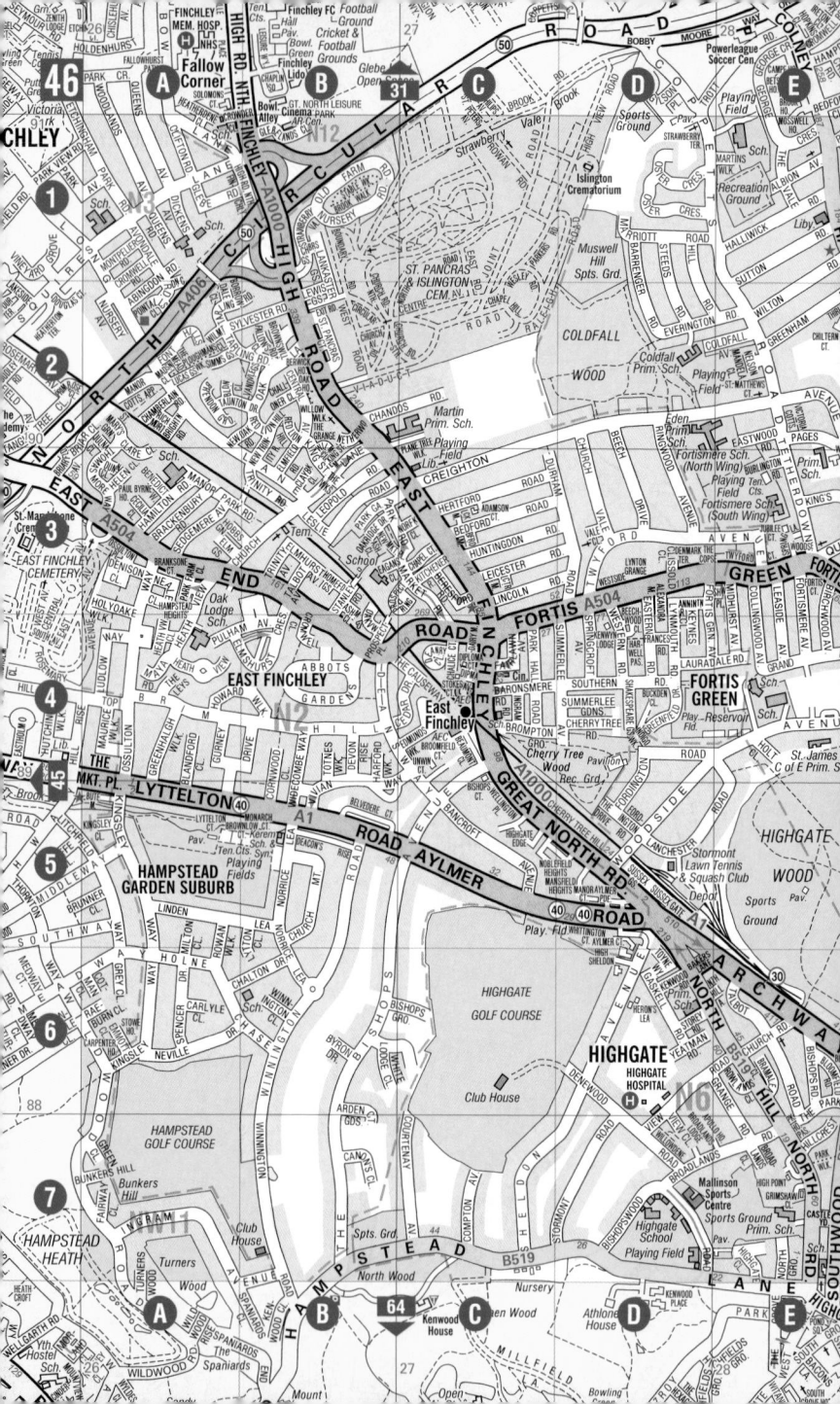

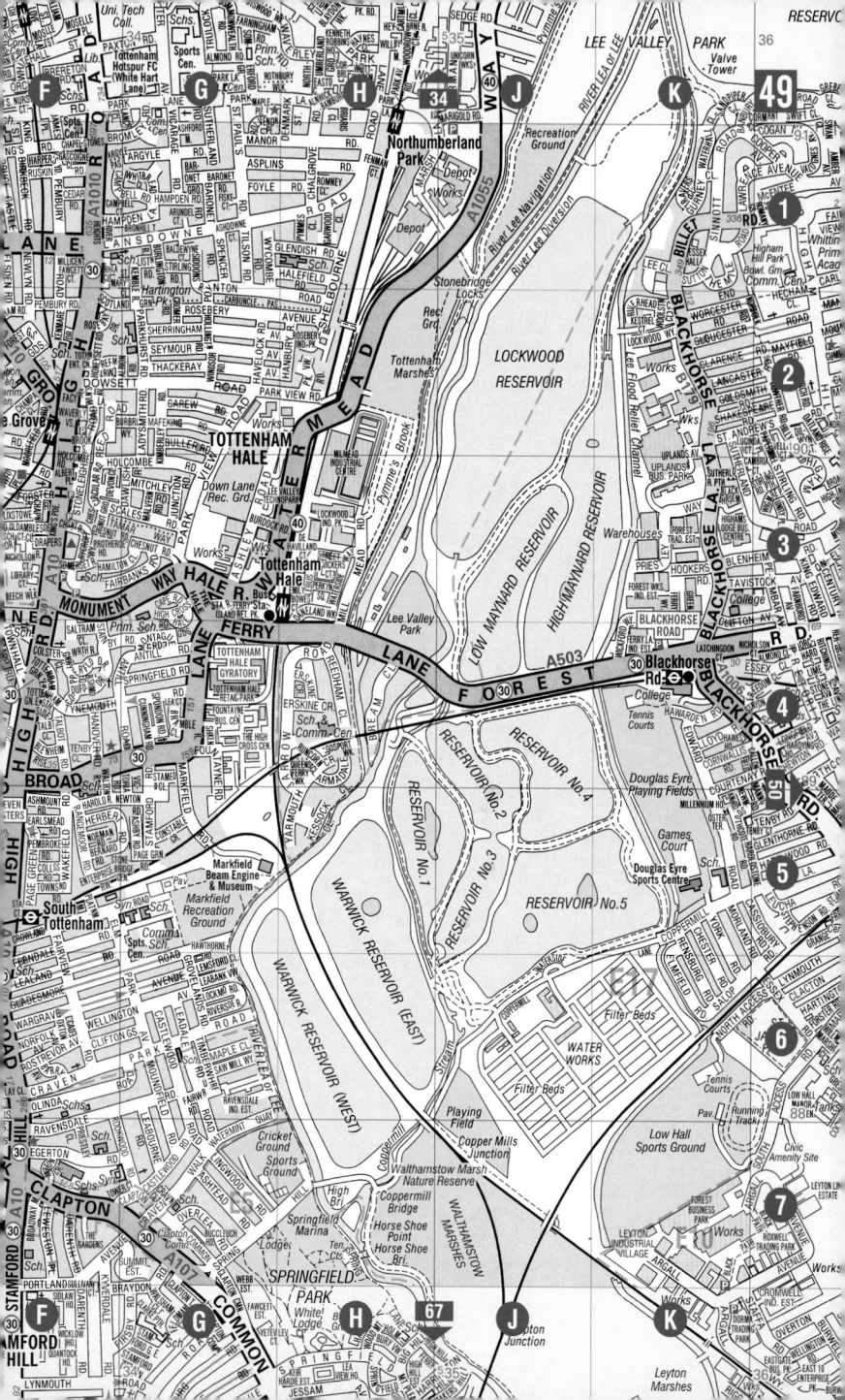

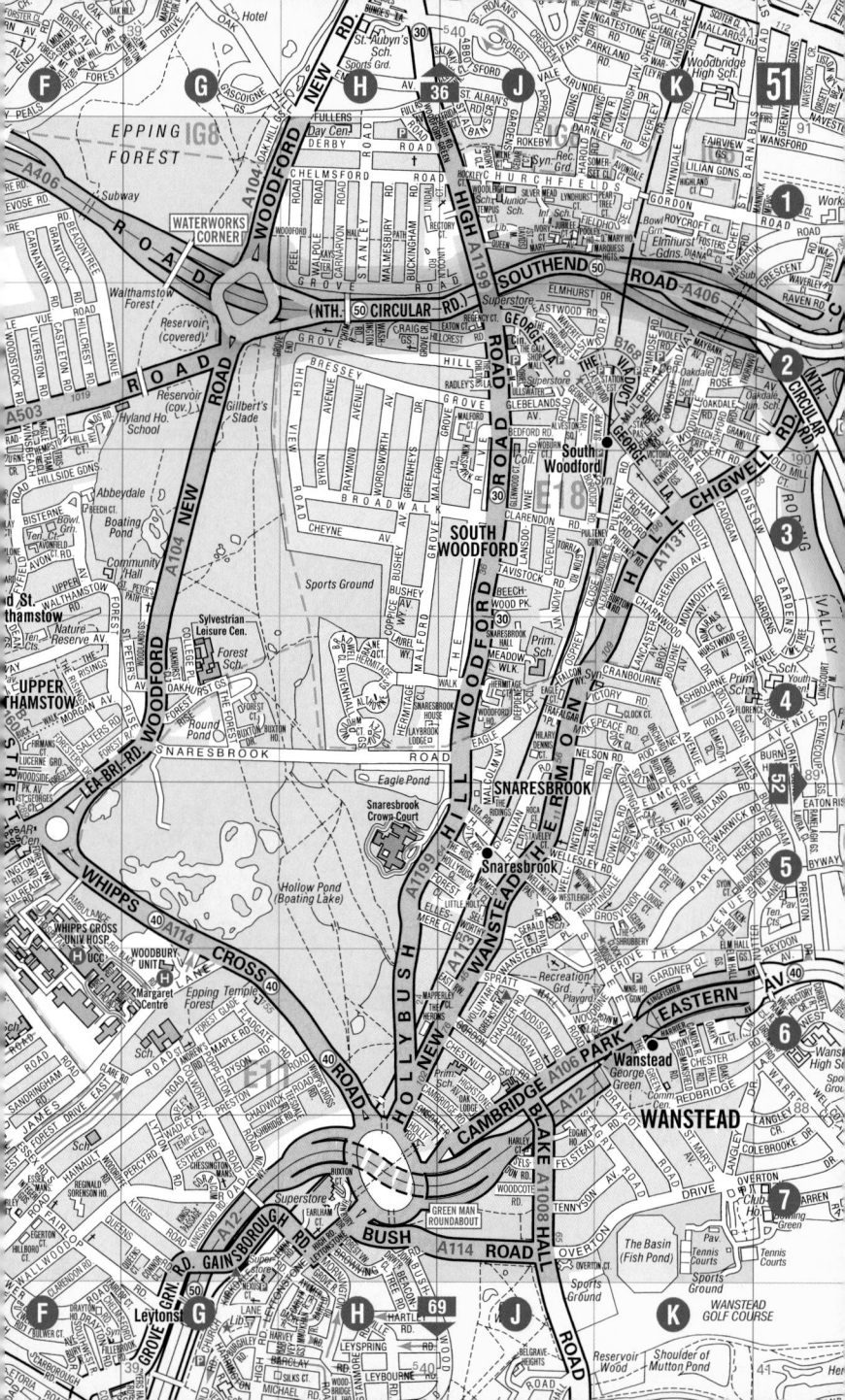

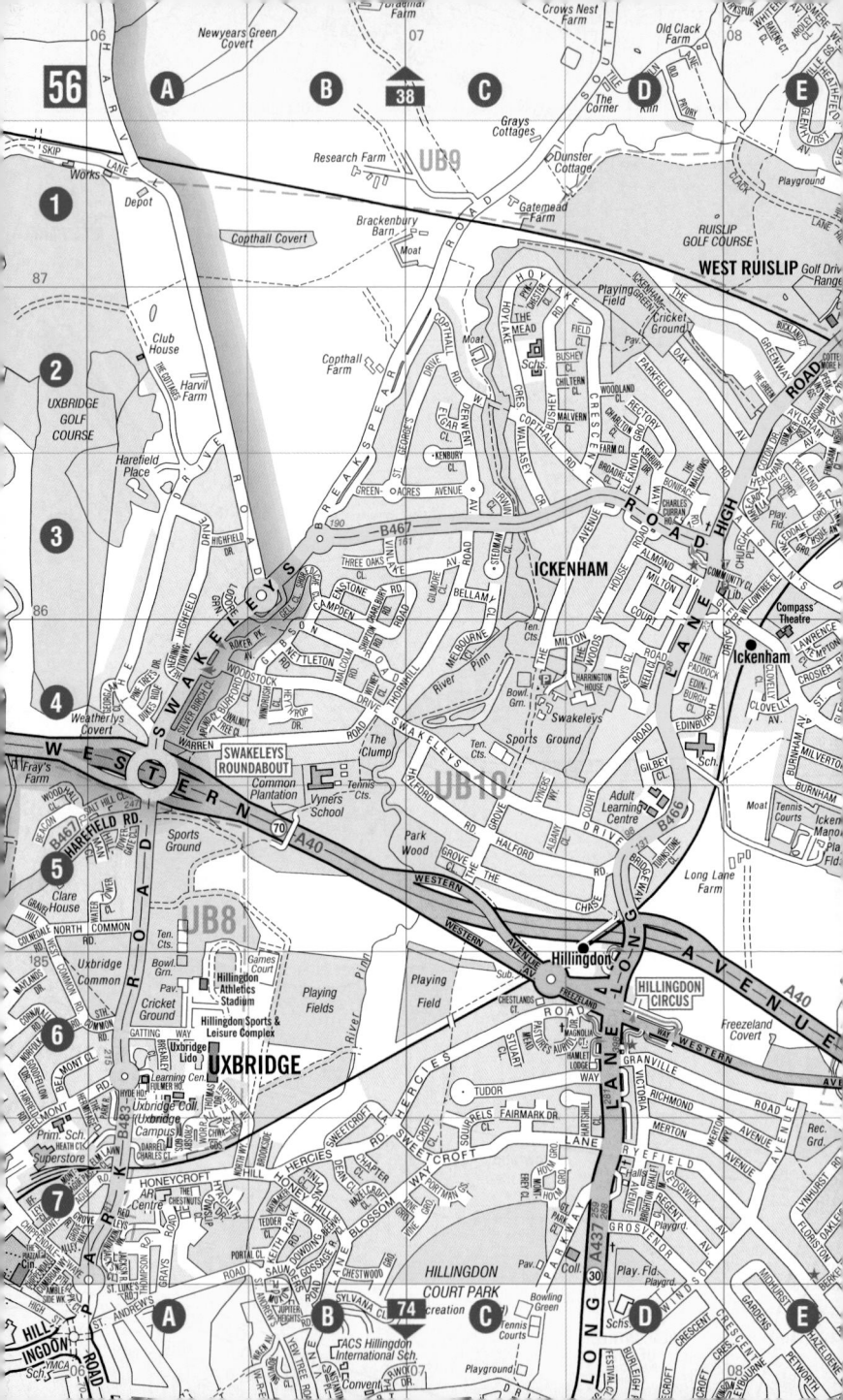

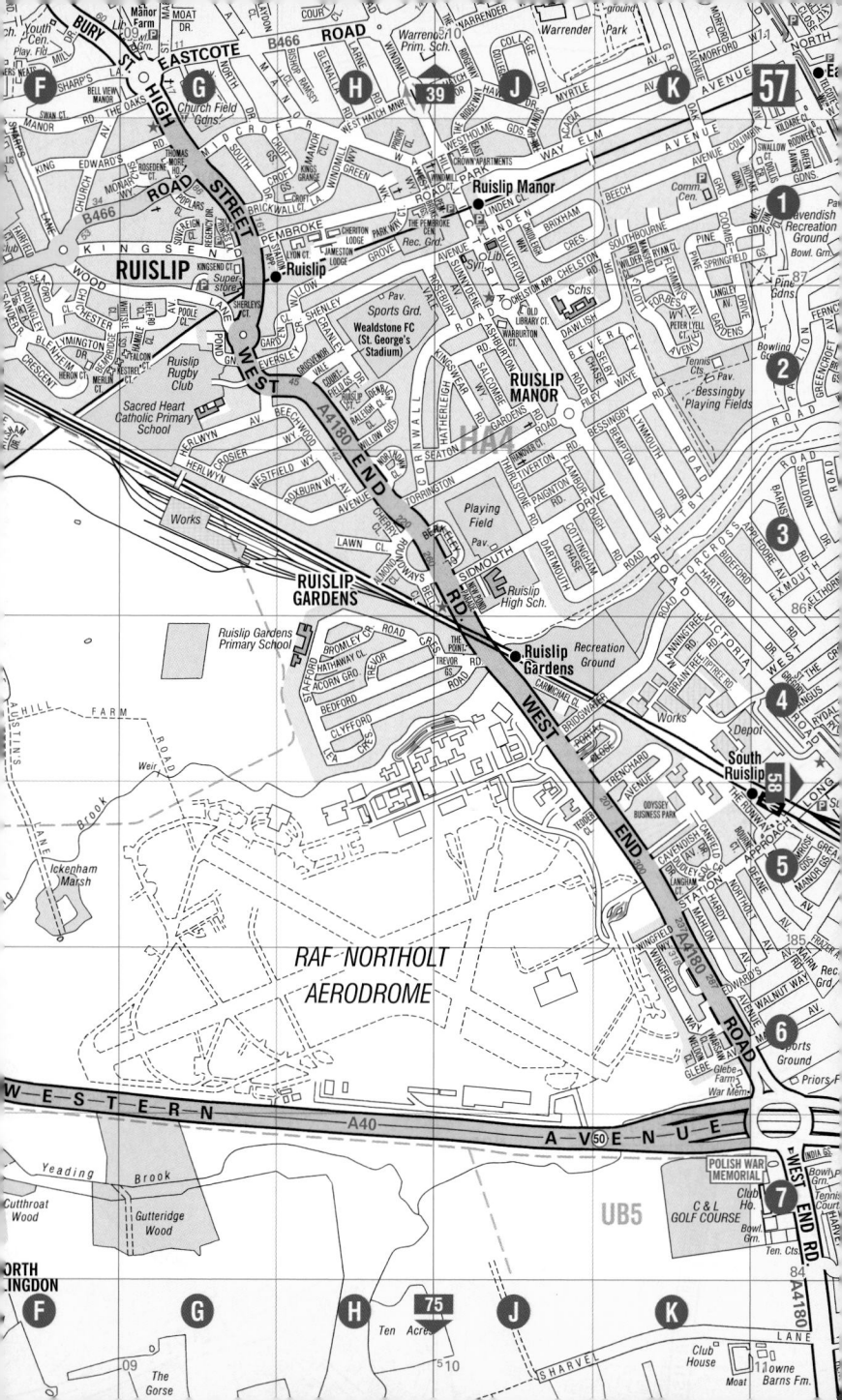

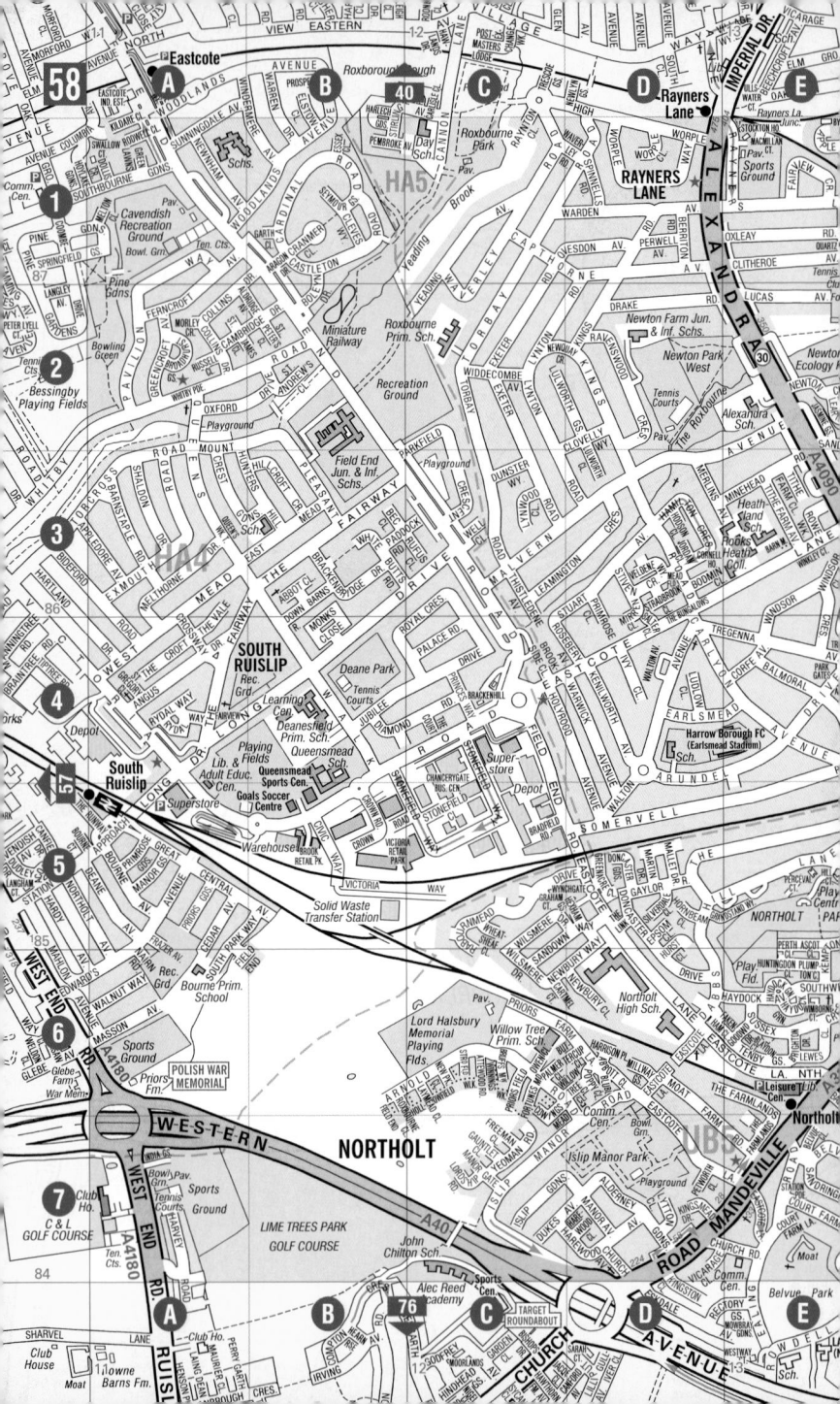

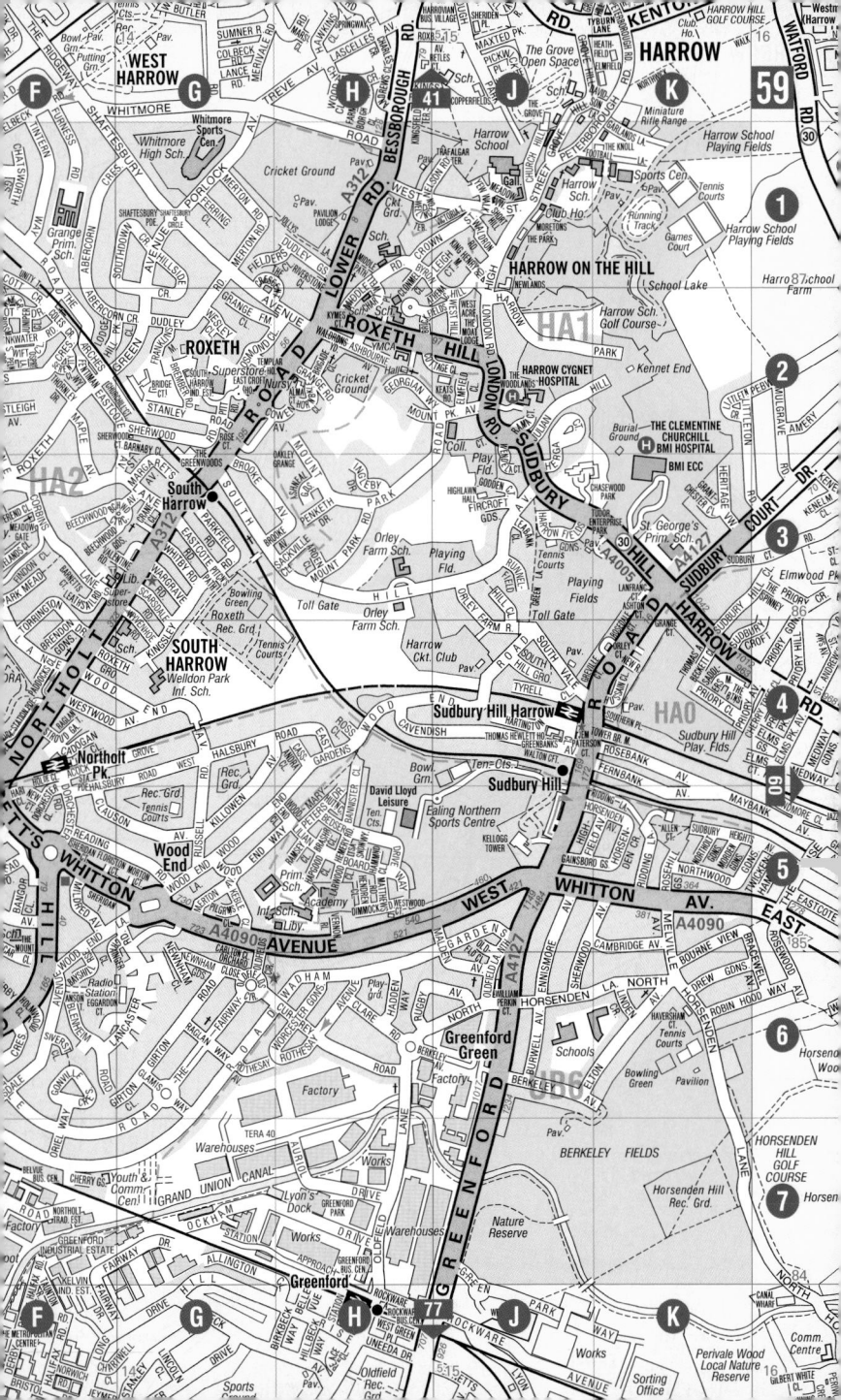

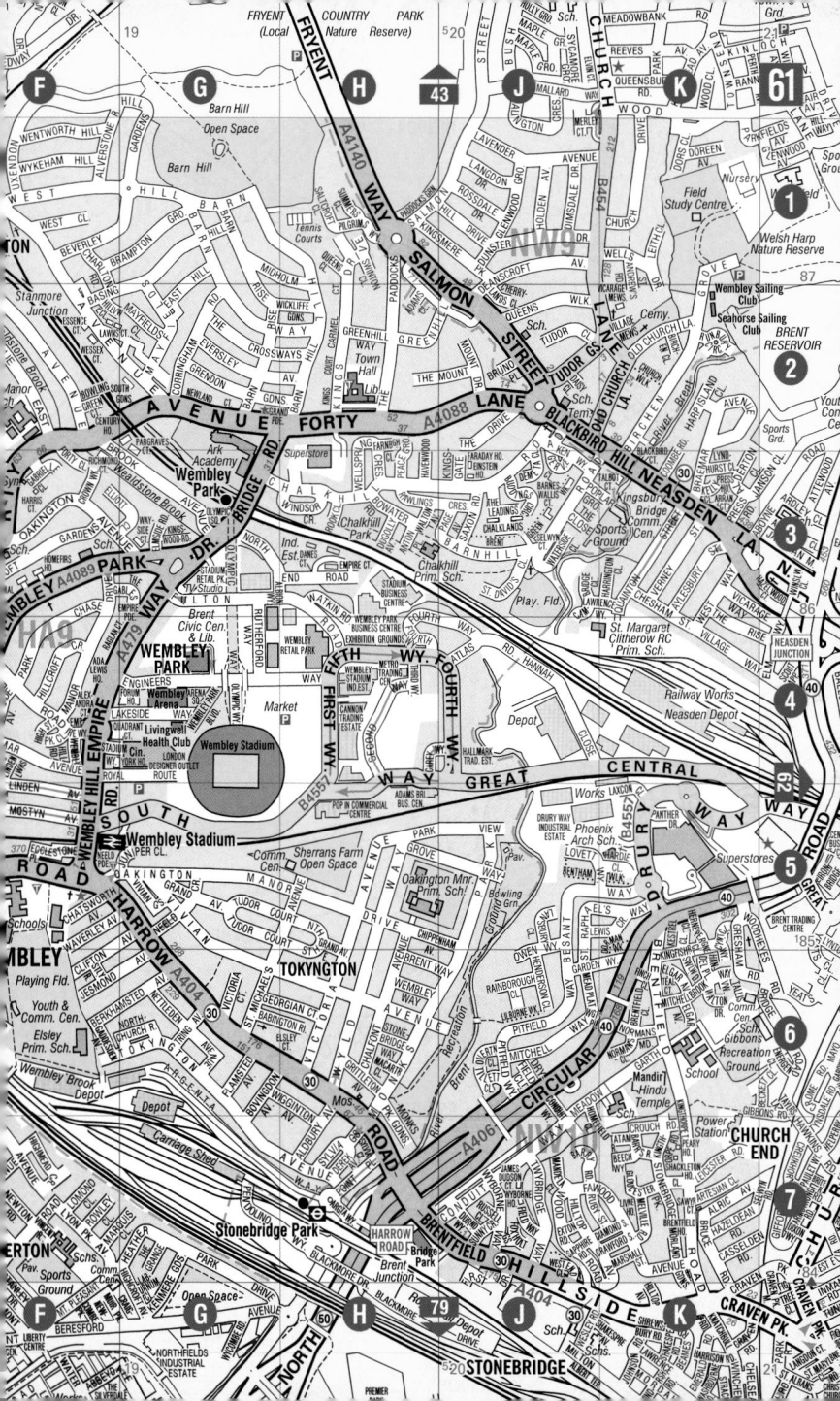

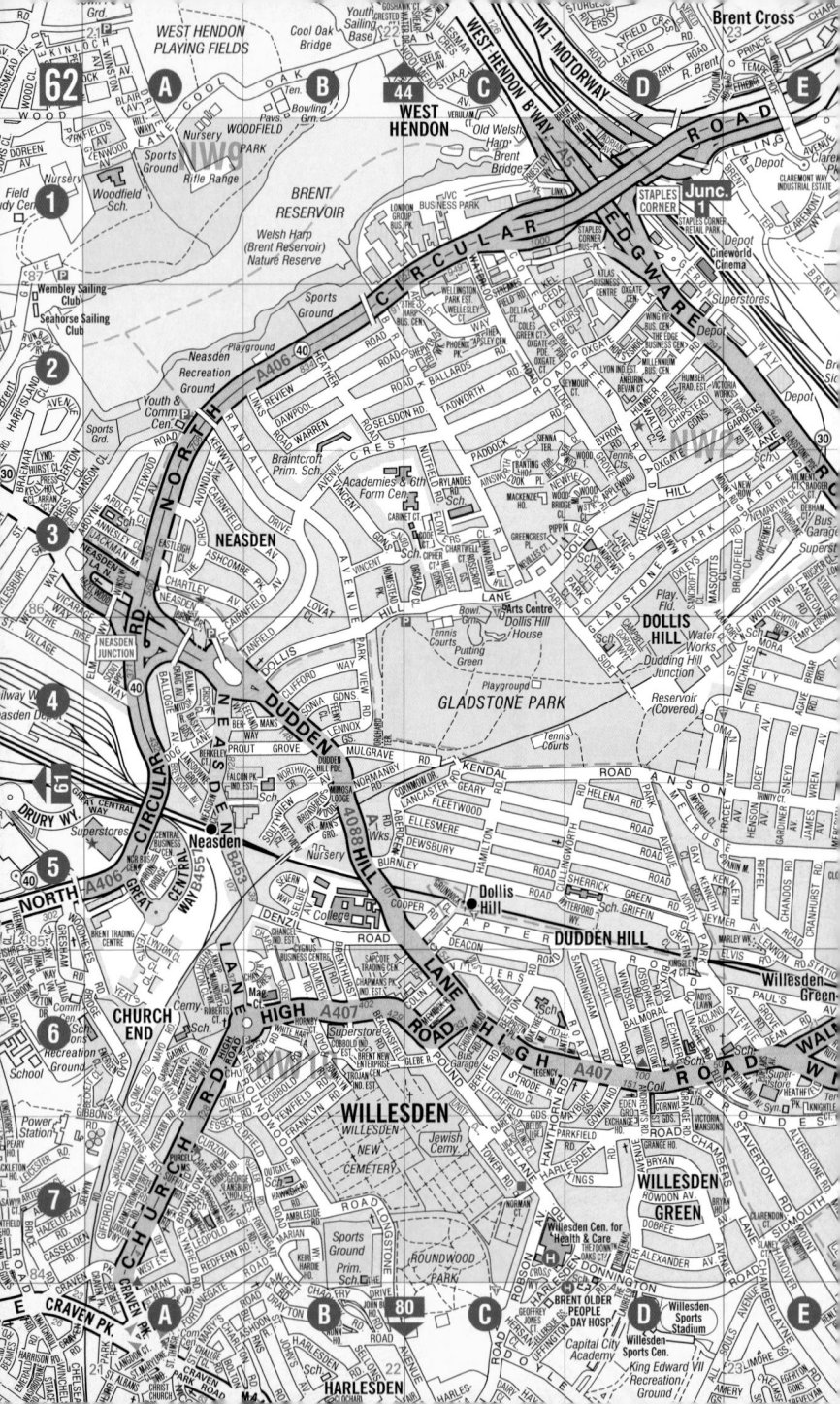

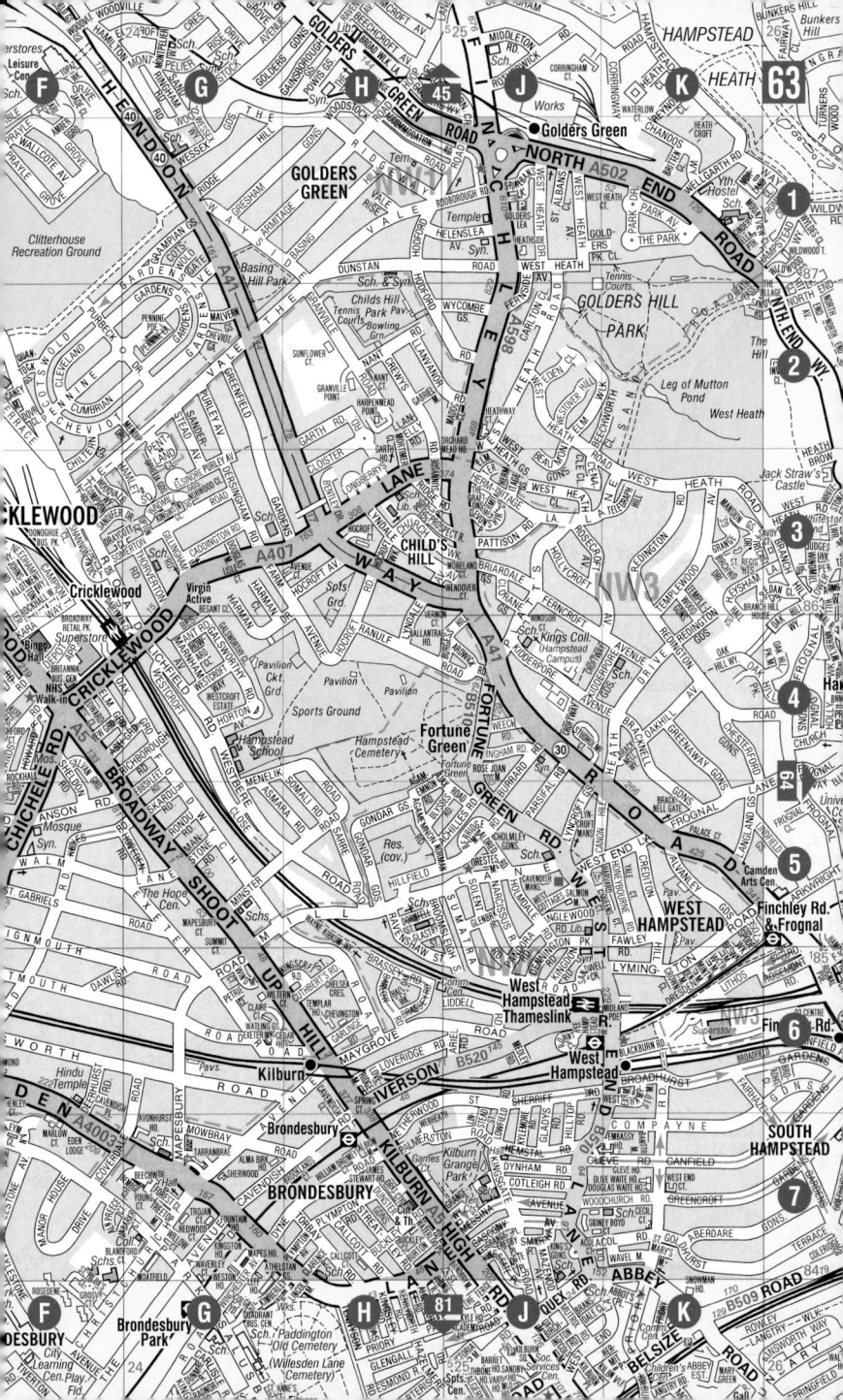

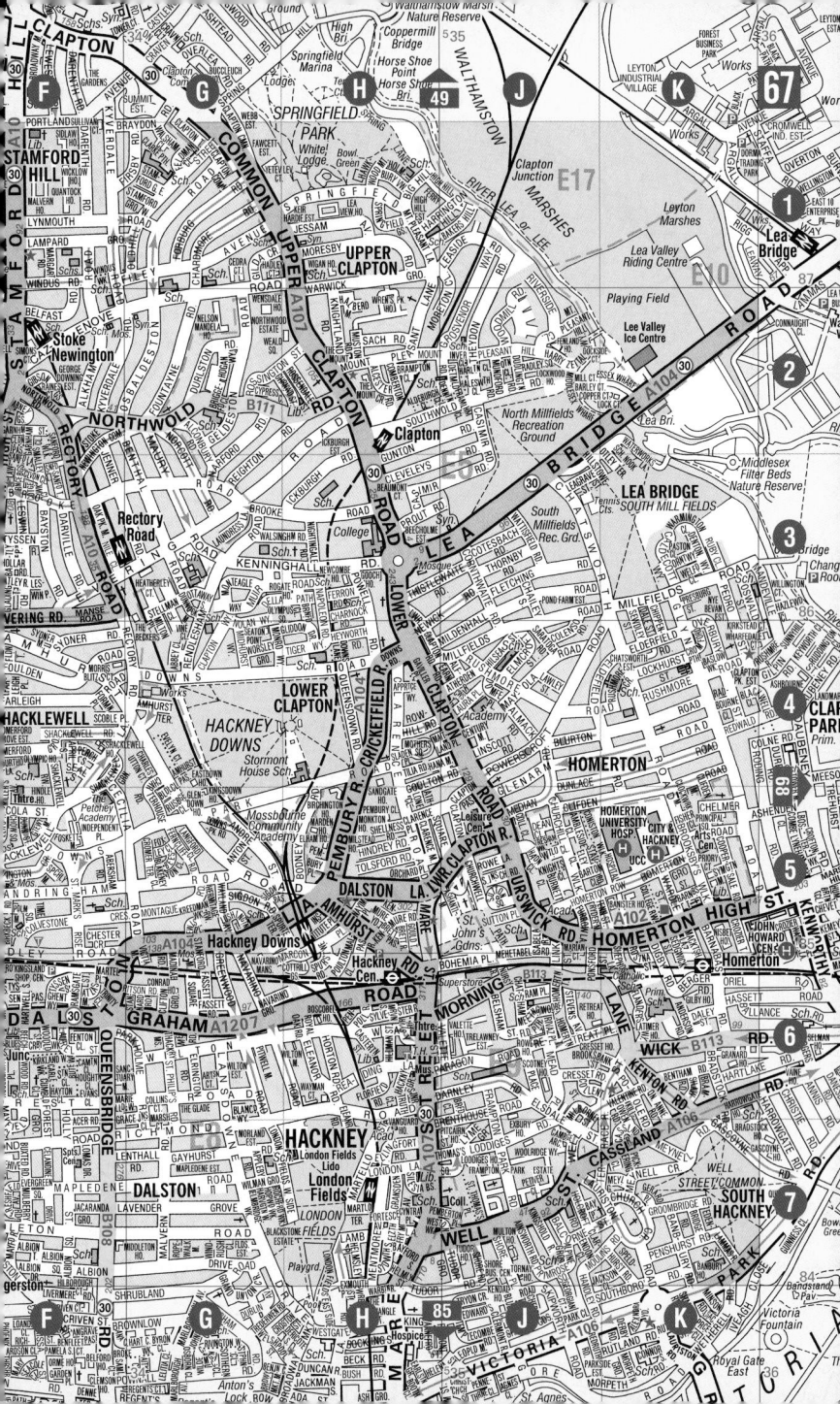

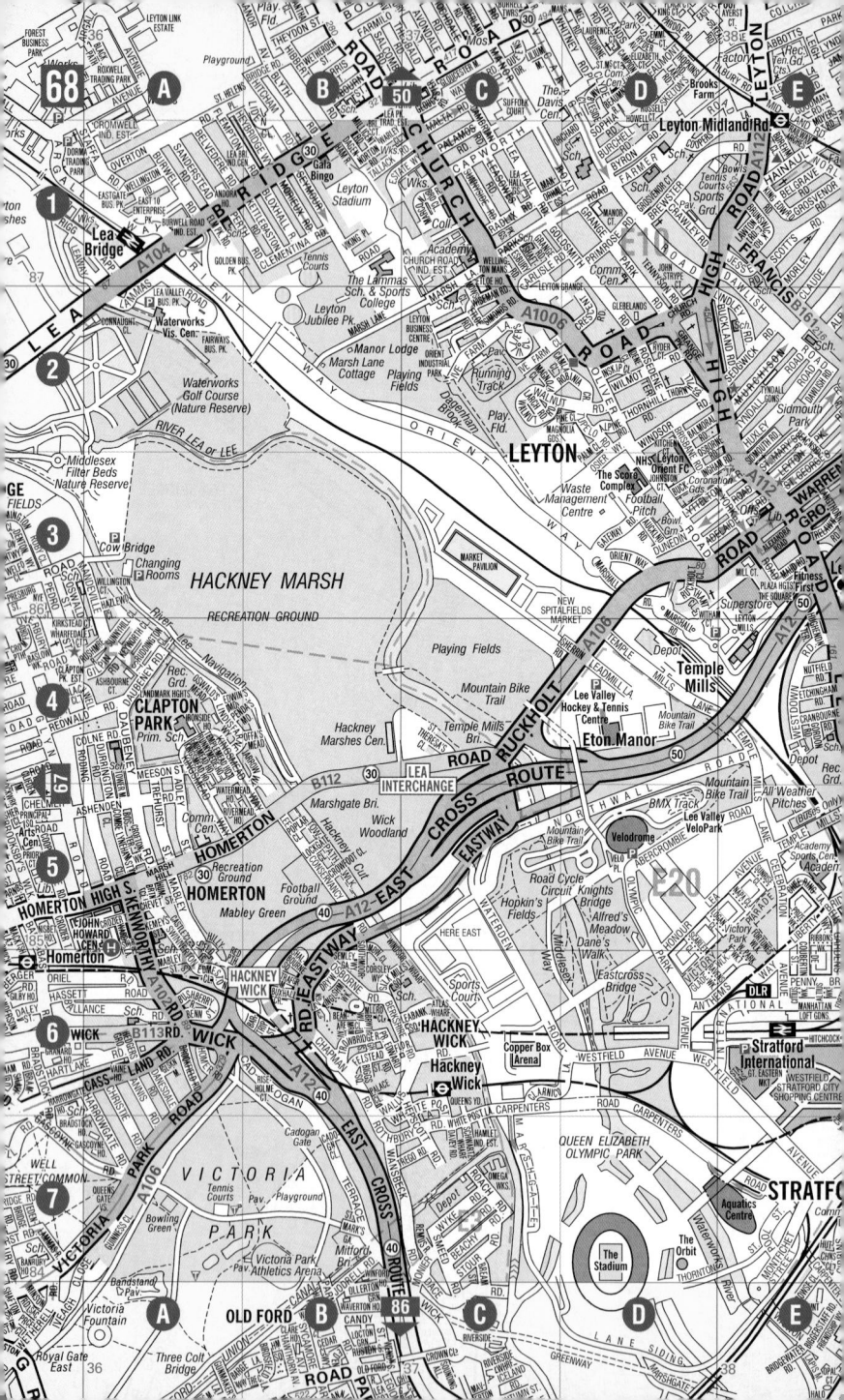

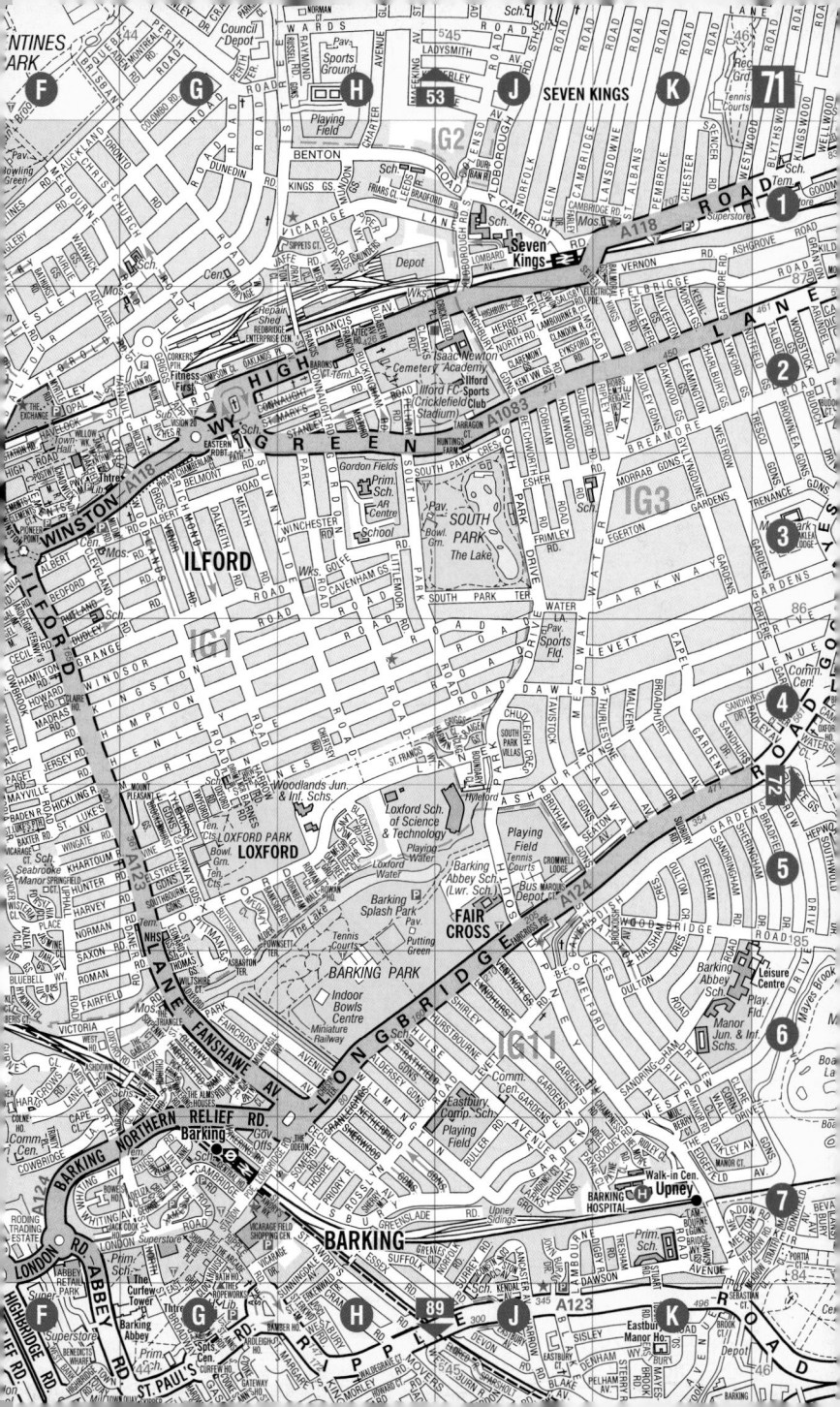

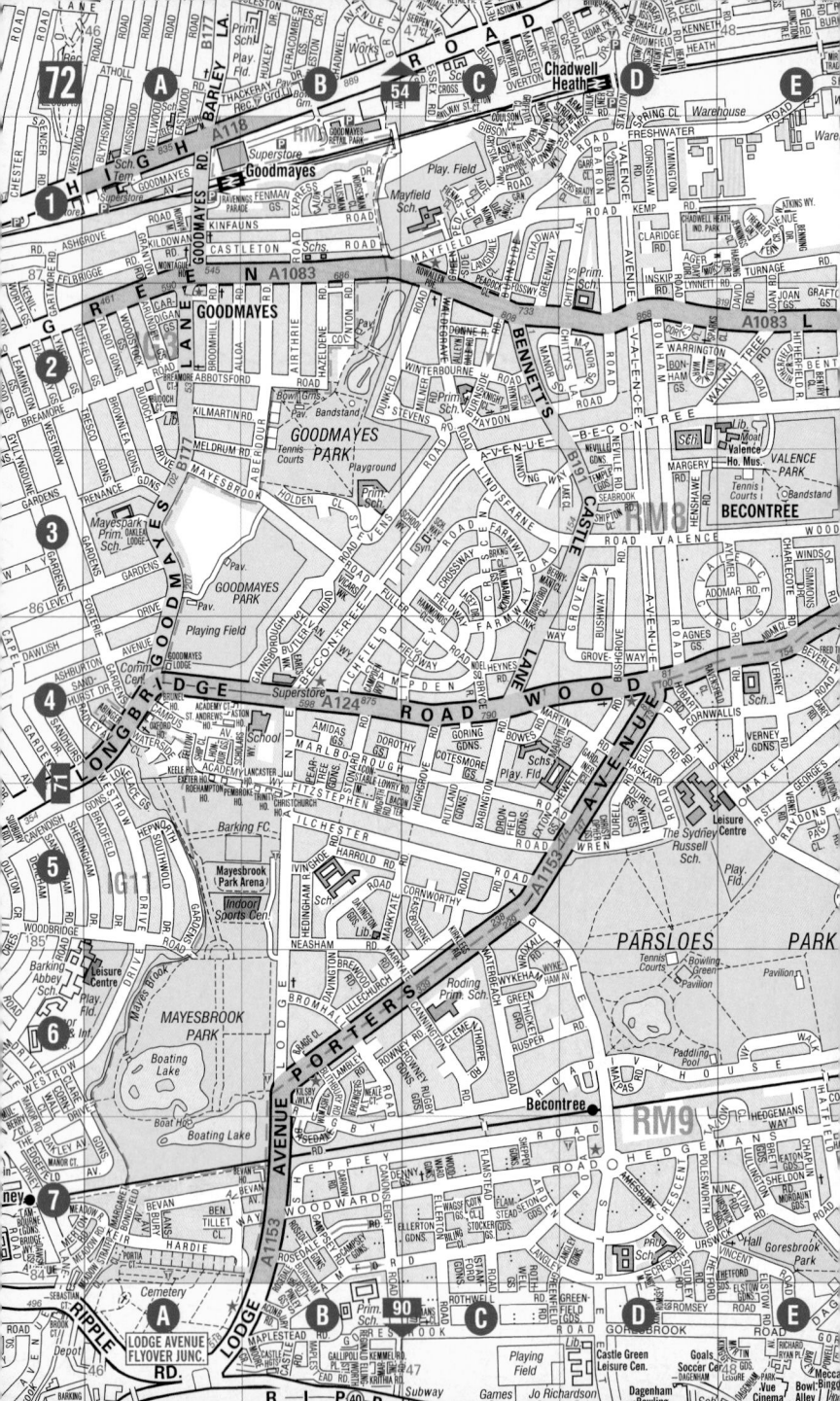

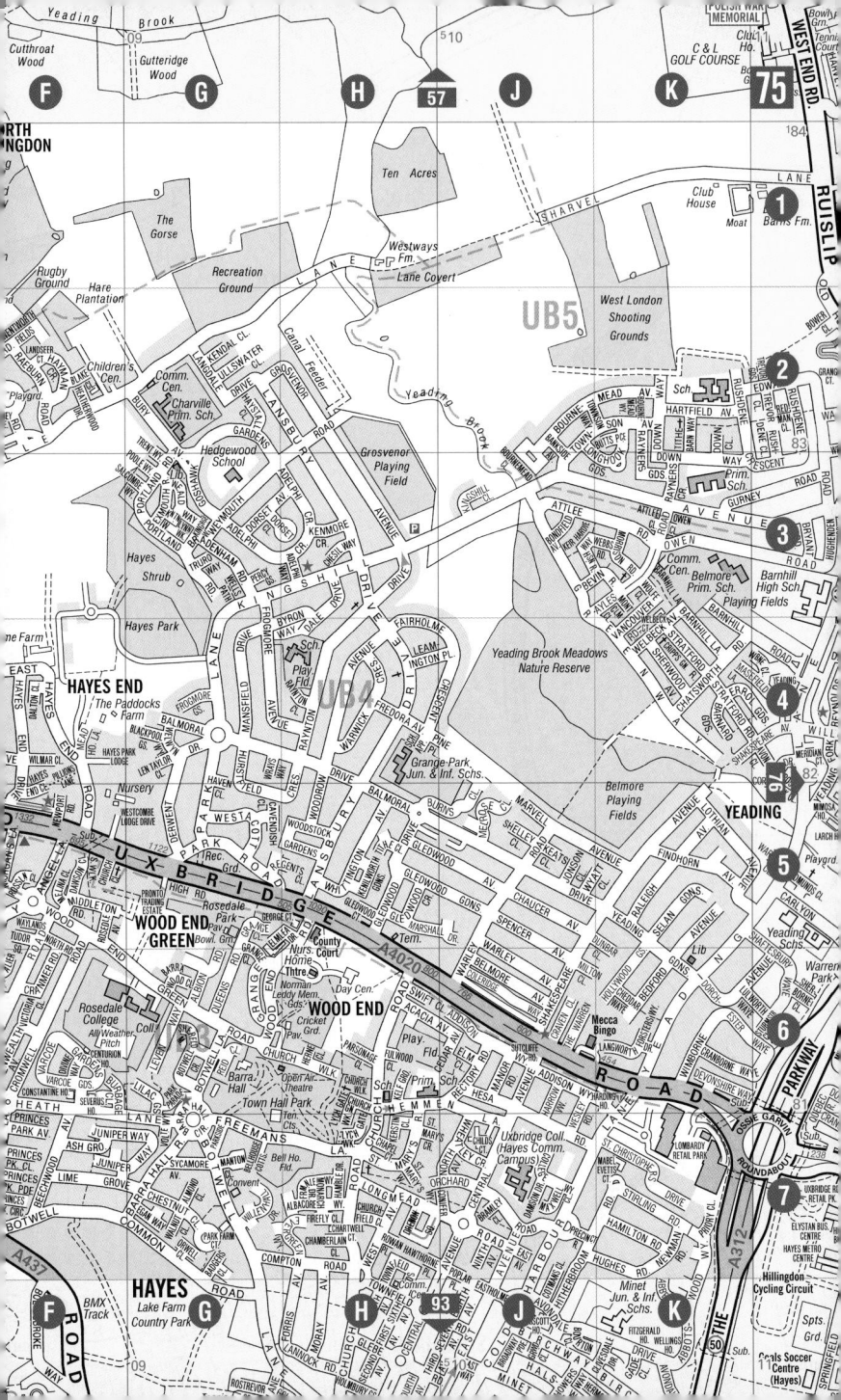

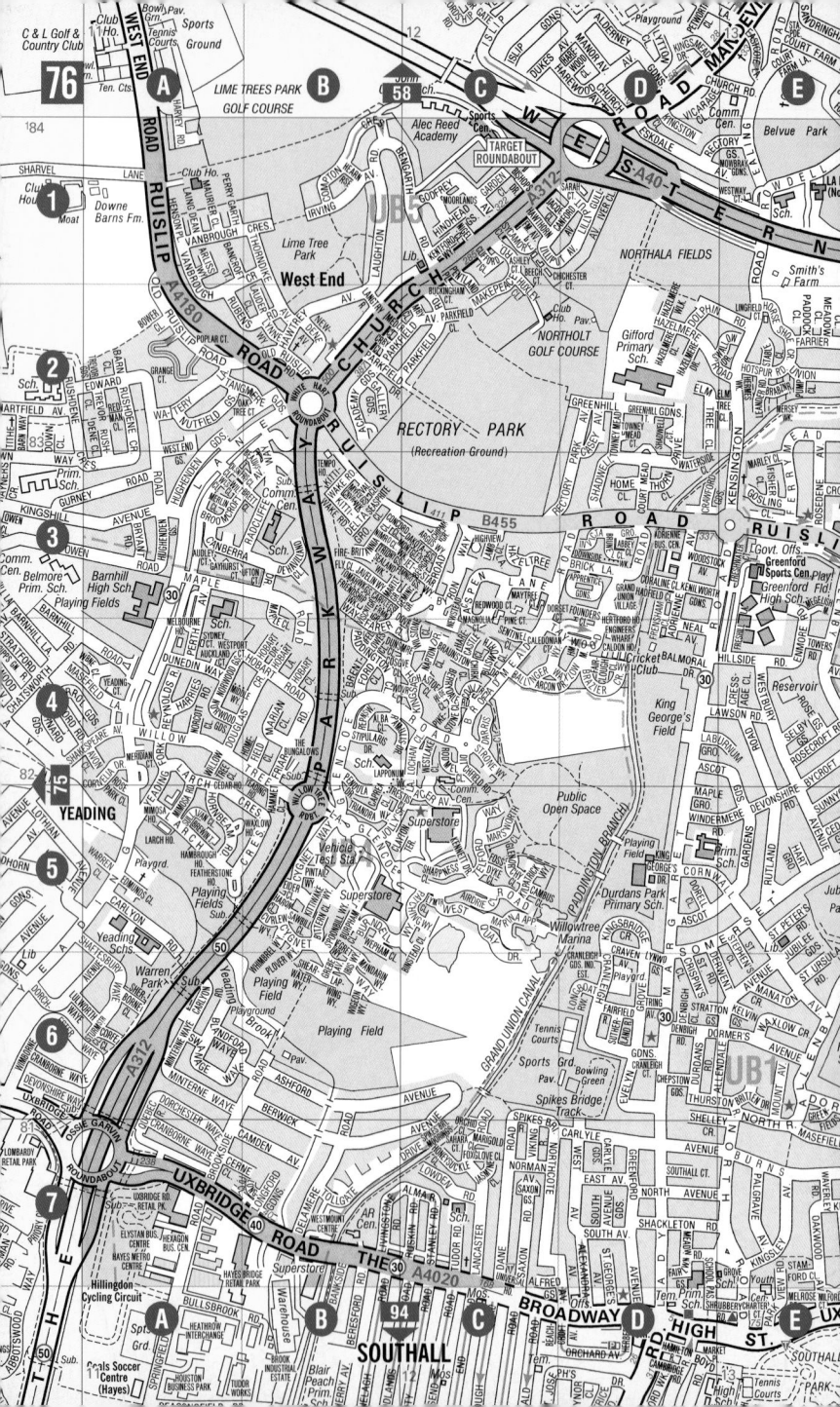

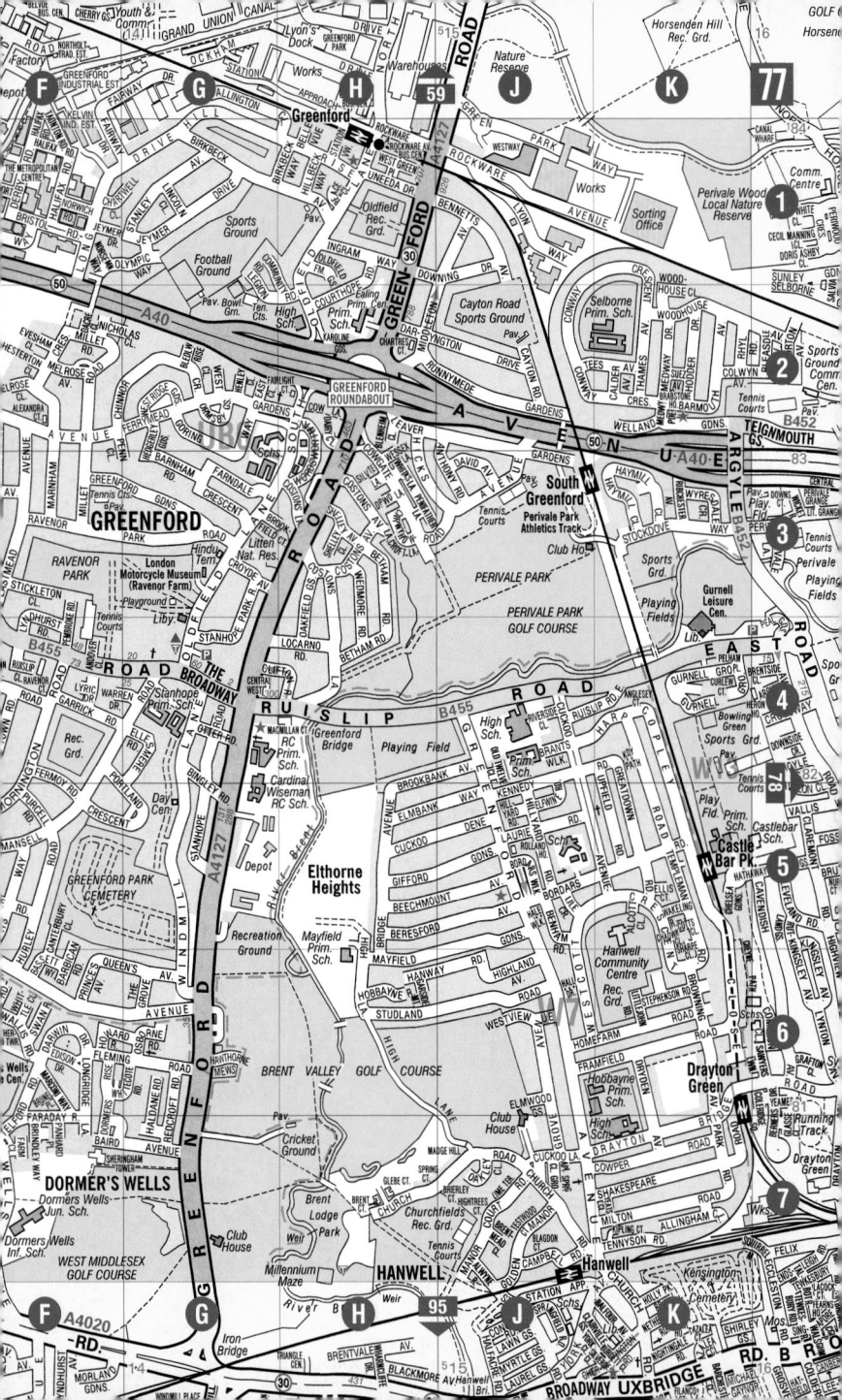

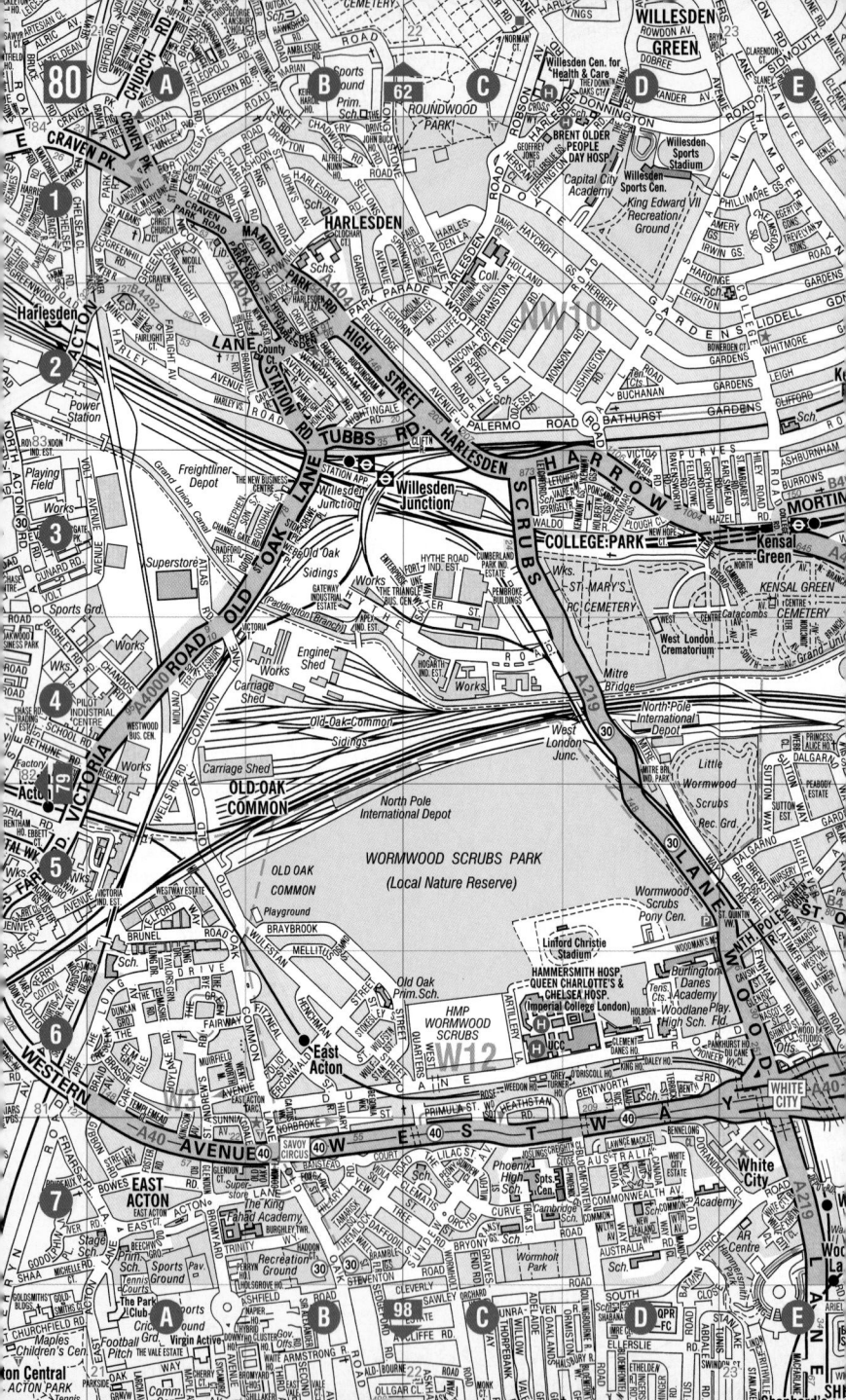

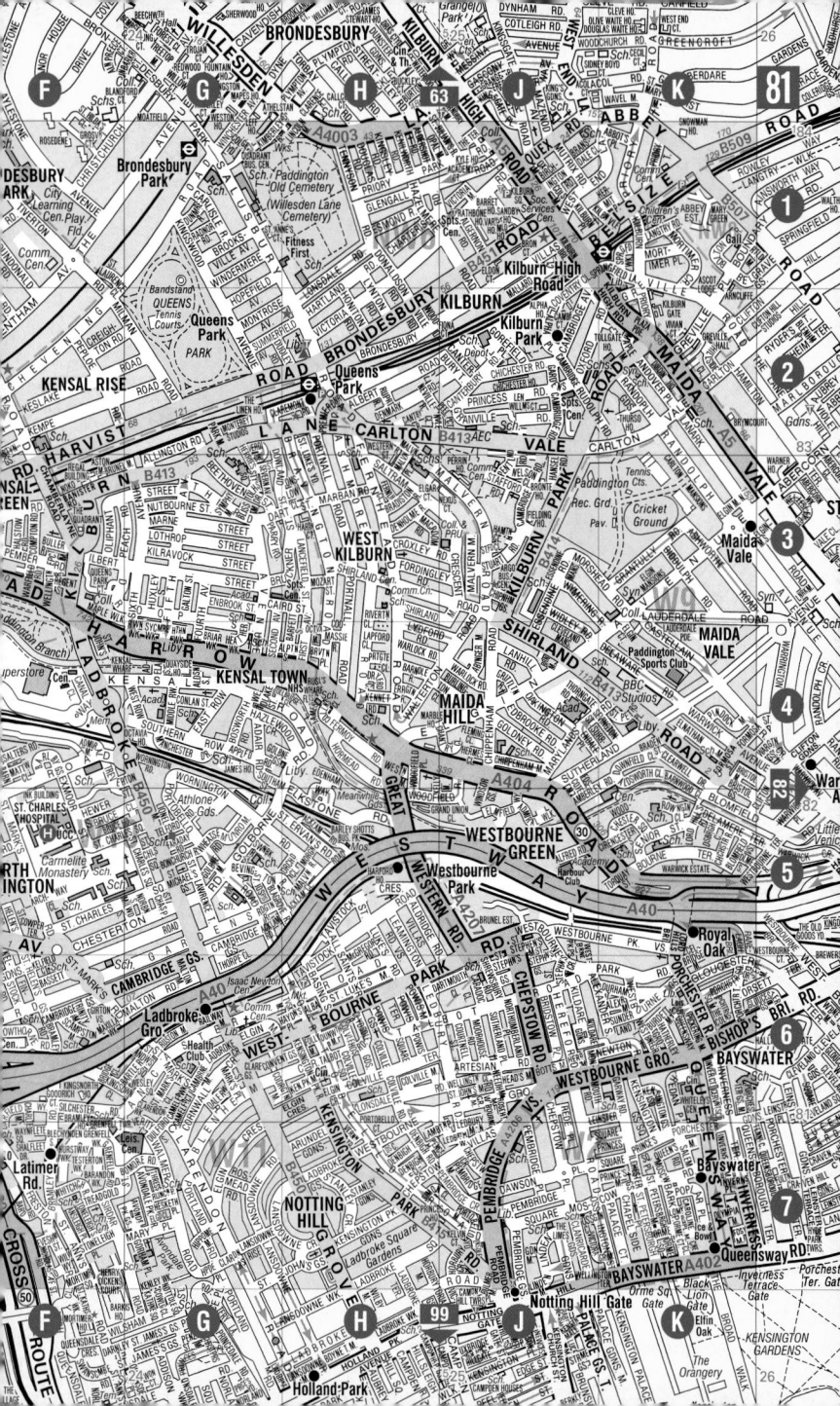

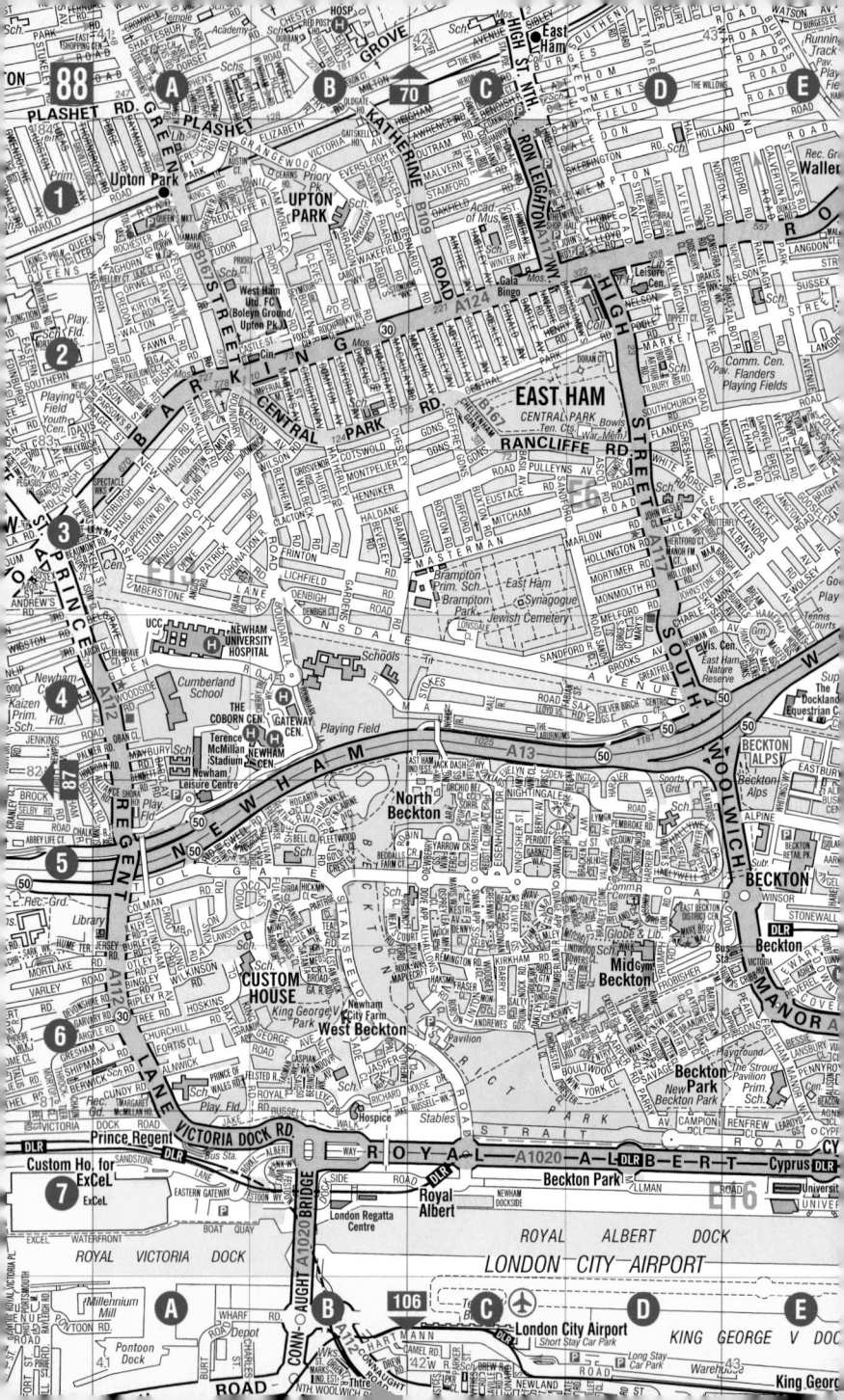

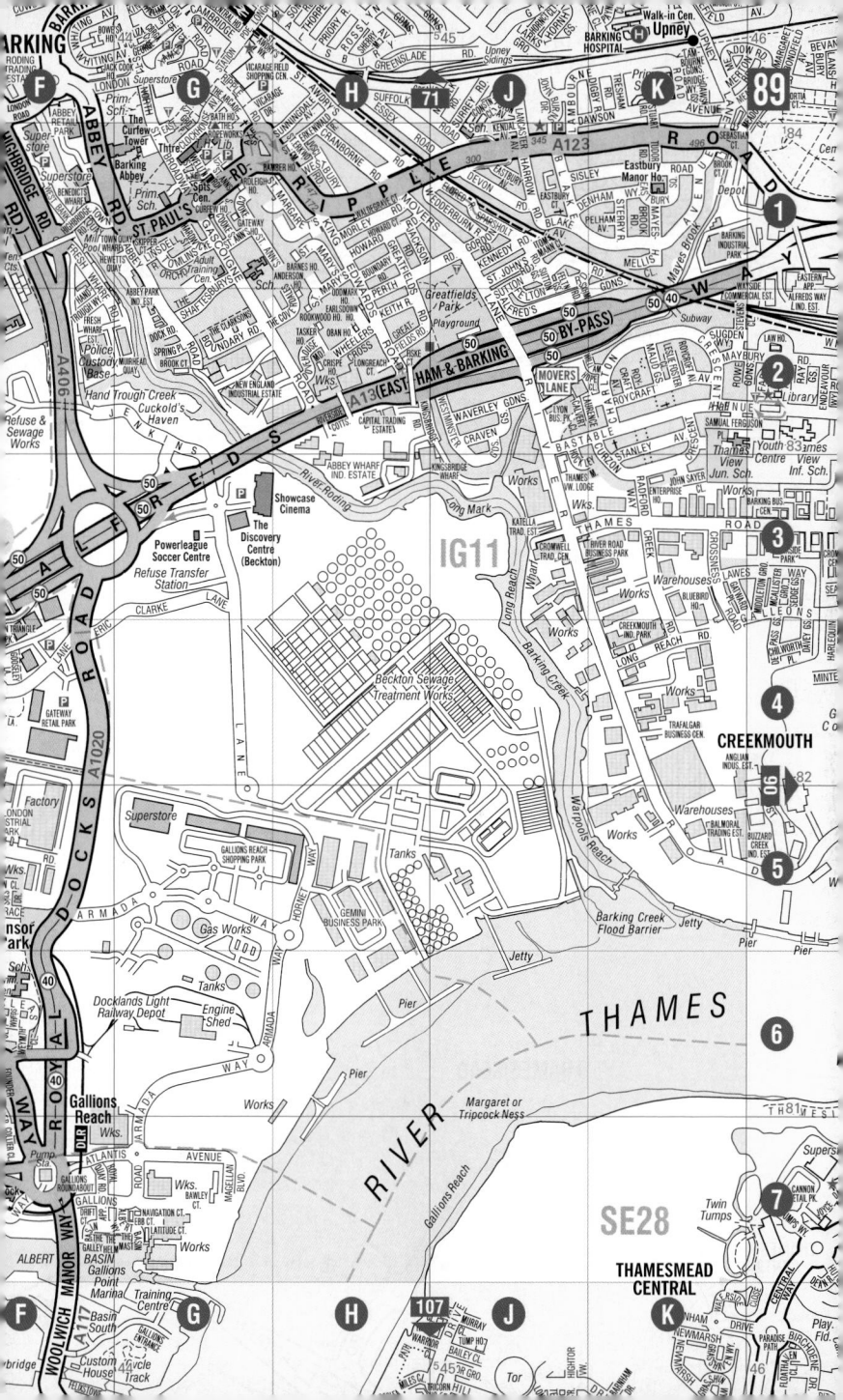

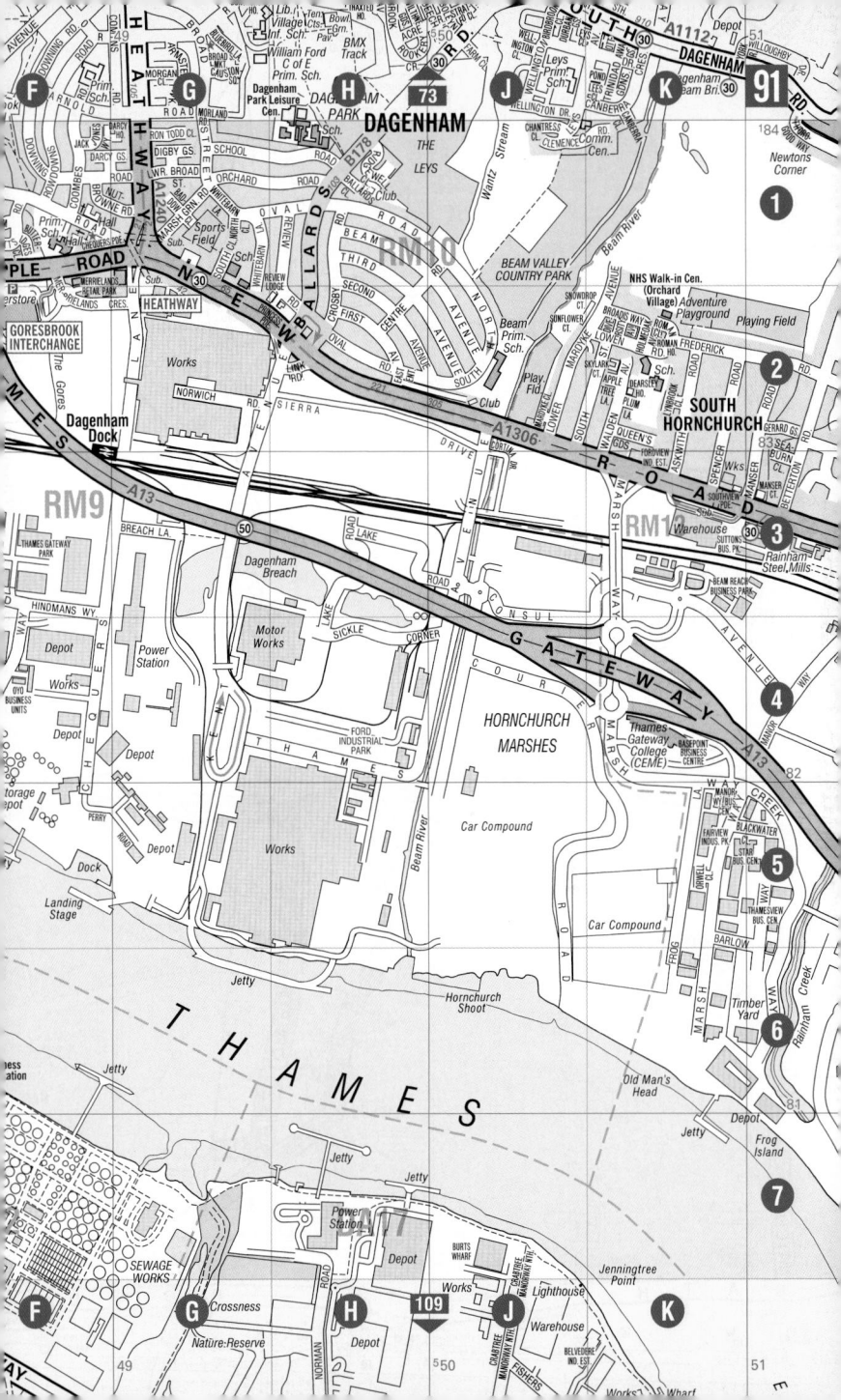

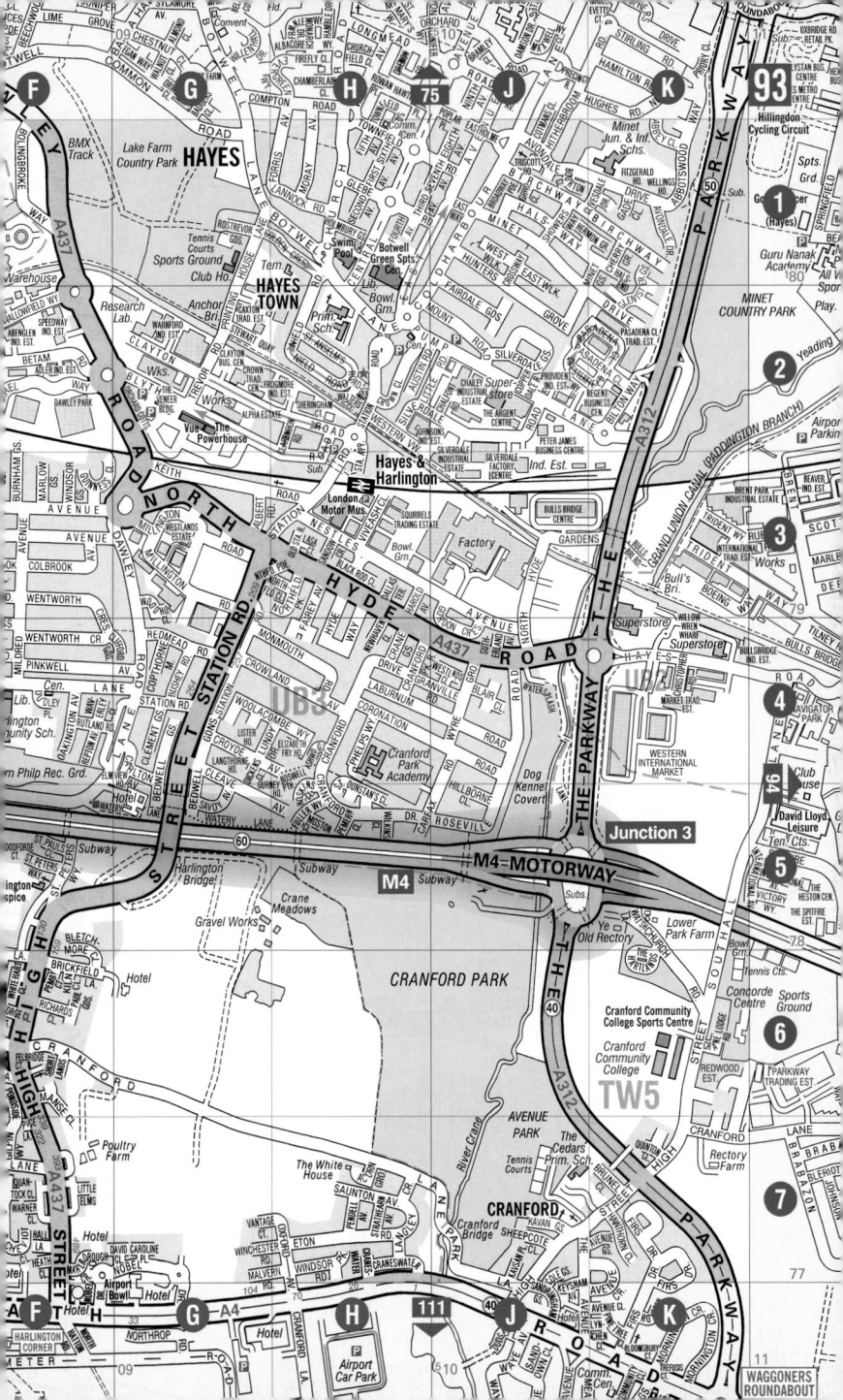

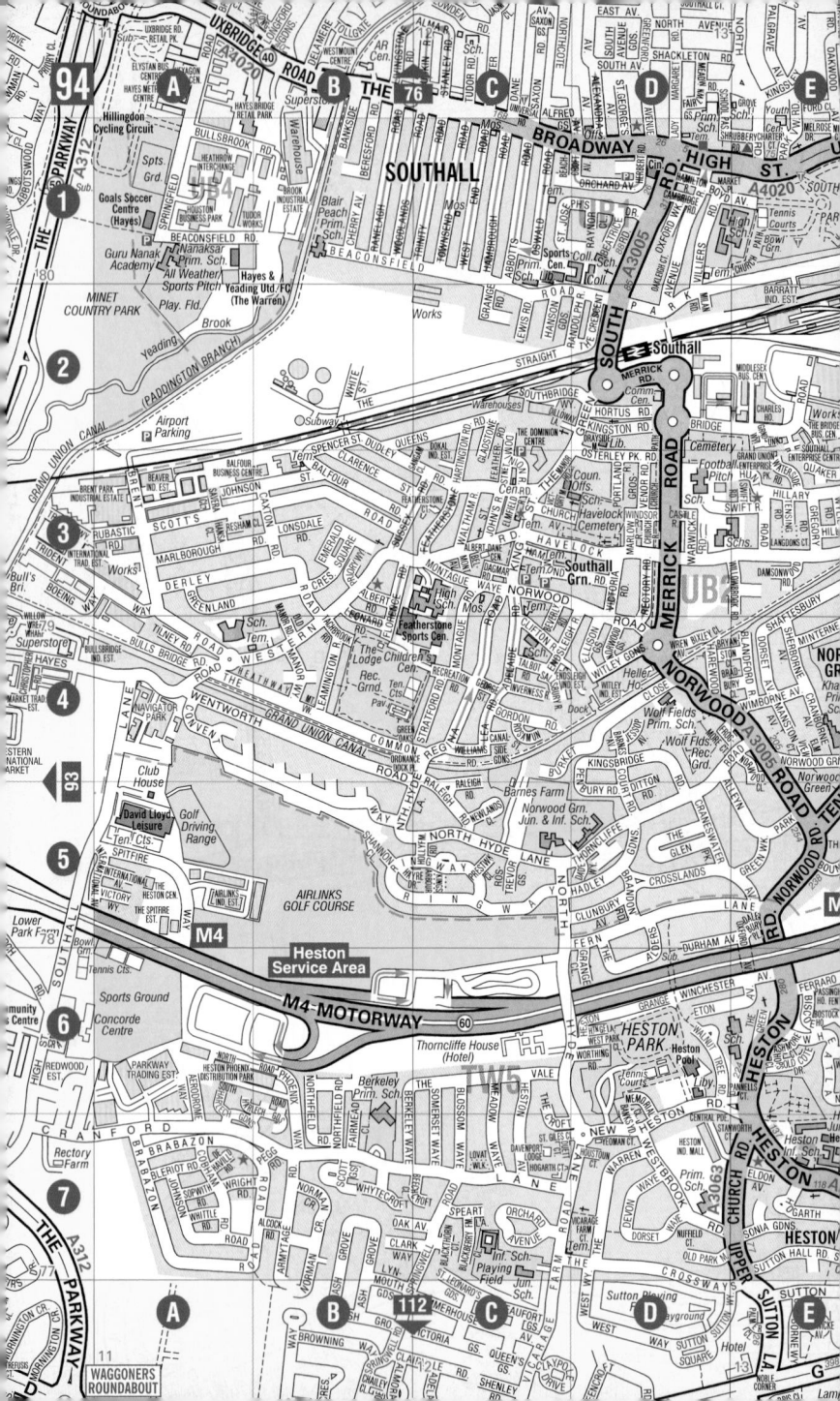

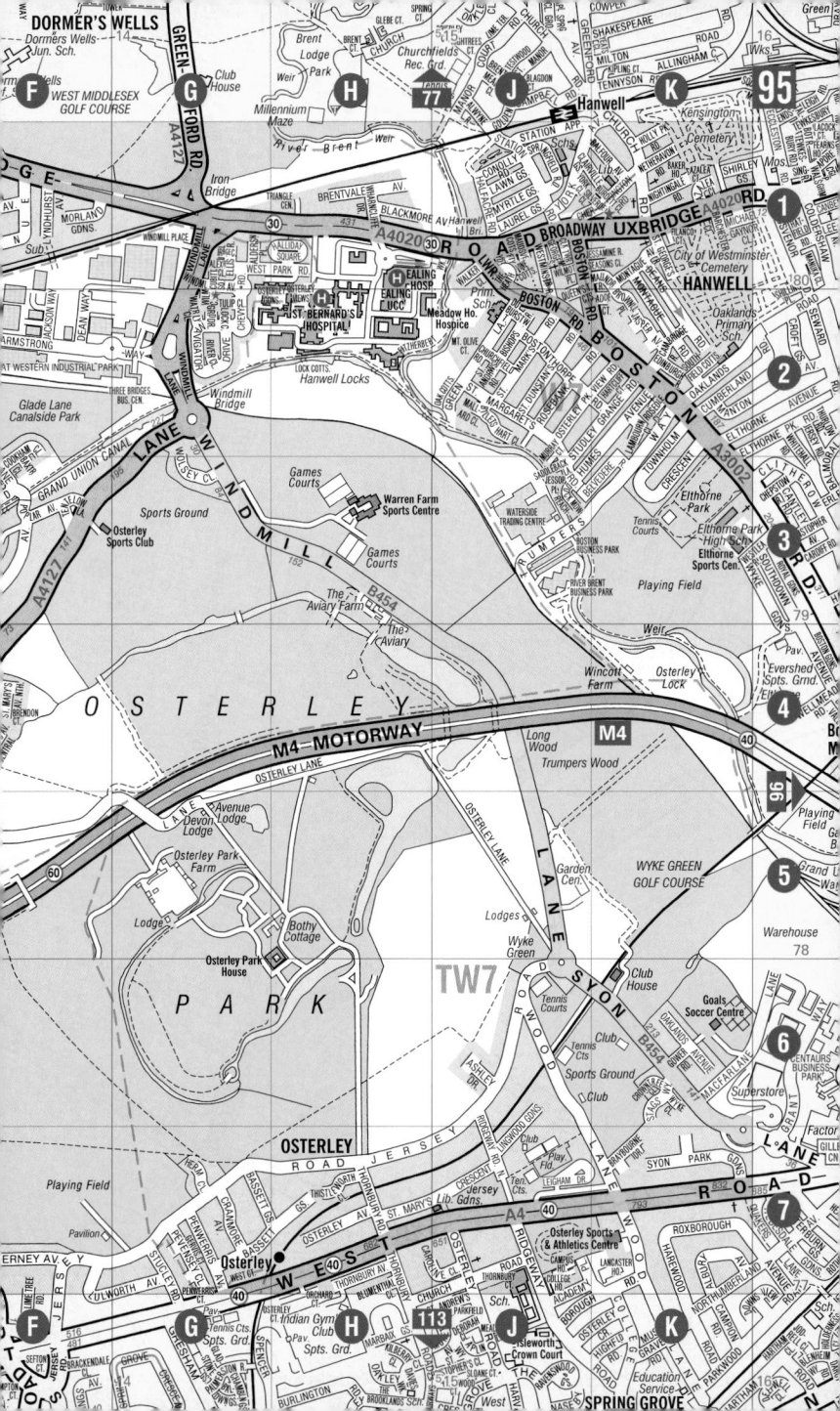

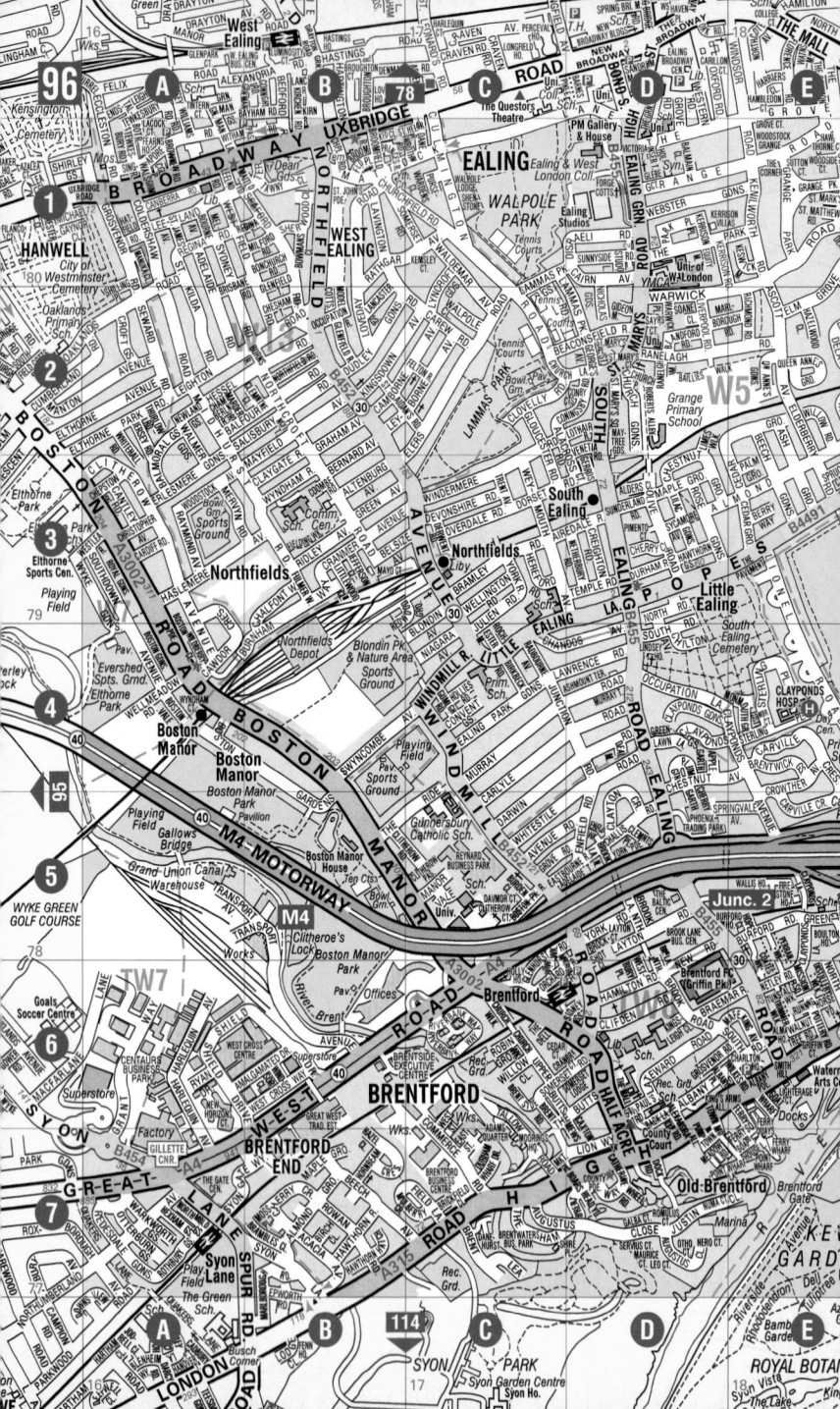

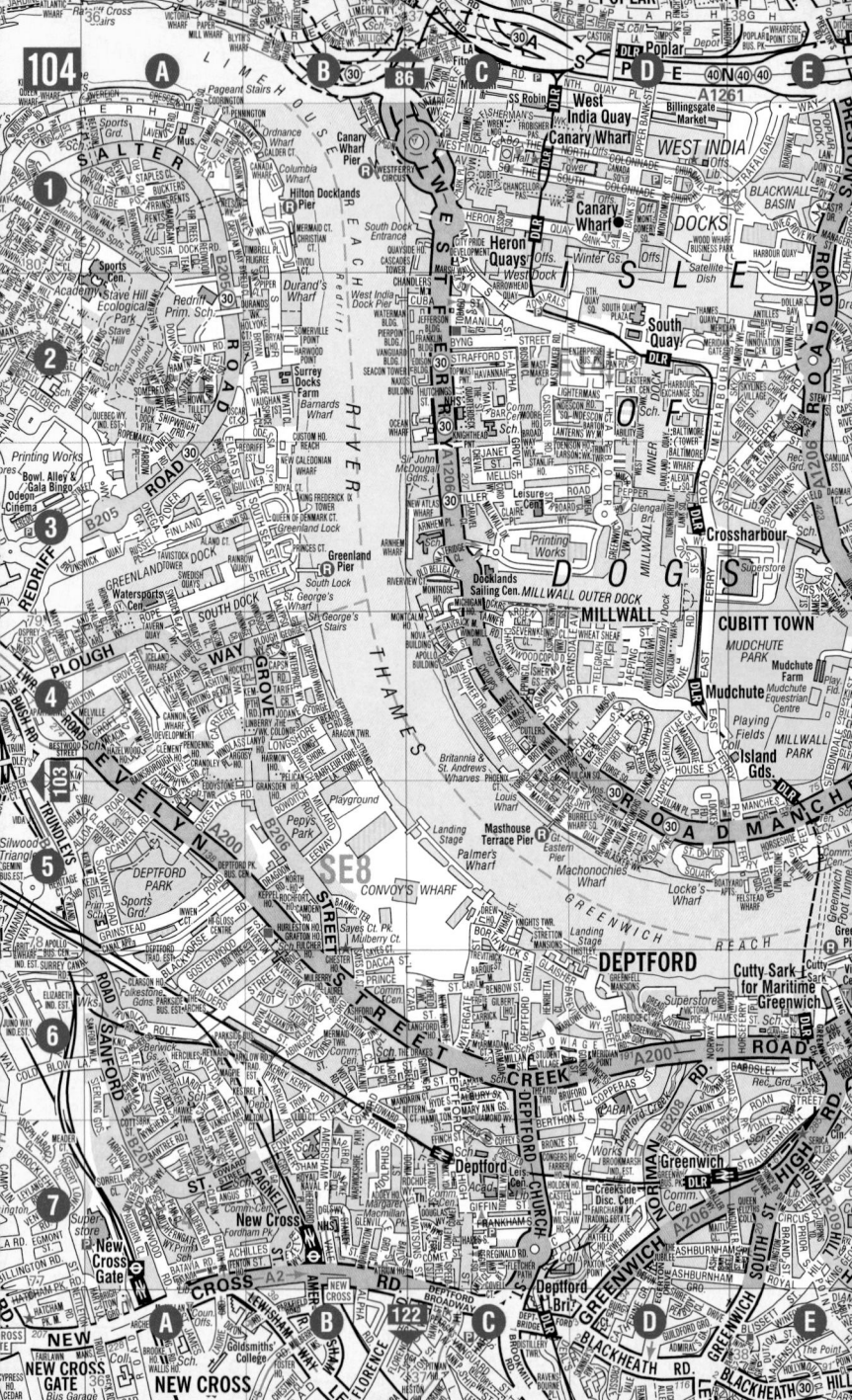

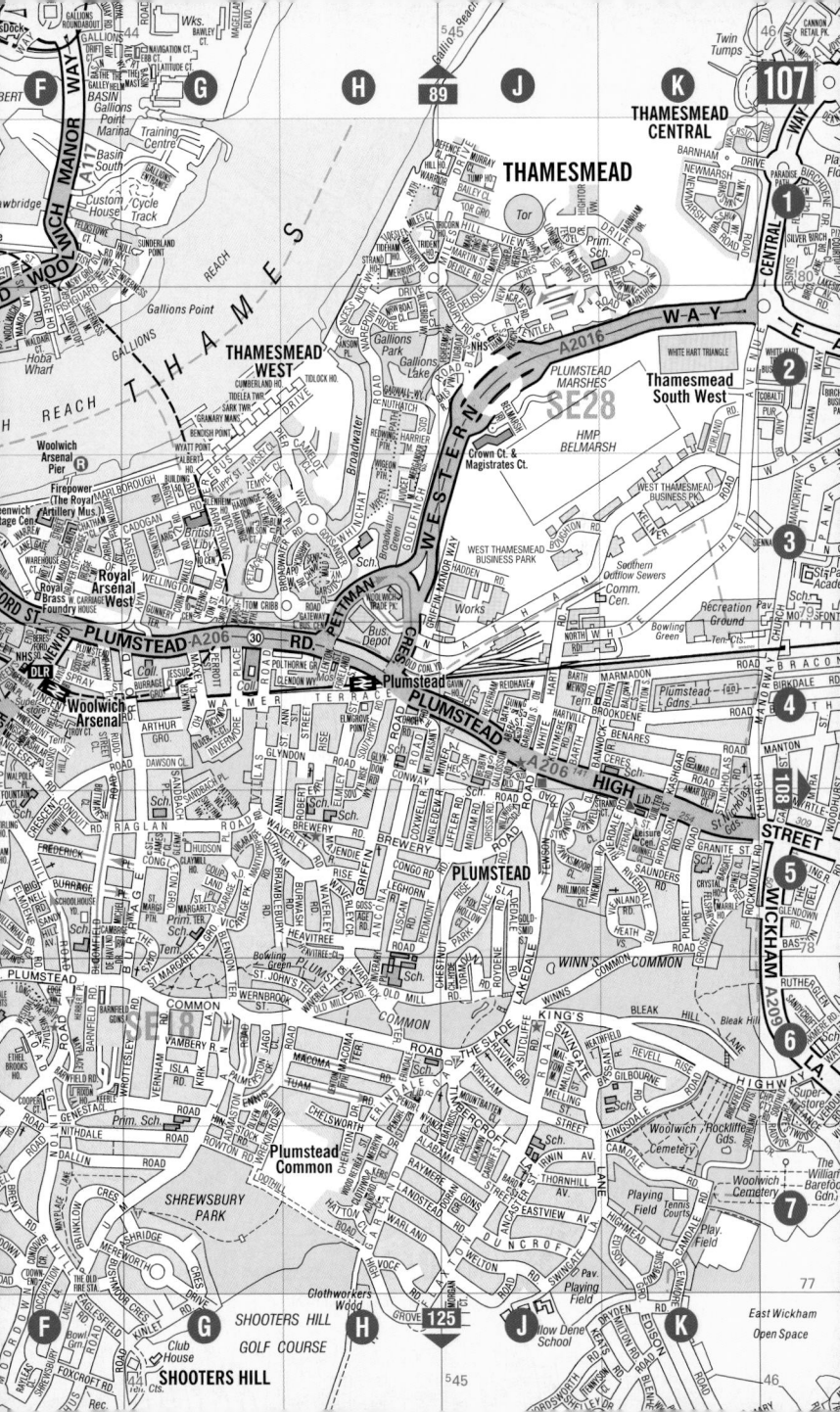

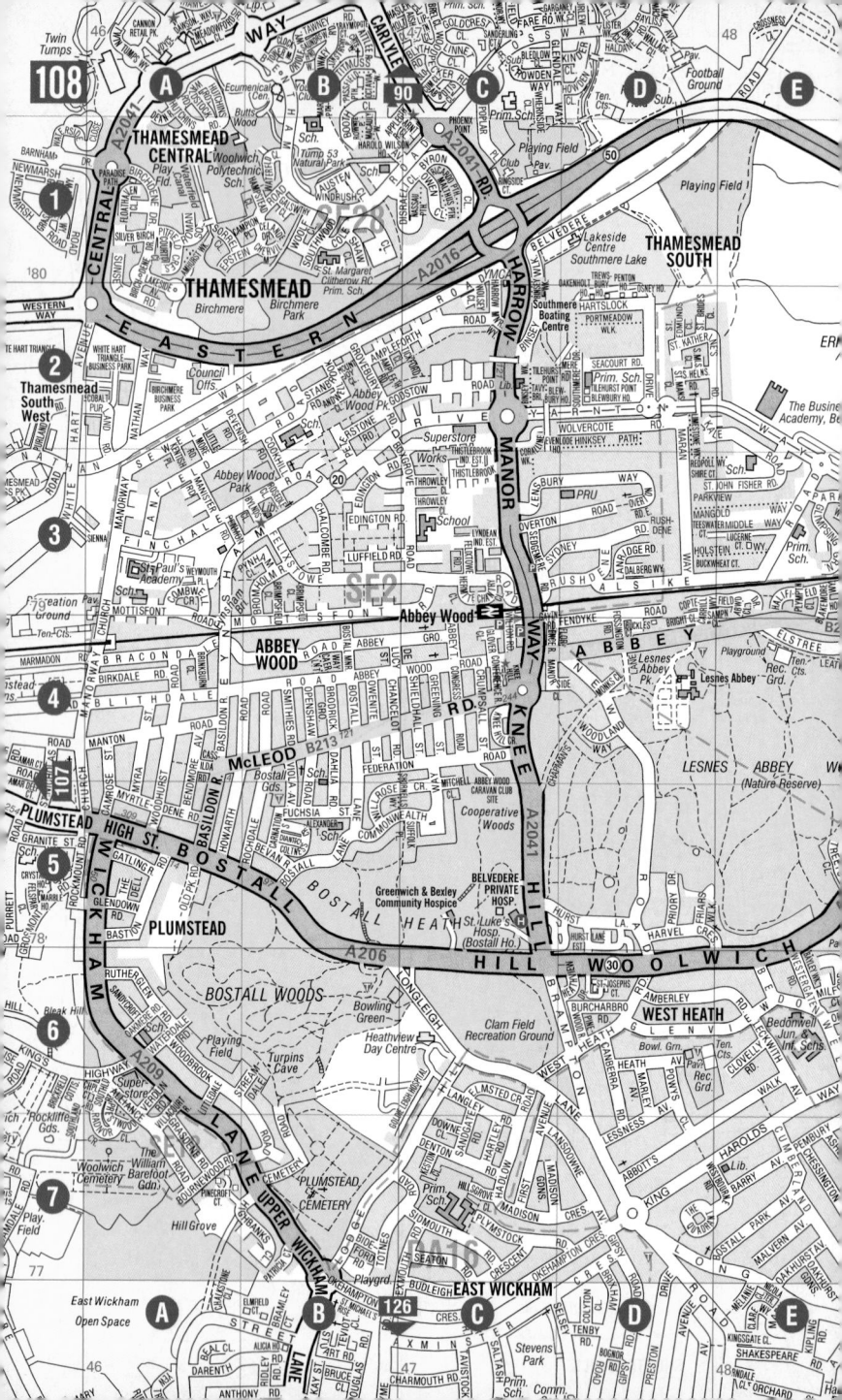

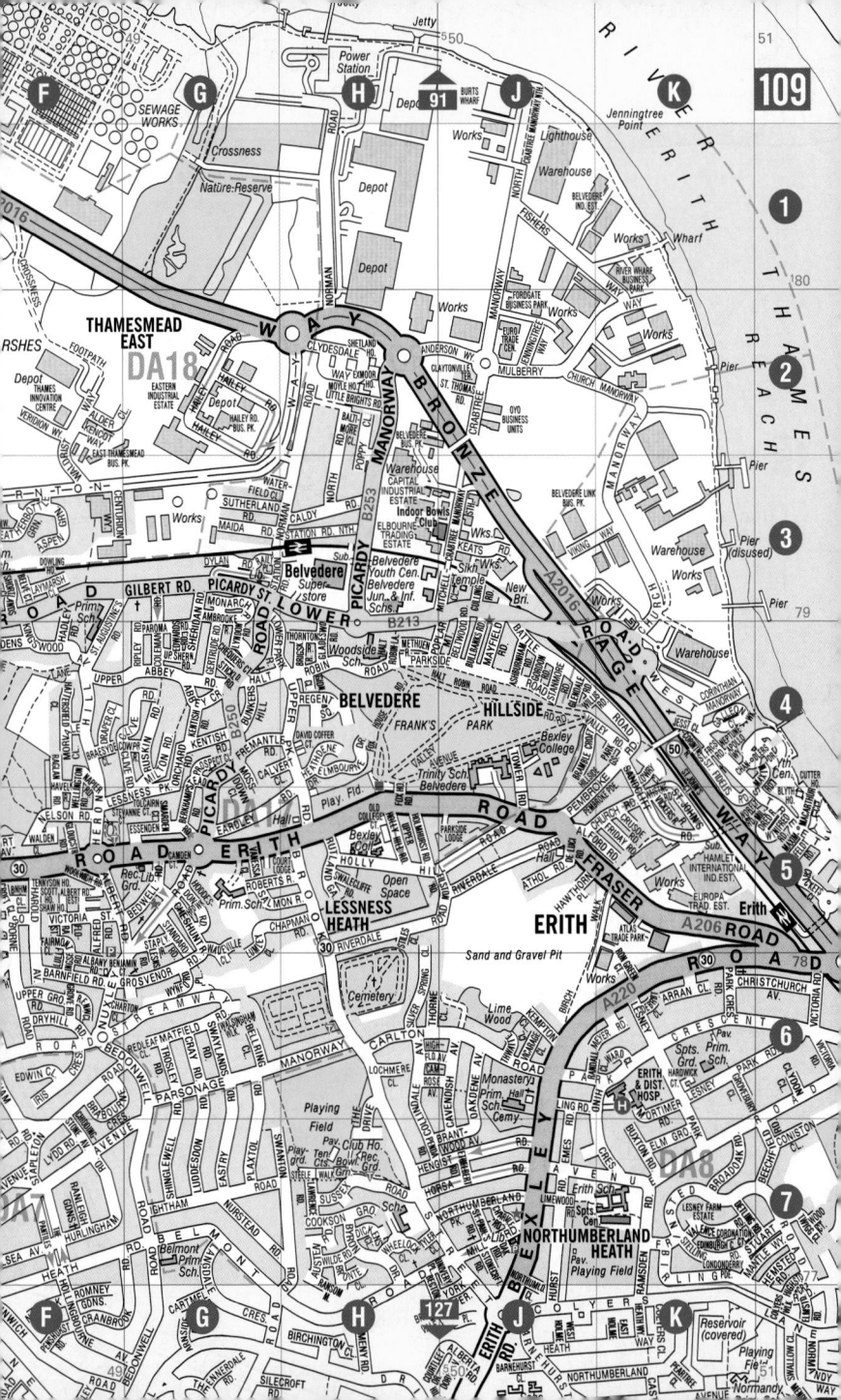

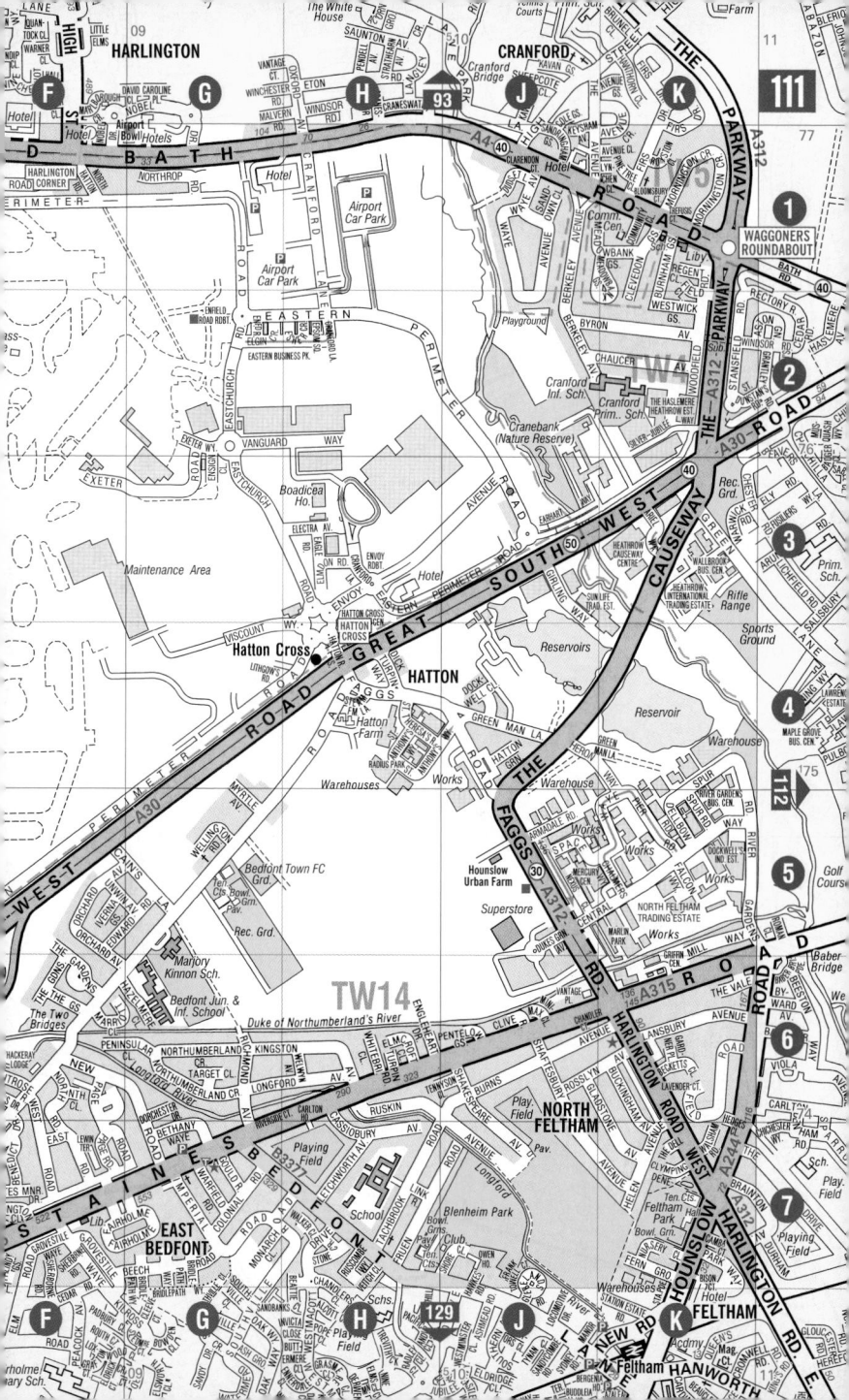

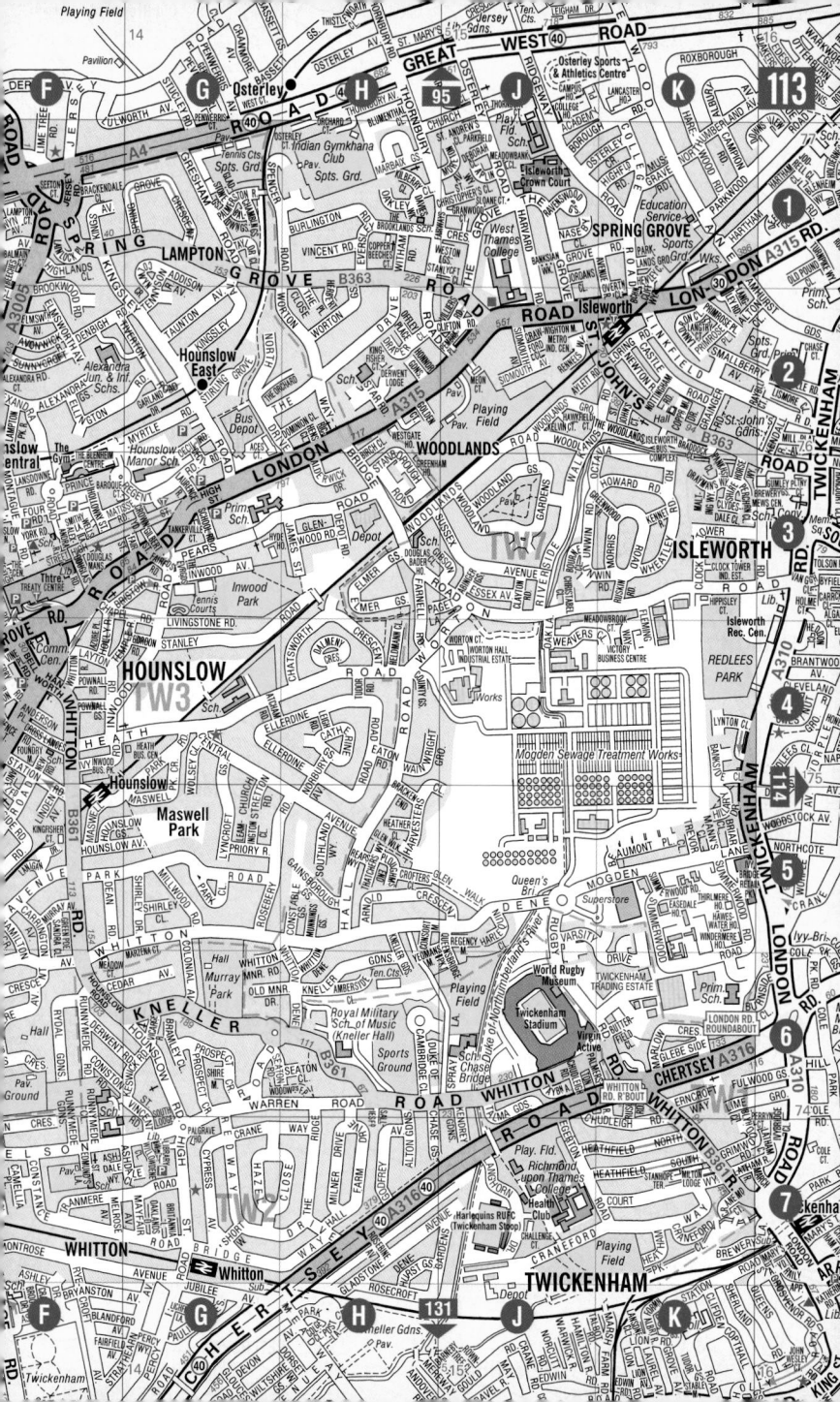

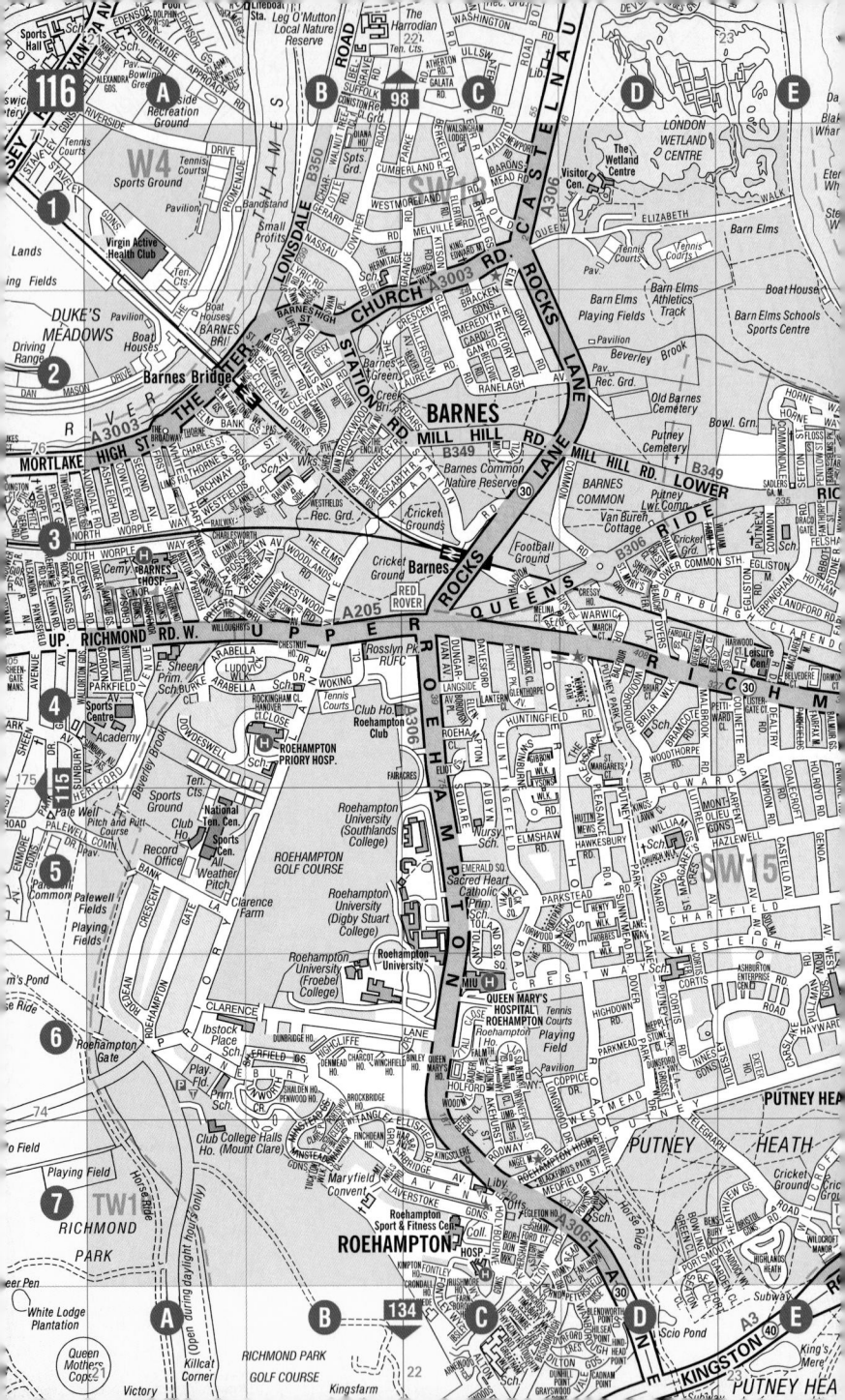

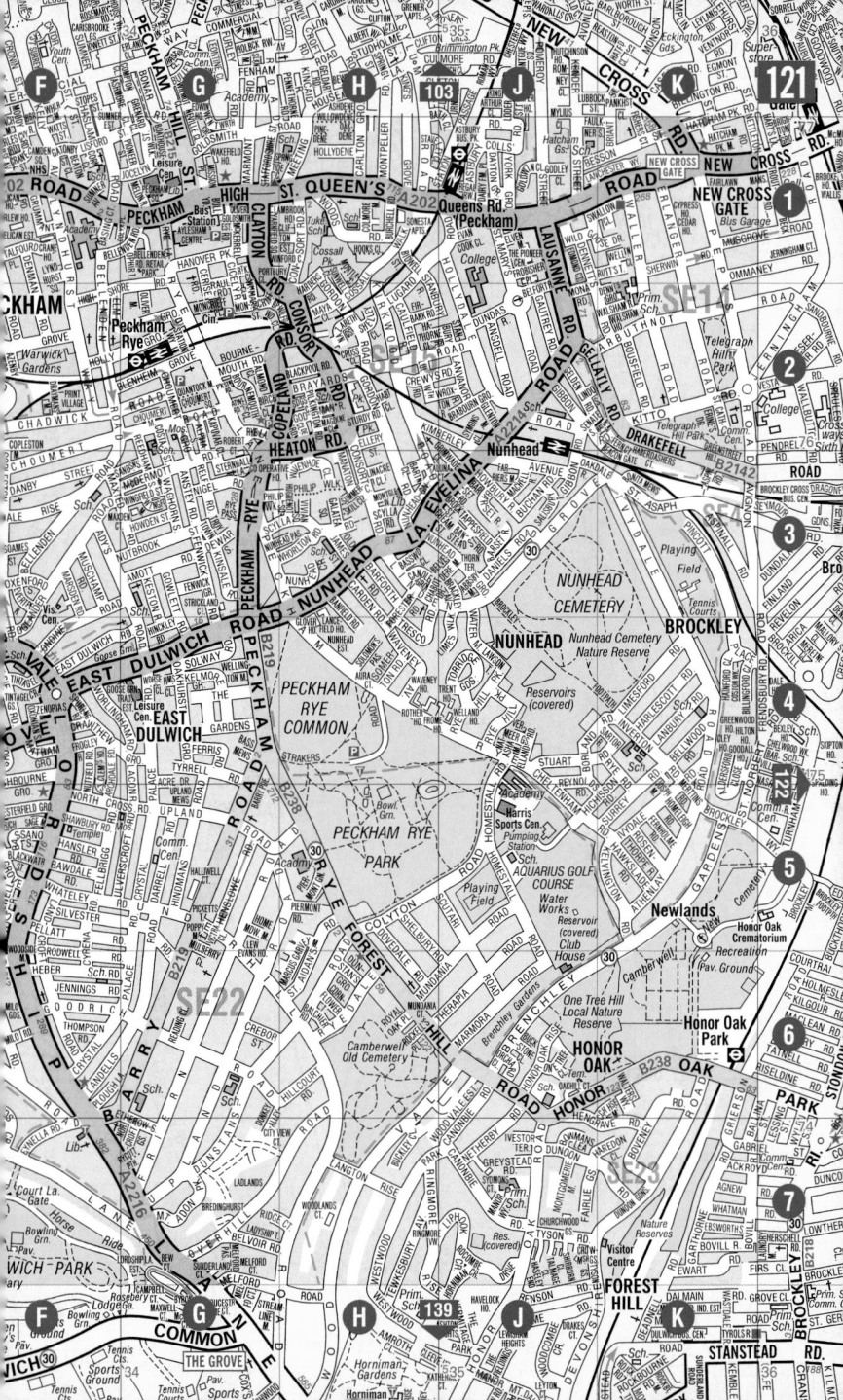

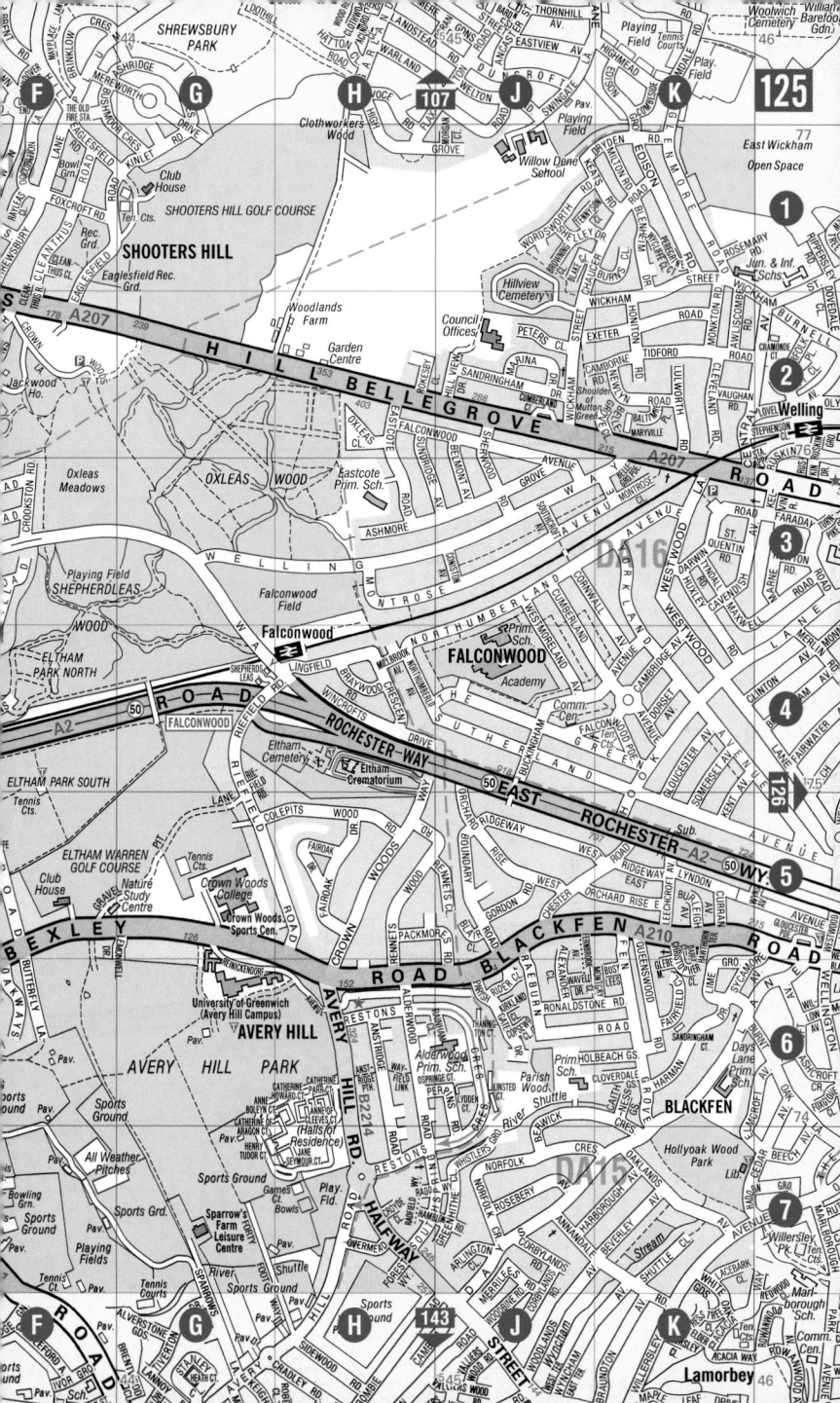

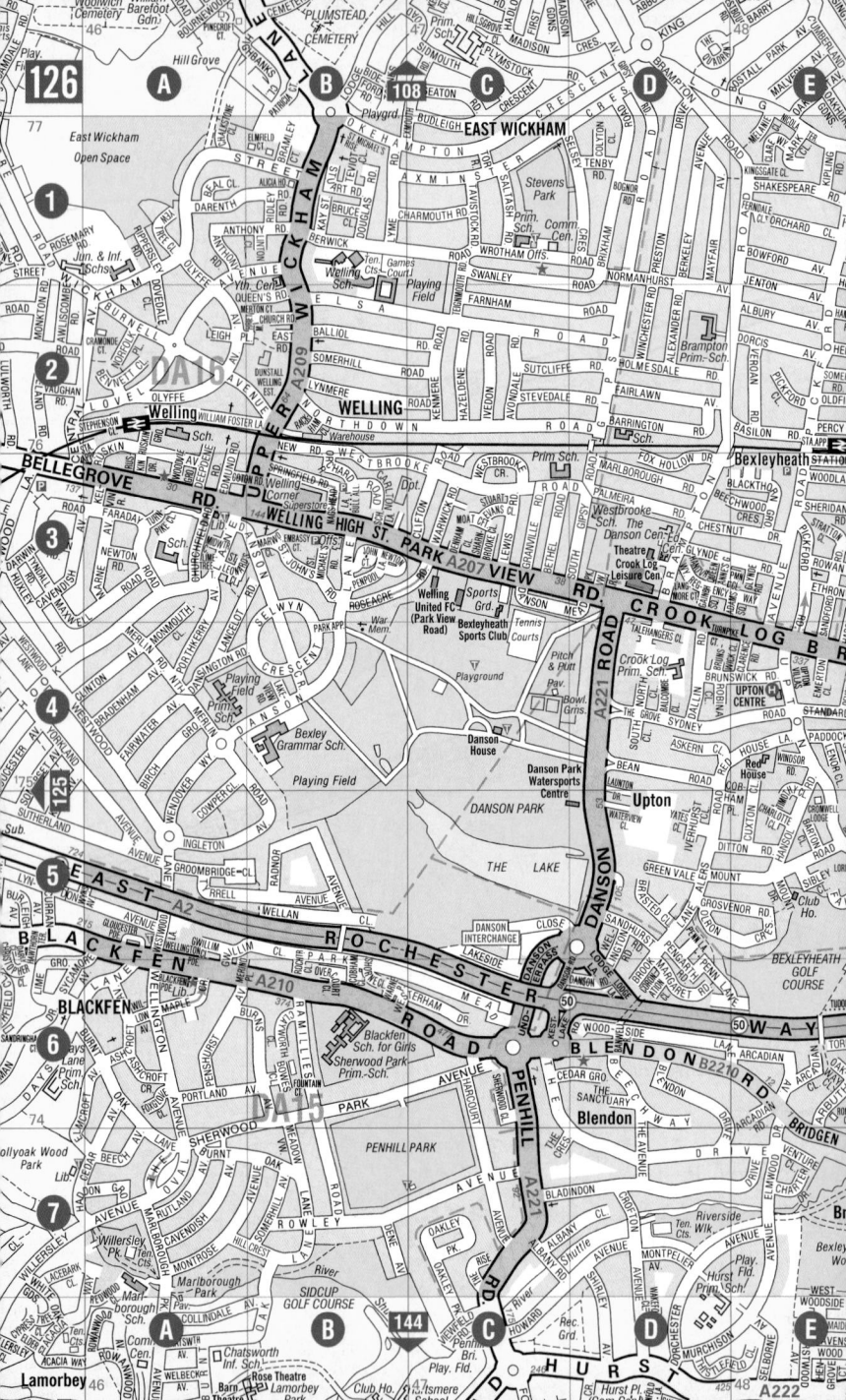

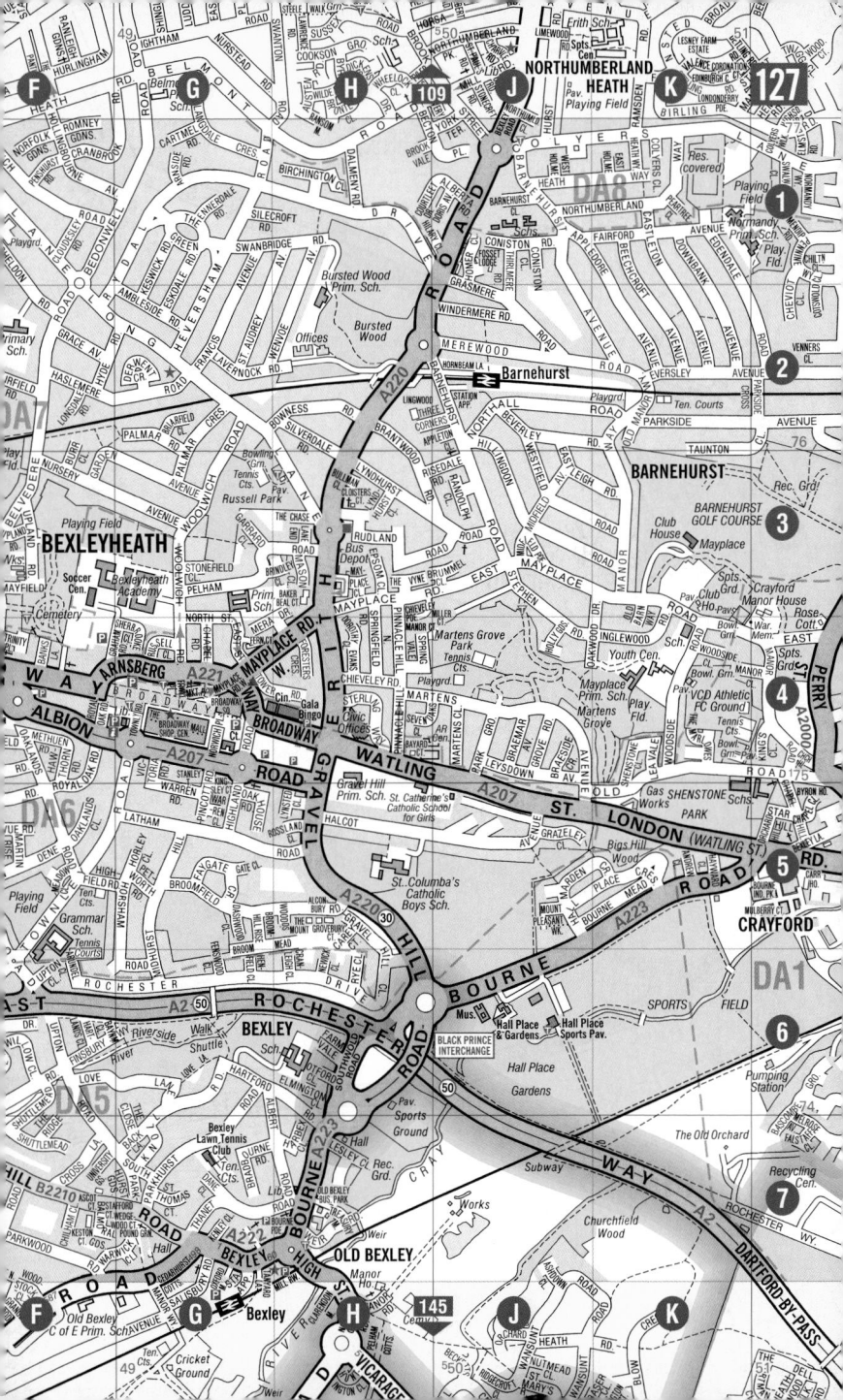

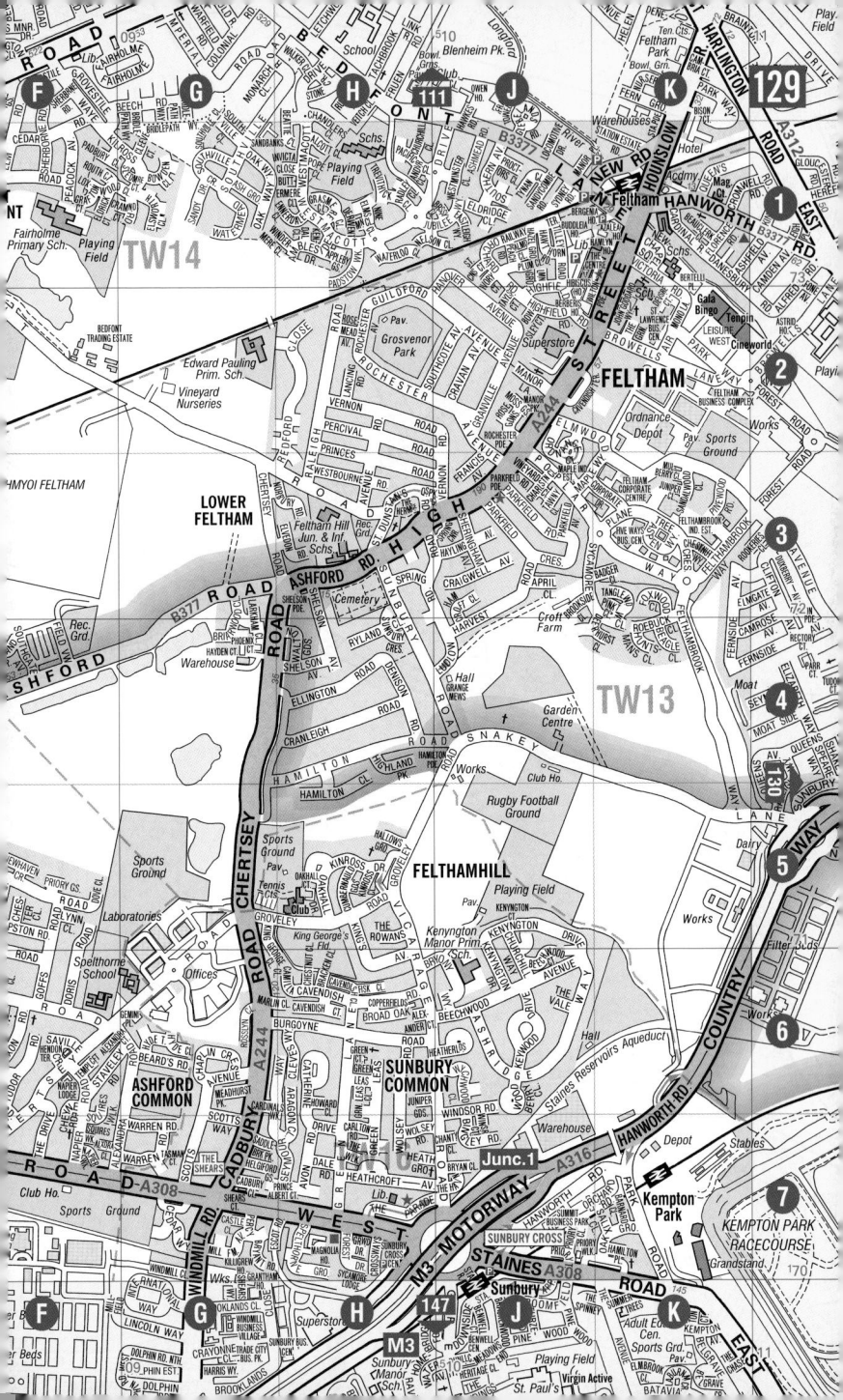

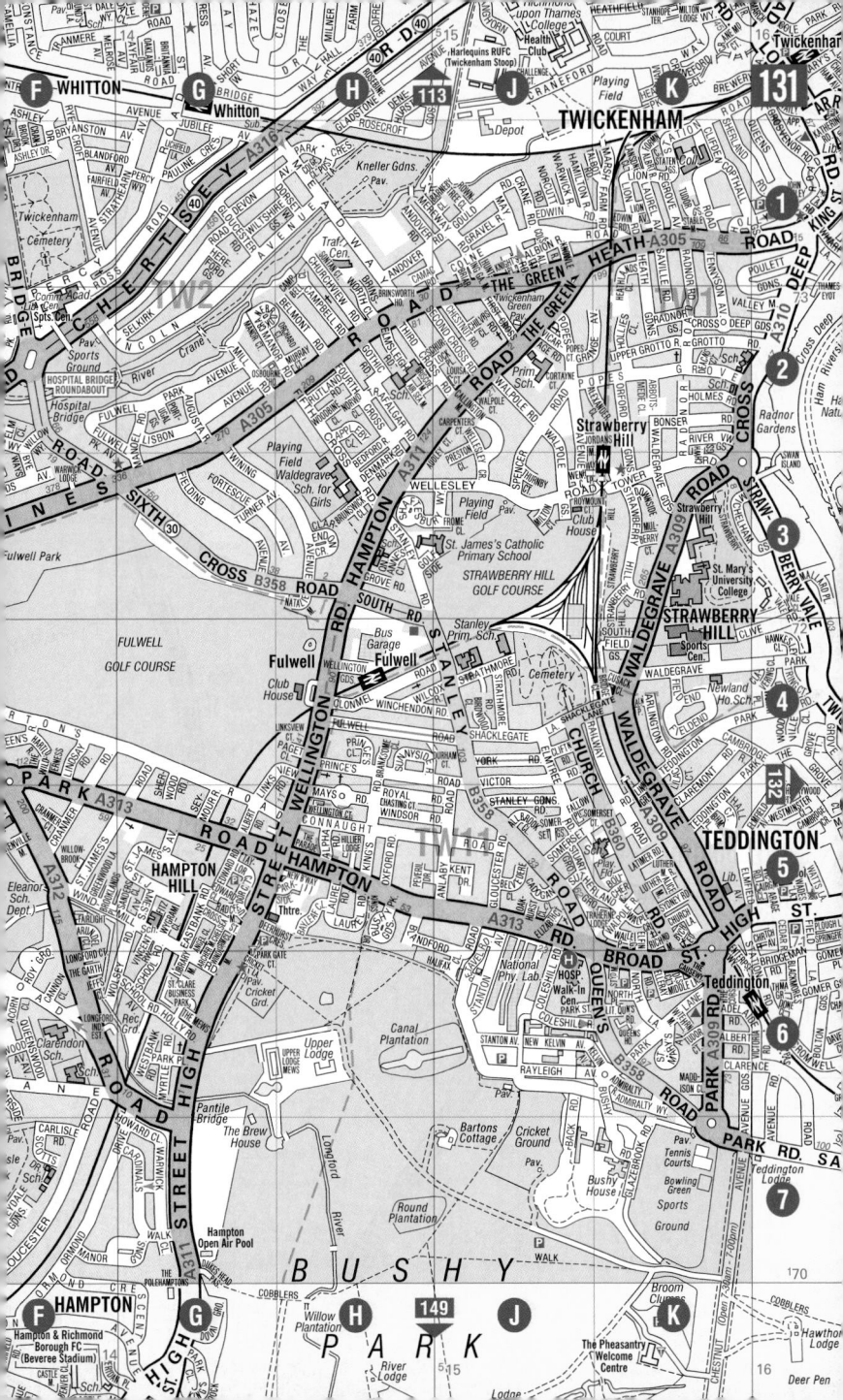

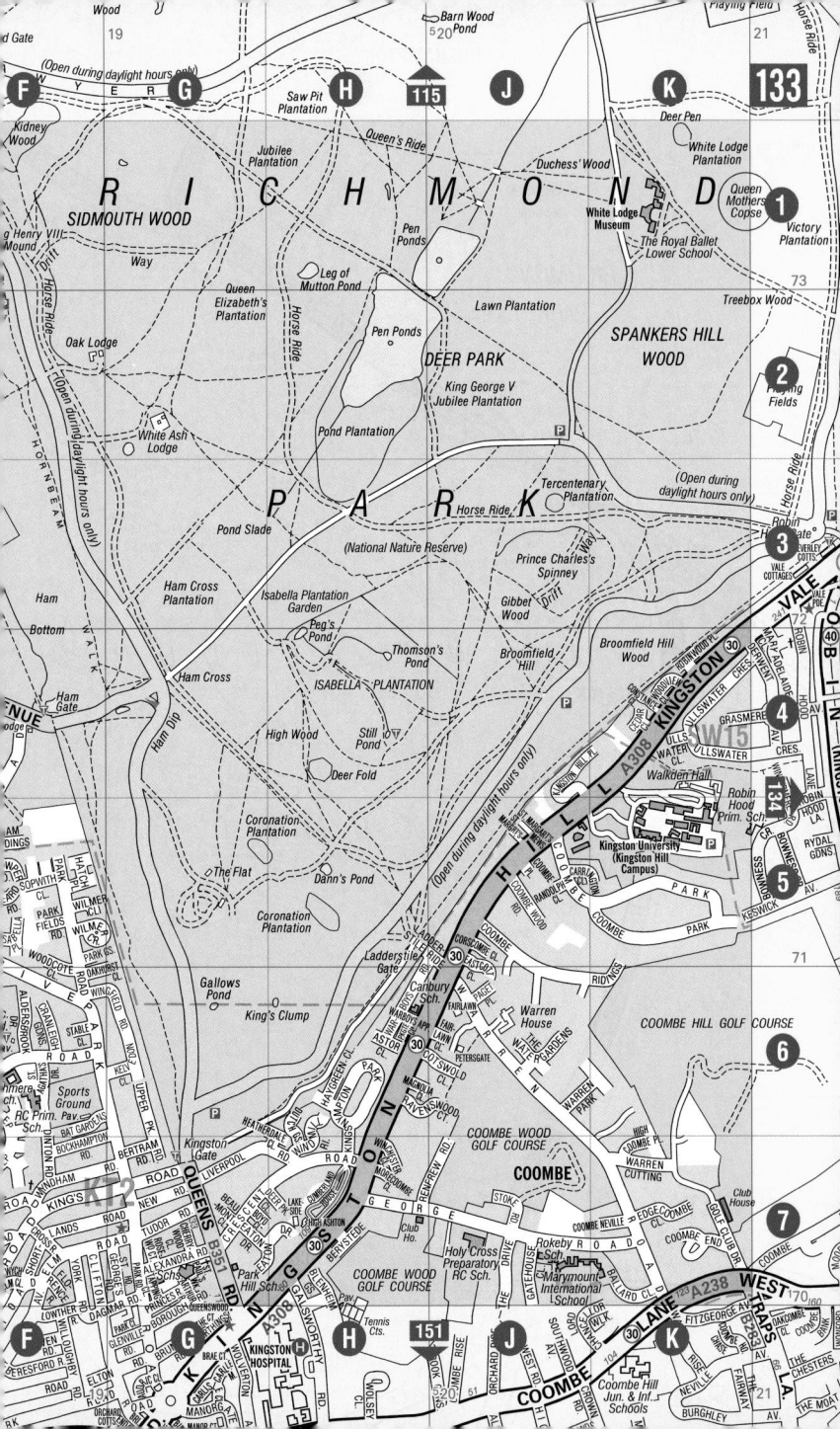

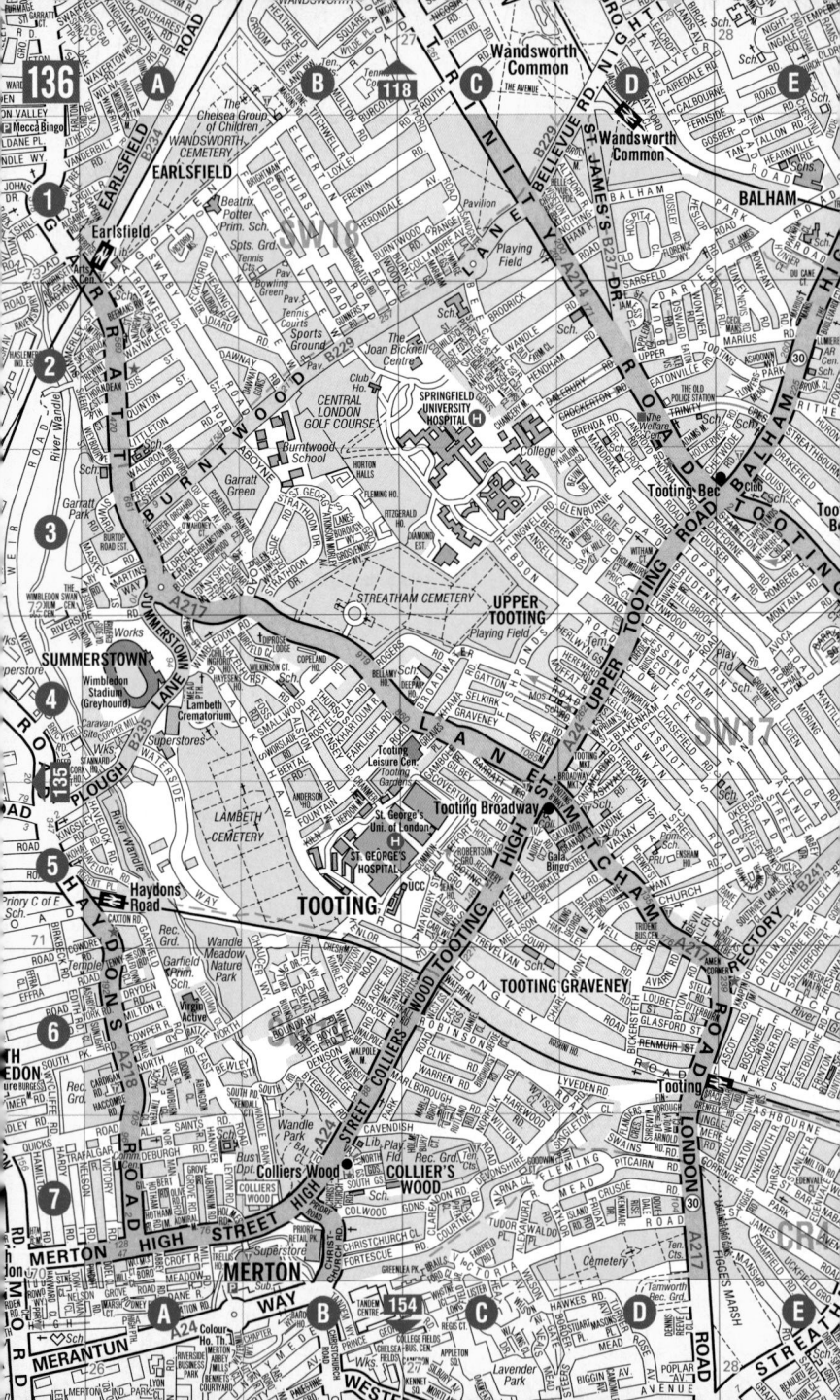

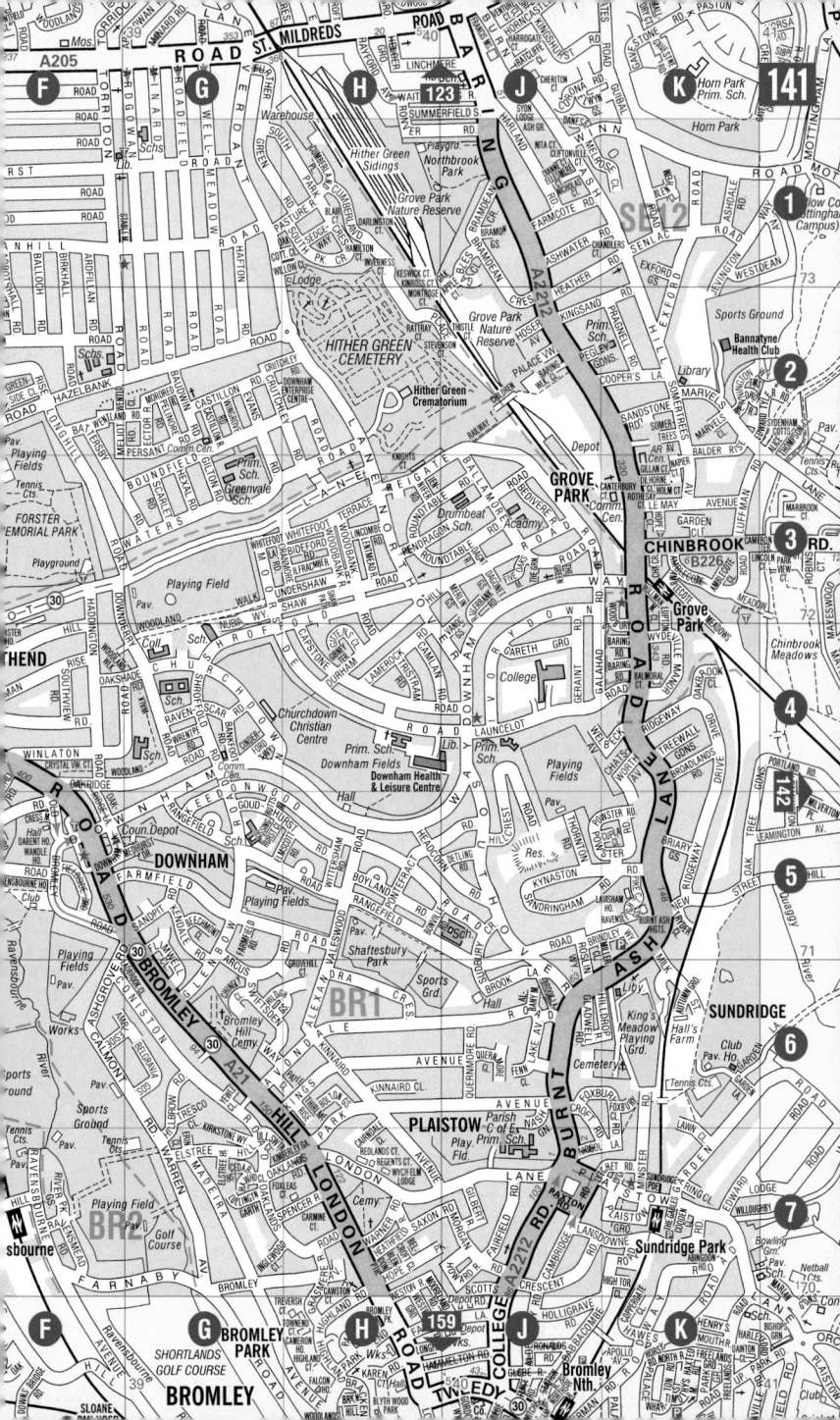

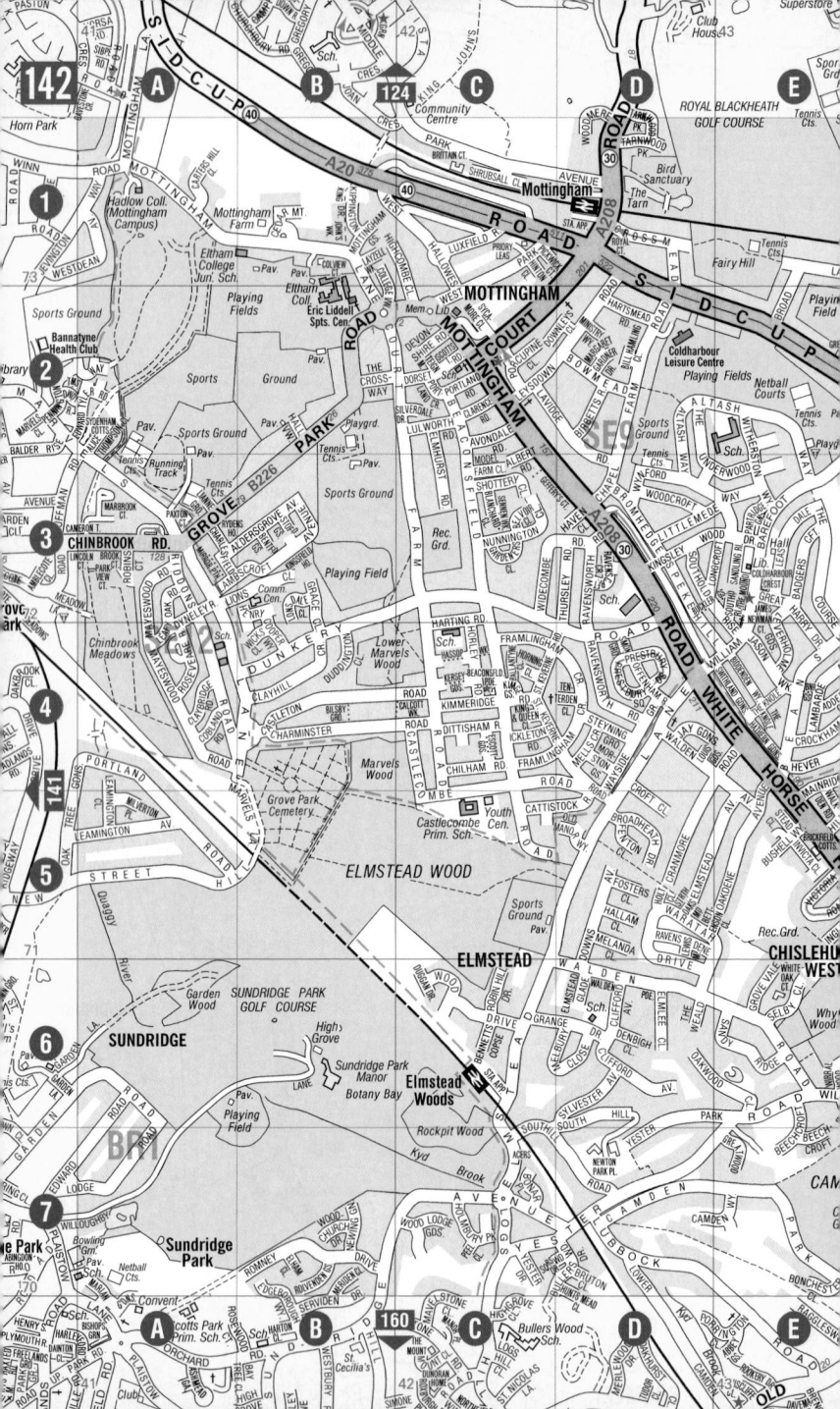

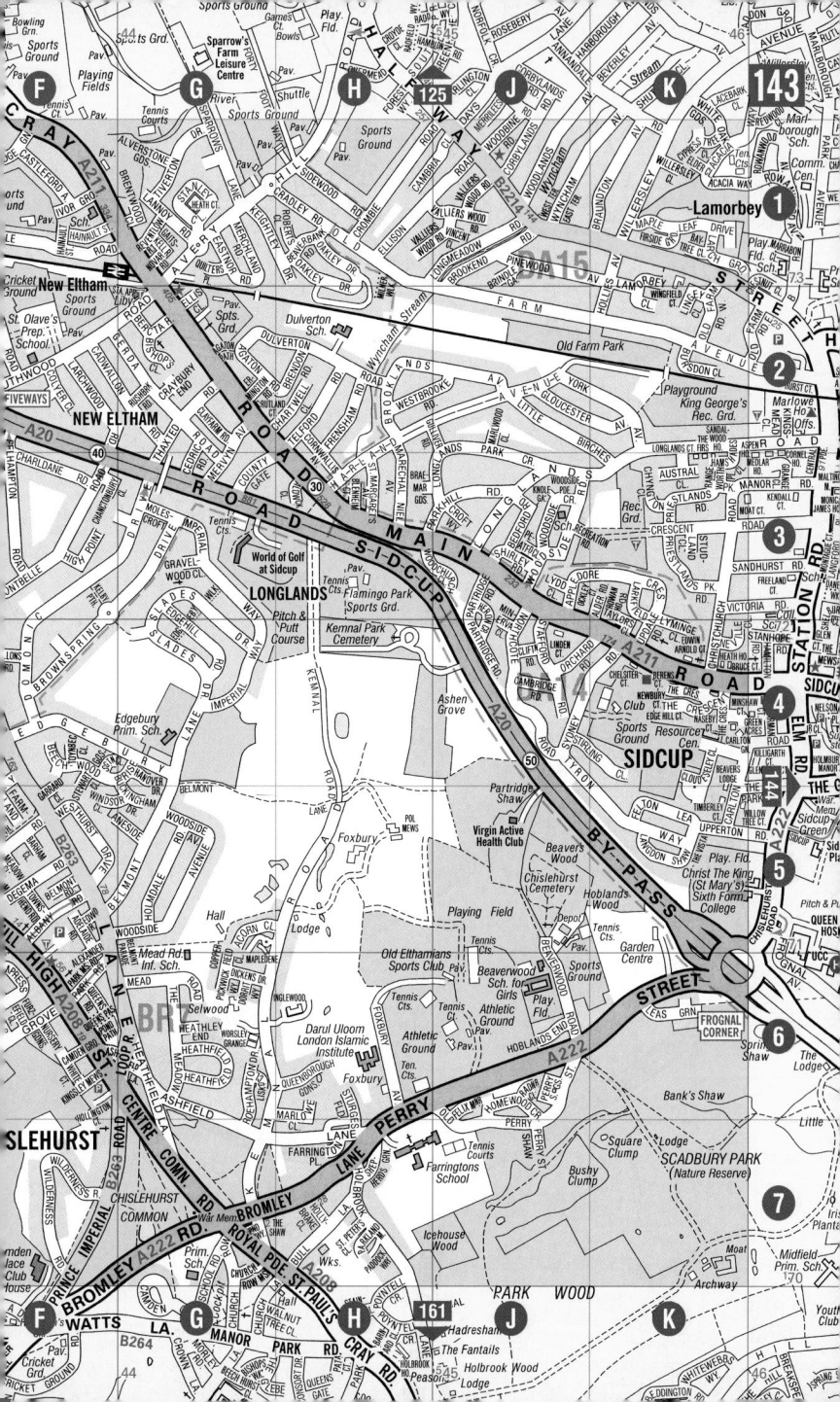

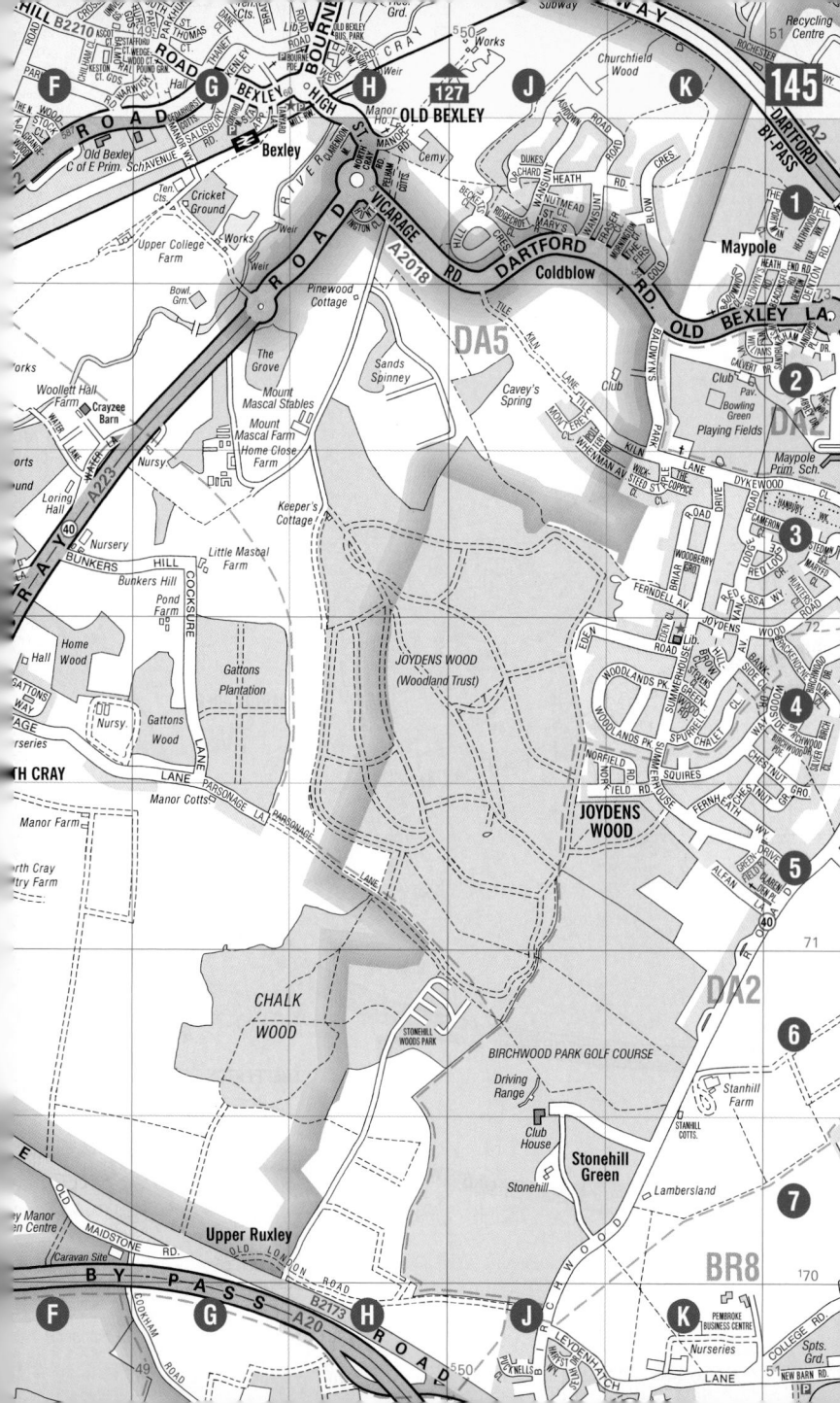

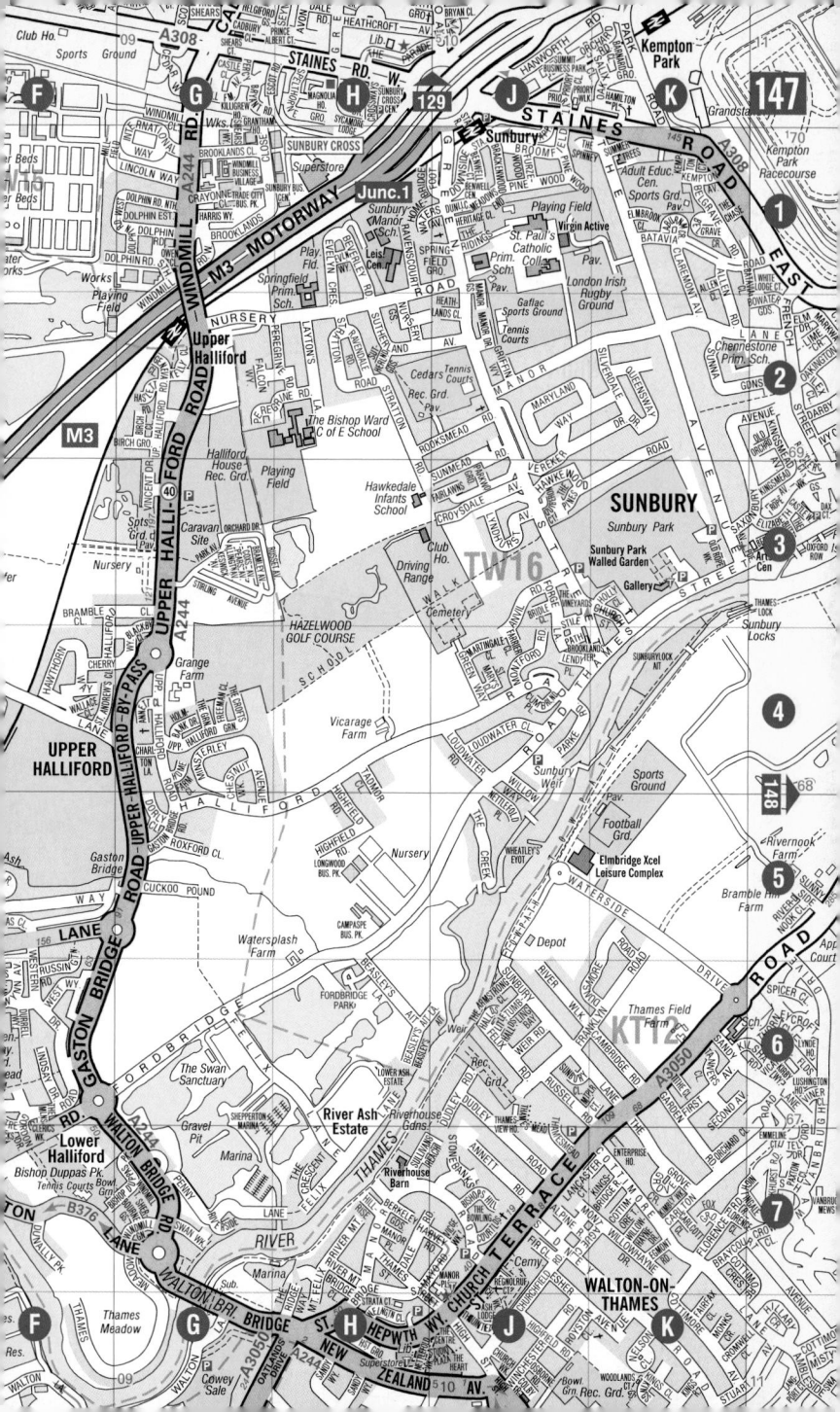

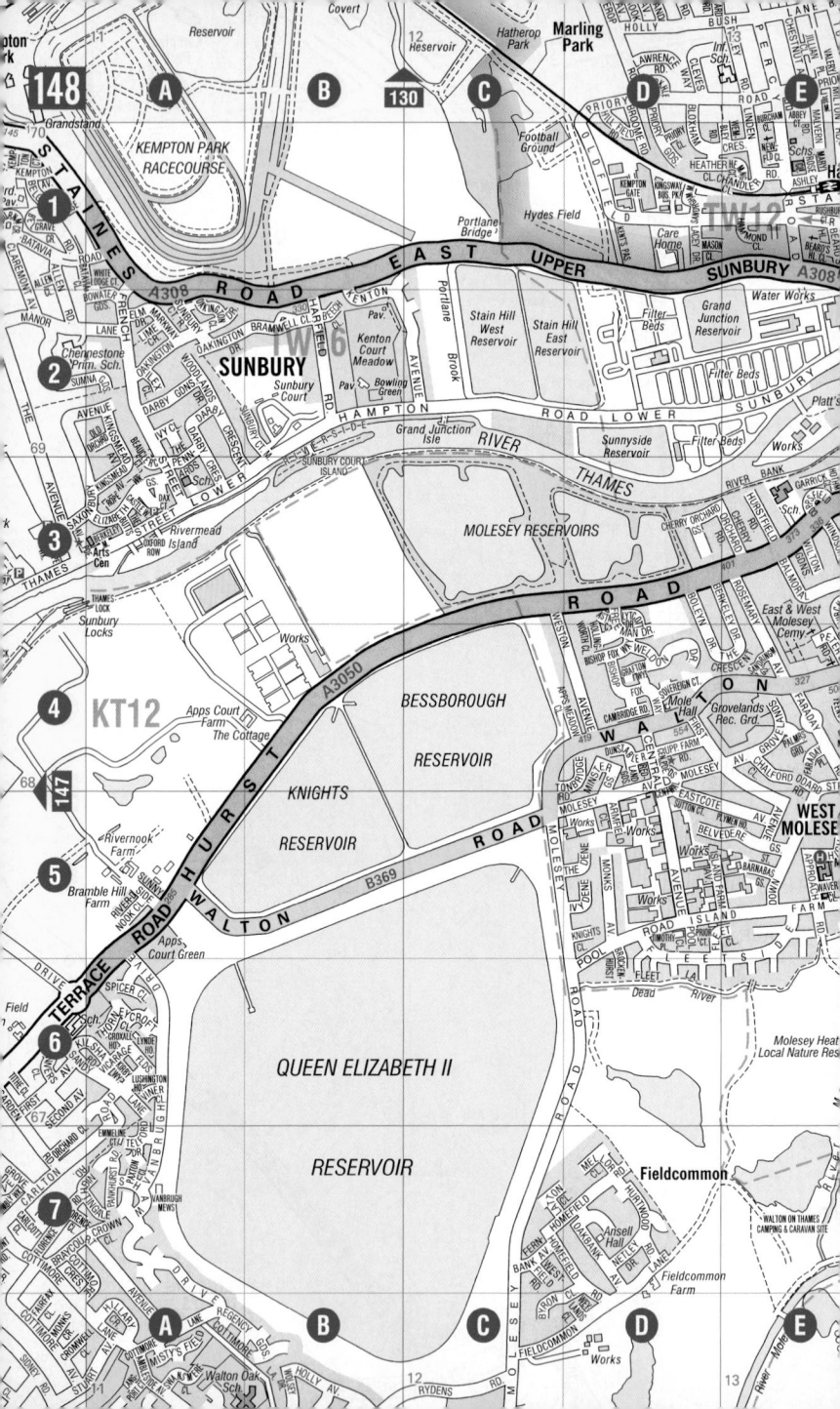

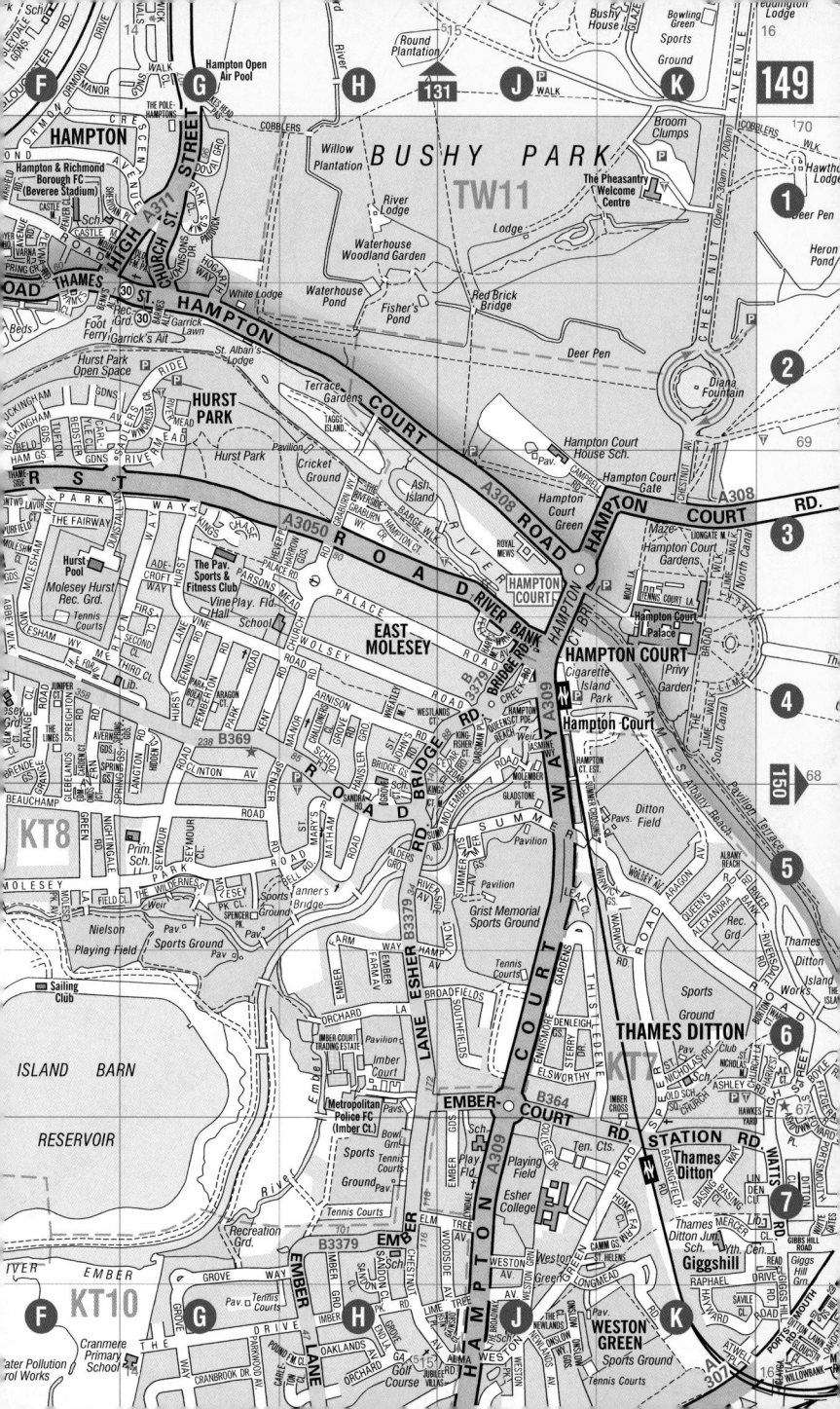

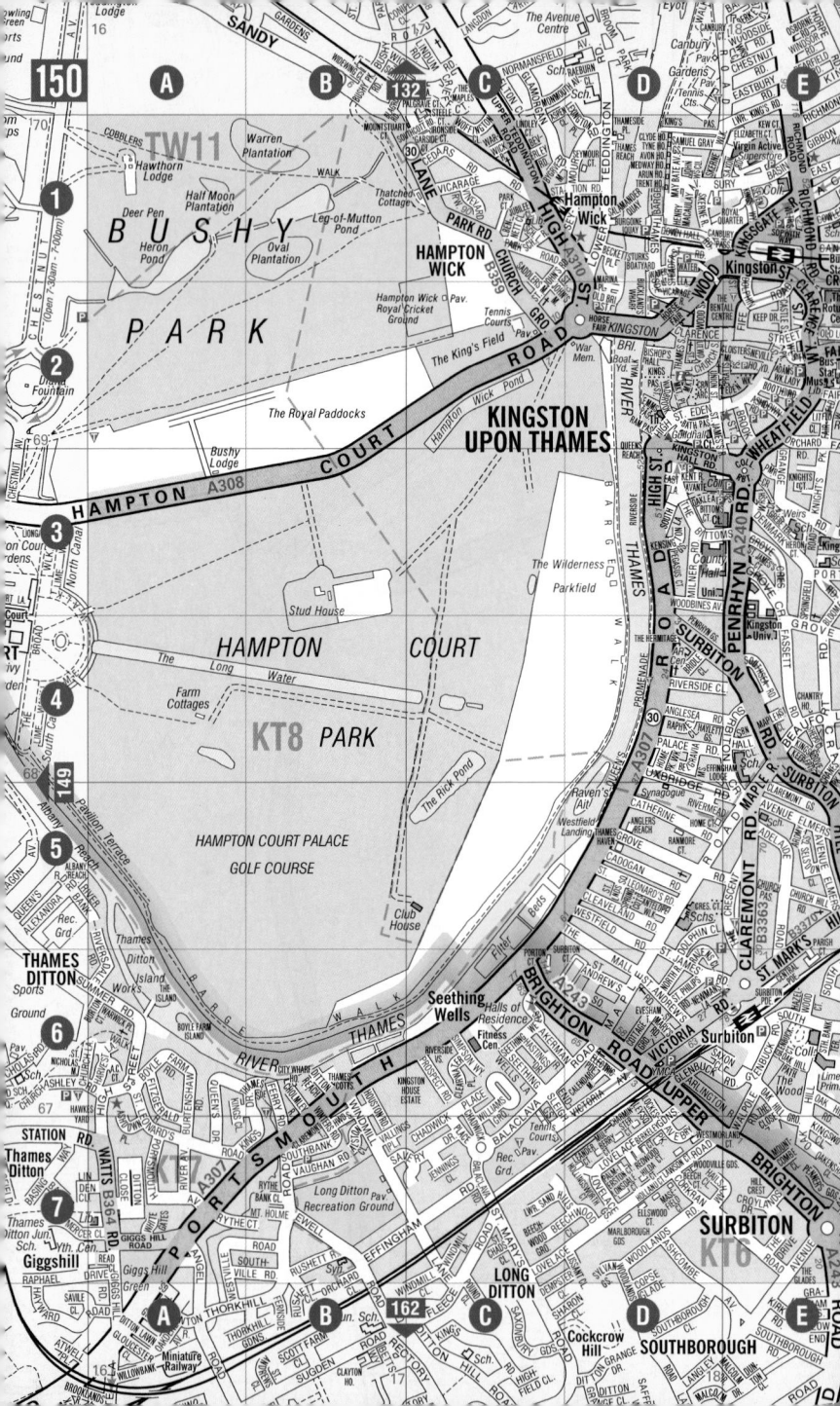

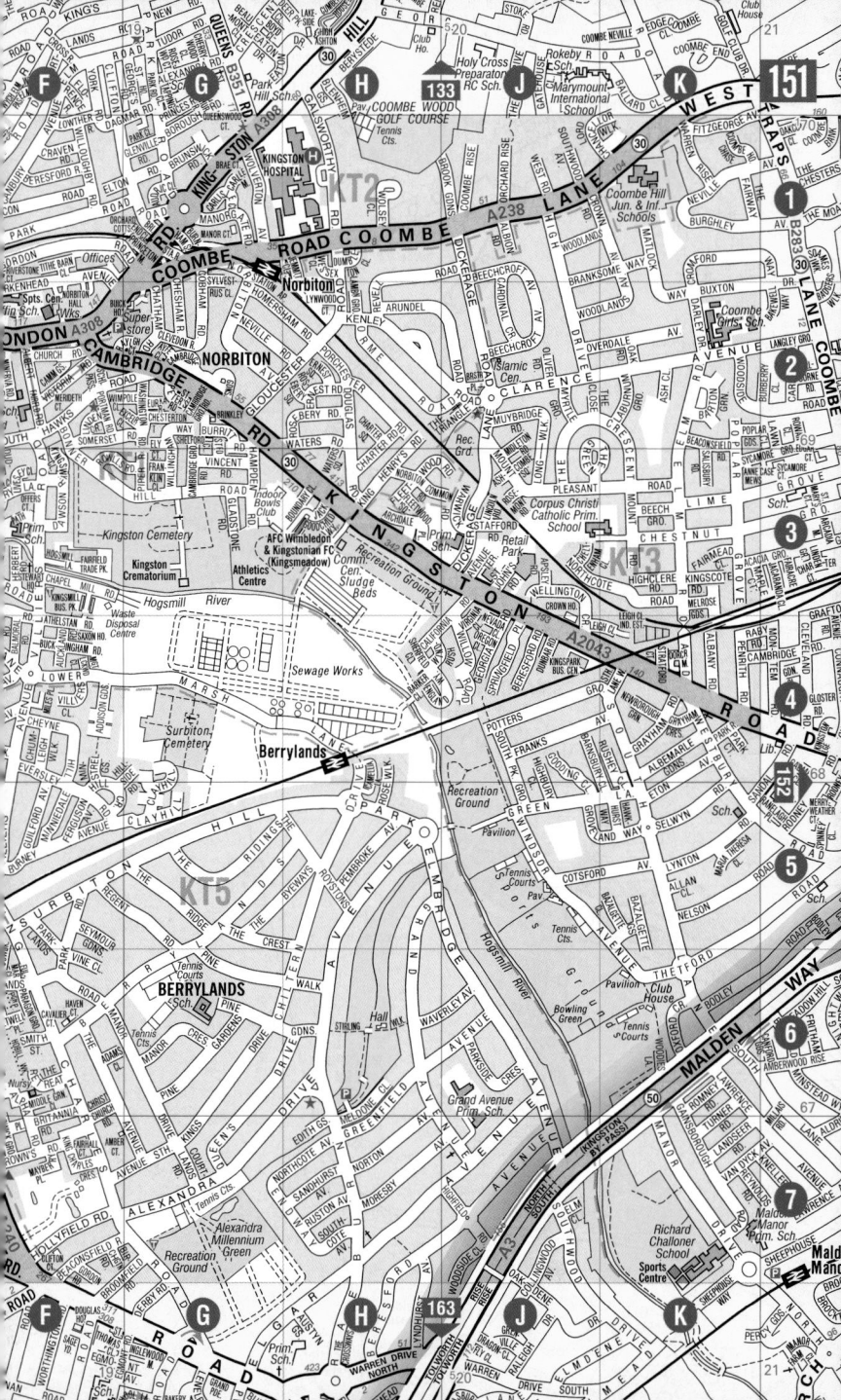

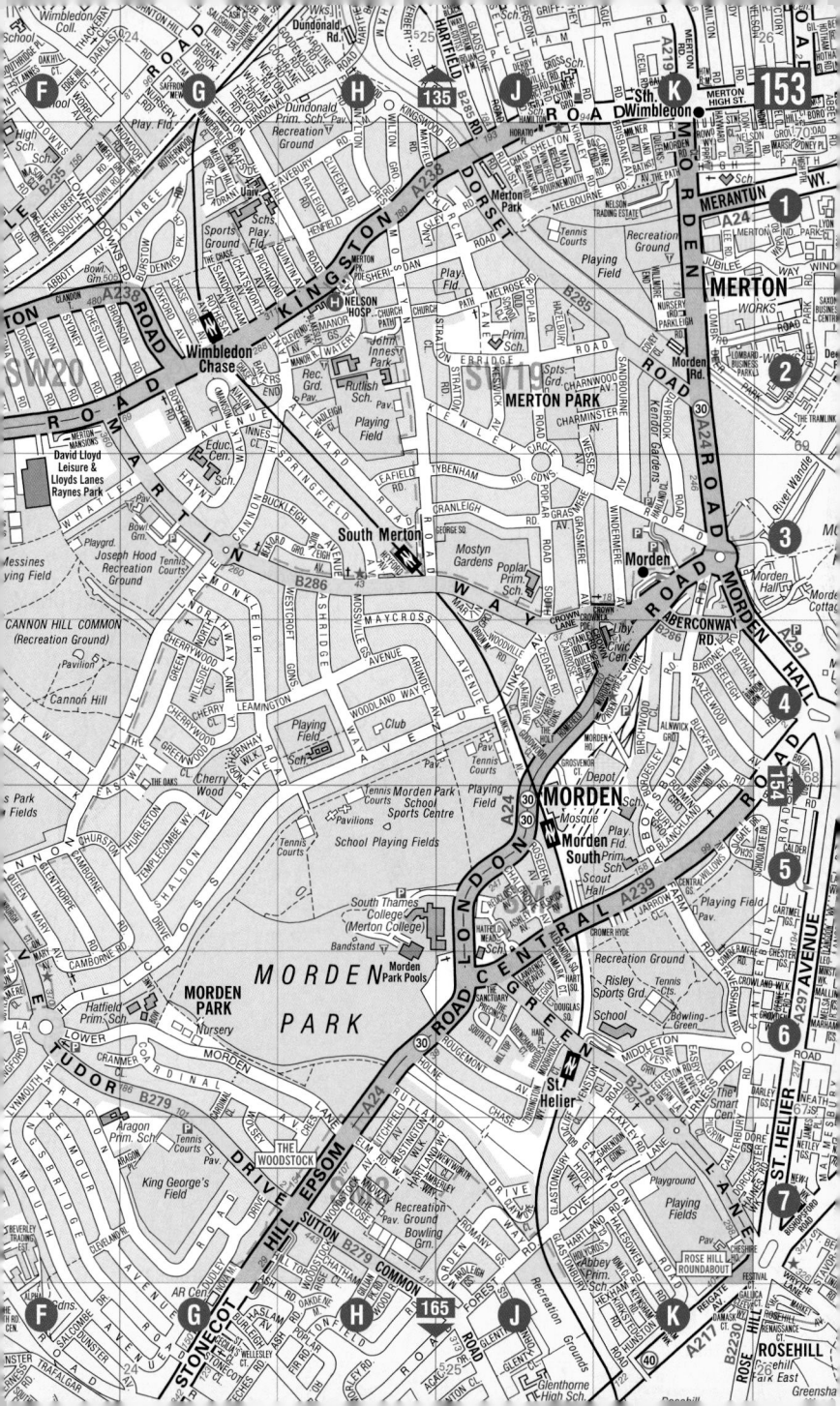

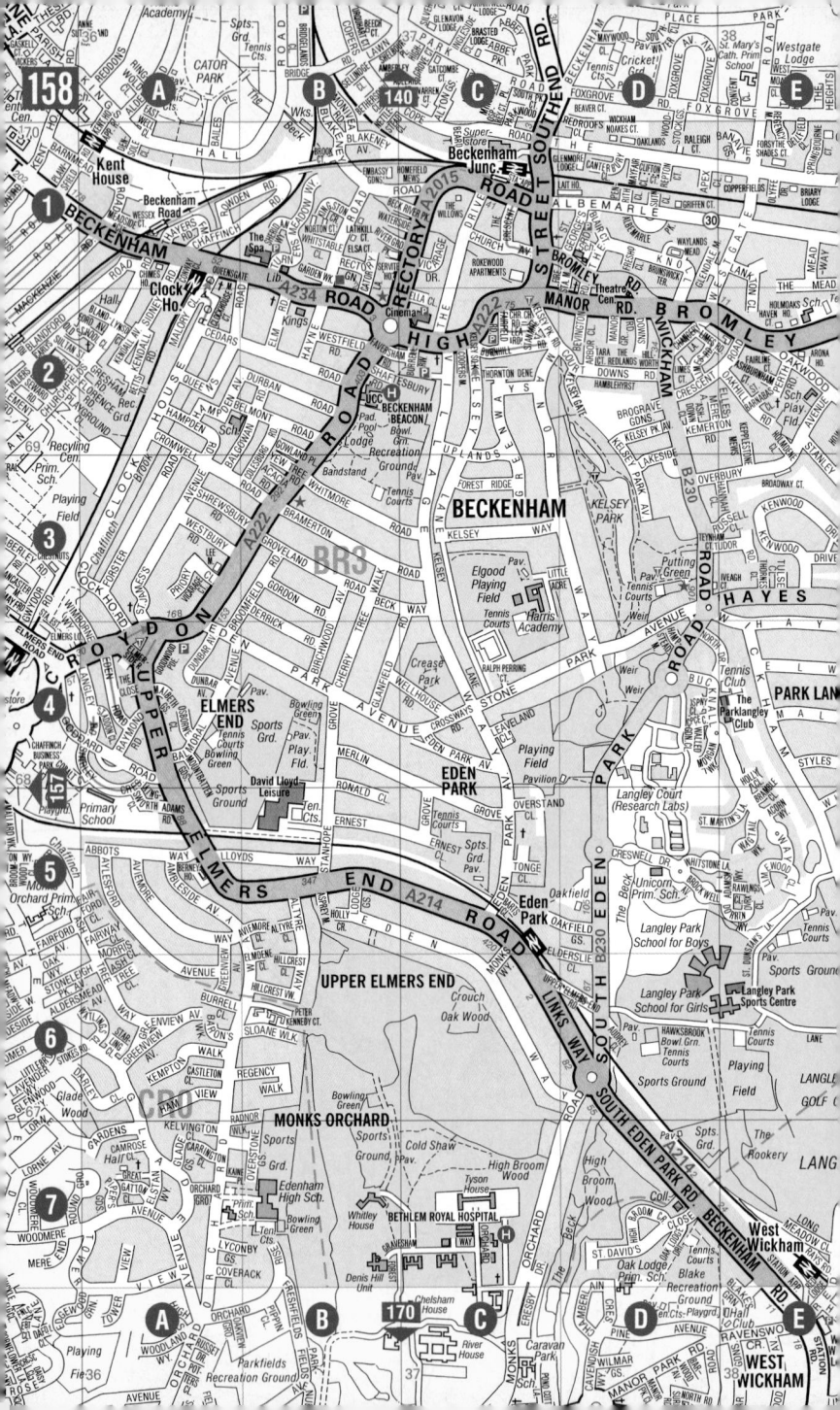

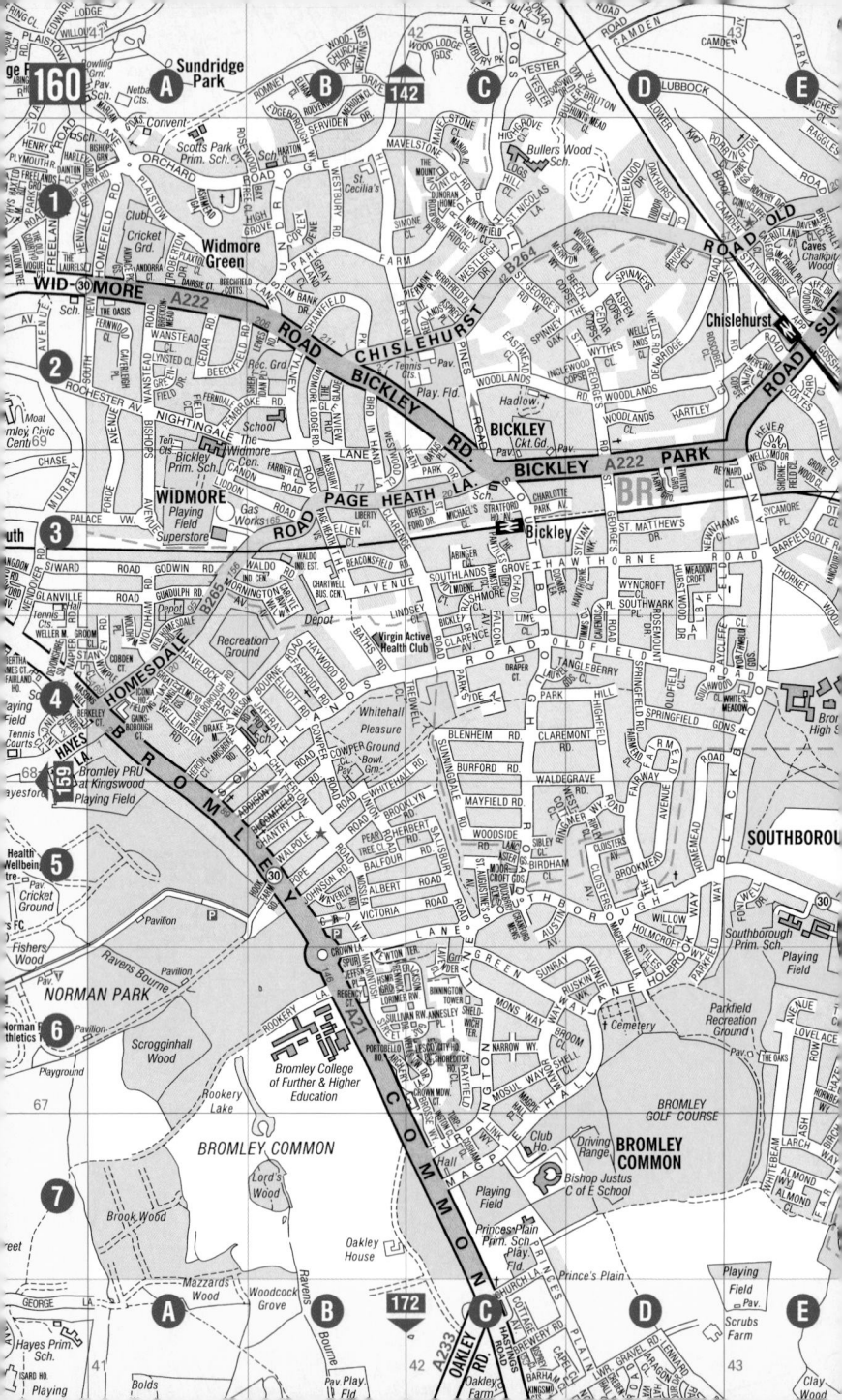

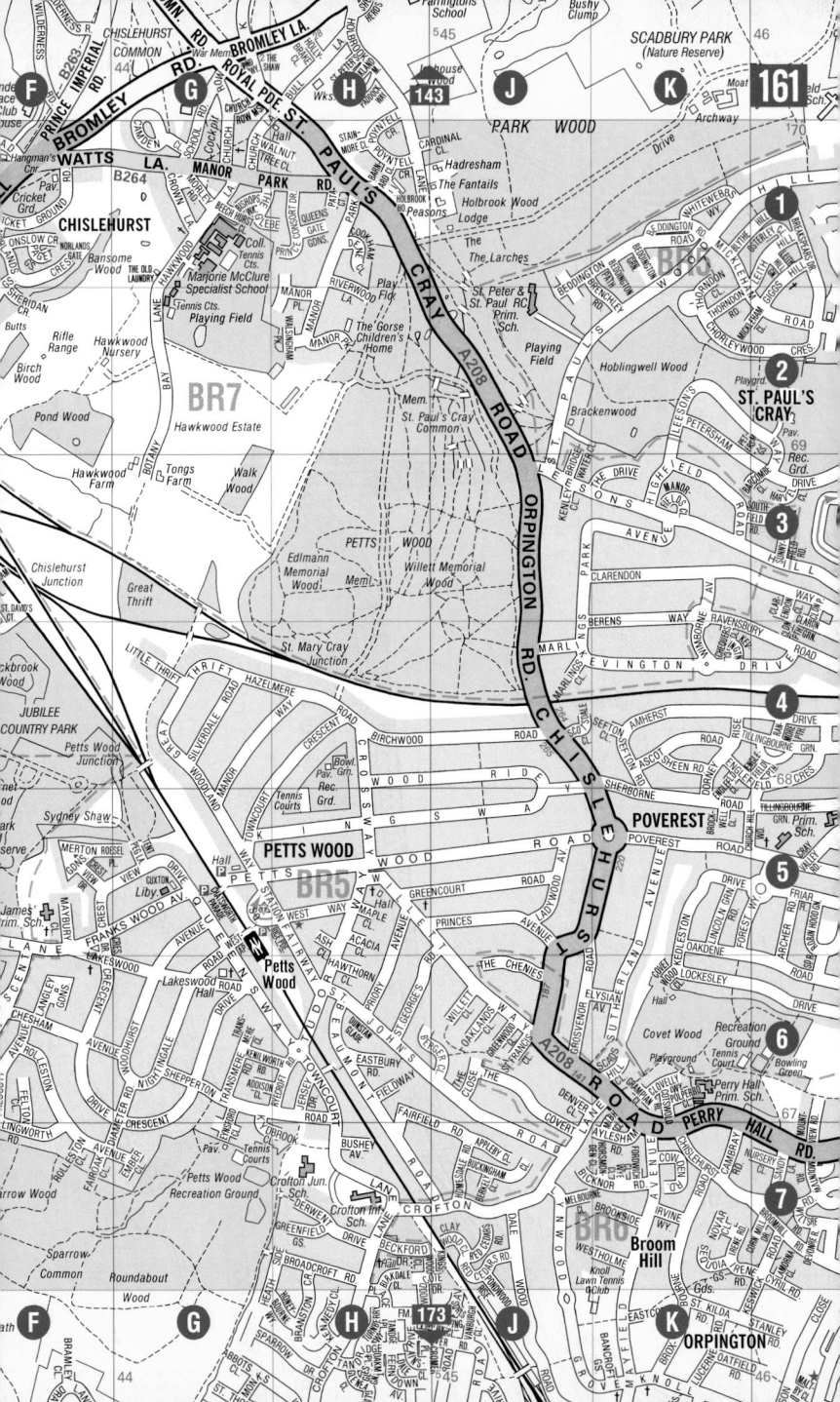

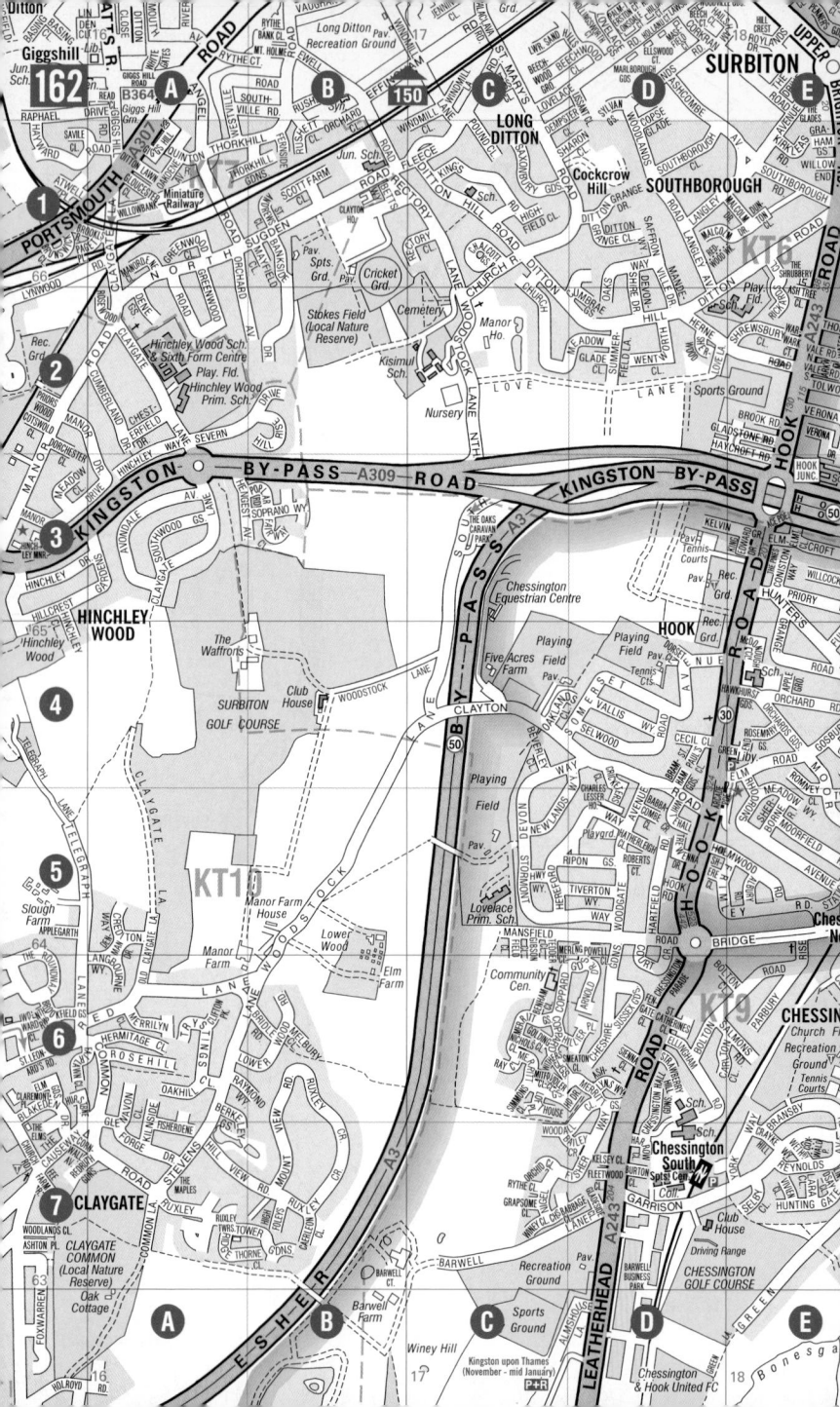

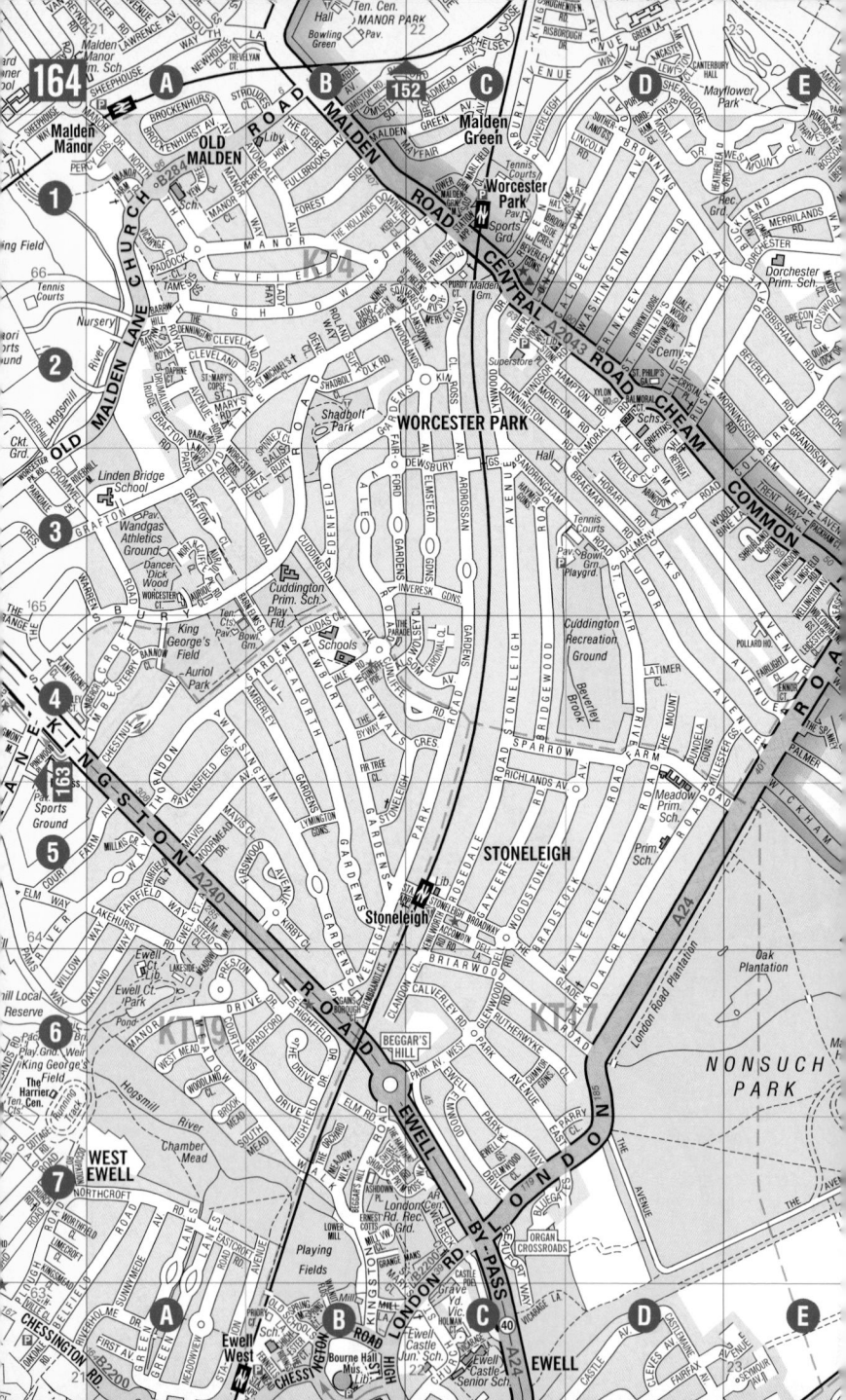

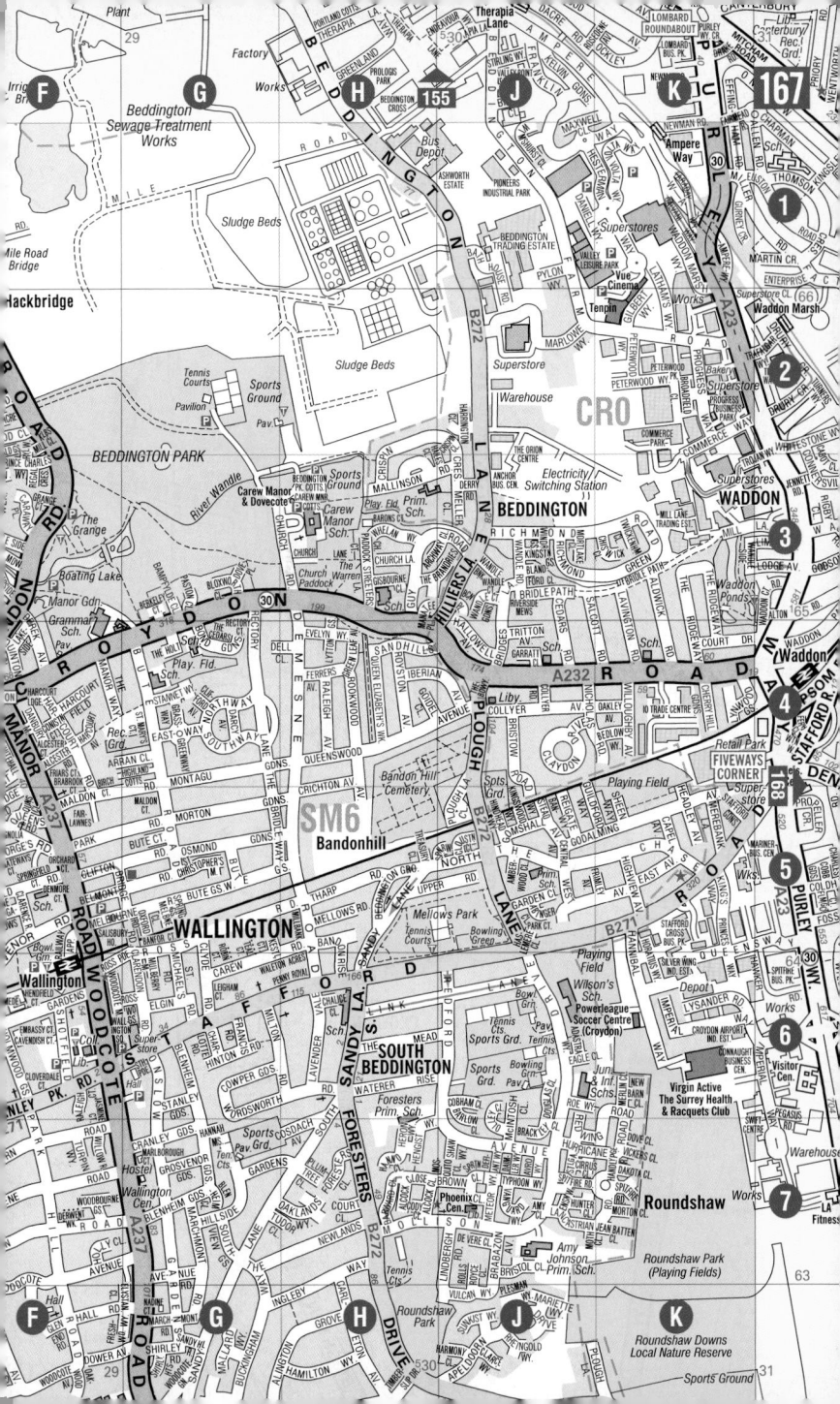

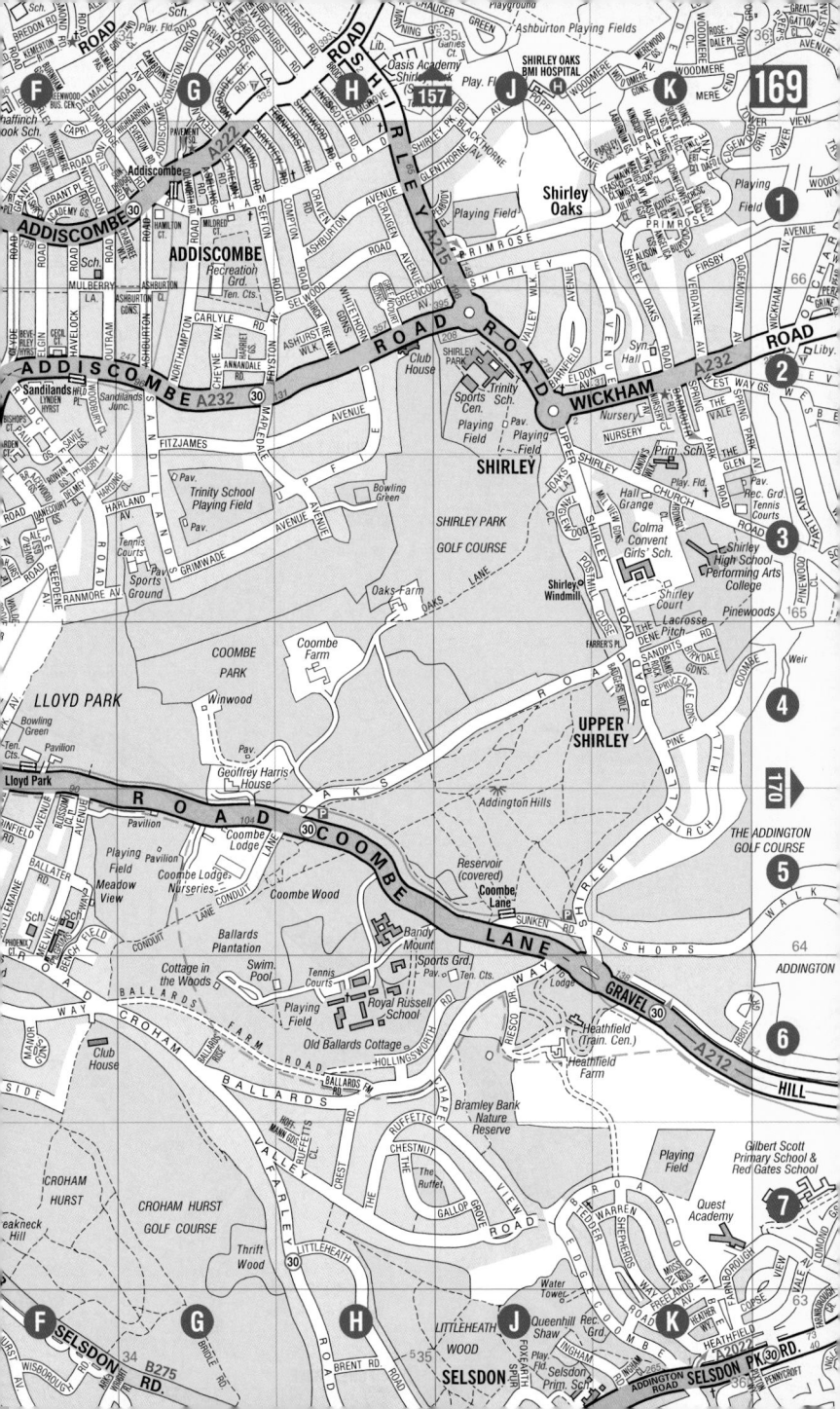

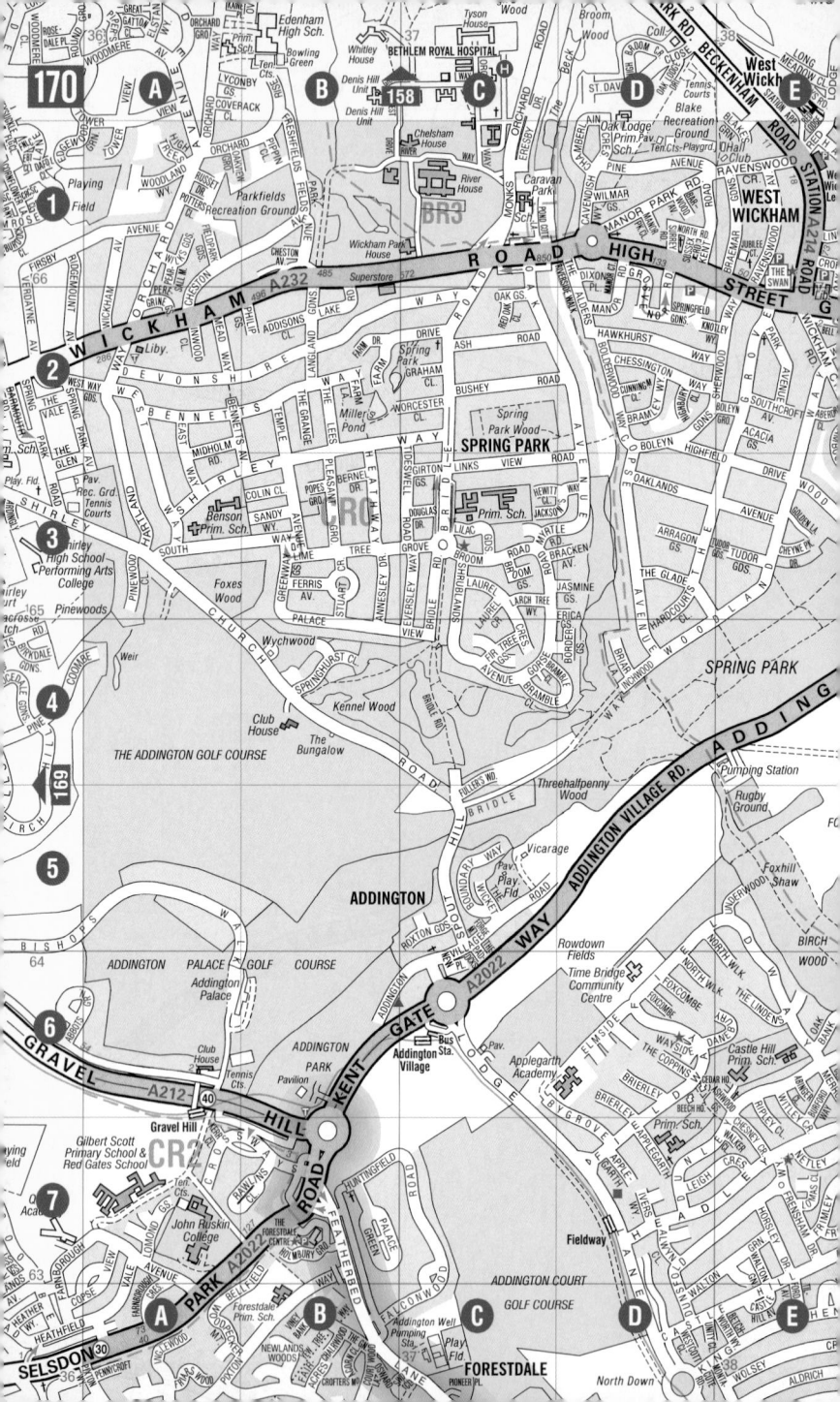

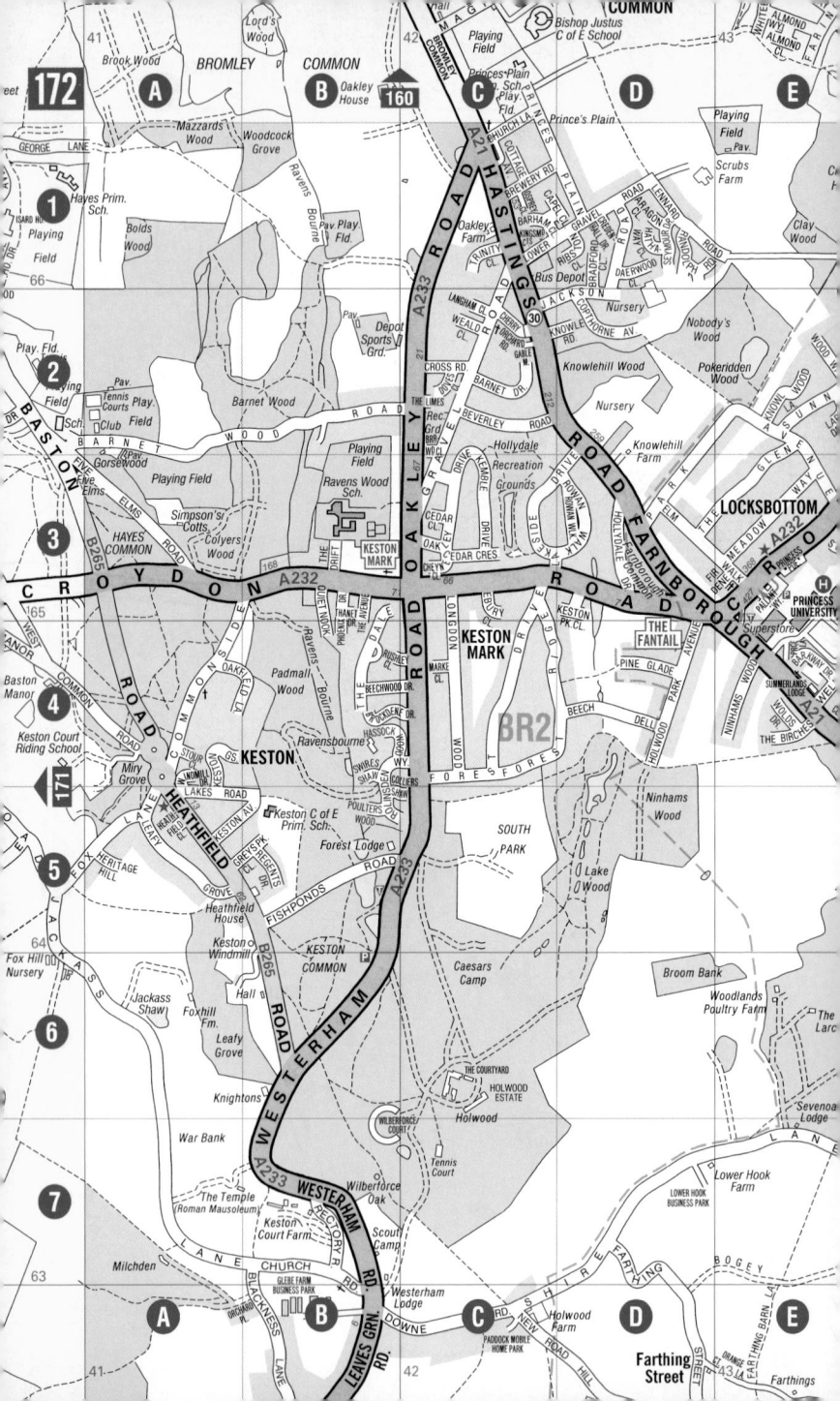

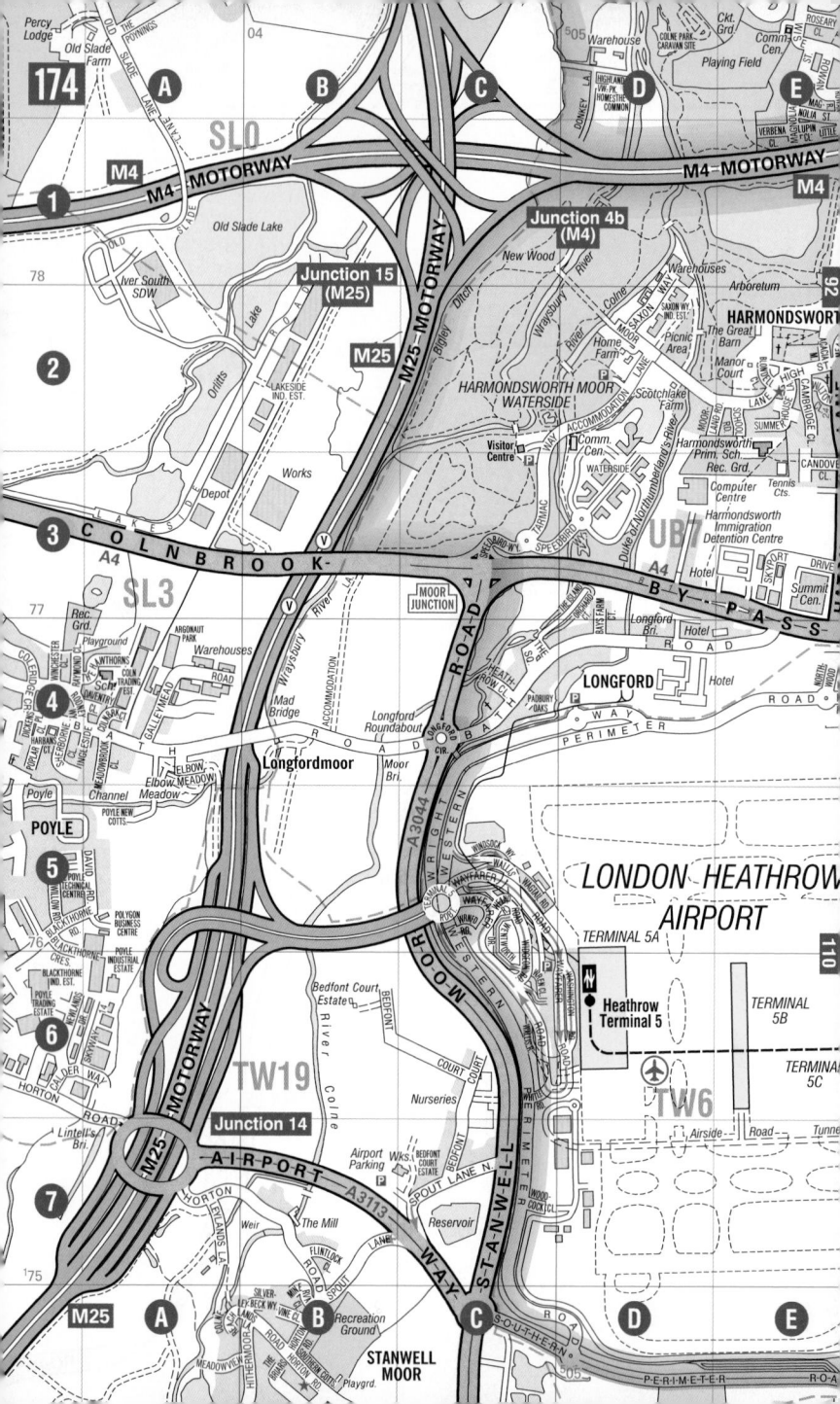

INDEX

Including Streets, Places & Areas, Industrial Estates, Selected Flats & Walkways,
Junction Names & Service Areas and Selected Places of Interest.

HOW TO USE THIS INDEX

1. Each street name is followed by its Postcode District (or, if outside the London Postcodes, by its Locality Abbreviation(s)) then by its map reference;
e.g. **Abbey Av.** HA0: Wemb . . . .2E **78** is in the HA0 Postcode District and the Wembley Locality and is to be found in square 2E on page **78**. The page number being shown in bold type.

2. A strict alphabetical order is followed in which Av., Rd., St., etc. (though abbreviated) are read in full and as part of the street name;
e.g. **Alder M.** appears after **Aldermary Rd.** but before **Aldermoor Rd.**

3. Streets and a selection of flats and walkways that cannot be shown on the mapping, appear in the index with the thoroughfare to which they are connected shown in brackets;
e.g. **Abady Ho.** SW1 . . . .3D **18** (off Page St.)

4. Addresses that are in more than one part are referred to as not continuous.

5. Places and areas are shown in the index in BLUE TYPE and the map reference is to the actual map square in which the town centre or area is located and not to the place name shown on the map;
e.g. ABBEY WOOD 4C **108**

6. An example of a selected place of interest is Barnet Mus. 4B **20**

7. Junction names and Service Areas are shown in the index in **BOLD CAPITAL TYPE**; e.g. **ANGEL EDMONTON 5B 34**

8. Map references for entries that appear on large scale pages **4-19** are shown first, with small scale map references shown in brackets; e.g. **Abbey St.** SE1 . . . .7H **15** (3E **102**)

GENERAL ABBREVIATIONS

All. : Alley	**Cl.** : Court	**Info.** : Information	**Pct.** : Precinct
App. : Approach	**Cres.** : Crescent	**Intl.** : International	**Prom.** : Promenade
Arc. : Arcade	**Cft.** : Croft	**Junc.** : Junction	**Quad.** : Quadrant
Av. : Avenue	**Dpt.** : Depot	**La.** : Lane	**Ri.** : Rise
Bk. : Back	**Dr.** : Drive	**Lit.** : Little	**Rd.** : Road
Blvd. : Boulevard	**E.** : East	**Lwr.** : Lower	**Rdbt.** : Roundabout
Bri. : Bridge	**Emb.** : Embankment	**Mnr.** : Manor	**Shop.** : Shopping
B'way. : Broadway	**Ent.** : Enterprise	**Mans.** : Mansions	**Sth.** : South
Bldg. : Building	**Est.** : Estate	**Mkt.** : Market	**Sq.** : Square
Bldgs. : Buildings	**Fld.** : Field	**Mdw.** : Meadow	**Sta.** : Station
Bus. : Business	**Flds.** : Fields	**Mdws.** : Meadows	**St.** : Street
C'way. : Causeway	**Gdn.** : Garden	**M.** : Mews	**Ter.** : Terrace
Cen. : Centre	**Gdns.** : Gardens	**Mt.** : Mount	**Twr.** : Tower
Chu. : Church	**Gth.** : Garth	**Mus.** : Museum	**Trad.** : Trading
Chyd. : Churchyard	**Ga.** : Gate	**Nth.** : North	**Up.** : Upper
Circ. : Circle	**Gt.** : Great	**Pal.** : Palace	**Va.** : Vale
Cir. : Circus	**Grn.** : Green	**Pde.** : Parade	**Vw.** : View
Cl. : Close	**Gro.** : Grove	**Pk.** : Park	**Vs.** : Villas
Coll. : College	**Hgts.** : Heights	**Pas.** : Passage	**Vis.** : Visitors
Comn. : Common	**Ho.** : House	**Pav.** : Pavilion	**Wlk.** : Walk
Cnr. : Corner	**Ho's.** : Houses	**Pl.** : Place	**W.** : West
Cott. : Cottage	**Ind.** : Industrial		**Yd.** : Yard
Cotts. : Cottages			

LOCALITY ABBREVIATIONS

Addtn : **Addington**	Clay : **Claygate**	Felt : **Feltham**	Kew : **Kew**
Ark : **Arkley**	Cockf : **Cockfosters**	G'frd : **Greenford**	King T : **Kingston upon Thames**
Ashf : **Ashford**	Col R : **Collier Row**	Had W : **Hadley Wood**	Lale : **Laleham**
Bark : **Barking**	Coln : **Colnbrook**	Ham : **Ham**	Lon : **London**
Barn : **Barnet**	Cowl : **Cowley**	Hamp : **Hampton**	H'row A : **London Heathrow Airport**
Beck : **Beckenham**	Cran : **Cranford**	Hamp H : **Hampton Hill**	Lford : **Longford**
Bedd : **Beddington**	Cray : **Crayford**	Hamp W : **Hampton Wick**	Lough : **Loughton**
Bedf : **Bedfont**	C'don : **Croydon**	Hanw : **Hanworth**	Mawney : **Mawney**
Belv : **Belvedere**	Dag : **Dagenham**	Hare : **Harefield**	Mitc : **Mitcham**
Bexl : **Bexley**	Dart : **Dartford**	Harl : **Harlington**	Mord : **Morden**
Bex : **Bexleyheath**	Downe : **Downe**	Harm : **Harmondsworth**	New Ad : **New Addington**
Bford : **Brentford**	E Barn : **East Barnet**	Harr : **Harrow**	New Bar : **New Barnet**
Brim : **Brimsdown**	E Mos : **East Molesey**	Hrw W : **Harrow Weald**	N Mald : **New Malden**
Brom : **Bromley**	Eastc : **Eastcote**	Hat E : **Hatch End**	N'olt : **Northolt**
Buck H : **Buckhurst Hill**	Edg : **Edgware**	Hayes : **Hayes**	Nwood : **Northwood**
Bush : **Bushey**	E'tree : **Elstree**	Hest : **Heston**	Orp : **Orpington**
B Hea : **Bushy Heath**	Enf : **Enfield**	Hext : **Hextable**	Pet W : **Petts Wood**
Cars : **Carshalton**	Enf H : **Enfield Highway**	Hil : **Hillingdon**	Pinn : **Pinner**
Chad H : **Chadwell Heath**	Enf L : **Enfield Lock**	Hin W : **Hinchley Wood**	Pond E : **Ponders End**
Cheam : **Cheam**	Enf W : **Enfield Wash**	Houn : **Hounslow**	Poyle : **Poyle**
Chels : **Chelsfield**	Eps : **Epsom**	Ick : **Ickenham**	Prat B : **Pratts Bottom**
Chert : **Chertsey**	Erith : **Erith**	Ilf : **Ilford**	Purl : **Purley**
Chess : **Chessington**	Esh : **Esher**	Isle : **Isleworth**	Rain : **Rainham**
Chig : **Chigwell**	Ewe : **Ewell**	Kenton : **Kenton**	Rich P : **Richings Park**
Chst : **Chislehurst**	Farnb : **Farnborough**	Kes : **Keston**	Rich : **Richmond**

1st Bowl—Abingdon Cl.

Rom : Romford
Ruis : Ruislip
Rush G : Rush Green
St M Cry : St Mary Cray
St P : St Pauls Cray
Sande : Sanderstead
Sels : Selsdon
Shep : Shepperton
Sidc : Sidcup
Sip : Sipson
S'hall : Southall
S Croy : South Croydon
Staines : Staines
Stan : Stanmore
Stanw : Stanwell
Stanw M : Stanwell Moor
Stock P : Stockley Park
Sun : Sunbury
Surb : Surbiton
Sutt : Sutton
Swan : Swanley
Tedd : Teddington
T Ditt : Thames Ditton
Thor H : Thornton Heath
Twick : Twickenham
Uxb : Uxbridge
Wadd : Waddon
Wall : Wallington
Walt T : Walton-on-Thames
W'stone : Wealdstone
Well : Welling
Wemb : Wembley
W Dray : West Drayton
W Mole : West Molesey
W W'ck : West Wickham
Weyb : Weybridge
Whitt : Whitton
Wilm : Wilmington
Wfd G : Woodford Green
Wor Pk : Worcester Park
Yead : Yeading
Yiew : Yiewsley

1st Bowl
Lewisham ... 3E 122
2 Temple Place ... *7A 84*
(off Temple Pl.)
2 Willow Road ... 4C 64
7/7 Memorial ... 5G 11 (1E 100)
10 Brock St. NW1 ... 3A 6
18 Stafford Terrace
The Sambourne Family Home ... *3J 99*
(off Stafford Ter.)
60 St Martins La. *WC2* ... *2E 12*
(off St Martin's La.)
198 Contemporary Arts and Learning ... *6B 120*
(off Railton Rd.)
201 Bishopsgate EC2 ... 5H 9

A

Aaron Hill Rd. E6 ... 5E 88
Abady Ho. *SW1* ... *3D 18*
(off Page St.)
Abberley M. SW4 ... 3F 119
Abbess Cl. E6 ... 5C 88
SW2 ... 1B 138
Abbeville M. SW4 ... 4H 119
Abbeville Rd. N8 ... 5H 47
SW4 ... 6G 119
Abbey Av. HA0: Wemb ... 2E 78
Abbey Cl. E5 ... 4G 67
HA5: Pinn ... 3K 39
SW8 ... 1H 119
UB3: Hayes ... 1K 93
UB5: N'olt ... 3D 76
Abbey Ct. *NW8* ... *2A 82*
(off Abbey Rd.)
SE17 ... *5C 102*
(off Macleod St.)
TW12: Hamp ... 7E 130
Abbey Cres. DA17: Belv ... 4G 109
Abbeydale Rd. HA0: Wemb ... 1F 79
Abbey Dr. DA2: Wilm ... 2K 145
SW17 ... 5E 136
Abbey Est. NW8 ... 1K 81
Abbeyfield Cl. CR4: Mitc ... 2C 154
Abbeyfield Est. SE16 ... 4J 103
Abbeyfield Rd. SE16 ... 4J 103
(not continuous)
Abbeyfields Cl. NW10 ... 3G 79
Abbey Gdns. BR7: Chst ... 1E 160
NW8 ... 2A 82
SE16 ... 4G 103
SW1 ... *1E 18*
(off Great College St.)
TW15: Ashf ... 5D 128
W6 ... 6G 99
Abbey Gro. SE2 ... 4B 108
Abbeyhill Rd. DA15: Sidc ... 2C 144
Abbey Ho. *E15* ... *2G 87*
(off Baker's Row)
NW8 ... 1A 4
Abbey Ind. Est. CR4: Mitc ... 5D 154
HA0: Wemb ... 1F 79
Abbey La. BR3: Beck ... 7C 140
E15 ... 2E 86
(not continuous)
Abbey La. Commercial Est. E15 ... 2G 87
Abbey Life Ct. E16 ... 5K 87
Abbey Lodge NW8 ... 2D 4
Abbey M. E17 ... 5C 50
TW7: Isle ... 1B 114
Abbey Mt. DA17: Belv ... 5F 109
Abbey Orchard St. SW1 ... 1D 18 (3H 101)
Abbey Orchard St. Est. SW1 ... 1D 18 (3H 101)
(not continuous)
Abbey Pde. *SW19* ... *7A 136*
(off Merton High St.)
W5 ... 3F 79
Abbey Pk. BR3: Beck ... 7C 140
Abbey Pk. Ind. Est. IG11: Bark ... 2G 89
Abbey Retail Pk. IG11: Bark ... 7F 71
Abbey Rd. CR0: C'don ... 3B 168
DA7: Bex ... 4E 126
DA17: Belv ... 4D 108
E15 ... 2F 87
EN1: Enf ... 5K 23
IG2: Ilf ... 5H 53
IG11: Bark ... 1F 89
NW6 ... 7K 63
NW8 ... 1A 4 (7K 63)
NW10 ... 1H 79
SE2 ... 4D 108
SW19 ... 7A 136
Abbey Rd. Apartments *NW8* ... *2A 82*
(off Abbey Rd.)
Abbey Sports Cen. ... 1G 89
Abbey St. E13 ... 4J 87
SE1 ... 7H 15 (3E 102)
SE16 ... 3G 103
Abbey Ter. SE2 ... 4C 108
Abbey Trad. Est. SE26 ... 5B 140
Abbey Vw. NW7 ... 3G 29
Abbey Wlk. KT8: W Mole ... 3F 149
Abbey Wharf Ind. Est. IG11: Bark ... 3H 89
ABBEY WOOD ... 4C 108
Abbey Wood Caravan Club Site SE2 ... 4C 108
Abbey Wood Rd. SE2 ... 4B 108
Abbot Cl. HA4: Ruis ... 3B 58
Abbot Ct. *SW8* ... *7J 101*
(off Hartington Rd.)
Abbot Ho. *E14* ... *7D 86*
(off Smythe St.)
Abbotsbury *NW1* ... *7H 65*
(off Camley St.)
Abbotsbury Cl. E15 ... 2E 86
W14 ... 2G 99
Abbotsbury Gdns. HA5: Eastc ... 7A 40
Abbotsbury Ho. W14 ... 2G 99
Abbotsbury M. SE15 ... 3J 121
Abbotsbury Rd. BR2: Hayes ... 2H 171
SM4: Mord ... 5K 153
W14 ... 1G 99
Abbots Cl. BR5: Farnb ... 1G 173
Abbots Ct. *W8* ... *2K 99*
(off Thackeray St.)
Abbots Dr. HA2: Harr ... 2E 58
Abbotsford Av. N15 ... 4C 48
Abbotsford Gdns. IG8: Wfd G ... 7D 36
Abbotsford Rd. IG3: Ilf ... 2A 72
Abbots Gdns. N2 ... 4B 46
Abbots Grn. CR0: Addtn ... 6K 169
Abbotshade Rd. SE16 ... 1K 103
Abbotshall Av. N14 ... 3B 32
Abbotshall Rd. SE6 ... 1F 141
Abbot's Ho. *W14* ... *3H 99*
(off St Mary Abbot's Ter.)
Abbotsleigh Cl. SM2: Sutt ... 7K 165
Abbotsleigh Rd. SW16 ... 4G 137
Abbots Mnr. SW1 ... 5J 17 (4F 101)
(not continuous)
Abbotsmede Cl. TW1: Twick ... 2K 131
Abbots Pk. SW2 ... 1A 138
Abbot's Pl. NW6 ... 1K 81
Abbots Rd. E6 ... 1B 88
HA8: Edg ... 7D 28
Abbots Ter. N8 ... 6J 47
Abbotstone Rd. SW15 ... 3E 116
Abbot St. E8 ... 6F 67
Abbots Wlk. W8 ... 3K 99
Abbots Way BR3: Beck ... 5A 158
Abbotswell Rd. SE4 ... 5B 122
Abbotswood Cl. DA17: Belv ... 3E 108
Abbotswood Gdns. IG5: Ilf ... 3D 52
Abbotswood Rd. SE22 ... 4E 120
SW16 ... 3H 137
Abbotswood Way
UB3: Hayes ... 1K 93
Abbott Av. SW20 ... 1F 153
Abbott Cl. TW12: Hamp ... 6C 130
UB5: N'olt ... 6D 58
Abbott Rd. E14 ... 5E 86
(not continuous)
Abbotts Cl. N1 ... 6C 66
RM7: Mawney ... 3H 55
SE28 ... 7C 90
UB8: Cowl ... 5A 74
Abbotts Cres. E4 ... 4A 36
EN2: Enf ... 2G 23
Abbotts Dr. HA0: Wemb ... 2B 60
Abbotts Ho. *SW1* ... *6C 18*
(off Aylesford St.)
Abbotts Mead TW10: Ham ... 4D 132
Abbotts Pk. Rd. E10 ... 7E 50
Abbotts Rd. CR4: Mitc ... 4G 155
EN5: New Bar ... 4E 20
SM3: Cheam ... 4G 165
UB1: S'hall ... 1C 94
Abbott's Wlk. DA7: Bex ... 7D 108
Abbott's Wharf *E14* ... *6C 86*
(off Stainsby Pl.)
Abbotts Wharf Moorings *E14* ... *6C 86*
(off Stainsby Rd.)
Abchurch La. EC4 ... 2F 15 (7D 84)
(not continuous)
Abchurch Yd. EC4 ... 2E 14 (7D 84)
Abdale Rd. W12 ... 1D 98
Abel Ho. *SE11* ... *7K 19*
(off Kennington Rd.)
Abenglen Ind. Est. UB3: Hayes ... 2F 93
Aberavon Rd. E3 ... 3A 86
Abercairn Rd. SW16 ... 7G 137
Aberconway Rd. SM4: Mord ... 4K 153
Abercorn Cl. NW7 ... 7B 30
NW8 ... 3A 82
Abercorn Commercial Cen.
HA0: Wemb ... 1D 78
Abercorn Cotts. *NW8* ... *3A 82*
(off Abercorn Pl.)
Abercorn Cres. HA2: Harr ... 1F 59
Abercorn Dell WD23: B Hea ... 2B 26
Abercorn Gdns. HA3: Kenton ... 7D 42
RM6: Chad H ... 6B 54
Abercorn Gro. HA4: Ruis ... 4F 39
Abercorn Mans. *NW8* ... *2A 82*
(off Abercorn Pl.)
Abercorn M. TW10: Rich ... 4F 115
Abercorn Pl. NW8 ... 3A 82
Abercorn Rd. HA7: Stan ... 7H 27
NW7 ... 7B 30
Abercorn Wlk. NW8 ... 3A 82
Abercorn Way SE1 ... 5G 103
Abercrombie Dr. EN1: Enf ... 1B 24
Abercrombie Rd. E20 ... 5D 68
Abercrombie St. SW11 ... 2C 118
Aberdale Ct. *SE16* ... *2K 103*
(off Garter Way)
Aberdare Cl. BR4: W W'ck ... 2E 170
Aberdare Gdns. NW6 ... 7K 63
NW7 ... 7A 30
Aberdare Rd. EN3: Pond E ... 4D 24
Aberdeen Cotts. HA7: Stan ... 7H 27
Aberdeen Ct. *W9* ... *4A 4*
(off Maida Vale)
Aberdeen La. N5 ... 5C 66
Aberdeen Mans. *WC1* ... *3E 6*
(off Kenton St.)
Aberdeen Pde. *N18* ... *5C 34*
(off Aberdeen Rd.)
Aberdeen Pk. N5 ... 5C 66
Aberdeen Pl. NW8 ... 4A 4 (4B 82)
Aberdeen Rd.
CR0: C'don ... 4C 168
HA3: W'stone ... 2K 41
N5 ... 4C 66
N18 ... 5B 34
(not continuous)
NW10 ... 5B 62
Aberdeen Sq. E14 ... 1B 104
Aberdeen Ter. SE3 ... 2F 123
Aberdeen Wharf *E1* ... *1H 103*
(off Wapping High St.)
Aberdour Rd. IG3: Ilf ... 3B 72
Aberdour St. SE1 ... 4E 102
Aberfeldy Ho. SE5 ... 7B 102
(not continuous)
Aberfeldy St. E14 ... 5E 86
(not continuous)
Aberford Gdns. SE18 ... 1C 124
Aberfoyle Rd. SW16 ... 6H 137
(not continuous)
Abergeldie Rd. SE12 ... 6K 123
Abernethy Rd. SE13 ... 4G 123
Abersham Rd. E8 ... 5F 67
Abery St. SE18 ... 4J 107
Ability Pl. E14 ... 2D 104
Ability Plaza *E8* ... *7F 67*
(off Arbutus St.)
Ability Towers *EC1* ... *1C 8*
(off Macclesfield Rd.)
Abingdon *W14* ... *4H 99*
(off Kensington Village)
Abingdon Cl. KT4: Wor Pk ... 3D 164
NW1 ... 6H 65
SE1 ... *4F 103*
(off Bushwood Dr.)
SW19 ... 6A 136
UB10: Hil ... 1B 74

Abingdon Ct. W8 . . . . .3J *99*
(off Abingdon Vs.)
Abingdon Gdns. W8 . . . . .3J *99*
Abingdon Ho. BR1: Brom 7K *141*
E2 . . . . .3J *9*
(off Boundary Rd.)
Abingdon Lodge BR2: Brom 2H *159*
(off Beckenham La.)
W8 . . . . .3J *99*
Abingdon Mans. W8 . . . . .3J *99*
(off Pater St.)
Abingdon Rd. N3 . . . . .2A *46*
SW16 . . . . .2J *155*
W8 . . . . .3J *99*
Abingdon St. SW1 . . . . . . .1E **18** (3J **101**)
Abingdon Vs. W8 . . . . .3J *99*
Abinger Cl. BR1: Brom 3C *160*
CR0: New Ad 6E *170*
IG11: Bark .4A *72*
SM6: Wall 5J *167*
Abinger Ct. SM6: Wall 5J *167*
(off Abinger Cl.)
W5 . . . . .7C *78*
Abinger Gdns. TW7: Isle 3J *113*
Abinger Gro. SE8 . . . . .6B *104*
Abinger Ho. SE1 . . . . .7E *14*
(off St. Dover St.)
Abinger M. W9 . . . . .4J *81*
Abinger Rd. W4 . . . . .3A *98*
Ablett St. SE16 . . . . .5J *103*
Abney Gdns. N16 . . . . .2F *67*
Abney Park Cemetery
(Local Nature Reserve) 2E *66*
Abney Pk. Ter. N16 . . . . .2F *67*
(off Cazenove Rd.)
Aborfield NW5 . . . . .5G *65*
Aboyne Dr. SW20 . . . . .2C *152*
Aboyne Rd. NW10 . . . . .3A *62*
SW17 . . . . .3B *136*
Abraham Fisher Ho. E12 . . . . .5E *70*
Abyssinia Cl. SW11 . . . . .4C *118*
Abyssinia Ct. N8 . . . . .5K *47*
Abyssinia Rd. SW11 . . . . .4C *118*
Acacia Av. HA4: Ruis 1J *57*
HA9: Wemb 5E *60*
N17 . . . . .7J *33*
TW8: Bford 7B *96*
TW17: Shep 5C *146*
UB3: Hayes 6H *75*
UB7: Yiew .7B *74*
Acacia Bus. Cen. E11 . . . . .3G *69*
Acacia Cl. BR5: Pet W 5H *161*
HA7: Stan .6D *26*
SE8 . . . . .4A *104*
SE20 . . . . .2G *157*
Acacia Ct. HA1: Harr 5F *41*
Acacia Dr. SM3: Sutt 1H *165*
Acacia Gdns. BR4: W W'ck 2E *170*
NW8 . . . . .2B *82*
SE21 . . . . .2D *138*
Acacia Gro. KT3: N Mald 3K *151*
SE21 . . . . .2D *138*
Acacia Ho. N22 . . . . .1A *48*
(off Douglas Rd.)
Acacia M. UB7: Harm 2E *174*
Acacia Pl. NW8 . . . . .2B *82*
Acacia Rd.
BR3: Beck 3B *158*
CR4: Mitc 3E *154*
E11 . . . . .2G *69*
E17 . . . . .6A *50*
EN2: Enf 1J *23*
N22 . . . . .1A *48*
NW8 . . . . .2B *82*
SW16 . . . . .1J *155*
TW12: Hamp 6E *130*
W3 . . . . .7J *79*
Acacias, The EN4: E Barn 5G *21*
Acacia Wlk. SW10 . . . . .7A *100*
(off Tadema Rd.)
Acacia Way DA15: Sidc 1K *143*
Academia Way N17 . . . . .6K *33*

The Academy
Middlesex County Cricket Club
. . . . .2K *45*
Academy, The SW8 . . . . . .7G **19** (6K **101**)
Academy Apartments E8 . . . . .5H *67*
(off Dalston La.)
Academy Bldgs. N1 . . . . .1G *9*
(off Fanshaw St.)
Academy Ct. DA5: Bexl 2K *145*
(off Beaconsfield Rd.)
E2 . . . . .3J *85*
(off Kirkwall Pl.)
NW6 . . . . .1J *81*
RM8: Dag .4A *72*
Academy Gdns. CR0: C'don 1F *169*
UB5: N'olt .2B *76*
W8 . . . . .2J *99*
Academy Ho. E3 . . . . .5D *86*
(off Violet Rd.)
Academy Pl. SE18 . . . . .1D *124*
TW7: Isle .1J *113*
Academy Rd. SE18 . . . . .1D *124*
Academy Way E17 . . . . .1C *50*
RM8: Dag .4A *72*
Acanthus Dr. SE1 . . . . .5G *103*
Acanthus Rd. SW11 . . . . .3E *118*
Accommodation La. UB7: Harm 2D *174*
UB7: Lford 4B *174*
Accommodation Rd. E4 . . . . .3A *36*
(off Ashwood Rd.)
KT17: Ewe 5C *164*
NW11 . . . . .1H *63*
AC Court KT7: T Ditt 6A *150*
Ace Pde. KT9: Chess 3E *162*
Acer Av. UB4: Yead 5C *76*
Acer Cl. EN3: Enf H 3F *25*
(off Enstone Rd.)
Acer Rd. E8 . . . . .7F *67*
Acers BR7: Chst 7C *142*
Aces Ct. TW3: Houn 2G *113*
Acfold Rd. SW6 . . . . .1K *117*
Achilles Cl. SE1 . . . . .5G *103*
Achilles Ho. E2 . . . . .2H *85*
(off Old Bethnal Grn. Rd.)
Achilles Rd. NW6 . . . . .5J *63*
Achilles Statue 5H **11** (1E **100**)
Achilles St. SE14 . . . . .7A *104*
Achilles Way W1 . . . . .5H **11** (1E **100**)
Acklam Rd. W10 . . . . .5G *81*
(not continuous)
Acklington Dr. NW9 . . . . .1A *44*
Ackmar Rd. SW6 . . . . .1J *117*
Ackroyd Dr. E3 . . . . .5B *86*
Ackroyd Rd. SE23 . . . . .7K *121*
Acland Cl. SE18 . . . . .7H *107*
Acland Cres. SE5 . . . . .3D *120*
Acland Ho. SW9 . . . . .1K *119*
Acland Rd. NW2 . . . . .6D *62*
Acle Cl. IG6: Ilf 1F *53*
Acme Studios E14 . . . . .5E *86*
(Gillender St.)
E14 . . . . .5E *86*
(off Leven Rd., Leven Rd.)
Acock Gro. UB5: N'olt 4F *59*
Acol Ct. NW6 .7J *63*
Acol Cres. HA4: Ruis 5K *57*
Acol Rd. NW6 . . . . .7J *63*
Aconbury Rd. RM9: Dag 1B *90*
Acorn Cl. BR7: Chst 5G *143*
E4 . . . . .5J *35*
EN2: Enf 1G *23*
HA7: Stan .7G *27*
TW12: Hamp 6F *131*
Acorn Ct. E3 .2C *86*
(off Morville St.)
E6 . . . . .7C *70*
IG2: Ilf 6J *53*
Acorn Gdns. SE19 . . . . .1F *157*
W3 . . . . .5K *79*
Acorn Gro. HA4: Ruis 4H *57*
UB3: Harl .7H *93*

Acorn Pde. SE15 . . . . .7H *103*
Acorn Production Cen. N7 . . . . .7J *65*
Acorn Wlk. SE16 . . . . .1A *104*
Acorn Way BR3: Beck 5E *158*
BR6: Farnb 4F *173*
SE23 . . . . .3K *139*
Acqua Ho. TW9: Kew 7H *97*
Acre Dr. SE22 . . . . .4G *121*
Acrefield Ho. NW4 . . . . .4F *45*
(off Belle Vue Est.)
Acre La. SM5: Cars 4E *166*
SM6: Wall 4E *166*
SW2 . . . . .4J *119*
Acre Path UB5: N'olt 6C *58*
(off Arnold Rd.)
Acre Rd. KT2: King T 1E *150*
RM10: Dag 7H *73*
SW19 . . . . .6B *136*
Acre Way HA6: Nwood 1H *39*
Acris St. SW18 . . . . .5A *118*
Acropolis Ho. KT1: King T 3F *151*
(off Winery La.)
Action Apartments N1 . . . . .1D *84*
(off Branch Pl.)
ACTON 1J *97*
Acton Central Ind. Est.
. . . . .1H *97*
Acton Cl. N9 .2B *34*
ACTON GREEN 3J *97*
Acton Hill M. W3 . . . . .1H *97*
Acton Ho. E8 .1F *85*
(off Lee St.)
W3 . . . . .6J *79*
Acton La. NW10 . . . . .3J *79*
W3 . . . . .2J *97*
W4 . . . . .4J *97*
(not continuous)
Acton M. E8 . . . . .1F *85*
Acton Pk. Est. W3 . . . . .2K *97*
Acton St. WC1 . . . . .2G **7** (3K **83**)
Acton Swimming Baths 1J *97*
(off Salisbury St.)
Acton Va. Ind. Pk. W3 . . . . .2B *98*
Acuba Rd. SW18 . . . . .2K *135*
Acworth Cl. N9 . . . . .7D *24*
Acworth Ho. SE18 . . . . .6F *107*
(off Barnfield Rd.)
Ada Cl. N11 . . . . .3J *31*
Ada Ct. N1 . . . . .1C *84*
(off Packington St.)
W9 . . . . .2A **4** (3A **82**)
Ada Gdns. E14 . . . . .6F *87*
E15 . . . . .1H *87*
Adagio Point SE8 . . . . .6D *104*
(off Copperas St.)
Ada Ho. E2 . . . . .1G *85*
(off Ada Pl.)
Adair Cl. SE25 . . . . .3H *157*
Adair Ho. SW3 . . . . .7D *16*
Adair Rd. W10 . . . . .4G *81*
Adair Twr. W10 . . . . .4G *81*
(off Appleford Rd.)
Ada Kennedy Ct. SE10 . . . . .7E *104*
(off Greenwich Sth. St.)
Adam & Eve Ct. W1 . . . . .7B *6*
Adam & Eve M. W8 . . . . .3J *99*
Ada Maria Ct. E1 . . . . .6H *85*
(off James Voller Way)
Adam Cl. SE6 . . . . .4B *140*
Adam Ct. SE11 . . . . .4K *19*
SW7 . . . . .4A *100*
(off Gloucester Rd.)
Adamfields NW3 . . . . .7B *64*
(off Adamson Rd.)
Adam Rd. E4 .6G *35*
Adams Bri. Bus. Cen. HA9: Wemb . . .5H *61*
Adams Cl. KT5: Surb 6F *151*
N3 . . . . .7D *30*
NW9 . . . . .2H *61*
RM5: Col R 1J *55*

Adams Ct. E17 . . . . .6A *50*
EC2 . . . . .7F **9** (6E **84**)
Adams Gdns. Est. SE16 . . . . .2J *103*
Adams Ho. E14 . . . . .6F *87*
(off Aberfeldy St.)
Adams M. N22 . . . . .7E *32*
SW17 . . . . .2D *136*
Adamson Ct. N2 . . . . .3C *46*
Adamson Rd. E16 . . . . .6J *87*
NW3 . . . . .7B *64*
Adamson Way BR3: Beck 5E *158*
Adams Pl. E14 . . . . .1D *104*
(off The Nth. Colonnade)
N7 . . . . .5K *65*
Adams Quarter TW8: Bford 7C *96*
Adamsrill Cl. EN1: Enf 6J *23*
Adamsrill Rd. SE26 . . . . .4K *139*
Adams Rd. BR3: Beck 5A *158*
N17 . . . . .2D *48*
Adam's Row W1 . . . . .3H **11** (7E **82**)
Adams Sq. DA6: Bex 3E *126*
Adams Ter. E3 . . . . .3C *86*
(off Rainhill Way)
Adam St. WC2 . . . . .3F **13** (7J **83**)
Adam Wlk. KT1: King T 2E *150*
Adams Way CR0: C'don 6F *157*
SE25 . . . . .5H *157*
Adam Wlk. SW6 . . . . .7E *98*
Adana SE13 .2E *122*
Ada Pl. E2 . . . . .1G *85*
Ada Wlk. SW16 . . . . .3K *137*
Ada Rd. HA0: Wemb 3D *60*
SE5 . . . . .7E *102*
Adastral Ho. WC1 . . . . .5G *7*
(off Harpur St.)
Adastra Way SM6: Wall 6J *167*
Ada St. E8 . . . . .1H *85*
Adcock Wlk. BR6: Orp 4K *173*
Adderley Gdns. SE9 . . . . .4E *142*
Adderley Gro. SW11 . . . . .5E *118*
Adderley Rd. HA3: W'stone 1K *41*
Adderley St. E14 . . . . .6E *86*
Addey Ho. SE8 . . . . .7B *104*
ADDINGTON .5C *170*
Addington Ct. SW14 . . . . .3K *115*
Addington Court Golf Course 7C *170*
Addington Dr. N12 . . . . .6G *31*
Addington Golf Course, The 4B *170*
Addington Gro. SE26 . . . . .4A *140*
Addington Ho. SW9 . . . . .2K *119*
(off Stockwell Rd.)
Addington Lofts SE5 . . . . .7C *102*
(off Bethwin Rd.)
Addington Palace Golf Course 6A *170*
Addington Rd. BR4: W W'ck 4E *170*
CR0: C'don 1A *168*
CR2: Sande, Sels 7K *169*
E3 . . . . .3C *86*
E16 . . . . .4G *87*
N4 . . . . .6A *48*
Addington Sq. SE5 . . . . .6D *102*
(not continuous)
Addington St. SE1 . . . . .7H **13** (2K **101**)
Addington Village Rd. CR0: Addtn 6B *170*
Addis Cl. EN3: Enf H 1E *24*
ADDISCOMBE 1G *169*
Addiscombe Av. CR0: C'don 1G *169*
Addiscombe Cl. HA3: Kenton 5C *42*
Addiscombe Ct. Rd.
CR0: C'don 1E *168*
Addiscombe Gro. CR0: C'don 2E *168*
Addiscombe Rd. CR0: C'don 2D *168*
(not continuous)
Addis Ho. E1 .5J *85*
(off Lindley St.)
Addisland Ct. W14 . . . . .2G *99*
(off Holland Vs. Rd.)
Addison Av. N14 . . . . .6A *22*
TW3: Houn 1G *113*
W11 . . . . .1G *99*

Addison Bri. Pl. W14 . . . . . 4H 99
Addison Cl. BR5: Pet W 6G 161
HA6: Nwood 1J 39
Addison Ct. *NW6* *1J 81*
(off Brondesbury Rd.)
Addison Cres. W14 . . . . . 3G 99
(not continuous)
Addison Dr. SE12 . . . . . 5K 123
Addison Gdns. KT5: Surb 4F 151
W14 . . . . . 3F 99
Addison Gro. W4 . . . . . 3A 98
Addison Ho. NW8 . . . . . 1A 4
Addison Pk. Mans. *W14* *3F 99*
(off Richmond Way)
Addison Pl. SE25 . . . . . 4G 157
UB1: S'hall 7E 76
W11 . . . . . 1G 99
Addison Rd.
BR2: Brom 5A 160
E11 . . . . . 6J 51
E17 . . . . . 5D 50
EN3: Enf H 1D 24
IG6: Ilf 1G 53
SE25 . . . . . 4G 157
TW11: Tedd 6B 132
W14 . . . . . 2G 99
Addisons Cl. CR0: C'don 2B 170
Addison Ter. *W4* *4J 97*
(off Chiswick Rd.)
Addison Way HA6: Nwood 1H 39
NW11 . . . . . 4H 45
UB3: Hayes 6J 75
Addle Hill EC4 . . . . . 1B 14 (6B 84)
Addlestone Ho. *W10* *5E 80*
(off Sutton Way)
Addle St. EC2 . . . . . 7D 8 (6C 84)
Addy Ho. SE16 . . . . . 4J 103
Adecroft Way
KT8: W Mole 3G 149
Adela Av. KT3: N Mald 5D 152
Adela Ho. *W6* *5E 98*
(off Queen Caroline St.)
Adelaide Av. SE4 . . . . . 4B 122
Adelaide Cl. EN1: Enf 1K 23
HA7: Stan 4F 27
SW9 . . . . . 4A 120
Adelaide Ct. BR3: Beck 7C 140
E9 . . . . . *5A 68*
(off Kenworthy Rd.)
NW8 . . . . . 1A 4
W7 . . . . . 2K 95
Adelaide Gdns.
RM6: Chad H 5E 54
Adelaide Gro. W12 . . . . . 1C 98
Adelaide Ho. E15 . . . . . 2H 87
E17 . . . . . 2B 50
SE5 . . . . . 2E 120
W11 . . . . . *6H 81*
(off Portobello Rd.)
Adelaide Rd. BR7: Chst 5F 143
E10 . . . . . 3D 68
IG1: Ilf 2F 71
KT6: Surb 5E 150
NW3 . . . . . 7B 64
SW18 . . . . . 5J 117
TW5: Hest 1C 112
TW9: Rich 4F 115
TW11: Tedd 6K 131
TW15: Ashf 5A 128
UB2: S'hall 4C 94
W13 . . . . . 1A 96
Adelaide St. WC2 . . . . . 3E 12 (7J 83)
(not continuous)
Adelaide Ter. TW8: Bford 5D 96
Adela St. W10 . . . . . 4G 81
Adelina Gro. E1 . . . . . 5J 85
Adelina M. SW12 . . . . . 1H 137
Adelina Yd. *E1* *5J 85*
(off Adelina Gro.)
Adeline Pl. WC1 . . . . . 6D 6 (5H 83)
Adeliza Cl. IG11: Bark 7G 71

Adelphi Ct. *E8* *7F 67*
(off Celandine Dr.)
SE16 . . . . . *2K 103*
(off Garter Way)
W4 . . . . . 6K 97
Adelphi Cres. UB4: Hayes 3G 75
Adelphi Ter. WC2 . . . . . 3F 13 (7J 83)
Adelphi Theatre *3F 13*
(off Strand)
Adelphi Way UB4: Hayes 3H 75
Adeney Cl. W6 . . . . . 6F 99
Aden Gro. N16 . . . . . 4D 66
Adenmore Rd. SE6 . . . . . 7C 122
Aden Rd. EN3: Brim 4F 25
IG1: Ilf 7G 53
Aden Ter. N16 . . . . . 4D 66
Adeyfield Ho. *EC1* *2F 9*
(off Cranwood St.)
Adie Rd. W6 . . . . . 3E 98
Adine Rd. E13 . . . . . 4K 87
Adler Ind. Est. UB3: Hayes 2F 93
Adler St. E1 . . . . . 6G 85
Adley St. E5 . . . . . 5A 68
Adlington Cl. N18 . . . . . 5J 33
Admaston Rd. SE18 . . . . . 7G 107
Admiral Ct. IG11: Bark 2B 90
SE5 . . . . . *1E 120*
(off Havil St.)
SM5: Cars 1C 166
SW10 . . . . . *1A 118*
(off Admiral Sq.)
W1 . . . . . *6G 5*
(off Blandford St.)
Admiral Ho. *SW1* *3B 18*
(off Willow Pl.)
TW11: Tedd 4A 132
Admiral Hyson Ind. Est. SE16 . . . . . 5H 103
Admiral M. SW19 . . . . . 7A 136
W10 . . . . . 4F 81
Admiral Pl. N8 . . . . . 4B 48
SE16 . . . . . 1A 104
Admirals Cl. E18 . . . . . 4K 51
Admirals Ct. *E6* *6F 89*
(off Trader Rd.)
SE1 . . . . . *5J 15*
(off Horselydown La.)
Admiral Seymour Rd. SE9 . . . . . 4D 124
Admiral's Ga. SE10 . . . . . 1D 122
Admiral Sq. SW10 . . . . . 1A 118
Admiral's Twr. *SE10* *6D 104*
(off Dowells St.)
Admiral St. SE8 . . . . . 2C 122
Admirals Wlk. NW3 . . . . . 3A 64
Admirals Way E14 . . . . . 2C 104
Admiralty Arch 4D 12 (1H 101)
Admiralty Cl. SE8 . . . . . 7C 104
UB7: W Dray 2A 92
Admiralty Rd. TW11: Tedd 6K 131
Admiralty Way
TW11: Tedd 6K 131
Admiral Wlk. W9 . . . . . 5J 81
Adolf St. SE6 . . . . . 4D 140
Adolphus Rd. N4 . . . . . 2B 66
Adolphus St. SE8 . . . . . 7B 104
Adomar Rd. RM8: Dag 3E 72
Adpar St. W2 . . . . . 5A 4 (5B 82)
Adrian Av. NW2 . . . . . 1D 62
Adrian Boult Ho. *E2* *3H 85*
(off Mansford St.)
Adrian Cl. EN5: Barn 6A 20
Adrian Ho. *E15* *7F 69*
(off Jupp Rd.)
N1 . . . . . *1K 83*
(off Barnsbury Est.)
SW8 . . . . . *7J 101*
(off Wyvil Rd.)
Adrian M. SW10 . . . . . 6K 99
Adriatic Apartments *E16* *7J 87*
(off Western Gateway)
Adriatic Bldg. *E14* *7A 86*
(off Horseferry Rd.)

Adriatic Ho. *E1* *4K 85*
(off Ernest St.)
Adrienne Av. UB1: S'hall 4D 76
Adrienne Bus. Cen.
UB1: S'hall 3D 76
Adron Ho. *SE16* *4J 103*
(off Millender Wlk.)
Adstock Ho. *N1* *7B 66*
(off The Sutton Est.)
Advance Rd. SE27 . . . . . 4C 138
Adventure Kingdom *2K 159*
(off Stockwell Cl.)
Adventurers Ct. *E14* *7F 87*
(off Newport Av.)
Advent Way N18 . . . . . 5D 34
Adys Lawn NW2 . . . . . 6D 62
Ady's Rd. SE15 . . . . . 3F 121
Aegean Apartments *E16* *7J 87*
(off Western Gateway)
Aegon Ho. *E14* *3D 104*
(off Lanark Sq.)
Aerodrome Rd. NW4 . . . . . 2B 44
NW9 . . . . . 2B 44
Aerodrome Way TW5: Hest 6A 94
Aeroville NW9 . . . . . 2A 44
AFC Wimbledon 3G 151
Affleck St. N1 . . . . . 1G 7 (2K 83)
Afghan Rd. SW11 . . . . . 2C 118
Afsil Ho. *EC1* *6K 7*
(off Viaduct Bldgs.)
Aftab Ter. *E1* *4H 85*
(off Tent St.)
Agamemnon Rd. NW6 . . . . . 4H 63
Agar Cl. KT6: Surb 2F 163
Agar Gro. NW1 . . . . . 7G 65
Agar Gro. Est. NW1 . . . . . 7H 65
Agar Ho. *KT1: King T* *3E 150*
(off Denmark Rd.)
Agar Pl. NW1 . . . . . 7G 65
Agar St. WC2 . . . . . 3E 12 (7J 83)
Agate Cl. E16 . . . . . 6B 88
NW10 . . . . . 3G 79
Agate Rd. W6 . . . . . 3E 98
Agatha Cl. E1 . . . . . 1H 103
Agaton Path SE9 . . . . . 2G 143
Agaton Rd. SE9 . . . . . 2G 143
Agave Rd. NW2 . . . . . 4E 62
Agdon St. EC1 . . . . . 3A 8 (4B 84)
Age Exchange 3H 123
Ager Av. RM8: Dag 1D 72
Agincourt Rd. NW3 . . . . . 4D 64
Agnes Av. IG1: Ilf 4E 70
Agnes Cl. E6 . . . . . 7E 88
Agnesfield Cl. N12 . . . . . 6H 31
Agnes Gdns. RM8: Dag 4D 72
Agnes George Wlk. E16 . . . . . 1B 106
Agnes Ho. *W11* *7F 81*
(off St Ann's Rd.)
Agnes Rd. W3 . . . . . 1B 98
Agnes St. E14 . . . . . 6B 86
Agnew Rd. SE23 . . . . . 7K 121
Agricola Ct. *E3* *1B 86*
(off Parnell Rd.)
Agricola Pl. EN1: Enf 5A 24
Ahoy Sailing Cen. *5C 104*
(off Stretton Mans.)
Aidan Cl. RM8: Dag 4E 72
Aigburth Mans. *SW9* *7A 102*
(off Mowll St.)
Ailantus Ct. HA8: Edg 5A 28
Aileen Wlk. E15 . . . . . 7H 69
Ailsa Av. TW1: Twick 5A 114
Ailsa Ho. *E16* *7E 88*
(off University Way)
Ailsa Rd. TW1: Twick 5B 114
Ailsa St. E14 . . . . . 5E 86
Ailsa Wlk. *E14* *2C 104*
(off Alpha Gro.)
Ainger M. *NW3* *7D 64*
(off Ainger Rd., not continuous)
Ainger Rd. NW3 . . . . . 7D 64

Ainsdale *NW1* *1A 6*
(off Harrington St.)
Ainsdale Cl. BR6: Orp 1H 173
Ainsdale Cres. HA5: Pinn 3E 40
Ainsdale Dr. SE1 . . . . . 5G 103
Ainsdale Rd. W5 . . . . . 4D 78
Ainsley Av. RM7: Rom 6H 55
Ainsley Cl. N9 . . . . . 1K 33
Ainsley St. E2 . . . . . 3H 85
Ainslie Ct. HA0: Wemb 2E 78
Ainslie Wlk. SW12 . . . . . 7F 119
Ainslie Wood Cres. E4 . . . . . 5J 35
Ainslie Wood Gdns. E4 . . . . . 4J 35
Ainslie Wood Nature Reserve 5J 35
Ainslie Wood Rd. E4 . . . . . 5H 35
Ainsty Est. SE16 . . . . . 2K 103
Ainsty St. SE16 . . . . . 2J 103
Ainsworth Cl. NW2 . . . . . 3C 62
SE15 . . . . . 2E 120
Ainsworth Ct. *NW10* *3D 80*
(off Plough Cl.)
Ainsworth Ho. *NW8* *1K 81*
(off Ainsworth Way)
W10 . . . . . *3G 81*
(off Kilburn La.)
Ainsworth Rd. CR0: C'don 1B 168
E9 . . . . . 7J 67
Ainsworth Way NW8 . . . . . 1A 82
Aintree Av. E6 . . . . . 1C 88
Aintree Cl. UB8: Hil 6D 74
Aintree Cres. IG6: Ilf 2G 53
Aintree Est. SW6 . . . . . 7G 99
Aintree Rd. UB6: G'frd 2B 78
Aintree St. SW6 . . . . . 7G 99
Airbourne Ho. *SM6: Wall* *4G 167*
(off Maldon Rd.)
Air Call Bus. Cen. NW9 . . . . . 3K 43
Airco Cl. NW9 . . . . . 3K 43
Aird Ho. *SE1* *3C 102*
(off Rockingham St.)
Airdrie Cl. N1 . . . . . 7K 65
UB4: Yead 5C 76
Airedale Av. W4 . . . . . 4B 98
Airedale Av. Sth. W4 . . . . . 5B 98
Airedale Rd. SW12 . . . . . 7D 118
W5 . . . . . 3C 96
Airedale Wlk. *E15* *7G 69*
(off Maiden Rd.)
Airlie Gdns. IG1: Ilf 1F 71
W8 . . . . . 1J 99
Airlinks Golf Course 5A 94
Air Links Ind. Est. TW13: Hanw 3C 130
Airlinks Ind. Est. TW5: Cran 5A 94
Air Pk. Way TW13: Felt 2K 129
Airport Bowl 1G 111
Airport Gate Bus. Cen. UB7: Sip 7B 92
Airport Way TW19: Stanw M 7A 174
Air Sea M. TW2: Twick 2H 131
Air St. W1 . . . . . 3B 12 (7G 83)
Airthrie Rd. IG3: Ilf 2B 72
Aisgill Av. W14 . . . . . 5H 99
(not continuous)
Aisher Rd. SE28 . . . . . 7C 90
Aislibie Rd. SE12 . . . . . 4G 123
Aiten Pl. W6 . . . . . 4C 98
Aithan Ho. *E14* *6B 86*
(off Copenhagen Pl.)
Aitken Cl. CR4: Mitc 7D 154
E8 . . . . . 1G 85
HA4: Eastc 6J 39
Aitken Rd. SE6 . . . . . 2D 140
Aitman Dr. TW8: Bford 5G 97
Aits Vw. KT8: W Mole 3F 149
Ajax Av. NW9 . . . . . 3A 44
Ajax Ho. *E2* *2H 85*
(off Old Bethnal Grn. Rd.)
Ajax Rd. NW6 . . . . . 4H 63
Akabusi Cl. CR0: C'don 6G 157
Akbar Ho. *E14* *4D 104*
(off Cahir St.)
Akehurst St. SW15 . . . . . 6C 116

Akenside Rd. NW3 . . . . .5B 64
Akerman Rd. KT6: Surb 6C 150
SW9 . . . . .2B 120
Akintero Ho. SE8 . . . . .6B 104
(off Alverton St.)
Alabama St. SE18 . . . . .7H 107
Alacross Rd. W5 . . . . .2C 96
Alamaro Lodge SE10 . . . . .3H 105
(off Teal St.)
Alana Hgts. E4 . . . . .7J 25
Alan Coren Cl. NW2 . . . . .4E 62
Alandale Dr. HA5: Pinn 1K 39
Aland Ct. SE16 . . . . .3A 104
Alander M. E17 . . . . .4E 50
Alan Dr. EN5: Barn 6B 20
Alan Gdns. RM7: Rush G 7G 55
Alan Hocken Way E15 . . . . .2G 87
Alan Preece Ct. NW6 . . . . .7F 63
Alan Rd. SW19 . . . . .5G 135
Alanthus Cl. SE12 . . . . .6J 123
Alaska Apartments E16 . . . . .7J 87
(off Western Gateway)
Alaska Bldg. SE13 . . . . .1D 122
(off Deal's Gateway)
Alaska Bldgs. SE1 . . . . .3J 13 (1A 102)
Alaska St. SE1 . . . . .5J 13 (1A 102)
Alastor Ho. E14 . . . . .3E 104
(off Strattondale St.)
Alba Cl. UB4: Yead 4B 76
Albacore Cres. SE13 . . . . .6D 122
Albacore Way UB3: Hayes 7H 75
Alba Gdns. NW11 . . . . .6G 45
Albain Cres. TW15: Ashf 2A 128
Alba M. SW18 . . . . .2J 135
Alban Highwalk EC2 . . . . .7D 8
(not continuous)
Albany, The 7C 104
Albany N12 . . . . .6E 30
W1 . . . . .3A 12 (7G 83)
Albany, The IG8: Wfd G 4C 36
Albany Cl. DA5: Bexl 7C 126
N15 . . . . .4B 48
SW14 . . . . .4H 115
UB10: Ick .5C 56
Albany Ct. E1 .6G 85
(off Plumber's Row)
E4 . . . . .6H 25
(Chelwood Cl.)
E4 . . . . .5G 35
(Westward Rd.)
E10 . . . . .7C 50
HA8: Edg .1K 43
NW8 . . . . .1A 4
(off Abbey Rd.)
NW10 . . . . .3D 80
(off Trenmar Gdns.)
TW15: Ashf 7E 128
Albany Pde. TW8: Bford 6E 96
Albany Cres. HA8: Edg 7B 28
Albany Ct. Ga. KT2: King T 6D 132
N1 . . . . .7A 66
SE5 . . . . .6C 102
SM1: Sutt .5K 165
Albany Pde. TW8: Bford 6E 96
Albany M. BR1: Brom 6J 141
KT2: King T 6D 132
N1 . . . . .7A 66
SE5 . . . . .6C 102
SM1: Sutt .5K 165
Albany Pde. TW8: Bford 6E 96
Albany Pk. Av. EN3: Enf W 1D 24
Albany Pk. Rd. KT2: King T 6D 132
Albany Pas. TW10: Rich 5E 114
Albany Pl. TW8: Bford 6D 96
Albany Reach KT7: T Ditt 5K 149
Albany Rd. BR7: Chst 5F 143
DA5: Bexl 7C 126
DA17: Belv 6F 109
E10 . . . . .7C 50
E12 . . . . .4B 70
E17 . . . . .6A 50
KT3: N Mald 4K 151
N4 . . . . .6A 48
N18 . . . . .5D 34
RM6: Chad H 6F 55

Albany Rd. SE5 . . . . .6D 102
SW19 . . . . .5K 135
TW8: Bford .6D 96
TW10: Rich 5F 115
W13 . . . . .7B 78
Albany St. NW1 . . . . .1K 5 (2F 83)
Albany Ter. NW1 . . . . .4K 5
TW10: Rich 5F 115
(off Albany Pas.)
Albany Vw. IG9: Buck H 1D 36
Albany Works E3 . . . . .1A 86
(off Gunmakers La.)
Alba Pl. W11 . . . . .6H 81
Albatross NW9 . . . . .2B 44
Albatross Cl. E6 . . . . .5D 88
Albatross St. SE18 . . . . .7J 107
Albatross Way SE16 . . . . .2K 103
Albemarle SW19 . . . . .2F 135
Albemarle App. IG2: Ilf 6F 53
Albemarle Av.
TW2: Whitt 1D 130
Albemarle Ct. N17 . . . . .3H 49
(off Perkyn Sq.)
Albemarle Gdns. IG2: Ilf 6F 53
KT3: N Mald 4K 151
Albemarle Ho. SE8 . . . . .4B 104
(off Foreshore)
SW9 . . . . .3A 120
Albemarle Pk. BR3: Beck 1D 158
HA7: Stan .5H 27
Albemarle Rd. BR3: Beck 1D 158
EN4: E Barn 7H 21
Albemarle St. W1 . . . . .3K 11 (7F 83)
Albemarle Way EC1 . . . . .4A 8 (4B 84)
Alberon Gdns. NW11 . . . . .4H 45
Alberta Av. SM1: Sutt 4G 165
Alberta Est. SE17 . . . . .5B 102
(off Alberta St.)
Alberta Ho. UB4: Yead 3K 75
(off Ayles Rd.)
Alberta Rd. DA8: Erith 1J 127
EN1: Enf 6A 24
Alberta St. SE17 . . . . .5B 102
Albert Av. E4 .4H 35
SW8 . . . . .7K 101
Albert Barnes Ho. SE1 . . . . .3C 102
(off New Kent Rd.)
Albert Basin Way E16 . . . . .7G 89
Albert Bigg Point E15 . . . . .2E 86
(off Godfrey St.)
Albert Bri. SW3 . . . . .7D 16 (6C 100)
Albert Bri. Rd. SW11 . . . . .7C 100
Albert Carr Gdns. SW16 . . . . .5J 137
Albert Cl. E9 . . . . .1H 85
N22 . . . . .1H 47
Albert Cotts. E1 . . . . .5G 85
(off Deal St.)
Albert Ct. E7 . . . . .4J 69
SW7 . . . . .7A 10 (3B 100)
Albert Ct. Ga. SW1 . . . . .7E 10
(off Knightsbridge)
Albert Cres. E4 . . . . .4H 35
Albert Dane Cen. UB2: S'hall 3C 94
Albert Dr. SW19 . . . . .2G 135
Albert Gdns. E1 . . . . .6K 85
Albert Ga. SW1 . . . . .6F 11 (2D 100)
Albert Gray Ho. SW10 . . . . .7B 100
(off Worlds End Est.)
Albert Gro. SW20 . . . . .1F 153
Albert Hall Mans. SW7 . . . . . . .7A 10 (2B 100)
Albert Ho. E18 .3K 51
(off Albert Rd.)
SE28 . . . . .3G 107
Albert Mans. CRO: C'don 1D 168
(off Lansdowne Rd.)
SW11 . . . . .1D 118
(off Albert Bri. Rd.)

Albert Memorial
Knightsbridge 7A 10 (2B 100)
Albert M. E14 .7A 86
(off Northey St.)
N4 . . . . .1K 65
SE4 . . . . .4A 122
W8 . . . . .3A 100
Albert Pal. Mans. SW11 . . . . .1F 119
(off Lurline Gdns.)
Albert Pl. N3 . . . . .1J 45
N17 . . . . .3F 49
W8 . . . . .3K 99
Albert Rd.
BR2: Brom 5B 160
CR4: Mitc .3D 154
DA5: Bexl .6G 127
DA17: Belv 5F 109
E10 . . . . .2E 68
E16 . . . . .1C 106
E17 . . . . .5C 50
E18 . . . . .3K 51
EN4: E Barn 4F 21
HA2: Harr 3G 41
IG1: Ilf 3F 71
IG9: Buck H 2G 37
KT1: King T 2F 151
KT3: N Mald 4B 152
N4 . . . . .1K 65
N15 . . . . .6E 48
N22 . . . . .1G 47
NW4 . . . . .4F 45
NW6 . . . . .2H 81
NW7 . . . . .5G 29
RM8: Dag .1G 73
SE9 . . . . .3C 142
SE20 . . . . .6K 139
SE25 . . . . .4G 157
SM1: Sutt .5B 166
TW1: Twick 1K 131
TW3: Houn 4E 112
TW10: Rich 5E 114
TW11: Tedd 6K 131
TW12: Hamp H 5G 131
TW15: Ashf 5B 128
UB2: S'hall 3B 94
UB3: Hayes 3G 93
UB7: View .1A 92
W5 . . . . .4B 78
Albert Rd. Est. DA17: Belv 5F 109
Alberts Cl. NW1 . . . . .3D 4
(off Colthurst Dr.)
Albert Sleet Ct. N9 . . . . .3C 34
Albert Sq. E15 .5G 69
SW8 . . . . .7K 101
Albert Starr Ho. SE8 . . . . .4K 103
(off Haddonfield)
Albert St. N12 .5F 31
NW1 . . . . .1F 83
Albert Studios SW11 . . . . .1D 118
Albert Ter. IG9: Buck H 2H 37
N1 . . . . .1E 82
NW10 . . . . .1J 79
W5 . . . . .4B 78
W6 . . . . .5C 98
(off Beavor La.)
Albert Ter. M. NW1 . . . . .1E 82
Albert Victoria Ho. N22 . . . . .1A 48
Albert Wlk. E16 . . . . .2E 106
Albert Way SE15 . . . . .7H 103
Albert Westcott Ho.
SE17 . . . . .5B 102
Albert Yd. SE19 . . . . .6F 139
Albery Cl. E8 . . . . .7F 67
(off Middleton Rd.)
Albion Av. N10 . . . . .1E 46
SW8 . . . . .2H 119
Albion Bldgs. N1 . . . . .2J 83
(off Albion Yd.)
Albion Cl. RM7: Rom 6K 55
W2 . . . . .2D 10 (7C 82)

Albion Ct. SE10 . . . . .4G 105
(off Azof St.)
SM2: Sutt .7B 166
W6 . . . . .4D 98
(off Albion Pl.)
Albion Dr. E8 . . . . .7F 67
Albion Est. SE16 . . . . .2K 103
Albion Gdns. W6 . . . . .4D 98
Albion Ga. W2 .2D 10
(not continuous)
Albion Gro. N16 . . . . .4E 66
Albion Ho. E16 . . . . .1F 107
(off Church St.)
SE8 . . . . .7C 104
(off Watsons St.)
Albion M. N1 . . . . .1A 84
NW6 . . . . .7H 63
W2 . . . . .2D 10 (7C 82)
W6 . . . . .4D 98
Albion Pde. N16 . . . . .4D 66
Albion Pl. EC1 . . . . .5A 8 (5B 84)
EC2 . . . . .6F 9 (5D 84)
W6 . . . . .4D 98
Albion Riverside Bldg. SW11 . . . . . . .7C 100
Albion Rd. DA6: Bex 4F 127
E17 . . . . .3E 50
KT2: King T 1J 151
N16 . . . . .4D 66
N17 . . . . .2G 49
SM2: Sutt .6B 166
TW2: Twick 1J 131
TW3: Houn 4E 112
UB3: Hayes 3G 93
Albion Sq. E8 .7F 67
(not continuous)
Albion St. CRO: C'don 1B 168
SE16 . . . . .2J 103
W2 . . . . .1D 10 (6C 82)
Albion Ter. E4 .4J 25
E8 . . . . .7F 67
Albion Vs. Rd. SE26 . . . . .3J 139
Albion Wlk. N1 .1F 7
(off York Way)
Albion Way EC1 . . . . .6C 8 (5C 84)
HA9: Wemb 3G 61
SE13 . . . . .4E 122
Albion Yd. E1 .5H 85
N1 . . . . .2J 83
Albon Ho. SW18 . . . . .6K 117
(off Neville Gill Cl.)
Albrighton Rd. SE22 . . . . .3E 120
Albuhera Cl. EN2: Enf 1F 23
Albury Av. DA7: Bex 2E 126
TW7: Isle 7K 95
Albury Cl. TW12: Hamp 6F 131
Albury Ct. CRO: C'don 4C 168
(off Tanfield Rd.)
CR4: Mitc .2B 154
SE8 . . . . .6C 104
(off Albury St.)
SM1: Sutt .4A 166
UB5: N'olt 3A 76
(off Canberra Dr.)
Albury Dr. HA5: Pinn . . . . .1A 40 & 1C 40
Albury Ho. SE1 .7B 14
(off Boyfield St.)
Albury M. E12 .2A 70
Albury Rd. KT9: Chess 5E 162
Albury St. SE8 . . . . .6C 104
Albyfield BR1: Brom 4D 160
Albyn Rd. SE8 . . . . .1C 122
Alcester Cl. SM6: Wall 4F 167
Alcester Cres. E5 . . . . .2H 67
Alcester Rd. SM6: Wall 4F 167
Alcock Cl. SM6: Wall 7H 167
Alcock Rd. TW5: Hest 7B 94
Alconbury DA6: Bex 5H 127
Alconbury Rd. E5 . . . . .2G 67
Alcorn Cl. SM3: Sutt 2J 165
Alcott Cl. TW14: Felt 1H 129
W7 . . . . .5K 77

Alcuin Ct. HA7: Stan 7H 27
Aldam Pl. N16 ....2F 67
Aldborough Ct. IG2: Ilf 5K 53
(off Aldborough Rd. Nth.)
ALDBOROUGH HATCH 4K 53
Aldborough Rd. RM10: Dag 6J 73
Aldborough Rd. Nth. IG2: Ilf 5K 53
Aldborough Rd. Sth. IG3: Ilf 1J 71
Aldbourne Rd. W12 ....1B 98
Aldbridge St. SE17 ....5E 102
Aldburgh M. W1 ....7H 5 (6E 82)
Aldbury Av. HA9: Wemb 7H 61
Aldbury Ho. SW3 ....5C 16
(off Cale St.)
Aldbury M. N9 ....7J 23
Aldebert Ter. SW8 ....7J 101
Aldeburgh Cl. E5 ....2H 67
Aldeburgh Pl. IG8: Wfd G 4D 36
SE10 ....4J 105
(off Aldeburgh St.)
Aldeburgh St. SE10 ....5J 105
Alden Av. E15 ....3H 87
Alden Ct. CRO: C'don 3E 168
Aldenham Dr. UB8: Hil 4D 74
Aldenham Ho. NW1 ....1B 6
(off Aldenham St.)
Aldenham St. NW1 ....1C 6 (2G 83)
Alden Ho. E8 ....1H 85
(off Duncan Rd.)
Aldensley Rd. W6 ....3D 98
Alderbrook Rd. SW12 ....6F 119
Alderbury Rd. SW13 ....6C 98
Alder Cl. DA18: Erith 2F 109
SE15 ....6F 103
Alder Ct. E7 ....5J 69
N11 ....6B 32
Alder Gro. NW2 ....2C 62
Aldergrove Gdns. TW3: Houn 2C 112
Alder Ho. E3 ....1B 86
(off Hornbeam Sq.)
NW3 ....6D 64
SE4 ....3C 122
SE15 ....6F 103
(off Alder Cl.)
Alder Lodge SW6 ....1E 116
Alderman Av. IG11: Bark 3A 90
Aldermanbury EC2 ....7D 8 (6C 84)
Aldermanbury Sq. EC2 ....6D 8 (5C 84)
Alderman Judge Mall KT1: King T 2E 150
(off Eden St.)
Aldermans Hill N13 ....4D 32
Aldermans Ho. E9 ....5A 68
(off Ward La.)
Aldermans Wlk. EC2 ....6G 9 (5E 84)
Aldermary Rd. BR1: Brom 1J 159
Alder M. N19 ....2G 65
Aldermoor Rd. SE6 ....3B 140
Alderney Av. TW5: Hest, Isle 7F 95
Alderney Ct. SE10 ....(off Trafalgar Rd.)
Alderney Gdns. UB5: N'olt 7D 58
Alderney Ho. EN3: Enf W 1E 24
N1 ....6C 66
(off Arran Wlk.)
Alderney M. SE1 ....3D 102
Alderney Rd. E1 ....4K 85
Alderney St. SW1 ....4K 17 (4F 101)
Alder Rd. DA14: Sidc 3K 143
SW14 ....3K 115
Alders, The BR4: W W'ck 1D 170
N21 ....6F 23
SW16 ....4G 137
TW5: Hest 6D 94
TW13: Hanw 4C 130
Alders Av. IG8: Wfd G 6B 36
ALDERSBROOK 2K 69
Aldersbrook Av. EN1: Enf 2K 23
Aldersbrook Dr. KT2: King T 6F 133
Aldersbrook La. E12 ....3D 70
Aldersbrook Rd. E11 ....2K 69
E12 ....2K 69

Alders Cl. E11 ....2K 69
HA8: Edg 5D 28
W5 ....3D 96
Aldersey Gdns. IG11: Bark 6H 71
Aldersford Cl. SE4 ....5K 121
Aldersgate St. EC1 ....6C 8
(off Bartholomew Cl.)
Aldersgate St. EC1 ....5C 8 (5C 84)
Alders Gro. KT8: E Mos 5H 149
Aldersgrove Av. SE9 ....3B 142
Aldershot Rd. NW6 ....1H 81
Aldershot Ter. SE18 ....7E 106
Aldersmead Av. CRO: C'don 6K 157
Aldersmead Rd. BR3: Beck 7A 140
Alderson Pl. UB2: S'hall 1G 95
Alderson St. W10 ....4G 81
Alders Rd. HA8: Edg 5D 28
Alderton Cl. NW10 ....3K 61
Alderton Ct. KT8: W Mole 4D 148
(off Dunstable Rd.)
Alderton Cres. NW4 ....5D 44
Alderton Rd. CRO: C'don 7F 157
SE24 ....3C 120
Alderton Way NW4 ....5D 44
Alderville Rd. SW6 ....2H 117
Alder Wlk. IG1: Ilf 5G 71
Alderwick Dr. N7 ....6K 65
(off Cornelia St.)
Alderwick Dr. TW3: Houn 3H 113
Alderwood M. EN4: Had W 1F 21
Alderwood Rd. SE9 ....6H 125
Aldford Ho. W1 ....4G 11
(off Park St.)
Aldford St. W1 ....4H 11 (1E 100)
ALDGATE 6F 85
Aldgate E1 ....6F 85
(off Whitechapel High St.)
EC3 ....1J 15 (6E 84)
Aldgate Av. E1 ....7J 9 (6F 85)
Aldgate Barrs E1 ....7H 9
Aldgate High St. EC3 ....1J 15 (6E 85)
Aldgate Pl. E1 ....7K 9 (6F 85)
Aldgate Twr. E1 ....6F 85
Aldham Ho. SE4 ....2B 122
(off Malpas Rd.)
Aldine Ct. W12 ....2E 98
(off Aldine St.)
Aldine Pl. W12 ....2E 98
Aldine St. W12 ....2E 98
Aldington Cl. RM8: Dag 1C 72
Aldington Ct. E8 ....7G 67
(off London Flds. W. Side)
Aldington Rd. SE18 ....3B 106
Aldis M. SW17 ....5C 136
Aldis St. SW17 ....5C 136
Aldren Rd. SW17 ....3A 136
Aldrich Cres. CRO: New Ad 7E 170
Aldriche Way E4 ....6K 35
Aldrich Gdns. SM3: Cheam 3H 165
Aldrich Ter. SW18 ....2A 136
Aldrick Ho. N1 ....1K 83
(off Barnsbury Est.)
Aldridge Av. HA4: Ruis 5K 39
HA7: Stan 1E 42
HA8: Edg 3C 28
Aldridge Cl. W11 ....5H 81
(off Aldridge Rd. Vs.)
Aldridge Ri. KT3: N Mald 7A 152
Aldridge Rd. Vs. W11 ....5H 81
Aldridge Wlk. N14 ....7D 22
Aldrington Rd. SW16 ....5G 137
Aldsworth Cl. W9 ....4K 81
Aldwick Cl. SE9 ....3H 143
Aldwick Rd. CRO: Bedd 3K 167
Aldworth Gro. SE13 ....6E 122
Aldworth Rd. E15 ....7G 69
Aldwych WC2 ....2G 13 (6K 83)
Aldwych Av. IG6: Ilf 4G 53
Aldwych Bldgs. WC2 ....7F 7
(off Parker M.)

Aldwych Ct. E8 ....7F 67
(off Middleton Rd.)
Aldwych Theatre 1G 13
(off Aldwych)
Aldwyn Ho. SW8 ....7J 101
(off Davidson Gdns.)
Alers Rd. DA6: Bex 5D 126
Alesia Cl. N22 ....7D 32
Alestan Beck Rd. E16 ....6B 88
Alexa Ct. SM2: Sutt 6A 166
W8 ....4J 99
Alexander Av. NW10 ....7D 62
Alexander Cl. BR2: Hayes 1J 171
DA15: Sidc 6J 125
EN4: E Barn 4G 21
TW2: Twick 2J 131
UB2: S'hall 1G 95
Alexander Ct. BR3: Beck 1F 159
HA7: Stan 3F 43
TW16: Sun 6H 129
Alexander Evans M. SE23 ....2K 139
Alexander Fleming Laboratory Mus.
....7B 4 (6B 82)
Alexander Ho. E14 ....3C 104
(off Tiller Rd.)
KT2: King T 1E 150
(off Seven Kings Way)
SE15 ....2H 121
(off Godman Rd.)
Alexander M. SW16 ....5G 137
W2 ....6K 81
Alexander Pl. SW7 ....3C 16 (4C 100)
Alexander Rd. BR7: Chst 6H 143
DA7: Bex 2D 126
N19 ....3H 65
Alexander Sq. SW3 ....3C 16 (4C 100)
Alexander St. W2 ....6J 81
Alexander Studios SW11 ....4B 118
(off Haydon Way)
Alexander Ter. SE2 ....5B 108
Alexandra Av. HA2: Harr 1D 58
N22 ....1H 47
SM1: Sutt 3J 165
SW11 ....1E 118
UB1: S'hall 7D 76
W4 ....7K 97
Alexandra Cl. HA2: Harr 3E 58
SE8 ....6B 104
TW15: Ashf 7F 129
Alexandra Cotts. SE14 ....1B 122
Alexandra Ct.
HA9: Wemb 4F 61
N14 ....5B 22
SE5 ....6C 102
(off Urlwin St.)
SW7 ....1A 16
TW3: Houn 2F 113
TW15: Ashf 6F 129
UB6: G'frd 2F 77
W2 ....7K 81
(off Moscow Rd.)
W9 ....4A 82
(off Maida Vale)
Alexandra Cres. BR1: Brom 6H 141
Alexandra Dr. KT5: Surb 7G 151
SE19 ....5E 138
Alexandra Gdns. N10 ....4F 47
SM5: Cars 7E 166
TW3: Houn 2F 113
W4 ....7A 98
Alexandra Gro. N4 ....1B 66
N12 ....5E 30
Alexandra Ho. E16 ....1K 105
(off Wesley Av.)
IG8: Wfd G 7K 37
W6 ....5E 98
(off Queen Caroline St.)
Alexandra Mans. SW3 ....7A 16
(off King's Rd.)
W12 ....1E 98
(off Stanlake Rd.)

Alexandra M. N2 ....3D 46
N4 ....2B 66
SW19 ....6H 135
Alexandra Palace 2H 47
Alexandra Pal. Way N22 ....4G 47
Alexandra Pde. HA2: Harr 4F 59
Alexandra Pk. Rd. N10 ....2F 47
N22 ....1G 47
Alexandra Pk. School Sports Cen. 1G 47
Alexandra Pl. CRO: C'don 1E 168
NW8 ....1A 82
SE25 ....5D 156
Alexandra Rd. CRO: C'don 1E 168
CR4: Mitc 7C 136
E6 ....3E 88
E10 ....3E 68
E17 ....6B 50
E18 ....3K 51
EN3: Pond E 4E 24
KT2: King T 7G 133
KT7: T Ditt 5K 149
N8 ....3A 48
N9 ....7C 24
N10 ....7A 32
N15 ....5D 48
NW4 ....4F 45
NW8 ....1A 82
RM6: Chad H 6E 54
SE26 ....6K 139
SW14 ....3K 115
SW19 ....6H 135
TW1: Twick 6C 114
TW3: Houn 2F 113
TW8: Bford 6D 96
TW9: Kew 2F 115
TW15: Ashf 7F 129
W4 ....2K 97
Alexandra Rd. Ind. Est. EN3: Pond E 4E 24
Alexandra Sq. SM4: Mord 5J 153
Alexandra St. E16 ....5J 87
SE14 ....7A 104
Alexandra Ter. E14 ....3C 104
(off Westferry Rd.)
Alexandra Wlk. SE19 ....5E 138
Alexandra Wharf E2 ....1H 85
(off Darwen Pl.)
Alexandra Yd. E9 ....1K 85
Alexandria Apartments SE17 ....4E 102
(off Townsend St.)
Alexandria Rd. W13 ....7A 78
Alexia Sq. E14 ....3D 104
Alexis St. SE16 ....4G 103
Alfan La. DA2: Wilm 5K 145
Alfearn Rd. E5 ....4J 67
Alford Ct. N1 ....1D 8
(off Shepherdess Wlk., not continuous)
Alford Grn. CRO: New Ad 6F 171
Alford Ho. N6 ....6G 47
Alford Pl. N1 ....1D 8 (2C 84)
Alford Rd. DA8: Erith 5J 109
Alfoxton Av. N15 ....4B 48
Alfreda St. SW11 ....1F 119
Alfred Cl. W4 ....4K 97
Alfred Ct. SE16 ....4H 103
(off Bombay St.)
Alfred Dickens Ho. E16 ....6H 87
(off Hallsville Rd.)
Alfred Finlay Ho. N22 ....2B 48
Alfred Gdns. UB1: S'hall 7C 76
Alfred Ho. E9 ....5A 68
(off Homerton Rd.)
E12 ....7C 70
(off Tennyson Av.)
Alfred M. W1 ....5C 6 (5H 83)
Alfred Nunn Ho. NW10 ....1B 80
Alfred Pl. WC1 ....5C 6 (5H 83)
Alfred Prior Ho. E12 ....4E 70
Alfred Rd. DA17: Belv 5F 109
E15 ....5H 69
IG9: Buck H 2G 37
KT1: King T 3E 150

Alfred Rd. SE25 .....5G 157
　SM1: Sutt 5A 166
　TW13: Felt 2A 130
　W2 .....5J 81
　W3 .....1J 97
Alfred Salter Ho. SE1 .....4F 103
　(off Fort Rd.)
Alfred's Gdns. IG11: Bark 2J 89
Alfred St. E3 .....3B 86
Alfreds Way IG11: Bark 3F 89
Alfreds Way Ind. Est. IG11: Bark 2A 90
Alfred Vs. E17 .....4E 50
Alfreton Cl. SW19 .....3F 135
Alfriston KT5: Surb 6F 151
Alfriston Av. CR0: C'don 7J 155
　HA2: Harr 6E 40
Alfriston Cl. KT5: Surb 5F 151
Alfriston Rd. SW11 .....5D 118
Algar Cl. HA7: Stan 5E 26
　TW7: Isle 3A 114
Algar Ho. SE1 .....7A 14
Algar Rd. TW7: Isle 3A 114
Algarve Rd. SW18 .....1K 135
Algernon Rd. NW4 .....6C 44
　NW6 .....1J 81
　SE13 .....4D 122
Algiers Rd. SE13 .....4C 122
Alibon Gdns. RM10: Dag 5G 73
Alibon Rd. RM9: Dag 5F 73
　RM10: Dag 5G 73
Alice Cl. EN5: New Bar 4F 21
　(off Station App.)
Alice Gilliatt Cl. W14 .....6H 99
　(off Star Rd.)
Alice La. E3 .....1B 86
Alice M. TW11: Tedd 5K 131
Alice Owen Technology Cen. EC1 .....1A 8
　(off Goswell Rd.)
Alice Shepherd Ho. E14 .....2E 104
　(off Manchester Rd.)
Alice St. SE1 .....3E 102
　(not continuous)
Alice Thompson Cl. SE12 .....2A 142
Alice Walker Cl. SE24 .....4B 120
Alice Way TW3: Houn 4F 113
Alicia Av. HA3: Kenton 4B 42
Alicia Cl. HA3: Kenton 4C 42
Alicia Gdns. HA3: Kenton 4B 42
Alicia Ho. DA16: Well 1B 126
Alie St. E1 .....1K 15 (6F 85)
Alington Cres. NW9 .....7J 43
Alington Gro. SM6: Wall 7G 167
Alison Cl.
　CR0: C'don 1K 169
　E6 .....6E 88
　HA5: Eastc 6K 39
Aliwal M. SW11 .....4C 118
Aliwal Rd. SW11 .....4C 118
Alkerden Rd. W4 .....5A 98
Alkham Rd. N16 .....2F 67
Alan Barclay Cl. N15 .....6E 49
Allan Cl. KT3: N Mald 5K 151
Allandale Av. N3 .....3G 45
Allanson Ct. E10 .....2C 68
　(off Leyton Grange Est.)
Allan Way W3 .....5J 79
Allard Cres. WD23: B Hea 1B 26
Allard Gdns. SW4 .....5H 119
Allard Ho. NW9 .....2B 44
　(off Boulevard Dr.)
Allardyce St. SW4 .....4K 119
Allbrook Cl.
　TW11: Tedd 5J 131
Allcroft Rd. NW5 .....5E 64
Allder Way CR2: S Croy 7B 168
Allenby Cl. UB6: G'frd 3E 76
Allenby Rd. SE23 .....3A 140
　SE28 .....3G 107
　UB1: S'hall 3E 76
Allen Cl. CR4: Mitc 1F 155
　TW16: Sun 1K 147

Allen Ct. E17 .....6C 50
　(off Yunus Khan Cl.)
　UB6: G'frd 5K 59
Allendale Av. UB1: S'hall 6E 76
Allendale Cl. SE5 .....2D 120
　SE26 .....5K 139
Allendale Rd. HA0: Wemb 6B 60
　UB6: G'frd 6B 60
Allen Edwards Dr. SW8 .....1J 119
Allenford Ho. SW15 .....6B 116
　(off Tunworth Cres.)
Allen Ho. W8 .....3J 99
　(off Allen St.)
Allen Mans. W8 .....3J 99
　(off Allen St.)
Allen Rd. BR3: Beck 2K 157
　CR0: C'don 1A 168
　E3 .....2B 86
　N16 .....4E 66
　TW16: Sun 1K 147
Allensbury Pl. NW1 .....7H 65
Allens Rd. EN3: Pond E 5D 24
Allen St. W8 .....3J 99
Allenswood SW19 .....1G 135
Allenswood Rd. SE9 .....3C 124
Allerford Cl. HA2: Harr 5G 41
Allerford Rd. SE6 .....3D 140
Allerton Ho. N1 .....1E 8
　(off Provost St.)
Allerton Rd. N16 .....2C 66
Allerton St. N1 .....1E 8 (3D 84)
Allerton Wlk. N7 .....2K 65
Allestree Rd. SW6 .....7G 99
Alleyn Cres. SE21 .....2D 138
Alleyndale Rd. RM8: Dag 2C 72
Alleyn Pk. SE21 .....2D 138
　UB2: S'hall 5E 94
Alleyn Rd. SE21 .....3D 138
Alley Way UB8: Uxb 7A 56
Allfarthing La. SW18 .....6K 117
Allgood Cl. SM4: Mord 6F 153
Allgood St. E2 .....1K 9 (2F 85)
Allhallows La. EC4 .....3E 14 (7D 84)
All Hallows Rd. N17 .....1E 48
Allhallows Rd. E6 .....5C 88
Alliance Cl.
　HA0: Wemb 4D 60
　TW4: Houn 5D 112
Alliance Ct. TW15: Ashf 4E 128
　W3 .....5H 79
Alliance Rd. E13 .....5A 88
　SE18 .....6A 108
　W3 .....4H 79
Allianz Park 7K 29
Allied Ct. N1 .....7E 66
　(off Enfield Rd.)
Allied Ind. Est. W3 .....2A 98
Allied Way W3 .....2A 98
Allingham Cl. W7 .....7K 77
Allingham Ct. BR2: Brom 4H 159
Allingham M. N1 .....2C 84
　(off Allingham St.)
Allingham St. N1 .....2C 84
Allington Av. N17 .....6K 33
　TW17: Shep 3G 147
Allington Cl. SW19 .....5F 135
　UB6: G'frd 7G 59
Allington Ct. CR0: C'don 6J 157
　(off Chart Cl.)
　EN3: Pond E 5E 24
　SW8 .....2G 119
Allington Rd. BR6: Orp 2H 173
　HA2: Harr 5G 41
　NW4 .....5D 44
　W10 .....3G 81
Allison Cl. SE10 .....1E 122
Allison Gro. SE21 .....1E 138
Allison Rd. N8 .....5A 48
　W3 .....6J 79

Alliston Ho. E2 .....2K 9
　(off Gibraltar Wlk.)
Allitsen Rd. NW8 .....2C 82
　(not continuous)
All Nations Ho. E8 .....7H 67
　(off Martello St.)
Allnutt Way SW4 .....5H 119
Alloa Rd. IG3: Ilf 2A 72
　SE8 .....5K 103
Allom Ho. W11 .....7G 81
　(off Clarendon Rd.)
Allonby Dr. HA4: Ruis 7D 38
Allonby Gdns. HA9: Wemb 1C 60
Allonby Ho. E14 .....5A 86
　(off Aston St.)
Allotment Way NW2 .....3F 63
Alloway Rd. E3 .....3A 86
Allport Ho. SE5 .....3D 120
　(off Champion Pk.)
Allport M. E1 .....4J 85
　(off Hayfield Pas.)
All Saints Cl. N9 .....2B 34
　SW8 .....1J 119
All Saints Ct. E1 .....7J 85
　(off Johnson St.)
　SW11 .....7F 101
　(off Prince of Wales Dr.)
　TW5: Hest 1B 112
All Saints Dr. SE3 .....2G 123
　(not continuous)
All Saints Ho. W11 .....5H 81
　(off All Saints Rd.)
All Saints M. HA3: Hrw W 6D 26
All Saints Pas. SW18 .....5J 117
All Saints Rd. SM1: Sutt 3K 165
　SW19 .....7A 136
　(not continuous)
　W3 .....3J 97
　W11 .....5H 81
All Saints St. N1 .....2K 83
Allsop Pl. NW1 .....4F 5 (4D 82)
All Souls Av. NW10 .....2D 80
All Souls' Pl. W1 .....6K 5 (5F 83)
Allum Way N20 .....1F 31
Alluvium Ct. SE1 .....7G 15
　(off Long La.)
Allwood Cl. SE26 .....4K 139
Alma Av. E4 .....7K 35
Alma Birk Ho. NW6 .....7G 63
Almack Rd. E5 .....4J 67
Alma Cl. N10 .....1F 47
Alma Ct. HA2: Harr 2H 59
Alma Cres. SM1: Sutt 5G 165
Alma Gro. SE1 .....4F 103
Alma Ho. N9 .....4B 34
　TW8: Bford 6E 96
Almanza Pl. IG11: Bark 2B 90
Alma Pl. CR7: Thor H 5A 156
　NW10 .....3D 80
　SE19 .....7F 139
Alma Rd. DA14: Sidc 3A 144
　EN3: Enf H, Pond E 5F 25
　KT10: Esh 7J 149
　N10 .....7A 32
　SM5: Cars 5C 166
　SW18 .....4A 118
　UB1: S'hall 7C 76
Alma Row HA3: Hrw W 1H 41
Alma Sq. E15 .....6F 69
　NW5 .....6F 65
Alma Ter. E3 .....1B 86
　(off Beale Rd.)
　SW18 .....7B 118
　W8 .....3J 99
Almeida St. N1 .....1B 84
Almeida Theatre 1B 84
　(off Almeida St.)
Almeric Rd. SW11 .....4D 118

Almer Rd. SW20 .....7C 134
Almington St. N4 .....1K 65
Almond Av. SM5: Cars 2D 166
　UB7: W Dray 3C 92
　UB10: Ick 3D 56
　W5 .....3D 96
Almond Cl.
　BR2: Brom 7E 160
　E17 .....4A 50
　HA4: Ruis 3H 57
　SE15 .....2G 121
　TW13: Felt 1J 129
　TW17: Shep 2E 146
　UB3: Hayes 7G 75
Almond Gro. TW8: Bford 7B 96
Almond Ho. E15 .....3G 87
　(off Teasel Way)
Almond Rd. N17 .....7B 34
　SE16 .....4H 103
Almonds Av. IG9: Buck H 2D 36
Almond Way BR2: Brom 7E 160
　CR4: Mitc 5H 155
　HA2: Harr 2F 41
Almorah Rd. N1 .....7D 66
　TW5: Hest 1B 112
Almshouse La. KT9: Chess 7C 162
Almshouses, The IG11: Bark 6G 71
　(off Fleming Rd.)
Alnwick N17 .....7C 34
Alnwick Gro. SM4: Mord 4K 153
Alnwick Rd. E16 .....6A 88
　SE12 .....6K 123
ALPERTON 2E 78
Alperton La. HA0: Wemb 3C 78
　UB6: G'frd 3C 78
Alperton St. W10 .....4H 81
Alphabet Gdns. SM5: Cars 6B 154
Alphabet Sq. E3 .....5C 86
Alpha Bus. Cen. E17 .....5B 50
Alpha Cl. NW1 .....2D 4 (4C 82)
Alpha Est. UB3: Hayes 2G 93
Alpha Gro. E14 .....2C 104
Alpha Ho. NW6 .....2J 81
　NW8 .....4D 4
　SW4 .....4K 119
Alpha Pl. NW6 .....2J 81
　SM4: Mord 1F 165
　SW3 .....7D 16 (6C 100)
Alpha Rd. CR0: C'don 1E 168
　E4 .....3H 35
　EN3: Pond E 4F 25
　KT5: Surb 6F 151
　N18 .....6B 34
　SE14 .....1B 122
　TW11: Tedd 5H 131
　UB10: Hil 4D 74
Alpha St. SE15 .....2G 121
Alphea Cl. SW19 .....7C 136
Alpine Av. KT5: Surb 2J 163
Alpine Bus. Cen. E6 .....5C 88
Alpine Cl. CR0: C'don 3E 168
　KT19: Ewe 5J 163
Alpine Copse BR1: Brom 2E 160
Alpine Gro. E9 .....7J 67
Alpine Rd. E10 .....2D 68
　KT12: Walt T 7J 147
　SE16 .....5K 103
Alpine Vw. SM5: Cars 5C 166
Alpine Wlk. HA7: Stan 2D 26
Alpine Way E6 .....5E 88
Alric Av. KT3: N Mald 3A 152
　NW10 .....7K 61
Alroy Rd. N4 .....7A 48
Alsace Rd. SE17 .....5E 102
Alscot Rd. SE1 .....4F 103
Alscot Way SE1 .....4F 103
Alsike Rd. DA18: Erith 3D 108
　SE2 .....3D 108
Alsom Av. KT4: Wor Pk 4C 164
Alston Cl. KT6: Surb 7B 150

Alston Rd. EN5: Barn 3B **20**
N18 . . . . .5C **34**
SW17 . . . . .4B **136**
Alston Works EN5: Barn 2B **20**
Altair Cl. N17 . . . . .6A **34**
Altash Way SE9 . . . . .2D **142**
Altenburg Av. W13 . . . . .3B **96**
Altenburg Gdns. SW11 . . . . .4D **118**
Alt Gro. SW19 .7H **135**
Altham Ct. HA2: Harr 1F **41**
Altham Rd. HA5: Pinn 1C **40**
Althea St. SW6 . . . . .2K **117**
Althorne Gdns. E18 . . . . .4H **51**
Althorne Way RM10: Dag 2G **73**
Althorp Cl. EN5: Ark 1H **29**
Althorpe M. SW11 . . . . .1B **118**
Althorpe Rd. HA1: Harr 5G **41**
Althorp Rd. SW17 . . . . .1D **136**
Altima Ct. SE22 . . . . .4G **121**
  (off E. Dulwich Rd.)
Altior Cl. N6 . . . . .6G **47**
Altissima Ho. SW8 . . . . .7F **101**
Altitude E1 . . . . .7K **9**
Altitude Apartments CR0: C'don 3D **168**
  (off Altyre Rd.)
Altius Apartments E3 . . . . .2C **86**
  (off Wick La.)
Altius Cl. E4 . . . . .6K **35**
Altius Wlk. E20 . . . . .6E **68**
Altmore Av. E6 . . . . .7D **70**
Alton Av. HA7: Stan 7E **26**
Alton Cl. DA5: Bexl 1E **144**
  TW7: Isle 2K **113**
Alton Gdns. BR3: Beck 7C **140**
  TW2: Whitt 7H **113**
Alton Ho. E3 . . . . .3D **86**
  (off Bromley High St.)
Alton Rd. CR0: Wadd 3A **168**
  N17 . . . . .3D **48**
  SW15 . . . . .1C **134**
  TW9: Rich 4E **114**
Alton St. E14 .5D **86**
Altura Twr. SW11 . . . . .2B **118**
Altus Ho. SE6 .4E **140**
Altyre Cl. BR3: Beck 5B **158**
Altyre Rd. CR0: C'don 2D **168**
Altyre Way BR3: Beck 5B **158**
Aluna Ct. SE15 . . . . .3J **121**
Alvanley Gdns. NW6 . . . . .5K **63**
Alverstone Av. EN4: E Barn 7H **21**
  SW19 . . . . .2J **135**
Alverstone Gdns. SE9 . . . . .1G **143**
Alverstone Ho. SE11 . . . . . .7J **19** (6A **102**)
Alverstone Rd. E12 . . . . .4E **70**
  HA9: Wemb 1F **61**
  KT3: N Mald 4B **152**
  NW2 . . . . .7E **62**
Alverston Gdns. SE25 . . . . .5E **156**
Alverton St. SE8 . . . . .5B **104**
  (not continuous)
Alveston Av. HA3: Kenton 3B **42**
Alveston Sq. E18 . . . . .2J **51**
Alvey St. SE17 . . . . .5D **102**
Alvia Gdns. SM1: Sutt 4A **166**
Alvington Cres. E8 . . . . .5F **67**
Alway Av. KT19: Ewe 5K **163**
Alwold Cres. SE12 . . . . .6K **123**
Alwyn Av. W4 .5K **97**
Alwyn Cl. CR0: New Ad 7D **170**
Alwyne La. N1 .7B **66**
Alwyne Pl. N1 .6C **66**
Alwyne Rd. N1 . . . . .7C **66**
  SW19 . . . . .6H **135**
  W7 . . . . .7J **77**
Alwyne Sq. N1 . . . . .6C **66**
Alwyne Vs. N1 . . . . .7B **66**
Alwyn Gdns. NW4 . . . . .4C **44**
  W3 . . . . .6H **79**
Alyth Gdns. NW11 . . . . .6J **45**
Aizette Ho. E2 .2K **85**
  (off Mace St.)

Amadeus Ho. BR1: Brom 3K **159**
  (off Elmfield Rd.)
Amalgamated Dr. TW8: Bford 6B **96**
Amanda Ct. TW15: Ashf 2B **128**
  (off Edward Way)
Amanda M. RM7: Rom 5J **55**
Amar Ct. SE18 . . . . .5K **107**
Amar Deep Ct. SE18 . . . . .5K **107**
Amarelle Apartments CR0: C'don 1D **168**
  (off Cherry Orchard Rd.)
Amazon Bldg. N8 . . . . .4K **47**
Amazon St. E1 . . . . .6G **85**
Ambassador Cl. TW3: Houn 2C **112**
Ambassador Gdns. E6 . . . . .5D **88**
Ambassador Ho. NW8 . . . . .1A **82**
Ambassadors Ct. E8 . . . . .7F **67**
  (off Holly St.)
  SW1 . . . . .5B **12**
Ambassador Sq. E14 . . . . .4D **104**
Ambassadors Theatre 2D **12**
  (off West St.)
Amber Av. E17 . . . . .1A **50**
Amber Cl. EN5: New Bar 6E **20**
Amber Ct. CR0: C'don 1E **168**
  E15 . . . . .1E **86**
  (off Warton Rd.)
  KT5: Surb 7F **151**
  N7 . . . . .4A **66**
  (off Bride St.)
Amberden Av. N3 . . . . .3J **45**
Ambergate St. SE17 . . . . .5B **102**
Amber Gro. NW2 . . . . .1F **63**
Amber Ho. E1 .6K **85**
  (off Aylward St.)
Amberley Cl. BR6: Chels 5K **173**
  HA5: Pinn 3D **40**
Amberley Ct. BR3: Beck 7B **140**
  DA14: Sidc 5C **144**
Amberley Gdns. EN1: Enf 7K **23**
  KT19: Ewe 4B **164**
Amberley Gro. CR0: C'don 7F **157**
  SE26 . . . . .5H **139**
Amberley Rd. E10 . . . . .7C **50**
  EN1: Enf .7A **24**
  IG9: Buck H 1F **37**
  N13 . . . . .2E **32**
  SE2 . . . . .6D **108**
  W9 . . . . .5J **81**
Amberley Way RM7: Mawney 4H **55**
  SM4: Mord 7H **153**
  TW4: Houn 5A **112**
  UB10: Uxb 2A **74**
Amberlith Ho. CR7: Thor H 3A **156**
  (off Thornton Rd.)
Amber M. N22 .3A **48**
  (off High Rd.)
Amberside Cl. TW7: Isle 6H **113**
Amber Way W3 . . . . .2A **98**
Amber Wharf E2 . . . . .1F **85**
  (off Nursery La.)
Amberwood Cl. SM6: Wall 5J **167**
Amberwood Ri. KT3: N Mald 6A **152**
Amblecote Cl. SE12 . . . . .3K **141**
Amblecote Mdws. SE12 . . . . .3K **141**
Amblecote Rd. SE12 . . . . .3K **141**
Ambler Rd. N4 . . . . .3B **66**
Ambleside BR1: Brom 6F **141**
  NW1 . . . . .1K **5**
  SW19 . . . . .1G **135**
Ambleside Av. BR3: Beck 5A **158**
  KT12: Walt T 7A **148**
  SW16 . . . . .4H **137**
Ambleside Cl. E9 . . . . .5J **67**
  E10 . . . . .7D **50**
  N17 . . . . .3F **49**
Ambleside Cres. EN3: Enf H 3E **24**
Ambleside Dr. TW14: Felt 1H **129**
Ambleside Gdns. HA9: Wemb 1D **60**
  IG4: IIf 4C **52**
  SM2: Sutt 6A **166**
  SW16 . . . . .5H **137**

Ambleside Point SE15 . . . . .7J **103**
  (off Tustin Est.)
Ambleside Rd. DA7: Bex 2G **127**
  NW10 . . . . .7B **62**
Ambleside Wlk. UB8: Uxb 1A **74**
Ambrooke Rd. DA17: Belv 3G **109**
Ambrosden Av. SW1 . . . . .2B **18** (3G **101**)
Ambrose Av. NW11 . . . . .7G **45**
Ambrose Cl. BR6: Orp 3K **173**
  E6 . . . . .5C **88**
Ambrose Ho. E14 . . . . .5C **86**
  (off Selsey St.)
Ambrose M. SW11 . . . . .2D **118**
Ambrose St. SE16 . . . . .4H **103**
Ambrose Wlk. E3 . . . . .2C **86**
Ambulance Rd. E11 . . . . .5F **51**
AMC Bus. Cen. NW10 . . . . .3H **79**
Amelia Cl. W3 . . . . .1H **97**
Amelia Ho. NW9 . . . . .2B **44**
  (off Boulevard Dr.)
  TW9: Kew 7H **97**
  W6 . . . . .5E **98**
  (off Queen Caroline St.)
Amelia Mans. E20 . . . . .6D **68**
  (off Olympic Pk. Av.)
Amelia St. SE17 . . . . .5C **102**
Amen Corner EC4 . . . . . . .1B **14** (6B **84**)
  SW17 . . . . .6D **136**
Amen Ct. EC4 . . . . .1B **14** (6B **84**)
Amenity Way SM4: Mord 7E **152**
American International University
in London, The
  Kensington Campus, Ansdell Street
  . . . . .3K **99**
  (off Ansdell St.)
  Kensington Campus, St Albans Grove
  . . . . .3K **99**
  Kensington Campus, Young Street
  . . . . .2K **99**
  Richmond Hill Campus 7E **114**
American University of London, The
America Sq. EC3 . . . . .2J **15** (7F **85**)
America St. SE1 . . . . .5C **14** (1C **102**)
Amerland Rd. SW18 . . . . .5H **117**
Amersham Av. N18 . . . . .6J **33**
Amersham Gro. SE14 . . . . .7B **104**
Amersham Rd. CR0: C'don 6C **156**
  SE14 . . . . .1B **122**
Amersham Va. SE14 . . . . .7B **104**
Amery Gdns. NW10 . . . . .1E **80**
Amery Ho. SE17 . . . . .5E **102**
  (off Kinglake St.)
Amery Rd. HA1: Harr 2A **60**
Amesbury Av. SW2 . . . . .2J **137**
Amesbury Cl. KT4: Wor Pk 1E **164**
  EN2: Enf .2F **23**
Amesbury Dr. E4 . . . . .6J **25**
Amesbury Rd.
  BR1: Brom 3B **160**
  RM9: Dag 7D **72**
  TW13: Felt 2B **130**
Amesbury Twr. SW8 . . . . .2G **119**
Ames Cls. E14 . . . . .5A **86**
  (off Maroon St.)
Ames Ho. E2 . . . . .2K **85**
  (off Mace St.)
Amethyst Cl. N11 . . . . .7C **32**
Amethyst Ct. BR6: Chels 5J **173**
  (off Farnborough Hill)
  EN3: Enf H 3F **25**
  (off Enstone Rd.)
Amethyst Rd. E15 . . . . .4F **69**
Amherst Av. W13 . . . . .6C **78**
Amherst Dr. BR5: St M Cry 4K **161**
Amherst Gdns. W13 . . . . .6C **78**
  (off Amherst Rd.)
Amherst Ho. SE16 . . . . .2K **103**
  (off Wolfe Cres.)
Amherst Rd. W13 . . . . .6C **78**
Amhurst Gdns. TW7: Isle 2A **114**

Amhurst Pde. N16 . . . . .7F **49**
  (off Amhurst Pk.)
Amhurst Pk. N16 . . . . .7D **48**
Amhurst Pas. E8 . . . . .4G **67**
Amhurst Rd. E8 . . . . .5H **67**
  N16 . . . . .4F **67**
Amhurst Ter. E8 . . . . .4G **67**
Amhurst Wlk. SE28 . . . . .1A **108**
Amias Dr. HA8: Edg 4K **27**
Amias Ho. EC1 .3C **8**
  (off Central St.)
Amidas Gdns. RM8: Dag 4B **72**
Amiel St. E1 . . . . .4J **85**
Amies St. SW11 . . . . .3D **118**
Amigo Ho. SE1 . . . . .1K **19**
  (off Morley St.)
Amina Way SE16 . . . . .3G **103**
Amiot Ho. NW9 . . . . .2B **44**
  (off Heritage Av.)
Amis Av. KT19: Ewe 6H **163**
Amisha Ct. SE1 . . . . .3F **103**
  (off Grange Rd.)
Amity Gro. SW20 . . . . .1D **152**
Amity Rd. E15 .7H **69**
Ammanford Grn. NW9 . . . . .6A **44**
Ammonite Ho. E15 . . . . .7H **69**
Amner Rd. SW11 . . . . .6E **118**
Amor Rd. W6 . . . . .3E **98**
Amory Ho. N1 .1K **83**
  (off Barnsbury Est.)
Amott Rd. SE15 . . . . .3G **121**
Amoy Pl. E14 .7C **86**
  (not continuous)
Ampere Way CR0: Wadd 7J **155**
Ampleforth Rd. SE2 . . . . .2B **108**
Amport Pl. NW7 . . . . .6B **30**
Ampthill Est. NW1 . . . . . . .1B **6** (2G **83**)
Ampthill Sq. NW1 . . . . . . .1B **6** (2G **83**)
Ampton Pl. WC1 . . . . .2G **7** (3K **83**)
Ampton St. WC1 . . . . .2G **7** (3K **83**)
Amroth Cl. SE23 . . . . .1H **139**
Amroth Grn. NW9 . . . . .6A **44**
Amstel Ct. SE15 . . . . .7F **103**
Amsterdam Rd. E14 . . . . .3E **104**
Amundsen Ct. E14 . . . . .5C **104**
  (off Napier Av.)
Amundsen Ho. NW10 . . . . .7K **61**
  (off Stonebridge Pk.)
Amwell Cl. EN2: Enf 5J **23**
Amwell Ct. Est. N4 . . . . .2C **66**
Amwell Ho. WC1 . . . . .1J **7**
  (off Cruikshank St.)
Amwell St. EC1 . . . . .1J **7** (3A **84**)
Amyand Cotts. TW1: Twick 6B **114**
Amyand La. TW1: Twick 7B **114**
Amyand Pk. Gdns. TW1: Twick 7B **114**
Amyand Pk. Rd. TW1: Twick 7A **114**
Amy Cl. SM6: Wall 7J **167**
Amy Johnson Ct. HA8: Edg 2H **43**
Amyruth Rd. SE4 . . . . .5C **122**
Amy Warne Cl. E6 . . . . .4C **88**
Anastasia M. N12 . . . . .5E **30**
Anatola Rd. N19 . . . . .2G **65**
Ancaster Cres. KT3: N Mald 6C **152**
Ancaster M. BR3: Beck 3K **157**
Ancaster Rd. BR3: Beck 3K **157**
Ancaster St. SE18 . . . . .7J **107**
Anchor SW18 .4K **117**
Anchorage Cl. SW19 . . . . .5J **135**
Anchorage Ho. E14 . . . . .7E **87**
  (off Clove Cres.)
Anchorage Point E14 . . . . .2B **104**
  (off Cuba St.)
Anchorage Point Ind. Est. SE7 . . . . . .3A **106**
Anchor & Hope La. SE7 . . . . .3K **105**
Anchor Brewhouse SE1 . . . . .5J **15** (1F **103**)
Anchor Bus. Cen. CR0: Bedd 3J **167**
Anchor Cl. IG11: Bark 3B **90**
Anchor Cl. EN1: Enf 5K **23**
  SW1 . . . . .4C **18**
  (off Vauxhall Bri. Rd.)

Anchor Dr. N15 . . . . .4E **48**
Anchor Ho. *E16* 5H **87**
   (off Barking Rd., Barking Rd.)
   E16 . . . . .6A **88**
   (off Prince Regent La., Prince Regent La.)
   EC1 . . . . .3C **8**
   (off Old St.)
   SW10 . . . . .6B **100**
   (off Cremorne Est.)
Anchor M. N1 . . . . .6E **66**
   SW12 . . . . .6F **119**
Anchor Retail Pk. E1 . . . . .4J **85**
Anchor St. SE16 . . . . .4H **103**
Anchor Ter. E1 . . . . .4J **85**
   SE1 . . . . .4D **14**
   (off Southwark Bri. Rd.)
Anchor Wharf *E3* 5D **86**
   (off Yeo St.)
Anchor Yd. EC1 . . . . .3D **8** (4C **84**)
Ancill Cl. W6 . . . . .6G **99**
Ancona Rd. NW10 . . . . .2C **80**
   SE18 . . . . .5H **107**
Andace Pk. Gdns. BR1: Brom 2A **160**
Andalus Rd. SW9 . . . . .3J **119**
Ander Cl. HA0: Wemb 4D **60**
Anderson Cl. N21 . . . . .5E **22**
   SM3: Sutt 1J **165**
   W3 . . . . .6K **79**
Anderson Ct. NW2 . . . . .1E **62**
Anderson Dr. TW15: Ashf 4E **128**
Anderson Hgts. SW16 . . . . .2K **155**
Anderson Ho. *E14* 7E **86**
   (off Woolmore St.)
   IG11: Bark 1H **89**
   SW17 . . . . .5B **136**
Anderson Pl. TW3: Houn 4F **113**
Anderson Rd. E9 . . . . .6K **67**
   IG8: Wfd G 3B **52**
Anderson Sq. *N1* 1B **84**
   (off Gaskin St.)
Anderson St. SW3 . . . . . .5E **16** (5D **100**)
Anderson Way DA17: Belv 2H **109**
Anderton Cl. SE5 . . . . .3D **120**
Anderton Ct. N22 . . . . .2H **47**
Andora Cl. *NW6* 7G **63**
   (off Brondesbury Pk.)
Andorra Ho. E10 . . . . .1A **68**
Andorra Ct. BR1: Brom 1A **160**
Andover Av. E16 . . . . .6B **88**
Andover Cl.
   TW14: Felt 1H **129**
   UB6: G'frd 4F **77**
Andover Ct. *E2* 4H **85**
   (off Thee Colts La.)
   TW19: Stanw 7A **110**
Andover Pl. NW6 . . . . .2K **81**
Andover Rd. BR6: Orp 7H **173**
   N7 . . . . .2K **65**
   TW2: Twick 1H **131**
Andoversford Ct. *SE15* 6E **102**
   (off Bibury Cl.)
Andover Ter. *W6* 4D **98**
   (off Raynham Rd.)
Andreck Ct. *BR3: Beck* 2E **158**
   (off Crescent Rd.)
Andre St. E8 . . . . .5G **67**
Andrew Cl. DA1: Cray 5K **127**
Andrew Ct. SE23 . . . . .2K **139**
Andrewes Gdns. E6 . . . . .6C **88**
Andrewes Highwalk EC2 . . . . .6D **8**
Andrewes Ho. EC2 . . . . .6D **8**
   SM1: Sutt 4J **165**
Andrew Fleming Memorial, The 1H **123**
Andrew Pl. SW8 . . . . .7H **101**
Andrew Reed Ho. *SW18* 7G **117**
   (off Linstead Way)
Andrews Cl. HA1: Harr 7H **41**
   IG9: Buck H 2F **37**
   KT4: Wor Pk 2E **164**
Andrews Crosse WC2 . . . . .1J **13**
Andrews Ga. TW17: Shep 2E **146**

Andrews Ho. CR2: S Croy 6C **168**
   NW3 .7D **64**
   (off Fellows Rd.)
Andrews Pl. DA2: Wilm 2K **145**
   SE9 .6F **125**
Andrew's Rd. E8 . . . . .1H **85**
Andrew St. E14 . . . . .6E **86**
Andrews Wlk. SE17 . . . . .6B **102**
Andringham Lodge *BR1: Brom* 1K **159**
   (off Palace Gro.)
Andrula Ct. N22 . . . . .1B **48**
Andwell Cl. SE2 . . . . .2B **108**
ANERLEY .1H **157**
Anerley Gro. SE19 . . . . .7F **139**
Anerley Hill SE19 . . . . .6F **139**
Anerley Pk. SE20 . . . . .7G **139**
Anerley Pk. Rd. SE20 . . . . .7H **139**
Anerley Rd. SE19 . . . . .7G **139**
   SE20 . . . . .7G **139**
Anerley Sta. Rd. SE20 . . . . .1H **157**
Anerley Va. SE19 . . . . .7F **139**
Aneurin Bevan Ct. NW2 . . . . .2D **62**
Aneurin Bevan Ho. N11 . . . . .7C **32**
Anfield Cl. SW12 . . . . .7G **119**
ANGEL 2A **84**
Angela Carter Cl. SW9 . . . . .3A **120**
Angela Davies Ind. Est. SE24 . . . . .4B **120**
Angel All. E1 . . . . .7K **9**
Angel Centre, The N1 . . . . .1K **7**
Angel Cl. N18 . . . . .5A **34**
   TW12: Hamp H 5G **131**
Angel Cnr. Pde. N18 . . . . .4B **34**
Angel Ct. EC2 . . . . .7F **9** (6D **84**)
   SW1 . . . . .5B **12** (1G **101**)
ANGEL EDMONTON 5B **34**
Angelfield TW3: Houn 4F **113**
Angel Ga. EC1 . . . . .1B **8** (3B **84**)
   (not continuous)
Angel Hill SM1: Sutt 3K **165**
Angel Hill Dr. SM1: Sutt 3K **165**
Angel Ho. *E3* 3C **86**
   (off Campbell Rd.)
Angelica Cl. UB7: Yiew 6A **74**
Angelica Dr. E6 . . . . .5E **88**
Angelica Gdns. CR0: C'don 1K **169**
Angelica Ho. *E3* 1B **86**
   (off Sycamore Av.)
Angelina Ho. *SE15* 1G **121**
   (off Goldsmith Rd.)
Angelis Apartments *N1* 1B **8**
   (off Graham St.)
Angel La. E15 . . . . .6F **69**
   EC4 . . . . .3E **14** (7D **84**)
   UB3: Hayes 5F **75**
Angell Pk. Gdns. SW9 . . . . .3A **120**
Angell Rd. SW9 . . . . .3A **120**
ANGELL TOWN 1A **120**
Angell Town Est. SW9 . . . . .2A **120**
Angel M. E1 . . . . .7H **85**
   N1 . . . . .2A **84**
   SW15 . . . . .7C **116**
Angelo M. SW16 . . . . .3K **155**
Angel Pl. N18 . . . . .4B **34**
   SE1 . . . . .6E **14** (2D **102**)
Angel Rd. HA1: Harr 6J **41**
   KT7: T Ditt 7A **150**
   N18 .5B **34**
Angel Rd. Works N18 . . . . .5D **34**
Angel Sq. EC1 . . . . .2B **84**
Angel St. EC1 . . . . .7C **8** (6B **84**)
Angel Wlk. W6 . . . . .4E **98**
Angel Way RM1: Rom 5K **55**
Angel Wharf N1 . . . . .2C **84**
Angel Yd. N6 . . . . .1E **64**
Angerstein Bus. Pk. SE10 . . . . .4J **105**
Angerstein La. SE3 . . . . .1H **123**
Anglais M. *NW9* 4A **44**
   (off Colin Cl.)
Anglebury *W2* 6J **81**
   (off Talbot Rd.)
Angle Cl. UB10: Hil 1C **74**

Angle Grn. RM8: Dag 1C **72**
Anglers, The *KT1: King T* 3D **150**
   (off High St.)
Anglers Cl. TW10: Ham 4C **132**
Angler's La. NW5 . . . . .6F **65**
Anglers Reach KT6: Surb 5D **150**
Anglesea Av. SE18 . . . . .4F **107**
Anglesea Ho. *KT1: King T* 4D **150**
   (off Anglesea Rd.)
Anglesea M. SE18 . . . . .4F **107**
Anglesea Rd. KT1: King T 4D **150**
   SE18 . . . . .4F **107**
Anglesea Ter. *W6* 3D **98**
   (off Wellesley Av.)
Anglesey Cl. TW15: Ashf 3C **128**
Anglesey Ct. W7 . . . . .4K **77**
Anglesey Ct. Rd. SM5: Cars 6E **166**
Anglesey Gdns. SM5: Cars 6E **166**
Anglesey Ho. *E14* 6C **86**
   (off Lindfield St.)
Anglesey Rd. EN3: Pond E 4C **24**
Anglesmede Cres. HA5: Pinn 3E **40**
Anglesmede Way HA5: Pinn 3E **40**
Angles Rd. SW16 . . . . .4J **137**
Anglia Ct. N17 . . . . .7C **34**
Anglia Ct. *RM8: Dag* 1D **72**
   (off Spring Cl.)
Anglia Ho. *E14* 6A **86**
   (off Salmon La.)
Anglian Ind. Est. IG11: Bark 4K **89**
Anglian Rd. E11 . . . . .3F **69**
Anglia Wlk. *E6* 1E **88**
   (off Napier Rd.)
Anglo Rd. E3 . . . . .2B **86**
Angrave Ct. *E8* 1F **85**
   (off Scriven St.)
Angrave Pas. E8 . . . . .1F **85**
Angus Cl. KT9: Chess 5G **163**
Angus Dr. HA4: Ruis 4A **58**
Angus Gdns. NW9 . . . . .1K **43**
Angus Ho. SW2 . . . . .7H **119**
Angus Rd. E13 . . . . .3A **88**
Angus St. SE14 . . . . .7A **104**
Anhalt Rd. SW11 . . . . .7C **100**
Ankerdine Cres. SE18 . . . . .7F **107**
Anlaby Rd. TW11: Tedd 5J **131**
Anley Rd. W14 . . . . .2F **99**
Anmersh Gro. HA7: Stan 1D **42**
Annabel Ct. E14 . . . . .6D **86**
Annabels M. W5 . . . . .4D **78**
Anna Cl. E8 . . . . .1F **85**
Annandale Gro. UB10: Ick 3E **56**
Annandale Rd. CR0: C'don 2G **169**
   DA15: Sidc 7J **125**
   SE10 . . . . .6H **105**
   W4 . . . . .5A **98**
Anna Neagle Cl. E7 . . . . .4J **69**
Annan Way RM1: Rom 1K **55**
Anne Boleyn Ct. SE9 . . . . .6G **125**
Anne Boleyn's Wlk. KT2: King T 5E **132**
   SM3: Cheam 7F **165**
Anne Case M. KT3: N Mald 3K **151**
Anne Compton M. SE12 . . . . .7H **123**
Anne Goodman Ho. *E1* 6J **85**
   (off Jubilee St.)
Anne Matthews Ct. *E14* 5C **86**
   (off Selsey St.)
Anne M. IG11: Bark 7G **71**
Anne of Cleeves Ct. SE9 . . . . .6H **125**
Annes Ct. NW1 . . . . .3D **4**
Annesley Av. NW9 . . . . .3K **43**
Annesley Cl. NW10 . . . . .3A **62**
Annesley Dr. CR0: C'don 3B **170**
Annesley Ho. SW9 . . . . .1A **120**
Annesley Pl. BR2: Brom 6C **160**
Annesley Rd. SE3 . . . . .1K **123**
Annesley Wlk. N19 . . . . .2G **65**
Annesmere Gdns. SE3 . . . . .3B **124**
Anne St. E13 . . . . .4J **87**
Anne Sutherland Ho. BR3: Beck 7K **139**
Annett Cl. TW17: Shep 4G **147**

Annette Cl. HA3: W'stone 2J **41**
Annette Cres. N1 . . . . .7C **66**
Annette Rd. N7 . . . . .3K **65**
   (not continuous)
Annett Rd. KT12: Walt T 7J **147**
Anne Way KT8: W Mole 4F **149**
Annexe Mkt. *E1* 5J **9**
   (off Spital Sq.)
Annie Besant Cl. E3 . . . . .1B **86**
Annie Taylor Ho. *E12* 4E **70**
   (off Walton Rd.)
Annington Rd. SC2 . . . . .3H **9** (4E **84**)
Annington Rd. N2 . . . . .3D **46**
Annis Rd. E9 . . . . .6A **68**
Ann La. SW10 . . . . .6B **100**
Ann Moss Way SE16 . . . . .3J **103**
Ann's Cl. SW1 . . . . .7F **11**
Ann's Pl. E1 .6J **9**
Ann St. SE18 . . . . .5G **107**
   (not continuous)
Ann Stroud Ct. SE12 . . . . .5J **123**
Annsworthy Av. CR7: Thor H 3D **156**
Annsworthy Cres. SE25 . . . . .2D **156**
Ansar Gdns. E17 . . . . .5B **50**
Ansdell Rd. SE15 . . . . .2J **121**
Ansdell St. W8 . . . . .3K **99**
Ansdell Ter. W8 . . . . .3K **99**
Ansell Gro. SM5: Cars 1E **166**
Ansell Ho. *E1* 5J **85**
   (off Mile End Rd.)
Ansell Rd. SW17 . . . . .3C **136**
Anselm Cl. CR0: C'don 3F **169**
Anselm Rd. HA5: Hat E 1D **40**
   SW6 .6J **99**
Ansford Rd. BR1: Brom 5E **140**
Ansleigh Pl. W11 . . . . .7F **81**
Anson Cl. RM7: Mawney 2H **55**
Anson Ho. *E1* 4A **86**
   (off Shandy St.)
   SW1 .7A **18**
   (off Churchill Gdns.)
Anson Pl. SE28 . . . . .2H **107**
Anson Rd. N7 . . . . .4G **65**
   NW2 .4D **62**
Anson Ter. UB5: N'olt 5F **59**
Anstey Dr. W3 . . . . .2H **97**
Anstey Ho. E9 . . . . .1J **85**
   (off Templecombe Rd.)
Anstey Rd. SE15 . . . . .3G **121**
Anstey Wlk. N15 . . . . .4B **48**
Anstice Cl. W4 . . . . .7A **98**
Anstridge Path SE9 . . . . .6H **125**
Anstridge Rd. SE9 . . . . .6H **125**
Antelope Rd. SE18 . . . . .3D **106**
Antelope Wlk. KT6: Surb 5D **150**
Antenor Ho. *E2* 2H **85**
   (off Old Bethnal Grn. Rd.)
Anthems Way E20 . . . . .6D **68**
Anthony Cl. NW7 . . . . .4F **29**
Anthony Cope Ct. *N1* 1F **9**
   (off Chart St.)
Anthony Cl. W3 . . . . .2A **98**
Anthony Ho. *NW8* 4C **4**
   (off Ashbridge St.)
Anthony Rd. DA16: Well 1A **126**
   SE25 . . . . .6G **157**
   UB6: G'frd 3J **77**
Anthony St. E1 . . . . .6H **85**
Anthony Way N18 . . . . .6E **34**
Antigua M. E13 . . . . .3K **87**
Antigua Wlk. SE19 . . . . .5D **138**
Antila Ct. *E1* 3K **9**
   (off Sclater St.)
Antilles Bay E14 . . . . .2E **104**
Antill Rd. E3 . . . . .3A **86**
   N15 . . . . .4G **49**
Antill Ter. E1 . . . . .6K **85**
Antlers Hill E4 . . . . .5J **25**
Antoinette M. NW2 . . . . .6C **62**
Anton Cres. SM1: Sutt 3J **165**
Antoneys Cl. HA5: Pinn 2B **40**

Antonine Hgts. SE1 . . . . .7G **15**
Anton Pl. HA9: Wemb 3H **61**
Anton St. E8 . . . . .5G **67**
Antony Ho. SE16 . . . . .4J **103**
. . . . (off Raymouth Rd.)
Antrim Gro. NW3 . . . . .6D **64**
Antrim Rd. NW3 . . . . .6D **64**
Antrobus Cl. SM1: Sutt 5H **165**
Antrobus Rd. W4 . . . . .4J **97**
Antwerp Way E16 . . . . .2E **106**
Anvil Cl. SW16 . . . . .7G **137**
Anvil Rd. TW16: Sun 3J **147**
Anworth Cl. IG8: Wfd G 6E **36**
Apeldoorn Dr. SM6: Wall 7J **167**
Apex Cl. BR3: Beck 1D **158**
APEX CORNER
   FELTHAM 3D **130**
   MILL HILL 4F **29**
Apex Cl. W13 . . . . .7A **78**
Apex Ho. E1 .3K **9**
. . . . (off Bacon St.)
Apex Ind. Est. NW10 . . . . .4B **80**
Apex Pde. NW7 . . . . .4E **28**
. . . . (off Selvage La.)
Apex Retail Pk. TW13: Hanw 3D **130**
Aphrodite Ct. E14 . . . . .4C **104**
. . . . (off Homer Dr.)
   E15 . . . . .1E **86**
. . . . (off Warton Rd.)
Aplin Way TW7: Isle 1J **113**
Apollo Av. BR1: Brom 1K **159**
Apollo Bldg. E14 . . . . .4C **104**
Apollo Bus. Cen. SE8 . . . . .5K **103**
Apollo Ct. E1 . . . . .7G **85**
. . . . (off Thomas More St.)
   E15 . . . . .1E **86**
. . . . (off High St.)
   SW9 . . . . .1A **120**
. . . . (off Southey Rd.)
Apollo Ho. E2 . . . . .2H **85**
. . . . (off St Jude's Rd.)
   E3 . . . . .2C **86**
. . . . (off Garrison Rd.)
   N6 . . . . .7D **46**
   SW10 . . . . .7B **100**
. . . . (off Milman's St.)
Apollo Pl. E11 . . . . .3G **69**
   SW10 . . . . .7B **100**
Apollo Theatre
   Soho 2C **12**
. . . . (off Shaftesbury Av.)
Apollo Victoria Theatre 2A **18**
. . . . (off Wilton Rd.)
Apollo Way DA8: Erith 4K **109**
   SE28 . . . . .3H **107**
Apostle Ct. SE20 . . . . .7K **139**
Apostles, The SE23 . . . . .2K **139**
. . . . (off Church Ri.)
Apostle Way CR7: Thor H 2B **156**
Apothecary St. EC4 . . . . .1A **14** (6B **84**)
Appach Rd. SW2 . . . . .5A **120**
Appian Ct. E3 . . . . .2B **86**
. . . . (off Parnell Rd.)
Apple Blossom Ct. SW8 . . . . .7H **101**
. . . . (off Pascal St.)
Appleby Cl. BR5: Pet W 7J **161**
   E4 . . . . .6K **35**
   N15 . . . . .5D **48**
   TW2: Twick 2H **131**
   UB8: Hil 6E **74**
Appleby Ct. W3 . . . . .2J **97**
. . . . (off Newport Rd.)
Appleby Gdns. TW14: Felt 1H **129**
Appleby Rd. E8 . . . . .7G **67**
   E16 . . . . .6H **87**
Appleby St. E2 . . . . .2F **85**
Appledore Av. DA7: Bex 1J **127**
   HA4: Ruis .3K **57**
Appledore Cl. BR2: Brom 5H **159**
   HA8: Edg .1G **43**
   SW17 . . . . .2D **136**

Appledore Cres. DA14: Sidc 3J **143**
Appledore Way NW7 . . . . .7A **30**
Appleford Ho. W10 . . . . .4G **81**
. . . . (off Bosworth Rd.)
Appleford Rd. W10 . . . . .4G **81**
Apple Gth. TW8: Bford 4D **96**
Applegarth CRO: New Ad 7D **170**
. . . . (not continuous)
   KT10: Clay 5A **162**
Applegarth Dr. IG2: Ilf 4K **53**
Applegarth Ho. SE1 . . . . .6B **14**
   SE15 . . . . .7G **103**
. . . . (off Bird in Bush Rd.)
Applegarth Rd. SE28 . . . . .1B **108**
   W14 . . . . .3F **99**
Applegate Ho. E20 . . . . .5E **68**
. . . . (off Victory Pde.)
Apple Gro. EN1: Enf 3K **23**
   HA2: Harr .1E **58**
   KT9: Chess 4E **162**
   TW1: Twick 6A **114**
Apple Mkt. KT1: King T 2D **150**
. . . . (off Market Pl.)
Apple Rd. E11 . . . . .3G **69**
Appleshaw Ho. SE5 . . . . .3E **120**
Appleton Cl. DA7: Bex 2J **127**
Appleton Gdns. KT3: N Mald 6C **152**
Appleton Rd. SE9 . . . . .3C **124**
Appleton Sq. CR4: Mitc 1C **154**
Apple Tree Av. UB7: View 5B **74**
   UB8: Hil 5B **74**
Appletree Cl. SE20 . . . . .1H **157**
Appletree Gdns. EN4: E Barn 4H **21**
Apple Tree La. RM13: Rain 2K **91**
APPLE TREE RDBT. 6B **74**
Apple Tree Yd. E1 . . . . .3K **85**
. . . . (off Longnor Rd.)
   SW1 . . . . .4B **12** (1G **101**)
Applewood Cl. N20 . . . . .1H **31**
   NW2 . . . . .3D **62**
   UB10: Ick .4A **56**
Applewood Dr. E13 . . . . .4K **87**
Appold St. EC2 . . . . .5G **9** (5E **84**)
Apprentice Gdns. UB5: N'olt 3D **76**
Apprentice Way E5 . . . . .4H **67**
Approach, The BR6: Orp 2K **173**
   EN1: Enf 2C **24**
   NW4 . . . . .5F **45**
   W3 . . . . .6K **79**
Approach Cl. N16 . . . . .4E **66**
Approach Rd. E2 . . . . .2J **85**
   EN4: E Barn 4G **21**
   HA8: Edg .6B **28**
   KT8: W Mole 5E **148**
   SW20 . . . . .2E **152**
   TW15: Ashf 6E **128**
Apps Mdw. Cl. KT8: W Mole 4D **148**
Aprey Gdns. NW4 . . . . .4E **44**
April Cl. BR6: Chels 5K **173**
   TW13: Felt 3J **129**
   W7 . . . . .7J **77**
April Ct. E2 . . . . .2G **85**
. . . . (off Teale St.)
April Glen SE23 . . . . .3K **139**
April St. E8 . . . . .4F **67**
Apsley Centre, The NW2 . . . . .2C **62**
Apsley Cl. HA2: Harr 5G **41**
Apsley Ho. E1 . . . . .5J **85**
. . . . (off Stepney Way)
   NW8 . . . . .2B **82**
. . . . (off Finchley Rd.)
   SW15 . . . . .6C **116**
. . . . (off Holford Way)
   TW4: Houn 4D **112**
Apsley House (Wellington Mus.) 2E **100**
Apsley Rd. KT3: N Mald 3J **151**
   SE25 . . . . .4H **157**
Apsley Way NW2 . . . . .2C **62**
   W1 . . . . .6H **11** (2E **100**)
Aqua Ho. NW10 . . . . .3G **79**

Aquarelle Ho. EC1 . . . . .1C **8**
Aquarius TW1: Twick 1B **132**
Aquarius Bus. Pk. NW2 . . . . .1C **62**
. . . . (off Priestley Way)
Aquarius Golf Course 6J **121**
Aquatics Centre
   Queen Elizabeth Olympic Pk. . .7E **68**
Aqua Vista Sq. E3 . . . . .5C **86**
. . . . (off Bow Comn. La.)
Aquila St. NW8 . . . . .2B **82**
Aquinas St. SE1 . . . . .5K **13** (1A **102**)
Arabella Ct. NW8 . . . . .2A **82**
. . . . (off Marlborough Pl.)
Arabella Dr. SW15 . . . . .4A **116**
Arabella St. SE16 . . . . .7K **15** (3G **103**)
Arabia Cl. E4 . . . . .7K **25** & 1A **36**
Arabian Ho. E1 . . . . .4A **86**
. . . . (off Ernest St.)
Arabin Rd. SE4 . . . . .4A **122**
Arado Ho. NW9 . . . . .2B **44**
. . . . (off Boulevard Dr.)
Aragon Av. KT7: T Ditt 5K **149**
Aragon Cl. BR2: Brom 1D **172**
   EN2: Enf 1E **22**
   TW16: Sun 6H **129**
Aragon Ct. KT8: E Mos 4G **149**
   SE11 . . . . .5J **19**
. . . . (off Hotspur St.)
Aragon Dr. HA4: Ruis 1B **58**
Aragon Ho. E16 . . . . .1J **105**
. . . . (off Capulet M.)
Aragon Pl. SM4: Mord 7G **153**
Aragon Rd. KT2: King T 5E **132**
   SM4: Mord 6F **153**
Aragon Twr. SE8 . . . . .4B **104**
Aral Ho. E1 . . . . .4K **85**
. . . . (off Ernest St.)
Arandora Cres. RM6: Chad H 7B **54**
Aran Dr. HA7: Stan 4H **27**
Aran Lodge NW6 . . . . .1C **82**
. . . . (off Woodchurch Rd.)
Aran M. N7 . . . . .7A **66**
. . . . (off St Clements St.)
Arapiles Ho. E14 . . . . .6F **87**
. . . . (off Blair St.)
Arbery Rd. E3 .3A **86**
Arbon Ct. N1 .1C **84**
. . . . (off Linton St.)
Arbor Cl. BR3: Beck 2D **158**
Arbor Ct. N16 .2D **66**
Arboretum Cl. N1 . . . . .6D **66**
. . . . (off Dove Rd.)
Arboretum Pl. IG11: Bark 7G **71**
. . . . (off Clockhouse Av.)
Arborfield Cl. SW2 . . . . .1K **137**
Arborfield Ho. E14 . . . . .7C **86**
. . . . (off E. India Dock Rd.)
Arbor Ho. BR6: Orp 2K **173**
. . . . (off Orchard Gro.)
Arbor Rd. E4 .3A **36**
Arbour Ho. E1 .6K **85**
. . . . (off Arbour St.)
Arbour Rd. EN3: Pond E 3E **24**
Arbour Sq. E1 .6K **85**
Arbroath Rd. SE9 . . . . .3C **124**
Arbury Ter. SE26 . . . . .3G **139**
Arbuthnot La. DA5: Bexl 6E **126**
Arbuthnot Rd. SE14 . . . . .2K **121**
Arbutus St. E8 . . . . .1F **85**
Arcade CRO: C'don 2C **168**
Arcade, The CRO: C'don 3C **168**
. . . . (off High St.)
   E20 . . . . .6E **68**
. . . . (within Westfield Stratford City Shop. Cen.)
   EC2 . . . . .6G **9**
   IG11: Bark .7G **71**
   N7 . . . . .4J **65**
. . . . (off Macready Pl.)
   SE9 . . . . .6E **124**
. . . . (off High St.)
Arcade Chambers SE9 . . . . .6E **124**

Arcade Ct. N11 . . . . .4A **32**
Arcade Pde. KT9: Chess 5D **162**
Arcadia Av. N3 . . . . .2J **45**
Arcadia Cl. SM5: Cars 4E **166**
Arcadia Ct. E1 .7J **9**
Arcadia M. KT3: N Mald 3A **152**
Arcadian Av. DA5: Bexl 6E **126**
Arcadian Cl. DA5: Bexl 6E **126**
Arcadian Gdns. N22 . . . . .7E **32**
Arcadian Pl. SW18 . . . . .7H **117**
Arcadian Rd. DA5: Bexl 6E **126**
Arch, The SE14 . . . . .6C **86**
Archangel St. SE16 . . . . .2K **103**
Archbishop Lanfranc School Sports Cen.
. . . . .6J **155**
Archbishop's Pl. SW2 . . . . .7K **119**
Archdale Ct. W12 . . . . .1D **98**
Archdale Ho. SE1 . . . . .7G **15**
. . . . (off Long La.)
Archdale Pl. KT3: N Mald 3H **151**
Archdale Rd. SE22 . . . . .5F **121**
Archel Rd. W14 . . . . .6H **99**
Archer Apartments N1 . . . . .2E **84**
. . . . (off Fern Cl.)
Archer Cl. EN5: Barn 6C **20**
   KT2: King T 7E **132**
Archer Ho. N1 .1E **84**
. . . . (off Whitmore Est.)
   SE14 . . . . .1A **122**
   SW11 . . . . .1B **118**
   W11 . . . . .7H **81**
. . . . (off Westbourne Gro.)
   W13 . . . . .1B **96**
. . . . (off Sherwood Cl.)
Archer M. SW9 . . . . .3J **119**
   TW12: Hamp H 6G **131**
Archer Rd.
   BR5: St M Cry 5K **161**
   SE25 . . . . .4H **157**
Archers Ct. CR2: S Croy 5C **168**
. . . . (off Nottingham Rd.)
Archers Dr. EN3: Enf H 2D **24**
Archers Lodge SE16 . . . . .5G **103**
. . . . (off Culloden St.)
Archer Sq. SE14 . . . . .6A **104**
Archer St. W1 . . . . .2C **12** (7H **83**)
Archer Ter. UB7: Yiew 7A **74**
Archery Cl. HA3: W'stone 3K **41**
   W2 . . . . .1D **10** (6C **82**)
Archery Flds. Ho. WC1 . . . . .1H **7**
. . . . (off Wharton St.)
Archery La. BR2: Brom 6B **160**
Archery Rd. SE9 . . . . .5D **124**
Archery Steps W2 . . . . .2D **10**
Arches SW8 . . . . .7F **19** (6J **101**)
Arches, The E16 . . . . .4G **87**
   HA2: Harr .2F **59**
   NW1 . . . . .7F **65**
   SE8 . . . . .6A **104**
   SW8 . . . . .7H **101**
   WC2 . . . . .4F **13**
. . . . (off Villiers St.)
Arches Bus. Centre, The UB2: S'hall . . .2D **94**
. . . . (off Merrick Rd.)
Arches Leisure Cen. 6G **105**
Archgate Bus. Cen. N12 . . . . .5F **31**
Archibald M. W1 . . . . .3J **11** (7F **83**)
Archibald Rd. N7 . . . . .4H **65**
Archibald St. E3 . . . . .3C **86**
Archie Cl. UB7: W Dray 2C **92**
Archie St. SE1 . . . . .7H **15** (2E **102**)
Arc Ho. SE1 . . . . .7J **15**
Arch St. SE1 .3C **102**
ARCHWAY 2G **65**
Archway Bus. Cen. N19 . . . . .3H **65**
Archway Cl. N19 . . . . .2G **65**
   SM6: Bedd 3H **167**
   SW19 . . . . .3K **135**
   W10 . . . . .5F **81**
Archway Leisure Cen. 2G **65**
Archway Mall N19 . . . . .2G **65**

Archway M. SW15 .....4G 117
  (off Putney Bri. Rd.)
Archway Rd. N6 .....6E 46
  N19 .....6E 46
Archway St. SW13 .....3A 116
Arcola St. E8 .....5F 67
Arcola Theatre 5F 67
Arcon Dr. UB5: N'olt 4C 76
Arcon Ter. N9 .....7B 24
Arctic Ho. NW9 .....2B 44
  (off Heritage Av.)
Arctic St. NW5 .....2F 65
Arcus Rd. BR1: Brom 6G 141
Ardbeg Rd. SE24 .....5D 120
Arden Cl. HA1: Harr 3H 59
  SE28 .....6D 90
  TW2: Whitt 7D 112
Arden Ct. Gdns. N2 .....6B 46
Arden Cres. E14 .....4C 104
  RM9: Dag 7C 72
Arden Est. N1 .....2E 84
Arden Grange N12 .....4F 31
Arden Gro. BR6: Farnb 4F 173
Arden Ho. N1 .....1G 9
  SE11 .....4G 19
  SE13 .....3D 122
  (off Thurston Rd.)
  SW9 .....2J 119
  (off Grantham Rd.)
Arden M. E17 .....5D 50
Arden Mhor HA5: Eastc 4K 39
Arden Rd. N3 .....3H 45
  W13 .....7C 78
Ardent Cl. SE25 .....3E 156
Ardent Ho. E3 .....2A 86
  (off Roman Rd.)
Ardfern Av. SW16 .....3A 156
Ardfillan Rd. SE6 .....1F 141
Ardgowan Rd. SE6 .....7G 123
Ardilaun Rd. N5 .....4C 66
Ardingly Cl. CR0: C'don 3K 169
Ardleigh Ct. BR1: Brom 7H 141
  (off London Rd.)
Ardleigh Gdns. SM3: Sutt 7J 153
Ardleigh Ho. IG11: Bark 1G 89
Ardleigh M. IG1: Ilf 3F 71
Ardleigh Rd. E17 .....1B 50
  N1 .....6E 66
Ardleigh Ter. E17 .....1B 50
Ardley Cl. HA4: Ruis 7E 38
  NW10 .....3A 62
  SE6 .....3A 140
Ardlui Rd. SE27 .....2C 138
Ardmay Gdns. KT6: Surb 5E 150
Ardmere Rd. SE13 .....6F 123
Ardmore La. IG9: Buck H 1E 36
Ardmore Pl. IG9: Buck H 1E 36
Ardoch Rd. SE6 .....2F 141
Ardra Rd. N9 .....3E 34
Ardrossan Gdns. KT4: Wor Pk 3C 164
Ardshiel Cl. SW15 .....3F 117
Ardwell Av. IG6: Ilf 5G 53
Ardwell Rd. SW2 .....2J 137
Ardwick Rd. NW2 .....4J 63
Arena, The EN3: Enf L 1G 25
Arena Bus. Cen. N4 .....2C 66
Arena Ho. E3 .....2C 86
  (off Lefevre Wlk.)
Arena Shop. Pk. N4 .....2C 66
Arena Sq. HA9: Wemb 4G 61
Ares Ct. E14 .....4C 104
  (off Homer Dr.)
Arethusa Ho. E14 .....4C 104
  (off Cahir St.)
Argali Ho. DA18: Erith 3E 109
  (off Kale Rd.)
Argall Av. E10 .....7K 49
Argall Way E10 .....1K 67
Argan Cl. EN5: Barn 3C 20
Argenta Way HA0: Wemb 6G 61
  NW10 .....7H 61

Argent Centre, The UB3: Hayes 2J 93
Argent Ct. E14 .....5C 86
  (off Thomas Rd.)
  EN5: New Bar 4F 21
  (off Leicester Rd.)
  KT6: Surb 3G 163
Argenton Twr. SW18 .....6K 117
  (off Mapleton Cres.)
Argo Bus. Cen. NW6 .....3J 81
Argonaut Pk. SL3: Poyle 4A 174
Argon M. SW6 .....7J 99
Argon Rd. N18 .....5D 34
Argos Ct. SW9 .....1A 120
  (off Caldwell St.)
Argos Ho. E2 .....2H 85
  (off Old Bethnal Grn. Rd.)
Argosy Ho. SE8 .....4A 104
Argosy La. TW19: Stanw 7A 110
Argus Cl. RM7: Mawney 1H 55
Argus Way UB5: N'olt 3C 76
Argyle Av. TW3: Houn 6E 112
Argyle Cl. W13 .....4A 78
Argyle Ho. E14 .....3E 104
Argyle Pas. N17 .....1F 49
Argyle Pl. W6 .....4D 98
Argyle Rd.
  E1 .....4K 85
  E15 .....4G 69
  E16 .....6K 87
  EN5: Barn 4A 20
  HA2: Harr 6F 41
  IG1: Ilf 2E 70
  N12 .....5E 30
  N17 .....1G 49
  N18 .....4B 34
  TW3: Houn 5F 113
  UB6: G'frd 3K 77
  W13 .....5A 78
Argyle Sq. WC1 .....1F 7 (3J 83)
  (not continuous)
Argyle St. WC1 .....1E 6 (3J 83)
Argyle Wlk. WC1 .....2F 7 (3J 83)
Argyle Way SE16 .....5G 103
Argyll Av. UB1: S'hall 1F 95
Argyll Cl. SW9 .....3K 119
Argyll Ct. SW2 .....7J 119
  (off New Pk. Rd.)
Argyll Gdns. HA8: Edg 2H 43
Argyll Mans. SW3 .....7B 16 (6B 100)
  W14 .....4G 99
  (off Hammersmith Rd.)
Argyll Rd. SE18 .....3G 107
  W8 .....2J 99
Argyll St. W1 .....1A 12 (6G 83)
Aria Ct. IG2: Ilf 6G 53
Arica Ho. SE16 .....3H 103
  (off Slippers Pl.)
Arica Rd. SE4 .....4A 122
Ariel Apartments E16 .....6J 87
Ariel Cl. SE11 .....4K 19 (4B 102)
Ariel Rd. NW6 .....6J 63
Ariel Way TW4: Houn 3K 111
  W12 .....1E 98
Aristotle Rd. SW4 .....3H 119
Arizona Bldg. SE13 .....1D 122
  (off Deal's Gateway)
Ark, The W6 .....5F 99
  (off Talgarth Rd.)
Arkell Gro. SE19 .....7B 138
Arkindale Rd. SE6 .....3E 140
Arklay Cl. UB8: Hil 4B 74
Arkley Cres. E17 .....5B 50
Arkley Rd. E17 .....5B 50
Arklow Ho. SE17 .....6D 102
Arklow M. KT6: Surb 2E 162
Arklow Rd. SE14 .....6B 104
Arklow Rd. Trad. Est. SE14 .....6A 104
Arkwright Rd. CR2: Sande 7F 169
  NW3 .....5A 64
Arlesey Cl. SW15 .....5G 117
Arlesford Rd. SW9 .....3J 119

Arlidge Ho. EC1 .....5K 7
  (off Kirby St.)
Arlingford Rd. SW2 .....5A 120
Arlington N12 .....3D 30
Arlington Av. N1 .....2C 84
Arlington Bldg. E3 .....2C 86
Arlington Cl. DA15: Sidc 7J 125
  SE13 .....5F 123
  SM1: Sutt 2J 165
  TW1: Twick 6C 114
Arlington Ct. W3 .....2H 97
  (off Mill Hill Rd.)
Arlington Dr. HA4: Ruis 6F 39
  SM5: Cars 2D 166
Arlington Gdns. IG1: Ilf 1E 70
  W4 .....5J 97
Arlington Grn. NW7 .....7A 30
Arlington Ho. EC1 .....1K 7
  (off Arlington Way)
  SE8 .....6B 104
  (off Evelyn St.)
  SW1 .....4A 12 (1G 101)
  TW9: Kew 7H 97
  UB7: W Dray 2B 92
  W12 .....1D 98
  (off Tunis Rd.)
Arlington Lodge SW2 .....4K 119
Arlington M. SE13 .....5F 123
Arlington Pk. Mans. W4 .....5J 97
  (off Sutton La. Nth.)
Arlington Pas. TW11: Tedd 4K 131
Arlington Pl. SE10 .....7E 104
Arlington Rd. IG8: Wfd G 1J 51
  KT6: Surb 6D 150
  N14 .....2A 32
  NW1 .....1F 83
  TW1: Twick 6C 114
  TW10: Ham 2D 132
  TW11: Tedd 4K 131
  TW15: Ashf 5B 128
  W13 .....6B 78
Arlington Sq. N1 .....1C 84
Arlington St. SW1 .....4A 12 (1G 101)
Arlington Way EC1 .....1K 7 (3A 84)
Arliss Ho. HA1: Harr 5K 41
Arliss Way UB5: N'olt 1A 76
Arlow Rd. N21 .....1F 33
Armada Ct. SE8 .....6C 104
Armadale Cl. N17 .....4H 49
Armadale Rd. SW6 .....7J 99
  TW14: Felt 5J 111
Armada St. SE8 .....6C 104
Armada Way E6 .....5F 89
Armagh Rd. E3 .....1B 86
Arments Cl. SE5 .....6D 102
  (off Albany Rd.)
Armfield Cl. KT8: W Mole 5D 148
Armfield Cres. CR4: Mitc 2D 154
Armfield Rd. EN2: Enf 1J 23
Arminger Rd. W12 .....1D 98
Armistice Gdns. SE25 .....3G 157
Armitage Ho. NW1 .....5D 4
  (off Lisson Gro.)
Armitage Rd. NW11 .....1G 63
  SE10 .....5H 105
Armour Cl. N7 .....6K 65
Armoury, The 4C 64
  (off Pond St.)
Armoury Ho. E3 .....1A 86
  (off Gunmakers La.)
Armoury Rd. SE8 .....2D 122
Armoury Way SW18 .....5J 117
Armsby Ho. E1 .....5J 85
  (off Stepney Way)
Armstead Wlk. RM10: Dag 7G 73
Armstrong Av. IG8: Wfd G 6B 36
Armstrong Cl.
  BR1: Brom 3C 160
  E6 .....6D 88
  HA5: Eastc 6J 39
  KT12: Walt T 6J 147

Armstrong Cl. RM8: Dag 7D 54
  SE3 .....4K 123
Armstrong Cres. EN4: Cockf 3G 21
Armstrong Ho. E14 .....6A 86
  (off Commercial Rd.)
Armstrong Rd. NW10 .....7A 62
  SE18 .....3G 107
  SW7 .....2A 16 (3B 100)
  TW13: Hanw 5C 130
  W3 .....1B 98
Armstrong Way UB2: S'hall 2F 95
Armytage Rd. TW5: Hest 7B 94
Arnal Cres. SW18 .....7G 117
Arncliffe NW6 .....2K 81
Arncliffe Cl. N11 .....6K 31
Arncroft Ct. IG11: Bark 3B 90
Arndale Wlk. SW18 .....5K 117
Arne Gro. BR6: Orp 3K 173
Arne Ho. SE11 .....5G 19
Arne St. WC2 .....1F 13 (6J 83)
Arnett Sq. E4 .....6G 35
Arne Wlk. SE3 .....4H 123
Arneways Av.
  RM6: Chad H 3D 54
Arneway St. SW1 .....2D 18 (3H 101)
Arnewood Cl. SW15 .....1C 134
Arneys La. CR4: Mitc 6E 154
Arngask Rd. SE6 .....7F 123
Arnhem Pl. E14 .....3C 104
Arnhem Way SE22 .....5E 120
Arnhem Wharf E14 .....3B 104
Arnison Rd. KT8: E Mos 4H 149
Arnold Bennett Way N8 .....3A 48
Arnold Cir. E2 .....2J 9 (3F 85)
Arnold Cl. HA3: Kenton 7F 43
Arnold Ct. N22 .....7D 32
Arnold Cres. TW7: Isle 5H 113
Arnold Dr. KT9: Chess 6D 162
Arnold Est. SE1 .....7K 15 (2F 103)
  (not continuous)
Arnold Ho. SE3 .....7A 106
  (off Shooters Hill Rd.)
  SE17 .....5B 102
  (off Doddington Gro.)
Arnold Mans. W14 .....6H 99
  (off Queen's Club Gdns.)
Arnold Rd. E3 .....3C 86
  N15 .....3F 49
  RM9: Dag 7F 73
  RM10: Dag 7F 73
  SW17 .....7D 136
  UB5: N'olt 6B 58
Arnold Ter. HA7: Stan 5E 26
Arnos Gro. N14 .....4C 32
Arnos Gro. Ct. N11 .....5B 32
  (off Palmer's Rd.)
Arnos Rd. N11 .....5B 32
Arnos Swimming Pool 5C 32
Arnot Ho. SE5 .....7C 102
  (off Comber Gro.)
Arnott Cl. SE28 .....1C 108
  W4 .....4K 97
Arnould Av. SE5 .....4D 120
Arnsberg Way
  DA6: Bex 4G 127
  DA7: Bex 4G 127
Arnside Gdns. HA9: Wemb 1D 60
Arnside Ho. SE17 .....6D 102
  (off Arnside St.)
Arnside Rd. DA7: Bex 1G 127
Arnside St. SE17 .....6D 102
Arnulf St. SE6 .....4D 140
Arnulls Rd. SW16 .....6B 138
Arodene Rd. SW2 .....6K 119
Arona Ho. BR3: Beck 2E 158
Arosa Rd. TW1: Twick 6D 114
Arpley Sq. SE20 .....7J 139
  (off High St.)
Arragon Gdns. BR4: W W'ck 3D 170
  SW16 .....7J 137

Arragon Rd.—Ashcroft Sq.

Arragon Rd. E6 ... 1B 88
SW18 ... 1J 135
TW1: Twick ... 7A 114
Arran Cl. DA8: Erith ... 6K 109
SM6: Wall ... 4F 167
Arran Ct. NW9 ... 2B 44
NW10 ... 3K 61
Arran Dr. E12 ... 1B 70
Arran Ho. E14 ... 1E 104
(off Raleana Rd.)
Arran M. W5 ... 1F 97
Arran Rd. SE6 ... 2D 140
Arran Wlk. N1 ... 7C 66
Arras Av. SM4: Mord ... 5A 154
Arrol Ho. SE1 ... 3C 102
Arrol Rd. BR3: Beck ... 3J 157
Arrow Ct. SW5 ... 4J 99
(off W. Cromwell Rd.)
Arrowhead Quay E14 ... 2C 104
Arrow Ho. N1 ... 1E 84
(off Wilmer Gdns.)
Arrow Rd. E3 ... 3D 86
Arrowscout Wlk. UB5: N'olt ... 3C 76
(off Argus Way)
Arrows Ho. SE15 ... 7J 103
(off Clifton Way)
Arrowsmith Ho. SE11 ... 5G 19
Arsenal FC ... 4A 66
Arsenal Rd. SE9 ... 2D 124
Arsenal Way SE18 ... 3G 107
Arta Ho. E1 ... 6J 85
(off Devonport St.)
Artbrand Ho. SE1 ... 7G 15
(off Leathermarket St.)
Artemis SW11 ... 2D 118
Artemis Ct. E14 ... 4C 104
(off Homer Dr.)
Artemis Pl. SW18 ... 7H 117
Arterberry Rd. SW20 ... 7E 134
Artesian Cl. NW10 ... 7K 61
Artesian Gro. EN5: New Bar ... 4F 21
Artesian Ho. SE1 ... 3F 103
(off Grange Rd.)
Artesian Rd. W2 ... 6J 81
Artesian Wlk. E11 ... 3G 69
Arthaus Apartments E8 ... 6H 67
(off Richmond Rd.)
Arthingworth St. E15 ... 1G 87
Arthouse
Crouch End ... 5J 47
Arthur Ct. CR0: C'don ... 3E 168
(off Fairfield Path)
SW11 ... 1E 118
W2 ... 6K 81
(off Queensway)
W10 ... 6F 81
(off Silchester Rd.)
Arthur Deakin Ho. E1 ... 5K 9
(off Hunton St.)
Arthurdon Rd. SE4 ... 5C 122
Arthur Gro. SE18 ... 4G 107
Arthur Henderson Ho. SW6 ... 2H 117
(off Fulham Rd.)
Arthur Horsley Wlk. E7 ... 5H 69
(off Tower Hamlets Rd.)
Arthur Ho. N1 ... 1E 84
(off Halcomb St.)
Arthur Lovell Ct. E14 ... 6B 86
(off Lovat Cl.)
Arthur Newton Ho. SW11 ... 3B 118
(off Winstanley Est.)
Arthur Rd. E6 ... 2D 88
KT2: King T ... 7G 133
KT3: N Mald ... 5D 152
N7 ... 4K 65
N9 ... 2A 34
RM6: Chad H ... 6C 54
SW19 ... 5H 135
Arthur St. EC4 ... 2F 15 (7D 84)
Arthur Wade Ho. E2 ... 1K 9
(off Baroness Rd.)
Arthur Wallis Ho. E12 ... 3E 70
(off Grantham Rd.)
Artichoke Hill E1 ... 7H 85
Artichoke M. SE5 ... 1D 120
(off Artichoke Pl.)
Artichoke Pl. SE5 ... 1D 120
Artillery Building, The E1 ... 6H 9
(off Artillery La.)
Artillery Cl. IG2: Ilf ... 6G 53
Artillery Ho. E3 ... 1A 86
(off Barge La.)
E15 ... 6G 69
SE18 ... 5E 106
(off Connaught M.)
Artillery La. E1 ... 6H 9 (5E 84)
W12 ... 6C 80
Artillery Mans. SW1 ... 1C 18
Artillery Pas. E1 ... 6J 9
Artillery Pl. HA3: Hrw W ... 7B 26
SE18 ... 4D 106
SW1 ... 2C 18 (3H 101)
Artillery Row SW1 ... 2C 18 (3G 101)
Artillery Sq. SE18 ... 3F 107
(off No 1 St.)
Artington Cl. BR6: Farnb ... 4G 173
Artisan Cl. E6 ... 6F 89
Artisan Ct. E8 ... 6G 67
Artisan M. NW10 ... 3F 81
(off Warfield Rd.)
Artisan Quarter NW10 ... 3F 81
(off Wellington Rd.)
Artizan St. E1 ... 7J 9
Arts Depot ... 5F 31
Arts Sq. E1 ... 4A 86
Arts Theatre ... 2E 12
(off Gt. Newport St.)
Arun Ct. SE25 ... 5G 157
Arundale KT1: King T ... 4D 150
(off Anglesea Rd.)
Arundel Av. SM4: Mord ... 4H 153
Arundel Bldgs. SE1 ... 3E 102
Arundel Cl. CR0: Wadd ... 3B 168
DA5: Bexl ... 6F 127
E15 ... 4G 69
SW11 ... 5C 118
TW12: Hamp H ... 5F 131
Arundel Ct. BR2: Brom ... 2G 159
HA2: Harr ... 4E 58
N12 ... 6H 31
N17 ... 1G 49
SE16 ... 5H 103
(off Verney Rd.)
SW3 ... 5D 16
(off Jubilee Pl.)
SW13 ... 6D 98
(off Arundel Ter.)
W11 ... 7H 81
(off Arundel Gdns.)
Arundel Dr. HA2: Harr ... 4D 58
IG8: Wfd G ... 7D 36
Arundel Gdns. HA8: Edg ... 7E 28
IG3: Ilf ... 2A 72
N21 ... 1F 33
W11 ... 7H 81
Arundel Gt. Ct. WC2 ... 2H 13 (7K 83)
Arundel Gro. N16 ... 5E 66
Arundel Ho. CR0: C'don ... 5D 168
(off Heathfield Rd.)
E17 ... 1B 50
W3 ... 2H 97
(off Park Rd. Nth.)
Arundel Mans. SW6 ... 1H 117
(off Kelvedon Rd.)
Arundel Pl. N1 ... 6A 66
Arundel Rd. CR0: C'don ... 6D 156
EN4: Cockf ... 3H 21
KT1: King T ... 2H 151
SM2: Cheam, Sutt ... 7H 165
(not continuous)
TW4: Houn ... 3A 112
Arundel Sq. N7 ... 6A 66
Arundel St. WC2 ... 2H 13 (7K 83)
Arundel Ter. SW13 ... 6D 98
Arun Ho. KT2: King T ... 1D 150
Arvon Rd. N5 ... 5A 66
(not continuous)
Asa Ct. UB3: Harl ... 3H 93
Asbaston Ter. IG1: Ilf ... 6G 71
Asbridge Ct. W6 ... 3D 98
(off Dalling Rd.)
Asbury Ct. N21 ... 5D 22
(off Pennington Dr.)
Ascalon Ho. SW8 ... 7G 101
(off Thessaly Rd.)
Ascalon St. SW8 ... 7G 101
Ascensis Twr. SW18 ... 4A 118
Ascent Ho. NW9 ... 2B 44
(off Boulevard Dr.)
Ascham Dr. E4 ... 7J 35
Ascham End E17 ... 1A 50
Ascham St. NW5 ... 5G 65
Aschurch Rd. CR0: C'don ... 7F 157
Ascot Cl. UB5: N'olt ... 5E 58
Ascot Ct. DA5: Bexl ... 7F 127
NW8 ... 2A 4
Ascot Gdns. UB1: S'hall ... 4D 76
Ascot Ho. NW1 ... 1K 5
(off Redhill St.)
W9 ... 4J 81
(off Harrow Rd.)
Ascot Lodge NW6 ... 1K 81
Ascot Pl. HA7: Stan ... 5H 27
Ascot Rd. BR5: St M Cry ... 4K 161
E6 ... 3D 88
N15 ... 5D 48
N18 ... 4B 34
SW17 ... 6E 136
TW14: Bedf ... 1C 128
Ascott Av. W5 ... 2E 96
Ascott Cl. HA5: Eastc ... 4J 39
Ashanti M. E8 ... 5J 67
Ashbee Ho. E2 ... 3J 85
(off Portman Pl.)
Ashbourne Av. DA7: Bex ... 7E 108
E18 ... 4K 51
HA2: Harr ... 2H 59
N20 ... 2J 31
NW11 ... 5H 45
Ashbourne Cl. N12 ... 4E 30
W5 ... 5G 79
Ashbourne Ct. E5 ... 4A 68
N12 ... 4E 30
(off Ashbourne Cl.)
Ashbourne Gro. NW7 ... 5E 28
SE22 ... 4F 121
W4 ... 5A 98
Ashbourne Pde. NW11 ... 4H 45
W5 ... 4F 79
Ashbourne Ri. BR6: Orp ... 4J 173
Ashbourne Rd. CR4: Mitc ... 7E 136
W5 ... 4F 79
Ashbourne Ter. SW19 ... 7H 135
Ashbourne Way NW11 ... 4H 45
Ashbridge Rd. E11 ... 7G 51
Ashbridge St. NW8 ... 4C 4 (4C 82)
Ashbrook HA8: Edg ... 6A 28
Ashbrook Rd. N19 ... 1H 65
RM10: Dag ... 3H 73
Ashburn Gdns. SW7 ... 4A 100
Ashburnham Av. HA1: Harr ... 6K 41
Ashburnham Cl. N2 ... 3B 46
Ashburnham Ct. BR3: Beck ... 2E 158
Ashburnham Gdns. HA1: Harr ... 6K 41
Ashburnham Gro. SE10 ... 7D 104
Ashburnham Mans. SW10 ... 7A 100
(off Ashburnham Rd.)
Ashburnham Pl. SE10 ... 7D 104
Ashburnham Retreat SE10 ... 7D 104
Ashburnham Rd. DA17: Belv ... 4J 109
NW10 ... 3E 80
SW10 ... 7A 100
TW10: Ham ... 3B 132
Ashburnham Twr. SW10 ... 7B 100
(off Worlds End Est.)
Ashburn Pl. SW7 ... 4A 100
Ashburton Av. CR0: C'don ... 1H 169
IG3: Ilf ... 5J 71
Ashburton Cl. CR0: C'don ... 1G 169
Ashburton Ent. Cen. SW15 ... 6E 116
Ashburton Gdns. CR0: C'don ... 2G 169
ASHBURTON GROVE ... 4A 66
Ashburton Ho. W9 ... 4H 81
(off Fernhead Rd.)
Ashburton Memorial Homes
CR0: C'don ... 7H 155
Ashburton Rd. CR0: C'don ... 2G 169
E16 ... 6J 87
HA4: Ruis ... 2J 57
Ashburton Ter. E13 ... 2J 87
Ashburton Triangle N5 ... 4A 66
Ashbury Dr. UB10: Ick ... 3D 56
Ashbury Gdns. RM6: Chad H ... 5D 54
Ashbury Pl. SW19 ... 6A 136
Ashbury Rd. SW11 ... 3D 118
Ashby Av. KT9: Chess ... 6G 163
Ashby Cl. BR4: W W'ck ... 3F 171
Ashby Ct. NW8 ... 3B 4
(off Pollitt Dr.)
Ashby Gro. N1 ... 7C 66
(not continuous)
Ashby Ho. N1 ... 7C 66
(off Essex Rd.)
SW9 ... 2B 120
UB5: N'olt ... 4D 76
(off Waxlow Way)
Ashby M. SE4 ... 2B 122
SW2 ... 5J 119
(off Prague Pl.)
Ashby Rd. N15 ... 5G 49
SE4 ... 2B 122
Ashbys Ct. E3 ... 2B 86
(off Centurion La.)
Ashby St. EC1 ... 2B 8 (3B 84)
Ashby Wlk. CR0: C'don ... 6C 156
Ashby Way UB7: Sip ... 7C 92
Aschurch Gro. W12 ... 3C 98
Aschurch Pk. Vs. W12 ... 3C 98
Aschurch Ter. W12 ... 3C 98
Ash Cl.
BR5: Pet W ... 5H 161
DA14: Sidc ... 3B 144
HA7: Stan ... 6F 27
HA8: Edg ... 4D 28
KT3: N Mald ... 2K 151
RM5: Col R ... 1H 55
SE20 ... 2J 157
SM5: Cars ... 2D 166
UB9: Hare ... 1A 38
Ashcombe Av. KT6: Surb ... 7D 150
Ashcombe Cl. TW15: Ashf ... 3A 128
Ashcombe Ct. TW15: Ashf ... 2B 128
Ashcombe Gdns. HA8: Edg ... 4B 28
Ashcombe Ho. E3 ... 3D 86
(off Bruce Rd.)
EN3: Pond E ... 3E 24
Ashcombe Pk. NW2 ... 3A 62
Ashcombe Rd. SM5: Cars ... 6E 166
SW19 ... 5J 135
Ashcombe Sq.
KT3: N Mald ... 3J 151
Ashcombe St. SW6 ... 2K 117
Ash Ct. KT19: Ewe ... 4J 163
N11 ... 6B 32
SW19 ... 7G 135
Ashcroft HA5: Hat E ... 6A 26
N14 ... 2C 32
Ashcroft Av. DA15: Sidc ... 6A 126
Ashcroft Ct. N20 ... 2G 31
Ashcroft Cres. DA15: Sidc ... 6A 126
Ashcroft Ho. SW8 ... 1G 119
(off Wadhurst Rd.)
Ashcroft Rd. KT9: Chess ... 3F 163
Ashcroft Sq. W6 ... 4E 98

Ashcroft Theatre
Croydon 3D 168
(within Fairfield Halls)
Ashdale Cl. TW2: Whitt 7G 113
TW19: Stanw 2A 128
Ashdale Gro. HA7: Stan 6E 26
Ashdale Ho. N4 . . . . .7D 48
Ashdale Rd. SE12 . . . . .1K 141
Ashdene HA5: Pinn 3A 24
SE15 . . . . .7H 103
Ashdene Cl. TW15: Ashf 7E 128
Ashdon Cl. IG8: Wfd G 6E 36
Ashdon Rd. NW10 . . . . .1B 80
Ashdown W13 . . . . .5B 78
(off Clivedon Ct.)
Ashdown Cl. BR3: Beck 2D 158
DA5: Bexl 7J 127
Ashdown Ct. E17 . . . . .2E 50
IG11: Bark 6F 71
SM2: Sutt 6A 166
Ashdown Cres. NW5 . . . . .5E 64
Ashdown Ct. N17 . . . . .1G 49
Ashdown Pl. KT7: T Ditt 7A 150
KT17: Ewe 7B 164
Ashdown Rd. EN3: Enf H 2D 24
KT1: King T 2E 150
UB10: Hil 2C 74
Ashdown Wlk. E14 . . . . .4C 104
RM7: Mawney 1H 55
Ashdown Way SW17 . . . . .2E 136
Ashe Ho. TW1: Twick 6D 114
(off Clevedon Rd.)
Ashen E6 . . . . .6E 88
Ashenden Rd. E5 . . . . .5A 68
Ashen Gro. SW19 . . . . .3J 135
Ashentree Ct. EC4 . . . . .1K 13
Asher Loftus Way N11 . . . . .6J 31
Asher Way E1 . . . . .1G 103
Ashfield Av. TW13: Felt 1K 129
WD23: Bush 1B 26
Ashfield Cl. BR3: Beck 7C 140
TW10: Ham 1E 132
Ashfield Ct. SW9 . . . . .2J 119
(off Clapham Rd.)
Ashfield Ho. W14 . . . . .5H 99
(off W. Cromwell Rd.)
Ashfield La. BR7: Chst 6F 143
(not continuous)
Ashfield Pde. N14 . . . . .1C 32
Ashfield Rd. N4 . . . . .6C 48
N14 .3B 32
W3 .1B 98
Ashfield St. E1 . . . . .5H 85
(not continuous)
Ashfield Yd. E1 . . . . .5J 85
ASHFORD 4B 128
Ashford Av. N8 . . . . .4J 47
TW15: Ashf 6D 128
UB4: Yead 6B 76
Ashford Bus. Complex TW15: Ashf . .5E 128
Ashford Cl. E17 . . . . .6A 50
TW15: Ashf 4A 128
ASHFORD COMMON 7F 129
Ashford Ct. HA8: Edg 3C 28
NW2 . . . . .4F 63
Ashford Cres. EN3: Enf H 2D 24
TW15: Ashf 3A 128
Ashford Ho. SE8 . . . . .6B 104
SW9 . . . . .4B 120
Ashford Ind. Est. TW15: Ashf 4E 128
Ashford Manor Golf Course 6B 128
Ashford M. N17 . . . . .1G 49
Ashford Pas. NW2 . . . . .4F 63
Ashford Rd. E6 . . . . .7E 70
E18 . . . . .2K 51
NW2 . . . . .4F 63
TW13: Felt 4F 129
TW15: Ashf 7E 128
TW18: Lale, Staines 7A 128
Ashford St. N1 . . . . .1G 9 (3E 84)
Ashford Tennis Club 4A 128

Ash Gro. BR4: W W'ck 2E 170
E8 . . . . .1H 85
(not continuous)
EN1: Enf 7K 23
HA0: Wemb 4A 60
N10 .4F 47
N13 .3H 33
NW2 . . . . .4F 63
SE12 . . . . .1J 141
SE20 . . . . .2J 157
TW5: Hest 1B 112
TW14: Felt 1G 129
UB1: S'hall 5E 76
UB3: Hayes 7F 75
UB7: Yiew 7B 74
UB9: Hare 1A 38
W5 .2E 96
Ashgrove Ct. W9 . . . . .5J 81
(off Elmfield Way)
Ashgrove Ho. SW1 . . . . .5D 18
(off Lindsay Sq.)
Ashgrove Rd. BR1: Brom 6F 141
IG3: Ilf 1K 71
TW15: Ashf 5E 128
Ash Hill Cl. WD23: Bush 1A 26
Ash Hill Dr. HA5: Pinn 3A 40
Ash Ho. E14 . . . . .2E 104
(off E. Ferry Rd.)
SE1 . . . . .4F 103
(off Longfield Est.)
W10 .4G 81
(off Heather Wlk.)
Ashingdon Cl. E4 . . . . .3K 35
Ashington Ho. E1 . . . . .4H 85
(off Barnsley St.)
Ashington Rd. SW6 . . . . .2H 117
Ash Island KT8: E Mos 3H 149
Ashlake Rd. SW16 . . . . .4J 137
Ashland Pl. W1 . . . . .5G 5 (5E 82)
Ashlar Pl. SE18 . . . . .4F 107
Ashleigh Commercial Est. SE7 . . . .3A 106
Ashleigh Ct. N14 . . . . .7B 22
W5 .4D 96
(off Murray Rd.)
Ashleigh Gdns. SM1: Sutt 2K 165
Ashleigh Rd. SE20 . . . . .3H 157
SW14 . . . . .3A 116
Ashley Av. IG6: Ilf 2F 53
SM4: Mord 5J 153
Ashley Cl. HA5: Pinn 2K 39
NW4 . . . . .2E 44
Ashley Ct. EN5: New Bar 5F 21
NW4 . . . . .2E 44
SW1 . . . . .2A 18
(off Morpeth Ter.)
UB5: N'olt 1C 76
Ashley Cres. N22 . . . . .2A 48
SW11 . . . . .3E 118
Ashley Dr. TW2: Whitt 7F 113
TW7: Isle 6J 95
Ashley Gdns. BR6: Orp 5J 173
HA9: Wemb 2E 60
N13 .4H 33
SW1 . . . . .2B 18 (3G 101)
(not continuous)
TW10: Ham 2D 132
Ashley La. CR0: Wadd 4B 168
NW4 . . . . .2E 44
Ashley Pl. SW1 . . . . .2A 18 (3G 101)
(not continuous)
Ashley Rd. CR7: Thor H 4K 155
E4 . . . . .6H 35
E7 . . . . .7A 70
EN3: Enf H 2D 24
KT7: T Ditt 6K 149
N17 .3G 49
N19 .1J 65
SW19 . . . . .6K 135

Ashley Rd. TW9: Rich 3E 114
TW12: Hamp 1E 148
Ashley Wlk. NW7 . . . . .7K 29
Ashling Rd. CR0: C'don 1G 169
Ashlin Rd. E15 . . . . .4F 69
Ash Lodge KT12: Walt T 7J 147
TW16: Sun 3J 147
(off Forest Dr.)
Ashlone Rd. SW15 . . . . .3E 116
Ashlyns Way KT9: Chess 6D 162
Ashmead N14 . . . . .5B 22
Ashmead Bus. Cen. E16 . . . . .4F 87
Ashmead Ga. BR1: Brom 1A 160
Ashmead Ho. E9 . . . . .5A 68
(off Homerton Rd.)
W13 .1A 96
(off Tewkesbury St.)
Ashmead M. SE8 . . . . .2C 122
Ashmead Rd. SE8 . . . . .2C 122
TW14: Felt 1J 129
Ashmere Av. BR3: Beck 2F 159
Ashmere Cl. SM3: Cheam 5F 165
Ashmere Gro. SW2 . . . . .4J 119
Ash M. NW5 . . . . .5G 65
Ashmill St. NW1 . . . . . . .5C 4 (5C 82)
Ashmole Pl. SW8 . . . . .6K 101
Ashmole St. SW8 . . . . .6K 101
Ashmore NW1 . . . . .7H 65
(off Agar Gro.)
Ashmore Cl. SE15 . . . . .7F 103
Ashmore Ct. N11 . . . . .6J 31
TW5: Hest 6E 94
Ashmore Gro. DA16: Well 3H 125
Ashmore Ho. W14 . . . . .3G 99
(off Russell Rd.)
Ashmore Rd. SE18 . . . . .7D 106
W9 . . . . .2H 81
Ashmount Est. N19 . . . . .7H 47
Ashmount Rd. N15 . . . . .5F 49
N19 .7G 47
Ashmount Ter. W5 . . . . .4D 96
Ashmour Gdns. RM1: Rom 2K 55
Ashneal Gdns. HA1: Harr 3H 59
Ashness Gdns. UB6: G'frd 6B 60
Ashness Rd. SW11 . . . . .5D 118
Ashpark Ho. E14 . . . . .6B 86
(off Norbiton Rd.)
Ashridge Cl. HA3: Kenton 6C 42
Ashridge Ct. N14 . . . . .5B 22
UB1: S'hall 6G 77
(off Redcroft Rd.)
Ashridge Cres. SE18 . . . . .7G 107
Ashridge Gdns. HA5: Pinn 4C 40
N13 .5C 32
Ashridge Way SM4: Mord 3H 153
TW16: Sun 6J 129
Ash Rd. BR6: Chels 7K 173
CR0: C'don 2C 170
E15 .5G 69
SM3: Sutt 7G 153
TW17: Shep 4C 146
Ash Row BR2: Brom 7E 160
Ashtead Rd. E5 . . . . .7G 49
Ashton Cl. SM1: Sutt 4J 165
Ashton Ct. E4 . . . . .3B 36
HA1: Harr 3K 59
Ashton Gdns. RM6: Chad H 6E 54
TW4: Houn 4D 112
Ashton Hgts. SE23 . . . . .1J 139
Ashton Ho. SE11 . . . . .5K 19
SW9 . . . . .7A 102
Ashton Pl. KT10: Clay 7A 162
Ashton Reach SE8 . . . . .4A 104
Ashton Rd. E15 . . . . .5F 69
Ashton St. E14 . . . . .7E 86
Ashtree Av. CR4: Mitc 2B 154
Ash Tree Cl.
CR0: C'don 6A 158
KT6: Surb 2E 162
Ashtree Cl. BR6: Farnb 4F 173

Ash Tree Ct. TW15: Ashf 5D 128
(off Feltham Hill Rd.)
Ash Tree Dell NW9 . . . . .5J 43
Ash Tree Ho. SE5 . . . . .7C 102
(off Pitman St.)
Ash Tree Way CR0: C'don 5K 157
Ashurst Cl. SE20 . . . . .1H 157
Ashurst Dr. IG2: Ilf 6F 53
IG6: Ilf 5G 53
TW17: Shep 5A 146
Ashurst Gdns. SW2 . . . . .1A 138
Ashurst Rd. EN4: Cockf 5J 21
N12 .5H 31
Ashvale Cl. E3 . . . . .2C 86
(off Matilda Gdns.)
Ashvale Rd. SW17 . . . . .5D 136
Ashview Apartments N4 . . . . .7C 48
(off Katherine Cl.)
Ashview Cl. TW15: Ashf 5A 128
Ashview Gdns. TW15: Ashf 5A 128
Ashville Rd. E11 . . . . .2F 69
Ash Wlk. HA0: Wemb 4C 60
Ashwater Rd. SE12 . . . . .1J 141
Ashway Centre, The KT2: King T . . .1E 150
Ashwell Cl. E6 . . . . .6C 88
Ashwell Ct. TW15: Ashf 2A 128
Ashwin St. E8 . . . . .6F 67
Ashwood Av. UB8: Hil 6C 74
Ashwood Gdns. CR0: New Ad 6E 170
UB3: Harl 4H 93
Ashwood Ho. NW4 . . . . .4E 44
(off Belle Vue Est.)
Ashwood Rd. E4 . . . . .3A 36
Ashworth Cl. SE5 . . . . .2D 120
Ashworth Est. CR0: Bedd 1J 167
Ashworth Mans. W9 . . . . .3K 81
(off Elgin Av.)
Ashworth Rd. W9 . . . . .3K 81
Aske Ho. N1 . . . . .1G 9
Asker Ho. N7 . . . . .4J 65
Askern Cl. DA6: Bex 4D 126
Aske St. N1 . . . . .1G 9 (3E 84)
Askew Cres. W12 . . . . .2B 98
Askew Est. W12 . . . . .1B 98
(off Uxbridge Rd.)
Askew Rd. W12 . . . . .2B 98
Askham Ct. W12 . . . . .1C 98
Askham Rd. W12 . . . . .1C 98
Askill Dr. SW15 . . . . .5G 117
Askwith Rd. RM13: Rain 3K 91
Asland Rd. E15 . . . . .1G 87
Aslett St. SW18 . . . . .7K 117
Asman Ho. N1 . . . . .2B 84
(off Colebrooke Rd.)
Asmara Rd. NW2 . . . . .5G 63
Asmuns Hill NW11 . . . . .5J 45
Asmuns Pl. NW11 . . . . .5H 45
Asolando Dr. SE17 . . . . .4C 102
Aspect Ct. E14 . . . . .2E 104
(off Manchester Rd.)
SW6 . . . . .2A 118
Aspects SM1: Sutt 5K 165
Aspen Cl. KT1: Hamp W 1C 150
N19 .2G 65
UB7: Yiew 1B 92
W5 . . . . .2F 97
Aspen Copse BR1: Brom 2D 160
Aspen Ct. NW4 . . . . .2G 45
Aspen Dr. HA0: Wemb 3A 60
Aspen Gdns. CR4: Mitc 5E 154
TW15: Ashf 5E 128
W6 . . . . .5D 98
Aspen Grn. DA18: Erith 3F 109
Aspen Gro. HA5: Eastc 3H 39
Aspen Ho. DA15: Sidc 2A 144
E15 .3G 87
(off Teasel Way)
SE15 . . . . .6J 103
(off Sharratt St.)
Aspen La. UB5: N'olt 3C 76

Aspenlea Rd. W6 . . . . .6F 99
Aspen Lodge W8 . . . . .3K 99
   (off Abbots Wlk.)
Aspen Way E14 . . . . .7D 86
   TW13: Felt 3K 129
Aspern Gro. NW3 . . . . .5C 64
Aspinall Rd. SE4 . . . . .3K 121
   (not continuous)
Aspinden Rd. SE16 . . . . .4H 103
ASPIRE National Training Cen. 2G 27
Aspire Sport & Fitness Cen. 1K 33
Aspley Rd. SW18 . . . . .5K 117
Asplins Rd. N17 . . . . .1G 49
Asprey M. BR3: Beck 5B 158
Asprey Pl. BR1: Brom 2C 160
Asquith Cl. RM8: Dag 1C 72
Asquith Ho. SW1 . . . . .2D 18
   (off Monck St.)
Assam St. E1 .6G 85
   (off White Church La.)
Assata M. N1 . . . . .6B 66
Assembly Apartments SE15 . . . . . . .1J 121
   (off York Gro.)
Assembly Pas. E1 . . . . .5J 85
Assembly Wlk. SM5: Cars 7C 154
Ass Ho. La. HA3: Hrw W 4A 26
Astall Cl. HA3: Hrw W 1J 41
Astbury Bus. Pk. SE15 . . . . .1J 121
Astbury Ho. SE11 . . . . .2J 19
Astbury Rd. SE15 . . . . .1J 121
Astell Ho. SW3 . . . . .5D 16
   (off Astell St.)
Astell Rd. SE3 . . . . .4A 124
Astell St. SW3 . . . . .5D 16 (5C 100)
Aster Ct. E5 . . . . .2J 67
   (off Woodmill Rd.)
Asterid Hgts. E20 . . . . .5E 68
   (off Liberty Bri. Rd.)
Aster Pl. E9 . . . . .7J 67
   (off Frampton Pk. Rd.)
Aste St. E14 . . . . .2E 104
Astey's Row N1 . . . . .7C 66
Asthall Gdns. IG6: Ilf 4G 53
Astins Ho. E17 . . . . .4D 50
Astleham Rd.
   TW17: Shep 3A 146
Astle St. SW11 . . . . .2E 118
Astley Av. NW2 . . . . .5E 62
Astley Ho. SE1 . . . . .5F 103
   (off Rowcross St.)
   SW13 .6D 98
   (off Wyatt Dr.)
   W2 . . . . .5J 81
   (off Alfred Rd.)
Aston Av. HA3: Kenton 7C 42
Aston Cl. DA14: Sidc 3A 144
Aston Cl. IG8: Wfd G 6D 36
Aston Grn. TW4: Cran 2A 112
Aston Ho. EC4 .6J 7
   (off Furnival St.)
   RM8: Dag 4A 72
   SW8 . . . . .1H 119
   W11 . . . . .7H 81
   (off Westbourne Gro.)
Aston M. RM6: Chad H 7C 54
   W10 . . . . .3F 81
Aston Pl. SW16 . . . . .6B 138
Aston Rd. SW20 . . . . .2E 152
   W5 . . . . .6D 78
Aston St. E14 .5A 86
Aston Ter. SW12 . . . . .6F 119
Astonville St. SW18 . . . . .1J 135
Aston Webb Ho. SE1 . . . . .5G 15
Astor Av. RM7: Rom 6J 55
Astor Cl. KT2: King T 6H 133
Astor Ct. E16 . . . . .6A 88
   (off Ripley Rd.)
   SW6 . . . . .7A 100
   (off Maynard Cl.)
Astoria Ct. E8 .7F 67
   (off Queensbridge Rd.)

Astoria Ho. NW9 . . . . .2B 44
   (off Boulevard Dr.)
Astoria Mans. SW16 . . . . .3J 137
Astoria Wlk. SW9 . . . . .3A 120
Astra Ho. E3 . . . . .3B 86
   (off Alfred St.)
   SE14 . . . . .6B 104
   (off Arklow Rd.)
Astral Ho. E1 . . . . .6H 9
   (off Middlesex Rd.)
   SE6 . . . . .4E 140
Astrid Ho. TW13: Felt 2A 130
Astrop M. W6 . . . . .3E 98
Astrop Ter. W6 . . . . .2E 98
Astwood M. SW7 . . . . .4A 100
Asylum Rd. SE15 . . . . .7H 103
Atalanta St. SW6 . . . . .1F 117
Atbara Rd. TW11: Tedd 6B 132
Atcham Rd. TW3: Houn 4G 113
Atcost Rd. IG11: Bark 5A 90
Atcraft Cen. HA0: Wemb 1E 78
Atelier Ct. Central E14 . . . . .5E 86
   (off Leven Rd.)
Atelier Ct. Nth. E14 . . . . .5E 86
   (off Leven Rd.)
Atelier Ct. Sth. E14 . . . . .5E 86
   (off Leven Rd.)
Atheldene Rd. SW18 . . . . .1K 135
Athelney St. SE6 . . . . .3C 140
Athelstane Gro. E3 . . . . .2B 86
Athelstane M. N4 . . . . .1A 66
Athelstan Gdns. NW6 . . . . .7G 63
Athelstan Ho. E9 . . . . .5B 68
   (off Homerton Rd.)
   KT1: King T 4F 151
   (off Athelstan Rd.)
Athelstan Rd. KT1: King T 4F 151
Athelstan Rd. HA3: W'stone 2H 41
Athena Cl. HA2: Harr 2H 59
   KT1: King T 4F 151
Athena Ct. SE1 . . . . .7G 15
   (off City Wlk.)
Athenaeum Ct. N5 . . . . .4C 66
Athenaeum Pl. N10 . . . . .3F 47
Athenaeum Rd. N20 . . . . .1F 31
Athena Pl. HA6: Nwood 1H 39
Athene Pl. EC4 . . . . .7K 7
   (off Thavie's Inn)
Athenia Ho. E14 . . . . .6F 87
   (off Blair St.)
Athenlay Rd. SE15 . . . . .5K 121
Athens Gdns. W9 . . . . .4J 81
   (off Harrow Rd.)
Atherden Rd. E5 . . . . .4J 67
Atherfold Rd. SW9 . . . . .3J 119
Atherley Way TW4: Houn 7D 112
Atherstone Ct. W2 . . . . .5K 81
   (off Delamere Ter.)
Atherstone M. SW7 . . . . .4A 100
Atherton Hgts. HA0: Wemb 7C 60
Atherton Leisure Cen. 6H 69
Atherton M. E7 . . . . .6H 69
Atherton Pl. HA2: Harr 3H 41
   UB1: S'hall 7E 76
Atherton Rd. E7 . . . . .6H 69
   IG5: Ilf .2C 52
   SW13 .7C 98
Atherton St. SW11 . . . . .2C 118
Athlone Cl. E5 .5H 67
Athlone Ct. E17 . . . . .3F 51
Athlone Ho. E1 . . . . .6J 85
   (off Sidney St.)
Athlone Rd. SW2 . . . . .7K 119
Athlone St. NW5 . . . . .6E 64
Athlon Ind. Est.
   HA0: Wemb 1D 78
Athlon Rd. HA0: Wemb 2D 78
Athol Cl. HA5: Pinn 1K 39
Athole Gdns. EN1: Enf 5K 23
Athol Gdns. HA5: Pinn 1K 39

Atholl Ho. W9 .3A 82
   (off Maida Vale)
Atholl Rd. IG3: Ilf 7A 54
Athol Rd. DA8: Erith 5J 109
Athol Sq. E14 .6E 86
Athol Way UB10: Hil 3C 74
Atkin Bldg. WC1 . . . . .4J 7
   (off Raymond Bldgs.)
Atkins Ct. E3 . . . . .1B 86
   (off Willow Tree Cl.)
Atkins Dr. BR4: W W'ck 2F 171
Atkins Lodge W8 . . . . .2J 99
   (off Thornwood Gdns.)
Atkinson Cl. BR6: Chels 5K 173
Atkinson Ct. E10 . . . . .7D 50
   (off Kings Cl.)
Atkinson Ho. E2 . . . . .2G 85
   (off Pritchards Rd.)
   E13 . . . . .4H 87
   (off Sutton Rd.)
   SE17 . . . . .4D 102
   (off Catesby St.)
   SW11 .1E 118
   (off Austin Rd.)
Atkinson Morley Av. SW17 . . . . .3B 136
Atkinson Rd. E16 . . . . .5A 88
Atkins Rd. E10 . . . . .6D 50
   SW12 .7G 119
Atlanta Bldg. SE13 . . . . .1D 122
   (off Deal's Gateway)
Atlanta Ct. CR7: Thor H 3C 156
Atlanta Ho. SE16 . . . . .3A 104
   (off Brunswick Quay)
Atlantic Apartments E16 . . . . .7J 87
   (off Seagull La.)
Atlantic Ct. E14 . . . . .7F 87
   (off Jamestown Way)
   SW3 . . . . .5E 16 (5D 100)
Atlantic Rd. SW9 . . . . .4A 120
Atlantic Wharf E1 . . . . .7K 85
Atlantis Av. E16 . . . . .7F 89
Atlantis Cl. IG11: Bark 3B 90
Atlas Bus. Cen. NW2 . . . . .1D 62
Atlas Cres. HA8: Edg 2C 28
Atlas Gdns. SE7 . . . . .4A 106
Atlas M. E8 . . . . .6F 67
   N7 . . . . .6K 65
Atlas Rd. E13 .2J 87
   HA9: Wemb 4J 61
   N11 . . . . .7K 31
   NW10 . . . . .3A 80
Atlas Trade Pk. DA8: Erith 5K 109
Atlas Wharf E9 . . . . .6C 68
Atlip Rd. HA0: Wemb 1E 78
Altitude E1 . . . . .6G 85
   (off Alie St.)
Atney Rd. SW15 . . . . .4G 117
Atrium, The IG9: Buck H 2G 37
   W12 . . . . .1F 99
Atrium Apartments N1 . . . . .1D 84
   (off Felton St.)
Atrium Hgts. SE8 . . . . .6D 104
   (off Creekside)
Atrium Ho. SE8 . . . . .7B 104
Atterbury Rd. N4 . . . . .6A 48
Atterbury St. SW1 . . . . .4D 18 (4J 101)
Attewood Av. NW10 . . . . .3A 62
Attewood Rd. UB5: N'olt 6C 58
Attfield Cl. N20 . . . . .2G 31
Attfield Ct. KT1: King T 2F 151
   (off Albert Rd.)
Attilburgh Ho. SE1 . . . . .7J 15
   (off St Saviour's Est.)
Attleborough Ct. SE23 . . . . .2G 139
Attle Cl. UB10: Hil 2C 74
Attlee Cl. CR7: Thor H 5C 156
   UB4: Yead 3K 75
   UB5: N'olt 3K 75
Attlee Rd. SE28 . . . . .7B 90
   UB4: Yead 3J 75
Attlee Ter. E17 . . . . .4D 50

Attneave St. WC1 . . . . .2J 7 (3A 84)
Attock M. E17 .5D 5_
Atunbi Ct. NW1 . . . . .7G 6_
   (off Farrier S_)
Atwater Cl. SW2 . . . . .1A 13_
Atwell Cl. E10 .6D 5_
Atwell Pl. KT7: T Ditt . . . . .7K 14_
Atwell Rd. SE15 . . . . .2G 12_
Atwood Av. TW9: Kew . . . . .2G 11_
Atwood Ho. W14 . . . . .4H 9_
   (off Beckford C_)
Atwood Rd. W6 . . . . .4D 9_
Atwoods All. TW9: Kew . . . . .1G 11_
Aube Ho. SE6 .4E 14_
Aubert Ct. N5 .4B 6_
Aubert Pk. N5 .4B 6_
Aubert Rd. N5 .4B 6_
Aubrey Beardsley Ho. SW1 . . . . .4B 1_
   (off Vauxhall Bri. Ro_)
Aubrey Mans. NW1 . . . . .5C _
   (off Lisson St_)
Aubrey Moore Point E15 . . . . .2E 8_
   (off Abbey La_)
Aubrey Pl. NW8 . . . . .2A 8_
Aubrey Rd. E17 . . . . .3C 5_
   N8 . . . . .5J 4_
   W8 . . . . .1H 9_
Aubrey Wlk. W8 . . . . .1H 9_
Auburn Cl. SE14 . . . . .7A 10_
Aubyn Hill SE27 . . . . .4C 13_
Aubyn Sq. SW15 . . . . .5C 11_
Auckland Cl. SE19 . . . . .1F 15_
Auckland Ct. UB4: Yead . . . . .4A 7_
Auckland Gdns. SE19 . . . . .1E 15_
Auckland Hill SE27 . . . . .4C 13_
Auckland Ho. W12 . . . . .7D 8_
   (off White City Est_)
Auckland Ri. SE19 . . . . .1E 15_
Auckland Rd. E10 . . . . .3D 6_
   IG1: Ilf .1F 7_
   KT1: King T . . . . .4F 15_
   SE19 . . . . .1F 15_
   SW11 .4C 11_
Auckland St. SE11 . . . . .6G 19 (5K 101)
Audax NW9 . . . . .2B 4_
Auden Pl. NW1 . . . . .1E 8_
   SM3: Cheam . . . . .4E 16_
Audleigh Pl. IG7: Chig . . . . .6K 3_
Audley Cl. N10 . . . . .7A 3_
   SW11 .3E 11_
Audley Ct. E18 . . . . .4H 5_
   HA5: Pinn . . . . .2A 4_
   TW2: Twick . . . . .3H 13_
   UB5: N'olt . . . . .3A 7_
Audley Dr. E16 . . . . .1K 10_
Audley Gdns. IG3: Ilf . . . . .2K 7_
Audley Pl. SM2: Sutt . . . . .7K 16_
Audley Rd. EN2: Enf . . . . .2G 23_
   NW4 . . . . .5C 4_
   TW10: Rich . . . . .5F 11_
   W5 . . . . .5F 7_
Audley Sq. W1 . . . . .4H 11 (1E 100)
Audrey Cl. BR3: Beck . . . . .6D 15_
Audrey Gdns. HA0: Wemb . . . . .2B 6_
Audrey Rd. IG1: Ilf . . . . .3F 7_
Audrey St. E2 .2G 8_
Audric Cl. KT2: King T . . . . .1G 15_
Augurs La. E13 . . . . .3K 8_
Augusta Cl. KT8: W Mole . . . . .3D 14_
Augusta Rd. TW2: Twick . . . . .2G 13_
Augustas La. N1 . . . . .7A 6_
Augusta St. E14 . . . . .6D 8_
Augustine Bell Twr. E3 . . . . .2C 8_
   (off Pancras Way)
Augustine Rd. HA3: Hrw W 1F 41
   W14 . . . . .3F 99
Augustus Bldg. E1 . . . . .6H 85
   (off Tarling St.)
Augustus Cl. HA7: Stan 3J 27
   TW8: Bford 7C 96
   W12 . . . . .2D 98

Augustus Ct. *SE1* . . . *4E **102***
(off Old Kent Rd.)
SW16 . . . 2H **137**
TW13: Hanw . . . 4D **130**
Augustus Ho. *NW1* . . . *1A **6***
(off Augustus St.)
Augustus La. BR6: Orp . . . 2K **173**
Augustus Rd. SW19 . . . 1F **135**
Augustus St. NW1 . . . 1K **5** (2F **83**)
Aulay Ho. SE16 . . . 3F **103**
Aultone Way SM1: Sutt . . . 2K **165**
SM5: Cars . . . 3D **166**
Aultone Yd. Ind. Est. SM5: Cars . . . 3D **166**
Aulton Pl. SE11 . . . 6K **19** (5A **102**)
Aura Ct. SE15 . . . 4H **121**
Aura Ho. TW9: Kew . . . 1H **115**
Aurelia Gdns. CR0: C'don . . . 5K **155**
Aurelia Ho. *E20* . . . *5E **68***
(off Sunrise Cl.)
Aurelia Rd. CR0: C'don . . . 6J **155**
Auriel Av. RM10: Dag . . . 6K **73**
Auriga M. N1 . . . 5D **66**
Auriol Cl. KT4: Wor Pk . . . 3A **164**
Auriol Dr. UB6: G'frd . . . 7H **59**
UB10: Hil . . . 6C **56**
Auriol Ho. *W12* . . . *1D **98***
(off Ellerslie Rd.)
Auriol Mans. *W14* . . . *4G **99***
(off Edith Rd.)
Auriol Pk. Rd. KT4: Wor Pk . . . 3A **164**
Auriol Rd. W14 . . . 4G **99**
Aurora Apartments *SW18* . . . *5J **117***
(off Buckhold Rd.)
Aurora Bldg. *E14* . . . *1E **104***
(off Blackwall Way)
Aurora Bldg., The N1 . . . 1F **9**
Aurora Ho. *E14* . . . *6D **86***
(off Kerbey St.)
SE6 . . . 4E **140**
Austell Gdns. NW7 . . . 3F **29**
Austell Hgts. *NW7* . . . *3F **29***
(off Austell Gdns.)
Austen Apartments SE20 . . . 2H **157**
Austen Cl. SE28 . . . 1B **108**
Austen Ho. *NW6* . . . *3J **81***
(off Cambridge Rd.)
SW17 . . . *3B **136***
(off St George's Gro.)
Austen Rd. DA8: Erith . . . 7H **109**
HA2: Harr . . . 2F **59**
Austin Av. BR2: Brom . . . 5C **160**
Austin Cl. SE23 . . . 7A **122**
TW1: Twick . . . 5C **114**
Austin Ct. E6 . . . 1A **88**
EN1: Enf . . . 5K **23**
SE15 . . . *3G **121***
(off Peckham Rye)
Austin Friars EC2 . . . 7F **9** (6D **84**)
Austin Friars Pas. EC2 . . . 7F **9**
Austin Friars Sq. *EC2* . . . *7F **9***
(off Austin Friars)
Austin Ho. *SE14* . . . *7B **104***
(off Achilles St.)
Austin Rd. SW11 . . . 1E **118**
UB3: Hayes . . . 2H **93**
Austin's La. HA4: Ruis . . . 4F **57**
UB10: Ick . . . 3E **56**
Austin St. E2 . . . 2J **9** (3F **85**)
Austin Ter. *SE1* . . . *1K **19***
(off Morley St.)
Austral Cl. DA15: Sidc . . . 3K **143**
Australian War Memorial . . . *6H **11***
(off Duke of Wellington Pl.)
Australia Rd. W12 . . . 7D **80**
Austral St. SE11 . . . 3K **19** (4B **102**)
Austyn Gdns. KT5: Surb . . . 1H **163**
Autumn Cl. EN1: Enf . . . 1B **24**
SW19 . . . 6A **136**
Autumn Gro. BR1: Brom . . . 6K **141**
Autumn Lodge *CR2: S Croy* . . . *4E **168***
(off South Pk. Hill Rd.)

Autumn St. E3 . . . 1C **86**
Autumn Way UB7: W Dray . . . 2B **92**
Avalon Cl. EN2: Enf . . . 2F **23**
SW20 . . . 2G **153**
W13 . . . 5A **78**
Avalon Ct. CR0: C'don . . . 7F **157**
Avalon Rd. SW6 . . . 1K **117**
W13 . . . 4A **78**
Avante KT1: King T . . . 3D **150**
Avantgarde Pl. *E1* . . . *3K **9***
(off Sclater St.)
Avantgarde Twr. *E1* . . . *3J **9***
(off Sclater St.)
Avard Gdns. BR6: Farnb . . . 4G **173**
Avarn Rd. SW17 . . . 6D **136**
Avebury Ct. *N1* . . . *1D **84***
(off Imber St.)
SE16 . . . *4J **103***
(off Debnams Rd.)
Avebury Pk. KT6: Surb . . . 7D **150**
Avebury Rd. BR6: Orp . . . 3H **173**
E11 . . . 1F **69**
SW19 . . . 1H **153**
Avebury St. N1 . . . 1D **84**
Aveley Mans. *IG11: Bark* . . . *7F **71***
(off Whiting Av.)
Aveley Rd. RM1: Rom . . . 4K **55**
Aveline St. SE11 . . . 5H **19** (5A **102**)
Aveling Pk. Rd. E17 . . . 2C **50**
Ave Maria La. EC4 . . . 1B **14** (6B **84**)
Avenell Mans. N5 . . . 4B **66**
Avenell Rd. N5 . . . 3B **66**
Avenfield Ho. *W1* . . . *2F **11***
(off Park La.)
Avening Rd. SW18 . . . 7J **117**
Avening Ter. SW18 . . . 7J **117**
Avenons Rd. E13 . . . 4J **87**
Aventine Av. CR4: Mitc . . . 3F **155**
Avenue, The BR1: Brom . . . 3B **160**
BR2: Kes . . . 4B **172**
BR3: Beck . . . 1D **158**
BR4: W W'ck . . . 7E **158**
BR5: St P . . . 7B **144**
BR6: Orp . . . 2K **173**
CR0: C'don . . . 3E **168**
DA5: Bexl . . . 7D **126**
Av., The *E3* . . . *4E **86***
(off Devas St.)
Avenue, The E4 . . . 6A **36**
E11 . . . 6K **51**
EC2 . . . 7H **9** (6E **84**)
EN5: Barn . . . 3B **20**
HA3: Hrw W . . . 1K **41**
HA5: Pinn . . . 6D **40**
HA9: Wemb . . . 1E **60**
IG9: Buck H . . . 2F **37**
KT4: Wor Pk . . . 2B **164**
KT5: Surb . . . 6F **151**
KT17: Ewe . . . 7D **164**
N3 . . . 2J **45**
N8 . . . 3A **48**
N10 . . . 2G **47**
N11 . . . 5A **32**
N17 . . . 3D **48**
NW6 . . . 1F **81**
RM1: Rom . . . 4K **55**
SE10 . . . 7F **105**
SM2: Cheam . . . 7G **165**
SM3: Cheam . . . 7E **164**
SM5: Cars . . . 7E **166**
SW4 . . . 4E **118**
SW18 . . . 7C **118**
TW1: Twick . . . 5B **114**
TW3: Houn . . . 5F **113**
TW5: Cran . . . 7J **93**
TW9: Kew . . . 2F **115**
TW12: Hamp . . . 6D **130**
TW16: Sun . . . 1K **147**
UB10: Ick . . . 4C **56**
W4 . . . 3A **98**
W13 . . . 6B **78**

Avenue Cl. N14 . . . 6B **22**
NW8 . . . 1C **82**
(not continuous)
TW5: Cran . . . 1K **111**
UB7: W Dray . . . 3A **92**
Avenue Ct. IG5: Ilf . . . 3C **52**
N14 . . . 6B **22**
NW2 . . . 3H **63**
SW3 . . . *4E **16***
(off Draycott Av.)
Avenue Cres. TW5: Cran . . . 1K **111**
W3 . . . 2H **97**
Avenue Elmers KT6: Surb . . . 5E **150**
Avenue Gdns. SE25 . . . 2G **157**
SW14 . . . 3A **116**
TW5: Cran . . . 7K **93**
TW11: Tedd . . . 7K **131**
W3 . . . 2H **97**
Avenue Ho. *NW6* . . . *7G **63***
(off The Avenue)
NW8 . . . *2C **82***
(off Allitsen Rd.)
NW10 . . . *2D **80***
(off All Souls Av.)
Avenue Ind. Est. E4 . . . 6H **35**
Avenue Lodge *NW8* . . . *7B **64***
(off Avenue Rd.)
Avenue Mans. *NW3* . . . *5K **63***
(off Finchley Rd.)
Avenue M. N10 . . . 3F **47**
Avenue Pde. N21 . . . 7J **23**
TW16: Sun . . . 3K **147**
Avenue Pk. Rd. SE27 . . . 2B **138**
Avenue Rd. BR3: Beck . . . 2K **157**
DA7: Bex . . . 3E **126**
DA8: Erith . . . 7J **109**
DA17: Belv, Erith . . . 4J **109**
E7 . . . 4K **69**
HA5: Pinn . . . 3C **40**
IG8: Wfd G . . . 6F **37**
KT1: King T . . . 3E **150**
KT3: N Mald . . . 4A **152**
N6 . . . 7G **47**
N12 . . . 4F **31**
N14 . . . 7B **22**
N15 . . . 5D **48**
NW3 . . . 7B **64**
NW8 . . . 7B **64**
NW10 . . . 2B **80**
RM6: Chad H . . . 7B **54**
SE20 . . . 1J **157**
SE25 . . . 2F **157**
SM6: Wall . . . 7G **167**
SW16 . . . 2H **155**
SW20 . . . 2D **152**
TW7: Isle . . . 1K **113**
TW8: Bford . . . 5C **96**
TW11: Tedd . . . 7A **132**
TW12: Hamp . . . 1F **149**
TW13: Felt . . . 3H **129**
UB1: S'hall . . . 1D **94**
W3 . . . 2H **97**
Avenue Sth. KT5: Surb . . . 7G **151**
Avenue Studios *SW3* . . . *4B **16***
(off Sydney Cl.)
Avenue Ter. KT3: N Mald . . . 3J **151**
Averil Gro. SW16 . . . 6B **138**
Averill St. W6 . . . 6F **99**
Avern Gdns. KT8: W Mole . . . 4F **149**
Avern Rd. KT8: W Mole . . . 4F **149**
Avershaw Ho. SW15 . . . 5F **117**
Avery Farm Row SW1 . . . 4J **17** (4E **100**)
Avery Gdns. IG2: Ilf . . . 5D **52**
AVERY HILL . . . 6H **125**
Avery Hill Rd. SE9 . . . 6H **125**
Avery Row W1 . . . 2J **11** (7F **83**)
Aviary Cl. E16 . . . 5H **87**
Aviation Dr. NW9 . . . 2C **44**
Aviemore Cl. BR3: Beck . . . 5B **158**
Aviemore Way BR3: Beck . . . 5A **158**
Avigdor M. N16 . . . 2D **66**

Avignon Rd. SE4 . . . 3K **121**
Avingdor Ct. *W3* . . . *1J **97***
(off Horn La.)
Avington Ct. *SE1* . . . *4E **102***
(off Old Kent Rd.)
Avington Gro. SE20 . . . 7J **139**
Avion Cres. NW9 . . . 1C **44**
Avis Sq. E1 . . . 6K **85**
Avoca Rd. SW17 . . . 4E **136**
Avocet Cl. SE1 . . . 5G **103**
Avocet M. SE28 . . . 3H **107**
Avon Cl.
KT4: Wor Pk . . . 2C **164**
SM1: Sutt . . . 4A **166**
UB4: Yead . . . 4A **76**
Avon Ct. E4 . . . 1K **35**
IG9: Buck H . . . 1E **36**
N12 . . . 5E **30**
SW15 . . . 5G **117**
UB6: G'frd . . . 4F **77**
W9 . . . *5J **81***
(off Elmfield Way)
Avondale Av. EN4: E Barn . . . 1J **31**
KT4: Wor Pk . . . 1B **164**
KT10: Hin W . . . 3A **162**
N12 . . . 5E **30**
NW2 . . . 3A **62**
Avondale Ct. E11 . . . 1G **69**
E16 . . . 5G **87**
E18 . . . 1K **51**
SM2: Sutt . . . *7A **166***
(off Brighton Rd.)
Avondale Cres. EN3: Enf H . . . 3F **25**
IG4: Ilf . . . 5B **52**
Avondale Dr. UB3: Hayes . . . 1J **93**
Avondale Gdns. TW4: Houn . . . 5D **112**
Avondale Ho. *SE1* . . . *5G **103***
(off Avondale Sq.)
Avondale Mans. *SW6* . . . *1H **117***
(off Rostrevor Rd.)
Avondale Pk. Gdns. W11 . . . 7G **81**
Avondale Pk. Rd. W11 . . . 7G **81**
Avondale Pavement SE1 . . . 5G **103**
Avondale Ri. SE15 . . . 3F **121**
Avondale Rd. BR1: Brom . . . 6G **141**
CR2: S Croy . . . 6C **168**
DA16: Well . . . 2C **126**
E16 . . . 5G **87**
E17 . . . 7C **50**
HA3: W'stone . . . 3K **41**
N3 . . . 1A **46**
N13 . . . 2F **33**
N15 . . . 5B **48**
SE9 . . . 2C **142**
SW14 . . . 3A **116**
SW19 . . . 5K **135**
TW15: Ashf . . . 3A **128**
Avondale Sq. SE1 . . . 5G **103**
Avonfield Ct. E17 . . . 3F **51**
Avon Ho. KT2: King T . . . 1D **150**
W8 . . . *3J **99***
(off Allen St.)
W14 . . . *4H **99***
(off Kensington Village)
Avonhurst Ho. NW2 . . . 7G **63**
Avonley Rd. SE14 . . . 7J **103**
Avon M. HA5: Hat E . . . 1D **40**
Avonmore Gdns. W14 . . . 4H **99**
Avonmore Mans. *W14* . . . *4G **99***
(off Avonmore Rd.)
Avonmore Pl. W14 . . . 4G **99**
Avonmore Rd. W14 . . . 4G **99**
Avonmouth Apartments *SW11* . . . *4C **118***
(off Monarch Sq.)
Avonmouth St. SE1 . . . 7C **14** (3C **102**)
Avon Path CR2: S Croy . . . 6C **168**
Avon Pl. SE1 . . . 7D **14** (2C **102**)
Avon Rd. E17 . . . 3F **51**
SE4 . . . 3C **122**
TW16: Sun . . . 7H **129**
UB6: G'frd . . . 4E **76**

Avonstowe Cl. BR6: Farnb 3G 173
Avon Way E18 . . . . .3J 51
Avonwick Rd. TW3: Houn 2F 113
Avril Way E4 . . . . .5K 35
Avro Ct. E9 . . . . .5A 68
(off Mabley St.)
Avro Ho. NW9 . . . . .2B 44
(off Boulevard Dr.)
SW8 . . . . .7F 101
(off Havelock St.)
Avro Way SM6: Wall 7J 167
Awfield Av. N17 . . . . .1D 48
Awliscombe Rd. DA16: Well 2K 125
Axe St. IG11: Bark 1g 89
(not continuous)
Axholme Av. HA8: Edg 1G 43
Axiom Apartments BR2: Brom 4K 159
(off Masons Hill)
Axio Way E3 . . . . .5C 86
Axis Apartments E1 . . . . .3J 9
(off Sclater St.)
Axis Ct. SE10 . . . . .6G 105
(off Woodland Cres.)
SE16 . . . . .2G 103
(off East La.)
Axis Ho. SE13 . . . . .4E 122
(off Lewisham High St.)
Axminster Cres. DA16: Well 1C 126
Axminster Rd. N7 . . . . .3J 65
Axon Pl. IG1: Ilf 2G 71
Aybrook St. W1 . . . . .6G 5 (5E 82)
Aycliffe Ho. SE17 . . . . .6D 102
(off Portland St.)
Aycliffe Rd. W12 . . . . .1C 98
Ayerst Ct. E10 . . . . .7E 50
Aylands Cl. HA9: Wemb 2E 60
Aylesbury Cl. E7 . . . . .6H 69
Aylesbury Ct. SM1: Sutt 3A 166
Aylesbury Ho. SE15 . . . . .6G 103
(off Friary Est.)
Aylesbury Rd. BR2: Brom 3J 159
SE17 . . . . .5D 102
Aylesbury St. EC1 . . . . .4A 8 (4B 84)
NW10 . . . . .3K 61
Aylesford Av. BR3: Beck 5A 158
Aylesford Ho. SE1 . . . . .7F 15
(off Long La.)
Aylesford St. SW1 . . . . . . .5C 18 (5H 101)
Aylesham Cen. SE15 . . . . .1G 121
Aylesham Cl. NW7 . . . . .7H 29
Aylesham Rd. BR6: Orp 7K 161
Ayles Rd. UB4: Yead 3K 75
Aylestone Av. NW6 . . . . .7F 63
Aylett Rd. SE25 . . . . .4H 157
TW7: Isle 2J 113
Ayley Cft. EN1: Enf 5B 24
Ayliffe Cl. KT1: King T 2G 151
Aylmer Cl. HA7: Stan 4F 27
Aylmer Ct. N2 . . . . .5D 46
Aylmer Dr. HA7: Stan 4F 27
Aylmer Ho. SE10 . . . . .5F 105
Aylmer Pde. N2 . . . . .5D 46
Aylmer Rd. E11 . . . . .1H 69
N2 . . . . .5C 46
RM8: Dag 3E 72
W12 . . . . .2B 98
Ayloffe Rd. RM9: Dag 6F 73
Aylsham Dr. UB10: Ick 2E 56
Aylton Est. SE16 . . . . .2J 103
Aylward Rd. SE23 . . . . .2K 139
SW20 . . . . .2H 153
Aylwards Ri. HA7: Stan 4F 27
Aylward St. E1 . . . . .6J 85
(Jamaica St.)
E1 .6J 85
(Jubilee St.)
Aylwin Est. SE1 . . . . .3E 102
Aynhoe Mans. W14 . . . . .4F 99
(off Aynhoe Rd.)
Aynho Rd. W14 . . . . .4F 99

Ayrscombe Path SW14 . . . . .2J 115
Ayr Ct. W3 . . . . .5G 79
Ayres Cl. E13 . . . . .3J 87
Ayres St. SE1 . . . . .6D 14 (2C 102)
Ayr Grn. RM1: Rom 1K 55
Ayrsome Rd. N16 . . . . .3E 66
Ayrton Gould Ho. E2 . . . . .3K 85
(off Roman Rd.)
Ayrton Rd. SW7 . . . . .1A 16 (3B 100)
Ayr Way RM1: Rom 1K 55
Aysgarth Ct. SM1: Sutt 3K 165
Aysgarth Rd. SE21 . . . . .7E 120
Ayston Ho. SE16 . . . . .4K 103
(off Plough Way)
Aytoun Pl. SW9 . . . . .2K 119
Aytoun Rd. SW9 . . . . .2K 119
Azalea Cl. IG1: Ilf 5F 71
W7 . . . . .1K 95
Azalea Ct. IG8: Wfd G 6B 36
W7 . . . . .1K 95
Azalea Ho. SE14 . . . . .7B 104
(off Achilles St.)
TW13: Felt 1K 129
Azalea Wlk. HA5: Eastc 5K 39
Azania M. NW5 . . . . .6F 65
Azenby Rd. SE15 . . . . .2F 121
Azof St. SE10 . . . . .4G 105
Azov Ho. E1 . . . . .4A 86
(off Commodore St.)
Aztec Ho. IG1: Ilf 2H 71
IG6: Ilf 1G 53
Azura Ct. E15 . . . . .1E 86
(off Warton Rd.)
Azure Bldg. E15 . . . . .7F 69
(off St. Eastern Rd.)
Azure Cl. NW9 . . . . .5G 43
Azure Ho. E2 . . . . .3G 85
(off Buckfast St.)
Azure Pl. TW3: Houn 4F 113

B

Baalbec Rd. N5 . . . . .5B 66
Babbacombe Cl. KT9: Chess 5D 162
Babbacombe Gdns. IG4: Ilf 4C 52
Babbacombe Ho. BR1: Brom 1J 159
(off Babbacombe Rd.)
Babbacombe Rd. BR1: Brom 1J 159
Babbage Cl. SE17 . . . . .6B 102
(off Cook's Rd.)
Babell Ho. N1 . . . . .6B 66
(off Canonbury Rd.)
Baber Bri. Caravan Site
TW14: Felt 5A 112
Baber Bri. Pde. TW14: Felt 6A 112
Baber Dr. TW14: Felt 6A 112
Babington Ct. WC1 . . . . .5G 7
Babington Ho. SE1 . . . . .6D 14
(off Disney St.)
Babington Ri. HA9: Wemb 6G 61
Babington Rd. NW4 . . . . .4D 44
RM8: Dag 5C 72
SW16 . . . . .5H 137
Babmaes St. SW1 . . . . .3C 12 (7H 83)
Bacchus Wlk. N1 . . . . .2E 84
(off Regan Way)
Bache's St. N1 . . . . .2F 9 (3D 84)
Back All. EC3 . . . . .1H 15
Bk. Church La. E1 . . . . .6G 85
Back Hill EC1 . . . . .4K 7 (4A 84)
Backhouse Pl. SE17 . . . . .4E 102
Back La. DA5: Bexl 7G 127
HA8: Edg 1J 43
IG9: Buck H 2G 37
N8 . . . . .5J 47
NW3 . . . . .4A 64
RM6: Chad H 7D 54
TW8: Bford 6D 96
TW10: Ham 3C 132
Backley Gdns. SE25 . . . . .6G 157

Back Pas. EC1 . . . . .5B 8
(off Long La.)
Back Rd. DA14: Sidc 4A 144
E17 . . . . .4E 50
TW11: Tedd 7J 131
Bacon Gro. SE1 . . . . .3F 103
Bacon La. HA8: Edg 1G 43
NW9 . . . . .4H 43
(not continuous)
Bacon's College Sports Cen. 1A 104
Bacons La. N6 . . . . .1E 64
Bacon St. E1 . . . . .3K 9 (4F 85)
E2 . . . . .3K 9 (4F 85)
Bacton Ter. RM8: Dag 5B 72
Bacton NW5 . . . . .5E 64
Bacton St. E2 . . . . .3J 85
Baddeley Ho. KT8: W Mole 5E 148
(off Down St.)
Baddesley Ho. SE11 . . . . .5H 19
Baddow Cl. IG8: Wfd G 6F 37
RM10: Dag 1G 91
Baddow Wlk. N1 . . . . .1C 84
(off New North Rd.)
Baden Dr. E4 . . . . .4J 25
Baden Pl. SE1 . . . . .6E 14 (2D 102)
Baden Powell Cl. KT6: Surb 2F 163
RM9: Dag 1e 90
Baden Powell Ho. DA17: Belv 3G 109
(off Ambrooke Rd.)
SW7 . . . . .2A 16
Baden Rd. IG1: Ilf 5F 71
N8 . . . . .4H 47
Bader Cl. NW9 . . . . .2B 44
(off Runway Cl.)
Bader Way SW15 . . . . .6C 116
Badgemore Path SE18 . . . . .5H 107
(off Tuscan Rd.)
Badger Cl. IG2: Ilf 6G 53
TW4: Houn 3A 112
TW13: Felt 3K 129
Badger Ct. NW2 . . . . .3E 62
Badgers Cl. HA1: Enf 3G 23
HA1: Harr 6H 41
TW15: Ashf 5B 128
UB3: Hayes 7G 75
Badgers Copse BR6: Orp 2K 173
KT4: Wor Pk 2B 164
Badgers Cft. N20 . . . . .7B 20
SE9 . . . . .3E 142
Badgers Hole CRO: C'don 4K 169
Badgers Wlk. KT3: N Mald 2A 152
Badlis Rd. E17 . . . . .3C 50
Badma Cl. N9 . . . . .3D 34
Badminton Cl. HA1: Harr 4J 41
UB5: N'olt 6E 58
Badminton M. E16 . . . . .1J 105
Badminton Rd. SW12 . . . . .6E 118
Badsworth Rd. SE5 . . . . .1C 120
Baffin Way E14 . . . . .1E 104
Bafton Ga. BR2: Hayes 1K 171
Bagley Cl. UB7: W Dray 2A 92
Bagley's La. SW6 . . . . .1K 117
Bagleys Spring RM6: Chad H 4E 54
Bagnigge Ho. WC1 . . . . .2J 7
(off Margery St.)
Bagshot Ct. SE18 . . . . .1E 124
Bagshot Ho. NW1 . . . . .1K 5
Bagshot Rd. EN1: Enf 7A 24
Bagshot St. SE17 . . . . .5E 102
Baildon E2 .2J 85
(off Cyprus St.)
Baildon St. SE8 . . . . .7B 104
Bailes Pl. BR3: Beck 1A 158
Bailey Cl. E4 . . . . .4K 35
N11 . . . . .7C 32
SE28 . . . . .1J 107
Bailey Cotts. E14 . . . . .5A 86
(off Maroon St.)
Bailey Ct. NW9 . . . . .3A 44
(off Lingard Av.)

Bailey Cres. KT9: Chess 7D 162
Bailey Ho. E3 . . . . .3D 86
(off Talwin St.)
SW10 . . . . .7K 99
(off Coleridge Gdns.)
Bailey M. SW2 . . . . .5A 120
W4 . . . . .6H 97
Bailey Pl. N16 . . . . .5E 66
SE26 . . . . .6K 139
Bailey Twr. E1 . . . . .7H 85
Baillies Wlk. W5 . . . . .2D 96
Bainbridge Cl. TW10: Ham 5E 132
Bainbridge Rd. RM9: Dag 4F 73
Bainbridge St. WC1 . . . . . . .7D 6 (6H 83)
Baines Cl. CR2: S Croy 5D 168
Baird Cl. E10 . . . . .1C 68
NW9 . . . . .6J 43
Baird Gdns. SE19 . . . . .4E 138
Baird Ho. W12 . . . . .7D 80
(off White City Est.)
Baird Memorial Cotts. N14 . . . . .2C 32
(off Balaams La.)
Baird Rd. EN1: Enf 3C 24
Baird St. EC1 . . . . .3D 8 (4C 84)
Bairny Wood App. IG8: Wfd G 6E 36
Baizdon Rd. SE3 . . . . .2G 123
Bakehouse M. TW12: Hamp 7E 130
Baker Beal Ct. DA7: Bex 3H 127
Baker Ho. E3 . . . . .3D 86
(off Bromley High St.)
W7 . . . . .1K 95
WC1 . . . . .4F 7
(off Colonnade)
Baker La. CR4: Mitc 2E 154
Baker Pas. NW10 . . . . .1A 80
Baker Path. KT19: Ewe 6J 163
Baker Rd. NW10 . . . . .1A 80
SE18 . . . . .7C 106
Bakers Av. E17 . . . . .6D 50
Bakers Ct. SE25 . . . . .3E 156
Bakers End SW20 . . . . .2G 153
Baker's Fld. N7 . . . . .4H 65
Bakers Gdns. SM5: Cars 2C 166
Bakers Hall Ct. EC3 . . . . .3G 15
Bakers Hill E5 . . . . .1J 67
EN5: New Bar 2E 20
Bakers La. N6 . . . . .6D 46
Bakers M. BR6: Chels 6K 173
W1 . . . . .7G 5 (6E 82)
Bakers Pas. NW3 . . . . .4A 64
(off Heath St.)
Baker's Rents E2 . . . . .2J 9 (3F 85)
Baker's Row E15 . . . . .2G 87
EC1 . . . . .4J 7 (4A 84)
BAKER STREET 5D 82
Baker St. EN1: Enf 3J 23
NW1 . . . . .4F 5 (4D 82)
W1 . . . . .4F 5 (4D 82)
Baker's Yd. EC1 . . . . .4J 7
Bakery Cl. SW9 . . . . .7K 101
Bakery M. KT6: Surb 1G 163
Bakery Path HA8: Edg 5C 28
(off St Margaret's Rd.)
Bakery Pl. SW11 . . . . .4D 118
Bakewell Way KT3: N Mald 2A 152
Balaam Ho. SM1: Sutt 4J 165
Balaam Leisure Cen. 4J 87
Balaams La. N14 . . . . .2C 32
Balaam St. E13 . . . . .4J 87
Balaclava Rd.
KT6: Surb 7C 150
SE1 . . . . .4F 103
Bala Grn. NW9 . . . . .6A 44
(off Ruthin Cl.)
Balcaskie Rd. SE9 . . . . .5D 124
Balchen Rd. SE3 . . . . .2B 124
Balchier Rd. SE22 . . . . .6H 121
Balcombe Cl. DA6: Bex 4D 126

Balcombe Ho.—Banstead Rd. Sth.

Balcombe Ho. *NW1* *3E 4*
(off Taunton Pl.)
Balcombe St. NW1 . . . . . 3E **4** (4D **82**)
Balcon Ct. W5 . . . . 6F **79**
Balcony, The W12 . . . . 1F **99**
Balcorne St. E9 . . . . 7J **67**
Balder Ri. SE12 . . . . 2K **141**
Balderton Flats *W1* *1H 11*
(off Balderton St.)
Balderton St. W1 . . . . . 1H **11** (6E **82**)
Baldewyne Ct. N17 . . . . 1G **49**
Baldock St. E3 . . . . 2D **86**
Baldrey Ho. *SE10* *5H 105*
(off Blackwall La.)
Baldry Gdns. SW16 . . . . 6J **137**
Baldwin Cres. SE5 . . . . 1C **120**
Baldwin Gdns. TW3: Houn 1G **113**
Baldwin Ho. SW2 . . . . 1A **138**
Baldwin Rd. SW11 . . . . 6E **118**
Baldwins Gdns. EC1 . . . . . 5J **7** (5A **84**)
Baldwin St. EC1 . . . . . 2E **8** (3D **84**)
Baldwin Ter. N1 . . . . 2C **84**
Baldwyn Gdns. W3 . . . . 7K **79**
Baldwyn's Pk. DA5: Bexl 2K **145**
Baldwyn's Rd. DA5: Bexl 2K **145**
Balearic Apartments *E16* *7J 87*
(off Western Gateway)
Bale Rd. E1 . . . . 5A **86**
Bales Ter. N9 . . . . 3A **34**
Balfern Gro. W4 . . . . 5A **98**
Balfern St. SW11 . . . . 2C **118**
Balfe St. N1 . . . . 2J **83**
Balfour Av. W7 . . . . 1K **95**
Balfour Bus. Cen. UB2: S'hall 3A **94**
Balfour Gro. N20 . . . . 3J **31**
Balfour Ho. *SW11* *1E 118*
(off Forfar Rd.)
W10 . . . . *5F 81*
(off St Charles Sq.)
Balfour M. N9 . . . . 3B **34**
W1 . . . . . 4H **11** (1E **100**)
Balfour Pl. SW15 . . . . 4D **116**
W1 . . . . . 3H **11** (7E **82**)
Balfour Rd. BR2: Brom 5B **160**
HA1: Harr 5H **41**
IG1: Ilf 2F **71**
N5 . . . . 4C **66**
SE25 . . . . 5G **157**
SM5: Cars 7D **166**
SW19 . . . . 7K **135**
TW3: Houn 3F **113**
UB2: S'hall 3B **94**
W3 . . . . 5J **79**
W13 . . . . 2A **96**
Balfour St. SE17 . . . . 4D **102**
Balfour Ter. N3 . . . . 2K **45**
Balfron Twr. E14 . . . . 6E **86**
Balgonie Rd. E4 . . . . 1A **36**
Balgove Ct. *NW10* *6D 62*
(off Eden Gro.)
Balgowan Cl. KT3: N Mald 5A **152**
Balgowan Rd. BR3: Beck 3A **158**
Balgowan St. SE18 . . . . 4K **107**
BALHAM 1E **136**
Balham Continental Mkt. *SW12* *1F 137*
(off Shipka Rd.)
Balham Gro. SW12 . . . . 7E **118**
Balham High Rd. SW12 . . . . 3E **136**
SW17 . . . . 3E **136**
Balham Hill SW12 . . . . 7F **119**
Balham Leisure Cen. 2F **137**
Balham New Rd. SW12 . . . . 7F **119**
Balham Pk. Rd. SW12 . . . . 1D **136**
Balham Rd. N9 . . . . 2B **34**
Balham Sta. Rd. SW12 . . . . 1F **137**
Balin Ho. *SE1* *6E 14*
(off Long La.)
Balkan Wlk. E1 . . . . 7H **85**
Balladier Wlk. E14 . . . . 5D **86**
Ballamore Rd. BR1: Brom 3J **141**
Ballance Rd. E9 . . . . 6K **67**
Ballantine St. SW18 . . . . 4A **118**
Ballantrae Ho. NW2 . . . . 4H **63**
Ballantyne Cl. SE9 . . . . 4C **142**
Ballard Cl. KT2: King T 7K **133**
Ballard Ho. *SE10* *6D 104*
(off Thames St.)
Ballards Cl. RM10: Dag 1H **91**
Ballards Farm Rd. CR0: C'don 6G **169**
CR2: S Croy 6G **169**
Ballards La. N3 . . . . 1J **45**
N12 . . . . 1J **45**
Ballards M. HA8: Edg 6B **28**
Ballards Ri. CR2: Sels 6G **169**
Ballards Rd. NW2 . . . . 2C **62**
RM10: Dag 2H **91**
Ballards Way CR0: C'don 6G **169**
CR2: Sels 6G **169**
Ballast Quay SE10 . . . . 5F **105**
Ballater Rd. CR2: S Croy 5F **169**
SW2 . . . . 4J **119**
Ball Ct. *EC3* *1F 15*
(off Birchin La.)
Balletica Apartments *WC2* *1F 13*
(off Long Acre)
Ball Ho. *NW9* *3B 44*
(off Aerodrome Rd.)
Ballina St. SE23 . . . . 7K **121**
Ballin Ct. *E14* *2E 104*
(off Stewart St.)
Ballingdon Rd. SW11 . . . . 6E **118**
Ballinger Point *E3* *3D 86*
(off Bromley High St.)
Ballinger Way UB5: N'olt 4C **76**
Balliol Av. E4 . . . . 4B **36**
Balliol Rd. DA16: Well 2B **126**
N17 . . . . 1E **48**
W10 . . . . 6E **80**
Balloch Rd. SE6 . . . . 1F **141**
Ballogie Av. NW10 . . . . 4A **62**
Ballow Cl. SE5 . . . . 7E **102**
Balls Pond Pl. N1 . . . . 6D **66**
Balls Pond Rd. N1 . . . . 6D **66**
Balmain Cl. W5 . . . . 1D **96**
Balmain Ct. TW3: Houn 1F **113**
Balmain Lodge *KT5: Surb* *4E 150*
(off Cranes Pk. Av.)
Balman Ho. *SE16* *4K 103*
(off Rotherhithe New Rd.)
Balmer Rd. E3 . . . . 2B **86**
Balmes Rd. N1 . . . . 1D **84**
Balmoral Apartments *W2* *6C 4*
(off Praed St.)
Balmoral Av. BR3: Beck 4A **158**
N11 . . . . 6K **31**
Balmoral Cl. SW15 . . . . 6F **117**
Balmoral Ct. *BR3: Beck* *1E 158*
(off The Avenue)
HA9: Wemb 3F **61**
KT4: Wor Pk 2D **164**
NW8 . . . . *2B 82*
(off Queen's Ter.)
SE12 . . . . 4K **141**
SE16 . . . . *1K 103*
(off King & Queen Wharf)
SE17 . . . . *5D 102*
(off Merrow St.)
SE27 . . . . 4C **138**
SM2: Sutt 7J **165**
Balmoral Cres. KT8: W Mole 3E **148**
Balmoral Dr. UB1: S'hall 4D **76**
UB4: Hayes 4G **75**
Balmoral Gdns. DA5: Bexl 7F **127**
IG3: Ilf 1K **71**
W13 . . . . 3A **96**
Balmoral Gro. N7 . . . . 6K **65**
Balmoral Ho. *E14* *3D 104*
(off Lanark Sq.)
E16 . . . . *1K 105*
(off Keats Av.)
W14 . . . . *4G 99*
(off Windsor Way)
Balmoral M. W12 . . . . 3B **98**
Balmoral Rd. E7 . . . . 4A **70**
E10 . . . . 2D **68**
HA2: Harr 4E **58**
KT1: King T 4F **151**
KT4: Wor Pk 3D **164**
NW2 . . . . 6D **62**
Balmoral Trad. Est.
IG11: Bark 5K **89**
Balmore Cl. E14 . . . . 6E **86**
Balmore Cres. EN4: Cockf 5K **21**
Balmore St. N19 . . . . 2F **65**
Balmuir Gdns. SW15 . . . . 4E **116**
Balnacraig Av. NW10 . . . . 4A **62**
Balniel Ga. SW1 . . . . . 5D **18** (5H **101**)
Balsam Ho. *E14* *7D 86*
(off E. India Dock Rd.)
Baltic Apartments *E16* *7J 87*
(off Western Gateway)
Baltic Centre, The TW8: Bford 5D **96**
Baltic Cl. SW19 . . . . 7B **136**
Baltic Ct. *E1* *1J 103*
(off Clave St.)
SE16 . . . . 2K **103**
Baltic Ho. SE5 . . . . 2C **120**
Baltic Pl. N1 . . . . 1E **84**
Baltic St. E. EC1 . . . . . 4C **8** (4C **84**)
Baltic St. W. EC1 . . . . . 4C **8** (4C **84**)
Baltimore Cl. DA17: Belv 2H **109**
Baltimore Ct. *SW1* *4C 18*
(off Vauxhall Bri. Rd.)
Baltimore Ho. SE11 . . . . 5J **19**
SW18 . . . . 3A **118**
Baltimore Pl. DA16: Well 2K **125**
Baltimore Twr. E14 . . . . 2D **104**
Baltimore Wharf E14 . . . . 3D **104**
Balvaird Pl. SW1 . . . . . 6D **18** (5H **101**)
Balvernie Gro. SW18 . . . . 7H **117**
Balvernie M. SW18 . . . . 7J **117**
Bamber Ho. IG11: Bark 1G **89**
Bamber Rd. SE15 . . . . 1F **121**
Bamborough Gdns. W12 . . . . 2E **98**
Bamburgh N17 . . . . 7C **34**
Bamford Av. HA0: Wemb 1F **79**
Bamford Rd. BR1: Brom 5E **140**
IG11: Bark 6G **71**
Bampfylde Cl. SM6: Wall 3G **167**
Bampton Ct. W5 . . . . 6D **78**
Bampton Dr. NW7 . . . . 7H **29**
Bampton Rd. SE23 . . . . 3K **139**
Banavie Gdns. BR3: Beck 1E **158**
Banbury Cl. EN2: Enf 1G **23**
Banbury Ct. SM2: Sutt 7J **165**
WC2 . . . . 2E **12**
Banbury Ho. E9 . . . . 7K **67**
Banbury Rd. E9 . . . . 7K **67**
E17 . . . . 7E **34**
Banbury St. SW11 . . . . 2C **118**
Banbury Wlk. *UB5: N'olt* *2E 76*
(off Brabazon Rd.)
Banchory Rd. SE3 . . . . 7K **105**
Bancroft Av. IG9: Buck H 2D **36**
N2 . . . . 5C **46**
Bancroft Cl. TW15: Ashf 5C **128**
Bancroft Ct. *SW8* *7J 101*
(off Allen Edwards Dr.)
UB5: N'olt 1A **76**
Bancroft Gdns. BR6: Orp 1K **173**
HA3: Hrw W 1G **41**
Bancroft Ho. *E1* *4J 85*
(off Cephas St.)
Bancroft Rd. E1 . . . . 3J **85**
HA3: Hrw W 2G **41**
Bandon Cl. UB10: Uxb 2B **74**
BANDONHILL 5H **167**
Bandon Ri. SM6: Wall 5H **167**
Banfield Rd. SE15 . . . . 3H **121**
Banfor Ct. SM6: Wall 5G **167**
Bangalore St. SW15 . . . . 3E **116**
Bangla Ho. *E8* *1F 85*
(off Clarissa St.)
Bangor Cl. UB5: N'olt 5F **59**
Banim St. W6 . . . . 4D **98**
Banister Ho. E9 . . . . 5K **67**
SW8 . . . . *1G 119*
(off Wadhurst Rd.)
W10 . . . . *3G 81*
(off Bruckner St.)
Banister M. NW6 . . . . 7K **63**
Banister Rd. W10 . . . . 3F **81**
Bank, The N6 . . . . 1F **65**
Bank Av. CR4: Mitc 2B **154**
Bank Bldgs. *E4* *6A 36*
(off The Avenue)
Bank Ct. E17 . . . . 4E **50**
Bank End SE1 . . . . . 4D **14** (1C **102**)
Bankfoot Rd. BR1: Brom 4G **141**
Bankhurst Rd. SE6 . . . . 7B **122**
Bank La. KT2: King T 7E **132**
SW15 . . . . 5A **116**
Bank M. SM1: Sutt 6A **166**
Bank of England 1E **14** (6D **84**)
Bank of England Mus. 1F **15**
Bank of England Sports Cen. 5A **116**
Banks Ho. *SE1* *3C 102*
(off Rockingham St.)
Banksian Wlk. TW7: Isle 1J **113**
Banksia Rd. N18 . . . . 5E **34**
Bankside CR2: S Croy 6F **169**
EN2: Enf 1G **23**
SE1 . . . . . 3C **14** (7C **84**)
(not continuous)
UB1: S'hall 1B **94**
Bankside Av. SE13 . . . . 3E **122**
UB5: N'olt 2J **75**
Bankside Cl. DA5: Bexl 4K **145**
SM5: Cars 6C **166**
TW7: Isle 4K **113**
Bankside Dr. KT7: T Ditt 1B **162**
Bankside Gallery 3B **14** (7B **84**)
Bankside Lofts SE1 . . . . 4B **14**
Bankside Mix SE1 . . . . . 4C **14** (1C **102**)
Bankside Pk. IG11: Bark 3A **90**
Bankside Pl. N4 . . . . 6C **48**
Bankside Rd. IG1: Ilf 5G **71**
Bankside Way SE19 . . . . 6E **138**
Banks La. DA6: Bex 4F **127**
Bank St. E14 . . . . 1D **104**
Banks Way E12 . . . . 4E **70**
Banks Yd. TW5: Hest 6D **94**
Bankton Rd. SW2 . . . . 4A **120**
Bankwell Rd. SE13 . . . . 4G **123**
Bannatyne Health Club
Chingford 6H **35**
Grove Park 2K **141**
Maida Vale *2K 81*
(off Greville Rd.)
Russell Square *3D 6*
(off Woburn Pl.)
Banner Ct. *SE16* *4J 103*
(off Rotherhithe New Rd.)
Banner Ho. *EC1* *4D 8*
(off Roscoe St.)
Bannerman Ho. SW8 . . . . . 7G **19** (6K **101**)
Banner St. EC1 . . . . . 4D **8** (4C **84**)
Banning St. SE10 . . . . 5G **105**
Bannister Cl. SW2 . . . . 1A **138**
UB6: G'frd 5H **59**
Bannister Ho. *HA3: W'stone* *3J 41*
(off Headstone Dr.)
SE14 . . . . *6K 103*
(off John Williams Cl.)
Bannister Sports Centre 6B **26**
Bannockburn Rd. SE18 . . . . 4J **107**
Bannon Ct. *SW6* *1K 117*
(off Michael Rd.)
Bannow Cl. KT19: Ewe 4A **164**
Banqueting House 5E **12** (1J **101**)
Banstead Ct. W12 . . . . 7B **80**
Banstead Gdns. N9 . . . . 3K **33**
Banstead Rd. SM5: Cars 7B **166**
Banstead Rd. Sth. SM2: Sutt 7B **166**

Banstead St. SE15 . . . .3J 121
Banstead Way SM6: Wall 5J 167
Banstock Rd. HA8: Edg 6C 28
Bantam Ho. NW9 . . . .2B 44
  (off Heritage Av.)
Banting Dr. N21 . . . .5E 22
Banting Ho. NW2 . . . .3C 62
Bantock Ho. W10 . . . .3G 81
  (off Third Av.)
Banton Cl. EN1: Enf 2C 24
Bantry Ho. E1 . . . .4K 85
  (off Ernest St.)
Bantry St. SE5 . . . .7D 102
Banwell Rd. DA5: Bexl 6D 126
Banyard Rd. SE16 . . . .3H 103
Baptist Gdns. NW5 . . . .6E 64
Baquba SE13 . . . .2D 122
Barandon Rd. W11 . . . .7F 81
  (off Grenfell Rd.)
Barbanel Ho. E1 . . . .4J 85
  (off Cephas St.)
Barbara Brosnan Ct. NW8 . . . .1A 4 (2B 82)
Barbara Castle Cl. SW6 . . . .6H 99
Barbara Cl. TW17: Shep 5D 146
Barbara Hucklesby Cl. N22 . . . .2B 48
Barbauld Rd. N16 . . . .3E 66
Barber Beaumont Ho. E1 . . . .3K 85
  (off Bancroft Rd.)
Barber Cl. N21 . . . .7F 23
Barberry Ct. E15 . . . .6G 69
Barbers All. E13 . . . .3K 87
Barbers Rd. E15 . . . .2D 86
Barbican EC2 . . . .5D 8
Barbican Arts Cen. 5D 8 (5C 84)
Barbican Cinema
  Beech St. 5D 8
  (off Beech St.)
  Whitecross St. 5C 84
  (off Whitecross St.)
Barbican Rd. UB6: G'frd 6F 77
Barbican Theatre
  Silk St. 5D 8
  (within Barbican Arts Cen.)
Barb M. W6 . . . .3E 98
Barbon All. EC2 . . . .7H 9
  (off Devonshire Sq.)
Barbon Cl. WC1 . . . .5F 7 (5K 83)
Barbot Cl. N9 . . . .3B 34
Barchard St. SW18 . . . .5K 117
Barchester Cl. W7 . . . .1K 95
Barchester Rd. HA3: Hrw W 2H 41
Barchester St. E14 . . . .5D 86
Barclay Cl. SW6 . . . .7J 99
Barclay Ho. E9 . . . .7J 67
  (off Well St.)
Barclay Oval IG8: Wfd G 4D 36
Barclay Path E17 . . . .5E 50
Barclay Rd. CR0: C'don 3D 168
  E11 . . . .1H 69
  E13 . . . .4A 88
  E17 . . . .5E 50
  N18 . . . .6J 33
  SW6 . . . .7J 99
Barcombe Av. SW2 . . . .2J 137
Barcombe Cl. BR5: St P 3K 161
Bardell Ho. SE1 . . . .7K 15
  (off Parkers Row)
Barden St. SE18 . . . .7J 107
Bardfield Av. RM6: Chad H 3D 54
Bardney Rd. SM4: Mord 4K 153
Bardolph Rd. N7 . . . .4J 65
  TW9: Rich 3F 115
Bard Rd. W10 . . . .7F 81
Bardsey Pl. E1 . . . .5J 85
Bardsey Wlk. N1 . . . .6C 66
  (off Douglas Rd. Nth.)
Bardsley Cl. CR0: C'don 3F 169
Bardsley Ho. SE10 . . . .6E 104
  (off Bardsley La.)
Bardsley La. SE10 . . . .6E 104

Barents Ho. E1 . . . .4K 85
  (off White Horse La.)
Barfett St. W10 . . . .4H 81
Barfield Av. N20 . . . .2J 31
Barfield Rd. BR1: Brom 3E 160
  E11 . . . .1H 69
Barfleur La. SE8 . . . .4B 104
Barford Cl. NW4 . . . .2C 44
Barford Ho. E3 . . . .2B 86
  (off Tredegar Rd.)
Barford St. N1 . . . .1A 84
Barforth Rd. SE15 . . . .3H 121
Barfreston Way SE20 . . . .1H 157
Bargate Cl. KT3: N Mald 7C 152
  SE18 . . . .5K 107
Barge Ho. Rd. E16 . . . .2F 107
Barge Ho. St. SE1 . . . .4K 13 (1A 102)
Barge La. E3 . . . .1A 86
Bargery Rd. SE6 . . . .1D 140
Barge Wlk.
  KT1: Hamp W 3D 150
  KT1: King T 1D 150
  KT8: E Mos 6A 150
  (Boyle Farm Island)
  KT8: E Mos 3H 149
  (Hampton Ct. Cres.)
  SE10 . . . .3H 105
Bargrove Cl. SE20 . . . .7G 139
Bargrove Cres. SE6 . . . .2B 140
Barham Cl. BR2: Brom 1C 172
  BR7: Chst 5F 143
  HA0: Wemb 6B 60
  RM7: Mawney 2H 55
Barham Ct. CR2: S Croy 4C 168
  (off Barham Rd.)
Barham Ho. SE17 . . . .5E 102
  (off Kinglake Est.)
Barham Rd. BR7: Chst 5F 143
  CR2: S Croy 4C 168
  SW20 . . . .7C 134
Baring Cl. SE12 . . . .2J 141
Baring Ct. N1 . . . .1D 84
  (off Baring St.)
Baring Ho. E14 . . . .6C 86
  (off Canton St.)
Baring Rd. CR0: C'don 1G 169
  EN4: Cockf 4G 21
  SE12 . . . .7J 123
Baring St. N1 . . . .1D 84
Baritone Ct. E15 . . . .1H 87
  (off Church St.)
Barker Cl. HA6: Nwood 1H 39
  KT3: N Mald 4H 151
  TW9: Kew 2H 115
Barker Dr. NW1 . . . .7G 65
Barker Ho. SE17 . . . .4E 102
  (off Congreve St.)
Barker M. SW4 . . . .4F 119
Barkers Arc. W8 . . . .2K 99
Barker St. SW10 . . . .6A 100
Barker Wlk. SW16 . . . .3H 137
Barkham Rd. N17 . . . .7J 33
Barkham Ter. SE1 . . . .1K 19
BARKING 1G 89
Barking Abbey 1G 89
Barking Abbey School Leisure Cen. 6A 72
Barking Bus. Cen. IG11: Bark 3A 90
Barking Ind. Pk. IG11: Bark 1K 89
Barking Northern Relief Rd.
  IG11: Bark 7F 71
BARKING RIVERSIDE 3B 90
BARKINGSIDE 3G 53
Barking Splash Pk. 5H 71
Barkis Ho. W11 . . . .1F 99
Bark Pl. W2 . . . .7K 81
Barkston Gdns. SW5 . . . .4K 99
Barkway Ct. N4 . . . .2C 66
Barkway Dr. BR6: Farnb 4E 172

Barkwith Ho. SE14 . . . .6K 103
  (off Cold Blow La.)
Barkwood Cl. RM7: Rom 5J 55
Barkworth Rd. SE16 . . . .5H 103
Barlborough St. SE14 . . . .7K 103
Barlby Gdns. W10 . . . .4F 81
Barlby Rd. W10 . . . .5E 80
Barley Cl. HA0: Wemb 4D 60
Barleycorn Way E14 . . . .7B 86
  (not continuous)
Barley Ct. E5 . . . .2J 67
  RM13: Rain 2K 91
  (off Lwr Mardyke Av.)
Barleyfields Cl. RM6: Chad H 6B 54
Barley La. IG3: Ilf 7A 54
  RM6: Chad H 7A 54
Barley Mow Pas. EC1 . . . .5B 8
  W4 . . . .5K 97
Barley Mow Way
  TW17: Shep 4C 146
Barley Shotts Bus. Pk. W10 . . . .5H 81
Barling NW1 . . . .6F 65
  (off Castlehaven Rd.)
Barlow Cl. SM6: Wall 6J 167
Barlow Dr. SE18 . . . .1C 124
Barlow Ho. N1 . . . .1E 8
  (off Provost St.)
  SE16 . . . .4H 103
  (off Rennie Est.)
  W11 . . . .7G 81
Barlow Pl. W1 . . . .3K 11 (7F 83)
Barlow Rd. NW6 . . . .6H 63
  TW12: Hamp 7E 130
  W3 . . . .1H 97
Barlow St. SE17 . . . .4D 102
Barlow Way RM13: Rain 5K 91
Barmeston Rd. SE6 . . . .2D 140
Barmor Cl. HA2: Harr 2F 41
Barmouth Av. UB6: G'frd 2K 77
Barmouth Rd. CR0: C'don 2K 169
  SW18 . . . .6A 118
Barnabas Cl. EN2: Enf 4F 23
Barnabas Ho. EC1 . . . .2C 8
Barnabas Lodge SW8 . . . .1J 119
  (off Guildford Rd.)
Barnabas Rd. E9 . . . .5K 67
Barnaby Cl. HA2: Harr 2G 59
Barnaby Ct. NW9 . . . .3A 44
  SE16 . . . .2G 103
  (off Scott Lidgett Cres.)
Barnaby Ho. SE15 . . . .6J 103
Barnaby Pl. SW7 . . . .4A 16
Barnaby Way IG7: Chig 3K 37
Barnard Cl. BR7: Chst 1H 161
  SE18 . . . .3E 106
  SM6: Wall 7H 167
  TW16: Sun 7K 129
Barnard Gdns. KT3: N Mald 4C 152
  UB4: Yead 4K 75
Barnard Gro. E15 . . . .7H 69
Barnard Hill N10 . . . .1F 47
Barnard Ho. E2 . . . .3H 85
  (off Ellsworth St.)
Barnard Lodge EN5: New Bar 4F 21
  W9 . . . .5J 81
  (off Admiral Wlk.)
Barnard M. SW11 . . . .4C 118
Barnardo Dr. IG6: Ilf 4G 53
Barnardo Gdns. E1 . . . .7K 85
Barnardo St. E1 . . . .6K 85
Barnardos Village IG6: Ilf 3G 53
Barnard Rd. CR4: Mitc 3E 154
  EN1: Enf 2C 24
  SW11 . . . .4C 118
Barnards Ho. SE16 . . . .2B 104
  (off Wyatt Cl.)
Barnard's Inn EC1 . . . .6J 7
Barnbrough NW1 . . . .1G 83
  (off Camden St.)
Barnby Sq. E15 . . . .1G 87

Barnby St. E15 . . . .1G 87
  NW1 . . . .1B 6 (2G 83)
Barn Cl. NW5 . . . .5F 65
  (off Torriano Av.)
  TW15: Ashf 5D 128
  UB5: N'olt 2A 76
Barn Cres. HA7: Stan 6H 27
Barncroft Cl. UB8: Hil 5D 74
Barneby Cl. TW2: Twick 1J 131
BARNEHURST 3J 127
Barnehurst Av. DA7: Bex 1J 127
  DA8: Erith 1J 127
Barnehurst Cl. DA8: Erith 1J 127
Barnehurst Golf Course 3K 127
Barnehurst Rd. DA7: Bex 2J 127
Barn Elms Athletics Track 2D 117
Barn Elms Cl. KT4: Wor Pk 3B 164
Barn Elms Pk. SW15 . . . .3E 117
BARNES 2B 116
Barnes All. TW12: Hamp 2G 149
Barnes Av. SW13 . . . .7C 98
  UB2: S'hall 4D 94
Barnes Bri. W4 . . . .2A 116
Barnes Cl. E12 . . . .4B 70
Barnes Common Nature Reserve 3C 116
Barnes Ct. CR7: Thor H 3C 156
  E16 . . . .5A 88
  EN5: New Bar 4E 20
  IG8: Buck H, Wfd G 5G 37
  N1 . . . .7A 66
Barnes End KT3: N Mald 5C 152
Barnes High St. SW13 . . . .2B 116
Barnes Ho. E2 . . . .2J 85
  (off Wadeson St.)
  IG11: Bark 1H 89
  SE14 . . . .6K 103
  (off John Williams Cl.)
Barnes Pikle W3 . . . .7D 79
Barnes Rd. IG1: Ilf 5G 71
  N18 . . . .4D 34
Barnes St. E14 . . . .6A 86
Barnes Ter. SE8 . . . .5B 104
Barnes Wallis Ct. HA9: Wemb 3J 61
BARNET 3B 20
Barnet Burnt Oak Leisure Cen. 1K 43
Barnet Bus. Cen. EN5: Barn 3B 20
Barnet By-Pass NW4 . . . .2E 44
  NW7 . . . .6G 29
Barnet Copthall Sports Cen. 1D 44
Barnet Dr. BR2: Brom 2C 172
Barnet FC 1E 42
Barnet Ga. La. EN5: Ark 1H 29
Barnet Gro. E2 . . . .1K 9 (3G 85)
Barnet Hill EN5: Barn 4C 20
Barnet Ho. N20 . . . .2F 31
Barnet La. EN5: Barn 1C 30
  N20 . . . .1C 30
Barnet Mus. 4B 20
Barnetts Ct. HA2: Harr 3F 59
BARNET VALE 5E 20
Barnett St. E1 . . . .6H 85
Barnet Way NW7 . . . .3E 28
Barnet Wood Rd. BR2: Brom 2A 172
Barney Cl. SE7 . . . .5A 106
Barn Fld. NW3 . . . .5D 64
Barnfield KT3: N Mald 6A 152
Barnfield Av. CR0: C'don 2J 169
  CR4: Mitc 4F 155
  KT2: King T 4D 132
Barnfield Cl. N4 . . . .7J 47
  SW17 . . . .3B 136
Barnfield Gdns. KT2: King T 4E 132
  SE18 . . . .6F 107
Barnfield Pl. E14 . . . .4C 104
Barnfield Rd. DA17: Belv 6F 109
  HA8: Edg 1J 43
  SE18 . . . .6F 107
  (not continuous
  W5 . . . .4C 78
Barnfield Wood Cl. BR3: Beck 6F 159

Barnfield Wood Rd. BR3: Beck 6F 159
Barnham Dr. SE28 . . . . .1K 107
(not continuous)
Barnham Rd. UB6: G'frd 3G 77
Barnham St. SE1 . . . . .6H 15 (2E 102)
Barn Hill HA9: Wemb 1G 61
Barnhill HA5: Eastc 5A 40
Barnhill Av. BR2: Brom 5H 159
Barnhill La. UB4: Yead 3K 75
Barnhill Rd. HA9: Wemb 3J 61
UB4: Yead 3K 75
Barningham Way NW9 . . . . .6K 43
Barnlea Cl. TW13: Hanw 2C 130
Barnmead Ct. RM9: Dag 5F 73
Barnmead Gdns. RM9: Dag 5F 73
Barnmead Rd. BR3: Beck 1K 157
RM9: Dag 5F 73
Barn M. HA2: Harr 3E 58
Barn Ri. HA9: Wemb 1G 61
BARNSBURY .7K 65
Barnsbury Cl. KT3: N Mald 4J 151
Barnsbury Cres. KT5: Surb 1J 163
Barnsbury Est. N1 . . . . .1K 83
(not continuous)
Barnsbury Gro. N7 . . . . .7K 65
Barnsbury Ho. SW4 . . . . .6H 119
Barnsbury La. KT5: Surb 2H 163
Barnsbury Pk. N1 . . . . .7A 66
Barnsbury Rd. N1 . . . . .2A 84
Barnsbury Sq. N1 . . . . .7A 66
Barnsbury St. N1 . . . . .7A 66
Barnsbury Ter. N1 . . . . .7K 65
Barnscroft SW20 . . . . .3D 152
Barnsdale Av. E14 . . . . .4D 104
Barnsdale Rd. W9 . . . . .4H 81
Barnsley St. E1 . . . . .4H 85
Barnstable La. SE13 . . . . .4E 122
Barnstaple Ho. *SE10* *7D 104*
(off Devonshire Dr.)
SE12 . . . .*5H 123*
(off Taunton Rd.)
Barnstaple Rd. HA4: Ruis 3A 58
Barnston Wlk. *N1* *1C 84*
(off Popham St.)
Barn St. N16 . . . . .2E 66
Barn Theatre, The
Sidcup 1A 144
West Molesey 4E 148
Barn Way HA9: Wemb 1G 61
Barnwell Cl. HA8: Edg 4A 28
Barnwell Ho. *SE5* *1E 120*
(off St Giles Rd.)
Barnwell Rd. SW2 . . . . .5A 120
Barnwood Cl. HA4: Ruis 2F 57
N20 . . . . .1C 30
W9 . . . . .4K 81
Baron Cl. N1 .2A 84
N11 . . . . .5K 31
Baroness Rd. E2 . . . . .1K 9 (3F 85)
Baronet Gro. N17 . . . . .1G 49
Baronet Rd. N17 . . . . .1G 49
Baron Gdns. IG6: Ilf 3G 53
Baron Gro. CR4: Mitc 4C 154
Baron Ho. SW19 . . . . .1B 154
Baron Rd. RM8: Dag 1D 72
Barons, The TW1: Twick 6B 114
Baronsclere Ct. N6 . . . . .7G 47
BARONS COURT 5G 99
Barons Ct. IG1: Ilf 2H 71
NW9 . . . . .6K 43
SM6: Bedd 3H 167
Baron's Ct. Rd. W14 . . . . .5G 99
Barons Court Theatre *5G 99*
(off Comeragh Rd.)
Baronsfield Rd. TW1: Twick 6B 114
Barons Ga. EN4: E Barn 6H 21
W4 . . . . .3J 97
Barons Keep W14 . . . . .5G 99
Barons Lodge *E14* *4F 105*
(off Manchester Rd.)
Barons Mead HA1: Harr 4J 41
Baronsmead Rd. SW13 . . . . .1C 116
Baronsmede W5 . . . . .2F 97
Baronsmere Ct. EN5: Barn 4B 20
Baronsmere Rd. N2 . . . . .4C 46
Baron's Pl. SE1 . . . . .7K 13 (2A 102)
Baron St. N1 . . . . .2A 84
Baron's Wlk. CR0: C'don 6A 158
Baron Wlk. CR4: Mitc 4C 154
E16 . . . . .5H 87
Baroque Ct. TW3: Houn 3F 113
Baroque Gdns. *SE8* *4A 104*
(off Grand Canal Av.)
Barque M. SE8 . . . . .6C 104
Barrack Rd. TW4: Houn 4B 112
Barracks La. EN5: Barn 3B 20
Barra Hall Cir. UB3: Hayes 7G 75
Barra Hall Rd. UB3: Hayes 7G 75
Barratt Av. N22 . . . . .2K 47
Barratt Ho. *N1* *7B 66*
(off Sable St.)
Barratt Ind. Est. UB1: S'hall 2E 94
Barratt Ind. Pk. E3 . . . . .4E 86
Barratt Way HA3: W'stone 2H 41
Barra Wood Cl. UB3: Hayes 6G 75
Barrenger Rd. N10 . . . . .1D 46
Barret Ho. NW6 . . . . .1J 81
SW9 . . . .*3K 119*
(off Benedict Rd.)
Barrett Ho. *SE17* *5C 102*
(off Browning St.)
Barrett Rd. E17 . . . . .4E 50
Barrett's Grn. Rd. NW10 . . . . .3J 79
Barrett's Gro. N16 . . . . .5E 66
Barrett St. W1 . . . . .1H 11 (6E 82)
Barrhill Rd. SW2 . . . . .2J 137
Barrie Ct. *EN5: New Bar* *5F 21*
(off Lyonsdown Rd.)
Barriedale SE14 . . . . .2A 122
Barrie Est. W2 . . . . .2A 10 (7B 82)
Barrie Ho. *NW8* *1C 82*
(off St Edmund's Ter.)
W2 . . . .*7A 82*
(off Lancaster Ga.)
Barrier App. SE7 . . . . .3B 106
Barrier Point Rd. E16 . . . . .1A 106
Barringers Ct. HA4: Ruis 7F 39
Barringer Sq. SW17 . . . . .4E 136
Barrington Cl. IG5: Ilf 1D 52
NW5 . . . . .5E 64
Barrington Ct. N10 . . . . .2E 46
SW4 . . . . .2J 119
W3 . . . .*2H 97*
(off Cheltenham Pl.)
Barrington Rd. DA7: Bex 2D 126
E12 . . . . .6E 70
N8 . . . . .5H 47
SM3: Sutt 2J 165
SW9 . . . . .3B 120
Barrington Vs. SE18 . . . . .1E 124
Barrington Wlk. SE19 . . . . .6E 138
Barrow Av. SM5: Cars 7D 166
Barrow Cl. N21 . . . . .3G 33
Barrow Ct. *SE6* *1H 141*
(off Cumberland Pl.)
Barrowdene Cl. HA5: Pinn 2C 40
Barrowell Grn. N21 . . . . .2G 33
Barrowfield Cl. N9 . . . . .3C 34
Barrowgate Rd. W4 . . . . .5J 97
Barrow Hedges Cl. SM5: Cars 7C 166
Barrow Hedges Way SM5: Cars 7C 166
Barrow Hill KT4: Wor Pk 2A 164
Barrow Hill Cl. KT4: Wor Pk 2A 164
Barrow Hill Est. *NW8* *2C 82*
(off Barrow Hill Rd.)
Barrow Hill Rd. NW8 . . . . .1C 4 (2C 82)
Barrow Point Av. HA5: Pinn 2C 40
Barrow Point La. HA5: Pinn 2C 40
Barrow Rd. CR0: Wadd 5A 168
SW16 . . . . .6H 137
Barrow Store Ct. *SE1* *7G 15*
(off Decima St.)
Barrow Wlk. TW8: Bford 6C 96
Barrs Rd. NW10 . . . . .7K 61
Barry Av. DA7: Bex 7E 108
N15 . . . . .6F 49
Barry Cl. BR6: Orp 3J 173
Barrydene N20 . . . . .1G 31
Barry Ho. *SE16* *4H 103*
(off Rennie Est.)
Barry Pde. SE22 . . . . .5G 121
Barry Rd. E6 . . . . .6C 88
NW10 . . . . .7J 61
SE22 . . . . .6G 121
Barry Ter. *TW15: Ashf* *2B 128*
(off Orchard Way)
Barset Rd. SE15 . . . . .3J 121
(not continuous)
Barson Cl. SE20 . . . . .7J 139
Barston Rd. SE27 . . . . .3C 138
Barstow Cres. SW2 . . . . .1K 137
Barter St. WC1 . . . . .6F 7 (5J 83)
Barters Wlk. HA5: Pinn 3C 40
Barth M. SE18 . . . . .4J 107
Bartholomew Cl. EC1 . . . . .6B 8 (5C 84)
(not continuous)
SW18 . . . . .4A 118
Bartholomew Ct. *E14* *7F 87*
(off Newport Av.)
EC1 . . . .*3D 8*
(off Old St.)
HA8: Edg .7J 27
Bartholomew Ho. IG8: Wfd G . . .7K 37 & 1F 53
W10 . . . .*4G 81*
(off Appleford Rd.)
Bartholomew La. EC2 . . . . .1F 15 (6D 84)
Bartholomew Pl. EC1 . . . . .6C 8
Bartholomew Rd. NW5 . . . . .6G 65
Bartholomew Sq. E1 . . . . .4H 85
EC1 . . . . .3D 8 (3C 84)
Bartholomew St. SE1 . . . . .3D 102
Bartholomew Vs. NW5 . . . . .6G 65
Barth Rd. SE18 . . . . .4J 107
Bartle Av. E6 .2C 88
Bartle Rd. W11 . . . . .6G 81
Bartlett Cl. E14 . . . . .6C 86
Bartlett Ct. EC4 . . . . .7K 7 (6A 84)
Bartlett Ho. *KT4: Wor Pk* *2B 164*
(off The Avenue)
Bartlett Ho's. *RM10: Dag* *7H 73*
(off Vicarage Rd.)
Bartlett M. E14 . . . . .5D 104
Bartletts Pas. *EC4* *7K 7*
(off Fetter La.)
Bartlett St. CR2: S Croy 5D 168
Bartlow Gdns. RM5: Col R 1K 55
Bartok Ho. *W11* *1H 99*
(off Lansdowne Wlk.)
Barton Av. RM7: Rush G 1H 73
Barton Cl. DA6: Bex 5E 126
E6 . . . . .6D 88
E9 . . . . .5J 67
NW4 . . . . .5C 44
SE15 . . . . .3H 121
TW17: Shep 6D 146
Barton Ct. *W14* *5G 99*
(off Baron's Ct. Rd.)
Barton Grn. KT3: N Mald 2K 151
Barton Ho. *E3* *3D 86*
(off Bow Rd.)
N1 . . . .*7B 66*
(off Sable St.)
SW6 . . . .*3K 117*
(off Wandsworth Bri. Rd.)
Barton Mdws. IG6: Ilf 4F 53
Barton M. E14 . . . . .2D 104
Barton Rd. DA14: Sidc 6E 144
W14 . . . . .5G 99
Barton St. SW1 . . . . .1E 18 (3J 101)
Bartonway *NW8* *1B 82*
(off Queen's Ter.)
Bartram Cl. UB8: Hil 4D 74
Bartram Rd. SE4 . . . . .5A 122
Bartrams La. EN4: Had W 1F 21
Bartrip St. E9 .6B 68
Barts Cl. BR3: Beck 5C 158
Barville Cl. SE4 . . . . .4A 122
Barwell Bus. Pk. KT9: Chess 7D 162
Barwell Ct. KT9: Chess 7B 162
Barwell Ho. *E2* *4G 85*
(off Menotti St.)
Barwell La. KT9: Chess 7C 162
Barwick Dr. UB8: Hil 5D 74
Barwick Ho. *W3* *2J 97*
(off Strafford Rd.)
Barwick Rd. E7 . . . . .4K 69
Barwood Av. BR4: W W'ck 1D 170
Bascombe Gro. DA1: Bexl, Cray 7K 127
Bascombe St. SW2 . . . . .6A 120
Basden Gro. TW13: Hanw 2E 130
Basden Ho. TW13: Hanw 2E 130
Basedale Rd. RM9: Dag 7B 72
Baseing Cl. E6 . . . . .7E 88
Baseline Bus. Studios *W11* *7F 81*
(off Barandon Wlk.)
Basepoint Bus. Cen. RM13: Rain 4K 91
Basevi Way SE8 . . . . .6D 104
Bashley Rd. NW10 . . . . .4K 79
Basil Av. E6 . . . . .3C 88
Basildene Rd. TW4: Houn 3B 112
Basildon Av. IG5: Ilf 1E 52
Basildon Cl. SM2: Sutt 7K 165
Basildon Ct. *W1* *5H 5*
(off Devonshire Rd.)
Basildon Rd. SE2 . . . . .5A 108
Basil Gdns. CR0: C'don 1K 169
SE27 . . . . .5C 138
Basil Ho. *E1* *6G 85*
(off Henriques St.)
SW8 . . . .*7J 101*
(off Wyvil Rd.)
Basil Mans. *SW3* *7E 10*
(off Basil St.)
Basilon Rd. DA7: Bex 2E 126
Basil Spence Ho. N22 . . . . .1K 47
Basil St. SW3 . . . . .1E 16 (3D 100)
Basin App. E14 . . . . .6A 86
E16 . . . . .7F 89
Basing Cl. KT7: T Ditt 7K 149
Basing Ct. SE15 . . . . .1F 121
Basingdon Way SE5 . . . . .4D 120
Basing Dr. DA5: Bexl 6F 127
Basingfield Rd. KT7: T Ditt 7K 149
Basinghall Av. EC2 . . . . .7E 8 (6D 84)
Basinghall Gdns. SM2: Sutt 7K 165
Basinghall St. EC2 . . . . .7E 8 (6D 84)
Basing Hill HA9: Wemb 2F 61
NW11 . . . . .1H 63
Basing Ho. Yd. E2 . . . . .1H 9
Basing Pl. E2 . . . . .1H 9 (3E 84)
Basing St. W11 . . . . .6H 81
Basing Way KT7: T Ditt 7K 149
N3 . . . . .3J 45
Basin Mill Apartments *E2* *1F 85*
(off Laburnum St.)
Basin South .1F 107
Basire St. N1 .1C 84
Baskerville Gdns. NW10 . . . . .4A 62
Baskerville Rd. SW18 . . . . .7C 118
Basket Gdns. SE9 . . . . .5C 124
Baslow Cl. HA3: Hrw W 1H 41
Baslow Wlk. E5 . . . . .4K 67
Basnett Rd. SW11 . . . . .3E 118
Basque Ct. *SE16* *2K 103*
(off Garter Way)
Bassano St. SE22 . . . . .5F 121
Bassant Rd. SE18 . . . . .6K 107
Bass Ct. *E15* *1H 87*
(off Plaistow Rd.)
Bassein Pk. Rd. W12 . . . . .2B 98
Bassett Gdns. TW7: Isle 7G 95
Bassett Ho. SW19 . . . . .5K 135
Bassett Rd. W10 . . . . .6F 81
Bassett's Cl. BR6: Farnb 4F 173

Bassett St.—Beagle Cl.

Bassett St. NW5 . . . . . . 6E 64
Bassett's Way BR6: Farnb 4F 173
Bassett Way UB6: G'frd 6F 77
Bassingbourn Ho. *N1* *7A 66*
(off The Sutton Est.)
Bassingham Rd. HA0: Wemb 6D 60
SW18 . . . . . . 7A 118
Bassishaw Highwalk EC2 . . . . . . 6E 8
Bass M. SE22 . . . . . . 4G 121
Basswood Cl. SE15 . . . . . . 3H 121
Bastable Av. IG11: Bark 2J 89
Basterfield Ho. *EC1* *4C 8*
(off Golden La. Est.)
Bastion Highwalk EC2 . . . . . . 6C 8
Bastion Ho. *EC2* *6D 8*
(off London Wall)
Bastion Rd. SE2 . . . . . . 5A 108
Baston Mnr. Rd.
BR2: Hayes, Kes 3K 171
Baston Rd. BR2: Hayes 2K 171
Bastwick St. EC1 . . . . . . 3C 8 (4C 84)
Basuto Rd. SW6 . . . . . . 1J 117
Batavia Cl. TW16: Sun 1K 147
Batavia Ho. *SE14* *7A 104*
(off Batavia Rd.)
Batavia M. SE14 . . . . . . 7A 104
Batavia Rd. SE14 . . . . . . 7A 104
TW16: Sun 1K 147
Batchelor St. N1 . . . . . . 1A 84
Bateman Cl. IG11: Bark 6G 71
Bateman Ho. *SE17* *6B 102*
(off Otto St.)
Bateman M. SW4 . . . . . . 6H 119
Bateman Rd. E4 . . . . . . 6H 35
Bateman's Bldgs. W1 . . . . . . 1C 12
Bateman's Row EC2 . . . . . . 3H 9 (4E 84)
Bateman St. W1 . . . . . . 1C 12 (6H 83)
Bates Cres. CR0: Wadd 5A 168
SW16 . . . . . . 7G 137
Bateson St. SE18 . . . . . . 4J 107
Bates Point *E13* *1J 87*
(off Pelly Rd.)
Bate St. E14 . . . . . . 7B 86
Bat Gdns. KT2: King T 6F 133
Bath Cl. SE15 . . . . . . 7H 103
Bath Ct. EC1 . . . . . . 2E 8
(St Luke's Est.)
EC1 . . . . . . 4J 7
(Warner St.)
SE26 . . . . . . *3G 139*
(off Droitwich Cl.)
Bathgate Ho. *SW9* *1B 120*
(off Lothian Rd.)
Bathgate Rd. SW19 . . . . . . 3F 135
Bath Gro. *E2* *2G 85*
(off Horatio St.)
Bath Ho. *E2* *4G 85*
(off Ramsey St.)
IG11: Bark 7G 71
SE1 . . . . . . *3C 102*
(off Bath Ter.)
Bath Ho. Rd. CR0: Bedd 1J 167
Bath Pas. KT1: King T 2D 150
Bath Pl. EC2 . . . . . . 2G 9 (3E 84)
EN5: Barn 3C 20
W6 . . . . . . *5E 98*
(off Peabody Est.)
Bath Rd. E7 . . . . . . 6B 70
N9 . . . . . . 2C 34
RM6: Chad H 6E 54
SL3: Coln, Poyle 4A 174
TW3: Houn 2B 112
TW4: Houn 2B 112
TW5: Cran 1G 111
TW6: H'row A 1G 111
UB3: Harl 1G 111
UB7: Lford, Harm, Sip 4C 174
W4 . . . . . . 4A 98
Baths Ct. W12 . . . . . . 2D 98
Baths Rd. BR2: Brom 4B 160
Bath St. EC1 . . . . . . 2D 8 (3C 84)
Bath Ter. SE1 . . . . . . 3C 102
Bathurst Av. SW19 . . . . . . 1K 153
Bathurst Gdns. NW10 . . . . . . 2D 80
Bathurst Ho. *W12* *7D 80*
(off White City Est.)
Bathurst M. W2 . . . . . . 2B 10 (6B 82)
Bathurst Rd. IG1: Ilf 1F 71
Bathurst St. W2 . . . . . . 2B 10 (7B 82)
Bathway SE18 . . . . . . 4E 106
Batley Cl. CR4: Mitc 7D 154
Batley Pl. N16 . . . . . . 3F 67
Batley Rd. EN2: Enf 1H 23
N16 . . . . . . 3F 67
Batman Cl. W12 . . . . . . 1D 98
Batoum Gdns. W6 . . . . . . 3E 98
Batsford Ho. *SW19* *4K 135*
(off Durnsford Rd.)
Batson Ho. *E1* *6G 85*
(off Fairclough St.)
Batson St. W12 . . . . . . 2C 98
Batsworth Rd. CR4: Mitc 3B 154
Battenberg Wlk. SE19 . . . . . . 6E 138
Batten Cl. E6 . . . . . . 6D 88
Batten Cotts. *E14* *5A 86*
(off Maroon St.)
Batten Ho. SW4 . . . . . . 5G 119
W10 . . . . . . *3G 81*
(off Third Av.)
Batten St. SW11 . . . . . . 3C 118
Battersby Rd. SE6 . . . . . . 2F 141
BATTERSEA 1E 118
Battersea Arts Cen. *3D 118*
(off Lavender Hill)
Battersea Bri. SW3 . . . . . . 7B 100
Battersea Bri. Rd. SW11 . . . . . . 7C 100
Battersea Bus. Cen. SW11 . . . . . . 3E 118
Battersea Bus. Pk. SW8 . . . . . . 1G 119
Battersea Church Rd. SW11 . . . . . . 1B 118
Battersea High St. SW11 . . . . . . 1B 118
(not continuous)
BATTERSEA PARK 7F 101
Battersea Park 7D 100
Battersea Park Children's Zoo 7E 100
Battersea Pk. Rd. SW8 . . . . . . 1E 118
SW11 . . . . . . 2C 118
Battersea Ri. SW11 . . . . . . 5C 118
Battersea Sports Cen. 3B 118
Battersea Sq. SW11 . . . . . . 1B 118
Battery Rd. SE28 . . . . . . 2J 107
Battilion Ho. *NW9* *2B 44*
(off Heritage Av.)
Battishill St. N1 . . . . . . 7B 66
Battlebridge Ct. *N1* *2J 83*
(off Wharfdale Rd.)
Battle Bri. La. SE1 . . . . . . 5G 15 (1E 102)
Battle Cl. SW19 . . . . . . 6A 136
Battledean Rd. N5 . . . . . . 5B 66
Battle Ho. *SE15* *6G 103*
(off Haymerle Rd.)
Battle Rd.
DA8: Erith 4J 109
DA17: Belv, Erith 4J 109
Batty St. E1 . . . . . . 6G 85
Batwa Ho. SE16 . . . . . . 5H 103
Baudwin Rd. SE6 . . . . . . 2G 141
Baugh Rd. DA14: Sidc 5C 144
Baulk, The SW18 . . . . . . 7J 117
Bavant Rd. SW16 . . . . . . 2J 155
Bavaria Rd. N19 . . . . . . 2J 65
Bavdene M. *NW4* *4D 44*
(off The Burroughs)
Bavent Rd. SE5 . . . . . . 2C 120
Bawdale Rd. SE22 . . . . . . 5F 121
Bawdsey Av. IG2: Ilf 4K 53
Bawley Ct. E16 . . . . . . 7G 89
Bawley Ter. *E15* *1F 87*
(off Rick Roberts Way)
Bawtree Rd. SE14 . . . . . . 7A 104
Bawtry Rd. N20 . . . . . . 3J 31
Baxendale N20 . . . . . . 2F 31
Baxendale St. E2 . . . . . . 3G 85
Baxter Cl. BR1: Brom 3F 161
UB2: S'hall 3F 95
UB10: Hil 3D 74
Baxter Ho. *E3* *3D 86*
(off Bromley High St.)
Baxter Rd. E16 . . . . . . 6A 88
IG1: Ilf 5F 71
N1 . . . . . . 6D 66
N18 . . . . . . 4C 34
Baxter Wlk. SW16 . . . . . . 2H 137
Bayard Ct. DA6: Bex 4H 127
Bay Ct. *E1* *4K 85*
(off Frimley Way)
W5 . . . . . . 3E 96
Baycroft Cl. HA5: Eastc 3A 40
Baydon Ct. BR2: Brom 3H 159
Bayer Ho. *EC1* *4C 8*
(off Golden La. Est.)
Bayes Cl. SE26 . . . . . . 5J 139
Bayes Ct. *NW3* *7D 64*
(off Primrose Hill Rd.)
Bayes Ho. *N1* *7A 66*
(off Augustas La.)
Bayfield Ho. *SE4* *4K 121*
(off Coston Wlk.)
Bayfield Rd. SE9 . . . . . . 4B 124
Bayford M. *E8* *7H 67*
(off Bayford St.)
Bayford Rd. NW10 . . . . . . 3F 81
Bayford St. E8 . . . . . . 7H 67
Bayford St. Bus. Cen. *E8* *7H 67*
(off Sidworth St.)
Baygrove M. KT1: Hamp W 1C 150
Bayham Pl. NW1 . . . . . . 1G 83
Bayham Rd. SM4: Mord 4K 153
W4 . . . . . . 3K 97
W13 . . . . . . 7B 78
Bayham St. NW1 . . . . . . 1G 83
Bayhurst Wood Country Pk. 5B 38
Bayleaf Cl.
TW12: Hamp H 5H 131
Bayley St. WC1 . . . . . . 6C 6 (5H 83)
Bayley Wlk. SE2 . . . . . . 6E 108
Baylis M. TW1: Twick 7A 114
Baylis Pl. BR1: Brom 3C 160
Baylis Rd. SE1 . . . . . . 7J 13 (2A 102)
Bayliss Av. SE28 . . . . . . 7D 90
Bayliss Cl. N21 . . . . . . 5D 22
UB1: S'hall *6F 77*
(off Whitecote Rd.)
Bayne Cl. E6 . . . . . . 6D 88
Baynes Cl. EN1: Enf 1B 24
Baynes M. NW3 . . . . . . 6B 64
Baynes St. NW1 . . . . . . 7G 65
Baynham Cl. DA5: Bexl 6F 127
Bayonne Rd. W6 . . . . . . 6G 99
Bays Ct. HA8: Edg 5C 28
Bays Farm Ct. UB7: Lford 4D 174
Bayshill Ri. UB5: N'olt 6F 59
Bayston Rd. N16 . . . . . . 3F 67
BAYSWATER 7A 82
Bayswater Cl. N13 . . . . . . 4G 33
Bayswater Rd. W2 . . . . . . 3A 10 (7K 81)
Baythorne Ho. *E16* *6H 87*
(off Turner St.)
Baythorne St. E3 . . . . . . 5B 86
Bayton Ct. *E8* *7G 67*
(off Lansdowne Dr.)
Bay Tree Cl. BR1: Brom 1B 160
Baytree Cl. DA15: Sidc 1K 143
Baytree Ct. SW2 . . . . . . 4K 119
Bay Tree Ho. *EC1* *4J 7*
(off Baker's Row)
Baytree Ho. E4 . . . . . . 7J 25
Baytree M. SE17 . . . . . . 4D 102
Baytree Rd. SW2 . . . . . . 4K 119
Baywillow Av. SM5: Cars 1D 166
Bazalgette Cl. KT3: N Mald 5K 151
Bazalgette Gdns. KT3: N Mald 5K 151
Bazalgette Ho. *NW8* *3B 4*
(off Orchardson St.)
Bazeley Ho. *SE1* *7A 1*
(off Library St.
Bazely St. E14 . . . . . . 7E 8
Bazile Rd. N21 . . . . . . 6F 2
BBC Broadcasting House 6K 5 (5F 83)
BBC Maida Vale Studios *4K 8*
(off Delaware Rd.
BDA Dental Mus. 6J 5 (5F 83)
Beacham Cl. SE7 . . . . . . 5B 10
Beachborough Rd. BR1: Brom 4E 14
Beach Ct. SE9 . . . . . . 6C 12
Beachcroft Av. UB1: S'hall 1C 94
Beachcroft Rd. E11 . . . . . . 3G 69
Beachcroft Way N19 . . . . . . 1H 65
Beach Gro. TW13: Hanw 2E 130
Beach Ho. *SW5* *5J 9*
(off Philbeach Gdns.
TW13: Hanw 2E 130
Beachy Rd. E3 . . . . . . 7C 68
Beacon Bingo
Cricklewood 4F 6
Streatham 2J 13
Beacon Cl. UB8: Uxb 5A 5
Beacon Ga. SE14 . . . . . . 3K 12
Beacon Gro. SM5: Cars 4E 16
Beacon Hill N7 . . . . . . 5J 6
Beacon Ho. *E14* *5D 10*
(off Burrells Wharf Sq.
SE5 . . . . . . *7E 10*
(off Southampton Way
Beacon Pl. CR0: Bedd 3J 16
Beacon Point *SE10* *6D 10*
(off Dowells St.)
Beacon Rd. SE13 . . . . . . 6F 12
TW6: H'row A 6C 11
Beacons Cl. E6 . . . . . . 5C 8
Beaconsfield *WC1* *6G 7*
(off Red Lion St.)
Beaconsfield Cl. N11 . . . . . . 5K 31
SE3 . . . . . . 6J 105
W4 . . . . . . 5J 97
Beaconsfield Pde. SE9 . . . . . . 4C 142
Beaconsfield Rd. BR1: Brom 3B 160
CR0: C'don 6D 156
DA5: Bexl 2K 145
E10 . . . . . . 2E 68
E16 . . . . . . 4H 87
E17 . . . . . . 6B 50
KT3: N Mald 2K 151
KT5: Surb 7F 151
N9 . . . . . . 3B 34
N11 . . . . . . 3K 31
N15 . . . . . . 4E 48
NW10 . . . . . . 6B 62
SE3 . . . . . . 7H 105
SE9 . . . . . . 2C 142
SE17 . . . . . . 5D 102
TW1: Twick 6B 114
UB1: S'hall 1B 94
UB4: Yead 1A 94
W4 . . . . . . 3K 97
W5 . . . . . . 2C 96
Beaconsfield St. N1 . . . . . . 1J 83
Beaconsfield Ter. RM6: Chad H 6D 54
Beaconsfield Ter. Rd. W14 . . . . . . 3G 99
Beaconsfield Wlk. E6 . . . . . . 6E 88
SW6 . . . . . . 1H 117
Beacontree Av. E17 . . . . . . 1F 51
BEACONTREE HEATH 1G 73
Beacontree Rd. E11 . . . . . . 1H 69
Beadle's Pde. RM10: Dag 6J 73
Beadlow Cl. SM5: Cars 6B 154
Beadman Pl. SE27 . . . . . . 4B 138
Beadman St. SE27 . . . . . . 4B 138
Beadnell Ct. *E1* *7G 85*
(off Cable St.)
Beadnell Rd. SE23 . . . . . . 1K 139
Beadon Rd. BR2: Brom 4J 159
W6 . . . . . . 4E 98
Beaford Gro. SW20 . . . . . . 3G 153
Beagle Cl. TW13: Felt 4K 129

194 A-Z London

Beak St. W1 . . . . .2B **12** (7G **83**)
Beal Cl. DA16: Well 1A **126**
Beale Arboretum, The 1J **21**
Beale Cl. N13 . . . . .5G **33**
Beale Pl. E3 .2B **86**
Beale Rd. E3 . . . . .1B **86**
Beal Rd. IG1: Ilf 2E **70**
Beam Av. RM10: Dag 1H **91**
Beames Rd. NW10 . . . . .1K **79**
Beaminster Gdns. IG6: Ilf 2F **53**
Beaminster Ho. SW8 . . . . .7K **101**
(off Dorset Rd.)
Beamish Dr. WD23: B Hea 1B **26**
Beamish Ho. SE16 . . . . .4H **103**
(off Rennie Est.)
Beamish Rd. N9 . . . . .1B **34**
Beam Reach Bus. Pk. RM13: Rain 3K **91**
Beam Valley Country Pk. 1J **91**
Beamway RM10: Dag 7K **73**
Beanacre Cl. E9 . . . . .6B **68**
Bean Rd. DA6: Bex 4D **126**
Beanshaw SE9 . . . . .4E **142**
Beansland Gro. RM6: Chad H 3E **54**
Bear All. EC4 . . . . .7A **8** (6B **84**)
Bear Cl. RM7: Rom 6H **55**
Beardell St. SE19 . . . . .6F **139**
Beardow Gro. N14 . . . . .6B **22**
Beard Rd. KT2: King T 5F **133**
Beardsfield E13 . . . . .2J **87**
Beard's Hill TW12: Hamp 1E **148**
Beard's Hill Cl. TW12: Hamp 1E **148**
Beardsley Ter. RM8: Dag 5B **72**
(off Stonard Rd.)
Beardsley Way W3 . . . . .2K **97**
Beard Rd. TW15: Ashf 6G **129**
Bearfield Rd. KT2: King T 7E **132**
Bear Gdns. SE1 . . . . .4C **14** (1C **102**)
Bear La. SE1 . . . . .4B **14** (1B **102**)
Bear Pit Apartments SE1 . . . . .4C **14**
(off New Globe Wlk.)
Bear Rd. TW13: Hanw 4B **130**
Bearstead Ri. SE4 . . . . .5B **122**
Bearstead Ter. BR3: Beck 1C **158**
Bear St. WC2 . . . . .2D **12** (7H **83**)
Beasley's Ait TW16: Sun 6H **147**
Beasley's Ait La. TW16: Sun 6H **147**
Beaton Cl. SE15 . . . . .1F **121**
Beatrice Av. HA9: Wemb 5E **60**
SW16 . . . . .3K **155**
Beatrice Cl. E13 . . . . .4J **87**
HA5: Eastc 4J **39**
Beatrice Ct. IG9: Buck H 2G **37**
Beatrice Ho. W6 . . . . .5E **98**
(off Queen Caroline St.)
Beatrice Pl. W8 . . . . .3K **99**
Beatrice Rd. E17 . . . . .5C **50**
N4 . . . . .7A **48**
N9 . . . . .7D **24**
SE1 . . . . .4G **103**
TW10: Rich 5F **115**
UB1: S'hall 1D **94**
Beatrice Webb Ho. E3 . . . . .2A **86**
(off Chisenhale Rd.)
Beatrix Apartments E3 . . . . .4B **86**
(off English St.)
Beatrix Ho. SW5 . . . . .5K **99**
(off Old Brompton Rd.)
Beatson Wlk. SE16 . . . . .1A **104**
(not continuous)
Beattie Cl. TW14: Felt 7H **111**
Beattie Ho. SW8 . . . . .1G **119**
Beattock Ri. N10 . . . . .4F **47**
Beatty Ho. E14 . . . . .2C **104**
(off Admirals Way)
SW1 . . . . .6B **18**
(off Dolphin Sq.)
Beatty Rd. HA7: Stan 6H **27**
N16 . . . . .4E **66**
Beatty St. NW1 . . . . .2G **83**
Beattyville Gdns. IG6: Ilf 4E **52**
Beauchamp Cl. W4 . . . . .3J **97**

Beauchamp Ct. EN5: Barn 4C **20**
(off Victors Way)
HA7: Stan 5H **27**
Beauchamp Pl. SW3 . . .1D **16** (3D **100**)
Beauchamp Rd. E7 . . . . .7K **69**
KT8: W Mole, E Mos 5F **149**
SE19 . . . . .1D **156**
SM1: Sutt 4J **165**
SW11 . . . . .4C **118**
TW1: Twick 7A **114**
Beauchamp St. EC1 . . . . .6J **7** (5A **84**)
Beauchamp Ter. SW15 . . . . .3D **116**
Beauclerc Ct. TW16: Sun 2A **148**
Beauclerc Rd. W6 . . . . .3D **98**
Beauclerc Ho. SM2: Sutt 6A **166**
Beauclerk Cl. TW13: Felt 1K **129**
Beaudesert M. UB7: W Dray 2A **92**
Beaufort E6 .5E **88**
Beaufort Av. HA3: Kenton 4A **42**
Beaufort Cl. E4 . . . . .6J **35**
RM7: Mawney 4J **55**
SW15 . . . . .7D **116**
W5 . . . . .5F **79**
Beaufort Ct. E14 . . . . .2C **104**
(off Admirals Way)
EN5: New Bar 5F **21**
N11 . . . . .5A **32**
(off The Limes Av.)
SW6 . . . . .6J **99**
TW10: Ham 4C **132**
Beaufort Dr. NW11 . . . . .4J **45**
Beaufort Gdns. E1 . . . . .5K **85**
IG1: Ilf 1E **70**
NW4 . . . . .6E **44**
SW3 . . . . .1D **16** (3C **100**)
SW16 . . . . .7K **137**
TW5: Hest 1C **112**
Beaufort Ho. E16 . . . . .1K **105**
(off Fairfax M.)
SW1 . . . . .6C **18**
(off Aylesford St.)
SW3 . . . . .7B **16**
(off Beaufort St.)
Beaufort Mans. SW3 . . . .7B **16** (6B **100**)
Beaufort M. SW6 . . . . .6H **99**
Beaufort Pk. NW11 . . . . .4J **45**
Beaufort Rd. HA4: Ruis 2F **57**
KT1: King T 4E **150**
TW1: Twick 7C **114**
TW10: Ham 4C **132**
W5 . . . . .5D **78**
Beaufort St. SW3 . . . . .7A **16** (6B **100**)
Beaufort Ter. E14 . . . . .5E **104**
(off Ferry St.)
Beaufoy Ho. SE27 . . . . .3B **138**
SW8 . . . . .7K **101**
(off Rita Rd.)
Beaufoy Rd. N17 . . . . .7K **33**
(not continuous)
Beaufoy Wlk. SE11 . . . . .4H **19** (4K **101**)
SE26 . . . . .4H **139**
Beaulieu Cl. CR4: Mitc 1E **154**
NW9 . . . . .4A **44**
SE5 . . . . .3D **120**
TW1: Twick 6D **114**
TW4: Houn 5D **112**
Beaulieu Dr. W5 . . . . .5E **78**
Beaulieu Dr. HA5: Pinn 6B **40**
Beaulieu Gdns. N21 . . . . .7H **23**
Beaulieu Hgts. SE25 . . . . .1E **156**
Beaulieu Lodge E14 . . . . .3F **105**
(off Schooner Cl.)
Beaulieu Pl. W4 . . . . .3J **97**
Beaumanor Gdns. SE9 . . . . .4E **142**
Beaumanor Mans. W2 . . . . .7K **81**
(off Queensway)

Beaumans Dr. E17 . . . . .1B **50**
Beaumaris Dr. IG8: Wfd G 7G **37**
Beaumaris Gdns. SE19 . . . . .7C **138**
Beaumaris Grn. NW9 . . . . .6A **44**
Beaumaris Twr. W3 . . . . .2A **97**
(off Park Rd. Nth.)
Beaumont W14 . . . . .4H **99**
(off Kensington Village)
Beaumont Av. HA0: Wemb 5C **60**
HA2: Harr 6F **41**
TW9: Rich 3F **115**
W14 . . . . .5H **99**
Beaumont Bldgs. WC2 . . . . .1F **13**
(off Martlett Ct.)
Beaumont Cl. KT2: King T 7G **133**
N2 . . . . .4C **46**
Beaumont Ct. E1 . . . . .3K **85**
E5 . . . . .3H **67**
HA0: Wemb 5C **60**
NW1 . . . . .1H **83**
NW9 . . . . .2B **44**
(off Cherry Cl.)
W1 . . . . .5H **5**
(off Beaumont St.)
W4 . . . . .5J **97**
Beaumont Cres. W14 . . . . .5H **99**
Beaumont Dr. KT4: Wor Pk 7D **152**
TW15: Ashf 5F **129**
Beaumont Gdns. NW3 . . . . .3J **63**
Beaumont Gro. E1 . . . . .4K **85**
Beaumont Ho. E10 . . . . .7D **50**
(off Skelton's La.)
W9 . . . . .3H **81**
(off Fernhead Rd.)
Beaumont Lodge E8 . . . . .6G **67**
(off Greenwood Rd.)
Beaumont M. HA5: Pinn 3C **40**
NW5 . . . . .5H **65**
(off Charlton King's Rd.)
W1 . . . . .5H **5** (5E **82**)
Beaumont Pl. EN5: Barn 1C **20**
TW7: Isle 5K **113**
W1 . . . . .3B **6** (4G **83**)
Beaumont Ri. N19 . . . . .1H **65**
Beaumont Rd. BR5: Pet W 6H **161**
E10 . . . . .7D **50**
(not continuous)
E13 . . . . .3K **87**
SE19 . . . . .6C **138**
SW19 . . . . .7G **117**
W4 . . . . .3J **97**
Beaumont Sq. E1 . . . . .5K **85**
Beaumont St. W1 . . . . .5H **5** (5E **82**)
Beaumont Ter. SE13 . . . . .7G **123**
(off Wellmeadow Rd.)
Beaumont Wlk. NW3 . . . . .7D **64**
Beauvais Ter. UB5: N'olt 3B **76**
Beauvale NW1 . . . . .7E **64**
(off Ferdinand St.)
Beauval Rd. SE22 . . . . .6F **121**
Beaux Arts Building, The N7 . . . . .3J **65**
Beaverbank Rd. SE9 . . . . .1H **143**
Beaver Cl. SE20 . . . . .7G **139**
SM4: Mord 7E **152**
TW12: Hamp 1F **149**
Beaver Ct. BR3: Beck 7D **140**
Beaver Gro. UB5: N'olt 3C **76**
Beaver Ind. Est. UB2: S'hall 3A **94**
Beavers Cres. TW4: Houn 4A **112**
Beavers La. TW4: Houn 2A **112**
Beavers La. Campsite TW4: Houn 4B **112**
Beavers Lodge DA14: Sidc 4K **143**
Beaverwood Rd. BR7: Chst 6J **143**
Beavor Gro. W6 . . . . .5C **98**
(off Beavor La.)
Beavor La. W6 . . . . .5C **98**
Bebbington Rd. SE18 . . . . .4J **107**
Beblets Cl. BR6: Chels 5K **173**
Beccles Dr. IG11: Bark 6J **71**
Beccles St. E14 . . . . .6B **86**
Bec Cl. HA4: Ruis 3B **58**

Bechervaise Ct. E10 . . . . .1D **68**
(off Leyton Grange Est.)
Bechtel Ho. W6 . . . . .4F **99**
(off Hammersmith Rd.)
Beck Cl. SE13 . . . . .1D **122**
Beck Ct. BR3: Beck 3K **157**
BECKENHAM 2C **158**
Beckenham Bus. Cen.
BR3: Beck 6A **140**
Beckenham Crematorium
BR3: Beck 3J **157**
Beckenham Gdns. N9 . . . . .3K **33**
Beckenham Gro. BR2: Brom 2F **159**
Beckenham Hill Est. BR3: Beck 5D **140**
Beckenham Hill Rd. BR3: Beck 7D **140**
SE6 . . . . .6D **140**
Beckenham La. BR2: Brom 2G **159**
Beckenham Pl. Pk. BR3: Beck 7D **140**
Beckenham Place Pk. Golf Course
. . . . .6D **140**
Beckenham Place Pk. Local Nature Reserve
. . . . .6E **140**
Beckenham Rd. BR3: Beck 1K **157**
BR4: W W'ck 7D **158**
Beckenham Theatre Centre, The 2D **158**
Beckers, The N16 . . . . .4G **67**
Becket Av. E6 . . . . .3E **88**
Becket Cl. SE25 . . . . .6G **157**
SW19 . . . . .1K **153**
(off High Path)
Becket Ho. E16 . . . . .1K **105**
(off Constable Av.)
SE1 . . . . .7E **14**
Becket Rd. N18 . . . . .4D **34**
Becket St. SE1 . . . . .7E **14** (3D **102**)
Beckett Cl. DA17: Belv 3F **109**
IG5: Ilf 1C **52**
NW10 . . . . .6A **62**
SW16 . . . . .2H **137**
Beckett Ho. E1 . . . . .5J **85**
(off Jubilee St.)
SW9 . . . . .2J **119**
Becketts Cl. BR6: Orp 3K **173**
DA5: Bexl 1J **145**
TW14: Felt 6K **111**
Becketts Ho. IG1: Ilf 3E **70**
Becketts Pl. KT1: Hamp W 1D **150**
Becketts Wharf KT1: Hamp W 1D **150**
(off Lwr. Teddington Rd.)
Beckett Wlk. BR3: Beck 6A **140**
Beckfoot NW1 . . . . .1B **6**
(off Ampthill Est.)
Beckford Dr. BR5: Orp 7H **161**
Beckford Ho. N16 . . . . .5E **66**
Beckford Pl. SE17 . . . . .5C **102**
Beckford Rd. CR0: C'don 6F **157**
Beckham Ho. SE11 . . . . .4H **19** (4K **101**)
Beckhaven Ho. SE11 . . . . .4K **19**
(off Gilbert Rd.)
Beck Ho. N18 . . . . .5C **34**
(off Upton Rd.)
Beck La. BR3: Beck 3K **157**
Beckley Ho. E3 . . . . .4B **86**
(off Hamlets Way)
Becklow Gdns. W12 . . . . .2C **98**
(off Becklow Rd.)
Becklow M. W12 . . . . .2C **98**
(off Becklow Rd.)
Becklow Rd. W12 . . . . .2B **98**
Beck River Pk. BR3: Beck 1B **158**
Beck Rd. CR4: Mitc 6D **154**
E8 . . . . .1H **85**
Becks Rd. DA14: Sidc 3A **144**
Beck Theatre, The 6H **75**
BECKTON 5E **88**
BECKTON ALPS 4D **88**
BECKTON PARK 6D **88**
Beckton Retail Pk. E6 . . . . .5E **88**
Beckton Rd. E16 . . . . .5H **87**

Beckton Triangle Retail Pk.
E6 . . . . .4F **89**
Beck Way BR3: Beck 3B **158**
Beckway Rd. SW16 . . . . .2H **155**
Beckway St. SE17 . . . . .4E **102**
(not continuous)
Beckwith Cl. EN2: Enf 1G **23**
Beckwith Ho. E2 . . . . .2H **85**
(off Wadeson St.)
Beckwith Rd. SE24 . . . . .5D **120**
Beclands Rd. SW17 . . . . .6E **136**
Becmead Av. HA3: Kenton 5B **42**
SW16 . . . . .4H **137**
Becondale Rd. SE19 . . . . .5E **138**
BECONTREE 4D **72**
Becontree Av. RM8: Dag 4B **72**
Becontree Heath Leisure Cen. 2G **73**
Becquerel Ct. SE10 . . . . .3H **105**
(off West Parkside)
Bective Pl. SW15 . . . . .4H **117**
Bective Rd. E7 . . . . .4J **69**
SW15 . . . . .4H **117**
Becton Pl. DA8: Erith 7H **109**
Bedale Rd. EN2: Enf 1H **23**
Bedale St. SE1 . . . . . .5E **14** (1D **102**)
Beddalls Farm Ct. E6 . . . . .5B **88**
BEDDINGTON 4J **167**
BEDDINGTON CORNER 7E **154**
Beddington Cross CRO: Bedd 7H **155**
Beddington Farm Rd.
CRO: Bedd, Wadd 7J **155**
Beddington Gdns. SM5: Cars 6E **166**
SM6: Wall 6E **166**
Beddington Grn. BR5: St P 1K **161**
Beddington Gro. SM6: Wall 5H **167**
Beddington La. CRO: Bedd, C'don . .5G **155**
Beddington Park 3F **167**
Beddington Pk. Cotts. SM6: Bedd . .3H **167**
Beddington Path BR5: St P 1K **161**
Beddington Rd. BR5: St P 2J **161**
IG3: Ilf 7K **53**
Beddington Ter. CRO: C'don 7K **155**
Beddington Trad. Est.
CRO: Bedd 1J **167**
Bede Cl. HA5: Pinn 1B **40**
Bedefield WC1 . . . . .2F **7** (3J **83**)
Bede Ho. SE14 . . . . .1B **122**
(off Clare Rd.)
Bedens Rd. DA14: Sidc 6E **144**
Bede Rd. RM6: Chad H 6C **54**
Bede Sq. E3 . . . . .4B **86**
(off Joseph St.)
Bedevere Rd. N9 . . . . .3B **34**
Bedfont Cl. CR4: Mitc 2E **154**
TW14: Bedf 6E **110**
Bedfont Ct. TW19: Stanw M 6B **174**
Bedfont Ct. Est. TW19: Stanw M . . .7C **174**
Bedfont Grn. Cl. TW14: Bedf 1E **128**
Bedfont Ind. Pk. TW15: Ashf 3E **128**
Bedfont Ind. Pk. Nth. TW15: Ashf . . .3E **128**
Bedfont Lakes Country Pk. 2E **128**
Bedfont Lakes Country Pk. Vis. Cen.
. . . . .3D **128**
Bedfont La. TW13: Felt 7G **111**
TW14: Felt 7G **111**
Bedfont Rd. TW13: Felt 1E **128**
TW14: Bedf 1E **128**
TW19: Stanw 6A **110**
Bedfont Trad. Est. TW14: Bedf 2F **129**
Bedford Av. EN5: Barn 5C **20**
UB4: Yead 6K **75**
WC1 . . . . .6D **6** (5H **83**)
Bedfordbury WC2 . . . . . . .2E **12** (7J **83**)
(not continuous)
Bedford Cl. N10 . . . . .7K **31**
W4 . . . . .6A **98**
Bedford Cnr. W4 . . . . .4A **98**
(off South Pde.)
Bedford Ct. CRO: C'don 1D **168**
(off Tavistock Rd.)
WC2 . . . . .3E **12** (7J **83**)

Bedford Ct. Mans. WC1 . . . . .6D **6**
Bedford Gdns. W8 . . . . .1J **99**
Bedford Gdns. Ho. W8 . . . . .1J **99**
(off Bedford Gdns.)
Bedford Hill SW12 . . . . .1F **137**
SW16 . . . . .1F **137**
Bedford Ho. CRO: C'don 7B **156**
SW4 . . . . .4J **119**
(off Solon New Rd. Est.)
Bedford M. N2 . . . . .3C **46**
SE6 . . . . .2D **140**
BEDFORD PARK 3K **97**
Bedford Pk. CRO: C'don 1C **168**
Bedford Pk. Cnr. W4 . . . . .4A **98**
Bedford Pk. Mans. W4 . . . . .4K **97**
Bedford Pas. SW6 . . . . .7G **99**
(off Dawes Rd.)
W1 . . . . .5B **6** (5G **83**)
Bedford Pl. CRO: C'don 1D **168**
WC1 . . . . .5E **6** (5J **83**)
Bedford Rd. DA15: Sidc 3J **143**
E6 . . . . .1E **88**
E17 . . . . .2C **50**
E18 . . . . .2J **51**
HA1: Harr 6G **41**
HA4: Ruis 4H **57**
IG1: Ilf 3F **71**
KT4: Wor Pk 2E **164**
N2 . . . . .3C **46**
N8 . . . . .6H **47**
N9 . . . . .7C **24**
N15 . . . . .4E **48**
N22 . . . . .2J **47**
NW7 . . . . .7F **29**
SW4 . . . . .4J **119**
TW2: Twick 3H **131**
W4 . . . . .3K **97**
W13 . . . . .7B **78**
Bedford Row SE1 . . . .7D **14** (3C **102**)
WC1 . . . . .5H **7** (5K **83**)
Bedford Sq. WC1 . . . . . . .6D **6** (5H **83**)
Bedford St. SM2: Sutt 2E **12** (7J **83**)
Bedford Ter. SM2: Sutt 6A **166**
SW2 . . . . .5J **119**
Bedford Way WC1 . . . . . . .4D **6** (4H **83**)
Bedgebury Ct. E17 . . . . .2E **50**
Bedgebury Gdns. SW19 . . . . .2G **135**
Bedgebury Rd. SE9 . . . . .4B **124**
Bedham Rd. BR1: Brom 3J **141**
Bedlam M. SE11 . . . . .3J **19**
Bedlow Way CRO: Bedd 4K **167**
Bedmond Ho. SW3 . . . . .5C **16**
(off Cale St.)
Bedonwell Rd.
DA7: Belv, Bex, Erith 6F **109**
DA17: Belv 6E **108**
SE2 . . . . .6E **108**
Bedser Cl. CR7: Thor H 3C **156**
SE11 . . . . .7H **19** (6K **101**)
Bedser Dr. UB6: G'frd 5H **59**
Bedster Gdns. KT8: W Mole 2F **149**
Bedwardine Rd. SE19 . . . . .7E **138**
Bedwell Cl. CRO: C'don 5D **156**
Bedwell Ct. RM6: Chad H 7D **54**
(off Chapel La.)
Bedwell Gdns. UB3: Harl 5G **93**
(not continuous)
Bedwell Ho. SW9 . . . . .2A **120**
Bedwell Rd. DA17: Belv 5G **109**
N17 . . . . .1E **48**
Beeby Rd. E16 . . . . .5K **87**
Beech Av. DA15: Sidc 7A **126**
HA4: Ruis 1K **57**
IG9: Buck H 2E **36**
N20 . . . . .1H **31**
TW8: Bford 7B **96**
W3 . . . . .1A **98**
Beech Cl. N9 . . . . .6B **24**
SE8 . . . . .6C **104**
SM5: Cars 2D **166**
SW15 . . . . .7C **116**

Beech Cl. SW19 . . . . .6E **134**
TW15: Ashf 5F **129**
TW16: Sun 2B **148**
UB7: W Dray 3C **92**
Beech Copse BR1: Brom 1D **160**
CR2: S Croy 5C **168**
Beech Ct. BR1: Brom 1H **159**
(off Blyth Rd.)
BR3: Beck 7B **140**
E17 . . . . .3F **51**
IG1: Ilf 3E **70**
(off Riverdene Rd.)
KT6: Surb 7D **150**
UB5: N'olt 1C **76**
W9 . . . . .5J **81**
(off Elmfield Way)
Beech Cres. Ct. N5 . . . . .4B **66**
Beechcroft BR7: Chst 7E **142**
Beechcroft Av. DA7: Bex 1K **127**
HA2: Harr 7E **40**
KT3: N Mald 1J **151**
NW11 . . . . .7H **45**
Beechcroft Cl. BR6: Orp 4H **173**
SW16 . . . . .5K **137**
TW5: Hest 7C **94**
Beechcroft Ct. N12 . . . . .4E **30**
NW11 . . . . .7H **45**
(off Beechcroft Av.)
Beechcroft Gdns. HA9: Wemb 3F **61**
Beechcroft Lodge SM2: Sutt 7A **166**
Beechcroft Rd. BR6: Orp 4H **173**
E18 . . . . .2K **51**
KT9: Chess 3F **163**
SW14 . . . . .3J **115**
SW17 . . . . .2C **136**
Beechdale N21 . . . . .2E **32**
Beechdale Rd. SW2 . . . . .6K **119**
Beech Dell BR2: Kes 4D **172**
Beechdene SE15 . . . . .1H **121**
(off Carlton Gro.)
Beech Dr. N2 . . . . .2D **46**
Beechen Cliff Way TW7: Isle 2K **113**
Beechen Gro. HA5: Pinn 3D **40**
Beechen Pl. SE23 . . . . .2K **139**
Beeches, The CR2: S Croy 5D **168**
(off Blunt Rd.)
E12 . . . . .7C **70**
TW3: Houn 1F **113**
Beeches Av. SM5: Cars 7C **166**
Beeches Cl. SE20 . . . . .1J **157**
Beeches Rd. SM3: Sutt 1G **165**
SW17 . . . . .3C **136**
Beeches Wlk. SM5: Cars 7B **166**
Beechey Ho. E1 . . . . .1H **103**
(off Watts St.)
Beechfield Cotts. BR1: Brom 1A **160**
Beechfield Ct. CR2: S Croy 4C **168**
(off Bramley Hill)
Beechfield Gdns. RM7: Rush G 7J **55**
Beechfield Rd. BR1: Brom 2A **160**
DA8: Erith 7K **109**
N4 . . . . .6C **48**
SE6 . . . . .1B **140**
Beech Gdns. EC2 . . . . .5C **8**
(off Beech St.)
RM10: Dag 7J **73**
W5 . . . . .2E **96**
Beech Gro. CR4: Mitc 5H **155**
KT3: N Mald 3K **151**
Beech Hall Cres. E4 . . . . .7A **36**
Beech Hall Rd. E4 . . . . .7K **35**
Beech Haven Ct. DA1: Cray 5K **127**
(off London Rd.)
Beech Hill EN4: Had W 1G **21**
Beech Hill Av. EN4: Had W 1F **21**
Beechhill Rd. SE9 . . . . .5E **124**
Beech Ho. CRO: New Ad 6D **170**
SE16 . . . . .2J **103**
(off Ainsty Est.)
Beech Ho. Rd. CRO: C'don 3D **168**

Beech Hurst Cl. BR7: Chst 1G **161**
Beeching Ct. W3 . . . . .3J **97**
(off Bollo Bri. Rd.)
Beech La. IG9: Buck H 2E **36**
Beech Lawns N12 . . . . .5G **31**
Beechmont Cl. BR1: Brom 5G **141**
Beechmore Gdns. SM3: Cheam 2F **165**
Beechmore Rd. SW11 . . . . .1D **118**
Beechmount Av. W7 . . . . .5H **77**
Beecholme N12 . . . . .5E **30**
Beecholme Av. CR4: Mitc 1F **155**
Beecholme Est. E5 . . . . .3H **67**
Beech Rd. N11 . . . . .6D **32**
SE16 . . . . .2J **155**
TW14: Bedf 7G **111**
Beechrow TW10: Ham 4E **132**
Beech St. EC2 . . . . .5C **8** (5C **84**)
RM7: Rom 4J **55**
Beech Tree Cl. HA7: Stan 5H **27**
N1 . . . . .7A **66**
Beech Tree Glade E4 . . . . .1C **36**
Beech Tree Pl. SM1: Sutt 5K **165**
Beechvale Cl. N12 . . . . .5H **31**
Beech Wlk. N17 . . . . .3F **49**
NW7 . . . . .6F **29**
Beech Way NW10 . . . . .7K **61**
TW2: Twick 3E **130**
Beechway DA5: Bexl 6D **126**
Beechwood Av. BR6: Chels 5J **173**
CR7: Thor H 4B **156**
HA2: Harr 3F **59**
HA4: Ruis 2H **57**
N3 . . . . .3H **45**
TW9: Kew 1G **115**
TW16: Sun 6J **129**
UB3: Hayes 7F **75**
UB6: G'frd 3F **77**
UB8: Hil 6C **74**
Beechwood Centre, The
BR2: Brom 1D **172**
(off Lwr. Gravel Rd.)
Beechwood Circ. HA2: Harr 3F **59**
Beechwood Cl. KT6: Surb 7C **150**
N2 . . . . .3D **46**
NW7 . . . . .5F **29**
SM5: Cars 4D **166**
TW16: Sun 6J **129**
W4 . . . . .6K **97**
Beechwood Cres. DA7: Bex 3D **126**
Beechwood Dr. BR2: Kes 4B **172**
IG8: Wfd G 5C **36**
Beechwood Gdns. HA2: Harr 3F **59**
IG5: Ilf 5D **52**
NW10 . . . . .3C **79**
Beechwood Gro. KT6: Surb 7C **150**
W3 . . . . .7A **80**
Beechwood Hall N3 . . . . .3H **45**
Beechwood Ho. E2 . . . . .2G **85**
(off Teale St.)
Beechwood M. N9 . . . . .2B **34**
Beechwood Pk. E18 . . . . .3J **51**
Beechwood Ri. BR7: Chst 4F **143**
Beechwood Rd. CR2: Sande 7E **168**
E8 . . . . .6F **67**
N8 . . . . .4H **47**
Beechwoods Ct. SE19 . . . . .5F **139**
Beechworth NW6 . . . . .7G **63**
Beechworth Cl. NW3 . . . . .2J **63**
Beecroft La. SE4 . . . . .5A **122**
Beecroft M. SE4 . . . . .5A **122**
Beecroft Rd. SE4 . . . . .5A **122**
Beehive Cl. E8 . . . . .7F **67**
UB10: Uxb 7B **56**
Beehive Ct. HA8: Edg 5C **28**
IG1: Ilf 6D **52**
Beehive La. IG1: Ilf 5D **52**
IG4: Ilf 5D **52**
Beehive Pas. EC3 . . . . .1G **15**
(off Lime St.)
Beehive Pl. SW9 . . . . .3A **120**
Beeken Dene BR6: Farnb 4G **173**

Beeleigh Rd. SM4: Mord 4K **153**
Beemans Row SW18 . . . . .2A **136**
Beeston Cl. E8 . . . . .5G **67**
Beeston Ho. SE1 . . . . .3D **102**
(off Burbage Cl.)
Beeston Pl. SW1 . . . . .1K **17** (3F **101**)
Beeston Rd. EN4: E Barn 6G **21**
Beeston Way TW14: Felt 6A **112**
Beethoven St. W10 . . . . .3G **81**
Beeton Cl. HA5: Hat E 1E **40**
Beeton Way SE27 . . . . .4D **138**
Begbie Rd. SE3 . . . . .1A **124**
BEGGAR'S HILL 6B **164**
Beggar's Hill KT17: Ewe 7B **164**
Beggars Roost La. SM1: Sutt 6J **165**
Begonia Cl. E6 . . . . .5D **88**
Begonia Pl. TM12: Hamp 6E **130**
Begonia Wlk. W12 . . . . .6B **80**
Beira St. SW12 . . . . .7F **119**
Bejun Ct. EN5: New Bar 4F **21**
Bekesbourne St. E14 . . . . .6A **86**
Belcroft Cl. BR1: Brom 7H **141**
Beldam Way TW3: Houn 3D **112**
Beldanes Lodge NW10 . . . . .7C **62**
Beldham Gdns.
  KT8: W Mole 2F **149**
Belfairs Dr. RM6: Chad H 7C **54**
Belfast Rd. N16 . . . . .2F **67**
  SE25 . . . . .4H **157**
Belfield Rd. KT19: Ewe 7K **163**
Belfont Wlk. N7 . . . . .4J **65**
(not continuous)
Belford Gro. SE18 . . . . .4E **106**
Belford Ho. E8 . . . . .1F **85**
Belfort Rd. SE15 . . . . .2J **121**
Belfry Cl. BR1: Brom 4F **161**
  SE16 . . . . .5H **103**
Belgrade Rd. N16 . . . . .4E **66**
  TW12: Hamp 1F **149**
Belgrave Ct. N14 . . . . .5B **22**
  NW7 . . . . .5E **28**
  W3 . . . . .2H **97**
Belgrave Ct. E2 . . . . .2H **85**
(off Temple St.)
  E13 . . . . .4A **88**
  E14 . . . . .7B **86**
(off Westferry Cir.)
  SW8 . . . . .7G **101**
(off Ascalon St.)
  W4 . . . . .5J **97**
Belgrave Cres. TW16: Sun 1K **147**
Belgrave Gdns. HA7: Stan 5H **27**
  N14 . . . . .5C **22**
  NW8 . . . . .1K **81**
Belgrave Hgts. E11 . . . . .1J **69**
Belgrave Ho. SW9 . . . . .7A **102**
Belgrave Mans. NW8 . . . . .1K **81**
(off Belgrave Gdns.)
Belgrave M. Nth. SW1 . . . . . .7G **11** (2E **100**)
Belgrave M. Sth. SW1 . . . . . .1H **17** (3E **100**)
Belgrave M. W. SW1 . . . . . .1G **17** (3E **100**)
Belgrave Pl. SW1 . . . . .1H **17** (3E **100**)
Belgrave Rd. CR4: Mitc 3B **154**
  E10 . . . . .1E **68**
  E11 . . . . .2J **69**
  E13 . . . . .4A **88**
  E17 . . . . .5C **50**
  IG1: Ilf 1D **70**
  SE25 . . . . .4F **157**
  SW1 . . . . .3K **17** (4F **101**)
  SW13 . . . . .7B **98**
  TW4: Houn 3D **112**
  TW16: Sun 1J **147**
Belgrave Sq. SW1 . . . . .1G **17** (3E **100**)
Belgrave St. E1 . . . . .5K **85**
Belgrave Ter. IG8: Wfd G 3D **36**
Belgrave Wlk. CR4: Mitc 3B **154**
Belgrave Yd. SW1 . . . . .2J **17**
BELGRAVIA 2H **17** (3E **100**)
Belgravia Cl. EN5: Barn 3C **20**
Belgravia Ct. SW1 . . . . .2J **17**

Belgravia Gdns.
  BR1: Brom 6G **141**
Belgravia Ho. SW1 . . . . .1G **17**
(off Halkin Pl.)
  SW4 . . . . .6H **119**
Belgravia M. KT1: King T 4D **150**
Belgravia Workshops N19 . . . . .2J **65**
(off Marlborough Rd.)
Belgrove St. WC1 . . . . .1F **7** (3J **83**)
Belham Wlk. SE5 . . . . .1D **120**
Belinda Rd. SW9 . . . . .3B **120**
Belitha Vs. N1 . . . . .7K **65**
BELL, THE 3C **50**
Bella Best Ho. SW1 . . . . .5K **17**
(off Westmoreland Ter.)
Bellamy Cl. E14 . . . . .2C **104**
  HA8: Edg .2D **28**
  UB10: Ick .3C **56**
  W14 . . . . .5H **99**
Bellamy Dr. HA7: Stan 1B **42**
Bellamy Dr. HA7: Stan 1B **42**
Bellamy Ho. SW17 . . . . .4B **136**
  TW5: Hest .6E **94**
Bellamy Rd. E4 . . . . .6J **35**
  EN2: Enf 2J **23**
Bellamy's Ct. SE16 . . . . .1K **103**
(off Abbotshade Rd.)
Bellamy St. SW12 . . . . .7F **119**
Bel La. TW13: Hanw 3C **130**
Bellarmine Ct. SE28 . . . . .1K **107**
Bellasis Av. SW2 . . . . .2J **137**
Bell Av. UB7: W Dray 4B **92**
Bell Brook Ri. N11 . . . . .4A **32**
Bell Cl. HA4: Ruis 3H **57**
  HA5: Pinn .2A **40**
Bellclose Rd. UB7: W Dray 2A **92**
Bell Cl. NW4 .4E **44**
Bell Dr. SW18 . . . . .7G **117**
Bellefields Rd. SW9 . . . . .3K **119**
Bellegrove Cl. DA16: Well 2K **125**
Bellegrove Pde. DA16: Well 3K **125**
Bellegrove Rd. DA16: Well 2H **125**
Bellenden Rd. SE15 . . . . .1F **121**
Bellenden Rd. Retail Pk. SE15 . . . . . . .1G **121**
Bellestaines Pleasaunce E4 . . . . .2H **35**
Belleville Rd. SW11 . . . . .5C **118**
Belle Vue UB6: G'frd 1H **77**
Bellevue Ct. TW3: Houn 4E **112**
Belle Vue Est. NW4 . . . . .4F **45**
Belle Vue La. WD23: B Hea 1C **26**
Bellevue M. N11 . . . . .5K **31**
Belle Vue Pde. SW17 . . . . .1D **136**
Belle Vue Pk. CR7: Thor H 3C **156**
Bellevue Pl. E1 . . . . .4J **85**
Belle Vue Rd. E17 . . . . .2F **51**
  NW4 . . . . .4E **44**
Bellevue Rd. DA6: Bex 5F **127**
  KT1: King T 3E **150**
(not continuous)
  N11 . . . . .4K **31**
  SW13 . . . . .2C **116**
  SW17 . . . . .1C **136**
  W13 . . . . .4B **78**
Bellew St. SW17 . . . . .3A **136**
Bell Farm Av. RM10: Dag 3J **73**
Bellfield CR0: Sels 7A **170**
Bellfield Av. HA3: Hrw W 6C **26**
Bellfield Cl. SE3 . . . . .7K **105**
Bellflower Cl. E6 . . . . .5C **88**
Bell Gdns. E10 . . . . .1C **68**
(off Church Rd.)
Bellgate M. NW5 . . . . .4F **65**
BELL GREEN 4B **140**
Bell Grn. SE26 . . . . .4B **140**
Bell Grn. La. SE26 . . . . .5B **140**
Bell Grn. Retail Pk. SE6 . . . . .3B **140**
Bellhaven E15 . . . . .6F **69**
Bell Hill CR0: C'don 2C **168**
Bell Ho. HA9: Wemb 3E **60**
  SE10 . . . . .6E **104**
(off Haddo St.)

Bellhouse Cotts. UB3: Hayes 7G **75**
Bell Ho. Rd. RM7: Rush G 1J **73**
Bellina M. NW5 . . . . .4F **65**
Bell Ind. Est. W4 . . . . .4J **97**
BELLINGHAM 3D **140**
Bellingham N17 . . . . .7C **34**
(off Park La.)
Bellingham Ct. IG11: Bark 3B **90**
Bellingham Grn. SE6 . . . . .3C **140**
Bellingham Leisure & Lifestyle Cen.
  . . . . .3D **140**
Bellingham Rd. SE6 . . . . .3D **140**
Bellingham Trad. Est. SE6 . . . . .3D **140**
Bell Inn Yd. EC3 . . . . .1F **15** (6D **84**)
Bell La. E1 . . . . .6J **9** (5F **85**)
  E16 . . . . .1H **105**
  EN3: Enf H, Enf W 1E **24**
  HA9: Wemb 2D **60**
  NW4 . . . . .4F **45**
  TW1: Twick 1A **132**
  TW14: Bedf 7F **111**
Bellmaker Ct. E3 . . . . .5C **86**
Bell Mdw. SE19 . . . . .5E **138**
Bell Moor NW3 . . . . .3A **64**
Bello Cl. SE24 . . . . .7B **120**
Bellot Gdns. SE10 . . . . .5G **105**
(off Bellot St.)
Bellot St. SE10 . . . . .5G **105**
Bell Pde. BR4: W W'ck 2E **170**
Bellring Cl. DA17: Belv 6G **109**
Bell Rd.
  EN1: Enf 1J **23**
  KT8: E Mos 5H **149**
  TW3: Houn 3F **113**
Bells All. NW6 . . . . .2J **117**
Bellscroft Rd. UB7: W Dray 2A **92**
Bellsize Ct. NW3 . . . . .5B **64**
Bell St. NW1 . . . . .5C **4** (5C **82**)
  SE18 . . . . .1C **124**
Belltrees Gro. SW16 . . . . .5K **137**
Bell Vw. Mnr.
  HA4: Ruis .7F **39**
Bell Water Ga. SE18 . . . . .3E **106**
Bell Wharf La. EC4 . . . . .3D **14** (7C **84**)
Bellwood Rd. SE15 . . . . .4K **121**
Bell Yd. WC2 . . . . .1J **13** (6A **84**)
Bell Yd. M. SE1 . . . . .7H **15** (2E **102**)
Belmarsh Rd. SE28 . . . . .2J **107**
BELMONT
  HA3 . . . . .2A **42**
  SM2 . . . . .7J **165**
Belmont Av. DA16: Well 3J **125**
  EN4: Cockf 5J **21**
  HA0: Wemb 1F **79**
  KT3: N Mald 5C **152**
  N9 . . . . .1B **34**
  N13 . . . . .5E **32**
  N17 . . . . .3C **48**
  UB2: S'hall 3C **94**
Belmont Circ. HA3: Kenton 1B **42**
Belmont Cl. E4 . . . . .5A **36**
  EN4: Cockf 4J **21**
  IG8: Wfd G 4E **36**
  N20 . . . . .1E **30**
  SW4 . . . . .3G **119**
  UB8: Uxb .6A **56**
Belmont Ct. N5 . . . . .4C **66**
  NW11 . . . . .5H **45**
Belmont Gro. SE13 . . . . .3F **123**
  W4 . . . . .4K **97**
Belmont Hall Ct. SE13 . . . . .3F **123**
Belmont Hill SE13 . . . . .3F **123**
Belmont La. BR7: Chst 5G **143**
  HA7: Stan .1C **42**
Belmont Lodge HA3: Hrw W 7C **26**
Belmont M. SW19 . . . . .2F **135**
Belmont Pde. BR7: Chst 5G **143**
  NW11 . . . . .5H **45**
Belmont Pk. SE13 . . . . .4F **123**
Belmont Pk. Cl. SE13 . . . . .4G **123**
Belmont Pk. Rd. E10 . . . . .6D **50**

Belmont Ri. SM2: Sutt 6H **165**
Belmont Rd. BR3: Beck 2A **158**
  BR7: Chst .5F **143**
  DA8: Erith .7G **109**
  HA3: W'stone 3K **41**
  IG1: Ilf 3G **71**
  N15 . . . . .4C **48**
  N17 . . . . .4C **48**
  SE25 . . . . .5H **157**
  SM6: Wall .5F **167**
  SW4 . . . . .3G **119**
  TW2: Twick 2H **131**
  UB8: Uxb .7A **56**
  W4 . . . . .4K **97**
Belmont St. NW1 . . . . .7E **64**
Belmont Ter. W4 . . . . .4K **97**
Belmore Av. UB4: Hayes 6J **75**
Belmore Ho. N7 . . . . .5H **65**
Belmore La. N7 . . . . .5H **65**
Belmore St. SW8 . . . . .1H **119**
Beloe Cl. SW15 . . . . .4C **116**
Belsham St. E9 . . . . .6J **67**
Belsize Av. N13 . . . . .6E **32**
  NW3 . . . . .6B **64**
  W13 . . . . .3B **96**
Belsize Ct. SM1: Sutt 4K **165**
Belsize Ct. Garages NW3 . . . . .5B **64**
(off Belsize La.)
Belsize Cres. NW3 . . . . .5B **64**
Belsize Gdns. SM1: Sutt 4K **165**
Belsize Gro. NW3 . . . . .6C **64**
Belsize La. NW3 . . . . .6B **64**
Belsize M. NW3 . . . . .6B **64**
Belsize Pk. NW3 . . . . .6B **64**
Belsize Pk. Gdns. NW3 . . . . .6B **64**
Belsize Pk. M. NW3 . . . . .6B **64**
Belsize Pl. NW3 . . . . .5B **64**
Belsize Rd. HA3: Hrw W 7C **26**
  NW6 . . . . .1K **81**
Belsize Sq. NW3 . . . . .6B **64**
Belsize Ter. NW3 . . . . .6B **64**
Belson Rd. SE18 . . . . .4D **106**
Beltane Dr. SW19 . . . . .3F **135**
Belthorn Cres. SW12 . . . . .7G **119**
Belton Rd. DA14: Sidc 4A **144**
  E7 . . . . .7K **69**
  E11 . . . . .4G **69**
  N17 . . . . .3E **48**
  NW2 . . . . .6C **62**
Belton Way E3 . . . . .5C **86**
Beltran Rd. SW6 . . . . .2K **117**
Beltwood Rd. DA17: Belv 4J **109**
BELVEDERE .4G **109**
Belvedere, The SW10 . . . . .1A **118**
(off Chelsea Harbour)
Belvedere Av. IG5: Ilf 2F **53**
  SW19 . . . . .5G **135**
Belvedere Bldgs. SE1 . . . . . . .7B **14** (2B **102**)
Belvedere Bus. Pk. DA17: Belv 2H **109**
Belvedere Cl. TW11: Tedd 5J **131**
Belvedere Ct. DA17: Belv 3F **109**
  N1 . . . . .1E **84**
(off De Beauvoir Cres.)
  N2 . . . . .5B **46**
  NW2 . . . . .6F **63**
(off Willesden La.)
  SW15 . . . . .4E **116**
Belvedere Dr. SW19 . . . . .5G **135**
Belvedere Gdns. KT8: W Mole 5D **148**
Belvedere Gro. SW19 . . . . .5G **135**
Belvedere Ho. TW13: Felt 1J **129**
(off Lemon Gro.)
Belvedere Ind. Est. DA17: Belv 1J **109**
Belvedere Link Bus. Pk.
  DA8: Erith .3J **109**
Belvedere M. SE3 . . . . .7K **105**
  SE15 . . . . .3J **121**
Belvedere Pl. SE1 . . . . .7B **14** (2B **102**)
  SW2 . . . . .4K **119**
Belvedere Rd. DA7: Bex 3F **127**
  E10 . . . . .1A **68**

Belvedere Rd. SE1 . . . . . . .7G **13** (2K **101**)
  SE2 . . . . .1C **108**
  SE19 .7F **139**
  W7 . . . . .3K **95**
Belvedere Sq. SW19 . . . . .5G **135**
Belvedere Strand NW9 . . . . .2B **44**
Belvedere Way HA3: Kenton 6E **42**
Belvoir Cl. SE9 . . . . .3C **142**
Belvoir Ho. SW1 . . . . .4G **101**
Belvoir Rd. SE22 . . . . .7G **121**
Belvue Bus. Cen. UB5: N'olt 7F **59**
Belvue Cl. UB5: N'olt 7E **58**
Belvue Rd. UB5: N'olt 7E **58**
Bembridge Cl. NW6 . . . . .7G **63**
Bembridge Gdns. HA4: Ruis 2F **57**
Bembridge Ho. KT2: King T 2G **151**
  (off Coombe Rd.)
  SE8 . . . . .4B **104**
  (off Longshore)
  SW18 .6K **117**
  (off Iron Mill Rd.)
Bemersyde Point E13 . . . . .3K **87**
  (off Dongola Rd. W.)
Bemerton Est. N1 . . . . .7J **65**
Bemerton St. N1 . . . . .1K **83**
Bemish Rd. SW15 . . . . .3F **117**
Bempton Dr. HA4: Ruis 2K **57**
Bemsted Rd. E17 . . . . .3B **50**
Benares Rd. SE18 . . . . .4K **107**
Benbow Ct. W6 . . . . .3E **98**
  (off Benbow Rd.)
Benbow Ho. SE8 . . . . .6C **104**
  (off Benbow St.)
Benbow Rd. W6 . . . . .3D **98**
Benbow St. SE8 . . . . .6C **104**
Benbury Cl. BR1: Brom 5E **140**
Bence Ho. SE8 . . . . .4A **104**
  (off Rainsborough Av.)
Bench, The TW10: Ham 3C **132**
Bench Fld. CR2: S Croy 6F **169**
Bencroft Rd. SW16 . . . . .7G **137**
Bencurtis Pk. BR4: W W'ck 3F **171**
Bendall Ho. NW1 . . . . .5D **4**
  (off Penfold St.)
Bendall M. NW1 . . . . .5D **4**
Benden Ho. SE13 . . . . .5E **122**
  (off Monument Gdns.)
Bendish Point SE28 . . . . .2G **107**
Bendish Rd. E6 . . . . .7C **70**
Bendmore Av. SE2 . . . . .5A **108**
Bendon Valley SW18 . . . . .7K **117**
Benedict Cl. BR6: Orp 3J **173**
  DA17: Belv 3E **108**
Benedict Ct. RM6: Chad H 6F **55**
Benedict Dr. TW14: Bedf 7F **111**
Benedict Rd. CR4: Mitc 3B **154**
  SW9 .3K **119**
Benedicts Wharf IG11: Bark 1F **89**
Benedict Way N2 . . . . .3A **46**
Benedict Wharf CR4: Mitc 3C **154**
Benenden Grn. BR2: Brom 5J **159**
Benenden Ho. SE17 . . . . .5E **102**
  (off Mina Rd.)
Benett Gdns. SW16 . . . . .2J **155**
Ben Ezra Ct. SE17 . . . . .4C **102**
  (off Asolando Dr.)
Benfleet Cl. SM1: Sutt 3A **166**
Benfleet Ct. E8 . . . . .1F **85**
Benfleet Way N11 . . . . .2K **31**
Bengal Ct. EC3 . . . . .1F **15**
  (off Birchin La.)
Bengal Rd. IG1: Ilf 4F **71**
Bengarth Dr. HA3: Hrw W 2H **41**
Bengarth Rd. UB5: N'olt 1C **76**
Bengeo Gdns. RM6: Chad H 6C **54**
Bengeworth Rd. HA1: Harr 2A **60**
  SE5 . . . . .3C **120**
Ben Hale Cl. HA7: Stan 5G **27**
Benham Cl. KT9: Chess 6C **162**
  SW11 .3B **118**

Benham Gdns. TW4: Houn 5D **112**
Benham Ho. SW10 . . . . .7K **99**
  (off Coleridge Gdns.)
Benham Rd. W7 . . . . .5J **77**
Benham's Pl. NW3 . . . . .4A **64**
Benhill Av. SM1: Sutt 4K **165**
  (not continuous)
Benhill Rd. SE5 . . . . .7D **102**
  SM1: Sutt 3A **166**
Benhill Wood Rd. SM1: Sutt 3A **166**
BENHILTON 2K **165**
Benhilton Gdns. SM1: Sutt 3K **165**
Benhurst Ct. SW16 . . . . .5A **138**
Benhurst La. SW16 . . . . .5A **138**
Benina Cl. IG2: Ilf 5K **53**
Benin Ho. WC1 . . . . .6G **7**
  (off Procter St.)
Benin St. SE13 . . . . .7F **123**
Benjafield Cl. N18 . . . . .4C **34**
Benjamin Cl. E8 . . . . .1G **85**
Benjamin Ct. DA17: Belv 6F **109**
  TW15: Ashf 7F **128**
Benjamin Franklin House 4E **12**
  (off Craven St.)
Benjamin M. SW12 . . . . .7G **119**
Benjamin St. EC1 . . . . .5A **8** (5B **84**)
Ben Jonson Ct. N1 . . . . .2E **84**
Ben Jonson Ho. EC2 . . . . .5D **8**
Ben Jonson Pl. EC2 . . . . .5D **8**
Ben Jonson Rd. E1 . . . . .5K **85**
Benkart M. SW15 . . . . .6C **116**
Benledi Rd. E14 . . . . .6F **87**
Benlow Works UB3: Hayes 2H **93**
  (off Silverdale Rd.)
Bennelong Cl. W12 . . . . .7D **80**
Bennerley Rd. SW11 . . . . .5C **118**
Bennet M. N19 . . . . .3H **65**
  (off Wedmore St.)
Bennets Courtyard SW19 . . . . . . .1A **154**
Bennets Fld. Rd.
  UB11: Stock P 1D **92**
Bennet's Hill EC4 . . . . . . .2B **14** (7C **84**)
Bennets Lodge EN2: Enf 3G **23**
Bennet St. SW1 . . . . .4A **12** (1G **101**)
Bennett Ct. DA16: Well 2A **126**
  HA6: Nwood 1H **39**
  KT1: Hamp W 1C **150**
  TW4: Houn 5C **112**
Bennett Ct. N7 . . . . .3K **65**
Bennett Gro. SE13 . . . . .1D **122**
Bennett Ho. SW1 . . . . .3D **18**
  (off Page St.)
Bennett Pk. SE3 . . . . .3H **123**
Bennett Rd. E13 . . . . .4A **88**
  N16 . . . . .4E **66**
  RM6: Chad H 6E **54**
  SW9 .2A **120**
Bennetts Av. CR0: C'don 2A **170**
  UB6: G'frd 1J **77**
Bennett's Castle La. RM8: Dag . . .2C **72**
Bennetts Cl. CR4: Mitc 1F **155**
  N17 . . . . .6A **34**
Bennetts Copse BR7: Chst 6C **142**
Bennett St. W4 . . . . .6A **98**
Bennett's Way CR0: C'don 2A **170**
Bennett's Yd. SW1 . . . . . .2D **18** (3H **101**)
Benning Dr. RM8: Dag 1E **72**
Benningholme Rd. HA8: Edg 6F **29**
Bennington Rd. IG8: Wfd G 7B **36**
  N17 . . . . .1E **48**
Benn's All. TW12: Hamp 2F **149**
Benn St. E9 . . . . .6A **68**
Benns Wlk. TW9: Rich 4E **114**
  (off Michelsdale Dr.)
Benrek Cl. IG6: Ilf 1G **53**
Bensbury Cl. SW15 . . . . .7D **116**
Bensham Cl. CR7: Thor H 4C **156**
Bensham Gro. CR7: Thor H 2C **156**
Bensham La. CR0: C'don 7B **156**
  CR7: Thor H 5B **156**
Bensham Mnr. Rd. CR7: Thor H . . .4C **156**

Bensham Mnr. Rd. Pas.
  CR7: Thor H 4C **156**
Bensley Cl. N11 . . . . .5J **31**
Ben Smith Way SE16 . . . . .3G **103**
Benson Av. E6 . . . . .2A **88**
Benson Ct. TW3: Houn 4E **112**
  UB8: Hil 5A **74**
Benson Ct. SW8 . . . . .1J **119**
  (off Hartington Rd.)
Benson Ho. E2 . . . . .3J **9**
  (off Ligonier St.)
  SE1 . . . . .5K **13**
  (off Hatfields)
Benson Quay E1 . . . . .7J **85**
Benson Rd. CR0: Wadd 3A **168**
  SE23 .1J **139**
Bentall Centre, The KT1: King T . . .2D **150**
Bentfield Gdns. SE9 . . . . .3B **142**
Bentfield Ho. NW9 . . . . .4B **44**
  (off Heritage Av.)
Bentham Rd. N16 . . . . .2G **67**
Bentham Ct. N1 . . . . .7C **66**
  (off Ecclesbourne Rd.)
Bentham Ho. SE1 . . . . .3D **102**
  (off Falmouth Rd.)
Bentham Rd. E9 . . . . .6K **67**
  SE28 .7B **90**
Bentham Wlk. NW10 . . . . .5J **61**
Ben Tillet Cl.
  E16 . . . . .1D **106**
  IG11: Bark 7A **72**
Ben Tillet Ho. N15 . . . . .3B **48**
Bentinck Cl. NW8 . . . . .2C **82**
Bentinck Ho. SW1 . . . . .2D **18**
  (off Monck St.)
  W12 . . . . .7D **80**
  (off White City Est.)
Bentinck Mans. W1 . . . . .7H **5**
  (off Bentinck St.)
Bentinck M. W1 . . . . .7H **5** (6E **82**)
Bentinck Rd. UB7: View 1A **92**
Bentinck St. W1 . . . . .7H **5** (6E **82**)
Bentley Cl. SW19 . . . . .3J **135**
Bentley Ct. SE13 . . . . .4E **122**
  (off Whitburn Rd.)
Bentley Dr. IG2: Ilf 6G **53**
  NW2 .3H **63**
Bentley Ho. E3 . . . . .4C **86**
  (off Wellington Way)
  SE5 .1E **120**
  (off Peckham Rd.)
Bentley Lodge WD23: B Hea 2D **26**
Bentley M. EN1: Enf 6J **23**
Bentley Priory Local Nature Reserve
  . . . . .4D **26**
Bentley Priory Mus. 3D **26**
Bentley Rd. N1 . . . . .6E **66**
Bentley Way
  EN5: New Bar 4F **21**
  HA7: Stan 5F **27**
  IG8: Buck H, Wfd G 2D **36**
Benton Rd. IG1: Ilf 1H **71**
  E17 . . . . .4C **138**
Benton's Ri. SE27 . . . . .5D **138**
Bentry Cl. RM8: Dag 2E **72**
Bentry Rd. RM8: Dag 2E **72**
Bentworth Ct. E2 . . . . .3K **9**
  (off Granby St.)
Bentworth Rd. W12 . . . . .6D **80**
Ben Uri Gallery 1K **81**
Benville Ho. SW8 . . . . .7K **101**
  (off Dorset Rd.)
Benwell Cen. TW16: Sun 1J **147**
Benwell Ct. TW16: Sun 1J **147**
Benwell Rd. N7 . . . . .4A **66**
Benwick Cl. SE16 . . . . .4H **103**
Benwick M. SE20 . . . . .1J **157**
Benwood Ct. SM1: Sutt 3A **166**
Benworth St. E3 . . . . .3B **86**
Benyon Ct. N1 . . . . .1E **84**
  (off De Beauvoir Est.)

Benyon Ho. EC1 . . . . .1K **7**
  (off Myddelton Pas.)
Benyon Rd. N1 . . . . .1D **84**
Benyon Wharf N1 . . . . .1E **84**
  (off Kingsland Rd.)
Berberis Ct. IG1: Ilf 6F **71**
Berberis Ho. E3 . . . . .5C **86**
  (off Gale St.)
  TW13: Felt 2J **129**
Berberis Wlk. SW7: W Dray 4A **92**
Berber Pde. SE18 . . . . .1C **124**
Berber Pl. E14 . . . . .7C **86**
Berber Rd. SW11 . . . . .5D **118**
Berberry Cl. HA8: Edg 4D **28**
Bercta Rd. SE9 . . . . .2G **143**
Berebinder Ho. E3 . . . . .2B **86**
  (off Tredegar Rd.)
Beregaria Ct. SE11 . . . . .7K **19**
  (off Kennington Pk. Rd.)
Berengers Ct. RM6: Chad H 7F **55**
  (off Whalebone La. Sth.)
Berengers Pl. RM9: Dag 6B **72**
Berenger Twr. SW10 . . . . .7B **100**
  (off Worlds End Est.)
Berenger Wlk. SW10 . . . . .7B **100**
  (off Worlds End Est.)
Berens Ct. DA14: Sidc 4K **143**
Berens Rd. NW10 . . . . .3F **81**
Berens Way BR7: Chst 3K **161**
Beresford Av. HA0: Wemb 1F **79**
  KT5: Surb 1H **163**
  N20 . . . . .2J **31**
  TW1: Twick 6C **114**
  W7 . . . . .5H **77**
Beresford Ct. E9 . . . . .5A **68**
  (off Mabley St.)
Beresford Dr. BR1: Brom 3C **160**
  IG8: Wfd G 4F **37**
Beresford Gdns. EN1: Enf 4K **23**
  RM6: Chad H 5E **54**
  TW4: Houn 5D **112**
Beresford Rd. E4 . . . . .1B **36**
  E17 . . . . .1D **50**
  HA1: Harr 5H **41**
  KT2: King T 1F **151**
  KT3: N Mald 4J **151**
  N2 . . . . .3C **46**
  N5 . . . . .5D **66**
  N8 . . . . .5A **48**
  SM2: Sutt 7H **165**
  UB1: S'hall 1B **94**
Beresford Sq. SE18 . . . . .4F **107**
Beresford St. SE18 . . . . .3F **107**
Beresford Ter. N5 . . . . .5C **66**
Berestede Rd. W6 . . . . .5B **98**
Bere St. E1 . . . . .7K **85**
Berge Ho. SE5 . . . . .2C **120**
  (off Carew St.)
Bergenia Ho. TW13: Felt 1J **129**
Bergen Sq. SE16 . . . . .3A **104**
Berger Cl. BR5: Pet W 6H **161**
Berger Rd. E9 . . . . .6K **67**
Berghem M. W14 . . . . .3F **99**
Bergholt Av. IG4: Ilf 5C **52**
Bergholt Cres. N16 . . . . .7E **48**
Bergholt M. NW1 . . . . .7H **65**
Berglen Ct. E14 . . . . .6A **86**
Bergman Ho. E17 . . . . .4C **50**
  (off Hoe St.)
Bering Sq. E14 . . . . .5C **104**
Bering Wlk. E16 . . . . .6B **88**
Berisford M. SW18 . . . . .6A **118**
Berkeley Av. DA7: Bex 1D **126**
  IG5: Ilf 2E **52**
  RM5: Col R 1J **55**
  TW4: Cran 1J **111**
  UB6: G'frd 6H **59**
  (not continuous)
Berkeley Cl. BR5: Pet W 7J **161**
  HA4: Ruis 3J **57**
  KT2: King T 7E **132**

Berkeley Ct.—Beverley Av.

Berkeley Ct. BR2: Brom ...4K 159
CR0: C'don ...*4D 168*
(off Coombe Rd.)
KT6: Surb ...7D 150
N3 ...1K 45
N14 ...6B 22
NW1 ...4F 5
NW10 ...4A 62
NW11 ...*7H 45*
(off Ravenscroft Av.)
SM6: Wall ...3G 167
W5 ...7C 78
Berkeley Cres. EN4: E Barn ...5G 21
Berkeley Dr. KT8: W Mole ...3D 148
Berkeley Gdns. KT10: Clay ...6A 162
KT12: Walt T ...7H 147
N21 ...7J 23
W8 ...1J 99
Berkeley Ho. *E3* ...*3C 86*
(off Wellington Way)
SE8 ...*5B 104*
(off Grove St.)
W8: Bford ...*6D 96*
(off Albany Rd.)
Berkeley M. TW16: Sun ...3A 148
W1 ...1F 11 (6D 82)
Berkeley Pl. SW19 ...6F 135
Berkeley Rd. E12 ...5C 70
N8 ...5H 47
N15 ...6D 48
NW9 ...4G 43
SW13 ...1C 116
UB10: Hil ...7E 56
Berkeleys, The SE25 ...4G 157
Berkeley Sq. W1 ...3K 11 (7F 83)
Berkeley St. W1 ...3K 11 (7F 83)
Berkeley Twr. *E14* ...*1B 104*
(off Westferry Cir.)
Berkeley Wlk. *N7* ...*2K 65*
(off Durham Rd.)
Berkeley Waye TW5: Hest ...6B 94
Berkhampstead Rd.
DA17: Belv ...5G 109
Berkhamsted Av. HA9: Wemb ...6F 61
Berkley Cl. *TW2: Twick* ...*3J 131*
(off Wellesley Rd.)
Berkley Gro. NW1 ...7E 64
Berkley Rd. NW1 ...7D 64
Berkshire Ct. *W7* ...*4K 77*
(off Copley Cl.)
Berkshire Gdns. N13 ...6F 33
N18 ...5C 34
Berkshire Ho. SE6 ...4C 140
Berkshire Rd. E9 ...6B 68
Berkshire Way CR4: Mitc ...4J 155
Berley Rd. E17 ...1B 50
Bermans Way NW10 ...4A 62
BERMONDSEY ...7K 15 (2G 103)
Bermondsey Exchange *SE1* ...*7H 15*
(off Bermondsey St.)
Bermondsey Sq. SE1 ...7H 15 (3E 102)
Bermondsey St. SE1 ...5G 15 (1E 102)
Bermondsey Trad. Est. SE16 ...5J 103
Bermondsey Wall E. SE16 ...2G 103
Bermondsey Wall W. SE16 ...2G 103
Bermuda Way *E1* ...*5A 86*
(off Dongola Rd.)
Bernal Cl. SE28 ...7D 90
Bernard Angell Ho. *SE10* ...*6F 105*
(off Trafalgar Rd.)
Bernard Ashley Dr. SE7 ...5K 105
Bernard Av. W13 ...3B 96
Bernard Cassidy St. E16 ...5H 87
Bernard Gdns. SW19 ...5H 135
Bernard Hegarty Lodge *E8* ...*7G 67*
(off Lansdowne Dr.)
Bernard Ho. E1 ...6J 9
Bernard Mans. *WC1* ...*4E 6*
(off Bernard St.)
Bernard Myers Ho. *SE5* ...*7E 102*
(off Havil St.)
Bernard Rd. N15 ...5F 49
RM7: Rush G ...7J 55
SM6: Wall ...4F 167
Bernard Shaw Ct. *NW1* ...*7G 65*
(off St Pancras Way)
Bernard Shaw Ho. *NW10* ...*1K 79*
(off Knatchbull Rd.)
Bernard St. WC1 ...4E 6 (4J 83)
Bernard Sunley Ho. *SW9* ...*7A 102*
(off Sth. Island Pl.)
Bernays Cl. HA7: Stan ...6H 27
Bernays Gro. SW9 ...4K 119
Bernel Dr. CR0: C'don ...3B 170
Berne Rd. CR7: Thor H ...5C 156
Berners Dr. W13 ...7A 78
Berners Ho. *N1* ...*2A 84*
(off Barnsbury Est.)
Berners M. W1 ...6B 6 (5G 83)
Berners Pl. W1 ...7B 6 (6G 83)
Berners Rd. N1 ...1B 84
N22 ...1A 48
Berners St. W1 ...6B 6 (5G 83)
Berner Ter. *E1* ...*6G 85*
(off Fairclough St.)
Berney Ho. BR3: Beck ...5A 158
Berney Rd. CR0: C'don ...7D 156
Bernhard Baron Ho. *E1* ...*6G 85*
(off Henriques St.)
Bernhardt Cres. NW8 ...3C 4 (4C 82)
Bernhart Cl. HA8: Edg ...7D 28
Bernie Grant Arts Cen. ...4F 49
Bernville Way HA3: Kenton ...5F 43
Bernwell Rd. E4 ...3B 36
Berridge Grn. HA8: Edg ...7B 28
Berridge M. NW6 ...5J 63
Berridge Rd. SE19 ...5D 138
Berriman Rd. N7 ...3K 65
Berrington Ho. *W2* ...*7J 81*
(off Herrington Rd.)
Berriton Rd. HA2: Harr ...1D 58
Berrybank Cl. E4 ...2K 35
Berry Cl. N21 ...1G 33
RM10: Dag ...5G 73
Berry Cotts. *E14* ...*6A 86*
(off Maroon St.)
Berry Ct. TW4: Houn ...5D 112
Berrydale Rd. UB4: Yead ...4C 76
Berryfield Cl.
BR1: Brom ...1C 160
E17 ...4D 50
Berryfield Rd. SE17 ...5B 102
Berry Hill HA7: Stan ...4J 27
Berryhill SE9 ...4F 125
Berryhill Gdns. SE9 ...4F 125
Berry Ho. *E1* ...*4H 85*
(off Headlam St.)
SW11 ...*2D 118*
(off Culvert Rd.)
BERRYLANDS ...6G 151
Berrylands KT5: Surb ...6F 151
SW20 ...3E 152
Berrylands Rd. KT5: Surb ...6F 151
Berry La. SE21 ...4D 138
Berryman Cl. RM8: Dag ...3C 72
Berryman's La. SE26 ...4K 139
Berrymead Gdns. W3 ...1J 97
Berrymede Rd. W4 ...3K 97
Berry Pl. EC1 ...2B 8 (3B 84)
Berry St. EC1 ...3B 8 (4B 84)
Berry Way W5 ...3E 96
Bertal Rd. SW17 ...4B 136
Bertelli Pl. TW13: Felt ...1K 129
Bertha Hollamby Ct. *DA14: Sidc* ...*5C 144*
(off Sidcup Hill)
Bertha James Ct. BR2: Brom ...4K 159
Berthons Gdns. *E17* ...*5F 51*
(off Wood St.)
Berthon St. SE8 ...7C 104
Bertie Rd. NW10 ...6C 62
SE26 ...6K 139
Bertram Cotts. SW19 ...7J 135
Bertram Rd. EN1: Enf ...4B 24
KT2: King T ...7G 133
NW4 ...6C 44
Bertram St. N19 ...2F 65
Bertrand Ho. *E16* ...*6K 87*
(off Russell Rd.)
SW16 ...*3J 137*
(off Leigham Av.)
Bertrand St. SE13 ...3D 122
Bertrand Way SE28 ...7B 90
Bert Rd. CR7: Thor H ...5C 156
Bert Way EN1: Enf ...4A 24
Berwick Av. UB4: Yead ...6B 76
Berwick Cl. HA7: Stan ...6E 26
TW2: Whitt ...1E 130
Berwick Ct. SE1 ...7D 14
Berwick Cres. DA15: Sidc ...7J 125
Berwick Gdns. SM1: Sutt ...3A 166
Berwick Ho. N2 ...2B 46
Berwick Rd. DA16: Well ...1B 126
E16 ...6K 87
N22 ...1B 48
Berwick St. W1 ...7B 6 (6G 83)
Berwick Way BR6: Orp ...1K 173
Berwyn Av. TW3: Houn ...1F 113
Berwyn Rd. SE24 ...1B 138
TW10: Rich ...4H 115
Beryl Av. E6 ...5C 88
Beryl Ho. *SE18* ...*5K 107*
(off Spinel Cl.)
Beryl Rd. W6 ...5F 99
Berystede KT2: King T ...7H 133
Besant Cl. NW2 ...3G 63
Besant Ct. N1 ...5D 66
SE28 ...*1B 108*
(off Titmuss Av.)
Besant Ho. *NW8* ...*1A 82*
(off Boundary Rd.)
Besant Pl. SE22 ...4F 121
Besant Rd. NW2 ...4G 63
Besant Wlk. N7 ...2K 65
Besant Way NW10 ...5J 61
Besford Ho. *E2* ...*2G 85*
(off Pritchard's Rd.)
Besley St. SW16 ...6G 137
Bessant Dr. TW9: Kew ...1H 115
Bessborough Gdns. SW1 ...5D 18 (5H 101)
Bessborough Pl. SW1 ...5D 18 (5H 101)
Bessborough Rd. HA1: Harr ...1H 59
SW15 ...1C 134
Bessborough St. SW1 ...5C 18 (5H 101)
Bessemer Ct. *NW1* ...*7G 65*
(off Rochester Sq.)
Bessemer Pk. Ind. Est. SE24 ...4B 120
Bessemer Pl. SE10 ...3H 105
Bessemer Rd. SE5 ...2C 120
Bessie Lansbury Cl. E6 ...6E 88
Bessingby Rd. HA4: Ruis ...2K 57
Bessingham Wlk. *SE4* ...*4K 121*
(off Aldersford Cl.)
Besson St. SE14 ...1J 121
Bessy St. E2 ...3J 85
Bestwood St. SE8 ...4K 103
Beswick M. NW6 ...6K 63
Beta Ct. *CR0: C'don* ...*1D 168*
(off Sydenham Rd.)
Betam Rd. UB3: Hayes ...2F 93
Beta Pl. SW4 ...4K 119
Betchworth Cl. SM1: Sutt ...5B 166
Betchworth Rd. IG3: Ilf ...2J 71
Betchworth Way CR0: New Ad ...7E 170
Betham Rd. UB6: G'frd ...3H 77
Bethany Waye TW14: Bedf ...7G 111
Bethecar Rd. HA1: Harr ...5J 41
Bethel Cl. NW4 ...5F 45
Bethell Av. E16 ...4H 87
IG1: Ilf ...7E 52
Bethel Rd. DA16: Well ...3C 126
Bethersden Cl. BR3: Beck ...7B 140
Bethersden Ho. *SE17* ...*5E 102*
(off Kinglake Est.)
Bethlehem Ho. *E14* ...*7B 86*
(off Limehouse C'way.)
BETHNAL GREEN ...3H 85
Bethnal Green Centre for Sports
& Performing Arts ...2K 9 (3F 85)
Bethnal Grn. Rd. E1 ...3J 9 (4F 85)
E2 ...3J 9 (4F 85)
Bethune Av. N11 ...4J 31
Bethune Rd. N16 ...7D 48
NW10 ...4K 79
Bethwin Rd. SE5 ...7B 102
Betjeman Cl. HA5: Pinn ...4E 40
Betjeman Ct. UB7: Yiew ...1A 92
Betony Cl. CR0: C'don ...1K 169
Betoyne Av. E4 ...4B 36
Betsham Ho. *SE1* ...*6E 14*
(off Newcomen St.)
Betstyle Cir. N11 ...4A 32
Betstyle Ho. N10 ...7K 31
Betstyle Rd. N11 ...4A 32
Bettenson Cl. BR7: Chst ...5D 142
Betterton Dr. DA14: Sidc ...2E 144
Betterton Ho. *WC2* ...*1F 13*
(off Betterton St.)
Betterton Rd. RM13: Rain ...3K 91
Betterton St. WC2 ...1E 12 (6J 83)
Bettons Pk. E15 ...1G 87
Bettridge Rd. SW6 ...2H 117
Betts Cl. BR3: Beck ...2A 158
Betts Ho. *E1* ...*7H 85*
(off Betts St.)
Betts M. E17 ...6B 50
Betts Rd. E16 ...7K 87
Betts St. E1 ...7H 85
Betts Way KT6: Surb ...1B 162
SE20 ...1H 157
Betty Brooks Ho. E11 ...3F 69
Betty May Gray Ho. *E14* ...*4E 104*
(off Pier St.)
Beulah Av. CR7: Thor H ...2C 156
Beulah Cl. HA8: Edg ...3C 28
Beulah Cres. CR7: Thor H ...2C 156
Beulah Gro. CR0: C'don ...6C 156
Beulah Hill SE19 ...6B 138
Beulah Path E17 ...5E 50
Beulah Rd.
CR7: Thor H ...3C 156
E17 ...5D 50
SM1: Sutt ...4J 165
SW19 ...7H 135
Bevan Av. IG11: Bark ...7A 72
Bevan Ct. CR0: Wadd ...5A 168
E3 ...*2C 86*
(off Tredegar Rd.)
Bevan Ho. IG11: Bark ...7B 72
N1 ...*1E 84*
(off Halcomb St.)
TW1: Twick ...6D 114
WC1 ...*5F 7*
(off Boswell St.)
Bevan M. W12 ...2C 98
Bevan Rd. EN4: Cockf ...4J 21
SE2 ...5B 108
Bevans Ho. *SW18* ...*4A 118*
(off Eltringham St.)
Bevan St. N1 ...1C 84
Bev Callender Cl. SW8 ...3F 119
Bevenden St. N1 ...1F 9 (3D 84)
Bevercote Wlk. *DA17: Belv* ...*6F 109*
(off Osborne Rd.)
Beveree Stadium ...1F 149
Beveridge Ct. *N21* ...*5D 22*
(off Pennington Dr.)
SE28 ...*7B 90*
(off Saunders Way)
Beveridge M. E1 ...5J 85
Beveridge Rd. NW10 ...7A 62
Beverley Av.
DA15: Sidc ...7K 125
SW20 ...1B 152
TW4: Houn ...4D 112

Beverley Cl. EN1: Enf 4K 23
  KT9: Chess 4C 162
  N21 . . . .1H 33
  SW11 . . . .4B 118
  SW13 . . . .2C 116
Beverley Cotts. SW15 . . . .3A 134
Beverley Ct. HA2: Harr 3H 41
  HA3: Kenton 4C 42
  N2 . . . .4D 46
  (off Western Rd.)
  N14 . . . .7B 22
  NW6 . . . .7A 64
  (off Fairfax Rd.)
  SE4 . . . .3B 122
  (not continuous)
  TW4: Houn 4D 112
  W4 . . . .5J 97
Beverley Cres. IG8: Wfd G 1K 51
Beverley Dr. HA8: Edg 3G 43
Beverley Gdns. HA7: Stan 1A 42
  HA9: Wemb 1F 61
  KT4: Wor Pk 1C 164
  NW11 . . . .7G 45
  SW13 . . . .3B 116
Beverley Ho. BR1: Brom 5F 141
  (off Brangbourne Rd.)
Beverley Hyrst CR0: C'don 2F 169
Beverley La. KT2: King T 7A 134
  SW15 . . . .3B 134
Beverley Meads & Fishpond Woods
  Nature Reserve 6B 134
Beverley M. E4 . . . .6A 36
Beverley Path SW13 . . . .2B 116
Beverley Rd. BR2: Brom 2C 172
  CR4: Mitc 4H 155
  DA7: Bex 2J 127
  E4 . . . .6A 36
  E6 . . . .3B 88
  HA4: Ruis 2J 57
  KT1: Hamp W 1C 150
  KT3: N Mald 4C 152
  KT4: Wor Pk 2E 164
  RM9: Dag 4E 72
  SE20 . . . .2H 157
  SW13 . . . .3B 116
  TW16: Sun 1H 147
  UB2: S'hall 4C 94
  W4 . . . .5B 98
Beverley Trad. Est. SM4: Mord 7F 153
Beverley Way KT3: N Mald 1B 152
  SW20 . . . .1B 152
Beversbrook Rd. N19 . . . .3H 65
Beverstone Rd. CR7: Thor H 4A 156
  SW2 . . . .5K 119
Beverston M. W1 . . . .6E 4
Bevill Allen Cl. SW17 . . . .5D 136
Bevill Cl. SE25 . . . .3G 157
Bevin Cl. SE16 . . . .1A 104
Bevin Ct. WC1 . . . .1H 7 (3K 83)
Bevington Path SE1 . . . .7J 15
Bevington Rd. BR3: Beck 2D 158
  W10 . . . .5G 81
Bevington St. SE16 . . . .2G 103
Bevin Ho. E2 . . . .3J 85
  (off Butler St.)
  E3 . . . .3C 86
  (off Alfred St.)
Bevin Rd. UB4: Yead 3J 75
Bevin Sq. SW17 . . . .3D 136
Bevin Way WC1 . . . .1J 7 (2A 84)
Bevis Marks EC3 . . . .7H 9 (6E 84)
Bewcastle Gdns. EN2: Enf 4D 22
Bew Ct. SE22 . . . .7G 121
Bewdley St. N1 . . . .7A 66
Bewick M. SE15 . . . .7H 103
Bewick St. SW8 . . . .2F 119
Bewley Ho. E1 . . . .7H 85
  (off Bewley St.)
Bewley St. E1 . . . .7J 85
  SW19 . . . .6A 136
Bewlys Rd. SE27 . . . .5B 138

Bexhill Cl. TW13: Felt 2C 130
Bexhill Rd. N11 . . . .5C 32
  SE4 . . . .6B 122
  SW14 . . . .3J 115
Bexhill Wlk. E15 . . . .1G 87
BEXLEY 7G 127
Bexley Gdns. N9 . . . .3J 33
  RM6: Chad H 5B 54
BEXLEYHEATH 4G 127
Bexleyheath Golf Course 5E 126
Bexleyheath Sports Club 4C 126
Bexley High St. DA5: Bexl 7K 127
Bexley Ho. SE4 . . . .4A 122
Bexley La. DA1: Cray 5K 127
  DA14: Sidc 4C 144
Bexley Lawn Tennis,
  Squash & Racketball Club 7G 127
Bexley Museum Collection, The 6J 127
Bexley Music & Dance Cen. 4A 144
  (off Station Rd.)
Bexley Rd. DA8: Erith 1J 127
  (not continuous)
  SE9 . . . .5F 125
Beynon Rd. SM5: Cars 5D 166
Bezier Apartments EC2 . . . .3F 9 (4D 84)
BFI Southbank 4H 13
Bianca Ho. N1 . . . .1G 9
  (off Crondall St.)
Bianca Rd. SE15 . . . .6G 103
Bibsworth Rd. N3 . . . .2H 45
Bibury Cl. SE15 . . . .6E 102
  (not continuous)
Bicester Rd. TW9: Rich 3G 115
Bickels Yd. SE1 . . . .7H 15
  (off Bermondsey St.)
Bickenhall Mans. W1 . . . .5F 5
  (not continuous)
Bickenhall St. W1 . . . .5F 5 (5D 82)
Bickersteth Rd. SW17 . . . .6D 136
Bickerton Rd. N19 . . . .2G 65
BICKLEY 3C 160
Bickley Cres. BR1: Brom 4C 160
Bickley Pk. Rd. BR1: Brom 3C 160
Bickley Rd. BR1: Brom 2B 160
  E10 . . . .7D 50
Bickley St. SW17 . . . .5C 136
Bicknell Ho. E1 . . . .6G 85
  (off Ellen St.)
Bicknell Rd. SE5 . . . .3C 120
Bicknoller Rd. EN1: Enf 1K 23
Bicknor Rd. BR6: Orp 7J 161
Bicycle M. SW4 . . . .3H 119
Bidborough Cl. BR2: Brom 5H 159
Bidborough St. WC1 . . . .2E 6 (3J 83)
Biddenden Way SE9 . . . .4E 142
Biddenham Ho. SE16 . . . .4K 103
  (off Plough Way)
Bidder St. E16 . . . .5G 87
  (not continuous)
Biddesden Ho. SW3 . . . .4E 16
  (off Cadogan St.)
Biddestone Rd. N7 . . . .4K 65
Biddulph Ho. SE18 . . . .4D 106
Biddulph Mans. W9 . . . .3K 81
  (off Elgin Av.)
Biddulph Rd. W9 . . . .3K 81
Bideford Av. UB6: G'frd 2B 78
Bideford Cl. HA8: Edg 1G 43
  TW13: Hanw 3D 130
Bideford Gdns. EN1: Enf 7K 23
Bideford Rd.
  BR1: Brom 3H 141
  DA16: Well 7B 108
  EN3: Enf L 1G 25
  HA4: Ruis 3K 57
Bidwell Gdns. N11 . . . .7B 32
Bidwell St. SE15 . . . .1H 121
Big Ben 7F 13 (2J 101)
Bigbury Cl. N17 . . . .7J 33
Biggerstaff Rd. E15 . . . .1E 86
Biggerstaff St. N4 . . . .2A 66

Biggin Av. CR4: Mitc 1D 154
Biggin Hill SE19 . . . .7B 138
Biggin Hill Cl. KT2: King T 5C 132
Biggin Way SE19 . . . .7B 138
Bigginwood Rd. SW16 . . . .7B 138
Biggs Ct. NW9 . . . .2A 44
  (off Harvey Cl.)
Biggs Row SW15 . . . .3F 117
Biggs Sq. E9 . . . .6B 68
Big Hill E5 . . . .1H 67
Bigland St. E1 . . . .6H 85
Bignell Rd. SE18 . . . .5F 107
Bignold Rd. E7 . . . .4J 69
Bigwood Ct. SE20 . . . .1H 157
Bigwood Rd. NW11 . . . .5K 45
Bike Shed, The IG11: Bark 7G 71
  (off Ripple Rd.)
Bilberry Ho. E3 . . . .5C 86
  (off Watts Gro.)
Billet Cl. RM6: Chad H 3D 54
Billet Rd. E17 . . . .1K 49
  RM6: Chad H 3B 54
Billets Hart Cl. W7 . . . .2J 95
Bill Hamling Cl. SE9 . . . .2D 142
Billing Cl. RM9: Dag 7C 72
Billingford Cl. SE4 . . . .4K 121
Billing Ho. E1 . . . .6K 85
  (off Bower St.)
Billingley NW1 . . . .1G 83
  (off Pratt St.)
Billing Pl. SW10 . . . .7K 99
Billing Rd. SW10 . . . .7K 99
Billingsgate Market 1D 104
Billing St. SW10 . . . .7K 99
Billington M. W3 . . . .1H 97
  (off High St.)
Billington Rd. SE14 . . . .7K 103
Billinton Hill CR0: C'don 2D 168
Billiter Sq. EC3 . . . .1H 15
Billiter St. EC3 . . . .1H 15 (6E 84)
Bill Nicholson Way N17 . . . .7A 34
  (off High Rd.)
Billockby Cl. KT9: Chess 6F 163
Billson St. E14 . . . .4E 104
Bilsby Gro. SE9 . . . .4B 142
Bilsby Lodge HA9: Wemb 3J 61
  (off Chalklands)
Bilton Centre, The UB6: G'frd 1B 78
Bilton Rd. UB6: G'frd 1A 78
Bilton Towers W1 . . . .1F 11
  (off Gt. Cumberland Pl.)
Bilton Way EN3: Enf L 1F 25
  UB3: Hayes 2J 93
Bina Gdns. SW5 . . . .4A 100
Binbrook Ho. W10 . . . .5E 80
  (off Sutton Way)
Bincote Rd. EN2: Enf 3E 22
Binden Rd. W12 . . . .3B 98
Bindon Grn. SM4: Mord 4K 153
Binfield Rd. CR2: S Croy 5F 169
  SW4 . . . .1J 119
Bingfield St. N1 . . . .1J 83
  (not continuous)
Bingham Ct. N1 . . . .7B 66
  (off Halton Rd.)
Bingham Pl. W1 . . . .5G 5 (5E 82)
Bingham Point SE18 . . . .4F 107
  (off Wilmount St.)
Bingham Rd. CR0: C'don 1G 169
Bingham St. N1 . . . .6D 66
Bingley Rd. E16 . . . .6A 88
  TW16: Sun 7J 129
  UB6: G'frd 4G 77
Binley Ho. SW15 . . . .6C 116
Binnacle Ho. E1 . . . .1H 103
  (off Cobblestone Sq.)
Binney St. W1 . . . .1H 11 (6E 82)
Binnie Ho. SE1 . . . .3C 102
  (off Bath Ter.)
Binnington Twr. BR2: Brom 6C 160

Binns Rd. W4 . . . .5A 98
Binns Ter. W4 . . . .5A 98
Binsey Wlk. SE2 . . . .2C 108
  (not continuous)
Binstead Cl. UB4: Yead 6C 76
Binyon Cres. HA7: Stan 5E 26
Bioko Ct. E1 . . . .5A 86
  (off Ocean Est.)
Biraj Ho. E6 . . . .1D 88
Birbetts Rd. SE9 . . . .2D 142
Bircham Path SE4 . . . .4K 121
  (off Aldersford Cl.)
Birchanger Rd. SE25 . . . .5G 157
Birch Av. N13 . . . .3H 33
  UB7: Yiew 6B 74
Birch Cl. E16 . . . .5G 87
  IG9: Buck H 3G 37
  N19 . . . .2G 65
  RM7: Mawney 3H 55
  SE15 . . . .2G 121
  TW3: Houn 2H 113
  TW8: Bford 7B 96
  TW11: Tedd 5A 132
  TW17: Shep 3G 147
Birch Ct. N12 . . . .4E 30
  RM6: Chad H 6C 54
  SM1: Sutt 4A 166
  SM6: Wall 4F 167
Birch Cres. UB10: Uxb 1B 74
Birchdale Gdns. RM6: Chad H 7D 54
Birchdale Rd. E7 . . . .5A 70
Birchden Dr. SE28 . . . .1A 108
Birchdown Ho. E3 . . . .3D 86
  (off Rainhill Way)
Birchen Cl. NW9 . . . .2K 61
Birchend Cl. CR2: S Croy 6D 168
Birchen Gro. NW9 . . . .2K 61
Birches, The BR2: Brom 4H 159
  (off Durham Rd.)
  BR6: Farnb 4E 172
  E12 . . . .4C 70
  N21 . . . .6E 22
  SE5 . . . .2E 120
  SE7 . . . .6K 105
  TW4: Houn 7D 112
Birches Cl. CR4: Mitc 3D 154
  HA5: Pinn 5C 40
Birchfield Ct. KT12: Walt T 7K 147
  (off Grove Cres.)
Birchfield Ho. E14 . . . .7C 86
  (off Birchfield St.)
Birchfield St. E14 . . . .7C 86
Birch Gdns. RM10: Dag 3J 73
Birch Grn. NW9 . . . .7F 29
Birch Gro. DA16: Well 4A 126
  E11 . . . .4G 69
  SE12 . . . .7H 123
  TW17: Shep 2G 147
  W3 . . . .1G 97
Birchgrove Ho. TW9: Kew 7H 97
Birch Hill CR0: C'don 5K 169
Birch Ho. N22 . . . .1A 48
  (off Acacia Rd.)
  SE14 . . . .1B 122
  SW2 . . . .6A 120
  UB7: W Dray 2B 92
  (off Park Lodge Av.)
  W10 . . . .4G 81
  (off Droop St.)
Birchington Cl. DA7: Bex 1H 127
Birchington Ct. NW6 . . . .1K 81
  (off West End La.)
Birchington Ho. E5 . . . .5H 67
Birchington Rd. KT5: Surb 7F 151
  N8 . . . .6H 47
  NW6 . . . .1J 81
Birchin La. EC3 . . . .1F 15 (6D 84)
Birchlands Av. SW12 . . . .7D 118
Birch Mead BR6: Farnb 2E 172
Birchmead Av. HA5: Pinn 4A 40
Birchmere Bus. Pk. SE28 . . . .2A 108

Birchmere Lodge SE16 . . . . .5H 103
(off Sherwood Gdns.)
Birchmere Row SE3 . . . . .2H 123
Birchmere Hall N5 . . . . .3C 66
Birchmere Wlk. N5 . . . . .3C 66
(not continuous)
Birch Pk. HA3: Hrw W 7B 26
Birch Rd. RM7: Mawney 3H 55
　TW13: Hanw 5B 130
Birch Row BR2: Brom 7E 160
Birch Tree Av. BR4: W W'ck 5H 171
Birch Tree Way CR0: C'don 2H 169
Birch Va. Ct. NW8 . . . . .3B 4
(off Pollitt Dr.)
Birch View HA1: Harr 5H 41
Birchville Ct. WD23: B Hea 1D 26
Birch Wlk.
　CR4: Mitc 1F 155
　DA8: Erith 6J 109
　IG3: Ilf 4J 71
(off Loxford La.)
Birchway UB3: Hayes 1J 93
Birchwood Apartments N4 . . . .7C 48
(off Woodberry Gro.)
Birchwood Av. BR3: Beck 4B 158
　DA14: Sidc 2B 144
　N10 . . . . .3E 46
　SM6: Wall 3E 166
Birchwood Cl. SM4: Mord 4K 153
Birchwood Ct. HA8: Edg 2J 43
　N13 . . . . .5G 33
Birchwood Dr. DA2: Wilm 4K 145
　NW3 . . . . .3K 63
Birchwood Gro. TW12: Hamp . .6E 130
Birchwood Pde. DA2: Wilm 4K 145
Birchwood Park Golf Course . . .7J 145
Birchwood Rd.
　BR5: Pet W 4H 161
　BR8: Swan 4H 161
　DA2: Wilm 7J 145
　SW17 . . . . .5F 137
Birdbrook Cl. RM10: Dag 7J 73
Birdbrook Ho. N1 . . . . .7C 66
(off Popham Rd.)
Birdbrook Rd. SE3 . . . . .4A 124
Birdcage Wlk. SW1 . . . .7A 12 (2G 101)
Birdham Cl. BR1: Brom 5C 160
Birdhurst Av. CR2: S Croy 4D 168
Birdhurst Ct. SM6: Wall 7G 167
(off Woodcote Av.)
Birdhurst Gdns. CR2: S Croy . . .4D 168
Birdhurst Ri. CR2: S Croy 5E 168
Birdhurst Rd. CR2: S Croy 5E 168
　SW18 . . . . .5A 118
　SW19 . . . . .6C 136
Bird in Bush BMX Track 7H 103
(off Bird in Bush Rd.)
Bird in Bush Rd. SE15 . . . . .7G 103
Bird in Hand La. BR1: Brom 2B 160
Bird-in-Hand M. SE23 . . . . .2J 139
(off Bird-in-Hand Pas.)
Bird-in-Hand Pas. SE23 . . . . . . .2J 139
Bird in Hand Path CR0: C'don . .7D 156
(off Sydenham Rd.)
Bird in Hand Yd. NW3 . . . . .4A 64
Birdsall Ho. SE5 . . . . .3E 120
Birds Farm Av. RM5: Col R 1H 55
Birdsfield La. E3 . . . . .1B 86
Bird St. W1 . . . . .1H 11 (6E 82)
Bird Wlk. TW2: Whitt 1D 130
Birdwood Av. SE13 . . . . .6F 123
Birdwood Cl. TW11: Tedd 4J 131
Birkbeck Av. UB6: G'frd 1G 77
　W3 . . . . .7J 79
Birkbeck Ct. W3 . . . . .1K 97
Birkbeck Gdns. IG8: Wfd G 2D 36
Birkbeck Gro. W3 . . . . .2K 97
Birkbeck Hill SE21 . . . . .1B 138
Birkbeck M. E8 . . . . .5F 67
　W3 . . . . .1K 97
Birkbeck Pl. SE21 . . . . .2C 138

Birkbeck Rd. BR3: Beck 2J 157
　DA14: Sidc 3A 144
　E8 . . . . .5F 67
　EN2: Enf 1J 23
　IG2: Ilf 5H 53
　N8 . . . . .4J 47
　N12 . . . . .5F 31
　N17 . . . . .1F 49
　NW7 . . . . .5G 29
　RM7: Rush G 1K 73
　SW19 . . . . .5K 135
　W3 . . . . .1K 97
　W5 . . . . .4C 96
Birkbeck St. E2 . . . . .3H 85
Birkbeck Way UB6: G'frd 1H 77
Birkdale Av. HA5: Pinn 3E 40
Birkdale Cl. BR6: Orp 7H 161
　SE16 . . . . .5H 103
　SE28 . . . . .6D 90
Birkdale Ct. UB1: S'hall 6G 77
(off Redcroft Rd.)
Birkdale Gdns. CR0: C'don 4K 169
Birkdale Rd. SE2 . . . . .4A 108
　W5 . . . . .4E 78
Birkenhead Av. KT2: King T 2F 151
Birkenhead St. WC1 . . . .1F 7 (3J 83)
Birkhall Rd. SE6 . . . . .1F 141
Birkwood Cl. SW12 . . . . .7H 119
Birley Lodge NW8 . . . . .2B 82
(off Acacia Rd.)
Birley Rd. N20 . . . . .2F 31
Birley St. SW11 . . . . .2E 118
Birling Rd. DA8: Erith 7K 109
Birnam Rd. N4 . . . . .2K 65
Birnbeck Ct. EN5: Barn 4A 20
　NW11 . . . . .5H 45
Birrell Ho. SW9 . . . . .2K 119
(off Stockwell Rd.)
Birse Cres. NW10 . . . . .3A 62
Birstall Rd. N15 . . . . .5E 48
Birtwhistle Ho. E3 . . . . .1B 86
(off Parnell Rd.)
Biscay Ho. E1 . . . . .4K 85
(off Mile End Rd.)
Biscayne Av. E14 . . . . .1F 105
Biscay Rd. W6 . . . . .5F 99
Biscoe Cl. TW5: Hest 6E 94
Biscoe Way SE13 . . . . .3F 123
Biscott Ho. E3 . . . . .4D 86
Bisenden Rd. CR0: C'don 2E 168
Bisham Cl. SM5: Cars 1D 166
Bisham Gdns. N6 . . . . .1E 64
Bishop Butt Cl. BR6: Orp 3K 173
Bishop Duppas Pk.
　TW17: Shep 7G 147
Bishop Fox Way KT8: W Mole . .4D 148
Bishop Ken Rd. HA3: W'stone . . .2K 41
Bishop King's Rd. W14 . . . . .4G 99
Bishop Ramsey Cl. HA4: Ruis . . .7H 39
Bishop Rd. N14 . . . . .7A 22
Bishops Av.
　BR1: Brom 2A 160
　E13 . . . . .1K 87
　RM6: Chad H 6C 54
　SW6 . . . . .2F 117
Bishops Avenue, The N2 . . . . . . .7B 46
Bishop's Bri. Rd. W2 . . . .6A 4 (6K 81)
Bishops Cl. E17 . . . . .4D 50
　EN1: Enf 2C 24
　EN5: Barn 6A 20
　N19 . . . . .3G 65
　SE9 . . . . .2G 143
　SM1: Sutt 3J 165
　TW10: Ham 3D 132
　UB10: Hil 2C 74
　W4 . . . . .5J 97
Bishops Ct. CR0: C'don 2F 169
　EC4 . . . . .7A 8
　HA0: Wemb 4B 60
　N2 . . . . .5C 46

Bishops Ct. W2 . . . . .6K 81
(off Bishop's Bri. Rd.)
　WC2 . . . . .7J 7
Bishopsdale Ho. NW6 . . . . .1J 81
(off Kilburn Vale)
Bishops Dr. TW14: Bedf 6F 111
　UB5: N'olt 1C 76
Bishopsford Ho. SM5: Cars 6C 154
Bishopsford Rd. SM4: Mord 7A 154
Bishopsgate EC2 . . . .1G 15 (6E 84)
Bishopsgate Arc. EC2 . . . . .6H 9
Bishopsgate Chyd. EC2 . . .7G 9 (5E 84)
Bishopsgate Institute & Libraries . . .6H 9
(off Bishopsgate)
Bishops Grn. BR1: Brom 1A 160
Bishops Gro. N2 . . . . .6C 46
　TW12: Hamp 4D 130
Bishops Gro. Caravan Site
　TW12: Hamp 4E 130
Bishop's Hall KT1: King T 2D 150
Bishops Hill KT12: Walt T 7J 147
Bishops Ho. SW8 . . . . .7J 101
(off Sth. Lambeth Rd.)
Bishop's Mans. SW6 . . . . .2F 117
Bishops Mead SE5 . . . . .7C 102
(off Camberwell Rd.)
Bishops Pk. Rd. SW6 . . . . .2F 117
　SW16 . . . . .1J 155
Bishops Pl. SM1: Sutt 5A 166
Bishops Rd. CR0: C'don 7B 156
　N6 . . . . .6E 46
　SW6 . . . . .1G 117
　SW11 . . . . .7C 100
　UB3: Hayes 6E 74
　W7 . . . . .2J 95
Bishops Sq. E1 . . . . . . .5H 9 (5E 84)
Bishop's Ter. SE11 . . . .3K 19 (4A 102)
Bishopsthorpe Rd. SE26 . . . . . .4K 139
Bishop St. N1 . . . . .1C 84
Bishops Vw. Ct. N10 . . . . .4F 47
Bishops Wlk. BR7: Chst 1G 161
　CR0: Addtn 5K 169
　HA5: Pinn 3C 40
Bishop's Way E2 . . . . .2H 85
Bishops Wharf Ho. SW11 . . . . . .7C 100
(off Parkgate Rd.)
Bishops Wood Almshouses E5 . . .4H 67
(off Lwr. Clapton Rd.)
Bishopswood Rd. N6 . . . . .7D 46
Bishop Wilfred Wood Cl. SE15 . .2G 121
Bishop Wilfred Wood Ct. E13 . . .2A 88
(off Pragel St.)
Bisley Cl. KT4: Wor Pk 1E 164
Bison Ct. TW14: Felt 7K 111
Bispham Rd. NW10 . . . . .3F 79
Bissagos Ct. E1 . . . . .5A 86
(off Ocean Est.)
Bissextile Ho. SE13 . . . . .2D 122
Bisson Rd. E15 . . . . .2E 86
Bisterne Av. E17 . . . . .3F 51
Bittacy Bus. Cen. NW7 . . . . .7A 30
Bittacy Cl. NW7 . . . . .6A 30
Bittacy Ct. NW7 . . . . .7B 30
Bittacy Hill NW7 . . . . .6K 29
Bittacy Pk. Av. NW7 . . . . .5A 30
Bittacy Ri. NW7 . . . . .6A 30
Bittacy Rd. NW7 . . . . .6A 30
Bittern Cl. UB4: Yead 5B 76
Bittern Ct. NW9 . . . . .2A 44
　SE8 . . . . .6C 104
Bittern Ho. SE1 . . . . .7C 14
(off Gt. Suffolk St.)
Bittern Pl. N22 . . . . .2K 47
Bittern St. SE1 . . . . . . .7C 14 (2C 102)
Bittoms, The KT1: King T 3D 150
Bittoms Ct. KT1: King T 3D 150
Bixley Cl. UB2: S'hall 4D 94
Blackall St. EC2 . . . . . . .3G 9 (4E 84)
Blackberry Cl. E17 . . . . .3D 50
　TW17: Shep 4G 147
Blackberry Ho. HA9: Wemb 7E 42

Blackberry Farm Cl. TW5: Hest . .7C 94
Blackberry Fld. BR5: St P 7A 144
Blackbird Cl. NW9 . . . . .3K 61
Blackbird Hill NW9 . . . . .2J 61
Blackbird Yd. E2 . . . . . . .1K 9 (3F 85)
Blackborne Rd. RM10: Dag 6G 73
Blackborough Ho. IG9: Buck H . . .2G 37
(off Beatrice Ct.)
Black Boy La. N15 . . . . .5C 48
Blackbrook La. BR1: Brom 5D 160
　BR2: Brom 5E 160
Black Bull Yd. EC1 . . . . .5K 7
(off Hatton Wall)
Blackburn NW9 . . . . .2B 44
Blackburn M. W1 . . . . .2G 11 (7E 82)
Blackburn Rd. NW6 . . . . .6K 63
Blackburn Trad. Est. TW19: Stanw . .6B 110
Blackburn Way TW4: Houn 5C 112
Blackbush Av. RM6: Chad H 5D 54
Blackbush Cl. SM2: Sutt 7K 165
Blackdown Cl. N2 . . . . .2A 46
Blackdown Ter. SE18 . . . . .1D 124
Blackett Apartments E3 . . . . .4B 86
(off Hamlets Way)
Blackett St. SW15 . . . . .3F 117
Black Fan Cl. EN2: Enf 1H 23
BLACKFEN 6A 126
Blackfen Pde. DA15: Sidc 6A 126
Blackfen Rd. DA15: Sidc 5J 125
Blackford Cl. CR2: S Croy 7B 168
Blackford's Path SW15 . . . . .7C 116
Blackfriars Bri. EC4 . . . .2A 14 (7B 84)
Blackfriars Ct. EC4 . . . . .2A 14
Black Friars La. EC4 . . . .3A 14 (6B 84)
(not continuous)
Blackfriars Pas. EC4 . . . .2A 14 (7B 84)
Blackfriars Rd. SE1 . . . .4A 14 (2B 102)
Blackfriars Underpass EC4 . .2A 14 (7A 84)
Black Gates HA5: Pinn 3D 40
BLACKHEATH 2H 123
Blackheath Av. SE10 . . . . .7F 105
Blackheath Bus. Est. SE10 . . . . . .1F 122
(off Blackheath Hill)
Blackheath Concert Halls 3H 123
Blackheath Gro. SE3 . . . . .2H 123
Blackheath Hill SE10 . . . . .1E 122
BLACKHEATH PARK 3J 123
Blackheath Pk. SE3 . . . . .3H 123
Blackheath Ri. SE13 . . . . .2E 122
(not continuous)
Blackheath Rd. SE10 . . . . .1D 122
Blackheath RUFC 7K 105
BLACKHEATH VALE 2H 123
Blackheath Va. SE3 . . . . .2G 123
Blackheath Village SE3 . . . . .2H 123
Black Horse Ct. SE1 . . . . .7G 15
Black Horse La. CR0: C'don 7G 157
　E17 . . . . .2K 49
Blackhorse M. E17 . . . . .3K 49
Black Horse Pde. HA5: Eastc 5K 39
BLACKHORSE ROAD 4K 49
Blackhorse Rd. DA14: Sidc 4A 144
　E17 . . . . .4K 49
　SE8 . . . . .6A 104
Blacklands Dr. UB4: Hayes 4E 74
Blacklands Rd. SE6 . . . . .4E 140
Blacklands Ter. SW3 . . . .4E 16 (4D 100)
Black Lion La. W6 . . . . .4C 98
Black Lion M. W6 . . . . .4C 98
Blackmans Yd. E2 . . . . .2G 85
Blackmore Av. UB1: S'hall 1H 95
Blackmore Dr. NW10 . . . . .7H 61
Blackmore Ho. N1 . . . . .1K 83
(off Barnsbury Est.)
Blackmore Rd. IG9: Buck H 1H 37
Blackmore's Gro. TW11: Tedd . . .6A 132
Blackness La. BR2: Kes 7B 172
Black Path E10 . . . . .7A 50
Blackpool Gdns. UB4: Hayes 4G 75
Blackpool Rd. SE15 . . . . .2H 121
BLACK PRINCE INTERCHANGE . .6H 127

Black Prince Rd.—Bloomfield Rd.

Black Prince Rd. SE1 4G 19 (4K 101)
SE11 4G 19 (4K 101)
Black Rd. E11 6G 51
Black Rod Cl. UB3: Hayes 3H 93
Blackshaw Rd. SW17 4A 136
Blacksmiths Cl. RM6: Chad H 6C 54
Blacksmiths Ho. *E17* *4C 50*
(off Gillards M.)
Blacks Rd. W6 5E 98
Blackstock M. N4 2B 66
Blackstock Rd. N4 2B 66
N5 2B 66
Blackstone Est. E8 7G 67
Blackstone Ho. *SW1* *6A 18*
(off Churchill Gdns.)
Blackstone Rd. NW2 5E 62
Black Swan Yd. SE1 6H 15 (2E 102)
Blackthorn Av. N7 6A 66
UB7: W Dray 4C 92
Blackthorn Ct. *E15* *4F 69*
(off Hall Rd.)
TW5: Hest 7C 94
Blackthorne Av. CR0: C'don 1J 169
Blackthorne Ct. *SE15* *7F 103*
(off Cator St.)
TW15: Ashf 7E 128
Blackthorne Ct. *UB1: S'hall* *1F 95*
(off Dormer's Wells La.)
Blackthorne Cres. SL3: Poyle 5A 174
Blackthorne Dr. E4 4A 36
Blackthorne Ind. Est. SL3: Poyle 6A 174
Blackthorne Rd. SL3: Poyle 5A 174
Blackthorn Gro. DA7: Bex 3E 126
Blackthorn Rd. IG1: Ilf 5H 71
Blackthorn St. E3 4C 86
Blacktree M. SW9 3A 120
BLACKWALL 1E 104
Blackwall La. SE10 5G 105
Blackwall Trad. Est. E14 5F 87
Blackwall Tunnel E14 1F 105
(not continuous)
Blackwall Tunnel App. E14 7E 86
Blackwall Tunnel Northern App. E3 2C 86
E14 4E 86
Blackwall Tunnel Southern App. SE10 3G 105
Blackwall Way E14 1E 104
Blackwater Cl. E7 4H 69
RM13: Rain 5K 91
Blackwater Ho. *NW8* *5B 4*
(off Church St.)
Blackwater St. SE22 5F 121
Blackwell Cl. E5 4K 67
HA3: Hrw W 7C 26
N21 5D 22
Blackwell Gdns. HA8: Edg 4B 28
Blackwell Ho. SW4 6H 119
Blackwood Av. N18 5E 34
Blackwood Ho. *E1* *4H 85*
(off Collingwood St.)
Blackwood St. SE17 5D 102
Blade M. SW15 4H 117
Bladen Ho. *E1* *6K 85*
(off Dunelm St.)
Blades Ct. SW15 4H 117
W6 *5D 98*
(off Lower Mall)
Blades Ho. *SE11* *7J 19*
(off Kennington Oval)
Bladindon Dr. DA5: Bexl 7C 126
Bladon Ct. SW16 6J 137
Bladon Gdns. HA2: Harr 6F 41
Blagdens Cl. N14 2C 32
Blagdens La. N14 2B 32
Blagdon Ct. W7 7J 77
Blagdon Rd. KT3: N Mald 4B 152
SE13 6D 122
Blagdon Wlk. TW11: Tedd 6C 132
Blagrove Cres. HA4: Eastc 6K 39
Blagrove Rd. TW11: Hamp W 7B 132
W10 5G 81
Blair Av. NW9 7A 44
Blair Cl. DA15: Sidc 5J 125
N1 6C 66
UB3: Harl 4J 93
Blair Ct. BR3: Beck 1D 158
NW8 1B 82
SE6 1H 141
Blairderry Rd. SW2 2J 137
Blairgowrie Ct. *E14* *6F 87*
(off Blair St.)
Blair Ho. SW9 2K 119
Blair St. E14 6E 86
Blake Av. IG11: Bark 1J 89
Blake Bldg. N8 3K 47
Blake Cl. DA16: Well 1J 125
SM5: Cars 1C 166
UB4: Hayes 2F 75
W10 5E 80
Blake Ct. N21 5E 22
NW6 *3J 81*
(off Malvern Rd.)
SE16 *5H 103*
(off Stubbs Dr.)
Blakeden Dr. KT10: Clay 6A 162
Blake Gdns. SW6 1K 117
Blake Hall Cres. E11 1J 69
Blake Hall Rd. E11 7J 51
Blakehall Rd. SM5: Cars 6D 166
Blake Ho. *E14* *2C 104*
(off Admirals Way)
SE1 1J 19 (3A 102)
SE8 *6C 104*
(off New King St.)
Blake M. TW9: Kew 1G 115
Blakemore Gdns. SW13 6D 98
Blakemore Rd. CR7: Thor H 5K 155
SW16 3J 137
Blakemore Way DA17: Belv 3E 108
Blakeney Av. BR3: Beck 1B 158
Blakeney Cl. E8 5G 67
N20 1F 31
NW1 7H 65
Blakeney Rd. BR3: Beck 7B 140
Blakenham Rd. SW17 4D 136
Blaker Ct. SE7 7A 106
(not continuous)
Blake Rd. CR0: C'don 2E 168
CR4: Mitc 3C 154
E16 4H 87
N11 7B 32
Blaker Rd. E15 2E 86
Blakes Av. KT3: N Mald 5B 152
Blake's Grn. BR4: W W'ck 1E 170
Blakes La. KT3: N Mald 5B 152
Blakesley Av. W5 6C 78
Blakesley Ho. *E12* *3E 70*
(off Grantham Rd.)
Blakesley Wlk. SW20 2H 153
Blake's Rd. SE15 7E 102
Blakes Ter. KT3: N Mald 5C 152
Blakesware Gdns. N9 7J 23
Blakewood Cl. TW13: Hanw 4A 130
Blakewood Ct. *SE20* *7H 139*
(off Anerley Pk.)
Blanchard Cl. SE9 3C 142
Blanchard Ho. *TW1: Twick* *6D 114*
(off Clevedon Rd.)
Blanchard Way E8 6G 67
Blanch Cl. SE15 7J 103
Blanchedowne SE5 4D 120
Blanche St. E16 4H 87
Blanchland Rd. SM4: Mord 5K 153
Blandfield Rd. SW12 7E 118
Blandford Av. BR3: Beck 2A 158
TW2: Whitt 1F 131
Blandford Cl. CR0: Bedd 3J 167
N2 4A 46
RM7: Mawney 4H 55
Blandford Ct. *N1* *7E 66*
(off St Peter's Way)
NW6 7F 63
Blandford Cres. E4 7K 25
Blandford Ho. *SW8* *7K 101*
(off Richborne Ter.)
Blandford Rd. BR3: Beck 2J 157
TW11: Tedd 5H 131
UB2: S'hall 4E 94
W4 3A 98
W5 2D 96
Blandford Sq. NW1 4D 4 (4C 82)
Blandford St. W1 7F 5 (6D 82)
Blandford Waye UB4: Yead 6A 76
Bland Ho. SE11 5H 19
Bland St. SE9 4B 124
Blaney Cres. E6 3F 89
Blanmerle Rd. SE9 1F 143
Blann Cl. SE9 6B 124
Blantyre St. SW10 7B 100
Blantyre Twr. *SW10* *7B 100*
(off Blantyre St.)
Blantyre Wlk. *SW10* *7B 100*
(off Worlds End Est.)
Blashford *NW3* *7D 64*
(off Adelaide Rd.)
Blashford St. SE13 7F 123
Blasker Wlk. E14 5D 104
Blaven Path E16 4H 87
Blawith Rd. HA1: Harr 4J 41
Blaxland Ho. *W12* *7D 80*
(off White City Est.)
Blaydon Cl. HA4: Ruis 7G 39
N17 7C 34
Blaydon Ct. UB5: N'olt 6E 58
Blaydon Wlk. N17 7C 34
Blazer Ct. NW8 2B 4
Bleak Hill La. SE18 6K 107
Bleak Ho. La. *W4* *5K 97*
(off Chiswick High Rd.)
Blean Gro. SE20 7J 139
Bleasdale Av. UB6: G'frd 2A 78
Blechynden Ho. *W10* *6F 81*
(off Kingsdown Cl.)
Blechynden St. W10 7F 81
Bledlow Cl. NW8 4B 4 (4B 82)
SE28 7C 90
Bledlow Ri. UB6: G'frd 2G 77
Bleeding Heart Yd. EC1 6K 7
Blegborough Rd. SW16 6G 137
Blemundsbury *WC1* *5G 7*
(off Dombey St.)
BLENDON 6D 126
Blendon Dr. DA5: Bexl 6D 126
Blendon Path BR1: Brom 7H 141
Blendon Rd. DA5: Bexl 6D 126
Blendon Row *SE17* *4D 102*
(off Orb St.)
Blendon Ter. SE18 5G 107
Blendworth Point SW15 1D 134
Blenheim Av. IG2: Ilf 6E 52
Blenheim Bus. Cen. *CR4: Mitc* *2D 154*
(off London Rd.)
Blenheim Centre, The
TW3: Houn 3F 113
Blenheim Cl. N21 1H 33
RM7: Mawney 4J 55
SE12 1K 141
SM6: Wall 7G 167
SW20 3E 152
UB6: G'frd 2H 77
Blenheim Ct.
BR2: Brom 4H 159
DA14: Sidc 3H 143
HA3: Kenton 6A 42
IG8: Wfd G 7E 36
N7 6J 65
N19 2J 65
RM13: Rain *2K 91*
(off Lowen Rd.)
SE10 *5J 105*
(off Denham St.)
SE16 *1K 103*
(off King & Queen Wharf)
SM2: Sutt 6A 166
Blenheim Cres. CR2: S Croy 7C 168
HA4: Ruis 2F 57
W11 7G 81
Blenheim Dr. DA16: Well 1K 125
Blenheim Gdns. HA9: Wemb 3E 60
KT2: King T 7H 133
NW2 6E 62
SM6: Wall 6G 167
SW2 6K 119
Blenheim Gro. SE15 2G 121
Blenheim Ho. *E16* *1K 105*
(off Constable Av.)
SE18 3G 107
SW3 *6D 16*
(off Kings Rd.)
TW3: Houn 3E 112
Blenheim Pde. UB10: Hil 4D 74
Blenheim Pk. Rd. CR2: S Croy 7C 168
Blenheim Pas. NW8 2A 82
Blenheim Pl. TW11: Tedd 5K 131
Blenheim Ri. N15 4F 49
Blenheim Rd. BR1: Brom 4C 160
DA15: Sidc 1C 144
E6 3B 88
E15 4G 69
E17 3K 49
EN5: Barn 3A 20
HA2: Harr 6F 41
NW8 2A 82
SE20 7J 139
SM1: Sutt 3J 165
SW20 3E 152
UB5: N'olt 6F 59
W4 3A 98
Blenheim Shop. Cen. SE20 7J 139
Blenheim St. W1 1J 11 (6F 83)
Blenheim Ter. NW8 2A 82
Blenheim Twr. *SE14* *7A 104*
(off Batavia Rd.)
Blenheim Way TW7: Isle 1A 114
Blenkarne Rd. SW11 6D 118
Bleriot Rd. TW5: Hest 7A 94
Blessbury Rd. HA8: Edg 1J 43
Blessington Cl. SE13 3F 123
Blessington Rd. SE13 3F 123
Blessing Way IG11: Bark 3C 90
Bletchingley Cl. CR7: Thor H 4B 156
Bletchley Ct. *HA7: Stan* *7K 27*
(off Hitchin Way)
N1 1E 8
Bletchley St. N1 1D 8 (2D 84)
Bletchmore Cl. UB3: Harl 5F 93
Bletsoe Wlk. N1 2C 84
Blewbury Ho. SE2 2C 108
(not continuous)
Blick Ho. *SE16* *3J 103*
(off Neptune St.)
Blincoe Cl. SW19 2F 135
Bliss Cres. SE13 2D 122
Blissett St. SE10 1E 122
Bliss Ho. EN1: Enf 1B 24
Bliss M. W10 3G 81
Blisworth Cl. UB4: Yead 4C 76
Blisworth Ho. *E2* *1G 85*
(off Whiston Rd.)
Blithbury Rd. RM9: Dag 6B 72
Blithdale Rd. SE2 4A 108
Blithehale Ct. *E2* *3H 85*
(off Withan St.)
Blithfield St. W8 3K 99
Blockley Rd. HA0: Wemb 2B 60
Block Wharf *E14* *2C 104*
(off Cuba St.)
Bloemfontein Av. W12 1D 98
Bloemfontein Rd. W12 7D 80
Bloemfontein Way W12 1D 98
Blomfield Ct. *W9* *3A 4*
(off Maida Vale)
Blomfield Mans. *W12* *1E 98*
(off Stanlake Rd.)
Blomfield Rd. W9 4A 4 (5K 81)

202 A-Z London

Blomfield St. EC2 . . . . . . .6F **9** (5D **84**)
Blomfield Vs. W2 . . . . .5K **81**
Blomville Rd. RM8: Dag 3E **72**
Blondell Cl. UB7: Harm 2E **174**
Blondel St. SW11 . . . . .2E **118**
Blondin Av. W5 . . . . .4C **96**
Blondin Park & Nature Area 4B **96**
Blondin St. E3 . . . . .2C **86**
Bloomberg Arc. EC4 . . . . .1E **14**
(off Queen Victoria St.)
Bloomberg Ct. SW1 . . . . .4C **18**
(off Vauxhall Bri. Rd.)
Bloomburg St. SW1 . . . .4B **18** (4H **101**)
Bloomfield Ct. E10 . . . . .3D **68**
(off Brisbane Rd.)
N6 . . . . .6E **46**
Bloomfield Cres. IG2: Ilf 6F **53**
Bloomfield Ho. E1 . . . . .5G **85**
(off Old Montague St.)
Bloomfield Pl. W1 . . . . .2K **11**
Bloomfield Rd. BR2: Brom 5B **160**
KT1: King T 4E **150**
N6 . . . . .6E **46**
SE18 . . . . .6F **107**
Bloomfield Ter. SW1 . . . . .5H **17** (5E **100**)
Bloom Gro. SE27 . . . . .3B **138**
Bloomhall Rd. SE19 . . . . .5D **138**
Bloom Pk. Rd. SW6 . . . . .7H **99**
BLOOMSBURY 5E **6** (5J **83**)
Bloomsbury Cl. NW7 . . . . .7H **29**
W5 . . . . .7F **79**
Bloomsbury Ct. HA5: Pinn 3D **40**
TW5: Cran 1K **111**
WC1 . . . . .6F **7**
Bloomsbury Ho. SW4 . . . . .6H **119**
Bloomsbury Mans. BR1: Brom 1K **159**
(off Widmore Rd.)
Bloomsbury M. IG8: Wfd G 6H **37**
Bloomsbury Pl. SW18 . . . . .5A **118**
WC1 . . . . .5F **7** (5J **83**)
Bloomsbury Sq. WC1 . . . . . .6F **7** (5J **83**)
Bloomsbury St. WC1 . . . . .6D **6** (5H **83**)
Bloomsbury Theatre 3C **6**
Bloomsbury Way WC1 . . . . .6E **6** (5J **83**)
Blore Cl. SW8 . . . . .1H **119**
Blore Ct. W1 . . . . .1C **12**
Blore Ho. SW10 . . . . .7K **99**
(off Coleridge Gdns.)
Blossom Av. HA2: Harr 2F **59**
Blossom Cl. CR2: S Croy 5F **169**
RM9: Dag 1F **91**
W5 . . . . .2E **96**
Blossom Dr. BR6: Orp 2K **173**
Blossom La. EN2: Enf 1H **23**
Blossom Pl. SE28 . . . . .3G **107**
Blossom St. E1 . . . . .4H **9** (4E **84**)
Blossom Way UB7: W Dray 4C **92**
UB10: Hil 7B **56**
Blossom Waye TW5: Hest 6C **94**
Blount St. E14 . . . . .6A **86**
Bloxam Gdns. SE9 . . . . .5C **124**
Bloxhall Rd. E10 . . . . .1B **68**
Bloxham Cres. TW12: Hamp 7D **130**
Bloxworth Cl. SM6: Wall 3G **167**
Blucher Rd. SE5 . . . . .7C **102**
Blue Anchor All. TW9: Rich 4E **114**
Blue Anchor La. SE16 . . . . .4G **103**
Blue Anchor Yd. E1 . . . . . .2K **15** (7G **85**)
Blue Ball Yd. SW1 . . . . .5A **12** (1G **101**)
Bluebell Av. E12 . . . . .5B **70**
Bluebell Cl. BR6: Farnb 2G **173**
E9 . . . . .1J **85**
RM7: Rush G 2K **73**
SE26 . . . . .4F **139**
SM6: Wall 1F **167**
UB5: N'olt 6D **58**
Bluebell Cl. NW9 . . . . .1A **44**
(off Heybourne Cres.)
Bluebell Way IG1: Ilf 6F **71**
Blueberry Cl. IG8: Wfd G 6D **36**
Bluebird Ho. IG11: Bark 3K **89**

Bluebird La. RM10: Dag 7G **73**
Bluebird Way SE28 . . . . .2H **107**
Blue Bldg. SE10 . . . . .5H **105**
(off Glenforth St.)
Blue Ct. N1 . . . . .1D **84**
(off Sherborne St.)
Blue Elephant Theatre 7C **102**
(off Bethwin Rd.)
Bluefield Cl. TW12: Hamp 5E **130**
Blue Fin Bldg. SE1 . . . . .4B **14**
Bluegate M. E1 . . . . .7H **85**
Bluegates KT17: Ewe 7C **164**
Bluehouse Rd. E4 . . . . .2B **36**
Blue Lion Pl. SE1 . . . . . .7G **15** (3E **102**)
Blueprint Apartments SW12 . . . . . .7F **119**
(off Balham Gro.)
Blue Riband Ind. Est. CR0: C'don . . .2B **168**
Blues St. E8 . . . . .6F **67**
Blue Water SW18 . . . . .4K **117**
Blumenthal Cl. TW7: Isle 7H **95**
Blundell Cl. E8 . . . . .5G **67**
Blundell Rd. HA8: Edg 1K **43**
Blundell St. N7 . . . . .7J **65**
Blunden Cl. RM8: Dag 1C **72**
Blunden Ct. SW6 . . . . .7J **99**
(off Farm La.)
Blunt Rd. CR2: S Croy 5D **168**
Blunts Av. UB7: Sip 7C **92**
Blunts Rd. SE9 . . . . .5E **124**
Blurton Rd. E5 . . . . .4J **67**
Blydon Ct. N21 . . . . .5E **22**
(off Chaseville Pk. Rd.)
Blythe Cl. E14 . . . . .4F **105**
TW1: Twick 6K **113**
Blythe Ct. BR1: Brom 1H **159**
(off Blyth Rd.)
Blythe Cl. SE6 . . . . .7B **122**
BLYTHE HILL 7B **122**
Blythe Hill BR5: St P 1K **161**
SE6 .7B **122**
Blythe Hill La. SE6 . . . . .7B **122**
Blythe Hill Pl. SE23 . . . . .7A **122**
Blythe Ho. SE11 . . . . . . .7J **19** (6A **102**)
Blythe M. W14 . . . . .3F **99**
Blythendale Ho. E2 . . . . .2G **85**
(off Mansford St.)
Blythe Rd. W14 . . . . .3F **99**
Blythe St. E2 . . . . .3H **85**
Blytheswood Pl. SW16 . . . . .4K **137**
Blythe Va. SE6 . . . . .1B **140**
Blyth Hill Pl. SE23 . . . . .7A **122**
(off Brockley Pk.)
Blyth Ho. DA8: Erith 5K **109**
Blyth Rd. BR1: Brom 1H **159**
E17 .7B **50**
SE28 . . . . .7C **90**
UB3: Hayes 2G **93**
Blyth's Wharf E14 . . . . .7A **86**
Blythswood Rd. IG3: Ilf 1A **72**
Blyth Wood Pk. BR1: Brom 1H **159**
Blythwood Rd. HA5: Pinn 1B **40**
N4 . . . . .7J **47**
Boades M. NW3 . . . . .4B **64**
Boadicea St. N1 . . . . .1K **83**
Boakes Cl. NW9 . . . . .4J **43**
Boardman Av. E4 . . . . .5J **25**
Boardman Cl. EN5: Barn 5B **20**
Boardwalk Pl. E14 . . . . .1E **104**
Boarley Ho. SE17 . . . . .4E **102**
(off Massinger St.)
Boars Head Yd. TW8: Bford 7D **96**
Boatemah Wlk. SW9 . . . . .2A **120**
(off Peckford Pl.)
Boathouse, The E14 . . . . .6C **86**
Boathouse Centre, The W10 . . . . .4F **81**
(off Canal Cl.)
Boathouse Wlk. SE15 . . . . .7F **103**
(not continuous)
Boat Lifter Way SE16 . . . . .4A **104**
Boat Quay E16 . . . . .7A **88**
Boatyard Apartments E14 . . . . . . .5D **104**

Bob Anker Cl. E13 . . . . .3J **87**
Bobbin Cl. SW4 . . . . .3G **119**
Bobby Moore Way N10 . . . . .7J **31**
Bob Hope Theatre, The 6D **124**
Bob Marley Way SE24 . . . . .4A **120**
Bockhampton Rd. KT2: King T 7F **133**
Bocking St. E8 . . . . .1H **85**
Boddicott Cl. SW19 . . . . .2G **135**
Boddington Gdns. W3 . . . . .2G **97**
Boddington Ho. SE14 . . . . .1J **121**
(off Pomeroy St.)
SW13 . . . . .6D **98**
(off Wyatt Dr.)
Bodeney Ho. SE5 . . . . .1E **120**
(off Peckham Rd.)
Boden Ho. E1 . . . . .5K **9**
(off Woodseer St.)
Bodiam Cl. EN1: Enf 2K **23**
Bodiam Rd. SW16 . . . . .7H **137**
Bodiam Way NW10 . . . . .3F **79**
Bodicea M. TW4: Houn 6D **112**
Bodington Cl. W12 . . . . .2F **99**
Bodium Ct. E17 . . . . .1B **50**
(off Thornbury Way)
Bodleian Ho. SE20 . . . . .1G **157**
Bodley Cl. KT3: N Mald 5A **152**
Bodley Mnr. Way SW2 . . . . .7A **120**
Bodley Rd. KT3: N Mald 6K **151**
Bodmin Cl. HA2: Harr 3D **58**
Bodmin Gro. SM4: Mord 5K **153**
Bodmin St. SW18 . . . . .1J **135**
Bodnant Gdns. SW20 . . . . .3C **152**
Bodney Rd. E8 . . . . .5H **67**
Boeing Way UB2: S'hall 3K **93**
Boevey Path DA17: Belv 5F **109**
Bogart Ct. E14 . . . . .7C **86**
(off Premiere Pl.)
Bogey La. BR6: Downe 7E **172**
Bognor Rd. DA16: Well 1D **126**
Bohemia Pl. E8 . . . . .6J **67**
Bohn Rd. E1 . . . . .5A **86**
Bohun Gro. EN4: E Barn 6H **21**
Boileau Pde. W5 . . . . .6F **79**
(off Boileau Rd.)
Boileau Rd. SW13 . . . . .7C **98**
W5 . . . . .6F **79**
Boisseau Ho. E1 . . . . .5J **85**
(off Stepney Way)
Bolanachi Bldg. SE16 . . . . .3F **103**
Bolander Gro. Nth. SW6 . . . . .6J **99**
(off Seagrave Rd.)
Bolander Gro. Sth. SW6 . . . . .6J **99**
(off Seagrave Rd.)
Bolden St. SE8 . . . . .2D **122**
Boldero Pl. NW8 . . . . .4C **4**
Bolderwood Way BR4: W W'ck 2D **170**
Boldmere Rd. HA5: Eastc 7A **40**
Boleyn Av. EN1: Enf 1C **24**
Boleyn Cl. E17 . . . . .4C **50**
IG9: Buck H 1D **36**
KT8: E Mos 4H **149**
(off Bridge Rd.)
Boleyn Dr. HA4: Ruis 2B **58**
KT8: W Mole 3D **148**
Boleyn Gdns. BR4: W W'ck 2D **170**
RM10: Dag 7J **73**
Boleyn Ground / Upton Park 2A **88**
Boleyn Gro. BR4: W W'ck 2E **170**
Boleyn Ho. E16 . . . . .1J **105**
(off Southey M.)
Boleyn Rd. E6 . . . . .2B **88**
E7 . . . . .7J **69**
N16 .5E **66**
Boleyn Way EN5: New Bar 3F **21**
Bolina Rd. SE16 . . . . .5J **103**
Bolingbroke Cl. EN4: Cockf 3J **21**
Bolingbroke Gro. SW11 . . . . .4C **118**
Bolingbroke Rd. W14 . . . . .3F **99**
Bolingbroke Wlk. SW11 . . . . .1B **118**
Bolingbroke Way UB3: Hayes 1F **93**
Bolliger Ct. NW10 . . . . .4J **79**

Bollo Bri. Rd. W3 . . . . .3H **97**
Bollo La. W3 . . . . .2H **97**
W4 . . . . .4J **97**
Bolney Ga. SW7 . . . . . . .7C **10** (2C **100**)
Bolney St. SW8 . . . . .7K **101**
Bolney Way TW13: Hanw 3C **130**
Bolsover St. W1 . . . . .4K **5** (4F **83**)
Bolstead Rd. CR4: Mitc 1F **155**
Bolster Gro. N22 . . . . .7C **32**
Bolt Ct. EC4 . . . . .6A **84**
Bolt Ho. N1 . . . . .1E **84**
(off Phillipp St.)
Boltmore Cl. NW4 . . . . .3F **45**
Bolton Cl. KT9: Chess 6D **162**
SE20 . . . . .2G **157**
Bolton Cres. SE5 . . . . .7B **102**
Bolton Dr. SM4: Mord 7A **154**
Bolton Gdns. BR1: Brom 6H **141**
NW10 . . . . .2F **81**
SW5 .5K **99**
TW11: Tedd 6A **132**
Bolton Gdns. M. SW10 . . . . .5A **100**
Bolton Ho. SE10 . . . . .5G **105**
(off Trafalgar Rd.)
SE11 . . . . .4B **102**
(off George Mathers Rd.)
Bolton Pl. NW8 . . . . .1K **81**
(off Bolton Rd.)
Bolton Rd. E15 . . . . .6H **69**
HA1: Harr 4G **41**
KT9: Chess 6D **162**
N18 .5A **34**
NW8 .1K **81**
NW10 . . . . .1A **80**
W4 . . . . .7J **97**
Boltons, The HA0: Wemb 4K **59**
IG8: Wfd G 4D **36**
SW10 . . . . .5A **100**
Boltons Ct. SW5 . . . . .5K **99**
(off Old Brompton Rd.)
Bolton St. W1 . . . . .4K **11** (1F **101**)
Bolton Studios SW10 . . . . .5A **100**
Bolton Wlk. N7 . . . . .2K **65**
(off Durham Rd.)
Bombay Ct. SE16 . . . . .2J **103**
(off St Marychurch St.)
Bombay St. SE16 . . . . .4H **103**
Bomer Cl. UB7: Sip 7C **92**
Bomore Rd. W11 . . . . .7G **81**
Bonar Pl. BR7: Chst 7C **142**
Bonar Rd. SE15 . . . . .7G **103**
Bonchester Cl. BR7: Chst 7E **142**
Bonchurch Cl. SM2: Sutt 7K **165**
Bonchurch Rd. W10 . . . . .5G **81**
W13 .1B **96**
Bond Cl. UB7: Yiew 6B **74**
Bondfield Av. UB4: Yead 3J **75**
Bondfield Rd. E6 . . . . .5D **88**
Bond Gdns. SM6: Wall 4G **167**
Bond Ho. NW6 . . . . .2H **81**
(off Rupert Rd.)
SE14 . . . . .7A **104**
(off Goodwood Rd.)
Bonding Yd. Wlk. SE16 . . . . .3A **104**
Bond Rd. CR4: Mitc 2C **154**
KT6: Surb 2F **163**
Bond St. E15 . . . . .5G **69**
W4 . . . . .4K **97**
W5 . . . . .7D **78**
Bondway SW8 . . . . .7F **19** (6J **101**)
Bonesgate Open Space
Local Nature Reserve 6G **163**
Boneta Rd. SE18 . . . . .3D **106**
Bonfield Rd. SE13 . . . . .4E **122**
Bonham Cl. DA17: Belv 5F **109**
Bonham Gdns. RM8: Dag 2D **72**
Bonham Ga. KT12: Walt T 7H **147**
(off New Zealand Av.)

Bonham Ho. W11 ....1H 99
Bonham Rd. RM8: Dag 2D 72
SW2 ....5K 119
Bonheur Rd. W4 ....2K 97
Bonhill St. EC2 ....4F 9 (4D 84)
Boniface Gdns. HA3: Hrw W 7A 26
Boniface Rd. UB10: Ick 3D 56
Boniface Wlk. HA3: Hrw W 7A 26
Bonington Ho. EN1: Enf 5B 24
Bonita M. SE4 ....3K 121
Bon Marche Ter. M. SE27 ....4E 138
(off Gypsy Rd.)
Bonner Hill Rd. KT1: King T 2F 151
Bonner Rd. E2 ....2J 85
Bonnersfield Cl. HA1: Harr 6K 41
Bonnersfield La. HA1: Harr 6K 41
(not continuous)
Bonner St. E2 ....2J 85
Bonneville Gdns. SW4 ....6G 119
Bonnington Ct. UB5: N'olt 2B 76
(off Gallery Gdns.)
Bonnington Ho. N1 ....2K 83
Bonnington Sq. SW8 ....7G 19 (6K 101)
Bonny St. NW1 ....7G 65
Bonser Rd. TW1: Twick 2K 131
Bonsor Ho. SW8 ....1G 119
Bonsor St. SE5 ....7E 102
Bonville Gdns. NW4 ....4D 44
Bonville Rd. BR1: Brom 5H 141
Bookbinders Cott. Homes N20 ....3J 31
Bookbinders Ct. E1 ....4H 85
(off Cudworth St.)
Booker Cl. E14 ....5B 86
Booker Rd. N18 ....5B 34
Bookham Ct. CR4: Mitc 3B 154
Boone Cl. N9 ....3D 34
Boones Rd. SE13 ....4G 123
Boord St. SE10 ....3G 105
Boothby Cl. E4 ....3K 35
Boothby Rd. N19 ....2H 65
Booth Cl. E9 ....1H 85
SE28 ....1B 108
Booth Ct. SE13 ....3D 122
Booth Dr. TW18: Staines 6A 128
Booth Ho. TW8: Bford 7C 96
(off High St.)
Booth La. EC4 ....2C 14
Boothman Ho. HA3: Kenton 3D 42
Booth Rd. CR0: C'don 2B 168
E16 ....2A 106
NW9 ....2K 43
Booth's Pl. W1 ....6B 6 (5G 83)
Boot Pde. HA8: Edg 6B 28
(off High St.)
Boot St. N1 ....2G 9 (3E 84)
Bordars Rd. W7 ....5J 77
Bordars Wlk. W7 ....5J 77
Bordeaux Ho. E15 ....5G 69
(off Luxembourg M.)
Borden Av. EN1: Enf 6J 23
Border Cres. SE26 ....5H 139
Border Gdns. CR0: C'don 4D 170
Bordergate CR4: Mitc 1D 154
Border Rd. SE26 ....5H 139
Bordesley Rd. SM4: Mord 5K 153
Bordeston Ct. TW8: Bford 7C 96
(off The Ham)
Bordon Wlk. SW15 ....7C 116
Boreas Wlk. N1 ....1B 8
Boreham Av. E16 ....6J 87
Boreham Cl. E11 ....1E 68
Boreham Rd. N22 ....2C 48
Boreman Ho. SE10 ....6E 104
(off Thames St.)
Borgard Rd. SE18 ....4D 106
Borkwood Pk. BR6: Orp 4K 173
Borkwood Way BR6: Orp 4J 173
Borland Rd. SE15 ....4J 121
TW11: Tedd 7B 132

Borley Ct. TW19: Stanw 1A 128
Borneo St. SW15 ....3E 116
BOROUGH, THE 7D 14 (2D 102)
Borough High St. SE1 ....7D 14 (2C 102)
Borough Hill CR0: Wadd 3B 168
Borough Mkt. SE1 ....5E 14
Borough Rd. CR4: Mitc 2C 154
KT2: King T 1G 151
SE1 ....7B 14 (3B 102)
TW7: Isle 1J 113
Borough Sports Ground 4J 165
Borough Sq. SE1 ....7C 14
Borrett Cl. SE17 ....5C 102
Borrodaile Rd. SW18 ....6K 117
Borrowdale NW1 ....2A 6
(off Robert St.)
Borrowdale Av. HA3: W'stone 2A 42
Borrowdale Cl. IG4: Ilf 4C 52
N2 ....2A 46
Borrowdale Ct. EN2: Enf 1H 23
Borthwick M. E15 ....4G 69
Borthwick Rd. E15 ....4G 69
NW9 ....6B 44
Borthwick St. SE8 ....5C 104
Borwick Av. E17 ....3B 50
Bosanquet Cl. UB8: Cowl 4A 74
Bosbury Rd. SE6 ....3E 140
Boscastle Rd. NW5 ....3F 65
Boscobel Cl. BR1: Brom 2D 160
Boscobel Ho. E8 ....6H 67
Boscobel Pl. SW1 ....3H 17 (4E 100)
Boscobel St. NW8 ....4B 4 (4B 82)
Bosco Cl. BR6: Orp 4K 173
Boscombe Av. E10 ....7F 51
Boscombe Cir. NW9 ....1K 43
Boscombe Cl. E5 ....5A 68
Boscombe Gdns. SW16 ....6J 137
Boscombe Ho. CR0: C'don 1D 168
(off Sydenham Rd.)
Boscombe Rd. KT4: Wor Pk 1E 164
SW17 ....6E 136
SW19 ....1K 153
W12 ....1C 98
Bose Cl. N3 ....1G 45
Bosgrove E4 ....2K 35
Boss Ho. SE1 ....6J 15
(off Boss St.)
Boss St. SE1 ....6J 15 (2F 103)
Bostall Hill SE2 ....5A 108
Bostall La. SE2 ....4B 108
Bostall Mnr. Way SE2 ....4B 108
Bostall Pk. Av. DA7: Bex 7E 108
Bostall Rd. BR5: St P 7B 144
Boston Bus. Pk. W7 ....3J 95
Boston Ct. SE25 ....4F 157
SM2: Sutt 7A 166
Boston Gdns.
TW8: Bford 4A 96
W4 ....6A 98
W7 ....3J 95
Boston Gro. HA4: Ruis 6E 38
Boston Ho. SW5 ....4K 99
(off Collingham Rd.)
BOSTON MANOR 4A 96
Boston Manor House 5B 96
Boston Mnr. Rd.
TW8: Bford 4B 96
Boston Pde. W7 ....3A 96
Boston Pk. Rd.
TW8: Bford 5C 96
Boston Pl. NW1 ....4E 4 (4D 82)
Boston Rd.
CR0: C'don 6K 155
E6 ....3C 88
E17 ....6C 50
HA8: Edg 7D 28
W7 ....1J 95
Bostonthorpe Rd. W7 ....2J 95
Boston Va. W7 ....4A 96
Bosun Cl. E14 ....2C 104

Boswell Ct. KT2: King T 1F 151
(off Clifton Rd.)
W14 ....3F 99
(off Blythe Rd.)
WC1 ....5F 7 (5J 83)
Boswell Ho. WC1 ....5F 7
(off Boswell St.)
Boswell Path UB3: Harl 4H 93
Boswell Rd. CR7: Thor H 4C 156
Boswell St. WC1 ....5F 7 (5J 83)
Bosworth Cl. E17 ....1B 50
Bosworth Ho. W10 ....4G 81
(off Bosworth Rd.)
Bosworth Rd. EN5: New Bar 3D 20
N11 ....6C 32
RM10: Dag 3G 73
W10 ....4G 81
Botany Bay La. BR7: Chst 3G 161
Botany Cl. EN4: E Barn 4H 21
Boteley Cl. E4 ....2A 36
Botham Cl. HA8: Edg 7D 28
Botha Rd. E13 ....5K 87
Bothwell Cl. E16 ....5H 87
Bothwell St. W6 ....6F 99
Botolph All. EC3 ....2G 15
Botolph La. EC3 ....3G 15 (7E 84)
Botsford Rd. SW20 ....2G 153
Botts M. W2 ....6J 81
Botwell Comn. Rd. UB3: Hayes 7F 75
Botwell Cres. UB3: Hayes 6G 75
Botwell Green Sports & Leisure Cen. 1H 93
Botwell La. UB3: Hayes 7G 75
Boucher Cl. TW11: Tedd 5K 131
Bouchier Ho. N2 ....2B 46
(off The Grange)
Boughton Av. BR2: Hayes 7H 159
Boughton Ho. SE1 ....6E 14
(off Tennis St.)
Boughton Rd. SE28 ....3J 107
Boulcott St. E1 ....6K 85
Boulevard, The IG8: Wfd G 6K 37
SW6 ....1A 118
SW17 ....2E 136
SW18 ....4K 117
Boulevard Dr. NW9 ....2B 44
Boulevard Walkway E1 ....1K 15
(off Piazza Wlk.)
Boulogne Cl. SE1 ....7J 15
(off St Saviour's Est.)
Boulogne Rd. CR0: C'don 6C 156
Boulter Cl. BR1: Brom 3E 160
Boulter Ho. SE14 ....1J 121
(off Kender St.)
Boulton Ho. TW8: Bford 5E 96
Boulton Rd. RM8: Dag 2E 72
Boultwood Rd. E6 ....6D 88
Bounces La. N9 ....2C 34
Bounces Rd. N9 ....2C 34
Boundaries Rd. SW12 ....2D 136
TW13: Felt 1A 130
Boundary Av. E17 ....7B 50
Boundary Bus. Ct. CR4: Mitc 3B 154
Boundary Cl. EN5: Barn 1C 20
IG3: Ilf 4J 71
KT1: King T 3H 151
SE20 ....2G 157
UB2: S'hall 5E 94
Boundary Ct. N18 ....6A 34
(off Snells Pk.)
Boundary Ho. SE5 ....7C 102
W11 ....1F 99
(off Queensdale Cres.)
Boundary La. E13 ....3B 88
SE17 ....6C 102
Boundary Pas. E2 ....3J 9 (4F 85)
Boundary Rd. DA15: Sidc 5J 125
E13 ....2A 88
E17 ....7B 50
HA5: Eastc 7B 40

Boundary Rd. HA9: Wemb 3E 60
IG11: Bark 1H 89
(King Edwards Rd.)
IG11: Bark 2G 89
(The Clarksons)
N2 ....1B 46
N9 ....6D 24
N22 ....3B 48
NW8 ....1K 81
SM5: Cars 6F 167
SM6: Wall 6F 167
SW19 ....6B 136
Boundary Row SE1 ....6A 14 (2B 102)
Boundary St. E2 ....2J 9 (3F 85)
Boundary Way CR0: Addtn 5C 170
Boundfield Rd. SE6 ....3G 141
BOUNDS GREEN 6C 32
Bounds Grn. Ct. N11 ....6C 32
(off Bounds Grn. Rd.)
Bounds Grn. Ind. Est. N11 ....6B 32
Bounds Grn. Rd. N11 ....6B 32
N22 ....6B 32
Bourbon Ho. SE6 ....5E 140
Bourdon La. W12 ....1F 99
Bourdon Rd. SW9 ....1A 120
Bourchier St. W1 ....2C 12 (7H 83)
Bourdon Pl. W1 ....2K 11
Bourdon Rd. SE20 ....2J 157
Bourdon St. W1 ....3J 11 (7F 83)
Bourke Cl. NW10 ....4A 62
SW4 ....6J 119
Bourlet Cl. W1 ....6A 6 (5G 83)
Bourn Av. EN4: E Barn 5G 21
N15 ....4D 48
UB8: Hil 4C 74
Bournbrook Rd. SE3 ....3B 124
Bourne, The N14 ....1C 32
Bourne Av. HA4: Ruis 5A 58
N14 ....2D 32
UB3: Harl 3E 92
Bournebrook Gro. RM7: Rush G 6K 55
Bourne Cir. UB3: Harl 3E 92
Bourne Cl. TW7: Isle 3J 113
Bourne Ct. HA4: Ruis 5K 57
IG8: Wfd G 3B 52
W4 ....6J 97
Bourne Dr. CR4: Mitc 2B 154
Bourne Est. EC1 ....5J 7 (5A 84)
Bourne Gdns. E4 ....4J 35
Bourne Hall Mus. 7B 164
Bourne Hill N13 ....2D 32
Bourne Hill Cl. N13 ....2E 32
Bourne Ho. IG9: Buck H 3G 37
TW15: Ashf 5C 128
Bourne Ind. Pk. DA1: Cray 5K 127
Bourne Mead DA5: Bexl 5K 127
Bournemead Av. UB5: N'olt 2J 75
Bournemead Cl. UB5: N'olt 3J 75
Bournemead Way UB5: N'olt 2K 75
Bournemouth Cl. SE15 ....2G 121
Bournemouth Rd. SE15 ....2G 121
SW19 ....1J 153
Bourne Pde. DA5: Bexl 7H 127
Bourne Pl. W4 ....5A 98
Bourne Rd. BR2: Brom 4B 160
DA1: Cray 6J 127
DA5: Bexl, Dart 7H 127
E7 ....3H 69
N8 ....6J 47
Bournes Ho. N15 ....6E 48
(off Chisley Rd.)
Bourneside Cres. N14 ....1C 32
Bourneside Gdns. SE6 ....5E 140
Bourne St. CR0: C'don 2B 168
SW1 ....4G 17 (4E 100)
Bourne Ter. W2 ....5K 81
Bourne Va. BR2: Hayes 1H 171
Bournevale Rd. SW16 ....4J 137
Bourne Vw. UB6: G'frd 6K 59
Bourneville Rd. SE6 ....7C 122

Bourne Way BR2: Hayes 2H **171**
  KT19: Ewe 4J **163**
  SM1: Sutt 5H **165**
Bournewood Rd. SE18 ....7A **108**
Bournwell Cl. EN4: Cockf 3J **21**
Bourton Cl. UB3: Hayes 1J **93**
Bousfield Rd. SE14 ....2K **121**
Boutflower Rd. SW11 ....4C **118**
Boutique Hall SE13 ....4E **122**
Bouton Pl. N1 ....7B **66**
  (off Waterloo Ter.)
Bouverie Gdns. HA3: Kenton 6D **42**
Bouverie M. N16 ....2E **66**
Bouverie Pl. W2 ....7B **4** (6B **82**)
Bouverie Rd. HA1: Harr 6G **41**
  N16 ....2E **66**
Bouverie St. EC4 ....1K **13** (6A **84**)
Bouvier Rd. EN3: Enf W 1D **24**
Boveney Rd. SE23 ....7K **121**
Bovet Ct. E1 ....5A **86**
  (off Ocean Est.)
Bovill Rd. SE23 ....7K **121**
Bovingdon Av. HA9: Wemb 6G **61**
Bovingdon Cl. N19 ....2G **65**
Bovingdon La. NW9 ....1A **44**
Bovingdon Rd. SW6 ....1K **117**
Bovril Cl. SW6 ....7K **99**
  (off Fulham Rd.)
BOW 3B **86**
Bowater Cl. NW9 ....5K **43**
  SW2 ....6J **119**
Bowater Gdns. TW16: Sun 2A **148**
Bowater Ho. EC1 ....4C **8**
  (off Golden La.)
Bowater Pl. SE3 ....7K **105**
Bowater Rd. HA9: Wemb 3H **61**
  SE18 ....3B **106**
Bow Bell Twr. E3 ....1C **86**
  (off Pancras Way)
Bow Bri. Est. E3 ....3D **86**
Bow Brook, The E2 ....2K **85**
  (off Mace St.)
Bow Chyd. EC4 ....1D **14**
BOW COMMON 5C **86**
Bow Comn. La. E3 ....4B **86**
Bow Creek Ecology Pk. 6G **87**
Bowden Cl. TW14: Bedf 1G **129**
Bowden Ho. E3 ....3D **86**
  (off Rainhill Way)
Bowden St. SE11 ....6K **19** (5A **102**)
Bowditch SE8 ....4B **104**
Bowdon Rd. E17 ....7C **50**
Bowen Ct. SE16 ....4J **103**
  (off Debnams Rd.)
Bowen Dr. SE21 ....3E **138**
Bowen Rd. HA1: Harr 7G **41**
Bowen St. E14 ....6D **86**
Bower Av. SE10 ....1G **123**
Bower Cl. RM5: Col R 1K **55**
  UB5: N'olt 2A **76**
Bower Ct. E4 ....1K **35**
  (off The Ridgeway)
Bowerdean St. SW6 ....1K **117**
Bowerden Cl. NW10 ....2D **80**
Bowerman Av. SE14 ....6A **104**
Bowerman Ct. N19 ....3G **65**
  (off St John's Way)
Bower St. E1 ....6K **85**
Bowers Wlk. E6 ....6D **88**
Bowery Ct. RM10: Dag 6H **73**
Bowes Cl. DA15: Sidc 6B **126**
Bowe's Ho. IG11: Bark 7F **71**
Bowes-Lyon Hall E16 ....1J **105**
  (off Wesley Av.)
BOWES PARK 6D **32**
Bowes Rd. N11 ....5B **32**
  N13 ....5B **32**
  RM8: Dag 4C **72**
  W3 ....7A **80**
Bow Exchange E3 ....5D **86**
  (off Yeo St.)

Bow Fair E3 ....2C **86**
  (off Fairfield Rd.)
Bowfell Rd. W6 ....6E **98**
Bowford Av. DA7: Bex 1E **126**
Bowhill Cl. SW9 ....7A **102**
Bow Ho. N1 ....1E **84**
  (off Wilmer Gdns.)
Bowie Cl. SW4 ....7H **119**
BOW INTERCHANGE 2D **86**
Bowland Rd. IG8: Wfd G 6F **37**
  SW4 ....4H **119**
Bowland Yd. SW1 ....7F **11**
Bow La. EC4 ....1D **14** (6C **84**)
  N12 ....7F **31**
  SM4: Mord 6G **153**
Bowly Ho. SE4 ....4K **121**
  (off Frendsbury Rd.)
Bowl Ct. EC2 ....4H **9** (4E **84**)
Bowles Ct. N12 ....7H **31**
Bowles Rd. SE1 ....6G **103**
Bowley Cl. SE19 ....6F **139**
Bowley Ho. SE16 ....3G **103**
Bowley La. SE19 ....5F **139**
Bowling, The KT12: Walt T 7J **147**
Bowling Cl. UB10: Uxb 1B **74**
Bowling Grn. Cl. SW15 ....7D **116**
Bowling Grn. Ct. HA9: Wemb 2F **61**
Bowling Grn. Ho. SW10 ....3B **100**
  (off Riley St.)
Bowling Grn. La. EC1 ....3K **7** (4A **84**)
Bowling Grn. Pl. SE1 ....6E **14** (2D **102**)
Bowling Grn. Row SE18 ....3D **106**
Bowling Grn. St. SE11 ...7J **19** (6A **102**)
Bowling Grn. Wlk. N1 ....1G **9** (3E **84**)
Bow Locks E3 ....4E **86**
Bowls Cl. HA7: Stan 5G **27**
Bowman Av. E16 ....7H **87**
Bowman Ho. N1 ....1E **84**
  (off Nuttall St.)
Bowman M. SW18 ....1H **135**
Bowman's Bldgs. NW1 ....5C **4**
  (off Penfold Pl.)
Bowmans Cl. W13 ....1B **96**
Bowmans Lea SE23 ....7J **121**
Bowmans Mdw. SM6: Wall 3F **167**
Bowman's M. E1 ....6G **85**
  N7 ....3J **65**
Bowman's Pl. N7 ....3J **65**
Bowman Trad. Est. NW9 ....3G **43**
Bowmead SE9 ....2D **142**
Bowmore Wlk. NW1 ....7H **65**
Bowness Cl. E8 ....6F **67**
  (off Beechwood Rd.)
Bowness Cres. SW15 ....5A **134**
Bowness Dr. TW4: Houn 4C **112**
Bowness Ho. SE15 ....7J **103**
  (off Hillbeck Cl.)
Bowness Rd. DA7: Bex 2H **127**
  SE6 ....7D **122**
Bowood Rd. EN3: Enf H 2E **24**
  SW11 ....5E **118**
Bow Rd. E3 ....3B **86**
Bowrons Av. HA0: Wemb 7D **60**
Bowry Ho. E14 ....5B **86**
  (off Wallwood St.)
Bowsley Cl. TW13: Felt 2J **129**
Bowsprit Point E14 ....3C **104**
  (off Westferry Rd.)
Bow St. E15 ....5G **69**
  WC2 ....1F **13** (6J **83**)
Bow Triangle Bus. Cen. E3 ....4C **86**
  (not continuous)
Bowyer Cl. E6 ....5D **88**
Bowyer Ho. N1 ....1E **84**
  (off Whitmore Est.)
Bowyer Pl. SE5 ....7C **102**
Bowyers Ct. TW1: Isle 4B **114**
Bowyer St. SE5 ....7C **102**
Boxall Rd. SE21 ....6E **120**
Boxelder Cl. HA8: Edg 5D **28**
Boxgrove Rd. SE2 ....3C **108**

Box La. IG11: Bark 2B **90**
Boxley Rd. SM4: Mord 4A **154**
Boxley St. E16 ....1K **105**
Boxmoor Ho. E2 ....1G **85**
  (off Whiston Rd.)
  W11 ....1F **99**
  (off Queensdale Cres.)
Boxmoor Rd. HA3: Kenton 4B **42**
Boxoll Rd. RM9: Dag 4F **73**
Boxted Cl. IG9: Buck H 1H **37**
Box Tree Ho. SE8 ....6A **104**
Boxtree La. HA3: Hrw W 1G **41**
Boxtree Rd. HA3: Hrw W 7C **26**
Boxwood Cl. UB7: W Dray 2B **92**
Boxworth Cl. N12 ....5G **31**
Boxworth Gro. N1 ....1K **83**
Boyard Rd. SE18 ....5F **107**
Boyce Ho. SW16 ....5G **137**
  W10 ....3H **81**
  (off Bruckner St.)
Boyce Way E13 ....4J **87**
Boycroft Av. NW9 ....6J **43**
Boyd Av. UB1: S'hall 1D **94**
Boyd Cl. KT2: King T 7G **133**
Boydell Ct. NW8 ....7B **64**
  (not continuous)
Boyden Ho. E17 ....3E **50**
Boyd Rd. SW19 ....6B **136**
Boyd St. E1 ....6G **85**
Boyd Way SE3 ....4A **124**
Boyfield St. SE1 ....7B **14** (2B **102**)
Boyland Rd. BR1: Brom 5H **141**
Boyle Av. HA7: Stan 6F **27**
Boyle Cl. UB10: Uxb 2B **74**
Boyle Farm Island KT7: T Ditt ...6A **150**
Boyle Farm Rd. KT7: T Ditt 6A **150**
Boyle St. W1 ....2A **12** (7G **83**)
Boyne Av. NW4 ....4F **45**
Boyne Rd. RM10: Dag 3G **73**
  SE13 ....3E **122**
Boyne Ter. M. W11 ....1H **99**
Boyseland Ct. HA8: Edg 2D **28**
Boyson Rd. SE17 ....6C **102**
  (not continuous)
Boyson Wlk. SE17 ....6D **102**
Boyton Cl. E1 ....4J **85**
  N8 ....3J **47**
Boyton Ho. NW8 ....2B **82**
  (off Wellington Rd.)
Boyton Rd. N8 ....3J **47**
Brabant Ct. EC3 ....2G **15**
Brabant Rd. N22 ....2K **47**
Brabazon Av. SM6: Wall 7J **167**
Brabazon Ct. SW1 ....5C **18**
  (off Moreton St.)
Brabazon Rd. TW5: Hest 7A **94**
  UB5: N'olt 2E **76**
Brabazon St. E14 ....6D **86**
Brabner Ho. E2 ....1K **9**
  (off Wellington Row)
Brabourne Cl. SE19 ....5E **138**
Brabourne Cres. DA7: Bex 6F **109**
Brabourne Hgts. NW7 ....3F **29**
Brabourne Ri. BR3: Beck 5E **158**
Brabourn Gro. SE15 ....2J **121**
Brabrook Ct. SM6: Wall 4F **167**
Brabstone Ho. UB6: G'frd 2K **77**
Bracer Ho. N1 ....2E **84**
  (off Whitmore Est.)
Bracewell Av. UB6: G'frd 5K **59**
Bracewell Rd. W10 ....5E **80**
Bracewood Gdns. CR0: C'don 3F **169**
Bracey M. N4 ....2J **65**
Bracey St. N4 ....2J **65**
Bracken, The E4 ....2K **35**
Bracken Av. CR0: C'don 3D **170**
  SW12 ....6E **118**
Brackenbridge Dr. HA4: Ruis 3A **58**
Brackenbury N4 ....1A **66**
  (off Osborne Rd.)
Brackenbury Gdns. W6 ....3D **98**

Brackenbury Rd. N2 ....3A **46**
  W6 ....3D **98**
Bracken Cl. E6 ....5D **88**
  TW2: Whitt 7E **112**
  TW16: Sun 6H **129**
Brackendale N21 ....2E **32**
Brackendale Cl. TW3: Houn 1F **113**
  HA4: Ruis 4K **145**
Brackendene DA2: Wilm 4K **145**
Bracken End TW7: Isle 5H **113**
Brackenfield Cl. E5 ....3H **67**
Bracken Gdns. SW13 ....2C **116**
Brackenhill HA4: Ruis 4C **58**
Bracken Hill Cl. BR1: Brom 1H **159**
Bracken Hill La. BR1: Brom 1H **159**
Bracken Ho. E3 ....5C **86**
  (off Devons Rd.)
Bracken Ind. Est. IG6: Ilf 1J **53**
Bracken M. E4 ....1K **35**
  RM7: Rom 6H **55**
Brackens BR3: Beck 7C **140**
Brackens, The EN1: Enf 7K **23**
Brackenwood TW16: Sun 1J **147**
Brackenwood Lodge EN5: New Bar ...4D **20**
  (off Prospect Rd.)
Brackley Av. SE15 ....3J **121**
Brackley Cl. HA8: Edg 7C **28**
  SM6: Wall 7J **167**
Brackley Ct. NW8 ....3B **4**
  (off Pollitt Dr.)
Brackley Rd. BR3: Beck 7B **140**
  W4 ....5A **98**
Brackley Sq. IG8: Wfd G 7G **37**
Brackley St. EC1 ....5D **8** (4C **84**)
Brackley Ter. W4 ....5A **98**
Bracklyn Ct. N1 ....2D **84**
  (not continuous)
Bracklyn St. N1 ....2D **84**
Bracknell Cl. N22 ....1A **48**
Bracknell Gdns. NW3 ....4K **63**
Bracknell Ga. NW3 ....5K **63**
Bracknell Way NW3 ....4K **63**
Bracondale Rd. SE2 ....4A **108**
Bradbeer Ho. E2 ....2J **85**
  (off Cornwall Av.)
Bradbourne Rd. DA5: Bexl 7G **127**
Bradbourne St. SW6 ....2J **117**
Bradbury Cl. UB2: S'hall 4D **94**
Bradbury M. N16 ....5E **66**
Bradbury St. N16 ....5E **66**
Bradby Ho. NW8 ....2K **81**
  (off Hamilton Ter.)
Bradby's HA1: Harr 1J **59**
  (off High St.)
Braddock Cl. TW7: Isle 2K **113**
Braddon Cl. EN5: Barn 3B **20**
Braddon Rd. TW9: Rich 3F **115**
Braddyll St. SE10 ....5G **105**
Bradenham Av. DA16: Well 4A **126**
Bradenham Cl. SE17 ....6D **102**
Bradenham Rd. HA3: Kenton 4B **42**
  UB4: Hayes 3G **75**
Braden St. W9 ....4K **81**
Bradfield Ct. NW1 ....7F **65**
  (off Hawley Rd.)
Bradfield Dr. IG11: Bark 5A **72**
Bradfield Ho. IG8: Wfd G 6K **37**
Bradfield Rd. E16 ....2J **105**
  HA4: Ruis 5C **58**
Bradford Cl. BR2: Brom 1D **172**
  N17 ....6A **34**
  SE26 ....4H **139**
Bradford Dr. KT19: Ewe 6B **164**
Bradford Ho. W14 ....3F **99**
  (off Spring Va. Ter.)
Bradford Rd. IG1: Ilf 1H **71**
  W3 ....2A **98**
Bradfords Cl. IG9: Buck H 4G **37**
Bradford Rd. SE6 ....6D **122**
Brading Cres. E11 ....2K **69**
Brading Rd. CR0: C'don 6K **155**
  SW2 ....7K **119**

Brading Ter. W12 ....3C 98
Bradiston Rd. W9 ....3H 81
Bradley Cl. N7 ....6J 65
Bradley Gdns. W13 ....6B 78
Bradley Ho. E3 ....3D 86
  (off Bromley High St.)
  IG8: Wfd G 7D 36
  SE16 ....4J 103
  (off Raymouth Rd.)
Bradley M. SW17 ....1D 136
Bradley Rd. N22 ....2K 47
  SE19 ....6C 138
Bradley's Cl. N1 ....2A 84
Bradley Stone Rd. E6 ....5D 88
Bradman Ho. NW8 ....3A 82
  (off Abercorn Pl.)
Bradmore Ct. EN3: Enf H 3F 25
  (off Enstone Rd.)
Bradmore Pk. Rd. W6 ....4D 98
Brad Rd. NW7 ....6A 30
Bradshaw Cl. SW19 ....6J 135
Bradshaw Cotts. E14 ....6A 86
  (off Repton St.)
Bradshaw Dr. NW7 ....7A 30
Bradshaw Waye UB8: Hil 5B 74
Bradshaws Cl. SE25 ....3G 157
Bradstock Ho. E9 ....7K 67
Bradstock Rd. E9 ....6K 67
  KT17: Ewe 5C 164
Brad St. SE1 ....5K 13 (1A 102)
Bradwell Av. RM10: Dag 2G 73
Bradwell Cl. E18 ....4H 51
Bradwell Ho. NW6 ....1K 81
  (off Mortimer Cres.)
Bradwell M. N18 ....4B 34
Bradwell Rd. IG9: Buck H 1H 37
Brady Ct. RM8: Dag 1D 72
Brady Dr. BR1: Brom 3E 160
Brady Ho. SW8 ....1G 119
  (off Corunna Rd.)
Bradymead E6 ....6E 88
Brady St. E1 ....4H 85
Braeburn Cl. BR6: Orp 2K 173
  (off Blossom Dr.)
  EN4: E Barn 4G 21
  RM13: Rain 2K 91
  (off Broadis Way)
Brae Cl. KT2: King T 1G 151
Braemar SW15 ....6F 117
Braemar Av. CR2: S Croy 7C 168
  CR7: Thor H 3A 156
  DA7: Bex 4J 127
  HA0: Wemb 7D 60
  N22 ....1J 47
  NW10 ....3K 61
  SW19 ....2J 135
Braemar Cl. SE16 ....5H 103
  (off Masters Dr.)
Braemar Ct. SE6 ....1H 141
  (off Cumberland Pl.)
Braemar Gdns. BR4: W W'ck 1E 170
  DA15: Sidc 3H 143
  NW9 ....1K 43
Braemar Ho. W9 ....3A 82
  (off Maida Vale)
Braemar Mans. SW7 ....3K 99
  (off Cornwall Gdns.)
Braemar Rd. E13 ....4H 87
  KT4: Wor Pk 3D 164
  N15 ....5E 48
  TW8: Bford 6D 96
Braeside BR3: Beck 5C 140
Braeside Av. SW19 ....1G 153
Braeside Cres. DA7: Bex 4J 127
Braeside Rd. SW16 ....7G 137
Braes St. N1 ....7B 66
Braesyde Cl. DA17: Belv 4F 109
Brafferton Rd. CR0: C'don 4C 168
Braganza St. SE17 ....5B 102

Bragg Cl. RM8: Dag 6B 72
Braham Ct. E2 ....4H 85
  (off Three Colts La.)
Braham Ho. SE11 ....6H 19 (5K 101)
Braham St. E1 ....1K 15 (6F 85)
Braid Av. W3 ....6A 80
Braid Cl. TW13: Hanw 2D 130
Braid Ho. SE10 ....1E 122
  (off Blackheath Hill)
Braidwood Pas. EC1 ....5C 8
  (off Aldersgate St.)
Braidwood Rd. SE6 ....1F 141
Braidwood St. SE1 ....5G 15 (1E 102)
Brailsford Cl. CR4: Mitc 7C 136
Brailsford Rd. SW2 ....5A 120
Brainton Av. TW14: Felt 7K 111
Braintree Av. IG4: Ilf 4C 52
Braintree Ho. E1 ....4J 85
  (off Malcolm Rd.)
Braintree Rd. HA4: Ruis 4K 57
  RM10: Dag 3G 73
Braintree St. E2 ....3J 85
Braithwaite Av. RM7: Rush G 7G 55
Braithwaite Gdns. HA7: Stan 1C 42
Braithwaite Ho. EC1 ....3E 8
  (off Bunhill Row)
Braithwaite Rd. EN3: Brim 3G 25
Braithwaite St. E1 ....4J 9 (4F 85)
Braithwaite Twr. W2 ....5B 4
  (off Hall Pl.)
Bramah Ho. SW1 ....6J 17 (5F 101)
  (off Broadis Way)
Bramah Rd. SW9 ....1A 120
Bramalea Cl. N6 ....6E 46
Bramall Cl. E15 ....5H 69
Bramall Ct. N7 ....6K 65
  (off Watkinson Rd.)
Bramber WC1 ....2E 6
Bramber Ct. TW8: Bford 4E 96
  W14 ....6H 99
  (off Bramber Rd.)
Bramber Ho. KT2: King T 1G 151
  (off Seven Kings Way)
Bramber Rd. N12 ....5H 31
  W14 ....6H 99
Brambleacres Cl. SM2: Sutt 7J 165
Brambledown Cl. BR4: W W'ck 5G 159
Brambledown Rd. CR2: Sande 7E 168
  SM5: Cars 7E 166
  SM6: Wall 7E 166
Bramble Gdns. W12 ....7B 80
Bramble Ho. E3 ....5C 86
  (off Devons Rd.)
Bramble La. TW12: Hamp 6D 130
Brambles, The SM1: Sutt 2B 166
  SW19 ....5H 135
  (off Woodside)
  UB7: W Dray 4A 92
Brambles Cl. TW7: Isle 7B 96
Brambles Farm Dr. UB10: Hil 3C 74
Bramblewood Cl. SM5: Cars 1C 166
Brambling Ct. SE8 ....6B 104
  (off Abinger Gro.)
Bramblings, The E4 ....4A 36
Bramcote Av. CR4: Mitc 4D 154
Bramcote Ct. CR4: Mitc 4D 154
  (off Bramcote Av.)
Bramcote Gro. SE16 ....5J 103
Bramcote Rd. SW15 ....4D 116
Bramdean Cres. SE12 ....1J 141
Bramdean Gdns. SE12 ....1J 141
Bramerton NW6 ....7F 63
  (off Willesden La.)
Bramerton Rd. BR3: Beck 3B 158

Bramerton St. SW3 ....7C 16 (6C 100)
Bramfield Ct. N4 ....2C 66
  (off Queen's Dr.)
Bramfield Rd. SW11 ....6C 118
Bramford Ct. N14 ....2C 32
Bramford Rd. SW18 ....4A 118
Bramham Gdns.
  KT9: Chess 4D 162
  SW5 ....5K 99
Bramhope La. SE7 ....6K 105
Bramlands Cl. SW11 ....3C 118
Bramley Av. TW17: Shep 3G 147
Bramley Bank Nature Reserve 6J 169
Bramley Cl. BR6: Farnb 1F 173
  CR2: S Croy 5C 168
  E17 ....2A 50
  HA5: Eastc 3H 39
  IG8: Wfd G 7F 37
  N14 ....5A 22
  NW7 ....3F 29
  TW2: Whitt 6G 113
  UB3: Hayes 7J 75
Bramley Ct. BR6: Orp 2K 173
  (off Blossom Dr.)
  CR4: Mitc 2B 154
  DA16: Well 1B 126
  E4 ....1K 35
  (off The Ridgeway)
  EN4: E Barn 4H 21
  RM13: Rain 2K 91
  (off Broadis Way)
  UB1: S'hall 7G 77
  (off Haldane Rd.)
Bramley Cres. IG2: Ilf 6E 52
  SW8 ....7H 101
Bramley Hill CR2: S Croy 5B 168
Bramley Ho. SW15 ....6B 116
  (off Tunworth Cres.)
  TW4: Houn 4D 112
Bramley Hyrst CR2: S Croy 5C 168
Bramley Lodge HA0: Wemb 4D 60
Bramley Pde. N14 ....4C 22
Bramley Rd. N14 ....5K 21
  SM1: Sutt 5B 166
  SM2: Cheam 7F 165
  W5 ....3C 96
  W10 ....6F 81
Bramley Sports Ground 5K 21
Bramley Way BR4: W W'ck 2D 170
  TW4: Houn 5D 112
Brampton WC1 ....1G 7
  (off Red Lion Sq.)
Brampton Cl. E5 ....2H 67
Brampton Ct. NW4 ....4D 44
  RM7: Rush G 6K 55
  (off Union Rd.)
Brampton Gro. HA3: Kenton 4A 42
  HA9: Wemb 1G 61
  NW4 ....4D 44
Brampton Ho. SE16 ....2J 103
  (off Albatross Way)
Brampton La. NW4 ....4E 44
Brampton Pk. Rd. N22 ....3A 48
Brampton Rd. CR0: C'don 7F 157
  DA7: Bex 3D 126
  E6 ....3B 88
  N15 ....5C 48
  NW9 ....4G 43
  SE2 ....6C 108
  UB10: Hil 2D 74
Bramshaw Ri. KT3: N Mald 6A 152
Bramshaw Rd. E9 ....6K 67
Bramshill Gdns. NW5 ....3F 65
Bramshill Rd. NW10 ....2B 80
Bramshot Av. SE7 ....6J 105
Bramshurst NW8 ....1K 81
  (off Abbey Rd.)
Bramston Rd. NW10 ....2C 80
  SW17 ....3A 136
Bramwell Cl. TW16: Sun 2B 148

Bramwell Ho. SE1 ....3C 102
  SW1 ....6A 18
  (off Churchill Gdns.)
Bramwell M. N1 ....1K 83
Bramwell Way E16 ....1A 106
Brancaster Dr. NW7 ....7H 29
Brancaster Ho. E1 ....3K 85
  (off Moody St.)
Brancaster Rd. E12 ....4D 70
  IG2: Ilf 6J 53
  SW16 ....3J 137
Brancepeth Gdns. IG9: Buck H 2D 36
Branch Hill NW3 ....3A 64
Branch Hill Ho. NW3 ....3K 63
Branch Pl. N1 ....1D 84
Branch Rd. E14 ....7A 86
Branch St. SE15 ....7E 102
Brancker Rd. HA3: Kenton 3D 42
Brancroft Way EN3: Brim 1F 25
Brand Cl. N4 ....1B 66
Brandesbury Sq. IG8: Wfd G 7K 37
Brandlehow Rd. SW15 ....4H 117
Brandon Cl. E16 ....4H 87
Brandon Est. SE17 ....6B 102
Brandon Ho. BR3: Beck 5D 140
  (off Beckenham Hill Rd.)
Brandon Mans. W14 ....6G 99
  (off Queen's Club Gdns.)
Brandon M. EC2 ....6E 8
  SE17 ....4C 102
  (off Brandon St.)
Brandon Rd. E17 ....4E 50
  N7 ....7J 65
  SM1: Sutt 4K 165
  UB2: S'hall 5D 94
Brandon St. SE17 ....4C 102
  (not continuous)
Brandram M. SE13 ....4G 123
  (off Brandram Rd.)
Brandram Rd. SE13 ....3G 123
Brandrams Wharf SE16 ....2J 103
Brandreth Ct. HA1: Harr 6K 41
Brandreth Rd. E6 ....6D 88
  SW17 ....2F 137
Brandries, The SM6: Bedd 3H 167
Brands Ho. NW6 ....1H 81
  (off Lincoln M.)
Brand St. SE10 ....7E 104
Brandville Gdns. IG6: Ilf 4F 53
Brandville Rd. UB7: W Dray 2A 92
Brandy Way SM2: Sutt 7J 165
Brangbourne Rd. BR1: Brom 5E 141
Brangton Rd. SE11 ....6H 19 (5K 101)
Brangwyn Cl. W14 ....3G 99
  (off Blythe Rd.)
Brangwyn Cres. SW19 ....1A 154
Branham Ho. SE18 ....5F 107
Branksea St. SW6 ....7G 99
Branksome Av. N18 ....6A 34
Branksome Cl. TW11: Tedd 4H 131
Branksome Ho. SW8 ....7K 101
  (off Meadow Rd.)
Branksome Rd. SW2 ....5J 119
  SW19 ....1J 153
Branksome Way HA3: Kenton 6F 43
  KT3: N Mald 1J 151
Bransby Rd. KT9: Chess 6E 162
Branscombe NW1 ....1G 83
  (off Plender St.)
Branscombe Ct. BR2: Brom 5H 159
Branscombe Gdns. N21 ....7F 23
Branscombe St. SE13 ....3D 122
Bransdale Cl. NW6 ....1J 81
Bransgrove Rd. HA8: Edg 1H 43
Branston Cres. BR5: Pet W 1H 173
Branstone Rd. TW9: Kew 1F 115
Brants Wlk. W7 ....4J 77
Brantwood Av. DA8: Erith 7J 109
  TW7: Isle 4A 114
Brantwood Cl. E17 ....3D 50

Brantwood Gdns. EN2: Enf	.4D 22
IG4: Ilf	.4C 52
Brantwood Ho. SE5	.7C 102
	(off Wyndham Est.)
Brantwood Rd. CR2: S Croy	.7C 168
DA7: Bex	.2H 127
N17	.6B 34
SE24	.5C 120
Branxholme Ct. BR1: Brom	.1H 159
	(off Highland Rd.)
Braque Bldg. SE1	.5C 14
	(off Union St.)
Brasenose Dr. SW13	.6E 98
Brasher Cl. UB6: G'frd	.5H 59
Brassett Point E15	.1G 87
	(off Abbey Rd.)
Brassey Cl. TW14: Felt	.1J 129
Brassey Ho. E14	.4D 104
	(off Cahir St.)
Brassey Rd. NW6	.6H 63
Brassey Sq. SW11	.3E 118
Brassie Av. W3	.6A 80
Brass Talley All. SE16	.2K 103
Brasted Cl. BR6: Orp	.2K 173
DA6: Bex	.5D 126
SE26	.4J 139
Brasted Lodge BR3: Beck	.7C 140
Brathay NW1	.1B 6
	(off Ampthill Est.)
Brathway Rd. SW18	.7J 117
Bratley St. E1	.4G 85
Bratten Ct. CRO: C'don	.6D 156
Braund Av. UB6: G'frd	.4F 77
Braundton Av. DA15: Sidc	.1K 143
Braunston Dr. UB4: Yead	.4C 76
Bravingtons Cl. TW17: Shep	.5B 146
Bravington Pl. W9	.4H 81
Bravington Rd. W9	.2H 81
Bravingtons Wlk. N1	.1F 7
	(off York Way)
Brawne Ho. SE17	.6B 102
	(off Brandon Est.)
Braxfield Rd. SE4	.4A 122
Braxted Pk. SW16	.6K 137
Bray NW3	.7C 64
Brayards Rd. SE15	.2H 121
Brayards Rd. Est. SE15	.2H 121
	(off Caulfield Rd.)
Braybourne Dr. TW7: Isle	.7K 95
Braybrooke Gdns. SE19	.7E 138
Braybrook St. W12	.5B 80
Brayburne Av. SW4	.2G 119
Bray Ct. E2	.3K 85
	(off Meath Cres.)
SW16	.5J 137
Braycourt Av. KT12: Walt T	.7K 147
Bray Cres. SE16	.2K 103
Braydon Rd. N16	.1G 67
Bray Dr. E16	.7H 87
Brayfield Ter. N1	.7A 66
Brayford Sq. E1	.6J 85
Bray Pas. E16	.7J 87
Bray Pl. SW3	.4E 16 (4D 100)
Brayton Gdns. EN2: Enf	.4H 22
Braywood Rd. SE9	.4H 125
Brazier Cres. UB5: N'olt	.4D 76
Brazil Cl. CRO: Bedd	.7J 155
Breach La. RM9: Dag	.3G 91
Bread St. EC4	.1D 14 (6C 84)
	(not continuous)
Breakspear Crematorium (Ruislip)
HA4: Ruis	.5E 38
Breakspear Ho. UB9: Hare	.3A 38
Breakspear M. UB9: Hare	.3A 38
Breakspear Rd. HA4: Ruis	.7D 38
Breakspear Rd. Nth.
UB9: Hare	.3A 38
Breakspear Rd. Sth. UB9: Hare	.3B 56
UB10: Ick	.3B 56
Breakspears Dr. BR5: St P	.7A 144 & 1K 161
Breakspears M. SE4	.2B 122

Breakspears Rd. SE4	.4B 122
	(not continuous)
Breakwell Ct. W10	.4G 81
	(off Wornington Rd.)
Bream Cl. N17	.4H 49
Bream Gdns. E6	.3E 88
Breamore Cl. SW15	.1C 134
Breamore Cl. IG3: Ilf	.2A 72
Breamore Ho. SE15	.7G 103
	(off Friary Est.)
Breamore Rd. IG3: Ilf	.2K 71
Bream's Bldgs. EC4	.7J 7 (6A 84)
Bream St. E3	.7C 68
Breamwater Gdns. TW10: Ham	.3B 132
Brearley Cl. HA8: Edg	.7D 28
UB8: Uxb	.6A 56
Breasley Cl. SW15	.4D 116
Breasy Pl. NW4	.4D 44
	(off Burroughs Gdns.)
Brechin Pl. SW7	.4A 100
Brecknock Rd. N7	.5H 65
N19	.4G 65
Brecknock Rd. Est. N19	.4G 65
Breckonmead BR1: Brom	.2A 160
Brecon Cl. CR4: Mitc	.3J 155
KT4: Wor Pk	.2E 164
Brecon Grn. NW9	.6A 44
Brecon Ho. E3	.2B 86
	(off Ordell Rd.)
UB5: N'olt	.3D 76
	(off Taywood Rd.)
W2	.6A 82
	(off Hallfield Est.)
Brecon Lodge UB7: W Dray	.2B 92
Brecon M. N7	.5H 65
Brecon Rd. EN3: Pond E	.4D 24
W6	.6G 99
Brede Cl. E6	.3E 88
Bredel Ho. E14	.5C 86
	(off St Paul's Way)
Bredgar SE13	.5D 122
Bredgar Rd. N19	.2G 65
Bredhurst Cl. SE20	.6J 139
Bredinghurst SE22	.7G 121
Bredin Ho. SW10	.7K 99
	(off Coleridge Gdns.)
Bredon Rd. CRO: C'don	.7F 157
Breer St. SW6	.3K 117
Breezers Ct. E1	.7G 85
	(off The Highway)
Breezer's Hill E1	.7G 85
Brember Rd. HA2: Harr	.2G 59
Bremer M. E17	.4D 50
Bremner Rd. SW7	.1A 16 (3A 100)
Brenchley Cl. BR2: Brom	.6H 159
BR7: Chst	.1E 160
Brenchley Gdns. SE23	.6J 121
Brenchley Rd. BR5: St P	.2K 161
Brenda Rd. SW17	.2D 136
Brende Gdns. KT8: W Mole	.4F 149
Brendon Av. NW10	.4A 62
Brendon Cl. UB3: Harl	.7E 92
UB2: S'hall	.4F 95
Brendon Gdns. HA2: Harr	.4F 59
IG2: Ilf	.5J 53
Brendon Gro. N2	.2A 46
Brendon Ho. RM8: Dag	.1F 73
SE9	.2H 143
Brendon St. W1	.7D 4 (6C 82)
Brendon Vs. N21	.1H 33
Brendon Way EN1: Enf	.7K 23
Brenley Cl. CR4: Mitc	.3E 154
Brenley Gdns. SE9	.4B 124
Brenley Ho. SE1	.6E 14
	(off Tennis St.)
Brennand Ct. N19	.3G 65
Brent Cl. DA5: Bexl	.1E 144
Brentcot Cl. W13	.4B 78
Brent Cl. NW11	.7F 45
W7	.1H 77
Brent Cres. NW10	.2F 79

BRENT CROSS	.7E 44
Brent Cross Fly-Over NW2	.7F 45
NW4	.7F 45
Brent Cross Gdns. NW4	.6F 45
BRENT CROSS INTERCHANGE	.6E 44
Brent Cross Shop. Cen. NW4	.7E 44
Brentfield NW10	.7H 61
Brentfield Cl. NW10	.6K 61
Brentfield Gdns. NW2	.7F 45
Brentfield Ho. NW10	.7K 61
Brentfield Rd. NW10	.6K 61
BRENTFORD	.6D 96
Brentford Bus. Cen.
TW8: Bford	.7C 96
Brentford Cl. UB4: Yead	.4B 76
BRENTFORD END	.7B 96
Brentford FC	.6D 96
Brentford Fountain Leisure Cen.	.5G 97
Brentford Ho. TW1: Twick	.7B 114
Brent Grn. NW4	.5E 44
Brent Grn. Wlk. HA9: Wemb	.3J 61
Brentham Club	.3C 78
Brentham Way W5	.4D 78
Brent Ho. E9	.6J 67
	(off Brenthouse Rd.)
Brenthouse Rd. E9	.7J 67
Brenthurst Rd. NW10	.6B 62
Brent Lea TW8: Bford	.7C 96
Brentmead Cl. W7	.7J 77
Brentmead Gdns. NW10	.2F 79
Brentmead Pl. NW11	.6F 45
Brent Mus.	.6D 62
	(off High Rd.)
Brent New Ent. Cen. NW10	.6B 62
Brenton Ct. E9	.5A 68
	(off Mabley St.)
Brenton St. E14	.6A 86
Brent Pk. Ind. Est. UB2: S'hall	.3K 93
Brent Pk. Rd. NW4	.7D 44
NW9	.7D 44
Brent Pl. EN5: Barn	.5C 20
Brent Rd. CR2: Sels	.7H 169
E16	.6J 87
SE18	.7F 107
TW8: Bford	.6C 96
UB2: S'hall	.3A 94
Brent Side TW8: Bford	.6C 96
Brentside Cl. W13	.4A 78
Brentside Executive Cen.
TW8: Bford	.6B 96
Brent St. NW4	.4E 44
Brent Ter. NW2	.1E 62
	(not continuous)
Brent Trad. Cen. NW10	.5A 62
Brentvale Av. HA0: Wemb	.1F 79
UB1: S'hall	.1H 95
Brent Valley Golf Course	.7J 77
Brent Vw. Rd. NW9	.6C 44
Brentwaters Bus. Pk.
TW8: Bford	.7C 96
Brent Way HA9: Wemb	.6H 61
N3	.6D 30
TW8: Bford	.7D 96
Brentwick Gdns. TW8: Bford	.4E 96
Brentwood Cl. SE9	.1G 143
Brentwood Ho. SE18	.7B 106
	(off Portway Gdns.)
Brentwood Lodge NW4	.5F 45
	(off Holmdale Gdns.)
Brereton Rd. N17	.7A 34
Bressay Dr. NW7	.7H 29
Bressenden Pl. SW1	.1K 17 (3F 101)
Bressey Av. EN1: Enf	.1B 24
Bressey Gro. E18	.2H 51
Bresslaw Ct. E3	.5B 86
	(off Wager St.)
Breton Highwalk EC2	.5D 8
	(off Golden La.)
Breton Ho. EC2	.5D 8
SE1	.7J 15
	(off St Saviour's Est.)

Brett Cl. N16	.2E 66
UB5: N'olt	.3B 76
Brett Cl. N9	.2D 34
Brettell St. SE17	.5D 102
Brettenham Av. E17	.1C 50
Brettenham Rd. E17	.2C 50
N18	.4B 34
Brett Gdns. RM9: Dag	.7E 72
Brett Ho. Cl. SW15	.7F 117
Brettinghurst SE1	.5G 103
	(off Avondale Sq.)
Brett Pas. E8	.5H 67
Brett Rd. E8	.5H 67
Brewers Bldgs. EC1	.1A 8
	(off Rawstorne St.)
Brewers Ct. W2	.5A 82
Brewer's Grn. SW1	.1C 18
Brewer's Hall Gdn. EC2	.6D 8
	(off Aldermanbury Sq.)
Brewers La. TW9: Rich	.5D 114
Brewer St. W1	.2B 12 (7G 83)
Brewery, The EC2	.5E 8 (5C 84)
RM1: Rom	.5K 55
Brewery Cl. HA0: Wemb	.5A 60
Brewery Ind. Estate, The N1	.1D 8
	(off Wenlock Rd.)
Brewery La. TW1: Twick	.7K 113
Brewery M. Cen. TW7: Isle	.3A 114
Brewery Rd. BR2: Brom	.1C 172
N7	.7J 65
SE18	.5G 107
Brewery Sq. EC1	.3B 8 (4B 84)
SE1	.5J 15
Brewery Wlk. RM1: Rom	.5K 55
Brewhouse La. E1	.1H 103
SW15	.3G 117
Brewhouse Rd. SE18	.4D 106
Brewhouse Wlk. SE16	.1A 104
Brewhouse Yd. EC1	.3A 8 (4B 84)
Brewin Ter. UB4: Yead	.5A 76
Brewood Rd. RM8: Dag	.6B 72
Brewster Gdns. W10	.5E 80
Brewster Ho. E14	.7B 86
	(off Three Colt St.)
SE1	.4F 103
	(off Dunton Rd.)
Brewster Pl. KT1: King T	.2J 151
Brewster Rd. E10	.1D 68
Brian Rd. RM6: Chad H	.5C 54
Briant Ho. SE1	.2J 19
Briants Cl. HA5: Pinn	.2D 40
Briant St. SE14	.1K 121
Briar Av. SW16	.7K 137
Briarbank Rd. W13	.6A 78
Briar Cl. IG9: Buck H	.2G 37
N2	.3K 45
N13	.3H 33
TW7: Isle	.5K 113
TW12: Hamp	.5D 130
Briar Ct. E3	.2C 86
	(off Morville St.)
SM3: Cheam	.4E 164
SW15	.4D 116
Briar Cres. UB5: N'olt	.6F 59
Briardale HA8: Edg	.4E 28
Briardale Gdns. NW3	.3J 63
Briarfield Av. N3	.2K 45
	(not continuous)
Briarfield Cl. DA7: Bex	.2G 127
Briar Gdns. BR2: Hayes	.1H 171
Briaris Cl. N17	.7C 34
Briar La. BR4: Addtn	.4D 170
Briar Rd. DA5: Bexl	.3K 145
HA3: Kenton	.5C 42
NW2	.4E 62
SW16	.3J 155
TW2: Twick	.1J 131
TW17: Shep	.5B 146
Briars, The TW19: Stanw M	.7B 174
WD23: B Hea	.1D 26
Briarswood Way BR6: Chels	.5K 173

Briar Wlk. HA8: Edg 7D **28**
   SW15 . . . . .4D **116**
   W10 . . . . .4G **81**
Briar Way UB7: W Dray 2C **92**
Briar Wood Cl. BR2: Brom 2C **172**
Briarwood Cl. NW9 . . . . .6J **43**
   TW13: Felt .4G **129**
Briarwood Ct. KT4: Wor Pk 1C **164**
   (off The Avenue)
Briarwood Dr. HA6: Nwood 2J **39**
Briarwood Rd. KT17: Ewe 6C **164**
   SW4 . . . . .5H **119**
Briary Cl. NW3 .7C **64**
Briary Ct. DA14: Sidc 5B **144**
   E16 . . . . .6H **87**
Briary Gdns. BR1: Brom 5K **141**
Briary Gro. HA8: Edg 2H **43**
Briary La. N9 . . . . .3A **34**
Briary Lodge BR3: Beck 1E **158**
Brickbarn Cl. SW10 . . . . .7A **100**
   (off King's Barn)
Brick Ct. EC4 . . . . .1J **13** (6A **84**)
Brickett Cl. HA4: Ruis 5E **38**
Brick Farm Cl. TW9: Kew 1H **115**
Brickfield Cl. E9 . . . . .6J **67**
   TW8: Bford .7C **96**
Brickfield Cotts. BR7: Chst 5E **142**
   SE18 . . . . .6K **107**
Brickfield Farm Gdns.
   BR6: Farnb 4G **173**
Brickfield Ho. N1 . . . . .1E **84**
   (off Hertford Rd.)
Brickfield La. UB3: Harl 6F **93**
Brickfield Rd. CR4: Mitc 3C **154**
   CR7: Thor H 1B **156**
   SW4 . . . . .6H **119**
   (off Parkfield Rd.)
   SW19 . . . . .4K **135**
Brickfields HA2: Harr 2H **59**
   (not continuous)
Brickfields Way UB7: W Dray 3B **92**
Brick La. E1 . . . . .3K **9** (4F **85**)
   E2 . . . . .3F **85**
   EN1: Enf 2C **24**
   EN3: Enf H .2C **24**
   HA7: Stan 7J **27**
   UB5: N'olt 3D **76**
Brick Lane Music Hall 1B **106**
BRICKLAYER'S ARMS 4D **102**
Bricklayers Arms Distribution Cen.
   SE1 . . . . .4E **102**
   (not continuous)
Brick St. W1 . . . . .5J **11** (1F **101**)
Brickwall La. HA4: Ruis 1G **57**
Brickwood Cl. SE26 . . . . .3H **139**
Brickwood Rd. CR0: C'don 2E **168**
Brideale Cl. SE15 . . . . .6F **103**
Bride Ct. EC4 .1A **14**
Bride La. EC4 . . . . .1A **14** (6B **84**)
Bridel M. N1 . . . . .1B **84**
   (off Colebrook Row)
Brides M. N7 . . . . .6K **65**
Brides Pl. N1 . . . . .7E **66**
Bride St. N7 . . . . .6K **65**
Bridewain St. SE1 . . . . .7J **15** (3F **103**)
Bridewell Pl. E1 . . . . .1H **103**
   EC4 . . . . .1A **14** (6B **84**)
Bridford M. W1 . . . . .5K **5** (5F **83**)
Bridge, The HA3: W'stone 4K **41**
   SW8 . . . . .7F **101**
Bridge App. NW1 . . . . .7E **64**
Bridge Av. W6 .4E **98**
   W7 . . . . .5H **77**
Bridge Av. Mans. W6 . . . . .5E **98**
   (off Bridge Av.)
Bridge Bus. Centre, The
   UB2: S'hall 2E **94**
Bridge Cl. EN1: Enf 2C **24**
   KT12: Walt T 7H **147**
   TW11: Tedd 4K **131**
   W10 . . . . .6F **81**

Bridge Ct. E10 .1B **68**
   E14 . . . . .7F **87**
   (off Newport Av.)
   HA2: Harr 2G **59**
   KT12: Walt T 7H **147**
   (off Bridge St.)
Bridge Dr. N13 .4E **32**
Bridge End E17 . . . . .1E **50**
Bridge End Cl. KT2: King T 1G **151**
Bridgefield Ho. W2 . . . . .6K **81**
   (off Queensway)
Bridgefield Rd. SM1: Sutt 6J **165**
Bridgefoot SE1 . . . . .6F **19** (5J **101**)
   TW16: Sun 1H **147**
Bridge Gdns. KT8: E Mos 4H **149**
   N16 . . . . .4D **66**
   TW15: Ashf 7E **128**
Bridge Ga. N21 . . . . .7H **23**
Bridgehill Cl. HA0: Wemb 1D **78**
Bridge Ho. CR0: C'don 3C **168**
   (off Surrey St.)
   E9 . . . . .6K **67**
   (off Shepherds La.)
   NW3 . . . . .7C **64**
   (off Adelaide Rd.)
   NW10 . . . . .2F **81**
   (off Chamberlayne Rd.)
   SE4 . . . . .4B **122**
   SM2: Sutt .6K **165**
   (off Bridge Rd.)
   SW1 . . . . .5J **17**
   (off Ebury Bri.)
   UB7: W Dray 1A **92**
   W2 . . . . .6A **4**
Bridgehouse Ct. SE1 . . . . .7A **14**
   (off Blackfriars Rd.)
Bridge Ho. Quay E14 . . . . .1E **104**
Bridgeland Rd. E16 . . . . .7J **87**
Bridgelands Cl. BR3: Beck 7B **140**
Bridge La. NW11 . . . . .4G **45**
   SW11 . . . . .1C **118**
Bridge Leisure Centre, The 4B **140**
Bridgeman Ho. E9 . . . . .7J **67**
   (off Frampton Pk. Rd.)
   W14 . . . . .4H **99**
   (off Radnor Ter.)
Bridgeman Rd. N1 . . . . .7K **65**
   TW11: Tedd 6A **132**
Bridgeman St. NW8 . . . . .2C **82**
Bridge Mdws. SE14 . . . . .6K **103**
Bridgemount M. N4 . . . . .7K **47**
BRIDGEN 7E **126**
Bridgend Rd. SW18 . . . . .4A **118**
Bridgenhall Rd. EN1: Enf 1A **24**
Bridgen Ho. E1 . . . . .6H **85**
   (off Nelson St.)
Bridgen Rd. DA5: Bexl 7E **126**
Bridge Pde. N21 . . . . .7H **23**
   (off Ridge Av.)
Bridgepark SW18 . . . . .5J **117**
Bridge Pk. Community Leisure Cen.
   . . . . .7H **61**
Bridge Pl. CR0: C'don 1D **168**
   SW1 . . . . .3K **17** (4F **101**)
Bridgepoint Lofts E7 . . . . .7A **70**
Bridgepoint Pl. N6 . . . . .1F **65**
   (off Hornsey La.)
Bridgeport Pl. E1 . . . . .1G **103**
Bridge Rd. BR3: Beck 7B **140**
   DA7: Bex 2E **126**
   E6 . . . . .7D **70**
   E11 . . . . .6F **51**
   E15 . . . . .7F **69**
   E17 . . . . .7B **50**
   HA9: Wemb 3G **61**
   KT8: E Mos 4H **149**
   KT9: Chess 5E **162**
   N9 . . . . .3B **34**
   N22 . . . . .1J **47**
   NW10 . . . . .6A **62**
   SM2: Sutt .6K **165**

Bridge Rd. SM6: Wall 5F **167**
   TW1: Twick 6B **114**
   TW3: Houn, Isle 3H **113**
   TW7: Isle 3H **113**
   UB2: S'hall .2D **94**
Bridge Rd. Depot E15 . . . . .1G **87**
Bridge Row CR0: C'don 1D **168**
Bridges Cl. Rd. SW11 . . . . .3B **118**
Bridges Ho. SE5 . . . . .7D **102**
   (off Elmington Est.)
Bridgeside Lodge N1 . . . . .2C **84**
   (off Wharf Rd.)
Bridges La. CR0: Bedd 4J **167**
Bridges Pl. SW6 . . . . .1H **117**
Bridges Rd. HA7: Stan 5E **26**
   SW19 . . . . .6K **135**
Bridges Rd. M. SW19 . . . . .6K **135**
Bridge St. HA5: Pinn 3C **40**
   KT12: Walt T 7G **147**
   SW1 . . . . .7E **12** (2J **101**)
   TW9: Rich .5D **114**
   W4 . . . . .4K **97**
Bridges Wharf SW11 . . . . .3B **118**
Bridge Ter. E15 . . . . .7F **69**
Bridgetown Cl. SE19 . . . . .5E **138**
Bridge Vw. W6 .5E **98**
Bridge Vw. Ct. SE1 . . . . .3E **102**
   (off Grange Rd.)
Bridge Wlk. IG1: Ilf 2F **71**
   (within The Exchange)
   SE8 . . . . .6D **104**
   (off Copperas St.)
Bridgewalk Hgts. SE1 . . . . .6F **15**
   (off Weston St.)
Bridgewater Cl. BR7: Chst 3J **161**
Bridgewater Gdns. HA8: Edg 2F **43**
Bridgewater Highwalk EC2 . . . . .5C **8**
Bridgewater Rd. E15 . . . . .1E **86**
   HA0: Wemb 6C **60**
Bridgewater Sq. EC2 . . . . . .5C **8** (5C **84**)
Bridgewater St. EC2 . . . . . . .5C **8** (5C **84**)
Bridge Way N11 . . . . .3B **32**
   NW11 . . . . .5H **45**
   TW2: Whitt 7G **113**
   UB10: Ick 5D **56**
Bridgeway HA0: Wemb 7E **60**
   IG11: Bark .7K **71**
Bridgeway St. NW1 . . . . .2G **83**
Bridge Wharf E2 . . . . .2K **85**
   N1 . . . . .2K **83**
   (off Calshot St.)
Bridge Wharf Rd. TW7: Isle 3B **114**
Bridgewood Cl. SE20 . . . . .7H **139**
Bridgewood Rd. KT4: Wor Pk 4C **164**
   SW16 . . . . .7H **137**
Bridge Yd. SE1 . . . . .4F **15** (1D **102**)
Bridgford St. SW18 . . . . .3A **136**
Bridgman Rd. W4 . . . . .3J **97**
Bridgnorth Ho. SE15 . . . . .6G **103**
   (off Friary Est.)
Bridgwater Ho. W2 . . . . .6A **82**
   (off Hallfield Est.)
Bridgwater Rd. HA4: Ruis 4J **57**
Bridle Cl. KT1: King T 4D **150**
   KT19: Ewe 5K **163**
   TW16: Sun 3J **147**
Bridle La. TW1: Twick 6B **114**
   W1 . . . . .2B **12** (7G **83**)
Bridle M. EN5: Barn 4C **20**
Bridle Path CR0: Bedd 3J **167**
Bridle Path, The IG8: Wfd G 7B **36**
Bridlepath Way TW14: Bedf 7G **111**
Bridle Rd.
   CR0: C'don 3C **170**
   CR2: Sande 7G **169**
   HA5: Eastc 6K **39**
   KT10: Clay 6B **162**
Bridle Way BR6: Farnb 4G **173**
   CR0: C'don 5C **170**
Bridleway, The SM6: Wall 4G **167**
Bridlington Rd. N9 . . . . .7C **24**

Bridport SE17 . . . . .5D **102**
   (off Cadiz St.)
Bridport Av. RM7: Rom 6H **55**
Bridport Ho. N1 . . . . .1D **84**
   (off Bridport Pl.)
   N18 . . . . .5A **34**
   (off College Gdns.)
Bridport Pl. N1 .1D **84**
   (not continuous)
Bridport Rd. CR7: Thor H 3A **156**
   N18 . . . . .5K **33**
   UB6: G'frd .1F **77**
Bridport Ter. SW8 . . . . .1H **119**
   (off Deeley Rd.)
Bridstow Pl. W2 . . . . .6J **81**
Brief St. SE5 .1B **120**
Brierfield NW1 .1G **83**
   (off Arlington Rd.)
Brierley CR0: New Ad 6D **170**
   (not continuous)
Brierley Av. N9 .1D **34**
Brierley Cl. SE25 . . . . .4G **157**
Brierley Ct. W7 . . . . .7J **77**
Brierley Rd. E11 . . . . .4F **69**
   SW12 . . . . .2G **137**
Brierly Gdns. E2 . . . . .2J **85**
Brigade Cl. HA2: Harr 2H **59**
Brigade St. SE3 . . . . .2H **123**
   (off Tranquil Va.)
Brigadier Av. EN2: Enf 1H **23**
Brigadier Hill EN2: Enf 1H **23**
Brigadier Ho. NW9 . . . . .2B **44**
   (off Heritage Av.)
Briggeford Cl. E5 . . . . .2G **67**
Briggs Cl. CR4: Mitc 1F **155**
Briggs Ho. E2 . . . . .1K **9**
   (off Chambord St.)
Bright Cl. DA17: Belv 4D **108**
Brightfield Rd. SE12 . . . . .5G **123**
Brightling Rd. SE4 . . . . .6B **122**
Brightlingsea Pl. E14 . . . . .7B **86**
Brightman Rd. SW18 . . . . .1B **136**
Brighton Av. E17 . . . . .5B **50**
Brighton Bldgs. SE1 . . . . .3E **102**
   (off Tower Bri. Rd.)
Brighton Cl. UB10: Hil 7D **56**
Brighton Dr. UB5: N'olt 6E **58**
Brighton Gro. SE14 . . . . .1A **122**
Brighton Ho. SE5 . . . . .1D **120**
   (off Camberwell Grn.)
Brighton Rd. CR2: S Croy 5C **168**
   E6 . . . . .3E **88**
   (not continuous)
   KT6: Surb .6C **150**
   N2 . . . . .2A **46**
   N16 . . . . .4E **66**
   SM2: Sutt .7K **165**
Brighton Ter. SW9 . . . . .4K **119**
Brightside, The EN3: Enf H 1E **24**
Brightside Rd. SE13 . . . . .6F **123**
Bright St. E14 .5D **86**
Brightwell Cl. CR0: C'don 1A **168**
Brightwell Ct. N7 . . . . .5K **65**
   (off Mackenzie Rd.)
Brightwell Cres. SW17 . . . . .5D **136**
Brightwen Gro. HA7: Stan 2F **27**
Brig M. SE8 . . . . .6C **104**
Brigstock Ho. SE5 . . . . .2C **120**
Brigstock Rd. CR7: Thor H 5A **156**
   DA17: Belv 4H **109**
Brill Pl. NW1 . . . . .1D **6** (2H **83**)
Brim Hill N2 . . . . .4A **46**
Brimpsfield Cl. SE2 . . . . .3B **108**
   (not continuous)
BRIMSDOWN .2G **25**
Brimsdown Av. EN3: Enf H 2F **25**
Brimsdown Ho. E3 . . . . .4D **86**
Brimsdown Ind. Est. EN3: Brim 1G **25**
   (Lockfield Av.)
   EN3: Brim .2G **25**
   (Stockingswater La.)

Brimstone Ho. E15 . . . . .7G 69
(off Victoria St.)
Brindle Ga. DA15: Sidc 1J 143
Brindlewick Gdns. BR3: Beck 6C 140
Brindley Cl. DA7: Bex 3H 127
HA0: Wemb 1D 78
Brindley Ct. HA7: Stan 7J 27
UB1: S'hall 7F 77
Brindley Ho. W2 . . . . .5J 81
(off Alfred Rd.)
Brindley St. SE14 . . . . .1B 122
Brindley Way BR1: Brom 5J 141
UB1: S'hall 7F 77
Brindwood Rd. E4 . . . . .3G 35
Brine Ho. E3 . . . . .2A 86
(off St Stephen's Rd.)
Brinkburn Cl. HA8: Edg 3H 43
SE2 .4A 108
Brinkburn Gdns. HA8: Edg 3G 43
Brinkley KT1: King T 2G 151
Brinkley Rd. KT4: Wor Pk 2D 164
Brinklow Cres. SE18 . . . . .7F 107
Brinklow Ho. W2 . . . . .5K 81
(off Torquay St.)
Brinkworth Rd. IG5: Ilf 3C 52
Brinkworth Way E9 . . . . .6B 68
Brinsdale Rd. NW4 . . . . .3F 45
Brinsley Ho. E1 . . . . .6J 85
(off Tarling St.)
Brinsley Rd. HA3: Hrw W 2H 41
Brinsworth Cl. TW2: Twick 1H 131
Brinsworth Ho. TW2: Twick 2H 131
Brinton Wlk. SE1 . . . . .5A 14
Brion Pl. E14 . . . . .5E 86
Brisbane Av. SW19 . . . . .1K 153
Brisbane Ho. W12 . . . . .7D 80
(off White City Est.)
Brisbane Rd. E10 . . . . .2D 68
IG1: Ilf 7F 53
W13 .2A 96
Brisbane St. SE5 . . . . .7D 102
Briscoe Cl. E11 . . . . .2H 69
Briscoe M. TW2: Twick 2H 131
Briscoe Rd. SW19 . . . . .6B 136
Briset Rd. SE9 . . . . .3B 124
Briset St. EC1 . . . . .5A 8 (4B 84)
Briset Way N7 . . . . .2K 65
Bristol Cl. SM6: Wall 7J 167
TW4: Houn 7E 112
TW19: Stanw 6A 110
Bristol Ct. TW19: Stanw 6A 110
Bristol Gdns. SW15 . . . . .7E 116
W9 . . . . .4K 81
Bristol Ho. IG11: Bark 7A 72
(off Margaret Bondfield Av.)
SE11 . . . . .2J 19
SW1 . . . . .5G 17
(off Lwr. Sloane St.)
WC1 . . . . .5F 7
(off Southampton Row)
Bristol M. W9 . . . . .4K 81
Bristol Pk. Rd. E17 . . . . .4A 50
Bristol Rd. E7 . . . . .6A 70
SM4: Mord 5A 154
UB6: G'frd 1F 77
Briston Gro. N8 . . . . .6J 47
Briston M. NW7 . . . . .7H 29
Bristow Ct. E8 . . . . .1H 85
(off Triangle Rd.)
Bristowe Cl. SW2 . . . . .6A 120
Bristow Rd. CR0: Bedd 4J 167
DA7: Bex 1E 126
SE19 . . . . .5E 138
TW3: Houn 3G 113
Britannia Bldg. N1 . . . . .1E 8
(off Ebenezer St.)
Britannia Bus. Cen. NW2 . . . . .4F 63
Britannia Cl. SW4 . . . . .4H 119
UB5: N'olt 3B 76
Britannia Ct. KT2: King T 1D 150
(off Skerne Wlk.)
UB7: W Dray 3A 92

Britannia Ga. E16 . . . . .1J 105
BRITANNIA JUNC. 1F 83
Britannia La. TW2: Whitt 7G 113
Britannia Leisure Cen. 1D 84
Britannia Rd. E14 . . . . .4C 104
IG1: Ilf 3F 71
KT5: Surb 7F 151
N12 .3F 31
SW6 . . . . .7K 99
Britannia Row N1 . . . . .1B 84
Britannia St. WC1 . . . . .1G 7 (3K 83)
Britannia Wlk. N1 . . . . . . .1E 8 (2D 84)
(not continuous)
Britannia Way NW10 . . . . .4H 79
SW6 . . . . .7K 99
(off Britannia Rd.)
TW19: Stanw 7A 110
Britannic Highwalk EC2 . . . . .6E 8
(off Moor La.)
British Genius Site 7E 100
British Gro. W4 . . . . .5B 98
British Gro. Pas. W4 . . . . .5B 98
British Gro. Sth. W4 . . . . .5B 98
British Legion Rd. E4 . . . . .2C 36
British Library 1D 6 (3H 83)
British Mus. 6D 6 (5J 83)
British Music Experience 1G 105
British Postal Museum and Archive, The
. . . . .3J 7 (4A 84)
British St. E3 . . . . .3B 86
British Telecom Cen. EC1 . . . . .7C 8
British Wharf Ind. Est. SE14 . . . . . . .5K 103
Britley Ho. E14 . . . . .6B 86
(off Copenhagen Pl.)
Brittain Ct. SE9 . . . . .1C 142
Brittain Rd. RM8: Dag 3E 72
Brittany Ho. EN2: Enf 1H 23
Brittany Point SE11 . . . . . . .4J 19 (4A 102)
Britten Cl. NW11 . . . . .1K 63
Britten Cl. E15 . . . . .2F 87
Brittenden Cl. BR6: Chels 6K 173
Brittenden Pde. BR6: Chels 6K 173
Britten Dr. UB1: S'hall 6E 76
Britten Ho. SW3 . . . . .5D 16
(off Britten St.)
Britten St. SW3 . . . . .6C 16 (5C 100)
Britten Theatre 3B 100
(off Prince Consort Rd.)
Brittidge Rd. NW10 . . . . .7A 62
Brittion Cl. SE6 . . . . .7F 123
Britton St. EC1 . . . . .4A 8 (4B 84)
Brixham Cres. HA4: Ruis 1J 57
Brixham Gdns. IG3: Ilf 5J 71
Brixham Rd. DA16: Well 1D 126
Brixham St. E16 . . . . .1E 106
BRIXTON 4K 119
Brixton Hill SW2 . . . . .7J 119
Brixton Hill Ct. SW2 . . . . .5K 119
Brixton Hill Pl. SW2 . . . . .7J 119
Brixton Oval SW2 . . . . .4A 120
Brixton Recreation Cen. 3A 120
(off Brixton Sta. Rd.)
Brixton Rd. SE11 . . . . .7J 19 (6A 102)
SW9 . . . . .4A 120
Brixton Sta. Rd. SW9 . . . . .3A 120
Brixton Water La. SW2 . . . . .5K 119
Broadacre CI. UB10: Ick 3D 56
Broadbent Cl. N6 . . . . .1F 65
Broadbent St. W1 . . . . .2J 11 (7F 83)
Broadberry CI. N18 . . . . .6C 34
Broadbridge CI. SE3 . . . . .7J 105
Broad Comn. Est. N16 . . . . .1G 67
(off Osbaldeston Rd.)
Broadcoombe CR2: Sels 7J 169
Broad Ct. WC2 . . . . .1F 13 (6J 83)
Broadcroft Av. HA7: Stan 2D 42
Broadcroft Rd. BR5: Pet W 7H 161
Broadeaves CI. CR2: S Croy 5E 168
Broadfield NW6 . . . . .6K 63
Broadfield CI. CR0: Wadd 2K 167
NW2 .3E 62

Broadfield CI. HA2: Harr 1F 41
(off Broadfields)
WD23: B Hea 2D 26
Broadfield La. NW1 . . . . .7J 65
Broadfield Pde. HA8: Edg 3C 28
(off Glengall Rd.)
Broadfield Rd. SE6 . . . . .7G 123
Broadfields HA2: Harr 2F 41
KT8: E Mos 6J 149
Broadfields Av. HA8: Edg 4C 28
N21 .6F 23
Broadfields Hgts. HA8: Edg 4C 28
Broadfield Sq. EN1: Enf 2C 24
Broadfields Way NW10 . . . . .5B 62
Broadfield Way IG9: Buck H 3F 37
Bradford Ho. E1 . . . . .4A 86
(off Commodore St.)
Broadgate EC2 . . . . .6F 9
Broadgate Arena 6G 9 (5E 84)
Broadgate Circ. EC2 . . . . . . .5G 9 (5E 84)
Broadgate Ice Rink 6G 9
(off Broadgate Circ.)
Broadgate Plaza EC2 . . . . .5E 84
Broadgate Rd. E16 . . . . .6B 88
Broadgates Av. EN4: Had W 1E 20
Broadgates Rd. SW11 . . . . .6K 19
(off Cleaver St.)
Broadgates Rd. SW18 . . . . .1B 136
Broadgate Twr. EC2 . . . . . . .4H 9 (4E 84)
BROAD GREEN 7B 156
Broad Grn. Av. CR0: C'don 7B 156
Broadhead Strand NW9 . . . . .1B 44
Broadheath Dr. BR7: Chst 5D 142
Broadhinton Rd. SW4 . . . . .3F 119
Broadhurst Av. HA8: Edg 4C 28
IG3: Ilf 4K 71
Broadhurst Cl. NW6 . . . . .6A 64
TW10: Rich 5F 115
Broadhurst Gdns. HA4: Ruis 2A 58
NW6 . . . . .6K 63
Broadis Way RM13: Rain 2K 91
Broadlands E17 . . . . .3A 50
TW13: Hanw 3E 130
Broadlands Av. EN3: Enf H 3C 24
SW16 . . . . .2J 137
Broadlands Cl. EN3: Enf H 3D 24
N6 . . . . .7E 46
SW16 . . . . .2J 137
Broadlands Ct. TW9: Kew 7G 97
(off Kew Gdns. Rd.)
Broadlands Lodge N6 . . . . .7D 46
Broadlands Rd. BR1: Brom 4K 141
N6 . . . . .7D 46
Broadlands Way KT3: N Mald 6B 152
Broad La. EC2 . . . . .5G 9 (5E 84)
N8 . . . . .5K 47
N15 .4F 49
N17 .4G 49
TW12: Hamp 7D 130
Broad Lawn SE9 . . . . .2E 142
Broadlawns Ct.
HA3: Hrw W 1K 41
Broadley St. NW8 . . . . .5B 4 (5B 82)
Broadley Ter. NW1 . . . . .4D 4 (4C 82)
Broadmayne SE17 . . . . .5D 102
(off Portland St.)
Broadmead SE6 . . . . .3C 140
W14 .4G 99
Broadmead Av. KT4: Wor Pk 7C 152
Broadmead Cen. IG8: Wfd G 7F 37
(off Navestock Cres.)
Broadmead CI. HA5: Hat E 1C 40
TW12: Hamp 6E 130
Broadmead CI. IG8: Wfd G 6D 36
Broadmead Rd. IG8: Wfd G 6D 36
(not continuous)
UB4: Yead 4C 76
UB5: N'olt 4C 76
Broad Oak IG8: Wfd G 5E 36
TW16: Sun 6H 129

Broad Oak CI. E4 . . . . .5H 35
Broadoak Ct. SW9 . . . . .3A 120
(off Gresham Rd.)
Broadoak Ho. NW6 . . . . .1K 81
(off Mortimer Cres.)
Broadoak Rd. DA8: Erith 7K 109
Broadoaks KT6: Surb 2H 163
Broadoaks Way BR2: Brom 5H 159
Broad Sanctuary SW1 . . . . . .7D 12 (2H 101)
Broadstone NW1 . . . . .7H 65
(off Agar Gro.)
Broadstone Ho. SW8 . . . . .7K 101
(off Dorset Rd.)
Broadstone Pl. W1 . . . . .6G 5 (5E 82)
Broad St. RM10: Dag 7G 73
TW11: Tedd 6K 131
Broad St. Av. EC2 . . . . .6G 9 (5E 84)
Broad St. Mkt. RM10: Dag 7G 73
Broad St. Pl. EC2 . . . . .6G 9
Broadview NW9 . . . . .6G 43
Broadview Rd. SW16 . . . . .7H 137
Broad Wlk. N21 . . . . .2E 32
NW1 . . . . .1H 5 (1E 82)
SE3 .2A 124
TW5: Hest 1B 112
TW9: Kew 7F 97
W1 . . . . .3F 11 (7D 82)
Broad Walk, The KT8: E Mos 4K 149
W8 . . . . .1K 99
Broadwalk E18 . . . . .3H 51
HA2: Harr 5E 40
Broadwalk, The HA6: Nwood 2E 38
Broadwalk Ct. W8 . . . . .1J 99
(off Palace Gdns. Ter.)
Broadwalk Ho. EC2 . . . . .5G 9
SW7 . . . . .2A 100
(off Hyde Pk. Ga.)
Broad Wlk. La. NW11 . . . . .7H 45
Broadwalk Shop. Cen. HA8: Edg 6C 28
Broadwall SE1 . . . . .4K 13 (1A 102)
Broadwater Farm Est. N17 . . . . .2D 48
Broadwater Gdns. BR6: Farnb 4F 173
Broadwater Rd. N17 . . . . .1E 48
SE28 . . . . .3H 107
SW17 . . . . .4C 136
Broadway DA6: Bex 4E 126
(not continuous)
DA7: Bex 4G 127
E13 .2K 87
E15 .7F 69
IG11: Bark 1G 89
SW1 . . . . .7C 12 (1H 101)
W7 . . . . .1J 95
W13 .1A 96
Broadway, The CR0: Bedd 4J 167
E4 . . . . .6A 36
HA3: W'stone 2J 41
HA6: Nwood 2J 39
HA7: Stan 5H 27
HA9: Wemb 3E 60
IG8: Wfd G 6E 36
KT7: T Ditt 7J 149
N8 . . . . .6J 47
N9 . . . . .3B 34
N11 .5J 31
N14 .1C 32
(off The Bourne)
N22 .2A 48
NW7 .5F 29
RM8: Dag 1F 73
SM1: Sutt 5A 166
SM3: Cheam 6G 165
SW13 . . . . .3A 116
SW19 . . . . .6H 135
UB1: S'hall 7B 76
UB6: G'frd 4G 77
W3 . . . . .2G 97
(off Ridgeway Dr.)
W5 . . . . .7D 78
Broadway Arc. W6 . . . . .4E 98
(off Hammersmith B'way.)

Broadway Av. CR0: C'don 5D 156
  TW1: Twick 6B 114
Broadway Centre, The W6 . . . . .4E 98
Broadway Chambers W6 . . . . .4E 98
  (off Hammersmith B'way.)
Broadway Cl. IG8: Wfd G 6E 36
Broadway Ct. BR3: Beck 3E 158
  SW19 . . . . .6J 135
Broadway Gdns. CR4: Mitc 4C 154
  IG8: Wfd G 6E 36
Broadway Ho. BR1: Brom 5F 141
  (off Bromley Rd.)
  E8 . . . . .1H 85
  (off Ada St.)
Broadway Mans. SW6 . . . . .7J 99
  (off Fulham Rd.)
Broadway Mkt. E8 . . . . .1H 85
  (not continuous)
  IG6: Ilf .1H 53
  (not continuous)
  SW17 . . . . .4D 136
Broadway Mkt. M. E8 . . . . .1G 85
Broadway M. E5 . . . . .7F 49
  N13 . . . . .5E 32
  N21 . . . . .1G 33
Broadway Pde. E4 . . . . .6K 35
  (off The Broadway)
  HA2: Harr 5F 41
  N8 . . . . .6J 47
  UB3: Hayes 1J 93
Broadway Pl. SW19 . . . . .6H 135
Broadway Retail Pk. NW2 . . . . .4F 63
Broadway Shop. Cen. DA6: Bex 4G 127
Broadway Shop. Mall SW1 . . .1C 18 (3H 101)
Broadway Sq. DA6: Bex 4G 127
Broadway Theatre, The
  Barking .1G 89
  Catford .7D 122
Broadway W5, The W5 . . . . .7D 78
Broadway Wlk. E14 . . . . .2C 104
Broadwell Ct. TW5: Hest 1B 112
  (off Springwell Rd.)
Broadwell Pde. NW6 . . . . .6K 63
  (off Broadhurst Gdns.)
Broadwick St. W1 . . . . .2B 12 (7G 83)
Broadwood Av. HA4: Ruis 6F 39
Broadwood Ter. W8 . . . . .4H 99
Broad Yd. EC1 . . . . .4A 8 (4B 84)
Brocas Cl. NW3 . . . . .7C 64
Brockbridge Ho. SW15 . . . . .6B 116
Brockdene Dr. BR2: Kes 4B 172
Brockdish Av. IG11: Bark 5K 71
Brockenhurst KT8: W Mole 5D 148
Brockenhurst Av. KT4: Wor Pk 1A 164
Brockenhurst Gdns. IG1: Ilf 5G 71
  NW7 . . . . .5F 29
Brockenhurst M. N18 . . . . .4B 34
Brockenhurst Rd. CR0: C'don 7H 157
Brockenhurst Way SW16 . . . . .2H 155
Brocket Ho. SW8 . . . . .2H 119
Brockham Cl. SW19 . . . . .5H 135
Brockham Ct. CR2: S Croy 5C 168
Brockham Cres. CR0: New Ad 7F 171
Brockham Dr. IG2: Ilf 6F 53
  SW2 . . . . .7K 119
Brockham Ho. NW1 . . . . .1G 83
  (off Bayham Pl.)
  SW2 . . . . .7K 119
  (off Brockham Dr.)
Brockham St. SE1 . . . . .7D 14 (3C 102)
Brockhurst Cl. HA7: Stan 6E 26
Brockill Cres. SE4 . . . . .4A 122
Brocklebank Ho. E16 . . . . .1E 106
  (off Glenister St.)
Brocklebank Ind. Est. SE7 . . . . .4J 105
Brocklebank Rd. SE7 . . . . .4K 105
  SW18 . . . . .7A 118
Brocklehurst St. SE14 . . . . .7K 103
Brocklesby Rd. SE25 . . . . .4H 157
BROCKLEY 4K 121
Brockley Av. HA7: Stan 3K 27

Brockley Cl. HA7: Stan 4K 27
Brockley Cres. RM5: Col R 1J 55
Brockley Cross SE4 . . . . .3A 122
Brockley Cross Bus. Cen. SE4 . . . . . .3A 122
Brockley Footpath SE4 . . . . .5A 122
  (not continuous)
  SE15 . . . . .3J 121
Brockley Gdns. SE4 . . . . .2B 122
Brockley Gro. SE4 . . . . .5B 122
Brockley Hall Rd. SE4 . . . . .5A 122
Brockley Hill HA7: Stan 1H 27
Brockley Jack Theatre 5A 122
Brockley M. SE4 . . . . .5A 122
Brockley Pk. SE23 . . . . .7A 122
Brockley Ri. SE23 . . . . .1A 140
Brockley Rd. SE4 . . . . .5A 122
Brockleyside HA7: Stan 4K 27
Brockley Vw. SE23 . . . . .7A 122
Brockley Way SE4 . . . . .5K 121
Brockman Ri. BR1: Brom 4F 141
Brockmer Ho. E1 . . . . .7H 85
  (off Crowder St.)
Brock Pl. E3 . . . . .4D 86
Brock Rd. E13 .5K 87
Brocks Dr. SM3: Cheam 3G 165
Brockshot Cl. TW8: Bford 5D 96
Brock St. SE15 . . . . .3J 121
Brockway Cl. E11 . . . . .2G 69
Brockweir E2 . . . . .2J 85
  (off Cyprus St.)
Brockwell Av. BR3: Beck 5D 158
Brockwell Cl. BR5: St M Cry 5K 161
Brockwell Ct. SW2 . . . . .5A 120
Brockwell Ho. SE11 . . . . .7H 19
  (off Vauxhall St.)
Brockwell Park 6B 120
Brockwell Pk. Gdns. SE24 . . . . .7A 120
Brockwell Park Lido 6B 120
Brockwell Pk. Row SW2 . . . . .7A 120
Brockwell Pas. SE24 . . . . .6B 120
Brodia Rd. N16 .3E 66
Brodick Ho. E3 .2B 86
  (off Saxon Rd.)
Brodie Ho. SE1 .5F 103
  (off Cooper's Rd.)
Brodie Rd. E4 . . . . .1K 35
  EN2: Enf 1H 23
Brodie St. SE1 .5F 103
Brodlove La. E1 .7K 85
Brodrick Gro. SE2 . . . . .4B 108
Brodrick Rd. SW17 . . . . .2C 136
Brody Ho. E1 . . . . .6J 9
  (off Strype St.)
Brograve Gdns. BR3: Beck 2D 158
Broken Wharf EC4 . . . . .2C 14 (7C 84)
Brokesley St. E3 . . . . .3B 86
Broke Wlk. E8 . . . . .1F 85
Bromar Rd. SE5 . . . . .3E 120
Bromefield HA7: Stan 1C 42
Bromehead Rd. E1 . . . . .6J 85
Bromell's Rd. SW4 . . . . .4G 119
Brome Rd. SE9 . . . . .3D 124
Bromfelde Rd. SW4 . . . . .3H 119
Bromfelde Wlk. SW4 . . . . .2H 119
Bromfield Ct. SE16 . . . . .3G 103
  (off Ben Smith Way)
Bromfield St. N1 . . . . .1A 84
Bromhall Rd. RM8: Dag 6B 72
  RM9: Dag 6B 72
Bromhead Rd. E1 . . . . .6J 85
  (off Jubilee St.)
Bromhedge SE9 . . . . .3D 142
Bromholm Rd. SE2 . . . . .3B 108
Bromleigh Cl. SE23 . . . . .2G 139
Bromleigh Ho. SE1 . . . . .7J 15
  (off St Saviour's Est.)
BROMLEY 2J 159
  . . . . .3D 86
Bromley Av. BR1: Brom 7G 141
Bromley Coll. BR1: Brom 1J 159
BROMLEY COMMON 7C 160

Bromley Comn. BR2: Brom 4A 160
Bromley Cres. BR2: Brom 3H 159
  HA4: Ruis .4H 57
Bromley Environmental Education Centre
  at High Elms (BEECHE) 6H 173
Bromley FC 5K 159
Bromley Gdns. BR2: Brom 3H 159
Bromley Gro. BR2: Brom 2F 159
Bromley Hall Rd. E14 . . . . .5E 86
Bromley High St. E3 . . . . .3D 86
Bromley Hill BR1: Brom 6G 141
Bromley Ho. BR1: Brom 1J 159
  (off North St.)
Bromley Ind. Cen. BR1: Brom 3B 160
Bromley La. BR7: Chst 7G 143
Bromley Little Theatre 1J 159
BROMLEY PARK 1G 159
Bromley Pk. BR1: Brom 1H 159
Bromley Pl. W1 . . . . .5A 6 (5G 83)
Bromley Rd. BR1: Brom 1D 140
  BR2: Brom 2D 158
  BR3: Beck 1D 158
  BR7: Chst .1F 161
  E10 . . . . .6D 50
  E17 . . . . .3C 50
  N17 . . . . .1F 49
  N18 . . . . .3J 33
  SE6 . . . . .1D 140
Bromley Ski Cen. 7E 144
Bromley St. E1 . . . . .5K 85
Bromley Tennis Cen. 3H 173
BROMPTON 2D 16 (3C 100)
Brompton Arc. SW3 . . . . .7E 10
Brompton Cemetery 6K 99
Brompton Cl. SE20 . . . . .2G 157
  TW4: Houn 5D 112
Brompton Cotts. SW10 . . . . .6A 100
  (off Hollywood Rd.)
Brompton Ct. BR1: Brom 1J 159
  (off Tweedy Rd.)
Brompton Gro. N2 . . . . .4C 46
Brompton M. N12 . . . . .6F 31
Brompton Oratory 2C 16 (3C 100)
Brompton Pk. Cres. SW6 . . . . .6K 99
Brompton Pl. SW3 . . . . .1D 16 (3C 100)
Brompton Rd. SW1 . . . . .3C 16 (4C 100)
  SW3 . . . . .3C 16 (4C 100)
  SW7 . . . . .3C 100
Brompton Sq. SW3 . . . . .1C 16 (3C 100)
Brompton Ter. SE18 . . . . .1D 124
Brompton Vs. SW6 . . . . .6J 99
  (off Lillie Rd.)
Bromwich Av. N6 . . . . .2E 64
Bromyard Av. W3 . . . . .7A 80
Bromyard Ho. SE15 . . . . .7H 103
  (off Commercial Way)
Bromyard Ho. W3 . . . . .1B 98
Bron Ct. NW6 . . . . .1J 81
BRONDESBURY .7H 63
Brondesbury Ct. NW2 . . . . .6F 63
Brondesbury M. NW6 . . . . .7J 63
BRONDESBURY PARK 1E 80
Brondesbury Pk. NW2 . . . . .6E 62
  NW6 . . . . .6E 62
Brondesbury Pk. Mans. NW6 . . . . .1G 81
  (off Salusbury Rd.)
Brondesbury Rd. NW6 . . . . .2H 81
Brondesbury Vs. NW6 . . . . .2H 81
Bronhill Ter. N17 . . . . .1G 49
Bronsart Rd. SW6 . . . . .7G 99
Bronson Rd. SW20 . . . . .2F 153
Bronte Cl. DA8: Erith 7H 109
  E7 . . . . .4J 69
  IG2: Ilf 4E 52
Bronte Ct. W3 .2G 97
  W14 . . . . .3F 99
  (off Girdler's Rd.)
Bronte Ho. N16 .5E 66
  NW6 . . . . .3J 81
  SW4 . . . . .7G 119

Bronte Ho. SW17 . . . . .3B 136
  (off Grosvenor Way)
Bronti Cl. SE17 . . . . .5C 102
Bronwen Ct. NW8 . . . . .2A 4
  (off Grove End Rd.)
Bronze Age Way DA8: Erith 2H 109
  DA17: Belv 2H 109
Bronze St. SE8 .7C 104
Brook Av. HA8: Edg 6C 28
  HA9: Wemb 2F 61
  RM10: Dag 7H 73
Brookbank Av. W7 . . . . .5H 77
Brookbank Rd. SE13 . . . . .3C 122
Brook Cl. HA4: Ruis 7G 39
  NW7 . . . . .7B 30
  SW17 . . . . .2E 136
  SW20 . . . . .3D 152
  TW19: Stanw 7B 110
  W3 . . . . .1G 97
Brook Ct. BR3: Beck 1B 158
  E11 . . . . .3G 69
  E17 . . . . .3A 50
  EC4 . . . . .2E 14
  (off Laurence Pountney La.)
  HA8: Edg .5C 28
  IG11: Bark 1K 89
  (Sebastian Ct.)
  IG11: Bark 2G 89
  (Spring Pl.)
  SE12 . . . . .3A 142
Brook Cres. E4 .4H 35
  N9 . . . . .4C 34
Brookdale N11 . . . . .4K 31
Brookdale Rd. DA5: Bexl 6E 126
  E17 . . . . .3C 50
  SE6 . . . . .7D 122
  (Catford B'way.)
  SE6 . . . . .6D 122
  (Medusa Rd.)
Brookdales NW11 . . . . .4G 45
Brookdene Rd. SE18 . . . . .4J 107
Brook Dr. HA1: Harr 4G 41
  HA4: Ruis .7G 39
  SE11 . . . . .2K 19 (3A 102)
Brooke Av. HA2: Harr 3G 59
Brooke Cl. WD23: Bush 1B 26
Brooke Cl. W10 .2G 81
  (off Kilburn La.)
Brooke Ho. SE14 . . . . .1A 122
  WD23: Bush 1B 26
Brookehowse Rd. SE6 . . . . .2C 140
Brookend Rd. DA15: Sidc 1J 143
Brooke Rd. E5 . . . . .3G 67
  E17 . . . . .4E 50
  N16 . . . . .3F 67
Brooke's Ct. EC1 . . . . .6J 7 (5A 84)
Brooke's Mkt. EC1 . . . . .5K 7
Brooke St. EC1 . . . . .6J 7 (5A 84)
Brooke Way WD23: Bush 1B 26
Brookfield N6 . . . . .3E 64
Brookfield Av. E17 . . . . .4E 50
  NW7 . . . . .6J 29
  SM1: Sutt 4B 166
  W5 . . . . .4D 78
Brookfield Cl. NW7 . . . . .6J 29
Brookfield Ct. N12 . . . . .4E 30
  UB6: G'frd .3G 77
Brookfield Cres. HA3: Kenton 5E 42
  NW7 . . . . .6J 29
Brookfield Gdns. KT10: Clay 6A 162
Brookfield Pk. NW5 . . . . .3F 65
Brookfield Path IG8: Wfd G 6B 36
Brookfield Rd. E9 . . . . .6A 68
  N9 . . . . .3B 34
  W4 . . . . .2K 97
Brookfields EN3: Pond E 4E 24
Brookfields Av. CR4: Mitc 5C 154
Brook Gdns. E4 .4J 35
  KT2: King T 1J 151
  SW13 . . . . .3B 116
Brook Ga. W1 . . . . .3F 11 (7D 82)

BROOK GREEN 4F 99
Brook Grn. W6 . . . . .3F 99
Brook Grn. Flats W14 . . . . .3F 99
(off Dunsany Rd.)
Brookhill Cl. EN4: E Barn 5H 21
SE18 . . . . .5F 107
Brookhill Rd. EN4: E Barn 5H 21
SE18 . . . . .6F 107
Brook Ho. E1 .7G 85
(off Fletcher St.)
W6 . . . . .4E 98
(off Shepherd's Bush Rd.)
Brookhouse Gdns. E4 . . . . .4B 36
Brook Ho's. NW1 . . . . .2G 83
(off Cranleigh St.)
Brook Ind. Est. UB4: Yead 1B 94
Brooking Cl. RM8: Dag 3C 72
Brooking Rd. E7 . . . . .5J 69
Brookland Cl. NW11 . . . . .4J 45
Brookland Gth. NW11 . . . . .4J 45
Brookland Hill NW11 . . . . .4K 45
Brookland Ri. NW11 . . . . .4J 45
Brooklands, The TW7: Isle 1H 113
Brooklands App.
RM1: Rom 4K 55
Brooklands Av. DA15: Sidc 2H 143
SW19 . . . . .2K 135
Brooklands Cl. RM7: Rom 4K 55
TW16: Sun 1G 147
Brooklands Ct. CR4: Mitc 2B 154
KT1: King T 4D 150
(off Surbiton Rd.)
N21 . . . . .5J 23
NW6 . . . . .7H 63
Brooklands Dr. UB6: G'frd 1C 78
Brooklands La. RM7: Rom 4K 55
(not continuous)
Brooklands Pk. SE3 . . . . .3J 123
Brooklands Pas. SW8 . . . . .1H 119
Brooklands Pl. TW12: Hamp H 5F 131
Brooklands Rd. KT7: T Ditt 1A 162
RM7: Rom 4K 55
Brooklands Ter. TW16: Sun 4J 147
Brook La. BR1: Brom 6J 141
DA5: Bexl, Bex 6D 126
SE3 . . . . .2K 123
Brook La. Bus. Cen. TW8: Bford 5D 96
Brook La. Nth. TW8: Bford 5D 96
(not continuous)
Brooklea Cl. NW9 . . . . .1A 44
Brook Lodge NW11 . . . . .5F 45
(off Nth. Circular Rd.)
RM7: Rom 4K 55
(off Brooklands Rd.)
Brooklyn SE20 . . . . .7G 139
Brooklyn Av. SE25 . . . . .4H 157
Brooklyn Cl. SM5: Cars 2C 166
Brooklyn Ct. W12 . . . . .1E 98
(off Frithville Gdns.)
Brooklyn Gro. SE25 . . . . .4H 157
Brooklyn Pas. W12 . . . . .2E 98
(off Lime Gro.)
Brooklyn Rd. BR2: Brom 5B 160
SE25 . . . . .4H 157
Brookman Ho. E3 . . . . .2B 86
(off Mostyn Gro.)
Brookmarsh Ind. Est. SE10 . . . . .7D 104
Brook Mead KT19: Ewe 6A 164
Brookmead CR0: Bedd 6G 155
Brookmead Av. BR1: Brom 5D 160
Brookmead Ind. Est. CR0: Bedd 6G 155
Brook Mdw. N12 . . . . .3E 30
Brook Mdw. Cl. IG8: Wfd G 6B 36
Brookmead Rd. CR0: C'don 6G 155
Brook M. IG7: Chig 3K 37
N13 . . . . .5F 33
WC2 . . . . .6H 83
Brook M. Nth. W2 . . . . . .2A 10 (7A 82)
Brookmill Rd. SE8 . . . . .1C 122
Brook Pde. IG7: Chig 3K 37
Brook Pk. Cl. N21 . . . . .5G 23

Brook Pl. EN5: Barn 5D 20
Brook Retail Pk. HA4: Ruis 5B 58
Brook Ri. IG7: Chig 3K 37
Brook Rd. CR7: Thor H 4C 156
IG2: Ilf 6J 53
IG9: Buck H, Wfd G 2D 36
KT6: Surb 2E 162
N8 . . . . .4J 47
N22 . . . . .3K 47
NW2 . . . . .2B 62
TW1: Twick 6A 114
Brook Rd. Sth. TW8: Bford 6D 96
Brooks Apartments E3 . . . . .5C 86
(off Geoff Cade Way)
Brooks Av. E6 . . . . .4D 88
Brooksbank Ho. E9 . . . . .6J 67
(off Retreat Pl.)
Brooksbank St. E9 . . . . .6J 67
Brooksby Ho. N1 . . . . .7A 66
(off Liverpool Rd.)
Brooksby M. N1 . . . . .7A 66
Brooksby St. N1 . . . . .7A 66
Brooksby's Wlk. E9 . . . . .5K 67
Brooks Cl. SE9 . . . . .2E 142
Brooks Ct. SW8 . . . . .7G 101
Brookscroft E17 . . . . .3D 50
Brookscroft Rd. E17 . . . . .1D 50
(not continuous)
Brooks Farm .7D 50
Brookshill HA3: Hrw W 5C 26
Brookshill Av. HA3: Hrw W 5C 26
Brookshill Dr. HA3: Hrw W 5C 26
Brookshill Ga. HA3: Hrw W 5C 26
Brookside BR6: Orp 7K 161
EN4: E Barn 6H 21
N21 . . . . .6E 22
SM5: Cars 5E 166
UB10: Uxb 7B 56
Brookside Cl.
EN5: Barn 6B 20
HA2: Harr 4C 58
HA3: Kenton 5D 42
TW13: Felt 3J 129
Brookside Cres. KT4: Wor Pk 1C 164
Brookside Rd. N9 . . . . .4C 34
(not continuous)
N19 . . . . .2G 65
NW11 . . . . .6G 45
UB4: Yead 7A 76
Brookside Sth. EN4: E Barn 7K 21
Brookside Wlk. N3 . . . . .3G 45
N12 . . . . .6D 30
NW11 . . . . .4G 45
Brookside Way CR0: C'don 6K 157
Brooks La. W4 . . . . .6G 97
Brooks Lodge N1 . . . . .2E 84
Brook's M. W1 . . . . .2J 11 (7F 83)
Brook Sq. SE18 . . . . .1C 124
Brooks Rd. E13 . . . . .1J 87
W4 . . . . .5G 97
Brook St. DA8: Erith 5H 109
DA17: Belv, Erith 5H 109
KT1: King T 2E 150
N17 . . . . .2F 49
W1 . . . . .2H 11 (7E 83)
W2 . . . . .2B 10 (7B 82)
Brooksville Av. NW6 . . . . .1G 81
Brook Va. DA8: Erith 1H 127
Brookview Ct. EN1: Enf 5K 23
Brookview Rd. SW16 . . . . .5G 137
Brookville Rd. SW6 . . . . .7H 99
Brook Wlk. HA8: Edg 6B 28
N2 . . . . .1B 46
Brook Way IG7: Chig 3K 37
Brookway SE3 . . . . .3J 123
Brookwood Av. SW13 . . . . .2B 116
Brookwood Cl. BR2: Brom 4H 159
Brookwood Ho. SE1 . . . . .7B 14
(off Webber St.)
Brookwood Rd. SW18 . . . . .1H 135
TW3: Houn 2F 113

Brook Cl. BR2: Brom 6C 160
TW11: Tedd 7D 132
Broomcroft Av. UB5: N'olt 3A 76
Broome Rd. TW12: Hamp 7D 130
Broome Way SE5 . . . . .7D 102
Broomfield E17 . . . . .7B 50
NW1 . . . . .7E 64
(off Ferdinand St.)
Broomfield Av. N13 . . . . .5E 32
Broomfield Cl. N2 . . . . .4C 46
Broomfield Ho. HA7: Stan 4B 26
(off Stanmore Hill)
SE17 . . . . .4E 102
(off Massinger St.)
Broomfield La. N13 . . . . .4D 32
Broomfield Pl. W13 . . . . .1B 96
Broomfield Rd. BR3: Beck 3A 158
DA6: Bex 5G 127
KT5: Surb 1F 163
N13 . . . . .5D 32
RM6: Chad H 7D 54
TW9: Kew 1F 115
TW11: Tedd 6C 132
W13 . . . . .1B 96
Broomfield St. E14 . . . . .5C 86
Broom Gdns. CR0: C'don 3C 170
Broomgrove Gdns. HA8: Edg 1G 43
Broomgrove Rd. SW9 . . . . .2K 119
Broomhall Rd. CR2: Sande 7D 168
BROOM HILL 7K 161
Broomhill Cl. IG8: Wfd G 6D 36
Broomhill Ri. DA6: Bex 5G 127
Broomhill Rd. BR6: Orp 7K 161
IG3: Ilf 2A 72
IG8: Wfd G 6D 36
(not continuous)
SW18 . . . . .5J 117
Broomhill Wlk. IG8: Wfd G 6C 36
Broomhouse La. SW6 . . . . .2J 117
Broomhouse Rd. SW6 . . . . .2J 117
Broomloan La. SM1: Sutt 2J 165
Broom Lock TW11: Tedd 6C 132
Broom Mead DA6: Bex 6G 127
Broom Pk. TW11: Tedd 7D 132
Broom Rd. CR0: C'don 3C 170
TW11: Tedd 5B 132
Broomsleigh Bus. Pk. SE26 . . . . .5B 140
Broomsleigh St. NW6 . . . . .5H 63
Broom Water TW11: Tedd 6C 132
Broom Water W. TW11: Tedd 5C 132
Broomwood Cl. CR0: C'don 5K 157
DA5: Bexl 2K 145
Broomwood Rd. SW4 . . . . .5E 118
SW11 . . . . .6D 118
Broseley Gro. SE26 . . . . .5A 140
Brosse Way BR2: Brom 6C 160
Broster Gdns. SE25 . . . . .3F 157
Brougham Rd. E8 . . . . .1G 85
W3 . . . . .6J 79
Brougham St. SW11 . . . . .2D 118
Brough Cl. KT2: King T 5D 132
SW8 . . . . .7J 101
Broughton Av. N3 . . . . .3G 45
TW10: Ham 3B 132
Broughton Ct. W13 . . . . .7B 78
Broughton Dr. SW9 . . . . .4A 120
Broughton Gdns. N6 . . . . .6G 47
Broughton Pl. E17 . . . . .1B 50
Broughton Rd. BR6: Orp 2H 173
CR7: Thor H 6A 156
SW6 . . . . .2K 117
W13 . . . . .7B 78
Broughton Rd. App. SW6 . . . . .2K 117
Broughton St. SW8 . . . . .2E 118
Broughton St. Ind. Est.
SW11 . . . . .2E 118
Brouncker Rd. W3 . . . . .2J 97
Browells La. TW13: Felt 2K 129
(not continuous)
Brown Bear Ct. TW13: Hanw 4B 130

Brown Cl. SM6: Wall 7J 167
Browne Ho. SE8 . . . . .7C 104
(off Deptford Chu. St.)
Brownell Pl. W7 . . . . .2K 95
Brownfield Area E14 . . . . .6D 86
Brownfield St. E14 . . . . .6D 86
Browngraves Rd. UB3: Harl 7E 92
Brown Hart Gdns. W1 . . . . . .2H 11 (7E 82)
Brownhill Rd. SE6 . . . . .7D 122
Browning Apartments E3 . . . . .4B 86
(off Hamlets Way)
Browning Av. KT4: Wor Pk 1D 164
SM1: Sutt 4C 166
W7 . . . . .6K 77
Browning Cl. DA16: Well 1J 125
E17 . . . . .4E 50
RM5: Col R 1F 55
TW12: Hamp 4D 130
W9 . . . . .4A 4 (4A 82)
Browning Ct. W14 . . . . .6H 99
(off Turneville Rd.)
Browning Ho. N16 . . . . .4E 66
(off Shakspeare Wlk.)
SE14 . . . . .1A 122
(off Loring Rd.)
W12 . . . . .6D 80
(off Wood La.)
Browning M. W1 . . . . .6H 5 (5F 83)
Browning Rd. E11 . . . . .7H 51
E12 . . . . .5D 70
EN2: Enf 1J 23
Browning St. SE17 . . . . .5C 102
Browning Way TW5: Hest 1B 112
Brownlea Gdns. IG3: Ilf 2A 72
Brownlow Cl. EN4: E Barn 5G 21
Brownlow Ct. N2 . . . . .5A 46
N11 . . . . .6D 32
(off Brownlow Rd.)
Brownlow Ho. SE16 . . . . .2G 103
(off George Row)
Brownlow M. WC1 . . . . .4H 7 (4K 83)
Brownlow Rd. CR0: C'don 4E 168
E7 . . . . .4J 69
E8 . . . . .1F 85
N3 . . . . .7E 30
N11 . . . . .6D 32
NW10 . . . . .7A 62
W13 . . . . .1A 96
Brownlow St. WC1 . . . . .6H 7 (5K 83)
Brownrigg Rd. TW15: Ashf 4C 128
Brown's Bldgs. EC3 . . . . . .1H 15 (6E 84)
Brownswood Wlk. NW7 . . . . .6A 30
Browns La. NW5 . . . . .5F 65
Brownspring Dr. SE9 . . . . .4F 143
Browns Rd. E17 . . . . .3C 50
KT5: Surb 7F 151
Brown St. W1 . . . . .7E 4 (6D 82)
Brownswell Rd. N2 . . . . .2B 46
BROWNSWOOD PARK 2B 66
Brownswood Rd. N4 . . . . .3B 66
Broxash Rd. SW11 . . . . .6E 118
Broxbourne Av. E18 . . . . .4K 51
Broxbourne Gdns. BR6: Orp 1K 173
(off Broxbourne Rd.)
Broxbourne Ho. E3 . . . . .4D 86
(off Empson St.)
Broxbourne Rd. BR6: Orp 1K 173
E7 . . . . .3J 69
Broxholme Cl. SE25 . . . . .4D 156
Broxholme Ho. SW6 . . . . .1K 117
(off Harwood Rd.)
Broxholm Rd. SE27 . . . . .3A 138
Broxted Rd. SE6 . . . . .2B 140
Broxwood Way NW8 . . . . .1C 82
Bruce Av. TW17: Shep 6E 146
Bruce Castle Ct. N17 . . . . .1F 49
(off Lordship La.)
Bruce Castle Mus. 1E 48
Bruce Castle Rd. N17 . . . . .1F 49
Bruce Cl. DA16: Well 1B 126
W10 . . . . .5F 81

Bruce Ct. DA15: Sidc 4K **143**
Bruce Gdns. N20 . . . . .3J **31**
Bruce Gro. N17 . . . . .1E **48**
Bruce Hall M. SW17 . . . . . . .4E **136**
Bruce Ho. W10 . . . . .5F **81**
Bruce Rd. CR4: Mitc 7E **136**
   E3 . . . . .3D **86**
   EN5: Barn 3B **20**
   HA3: W'stone 2J **41**
   NW10 . . . . .7K **61**
   SE25 . . . . .4D **156**
Bruckner St. W10 . . . . .3G **81**
Brudenell Rd. SW17 . . . . . . .3D **136**
Bruffs Mdw. UB5: N'olt 6C **58**
Bruford Ct. SE8 . . . . .6C **104**
Bruges Pl. NW1 . . . . .7G **65**
   (off Randolph St.)
Brumfield Rd. KT19: Ewe 5J **163**
Brummel Cl. DA7: Bex 3J **127**
Brune Ho. E1 . . . . .6J **9**
Brunei Gallery 5D **6** (5H **83**)
Brunel Cl. SE19 . . . . .6F **139**
   TW5: Cran 7K **93**
   UB5: N'olt 3D **76**
Brunel Ct. HA8: Edg 4A **28**
   SE16 . . . . .2J **103**
   (off Canon Beck Rd.)
   SW13 . . . . .2B **116**
   (off Westfields Av.)
Brunel Est. W2 . . . . .5J **81**
Brunel Ho. BR2: Brom 6C **160**
   (off Wells Vw. Dr.)
   E14 . . . . .5D **104**
   (off Ship Yd.)
   RM8: Dag 4A **72**
Brunel M. W10 . . . . .3F **81**
Brunel Mus. 2J **103**
Brunel Pl. UB1: S'hall 6F **77**
Brunel Rd. E17 . . . . .6A **50**
   IG8: Wfd G 5J **37**
   SE16 . . . . .2J **103**
   W3 . . . . .5A **80**
Brunel Science Pk. UB8: Cowl 3A **74**
Brunel St. E16 . . . . .6H **87**
Brunel University
   Indoor Athletics Cen. 3A **74**
   Sports Pk. 4B **74**
Brunel University
   Uxbridge Campus 3A **74**
Brunel Wlk. N15 . . . . .5E **48**
   SW10 . . . . .7B **100**
   (off Cheyne Rd.)
   TW2: Whitt 7E **112**
Brune St. E1 . . . . . . .6J **9** (5F **85**)
Brunlees Ho. SE1 . . . . .3C **102**
   (off Bath Ter.)
Brunner Cl. NW11 . . . . .5K **45**
Brunner Ho. SE6 . . . . .4E **140**
Brunner Rd. E17 . . . . .5A **50**
   W5 . . . . .4D **78**
Bruno Pl. NW9 . . . . .2J **61**
Brunswick Av. N11 . . . . .3K **31**
Brunswick Cen. WC1 . . . . .3E **6** (4J **83**)
Brunswick Cl. DA6: Bex 4D **126**
   HA5: Pinn 6C **40**
   KT7: T Ditt 1A **162**
   TW2: Twick 3H **131**
Brunswick Cl. Est. EC1 . . . .2A **8** (3B **84**)
Brunswick Ct. EC1 . . . . .2A **8**
   (off Tompion St.)
   EN4: E Barn 5G **21**
   SE1 . . . . .7H **15** (2E **102**)
   SM1: Sutt 4K **165**
   SW1 . . . . .4D **18**
   (off Regency St.)
Brunswick Cres. N11 . . . . .3K **31**
Brunswick Flats W11 . . . . .6J **81**
   (off Westbourne Gro.)
Brunswick Gdns. IG6: Ilf 1G **53**
   W5 . . . . .4E **78**
   W8 . . . . .1J **99**

Brunswick Gro. N11 . . . . .3K **31**
Brunswick Ho. E2 . . . . .2F **85**
   (off Thurtle Rd.)
   N3 . . . . .1H **45**
   SE16 . . . . .3A **104**
   (off Brunswick Quay)
   W6 . . . . .5E **98**
   (off Parrs Way)
Brunswick Ind. Pk. N11 . . . . . .4A **32**
Brunswick Mans. WC1 . . . . .3F **7**
   (off Handel St.)
Brunswick M. SW16 . . . . .6H **137**
   W1 . . . . .7F **5** (6D **82**)
BRUNSWICK PARK 3J **31**
Brunswick Pk. SE5 . . . . .1E **120**
Brunswick Pk. Gdns. N11 . . . . .2K **31**
Brunswick Pk. Rd. N11 . . . . . . .2K **31**
Brunswick Pl. N1 . . . . . .2F **9** (3D **84**)
   NW1 . . . . .4H **5** (4E **82**)
   (not continuous)
   SE19 . . . . .7G **139**
Brunswick Quay SE16 . . . . . . .3K **103**
Brunswick Rd. DA6: Bex 4D **126**
   E10 . . . . .1E **68**
   E14 . . . . .6E **86**
   EN3: Enf L 1H **25**
   KT2: King T 1G **151**
   N15 . . . . .5E **48**
   SM1: Sutt 4K **165**
   W5 . . . . .4D **78**
Brunswick Sq. N17 . . . . .6A **34**
   WC1 . . . . .3F **7** (4J **83**)
   (not continuous)
Brunswick St. E17 . . . . .5E **50**
Brunswick Ter. BR3: Beck 1D **158**
Brunswick Vs. SE5 . . . . .1E **120**
Brunswick Way N11 . . . . .4A **32**
Brunton Pl. E14 . . . . .6A **86**
Brushfield St. E1 . . . . .5H **9** (5E **84**)
Brushwood Cl. E14 . . . . .5D **86**
Brussels Rd. SW11 . . . . .4B **118**
Bruton Cl. BR7: Chst 7D **142**
Bruton La. W1 . . . . . . .3K **11** (7F **83**)
Bruton Pl. W1 . . . . . . .3K **11** (7F **83**)
Bruton Rd. SM4: Mord 4A **154**
Bruton St. W1 . . . . . . .3K **11** (7F **83**)
Bruton Way W13 . . . . .5A **78**
Brutus Ct. SE11 . . . . .4B **102**
   (off Kennington La.)
Bryan Av. NW10 . . . . .7D **62**
Bryan Cl. TW16: Sun 7J **129**
Bryan Ho. NW10 . . . . .7D **62**
   SE16 . . . . .2B **104**
Bryan Rd. SE16 . . . . .2B **104**
Bryan's All. SW6 . . . . .2K **117**
Bryanston Av. TW2: Whitt 1F **131**
Bryanston Cl. UB2: S'hall 4D **94**
Bryanston Ct. W1 . . . . .7E **4**
   (not continuous)
Bryanstone Ct. SM1: Sutt 3A **166**
Bryanstone Rd. N8 . . . . .5H **47**
Bryanston Mans. W1 . . . . .5E **4**
   (off York St.)
Bryanston M. E. W1 . . . . .6E **4** (5D **82**)
Bryanston M. W. W1 . . . . .6E **4** (5D **82**)
Bryanston Pl. W1 . . . . . . .6E **4** (5D **82**)
Bryanston Sq. W1 . . . . . . .6E **4** (6D **82**)
Bryanston St. W1 . . . . . .1E **10** (6D **82**)
Bryan St. N1 . . . . .1K **83**
Bryant Cl. EN5: Barn 5C **20**
Bryant Ct. E2 . . . . .2F **85**
   (off Whiston Rd., not continuous)
   W3 . . . . .1K **97**
Bryant Ho. E3 . . . . .2C **86**
   (off Thomas Fyre Dr.)
Bryant Rd. UB5: N'olt 3A **76**
Bryant St. E15 . . . . .7F **69**
Bryantwood Rd. N7 . . . . .5A **66**
Brycedale Cres. N14 . . . . .4C **32**
Bryce Ho. SE14 . . . . .6K **103**
   (off John Williams Cl.)

Bryce Rd. RM8: Dag 4C **72**
Brydale Ho. SE16 . . . . .4K **103**
   (off Rotherhithe New Rd.)
Bryden Cl. SE26 . . . . .5A **140**
Brydges Pl. WC2 . . . . . .3E **12** (7J **83**)
Brydges Rd. E15 . . . . .5F **69**
Brydon Wlk. N1 . . . . .1J **83**
Bryer Ct. EC2 . . . . .5C **8**
Bryett Rd. N7 . . . . .3J **65**
Bryher Ct. SE11 . . . . .5J **19**
Brymay Cl. E3 . . . . .2C **86**
Brymcourt W9 . . . . .2K **81**
Brynmaer Rd. SW11 . . . . .1D **118**
Bryn-y-mawr Rd. EN1: Enf 4A **24**
Bryony Cl. UB8: Hil 5B **74**
Bryony Rd. W12 . . . . .7C **80**
Bryony Way TW16: Sun 6J **129**
Buccleugh Ho. E5 . . . . .7G **49**
Buchanan Cl. N21 . . . . .5E **22**
Buchanan Ct. SE16 . . . . .4K **103**
   (off Worgan St.)
Buchanan Gdns. NW10 . . . . . .2D **80**
Buchan Ho. W3 . . . . .2H **97**
   (off Hanbury Rd.)
Buchan Rd. SE15 . . . . .3J **121**
Bucharest Rd. SW18 . . . . .7A **118**
Buckden Cl. N2 . . . . .4D **46**
   SE12 . . . . .6J **123**
Buckfast Cl. W13 . . . . .7A **78**
   (off Romsey Rd.)
Buckfast Ho. N14 . . . . .5B **22**
Buckfast Rd. SM4: Mord 4K **153**
Buckfast St. E2 . . . . .3G **85**
Buck Hill Wlk. W2 . . . . .3B **10** (7B **82**)
Buckhold Rd. SW18 . . . . .6J **117**
Buckhurst Av. SM5: Cars 1C **166**
Buckhurst Ct. IG9: Buck H 1G **37**
BUCKHURST HILL 2G **37**
Buckhurst Hill Ho. IG9: Buck H 2E **36**
Buckhurst Ho. N7 . . . . .5H **65**
Buckhurst St. E1 . . . . .4H **85**
Buckhurst Way IG9: Buck H 4G **37**
Buckingham Arc. WC2 . . . . .3E **12**
Buckingham Av. CR7: Thor H . . .1A **156**
   DA16: Well 4J **125**
   KT8: W Mole 2F **149**
   N20 . . . . .7F **21**
   TW14: Felt 6K **111**
   UB6: G'frd 1A **78**
Buckingham Chambers SW1 . . . . .3B **18**
   (off Greencoat Pl.)
Buckingham Cl. BR5: Pet W 7J **161**
   EN1: Enf 2K **23**
   TW12: Hamp 5D **130**
   W5 . . . . .5C **78**
Buckingham Ct. NW4 . . . . .3C **44**
   UB5: N'olt 2C **76**
   W7 . . . . .4K **77**
   (off Copley Cl.)
   W11 . . . . .7J **81**
   (off Kensington Pk. Rd.)
Buckingham Dr. BR7: Chst 4G **143**
Buckingham Gdns. CR7: Thor H . . .2A **156**
   HA8: Edg 7K **27**
   KT8: W Mole 2F **149**
Buckingham Ga. SW1 . . . .1A **18** (3G **101**)
Buckingham Gro. UB10: Hil 2C **74**
Buckingham La. SE23 . . . . . . .7A **122**
Buckingham Mans. NW6 . . . . . .5K **63**
   (off West End La.)
Buckingham M. N1 . . . . .6E **66**
   NW10 . . . . .2B **80**
   SW1 . . . . .1A **18**
Buckingham Palace 7K **11** (2F **101**)
Buckingham Pal. Rd. SW1 . . .4J **17** (4F **101**)
Buckingham Pde. HA7: Stan 5H **27**
Buckingham Pl. SW1 . . . .1A **18** (3G **101**)
Buckingham Rd. CR4: Mitc 4J **155**
   E10 . . . . .3D **68**
   E11 . . . . .5A **52**
   E15 . . . . .5H **69**

Buckingham Rd. E18 . . . . .1H **51**
   HA1: Harr 5H **41**
   HA8: Edg 7A **28**
   IG1: Ilf 2H **71**
   KT1: King T 4F **151**
   N1 . . . . .6E **66**
   N22 . . . . .1J **47**
   NW10 . . . . .2B **80**
   TW10: Ham 2D **132**
   TW12: Hamp 4D **130**
Buckingham St. WC2 . . . .4F **13** (7J **83**)
Buckingham Way SM6: Wall . . .7G **167**
Buckland Cl. NW7 . . . . .4H **29**
Buckland Ct. N1 . . . . .2E **84**
   (off St John's Est.)
   UB10: Ick 2E **56**
Buckland Cres. NW3 . . . . .7B **64**
Buckland Ho. SW1 . . . . .5J **17**
   (part of Abbots Mnr.)
Buckland Ri. HA5: Pinn 1A **40**
Buckland Rd. BR6: Orp 4J **173**
   E10 . . . . .2E **68**
   KT9: Chess 5F **163**
Bucklands Rd. TW11: Tedd 6C **132**
Buckland St. N1 . . . . .2D **84**
Buckland's Wharf KT1: King T . . .2D **150**
Buckland Wlk. SM4: Mord 4A **154**
   W3 . . . . .2J **97**
Buckland Way KT4: Wor Pk 1E **164**
Buck La. NW9 . . . . .5K **43**
Bucklebury NW1 . . . . .3A **6**
   (off Stanhope St.)
Buckleigh Av. SW20 . . . . .3G **153**
Buckleigh Ho. SW16 . . . . .6H **137**
Buckleigh Way SE19 . . . . .7F **139**
Buckler Cl. N7 . . . . .5K **65**
Buckler Gdns. SE9 . . . . .3D **142**
Bucklers All. SW6 . . . . .6H **99**
Bucklersbury EC4 . . . . .1E **14** (6D **84**)
Bucklersbury Pas. EC4 . . . . . . .6D **84**
Buckler's Way SM5: Cars 3D **166**
Buckles Ct. DA17: Belv 4D **108**
Buckle St. E1 . . . . .7K **9** (6F **85**)
Buckley Cl. SE23 . . . . .7H **121**
Buckley Ct. NW6 . . . . .7H **63**
   SE1 . . . . .3F **103**
Buckley Ho. W14 . . . . .2G **99**
   (off Holland Pk. Av.)
Buckley Rd. NW6 . . . . .7H **63**
Buckmaster Cl. SW9 . . . . .3A **120**
   (off Stockwell Pk. Rd.)
Buckmaster Ho. N7 . . . . .4K **65**
Buckmaster Rd. SW11 . . . . . . .4C **118**
Bucknall St. WC2 . . . . . .7D **6** (6J **83**)
Bucknall Way BR3: Beck 4D **158**
Bucknell Cl. SW2 . . . . .4K **119**
Bucknell Ho. SW2 . . . . .4K **119**
Bucknill Ho. SW1 . . . . .5J **17**
   (off Ebury Bri. Rd.)
Buckrell Rd. E4 . . . . .2A **36**
Buckridge Ho. EC1 . . . . .5J **7**
   (off Portpool La.)
Buckshead Ho. W2 . . . . .5J **81**
   (off Gt. Western Rd.)
Buckstone Cl. SE23 . . . . .6J **121**
Buckstone Rd. N18 . . . . .5B **34**
Buck St. NW1 . . . . .7F **65**
Buckters Rents SE16 . . . . .1A **104**
Buckthorne Rd. SE4 . . . . .5A **122**
Buckthorn Ho. DA15: Sidc 3K **143**
   E15 . . . . .3G **87**
   (off Manor Rd.)
Buck Wlk. E17 . . . . .4F **51**
Buckwheat Ct. DA18: Erith 3D **108**
Budd Cl. N12 . . . . .4E **30**
Buddings Circ. HA9: Wemb 3J **61**
Buddleia Ho. TW13: Felt 1J **129**
Budd's All. TW1: Twick 5C **114**
Bude Cl. E17 . . . . .5B **50**
Budge La. CR4: Mitc 7D **154**

Budge Row—Burney St.

Budge Row EC4 . . . . . 1E **14** (7D **84**)
Budge's Wlk. W2 . . . . . 3A **10**
Budleigh Cres. DA16: Well 1C **126**
Budleigh Ho. *SE15* *7G* ***103***
(off Bird in Bush Rd.)
Budoch Ct. IG3: Ilf 2A **72**
Budoch Dr. IG3: Ilf 2A **72**
Buer Rd. SW6 . . . . . 2G **117**
Bugsby's Way SE7 . . . . . 4H **105**
SE10 . . . . . 4H **105**
Buick Ho. *E3* *4C* ***86***
(off Wellington Way)
KT2: King T 2F **151**
Building 50 SE18 . . . . . 3G **107**
Bulbarrow *NW8* *1K* ***81***
(off Abbey Rd.)
Bulganak Rd. CR7: Thor H 4C **156**
Bulinga St. SW1 . . . . . 4E **18**
Bullace Row SE5 . . . . . 1D **120**
Bull All. DA16: Well 3B **126**
Bullard's Pl. E2 . . . . . 3K **85**
Bullbanks Rd. DA17: Belv 4J **109**
Bulleid Way SW1 . . . . . 4K **17** (4F **101**)
Bullen Ho. *E1* *4H* ***85***
(off Collingwood St.)
Bullen St. SW11 . . . . . 2C **118**
Buller Cl. SE15 . . . . . 7G **103**
Buller Rd. CR7: Thor H 2D **156**
IG11: Bark 7J **71**
N17 . . . . . 2G **49**
N22 . . . . . 2A **48**
NW10 . . . . . 3F **81**
Bullers Cl. DA14: Sidc 5E **144**
Bullers Wood Dr. BR7: Chst 7D **142**
Bullescroft Rd. HA8: Edg 3B **28**
Bullfinch Ho. *NW9* *6B* ***44***
(off Perryfield Way)
Bullingham Mans. *W8* *2J* ***99***
(off Pitt St.)
Bull Inn Ct. WC2 . . . . . 3F **13**
Bullivant St. E14 . . . . . 7E **86**
Bull La. BR7: Chst 7H **143**
N18 . . . . . 5K **33**
RM10: Dag 3H **73**
Bullman Cl. DA7: Bex 3H **127**
Bull Rd. E15 . . . . . 2H **87**
Bullrush Cl. CR0: C'don 6E **156**
SM5: Cars 2C **166**
Bull's All. SW14 . . . . . 2K **115**
Bulls Bri. Cen. UB3: Hayes 3J **93**
Bullsbridge Ind. Est.
UB2: S'hall 4A **94**
Bulls Bri. Rd.
UB2: S'hall 4A **94**
UB3: Hayes 3K **93**
Bullsbrook Rd. UB4: Yead 1A **94**
Bulls Gdns. SW3 . . . . . 3D **16** (4C **100**)
Bulls Head Pas. EC3 . . . . . 1G **15**
Bull Theatre, The 4C **20**
Bull Yd. SE15 . . . . . 1G **121**
Bulmer Gdns. HA3: Kenton 7D **42**
Bulmer M. W11 . . . . . 7J **81**
Bulmer Pl. W11 . . . . . 1J **99**
Bulow Est. *SW6* *1K* ***117***
(off Pearscroft Rd.)
Bulstrode Av. TW3: Houn 2D **112**
Bulstrode Gdns. TW3: Houn 3E **112**
Bulstrode Pl. W1 . . . . . 6H **5** (5E **82**)
Bulstrode Rd. TW3: Houn 3E **112**
Bulstrode St. W1 . . . . . 7H **5** (6E **82**)
Bulwer Ct. E11 . . . . . 1F **69**
Bulwer Ct. Rd. E11 . . . . . 1F **69**
Bulwer Gdns. EN5: New Bar 4F **21**
Bulwer Rd. E11 . . . . . 7F **51**
EN5: New Bar 4E **20**
N18 . . . . . 4K **33**
Bulwer St. W12 . . . . . 1E **98**
Bunbury Ho. *SE15* *7G* ***103***
(off Fenham Rd.)
Bunce's La. IG8: Wfd G 7C **36**
Bungalow Rd. SE25 . . . . . 4E **156**
Bungalows, The E10 . . . . . 6E **50**
HA2: Harr 4D **58**
IG6: Ilf 1J **53**
SM6: Wall 5F **167**
SW16 . . . . . 7F **137**
UB4: Yead 4B **76**
Bunhill Row EC1 . . . . . 3E **8** (4D **84**)
Bunhouse Pl. SW1 . . . . . 5H **17** (5E **100**)
Bunkers Hill DA14: Sidc 3F **145**
DA17: Belv 4G **109**
NW11 . . . . . 7A **46**
Bunning Way N7 . . . . . 7J **65**
Bunns La. NW7 . . . . . 6F **29**
(not continuous)
Bunsen Ho. *E3* *2A* ***86***
(off Grove Rd.)
Bunsen St. E3 . . . . . 2A **86**
Buntingbridge Rd. IG2: Ilf 5H **53**
Bunting Cl. CR4: Mitc 5D **154**
N9 . . . . . 1E **34**
Bunting Ct. NW9 . . . . . 2A **44**
Bunting Ho. *UB10: Ick* *2E* ***56***
(off Coyle Dr.)
Bunton St. SE18 . . . . . 3E **106**
Bunwell Ho. *E3* *4B* ***86***
(off William Whiffin Sq.)
Bunyan Ct. EC2 . . . . . 5C **8**
Bunyan Rd. E17 . . . . . 3A **50**
Buonaparte M. SW1 . . . . . 5C **18** (5H **101**)
Burbage Cl. SE1 . . . . . 3D **102**
UB3: Hayes 6F **75**
Burbage Ho. *N1* *1D* ***84***
(off Poole St.)
SE14 . . . . . *6K* ***103***
(off Samuel Cl.)
Burbage Rd. SE21 . . . . . 6C **120**
SE24 . . . . . 6C **120**
Burberry Cl. KT3: N Mald 2A **152**
Burbidge Rd. TW17: Shep 4C **146**
Burbridge Way N17 . . . . . 2G **49**
Burcham Cl. TW12: Hamp 7E **130**
Burcham St. E14 . . . . . 6D **86**
Burcharbro Rd. SE2 . . . . . 6D **108**
Burchell Ct. WD23: Bush 1B **26**
Burchell Ho. *SE11* *5H* ***19***
(off Jonathan St.)
Burchell Rd. E10 . . . . . 1D **68**
SE15 . . . . . 1H **121**
Burcher Gale Gro. SE15 . . . . . 7F **103**
Burchetts Way TW17: Shep 6D **146**
Burchett Way RM6: Chad H 6F **55**
Burchwall Cl. RM5: Col R 1J **55**
Burcote Rd. SW18 . . . . . 7B **118**
Burden Cl. TW8: Bford 5C **96**
Burden Ho. *SW8* *7J* ***101***
(off Thorncroft St.)
Burdenshott Av. TW10: Rich 4H **115**
Burden Way E11 . . . . . 2K **69**
Burder Cl. N1 . . . . . 6E **66**
Burder Rd. N1 . . . . . 6E **66**
Burdett Av. SW20 . . . . . 1C **152**
Burdett Cl. DA14: Sidc 5E **144**
W7 . . . . . 1K **95**
Burdett M. NW3 . . . . . 6B **64**
W2 . . . . . 6K **81**
Burdett Rd. CR0: C'don 6D **156**
E3 . . . . . 4A **86**
E14 . . . . . 4A **86**
TW9: Rich 2F **115**
Burdetts Rd. RM9: Dag 1F **91**
Burdock Cl. CR0: C'don 1K **169**
Burdock Rd. N17 . . . . . 3G **49**
Burdon La. SM2: Cheam 7G **165**
Burdon Pk. SM2: Cheam 7H **165**
Bure Ct. EN5: New Bar 5E **20**
Burfield Cl. SW17 . . . . . 4B **136**
Burford Cl. IG6: Ilf 4G **53**
RM8: Dag 3C **72**
UB10: Ick 4A **56**
Burford Gdns. N13 . . . . . 3E **32**
Burford Ho. TW8: Bford 5D **96**
Burford Rd. BR1: Brom 4C **160**
E6 . . . . . 3C **88**
E15 . . . . . 1F **87**
KT4: Wor Pk 7B **152**
SE6 . . . . . 2B **140**
SM1: Sutt 2J **165**
TW8: Bford 5E **96**
Burford Wlk. SW6 . . . . . 7A **100**
Burford Way CR0: New Ad 6E **170**
Burford Wharf Apartments *E15* *1F* ***87***
(off Cam Rd.)
Burges Gro. SW13 . . . . . 7D **98**
Burges Rd. E6 . . . . . 7C **70**
Burgess Av. NW9 . . . . . 6K **43**
Burgess Bus. Pk. SE5 . . . . . 7D **102**
Burgess Cl. TW13: Hanw 4C **130**
Burgess Ct. E6 . . . . . 7E **70**
UB1: S'hall *6F* ***77***
(off Fleming Rd.)
Burgess Hill NW2 . . . . . 4J **63**
Burgess Ho. *SE5* *7C* ***102***
(off Bethwin Rd.)
Burgess Lofts *SE5* *7C* ***102***
(off Bethwin Rd.)
Burgess M. SW19 . . . . . 6K **135**
Burgess Pk. 6D **102**
Burgess Pk. Kart Track 6D **102**
Burgess Rd. E6 . . . . . 7E **70**
E15 . . . . . 4G **69**
SM1: Sutt 4K **165**
Burgess St. E14 . . . . . 5C **86**
Burge St. SE1 . . . . . 3D **102**
Burgh House 4B **64**
Burghill Rd. SE26 . . . . . 4A **140**
Burghley Av.
KT3: N Mald 1K **151**
Burghley Hall Cl. SW19 . . . . . 1G **135**
Burghley Ho. SW19 . . . . . 3G **135**
Burghley Pas. *E11* *1G* ***69***
(off Burghley Rd.)
Burghley Pl. CR4: Mitc 5D **154**
Burghley Rd. E11 . . . . . 1G **69**
N8 . . . . . 3A **48**
NW5 . . . . . 4F **65**
SW19 . . . . . 4F **135**
Burghley Twr. W3 . . . . . 7B **80**
Burgh St. N1 . . . . . 2B **84**
Burgoine Quay KT1: Hamp W 1D **150**
Burgon St. EC4 . . . . . 1B **14** (6B **84**)
Burgos Cl. CR0: Wadd 6A **168**
Burgos Gro. SE10 . . . . . 1D **122**
Burgoyne Ho. *TW8: Bford* *5D* ***96***
(off Ealing Rd.)
Burgoyne Rd. N4 . . . . . 6B **48**
SE25 . . . . . 4F **157**
SW9 . . . . . 3K **119**
TW16: Sun 6H **129**
Burgundy Ho. *E20* *5E* ***68***
(off Liberty Bri. Rd.)
EN2: Enf *1H* ***23***
(off Bedale Rd.)
Burgundy Pl. W12 . . . . . 1F **99**
Burham Cl. SE20 . . . . . 7J **139**
Burhill Gro. HA5: Pinn 2C **40**
Burke Cl. SW15 . . . . . 4A **116**
Burke Lodge E13 . . . . . 3K **87**
Burke St. E16 . . . . . 5H **87**
(not continuous)
Burket Cl. UB2: S'hall 4C **94**
Burland Rd. SW11 . . . . . 5D **118**
Burleigh Av. DA15: Sidc 5K **125**
SM6: Wall 3E **166**
Burleigh Cl.
RM7: Mawney 4H **55**
Burleigh Gdns. N14 . . . . . 1B **32**
TW15: Ashf 5E **128**
Burleigh Ho. SW3 . . . . . 7B **16**
W10 . . . . . *5G* ***81***
(off St Charles Sq.)
Burleigh Pde. N14 . . . . . 1C **32**
Burleigh Pl. SW15 . . . . . 5F **117**
Burleigh Rd. EN1: Enf 4K **23**
SM3: Sutt 1G **165**
UB10: Hil 1D **74**
Burleigh St. WC2 . . . . . 2G **13** (7K **83**)
Burleigh Wlk. SE6 . . . . . 1E **140**
Burleigh Way EN2: Enf 3J **23**
Burley Cl. E4 . . . . . 5H **35**
SW16 . . . . . 2H **155**
Burley Ho. *E1* *6K* ***85***
(off Chudleigh St.)
Burley Rd. E16 . . . . . 6A **88**
Burlington Arc. W1 . . . . . 3A **12** (7G **83**)
Burlington Av. RM7: Rom 6H **55**
TW9: Kew 1G **115**
Burlington Cl. BR6: Farnb 2F **173**
E6 . . . . . 6C **88**
HA5: Eastc 3K **39**
TW14: Bedf 7F **111**
W9 . . . . . 4J **81**
Burlington Cnr. *NW1* *7G* ***65***
(off Camden Rd.)
Burlington Ct. *E1* *7G* ***85***
(off Cable St.)
Burlington Gdns. RM6: Chad H 7E **54**
SW6 . . . . . 2G **117**
W1 . . . . . 3A **12** (7G **83**)
W3 . . . . . 1J **97**
W4 . . . . . 5J **97**
Burlington Ho. *N15* *6D* ***48***
(off Tewkesbury Rd.)
SE16 . . . . . *2K* ***103***
(off Province Dr.)
UB7: W Dray *2B* ***92***
(off Park Lodge Av.)
Burlington La. W4 . . . . . 7J **97**
Burlington M. SW15 . . . . . 5H **117**
W3 . . . . . 1J **97**
Burlington Pl. IG8: Wfd G 3E **36**
SW6 . . . . . 2G **117**
Burlington Ri. EN4: E Barn 1H **31**
Burlington Rd. CR7: Thor H 2C **156**
EN2: Enf 1J **23**
KT3: N Mald 4B **152**
N10 . . . . . 3E **46**
N17 . . . . . 1G **49**
SW6 . . . . . 2G **117**
TW7: Isle 1H **113**
W4 . . . . . 5J **97**
Burma M. N16 . . . . . 4D **66**
Burma Rd. N16 . . . . . 4D **66**
Burmarsh NW5 . . . . . 6E **64**
Burmarsh Ct. SE20 . . . . . 1J **157**
Burma Ter. SE19 . . . . . 5E **138**
Burmester Rd. SW17 . . . . . 3A **136**
Burnaby Cres. W4 . . . . . 6J **97**
Burnaby Gdns. W4 . . . . . 6H **97**
Burnaby St. SW10 . . . . . 7A **100**
Burnand Ho. *W14* *3F* ***99***
(off Redan St.)
Burnbrae Cl. N12 . . . . . 6E **30**
Burnbury Rd. SW12 . . . . . 1G **137**
Burncroft Av. EN3: Enf H 2D **24**
Burndell Way UB4: Yead 5B **76**
Burne Jones Ho. W14 . . . . . 4G **99**
Burnell Av. DA16: Well 2A **126**
TW10: Ham 5C **132**
Burnell Gdns. HA7: Stan 2D **42**
Burnelli Bldg. *SW8* *7F* ***101***
(off Sopwith Way)
Burnell Rd. SM1: Sutt 4K **165**
Burnell Wlk. *SE1* *5F* ***103***
(off Cadet Dr.)
Burnels Av. E6 . . . . . 3E **88**
Burness Cl. N7 . . . . . 6K **65**
Burne St. NW1 . . . . . 5C **4** (5C **82**)
Burnett Cl. E9 . . . . . 5J **67**
Burnett Ho. *SE13* *2E* ***122***
(off Lewisham Hill)
Burnett Rd. IG6: Ilf 7K **37**
Burney Av. KT5: Surb 5F **151**
Burney St. SE10 . . . . . 7E **104**

Burnfoot Av. SW6	1G 117
Burnham NW3	7C 64
Burnham Av. UB10: Ick	4E 56
Burnham Cl. EN1: Enf	1K 23
HA3: W'stone	4A 42
NW7	7H 29
SE1	4F 103
Burnham Ct. NW4	4E 44
(off Brent St.)	
NW6	7A 64
(off Fairhazel Gdns.)	
W2	7K 81
(off Moscow Rd.)	
Burnham Cres. E11	4A 52
Burnham Dr. KT4: Wor Pk	2F 165
Burnham Est. E2	3J 85
(off Burnham St.)	
Burnham Gdns. CR0: C'don	7F 157
TW4: Cran	1K 111
UB3: Harl	3F 93
Burnham Rd. DA14: Sidc	2E 144
E4	5G 35
RM7: Rom	3K 55
RM9: Dag	7B 72
SM4: Mord	4K 153
Burnham St. E2	3J 85
KT2: King T	1G 151
Burnham Way SE26	5B 140
W13	4B 96
Burnhill Cl. SE15	7H 103
Burnhill Ho. EC1	2C 8
(off Norman St.)	
Burnhill Rd. BR3: Beck	2C 158
Burnley Rd. NW10	5B 62
SW9	2K 119
Burnsall St. SW3	6D 16 (5C 100)
Burns Av. DA15: Sidc	6B 126
RM6: Chad H	7C 54
TW14: Felt	6J 111
UB1: S'hall	7E 76
Burns Cl. DA16: Well	1K 125
E17	4E 50
SM5: Cars	7E 166
SW19	6B 136
UB4: Hayes	5H 75
Burns Ho. E2	3J 85
(off Cornwall Av.)	
SE17	5B 102
(off Doddington Gro.)	
Burnside Av. E4	6G 35
Burnside Cl. EN5: New Bar	3D 20
SE16	1K 103
TW1: Twick	6A 114
Burnside Ct. SM5: Cars	3E 166
Burnside Rd. RM8: Dag	2C 72
Burns Rd. HA0: Wemb	2E 78
NW10	1B 80
SW11	2D 118
W13	2B 96
Burns Way TW5: Hest	2B 112
Burnt Ash Hgts. BR1: Brom	5K 141
Burnt Ash Hill SE12	6H 123
Burnt Ash La. BR1: Brom	7J 141
Burnt Ash Rd. SE12	5H 123
Burnthwaite Rd. SW6	7H 99
BURNT OAK	1H 43
Burnt Oak Apartments E16	6J 87
(off Pacific Rd.)	
Burnt Oak B'way. HA8: Edg	7B 28
Burnt Oak Flds. HA8: Edg	1J 43
Burnt Oak La. DA15: Sidc	6A 126
(not continuous)	
Burntwood Cl. SW18	1C 136
Burntwood Grange Rd. SW18	1B 136
Burntwood La. SW17	3A 136
Burntwood Vw. SE19	5F 139
Buross St. E1	6H 85
Burpham Cl. UB4: Yead	5B 76
Burrage Cl. SE16	4K 103
(off Worgan St.)	
Burrage Gro. SE18	4G 107
Burrage Pl. SE18	5F 107
Burrage Rd. SE18	5G 107
Burrard Ho. E2	2J 85
(off Bishop's Way)	
Burrard Rd. E16	6K 87
NW6	5J 63
Burr Cl. DA7: Bex	3F 127
E1	4K 15 (1G 103)
Burrell Cl. CR0: C'don	6A 158
HA8: Edg	2C 28
Burrell Row BR3: Beck	2C 158
Burrell St. SE1	4A 14 (1B 102)
Burrells Wharf Sq. E14	5D 104
Burrell Towers E10	7C 50
Burrfield St. SE16	3K 103
(off Worgan St.)	
Burritt Rd. KT1: King T	2G 151
Burroughs, The NW4	4D 44
Burroughs Club, The	4D 44
Burroughs Cotts. E14	5A 86
(off Halley St.)	
Burroughs Gdns. NW4	4D 44
Burroughs Pde. NW4	4D 44
Burrow Ho. SW9	2A 120
(off Stockwell Pk. Rd.)	
Burrow Rd. SE22	4E 120
Burrows M. SE1	6A 14 (2B 102)
Burrows Rd. NW10	3E 80
Burrow Wlk. SE21	7C 120
Burr Rd. SW18	1J 135
Bursar St. SE1	5G 15 (1E 102)
Bursdon Cl. DA15: Sidc	2K 143
Bursland Rd. EN3: Pond E	4E 24
Burslem St. E1	6G 85
Burstock Rd. SW15	4G 117
Burston Rd. SW15	5F 117
Burston Vs. SW15	5F 117
(off St John's Av.)	
Burstow Rd. SW20	1G 153
Burtenshaw Rd. KT7: T Ditt	7A 150
Burtley Cl. N4	1C 66
Burton Bank N1	7D 66
(off Yeate St.)	
Burton Cl. CR7: Thor H	3D 156
KT9: Chess	7D 162
Burton Ct. KT7: T Ditt	6A 150
SE20	2J 157
SW3	5F 17
(not continuous)	
Burton Gdns. TW5: Hest	1D 112
Burton Gro. SE17	5D 102
Burtonhole Cl. NW7	4A 30
Burtonhole La. N12	4B 30
NW7	5K 29
Burton Ho. SE16	2H 103
(off Cherry Gdn. St.)	
Burton La. SW9	2A 120
(not continuous)	
Burton M. SW1	4H 17 (4E 100)
Burton Pl. WC1	2D 6 (3H 83)
Burton Rd. E18	3K 51
KT2: King T	7E 132
NW6	7H 63
SW9	2B 120
(Akerman Rd.)	
SW9	2A 120
(Evesham Wlk.)	
Burtons Ct. E15	7F 69
Burton St. WC1	2D 6 (3H 83)
Burtonwood Ho. N4	7D 48
Burtop Rd. Est. SW17	3A 136
Burt Rd. E16	1A 106
Burts Wharf DA17: Belv	7J 91
Burt Ho. N1	1G 9
(off Aske St.)	
Burtwell La. SE27	4D 138
Burwash Ho. SE1	7E 15
(off Kipling Est.)	
Burwash Rd. SE18	5H 107
Burway Cl. CR2: S Croy	6E 168
Burwell KT1: King T	2G 151
(off Excelsior Cl.)	
Burwell Av. UB6: G'frd	6J 59
Burwell Cl. E1	6H 85
Burwell Rd. E10	1A 68
Burwell Rd. Ind. Est. E10	1A 68
Burwell Wlk. E3	4C 86
Burwood Av. BR2: Hayes	2K 171
HA5: Eastc	5K 39
Burwood Cl. KT6: Surb	1G 163
Burwood Ho. SW9	4B 120
Burwood Pl. EN4: Had W	1F 21
W2	7D 4 (6C 82)
Bury Av. HA4: Ruis	6E 38
UB4: Hayes	2G 75
Bury Cl. SE16	1K 103
Bury Ct. EC3	7H 9 (6E 84)
Buryfield Ct. SE8	4K 103
(off Lower Rd.)	
Bury Gro. SM4: Mord	5K 153
Bury Hall Vs. N9	7A 24
Bury Pl. WC1	6E 6 (5J 83)
Bury Rd. E4	1B 36
N22	2A 48
RM10: Dag	5H 73
Buryside Cl. IG2: Ilf	4K 53
Bury St. EC3	1H 15 (6E 84)
HA4: Ruis	5E 38
N9	7A 24
SW1	4B 12 (1G 101)
Bury St. W. N9	7J 23
Bury Wlk. SW3	4C 16 (4C 100)
Busbridge Ho. E14	5C 86
(off Brabazon St.)	
Busby Ho. SW16	4G 137
Busby M. NW5	6H 65
Busby Pl. NW5	6H 65
Busch Cl. TW7: Isle	1B 114
Bushbaby Cl. SE1	3E 102
Bushberry Rd. E9	6A 68
Bush Cl. IG2: Ilf	5H 53
Bush Cotts. SW18	5J 117
Bush Ct. N14	1C 32
W12	2F 99
Bushell Cl. SW2	2K 137
Bushell Grn. WD23: B Hea	2C 26
Bushell St. E1	1G 103
Bushell Way BR7: Chst	5E 142
BUSHEY	1C 26
Bushey Av. BR5: Pet W	7H 161
E18	3H 51
Bushey Cl. E4	3K 35
UB10: Ick	2C 56
Bushey Ct. SW20	3D 152
Bushey Down SW12	2F 137
Bushey Golf Course	1A 26
BUSHEY HEATH	1C 26
Bushey Hill Rd. SE5	1E 120
Bushey La. SM1: Sutt	4J 165
Bushey Lees DA15: Sidc	6K 125
BUSHEY MEAD	2F 153
Bushey Rd. CR0: C'don	2C 170
E13	2A 88
N15	6E 48
SM1: Sutt	4J 165
(not continuous)	
SW20	3D 152
UB3: Harl	4G 93
UB10: Ick	2C 56
Bushey Way BR3: Beck	6E 159
Bush Fair Ct. N14	6A 22
Bushfield Cl. HA8: Edg	2C 28
Bushfield Cres. HA8: Edg	2C 28
Bush Gro. HA7: Stan	1D 42
NW9	7J 43
Bushgrove Rd. RM8: Dag	4D 72
Bush Hill N21	7H 23
Bush Hill Pde. EN1: Enf	7J 23
N9	7J 23
BUSH HILL PARK	6A 24
Bush Hill Park Golf Course	5H 23
Bush Hill Rd. HA3: Kenton	6F 43
N21	6J 23
Bush Ind. Est. N19	3G 65
NW10	4K 79
Bushmead Cl. N15	4F 49
Bushmoor Cres. SE18	7F 107
Bushnell Rd. SW17	2F 137
Bush Rd. E8	1H 85
E11	7H 51
IG9: Buck H	4G 37
SE8	4K 103
TW9: Kew	6F 97
TW17: Shep	5B 146
Bush Theatre	2E 98
Bushway RM8: Dag	4D 72
Bushwood E11	7H 51
Bushwood Dr. SE1	4F 103
Bushwood Rd. TW9: Kew	6G 97
Bushy Cl. KT1: Hamp W	1C 150
(off Beverley Rd.)	
Bushy Park	7H 131
Bushy Pk. Gdns. TW11: Tedd	5H 131
Bushy Pk. Rd. TW11: Tedd	7B 132
(not continuous)	
Bushy Rd. TW11: Tedd	6K 131
Business Design Cen. N1	1A 84
(off Upper St.)	
Buspace Studios W10	4G 81
(off Conlan St.)	
Butcher Row E14	7K 85
Butchers M. UB3: Hayes	7H 75
(off Hemmen La.)	
Butchers Rd. E16	6J 87
Bute Av. TW10: Ham	2E 132
Bute Ct. SM6: Wall	5G 167
Bute Gdns. SM6: Wall	5G 167
TW10: Ham	1E 132
W6	4F 99
Bute Gdns. W. SM6: Wall	5G 167
Bute M. NW11	5A 46
Bute Rd. CR0: C'don	1A 168
IG6: Ilf	5F 53
SM6: Wall	4G 167
Bute St. SW7	3A 16 (4B 100)
Bute Wlk. N1	6D 66
Butfield Ho. E9	6J 67
(off Stevens Av.)	
Butler Av. HA1: Harr	7H 41
Butler Cl. HA8: Edg	2H 43
Butler Ct.	
HA0: Wemb	4A 60
RM8: Dag	2G 73
(off Gosfield Rd.)	
Butler Farm Cl. TW10: Ham	4D 132
Butler Ho. E2	3J 85
(off Bacton St.)	
E3	5B 86
(off Geoffrey Chaucer Way)	
E14	6B 86
(off Burdett St.)	
SW9	1B 120
(off Lothian Rd.)	
Butler Pl. SW1	1C 18 (3H 101)
Butler Rd.	
HA1: Harr	7G 41
NW10	7B 62
RM8: Dag	4B 72
Butlers & Colonial Wharf SE1	6K 15
(off Shad Thames)	
Butlers Ct. TW4: Houn	3D 112
Butlers Dr. E4	1K 25
Butler St. E2	3J 85
UB10: Hil	4D 74
Butlers Wharf SE1	5K 15 (1F 103)
Butlers Wharf W. SE1	2A 86
(off Shad Thames)	
Butley Ct. E3	2A 86
(off Ford St.)	
Buttercup Cl. UB5: N'olt	6D 58

Butterfield Cl. N17 ....6H **33**
  SE16 ....2H **103**
  TW1: Twick 6K **113**
Butterfields E17 ....5E **50**
Butterfield Sq. E6 ....6D **88**
Butterfly Apartments SW11 ....4C **118**
  (off Comyn Rd.)
Butterfly Ct. E6 ....3D **88**
  NW9 ....1A **44**
Butterfly La. SE9 ....6F **125**
Butterfly Wlk. SE5 ....1D **120**
  (off Denmark Hill)
Butter Hill SM5: Cars 3E **166**
  SM6: Wall 3E **166**
Butteridges Cl. RM9: Dag 1F **91**
Buttermere NW1 ....1K **5**
  (off Augustus St.)
Buttermere Cl. E15 ....4F **69**
  SE1 ....4F **103**
  SM4: Mord 6F **153**
  TW14: Felt 1H **129**
Buttermere Ct. NW8 ....1B **82**
  (off Boundary Rd.)
Buttermere Dr. SW15 ....5G **117**
Buttermere Ho. E3 ....3B **86**
  (off Mile End Rd.)
Buttermere Wlk. E8 ....6F **67**
Butterwick W6 ....4F **99**
Butterworth Gdns. IG8: Wfd G 6D **36**
Butterworth Ter. SE17 ....5C **102**
  (off Sutherland Wlk.)
Buttery M. N14 ....3D **32**
Buttesland St. N1 ....1F **9** (3D **84**)
Buttfield Cl. RM10: Dag 6H **73**
Buttmarsh Cl. SE18 ....5F **107**
Button Lodge E17 ....4C **50**
Buttonscroft Cl. CR7: Thor H 3C **156**
Butts, The TW8: Bford 6C **96**
  TW16: Sun 3A **148**
Buttsbury Rd. IG1: Ilf 5G **71**
Butts Cotts TW13: Hanw 3C **130**
Butts Cres. TW13: Hanw 3E **130**
Buttsmead HA6: Nwood 1E **38**
Butts Piece UB5: N'olt 2K **75**
Butts Rd. BR1: Brom 5G **141**
Buxhall Cres. E9 ....6B **68**
Buxted Rd. E8 ....7F **67**
  N12 ....5H **31**
  SE22 ....4E **120**
Buxton Cl. IG8: Wfd G 6G **37**
  N9 ....2D **34**
Buxton Ct. E11 ....7H **51**
  N1 ....1D **8**
  (not continuous)
Buxton Cres. SM3: Cheam 4G **165**
Buxton Dr. E11 ....4G **51**
  KT3: N Mald 2K **151**
Buxton Gdns. W3 ....7H **79**
Buxton Ho. E11 ....4G **51**
Buxton M. SW4 ....2H **119**
Buxton Rd. CR7: Thor H 5B **156**
  DA8: Erith 7K **109**
  E4 ....1A **36**
  E6 ....3C **88**
  E15 ....5G **69**
  E17 ....4A **50**
  (not continuous)
  IG2: Ilf 6J **53**
  N19 ....1H **65**
  NW2 ....6D **62**
  SW14 ....3A **116**
  TW15: Ashf 5A **128**
Buxton St. E1 ....4K **9** (4G **85**)
Buzzard Creek Ind. Est. IG11: Bark 5A **90**
Byam St. SW6 ....2A **118**
Byards Ct. SE16 ....4K **103**
  (off Worgan St.)
Byards Cft. SW16 ....1H **155**
Byas Ho. E3 ....3B **86**
  (off Benworth St.)
Byatt Wlk. TW12: Hamp 6C **130**

Bychurch End TW11: Tedd 5K **131**
Bycroft Rd. UB1: S'hall 4E **76**
Bycroft St. SE20 ....7K **139**
Bycullah Av. EN2: Enf 3G **23**
Bycullah Rd. EN2: Enf 2G **23**
Bye, The W3 ....6A **80**
Byegrove Rd. SW19 ....6B **136**
Byelands Cl. SE16 ....1K **103**
Bye Way, The
  HA3: W'stone 1J **41**
Byeway, The SW14 ....3J **115**
Byeways TW2: Twick 3F **131**
Byeways, The KT5: Surb 5G **151**
Byfield Gdns. SW13 ....1C **116**
Byfield Cl. SE16 ....2B **104**
Byfield Rd. TW7: Isle 3A **114**
Byford Cl. E15 ....7G **69**
Byford Ho. EN5: Barn 4A **20**
  HA2: Harr 1E **58**
Bygrove CR0: New Ad 6D **170**
Bygrove St. E14 ....6D **86**
  (not continuous)
Byland Cl. N21 ....7E **22**
  SM4: Mord 7A **154**
Bylands Cl. SE2 ....3B **108**
Byne Rd. SE26 ....6J **139**
  SM5: Cars 2C **166**
Bynes Rd. CR2: S Croy 7D **168**
Byng Pl. WC1 ....4D **6** (4H **83**)
Byng Rd. EN5: Barn 2A **20**
Byng St. E14 ....2C **104**
Bynon Av. DA7: Bex 3F **127**
Byrne Ho. N14 ....6A **22**
Byrne Cl. CR0: C'don 6C **156**
Byrne Rd. SW12 ....1F **137**
Byron Av. E12 ....6C **70**
  E18 ....3H **51**
  KT3: N Mald 5C **152**
  NW9 ....4H **43**
  SM1: Sutt 4B **166**
  TW4: Cran 2J **111**
Byron Av. E. SM1: Sutt 4B **166**
Byron Cl. E8 ....1G **85**
  KT12: Walt T 7C **148**
  SE20 ....3H **157**
  SE26 ....4A **140**
  SE28 ....1C **108**
  SW16 ....6J **137**
  TW12: Hamp 4D **130**
Byron Ct. E11 ....4K **51**
  (off Makepeace Rd.)
  EN2: Enf 2G **23**
  HA1: Harr 6J **41**
  NW6 ....7A **64**
  (off Fairfax Rd.)
  SE22 ....1G **139**
  SW3 ....4D **16**
  (off Elystan St.)
  W7 ....4A **96**
  (off Boston Rd.)
  W9 ....4J **81**
  (off Lanhill Rd.)
  WC1 ....3G **7**
  (off Mecklenburgh Sq.)
Byron Dr. DA8: Erith 7H **109**
  N2 ....6B **46**
Byron Gdns. SM1: Sutt 4B **166**
Byron Hill Rd. HA2: Harr 1H **59**
Byron Ho. DA1: Cray 5K **127**
Byron M. NW3 ....4C **64**
  W9 ....4J **81**
Byron Pde. UB10: Hil 4E **74**
Byron Rd. E10 ....1D **68**
  E17 ....3C **50**
  HA0: Wemb 2C **60**
  HA1: Harr 6J **41**
  HA3: W'stone 2K **41**
  NW2 ....2D **62**
  NW7 ....5H **29**
  W5 ....1F **97**
Byron St. E14 ....6E **86**

Byron Ter. N9 ....6D **24**
  SE7 ....7A **106**
Byron Way UB4: Hayes 4H **75**
  UB5: N'olt 3C **76**
  UB7: W Dray 4B **92**
Bysouth Cl. IG5: Ilf 1F **53**
  N15 ....4D **48**
Bythorn St. SW9 ....3K **119**
Byton Rd. SW17 ....6D **136**
Byward Av. TW14: Felt 6A **112**
Byward St. EC3 ....3H **15** (7E **84**)
Bywater Ho. SE18 ....3C **106**
Bywater Pl. SE16 ....1A **104**
Bywater St. SW3 ....5E **16** (5D **100**)
Byway E11 ....5A **52**
Byway, The KT19: Ewe 4B **164**
  SM2: Sutt 7B **166**
Bywell Pl. E16 ....5H **87**
  W1 ....6A **6**
Bywood Av. CR0: C'don 6J **157**
Byworth Wlk. N19 ....1J **65**

C

Cabbell St. NW1 ....6C **4** (5C **82**)
Cabinet Cl. NW2 ....3C **62**
Cabinet Way E4 ....6G **35**
Cable Car
  Emirates Air Line 2H **105**
Cable Cl. SE16 ....4A **104**
  (off Rope St.)
Cable Ho. WC1 ....1J **7**
  (off St. Percy St.)
Cable Pl. SE10 ....1E **122**
Cable St. E1 ....7G **85**
Cable Trade Pk. SE7 ....4A **106**
Cabot Cl. CR0: Wadd 3A **168**
Cabot Ct. SE16 ....4K **103**
  (off Worgan St.)
Cabot Sq. E14 ....1C **104**
Cabot Way E6 ....1B **88**
Cab Rd. SE1 ....5H **13**
Cabul Rd. SW11 ....2C **118**
Caci Ho. W14 ....4H **99**
  (off Kensington Village)
Cactus Cl. SE15 ....2E **120**
Cactus Wlk. W12 ....6B **80**
Cadbury Cl. TW7: Isle 1A **114**
  TW16: Sun 7G **129**
Cadbury Rd. TW16: Sun 7G **129**
Cadbury Way SE16 ....3F **103**
Caddington Cl.
  EN4: E Barn 5H **21**
Caddington Rd. NW2 ....3G **63**
Caddis Cl. HA7: Stan 7E **26**
Cadell Cl. E2 ....1K **9** (2F **85**)
Cade Rd. SE10 ....1F **123**
Cader Rd. SW18 ....6A **118**
Cadet Dr. SE1 ....4F **103**
Cadet Pl. SE10 ....5G **105**
Cadiz Ct. RM10: Dag 7K **73**
Cadiz Rd. RM10: Dag 7J **73**
Cadiz St. SE17 ....5C **102**
Cadley Ter. SE23 ....2J **139**
Cadman Cl. SW9 ....7B **102**
Cadman Cl. W4 ....5H **97**
  (off Chaseley Dr.)
Cadmer Cl. KT3: N Mald 4A **152**
Cadmore Ho. N1 ....7B **66**
  (off The Sutton Est.)
Cadmus Cl. SW4 ....3H **119**
Cadmus Ct. SE8 ....4A **104**
  (off Seafarer Way)
  SW9 ....1A **120**
  (off Southey Rd.)
Cadnam Lodge E14 ....3E **104**
  (off Schooner Cl.)
Cadnam Point SW15 ....1D **134**
Cadogan Cl. BR3: Beck 1F **159**
  E9 ....7B **68**

Cadogan Cl. HA2: Harr 4F **59**
  TW11: Tedd 5J **131**
Cadogan Ct. E9 ....7B **68**
  (off Cadogan Ter.)
  SM2: Sutt 6K **165**
  SW3 ....4E **16**
  (off Draycott Av.)
Cadogan Ct. Gdns. SW1 ....3G **17**
  (off D'Oyley St.)
Cadogan Gdns. E18 ....3K **51**
  N3 ....1K **45**
  N21 ....5F **23**
  SW3 ....3F **17** (4D **100**)
Cadogan Ga. SW1 ....3F **17** (4D **100**)
Cadogan Hall 3G **17**
  (off Sloane Ter.)
Cadogan Ho. IG8: Wfd G 7K **37**
  SW3 ....7B **16**
Cadogan La. SW1 ....2G **17** (3E **100**)
Cadogan Mans. SW3 ....4F **17**
  (off Cadogan Gdns.)
Cadogan Pl. SW1 ....1F **17** (3D **100**)
Cadogan Rd. KT6: Surb 5D **150**
  SE18 ....3G **107**
Cadogan Sq. SW1 ....2E **16** (3D **100**)
Cadogan St. SW3 ....4E **16** (4D **100**)
Cadogan Ter. E9 ....6B **68**
Cadoxton Av. N15 ....6F **49**
Cadwallon Rd. SE9 ....2F **143**
Caedmon Rd. N7 ....4K **65**
Caerleon Cl. DA14: Sidc 5C **144**
  KT10: Clay 7B **162**
Caerleon Ter. SE2 ....4B **108**
Caernarfon Ho. HA7: Stan 5F **27**
Caernarvon Cl. CR4: Mitc 3J **155**
Caernarvon Dr. IG5: Ilf 1E **52**
Caernarvon Ho. E16 ....1K **105**
  (off Audley Dr.)
  W2 ....6A **82**
  (off Hallfield Est.)
Caesar Ct. E2 ....2K **85**
  (off Palmer's Rd.)
Caesars Wlk. CR4: Mitc 5D **154**
Caesars Way TW17: Shep 6F **147**
Café Gallery W14
Cahill St. EC1 ....4D **8** (4C **84**)
Cahir St. E14 ....4D **104**
Cain Cl. W5 ....5C **78**
  (off Castlebar M.)
Caine Ho. W3 ....2H **97**
  (off Hanbury Rd.)
Cain's La. TW14: Felt 5G **111**
Caird St. W10 ....3G **81**
Cairn Av. W5 ....1D **96**
Cairncross M. N8 ....6J **47**
Cairndale Cl. BR1: Brom 7H **141**
Cairnfield Av. NW2 ....3A **62**
Cairngorm Cl. TW11: Tedd 5A **132**
Cairns Av. IG8: Wfd G 6H **37**
  SW16: Mitc 3G **155**
Cairns M. SE18 ....1C **124**
Cairns Pl. SW16 ....2G **155**
Cairns Rd. SW11 ....5C **118**
Cairn Way HA7: Stan 6E **26**
Cairo New Rd. CR0: C'don 2B **168**
Cairo Rd. E17 ....4C **50**
Caister Ho. N7 ....6K **65**
Caistor Ho. E15 ....1H **87**
  (off Caistor Pk. Rd.)
Caistor M. SW12 ....7F **119**
Caistor Pk. Rd. E15 ....1H **87**
Caistor Rd. SW12 ....7F **119**
Caithness Gdns. DA15: Sidc 6K **125**
Caithness Ho. N1 ....1K **83**
  (off Twyford St.)
Caithness Rd. CR4: Mitc 7F **137**
  W14 ....3F **99**
Calabria Rd. N5 ....6B **66**
Calais Ga. SE5 ....1B **120**
Calais St. SE5 ....1B **120**
Calbourne Rd. SW12 ....7D **118**

Calcott Ct. *W14* 3G **99**
(off Blythe Rd.)
Calcott Wlk. SE9 . . . . .4C **142**
Calcraft Ho. *E2* 2J **85**
(off Bonner Rd.)
Caldbeck Av. KT4: Wor Pk 2C **164**
Caldecote *KT1: King T* 2G **151**
(off Excelsior Cl.)
Caldecote Gdns. WD23: Bush 1D **26**
CALDECOTE HILL 1E **26**
Caldecot Rd. SE5 . . . . .2C **120**
Caldecott Way E5 . . . . .3K **67**
Calder Av. UB6: G'frd 2K **77**
Calder Cl. EN1: Enf 3K **23**
Calder Cl. SE16 . . . . .1B **104**
Calder Gdns. HA8: Edg 3G **43**
Calderon Ho. *NW8* 2C **82**
(off Townshend Est.)
Calderon Pl. W10 . . . . .5E **80**
Calderon Rd. E11 . . . . .4E **68**
Calder Rd. SM4: Mord 5A **154**
Caldervale Rd. SW4 . . . . .5H **119**
Calder Way SL3: Poyle 6A **174**
Calderwood Pl. EN4: Had W 1E **20**
Calderwood St. SE18 . . . . .4E **106**
Caldew Cl. NW7 . . . . .7H **29**
Caldew St. SE5 . . . . .7D **102**
Caldicote Grn. NW9 . . . . .6A **44**
Caldon Ho. UB5: N'olt 4D **76**
Caldwell Cl. SE18 . . . . .5E **106**
Caldwell Ho. *SW13* 7E **98**
(off Trinity Chu. Rd.)
Caldwell St. SW9 . . . . .7K **101**
Caldy Rd. DA17: Belv 3H **109**
Caldy Wlk. N1 . . . . .7C **66**
Caleb St. SE1 . . . . . .6C **14** (2C **102**)
Caledonia Cl. *IG11: Bark* 2C **90**
(off Keel Cl.)
Caledonia Ho. *E14* 6A **86**
(off Salmon La.)
Caledonian Cl. IG3: Ilf 1B **72**
Caledonian Ct. *BR2: Brom* 6C **160**
(off Wells Vw. Dr.)
UB5: N'olt 4C **76**
Caledonian Rd. N1 . . . . .1F **7** (2J **83**)
N7 . . . . .4K **65**
Caledonian Sq. NW1 . . . . .6H **65**
Caledonian Wharf E14 . . . . .4F **105**
Caledonia Rd. TW19: Stanw 1A **128**
Caledonia St. N1 . . . . .1F **7** (2J **83**)
Caledon Rd. E6 . . . . .1D **88**
SM6: Wall 4E **166**
Calendar M. KT6: Surb 6D **150**
Cale St. SW3 . . . . .5C **16** (5C **100**)
Caletock Way SE10 . . . . .5H **105**
Calgarth *NW1* 2G **83**
(off Ampthill Est.)
Calgary Ct. RM7: Mawney 4H **55**
SE16 .2J **103**
(off Canada Est.)
Calia Ho. *E20* 6E **68**
(off Anthems Way)
Caliban Twr. *N1* 2E **84**
(off Arden Est.)
Calico Ct. *SE16* 3G **103**
(off Marine St.)
Calico Ho. *E20* 6E **68**
(off Mirabelle Gdns.)
EC4 . . . . .1D **14**
(off Well Ct.)
SE1 . . . . .7G **15**
(off Long La.)
Calico Row SW11 . . . . .3A **118**
Calidore Cl. SW2 . . . . .6K **119**
California Bldg. *SE13* 1D **122**
(off Deal's Gateway)
California La. WD23: B Hea 1C **26**
California Pl. *WD23: B Hea* 1C **26**
(off High Rd.)
California Rd. KT3: N Mald 4H **151**
Callaby Ter. *N1* 6D **66**

Callaghan Cl. SE13 . . . . .4G **123**
Callahan Cotts. *E1* 5J **85**
(off Lindley St.)
Callander Rd. SE6 . . . . .2D **140**
Callanders, The WD23: B Hea 1D **26**
Callard Av. N13 . . . . .4G **33**
Callcott Cl. NW6 . . . . .7H **63**
Callcott Rd. NW6 . . . . .7H **63**
Callcott St. W8 . . . . .1J **99**
Callendar Rd. SW7 . . . . . . .1A **16** (3B **100**)
Callender Ct. *CR0: C'don* 6C **156**
(off Harry Cl.)
Callingham Cl. E14 . . . . .5B **86**
Callingham M. TW2: Twick 2J **131**
Callis Farm Cl. TW19: Stanw 6A **110**
Callisons Pl. SE10 . . . . .5G **105**
Callis Rd. E17 . . . . .6B **50**
Calliston Cl. *E16* 5J **87**
(off Hammersley Rd.)
Callonfield E17 . . . . .4K **49**
Callow St. SW3 . . . . .7A **16** (6B **100**)
Cally Swimming Pool 1K **83**
Calmont Rd. BR1: Brom 6F **141**
Calne Av. IG5: Ilf 1F **53**
Calonne Rd. SW19 . . . . .4F **135**
Calshot Ho. *N1* 2K **83**
(off Calshot St.)
Calshot Rd. TW6: H'row A 2C **110**
Calshot St. N1 . . . . .1G **7** (2K **83**)
Calshot Way EN2: Enf 3G **23**
TW6: H'row A 2C **110**
Calstock *NW1* 1G **83**
(off Royal Coll. St.)
Calstock Ho. SE11 . . . . .5K **19**
Calthorpe Gdns. HA8: Edg 5K **27**
SM1: Sutt 3A **166**
Calthorpe St. WC1 . . . . . . .3H **7** (4K **83**)
Calton Av. SE21 . . . . .6E **120**
Calton Rd. EN5: New Bar 6F **21**
Calverley Cl. BR3: Beck 6D **140**
Calverley Ct. KT19: Ewe 4K **163**
Calverley Cres. RM10: Dag 2G **73**
Calverley Gdns. HA3: Kenton 7D **42**
Calverley Gro. N19 . . . . .1H **65**
Calverley Rd. KT17: Ewe 6C **164**
Calvert Av. E2 . . . . .2H **9** (3E **84**)
Calvert Cl. DA14: Sidc 6E **144**
DA17: Belv 4G **109**
Calvert Dr. DA2: Wilm 2K **145**
Calvert Ho. *W12* 7D **80**
(off White City Est.)
Calverton *SE5* 6E **102**
(off Albany Rd.)
Calverton Rd. E6 . . . . .1E **88**
Calvert Rd. EN5: Barn 2A **20**
SE10 . . . . .5H **105**
Calvert's Bldgs. SE1 . . . . .5E **14** (1D **102**)
Calvert St. NW1 . . . . .1E **82**
Calydon Rd. SE7 . . . . .5K **105**
Calypso Cres. SE15 . . . . .7F **103**
Calypso Way SE16 . . . . .3B **104**
Camac Rd. TW2: Twick 1H **131**
Camarthen Grn. NW9 . . . . .5A **44**
Cambalt Rd. SW15 . . . . .5F **117**
Cambay Ho. *E1* 4A **86**
(off Harford St.)
Camber Ho. SE15 . . . . .6J **103**
Camberley Av. EN1: Enf 4K **23**
SW20 . . . . .2D **152**
Camberley Cl. SM3: Cheam 3F **165**
Camberley Ho. NW1 . . . . .1K **5**
Camberley Rd.
TW6: H'row A 3C **110**
Cambert Way SE3 . . . . .4K **123**
CAMBERWELL 1D **120**
Camberwell Bus. Cen. SE5 . . . . . . .7D **102**
Camberwell Chu. St. SE5 . . . . .1D **120**
Camberwell Glebe SE5 . . . . .1E **120**
CAMBERWELL GREEN 1C **120**

Camberwell Grn. SE5 . . . . .1D **120**
Camberwell Gro. SE5 . . . . .1D **120**
Camberwell Leisure Cen. 1D **120**
Camberwell New Rd. SE5 . . . . .6A **102**
Camberwell Pl. SE5 . . . . .1C **120**
Camberwell Rd. SE5 . . . . .6C **102**
Camberwell Sta. Rd. SE5 . . . . .1C **120**
Camberwell Trad. Est. SE5 . . . . . . .1B **120**
Cambeys Rd. RM10: Dag 5H **73**
Camborne Av. W13 . . . . .2B **96**
Camborne Cl. TW6: H'row A 3C **110**
Camborne Cres. TW6: H'row A 3C **110**
(off Camborne Rd.)
Camborne M. SW18 . . . . .7J **117**
W11 .6G **81**
Camborne Rd. CR0: C'don 7G **157**
DA14: Sidc 3C **144**
DA16: Well 2K **125**
SM2: Sutt 7J **165**
SM4: Mord 5F **153**
SW18 . . . . .7J **117**
TW6: H'row A 3C **110**
Camborne Way TW5: Hest 1E **112**
TW6: H'row A 3C **110**
Cambourne Av. N9 . . . . .7E **24**
Cambourne Rd. HA8: Edg 4A **28**
Cambourne Wlk. TW10: Rich 6D **114**
Cambrai Cl. N13 . . . . .3D **32**
Cambray Rd. BR6: Orp 7K **161**
SW12 . . . . .1G **137**
Cambria Cl. DA15: Sidc 1H **143**
TW3: Houn 4E **112**
Cambria Ct. E17 . . . . .3A **50**
TW14: Felt 7K **111**
Cambria Gdns. TW19: Stanw 7A **110**
(not continuous)
Cambria Ho. *E14* 6A **86**
(off Salmon La.)
SE26 . . . . .4G **139**
(off High Level Dr.)
Cambrian Av. IG2: Ilf 5J **53**
Cambrian Cl. SE27 . . . . .3B **138**
Cambrian Grn. *NW9* 5A **44**
(off Snowdon Dr.)
Cambrian Rd. E10 . . . . .7C **50**
TW10: Rich 6F **115**
Cambria Rd. SE5 . . . . .3C **120**
Cambria St. SW6 . . . . .7K **99**
Cambridge Arc. E9 . . . . .7J **67**
Cambridge Av. DA16: Well 4K **125**
KT3: N Mald 3A **152**
(not continuous)
NW6 .2J **81**
UB6: G'frd 5K **59**
Cambridge Barracks Rd. SE18 . . . .4D **106**
Cambridge Cir. WC2 . . . . .1D **12** (6H **83**)
Cambridge Cl. E17 . . . . .6B **50**
EN4: E Barn 1K **31**
N22 .1A **48**
NW10 . . . . .3J **61**
SW20 . . . . .1D **152**
TW4: Houn 4C **112**
UB7: Harm 2E **174**
Cambridge Cotts. TW9: Kew 6G **97**
Cambridge Ct. *E2* 2H **85**
(off Cambridge Heath Rd.)
N16 .7E **48**
(off Amhurst Pk.)
NW6 .2J **81**
(not continuous)
W2 . . . . .6C **4**
(off Edgware Rd.)
W6 . . . . .4E **98**
(off Shepherd's Bush Rd.)
Cambridge Cres. E2 . . . . .2H **85**
TW11: Tedd 5A **132**
Cambridge Dr. HA4: Ruis 2A **58**
SE12 . . . . .5J **123**
Cambridge Gdns. EN1: Enf 2B **24**
KT1: King T 2G **151**
N10 .1E **46**

Cambridge Gdns. N17 . . . . .7J **33**
N21 .7J **23**
NW6 .2J **81**
W10 .6F **81**
Cambridge Ga. NW1 . . . . .3J **5** (4F **83**)
Cambridge Ga. M. NW1 . . .3K **5** (4F **83**)
Cambridge Grn. SE9 . . . . .1F **143**
Cambridge Gro. SE20 . . . . .1H **157**
W6 .4D **98**
Cambridge Gro. Rd. KT1: King T . . .3G **151**
(not continuous)
Cambridge Heath Rd. E1 . . . . .5H **85**
E2 .5H **85**
Cambridge Ho. *W6* 4D **98**
(off Cambridge Gro.)
W13 . . . . .6A **78**
Cambridge Pde. EN1: Enf 1B **24**
Cambridge Pk. E11 . . . . .7J **51**
TW1: Twick 6C **114**
Cambridge Pk. Ct. TW1: Twick 7D **114**
Cambridge Pk. Rd. *E11* 7J **51**
(off Lonsdale Rd.)
Cambridge Pl. W8 . . . . .2K **99**
Cambridge Rd. BR1: Brom 7J **141**
CR4: Mitc 3G **155**
DA14: Sidc 4J **143**
E4 . . . . .1A **36**
E11 .6H **51**
HA2: Harr 5E **40**
IG3: Ilf 1J **71**
IG11: Bark 7G **71**
KT1: King T 2F **151**
KT2: King T 2F **151**
KT3: N Mald 4K **151**
KT8: W Mole 4D **148**
KT12: Walt T 6K **147**
NW6 .2J **81**
(not continuous)
SE20 . . . . .3H **157**
SM5: Cars 6C **166**
SW11 . . . . .1D **118**
SW13 . . . . .2B **116**
SW20 . . . . .1C **152**
TW1: Twick 6D **114**
TW4: Houn 4C **112**
TW9: Kew 7G **97**
TW11: Tedd 4K **131**
TW12: Hamp 7D **130**
TW15: Ashf 7E **128**
UB1: S'hall 1D **94**
W7 .2K **95**
Cambridge Rd. Nth. W4 . . . . .5H **97**
Cambridge Rd. Sth. W4 . . . . .5H **97**
Cambridge Row SE18 . . . . .5F **107**
Cambridge Sq. W2 . . . . . . .7C **4** (6C **82**)
Cambridge St. SW1 . . . . . .4K **17** (4F **101**)
Cambridge Ter. N9 . . . . .7K **23**
NW1 . . . . .2J **5** (3F **83**)
Cambridge Ter. M. NW1 . . .2K **5** (3F **83**)
Cambridge Theatre 1E **12**
(off Earlham St.)
Cambstone Cl. N11 . . . . .2K **31**
Cambus Cl. UB4: Yead 5C **76**
Cambus Rd. E16 . . . . .5J **87**
Cam Ct. SE15 . . . . .6F **103**
Camdale Rd. SE18 . . . . .7K **107**
Camden Arts Cen. 5K **63**
Camden Av. TW13: Felt 1A **130**
UB4: Yead 7B **76**
Camden Cl. BR7: Chst 1G **161**
Camden Ct. DA17: Belv 5G **109**
NW1 .7G **65**
(off Rousden St.)
Camden Gdns. CR7: Thor H 3B **156**
NW1 .7F **65**
SM1: Sutt 5K **165**
Camden Gro. BR7: Chst 6F **143**
Camden High St. NW1 . . . . .7F **65**
Camden Hill Rd. SE19 . . . . .6E **138**
Camden Ho. SE8 . . . . .5B **104**
Camdenhurst St. E14 . . . . .6A **86**

Camden La. N7 . . . . .5H 65
Camden Lock Market 7F 65
Camden Lock Pl. NW1 . . . . .7F 65
Camden Markets 7F 65
Camden M. NW1 . . . . .7G 65
Camden Pk. Rd. BR7: Chst 7D 142
NW1 . . . . .6H 65
Camden Pas. N1 . . . . .2B 84
Camden Peoples Theatre 3A 6
(off Hampstead Rd.)
Camden Rd. DA5: Bexl 1E 144
E11 . . . . .6K 51
E17 . . . . .6B 50
N7 . . . . .4J 65
NW1 . . . . .7G 65
SM1: Sutt 5K 165
SM5: Cars 4D 166
Camden Row HA5: Pinn 3A 40
SE3 . . . . .2G 123
Camden Sq. NW1 . . . . .7H 65
(not continuous)
SE15 . . . . .1F 121
Camden St. NW1 . . . . .7G 65
Camden Studios NW1 . . . . .1G 83
(off Camden St.)
Camden Ter. NW1 . . . . .6H 65
CAMDEN TOWN 1F 83
Camden Wlk. N1 . . . . .1B 84
Camden Way BR7: Chst 7D 142
CR7: Thor H 3B 156
Cameford Cl. SW2 . . . . .7J 119
Cameford NW1 . . . . .1G 83
(off Royal Coll. St.)
Cameford Ct. W11 . . . . .6G 81
Cameford Ho. SE1 . . . . . . .5F 19 (5J 101)
Cameford Wlk. W11 . . . . .6G 81
Camel Gro. KT2: King T 5D 132
Camellia Cl. E10 . . . . .2C 68
Camellia Ho. SE8 . . . . .7B 104
(off Idonia St.)
TW13: Felt 1J 129
(off Bedfont La.)
Camellia La. KT5: Surb 4H 151
Camellia Pl. TW2: Whitt 7F 113
Camellia St. SW8 . . . . .7J 101
(not continuous)
Camelot Cl. SE28 . . . . .2H 107
SW19 . . . . .4H 135
Camelot Ho. NW1 . . . . .6H 65
Camel Rd. E16 . . . . .1C 106
Camera Pl. SW10 . . . . .7A 16 (6B 100)
Camera Press Gallery, The 6J 15
(off Queen Elizabeth St.)
Cameret Ct. W11 . . . . .2F 99
(off Holland Rd.)
Cameron Cl. DA5: Bexl 3K 145
N18 . . . . .4C 34
N20 . . . . .2G 31
N22 . . . . .7E 32
Cameron Cres. HA8: Edg 1H 43
Cameron Ho. BR1: Brom 1H 159
NW8 . . . . .2C 82
(off St John's Wood Ter.)
SE5 . . . . .7C 102
Cameron Pl. E1 . . . . .6H 85
SW16 . . . . .2A 138
Cameron Rd. BR2: Brom 5J 159
CR0: C'don 6B 156
IG3: Ilf 1J 71
SE6 . . . . .2B 140
Cameron Sq. CR4: Mitc 1C 154
Cameron Ter. SE12 . . . . .3K 141
Camerton Cl. E8 . . . . .6F 67
Camgate Centre, The TW19: Stanw . .6B 110
Camgate Mans. SE5 . . . . .6C 102
(off Camberwell Rd.)
Camilla Cl. TW16: Sun 6H 129
Camilla Rd. SE16 . . . . .4H 103
Camille Cl. SE25 . . . . .3G 157
Camlan Rd. BR1: Brom 4H 141
Camlet St. E2 . . . . .3J 9 (4F 85)

Camlet Way EN4: Barn, Had W 2D 20
Camley St. N1 . . . . .7H 65
Camley Street Natural Pk. 2J 83
Camley Street Natural Pk. Vis. Cen. . .2H 83
Camm Gdns. KT1: King T 2F 151
KT7: T Ditt 7K 149
Camms Ter. RM10: Dag 5J 73
(off Cambeys Rd.)
Camomile Av. CR4: Mitc 1D 154
Camomile Rd. RM7: Rush G 2K 73
Camomile St. EC3 . . . . .7H 9 (6E 84)
Camomile Way UB7: View 6A 74
Campaign Ct. W9 . . . . .4H 81
(off Chantry Cl.)
Campana Bldg. E1 . . . . .7K 85
(off Jardine Rd.)
Campaspe Bus. TW16: Sun 5H 147
Campbell Av. IG6: Ilf 4F 53
Campbell Cl. HA4: Ruis 6J 39
SE18 . . . . .1E 124
SW16 . . . . .4H 137
TW2: Twick 1H 131
Campbell Ct. N17 . . . . .1F 49
NW9 . . . . .6J 43
SE22 . . . . .1G 139
SW7 . . . . .3A 100
(off Gloucester Rd.)
Campbell Cft. HA8: Edg 5B 28
Campbell Gordon Way NW2 . . . . . . .4D 62
Campbell Ho. SW1 . . . . .6A 18
(off Churchill Gdns.)
W2 . . . . .4A 4
(off Hall Pl.)
W12 . . . . .7D 80
(off White City Est.)
Campbell Rd. CR0: C'don 7B 156
E3 . . . . .3C 86
E6 . . . . .1C 88
E15 . . . . .4H 69
E17 . . . . .4B 50
KT8: E Mos 3J 149
N17 . . . . .1F 49
TW2: Twick 2H 131
W7 . . . . .7J 77
Campbell Wlk. N1 . . . . .1J 83
(off Outram Pl.)
Campdale Rd. N7 . . . . .3H 65
Campden Cres. HA0: Wemb 3B 60
RM8: Dag 4B 72
Campden Gro. W8 . . . . .2J 99
Campden Hill W8 . . . . .2J 99
Campden Hill Ct. W8 . . . . .2J 99
Campden Hill Gdns. W8 . . . . .1J 99
Campden Hill Ga. W8 . . . . .2J 99
Campden Hill Mans. W8 . . . . .1J 99
(off Edge St.)
Campden Hill Pl. W11 . . . . .1H 99
Campden Hill Rd. W8 . . . . .1J 99
Campden Hill Sq. W8 . . . . .1H 99
Campden Hill Towers W11 . . . . .1J 99
Campden Ho. NW6 . . . . .7B 64
(off Harben Rd.)
W8 . . . . .1J 99
(off Sheffield Ter.)
Campden Ho. Cl. W8 . . . . .2J 99
Campden Ho's. W8 . . . . .1J 99
Campden Ho. Ter. W8 . . . . .1J 99
(off Kensington Chu. St.)
Campden Mans. W8 . . . . .1J 99
(off Kensington Mall)
Campden Rd. CR2: S Croy 5E 168
UB10: Ick 3B 56
Campden St. W8 . . . . .1J 99
Campden Way RM8: Dag 4B 72
Campe Ho. N10 . . . . .7K 31
Campen Cl. SW19 . . . . .2G 135
Camperdown St. E1 . . . . . . .1K 15 (6F 85)
Campfield Rd. SE9 . . . . .7B 124
Campion Cl. CR0: C'don 4E 168
E6 . . . . .7D 88

Campion Cl. HA3: Kenton 6F 43
RM7: Rush G 2K 73
UB8: Hil 5B 74
Campion Ct. HA0: Wemb 2E 78
Campion Gdns. IG8: Wfd G 5D 36
Campion Ho. E14 . . . . .6B 86
(off Frances Wharf)
Campion Pl. SE28 . . . . .1A 108
Campion Rd. E10 . . . . .7D 50
SW15 . . . . .4E 116
TW7: Isle .1K 113
Campion Ter. NW2 . . . . .3F 63
Campion Way HA8: Edg 4D 28
Camplin Rd. HA3: Kenton 5E 42
Camplin St. SE14 . . . . .7K 103
Camp Rd. SW19 . . . . .5D 134
Campsbourne, The N8 . . . . .4J 47
Campsbourne Ho. N8 . . . . .4J 47
(off Pembroke Rd.)
Campsbourne Pde. N8 . . . . .4J 47
(off High St.)
Campsbourne Rd. N8 . . . . .3J 47
(not continuous)
Campsey Gdns. RM9: Dag 7B 72
Campsey Rd. RM9: Dag 7B 72
Campsfield Ho. N8 . . . . .4J 47
(off Campsfield Rd.)
Campsfield Rd. N8 . . . . .3J 47
Campshill Pl. SE13 . . . . .5E 122
Campshill Rd. SE13 . . . . .5E 122
Campus Av. RM8: Dag 4A 72
Campus Ho. TW7: Isle 7J 95
Campus Rd. E17 . . . . .6B 50
Campus Way NW4 . . . . .3D 44
Camp Vw. SW19 . . . . .5D 134
Cam Rd. E15 . . . . .1F 87
Camrose Av. DA8: Erith 6H 109
HA8: Edg 2E 42
TW13: Felt 4A 130
Camrose Cl. CR0: C'don 7A 158
SM4: Mord 4J 153
Camrose St. SE2 . . . . .5A 108
Camwal Cl. CR4: Mitc 2C 154
Canada Av. N18 . . . . .6H 33
Canada Cres. W3 . . . . .5J 79
Canada Est. SE16 . . . . .3J 103
Canada Gdns. SE13 . . . . .5E 122
Canada House 4D 12
Canada Ho. SE16 . . . . .3A 104
(off Brunswick Quay)
SW1 . . . . .1H 101
(off Trafalgar Sq.)
Canada Memorial 6A 12
(within Green Park)
Canada Pl. E14 . . . . .1D 104
(off Canada Sq.)
Canada Rd. W3 . . . . .5J 79
Canada Sq. E14 . . . . .1D 104
Canada St. SE16 . . . . .2K 103
Canada Way W12 . . . . .7D 80
Canada Wharf SE16 . . . . .1B 104
Canadian Av. SE6 . . . . .1D 140
Canal App. SE8 . . . . .5A 104
Canal Blvd. NW1 . . . . .6H 65
CANAL BRIDGE 6G 103
Canal Bldg. N1 . . . . .2C 84
Canal Cl. E1 . . . . .4A 86
W10 . . . . .4F 81
Canal Cotts. E3 . . . . .1B 86
(off Parnell Rd.)
Canal Gro. SE15 . . . . .6H 103
Canal Market 7F 65
(off Castlehaven Rd.)
Canal Path E2 . . . . .1F 85
Canal Reach N1 . . . . .1J 83
Canalside SE28 . . . . .7D 90
Canalside Activity Cen. 4F 81
Canalside Gdns. . . . .
UB2: S'hall 4C 94
Canalside N1 . . . . .2C 84
(off Arlington Av.)

Canal Side Studios NW1 . . . . .1H 83
(off St Pancras Way)
Canalside Studios N1 . . . . .1E 84
(off Orsman Rd.)
Canal St. SE5 . . . . .6D 102
Canal Wlk. CR0: C'don 6E 156
N1 . . . . .1D 84
NW10 . . . . .7J 61
(off Westend Cl.)
SE26 . . . . .5J 139
Canal Way W10 . . . . .4F 81
Canal Wharf E8 . . . . .1E 84
(off Kingsland Rd.)
UB6: G'frd 1A 78
Canary Vw. SE10 . . . . .6D 104
(off Dowells St.)
Canberra Cl. NW4 . . . . .3C 44
RM10: Dag 1K 91
Canberra Cres. RM10: Dag 7K 73
Canberra Dr. UB4: N'olt 3B 76
UB5: N'olt 3A 76
Canberra Path E10 . . . . .7D 50
(off Whitney Rd.)
Canberra Pl. TW9: Rich 3G 115
Canberra Rd. DA7: Bex 6D 108
E6 . . . . .1D 88
SE7 . . . . .6A 106
TW6: H'row A 3C 110
W13 . . . . .1A 96
Canbury Av. KT2: King T 1F 151
Canbury Bus. Cen. KT2: King T 1E 150
Canbury Bus. Pk. KT2: King T 1E 150
(off Canbury Pk. Rd.)
Canbury Ct. KT2: King T 7D 132
Canbury M. SE26 . . . . .3G 139
Canbury Pk. Rd. KT2: King T 1E 150
Canbury Pas. KT2: King T 1D 150
Cancell Rd. SW9 . . . . .1A 120
Candahar Rd. SW11 . . . . .2C 118
Candida Ct. NW1 . . . . .7F 65
Candid Ho. NW10 . . . . .3D 80
(off Trenmar Gdns.)
Candle Gro. SE15 . . . . .3H 121
Candlelight Ct. E15 . . . . .6H 69
(off Romford Rd.)
Candler M. TW1: Twick 7A 114
Candler St. N15 . . . . .6D 48
Candle St. E1 . . . . .5A 86
C & L Golf Course 7K 57
Candover Cl. UB7: Harm 3E 174
Candover St. W1 . . . . .6A 6 (5G 83)
Candy St. E3 . . . . .1B 86
Candy Wharf E3 . . . . .4A 86
Caney M. NW2 . . . . .2F 63
Canfield Dr. HA4: Ruis 5K 57
Canfield Gdns. NW6 . . . . .7K 63
Canfield Ho. N15 . . . . .6E 48
(off Albert Rd.)
Canfield Pl. NW6 . . . . .6A 64
Canfield Rd. IG8: Wfd G 7H 37
Canford Av. UB5: N'olt 1D 76
Canford Cl. EN2: Enf 2F 23
Canford Gdns. KT3: N Mald 6A 152
Canford Pl. TW11: Tedd 6C 132
Canford Rd. SW11 . . . . .5E 118
Canham Gdns. TW4: Houn 7D 112
Canham Rd. SE25 . . . . .3E 156
W3 . . . . .2A 98
Canmore Gdns. SW16 . . . . .7G 137
CANN HALL 4G 69
Cann Hall Rd. E11 . . . . .4G 69
Cann Ho. W14 . . . . .3G 99
(off Russell Rd.)
Canning Cres. N22 . . . . .1K 47
Canning Cross SE5 . . . . .2E 120
Canning Ho. W12 . . . . .7D 80
(off Australia Rd.)
Canning Pas. W8 . . . . .3A 100
Canning Pl. W8 . . . . .3A 100
Canning Pl. M. W8 . . . . .3A 100
(off Canning Pl.)

Canning Rd.—Carey Rd.

Canning Rd. CR0: C'don 2F **169**
E15 2G **87**
E17 4A **50**
HA3: W'stone 3J **41**
N5 3B **66**
Cannington Rd. RM9: Dag 6C **72**
CANNING TOWN 6H **87**
CANNING TOWN 5G **87**
Cannizaro Rd. SW19 6E **134**
Cannock Ct. E17 2E **50**
Cannock Ho. N4 7C **48**
Cannonbury Av. HA5: Pinn 6B **40**
Cannon Cl. SW20 3E **152**
TW12: Hamp 6F **131**
Cannon Ct. *EC1* *3B 8*
(off Brewhouse Yd.)
Cannon Dr. E14 7C **86**
Cannon Hill N14 3D **32**
NW6 5J **63**
Cannon Hill La. SW20 5F **153**
Cannon Hill M. N14 3D **32**
Cannon Ho. SE11 4H **19**
Cannon La. HA5: Pinn 5C **40**
NW3 3B **64**
Cannon Pl. NW3 3B **64**
SE7 5C **106**
Cannon Retail Pk. SE28 7A **90**
Cannon Rd. DA7: Bex 1E **126**
N14 3D **32**
Cannons Health Club
Richmond 4D **114**
Cannon St. EC4 1C **14** (6C **84**)
Cannon St. Rd. E1 6H **85**
Cannon Trad. Est. HA9: Wemb 4H **61**
Cannon Way KT8: W Mole 4E **148**
Cannon Wharf Development
SE8 4A **104**
Cannon Workshops *E14* *7C 86*
(off Cannon Dr.)
Canon All. *EC4* *1C 14*
(off Queen's Head Pas.)
Canon Av. RM6: Chad H 5C **54**
Canon Beck Rd. SE16 2J **103**
Canonbie Rd. SE23 7J **121**
CANONBURY 6C **66**
Canonbury Bus. Cen. N1 1C **84**
Canonbury Cotts. EN1: Enf 1K **23**
Canonbury Ct. *N1* *7B 66*
(off Hawes St.)
Canonbury Cres. N1 7C **66**
Canonbury Gro. N1 7C **66**
Canonbury Hgts. *N1* *6D 66*
(off Dove Rd.)
Canonbury La. N1 7B **66**
Canonbury Pk. Nth. N1 6C **66**
Canonbury Pk. Sth. N1 6C **66**
Canonbury Pl. N1 6B **66**
(not continuous)
Canonbury Rd. EN1: Enf 1K **23**
N1 6B **66**
Canonbury Sq. N1 7B **66**
Canonbury St. N1 7C **66**
Canonbury Vs. N1 7B **66**
Canon Mohan Cl. N14 6K **21**
Canon Rd. BR1: Brom 3A **160**
Canon Row SW1 7E **12** (2J **101**)
(not continuous)
Canons Cl. CR4: Mitc 4D **154**
HA8: Edg 6A **28**
N2 7B **46**
Canons Cnr. HA8: Edg 4K **27**
Canons Ct. E15 4G **69**
HA8: Edg 6A **28**
Canons Dr. HA8: Edg 6K **27**
Canonsleigh Rd. RM9: Dag 7B **72**
Canons Leisure Cen.
Mitcham 4D **154**
CANONS PARK 7J **27**
Canons Pk. HA7: Stan 6J **27**
Canons Pk. Cl. HA8: Edg 7K **27**
Canon St. N1 1C **84**
Canon's Wlk. CR0: C'don 3K **169**
Canopus Way TW19: Stanw 7A **110**
Canrobert St. E2 2H **85**
Cantelowes Rd. NW1 6H **65**
Canterbury Av. DA15: Sidc 2B **144**
IG1: Ilf 7C **52**
Canterbury Cl. BR3: Beck 1D **158**
E6 6D **88**
KT4: Wor Pk 2F **165**
SE5 *2C 120*
(off Lilford Rd.)
UB6: G'frd 5F **77**
Canterbury Ct. *CR2: S Croy* *7C 168*
(off St Augustine's Av.)
NW6 *2J 81*
(off Canterbury Rd.)
NW9 2A **44**
SE5 7A **102**
SE12 3K **141**
TW15: Ashf 4B **128**
Canterbury Cres. SW9 3A **120**
Canterbury Gro. SE27 4A **138**
Canterbury Hall
KT4: Wor Pk 7D **152**
Canterbury Ho. *CR0: C'don* *1D 168*
(off Sydenham Rd.)
E3 *3D 86*
(off Bow Rd.)
IG11: Bark *7A 72*
(off Margaret Bondfield Av.)
RM8: Dag *4A 72*
(off Academy Way)
SE1 1H **19** (3K **101**)
SE8 *5C 104*
(off Wharf St.)
Canterbury Ind. Pk. SE15 6J **103**
Canterbury Pl. SE17 5B **102**
Canterbury Rd. CR0: C'don 7K **155**
E10 7E **50**
HA1: Harr 5F **41**
HA2: Harr 5F **41**
NW6 2H **81**
(Carlton Va.)
NW6 2J **81**
(Princess Rd.)
SM4: Mord 7K **153**
TW13: Hanw 2C **130**
Canterbury Ter. NW6 2J **81**
Cantium Retail Pk. SE1 6G **103**
Cantley Gdns. IG2: Ilf 6G **53**
SE19 1F **157**
Cantley Rd. W7 3A **96**
Canto Ct. *EC1* *3D 8*
(off Old St.)
Canton St. E14 6C **86**
Cantrell Rd. E3 4B **86**
Cantwell Rd. SE18 7F **107**
Canute Gdns. SE16 4K **103**
Canvey St. SE1 4C **14** (1C **102**)
Cape Cl. IG11: Bark 7F **71**
Cape Henry Ct. *E14* *7F 87*
(off Jamestown Way)
Cape Ho. *E8* *6F 67*
(off Dalston La.)
Capel Av. SM6: Wall 5K **167**
Capel Cl. BR2: Brom 1C **172**
N20 3F **31**
Capel Ct. *EC2* *1F 15*
(off Bartholomew La.)
SE20 1J **157**
Capel Cres. HA7: Stan 2F **27**
Capel Gdns. HA5: Pinn 4D **40**
IG3: Bark, Ilf 4K **71**
Capel Ho. *E9* *7J 67*
(off Loddiges Rd.)
Capel Rd. E7 4K **69**
E12 4K **69**
EN4: E Barn 6H **21**
Capener's Cl. SW1 7F **11**
Capern Rd. SW18 1A **136**
Cape Rd. N17 3G **49**
Cape Yd. E1 1G **103**
Capital Bus. Cen. CR2: S Croy 7D **168**
HA0: Wemb 2D **78**
Capital E. Apartments *E16* *7J 87*
(off Western Gateway)
Capital Ho. *SW15* *5G 117*
(off Plaza Gdns.)
Capital Ind. Est. CR4: Mitc 5D **154**
DA17: Belv 3H **109**
Capital Interchange Way
TW8: Bford 5G **97**
Capital Trad. Est. IG11: Bark 2H **89**
Capital Wharf E1 1G **103**
Capitol Ind. Pk. NW9 3J **43**
Capitol Way NW9 3J **43**
Capland Ho. *NW8* *3B 4*
(off Capland St.)
Capland St. NW8 3B **4** (4B **82**)
Caple Ho. *SW10* *7A 100*
(off King's Rd.)
Caple Rd. NW10 2B **80**
Capper St. WC1 4B **6** (4G **83**)
Caprea Cl. UB4: Yead 5B **76**
Capricorn Cen. RM8: Dag 7F **55**
Capri Ho. E17 2B **50**
Capri Rd. CR0: C'don 1F **169**
Capstan Cl. RM6: Chad H 6B **54**
Capstan Ct. *E1* *7J 85*
(off Wapping Wall)
Capstan Ho. *E14* *7F 87*
(off Clove Cres., Clove Cres.)
E14 *4E 104*
(off Stebondale St., Stebondale St.)
Capstan Ride EN2: Enf 2F **23**
Capstan Rd. SE8 4B **104**
Capstan Sq. E14 2E **104**
Capstan Way SE16 1A **104**
Capstone Rd. BR1: Brom 4H **141**
Captain Cook Statue *4D 12*
(in The Mall)
Capthorne Av. HA2: Harr 1C **58**
Capuchin Cl. HA7: Stan 6G **27**
Capulet M. E16 1J **105**
Capulet Sq. *E3* *3D 86*
(off Talwin St.)
Capworth St. E10 1C **68**
Caradoc Cl. W2 6J **81**
Caradoc Evans Cl. *N11* *5A 32*
(off Springfield Rd.)
Caradoc St. SE10 5G **105**
Caradon Cl. E11 1G **69**
Caradon Way N15 4D **48**
Cara Ho. *N1* *7A 66*
(off Liverpool Rd.)
Caramel Ct. *E3* *2D 86*
(off Taylor Pl.)
Caranday Vs. *W11* *1F 99*
(off Norland Rd.)
Carat Ho. *E14* *5C 86*
(off Ursula Gould Way)
Caravel Cl. E14 3C **104**
Caravelle Gdns.
UB5: N'olt 3B **76**
Caravel M. SE8 6C **104**
Caraway Apartments *SE1* *6K 15*
(off Cayenne Ct.)
Caraway Cl. E13 5K **87**
Caraway Hgts. *E14* *7E 86*
(off Poplar High St.)
Caraway Pl. SM6: Wall 3F **167**
Carberry Rd. SE19 6E **138**
Carbery Av. W3 2F **97**
Carbis Cl. E4 1A **36**
Carbis Rd. E14 6B **86**
Carbrooke Ho. *E9* *1J 85*
(off Templecombe Rd.)
Carbuncle Pas. N17 2G **49**
Carburton St. W1 5K **5** (5F **83**)
Cardale St. E14 2E **104**
Cardamon Bldg. *SE1* *5K 15*
(off Shad Thames)
Carden Ct. KT8: W Mole 4F **149**
Carden Rd. SE15 3H **121**
Cardiff Ho. *SE15* *6G 103*
(off Friary Est.)
Cardiff Rd. EN3: Pond E 4C **24**
W7 3A **96**
Cardiff St. SE18 7J **107**
Cardigan Ct. *W7* *4K 77*
(off Copley Cl.)
Cardigan Gdns. IG3: Ilf 2A **72**
Cardigan Pl. SE3 2F **123**
Cardigan Rd. E3 2B **86**
SW13 2C **116**
SW19 6A **136**
TW10: Rich 6E **114**
Cardigan St. SE11 5J **19** (5A **102**)
Cardigan Wlk. *N1* *7C 66*
(off Ashby Gro.)
Cardinal Av. KT2: King T 5E **132**
SM4: Mord 6G **153**
Cardinal Bourne St. SE1 3D **102**
Cardinal Cap All. SE1 1C **102**
Cardinal Cl. BR7: Chst 1J **161**
HA8: Edg 7D **28**
KT4: Wor Pk 4C **164**
SM4: Mord 6G **153**
Cardinal Ct. *E1* *7G 85*
(off Thomas More St.)
Cardinal Cres. KT3: N Mald 2J **151**
Cardinal Hinsley Cl. NW10 2C **80**
Cardinal Mans. *SW1* *3A 18*
(off Carlisle Pl.)
Cardinal Pl. SW1 1A **18** (3G **101**)
(not continuous)
SW15 4F **117**
Cardinal Rd. HA4: Ruis 1B **58**
TW13: Felt 1K **129**
Cardinals Wlk. TW12: Hamp 7G **131**
TW16: Sun 6G **129**
Cardinals Way N19 1H **65**
Cardinal Wlk. SW1 2A **18**
Cardinal Way HA3: W'stone 3J **41**
Cardine M. SE15 7H **103**
Cardington Sq. TW4: Houn 4B **112**
Cardington St. NW1 1B **6** (3G **83**)
Cardinham Rd. BR6: Chels 4K **173**
Cardozo Rd. N7 5J **65**
Cardrew Av. N12 5G **31**
Cardrew Cl. N12 5H **31**
Cardrew Ct. N12 5G **31**
Cardross Ho. *W6* *3D 98*
(off Cardross St.)
Cardross St. W6 3D **98**
Cardwell Rd. N7 4J **65**
Cardwell Ter. *N7* *4J 65*
(off Cardwell Rd.)
Career Ct. *SE16* *2K 103*
(off Christopher Cl.)
Carew Cl. N7 2K **65**
Carew Ct. *RM6: Chad H* *6B 54*
(off Quarles Pk. Rd.)
SE14 *6K 103*
(off Samuel Cl.)
SM2: Sutt 7K **165**
Carew Manor & Dovecote 3G **167**
Carew Mnr. Cotts. SM6: Bedd 3H **167**
Carew Rd. CR4: Mitc 2E **154**
CR7: Thor H 4B **156**
N17 2G **49**
SM6: Wall 6G **167**
TW15: Ashf 6E **128**
W13 2C **96**
Carew St. SE5 2C **120**
Carey Ct. DA6: Bex 5H **127**
SE5 7C **102**
Carey Gdns. SW8 1G **119**
Carey La. EC2 7C **8** (6C **84**)
Carey Mans. *SW1* *3C 18*
(off Rutherford St.)
Carey Pl. SW1 4C **18** (4H **101**)
Carey Rd. RM9: Dag 4E **72**

Carey St. WC2 . . . . .1H 13 (6K 83)
Carey Way HA9: Wemb 4H 61
Carfax Ho. SE20 . . . . .1G 157
Carfax Pl. SW4 . . . . .4H 119
Carfax Rd. UB3: Harl 5H 93
Carfree Cl. N1 . . . . .7A 66
Cargill Rd. SW18 . . . . .1K 135
Cargo Point TW19: Stanw 6B 110
Cargreen Pl. SE25 . . . . .4F 157
                        (off Cargreen Rd.)
Cargreen Rd. SE25 . . . . .4F 157
Cargrey Ho. HA7: Stan 5H 27
Carholme Rd. SE23 . . . . .1B 140
Carillon Ct. E1 . . . . .5G 85
                      (off Greatorex St.)
    W5 . . . . .7D 78
Carina Ho. E20 . . . . .5E 68
                        (off Cheering La.)
Carinthia Ct. SE16 . . . . .4A 104
                         (off Plough Way)
Carisbrook N10 . . . . .2F 47
Carisbrook Cl. EN1: Enf 1A 24
Carisbrooke Av. DA5: Bexl 1D 144
Carisbrooke Cl. HA7: Stan 2D 42
    TW4: Houn 7C 112
Carisbrooke Cl. SM2: Cheam 7H 165
    UB5: N'olt .1D 76
                       (off Eskdale Av.)
    W1 . . . . .6H 5
                      (off Weymouth St.)
    W3 . . . . .2J 97
                      (off Brouncker Rd.)
Carisbrooke Gdns. SE15 . . . . .7F 103
Carisbrooke Ho. KT2: King T 1E 150
                    (off Seven Kings Way)
    TW10: Rich 5G 115
    UB7: W Dray 2B 92
                     (off Park Lodge Av.)
Carisbrooke Rd. BR2: Brom 4A 160
    CR4: Mitc .4H 155
    E17 . . . . .4A 50
Carker's La. NW5 . . . . .5F 65
Carlcott Cl. KT12: Walt T 7K 147
Carleton Av. SM6: Wall 7J 167
Carleton Cl. KT10: Esh 7H 149
Carleton Gdns. N19 . . . . .5G 65
Carleton Rd. N7 . . . . .5H 65
Carleton Vs. NW5 . . . . .5G 65
Carlile Cl. E3 .2B 86
Carlile Ho. SE1 . . . . .3D 102
                         (off Tabard St.)
Carlina Gdns. IG8: Wfd G 5E 36
Carlingford Gdns.
                    CR4: Mitc 7D 136
Carlingford Rd. N15 . . . . .3B 48
    NW3 . . . . .4B 64
    SM4: Mord 6F 153
Carlisle Av. EC3 . . . . .1J 15 (6F 85)
    W3 . . . . .6A 80
Carlisle Cl. HA5: Pinn 7C 40
    KT2: King T 1G 151
Carlisle Gdns. HA3: Kenton 7D 42
    IG1: Ilf 6C 52
Carlisle Ho. IG1: Ilf 6C 52
Carlisle La. SE1 . . . . .2H 19 (3K 101)
Carlisle Mans. SW1 . . . . .3A 18
                         (off Carlisle Pl.)
Carlisle M. KT2: King T 1G 151
Carlisle Pl. N11 . . . . .4A 32
    SW1 . . . . .2A 18 (3G 101)
Carlisle Rd. E10 . . . . .1C 68
    N4 . . . . .7A 48
    NW6 . . . . .1G 81
    NW9 . . . . .3J 43
    SM1: Sutt .6H 165
    TW12: Hamp 7F 131
Carlisle St. W1 . . . . .1C 12 (6H 83)
Carlisle Wlk. E8 . . . . .6F 67
Carlisle Way SW17 . . . . .5E 136
Carlos Pl. W1 . . . . .3H 11 (7E 82)

Carlow St. NW1 . . . . .2G 83
Carlson Ct. SW15 . . . . .4H 117
Carlton Av. CR2: S Croy 7E 168
    HA3: Kenton 5B 42
    N14 . . . . .5C 22
    TW14: Felt 6A 112
    W5 . . . . .4G 93
Carlton Av. E. HA9: Wemb 2D 60
Carlton Av. W. HA0: Wemb 2B 60
Carlton Cl. HA8: Edg 5B 28
    KT9: Chess 6D 162
    NW3 . . . . .2J 63
    UB5: N'olt .5G 59
Carlton Ct. IG6: Ilf 3H 53
    N3 . . . . .7D 30
    SE20 . . . . .1H 157
    UB8: Cowl .5A 74
    W9 . . . . .2K 81
                         (off Maida Vale)
Carlton Cres. SM3: Cheam 4G 165
Carlton Dr. IG6: Ilf 3H 53
    SW15 . . . . .5F 117
Carlton Gdns. SW1 . . . . . . .5C 12 (1H 101)
    W5 . . . . .6C 78
Carlton Grn. DA14: Sidc 4K 143
Carlton Gro. SE15 . . . . .1H 121
Carlton Hill NW8 . . . . .2K 81
Carlton Ho. 2J 81
            (off Canterbury Ter., not continuous)
    SE16 . . . . .2K 103
                        (off Wolfe Cres.)
    TW4: Houn 6E 112
    TW14: Felt 6H 111
Carlton Ho. Ter. SW1 . . . . . .5C 12 (1H 101)
                       (off Carlton Rd.)
Carlton Lodge N4 . . . . .7A 48
                        (off Carlton Rd.)
Carlton Mans. N16 . . . . .1F 67
    NW6 . . . . .7J 63
                      (off West End La.)
    W9 . . . . .3K 81
    W14 . . . . .2G 99
                     (off Holland Pk. Gdns.)
Carlton M. NW6 . . . . .5J 63
                        (off West Cotts.)
Carlton Pde. HA9: Wemb 2E 60
Carlton Pk. Av. SW20 . . . . .2F 153
Carlton Rd.
    CR2: S Croy 6D 168
    DA8: Erith .6H 109
    DA14: Sidc 5K 143
    DA16: Well 3B 126
    E11 . . . . .1H 69
    E12 . . . . .4B 70
    E17 . . . . .1A 50
    KT3: N Mald 2A 152
    KT12: Walt T 7K 147
    N4 . . . . .7A 48
    N11 . . . . .5K 31
    SW14 . . . . .3J 115
    TW16: Sun 7H 129
    W4 . . . . .2K 97
    W5 . . . . .7C 78
Carlton Sq. E1 . . . . .4K 85
                        (not continuous)
Carlton St. SW1 . . . . .3C 12 (7H 83)
Carlton Ter. E7 . . . . .7A 70
    E11 . . . . .5K 51
                        (not continuous)
    N18 . . . . .3J 33
    SE26 . . . . .3J 139
Carlton Twr. Pl. SW1 . . . . . .1F 17 (3D 100)
Carlton Va. NW6 . . . . .2H 81
Carlton Vs. SW15 . . . . .5G 117
Carlton Works, The SE15 . . . . .7H 103
                        (off Asylum Rd.)
Cartwell St. SW17 . . . . .5C 136
Carlyle Av. BR1: Brom 3B 160
    UB1: S'hall 7D 76
Carlyle Cl. KT8: W Mole 2F 149
    N2 . . . . .6A 46

Carlyle Ct. SW6 . . . . .1K 117
                       (off Imperial Rd.)
    SW10 . . . . .1A 118
                   (off Chelsea Harbour Dr.)
Carlyle Gdns. UB1: S'hall 7D 76
Carlyle Ho. KT8: W Mole 5E 148
                         (off Down St.)
    N16 . . . . .3E 66
    SE5 . . . . .7C 102
                       (off Bethwin Rd.)
    SW3 . . . . .7B 16
                     (off Old Church St.)
Carlyle Mans. SW3 . . . . .7C 16
                        (off Cheyne Wlk.)
    W8 . . . . .1J 99
                    (off Kensington Mall)
Carlyle M. E1 . . . . .4K 85
Carlyle Pl. SW15 . . . . .4F 117
Carlyle Rd.
    CR0: C'don 2G 169
    E12 . . . . .4C 70
    NW10 . . . . .1K 79
    SE28 . . . . .7B 90
    W5 . . . . .4C 96
Carlyle's House 7C 16
Carlyle Sq. SW3 . . . . . . .6B 16 (5B 100)
Carly M. E2 . . . . .3G 85
                        (off Barnet Gro.)
Carlyon Av. HA2: Harr 4D 58
Carlyon Cl. HA0: Wemb 1E 78
Carlyon Rd. HA0: Wemb 2E 78
    UB4: Yead .5A 76
                        (not continuous)
Carlys Cl. BR3: Beck 2K 157
Carmalt Gdns. SW15 . . . . .4E 116
Carmarthen Ct. W7 . . . . .4K 77
                         (off Copley Cl.)
Carmarthen Pl. SE1 . . . . . . .6G 15 (2E 102)
Carmel Ct. HA9: Wemb 2H 61
    W8 . . . . .2K 99
                       (off Holland St.)
Carmelite Cl. HA3: Hrw W 1G 41
Carmelite Rd. HA3: Hrw W 1G 41
Carmelite St. EC4 . . . . .2K 13 (7A 84)
Carmelite Wlk. HA3: Hrw W 1G 41
Carmelite Way HA3: Hrw W 2G 41
Carmel Lodge SW6 . . . . .6J 99
                         (off Lillie Rd.)
Carmelo M. E1 . . . . .5K 85
                        (off Maria Ter.)
Carmel Way TW9: Rich 2H 115
Carmen St. E14 . . . . .6D 86
Carmichael Cl. HA4: Ruis 4J 57
    SW11 . . . . .3B 118
Carmichael Ct. SW13 . . . . .2B 116
                        (off Grove Rd.)
Carmichael Ho. E14 . . . . .7E 86
                     (off Poplar High St.)
Carmichael M. SW18 . . . . .7B 118
Carmichael Rd. SE25 . . . . .5F 157
Carmine W2 . . . . .6B 4 (5B 82)
Carminia Ct. BR1: Brom 7H 141
Carmine Wharf E14 . . . . .6B 86
Carminia Rd. SW17 . . . . .2F 137
Carnaby St. W1 . . . . .1A 12 (6G 83)
Carnac St. SE27 . . . . .4D 138
Carnanton Rd. E17 . . . . .1F 51
Carnarvon Av. EN1: Enf 3A 24
Carnarvon Dr. UB3: Harl 3E 92
Carnarvon Rd. E10 . . . . .5E 50
    E15 . . . . .6H 69
    E18 . . . . .1H 51
    EN5: Barn .3B 20
Carnation Cl. RM7: Rush G 2K 73
Carnation St. SE2 . . . . .5B 108
Carnbrook M. SE3 . . . . .3B 124
Carnbrook Rd. SE3 . . . . .3B 124
Carnecke Gdns. SE9 . . . . .5C 124
Carnegie Cl. KT6: Surb 2F 163
Carnegie Pl. SW19 . . . . .3F 135
Carnegie Rd. HA1: Harr 7K 41

Carnegie St. N1 . . . . .1K 83
Carnell Apartments E14 . . . . .6B 86
                      (off St Anne's Row)
Carney Pl. SW9 . . . . .4A 120
Carnforth Cl. KT19: Ewe 6H 163
Carnforth Rd. SW16 . . . . .7H 137
                        (not continuous)
Carnie Lodge SW17 . . . . .3F 137
Carnival Ho. SE1 . . . . .6K 15
                       (off Gainsford St.)
Carnoustie Cl. SE28 . . . . .6D 90
Carnoustie Dr. N1 . . . . .7K 65
                        (not continuous)
Carnwath Rd. SW6 . . . . .3J 117
Caroe Ct. N9 .1C 34
Carol Cl. NW4 . . . . .4F 45
Carole Ho. NW1 . . . . .1D 82
                     (off Regent's Pk. Rd.)
Carolina Cl. E15 . . . . .5G 69
Carolina Rd. CR7: Thor H 2B 156
Caroline Cl. CR0: C'don 4E 168
    N10 . . . . .2F 47
    SW16 . . . . .3K 137
    TW7: Isle .7H 95
    UB7: W Dray 2A 92
    W2 . . . . .7K 81
Caroline Cl. HA7: Stan 6F 27
    SE6 . . . . .4F 141
    TW15: Ashf 6D 128
Caroline Gdns. E2 . . . . .1H 9 (3E 84)
    SE15 . . . . .7H 103
                        (not continuous)
Caroline Ho. W2 . . . . .7K 81
                      (off Bayswater Rd.)
    W6 . . . . .5E 98
                    (off Queen Caroline St.)
Caroline Pl. SW11 . . . . .2E 118
    UB3: Harl .7G 93
    W2 . . . . .7K 81
Caroline Pl. M. W2 . . . . .7K 81
Caroline St. E1 . . . . .6K 85
Caroline Ter. SW1 . . . . .4G 17 (4E 100)
Caroline Wlk. W6 . . . . .6G 99
                         (off Lillie Rd.)
Carol St. NW1 . . . . .1G 83
Caronia Ct. SE16 . . . . .4A 104
                        (off Plough Way)
Caro Pl. KT3: N Mald 4B 152
Carpenter Gdns. N21 . . . . .2G 33
Carpenter Ho. E1 . . . . .5K 85
                      (off Trafalgar Gdns.)
    E14 . . . . .5C 86
                        (off Burgess St.)
    NW11 . . . . .6A 46
Carpenters Arms Apartments SE1 . . .4G 103
                        (off Welsford St.)
Carpenters Arms Path SE9 . . . . .6D 124
                      (off Eltham High St.)
Carpenters Cl. EN5: New Bar 6E 20
Carpenters Cl. NW1 . . . . .1G 83
                         (off Pratt St.)
    TW2: Twick 2J 131
Carpenters M. N7 . . . . .5J 65
Carpenters Pl. SW4 . . . . .4H 119
Carpenters Rd. E15 . . . . .7E 68
    E20 . . . . .6C 68
Carpenter St. W1 . . . . .3J 11 (7F 83)
Carp Ho. E3 . . . . .1B 86
                       (off Old Ford Rd.)
Carradale Ho. E14 . . . . .6E 86
                     (off St Leonard's Rd.)
Carrara Cl. SE24 . . . . .4A 120
    SW9 . . . . .4B 120
Carrara M. E8 .6G 67
                        (off Dalston La.)
Carrara Wharf SW6 . . . . .3G 117
Carr Ho. HA7: Stan 6F 27
Carre M. SE5 . . . . .1B 120
                         (off Calais St.)
Carr Gro. SE18 . . . . .4C 106

Carr Ho. DA1: Cray 5K 127
Carriage Dr. E. SW11 . . . . .7E 100
Carriage Dr. Nth. SW11 . . . .7H 17 (6E 100)
(Carriage Dr. E.)
SW11 .7D 100
(The Parade)
Carriage Dr. Sth. SW11 . . . . .1D 118
(not continuous)
Carriage Dr. W. SW11 . . . . .7D 100
Carriage M. IG1: Ilf 2G 71
Carriage Pl. N16 . . . . .3D 66
SW16 .5G 137
Carriage St. SE18 . . . . .3F 107
Carriage Way SE8 . . . . .7C 104
(off Deptford High St.)
Carrick Cl. TW7: Isle 3A 114
Carrick Dr. IG6: Ilf 1G 53
Carrick Gdns. N17 . . . . .7K 33
Carrick Ho. N7 . . . . .6K 65
(off Caledonian Rd.)
SE11 . . . . .5K 19 (5A 102)
Carrick M. SE8 . . . . .6C 104
Carrill Way DA17: Belv 3D 108
Carrington Av. TW3: Houn 5F 113
Carrington Cl. CRO: C'don 7A 158
KT2: King T 5J 133
Carrington Ct. SW11 . . . . .4C 118
(off Barnard Rd.)
Carrington Gdns. E7 . . . . .4J 69
Carrington Ho. W1 . . . . .5J 11
(off Carrington St.)
Carrington Rd. TW10: Rich 4G 115
Carrington Sq. HA3: Hrw W 6B 26
Carrington St. W1 . . . . .5J 11 (1F 101)
Carrock Ct. RM7: Rush G 6K 55
(off Union Rd.)
Carrol Cl. NW5 . . . . .4F 65
Carroll Cl. E15 . . . . .5H 69
Carroll Ct. W3 . . . . .3H 97
(off Osborne Rd.)
Carroll Ho. W2 . . . . .2A 10
(off Craven Ter.)
Carronade Ct. N7 . . . . .5K 65
Carronade Pl. SE28 . . . . .3G 107
Carron Cl. E14 . . . . .6D 86
Carroun Rd. SW8 . . . . .7K 101
Carroway La. UB6: G'frd 3H 77
Carrow Rd. RM9: Dag 7B 72
Carr Rd. E17 . . . . .2B 50
UB5: N'olt 6E 58
Carrs La. N21 . . . . .5H 23
Carr St. E14 . . . . .5A 86
CARSHALTON 4E 166
Carshalton Athletic 4C 166
CARSHALTON BEECHES 7C 166
Carshalton Gro. SM1: Sutt 4B 166
CARSHALTON ON THE HILL 7E 166
Carshalton Pk. Rd. SM5: Cars 5D 166
Carshalton Pl. SM5: Cars 5E 166
Carshalton Rd. CR4: Mitc 4E 154
SM1: Sutt 5A 166
SM5: Cars 5A 166
Carslake Rd. SW15 . . . . .6E 116
Carson Rd. E16 . . . . .4J 87
EN4: Cockf 4J 21
SE21 .2D 138
Carson Ter. W11 . . . . .1G 99
(off Princes Pl.)
Carstairs Rd. SE6 . . . . .3E 140
Carston Cl. SE12 . . . . .5H 123
Carswell Cl. IG4: Ilf 4B 52
Carswell Rd. SE6 . . . . .7E 122
Carter Cl. EN5: Barn 5B 20
NW9 . . . . .6K 43
Carter Ct. EC4 . . . . .1A 14
Carter Dr. RM5: Col R 1H 55
Carteret Ho. W12 . . . . .7D 80
(off White City Est.)
Carteret St. SW1 . . . . . .7C 12 (2H 101)
Carteret Way SE8 . . . . .4A 104
Carterhatch La. EN1: Enf 1A 24

Carterhatch Rd. EN3: Enf H 1D 24
Carter Ho. E1 . . . . .6J 9
Carter La. EC4 . . . . .1B 14 (6B 84)
Carter Pl. SE17 . . . . .5C 102
Carter Rd. E13 . . . . .1K 87
SW19 .6B 136
Carters Cl. KT4: Wor Pk 2F 165
NW5 . . . . .5H 65
(off Torriano Av.)
Carters Hill Cl. SE9 . . . . .1A 142
Carters La. SE23 . . . . .2A 140
Carter St. SE17 . . . . .6C 102
Carter's Yd. SW18 . . . . .5J 117
Carthew Rd. W6 . . . . .3D 98
Carthew Vs. W6 . . . . .3D 98
Carthusian Ct. EC1 . . . . .5C 8
(off Carthusian St.)
Carthusian St. EC1 . . . . . . .5C 8 (5C 84)
Cartier Circ. E14 . . . . .1D 104
Carting La. WC2 . . . . .3F 13 (7J 83)
Cart La. E4 .1K 36
Cart Lodge M. CRO: C'don 1E 168
Cartmel NW1 . . . . .1A 6
(off Harrington St.)
Cartmel Cl. N17 . . . . .7C 34
Cartmel Ct. UB5: N'olt 6C 58
Cartmel Gdns. SM4: Mord 5A 154
Cartmel Rd. DA7: Bex 1G 127
Carton Ho. W11 . . . . .7F 81
(off St Ann's Rd.)
SE16 . . . . .8E 6
(off Lit. Russell St.)
Cartoon Mus. 6E 6
(off Lit. Russell St.)
Cartridge Pl. SE18 . . . . .3F 107
Cartwright Gdns. WC1 . . . . .2E 6 (3J 83)
Cartwright Ho. SE1 . . . . .3C 102
(off County St.)
Cartwright Rd. RM9: Dag 7F 73
Cartwright St. E1 . . . . .2K 15 (7F 85)
Cartwright Way SW13 . . . . .7D 98
Carvel Ho. E14 . . . . .5E 104
(off Manchester Rd.)
Carver Cl. W4 . . . . .3J 97
Carver Rd. SE24 . . . . .6C 120
Carville Cres. TW8: Bford 4E 96
Carville St. N4 . . . . .2A 66
Cary Av. SE16 . . . . .4A 104
Cary Rd. E11 . . . . .4G 69
Carysfort Rd. N8 . . . . .5H 47
N16 . . . . .3D 66
Casby Ho. SE16 . . . . .3G 103
(off Marine St.)
Cascade Av. N10 . . . . .4G 47
Cascade Cl. IG9: Buck H 2G 37
Cascade Ct. SW8 . . . . .7F 101
Cascade Rd. IG9: Buck H 2G 37
Cascades Ct. SW19 . . . . .7H 135
Cascades Twr. E14 . . . . .1B 104
Casel Ct. HA7: Stan 2F 27
(off Brightwen Gro.)
Casella Rd. SE14 . . . . .7K 103
Casewick Rd. SE27 . . . . .5A 138
Casey Av. UB5: N'olt 2D 76
Casey Cl. NW8 . . . . .2C 4 (3C 82)
Casey Ct. SE14 . . . . .1K 121
(off Besson St.)
Cashmere Ho. E8 . . . . .1F 85
(off Pamela St.)
Casimir Rd. E5 . . . . .2J 67
Casino Av. SE24 . . . . .5C 120
Caspian St. SE5 . . . . .7D 102
Caspian Wlk. E16 . . . . .6B 88
Caspian Wharf E3 . . . . .5D 86
(off Violet Rd.)
Cassander Pl. HA5: Pinn 1C 40
(off Holly Gro.)
Cassandra Cl. UB5: N'olt 4H 59
Cassel Dden Rd. NW10 . . . . .7K 61
Cassell Ho. SW9 . . . . .2K 119
(off Stockwell Gdns. Est.)
Cass Ho. E9 .6K 67
(off Harrowgate Rd.)

Cassidy Rd. SW6 . . . . .7J 99
(not continuous)
Cassilda Rd. SE2 . . . . .4A 108
Cassilis Rd. E14 . . . . .2C 104
TW1: Twick 5B 114
Cassini Apartments E16 . . . . .6J 87
Cassiobury Av. TW14: Felt 7H 111
Cassiobury Rd. E17 . . . . .5A 50
Cassland Rd. CR7: Thor H 4D 156
E9 . . . . .7K 67
Casslee Rd. SE6 . . . . .7B 122
Cassocks Sq. TW17: Shep 7F 147
Casson Apartments E14 . . . . .6C 86
(off Upper Nth. St.)
Casson Ho. E1 . . . . .5K 9
(off Hanbury St.)
Casson St. E1 . . . . .5G 85
Castalia Sq. E14 . . . . .2E 104
Castellain Mans. W9 . . . . .4K 81
(off Castellain Rd., not continuous)
Castellain Rd. W9 . . . . .4K 81
Castellane Cl. HA7: Stan 7E 26
Castello Av. SW15 . . . . .5E 116
Castell Ho. SE8 . . . . .7C 104
CASTELNAU 6D 98
Castelnau SW13 . . . . .1C 116
Castelnau Gdns. SW13 . . . . .6D 98
Castelnau Mans. SW13 . . . . .6D 98
(off Castelnau, not continuous)
Castelnau Row SW13 . . . . .6D 98
Casterbridge NW6 . . . . .1K 81
(off Abbey Rd.)
W11 . . . . .6H 81
(off Dartmouth Cl.)
Casterbridge Rd. SE3 . . . . .3J 123
Casterton St. E8 . . . . .6H 67
Castile Rd. SE18 . . . . .4E 106
Castillon Rd. SE6 . . . . .2G 141
Castlands Rd. SE6 . . . . .2B 140
Castleacre W2 . . . . .1C 10
(off Hyde Pk. Cres.)
Castle Av. E4 . . . . .5A 36
KT17: Ewe 7D 164
UB7: Yiew 7A 74
Castlebar Ct. W5 . . . . .5C 78
Castlebar Hill W5 . . . . .5C 78
Castlebar M. W5 . . . . .5C 78
Castlebar Pk. W5 . . . . .5B 78
Castlebar Rd. W5 . . . . .5C 78
Castle Baynard St. EC4 . . . .2B 14 (7B 84)
Castlebrook Cl. SE11 . . . . .4B 102
Castle Bus. Cen. TW12: Hamp 1F 149
(off Castle M.)
Castle Climbing Centre, The 2C 66
Castle Cl. BR2: Brom 3G 159
E9 . . . . .5A 68
SW19 .3F 135
TW16: Sun 7G 129
W3 . . . . .2H 97
Castlecombe Dr. SW19 . . . . .7F 117
Castlecombe Rd. SE9 . . . . .4C 142
Castle Ct. EC3 . . . . .1F 15
(off Birchin La.)
SE26 . . . . .4A 140
SW15 .3G 117
(off Brewhouse La.)
Castleden Ho. NW3 . . . . .7B 64
(off Hilgrove Rd.)
Castledine Rd. SE20 . . . . .7H 139
Castle Dr. IG4: Ilf 6C 52
Castleford Av. SE9 . . . . .1F 143
Castleford Cl. N17 . . . . .6A 34
Castleford Ct. NW8 . . . . .3B 4
(off Henderson St.)
Castlegate TW9: Rich 3F 115
Castle Green Leisure Cen. 1D 90
Castlehaven Rd. NW1 . . . . .7F 65
Castle Hgts. RM9: Dag 1B 90
Castle Hill Av.
CRO: New Ad 7D 170
Castle Hill Local Nature Reserve 6G 163

Castle Hill Pde. W13 . . . . .7B 78
(off The Avenue)
Castle Ho. SM2: Sutt 6J 165
SW8 . . . . .7J 101
(off Sth. Lambeth Rd.)
Castle Ind. Est. SE17 . . . . .4C 102
Castle La. SW1 . . . . .1B 18 (3G 101)
Castleleigh Ct. EN2: Enf 5J 23
Castlemaine Av. CR2: S Croy 5F 169
KT17: Ewe 7D 164
Castlemain St. E1 . . . . .5H 85
Castle Mead SE5 . . . . .7C 102
Castle M. N12 . . . . .5F 31
NW1 . . . . .7F 65
SW17 .4C 136
TW12: Hamp 1F 149
(not continuous)
Castle Pde. KT17: Ewe 7C 164
Castle Pl. NW1 . . . . .6F 65
W4 . . . . .4A 98
Castle Point E13 . . . . .2A 88
(off Boundary Rd.)
Castlereagh Ho. HA7: Stan 6G 27
Castlereagh St. W1 . . . . . . .7E 4 (6D 82)
Castle Rd. EN3: Enf H 1F 25
N12 . . . . .5F 31
NW1 . . . . .6F 65
RM9: Dag 1B 90
TW7: Isle 2K 113
UB2: S'hall 3D 94
UB5: N'olt 6F 59
Castle Row W4 . . . . .5K 97
Castle St. E6 . . . . .2A 88
KT1: King T 2E 150
Castleton Av. DA7: Bex 1K 127
HA9: Wemb 4E 60
Castleton Cl. CRO: C'don 6A 158
Castleton Gdns. HA9: Wemb 3E 60
Castleton Ho. E14 . . . . .4E 104
(off Pier St.)
Castleton Rd. CR4: Mitc 4H 155
E17 . . . . .2F 51
HA4: Ruis 1B 58
IG3: Ilf .1A 72
SE9 . . . . .4B 142
Castletown Rd. W14 . . . . .5G 99
Castleview Cl. N4 . . . . .2C 66
Castleview Gdns. IG1: Ilf 6C 52
Castle Wlk. TW16: Sun 3A 148
Castle Way SW19 . . . . .3F 135
TW13: Hanw 4A 130
Castle Wharf E14 . . . . .7G 87
(off Orchard Pl.)
Castlewood Dr. SE9 . . . . .2D 124
Castlewood Rd. EN4: Cockf 3G 21
N15 . . . . .6G 49
N16 . . . . .6G 49
Castle Yd. N6 . . . . .7E 46
SE1 . . . . .4B 14 (1B 102)
TW10: Rich 5D 114
Castor La. E14 . . . . .7D 86
Catalina Ho. E1 . . . . .1K 15
Catalina Rd. TW6: H'row A 2D 110
Catalpa Ct. SE13 . . . . .6F 123
Caterham Av. IG5: Ilf 2D 52
Caterham High School Fitness Cen.
. . . . .2D 52
Caterham Rd. SE13 . . . . .3F 123
Catesby Ho. E9 . . . . .7J 67
(off Frampton Pk. Rd.)
Catesby St. SE17 . . . . .4D 102
Catford B'way. SE6 . . . . .7D 122
CATFORD 7D 122
CATFORD GYRATORY 7D 122
Catford Hill SE6 . . . . .1B 140
Catford Island SE6 . . . . .7D 122
Catford M. SE6 . . . . .7D 122
Catford Rd. SE6 . . . . .7C 122
Catford Trad. Est. SE6 . . . . .2D 140
Cathall Leisure Cen. 2G 69
Cathall Rd. E11 . . . . .2F 69

Cathay Ho. SE16 . . . . .2H **103**
Cathay St. SE16 . . . . .2H **103**
Cathay Wlk. UB5: N'olt 2E **76**
    (off Brabazon Rd.)
Cathcart Dr. BR6: Orp 2J **173**
Cathcart Hill N19 . . . . .3G **65**
Cathcart Ho. SW10 . . . . .5A **100**
    (off Cathcart Rd.)
Cathcart Rd. SW10 . . . . .6K **99**
Cathcart St. NW5 . . . . .6F **65**
Cathedral Lodge EC1 . . . . .5C **8**
    (off Aldersgate St.)
Cathedral Mans. SW1 . . . . .3A **18**
    (off Vauxhall Bri. Rd.)
Cathedral Piazza SW1 . . . .2A **18** (3G **101**)
Cathedral St. SE1 . . . . . .4E **14** (1D **102**)
Cathedral Wlk. SW1 . . . . .1A **18**
Catherall Rd. N5 . . . . .3C **66**
Catherine Cl. NW4 . . . . .4D **44**
Catherine Cl. IG2: Ilf 5G **53**
N14 . . . . .5B **22**
SW3 . . . . .7A **16**
    (off Callow St.)
SW19 . . . . .5H **135**
Catherine Dr. TW9: Rich 4E **114**
TW16: Sun 6H **129**
Catherine Gdns. TW3: Houn 4H **113**
Catherine Griffiths Ct. EC1 . . . . .3K **7**
    (off Northampton Rd.)
Catherine Gro. SE10 . . . . .1D **122**
Catherine Ho. E3 . . . . .2C **86**
    (off Thomas Fyre Dr.)
N1 . . . . .1E **84**
    (off Whitmore Est.)
Catherine Howard Ct. SE9 . . . . .6H **125**
Catherine of Aragon Ct. SE9 . . . . . . .6G **125**
Catherine Parr Ct. SE9 . . . . .6H **125**
Catherine Pl. HA1: Harr 5K **41**
SW1 . . . . .1A **18** (3G **101**)
Catherine Rd. KT6: Surb 5D **150**
Catherine St. WC2 . . . . .2G **13** (7K **83**)
Catherine Wheel All. E1 . . . .1H **9** (5E **84**)
Catherine Wheel Rd.
TW8: Bford 7D **96**
Catherine Wheel Yd. SW1 . . . . .5A **12**
Catherwood Ct. N1 . . . . .1E **8**
Cat Hill EN4: E Barn 6H **21**
Cathles Rd. SW12 . . . . .6F **119**
Cathnor Rd. W12 . . . . .2D **98**
Catlin Cres. TW17: Shep 5F **147**
Catling Cl. SE23 . . . . .3J **139**
Catlin's La. HA5: Eastc 3K **39**
Catlin St. SE16 . . . . .5G **103**
Cator La. BR3: Beck 1B **158**
Cato Rd. SW4 . . . . .3H **119**
Cator Park Sports Cen. 6A **140**
Cator Rd. SE26 . . . . .6K **139**
SM5: Cars 5D **166**
Cator St. SE15 . . . . .7F **103**
    (Commercial Way)
SE15 . . . . .6F **103**
    (Ebley Cl.)
Cato St. W1 . . . . .6D **4** (5C **82**)
Catsey La. WD23: Bush 1B **26**
Catsey Woods WD23: Bush 1B **26**
Catterick Cl. N11 . . . . .6K **31**
Cattistock Rd. SE9 . . . . .5C **142**
Cattley Cl. EN5: Barn 4B **20**
Catton St. WC1 . . . . .6G **7** (5K **83**)
Catwalk Pl. N15 . . . . .6D **48**
Caudwell Ter. SW18 . . . . .6B **118**
Caughley Ho. SE11 . . . . .2J **19**
Caulfield Ct. NW1 . . . . .7G **65**
    (off Baynes St.)
Caulfield Gdns. HA5: Pinn 2A **40**
Caulfield Rd. E6 . . . . .1C **88**
SE15 . . . . .2H **121**
W3 . . . . .3J **97**
Causeway, The KT9: Chess 4E **162**
KT10: Clay 7A **162**
N2 . . . . .4C **46**

Causeway, The SM2: Sutt 7A **166**
SM5: Cars 3E **166**
SW18 . . . . .5K **117**
SW19 . . . . .5E **134**
TW4: Houn 4J **111**
TW11: Tedd 6K **131**
TW14: Felt, Houn 4J **111**
Causeyware Rd. N9 . . . . .7D **24**
Causton Cotts. E14 . . . . .6A **86**
    (off Galsworthy Av.)
Causton Ho. SE5 . . . . .6C **102**
SW9 . . . . .1K **119**
Causton Rd. N6 . . . . .7F **47**
Causton Sq. RM10: Dag 7G **73**
Causton St. SW1 . . . . . .4D **18** (4H **101**)
Cautley Av. SW4 . . . . .5G **119**
Cavalier Cl. RM6: Chad H 4D **54**
Cavalier Ct. KT5: Surb 6F **151**
Cavalier Gdns. UB3: Hayes 6F **75**
Cavalry Cres. TW4: Houn 4B **112**
Cavalry Gdns. SW15 . . . . .5H **117**
Cavalry Memorial 1E **100**
Cavalry Sq. SW3 . . . . . . .5F **17** (5D **100**)
Cavan Pl. HA5: Hat E 1D **40**
Cavatina Point SE8 . . . . .6D **104**
    (off Copperas St.)
Cavaye Ho. SW10 . . . . .7A **16**
    (off Cavaye Pl.)
Cavaye Pl. SW10 . . . . . .6A **16** (5A **100**)
Cavell Dr. EN2: Enf 2F **23**
Cavell Ho. N1 . . . . .1E **84**
    (off Colville Est.)
Cavell Rd. N17 . . . . .7J **33**
Cavell St. E1 . . . . .5H **85**
Cavendish Av. DA8: Erith 6J **109**
DA15: Sidc 7A **126**
DA16: Well 3K **125**
HA1: Harr 4H **59**
HA4: Ruis 5K **57**
IG8: Wfd G 1K **51**
KT3: N Mald 5C **152**
N3 . . . . .2J **45**
NW8 . . . . .1B **4** (2B **82**)
W13 . . . . .5A **78**
Cavendish Cl. N18 . . . . .5C **34**
NW6 . . . . .6H **63**
NW8 . . . . .1B **4** (3B **82**)
TW16: Sun 6H **129**
UB4: Hayes 5G **75**
Cavendish Ct. EC3 . . . . .7H **9**
SE6 . . . . .1D **140**
    (off Bromley Rd.)
SM6: Wall 6F **167**
TW16: Sun 6H **129**
Cavendish Dr. E11 . . . . .1F **69**
HA8: Edg 6A **28**
Cavendish Gdns. IG1: Ilf 1E **70**
IG11: Bark 5J **71**
RM6: Chad H 5E **54**
SW4 . . . . .6G **119**
Cavendish Ho. CR0: C'don 1D **168**
    (off Tavistock Rd.)
NW8 . . . . .1B **4**
    (off Wellington Rd.)
NW9 . . . . .3B **44**
SW1 . . . . .2D **18**
    (off Monck St.)
UB7: W Dray 2B **92**
    (off Park Lodge Av.)
W1 . . . . .6A **6**
    (off Mortimer St.)
Cavendish Mans. EC1 . . . . .4J **7**
    (off Rosebery Av.)
NW6 . . . . .5J **63**
Cavendish M. Nth. W1 . . . . .5K **5** (5F **83**)
Cavendish M. Sth. W1 . . . . .6K **5** (5F **83**)
Cavendish Pde. SW4 . . . . .6F **119**
    (off Clapham Comn. Sth. Side)
TW4: Houn 2C **112**
Cavendish Pl. BR1: Brom 4D **160**
NW2 . . . . .6F **63**

Cavendish Pl. SW4 . . . . .5H **119**
W1 . . . . .7K **5** (6F **83**)
Cavendish Rd. CR0: C'don 1B **168**
E4 . . . . .6K **35**
EN5: Barn 3A **20**
KT3: N Mald 4B **152**
N4 . . . . .6B **48**
N18 . . . . .5C **34**
NW6 . . . . .7G **63**
SM2: Sutt 7A **166**
SW12 . . . . .6F **119**
SW19 . . . . .7B **136**
TW16: Sun 6H **129**
W4 . . . . .1J **115**
Cavendish Sq. W1 . . . . . . .7K **5** (6F **83**)
Cavendish St. N1 . . . . .2D **84**
Cavendish Ter. E3 . . . . .3B **86**
TW13: Felt 2J **129**
Cavendish Way BR4: W W'ck 1D **170**
Cavenham Gdns. IG1: Ilf 3H **71**
Caverleigh Pl. BR1: Brom 2A **160**
Caverleigh Way KT4: Wor Pk 1C **164**
Cave Rd. E13 . . . . .3K **87**
TW10: Ham 4C **132**
Caversham Av. N13 . . . . .3F **33**
SM3: Cheam 2G **165**
Caversham Ct. N11 . . . . .3K **31**
    (off Brunswick Pk. Rd.)
Caversham Ho. KT1: King T 2E **150**
    (off Lady Booth Rd.)
N15 . . . . .4C **48**
    (off Caversham Rd.)
SE15 . . . . .6G **103**
    (off Haymerle Rd.)
Caversham M. SW3 . . . . .7E **16**
Caversham Rd. KT1: King T 2F **151**
N15 . . . . .4C **48**
NW5 . . . . .6G **65**
Caversham St. SW3 . . . . .7E **16** (6D **100**)
Caverswall St. W12 . . . . .6E **80**
Caveside Cl. BR7: Chst 1E **160**
Cavesson Ho. E20 . . . . .5E **68**
    (off Ribbons Wlk.)
Cavour Ho. SE17 . . . . .5B **102**
    (off Alberta Est.)
Cawdor Cres. W7 . . . . .4A **96**
Cawnpore St. SE19 . . . . .5E **138**
Cawston Ct. BR1: Brom 7H **141**
Caxton Cl. SW11 . . . . .2C **118**
Caxton Gro. E3 . . . . .3C **86**
Caxton Hall SW1 . . . . .3H **101**
    (off Caxton St.)
Caxton M. TW8: Bford 6D **96**
Caxton Pl. IG1: Ilf 3E **70**
Caxton Rd. N22 . . . . .2K **47**
SW19 . . . . .5A **136**
UB2: S'hall 3B **94**
W12 . . . . .2F **99**
Caxtons, The SW9 . . . . .7B **102**
    (off Langton Rd.)
Caxton St. SW1 . . . . . . .1C **18** (3G **101**)
Caxton St. Nth. E16 . . . . .6H **87**
Caxton Trad. Est. UB3: Hayes 2G **93**
Caxton Wlk. WC2 . . . . . .1D **12** (6H **83**)
Cayenne Ct. SE1 . . . . . .5K **15** (2F **103**)
Caygill Cl. BR2: Brom 4H **159**
Cayley Rd. UB2: S'hall 3F **95**
Cayton Pl. EC1 . . . . .2E **8**
Cayton Rd. UB6: G'frd 2J **77**
Cayton St. EC1 . . . . .2E **8** (3D **84**)
Cazenove Rd. E17 . . . . .1C **50**
N16 . . . . .2F **67**
Cearns Ho. E6 . . . . .1B **88**
Cecil Av. EN1: Enf 4A **24**
HA9: Wemb 5F **61**
IG11: Bark 7H **71**
Cecil Cl. KT9: Chess 4D **162**
TW15: Ashf 7E **128**
W5 . . . . .5D **78**
Cecil Ct. CR0: C'don 2F **169**
EN2: Enf .4J **23**

Cecil Ct. EN5: Barn 3A **20**
NW6 . . . . .7K **63**
SW10 . . . . .6A **100**
    (off Fawcett St.)
WC2 . . . . .3E **12** (7J **83**)
Cecile Pk. N8 . . . . .6J **47**
Cecil Gro. NW8 . . . . .1C **82**
Cecil Hepworth Playhouse, The 7H **147**
    (off Hepworth Way)
Cecil Ho. E17 . . . . .1C **50**
Cecilia Cl. N2 . . . . .3A **46**
Cecilia Rd. E8 . . . . .5F **67**
Cecil Manning Cl. UB6: G'frd 1A **78**
Cecil Mans. SW17 . . . . .2E **136**
Cecil Pk. HA5: Pinn 4C **40**
Cecil Pl. CR4: Mitc 5D **154**
Cecil Rhodes Ho. NW1 . . . . .2H **83**
    (off Goldington St.)
Cecil Rd. CR0: C'don 6J **155**
E11 . . . . .3H **69**
E13 . . . . .1J **87**
E17 . . . . .1C **50**
EN2: Enf .3H **23**
HA3: W'stone 3J **41**
IG1: Ilf 4F **71**
N10 . . . . .2F **47**
N14 . . . . .1B **32**
NW9 . . . . .3A **44**
NW10 . . . . .1A **80**
RM6: Chad H 7D **54**
SM1: Sutt 6H **165**
SW19 . . . . .7K **135**
TW3: Houn 2G **113**
TW15: Ashf 7E **128**
W3 . . . . .5J **79**
Cecil Rosen Ct. HA0: Wemb 3B **60**
Cecil Sharp House 1E **82**
    (off Gloucester Av.)
Cecil Way BR2: Hayes 1J **171**
Cedar Av. DA15: Sidc 7A **126**
EN3: Enf H 2D **24**
EN4: E Barn 7H **21**
HA4: Ruis 5A **58**
RM6: Chad H 5E **54**
TW2: Whitt 6F **113**
UB3: Hayes 6J **75**
UB7: Yiew 7B **74**
Cedar Cl. BR2: Brom 3C **172**
E3 . . . . .1B **86**
IG1: Ilf 5H **71**
IG9: Buck H 2G **37**
KT8: E Mos 4J **149**
RM7: Rom 4J **55**
SE21 . . . . .1C **138**
SM5: Cars 6D **166**
SW15 . . . . .4K **133**
Cedar Copse BR1: Brom 2D **160**
Cedar Ct. E11 . . . . .5K **51**
E18 . . . . .1J **51**
N1 . . . . .7C **66**
N10 . . . . .2E **46**
N11 . . . . .5B **32**
N20 . . . . .1G **31**
SE1 . . . . .7G **15**
    (off Royal Oak Yd.)
SE7 . . . . .6A **106**
SE9 . . . . .6C **124**
SE13 . . . . .4F **123**
SM2: Sutt 6A **166**
SW19 . . . . .3F **135**
TW8: Bford 6C **96**
Cedar Cres. BR2: Brom 3C **172**
Cedarcroft Rd.
KT9: Chess 4F **163**
Cedar Dr. HA5: Hat E 6A **26**
N2 . . . . .4C **46**
Cedar Gdns. SM2: Sutt 6A **166**
Cedar Grange EN1: Enf 5K **23**
Cedar Gro. DA5: Bexl 6D **126**
UB1: S'hall 5E **76**
W5 . . . . .3E **96**

Cedar Hgts. NW2 . . . . .6H 63
TW10: Ham 1E 132
Cedar Ho. E2 . . . . .2H 85
(off Mowlem St.)
E14 . . . . .2E 104
(off Manchester St.)
N22 . . . . .1A 48
(off Acacia Rd.)
SE14 . . . . .1K 121
SE16 . . . . .2K 103
(off Woodland Cres.)
SW6 . . . . .2A 118
(off Lensbury Av.)
TW9: Kew 1H 115
TW16: Sun 7H 129
(off Spelthorne Gro.)
UB4: Yead 4A 76
W8 .3K 99
(off Marloes Rd.)
Cedarhurst BR1: Brom 7G 141
Cedarhurst Cotts. DA5: Bexl 7G 127
Cedarhurst Dr. SE9 . . . . .5A 124
Cedarland Ter. SW20 . . . . .7D 134
Cedar Lawn Av. EN5: Barn 5B 20
Cedar M. SE4 . . . . .3B 122
SW15 . . . . .5F 117
Cedar Mt. SE9 . . . . .1B 142
Cedarne Rd. SW6 . . . . .7K 99
Cedar Pk. IG7: Chig 4K 37
Cedar Pk. Gdns.
RM6: Chad H 7D 54
SW19 . . . . .5D 134
Cedar Pk. Rd. EN2: Enf 1H 23
Cedar Pl. SE7 . . . . .5A 106
Cedar Ri. N14 . . . . .7K 21
Cedar Rd. BR1: Brom 2A 160
CR0: C'don 2D 168
EN2: Enf 1G 23
KT8: E Mos 4J 149
N17 . . . . .1F 49
NW2 . . . . .4E 62
RM7: Rom 4J 55
SM2: Sutt 6A 166
TW4: Cran 2A 112
TW11: Tedd 5A 132
TW14: Bedf 1F 129
Cedars, The E9 . . . . .7K 67
(off Banbury Rd.)
E15 . . . . .7H 69
IG9: Buck H 1D 36
SM6: Wall 4G 167
TW11: Tedd 6K 131
W13 . . . . .6C 78
Cedars Av. CR4: Mitc 4E 154
E17 . . . . .5C 50
Cedars Cl. NW4 . . . . .3F 45
SE13 . . . . .3F 123
Cedars Ct. N9 . . . . .2K 33
Cedars Dr. UB10: Hil 2B 74
Cedars Ho. E17 . . . . .3D 50
Cedars M. SW4 . . . . .4F 119
(not continuous)
Cedars Rd. BR3: Beck 2A 158
CR0: Bedd 3J 167
E15 . . . . .6G 69
KT1: Hamp W 1C 150
N9 .2B 34
N21 . . . . .2G 33
SM4: Mord 4J 153
SW4 . . . . .3F 119
SW13 . . . . .2C 116
W4 .5J 97
Cedar Ter. TW9: Rich 4E 114
Cedar Tree Gro. SE27 . . . . .5B 138
Cedar Vw. KT1: King T 3D 150
(off Milner Rd.)
Cedarville Gdns. SW16 . . . . .6K 137
Cedar Way N1 . . . . .7H 65
TW16: Sun 7G 129
Cedar Way Ind. Est. N1 . . . . .7H 65
Cedra Ct. N16 . . . . .1G 67

Cedric Chambers NW8 . . . . .3A 4
(off Northwick Cl.)
Cedric Rd. SE9 . . . . .3G 143
Celadon Cl. EN3: Enf H 3F 25
Celandine Cl. E14 . . . . .5C 86
Celandine Ct. E4 . . . . .3J 35
Celandine Dr. E8 . . . . .7F 67
SE28 . . . . .1B 108
Celandine Gro. N14 . . . . .5B 22
Celandine Way E15 . . . . .3G 87
Celbridge M. W2 . . . . .5K 81
Celebration Av. E20 . . . . .5E 68
Celebration Way E4 . . . . .6K 35
Celestial Gdns. SE13 . . . . .4F 123
Celia Cres. TW15: Ashf 6A 128
Celia Ho. N1 . . . . .2E 84
(off Arden Est.)
Celia Rd. N19 . . . . .4G 65
Celtic Av. BR2: Brom 3G 159
Celtic St. E14 . . . . .5D 86
Cemetery La. SE7 . . . . .6C 106
TW17: Shep 7D 146
Cemetery Rd. E7 . . . . .5H 69
N17 . . . . .7K 33
SE2 . . . . .7B 108
Cemetery Way E4 . . . . .3H 35
Cenacle Cl. NW3 . . . . .3J 63
Cenotaph 6E 12 (2J 101)
Centaur Ct. TW8: Bford 5E 96
Centaurs Bus. Pk. TW7: Isle 6A 96
Centaur St. SE1 . . . . . .1H 19 (3K 101)
Centenary Rd. EN3: Brim 4G 25
Centenary Trad. Est. EN3: Brim 3G 25
Central Av. W3 . . . . .1K 97
Central Comn. Rd. BR7: Chst 6G 143
Central Ct. Shop. Cen. SW19 . . . . . .6H 135
Central Apartments HA9: Wemb 5E 60
Central Arc. TW15: Ashf 4B 128
(off Woodthorpe Rd.)
Central Av. DA16: Well 2K 125
E11 . . . . .2F 69
EN1: Enf 2C 24
HA5: Pinn 6D 40
KT8: W Mole 4D 148
N2 .2B 46
N9 .3K 33
SM6: Wall 5J 167
SW11 . . . . .7D 100
TW3: Houn 4G 113
UB3: Hayes 1H 93
Central Bus. Cen. NW10 . . . . .5A 62
Central Cir. NW4 . . . . .5D 44
Central Courtyard EC2 . . . . .7H 9
(off Cutlers Gdns.)
Central Criminal Court
Old Bailey 7B 8 (6B 84)
Centrale Shop. Cen.
CR0: C'don 2C 168
Central Gallery IG1: IIf 2F 71
(within The Exchange)
Central Ho. E15 . . . . .2D 86
IG11: Bark 7G 71
Central London Golf Course 2B 136
Central Mall SW18 . . . . .6K 117
(within Southside Shop. Cen.)
Central Mans. NW4 . . . . .5D 44
(off Watford Way)
Central Markets (Smithfield) 6A 8
Central Pde. DA15: Sidc 3A 144
E17 . . . . .4C 50
EN3: Enf H 2D 24
HA1: Harr 5K 41
IG2: IIf 6H 53
KT6: Surb 6E 150
KT8: W Mole 4D 148
SE20 . . . . .7H 139
(off High St.)
TW5: Hest 7D 94
TW14: Felt 7A 112

Central Pde. UB6: G'frd 3A 78
W3 .2H 97
Central Pk. NW10 . . . . .3J 79
Central Pk. Av. RM10: Dag 3H 73
Central Pk. Est. TW4: Houn 5B 112
Central Pk. Rd. E6 . . . . .2B 88
Central Pl. SE25 . . . . .5G 157
Central Rd.
HA0: Wemb 5B 60
KT4: Wor Pk 1C 164
SM4: Mord 6J 153
Central St Giles Piazza WC2 . . . . . . .7E 6
Central St Martins College of Art & Design
Byam Shaw Campus 2H 65
Central School Path SW14 . . . . .3J 115
Central Sq. HA9: Wemb 5E 60
(off High Rd.)
KT8: W Mole 5D 148
NW11 . . . . .6K 45
Central St. EC1 . . . . .1C 8 (3C 84)
Central Ter. BR3: Beck 3K 157
Central Walkway N19 . . . . .4H 65
(off Pleshey Rd.)
Central Way NW10 . . . . .3J 79
SE28 . . . . .1A 108
SM5: Cars 7C 166
TW14: Felt 5J 111
Central West SE8: G'frd 4G 77
Central Wharf E14 . . . . .6C 86
(off Thomas Rd.)
Centre, The KT12: Walt T 7J 147
TW3: Houn 3F 113
TW13: Felt 1K 129
Centre Av. W3 . . . . .1K 97
Centre Comn. Rd. BR7: Chst 6G 143
Centre Ct. Shop. Cen. SW19 . . . . . .6H 135
Centre for the Magic Arts, The 3B 6
(off Stephenson Way)
Centre for Wildlife Gardening Vis. Cen.
. . . . .3F 121
Centre Hgts. NW3 . . . . .7B 64
(off Finchley Rd.)
Centre of Cell 5H 85
(off Newark St.)
Centre Point SE1 . . . . .5G 103
Centrepoint WC2 . . . . .7D 6
Centre Point Ho. WC2 . . . . .7D 6
(off St Giles High St.)
Centre Rd. E7 . . . . .2J 69
E11 . . . . .2J 69
RM10: Dag 2H 91
Centre Sq. SW18 . . . . .5J 117
(off Buckhold Rd.)
Centre St. E2 . . . . .2H 85
Centre Vw. Apartments CR0: C'don . .3C 168
(off Whitgift St.)
Centre Way E17 . . . . .7K 35
N9 .2D 34
Centreway IG1: IIf 2G 71
(off High Rd.)
Centreway Apartments IG1: IIf 2G 71
(off Axon Pl.)
Centric Cl. NW1 . . . . .1E 82
Centrillion Point CR0: C'don 4C 168
(off Mason's Av.)
Centro Ct. E6 . . . . .4D 88
Centurion Bldg. SW8 . . . . . .7J 17 (6F 101)
Centurion Cl. N7 . . . . .7K 65
Centurion Ct. SE18 . . . . .4E 106
SM6: Wall 2F 167
Centurion Ho. UB3: Hayes 6F 75
Centurion La. E3 . . . . .1B 86
Centurion Sq. SE18 . . . . .1C 124
Centurion Way DA18: Erith 3F 109
Centurion Cl. NW4 . . . . .5F 45
Century Ct. NW8 . . . . .2B 4
Century Ho. HA9: Wemb 2F 61
SW15 . . . . .4F 117
Century M. E5 . . . . .4J 67
N5 .3B 66
(off Conewood St.)

Century Plaza HA8: Edg 6B 28
(off Station Rd.)
Century Rd. E17 . . . . .3A 50
Century Way BR3: Beck 6B 140
Century Yd. SE23 . . . . .2J 139
(not continuous)
Cephas Av. E1 . . . . .4J 85
Cephas St. E1 . . . . .4J 85
(off Doveton St.)
Ceres Rd. SE18 . . . . .4K 107
Cerise Apartments E3 . . . . .1A 86
(off Gunmaker's La.)
Cerise Rd. SE15 . . . . .1G 121
Cerne Cl. UB4: Yead 7A 76
Cerne Rd. SM4: Mord 6A 154
Cerney M. W2 . . . . .2A 10 (7B 82)
Cervantes Ct. W2 . . . . .6K 81
W11 . . . . .6G 81
(off Rushton M.)
Cester St. E2 . . . . .1G 85
Ceylon Rd. W14 . . . . .3F 99
Ceylon Wharf Apartments SE16 . . . . .2J 103
(off St Marychurch St.)
CFGS Community Performing Arts &
Sports Cen. 3B 86
Chabot Dr. SE15 . . . . .3H 121
Chadacre Av. IG5: IIf 3D 52
Chadacre Ct. E15 . . . . .1J 87
(off Vicars Cl.)
Chadacre Ho. SW9 . . . . .4B 120
(off Loughborough Pk.)
Chadacre Rd. KT17: Ewe 6D 164
Chadbourn St. E14 . . . . .5D 86
Chadbury Ct. NW7 . . . . .1C 44
Chad Cres. N9 . . . . .3D 34
Chadd Dr. BR1: Brom 3C 160
Chadd Grn. E13 . . . . .1J 87
(not continuous)
Chadston Ho. N1 . . . . .7B 66
(off Halton Rd.)
Chadswell WC1 . . . . .2F 7
(off Cromer St.)
Chadview Ct. RM6: Chad H 7D 54
Chadville Gdns. RM6: Chad H 5D 54
Chadway RM8: Dag 1C 72
Chadwell Av. RM6: Chad H 7B 54
CHADWELL HEATH 7D 54
Chadwell Heath Ind. Pk. RM8: Dag . . .1D 72
Chadwell Heath La. RM6: Chad H . . .4B 54
Chadwell Ho. SE17 . . . . .5D 102
(off Inville Rd.)
Chadwell La. N8 . . . . .3K 47
Chadwell St. EC1 . . . . .1K 7 (3A 84)
Chadwick Av. E4 . . . . .4A 36
N21 . . . . .5E 22
SW19 . . . . .6J 135
Chadwick Cl. SW15 . . . . .7B 116
TW11: Tedd 6A 132
W7 .5K 77
Chadwick Ct. E14 . . . . .6C 86
(off Jonzen Wlk.)
Chadwick Gdns. UB8: Uxb 7A 56
Chadwick M. W4 . . . . .6H 97
Chadwick Pl. KT6: Surb 7C 150
Chadwick Rd. E11 . . . . .6G 51
IG1: IIf 3F 71
NW10 . . . . .1B 80
SE15 . . . . .2F 121
Chadwick St. SW1 . . . . . . .2C 18 (3H 101)
Chadwick Way SE28 . . . . .7D 90
Chadwin Rd. E13 . . . . .5K 87
Chadworth Ho. EC1 . . . . .2C 8
(off Lever St.)
N4 .1C 66
Chaffinch Av. CR0: C'don 6K 157
Chaffinch Bus. Pk. BR3: Beck 4K 157
Chaffinch Cl. CR0: C'don 5K 157
KT6: Surb 3G 163
N9 .1E 34
Chaffinch Rd. BR3: Beck 1A 158

Chafford Way. RM6: Chad H 4C 54
Chagford Ho. E3 . . . . .3D 86
                                    (off Talwin St.)
Chagford St. NW1 . . . . .4E 4 (4D 82)
Chailey Av. EN1: Enf 2A 24
Chailey Cl. TW5: Hest 1B 112
Chailey Ind. Est. UB3: Hayes 2J 93
Chailey St. E5 . . . . .3J 67
Chalbury Wlk. N1 . . . . .2K 83
Chalcombe Rd. SE2 . . . . .3B 108
Chalcot Cl. SM2: Sutt 7J 165
Chalcot Cres. NW1 . . . . .1D 82
Chalcot Gdns. NW3 . . . . .6D 64
Chalcot M. SW16 . . . . .3J 137
Chalcot Rd. NW1 . . . . .7E 64
Chalcot Sq. NW1 . . . . .7E 64
                                    (not continuous)
Chalcott Gdns. KT6: Surb 1C 162
Chalcroft Rd. SE13 . . . . .5G 123
Chaldon Ct. SE19 . . . . .2D 156
Chaldon Path CR7: Thor H 4B 156
Chaldon Rd. SW6 . . . . .7G 99
Chale Rd. SW2 . . . . .6J 119
Chalet Cl. DA5: Bexl 4K 145
    TW15: Ashf 6F 129
Chalet Ct. CR7: Thor H 5C 156
Chalet Est. NW7 . . . . .4H 29
Chalfont Av. HA9: Wemb 6H 61
Chalfont Ct. HA1: Harr 6K 41
                                (off Northwick Pk. Rd.)
    NW1 . . . . .4F 5
                                    (off Baker St.)
    NW9 . . . . .3B 44
Chalfont Grn. N9 . . . . .3K 33
Chalfont Ho. SE16 . . . . .3H 103
                                    (off Keetons Rd.)
Chalfont M. SW19 . . . . .1H 135
    UB10: Hil 7D 56
Chalfont Rd. N9 . . . . .3K 33
    SE25 . . . . .3F 157
    UB3: Hayes 2J 93
Chalfont Wlk. HA5: Pinn 2A 40
Chalfont Way. W13 . . . . .3B 96
Chalford NW6 . . . . .6A 64
                                    (off Finchley Rd.)
Chalford Cl. KT8: W Mole 4E 148
Chalford Rd. SE21 . . . . .4D 138
Chalford Wlk. IG8: Wfd G 1B 52
Chalgrove Av. SM4: Mord 5J 153
Chalgrove Cres. IG5: Ilf 2C 52
Chalgrove Gdns. N3 . . . . .3G 45
Chalgrove Rd. N17 . . . . .1H 49
    SM2: Sutt 7B 166
Chalice Cl. SM6: Wall 6H 167
Chalice Cl. N2 . . . . .4C 46
    SE19 . . . . .6D 138
Chalkenden Cl. SE20 . . . . .7H 139
CHALKER'S CORNER 3H 115
CHALK FARM 7E 64
Chalk Farm Pde. NW3 . . . . .7E 64
                                    (off Adelaide Rd.)
Chalk Farm Rd. NW1 . . . . .7E 64
Chalk Hill Rd. W6 . . . . .4F 99
Chalkhill Rd. HA9: Wemb 3H 61
Chalklands HA9: Wemb 3J 61
Chalk La. EN4: Cockf 3J 21
Chalkley Cl. CR4: Mitc 2D 154
Chalkmill Dr. EN1: Enf 3C 24
Chalk Pit Way SM1: Sutt 5A 166
Chalk Rd. E13 . . . . .5K 87
Chalkstone Cl. DA16: Well 1A 126
Chalkwell Ho. E1 . . . . .6K 85
                                    (off Pitsea St.)
Chalkwell Pk. Av. EN1: Enf 4K 23
Challenge Cl. NW10 . . . . .1A 80
Challenge Cl. TW2: Twick 7J 113
Challenger Ho. E14 . . . . .7A 86
                                    (off Victory Pl.)
Challenge Rd. TW15: Ashf 3F 129
Challice Way SW2 . . . . .1K 137
Challin St. SE20 . . . . .1J 157

Challis Rd. TW8: Bford 5D 96
Challoner Cl. N2 . . . . .2B 46
Challoner Ct. BR2: Brom 2F 159
    W14 . . . . .5H 99
                                    (off Challoner St.)
Challoner Cres. W14 . . . . .5H 99
Challoner Mans. W14 . . . . .5H 99
                                    (off Challoner St.)
Challoners Cl. KT8: E Mos 4H 149
Challoner St. W14 . . . . .5H 99
Chalmers Ho. E17 . . . . .5D 50
Chalmers Rd. TW15: Ashf 5D 128
Chalmers Rd. E. TW15: Ashf 4D 128
Chalmers Wlk. SE17 . . . . .6B 102
                                    (off Hillingdon St.)
Chalmers Way TW1: Isle 4B 114
    TW14: Felt 5K 111
Chaloner Ct. SE1 . . . . .6E 14
Chalsey Rd. SE4 . . . . .4B 122
Chalton Dr. N2 . . . . .6B 46
Chalton Ho. NW1 . . . . .1C 6
                                    (off Chalton St.)
Chalton St. NW1 . . . . .1C 6 (2G 83)
                                    (not continuous)
Chamberlain Cl. IG1: Ilf 3G 71
    SE28 . . . . .3H 107
    UB3: Hayes 7H 75
Chamberlain Cotts. SE5 . . . . .1D 120
Chamberlain Ct. SE16 . . . . .4J 103
                                    (off Silwood St.)
Chamberlain Cres. BR4: W W'ck 1D 170
Chamberlain Gdns. TW3: Houn 1G 113
Chamberlain Ho. E1 . . . . .7J 85
                                    (off Cable St.)
    EC2 . . . . .3G 9
                                    (off Blackall St.)
    NW1 . . . . .1D 6
    SE1 . . . . .7J 13
                                (off Westminster Bri. Rd.)
Chamberlain La. HA5: Eastc 3J 39
Chamberlain Pl. E17 . . . . .3A 50
Chamberlain Rd. N2 . . . . .2A 46
    W13 . . . . .2A 96
Chamberlain St. NW1 . . . . .7D 64
Chamberlain Wlk. TW13: Hanw 4C 130
Chamberlain Way HA5: Eastc 3K 39
    KT6: Surb 7E 150
Chamberlayne Av. HA9: Wemb 3E 60
Chamberlayne Mans. NW10 . . . . .3F 81
                                (off Chamberlayne Rd.)
Chamberlayne Rd. NW10 . . . . .1E 80
Chamberlens Garages W6 . . . . .4D 98
                                    (off Dalling Rd.)
Chambers, The SW10 . . . . .1A 118
                                (off Chelsea Harbour Dr.)
Chambers Av. DA14: Sidc 6E 144
Chambers Bus. Pk. UB7: Sip 6C 92
Chambers Gdns. N2 . . . . .1B 46
Chambers La. NW10 . . . . .7D 62
Chambers Pl. CR2: S Croy 7D 168
Chambers St. SE16 . . . . .2G 103
Chamber St. E1 . . . . .2K 15 (7F 85)
Chambers Wlk. HA7: Stan 5G 27
Chambers Wharf SE16 . . . . .2G 103
Chambon Pl. W6 . . . . .4C 98
Chambord Ho. E2 . . . . .2K 9
                                    (off Chambord St.)
Chambord St. E2 . . . . .2K 9 (3F 85)
Chamomile Ct. E17 . . . . .6C 50
                                    (off Yunus Khan Cl.)
Champa Cl. N17 . . . . .2F 49
Champion Cres. SE26 . . . . .4A 140
Champion Gro. SE5 . . . . .3D 120
Champion Hill SE5 . . . . .3D 120
Champion Hill Est. SE5 . . . . .3E 120
Champion Hill Stadium 4E 120
Champion Ho. SE7 . . . . .6A 106
                                    (off Charlton Rd.)
Champion Pk. SE5 . . . . .2D 120
Champion Rd. SE26 . . . . .4A 140

Champions Wlk. E20 . . . . .5E 68
Champions Way NW4 . . . . .1D 44
    NW7 . . . . .1D 44
Champlain Ho. W12 . . . . .7D 80
                                    (off White City Est.)
Champness Cl. SE27 . . . . .4D 138
Champness Rd. IG11: Bark 6K 71
Champneys Cl. SM2: Cheam 7H 165
Chancel Ct. W1 . . . . .7H 83
                                    (off Old Compton St.)
Chancel Ind. Est. NW10 . . . . .5B 62
Chancellor Gdns. CR2: S Croy 7B 168
Chancellor Gro. SE21 . . . . .2C 138
Chancellor Ho. E1 . . . . .1H 103
                                    (off Green Bank)
    SW7 . . . . .3A 100
                                    (off Hyde Pk. Ga.)
Chancellor Pas. E14 . . . . .1C 104
Chancellor Pl. NW9 . . . . .2B 44
Chancellors Ct. WC1 . . . . .5G 7
Chancellor's Rd. W6 . . . . .5E 98
Chancellor's St. W6 . . . . .5E 98
Chancellors Wharf W6 . . . . .5E 98
Chancelot Rd. SE2 . . . . .4B 108
Chancel St. SE1 . . . . .5A 14 (1B 101)
Chancery Bldg. SW8 . . . . .7D 18 (6H 101)
Chancery Bldgs. E1 . . . . .7H 85
                                    (off Lowood St.)
Chancerygate UB7: Yiew 1C 92
Chancerygate Bus. Cen. HA4: Ruis . . .4C 58
Chancery Gate Bus. Pk.
    KT6: Surb 2F 163
Chancery La. BR3: Beck 2D 158
    WC2 . . . . .6H 7 (6A 84)
Chancery M. SW17 . . . . .2C 136
Chance St. E1 . . . . .3J 9 (4F 85)
    E2 . . . . .3J 9 (4F 85)
Chanctonbury Cl. SE9 . . . . .3F 143
Chanctonbury Gdns. SM2: Sutt 7K 165
Chanctonbury Way N12 . . . . .4C 30
Chandaria Ct. CR0: C'don 3C 168
                                    (off Church Rd.)
Chandler Av. E16 . . . . .5J 87
Chandler Cl. TW12: Hamp 1E 148
Chandler Ct. TW14: Felt 6J 111
Chandler Ho. NW6 . . . . .1H 81
                                    (off Willesden La.)
    WC1 . . . . .4F 7
                                    (off Colonnade)
Chandlers Av. SE10 . . . . .3H 105
Chandlers Cl. KT8: W Mole 5F 149
    TW14: Felt 7H 111
Chandlers Dr. SE12 . . . . .1K 141
Chandlers Dr. DA8: Erith 4K 109
Chandlers M. E14 . . . . .2C 104
Chandler St. E1 . . . . .1H 103
Chandlers Way SW2 . . . . .7A 120
Chandler Way SE15 . . . . .6E 102
Chandlery, The SE1 . . . . .1K 19
                                    (off Gerridge St.)
Chandlery Ho. E1 . . . . .6G 85
                                    (off Gowers Wlk.)
Chandon Lodge SM2: Sutt 7A 166
Chandos Av. E17 . . . . .2C 50
    N14 . . . . .3B 32
    N20 . . . . .1F 31
    W5 . . . . .4C 96
Chandos Cl. IG9: Buck H 2E 36
Chandos Ct. HA7: Stan 6G 27
    HA8: Edg 7A 28
    N14 . . . . .2C 32
Chandos Cres. HA8: Edg 7A 28
Chandos Pde. HA8: Edg 7A 28
Chandos Pl. WC2 . . . . .3E 12 (7J 83)
Chandos Rd. E15 . . . . .5F 69
    HA1: Harr 5G 41
    HA5: Eastc 7B 40
    N2 . . . . .2A 46
    N17 . . . . .2E 48
    NW2 . . . . .5E 62
    NW10 . . . . .4A 80

Chandos St. W1 . . . . .6K 5 (5F 83)
Chandos Way NW11 . . . . .1K 63
Change All. EC3 . . . . .1F 15 (6D 84)
Chanin M. NW2 . . . . .5E 62
Channel 4 TV 2C 18
Channel Cl. TW5: Hest 1E 112
Channel Ga. Rd. NW10 . . . . .3A 80
Channel Ho. E14 . . . . .5A 86
                                    (off Aston St.)
    SE16 . . . . .2K 103
                                    (off Water Gdns. Sq.)
Channel Islands Est. N1 . . . . .6C 66
Channelsea Bus. Cen. E15 . . . . .2F 87
Channelsea Path E15 . . . . .1F 87
Channelsea Rd. E15 . . . . .1F 87
Channon Ct. KT6: Surb 6D 150
                                    (off Maple Rd)
Chantress Cl. RM10: Dag 1J 91
Chantrey Ho. SW1 . . . . .3K 17
Chantrey Rd. SW9 . . . . .3K 119
Chantry, The E4 . . . . .1K 35
    UB8: Hil 3B 74
Chantry Cl. DA14: Sidc 5E 144
    EN2: Enf .1H 23
    HA3: Kenton 5F 43
    SE2 . . . . .3C 108
    TW16: Sun 7J 129
    UB7: Yiew 7A 74
    W9 . . . . .4J 81
Chantry Ct. SM5: Cars 3C 166
Chantry Cres. NW10 . . . . .6B 62
Chantry Ho. KT1: King T 4E 150
Chantry La. BR2: Brom 5B 160
Chantry Pl. HA3: Hrw W 1F 41
Chantry Rd. HA3: Hrw W 1F 41
    KT9: Chess 5F 163
Chantry Sq. W8 . . . . .3K 99
Chantry St. N1 . . . . .1B 84
Chantry Way CR4: Mitc 3B 154
Chant Sq. E15 . . . . .7F 69
Chant St. E15 . . . . .7F 69
                                    (not continuous)
Chapel, The SW15 . . . . .6G 117
Chapel Cl. DA1: Cray 5K 127
    NW10 . . . . .5B 62
Chapel Ct. E10 . . . . .2D 68
                                    (off Rosedene Ter.)
    N2 . . . . .3C 46
    RM7: Rush G 6K 55
    SE1 . . . . .6E 14 (2D 102)
    SE18 . . . . .6A 108
    UB3: Hayes 7H 75
CHAPEL END 1D 50
Chapel Farm Rd. SE9 . . . . .3D 142
Chapel Ga. M. SW4 . . . . .3J 119
                                    (off Bedford Rd.)
Chapel Ga. Pl. BR7: Chst 6F 143
Chapel Hill DA1: Cray 5K 127
Chapel Ho. St. E14 . . . . .5D 104
Chapelier Ho. SW18 . . . . .4J 117
Chapel La. HA5: Pinn 3B 40
    RM6: Chad H 7D 54
    UB8: Hil 6C 74
Chapel Mkt. N1 . . . . .2A 84
Chapel M. IG8: Wfd G 6K 37
Chapel Mill Rd. KT1: King T 3F 151
Chapelmount Rd. IG8: Wfd G 6J 37
Chapel of St John the Evangelist 3J 15
                                (within The Tower of London)
Chapel of St Peter & St Paul 6F 105
                                (in University of Greenwich)
Chapel Path E11 . . . . .6K 51
                                    (off Woodbine Pl.)
Chapel Pl. EC2 . . . . .2G 9 (3E 84)
    N1 . . . . .2A 84
    N17 . . . . .7A 34
    W1 . . . . .1J 11 (6F 83)
Chapel Rd. DA7: Bex 4G 127
    IG1: Ilf 3E 70
    SE27 . . . . .4B 138
    TW1: Twick 7B 114

Chapel Rd. TW3: Houn 3F 113
   W13 . . . . .1B 96
Chapel Side W2 . . . . .7K 81
Chapel Stones N17 . . . . .1F 49
Chapel St. EN2: Enf 3H 23
   NW1 . . . . .6C 4 (5C 82)
   SW1 . . . . .1H 17 (3E 100)
Chapel Vw. CR2: Sels 6J 169
Chapel Wlk. CR0: C'don 2C 168
   NW4 . . . . .4D 44
               (not continuous)
Chapel Way N7 . . . . .3K 65
Chapel Yd. SW18 . . . . .5K 117
       (off Wandsworth High St.)
Chaplin Cl. HA0: Wemb 6D 60
   SE1 . . . . .6K 13 (2A 102)
Chaplin Ct. E3 . . . . .4B 86
             (off Joseph St.)
   SE14 .1K 121
             (off Besson St.)
   SE17 . . . . .6B 102
             (off Royal Rd.)
Chaplin Cres. TW16: Sun 6G 129
Chaplin Ho. DA14: Sidc 4A 144
       (off Sidcup High St.)
   E17 . . . . .4C 50
             (off Hoe St.)
   N1 . . . . .1D 84
        (off Shepperton Rd.)
   W3 . . . . .3J 97
         (off All Saints Rd.)
Chaplin Rd. E15 . . . . .2H 87
   HA0: Wemb 6C 60
   N17 . . . . .3F 49
   NW2 . . . . .6E 62
   RM9: Dag 7E 72
Chaplin Sq. N12 . . . . .7G 31
Chapman Av. UB7: W Dray 3B 92
Chapman Cres. HA3: Kenton 6E 42
Chapman Grn. N22 . . . . .1A 48
Chapman Ho. E1 . . . . .6H 85
             (off Bigland St.)
Chapman Pl. N4 . . . . .2B 66
Chapman Rd. CR0: C'don 1A 168
   DA17: Belv 5G 109
   E9 . . . . .6B 68
Chapman's La. DA17: Belv 4D 108
   SE2 . . . . .4C 108
Chapmans Pk. Ind. Est. NW10 . . . . .6B 62
Chapman Sq. SW19 . . . . .2F 135
Chapman's Ter. N22 . . . . .1B 48
Chapman St. E1 . . . . .7H 85
Chapone Pl. W1 . . . . . . .1C 12 (6H 83)
Chapter Chambers SW1 . . . . .4C 18
             (off Chapter St.)
Chapter Cl. UB10: Hil 7B 56
   W4 . . . . .3J 97
Chapter House 1C 14
Chapter Ho. E2 . . . . .4G 85
           (off Dunbridge St.)
Chapter Rd. NW2 . . . . .5C 62
   SE17 . . . . .5B 102
Chapter St. SW1 . . . . . . .4C 18 (4H 101)
Chapter Way SW19 . . . . .1B 154
   TW12: Hamp 4E 130
Chara Pl. W4 . . . . .6K 97
Charcot Ho. SW15 . . . . .6B 116
Charcot Rd. NW9 . . . . .2K 43
Charcroft Ct. W14 . . . . .2F 99
           (off Minford Gdns.)
Charcroft Gdns. EN3: Pond E 4E 24
Chardin Ho. SW9 . . . . .1A 120
           (off Gosling Way)
Chardin Rd. W4 . . . . .4A 98
Chardmore Rd. N16 . . . . .1G 67
Chard Rd. TW6: H'row A 2D 110
Chardwell Cl. E6 . . . . .6D 88
Charecroft Way W12 . . . . .2F 99
   W14 . . . . .2F 99
Charfield Ct. W9 . . . . .4K 81
           (off Shirland Rd.)

Charford Rd. E16 . . . . .5J 87
Chargeable La. E13 . . . . .4H 87
Chargeable St. E16 . . . . .4H 87
Chargrove Cl. SE16 . . . . .2K 103
Charing Cl. BR6: Orp 4K 173
Charing Ct. BR2: Brom 2G 159
Charing Cross SW1 . . . . .4E 12
Charing Cross Rd. WC2 . . . . .7D 6 (6H 83)
Charing Cross Sports Club 6F 99
Charing Cross Theatre 4F 13
           (off Villiers St.)
Charing Cross Underground Shop. Cen.
   WC2 . . . . .3E 12
Charing Ho. SE1 . . . . .6K 13
          (off Windmill Wlk.)
Chariot Cl. E3 . . . . .1C 86
Charis Ho. E3 . . . . .3D 86
             (off Grace St.)
Charlbert Ct. NW8 . . . . .2C 82
          (off Charlbert St.)
Charlbert St. NW8 . . . . .2C 82
Charlbury Av. HA7: Stan 5J 27
Charlbury Gdns. IG3: IIf 2K 71
Charlbury Gro. W5 . . . . .6C 78
Charlbury Rd. UB10: Ick 3B 56
Charldane Rd. SE9 . . . . .3F 143
Charlecote Gro. SE26 . . . . .3H 139
Charlecote Rd. RM8: Dag 3E 72
Charlemont Rd. E6 . . . . .4D 88
Charles II Pl. SW3 . . . . . .6E 16 (5D 100)
Charles II St. SW1 . . . . . . .4C 12 (1H 101)
Charles Auffray Ho. E1 . . . . .5J 85
             (off Smithy St.)
Charles Babbage Cl. KT9: Chess . . .7C 162
Charles Baker Pl. SW17 . . . . .1C 136
Charles Barry Cl. SW4 . . . . .3G 119
Charles Bradlaugh Ho. N17 . . . . . . .7C 34
          (off Haynes Cl.)
Charles Burton Ct. E5 . . . . .5A 68
          (off Ashenden Rd.)
Charles Chu. Wlk. IG1: IIf 6D 52
Charles Cl. DA14: Sidc 4B 144
Charles Cobb Gdns. CR0: Wadd 5A 168
Charles Coveney Rd. SE15 . . . . .1F 121
Charles Cres. HA1: Harr 7H 41
            (not continuous)
Charles Curran Ho. UB10: Ick 3D 56
Charles Darwin Ho. E2 . . . . .3H 85
           (off Canrobert St.)
Charles Dickens Ho. E2 . . . . .3G 85
          (off Mansford St.)
Charles Dickens Museum, The 4G 7
Charlesfield SE9 . . . . .3A 142
Charles Flemwell M. E16 . . . . .1J 105
Charles Gardner Ct. N1 . . . . .1F 9
        (off Haberdasher St.)
Charles Grinling Wlk. SE18 . . . . .4E 106
Charles Gro. N14 . . . . .1B 32
Charles Haller St. SW2 . . . . .7A 120
Charles Harrod Ct. SW13 . . . . .6E 98
         (off Somerville Av.)
Charles Hocking Ho. W3 . . . . .2J 97
         (off Bollo Bri. Rd.)
Charles Ho. N17 . . . . .7A 34
           (off Love La.)
   UB2: S'hall 2E 94
   W14 . . . . .4H 99
          (off Gerrard Rd.)
Charles La. NW8 . . . . .2C 82
Charles Lesser Ho. KT9: Chess 5D 162
Charles Mackenzie Ho. SE16 . . . . . .4G 103
          (off Linsey St.)
Charlesmere Gdns. SE28 . . . . .2J 107
         (off Thames Reach)
Charles Nex M. SE21 . . . . .2C 138
Charles Pl. E4 . . . . .7K 25 & 1A 36
   NW1 . . . . .2B 6 (3G 83)
Charles Rd. E7 . . . . .7A 70
   RM6: Chad H 6D 54
   RM10: Dag 6K 73

Charles Rd. SW19 . . . . .1J 153
   TW18: Staines 6A 128
   W13 . . . . .6A 78
Charles Rowan Ho. WC1 . . . . .2J 7
         (off Margery St.)
Charles Sevright Way NW7 . . . . .5A 30
Charles Simmons Ho. WC1 . . . . .2J 7
         (off Margery St.)
Charles Sq. N1 . . . . .2F 9 (3D 84)
Charles Sq. Est. N1 . . . . .2F 9
Charles St. CR0: C'don 3C 168
   E16 . . . . .1A 106
   EN1: Enf 5A 24
   N19 . . . . .1J 65
   SW13 . . . . .2A 116
   TW3: Houn 2D 112
   UB10: Hil 4D 74
   W1 . . . . .4J 11 (1F 101)
Charleston Cl. TW13: Felt 3J 129
Charleston St. SE17 . . . . .4C 102
Charles Townsend Ho. EC1 . . . . .3A 8
         (off Skinner St.)
Charles Uton Ct. E8 . . . . .4G 67
Charles Whincup Rd. E16 . . . . .1K 105
Charlesworth Ho. E14 . . . . .6C 86
            (off Dod St.)
Charlesworth Pl. SW13 . . . . .3A 116
Charleville Cir. SE26 . . . . .5G 139
Charleville Ct. W14 . . . . .5H 99
         (off Charleville Rd.)
Charleville Mans. W14 . . . . .5G 99
      (off Charleville Rd., not continuous)
Charleville M. TW7: Isle 4B 114
Charleville Rd. W14 . . . . .5G 99
CHARLIE BROWN'S RDBT. 2A 52
Charlie Chaplin Wlk. SE1 . . .4H 13 (1K 101)
Charlieville Rd. DA8: Erith 7J 109
Charlmont Rd. SW17 . . . . .6C 136
Charlotte Cl. DA6: Bex 5E 126
   IG6: IIf .1G 53
Charlotte Ct. IG2: IIf 6E 52
   N8 . . . . .6H 47
   SE1 . . . . .4E 102
         (off Old Kent Rd.)
   W6 . . . . .4C 98
Charlotte Despard Av. SW11 . . . . . . .1E 118
Charlotte Ho. E16 . . . . .1K 105
          (off Fairfax M.)
   W6 . . . . .5E 98
       (off Queen Caroline St.)
Charlotte M. W1 . . . . .5B 6 (5G 83)
   W10 . . . . .6F 81
   W14 . . . . .4G 99
Charlotte Pk. Av. BR1: Brom 3C 160
Charlotte Pl. NW9 . . . . .5J 43
   SW1 . . . . .4A 18 (4G 101)
   W1 . . . . .6B 6 (5G 83)
Charlotte Rd. EC2 . . . . .2G 9 (3E 84)
   RM10: Dag 6H 73
   SM6: Wall 6G 167
   SW13 . . . . .1B 116
Charlotte Row SW4 . . . . .3G 119
Charlotte Sq. TW10: Rich 6F 115
Charlotte St. W1 . . . . .5B 6 (5G 83)
Charlotte Ter. N1 . . . . .1K 83
Charlow Cl. SW6 . . . . .2A 118
CHARLTON 7B 106
   . . . . .3E 146
Charlton Athletic FC 5A 106
Charlton Chu. La. SE7 . . . . .5A 106
Charlton Cl. UB10: Ick 2D 56
Charlton Ct. E2 . . . . .1F 85
   NW5 . . . . .5H 65
Charlton Cres. IG11: Bark 2K 89
Charlton Dene SE7 . . . . .7A 106
Charlton Ga. Bus. Pk. SE7 . . . . .4A 106
Charlton Ho. TW8: Bford 6E 96
Charlton King's Rd. NW5 . . . . .5H 65
Charlton La. SE7 . . . . .4B 106
   TW17: Shep 3E 146
          (not continuous)

Charlton Lido 7B 106
Charlton Pk. La. SE7 . . . . .7B 106
Charlton Pk. Rd. SE7 . . . . .6B 106
Charlton Pl. N1 . . . . .2B 84
Charlton Rd.
   HA3: Kenton 4D 42
   HA9: Wemb 1F 61
   N9 . . . . .1E 34
   NW10 . . . . .1A 80
   SE3 . . . . .7J 105
   SE7 . . . . .7J 105
   TW17: Shep 3E 146
Charlton Way SE3 . . . . .1G 123
Charlwood CR0: Sels 7B 170
Charlwood Cl. HA3: Hrw W 6D 26
Charlwood Ho. SW1 . . . . .4C 18
         (off Vauxhall Bri. Rd.)
   TW9: Kew 7H 97
Charlwood Ho.'s. WC1 . . . . .2F 7
          (off Midhope St.)
Charlwood Pl. SW1 . . . . . . .4B 18 (4G 101)
Charlwood Rd. SW15 . . . . .4F 117
Charlwood St. SW1 . . . . . . .6A 18 (5G 101)
           (not continuous)
Charlwood Ter. SW15 . . . . .4F 117
Charmans Ho. SW8 . . . . .7J 101
         (off Wandsworth Rd.)
Charmeuse Ct. E2 . . . . .2H 85
         (off Silk Weaver Way)
Charmian Av. HA7: Stan 3D 42
Charmian Ho. N1 . . . . .1G 9
           (off Crondall St.)
Charminster Av. SW19 . . . . .2J 153
Charminster Ct. KT6: Surb 7D 150
Charminster Rd. KT4: Wor Pk 1F 165
   SE9 . . . . .4B 142
Charmouth Ct. TW10: Rich 5F 115
Charmouth Ho. SW8 . . . . .7K 101
Charmouth Rd. DA16: Well 1C 126
Charnock Ho. W12 . . . . .7D 80
         (off White City Est.)
Charnock Rd. E5 . . . . .3H 67
Charnwood Av. SW19 . . . . .2J 153
Charnwood Cl. KT3: N Mald 4A 152
Charnwood Dr. E18 . . . . .3K 51
Charnwood Gdns. E14 . . . . .4C 104
Charnwood Pl. N20 . . . . .3F 31
Charnwood Rd. SE25 . . . . .5D 156
   UB10: Hil 2C 74
Charnwood St. E5 . . . . .2H 67
Charrington Rd. CR0: C'don 2C 168
Charrington St. NW1 . . . . .2H 83
           (not continuous)
Charsley Rd. SE6 . . . . .2D 140
Chart Cl. BR2: Brom 1G 159
   CR0: C'don 6J 157
   CR4: Mitc 4D 154
Charter Av. IG2: IIf 1H 71
Charter Bldgs. SE10 . . . . .1D 122
         (off Catherine Gro.)
Charter Ct. KT3: N Mald 3A 152
   N4 . . . . .1A 66
   N22 . . . . .1H 47
   UB1: S'hall 1E 94
Charter Cres. TW4: Houn 4C 112
Charter Dr. DA5: Bexl 7E 126
Charterhouse 4B 8
Charter Ho. SM2: Sutt 6K 165
          (off Mulgrave Rd.)
   WC2 . . . . .1F 13
           (off Crown Ct.)
Charterhouse Apartments
   SW18 . . . . .4K 117
Charterhouse Av. HA0: Wemb 4C 60
Charterhouse Bldgs. EC1 . . . .4B 8 (4C 84)
Charterhouse M. EC1 . . . . . . .5B 8 (5B 84)
Charterhouse Rd. BR6: Chels 3K 173
   E8 . . . . .4G 67
Charterhouse Sq. EC1 . . . . . .5B 8 (5B 84)
Charterhouse St. EC1 . . . . . . .6K 7 (5A 84)
Charteris Community Sports Cen. 1J 89

Charteris Rd. IG8: Wfd G 7E **36**
   N4 . . . . .1A **66**
   NW6 . . . . .1H **81**
Charter Quay KT1: King T 2D **150**
   (off Wadbrook St.)
Charter Rd. KT1: King T 3H **151**
Charter Road, The IG8: Wfd G 6B **36**
Charters Cl. SE19 . . . . .5E **138**
Charter Sq. KT1: King T 2H **151**
Charter Way N3 . . . . .4H **45**
   N14 . . . . .6B **22**
Charles Ho. SE1 . . . . .7H **15**
   (off Stevens St.)
Chartfield Av. SW15 . . . . .5D **116**
Chartfield Sq. SW15 . . . . .5F **117**
Chartham Ct. SW9 . . . . .3A **120**
   (off Canterbury Cres.)
Chartham Gro. SE27 . . . . .3B **138**
Chartham Ho. SE1 . . . . .7F **15**
   (off Weston St.)
Chartham Rd. SE25 . . . . .3H **157**
Chart Hills Cl. SE28 . . . . .6E **90**
Chart Ho. CR4: Mitc 2D **154**
   E14 . . . . .5D **104**
   (off Burrells Wharf Sq.)
Chartley Av. HA7: Stan 6E **26**
   NW2 . . . . .3A **62**
Charlton Cl. DA17: Belv 6F **109**
Chartres Cl. UB6: G'frd 2H **77**
Chartridge SE17 . . . . .6D **102**
   (off Westmoreland Rd.)
Chart St. N1 . . . . .1F **9** (3D **84**)
Chartwell Bus. Cen. BR1: Brom 3B **160**
Chartwell Cl. CR0: C'don 1D **168**
   SE9 . . . . .2H **143**
   UB6: G'frd 1F **77**
Chartwell Cl. EN5: Barn 4B **20**
   IG8: Wfd G 7C **36**
   NW2 . . . . .3C **62**
   UB3: Hayes 7H **75**
Chartwell Dr. BR6: Farnb 5H **173**
Chartwell Gdns. SM3: Cheam 4G **165**
Chartwell Ho. W11 . . . . .1H **99**
   (off Ladbroke Rd.)
Chartwell Lodge BR3: Beck 7C **140**
Chartwell Pl. HA2: Harr 2H **59**
   SM3: Cheam 4G **165**
Chartwell Way SE20 . . . . .1H **157**
Charville Ct. HA1: Harr 6K **41**
   (off Gayton Rd.)
   SE10 . . . . .6F **105**
   (off Trafalgar Gro.)
Charville La. UB4: Hayes 3E **74**
Charville La. W. UB10: Hil 3D **74**
   (not continuous)
Charwood SW16 . . . . .4A **138**
Chase, The BR1: Brom 3K **159**
   DA7: Bex .3H **127**
   E12 . . . . .4B **70**
   HA5: Eastc 6A **40**
   HA5: Pinn 4D **40**
   HA7: Stan 6F **27**
   HA8: Edg 1H **43**
   RM1: Rom 3K **55**
   RM6: Chad H 6E **54**
   RM7: Rush G 3K **73**
   SM6: Wall 5J **167**
   SW4 . . . . .3F **119**
   SW16 . . . . .7K **137**
   SW20 . . . . .1G **153**
   TW16: Sun 1K **147**
   UB10: Ick 5C **56**
Chase Bank Ct. N14 . . . . .6B **22**
   (off Avenue Rd.)
Chase Centre, The NW10 . . . . .3K **79**
Chase Ct. SW3 . . . . .2E **16**
   (off Beaufort Gdns.)
   SW20 . . . . .2G **153**
   TW7: Isle 2A **114**
Chase Ct. Gdns. EN2: Enf 3H **23**
Chase Cross Rd. RM5: Col R 1J **55**

Chasefield Rd. SW17 . . . . .4D **136**
Chase Gdns. E4 . . . . .4H **35**
   TW2: Whitt 7H **113**
Chase Grn. EN2: Enf 3H **23**
Chase Grn. Av. EN2: Enf 2G **23**
Chase Hill EN2: Enf 3H **23**
Chase Ho. NW6 . . . . .3J **81**
   (off Hansel Rd.)
Chase La. IG2: Ilf 5H **53**
   IG6: Ilf 5H **53**
Chaseley Dr. W4 . . . . .5H **97**
Chaseley St. E14 . . . . .6A **86**
Chasemore Cl. CR4: Mitc 7D **154**
Chasemore Gdns. CR0: Wadd 5A **168**
Chasemore Ho. SW6 . . . . .7G **99**
   (off Williams Cl.)
Chase Ridings EN2: Enf 2F **23**
Chase Rd. N14 . . . . .5B **22**
   NW10 . . . . .4K **79**
Chase Rd. Trad. Est. NW10 . . . . .4K **79**
CHASE SIDE .1J **23**
Chase Side EN2: Enf 3H **23**
   N14 . . . . .5K **21**
Chase Side Av. EN2: Enf 2H **23**
   SW20 . . . . .1G **153**
Chase Side Cres. EN2: Enf 1H **23**
Chase Side Pl. EN2: Enf 2H **23**
Chaseville Pde. N21 . . . . .5E **22**
Chaseville Pk. Rd. N21 . . . . .5D **22**
Chase Way N14 . . . . .2A **32**
Chaseway Lodge E16 . . . . .6J **87**
   (off Butchers Rd.)
Chaseways Vs. RM5: Col R 1F **55**
Chasewood Av. EN2: Enf 2G **23**
Chasewood Cl. NW7 . . . . .5E **28**
Chasewood Pk. HA1: Harr 3K **59**
Chaston Pl. NW5 . . . . .5E **64**
   (off Grafton Ter.)
Chater Ho. E2 . . . . .3K **85**
   (off Roman Rd.)
Chatfield Rd. CR0: C'don 1B **168**
   SW11 . . . . .3A **118**
Chatham Av. BR2: Hayes 7H **159**
Chatham Cl. NW11 . . . . .5J **45**
   SE18 . . . . .3F **107**
   SM3: Sutt 7H **153**
Chatham Ho. SM6: Wall 5F **167**
   (off Melbourne Rd.)
Chatham Pl. E9 . . . . .6J **67**
Chatham Rd. E17 . . . . .3A **50**
   E18 . . . . .2H **51**
   KT1: King T 2G **151**
   SW11 . . . . .6D **118**
Chatham St. SE17 . . . . .4D **102**
Chatsfield Pl. W5 . . . . .6E **78**
Chats Palace Arts Cen. 5K **67**
Chatsworth Av. BR1: Brom 4K **141**
   DA15: Sidc 1A **144**
   HA9: Wemb 5F **61**
   NW4 . . . . .2E **44**
   SW20 . . . . .1G **153**
Chatsworth Cl. BR4: W W'ck 2H **171**
   NW4 . . . . .2E **44**
   W4 . . . . .6J **97**
Chatsworth Ct. HA7: Stan 5H **27**
   SW16 . . . . .3K **155**
   W8 . . . . .4J **99**
   (off Pembroke Rd.)
Chatsworth Cres. TW3: Houn 4H **113**
Chatsworth Dr. EN1: Enf 7B **24**
Chatsworth Est. E5 . . . . .4K **67**
Chatsworth Gdns. HA2: Harr 1F **59**
   KT3: N Mald 5B **152**
   W3 . . . . .1H **97**
Chatsworth Ho. BR2: Brom 4J **159**
   (off Westmoreland Rd.)
   E16 . . . . .1K **105**
   (off Wesley Av.)
Chatsworth Lodge W4 . . . . .5K **97**
   (off Bourne Pl.)
Chatsworth Pde. BR5: Pet W 5G **161**

Chatsworth Pl. CR4: Mitc 3D **154**
   TW11: Tedd 4A **132**
Chatsworth Ri. W5 . . . . .4F **79**
Chatsworth Rd. CR0: C'don 4D **168**
   E5 . . . . .3J **67**
   E15 . . . . .5H **69**
   NW2 . . . . .6E **62**
   SM3: Cheam 5F **165**
   UB4: Yead 4K **75**
   W4 . . . . .6J **97**
   W5 . . . . .4F **79**
Chatsworth Way SE27 . . . . .3B **138**
CHATTERN HILL 4D **128**
Chattern Hill TW15: Ashf 4D **128**
Chattern Rd. TW15: Ashf 4E **128**
Chatterton Ct. TW9: Kew 2F **115**
Chatterton M. N4 . . . . .3B **66**
   (off Chatterton Rd.)
Chatterton Rd. BR2: Brom 4B **160**
   N4 . . . . .3B **66**
Chatto Rd. SW11 . . . . .5D **118**
Chaucer Av. TW4: Cran 2K **111**
   TW9: Rich 3G **115**
   UB4: Hayes 5J **75**
Chaucer Cl. N11 . . . . .5B **32**
Chaucer Ct. EN5: New Bar 5E **20**
   N16 . . . . .4E **66**
   SW17 . . . . .3B **136**
   (off Lanesborough Way)
Chaucer Dr. SE1 . . . . .4F **103**
Chaucer Gdns. SM1: Sutt 3J **165**
Chaucer Grn. CR0: C'don 7H **157**
Chaucer Ho. EN5: Barn 4A **20**
   SM1: Sutt 3J **165**
   EA **18**
   SW1 . . . . .4A **18**
   (off Churchill Gdns.)
Chaucer Mans. W14 . . . . .6G **99**
   (off Queen's Club Gdns.)
Chaucer Rd. DA15: Sidc 1C **144**
   DA16: Well 1J **125**
   E7 . . . . .6J **69**
   E11 . . . . .6J **51**
   E17 . . . . .2E **50**
   SE24 . . . . .5A **120**
   SM1: Sutt 4J **165**
   TW15: Ashf 4A **128**
   W3 . . . . .1J **97**
Chaucer Way SW19 . . . . .6B **136**
Chaulden Ho. EC1 . . . . .2F **9**
   (off Cranwood St.)
Chauncey Cl. N9 . . . . .3B **34**
Chaundrye Cl. SE9 . . . . .6D **124**
Chauntler Cl. E16 . . . . .6K **87**
Chaville Cl. N11 . . . . .4K **31**
Chaville Way N3 . . . . .1J **45**
Cheadle Cl. NW8 . . . . .3B **4**
   (off Henderson Dr.)
Cheadle Ho. E14 . . . . .6B **86**
   (off Copenhagen Pl.)
CHEAM 6G **165**
Cheam Comn. Rd. KT4: Wor Pk 2D **164**
Cheam Leisure Cen. 4F **165**
Cheam Mans. SM3: Cheam 7G **165**
Cheam Pk. Way SM3: Cheam 6G **165**
Cheam Rd. SM1: Sutt 6H **165**
   SM2: Cheam 7F **165**
Cheam St. SE15 . . . . .3J **121**
CHEAM VILLAGE 6G **165**
Cheapside EC2 . . . . .1D **14** (6C **84**)
   N13 . . . . .4J **33**
   N22 . . . . .3A **48**
Cheapside Pas. EC2 . . . . .1C **14**
   (off One New Change)
Cheddar Cl. N11 . . . . .6J **31**
Cheddar Waye UB4: Yead 6K **75**
Cheddington Ho. E2 . . . . .1G **85**
   (off Whiston Rd.)
Cheddington Rd. N18 . . . . .3K **33**
Chedworth Cl. E16 . . . . .6H **87**
   (off Wouldham Rd.)

Chedworth Ho. N15 . . . . .4D **48**
   (off West Grn. Rd.)
Cheering La. E20 . . . . .5E **68**
Cheesegrater, The 1G **15**
Cheeseman Cl. TW12: Hamp 6C **130**
Cheesemans Ter. W14 . . . . .5H **99**
   (not continuous)
Cheffery Ct. TW15: Ashf 6D **128**
Cheldon Av. NW7 . . . . .7A **30**
Chelford Rd. BR1: Brom 5F **141**
Chelmer Cres. IG11: Bark 2B **90**
Chelmer Rd. E9 . . . . .5K **67**
Chelmsford Cl. E6 . . . . .6D **88**
   W6 . . . . .6F **99**
Chelmsford Ct. N14 . . . . .7C **22**
   (off Chelmsford Rd.)
Chelmsford Gdns. IG1: Ilf 7C **52**
Chelmsford Ho. N7 . . . . .4K **65**
   (off Holloway Rd.)
Chelmsford Rd. E11 . . . . .1F **69**
   E17 . . . . .6C **50**
   E18 . . . . .1H **51**
   N14 . . . . .7B **22**
Chelmsford Sq. NW10 . . . . .1E **80**
Chelmsine Ct. HA4: Ruis 5E **38**
CHELSEA 6D **16** (5C **100**)
Chelsea Bri. SW1 . . . . .7J **17** (6F **101**)
Chelsea Bri. Rd. SW1 . . . . .5G **17** (5E **100**)
Chelsea Bri. Wharf SW8 . . . . .6F **101**
Chelsea Cinema 6D **16** (5C **100**)
Chelsea Cloisters SW3 . . . .4D **16** (4C **100**)
Chelsea Cl. . . . .
   HA8: Edg 2G **43**
   KT4: Wor Pk 7C **152**
   NW10 . . . . .1K **79**
   TW12: Hamp H 5G **131**
Chelsea Ct. BR1: Brom 3C **160**
   (off Holmdene Cl.)
   SW3 . . . . .7G **17**
   (off Embankment Gdns.)
Chelsea Cres. NW2 . . . . .6H **63**
   SW10 . . . . .1A **118**
Chelsea Emb. SW3 . . . . . . .7D **16** (6D **100**)
Chelsea Farm Ho. Studios SW10 . . . .6B **100**
   (off Cremorne Est.)
Chelsea FC 7K **99**
Chelsea Flds. SW19 . . . . .1B **154**
Chelsea Gdns. SM3: Cheam 4G **165**
   SW1 . . . . .6H **17** (5E **100**)
   W13 . . . . .5K **77**
Chelsea Ga. SW1 . . . . .6H **17**
Chelsea Harbour SW10 . . . . .1A **118**
   (off Chelsea Harbour Dr.)
Chelsea Harbour Design Cen. SW10 . .1A **118**
Chelsea Harbour Dr. SW10 . . . . .1A **118**
Chelsea Lodge SW3 . . . . .7F **17**
   (off Tite St.)
Chelsea Mnr. Ct. SW3 . . . . .7D **16** (6C **100**)
Chelsea Mnr. Gdns. SW3 . . .6D **16** (5C **100**)
Chelsea Mnr. St. SW3 . . . . .6D **16** (5C **100**)
Chelsea Mnr. Studios SW3 . . . . .6D **16**
   (off Flood St.)
Chelsea Pk. Gdns. SW3 . . . .7A **16** (6B **100**)
Chelsea Physic Garden 7E **16** (6D **100**)
Chelsea Reach Twr. SW10 . . . . .7B **100**
   (off Worlds End Est.)
Chelsea Sports Cen. 6D **16** (5C **100**)
Chelsea Sq. SW3 . . . . .5B **16** (5B **100**)
Chelsea Studios SW6 . . . . .7K **99**
   (off Fulham Rd.)
Chelsea Theatre, The 7A **100**
Chelsea Towers SW3 . . . . .7D **16**
Chelsea Village SW6 . . . . .7K **99**
   (off Fulham Rd.)
Chelsea Vista SW6 . . . . .1A **118**
Chelsea Wharf SW10 . . . . .7B **100**
   (off Lots Rd.)
Chelsfield Av. N9 . . . . .7E **24**
Chelsfield Gdns. SE26 . . . . .3J **139**
Chelsfield Grn. N9 . . . . .7E **24**
   (not continuous)

Chelsfield Ho. *SE17* 4E *102*
    (off Massinger St.)
Chelsfield Point *E9* 5D *7*
    (off Penshurst Rd.)
Chelsham Rd. CR2: S Croy 7D *168*
  SW4 . . . . .3H *119*
Chelsiter Cl. DA14: Sidc 4K *143*
Chelston App. HA4: Ruis 2J *57*
Chelston Ct. E11 . . . . .5K *51*
Chelston Rd. HA4: Ruis 1J *57*
Chelsworth Dr. SE18 . . . . .6H *107*
Cheltenham Av. TW1: Twick 7A *114*
Cheltenham Cl. KT3: N Mald 3J *151*
  UB5: N'olt .6F *59*
Cheltenham Cl. *HA7: Stan* 5H *27*
    (off Marsh La.)
Cheltenham Gdns. E6 . . . . .2C *88*
Cheltenham Ho. IG8: Wfd G 6K *37*
  UB3: Harl 3E *92*
    (off Skipton Dr.)
Cheltenham Pl. HA3: Kenton 4E *42*
  W3 . . . . .1H *97*
Cheltenham Rd. BR6: Chels 3K *173*
  E10 . . . . .6E *50*
  SE15 . . . . .4J *121*
Cheltenham Ter. SW3 . . . . .5F *17* (5D *100*)
Chelverton Rd. SW15 . . . . .4F *117*
Chelwood N20 . . . . .2G *31*
Chelwood Cl. E4 . . . . .6J *25*
Chelwood Ct. CR2: S Croy 5C *168*
  SW11 . . . . .1B *118*
    (off Westbridge Rd.)
Chelwood Gdns. TW9: Kew 2G *115*
Chelwood Gdns. Pas. TW9: Kew 2G *115*
Chelwood Ho. *W2* 1B *10*
    (off Gloucester Sq.)
Chelwood Wlk. SE4 . . . . .4A *122*
Chenappa Cl. E13 . . . . .3J *87*
Chenduit Way HA7: Stan 5E *26*
Cheney Cl. SE23 . . . . .1K *139*
Cheney Row E17 . . . . .1B *50*
Cheneys Rd. E11 . . . . .3G *69*
Cheney St. HA5: Eastc 4A *40*
Chenies, The BR6: Pet W 6J *161*
  NW1 . . . . .2H *83*
    (off Pancras Rd.)
Chenies Ho. *W2* 7K *81*
    (off Moscow Rd.)
  W4 . . . . .7B *98*
    (off Corney Reach Way)
Chenies M. WC1 . . . . .4C *6* (4H *83*)
Chenies Pl. NW1 . . . . .2H *83*
Chenies St. WC1 . . . . .5C *6* (5H *83*)
Cheniston Gdns. W8 . . . . .3K *99*
Chenla SE13 . . . . .2D *122*
Chepstow Cl. SW15 . . . . .5G *117*
Chepstow Cnr. *W2* 6J *81*
    (off Chepstow Pl.)
Chepstow Ct. *W11* 7J *81*
    (off Chepstow Vs.)
Chepstow Cres. IG3: Ilf 6J *53*
  W11 . . . . .7J *81*
Chepstow Gdns. UB1: S'hall 6D *76*
Chepstow Pl. W2 . . . . .6J *81*
Chepstow Ri. CR0: C'don 3E *168*
Chepstow Rd.
  CR0: C'don 3E *168*
  W2 . . . . .6J *81*
  W7 . . . . .3A *96*
Chepstow Vs. W11 . . . . .7H *81*
Chequers IG9: Buck H 1E *36*
Chequers, The HA5: Pinn 3B *40*
Chequers Cl. BR5: St P 4K *161*
  NW9 . . . . .3A *44*
Chequers Ct. DA17: Belv 4G *109*
  EC1 . . . . .4D *8*
    (off Chequer St.)
Chequers Ho. *NW8* 3C *4*
    (off Jerome Cres.)
Chequers La. RM9: Dag 4F *91*
    (not continuous)

Chequers Pde. N13 . . . . .5H *33*
  RM9: Dag .1F *91*
  SE9 . . . . .6D *124*
    (off Eltham High St.)
Chequer St. EC1 . . . . .4D *8* (4C *84*)
    (not continuous)
Chequers Way N13 . . . . .5G *33*
Cherbury Cl. SE28 . . . . .6D *90*
Cherbury Ct. *N1* 2D *84*
    (off St John's Est.)
Cherbury St. N1 . . . . .2D *84*
Cherchefelle M. HA7: Stan 5G *27*
Cherimoya Gdns.
  KT8: W Mole 3F *149*
Cherington Rd. W7 . . . . .1J *95*
Cheriton Av. BR2: Brom 5H *159*
  IG5: Ilf 2D *52*
Cheriton Cl. EN4: Cockf 3J *21*
  W5 . . . . .5C *78*
Cheriton Ct. SE12 . . . . .7J *123*
  SE25 . . . . .5E *156*
Cheriton Dr. SE18 . . . . .7H *107*
Cheriton Lodge HA4: Ruis 1H *57*
Cheriton Sq. SW17 . . . . .2E *136*
Cherry Av. UB1: S'hall 1B *94*
Cherry Blossom Cl. N13 . . . . .5G *33*
Cherry Cl. E17 . . . . .5D *50*
  HA0: Wemb 3D *60*
  HA4: Ruis 3H *57*
  NW9 . . . . .2A *44*
  SM4: Mord 4G *153*
  SM5: Cars 2D *166*
  SW2 . . . . .7A *120*
  W5 . . . . .3D *96*
Cherrycot Hill BR6: Farnb 4G *173*
Cherrycot Ri. BR6: Farnb 4G *173*
Cherry Ct. HA5: Pinn 2B *40*
  IG6: Ilf 3F *53*
  W3 . . . . .1A *98*
Cherry Cres. TW8: Bford 7B *96*
Cherrydown Av. E4 . . . . .3G *35*
Cherrydown Cl. E4 . . . . .3H *35*
Cherrydown Rd. DA14: Sidc 2D *144*
Cherrydown Wlk. RM7: Mawney 2H *55*
Cherry Gdn. Ho. *SE16* 2H *103*
    (off Cherry Gdn. St.)
Cherry Gdns. RM9: Dag 5F *73*
  UB5: N'olt .7F *59*
Cherry Gdn. St. SE16 . . . . .2H *103*
Cherry Gth. TW8: Bford 5D *96*
Cherry Gro. UB3: Hayes 1K *93*
  UB8: Hil 5D *74*
Cherry Hill EN5: New Bar 6E *20*
  HA3: Hrw W 6E *26*
Cherry Hill Gdns. CR0: Wadd 4K *167*
Cherrylands Cl. NW9 . . . . .2J *61*
Cherry La. UB7: W Dray 4B *92*
Cherry Laurel Wlk. SW2 . . . . .6K *119*
Cherry Orchard SE7 . . . . .6A *106*
  UB7: W Dray 2A *92*
Cherry Orchard Gdns. CR0: C'don . . .1D *168*
  KT8: W Mole 3D *148*
Cherry Orchard Rd. BR2: Brom 2C *172*
  CR0: C'don 2D *168*
  KT8: W Mole 3E *148*
Cherry Pk. La. E20 . . . . .7E *68*
Cherry Red Records Stadium (Kingsmeadow)
  . . . . .3H *151*
Cherry Rd. EN3: Enf W 1D *24*
Cherry St. RM7: Rom 5K *55*
Cherry Tree Av. UB7: Yiew 6B *74*
Cherry Tree Cl. E9 . . . . .1J *85*
  HA0: Wemb 4A *60*
Cherry Tree Ct. *NW1* 7G *65*
    (off Camden Rd.)
  NW9 . . . . .4J *43*
  SE7 . . . . .6A *106*
Cherry Tree Dr. SW16 . . . . .3J *137*
Cherry Tree Hill N2 . . . . .5C *46*
Cherry Tree Ho. N22 . . . . .7D *32*
Cherry Tree Ri. IG9: Buck H 4F *37*

Cherry Tree Rd. E15 . . . . .5G *69*
  N2 . . . . .4D *46*
Cherry Tree Ter. *SE1* 7H *15*
    (off Whites Grounds)
Cherry Tree Wlk. BR3: Beck 4B *158*
  BR4: W W'ck 4H *171*
  EC1 . . . . .4D *8* (4C *84*)
Cherry Tree Way E13 . . . . .4B *88*
  HA7: Stan .6G *27*
Cherry Way BR2: Hayes 1J *171*
Cherry Way KT19: Ewe 6K *163*
  TW17: Shep 4F *147*
Cherrywood Cl. E3 . . . . .3A *86*
  KT2: King T 7G *133*
Cherrywood Dr. SW15 . . . . .5F *117*
Cherrywood La. SM4: Mord 4G *153*
Cherrywood Lodge *SE13* 6F *123*
    (off Birdwood Av.)
Cherry Wood Way W5 . . . . .5G *79*
Chertsey Bri. Rd. KT16: Chert 7A *146*
Chertsey Ct. SW14 . . . . .3H *115*
Chertsey Dr. SM3: Cheam 2G *165*
Chertsey Ho. *E2* 2J *9*
    (off Arnold Cir.)
CHERTSEY MEADS 7A *146*
Chertsey Meads Local Nature Reserve
  . . . . .7A *146*
Chertsey Rd. E11 . . . . .2F *69*
  IG1: Ilf 4H *71*
  TW1: Twick 6K *113*
  TW2: Twick 2F *131*
  TW13: Felt 3G *129*
  TW15: Ashf 7F *129*
  TW16: Sun 7F *129*
  TW17: Shep 7A *146*
Chertsey St. SW17 . . . . .5E *136*
Cherwell Cl. TW13: Felt 3J *129*
Chervil M. SE28 . . . . .1B *108*
Cherwell Ct. KT19: Ewe 4J *163*
Cherwell Ho. NW8 . . . . .4B *4*
Cherwell M. SW11 . . . . .4C *118*
Cherwell Way HA4: Ruis 6E *38*
Cheryls Cl. SW6 . . . . .1K *117*
Cheseman St. SE26 . . . . .3H *139*
Chesfield Rd. KT2: King T 7E *132*
Chesham Apartments E4 . . . . .7J *35*
Chesham Av. BR5: Pet W 6F *161*
Chesham Cl. NW7 . . . . .4F *29*
  RM7: Rom 4K *55*
  SW1 . . . . .2G *17*
Chesham Cres. SE20 . . . . .1J *157*
Chesham Flats *W1* 2H *11*
    (off Brown Hart Gdns.)
Chesham Ho. *SE8* 1C *122*
    (off Brookmill Rd.)
Chesham M. SW1 . . . . .1G *17*
Chesham Pl. SW1 . . . . .2G *17* (3E *100*)
    (not continuous)
Chesham Rd. KT1: King T 2G *151*
  SE20 . . . . .2J *157*
  SW19 . . . . .5B *136*
  SW1 . . . . .2G *17* (3E *100*)
Chesham St. NW10 . . . . .3K *61*
  SW1 . . . . .2G *17* (3E *100*)
Chesham Ter. W13 . . . . .2B *96*
Cheshire Cl. CR4: Mitc 3J *155*
  E17 . . . . .1D *50*
  SE4 . . . . .2B *122*
Cheshire Ct. *EC4* 1K *13*
    (off Fleet St.)
Cheshire Gdns. KT9: Chess 6D *162*
Cheshire Ho. N18 . . . . .4C *34*
  SM4: Mord 7K *153*
Cheshire Rd. N22 . . . . .7E *32*
Cheshire St. E2 . . . . .3K *9* (4F *85*)
Cheshir Ho. NW4 . . . . .4E *44*
Chesholm Rd. N16 . . . . .3E *66*
Cheshunt Ho. *NW6* 1K *81*
    (off Mortimer Cres.)
Cheshunt Rd. DA17: Belv 5G *109*
  E7 . . . . .6K *69*

Chesil Ct. E2 . . . . .2J *85*
  SW3 . . . . .7D *16* (6C *100*)
Chesilton Rd. SW6 . . . . .1H *117*
Chesil Way UB4: Hayes 3H *75*
Chesley Gdns. E6 . . . . .2B *88*
Chesney Ct. *W9* 4J *81*
    (off Shirland Rd.)
Chesney Cres. CR0: New Ad 7E *170*
Chesney Ho. *SE13* 4F *123*
    (off Mercator Rd.)
Chesney St. SW11 . . . . .1E *118*
Chesnut Gro. N17 . . . . .3F *49*
Chesnut Rd. N17 . . . . .3F *49*
Chesnut Row *N3* 7D *30*
    (off Nether St.)
Chessell Cl. CR7: Thor H 4B *156*
Chessholme Cl. TW16: Sun 7G *129*
    (off Scotts Av.)
Chessholme Rd. TW15: Ashf 6E *128*
Chessing Cl. *N2* 3D *46*
    (off Fortis Grn.)
CHESSINGTON 5E *162*
Chessington Av. DA7: Bex 7E *108*
  N3 . . . . .3G *45*
Chessington Cl. KT19: Ewe 6J *163*
Chessington Ct. HA5: Pinn 4D *40*
  N3 . . . . .3H *45*
    (off Charter Way)
Chessington Golf Course 7D *162*
Chessington Hall Gdns. KT9: Chess . .7D *162*
Chessington Hill Pk. KT9: Chess 5G *163*
Chessington Ho. SW8 . . . . .2H *119*
Chessington Lodge N3 . . . . .3H *45*
Chessington Mans. E10 . . . . .7C *50*
  E11 . . . . .7G *51*
Chessington Pde. KT9: Chess 6D *162*
Chessington Pk. KT9: Chess 4G *163*
Chessington Rd. KT17: Ewe 7B *164*
  KT19: Ewe 6G *163*
Chessington Sports Cen. 7D *162*
Chessington Trade Pk. KT9: Chess . .4G *163*
Chessington Way BR4: W W'ck 2D *170*
Chesson Rd. W14 . . . . .6H *99*
Chesswood Way HA5: Pinn 2B *40*
Chestbrook Ct. *EN1: Enf* 5K *23*
    (off Forsyth Pl.)
Chester Av. TW2: Whitt 1D *130*
  TW10: Rich 6F *115*
Chester Cl. SM1: Sutt 2J *165*
  SW1 . . . . .7J *11* (2F *101*)
  SW13 . . . . .3D *116*
  TW10: Rich 6F *115*
  TW15: Ashf 5F *129*
  UB8: Hil 6D *74*
Chester Cl. Nth. NW1 . . . . .1K *5* (3F *83*)
Chester Cl. Sth. NW1 . . . . .2K *5* (3F *83*)
Chester Cotts. SW1 . . . . .4G *17*
Chester Ct. BR2: Brom 4H *159*
    (off Durham Rd.)
  NW1 . . . . .1K *5* (3F *83*)
    (not continuous)
  SE5 . . . . .7D *102*
    (off Lomond Gro.)
  SE8 . . . . .5K *103*
  W6 . . . . .4F *99*
    (off Wolverton Gdns.)
Chester Cres. E8 . . . . .5F *67*
Chester Dr. HA2: Harr 6D *40*
Chesterfield Cl. SE13 . . . . .2F *123*
Chesterfield Ct. KT5: Surb 5E *150*
    (off Cranes Pk.)
Chesterfield Dr. KT10: Hin W 2A *162*
Chesterfield Flats *EN5: Barn* 5A *20*
    (off Bells Hill)
Chesterfield Gdns. N4 . . . . .5B *48*
  SE10 . . . . .1F *123*
  W1 . . . . .4J *11* (1F *101*)
Chesterfield Gro. SE22 . . . . .5F *121*
Chesterfield Hill W1 . . . . . . .4J *11* (1F *101*)
Chesterfield Ho. *W1* 4H *11*
    (off Chesterfield Gdns.)

Chesterfield Lodge *N21* 7E **22**
     (off Church Hill)
Chesterfield M. N4 . . . . .5B **48**
  TW15: Ashf 4A **128**
Chesterfield Rd. E10 . . . . .6E **50**
  EN5: Barn 5A **20**
  KT19: Ewe 7K **163**
  N3 . . . . .6D **30**
  TW15: Ashf 4A **128**
  W4 . . . . .6J **97**
Chesterfield St. W1 . . . . . .4J **11** (1F **101**)
Chesterfield Wlk. SE10 . . . . .1F **123**
Chesterfield Way SE15 . . . . .7J **103**
  UB3: Hayes 2J **93**
Chesterford Gdns. NW3 . . . . .4K **63**
Chesterford Ho. *SE18* 1B **124**
     (off Tellson Av.)
Chesterford Rd. E12 . . . . .5D **70**
Chester Gdns. EN3: Pond E 6C **24**
  SM4: Mord 6A **154**
  W13 . . . . .6B **78**
Chester Ga. NW1 . . . . .2J **5** (3F **83**)
Chester Ho. N10 . . . . .2F **47**
  SE8 . . . . .6B **104**
  SW1 . . . . .3J **17**
     (off Eccleston Pl.)
  SW9 . . . . .7A **102**
     (off Cranmer Rd.)
Chesterman Ct. *W4* 7A **98**
     (off Corney Reach Way)
Chester M. E17 . . . . .2C **50**
  SW1 . . . . .1J **17** (3F **101**)
Chester Pl. NW1 . . . . .1J **5** (3F **83**)
Chester Rd. DA15: Sidc 5J **125**
  E7 . . . . .7B **70**
  E11 . . . . .6K **51**
  E16 . . . . .4G **87**
  E17 . . . . .5K **49**
  HA6: Nwood 1H **39**
  IG3: Ilf 1K **71**
  IG7: Chig 3K **37**
  N9 . . . . .1C **34**
  N17 . . . . .3D **48**
  N19 . . . . .2F **65**
  NW1 . . . . .2H **5** (3E **82**)
  SW19 . . . . .6E **134**
  TW4: Houn 3K **111**
  TW6: H'row A 3C **110**
Chester Row SW1 . . . . .4G **17** (4E **100**)
Chesters, The KT3: N Mald 1A **152**
Chester Sq. SW1 . . . . .3H **17** (4E **100**)
Chester Sq. M. SW1 . . . . .2J **17**
Chester St. E2 . . . . .4G **85**
  SW1 . . . . .1H **17** (3E **100**)
Chester Ter. IG11: Bark 6H **71**
  NW1 . . . . .1J **5** (3F **83**)
     (not continuous)
Chesterton Cl. SW18 . . . . .5J **117**
  UB6: G'frd 2F **77**
Chesterton Ct. *W3* 3H **97**
     (off Bollo Bri. Rd.)
  W5 . . . . .5D **78**
Chesterton Dr. TW19: Stanw 1B **128**
Chesterton Ho. *CR0: C'don* 4D **168**
     (off Heathfield Rd.)
  SW11 . . . . .3B **118**
     (off Ingrave St.)
  W10 . . . . .5G **81**
     (off Portobello Rd.)
Chesterton Rd. E13 . . . . .3J **87**
  W10 . . . . .5F **81**
Chesterton Sq. W8 . . . . .4J **99**
Chesterton Ter. E13 . . . . .3J **87**
  KT1: King T 2G **151**
Chester Way SE11 . . . . . .4K **19** (4A **102**)
Chesthunte Rd. N17 . . . . .1C **48**
Chestlands Ct. UB10: Hil 6C **56**
Chestnut All. SW6 . . . . .6H **99**
Chestnut Av. BR4: W W'ck 5G **171**
  E7 . . . . .4K **69**
  HA0: Wemb 5B **60**

Chestnut Av. HA6: Nwood 2H **39**
  HA8: Edg 6K **27**
  IG9: Buck H 3G **37**
  KT8: E Mos 3K **149**
  KT10: Esh 7H **149**
  KT19: Ewe 4A **164**
  N8 . . . . .5J **47**
  SW14 . . . . .3K **115**
  TW8: Bford 4D **96**
  TW11: Tedd 2K **149**
  TW12: Hamp 7E **130**
  TW7: Yiew 7B **74**
Chestnut Av. Nth. E17 . . . . .4F **51**
Chestnut Av. Sth. E17 . . . . .5E **50**
Chestnut Cl. BR6: Chels 5K **173**
  DA15: Sidc 1A **144**
  IG9: Buck H 3G **37**
  N14 . . . . .5B **22**
  N16 . . . . .2D **66**
  SE6 . . . . .5E **140**
  SE14 . . . . .1B **122**
  SM5: Cars 1D **166**
  TW15: Ashf 4D **128**
  TW16: Sun 6H **129**
  UB3: Hayes 7G **75**
  UB7: Harl, Sip 7D **92**
Chestnut Ct. *CR2: S Croy* 4C **168**
     (off Bramley Hill)
  N8 . . . . .5J **47**
  SW6 . . . . .6H **99**
  TW13: Hanw 5B **130**
  TW19: Stanw 1A **128**
     (off Mulberry Av.)
  W8 . . . . .3K **99**
     (off Abbots Wlk.)
Chestnut Dr. DA7: Bex 3D **126**
  E11 . . . . .6J **51**
  HA3: Hrw W 7E **26**
  HA5: Pinn 6B **40**
Chestnut Gro. CR2: Sels 7H **169**
  CR4: Mitc 5H **155**
  DA2: Wilm 4K **145**
  EN4: E Barn 5J **21**
  HA0: Wemb 5B **60**
  KT3: N Mald 3K **151**
  SE20 . . . . .7H **139**
  SW12 . . . . .7E **118**
  TW7: Isle 4A **114**
  W5 . . . . .3D **96**
Chestnut Ho. *E3* 1B **86**
     (off Sycamore Av.)
  SW15 .4B **116**
  W4 . . . . .4A **98**
     (off The Orchard)
Chestnut La. N20 . . . . .1B **30**
Chestnut M. SW14 . . . . .4J **115**
Chestnut Pl. SE26 . . . . .4F **139**
Chestnut Plaza *E20* 6E **68**
     (within Westfield Stratford City Shop. Cen.)
Chestnut Rd. SE18 . . . . .6H **107**
  WD23: Bush 1A **26**
Chestnut Rd.
  KT2: King T 7E **132**
  SE27 . . . . .3B **138**
  SW20 . . . . .2F **153**
  TW2: Twick 2J **131**
  TW15: Ashf 4D **128**
Chestnuts, The HA5: Hat E 1D **40**
  N5 . . . . .4C **66**
     (off Highbury Grange)
  UB10: Uxb 7A **56**
The Chestnuts BR3: Beck 3K **157**
Chestnut Ter. SM1: Sutt 4K **165**
Chestnut Wlk. IG8: Wfd G 5D **36**
  TW17: Shep 4G **147**
Chestnut Way TW13: Felt 3K **129**
Cheston Av. CR0: C'don 2A **170**
Chestwood Gro. UB10: Hil 7B **56**
Chettle Cl. *SE1* 3D **102**
     (off Spurgeon St.)

Chettle Ct. N8 . . . . .6A **48**
Chetwode Ho. NW8 . . . . .3C **4**
Chetwode Rd. SW17 . . . . .3D **136**
Chetwood Wlk. *E6* 5C **88**
     (off Greenwich Cres.)
Chetwynd Av. EN4: E Barn 1J **31**
Chetwynd Dr. UB10: Hil 2B **74**
Chetwynd Rd. NW5 . . . . .4F **65**
Chetwynd Vs. *NW5* 4F **65**
     (off Chetwynd Rd.)
Chevalier Cl. HA7: Stan 4K **27**
Cheval Pl. SW7 . . . . . . .1D **16** (3C **100**)
Cheval St. E14 . . . . .3C **104**
Cheveney Wlk. BR2: Brom 3J **159**
Chevening Rd. NW6 . . . . .2F **81**
  SE10 . . . . .5H **105**
  SE19 . . . . .6D **138**
Chevenings, The DA14: Sidc 3C **144**
Cheverell Ho. *E2* 2G **85**
     (off Pritchard's Rd.)
Cheverton Rd. N19 . . . . .1H **65**
Chevet St. E9 . . . . .5A **68**
Chevington NW2 . . . . .6H **63**
Cheviot *N17* 7C **34**
     (off Northumberland Gro.)
Cheviot Cl. DA7: Bex 2K **127**
  EN1: Enf .2J **23**
  UB3: Harl 7F **93**
Cheviot Ct. *SE14* 6J **103**
     (off Avonley Rd.)
  UB2: S'hall 4F **95**
Cheviot Gdns. NW2 . . . . .2F **63**
  SE27 . . . . .4B **138**
Cheviot Ga. NW2 . . . . .2G **63**
Cheviot Ho. *E1* 3K **85**
     (off Commercial Rd.)
Cheviot Rd. SE27 . . . . .5A **138**
Cheviot Way IG2: Ilf 4J **53**
Chevron Cl. E16 . . . . .6J **87**
Chevy Rd. UB2: S'hall 2G **95**
Chewton Rd. E17 . . . . .4A **50**
Cheylesmore Ho. *SW1* 5J **17**
     (off Ebury Bri. Rd.)
Cheyne Av. E18 . . . . .3H **51**
  TW2: Whitt 1D **130**
Cheyne Cl. BR2: Brom 3C **172**
  NW4 . . . . .5E **44**
Cheyne Ct. SW3 . . . . .7E **16** (6D **100**)
Cheyne Gdns. SW3 . . . . . .7D **16** (6C **100**)
Cheyne Hill KT5: Surb 4F **151**
Cheyne Ho. *SW3* 7E **16**
     (off Chelsea Emb.)
Cheyne M. SW3 . . . . .7D **16** (6C **100**)
Cheyne Pk. Dr. BR4: W W'ck 3E **170**
Cheyne Path W7 . . . . .5K **77**
Cheyne Pl. SW3 . . . . .7E **16** (6D **100**)
Cheyne Rd. TW15: Ashf 7F **129**
Cheyne Row SW3 . . . . .7C **16** (6C **100**)
Cheyne Wlk. CR0: C'don 2G **169**
  N21 . . . . .5G **23**
  NW4 . . . . .6E **44**
  SW3 . . . . .7C **16** (6B **100**)
     (not continuous)
  SW10 . . . . .7B **100**
Cheyneys Av. HA8: Edg 6J **27**
Chichele Gdns. CR0: C'don 4E **168**
Chichele Rd. NW2 . . . . .5F **63**
Chicheley Gdns. HA3: Hrw W 7B **26**
     (not continuous)
Chicheley Rd. HA3: Hrw W 7B **26**
Chicheley St. SE1 . . . . . .6H **13** (2K **101**)
Chichester Av. HA4: Ruis 2F **57**
Chichester Cl. E6 . . . . .6C **88**
  SE3 . . . . .7A **106**
  TW12: Hamp 6D **130**
Chichester Ct. HA7: Stan 3E **42**
  HA8: Edg 6B **28**
     (off Whitchurch La.)
  KT17: Ewe 7B **164**
  NW1 . . . . .7J **65**
     (off Royal Coll. St.)

Chichester Ct. TW19: Stanw 1A **128**
  UB5: N'olt 1D **76**
Chichester Gdns. IG1: Ilf 7C **52**
Chichester Ho. NW6 . . . . .2J **81**
  SW9 . . . . .7A **102**
     (off Cranmer Rd.)
Chichester M. SE27 . . . . .4A **138**
Chichester Rents WC2 . . . . .7J **7**
Chichester Rd. CR0: C'don 3E **168**
  E11 . . . . .3G **69**
  N9 . . . . .1B **34**
  NW6 . . . . .2J **81**
  W2 . . . . .5K **81**
Chichester St. SW1 . . . . .6B **18** (5G **101**)
Chichester Way E14 . . . . .4F **105**
  TW14: Felt 7A **112**
Chickenshed Theatre 5K **21**
Chicksand Ho. *E1* 5K **9**
     (off Chicksand St.)
Chicksand St. E1 . . . . .6K **9** (5F **85**)
     (not continuous)
Chiddingfold N12 . . . . .3D **30**
Chiddingstone SE13 . . . . .5E **122**
Chiddingstone Av. DA7: Bex 7F **109**
Chiddingstone St. SW6 . . . . .2J **117**
Chieveley Pde. DA7: Bex 3H **127**
Chieveley Rd. DA7: Bex 4H **127**
Chignell Pl. W13 . . . . .1A **96**
CHIGWELL 3K **37**
Chigwell Ct. *E9* 6A **68**
     (off Ballance Rd.)
Chigwell Golf Course 4K **37**
Chigwell Hill E1 . . . . .7H **85**
Chigwell Hurst Cl. HA5: Pinn 3B **40**
Chigwell Pk. IG7: Chig 4K **37**
Chigwell Pk. Dr. IG7: Chig 3K **37**
Chigwell Ri. IG7: Chig 2K **37**
Chigwell Rd. E18 . . . . .3K **51**
  IG8: Wfd G 2A **52**
Chilcombe Ho. *SW15* 7C **116**
     (off Fontley Way)
Chilcot Cl. E14 . . . . .6D **86**
Chilcott Cl. HA0: Wemb 4C **60**
Childebert Rd. SW17 . . . . .2F **137**
Childeric Rd. SE14 . . . . .7A **104**
Childerley *KT1: King T* 3G **151**
     (off Burritt Rd.)
Childerley St. SW6 . . . . .1G **117**
Childers, The IG8: Wfd G 5J **37**
Childers St. SE8 . . . . .6A **104**
Child La. SE10 . . . . .3H **105**
Childs Ct. UB3: Hayes 7J **75**
CHILD'S HILL .3H **63**
Childs Hill Wlk. *NW2* 3H **63**
     (off Cricklewood La.)
Child's La. SE19 . . . . .6E **138**
Child's M. *SW5* 4J **99**
     (off Child's Pl.)
Child's Pl. SW5 . . . . .4J **99**
Child's St. SW5 . . . . .4J **99**
Child's Wlk. *SW5* 4J **99**
     (off Child's St.)
Childs Way NW11 . . . . .5H **45**
Chilham Cl. DA5: Bexl 7F **127**
  UB6: G'frd 2A **78**
Chilham Ho. SE1 . . . . .3D **102**
  SE15 . . . . .6J **103**
Chilham Rd. SE9 . . . . .4C **142**
Chilham Way BR2: Hayes 7J **159**
Chilianwalla Memorial 7G **17** (6E **100**)
Chillerton Rd. SW17 . . . . .5E **136**
Chillingford Ho. SW17 . . . . .4A **136**
Chillington Dr. SW11 . . . . .4B **118**
Chillingworth Gdns.
  TW1: Twick 3K **131**
Chillingworth Rd. N7 . . . . .5A **66**
Chilmark Gdns. KT3: N Mald 6C **152**
Chilmark Rd. SW16 . . . . .2H **155**
Chiltern Av. TW2: Whitt 1E **130**
Chiltern Cl. CR0: C'don 3E **168**
  DA7: Bex 1K **127**

Chiltern Cl. KT4: Wor Pk 1E 164
   UB10: Ick 2C 56
Chiltern Cl. BR2: Brom 2C 172
   (off Gravel Rd.)
   EN5: New Bar 5F 21
   HA1: Harr 5H 41
   N10 . . . . .2E 46
   NW1 . . . . .4F 5
   (off Baker St.)
   SE14 . . . . .7J 103
   (off Avonley Rd.)
   UB8: Hil .4D 74
Chiltern Dene EN2: Enf 4E 22
Chiltern Dr. KT5: Surb 6G 151
Chiltern Gdns. BR2: Brom 4H 159
   NW2 . . . . .3F 63
Chiltern Ho. N9 . . . . .3B 34
   SE17 . . . . .6D 102
   (off Portland St.)
   W5 . . . . .5E 78
   W10 . . . . .5G 81
   (off Telford Rd.)
Chiltern Rd. E3 . . . . .4C 86
   HA5: Eastc 5A 40
   IG2: Ilf 5J 53
Chilterns, The BR1: Brom 2K 159
   (off Murray Av.)
Chiltern St. W1 . . . . .5G 5 (5E 82)
Chiltern Way IG8: Wfd G 3D 36
Chilthorne Cl. SE6 . . . . .7B 122
Chilton Av. W5 . . . . .4D 96
Chilton Ct. N22 . . . . .7D 32
   (off Truro Rd.)
Chilton Gro. SE8 . . . . .4K 103
Chiltonian Ind. Est. SE12 . . . . . . .6H 123
Chiltonian M. SE13 . . . . .5F 123
Chilton Rd. HA8: Edg 6B 28
   TW9: Rich 3G 115
Chiltons, The E18 . . . . .2J 51
Chilton St. E2 . . . . .3K 9 (4F 85)
Chilvers Cl. TW2: Twick 2J 131
Chilver St. SE10 . . . . .5H 105
Chilworth Ct. SW19 . . . . .1F 135
Chilworth Gdns. SM1: Sutt 3A 166
Chilworth M. W2 . . . . .1A 10 (6B 82)
Chilworth Pl. IG11: Bark 4A 90
Chilworth St. W2 . . . . .1A 10 (6A 82)
Chimes Av. N13 . . . . .5F 33
Chimes Ho. BR3: Beck 1A 158
Chimes Ter. N8 . . . . .5J 47
Chimney Ct. E1 . . . . .1H 103
   (off Brewhouse La.)
China Ct. E1 . . . . .1H 103
   (off Asher Way)
China Hall M. SE16 . . . . .3J 103
China M. SW2 . . . . .7K 119
China Town 2D 12
   (off Gerrard St.)
China Wharf SE1 . . . . .6K 15 (2G 103)
Chinbrook Cres. SE12 . . . . .3K 141
Chinbrook Rd. SE12 . . . . .3K 141
Chinchilla Dr. TW4: Houn 2A 112
Chine, The HA0: Wemb 5B 60
   N10 . . . . .4G 47
   N21 . . . . .6G 23
Ching Ct. WC2 . . . . .1E 12
   (off Monmouth St.)
Chingdale Rd. E4 . . . . .3B 36
CHINGFORD 1K 35
Chingford Av. E4 . . . . .3H 35
Chingford Fitness & Wellbeing Cen.
. . . . .4K 35
Chingford Golf Range 1H 35
CHINGFORD GREEN 1A 36
CHINGFORD HATCH 4A 36
Chingford Ind. Cen. E4 . . . . .5F 35
Chingford La. IG8: Wfd G 4B 36
CHINGFORD MOUNT 4H 35
Chingford Mt. Rd. E4 . . . . .4H 35
Chingford Rd. E4 . . . . .6H 35
   E17 . . . . .1D 50

Chingley Cl. BR1: Brom 6G 141
Chingstone Ter. E4 . . . . .1K 35
Ching Way E4 . . . . .6G 35
   (not continuous)
Chinnery Cl. EN1: Enf 1A 24
Chinnock's Wharf E14 . . . . .7A 86
   (off Narrow St.)
Chinnor Cres. UB6: G'frd 2F 77
Chipka St. E14 . . . . .2E 104
   (not continuous)
Chipley St. SE14 . . . . .6A 104
Chipmunk Gro. UB5: N'olt 3C 76
Chippendale All. UB8: Uxb 7A 56
Chippendale Ho. SW1 . . . . .6K 17
   (off Churchill Gdns.)
Chippendale St. E5 . . . . .3K 67
Chippendale Waye UB8: Uxb 7A 56
Chippenham KT1: King T 2F 151
   (off Excelsior Cl.)
Chippenham Av. HA9: Wemb 5H 61
Chippenham Cl. HA5: Eastc 4H 39
Chippenham Gdns. NW6 . . . . .3J 81
Chippenham M. W9 . . . . .4J 81
Chippenham Rd. W9 . . . . .4J 81
Chipperfield Ho. SW3 . . . . .5C 16
   (off Cale St.)
Chipperfield Rd. BR5: St P 7A 144
   (not continuous)
CHIPPING BARNET 4B 20
Chipping Cl. EN5: Barn 3B 20
Chipstead Av. CR7: Thor H 4B 156
Chipstead Cl. SE19 . . . . .7F 139
   SM2: Sutt 7K 165
Chipstead Gdns. NW2 . . . . .2D 62
Chipstead St. SW6 . . . . .1J 117
Chip St. SW4 . . . . .3H 119
Chirk Cl. UB4: Yead 4C 76
Chisenhale Rd. E3 . . . . .2A 86
Chisholm Ct. W6 . . . . .5C 98
Chisholm Rd. CR0: C'don 2E 168
   TW10: Rich 6F 115
Chisledon Wlk. E9 . . . . .6B 68
   (off Osborne Rd.)
CHISLEHURST 6F 143
Chislehurst Av. N12 . . . . .7F 31
Chislehurst Caves 1E 160
Chislehurst Golf Course 7F 143
Chislehurst Rd. BR1: Brom 2B 160
   BR5: Pet W 4J 161
   BR6: Orp, Pet W, St M Cry 4J 161
   BR7: Chst 2B 160
   DA14: Sidc 5A 144
   TW10: Rich 5E 114
CHISLEHURST WEST 6E 142
Chislet Cl. BR3: Beck 7C 140
Chisley Rd. N15 . . . . .6E 48
Chiswell Sq. SE3 . . . . .2K 123
Chiswell St. EC1 . . . . .5E 8 (5C 84)
   SE5 . . . . .7D 102
   (off Edmund St.)
CHISWICK .5K 97
Chiswick Bri. SW14 . . . . .2J 115
Chiswick Cl. CR0: Bedd 3K 167
Chiswick Comn. Rd. W4 . . . . .4K 97
Chiswick Community Sports Hall . . .7K 97
Chiswick Ct.
   HA5: Pinn 3D 40
   W4 . . . . .4H 97
Chiswick High Rd. W4: Bford, Lon . . .5G 97
Chiswick House & Gardens 6K 97
Chiswick Ho. Grounds W4 . . . . .6A 98
Chiswick La. W4 . . . . .5A 98
Chiswick La. Sth. W4 . . . . .6B 98
Chiswick Lifeboat Station 7B 98
Chiswick Mall W4 . . . . .6B 98
   W6 . . . . .5C 98
Chiswick Pk. W4 . . . . .4H 97
Chiswick Plaza W4 . . . . .6J 97
Chiswick Quay W4 . . . . .1J 115
Chiswick Rd. N9 . . . . .2B 34
   W4 . . . . .4J 97

CHISWICK RDBT. 5G 97
Chiswick Sq. W4 . . . . .6A 98
Chiswick Staithe W4 . . . . .1J 115
Chiswick Ter. W4 . . . . .4J 97
   (off Chiswick High Rd.)
Chiswick Village W4 . . . . .6G 97
Chiswick Wharf W4 . . . . .6B 98
Chitterfield Ga. UB7: Sip 7C 92
Chitty's La. RM8: Dag 2D 72
Chitty St. W1 . . . . .5B 6 (5G 83)
Chivalry Rd. SW11 . . . . .5C 118
Chivelston SW19 . . . . .1F 135
Chivenor Gro. KT2: King T 5D 132
Chivers Rd. E4 . . . . .3J 35
Choats Mnr. Way RM9: Dag 2E 90
Choats Rd. IG11: Bark 2C 90
   RM9: Dag 2C 90
Chobham Gdns. SW19 . . . . .2F 135
Chobham Rd. E15 . . . . .5F 69
Chocolate Factory 1, The 2K 47
   (off Clarendon Rd.)
Chocolate Factory 2, The 2K 47
   (off Coburg Rd.)
Chocolate Studios N1 . . . . .1E 8
   (off Shepherdess Pl.)
Choice Vw. IG1: Ilf 2G 71
   (off Axon Pl.)
Cholmeley Cl. N6 . . . . .7F 47
Cholmeley Cres. N6 . . . . .7F 47
Cholmeley Lodge N6 . . . . .1F 65
Cholmeley Pk. N6 . . . . .1F 65
Cholmley Gdns. NW6 . . . . .5J 63
Cholmley Rd. KT7: T Ditt 6B 150
Cholmley Ter. KT7: T Ditt 7B 150
   (off Portsmouth Rd.)
Cholmley Vs. KT7: T Ditt 6B 150
   (off Portsmouth Rd.)
Cholmondeley Av. NW10 . . . . .2C 80
Cholmondeley Wlk. TW9: Rich 5C 114
Choppin's Ct. E1 . . . . .1H 103
Chopwell Cl. E15 . . . . .7F 69
Chorleywood Cres. BR5: St P 2K 161
Choudhury Mans. N1 . . . . .7J 65
   (off Pembroke St.)
Choumert Gro. SE15 . . . . .2G 121
Choumert M. SE15 . . . . .2G 121
Choumert Rd. SE15 . . . . .3F 121
Choumert Sq. SE15 . . . . .2G 121
Chow Sq. E8 . . . . .5F 67
Chrisp Ho. SE10 . . . . .6G 105
   (off Maze Hill)
Chrisp St. E14 . . . . .5D 86
   (not continuous)
Chrisp St. E14 . . . . .6D 86
Christabel Cl. TW7: Isle 3J 113
Christabel Pankhurst Ct. SE5 . . . . . .7D 102
   (off Brisbane St.)
Christchurch Av. DA8: Erith 6K 109
   HA0: Wemb 6E 60
   HA3: Kenton, W'stone 4K 41
   N12 . . . . .6F 31
   NW6 . . . . .1F 81
   TW11: Tedd 5A 132
Christchurch Cl. EN2: Enf 2H 23
   N12 . . . . .7G 31
   SW19 . . . . .7B 136
Christ Church Ct. NW10 . . . . .1A 80
Christchurch Ct. EC4 . . . . .7B 8
   (off Warwick La.)
   NW6 . . . . .7G 63
   (off Willesden La.)
   UB4: Yead 4A 76
   (off Dunedin Way)
Christchurch Flats TW9: Rich 3E 114
Christchurch Gdns. HA3: W'stone . . .4A 42
Christchurch Grn. HA0: Wemb 6E 60
Christchurch Hill NW3 . . . . .3B 64
Christchurch Ho. RM8: Dag 5B 72
   SW2 . . . . .1K 137
   (off Christchurch Rd.)
Christchurch La. EN5: Barn 2B 20

Christchurch Lodge EN4: Cockf 4J 21
Christchurch Pk. SM2: Sutt 7A 166
Christchurch Pas. EN5: Barn 2B 20
   NW3 . . . . .3A 64
Christchurch Path UB3: Harl 3E 92
Christchurch Pl. SW8 . . . . .2H 119
Christ Chu. Rd. BR3: Beck 2C 158
   KT5: Surb 6F 151
Christchurch Rd. DA15: Sidc 4K 143
   IG1: Ilf 1F 71
   N8 . . . . .6J 47
   SW2 . . . . .1K 137
   SW14 . . . . .5H 115
   SW19 . . . . .7B 136
   TW6: H'row A 3C 110
Christchurch Sq. E9 . . . . .1J 85
Christchurch St. SW3 . . . . . . .7E 16 (6D 100)
Christchurch Ter. SW3 . . . . .7E 16
Christchurch Way SE10 . . . . .5G 105
Christian Ct. SE16 . . . . .1B 104
Christian Flds. SW16 . . . . .7A 138
Christian Pl. E1 . . . . .6G 85
   (off Burslem St.)
Christian St. E1 . . . . .6G 85
Christie Ct. N19 . . . . .2J 65
Christie Dr. CR0: C'don 5G 157
Christie Gdns. RM6: Chad H 6B 54
Christie Ho. E16 . . . . .5J 87
   (off Hammersley Rd.)
   SE10 . . . . .5H 105
   (off Blackwall La.)
   W12 . . . . .6D 80
   (off Du Cane Rd.)
Christie Rd. E9 . . . . .6A 68
Christina Sq. N4 . . . . .1B 66
Christina St. EC2 . . . . .3G 9 (4E 84)
Christine Worsley Cl. N21 . . . . .1G 33
Christopher Av. W7 . . . . .3A 96
Christopher Bell Twr. E3 . . . . .2C 86
   (off Pancras Way)
Christopher Cl. DA15: Sidc 5K 125
   SE16 . . . . .2K 103
Christopher Ct. E1 . . . . .6G 85
   (off Leman St.)
   TW15: Ashf 5A 128
Christopher Gdns. RM9: Dag 5D 72
Christopher Ho. DA15: Sidc 2A 144
   (off Station Rd.)
Christopher Pl. N22 . . . . .7D 32
   (off Myddleton Rd.)
   NW1 . . . . .1D 6 (3H 83)
Christophers M. W11 . . . . .1G 99
Christopher Rd. UB2: S'hall 4K 93
Christophers St. EC2 . . . . . . .4F 9 (4D 84)
Chroma Mans. E20 . . . . .6E 68
   (off Penny Brookes St.)
Chryssell Rd. SW9 . . . . .7A 102
Chubworthy St. SE14 . . . . .6A 104
Chudleigh DA14: Sidc 4B 144
Chudleigh Cres. IG3: Ilf 4J 71
Chudleigh Gdns. SM1: Sutt 3A 166
Chudleigh Rd. NW6 . . . . .7F 63
   SE4 . . . . .5B 122
   TW2: Twick 6J 113
Chudleigh St. E1 . . . . .6K 85
Chudleigh Way HA4: Ruis 1J 57
Chulsa Rd. SE26 . . . . .5H 139
Chumleigh Gdns. SE5 . . . . .6E 102
   (off Chumleigh St.)
Chumleigh St. SE5 . . . . .6E 102
Chumleigh Wlk. KT5: Surb 4F 151
Church All. CR0: C'don 1A 168
Church App. SE21 . . . . .3D 138
Church Av. BR3: Beck 1C 158
   DA14: Sidc 5A 144
   E4 . . . . .6A 36
   (not continuous)
   HA4: Ruis 1F 57
   HA5: Pinn 6C 40
   NW1 . . . . .6F 65
   SW14 . . . . .3K 115

Church Av. UB2: S'hall 3C 94
  UB5: N'olt 7D 58
Churchbank E17 .4C 50
  (off Eastfield Rd.)
Churchbury Cl. EN1: Enf 2K 23
Churchbury La. EN1: Enf 3J 23
Churchbury Rd. EN1: Enf 2K 23
  SE9 . . . . .7B 124
Church Cloisters EC3 . . . . .3G 15
Church Cl. HA6: N'wood 1H 39
  HA8: Edg 5D 28
  N20 . . . . .3H 31
  TW3: Houn 2C 112
  UB4: Hayes 5F 75
  UB7: W Dray 3A 92
  W8 . . . . .2K 99
Church Ct. EC4 .6A 84
  SE16 . . . . .2B 104
  (off Rotherhithe St.)
  TW9: Rich 5D 114
Church Cres. E9 .7K 67
  N3 . . . . .1H 45
  N10 . . . . .4F 47
  N20 . . . . .3H 31
Churchcroft Cl. SW12 . . . . .7E 118
Churchdown BR1: Brom 4G 141
Church Dr. BR4: W W'ck 3G 171
  HA2: Harr 6E 40
  NW9 . . . . .1K 61
Church Elm La. RM10: Dag 6G 73
CHURCH END .1H 45
  . . . . .7A 62
Church End E17 .4D 50
  NW4 . . . . .3D 44
Church Entry EC4 . . . . .1B 14
Church Est. Almshouses TW9: Rich . . .4F 115
  (off Sheen Rd.)
Church Farm La. SM3: Cheam 6G 165
Church Farm Pool 7J 21
Churchfield Av. N12 . . . . .6G 31
Churchfield Cl. HA2: Harr 4G 41
  UB3: Hayes 7H 75
Churchfield Ho. W2 . . . . .4A 4
  (off Hall Pl.)
Churchfield Mans. SW6 . . . . .2H 117
  (off New Kings Rd.)
Churchfield Pl. TW17: Shep 7D 146
Churchfield Rd. DA16: Well 3A 126
  KT12: Walt T 7J 147
  W3 . . . . .1J 97
  W7 . . . . .2J 95
  W13 . . . . .1B 96
Churchfields E18 . . . . .1J 51
  KT8: W Mole 3E 148
  SE10 . . . . .6E 104
Churchfields Av. TW13: Hanw 3D 130
Churchfields Rd. BR3: Beck 2K 157
Churchfield Way N12 . . . . .6F 31
Church Gdns. HA0: Wemb 4A 60
  W5 . . . . .2D 96
Church Gth. N19 . . . . .2H 65
  (off St John's Gro.)
Church Ga. SW6 . . . . .3G 117
Church Grn. SW9 . . . . .1A 120
  UB3: Hayes 6H 75
Church Gro. KT1: Hamp W 1C 150
  SE13 . . . . .5D 122
Church Hill DA1: Cray 4K 127
  E17 . . . . .4C 50
  HA1: Harr 1J 59
  N21 . . . . .7E 22
  SE18 . . . . .3D 106
  SM5: Cars 5D 166
  SW19 . . . . .5H 135
Church Hill Rd. E17 . . . . .4D 50
  EN4: E Barn 6H 21
  KT6: Surb 5E 150
  SM3: Cheam 3F 165
Church Hill Wood BR5: St M Cry 5K 161
Church Ho. EC1 .3B 8
  (off Compton St.)

Church Ho. SW1 . . . . .1D 18
  (off Gt. Smith St.)
Church Hyde SE18 . . . . .6J 107
Churchill Av. HA3: Kenton 6B 42
  UB10: Hil 3D 74
Churchill Cl. TW14: Felt 1H 129
  UB10: Hil 3D 74
Churchill Ct. BR6: Farnb 5G 173
  HA2: Harr 2F 59
  (Eastcote La.)
  HA2: Harr 5F 41
  (Montrose Ct.)
  HA5: Hat E 1C 40
  N4 . . . . .7A 48
  N9 . . . . .1K 33
  SE18 . . . . .4D 106
  UB5: N'olt 5E 58
  (off Newmarket Av.)
  W5 . . . . .4F 79
Churchill Gdns. SW1 . . . . .6A 18
  (not continuous)
  W3 . . . . .6G 79
Churchill Gdns. Rd. SW1 . . . .6K 17 (5F 101)
Churchill Lodge IG6: Ilf 4G 53
Churchill Pl. E14 . . . . .1D 104
  HA1: Harr 4J 41
  NW7 . . . . .6G 29
Churchill Rd. CR2: S Croy 7C 168
  E16 . . . . .6A 88
  HA8: Edg 6A 28
  NW2 . . . . .6D 62
  NW5 . . . . .4F 65
Churchills M. IG8: Wfd G 6C 36
Churchill Ter. E4 . . . . .4H 35
Churchill Theatre 2J 159
Churchill Wlk. E9 . . . . .5J 67
Churchill War Rooms 6D 12 (2H 101)
Churchill Way BR1: Brom 2J 159
  TW16: Sun 5J 129
Churchlands Way KT4: Wor Pk 2F 165
Church La. BR2: Brom 1C 172
  BR7: Chst 1G 161
  E11 . . . . .1G 69
  E17 . . . . .4D 50
  EN1: Enf 3J 23
  HA3: W'stone 1K 41
  HA5: Pinn 3C 40
  KT7: T Ditt 6K 149
  KT9: Chess 6F 163
  N2 . . . . .3B 46
  N8 . . . . .4K 47
  N9 . . . . .2B 34
  N17 . . . . .1E 48
  NW9 . . . . .6J 43
  RM10: Dag 7J 73
  SM6: Bedd 3H 167
  (not continuous)
  SW17 . . . . .5D 136
  SW19 . . . . .1H 153
  TW1: Twick 1A 132
  TW10: Ham 1E 132
  TW11: Tedd 5K 131
  W5 . . . . .2C 96
Churchley Rd. SE26 . . . . .4H 139
Church Manorway DA8: Erith 4K 109
  DA17: Belv 2J 109
  SE2 . . . . .5A 108
Church Mead SE5 . . . . .7C 102
  (off Camberwell Rd.)
Churchmead Cl. EN4: E Barn 6H 21
Church Mdw. KT6: Surb 2C 162
Churchmead Rd. NW10 . . . . .6C 62
Churchmore Rd. SW16 . . . . .1G 155
Church Mt. N2 . . . . .5B 46
Church Paddock Ct. SM6: Bedd 3H 167
Church Pde. TW15: Ashf 4B 128
Church Pas. EC2 . . . . .7D 8
  (off Gresham St.)
  EN5: Barn 3B 20
  KT6: Surb 5E 150
  TW1: Twick 1B 132

Church Path CR0: C'don 2C 168
  CR4: Mitc 3C 154
  (not continuous)
  E11 . . . . .5J 51
  E17 . . . . .4D 50
  N5 . . . . .5B 66
  N8 . . . . .5K 47
  (off Tottenham La.)
  N12 . . . . .3F 31
  (Woodside La.)
  N12 . . . . .4F 31
  (Woodside Pk. Rd.)
  N17 . . . . .7K 33
  N10 . . . . .7A 62
  SW14 . . . . .3K 115
  (not continuous)
  SW19 . . . . .2H 153
  UB1: S'hall 1E 94
  UB2: S'hall 3D 94
  (not continuous)
  W3 . . . . .2J 97
  (not continuous)
  W4 . . . . .3J 97
Church Pl. CR4: Mitc 3C 154
  SW1 . . . . .3B 12 (7G 83)
  UB10: Ick 3E 56
  W5 . . . . .2D 96
Church Ri. KT9: Chess 6F 163
  SE23 . . . . .2K 139
Church Rd. BR2: Brom 2J 159
  (Edison Rd.)
  BR2: Brom 3G 159
  (Hazelwood Ho's.)
  BR2: Kes 7B 172
  BR6: Farnb 5G 173
  CR0: C'don 3C 168
  CR4: Mitc 1B 154
  DA7: Bex 2F 127
  DA8: Erith 5K 109
  DA14: Sidc 4A 144
  DA16: Well 2B 126
  E10 . . . . .1C 68
  E12 . . . . .5C 70
  E17 . . . . .2A 50
  EN3: Pond E 6D 24
  HA6: N'wood 1H 39
  HA7: Stan 5G 27
  IG2: Ilf .6J 53
  IG9: Buck H 1E 36
  IG11: Bark 6G 71
  KT1: King T 2F 151
  KT4: Wor Pk 1A 164
  KT6: Surb 1C 162
  KT8: E Mos 4H 149
  KT10: Clay 7A 162
  KT19: Ewe 7K 163
  N1 . . . . .1C 66
  N6 . . . . .6E 46
  N17 . . . . .1E 48
  (not continuous)
  NW4 . . . . .4D 44
  NW10 . . . . .7A 62
  SE19 . . . . .1E 156
  SM3: Cheam 6G 165
  SM6: Bedd 3H 167
  SW13 . . . . .2B 116
  SW19 . . . . .5G 135
  (Courthorpe Rd.)
  SW19 . . . . .1B 154
  (Reynolds Cl.)
  TW5: Cran 5K 93
  TW5: Hest 7E 94
  TW7: Isle 1H 113
  TW9: Rich 4E 114
  TW10: Ham 4D 132
  TW10: Rich 5E 114
  TW11: Tedd 4J 131
  TW13: Hanw 5B 130
  TW15: Ashf 3B 128
  TW17: Shep 7D 146

Church Rd. UB2: S'hall 3D 94
  UB3: Hayes 1H 93
  UB5: N'olt 2B 76
  UB7: W Dray 3A 92
  UB8: Cowl 4A 74
  W3 . . . . .1J 97
  W7 . . . . .7H 77
Church Rd. Almshouses E10 . . . . .2D 68
  (off Church Rd.)
Church Rd. Ind. Est. E10 . . . . .1C 68
Church Rd. Row BR7: Chst 1G 161
  NW3 . . . . .4A 64
  SW6 . . . . .7K 99
  (off Moore Pk. Rd.)
Church Row M. BR7: Chst 7G 143
Church Sq. TW17: Shep 7D 146
Church St. CR0: C'don 3B 168
  E15 . . . . .1G 87
  E16 . . . . .1F 107
  EN2: Enf 3H 23
  KT1: King T 2D 150
  KT12: Walt T 7J 147
  KT17: Ewe 7C 164
  N9 . . . . .2B 34
  NW8 . . . . .5B 4 (5B 82)
  (not continuous)
  RM10: Dag 6H 73
  SM1: Sutt 5K 165
  TW1: Twick 1A 132
  TW7: Isle 3B 114
  TW12: Hamp 1G 149
  TW16: Sun 3K 147
  W2 . . . . .5B 4 (5B 82)
  (not continuous)
  W4 . . . . .6B 98
Church St. Est. NW8 . . . . .4B 4 (4B 82)
Church St. Nth. E15 . . . . .1G 87
Church St. Pas. E15 . . . . .1G 87
  (off Church St.)
Church Stretton Rd. TW3: Houn 5G 113
Church Ter. NW4 . . . . .3D 44
  SE13 . . . . .3G 123
  TW10: Rich 5D 114
Church Va. N2 . . . . .3D 46
  SE23 . . . . .2K 139
Church Vw. TW10: Rich 5E 114
Church Vw. Gro. SE26 . . . . .6K 139
Churchview Rd.
  TW2: Twick 1H 131
Church Wlk. EN2: Enf 3J 23
  KT7: T Ditt 6K 149
  KT12: Walt T 7J 147
  (not continuous)
  N6 . . . . .3E 64
  N16 . . . . .3D 66
  (not continuous)
  NW2 . . . . .3H 63
  NW4 . . . . .3E 44
  NW9 . . . . .2K 61
  SW13 . . . . .1C 116
  SW15 . . . . .5D 116
  SW16 . . . . .2G 155
  SW20 . . . . .3E 152
  TW8: Bford 6C 96
  (not continuous)
  TW9: Rich 5D 114
  UB3: Hayes 6G 75
Churchward Ho. SE17 . . . . .6B 102
  (off Lorrimore Sq.)
  W14 . . . . .5H 99
  (off Ivatt Pl.)
Church Way EN4: Cockf 4J 21
  HA8: Edg 6B 28
  N20 . . . . .3H 31
Churchway NW1 . . . . .1D 6 (3H 83)
Churchwell Path E9 . . . . .5J 67
Churchwood Gdns. IG8: Wfd G 4D 36
  SE23 . . . . .7J 121
Churchyard Pas. SE5 . . . . .2D 120
Churchyard Row SE11 . . . . .4B 102

Church Yd. Wlk. *W2* *5A 4*
    (off St Mary's Sq.)
Churston Av. E13 . . . . .1K **87**
Churston Cl. SW2 . . . . .1A **138**
Churston Dr. SM4: Mord 5F **153**
Churston Gdns. N11 . . . . .6B **32**
Churston Mans. *WC1* *4H 7*
    (off Gray's Inn Rd.)
Churton Pl. SW1 . . . . .4B 18 (4G **101**)
Churton St. SW1 . . . . .4B 18 (4G **101**)
Chusan Pl. E14 .6B **86**
Chute Ho. *SW9* *2A 120*
    (off Stockwell Pk. Rd.)
Chuter Ede Ho. *SW6* *6H 99*
    (off Clem Attlee Ct.)
Chyngton Cl. DA15: Sidc 3K **143**
Cibber Rd. SE23 . . . . .2K **139**
Cicada Rd. SW18 . . . . .6A **118**
Cicely Ho. *NW8* *2B 82*
    (off Cochrane St.)
Cicely Rd. SE15 . . . . .1G **121**
Cinderella Path NW11 . . . . .1K **63**
Cinderford Way BR1: Brom 4G **141**
Cine Lumiere *3A 16*
    (off Queensberry Pl.)
Cineworld Cinema
  Bexleyheath 4H **127**
  Chelsea, Fulham Rd. 5A **100**
  Chelsea, King's Rd. 6B **100**
  Enfield 4B **24**
  Feltham 2K **129**
  Hammersmith 4D **98**
  Haymarket *3C 12*
    (off Haymarket)
  Ilford *3F 71*
    (off Clements Rd.)
  Shaftesbury Av. *3C 12*
    (off Shaftesbury Av.)
  Staples Corner 1D **62**
  The O2 . . . . .1G **105**
    (within The O2)
  Wandsworth 5K **117**
  Wembley .4G **61**
  West India Quay 7C **86**
  Wood Green 2A **48**
    (within Wood Green Shop. City)
Cinnabar Wharf Central *E1* *1G 103*
    (off Wapping High St.)
Cinnabar Wharf E. *E1* *1G 103*
    (off Wapping High St.)
Cinnabar Wharf W. *E1* *1G 103*
    (off Wapping High St.)
Cinnamon Cl. CR0: C'don 7J **155**
  SE15 . . . . .7F **103**
Cinnamon M. N13 . . . . .2F **33**
Cinnamon Row SW11 . . . . .3A **118**
Cinnamon St. E1 . . . . .1H **103**
Cinnamon Wharf *SE1* *6K 15*
    (off Shad Thames)
Cintra Pk. SE19 . . . . .7F **139**
Cipher Cl. NW2 . . . . .3C **62**
Circa Apartments NW1 . . . . .7E **64**
Circle, The NW2 . . . . .3A **62**
  NW7 . . . . .6E **28**
  SE1 . . . .*6J 15*
    (off Queen Elizabeth St.)
Circle Gdns. SW19 . . . . .2J **153**
Circuits, The HA5: Pinn 4A **40**
Circular Rd. N17 . . . . .3F **49**
Circular Way SE18 . . . . .6D **106**
Circus Lodge NW8 . . . . .1A **4**
Circus M. W1 . . . . .5E **4**
Circus Pl. EC2 . . . . .6F **9** (5D **84**)
Circus Rd. NW8 . . . . .1A **4** (3B **82**)
Circus St. SE10 . . . . .7E **104**
Cirencester St. W2 . . . . .5K **81**
Cirrus Apartments *E1* *3K 9*
    (off Bacon St.)
Cirrus Cl. SM6: Wall 7J **167**
Cissbury Ho. SE26 . . . . .3G **139**
Cissbury Ring Nth. N12 . . . . .5C **30**

Cissbury Ring Sth. N12 . . . . .5C **30**
Cissbury Rd. N15 . . . . .5D **48**
Citadel Pl. SE11 . . . . . . .5G **19** (5K **101**)
Citius Apartments *E3* *2C 86*
    (off Tredegar La.)
Citius Ct. E4 . . . . .6K **35**
Citius Wlk. E20 . . . . .6E **68**
Citizen Ho. N7 .4A **66**
Citizen Rd. N7 .4A **66**
Citrine Apartments *E3* *1A 86*
    (off Gunmaker's La.)
Citrus Ho. SE8 . . . . .5B **104**
    (off Alverton St.)
City Apartments *E1* *7K 9*
    (off White Church La.)
City Bus. Cen. SE16 . . . . .3J **103**
City Ct. CR0: C'don 7B **156**
City Cross Bus. Pk. SE10 . . . . .4G **105**
City East Bldg. *E1* *7H 85*
    (off Cable St.)
City Forum EC1 . . . . .1C **8** (3C **84**)
City Gdn. Row N1 . . . . .1C **8** (2B **84**)
City Gate Ho. IG2: Ilf 6E **52**
    (off Eastern Av.)
City Gateway *E1* *7G 85*
    (off Ensign St.)
City Hall 5H **15** (1E **102**)
City Harbour *E14* *3D 104*
    (off Selsdon Way)
City Hgts. *E8* *1F 85*
    (off Kingsland Rd.)
City Ho. BR2: Brom 6C **160**
City Lights Ct. *SE11* *5K 19*
    (off Bowden St.)
City Mill Apartments *E8* *1F 85*
    (off Lovelace St.)
City Mill River Path E15 . . . . .1E **86**
CITY OF LONDON 1E **14** (6D **84**)
City of London Almshouses
  SW9 . . . . .4K **119**
City of London Crematorium E12 . . . .3C **70**
City of London Distillery 6B **84**
City of London Point *N7* *6H 65*
    (off York Way)
City of London Police Mus. 6C **84**
City of Westminster College
  Paddington Green Campus 5A **4**
City Pavilion, The
  Marks Gate 2F **55**
City Pav. *EC1* *5A 8*
    (off Britton St.)
City Pl. Ho. *EC2* *6D 8*
    (off Basinghall St.)
Citypoint EC2 . . . . .5E **8**
City Pride Development E14 . . . . .1C **104**
City Rd. EC1 . . . . .1A **8** (2B **84**)
City Tower *EC2* *6E 8*
    (off Basinghall St.)
City University London
  Goswell Pl. 3B **84**
  Northampton Square Campus
    . . . . .2A **8** (3B **84**)
City University London
  Saddlers Sports Centre, The
    . . . . .3B **8** (4B **84**)
City Vw. IG1: Ilf 2G **71**
    (off Axon Pl.)
Cityview SE7 . . . . .6A **106**
City Vw. Apartments *N1* *7C 66*
    (off Essex Rd.)
City Vw. Ct. SE22 . . . . .7G **121**
City Wlk. SE1 . . . . .7G **15** (2E **102**)
City Wlk. Apartments *EC1* *2C 8*
    (off Seward St.)
City Wharf Ho. KT7: T Ditt 6B **150**
Civic Way HA4: Ruis 5B **58**
  IG6: Ilf 4G **53**
Civil and Family Courts
  Barnet 1J **45**
Civil Justice Cen.
  Central London 4J **5**

Clabon M. SW1 . . . . .2E **16** (3D **100**)
Clack La. HA4: Ruis 1E **56**
Clack St. SE16 . . . . .2J **103**
Clacton Rd. E6 . . . . .3B **88**
  E17 . . . . .6A **50**
  N17 . . . . .2F **49**
Claigmar Gdns. N3 . . . . .1K **45**
Claire Ct. HA5: Hat E 1D **40**
  N12 . . . . .3F **31**
  NW2 . . . . .6G **63**
  WD23: B Hea 1C **26**
Claire Gdns. HA7: Stan 5H **27**
Claire Ho. IG1: Ilf 4F **71**
Claire Pl. E14 .3C **104**
Clairvale Rd. TW5: Hest 1B **112**
Clairview Rd. SW16 . . . . .5F **137**
Clairville Gdns. W7 . . . . .1J **95**
Clairville Point SE23 . . . . .3K **139**
    (off Dacres Rd.)
Clamp Hill HA7: Stan 4C **26**
Clancarty Rd. SW6 . . . . .2J **117**
Clandon Cl. KT17: Ewe 6B **164**
  W3 . . . . .2H **97**
Clandon Gdns. N3 . . . . .3J **45**
Clandon Ho. SE1 . . . . .7B **14**
    (off Webber St.)
Clandon Rd. IG3: Ilf 2J **71**
Clandon St. SE8 . . . . .2C **122**
Clandon Ter. SW20 . . . . .2F **153**
Clanricarde Gdns. W2 . . . . .7J **81**
CLAPHAM 4H **119**
CLAPHAM COMMON 4H **119**
Clapham Comn. Nth. Side SW4 . . . . .4D **118**
Clapham Comn. Sth. Side SW4 . . . . .6F **119**
Clapham Comn. W. Side SW4 . . . . . .4D **118**
    (not continuous)
Clapham Cres. SW4 . . . . .4H **119**
Clapham High St. SW4 . . . . .4H **119**
CLAPHAM JUNCTION 3C **118**
Clapham Leisure Cen. 3H **119**
Clapham Mnr. Ct. SW4 . . . . .3G **119**
Clapham Mnr. St. SW4 . . . . .3G **119**
CLAPHAM PARK 7H **119**
Clapham Pk. Est. SW4 . . . . .6H **119**
Clapham Pk. Rd. SW4 . . . . .4G **119**
Clapham Pk. Ter. SW2 . . . . .5J **119**
    (off Lyham Rd.)
Clapham Picturehouse 4G **119**
Clapham Rd. SW9 . . . . .3J **119**
Clapham Rd. Est. SW4 . . . . .3J **119**
Clap La. RM10: Dag, Rush G 2H **73**
Clapps Ga. La. E6 . . . . .4E **88**
Clapton Comn. E5 . . . . .7F **49**
    (not continuous)
CLAPTON PARK 4K **67**
Clapton Pk. Est. E5 . . . . .4K **67**
Clapton Pas. E5 . . . . .5J **67**
Clapton Sq. E5 . . . . .5J **67**
Clapton Ter. E5 . . . . .1G **67**
Clapton Way E5 . . . . .4G **67**
Clara Grant Ho. *E14* *3C 104*
    (off Mellish St.)
Clara Nehab Ho. *NW11* *5H 45*
    (off Leeside Cres.)
Clara Pl. SE18 . . . . .4E **106**
Clare Cl. N2 . . . . .3A **46**
Clare Ct. *W11* *7G 81*
    (off Clarendon Rd.)
  WC1 . . . .*2F 7*
    (off Judd St.)
Claredale Ho. *E2* *2H 85*
    (off Claredale St.)
Claredale St. E2 . . . . .2G **85**
Clare Gdns. E7 . . . . .4J **69**
  IG11: Bark 6K **71**
  W11 . . . . .6G **81**
Clare Ho.
  E3 . . . . .1B **86**
  E16 . . . . .7E **88**
    (off University Way)

Clare Ho. *HA8: Edg* *2J 43*
    (off Burnt Oak B'way.)
  SE1 . . . .*5F 103*
    (off Cooper's Rd.)
Clare La. N1 . . . . .7C **66**
Clare Lawn Av. SW14 . . . . .5K **115**
Clare Mkt. WC2 . . . . .1H **13** (6K **83**)
Clare M. SW6 .7K **99**
Claremont *TW17: Shep* *6D 146*
    (off Laleham Rd.)
Claremont Av. HA3: Kenton 5E **42**
  KT3: N Mald 5C **152**
  TW16: Sun 1K **147**
Claremont Cl. BR6: Farnb 4E **172**
  E16 . . . . .1E **106**
  N1 . . . . .1K **7** (2A **84**)
  SW2 . . . . .1J **137**
Claremont Ct. *E2* *2H 85*
  (off Cambridge Heath Rd., Cambridge Heath
    Rd.)
  E2 . . . .*2G 85*
    (off Claredale St., Claredale St.)
  W2 . . . .*6K 81*
    (off Queensway)
  W9 . . . .*2H 81*
    (off Claremont Rd.)
Claremont Dr. TW17: Shep 6D **146**
Claremont Gdns. IG3: Ilf 2J **71**
  KT6: Surb 5E **150**
Claremont Gro. IG8: Wfd G 6F **37**
  W4 . . . . .7A **98**
Claremont Ho. SM2: Sutt 7K **165**
Claremont Pk. N3 . . . . .1G **45**
Claremont Pl. KT10: Clay 6A **162**
Claremont Rd. BR1: Brom 4C **160**
  CR0: C'don 1G **169**
  E7 . . . . .5K **69**
  E11 . . . . .3F **69**
  E17 . . . . .2A **50**
  HA3: W'stone 2J **41**
  KT6: Surb 5E **150**
  N6 . . . . .7G **47**
  NW2 . . . . .7F **45**
  TW1: Twick 6B **114**
  TW11: Tedd 5K **131**
  W9 . . . . .2G **81**
  W13 . . . . .5A **78**
Claremont Sq. N1 . . . . .1J **7** (2A **84**)
Claremont St. E16 . . . . .2E **106**
  N18 . . . . .6B **34**
  SE10 . . . . .6D **104**
Claremont Ter. KT7: T Ditt 7B **150**
Claremont Vs. *SE5* *7D 102*
    (off Southampton Way)
Claremont Way NW2 . . . . .1F **62**
    (not continuous)
Claremont Way Ind. Est. NW2 . . . . . .1E **62**
Clarence Av. BR1: Brom 4C **160**
  IG2: Ilf 6E **52**
  KT3: N Mald 2J **151**
  SW4 . . . . .7H **119**
Clarence Cl. EN4: E Barn 5G **21**
  WD23: B Hea 1E **26**
Clarence Ct. NW7 . . . . .5F **29**
  W6 . . . .*4D 98*
    (off Cambridge Gro.)
Clarence Cres. DA14: Sidc 3B **144**
  SW4 . . . . .6H **119**
Clarence Gdns. NW1 . . . . . . .2K **5** (3F **83**)
Clarence Ga. IG8: Ilf, Wfd G 6K **37**
Clarence Ga. Gdns. *NW1* *4F 5*
    (off Glentworth St.)
Clarence House 6B **12**
Clarence Ho. *SE17* *6D 102*
    (off Merrow St.)
Clarence La. SW15 . . . . .6A **116**
Clarence M. E5 . . . . .5H **67**
  SE16 . . . . .1K **103**
  SW12 . . . . .7F **119**
Clarence Pk. Cres. HA7: Stan 3D **26**

Clarence Pl. E5 . . . . .5H 67
Clarence Rd. BR1: Brom 3B 160
  CR0: C'don 7D 156
  DA6: Bex 4E 126
  DA14: Sidc 3B 144
  E5 . . . . .4H 67
  E12 . . . . .4A 70
  E16 . . . . .4G 87
  E17 . . . . .2K 49
  EN3: Pond E 5C 24
  N15 . . . . .5C 48
  N22 . . . . .7D 32
  NW6 . . . . .7H 63
  SE8 . . . . .6D 104
  SE9 . . . . .2D 142
  SM1: Sutt 5K 165
  SM6: Wall 5F 167
  SW19 .6K 135
  TW9: Kew 1F 115
  TW11: Tedd 6K 131
  W4 . . . . .5G 97
Clarence St. KT1: King T 2D 150
  TW9: Rich 4E 114
  UB2: S'hall 3B 94
Clarence Ter. NW1 . . . . . . .3F 5 (4D 82)
  W2 . . . . .4F 113
Clarence Wlk. SW4 . . . . .2J 119
Clarence Way NW1 . . . . .7F 65
Clarendon Pl. DA2: Wilm 5K 145
Clarendon Cl. BR5: St P 3K 161
  E9 . . . . .7J 67
  W2 . . . . .2C 10 (7C 82)
Clarendon Cl. BR3: Beck 1D 158
    (off Albemarle Rd.)
  NW2 . . . . .7E 62
  NW11 .4H 45
  TW5: Cran 1J 111
  TW9: Kew 1F 115
  W9 . . . . .3A 4
    (off Maida Vale)
Clarendon Cres. TW2: Twick 3H 131
Clarendon Cross W11 . . . . .7G 81
Clarendon Dr. SW15 . . . . .4E 116
Clarendon Flats W1 . . . . .1H 11
    (off Balderton St.)
Clarendon Gdns. HA9: Wemb 3D 60
  IG1: Ilf 7D 52
  NW4 . . . . .3C 44
  W9 . . . . .4A 82
Clarendon Grn. BR5: St P 4K 161
Clarendon Gro. CR4: Mitc 3D 154
  NW1 . . . . .1C 6 (3H 83)
Clarendon Ho. KT2: King T 1E 150
    (off Cowleaze Rd.)
  NW1 . . . . .1B 6
    (off Werrington St.)
  W2 . . . . .2C 10
    (off Strathearn Pl.)
Clarendon Lodge W11 . . . . .7G 81
    (off Clarendon Rd.)
Clarendon M. DA5: Bexl 1H 145
  W2 . . . . .2C 10 (7C 82)
Clarendon Path BR5: St P 4K 161
    (not continuous)
Clarendon Pl. W2 . . . . . . .2C 10 (7C 82)
Clarendon Ri. SE13 . . . . .4E 122
Clarendon Rd. CR0: C'don 2B 168
  E11 . . . . .1F 69
  E17 . . . . .6D 50
  E18 . . . . .3J 51
  HA1: Harr 6J 41
  N8 . . . . .3K 47
  N15 . . . . .4C 48
  N18 . . . . .6B 34
  N22 . . . . .2H 47
  SM6: Wall 6G 167
  SW19 .7C 136
  TW15: Ashf 4B 128
  UB3: Hayes 2H 93
  W5 . . . . .3E 78
  W11 . . . . .7G 81

Clarendon St. SW1 . . . . . . .5K 17 (5F 101)
Clarendon Ter. W9 . . . . .3A 4 4 (4A 82)
Clarendon Wlk. W11 . . . . .6G 81
Clarendon Way BR5: St P 3K 161
  BR7: Chst 3K 161
  N21 . . . . .1G 23
Clarens St. SE6 . . . . .2B 140
Clare Pl. SW15 . . . . .7B 116
Clare Point NW2 . . . . .1F 63
    (off Whitefield Av.)
Clare Rd. E11 . . . . .6F 51
  NW10 . . . . .7C 62
  SE14 . . . . .1B 122
  TW4: Houn 3D 112
  TW19: Stanw 1A 128
  UB6: G'frd 6H 59
Clare St. E2 . . . . .2H 85
Claret Gdns. SE25 . . . . .3E 156
Clareville Gro. SW7 . . . . .4A 16
    (off Clareville St.)
Clareville Gro. SW7 . . . . .4A 16 (4A 100)
Clareville Gro. M. SW7 . . . .4A 16 (4A 100)
Clareville Rd. BR5: Farnb 2G 173
Clareville St. SW7 . . . . . .4A 16 (4A 100)
Clare Way DA7: Bex 1E 126
Clarewood Ct. W1 . . . . .6E 4
    (off Seymour Pl.)
Clarewood Wlk. SW9 . . . . .4A 120
Clarges M. W1 . . . . .4J 11 (1F 101)
Clarges St. W1 . . . . .4K 11 (1F 101)
Claribel Rd. SW9 . . . . .2B 120
Clarice Way SM6: Wall 7J 167
Claridge Cl. SW6 . . . . .2H 117
Claridge Rd. RM8: Dag 1D 72
Clarinet Cl. HA8: Edg 7C 28
Clarion Ho. E3 . . . . .2A 86
    (off Roman Rd.)
  SW1 . . . . .5B 18
    (off Moreton Pl.)
  W1 . . . . .1C 12
    (off St Anne's Ct.)
Clarissa Ho. E14 . . . . .6D 86
    (off Cordela St.)
Clarissa Rd. RM6: Chad H 7D 54
Clarissa St. E8 . . . . .1F 85
Clarke Cl. CR0: C'don 6C 156
Clarke Mans. IG11: Bark 7K 71
    (off Upney La.)
Clarke M. N9 . . . . .3C 34
Clarke Path N16 . . . . .1G 67
Clarkes Av.
  KT4: Wor Pk 1F 165
Clarkes Dr. UB8: Hil 5A 74
Clarke's M. W1 . . . . .5H 5 (5E 82)
Clark Gro. IG3: Ilf 4J 71
Clark Ho. SW10 . . . . .7A 100
    (off Coleridge Gdns.)
Clarks Mead WD23: Bush 1B 26
Clarkson Rd. E16 . . . . .6H 87
Clarkson Row NW1 . . . . .2G 83
    (off Mornington Ter.)
Clarksons, The IG11: Bark 2G 89
Clarkson St. E2 . . . . .3H 85
Clarks Rd. IG1: Ilf 2H 71
Clark St. E1 . . . . .5H 85
    (not continuous)
Clark Way TW5: Hest 7B 94
Clarnico Rd. E20 . . . . .6C 68
Clarson Ho. SE5 . . . . .7B 102
    (off Midnight Av.)
  SE8 . . . . .6A 104
Classic Mans. E9 . . . . .7H 67
    (off Wells St.)
Classon Cl. UB7: W Dray 2A 92
Claude Rd. E10 . . . . .2E 68
  E13 . . . . .1K 87
  SE15 . . . . .2H 121
Claude St. E14 . . . . .4C 104
Claudia Jones Ho. N17 . . . . .1C 48
Claudia Jones Way SW2 . . . . .6J 119
Claudia Pl. SW19 . . . . .1G 135

Claudius Cl. HA7: Stan 3J 27
Claughton Rd. E13 . . . . .2A 88
Clauson Av. UB5: N'olt 5F 59
Clavell St. SE10 . . . . .6E 104
Claverdale Rd. SW2 . . . . .7K 119
Clavering Av. SW13 . . . . .6D 98
Clavering Cl. TW1: Twick 4A 132
Clavering Ho. SE13 . . . . .4F 123
    (off Blessington Rd.)
Clavering Pl. SW12 . . . . .6E 118
Clavering Rd. E12 . . . . .1B 70
Claverings Ind. Est. N9 . . . . .2D 34
    (off Centre Way)
Claverley Gro. N3 . . . . .1K 45
Claverley Vs. N3 . . . . .7E 30
Claverton St. SW1 . . . . . .6B 18 (5G 101)
Clave St. E1 . . . . .1J 103
Claxton Gro. W6 . . . . .5F 99
Claxton Path SE4 . . . . .4K 121
    (off Coston Wlk.)
Clay Av. CR4: Mitc 2F 155
Claybank Gro. SE13 . . . . .3D 122
Claybourne M. SE19 . . . . .7E 138
Claybridge Rd. SE12 . . . . .4A 142
Claybrook Cl. N2 . . . . .3B 46
Claybrook Rd. W6 . . . . .6F 99
Claybury WD23: Bush 1A 26
Claybury B'way. IG5: Ilf 3C 52
Claybury Hall IG8: Wfd G 7J 37
Claybury Rd. IG8: Wfd G 7H 37
Clay Ct. E17 . . . . .3F 51
  SE1 . . . . .7G 15
    (off Long La.)
Claydon Dr. CR0: Bedd 4J 167
Claydon Ho. NW4 . . . . .2F 45
    (off Holders Hill Rd.)
Claydown M. SE18 . . . . .5E 106
Clayfarm Rd. SE9 . . . . .2G 143
CLAYGATE .7A 162
Claygate Common (Local Nature Reserve)
  . . . . .7A 162
Claygate Cres. CR0: New Ad 6E 170
Claygate La. KT7: T Ditt 1A 162
  KT10: Clay, Hin W 2A 162
Claygate Rd. W13 . . . . .3B 96
CLAYHALL .3C 52
Clayhall Av. IG5: Ilf 3C 52
Clayhall Ct. E3 . . . . .2B 86
    (off St Stephen's Rd.)
Clay Hill EN2: Enf 1K 23
Clayhill KT5: Surb 5G 151
Clayhill Cres. SE9 . . . . .4B 142
Claylands Pl. SW8 . . . . .7A 102
Claylands Rd. SW8 . . . . . . .7H 19 (6K 101)
Clay La. HA3: Kenton 4D 42
  HA8: Edg 2B 28
  TW19: Stanw 7B 110
  WD23: B Hea 1D 26
Claymill Ho. SE18 . . . . .5G 107
Claymore Cl. SM4: Mord 7J 153
Clay Path E17 . . . . .2C 50
Claypole Ct. E17 . . . . .5C 50
    (off Yunus Khan Cl.)
Claypole Dr. TW5: Hest 1C 112
Claypole Rd. E15 . . . . .2E 86
Claypools Av. TW8: Bford 4D 96
Claypools Gdns. W5 . . . . .4D 96
    (not continuous)
Claypools La. TW8: Bford 5E 96
    (not continuous)
Clay St. W1 . . . . .6F 5 (5D 82)
Clayton Av. HA0: Wemb 7E 60
Clayton Bus. Cen. UB3: Hayes 2G 93
Clayton Cl. E6 . . . . .6D 88
Clayton Cres. N1 . . . . .1J 83
  TW8: Bford 5D 96
Clayton Dr. SE8 . . . . .5A 104
Clayton Fld. NW9 . . . . .7F 29
Clayton Ho. E9 . . . . .7J 67
    (off Frampton Pk. Rd.)
  KT7: T Ditt 1B 162

Clayton Ho. SW13 . . . . .7E 98
    (off Trinity Chu. Rd.)
Clayton M. SE10 . . . . .1F 123
Clayton Rd. KT9: Chess 4C 162
  RM7: Rush G 1J 73
  SE15 . . . . .1G 121
  TW7: Isle 3J 113
  UB3: Hayes 2G 93
Clayton St. SE11 . . . . .7J 19 (6A 102)
Clayton Ter. UB4: Yead 5C 76
Claytonville Ter. DA17: Belv 2J 109
Clay Wood Cl. BR6: Orp 7J 161
Clayworth Cl. DA15: Sidc 6B 126
Cleanthus Cl. SE18 . . . . .2F 125
Cleanthus Rd. SE18 . . . . .2F 125
    (not continuous)
Clearbrook Way E1 . . . . .6J 85
Clearwater Pl. KT6: Surb 6C 150
Clearwater Ter. W11 . . . . .2F 99
Clearwater Yd. NW1 . . . . .1F 83
    (off Inverness St.)
Clearwell Dr. W9 . . . . .4K 81
Cleave Av. BR6: Chels 6J 173
  UB3: Harl 4G 93
Cleaveland Rd. KT6: Surb 5D 150
Cleaverholme Cl. SE25 . . . . .6H 157
Cleaver Ho. NW3 . . . . .7D 64
    (off Adelaide Rd.)
Cleaver Sq. SE11 . . . . .5K 19 (5A 102)
Cleaver St. SE11 . . . . .5K 19 (5A 102)
Cleaves Almshouses KT2: King T 2E 150
    (off London Rd.)
Cleeve Ct. TW14: Bedf 1G 129
Cleeve Hill SE23 . . . . .1H 139
Cleeve Ho. E2 . . . . .2H 9
    (off Calvert Av.)
Cleeve Pk. Gdns. DA14: Sidc 2B 144
Cleeve Way SM1: Sutt 1K 165
  SW15 .7B 116
Cleeve Workshops E2 . . . . .2H 9
    (off Boundary Rd.)
Clegg Ho. SE16 . . . . .3J 103
    (off Moodkee St.)
Clegg St. E1 . . . . .1H 103
  E13 . . . . .2J 87
Cleland Ho. E2 . . . . .2J 85
    (off Sewardstone Rd.)
Clematis Apartments E3 . . . . .3B 86
    (off Merchant St.)
Clematis Gdns. IG8: Wfd G 5D 36
Clematis St. W12 . . . . .7C 80
Clem Attlee Ct. SW6 . . . . .6H 99
Clem Attlee Pde. SW6 . . . . .6H 99
    (off North End Rd.)
Clemence Rd. RM10: Dag 1J 91
Clemence St. E14 . . . . .5B 86
Clement Av. SW4 . . . . .4H 119
Clement Cl. NW6 . . . . .7E 62
  W4 . . . . .4K 97
Clement Danes Ho. W12 . . . . .6D 80
Clement Gdns. UB3: Harl 4G 93
Clementhorpe Rd. RM9: Dag 6C 72
Clement Ho. SE8 . . . . .4A 104
  W10 . . . . .5E 80
    (off Dalgarno Gdns.)
Clementina Ct. E3 . . . . .4A 86
    (off Copperfield Rd.)
Clementina Rd. E10 . . . . .1B 68
Clementine Cl. W13 . . . . .2B 96
Clementine Wlk. IG8: Wfd G 7D 36
Clement Rd. BR3: Beck 2K 157
  SW19 .5G 135
Clement's Av. E16 . . . . .7J 87
Clements Cl. N12 . . . . .4E 30
Clements Ct. IG1: Ilf 3F 71
  TW4: Houn 4B 112
Clement's Inn WC2 . . . . . . .1H 13 (6K 83)
Clement's Inn Pas. WC2 . . . . .1H 13
Clements La. EC4 . . . . .2F 15 (7D 84)
  IG1: Ilf 3F 71
Clements Pl. TW8: Bford 5D 96

Clements Rd. E6 . . . . .7C 70
　IG1: Ilf .3F 71
　SE16 .3G 103
Clemson Ho. E8 . . . . .1F 85
Clendon Way SE18 . . . . .4H 107
Clennam St. SE1 . . . . . .6D 14 (2C 102)
Clensham Ct. SM1: Sutt 2J 165
Clensham La. SM1: Sutt 2J 165
Clenston M. W1 . . . . .7E 4 (6D 82)
Cleopatra Cl. HA7: Stan 3J 27
Cleopatra's Needle 4G 13 (1J 101)
Clephane Rd. N1 . . . . .6C 66
Clephane Rd. Nth. N1 . . . . .6C 66
Clere Pl. EC2 . . . . .3F 9 (4D 84)
Clere St. EC2 . . . . .3F 9 (4D 84)
CLERKENWELL 4K 7 (4A 84)
Clerkenwell Cl. EC1 . . . . . .3K 7 (4A 84)
　(not continuous)
Clerkenwell Cl. N1 . . . . .2B 84
　(off Duncan St.)
Clerkenwell Grn. EC1 . . . . . .4K 7 (4A 84)
Clerkenwell Rd. EC1 . . . . . .4J 7 (4A 84)
Clerk's Pl. EC2 . . . . .7G 9 (6E 84)
Clermont Rd. E9 . . . . .1J 85
Clevedon Cl. N16 . . . . .3F 67
Clevedon Ct. CR2: S Croy 5E 168
　SW11 .1C 118
　(off Bolingbroke Wlk.)
Clevedon Gdns. TW5: Cran 1K 111
　UB3: Harl 3F 93
Clevedon Ho. SM1: Sutt 4A 166
Clevedon Mans. NW5 . . . . .4E 64
Clevedon Pas. N16 . . . . .2F 67
Clevedon Rd. KT1: King T 2G 151
　SE20 . . . . .1K 157
　TW1: Twick 6D 114
Cleve Ho. NW6 . . . . .7K 63
Cleveland Av. SW20 . . . . .2H 153
　TW12: Hamp 7D 130
　W4 . . . . .4B 98
Cleveland Ct. W13 . . . . .5B 78
Cleveland Gdns. KT4: Wor Pk 2A 164
　N4 . . . . .5C 48
　NW2 . . . . .2F 63
　SW13 .2B 116
　W2 . . . . .6A 82
Cleveland Gro. E1 . . . . .4J 85
Cleveland Ho. N2 . . . . .2B 46
　(off The Grange)
Cleveland Mans. NW6 . . . . .7H 63
　(off Willesden La.)
　SW9 . . . . .7A 102
　(off Mowll St.)
　W9 . . . . .4J 81
Cleveland M. W1 . . . . .5A 6 (5G 83)
Cleveland Pk. TW19: Stanw 6A 110
Cleveland Pk. Av. E17 . . . . .4C 50
Cleveland Pk. Cres. E17 . . . . .4C 50
Cleveland Pl. SW1 . . . . . .4B 12 (1G 101)
Cleveland Ri. SM4: Mord 7F 153
Cleveland Rd. DA16: Well 2K 125
　E18 . . . . .3J 51
　IG1: Ilf .3F 71
　KT3: N Mald 4A 152
　KT4: Wor Pk 2A 164
　N1 . . . . .7D 66
　N9 . . . . .7C 24
　SW13 .2B 116
　TW7: Isle 4A 114
　W4 . . . . .3J 97
　W13 . . . . .5A 78
Cleveland Row SW1 . . . .5A 12 (1G 101)
Cleveland Sq. W2 . . . . .6A 82
Cleveland St. W1 . . . . .4K 5 (4F 83)
Cleveland Ter. W2 . . . . .6A 82
Cleveland Way E1 . . . . .4J 85
Cleveley Cl. SE7 . . . . .4B 106
Cleveley Ct. SE8 . . . . .4A 104
　(off Ashton Reach)
Cleveley Cres. W5 . . . . .2E 78

Cleveleys Rd. E5 . . . . .3H 67
Cleverly Est. W12 . . . . .1C 98
Cleve Rd. DA14: Sidc 3D 144
　NW6 . . . . .7J 63
Cleves Av. KT17: Ewe 7D 164
Cleves Ho. E16 . . . . .1J 105
　(off Southey M.)
Cleves Rd. E6 . . . . .1B 88
　TW10: Ham 3C 132
Cleves Wlk. IG6: Ilf 1G 53
Cleves Way HA4: Ruis 1B 58
　TW12: Hamp 7D 130
　TW16: Sun 6H 129
Clewer Ct. E10 . . . . .1C 68
　(off Leyton Grange Est.)
Clewer Cres. HA3: Hrw W 1H 41
Clewer Ho. SE2 . . . . .2D 108
　(off Wolvercote Rd.)
Cley Ho. SE4 . . . . .4K 121
Clichy Est. E1 . . . . .5J 85
Clichy Ho. E1 . . . . .5J 85
　(off Stepney Way)
Clifden M. E5 . . . . .4K 67
Clifden Rd. E5 . . . . .5J 67
　TW1: Twick 1K 131
　TW8: Bford 6D 96
Cliffe Ho. SE10 . . . . .5H 105
　(off Blackwall La.)
Cliffe Rd. CR2: S Croy 5D 168
Cliffe Wlk. SM1: Sutt 5A 166
　(off Greyhound Rd.)
Clifford Av. BR7: Chst 6D 142
　IG5: Ilf 1F 53
　SM6: Wall 4G 167
　SW14 . . . . .3H 115
Clifford Cl. UB5: N'olt 1C 76
Clifford Ct. W2 . . . . .5K 81
　(off Westbourne Pk. Vs.)
Clifford Dr. SW9 . . . . .4B 120
Clifford Gdns. NW10 . . . . .2E 80
　UB3: Harl 4G 93
Clifford Gro. TW15: Ashf 4C 128
Clifford Haigh Ho. SW6 . . . . .7F 99
Clifford Ho. BR3: Beck 6D 140
　(off Calverley Cl.)
　W14 . . . . .4H 99
　(off Edith Vs.)
Clifford Rd. E16 . . . . .4H 87
　E17 . . . . .2E 50
　EN5: New Bar 3E 20
　HA0: Wemb 7D 60
　N1 . . . . .1E 84
　N9 . . . . .6D 24
　SE25 . . . . .4G 157
　TW4: Houn 3B 112
　TW10: Ham 2D 132
Clifford's Inn EC4 . . . . .1J 13
Clifford's Inn Pas. EC4 . . . . .1J 13 (6A 84)
Clifford St. W1 . . . . .3A 12 (7G 83)
Clifford Way NW10 . . . . .4B 62
　UB3: Harl 6H 65
Clifford Rd. NW1 . . . . .6H 65
Cliffsend Ho. SW9 . . . . .1A 120
　(off Cowley Rd.)
Cliff Ter. SE8 . . . . .2C 122
Cliffview Rd. SE13 . . . . .3C 122
Cliff Vs. NW1 . . . . .6H 65
Cliff Wlk. E16 . . . . .5H 87
Clifton Av. E17 . . . . .3K 49
　HA7: Stan 2B 42
　HA9: Wemb 6F 61
　N3 . . . . .1H 45
　TW13: Felt 3A 130
　W12 . . . . .1B 98
Clifton Cl. BR6: Farnb 5G 173
Clifton Ct. BR3: Beck 1C 158
　IG8: Wfd G 6D 36
　KT5: Surb 7F 151
　N4 . . . . .2A 66
　NW8 . . . . .3A 4
　SE15 . . . . .7H 103
　TW19: Stanw 6A 110

Clifton Cres. SE15 . . . . .7H 103
Clifton Est. SE15 . . . . .1H 121
Clifton Gdns. EN2: Enf 4D 22
　N15 . . . . .6F 49
　NW11 . . . . .6H 45
　UB10: Hil 2D 74
　W4 . . . . .4K 97
　(not continuous)
　W9 . . . . .4A 82
Clifton Ga. SW10 . . . . .6A 100
Clifton Gro. E8 . . . . .6G 67
Clifton Hill NW8 . . . . .2A 82
Clifton Hill Studios NW8 . . . . .2A 82
Clifton Ho. E2 . . . . .3J 9
　(off Club Row)
　E11 . . . . .2G 69
Clifton M. SE25 . . . . .4E 156
Clifton Pde. TW13: Felt 3A 130
Clifton Pk. Av. SW20 . . . . .2E 152
Clifton Pl. SE16 . . . . .2J 103
　SW10 .6A 100
　(off Hollywood Rd.)
　W2 . . . . .1B 10 (6B 82)
Clifton Ri. SE14 . . . . .7A 104
　(not continuous)
Clifton Rd. DA14: Sidc 4K 143
　DA16: Well 3C 126
　E7 . . . . .6B 70
　E16 . . . . .5G 87
　HA3: Kenton 4F 43
　IG2: Ilf 6H 53
　KT2: King T 7F 133
　N1 . . . . .6C 66
　N3 . . . . .1A 46
　N8 . . . . .6H 47
　N22 . . . . .1G 47
　NW10 . . . . .2C 80
　SE25 . . . . .4E 156
　SM6: Wall 5F 167
　SW19 . . . . .6F 135
　TW7: Isle 2J 113
　TW11: Tedd 4J 131
　UB2: S'hall 4C 94
　UB6: G'frd 4G 77
　W9 . . . . .3A 4 (4A 82)
Clifton St. EC2 . . . . .4G 9 (4E 84)
Clifton Ter. N4 . . . . .2A 66
Clifton Vs. W9 . . . . .5A 82
Cliftonville Ct. SE12 . . . . .1J 141
Clifton Wlk. W6 . . . . .4D 98
　(off King St.)
Clifton Way HA0: Wemb 1E 78
　SE15 . . . . .7H 103
　TW6: H'row A 3E 110
Climsland Ho. SE1 . . . . . .4K 13 (1A 102)
Cline Rd. N11 . . . . .6B 32
Clinger Ct. N1 . . . . .1E 84
　(off Hobbs Pl. Est.)
Clink Prison Mus. 4E 14
Clink St. SE1 . . . . .4D 14 (1D 102)
Clink Wharf SE1 . . . . .4E 14
　(off Clink St.)
Clinton Av. DA16: Well 4A 126
　KT8: E Mos 4G 149
Clinton Ho. KT6: Surb 7D 150
　(off Lovelace Gdns)
Clinton Rd. E3 . . . . .3A 86
　E7 . . . . .4J 69
　N15 . . . . .4D 48
Clinton Ter. SE8 . . . . .6C 104
　(off Watergate St.)
　SM1: Sutt 4A 166
Clipper Apartments SE10 . . . . .6E 104
　(off Welland St.)
Clipper Cl. SE16 . . . . .2K 103
Clipper Ho. E14 . . . . .5E 104
　(off Manchester Rd.)
Clipper Way SE13 . . . . .4E 122
Clippesby Cl. KT9: Chess 6F 163
Clipstone M. W1 . . . . .5A 6 (5G 83)
Clipstone Rd. TW3: Houn 3E 112

Clipstone St. W1 . . . . .5K 5 (5F 83)
Clissold Cl. N2 . . . . .3D 46
Clissold Ct. N4 . . . . .2C 66
Clissold Cres. N16 . . . . .3D 66
Clissold Leisure Cen. 3D 66
Clissold Rd. N16 . . . . .3D 66
Clitheroe Av. HA2: Harr 1E 58
Clitheroe Rd. SW9 . . . . .2A 120
Clitherow Av. W7 . . . . .3A 96
Clitherow Ct. TW8: Bford 5C 96
Clitherow Pas. TW8: Bford 5C 96
Clitherow Rd. TW8: Bford 5B 96
Clitterhouse Cres. NW2 . . . . .1E 62
Clitterhouse Rd. NW2 . . . . .1E 62
Clive Av. N18 . . . . .6B 34
Clive Ct. W9 .4A 82
Cliveden Cl. N12 . . . . .4F 31
Cliveden Ho. E16 . . . . .1J 105
　(off Fitzwilliam M.)
　SW1 . . . . .3G 17
　(off Cliveden Pl.)
Cliveden Pl. SW1 . . . . . . .3G 17 (4E 100)
　TW17: Shep 5E 146
Clivedon Ct. W13 . . . . .5B 78
Clivedon Rd. E4 . . . . .5B 36
Clive Ho. SE10 . . . . .6E 104
　(off Haddo St.)
Clive Lloyd Ho. N15 . . . . .5C 48
　(off Woodlands Pk. Rd.)
Clive Pas. SE21 . . . . .3D 138
Clive Rd. DA17: Belv 4G 109
　EN1: Enf .4B 24
　SE21 . . . . .3D 138
　SW19 . . . . .6C 136
　TW1: Twick 4K 131
　TW14: Felt 6J 111
Clivesdale Dr. UB3: Hayes 1K 93
Clive Way EN1: Enf 4B 24
Cloak La. EC4 . . . . .2D 14 (7C 84)
Clochar Ct. NW10 . . . . .1B 80
Clock Ct. E11 . . . . .3K 51
Clock Ho. E3 .3E 86
　E17 . . . . .4F 51
　(off Wood St.)
Clockhouse, The SW19 . . . . .3E 134
Clockhouse Av. IG11: Bark 1G 89
Clockhouse Cl. SW19 . . . . .2E 134
Clockhouse Ct. BR3: Beck 2A 158
CLOCKHOUSE JUNC. 5E 32
Clockhouse La. RM5: Col R 1H 55
　TW14: Bedf 4C 128
　TW15: Ashf 4C 128
Clock Ho. Pde. E11 . . . . .6K 51
Clockhouse Pde. N13 . . . . .5F 33
Clockhouse Pl. SW15 . . . . .6G 117
Clock Ho. Rd. BR3: Beck 3A 158
CLOCKHOUSE RDBT. 1D 128
Clock Pde. EN2: Enf 5J 23
Clock Pl. SE1 . . . . .4B 102
　(off Newington Butts)
Clock Twr. Ind. Est. TW7: Isle 3K 113
Clock Twr. M. N1 . . . . .1C 84
　SE28 . . . . .7B 90
　W7 . . . . .1J 95
Clock Twr. Rd. TW7: Isle 3K 113
Clock Vw. Cres. N7 . . . . .6J 65
　(not continuous)
Clockwork M. E9 . . . . .5K 67
Cloister Cl. TW11: Tedd 5B 132
Cloister Gdns. HA8: Edg 5D 28
　SE25 . . . . .6H 157
Cloister Rd. NW2 . . . . .3H 63
　W3 . . . . .5J 79
Cloisters, The E1 . . . . .1E 18
Cloisters, The E1 . . . . .1J 85
　SW9 . . . . .1A 120
　TW7: Isle 3A 114
　(off Pulteney Cl.)

Cloisters Av. BR2: Brom 5D 160
Cloisters Bus. Cen. SW8 . . . . .7F 101
   (off Battersea Pk. Rd.)
Cloisters Ct. DA7: Bex 3H 127
Cloisters Mall KT1: King T 2E 150
Clonard Way HA5: Hat E 6A 26
Clonbrock Rd. N16 . . . . .4E 66
Cloncurry St. SW6 . . . . .2F 117
Clonmel CI. HA2: Harr 2H 59
Clonmell Rd. N17 . . . . .3D 48
Clonmel Rd. SW6 . . . . .7H 99
   TW11: Tedd 4H 131
Clonmore St. SW18 . . . . .1H 135
Cloonmore Av. BR6: Chels 4K 173
Clorane Gdns. NW3 . . . . .3J 63
Close, The BR3: Beck 4A 158
   BR5: Pet W 6J 161
   CR4: Mitc 4D 154
   DA5: Bexl 6G 127
   DA14: Sidc 4B 144
   E4 . . . . .7K 35
   EN4: E Barn 6J 21
   HA0: Wemb 6E 60
   HA2: Harr 2G 41
   HA5: Eastc 7A 40
   HA5: Pinn 7D 40
   HA9: Wemb 3J 61
   IG2: Ilf 6J 53
   KT3: N Mald 2J 151
   KT6: Surb 6E 150
   N10 . . . . .2F 47
   N14 . . . . .2C 32
   N20 . . . . .2C 30
   RM6: Chad H 6E 54
   SE3 . . . . .2F 123
   SE25 . . . . .6G 157
   SM3: Sutt 7H 153
   SM5: Cars 7C 166
   TW7: Isle .2H 113
   TW9: Rich 3H 115
   UB10: Hil .1C 74
Cloth CI. EC1 . . . . .6B 8
Cloth Fair EC1 . . . . .6B 8 (5B 84)
Clothier St. E1 . . . . .7H 9 (6E 84)
Cloth St. EC1 . . . . .5C 8 (5C 84)
Clothworkers Rd. SE18 . . . . .7H 107
Cloudesdale Rd. SW17 . . . . .2F 137
Cloudesley CI. DA14: Sidc 4K 143
Cloudesley Ho. N1 . . . . .1A 84
   (off Cloudesley St.)
Cloudesley Mans. N1 . . . . .1A 84
   (off Cloudesley Pl.)
Cloudesley Pl. N1 . . . . .1A 84
Cloudesley Rd. DA7: Bex 1F 127
   N1 . . . . .1A 84
   (not continuous)
Cloudesley Sq. N1 . . . . .1A 84
Cloudesley St. N1 . . . . .1A 84
Clouston CI. SM6: Wall 5J 167
Clova Rd. E7 . . . . .6H 69
Clove Cres. E14 . . . . .7E 86
Clove Hitch Quay SW11 . . . . .3A 118
Clovelly Av. NW9 . . . . .4B 44
   UB10: Ick 4E 56
Clovelly CI. HA5: Eastc 3K 39
   UB10: Ick 4E 56
Clovelly Ct. NW2 . . . . .5E 62
Clovelly Gdns. EN1: Enf 7K 23
   RM7: Mawney 1H 55
   SE19 . . . . .1F 157
Clovelly Ho. W2 . . . . .6A 82
   (off Hallfield Est.)
Clovelly Rd. DA7: Bex 6E 108
   N8 . . . . .4H 47
   TW3: Houn 2E 112
   W4 . . . . .2K 97
   W5 . . . . .2C 96
Clovelly Way BR6: St M Cry 6K 161
   E1 . . . . .6J 85
   HA2: Harr 2D 58
Clover CI. E11 . . . . .2F 69

Cloverdale Ct. SM6: Wall 6F 167
Cloverdale Gdns. DA15: Sidc 6K 125
Clover M. SW3 . . . . .7F 17 (6D 100)
Clover Way SM6: Wall 1E 166
Clove St. E13 . . . . .4J 87
Clowders Rd. SE6 . . . . .3B 140
Clowser CI. SM1: Sutt 5A 166
Cloysters Grn. E1 . . . . .1G 103
Cloyster Wood HA8: Edg 7J 27
Club Gdns. Rd. BR2: Hayes 7J 159
Clubhouse, The E14 . . . . .6C 86
Club Row E1 . . . . .3J 9 (4F 85)
   E2 . . . . .3J 9 (4F 85)
Clumps, The TW15: Ashf 4F 129
Clunbury Av. UB2: S'hall 5D 94
Clunbury St. N1 . . . . .2D 84
Clunie Ho. SW1 . . . . .1F 17
   (off Hans Pl.)
Cluny Est. SE1 . . . . .7G 15 (3E 102)
Cluny M. SW5 . . . . .4J 99
Cluny PI. SE1 . . . . .7G 15 (3E 102)
Cluse CI. N1 .2C 84
   (off St Peters St., not continuous)
Cluster Ho. W3 . . . . .1B 98
Clutton St. E14 . . . . .5D 86
Clydach Rd. EN1: Enf 4A 24
Clyde Cir. N15 . . . . .4E 48
Clyde Ct. NW1 . . . . .2H 83
   (off Hampden Cl.)
Clyde Flats SW6 . . . . .7H 99
   (off Rylston Rd.)
Clyde Ho. KT2: King T 1D 150
   SW18 . . . . .4J 117
   (off Enterprise Way)
Clyde PI. E10 . . . . .7D 50
Clyde Rd. CR0: C'don 2F 169
   N15 . . . . .4E 48
   N22 . . . . .1H 47
   SM1: Sutt 5J 165
   SM6: Wall 6G 167
   TW19: Stanw 1A 128
Clydesdale EN3: Pond E 4E 24
Clydesdale Av. HA7: Stan 3D 42
Clydesdale CI. TW7: Isle 3K 113
Clydesdale Ct. N20 . . . . .1G 31
Clydesdale Gdns.
   TW10: Rich 4H 115
Clydesdale Ho. DA18: Erith 2E 108
   (off Kale Rd.)
   W11 . . . . .6H 81
   (off Clydesdale Rd.)
Clydesdale Rd. W11 . . . . .6H 81
Clydesdale Way DA17: Belv 2H 109
Clyde St. SE8 . . . . .6B 104
Clyde Ter. SE23 . . . . .2J 139
Clyde Va. SE23 . . . . .2J 139
Clyde Way RM1: Rom 1K 55
Clyde Wharf E16 . . . . .1J 105
Clydon Cl. DA8: Erith 6K 109
Clyfford Rd. HA4: Ruis 4H 57
Clymping Dene TW14: Felt 7K 111
Clynes Ho. E2 . . . . .3K 85
   (off Knottisford St.)
   RM10: Dag 3G 73
   (off Uvedale Rd.)
Clyston St. SW8 . . . . .2G 119
Coach & Horses Yd. W1 . . . . .2K 11 (7G 83)
Coach Ho. La. N5 . . . . .4B 66
   SW19 . . . . .4F 135
Coach Ho. M. SE1 . . . . .7G 15
   (off Long La.)
   SE23 . . . . .6K 121
   SM2: Sutt 6K 165
Coachhouse M. SE20 . . . . .7H 139
Coach Ho. Yd. NW3 . . . . .4A 64
   (off Heath St.)
   SW18 . . . . .4K 117
Coachmaker M. SW4 . . . . .3J 119
   (off Bedford Rd.)
   W4 . . . . .3K 97
   (off Berrymede Rd.)

Coach Yd. M. N19 . . . . .1J 65
Coalbrookdale Gates 6A 10 (2B 100)
Coaldale Wlk. SE21 . . . . .7C 120
Coal Drops N1 . . . . .1J 83
Coalecroft Rd. SW15 . . . . .4E 116
Coalport Ho. SE11 . . . . .2J 19
Coal Post CI. BR6: Chels 6K 173
Coalstore Ct. E1 . . . . .5A 86
Coatbridge Ho. N1 . . . . .7K 65
   (off Carnoustie Dr.)
Coates Av. SW18 . . . . .6C 118
Coates CI. CR7: Thor H 3C 156
Coates Hill Rd. BR1: Brom 2E 160
Coate St. E2 .2G 85
Coates Wlk. TW8: Bford 6E 96
Cobalt SE28 . . . . .2A 108
Cobalt Building, The EC2 . . . . .5C 8
   (off Bridgewater Sq.)
Cobalt CI. BR3: Beck 4K 157
Cobalt PI. SW11 . . . . .1B 118
Cobalt Sq. SW8 . . . . .7G 19
Cobbett Rd. SE9 . . . . .3C 124
   TW2: Whitt 1E 130
Cobbetts Av. IG4: Ilf 5B 52
Cobbett St. SW8 . . . . .7K 101
Cobble La. N1 . . . . .7B 66
Cobble M. N5 . . . . .3C 66
   N6 . . . . .1E 64
   (off Highgate West Hill)
Cobble Path E17 . . . . .5C 50
   (off Cedars Av.)
Cobblers Wlk. KT1: Hamp W 1A 150
   KT8: E Mos 1A 150
   TW11: Tedd 1A 150
   TW12: Hamp 1G 149
Cobblestone PI. CR0: C'don 1C 168
Cobblestone Sq. E1 . . . . .1H 103
Cobbold Ct. SW1 . . . . .3C 18
   (off Elverton St.)
Cobbold Ind. Est. NW10 . . . . .6B 62
Cobbold Rd. E11 . . . . .3H 69
   NW10 . . . . .6B 62
   W12 . . . . .2A 98
Cobb's CI. EC4 . . . . .1B 14
Cobb's Hall SW6 . . . . .6F 99
   (off Fulham Pal. Rd.)
Cobb's Rd. TW4: Houn 4D 112
Cobbsthorpe Vs. SE26 . . . . .4K 139
Cobb St. E1 . . . . .6J 9 (5F 85)
Cobden Bldgs. WC1 . . . . .1G 7
   (off King's Cross Rd.)
Cobden Ct. BR2: Brom 4A 160
Cobden Ho. E2 . . . . .3G 85
   (off Nelson Gdns.)
   NW1 . . . . .2G 83
   (off Arlington Rd.)
Cobden M. SE26 . . . . .5H 139
Cobden Rd. BR6: Farnb 4H 173
   E11 . . . . .3G 69
   SE25 . . . . .5G 157
Cobham Av. KT3: N Mald 5C 152
Cobham CI. BR2: Brom 7C 160
   DA15: Sidc 6B 126
   EN1: Enf .3B 24
   HA8: Edg .2H 43
   SM6: Wall 6J 167
   SW11 . . . . .6C 118
Cobham Ct. CR4: Mitc 2B 154
Cobham M. NW1 . . . . .7H 65
Cobham PI. DA6: Bex 5E 126
Cobham Rd. E17 . . . . .1E 50
   IG3: Ilf 2J 71
   KT1: King T 2G 151
   N22 . . . . .3B 48
   TW5: Hest 7A 94
Coborn M. E3 . . . . .3B 86
   (off Coborn St.)
Coborn Rd. E3 . . . . .2B 86
Coborn St. E3 . . . . .3B 86

Coburg Rd. SE5 . . . . .6F 103
Coburg St. NW1 . . . . .2B 6 (3G 83)
Coburg CI. SW1 . . . . .3B 18 (4G 101)
Coburg Cres. SW2 . . . . .1K 137
Coburg Dwellings E1 . . . . .6J 85
   (off Hardinge St.)
Coburg Gdns. IG5: Ilf 2B 52
Coburg Rd. N22 . . . . .3K 47
Cochrane CI. NW8 . . . . .1B 4
Cochrane Ct. E10 . . . . .1C 68
   (off Leyton Grange Est.)
Cochrane Ho. E14 . . . . .2C 104
   (off Admirals Way)
Cochrane M. NW8 . . . . .2B 82
Cochrane Rd. SW19 . . . . .7G 135
Cochrane St. NW8 . . . . .1B 4 (2B 82)
Cockburn Ho. SW1 . . . . .6D 18
   (off Aylesford St.)
COCKCROW HILL 1D 162
Cockerell Rd. E17 . . . . .7A 50
COCKFOSTERS 4J 21
Cockfosters Pde. EN4: Cockf 4K 21
Cockfosters Rd. EN4: Cockf, Had W . .1H 21
Cock Hill E1 . . . . .6H 9 (5E 84)
Cock La. EC1 . . . . .6A 8 (5B 84)
Cockpit Steps SW1 . . . . .7C 12
Cockpit Theatre 4C 4
   (off Gateforth St.)
Cockpit Yd. WC1 . . . . .5H 7 (5K 83)
Cocks Cres. KT3: N Mald 4B 152
Cocksett Av. BR6: Chels 6J 173
Cockspur Ct. SW1 . . . . .4D 12 (1H 101)
Cockspur St. SW1 . . . . .4D 12 (1H 101)
Cocksure La. DA14: Sidc 3G 145
Coda Centre, The SW6 . . . . .7G 99
Code CI. NW2 . . . . .3C 62
Code St. E1 . . . . .4K 9
Codicote Ho. SE8 . . . . .4K 103
   (off Chilton Gro.)
Codicote Ter. N4 . . . . .2C 66
Codling CI. E1 . . . . .1G 103
Codling Way HA0: Wemb 4D 60
Codrington Ct. E1 . . . . .4H 85
   SE16 . . . . .7A 86
Codrington Hill SE23 . . . . .7A 122
Codrington M. W11 . . . . .6G 81
Cody CI. HA3: Kenton 3D 42
   SM6: Wall 7H 167
Cody Rd. E16 .4F 87
Coe Av. SE25 . . . . .6G 157
Coe's All. EN5: Barn 4B 20
Coffey St. SE8 . . . . .7C 104
Cogan Av. E17 . . . . .1A 50
Coin St. SE1 . . . . .4J 13 (1A 102)
   (not continuous)
Coity Rd. NW5 . . . . .6E 64
Cokers La. SE21 . . . . .1D 138
Coke St. E1 . . . . .6G 85
Colas M. NW6 . . . . .1J 81
Colbeck M. SW7 . . . . .4K 99
Colbeck Rd. HA1: Harr 7G 41
Colberg PI. N16 . . . . .7F 49
Colbert SE5 .1C 120
   (off Sceaux Gdns.)
Colborne Ho. E14 . . . . .7C 86
   (off E. India Dock Rd.)
Colborne Way KT4: Wor Pk 3E 164
Colbrook Av. UB3: Harl 3F 93
Colbrook CI. UB3: Harl 3F 93
Colburn Way SM1: Sutt 3B 166
Colby M. SE19 . . . . .5E 138
Colby Rd. KT12: Walt T 7J 147
   SE19 . . . . .5E 138
Colchester Av. E12 . . . . .4D 70
Colchester Dr. HA5: Pinn 5B 40
Colchester Ho. E3 . . . . .1B 86
   (off Parnell Rd.)
Colchester Rd. E10 . . . . .7E 50
   E17 . . . . .6C 50
   HA6: Nwood 2J 39
   HA8: Edg .7D 28

Colclough Ct. CR0: C'don ...6C 156
  (off Simpson Cl.)
Coldbath Sq. EC1 ...3J 7 (4A 84)
Coldbath St. SE13 ...1D 122
COLDBLOW ...1J 145
Cold Blow Cres. DA5: Bexl ...1K 145
Cold Blow La. SE14 ...7K 103
  (not continuous)
Cold Blows CR4: Mitc ...3D 154
Coldershaw Rd. W7 ...1A 96
  W13 ...1A 96
Coldfall Av. N10 ...2E 46
Coldham Ct. N22 ...1B 48
Coldharbour E14 ...2E 104
Coldharbour Crest SE9 ...3E 142
Coldharbour Ind. Est. SE5 ...2C 120
Coldharbour La. SE5 ...3C 120
  SW9 ...4A 120
  UB3: Hayes ...1J 93
Coldharbour Leisure Cen. ...2D 142
Coldharbour Pl. SE5 ...2C 120
Coldharbour Rd. CR0: Wadd ...5A 168
Coldharbour Way
  CR0: Wadd ...5A 168
Coldstream Gdns. SW18 ...6H 117
Colebeck M. N1 ...6B 66
Colebert Av. E1 ...4J 85
Colebert Ho. E1 ...4J 85
  (off Colebert Av.)
Colebrook Cl. NW7 ...6A 30
  SW15 ...7F 117
Colebrook Ct. SW3 ...4D 16
  (off Makins St.)
Colebrooke Av. W13 ...6B 78
Colebrooke Ct. DA14: Sidc ...3B 144
Colebrooke Dr. E11 ...7A 52
Colebrooke Pl. N1 ...1B 84
Colebrooke Ri. BR2: Brom ...2G 159
Colebrooke Row N1 ...2B 84
Colebrook Ho. E14 ...6D 86
  (off Ellesmere St.)
  SE18 ...7E 106
Colebrook Rd. SW16 ...1J 155
Colebrook Way N11 ...5A 32
Coleby Path SE5 ...7D 102
Colechurch Ho. SE1 ...5G 103
  (off Avondale Sq.)
Cole Cl. SE28 ...1B 108
Cole Ct. TW1: Twick ...7A 114
Coledale Dr. HA7: Stan ...1C 42
Colefax Bldgs. E1 ...6G 85
  (off Plumber's Row)
Coleford Rd. SW18 ...5A 118
Cole Gdns. TW5: Cran ...7J 93
Colegrave Rd. E15 ...5F 69
Colegrove Rd. SE15 ...6F 103
Coleherne Ct. SW5 ...5K 99
Coleherne Mans. SW5 ...5K 99
  (off Old Brompton Rd.)
Coleherne M. SW10 ...5K 99
Coleherne Rd. SW10 ...5K 99
Colehill Gdns. SW6 ...2G 117
Colehill La. SW6 ...1G 117
Cole Ho. SE1 ...7K 13
  (off Baylis Rd.)
Coleman Cl. SE25 ...2G 157
Coleman Ct. SW18 ...7J 117
Coleman Flds. N1 ...1C 84
Coleman Mans. N8 ...7J 47
Coleman Rd. DA17: Belv ...4G 109
  RM9: Dag ...6E 72
  SE5 ...7E 102
Colemans Heath SE9 ...3E 142
Coleman St. EC2 ...7E 8 (6D 84)
Coleman St. Bldgs. EC2 ...7E 8
Colenso Dr. NW7 ...7H 29
Colenso Rd. E5 ...4J 67
  IG2: Ilf ...1J 71
COLE PARK ...6A 114
Cole Pk. Gdns. TW1: Twick ...5A 114
Cole Pk. Rd. TW1: Twick ...6A 114

Cole Pk. Vw. TW1: Twick ...6A 114
Colepits Wood Rd. SE9 ...5H 125
Coleraine Rd. N8 ...3A 48
  SE3 ...6H 105
Coleridge Av. E12 ...6C 70
  SM1: Sutt ...4C 166
Coleridge Cl. SW8 ...2F 119
Coleridge Cl. EN5: New Bar ...5E 20
  (off Station Rd.)
  N1 ...1C 84
  (off Dibden St.)
  SW1 ...3C 18
  (off Regency St.)
  W14 ...3F 99
  (off Blythe Rd.)
Coleridge Cres. SL3: Poyle ...4A 174
Coleridge Dr. HA4: Ruis ...6K 39
Coleridge Gdns. NW6 ...7K 64
  SW10 ...7K 99
Coleridge Ho. SE17 ...5C 102
  (off Browning St.)
  SW1 ...6B 18
  (off Churchill Gdns.)
Coleridge La. N8 ...6J 47
Coleridge Rd. CR0: C'don ...7J 157
  E17 ...4B 50
  N4 ...2A 66
  N8 ...6H 47
  N12 ...5F 31
  TW15: Ashf ...4A 128
Coleridge Sq. SW10 ...7A 100
  (off Coleridge Gdns.)
  W13 ...6A 78
Coleridge Wlk. NW11 ...4J 45
Coleridge Way UB4: Hayes ...6J 75
  UB7: W Dray ...4A 92
Cole Rd. TW1: Twick ...6A 114
Colesburg Rd. BR3: Beck ...3B 158
Coles Cres. HA2: Harr ...2F 59
Coles Grn. WD23: B Hea ...1B 26
Coles Grn. Ct. NW2 ...2C 62
Coles Grn. Rd. NW2 ...1C 62
Coleshill Flats SW1 ...4H 17
Coleshill Rd. TW11: Tedd ...6J 131
Colestown St. SW11 ...2C 118
Cole St. SE1 ...7D 14 (2C 102)
Colesworth Ho. HA8: Edg ...2J 43
  (off Burnt Oak B'way.)
Colet Cl. N13 ...6G 33
Colet Ct. W6 ...4F 99
  (off Hammersmith Rd.)
Colet Flats E1 ...6A 86
  (off Troon St.)
Colet Gdns. W14 ...4F 99
Colet Ho. SE17 ...5B 102
  (off Doddington Gro.)
Colette Ct. SE16 ...2K 103
  (off Eleanor Cl.)
Coley St. WC1 ...4H 7 (4K 83)
Colfe & Hatcliffe Glebe SE13 ...5D 122
  (off Lewisham High St.)
Colfe Rd. SE23 ...1A 140
Colfes Leisure Cen. ...6J 123
Colham Av. UB7: Yiew ...1A 92
COLHAM GREEN ...5C 74
Colham Grn. Rd. UB8: Hil ...5C 74
Colham Mill Rd. UB7: W Dray ...2A 92
Colham Rd. UB8: Hil ...4B 74
COLHAM RDBT. ...6C 74
Colina M. N15 ...5B 48
Colina Rd. N15 ...5B 48
Colin Cl. BR4: W W'ck ...3H 171
  CR0: C'don ...3B 170
  NW9 ...4A 44
Colin Ct. SE6 ...7B 122
Colin Cres. NW9 ...4B 44
COLINDALE ...3K 43
Colindale Av. NW9 ...3K 43
Colindale Bus. Pk. NW9 ...3J 43
Colindale Retail Pk. NW9 ...4K 43
Colindeep Gdns. NW4 ...4C 44

Colindeep La. NW4 ...3A 44
  NW9 ...3A 44
Colin Dr. NW9 ...5B 44
Colinette Rd. SW15 ...4E 116
Colin Gdns. NW9 ...4B 44
Colin Pde. NW9 ...4A 44
Colin Pk. Rd. NW9 ...4A 44
Colin Pond Ct. RM6: Chad H ...4D 54
Colinsdale N1 ...1B 84
  (off Camden Wlk.)
Colinton Rd. IG3: Ilf ...2B 72
Colin Winter Ho. E1 ...4J 85
  (off Nicholas Rd.)
Coliseum Theatre ...3E 12
  (off St Martin's La.)
Coliston Pas. SW18 ...7J 117
  (off Coliston Rd.)
Coliston Rd. SW18 ...7J 117
Collamore Av. SW18 ...1C 136
Collapit Cl. HA1: Harr ...6F 41
Collard Pl. NW1 ...7F 65
Collards Almshouses E17 ...5E 50
  (off Maynard Rd.)
Collection Pl. NW8 ...1K 81
  (off Bolton Pl.)
College App. SE10 ...6E 104
College Av. HA3: Hrw W ...1J 41
College Cl. E9 ...5J 67
  HA3: Hrw W ...7D 26
  N18 ...5A 34
  TW2: Twick ...1H 131
College Ct. EN3: Pond E ...5D 24
  NW3 ...6B 64
  (off College Cres.)
  SW3 ...6F 17
  W5 ...7E 78
  W6 ...5E 98
  (off Queen Caroline St.)
College Cres. NW3 ...7A 64
College Cross N1 ...7A 66
College Dr. HA4: Ruis ...7J 39
  KT7: T Ditt ...7J 149
College East E1 ...6K 9 (5F 85)
College Flds. Bus. Cen. SW19 ...1C 154
College Gdns. E4 ...7J 25
  EN2: Enf ...1J 23
  IG4: Ilf ...5C 52
  KT3: N Mald ...5B 152
  N18 ...5B 34
  SE21 ...1E 138
  SW17 ...2C 136
College Grn. SE19 ...7E 138
College Gro. NW1 ...1G 83
College Hill EC4 ...2D 14 (7C 84)
College Hill Rd. HA3: Hrw W ...7D 26
College Ho. SW15 ...5F 117
  TW7: Isle ...7J 95
College La. NW5 ...4F 65
College Mans. NW6 ...1G 81
  (off Salusbury Rd.)
College M. N1 ...7A 66
  (off College Cross, not continuous)
  SW1 ...1E 18
  SW18 ...5K 117
College of Arms ...2C 14
College Pde. NW6 ...1G 81
  (off Salusbury Rd.)
College Pk. Cl. SE13 ...4F 123
College Pk. Rd. N17 ...6A 34
College Pl. E17 ...4G 51
  NW1 ...1G 83
  SW10 ...7A 100
College Point E15 ...6H 69
College Rd. BR1: Brom ...1J 159
  BR8: Hext ...7K 145
  CR0: C'don ...2D 168
  E17 ...5E 50
  EN2: Enf ...2J 23
  HA1: Harr ...6J 41

College Rd. HA3: Hrw W ...1J 41
  HA9: Wemb ...1D 60
  N17 ...6A 34
  N21 ...2F 33
  NW10 ...2C 80
  SE19 ...5F 139
  SE21 ...7E 120
  SW19 ...6B 136
  TW7: Isle ...1K 113
  W13 ...6B 78
COLLEGE RDBT. ...3E 150
College Row E9 ...5K 67
College Slip BR1: Brom ...1J 159
College St. EC4 ...2D 14 (7C 84)
College Ter. E3 ...3B 86
  N3 ...2H 45
College Vw. SE9 ...1B 142
College Wlk. KT1: King T ...3E 150
College Way TW15: Ashf ...4B 128
  UB3: Hayes ...7J 75
College Yd. NW5 ...4F 65
  NW6 ...1G 81
Collent St. E9 ...6J 67
Collerston Ho. SE10 ...5H 105
  (off Armitage Rd.)
Colless Rd. N15 ...5F 49
Collett Rd. SE16 ...3G 103
Collett Way UB2: S'hall ...2F 95
Collett Cl. E6 ...7F 89
  KT19: Ewe ...6G 163
Collett Dr. DA8: Edg ...2G 43
COLLIER ROW ...1H 55
Collier Row La. RM5: Col R ...1H 55
Collier Row Rd. RM5: Col R ...1F 55
Colliers Cl. CR0: C'don ...4D 168
  (off St Peter's Rd.)
Colliers Shaw BR2: Kes ...4B 172
Collier St. N1 ...2K 83
Colliers Water La. CR7: Thor H ...5A 156
COLLIERS WOOD ...7B 136
COLLIERS WOOD ...7B 136
Collindale Av. DA8: Erith ...7H 109
  DA15: Sidc ...1A 144
Collingbourne Rd. W12 ...1D 98
Collingham Gdns. SW5 ...4K 99
Collingham Pl. SW5 ...4K 99
Collingham Rd. SW5 ...4K 99
Collings Cl. N22 ...6E 32
Collington St. SE10 ...5F 105
Collingtree Rd. SE26 ...4J 139
Collingwood Av. KT5: Surb ...1J 163
  N10 ...3E 46
Collingwood Cl. SE20 ...1H 157
  TW2: Whitt ...7E 112
Collingwood Ct. EN5: New Bar ...5E 20
  W5 ...5F 79
Collingwood Ho. E1 ...4H 85
  (off Darling Row)
  SE16 ...1A 104
  (off Cherry Gdn. St.)
  SW1 ...6C 18
  (off Dolphin Sq.)
  W1 ...5A 6
  (off Clipstone St.)
Collingwood Rd. CR4: Mitc ...3C 154
  E17 ...6C 50
  N15 ...4E 48
  SM1: Sutt ...3J 165
  UB8: Hil ...4D 74
Collingwood St. E1 ...4H 85
Collins Av. HA7: Stan ...2E 42
Collins Ct. E8 ...6G 67
Collins Dr. HA4: Ruis ...2A 58
Collins Ho. E14 ...7E 86
  (off Newby Pl.)
  SE10 ...5H 105
  (off Armitage Rd.)
Collinson Ct. SE1 ...7C 14
  (off Gt. Suffolk St.)
Collinson Ho. SE3 ...4K 123
  (off Wallace Cl.)

Collinson Ho. *SE15* 7G *103*
   (off Peckham Pk. Rd.)
Collinson St. SE1 . . . . .7C 14 (2C 102)
Collinson Wlk. SE1 . . . . . . .7C 14 (2C 102)
Collins Path TW12: Hamp 6D 130
Collins Rd. N5 . . . . .4C 66
Collins Sq. SE3 . . . . .2H 123
Collins St. SE3 . . . . .2G 123
   (not continuous)
Collin's Yd. N1 . . . . .1B 84
Collinwood Av. EN3: Enf H 3D 24
Collinwood Gdns. IG5: Ilf 5D 52
Collis All. TW2: Twick 1J 131
Collison Pl. N16 . . . . .1E 66
Coll's Rd. SE15 . . . . .1J 121
Collyer Av. CR0: Bedd 4J 167
Collyer Pl. SE15 . . . . .1G 121
Collyer Rd. CR0: Bedd 4J 167
Colman Ct. HA7: Stan 6G 27
   N12 . . . . .6F 31
Colman Pde. EN1: Enf 3K 23
Colman Rd. E16 . . . . .5A 88
Colmans Wharf *E14* 5D *86*
   (off Morris Rd.)
Colmar Cl. E1 .4K 85
Colmer Pl. HA3: Hrw W 7C 26
Colmer Rd. SW16 . . . . .1J 155
Colmore M. SE15 . . . . .1H 121
Colmore Rd. EN3: Pond E 4D 24
Colnbrook By-Pass SL3: Coln 3A 174
   UB7: Harm 3A 174
Colnbrook Ct. SL3: Poyle 4A 174
Colnbrook St. SE1 . . . . .3B 102
Colne Cl. KT19: Ewe 4J 163
   W7 . . . . .6H 77
   (off High La.)
Colnedale Rd. UB8: Uxb 5A 56
Colne Ho. IG11: Bark 7F 71
   NW8 . . . . .4B 4
   (off Penfold St.)
Colne Pk. Caravan Site
   UB7: W Dray 1D 174
Colne Reach TW19: Stanw M 7A 174
Colne Rd. E5 .4A 68
   N21 . . . . .7J 23
   TW1: Twick 1J 131
   TW2: Twick 1J 131
Colne St. E13 .3J 87
COLNEY HATCH 6J 31
Colney Hatch La. N10 . . . . .6J 31
   N11 . . . . .6J 31
Colnmore Ct. E2 . . . . .3K *85*
   (off Meath Cres.)
Coln Trad. Est. SL3: Poyle 4A 174
Cologne Rd. SW11 . . . . .4B 118
Coloma Ct. BR4: W W'ck 4G 171
Colombo Rd. IG1: Ilf 1G 71
Colombo St. SE1 . . . . .5A 14 (1B 102)
Colombo Street Sports & Community Cen.
   . . . . .5A 14
Colomb St. SE10 . . . . .5G 105
Colonel's Wlk. EN2: Enf 3G 23
Colonial Av. TW2: Whitt 6G 113
Colonial Ct. N7 . . . . .3K 65
Colonial Dr. W4 . . . . .4J 97
Colonial Rd. TW14: Felt 7G 111
Colonnade WC1 . . . . .4F 7 (4J 83)
Colonnade, The *SE1* 6J *13*
   (off Waterloo Rd.)
Colonnades, The W2 . . . . .6K 81
Colonnades Leisure Park, The 6A 168
Colonnade Wlk. SW1 . . . .4J 17 (4F 101)
Colony Mans. *SW5* 5K *99*
   (off Earl's Ct. Rd.)
Colony M. *N1* .5D *66*
   (off Mildmay Gro. Nth.)
Colorado Apartments *N8* 3K *47*
   (off Gt. Amwell La.)
Colorado Bldg. *SE13* 1D *122*
   (off Deal's Gateway)

Colosseum Apartments *E2* 2K *85*
   (off Palmers Rd.)
Colosseum Ter. NW1 . . . . .2K 5
Colour Cl. SW1 . . . . .5B 12
Colour Ho. *SE1* 7H *15*
   (off Bell Yd M.)
Colour House Theatre
   Merton 1A 154
Colroy Ct. NW11 . . . . .5G 45
Colson Rd. CR0: C'don 2E 168
Colson Way SW16 . . . . .4G 137
Colstead Ho. *E1* 6H *85*
   (off Watney Mkt.)
Colsterworth Rd. N15 . . . . .4F 49
   (not continuous)
Colston Av. SM5: Cars 4C 166
Colston Ct. SM5: Cars 4D 166
Colston Rd. E7 . . . . .6B 70
   SW14 . . . . .4J 115
Coltash Ct. *EC1* 3D *8*
   (off Whitecross St.)
Colthurst Cres. N4 . . . . .2B 66
Colthurst Dr. N9 . . . . .3C 34
Coltham Ho. *SE10* 6E *104*
   (off Welland St.)
Coltman St. E14 . . . . .5A 86
Coltness Cres. SE2 . . . . .5B 108
Colton Gdns. N17 . . . . .3C 48
Colton Rd. HA1: Harr 5J 41
Coltsfoot Dr. UB7: Yiew 6A 74
Coltstead Dr. UB7: Yiew 6A 74
Columbas Dr. NW3 . . . . .1B 64
Columbia Av. HA4: Ruis 1K 57
   HA8: Edg 1H 43
   KT4: Wor Pk 7B 152
Columbia Gdns. Nth. *SW6* 6J *99*
   (off Rickett St.)
Columbia Gdns. Sth. *SW6* 6J *99*
   (off Rickett St.)
Columbia Ho. *E3* 4B *86*
   (off Hamlets Way)
Columbia Point *SE16* 3J *103*
   (off Canada Est.)
Columbia Rd. E2 . . . . .1J 9 (3F 85)
   E13 . . . . .4H 87
Columbia Road Flower Market 1K *9*
   (off Columbia Rd.)
Columbia Sq. SW14 . . . . .4J 115
Columbia Wharf EN3: Pond E 6F 25
Columbine Av. CR2: S Croy 7B 168
   E6 . . . . .5C 88
Columbine Way SE13 . . . . .2E 122
Columbus Ct. *SE16* 1J *103*
   (off Rotherhithe St.)
Columbus Courtyard E14 . . . . .1C 104
Columbus Gdns. HA6: Nwood 1J 39
Colva Wlk. N19 . . . . .2F 65
Colvern Ho. RM7: Rom 5J 55
Colverson Ho. *E1* 5J *85*
   (off Lindley St.)
Colvestone Cres. E8 . . . . .5F 67
Colview Ct. SE9 . . . . .1B 142
Colville Est. N1 . . . . .1E 84
Colville Est. W. E2 . . . . .2K 9
Colville Gdns. W11 . . . . .6H 81
   (not continuous)
Colville Ho. *E2* 2J *85*
   (off Waterloo Gdns.)
Colville Ho's. W11 . . . . .6H 81
Colville Mans. *E20* 5D *68*
   (off Victory Pde.)
Colville M. W11 . . . . .6H 81
Colville Pl. W1 . . . . .6B 6 (5H 83)
Colville Rd.
   E11 . . . . .3E 68
   E17 . . . . .2A 50
   N9 . . . . .1C 34
   W3 . . . . .3H 97
   W11 . . . . .6H 81
Colville Sq. W11 . . . . .6H 81
Colville Ter. W11 . . . . .6H 81
Colvin Cl. SE26 . . . . .5J 139

Colvin Gdns. E4 . . . . .3K 35
   E11 . . . . .4K 51
   IG6: Ilf 1G 53
Colvin Ho. *W10* 6F *81*
   (off Kingsdown Cl.)
Colvin Rd. CR7: Thor H 5A 156
   E6 . . . . .6C 70
Colwall Gdns. IG8: Wfd G 5D 36
Colwell Rd. SE22 . . . . .5F 121
Colwick Cl. N6 . . . . .7H 47
Colwith Rd. W6 . . . . .6E 98
Colwood Gdns. SW19 . . . . .7B 136
Colworth Gro. SE17 . . . . .4C 102
Colworth Rd. CR0: C'don 1G 169
   E11 . . . . .6G 51
Colwyn Av. UB6: G'frd 2K 77
Colwyn Cl. SW16 . . . . .5G 137
Colwyn Cres. TW3: Houn 1G 113
Colwyn Grn. *NW9* 6A *44*
   (off Snowdon Dr.)
Colwyn Ho. SE1 . . . . .2J 19 (3A 102)
Colwyn Rd. NW2 . . . . .3D 62
Colyer Cl. SE9 . . . . .2F 143
Colyers Cl. DA8: Erith 1K 127
Colyers La. DA8: Erith 1J 127
Colyers Wlk. DA8: Erith 1K 127
Colyton Cl. DA16: Well 1D 126
   HA0: Wemb 6C 60
Colyton La. SW16 . . . . .5A 138
Colyton Rd. SE22 . . . . .5H 121
Colyton Way N18 . . . . .5B 34
Combe, The NW1 . . . . .2K 5 (3F 83)
Combe Av. SE3 . . . . .7H 105
Combedale Rd. SE10 . . . . .5J 105
Combe Ho. *W2* 5J *81*
   (off Gt. Western Rd.)
Combemartin Rd. SW18 . . . . .7G 117
Combe M. SE3 . . . . .7H 105
Comber Cl. NW2 . . . . .3D 62
Comber Gro. SE5 . . . . .7C 102
Comber Ho. SE5 . . . . .7C 102
Combermere Rd.
   SM4: Mord 6K 153
   SW9 . . . . .3K 119
Comberton *KT1: King T* 2G *151*
   (off Eureka Rd.)
Comberton Rd. E5 . . . . .2H 67
Combeside SE18 . . . . .7K 107
Combwell Cres. SE2 . . . . .3A 108
Comedy Store 3C *12*
   (off Oxendon St.)
Comely Bank Rd. E17 . . . . .5E 50
Comeragh M. W14 . . . . .5G 99
Comeragh Rd. W14 . . . . .5G 99
Comer Cres. *UB2: S'hall* 2G *95*
   (off Windmill Av.)
Comerell Pl. SE10 . . . . .5H 105
Comerford Rd. SE4 . . . . .4A 122
Comer Ho. EN5: New Bar 4F 21
Comet Cl. E12 . . . . .4B 70
Comet Ho. UB3: Harl 7E 92
Comet Pl. SE8 . . . . .7C 104
   (not continuous)
Comet Rd. TW19: Stanw 7A 110
Comet St. SE8 . . . . .7C 104
Comfort St. SE15 . . . . .6E 102
Commander Av. NW9 . . . . .3C 44
Commerce Pk. CR0: Wadd 2K 167
Commerce Rd. N22 . . . . .1K 47
   TW8: Bford 6C 96
Commerce Way CR0: Wadd 2K 167
Commercial Dock Path *SE16* 3B *104*
   (off Gulliver St.)
Commercial Rd. E1 . . . . . . .7K 9 (6G 85)
   E14 . . . . .6G 85
   N18 . . . . .5K 33
Commercial Rd. Ind. Est. N18 . . . . . .6A 34
Commercial St. E1 . . . . .4J 9 (4F 85)
Commercial Way NW10 . . . . .2H 79
   SE10 . . . . .4H 105
   SE15 . . . . .7F 103

Commercial Wharf *E8* 1E *84*
   (off Kingsland Rd.)
Commerell St. SE10 . . . . .5G 105
Commodity Quay E1 . . . . . .3K 15 (7F 85)
Commodore Ct. *SE8* 1C *122*
   (off Albyn Rd.)
Commodore Ho. *E14* 7E *86*
   (off Poplar High St.)
   SW18 . . . . .3A 118
Commodore Sq. SW10 . . . . .1A 118
Commodore St. E1 . . . . .4A 86
Common, The E15 . . . . .6G 69
   HA7: Stan 2D 26
   UB2: S'hall 4A 94
   UB7: W Dray 1D 174
   W5 . . . . .7E 78
   (not continuous)
Commondale SW15 . . . . .2E 116
Commonfield La. SW17 . . . . .5C 136
Common La. KT10: Clay 7A 162
Common Mile Cl. SW4 . . . . .5H 119
Common Rd. HA7: Stan 4C 26
   KT10: Clay 6A 162
   SW13 . . . . .3D 116
Commonside BR2: Kes 4A 172
Commonside E. CR4: Mitc 3E 154
Commonside W. CR4: Mitc 3D 154
Commonwealth Av. UB3: Hayes 6F 75
   W12 . . . . .7D 80
   (not continuous)
Commonwealth Conference Cen. 5B 12
Commonwealth Rd. N17 . . . . .7B 34
Commonwealth Way SE2 . . . . .5B 108
Community Cl. TW5: Cran 1K 111
   UB10: Ick 3D 56
Community La. N7 . . . . .5H 65
Community Rd. E15 . . . . .5F 69
   UB6: G'frd 1G 77
Como Rd. SE23 . . . . .2A 140
Como St. RM7: Rom 5K 55
Compass Cl. *SE1* 5J *15*
   (off Shad Thames)
Compass Hill TW10: Rich 6D 114
Compass Ho. *E1* 1H *103*
   (off Raine St.)
   SW18 . . . . .4K 117
Compass La. *BR1: Brom* 1J *159*
   (off North St.)
Compass Point *E14* 7B *86*
   (off Grenade St.)
Compass Theatre 3E 56
Compayne Gdns. NW6 . . . . .7K 63
Compayne Mans. *NW6* 6K *63*
   (off Fairhazel Gdns.)
Complter Pas. EC2 . . . . .1D 14
Compton Av. E6 . . . . .2B 88
   HA0: Wemb 4C 60
   N1 . . . . .6B 66
   N6 . . . . .7C 46
Compton Cl. E3 . . . . .5C 86
   HA8: Edg 7D 28
   NW1 . . . . .2K 5
   NW11 . . . . .3F 63
   SE15 . . . . .7G 103
   W13 . . . . .6A 78
Compton Ct. SE19 . . . . .6E 138
   SM1: Sutt 4A 166
Compton Cres. KT9: Chess 5E 162
   N17 . . . . .7H 33
   UB5: N'olt 1B 76
   W4 . . . . .6J 97
Compton Ho. SW11 . . . . .1C 118
Compton Leisure Cen. 6H 31
Compton Pas. EC1 . . . . . . .3B 8 (4B 84)
Compton Pl. WC1 . . . . .3E 6 (4J 83)
Compton Ri. HA5: Pinn 5C 40
Compton Rd. CR0: C'don 1H 169
   N1 . . . . .6B 66
   N21 . . . . .1G 33

Compton Rd. NW10 . . . . .3F **81**
  SW19 . . . . .6H **135**
  UB3: Hayes 1B **75**
Compton St. EC1 . . . . .3A **8** (4B **84**)
Compton Ter. N1 . . . . .6B **66**
  N21 .1F **33**
Comreddy Cl. EN2: Enf 1G **23**
Comus Ho. SE17 . . . . .4E **102**
                 (off Comus Pl.)
Comus Pl. SE17 . . . . .4E **102**
Comyn Rd. SW11 . . . . .4C **118**
Comyns, The WD23: B Hea 1B **26**
Comyns Cl. E16 . . . . .5H **87**
Comyns Rd. RM9: Dag 7G **73**
Conant Ho. SE11 . . . . .7K **19**
               (off St Agnes Pl.)
Conant M. E1 . . . . .7G **85**
Concanon Rd. SW2 . . . . .4K **119**
Concert Hall App. SE1 . . . .5H **13** (1K **101**)
Concord Bus. Cen. W3 . . . . .4H **79**
Concord Cl. UB5: N'olt 3B **76**
Concord Ct. KT1: King T 3F **151**
                 (off Winery La.)
Concorde Cl. TW3: Houn 2F **113**
  UB10: Uxb 2A **74**
Concorde Dr. E6 . . . . .5D **88**
Concorde Way SE16 . . . . .4K **103**
Concord Ho. KT3: N Mald 3A **152**
  N17 . . . . .7A **34**
                  (off Park La.)
Concordia Wharf E14 . . . . .1E **104**
             (off Coldharbour)
Concord Rd. EN3: Pond E 5C **24**
  W3 . . . . .4H **79**
Concord Ter. HA2: Harr 2F **59**
               (off Coles Cres.)
Concourse, The N9 . . . . .2B **34**
  (within Edmonton Grn. Shop. Cen.)
  NW9 .1B **44**
            (off Quakers Course)
Condell Rd. SW8 . . . . .1G **119**
Conder St. E14 . . . . .6A **86**
Condor Path UB5: N'olt 2E **76**
                (off Union Rd.)
Condover Cres. SE18 . . . . .7F **107**
Condray Pl. SW11 . . . . .7C **100**
Conduit Av. SE10 . . . . .1F **123**
Conduit Ct. WC2 . . . . .2E **12**
Conduit La. CR0: C'don 5G **169**
  CR2: S Croy 5G **169**
  EN3: Pond E 6F **25**
  N18 . . . . .5D **34**
Conduit M. SE18 . . . . .5F **107**
  W2 . . . . .1A **10** (6B **82**)
Conduit Pas. W2 . . . . .1A **10**
Conduit Pl. W2 . . . . .1A **10** (6B **82**)
Conduit Rd. SE18 . . . . .5F **107**
Conduit St. W1 . . . . .2K **11** (7F **83**)
Conduit Way NW10 . . . . .7J **61**
Conewood St. N5 . . . . .3B **66**
Coney Acre SE21 . . . . .1C **138**
Coney Burrows E4 . . . . .2B **36**
Coney Gro. UB8: Hil 3C **74**
Coneygrove Path UB5: N'olt 6C **58**
                (off Arnold Rd.)
CONEY HALL 3G **171**
Coney Hall Pde. BR4: W W'ck 3G **171**
Coney Hill Rd. BR4: W W'ck 2G **171**
Coney Way SW8 . . . . .6K **101**
Conference Cl. E4 . . . . .2K **35**
Conference Rd. SE2 . . . . .4C **108**
Congers Ho. SE8 . . . . .7C **104**
Congleton Gro. SE18 . . . . .5G **107**
Congo Dr. N9 .3D **34**
Congo Rd. SE18 . . . . .5H **107**
Congress Rd. SE2 . . . . .4C **108**
Congreve Ho. N16 . . . . .5E **66**
Congreve Rd. SE9 . . . . .3D **124**
Congreve St. SE17 . . . . .4E **102**
Congreve Wlk. E16 . . . . .5B **88**
               (off Fulmer Rd.)

Conical Cnr. EN2: Enf 2H **23**
Conifer Cl. BR6: Orp 4H **173**
Conifer Ct. TW15: Ashf 5B **128**
               (off The Crescent)
Conifer Gdns. EN1: Enf 6K **23**
  SM1: Sutt 2K **165**
  SW16 . . . . .3K **137**
Conifer Ho. SE4 . . . . .4B **122**
             (off Brockley Rd.)
Conifers Cl. TW11: Tedd 7B **132**
Conifer Way HA0: Wemb 3C **60**
  UB3: Hayes 7J **75**
Coniger Rd. SW6 . . . . .2J **117**
Coningham Ct. SW10 . . . . .7A **100**
               (off King's Rd.)
Coningham M. W12 . . . . .1C **98**
Coningham Rd. W12 . . . . .2D **98**
Coningsby Av. NW9 . . . . .2A **44**
Coningsby Cotts. W5 . . . . .2D **96**
Coningsby Ct. CR4: Mitc 2E **154**
Coningsby Gdns. E4 . . . . .6J **35**
Coningsby Rd. CR2: S Croy 7C **168**
  N4 . . . . .7B **48**
  W5 . . . . .2D **96**
Conington Rd. SE13 . . . . .2D **122**
Conisbee Ct. N14 . . . . .5B **22**
Conisborough Cres. SE6 . . . . .3E **140**
Conisbrough NW1 . . . . .1G **83**
               (off Bayham St.)
Coniscliffe Cl. BR7: Chst 1E **160**
Coniscliffe Rd. N13 . . . . .3H **33**
Coniston NW1 .1A **6**
             (off Harrington St.)
Coniston Av. DA16: Well 3J **125**
  IG11: Bark 7J **71**
  UB6: G'frd 3B **78**
Coniston Cl. DA7: Bex 1J **127**
  DA8: Erith 7K **109**
  IG11: Bark 7J **71**
  N20 . . . . .3F **31**
  SW13 .7B **98**
  SW20 .6F **153**
  W4 . . . . .7J **97**
Coniston Ct. NW7 . . . . .7B **30**
             (off Langstone La.)
  SE16 .2K **103**
              (off Eleanor Cl.)
  SM6: Wall 4F **167**
  TW15: Ashf 3A **128**
  W2 . . . . .1D **10**
              (off Kendal St.)
Coniston Way N7 . . . . .7J **65**
Coniston Gdns. HA5: Eastc 4J **39**
  HA9: Wemb 1C **60**
  IG4: Ilf .4C **52**
  N9 . . . . .1D **34**
  NW9 . . . . .5K **43**
  SM2: Sutt 6B **166**
Coniston Ho. E3 . . . . .4B **86**
             (off Southern Gro.)
  SE5 . . . . .7C **102**
             (off Wyndham Rd.)
Coniston Rd. BR1: Brom 6G **141**
  CR0: C'don 7G **157**
  DA7: Bex 1J **127**
  N10 . . . . .2F **47**
  N17 . . . . .6B **34**
  TW2: Whitt 6F **113**
Coniston Wlk. E9 . . . . .5J **67**
Coniston Way KT9: Chess 3E **162**
Conlan St. W10 . . . . .4G **81**
Conley Rd. NW10 . . . . .6A **62**
Conley St. SE10 . . . . .5G **105**
Connaught Av.
  E4 . . . . .7K **25** & 1A **36**
  EN1: Enf 2K **23**
  EN4: E Barn 1J **31**
  SW14 .3J **115**
  TW4: Houn 4C **112**
  TW15: Ashf 4A **128**
Connaught Bri. E16 . . . . .1B **106**

Connaught Bus. Cen.
  CR0: Wadd 6K **167**
  CR4: Mitc 5D **154**
  NW9 . . . . .5B **44**
Connaught Cl. E10 . . . . .2A **68**
  EN1: Enf 2K **23**
  SM1: Sutt 2B **166**
  UB8: Hil 4E **74**
  W2 . . . . .1D **10** (6C **82**)
Connaught Club, The 1C **36**
Connaught Ct. E17 . . . . .4D **50**
               (off Orford Rd.)
  W2 . . . . .2E **10**
             (off Connaught St.)
Connaught Dr. NW11 . . . . .4J **45**
Connaught Gdns. N10 . . . . .5F **47**
  N13 . . . . .4G **33**
  SM4: Mord 4A **154**
Connaught Hgts. E16 . . . . .1B **106**
       (off Agnes George Wlk.)
  UB10: Hil 4E **74**
             (off Uxbridge Rd.)
Connaught Ho. NW10 . . . . .3D **80**
             (off Trenmar Gdns.)
  W1 . . . . .3J **11**
             (off Davies St.)
Connaught La. IG1: Ilf 2G **71**
Connaught Lodge N4 . . . . .7A **48**
             (off Connaught Rd.)
Connaught M. NW3 . . . . .4C **64**
  SE18 . . . . .5E **106**
  SW6 . . . . .1G **117**
Connaught Pl. W2 . . . . .2E **10** (7D **82**)
Connaught Rd. E4 . . . . .1B **36**
  E11 . . . . .1F **69**
  E16 . . . . .1B **106**
  E17 . . . . .5C **50**
  EN5: Barn 6A **20**
  HA3: W'stone 1K **41**
  IG1: Ilf .2H **71**
  KT3: N Mald 4A **152**
  N4 . . . . .7A **48**
  NW10 .1A **80**
  SE18 . . . . .5E **106**
  SM1: Sutt 2B **166**
  TW10: Rich 5F **115**
  TW11: Tedd 5H **131**
  W13 . . . . .7B **78**
CONNAUGHT RDBT. 7B **88**
       (off Victoria Dock Rd.)
Connaught Sq. W2 . . . . .1D **10** (6D **82**)
Connaught St. W2 . . . . .1D **10** (6C **82**)
Connaught Way N13 . . . . .4G **33**
Connaught Works E3 . . . . .1A **86**
             (off Old Ford Rd.)
Connect La. IG6: Ilf 2G **53**
Connell Ct. SE14 . . . . .6K **103**
             (off Myers La.)
Connell Cres. W5 . . . . .4F **79**
Connersville Way CR0: Wadd 3A **168**
Conniffe Ct. SE9 . . . . .5F **125**
Cunningham Ct. SE9 . . . . .5A **124**
Connington Cres. E4 . . . . .3A **36**
Connolly Ct. RM7: Rush G 6K **55**
               (off Union Rd.)
Connor Cl. E11 . . . . .7G **51**
  IG6: Ilf .1G **53**
Connor Ct. SW11 . . . . .1F **119**
Connor Rd. RM9: Dag 4F **73**
Connor St. E9 . . . . .1K **85**
Conolly Dell W7 . . . . .1J **95**
              (off Conolly Rd.)
Conolly Rd. W7 . . . . .1J **95**
Conrad Ct. NW9 . . . . .2A **44**
             (off Needleman Cl.)
  SE8 . . . . .4A **104**
               (off Cary Av.)
Conrad Dr. KT4: Wor Pk 1E **164**
Conrad Ho. E8 . . . . .6G **67**
  E14 . . . . .7A **86**
               (off Victory Pl.)

Conrad Ho. E16 . . . . .1K **105**
               (off Wesley Av.)
  N16 . . . . .5E **66**
             (off Matthias Rd.)
  SW8 . . . . .7J **101**
               (off Wyvil Rd.)
Conrad Twr. W3 . . . . .3H **97**
Consfield Av. KT3: N Mald 4C **152**
Consort Cl. W8 . . . . .3K **99**
               (off Wright's La.)
Consort Ho. E14 . . . . .5D **104**
             (off St Davids Sq.)
  SW6 . . . . .2A **118**
             (off Lensbury Av.)
  W2 . . . . .7K **81**
              (off Queensway)
Consort Lodge NW8 . . . . .1D **82**
            (off Prince Albert Rd.)
Consort M. TW7: Isle 5H **113**
Consort Rd. SE15 . . . . .1H **121**
Cons St. SE1 . . . . .6K **13** (2A **102**)
Constable Av. E16 . . . . .1K **105**
Constable Cl. N11 . . . . .5J **31**
  NW11 .6K **45**
  UB4: Hayes 2E **74**
Constable Ct. SE16 . . . . .5H **103**
              (off Stubbs Dr.)
  W4 . . . . .5H **97**
             (off Chaseley Dr.)
Constable Cres. N15 . . . . .5G **49**
Constable Gdns. HA8: Edg 1G **43**
  TW7: Isle 5H **113**
Constable Ho. NW3 . . . . .7D **64**
  UB5: N'olt 2B **76**
              (off Gallery Gdns.)
Constable Ho's. E14 . . . . .2C **104**
              (off Cassilis Rd.)
Constable M. BR1: Brom 2K **159**
  RM8: Dag 4B **72**
Constable Wlk. SE21 . . . . .3E **138**
Constance Allen Ho. W10 . . . . .6F **81**
               (off Bridge Cl.)
Constance Cl. SW15 . . . . .4K **133**
Constance Cres. BR2: Hayes 7H **159**
Constance Rd. CR0: C'don 7B **156**
  EN1: Enf 6K **23**
  SM1: Sutt 4A **166**
  TW2: Whitt 7F **113**
Constance St. E16 . . . . .1C **106**
Constant Ho. E14 . . . . .7D **86**
               (off Harrow La.)
Constantine Ct. E1 . . . . .6G **85**
             (off Fairclough St.)
Constantine Ho. UB3: Hayes 6F **75**
Constantine Pl. UB10: Hil 1B **74**
Constantine Rd. NW3 . . . . .4C **64**
Constitution Hill SW1 . . . . . .6J **11** (2F **101**)
Constitution Ri. SE18 . . . . .1E **124**
Consul Av.
  RM9: Dag, Rain 3J **91**
  RM13: Rain 3J **91**
Consul Ho. E3 . . . . .4C **86**
           (off Wellington Way)
Content St. SE17 . . . . .4D **102**
Contessa Cl. BR6: Farnb 5J **173**
Control Twr. Rd. TW6: H'row A 3C **110**
Convair Wlk. UB5: N'olt 3B **76**
Convent Cl. BR3: Beck 7E **140**
  EN5: Barn 2C **20**
Convent Gdns. W5 . . . . .4C **96**
  W11 . . . . .6G **81**
Convent Hill SE19 . . . . .6C **138**
Convent Rd. TW15: Ashf 5D **128**
Convent Way UB2: S'hall 4A **94**
Conway Cl. BR3: Beck 1A **158**
  HA7: Stan 6F **27**
Conway Cres. RM6: Chad H 6C **54**
  UB6: G'frd 2J **77**
Conway Dr. SM2: Sutt 6K **165**
  TW15: Ashf 6E **128**
  UB3: Harl 3E **92**

Conway Gdns. CR4: Mitc 4J **155**
  EN2: Enf 1K **23**
  HA9: Wemb 7C **42**
Conway Gro. W3 . . . . .5K **79**
Conway Ho. E14 . . . . .4C **104**
                 (off Cahir St.)
  SW3 . . . . .6F **17**
           (off Ormonde Ga.)
Conway M. W1 . . . . .4A **6**
Conway Rd. N14 . . . . .3D **32**
  N15 . . . . .5B **48**
  NW2 . . . . .2E **62**
  SE18 . . . . .4H **107**
  SW20 . . . . .1E **152**
  TW4: Houn 7D **112**
  TW6: H'row A 3D **110**
  TW13: Hanw 5B **130**
Conway St. W1 . . . . .4A **6** (4G **83**)
          (not continuous)
Conway Wlk. TW12: Hamp 6D **130**
Conybeare NW3 . . . . .7C **64**
Conyers Cl. IG8: Wfd G 6B **36**
Conyer's Rd. SW16 . . . . .5H **137**
Conyer St. E3 . . . . .2A **86**
Cooden Cl. BR1: Brom 7K **141**
Cook Cl. SE8 . . . . .5A **104**
          (off Evelyn St.)
  SE16 . . . . .1K **103**
        (off Rotherhithe St.)
Cookes Cl. E11 . . . . .2H **69**
Cookes La. SM3: Cheam 6G **165**
Cooke St. IG11: Bark 1G **89**
          (not continuous)
Cookham Cl. UB2: S'hall 3F **95**
Cookham Cres. SE16 . . . . . . .2K **103**
Cookham Dene Cl. BR7: Chst . .1H **161**
Cookham Ho. E2 . . . . .3J **9**
        (off Montclare St.)
Cookham Rd. BR8: Swan 7G **145**
Cookhill Rd. SE2 . . . . .2B **108**
Cook Rd. RM9: Dag 1E **90**
Cooks Cl. E14 . . . . .1C **104**
        (off Cabot Sq.)
  RM5: Col R 1J **55**
Cooks Hole Rd. EN2: Enf 1H **23**
Cookson Gro. DA8: Erith 7H **109**
Cooks Rd. E15 . . . . .2D **86**
  SE17 . . . . .6B **102**
Coolfin Rd. E16 . . . . .6J **87**
Coolgardie Av. E4 . . . . .5A **36**
  IG7: Chig 3K **37**
Coolgardie Rd. TW15: Ashf . . .5E **128**
Coolhurst Rd. N8 . . . . .6H **47**
Coolhurst Tennis & Squash Club 6H **47**
Cool Oak La. NW9 . . . . .7A **44**
Coomassie Rd. W9 . . . . .4H **81**
COOMBE 7J **133**
Coombe Av. CR0: C'don 4E **168**
Coombe Bank KT2: King T 1A **152**
Coombe Cl. HA8: Edg 2F **43**
  TW3: Houn 4E **112**
Coombe Cnr. N21 . . . . .1G **33**
Coombe Ct. CR0: C'don 4D **168**
        (off Coombe Rd.)
Coombe Cres. TW12: Hamp . . .7D **130**
Coombe Dene BR2: Brom 4H **159**
       (off Cumberland Rd.)
Coombe Dr. HA4: Ruis 1K **57**
Coombefield Cl. KT3: N Mald . .5A **152**
Coombe Gdns. KT3: N Mald . . .4B **152**
  SW20 . . . . .2C **152**
Coombe Hill Glade KT2: King T .7A **134**
Coombe Hill Golf Course 7K **133**
Coombe Hill Rd. KT2: King T . . .7A **134**
Coombe Ho. N7 . . . . .5H **65**
Coombe Ho. Chase KT3: N Mald .1K **151**
Coombehurst Cl. EN4: Cockf . . .2J **21**
COOMBE LANE 1B **152**
Coombe La. CR0: C'don 5H **169**
  SW20 . . . . .1B **152**

Coombe La. Flyover SW20 . . . . . .1B **152**
Coombe La. W. KT2: King T 1H **151**
Coombe Lea BR1: Brom 3C **160**
Coombe Lodge SE7 . . . . .6A **106**
Coombe Neville KT2: King T . . .7K **133**
Coombe Pk. KT2: King T 5J **133**
Coombe Pl. KT2: King T 5J **133**
Coomber Ho. SW6 . . . . .3K **117**
     (off Wandsworth Bri. Rd.)
Coombe Ridings KT2: King T . . .5J **133**
Coombe Ri. KT2: King T 1J **151**
Coombe Rd. CR0: C'don 4D **168**
  KT2: King T 1G **151**
  KT3: N Mald 2A **152**
  N22 . . . . .2A **48**
  NW10 . . . . .3K **61**
  SE26 . . . . .4H **139**
  TW12: Hamp 6D **130**
  W4 . . . . .5A **98**
  W13 . . . . .3B **96**
Coomber Way CR0: Bedd 7H **155**
Coombes Rd. RM9: Dag 1F **91**
Coombe Wlk. SM1: Sutt 3K **165**
Coombewood Dr. RM6: Chad H . .6F **55**
Coombe Wood Golf Course 7H **133**
Coombe Wood Local Nature Reserve
  . . . . .7B **134**
Coombe Wood Rd. KT2: King T .5J **133**
Coombrook Ct. SE16 . . . . .2A **104**
        (off Elgar St.)
Coombs St. N1 . . . . .1B **8** (2B **84**)
Coomer M. SW6 . . . . .6H **99**
Coomer Pl. SW6 . . . . .6H **99**
Coomer Rd. SW6 . . . . .6H **99**
Coomer Rd. SW6 . . . . .6H **99**
Cooms Wlk. HA8: Edg 1J **43**
Coope Ct. RM7: Rush G 6K **55**
        (off Union Rd.)
Cooperage, The SE1 . . . . .6J **15**
       (off Gainsford St.)
  SW8 . . . . .7K **101**
      (off Regent's Bri. Gdns.)
Cooperage Cl. N17 . . . . .6A **34**
Co-operative Ho. SE15 . . . . . . .3G **121**
Cooper Av. E17 . . . . .1A **50**
Cooper Cl. SE1 . . . . .7K **13** (2A **102**)
Cooper Ct. SE18 . . . . .6F **107**
Cooper Cres. SM5: Cars 3D **166**
Cooper Ho. NW8 . . . . .4A **4**
        (off Lyons Pl.)
  SE4 . . . . .5K **121**
       (off St Norbert Rd.)
  TW4: Houn 3D **112**
Cooper Rd. CR0: Wadd 4B **168**
  NW4 . . . . .6F **45**
  NW10 . . . . .5C **62**
Coopersale Cl. IG8: Wfd G 7F **37**
Coopersale Rd. E9 . . . . .5K **67**
Coopers Cl. E1 . . . . .4J **85**
  RM10: Dag 6H **73**
Coopers Cl. E3 . . . . .4B **86**
        (off Eric St.)
  TW7: Isle 2K **113**
      (off Woodlands Rd.)
  W3 . . . . .1J **97**
       (off Church Rd.)
Coopers La. E10 . . . . .1D **68**
  NW1 . . . . .2H **83**
  SE12 . . . . .2K **141**
Coopers Lodge SE1 . . . . .6J **15**
        (off Tooley St.)
Coopers M. BR3: Beck 2C **158**
Cooper M. W4 . . . . .3J **97**
Cooper's Rd. SE1 . . . . .5F **103**
Coopers Row EC3 . . . . .2J **15** (7F **85**)
Cooper St. E16 . . . . .5H **87**
Coopers Wlk. E15 . . . . .5G **69**
Coopers Yd. N1 . . . . .7B **66**
        (off Upper St.)
  SE19 . . . . .6E **138**
Coote Gdns. RM8: Dag 3F **73**
Coote Rd. DA7: Bex 1F **127**
  RM8: Dag 3F **73**

Cope Ho. EC1 . . . . .2D **8**
Copeland Dr. E14 . . . . .4C **104**
Copeland Ho. SE11 . . . . .2H **19**
  SW17 . . . . .4B **136**
Copeland Rd. E17 . . . . .6D **50**
  SE15 . . . . .2G **121**
Copeman Cl. SE26 . . . . .5J **139**
Copenhagen Gdns. W4 . . . . . . .2K **97**
Copenhagen Ho. N1 . . . . .1K **83**
       (off Barnsbury Est.)
Copenhagen Pl. E14 . . . . .6B **86**
        (not continuous)
Copenhagen St. N1 . . . . .1J **83**
Cope Pl. W8 . . . . .3J **99**
Copers Cope Rd. BR3: Beck . . .7B **140**
Cope St. SE16 . . . . .4K **103**
Copford Cl. IG8: Wfd G 6H **37**
Copford Wlk. N1 . . . . .1C **84**
       (off Popham St.)
Copgate Path SW16 . . . . .6K **137**
Copinger Wlk. HA8: Edg 1H **43**
Copland Av. HA0: Wemb 5D **60**
Copland Cl. HA0: Wemb 5C **60**
Copland M. HA0: Wemb 6E **60**
Copland Rd. HA0: Wemb 6E **60**
Copleston Pas. SE5 . . . . .2F **121**
Copleston M. SE15 . . . . .2F **121**
Copleston Pas. SE5 . . . . .2F **121**
Copleston Rd. SE15 . . . . .3F **121**
Copley Cl. SE17 . . . . .6C **102**
  W7 . . . . .4K **77**
Copley Dene BR1: Brom 1B **160**
Copley Pk. SW16 . . . . .6K **137**
Copley Rd. HA7: Stan 5H **27**
Copley St. E1 . . . . .5K **85**
Coppard Gdns. KT9: Chess . . .6C **162**
Coppelia Rd. SE3 . . . . .4H **123**
Coppen Rd. RM8: Dag 7F **55**
Copperas St. SE8 . . . . .6D **104**
Copper Beech Cl. IG5: Ilf 1E **52**
Copperbeech Cl. NW3 . . . . .5B **64**
Copper Beeches Ct. TW7: Isle . .1H **113**
Copper Box Arena 6C **68**
Copper Cl. N17 . . . . .7C **34**
  SE19 . . . . .7F **139**
Copper Ct. E5 . . . . .2J **67**
Copperdale Rd. UB3: Hayes . . .2J **93**
Copperfield Av. UB8: Hil 5C **74**
Copperfield Dr. N15 . . . . .4F **49**
Copperfield Ho. SE1 . . . . .7K **15**
       (off Wolseley St.)
  W1 . . . . .5H **5**
      (off Marylebone High St.)
  W11 . . . . .1F **99**
       (off St Ann's Rd.)
Copperfield M. E2 . . . . .2G **85**
  N18 . . . . .4K **33**
Copperfield Rd. E3 . . . . .4A **86**
  SE28 . . . . .6C **90**
Copperfields BR3: Beck 1E **158**
  HA1: Harr 7J **41**
  TW16: Sun 6H **129**
Copperfields Ct. W3 . . . . .2G **97**
Copperfield St. SE1 . . . . .6B **14** (2B **102**)
Copperfield Way BR7: Chst 6G **143**
  HA5: Pinn 4D **40**
Coppergate Cl. BR1: Brom 1K **159**
Copperlight Apartments SW18 . . . .5J **117**
       (off Buckhold Rd.)
Coppermead Cl. NW2 . . . . .3E **62**
Copper M. W4 . . . . .3J **97**
Copper Mill Dr. TW7: Isle 2K **113**
Coppermill Hgts. N17 . . . . .3H **49**
       (off Daneland Wlk.)
Copper Mill La. SW17 . . . . .4A **136**
Coppermill La. E17 . . . . .6J **49**
Copper Row SE1 . . . . .5J **15**
Copperworks, The N1 . . . . .2J **83**
       (off Railway St.)
Coppetts Cen. N12 . . . . .7J **31**
Coppetts Cl. N12 . . . . .7H **31**

Coppetts Rd. N10 . . . . .7J **31**
Coppetts Wood & Glebelands
  Local Nature Reserve 6J **31**
Coppice, The DA5: Bexl 3K **145**
  EN2: Enf 4G **23**
  EN5: New Bar 6E **20**
      (off Great Nth. Rd.)
  TW15: Ashf 6D **128**
  UB7: Yiew 6A **74**
Coppice Cl. BR3: Beck 4D **158**
  HA4: Ruis 6F **39**
  HA7: Stan 6E **26**
  SW20 . . . . .3E **152**
Coppice Dr. SW15 . . . . .6D **116**
Coppice Wlk. N20 . . . . .3D **30**
Coppice Way E18 . . . . .4H **51**
Coppies Gro. N11 . . . . .4A **32**
Copping Cl. CR0: C'don 4E **168**
Coppins, The CR0: New Ad . . .6D **170**
  HA3: Hrw W 6D **26**
Coppock Cl. SW11 . . . . .2C **118**
Coppsfield KT8: W Mole 3E **148**
Copse, The E4 . . . . .1C **36**
  N2 . . . . .3D **46**
Copse Av. BR4: W W'ck 2D **170**
Copse Cl. HA6: Nwood 2E **38**
  SE7 . . . . .6K **105**
Copse Glade KT6: Surb 7D **150**
COPSE HILL 7C **134**
Copse Hill SM2: Sutt 7K **165**
  SW20 . . . . .1C **152**
Copse Vw. CR2: Sels 7K **169**
Copsewood Cl. DA15: Sidc 6J **125**
Copse Wood Way HA6: Nwood . .1D **38**
Captain Ho. SW18 . . . . .4J **117**
Coptefield Dr. DA17: Belv 3D **108**
Copthall Av. EC2 . . . . . . .7F **9** (6D **84**)
        (not continuous)
Copthall Bldgs. EC2 . . . . .7F **9**
Copthall Cl. EC2 . . . . . . .7E **8** (6D **84**)
Copthall Dr. NW7 . . . . .7H **29**
Copthall Gdns. NW7 . . . . .7H **29**
  TW1: Twick 1K **131**
Copthall Leisure Cen. 7J **29**
Copthall Rd. E. UB10: Ick 2C **56**
Copthall Rd. W. UB10: Ick 2C **56**
Copthorne Av.
  BR2: Brom 2D **172**
  SW12 . . . . .7H **119**
Copthorne Chase TW15: Ashf . .4B **128**
Copthorne Cl. TW17: Shep 6E **146**
Copthorne M. UB3: Harl 4G **93**
Coptic St. WC1 . . . . .6E **6** (5J **83**)
Copwood Cl. N12 . . . . .4G **31**
Coral Apartments E16 . . . . .7J **87**
     (off Western Gateway)
Coral Cl. RM6: Chad H 3D **54**
Coral Ho. E1 . . . . .4A **86**
       (off Harford St.)
  NW10 . . . . .3G **79**
Coraline Cl. UB1: S'hall 3D **76**
Coralline Wlk. SE2 . . . . .3C **108**
Coral Mans. NW6 . . . . .1J **81**
      (off Kilburn High Rd.)
Coral Row SW11 . . . . .3A **118**
Coral St. SE1 . . . . .7K **13** (2A **102**)
Coram Ho. W4 . . . . .5A **98**
        (off Wood St.)
  WC1 . . . . .3E **6**
Coram Mans. WC1 . . . . .4G **7**
       (off Millman St.)
Coram St. WC1 . . . . .4E **6** (4J **83**)
Coran Cl. N9 . . . . .7E **24**
Corban Rd. TW3: Houn 3E **112**
Corbar Cl. EN4: Had W 1G **21**
Corbden Cl. SE15 . . . . .1F **121**
Corben M. SW8 . . . . .2G **119**
Corbet Cl. SM6: Wall 1E **166**
Corbet Ct. EC3 . . . . . . .1F **15** (6D **84**)
Corbet Ho. N1 . . . . .2A **84**
       (off Barnsbury Est.)

Corbet Ho. *SE5* 7C *102*
    (off Wyndham Rd.)
Corbet Pl. E1 . . . . .5J 9 (5F **85**)
Corbett Cl. SE26 . . . . .4B **140**
Corbett Gro. N22 . . . . .7D **32**
Corbett Ho. *SW10* 6A *100*
    (off Cathcart Rd.)
Corbett Rd. E11 . . . . .6A **52**
    E17 . . . . .3E **50**
Corbetts La. SE16 . . . . .4J **103**
    (not continuous)
Corbetts Pas. *SE16* 4J *103*
    (off Corbetts La.)
Corbetts Wharf *SE16* 2H *103*
    (off Bermondsey Wall E.)
Corbicum E11 . . . . .7G **51**
Corbridge Ct. SE8 . . . . .6D **104**
Corbiere Ct. SW19 . . . . .6F **135**
Corbiere Ho. *N1* 1D *84*
    (off De Beauvoir Est.)
Corbin Ho. *E3* 3D *86*
    (off Bromley High St.)
Corbins La. HA2: Harr 3F **59**
Corbould Cl. SM5: Cars 6D **166**
Corbridge N17 . . . . .7C **34**
Corbridge Cres. E2 . . . . .2H **85**
Corby Cres. EN2: Enf 4D **22**
Corbylands Rd. DA15: Sidc 7J **125**
Corbyn St. N4 . . . . .1J **65**
Corby Rd. NW10 . . . . .2K **79**
Corby Way E3 . . . . .4C **86**
Cordage Ho. *E1* 1H *103*
    (off Cobblestone Sq.)
Cordelia Cl. SE24 . . . . .4B **120**
Cordelia Gdns. TW19: Stanw 7A **110**
Cordelia Ho. *N1* 2E *84*
    (off Arden Est.)
Cordelia Rd. TW19: Stanw 7A **110**
Cordelia St. E14 . . . . .6D **86**
Cordell Ho. *N15* 5F *49*
    (off Newton Rd.)
Cordingley Rd. HA4: Ruis 2F **57**
Cording St. E14 . . . . .5D **86**
Cordwainer Ho. E8 . . . . .1H **85**
Cordwainers Ct. *E9* 7J *67*
    (off St Thomas's Sq.)
Cordwainers Wlk. E13 . . . . .2J **87**
Cord Way E14 . . . . .3C **104**
Cordwell Rd. SE13 . . . . .5G **123**
Corefield Cl. N11 . . . . .2K **31**
Corelli Ct. SE1 . . . . .4H **103**
    SW5 . . . . .4J *99*
    (off W. Cromwell Rd.)
Corelli Rd. SE3 . . . . .2C **124**
Corfe Av. HA2: Harr 4E **58**
Corfe Cl. TW4: Houn 1C **130**
    UB4: Yead 6A **76**
Corfe Ho. *SW8* 7K *101*
    (off Dorset Rd.)
Corfe Twr. W3 . . . . .2H **97**
Corfield Rd. N21 . . . . .5E **22**
Corfield St. E2 . . . . .3H **85**
Corfton Lodge W5 . . . . .5E **78**
Corfton Rd. W5 . . . . .6E **78**
Coriander Av. E14 . . . . .6F **87**
Coriander Ct. *SE1* 6K *15*
    (off Gainsford St.)
Caries Cl. RM8: Dag 2D **72**
Corinium Cl. HA9: Wemb 4F **61**
Corinne Rd. N19 . . . . .4G **65**
Corinthian Manorway DA8: Erith 4K **109**
Corinthian Rd. DA8: Erith 4K **109**
Corinthian Way TW19: Stanw 7A **110**
Corkers Path IG1: Ilf 2G **71**
Corker Wlk. N7 . . . . .2K **65**
Cork Ho. SW19 . . . . .4K **135**
Corkran Rd. KT6: Surb 7D **150**
Corkscrew Hill BR4: W W'ck 2E **170**
Cork Sq. E1 . . . . .1H **103**
Cork St. W1 . . . . .3A **12** (7G **83**)
Cork St. M. W1 . . . . .3A **12**

Cork Tree Ho. *SE27* 5B *138*
    (off Lakeview Rd.)
Cork Tree Retail Pk. E4 . . . . .5F **35**
Cork Tree Way E4 . . . . .5F **35**
Corlett St. NW1 . . . . .5C **4** (5C **82**)
Cormont Rd. SE5 . . . . .1B **120**
Cormorant Cl. E17 . . . . .7F **35**
Cormorant Ct. *SE8* 6B *104*
    (off Pilot Cl.)
Cormorant Ho. EN3: Pond E 5E **24**
Cormorant Lodge *E1* 1G *103*
    (off Thomas More St.)
Cormorant Pl. SM1: Sutt 5H **165**
Cormorant Rd. E7 . . . . .5H **69**
Cornbury Ho. *SE8* 6B *104*
    (off Evelyn St.)
Cornbury Rd. HA8: Edg 7J **27**
Cornel Ho. DA15: Sidc 3A **144**
Cornelia Dr. UB4: Yead 4A **76**
Cornelia Ho. *TW1: Twick* 6D *114*
    (off Denton Rd.)
Cornelia St. N7 . . . . .6K **65**
Cornell Bldg. *E1* 6G *85*
    (off Coke St.)
Cornell Cl. DA14: Sidc 6E **144**
Cornell Ct. EN3: Enf H 3F **25**
Cornell Ho. HA2: Harr 3D **58**
Cornell Sq. SW8 . . . . .1H **119**
Corner, The W5 . . . . .1E **96**
Corner Ct. *E2* 4H *85*
    (off Three Colts La.)
Cornercroft SM3: Cheam 5G *165*
    (off Wickham Av.)
Corner Fielde SW2 . . . . .1K **137**
Corner Grn. SE3 . . . . .2J **123**
Corner Ho. NW6 . . . . .2K **81**
    (off Quex Rd.)
Corner House Arts Centre, The 1F **163**
Cornerstone Ho. CRO: C'don 7C **156**
Corney Reach Way W4 . . . . .7A **98**
Corney Rd. W4 . . . . .6A **98**
Cornfield Cl. UB8: Uxb 2A **74**
Cornflower La. CRO: C'don 1K **169**
Cornflower Ter. SE22 . . . . .6H **121**
Cornford Cl. BR2: Brom 5J **159**
Cornford Gro. SW12 . . . . .2F **137**
Cornhill EC3 . . . . .1F **15** (6D **84**)
Cornick Ho. *SE16* 3H *103*
    (off Slippers Pl.)
Cornish Ct. N9 . . . . .7C **24**
Cornish Gro. SE20 . . . . .1H **157**
Cornish Ho. *SE17* 6B *102*
    (off Brandon Est.)
    TW8: Bford 5F **97**
Corn Mill Dr. BR6: Orp 7K **161**
Cornmill Ho. *SE8* 5C *104*
    (off Wharf St.)
Cornmill La. SE13 . . . . .3E **122**
Cornmow Dr. NW10 . . . . .5B **62**
Cornshaw Rd. RM8: Dag 1D **72**
Cornthwaite Rd. E5 . . . . .3J **67**
Cornwall Av. DA16: Well 3J **125**
    E2 . . . . .3J **85**
    KT10: Clay 7A **162**
    N3 . . . . .6G **30**
    N22 . . . . .1J **47**
    UB1: S'hall 5D **76**
Cornwall Cl. IG11: Bark 6K **71**
Cornwall Cl. HA5: Hat E 1D **40**
    W7 . . . . .4K **77**
    (off Copley Cl.)
Cornwall Cres. W11 . . . . .6G **81**
Cornwall Dr. BR5: St P 7C **144**
Cornwall Gdns. NW10 . . . . .6D **62**
    SE25 . . . . .4F **157**
    SW7 . . . . .3K **99**
Cornwall Gdns. Wlk. SW7 . . . . .3K **99**
Cornwall Gro. W4 . . . . .5A **98**

Cornwall Ho. SW7 . . . . .3K **99**
    (off Cornwall Gdns.)
Cornwallis Av. N9 . . . . .2C **34**
    SE9 . . . . .2H **143**
Cornwallis Ct. *SW8* 1J *119*
    (off Lansdowne Grn.)
Cornwallis Gro. N9 . . . . .2C **34**
Cornwallis Ho. *SE16* 2H *103*
    (off Cherry Gdn. St.)
    W12 . . . . .7D *80*
    (off India Way)
Cornwallis Rd. E17 . . . . .4K **49**
    N9 . . . . .2C **34**
    N19 . . . . .2J **65**
    RM9: Dag 4D **72**
    SE18 . . . . .3G **107**
Cornwallis Sq. N19 . . . . .2J **65**
Cornwallis Wlk. SE9 . . . . .3D **124**
Cornwall Mans. SW10 . . . . .7A *100*
    (off Cremorne Rd.)
    W8 . . . . .3F *99*
    (off Kensington Ct.)
    W14 . . . . .3F *99*
    (off Blythe Rd.)
Cornwall M. Sth. SW7 . . . . .3A **100**
Cornwall M. W. SW7 . . . . .3K **99**
Cornwall Pl. E4 . . . . .4J **25**
Cornwall Rd. CRO: C'don 2B **168**
    HA1: Harr 6G **41**
    HA4: Ruis 3H **57**
    HA5: Hat E 1D **40**
    N4 . . . . .7A **48**
    N15 . . . . .5D **48**
    N18 . . . . .5B **34**
    SE1 . . . . .4J **13** (1A **102**)
    SM2: Sutt 7H **165**
    TW1: Twick 7A **114**
    UB8: Uxb 6A **56**
Cornwall Sq. SE11 . . . . .5K **19**
Cornwall St. E1 . . . . .7H **85**
Cornwall Ter. NW1 . . . . .4F **5** (4D **82**)
Cornwall Ter. M. NW1 . . . . .4F **5**
Corn Way E11 . . . . .3F **69**
Cornwood Cl. N2 . . . . .5B **46**
Cornwood Dr. E1 . . . . .6J **85**
Cornworthy Rd. RM8: Dag 5C **72**
Corona Bldg. *E14* 1E *104*
    (off Blackwall Way)
Corona Rd. SE12 . . . . .7J **123**
Coronation Av. N16 . . . . .4F **67**
Coronation Cl. DA5: Bexl 6D **126**
    IG6: Ilf .4G **53**
Coronation Ct. DA8: Erith 7K **109**
    E15 . . . . .6H **69**
    KT1: King T 4E *150*
    (off Surbiton Rd.)
    W10 . . . . .5E *80*
    (off Brewster Gdns.)
Coronation Rd. E13 . . . . .3A **88**
    NW10 .3G **79**
    UB3: Harl 4H **93**
Coronation Vs. NW10 . . . . .4H **79**
Coronation Wlk. TW2: Whitt 1E **130**
Coroners Court
    City of London 2E **14** (7D **84**)
    North London 4C **20**
    Poplar .7D *86*
    (off Poplar High St.)
    St Pancras 1H **83**
    South London 3D *168*
    (off Barclay Rd.)
    Southwark 2D **102**
    West London 1A **118**
    Westminster 3D **18** (4H **101**)
Coronet Cinema 1J *99*
    (off Notting Hill Ga.)
Coronet Pde. HA0: Wemb 6E **60**
Coronet St. N1 . . . . .2G **9** (3E **84**)
Coronet Theatre 3C *102*
    (off New Kent Rd.)
Corporate Dr. TW13: Felt 3K **129**

Corporate Ho. HA3: Hrw W 1H **41**
Corporation Av. TW4: Houn 4C **112**
Corporation Row EC1 . . . . .3K **7** (4A **84**)
Corporation St. E15 . . . . .2G **87**
    N7 . . . . .5J **65**
Corrance Rd. SW2 . . . . .4J **119**
Corri Av. N14 . . . . .4C **32**
Corrib Ct. N13 . . . . .3E **32**
Corrib Dr. SM1: Sutt 5C **166**
Corrigan Cl. NW4 . . . . .3E **44**
Corringham Ct. NW11 . . . . .7J **45**
Corringham Ho. *E1* 6K *85*
    (off Pitsea St.)
Corringham Rd. HA9: Wemb 2G **61**
    NW11 .7J **45**
Corringway NW11 . . . . .7K **45**
    W5 . . . . .4G **79**
Corris Grn. NW9 . . . . .5A **44**
Corry Dr. SW9 . . . . .4B **120**
Corry Ho. *E14* 7D *86*
    (off Wade's Pl.)
Corsair Cl. TW19: Stanw 7A **110**
Corsair Rd. TW19: Stanw 7A **110**
Corscombe Cl. KT2: King T 5J **133**
Corsehill St. SW16 . . . . .6G **137**
Corsellis Sq. *TW1: Isle* 4B *114*
    (off Varley Dr.)
Corsham St. N1 . . . . .2F **9** (3D **84**)
Corsica St. N5 . . . . .6B **66**
Corsley Way E9 . . . . .6B **68**
Cortayne Ct. TW2: Twick 2J **131**
Cortayne Rd. SW6 . . . . .2H **117**
Cortina Dr. RM13: Rain 2J **91**
Cortis Rd. SW15 . . . . .6D **116**
Cortis Ter. SW15 . . . . .6D **116**
Cortland Cl. IG8: Wfd G 1A **52**
Corunna Rd. SW8 . . . . .1G **119**
Corunna Ter. SW8 . . . . .1G **119**
Corvette Sq. SE10 . . . . .6F **105**
Corwell Gdns. UB8: Hil 6E **74**
Corwell La. UB8: Hil 6E **74**
Coryton Path *W9* 4H *81*
    (off Ashmore Rd.)
Cosbycote Av. SE24 . . . . .5C **120**
Cosdach Av. SM6: Wall 7H **167**
Cosedge Cres. CRO: Wadd 5A **168**
Cosgrove Cl. N21 . . . . .2H **33**
    UB4: Yead 4B **76**
Cosgrove Ho. *E2* 1G *85*
    (off Whiston Rd.)
Cosmo Pl. WC1 . . . . .5F **7** (5J **83**)
Cosmopolitan Ct. EN1: Enf 5B **24**
Cosmur Cl. W12 . . . . .3B **98**
Cossall Wlk. SE15 . . . . .2H **121**
Cossar M. SW2 . . . . .5A **120**
Cosser St. SE1 . . . . .1J **19** (3A **102**)
Costa St. SE15 . . . . .2G **121**
Costons Av. UB6: G'frd 3H **77**
Costons La. UB6: G'frd 3H **77**
    (not continuous)
Coston Wlk. SE4 . . . . .4K **121**
Cosway Mans. *NW1* 5D *4*
    (off Shroton St.)
Cosway St. NW1 . . . . .5D **4** (5C **82**)
Cotall St. E14 . . . . .5C **86**
Coteford Cl. HA5: Eastc 5J **39**
Coteford St. SW17 . . . . .4D **136**
Cotelands CRO: C'don 3E **168**
Cotesbach Rd. E5 . . . . .3J **67**
Cotes Ho. *NW8* 4C *4*
    (off Broadley St.)
Cotesmore Gdns. RM8: Dag 4C **72**
Cotford Rd. CR7: Thor H 4C **156**
Cotham St. SE17 . . . . .4C **102**
Cotherstone Ct. *E2* 4H *85*
    (off Three Colts La.)
Cotherstone Rd. SW2 . . . . .1K **137**
Cotleigh Av. DA5: Bexl 2D **144**
Cotleigh Rd.
    NW6 . . . . .7J **63**
    RM7: Rom 6K **55**

Cotman Cl. NW11 . . . . .6A **46**
   SW15 . . . . .6F **117**
Cotman Gdns. HA8: Edg 2G **43**
Cotman Ho. *NW8* 2C **82**
          (off Townshend Est.)
   UB5: N'olt 2B **76**
          (off Academy Gdns.)
Cotman M. *RM8*: Dag 5C **72**
          (off Highgrove Rd.)
Cotmans Cl. UB3: Hayes 1J **93**
Coton Dr. UB10: Ick 3E **56**
Coton Rd. DA16: Well 3A **126**
Cotsford Av. KT3: N Mald 5J **151**
Cotswold Cl.
   DA7: Bex 2K **127**
   KT2: King T 6J **133**
   KT10: Hin W 2A **162**
   N11 . . . . .4K **31**
Cotswold Cl. EC1 . . . . .3C **8**
   UB6: G'frd 2K **77**
          (off Hodder Dr.)
Cotswold Gdns. E6 . . . . .3B **88**
   IG2: Ilf 7H **53**
   NW2 . . . . .2F **63**
Cotswold Ga. NW2 . . . . .1G **63**
Cotswold Grn. EN2: Enf 4E **22**
Cotswold M. SW11 . . . . .1B **118**
Cotswold Ri. BR6: St M Cry 6K **161**
Cotswold Rd. TW12: Hamp 5E **130**
Cotswold St. SE27 . . . . .4B **138**
Cotswold Way EN2: Enf 3E **22**
   KT4: Wor Pk 2E **164**
Cottage Av. BR2: Brom 1C **172**
Cottage Cl. *E1* .4J **85**
          (off Mile End Rd.)
   HA2: Harr 2H **59**
   HA4: Ruis 1F **57**
Cottage Fld. Cl. DA14: Sidc 1C **144**
Cottage Grn. SE5 . . . . .7D **102**
Cottage Gro. KT6: Surb 6D **150**
   SW9 . . . . .3J **119**
Cottage Pl. SW3 . . . . .1C **16** (3C **100**)
Cottage Rd. KT19: Ewe 7K **163**
   N7 . . . . .5K **65**
          (not continuous)
Cottages, The UB10: Ick 2A **56**
Cottage St. E14 . . . . .7D **86**
Cottage Wlk. N16 . . . . .3F **67**
Cottenham Dr. NW9 . . . . .3B **44**
   SW20 . . . . .7D **134**
Cottenham Pde. SW20 . . . . .2D **152**
COTTENHAM PARK 1D **152**
Cottenham Pk. Rd. SW20 . . . . .1C **152**
          (not continuous)
Cottenham Pl. SW20 . . . . .7D **134**
Cottenham Rd. E17 . . . . .4B **50**
Cotterill Rd. KT6: Surb 2E **162**
Cottesbrook St. SE14 . . . . .7A **104**
Cottesloe Ho. *NW8* 3C **4**
Cottesloe M. *SE1* 1K **19**
          (off Emery St.)
Cottesmore Av. IG5: Ilf 2E **52**
Cottesmore Ct. *W8* 3K **99**
          (off Stanford Rd.)
Cottesmore Gdns. W8 . . . . .3K **99**
Cottesmore Ho. UB10: Ick 2E **56**
Cottimore Av. KT12: Walt T 7K **147**
Cottimore Cres. KT12: Walt T 7K **147**
Cottimore La. KT12: Walt T 7K **147**
Cottimore Ter. KT12: Walt T 7K **147**
Cottingham Chase HA4: Ruis 3J **57**
Cottingham Rd.
   SE20 . . . . .7K **139**
   SW8 . . . . .7K **101**
Cottington Rd. TW13: Hanw 4B **130**
Cottington St. SE11 . . . . . .5K **19** (5A **102**)
Cottle Way *SE16* 2H **103**
          (off Paradise St.)
Cotton Apartments *E1* 5K **85**
          (off Killick Way)
Cotton Av. W3 .6K **79**

Cotton Cl. CR4: Mitc 3C **154**
   E11 . . . . .2G **69**
   RM9: Dag 7C **72**
Cottongrass Cl. CR0: C'don 1K **169**
Cottonham Cl. N12 . . . . .5G **31**
Cotton Hill BR1: Brom 4E **140**
Cotton Ho. SW2 . . . . .7J **119**
Cotton Row SW11 . . . . .3A **118**
Cottons App. RM7: Rom 5K **55**
Cottons Cen. SE1 . . . . .4G **15** (1E **102**)
Cottons Ct. RM7: Rom 5K **55**
Cotton's Gdns. E2 . . . . .1H **9** (3E **84**)
Cottons La. SE1 . . . . .4F **15** (1D **102**)
Cotton St. E14 .7E **86**
Cottrell Ct. *SE10* 4H **105**
          (off Hop St.)
Cottrill Gdns. E8 . . . . .6H **67**
Cotts Cl. W7 . . . . .5K **77**
Couchmore Av. IG5: Ilf 2D **52**
Coulgate St. SE4 . . . . .3A **122**
Coulson Cl. RM8: Dag 1C **72**
Coulson St. SW3 . . . . .5E **16** (5D **100**)
Coulter Cl. UB4: Yead 4C **76**
Coulter Rd. W6 . . . . .3D **98**
Coulthurst Ct. *SW16* 7J **137**
          (off Heybridge Av.)
Councillor St. SE5 . . . . .7C **102**
Counter Ct. *SE1* 5E **14**
          (off Borough High St.)
Counters Cl. *W14* 3G **99**
          (off Holland Rd.)
Counter St. SE1 . . . . .5G **15** (1E **102**)
Countess Rd. NW5 . . . . .5G **65**
Countisbury Av. EN1: Enf 7A **24**
Country Court

   Bow 6H **69**
   Brentford 6D **96**
   Bromley .1J **159**
   Central London 4J **5**
   Clerkenwell and Shoreditch

             . . . . .3C **8** (4C **84**)
   Croydon .2D **168**
   Edmonton 6B **34**
   Kingston upon Thames 2D **150**
   Lambeth 5K **19** (5A **102**)
   Uxbridge 5H **75**
   Wandsworth 5G **117**
   West London 5F **99**
          (off Talgarth Rd.)
   Willesden 2B **80**
   Woolwich 3E **106**
County Gdns. TW7: Isle 4H **113**
County Ga. EN5: New Bar 6E **20**
   SE9 . . . . .3G **143**
County Ground, The
   Beckenham 6C **140**
County Gro. SE5 . . . . .1C **120**
County Hall Apartments SE1 . . . . .6G **13**
County Hall (Former) 6G **13**
County Ho. *SW9* 1A **120**
          (off Brixton Rd.)
County Pde. TW8: Bford 7D **96**
County Rd.
   CR7: Thor H 2B **156**
   E6 . . . . .5F **89**
County St. SE1 .3C **102**
Coupland Pl. SE18 . . . . .5G **107**
Courcy Rd. N8 .3A **48**
Courier Rd. RM9: Dag 4J **91**
Courland Gro. SW8 . . . . .1H **119**
Courland St. SW8 . . . . .1H **119**
Course, The SE9 . . . . .3E **142**
Court, The HA4: Ruis 4C **58**
Court Annexe 7D **14** (2C **102**)
Courtauld Cl. SE28 . . . . .1A **108**
Courtauld Gallery 2G **13**
Courtauld Ho. *E2* 1G **85**
          (off Goldsmiths Row)
Courtauld Rd. N19 . . . . .1J **65**
Court Av. DA17: Belv 5F **109**

Court Cl. HA3: Kenton 3E **42**
   NW8 . . . . .7B **64**
       (off Boydell Ct., not continuous)
   SM6: Wall 7H **167**
   TW2: Twick 3F **131**
Court Cl. Av. TW2: Twick 3F **131**
Court Cres. KT9: Chess 5D **162**
Court Downs Rd. BR3: Beck 2D **158**
Court Dr. CR0: Wadd 4K **167**
   HA7: Stan 4K **27**
   SM1: Sutt 4C **166**
   UB10: Hil 1B **74**
   SM2: Sutt 7J **165**
Courtenay Dr. BR3: Beck 2F **159**
Courtenay Gdns. HA3: Hrw W 2G **41**
Courtenay Ho. *CR0: C'don* 7C **156**
          (off Oakfield Rd.)
Courtenay M. E17 . . . . .5A **50**
Courtenay Pl. E17 . . . . .5A **50**
Courtenay Rd. E11 . . . . .3H **69**
   E17 . . . . .4K **49**
   HA9: Wemb 3D **60**
   KT4: Wor Pk 3E **164**
   SE20 . . . . .6K **139**
Courtenay Sq. SE11 . . . . . . .6J **19** (5A **102**)
Courtenay St. SE11 . . . . . . .5J **19** (5A **102**)
Courtens M. HA7: Stan 7H **27**
Court Farm Av. KT19: Ewe 5K **163**
Court Farm La. UB5: N'olt 7E **58**
Court Farm Rd. SE9 . . . . .2B **142**
   UB5: N'olt 7E **58**
Courtfield W5 . . . . .5C **78**
Courtfield Av. HA1: Harr 5K **41**
Courtfield Cres. HA1: Harr 5K **41**
Courtfield Gdns. HA4: Ruis 2H **57**
   SW5 . . . . .4K **99**
   W13 . . . . .6A **78**
Courtfield M. *EC1* 5J **7**
          (off Baldwins Gdns.)
Courtfield M. SW5 . . . . .4A **100**
Courtfield Ri.
   BR4: W W'ck 3F **171**
Courtfield Rd. SW7 . . . . .4A **100**
   TW15: Ashf 6D **128**
Court Gdns. N1 . . . . .6A **66**
   N7 . . . . .6A **66**
Courtgate St. N7 . . . . .6G **29**
Courthill Rd. SE13 . . . . .4E **122**
Courthope Ho. *SE16* 3J **103**
          (off Lower Rd.)
   SW8 . . . . .7J **101**
          (off Hartington Rd.)
Courthope Rd. NW3 . . . . .4D **64**
   SW19 . . . . .5G **135**
   UB6: G'frd 2H **77**
Courthope Vs. SW19 . . . . .7G **135**
Courthouse, The *SW1* 2D **18**
          (off Horseferry Rd.)
Courthouse Gdns. N3 . . . . .6D **30**
Courthouse La. N16 . . . . .4F **67**
Courthouse Rd. N12 . . . . .6E **30**
Courtland Av. E4 . . . . .2C **36**
   IG1: Ilf 2D **70**
   NW7 . . . . .3E **28**
   SW16 . . . . .7K **137**
Courtland Gro. SE28 . . . . .6D **90**
Courtland Rd. E6 . . . . .1C **88**
Courtlands KT12: Walt T 7J **147**
   TW10: Rich 5G **115**
Courtlands Av. BR2: Hayes 1G **171**
   SE12 . . . . .5H **123**
   TW9: Kew 2H **115**
   TW12: Hamp 6D **130**
Courtlands Cl. HA4: Ruis 7H **39**
Courtlands Dr. KT19: Ewe 6A **164**
Courtlands Rd. KT5: Surb 7G **151**
Court La. SE21 . . . . .6E **120**
Court La. Gdns. SE21 . . . . .7E **120**
Courtleet Dr. DA8: Erith 1H **127**

Courtleigh NW11 . . . . .5H **45**
Courtleigh Gdns. NW11 . . . . .4G **45**
Court Lodge DA17: Belv 5G **109**
   SW1 . . . . .4G **17**
          (off Sloane Sq.)
Courtman Rd. N17 . . . . .7H **33**
Court Mead UB5: N'olt 3D **76**
Courtmead Cl. SE24 . . . . .6C **120**
Cournell St. W2 .6J **81**
Courtney Cl. SE19 . . . . .6E **138**
Courtney Ct. N7 . . . . .5A **66**
Courtney Cres. SM5: Cars 7D **166**
Courtney Ho. *NW4* 3E **44**
          (off Mulberry Cl.)
   W14 . . . . .3G **99**
          (off Russell Rd.)
Courtney Pl. CR0: Wadd 3A **168**
Courtney Rd. CR0: Wadd 3A **168**
   N7 . . . . .5A **66**
   SW19 . . . . .7C **136**
   TW6: H'row A 3C **110**
Courtney Way
   TW6: H'row A 2C **110**
Court Pde. HA0: Wemb 3B **60**
Courtrai Rd. SE23 . . . . .6A **122**
Court Rd. SE9 .6D **124**
   SE25 . . . . .2F **157**
   UB2: S'hall 4D **94**
   UB10: Ick 5D **56**
Court Royal SW15 . . . . .5G **117**
Courtside N8 . . . . .6H **47**
   SE26 . . . . .3H **139**
Court St. BR1: Brom 2J **159**
   E1 . . . . .5H **85**
Courtville Ho. *W10* 3G **81**
          (off Third Av.)
Court Way NW9 . . . . .4A **44**
   TW2: Twick 7K **113**
   W3 . . . . .5J **79**
Courtway IG6: Ilf 3G **53**
   IG8: Wfd G 5F **37**
Courtwood La. CR0: Sels 7B **170**
Court Yd. SE9 .6D **124**
Courtyard *SW3* .5E **16**
          (off Smith St.)
Courtyard, The BR2: Kes 6C **172**
   E2 . . . . .1K **9**
          (off Ezra St.)
   EC3 . . . . .1F **15**
       (within Royal Exchange)
   N1 . . . . .7K **65**
   NW1 . . . . .7E **64**
   SE14 . . . . .1K **121**
          (off Besson St.)
   SW3 . . . . .7B **16**
          (off Trident Pl.)
Courtyard Apartments *E1* 3K **9**
          (off Sclater St.)
Courtyard Ho. *SW6* 2A **118**
          (off Lensbury Av.)
Courtyard M. BR5: St P 7A **144**
Courtyard Theatre
   Shoreditch 2G **9** (3E **84**)
Cousin La. EC4 . . . . .3E **14** (7D **84**)
Cousins Cl. UB7: Yiew 7A **74**
Coulthurst Rd. SE3 . . . . .3K **105**
Coutts Av. KT9: Chess 5E **162**
Coutt's Cres. NW5 . . . . .3E **64**
Couzens Ho. *E3* 5B **86**
          (off Weatherley Cl.)
Coval Gdns. SW14 . . . . .4H **115**
Coval La. SW14 . . . . .4H **115**
Coval Pas. SW14 . . . . .4J **115**
Coval Rd. SW14 . . . . .4H **115**
Coveleees Wall E6 . . . . .6E **88**
Covell Ct. *EN2: Enf* 1E **22**
          (off The Ridgeway)
   SE8 . . . . .7C **104**
COVENT GARDEN 2F **13** (7J **83**)
Covent Garden 2F **13** (7J **83**)
Covent Gdn. WC2 . . . . .2F **13** (7J **83**)

Coventry Cl. E6 . . . . .6D **88**
 NW6 . . . . .2J **81**
Coventry Hall SW16 . . . . .5J **137**
Coventry Rd. E1 . . . . .4H **85**
 E2 . . . . .4H **85**
 IG1: Ilf 2F **71**
 SE25 . . . . .4G **157**
Coventry St. W1 . . . . . .3C **12** (7H **83**)
Coverack Cl. CR0: C'don 7A **158**
 N14 . . . . .6B **22**
Coverdale Cl. HA7: Stan 5G **27**
Coverdale Gdns. CR0: C'don 3F **169**
Coverdale Rd. N11 . . . . .6K **31**
 NW2 . . . . .7F **63**
 W12 . . . . .2D **98**
Coverdales, The IG11: Bark 2H **89**
Coverham Ho. SE4 . . . . .4K **121**
                              (off Billingford Cl.)
Coverley Cl. E1 . . . . .5G **85**
Coverley Point SE11 . . . . .4G **19**
Covert, The BR6: Pet W 6J **161**
 HA6: N'wood 1E **38**
 SE19 . . . . .7F **139**
                                     (off Fox Hill)
Coverton Rd. SW17 . . . . .5C **136**
Covert Way EN4: Had W 2F **21**
Covet Wood Cl. BR5: St M Cry . . .6K **161**
Covey Cl. SW19 . . . . .2K **153**
Covey Rd. KT4: Wor Pk 2F **165**
Covington Gdns. SW16 . . . . .7B **138**
Covington Way SW16 . . . . .6K **137**
                               (not continuous)

Cowan Cl. E6 . . . . .5C **88**
Cowbridge La. IG11: Bark 7F **71**
Cowbridge Rd. HA3: Kenton 4F **43**
Cowcross St. EC1 . . . . .5A **8** (5B **84**)
Cowdenbeath Path N1 . . . . .1K **83**
Cowden Rd. BR6: Orp 7K **161**
Cowden St. SE6 . . . . .4C **140**
Cowdray Rd. UB10: Hil 1E **74**
Cowdrey Cl. EN1: Enf 2K **23**
Cowdrey M. SE6 . . . . .4C **140**
Cowdrey Rd. SW19 . . . . .5K **135**
Cowen Av. HA2: Harr 2H **59**
Cowgate Rd. UB6: G'frd 3H **77**
Cowick Rd. SW17 . . . . .4D **136**
Cowings Mead N'olt 6C **58**
Cowland Av. EN3: Pond E 4D **24**
Cow La. UB6: G'frd 2H **77**
Cow Leaze E6 . . . . .6E **88**
Cowleaze Rd.
 KT2: King T 1E **150**
COWLEY .4A **74**
Cowley La. E11 . . . . .3G **69**
COWLEY PEACHEY 6A **74**
Cowley Pl. NW4 . . . . .5E **44**
Cowley Rd. E11 . . . . .5K **51**
 IG1: Ilf 7D **52**
 SW9 . . . . .1A **120**
                               (not continuous)
 SW14 . . . . .3A **116**
 W3 . . . . .1B **98**
Cowley St. SW1 . . . . . . .1E **18** (3J **101**)
Cowling Cl. W11 . . . . .1G **99**
Cowper Av. E6 . . . . .7C **70**
 SM1: Sutt 4B **166**
Cowper Cl. BR2: Brom 4B **160**
 DA16: Well 5A **126**
Cowper Gdns. N14 . . . . .6A **22**
 SM6: Wall 6G **167**
Cowper Ho. SE17 . . . . .5C **102**
                               (off Browning St.)
 SW1 . . . . .6C **18**
                               (off Aylesford St.)
Cowper Rd. BR2: Brom 4B **160**
 DA17: Belv 4G **109**
 KT2: King T 5F **133**
 N14 . . . . .1A **32**
 N16 . . . . .5E **66**
 N18 . . . . .5B **34**
 SW19 .6A **136**

Cowper Rd. W3 . . . . .1K **97**
 W7 . . . . .7K **77**
Cowper's Ct. EC3 . . . . .1F **15**
                               (off Birchin La.)
Cowper St. EC2 . . . . . . .3F **9** (4D **84**)
Cowper Ter. W10 . . . . .5F **81**
Cowslip Cl. UB10: Uxb 7A **56**
Cowslip Rd. E18 . . . . .2K **51**
Cowthorpe Rd. SW8 . . . . .1H **119**
Cox Ct. EN4: E Barn 4H **21**
Coxe Pl. HA3: W'stone 4A **42**
Cox Ho. W6 . . . . .6G **99**
                               (off Field Rd.)
Cox La. KT9: Chess 4F **163**
 KT19: Ewe 5H **163**
                               (not continuous)
Coxmount Rd. SE7 . . . . .5B **106**
Coxs Av. TW17: Shep 3G **147**
Coxson Way SE1 . . . . . . .7J **15** (2F **103**)
Cox's Wlk. SE21 . . . . .1G **139**
Coxwell Rd. SE18 . . . . .5H **107**
 SE19 . . . . .7E **138**
Coxwold Path KT9: Chess 7E **162**
Coyle Dr. UB10: Ick 2E **56**
Crabbs Cft. Cl. BR6: Farnb 5G **173**
Crab Hill BR3: Beck 7F **141**
Crabtree Av.
 HA0: Wemb 2E **78**
 RM6: Chad H 4D **54**
Crabtree Cl. E2 . . . . .2F **85**
Crabtree Ct. EN5: New Bar 4E **20**
Crabtree Hall SW6 . . . . .7E **98**
                               (off Crabtree La.)
Crabtree La. SW6 . . . . .7E **98**
                               (not continuous)
Crabtree Manorway Nth.
 DA17: Belv, Erith 2J **109**
Crabtree Manorway Sth.
 DA17: Belv 3J **109**
Crabtree Pl. W1 . . . . . . .6C **6** (5G **83**)
Crabtree Wlk. CR0: C'don 1G **169**
Crace St. NW1 . . . . .1C **6** (3H **83**)
Craddock Rd. EN1: Enf 3A **24**
Craddock St. NW5 . . . . .6E **64**
Cradford Ho. Nth. E2 . . . . .3K **85**
Cradford Ho. Sth. E2 . . . . .3K **85**
Cradley Rd. SE9 . . . . .1H **143**
Crafts Council & Gallery 2A **84**
Cragie Ho. SE1 . . . . .4F **103**
                               (off Balaclava Rd.)
Craig Dr. UB8: Hil 6D **74**
Craigen Av. CR0: C'don 1H **169**
Craigerne Rd. SE3 . . . . .7K **105**
Craig Gdns. E18 . . . . .2H **51**
Craigholm SE18 . . . . .2E **124**
Craig Ho. E17 . . . . .4C **50**
                               (off High St.)
Craigmore Ct. HA6: N'wood 1G **39**
Craigmuir Pk. HA0: Wemb 1F **79**
Craignair Rd. SW2 . . . . .7A **120**
Craignish Av. SW16 . . . . .2K **155**
Craig Pk. Rd. N18 . . . . .4C **34**
Craig Rd. TW10: Ham 4C **132**
Craig's Ct. SW1 . . . . . . .4E **12** (1J **101**)
Craigton Rd. SE9 . . . . .4D **124**
Craigweil Cl. HA7: Stan 5J **27**
Craigweil Dr. HA7: Stan 5J **27**
Craigwell Av. TW13: Felt 3J **129**
Craik Ct. NW6 . . . . .2H **81**
                               (off Carlton Vale)
Crail Row SE17 . . . . .4D **102**
Crales Ho. SE18 . . . . .3C **106**
Cramer St. W1 . . . . .6H **5** (5E **82**)
Crammond Cl. W6 . . . . .6G **99**
Cramond Ct. TW14: Bedf 1G **129**
Cramonde Cl. DA16: Well 2A **126**
Crampton Ho. SW8 . . . . .1G **119**
Crampton Rd. SE20 . . . . .6J **139**
Crampton St. SE17 . . . . .4C **102**
Cranberry Cl. UB5: N'olt 2B **76**

Cranberry Ent. Pk. N17 . . . . .7A **34**
                               (off White Hart La.)
Cranberry La. E16 . . . . .4G **87**
Cranborne Av. KT6: Surb 3G **163**
 UB2: S'hall 4E **94**
Cranborne Rd. IG11: Bark 1H **89**
Cranborne Waye UB4: Yead 6K **75**
                               (not continuous)
Cranbourn All. WC2 . . . . .2D **12**
                               (off Cranbourn St.)
Cranbourne NW1 . . . . .7H **65**
                               (off Agar Gro.)
Cranbourne Av. E11 . . . . .4K **51**
Cranbourne Cl. SW16 . . . . .3J **155**
Cranbourne Ct. SW11 . . . . .7C **100**
                               (off Albert Bri. Rd.)
Cranbourne Dr. HA5: Pinn 5B **40**
Cranbourne Gdns. IG6: Ilf 3G **53**
 NW11 . . . . .5G **45**
Cranbourne Pas. SE16 . . . . .2H **103**
Cranbourne Rd. E12 . . . . .5C **70**
 E15 . . . . .4E **68**
 HA6: N'wood 3H **39**
 N10 . . . . .2F **47**
Cranbourne Ho. SE16 . . . . .2H **103**
                               (off Marigold St.)
Cranbourn St. WC2 . . . . .2D **12** (7H **83**)
CRANBROOK 1D **70**
Cranbrook NW1 . . . . .1G **83**
                               (off Camden St.)
Cranbrook Cl. BR2: Hayes 6J **159**
Cranbrook Ct. CR2: S Croy 5E **168**
 TW8: Bford 6C **96**
Cranbrook Dr. KT10: Esh 7G **149**
 TW2: Whitt 1F **131**
Cranbrook Est. E2 . . . . .2K **85**
Cranbrook La. N11 . . . . .4A **32**
Cranbrook M. E17 . . . . .5B **50**
Cranbrook Pk. N22 . . . . .1A **48**
Cranbrook Ri. IG1: Ilf 6D **52**
Cranbrook Rd. CR7: Thor H 2C **156**
 DA7: Bex 1F **127**
 EN4: E Barn 6G **21**
 IG1: Ilf 7E **52**
 IG2: Ilf 5E **52**
 IG6: Ilf 5E **52**
 SE8 . . . . .1C **122**
 SW19 .7G **135**
 TW4: Houn 4D **112**
 W4 . . . . .5A **98**
Cranbrook St. E2 . . . . .2K **85**
Cranbury Rd. SW6 . . . . .2K **117**
Crandley Ct. SE8 . . . . .4A **104**
                               (not continuous)
Crane Av. TW7: Isle 5A **114**
 W3 . . . . .7J **79**
Cranebank M. TW1: Twick 4A **114**
Cranebrook TW2: Twick 2G **131**
Crane Cl. HA2: Harr 3G **59**
 RM10: Dag 6G **73**
Crane Ct. EC4 . . . . .1A **14**
 KT19: Ewe 4J **163**
 SW14 . . . . .4J **115**
Craneford Cl. TW2: Twick 7K **113**
Craneford Way
 TW2: Twick 7J **113**
Crane Gdns. UB3: Harl 4H **93**
Crane Gro. N7 . . . . .6A **66**
Crane Hgts. N17 . . . . .3H **49**
                               (off Waterside Way)
Crane Ho. E3 . . . . .2A **86**
                               (off Roman Rd.)
 SE15 . . . . .1F **121**
 TW13: Hanw 3E **130**
Crane Lodge Rd. TW5: Cran 6K **93**
Crane Mead SE16 . . . . .5J **103**
Crane Mead Ct. TW1: Twick 7K **113**
Crane Pk. Island Nature Reserve . . .2D **130**
Crane Pk. Rd. TW2: Whitt 2F **131**

Crane Rd. TW2: Twick 1J **131**
 TW1: Stanw 6C **110**
Cranesbill Cl. NW9 . . . . .3K **43**
 SW16 .2H **155**
Cranes Dr. KT5: Surb 4E **150**
Cranes Pk. KT5: Surb 4E **150**
Cranes Pk. Av. KT5: Surb 4E **150**
Cranes Pk. Cres. KT5: Surb 4F **151**
Crane St. SE10 . . . . .5F **105**
 SE15 . . . . .1F **121**
Craneswater UB3: Harl 7H **93**
Craneswater Pk. UB2: S'hall 5D **94**
Crane Way TW2: Whitt 7G **113**
Cranfield Cl. SE27 . . . . .3C **138**
Cranfield Ct. W1 . . . . .6D **4**
Cranfield Dr. NW9 . . . . .7F **29**
Cranfield Ho. WC1 . . . . .5E **6**
Cranfield Rd. SE4 . . . . .3B **122**
Cranfield Rd. E. SM5: Cars 7E **166**
Cranfield Rd. W. SM5: Cars 7E **166**
Cranfield Row SE1 . . . . .1K **19**
Cranfield Wlk. SE3 . . . . .3K **123**
CRANFORD 7J **93**
Cranford Av. N13 . . . . .5D **32**
 TW19: Stanw 7A **110**
Cranford Cl. SW20 . . . . .7D **134**
 TW19: Stanw 7A **110**
Cranford Community College Sports Cen.
 . . . . .6K **93**
Cranford Cotts. E1 . . . . .7K **85**
                               (off Cranford St.)
Cranford Dr. UB3: Harl 4H **93**
Cranford La. TW5: Cran, Hest 7K **93**
 TW6: H'row A 1H **111**
                               (Bath Rd.)
 TW6: H'row A 3H **111**
                               (Elmdon Rd.)
 UB3: Cran, Harl 6F **93**
Cranford M. BR2: Brom 5C **160**
Cranford Pk. Rd. UB3: Harl 4H **93**
Cranford St. E1 . . . . .7K **85**
Cranford Way N8 . . . . .4K **47**
Cranhurst Rd. NW2 . . . . .5E **62**
Cranleigh W11 . . . . .1H **99**
                               (off Ladbroke Rd.)
Cranleigh Cl. BR6: Chels 3K **173**
 DA5: Bexl 6H **127**
 SE20 .2H **157**
Cranleigh Ct. CR4: Mitc 3B **154**
 TW9: Rich 3G **115**
 UB1: S'hall 6D **76**
Cranleigh Gdns. HA3: Kenton 5E **42**
 IG11: Bark 7H **71**
 KT2: King T 6F **133**
 N21 . . . . .5F **23**
 SE25 . . . . .3E **156**
 SM1: Sutt 2K **165**
 UB1: S'hall 6D **76**
Cranleigh Gdns. Ind. Est. UB1: S'hall . .6D **76**
Cranleigh Ho's. NW1 . . . . .2G **83**
                               (off Cranleigh St.)
Cranleigh M. SW11 . . . . .2C **118**
Cranleigh Rd. N15 . . . . .5C **48**
 SW19 .3J **153**
 TW13: Felt 4H **129**
Cranleigh St. NW1 . . . . .2G **83**
Cranley Dene Ct. N10 . . . . .4F **47**
Cranley Dr. HA4: Ruis 2H **57**
 IG2: Ilf 7G **53**
CRANLEY GARDENS 4F **47**
Cranley Gdns. N10 . . . . .4F **47**
 N13 . . . . .3E **32**
 SM6: Wall 7G **167**
 SW7 . . . . .5A **16** (5A **100**)
Cranley M. SW7 . . . . . . .5A **16** (5A **100**)
Cranley Pde. SE9 . . . . .4C **142**
                               (off Beaconsfield Rd.)
Cranley Pl. SW7 . . . . . . .4A **16** (4B **100**)
Cranley Rd. E13 . . . . .5K **87**
 IG2: Ilf 6G **53**
Cranmer Av. W13 . . . . .3B **96**

Cranmer Cl. HA4: Ruis 1B 58
   HA7: Stan 7H 27
   SM4: Mord 6F 153
Cranmer Cl. N3 . . . . .2G 45
   SW3 . . . . .4D 16 (4C 100)
   SW4 . . . . .3H 119
   TW12: Hamp H 5F 131
Cranmere Cl. EN2: Enf 2F 23
Cranmer Farm Cl. CR4: Mitc 4D 154
Cranmer Gdns. RM10: Dag 4J 73
Cranmer Ho. SW9 . . . . .7A 102
        (off Cranmer Rd.)
   SW11 . . . . .1C 118
        (off Surrey La. Est.)
Cranmer Rd. CR0: C'don 3B 168
   CR4: Mitc 4D 154
   E7 . . . . .4K 69
   HA8: Edg 3C 28
   KT2: King T 5E 132
   SW9 .7A 102
   TW12: Hamp H 5F 131
   UB3: Hayes 6F 75
Cranmer Ter. SW17 . . . . .5B 136
Cranmore Av. TW7: Isle 7G 95
Cranmore Rd. BR1: Brom 3H 141
   BR7: Chst 5D 142
Cranmore Way N10 . . . . .4G 47
Cranston Cl. TW3: Houn 2C 112
   UB10: Ick 2F 57
Cranston Est. N1 . . . . .2D 84
Cranston Gdns. E4 . . . . .6J 35
Cranston Rd. SE23 . . . . .1A 140
Cranswick Rd. SE16 . . . . .5H 103
Crantock Rd. SE6 . . . . .2D 140
Cranwell Cl. E3 . . . . .4D 86
Cranwell Gro. TW17: Shep 4B 146
Cranwell Rd. TW6: H'row A 2D 110
Cranwich Av. N21 . . . . .7J 23
Cranwich Rd. N16 . . . . .7D 48
Cranwood Ct. EC1 . . . . .2F 9
Cranwood St. EC1 . . . . .2E 8 (3D 84)
Cranworth Cres. E4 . . . . .1A 36
Cranworth Gdns. SW9 . . . . .1A 120
Craster Rd. SW2 . . . . .7K 119
Crathie Rd. SE12 . . . . .6K 123
Cravan Av. TW13: Felt 2J 129
Craven Av. UB1: S'hall 5D 76
   W5 . . . . .7C 78
Craven Cl. N16 . . . . .7G 49
   UB4: Hayes 6J 75
Craven Cottage 2F 117
Craven Ct. NW10 . . . . .1A 80
   RM6: Chad H 6E 54
Craven Gdns. IG6: Ilf 2H 53
   IG11: Bark 2J 89
   SW19 . . . . .5J 135
Craven Hill W2 . . . . .7A 82
Craven Hill Gdns. W2 . . . . .7A 82
        (not continuous)
Craven Hill M. W2 . . . . .7A 82
Craven Ho. N2 . . . . .2B 46
      (off High Rd. E. Finchley)
Craven Lodge SW6 . . . . .1F 117
        (off Harbord St.)
   W2 . . . . .7A 82
        (off Craven Hill)
Craven M. SW11 . . . . .3E 118
Craven Pk. NW10 . . . . .1K 79
Craven Pk. M. NW10 . . . . .7A 62
Craven Pk. Rd. N15 . . . . .6E 49
   NW10 .1A 80
Craven Pas. WC2 . . . . .4E 12
        (off Craven St.)
Craven Rd. CR0: C'don 1H 169
   KT2: King T 1F 151
   NW10 .1K 79
   W2 . . . . .1A 10 (7A 82)
   W5 . . . . .7C 78
Craven St. WC2 . . . . . . .4E 12 (1J 101)
Craven Ter. W2 . . . . .2A 10 (7A 82)
Craven Wlk. N16 . . . . .7G 49

Crawford Av. HA0: Wemb 5D 60
Crawford Bldgs. W1 . . . . .6D 4
        (off Homer St.)
Crawford Cl. TW7: Isle 2J 113
Crawford Ct. NW9 . . . . .3A 44
        (off Charcot Rd.)
Crawford Est. SE5 . . . . .2C 120
Crawford Gdns. N13 . . . . .3G 33
   UB5: N'olt 3D 76
Crawford Mans. W1 . . . . .6D 4
        (off Crawford St.)
Crawford M. W1 . . . . .6E 4 (5D 82)
Crawford Pas. EC1 . . . . . . .4K 7 (4A 84)
Crawford Pl. W1 . . . . .7D 4 (6C 82)
Crawford Rd. SE5 . . . . .1C 120
Crawford St. NW10 . . . . .7K 61
   W1 . . . . .6E 4 (5C 82)
Crawley Rd. E10 . . . . .1D 68
   EN1: Enf 7K 23
   N22 . . . . .2C 48
Crawshay Rd. SW9 . . . . .1A 120
Crawthew Gro. SE22 . . . . .4F 121
Craybrooke Rd. DA14: Sidc 4B 144
Craybury End SE9 . . . . .2G 143
Crayfields Bus. Pk. BR5: St P 7C 144
CRAYFORD 5K 127
Crayford Cl. E6 . . . . .6C 88
Crayford Ho. SE1 . . . . .7F 15
        (off Long La.)
Crayford M. N7 . . . . .4J 65
Crayford Rd. N7 . . . . .4H 65
Cray Ho. NW8 . . . . .5B 4
        (off Penfold St.)
Crayke Hill KT9: Chess 7E 162
Crayle Ho. EC1 . . . . .3B 8
        (off Malta St.)
Crayleigh Ter. DA14: Sidc 6C 144
Crayonne Cl. TW16: Sun 1G 147
Cray Rd. DA14: Sidc 6C 144
   DA17: Belv 6G 109
Cray Valley Golf Course 7E 144
Cray Valley Rd. BR5: St M Cry 5K 161
Cray Wanderers FC 5K 159
Crayzee Barn .2F 145
Crealock Gro. IG8: Wfd G 5C 36
Crealock St. SW18 . . . . .6K 117
Creasy Est. SE1 . . . . .3E 102
Creative Ho. SW8 . . . . .7F 101
      (off Prince of Wales Dr.)
Crebor St. SE22 . . . . .6G 121
Crecy Ct. SE11 . . . . .5J 19
        (off Hotspur St.)
Credenhall Dr. BR2: Brom 1D 172
Credenhill Ho. SE15 . . . . .7H 103
Credenhill St. SW16 . . . . .6G 137
Crediton Hgts. NW10 . . . . .1F 81
      (off Okehampton Rd.)
Crediton Hill NW6 . . . . .5K 63
Crediton Rd. E16 . . . . .6J 87
   NW10 .1F 81
Crediton Way KT10: Clay 5A 162
Credon Rd. E13 . . . . .2A 88
   SE16 .5H 103
Creechurch La. EC3 . . . .1H 15 (6E 84)
        (not continuous)
Creechurch Pl. EC3 . . . . .1H 15
Creed Ct. E1 .3A 86
   EC4 . . . . .1B 14
Creed La. EC4 . . . . .1B 14 (6B 84)
Creek, The TW16: Sun 5J 147
Creek Cotts. KT8: E Mos 4J 149
        (off Creek Rd.)
Creek Ho. W14 . . . . .3G 99
        (off Russell Rd.)
CREEKMOUTH 4K 89
Creekmouth Ind. Pk. IG11: Bark 4K 89
Creek Rd. IG11: Bark 3K 89
   KT8: E Mos 4J 149
   SE8 . . . . .6C 104
   SE10 .6C 104
Creekside SE8 . . . . .7D 104

Creekside Discovery Cen. 7D 104
Creekside Foyer SE8 . . . . .6D 104
        (off Stowage)
Creek Way RM13: Rain 5K 91
Creeland Gro. SE6 . . . . .1B 140
Crefeld Cl. W6 . . . . .6G 99
Creffield Rd. W3 . . . . .7F 79
   W5 . . . . .7F 79
Creighton Av. E6 . . . . .2B 88
   N2 . . . . .3C 46
   N10 . . . . .3C 46
Creighton Cl. W12 . . . . .7C 80
Creighton Rd. N17 . . . . .7K 33
   NW6 . . . . .2F 81
   W5 . . . . .3D 96
Cremer Bus. Cen. E2 . . . . .1J 9
        (off Cremer St.)
Cremer Ho. SE8 . . . . .7C 104
       (off Deptford Chu. St.)
Cremer St. E2 . . . . .1J 9 (2F 85)
Cremorne Est. SW10 . . . . .6B 100
        (not continuous)
Cremorne Riverside Cen. 7B 100
Cremorne Rd. SW10 . . . . .7A 100
Creon Ct. SW9 . . . . .7A 102
        (off Caldwell St.)
Crescent EC3 . . . . .2J 15 (7F 85)
Crescent, The BR3: Beck 1C 158
   BR4: W W'ck 6G 159
   CR0: C'don 5D 156
   DA5: Bexl 7C 126
   DA14: Sidc 4K 143
   E17 . . . . .6A 50
   EN5: New Bar 2E 20
   HA0: Wemb 2B 60
   HA2: Harr 1G 59
   IG2: Ilf 6E 52
   KT3: N Mald 3J 151
   KT6: Surb 5E 150
   KT8: W Mole 4E 148
   N9 . . . . .2C 34
   N11 . . . . .4J 31
   NW2 . . . . .3D 62
   SM1: Sutt 5B 166
   SW13 . . . . .2B 116
   SW19 . . . . .3J 135
   TW15: Ashf 5B 128
   TW17: Shep 7H 147
   UB1: S'hall 2D 94
   UB3: Harl 7E 92
   W3 . . . . .6A 80
Crescent Arc. SE10 . . . . .6E 104
        (off Creek Rd.)
Crescent Ct. KT6: Surb 5D 150
   SW4 .5H 119
        (off Park Hill)
Crescent Ct. Bus. Cen. E16 . . . . .4F 87
Crescent Dr. BR5: Pet W 5F 161
Crescent East EN4: Had W 1F 21
Crescent Gdns. HA4: Ruis 7K 39
   SW19 . . . . .3J 135
Crescent Gro. CR4: Mitc 4C 154
   SW4 .4G 119
Crescent Ho. EC1 . . . . .4C 8
        (off Golden La. Est.)
   SE13 .2D 122
Crescent La. SW4 . . . . .4G 119
Crescent Mans. SW3 . . . . .4C 16
        (off Fulham Rd.)
   W11 . . . . .7G 81
        (off Elgin Cres.)
Crescent M. N22 . . . . .1J 47
Crescent Pde. UB10: Hil 3C 74
Crescent Pl. SW3 . . . . . .3D 16 (4C 100)
Crescent Ri. EN4: E Barn 5H 21
   N3 . . . . .1H 45
   N22 . . . . .1H 47
Crescent Rd.
   BR1: Brom 7J 141
   BR3: Beck 2D 158
   DA15: Sidc 3K 143

Crescent Rd. E4 . . . . .1B 36
   E6 . . . . .1A 88
   E10 . . . . .2D 68
   E13 . . . . .1J 87
   E18 . . . . .1A 52
   EN2: Enf 4G 23
   EN4: E Barn 4G 21
   KT2: King T 7G 133
   N3 . . . . .1H 45
   N8 . . . . .6H 47
   N9 . . . . .1B 34
   N11 . . . . .4J 31
   N15 . . . . .3B 48
   N22 . . . . .1H 47
   RM10: Dag 3H 73
   SE18 .5F 107
   SW20 . . . . .1F 153
   TW17: Shep 5E 146
Crescent Row EC1 . . . . . . .4C 8 (4C 84)
Crescent Stables SW15 . . . . .5G 117
Crescent St. N1 . . . . .7K 65
Crescent Way BR6: Orp 5J 173
   N12 . . . . .6H 31
   SE4 . . . . .3C 122
   SW16 . . . . .6K 137
Crescent West EN4: Had W 1F 21
Crescent Wharf E16 . . . . .2K 105
        (not continuous)
Crescent Wood Rd. SE26 . . . . .3G 139
Cresford Rd. SW6 . . . . .1K 117
Crespigny Rd. NW4 . . . . .6D 44
Cressage Cl. UB1: S'hall 4E 76
Cressage Ho. TW8: Bford 6E 96
        (off Ealing Rd.)
Cressall Ho. E14 . . . . .3C 104
        (off Tiller Rd.)
Cresset Ho. E9 . . . . .6J 67
Cresset Rd. E9 . . . . .6J 67
Cresset St. SW4 . . . . .3H 119
Cressida Rd. N19 . . . . .1G 65
Cressingham Gro. SM1: Sutt 4A 166
Cressingham Rd.
   HA8: Edg 6E 28
   SE13 .3E 122
Cressington Cl. N16 . . . . .5E 66
Cross M. BR1: Brom 5F 141
Cresswell Gdns. SW5 . . . . .5A 100
Cresswell Ho. HA9: Wemb 3E 60
   TW19: Stanw 6A 110
        (off Douglas Rd.)
Cresswell Pk. SE3 . . . . .3H 123
Cresswell Pl. SW10 . . . . .5A 100
Cresswell Rd. SE25 . . . . .4G 157
   TW1: Twick 6D 114
   TW13: Hanw 3C 130
Cresswell Way N21 . . . . .7F 23
Cressy Ct. E1 .5J 85
   W6 . . . . .3D 98
Cressy Ho. SW15 . . . . .3D 116
Cressy Ho's. E1 . . . . .5J 85
        (off Hannibal Rd.)
Cressy Pl. E1 .5J 85
Cressy Rd. NW3 . . . . .5D 64
Crest, The KT5: Surb 5G 151
   N13 . . . . .4F 33
   NW4 . . . . .5E 44
Cresta Ct. W5 . . . . .4F 79
Cresta Ho. E3 . . . . .4C 86
        (off Dimson Cres.)
   NW3 . . . . .7B 64
        (off Finchley Rd.)
Crestbrook Av. N13 . . . . .3G 33
Crestbrook Pl. N13 . . . . .3G 33
        (off Green Lanes)
Crest Ct. NW4 . . . . .5E 44
Crest Dr. EN3: Enf W 1D 24
Crested Ct. NW9 . . . . .7B 44
Crestfield St. WC1 . . . . .1F 7 (3J 83)
Crest Gdns. HA4: Ruis 3A 58
Creston Way KT4: Wor Pk 1F 165

Crest Rd.—Cross Deep

Crest Rd. BR2: Hayes .7H 159
CR2: Sels .7H 169
NW2 .2B 62
Crest Vw. HA5: Pinn .4B 40
Crest Vw. Dr. BR5: Pet W .5F 161
Crestway SW15 .6C 116
Crestwood Way TW4: Houn .5C 112
Creswell Dr. BR3: Beck .5D 158
Creswick Ct. W3 .7H 79
Creswick Rd. W3 .7H 79
Creswick Wlk. E3 .3C 86
NW11 .4H 45
Creton St. SE18 .3E 106
Creukhorne Rd. NW10 .7A 62
Crewdson Rd. SW9 .7A 102
Crewe Pl. NW10 .3B 80
Crewkerne Ct. *SW11* *.1B 118*
(off Bolingbroke Wlk.)
Crews St. E14 .4C 104
Crewys Rd. NW2 .2H 63
SE15 .2H 121
Crichton Av. SM6: Bedd .5H 167
Crichton Ho. DA14: Sidc .6D 144
Crichton Rd. SM5: Cars .6D 166
Crichton St. SW8 .2G 119
Crick Ct. *IG11: Bark* *.2G 89*
(off Spring Pl.)
Cricketers Arms Rd. EN2: Enf .2H 23
Cricketers Cl. DA8: Erith .5K 109
KT9: Chess .4D 162
N14 .7B 22
Cricketers Ct. *SE11* *.4B 102*
(off Kennington La.)
Cricketers M. SW18 .5K 117
Cricketers Ter. SM5: Cars .3C 166
Cricketers Wlk. SE26 .5J 139
Cricketfield Rd. E5 .4H 67
Cricket Grn. CR4: Mitc .3D 154
Cricket Ground Rd. BR7: Chst .1F 161
Cricket La. BR3: Beck .6A 140
TW12: Hamp H .6G 131
Cricklade Av. SW2 .2J 137
Cricklefield Pl. IG1: Ilf .2J 71
CRICKLEWOOD .4F 63
Cricklewood B'way. NW2 .3E 62
Cricklewood La. NW2 .4F 63
Cridland St. E15 .1H 87
Crieff Ct. TW11: Tedd .7C 132
Crieff Rd. SW18 .6A 118
Criffel Av. SW2 .2H 137
Crimscott St. SE1 .3E 102
Crimsworth Rd. SW8 .1H 119
Crinan St. N1 .2J 83
Cringle St. SW8 .7G 101
Cripplegate St. EC2 .5D 8 (5C 84)
Cripps Grn. UB4: Yead .4K 75
Crispe Ho. IG11: Bark .2H 89
N1 *.1K 83*
(off Barnsbury Est.)
Crispen Rd. TW13: Hanw .4C 130
Crispian Cl. NW10 .4A 62
Crispin Cl. CR0: Bedd .2J 167
Crispin Ct. SE17 .4E 102
Crispin Cres. CR0: Bedd .3H 167
Crispin Ind. Cen. N18 .5D 34
Crispin Lodge N11 .5J 31
Crispin M. NW11 .5H 45
Crispin Pl. E1 .5J 9 (5F 85)
Crispin Rd. HA8: Edg .6D 28
Crispin St. E1 .6J 9 (5F 85)
Crispin Way UB8: Hil .4B 74
Crisp Rd. W6 .5E 98
Cristie Ct. E16 .4H 87
Cristowe Rd. SW6 .2H 117
Criterion Bldgs. *KT7: T Ditt* *.7B 150*
(off Portsmouth Rd.)
Criterion Ct. *E8* *.7F 67*
(off Middleton Rd.)
Criterion M. N19 .2H 65
SE24 *.5B 120*
(off Shakespeare Rd.)
Criterion Theatre *.3C 12*
(off Piccadilly Cir.)
CRITTALLS CORNER .7C 144
Crockerton Rd. SW17 .2D 136
Crockham Way SE9 .4E 142
Crocus Cl. CR0: C'don .1K 169
Crocus Fld. EN5: Barn .6C 20
Croft, The CR0: C'don .3F 169
E4 .2B 36
EN5: Barn .4B 20
HA0: Wemb .5C 60
HA4: Ruis .4A 58
HA5: Pinn .7D 40
HA8: Edg .7C 28
NW10 .2B 80
TW5: Hest .6C 94
W5 .5E 78
Croft Av. BR4: W W'ck .1E 170
Croft Cl. BR7: Chst .5D 142
DA17: Belv .5F 109
NW7 .3F 29
UB3: Harl .7E 92
UB10: Hil .7C 56
Croft Ct. HA4: Ruis .1H 57
SE13 .6E 122
SM1: Sutt .2B 166
Croftdown Rd. NW5 .3E 64
Croft End Cl. KT9: Chess .3F 163
Crofters Cl. TW7: Isle .5H 113
Crofters Ct. *SE8* *.4A 104*
(off Croft St.)
Crofters Mead CR0: Sels .7B 170
Crofters Way NW1 .1H 83
Croft Gdns. HA4: Ruis .1H 57
W7 .2A 96
Croft Ho. E17 .4D 50
NW9 .3B 44
W10 *.3G 81*
(off Third Av.)
Croft Lodge Cl. IG8: Wfd G .6E 36
Croft M. N12 .3F 31
CROFTON .2G 173
Crofton Av. BR6: Farnb .2G 173
DA5: Bexl .7D 126
W4 .7J 97
Croftongate Way SE4 .5A 122
Crofton Gro. E4 .4A 36
Crofton Ho. *SW3* *.7C 16*
(off Old Church St.)
Crofton La. BR5: Farnb, Orp, Pet W .2H 173
BR6: Pet W .7H 161
CROFTON PARK .5B 122
Crofton Pk. Rd. SE4 .6B 122
Crofton Rd. BR6: Farnb, Orp .3E 172
E13 .4K 87
SE5 .1E 120
Crofton Roman Villa .2J 173
Crofton Ter. E5 .5A 68
TW9: Rich .4F 115
Crofton Way EN2: Enf .2F 23
EN5: New Bar .6E 20
Croft Rd. BR1: Brom .6J 141
EN3: Enf H .1F 25
SM1: Sutt .5C 166
SW16 .1A 156
SW19 .7A 136
Crofts, The TW17: Shep .4G 147
Crofts Ho. *E2* *.2G 85*
(off Teale St.)
Croftside, The SE25 .3G 157
Crofts La. N22 .7F 33
Crofts Rd. HA1: Harr .6A 42
Crofts St. E1 .3K 15 (7G 85)
Croft St. SE8 .4A 104
Crofts Vs. HA1: Harr .6A 42
Croft Way DA15: Sidc .3J 143
Croftway NW3 .4J 63
TW10: Ham .3B 132
Crogsland Rd. NW1 .7E 64
Croham Cl. CR2: S Croy .7E 168
Croham Hurst Golf Course .6F 169
Croham Mnr. Rd. CR2: S Croy .7E 168
Croham Mt. CR2: S Croy .7E 168
Croham Pk. Av. CR2: S Croy .5E 168
Croham Rd. CR2: S Croy .5D 168
Croham Valley Rd. CR2: Sels .6G 169
Croindene Rd. SW16 .1J 155
Crokesley Ho. *HA8: Edg* *.2J 43*
(off Burnt Oak B'way.)
Cromartie Rd. N19 .7H 47
Cromarty Ct. SW2 .5K 119
Cromarty Ho. *E1* *.5A 86*
(off Ben Jonson Rd.)
Cromarty Rd. HA8: Edg .2C 28
Cromberdale Ct. *N17* *.1G 49*
(off Spencer Rd.)
Crombie Cl. IG4: Ilf .5D 52
Crombie M. SW11 .2C 118
Crombie Rd. DA15: Sidc .1H 143
Crome Ho. *UB5: N'olt* *.2C 76*
(off Parkfield Dr.)
Cromer Cl. UB8: Hil .6E 74
Cromer Hyde SM4: Mord .5K 153
Crome Rd. NW10 .6A 62
Cromer Pl. BR6: Orp .1J 173
Cromer Rd. E10 .7F 51
EN5: New Bar .4F 21
IG8: Wfd G .4D 36
N17 .2G 49
RM6: Chad H .6E 54
RM7: Rom .6J 55
SE25 .3H 157
SW17 .6E 136
TW6: H'row A .2C 110
Cromer St. WC1 .2E 6 (3J 83)
Cromer Ter. E8 .5G 67
RM6: Chad H .5B 54
Cromer Vs. Rd. SW18 .6H 117
Cromford Cl. BR6: Orp .3J 173
Cromford Path E5 .4K 67
Cromford Rd. SW18 .5J 117
Cromford Way KT3: N Mald .1K 151
Cromlix Cl. BR7: Chst .2F 161
Crompton Ct. SW3 .3C 16 (4C 100)
Crompton Ho. *SE1* *.3C 102*
(off County St.)
W2 *.4A 4*
(off Hall Pl.)
Crompton Pl. EN3: Enf L .1H 25
Crompton St. W2 .4A 4 (4B 82)
Cromwell Av. BR2: Brom .4K 159
KT3: N Mald .5B 152
N6 .1F 65
W6 .5D 98
Cromwell Cen. IG11: Bark .3A 90
NW10 .3K 79
Cromwell Centre, The *RM8: Dag* *.7F 55*
(off Coppen Rd.)
Cromwell Cl. BR2: Brom .4K 159
E1 .1G 103
KT12: Walt T .7K 147
N2 .4B 46
W3 .1J 97
(not continuous)
W4 *.5H 97*
(off Harvard Rd.)
Cromwell Ct. EN3: Pond E .5E 24
Cromwell Cres. SW5 .4J 99
Cromwell Gdns. SW7 .2B 16 (3B 100)
Cromwell Gro. W6 .3E 98
Cromwell Highwalk EC2 .5D 8
Cromwell Ho. CR0: C'don .3B 168
SW11 *.1E 118*
(off Charlotte Despard Av.)
Cromwell Ind. Est. E10 .1A 68
Cromwell Lodge DA6: Bex .5E 126
E1 *.4J 85*
(off Cleveland Gro.)
IG11: Bark .5J 71
Cromwell Mans. *SW5* *.4J 99*
(off Cromwell Rd.)
Cromwell M. SW7 .3B 16 (4B 100)
Cromwell Pl. *EC2* *.5D 8*
(off Silk St.)
N6 .1F 65
SW7 .3B 16 (4B 100)
SW14 .3J 115
Cromwell Rd. BR3: Beck .2A 158
CR0: C'don .7D 156
E7 .7A 70
E17 .5E 50
HA0: Wemb .2E 78
KT2: King T .1E 150
KT4: Wor Pk .3K 163
N3 .1A 46
N10 .7K 31
(not continuous)
SW5 .4J 99
SW7 .3A 16 (4J 99)
SW9 .1A 120
SW19 .5J 135
TW3: Houn .4E 112
TW11: Tedd .6A 132
TW13: Felt .1K 129
UB3: Hayes .6F 75
Cromwell St. TW3: Houn .4E 112
Cromwell Twr. EC2 .5D 8
Cromwell Trad. Cen. IG11: Bark .3J 89
Crondace Rd. SW6 .1J 117
Crondall Ct. N1 .1F 9
Crondall Ho. SW15 .7C 116
Crondall St. N1 .1F 9 (2D 84)
Crone Ct. *NW6* *.2H 81*
(off Denmark Rd.)
Cronin St. SE15 .7F 103
CROOKED BILLET .7H 35
Crooked Billet SW19 .6E 134
Crooked Billet Yd. E2 .1H 9
Crooked Usage N3 .3G 45
Crooke Rd. SE8 .5A 104
Crookham Rd. SW6 .1H 117
Crook Log DA6: Bex .3D 126
Crook Log Leisure Cen. .3D 126
Crookston Rd. SE9 .3E 124
Croombs Rd. E16 .5A 88
Croom's Hill SE10 .7E 104
Croom's Hill Gro. SE10 .7E 104
Cropley Ct. *N1* *.2D 84*
(off Cropley St., not continuous)
Cropley St. N1 .1E 8 (2D 84)
Croppath Rd. RM10: Dag .4G 73
Cropthorne Ct. W9 .3A 82
Crosbie Ho. *E17* *.3E 50*
(off Prospect Hill)
Crosby Cl. TW13: Hanw .3C 130
Crosby Ct. SE1 .6E 14 (2D 102)
Crosby Gdns. UB8: Uxb .7A 56
Crosby Ho. E7 .6J 69
E14 *.3E 104*
(off Manchester Rd.)
Crosby Rd. E7 .6J 69
RM10: Dag .2H 91
Crosby Row SE1 .7E 14 (2D 102)
Crosby Sq. EC3 .1G 15 (6E 84)
Crosby Wlk. E8 .6F 67
SW2 .7A 120
Crosby Way SW2 .7A 120
Crosier Cl. SE3 .1C 124
Crosier Rd. UB10: Ick .4E 56
Crosier Way HA4: Ruis .3G 57
Crosland Pl. SW11 .3E 118
Cross Av. SE10 .6F 105
Crossbones Graveyard *.5D 14*
(off Redcross Way)
Crossbow Ho. *N1* *.1E 84*
(off Whitmore Est.)
W13 *.1B 96*
(off Sherwood Cl.)
Crossbrook Rd. SE3 .2C 124
Cross Cl. SE15 .2H 121
Cross Ct. *SE28* *.7B 90*
(off Titmuss Av.)
Cross Deep TW1: Twick .2K 131

Cross Deep Gdns. TW1: Twick 2K 131
Crossfield Ct. W10 . . . . .6F 81
   (off Cambridge Gdns.)
Crossfield Ho. W11 . . . . .7G 81
   (off Mary Pl.)
Crossfield Rd. N17 . . . . .3C 48
  NW3 . . . . .6B 64
Crossfield St. SE8 . . . . .7C 104
   (not continuous)
Crossford St. SW9 . . . . .2K 119
Cross Ga. HA8: Edg 3B 28
Crossgate UB6: G'frd 6B 60
Cross Keys Cl. N9 . . . . .2B 34
  W1 . . . . .6H 5 (5E 82)
Cross Keys Sq. EC1 . . . . .6C 8
   (off Little Britain)
Cross Lances Rd. TW3: Houn 4F 113
Crossland Rd. CR7: Thor H 6B 156
Crosslands Av. UB2: S'hall 5D 94
  W5 . . . . .1F 97
Crosslands Rd. KT19: Ewe 6K 163
Cross La. DA5: Bexl 7F 127
  EC3 . . . . .3G 15 (7E 84)
   (not continuous)
  N8 . . . . .3K 47
   (not continuous)
Crossleigh Ct. SE14 . . . . .7B 104
   (off New Cross Rd.)
Crosslet St. SE17 . . . . .4D 102
Crosslet Va. SE10 . . . . .1D 122
Crossley St. N7 . . . . .6A 66
Crossmead SE9 .1D 142
Crossmead Av. UB6: G'frd 3E 76
Crossmount Ho. SE5 . . . . .7C 102
   (off Bowyer St.)
Crossness Footpath DA18: Erith . . .1F 109
Crossness La. SE2 . . . . .7E 90
Crossness Nature Reserve 1G 109
Crossness Pumping Station, The . . .6E 90
Crossness Rd. IG11: Bark 3K 89
Cross Rd. BR2: Brom 2C 172
  CR0: C'don 1D 168
  DA14: Sidc 4B 144
  E4 . . . . .1A 36
  EN1: Enf 4K 23
  HA1: Harr 4H 41
  HA2: Harr 3F 59
  HA3: W'stone .2A 42
  IG8: Wfd G 6J 37
  KT2: King T 7F 133
  N11 . . . . .5A 32
  N22 . . . . .7F 33
  RM6: Chad H .7C 54
  RM7: Mawney 4G 55
  SE5 . . . . .2E 120
  SM1: Sutt 5B 166
  SW19 . . . . .7J 135
  TW13: Hanw .4C 130
Cross St. N1 . . . . .1B 84
  N18 . . . . .5B 34
  SE5 . . . . .3D 120
  SW13 . . . . .2A 116
  TW12: Hamp H 5G 131
Crossthwaite Av. SE5 . . . . .4D 120
Crosstrees Ho. E14 . . . . .3C 104
   (off Cassilis Rd.)
Crosswall EC3 . . . . .2J 15 (7F 85)
Cross Way NW10 . . . . .7C 62
Cross Way, The HA3: W'stone 2J 41
Crossway
  BR5: Pet W 4H 161
  EN1: Enf 7K 23
  HA4: Ruis 4A 58
  HA5: Pinn 2K 39
  IG8: Wfd G 4F 37
  N12 . . . . .6G 31
  N16 . . . . .5E 66
  NW9 . . . . .4B 44
  RM8: Dag 3C 72
  SE28 . . . . .6B 90
  SW20 . . . . .4E 152

Crossway UB3: Hayes 1J 93
  W13 . . . . .4A 78
Crossway, The N22 . . . . .7G 33
  SE9 . . . . .2B 142
  UB10: Hil 2B 74
Crossway Ct. SE4 . . . . .2A 122
Crossway Pde. N22 . . . . .7G 33
   (off The Crossway)
Crossways CR2: Sels 7A 170
  N21 . . . . .6H 23
  SM2: Sutt 7B 166
  TW16: Sun 7H 129
Crossways, The HA9: Wemb 2G 61
  KT5: Surb 1H 163
  TW5: Hest 7D 94
Crossways Rd. BR3: Beck 4C 158
  CR4: Mitc 3F 155
Crossways Ter. E5 . . . . .4J 67
Crosswell CW17: Shep 2E 146
Croston St. E8 . . . . .1G 85
Crothall Cl. N13 .3E 32
Crouch Av. IG11: Bark 2B 90
Crouch Cl. BR3: Beck 6C 140
Crouch Cft. SE9 .3E 142
CROUCH END 7H 47
Crouch End Hill N8 . . . . .7H 47
Crouch Hall Ct. N19 . . . . .1J 65
Crouch Hall Rd. N8 . . . . .6H 47
Crouch Hill N4 . . . . .6J 47
  N8 . . . . .6J 47
Crouchman's Cl. SE26 . . . . .3F 139
Crouch Rd. NW10 . . . . .7K 61
Crowborough Rd. SW17 . . . . .6E 136
Crowden Way SE28 . . . . .7C 90
Crowder Cl. N12 .1A 46
Crowder St. E1 . . . . .7H 85
Crowfield Ho. N5 . . . . .4C 66
Crowfoot Cl. E9 .5B 68
  SE28 . . . . .1J 107
Crowhurst Cl. SW9 . . . . .2A 120
Crowhurst Ho. SW9 . . . . .2K 119
   (off Aytoun Rd.)
Crowland Av. UB3: Harl 4G 93
Crowland Gdns. N14 . . . . .7D 22
Crowland Ho. NW8 . . . . .1A 82
   (off Springfield Rd.)
Crowland Rd. CR7: Thor H 4D 156
  N15 . . . . .5F 49
CROWLANDS 7H 55
Crowlands Av. RM7: Rom 6H 55
Crowlands Heath Golf Course 1H 73
Crowland Ter. N1 . . . . .7D 66
Crowland Wlk. SM4: Mord 6K 153
Crow La. RM7: Rush G 7F 55
Crowley Cres. CR0: Wadd 5A 168
Crowley M. SW16: Mitc 3G 155
Crowline Wlk. N1 . . . . .6C 66
Crowmarsh Gdns. SE23 . . . . .7J 121
Crown All. SE9 .6D 124
   (off Court Yd.)
Crown Apartments HA4: Ruis 1J 57
Crown Arc. KT1: King T 2D 150
Crownbourne Ct. SM1: Sutt 4K 165
   (off St Nicholas Way)
Crown Bldgs. E4 . . . . .1K 35
Crown Cl. E3 . . . . .1C 86
  IG9: Buck H 1E 36
  KT12: Walt T 7A 148
  N22 . . . . .1A 48
  N46 . . . . .6K 63
  NW6 . . . . .6K 63
  NW7 . . . . .2G 29
  UB3: Hayes 2H 93
Crown Cl. Bus. Cen. E3 . . . . .1C 86
   (off Crown Cl.)
Crown Cotts. RM5: Col R 1G 55
Crown Court
  Blackfriars 6B 14 (2B 102)
  Croydon 2D 168
  Harrow 3H 41
  Inner London 7C 14 (3C 102)
  Isleworth 1J 113

Crown Court
  Kingston upon Thames 3D 150
  Snaresbrook 5H 51
  Southwark 4G 15 (1E 102)
  Wood Green .1A 48
  Woolwich 2J 107
Crown Ct. EC2 . . . . .1D 14
  N10 . . . . .7K 31
  NW8 . . . . .2D 4
   (off Park Rd.)
  SE12 . . . . .6K 123
  WC2 . . . . .1F 13 (6J 83)
Crown Dale SE19 . . . . .6B 138
   (not continuous)
Crowndale Ct. NW1 . . . . .2H 83
   (off Crowndale Rd.)
Crowndale Pl. E17 . . . . .2E 50
Crowndale Rd. NW1 . . . . .2G 83
Crown Dr. RM7: Rush G 6K 55
Crownfield Av. IG2: Ilf 6J 53
Crownfield Rd. E15 . . . . .4F 69
Crowngate Ho. E3 . . . . .2B 86
   (off Hereford Rd.)
Crown Grn. M. HA9: Wemb 2E 60
Crown Hill CR0: C'don 2C 168
Crownhill Rd. IG8: Wfd G 7H 37
  NW10 . . . . .1B 80
  NW10 . . . . .2G 79
Crown Ho. KT3: N Mald 3J 151
Crown La. BR2: Brom 5B 160
  BR7: Chst 1G 161
  N14 . . . . .1B 32
  SM4: Mord 4J 153
  SW16 . . . . .5A 138
Crown La. Gdns. SW16 . . . . .5A 138
Crown La. Spur BR2: Brom 6B 160
Crown Lodge SW3 . . . . .4D 16
Crown Mdw. Ct. BR2: Brom 6C 160
Crownmead Way
  RM7: Mawney 4H 55
Crown M. E1 . . . . .5K 85
   (off White Horse La.)
  E13 . . . . .1A 88
  W6 . . . . .4C 98
Crown Mill CR4: Mitc 5C 154
Crown Office Row EC4 . . . .2J 13 (7A 84)
Crown Pde. N14 . . . . .1B 32
  SM4: Mord 3J 153
Crown Pas. KT1: King T 2D 150
   (off Church St.)
  SW1 . . . . .5B 12 (1G 101)
Crown Pl. EC2 . . . . .5G 9 (5E 84)
  NW5 . . . . .6F 65
  SE16 . . . . .5H 103
Crown Point SE19 . . . . .6B 138
Crown Point Pde. SE19 . . . . .6B 138
   (off Crown Dale)
Crown Reach SW1 . . . . .6D 18 (5H 101)
Crown Rd. EN1: Enf 3B 24
  HA4: Ruis 5B 58
   (not continuous)
  IG6: Ilf 4H 53
  KT3: N Mald 1J 151
  N10 . . . . .7K 31
  SM1: Sutt 4K 165
  SM4: Mord 4K 153
  TW1: Twick 6B 114
Crownstone Ct. SW2 . . . . .5A 120
Crownstone Rd. SW2 . . . . .5A 120
Crown St. HA2: Harr 1H 59
  RM10: Dag 6H 73
   (not continuous)
  SE5 . . . . .7C 102
  W3 . . . . .1H 97
Crown Ter. N14 .1C 32
   (off Crown La.)
  TW9: Rich 4F 115
Crown Trad. Cen. UB3: Hayes 2G 93
Crowntree Cl. TW7: Isle 6K 95
Crown Wlk. HA9: Wemb 3F 61
Crown Way UB7: Yiew 1B 92

Crown Wharf E14 . . . . .1E 104
   (off Coldharbour)
  SE8 . . . . .5B 104
   (off Grove St.)
Crown Woods SE18 . . . . .2F 125
Crown Woods Sports Cen. 5G 125
Crown Woods Way SE9 . . . . .5H 125
Crown Yd. E2 . . . . .2H 85
  SW6 . . . . .2J 117
  TW3: Houn 3G 113
Crowshott Av. HA7: Stan 2C 42
Crows Rd. E3 . . . . .3F 87
  E15 . . . . .3F 87
  IG11: Bark 6F 71
Crowther Av. TW8: Bford 4E 96
Crowther Cl. SW6 . . . . .6H 99
   (off Bucklers All.)
Crowther Rd. SE25 . . . . .5G 157
Crowthorne Cl. SW18 . . . . .7H 117
Crowthorne Rd. W10 . . . . .6F 81
Croxall Ho. KT12: Walt T 6A 148
Croxden Cl. HA8: Edg 3G 43
Croxden Wlk. SM4: Mord 6A 154
Croxford Gdns. N22 . . . . .7G 33
Croxford Way RM7: Rush G 1K 73
Croxley Grn. BR5: St P 7B 144
Croxley Rd. W9 . . . . .3H 81
Croxted Cl. SE21 . . . . .7C 120
Croxted M. SE24 . . . . .6C 120
Croxted Rd. SE21 . . . . .7C 120
  SE24 . . . . .7C 120
Croxteth Ho. SW8 . . . . .2H 119
Croyde Av. UB3: Harl 4G 93
  UB6: G'frd 3G 77
Croyde Cl. DA15: Sidc 7H 125
CROYDON 2C 168
Croydon N17 . . . . .2D 48
   (off Gloucester Rd.)
Croydon Airport Ind. Est.
  CR0: Wadd 6K 167
Croydon Airport Vis. Cen. 6A 168
Croydon Clocktower 3C 168
   (off Katharine St.)
Croydon Crematorium CR0: C'don . .5K 155
Croydon Flyover, The CR0: C'don . . .4B 168
Croydon Gro. CR0: C'don 1B 168
Croydon Ho. SE1 . . . . .6K 13
   (off Wootton St.)
Croydon Rd. BR2: Hayes, Kes 3G 171
  BR3: Beck 4K 157
  BR4: Hayes, W W'ck 3G 171
  CR0: Bedd, Wadd 4F 167
  CR0: C'don 4E 154
  CR4: Mitc 4E 154
  E13 . . . . .4H 87
  SE20 . . . . .2H 157
  SM6: Bedd, Wall 4F 167
  TW6: H'row A .2D 110
Croydon Rd. Ind. Est. BR3: Beck 4K 157
Croydon Sailing Club 2F 157
Croydon Sports Arena 5J 157
Croydon Valley Trade Pk. CR0: Bedd . . .7J 155
   (off Therapia La.)
Croyland Rd. N9 . . . . .1B 34
Croylands Dr. KT6: Surb 7E 150
Croysdale Av. TW16: Sun 3J 147
Crozier Ho. SW8 . . . . .7K 101
   (off Wilkinson St.)
Crozier Ter. E9 . . . . .5K 67
   (not continuous)
Crucible Cl. RM6: Chad H 6B 54
Crucifix La. SE1 . . . . .6H 15 (2E 102)
Cruden Ho. E3 . . . . .2B 86
   (off Vernon Rd.)
  SE17 . . . . .6B 102
   (off Brandon Est.)
Cruden St. N1 . . . . .1B 84
Cruikshank Ho. NW8 . . . . .2C 82
   (off Townshend Rd.)
Cruikshank Rd. E15 . . . . .4G 69
Cruikshank St. WC1 . . . . .1J 7 (3A 84)

Crummock Gdns. NW9 . . . . .5A **44**
Crumpsall St. SE2 . . . . .4C **108**
Crundale Av. NW9 . . . . .5G **43**
Crunden Rd. CR2: S Croy 7D **168**
Crusader Gdns. CR0: C'don 3E **168**
Crusader Ind. Est. N4 . . . . .6C **48**
Crusoe M. N16 . . . . .2D **66**
Crusoe Rd. CR4: Mitc 7D **136**
DA8: Erith 5K **109**
Crutched Friars EC3 . . . . .2H **15** (7E **84**)
Crutchley Rd. SE6 . . . . .2G **141**
Crypt, The 1D **120**
Crystal, The 7J **87**
Crystal Ct. E8 . . . . .1H **85**
SE19 . . . . .5F **139**
(off College Rd.)
Crystal Ho. SE18 . . . . .5K **107**
CRYSTAL PALACE 6F **139**
Crystal Palace Athletics Stadium . .6G **139**
Crystal Palace Dinosaurs 6G **139**
Crystal Palace FC 4E **156**
Crystal Palace Indoor Bowling Club
. . . . .1H **157**
Crystal Palace Mus. 6F **139**
Crystal Palace National Sports Cen.
. . . . .5G **139**
Crystal Palace Pde. SE19 . . . . .6F **139**
Crystal Palace Pk. 5G **139**
Crystal Palace Pk. Farm 6G **139**
Crystal Palace Pk. Rd. SE26 . . . . . .5G **139**
Crystal Palace Rd. SE22 . . . . .6F **121**
Crystal Palace Sta. Rd. SE19 . . . . .6G **139**
Crystal Pl. KT4: Wor Pk 2D **164**
Crystal Ter. SE19 . . . . .6D **138**
Crystal Vw. Ct. BR1: Brom 4F **141**
Crystal Way HA1: Harr 5K **41**
RM8: Dag 1C **72**
Crystal Wharf N1 . . . . .2B **84**
Cuba Dr. EN3: Enf H 2D **24**
Cuba St. E14 . . . . .2C **104**
Cube, The
North East London Gymnastic Club
. . . . .4D **66**
Cube Ho. SE16 . . . . .3F **103**
Cubitt Apartments SW11 . . . . .3A **118**
(off Chatfield Rd.)
Cubitt Bldg. SW1 . . . . . . .7J **17** (5F **101**)
Cubitt Cl. NW1 . . . . .1A **6**
(off Park Village E.)
Cubitt Ho. SW4 . . . . .6G **119**
Cubitt Sq. UB2: S'hall 1G **95**
Cubitt Steps E14 . . . . .1C **104**
Cubitt St. WC1 . . . . .2H **7** (3K **83**)
Cubitt's Yd. WC2 . . . . .2F **13**
Cubitt Ter. SW4 . . . . .3G **119**
CUBITT TOWN 4E **104**
Cuckoo Av. W7 . . . . .4J **77**
Cuckoo Dene W7 . . . . .5H **77**
Cuckoo Hall La. N9 . . . . .7D **24**
Cuckoo Hall Rd. N9 . . . . .7D **24**
Cuckoo Hill HA5: Eastc, Pinn 3A **40**
Cuckoo Hill Dr. HA5: Pinn 3A **40**
Cuckoo Hill Rd. HA5: Pinn 4A **40**
Cuckoo La. W7 . . . . .7J **77**
Cuckoo Pound TW17: Shep 5G **147**
Cudas Cl. KT19: Ewe 4B **164**
Cuddington Av. KT4: Wor Pk 3B **164**
Cudham La. Nth.
BR6: Downe 7J **173**
Cudham St. SE6 . . . . .7E **122**
Cudworth Ho. SW8 . . . . .1G **119**
Cudworth St. E1 . . . . .4H **85**
Cuff Cres. SE9 . . . . .6B **124**
Cuffley Ho. W10 . . . . .5E **80**
(off Sutton Way)
Cuff Point E2 . . . . .1J **9**
(off Columbia Rd.)
Culand Ho. SE17 . . . . .4E **102**
(off Congreve St.)
Culford Gdns. SW3 . . . . . .4F **17** (4D **100**)
Culford Gro. N1 . . . . .6E **66**

Culford Mans. SW3 . . . . .4F **17**
(off Culford Gdns.)
Culford M. N1 . . . . .6E **66**
Culford Rd. N1 . . . . .7E **66**
Culford Ter. N1 . . . . .6E **66**
(off Balls Pond Rd.)
Culgaith Gdns. EN2: Enf 4D **22**
Culham Ho. E2 . . . . .2J **9**
(off Palissy St.)
W2 . . . . .5J **81**
(off Gt. Western Rd.)
Cullen Way NW10 . . . . .4J **79**
Culling Rd. DA17: Belv 3J **109**
SE16 .3J **103**
Cullington Cl. HA3: W'stone 4A **42**
Cullingworth Rd. NW10 . . . . .5C **62**
Culloden Cl. SE7 . . . . .6K **105**
SE16 .5G **103**
Culloden Ho. SE14 . . . . .7A **104**
(off Batavia Rd.)
Culloden Rd. EN2: Enf 2G **23**
Cullum St. EC3 . . . . .2G **15** (7E **84**)
Cullum Welch Ct. N1 . . . . .1F **9**
(off Haberdasher St.)
Cullum Welch Ho. EC1 . . . . .4C **8**
(off Golden La. Est.)
Culmington Pde. W13 . . . . .1C **96**
(off Uxbridge Rd.)
Culmington Rd. CR2: S Croy 7C **168**
W13 . . . . .1C **96**
Culmore Rd. SE15 . . . . .7H **103**
Culmstock Rd. SW11 . . . . .5E **118**
Culpepper Cl. N18 . . . . .5C **34**
Culpepper Cl. SE11 . . . . .3J **19**
Culross Cl. N15 . . . . .4C **48**
Culross Ho. W10 . . . . .6F **81**
(off Bridge Cl.)
Culross St. W1 . . . . .3G **11** (7E **82**)
Culsac Rd. KT6: Surb 2E **162**
Culverden Rd. SW12 . . . . .2G **137**
Culver Gro. HA7: Stan 2C **42**
Culverhouse WC1 . . . . .6G **7**
(off Red Lion Sq.)
Culverhouse Gdns. SW16 . . . . . . .3K **137**
Culverlands Cl. HA7: Stan 4G **27**
Culverley Rd. SE6 . . . . .1D **140**
Culvers Av. SM5: Cars 2D **166**
Culvers Retreat SM5: Cars 1D **166**
Culvers Way SM5: Cars 2D **166**
Culvert Pl. SW11 . . . . .2E **118**
Culvert Rd. N15 . . . . .5E **48**
(not continuous)
SW11 . . . . .2D **118**
Culworth Ho. NW8 . . . . .2C **82**
(off Allitsen Rd.)
Culworth St. NW8 . . . . .2C **82**
Culzean Cl. SE27 . . . . .3B **138**
Cumberland Av. DA16: Well 3J **125**
NW10 . . . . .3H **79**
Cumberland Bus. Pk. NW10 . . . . . .3H **79**
Cumberland Cl. E8 . . . . .6F **67**
IG6: Ilf 1G **53**
SW20 . . . . .7F **135**
TW1: Twick 6B **114**
Cumberland Cres. CR0: C'don 1D **168**
DA16: Well 2J **125**
HA1: Harr 3J **41**
(off Princes Dr.)
SW1 . . . . .5K **17**
(off Cumberland St.)
W1 . . . . .1F **11**
(off Gt. Cumberland Pl.)
Cumberland Cres. W14 . . . . .4G **99**
(not continuous)
Cumberland Dr. DA7: Bex 7E **108**
KT9: Chess 3E **162**
KT10: Hin W 2A **162**
Cumberland Gdns. NW4 . . . . .2G **45**
WC1 . . . . .1J **7** (3A **84**)
Cumberland Ga. W1 . . . . .2E **10** (7D **82**)

Cumberland Ho. E16 . . . . .1J **105**
(off Wesley Av.)
KT2: King T 7H **133**
N9 . . . . .1D **34**
(off Cumberland Rd.)
SE28 .2G **107**
W8 . . . . .2K **99**
(off Kensington Ct.)
Cumberland Mans. W1 . . . . .7E **4**
Cumberland Mkt. NW1 . . .1K **5** (3F **83**)
Cumberland M. SE11 . . . .6K **19** (5A **102**)
Cumberland Mills Sq. E14 . . . . . . .5F **105**
Cumberland Pk. Ind. Est. NW10 . . . .3C **80**
Cumberland Pl. NW1 . . . . .1J **5** (3F **83**)
SE6 .1H **141**
TW16: Sun 4J **147**
Cumberland Rd. BR2: Brom 4G **159**
E12 . . . . .4B **70**
E13 . . . . .5K **87**
E17 . . . . .2A **50**
HA1: Harr 5F **41**
HA7: Stan 3F **43**
N9 . . . . .1D **34**
N22 . . . . .2K **47**
SE25 . . . . .6H **157**
SW13 . . . . .1B **116**
TW9: Kew 7G **97**
TW15: Ashf 3A **128**
W3 . . . . .7J **79**
W7 . . . . .2K **95**
Cumberland St. SW1 . . . . .5K **17** (5F **101**)
Cumberland Ter. NW1 . . . .1J **5** (2F **83**)
Cumberland Ter. M. NW1 . . . . .1J **5**
(not continuous)
Cumberland Vs. W3 . . . . .7J **79**
(off Cumberland Rd.)
Cumberland Wharf SE16 . . . . .2J **103**
(off Rotherhithe St.)
Cumberlow Av. SE25 . . . . .3F **157**
Cumbernauld Gdns. TW16: Sun . . .5H **129**
Cumberton Rd. N17 . . . . .1D **48**
Cumbrae Gdns. KT6: Surb 2D **162**
Cumbrian Gdns. NW2 . . . . .2F **63**
Cumbrian Way UB8: Uxb 1A **74**
Cumming St. N1 . . . . .1H **7** (2K **83**)
Cumnor Cl. SW9 . . . . .2K **119**
(off Robsart St.)
Cumnor Gdns. KT17: Ewe 6C **164**
Cumnor Rd. SM2: Sutt 6A **166**
Cunard Ct. HA7: Stan 2F **27**
(off Brightwen Gro.)
Cunard Cres. N21 . . . . .6J **23**
Cunard Pl. EC3 . . . . .1H **15** (6E **84**)
Cunard Rd. NW10 . . . . .3K **79**
Cunard Wlk. SE16 . . . . .4K **103**
Cundy Rd. E16 . . . . .6A **88**
Cundy St. SW1 . . . . .4H **17** (4E **100**)
Cunliffe Pde. KT19: Ewe 4B **164**
Cunliffe Rd. KT19: Ewe 4B **164**
Cunliffe St. SW16 . . . . .6G **137**
Cunningham Cl. BR4: W W'ck 2D **170**
RM6: Chad H 5C **54**
Cunningham Ct. E10 . . . . .3D **68**
(off Oliver Rd.)
W9 . . . . .4A **4**
(off Maida Vale)
Cunningham Ho. SE5 . . . . .7D **102**
(off Elmington Est.)
Cunningham Pk. HA1: Harr 5G **41**
Cunningham Pl. NW8 . . . . . .3A **4** (4B **82**)
Cunningham Rd. N15 . . . . .4G **49**
Cunnington St. W4 . . . . .3J **97**
Cupar Rd. SW11 . . . . .1E **118**
Cupola Cl. BR1: Brom 5K **141**
Cureton St. SW1 . . . . . . .4D **18** (4H **101**)
Curie Ho. IG11: Bark 1G **89**
Curlew Tower, The 1G **89**
Curie Ct. HA1: Harr 7B **42**
Curie Gdns. NW9 . . . . .2A **44**
Curlew Cl. SE28 . . . . .7D **90**

Curlew Ct. KT6: Surb 3G **163**
W13 .4K **77**
Curlew Ho. EN3: Pond E 5E **24**
SE4 . . . . .4A **122**
(off St Norbert Rd.)
SE15 .1F **121**
Curlew St. SE1 . . . . .6K **15** (2F **103**)
Curlew Way UB4: Yead 5B **76**
Curness St. SE13 . . . . .4E **122**
Curnick's La. SE27 . . . . .4C **138**
Curran Av. DA15: Sidc 5K **125**
SM6: Wall 3E **166**
Curran Ho. SW3 . . . . .4C **16**
(off Lucan Pl.)
Currey Rd. UB6: G'frd 6H **59**
Curricle St. W3 . . . . .1A **98**
Currie Hill Cl. SW19 . . . . .4H **135**
Curry Ri. NW7 . . . . .6A **30**
Cursitor St. EC4 . . . . .7J **7** (6A **84**)
Curtain Pl. EC2 . . . . .3H **9** (3E **84**)
Curtain Rd. EC2 . . . . .2H **9** (4E **84**)
Curthwaite Gdns. EN2: Enf 4C **22**
Curtis Dr. W3 . . . . .6K **79**
Curtis Fld. Rd. SW16 . . . . .4K **137**
Curtis Ho. N11 . . . . .5B **32**
(off Ladderswood Way)
SE17 . . . . .5D **102**
(off Morecambe St.)
Curtis La. HA0: Wemb 6E **60**
Curtis Rd. KT19: Ewe 4J **163**
TW4: Houn 7D **112**
Curtiss Ho. NW9 . . . . .3B **44**
Curtis St. SE1 . . . . .4F **103**
Curtis Way SE1 . . . . .4F **103**
SE28 .7B **90**
Curtlington Ho. HA8: Edg 2J **43**
(off Burnt Oak B'way.)
Curve, The W12 . . . . .7C **80**
Curwen Av. E7 . . . . .4K **69**
Curwen Rd. W12 . . . . .2C **98**
Curzon Av. EN3: Pond E 5E **24**
HA7: Stan 1A **42**
Curzon Cinema
Mayfair 5J **11**
(off Curzon St.)
Richmond 5D **114**
Soho .2D **12**
(off Shaftesbury Av.)
Curzon Cl. BR6: Orp 4H **173**
Curzon Ct. SW6 . . . . .1A **118**
(off Imperial Rd.)
Curzon Cres. IG11: Bark 2K **89**
NW10 . . . . .7A **62**
Curzon Ga. W1 . . . . .5H **11** (1E **100**)
Curzon Pl. HA5: Eastc 5A **40**
Curzon Rd.
CR7: Thor H 6A **156**
N10 . . . . .2F **47**
W5 . . . . .4B **78**
Curzon Sq. W1 . . . . .5H **11** (1E **100**)
Curzon St. W1 . . . . .5H **11** (1E **100**)
Cusack Cl. TW1: Tedd 4K **131**
Custance Ho. N1 . . . . .1E **8**
(off Provost St.)
Custance St. N1 . . . . .1E **8** (3D **84**)
CUSTOM HOUSE 6A **88**
Custom Ho. EC3 . . . . .3G **15** (7E **84**)
Custom Ho. Reach
SE16 .2B **104**
Custom Ho. Wlk. EC3 . . . .3G **15** (7E **84**)
Cut, The SE1 . . . . .6K **13** (2A **102**)
Cutbush Ho. N7 . . . . .5H **65**
Cutcombe Rd. SE5 . . . . .2C **120**
Cuthberga Cl. IG11: Bark 7G **71**
Cuthbert Ho. W2 . . . . .2C **86**
(off Hall Pl.)
Cuthbert Bell Twr. E3 . . . . .2C **86**
(off Pancras Way)
Cuthbert Gdns. SE25 . . . . .3E **156**
Cuthbert Harrowing Ho. EC1 . . . . . . .4C **8**
(off Golden La. Est.)
Cuthbert Ho. W2 . . . . .5A **4**
(off Hall Pl.)

Cuthbert Rd.
CR0: C'don 2B **168**
E17 .3E **50**
N18 .5B **34**
Cuthbert St. W2 . . . . .5A **4** (5B **82**)
Cuthill Wlk. SE5 . . . . .1D **120**
Cutlers Gdns. EC2 . . . . . .6H **9** (5E **84**)
Cutlers Gdns. Arc. EC2 . . . . .7H **9**
(off Devonshire Sq.)
Cutlers Sq. E14 . . . . .4C **104**
Cutlers Ter. N1 . . . . .6E **66**
(off Balls Pond Rd.)
Cutler St. E1 . . . . .7H **9** (6E **84**)
Cutter Ho. DA8: Erith 4K **109**
Cutter La. SE10 . . . . .2G **105**
Cutthroat All. TW10: Ham 2C **132**
Cutty Sark 6E **104**
Cutty Sark Gdns. SE10 . . . . .6E **104**
(off King William Wlk.)
Cutty Sark Hall SE10 . . . . .6E **104**
(off Welland St.)
Cuxton BR5: Pet W 5G **161**
Cuxton Cl. DA6: Bex 5E **126**
Cuxton Ho. SE17 . . . . .5E **102**
(off Mina Rd.)
Cyan Apartments E3 . . . . .1A **86**
(off Gunmaker's La.)
Cyclamen Ct. TW12: Hamp 6E **130**
Cyclamen Way
KT19: Ewe 5J **163**
Cyclops M. E14 . . . . .4C **104**
Cygnet Av. TW14: Felt 7A **112**
Cygnet Cl. NW10 . . . . .5K **61**
Cygnet Ho. SE15 . . . . .6G **103**
SW3 . . . . .6D **16**
(off King's Rd.)
Cygnet Ho. Nth. E14 . . . . .6D **86**
(off Chrisp St.)
Cygnet Ho. Sth. E14 . . . . .6D **86**
(off Chrisp St.)
Cygnets, The
TW13: Hanw 4C **130**
Cygnet St. E1 . . . . .3K **9** (4F **85**)
Cygnet Way UB4: Yead 5B **76**
Cygnus Bus. Cen. NW10 . . . . . . .5B **62**
Cymbeline Ct. HA1: Harr 6K **41**
Cynthia St. N1 . . . . .1H **7** (2K **83**)
Cyntra Pl. E8 . . . . .7H **67**
Cypress Av. TW2: Whitt 7G **113**
Cypress Cl. E5 . . . . .2G **67**
KT19: Eps 7K **163**
Cypress Ct. E15 . . . . .4F **69**
(off Langthorne Rd.)
SM1: Sutt 5J **165**
Cypress Gdns. SE4 . . . . .5A **122**
Cypress Ho. SE14 . . . . .1K **121**
SE16 . . . . .2K **103**
(off Woodland Cres.)
Cypress Pl. W1 . . . . .4B **6** (4G **83**)
Cypress Rd. HA3: Hrw W 2H **41**
SE25 . . . . .2E **156**
Cypress Tree Cl. DA15: Sidc 1K **143**
CYPRUS .7E **88**
Cyprus Av. N3 . . . . .2G **45**
Cyprus Cl. N4 . . . . .6B **48**
Cyprus Gdns. N3 . . . . .2G **45**
Cyprus Pl. E2 . . . . .2J **85**
E6 . . . . .7E **88**
Cyprus Rd. N3 . . . . .2H **45**
N9 . . . . .2A **34**
Cyprus St. E2 . . . . .2J **85**
(not continuous)
Cyrena Rd. SE22 . . . . .6F **121**
Cyril Lodge DA14: Sidc 4A **144**
Cyril Mans. SW11 . . . . .1D **118**
Cyril Rd. BR6: Orp 7K **161**
DA7: Bex 2E **126**
Cyrus Ho. EC1 . . . . .3B **8**
Cyrus St. EC1 . . . . .3B **8**
Cyrus Ter. UB10: Ick 3E **56**
(off Pentland Way)

Czar St. SE8 . . . . .6C **104**

D

Dabbs Hill La. UB5: N'olt 6D **58**
(not continuous)
Dabbs La. EC1 . . . . .4K **7**
(off Farringdon Rd.)
Dabin Cres. SE10 . . . . .1E **122**
Dacca St. SE8 . . . . .6B **104**
Dace Rd. E3 . . . . .1C **86**
Dacre Av. IG5: Ilf 2E **52**
Dacre Cl. UB6: G'frd 2F **77**
Dacre Gdns. SE13 . . . . .4G **123**
Dacre Ho. SW3 . . . . .7B **16**
Dacre Pk. SE13 . . . . .3G **123**
Dacre Pl. SE13 . . . . .3G **123**
Dacre Rd. CR0: C'don 7J **155**
E11 . . . . .1H **69**
E13 . . . . .1K **87**
Dacres Gdns. SE23 . . . . .3K **139**
Dacres Ho. SW4 . . . . .3F **119**
Dacres Rd. SE23 . . . . .2K **139**
Dacre St. SW1 . . . . . .1C **18** (3H **101**)
Dade Way UB2: S'hall 5D **94**
Daerwood Cl. BR2: Brom 1D **172**
Daffodil Gdns. IG1: Ilf 5F **71**
Daffodil Pl. TW12: Hamp 6E **130**
Daffodil St. W12 . . . . .7B **80**
Dafforne Rd. SW17 . . . . .3E **136**
Da Gama Pl. E14 . . . . .5C **104**
DAGENHAM 6G **73**
Dagenham & Redbridge FC 5H **73**
Dagenham Av. RM9: Dag 1H **91**
(not continuous)
Dagenham Bowl 1E **90**
Dagenham Bowling 1D **90**
Dagenham Leisure Park 1D **90**
Dagenham Leisure Pk. RM9: Dag . . .1E **90**
Dagenham Leisure Cen. 7G **73**
Dagenham Rd. E10 . . . . .1B **68**
RM7: Rush G 7K **55**
RM13: Rain 7K **73**
Dagmar Av. HA9: Wemb 4F **61**
Dagmar Ct. E14 . . . . .3E **104**
Dagmar Gdns. NW10 . . . . .2F **81**
Dagmar M. UB2: S'hall 3C **94**
(off Dagmar Rd.)
Dagmar Pas. N1 . . . . .1B **84**
(off Cross St.)
Dagmar Rd. KT2: King T 1F **151**
N4 . . . . .7A **48**
N15 . . . . .4D **48**
N22 . . . . .1H **47**
RM10: Dag 7J **73**
SE5 . . . . .1E **120**
SE25 . . . . .5E **156**
UB2: S'hall 3C **94**
Dagmar Ter. N1 . . . . .1B **84**
Dagnall Pk. SE25 . . . . .6E **156**
Dagnall Rd. SE25 . . . . .5E **156**
Dagnall St. SW11 . . . . .2D **118**
Dagnan Rd. SW12 . . . . .7F **119**
Dagobert Ho. E1 . . . . .5J **85**
(off Smithy St.)
Dagonet Gdns. BR1: Brom 3J **141**
Dagonet Rd. BR1: Brom 3J **141**
Dahlia Gdns. CR4: Mitc 4H **155**
IG1: Ilf 6F **71**
Dahlia Rd. SE2 . . . . .4B **108**
Dahomey Rd. SW16 . . . . .6G **137**
Daimler Ho. E3 . . . . .4C **86**
(off Wellington Way)
Daimler Way SM6: Wall 7J **167**
Dain Cl. W8 . . . . .4J **99**
(off Lexham Gdns.)
Daines Cl. E12 . . . . .3D **70**
Dainford Cl. BR1: Brom 5F **141**

Dainton Cl. BR1: Brom 1K **159**
Dainton Ho. W2 . . . . .5J **81**
(off Gt. Western Rd.)
Daintry Cl. HA3: W'stone 4A **42**
Daintry Way E9 . . . . .6B **68**
Dairsie Ct. BR1: Brom 1A **160**
Dairsie Rd. SE9 . . . . .3E **124**
Dairy Cl. BR1: Brom 7K **141**
CR7: Thor H 2C **156**
NW10 . . . . .1C **80**
SW6 . . . . .1J **117**
UB6: G'frd 2H **77**
Dairy La. SE18 . . . . .4D **106**
Dairyman Cl. NW2 . . . . .3F **63**
Dairy M. N2 . . . . .4C **46**
RM6: Chad H 7D **54**
SW9 . . . . .3J **119**
Dairy Wlk. SW19 . . . . .4G **135**
Daisy Cl. CR0: C'don 1K **169**
NW9 . . . . .2J **61**
Daisy Dobbings Wlk. N19 . . . . . . .7J **47**
(off Jessie Blythe La.)
Daisy La. SW6 . . . . .3J **117**
Daisy Rd. E16 . . . . .4G **87**
E18 . . . . .2K **51**
Dakin Pl. E1 . . . . .5A **86**
Dakota Bldg. SE13 . . . . .1D **122**
(off Deal's Gateway)
Dakota Cl. SM6: Wall 7K **167**
UB5: N'olt 3C **76**
Dakota Gdns. E6 . . . . .4C **88**
UB5: N'olt 3C **76**
Dakota Ho. CR7: Thor H 6B **156**
Dalberg Rd. SW2 . . . . .4A **120**
(not continuous)
Dalberg Way SE2 . . . . .3D **108**
Dalby Rd. SW18 . . . . .4A **118**
Dalbys Cres. N17 . . . . .6K **33**
Dalby St. NW5 . . . . .6F **65**
Dalcross Rd. TW4: Houn 2C **112**
Dale, The BR2: Kes 4B **172**
Dale Av. HA8: Edg 1F **43**
TW4: Houn 3C **112**
Dalebury Cl. TW5: Hest 5E **94**
Dalebury Rd. SW17 . . . . .2D **136**
Dale Cl. EN5: New Bar 6F **21**
HA5: Pinn 1K **39**
SE3 . . . . .3J **123**
Dale Ct. EN2: Enf 1H **23**
KT2: King T 7F **133**
(off York Rd.)
Dale Dr. UB4: Hayes 4H **75**
Dalefield IG9: Buck H 1F **37**
(off Roebuck La.)
Dale Gdns. IG8: Wfd G 4E **36**
Dale Grn. Rd. N11 . . . . .3A **32**
Dale Gro. N12 . . . . .5F **31**
Daleham Dr. UB8: Hil 6D **74**
Daleham Gdns. NW3 . . . . .5B **64**
Daleham M. NW3 . . . . .6B **64**
Dalehead NW1 . . . . .1A **6**
(off Hampstead Rd.)
Dale Ho. N1 . . . . .1E **84**
(off Halcomb St.)
NW8 . . . . .1A **82**
(off Boundary Rd.)
SE4 . . . . .4A **122**
Dale Lodge N6 . . . . .6G **47**
Dalemain M. E16 . . . . .1J **105**
Dale Pk. Av. SM5: Cars 2D **166**
Dale Pk. Rd. SE19 . . . . .1C **156**
Dale Rd. KT12: Walt T 7H **147**
NW5 . . . . .5E **64**
SE17 . . . . .6B **102**
SM1: Sutt 4H **165**
TW16: Sun 7H **129**
UB6: G'frd 5F **77**
Dale Row W11 . . . . .6G **81**
Daleside Rd. KT19: Ewe 6K **163**
SW16 . . . . .5F **137**
Dale St. W4 . . . . .5A **98**
Dale Vw. Av. E4 . . . . .2K **35**

Dale Vw. Cres. E4 . . . . .2K **35**
Dale Vw. Gdns. E4 . . . . .3A **36**
Daleview Rd. N15 . . . . .6E **48**
Dalewood Gdns. KT4: Wor Pk 2D **164**
Dale Wood Rd. BR6: Orp 7J **161**
Daleworth Cl. BR3: Beck 6C **140**
Daley Ho. W12 . . . . .6D **80**
Daley St. E9 . . . . .6K **67**
Daley Thompson Way SW8 . . . . . . .2F **119**
Dalgarno Gdns. W10 . . . . .5E **80**
Dalgarno Way W10 . . . . .4E **80**
Dalgleish St. E14 . . . . .6A **86**
Daling Way E3 . . . . .1A **86**
Dalkeith Ct. SW1 . . . . .3D **18**
(off Vincent St.)
Dalkeith Gro. HA7: Stan 5J **27**
Dalkeith Ho. SW9 . . . . .1B **120**
(off Lothian Rd.)
Dalkeith Rd. IG1: Ilf 3G **71**
SE21 . . . . .1C **138**
Dallas Rd. NW4 . . . . .7C **44**
SE26 . . . . .3H **139**
SM3: Cheam 6G **165**
W5 . . . . .5F **79**
Dallas Ter. UB3: Harl 3H **93**
Dallega Cl. UB3: Hayes 7F **75**
Dallinger Rd. SE12 . . . . .6H **123**
Dalling Rd. W6 . . . . .4D **98**
Dallington Sq. EC1 . . . . .3B **8**
(off Dallington St.)
Dallington St. EC1 . . . . . . .3B **8** (4B **84**)
Dallin Rd. DA6: Bex 4D **126**
SE18 . . . . .7F **107**
Dalmain Rd. SE23 . . . . .1K **139**
Dalmally Rd. CR0: C'don 7F **157**
Dalmany Pas. CR0: C'don 7F **157**
Dalmeny Av. N7 . . . . .4H **65**
SW16 . . . . .2A **156**
Dalmeny Cl. HA0: Wemb 6C **60**
Dalmeny Cres. TW3: Houn 4H **113**
Dalmeny Rd. DA8: Erith 1H **127**
EN5: New Bar 6F **21**
KT4: Wor Pk 3D **164**
N7 . . . . .3H **65**
(not continuous)
SM5: Cars 7E **166**
Dalmeyer Rd. NW10 . . . . .6B **62**
Dalmore Rd. SE21 . . . . .2C **138**
Dalo Lodge E3 . . . . .5C **86**
(off Gale St.)
Dalrymple Cl. N14 . . . . .7C **22**
Dalrymple Rd. SE4 . . . . .4A **122**
DALSTON .6F **67**
Dalston Gdns. HA7: Stan 1E **42**
Dalston La. E8 . . . . .6F **67**
Dalston Sq. E8 . . . . .6F **67**
(not continuous)
Dalton Av. CR4: Mitc 2C **154**
Dalton Cl. BR6: Orp 3J **173**
UB4: Hayes 4F **75**
Dalton Ho. E3 . . . . .2A **86**
(off Ford St.)
HA7: Stan 5F **27**
SE14 . . . . .6K **103**
(off John Williams Cl.)
SW1 . . . . .5J **17**
(off Ebury Bri. Rd.)
Dalton Rd. HA3: W'stone 2H **41**
Dalton St. SE27 . . . . .3B **138**
Dalwood St. SE5 . . . . .1E **120**
Daly Dr. BR1: Brom 3E **160**
Dalyell Rd. SW9 . . . . .3K **119**
Damascene Wlk. SE21 . . . . .1C **138**
Damask Ct. SM1: Sutt 1K **165**
Damask Cres. E16 . . . . .4G **87**
Damer Ter. SW10 . . . . .7A **100**
Dames Rd. E7 . . . . .3J **69**
Dame St. N1 . . . . .2C **84**
Damien Ct. E1 . . . . .6H **85**
(off Damien St.)
Damien St. E1 . . . . .6H **85**

Damon Cl. DA14: Sidc 3B 144
Damory Ho. SE16 . . . . .4H 103
(off Abbeyfield Est.)
Damsel Ho. SE4 . . . . .3A 122
(off Dragonfly Pl.)
Damson Dr. UB3: Hayes 7J 75
Damson Way SM5: Cars 7D 166
Damsonwood Ho. UB2: S'hall 3E 94
Danbrook Rd. SW16 . . . . .1J 155
Danbury Cl. RM6: Chad H 3D 54
Danbury Mans. IG11: Bark 7F 71
(off Whiting Av.)
Danbury M. SM6: Wall 4F 167
Danbury St. N1 .2B 84
Danbury Way IG8: Wfd G 6F 37
Danby Cl. EN2: Enf 3H 23
Danby Ho. E9 . . . . .7J 67
(off Frampton Pk. Rd.)
W10 . . . . .3G 81
(off Bruckner St.)
Danby St. SE15 .3F 121
Dance Ho. SE4 .5K 121
(off St Norbert Rd.)
Dancer Rd. SW6 . . . . .1H 117
TW9: Rich 3G 115
Dancers Way SE8 . . . . .6D 104
Dance Sq. EC1 . . . . .2C 8 (3C 84)
Dandridge Cl. SE10 . . . . .5H 105
Dandridge Ho. E1 . . . . .5J 9
(off Lamb St.)
Danebury CR0: New Ad 6E 170
Danebury Av. SW15 . . . . .6A 116
Daneby Rd. SE6 . . . . .3D 140
Dane Cl. BR6: Farnb 5H 173
DA5: Bexl 7G 127
Danecourt Gdns. CR0: C'don 3F 169
Danecroft Rd. SE24 . . . . .5C 120
Danehill Wlk. DA14: Sidc 3A 144
Danehurst TW8: Bford 7C 96
Danehurst Gdns. IG4: Ilf 5C 52
Danehurst St. SW6 . . . . .1G 117
Daneland EN4: E Barn 6J 21
Daneland Wlk. N17 . . . . .3H 49
Danemead Gro. UB5: N'olt 5F 59
Danemere St. SW15 . . . . .3E 116
Dane Pl. E3 . . . . .2A 86
Dane Rd. IG1: Ilf 5G 71
N18 . . . . .3D 34
SW19 . . . . .1A 154
TW15: Ashf .6E 128
UB1: S'hall .7C 76
W13 . . . . .1C 96
Danesbury Rd. TW13: Felt 1K 129
Danescombe SE12 . . . . .1J 141
Danes Cl. HA9: Wemb 3H 61
NW8 . . . . .1D 82
(off St Edmund's Ter.)
Danescourt Cres. SM1: Sutt 2A 166
Danescroft NW4 . . . . .5F 45
Danescroft Av. NW4 . . . . .5F 45
Danescroft Gdns. NW4 . . . . .5F 45
Danesdale Rd. E9 . . . . .6A 68
Danesfield SE5 .6E 102
(off Albany Rd.)
Danes Ga. HA1: Harr 3J 41
Danes Ho. W10 .5E 80
(off Sutton Way)
Danes Rd. RM7: Rush G 7J 55
Dane St. WC1 . . . . .6G 7 (5K 83)
Daneswood Av. SE6 . . . . .3E 140
Danethorpe Rd. HA0: Wemb 6D 60
Danetree Cl. KT19: Ewe 7J 163
Danetree Rd. KT19: Ewe 7J 163
Danette Gdns. RM10: Dag 2G 73
Daneville Rd. SE5 . . . . .1D 120
Dangan Rd. E11 .6J 51
Daniel Bolt Cl. E14 . . . . .5D 86
Daniel Cl. N18 . . . . .4D 34
SW17 . . . . .6C 136
TW4: Houn .7D 112
Daniel Ct. NW9 .1A 44

Daniel Gdns. SE15 . . . . .7F 103
Daniell Ho. N1 . . . . .2D 84
(off Cranston Est.)
Daniell Way CR0: Wadd 1J 167
Daniel Pl. NW4 .7D 44
Daniel Rd. W5 . . . . .7F 79
Daniels Rd. SE15 . . . . .3J 121
Danleigh Ct. N14 . . . . .7C 22
Dan Leno Wlk. SW6 . . . . .7K 99
Dan Mason Dr. W4 . . . . .2J 115
Danny Fiszman Bri. N5 . . . . .4A 66
N7 . . . . .4A 66
Dansey Pl. W1 . . . . .2C 12
Dansington Rd. DA16: Well 4A 126
Danson Cres. DA16: Well 3B 126
DANSON INTERCHANGE 5D 126
Danson La. DA16: Well 4B 126
Danson Mead DA16: Well 3C 126
Danson Park 5C 126
Danson Park Watersports Cen. 4C 126
Danson Rd. DA5: Bexl, Bex 6C 126
DA6: Bex 5D 126
SE17 . . . . .5B 102
Dante Pl. SE11 . . . . .4B 102
Dante Rd. SE11 .4B 102
Danube Apartments N8 . . . . .3K 47
(off Gt. Amwell La.)
Danube Cl. N9 . . . . .3D 34
Danube Ct. SE15 . . . . .7F 103
(off Daniel Gdns.)
Danube St. SW3 . . . . .5D 16 (5C 100)
Danvers Av. SW11 . . . . .4C 118
Danvers Ho. E1 . . . . .6G 85
(off Christian St.)
Danvers Rd. N8 .4H 47
Danvers St. SW3 . . . . .7B 16 (6B 100)
Dao Cl. E13 . . . . .1K 87
Da Palma Ct. SW6 . . . . .6J 99
(off Anselm Rd.)
Daphne Cl. KT4: Wor Pk 2A 164
Daphne Gdns. E4 . . . . .3K 35
Daphne Ho. N22 .1A 48
(off Acacia Rd.)
Daphne St. SW18 . . . . .6A 118
Daplyn St. E1 . . . . .5K 9 (5G 85)
D'Arblay St. W1 . . . . .1B 12 (6G 83)
Darby Cres. TW16: Sun 2A 148
Darby Rd. TW16: Sun 2A 148
Darcy Av. SM6: Wall 4G 167
Darcy Cl. N20 . . . . .2G 31
D'Arcy Dr. HA3: Kenton 4D 42
Darcy Gdns. HA3: Kenton 4D 42
RM9: Dag 1F 91
Darcy Ho. E8 . . . . .1H 85
(off London Flds. E. Side)
D'Arcy Pl. BR2: Brom 4J 159
Darcy Rd. SM3: Cheam 4F 165
SW16 . . . . .2J 155
TW7: Isle 1A 114
Dare Gdns. RM8: Dag 3E 72
Darell Rd. TW9: Rich 3G 115
Darent Ho. BR1: Brom 5F 141
NW8 . . . . .5B 4
(off Church St. Est.)
Darenth Rd. DA16: Well 1A 126
N16 . . . . .7F 49
Darfield NW1 . . . . .1G 83
(off Bayham St.)
Darfield Rd. SE4 . . . . .5B 122
Darfield Way W10 . . . . .6F 81
Darfur St. SW15 . . . . .3F 117
Dargate Cl. SE19 . . . . .7F 139
Darien Rd. SW11 . . . . .3B 118
Daring Ho. E3 . . . . .2A 86
(off Roman Rd.)
Dark Ho. Wlk. EC3 . . . . .3F 15 (7D 84)
Darlands Dr. EN5: Barn 5A 20
Darlan Rd. SW6 .7H 99

Darlaston Rd. SW19 . . . . .7F 135
Darley Cl. CR0: C'don 6A 158
Darley Dr. KT3: N Mald 2K 151
Darley Gdns. SM4: Mord 6A 154
Darley Ho. SE11 .6G 19
Darley Rd. N9 . . . . .1A 34
SW11 . . . . .6D 118
Darling Ho. TW1: Twick 6D 114
Darling Rd. SE4 .3C 122
Darling Row E1 .4H 85
Darlington Ct. SE6 . . . . .1H 141
Darlington Ho. SW8 . . . . .7H 101
(off Hemans St.)
Darlington Rd. SE27 . . . . .5B 138
Darmaine Cl. CR2: S Croy 7C 168
Darnall Ho. SE10 . . . . .1E 122
(off Royal Hill)
Darnaway Pl. E14 . . . . .5E 86
(off Aberfeldy St.)
Darnay Apartments E15 . . . . .6F 69
Darndale Cl. E17 . . . . .2B 50
Darnley Cl. DA15: Sidc 5K 125
Darnley Ho. E14 .6A 86
(off Camdenhurst St.)
Darnley Rd. E9 . . . . .6J 67
IG8: Wfd G .1J 51
Darnley Ter. W11 . . . . .1F 99
Darrell Charles Ct. UB8: Uxb 7A 56
Darrell Rd. SE22 . . . . .5G 121
Darren Cl. N4 . . . . .7K 47
Darren Ct. N7 . . . . .4J 65
Darrick Wood Rd. BR6: Orp 2H 173
Darrick Wood Sports Cen. 3G 173
Darrick Wood Swimming Pool 3G 173
Darris Cl. UB4: Yead 4C 76
Darsley Dr. SW8 .1H 119
Dartford Av. N9 . . . . .6D 24
Dartford By-Pass DA5: Bexl, Dart 7K 127
Dartford Gdns. RM6: Chad H 5B 54
Dartford Ho. SE1 . . . . .4F 103
(off Longfield Est.)
Dartford Rd. DA5: Bexl 1J 145
Dartford St. SE17 . . . . .6C 102
Dartington NW1 . . . . .1G 83
(off Plender St.)
Dartington Ho. SW8 . . . . .2H 119
(off Union Gro.)
W2 . . . . .5K 81
(off Senior St.)
Dartle Ct. SE16 . . . . .2G 103
(off Scott Lidgett Cres.)
Dartmoor Wlk. E14 . . . . .4C 104
(off Severnake Cl.)
Dartmouth Cl. W11 . . . . .6H 81
Dartmouth Ct. SE10 . . . . .1E 122
Dartmouth Gro. SE10 . . . . .1E 122
Dartmouth Hill SE10 . . . . .1E 122
Dartmouth Ho. KT2: King T 1F 150
(off Seven Kings Way)
SE10 . . . . .1D 122
(off Catherine Gro.)
DARTMOUTH PARK 3F 65
Dartmouth Pk. Av. NW5 . . . . .3F 65
Dartmouth Pk. Hill N19 . . . . .1F 65
NW5 . . . . .1F 65
Dartmouth Pk. Rd. NW5 . . . . .4E 64
Dartmouth Rd. SE23 . . . . .2J 139
W4 . . . . .6A 98
Dartmouth Rd. BR2: Hayes 7J 159
HA4: Ruis 3J 57
NW2 . . . . .6F 63
NW4 . . . . .6C 44
SE23 . . . . .3H 139
SE26 . . . . .3H 139
Dartmouth Row SE10 . . . . .2E 122
Dartmouth St. SW1 . . . . .7D 12 (2H 101)
Dartmouth Ter. SE10 . . . . .1F 123
Dartnell Rd. CR0: C'don 7F 157
Darton Ct. W3 . . . . .1J 97
Dartrey Twr. SW10 . . . . .7A 100
(off Worlds End Est.)

Dartrey Wlk. SW10 . . . . .7A 100
Dart St. W10 . . . . .3G 81
Darvell Ho. SE17 . . . . .5D 102
(off Inville Rd.)
Darville Rd. N16 .3F 67
Darwell Cl. E6 . . . . .2E 88
Darwen Pl. E2 . . . . .2H 85
Darwin Cl. BR6: Farnb 5H 173
N11 . . . . .3A 32
Darwin Ct. CR2: S Croy 5B 168
(off Warham Rd.)
E13 . . . . .3K 87
NW1 . . . . .1F 83
(not continuous)
SE17 . . . . .4D 102
(off Barlow St.)
Darwin Dr. UB1: S'hall 6F 77
Darwin Ho. SE20 . . . . .1G 157
SW1 . . . . .7A 18
Darwin Rd. DA16: Well 3K 125
N22 . . . . .1B 48
W5 . . . . .5C 96
Darwin St. SE17 .4D 102
(not continuous)
Darwood Ct. NW6 . . . . .7A 64
(off Belsize Rd.)
Daryngton Dr. UB6: G'frd 2H 77
Daryngton Ho. SE1 . . . . .7F 15
(off Hankey Pl.)
SW8 . . . . .7J 101
(off Hartington Rd.)
Dashwood Cl. DA6: Bex 5G 127
Dashwood Rd. N8 . . . . .6K 47
Dashwood Studios SE17 . . . . .4C 102
(off Walworth Rd.)
Dassett Rd. SE27 . . . . .5B 138
Data Point Bus. Cen. E16 . . . . .4F 87
Datchelor Pl. SE5 . . . . .1D 120
Datchet Ho. E2 . . . . .3F 85
(off Virginia Rd.)
NW1 . . . . .1K 5
(off Augustus St.)
Datchet Rd. SE6 .2B 140
Datchworth Ct. EN1: Enf 5K 23
Datchworth Ho. N1 . . . . .7B 66
(off The Sutton Est.)
Date St. SE17 . . . . .5D 102
Daubeney Gdns. N17 . . . . .7H 33
Daubeney Pl. TW12: Hamp 1G 149
(off High St.)
Daubeney Rd. E5 . . . . .4A 68
N17 . . . . .7H 33
Daubeney Twr. SE8 . . . . .5B 104
(off Bowditch)
Dault Rd. SW18 .7A 118
Dauncey Ho. SE1 . . . . .7A 14
Dave Adams Ho. E3 . . . . .2B 86
(off Norman Gro.)
Davema Cl. BR7: Chst 1E 160
Davenant Ho. E1 .5G 85
(off Old Montague St.)
Davenant Rd. CR0: C'don 4B 168
N19 . . . . .2H 65
Davenant St. E1 .5G 85
Davenport Cen. IG11: Bark 1B 90
Davenport Cl. TW11: Tedd 6A 132
Davenport Ct. CR0: C'don 7B 156
Davenport Ho. SE11 . . . . .3J 19
(off Walnut Tree Wlk.)
UB7: W Dray 2B 92
Davenport Lodge
TW5: Hest 7C 94
Davenport Rd. DA14: Sidc 2E 144
SE6 . . . . .6D 122
Daventer Dr. HA7: Stan 7E 26
Daventry Av. E17 . . . . .6C 50
Daventry Cl. SL3: Poyle 4A 174
Daventry St. NW1 . . . . .5C 4 (5C 82)
Daver Ct. SW3 . . . . .5D 16 (5C 100)
W5 . . . . .4D 78
Davern Cl. SE10 .4H 105

Davey Cl. N7 . . . . .6K 65
   N13 . . . . .5E 32
Davey Gdns. IG11: Bark 4A 90
Davey Rd. E9 . . . . .7C 68
Davey's Ct. WC2 . . . . .2E 12
Davey St. SE15 . . . . .6F 103
David Av. UB6: G'frd 3J 77
David Cl. UB3: Harl 7G 93
David Ct. E14 . . . . .7D 86
                       (off Hillary M.)
   N20 . . . . .3F 31
Davidge Ho. SE1 . . . . .7K 13
                       (off Coral St.)
Davidge St. SE1 . . . . .7A 14 (2B 102)
David Hewitt Ho. E3 . . . . .5D 86
                    (off Watts Gro.)
David Ho. DA15: Sidc 3A 144
   SW8 . . . . .7J 101
                    (off Wyvil Rd.)
David Lean Cinema
   Croydon .3D 168
            (within Fairfield Halls)
David Lee Point E15 . . . . .1G 87
               (off Leather Gdns.)
David Lloyd Leisure
   Barnet 7G 31
   Beckenham 4B 158
   Cheam 7F 165
   Chigwell 1J 37
   Enfield 2B 24
   Fulham 7J 99
   (within Fulham Broadway Shop. Cen.)
   Hampton .3E 130
   Hounslow 5A 94
   Kidbrooke .4K 123
   Kingston upon Thames 2E 150
          (within The Rotunda Cen.)
   Raynes Park 3F 153
   Sidcup 5C 144
   South Kensington 4K 99
               (off Point West)
   Sudbury Hill 5H 59
David M. SE10 . . . . .7E 104
   W1 . . . . .5F 5 (5D 82)
David Rd. RM8: Dag 2E 72
Davids Ct. CR0: C'don 6G 157
   SL3: Poyle 5A 174
David's Ct. UB1: S'hall 6G 77
              (off Whitecote St.)
Davidson Gdns. SW8 . . . . .7J 101
Davidson La. HA1: Harr 7K 41
Davidson Rd. CR0: C'don 1E 168
Davidson Terraces E7 . . . . .5K 69
             (off Claremont Rd.)
David's Rd. SE23 . . . . .1J 139
David St. E15 . . . . .6F 69
David Twigg Cl. KT2: King T 1E 150
David Wildman La. NW7 . . . . .6B 30
Davies Cl. CR0: C'don 6G 157
Davies La. E11 .2G 69
Davies M. W1 . . . . .2J 11 (7F 83)
Davies St. W1 . . . . .1J 11 (6F 83)
Davies Wlk. TW7: Isle 1H 113
Da Vinci Ct. SE16 . . . . .5H 103
               (off Rossetti Rd.)
Da Vinci Lodge SE10 . . . . .3H 105
              (off West Parkside)
Da Vinci Torre SE13 . . . . .3D 122
              (off Loampit Va.)
Davington Gdns. RM8: Dag 5B 72
Davington Rd. RM8: Dag 6B 72
Davinia Cl. IG8: Wfd G 6J 37
Davis Ho. W12 .7D 80
            (off White City Est.)
Davis Rd. KT9: Chess 4G 163
   W3 . . . . .1B 98
Davis Rd. Ind. Pk. KT9: Chess 4G 163
Davis St. E13 . . . . .2K 87
Davisville Rd. W12 . . . . .2C 98
Davis Way DA14: Sidc 6E 144
Davmor Ct. TW8: Bford 5C 96

Dawes Av. TW7: Isle 5A 114
Dawes Ho. SE17 . . . . .4D 102
                 (off Orb St.)
Dawes Rd. SW6 . . . . .7G 99
   UB10: Uxb 2A 74
Dawes St. SE17 . . . . .5D 102
Dawkins Ct. SE1 . . . . .3D 102
Dawley Av. UB8: Hil 5E 74
Dawley Pde. UB3: Hayes 7E 74
Dawley Pk. UB3: Hayes 2F 93
Dawley Rd. UB3: Harl, Hayes 7E 74
Dawlish Av. N13 . . . . .4D 32
   SW18 . . . . .2K 135
   UB6: G'frd 2A 78
Dawlish Dr. HA4: Ruis 2J 57
   HA5: Pinn .5C 40
   IG3: Ilf 4J 71
Dawlish Rd. E10 . . . . .1E 68
   N17 . . . . .3G 49
   NW2 . . . . .6F 63
Dawnay Gdns. SW18 . . . . .2B 136
Dawnay Rd. SW18 . . . . .2A 136
Dawn Cl. TW4: Houn 3C 112
Dawn Cres. E15 . . . . .1F 87
Dawpool Rd. NW2 . . . . .2B 62
Daws Hill E4 . . . . .2K 25
Daws La. NW7 .5G 29
Dawson Av. IG11: Bark 7K 71
Dawson Cl. SE18 . . . . .4G 107
   UB3: Hayes 5F 75
Dawson Ct. W3 . . . . .3J 97
             (off Palmerston Rd.)
Dawson Gdns. IG11: Bark 7K 71
Dawson Ho. E2 . . . . .3J 85
                (off Sceptre Rd.)
Dawson Pl. W2 . . . . .7J 81
Dawson Rd. KT1: King T 3F 151
   NW2 . . . . .5E 62
Dawson St. E2 . . . . .1K 9 (2F 85)
Dawson Ter. N9 . . . . .7D 24
Daybrook Rd. SW19 . . . . .2K 153
Day Dr. RM8: Dag 1D 72
Day Ho. SE5 . . . . .7C 102
               (off Bethwin Rd.)
Daylesford Av. SW15 . . . . .4C 116
Daymer Gdns. HA5: Eastc 4K 39
Daynor Ho. NW6 . . . . .1J 81
                (off Quex Ho.)
Daysbrook Rd. SW2 . . . . .1K 137
Days La. DA15: Sidc 7J 125
Dayton Gro. SE15 . . . . .1J 121
Deaconess Ct. N15 . . . . .4F 49
           (off Tottenham Grn. E.)
Deacon Estate, The E4 . . . . .6G 35
Deacon Ho. SE11 . . . . .4H 19
             (off Black Prince Rd.)
Deacon M. N1 .7D 66
Deacon Rd. KT2: King T 1F 151
   NW2 . . . . .5C 62
Deacons Cl. HA5: Pinn 2K 39
Deacons Ct. TW1: Twick 2K 131
Deacons Leas BR6: Orp 4H 173
Deacon's Ri. N2 . . . . .5B 46
Deacon Ter. N1 . . . . .6C 66
             (off Harecourt Rd.)
Deacons Wlk. TW12: Hamp 4E 130
Deacon Way IG8: Wfd G 7J 37
   SE17 . . . . .4C 102
Deal Ct. NW9 .2B 44
               (off Hazel Cl.)
   UB1: S'hall 6G 77
              (off Haldane Rd.)
Deal Ho. SE15 . . . . .6K 103
             (off Lovelinch La.)
   SE17 . . . . .5E 102
               (off Mina Rd.)
Deal M. W5 . . . . .4D 96
Deal Porters Wlk. SE16 . . . . .2K 103
Deal Porters Way SE16 . . . . .3J 103
Deal Rd. SW17 . . . . .6E 136

Deal's Gateway SE13 . . . . .1C 122
Deal St. E1 . . . . .5G 85
Dealtry Rd. SW15 . . . . .4E 116
Deal Wlk. SW9 . . . . .7A 102
Dean Abbott Ho. SW1 . . . . .3C 18
               (off Vincent St.)
Dean Bradley St. SW1 . . . . .2E 18 (3J 101)
Dean Cl. E9 . . . . .5J 67
   SE16 . . . . .1K 103
   UB10: Hil .7B 56
Dean Ct. HA0: Wemb 3B 60
   HA8: Edg .6D 28
   RM7: Rom .5K 55
   SW8 . . . . .7J 101
              (off Thorncroft St.)
   W3 . . . . .6K 79
Deancross St. E1 . . . . .6J 85
Dean Dr. HA7: Stan 2E 42
Deane Av. HA4: Ruis 5A 58
Deane Ct. HA6: Nwood 1G 39
Deane Cft. Rd. HA5: Eastc 6A 40
Deanery Cl. N2 . . . . .4C 46
Deanery M. W1 . . . . .4H 11
Deanery Rd. E15 . . . . .6G 69
Deanery St. W1 . . . . .4H 11 (1E 100)
Dean Farrar St. SW1 . . . . . .1D 18 (3H 101)
Deanfield Gdns. CR0: C'don 4D 168
Dean Gdns. E17 . . . . .4F 51
Deanhill Ct. SW14 . . . . .4H 115
Deanhill Rd. SW14 . . . . .4H 115
Dean Ho. E1 . . . . .6J 85
               (off Tarling St.)
   SE14 . . . . .7A 104
            (off New Cross Rd.)
Dean Rd. CR0: C'don 4D 168
   NW2 . . . . .6E 62
   SE28 . . . . .1A 108
   TW3: Houn 5F 113
   TW12: Hamp 5E 130
Dean Ryle St. SW1 . . . . .3E 18 (4J 101)
Deansbrook Cl. HA8: Edg 7D 28
Deansbrook Rd. HA8: Edg 7C 28
Dean's Bldgs. SE17 . . . . .4D 102
Deans Cl. CR0: C'don 3F 169
   HA8: Edg .6D 28
   W4 . . . . .6H 97
Dean's Ct. EC4 . . . . .1B 14 (6B 84)
Deanscroft Av. NW9 . . . . .1J 61
Deans Dr. HA8: Edg 5E 28
   N13 . . . . .6G 33
Deans Ga. CL. SE23 . . . . .3K 139
Deanshanger Ho. SE8 . . . . .4K 103
              (off Chilton Gro.)
Deans La. HA8: Edg 5D 28
   W4 . . . . .6H 97
               (off Deans Cl.)
Dean's M. W1 . . . . .7K 5 (6F 83)
Deans Rd. SM1: Sutt 3K 165
   W7 . . . . .1K 95
Dean Stanley St. SW1 . . . . .2E 18 (3J 101)
Deanston Wharf E16 . . . . .2K 105
               (not continuous)
Dean St. E7 . . . . .5J 69
   W1 . . . . .7C 6 (6H 83)
Deans Way HA8: Edg 5D 28
Deansway N2 . . . . .4B 46
   N9 . . . . .3K 33
Deanswood N11 . . . . .6C 32
Dean's Yd. SW1 . . . . .1D 18 (3H 101)
Dean Trench St. SW1 . . . . . .2E 18 (3J 101)
Dean Wlk. HA8: Edg 6D 28
Dean Way UB2: S'hall 2F 95
Dearne Cl. HA7: Stan 5F 27
De'Arn Gdns. CR4: Mitc 3C 154
Dearsley Ho. RM13: Rain 2K 91
Dearsley Rd. EN1: Enf 3B 24
Death Trap, London's 7G 13
Deauville Ct. SE16 . . . . .2K 103
              (off Eleanor Cl.)
   SW4 . . . . .6G 119

De Barowe M. N5 . . . . .4B 66
Debdale Ho. E2 . . . . .1G 85
               (off Whiston Rd.)
Debden N17 . . . . .2D 48
             (off Gloucester Rd.)
Debden Cl. IG8: Wfd G 7G 37
   KT2: King T 5D 132
   NW9 . . . . .1A 44
De Beauvoir Ct. N1 . . . . .7D 66
             (off Northchurch Rd.)
De Beauvoir Cres. N1 . . . . .1E 84
De Beauvoir Est. N1 . . . . .1E 84
De Beauvoir Pl. N1 . . . . .6E 66
De Beauvoir Rd. N1 . . . . .1E 84
De Beauvoir Sq. N1 . . . . .7E 66
DE BEAUVOIR TOWN 1E 84
De Beauvoir Wharf N1 . . . . .1E 84
              (off Hertford Rd.)
Debenham Ct. E8 . . . . .1G 85
               (off Pownall Rd.)
Debham Ct. NW2 . . . . .3E 62
Debnams Rd. SE16 . . . . .4J 103
De Bohun Av. N14 . . . . .6A 22
Deborah Cl. TW7: Isle 1J 113
Deborah Ct. E18 . . . . .3K 51
              (off Victoria Rd.)
Deborah Cres. HA4: Ruis 7F 39
Deborah Lodge HA8: Edg 1H 43
Debrabant Cl. DA8: Erith 6K 109
De Brome Rd.
   TW13: Felt 1A 130
De Bruin Ct. E14 . . . . .5E 104
               (off Ferry St.)
Deburgh Rd. SW19 . . . . .7A 136
Debussy NW9 .2B 44
Decima St. SE1 . . . . .7G 15 (3E 102)
Decima Studios SE1 . . . . .7G 15
               (off Decima St.)
Decimus Cl. CR7: Thor H 4D 156
Deck Cl. SE16 .1K 103
De Coubertin St. E20 . . . . .6E 68
Decoy Av. NW11 . . . . .5G 45
De Crespigny Pk. SE5 . . . . .2D 120
Dee Ct. W7 . . . . .6H 77
              (off Hobbayne Rd.)
Dee Ho. KT2: King T 1D 150
             (off May Bate Av.)
Deeley Rd. SW8 . . . . .1H 119
Deena Cl. W3 . . . . .6F 79
Deen City Farm 2A 154
Deepak Ho. SW17 . . . . .4C 136
Deepdale SW19 . . . . .4F 135
Deepdale Av. BR2: Brom 4H 159
Deepdale Cl. N11 . . . . .6K 31
Deepdale Ct. CR2: S Croy 4D 168
              (off Birdhurst Av.)
Deep Dene W5 .4F 79
Deepdene Av. CR0: C'don 3F 169
Deepdene Cl. E11 . . . . .4J 51
Deepdene Ct. BR2: Brom 3G 159
   N21 . . . . .6G 23
Deepdene Gdns. SW2 . . . . .7K 119
Deepdene Mans. SW6 . . . . .1H 117
              (off Rostrevor Rd.)
Deepdene Point SE23 . . . . .3K 139
Deepdene Rd. DA16: Well 3A 126
   SE5 . . . . .4D 120
Deepwell Cl. TW7: Isle 1A 114
Deepwood La. UB6: G'frd 3H 77
Deerbrook Rd. SE24 . . . . .1B 138
Deerdale Rd. SE24 . . . . .4C 120
Deerfield Cl. NW9 . . . . .5B 44
Deerfield Cotts. NW9 . . . . .5B 44
Deerhurst Cl. TW13: Felt 4K 129
Deerhurst Ct. CR0: C'don 1B 168
             (off Parson's Mead)
Deerhurst Cres. TW12: Hamp H 5G 131
Deerhurst Ho. SE15 . . . . .6G 103
             (off Haymerle Rd.)
Deerhurst Rd. NW2 . . . . .6F 63
   SW16 . . . . .5K 137

Deerings Dr.—Densole Cl.

Deerings Dr. HA5: Eastc 5J 39
Deerleap Gro. E4 5J 25
Dee Rd. TW9: Rich 4F 115
Deer Pk. Cl. KT2: King T 7H 133
Deer Pk. Gdns. CR4: Mitc 4B 154
Deer Pk. Rd. SW19 2K 153
Deer Pk. Way BR4: W W'ck 2H 171
Deeside Rd. SW17 3B 136
Dee St. E14 6E 86
Defence Cl. SE28 1J 107
Defiance Wlk. SE18 3D 106
Defiant Way SM6: Wall 7J 167
Defoe Av. TW9: Kew 7G 97
Defoe Cl. SE16 2B 104
SW17 6C 136
Defoe Ho. EC2 5D 8
Defoe Pl. EC2 5C 8
(off Beech St.)
SW17 4D 136
Defoe Rd. N16 3E 66
De Frene Rd. SE26 4K 139
Degema Rd. BR7: Chst 5F 143
Dehar Cres. NW9 7B 44
Dehavilland Cl. UB5: N'olt 3B 76
De Havilland Ct. N17 3H 49
De Havilland Dr. SE18 6F 107
De Havilland Rd. HA8: Edg 2G 43
TW5: Hest 7A 94
Dehavilland Studios E5 2J 67
(off Theydon Rd.)
De Havilland Way TW19: Stanw 6A 110
Dekker Ho. SE5 7D 102
(off Elmington Est.)
Dekker Rd. SE21 6E 120
Delacourt Rd. SE3 7K 105
Delafield Ho. E1 6G 85
(off Christian St.)
Delafield Rd. SE7 5K 105
Delaford Rd. SE16 5H 103
Delaford St. SW6 7G 99
Delahay Ho. SW3 7E 16
(off Chelsea Emb.)
Delamare Ct. SE6 3D 140
Delamare Cres. CR0: C'don 6J 157
Delamere Ct. E17 2E 50
Delamere Gdns. NW7 6E 28
Delamere Rd. SW20 1F 153
UB4: Yead 7B 76
W5 2E 96
Delamere St. W2 5K 81
Delamere Ter. W2 5K 81
Delancey Pas. NW1 1F 83
(off Delancey St.)
Delancey St. NW1 1F 83
Delancey Studios NW1 1F 83
Delany Ho. SE10 6E 104
(off Thames St.)
Delarch Ho. SE1 7A 14
De Laune St. SE17 6K 19 (5B 102)
Delaware Mans. W9 4K 81
(off Delaware Rd.)
Delaware Rd. W9 4K 81
Delawyk Cres. SE24 6C 120
Delcombe Av. KT4: Wor Pk 1E 164
Delderfield Ho. RM1: Rom 2K 55
(off Portnoi Cl.)
Delft Ho. KT2: King T 7F 133
(off Acre Rd.)
Delft Way SE22 5E 120
Delhi Rd. EN1: Enf 7A 24
Delhi St. N1 1J 83
Delia St. SW18 7K 117
Delisle Rd. SE28 1J 107
Delius Gro. E15 2F 87
Dell, The DA5: Bexl 1K 145
HA0: Wemb 5B 60
HA5: Pinn 2B 40
IG8: Wfd G 3E 36
SE2 5A 108
SE19 1F 157
TW8: Bford 6C 96
Dell, The TW14: Felt 7K 111
Della Path E5 3G 67
Dellbow Rd. TW14: Felt 5K 111
Dell Cl. E15 1F 87
IG8: Wfd G 3E 36
SM6: Wall 4G 167
Dell Farm Rd. HA4: Ruis 5F 39
Dellfield Cl. BR3: Beck 1E 158
Dell La. KT17: Ewe 5C 164
Dellors Cl. EN5: Barn 5A 20
Dellow Cl. IG2: Ilf 7H 53
Dellow Ho. E1 7H 85
(off Dellow St.)
Dellow St. E1 7H 85
Dell Rd. KT17: Ewe 6C 164
UB7: W Dray 4B 92
Dells Cl. E4 7J 25
TW11: Tedd 6K 131
Dell's M. SW1 4B 18
Dell Wlk. KT3: N Mald 2A 152
Dell Way W13 6C 78
Dellwood Gdns. IG5: Ilf 3E 52
Delmare Cl. SW9 4K 119
Delme Cres. SE3 2K 123
Delmerend Ho. SW3 5C 16
(off Cale St.)
Delmey Cl. CR0: C'don 3F 169
Deloraine Ho. SE8 1C 122
Delorme St. W6 6F 99
Delroy Ct. N20 7F 21
Delta Bldg. E14 6E 86
(off Ashton St.)
Delta Building, The RM7: Rush G 6K 55
Delta Cen. HA0: Wemb 1F 79
Delta Cl. KT4: Wor Pk 3B 164
Delta Ct. NW2 2C 62
SE8 6A 104
(off Trundleys Rd.)
Delta Gro. UB5: N'olt 3B 76
Delta Ho. N1 1E 8
(off Nile St.)
Delta Pk. SW18 4K 117
Delta Pk. Ind. Est. EN3: Brim 3G 25
Delta Point CR0: C'don 1C 168
(off Wellesley Rd.)
E2 3G 85
(off Delta St.)
Delta Rd. KT4: Wor Pk 3A 164
Delta St. E2 3G 85
De Luci Rd. DA8: Erith 5J 109
De Lucy St. SE2 4B 108
Delvan Cl. SE18 7E 106
Delvers Mead RM10: Dag 4J 73
Delverton Ho. SE17 5B 102
(off Delverton Rd.)
Delverton Rd. SE17 5B 102
Delvino Rd. SW6 1J 117
Demesne Rd. SM6: Wall 4H 167
Demeta Cl. HA9: Wemb 3J 61
De Montfort Pde. SW16 3J 137
De Montfort Rd. SW16 3J 137
De Morgan Rd. SW6 3K 117
Dempster Cl. KT6: Surb 1C 162
Dempster Rd. SW18 5A 118
Den, The 5J 103
Denbar Pde. RM7: Rom 4J 55
Denberry Dr. DA14: Sidc 3B 144
Denbigh Cl. BR7: Chst 6D 142
HA4: Ruis 2H 57
SM1: Sutt 5H 165
UB1: S'hall 6D 76
W11 7H 81
Denbigh Ct. E6 3B 88
W7 5K 77
(off Copley Cl.)
Denbigh Dr. UB3: Harl 2E 92
Denbigh Gdns. TW10: Rich 5F 115
Denbigh Ho. SW1 1F 17
(off Hans Pl.)
W11 7H 81
(off Westbourne Gro.)
Denbigh M. SW1 4A 18
Denbigh Pl. SW1 5A 18 (5G 101)
Denbigh Rd. E6 3B 88
TW3: Houn 2F 113
UB1: S'hall 6D 76
W11 7H 81
W13 7B 78
Denbigh St. SW1 4A 18 (4G 101)
(not continuous)
Denbigh Ter. W11 7H 81
Denbridge Rd. BR1: Brom 2D 160
Denbury Ho. E3 3D 86
(off Talwin St.)
Denby Ct. SE11 3H 19
Dence Ho. E2 2K 9
(off Turin St.)
Denchworth Ho. SW9 2A 120
Dencliffe TW15: Ashf 5C 128
Den Cl. BR3: Beck 3F 159
Dencora Centre, The EN3: Brim 3F 25
Dene, The CR0: C'don 4K 169
HA9: Wemb 4E 60
KT8: W Mole 5D 148
W13 5B 78
Dene Av. DA15: Sidc 7B 126
TW3: Houn 3D 112
Dene Cl. BR2: Hayes 1H 171
DA2: Wilm 4K 145
E10 2D 68
KT4: Wor Pk 2B 164
SE4 3A 122
Dene Ct. CR2: S Croy 5C 168
(off Warham Rd.)
W5 5C 78
Denecroft Cres. UB10: Hil 1D 74
Dene Gdns. HA7: Stan 5H 27
KT7: T Ditt 2A 162
Dene Ho. N14 7C 22
Denehurst Gdns. IG8: Wfd G 4E 36
NW4 6E 44
TW2: Twick 7H 113
TW10: Rich 4G 115
W3 1H 97
Dene Rd. IG9: Buck H 1G 37
N11 1J 31
Denesmead SE24 5C 120
Denewood EN5: New Bar 5F 21
Denewood Rd. N6 6D 46
Denford St. SE10 5H 105
(off Glenforth St.)
Dengie Wlk. N1 1C 84
(off Basire St.)
Denham Cl. DA16: Well 3C 126
Denham Ct. NW6 7A 64
(off Fairfax Rd.)
SE26 3H 139
(off Kirkdale)
UB1: S'hall 7G 77
(off Baird Av.)
Denham Cres. CR4: Mitc 4D 154
Denham Dr. IG2: Ilf 6G 53
Denham Ho. UB7: W Dray 2B 92
(off Park Lodge Av.)
W12 7D 80
(off White City Est.)
Denham Rd. N20 3J 31
TW14: Felt 7A 112
Denham St. SE10 5J 105
Denham Way IG11: Bark 1J 89
Denholme Rd. W9 3H 81
Denison Cl. N2 3A 46
Denison Ho. E14 3D 104
Denison Rd. SW19 6B 136
TW13: Felt 4H 129
W5 4C 78
Deniston Av. DA5: Bexl 1E 144
Denis Way SW4 3H 119
Denland Ho. SW8 7K 101
(off Dorset Rd.)
Denleigh Gdns. KT7: T Ditt 6J 149
N21 1F 33
Denman Dr. KT10: Clay 5A 162
NW11 5J 45
TW15: Ashf 6D 128
Denman Dr. Nth. NW11 5J 45
Denman Dr. Sth. NW11 5J 45
Denman Ho. N16 2E 66
Denman Rd. SE15 1F 121
Denman St. W1 3C 12 (7H 83)
Denmark Av. SW19 7G 135
Denmark Ct. SM4: Mord 6J 153
Denmark Gdns. SM5: Cars 3D 166
Denmark Gro. N1 2A 84
DENMARK HILL 3C 120
Denmark Hill SE5 1D 120
Denmark Hill Dr. NW9 3C 44
Denmark Hill Est. SE5 4D 120
Denmark Ho. SE7 4C 106
Denmark Mans. SE5 2C 120
(off Coldharbour La.)
Denmark Path SE25 5H 157
Denmark Pl. E3 3C 86
WC2 7D 6 (6H 83)
Denmark Rd. BR1: Brom 1K 159
KT1: King T 3E 150
N8 4A 48
NW6 2H 81
SE5 1C 120
SE25 5G 157
SM5: Cars 3D 166
SW19 6F 135
TW2: Twick 3H 131
W13 7B 78
Denmark St. E11 3G 69
E13 5K 87
N17 1H 49
WC2 7D 6 (6H 83)
Denmark Ter. N2 3D 46
Denmark Wlk. SE27 4C 138
Denmead Ho. SW15 6B 116
Denmead Rd. CR0: C'don 1B 168
Denmore Ct. SM6: Wall 5F 167
Dennan Rd. KT6: Surb 1F 163
Dennard Way BR6: Farnb 4F 173
Denner Rd. E4 2H 35
Denne Ter. E8 1F 85
Dennett Rd. CR0: C'don 1A 168
Dennett's Gro. SE14 2K 121
Dennett's Rd. SE14 1J 121
Denning Av. CR0: Wadd 4A 168
Denning Cl. NW8 1A 4 (3A 82)
TW12: Hamp 5D 130
Denning M. SW12 6E 118
Denning Point E1 7K 9
(off Commercial St.)
Denning Rd. NW3 4B 64
Dennington Cl. E5 2J 67
Dennington Pk. Rd. NW6 6J 63
Denningtons, The KT4: Wor Pk 2A 164
Dennis Av. HA9: Wemb 5F 61
Dennis Cl. TW15: Ashf 7F 129
Dennis Gdns. HA7: Stan 5H 27
Dennis Ho. E3 2B 86
(off Roman Rd.)
SM1: Sutt 4K 165
Dennis La. HA7: Stan 3G 27
Dennison Point E15 7E 68
Dennis Pde. N14 1C 32
Dennis Pk. Cres. SW20 1G 153
Dennis Reeve Cl. CR4: Mitc 1D 154
Dennis Rd. KT8: E Mos 4G 149
Dennis Way SW4 3H 119
Denny Cl. E6 5C 88
Denny Cres. SE11 5K 19 (5A 102)
Denny Gdns. RM9: Dag 7B 72
Denny Rd. N9 1C 34
Denny St. SE11 5K 19 (5A 102)
Den Rd. BR2: Brom 3F 159
Densham Ho. NW8 1B 4
(off Cochrane St.)
Densham Rd. E15 1G 87
Densole Cl. BR3: Beck 1A 158

Denstone Ho. SE15 ....6G 103
(off Haymerle Rd.)
Densworth Gro. N9 ....2D 34
Dent Ho. SE17 ....4E 102
(off Peacock St.)
Denton NW1 ....6E 64
Denton Ho. N1 ....7B 66
(off Halton Rd.)
Denton Rd. DA5: Bexl 2K 145
DA16: Well 7C 108
N8 ....5K 47
N18 ....4K 33
TW1: Twick 6D 114
Denton St. SW18 ....6K 117
Denton Ter. DA5: Bexl 2K 145
Denton Way E5 ....3K 67
Dents Rd. SW11 ....6D 118
Denver Cl. BR6: Pet W 6J 161
Denver Rd. N16 ....7E 48
Denwood SE23 ....3K 139
Denyer St. SW3 .....4D 16 (4C 100)
Denys Ho. EC1 ....5J 7
(off Bourne Est.)
Denziloe Av. UB10: Hil 3D 74
Denzil Rd. NW10 ....5B 62
Deodar Rd. SW15 ....4G 117
Deodora Cl. N20 ....3H 31
Department for Communities 1A 18
De Pass Gdns. IG11: Bark 4A 90
Depot App. NW2 ....4F 63
Depot Rd. TW3: Houn 3H 113
W12 ....7E 80
Depot St. SE5 ....6D 102
DEPTFORD 7C 104
Deptford Bri. SE8 ....1C 122
Deptford B'way. SE8 ....1C 122
Deptford Bus. Pk. SE15 ....6J 103
Deptford Chu. St. SE8 ....6C 104
Deptford Creek Bri. SE8 ....6D 104
(off Creek Rd.)
Deptford Ferry Rd. E14 ....4C 104
Deptford Grn. SE8 ....6C 104
Deptford High St. SE8 ....6C 104
Deptford Pk. Bus. Cen. SE8 .....5A 104
Deptford Strand SE8 ....4B 104
Deptford Trad. Est. SE8 ....5A 104
Deptford Wharf SE8 ....4B 104
De Quincey Ho. SW1 ....6A 18
(off Lupus St.)
De Quincey M. E16 ....1J 105
De Quincey Rd. N17 ....1D 48
Derby Av. HA3: Hrw W 1H 41
N12 ....5F 31
RM7: Rom 6J 55
Derby Ga. SW1 ....6E 12 (2J 101)
(not continuous)
Derby Hill SE23 ....2J 139
Derby Hill Cres. SE23 ....2J 139
Derby Ho. HA5: Pinn 2B 40
SE11 ....3J 19
Derby Lodge N3 ....2H 45
WC1 ....1G 7
(off Britannia St.)
Derby Rd. CR0: C'don 1B 168
E7 ....7B 70
E9 ....1K 85
E18 ....1H 51
EN3: Pond E 5C 24
KT5: Surb 1G 163
N18 ....5D 34
SM1: Sutt 6H 165
SW14 ....4H 115
SW19 ....7J 135
TW3: Houn 4F 113
Derby Rd. Ind. Est.
TW3: Houn 4F 113
Derbyshire St. E2 ....3G 85
(not continuous)
Derby St. W1 ....5H 11 (1E 100)
Dere Cl. SW6 ....1G 117

Dereham Ho. SE4 ....4K 121
(off Frendsbury Rd.)
Dereham Pl. EC2 ....2H 9 (3E 84)
Dereham Rd. IG11: Bark 5K 71
Derek Av. HA9: Wemb 7H 61
KT19: Ewe 6G 163
SM6: Wall 4F 167
Derek Cl. KT19: Ewe 5H 163
Derek Walcott Cl. SE24 ....5B 120
Dericote St. E8 ....1H 85
Deri Dene Cl. TW19: Stanw 6A 110
Dering Pl. CR0: C'don 4C 168
Dering Rd. CR0: C'don 4C 168
Dering St. W1 ....1K 11 (6F 83)
Dering Yd. W1 ....1K 11 (6F 83)
Derinton Rd. SW17 ....4D 136
Derley Rd. UB2: S'hall 3A 94
Dermody Gdns. SE13 ....5F 123
Dermody Rd. SE13 ....5F 123
Deronda Rd. SE24 ....1B 138
Deroy Cl. SM5: Cars 6D 166
Derrick Gdns. SE7 ....3A 106
Derrick Rd. BR3: Beck 3B 158
Derrycombe Ho. W2 ....5J 81
(off Gt. Western Rd.)
Derry Ho. NW8 ....4B 4
(off Church St. Est.)
Derry M. N19 ....2J 65
Derry Rd. CR0: Bedd 3J 167
Derry St. W8 ....2K 99
Dersingham Av. E12 ....4D 70
Dersingham Rd. NW2 ....3G 63
Derwent NW1 ....2A 6
(off Robert St.)
Derwent Av. EN4: E Barn 1J 31
N18 ....5J 33
NW7 ....6E 28
NW9 ....5A 44
SW15 ....4A 134
UB10: Ick 2C 56
Derwent Cl. TW14: Felt 1H 129
Derwent Ct. SE16 ....2K 103
(off Eleanor Cl.)
Derwent Cres. DA7: Bex 2G 127
HA7: Stan 2C 42
N20 ....3F 31
Derwent Dr. BR5: Pet W 7H 161
UB4: Hayes 5G 75
Derwent Gdns. HA9: Wemb 7C 42
IG4: Ilf 4C 52
Derwent Gro. SE22 ....4F 121
Derwent Ho. E3 ....4B 86
(off Southern Gro.)
KT2: King T 1D 150
(off May Bate Av.)
SW7 ....3A 16
(off Cromwell Rd.)
Derwent Lodge KT4: Wor Pk 2D 164
TW7: Isle 2H 113
Derwent Point EC1 ....1A 8
(off Goswell Rd.)
Derwent Ri. NW9 ....6A 44
N13 ....4E 32
SE20 ....2G 157
SW20 ....6F 153
TW2: Whitt 6F 113
UB1: S'hall 6D 76
W5 ....3C 96
Derwent St. SE10 ....5G 105
Derwent Wlk. SM6: Wall 7F 167
Derwentwater Rd. W3 ....1J 97
Derwent Yd. W5 ....3C 96
(off Derwent Rd.)
De Salis Rd. UB10: Hil 4E 74
Desborough Cl. TW17: Shep 7C 146
W2 ....5K 81
Desborough Ho. W14 ....6H 99
(off North End Rd.)
Desborough Sailing Club 7D 146

Desborough St. W2 ....5K 81
(off Cirencester St.)
Desenfans Rd. SE21 ....6E 120
Desford Rd. E16 ....4G 87
Desford Way TW15: Ashf 2B 128
Design Mus.
Kensington 3H 99
Southwark 6K 15 (2F 103)
Desmond Ho. EN4: E Barn 6H 21
Desmond St. SE14 ....6A 104
Desmond Tutu Dr. SE23 ....1B 140
Despard Rd. N19 ....1G 65
Desvignes Dr. SE13 ....6F 123
Dethick Ct. E3 ....1A 86
Detling Ho. SE17 ....4E 102
(off Congreve St.)
Detling Rd. BR1: Brom 5J 141
DA8: Erith 7K 109
Detmold Rd. E5 ....2J 67
Dettingen Pl. IG11: Bark 2B 90
Devalls Cl. E6 ....7F 89
Devana End SM5: Cars 3D 166
Devane Way SE27 ....3B 138
Devas Rd. SW20 ....1E 152
Devas St. E3 ....4D 86
Devenay Rd. E15 ....7H 69
Devenish Rd. SE2 ....2A 108
Deventer Cres. SE22 ....5E 120
Deveraux Cl. BR3: Beck 5E 158
De Vere Cl. SM6: Wall 7J 167
De Vere Cotts. W8 ....3A 100
(off Canning Pl.)
De Vere Gdns. IG1: Ilf 2D 70
W8 ....2A 100
Deverell St. SE1 ....3D 102
De Vere M. W8 ....3A 100
(off Canning Pl.)
Devereux Ct. WC2 ....1J 13
Devereux La. SW13 ....7D 98
Devereux Rd. SW11 ....6D 118
Deveron Way RM1: Rom 1K 55
Devey Cl. KT2: King T 7B 134
Devitt Ho. E14 ....7D 86
(off Wade's Pl.)
Devizes St. N1 ....1D 84
Devon Av. TW2: Twick 1G 131
Devon Cl. IG9: Buck H 2E 36
N17 ....3F 49
UB6: G'frd 1C 78
Devon Ct. TW12: Hamp 7E 130
W7 ....5K 77
(off Copley Cl.)
Devoncroft Gdns. TW1: Twick 7A 114
Devon Gdns. N4 ....6B 48
Devon Ho. E17 ....2B 50
N1 ....1B 84
(off Upper St.)
Devonhurst Pl. W4 ....5K 97
Devonia Gdns. N18 ....6H 33
Devonia Rd. N1 ....2B 84
Devon Mans. HA3: Kenton 5C 42
(off Woodcock Hill)
SE1 ....3C 102
(off Tooley St.)
Devon Pde. HA3: Kenton 5C 42
Devonport W2 ....1C 10 (6C 82)
Devonport Gdns. IG1: Ilf 6D 52
Devonport Ho. W2 ....5J 81
(off Gt. Western Rd.)
Devonport M. W12 ....2D 98
Devonport Rd. W12 ....1D 98
(not continuous)
Devonport St. E1 ....6J 85
Devon Ri. N2 ....4B 46
Devon Rd. IG11: Bark 1J 89
SM2: Cheam 7G 165
Devons Est. E3 ....3D 86
Devonshire Av. SM2: Sutt 7A 166
Devonshire Cl. E15 ....4G 69
N13 ....3F 33
W1 ....5J 5 (5F 83)

Devonshire Ct. E1 ....3J 85
(off Bancroft Rd.)
HA5: Hat E 1D 40
(off Devonshire Rd.)
N17 ....6H 33
TW13: Felt 2K 129
WC1 ....5F 7
(off Boswell St.)
Devonshire Cres. NW7 ....7A 30
Devonshire Dr. KT6: Surb 1D 162
SE10 ....7D 104
Devonshire Gdns. N17 ....6H 33
N21 ....7H 23
W4 ....7J 97
Devonshire Gro. SE15 ....6H 103
Devonshire Hall E9 ....6J 67
(off Frampton Pk. Rd.)
Devonshire Hill La. N17 ....6G 33
Devonshire Ho. E14 ....4C 104
(off Westferry Rd.)
IG8: Wfd G 7K 37
NW6 ....6H 63
(off Kilburn High Rd.)
SE1 ....3C 102
(off Bath Ter.)
SM2: Sutt 7A 166
SW1 ....5D 18
(off Lindsay Sq.)
SW15 ....5F 117
W2 ....5B 4
(off Adpar St.)
Devonshire Ho. Bus. Cen. BR2: Brom .4K 159
(off Devonshire Sq.)
Devonshire M. N13 ....4F 33
SW10 ....7A 16
(off Park Wlk.)
W4 ....5A 98
Devonshire M. Nth. W1 ....5J 5 (5F 83)
Devonshire M. Sth. W1 ....5J 5 (5F 83)
Devonshire M. W. W1 ......4H 5 (4E 82)
Devonshire Pas. W4 ....5A 98
Devonshire Pl. NW2 ....3J 63
W1 ....4H 5 (4E 82)
W8 ....3K 99
Devonshire Pl. M. W1 .....4H 5 (5E 82)
Devonshire Point TW15: Ashf 3E 128
Devonshire Rd. BR6: Orp 7K 161
CR0: C'don 7D 156
DA6: Bex 4E 126
E16 ....6K 87
E17 ....6C 50
HA1: Harr 6H 41
HA5: Eastc 6A 40
HA5: Hat E 1D 40
IG2: Ilf 7J 53
N9 ....1D 34
N13 ....4E 32
N17 ....6H 33
NW7 ....7A 30
SE9 ....2C 142
SE23 ....1J 139
SM2: Sutt 7A 166
SM5: Cars 4E 166
SW19 ....7C 136
TW13: Hanw 3C 130
UB1: S'hall 5E 76
W4 ....5A 98
W5 ....4D 96
Devonshire Road Nature Reserve .7K 121
Devonshire Road Nature Reserve Vis. Cen.
...............................7K 121
Devonshire Row EC2 ......6H 9 (5E 84)
Devonshire Row M. W1 ....4K 5
Devonshire Sq. BR2: Brom 4K 159
EC2 ....6H 9 (6E 84)
Devonshire St. W1 ......5H 5 (5E 82)
W4 ....5A 98
Devonshire Ter. W2 ....6A 82
Devonshire Way CR0: C'don 2A 170
UB4: Yead 6K 75
Devons Rd. E3 ....3D 86

Devon St.—Dolland St.

Devon St. SE15 .6H **103**
Devon Way KT9: Chess .5C **162**
KT19: Ewe .5H **163**
UB10: Hil .2B **74**
Devon Waye TW5: Hest .7D **94**
Devon Wharf E14 .5F **87**
De Walden Ho. *NW8* .*2C* ***82***
(off Allitsen Rd.)
De Walden St. W1 .6H **5** (5E **82**)
Dewar St. SE15 .3G **121**
Dewberry Gdns. E6 .5C **88**
Dewberry St. E14 .5E **86**
Dewey La. *SW2* .*6A* ***120***
(off Tulse Hill)
Dewey Rd. N1 .2A **84**
RM10: Dag .6H **73**
Dewey St. SW17 .5D **136**
Dewhurst Ct. TW3: Houn .4E **112**
Dewhurst Rd. W14 .3F **99**
Dewsbury Cl. HA5: Pinn .6C **40**
Dewsbury Ct. W4 .4J **97**
Dewsbury Gdns. KT4: Wor Pk .3C **164**
Dewsbury Rd. NW10 .5C **62**
Dewsbury Ter. NW1 .1F **83**
Dews Farm Sand Pits Nature Reserve .6A **38**
Dexter Apartments *SE15* .*1H* ***121***
(off Queen's Rd.)
Dexter Ho. *DA18: Erith* .*3E* ***108***
(off Kale Rd.)
Dexter Rd. EN5: Barn .6A **20**
Deyncourt Rd. N17 .1C **48**
Deynecourt Gdns. E11 .4A **52**
D'Eynsford Rd. SE5 .1D **120**
Dhonau Ho. *SE1* .*4F* ***103***
(off Longfield Est.)
Diadem Ct. W1 .7C **6**
Dial Walk, The W8 .2K **99**
Diameter Rd. BR5: Pet W .7F **161**
Diamond Cl. RM8: Dag .1C **72**
Diamond Est. SW17 .3C **136**
Diamond Gdns. E3 .5B **86**
Diamond Ho. *E3* .*2A* ***86***
(off Roman Rd.)
Diamond Jubilee Way SM5: Cars .7D **166**
Diamond Rd. HA4: Ruis .4B **58**
Diamond St. NW10 .7K **61**
SE15 .7E **102**
Diamond Ter. SE10 .1E **122**
Diamond Way SE8 .6C **104**
Diana Cl. DA14: Sidc .2E **144**
E18 .1K **51**
SE8 .6B **104**
Diana Gdns. KT6: Surb .2F **163**
Diana Ho. SW13 .1B **116**
Diana, Princess of Wales Memorial Playground .1K **99**
Diana, Princess of Wales Memorial Walk .*1A* ***100***
(within Kensington Gdns.)
Diana Rd. E17 .3B **50**
Dianne Ct. SE12 .1J **141**
Dianne Way EN4: E Barn .4H **21**
Dianthus Cl. SE2 .5B **108**
Dibden Ho. SE5 .7E **102**
Dibden St. N1 .1C **84**
Dibdin Cl. SM1: Sutt .3J **165**
Dibdin Ho. W9 .2K **81**
Dibdin Rd. SM1: Sutt .3J **165**
Dibdin Row SE1 .1K **19** (3A **102**)
Dicey Av. NW2 .4E **62**
Dickens Av. N3 .1A **46**
UB8: Hil .6D **74**
Dickens Cl. DA8: Erith .7H **109**
TW10: Ham .2E **132**
UB3: Harl .4G **93**
Dickens Ct. *E11* .*4J* ***51***
(off Makepeace Rd.)
SW17 .*3B* ***136***
(off Grosvenor Way)
Dickens Dr. BR7: Chst .6G **143**
Dickens Est. SE1 .2G **103**
SE16 .3G **103**
Dickens Ho. *NW6* .*3J* ***81***
(off Malvern Rd.)
NW8 .3B **4**
SE17 .*5B* ***102***
(off Doddington Gro.)
WC1 .3E **6**
Dickens La. N18 .5K **33**
Dickens M. *EC1* .*5A* ***8***
(off Turnmill St.)
Dickenson Cl. N9 .1B **34**
Dickenson Rd. N8 .7J **47**
TW13: Hanw .5A **130**
Dickensons La. SE25 .5G **157**
(not continuous)
Dickensons Pl. SE25 .6G **157**
Dickens Pl. SL3: Poyle .4A **174**
Dickens Ri. IG7: Chig .3K **37**
Dickens Rd. E6 .2B **88**
Dickens Sq. SE1 .7D **14** (3C **102**)
Dickens St. SW8 .2F **119**
Dickenswood Cl. SE19 .7B **138**
Dickerage La. KT3: N Mald .3J **151**
Dickerage Rd. KT1: King T .1J **151**
KT3: N Mald .1J **151**
Dickinson Ct. *EC1* .*3B* ***8***
(off Brewhouse Yd.)
Dicksee Ho. *NW8* .*4A* ***4***
(off Lyons Pl.)
Dickson Fold HA5: Pinn .4B **40**
Dickson Ho. *E1* .*6H* ***85***
(off Philpot St.)
N1 .*7A* ***66***
(off Drummond Way)
Dickson Rd. SE9 .3C **124**
Dick Turpin Way TW14: Felt .4H **111**
Didsbury Cl. E6 .1D **88**
Dieppe Cl. W14 .5H **99**
Digby Bus. Cen. *E9* .*6K* ***67***
(off Digby Rd.)
Digby Cres. N4 .2C **66**
Digby Gdns. RM10: Dag .1G **91**
Digby Mans. *W6* .*5D* ***98***
(off Hammersmith Bri. Rd.)
Digby Pl. CR0: C'don .3F **169**
Digby Rd. E9 .6K **67**
IG11: Bark .7K **71**
Digby St. E2 .3J **85**
Diggon St. E1 .5K **85**
Dighton Ct. SE5 .6C **102**
Dighton Rd. SW18 .5A **118**
Dignum St. N1 .2A **84**
Digswell St. N7 .6A **66**
Dilhorne Cl. SE12 .3K **141**
Dilke St. SW3 .7F **17** (6D **100**)
Dilloway La. UB2: S'hall .2C **94**
Dillwyn Cl. SE26 .4A **140**
Dilston Cl. UB5: N'olt .3A **76**
Dilston Gro. SE16 .4J **103**
Dilton Gdns. SW15 .1C **134**
Dilwyn Ct. E17 .2A **50**
Dimes Pl. W6 .4D **98**
Dimmock Dr. UB6: G'frd .5H **59**
Dimond Cl. E7 .4J **69**
Dimsdale Dr. EN1: Enf .7B **24**
NW9 .1J **61**
Dimsdale Hgts. *E1* .*6H* ***85***
(off Spencer Way)
Dimsdale Wlk. E13 .2J **87**
Dimson Cres. E3 .3C **86**
Dinerman Ct. NW8 .1A **82**
Dingle, The UB10: Hil .3D **74**
Dingle Gdns. E14 .7C **86**
Dingle Rd. TW15: Ashf .5D **128**
Dingles Ct. HA5: Pinn .1B **40**
Dingley La. SW16 .2H **137**
Dingley Pl. EC1 .1D **8** (3C **84**)
Dingley Rd. EC1 .2C **8** (3C **84**)
Dingwall Av. CR0: C'don .2C **168**
Dingwall Gdns. NW11 .6J **45**
Dingwall Rd. CR0: C'don .1D **168**
SM5: Cars .7D **166**
SW18 .7A **118**
Dinmont Est. E2 .2G **85**
Dinmont Ho. *E2* .*2G* ***85***
(off Pritchard's Rd.)
Dinmont St. E2 .2H **85**
Dinmore Ho. *E9* .*1J* ***85***
(off Templecombe Rd.)
Dinnington Ho. *E1* .*4H* ***85***
(off Coventry Rd.)
Dinsdale Gdns. EN5: New Bar .5E **20**
SE25 .5E **156**
Dinsdale Rd. SE3 .6H **105**
Dinsmore Rd. SW12 .7F **119**
Dinton Ho. *NW8* .*3D* ***4***
(off Lilestone St.)
Dinton Rd. KT2: King T .7F **133**
SW19 .6B **136**
Diploma Av. N2 .4C **46**
Diploma Ct. N2 .4C **46**
Diprose Lodge SW17 .4B **136**
Dirleton Rd. E15 .1H **87**
Disbrowe Rd. W6 .6G **99**
Discover Stratford .7F **69**
Discover Greenwich Vis. Cen. .6E **104**
Discovery Bus. Pk. *SE16* .*3G* ***103***
(off St James's Rd.)
Discovery Cen. (Beckton), The .3G **89**
Discovery Dock Apartments E. *E14* .*2D* ***104***
(off Sth. Quay Sq.)
Discovery Dock Apartments W. *E14* .*2D* ***104***
(off Sth. Quay Sq.)
Discovery Ho. *E14* .*7E* ***86***
(off Newby Pl.)
Discovery Wlk. E1 .1H **103**
Dishforth La. NW9 .7F **29**
Disley Ct. *UB1: S'hall* .*6F* ***77***
(off Howard Rd.)
Disney Pl. SE1 .6D **14** (2C **102**)
Disney St. SE1 .6D **14** (2C **102**)
Dison Cl. EN3: Enf H .1E **24**
Disraeli Cl. SE28 .1C **108**
W4 .3K **97**
Disraeli Gdns. SW15 .4H **117**
Disraeli Rd. E7 .6J **69**
NW10 .2K **79**
SW15 .4G **117**
W5 .1D **96**
Diss St. E2 .1J **9** (3F **85**)
Distaff La. EC4 .2C **14** (7C **84**)
Distillery La. W6 .5E **98**
Distillery Rd. W6 .5E **98**
Distillery Twr. SE8 .1C **122**
Distillery Wlk. TW8: Bford .6E **96**
Distillery Wharf W6 .6E **98**
Distin St. SE11 .4J **19** (4A **102**)
District Rd. HA0: Wemb .5B **60**
Ditch All. SE13 .1D **122**
Ditchburn St. E14 .7E **86**
Ditchfield Rd. UB4: Yead .4C **76**
Ditchley Ct. *W7* .*5K* ***77***
(off Templeman Rd.)
Dittisham Rd. SE9 .4C **142**
Ditton Cl. KT7: T Ditt .7A **150**
Dittoncroft Cl. CR0: C'don .4E **168**
Ditton Grange Cl. KT6: Surb .1D **162**
Ditton Grange Dr. KT6: Surb .1D **162**
Ditton Hill KT6: Surb .1C **162**
Ditton Hill Rd. KT6: Surb .1C **162**
Ditton Lawn KT7: T Ditt .1A **162**
Ditton Pl. SE20 .1H **157**
Ditton Reach KT7: T Ditt .6B **150**
Ditton Rd. DA6: Bex .5D **126**
KT6: Surb .2D **162**
UB2: S'hall .5D **94**
Diversity Av. RM13: Rain .2K **91**
Divine Way UB3: Hayes .6F **75**
Divis Way *SW15* .*6D* ***116***
(off Dover Pk. Dr.)
Dixon Clark Ct. N1 .6B **66**
Dixon Cl. E6 .6D **88**
Dixon Ho. *W10* .*6F* ***81***
(off Darfield Way)
Dixon Pl. BR4: W W'ck .1D **170**
Dixon Rd. SE14 .1A **122**
SE25 .3E **156**
Dixon's All. SE16 .2H **103**
Dixon Way NW10 .7A **62**
Dobbin Cl. HA3: Kenton .2A **42**
Dobell Rd. SE9 .5D **124**
Dobree Av. NW10 .7D **62**
Dobson Cl. NW6 .7B **64**
Dobson Ho. *SE14* .*6K* ***103***
(off John Williams Cl.)
Doby Ct. EC4 .2D **14**
Dock Cotts. *E1* .*7J* ***85***
(off The Highway)
Dockers Tanner Rd. E14 .3C **104**
Dockett Eddy KT16: Chert .7A **146**
Dockett Eddy La. TW17: Shep .7B **146**
Dockett Moorings KT16: Chert .7A **146**
Dockhead SE1 .7K **15** (2F **103**)
Dockhead Wharf *SE1* .*7K* ***15***
(off Shad Thames)
Dock Hill Av. SE16 .1K **103**
Docklands Ct. *E14* .*6B* ***86***
(off Wharf La.)
Docklands Equestrian Centre, The .4E **88**
Docklands Sailing & Watersports Cen. .3C **104**
Dockland St. E16 .1E **106**
(not continuous)
Dockley Rd. SE16 .3G **103**
Dockley Rd. Ind. Est. *SE16* .*3G* ***103***
(off Dockley Rd.)
Dock Mdw. Reach W7 .3J **95**
Dock Offices *SE16* .*3J* ***103***
(off Surrey Quays Rd.)
Dock Rd. E16 .7H **87**
IG11: Bark .2G **89**
TW8: Bford .7D **96**
Dockside Ct. E5 .2J **67**
Dockside Rd. E16 .7B **88**
Dock St. E1 .7G **85**
Dockwell Cl. TW14: Felt .4J **111**
Dockwell's Ind. Est.
TW14: Felt .5K **111**
Doctor Johnson Av. SW17 .3F **137**
Doctors Cl. SE26 .5J **139**
Docura Ho. N7 .2K **65**
Docwra's Bldgs. N1 .6E **66**
Dodbrooke Rd. SE27 .3A **138**
Dodd Ho. *SE16* .*4H* ***103***
(off Rennie Est.)
Doddington Gro. SE17 .6B **102**
Doddington Pl. SE17 .6B **102**
Dodsley Pl. N9 .3D **34**
Dodson St. SE1 .7K **13** (2A **102**)
Dod St. E14 .6B **86**
Doebury Wlk. *SE18* .*7A* ***108***
(off Prestwood Cl.)
Doel Cl. SW19 .7A **136**
Dog & Duck Yd. WC1 .5H **7**
Doggett Rd. SE6 .7C **122**
Doggetts Cl. EN4: E Barn .5H **21**
Doghurst Av. UB3: Harl .7D **92**
Doghurst Dr. UB7: Sip .7D **92**
Dog Kennel Hill SE22 .3E **120**
Dog Kennel Hill Est. *SE22* .*3E* ***120***
(off Albrighton Rd.)
Dog La. NW10 .4A **62**
Doherty Rd. E13 .4J **87**
Dokal Ind. Est. UB2: S'hall .2C **94**
Dolben Ct. *SW1* .*4D* ***18***
(off Montaigne Cl.)
Dolben St. SE1 .5A **14** (1B **102**)
(not continuous)
Dolby Rd. SW6 .2H **117**
Dolland Ho. SE11 .6H **19**
Dolland St. SE11 .6H **19** (5K **101**)

Dollar Bay E14 . . . . .2E **104**
Dollar Bay Ct. E14 . . . . .2E **104**
 (off Lawn Ho. Cl.)
Dollary Pde. KT1: King T 3H **151**
 (off Kingston Rd.)
Dolliffe Cl. CR4: Mitc 2C **154**
Dollis Av. N3 . . . . .1H **45**
Dollis Brook Wlk. EN5: Barn 6B **20**
Dollis Cres. HA4: Ruis 1A **58**
Dolliscroft NW7 . . . . .7B **30**
DOLLIS HILL 2D **62**
Dollis Hill Av. NW2 . . . . .3D **62**
Dollis Hill La. NW2 . . . . .4B **62**
Dollis M. N3 . . . . .1J **45**
Dollis Pk. N3 . . . . .1H **45**
Dollis Rd. N3 . . . . .7B **30**
 NW7 .7B **30**
Dollis Valley Dr. EN5: Barn 6C **20**
Dollis Valley Way EN5: Barn 6C **20**
Dolman Cl. N3 . . . . .2A **46**
Dolman Rd. W4 . . . . .4K **97**
Dolman St. SW4 . . . . .4K **119**
Dolphin Cl. KT6: Surb 5D **150**
 SE16 .2K **103**
 SE28 .6D **90**
Dolphin Ct. NW11 . . . . .6G **45**
Dolphin Ho. SW6 . . . . .2A **118**
 (off Lensbury Av.)
 SW18 . . . . .4K **117**
Dolphin La. E14 . . . . .7D **86**
Dolphin Rd. TW16: Sun 1G **147**
 UB5: N'olt 2D **76**
Dolphin Rd. Nth. TW16: Sun 1G **147**
Dolphin Rd. Sth. TW16: Sun 1G **147**
Dolphin Rd. W. TW16: Sun 1G **147**
Dolphin Sq. SW1 . . . . .6B **18** (5G **101**)
 W4 . . . . .7A **98**
Dolphin St. KT1: King T 2E **150**
Dolphin Twr. SE8 . . . . .6B **104**
 (off Abinger Gro.)
Dombey Ho. SE1 . . . . .7K **15**
 (off Wolseley St.)
 W11 .1F **99**
 (off St Ann's Rd.)
Dombey St. WC1 . . . . .5G **7** (5K **83**)
 (not continuous)
Domecq Ho. EC1 . . . . .3B **8**
 (off Dallington St.)
Dome Hill Pk. SE26 . . . . .4F **139**
Domelton Ho. SW18 . . . . .6K **117**
 (off Iron Mill Rd.)
Domett Cl. SE5 . . . . .4D **120**
Domfe Pl. E5 . . . . .4J **67**
Domingo St. EC1 . . . . . . .3C **8** (4C **84**)
Dominica Cl. E13 . . . . .2B **88**
Dominion Bus. Pk. N9 . . . . .2E **34**
Dominion Centre, The UB2: S'hall . . .2C **94**
Dominion Cl. TW3: Houn 2H **113**
Dominion Ct. E8 . . . . .7F **67**
 (off Middleton Rd.)
Dominion Dr. SE16 . . . . .2K **103**
Dominion Ho. E14 . . . . .5D **104**
 (off St Davids Sq.)
Dominion Ind. Est. UB2: S'hall 2C **94**
 (off Feather Rd.)
Dominion Pde. HA1: Harr 5K **41**
Dominion Rd. CRO: C'don 7F **157**
 UB2: S'hall 2C **94**
Dominion St. EC2 . . . . . .5F **9** (5D **84**)
Dominion Theatre 7D **6**
 (off Tottenham Ct. Rd.)
Domonic Dr. SE9 . . . . .4F **143**
Domville Cl. N20 . . . . .2G **31**
Domville Ct. SE17 . . . . .5E **102**
 (off Bagshott St.)
Donald Dr. RM6: Chad H 5C **54**
Donald Hunter Ho. E7 . . . . .5K **69**
 (off Woodgrange Rd.)
Donald Rd. CRO: C'don 7A **156**
 E13 .1K **87**

Donaldson Rd. NW6 . . . . .1H **81**
 SE18 .1E **124**
Donald Woods Gdns. KT5: Surb . . .2H **163**
Donato Dr. SE15 . . . . .6E **102**
Doncaster Dr. UB5: N'olt 5D **58**
Doncaster Gdns. N4 . . . . .6C **48**
 UB5: N'olt 5D **58**
Doncaster Rd. N9 . . . . .7C **24**
Donegal Ho. E1 . . . . .4H **85**
 (off Cambridge Heath Rd.)
Donegal St. N1 . . . . .2K **83**
Doneraile Ho. SW1 . . . . .5J **17**
 (off Ebury Bri. Rd.)
Doneraile St. SW6 . . . . .2F **117**
Dongola Rd. E1 . . . . .5A **86**
 E13 .3K **87**
 N17 . . . . .3E **48**
Dongola Rd. W. E13 . . . . .3K **87**
Don Gratton Ho. E1 . . . . .5G **85**
 (off Old Montague St.)
Donington Av. IG2: Ilf 5G **53**
 IG6: Ilf 5G **53**
Donkey All. SE22 . . . . .7G **121**
Donkey La. EN1: Enf 2B **24**
 UB7: W Dray 1D **174**
Donkin Ho. SE16 . . . . .4H **103**
 (off Rennie Est.)
Donmar Warehouse Theatre 1E **12**
 (off Earlham St.)
Donnatt's Rd. SE14 . . . . .1B **122**
Donne Ct. SE24 . . . . .6C **120**
Donnefield Av. HA8: Edg 7K **27**
Donne Ho. E14 . . . . .6C **86**
 (off Dod St.)
 SE14 .6K **103**
 (off Samuel Cl.)
Donnelly Ct. SW6 . . . . .7G **99**
 (off Dawes Rd.)
Donnelly Ho. SE1 . . . . .3A **102**
 (off McAuley Cl.)
Donne Pl. CR4: Mitc 4F **155**
 SW3 . . . . .3D **16** (4C **100**)
Donne Rd. RM8: Dag 2C **72**
Donnington Ct. NW1 . . . . .7F **65**
 (off Castlehaven Rd.)
 NW10 .7D **62**
 (off Donnington Rd.)
Donnington Mans. NW10 . . . . .1E **80**
 (off Donnington Rd.)
Donnington Rd. HA3: Kenton 5D **42**
 KT4: Wor Pk 2C **164**
 NW10 .7D **62**
Donnybrook Ct. E3 . . . . .1B **86**
 (off Old Ford Rd.)
Donnybrook Rd. SW16 . . . . .7G **137**
Donoghue Bus. Pk.
 NW2 . . . . .3F **63**
Donoghue Cotts. E14 . . . . .5A **86**
 (off Galsworthy Av.)
Donovan Av. N10 . . . . .2F **47**
Donovan Ct. SW10 . . . . .6A **16**
 (off Drayton Gdns.)
Donovan Ho. E1 . . . . .7J **85**
 (off Cable St.)
Donovan Pl. N21 . . . . .5E **22**
Don Phelan Cl. SE5 . . . . .1D **120**
Doon St. SE1 . . . . .5J **13** (1A **102**)
Dora Ho. E14 . . . . .6B **86**
 (off Rhodeswell Rd.)
 W11 .7F **81**
 (off St Ann's Rd.)
Doral Way SM5: Cars 5D **166**
Doran Ct. E6 . . . . .2D **88**
Dorando Cl. W12 . . . . .7D **80**
Doran Gro. SE18 . . . . .7J **107**
Doran Mnr. N2 . . . . .5D **46**
 (off Great Nth. Rd.)
Doran Wlk. E15 . . . . .7E **68**
Dora Rd. SW19 . . . . .5J **135**
Dora St. E14 . . . . .6B **86**

Dora Way SW9 . . . . .2A **120**
Dorchester Av. DA5: Bexl 1D **144**
 HA2: Harr 6G **41**
 N13 . . . . .4H **33**
Dorchester Cl. BR5: St P 7B **144**
 KT10: Hin W 2A **162**
 UB5: N'olt 5F **59**
Dorchester Ct. E18 . . . . .1H **51**
 (off Buckingham Rd.)
 N1 . . . . .7E **66**
 (off Englefield Rd.)
 N10 . . . . .3F **47**
 N14 . . . . .7A **22**
 NW2 . . . . .3F **63**
 SE24 .5C **120**
 SW1 . . . . .2F **17**
 (off Sloane St.)
Dorchester Dr. SE24 . . . . .5C **120**
 TW14: Bedf 6G **111**
Dorchester Gdns. E4 . . . . .4H **35**
 NW11 .4J **45**
Dorchester Gro. W4 . . . . .5A **98**
Dorchester Ho. TW9: Kew 7H **97**
Dorchester M. KT3: N Mald 4K **151**
 TW1: Twick 6C **114**
Dorchester Rd. KT4: Wor Pk 1E **164**
 SM4: Mord 7K **153**
 UB5: N'olt 5F **59**
Dorchester Ter. NW2 . . . . .3F **63**
 (off Needham Ter.)
Dorchester Way HA3: Kenton 6F **43**
Dorchester Waye UB4: Yead 6K **75**
 (not continuous)
Dorcis Av. DA7: Bex 2E **126**
Dordrecht Rd. W3 . . . . .1A **98**
Dore Av. E12 . . . . .5E **70**
Doreen Av. NW9 . . . . .1K **61**
Doreen Capstan Ho. E11 . . . . .3G **69**
 (off Apollo Pl.)
Dore Gdns. SM4: Mord 7K **153**
Dorell Cl. UB1: S'hall 5D **76**
Dorey Ho. TW8: Bford 7C **96**
 (off High St.)
Dorman Theatre 1A **102**
 (within National Theatre)
Doria Rd. SW6 . . . . .2H **117**
Doric Ho. E2 . . . . .2K **85**
 (off Mace St.)
Doric Way NW1 . . . . .1C **6** (3H **83**)
Dorie M. N12 . . . . .4E **30**
 (off Ashbourne Cl.)
Dorien Rd. SW20 . . . . .2F **153**
Doris Ashby Cl. UB6: G'frd 1A **78**
Doris Av. DA8: Erith 1J **127**
Doris Emmerton Ct. SW11 . . . . . . .4A **118**
Doris Rd. E7 . . . . .7J **69**
 TW15: Ashf 6F **129**
Dorking Cl. KT4: Wor Pk 2D **164**
 SE8 . . . . .6B **104**
Dorking Ct. N17 . . . . .1G **49**
 (off Hampden La.)
Dorking Ho. SE1 . . . . .3D **102**
Dorlcote Rd. SW18 . . . . .7C **118**
Dorly Cl. TW17: Shep 5G **147**
Dorman Pl. N9 . . . . .2B **34**
Dormans Cl. HA6: Nwood 1F **39**
Dorman Wlk. NW10 . . . . .5K **61**
Dorman Way NW8 . . . . .1B **82**
Dorma Trad. Pk. E10 . . . . .1K **67**
Dormay St. SW18 . . . . .5K **117**
Dormer Cl. E15 . . . . .6H **69**
 EN5: Barn 5A **20**
Dormer's Av. UB1: S'hall 6E **76**
Dormers Ri. UB1: S'hall 7F **77**
DORMER'S WELLS 6E **76**
Dormer's Wells La. UB1: S'hall 6E **76**
Dormers Wells Leisure Cen. 6F **77**
Dormstone Ho. SE17 . . . . .4E **102**
 (off Congreve St.)
Dormywood HA4: Ruis 5H **39**
Dornberg Cl. SE3 . . . . .7J **105**

Dornberg Rd. SE3 . . . . .7K **105**
Dorncliffe Rd. SW6 . . . . .2G **117**
Dorney NW3 . . . . .7C **64**
Dorney Ri. BR5: St M Cry 4K **161**
Dorney Way TW4: Houn 5C **112**
Dornfell St. NW6 . . . . .5H **63**
Dornoch Ho. E3 . . . . .2B **86**
 (off Anglo Rd.)
Dornton Rd. CR2: S Croy 5D **168**
 SW12 . . . . .2F **137**
Dorothy Av. HA0: Wemb 7E **60**
Dorothy Evans Cl. DA7: Bex 4H **127**
Dorothy Gdns. RM8: Dag 4B **72**
Dorothy Pettingell Ho. SM1: Sutt 3K **165**
 (off Vermont Rd.)
Dorothy Rd. SW11 . . . . .3D **118**
Dorothy Smith La. N17 . . . . .7J **33**
Dorrell Pl. SW9 . . . . .3A **120**
Dorrien Wlk. SW16 . . . . .2H **137**
Dorrington Cl. SE25 . . . . .2E **156**
Dorrington Point E3 . . . . .3D **86**
 (off Bromley High St.)
Dorrington St. EC1 . . . . .5J **7** (5A **84**)
Dorrington Way BR3: Beck 5E **158**
Dorrit Ho. W11 . . . . .1F **99**
 (off St Ann's Rd.)
Dorrit M. N18 . . . . .5K **33**
Dorrit St. SE1 . . . . .6D **14** (2C **102**)
Dorrit Way BR7: Chst 6G **143**
Dorryn Ct. SE26 . . . . .5K **139**
Dors Cl. NW9 . . . . .1K **61**
Dorset Av. DA16: Well 4K **125**
 RM1: Rom 4K **55**
 UB2: S'hall 4E **94**
 UB4: Hayes 3G **75**
Dorset Bldgs. EC4 . . . . . . .1A **14** (6B **84**)
Dorset Cl. KT9: Chess 4D **162**
 NW1 . . . . .5E **4** (5D **82**)
 UB4: Hayes 3G **75**
Dorset Ct. HA6: Nwood 1H **39**
 N1 . . . . .7E **66**
 (off Hertford Rd.)
 UB5: N'olt 3C **76**
 W7 . . . . .5K **77**
 (off Copley Cl.)
Dorset Dr. HA8: Edg 6A **28**
Dorset Gdns. CR4: Mitc 4K **155**
 HA0: Wemb 5C **60**
Dorset Ho. NW1 . . . . .5F **5**
 (off Gloucester Pl.)
Dorset Mans. SW6 . . . . .6F **99**
 (off Lille Rd.)
Dorset M. N3 . . . . .1J **45**
 SW1 . . . . .1J **17** (3F **101**)
Dorset Pl. E15 . . . . .6F **69**
Dorset Ri. EC4 . . . . .1A **14** (6B **84**)
Dorset Rd. BR3: Beck 3K **157**
 CR4: Mitc 2C **154**
 E7 . . . . .7A **70**
 HA1: Harr 6G **41**
 N15 . . . . .4D **48**
 N22 . . . . .1J **47**
 SE9 . . . . .2C **142**
 SW8 . . . . .7J **101**
 SW19 . . . . .1J **153**
 TW15: Ashf 3A **128**
 W5 . . . . .3C **96**
Dorset Sq. NW1 . . . . .4E **4** (4D **82**)
Dorset St. W1 . . . . .6F **5** (5D **82**)
Dorset Way TW2: Twick 1H **131**
 UB10: Hil 2B **74**
Dorset Waye TW5: Hest 7D **94**
Dorset Wharf W6 . . . . .7E **98**
 (off Rainville Rd.)
Dorsey Ho. N1 . . . . .6B **66**
 (off Canonbury Rd.)
Dorton Cl. SE15 . . . . .7E **102**
Dorton Vs. UB7: Sip 7C **92**
Dorville Cres. W6 . . . . .3D **98**
Dorville Rd. SE12 . . . . .5H **123**
Dothill Rd. SE18 . . . . .7G **107**

Douai Gro. TW12: Hamp 1G **149**
Doughty Ct. *E1* 1H **103**
(off Prusom St.)
Doughty Ho. SW10 . . . . .6A **100**
(off Netherton Gro.)
Douglas Av. E17 . . . . .1B **50**
HA0: Wemb 7E **60**
KT3: N Mald 4D **152**
Douglas Bader Ho. TW7: Isle 3H **113**
Douglas Cl. HA7: Stan 5F **27**
IG6: Ilf 7K **37**
SM6: Wall 6J **167**
Douglas Ct. *KT1: King T* 4E **150**
(off Geneva Rd.)
N3 . . . . .2K **45**
NW6 . . . . .7J **63**
(off Quex Rd.)
Douglas Cres. UB4: Yead 4A **76**
Douglas Dr. CR0: C'don 3C **170**
Douglas Est. *N1* 6C **66**
(off Oransay Rd.)
Douglas Eyre Sports Cen. 5K **49**
Douglas Ho. KT6: Surb 1F **163**
Douglas Johnstone Ho. *SW6* 6H **99**
(off Clem Attlee Ct.)
Douglas Mans. TW3: Houn 3F **113**
Douglas M. NW2 . . . . .3G **63**
Douglas Path *E14* 5E **104**
(off Manchester Rd.)
Douglas Rd. DA16: Well 1B **126**
E4 . . . . .1B **36**
E16 . . . . .5J **87**
IG3: Ilf 7A **54**
KT1: King T 2H **151**
KT6: Surb 2F **163**
N1 . . . . .7C **66**
N22 . . . . .1A **48**
NW6 . . . . .1H **81**
TW3: Houn 3F **113**
TW19: Stanw 6A **110**
Douglas Rd. Nth. N1 . . . . .6C **66**
Douglas Rd. Sth. N1 . . . . .6C **66**
Douglas Robinson Ct. *SW16* 7J **137**
(off Streatham High Rd.)
Douglas Sq. SM4: Mord 6J **153**
Douglas Sq. SW1 . . . . .4C **18** (4H **101**)
Douglas Ter. E17 . . . . .1B **50**
Douglas Waite Ho. NW6 . . . . .7J **63**
(Stanley St.)
SE8 . . . . .7C **104**
(Watsons St.)
Douglas Way SE8 . . . . .7B **104**
Doulton Ho. SE11 . . . . .2H **19**
Doulton M. NW6 . . . . .6K **63**
Dounesforth Gdns. SW18 . . . . .1K **135**
Douro Pl. W8 . . . . .3K **99**
Douro St. E3 . . . . .2C **86**
Douthwaite Sq. E1 . . . . .1G **103**
Dove App. E6 . . . . .5C **88**
Dove Cl. NW7 . . . . .7G **29**
SM6: Wall 7K **167**
UB5: N'olt 4B **76**
Dove Commercial Cen.
NW5 . . . . .5G **65**
Dovecot Cl. HA5: Eastc 5A **40**
Dovecote Av. N22 . . . . .3A **48**
Dovecote Gdns. SW14 . . . . .3K **115**
Dovecote Ho. *SE16* 2K **103**
(off Water Gdns. Sq.)
Dovecote M. UB9: Hare 3A **38**
Dove Ct. TW19: Stanw 7A **110**
Dovedale Av. HA3: Kenton 6C **42**
IG5: Ilf 2E **52**
Dovedale Bus. Est. SE15 . . . . .2G **121**
(off Blenheim Gro.)
Dovedale Cl. DA16: Well 2A **126**
Dovedale Ri. CR4: Mitc 7D **136**
Dovedale Rd. SE22 . . . . .5H **121**
Dovedon Cl. N14 . . . . .2D **32**

Dovehouse Ct. *UB5: N'olt* 3B **76**
(off Delta Gro.)
Dove Ho. Gdns. E4 . . . . .2H **35**
Dovehouse Mead IG11: Bark 2H **89**
Dovehouse St. SW3 . . . . . .5B **16** (5B **100**)
Dove M. SW5 . . . . .4A **100**
Dove Pk. HA5: Hat E 1E **40**
Dover Cl. NW2 .2F **63**
RM5: Col R 2J **55**
Dover Ct. *EC1* .3A **8**
(off St John St.)
N1 . . . . .7D **66**
(off Southgate Rd.)
Dovercourt Av. CR7: Thor H 5A **156**
Dovercourt Est. N1 . . . . .6D **66**
Dovercourt Gdns. HA7: Stan 5K **27**
Dovercourt La. SM1: Sutt 3A **166**
Dovercourt Rd. SE22 . . . . .6E **120**
Doverfield Rd. SW2 . . . . .7J **119**
Dover Flats SE1 . . . . .4E **102**
Dover Gdns. SM5: Cars 3D **166**
Dover Ho. N18 .5A **34**
SE15 . . . . .6J **103**
Dover Ho. Rd. SW15 . . . . .4C **116**
Doveridge Gdns. N13 . . . . .4G **33**
Dove Rd. N1 . . . . .6D **66**
Dove Row E2 . . . . .1G **85**
Dover Pk. Dr. SW15 . . . . .6D **116**
Dover Patrol SE3 . . . . .2K **123**
Dover Rd. E12 . . . . .2A **70**
N9 . . . . .2D **34**
RM6: Chad H 6E **54**
SE19 . . . . .6D **138**
Dover St. W1 . . . . .3K **11** (7F **83**)
Dover Ter. *TW9: Rich* 2F **115**
(off Sandycombe Rd.)
Dover Yd. W1 . . . . .4A **12**
Doves Cl. BR2: Brom 2C **172**
Doves Yd. N1 . . . . .1A **84**
Dove Ct. SW9 . . . . .1K **119**
Doveton Ho. *E1* 4J **85**
(off Doveton St.)
Doveton Rd. CR2: S Croy 5D **168**
Doveton St. E1 .4J **85**
Dove Wlk. SW1 . . . . .5G **17** (5E **100**)
Dovey Lodge *N1* 7A **66**
(off Bewdley St.)
Dovill Ct. *SE16* 3G **103**
(off Old Jamaica Rd.)
Dowanhill Rd. SE6 . . . . .1F **141**
Dowd Cl. N11 . . . . .2K **31**
Dowdeswell Cl. SW15 . . . . .4A **116**
Dowding Dr. SE9 . . . . .5A **124**
Dowding Ho. *N6* 7E **46**
(off Hillcrest)
Dowding Pl. HA7: Stan 6F **27**
Dowding Rd. UB10: Uxb 7B **56**
Dowdney Cl. NW5 . . . . .5G **65**
Dowe Ho. SE3 . . . . .3G **123**
Dowells St. SE10 . . . . .6D **104**
Dower Av. SM6: Wall 7F **167**
Dower Ct. *SE16* 4J **103**
(off Silwood St.)
Dowes Ho. SW16 . . . . .3J **137**
Dowgate Hill EC4 . . . . .2E **14** (7D **84**)
Dowland St. W10 . . . . .3G **81**
Dowlas St. SE5 .7E **102**
Dowler Cl. KT2: King T 1B **58**
Dowler Ho. *E1* .6G **85**
(off Burslem St.)
Dowlerville Rd. BR6: Chels 6K **173**
Dowling Ho. DA17: Belv 3F **109**
Dowman Cl. SW19 . . . . .7K **135**
Downage NW4 .3E **44**
(not continuous)
Downalong WD23: B Hea 1C **26**
Downbank Av. DA7: Bex 1K **127**
Down Barns Rd. HA4: Ruis 3B **58**
Downbarton Ho. *SW9* 1A **120**
(off Gosling Way)
Downbury M. SW18 . . . . .5J **117**

Down Cl. UB5: N'olt 2K **75**
Downderry Rd. BR1: Brom 3F **141**
Downe Cl. DA16: Well 7C **108**
Downend SE18 .7F **107**
Downend Ct. *SE15* 6E **102**
(off Bibury Cl.)
Downe Rd. BR2: Kes 7C **172**
CR4: Mitc 2D **154**
Downer's Cott. SW4 . . . . .4G **119**
Downesbury *NW3* 6D **64**
(off Steele's Rd.)
Downes Cl. TW1: Twick 6B **114**
Downes Ct. N21 . . . . .1F **33**
Downes Ho. CR0: Wadd 4B **168**
(off Violet La.)
Downe Ter. TW10: Rich 6E **114**
Downey Ho. *E1* 4K **85**
(off Globe Rd.)
Downfield KT4: Wor Pk 1B **164**
Downfield Cl. W9 . . . . .4K **81**
Down Hall Rd. KT2: King T 1D **150**
DOWNHAM 5F **141**
Downham Cl. RM5: Col R 1G **55**
Downham Ct. *N1* 7D **66**
(off Downham Rd.)
Downham Ent. Cen. SE6 . . . . .2H **141**
Downham Health & Leisure Cen. 4H **141**
Downham La. BR1: Brom 5F **141**
Downham Rd. N1 . . . . .7D **66**
Downham Way BR1: Brom 5F **141**
Downham Wharf *N1* 1E **84**
(off Hertford Rd.)
Downhills Av. N17 . . . . .3D **48**
Downhills Pk. Rd. N17 . . . . .3C **48**
Downhills Way N17 . . . . .3C **48**
Downhurst Av. NW7 . . . . .5E **28**
Downhurst Ct. NW4 . . . . .3E **44**
Downing Cl. HA2: Harr 3G **41**
Downing Ho. *W10* 6F **81**
(off Cambridge Gdns.)
Downing Dr. UB6: G'frd 1H **77**
Downing Rd. RM9: Dag 7F **73**
Downings E6 . . . . .6E **88**
Downing St. SW1 . . . . .6E **12** (2J **101**)
Downland Cl. N20 . . . . .1F **31**
Downland Ct. E11 . . . . .2G **69**
Downleys Cl. SE9 . . . . .2C **142**
Downman Rd. SE9 . . . . .3C **124**
Down Pl. W6 . . . . .4D **98**
Down Rd. TW11: Tedd 6B **132**
Downs, The SW20 . . . . .7F **135**
Downs Av. BR7: Chst 5D **142**
HA5: Pinn 6C **40**
Downs Bri. Rd. BR3: Beck 1F **159**
Downs Ct. UB6: G'frd 3A **78**
Downs Ct. Pde. *E8* 5H **67**
(off Amhurst Rd.)
Downsell Rd. E15 . . . . .4E **68**
Downsfield Rd. E17 . . . . .6A **50**
Downshall Av. IG3: Ilf 6J **53**
Downs Hill BR3: Beck 7F **141**
Downshire Hill NW3 . . . . .4B **64**
Downside TW1: Twick 3K **131**
TW16: Sun 1J **147**
Downside Cl. SW19 . . . . .6A **136**
Downside Cres. NW3 . . . . .5C **64**
W13 . . . . .4A **78**
Downside Rd. SM2: Sutt 6B **166**
Downside Wlk. *TW8: Bford* 6D **96**
(off Windmill Rd.)
UB5: N'olt 3D **76**
Downs La. E5 . . . . .4H **67**
Downs Pk. Rd. E5 . . . . .5F **67**
E8 . . . . .5F **67**
Downs Rd.
BR3: Beck 2D **158**
CR7: Thor H 1C **156**
E5 . . . . .4G **67**
EN1: Enf 4K **23**

Down St. KT8: W Mole 5E **148**
W1 . . . . .5J **11** (1F **101**)
Down St. M. W1 . . . . .5J **11** (1K **101**)
Downs Vw. TW7: Isle 1K **113**
Downsview Gdns. SE19 . . . . .7B **138**
Downsview Rd. SE19 . . . . .7C **138**
Downsway BR6: Orp 5J **173**
Downsway, The SM2: Sutt 7A **166**
Downton Av. SW2 . . . . .2J **137**
Downtown Rd. SE16 . . . . .2A **104**
Down Way UB5: N'olt 3K **75**
Downy Ho. W3 .1A **98**
Dowrey St. N1 .1A **84**
Dowsett Rd. N17 . . . . .2F **49**
Dowson Cl. SE5 . . . . .4D **120**
Dowson Ho. *E1* 6K **85**
(off Bower St.)
Do Wyndsor Ct. *SE16* 3G **103**
(off Jamaica Rd.)
Doyce St. SE1 . . . . .6C **14** (2C **102**)
Doyle Gdns. NW10 . . . . .1C **80**
Doyle Ho. SW13 . . . . .7F **98**
(off Trinity Chu. Rd.)
Doyle Rd. SE25 .4G **157**
D'Oyley St. SW1 . . . . .3G **17** (4E **100**)
Doynton St. N19 . . . . .2F **65**
Draco Gate SW15 . . . . .3E **116**
Draco St. SE17 .6C **102**
Dragmore St. SW4 . . . . .6H **119**
Dragonfly Cl. E13 . . . . .3K **87**
KT5: Surb 1J **163**
Dragonfly Ct. NW9 . . . . .1A **44**
(off Heybourne Cres.)
Dragonfly Pl. SE4 . . . . .3A **122**
Dragon Rd. SE15 . . . . .6E **102**
Dragon Yd. WC1 . . . . .7F **7** (6J **83**)
Dragoon Rd. SE8 . . . . .5B **104**
Dragor Rd. NW10 . . . . .4J **79**
Drake Cl. IG11: Bark 4A **90**
SE16 . . . . .2K **103**
Drake Ct. *KT5: Surb* 4E **150**
(off Cranes Pk. Av.)
SE1 . . . . .7D **14**
(off Swan St.)
SE19 . . . . .5F **139**
W12 . . . . .2E **98**
(off Scott's Rd.)
Drake Cres. SE28 . . . . .6C **90**
Drakefell Rd. SE4 . . . . .2K **121**
SE14 . . . . .2K **121**
Drakefield Rd. SW17 . . . . .3E **136**
Drake Hall *E16* 1K **106**
(off Wesley Av.)
Drake Ho. *E1* 5J **85**
(off Stepney Way)
E14 . . . . .7A **86**
(off Victory Pl.)
SW1 . . . . .7C **18**
(off Dolphin Sq.)
Drakeland Ho. *W9* 4H **81**
(off Fernhead Rd.)
Drakeley Ct. N5 . . . . .4B **66**
Drake M. BR2: Brom 4A **160**
Drake Rd. CR0: C'don 7K **155**
CR4: Mitc 6E **154**
HA2: Harr 2D **58**
KT9: Chess 5G **163**
SE4 . . . . .3C **122**
Drakes, The SE8 . . . . .6C **104**
Drakes Ct. SE23 . . . . .1J **139**
Drakes Courtyard NW6 . . . . .7H **63**
Drakes Dr. HA6: Nwood 1D **38**
Drake St. EN2: Enf 1J **23**
WC1 . . . . .6G **7** (5K **83**)
Drakes Wlk. E6 .1D **88**
Drakewood Rd. SW16 . . . . .7H **137**
Draper Cl. DA17: Belv 4F **109**
TW7: Isle 2H **113**
Draper Ct. BR1: Brom 4C **160**
Draper Ho. *SE1* 4B **102**
(off Newington Butts)

Draper Pl. N1 .1B 84
   (off Dagmar Ter.)
Drapers Almshouses E3 . . . . .3D 86
   (off Rainhill Way)
Drapers Cott. Homes NW7 . . . . .4G 29
   (not continuous)
Draper's Ct. SW11 . . . . .1E 118
   (off Battersea Pk. Rd.)
Drapers Gdns. EC2 . . . . .7F 9 (6D 84)
Drapers Rd. E15 . . . . .4F 69
  EN2: Enf 2G 23
  N17 . . . . .3F 49
Drapers Way SE16 . . . . .4G 103
Draven Cl. BR2: Hayes 7H 159
Drawell Cl. SE18 . . . . .5J 107
Drax Av. SW20 . . . . .7C 134
Draxmont SW19 . . . . .6G 135
Draycot Rd. E11 . . . . .6K 51
  KT6: Surb .1G 163
Draycott Av. HA3: Kenton 6B 42
  SW3 . . . . .3D 16 (4C 100)
Draycott Cl. HA3: Kenton 6B 42
  NW2 . . . . .3F 63
  SE5 . . . . .7D 102
   (not continuous)
Draycott M. SW6 . . . . .2H 117
   (off Laurel Bank Gdns.)
Draycott Pl. SW3 . . . . .4E 16 (4D 100)
Draycott Ter. SW3 . . . . .4F 17 (4D 100)
Dray Ct. HA0: Wemb 5A 60
   (off Brewery Cl.)
Drayford Cl. W9 . . . . .4H 81
Dray Gdns. SW2 . . . . .5K 119
Draymans M. SE15 . . . . .2F 121
Draymans Way TW7: Isle 3K 113
Drayside M. UB2: S'hall 2D 94
Drayson M. W8 . . . . .2J 99
Drayton Av. BR6: Farnb 1F 173
  W13 . . . . .7A 78
Drayton Bri. Rd. W7 . . . . .7K 77
  W13 . . . . .7K 77
Drayton Cl. IG1: Ilf 1H 71
  TW4: Houn 5D 112
Drayton Ct. UB7: W Dray 4B 92
Drayton Gdns. N21 . . . . .7G 23
  SW10 . . . . .6A 16 (5A 100)
  UB7: W Dray 2A 92
  W13 . . . . .7A 78
Drayton Grn. W13 . . . . .7A 78
Drayton Grn. Rd. W13 . . . . .7B 78
Drayton Gro. W13 . . . . .7A 78
Drayton Ho. E11 . . . . .1F 69
  SE5 . . . . .7D 102
   (off Elmington Rd.)
Drayton Pk. N5 . . . . .4A 66
Drayton Pk. M. N5 . . . . .5A 66
Drayton Rd. CR0: C'don 2B 168
  E11 . . . . .1F 69
  N17 . . . . .2E 48
  NW10 . . . . .1B 80
  W13 . . . . .7A 78
Drayton Waye HA3: Kenton 6B 42
Dray Wlk. E1 . . . . .4K 9 (4F 85)
Dreadnought Cl. SW19 . . . . .2B 154
Dreadnought St. SE10 . . . . .3G 105
Dreadnought Wlk. SE10 . . . . .6D 104
Drenon Sq. UB3: Hayes 7H 75
Dresden Cl. NW6 . . . . .6K 63
Dresden Ho. SE11 . . . . .3H 19
  SW11 . . . . .2E 118
   (off Dagnall St.)
Dresden Rd. N19 . . . . .1G 65
Dressington Av. SE4 . . . . .6C 122
Drewery Cl. SE3 . . . . .3G 123
Drewett Ho. E1 . . . . .6G 85
   (off Christian St.)
Drew Gdns. UB6: G'frd 6K 59
Drew Ho. SE8 .5C 104
  SW16 . . . . .3J 137

Drew Rd. E16 .1B 106
   (not continuous)
Drewstead La. SW16 . . . . .2H 137
Drewstead Rd. SW16 . . . . .2H 137
Drey Cl. KT4: Wor Pk 2C 164
   (off The Avenue)
Driffield Ct. NW9 . . . . .1A 44
   (off Pageant Av.)
Driffield Rd. E3 . . . . .2A 86
Drift, The BR2: Brom 3B 172
Drift Ct. E16 . . . . .7F 89
Driftway, The CR4: Mitc 1E 154
Driftway Ho. E3 . . . . .2B 86
   (off Stafford Rd.)
Drinkwater Ho. SE5 . . . . .7D 102
   (off Picton St.)
Drinkwater Rd. HA2: Harr 2F 59
Drive, The BR3: Beck 2C 158
  BR4: W W'ck 7F 159
  BR6: Orp 2K 173
  BR7: Chst .3K 161
  CR7: Thor H 4D 156
  DA5: Bexl .6C 126
  DA8: Erith .7H 109
  DA14: Sidc 3B 144
  E4 . . . . .1A 36
  E17 . . . . .3D 50
  E18 . . . . .4J 51
  EN2: Enf 1J 23
  EN5: Barn .3B 20
  EN5: New Bar 6F 21
  HA2: Harr .7E 40
  HA6: Nwood 2G 39
  HA8: Edg .5B 28
  HA9: Wemb 2J 61
  IG1: Ilf 6C 52
  IG5: Ilf 1F 37
  IG11: Bark 7K 71
  KT2: King T 7J 133
  KT6: Surb .7E 150
  KT10: Esh .7G 149
  KT19: Ewe 6B 164
  N3 . . . . .7D 30
  N6 . . . . .5D 46
  N7 . . . . .6K 65
   (not continuous)
  N11 . . . . .6B 32
  NW10 . . . . .1B 80
  NW11 . . . . .7G 45
  RM5: Col R 1J 55
  SM4: Mord 5A 154
  SW6 . . . . .2G 117
  SW20 . . . . .7E 134
  TW3: Houn 2H 113
  TW7: Isle .2H 113
  TW14: Felt 7A 112
  TW15: Ashf 7F 129
  UB10: Ick .4A 56
  W3 . . . . .6J 79
Drive Ct. HA8: Edg 5B 28
Drive Mans. SW6 . . . . .2G 117
   (off Fulham Rd.)
Driveway, The E17 . . . . .7D 50
   (off Hoe St.)
Dr Johnson's House 1K 13
   (off Pemberton Row)
Droitwich Cl. SE26 . . . . .3G 139
Dromey Gdns. HA3: Hrw W 7E 26
Dromore Rd. SW15 . . . . .6G 117
Dronfield Gdns. RM8: Dag 5C 72
Dron Ho. E1 . . . . .5J 85
   (off Adelina Gro.)
Droop St. W10 .3F 81
Drovers Cl. KT1: King T 2E 150
   (off Fairfield E.)
Drovers Pl. SE15 . . . . .7J 103
Drovers Rd. CR2: S Croy 5D 168
Drovers Way N7 . . . . .6J 65
Druce Rd. SE21 . . . . .6E 120
Druid St. SE1 . . . . .6H 15 (2E 102)
   (not continuous)

Druids Way BR2: Brom 4F 159
Drumaline Ridge KT4: Wor Pk 2A 164
Drummond Av. RM7: Rom 4K 55
Drummond Ct. N12 . . . . .7H 31
  W3 . . . . .3J 97
   (off Palmerston Rd.)
Drummond Cres. NW1 . . . . .1C 6 (3H 83)
Drummond Dr. HA7: Stan 7E 26
Drummond Ga. SW1 . . . . . . .5D 18 (5H 101)
Drummond Ho. E2 . . . . .2G 85
   (off Goldsmiths Row)
  N2 . . . . .2A 46
   (off Font Hills)
Drummond Pl. TW1: Twick 7B 114
Drummond Rd. CR0: C'don 2C 168
  E11 . . . . .6A 52
  RM7: Rom .4K 55
  SE16 . . . . .3H 103
Drummonds, The IG9: Buck H 2E 36
Drummonds Pl. TW9: Rich 4E 114
Drummond St. NW1 . . . . . . .3A 6 (4G 83)
Drummond Way N1 . . . . .7A 66
Druries HA1: Harr 1J 59
   (off High St.)
Drury Cl. SW15 . . . . .6C 116
Drury Cres. CR0: Wadd 2A 168
Drury Ho. SW8 . . . . .1G 119
Drury La. WC2 . . . . .7F 7 (6J 83)
Drury Lane Theatre Royal 2G 13
Drury Rd. HA1: Harr 7G 41
Drury Way NW10 . . . . .5K 61
Drury Way Ind. Est. NW10 . . . . .5J 61
Dryad St. SW15 . . . . .3F 117
Dryburgh Gdns. NW9 . . . . .3G 43
Dryburgh Ho. SW1 . . . . .5B 18
   (part of Abbots Mnr.)
Dryburgh Rd. SW15 . . . . .3D 116
Dryden Av. W7 . . . . .6K 77
Dryden Bldg. E1 . . . . .6G 85
   (off Commercial Rd.)
Dryden Cl. SW4 . . . . .5H 119
Dryden Ct. SE11 . . . . .4K 19 (4A 102)
Dryden Mans. W14 . . . . .6G 99
   (off Queen's Club Gdns.)
Dryden Rd. DA16: Well 1K 125
  EN1: Enf 6K 23
  HA3: W'stone 1K 41
  SW19 . . . . .6A 136
Dryden St. WC2 . . . . .1F 13 (6J 83)
Dryfield Cl. NW10 . . . . .6J 61
Dryfield Rd. HA8: Edg 6D 28
Dryfield Wlk. SE8 . . . . .6C 104
Dryhill Rd. DA17: Belv 6F 109
Dryland Av. BR6: Orp 4K 173
Drylands Rd. N8 . . . . .6J 47
Drysdale Av. E4 . . . . .7J 25
Drysdale Dwellings E8 . . . . .5F 67
   (off Dunn St.)
Drysdale Pl. N1 . . . . .1H 9 (3E 84)
Drysdale St. N1 . . . . .1H 9 (3E 84)
Dublin Av. E8 . . . . .1G 85
Dublin Ct. HA2: Harr 2H 59
   (off Northolt Rd.)
Du Burstow Ter. W7 . . . . .2J 95
Ducaine Apartments E3 . . . . .3B 86
   (off Merchant St.)
Ducal St. E2 . . . . .2K 9 (3F 85)
Du Cane Cl. W12 . . . . .6E 80
Du Cane Ct. SW17 . . . . .1E 136
Du Cane Rd. W12 . . . . .6B 80
Ducavel Ho. SW2 . . . . .1K 137
Duchess Cl. N11 . . . . .5A 32
  SM1: Sutt .4A 166
Duchess Cres. HA7: Stan 3E 26
Duchess Gro.
  IG9: Buck H 2E 36
Duchess M. W1 . . . . .6K 5 (5F 83)
Duchess of Bedford Ho. W8 . . . . .2J 99
   (off Duchess of Bedford's Wlk.)
Duchess of Bedford's Wlk. W8 . . . . .2J 99
Duchess St. W1 . . . . .6K 5 (5F 83)

Duchess Theatre 2G 13
   (off Catherine St.)
Duchy Rd. EN4: Had W 1G 21
Duchy St. SE1 . . . . .4K 13 (1A 102)
   (not continuous)
Ducie St. SW4 .4K 119
Duckett M. N4 .6B 48
Duckett Rd. N4 .6B 48
Duckett's Apartments E3 . . . . .7B 68
   (off Wick La.)
Duckett St. E1 .4K 85
Duck La. W1 . . . . .1C 12
Duck Lees La. EN3: Pond E 4F 25
Duck's Hill Rd. HA4: Ruis 1D 38
  HA6: Nwood 1D 38
DUCKS ISLAND 6A 20
Ducks Wlk. TW1: Twick 5C 114
Du Cros Dr. HA7: Stan 6J 27
Du Cros Rd. W3 . . . . .1A 98
DUDDEN HILL .5D 62
Dudden Hill La. NW10 . . . . .4B 62
Dudden Hill Pde. NW10 . . . . .4B 62
Duddington Cl. SE9 . . . . .4B 142
Dudley Av. HA3: Kenton 3C 42
Dudley Ct. NW11 . . . . .4H 45
  W1 . . . . .1E 10
   (off Up. Berkeley St.)
  WC2 . . . . .7E 6 (6J 83)
Dudley Dr. HA4: Ruis 5K 57
  SM4: Mord 1G 165
Dudley Gdns. HA2: Harr 1H 59
  W13 . . . . .2B 96
Dudley Ho. W2 .6A 4
   (off Nth. Wharf Rd.)
Dudley M. SW2 . . . . .6A 120
Dudley Pl. TW19: Stanw 6B 110
  UB3: Harl .4F 93
Dudley Rd. E17 . . . . .2C 50
  HA2: Harr .2G 59
  IG1: Ilf 4F 71
  KT1: King T 3F 151
  KT12: Walt T 6J 147
  N3 . . . . .2K 45
  NW6 . . . . .2G 81
  SW19 . . . . .6J 135
  TW9: Rich .2F 115
  TW14: Bedf 1E 128
  TW15: Ashf 5B 128
  UB2: S'hall 2B 94
Dudley St. W2 . . . . .6A 4 (5B 82)
Dudlington Rd. E5 . . . . .2J 67
Dudmaston M. SW3 . . . . .5B 16
Dudrich Cl. N11 . . . . .6J 31
Dudrich M. EN2: Enf 1F 23
  SE22 . . . . .5F 121
Dudsbury Rd. DA14: Sidc 6B 144
Dudset La. TW5: Cran 1J 111
Duett Ct. TW5: Hest 7C 94
Duffell Ho. SE11 . . . . .6H 19
Dufferin Av. EC1 . . . . .4E 8
Dufferin Ct. EC1 . . . . .4E 8
   (off Dufferin St.)
Dufferin St. EC1 . . . . .4D 8 (4C 84)
Duffield Cl. HA1: Harr 5K 41
Duffield Dr. N15 . . . . .4F 49
Duff St. E14 . . . . .6D 86
Dufour's Pl. W1 . . . . .1B 12 (6G 83)
Dufton Dwellings E15 . . . . .4G 69
   (off High Rd. Leyton)
Dugard Way SE11 . . . . .4B 102
Dugdale Cen.
  Enfield 4J 23
Dugdale Cl. NW10 . . . . .3D 80
   (off Harrow Rd.)
Duggan Dr. BR7: Chst 6C 142
Dugolly Av. HA9: Wemb 3H 61
Duke Cl. TW3: Houn 4D 112
Duke Gdns. IG6: Ilf 4H 53
Duke Humphrey Rd. SE3 . . . . .1G 123
Duke of Cambridge Cl.
  TW2: Whitt 6H 113

Duke of Clarence Ct. SE17 . . . . .5C 102
(off Manor Pl.)
Duke of Edinburgh Rd. SM1: Sutt 2B 166
Duke of Wellington Av. SE18 . . . . . .3F 107
Duke of Wellington Pl.
SW1 . . . . .6H 11 (2E 100)
Duke of York Column (Memorial) 5C 12
Duke of York Sq. SW3 . . . .4F 17 (5D 100)
Duke of York's Theatre 3E 12
(off St Martin's La.)
Duke of York St. SW1 . . . . .4B 12 (1G 101)
Duke Rd. IG6: Ilf 4H 53
W4 . . . . .5K 97
Dukes Av. HA1: Harr 4J 41
HA2: Harr 6D 40
HA8: Edg 6A 28
KT2: King T 4C 132
KT3: N Mald 3A 152
N3 .1K 45
N10 .3F 47
TW4: Houn 4C 112
TW10: Ham 4C 132
UB5: N'olt 7C 58
W4 .5K 97
Dukes Cl. TW12: Hamp 5D 130
TW15: Ashf 4E 128
Dukes Ct. E6 . . . . .1E 88
(not continuous)
SE13 . . . . .2E 122
SW14 . . . . .2K 115
W2 . . . . .7K 81
(off Moscow Rd.)
Dukes Ga. W4 . . . . .4J 97
Dukes Grn. Av. TW14: Felt 5J 111
Dukes Head Pas. TW12: Hamp 7G 131
Duke's Head Yd. N6 . . . . .1F 65
Duke Shore Wharf E14 . . . . .7B 86
Duke's Ho. SW1 . . . . .3D 18
(off Vincent St.)
Dukes La. W8 . . . . .2K 99
Duke's La. Chambers W8 . . . . .2K 99
(off Dukes La.)
Duke's La. Mans. W8 . . . . .2K 99
(off Dukes La.)
Dukes Lodge W8 . . . . .1H 99
(off Holland Wlk.)
Dukes Meadow Golf & Tennis 2K 115
Dukes Meadow Golf Course 2K 115
Duke's Meadows 2K 115
Dukes M. N10 . . . . .3F 47
W1 . . . . .7H 5
Dukes Orchard DA5: Bexl 1J 145
Duke's Pas. E17 . . . . .4E 50
Duke's Pl. EC3 . . . . .1H 15 (6E 84)
Dukes Point N6 . . . . .1F 65
(off Dukes Head Yd.)
Dukes Ride UB10: Ick 4A 56
Dukes Rd. E6 . . . . .1E 88
W3 . . . . .4G 79
WC1 . . . . .2D 6 (3H 83)
Dukesthorpe Rd. SE26 . . . . .4K 139
Duke St. SM1: Sutt 4B 166
TW9: Rich 4D 114
W1 . . . . .7H 5 (6E 82)
Duke St. Hill SE1 . . . . . .4F 15 (1D 102)
Duke St. Mans. W1 . . . . .1H 11
(off Duke St.)
Duke St. St James's SW1 . . .4B 12 (1G 101)
Dukes Way
BR4: W W'ck 3G 171
HA9: Wemb 5E 60
Duke's Yd. W1 . . . . .2H 11 (7E 82)
Dulas St. N4 . . . . .1K 65
Dulford St. W11 . . . . .7G 81
Dulka Rd. SW11 . . . . .5D 118
Dulverton NW1 . . . . .1G 83
(off Royal College St.)
Dulverton Mans. WC1 . . . . .4H 7
Dulverton Rd. HA4: Ruis 1J 57
SE9 . . . . .2G 143
DULWICH .2E 138

Dulwich & Sydenham Hill Golf Course
. . . . .2F 139
Dulwich Bus. Cen. SE23 . . . . .1K 139
Dulwich Comn. SE21 . . . . .1E 138
SE22 . . . . .1E 138
Dulwich Hamlet FC 4E 120
Dulwich Lawn Cl. SE22 . . . . .5F 121
Dulwich Leisure Cen. 4G 121
Dulwich Oaks, The SE21 . . . . .3F 139
Dulwich Picture Gallery 7D 120
Dulwich Ri. Gdns. SE22 . . . . .5F 121
Dulwich Rd. SE24 . . . . .5A 120
Dulwich Upper Wood Nature Pk. 5F 139
DULWICH VILLAGE 7E 120
Dulwich Village SE21 . . . . .6D 120
Dulwich Wood Av. SE19 . . . . .4E 138
Dulwich Wood Pk. SE19 . . . . .4E 138
Dumain Ct. SE11 . . . . .4B 102
(off Opal St.)
Dumbarton Ct. SW2 . . . . .6J 119
Dumbarton Rd. SW2 . . . . .6J 119
Dumbleton Cl. KT1: King T 1H 151
Dumbreck Rd. SE9 . . . . .4D 124
Dumont Rd. N16 . . . . .3E 66
Dumpton Pl. NW1 . . . . .7E 64
Dumsey Eyot KT16: Chert 7A 146
Dunally Pk. TW17: Shep 7F 147
Dunbar Av. BR3: Beck 4A 158
RM10: Dag 3G 73
SW16 . . . . .2A 156
Dunbar Cl. UB4: Hayes 5K 75
Dunbar Ct. BR2: Brom 3H 159
(off Durham Rd.)
SM1: Sutt 5B 166
Dunbar Gdns. RM10: Dag 5G 73
Dunbar Rd. E7 . . . . .6J 69
KT3: N Mald 4J 151
N22 .1A 48
Dunbar St. SE27 . . . . .3C 138
Dunbar Ter. E8 . . . . .6F 67
(off Dalston Sq.)
Dunbar Wharf E14 . . . . .7B 86
(off Narrow St.)
Dunblane Cl. HA8: Edg 2C 28
Dunblane Rd. SE9 . . . . .3D 124
Dunboe Pl. TW17: Shep 7E 146
Dunboyne Rd. NW3 . . . . .5D 64
Dunbridge Ho. SW15 . . . . .6B 116
Dunbridge St. E2 . . . . .4G 85
Duncan Cl.
EN5: New Bar 4F 21
Duncan Ct. E14 . . . . .5E 86
(off Teviot St.)
N21 .1G 33
Duncan Gro. W3 . . . . .6A 80
Duncan Ho. NW3 . . . . .7D 64
(off Fellows Rd.)
SW1 . . . . .6D 18
(off Dolphin Sq.)
Duncannon Ho. SW1 . . . . .6D 18
(off Lindsay Sq.)
Duncannon St. WC2 . . . . . . .3E 12 (7J 83)
Duncan Rd. E8 . . . . .1H 85
TW9: Rich 4E 114
Duncan St. N1 . . . . .2B 84
Duncan Ter. N1 . . . . .2B 84
(not continuous)
Dunch St. E1 . . . . .6H 85
Dunchurch Ho. RM10: Dag 6G 73
Duncombe Hill SE23 . . . . .7A 122
Duncombe Rd. N19 . . . . .1H 65
Duncrievie Rd. SE13 . . . . .6F 123
Duncroft SE18 . . . . .7J 107
Dundalk Ho. E1 . . . . .6J 85
(off Clark St.)
Dundalk Rd. SE4 . . . . .3A 122
Dundas Ct. SE10 . . . . .6D 104
(off Dowells St.)
Dundas Gdns. KT8: W Mole 3F 149
Dundas Ho. E2 . . . . .2J 85
(off Bishop's Way)

Dundas Rd. SE15 . . . . .2J 121
SW9 . . . . .1A 120
Dundee Ct. E1 . . . . .1H 103
(off Wapping High St.)
SE1 .7F 15
(off Long La.)
Dundee Ho. W9 . . . . .3A 82
(off Maida Vale)
Dundee Rd. E13 . . . . .2K 87
SE25 . . . . .5H 157
Dundee St. E1 . . . . .1H 103
Dundee Way EN3: Brim 3F 25
Dundee Wharf E14 . . . . .7B 86
Dundela Gdns. KT4: Wor Pk 4D 164
Dundonald Cl. E6 . . . . .6C 88
Dundonald Rd. NW10 . . . . .1F 81
SW19 . . . . .7G 135
Dundry Ho. SE26 . . . . .3G 139
Dunedin Ho. E16 . . . . .1D 106
(off Manwood St.)
Dunedin M. SW2 . . . . .1J 137
Dunedin Rd. E10 . . . . .3D 68
IG1: Ilf 1G 71
Dunedin Way UB4: Yead 4A 76
Dunelm Gro. SE27 . . . . .3C 138
Dunelm St. E1 . . . . .6K 85
Dunfield Gdns. SE6 . . . . .5D 140
Dunfield Rd. SE6 . . . . .5D 140
(not continuous)
Dunford Ct. HA5: Hat E 1D 40
Dunford Rd. N7 . . . . .4K 65
Dungannon Ho. SW6 . . . . .7J 99
(off Vanston Pl.)
Dungarvan Av. SW15 . . . . .4C 116
Dunheved Cl. CR7: Thor H 6A 156
Dunheved Rd. Nth. CR7: Thor H 6A 156
Dunheved Rd. Sth. CR7: Thor H 6A 156
Dunheved Rd. W. CR7: Thor H 6A 156
Dunhill Point SW15 . . . . .1C 134
Dunholme Grn. N9 . . . . .3A 34
Dunholme La. N9 . . . . .3A 34
Dunholme Rd. N9 . . . . .3A 34
Dunkeld Rd. RM8: Dag 2B 72
SE25 . . . . .4D 156
Dunkery Rd. SE9 . . . . .4B 142
Dunkirk Ho. SE1 . . . . .2D 102
Dunkirk St. SE27 . . . . .4C 138
Dunlace Rd. E5 . . . . .4J 67
Dunleary Cl. TW4: Houn 7D 112
Dunley Dr. CR0: New Ad 7D 170
Dunlin Ho. SE16 . . . . .4K 103
(off Tawny Way)
Dunloe Av. N17 . . . . .3D 48
Dunloe Ct. E2 . . . . .2F 85
Dunloe Pas. E2 . . . . .2F 85
(off Dunloe St.)
Dunloe St. E2 . . . . .2F 85
Dunlop Pl. SE16 . . . . .3F 103
Dunmore Point E2 . . . . .2J 9
(off Gascoigne Pl.)
Dunmore Rd. NW6 . . . . .1G 81
SW20 . . . . .1E 152
Dunmow Cl. RM6: Chad H 5C 54
TW13: Hanw 3C 130
Dunmow Ho. SE11 . . . . .5H 19
(off Newburn St.)
Dunmow Rd. E15 . . . . .4F 69
Dunmow Wlk. N1 . . . . .1C 84
(off Popham St.)
Dunnage Cres. SE16 . . . . .4A 104
(not continuous)
Dunnell Cl. TW16: Sun 1J 147
Dunnett Ho. E3 . . . . .2B 86
(off Vernon Rd.)
Dunnico Ho. SE17 . . . . .5E 102
(off East St.)
Dunn Mead NW9 . . . . .7G 29
Dunnock Cl. N9 . . . . .1E 34
Dunnock Ho. NW9 . . . . .6B 44
Dunnock M. E5 . . . . .3G 67
Dunnock Rd. E6 . . . . .6C 88

Dunn's Pas. WC1 . . . . .7F 7
Dunn St. E8 .5F 67
Dunollie Pl. NW5 . . . . .5G 65
Dunollie Rd. NW5 . . . . .5G 65
Dunoon Gdns. SE23 . . . . .7K 121
Dunoon Ho. N1 . . . . .1K 83
(off Bemerton Est.)
Dunoon Rd. SE23 . . . . .7J 121
Dunoran Home BR1: Brom 1C 160
Dunraven Dr. EN2: Enf 2G 23
Dunraven Rd. W12 . . . . .1C 98
Dunraven St. W1 . . . . .2F 11 (7D 82)
Dunsany Rd. W14 . . . . .3F 99
Dunsfold Cl. SM2: Sutt 7K 165
(off Blackbush Cl.)
Dunsfold Way CR0: New Ad 7D 170
Dunsford Way SW15 . . . . .6D 116
Dunsmore Cl. UB4: Yead 4B 76
Dunsmore Rd. KT12: Walt T 6K 147
Dunsmure Rd. N16 . . . . .1E 66
Dunspring La. IG5: Ilf 2F 53
Dunstable M. W1 . . . . .5H 5 (5E 82)
Dunstable Rd. KT8: W Mole 4D 148
TW9: Rich 4E 114
Dunstall Rd. SW20 . . . . .6D 134
Dunstall Way KT8: W Mole 3F 149
Dunstall Welling Est. DA16: Well 2B 126
Dunstan Cl. N2 . . . . .3A 46
Dunstan Glade BR5: Pet W 6H 161
Dunstan Ho's. E1 . . . . .5J 85
(off Stepney Grn.)
Dunstan M. EN1: Enf 3K 23
Dunstan's Gro. SE22 . . . . .6H 121
Dunstan's Rd. SE22 . . . . .7G 121
Dunster Av. SM4: Mord 1F 165
Dunster Cl. EN5: Barn 4A 20
RM5: Col R 2J 55
Dunster Ct. EC3 . . . . .2H 15 (7E 84)
Dunster Dr. NW9 . . . . .1J 61
Dunster Gdns. NW6 . . . . .7H 63
Dunster Ho. SE6 . . . . .3E 140
Dunsterville Way SE1 . . . . . .7F 15 (2D 102)
Dunster Way HA2: Harr 3C 58
SM6: Wall 1E 166
Dunston Rd. E8 . . . . .1F 85
SW11 . . . . .2E 118
Dunston St. E8 . . . . .1E 84
Dunton Cl. KT6: Surb 1E 162
Dunton Ct. SE23 . . . . .2H 139
Dunton Rd. E10 . . . . .7D 50
RM1: Rom 4K 55
SE1 .5F 103
Duntshill Rd. SW18 . . . . .1K 135
Dunvegan Cl. KT8: W Mole 4E 148
Dunvegan Rd. SE9 . . . . .4D 124
Dunwich Ct. RM6: Chad H 5B 54
(off Glandford Way)
Dunwich Rd. DA7: Bex 1F 127
Dunworth M. W11 . . . . .6H 81
Duplex Side SW1 . . . . .7F 11 (2D 100)
Dupont Rd. SW20 . . . . .2F 153
Duppas Av. CR0: Wadd 4B 168
Duppas Cl. TW17: Shep 5F 147
Duppas Ct. CR0: C'don 3B 168
(off Duppas Hill Ter.)
Duppas Hill La. CR0: C'don 4B 168
Duppas Hill Rd. CR0: Wadd 4A 168
Duppas Hill Ter. CR0: C'don 3B 168
Duppas Rd. CR0: Wadd 3A 168
Dupree Rd. SE7 . . . . .5K 105
Dura Den Cl. BR3: Beck 7D 140
Durand Cl. SM5: Cars 1D 166
Durand Gdns. SW9 . . . . .1K 119
Durands Wlk. SE16 . . . . .2B 104
Durand Way NW10 . . . . .7J 61
Durants Park 3D 24
Durants Pk. Av. EN3: Pond E 4E 24
Durants Rd. EN3: Pond E 4D 24
Durant St. E2 . . . . .2G 85
Durban Ct. E7 . . . . .7B 70

Durban Gdns. RM10: Dag 7J 73
Durban Ho. W12 . . . . .7D 80
(off White City Est.)
Durban Rd. BR3: Beck 2B 158
E15 . . . . .3G 67
E17 . . . . .1B 50
IG2: Ilf 1J 71
N17 . . . . .6K 33
SE27 . . . . .4C 138
Durbin Rd. KT9: Chess 4E 162
Durdan Cotts. UB1: S'hall 6D 76
(off Denbigh Rd.)
Jurdans Ho. NW1 . . . . .7F 65
(off Farrier Cl.)
Jurdans Rd. UB1: S'hall 6D 76
(off Wolfe Cres.)
Jurell Gdns. RM9: Dag 5D 72
Jurell Ho. SE16 . . . . .2K 103
(off Wolfe Cres.)
Jurell Rd. RM9: Dag 5D 72
Jurley Pl. SE5 . . . . .7D 102
Jurlford Cres. SW15 . . . . . . .1D 134
Jurham Av. BR2: Brom 4H 159
IG8: Buck H, Wfd G 5G 37
TW5: Hest 5D 94
Jurham Cl. SW20 . . . . .2D 152
Jurham Ct. NW6 . . . . .2J 81
(off Kilburn Pk. Rd.)
TW11: Tedd 4J 131
Jurham Hill BR1: Brom 4H 141
Jurham Ho. BR2: Brom 4G 159
IG11: Bark 7A 72
(off Margaret Bondfield Av.)
NW8 . . . . .2D 4
(off Lorne Cl.)
RM10: Dag 5J 73
Jurham Ho. St. WC2 . . . . . . .3F 13
SW3 . . . . .6E 16 (5D 100)
Jurham Ri. SE18 . . . . .5G 107
Jurham Rd. BR2: Brom 3H 159
DA14: Sidc 5B 144
E12 . . . . .4B 70
E16 . . . . .4G 87
HA1: Harr 5F 41
N2 . . . . .3C 46
N7 . . . . .2K 65
N9 . . . . .2B 34
RM10: Dag 5J 73
SW20 . . . . .1D 152
TW14: Felt 7A 112
W5 . . . . .3D 96
Jurham Row E1 . . . . .5J 85
Jurham St. SE11 . . . . .6G 19 (5K 101)
Jurham Ter. W2 . . . . .6K 81
Jurham Wharf Dr. TW8: Bford 7C 96
Jurham Yd. E2 . . . . .3H 85
Jurley Av. HA5: Pinn 7C 40
Jurley Rd. N16 . . . . .7E 48
Jurlston Rd. E5 . . . . .2G 67
KT2: King T 6E 132
Jurnford Ho. SE6 . . . . .3E 140
Jurnford St. N15 . . . . .5E 48
SE10 . . . . .6E 104
Jurning Rd. SE19 . . . . .5D 138
Jurnsford Av. SW19 . . . . .2J 135
Jurnsford Ct. EN3: Enf H 3F 25
(off Enstone Rd.)
Jurnsford Rd. N11 . . . . .1H 47
SW19 . . . . .2J 135
Jurrant Cl. HA3: Hrw W 2J 41
Jurrant Ho. EC1 . . . . .5E 8
(off Chiswell St.)
Jurrant Way BR6: Farnb 5H 173
Jurrell Rd. SW6 . . . . .1H 117
Jurrell Way TW17: Shep 4F 147
Jurrels Ho. W14 . . . . .4H 99
(off Warwick Gdns.)
Jurrington Av. SW20 . . . . .7E 134
Jurrington Pk. Rd. SW20 . . . . . .1E 152
Jurrington Rd. E5 . . . . .4A 68
Jurrington Twr. SW8 . . . . .2G 119

Durrisdeer Ho. NW2 . . . . .4H 63
(off Lyndale)
Dursley Cl. SE3 . . . . .2A 124
Dursley Gdns. SE3 . . . . .1B 124
Dursley Rd. SE3 . . . . .2A 124
Durward Ho. W8 . . . . .2K 99
(off Kensington Ct.)
Durward St. E1 . . . . .5H 85
Durweston M. W1 . . . . .5F 5
Durweston St. W1 . . . . . .6F 5 (5D 82)
Dury Falls Cl. RM5: Col R 2J 55
Dury Rd. EN5: Barn 1C 20
Dutch Barn Cl. TW19: Stanw 6A 110
Dutch Gdns. KT2: King T 6H 133
Dutch Yd. SW18 . . . . .5J 117
Dutton St. SE10 . . . . .1E 122
Duval Ho. N19 . . . . .2H 65
(off Ashbrook Rd.)
Duxberry Av. TW13: Felt 3A 130
Duxberry Cl. BR2: Brom 5C 160
Duxford Ho. SE2 . . . . .2D 108
(off Wolvercote Rd.)
Dye Ho. La. E3 . . . . .1C 86
Dyer Ho. TW12: Hamp 1F 149
Dyer's Bldgs. EC1 . . . . . .6J 7 (5A 84)
Dyers Hall Rd. E11 . . . . .1G 69
Dyers Hill Rd. E11 . . . . .2F 69
Dyers La. SW15 . . . . .4D 116
Dykes Way BR2: Brom 3H 159
Dykewood Cl. DA5: Bexl 3K 145
Dylan Rd. DA17: Belv 3G 109
SE24 . . . . .4B 120
Dylways SE5 . . . . .4D 120
Dymchurch Cl. BR6: Orp 4J 173
IG5: Ilf 2E 52
Dymes Path SW19 . . . . .2F 135
Dymock St. SW6 . . . . .3K 117
Dyneley Rd. SE12 . . . . .3A 142
Dyne Rd. NW6 . . . . .7G 63
Dynevor Rd. N16 . . . . .3E 66
TW10: Rich 5E 114
Dynham Rd. NW6 . . . . .7J 63
Dyott St. WC1 . . . . .7D 6 (6H 83)
Dysart Av. KT2: King T 5C 132
Dysart St. EC2 . . . . . .4G 9 (4D 84)
Dyson Cl. HA0: Wemb 6A 60
NW2 . . . . .1E 62
Dyson Ho. SE10 . . . . .5H 105
(off Blackwall La.)
Dyson Rd. E11 . . . . .6G 51
E15 . . . . .6H 69
Dysons Rd. N18 . . . . .5C 34

E

Eade Rd. N4 . . . . .7C 48
Eagans Cl. N2 . . . . .3B 46
Eagle Av. RM6: Chad H 6E 54
Eagle Cl. EN3: Pond E 4D 24
SE16 . . . . .5J 103
SM6: Wall 6J 167
Eagle Ct. E11 . . . . .4J 51
EC1 . . . . .5A 8 (5B 84)
Eagle Dr. NW9 . . . . .2A 44
Eagle Dwellings EC1 . . . . .1D 8
(off City Rd.)
Eagle Hgts. SW11 . . . . .3C 118
Eagle Hill SE19 . . . . .6D 138
Eagle Ho. E1 . . . . .4H 85
(off Headlam St.)
N1 . . . . .2D 84
(off Eagle Wharf Rd.)
Eagle Ho. M. SW4 . . . . .5G 119
Eagle La. E11 . . . . .4J 51
Eagle Lodge NW11 . . . . .7H 45
Eagle Mans. N16 . . . . .5F 67
(off Salcombe Rd.)
Eagle M. N1 . . . . .6E 66
Eagle Pl. SW1 . . . . .3B 12
SW7 . . . . .5A 100

Eagle Rd. HA0: Wemb 7D 60
TW6: H'row A 3H 111
Eaglesfield Rd. SE18 . . . . .1F 125
Eagle St. WC1 . . . . . . .6G 7 (5K 83)
Eagle Ter. IG8: Wfd G 7E 36
Eagle Trad. Est. CR4: Mitc 6D 154
Eagle Wharf Ct. SE1 . . . . .5J 15
(off Lafone St.)
Eagle Wharf E. E14 . . . . .7A 86
(off Narrow St.)
Eagle Wharf Rd. N1 . . . . .2C 84
Eagle Wharf W. E14 . . . . .7A 86
(off Narrow St.)
Eagle Works E. E1 . . . . .4K 9
Eagle Works W. E1 . . . . .4J 9
Eagling Cl. E3 . . . . .3C 86
Ealdham Sq. SE9 . . . . .4A 124
EALING 7D 78
Ealing B'way. Cen. W5 . . . . .7D 78
EALING COMMON 7F 79
Ealing Golf Course 3B 78
Ealing Grn. W5 . . . . .1D 96
Ealing Pk. Gdns. W5 . . . . .4C 96
Ealing Pk. Mans. W5 . . . . .3D 96
(off Sth. Ealing Rd.)
Ealing Rd. HA0: Wemb 6E 60
TW8: Bford 5D 96
UB5: N'olt 1E 76
Ealing Squash & Fitness Club . . .6E 78
Ealing Studios 1D 96
Ealing Village W5 . . . . .6E 78
Eamont Cl. HA4: Ruis 7D 38
Eamont Ct. NW8 . . . . .2C 82
(off Eamont St.)
Eamont St. NW8 . . . . .2C 82
Eardley Cres. SW5 . . . . .5J 99
Eardley Point SE18 . . . . .4F 107
(off Wilmount St.)
Eardley Rd. DA17: Belv 5G 109
SW16 . . . . .5G 137
Earhart Ho. NW9 . . . . .3C 44
(off East Dr.)
Earhart Way TW6: Cran, H'row A . . .3J 111
Earl Cl. N11 . . . . .5A 32
Earldom Rd. SW15 . . . . .4E 116
Earle Gdns. KT2: King T 7E 132
Earle Ho. SW1 . . . . .4D 18
(off Montaigne Cl.)
Earlham Ct. E11 . . . . .7H 51
Earlham Gro. E7 . . . . .5H 69
N22 . . . . .7E 32
Earlham St. WC2 . . . . . .1D 12 (6J 83)
Earl Ho. NW1 . . . . .4D 4
(off Lisson Gro.)
Earlom Ho. WC1 . . . . .2J 7
(off Margery St.)
Earl Ri. SE18 . . . . .5H 107
Earl Rd. SW14 . . . . .4J 115
Earlsbury Gdns. HA8: Edg 4B 28
EARL'S COURT 4K 99
Earl's Ct. Gdns. SW5 . . . . .4K 99
Earl's Ct. Rd. SW5 . . . . .3J 99
W8 . . . . .3J 99
Earl's Ct. Sq. SW5 . . . . .5K 99
Earls Cres. HA1: Harr 4J 41
Earlsdown Ho. IG11: Bark 2H 89
Earlsferry Way N1 . . . . .7J 65
(not continuous)
EARLSFIELD 1A 136
Earlsfield Ho. KT2: King T 1D 150
(off Seven Kings Way)
Earlsfield Rd. SW18 . . . . .1A 136
Earlshall Rd. SE9 . . . . .4D 124
Earls Ho. TW9: Kew 7H 97
Earlsmead HA2: Harr 4D 58
Earlsmead Rd. N15 . . . . .5F 49
NW10 . . . . .3E 80
Earlsmead Stadium 4D 58
Earls Ter. W8 . . . . .3H 99
Earlsthorpe M. SW12 . . . . .6E 118
Earlsthorpe Rd. SE26 . . . . .4K 139

Earlstoke St. EC1 . . . . .1A 8 (3B 84)
Earlston Gro. E9 . . . . .1H 85
Earl St. EC2 . . . . .5G 9 (5D 84)
Earls Wlk. RM8: Dag 4B 72
W8 . . . . .3J 99
Earlswood Av. CR7: Thor H 5A 156
Earlswood Cl. SE10 . . . . .6G 105
Earlswood Gdns. IG5: Ilf 3E 52
Earlswood St. SE10 . . . . .5G 105
Early M. NW1 . . . . .1F 83
Early Rivers Ho. E20 . . . . .5E 68
(off Ellis Way)
Earnshaw Ho. EC1 . . . . .2B 8
(off Percival St.)
Earnshaw St. WC2 . . . . . .7D 6 (6H 83)
Earsby St. W14 . . . . .4G 99
(not continuous)
Easby Cres. SM4: Mord 6K 153
Easebourne Rd. RM8: Dag 5C 72
Easedale Ho. TW7: Isle 5K 113
Eashing Point SW15 . . . . .1D 134
(off Wanborough Dr.)
Easleys M. W1 . . . . . . .7H 5 (6E 82)
East 10 Ent. Pk. E10 . . . . .1A 68
EAST ACTON 7B 80
E. Acton Arc. W3 . . . . .6A 80
E. Acton Ct. W3 . . . . .7A 80
E. Acton La. W3 . . . . .1A 98
E. Arbour St. E1 . . . . .6K 85
East Av. E12 . . . . .7C 70
E17 . . . . .4D 50
SM6: Wall 5K 167
UB1: S'hall 7D 76
UB3: Hayes 1H 93
East Bank N16 . . . . .7E 48
Eastbank Rd. TW12: Hamp H 5G 131
EAST BARNET 6H 21
East Barnet Golf Course 3F 21
E. Barnet Rd. EN4: E Barn 4G 21
E. Beckton District Cen. E6 . . . . .5D 88
EAST BEDFONT 7G 111
East Block SE1 . . . . .6H 13
(off York Rd.)
Eastbourne Av. W3 . . . . .6K 79
Eastbourne Gdns. SW14 . . . . . .3J 115
Eastbourne M. W2 . . . . . .7A 4 (6A 82)
Eastbourne Rd. E6 . . . . .3E 88
(not continuous)
E15 . . . . .1G 87
N15 . . . . .6E 48
SW17 . . . . .6E 136
TW8: Bford 5C 96
TW13: Felt 2B 130
W4 . . . . .6J 97
Eastbourne Ter. W2 . . . . . .7A 4 (6A 82)
Eastbournia Av. N9 . . . . .3C 34
Eastbrook Av. N9 . . . . .7D 24
RM10: Dag 4J 73
Eastbrook Cl. RM10: Dag 4J 73
Eastbrook Dr. RM7: Rush G 3K 73
Eastbrookend Country Pk. 3K 73
Eastbrook Rd. SE3 . . . . .1K 123
Eastbury Av. EN1: Enf 1A 24
IG11: Bark 1J 89
Eastbury Ct. EN5: New Bar 5F 21
(off Lyonsdown Rd.)
IG11: Bark 1J 89
Eastbury Gro. W4 . . . . .5A 98
Eastbury Manor House 1K 89
Eastbury Rd.
BR5: Pet W 6H 161
E6 . . . . .4E 88
KT2: King T 7E 132
RM7: Rom 6K 55
Eastbury Sq. IG11: Bark 1K 89
Eastbury Ter. E1 . . . . .4K 85
Eastcastle St. W1 . . . . . . .7A 6 (6G 83)
Eastcheap EC3 . . . . .2G 15 (7E 84)
E. Churchfield Rd. W3 . . . . .1K 97
Eastchurch Rd. TW6: H'row A . . .2G 111

East Cl. EN4: Cockf 4K 21
  UB6: G'frd 2G 77
  W5 . . . . .4G 79
Eastcombe Av. SE7 . . . . .6K 105
EASTCOTE 7K 39
Eastcote BR6: Orp 1K 173
Eastcote Av. HA2: Harr 2F 59
  KT8: W Mole 5D 148
  UB6: G'frd 5A 60
Eastcote Hockey & Badminton Club . . .6H 39
Eastcote Ind. Est. HA4: Ruis 7A 40
Eastcote La. HA2: Harr 4C 58
  UB5: N'olt 5D 58
      (not continuous)
Eastcote La. Nth. UB5: N'olt 6D 58
Eastcote Pl. HA5: Eastc 6K 39
Eastcote Rd. DA16: Well 2H 125
  HA2: Harr 3G 59
  HA4: Ruis 7G 39
  HA5: Pinn 5B 40
Eastcote St. SW9 . . . . .2K 119
Eastcote Vw. HA5: Pinn 4A 40
EASTCOTE VILLAGE 5K 39
Eastcott Cl. KT2: King T 5J 133
East Ct. HA0: Wemb 2C 60
East Cres. EN1: Enf 5A 24
  N11 . . . . .4J 31
East Cft. Ho. HA2: Harr 2G 59
Eastcroft Rd. KT19: Ewe 7A 164
E. Cross Route E3 . . . . .7B 68
  E9 . . . . .5B 68
      (Crowfoot Cl.)
  E9 . . . . .7B 68
      (Wansbeck Rd.)
  E10 . . . . .5B 68
Eastdown Ct. SE13 . . . . .4F 123
Eastdown Ho. E8 . . . . .4G 67
Eastdown Pk. SE13 . . . . .4F 123
East Dr. NW9 . . . . .3C 44
  SM5: Cars 7C 166
E. Duck Lees La. EN3: Pond E 4F 25
EAST DULWICH 4F 121
E. Dulwich Est. SE22 . . . . .3E 120
      (off Albrighton Rd.)
E. Dulwich Gro. SE22 . . . . .5E 120
E. Dulwich Rd. SE15 . . . . .4F 121
  SE22 . . . . .4F 121
      (not continuous)
East End Farm HA5: Pinn 3D 40
East End Rd. N2 . . . . .3K 45
  N3 . . . . .2J 45
East End Way HA5: Pinn 3C 40
East Entrance RM10: Dag 2H 91
Eastern App. IG11: Bark 1A 90
Eastern Av. E11 . . . . .6K 51
  HA5: Pinn 7B 40
  IG2: Ilf .6F 53
  IG4: Ilf .6C 52
  RM6: Chad H 4A 54
Eastern Av. E. RM1: Rom 3K 55
Eastern Av. Retail Pk. RM7: Rom 4J 55
Eastern Av. W. RM1: Rom 4E 54
  RM5: Rom 4E 54
  RM6: Chad H 4E 54
  RM7: Chad H, Mawney, Rom 4E 54
Eastern Bus. Pk. TW6: H'row A 2G 111
Eastern Ct. E15 . . . . .6G 69
      (off Gt. Eastern Rd.)
Eastern Gateway E16 . . . . .7A 88
Eastern Ho. E2 . . . . .3H 85
      (off Bethnal Grn. Rd.)
Eastern Ind. Est. DA18: Erith 2G 109
Eastern Perimeter Rd.
  TW6: H'row A 2H 111
Eastern Quay Apartments E16 . . . . . . .1K 105
      (off Portsmouth M.)
Eastern Rd. E13 . . . . .2K 87
  E17 . . . . .5E 50
  N2 . . . . .3D 46
  N22 . . . . .1J 47
  SE4 . . . . .4C 122

EASTERN RDBT. 2G 71
Easternville Gdns. IG2: Ilf 6G 53
Eastern Way DA17: Belv 2A 108
  DA18: Erith 2A 108
  SE2 . . . . .2A 108
  SE28 . . . . .2A 108
E. Ferry Rd. E14 . . . . .4D 104
Eastfield Gdns. RM10: Dag 4G 73
Eastfield Rd. E17 . . . . .4C 50
  EN3: Enf W 1E 24
  N8 . . . . .3J 47
  RM9: Dag 4F 73
  RM10: Dag 4G 73
Eastfields HA5: Eastc 5A 40
Eastfields Av. SW18 . . . . .4J 117
Eastfields Rd. CR4: Mitc 2E 154
  W3 . . . . .5J 79
Eastfield St. E14 . . . . .5A 86
EAST FINCHLEY 4C 46
East Gdns. SW17 . . . . .6C 136
Eastgate Bus. Pk. E10 . . . . .1A 68
Eastgate Cl. SE28 . . . . .6D 90
Eastglade HA5: Pinn 3D 40
EAST HAM 2D 88
East Ham & Barking By-Pass
  IG11: Bark 2H 89
Eastham Cl. EN5: Barn 5B 20
East Ham Ind. Est. E6 . . . . .4C 88
East Ham Leisure Cen. 1D 88
East Ham Mnr. Way E6 . . . . .6E 88
East Ham Nature Reserve 4D 88
East Ham Nature Reserve Vis. Cen.
  . . . . .4D 88
E. Handyside Canopy N1 . . . . .1J 83
E. Harding St. EC4 . . . . .7K 7 (6A 84)
E. Heath Rd. NW3 . . . . .3A 64
East Hill HA9: Wemb 2G 61
  SW18 .5K 117
Eastholm NW11 . . . . .4K 45
East Holme DA8: Erith 1K 127
Eastholme UB3: Hayes 1J 93
E. India Bldgs. E14 . . . . .7C 86
      (off Saltwell St.)
E. India Ct. SE16 . . . . .2J 103
      (off St Marychurch St.)
East India Dock Basin Nature Reserve
  . . . . .7G 87
E. India Dock Ho. E14 . . . . .6E 86
E. India Dock Rd. E14 . . . . .6C 86
E. India Way CR0: C'don 1F 169
Eastlake Ho. NW8 . . . . .4B 4
Eastlake Rd. SE5 . . . . .2C 120
Eastlands Cres. SE21 . . . . .6F 121
East La. HA0: Wemb 3B 60
  HA9: Wemb 3B 60
  KT1: King T 3D 150
  SE16 . . . . .2G 103
      (Chambers St.)
  SE16 . . . . .2G 103
      (Scott Lidgett Cres.)
East La. Bus. Pk. HA9: Wemb 2D 60
Eastlea M. E16 . . . . .4G 87
Eastleigh Av. HA2: Harr 2F 59
Eastleigh Cl. NW2 . . . . .3A 62
  SM2: Sutt 7K 165
Eastleigh Rd. DA7: Bex 3J 127
  E17 . . . . .2B 50
Eastleigh Wlk. SW15 . . . . .7C 116
Eastleigh Way TW14: Felt 1J 129
East Lodge E16 . . . . .1J 105
      (off Wesley Av.)
E. London Crematorium E13 . . . . .3H 87
East London Gymnastic Cen. 6D 88
Eastman Ho. SW4 . . . . .6G 119
Eastman Rd. W3 . . . . .2K 97
East Mead HA4: Ruis 3B 58
Eastmead Av. UB6: G'frd 3F 77
Eastmead Cl. BR1: Brom 2C 160
Eastmearn Rd. SE21 . . . . .2C 138
EAST MOLESEY 4H 149
Eastmoor Pl. SE7 . . . . .3B 106

Eastmoor St. SE7 . . . . .3B 106
East Mt. St. E1 . . . . .5H 85
      (not continuous)
Eastney Rd. CR0: C'don 1B 168
Eastney St. SE10 . . . . .5F 105
Eastnor Rd. SE9 . . . . .1G 143
Eastone Apartments E1 . . . . .6K 9
      (off Lolesworth Cl.)
Easton St. WC1 . . . . .3J 7 (4A 84)
East Pk. Cl. RM6: Chad H 5E 54
East Parkside SE10 . . . . .2G 105
East Pas. EC1 . . . . .5C 8
East Pl. SE27 . . . . .4C 138
East Point SE1 . . . . .5G 103
East Pole Cotts. N14 . . . . .4C 22
E. Poultry Av. EC1 . . . . .6A 8 (5B 84)
East Ramp TW6: H'row A 1D 110
East Rd. DA16: Well 2B 126
  E15 . . . . .1J 87
  EN3: Enf W 1D 24
  EN4: E Barn 1K 31
  HA1: Harr 7B 42
  HA8: Edg 1H 43
  KT2: King T 1E 150
  N1 . . . . .2E 8 (3D 84)
  RM6: Chad H 5E 54
  RM7: Rush G 7K 55
  SW3 . . . . .6G 17 (5E 100)
  SW19 .6A 136
  TW14: Bedf 7F 111
  UB7: W Dray 4B 92
E. Rochester Way DA5: Bexl 6F 127
  DA15: Sidc 5J 125
East Row E11 . . . . .6J 51
  W10 . . . . .4G 81
Eastry Av. BR2: Hayes 6H 159
Eastry Ho. SW8 . . . . .7J 101
      (off Hartington Rd.)
  W11 . . . . .7G 81
      (off Walmer Rd.)
Eastry Rd. DA8: Erith 7G 109
EAST SHEEN .4J 115
E. Sheen Av. SW14 . . . . .5K 115
East Shopping Cen. E7 . . . . .7K 69
East Side W12 . . . . .2E 98
      (off Shepherd's Bush Mkt.)
Eastside Halls SW7 . . . . .1B 16
      (off Prince's Gdns.)
Eastside M. E3 . . . . .2C 86
      (off Morville St.)
Eastside Rd. NW11 . . . . .4H 45
East Smithfield E1 . . . . .3K 15 (7F 85)
East Sq. E10 .7D 50
East Stand N5 . . . . .3B 66
East St. BR1: Brom 2J 159
  DA7: Bex 4G 127
  IG11: Bark 1G 89
  SE17 . . . . .5C 102
      (not continuous)
  TW8: Bford 7C 96
E. Surrey Gro. SE15 . . . . .7F 103
E. Tenter St. E1 . . . . .1K 15 (6F 85)
East Ter. DA15: Sidc 1J 143
E. Thamesmead Bus. Pk.
  DA18: Erith 2F 109
East Twr. E14 . . . . .2D 104
      (off Pan Peninsula Sq.)
East Towers HA5: Pinn 5B 40
East Va. W3 .1B 98
East Vw. E4 .5K 35
  EN5: Barn 2C 20
Eastview Av. SE18 . . . . .7J 107
Eastville Av. NW11 . . . . .6H 45
East Wlk.
  EN4: E Barn 7K 21
  UB3: Hayes 1J 93
East Way BR2: Hayes 7J 159
  CR0: C'don 2A 170
  E11 . . . . .5K 51
  HA4: Ruis 1J 57
  UB3: Hayes 1J 93

Eastway E9 . . . . .6B 68
      (not continuous)
  SM4: Mord 5F 153
  SM6: Wall 4G 167
Eastway Cres. HA2: Harr 2F 59
Eastwell Cl. BR3: Beck 7A 140
EAST WICKHAM 7F 107
Eastwell Ho. SE1 . . . . .7F 15
East Wintergarden E14 . . . . .1D 104
      (off Bank St.)
Eastwood Cl. E18 . . . . .2J 51
  N7 . . . . .5A 66
  N17 . . . . .7C 34
Eastwood Ho. E3 . . . . .5C 8
      (off Bow Comn. La.)
Eastwood Rd. E18 . . . . .2J 51
  IG3: Ilf .1A 72
  N10 . . . . .2E 46
  UB7: W Dray 2C 92
East Woodside DA5: Bexl 7E 126
Eastwood St. SW16 . . . . .6G 137
Eatington Rd. E10 . . . . .5F 51
Eaton Cl. HA7: Stan 4G 27
  SW1 . . . . .4G 17 (4E 100)
Eaton Ct. E18 . . . . .2J 51
  HA8: Edg 4B 28
Eaton Dr. KT2: King T 7G 133
  RM5: Col R 1H 55
  SW9 . . . . .4B 120
Eaton Gdns. RM9: Dag 7E 72
Eaton Ga. SW1 . . . . .3G 17 (4E 100)
Eaton Ho. E14 . . . . .7B 8
      (off Westferry Cir.)
  SW11 .1B 118
Eaton La. SW1 . . . . .2K 17 (3F 101)
Eaton Mans. SW1 . . . . .4G 17
      (off Bourne St.)
Eaton M. Nth. SW1 . . . . .3G 17 (4E 100)
Eaton M. Sth. SW1 . . . . .3H 17 (4E 100)
Eaton M. W. SW1 . . . . .3H 17 (4E 100)
Eaton Pk. Rd. N13 . . . . .2F 33
Eaton Pl. SW1 . . . . .2G 17 (4E 100)
Eaton Ri. E11 . . . . .5A 52
  W5 . . . . .5D 78
Eaton Rd. DA14: Sidc 2D 144
  EN1: Enf 4K 23
  NW4 . . . . .5E 44
  SM2: Sutt 6B 166
  TW3: Houn 4H 113
Eaton Row SW1 . . . . .2J 17 (3F 101)
Eatons Mead E4 . . . . .2H 35
Eaton Sq. SW1 . . . . .3G 17 (4E 100)
Eaton Ter. E3 .3A 86
  SW1 . . . . .3G 17 (4E 100)
Eaton Ter. M. SW1 . . . . .3G 17
Eatonville Rd. SW17 . . . . .2D 136
Eatonville Vs. SW17 . . . . .2D 136
Ebb Cl. E16 . . . . .5C 8
Ebbett Cl. W3 . . . . .5K 79
Ebbisham Dr. SW8 . . . . .7G 19 (6K 101)
Ebbisham Rd. KT4: Wor Pk 2E 164
Ebbsfleet Rd. NW2 . . . . .5G 63
Ebdon Way SE3 . . . . .3K 123
Ebenezer Ho. SE11 . . . . .4K 19 (4B 102)
Ebenezer Mussel Ho. E2 . . . . .2J 85
      (off Patriot Sq.)
Ebenezer St. N1 . . . . .1E 8 (3D 84)
Ebenezer Wlk. SW16 . . . . .1G 155
Ebley Cl. SE15 . . . . .6F 103
Ebner St. SW18 . . . . .5K 117
Ebony Ho. E2 .3G 8
      (off Buckfast St.)
Ebor Cotts. SW15 . . . . .3A 134
Ebor St. E1 . . . . .3J 9 (4F 85)
Ebrington Rd. HA3: Kenton 6D 42
Ebsworth St. SE23 . . . . .7K 121
Eburne Rd. N7 . . . . .3J 65
Ebury Bri. SW1 . . . . .5J 17 (5F 101)
Ebury Bri. Est. SW1 . . . . .5J 17 (5F 101)
Ebury Bri. Rd. SW1 . . . . .6H 17 (5E 100)
Ebury Cl. BR2: Kes 3C 172

Ebury M. N5 . . . . .3C **66**
   SE27 .3B **138**
   SW1 . . . . .3J **17** (4F **101**)
Ebury M. E. SW1 . . . . .2J **17** (3F **101**)
Ebury Sq. SW1 . . . . .4H **17** (4E **100**)
Ebury St. SW1 . . . . .4H **17** (4E **100**)
Ecclesbourne Apartments N1 . . . . . . .7D **66**
    (off Ecclesbourne Rd.)
Ecclesbourne Cl. N13 . . . . .5F **33**
Ecclesbourne Gdns. N13 . . . . .5F **33**
Ecclesbourne Rd. CR7: Thor H 5C **156**
   N1 . . . . .7C **66**
Eccleshill BR2: Brom 4H **159**
    (off Durham Rd.)
Eccles Rd. SW11 . . . . .4D **118**
Eccleston Bri. SW1 . . . . . . .3K **17** (4F **101**)
Eccleston Cl. BR6: Orp 1H **173**
   EN4: Cockf 4J **21**
Eccleston Cres. RM6: Chad H 7B **54**
Eccleston Ct. HA9: Wemb 5E **60**
Eccleston M. HA9: Wemb 5E **60**
Eccleston Pl. HA9: Wemb 5F **61**
Eccleston Ho. SW2 . . . . .6A **120**
Eccleston M. SW1 . . . . .2H **17** (3E **100**)
Eccleston Pl. SW1 . . . . .3J **17** (4F **101**)
Eccleston Rd. W13 . . . . .7A **78**
Eccleston Sq. SW1 . . . . .4K **17** (4F **101**)
    (not continuous)
Eccleston Sq. M. SW1 . . . . . .4A **18** (4F **101**)
Eccleston St. SW1 . . . . .2J **17** (3F **101**)
Echelforde Dr. TW15: Ashf 4C **128**
Echo Hgts. E4 . . . . .1J **35**
Eckford St. N1 . . . . .2A **84**
Eckington Ho. N15 . . . . .6D **48**
    (off Fladbury Rd.)
Eckstein Rd. SW11 . . . . .4C **118**
Eclipse Bldg. N1 . . . . .6A **66**
    (off Laycock St.)
Eclipse Ho. N22 . . . . .2K **47**
    (off Station Rd.)
Eclipse Rd. E13 . . . . .5K **87**
Ecology Centre and Arts Pavilion 3A **86**
Ector Rd. SE6 .2G **141**
Edam Ct. DA15: Sidc 3A **144**
Edans Ct. W12 . . . . .2B **98**
Edar Ho. CRO: New Ad 6D **170**
Edbrooke Rd. W9 . . . . .4J **81**
Eddington Ct. E16 . . . . .5H **87**
    (off Silvertown Sq.)
Eddinton Cl. CRO: New Ad 6E **170**
Eddisbury Ho. SE26 . . . . .3G **139**
Eddiscombe Rd. SW6 . . . . .2H **117**
Eddy Cl. RM7: Rom 6H **55**
Eddystone Rd. SE4 . . . . .5A **122**
Eddystone Twr. SE8 . . . . .5A **104**
Eddystone Wlk. TW19: Stanw 7A **110**
Ede Cl. TW3: Houn 3D **112**
Edenbridge Cl. SE16 . . . . .5H **103**
    (off Masters Dr.)
Edenbridge Rd. E9 . . . . .7K **67**
   EN1: Enf .6K **23**
Eden Cl. DA5: Bexl 4K **145**
   HA0: Wemb 1D **78**
   NW3 . . . . .2J **63**
   W8 . . . . .3J **99**
Eden Ct. IG6: Ilf 1H **53**
Edencourt Rd. SW16 . . . . .6F **137**
Edendale W3 .7H **79**
Edendale Rd. DA7: Bex 1K **127**
Edenfield Gdns. KT4: Wor Pk 3B **164**
Eden Gro. E17 . . . . .5D **50**
   N7 . . . . .5K **65**
   NW10 . . . . .6D **62**
Edenham Way W10 . . . . .4H **81**
Eden Ho. NW8 . . . . .4C **4**
    (off Church St.)
   SE8 . . . . .5C **104**
    (off Deptford High St.)
   SE16 . . . . .2K **103**
    (off Water Gdns. Sq.)
Edenhurst Av. SW6 . . . . .3H **117**

Eden Lodge NW6 . . . . .7F **63**
Eden M. SW17 . . . . .3A **136**
EDEN PARK .5C **158**
Eden Pk. Av. BR3: Beck 4A **158**
Eden Rd. BR3: Beck 4A **158**
   CRO: C'don 4D **168**
   DA5: Bexl 4J **145**
   E17 . . . . .5D **50**
   SE27 . . . . .4B **138**
Edensor Gdns. W4 . . . . .7A **98**
Edensor Rd. W4 . . . . .7A **98**
Eden St. KT1: King T 2D **150**
Edenvale Cl. CR4: Mitc 7E **136**
Edenvale Rd. CR4: Mitc 7E **136**
Edenvale St. SW6 . . . . .2A **118**
Eden Wlk. KT1: King T 2E **150**
Eden Way BR3: Beck 5B **158**
   E3 . . . . .1B **86**
Ederline Av. SW16 . . . . .3K **155**
Edgar Ct. KT3: N Mald 2A **152**
Edgar Ho. E9 .5A **68**
    (off Homerton Rd.)
   E11 . . . . .7J **51**
   SW8 . . . . .7J **101**
    (off Wyvil Rd.)
Edgar Kail Way SE22 . . . . .4E **120**
Edgarley Ter. SW6 . . . . .1G **117**
Edgar Myles Ho. E16 . . . . .5H **87**
    (off Ordnance Rd.)
Edgar Rd. E3 .3D **86**
   RM6: Chad H 7D **54**
   TW4: Houn 7D **112**
   UB7: Yiew .7A **74**
Edgar Wallace Cl. SE15 . . . . .7E **102**
Edgar Wright Ct. SW6 . . . . .7H **99**
    (off Dawes Rd.)
Edgcott Ho. W10 . . . . .5E **80**
    (off Sutton Way)
Edge, The SE8 . . . . .7B **104**
    (off Glenville Gro.)
Edge Apartments E15 . . . . .7F **69**
Edgeborough Way BR1: Brom 7B **142**
Edgebury BR7: Chst 4F **143**
Edgebury Wlk. BR7: Chst 4G **143**
Edge Bus. Centre, The NW2 . . . . .2D **62**
Edgecombe Ho. SE5 . . . . .2E **120**
   SW19 . . . . .1G **135**
Edgecombe CR2: Sels 7J **169**
Edgecombe Cl. KT2: King T 7K **133**
Edgecote Cl. W3 . . . . .1J **97**
Edgecot Gro. N15 . . . . .5E **48**
Edgefield Av. IG11: Bark 7K **71**
Edgefield Cl. BR3: Beck 6C **140**
Edgefield Ct. IG11: Bark 7K **71**
    (off Edgefield Av.)
Edge Hill SE18 . . . . .6F **107**
   SW19 . . . . .7F **135**
Edge Hill Av. N3 . . . . .4J **45**
Edge Hill Ct. DA14: Sidc 4K **143**
   SW19 . . . . .7F **135**
Edgehill Gdns. RM10: Dag 4G **73**
Edgehill Ho. SW9 . . . . .2B **120**
Edgehill Rd. BR7: Chst 3G **143**
   CR4: Mitc .1F **155**
   W13 . . . . .5C **78**
Edgeley La. SW4 . . . . .3H **119**
Edgeley Rd. SW4 . . . . .3H **119**
Edgel St. SW18 . . . . .4K **117**
Edge Point Cl. SE27 . . . . .5B **138**
Edge St. W8 . . . . .1J **99**
Edgewood Dr. BR6: Chels 5K **173**
Edgewood Grn. CRO: C'don 1K **169**
Edgeworth Av. NW4 . . . . .5C **44**
Edgeworth Cl. NW4 . . . . .5C **44**
Edgeworth Ct. EN4: Cockf 4H **21**
    (off Fordham Rd.)
Edgeworth Cres. NW4 . . . . .5C **44**
Edgeworth Ho. NW8 . . . . .1A **82**
    (off Boundary Rd.)
Edgeworth Rd. EN4: Cockf 4H **21**
   SE9 . . . . .4A **124**

Edgington Rd. SW16 . . . . .6H **137**
Edgington Way DA14: Sidc 7C **144**
Edgson Ho. SW1 . . . . .5J **17**
    (off Ebury Bri. Rd.)
EDGWARE 6B **28**
EDGWARE BURY 1A **28**
Edgwarebury Gdns.
   HA8: Edg 5B **28**
Edgwarebury La. HA8: Edg 1A **28**
    (not continuous)
   WD6: E'tree 1A **28**
Edgware Ct. HA8: Edg 6B **28**
Edgware Rd. NW2 . . . . .1D **62**
   NW9 . . . . .2J **43**
   W2 . . . . .4A **4** (4B **82**)
Edgware Way HA8: Edg 4A **28**
   NW7 . . . . .4A **28**
   WD6: E'tree 1J **27**
Edinburgh Cl. E2 . . . . .2J **85**
   HA5: Pinn .7B **40**
   UB10: Ick .4D **56**
Edinburgh Ct. DA8: Erith 7K **109**
   KT1: King T 3E **150**
    (off Watersplash Cl.)
   SE16 . . . . .1K **103**
    (off Rotherhithe St.)
   SW20 . . . . .5F **153**
Edinburgh Dr. UB10: Ick 4D **56**
Edinburgh Ga. SW1 . . . . . .7E **10** (2D **100**)
   NW4 . . . . .3E **44**
   W9 . . . . .3K **81**
    (off Maida Vale)
Edinburgh Rd. E13 . . . . .2K **87**
   E17 . . . . .5C **50**
   N18 . . . . .5B **34**
   SM1: Sutt .2A **166**
   W7 . . . . .2K **95**
Edington NW5 .6E **64**
Edington Rd. EN3: Enf H 2D **24**
   SE2 . . . . .3B **108**
Edison Bldg. E14 . . . . .2C **104**
Edison Cl. E17 .5C **50**
   UB7: W Dray 2B **92**
Edison Ct. CRO: C'don 7B **156**
    (off Campbell Rd.)
   SE10 . . . . .3H **105**
    (off Schoolbank Rd.)
   W3 . . . . .2A **98**
Edison Dr. HA9: Wemb 3E **60**
   UB1: S'hall 6F **77**
Edison Gro. SE18 . . . . .7K **107**
Edison Hgts. E1 . . . . .3K **9**
    (off Cygnet St.)
Edison Ho. HA9: Wemb 3J **61**
    (off Barnhill Rd.)
   SE1 . . . . .4D **102**
    (off New Kent Rd.)
Edison M. SW18 . . . . .6K **117**
Edison Rd. BR2: Brom 2J **159**
   DA16: Well 1K **125**
   EN3: Brim .2G **25**
   N8 . . . . .6H **47**
Edis St. NW1 .1E **82**
Editha Mans. SW10 . . . . .6A **100**
    (off Edith Gro.)
Edith Brinson Ho. E14 . . . . .6F **87**
    (off Oban St.)
Edith Cavell Cl. N19 . . . . .7J **47**
Edith Cavell Ho. E14 . . . . .6D **86**
    (off Sturry St.)
Edith Cavell Way SE18 . . . . .1C **124**
Edith Gdns. KT5: Surb 7H **151**
Edith Gro. SW10 . . . . .6A **100**
Edith Ho. W6 . . . . .5E **98**
    (off Queen Caroline St.)
Edithna St. SW9 . . . . .3J **119**
Edith Nesbit Wlk. SE9 . . . . .5D **124**
Edith Neville Cotts. NW1 . . . . .1C **6**
    (off Drummond Cres.)
Edith Ramsay Ho. E1 . . . . .5A **86**
    (off Duckett St.)

Edith Rd. E6 . . . . .7B **70**
   E15 . . . . .5F **69**
   N11 . . . . .7C **32**
   RM6: Chad H 7D **54**
   SE25 . . . . .5D **156**
   SW19 . . . . .6K **135**
   W14 . . . . .4G **99**
Edith Row SW6 . . . . .1K **117**
Edith St. E2 . . . . .2G **85**
Edith Summerskill Ho. SW6 . . . . .7H **99**
    (off Clem Attlee Ct.)
Edith Ter. SW10 . . . . .7A **100**
Edith Vs. W14 .4H **99**
Edith Yd. SW10 . . . . .7A **100**
Edmansons Cl. N17 . . . . .1F **49**
Edmeston Cl. E9 . . . . .6A **68**
Edmond Ct. SE14 . . . . .1J **121**
Edmonds Ct. KT8: W Mole 5F **149**
Edmonscote W13 . . . . .5A **78**
EDMONTON 3B **34**
Edmonton Cl. SE16 . . . . .3J **103**
    (off Canada Est.)
Edmonton Grn. Shop. Cen. N9 . . . . . .2B **34**
Edmonton Leisure Cen. 3B **34**
Edmund Gro. TW13: Hanw 2D **130**
Edmund Halley Way SE10 . . . . .2G **105**
Edmund Ho. SE17 . . . . .6B **102**
Edmund Hurst Dr. E6 . . . . .5F **89**
Edmund Rd. CR4: Mitc 3C **154**
   DA16: Well 3A **126**
Edmundsbury Ct. Est. SW9 . . . . .4K **119**
Edmunds Cl. UB4: Yead 5A **76**
Edmund St. SE5 . . . . .7D **102**
Edmunds Wlk. N2 . . . . .4C **46**
Ednam Ho. SE15 . . . . .6G **103**
    (off Haymerle Rd.)
Edna Rd. SW20 . . . . .2F **153**
Edna St. SW11 . . . . .1C **118**
Edred Ho. E9 . . . . .4A **68**
    (off Lindisfarne Way)
Edrich Ho. SW4 . . . . .1J **119**
Edric Ho. SW1 . . . . .3D **18**
    (off Page St.)
Edrick Rd. HA8: Edg 6D **28**
Edrick Wlk. HA8: Edg 6D **28**
Edric Rd. SE14 . . . . .7K **103**
Edridge Rd. CRO: C'don 3C **168**
Edward VII Mans. NW10 . . . . .3F **81**
    (off Chamberlayne Rd.)
Edward Alderton Theatre 3D **126**
Edward Av. E4 .6J **35**
   SM4: Mord 5B **154**
Edward Bond Ho. WC1 . . . . .2F **7**
    (off Cromer St.)
Edward Clifford Ho. SE17 . . . . .4D **102**
    (off Elsted St.)
Edward Cl. N9 .7A **24**
   NW2 . . . . .4F **63**
   TW12: Hamp H 5G **131**
Edward Ct. E16 . . . . .5J **87**
Edward Dodd Ct. N1 . . . . .1F **9**
    (off Chart St.)
Edward Edwards Ho. SE1 . . . . .5A **14**
Edwardes Pl. W8 . . . . .3H **99**
Edwardes Sq. W8 . . . . .3H **99**
Edward Gro. EN4: E Barn 5G **21**
Edward Heylin Ho. E15 . . . . .2D **86**
    (off Thomas Fyre Dr.)
Edward Heylyn Ho. E3 . . . . .2C **86**
    (off Thomas Fyre Dr.)
Edward Ho. SE11 . . . . .5H **19**
   W2 . . . . .4A **4**
    (off Hall Pl.)
   W14 . . . . .4H **99**
Edward Kennedy Ho. W10 . . . . .4G **81**
    (off Wornington Rd.)
Edward Mann Cl. E1 . . . . .6K **85**
    (off Pitsea St.)
Edward M. NW1 . . . . .1K **5** (3F **83**)
Edward Mills Way E14 . . . . .6C **86**
Edward Pl. SE8 . . . . .6B **104**

Edward Rd.—Elgin M. Sth.

Edward Rd.
BR1: Brom 7K **141**
BR7: Chst 5F **143**
CR0: C'don 7E **156**
E17 4K **49**
EN4: E Barn 5G **21**
HA2: Harr 3G **41**
RM6: Chad H 6E **54**
SE20 7K **139**
TW12: Hamp H 5G **131**
TW14: Felt 5F **111**
UB5: N'olt 2A **76**
Edward's Av. HA4: Ruis 6K **57**
Edwards Cl. KT4: Wor Pk 2F **165**
Edward's Cotts. N1 6B **66**
Edwards Ct. *CR0: C'don* *4E* ***168***
(off South Pk. Hill Rd.)
Edwards Dr. N11 7C **32**
Edward's La. N16 2E **66**
Edwards Mans. *IG11: Bark* *7K* ***71***
(off Upney La.)
Edwards M. N1 7B **66**
W1 1G **11** (6E **82**)
Edward Sq. N1 1K **83**
SE16 1A **104**
Edwards Rd. DA17: Belv 4G **109**
Edward St. E16 4J **87**
(not continuous)
SE8 6B **104**
SE14 7A **104**
Edwards Yd. HA0: Wemb 1E **78**
Edward Temme Av. E15 7H **69**
Edward Tyler Rd. SE12 2A **142**
Edward Way TW15: Ashf 2B **128**
Edwina Gdns. IG4: Ilf 5C **52**
Edwin Arnold Ct. DA14: Sidc 4K **143**
Edwin Av. E6 2E **88**
(not continuous)
Edwin Cl. DA7: Bex 6F **109**
Edwin Hall Pl. SE13 6F **123**
Edwin Ho. SE15 7G **103**
Edwin Pl. *CR0: C'don* *1E* ***168***
(off Leslie Gro.)
Edwin Rd. HA8: Edg 6E **28**
TW1: Twick 1K **131**
TW2: Twick 1J **131**
Edwin's Mead E9 4A **68**
Edwin Stray Ho. TW13: Hanw 2E **130**
Edwin St. E1 4J **85**
E16 5J **87**
Edwin Ware Ct. HA5: Pinn 2A **40**
Edwy Ho. *E9* *4B* ***68***
(off Homerton Rd.)
Edwyn Cl. EN5: Barn 6A **20**
Edwyn Ho. *SW18* *6K* ***117***
(off Neville Gill Cl.)
Eel Brook Cl. SW6 1K **117**
Eel Pie Island TW1: Twick 1A **132**
Effie Pl. SW6 7J **99**
Effie Rd. SW6 7J **99**
Effingham Cl. SM2: Sutt 7K **165**
Effingham Lodge KT1: King T 4D **150**
Effingham Rd. CR0: C'don 7K **155**
KT6: Surb 7B **150**
N8 5A **48**
SE12 5G **123**
Effort St. SW17 5C **136**
Effra Cl. SW19 6K **135**
Effra Ct. *SW2* *5K* ***119***
(off Brixton Hill)
Effra Pde. SW2 5A **120**
Effra Rd. SW2 4A **120**
SW19 6K **135**
Effra Rd. Retail Pk. SW2 5A **120**
Egan Way UB3: Hayes 7G **75**
Egbert Ho. *E9* *5A* ***68***
(off Homerton Rd.)
Egbert St. NW1 1E **82**
Egbury Ho. *SW15* *6B* ***116***
(off Tangley Gro.)
Egeremont Rd. SE13 2D **122**
Egerton Cl. HA5: Eastc 4J **39**
Egerton Ct. E11 7F **51**
Egerton Cres. SW3 3D **16** (4C **100**)
Egerton Dr. SE10 1D **122**
Egerton Gdns. IG3: Ilf 3K **71**
NW4 4D **44**
NW10 1E **80**
SW3 2C **16** (4C **100**)
W13 6B **78**
Egerton Gdns. M. SW3 2D **16** (3C **100**)
Egerton Pl. SW3 2D **16** (3C **100**)
Egerton Rd. HA0: Wemb 7F **61**
KT3: N Mald 4B **152**
N16 7F **49**
SE25 3E **156**
TW2: Twick 7J **113**
Egerton Ter. SW3 2D **16** (3C **100**)
Egerton Way UB3: Harl 7D **92**
Eggardon Ct. UB5: N'olt 6F **59**
Egham Cl. SM3: Cheam 2G **165**
SW19 2G **135**
Egham Cres. SM3: Cheam 3G **165**
Egham Rd. E13 5K **87**
Eglantine Rd. SW18 5A **118**
Egleston Rd. SM4: Mord 6K **153**
Egleton Ho. SW15 7C **116**
Eglington Ct. SE17 6C **102**
Eglington Rd. E4 7K **25**
Eglinton Hill SE18 6F **107**
Eglinton Rd. SE18 6E **106**
Egliston M. SW15 3E **116**
Egliston Rd. SW15 3E **116**
Eglon M. NW1 7D **64**
Egmont Av. KT6: Surb 1F **163**
Egmont Ct. *KT12: Walt T* *7K* ***147***
(off Egmont Rd.)
Egmont M. KT19: Ewe 4K **163**
Egmont Rd. KT3: N Mald 4B **152**
KT6: Surb 1F **163**
KT12: Walt T 7K **147**
SM2: Sutt 7A **166**
Egmont St. SE14 7K **103**
Egremont Ho. *E20* *5E* ***68***
(off Medals Way)
SE13 *2D* ***122***
(off Russett Way)
Egremont Rd. SE27 3A **138**
Egret Ho. *SE16* *4K* ***103***
(off Tawny Way)
Egret Way UB4: Yead 5B **76**
Eider Cl. E7 5H **69**
UB4: Yead 5B **76**
Eider Ct. *SE8* *6B* ***104***
(off Pilot Cl.)
Eighteenth Rd. CR4: Mitc 4J **155**
Eighth Av. E12 4D **70**
UB3: Hayes 1J **93**
Eileen Rd. SE25 5D **156**
Eindhoven Cl. SM5: Cars 1E **166**
Einstein Ho. HA9: Wemb 3J **61**
Eisenhower Dr. E6 5C **88**
Ekarro Ho. *SW8* *1J* ***119***
(off Guildford Rd.)
Elaine Gro. NW5 5E **64**
Elam Cl. SE5 2B **120**
Elam St. SE5 2B **120**
Elan Ct. E1 5H **85**
Eland Pl. CR0: Wadd 3B **168**
Eland Rd. CR0: Wadd 3B **168**
SW11 3D **118**
Elba Pl. SE17 4C **102**
Elberon Av. CR0: Bedd 6G **155**
Elbe St. SW6 2A **118**
Elborough Rd. SE25 5G **157**
Elborough St. SW18 1J **135**
Elbourne Ct. *SE16* *3K* ***103***
(off Worgan St.)
Elbourne Trad. Est. DA17: Belv 3H **109**
Elbourn Ho. *SW3* *5C* ***16***
(off Cale St.)
Elbow Mdw. SL3: Poyle 4A **174**
Elbury Dr. E16 6J **87**
Elcho St. SW11 7C **100**
Elcot Av. SE15 7H **103**
Elden Ho. *SW3* *3C* ***16***
(off Sloane Av.)
Eldenwall Ind. Est. RM8: Dag 1E **72**
Elder Av. N8 5J **47**
Elderberry Gro. SE27 4C **138**
Elderberry Rd. W5 2E **96**
Elderberry Way E6 3D **88**
Elder Cl. DA15: Sidc 1K **143**
N20 2E **30**
UB7: Yiew 7A **74**
Elder Ct. WD23: B Hea 2D **26**
Elderfield Ho. *E14* *7C* ***86***
(off Pennyfields)
Elderfield Pl. SW17 4F **137**
Elderfield Rd. E5 4K **67**
Elderfield Wlk. E11 5K **51**
Elderflower Way E15 7G **69**
Elder Gdns. SE27 5C **138**
Elder Ho. *E15* *3G* ***87***
(off Manor Rd.)
KT1: King T *1D* ***150***
(off Water La.)
Elder Oak Cl. SE20 1H **157**
Elder Oak Ct. *SE20* *1H* ***157***
(off Anerley Rd.)
Elder Pl. CR2: S Croy 6B **168**
Elder Rd. SE27 5C **138**
Elderslie Cl. BR3: Beck 5C **158**
Elderslie Rd. SE9 5E **124**
Elder St. E1 5J **9** (4F **85**)
(not continuous)
Elderton Rd. SE26 4A **140**
Eldertree Pl. CR4: Mitc 1G **155**
Eldertree Way
CR4: Mitc 1G **155**
Elder Wlk. *N1* *1B* ***84***
(off Popham St.)
SE13 3E **122**
Elderwood Pl. SE27 5C **138**
Eldon Av. CR0: C'don 2J **169**
TW5: Hest 7E **94**
Eldon Ct. NW6 1J **81**
Eldon Gro. NW3 5B **64**
Eldon Ho. *NW9* *3C* ***44***
(off East Dr.)
Eldon Pk. SE25 4H **157**
Eldon Rd. E17 4B **50**
N9 1D **34**
N22 1B **48**
W8 3K **99**
Eldons Pas. *E1* *7G* ***85***
(off Cable St.)
Eldon St. EC2 6F **9** (5D **84**)
Eldon Way NW10 3H **79**
Eldred Rd. IG11: Bark 1J **89**
Eldrick Ct. TW14: Bedf 1F **129**
Eldridge Cl. TW14: Felt 1J **129**
Eldridge Ct. RM10: Dag 6H **73**
SE16 3G **103**
Eleanor Cl. N15 3F **49**
SE16 2K **103**
Eleanor Ct. *E2* *1G* ***85***
(off Whiston Rd.)
Eleanor Cres. NW7 5A **30**
Eleanor Gdns. EN5: Barn 5A **20**
RM8: Dag 2F **73**
Eleanor Gro. SW13 3A **116**
UB10: Ick 3D **56**
Eleanor Ho. *W6* *5E* ***98***
(off Queen Caroline St.)
Eleanor Rathbone Ho. *N6* *7H* ***47***
(off Avenue Rd.)
Eleanor Rd. E8 6H **67**
E15 6H **69**
N11 6D **32**
SW9 1A **120**
Eleanor St. E3 3C **86**
Eleanor Wlk. SE18 4C **106**
Electra Av. TW6: H'row A 3H **111**
Electra Bus. Pk. E16 5F **87**
Electric Av. SW9 4A **120**
Electric Cinema 6H **81**
Electric Empire, The *SE14* *1K* ***121***
(off New Cross Rd.)
Electric Ho. *E3* *3C* ***86***
(off Bow Rd.)
Electric La. SW9 4A **120**
(not continuous)
Electric Pde. *E18* *2J* ***51***
(off George La.)
IG3: Ilf 2J **71**
KT6: Surb 6D **150**
Elektron Twr. E14 7F **87**
Eleonora Ter. *SM1: Sutt* *5A* ***166***
(off Lind Rd.)
ELEPHANT & CASTLE **3B 102**
Elephant & Castle SE1 4B **102**
Elephant & Castle Leisure Cen. 4B **102**
Elephant & Castle Shop. Cen.
SE1 4C **102**
Elephant La. SE16 2J **103**
Elephant Rd. SE17 4C **102**
Elers Rd. UB3: Harl 4F **93**
W13 2C **96**
Eley Rd. N18 4E **34**
Eley Rd. Retail Pk. N18 5D **34**
Eleys Est. N18 3E **34**
(not continuous)
Elfindale Rd. SE24 5C **120**
Elfin Gro. TW11: Tedd 5K **131**
Elfin Oak 1K **99**
Elford Cl. SE3 4A **124**
Elford M. SW4 5G **119**
Elfort Rd. N5 4A **66**
Elfrida Cl. IG8: Wfd G 7D **36**
Elfrida Cres. SE6 4C **140**
Elf Row E1 7J **85**
Elfwine Rd. W7 5J **77**
Elgal Cl. BR6: Farnb 5F **173**
Elgar *N8* *3J* ***47***
(off Boyton Cl.)
Elgar Av. KT5: Surb 1G **163**
NW10 6K **61**
(not continuous)
SW16 3J **155**
W5 2E **96**
Elgar Cl. E13 2A **88**
IG9: Buck H 2G **37**
SE8 7C **104**
UB10: Ick 2C **56**
Elgar Ct. NW6 3J **81**
W14 *3G* ***99***
(off Blythe Rd.)
Elgar Ho. *NW6* *7A* ***64***
(off Fairfax Rd.)
SW1 *6K* ***17***
(off Churchill Gdns.)
Elgar St. SE16 3A **104**
Elgin Av. HA3: Kenton 2B **42**
TW15: Ashf 6E **128**
W9 4H **81**
W12 2C **98**
Elgin Cl. W12 2D **98**
Elgin Ct. *CR2: S Croy* *4C* ***168***
(off Bramley Hill)
W9 4K **81**
Elgin Cres. TW6: H'row A 2G **111**
W11 7G **81**
Elgin Dr. HA6: Nwood 1G **39**
Elgin Est. *W9* *4J* ***81***
(off Elgin Av.)
Elgin Ho. *E14* *6D* ***86***
(off Ricardo St.)
RM6: Chad H *6F* ***55***
(off High Rd.)
Elgin Mans. W9 3K **81**
Elgin M. W11 6G **81**
Elgin M. Nth. W9 3K **81**
Elgin M. Sth. W9 3K **81**

Elgin Rd. CR0: C'don 2F 169
  IG3: Ilf 1J 71
  N22 .....2G 47
  SM1: Sutt 3A 166
  SM6: Wall 6G 167
Elgood Cl. W11 .....7G 81
Elgood Ho. NW8 .....2B 82
  (off Wellington Rd.)
  SE1 .....7E 14
  (off Tabard St.)
Elham Cl. BR1: Brom 7B 142
Elham Ho. E5 .....5H 67
Elia M. N1 .....1A 8 (2B 84)
Elia Pl. SW8 .....6A 102
Elia St. N1 .....1B 8 (2B 84)
Elibank Rd. SE9 .....4D 124
Elim Est. SE1 .....7G 15 (3E 102)
Elim St. SE1 .....7G 15 (3D 102)
  (not continuous)
Elim Way E13 .....3H 87
Eliot Bank SE23 .....2H 139
Eliot Cotts. SE3 .....2G 123
Eliot Ct. SW18 .....6K 117
Eliot Dr. HA2: Harr 2F 59
Eliot Gdns. SW15 .....4C 116
Eliot Hill SE13 .....2E 122
Eliot M. NW8 .....2A 82
Eliot Pk. SE13 .....2E 122
Eliot Pl. SE3 .....2G 123
Eliot Rd. RM9: Dag 4D 72
Eliot Va. SE3 .....2F 123
Elis David Almshouses CR0: C'don 3B 168
Elis Way E20 .....5E 68
Elizabethan Cl. TW19: Stanw 7A 110
Elizabethan Way TW19: Stanw 7A 110
Elizabeth Av. EN2: Enf 3G 23
  IG1: Ilf 2H 71
  N1 .....1C 84
  TW18: Staines 7A 128
Elizabeth Barnes Ct. SW6 .....2K 117
  (off Marinefield Rd.)
Elizabeth Blackwell Ho. N22 .....1A 48
  (off Progress Way)
Elizabeth Blount Ct. E14 .....6A 86
  (off Carr St.)
Elizabeth Bri. SW1 .....4J 17 (4F 101)
Elizabeth Cl. E14 .....6D 86
  EN5: Barn 3A 20
  RM7: Mawney 1H 55
  SM1: Sutt 4H 165
  W9 .....4A 82
Elizabeth Clyde Cl. N15 .....4E 48
Elizabeth Cotts.
  TW9: Kew 1F 115
Elizabeth Ct. BR1: Brom 1H 159
  (off Highland Rd.)
  CR0: C'don 3E 168
  (off The Avenue)
  E4 .....5G 35
  E10 .....7D 50
  IG8: Wfd G 7F 37
  KT2: King T 1E 150
  NW1 .....3D 4
  SW1 .....2D 18
  SW10 .....6B 100
  (off Milman's St.)
  TW11: Tedd 5J 131
  TW16: Sun 7H 129
  (off Elizabeth Gdns.)
Elizabeth Croll Ho. WC1 .....1H 7
  (off Penton Ri.)
Elizabeth Fry Apartments
  IG11: Bark 7G 71
  (off Kings Rd.)
Elizabeth Fry Ho. UB3: Harl 4H 93
Elizabeth Fry M. E8 .....7H 67
Elizabeth Fry Pl. SE18 .....1C 124
Elizabeth Gdns. HA7: Stan 6H 27
  TW7: Isle 4A 114
  TW16: Sun 3A 148
  W3 .....1B 98

Elizabeth Garrett Anderson Ho.
  DA17: Belv 3G 109
  (off Ambrooke Rd.)
Elizabeth Ho. E3 .....3D 86
  (off St Leonard's St.)
  SE11 .....4K 19
  (off Reedworth St.)
  SM3: Cheam 6G 165
  (off Park La.)
  W6 .....5E 98
  (off Queen Caroline St.)
Elizabeth Ind. Est. SE14 .....6K 103
Elizabeth M. E2 .....2G 85
  (off Kay St.)
  HA1: Harr 6J 41
  NW3 .....6C 64
Elizabeth Newcomen Ho. SE1 .....6E 14
  (off Newcomen St.)
Elizabeth Pl. N15 .....4D 48
Elizabeth Ride N9 .....7C 24
Elizabeth Rd. E6 .....1B 88
  N15 .....5E 48
Elizabeth Sq. SE16 .....7A 86
  (off Sovereign Cres.)
Elizabeth St. SW1 .....3H 17 (4E 100)
Elizabeth Ter. SE9 .....6D 124
Elizabeth Way SE19 .....7D 138
  TW13: Hanw 4A 130
Elkanette M. N20 .....2F 31
Elkington Point SE11 .....4J 19
Elkington Rd. E13 .....4K 87
Ekstone Rd. W10 .....5H 81
Ella Cl. BR3: Beck 2C 158
Ellacott M. SW16 .....2H 137
Ellaline Rd. W6 .....6F 99
Ella M. NW3 .....4D 64
Ellanby Cres. N18 .....4C 34
Elland Cl. EN5: New Bar 5G 21
Elland Ho. E14 .....6B 86
  (off Copenhagen Pl.)
Elland Rd. SE15 .....4J 121
Ella Rd. N8 .....7J 47
Ellement Cl. HA5: Pinn 5B 40
Elena Ct. N14 .....3D 32
  (off Conway Rd.)
Ellenborough Ho. W12 .....7D 80
  (off White City Est.)
Ellenborough Pl. SW15 .....4C 116
Ellenborough Rd. DA14: Sidc 5D 144
  N22 .....1C 48
Ellenbridge Way CR2: Sande 7E 168
Ellen Cl. BR1: Brom 3B 160
Ellen Ct. E4 .....1K 35
  (off The Ridgeway)
  N9 .....2D 34
Ellen Julia Ct. E1 .....6J 85
  (off James Voller Way)
Ellen St. E1 .....6G 85
Ellen Terry Ct. NW1 .....7F 65
  (off Farrier St.)
Ellen Webb Dr. HA3: W'stone 3J 41
Ellen Wilkinson Ho. E2 .....3K 85
  (off Usk St.)
  RM10: Dag 3G 73
  SW6 .....6H 99
  (off Clem Attlee Ct.)
Elleray Rd. TW11: Tedd 6K 131
Ellerby St. SW6 .....1F 117
Ellerdale Cl. NW3 .....4A 64
Ellerdale Rd. NW3 .....5A 64
Ellerdale St. SE13 .....4D 122
Ellerdine Rd. TW3: Houn 4G 113
Ellerker Gdns. TW10: Rich 6E 114
Ellerman Av. TW2: Whitt 1D 130
Ellerslie Gdns. NW10 .....1C 80
Ellerslie Rd. W12 .....1D 98
Ellerslie Sq. Ind. Est. SW2 .....5J 119
Ellerton Gdns. RM9: Dag 7C 72
Ellerton Lodge N3 .....2J 45
Ellerton Rd. KT6: Surb 2F 163
  RM9: Dag 7C 72

Ellerton Rd. SW13 .....1C 116
  SW18 .....1B 136
  SW20 .....7C 134
Ellery Ho. SE17 .....4D 102
Ellery Rd. SE19 .....7D 138
Ellery St. SE15 .....2H 121
Ellesmere Av. BR3: Beck 2E 158
  NW7 .....3E 28
Ellesmere Cl. E11 .....5H 51
  HA4: Ruis 7E 38
Ellesmere Ct. SE12 .....1J 141
  W4 .....5K 97
Ellesmere Gdns. IG4: Ilf 5C 52
Ellesmere Gro. EN5: Barn 5C 20
Ellesmere Ho. SW10 .....6A 100
  (off Fulham Rd.)
Ellesmere Mans. NW6 .....6A 64
  (off Canfield Gdns.)
Ellesmere Rd. E3 .....2A 86
  NW10 .....5C 62
  TW1: Twick 6C 114
  UB6: G'frd 4G 77
  W4 .....6K 97
Ellesmere St. E14 .....6D 86
Ellies M. TW15: Ashf 2A 128
Ellingfort Rd. E8 .....7H 67
Ellingham Rd. E15 .....4F 69
  KT9: Chess 6D 162
  W12 .....2C 98
Ellington Cl. N14 .....2C 32
Ellington Ho. SE1 .....3C 102
  SE18 .....7E 106
Ellington Rd. N10 .....4F 47
  TW3: Houn 2F 113
  TW13: Felt 4H 129
Ellington St. N7 .....6A 66
Elliot Cl. E15 .....7G 69
Elliot Ct. IG8: Wfd G 6G 37
Elliot Ho. SW17 .....3B 136
  (off Grosvenor Way)
  W1 .....6D 4
  (off Cato St.)
Elliot Rd. NW4 .....6D 44
Elliott Av. HA4: Ruis 2K 57
Elliott Cl. HA9: Wemb 3F 61
Elliott Gdns. TW17: Shep 4C 146
Elliott Rd. BR2: Brom 4B 160
  CR7: Thor H 4B 156
  HA7: Stan 6F 27
  SW9 .....1B 120
  W4 .....4A 98
Elliott Sq. NW3 .....7C 64
Elliotts Row SE11 .....4B 102
Ellis Cl. HA4: Eastc 6J 39
  HA8: Edg 6F 29
  NW10 .....6D 62
  SE9 .....2G 143
Elliscombe Mt. SE7 .....6A 106
Elliscombe Rd. SE7 .....6A 106
Ellis Ct. E1 .....6J 85
  (off James Voller Way)
  W7 .....5K 77
Ellisfield Dr. SW15 .....7C 116
Ellis Franklin Ct. NW8 .....2A 82
  (off Abbey Rd.)
Ellis Ho. SE17 .....5D 102
  (off Brandon St.)
Ellison Gdns. UB2: S'hall 4D 94
Ellison Ho. SE13 .....2D 122
  (off Lewisham Rd.)
Ellison Rd. DA15: Sidc 1H 143
  SW13 .....2B 116
  SW16 .....7H 137
Ellis Rd. CR4: Mitc 6D 154
  UB2: S'hall 1G 95
Ellis St. SW1 .....3F 17 (4E 100)
Elliston Ho. SE18 .....4E 106
  (off Wellington St.)

Ellora Rd. SW16 .....5H 137
Ellsworth Cl. KT6: Surb 7D 150
Ellsworth St. E2 .....3H 85
Ellwood Ct. W9 .....4K 81
  (off Clearwell Dr.)
Elmar Rd. N15 .....4D 48
Elm Av. HA4: Ruis 1J 57
  TW19: Stanw 2A 128
  W5 .....1E 96
Elmbank N14 .....7D 22
Elmbank Av. EN5: Barn 4A 20
Elm Bank Dr. BR1: Brom 2B 160
Elm Bank Gdns. SW13 .....2A 116
Elmbank Way W7 .....5H 77
Elmbourne Dr. DA17: Belv 4H 109
Elmbourne Rd. SW17 .....3F 137
Elmbridge Av. KT5: Surb 5H 151
Elmbridge Cl. HA4: Ruis 6J 39
Elmbridge Dr. HA4: Ruis 5H 39
Elmbridge Wlk. E8 .....7G 67
Elmbridge Xcel Leisure Complex 5K 147
Elmbrook Cl. TW16: Sun 1K 147
Elmbrook Gdns. SE9 .....4C 124
Elmbrook Rd. SM1: Sutt 4H 165
Elm Cl. CR2: S Croy 6E 168
  E11 .....6K 51
  HA2: Harr 6F 41
  IG9: Buck H 2G 37
  KT5: Surb 7J 151
  N19 .....2G 65
  NW4 .....5F 45
  RM7: Mawney 1H 55
  SM5: Cars 1D 166
  SW20 .....4E 152
  TW2: Twick 2F 131
  UB3: Hayes 6J 75
Elmcote HA5: Pinn 2B 40
Elm Cotts. CR4: Mitc 2D 154
Elm Ct.
  CR4: Mitc 2D 154
  EC4 .....1J 13
  E Barn 7H 21
  KT8: W Mole 4F 149
  SE1 .....7G 15
  (off Royal Oak Yd.)
  SE13 .....3F 123
  SW9 .....1A 120
  (off Cranworth Gdns.)
  TW16: Sun 7H 129
  (off Grangewood Dr.)
  W9 .....5J 81
  (off Admiral Wlk.)
Elm Cres. KT2: King T 1E 150
  W5 .....1E 96
Elmcroft N6 .....7G 47
  N8 .....5K 47
Elmcroft Av. DA15: Sidc 7K 125
  E11 .....5K 51
  N9 .....6C 24
  NW11 .....7H 45
Elmcroft Cl. E11 .....4K 51
  KT9: Chess 3E 162
  TW14: Felt 6H 111
  W5 .....6D 78
Elmcroft Cres. HA2: Harr 3E 40
  NW11 .....7G 45
Elmcroft Dr. KT9: Chess 3E 162
  TW15: Ashf 5C 128
Elmcroft Gdns. NW9 .....4G 43
Elmcroft St. E5 .....4J 67
Elmcroft Ter. UB8: Hil 6C 74
Elmdale Rd. N13 .....5E 32
Elmdene KT5: Surb 1J 163
Elmdene Cl. BR3: Beck 6B 158
Elmdene Rd. SE18 .....5F 107
Elmdon Rd. TW4: Houn 2B 112
  TW6: H'row A 3H 111
  TW16: Sun 2A 148
Elmer Cl. EN2: Enf 3E 22

Elmer Gdns. HA8: Edg 7C **28**
   TW7: Isle 3H **113**
Elmer Ho. NW8 ....*5C **4***
   (off Penfold St.)
Elmer Rd. SE6 ....7E **122**
Elmers Dr. TW11: Tedd 6B **132**
ELMERS END 4A **158**
Elmers End Rd. BR3: Beck 2J **157**
   SE20 ....2J **157**
Elmerside Rd. BR3: Beck 4A **158**
Elmers Lodge BR3: Beck 4K **157**
Elmers Rd. SE25 ....7G **157**
Elmfield HA1: Harr 7K **41**
Elmfield Av. CR4: Mitc 1E **154**
   N8 ....5J **47**
   TW11: Tedd 5K **131**
Elmfield Cl. HA1: Harr 2J **59**
Elmfield Ct. DA16: Well 1B **126**
Elmfield Ho. N2 ....*2B **46***
   (off The Grange)
   NW8 ....*2K **81***
   (off Carlton Hill)
   W9 ....*4J **81***
   (off Goldney Rd.)
Elmfield Pk. BR1: Brom 3J **159**
Elmfield Rd. BR1: Brom 2J **159**
   E4 ....2K **35**
   E17 ....6C **50**
   N2 ....3B **46**
   SW17 ....2E **136**
   UB2: S'hall 3C **94**
Elmfield Way CR2: Sande 7F **169**
   W9 ....5J **81**
Elm Friars Wlk. NW1 ....7H **65**
Elm Gdns. CR4: Mitc 4H **155**
   KT10: Clay 6A **162**
   N2 ....3A **46**
Elmgate Av. TW13: Felt 3K **129**
Elmgate Gdns. HA8: Edg 5D **28**
Elm Grn. W3 ....6A **80**
Elmgreen Cl. E15 ....1G **87**
Elm Gro. BR6: Orp 1K **173**
   DA8: Erith 7K **109**
   HA2: Harr 7E **40**
   IG8: Wfd G 5C **36**
   KT2: King T 1E **150**
   N8 ....6J **47**
   NW2 ....4F **63**
   SE15 ....2F **121**
   SM1: Sutt 4K **165**
   SW19 ....7G **135**
   UB7: Yiew 7B **74**
Elmgrove Cres. HA1: Harr 5K **41**
Elmgrove Gdns. HA1: Harr 5A **42**
Elm Gro. Pde. SM6: Wall 3E **166**
Elmgrove Point SE18 ....4H **107**
Elm Gro. Rd. SW13 ....1C **116**
   W5 ....2E **96**
Elmgrove Rd. CR0: C'don 7H **157**
   HA1: Harr 5K **41**
   HA3: W'stone 5A **42**
Elm Hall Gdns. E11 ....5K **51**
   (not continuous)
Elm Ho. E3 ....*1B **86***
   (off Sycamore Av.)
   E14 ....*2E **104***
   (off E. Ferry Rd.)
   KT2: King T *7F **133***
   (off Elm Rd.)
   W10 ....*4G **81***
   (off Briar Wlk.)
Elmhurst DA17: Belv 6E **108**
Elmhurst Av. CR4: Mitc 7F **137**
   N2 ....3B **46**
Elmhurst Cl. CR0: C'don 4D **168**
Elmhurst Dr. E18 ....2J **51**
Elmhurst Lodge SM2: Sutt 7A **166**
Elmhurst Mans. SW4 ....3H **119**
Elmhurst Rd. E7 ....7K **69**
   N17 ....2F **49**
   SE9 ....2C **142**

Elmhurst St. SW4 ....3H **119**
Elmington Cl. DA5: Bexl 6H **127**
Elmington Est. SE5 ....7D **102**
Elmington Rd. SE5 ....7D **102**
Elmira St. SE13 ....3D **122**
Elm La. SE6 ....2B **140**
Elm Lawn Cl. UB8: Uxb 7A **56**
Elmlea Dr. UB3: Hayes 5G **75**
Elm Lea Trad. Est. N17 ....6C **34**
Elmlee Cl. BR7: Chst 6D **142**
Elmley Cl. E6 ....5C **88**
Elmley St. SE18 ....5H **107**
   (not continuous)
Elm Lodge SW6 ....1E **116**
Elmore Cl. HA0: Wemb 2E **78**
Elmore Ho. N1 ....*7D **66***
   (off Elmore St.)
   SW9 ....2B **120**
Elmore Rd. E11 ....3E **68**
   EN3: Enf W 1E **24**
Elmore St. N1 ....7C **66**
Elm Pde. DA14: Sidc 4A **144**
Elm Pk. HA7: Stan 5G **27**
   SW2 ....6K **119**
Elm Pk. Av. N15 ....5F **49**
Elm Pk. Chambers SW10 ....*6A **16***
   (off Fulham Rd.)
Elm Pk. Cl. HA5: Pinn 2A **40**
Elm Pk. Gdns. NW4 ....5F **45**
   SW10 ....6A **16** (5B **100**)
Elm Pk. Ho. SW10 ....6A **16** (5B **100**)
Elm Pk. La. SW3 ....6A **16** (5B **100**)
Elm Pk. Mans.
   SW10 ....7A **16** (6A **100**)
Elm Pk. Rd. E10 ....1A **68**
   HA5: Pinn 2A **40**
   N3 ....7C **30**
   N21 ....7H **23**
   SE25 ....3F **157**
   SW3 ....7A **16** (6B **100**)
Elm Pas. EN5: Barn 4C **20**
Elm Pl. SW7 ....5A **16** (5B **100**)
   TW15: Ashf 5C **128**
Elm Quay Ct. SW8 ....7C **18** (6H **101**)
Elm Rd. BR3: Beck 2B **158**
   BR6: Chels 7K **173**
   CR7: Thor H 4D **156**
   DA14: Sidc 4A **144**
   E7 ....6H **69**
   E11 ....2F **69**
   E17 ....5E **50**
   EN5: Barn 4C **20**
   HA9: Wemb 5E **60**
   KT2: King T 1F **151**
   KT3: N Mald 2K **151**
   KT9: Chess 4E **162**
   KT17: Ewe 6B **164**
   N22 ....1B **48**
   RM7: Mawney 2H **55**
   SM6: Wall 1E **166**
   SW14 ....3J **115**
   TW14: Bedf 1F **129**
Elm Rd. W. SM3: Sutt 7H **153**
Elm Row NW3 ....3A **64**
Elms, The CR0: C'don *1C **168***
   (off Tavistock Rd.)
   E12 ....6B **70**
   KT10: Clay 7A **162**
   SW13 ....3B **116**
   TW15: Ashf 5C **128**
Elms Av. N10 ....3F **47**
   NW4 ....5F **45**
Elmscott Gdns. N21 ....6H **23**
Elmscott Rd. BR1: Brom 5G **141**
Elms Ct. HA0: Wemb 4A **60**
Elms Cres. SW4 ....6G **119**
Elmsdale Rd. E17 ....4B **50**
Elms Gdns. HA0: Wemb 4A **60**
   RM9: Dag 4F **73**
Elmshaw Rd. SW15 ....5C **116**
Elmshurst Cres. N2 ....4B **46**

Elmside CR0: New Ad 6D **170**
Elmside Rd. HA9: Wemb 3G **61**
Elmslie Cl. IG8: Wfd G 6J **37**
Elmslie Point E3 ....*5B **86***
   (off Leopold St.)
Elms M. W2 ....2A **10** (7B **82**)
Elms Pk. Av. HA0: Wemb 4A **60**
Elms Rd. HA3: Hrw W 7C **26**
   SW4 ....5G **119**
ELMSTEAD 6D **142**
Elmstead Av. BR7: Chst 5D **142**
   HA9: Wemb 1E **60**
Elmstead Cl. SM1: Sutt 3K **165**
Elmstead Gdns. KT19: Ewe 5A **164**
   N20 ....2D **30**
Elmstead Glade BR7: Chst 6D **142**
Elmstead La. BR7: Chst 7C **142**
Elmstead Rd. DA8: Erith 1K **127**
   IG3: IIf 2J **71**
Elmsted Cres. DA16: Well 6C **108**
Elmstone Rd. SW6 ....1J **117**
Elm St. WC1 ....4H **7** (4K **83**)
Elmsway TW15: Ashf 5C **128**
Elmsworth Av. TW3: Houn 2F **113**
Elm Ter. HA3: Hrw W 1H **41**
   NW2 ....3J **63**
   NW3 ....4C **64**
   SE9 ....6E **124**
Elmton Ct. NW8 ....*3A **4***
   (off Cunningham Pl.)
Elm Tree Av. KT10: Esh 7H **149**
Elm Tree Cl. NW8 ....1A **4** (3B **82**)
   TW15: Ashf 5D **128**
   UB5: N'olt 2D **76**
Elm Tree Ct. NW8 ....1A **4**
   SE7 ....6A **106**
Elm Tree Rd. NW8 ....1A **4** (3B **82**)
Elmtree Rd. TW11: Tedd 4J **131**
Elm Vw. Ct. UB2: S'hall 4E **94**
Elm Vw. Ho. UB3: Harl 4F **93**
Elm Wlk. BR6: Farnb 3D **172**
   NW3 ....2J **63**
   SW20 ....4E **152**
Elm Way KT4: Wor Pk 3E **164**
   KT19: Ewe 5K **163**
   N11 ....6K **31**
   NW10 ....4A **62**
Elmwood Av. HA3: Kenton 5A **42**
   N13 ....5D **32**
   TW13: Felt, Hanw 2J **129**
Elmwood Cl. KT17: Ewe 7C **164**
   SM6: Wall 2F **167**
Elmwood Ct. E10 ....*1C **68***
   (off Goldsmith Rd.)
   HA0: Wemb 3D **60**
   SW11 ....1F **119**
Elmwood Cres. NW9 ....4J **43**
Elmwood Dr. DA5: Bexl 7E **126**
   KT17: Ewe 6C **164**
Elmwood Gdns. W7 ....6J **77**
Elmwood Ho. NW10 ....*2D **80***
   (off All Souls Av.)
Elmwood Rd. CR0: C'don 7B **156**
   CR4: Mitc 3D **154**
   SE24 ....5D **120**
   W4 ....6J **97**
Elmworth Gro. SE21 ....2D **138**
Elnathan M. W9 ....4K **81**
Elphinstone Ct. SW16 ....6J **137**
Elphinstone Rd. E17 ....2B **50**
Elphinstone St. N5 ....4B **66**
Elrington Rd. E8 ....6G **67**
   IG8: Wfd G 5D **36**
Elsa Cotts. E14 ....*5A **86***
   (off Halley St.)

Elsa Ct. BR3: Beck 1B **158**
Elsa Rd. DA16: Well 2B **126**
Elsa St. E1 ....5J **85**
   E14 ....5J **85**
Elsdale St. E9 ....6J **67**
Elsden M. E2 ....2J **85**
Elsden Rd. N17 ....1F **49**
Elsenham Rd. E12 ....5E **70**
Elsenham St. SW18 ....1H **135**
Elsham Rd. E11 ....3G **69**
   W14 ....2G **99**
Elsham Ter. W14 ....*3G **99***
   (off Elsham Rd.)
Elsiedene Rd. N21 ....7H **23**
Elsie La. Ct. W2 ....*5J **81***
   (off Westbourne Pk. Vs.)
Elsiemaud Rd. SE4 ....5B **122**
Elsie Rd. SE22 ....4F **121**
Elsinore Av. TW19: Stanw 7A **110**
Elsinore Gdns. NW2 ....3G **63**
Elsinore Ho. N1 ....*1A **84***
   (off Denmark Gro.)
   SE5 ....*2C **120***
   (off Denmark Rd.)
   SE7 ....4C **106**
   W6 ....*5F **99***
   (off Fulham Pal. Rd.)
Elsinore Rd. SE23 ....1A **140**
Elsinore Way TW9: Rich 3H **115**
Elsley Ct. HA9: Wemb 6H **61**
Elsley Rd. SW11 ....3D **118**
Elspeth Rd. HA0: Wemb 5E **60**
   SW11 ....4D **118**
Elsrick Av. SM4: Mord 5J **153**
Elstan Way CR0: C'don 7A **158**
Elstar Ct. RM13: Rain *2K **91***
   (off Lowen Rd.)
Elstead Ct. SM3: Sutt 1G **165**
Elstead Ho. SW2 ....*7K **119***
   (off Redlands Way)
Elsted St. SE17 ....4D **102**
Elstow Cl. HA4: Ruis 7B **40**
   SE9 ....5D **124**
   (not continuous)
Elstow Gdns. RM9: Dag 1E **90**
Elstow Grange NW6 ....7F **63**
Elstow Rd. RM9: Dag 1E **90**
Elstree Gdns. DA17: Belv 4E **108**
   IG1: IIf 5G **71**
   N9 ....1C **34**
Elstree Hill BR1: Brom 7G **141**
Elstree Hill Sth. WD6: E'tree 1H **27**
Elstree Rd. WD23: B Hea 1C **26**
Elswick Rd. SE13 ....2D **122**
Elswick St. SW6 ....2A **118**
Elsworth Cl. TW14: Bedf 1G **129**
Elsworthy KT7: T Ditt 6J **149**
Elsworthy Ct. NW3 ....*7D **64***
   (off Primrose Hill Rd.)
Elsworthy Ri. NW3 ....7C **64**
Elsworthy Rd. NW3 ....1C **82**
Elsworthy Ter. NW3 ....7C **64**
Elsynge Rd. SW18 ....5B **118**
ELTHAM 6D **124**
Eltham Cen. 5E **124**
Eltham Crematorium SE9 ....4H **125**
Eltham Grn. SE9 ....5B **124**
Eltham Grn. Rd. SE9 ....4A **124**
Eltham High St. SE9 ....6D **124**
Eltham Hill SE9 ....5B **124**
Eltham Palace & Gardens 7C **124**
Eltham Pal. Rd. SE9 ....6A **124**
ELTHAM PARK 4E **124**
Eltham Pk. Gdns. SE9 ....4E **124**
Eltham Rd. SE9 ....5H **123**
   SE12 ....5H **123**
Eltham Warren Golf Course 5F **125**
Elthiron Rd. SW6 ....1J **117**
Elthorne Av. W7 ....2K **95**
Elthorne Ct. TW13: Felt 1A **130**
ELTHORNE HEIGHTS 5J **77**
Elthorne Pk. Rd. W7 ....2J **95**

Elthorne Rd. N19 . . . . .2H 65
  NW9 . . . . .7K 43
Elthorne Sports Cen. 3K 95
Elthorne Way NW9 . . . . .6K 43
Elthruda Rd. SE13 . . . . .6F 123
Elitisley Rd. IG1: Ilf 4F 71
Elton Av. EN5: Barn 5C 20
  HA0: Wemb 5B 60
  UB6: G'frd 6J 59
Elton Cl. KT1: Hamp W 7C 132
Elton Ho. E3 . . . . .1B 86
                   (off Candy St.)
Elton Pl. N16 . . . . .5E 66
Elton Rd. KT2: King T 1F 151
Eltringham St. SW18 . . . . .4A 118
Eluna Apartments E1 . . . . .7H 85
             (off Wapping La.)
Elvaston M. SW7 . . . . . . .2A 16 (3A 100)
Elvaston Pl. SW7 . . . . . . .2A 16 (3A 100)
Elveden Ho. SE24 . . . . .5B 120
Elveden Pl. NW10 . . . . .2G 79
Elveden Rd. NW10 . . . . .2G 79
Elvedon Rd. TW13: Felt 3H 129
Elvendon Rd. N13 . . . . .6D 32
Elven M. SE15 . . . . .1J 121
Elver Gdns. E2 . . . . .3G 85
Elverson Rd. SE8 . . . . .2D 122
Elverton St. SW1 . . . . . .3C 18 (4H 101)
Elvin Cl. NW9 . . . . .7J 43
Elvington Grn. BR2: Brom 5H 159
Elvington La. NW9 . . . . .1A 44
Elvino Rd. SE26 . . . . .5A 140
Elvis Rd. NW2 . . . . .6E 62
Elwill Way BR3: Beck 4E 158
Elwin St. E2 . . . . .1K 9 (3G 85)
Elwood Cl. EN5: New Bar 4F 21
Elwood St. N5 . . . . .3B 66
Elworth Ho. SW8 . . . . .7K 101
                (off Oval Pl.)
Elwyn Gdns. SE12 . . . . .7J 123
Ely Cl. KT3: N Mald 2B 152
Ely Ct. EC1 . . . . .6K 7
  KT1: King T 2G 151
  NW6 . . . . .2J 81
          (off Chichester Rd.)
Ely Gdns. IG1: Ilf 7C 52
  RM10: Dag 3J 73
Ely Ho. SE15 . . . . .7G 103
             (off Friary Est.)
Elyne Rd. N4 . . . . .6A 48
Ely Pl. EC1 . . . . .6K 7 (5A 84)
  IG8: Wfd G 6K 37
  SW8 . . . . .7K 101
Ely Rd. CR0: C'don 5D 156
  E10 . . . . .6E 50
  TW4: Houn 3A 112
  TW6: H'row A 2H 111
           (off Esher Cres.)
Elysian Av. BR5: St M Cry 6K 161
Elysian Pl. CR2: S Croy 7C 168
Elysium Apartments E1 . . . . .4J 85
            (off Theven St.)
Elysium Pl. SW6 . . . . .2H 117
           (off Elysium St.)
Elysium St. SW6 . . . . .2H 117
Elystan Bus. Cen. UB4: Yead 7A 76
Elystan Cl. SM6: Wall 7G 167
Elystan Ho. SW3 . . . . .4C 16
           (off Elystan St.)
Elystan Pl. SW3 . . . . .5D 16 (5C 100)
Elystan St. SW3 . . . . .4C 16 (4C 100)
Elystan Wlk. N1 . . . . .1A 84
Ely's Yd. E1 . . . . .5K 9 (5F 85)
Emanuel Av. W3 . . . . .6J 79
Emanuel Dr. TW12: Hamp 5D 130
Emanuel Ho. SW1 . . . . .3H 101
Embankment SW15 . . . . .2F 117
Embankment, The TW1: Twick 1A 132
Embankment Galleries 2H 13
      (within Somerset House)
Embankment Gdns. SW3 . . .7F 17 (6D 100)

Embankment Pl. WC2 . . . . . .4F 13 (1J 101)
Embassy Apartments SE5 . . . . .2C 120
       (off Coldharbour La.)
Embassy Ct. DA14: Sidc 3B 144
  DA16: Well 3B 126
  E2 . . . . .4H 85
           (off Brady St.)
  N11 . . . . .6C 32
        (off Bounds Grn. Rd.)
  NW8 . . . . .1B 4
  SM6: Wall 6F 167
  W5 . . . . .7F 79
Embassy Gdns. BR3: Beck 1B 158
Embassy Ho. NW6 . . . . .7K 63
Embassy Lodge N3 . . . . .2H 45
           (off Cyprus Rd.)
Embassy Theatre
  Central School of Speech & Drama
  . . . . .7B 64
Embassy Way SW8 . . . . .6H 101
Emba St. SE16 . . . . .2G 103
Ember Cl. BR5: Pet W 7G 161
Ember Ct. NW9 . . . . .2B 44
Embercourt Rd. KT7: T Ditt 6J 149
Ember Farm Av. KT8: E Mos 6H 149
Ember Farm Way KT8: E Mos 6H 149
Ember Gdns. KT7: T Ditt 7J 149
Ember La. KT8: E Mos 7H 149
  KT10: Esh 7H 149
Emberton SE5 . . . . .6E 102
           (off Albany Rd.)
Emberton Ct. EC1 . . . . .2A 8
         (off Tompion St.)
Embleton Rd. SE13 . . . . .4D 122
Embleton Wlk. TW12: Hamp 5D 130
Embroidery World Bus. Cen.
  IG8: Wfd G 2B 52
Embry Cl. HA7: Stan 4F 27
Embry Dr. HA7: Stan 6F 27
Embry Rd. SE9 . . . . .4A 124
Embry Way HA7: Stan 5F 27
Emden Cl. UB7: W Dray 2C 92
Emden St. SW6 . . . . .1K 117
Emerald Cl. E16 . . . . .6B 88
Emerald Gdns. RM8: Dag 1G 73
Emerald Rd. NW10 . . . . .1K 79
Emerald Sq. SW15 . . . . .5C 116
  UB2: S'hall 3B 94
Emerald St. WC1 . . . . .5G 7 (5K 83)
Emerson Apartments N8 . . . . .3K 47
Emerson Gdns. HA3: Kenton 6F 43
Emerson Rd. IG1: Ilf 7E 52
Emerson St. SE1 . . . . . . .4C 14 (1C 102)
Emerton Cl. DA6: Bex 4E 126
Emery Hill St. SW1 . . . . . .2B 18 (3G 101)
Emery St. SE1 . . . . .1K 19 (3A 102)
Emery Theatre 6D 86
          (off Annabel Cl.)
Emery Walker Trust 5C 98
       (off Hammersmith Ter.)
Emes Rd. DA8: Erith 7J 109
Emilia Cl. EN3: Pond E 5C 24
Emily Bowes Ct. N17 . . . . .3H 49
Emily Ct. SE1 . . . . .7C 14
           (off Sudrey St.)
Emily Duncan Pl. E7 . . . . .4K 69
Emily Ho. W10 . . . . .4G 81
          (off Kensal Rd.)
Emily St. E16 . . . . .6H 87
           (off Jude St.)
Emirates Air Line
  Cable Car 2H 105
Emirates Stadium 4A 66
Emlyn Gdns. W12 . . . . .2A 98
Emlyn Rd. W12 . . . . .2A 98
Emma Ho. RM1: Rom 4K 55
Emmanuel Ct. E10 . . . . .7D 50
Emmanuel Ho. SE11 . . . . .4J 19 (4A 102)
Emmanuel Rd. HA6: Nwood 1H 39
  SW12 . . . . .1G 137
Emma Rd. E13 . . . . .2H 87

Emma St. E2 . . . . .2H 85
Emmaus Way IG7: Chig 5K 37
Emmeline Ct. KT12: Walt T 7A 148
Emminster NW6 . . . . .1K 81
           (off Abbey Rd.)
Emmott Av. IG6: Ilf 5G 53
Emmott Cl. E1 . . . . .4A 86
  NW11 . . . . .6A 46
Emms Pas. KT1: King T 2D 150
Emperor Ho. E20 . . . . .5E 68
           (off Napa Cl.)
  SE4 . . . . .3A 122
         (off Dragonfly Pl.)
Emperor's Ga. SW7 . . . . .3A 100
Empingham Ho. SE8 . . . . .4K 103
          (off Chilton Gro.)
Empire Av. N18 . . . . .5H 33
Empire Cinema
  Bromley .2J 159
           (off High St.)
  Leicester Square 2D 12
       (off Leicester Sq.)
  Sutton 5K 165
  Walthamstow 4C 50
Empire Ct. SE7 . . . . .6K 105
Empire Ct. HA9: Wemb 3H 61
Empire Ho. N18 . . . . .6J 33
  SW7 . . . . .2C 16
Empire M. SW16 . . . . .5J 137
Empire Pde. HA9: Wemb 3G 61
  N18 . . . . .6J 33
Empire Reach SE10 . . . . .6D 104
          (off Dowells St.)
Empire Rd. UB6: G'frd 1B 78
Empire Sq. N7 . . . . .3J 65
Empire Sq. SE1 . . . . .7E 14
          (off Tabard St.)
  SE20 . . . . .7K 139
           (off High St.)
Empire Sq. E. SE1 . . . . .7E 14
Empire Sq. Sth. SE1 . . . . .7E 14
Empire Sq. W. SE1 . . . . .7E 14
Empire Way HA9: Wemb 4F 61
Empire Wharf E3 . . . . .1A 86
         (off Old Ford Rd.)
Empire Wharf Rd. E14 . . . . .4F 105
Empress App. SW6 . . . . .5J 99
Empress Av. E4 . . . . .7J 35
  E12 . . . . .2A 70
  IG1: Ilf 2D 70
  IG8: Wfd G 7C 36
Empress Dr. BR7: Chst 6F 143
Empress M. SE5 . . . . .2C 120
Empress Pde. E4 . . . . .7H 35
Empress Pl. SW6 . . . . .5J 99
Empress State Bldg. SW6 . . . . .5J 99
Empress St. SE17 . . . . .6C 102
Empson St. E3 . . . . .4D 86
Emsworth Cl. N9 . . . . .1D 34
Emsworth Ct. SW16 . . . . .3J 137
Emsworth Rd. IG6: Ilf 2F 53
Emsworth St. SW2 . . . . .2K 137
EMT House E6 . . . . .5E 88
Emu Rd. SW8 . . . . .2F 119
Enard Ho. E3 . . . . .2B 86
         (off Cardigan Rd.)
Ena Rd. SW16 . . . . .3J 155
Enbrook St. W10 . . . . .3G 81
Enclave, The SW13 . . . . .2B 116
Enclave Ct. EC1 . . . . .3B 8
         (off Dallington St.)
Endale Cl. SM5: Cars 2D 166
Endeavour Ho. E14 . . . . .2C 104
           (off Cuba St.)
  SE8 . . . . .4A 104
         (off Ashton Reach)
Endeavour Way CR0: Bedd 7J 155
  IG11: Bark 2A 90
  SW19 . . . . .4K 135
Endell St. WC2 . . . . .7E 6 (6J 83)
Enderby St. SE10 . . . . .5F 105

Enderley Cl. HA3: Hrw W 2J 41
Enderley Rd. HA3: Hrw W 1J 41
Enders Cl. EN2: Enf 1F 23
Endersleigh Gdns. NW4 . . . . .4C 44
Endlebury Rd. E4 . . . . .2K 35
Endlesham Rd. SW12 . . . . .7E 118
Endsleigh Ct. WC1 . . . . .3D 6
Endsleigh Gdns. IG1: Ilf 2D 70
  KT6: Surb 6C 150
  NW1 . . . . .3C 6 (4H 83)
Endsleigh Ind. Est.
  UB2: S'hall 4C 94
Endsleigh Pl. WC1 . . . . . . .3D 6 (4H 83)
Endsleigh Rd. UB2: S'hall 4C 94
  W13 . . . . .7A 78
Endsleigh St. WC1 . . . . . . .3D 6 (4H 83)
Endway KT5: Surb 7H 151
Endwell Rd. SE4 . . . . .2A 122
Endymion Rd. N4 . . . . .7A 48
  SW2 . . . . .6K 119
Energen Cl. NW10 . . . . .6A 62
Energize Fitness Club
  Hammersmith 5G 99
          (off Gliddon Rd.)
Energy Centre, The N1 . . . . .1G 9
         (off Bowling Grn. Wlk.)
ENFIELD 3J 23
Enfield Bus. Cen. EN3: Enf H 2D 24
Enfield Cloisters N1 . . . . .1G 9
         (off Fanshaw St.)
Enfield Golf Course 4G 23
ENFIELD HIGHWAY 3D 24
Enfield Ho. SW9 . . . . .2J 119
         (off Stockwell Rd.)
ENFIELD ISLAND VILLAGE 1H 25
ENFIELD LOCK 1G 25
Enfield Lock EN3: Enf L 1H 25
Enfield Mus. .4J 23
         (off London Rd.)
Enfield Retail Pk. EN1: Enf 3B 24
Enfield Rd. EN2: Enf 4C 22
  N1 . . . . .7E 66
  TW6: H'row A 2G 111
  TW8: Bford 5D 96
  W3 . . . . .2H 97
ENFIELD ROAD RDBT. 2G 111
ENFIELD TOWN 4J 23
Enfield Town FC 2A 24
Enfield Wlk. TW8: Bford 5D 96
ENFIELD WASH 1F 25
Enford St. W1 . . . . .5E 4 (5D 82)
Engadine Cl. CR0: C'don 3F 169
Engadine St. SW18 . . . . .1H 135
Engate St. SE13 . . . . .4E 122
Engel Pk. NW7 . . . . .6K 29
Engine Cl. SW1 . . . . .5B 12
        (off Ambassador's Ct.)
Engineer Cl. SE18 . . . . .6E 106
Engineers Way HA9: Wemb 4G 61
Engineers Wharf UB5: N'olt 4D 76
England's La. NW3 . . . . .6D 64
England Way KT3: N Mald 4H 151
Englefield NW1 . . . . .2A 6
         (off Clarence Gdns.)
Englefield Cl. BR5: St M Cry 5K 161
  CR0: C'don 6C 156
  EN2: Enf .2F 23
Englefield Cres. BR5: St M Cry 4K 161
Englefield Path BR5: St M Cry 4K 161
Englefield Rd. N1 . . . . .7D 66
Engleheart Dr. TW14: Felt 6H 111
Engleheart Rd. SE6 . . . . .7D 122
Englewood Rd. SW12 . . . . .6F 119
English Grounds SE1 . . . . .5G 15 (1E 102)
English St. E3 . . . . .4B 86
Enid St. SE16 . . . . .7K 15 (3F 103)
Enmore Av. SE25 . . . . .5G 157
Enmore Gdns. SW14 . . . . .5K 115
Enmore Rd. SE25 . . . . .5G 157
  SW15 . . . . .4E 116
  UB1: S'hall 4E 76

Ennerdale NW1 . . . .1A **6**
  (off Varndell St.)
Ennerdale Av. HA7: Stan 3C **42**
  TW14: Felt 1H **129**
Ennerdale Cl. SM1: Sutt 4H **165**
Ennerdale Ct. E11 . . . .7J **51**
  (off Cambridge Rd.)
Ennerdale Dr. NW9 . . . .5A **44**
Ennerdale Gdns. HA9: Wemb 1C **60**
Ennerdale Ho. E3 . . . .4B **86**
Ennerdale Rd. DA7: Bex 1G **127**
  TW9: Kew, Rich 2F **115**
Ennersdale Rd. SE13 . . . .5F **123**
Ennis Ho. E14 . . . .6D **86**
  (off Vesey Path)
Ennismore Av. UB6: G'frd 6J **59**
  W4 . . . .4B **98**
Ennismore Gdns. KT7: T Ditt 6J **149**
  SW7 . . . .7C **10** (2C **100**)
Ennismore Gdns. M. SW7 . . . .1C **16** (3C **100**)
Ennismore M. SW7 . . . .7C **10** (3C **100**)
Ennismore St. SW7 . . . .1C **16** (3C **100**)
Ennis Rd. N4 . . . .1A **66**
  SE18 . . . .6G **107**
Ennor Ct. SM3: Cheam 4E **164**
Ensbury Ho. SW8 . . . .7K **101**
  (off Carroun Rd.)
Ensham Ho. SW17 . . . .5D **136**
Ensign Cl. TW6: H'row A 3G **111**
  TW19: Stanw 1A **128**
Ensign Dr. N13 . . . .3H **33**
Ensign Ho. E14 . . . .2C **104**
  (off Admirals Way)
  NW9 . . . .3C **44**
  (off East Dr.)
  SW18 . . . .3A **118**
Ensign St. E1 . . . .7G **85**
  SE3 . . . .4K **123**
Ensign Way SM6: Wall 7J **167**
  TW19: Stanw 1A **128**
Enslin Rd. SE9 . . . .6E **124**
Ensor M. SW7 . . . .5A **16** (5B **100**)
Enstone Rd. EN3: Enf H 3F **25**
  UB10: Ick 3B **56**
Enterprise Bus. Pk. E14 . . . .2D **104**
Enterprise Centre, The BR3: Beck 3A **140**
  (off Cricket La.)
Enterprise Cl. CR0: C'don 1A **168**
Enterprise Ho. E4 . . . .7K **25**
  E9 . . . .7J **67**
  (off Tudor Gro.)
  SE5 . . . .5D **104**
  (off St Davids Sq.)
  E14 . . . .3K **89**
  (off St Davids Sq.)
  IG11: Bark 5J **103**
  KT12: Walt T 7K **147**
Enterprise Ind. Est. SE16 . . . .5J **103**
Enterprise Row N15 . . . .5F **49**
Enterprise Trad. Est. UB2: S'hall 2F **95**
Enterprise Way NW10 . . . .3B **80**
  SW18 . . . .4J **117**
  TW11: Tedd 6K **131**
Enterprize Way SE8 . . . .4B **104**
Entertainment Av. SE10 . . . .1G **105**
Envoy Av. TW6: H'row A 3H **111**
Envoy Ho. NW9 . . . .3C **44**
  (off East Dr.)
ENVOY RDBT. 3H **111**
Epcot M. NW10 . . . .3F **81**
Epirus M. SW6 . . . .7J **99**
Epirus Rd. SW6 . . . .7H **99**
Epping Cl. E14 . . . .4C **104**
  RM7: Mawney 3H **55**
Epping Glade E4 . . . .6K **25**
Epping New Rd. IG9: Buck H 3D **36**
Epping Pl. N1 . . . .6A **66**
Epping Way E4 . . . .6J **25**
Epple Rd. SW6 . . . .1H **117**
Epsom Cl. DA7: Bex 3H **127**
  UB5: N'olt 5D **58**
Epsom Rd. CR0: Wadd 4A **168**

Epsom Rd. IG3: Ilf 6K **53**
  SM3: Sutt 7H **153**
  SM4: Mord 7H **153**
Epsom Sq. TW6: H'row A 2H **111**
Epstein Ct. N1 . . . .1B **84**
  (off Gaskin St.)
Epstein Rd. SE28 . . . .1A **108**
Epworth Rd. TW7: Isle 7B **96**
Epworth St. EC2 . . . .4F **9** (4D **84**)
Equana Apartments SE8 . . . .5A **104**
  (off Evelyn St.)
Equiano Ho. SW9 . . . .1K **119**
  (off Lett Rd.)
Equinox Ct. IG2: Ilf 5F **53**
Equinox Ho. IG11: Bark 6G **71**
  (off Wakering Rd.)
Equinox Sq. E14 . . . .6D **86**
Equity M. W5 . . . .1D **96**
Equity Sq. E2 . . . .2K **9**
  (off Shacklewell St.)
Erasmus St. SW1 . . . .4D **18** (4H **101**)
Erconwald St. W12 . . . .6B **80**
Erebus Dr. SE28 . . . .3G **107**
Eresby Dr. BR3: Beck 1C **170**
Eresby Ho. SW7 . . . .7D **10**
  (off Rutland Ga.)
Eresby Pl. NW6 . . . .7J **63**
Erica Gdns. CR0: C'don 3D **170**
Erica Ho. N22 . . . .1A **48**
  (off Acacia Rd.)
  SE4 . . . .3B **122**
Erica St. W12 . . . .7C **80**
Eric Clarke La. IG11: Bark 4F **89**
Eric Cl. E7 . . . .4J **69**
Ericcson Cl. SW18 . . . .5J **117**
Eric Fletcher Ct. N1 . . . .7C **66**
  (off Essex Rd.)
Erickson Gdns. BR2: Brom 6C **160**
Eric Liddell Sports Cen. 2B **142**
Eric Rd. E7 . . . .4J **69**
  NW10 . . . .6B **62**
  RM6: Chad H 7D **54**
Eric Shipman Ter. E13 . . . .4J **87**
  (off Balaam St.)
Ericson Ho. SE13 . . . .4F **123**
  (off Blessington Rd.)
Eric St. E3 . . . .4B **86**
  (not continuous)
Eric Wilkins Ho. SE1 . . . .5G **103**
  (off Old Kent Rd.)
Eridge Rd. W4 . . . .3K **97**
Erin Cl. BR1: Brom 7G **141**
  IG3: Ilf 6A **54**
  SW6 . . . .7J **99**
Erindale SE18 . . . .6H **107**
Erindale Ter. SE18 . . . .6H **107**
Erin M. N22 . . . .1B **48**
Erin's Vs. SE14 . . . .1K **121**
  (off New Cross Rd.)
ERITH 5K **109**
Erith Cres. RM5: Col R 1J **55**
Erith Rd. DA7: Bex 4H **127**
  DA8: Erith 5C **109**
  (Picardy Rd.)
  DA8: Erith 4H **127**
  (Watling St.)
  DA17: Belv, Erith 5C **109**
Erith School Community Sports Cen. 7J **109**
Erlanger Rd. SE14 . . . .1K **121**
Erlesmere Gdns. W13 . . . .3A **96**
Erlich Cotts. E1 . . . .5J **85**
  (off Sidney St.)
Ermine Cl. TW4: Houn 2A **112**
Ermine Ho. E3 . . . .1B **86**
  (off Parnell Rd.)
  N17 . . . .7A **34**
  (off Moselle St.)
Ermine M. E2 . . . .1F **85**
Ermine Rd. N15 . . . .6F **49**
  SE13 . . . .4D **122**

Ermine Side EN1: Enf 5B **24**
Ermington Rd. SE9 . . . .2G **143**
Ernald Av. E6 . . . .2C **88**
Erncroft Way TW1: Twick 6K **113**
Ernest Av. SE27 . . . .4B **138**
Ernest Cl. BR3: Beck 5C **158**
Ernest Cotts. KT17: Ewe 7B **164**
Ernest Gdns. W4 . . . .6H **97**
Ernest Gro. BR3: Beck 5B **158**
Ernest Harriss Ho. W9 . . . .4J **81**
  (off Elgin Av.)
Ernest Rd. KT1: King T 2H **151**
Ernest Shackleton Lodge SE10 . . . .4G **105**
  (off Christchurch Way)
Ernest Sq. KT1: King T 2H **151**
Ernest St. E1 . . . .4K **85**
Ernle Rd. SW20 . . . .7D **134**
Ernshaw Pl. SW15 . . . .5G **117**
Ernst Bldg. SE1 . . . .5C **14**
  (off Union St.)
Eros 3C **12** (7H **83**)
Eros Ho. Shops SE6 . . . .7D **122**
  (off Brownhill Rd.)
Erpingham Rd. SW15 . . . .3E **116**
Erridge Rd. SW19 . . . .2J **153**
Errington Rd. W9 . . . .4H **81**
Errol Gdns. KT3: N Mald 4C **152**
  UB4: Yead 4K **75**
Errol St. EC1 . . . .4D **8** (4C **84**)
Erskine Cl. SM1: Sutt 3C **166**
Erskine Cres. N17 . . . .4H **49**
Erskine Hill NW11 . . . .4J **45**
Erskine Ho. SW1 . . . .6A **18**
  (off Churchill Gdns.)
Erskine M. NW3 . . . .7D **64**
  (off Erskine Rd.)
Erskine Rd. E17 . . . .4B **50**
  NW3 . . . .7D **64**
  SM1: Sutt 4B **166**
Erwin Ho. NW9 . . . .3C **44**
  (off Commander Av.)
Erwood Rd. SE7 . . . .5C **106**
Esam Way SW16 . . . .5A **138**
Escot Rd. TW16: Sun 7G **129**
Escott Gdns. SE9 . . . .4C **142**
Escreet Gro. SE18 . . . .4E **106**
Esher Av. KT12: Walt T 7J **147**
  RM7: Rom 6J **55**
  SM3: Cheam 3F **165**
Esher By-Pass KT9: Chess 7B **162**
  KT10: Clay 7B **162**
Esher Cl. DA5: Bexl 1E **144**
Esher Cres. TW6: H'row A 2H **111**
Esher Gdns. SW19 . . . .2F **135**
Esher M. CR4: Mitc 3E **154**
Esher Rd. IG3: Ilf 3J **71**
  KT8: E Mos 6H **149**
Eskdale NW1 . . . .1A **6**
  (off Stanhope St.)
Eskdale Av. UB5: N'olt 1D **76**
Eskdale Cl. HA9: Wemb 2D **60**
Eskdale Rd. DA7: Bex 2G **127**
Esk Ho. E3 . . . .4B **86**
  (off British St.)
Eskmont Ridge SE19 . . . .7D **138**
Esk Rd. E13 . . . .4J **87**
Esk Way RM1: Rom 1K **55**
Esmar Cres. NW9 . . . .7C **44**
Esmeralda Rd. SE1 . . . .4G **103**
Esmond Ct. W8 . . . .3K **99**
  (off Thackeray St.)
Esmond Gdns. W4 . . . .4K **97**
Esmond Rd. NW6 . . . .1H **81**
  W4 . . . .4K **97**
Esmond St. SW15 . . . .4G **117**
Esparto St. SW18 . . . .7K **117**
Esprit Ct. E1 . . . .6J **9**
  (off Brune St.)
Esquiline La. CR4: Mitc 3F **155**
Essan Ho. W5 . . . .5B **78**

Essence E3 . . . .2B **86**
  (off Cardigan Rd.)
Essence Ct. HA9: Wemb 2F **61**
Essenden Rd. CR2: S Croy 7E **168**
  DA17: Belv 5G **109**
Essendine Mans. W9 . . . .3J **81**
Essendine Rd. W9 . . . .3J **81**
Essex Av. TW7: Isle 3J **113**
Essex Cl. E17 . . . .4A **50**
  HA4: Ruis 1B **58**
  RM7: Mawney 4H **55**
  SM4: Mord 7F **153**
Essex Ct. EC4 . . . .1J **13**
  SW13 . . . .2B **116**
  W6 . . . .3E **98**
  (off Hammersmith Gro.)
Essex Gdns. N4 . . . .6B **48**
Essex Gro. SE19 . . . .6D **138**
Essex Hall E17 . . . .1K **49**
Essex Ho. E14 . . . .6D **86**
  (off Giraud St.)
Essex Mans. E11 . . . .7F **51**
Essex M. SE19 . . . .6E **138**
Essex Pk. N3 . . . .6E **30**
Essex Pk. M. W3 . . . .1A **98**
Essex Pl. W4 . . . .4J **97**
  (not continuous)
Essex Pl. Sq. W4 . . . .4K **97**
Essex Rd.
  E4 . . . .1B **36**
  E10 . . . .6E **50**
  E12 . . . .5C **70**
  E17 . . . .6A **50**
  E18 . . . .2K **51**
  EN2: Enf 4J **23**
  IG11: Bark 7H **71**
  N1 . . . .1B **84**
  NW10 . . . .7A **62**
  RM6: Chad H 7C **54**
  RM7: Mawney 4H **55**
  RM10: Dag 5J **73**
  W3 . . . .7J **79**
  W4 . . . .4K **97**
Essex Rd. Sth. E11 . . . .7F **51**
Essex St. E7 . . . .6J **69**
  WC2 . . . .1J **13** (6A **84**)
Essex Twr. SE20 . . . .1H **157**
  (off Jasmine Gro.)
Essex Vs. W8 . . . .2J **99**
Essex Wharf E5 . . . .2K **67**
Essian St. E1 . . . .5A **86**
Essoldo Way HA8: Edg 3F **43**
Estate Way E10 . . . .1B **68**
Estcourt Rd. SE25 . . . .6H **157**
  SW6 . . . .7H **99**
Estella Apartments E15 . . . .6E **69**
  (off Grove Cres. Rd.)
Estella Av. KT3: N Mald 4D **152**
Estella Ho. W11 . . . .7F **81**
  (off St Ann's Rd.)
Estelle Rd. NW3 . . . .4D **64**
Esterbrooke St. SW1 . . . .4C **18** (4H **101**)
Este Rd. SW11 . . . .3C **118**
Esther Cl. N21 . . . .7F **23**
Esther M. BR1: Brom 1K **159**
  (off Freelands Rd.)
Esther Randall Ct. NW1 . . . .3K **5**
  (off Lit. Albany St.)
Esther Rd. E11 . . . .7G **51**
Estoria Cl. SW2 . . . .7A **120**
Estorick Collection of Modern Italian Art 6B **66**
Estreham Rd. SW16 . . . .6H **137**
Estridge Cl.
  TW3: Houn 4E **112**
Estuary Cl. IG11: Bark 3B **90**
Estuary Ho. E16 . . . .1B **106**
  (off Agnes George Wlk.)
Eswyn Rd. SW17 . . . .4D **136**
Etal Ho. N1 . . . .7B **66**
  (off The Sutton Est.)

Etcetera Theatre 7F 65
(off Camden High St.)
Etchingham Ct. N3 . . . . .7E 30
Etchingham Pk. Rd. N3 . . . . .7E 30
Etchingham Rd. E15 . . . . .4E 68
Eternit Wlk. SW6 . . . . .1E 116
Etfield Gro. DA14: Sidc 5B 144
Ethelbert Cl. BR1: Brom 2J 159
Ethelbert Ct. BR1: Brom 3J 159
(off Ethelbert Rd.)
Ethelbert Gdns. IG2: Ilf 5D 52
Ethelbert Ho. E9 . . . . .4A 68
(off Homerton Rd.)
Ethelbert Rd. BR1: Brom 3J 159
DA8: Erith 7J 109
SW20 . . . . .1F 153
Ethelbert St. SW12 . . . . .1F 137
Ethel Brooks Ho. SE18 . . . . .6F 107
Ethelburga St. SW11 . . . . .1C 118
Ethelburga Twr. SW11 . . . . .1C 118
(off Rosenau Rd.)
Etheldene Av. N10 . . . . .4G 47
Ethelden Rd. W12 . . . . .1D 98
Ethelred Ct. HA3 . . . . .5G 43
Ethel Rd. E16 . . . . .6K 87
TW15: Ashf 5A 128
Ethel St. SE17 . . . . .4C 102
Etheridge Rd. NW4 . . . . .7E 44
(not continuous)
Etherley Rd. N15 . . . . .5C 48
Etherow St. SE22 . . . . .7G 121
Etherstone Grn. SW16 . . . . .4A 138
Etherstone Rd. SW16 . . . . .4A 138
Ethnard Rd. SE15 . . . . .6H 103
Ethos Sport Imperial 7B 10 (2B 100)
Ethronvi Rd. DA7: Bex 3E 126
Etloe Ho. E10 . . . . .1C 68
Etloe Rd. E10 . . . . .2C 68
Eton Av. EN4: E Barn 6H 21
HA0: Wemb 4B 60
KT3: N Mald 5K 151
N12 .7F 31
NW3 . . . . .7B 64
TW5: Hest 6D 94
Eton Cl. SW18 . . . . .7K 117
Eton Coll. Rd. NW3 . . . . .6D 64
Eton Ct. HA0: Wemb 4C 60
NW3 . . . . .7B 64
Eton Garages NW3 . . . . .6C 64
Eton Gro. NW9 . . . . .3G 43
SE13 . . . . .3G 123
Eton Hall NW3 . . . . .6D 64
Eton Ho. N5 .4B 66
(off Leigh Rd.)
UB7: W Dray 2B 92
ETON MANOR 4D 68
Eton Mnr. Ct. E10 . . . . .2C 68
(off Leyton Grange Est.)
Eton Pl. NW3 . . . . .7E 64
Eton Ri. NW3 . . . . .6D 64
Eton Rd. IG1: Ilf 4G 71
NW3 . . . . .7D 64
UB3: Harl 7H 93
Eton St. TW9: Rich 5E 114
Eton Vs. NW3 . . . . .6D 64
Etta St. SE8 . . . . .6A 104
Ettrick St. E14 . . . . .6E 86
(not continuous)
Etwell Pl. KT5: Surb 6F 151
Eucalyptus M. SW16 . . . . .6H 137
Euesden Cl. N9 . . . . .3C 34
Eugene Cotter Ho. SE17 . . . . .4D 102
(off Tatum St.)
Eugenia Rd. SE16 . . . . .4J 103
Eugenie M. BR7: Chst 1F 161
Eureka Rd. KT1: King T 2G 151
Euro Cl. NW10 . . . . .6C 62
Eurolink Bus. Cen. SW2 . . . . .4A 120
Europa Pl. EC1 . . . . .2C 8 (3C 84)
Europa Trade Pk. E16 . . . . .4G 87
Europa Trad. Est. DA8: Erith 5K 109

European Bus. Cen. NW9 . . . . .3J 43
(not continuous)
European Design Cen. NW9 . . . . . . .3K 43
Europe Rd. SE18 . . . . .3D 106
Euro Trade Cen. DA17: Belv 2J 109
Eustace Bldg. SW8 . . . . .6F 101
Eustace Ho. SE11 . . . . .3G 19
Eustace Pl. SE18 . . . . .4D 106
Eustace Rd. E6 . . . . .3C 88
RM6: Chad H 7D 54
SW6 . . . . .7J 99
Euston Gro. NW1 . . . . .2C 6
Euston Rd. CR0: C'don 1A 168
N1 . . . . .3J 83
NW1 . . . . .4A 6 (4F 83)
Euston Sq. NW1 . . . . .2C 6 (3H 83)
(not continuous)
Euston Sta. Colonnade NW1 . .2C 6 (3H 83)
Euston St. NW1 . . . . .2B 6 (3G 83)
Euston Twr. NW1 . . . . .3A 6 (4G 83)
EUSTON UNDERPASS 4G 83
Eva Ct. CR2: S Croy 6E 168
Evan Cook Cl. SE15 . . . . .1J 121
Evandale Rd. SW9 . . . . .2A 120
Evangelist Ho. EC4 . . . . .1A 14
(off Black Friars La.)
Evangelist Rd. NW5 . . . . .4F 65
Evan Ho. E16 .5J 87
(off Exeter Rd.)
Evans Apartments E2 . . . . .3K 85
Evans Cl. E8 .6F 67
Evans Gro. TW13: Hanw 2E 130
Evans Ho. SW8 . . . . .7H 101
(off Wandsworth Rd.)
TW13: Hanw 2E 130
W12 .7D 80
(off White City Est.)
Evans Rd. SE6 . . . . .2G 141
Evanston Av. E4 . . . . .7K 35
Evanston Gdns. IG4: Ilf 6C 52
Eva Rd. RM6: Chad H 7C 54
Evedon Ho. N1 . . . . .1E 84
(off Halcomb St.)
Evelina Mans. SE5 . . . . .7D 102
Evelina Rd. SE15 . . . . .3J 121
SE20 . . . . .7J 139
Eveline Lowe Est. SE16 . . . . .3G 103
Eveline Rd. CR4: Mitc 1D 154
Evelyn Av. HA4: Ruis 7G 39
NW9 . . . . .4K 43
Evelyn Cl. TW2: Whitt 7F 113
Evelyn Ct. E3 . . . . .5B 86
(off Burdett Rd.)
E8 . . . . .4G 67
N1 . . . . .1E 8
(off Evelyn Wlk.)
Evelyn Cres. TW16: Sun 1H 147
(off The Sutton Est.)
Evelyn Denington Ct. N1 . . . . .7B 66
Evelyn Denington Rd. E6 . . . . .4C 88
Evelyn Dr. HA5: Pinn 1B 40
Evelyn Fox Ct. W10 . . . . .5E 80
Evelyn Gdns. SW7 . . . . . . .6A 16 (5A 100)
TW9: Rich 4E 114
Evelyn Gro. UB1: S'hall 6D 76
W5 . . . . .1F 97
Evelyn Ho. SE14 . . . . .1A 122
(off Loring Rd.)
W8 . . . . .2K 99
(off Hornton St.)
W12 .2B 98
(off Cobbold Rd.)
Evelyn Mans. SW1 . . . . .2A 18
(off Carlisle Pl.)
W14 .5H 99
(off Queen's Club Gdns.)
Evelyn Rd. E16 . . . . .1J 105
E17 .4E 50
EN4: Cockf 4J 21
SW19 . . . . .5K 135
TW9: Rich 3E 114

Evelyn Rd. TW10: Ham 3C 132
W4 . . . . .3K 97
Evelyns Cl. UB8: Hil 6C 74
Evelyn St. SE8 . . . . .4A 104
Evelyn Ter. TW9: Rich 3E 114
Evelyn Wlk. N1 . . . . .1E 8 (2D 84)
Evelyn Way SM6: Bedd 4H 167
TW16: Sun 1H 147
Evelyn Yd. W1 . . . . .7C 6 (6H 83)
Evening Hill BR3: Beck 7E 140
Evenlode Ho. SE2 . . . . .2C 108
Evenwood Cl. SW15 . . . . .5G 117
Everall Cl. E4 . . . . .6G 35
Everard Av. BR2: Hayes 1J 171
Everard Ct. N13 . . . . .3E 32
Everard Ho. E1 . . . . .6G 85
(off Boyd St.)
Everard Way HA9: Wemb 3E 60
Everatt Cl. SW18 . . . . .6H 117
Everdon Rd. SW13 . . . . .6C 98
Everest Pl. E14 . . . . .5E 86
Everest Rd. SE9 . . . . .5D 124
TW19: Stanw 7A 110
Everett Cl. HA5: Eastc 3H 39
WD23: B Hea 1D 26
Everett Ho. SE17 . . . . .5D 102
(off East St.)
Everett Wlk. DA17: Belv 5F 109
(off Osborne Rd.)
Everglade Ho. E17 . . . . .2B 50
Everglades, The TW3: Houn 3G 113
Everglade Strand NW9 . . . . .1B 44
Evergreen Apartments IG8: Wfd G . .1H 51
(off High Rd. Woodford Grn.)
Evergreen Cl. SE20 . . . . .7J 139
Evergreen Dr. UB7: W Dray 2B 92
UB10: Hil 2D 74
Evergreen Sq. E8 . . . . .7F 67
Evergreen Way UB3: Hayes 7H 75
Everilda St. N1 . . . . .1K 83
Evering Rd. E5 . . . . .3F 67
N16 .3F 67
Everington Rd. N10 . . . . .2D 46
Everington St. W6 . . . . .6F 99
Everitt Rd. NW10 . . . . .3K 79
Everleigh St. N4 . . . . .1K 65
Eve Rd. E11 .4G 69
E15 .2G 87
N17 .3E 48
TW7: Isle 4A 114
Eversfield Gdns. NW7 . . . . .6F 29
Eversfield Rd. TW9: Kew 2F 115
Evershed Ho. E1 . . . . .7K 9
(off Old Castle St.)
Evershed Wlk. W4 . . . . .3J 97
Eversholt Ct. EN5: New Bar 5F 21
Eversholt St. NW1 . . . . .1B 6 (2G 83)
Eversholt Rd. N4 . . . . .1K 65
Eversleigh Ct. N3 . . . . .7C 30
Eversleigh Pl. BR3: Beck 6C 140
Eversleigh Rd. E6 . . . . .1B 88
EN5: New Bar 5F 21
N3 . . . . .7C 30
SW11 . . . . .3D 118
Eversley Av. DA7: Bex 2K 127
HA9: Wemb 2G 61
Eversley Cl. N21 . . . . .6E 22
Eversley Cres.
HA4: Ruis 2G 57
N21 .6E 22
TW7: Isle 1H 113
Eversley Ho. E2 . . . . .2K 9
(off Gosset St.)
Eversley Mt. N21 . . . . .6E 22
Eversley Pk. SW19 . . . . .6D 134
Eversley Pk. Rd. N21 . . . . .6E 22
Eversley Rd. KT5: Surb 4F 151
SE7 .6K 105
SE19 . . . . .7D 138
Eversley Way CR0: C'don 3C 170
Everthorpe Rd. SE15 . . . . .3F 121

Everton Bldgs. NW1 . . . . .2A 6 (3G 83)
Everton Ct. HA7: Stan 3E 42
(off Honeypot La.)
Everton Dr. HA7: Stan 3E 42
Everton Rd. CR0: C'don 1G 169
Everyman Baker Street (Cinema) . . .5F 5
(off Baker St.)
Everyman Cinema
Belsize Park 5C 64
Evesham Av. E17 . . . . .2C 50
Evesham Cl. SM2: Sutt 7J 165
UB6: G'frd 2F 77
Evesham Ct. TW10: Rich 6F 115
W13 .1A 96
(off Tewkesbury Rd.)
Evesham Grn. SM4: Mord 6K 153
Evesham Ho. E2 . . . . .2J 85
(off Old Ford Rd.)
NW8 .1A 82
(off Abbey Rd.)
SW1 . . . . .5K 17
(part of Abbots Mnr.)
Evesham Rd. E15 . . . . .7H 69
N11 .5B 32
SM4: Mord 6K 153
Evesham St. W11 . . . . .7F 81
Evesham Ter. KT6: Surb 6D 150
Evesham Wlk. SE5 . . . . .2D 120
SW9 . . . . .2A 120
Evesham Way IG5: Ilf 3E 52
SW11 . . . . .3E 118
Evette M. IG5: Ilf 1E 52
Evry Rd. DA14: Sidc 6C 144
Ewald Rd. SW6 . . . . .2H 117
Ewanrigg Ter. IG8: Wfd G 5F 37
Ewart Gro. N22 . . . . .1K 47
Ewart Ho. HA1: Harr 5A 42
Ewart Pl. E3 .2B 86
Ewart Rd. SE23 . . . . .7K 121
Ewe Cl. N7 . . . . .6J 65
EWELL 7C 164
Ewell By-Pass KT17: Ewe 7C 164
Ewell Ct. Av. KT19: Ewe 5A 164
Ewellhurst Rd. IG5: Ilf 2C 52
Ewell Pk. Gdns. KT17: Ewe 7C 164
Ewell Pk. Way KT17: Ewe 6C 164
Ewell Rd. KT6: Surb 7B 150
(Mount Holme)
KT6: Surb 6E 150
(South Ter.)
SM3: Cheam 6F 165
Ewelme Rd. SE23 . . . . .1J 139
Ewen Cres. SW2 . . . . .7A 120
Ewen Henderson Ct. SE14 . . . . .7A 104
(off Goodwood Rd.)
Ewen Ho. N1 .1K 83
(off Barnsbury Est.)
Ewer St. SE1 . . . . .5C 14 (1C 102)
Ewhurst Av. CR2: Sande 7F 169
Ewhurst Cl. E1 . . . . .5J 85
Ewhurst Ct. CR4: Mitc 3B 154
Ewhurst Rd. SE4 . . . . .6B 122
Exbury Ho. E9 . . . . .7J 67
SW1 . . . . .5C 18
(off Rampayne St.)
Exbury Rd. SE6 . . . . .2C 140
ExCeL 7K 87
Excel Cl. WC2 . . . . .3D 12
Excel Marina E16 . . . . .7J 87
Excelsior Cl. KT1: King T 2G 151
Excelsior Gdns. SE13 . . . . .2E 122
Excelsior Ind. Est. SE15 . . . . .6J 103
Excel Waterfront E16 . . . . .7K 87
Exchange, The CR0: C'don 3C 168
(off Surrey St.)
IG1: Ilf 2F 71
Exchange Apartments BR2: Brom . . .4K 159
(off Sparkes Cl.)
Exchange Arc. EC2 . . . . .5H 9 (5E 84)
Exchange Bldg. E1 . . . . .4J 9
(off Commercial St.)

Exchange Cl. N11	2K 31
Exchange Ct. WC2	3F 13 (7J 83)
Exchange Garages N13	4F 33
Exchange Ho. EC2	5H 9
NW10	7D 62
SW1	4C 18
	(off Vauxhall Bri. Rd.)
Exchange Mans. NW11	7H 45
Exchange Pl. EC2	5G 9 (5E 84)
Exchange Sq. EC2	5G 9 (5E 84)
Exchange St. EC1	2C 8 (3C 84)
RM1: Rom	5K 55 & 6K 55
Exchange Wlk. HA5: Pinn	7C 40
Exeforde Av. TW15: Ashf	4C 128
Exeter Cl. E6	6D 88
Exeter Cl. KT6: Surb	5E 150
	(off Maple Rd.)
NW6	2J 81
	(off Cambridge Rd.)
Exeter Gdns. IG1: Ilf	1C 70
Exeter Ho. IG11: Bark	7A 72
	(off Margaret Bondfield Av.)
N1	1E 84
	(off New Era Est.)
RM8: Dag	4A 72
SE15	6G 103
	(off Friary Est.)
SW15	6E 116
TW13: Hanw	2D 130
	(off Watermill Way)
W2	6A 82
	(off Hallfield Est.)
Exeter Mans. NW2	6G 63
Exeter M. NW6	6K 63
SW6	7J 99
Exeter Rd. CR0: C'don	7E 156
DA16: Well	2K 125
E16	5J 87
E17	5C 50
EN3: Pond E	3E 24
HA2: Harr	2C 58
N9	2D 34
N14	1A 32
NW2	5G 63
RM10: Dag	6H 73
TW6: H'row A	3F 111
TW13: Hanw	3D 130
Exeter St. WC2	2F 13 (7J 83)
Exeter Way SE14	7B 104
TW6: H'row A	2G 111
Exford Ct. SW11	1B 118
	(off Bolingbroke Wlk.)
Exford Gdns. SE12	1K 141
Exford Rd. SE12	2K 141
Exhibition Cl. W12	7E 80
Exhibition Grounds	
HA9: Wemb	4H 61
Exhibition Rd. SW7	7B 10 (2B 100)
Exit Rd. N2	2B 46
Exmoor Cl. IG6: Ilf	1G 53
Exmoor Ho. DA17: Belv	2H 109
E3	2A 86
	(off Gernon Rd.)
Exmoor St. W10	4F 81
Exmouth Ho. E14	4D 104
	(off Cahir St.)
EC1	3J 7
	(off Pine St.)
Exmouth Mkt. EC1	3J 7 (4A 84)
Exmouth M. NW1	2B 6 (3G 83)
Exmouth Pl. E8	7H 67
Exmouth Rd. DA16: Well	1C 126
E17	5B 50
HA4: Ruis	3A 58
UB4: Hayes	3G 75
Exmouth St. E1	6J 85
Exning Rd. E16	4G 87
Exonbury NW8	1K 81
	(off Abbey Rd.)
Exon St. SE17	5E 102
Explorer Av. TW19: Stanw	1A 128
Explorers Ct. E14	7F 87
	(off Newport Av.)
Export Ho. SE1	7H 15
	(off Tower Bri. Rd.)
Express Dr. IG3: Ilf	1B 72
Express Ho. SE8	6A 104
	(off Rolt St.)
Express Newspapers SE1	4A 14
	(off Blackfriars Rd.)
Express Wharf E14	2C 104
	(off Hutchings St.)
Exton Gdns. RM8: Dag	5C 72
Exton Rd. NW10	7J 61
Exton St. SE1	5J 13 (1A 102)
Eyebright Cl. CR0: C'don	1K 169
Eyhurst Cl. NW2	2C 62
Eylewood Rd. SE27	5C 138
Eynella Rd. SE22	7F 121
Eynham Rd. W12	6E 80
Eynsford Cl. BR5: Pet W	7G 161
Eynsford Cres. DA5: Bexl	1C 144
Eynsford Ho. SE1	7E 14
	(off Crosby Row)
SE15	6J 103
SE17	4E 102
	(off East St.)
Eynsford Rd. IG3: Ilf	2J 71
Eynsford Ter. UB7: Yiew	6B 74
Eynsham Dr. SE2	4A 108
Eynswood Dr. DA14: Sidc	5B 144
Eyot Gdns. W6	5B 98
Eyot Grn. W4	5B 98
Eyot Ho. SE16	3G 103
	(off Frean St.)
Eyre Cl. NW8	2B 82
Eyre St. Hill EC1	4J 7 (4A 84)
Eysham Cl. EN5: New Bar	5E 20
Eythorne Rd. SW9	1A 120
Ezra St. E2	1K 9 (3F 85)

F

Faber Gdns. NW4	5C 44
Fabian Bell Twr. E3	2C 86
	(off Pancras Way)
Fabian Rd. SW6	7H 99
Fabian St. E6	4D 88
Facade, The SE23	2J 139
Factory La. CR0: C'don	1A 168
N17	2F 49
Factory Rd. E16	1B 106
Factory Yd. W7	1J 95
Faggs Rd. TW14: Felt	4H 111
Fairacre HA5: Eastc	4J 39
Fairacre Cl. HA6: Nwood	1G 39
Fair Acres BR2: Brom	5J 159
CR0: Sels	7B 170
Fairacres HA4: Ruis	7H 39
SW15	4B 116
Fairbank Av. BR6: Farnb	2F 173
Fairbank Est. N1	1F 9 (2D 84)
Fairbanks Ct. HA0: Wemb	1E 78
Fairbanks Rd. N17	3F 49
Fairbourne Ho. UB3: Harl	3E 92
Fairbourne Rd. N17	3E 48
SW4	6H 119
Fairbriar Residence SW7	4A 100
	(off Stanhope Gdns.)
Fairbridge Rd. N19	2H 65
Fairbrook Cl. N13	5F 33
Fairbrook Rd. N13	6F 33
Fairburn Ct. SW15	5G 117
Fairburn Ho. W14	5H 99
	(off Ivatt Pl.)
Fairby Ho. SE1	4F 103
	(off Longfield Est.)
Fairby Rd. SE12	5K 123
Faircharm Trad. Est. SE8	7D 104
Fairchild Cl. SW11	2B 118
Fairchild Ho. E2	2H 85
	(off Cambridge Cres.)
E9	7J 67
	(off Frampton Pk. Rd.)
N1	1G 9
	(off Fanshaw St.)
N3	1J 45
Fairchild Pl. EC2	4H 9
Fairchild St. EC2	3H 9 (4E 84)
Fair Cl. WD23: Bush	1A 26
Fairclough Cl. UB5: N'olt	4D 76
Fairclough St. E1	6G 85
Faircroft TW11: Tedd	6A 132
FAIR CROSS	5J 71
Faircross Av. IG11: Bark	6G 71
RM5: Col R	1K 55
Faircross Pde. IG11: Bark	5J 71
Fairdale Gdns. SW15	4D 116
UB3: Hayes	2J 93
Fairey Av. UB3: Harl	4H 93
Fairfax Av. KT17: Ewe	7D 164
Fairfax Cl. KT12: Walt T	7K 147
Fairfax Ct. NW6	7A 64
	(off Fairfax Rd.)
Fairfax Gdns. SE3	1A 124
Fairfax Ho. KT1: King T	3F 151
	(off Livesey Cl.)
Fairfax Mans. NW6	7A 64
	(off Finchley Rd.)
Fairfax M. E16	1K 105
N8	4B 48
SW15	4E 116
Fairfax Pl. NW6	7A 64
W14	3G 99
Fairfax Rd. N8	4A 48
NW6	7A 64
TW11: Tedd	6A 132
W4	3A 98
Fairfax Way N10	7K 31
Fairfield E1	5J 85
	(off Redman's Rd.)
KT1: King T	2F 151
N20	2G 31
NW1	1G 83
	(off Arlington Rd.)
Fairfield Av. HA4: Ruis	7E 38
HA8: Edg	6C 28
NW4	6D 44
TW2: Whitt	1F 131
Fairfield Cl. CR4: Mitc	7C 136
DA15: Sidc	6K 125
EN3: Pond E	4E 24
KT19: Ewe	5A 164
N12	4F 31
Fairfield Cl. HA4: Ruis	1F 57
HA6: Nwood	2J 39
NW10	1C 80
Fairfield Cres. HA8: Edg	6C 28
Fairfield Dr. HA2: Harr	3G 41
SW18	5K 117
UB6: G'frd	1C 78
Fairfield East KT1: King T	2E 150
Fairfield Gdns. N8	5J 47
Fairfield Gro. SE7	6B 106
Fairfield Halls	
Croydon	3D 168
Fairfield Nth. KT1: King T	2E 150
Fairfield Path CR0: C'don	3D 168
Fairfield Pl. KT1: King T	3E 150
Fairfield Rd. BR1: Brom	7J 141
BR3: Beck	2C 158
BR5: Pet W	6H 161
CR0: C'don	3D 168
DA7: Bex	2F 127
E3	2C 86
E17	2A 50
IG1: Ilf	6F 71
IG8: Wfd G	6D 36
KT1: King T	2E 150
N8	5J 47
N18	4B 34
Fairfield Rd. UB1: S'hall	6D 76
UB7: Yiew	7A 74
UB8: Uxb	6A 56
Fairfields Cl. NW9	5J 43
Fairfields Cres. NW9	4J 43
Fairfields Sth. KT1: King T	2E 150
Fairfields Rd. TW3: Houn	3G 113
Fairfield St. SW18	5K 117
Fairfield Trade Pk. KT1: King T	3F 151
Fairfield Way EN5: Barn	5D 20
KT19: Ewe	5A 164
Fairfield West KT1: King T	2E 150
Fairfoot Rd. E3	4C 86
Fairford SE6	1C 140
Fairford Av. CR0: C'don	5K 157
DA7: Bex	1K 127
Fairford Cl. CR0: C'don	5A 158
Fairford Ct. SM2: Sutt	7K 165
Fairford Gdns. KT4: Wor Pk	2B 164
Fairford Ho. SE11	4K 19 (4A 102)
Fairgreen EN4: Cockf	3J 21
Fairgreen Ct. EN4: Cockf	3J 21
Fairgreen E. EN4: Cockf	3J 21
Fairgreen Rd. CR7: Thor H	5B 156
Fairhall Cl. KT5: Surb	7F 151
Fairhaven Av. CR0: C'don	6K 157
Fairhaven Cl. CR2: S Croy	5C 168
	(off Warham Rd.)
Fairhazel Gdns. NW6	6K 63
Fairhazel Mans. NW6	7A 64
	(off Fairhazel Gdns.)
Fairholme TW14: Bedf	7F 111
Fairholme Cl. N3	4G 45
Fairholme Cres. UB4: Hayes	4H 75
Fairholme Gdns. N3	3G 45
Fairholme Rd. CR0: C'don	7A 156
HA1: Harr	5K 41
IG1: Ilf	7D 52
SM1: Sutt	6H 165
TW15: Ashf	5A 128
W14	5G 99
Fairholt Cl. N16	1E 66
Fairholt Rd. N16	1D 66
Fairholt St. SW7	1D 16 (3C 100)
Fairland Ho. BR2: Brom	4K 159
Fairland Rd. E15	6H 69
Fairlands Av.	
CR7: Thor H	4K 155
IG9: Buck H	2D 36
SM1: Sutt	2J 165
Fairlands Ct. SE9	6E 124
Fairlawn KT2: King T	6J 133
SE7	7A 106
Fairlawn Av. DA7: Bex	2D 126
N2	4C 46
W4	4J 97
Fairlawn Cl. KT2: King T	6J 133
KT10: Clay	6A 162
N14	6B 22
TW13: Hanw	4D 130
Fairlawn Ct. SE7	7A 106
	(not continuous)
W4	4J 97
Fairlawn Dr. IG8: Wfd G	7D 36
Fairlawnes SM6: Wall	5F 167
Fairlawn Gdns. UB1: S'hall	7D 76
Fairlawn Gro. W4	4J 97
Fairlawn Mans. SE14	1K 121
Fairlawn Pk. SE26	5A 140
Fairlawn Rd. SW19	7H 135
Fairlawns	
HA5: Pinn	2B 40
TW1: Twick	6C 114
TW16: Sun	3J 147
Fairlead Ho. E14	3C 104
	(off Alpha Gro.)
Fairlea Pl. W5	4C 78
Fairlie Cl. E3	3D 86
	(off Stroudley Wlk.)
Fairlie Gdns. SE23	7J 121
Fairlight TW12: Hamp H	5F 131

Fairlight Av. E4 . . . . . .2A 36
  IG8: Wfd G 6D 36
  NW10 . . . . . .2A 80
Fairlight Cl. E4 . . . . . .2A 36
  KT4: Wor Pk 4E 164
Fairlight Ct. NW10 . . . . . .2A 80
  UB6: G'frd 2G 77
Fairlight Rd. SW17 . . . . . .4B 136
Fairline Ct. BR3: Beck 2E 158
FAIRLOP 1J 53
Fairlop Ct. E11 . . . . . .1F 69
Fairlop Gdns. IG6: Ilf 1G 53
Fairlop Rd. E11 . . . . . .7F 51
  IG6: Ilf 2G 53
Fairlop Sailing Cen. 1K 53
Fairlop Waters Country Pk. 2K 53
Fairlop Waters Golf Course 1J 53
Fairmead Dr. UB10: Hil 6C 56
Fairmead BR1: Brom 4D 160
  (Amberley Way)
  KT5: Surb 1H 163
Fairmead Cl.
  BR1: Brom 4D 160
  KT3: N Mald 3K 151
  TW5: Hest 7B 94
Fairmead Ct. TW9: Rich 2H 115
Fairmead Cres. HA8: Edg 3D 28
Fairmead Gdns. IG4: Ilf 5C 52
Fairmead Ho. E9 . . . . . .4A 68
  CRO: C'don 7K 155
  N19 . . . . . .3H 65
Fairmile Av. SW16 . . . . . .5H 137
Fairmile Ho. TW11: Tedd 4A 132
Fairmont Av. E14 . . . . . .1F 105
Fairmont Cl. DA17: Belv 5F 109
Fairmont Ho. E3 . . . . . .2C 86
  (off Wellington Way)
  SE16 . . . . . .2K 103
  (off Needleman St.)
Fairmount Rd. SW2 . . . . . .6K 119
Fairoak Cl. BR5: Pet W 7F 161
Fairoak Dr. SE9 . . . . . .5H 125
Fairoak Gdns. RM1: Rom 2K 55
Fair Oak Pl. IG6: Ilf 2G 53
Fairseat Cl. WD23: B Hea 2D 26
Fairstead Lodge IG8: Wfd G 6D 36
  (off Snakes La. W.)
Fairstead Wlk. N1 . . . . . .1C 84
  (off Popham St.)
Fair St. SE1 . . . . . .6H 15 (2E 102)
  TW3: Houn 3G 113
Fairthorne Vs. SE7 . . . . . .5J 105
  (off Felltram Way)
Fairthorn Rd. SE7 . . . . . .5J 105
Fairview HA4: Ruis 4A 58
Fairview Av. HA0: Wemb 6D 60
Fairview Cl. E17 . . . . . .1A 50
  SE26 . . . . . .5A 140
Fairview Ct. NW4 . . . . . .2F 45
  TW15: Ashf 5C 128
Fairview Cres. HA2: Harr 1E 58
Fairview Dr. BR6: Orp 4H 173
  TW17: Shep 5B 146
Fairview Est. NW10 . . . . . .3J 79
Fairview Gdns. IG8: Wfd G 1K 51
Fairview Ho. SW2 . . . . . .7K 119
Fairview Ind. Pk. RM13: Rain 5K 91
Fairview Pl. SW2 . . . . . .7K 119
Fairview Rd. EN2: Enf 1F 23
  N15 . . . . . .5F 49
  SM1: Sutt 5B 166
  SW16 . . . . . .1K 155
Fairview Vs. E4 . . . . . .7H 35
Fairview Way HA8: Edg 4B 28
Fairwall Ho. SE5 . . . . . .1E 120
Fairwater Av. DA16: Well 4A 126
Fairwater Dr. TW17: Shep 5E 146
Fairwater Ho. TW11: Tedd 4A 132
Fairway BR5: Pet W 5H 161
  DA6: Bex 5E 126
  IG8: Wfd G 5F 37
  SW20 . . . . . .3E 152

Fairway, The BR1: Brom 5D 160
  EN5: New Bar 6E 20
  HA0: Wemb 3B 60
  HA4: Ruis 4A 58
  KT3: N Mald 1K 151
  KT8: W Mole 3F 149
  N13 . . . . . .3H 33
  N14 . . . . . .6A 22
  NW7 . . . . . .3E 28
  UB5: N'olt 6G 59
  UB10: Hil 3B 74
  W3 . . . . . .6A 80
Fairway Av. NW9 . . . . . .3H 43
Fairway Cl. CRO: C'don 5A 158
  KT10: Surb 3B 162
  KT19: Ewe 4J 163
  NW11 . . . . . .7A 46
  TW4: Houn 5A 112
  (Amberley Way)
  TW4: Houn 5B 112
  (Islay Gdns.)
Fairway Ct. EN5: New Bar 6E 20
  NW7 . . . . . .3E 28
  SE16 . . . . . .2K 103
  (off Christopher Cl.)
Fairway Dr. SE28 . . . . . .6D 90
  UB6: G'frd 7F 59
Fairway Gdns. BR3: Beck 6F 159
  IG1: Ilf 5G 71
Fairways E17 . . . . . .4E 50
  HA7: Stan 2E 42
  TW7: Isle 1H 113
  TW11: Tedd 7D 132
  TW15: Ashf 6D 128
Fairways Bus. Pk. E10 . . . . . .2A 68
Fairway Trad. Est. TW4: Houn 5A 112
Fairweather Cl. N15 . . . . . .4E 48
Fairweather Ct. N13 . . . . . .3E 32
Fairweather Ho. N7 . . . . . .4J 65
Fairweather Rd. N16 . . . . . .6G 49
Fairwyn Rd. SE26 . . . . . .4A 140
Faith Ct. E3 . . . . . .2C 86
  (off Lefevre Wlk.)
  SE1 . . . . . .5F 103
  (off Cooper's Rd.)
Faith M. E12 . . . . . .4B 70
Fakenham Cl. NW7 . . . . . .7H 29
  UB5: N'olt 6D 58
Fakruddin St. E1 . . . . . .4G 85
Falcon WC1 . . . . . .5F 7
  (off Old Gloucester St.)
Falcon Av. BR1: Brom 4C 160
Falconberg M. W1 . . . . . .7D 6 (6H 83)
Falcon Cl. HA6: Nwood 1G 39
  W4 . . . . . .6J 97
Falcon Ct. E18 . . . . . .3K 51
  (off Albert Rd.)
  EC4 . . . . . .1K 13 (6A 84)
  EN5: New Bar 4F 21
  HA4: Ruis 2G 57
  N1 . . . . . .1B 8
  (off City Gdn. Row)
Falcon Cres. EN3: Pond E 5E 24
Falcon Dr. TW19: Stanw 6A 110
Falconer Ct. N17 . . . . . .7H 33
  (off Compton Cres.)
Falconer Wlk. N7 . . . . . .2K 65
Falconet Ct. E1 . . . . . .1H 103
  (off Wapping High St.)
Falcon Gro. SW11 . . . . . .3C 118
Falcon Highwalk EC2 . . . . . .6C 8
Falcon Ho. BR1: Brom 1H 159
  E14 . . . . . .5D 104
  (off St Davids Sq.)
  NW6 . . . . . .1K 81
  (off Springfield Wlk.)
  SW5 . . . . . .5K 99
  (off Old Brompton Rd.)
Falcon La. SW11 . . . . . .3C 118
Falcon Lodge W9 . . . . . .5J 81
  (off Admiral Wlk.)

Falcon Pk. Ind. Est. NW10 . . . . . .4A 62
Falcon Point SE1 . . . . . .3B 14 (7B 84)
Falcon Rd. EN3: Pond E 5E 24
  SW11 . . . . . .2C 118
  TW12: Hamp 7D 130
Falconry Cl. KT1: King T 3E 150
  (off Fairfield Sth.)
Falcon St. E13 . . . . . .4J 87
Falcon Ter. SW11 . . . . . .3C 118
Falcon Way E11 . . . . . .4J 51
  E14 . . . . . .4D 104
  HA3: Kenton 5E 42
  NW9 . . . . . .2A 44
  TW14: Felt 5K 111
  TW16: Sun 2G 147
Falcon Wharf SW11 . . . . . .2B 118
FALCONWOOD 4K 125
Falconwood Av.
  DA16: Well 2H 125
Falconwood Cl. SE3 . . . . . .2H 123
  (off Montpelier Row)
Falconwood Pde. DA16: Well 4J 125
Falconwood Rd. CRO: Sels 7B 170
Falcourt Cl. SM1: Sutt 5K 165
Falkirk Ct. SE16 . . . . . .1K 103
  (off Rotherhithe St.)
Falkirk Ho. W9 . . . . . .2K 81
  (off Maida Vale)
Falkirk St. N1 . . . . . .1H 9 (2E 84)
Falkland Av. N3 . . . . . .7D 30
  N11 . . . . . .4A 32
Falkland Ho. SE6 . . . . . .4E 140
  W8 . . . . . .3K 99
  W14 . . . . . .5H 99
  (off Edith Vs.)
Falkland Pk. Av. SE25 . . . . . .3E 156
Falkland Pl. NW5 . . . . . .5G 65
Falkland Rd. EN5: Barn 2B 20
  N8 . . . . . .4A 48
  NW5 . . . . . .5G 65
Fallaize Av. IG1: Ilf 4F 71
Falling La. UB7: Yiew 7A 74
Fallodon Way NW11 . . . . . .4J 45
Fallodon Ho. W11 . . . . . .5H 81
  (off Tavistock Cres.)
FALLOW CORNER 7F 31
Fallow Ct. SE16 . . . . . .5G 103
  (off Argyle Way)
Fallow Ct. Av. N12 . . . . . .7F 31
Fallowfield HA7: Stan 4F 27
  HA7: Stan 3F 27
Fallowfields Dr. N12 . . . . . .6H 31
Fallowhurst Path N3 . . . . . .7F 31
Fallow Pl. TW11: Tedd 5J 131
Fallows Cl. N2 . . . . . .2B 46
Fallsbrook Rd. SW16 . . . . . .6F 137
Falman Cl. N9 . . . . . .1B 34
Falmer Rd. E17 . . . . . .3D 50
  EN1: Enf 4K 23
  N15 . . . . . .5C 48
Falmouth Av. E4 . . . . . .5A 36
Falmouth Cl. N22 . . . . . .7E 32
  SE12 . . . . . .5H 123
Falmouth Gdns. IG4: Ilf 4B 52
Falmouth Ho. HA5: Hat E 1D 40
  KT2: King T 1D 150
  (off Skerne Rd.)
  SE11 . . . . . .5K 19
  (off Seaton Cl.)
  W2 . . . . . .2C 10
  (off Clarendon Pl.)
Falmouth Rd. SE1 . . . . . .7E 14 (3C 102)
Falmouth St. E15 . . . . . .5F 69
Falmouth Wlk. SW15 . . . . . .6C 116
Falmouth Way E17 . . . . . .5B 50
Falstaff Bldg. E1 . . . . . .7H 85
  (off Cannon St. Rd.)
Falstaff Cl. DA1: Cray 7K 127
Falstaff Ho. SE11 . . . . . .4B 102
  (off Opal St.)

Falstaff Ho. N1 . . . . . .1G 9
  (off Regan Way)
Falstaff M. TW12: Hamp H 5H 131
  (off High St.)
Fambridge Cl. SE26 . . . . . .4B 140
Fambridge Ct. RM7: Rom 5K 55
  (off Marks Rd.)
Fambridge Rd. RM8: Dag 1G 73
Fancourt M. BR1: Brom 3E 160
Fan Museum, The 7E 104
Fann St. EC1 . . . . . .4C 8 (4C 84)
  EC2 . . . . . .4C 8 (4C 84)
  (not continuous)
Fanshawe Av. IG11: Bark 6G 71
Fanshawe Cres. RM9: Dag 5E 72
Fanshawe Rd. TW10: Ham 4C 132
Fanshaw St. N1 . . . . . .1G 9 (3E 84)
FANTAIL, THE 3D 172
Fantail Cl. SE28 . . . . . .6C 90
Fanthorpe St. SW15 . . . . . .3E 116
Faraday Av. DA14: Sidc 2A 144
Faraday Cl. N7 . . . . . .6K 65
Faraday Ho. E14 . . . . . .7B 86
  (off Brightlingsea Pl.)
  HA9: Wemb 3J 61
  SE1 . . . . . .7E 14
  (off Cole St.)
  W10 . . . . . .5G 81
  (off Wornington Rd.)
Faraday Lodge SE10 . . . . . .3H 105
Faraday Mans. W14 . . . . . .6G 99
  (off Queen's Club Gdns.)
Faraday Pl. KT8: W Mole 4E 148
  E15 . . . . . .6H 69
  KT8: W Mole 4E 148
  SW19 . . . . . .6J 135
  UB1: S'hall 7F 77
  W3 . . . . . .7J 79
  W10 . . . . . .5G 81
Faraday Way CRO: Wadd 1K 167
  SE18 . . . . . .3B 106
Fareham Rd. TW14: Felt 7A 112
Farewell Pl. CR4: Mitc 1C 154
Fari Ct. E17 . . . . . .4C 50
  (off Tower M.)
Faringdon Av. BR2: Brom 7E 160
Faringdon Rd. EN3 . . . . . .7G 69
Farjeon Ho. NW6 . . . . . .7B 64
  (off Hilgrove Rd.)
Farjeon Rd. SE3 . . . . . .1B 124
Farleigh Av. BR2: Hayes 7H 159
Farleigh Ct. CR2: S Croy 5C 168
Farleigh Ho. N1 . . . . . .7B 66
  (off Halton Rd.)
Farleigh Pl. N16 . . . . . .4F 67
Farleigh Rd. N16 . . . . . .4F 67
Farley Cl. NW1 . . . . . .6G 5
  (off Allsop Pl.)
Farley Dr. IG3: Ilf 1J 71
Farley Ho. SE26 . . . . . .3H 139
Farley M. SE6 . . . . . .7E 122
Farley Pl. SE25 . . . . . .4G 157
Farley Rd. CR2: Sels 7H 169
  SE6 . . . . . .7D 122
Farlington Pl. SW15 . . . . . .7D 116
Farlow Rd. SW15 . . . . . .3F 117
Farlton Rd. SW18 . . . . . .1K 135
Farman Gro. UB5: N'olt 3B 76
Farman Ter. HA3: Kenton 4D 42
Farm Av. HA0: Wemb 6C 60
  HA2: Harr 7D 40
  NW2 . . . . . .3G 63
  SW16 . . . . . .4J 137
Farnborough Cl. HA1: Harr 7H 41
Farm Cl. BR4: W W'ck 3H 171
  IG9: Buck H 3F 37
  RM10: Dag 7J 73
  SM2: Sutt 7B 166

Farm Cl. SW6 . . . . .7J **99**
TW17: Shep 7C **146**
UB1: S'hall 7F **77**
UB10: Ick 2D **56**
Farmcote Rd. SE12 . . . . .1J **141**
Farm Ct. NW4 . . . . .3C **44**
Farmdale Rd. SE10 . . . . .5J **105**
SM5: Cars 7C **166**
Farm Dr. CR0: C'don 2B **170**
Farm End HA6: Nwood 1D **38**
Farmer Rd. E10 . . . . .1D **68**
Farmer's Rd. SE5 . . . . .7B **102**
Farmer St. W8 . . . . .1J **99**
Farmfield Rd. BR1: Brom 5G **141**
Farm Ho. NW7 . . . . .7H **29**
Farmhouse Rd. SW16 . . . . .7G **137**
Farmilo Rd. E17 . . . . .7B **50**
Farmington Av. SM1: Sutt 3B **166**
Farmlands EN2: Enf 1F **23**
HA5: Eastc 4J **39**
Farmlands, The UB5: N'olt 6D **58**
Farmland Wlk. BR7: Chst 5F **143**
Farm La. CR0: C'don 2B **170**
N14 .7A **22**
SW6 .6J **99**
Farm La. Trad. Est. SW6 . . . . . . .6J **99**
Farmleigh N14 . . . . .7B **22**
Farmleigh Ho. SW9 . . . . .5B **120**
Farm M. CR4: Mitc 2F **155**
Farm Pl. W8 . . . . .1J **99**
Farm Rd. HA8: Edg 6C **28**
N21 . . . . .1H **33**
NW10 . . . . .1K **79**
SM2: Sutt 7B **166**
SM4: Mord 5K **153**
TW4: Houn 1C **130**
Farmstead Ct. SM6: Wall 5F **167**
                              (off Melbourne Rd.)
Farmstead Rd. HA3: Hrw W 1H **41**
SE6 .4D **140**
Farm St. W1 . . . . .3J **11** (7F **83**)
Farm Va. DA5: Bexl 6H **127**
Farm Wlk. NW11 . . . . .5H **45**
Farm Way IG9: Buck H 4F **37**
KT4: Wor Pk 3E **164**
Farmway RM8: Dag 3C **72**
Farnaby Ho. W10 . . . . .3H **81**
                              (off Bruckner St.)
Farnaby Rd. BR1: Brom 7F **141**
BR2: Brom 7F **141**
SE9 .4A **124**
Farnan Av. E17 . . . . .2C **50**
Farnan Lodge SW16 . . . . .5J **137**
Farnan Rd. SW16 . . . . .5J **137**
FARNBOROUGH 5G **173**
Farnborough Av. CR2: Sels 7K **169**
E17 .3A **50**
Farnborough Cl. HA9: Wemb 2H **61**
Farnborough Comn. BR6: Farnb . . .3D **172**
Farnborough Cres. BR2: Hayes . . .1H **171**
CR2: Sels 7A **170**
Farnborough Hill
BR6: Chels, Farnb 5H **173**
Farnborough Ho. SW15 . . . . .1C **134**
Farnborough Way
BR6: Chels, Farnb 5G **173**
Farncombe St. SE16 . . . . .2G **103**
Farndale Av. N13 . . . . .2G **33**
Farndale Ct. SE18 . . . . .7C **106**
Farndale Cres. UB6: G'frd 3G **77**
Farndale Ho. NW6 . . . . .1K **81**
                              (off Kilburn Vale)
Farnell M. SW5 . . . . .5K **99**
Farnell Pl. W3 . . . . .7H **79**
Farnell Rd. TW7: Isle 3H **113**
Farnfield Ct. CR2: S Croy 5B **168**
Farnham Cl. N20 . . . . .7F **21**
Farnham Ct. SM3: Cheam 6G **165**
UB1: S'hall 7G **77**
                              (off Redcroft Rd.)
Farnham Gdns. SW20 . . . . .2D **152**

Farnham Ho. NW1 . . . . .4D **4**
SE1 .5C **14**
                              (off Union St.)
Farnham Pl. SE1 . . . . . . .5B **14** (1B **102**)
Farnham Rd. DA16: Well 2C **126**
IG3: Ilf 7K **53**
Farnham Royal SE11 . . . . . .6H **19** (5K **101**)
Farningham Ct. SW16 . . . . .7H **137**
Farningham Ho. N4 . . . . .7D **48**
Farningham Rd. N17 . . . . .7B **34**
Farnley Ho. SW8 . . . . .2H **119**
Farnley Rd. E4 . . . . .1B **36**
SE25 . . . . .4D **156**
Farnsworth Ct. SE10 . . . . .3H **105**
                              (off West Parkside)
Farnworth Ho. E14 . . . . .4F **105**
                              (off Manchester Rd.)
Faro Cl. BR1: Brom 2E **160**
Faroe Rd. W14 . . . . .3F **99**
Farorna Wlk. EN2: Enf 1F **23**
Farquhar Rd. SE19 . . . . .5F **139**
SW19 . . . . .3J **135**
Farquharson Rd. CR0: C'don 1C **168**
Farrance Rd. HA3: Kenton 7A **42**
Farrance St. E14 . . . . .6C **86**
Farrans Ct. HA3: Kenton 7B **42**
Farrant Av. N22 . . . . .2A **48**
Farrant Cl. BR6: Chels 7K **173**
Farr Av. IG11: Bark 2A **90**
Farrell Ho. E1 . . . . .6J **85**
                              (off Ronald St.)
Farren Rd. SE23 . . . . .2A **140**
Farrer Ct. TW1: Twick 7D **114**
Farrer Ho. SE8 . . . . .7C **104**
Farrer M. N8 . . . . .4G **47**
Farrer Rd. HA3: Kenton 5E **42**
N8 . . . . .4G **47**
Farrer's Pl. CR0: C'don 4K **169**
Farrier Cl. BR1: Brom 3B **160**
TW16: Sun 4J **147**
UB8: Hil 6C **74**
Farrier Ct. E1 . . . . .5K **85**
                              (off White Horse La.)
RM13: Rain 2K **91**
                              (off Lowen Rd.)
Farrier Pl. SM1: Sutt 3K **165**
Farrier Rd. UB5: N'olt 2E **76**
Farriers Ho. EC1 . . . . .4D **8**
                              (off Errol St.)
Farriers M. SE15 . . . . .3J **121**
Farrier St. NW1 . . . . .7F **65**
Farrier Wlk. SW10 . . . . .6A **100**
Farringdon Ho. TW9: Kew 7H **97**
UB7: W Dray 2B **92**
Farringdon La. EC1 . . . . .4K **7** (4A **84**)
Farringdon Rd. EC1 . . . . .3J **7** (4A **84**)
Farringdon St. EC4 . . . . .6A **8** (5B **84**)
Farrington Ct. BR1: Brom 2K **159**
                              (off Widmore Rd.)
Farrington Pl. BR7: Chst 7H **143**
Farrins Rents SE16 . . . . .1A **104**
Farrow La. SE14 . . . . .7J **103**
Farrow Pl. SE16 . . . . .3A **104**
Farr Rd. EN2: Enf 1J **23**
Farthingale Wlk. E15 . . . . .7F **69**
Farthing All. SE1 . . . . .7K **15** (2G **103**)
Farthing Barn La. BR6: Downe 7E **172**
Farthing Ct. NW7 . . . . .7B **30**
Farthing Flds. E1 . . . . .1H **103**
Farthings, The KT2: King T 1G **151**
Farthings Cl. E4 . . . . .3B **36**
HA5: Eastc 6K **39**
FARTHING STREET 7D **172**
Farthing St. BR6: Downe 7D **172**
Farwell Rd. DA14: Sidc 4B **144**
Farwig La. BR1: Brom 1H **159**
Fashion & Textile Mus. 6H **15** (2E **102**)
Fashion St. E1 . . . . .6K **9** (5F **85**)
Fashoda Rd. BR2: Brom 4B **160**
Fassett Rd. E8 . . . . .6G **67**
KT1: King T 4E **150**

Fassett Sq. E8 . . . . .6G **67**
Fathom Ct. E16 . . . . .7F **89**
                              (off Basin App.)
Fauconberg Ct. W4 . . . . .6J **97**
                              (off Fauconberg Rd.)
Fauconberg Rd. W4 . . . . .6J **97**
Faulkner Cl. RM8: Dag 7D **54**
Faulkner Ho. W6 . . . . .6E **98**
Faulkner M. E17 . . . . .1A **50**
Faulkners All. EC1 . . . . . . .5A **8** (5B **84**)
Faulkner St. SE14 . . . . .1J **121**
Fauna Cl. HA7: Stan 4J **27**
RM6: Chad H 6C **54**
Faunce Ho. SE17 . . . . .6B **102**
                              (off Doddington Gro.)
Faunce St. SE17 . . . . .5B **102**
Favart Rd. SW6 . . . . .1J **117**
Faversham Av. E4 . . . . .1B **36**
EN1: Enf 6J **23**
Faversham Ho. NW1 . . . . .1G **83**
                              (off Bayham Pl.)
SE17 . . . . .5E **102**
                              (off Kinglake St.)
Faversham Rd. BR3: Beck 2B **158**
SE6 .7B **122**
SM4: Mord 5A **154**
Fawcett Cl. SW11 . . . . .2B **118**
SW16 . . . . .5A **138**
Fawcett Ct. SW10 . . . . .6A **100**
                              (off Fawcett St.)
Fawcett Est. E5 . . . . .1G **67**
Fawcett Rd. CR0: C'don 3C **168**
NW10 . . . . .7B **62**
Fawcett St. SW10 . . . . .6A **100**
Fawe Pk. M. SW15 . . . . .4H **117**
Fawe Pk. Rd. SW15 . . . . .4H **117**
Fawe St. E14 . . . . .5D **86**
Fawkham Ho. SE1 . . . . .4F **103**
                              (off Longfield Est.)
Fawley Lodge E14 . . . . .4F **105**
                              (off Millennium Dr.)
Fawley Rd. NW6 . . . . .5K **63**
Fawnbrake Av. SE24 . . . . .5B **120**
Fawn Hgts. IG9: Buck H 2E **36**
                              (off Stag La.)
Fawn Rd. E13 . . . . .2A **88**
Fawns Mnr. Cl. TW14: Bedf 1E **128**
Fawns Mnr. Rd. TW14: Bedf 1F **129**
Fawood Av. NW10 . . . . .7J **61**
Faygate Cres. DA6: Bex 5G **127**
Faygate Rd. SW2 . . . . .2K **137**
Fayland Av. SW16 . . . . .5G **137**
Fazeley Ct. W9 . . . . .5J **81**
                              (off Elmfield Way)
Fazeley Ho. UB5: N'olt 3D **76**
                              (off Taywood Rd.)
Fearley Cres. TW12: Hamp 5C **130**
Fearnley Ho. SE5 . . . . .2E **120**
Fearns Ho. W13 . . . . .1A **96**
Fearon St. SE10 . . . . .5J **105**
Featherbed La. CR0: Sels 7B **170**
Feather M. E1 . . . . .5G **85**
Feathers Pl. SE10 . . . . .6F **105**
Featherstone Av. SE23 . . . . .2H **139**
Featherstone Ct. UB2: S'hall 3B **94**
Featherstone Ho. UB4: Yead 5A **76**
Featherstone Ind. Est. UB2: S'hall . .3C **94**
                              (off Feather Rd.)
Featherstone Rd. NW7 . . . . .6J **29**
UB2: S'hall 3C **94**
Featherstone Sports Cen. 4B **94**
Featherstone St. EC1 . . . . . .3E **8** (4D **84**)
Featherstone Ter. UB2: S'hall 3C **94**
Featley Rd. SW9 . . . . .3B **120**
Federal Rd. UB6: G'frd 1C **78**
Federation Rd. SE2 . . . . .4B **108**
Fee Farm Rd. KT10: Clay 7A **162**
Feeny Cl. NW10 . . . . .4B **62**
Felbridge Av. HA7: Stan 1A **42**
Felbridge Cl. SM2: Sutt 7K **165**
SW16 . . . . .4A **138**

Felbridge Ct. TW13: Felt 1K **129**
                              (off High St.)
UB3: Harl 6F **93**
Felbridge Ho. SE22 . . . . .3E **120**
Felbridge Rd. IG3: Ilf 2K **71**
Felday Rd. SE13 . . . . .6D **122**
Felden Cl. HA5: Hat E 1C **40**
Felden St. SW6 . . . . .1H **117**
Feldman Cl. N16 . . . . .1G **67**
Feldspar Ct. EN3: Enf H 3F **25**
                              (off Enstone Rd.)
Felgate M. W6 . . . . .4D **98**
Felhampton Rd. SE9 . . . . .2F **143**
Felhurst Cres. RM10: Dag 4H **73**
Feline Cl. EN4: E Barn 6H **21**
Felix Av. N8 . . . . .6J **47**
Felix Ct. E17 . . . . .5D **50**
NW9 .2A **44**
Felix Ho. E16 . . . . .7E **88**
                              (off University Way)
Felix La. TW17: Shep 6G **147**
Felix Mnr. BR7: Chst 6J **143**
Felix Neubergh Ho. EN1: Enf 4K **23**
Felix Pl. SW2 . . . . .5A **120**
                              (off Talma Rd.)
Felix Rd. KT12: Walt T 6J **147**
W13 .7A **78**
Felixstowe Ct. E16 . . . . .1F **107**
Felixstowe Rd. N9 . . . . .3B **34**
N17 .3F **49**
NW10 . . . . .3D **80**
SE2 .3B **108**
Felix St. E2 . . . . .2H **85**
Fellbrigg Rd. SE22 . . . . .5F **121**
Fellbrigg St. E1 . . . . .4H **85**
Fellbrook TW10: Ham 3B **132**
Fellmongers Path SE1 . . . . .7J **15**
Fellmongers Yd. CR0: C'don 3C **168**
Fellowes Cl. UB4: Yead 4B **76**
Fellowes Rd. SM5: Cars 3C **166**
Fellows Cl. E2 . . . . .1J **9** (2F **85**)
                              (not continuous)
Fellowship Cl. RM8: Dag 4A **72**
Fellows Rd. NW3 . . . . .7B **64**
Fell Rd. CR0: C'don 3C **168**
                              (not continuous)
Feltham M. SE7 . . . . .5J **105**
Feltham Way SE7 . . . . .5J **105**
Fell Wlk. HA8: Edg 1J **43**
Felmersham Cl. SW4 . . . . .4J **119**
Felmingham Rd. SE20 . . . . .2J **157**
Felnex Trad. Est. NW10 . . . . .2K **79**
SM6: Wall 2E **166**
Felsberg Rd. SW2 . . . . .6J **119**
Fels Cl. RM10: Dag 3H **73**
Fels Farm Av. RM10: Dag 3J **73**
Felsham Rd. SW15 . . . . .3E **116**
Felspar Cl. SE18 . . . . .5K **107**
Felstead Av. IG5: Ilf 1E **52**
Felstead Cl. N13 . . . . .5F **33**
Felstead Gdns. E14 . . . . .5E **104**
Felstead Rd. E9 . . . . .6B **68**
E11 .7J **51**
Felstead St. E9 . . . . .6B **68**
Felstead Wharf E14 . . . . .5E **104**
Felsted Rd. E16 . . . . .6B **88**
FELTHAM 1K **129**
Feltham Av. KT8: E Mos 4J **149**
Felthambrook Ind. Est. TW13: Felt . .3K **129**
Felthambrook Way TW13: Felt 3K **129**
Feltham Bus. Complex TW13: Felt . .2K **129**
Feltham Corporate Cen.
TW13: Felt 3K **129**
FELTHAMHILL 5H **129**
Feltham Hill Rd. TW15: Ashf 5C **128**
Feltham Rd. CR4: Mitc 2D **154**
TW15: Ashf 4C **128**
Felton Cl. BR5: Pet W 6F **161**
Felton Gdns. IG11: Bark 1J **89**

Felton Hall Ho. SE16 . . . . .7K 15
   (off George Row)
Felton Ho. N1 .1D 84
   (off Colville Est.)
Felton Lea DA14: Sidc 5K 143
Felton Rd. IG11: Bark 2J 89
   W13 . . . . .2C 96
Felton St. N1 .1D 84
Fencepiece Rd. IG6: Chig, Ilf 1G 53
Fenchurch Av. EC3 . . . . .1G 15 (6E 84)
Fenchurch Bldgs. EC3 . . .1H 15 (6E 84)
Fenchurch Ho. EC3 . . . .
   (off Minories)
Fenchurch M. E3 . . . . .5B 86
   (off St Paul's Way)
Fenchurch Pl. EC3 . . . . .2H 15 (6E 84)
Fenchurch St. EC3 . . . . .2G 15 (7E 84)
Fen Ct. EC3 . . . . .2G 15 (6E 84)
Fendall Rd. KT19: Ewe 5J 163
Fendall St. SE1 . . . . .3E 102
   (not continuous)
Fendt Cl. E16 .6H 87
Fendyke Rd. DA17: Belv 4D 108
Fenelon Pl. W14 . . . . .4H 99
Fengate Cl. KT9: Chess 6D 162
Fen Gro. DA15: Sidc 5K 125
Fenham Rd. SE15 . . . . .7G 103
Fenland Ho. E5 . . . . .2J 67
Fen La. SW13 . . . . .1D 116
Fenman Ct. N17 . . . . .1H 49
Fenman Gdns. IG3: Ilf 1B 72
Fenn Cl. BR1: Brom 6J 141
Fennel Apartments SE1 . . . .
   (off Cayenne Ct.)
Fennel Cl. CR0: C'don 1K 169
   E16 . . . . .4G 87
Fennells Mead KT17: Ewe 7B 164
Fennell St. SE18 . . . . .6E 106
Fenner Cl. SE16 . . . . .4H 103
Fenner Ho. E1 . . . . .1H 103
   (off Watts St.)
Fenner Sq. SW11 . . . . .3B 118
Fenn Ho. TW7: Isle 1B 114
Fennings Rd. SW4 . . . . .6H 119
Fenning St. SE1 . . . . .6G 15 (2E 102)
Fenn St. E9 .5K 67
Fenstanton N4 . . . .
   (off Marquis Rd.)
Fenstanton Av. N12 . . . . .6G 31
Fen St. E16 . . . . .7H 87
Fenswood Cl. DA5: Bexl 6G 127
Fentiman Rd. SW8 . . . . .7F 19 (6J 101)
Fentiman Way HA2: Harr 2F 59
Fenton Cl. BR7: Chst 5D 142
   E8 . . . . .6F 67
   SW9 . . . . .2K 119
Fenton House 3A 64
   (off Hampstead Gro.)
Fenton Ho. SE14 . . . . .7A 104
   TW5: Hest 6E 94
Fenton Pde. SE10 . . . . .5H 105
   (off Woolwich Rd.)
Fenton Rd. N17 . . . . .7H 33
Fentons Av. E13 . . . . .3K 87
Fenton St. E1 . . . . .6H 85
Fenwick Cl. SE18 . . . . .6E 106
Fenwick Gro. SE15 . . . . .3G 121
Fenwick Pl. CR2: S Croy 7B 168
   SW9 . . . . .3J 119
Fenwick Rd. SE15 . . . . .3G 121
Ferby Ct. DA14: Sidc 4K 143
   (off Main Rd.)
Ferdinand Dr. SE15 . . . . .7E 102
Ferdinand Ho. NW1 . . . . .7E 64
   (off Ferdinand Pl.)
Ferdinand Pl. NW1 . . . . .7E 64
Ferdinand St. NW1 . . . . .7E 64
Ferguson Av. KT5: Surb 5F 151
Ferguson Centre, The E17 . . . . .6A 50
Ferguson Cl. BR2: Brom 3F 159
   E14 . . . . .4C 104

Ferguson Dr. W3 . . . . .6K 79
Ferguson Ho. SE10 . . . . .1E 122
   (off Sparta St.)
Fergus Rd. N5 . . . . .5B 66
Ferial Ct. SE15 . . . . .7G 103
   (off Fenham Rd.)
Fermain Ct. E. N1 . . . . .1E 84
   (off Hertford Rd.)
Fermain Ct. Nth. N1 . . . . .1E 84
   (off De Beauvoir Est.)
Fermain Ct. W. N1 . . . . .1E 84
   (off De Beauvoir Est.)
Ferme Pk. Rd. N4 . . . . .5J 47
   N8 . . . . .5J 47
Fermor Rd. SE23 . . . . .1A 140
Fermoy Ho. W9 . . . . .4H 81
   (off Fermoy Rd.)
Fermoy Rd. UB6: G'frd 4F 77
   W9 . . . . .4H 81
   (not continuous)
Fern Av. CR4: Mitc 4H 155
Fernbank IG9: Buck H 1E 36
Fernbank Av. HA0: Wemb 4K 59
   KT12: Walt T 7C 148
Fernbank M. SW12 . . . . .6G 119
Fernbrook Av. DA15: Sidc 5J 125
Fernbrook Cres. SE13 . . . . .6G 123
   (off Leahurst Rd.)
Fernbrook Dr. HA2: Harr 7F 41
Fernbrook Rd. SE13 . . . . .5G 123
Ferncliff Rd. E8 . . . . .5G 67
Fern Cl. N1 . . . . .2E 84
Fern Ct. DA7: Bex 4G 127
   RM7: Rom 5K 55
   SE14 . . . . .2K 121
Ferncroft Av. HA4: Ruis 2A 58
   N12 . . . . .6J 31
   NW3 . . . . .3J 63
Ferndale BR1: Brom 2A 160
Ferndale Av. E17 . . . . .5F 51
   TW4: Houn 3C 112
Ferndale Cl. DA7: Bex 1E 126
Ferndale Community Sports Cen. . . .3K 119
Ferndale Cres. SM5: Cars 1D 166
Ferndale Rd. E7 . . . . .7K 69
   E11 . . . . .2G 69
   N15 . . . . .6F 49
   RM5: Col R 2J 55
   SE25 . . . . .5H 157
   SW4 . . . . .4J 119
   SW9 . . . . .4J 119
   TW15: Ashf 5A 128
Ferndale St. E6 . . . . .7F 89
Ferndale Ter. HA1: Harr 4K 41
Ferndale Way BR6: Farnb 5H 173
Ferndell Av. DA5: Bexl 3K 145
Fern Dene W13 . . . . .5B 78
Ferndene Rd. SE24 . . . . .4C 120
Ferndown HA6: Nwood 2J 39
   NW1 . . . . .7H 65
   (off Camley St.)
Ferndown Av. BR6: Orp 1H 173
Ferndown Cl. HA5: Pinn 1C 40
   SM2: Sutt 6B 166
Ferndown Ct. UB1: S'hall 6G 77
   (off Haldane Rd.)
Ferndown Lodge E14 . . . . .3E 104
   (off Manchester Rd.)
Ferndown Rd. SE9 . . . . .7B 124
Ferney Meade Way TW7: Isle 2A 114
Ferney Rd. EN4: E Barn 7K 21
Fern Gro. TW14: Felt 7K 111
Fernhall Dr. IG4: Ilf 5B 52
Fernham Rd. CR7: Thor H 3C 156
Fernhead Rd. W9 . . . . .3H 81
Fernheath Way DA2: Wilm 5K 145
Fernhill Ct. E17 . . . . .2F 51
Fernhill Gdns. KT2: King T 5D 132
Fern Hill Pl. BR6: Farnb 5G 173
Fernhill St. E16 . . . . .1D 106

Fernholme Rd. SE15 . . . . .5K 121
Fernhurst Gdns. HA8: Edg 6B 28
Fernhurst Rd. . . . .
   CR0: C'don 7H 157
   SW6 . . . . .1G 117
   TW15: Ashf 4E 128
Fern La. TW5: Hest 5D 94
Fernlea Rd. CR4: Mitc 2E 154
   SW12 . . . . .1F 137
Fernleigh Cl. CR0: Wadd 4A 168
   W9 . . . . .3H 81
Fernleigh Ct. HA2: Harr 2F 41
   HA9: Wemb 2E 60
   RM7: Rom 5J 55
Fernleigh Rd. N21 . . . . .2F 33
Fernly Cl. HA5: Eastc 4J 39
Fernsbury St. WC1 . . . . .2J 7 (3A 84)
Fernshaw Cl. SW10 . . . . .6A 100
Fernshaw Mans. SW10 . . . . .6A 100
   (off Fernshaw Rd.)
Fernshaw Rd. SW10 . . . . .6A 100
Fernside IG9: Buck H 1E 36
   KT7: T Ditt 1B 162
   NW11 . . . . .2J 63
Fernside Av. NW7 . . . . .3E 28
   TW13: Felt 4K 129
Fernside Ct. NW4 . . . . .2F 45
Fernside Rd. SW12 . . . . .1D 136
Ferns Rd. E15 . . . . .6H 69
Fern St. E3 . . . . .4C 86
Fernthorpe Rd. SW16 . . . . .6G 137
Ferntower Rd. N5 . . . . .5D 66
Fern Wlk. SE16 . . . . .5G 103
   TW15: Ashf 5A 128
Fernways IG1: Ilf 4F 71
Fernwood SW19 . . . . .1H 135
Fernwood Av. HA0: Wemb 6C 60
   SW16 . . . . .4H 137
Fernwood Cl. BR1: Brom 2A 160
Fernwood Cl. N14 . . . . .7B 22
Fernwood Cres. N20 . . . . .3J 31
Ferny Hill EN4: Had W 1J 21
Ferranti Cl. SE18 . . . . .3B 106
Ferrers Av. SM6: Bedd 4H 167
   UB7: W Dray 2A 92
Ferrers Rd. SW16 . . . . .5H 137
Ferrestone Rd. N8 . . . . .4K 47
Ferrey M. SW9 . . . . .2A 120
Ferriby Cl. N1 .7A 66
Ferrier Ind. Est. SW18 . . . . .4K 117
   (off Ferrier St.)
Ferrier Point E16 . . . . .5J 87
   (off Forty Acre La.)
Ferrier St. SW18 . . . . .4K 117
Ferring Cl. HA2: Harr 1G 59
Ferrings SE21 . . . . .3E 138
Ferris Av. CR0: C'don 3B 170
Ferris Rd. SE22 . . . . .4G 121
Ferron Rd. E5 . . . . .3H 67
Ferry App. SE18 . . . . .3E 106
Ferrybridge Ho. SE11 . . . . .2H 19
Ferrydale Lodge NW4 . . . . .4E 44
   (off Parson St.)
Ferry Ho. E5 . . . . .1H 67
   (off Harrington Hill)
Ferry Island Retail Pk. N17 . . . . .3G 49
Ferry La. N17 .4G 49
   SW13 . . . . .6B 98
   TW8: Bford 6E 96
   TW9: Kew 6F 97
   TW17: Shep 7C 146
Ferry La. Ind. Est. E17 . . . . .4K 49
Ferryman's Quay SW6 . . . . .2A 118
Ferrymead Av. UB6: G'frd 3E 76
Ferrymead Dr. UB6: G'frd 2E 76
Ferrymead Gdns. UB6: G'frd 2G 77
Ferrymoor TW10: Ham 3B 132
Ferry Pl. SE18 . . . . .3E 106
Ferry Quays TW8: Bford 6E 96
   (Ferry La.)

Ferry Quays TW8: Bford 7D 96
   (off Point Wharf La., Point Wharf La.)
Ferry Rd. KT7: T Ditt 6B 150
   KT8: W Mole 3E 148
   SW13 . . . . .7C 98
   TW1: Twick 1B 132
   TW11: Tedd 5B 132
Ferry Sq. TW8: Bford 7E 96
Ferry St. E14 . . . . .5E 104
Ferry Wharf TW8: Bford 7E 96
Festing Rd. SW15 . . . . .3F 117
Festival Cl. DA5: Bexl 1D 144
   UB10: Hil .1D 74
Festival Ct. E8 . . . . .7F 67
   (off Holly St.)
   SM1: Sutt 7K 153
Festival Wlk. SM5: Cars 4D 166
Festival Way E4 . . . . .6K 35
Festive Mans. E20 . . . . .5E 68
   (off Napa Cl.)
Festoon Way E16 . . . . .7B 88
Festuca Ho. E20 . . . . .5E 68
   (off Mirabelle Gdns.)
Fetherstone Ct. RM6: Chad H 6F 55
   (off High Rd.)
Fetherton Cl. IG11: Bark 2G 89
   (off Spring Pl.)
Fetter La. EC4 . . . . .1K 13 (6A 84)
Fetter La. Apartments EC4 . . . . .1J 13
   (off Fetter La.)
Fettes Ho. NW8 . . . . .2B 82
   (off Wellington Rd.)
Fews Lodge RM6: Chad H 4D 54
Ffinch St. SE8 . . . . .7C 104
Fidelis Ho. E1 . . . . .6J 9
   (off Gun St.)
Fidgeon Cl. BR1: Brom 3E 160
Field Cl. BR1: Brom 2A 160
   E4 . . . . .6J 35
   HA4: Ruis .1E 56
   IG9: Buck H 3F 37
   KT8: W Mole 5F 149
   KT9: Chess 5C 162
   NW2 . . . . .2C 62
   TW4: Cran 1K 111
   UB3: Harl .7F 92
   UB10: Ick .2D 56
FIELDCOMMON 7D 148
Fieldcommon La. . . . .
   KT12: Walt T 7C 148
Field Ct. SW19 . . . . .3J 135
   WC1 . . . . .6H 7 (5K 83)
Field End HA4: Ruis 6A 58
   UB5: N'olt .6B 58
Fieldend TW1: Twick 4K 131
Field End Rd. HA4: Ruis 1B 58
   HA5: Eastc 5K 39
Fieldend Rd. SW16 . . . . .1G 155
Fielders Cl. EN1: Enf 4K 23
   HA2: Harr .1G 59
Fieldfare Rd. SE28 . . . . .7C 90
Fieldgate La. CR4: Mitc 2C 154
Fieldgate Mans. E1 . . . . .5G 85
   (off Fieldgate St., not continuous)
Fieldgate St. E1 . . . . .5G 85
Field Ho. NW6 .3F 81
   (off Harvist Rd.)
   SM4: Mord 5K 153
   (off School Ga. Dr.)
Fieldhouse Cl. E18 . . . . .1J 51
Fieldhouse Rd. SW12 . . . . .1G 137
Fielding Av. TW2: Twick 3G 131
Fielding Ct. WC2 . . . . .1E 12
   (off Earlham St.)
Fielding Ho. NW6 . . . . .3J 81
   NW8 . . . . .1A 82
   (off Ainsworth Way)
   W4 . . . . .6A 98
   (off Devonshire Rd.)
Fielding La. BR2: Brom 4A 160
Fielding M. SW13 . . . . .6D 98

Fielding Rd. W4 ... 3K 97
  W14 ... 3F 99
Fieldings, The SE23 ... 1J 139
Fielding St. SE17 ... 6C 102
Fielding Ter. W5 ... 7F 79
Fielding Wlk. W13 ... 3B 96
Field La. TW8: Bford ... 7C 96
  TW11: Tedd ... 5A 132
Field Maple M. RM5: Col R ... 1G 55
Field Mead NW7 ... 7F 29
  NW9 ... 7F 29
Fieldpark Gdns. CRO: C'don ... 1A 170
Field Pl. KT3: N Mald ... 6B 152
Field Point E7 ... 4J 69
Field Rd. E7 ... 4H 69
  N17 ... 3D 48
  TW14: Felt ... 6K 111
  W6 ... 5G 99
Fieldsend Rd. SM3: Cheam ... 5G 165
Fields Est. E8 ... 7G 67
Fieldside Cl. BR6: Farnb ... 4G 173
Fieldside Rd. BR1: Brom ... 5F 141
Fields Pk. Cres. RM6: Chad H ... 5D 54
Field St. WC1 ... 1G 7 (3K 83)
Fieldsway Ho. N5 ... 5A 66
Field Vw. TW13: Felt ... 4F 129
Fieldview SW18 ... 1B 136
Field Vw. Cl. RM7: Mawney ... 3G 55
Fieldview Cotts. N14 ... 2C 32
  (off Balaams La.)
Field Way HA4: Ruis ... 1E 56
  NW10 ... 7J 61
  UB6: G'frd ... 1F 77
Fieldway BR5: Pet W ... 6H 161
  CRO: New Ad ... 7D 170
  RM8: Dag ... 3C 72
Fieldway Cres. N5 ... 5A 66
Fiennes Cl. RM8: Dag ... 1C 72
Fifehead Cl. TW15: Ashf ... 6A 128
Fife Rd. E16 ... 5J 87
  KT1: King T ... 2E 150
  N22 ... 7G 33
  SW14 ... 5J 115
Fife Ter. N1 ... 2K 83
Fifield Path SE23 ... 3K 139
Fifth Av. E12 ... 4D 70
  UB3: Hayes ... 1H 93
  W10 ... 3G 81
Fifth Cross Rd. TW2: Twick ... 2H 131
Fifth Way HA9: Wemb ... 4H 61
Figges Rd. CR4: Mitc ... 7E 136
Fight for Peace Academy ... 1E 106
Fig Tree Cl. NW10 ... 1A 80
Figure Ct. SW3 ... 6F 17
Filanco Ct. W7 ... 1K 95
Filby Rd. KT9: Chess ... 6F 163
Filey Av. N16 ... 1G 67
Filey Cl. SM2: Sutt ... 7A 166
Filey Waye HA4: Ruis ... 2J 57
Filigree Ct. SE16 ... 1B 104
Fillebrook Av. EN1: Enf ... 2K 23
Fillebrook Rd. E11 ... 1F 69
Filmer Chambers SW6 ... 1G 117
  (off Filmer Rd.)
Filmer Ho. SW6 ... 1H 117
  (off Filmer Rd.)
Filmer M. SW6 ... 1H 117
Filmer Rd. SW6 ... 1G 117
Filston Rd. DA8: Erith ... 5J 109
Filton Cl. NW9 ... 1A 44
Filton Ct. SE14 ... 7J 103
  (off Farrow La.)
Finborough Ho. SW10 ... 6A 100
  (off Finborough Rd.)
Finborough Rd. SW10 ... 5K 99
  SW17 ... 6D 136
Finborough Theatre, The ... 6K 99
  (off Finborough Rd.)
Finchale Rd. SE2 ... 3A 108
Fincham Cl. UB10: Ick ... 3E 56
Finch Av. SE27 ... 4D 138

Finch Cl. EN5: Barn ... 5D 20
  NW10 ... 6K 61
Finch Ct. DA14: Sidc ... 3B 144
Finchdean Ho. SW15 ... 7B 116
Finch Dr. TW14: Felt ... 7B 112
Finch Gdns. E4 ... 5H 35
Finch Ho. E3 ... 1B 86
  (off Jasmine Sq.)
  SE8 ... 7D 104
  (off Bronze St.)
Finchingfield Av. IG8: Wfd G ... 7F 37
Finch La. EC3 ... 1F 15 (6D 84)
FINCHLEY ... 1J 45
Finchley Cl. N3 ... 6E 30
Finchley Golf Course ... 6C 30
Finchley Ind. Est. N12 ... 4F 31
Finchley La. NW4 ... 4E 44
Finchley Lido ... 7G 31
Finchley Manor Club ... 1H 45
Finchley Pk. N12 ... 4F 31
Finchley Pl. NW8 ... 2B 82
Finchley Rd. NW2 ... 4H 45
  NW3 ... 4H 45
  NW8 ... 1B 82
  NW11 ... 4H 45
Finchley Way N3 ... 7D 30
Finch Lodge W9 ... 5J 81
  (off Admiral Wlk.)
Finch M. SE15 ... 1F 121
Finch's Ct. E14 ... 7D 86
Finden Rd. E7 ... 5A 70
Findhorn Av. UB4: Yead ... 5K 75
Findhorn St. E14 ... 6E 86
Findlay Ho. E3 ... 3C 86
  (off Trevithick Way)
Findon Cl. HA2: Harr ... 3F 59
  SW18 ... 6J 117
Findon Rd. N9 ... 1C 34
  W12 ... 2C 98
Fine Bush La. UB9: Hare ... 6D 38
Fingal St. SE10 ... 5H 105
Fingest Ho. NW8 ... 3C 4
  (off Lilestone St.)
Finians Cl. UB10: Uxb ... 7B 56
Finland Rd. SE4 ... 3A 122
Finland St. SE16 ... 3A 104
Finlays Cl. KT9: Chess ... 5G 163
Finlay St. SW6 ... 1F 117
Finley Ct. SE5 ... 7C 102
  (off Redcar St.)
Finmere Ho. N4 ... 7C 48
Finmere Ho. N1 ... 1C 84
  (off Britannia Row)
Finney La. TW7: Isle ... 1A 114
Finn Ho. N1 ... 1F 9
  (off Bevenden St.)
Finnis St. E2 ... 3H 85
Finnymore Rd. RM9: Dag ... 7E 72
FINSBURY ... 3C 8 (3A 84)
Finsbury Av. EC2 ... 6F 9 (5D 84)
Finsbury Av. Sq. EC2 ... 5G 9 (5E 84)
Finsbury Cir. EC2 ... 6F 9 (5D 84)
Finsbury Cotts. N22 ... 7D 32
Finsbury Est. EC1 ... 2K 7 (3A 84)
Finsbury Ho. N22 ... 1J 47
Finsbury Leisure Cen. ... 3C 8 (3C 84)
Finsbury Mkt. EC2 ... 4G 9 (4E 84)
  (not continuous)
FINSBURY PARK ... 1A 66
Finsbury Pk. Av. N4 ... 6C 48
Finsbury Pk. Rd. N4 ... 2B 66
Finsbury Pavement EC2 ... 5F 9 (5D 84)
Finsbury Rd. N22 ... 7E 32
  (not continuous)
Finsbury Sq. EC2 ... 4F 9 (4D 84)
Finsbury St. EC2 ... 5E 8 (5D 84)
Finsbury Way DA5: Bexl ... 6F 127
Finsen Rd. SE5 ... 4C 120
Finstock Rd. W10 ... 6F 81
Finucane Ct. TW9: Rich ... 3F 115
  (off Lwr. Mortlake Rd.)

Finucane Ri. WD23: B Hea ... 2B 26
Finwhale Ho. E14 ... 3D 104
  (off Glengall Gro.)
Fiona Ct. EN2: Enf ... 3G 23
  NW6 ... 2J 81
Firbank Cl. E16 ... 5B 88
  EN2: Enf ... 4H 23
Firbank Rd. SE15 ... 2H 121
Fir Cl. KT12: Walt T ... 7J 147
Fircroft Gdns. HA1: Harr ... 3J 59
Fircroft Rd. KT9: Chess ... 4F 163
  SW17 ... 2D 136
Fir Dene BR6: Farnb ... 3D 172
Firdene KT5: Surb ... 1J 163
Fire Bell All. KT6: Surb ... 6E 150
Firecrest Dr. NW3 ... 3K 63
Firefly Cl. UB3: Hayes ... 7H 75
  UB5: N'olt ... 3B 76
Firefly Gdns. E6 ... 4C 88
Firehorn Ho. E15 ... 3G 87
  (off Teasel Way)
Firemans Flats N22 ... 7D 32
Firepower (The Royal Artillery Mus.)
  ... 3F 107
Fire Station All. EN5: Barn ... 3B 20
Fire Station M. BR3: Beck ... 1C 158
Firestone Ho. TW8: Bford ... 5E 96
Firethorn Cl. HA8: Edg ... 4D 28
Firewatch Cl. E1 ... 5A 86
  (off Candle St.)
Fir Gro. KT3: N Mald ... 6B 152
Fir Gro. Rd. SW9 ... 2A 120
Firhill Rd. SE6 ... 4C 140
Fir Ho. W10 ... 4G 81
  (off Droop St.)
Firle Ho. W10 ... 5E 80
  (off Sutton Way)
Firman Cl. KT3: N Mald ... 4A 152
Firmans Ct. E17 ... 4F 51
Fir Rd. SM3: Sutt ... 1H 165
  TW13: Hanw ... 5B 130
Firs, The DA5: Bexl ... 1K 145
  DA15: Sidc ... 2K 143
  E6 ... 7C 70
  HA8: Edg ... 4E 28
  (off Stoneyfields La.)
  IG8: Wfd G ... 7F 37
  N20 ... 1G 31
  SE26 ... 5H 139
  (Border Rd.)
  SE26 ... 5J 139
  (Waverley St.)
  W5 ... 5D 78
Firs Av. N10 ... 3E 46
  N11 ... 6J 31
  SW14 ... 4J 115
Firsby Av. CRO: C'don ... 1K 169
Firsby Rd. N16 ... 1G 67
Firs Cl. CR4: Mitc ... 2F 155
  N10 ... 4E 46
  SE23 ... 7A 122
Firscroft N13 ... 3H 33
Fir Dr. TW5: Cran ... 7K 93
Firs Ho. N22 ... 1A 48
  (off Acacia Rd.)
Firside Gro. DA15: Sidc ... 1K 143
Firs La. N13 ... 3H 33
  N21 ... 7H 23
Firs Pk. Av. N21 ... 1J 33
Firs Pk. Gdns. N21 ... 1H 33
First Av. DA7: Bex ... 7C 108
  E12 ... 4C 70
  E13 ... 3J 87
  E17 ... 5C 50
  EN1: Enf ... 5A 24
  HA9: Wemb ... 2D 60
  KT8: W Mole ... 4D 148
  KT12: Walt T ... 6K 147
  KT19: Ewe ... 7A 164
  N18 ... 4D 34
  NW4 ... 4E 44

First Av. RM6: Chad H ... 5C 54
  RM10: Dag ... 2H 91
  SW14 ... 3A 116
  UB3: Hayes ... 1H 93
  W3 ... 1B 98
  W10 ... 4H 81
First Cl. KT8: W Mole ... 3G 149
First Cross Rd. TW2: Twick ... 2J 131
First Dr. NW10 ... 7J 61
First St. SW3 ... 3D 16 (4C 100)
First Way HA9: Wemb ... 4H 61
Firstway SW20 ... 2E 152
Firs Wlk. IG8: Wfd G ... 5D 36
Firswood Av. KT19: Ewe ... 5A 164
Firth Gdns. SW6 ... 1G 117
Firth Ho. E2 ... 3G 85
  (off Turin St.)
Fir Tree Av. UB7: W Dray ... 3C 92
Firtree Av. CR4: Mitc ... 2E 154
Fir Tree Cl. BR6: Chels ... 5K 173
  KT19: Ewe ... 4B 164
  RM1: Rom ... 3K 55
  SW16 ... 5G 137
  W5 ... 6E 78
Fir Tree Gdns. CRO: C'don ... 4C 170
Fir Tree Gro. SM5: Cars ... 7D 166
Firtree Ho. SE13 ... 7F 123
  (off Birdwood Av.)
Fir Tree Pl. TW15: Ashf ... 5C 128
Fir Tree Rd. TW4: Houn ... 4C 112
Fir Trees Cl. SE16 ... 1A 104
Fir Tree Wlk. EN1: Enf ... 3J 23
  RM10: Dag ... 3J 73
Fir Wlk. SM3: Cheam ... 6F 165
Fisher Cl. CRO: C'don ... 1F 169
  E9 ... 5K 67
  UB6: G'frd ... 3E 76
Fisher Ho. E1 ... 1A 84
  (off Cable St.)
  N1 ... 1A 84
  (off Barnsbury Est.)
Fisherman Cl. TW10: Ham ... 4B 132
Fishermans Dr. SE16 ... 2K 103
Fishermans Pl. W4 ... 6B 98
Fishermans Wlk. E14 ... 1C 104
  SE28 ... 2J 107
Fisher Rd. HA3: W'stone ... 2K 41
Fisher's Cl. SW16 ... 3H 137
Fishers Ct. SE14 ... 1K 121
Fishersdene KT10: Clay ... 7A 162
Fisher's La. W4 ... 4K 97
Fisher St. E16 ... 5H 87
  WC1 ... 6G 7 (5K 83)
Fishers Way DA17: Belv ... 1J 109
  HA0: Wemb ... 5B 60
Fisherton St. NW8 ... 4A 4 (4B 82)
Fishguard Way E16 ... 1F 107
Fishmongers Hall Wharf EC4 ... 3E 14
Fishponds Rd. BR2: Kes ... 5B 172
  SW17 ... 4C 136
Fish St. Hill EC3 ... 3F 15 (7D 84)
Fish Wharf EC3 ... 3F 15 (7D 84)
Fisk Cl. TW16: Sun ... 6H 129
Fiske Ct. IG11: Bark ... 2H 89
  N17 ... 1G 49
  SM2: Sutt ... 7A 166
Fit4less
  Aldgate ... 2K 15
  (off Mansell St.)
  Sutton ... 6J 165
Fitch Cl. SW2 ... 5A 120
Fitness 4 Less
  Canning Town ... 5G 87
Fitness First
  America Square ... 2K 15
  Baker Street ... 5D 82
  Beckenham ... 5B 140
  Berkeley Square ... 3K 11 (7F 83)
  Bloomsbury ... 4E 6
  Brixton ... 3A 120
  Camden ... 1F 83

Fitness First
Chancery Lane 6K 7
Clapham Junction 4C 118
Covent Garden 3F 13
(off Bedford St.)
Embankment 4F 13
(off Embankment Pl.)
Fetter Lane 1K 13
(off Fetter La.)
Gracechurch Street 2G 15
(off Gracechurch St.)
Great Marlborough Street 1A 12
Hammersmith 4E 98
Harrow 6J 41
(within St George's Shop. & Leisure Cen.)
High Holborn 6G 7
(off High Holborn)
Highbury 3B 66
Ilford 2G 71
Islington 1A 8 (2B 84)
Kilburn 1H 81
Kingly Street 2A 12
Kingsbury 5G 43
Leyton Mills 3E 68
London Bridge 5F 15
(off London Bri. St.)
North Finchley 5F 31
Old Street 3E 8
(off Featherstone St.)
Paternoster Square 7B 8
Pinner 3B 40
Queen Victoria Street 2C 14
(off Queen Victoria St.)
South Kensington 3A 16
(off Harrington Rd.)
Streatham 2J 137
Thomas More Square 7G 85
(off Thomas More Sq.)
Tooting Bec 3E 136
Victoria 1A 18
Walworth Road 5C 102
Wembley 5E 60
Fitrooms 6H 99
(off North End Rd.)
FitSpace Gym 3F 107
Fitzalan Rd. N3 . . . . .3G 45
Fitzalan St. SE11 . . . . .3H 19 (4A 102)
Fitzclarence Ho. W11 . . . . . . .2G 99
(off Holland Park Av.)
Fitzgeorge Av. KT3: N Mald 1K 151
W14 . . . . .4G 99
Fitzgerald Av. SW14 . . . . . . .3A 116
Fitzgerald Ct. E10 . . . . .1D 68
(off Leyton Grange Est.)
Fitzgerald Ho. E14 . . . . .6D 86
(off E. India Dock Rd.)
SW9 . . . . .2A 120
SW17 . . . . .3B 136
UB3: Hayes 1K 93
Fitzgerald Rd. E11 . . . . .5J 51
KT7: T Ditt 6A 150
SW14 . . . . .3K 115
Fitzhardinge Ho. W1 . . . . .7G 5
(off Portman Sq.)
Fitzhardinge St. W1 . . . . .7G 5 (6E 82)
Fitzherbert Wlk. UB1: S'hall . . .2H 95
Fitzhugh Gro. SW18 . . . . .6B 118
Fitzjames Av. CR0: C'don 2G 169
W14 . . . . .4G 99
Fitzjohn Av. EN5: Barn 5B 20
Fitzjohn's Av. NW3 . . . . .4A 64
Fitzmaurice Ho. SE16 . . . . . . .4H 103
(off Rennie St.)
Fitzmaurice Pl. W1 . . . .4K 11 (1F 101)
Fitzneal St. W12 . . . . .6B 80
Fitzpatrick Rd. SW9 . . . . . . .1B 120
FITZROVIA 5K 5
Fitzrovia Apartments W1 . . . . . .4K 5
(off Bolsover St.)
Fitzroy Bri. NW1 . . . . .1E 82
Fitzroy Bus. Pk. BR5: St P 7D 144

Fitzroy Cl. N6 . . . . .1D 64
Fitzroy Ct. CR0: C'don 7D 156
N6 . . . . .6G 47
W1 . . . . .4B 6
Fitzroy Cres. W4 . . . . .7K 97
Fitzroy Gdns. SE19 . . . . .7E 138
Fitzroy Ho. E14 . . . . .5B 86
(off Wallwood St.)
SE1 . . . . .5F 103
(off Cooper's Rd.)
Fitzroy House Mus. 4A 6 (4G 83)
Fitzroy M. W1 . . . . .4A 6
Fitzroy Pk. N6 . . . . .1D 64
Fitzroy Rd. NW1 . . . . .1E 82
Fitzroy Sq. W1 . . . . .4A 6 (4G 83)
Fitzroy St. W1 . . . . .4A 6 (4G 83)
(not continuous)
Fitzroy Yd. NW1 . . . . .1E 82
Fitzstephen Rd. RM8: Dag 5B 72
Fitzwarren Gdns. N19 . . . . . . .1G 65
Fitzwilliam Av. TW9: Rich 2F 115
Fitzwilliam Cl. N20 . . . . .1K 31
Fitzwilliam Hgts. SE23 . . . . . .2J 139
Fitzwilliam Ho. TW9: Rich 4D 114
Fitzwilliam M. E16 . . . . .1J 105
Fitzwilliam Rd. SW4 . . . . .3G 119
Fitzwygram Cl. TW12: Hamp H . . .5G 131
Five Acre NW9 . . . . .1B 44
Fiveacre Cl. CR7: Thor H 6A 156
Five Bell All. E14 . . . . .6B 86
(off Three Colt St.)
Five Elms Rd. BR2: Hayes 3K 171
RM9: Dag 3F 73
Five Oaks M. BR1: Brom 3J 141
Fives Cl. SE11 . . . . .3B 102
FIVEWAYS 2F 143
Five Ways Bus. Cen. TW13: Felt . . .3K 129
FIVEWAYS CORNER
CROYDON 4A 168
HENDON 1C 44
Fiveways Rd. SW9 . . . . .2A 120
Flack Cl. E10 . . . . .7D 50
Fladbury Rd. N15 . . . . .6D 48
Fladgate Rd. E11 . . . . .6G 51
Flag Cl. CR0: C'don 1K 169
Flagon Ct. CR0: C'don 4C 168
(off St Andrew's Rd.)
Flag Wlk. HA5: Eastc 6J 39
Flambard Av. HA1: Harr 6A 42
Flamborough Ho. SE15 . . . . . . .1G 121
(off Clayton Rd.)
Flamborough Rd. HA4: Ruis 3J 57
Flamborough St. E14 . . . . .6A 86
Flamborough Wlk. E14 . . . . .6A 86
(off Flamborough St.)
Flamingo Ct. SE8 . . . . .7C 104
(off Hamilton St.)
SE17 . . . . .5C 102
(off Crampton St.)
Flamingo Gdns. UB5: N'olt 3C 76
Flamstead Gdns. RM9: Dag 7C 72
Flamstead Ho. SW3 . . . . .5C 16
(off Cale St.)
Flamstead Rd. RM9: Dag 7C 72
Flamsted Av. HA9: Wemb 6G 61
Flamsteed Rd. SE7 . . . . .5C 106
Flanaghan Apartments E3 . . . . . .4B 86
(off Portia Way)
Flanchford Ho. E12 . . . . .3B 98
Flanchford Rd. W12 . . . . .3E 98
Flanders Ct. E17 . . . . .7A 50
Flanders Cres. SW17 . . . . .7D 136
Flanders Mans. W4 . . . . .4B 98
Flanders Rd. E6 . . . . .2D 88
W4 . . . . .4A 98
Flanders Way E9 . . . . .6K 67
Flandrian Cl. EN3: Enf L 1J 25
Flank St. E1 . . . . .7G 85
Flannery Ct. SE16 . . . . .3H 103
Flansham Ho. E14 . . . . .6B 86
(off Clemence St.)

Flask Wlk. NW3 . . . . .4A 64
Flatford Ho. SE6 . . . . .4E 140
Flather Cl. SW16 . . . . .5G 137
Flat Iron Sq. SE1 . . . . .5D 14
(off Southwark Bri. Rd.)
Flatiron Yd. SE1 . . . . .5D 14
(off Ayres St.)
Flavell M. SE10 . . . . .5G 105
Flaxen Cl. E4 . . . . .3J 35
Flaxen Rd. E4 . . . . .3J 35
Flaxley Ho. SW1 . . . . .5J 17
(part of Abbots Mnr.)
Flaxley Rd. SM4: Mord 7K 153
Flaxman Ct. DA17: Belv 5G 109
(off Hoddesdon St.)
W1 . . . . .1C 12 (6H 83)
WC1 . . . . .2D 6
(off Flaxman Ter.)
Flaxman Ho. SE1 . . . . .3B 102
(off London Rd.)
W4 . . . . .5A 98
(off Devonshire St.)
Flaxman Rd. SE5 . . . . .3B 120
Flaxman Sports Cen. 3C 120
Flaxman Ter. WC1 . . . . .2D 6 (3H 83)
Flaxton Rd. SE18 . . . . .7H 107
Flecker Cl. HA7: Stan 5E 26
Flecker Ho. SE5 . . . . .7D 102
(off Lomond Gro.)
Fleece Dr. N9 . . . . .4B 34
Fleece Rd. KT6: Surb 1C 162
Fleece Wlk. N7 . . . . .6J 65
Fleeming Cl. E17 . . . . .2B 50
Fleeming Rd. E17 . . . . .2B 50
Fleetbank Ho. EC4 . . . . .1K 13
(off Salisbury Sq.)
Fleet Bldg. EC4 . . . . .7A 8
Fleet Cl. HA4: Ruis 6E 38
KT8: W Mole 5D 148
Fleetfield WC1 . . . . .1F 7
(off Birkenhead St.)
Fleet Ho. E14 . . . . .7A 86
(off Victory Pl.)
Fleet La. KT8: W Mole 6D 148
Fleet Pl. EC4 . . . . .7A 8 (6B 84)
Fleet Rd. NW3 . . . . .5C 64
Fleetside KT8: W Mole 5D 148
Fleet Sq. WC1 . . . . .2H 7 (3K 83)
Fleet St. EC4 . . . . .1J 13 (6A 84)
Fleetway WC1 . . . . .1F 7
(off Birkenhead St.)
Fleetway W. UB6: G'frd 2B 78
Fleetwood Cl. CR0: C'don 3F 169
E16 . . . . .5B 88
KT9: Chess 7D 162
Fleetwood Ct. E6 . . . . .5D 88
(off Evelyn Dennington Rd.)
TW19: Stanw 6A 110
(off Douglas Rd.)
Fleetwood Rd. KT1: King T 3H 151
NW10 . . . . .5C 62
Fleetwood Sq. KT1: King T 3H 151
Fleetwood St. N16 . . . . .2E 66
Fleming N8 . . . . .3J 47
(off Boyton Cl.)
Fleming Cl. SW10 . . . . .7A 16
(off Winterton Pl.)
W9 . . . . .4J 81
Fleming Collection, The 7F 83
(off Berkeley St.)
Fleming Ct. CR0: Wadd 5A 168
W2 . . . . .5A 4
Fleming Dr. N21 . . . . .5E 22
Fleming Ho. HA9: Wemb 3J 61
(off Barnhill Rd.)
N4 . . . . .1C 66
SE16 . . . . .2G 103
(off George Row)
SW17 . . . . .3B 136
Fleming Lodge W9 . . . . .5J 81
(off Admiral Wlk.)

Fleming Mead CR4: Mitc 7C 136
Fleming Rd. SE17 . . . . .6B 102
UB1: S'hall 6F 77
Fleming Wlk. NW9 . . . . .3A 44
Fleming Way SE28 . . . . .7D 90
TW7: Isle 4K 113
Flempton Av. HA4: Ruis 1K 57
Flempton Rd. E10 . . . . .1A 68
Fletcher Bldgs. WC2 . . . . .1F 13
(off Martlett Ct.)
Fletcher Cl. E6 . . . . .6F 89
NW9 . . . . .3A 44
Fletcher Ho. N1 . . . . .1E 84
(off Nuttall St.)
SE15 . . . . .7J 103
(off Clifton Way)
Fletcher La. E10 . . . . .7E 50
Fletcher Path SE8 . . . . .7C 104
Fletcher Rd. W4 . . . . .3J 97
Fletchers Cl. BR2: Brom 4K 159
Fletcher St. E1 . . . . .7G 85
Fletching Rd. E5 . . . . .3J 67
SE7 . . . . .6A 106
Fletton Rd. N11 . . . . .7D 32
Fleur de Lis St. E1 . . . . .4H 9 (4F 85)
Fleur Gates SW19 . . . . .7F 117
Flexmere Gdns. N17 . . . . .1D 48
Flexmere Rd. N17 . . . . .1D 48
Flight App. NW9 . . . . .2B 44
Flight Ho. N1 . . . . .1E 84
(off Phillipp St.)
Flimwell Cl. BR1: Brom 5G 141
Flinders Ho. E1 . . . . .1H 103
(off Green Bank)
Flint Cl. BR6: Chels 6K 173
CR0: C'don 6K 155
E15 . . . . .7H 69
Flintlock Cl. E1 . . . . .6H 85
Flintlock Ct. TW19: Stanw M 7B 174
Flintmill Cres. SE3 . . . . .2C 124
Flinton St. SE17 . . . . .5E 102
Flint St. SE17 . . . . .5D 102
Flitcroft St. WC2 . . . . . .1D 12 (6H 83)
Flitton Ho. N1 . . . . .7B 66
(off The Sutton Est.)
Floathaven Cl. SE28 . . . . .1A 108
Flock Mill Pl. SW18 . . . . .1K 135
Flockton St. SE16 . . . . .2G 103
Flodden Rd. SE5 . . . . .1C 120
Flood La. TW1: Twick 1A 132
Flood Pas. SE18 . . . . .3C 106
Flood St. SW3 . . . . . . .6D 16 (5C 100)
Flood Wlk. SW3 . . . . . .7D 16 (6C 100)
Flora Cl. E14 . . . . .6D 86
HA7: Stan 3K 27
Flora Gdns. RM6: Chad H 6C 54
W6 . . . . .4D 98
(off Albion Gdns.)
Flora Ho. E3 . . . . .1C 86
(off Garrison Rd.)
Floral Pl. N1 . . . . .5A 66
Floral St. WC2 . . . . . . .2E 12 (7J 83)
Flora St. DA17: Belv 5F 109
Florence Av. EN2: Enf 3H 23
SM4: Mord 5A 154
Florence Cantwell Wlk. N19 . . . . .7J 47
(off Jessie Blythe La.)
Florence Cl. KT12: Walt T 7K 147
Florence Cl. E11 . . . . .4K 51
N1 . . . . .7B 66
(off Florence St.)
SW19 . . . . .6G 135
W9 . . . . .3A 82
(off Maida Vale)
Florence Dr. EN2: Enf 3H 23
Florence Elson Cl. E12 . . . . . . .4E 70
Florence Gdns.
RM6: Chad H 7C 54
W4 . . . . .6J 97
Florence Ho. KT2: King T 7F 133
(off Florence Rd.)

Florence Ho.—Forge La.

Florence Ho. *SE16* 5H 103
(off Rotherhithe New Rd.)
W11 . . . . .7F 81
(off St Ann's Rd.)
Florence Mans. *NW4* 5D 44
(off Vivian Av.)
SW6 .1H 117
(off Rostrevor Rd.)
Florence Nightingale Mus. . . .7G 13 (2K 101)
Florence Rd. BR1: Brom 1J 159
BR3: Beck 2A 158
CR2: Sande 7D 168
E6 . . . . .1A 88
E13 . . . . .2J 87
KT2: King T 7F 133
KT12: Walt T 7K 147
N4 . . . . .7K 47
(not continuous)
SE2 . . . . .4C 108
SE14 .1B 122
SW19 .6K 135
TW13: Felt 1K 129
UB2: S'hall 4B 94
W4 . . . . .3K 97
W5 . . . . .7E 78
Florence Root Ho. IG4: Ilf 5C 52
Florence Sq. E3 . . . . .4D 86
Florence St. E16 . . . . .4H 87
N1 . . . . .7B 66
NW4 . . . . .4E 44
Florence Ter. SE14 . . . . .1B 122
SW15 .3A 134
Florence Way SW12 . . . . .1D 136
Florey Lodge *W9* 5J 81
(off Admiral Wlk.)
Florey Sq. N21 . . . . .5E 22
Florfield Pas. *E8* 6H 67
(off Reading La.)
Florfield Rd. E8 . . . . .6H 67
Florian SE5 .1E 120
Florian Av. SM1: Sutt 4B 166
Florian Ct. *E16* 5J 87
(off Hastings Rd.)
Florian Rd. SW15 . . . . .4G 117
Florida Cl. WD23: B Hea 2C 26
Florida Ct. *BR2: Brom* 4H 159
(off Westmoreland Rd.)
Florida Rd. CR7: Thor H 1B 156
Florida St. E2 . . . . .3G 85
Florin Ct. EC1 .5C 8
N18 . . . . .4K 33
SE1 . . . . .7J 15
(off Tanner St.)
Floris Pl. SW4 . . . . .3G 119
Floriston Av. UB10: Hil 7E 56
Floriston Cl. HA7: Stan 1B 42
Floriston Ct. UB5: N'olt 5F 59
Floriston Gdns. HA7: Stan 1B 42
Florys Ct. SW19 . . . . .1G 135
Floss St. SW15 . . . . .2E 116
Flotilla Ho. SW18 . . . . .3A 118
Flower & Dean Wlk. E1 . . . . .6K 9 (5F 85)
Flowerdown Ct. *HA4: Eastc* 6J 39
(off Lidgould Gro.)
Flower La. NW7 . . . . .5G 29
Flower M. NW11 . . . . .6G 45
Flower Pot Cl. N15 . . . . .6F 49
Flowers Av. HA4: Eastc, Ruis 6J 39
Flowers Cl. NW2 . . . . .3C 62
Flowersmead SW17 . . . . .2E 136
Flowers M. N19 . . . . .2G 65
Flower Walk, The SW7 . . . . . .6A 10 (2A 100)
Floyd Rd. SE7 . . . . .5A 106
Floyer Cl. TW10: Rich 5F 115
Fludyer St. SE13 . . . . .4G 123
Flying Angel Ho. *E16* 7K 87
(off Victoria Dock Rd.)
Flynn Ct. *E14* .7C 86
(off Garford St.)
Foley Ho. *E1* 6J 85
(off Tarling St.)
Foley St. W1 . . . . .6A 6 (5G 83)
Folgate St. E1 . . . . .5H 9 (5E 84)
(not continuous)
Foliot Ho. *N1* .2K 83
(off Priory Grn. Est.)
Foliot St. W12 . . . . .6B 80
Folkestone Ct. *UB5: N'olt* 5F 59
(off Newmarket Av.)
Folkestone Ho. *SE17* 5E 102
(off Upnor Way)
Folkestone Rd. E6 . . . . .2E 88
E17 . . . . .4D 50
N18 . . . . .4B 34
Folkingham La. NW9 . . . . .1K 43
Folkington Cnr. N12 . . . . .5C 30
Folland *NW9* 2B 44
(off Hundred Acre)
Follett Ho. *SW10* 7B 100
(off Worlds End Est.)
Follett St. E14 .6E 86
Follingham Ct. *N1* 1H 9
(off Drysdale Pl.)
Folly Brook & Darland's Lake Nature Reserve
. . . . .3B 30
Folly La. E4 . . . . .6G 35
E17 . . . . .1A 50
Folly M. W11 .6H 81
Folly Wall E14 . . . . .2E 104
Fonda Ct. *E14* .7C 86
(off Premiere Pl.)
Fondant Ct. *E3* 2D 86
(off Taylor Pl.)
Fontaine Ho. *E17* 4C 50
(off Hoe St.)
Fontaine Rd. SW16 . . . . .7K 137
Fontarabia Rd. SW11 . . . . .4E 118
Fontayne Av. RM1: Rom 2K 55
Fontenelle SE5 . . . . .1E 120
Fontenoy Ho. *SE11* 4B 102
(off Kennington La.)
Fontenoy Rd. SW12 . . . . .2F 137
Fonteyne Gdns. IG8: Wfd G 2B 52
Fonthill Cl. SE20 . . . . .2G 157
Fonthill Ho. *SW1* 5K 17
(part of Abbots Mnr.)
W14 . . . . .3G 99
(off Russell Rd.)
Fonthill M. N4 . . . . .2K 65
Fonthill Rd. N4 . . . . .1K 65
Font Hills N2 .2A 46
Fontley Way SW15 . . . . .7C 116
Fontmell Cl. TW15: Ashf 5C 128
Fontmell Pk. TW15: Ashf 5B 128
Fontwell Cl. HA3: Hrw W 7D 26
UB5: N'olt 6E 58
Fontwell Dr. BR2: Brom 5E 160
Football La. HA1: Harr 1K 59
Footpath, The SW15 . . . . .6C 116
FOOTS CRAY .6C 144
Foots Cray High St.
DA14: Sidc 6C 144
Foots Cray La. DA14: Sidc 1C 144
Foots Cray Meadows (Nature Reserve)
. . . . .4D 144
Footscray Rd. SE9 . . . . .6E 124
Forber Ho. *E2* .3J 85
(off Cornwall Av.)
Forbes Cl. NW2 . . . . .3C 62
Forbes Ho. *E7* .5A 70
(off Romford Rd.)
W4 . . . . .5G 97
(off Stonehill Rd.)
Forbes St. E1 .6G 85
Forbes Way HA4: Ruis 2K 57
Forburg Rd. N16 . . . . .1G 67
Fordbridge Ct. TW15: Ashf 6A 128
Fordbridge Pk. TW16: Sun 6H 147
Fordbridge Rd. TW15: Ashf 6A 128
TW16: Sun 6G 147
TW17: Shep 6G 147
FORDBRIDGE RDBT. 6A 128
Ford Cl. CR7: Thor H 5B 156
E3 . . . . .2A 86
HA1: Harr 7H 41
TW15: Ashf 6A 128
TW17: Shep 4C 146
Forde Av. BR1: Brom 3A 160
Fordel Rd. SE6 . . . . .1E 140
Ford End IG8: Wfd G 6E 36
Fordgate Bus. Pk. DA17: Belv 2J 109
Fordham *KT1: King T* 2G 151
(off Excelsior Cl.)
Fordham Cl. EN4: Cockf 3H 21
KT4: Wor Pk 1D 164
Fordham Ho. *SE14* 7A 104
(off Angus St.)
Fordham Rd. EN4: Cockf 3G 21
Fordham St. E1 . . . . .6G 85
Fordhook Av. W5 . . . . .1F 97
Ford Ho. EN5: New Bar 5E 20
Fordie Ho. *SW1* 2F 17
(off Sloane St.)
Ford Ind. Pk. RM9: Dag 4H 91
Fordingley Rd. W9 . . . . .3H 81
Fordington Ho. SE26 . . . . .3G 139
Fordington Rd. N6 . . . . .5D 46
Ford Lodge RM7: Rom 4K 55
Fordmill Rd. SE6 . . . . .2C 140
Ford Rd. E3 . . . . .2B 86
RM9: Dag 7F 73
RM10: Dag 7F 73
TW15: Ashf 4B 128
Fords Gro. N21 . . . . .1H 33
Fords Pk. Rd. E16 . . . . .5J 87
Ford Sq. E1 . . . . .5H 85
Ford St. E3 . . . . .1A 86
E16 . . . . .6H 87
Fordview Ind. Est. RM13: Rain 3K 91
Fordwich Cl. BR6: Orp 7K 161
Fordwych Rd. NW2 . . . . .4G 63
Fordyce Rd. SE13 . . . . .6E 122
Fordyke Rd. RM8: Dag 2F 73
Foreign St. SE5 . . . . .2B 120
Foreland Ct. NW4 . . . . .1F 45
Foreland Ho. *W11* 7G 81
(off Walmer Rd.)
Foreland St. SE18 . . . . .4H 107
Forelle Way SM5: Cars 7D 166
Foreman Ct. TW1: Twick 1K 131
Foreman Ho. *SE4* 4K 121
(off Billingford Cl.)
Foreshore SE8 . . . . .4B 104
Forest, The E11 . . . . .4G 51
Forest App. E4 .1B 36
IG8: Wfd G 7D 36
Forest Av. E4 . . . . .1B 36
IG7: Chig 5K 37
Forest Bus. Pk. E10 . . . . .7K 49
Forest Cl. BR7: Chst 1E 160
E11 . . . . .5J 51
IG8: Wfd G 3E 36
N10 . . . . .1F 47
NW6 . . . . .7G 63
Forest Ct. E4 . . . . .1C 36
E11 . . . . .4G 51
N12 . . . . .5E 30
Forest Cft. SE23 . . . . .2H 139
FORESTDALE 7B 170
Forestdale N14 . . . . .4C 32
Forestdale Centre, The CR0: Sels 7B 170
Forest Dene Ct. SM2: Sutt 6A 166
Forest Dr. BR2: Kes 4C 172
BR3: Beck 7B 158
E12 . . . . .3B 70
IG8: Wfd G 7A 36
TW16: Sun 7H 129
Forest Dr. E. E11 . . . . .7F 51
Forest Dr. W. E11 . . . . .7E 50
Forest Edge IG9: Buck H 4F 37
Forester Ho. *E14* 7A 86
(off Victory Pl.)
Forester Rd. SE15 . . . . .3H 121
Foresters Cl. SM6: Wall 7H 167
Foresters Cres. DA7: Bex 4H 127
Foresters Dr. E17 . . . . .4F 51
SM6: Wall 7H 167
Forest Gdns. N17 . . . . .2F 49
FOREST GATE .5J 69
Forest Ga. NW9 . . . . .4A 44
Forest Ga. Retreat *E7* 5J 69
(off Odessa Rd.)
Forest Glade E4 . . . . .4B 36
E11 . . . . .6G 51
Forest Gro. E8 .6F 67
Forest Hgts. IG9: Buck H 2D 36
FOREST HILL .2J 139
Forest Hill Bus. Cen. *SE23* 2J 139
(off Clyde Va.)
Forest Hill Ind. Est. SE23 . . . . .2J 139
Forest Hill Pool 2J 139
Forest Hill Rd. SE22 . . . . .5H 121
SE23 . . . . .5H 121
Forest Hill School Sports Cen. 3K 139
Forestholme Cl. SE23 . . . . .2J 139
Forest Ind. Pk. IG6: Ilf 1J 53
Forest La. E7 .5G 69
E15 . . . . .5G 69
IG7: Chig 5K 37
Forest Lodge *SE23* 3J 139
(off Dartmouth Rd.)
Forest Mt. Rd. IG8: Wfd G 7A 36
Forest Point *E7* .5K 69
(off Windsor Rd.)
Fore St. EC2 . . . . .6D 8 (5C 84)
HA5: Eastc 4H 39
N9 . . . . .4B 34
N18 . . . . .6A 34
Fore St. Av. EC2 . . . . .6E 8 (5D 84)
Forest Ridge BR2: Kes 4C 172
BR3: Beck 3C 158
Forest Ri. E17 .3F 51
Forest Rd. E7 . . . . .4J 69
E8 . . . . .6F 67
E11 . . . . .7F 51
E17 . . . . .4A 50
IG6: Chig, Ilf 2H 53
IG8: Wfd G 3D 36
N9 . . . . .1C 34
N17 . . . . .4J 49
RM7: Mawney 3H 55
SM3: Sutt 1J 165
TW9: Kew 7G 97
TW13: Felt 2A 130
Forest Side E4 .1C 36
E7 . . . . .4K 69
IG9: Buck H 1F 37
KT4: Wor Pk 1B 164
Forest St. E7 . . . . .5J 69
Forest Ter. IG7: Chig 5K 37
Forest Trad. Est. E17 . . . . .3K 49
Forest Vw. E4 . . . . .7K 25 & 1B 36
E11 . . . . .7H 51
Forest Vw. Av. E10 . . . . .5F 51
Forest Vw. Rd. E12 . . . . .4C 70
E17 . . . . .1E 50
Forest Wlk. N10 . . . . .1F 47
Forest Way BR5: St M Cry 5K 161
DA15: Sidc 7H 125
IG8: Wfd G 4E 36
N19 . . . . .2G 65
Forest Works Ind. Est. E17 . . . . .3K 49
Forfar Rd. N22 . . . . .1B 48
SW11 . . . . .1E 118
Forge Cl. BR2: Hayes 1J 171
UB3: Harl 6F 93
Forge Cotts. W5 . . . . .1D 96
Forge Dr. KT10: Clay 7A 162
Forge La.
HA6: Nwood 1G 39
SM3: Cheam 7G 165
TW10: Ham 1E 132
TW13: Hanw 5C 130
TW16: Sun 3J 147

Forge M. CR0: Addtn 5C 170
　TW16: Sun 3J 147
　　　　　　　　　　　　(off Forge La.)
Forge Pl. NW1 . . . . .6E 64
Forge Sq. E14 . . . . .4D 104
Forlong Path UB5: N'olt 6C 58
　　　　　　　　(off Cowings Mead)
Forman Pl. N16 . . . . .4F 67
Formation, The E16 . . . . .2F 107
　　　　　　　(off Woolwich Mnr. Way)
Formby Av. HA7: Stan 3C 42
Formby Ct. N7 . . . . .5A 66
　　　　　　　　　　　(off Morgan Rd.)
Formosa Ho. E1 . . . . .4A 86
　　　　　　　　　　　(off Ernest St.)
Formosa St. W9 . . . . .4K 81
Formunt Cl. E16 . . . . .5H 87
Forres Gdns. NW11 . . . . .6J 45
Forrester Path SE26 . . . . .4J 139
Forrester Way UB4: Yead 6K 75
Forston St. N1 . . . . .2C 84
Forsyte Cres. SE19 . . . . .1E 156
Forsyte Ho. SW3 . . . . .6D 16
Forsythe Shades Ct. BR3: Beck 1E 158
Forsyth Gdns. SE17 . . . . .6B 102
Forsyth Ho. E9 . . . . .7J 67
　　　　　　　　(off Frampton Pk. Rd.)
　SW1 . . . . .5B 18
　　　　　　　　　　(off Tachbrook St.)
Forsythia Cl. IG1: Ilf 5F 71
Forsyth Pl. EN1: Enf 5K 23
Forterie Gdns. IG3: Bark, Ilf 3A 72
Fortescue Av. E8 . . . . .7H 67
　　TW2: Twick 3G 131
Fortescue Rd. HA8: Edg 1K 43
　　SW19 . . . . .7B 136
Fortess Gro. NW5 . . . . .5G 65
Fortess Rd. NW5 . . . . .5F 65
Fortess Wlk. NW5 . . . . .5F 65
Fortess Yd. NW5 . . . . .4F 65
Forthbridge Rd. SW11 . . . . .4E 118
Forth Ho. E3 .2B 86
　　　　　　　　　　　(off Tredegar Rd.)
Fortis Cl. E16 .6A 88
Fortis Ct. N10 . . . . .3E 46
FORTIS GREEN 4D 46
Fortis Grn. N2 . . . . .4C 46
　　N10 . . . . .4C 46
Fortis Grn. Av. N2 . . . . .3D 46
Fortis Grn. Rd. N10 . . . . .3E 46
Fortismere Av. N10 . . . . .3E 46
Fortius Apartments E3 . . . . .2C 86
　　　　　　　　　　　(off Tredegar La.)
Fortius Wlk. E20 . . . . .6E 68
Fortnam Rd. N19 . . . . .2H 65
Fortnum's Acre HA7: Stan 6E 26
Fort Rd. SE1 . . . . .4F 103
　　UB5: N'olt 7E 58
Fortrose Cl. E14 . . . . .6F 87
Fortrose Gdns. SW2 . . . . .1J 137
　　　　　　　　　　　(not continuous)
Fort St. E1 . . . . .6H 9 (5E 84)
　　E16 . . . . .1K 105

Fortuna Cl. N7 . . . . .6K 65
Fortuna Ho. E20 . . . . .5D 68
　　　　　　　　　　　(off Scarlet Cl.)
Fortune Av. HA8: Edg 1H 43
Fortune Ct. E8 . . . . .7F 67
　　　　　　　　(off Queensbridge Rd.)
　　IG11: Bark 2C 90
Fortunegate Rd. NW10 . . . . .1A 80
FORTUNE GREEN 5J 63
Fortune Grn. Rd. NW6 . . . . .4J 63
Fortune Ho. EC1 . . . . .4D 8
　　　　　　　　　　　(off Fortune St.)
　SE11 . . . . .4J 19
Fortune Pl. SE1 . . . . .5F 103
Fortunes Mead UB5: N'olt 6C 58
Fortune St. EC1 . . . . .4D 8 (4C 84)
Fortunes Wlk. E20 . . . . .5E 68
Fortune Theatre 1F 13
　　　　　　　　　　　(off Russell St.)
Fortune Wlk. SE28 . . . . .3H 107
　　　　　　　　　(off Broadwater Rd.)
Fortune Way NW10 . . . . .3C 80
Forty Acre La. E16 . . . . .5J 87
Forty Av. HA9: Wemb 3F 61
Forty Cl. HA9: Wemb 3F 61
Forty Footpath SW14 . . . . .3J 115
Forty Foot Way SE9 . . . . .7G 125
FORTY HILL .1K 23
Forty Hill EN2: Enf 1K 23
Forty La. HA9: Wemb 2H 61
Forum, The KT8: W Mole 4F 149
Forum Cl. E3 .1C 86
Forum Ho. HA9: Wemb 4G 61
Forum Magnum Sq. SE1 . . . . .6H 13
　　　　　　　　　　　　　(off York Rd.)
Forumside HA8: Edg 6B 28
Forum Way HA8: Edg 6B 28
Forval Cl. CR4: Mitc 5D 154
Forward Bus. Centre, The E16 . . . . . .4F 87
Forward Dr. HA3: W'stone 4K 41
Fosbrooke Ho. SW8 . . . . .7J 101
　　　　　　　　　(off Davidson Gdns.)
Fosbury M. W2 . . . . .7K 81
Foscote Ct. W9 . . . . .4J 81
　　　　　　　　　　　(off Amberley Rd.)
Foscote M. W9 . . . . .4J 81
Foscote Rd. NW4 . . . . .6D 44
Foskett M. N2 . . . . .2B 46
　　　　　　　　　　　(off The Grange)
Foskett M. E8 .5F 67
Foskett Rd. SW6 . . . . .2H 117
Foss Av. CR0: Wadd 5A 168
Fosdene Rd. SE7 . . . . .5K 105
Fossdyke Cl. UB4: Yead 5C 76
Fosset Lodge DA7: Bex 1J 127
Fosse Way W13 . . . . .5A 78
Foss Ho. NW8 . . . . .2K 81
　　　　　　　　　　　(off Carlton Hill)
Fossil Ct. SE1 .7G 15
　　　　　　　　　　　　(off Long La.)
Fossil Rd. SE13 . . . . .3C 122
Fossington Rd. DA17: Belv 4D 108
Foss Rd. SW17 . . . . .4B 136
Fossway RM8: Dag 2C 72
Foster Ct. E16 . . . . .7H 87
　　　　　　　　　　　(off Tarling Rd.)
　　NW1 . . . . .7G 65
　　　　　　　　　(off Royal College St.)
　　NW4 . . . . .4E 44
Foster Ho. SE14 . . . . .1B 122
Foster La. EC2 . . . . .7C 8 (6C 84)
Foster Rd. E13 . . . . .4J 87
　　W3 . . . . .7A 80
　　W4 . . . . .5K 97
Fosters Cl. BR7: Chst 5D 142
　　E18 . . . . .1K 51
Foster St. NW4 . . . . .4E 44
Foster's Way SW18 . . . . .1K 135
Foster Wlk. NW4 . . . . .4E 44
Fothergill Cl. E13 . . . . .2J 87
Fothergill Dr. N21 . . . . .5D 22

Fotheringham Rd. EN1: Enf 4A 24
　　　　　　　　　　　(not continuous)
Foubert's Pl. W1 . . . . .1A 12 (6G 83)
Foulden Rd. N16 . . . . .4F 67
Foulden Ter. N16 . . . . .4F 67
Foulis Ter. SW7 . . . . .5B 16 (5B 100)
Foulser Rd. SW17 . . . . .3D 136
Foulsham Rd. CR7: Thor H 3C 156
Foundation Pl. SE9 . . . . .5E 124
　　　　　　　　　　　(off Archery Rd.)
Founder Cl. E6 . . . . .6F 89
Founders Cl. UB5: N'olt 3D 76
Founders Ct. EC2 . . . . .7E 8
Founders Gdns. SE19 . . . . .7C 138
Founders Ho. SW1 . . . . .6C 18
　　　　　　　　　　　(off Aylesford St.)
Foundling Ct. WC1 . . . . .3E 6
　　　　　　　　　　(off Brunswick Cen.)
Foundling Museum, The 3F 7
Foundry, The EC2 . . . . .2H 9
　　　　　　　　　　　(off Dereham Pl.)
Foundry Cl. SE16 . . . . .1A 104
Foundry Ho. E14 . . . . .5D 86
　　　　　　　　　　　(off Morris Rd.)
Foundry M. NW1 . . . . .3B 6 (4G 83)
　　TW3: Houn 4F 113
Foundry Pl. E1 . . . . .5J 85
　　　　　　　　　　　(off Jubilee St.)
　　SW18 . . . . .7K 117
Fountain Cl. SE18 . . . . .5F 107
　　UB8: Hil .5E 74
Fountain Ct. DA15: Sidc 6B 126
　　EC4 . . . . .2J 13 (7A 84)
　　SE23 . . . . .2K 139
　　SW1 . . . . .4J 17
　　　　　　　　(off Buckingham Pal. Rd.)
　　W11 . . . . .2F 99
　　　　　　　　　　　(off Clearwater Ter.)
Fountain Dr. SE19 . . . . .4F 139
　　SM5: Cars 7D 166
Fountain Grn. Sq. SE16 . . . . .2G 103
Fountain Ho. CR4: Mitc 2D 154
　　E2 . . . . .3J 9
　　　　　　　　　　　(off Redchurch St.)
　　NW6 . . . . .7G 63
　　SE16 . . . . .2G 103
　　　　　　　　　　(off Bermondsey Wall E.)
　　SW6 . . . . .2A 118
　　W1 . . . . .4G 11
　　　　　　　　　　　　　(off Park St.)
Fountain M. N5 . . . . .4C 66
　　　　　　　　　(off Highbury Grange)
　　NW3 . . . . .6D 64
Fountain Pl. SW9 . . . . .1A 120
Fountain Rd. CR7: Thor H 3C 156
　　SW17 . . . . .5B 136
FOUNTAIN RDBT. 4A 152
Fountains, The N3 . . . . .7E 30
　　　　　　　　　　　(off Ballards La.)
Fountains Av. TW13: Hanw 3D 130
Fountains Cl. TW13: Hanw 2D 130
　　　　　　　　　　　(not continuous)
Fountains Cres. N14 . . . . .7D 22
Fountain Sq. SW1 . . . . .3K 17 (4F 101)
Fountayne Bus. Cen. N15 . . . . .4G 49
Fountayne Rd. N15 . . . . .4G 49
　　N16 . . . . .2G 67
Fount St. SW8 . . . . .7H 101
Fouracre Path SE25 . . . . .6E 156
Four Acres N12 . . . . .3E 30
Fouracres EN3: Enf H 1F 25
Four Dials E20 . . . . .6E 68
　　　　　　(within Westfield Stratford City Shop. Cen.)
Fourland Wlk. HA8: Edg 6D 28
Fournier St. E1 . . . . .5J 9 (5F 85)
Fourscore Mans. E8 . . . . .7G 67
　　　　　　　　　　　(off Shrubland Rd.)
Four Seasons Cl. E3 . . . . .2C 86
Four Seasons Cres. SM3: Sutt 2H 165
Four Seasons Ter. UB7: W Dray 2C 92
Four Sq. Ct. TW3: Houn 6E 112

Fourth Av. E12 . . . . .4D 70
　　RM7: Rush G 1K 73
　　UB3: Hayes 1H 93
　　W10 . . . . .4G 81
Fourth Cross Rd. TW2: Twick 2H 131
Fourth Way HA9: Wemb 4H 61
Four Wents, The E4 . . . . .1A 36
Fovant Cl. SW8 . . . . .2G 119
Fowey Av. IG4: Ilf 5B 52
Fowey Cl. E1 . . . . .1H 103
Fowey Ho. SE11 . . . . .5K 19
Fowler Cl. SW11 . . . . .3B 118
Fowler Ho. N15 . . . . .5D 48
　　　　　　　　　　　(off South Gro.)
Fowler Rd. CR4: Mitc 2E 154
　　E7 . . . . .4J 69
　　N1 . . . . .1B 84
Fowlers Cl. DA14: Sidc 5E 144
Fowlers M. N19 . . . . .2G 65
　　　　　　　　　　　(off Holloway Rd.)
Fowler's Wlk. W5 . . . . .4D 78
Fox & Knot St. EC1 . . . . .5B 8
Foxberry Rd. SE4 . . . . .3A 122
Foxborough Gdns. SE4 . . . . .5C 122
Foxbourne Rd. SW17 . . . . .2E 136
Foxbury Av. BR7: Chst 6H 143
Foxbury Cl. BR1: Brom 6K 141
　　BR1: Brom 6J 141
Fox Cl. BR6: Chels 5K 173
　　E1 . . . . .4J 85
　　E16 . . . . .5J 87
Foxcombe CR0: New Ad 6D 170
　　　　　　　　　　　(not continuous)
Foxcombe Cl. E6 . . . . .2B 88
Foxcombe Rd. SW15 . . . . .1C 134
Foxcote SE5 .5E 102
Foxcroft WC1 .1H 7
　　　　　　　　　　　(off Penton Ri.)
Foxcroft Rd. SE18 . . . . .1F 125
Foxdene Cl. E18 . . . . .3K 51
Foxearth Spur CR2: Sels 7J 169
Foxes Dale BR2: Brom 3F 159
　　SE3 . . . . .3J 123
Foxfield NW1 .1F 83
　　　　　　　　　　　(off Arlington Rd.)
Foxfield Rd. BR6: Orp 2H 173
Foxglove Cl. DA15: Sidc 6A 126
　　N9 . . . . .1D 34
　　UB1: S'hall 7C 76
Foxglove Ct. E3 . . . . .2C 86
　　　　　　　　　(off Four Seasons Cl.)
　　HA0: Wemb 2E 78
Foxglove Gdns. E11 . . . . .4A 52
Foxglove La. KT9: Chess 4G 163
Foxglove Path SE28 . . . . .1J 107
　　　　　　　　　　　(off Martins Pl.)
Foxglove Rd. RM7: Rush G 2K 73
Foxglove St. W12 . . . . .7B 80
Foxglove Way SM6: Wall 1F 167
Fox Gro. KT12: Walt T 7K 147
Foxgrove N14 . . . . .3D 32
Foxgrove Av. BR3: Beck 7D 140
Foxgrove Rd. BR3: Beck 7D 140
Foxham Rd. N19 . . . . .3H 65
Fox Hill SE19 .7F 139
Fox Hill Gdns. SE19 . . . . .7F 139
Foxhole Rd. SE9 . . . . .5C 124
Fox Hollow Cl. SE18 . . . . .5J 107
Fox Hollow Dr. DA7: Bex 3D 126
Foxholt Gdns. NW10 . . . . .7J 61
Foxhome Cl. BR7: Chst 6E 142
Fox Ho. Rd. DA17: Belv 5H 109
　　　　　　　　　　　(not continuous)
Foxlands Cres. RM10: Dag 5J 73
Foxlands La. RM10: Dag 5K 73
Foxlands Rd. RM10: Dag 5J 73
Fox La. BR2: Kes 5K 171
　　N13 . . . . .2E 32
　　W5 . . . . .4E 78
Foxleas Ct. BR1: Brom 7G 141

Foxlees—Friars Av.

Foxlees HA0: Wemb 4A **60**
Foxley Cl. E8 .... 5G **67**
Foxley Ct. SM2: Sutt 7A **166**
Foxley Ho. *E3* *3D* ***86***
(off Bow Rd.)
Foxley Rd. CR7: Thor H 4B **156**
SW9 .... 7A **102**
Foxley Sq. SW9 .... 7B **102**
Foxmead Cl. EN2: Enf 3E **22**
Foxmore St. SW11 .... 1D **118**
Fox Rd. E16 .... 5H **87**
Fox's Path CR4: Mitc 2C **154**
Fox's Yd. E2 .... 3K **9**
Foxton Gro. CR4: Mitc 2B **154**
Foxton Ho. *E16* *2E* ***106***
(off Albert Rd.)
Foxwarren KT10: Clay 7A **162**
Foxwell M. SE4 .... 3A **122**
Foxwell St. SE4 .... 3A **122**
Foxwood Cl. NW7 .... 4F **29**
TW13: Felt 3K **129**
Foxwood Grn. Cl. EN1: Enf 6K **23**
Fox Wood Nature Reserve 4E **78**
Foxwood Rd. SE3 .... 4H **123**
Foyle Rd. N17 .... 1G **49**
SE3 .... 6H **105**
Framfield Cl. N12 .... 3D **30**
Framfield Ct. *EN1: Enf* *6K* ***23***
(off Queen Anne's Gdns.)
Framfield Rd. CR4: Mitc 7E **136**
N5 .... 5B **66**
W7 .... 6J **77**
Framlingham Cl. E5 .... 2J **67**
Framlingham Ct. *RM6: Chad H* *5B* ***54***
(off Norwich Cres.)
Framlingham Cres. SE9 .... 4C **142**
Frampton *NW1* *7H* ***65***
(off Wrotham Rd.)
Frampton Cl. IG6: Ilf 4H **53**
SM2: Sutt 7J **165**
Frampton Ct. *W3* *2J* ***97***
(off Avenue Rd.)
Frampton Ho. *NW8* *4B* ***4***
(off Frampton St.)
Frampton Pk. Est. E9 .... 7J **67**
Frampton Pk. Rd. E9 .... 6J **67**
Frampton Rd. TW4: Houn 5C **112**
Frampton St. NW8 .... 4B **4** (4B **82**)
Francemary Rd. SE4 .... 5C **122**
Frances Ct. E17 .... 6C **50**
SE25 .... 3F **157**
Frances Rd. E4 .... 6H **35**
Frances St. SE18 .... 3D **106**
Frances Wharf E14 .... 6B **86**
Franche Ct. Rd. SW17 .... 3A **136**
Francis & Dick James Ct. NW7 .... 7B **30**
Francis Av. DA7: Bex 2G **127**
IG1: Ilf 2H **71**
TW13: Felt 3J **129**
Francis Bacon Ct. *SE16* *4H* ***103***
(off Galleywall Rd.)
Francis Barber Cl. SW16 .... 5K **137**
Francis Bentley M. SW4 .... 3G **119**
Franciscan Rd. SW17 .... 5D **136**
Francis Chichester Way SW11 .... 1E **118**
Francis Cl. E14 .... 4F **105**
KT19: Ewe 4K **163**
TW17: Shep 4C **146**
Francis Ct. EC1 .... 5A **8**
KT5: Surb *4E* ***150***
(off Cranes Pk. Av.)
NW7 .... *5G* ***29***
(off Watford Way)
SE14 .... *6K* ***103***
(off Myers La.)
Francis Gro. SW19 .... 6H **135**
Francis Ho. E17 .... 6B **50**
N1 .... *1E* ***84***
(off Colville Est.)
SW10 .... *7K* ***99***
(off Coleridge Gdns.)
Francis Ho. *SW18* *4A* ***118***
(off Eltringham St.)
Francis M. SE12 .... 7J **123**
Francis Pl. *N6* *7F* ***47***
(off Shepherd's Cl.)
Francis Rd. CR0: C'don 7B **156**
E10 .... 1E **68**
HA1: Harr 5A **42**
HA5: Eastc 5A **40**
IG1: Ilf 2H **71**
N2 .... 4D **46**
SM6: Wall 6G **167**
TW4: Houn 2B **112**
UB6: G'frd 2B **78**
Francis St. E15 .... 5G **69**
IG1: Ilf 2H **71**
SW1 .... 3A **18** (4G **101**)
Francis Ter. N19 .... 3G **65**
Francis Ter. M. N19 .... 3G **65**
Francis Wlk. N1 .... 1K **83**
Francklyn Gdns. HA8: Edg 3B **28**
Franconia Rd. SW4 .... 5H **119**
Frank Bailey Wlk. E12 .... 6E **70**
Frank Beswick Ho. *SW6* *6H* ***99***
(off Clem Attlee Ct.)
Frank Burton Cl. SE7 .... 5K **105**
Frank Dixon Cl. SE21 .... 7E **120**
Frank Dixon Way SE21 .... 1E **138**
Frankfurt Rd. SE24 .... 5C **120**
Frank Godley Ct. DA14: Sidc 5B **144**
Frankham Ho. *SE8* *7C* ***104***
(off Frankham St.)
Frankham St. SE8 .... 7C **104**
Frank Ho. *SW8* *7J* ***101***
(off Wyvil Rd.)
Frankland Cl. IG8: Wfd G 5F **37**
SE16 .... 3H **103**
Frankland Rd. E4 .... 5H **35**
SW7 .... 2A **16** (3B **100**)
Franklin Bldg. E14 .... 2C **104**
Franklin Cl. KT1: King T 3G **151**
N20 .... 7F **21**
SE13 .... 1D **122**
SE27 .... 3B **138**
Franklin Cotts. HA7: Stan 4G **27**
Franklin Cres. CR4: Mitc 4G **155**
Franklin Ho.
BR2: Brom 3G **159**
E1 .... *1H* ***103***
(off Watts St.)
E14 .... *6F* ***87***
(off E. India Dock Rd.)
NW6 .... *3J* ***81***
(off Carlton Va.)
Franklin Ind. Est. *SE20* *1J* ***157***
(off Franklin Rd.)
Franklin Pas. SE9 .... 3C **124**
Franklin Pl. SE13 .... 1D **122**
Franklin Rd. DA7: Bex 1E **126**
SE20 .... 7J **139**
Franklins M. HA2: Harr 2G **59**
Franklin Sq. W14 .... 5H **99**
Franklin's Row SW3 .... 5F **17** (5D **100**)
Franklin St. E3 .... 3D **86**
N15 .... 6E **48**
Franklin Way CR0: Wadd 7J **155**
Franklyn Rd. KT12: Walt T 6J **147**
NW10 .... 6B **62**
Frank M. SE1 .... 4H **103**
Franks Av. KT3: N Mald 4J **151**
Frank Soskice Ho. *SW6* *6H* ***99***
(off Clem Attlee Ct.)
Frank St. E13 .... 4J **87**
Franks Wood Av. BR5: Pet W 5F **161**
Frankswood Av. UB7: Yiew 6B **74**
Frank Towell Ct. TW14: Felt 7J **111**
Frank Whymark Ho. *SE16* *2J* ***103***
(off Rupack St.)
Franlaw Cres. N13 .... 4H **33**
Fransfield Gro. SE26 .... 3H **139**
Frans Hals Ct. E14 .... 3F **105**
Franshams *WD23: B Hea* *2D* ***26***
(off Hartsbourne Rd.)
Frant Cl. SE20 .... 7J **139**
Franthorne Way SE6 .... 2D **140**
Frant Rd. CR7: Thor H 5B **156**
Fraserburgh Ho. *E3* *2B* ***86***
(off Vernon Rd.)
Fraser Cl. DA5: Bexl 1J **145**
E6 .... 6C **88**
Fraser Ct. *E14* *5E* ***104***
(off Ferry St.)
SE1 .... 7D **14**
SW11 .... *1C* ***118***
(off Surrey La. Est.)
Fraser Ho. TW8: Bford 5F **97**
Fraser Rd. DA8: Erith 5K **109**
E17 .... 5D **50**
N9 .... 3C **34**
UB6: G'frd 1B **78**
Fraser St. W4 .... 5A **98**
Frating Cres. IG8: Wfd G 6E **36**
Frazer Av. HA4: Ruis 5A **58**
Frazier St. SE1 .... 7J **13** (2A **102**)
Frean St. SE16 .... 3G **103**
Frearson Ho. *WC1* *1H* ***7***
(off Penton Ri.)
Freda Corbett Cl. SE15 .... 7G **103**
Frederica Ct. SW2 .... 1B **138**
Frederica Rd. E4 .... 1A **36**
Frederica St. N7 .... 7K **65**
Frederick Charrington Ho. *E1* *4J* ***85***
(off Wickford St.)
Frederick Cl. SM1: Sutt 4H **165**
W2 .... 2D **10** (7D **82**)
Frederick Ct. *SW3* *4F* ***17***
(off Duke of York Sq.)
Frederick Cres. EN3: Enf H 2D **24**
SW9 .... 7B **102**
Frederick Dobson Ho. *W11* *7G* ***81***
(off Cowling Cl.)
Frederick Gdns. CR0: C'don 6B **156**
SM1: Sutt 5H **165**
Frederick Ho. *SE18* *4C* ***106***
(off Pett St.)
Frederick Pl. *N8* *6H* ***47***
(off Crouch Hall Rd.)
SE18 .... 5F **107**
Frederick Rd. RM13: Rain 2K **91**
SE17 .... 6B **102**
SM1: Sutt 5H **165**
Fredericks Pl. EC2 .... 1E **14** (6D **84**)
N12 .... 4F **31**
Frederick Sq. *SE16* *7A* ***86***
(off Sovereign Cres.)
Frederick's Row EC1 .... 1A **8** (3B **84**)
Frederick St. WC1 .... 2G **7** (3K **83**)
Frederick Ter. E8 .... 7F **67**
Frederick Vs. *W7* *1J* ***95***
(off Lwr. Boston Rd.)
Frederic M. SW1 .... 7F **11**
Frederic St. E17 .... 5A **50**
Fredora Av. UB4: Hayes 4H **75**
Fred Styles Ho. SE7 .... 6A **106**
Fred Tibble Ct.
RM9: Dag 4E **72**
Fred White Wlk. N7 .... 6J **65**
Freedom Cl. E17 .... 4A **50**
Freedom Rd. N17 .... 2D **48**
Freedom St. SW11 .... 2D **118**
Freegrove Rd. N7 .... 5J **65**
(not continuous)
Freeland Ct. DA15: Sidc 3A **144**
Freeland Pk. NW4 .... 2G **45**
Freeland Rd. W5 .... 7F **79**
Freelands Av. CR2: Sels 7K **169**
Freelands Gro. BR1: Brom 1K **159**
Freelands Rd. BR1: Brom 1K **159**
Freeling Ho. *NW8* *1B* ***82***
(off Dorman Way)
Freeling St. N1 .... 7K **65**
(Carnoustie Dr.)
Freeling St. N1 .... 7J **65**
(Pembroke St.)
Freeman Cl. TW17: Shep 4G **147**
UB5: N'olt 7C **58**
Freeman Ct. N7 .... 3J **65**
SW16 .... 2J **155**
Freeman Dr. KT8: W Mole 3D **148**
Freeman Ho. *SE11* *4B* ***102***
(off George Mathers Rd.)
Freeman Rd. SM4: Mord 5B **154**
Freemans La. UB3: Hayes 7G **75**
Freemantle Av. EN3: Pond E 5E **24**
Freemantle St. SE17 .... 5E **102**
Freeman Wlk. SE9 .... 5A **124**
Freemasons' Hall 7F **7**
Freemasons Pl. *CR0: C'don* *1E* ***168***
(off Freemasons Rd.)
Freemasons Rd. CR0: C'don 1E **168**
E16 .... 5K **87**
Freesia Cl. BR6: Chels 5K **173**
Freethorpe Cl. SE19 .... 7D **138**
Free Trade Wharf E1 .... 7K **85**
Freezeland Way UB10: Hil 6D **56**
Freight La. N1 .... 7H **65**
Freightliners City Farm 6A **66**
Freke Rd. SW11 .... 3E **118**
Fremantle Ho. *E1* *4H* ***85***
(off Somerford St.)
Fremantle Rd. DA17: Belv 4G **109**
IG6: Ilf 2F **53**
Fremantle Way UB3: Hayes 7H **75**
Fremont St. E9 .... 1H **85**
(not continuous)
French Horn Yd. WC1 .... 6G **7**
French Ordinary Ct. EC3 .... 2H **15**
French Pl. E1 .... 2H **9** (3E **84**)
French St. TW16: Sun 2A **148**
Frendsbury Rd. SE4 .... 4A **122**
Frensham Cl. UB1: S'hall 4D **76**
Frensham Ct. SW19 .... 3A **154**
Frensham Dr. CR0: New Ad 7E **170**
SW15 .... 3B **134**
Frensham Rd. SE9 .... 2H **143**
Frensham St. SE15 .... 6G **103**
Frere St. SW11 .... 2C **118**
Fresham Ho. *BR2: Brom* *3H* ***159***
(off Durham Rd.)
Freshfield Av. E8 .... 7F **67**
Freshfield Cl. SE13 .... 4F **123**
Freshfield Dr. N14 .... 7A **22**
Freshfields CR0: C'don 1B **170**
Freshford St. SW18 .... 3A **136**
Freshill La. UB1: S'hall 4E **76**
Freshwater Cl. SW17 .... 6E **136**
Freshwater Ct. UB1: S'hall 3E **76**
W1 .... *6D* ***4***
(off Crawford St.)
Freshwater Rd. RM8: Dag 1D **72**
SW17 .... 6E **136**
Freshwell Av. RM6: Chad H 4C **54**
Fresh Wharf Est. IG11: Bark 2F **89**
Fresh Wharf Rd. IG11: Bark 1F **89**
Freshwood Cl. BR3: Beck 1D **158**
Freshwood Way SM6: Wall 7F **167**
Freston Gdns. EN4: Cockf 5K **21**
Freston Pk. N3 .... 2H **45**
Freston Rd. W10 .... 7F **81**
W11 .... 7F **81**
Freswick Ho. *SE8* *4A* ***104***
(off Chilton Gro.)
Freta Rd. DA6: Bex 5F **127**
Freud Mus. 6A **64**
Frewell Ho. *EC1* *5J* ***7***
(off Bourne Est.)
Frewin Rd. SW18 .... 1B **136**
Friar M. SE27 .... 3B **138**
Friar Rd.
BR5: St M Cry 5K **161**
UB4: Yead 4B **76**
Friars Av. N20 .... 3H **31**
SW15 .... 3B **134**

Friars Cl. E4 . . . . .3K **35**
  IG1: Ilf 1H **71**
  SE1 . . . . .5B **14**
  UB5: N'olt 3B **76**
Friars Ct. E17 . . . . .1B **50**
  RM7: Rush G 6K **55**
  SM6: Wall 4F **167**
Friars Gdns. W3 . . . . .6K **79**
Friarsgate NW10 . . . . .2H **79**
Friars Ga. Cl. IG8: Wfd G 4D **36**
Friars La. TW9: Rich 5D **114**
Friars Mead E14 . . . . .3E **104**
Friars M. SE9 . . . . .5E **124**
Friars Pl. La. W3 . . . . .7K **79**
Friars Rd. E6 . . . . .1B **88**
Friars Stile Pl. TW10: Rich 6E **114**
Friars Stile Rd. TW10: Rich 6E **114**
Friar St. EC4 . . . . .1B **14** (6B **84**)
Friars Wlk. N14 . . . . .7A **22**
  SE2 . . . . .5D **108**
Friars Way W3 . . . . .6K **79**
Friars Wood CRO: Sels 7A **170**
Friary Cl. N12 . . . . .5H **31**
Friary Ct. SW1 . . . . .5B **12**
Friary Est. SE15 . . . . .6G **103**
  (not continuous)
Friary La. IG8: Wfd G 4D **36**
Friary Pk. W3 . . . . .6K **79**
Friary Pk. Ct. W3 . . . . .6J **79**
Friary Rd. N12 . . . . .4G **31**
  N20 . . . . .4G **31**
  SE15 . . . . .7G **103**
  W3 . . . . .6J **79**
Friary Way N12 . . . . .4H **31**
FRIDAY HILL 2B **36**
Friday Hill E4 . . . . .2B **36**
Friday Hill E. E4 . . . . .3B **36**
Friday Hill W. E4 . . . . .2B **36**
Friday Rd. CR4: Mitc 7D **136**
  DA8: Erith 5K **109**
Friday St. EC4 . . . . .2C **14** (7C **84**)
Frideswide Pl. NW5 . . . . .5G **65**
Friendly Pl. SE13 . . . . .1D **122**
Friendly St. SE8 . . . . .2C **122**
Friendly St. M. SE8 . . . . .2C **122**
Friendship Ho. SE1 . . . . .7B **14**
  (off Belvedere Pl.)
Friendship Wlk. UB5: N'olt 3B **76**
Friendship Way E15 . . . . .1E **86**
Friends Rd. CRO: C'don 3D **168**
Friend St. EC1 . . . . .1A **8** (3B **84**)
FRIERN BARNET 5J **31**
Friern Barnet La. N11 . . . . .2G **31**
  N20 . . . . .2G **31**
Friern Barnet Rd. N11 . . . . .5J **31**
Friern Bri. Retail Pk.
  N11 . . . . .6A **32**
Friern Ct. N20 . . . . .3G **31**
Friern Mt. Dr. N20 . . . . .7F **21**
Friern Pk. N12 . . . . .5F **31**
Friern Rd. SE22 . . . . .7G **121**
  (not continuous)
Friern Watch Av. N12 . . . . .4F **31**
Frigate Ho. E14 . . . . .4E **104**
  (off Stebondale St.)
Frigate M. SE8 . . . . .6C **104**
Frimley Av. SM6: Wall 5J **167**
Frimley Cl. CRO: New Ad 7E **170**
  SW19 . . . . .2G **135**
Frimley Ct. DA14: Sidc 5C **144**
Frimley Cres. CRO: New Ad 7E **170**
Frimley Gdns. CR4: Mitc 3C **154**
Frimley Rd. IG3: Ilf 3J **71**
  KT9: Chess 5D **162**
Frimley St. E1 . . . . .4J **85**
  (off Frimley Way)
Frimley Way E1 . . . . .4K **85**
Fringewood Cl. HA6: N'wood 1D **38**
Frinstead Ho. W10 . . . . .7F **81**
  (off Freston Rd.)
Frinsted Rd. DA8: Erith 7K **109**

Frinton Cl. W13 . . . . .5B **78**
  (off Hardwick Grn.)
Frinton Dr. IG8: Wfd G 7A **36**
Frinton M. IG2: Ilf 6E **52**
Frinton Rd. DA14: Sidc 2E **144**
  E6 . . . . .3B **88**
  N15 . . . . .6E **48**
  SW17 . . . . .6E **136**
Friston St. SW6 . . . . .2K **117**
Friswell Pl. DA6: Bex 4G **127**
Fritham Cl. KT3: N Mald 6A **152**
Frith Cl. NW7 . . . . .7B **30**
Frith Ho. NW8 . . . . .4B **4**
  (off Frampton St.)
Frith La. NW7 . . . . .7B **30**
Frith Rd. CRO: C'don 2C **168**
  E11 . . . . .4E **68**
Frith St. W1 . . . . .1C **12** (6H **83**)
Frithville Ct. W12 . . . . .1E **98**
  (off Frithville Gdns.)
Frithville Gdns. W12 . . . . .1E **98**
Frizlands La. RM10: Dag 2H **73**
Frobisher Cl. HA5: Pinn 7B **40**
Frobisher Ct. NW9 . . . . .2A **44**
  SE8 .5A **104**
  (off Evelyn St.)
  SE10 . . . . .6F **105**
  (off Old Woolwich Rd.)
  SE23 . . . . .2H **139**
  SM3: Cheam 7G **165**
  W12 .2E **98**
  (off Lime Gro.)
Frobisher Cres. EC2 . . . . .5D **8**
  (off Silk St.)
  TW19: Stanw 7A **110**
Frobisher Gdns. E10 . . . . .7D **50**
  TW19: Stanw 7A **110**
Frobisher Ho. E1 . . . . .1H **103**
  (off Watts St.)
  SW1 .7C **18**
  (off Dolphin Sq.)
Frobisher M. EN2: Enf 4J **23**
Frobisher Pas. E14 . . . . .1C **104**
Frobisher Pl. SE15 . . . . .1J **121**
Frobisher Rd. E6 . . . . .6D **88**
  N8 . . . . .4A **48**
Frobisher St. SE10 . . . . .6G **105**
Frog La. RM13: Rain 6K **91**
Frogley Rd. SE22 . . . . .4F **121**
Frogmore SW18 . . . . .5J **117**
Frogmore Av. UB4: Hayes 4G **75**
Frogmore Ct. SM3: Cheam 3F **165**
Frogmore Gdns. SM3: Cheam 4G **165**
  UB4: Hayes 4G **75**
Frogmore Ind. Est. N5 . . . . .5C **66**
  NW10 . . . . .3J **79**
  UB3: Hayes 2G **93**
Frognal NW3 . . . . .4A **64**
Frognal Av. DA14: Sidc 6A **144**
  HA1: Harr 4K **41**
Frognal Cl. NW3 . . . . .5A **64**
FROGNAL CORNER 6K **143**
Frognal Ct. NW3 . . . . .6A **64**
Frognal Gdns. NW3 . . . . .4A **64**
Frognal La. NW3 . . . . .5K **63**
Frognal Pde. NW3 . . . . .6A **64**
Frognal Pl. DA14: Sidc 6A **144**
Frognal Ri. NW3 . . . . .3A **64**
Frognal Way NW3 . . . . .4A **64**
Frogwell Cl. N15 . . . . .6D **48**
Froissart Rd. SE9 . . . . .5B **124**
Frome Ho. SE15 . . . . .4H **121**
Frome Rd. N22 . . . . .3B **48**
Frome St. N1 . . . . .2C **84**
Fromondes Rd. SM3: Cheam 5G **165**
Frontenac NW10 . . . . .7D **62**
Frontier Works N17 . . . . .6K **33**
Frost Ct. NW9 . . . . .2A **44**
  (off Salk Cl.)
Frostic Wlk. E1 . . . . .6K **9** (5G **85**)

Froude St. SW8 . . . . .2F **119**
Fruen Rd. TW14: Felt 7H **111**
Fruiterers Pas. EC4 . . . . .3D **14**
  (off Queen St. Pl.)
Fryatt Rd. N17 . . . . .7J **33**
  (not continuous)
Fryday Gro. M. SW12 . . . . .7G **119**
  (off Weir Rd.)
Frye Ct. E3 .3B **86**
  (off Benworth St.)
Frye Ho. E20 . . . . .6E **68**
  (off Penny Brookes St.)
Fryent Cl. NW9 . . . . .6G **43**
Fryent Country Pk. (Local Nature Reserve)
  . . . . .7G **43**
Fryent Cres. NW9 . . . . .6A **44**
Fryent Flds. NW9 . . . . .6A **44**
Fryent Gro. NW9 . . . . .6A **44**
Fryent Way NW9 . . . . .5G **43**
Fryers Vw. SE4 . . . . .4K **121**
  (off Frendsbury Rd.)
Fry Ho. E6 .7A **70**
Frying Pan Alley E1 . . . . .6J **9**
Fry Rd. E6 .7B **70**
  NW10 . . . . .1B **80**
Fryston Av. CRO: C'don 2G **169**
Fuchsia Cl. RM7: Rush G 2K **73**
Fuchsia St. SE2 . . . . .5B **108**
Fulbeck Dr. NW9 . . . . .1A **44**
Fulbeck Ho. N7 . . . . .6K **65**
  (off Sutterton St.)
Fulbeck Rd. N19 . . . . .4G **65**
Fulbeck Wlk. HA8: Edg 2C **28**
Fulbeck Way HA2: Harr 2G **41**
Fulbourn KT1: King T 2G **151**
  (off Eureka Rd.)
Fulbourne Rd. E17 . . . . .1E **50**
Fulbourne St. E1 . . . . .5H **85**
Fulbrook M. N19 . . . . .4G **65**
Fulcher Ho. N1 . . . . .1E **84**
  (off Colville Est.)
  SE8 .5B **104**
Fulford Ho. KT19: Ewe 7K **163**
Fulford Rd. KT19: Ewe 7K **163**
Fulford St. SE16 . . . . .2H **103**
FULHAM .2G **117**
FULHAM BROADWAY 7J **99**
Fulham B'way. SW6 . . . . .7J **99**
Fulham Broadway Shop. Cen.
  SW6 . . . . .7J **99**
Fulham Bus. Exchange SW6 . . . . .1A **118**
  (off The Boulevard)
Fulham Cl. UB10: Hil 4E **74**
Fulham Ct. SW6 . . . . .1J **117**
Fulham FC 1F **117**
Fulham High St. SW6 . . . . .2G **117**
Fulham Island SW6 . . . . .7J **99**
  (off Fulham Rd.)
Fulham Palace 2G **117**
Fulham Pal. Rd. SW6 . . . . .5E **98**
  W6 . . . . .5E **98**
Fulham Pk. Gdns. SW6 . . . . .2H **117**
Fulham Pk. Rd. SW6 . . . . .2H **117**
Fulham Pools
  Virgin Active 6G **99**
Fulham Rd. SW3 . . . . .7A **16** (7K **99**)
  SW6 .7K **99**
  (Fulham B'way.)
  SW6 .2G **117**
  (Fulham High St.)
  SW10 . . . . .7A **16** (7K **99**)
Fullbrooks Av. KT4: Wor Pk 1B **164**
Fuller Cl. BR6: Chels 5K **173**
  E2 . . . . .4G **85**
  (off Cheshire St.)
  WD23: Bush 1C **26**
Fuller Ct. N8 . . . . .5H **47**
Fuller Rd. RM8: Dag 3B **72**
Fullers Av. IG8: Wfd G 7C **36**
  KT6: Surb 2F **163**
Fullers Cl. RM5: Col R 1J **55**

Fuller's Griffin Brewery & Vis. Cen.
  . . . . .6B **98**
Fullers La. RM5: Col R 1J **55**
Fullers Rd. E18 . . . . .7C **36**
Fuller St. NW4 . . . . .4E **44**
Fullers Way Nth. KT6: Surb 3F **163**
Fullers Way Sth. KT9: Chess 4E **162**
Fuller's Wood CRO: C'don 5C **170**
Fullerton Ct. TW11: Tedd 6A **132**
Fullerton Rd. CRO: C'don 7F **157**
  SM5: Cars 7C **166**
  SW18 . . . . .5K **117**
Fuller Way UB3: Harl 5H **93**
Fullwell Av. IG5: Ilf 1D **52**
  IG6: Ilf 1F **53**
FULLWELL CROSS 2G **53**
Fullwell Cross IG6: Ilf 2H **53**
Fullwell Cross Leisure Cen. 2G **53**
Fullwell Pde. IG5: Ilf 1E **52**
Fullwood's M. N1 . . . . .1F **9** (3D **84**)
Fulmar Cl. KT5: Surb 6F **151**
Fulmar Ho. SE16 . . . . .4K **103**
  (off Tawny Way)
Fulmead St. SW6 . . . . .1K **117**
Fulmer Cl. TW12: Hamp 5C **130**
Fulmer Ho. NW8 . . . . .4C **4**
  (off Mallory St.)
  UB8: Uxb 6A **56**
Fulmer Rd. E16 . . . . .5J **87**
Fulmer Way W13 . . . . .3B **96**
Fulneck E1 .5J **85**
  (off Mile End Rd.)
Fulready Rd. E10 . . . . .5F **51**
Fulstone Cl. TW4: Houn 4D **112**
Fulthorp Rd. SE3 . . . . .2H **123**
Fulton M. W2 . . . . .7A **82**
Fulton Rd. HA9: Wemb 3G **61**
FULWELL .4H **131**
Fulwell Ct. IG5: Ilf 1E **52**
  UB1: S'hall 1F **95**
  (off Baird Av.)
Fulwell Golf Course 4H **131**
Fulwell Pk. Av. TW2: Twick 2F **131**
Fulwell Rd. TW11: Tedd 4H **131**
Fulwood Av. HA0: Wemb 2F **79**
Fulwood Cl. UB3: Hayes 6H **75**
Fulwood Ct. HA3: Kenton 6A **42**
Fulwood Gdns. TW1: Twick 6K **113**
Fulwood Pl. WC1 . . . . .6H **7** (5K **83**)
Fulwood Wlk. SW19 . . . . .1G **135**
Funky Footprints Nature Reserve . .6C **146**
Furber St. W6 . . . . .3D **98**
Furham Fld. HA5: Hat E 7A **26**
Furley Ho. SE15 . . . . .7G **103**
  (off Peckham Pk. Rd.)
Furley Rd. SE15 . . . . .7G **103**
Furlong Av. CR4: Mitc 3C **154**
Furlong Cl. SM6: Wall 1F **167**
Furlong Rd. N7 . . . . .6A **66**
Furmage St. SW18 . . . . .7K **117**
Furneaux Av. SE27 . . . . .5B **138**
Furness Ho. SW1 . . . . .5J **17**
  (part of Abbots Mnr.)
Furness Rd. HA2: Harr 7F **41**
  NW10 . . . . .2C **80**
  SM4: Mord 6K **153**
  SW6 .2K **117**
Furnival Ct. E3 . . . . .6A **6**
  (off Four Seasons Cl.)
Furnival Mans. W1 . . . . .6A **6**
  (off Wells St.)
Furnival St. EC4 . . . . .7J **7** (6A **84**)
Furrow La. E9 . . . . .5J **67**
Fursby Av. N3 . . . . .6D **30**
Fursecroft W1 . . . . .7E **4**
Furtherfield Cl. CRO: C'don 6A **156**
Further Grn. Rd. SE6 . . . . .7G **123**
FURZEDOWN 5F **137**
Furzedown Dr. SW17 . . . . .5F **137**
Furzedown Recreation Cen. 5F **137**
Furzedown Rd. SW17 . . . . .5F **137**

Furze Farm Cl. RM6: Chad H 2E **54**
Furzefield Cl. BR7: Chst 6F **143**
Furzefield Rd. SE3 ....6K **105**
Furzeground Way UB11: Stock P 1E **92**
Furzeham Rd. UB7: W Dray 2A **92**
Furze Rd. CR7: Thor H 3C **156**
Furze St. E3 ....5C **86**
Furzewood TW16: Sun 1J **147**
Fusiliers Way TW4: Houn 3A **112**
(not continuous)
Fye Foot La. EC4 ....2C **14**
(off Queen Victoria St.)
Fyfe Apartments N8 ....3K **47**
Fyfe Way BR1: Brom 2J **159**
Fyfield N4 ....2A **66**
(off Six Acres Est.)
Fyfield Cl. BR2: Brom 4F **159**
Fyfield Ct. E7 ....6J **69**
Fyfield Ho. E6. ....1C **88**
(off Ron Leighton Way)
Fyfield Rd. E17 ....3F **51**
EN1: Enf 3K **23**
IG8: Wfd G 7F **37**
SW9 ....3A **120**
Fynes St. SW1 ....3C **18** (4H **101**)

G

Gable Cl. HA5: Hat E 1E **40**
Gable Cl. SE26 ....4H **139**
Gable M. BR2: Brom 2C **172**
Gables, The BR1: Brom 7K **141**
HA9: Wemb 3G **61**
IG11: Bark 6G **71**
N10 ....3E **46**
(off Fortis Grn.)
Gables Av. TW15: Ashf 5B **128**
Gables Cl. SE5 ....1E **120**
SE12 ....1J **141**
Gables Lodge EN4: Had W 1F **21**
Gabriel Cl. TW13: Hanw 4C **130**
Gabriel Ho. N1 ....1B **84**
(off Islington Grn.)
SE11 ....3G **19** (4K **101**)
SE16 ....3B **104**
(off Odessa St.)
Gabrielle Cl. HA9: Wemb 3F **61**
Gabrielle Ct. NW3 ....6B **64**
Gabriel M. NW2 ....2H **63**
Gabriel's M. BR3: Beck 1K **157**
Gabriel St. SE23 ....7K **121**
Gabriels Wharf SE1 ......4J **13** (1A **102**)
Gad Cl. E13 ....3K **87**
Gaddesden Av. HA9: Wemb 6F **61**
Gaddesden Ho. EC1 ....2F **9**
(off Cranwood St.)
Gadebridge Ho. SW3 ....5C **16**
(off Cale Gdns.)
Gade Cl. UB3: Hayes 1K **93**
Gadesden Rd. KT19: Ewe 6J **163**
Gadsbury Cl. NW9 ....6B **44**
Gadsden Ho. W10 ....4G **81**
(off Hazelwood Cres.)
Gadwall Cl. E16 ....6K **87**
Gadwall Ho. NW9 ....6C **44**
(off Perryfield Way)
Gadwall Way SE28 ....2H **107**
Gage Brown Ho. W10 ....6F **81**
(off Bridge Cl.)
Gage M. CR2: S Croy 5B **168**
Gage Rd. E16 ....5G **87**
Gage St. WC1 ....5F **7** (5J **83**)
Gainford Ho. E2 ....3H **85**
(off Ellsworth St.)
Gainford St. N1 ....1A **84**
Gainsboro Gdns. UB6: G'frd 5J **59**
Gainsborough Av. E12 ....5E **70**
Gainsborough Cl.
BR3: Beck 7C **140**
KT10: Esh 7J **149**
Gainsborough Ct. BR2: Brom 4A **160**
KT19: Ewe 6B **164**
N12 ....5E **30**
SE16 ....5H **103**
(off Stubbs Dr.)
SE21 ....2E **138**
W4 ....5H **97**
(off Chaseley Dr.)
W12 ....2E **98**
Gainsborough Gdns. HA8: Edg 2F **43**
NW3 ....3B **64**
NW11 ....7H **45**
TW7: Isle 5H **113**
Gainsborough Ho. E14 ....2C **104**
(off Cassilis Rd., Cassilis Rd.)
E14 ....7A **86**
(off Victory Pl., Victory Pl.)
EN1: Enf 5B **24**
RM8: Dag 1D **72**
(off Longbridge Rd.)
SW1 ....4D **18**
(off Erasmus St.)
Gainsborough Lodge HA1: Harr 5K **41**
(off Hindes Rd.)
Gainsborough Mans. W14 ....6G **99**
(off Queen's Club Gdns.)
Gainsborough M. SE26 ....3H **139**
Gainsborough Rd.
E11 ....7G **51**
E15 ....3G **87**
IG8: Wfd G 6H **37**
KT3: N Mald 6K **151**
N12 ....5E **30**
RM8: Dag 4B **72**
TW9: Rich 2F **115**
UB4: Hayes 2E **74**
W4 ....4B **98**
Gainsborough Sq. DA6: Bex 3D **126**
Gainsborough St. E9 ....6B **68**
Gainsborough Studios E. N1 ......1D **84**
(off Poole St.)
Gainsborough Studios Nth. N1 ....1D **84**
(off Poole St.)
Gainsborough Studios Sth. N1 ....1D **84**
(off Poole St.)
Gainsborough Studios W. N1 ......1D **84**
(off Poole St.)
Gainsborough Ter. SM2: Sutt 7H **165**
(off Belmont Ri.)
Gainsborough Twr. UB5: N'olt 2B **76**
(off Academy Gdns.)
Gainsfield Ct. E11 ....3G **69**
Gainsford Rd. E17 ....4B **50**
Gainsford St. SE1 ....6J **15** (2F **103**)
Gairloch Ho. NW1 ....7H **65**
(off Stratford Vs.)
Gairloch Rd. SE5 ....2E **120**
Gaisford St. NW5 ....6G **65**
Gaitskell Ct. SW11 ....2C **118**
Gaitskell Rd. E6 ....1B **88**
E17 ....3D **50**
SE17 ....6E **102**
(off Villa St.)
Gaitskell Rd. SE9 ....1G **143**
Gaitskell Way SE1 ....6C **14**
(off Weller St.)
Gala Bingo
Acton 1K **97**
(off High St.)
Bexleyheath 4H **127**
Camberwell 7C **102**
East Ham 1C **88**
Enfield 4B **24**
Feltham 2K **129**
Harrow 5K **41**
Hounslow 4E **112**
Leyton 1B **68**
Stratford 1F **87**
Surrey Quays 3K **103**
Tooting 5C **136**
Gala Ct. CR7: Thor H 5A **156**
Galahad Rd. BR1: Brom 4J **141**
N9 ....3B **34**
Galata Rd. SW13 ....7C **98**
Galatea Sq. SE15 ....3H **121**
Galaxy Bldg. E14 ....4C **104**
(off Crews St.)
Galaxy Ho. EC2 ....3F **9**
(off Leonard St.)
Galba Ct. TW8: Bford 7D **96**
Galbraith St. E14 ....3E **104**
Galdana Av. EN5: New Bar 3F **21**
Galeborough Av. IG8: Wfd G 7A **36**
Gale Cl. CR4: Mitc 3B **154**
TW12: Hamp 6C **130**
Galena Arches W6 ....4D **98**
(off Galena Rd.)
Galena Hgts. E20 ....6E **68**
(off Mirabelle Gdns.)
Galena Ho. SE18 ....5K **107**
(off Grosmont Rd.)
Galena Rd. W6 ....4D **98**
Galen Pl. WC1 ....6F **7** (5J **83**)
Galesbury Rd. SW18 ....6A **118**
Gales Gdns. E2 ....3H **85**
Gale St. E3 ....5C **86**
RM9: Dag 5C **72**
Gales Way IG8: Wfd G 7H **37**
Galgate Cl. SW19 ....1F **135**
Gallants Farm Rd. EN4: E Barn 7H **21**
Galleon Cl. DA8: Erith 4K **109**
SE16 ....2K **103**
Galleon Ho. E14 ....4E **104**
(off Glengarnock Av.)
Galleons Dr. IG11: Bark 3A **90**
Galleons Vw. E14 ....2E **104**
(off Stewart St.)
Galleria Ct. SE15 ....6F **103**
Galleria Shop. Mall, The E18 ......2J **51**
Galleries, The NW8 ....1A **4**
(off Abbey Rd.)
Gallery, The 1G **99**
(off Clockhouse Av.)
Gallery, The E20 ....6E **68**
(within Westfield Stratford City Shop. Cen.)
SE14 ....7B **104**
(off New Cross Rd.)
Gallery Apartments E1 ....6J **85**
(off Commercial Rd.)
SE1 ....7G **15**
(off Lamb Wlk.)
Gallery at London Glassblowing, The
..............................6G **15**
Gallery Ct. E17 ....2E **50**
(off Fulbourne Rd.)
SE1 ....7E **14**
(off Pilgrimage St.)
SW10 ....6A **100**
(off Gunter Gro.)
Gallery Gdns. UB5: N'olt 2B **76**
Gallery Ho. E8 ....6H **67**
(off Hackney Gro.)
Gallery Rd. SE21 ....1D **138**
Galley, The E16 ....7F **89**
Galleymead Rd. SL3: Poyle 4A **174**
Galleywall Rd. SE16 ....4H **103**
Galleywall Rd. Trad. Est. SE16 ....4H **103**
Galleywood Ho. W10 ....3F **81**
(off Sutton Way)
Galliard Cl. N9 ....6D **24**
Galliard Rd. N9 ....6B **24**
Gallia Rd. N5 ....5B **66**
Gallica Ct. SM1: Sutt 1K **165**
Gallions Cl. IG11: Bark 3A **90**
Gallions Entrance E16 ....1G **107**
Gallions Reach Shop. Pk. E6 ......5G **89**
Gallions Rd. E16 ....7F **89**
SE7 ....4K **105**
(not continuous)
GALLIONS RDBT. 7F **89**
Gallions Vw. Rd. SE28 ....2J **107**
Gallipoli Pl. RM9: Dag 1B **90**
Gallon Cl. SE7 ....4A **106**
Gallop, The CR2: Sels 7H **169**
SM2: Sutt 7B **166**
Gallosson Rd. SE18 ....4J **107**
Galloway Path CR0: C'don 4D **168**
Galloway Rd. W12 ....1C **98**
Gallus Cl. N21 ....6E **22**
Gallus Sq. SE3 ....3K **123**
Galpins Rd. CR7: Thor H 5J **155**
Galsworthy Av. E14 ....6A **86**
RM6: Chad H 7B **54**
Galsworthy Cl. NW2 ....4G **63**
SE28 ....1B **108**
Galsworthy Ct. W3 ....3H **97**
(off Bollo Bri. Rd.)
Galsworthy Cres. SE3 ....7A **106**
Galsworthy Ho. W11 ....6G **81**
(off Elgin Cres.)
Galsworthy Rd. KT2: King T 7H **133**
NW2 ....4G **63**
Galsworthy Ter. N16 ....3D **66**
Galton Ct. NW9 ....3A **44**
(off Joslin Av.)
Galton St. W10 ....3G **81**
Galva Cl. EN4: Cockf 4K **21**
Galvani Way CR0: Wadd 1K **167**
Galveston Ho. E1 ....4A **86**
(off Harford St.)
Galveston Rd. SW15 ....5H **117**
Galway Cl. SE16 ....5H **103**
(off Masters Dr.)
Galway Ho. E1 ....5K **85**
(off White Horse La.)
EC1 ....2D **8**
Galway St. EC1 ....2D **8** (3C **84**)
Galy NW9 ....3A **44**
Gambado
Beckenham 6C **140**
Chelsea 1A **118**
(off Station Ct.)
Gambetta St. SW8 ....2F **119**
Gambia St. SE1 ....5B **14** (1B **102**)
Gambier Ho. EC1 ....2D **8**
(off Mora St.)
Gamble Rd. SW17 ....4C **136**
Games Rd. EN4: Cockf 3H **21**
Gamlen Rd. SW15 ....4F **117**
Gamma Ct. CR0: C'don 1D **168**
(off Sydenham Rd.)
Gamuel Cl. E17 ....6C **50**
GANTS HILL 6E **52**
Gants Hill IG2: Ilf 6E **52**
Gants Hill Cres. IG2: Ilf 5E **52**
Gantshill Cres. IG2: Ilf 5E **52**
Gap Rd. SW19 ....5J **135**
Garage Rd. W3 ....6G **79**
Garand Ct. N7 ....5K **65**
Garbett Ho. SE17 ....6B **102**
(off Doddington Gro.)
Garbutt Pl. W1 ....5H **5** (5E **82**)
Garden Av. CR4: Mitc 7F **137**
DA7: Bex 3F **127**
Garden City HA8: Edg 6B **28**
Garden Cl.
E4 ....5H **35**
HA4: Ruis 2G **57**
KT3: N Mald 4A **152**
SE12 ....3K **141**
SM6: Wall 5J **167**
SW15 ....7E **116**
TW12: Hamp 5D **130**
TW15: Ashf 6E **128**
UB5: N'olt 1C **76**

Garden Ct. CR0: C'don 2F 169
EC4 . . . . .2J 13
HA7: Stan 5H 27
N12 . . . . .5E 30
NW8 . . . . .1A 4
(off Garden Rd.)
TW9: Kew 1F 115
TW12: Hamp 5D 130
W4 . . . . .3J 97
W11 . . . . .7G 81
(off Clarendon Rd.)
Gardener Gro. TW13: Hanw 2D 130
Gardeners Cl. N11 . . . . .2K 31
SE9 . . . . .3C 142
Gardeners Rd. CR0: C'don 1B 168
Garden Ho. N2 . . . . .2B 46
(off The Grange)
NW6 . . . . .2K 81
(off Oxford Rd.)
SW7 . . . . .3K 99
(off Cornwall Gdns.)
Garden Houses, The W6 . . . . .6F 99
(off Bothwell St.)
Gardenia Rd. BR1: Brom 3E 160
EN1: Enf .6K 23
Gardenia Way IG8: Wfd G 6D 36
Garden La. BR1: Brom 6K 141
SW2 . . . . .1K 137
Garden M. W2 . . . . .7J 81
Garden Museum, The 2G 19 (3K 101)
Garden Pl. E8 . . . . .1F 85
Garden Rd. BR1: Brom 7K 141
KT12: Walt T 6K 147
NW8 . . . . .1A 4 (3A 82)
SE20 . . . . .1J 157
TW9: Rich 3G 115
Garden Row SE1 . . . . .3B 102
Garden Royal SW15 . . . . .6F 117
Gardens, The BR3: Beck 1E 158
E5 . . . . .7F 49
HA1: Harr 6G 41
HA5: Pinn 6D 40
N8 . . . . .4J 47
(not continuous)
SE22 . . . . .4G 121
TW14: Felt 5F 111
Garden St. E1 . . . . .5K 85
Garden Ter. SW1 . . . . .5C 18 (5H 101)
SW7 . . . . .7D 10
Garden Wlk. BR3: Beck 1B 158
EC2 . . . . .2G 9 (3E 84)
Garden Way NW10 . . . . .6J 61
Gardiner Av. NW2 . . . . .5E 62
Gardiner Cl. EN3: Pond E 6E 24
RM8: Dag 4D 72
Gardiner Ct. CR2: S Croy 6D 168
Gardiner Ho. SW11 . . . . .1C 118
Gardiner Cl. E11 . . . . .6K 51
Gardner Ct. EC1 . . . . .3A 8
(off Brewery Sq.)
N5 . . . . .4C 66
Gardner Ho. TW13: Hanw 2D 130
UB1: S'hall 7B 76
(off The Broadway)
Gardner Ind. Est. BR3: Beck 5B 140
Gardner Pl. TW14: Felt 6K 111
Gardner Rd. E13 . . . . .4K 87
Gardners La. EC4 . . . . .2C 14 (7C 84)
Gardnor Rd. NW3 . . . . .4B 64
Gard St. EC1 . . . . .1B 8 (3B 84)
Garendon Gdns. SM4: Mord 7K 153
Garendon Rd. SM4: Mord 7K 153
Garenne Cl. E4 . . . . .1K 35
Gareth Cl. KT4: Wor Pk 2F 165
Gareth Ct. SW16 . . . . .3H 137
Gareth Dr. N9 . . . . .2B 34
Gareth Gro. BR1: Brom 4J 141
Garfield EN2: Enf 5J 23
(off London Rd.)
Garfield Ct. NW6 . . . . .7G 63
(off Willesden La.)

Garfield M. SW11 . . . . .3E 118
Garfield Rd. E4 . . . . .1A 36
E13 . . . . .4H 87
EN3: Pond E 4D 24
SW11 . . . . .3E 118
SW19 . . . . .5A 136
TW1: Twick 1A 132
Garford St. E14 . . . . .7C 86
Garganey Ct. NW10 . . . . .6K 61
(off Elgar Av.)
Garganey Wlk. SE28 . . . . .7C 90
Garibaldi St. SE18 . . . . .4J 107
Garland Cl. SE1 . . . . .3C 102
Garland Ct. E14 . . . . .7C 86
(off Premiere Pl.)
SE17 . . . . .4C 102
(off Wansey St.)
Garland Dr. TW3: Houn 2G 113
Garland Ho. KT2: King T 1E 150
(off Skerne Rd.)
UB7: W Dray 2B 92
Garland Rd. HA7: Stan 1E 42
SE18 . . . . .7H 107
Garlands Ct. CR0: C'don 4D 168
(off Chatsworth Rd.)
Garlands Ho. NW8 . . . . .2A 82
(off Carlton Hill)
Garlands La. HA1: Harr 1K 59
Garlick Hill EC4 . . . . .2D 14 (7C 84)
Garlies Rd. SE23 . . . . .3A 140
Garlinge Ho. SW9 . . . . .1A 120
(off Gosling Way)
Garlinge Rd. NW2 . . . . .6H 63
Garman Cl. N18 . . . . .5J 33
Garman Rd. N17 . . . . .7C 34
(not continuous)
Garnault M. EC1 . . . . .2K 7
Garnault Pl. EC1 . . . . .2K 7 (3A 84)
Garnault Rd. EN1: Enf 1A 24
Garner Cl. RM8: Dag 1D 72
Garner Ct. TW19: Stanw 6A 110
(off Douglas Rd.)
Garner Rd. E17 . . . . .1E 50
Garner St. E2 . . . . .2G 85
Garnet Ho. E1 . . . . .1J 103
(off Garnet St.)
Garnet Rd. CR7: Thor H 4C 156
NW10 . . . . .6A 62
Garnet St. E1 . . . . .7J 85
Garnett Cl. SE9 . . . . .3D 124
Garnett Rd. NW3 . . . . .5D 64
Garnett Way E17 . . . . .1A 50
(off McEntee Av.)
Garnet Wlk. E6 . . . . .5C 88
Garnham Cl. N16 . . . . .2F 67
Garnham St. N16 . . . . .2F 67
Garnies Cl. SE15 . . . . .7F 103
Garrad's Rd. SW16 . . . . .3H 137
Garrard Cl. BR7: Chst 5F 143
DA7: Bex .3G 127
Garrard Wlk. NW10 . . . . .6A 62
Garratt Cl. CR0: Bedd 4J 167
Garratt Ct. SW18 . . . . .7K 117
Garratt La. SW17 . . . . .6K 117
SW18 . . . . .6K 117
Garratt Rd. HA8: Edg 7B 28
Garratts Rd. WD23: Bush 1B 26
Garratt Ter. SW17 . . . . .4C 136
Garraway Ct. SW13 . . . . .7E 98
(off Wyatt Dr.)
Garrett Cl. W3 . . . . .5K 79
Garrett Ho. SE1 . . . . .6A 14
(off Burrows M.)
Garrett St. EC1 . . . . .3D 8 (4C 84)
Garrick Av. NW11 . . . . .6G 45
Garrick Cl. SW18 . . . . .4A 118
TW9: Rich 5D 114
W5 . . . . .4E 78
Garrick Ct. E8 . . . . .7F 67
(off Jacaranda Gro.)
Garrick Cres. CR0: C'don 2E 168

Garrick Dr. NW4 . . . . .2E 44
SE28 . . . . .3H 107
Garrick Gdns. KT8: W Mole 3E 148
Garrick Ho. KT1: King T 4E 150
(off Surbiton Rd.)
W1 . . . . .5J 11
W4 . . . . .6A 98
Garrick Ind. Cen. NW9 . . . . .5B 44
Garrick Pk. NW4 . . . . .2F 45
Garrick Rd. NW9 . . . . .6B 44
TW9: Rich 2G 115
UB6: G'frd 4F 77
Garricks Ho. KT1: King T 2D 150
(off Wadbrook St.)
Garrick St. WC2 . . . . .2E 12 (7J 83)
Garrick Theatre 3E 12
(off Charing Cross Rd.)
Garrick Way NW4 . . . . .4F 45
Garrick Yd. WC2 . . . . .2E 12
Garrison Cl. SE18 . . . . .7E 106
TW4: Houn 5D 112
Garrison La. KT9: Chess 7D 162
Garrison Rd. E3 . . . . .1C 86
Garrowsfield EN5: Barn 6C 20
Garry Way RM1: Rom 1K 55
Garsdale Cl. N11 . . . . .6K 31
Garsdale Ter. W14 . . . . .5H 99
(off Aisgill Av.)
Garside Cl. SE28 . . . . .3H 107
TW12: Hamp 6F 131
Garside Ct. TW11: Hamp W 1C 150
Garsington M. SE4 . . . . .3B 122
Garson Ho. W2 . . . . .2A 10
(off Gloucester Ter.)
Garson Rd. N1 . . . . .7B 66
(off The Sutton Est.)
Garter Way SE16 . . . . .2K 103
Garth, The HA3: Kenton 6F 43
TW12: Hamp H 6F 131
Garth Cl. HA4: Ruis 1B 58
KT2: King T 5F 133
SM4: Mord 7F 153
Garth Ct. HA1: Harr 6K 41
(off Northwick Pk. Rd.)
W4 . . . . .5K 97
Garth M. W5 .4E 78
Garthorne Rd. SE23 . . . . .7K 121
Garthorne Road Nature Reserve . .7K 121
Garth Rd. KT2: King T 5F 133
NW2 . . . . .2H 63
SM4: Mord 6E 152
W4 . . . . .5K 97
Garth Rd. Ind. Centre, The
SM4: Mord 1F 165
Garthside TW10: Ham 5E 132
Garthway N12 . . . . .6H 31
Gartmoor Gdns. SW19 . . . . .1H 135
Gartmore Rd. IG3: Ilf 2K 71
Garton Pl. SW18 . . . . .6A 118
Gartons Cl. EN3: Pond E 4D 24
Gartons Way SW11 . . . . .3A 118
Garvary Rd. E16 . . . . .6K 87
Garway Ct. E3 . . . . .2C 86
(off Matilda Gdns.)
Garway Rd. W2 . . . . .6K 81
Garwood Cl. N17 . . . . .1H 49
Gascogne Pl. N17 . . . . .1F 49
Gascoigne Gdns. IG8: Wfd G 7B 36
Gascoigne Pl. E2 . . . . .1J 9 (3F 85)
(not continuous)
Gascoigne Rd. CR0: New Ad 7F 171
IG11: Bark 1G 89
Gascony Av. NW6 . . . . .7J 63
Gascony Pl. W12 . . . . .1F 99
Gascoyne Ho. E9 . . . . .7A 68
Gascoyne Rd. E9 . . . . .7K 67
Gaselee St. E14 . . . . .1E 104
(off Baffin Way)
Gaskarth Rd. HA8: Edg 1J 43
SW12 . . . . .6F 119

Gaskell Ct. SE20 . . . . .7K 139
Gaskell Rd. N6 . . . . .6D 46
Gaskell St. SW4 . . . . .2J 119
Gaskin St. N1 . . . . .1B 84
Gaspar M. SW5 . . . . .4K 99
Gaspar M. SW5 . . . . .4K 99
Gassiot Rd. SW17 . . . . .4D 136
Gassiot Way SM1: Sutt 3B 166
Gasson Ho. SE14 . . . . .6K 103
(off John Williams Cl.)
Gastein Rd. W6 . . . . .6F 99
Gastigny Ho. EC1 . . . . .2D 8
Gaston Bell Cl. TW9: Rich 3F 115
Gaston Bri. Rd. TW17: Shep 6F 147
Gaston Rd. CR4: Mitc 3E 154
Gaston Way TW17: Shep 5F 147
Gataker Ho. SE16 . . . . .3H 103
(off Slippers Pl.)
Gataker St. SE16 . . . . .3H 103
Gatcombe Cl. BR3: Beck 7C 140
Gatcombe Ho. SE22 . . . . .3E 120
Gatcombe M. W5 . . . . .7F 79
Gatcombe Rd. E16 . . . . .1J 105
N19 . . . . .3H 65
Gatcombe Way EN4: Cockf 3J 21
Gateacre Ct. DA14: Sidc 4B 144
Gate Centre, The TW8: Bford 7A 96
(off Notting Hill Ga.)
Gate Cinema .1J 99
(off Notting Hill Ga.)
Gateforth St. NW8 . . . . .4C 4 (4C 82)
Gate Hill Ct. W11 . . . . .1J 99
(off Ladbroke Ter.)
Gate Ho. E3 .1A 86
(off Gunmakers La.)
N1 . . . . .7D 66
(off Ufton Rd.)
NW6 . . . . .2K 81
(off Oxford Rd.)
Gatehouse Cl. KT2: King T 7J 133
Gatehouse Sq. SE1 . . . . .4D 14
Gatehouse Theatre
Highgate .1E 64
Gateley Ho. SE4 . . . . .4K 121
(off Coston Wlk.)
Gateley Rd. SW9 . . . . .3K 119
Gate Lodge W9 . . . . .5J 81
(off Admiral Wlk.)
Gately Ct. SE15 . . . . .7F 103
Gate M. SW7 . . . . .7D 10
Gater Dr. EN2: Enf 1J 23
Gates NW9 . . . . .2B 44
Gatesborough St. EC2 . . . . .3G 9 (4E 84)
Gates Cl. SE17 . . . . .5C 102
Gatesden WC1 . . . . .2G 7 (3J 83)
Gates Grn. Rd.
BR2: Kes .3H 171
BR4: W W'ck 3H 171
Gateside Rd. SW17 . . . . .3D 136
Gatestone Ct. SE19 . . . . .6E 138
(off Central Hill)
Gatestone Rd. SE19 . . . . .6E 138
Gate St. WC2 . . . . .7G 7 (6K 83)
Gate Theatre, The
London 1J 99
(off Pembridge Rd.)
Gateway SE17 . . . . .6C 102
Gateway Arc. N1 . . . . .2B 84
(off Upper St.)
Gateway Bus. Cen. SE26 . . . . .6A 140
SE28 . . . . .3H 107
Gateway Cl. IG2: Ilf 6E 52
(off Parham Dr.)
Gateway Ho. IG11: Bark 1G 89
Gateway Ind. Est. NW10 . . . . .3B 80
Gateway M.
E8 . . . . .5F 67
N11 . . . . .6B 32
Gateway Retail Pk. E6 . . . . .4F 89
Gateway Rd. E10 . . . . .3D 68
Gateways KT6: Surb 5E 150
(off Surbiton Hill Rd.)

Gateways, The SW3 . . . . .4D **16** (4C **100**)
  TW9: Rich 4D **114**
               (off Park La.)
Gateways Ct. SM6: Wall 5F **167**
Gatfield Gro. TW13: Hanw 2E **130**
Gatfield Ho. TW13: Hanw 2D **130**
Gathorne Rd. N22 . . . . .2A **48**
Gathorne St. E2 . . . . .2K **85**
Gatley Av. KT19: Ewe 5H **163**
Gatliff Cl. SW1 . . . . .6H **17**
Gatliff Rd. SW1 . . . . . .6J **17** (5F **101**)
Gatling Rd. SE2 . . . . .5A **108**
Gatonby St. SE15 . . . . .1F **121**
Gatting Cl. HA8: Edg 7D **28**
Gatting Way UB8: Uxb 6A **56**
Gattis Wharf N1 . . . . .2J **83**
       (off New Wharf Rd.)
Gatton Cl. SM2: Sutt 7K **165**
Gatton Rd. SW17 . . . . .4C **136**
Gattons Way DA14: Sidc 4F **145**
Gatward Cl. N21 . . . . .6G **23**
Gatward Grn. N9 . . . . .2A **34**
Gatward Pl. IG11: Bark 3K **89**
Gatwick Ho. E14 . . . . .6B **86**
      (off Clemence St.)
Gatwick Rd. SW18 . . . . .7H **117**
Gauden Cl. SW4 . . . . .3H **119**
Gauden Rd. SW4 . . . . .2H **119**
Gaudi Apartments N8 . . . . .3K **47**
      (off Gt. Amwell La.)
Gaugin Ct. SE16 . . . . .5H **103**
        (off Stubbs Dr.)
Gaumont Ter. W12 . . . . .2E **98**
       (off Lime Gro.)
Gaumont Twr. E8 . . . . .6F **67**
      (off Dalston Sq.)
Gauntlet NW9 . . . . .2B **44**
       (five Acre)
Gauntlet Cl. UB5: N'olt 7C **58**
Gauntlett Cl. HA0: Wemb 5B **60**
Gauntlett Rd. SM1: Sutt 5B **166**
Gaunt St. SE1 . . . . .3C **102**
Gautrey Rd. SE15 . . . . .2J **121**
Gautrey Sq. E6 . . . . .6D **88**
Gavel St. SE17 . . . . .4D **102**
Gaverick M. E14 . . . . .4C **104**
Gavestone Cres. SE12 . . . . .7A **124**
Gavestone Rd. SE12 . . . . .7K **123**
Gaviller Pl. E5 . . . . .4H **67**
Gavina Cl. SM4: Mord 5C **154**
Gavin Ho. SE18 . . . . .4J **107**
Gawain Wlk. N9 . . . . .3B **34**
Gawber St. E2 . . . . .3J **85**
Gawsworth Cl. E15 . . . . .5H **69**
Gawthorne Cl. E3 . . . . .2C **86**
Gay Cl. NW2 . . . . .5D **62**
Gaydon Ho. W2 . . . . .5K **81**
       (off Bourne Ter.)
Gaydon La. NW9 . . . . .1A **44**
Gayfere Pl. SE25 . . . . .2E **156**
     (off Grange Hill)
Gayfere Rd. IG5: Ilf 3D **52**
  KT17: Ewe 5C **164**
Gayfere St. SW1 . . . . . .2E **18** (3J **101**)
Gayford Rd. W12 . . . . .2B **98**
Gay Gdns. RM10: Dag 4J **73**
Gay Ho. N16 . . . . .5E **66**
Gayhurst SE17 . . . . .5D **102**
     (off Hopwood Rd.)
Gayhurst Ct. UB5: N'olt 3A **76**
Gayhurst Ho. NW8 . . . . .3C **4**
      (off Mallory St.)
Gayhurst Rd. E8 . . . . .7G **67**
Gaylor Rd. UB5: N'olt 5D **58**
Gaymead NW8 . . . . .1K **81**
      (off Abbey Rd.)
Gaynesford Rd. SE23 . . . . .2K **139**
  SM5: Cars 7D **166**
Gaynes Hill Rd. IG8: Wfd G 6H **37**
Gay Rd. E15 . . . . .2F **87**
Gaysham Av. IG2: Ilf 5E **52**

Gaysham Hall IG5: Ilf 3F **53**
Gaysley Ho. SE11 . . . . .4J **19**
Gay St. SW15 . . . . .3F **117**
Gayton HA1: Harr 7J **41**
      (off Grove Hill)
Gayton Cl. HA1: Harr 6K **41**
Gayton Cres. NW3 . . . . .4B **64**
Gayton Ho. E3 . . . . .4C **86**
      (off Chiltern Rd.)
Gayton Rd. HA1: Harr 6K **41**
  NW3 . . . . .4B **64**
  SE2 . . . . .3C **108**
Gayville Rd. SW11 . . . . .6D **118**
Gaywood Cl. SW2 . . . . .1K **137**
Gaywood Rd. E17 . . . . .3C **50**
Gaywood St. SE1 . . . . .3B **102**
Gaza St. SE17 . . . . .5B **102**
Gaze Ho. E14 . . . . .6F **87**
      (off Blair St.)
Gazelle Ho. E15 . . . . .6G **69**
Gean Ct. E11 . . . . .4F **69**
  N11 . . . . .6B **32**
      (off Cline Rd.)
Geariesville Gdns. IG6: Ilf 4F **53**
Gearing Cl. SW17 . . . . .4E **136**
Geary Rd. NW10 . . . . .5C **62**
Geary St. N7 . . . . .5K **65**
Geddes Pl. DA6: Bex 4G **127**
      (off Arnsberg Way)
Gedeney Rd. N17 . . . . .1C **48**
Gedling Ct. SE1 . . . . .7K **15**
      (off Sweeney Cres.)
Gedling Pl. SE1 . . . . .7K **15** (3F **103**)
Geere Rd. E15 . . . . .1H **87**
Gees Ct. W1 . . . . .1H **11** (6E **82**)
Gee St. EC1 . . . . .3C **8** (4C **84**)
Geffery's Ct. SE9 . . . . .3C **142**
Geffrye Ct. N1 . . . . .2E **84**
Geffrye Est. N1 . . . . .2E **84**
Geffrye Mus. 1J **9** (2F **85**)
Geffrye St. E2 . . . . .1J **9** (2F **85**)
Geldart Rd. SE15 . . . . .7H **103**
Geldeston Rd. E5 . . . . .2G **67**
Gellatly Rd. SE14 . . . . .2J **121**
Gell Cl. UB10: Ick 3B **56**
Gelsthorpe Rd. RM5: Col R 1H **55**
Gem Cl. SE10 . . . . .7D **104**
     (off Merryweather Pl.)
Gemini Apartments E1 . . . . .3K **9**
      (off Sclater St.)
Gemini Bus. Cen. E16 . . . . .4F **87**
Gemini Bus. Est. SE14 . . . . .5K **103**
Gemini Bus. Pk. E6 . . . . .5H **89**
Gemini Ct. E1 . . . . .7G **85**
      (off Vaughan Way)
Gemini Gro. UB5: N'olt 3C **76**
Gemini Ho. E3 . . . . .1C **86**
      (off Garrison Rd.)
Gemini Pl. TW15: Ashf 6G **129**
Genas Cl. IG6: Ilf 1F **53**
General Gordon Pl. SE18 . . . . . . .4F **107**
General Gordon Sq. SE18 . . . . . . .4F **107**
    (off Woolwich New Rd.)
General Wolfe Rd. SE10 . . . . .1F **123**
Genesis Bus. Pk. NW10 . . . . .2H **79**
Genesis Cl. TW19: Stanw 1B **128**
Genesta Rd. SE18 . . . . .6F **107**
Geneva Cl. TW17: Shep 2G **147**
Geneva Ct. NW9 . . . . .5B **44**
Geneva Dr. SW9 . . . . .4A **120**
Geneva Gdns. RM6: Chad H 5E **54**
Geneva Rd. CR7: Thor H 5C **156**
  KT1: King T 4E **150**
Genever Cl. E4 . . . . .5H **35**
Genista Rd. N18 . . . . .5C **34**
Genoa Av. SW15 . . . . .5E **116**
Genoa Ho. E1 . . . . .4K **85**
      (off Ernest St.)
  SW18 . . . . .3A **118**
Genoa Rd. SE20 . . . . .1J **157**
Genotin Rd. EN1: Enf 3J **23**

Genotin Ter. EN1: Enf 3J **23**
Gentlemans Row EN2: Enf 3H **23**
Gentry Gdns. E13 . . . . .4J **87**
Geoff Cade Way E3 . . . . .5B **86**
Geoffrey Chaucer Way E3 . . . . . . .5B **86**
Geoffrey Cl. SE5 . . . . .2C **120**
Geoffrey Ct. SE4 . . . . .2B **122**
Geoffrey Gdns. E6 . . . . .2C **88**
Geoffrey Ho. SE1 . . . . .7F **15**
     (off Pardoner St.)
Geoffrey Jones Ct. NW10 . . . . . . .1C **80**
Geoffrey Rd. SE4 . . . . .3B **122**
George V Av. HA5: Pinn 2D **40**
George V Cl. HA5: Pinn 3E **40**
George V Way UB6: G'frd 1B **78**
George Beard Rd. SE8 . . . . .4B **104**
George Belt Ho. E2 . . . . .3K **85**
      (off Smart St.)
George Comberton Wlk. E12 . . . . .5E **70**
George Ct. TW15: Ashf 4B **128**
      (off Church Rd.)
  UB3: Hayes 5H **75**
  WC2 . . . . .3F **13**
George Cres. N10 . . . . .7K **31**
George Davies Lodge IG6: Ilf 5G **53**
    (off Veronique Gdns.)
George Downing Est. N16 . . . . . . .2F **67**
George Eliot Ho. SE17 . . . . .5C **102**
      (off Thrush St.)
  SW1 . . . . .4B **18**
     (off Vauxhall Bri. Rd.)
George Elliston Ho. SE1 . . . . .5G **103**
     (off Old Kent Rd.)
George Eyre Ho. NW8 . . . . .2B **82**
     (off Cochrane St.)
George Furness Ho. NW10 . . . . . .6D **62**
      (off Grange Rd.)
George Gange Way HA3: W'stone . .3J **41**
George Gillett Ct. EC1 . . . . .3D **8**
George Groves Rd. SE20 . . . . .1G **157**
George Ho. NW6 . . . . .2H **81**
      (off Albert Rd.)
George Hudson Twr. E15 . . . . .2D **86**
      (off High St.)
George Inn Yd. SE1 . . . .5E **14** (1D **102**)
George La. BR2: Hayes 1K **171**
  E18 . . . . .2J **51**
  SE6 . . . . .6D **122**
  SE13 . . . . .6D **122**
George Lansbury Ho. E3 . . . . .3B **86**
       (off Bow Rd.)
  N22 . . . . .1A **48**
     (off Progress Way)
  NW10 . . . . .7A **62**
George Leybourne Ho. E1 . . . . . . .7G **85**
     (off Fletcher St.)
George Lindgren Ho. SW6 . . . . . . .7H **99**
     (off Clem Attlee Ct.)
George Loveless Ho. E2 . . . . .1K **9**
      (off Diss St.)
George Lowe Ct. W2 . . . . .5K **81**
     (off Bourne Ter.)
George Mathers Rd. SE11 . . . . . . .4B **102**
George M. EN2: Enf 3J **23**
  NW1 . . . . .2B **6**
  SW9 . . . . .2A **120**
George Padmore Ho. E8 . . . . .1G **85**
     (off Brougham Rd.)
George Peabody Ct. NW1 . . . . . . .5C **4**
      (off Burne St.)
George Peabody St. E13 . . . . .2A **88**
George Pl. N17 . . . . .3E **48**
George Potter Ho. SW11 . . . . .2B **118**
     (off George Potter Way)
George Potter Way SW11 . . . . . . .2B **118**
George Rd. E4 . . . . .6H **35**
  KT2: King T 7H **133**
  KT3: N Mald 4B **152**
George Row SE16 . . . . .2G **103**
George Scott Ho. E1 . . . . .6K **85**
     (off W. Arbour St.)

George Sq. SW19 . . . . .3J **153**
George's Rd. N7 . . . . .5K **65**
George's Sq. SW6 . . . . .6H **99**
     (off North End Rd.)
George St. CR0: C'don 2C **168**
  E16 . . . . .6H **87**
  IG11: Bark 7G **71**
  TW3: Houn 2D **112**
  TW9: Rich 5D **114**
  UB2: S'hall 4A **94**
  W1 . . . . .7E **4** (6D **82**)
  W7 . . . . .1J **95**
Georgetown Cl. SE19 . . . . .5E **138**
Georgette Pl. SE10 . . . . .7E **104**
George Vale Ho. E2 . . . . .2G **85**
     (off Mansford St.)
Georgeville Gdns. IG6: Ilf 4F **53**
George Walter Ct. SE16 . . . . .4J **103**
     (off Millender Wlk.)
George Wyver Cl. SW19 . . . . .7G **117**
George Yd. EC3 . . . . .1F **15** (6D **84**)
  W1 . . . . .2H **11** (7E **82**)
Georgia Ct. SE16 . . . . .3G **103**
      (off Priter Rd.)
Georgiana St. NW1 . . . . .1G **83**
Georgian Cl. BR2: Hayes 1K **171**
  HA7: Stan 7F **27**
  UB10: Ick 4A **56**
Georgian Ct. CR0: C'don 1D **168**
       (off Cross Rd.)
  E9 . . . . .1J **85**
  EN5: New Bar 4F **21**
  HA9: Wemb 6G **61**
  N3 . . . . .1H **45**
  NW4 . . . . .5D **44**
  SW16 . . . . .4J **137**
Georgian Ho. E16 . . . . .1J **105**
      (off Capulet M.)
  N1 . . . . .1E **84**
      (off Hertford Rd.)
Georgian Way HA1: Harr 2H **59**
Georgia Rd. CR7: Thor H 1B **156**
  KT3: N Mald 4J **151**
Geraldine Rd. SW18 . . . . .5A **118**
  W4 . . . . .6G **97**
Geraldine St. SE11 . . . . . .2K **19** (3B **102**)
Gerald M. SW1 . . . . .3H **17**
Gerald Pl. E8 . . . . .6F **67**
      (off Dalston Sq.)
Gerald Rd. E16 . . . . .4H **87**
  RM8: Dag 1F **73**
  SW1 . . . . .3H **17** (4E **100**)
Gerard Av. TW4: Houn 7E **112**
Gerard Gdns. RM13: Rain 2K **91**
Gerard Pl. E9 . . . . .7K **67**
Gerard Rd. HA1: Harr 6A **42**
  SW13 . . . . .1B **116**
Gerards Cl. SE16 . . . . .5J **103**
Gerards Pl. SW4 . . . . .4H **119**
Gerda Rd. SE9 . . . . .2G **143**
Germander Way E15 . . . . .3G **87**
Gernigan Ho. SW18 . . . . .6B **118**
Gernon Rd. E3 . . . . .2A **86**
Geron Way NW2 . . . . .1D **62**
Gerrard Gdns. HA5: Eastc 5J **39**
Gerrard Ho. SE14 . . . . .7J **103**
      (off Briant St.)
Gerrard Pl. W1 . . . . .2D **12** (7H **83**)
Gerrard Rd. N1 . . . . .2B **84**
Gerrards Cl. N14 . . . . .5B **22**
Gerrards St. W5 . . . . .3D **96**
Gerrard St. W1 . . . . .2D **12** (7H **83**)
Gerrard Way SE3 . . . . .4A **124**
Gerridge Ct. SE1 . . . . .1K **19**
      (off Gerridge St.)
Gerridge St. SE1 . . . . . . .1K **19** (3A **102**)
Gerry Raffles Sq. E15 . . . . .6F **69**
Gertrude Rd. DA17: Belv 4G **109**
Gertrude St. SW10 . . . . . .7A **16** (6A **100**)

Gervase Cl. HA9: Wemb 3J **61**
Gervase Rd. HA8: Edg 1J **43**
Gervase St. SE15 . . . . .7H **103**
Gervis Ct. TW7: Isle 7G **95**
Ghent St. SE6 . . . . .2C **140**
Ghent Way E8 . . . . .6F **67**
Gherkin, The 1H **15**
Giant Arches Rd. SE24 . . . . .7C **120**
Giant Tree Hill WD23: B Hea 1C **26**
Gibbfield Cl. RM6: Chad H 3E **54**
Gibbings Ho. SE1 . . . . .7B **14**
(off King James St.)
Gibbins Rd. E15 . . . . .7E **68**
Gibbon Ho. NW8 . . . . .4B **4**
(off Fisherton St.)
Gibbon Rd. KT2: King T 1E **150**
SE15 . . . . .2J **121**
W3 . . . . .7A **80**
Gibbons Rd. NW11 . . . . .5H **45**
Gibbon's Rents SE1 . . . . .5G **15**
Gibbons Rd. NW10 . . . . .6A **62**
Gibbon Wlk. SW15 . . . . .4C **116**
Gibbs Av. SE19 . . . . .5D **138**
Gibbs Cl. SE19 . . . . .6D **138**
Gibbs Grn. HA8: Edg 4D **28**
W14 . . . . .5H **99**
(not continuous)
Gibbs Ho. BR1: Brom 1H **159**
(off Longfield)
Gibb's Rd. N18 . . . . .4D **34**
Gibbs Sq. SE19 . . . . .5D **138**
Gibney Ter. BR1: Brom 4H **141**
Gibraltar Wlk. E2 . . . . .2K **9**
Gibson Cl. E1 . . . . .4J **85**
KT9: Chess 5C **162**
N21 . . . . .6F **23**
TW7: Isle 3J **113**
Gibson Ct. SE9 . . . . .5A **124**
Gibson Gdns. N16 . . . . .2F **67**
Gibson Ho. SM1: Sutt 4J **165**
Gibson M. TW1: Twick 6C **114**
Gibson Rd. RM8: Dag 1C **72**
SE11 . . . . .4H **19** (4K **101**)
SM1: Sutt 5K **165**
UB10: Ick 4B **56**
Gibsons Hill SW16 . . . . .7A **138**
(not continuous)
Gibson Sq. N1 . . . . .1A **84**
Gibson Sq. Gdns. N1 . . . . .1A **84**
(off Gibson Sq.)
Gibson St. SE10 . . . . .5G **105**
Gideon Cl. DA17: Belv 4H **109**
HA8: Edg 6B **28**
Gideon M. W5 . . . . .2D **96**
Gideon Rd. SW11 . . . . .3E **118**
Gielgud Theatre 2C **12**
(off Shaftesbury Av.)
Giesbach Rd. N19 . . . . .2H **65**
Giffard Rd. N18 . . . . .6K **33**
Giffin Sq. Mkt. SE8 . . . . .7C **104**
(off Giffin St.)
Giffin St. SE8 . . . . .7C **104**
Gifford Gdns. W7 . . . . .5H **77**
Gifford Ho. SE10 . . . . .5F **105**
(off Eastney St.)
SW1 . . . . .6A **18**
(off Churchill Gdns.)
Gifford Rd. NW10 . . . . .7A **62**
Gifford St. N1 . . . . .7J **65**
Gift La. E15 .1G **87**
GIGGSHILL 7A **150**
Giggs Hill BR5: St P 2K **161**
Giggs Hill Gdns. KT7: T Ditt 1A **162**
Giggs Hill Rd. KT7: T Ditt 7A **150**
Gilbert Bri. EC2 . . . . .5D **8**
(off Wood St.)
Gilbert Cl. SE18 . . . . .1D **124**
SW19 . . . . .1K **153**
(off Morden Rd.)
Gilbert Ct. W5 . . . . .6F **79**
(off Green Va.)

Gilbert Gro. HA8: Edg 1K **43**
Gilbert Ho. E2 . . . . .3K **85**
(off Usk St.)
E17 . . . . .3E **50**
EC2 . . . . .5D **8**
SE8 . . . . .6C **104**
SW1 . . . . .6K **17**
(off Churchill Gdns.)
SW8 . . . . .7J **101**
(off Wyvil Rd.)
SW13 . . . . .7D **98**
(off Trinity Chu. Rd.)
Gilbert Pl. WC1 . . . . .6E **6** (5J **83**)
Gilbert Rd. BR1: Brom 7J **141**
DA17: Belv 3G **109**
HA5: Pinn 4B **40**
SE11 . . . . .4K **19** (4A **102**)
SW19 . . . . .7A **136**
UB9: Hare 2A **38**
Gilbert Scott Bldg. SW15 . . . . .6G **117**
Gilbert Scott Cl. HA0: Wemb 5D **60**
Gilbert Sheldon Ho. W2 . . . . .5B **4**
(off Edgware Rd.)
Gilbertson Ho. E14 . . . . .3C **104**
(off Mellish St.)
Gilbert St. E15 . . . . .4G **69**
TW3: Houn 3G **113**
W1 . . . . .1H **11** (6E **82**)
Gilbert Way CR0: Wadd 2K **167**
Gilbert White Cl. UB6: G'frd 1A **78**
Gilby Ho. E9 . . . . .6K **67**
Gilbey Cl. UB10: Ick 4D **56**
Gilbey Ho. NW1 . . . . .7F **65**
Gilbey Rd. SW17 . . . . .4C **136**
Gilbeys Yd. NW1 . . . . .7E **64**
Gilbourne Rd. SE18 . . . . .6K **107**
Gilby Ho. E9 . . . . .6K **67**
Gilda Av. EN3: Pond E 5F **25**
Gilda Ct. NW7 . . . . .1C **44**
Gilda Cres. N16 . . . . .1G **67**
Gildea Cl. HA5: Hat E 1E **40**
Gildea St. W1 . . . . .6K **5** (5F **83**)
Gilden Cres. NW5 . . . . .5E **64**
Gildersome St. SE18 . . . . .6E **106**
Gilders Rd. KT9: Chess 7F **163**
Giles Coppice SE19 . . . . .4F **139**
Giles Ho. W11 . . . . .6J **81**
(off Westbourne Gro.)
Gilesmead SE5 . . . . .1D **120**
Gilford Ho. IG1: Ilf 2F **71**
(off Clements Rd.)
Gilfrid Cl. UB8: Hil 6D **74**
Gilkes Cres. SE21 . . . . .6E **120**
Gilkes Pl. SE21 . . . . .6E **120**
Gillam Ho. SE16 . . . . .4J **103**
(off Silwood St.)
Gillan Ct. SE12 . . . . .3K **141**
Gillan Grn. WD23: B Hea 2B **26**
Gillards M. E17 . . . . .4C **50**
Gillards Way E17 . . . . .4C **50**
Gill Av. E16 .6J **87**
Gillender St. E3 . . . . .4E **86**
E14 . . . . .4E **86**
Gillespie Pk. Local Nature Reserve . .3A **66**
Gillespie Rd. N5 . . . . .3A **66**
Gillett Av. E6 . . . . .2C **88**
GILLETTE CORNER 7A **96**
Gillett Ho. N8 . . . . .3J **47**
(off Campsfield Rd.)
Gillett Pl. N16 . . . . .5E **66**
Gillett Rd. CR7: Thor H 4D **156**
Gillett Sq. N16 . . . . .5E **66**
(off Gillett St.)
Gillett St. N16 . . . . .5E **66**
Gillfoot NW1 . . . . .1A **6**
(off Hampstead Rd.)
Gillham Ter. N17 . . . . .6B **34**
Gillian Ho. HA3: Hrw W 6D **26**
Gillian Pk. Rd. SM3: Sutt 1H **165**
Gillian St. SE13 . . . . .5D **122**
Gillies Ho. NW6 . . . . .7B **64**
(off Hilgrove Rd.)

Gillies St. NW5 . . . . .5E **64**
Gilling Ct. NW3 . . . . .6C **64**
Gillingham M. SW1 . . . . .3A **18** (4G **101**)
Gillingham Rd. NW2 . . . . .3G **63**
Gillingham Row SW1 . . . .3A **18** (4G **101**)
Gillingham St. SW1 . . . . .3A **18** (4G **101**)
Gillings Ct. EN5: Barn 4B **20**
(off Wood St.)
Gillison Wlk. SE16 . . . . .3H **103**
Gillis Sq. SW15 . . . . .6C **116**
Gillman Dr. E15 . . . . .1H **87**
Gillman Ho. E2 . . . . .2G **85**
(off Pritchard's Rd.)
Gillray Ho. SW10 . . . . .6B **100**
(off Ann La.)
Gill St. E14 .6B **86**
Gillum Cl. EN4: E Barn 1J **31**
Gilman Ho. N1 . . . . .7A **66**
(off Drummond Way)
Gilmore Cl. UB10: Ick 3C **56**
Gilmore Ct. N11 . . . . .5J **31**
Gilmore Cres. TW15: Ashf 5C **128**
Gilmore Rd. SE13 . . . . .4F **123**
Gilmour Ho. NW9 . . . . .2C **44**
Gilpin Av. SW14 . . . . .4K **115**
Gilpin Cl. CR4: Mitc 2C **154**
W2 . . . . .5A **4**
(off Porteus Rd.)
Gilpin Cres. N18 . . . . .5A **34**
TW2: Whitt 7F **113**
Gilpin Rd. E5 . . . . .4A **68**
Gilpin Way UB3: Harl 7F **93**
Gilray Ho. W2 . . . . .2A **10**
(off Gloucester Ter.)
Gilsland Pl. CR7: Thor H 4D **156**
Gilsland Rd. CR7: Thor H 4D **156**
Gilson Pl. N10 . . . . .7J **31**
Gilstead Rd. SW6 . . . . .2K **117**
Gilston Rd. SW10 . . . . .7A **16** (5A **100**)
Gilton Rd. SE6 . . . . .3G **141**
Giltspur St. EC1 . . . . .7B **8** (6B **84**)
Gilwell Cl. E4 . . . . .4J **25**
Gilwell La. E4 . . . . .4K **25**
(not continuous)
GILWELL PARK 4K **25**
Gilwell Pk. E4 . . . . .3K **25**
Ginger Apartments SE1 . . . . .6K **15**
(off Cayenne Ct.)
Ginsburg Yd. NW3 . . . . .4A **64**
Gippeswyck Cl. HA5: Pinn 1B **40**
Gipsy Hill SE19 . . . . .4E **138**
Gipsy La. SW15 . . . . .3D **116**
Gipsy Rd. DA16: Well 7D **108**
SE27 .4C **138**
Gipsy Rd. Gdns. SE27 . . . . .4C **138**
Giralda Cl. E16 . . . . .5B **88**
Giraud St. E14 . . . . .6D **86**
Girdler's Rd. W14 . . . . .4F **99**
Girdlestone Wlk. N19 . . . . .2G **65**
Girdwood Rd. SW18 . . . . .7G **117**
Girling Ho. N1 . . . . .1E **84**
(off Colville St.)
Girling Way TW14: Felt 3J **111**
Gironde Rd. SW6 . . . . .7H **99**
Girtin Ho. UB5: N'olt 2B **76**
(off Academy Gdns.)
Girton Av. NW9 . . . . .3G **43**
Girton Cl. UB5: N'olt 6G **59**
Girton Gdns. CR0: C'don 3C **170**
Girton Rd. SE26 . . . . .5K **139**
UB5: N'olt 6G **59**
Girton Vs. W10 . . . . .6F **81**
Gisbourne Cl. SM6: Bedd 3H **167**
Gisburn Ho. SE15 . . . . .6G **103**
(off Friary Est.)
Gisburn Rd. N8 . . . . .4K **47**
Gissing Wlk. N1 . . . . .7A **66**
Gittens Cl. BR1: Brom 4H **141**
Given Wilson Wlk. E13 . . . . .2H **87**
Giverny Ho. SE16 . . . . .2K **103**
(off Water Gdns. Sq.)

Glacier Way HA0: Wemb 2D **78**
Gladbeck Way EN2: Enf 4G **23**
Gladding Rd. E12 . . . . .4B **70**
Glade, The BR1: Brom 2B **160**
BR4: W W'ck 3D **170**
CR0: C'don 5K **157**
E8 . . . . .6G **67**
EN2: Enf 3F **23**
IG5: Ilf .1D **52**
IG8: Wfd G 3E **36**
KT17: Ewe 6C **164**
N12 . . . . .3G **31**
N21 . . . . .6E **22**
SE7 . . . . .7A **106**
SM2: Cheam 7G **165**
W12 . . . . .2D **98**
(off Coningham Rd.)
Glade Cl. KT6: Surb 2D **162**
Glade Ct. IG5: Ilf 1D **52**
Glade Gdns. CR0: C'don 7A **158**
Glade La. UB2: S'hall 2F **95**
Glades, The KT6: Surb 7E **150**
The Glades BR1: Brom 2J **159**
Gladeside CR0: C'don 6K **157**
N21 . . . . .6E **22**
Gladeside Cl. KT9: Chess 7D **162**
Gladesmore Community School
& Sports Cen. 5G **49**
Gladesmore Rd. N15 . . . . .6F **49**
Glades Pl. BR1: Brom 2J **159**
Gladeswood Rd. DA17: Belv 4H **109**
Glade Wlk. E20 . . . . .6D **68**
Gladiator St. SE23 . . . . .7A **122**
Glading Ter. N16 . . . . .3F **67**
Gladioli Cl. TW12: Hamp 6E **130**
Gladsdale Dr. HA5: Eastc 4J **39**
Gladsmuir Rd. EN5: Barn 2B **20**
N19 . . . . .1G **65**
Gladstone Av. E12 . . . . .7C **70**
N22 . . . . .2A **48**
TW2: Twick 1H **131**
TW14: Felt 6J **111**
Gladstone Ct. NW6 . . . . .7A **64**
(off Fairfax Rd.)
SW1 . . . . .4D **18**
(off Regency St.)
Gladstone Ct. Bus. Cen. SW8 . . . . . .1F **119**
(off Pagden St.)
Gladstone Gdns. TW3: Houn 1G **113**
Gladstone Ho. CR4: Mitc 2D **154**
E14 . . . . .6C **86**
(off E. India Dock Rd.)
Gladstone M. N22 . . . . .2A **48**
NW6 . . . . .7H **63**
(off Cavendish Rd.)
SE20 . . . . .7J **139**
Gladstone Pde. NW2 . . . . .2E **62**
Gladstone Pk. Gdns. NW2 . . . . .4D **62**
Gladstone Pl. E3 . . . . .2B **86**
EN5: Barn 4A **20**
KT8: E Mos 5J **149**
Gladstone Rd. BR6: Farnb 5G **173**
CR0: C'don 7D **156**
IG9: Buck H 1F **37**
KT1: King T 3G **151**
KT6: Surb 2D **162**
SW19 . . . . .7J **135**
UB2: S'hall 2C **94**
W4 . . . . .3K **97**
Gladstone St. SE1 . . . . .3B **102**
Gladstone Ter. SE27 . . . . .5C **138**
(off Bentons La.)
SW8 . . . . .1F **119**
Gladstone Way HA3: W'stone 3J **41**
Gladwell Rd. BR1: Brom 6J **141**
N8 . . . . .6K **47**
Gladwin Ho. NW1 . . . . .1B **6**
(off Werrington St.)
Gladwyn Rd. SW15 . . . . .3F **117**
Gladys Dimson Ho. E7 . . . . .5H **69**
Gladys Rd. NW6 . . . . .7J **63**

Glaisher St. SE8 . . . 6C 104
Glamis Ct. W3 . . . 2H 97
Glamis Cres. UB3: Harl . . . 3E 92
Glamis Pl. E1 . . . 7J 85
Glamis Rd. E1 . . . 7J 85
Glamis Way UB5: N'olt . . . 6G 59
Glamorgan Cl. CR4: Mitc . . . 3J 155
Glamorgan Cl. W7 . . . 5K 77
(off Copley Cl.)
Glamorgan Rd. KT1: Hamp W . . . 7C 132
Glandford Way RM6: Chad H . . . 5B 54
Glanfield Rd. BR3: Beck . . . 4B 158
Glanleam Rd. HA7: Stan . . . 4J 27
Glanville M. HA7: Stan . . . 5F 27
Glanville Rd. BR2: Brom . . . 3K 159
  SW2 . . . 5J 119
Glasbrook Av. TW2: Whitt . . . 1D 130
Glasbrook Rd. SE9 . . . 7B 124
Glaserton Rd. N16 . . . 7E 48
Glasford St. SW17 . . . 6D 136
Glaslyn Ct. HA2: Harr . . . 2H 59
(off Roxeth Hill)
Glaslryn Ho. HA2: Harr . . . 2H 59
(off Roxeth Hill)
Glasgow Ho. W9 . . . 2K 81
(off Maida Vale)
Glasgow Rd. E13 . . . 2K 87
  N18 . . . 5C 34
Glasgow Ter. SW1 . . . 6A 18 (5G 101)
Glasier Ct. E15 . . . 7G 69
Glaskin M. E9 . . . 6A 68
Glass Building, The NW1 . . . 1F 83
(off Jamestown Rd.)
Glasse Cl. W13 . . . 7A 78
Glass Foundry Yd. E13 . . . 5K 87
(off Denmark St.)
Glasshill St. SE1 . . . 6B 14 (2B 102)
Glass Ho. WC2 . . . 1E 12
(off Shaftesbury Av.)
Glass House, The SE1 . . . 7G 15
(off Royal Oak Yd.)
Glasshouse Cl. UB8: Hil . . . 5D 74
Glasshouse Flds. E1 . . . 7K 85
(not continuous)
Glasshouse St. W1 . . . 3B 12 (7G 83)
Glasshouse Wlk. SE11 . . . 5F 19 (5J 101)
Glasshouse Yd. EC1 . . . 4C 8 (4C 84)
Glasslyn Rd. N8 . . . 5H 47
Glassmill La. BR2: Brom . . . 2H 159
Glass Mill Leisure Cen. . . . 3E 122
Glass St. E2 . . . 4H 85
Glassworks Studios E2 . . . 1H 9
(off Basing Pl.)
Glass Yd. SE18 . . . 3E 106
Glastonbury Av. IG8: Wfd G . . . 7G 37
Glastonbury Ct. SE14 . . . 7J 103
(off Farrow La.)
  W13 . . . 1A 96
(off Talbot Rd.)
Glastonbury Ho. SE12 . . . 5H 123
(off Wantage Rd.)
  SW1 . . . 5J 17
(part of Abbots Mnr.)
Glastonbury Pl. E1 . . . 6J 85
Glastonbury Rd. N9 . . . 1B 34
  SM4: Mord . . . 7J 153
Glastonbury St. NW6 . . . 5H 63
Glaston Ct. W5 . . . 1D 96
(off Grange Rd.)
Glaucus St. E3 . . . 5D 86
Glazbury Rd. W14 . . . 4G 99
Glazebrook Cl. SE21 . . . 2D 138
Glazebrook Rd. TW11: Tedd . . . 7K 131
Glebe, The BR7: Chst . . . 1G 161
  KT4: Wor Pk . . . 1B 164
  SE3 . . . 3G 123
  SW16 . . . 4H 137
  UB7: W Dray . . . 4B 92
Glebe Av. CR4: Mitc . . . 2C 154
  EN2: Enf . . . 3G 23
  HA3: Kenton . . . 4E 42

Glebe Av. HA4: Ruis . . . 6K 57
  IG8: Wfd G . . . 6D 36
  UB10: Ick . . . 3E 56
Glebe Cl. UB10: Ick . . . 4E 56
  W4 . . . 5A 98
Glebe Cotts. TW13: Hanw . . . 3E 130
(off Twickenham Rd.)
Glebe Ct. CR4: Mitc . . . 3D 154
  E3 . . . 3D 86
(off Rainhill Way)
  HA7: Stan . . . 5H 27
  N13 . . . 3F 33
  SE3 . . . 3G 123
  W5 . . . 1D 96
  W7 . . . 7H 77
Glebe Cres. HA3: Kenton . . . 3E 42
  NW4 . . . 4E 44
Glebe Farm Pas. Pk. BR2: Kes . . . 7B 172
Glebe Gdns. KT3: N Mald . . . 7A 152
Glebe Ho. SE16 . . . 3H 103
(off Slippers Pl.)
Glebe Ho. Dr. BR2: Hayes . . . 1K 171
Glebe Hyrst SE19 . . . 4E 138
Glebe Knoll BR2: Brom . . . 2H 159
Glebeland Gdns. TW17: Shep . . . 6E 146
Glebelands E10 . . . 2D 68
  KT8: W Mole . . . 5F 149
Glebelands Av. E18 . . . 2J 51
  IG2: Ilf . . . 7H 53
Glebelands Cl. N12 . . . 1B 46
  SE5 . . . 3E 120
Glebelands Rd. TW14: Felt . . . 1J 129
Glebe La. HA3: Kenton . . . 4E 42
Glebe M. DA15: Sidc . . . 6K 125
Glebe Path CR4: Mitc . . . 3D 154
Glebe Pl. SW3 . . . 7C 16 (6C 100)
Glebe Rd. BR1: Brom . . . 1J 159
  E8 . . . 7F 67
  HA7: Stan . . . 5H 27
  N3 . . . 1J 45
  N8 . . . 4K 47
  NW10 . . . 6C 62
  RM10: Dag . . . 6H 73
  SM2: Cheam . . . 7G 165
  SM5: Cars . . . 6D 166
  SW13 . . . 2C 116
  UB3: Hayes . . . 1H 93
Glebe Side TW1: Twick . . . 6K 113
Glebe Sq. CR4: Mitc . . . 3D 154
Glebe St. W4 . . . 5A 98
Glebe Ter. W4 . . . 5A 98
Glebe Way BR4: W W'ck . . . 2E 170
  IG8: Wfd G . . . 5F 37
  TW13: Hanw . . . 3E 130
Gledhow Gdns. SW5 . . . 4A 100
Gledstanes Rd. W14 . . . 5G 99
Gledwood Av. UB4: Hayes . . . 5H 75
Gledwood Ct. UB4: Hayes . . . 5H 75
Gledwood Cres. UB4: Hayes . . . 5H 75
Gledwood Dr. UB4: Hayes . . . 5H 75
Gledwood Gdns. UB4: Hayes . . . 5H 75
Gleed Av. WD23: B Hea . . . 2C 26
Gleeson Dr. BR6: Chels . . . 5K 173
Glegg Pl. SW15 . . . 4F 117
Glen, The BR2: Brom . . . 2G 159
  BR6: Farnb . . . 3D 172
  CR0: C'don . . . 3K 169
  EN2: Enf . . . 4G 23
  HA5: Eastc . . . 5K 39
  HA5: Pinn . . . 7C 40
  HA9: Wemb . . . 4E 60
  UB2: S'hall . . . 5D 94
Glenaffric Av. E14 . . . 4E 104
Glen Albyn Rd. SW19 . . . 2F 135
Glenallan Ho. W14 . . . 4H 99
(off North End Cres.)
Glenalla Rd. HA4: Ruis . . . 7H 39
Glenalmond Ho. TW15: Ashf . . . 3A 128
Glenalmond Rd. HA3: Kenton . . . 4E 42
Glenalvon Way SE18 . . . 4C 106
Glena M. SM1: Sutt . . . 4A 166

Glenarm Rd. E5 . . . 4J 67
Glen Av. TW15: Ashf . . . 4C 128
Glenavon Cl. KT10: Clay . . . 6A 162
Glenavon Ct. KT4: Wor Pk . . . 2D 164
Glenavon Lodge BR3: Beck . . . 7C 140
Glenavon Rd. E15 . . . 7G 69
Glenbarr Cl. SE9 . . . 3F 125
Glenbow Rd. BR1: Brom . . . 6G 141
Glenbrook Nth. EN2: Enf . . . 4E 22
Glenbrook Rd. NW6 . . . 5J 63
Glenbrook Sth. EN2: Enf . . . 4E 22
Glenbuck Ct. KT6: Surb . . . 6E 150
Glenbuck Rd. KT6: Surb . . . 6D 150
Glenburnie Rd. SW17 . . . 3D 136
Glencairn Dr. W5 . . . 4C 78
Glencairne Cl. E16 . . . 5B 88
Glencairn Rd. SW16 . . . 1J 155
Glencar Ct. SE19 . . . 6B 138
Glen Cl. TW17: Shep . . . 4C 146
Glencoe Av. IG2: Ilf . . . 7H 53
Glencoe Dr. RM10: Dag . . . 4G 73
Glencoe Mans. SW9 . . . 7A 102
(off Mowll St.)
Glencoe Rd. UB4: Yead . . . 5B 76
Glen Ct. BR1: Brom . . . 7H 141
(off Bromley Av.)
  DA15: Sidc . . . 4A 144
Glen Cres. IG8: Wfd G . . . 6E 36
Glendale Av. HA8: Edg . . . 4A 28
  N22 . . . 7F 33
  RM6: Chad H . . . 7C 54
Glendale Cl. SE9 . . . 3E 124
Glendale Dr. SW19 . . . 5H 135
Glendale Gdns. HA9: Wemb . . . 1D 60
Glendale M. BR3: Beck . . . 1D 158
Glendale Rd. DA8: Erith . . . 4J 109
Glendale Way SE28 . . . 7C 90
Glendall St. SW9 . . . 4K 119
Glendarvon St. SW15 . . . 3F 117
Glendevon Cl. HA8: Edg . . . 3C 28
Glendish Rd. N17 . . . 1H 49
Glendor Gdns. NW7 . . . 4E 28
Glendower Gdns. SW14 . . . 3K 115
Glendower Pl. SW7 . . . 3A 16 (4B 100)
Glendower Rd. E4 . . . 1A 36
  SW14 . . . 3K 115
Glendown Ho. E8 . . . 5G 67
Glendown Rd. SE2 . . . 5A 108
Glendun Ct. W3 . . . 7A 80
Glendun Rd. W3 . . . 7A 80
Gleneagle M. SW16 . . . 5H 137
Gleneagle Rd. SW16 . . . 5H 137
Gleneagles HA7: Stan . . . 7G 27
  W13 . . . 5B 78
(off Malvern Way)
Gleneagles Cl. BR6: Orp . . . 1H 173
  SE16 . . . 5H 103
Gleneagles Grn. BR6: Orp . . . 1H 173
Gleneagles Twr. UB1: S'hall . . . 6D 76
(off Fleming Rd.)
Gleneldon M. SW16 . . . 4J 137
Gleneldon Rd. SW16 . . . 4J 137
Glenelg Rd. SW2 . . . 5J 119
Glenesk Rd. SE9 . . . 3E 124
Glenfarg Rd. SE6 . . . 1E 140
Glenfield Cres. HA4: Ruis . . . 7F 39
Glenfield Rd. SW12 . . . 1G 137
  TW15: Ashf . . . 6D 128
  W13 . . . 2B 96
Glenfield Ter. W13 . . . 2B 96
Glenfinlas Way SE5 . . . 7B 102
Glenforth St. SE10 . . . 5H 105
Glengall Bus. Cen. SE15 . . . 6F 103
Glengall Gro. E14 . . . 3D 104
Glengall Pas. NW6 . . . 1J 81
(off Priory Pk. Rd.)
Glengall Rd. DA7: Bex . . . 3E 126
  HA8: Edg . . . 3B 28
  IG8: Wfd G . . . 6D 36
  NW6 . . . 1H 81
  SE15 . . . 5F 103

Glengall Ter. SE15 . . . 6F 103
Glen Gdns. CR0: Wadd . . . 3A 168
Glengarnock Av. E14 . . . 4E 104
Glengarry Rd. SE22 . . . 5E 120
Glenham Dr. IG2: Ilf . . . 5F 53
Glenhead Cl. SE9 . . . 3F 125
Glenhill Cl. N3 . . . 2J 45
Glen Ho. E16 . . . 1E 106
(off Storey St.)
Glenhouse Rd. SE9 . . . 5E 124
Glenhurst BR3: Beck . . . 1E 158
Glenhurst Av. DA5: Bexl . . . 1F 145
  HA4: Ruis . . . 7E 38
  NW5 . . . 4E 64
Glenhurst Ct. SE19 . . . 5F 139
Glenhurst Ri. SE19 . . . 7C 138
Glenhurst Rd. N12 . . . 5G 31
  TW8: Bford . . . 6C 96
Glenilla Rd. NW3 . . . 6C 64
Glenister Gdns. UB3: Hayes . . . 2K 93
Glenister Ho. UB3: Hayes . . . 1K 93
(off Avondale Dr.)
Glenister Pk. Rd. SW16 . . . 7H 137
Glenister Rd. SE10 . . . 5H 105
Glenister St. E16 . . . 1E 106
Glenkerry Ho. E14 . . . 6E 86
(off Burcham St.)
Glenlea Rd. SE9 . . . 5D 124
Glenloch Rd. EN3: Enf H . . . 2D 24
  NW3 . . . 6C 64
Glenluce Rd. SE3 . . . 6J 105
Glenlyon Rd. SE9 . . . 5E 124
Glenmead IG9: Buck H . . . 1F 37
Glenmere Av. NW7 . . . 7H 29
Glenmere Row SE12 . . . 6J 123
Glenmill TW12: Hamp . . . 5D 130
Glenmore Lawns W13 . . . 6A 78
Glenmore Lodge BR3: Beck . . . 1D 158
Glenmore Pde. HA0: Wemb . . . 1E 78
Glenmore Rd. DA16: Well . . . 7K 107
  NW3 . . . 6C 64
Glenmore Way IG11: Bark . . . 2A 90
Glenmount Path SE18 . . . 5G 107
Glennie Ct. SE22 . . . 1G 139
Glennie Ho. SE10 . . . 1E 122
(off Blackheath Hill)
Glennie Rd. SE27 . . . 3A 138
Glenny Rd. IG11: Bark . . . 6G 71
Glenorchy Cl. UB4: Yead . . . 5C 76
Glenpark Ct. W13 . . . 7A 78
Glenparke Rd. E7 . . . 6K 69
Glenridding NW1 . . . 1B 6
(off Ampthill Est.)
Glen Ri. IG8: Wfd G . . . 6E 36
Glen Rd. E13 . . . 4A 88
  E17 . . . 5B 50
  KT9: Chess . . . 4F 163
Glen Rd. End SM6: Wall . . . 7F 167
Glenrosa St. SW6 . . . 2A 118
Glenrose Ct. DA14: Sidc . . . 5B 144
  SE1 . . . 7G 15
(off Long La.)
Glenroy St. W12 . . . 6E 80
Glensdale Rd. SE4 . . . 3B 122
Glenshaw Mans. SW9 . . . 7A 102
(off Brixton Rd.)
Glenshiel Rd. SE9 . . . 5E 124
Glentanner Way SW17 . . . 3B 136
Glen Ter. E14 . . . 2E 104
(off Manchester Rd.)
Glentham Gdns. SW13 . . . 6D 98
Glentham Rd. SW13 . . . 6C 98
Glenthorne Av. CR0: C'don . . . 1H 169
Glenthorne Cl. SM3: Sutt . . . 1J 165
  UB10: Hil . . . 3C 74
Glenthorne Gdns. IG6: Ilf . . . 3E 52
  SM3: Sutt . . . 1J 165
Glenthorne M. W6 . . . 4D 98

Glenthorne Rd. E17 ....5A 50
  KT1: King T 4F 151
  N11 ....5J 31
  W6 ....4D 98
Glenthorpe Av. SW15 ....4C 116
Glenthorpe Gdns. HA7: Stan 3E 26
Glenthorpe Rd. SM4: Mord 5F 153
Glenton M. SE15 ....2J 121
Glenton Rd. SE13 ....4G 123
Glentrammon Av. BR6: Chels 6K 173
Glentrammon Cl. BR6: Chels 5K 173
Glentrammon Gdns. BR6: Chels 6K 173
Glentrammon Rd. BR6: Chels 6K 173
Glentworth St. NW1 ....4F 5 (4D 82)
Glenure Rd. SE9 ....5E 124
Glenvern Ct. TW7: Isle 2A 114
  (off White Lodge Cl.)
Glenview SE2 ....6D 108
Glenview Rd. BR1: Brom 2B 160
Glenville Av. EN2: Enf 1H 23
Glenville Gro. SE8 ....7B 104
Glenville M. SW18 ....7K 117
Glenville Rd. KT2: King T 1G 151
Glen Wlk. TW7: Isle 5H 113
  (not continuous)
Glenwood Av. NW9 ....1A 62
Glenwood Cl. HA1: Harr 5K 41
Glenwood Ct. DA14: Sidc 4A 144
  E18 ....3J 51
Glenwood Gdns. IG2: Ilf 5E 52
Glenwood Gro. NW9 ....1J 61
Glenwood Rd. KT17: Ewe 6C 164
  N15 ....5B 48
  NW7 ....3F 29
  SE6 ....1B 140
  TW3: Houn 3H 113
Glenwood Way CRO: C'don 6K 157
Glenworth Av. E14 ....4F 105
Gliddon Dr. E5 ....4H 67
Gliddon Rd. W14 ....4G 99
Glimpsing Grn. DA18: Erith 3E 108
Glisson Rd. UB10: Hil 2C 74
Globe App. E3 ....2E 86
Globe Pond Rd. SE16 ....1A 104
Globe Rd. E1 ....3J 85
  E2 ....3J 85
  E15 ....5H 69
  IG8: Wfd G 6F 37
Globe Rope Wlk. E14 ....4D 104
  (off E. Ferry Rd.)
Globe St. SE1 ....7E 14 (3D 102)
Globe Ter. E2 ....3J 85
GLOBE TOWN 3K 85
Globe Town Mkt. E2 ....3K 85
Globe Vw. EC4 ....2C 14
  (off High Timber St.)
Globe Wharf SE16 ....7K 85
Globe Yd. W1 ....1J 11
Glossop Rd. CR2: Sande 7D 168
Gloster Ridley Ct. E14 ....6B 86
  (off St Anne's Row)
Gloster Rd. KT3: N Mald 4A 152
Gloucester W14 ....4H 99
  (off Kensington Village)
Gloucester Arc. SW7 ....4A 100
Gloucester Av. DA15: Sidc 2J 143
  DA16: Well 4K 125
  NW1 ....7E 64
Gloucester Cir. SE10 ....7E 104
Gloucester Cl. KT7: T Ditt 1A 162
  NW10 ....7K 61
Gloucester Ct. CR4: Mitc 5J 155
  EC3 ....3H 15 (7E 84)
  HA1: Harr 3J 41
  NW11 ....7H 45
  (off Golders Grn. Rd.)
  SE1 ....5F 103
  (off Rolls Rd., Rolls Rd.)
  SE1 ....7D 14
  (off Swan St., Swan St.)

Gloucester Ct. SE22 ....1G 139
  TW9: Kew 7G 97
  W7 ....5K 77
  (off Copley Cl.)
Gloucester Cres. NW1 ....1F 83
  TW18: Staines 6A 128
Gloucester Dr. N4 ....2B 66
  NW11 ....4J 45
Gloucester Gdns. EN4: Cockf 4K 21
  IG1: Ilf 7C 52
  NW11 ....7H 45
  SM1: Sutt 2K 165
  W2 ....6A 82
Gloucester Ga. NW1 ....2F 83
  (not continuous)
Gloucester Ga. Bri. NW1 ....1F 83
  (off Gloucester Gate)
Gloucester Ga. M. NW1 ....2F 83
Gloucester Gro. HA8: Edg 1K 43
Gloucester Ho. E16 ....1J 105
  (off Gatcombe Rd.)
  NW6 ....2J 81
  (off Cambridge Rd.)
  SW9 ....7A 102
  TW10: Rich 5G 115
Gloucester M. E10 ....7C 50
  W2 ....1A 10 (6A 82)
Gloucester M. W. W2 ....6A 82
Gloucester Pde. DA15: Sidc 5A 126
  UB3: Harl 3E 92
Gloucester Pk. Apartments SW7 ....4A 100
  (off Ashburn Pl.)
Gloucester Pl. NW1 ....4E 4 (4D 82)
  W1 ....4E 4 (4D 82)
Gloucester Pl. M. W1 ....6F 5 (5D 82)
Gloucester Rd. CRO: C'don 1D 168
  DA17: Belv 5F 109
  E10 ....7C 50
  E11 ....5K 51
  E12 ....3D 70
  E17 ....2K 49
  EN2: Enf 1H 23
  EN5: New Bar 5E 20
  HA1: Harr 5F 41
  KT1: King T 2G 151
  N17 ....2D 48
  N18 ....5A 34
  SW7 ....4A 16 (3A 100)
  TW2: Twick 1G 131
  TW4: Houn 4C 112
  TW9: Kew 7G 97
  TW11: Tedd 5J 131
  TW12: Hamp 7F 131
  TW13: Felt 1A 130
  W3 ....2J 97
  W5 ....2C 96
Gloucester Sq. E2 ....1G 85
  W2 ....1B 10 (6B 82)
  (not continuous)
Gloucester St. SW1 ....6A 18 (5G 101)
Gloucester Ter. N14 ....1C 32
  (off Crown La.)
  W2 ....1A 10 (6A 82)
Gloucester Wlk. W8 ....2J 99
Gloucester Way EC1 ....2K 7 (3A 84)
Glover Cl. SE2 ....4C 108
Glover Dr. N18 ....6D 34
Glover Ho. NW6 ....7A 64
  (off Harben Rd.)
  SE15 ....4H 121
Glover Rd. HA5: Pinn 6B 40
Glovers Gro. HA4: Ruis 7D 38
Gloxinia Wlk. TW12: Hamp 6E 130
Glycena Rd. SW11 ....3D 118
Glyn Av. EN4: E Barn 4G 21
Glyn Cl. SE25 ....2E 156
Glyn Ct. HA7: Stan 6G 27
  SW16 ....3A 138
Glyndale Grange SM2: Sutt 6K 165
Glyndebourne Ct. UB5: N'olt 3A 76
  (off Canberra Dr.)

Glyndebourne Pk. BR6: Farnb 2F 173
Glynde M. SW3 ....2D 16
Glynde Reach WC1 ....2F 7
Glynde Rd. DA7: Bex 3D 126
Glynde St. SE4 ....6B 122
Glyndon Rd. SE18 ....4G 107
  (not continuous)
Glyn Dr. DA14: Sidc 4B 144
Glynfield Rd. NW10 ....7A 62
Glyn Mans. W14 ....4G 99
  (off Hammersmith Rd.)
Glynne Rd. N22 ....2A 48
Glyn Rd. E5 ....3K 67
  EN3: Pond E 4D 24
  KT4: Wor Pk 2F 165
Glyn St. SE11 ....6G 19 (5K 101)
Glynswood Pl. HA6: Nwood 1D 38
Glynwood Ct. SE23 ....2J 139
Goals Soccer Cen.
  Bexleyheath 3F 127
  Chingford 6H 35
  Dagenham 1D 90
  Eltham 6A 124
  Gillette Corner 6K 95
  Hayes 1A 94
  Heathrow 4E 92
  Ruislip 5B 58
  Sutton 3F 165
  Tolworth 2J 163
  Wimbledon 3C 152
Go Ape
  Trent Park 3K 21
Goater's All. SW6 ....7G 99
  (off Dawes Rd.)
Goat Ho. Bri. SE25 ....3G 157
Goat La. EN1: Enf 1A 24
Goat Rd. CR4: Cars, Mitc 7D 154
Goat Wharf TW8: Bford 6E 96
Gobions Av. RM5: Col R 1K 55
Godalming Av. SM6: Wall 5J 167
Godalming Rd. E14 ....5D 86
Godbold Rd. E15 ....4G 87
Goddard Cl. TW17: Shep 3B 146
Goddard Ct. HA3: Kenton 2A 42
Goddard Ho. SE11 ....4B 102
  (off George Mathers Rd.)
Goddard Pl. N19 ....3G 65
Goddard Rd. BR3: Beck 4K 157
Goddards Way IG1: Ilf 1H 71
Goddarts Ho. E17 ....3C 50
Goddington La. BR6: Chels 3K 173
Godfree Ct. SE1 ....6E 14
  (off Long La.)
Godfrey Av. TW2: Whitt 7H 113
  UB5: N'olt 1C 76
Godfrey Hill SE18 ....4C 106
Godfrey Ho. EC1 ....2E 8
Godfrey Pl. E2 ....2J 9
  (off Austin St.)
Godfrey Rd. SE18 ....4D 106
Godfrey St. E15 ....2G 86
  SW3 ....5D 16 (5C 100)
Godfrey Way TW4: Houn 7C 112
Goding St. SE11 ....5F 19 (5J 101)
Godley Cl. SE14 ....1J 121
Godley Rd. SW18 ....1B 136
Godliman St. EC4 ....1B 14 (6B 84)
Godman Rd. SE15 ....2H 121
Godolphin Cl. N13 ....6G 33
Godolphin Ho. NW3 ....7C 64
  (off Fellows Rd.)
Godolphin Pl. W3 ....7K 79
Godolphin Rd. W12 ....1D 98
  (not continuous)
Godric Cres. CRO: New Ad 7F 171
Godson Rd. CRO: Wadd 3A 168
Godson St. N1 ....2A 84
Godson Yd. NW6 ....3J 81
  (off Kilburn Pk. Rd.)
Godstone Ho. SE1 ....7F 15
  (off Pardoner St.)

Godstone Rd. SM1: Sutt 4A 166
  TW1: Twick 6B 114
Godstone Rd. SE2 ....2B 108
Godwin Cl. E4 ....1K 25
  KT19: Ewe 6J 163
  N1 ....2C 84
Godwin Ct. NW1 ....2G 83
  (off Chalton St.)
Godwin Ho. E2 ....2F 85
  (off Thurtle Rd.)
  NW6 ....2K 81
  (off Tollgate Gdns., not continuous)
Godwin Rd. BR2: Brom 3A 160
  E7 ....4K 69
Goffers Rd. SE3 ....1G 123
Goffs Rd. TW15: Ashf 6F 129
Goidel Cl. SM6: Bedd 4H 167
Golborne Gdns. W10 ....4G 81
  (not continuous)
Golborne M. W10 ....5G 81
Golborne Rd. W10 ....5G 81
Golda Cl. EN5: Barn 6A 20
Golda Ct. N3 ....2H 45
Goldbeaters Gro. HA8: Edg 6F 29
Goldbeaters Ho. W1 ....1D 12
  (off Manette St.)
Goldcliff Cl. SM4: Mord 7J 153
Goldcrest Cl. E16 ....5B 88
  SE28 ....7C 90
Goldcrest M. W5 ....5D 78
Goldcrest Way CRO: New Ad 7F 171
  WD23: Bush 1B 26
Golden Bus. Pk. E10 ....1A 68
Golden Cl. EN4: E Barn 4H 21
  TW1: Isle 2H 113
  TW9: Rich 5D 114
Golden Cres. UB3: Hayes 1H 93
Golden Cross M. W11 ....6H 81
  (off Portobello Rd.)
Golden Hinde 4E 14 (1D 102)
Golden Hind Pl. SE8 ....4B 104
  (off Grove St.)
Golden Jubilee Bridges 5G 13
Golden La. BR4: W W'ck 3E 170
  EC1 ....3C 8 (4C 84)
Golden La. Campus EC1 ....4D 8
Golden La. Est. EC1 ....4C 8 (4C 84)
Golden Lane Leisure Cen. 4C 8
Golden Mnr. W7 ....7J 77
Golden M. SE20 ....1J 157
Golden Mile Ho. TW8: Bford 5E 96
  (off Clayponds La.)
Golden Pde. E17 ....3E 50
  (off Wood St.)
Golden Plover Cl. E16 ....6J 87
Golden Sq. W1 ....2B 12 (7G 83)
Golden Yd. NW3 ....4A 64
  (off Holly Mt.)
Golders Cl. HA8: Edg 5C 28
Golders Ct. NW11 ....7H 45
Golders Gdns. NW11 ....7G 45
GOLDERS GREEN 6G 45
Golders Grn. Crematorium NW11 ....7J 45
Golders Grn. Cres. NW11 ....7H 45
Golders Grn. Rd. NW11 ....6G 45
Golderslea NW11 ....1J 63
Golders Mnr. Dr. NW11 ....6F 45
Golders Pk. Cl. NW11 ....1J 63
Golders Ri. NW4 ....5F 45
Golders Way NW11 ....7H 45
Golderton NW4 ....4D 44
  (off Prince of Wales Cl.)
Goldfinch Cl. E3 ....2C 86
  (off Four Seasons Cl.)
Goldfinch Rd. SE28 ....3H 107
Goldhawk Ind. Est. W6 ....3D 98
Goldhawk M. W12 ....2D 98
Goldhawk Rd. W6 ....4B 98
  W12 ....3C 98
Goldhaze Cl. IG8: Wfd G 7F 37
Gold Hill HA8: Edg 6E 28

Goldhurst Ho. W6 . . . . .6E **98**
Goldhurst Mans. NW6 . . . . .6A **64**
   (off Goldhurst Ter.)
Goldhurst Ter. NW6 . . . . .7K **63**
Goldie Ho. N19 . . . . .7H **47**
Goldie Leigh Hospital SE2 . . . . .7B **108**
Golding Cl. KT9: Chess 6C **162**
  N18 . . . . .6J **33**
Golding Ct. IG1: Ilf 3E **70**
Golding St. E1 . . . . .6G **85**
   (not continuous)
Golding Ter. E1 . . . . .6G **85**
   (off Rope Wlk. Gdns.)
  SW11 .2E **118**
Goldington Bldgs. NW1 . . . . .1H **83**
   (off Royal College St.)
Goldington Cres. NW1 . . . . .2H **83**
Goldington St. NW1 . . . . .2H **83**
Gold La. HA8: Edg 6E **28**
Goldman Cl. E2 . . . . .3K **9** (4G **85**)
Goldney Rd. W9 . . . . .4J **81**
Goldrill Dr. N11 . . . . .2K **31**
Goldsboro' Rd. SW8 . . . . .1H **119**
Goldsborough Cres. E4 . . . . .2J **35**
Goldsborough Ho. E14 . . . . .5D **104**
   (off St Davids Sq.)
Goldsdown Cl. EN3: Enf H 2F **25**
Goldsdown Rd. EN3: Enf H 2E **24**
Goldsmid St. SE18 . . . . .5J **107**
Goldsmith Av. E12 . . . . .6C **70**
  NW9 . . . . .5A **44**
  RM7: Rush G 7G **55**
  W3 . . . . .7K **79**
Goldsmith Cl. HA2: Harr 1E **58**
Goldsmith Ct. WC2 . . . . .7F **7**
   (off Stukeley St.)
Goldsmith Est. SE15 . . . . .1G **121**
Goldsmith La. NW9 . . . . .4H **43**
Goldsmith Rd. E10 . . . . .1C **68**
  E17 . . . . .2K **49**
  N11 . . . . .5J **31**
  SE15 . . . . .1G **121**
  W3 . . . . .1K **97**
Goldsmith's Bldgs. W3 . . . . .1K **97**
Goldsmiths Cl. W3 . . . . .1K **97**
Goldsmiths College 1A **122**
Goldsmith's Pl. NW6 . . . . .1K **81**
   (off Springfield La.)
Goldsmith's Row E2 . . . . .2G **85**
Goldsmith's Sq. E2 . . . . .2G **85**
Goldsmith St. EC2 . . . . .7D **8** (6C **84**)
Goldsworthy Gdns. SE16 . . . . .5J **103**
Goldthorpe NW1 . . . . .1G **83**
   (off Camden St.)
Goldwell Ho. SE22 . . . . .3E **120**
   (off Quorn Rd.)
Goldwell Rd. CR7: Thor H 4K **155**
Goldwin Cl. SE14 . . . . .1J **121**
Goldwing Cl. E16 . . . . .6J **87**
Golf Cl. CR7: Thor H 1A **156**
  HA7: Stan 7H **27**
Golf Club Dr. KT2: King T 7K **133**
Golfe Rd. IG1: Ilf 3H **71**
Golf Kingdom
  Barking .5F **55**
Golf Rd. BR1: Brom 3E **160**
  W5 . . . . .6F **79**
Golf Side Tw2: Twick 3H **131**
Golfside Cl. KT3: N Mald 2A **152**
  N20 . . . . .3H **31**
Gollogly Ter. SE7 . . . . .5A **106**
Gomer Gdns. TW11: Tedd 6A **132**
Gomer Pl. TW11: Tedd 6A **132**
Gomm Rd. SE16 . . . . .3J **103**
Gomshall Av. SM6: Wall 5J **167**
Gondar Gdns. NW6 . . . . .5H **63**
Gonson St. SE8 . . . . .6D **104**
Gonston Cl. SW19 . . . . .2G **135**
Gonville Cres. UB5: N'olt 6F **59**
Gonville Rd. CR7: Thor H 5K **155**
Gonville St. SW6 . . . . .3G **117**

Gooch Ho. E5 . . . . .3H **67**
  EC1 . . . . .5J **7**
   (off Portpool La.)
Goodall Ho. SE4 . . . . .4K **121**
Goodall Rd. E11 . . . . .3G **69**
Goodchild Rd. N4 . . . . .1C **66**
Gooden Ct. HA1: Harr 3J **59**
Goodenough Rd. SW19 . . . . .7H **135**
Goodey Rd. IG11: Bark 7K **71**
Goodfaith Ho. E14 . . . . .7D **86**
   (off Simpson's Rd.)
Goodge Pl. W1 . . . . .6B **6** (5G **83**)
Goodge St. W1 . . . . .6B **6** (5G **83**)
Goodhall Cl. HA7: Stan 6F **27**
Goodhall St. NW10 . . . . .3B **80**
   (not continuous)
Goodhart Pl. E14 . . . . .7A **86**
Goodhart Way BR4: W W'ck 7G **159**
Goodhew Rd. CR0: C'don 6G **157**
Goodhope Ho. E14 . . . . .7D **86**
   (off Poplar High St.)
Gooding Cl. KT3: N Mald 4J **151**
Gooding Cl. N7 . . . . .6J **65**
Gooding Ho. SE7 . . . . .5A **106**
Goodman Cres. CR0: C'don 6B **156**
  SW2 . . . . .2J **137**
Goodman Rd. E10 . . . . .7E **50**
Goodmans Ct. E1 . . . . .2J **15** (7F **85**)
  HA0: Wemb 4D **60**
Goodman's Stile E1 . . . . .6G **85**
Goodmans Yd. E1 . . . . .2J **15** (7F **85**)
GOODMAYES 2A **72**
Goodmayes Av. IG3: Ilf 1A **72**
Goodmayes La. IG3: Ilf 4A **72**
Goodmayes Lodge RM8: Dag 4A **72**
Goodmayes Retail Pk. RM6: Chad H . .1B **72**
Goodmayes Rd. IG3: Ilf 1A **72**
Goodrich Cl. W10 . . . . .6F **81**
Goodrich Ho. E2 . . . . .2J **85**
   (off Sewardstone Rd.)
Goodrich Rd. SE22 . . . . .6F **121**
Goodridge Ho. E4 . . . . .7K **35**
Goodson Ho. SM4: Mord 7A **154**
   (off Green La.)
Goodson Rd. NW10 . . . . .7A **62**
Goodspeed Ho. E14 . . . . .7D **86**
   (off Simpson's Rd.)
Goods Way N1 . . . . .2J **83**
Goodward Sq. E1 . . . . .4K **85**
Goodway Gdns. E14 . . . . .6F **87**
Goodwill Dr. HA2: Harr 1E **58**
Goodwill Ho. E14 . . . . .7D **86**
   (off Simpson's Rd.)
Goodwin Cl. CR4: Mitc 3B **154**
  SE16 . . . . .3F **103**
Goodwin Ct. EN4: E Barn 6H **21**
  N8 . . . . .3J **47**
   (off Campsbourne Rd.)
  SW19 .7C **136**
Goodwin Dr. DA14: Sidc 3D **144**
Goodwin Gdns. CR0: Wadd 6B **168**
Goodwin Ho. N9 . . . . .1D **34**
Goodwin Rd. CR0: Wadd 5B **168**
  N9 . . . . .1E **34**
  W12 . . . . .2C **98**
Goodwins Ct. WC2 . . . . . . .2E **12** (7J **83**)
Goodwin St. N4 . . . . .2A **66**
Goodwood Apartments E4 . . . . .7J **35**
Goodwood Cl. HA7: Stan 5H **27**
  SM4: Mord 4J **153**
Goodwood Ct. W1 . . . . .5K **5**
   (off Devonshire St.)
Goodwood Dr. UB5: N'olt 6E **58**
Goodwood Ho. SE14 . . . . .7A **104**
   (off Goodwood Rd.)
Goodwood Pde. BR3: Beck 4A **158**
Goodwood Rd. SE14 . . . . .7A **104**
Goodwyn Av. NW7 . . . . .5F **29**
Goodwyns Va. N10 . . . . .1E **46**
Goodyear Ho. N2 . . . . .2B **46**
   (off The Grange)

Goodyear Pl. SE5 . . . . .6C **102**
Goodyer Ho. SW1 . . . . .5C **18**
   (off Tachbrook St.)
Goodyers Gdns. NW4 . . . . .5F **45**
Goosander Way SE28 . . . . .3H **107**
Gooseacre La. HA3: Kenton 5D **42**
Goose Grn. Trad. Est. SE22 . . . . . . .4F **121**
Gooseley La. E6 . . . . .4F **89**
   (Claps Ga. La.)
  E6 . . . . .3E **89**
   (Folkestone Rd.)
Goosens Cl. SM1: Sutt 5A **166**
Goose Sq. E6 . . . . .6D **88**
Gophir La. EC4 . . . . .2E **14** (7D **84**)
Gopsall St. N1 . . . . .1D **84**
Gordon Av. E4 . . . . .6B **36**
  HA7: Stan 7E **26**
  SW14 .4A **116**
  TW1: Twick 5A **114**
Gordonbrook Rd. SE4 . . . . .5C **122**
Gordon Cl. E17 . . . . .6C **50**
  N19 . . . . .1G **65**
Gordon Cotts. W8 . . . . .2K **99**
   (off Dukes La.)
Gordon Ct. HA8: Edg 5A **28**
Gordon Cres.
  CR0: C'don 1E **168**
  UB3: Hayes 4J **93**
Gordondale Rd. SW19 . . . . .2J **135**
Gordon Dr. TW17: Shep 7F **147**
Gordon Gro. SE5 . . . . .2B **120**
Gordon Hill EN2: Enf 1H **23**
Gordon Ho. E1 . . . . .7J **85**
   (off Glamis Rd.)
  SW1 . . . . .2B **18**
   (off Greencoat Pl.)
  W5 . . . . .3E **78**
Gordon Ho. Rd. NW5 . . . . .4E **64**
Gordon Mans. W14 . . . . .3F **99**
   (off Addison Gdns.)
  WC1 . . . . .4C **6**
   (off Torrington Pl.)
Gordon Pl. W8 . . . . .2J **99**
Gordon Rd. BR3: Beck 3B **158**
  DA15: Sidc 5J **125**
  DA17: Belv 4J **109**
  E4 . . . . .1B **36**
  E11 . . . . .6J **51**
  E15 . . . . .4E **68**
  E18 . . . . .1K **51**
  EN2: Enf 1H **23**
  HA3: W'stone 3J **41**
  IG1: Ilf 3H **71**
  IG11: Bark 1J **89**
  KT2: King T 1F **151**
  KT5: Surb 7F **151**
  N3 . . . . .7C **30**
  N9 . . . . .2C **34**
  N11 . . . . .7C **32**
  RM6: Chad H 6F **55**
  SE15 . . . . .2H **121**
  SM5: Cars 6D **166**
  TW3: Houn 4G **113**
  TW9: Rich 2F **115**
  TW15: Ashf 3A **128**
  TW17: Shep 6F **147**
  UB2: S'hall 4C **94**
  UB7: Yiew 7A **74**
  W4 . . . . .6H **97**
  W5 . . . . .7B **78**
  W13 . . . . .7B **78**
Gordon Sq. WC1 . . . . .3C **6** (4H **83**)
Gordon St. E13 . . . . .3J **87**
  WC1 . . . . .3C **6** (4H **83**)
Gordon Way BR1: Brom 1J **159**
  EN5: Barn 4C **20**
Gore Cl. UB9: Hare 5G **43**
Gorefield Ho. NW6 . . . . .2J **81**
   (off Gorefield Pl.)
Gorefield Pl. NW6 . . . . .2J **81**

Gore Ho. N1 .7A **66**
   (off Drummond Way)
Gore Rd. E9 .1J **85**
  SW20 .2E **152**
GORESBROOK INTERCHANGE 2F **91**
Goresbrook Rd. RM9: Dag 1B **90**
Gore St. SW7 . . . . .3A **100**
Gorham Ho. SE16 . . . . .2K **103**
   (off Wolfe Cres.)
Gorham Pl. W11 . . . . .7G **81**
Goring Cl. RM5: Col R 1J **55**
Goring Gdns. RM8: Dag 4C **72**
Goring Rd. N11 . . . . .6D **32**
  RM10: Dag 6K **73**
Goring St. EC3 . . . . .7H **9**
Goring Way UB6: G'frd 2G **77**
Gorleston Rd. N15 . . . . .5D **48**
Gorleston St. W14 . . . . .4G **99**
   (not continuous)
Gorman Rd. SE18 . . . . .4D **106**
Gorringe Pk. Av. CR4: Mitc 7D **136**
Gorse Cl. E16 . . . . .6J **87**
Gorsefield Ho. E14 . . . . .7C **86**
   (off E. India Dock Rd.)
Gorse Ri. SW17 . . . . .5E **136**
Gorse Rd. CR0: C'don 4C **170**
Gorse Wlk. UB7: Yiew 6A **74**
Gorseway RM7: Rush G . . . .1K **73** & 2K **73**
Gorst Rd. NW10 . . . . .4J **79**
  SW11 .6D **118**
Gorsuch Pl. E2 . . . . .1J **9** (3F **85**)
Gorsuch St. E2 . . . . .1J **9** (2F **85**)
Gosberton Rd. SW12 . . . . .1D **136**
Gosbury Hill KT9: Chess 4E **162**
Gosfield Rd. RM8: Dag 2G **73**
Gosfield St. W1 . . . . .6A **6** (5G **83**)
Gosford Gdns. IG4: Ilf 5D **52**
Gosford Ho. E3 . . . . .2B **86**
   (off Tredegar Rd.)
Goshawk Ct. NW9 . . . . .7B **44**
Goshawk Gdns. UB4: Hayes 3G **75**
Goslett Yd. WC2 . . . . .1D **12** (6H **83**)
Gosling Cl. UB6: G'frd 3E **76**
Gosling Ho. E1 . . . . .7J **85**
   (off Sutton St.)
Gosling Way SW9 . . . . .1A **120**
Gospatrick Rd. N17 . . . . .7H **33**
GOSPEL OAK 4E **64**
Gosport Rd. E17 . . . . .5B **50**
Gosport Wlk. N17 . . . . .4H **49**
Gossage Rd. SE18 . . . . .5H **107**
  UB10: Uxb 7B **56**
Gosse Ct. N1 .1E **84**
   (off Downham Rd.)
Gosset St. E2 . . . . .1K **9** (3F **85**)
Gosshill Rd. BR7: Chst 2E **160**
Gossington Cl. BR7: Chst 4F **143**
Gosterwood St. SE8 . . . . .6A **104**
Gostling Rd. TW2: Whitt 1E **130**
Goston Gdns. CR7: Thor H 3A **156**
Goston Ga. SW8 . . . . .1K **119**
   (off Hampson Way)
Goswell Pl. EC1 . . . . .2B **8**
Goswell Rd. EC1 . . . . .1A **8** (2B **84**)
Gothic Cotts. EN2: Enf 2H **23**
   (off Chase Grn. Av.)
Gothic Ct. SE5 . . . . .7C **102**
   (off Wyndham Rd.)
  UB3: Harl 6F **93**
Gothic Rd. TW2: Twick 2H **131**
Gottfried M. NW5 . . . . .4G **65**
Goudhurst Rd. BR1: Brom 5G **141**
Gough Ho. KT1: King T 2E **150**
   (off Eden St.)
  N1 . . . . .1B **84**
   (off Windsor St.)
Gough Rd. E15 . . . . .4H **69**
  EN1: Enf .2C **24**
Gough Sq. EC4 . . . . .1K **13** (6A **84**)
Gough St. WC1 . . . . .3H **7** (4K **83**)
Gough Wlk. E14 . . . . .6C **86**

Goulden Ho.—Grangeway

Goulden Ho. SW11 . . . . 2C **118**
Goulden Ho. App. SW11 . . . . 2C **118**
Goulding Gdns. CR7: Thor H 2C **156**
Gouldman Ho. *E1* *4J 85*
(off Wyllen Cl.)
Gould Rd. TW2: Twick 1J **131**
TW14: Felt 7G **111**
GOULDS GREEN 5D **74**
Gould's Grn. UB8: Hil 7D **74**
Gould Ter. E8 . . . . 5H **67**
Gould Way HA8: Edg 7C **28**
Goulston St. E1 . . . . 7J **9** (6F **85**)
Goulton Rd. E5 . . . . 4H **67**
Gourley Pl. N15 . . . . 5E **48**
Gourley St. N15 . . . . 5E **48**
Gourock Rd. SE9 . . . . 5E **124**
Govan St. E2 . . . . 1G **85**
Gover Ct. SW4 . . . . 2J **119**
Govett Av. TW17: Shep 5E **146**
Govier Cl. E15 . . . . 7G **69**
Gowan Av. SW6 . . . . 1G **117**
Gowan Ho. *E2* *2K 9*
(off Chambord St.)
Gowan Rd. NW10 . . . . 6D **62**
Gower Cl. SW4 . . . . 6G **119**
Gower Ct. WC1 . . . . 3C **6** (4H **83**)
Gower Ho. E17 . . . . 3D **50**
SE17 . . . . *5C 102*
(off Morecambe St.)
Gower M. WC1 . . . . 6D **6** (5H **83**)
Gower M. Mans. *WC1* *5D 6*
(off Gower M.)
Gower Pl. WC1 . . . . 3B **6** (4H **83**)
Gower Rd. E7 . . . . 6J **69**
TW7: Isle 6K **95**
Gower St. WC1 . . . . 3B **6** (4G **83**)
Gower's Wlk. E1 . . . . 6G **85**
Gowland Pl. BR3: Beck 2B **158**
Gowlett Rd. SE15 . . . . 3G **121**
Gowlland Cl. CR0: C'don 7G **157**
Gowrie Rd. SW11 . . . . 3E **118**
Graburn Way KT8: E Mos 3H **149**
Grace Av. DA7: Bex 2F **127**
Grace Bus. Cen. CR4: Mitc 6D **154**
Gracechurch St. EC3 . . . . 2F **15** (7D **84**)
Grace Cl. HA8: Edg 7D **28**
SE9 . . . . 3B **142**
Grace Ct. *CR0: C'don* *3B 168*
(off Waddon Rd.)
SM2: Sutt 7K **165**
Gracedale Rd. SW16 . . . . 5F **137**
Gracefield Gdns. SW16 . . . . 3J **137**
Gracehill *E1* *5J 85*
(off Hannibal Rd.)
Grace Ho. SE11 . . . . 7H **19**
Grace Jones Cl. E8 . . . . 6G **67**
Grace M. BR3: Beck 6C **140**
SE20 . . . . *2J 157*
(off Marlow Rd.)
Grace Path SE26 . . . . 4J **139**
Grace Pl. E3 . . . . 3D **86**
Grace Rd. CR0: C'don 6C **156**
Graces All. E1 . . . . 7G **85**
Graces M. NW8 . . . . 2A **82**
SE5 . . . . 2D **120**
Grace's Rd. SE5 . . . . 2E **120**
Grace St. E3 . . . . 3D **86**
Gradient, The SE26 . . . . 4G **139**
Graduate Pl. SE1 . . . . 7F **15**
Graeme Rd. EN1: Enf 2J **23**
Graemesdyke Av. SW14 . . . . 3H **115**
Grafton Chambers *NW1* *2D 6*
(off Grafton Pl.)
Grafton Cl. KT4: Wor Pk 3A **164**
TW4: Houn 1C **130**
W13 . . . . 6A **78**
Grafton Ct. TW14: Bedf 1F **129**
Grafton Cres. NW1 . . . . 6F **65**
Grafton Gdns.
N4 . . . . 6C **48**
RM8: Dag 2E **72**
Grafton Ho. *E3* *3C 86*
(off Wellington Way)
SE8 . . . . 5B **104**
Grafton M. W1 . . . . 4A **6** (4G **83**)
Grafton Pk. Rd. KT4: Wor Pk 2A **164**
Grafton Pl. NW1 . . . . 2D **6** (3H **83**)
Grafton Rd.
CR0: C'don 1A **168**
EN2: Enf 3E **22**
HA1: Harr 5G **41**
KT3: N Mald 3A **152**
KT4: Wor Pk 3K **163**
NW5 . . . . 5E **64**
RM8: Dag 2E **72**
W3 . . . . 7J **79**
Graftons, The NW2 . . . . 3J **63**
Grafton Sq. SW4 . . . . 3G **119**
Grafton St. W1 . . . . 3K **11** (7F **83**)
Grafton Ter. NW5 . . . . 5D **64**
Grafton Way KT8: W Mole 4D **148**
W1 . . . . 4A **6** (4G **83**)
(not continuous)
WC1 . . . . 4A **6** (4G **83**)
Grafton Yd. NW5 . . . . 6F **65**
Graham Av. CR4: Mitc 1E **154**
W13 . . . . 2B **96**
Graham Cl. CR0: C'don 2C **170**
Graham Ct. *SE14* *6K 103*
(off Myers La.)
UB5: N'olt 5C **58**
GRAHAME PARK 1A **44**
Grahame Pk. Way NW7 . . . . 7G **29**
NW9 . . . . 2B **44**
Grahame Twr. *W3* *3H 97*
(off Hanbury Rd.)
Grahame White Ho. HA3: Kenton 3D **42**
Graham Gdns. KT6: Surb 1E **162**
Graham Ho. *N9* *1D 34*
(off Cumberland Rd.)
Graham Lodge NW4 . . . . 6D **44**
Graham Mans. *IG11: Bark* *7A 72*
(off Lansbury Av.)
Graham Rd. CR4: Mitc 1E **154**
DA6: Bex 4F **127**
E8 . . . . 6G **67**
E13 . . . . 4J **87**
HA3: W'stone 3J **41**
N15 . . . . 3B **48**
NW4 . . . . 6D **44**
SW19 . . . . 7H **135**
TW12: Hamp H 4E **130**
W4 . . . . 3K **97**
Graham St. N1 . . . . 1B **8** (2B **84**)
Graham Ter. *DA15: Sidc* *6B 126*
(off Westerham Dr.)
SW1 . . . . 4G **17** (4E **100**)
Grainger Cl. UB5: N'olt 5F **59**
Grainger Ct. SE5 . . . . 7C **102**
Grainger Rd. N22 . . . . 1C **48**
TW7: Isle 2K **113**
Grainstore, The E16 . . . . 7J **87**
Gramer Cl. E11 . . . . 2F **69**
Grampian Cl. BR6: St M Cry 6K **161**
SM2: Sutt 7A **166**
UB3: Harl 7F **93**
Grampian Gdns. NW2 . . . . 1G **63**
Grampians, The *W6* *2F 99*
(off Shepherd's Bush Rd.)
Gramsci Way SE6 . . . . 3D **140**
Granada St. SW17 . . . . 5D **136**
Granard Av. SW15 . . . . 5D **116**
Granard Bus. Cen. NW7 . . . . 6F **29**
Granard Ho. E9 . . . . 6K **67**
Granard Rd. SW12 . . . . 7D **118**
Granary Cl. N9 . . . . 7D **24**
Granary Ct. *E15* *6F 69*
(off Millstone Cl.)
Granary Mans. SE28 . . . . 2G **107**
Granary Rd. E1 . . . . 4H **85**
Granary Sq. N1 . . . . 1J **83**
Granary St. NW1 . . . . 1H **83**
Granby Pl. *SE1* *7J 13*
(off Lower Marsh)
Granby Rd. SE9 . . . . 2D **124**
Granby St. E2 . . . . 3K **9** (4G **85**)
(not continuous)
Granby Ter. NW1 . . . . 1A **6** (2G **83**)
Grand Arc. N12 . . . . 5F **31**
Grand Av. EC1 . . . . 5B **8** (5B **84**)
(not continuous)
HA9: Wemb 5G **61**
KT5: Surb 5H **151**
N10 . . . . 4E **46**
Grand Av. E. HA9: Wemb 5H **61**
Grand Canal Apartments *N1* *1E 84*
(off De Beauvoir Cr.)
Grand Canal Av. SE8 . . . . 4A **104**
Grand Connaught Rooms 7G **7**
Grand Courts RM8: Dag 3E **72**
Grand Depot Rd. SE18 . . . . 5E **106**
Grand Dr. SW20 . . . . 2E **152**
UB2: S'hall 2G **95**
Granden Rd. SW16 . . . . 2J **155**
Grandfield Ct. W4 . . . . 6K **97**
Grandison Rd. KT4: Wor Pk 2E **164**
SW11 . . . . 5D **118**
Grand Junc. Wharf N1 . . . . 2C **84**
Grand Pde. HA9: Wemb 2G **61**
KT6: Surb 1G **163**
N4 . . . . 5B **48**
SW14 . . . . *4J 115*
(off Up. Richmond Rd. W.)
Grand Pde. M. SW15 . . . . 5G **117**
Grandstand Way UB5: N'olt 5D **58**
Grand Twr. *SW15* *5G 117*
(off Plaza Gdns.)
Grand Union Canal Wlk. *W10* *4E 80*
(off Canal Way)
Grand Union Cen. *W10* *4F 81*
(off West Row)
Grand Union Cl. W9 . . . . 5J **81**
Grand Union Cres. E8 . . . . 1G **85**
Grand Union Ent. Pk. UB2: S'hall 3E **94**
Grand Union Hgts. HA0: Wemb 1D **78**
Grand Union Ho. *N1* *1E 84*
(off Hertford Rd.)
Grand Union Ind. Est. NW10 . . . . 2H **79**
Grand Union Village UB5: N'olt 3D **76**
Grand Union Wlk. *NW1* *7F 65*
(off Kentish Town Rd.)
Grand Union Way UB2: S'hall 2E **94**
Grand Vitesse Ind. Cen. *SE1* *5B 14*
(off Gt. Suffolk St.)
Grand Wlk. E1 . . . . 4A **86**
Granfield St. SW11 . . . . 1B **118**
Grange, The CR0: C'don 2B **170**
E17 . . . . *5A 50*
(off Lynmouth Rd.)
HA0: Wemb 7G **61**
KT3: N Mald 5B **152**
KT4: Wor Pk 4K **163**
N2 . . . . 2B **46**
N20 . . . . 1F **31**
(Grangeview Rd.)
N20 . . . . 1G **31**
(Oxford Gdns.)
SE1 . . . . 3F **103**
SW19 . . . . 6F **135**
W3 . . . . 2H **97**
W4 . . . . 5H **97**
W13 . . . . 5C **78**
W14 . . . . 4H **99**
Grange Av. EN4: E Barn 1H **31**
HA7: Stan 2B **42**
IG8: Wfd G 6D **36**
N12 . . . . 5F **31**
N20 . . . . 7B **20**
SE25 . . . . 2E **156**
TW2: Twick 2J **131**
Grangecliffe Gdns. SE25 . . . . 2E **156**
Grange Cl. DA15: Sidc 3A **144**
HA8: Edg 5D **28**
Grange Cl. IG8: Wfd G 7D **36**
KT8: W Mole 4F **149**
TW5: Hest 6D **94**
UB3: Hayes 5G **75**
Grange Ct. HA1: Harr 4K **59**
HA5: Pinn 3C **40**
NW10 . . . . *3A 62*
(off Neasden La.)
SM2: Sutt 7K **165**
SM6: Wall 3F **167**
TW17: Shep 4C **146**
UB5: N'olt 2A **76**
WC2 . . . . 1H **13** (6K **83**)
Grangecourt Rd. N16 . . . . 1E **66**
Grange Cres. SE28 . . . . 6C **90**
Grangedale Cl. HA6: Nwood 1G **39**
Grange Dr. BR7: Chst 6C **142**
Grange Farm Cl. HA2: Harr 2G **59**
Grangefield *NW1* *7H 65*
(off Marquis Rd.)
Grange Gdns. HA5: Pinn 3C **40**
N14 . . . . 1C **32**
NW3 . . . . 3K **63**
SE25 . . . . 2E **156**
Grange Gro. N1 . . . . 6C **66**
Grange Hill HA8: Edg 5D **28**
SE25 . . . . 2E **156**
Grangehill Pl. SE9 . . . . 3D **124**
Grangehill Rd. SE9 . . . . 4D **124**
Grange Ho. NW10 . . . . 7D **62**
SE1 . . . . 3F **103**
Grange La. SE21 . . . . 2F **139**
Grange Lodge SW19 . . . . 6F **135**
Grange Mans. KT17: Ewe 7B **164**
Grange M. N21 . . . . 6G **23**
TW13: Felt 4J **129**
Grangemill Rd. SE6 . . . . 3C **140**
Grangemill Way SE6 . . . . 2C **140**
GRANGE PARK 6G **23**
Grange Pk. W5 . . . . 1E **96**
Grange Pk. Av. N21 . . . . 6H **23**
Grange Pk. Pl. SW20 . . . . 7D **134**
Grange Pk. Rd. CR7: Thor H 4D **156**
E10 . . . . 1D **68**
Grange Pl. NW6 . . . . 7J **63**
Grange Rd. BR6: Orp 2H **173**
CR2: S Croy 7C **168**
CR7: Thor H 4D **156**
E10 . . . . 1C **68**
E13 . . . . 3H **87**
E17 . . . . 5A **50**
(not continuous)
HA1: Harr 5A **42**
HA2: Harr 2H **59**
HA8: Edg 6E **28**
IG1: Ilf 4F **71**
KT1: King T 3E **150**
KT8: W Mole 4F **149**
KT9: Chess 4E **162**
N6 . . . . 6E **46**
N17 . . . . 6B **34**
N18 . . . . 6B **34**
NW10 . . . . 6D **62**
SE1 . . . . 3E **102**
SE19 . . . . 4D **156**
SE25 . . . . 4D **156**
SM2: Sutt 7J **165**
SW13 . . . . 1C **116**
UB1: S'hall 2C **94**
UB3: Hayes 6G **75**
W4 . . . . 5H **97**
W5 . . . . 1D **96**
Grange St. N1 . . . . 1D **84**
Grange Va. SM2: Sutt 7K **165**
Grange Vw. Rd. N20 . . . . 1F **31**
Grange Wlk. SE1 . . . . 3E **102**
Grange Wlk. M. *SE1* *3E 102*
(off Grange Wlk.)
Grange Way NW6 . . . . 7J **63**
Grangeway IG8: Wfd G 4F **37**
N12 . . . . 4E **30**

Grangeway, The—Gt. Western Ind. Pk.

Grangeway, The N21 .6G **23**
Grangeway Gdns. IG4: Ilf .5C **52**
Grangewood DA5: Bexl .1F **145**
Grangewood Cl.
HA5: Eastc .5J **39**
Grangewood Dr. TW16: Sun .7H **129**
Grangewood La. BR3: Beck .6B **140**
Grangewood St. E6 .1B **88**
Grangewood Ter. SE25 .2D **156**
Grange Yd. SE1 .3F **103**
Granham Gdns. N9 .2A **34**
Granite Apartments E15 .6G **69**
Granite St. SE18 .5K **107**
Granleigh Rd. E11 .2G **69**
Gransden Av. E8 .7H **67**
Gransden Ho. SE8 .5B **104**
Gransden Rd. W12 .2B **98**
Grantbridge St. N1 .2B **84**
Grantchester *KT1: King T* .*2G* ***151***
(off St Peters Rd.)
Grantchester Cl. HA1: Harr .3K **59**
Grant Cl. DA17: Belv .5F **109**
N14 .7B **22**
N17 .2E **48**
TW17: Shep .6D **146**
Grant Ct. *E4* .*1K* ***35***
(off The Ridgeway)
NW9 .*2B* ***44***
(off Hazel Cl.)
Grantham Cl. HA8: Edg .3K **27**
Grantham Ct. KT2: King T .5D **132**
RM6: Chad H .7F **55**
SE16 .*2K* ***103***
(off Eleanor Cl.)
Grantham Gdns. RM6: Chad H .6F **55**
Grantham Ho. *SE15* .*6G* ***103***
(off Friary Est.)
TW16: Sun .7G **129**
UB5: N'olt .*3D* ***76***
(off Taywood Rd.)
Grantham Pl. W1 .5J **11** (1F **101**)
Grantham Rd. E12 .4E **70**
SW9 .2J **119**
W4 .7A **98**
Grant Ho. *E17* .*4C* ***50***
(off High St.)
SW9 .*1K* ***119***
(off Liberty St.)
Grantley Ho. *SE14* .*6K* ***103***
(off Myers La.)
Grantley Rd. TW4: Cran .2A **112**
Grantley St. E1 .3K **85**
Grant Museum of Zoology .4C **6**
Grantock Rd. E17 .1F **51**
Granton Rd. DA14: Sidc .6C **144**
IG3: Ilf .1A **72**
SW16 .1G **155**
Grant Pl. CR0: C'don .1F **169**
Grant Rd. CR0: C'don .1F **169**
HA3: W'stone .3K **41**
SW11 .4B **118**
Grants Cl. NW7 .7K **29**
Grants Quay Wharf EC3 .3F **15** (7D **84**)
Grant St. E13 .3J **87**
N1 .2A **84**
Grant Ter. *N16* .*7G* ***49***
(off Castlewood Rd.)
Grantully Rd. W9 .3K **81**
Grant Way TW7: Isle .6A **96**
Granville Arc. SW9 .4A **120**
Granville Av. N9 .3D **34**
TW3: Houn .5E **112**
TW13: Felt .2J **129**
Granville Cl. CR0: C'don .2E **168**
Granville Ct. N1 .1E **84**
N4 .6K **47**
SE14 .*7A* ***104***
(off Nynehead St.)
Granville Gdns. SW16 .1K **155**
W5 .1F **97**
Granville Gro. SE13 .3E **122**
Granville Ho. *E14* .*6C* ***86***
(off E. India Dock Rd.)
Granville Mans. *W12* .*2E* ***98***
(off Shepherd's Bush Grn.)
Granville M. DA14: Sidc .4A **144**
Granville Pk. SE13 .3E **122**
Granville Pl. HA5: Pinn .3B **40**
N12 .7F **31**
SW6 .7K **99**
W1 .1G **11** (6E **82**)
Granville Point NW2 .2H **63**
Granville Rd. DA14: Sidc .4A **144**
DA16: Well .3C **126**
E17 .6D **50**
E18 .2K **51**
EN5: Barn .4A **20**
IG1: Ilf .1F **71**
N4 .6K **47**
N12 .7F **31**
N13 .6E **32**
N22 .1B **48**
NW2 .2H **63**
NW6 .2J **81**
(not continuous)
SW18 .7H **117**
SW19 .7J **135**
UB3: Harl .4H **93**
UB10: Hil .6D **56**
Granville Sq. SE15 .7E **102**
WC1 .2H **7** (3K **83**)
Granville St. WC1 .2H **7** (3K **83**)
Granwood Ct. TW7: Isle .1J **113**
Grape St. WC2 .7E **6** (6J **83**)
Graphite Apartments, The *N1* .*2D* ***84***
(off Provost St.)
Graphite Sq. SE11 .5G **19** (5K **101**)
Grapsome Cl. KT9: Chess .7C **162**
Grasdene Rd. SE18 .7A **108**
Grasgarth Cl. W3 .7J **79**
Grasmere *NW1* .*2K* ***5***
(off Osnaburgh St.)
Grasmere Av. BR6: Farnb .3F **173**
HA4: Ruis .7E **38**
HA9: Wemb .7C **42**
SW15 .4K **133**
SW19 .3J **153**
TW3: Houn .6F **113**
W3 .7K **79**
Grasmere Cl. TW14: Felt .1H **129**
Grasmere Ct. N22 .6E **32**
SE26 .5G **139**
SM2: Sutt .6A **166**
SW13 .*6C* ***98***
(off Verdun Rd.)
Grasmere Gdns. BR6: Farnb .3F **173**
HA3: W'stone .2A **42**
IG4: Ilf .5D **52**
Grasmere Point *SE15* .*7J* ***103***
(off Old Kent Rd.)
Grasmere Rd. BR1: Brom .1H **159**
BR6: Farnb .3F **173**
DA7: Bex .2J **127**
E13 .2J **87**
N10 .1F **47**
N17 .6B **34**
SE25 .6H **157**
SW16 .5J **137**
Graspan Royal Marines Memorial .1H **101**
Grasshaven Way SE28 .1K **107**
(not continuous)
Grassington Cl. N11 .6K **31**
Grassington Rd. DA14: Sidc .4A **144**
Grassmount SE23 .2H **139**
Grass Pk. N3 .1H **45**
Grassway SM6: Wall .4G **167**
Grasvenor Av. EN5: Barn .5D **20**
Gratton Rd. W14 .3G **99**
Gratton Ter. NW2 .3F **63**
Gravel Hill
CR0: Addtn .6K **169**
DA6: Bex .4H **127**
Gravel Hill N3 .2H **45**
UB8: Uxb .5A **56**
Gravel Hill Cl. DA6: Bex .5H **127**
Gravel La. E1 .7J **9** (6F **85**)
Gravel Pit La. SE9 .5F **125**
Gravel Pit Way BR6: Orp .2K **173**
Gravel Rd. BR2: Brom .3C **172**
TW2: Twick .1J **131**
Gravelwood Cl. BR7: Chst .3G **143**
Gravely Ho. *SE8* .*4A* ***104***
(off Chilton Gro.)
Gravenel Gdns. *SW17* .*5C* ***136***
(off Nutwell St.)
Graveney Gro. SE20 .7J **139**
Graveney Rd. SW17 .4C **136**
Gravesend Rd. W12 .7C **80**
Gravesham Way BR3: Beck .7B **158**
Gray Av. RM8: Dag .1F **73**
Gray Ct. E1 .5A **86**
HA5: Pinn .4C **40**
Grayham Cres. KT3: N Mald .4K **151**
Grayham Rd. KT3: N Mald .4K **151**
Gray Ho. *SE17* .*5C* ***102***
(off King & Queen St.)
Grayland Cl. BR1: Brom .1B **160**
Grayling Cl. E16 .4G **87**
Grayling Ct. *W5* .*1D* ***96***
(off Grange Rd.)
Grayling Rd. N16 .2D **66**
Grayling Sq. *E2* .*3G* ***85***
(off Nelson Gdns.)
Grayscroft Rd. SW16 .7H **137**
Grays Farm Production Village
BR5: St P .7B **144**
Grays Farm Rd. BR5: St P .7B **144**
Grayshott Rd. SW11 .2E **118**
Gray's Inn .5H **7** (5K **83**)
Gray's Inn Bldgs. *EC1* .*4J* ***7***
(off Rosebery Av.)
Gray's Inn Pl. WC1 .6H **7** (5K **83**)
Gray's Inn Rd. WC1 .1F **7** (3J **83**)
Gray's Inn Sq. WC1 .5J **7** (5K **83**)
Grays La. TW15: Ashf .4D **128**
Grayson Ho. EC1 .2D **8**
Grays Rd. UB10: Uxb .7A **56**
Grays Ter. E7 .6A **70**
Grayston Ho. SE3 .4A **124**
Gray St. SE1 .7K **13** (2A **102**)
Grayswood Gdns. SW20 .2D **152**
Grayswood Point SW15 .1C **134**
Gray's Yd. W1 .1H **11**
Graywood Ct. N12 .7F **31**
Grazebrook Rd. N16 .2D **66**
Grazeley Cl. DA6: Bex .5J **127**
Grazeley Ct. SE19 .5E **138**
Gt. Acre Ct. SW4 .4H **119**
Gt. Amwell La. N8 .3K **47**
Gt. Arthur Ho. *EC1* .*4C* ***8***
(off Golden La. Est.)
Gt. Bell All. EC2 .7E **8** (6D **84**)
Great Benty UB7: W Dray .4A **92**
Great Brownings SE21 .4F **139**
Gt. Bushey Dr. N20 .1E **30**
Gt. Cambridge Ind. Est. EN1: Enf .5C **24**
GREAT CAMBRIDGE JUNC. .4J **33**
Gt. Cambridge Rd. EN1: Enf .4J **33**
N9 .4J **33**
N17 .5J **33**
N18 .4J **33**
Gt. Castle St. W1 .7K **5** (6F **83**)
Gt. Central Av. HA4: Ruis .5A **58**
Gt. Central St. NW1 .5E **4** (5D **82**)
Gt. Central Way HA9: Wemb .4J **61**
NW10 .4J **61**
Gt. Chapel St. W1 .7C **6** (6H **83**)
Gt. Chart St. SW11 .4B **118**
Gt. Chertsey Rd. TW2: Twick .3D **130**
TW13: Hanw, Twick .3D **130**
W4 .1J **115**
(not continuous)
Gt. Church La. W6 .4F **99**
Gt. College St. SW1 .1E **18** (3J **101**)
Great Cft. *WC1* .*2F* ***7***
(off Cromer St.)
Gt. Cross Av. SE10 .7F **105**
Gt. Cumberland M. W1 .1E **10** (6D **82**)
Gt. Cumberland Pl. W1 .7E **4** (6D **82**)
Gt. Dover St. SE1 .7D **14** (2C **102**)
Greatdown Rd. W7 .4K **77**
Gt. Eastern Ent. Cen. E14 .2D **104**
Gt. Eastern Rd. E15 .7F **69**
Gt. Eastern St. EC2 .2G **9** (3E **84**)
Gt. Eastern Wlk. EC2 .6H **9**
Gt. Eastern Wharf SW11 .7C **100**
Gt. Elms Rd. BR2: Brom .4A **160**
Greater London Ho. *NW1* .*2G* ***83***
(off Hampstead Rd.)
Great Fld. NW9 .1A **44**
Greatfield NW5 .5G **65**
Greatfield Av. E6 .4D **88**
Greatfield Cl. N19 .4G **65**
SE4 .4C **122**
Greatfields Dr. UB8: Hil .5C **74**
Greatfields Rd. IG11: Bark .1H **89**
Gt. Fleete Way IG11: Bark .2C **90**
Gt. Galley Cl. IG11: Bark .3B **90**
Gt. Gatton Cl. CR0: C'don .7A **158**
Gt. George St. SW1 .7D **12** (2H **101**)
Gt. Guildford Bus. Sq. SE1 .5C **14** (1C **102**)
Gt. Guildford St. SE1 .4C **14** (1C **102**)
Great Hall .6F **17** (5D **100**)
Great Hall *SW11* .*1E* ***118***
(off Battersea Pk. Rd.)
Greatham Wlk. SW15 .1C **134**
Gt. Harry Dr. SE9 .3E **142**
Gt. James St. WC1 .5G **7** (5K **83**)
Gt. Marlborough St. W1 .1A **12** (6G **83**)
Gt. Maze Pond SE1 .6F **15** (2D **102**)
Great Minster Ho. *SW1* .*3D* ***18***
(off Marsham St.)
Gt. Newport St. WC2 .2E **12** (7J **83**)
Gt. New St. *EC4* .*7K* ***7***
(off New Fetter La.)
Great Nth. Leisure Pk. N12 .7G **31**
Great Nth. Rd. EN5: Barn .1C **20** & 2C **20**
EN5: New Bar .5D **20**
N2 .5C **46**
N6 .5C **46**
Great Nth. Way NW4 .2D **44**
Greatorex Ho. *E1* .*5G* ***85***
(off Greatorex St.)
Greatorex St. E1 .5G **85**
Gt. Ormond St. WC1 .5F **7** (5J **83**)
Gt. Owl Rd. IG7: Chig .3K **37**
Great Pk. Cl. UB10: Hil .7C **56**
Gt. Percy St. WC1 .1H **7** (3K **83**)
Gt. Peter St. SW1 .2C **18** (3H **101**)
Gt. Portland St. W1 .4K **5** (4F **83**)
Gt. Pulteney St. W1 .2B **12** (7G **83**)
Gt. Queen St. WC2 .1F **13** (6J **83**)
Gt. Russell Mans. *WC1* .*6E* ***6***
(off Gt. Russell St.)
Gt. Russell St. WC1 .7D **6** (6H **83**)
Great St Helen's EC3 .7G **9** (6E **84**)
Great St Thomas Apostle EC4 .2D **14** (7C **84**)
Gt. Scotland Yd. SW1 .5E **12** (1J **101**)
Gt. Smith St. SW1 .1D **18** (3H **101**)
Great Sth. West Rd. TW4: Houn .4H **111**
TW14: Bedf, Felt .7E **110**
Great Spilmans SE22 .5E **120**
Great Strand NW9 .1B **44**
Gt. Suffolk St. SE1 .5B **14** (1B **102**)
Gt. Sutton St. EC1 .4B **8** (4B **84**)
Gt. Swan All. EC2 .7E **8** (6D **84**)
Great Thrift BR5: Pet W .4G **161**
Gt. Titchfield St. W1 .4K **5** (4F **83**)
Gt. Tower St. EC3 .2G **15** (7E **84**)
Gt. Trinity La. EC4 .2D **14** (7C **84**)
Great Turnstile WC1 .6H **7** (5K **83**)
Gt. Turnstile Ho. *WC1* .*6H* ***7***
(off Great Turnstile)
Gt. Western Ind. Pk. UB2: S'hall .2F **95**

282 A-Z London

Gt. Western Rd. W9 . . . . .5H **81**
W11 . . . . .5H **81**
Gt. West Rd. TW5: Hest 2B **112**
TW7: Bford, Isle 2B **112**
TW8: Bford 2B **112**
W4 . . . . .5H **97**
(Cedars Rd.)
W4 . . . . .5B **98**
(Dorchester St.)
W6 . . . . .5B **98**
Gt. West Trad. Est. TW8: Bford 6B **96**
Gt. Winchester St. EC2 . . . .7F **9** (6D **84**)
Gt. Windmill St. W1 . . . . . .2C **12** (7H **83**)
Greatwood BR7: Chst 7E **142**
Great Yd. SE1 . . . . .6H **15**
Greaves Cl. IG11: Bark 7H **71**
Greaves Cotts. E14 . . . . .5A **86**
(off Maroon St.)
Greaves Pl. SW17 . . . . .4C **136**
Greaves Twr. SW10 . . . . .7A **100**
(off Worlds End Est.)
Grebe Av. UB4: Yead 6B **76**
Grebe Cl. E7 . . . . .5H **69**
E17 . . . . .7F **35**
IG11: Bark 4A **90**
Grebe Ct. E14 . . . . .2E **104**
(off River Barge Cl.)
SE8 . . . . .8B **104**
(off Dorking Cl.)
SM1: Sutt 5H **165**
Grebe Ter. KT1: King T 3E **150**
Grecian Cres. SE19 . . . . .6B **138**
Greek Ct. W1 . . . . .1D **12** (6H **83**)
Greek St. W1 . . . . .1D **12** (6H **83**)
Green, The BR1: Brom 3J **141**
(not continuous)
BR2: Hayes 7J **159**
BR5: St P 7B **144**
CR0: Sels 7B **170**
DA7: Bex 1G **127**
DA14: Sidc 4A **144**
DA16: Well 4J **125**
E4 . . . . .1K **35**
E11 . . . . .6K **51**
E15 . . . . .6G **69**
HA0: Wemb 2A **60**
IG8: Wfd G 5D **36**
IG9: Buck H 1E **36**
KT3: N Mald 3K **151**
N9 .2B **34**
N14 . . . . .2C **32**
N17 . . . . .6H **33**
N21 . . . . .7F **23**
SM1: Sutt 3K **165**
SM4: Mord 4G **153**
SM5: Cars 4E **166**
SM6: Wall 2E **166**
SW14 . . . . .3J **115**
SW19 . . . . .5F **135**
TW2: Twick 1J **131**
TW5: Hest 2B **112**
TW9: Rich 5D **114**
TW13: Felt 2K **129**
TW17: Shep 4G **147**
UB2: S'hall 3C **94**
UB7: W Dray 3A **92**
UB10: Ick 2E **56**
W3 .6A **80**
W5 .1D **96**
Greenacre Cl. EN5: Barn 1C **20**
UB5: N'olt 5D **58**
Greenacre Gdns. E17 . . . . .4E **50**
Greenacre Pl. SM6: Wall 2F **167**
Green Acres CR0: C'don 3F **169**
DA14: Sidc 4A **144**
Greenacres N3 . . . . .2H **45**
SE9 . . . . .6E **124**
WD23: B Hea 2C **26**
Greenacres Av. UB10: Ick 3B **56**
Greenacres Cl. BR6: Farnb 4G **173**
Greenacres Dr. HA7: Stan 6G **27**

Greenacre Sq. SE16 . . . . .2K **103**
Greenacre Wlk. N14 . . . . .3C **32**
Greenan Ct. E2 . . . . .3K **85**
(off Meath Cres.)
Green Arbour Ct. EC1 . . . . .7A **8**
W13 . . . . .3B **96**
Greenaway Av. N18 . . . . .6E **34**
Greenaway Gdns. NW3 . . . . .4K **63**
Greenaway Ho. NW8 . . . . .1A **82**
(off Boundary Rd.)
WC1 .2J **7**
(off Fernsbury St.)
Greenaway Ter. TW19: Stanw 1A **128**
(off Victory Cl.)
Green Bank E1 . . . . .1H **103**
N12 . . . . .4E **30**
Greenbank Av. HA0: Wemb 5A **60**
Greenbank Cl. E4 . . . . .2K **35**
Greenbank Ct. TW7: Isle 2K **113**
(off Lanadron Cl.)
Greenbank Cres. NW4 . . . . .4G **45**
Greenbank Lodge BR7: Chst 2E **160**
(off Forest Cl.)
Greenbanks HA1: Harr 4J **59**
Greenbanks Cl. SE13 . . . . .3D **122**
Greenbay Rd. SE7 . . . . .7B **106**
Greenberry St. NW8 . . . . . .1C **4** (2C **82**)
Greenbrook Av. EN4: Had W 1F **21**
Green Cl. BR2: Brom 3G **159**
NW9 . . . . .6J **43**
NW11 . . . . .7A **46**
SM5: Cars 2D **166**
TW13: Hanw 5C **130**
Greencoat Mans. SW1 . . . . .2B **18**
(off Greencoat Row)
Greencoat Pl. SW1 . . . . . .3B **18** (4G **101**)
Greencoat Row SW1 . . . . .2B **18** (3G **101**)
Green Ct. TW16: Sun 6H **129**
Greencourt Av. CR0: C'don 2H **169**
HA8: Edg 1H **43**
Greencourt Gdns.
CR0: C'don 1H **169**
Greencourt Ho. E1 . . . . .4K **85**
(off Mile End Rd.)
Greencourt Rd. BR5: Pet W 5H **161**
Greencrest Pl. NW2 . . . . .3C **62**
Greencroft HA8: Edg 5D **28**
Greencroft Av. HA4: Ruis 2A **58**
Greencroft Cl. E6 . . . . .5B **88**
Greencroft Gdns. EN1: Enf 3K **23**
NW6 . . . . .7K **63**
Greencroft Rd. TW5: Hest 1D **112**
Green Dale SE5 . . . . .4D **120**
SE22 . . . . .5E **120**
Greendale NW7 . . . . .4F **29**
Green Dale Cl. SE22 . . . . .5E **120**
Green Dragon Ct. SE1 . . . . .4E **14**
Green Dragon Ho. WC2 . . . . .7F **7**
(off Stukeley St.)
Green Dragon La. N21 . . . . .6F **23**
TW8: Bford 5E **96**
Green Dragon Yd. E1 . . . .6K **9** (5G **85**)
Greene Ct. UB1: S'hall 1E **94**
Greene Ct. SE14 . . . . .6K **103**
(off Samuel Cl.)
Greene Ho. SE1 . . . . .3D **102**
(off Burbage Cl.)
Green End KT9: Chess 4E **162**
N21 . . . . .2G **33**
Greenend Rd. W4 . . . . .2A **98**
Greener Ct. CR0: C'don 6C **156**
(off Goodman Cres.)
Greener Ho. SW4 . . . . .3H **119**
Green Farm Cl. BR6: Chels 5K **173**
Green Ferry Way E17 . . . . .3K **49**
Greenfield Av. KT5: Surb 7H **151**
Greenfield Dr.
BR1: Brom 2A **160**
N2 . . . . .4D **46**

Greenfield Gdns. BR5: Pet W 7H **161**
NW2 . . . . .2G **63**
RM9: Dag 1D **90**
Greenfield Ho. SW19 . . . . .1F **135**
Greenfield Rd. DA2: Wilm 5K **145**
E1 . . . . .5G **85**
N15 . . . . .5E **48**
RM9: Dag 1C **90**
Greenfields UB1: S'hall 6E **76**
Greenfield Way HA2: Harr 3F **41**
GREENFORD 3E **76**
Greenford Av. UB1: S'hall 7D **76**
W7 .4J **77**
Greenford Bus. Cen.
UB6: G'frd 7H **59**
Greenford Gdns. UB6: G'frd 3F **77**
GREENFORD GREEN 6J **59**
Greenford Ind. Est. UB6: G'frd 7F **59**
Greenford Pk. UB6: G'frd 7H **59**
Greenford Rd. HA1: Harr 2H **77**
SM1: Sutt 4K **165**
(not continuous)
UB1: S'hall 7G **77**
UB6: G'frd 2H **77**
Greenford Sports Cen. 3E **76**
Green Gdns. BR6: Farnb 5G **173**
Greengate UB6: G'frd 6B **60**
Greengate Lodge E13 . . . . .2K **87**
(off Hollybush St.)
Greengate St. E13 . . . . .2K **87**
Greenhalgh Wlk. N2 . . . . .4A **46**
Greenham Cl. SE1 . . . . . . .7J **13** (2A **102**)
Greenham Cres. E4 . . . . .6G **35**
Greenham Ho. E9 . . . . .1J **85**
(off Templecombe Rd.)
TW7: Isle 3H **113**
Greenham Rd. N10 . . . . .2E **46**
Greenhaven Dr. SE28 . . . . .6B **90**
Green Hedges TW1: Twick 5C **114**
Greenheys Cl. HA6: Nwood 1G **39**
Greenheys Dr. E18 . . . . .3H **51**
GREENHILL 5J **41**
Green Hill SE18 . . . . .5D **106**
Greenhill HA9: Wemb 2H **61**
IG9: Buck H 1F **37**
NW3 . . . . .4B **64**
SM1: Sutt 2A **166**
Greenhill Ct. EN5: New Bar 5E **20**
SE18 . . . . .5D **106**
Greenhill Gdns. UB5: N'olt 2D **76**
Greenhill Gro. E12 . . . . .4C **70**
Greenhill Pde. EN5: New Bar 5E **20**
Greenhill Pk. EN5: New Bar 5E **20**
NW10 . . . . .1A **80**
Greenhill Rd. HA1: Harr 6J **41**
NW10 . . . . .1A **80**
Greenhill's Rents EC1 . . . . .5A **8** (5B **84**)
Greenhills Ter. N1 . . . . .6D **66**
Greenhill Ter. SE18 . . . . .5D **106**
UB5: N'olt 2D **76**
Greenhill Way HA1: Harr 6J **41**
HA9: Wemb 2H **61**
Greenhithe Cl. DA15: Sidc 7J **125**
Greenholm Rd. SE9 . . . . .5F **125**
Green Hundred Rd. SE15 . . . . .6G **103**
Greenhurst Rd. SE27 . . . . .5A **138**
Greening St. SE2 . . . . .4C **108**
Greenland Cres. UB2: S'hall 3A **94**
Greenland Ho. E1 . . . . .4A **86**
(off Ernest St.)
Greenland M. SE8 . . . . .5K **103**
Greenland Pl. NW1 . . . . .1F **83**
Greenland Quay SE16 . . . . .4K **103**
Greenland Rd. EN5: Barn 6A **20**
NW1 . . . . .1G **83**
Greenlands KT19: Ewe 5H **163**
Greenlands La. NW4 . . . . .1D **44**
Greenland Way CR0: Bedd 7H **155**

Green La.
BR7: Chst 1F **143**
CR7: Thor H 7K **137**
HA1: Harr 3J **59**
HA7: Stan 4G **27**
HA8: Edg 4A **28**
(not continuous)
IG1: Ilf 2H **71**
IG3: Ilf 2H **71**
KT3: N Mald 5J **151**
KT4: Wor Pk 1C **164**
KT8: W Mole 5F **149**
KT9: Chess 7D **162**
NW4 . . . . .4F **45**
RM8: Dag 2H **71**
SE9 .1F **143**
SE20 . . . . .7K **139**
SM4: Mord 6J **153**
(Central Rd.)
SM4: Mord 7E **152**
(Lwr. Morden La.)
SW16 . . . . .7K **137**
TW4: Houn 3K **111**
TW13: Hanw 5C **130**
TW16: Sun 7H **129**
TW17: Shep 6E **146**
UB8: Hil 5E **74**
W7 .2J **95**
Green La. Bus. Pk. SE9 . . . . .2E **142**
Green La. Cotts. HA7: Stan 4G **27**
Green La. Gdns. CR7: Thor H 2C **156**
Green Lanes KT19: Ewe 7A **164**
N4 . . . . .1C **66**
N8 . . . . .3B **48**
N13 . . . . .6E **32**
N15 . . . . .3B **48**
N16 . . . . .1C **66**
N21 . . . . .7F **33**
Greenlaw Ct. W5 . . . . .6D **78**
(off Mount Pk. Rd.)
Greenlaw Gdns. KT3: N Mald 7B **152**
Greenlawn La. TW8: Bford 4D **96**
Green Lawns HA4: Ruis 1A **58**
Greenlawns N12 . . . . .6E **30**
Greenlawns, The SE18 . . . . .4F **107**
(off Vincent Rd.)
Greenlaw St. SE18 . . . . .3E **106**
Green Leaf Av. SM6: Bedd 4H **167**
Greenleaf Cl. SW2 . . . . .7A **120**
Greenleafe Dr. IG6: Ilf 3F **53**
Greenleaf Rd. E6 . . . . .1A **88**
E17 . . . . .3B **50**
Greenleaf Way HA3: W'stone 3K **41**
Greenlea Pk. SW19 . . . . .7B **136**
Green Leas KT1: King T 3E **150**
(off Mill St.)
Green Leas Cl. TW16: Sun 6H **129**
Greenleaves Ct. TW15: Ashf 6D **128**
Greenlink Wlk. TW9: Kew 1H **115**
Green Man Gdns. W13 . . . . .7A **78**
Green Man La. TW14: Felt 4J **111**
W13 . . . . .7A **78**
(not continuous)
Green Man Pas. W13 . . . . .7B **78**
(not continuous)
GREEN MAN RDBT. 7H **51**
Greenman St. N1 . . . . .7C **66**
Greenmead DA18: Erith 3E **108**
Greenmead Cl. SE25 . . . . .5G **157**
Green M. N1 . . . . .3D **84**
Green Moor Link N21 . . . . .7G **23**
Greenmoor Rd.
EN3: Enf H 2D **24**
Greenoak Pl. EN4: Cockf 2J **21**
Green Oaks UB2: S'hall 4B **94**
Greenoak Way SW19 . . . . .4F **135**
Greenock Rd. SW16 . . . . .1H **155**
W3 . . . . .3H **97**
Greeno Cres. TW17: Shep 5C **146**
Green Pde. TW3: Houn 5F **113**

Green Park
London 6K 11 (2F 101)
Greenpark Ct. HA0: Wemb 7C 60
Green Pk. Way UB6: G'frd 7J 59
Green Pl. SE10 . . . . .2G 105
Green Point E15 . . . . .6G 69
Green Pond Cl. E17 . . . . .3B 50
Green Pond Rd. E17 . . . . .3A 50
Green Rd. N14 . . . . .6A 22
N20 . . . . .3F 31
Green Rd. Nth. EN3: Pond E 4F 25
Greenrod Pl. TW8: Bford 5E 96
(off Clayponds La.)
Greenroof Way SE10 . . . . .3H 105
Green's Ct. W1 . . . . .2C 12
W11 . . . . .1H 99
(off Lansdowne M.)
Green's End SE18 . . . . .4F 107
Greenshank Cl. E17 . . . . .7F 35
Greenshank Ho. NW9 . . . . .6B 44
Greenshields Ind. Est. E16 . . . . . . .2J 105
Greenside DA5: Bexl 1E 144
RM8: Dag 1C 72
Greenside Cl. N20 . . . . .2G 31
SE6 .2F 141
Greenside Rd. CR0: C'don 7A 156
W12 . . . . .3C 98
Greenslade Rd. IG11: Bark 7H 71
Greenstead Av. IG8: Wfd G 7F 37
Greenstead Cl. IG8: Wfd G 6F 37
Greenstead Gdns. IG8: Wfd G 6F 37
SW15 . . . . .5D 116
Greensted Rd. IG10: Lough 1H 37
Greenstone M. E11 . . . . .6J 51
Green St. E7 . . . . .6K 69
E13 . . . . .6K 69
EN3: Brim, Enf H 2D 24
TW16: Sun 1J 147
W1 . . . . .2G 11 (7E 82)
GREEN STREET GREEN 5K 173
Greenstreet Hill SE14 . . . . .2K 121
Green Ter. EC1 . . . . .2K 7 (3A 84)
Green Vale DA6: Bex 5D 126
W5 . . . . .6F 79
Greenvale Rd. SE9 . . . . .4D 124
Green Verges HA7: Stan 7J 27
Green Vw. KT9: Chess 7F 163
Greenview Av. BR3: Beck 6A 158
CR0: C'don 6A 158
Greenview Cl. W3 . . . . .1A 98
Greenview Ct. TW15: Ashf 4B 128
Greenview Dr. SW20 . . . . .3E 152
Green Wlk.
HA4: Ruis 1H 57
IG8: Wfd G 6H 37
IG10: Lough 1H 37
NW4 .5F 45
SE1 .3E 102
TW12: Hamp 6D 130
UB2: S'hall 5E 94
Green Walk, The E4 . . . . .1A 36
Green Way BR2: Brom 6C 160
SE9 .5B 124
TW16: Sun 4J 147
Greenway BR7: Chst 5E 142
E6 . . . . .4E 88
E15 . . . . .2F 87
E20 . . . . .1D 86
HA3: Kenton 5E 42
HA5: Pinn 2K 39
IG8: Wfd G 5F 37
N14 . . . . .2D 32
N20 . . . . .2D 30
RM8: Dag 2C 72
SM6: Wall 4G 167
SW20 . . . . .4E 152
UB4: Yead 3J 75
Greenway, The HA3: W'stone 1J 41
HA5: Pinn 6D 40
NW9 .2K 43
TW4: Houn 4D 112

Greenway, The UB8: Uxb 2A 74
UB10: Ick 2D 56
Greenway Av. E17 . . . . .4F 51
Greenway Cl. N4 . . . . .2C 66
N11 . . . . .6K 31
N15 . . . . .4F 49
N20 . . . . .2D 30
NW9 .2K 43
Greenway Ct. IG1: Ilf 1E 70
Greenway Gdns. CR0: C'don 3B 170
HA3: W'stone 2J 41
NW9 .2K 43
UB6: G'frd 3E 76
Greenways BR3: Beck 3C 158
Greenways, The TW1: Twick 6A 114
Greenways Dr. TW4: Houn 4C 112
Greenwell St. W1 . . . . . . .4K 5 (4F 83)
GREENWICH 7E 104
Greenwich Bus. Pk. SE10 . . . . .7D 104
Greenwich Chu. St. SE10 . . . . .6E 104
Greenwich Ct. E1 . . . . .6H 85
(off Cavell St.)
Greenwich Cres. E6 . . . . .5C 88
Greenwich Foot Tunnel SE10 . . . . . . .5E 104
Greenwich Hgts. SE18 . . . . .7C 106
Greenwich Heritage Cen. 3F 107
Greenwich High Rd. SE10 . . . . .1D 122
Greenwich Ho. SE13 . . . . .6F 123
Greenwich Mkt. SE10 . . . . .6E 104

GREENWICH MILLENNIUM VILLAGE

. . . . .3H 105
Greenwich Park 7F 105
Greenwich Pk. St. SE10 . . . . .6F 105
Greenwich Peninsula Ecology Pk. . . .3J 105
Greenwich Picturehouse 7E 104
Greenwich Quay SE8 . . . . .6D 104
Greenwich Shop. Pk. SE7 . . . . .4K 105
Greenwich Sth. St. SE10 . . . . .1D 122
Greenwich Theatre 7E 104
Greenwich Vw. Pl. E14 . . . . .3D 104
Greenwich Yacht Club 3J 105
Greenwood NW5 . . . . .5G 65
(off Osney Cres.)
Greenwood Av. EN3: Enf H 2F 25
RM10: Dag 4H 73
Greenwood Bus. Cen. CR0: C'don . . .7F 157
Greenwood Cl. BR5: Pet W 6J 161
DA15: Sidc 2A 144
KT7: T Ditt 4J 151
SM4: Mord 4G 153
UB3: Hayes 1J 93
WD23: B Hea 1D 26
Greenwood Dr. E4 . . . . .5A 36
Greenwood Gdns. IG6: Ilf 1G 53
N13 . . . . .3G 33
Greenwood Ho. EC1 . . . . .2J 7
(off Rosebery Av.)
N22 . . . . .1K 47
SE4 .4K 121
Greenwood La. TW12: Hamp H 5F 131
Greenwood Mans. IG11: Bark 7A 72
(off Lansbury Av.)
Greenwood Pk. KT2: King T 7A 134
Greenwood Pl. NW5 . . . . .5F 65
Greenwood Rd. CR0: C'don 7B 156
CR4: Mitc 3H 155
DA5: Bexl 4K 145
E8 . . . . .6G 67
E13 . . . . .2H 87
KT7: T Ditt 1A 162
TW7: Isle 3K 113
Greenwoods, The HA2: Harr 3G 59
Greenwood Ter. NW10 . . . . .1K 79
Greenwood Theatre 2D 102
Green Wrythe Cres. SM5: Cars 1C 166
Green Wrythe La. SM5: Cars 6B 154
Green Yard, The EC3 . . . . .1G 15
Greer Rd. HA3: Hrw W 1G 41
Greet Ho. SE1 . . . . .7K 13
Greet St. SE1 . . . . .5K 13 (1A 102)

Greg Cl. E10 . . . . .6E 50
Gregor M. SE3 . . . . .7J 105
Gregory Cl. BR2: Brom 4G 159
Gregory Cres. SE9 . . . . .7B 124
Gregory Pl. W8 . . . . .2K 99
Gregory Rd. RM6: Chad H 4D 54
UB2: S'hall 3E 94
Greig Cl. N8 . . . . .5J 47
Greig Ter. SE17 . . . . .6B 102
Grenaby Av. CR0: C'don 7D 156
Grenaby Rd. CR0: C'don 7D 156
Grenada Ho. E14 . . . . .7B 86
(off Limehouse C'way.)
Grenada Rd. SE7 . . . . .7A 106
Grenade St. E14 . . . . .7B 86
Grenadier St. E16 . . . . .1E 106
Grena Gdns. TW9: Rich 4F 115
Grenard Cl. SE15 . . . . .7G 103
Grena Rd. TW9: Rich 4F 115
Grendon Gdns. HA9: Wemb 2G 61
Grendon Ho. E9 . . . . .7J 67
(off Shore Pl.)
N1 . . . . .2K 83
(off Calshot St.)
Grendon Lodge HA8: Edg 2D 28
Grendon St. NW8 . . . . .3C 4 (4C 82)
Grenfell Cl. NW7 . . . . .6J 29
Grenfell Gdns. HA3: Kenton 7E 42
IG3: Ilf 5K 53
Grenfell Ho. SE5 . . . . .7C 102
Grenfell Rd. CR4: Mitc 6D 136
W11 . . . . .7F 81
Grenfell Twr. W11 . . . . .7F 81
Grenfell Wlk. W11 . . . . .7F 81
Grenier Apartments SE15 . . . . .7H 103
Grenoch Cl. SM1: Sutt 2B 166
Grennell Rd. SM1: Sutt 2A 166
Grenoble Gdns. N13 . . . . .6F 33
Grenville Cl. KT5: Surb 1J 163
N3 . . . . .1G 45
Grenville Ct. W13 . . . . .5B 78
Grenville Gdns. IG8: Wfd G 1A 52
Grenville Ho. E3 . . . . .2A 86
(off Arbery Rd.)
SE8 . . . . .6C 104
(off New King St.)
SW1 . . . . .5B 18
(off Dolphin Sq.)
Grenville M. N19 . . . . .1J 65
SW7 .4A 100
TW12: Hamp H 5F 131
Grenville Pl. NW7 . . . . .5G 29
SW7 .3A 100
Grenville Rd. N19 . . . . .1J 65
Grenville St. WC1 . . . . .4F 7 (4J 83)
Gresham Av. N20 . . . . .4J 31
Gresham Cl. DA5: Bexl 6E 126
EN2: Enf 3H 23
Gresham Dr. RM6: Chad H 5B 54
Gresham Gdns. NW11 . . . . .1G 63
Gresham La. N19 . . . . .2H 65
Gresham Lodge E17 . . . . .5D 50
Gresham Pl. N19 . . . . .2H 65
Gresham Rd. BR3: Beck 2A 158
E6 . . . . .2D 88
E16 . . . . .6K 87
HA8: Edg 6A 28
NW10 .5K 61
SE25 .4G 157
SW9 .3A 120
TW3: Houn 1G 113
TW12: Hamp 6E 130
UB10: Hil 2C 74
Gresham St. EC2 . . . . .7C 8 (6C 84)
Gresham Way SW19 . . . . .3K 135
Gresham Way Ind. Est. SW19 . . . . . .3K 135
(off Gresham Way)
Gresley Cl. E17 . . . . .6A 50
N15 . . . . .4D 48
Gresley Ho. SW1 . . . . .5A 18
Gresley Rd. N19 . . . . .1G 65
Gressenhall Rd. SW18 . . . . .6H 117
Gresse St. W1 . . . . .6C 6 (6H 83)

Gresswell Cl. DA14: Sidc 3A 144
Greswell St. SW6 . . . . .1F 117
Gretton Ho. E2 . . . . .3J 85
(off Globe Rd.)
Gretton Rd. N17 . . . . .7A 34
Greville Cl. TW1: Twick 7B 114
Greville Ct. E5 . . . . .3H 67
(off Napoleon Rd.)
HA1: Harr 4J 59
Greville Hall NW6 . . . . .2K 81
Greville Ho. SW1 . . . . .1G 17
(off Kinnerton St.)
Greville Lodge E13 . . . . .1K 87
HA8: Edg 4C 28
(off Broadhurst Av.)
N12 . . . . .5E 30
Greville M. NW6 . . . . .1K 81
(off Greville Rd.)
Greville Pl. NW6 . . . . .2K 81
Greville Rd. E17 . . . . .4E 50
NW6 .2K 81
TW10: Rich 6F 115
Greville St. EC1 . . . . .6J 7 (5A 84)
(not continuous)
Grey Cl. NW11 . . . . .6A 46
Greycoat Gdns. SW1 . . . . .2C 18
(off Greycoat St.)
Greycoat Pl. SW1 . . . . .2C 18 (3H 101)
Greycoat St. SW1 . . . . .2C 18 (3H 101)
Greycot Rd. BR3: Beck 5C 140
Grey Eagle St. E1 . . . . .4K 9 (4F 85)
Greyfell Cl. HA7: Stan 5G 27
Greyfriars SE26 . . . . .3G 139
(off Wells Pk. Rd.)
Greyfriars Pas. EC1 . . . . . .7B 8 (6A 84)
Greyhound Ct. WC2 . . . . . .2H 13 (7K 83)
Greyhound Hill NW4 . . . . .3C 44
Greyhound La. SW16 . . . . .6H 137
Greyhound Mans. W6 . . . . .6G 99
(off Greyhound Rd.)
Greyhound Rd. N17 . . . . .3E 48
NW10 .3D 80
SM1: Sutt 5A 166
W6 . . . . .6F 99
W14 . . . . .6F 99
Greyhound Ter. SW16 . . . . .1G 155
Grey Ho. W12 . . . . .7D 80
(off White City Est.)
Greyladies Gdns. SE10 . . . . .2E 122
Greys Pk. Cl. BR2: Kes 5B 172
Greystead Rd. SE23 . . . . .7J 121
Greystoke Av. HA5: Pinn 3E 40
Greystoke Ct. W5 . . . . .4E 78
Greystoke Dr. HA4: Ruis 6D 38
Greystoke Gdns. EN2: Enf 4C 22
W5 . . . . .4E 78
Greystoke Ho. SE15 . . . . .6G 103
(off Peckham Pk. Rd.)
W5 . . . . .4E 78
Greystoke Lodge W5 . . . . .4F 79
(off Hanger La.)
Greystoke Pk. Ter. W5 . . . . .3D 78
Greystoke Pl. EC4 . . . . .7J 7 (6A 84)
Greystone Gdns. HA3: Kenton 6C 42
IG6: Ilf 2G 53
Greyswood Av. N18 . . . . .6E 34
Greyswood St. SW16 . . . . .6F 137
Grey Turner Ho. W12 . . . . .6C 80
Grierson Ho. SW16 . . . . .4G 137
Grierson Rd. SE23 . . . . .7K 121
Griffin Cl. BR3: Beck 1D 158
NW10 .5K 111
Griffin Cen. TW14: Felt 5K 111
Griffin Centre, The KT1: King T 2D 150
(off Market Rd.)
Griffin Cl. NW10 . . . . .5D 62
Griffin Ct. TW8: Bford 6E 96
W4 . . . . .5B 98
Griffin Ho.
CR0: C'don 7B 156
E14 . . . . .6D 86
(off Ricardo St.)

Griffin Ho. sN1 . . . . .1E 84
   (off Halcomb St.)
W6 . . . . .4F 99
   (off Hammersmith Rd.)
Griffin Mnr. Way SE28 . . . . .3H 107
Griffin M. SW12 . . . . .1G 137
Griffin Park 6D 96
Griffin Rd. N17 . . . . .2E 48
SE18 . . . . .5H 107
Griffins Cl. N21 . . . . .7J 23
Griffin Way TW16: Sun 2J 147
Griffith Cl. E17 .1F 51
RM8: Dag 7C 54
Griffiths Cl. KT4: Wor Pk 2D 164
Griffiths Rd. SW19 . . . . .7J 135
Griggs App. IG1: Ilf 2G 71
Griggs Cl. IG3: Ilf 4J 71
Grilse Cl. N9 . . . . .4C 34
Grimaldi Ho. N1 . . . . .2K 83
   (off Calshot St.)
Grimsby Gro. E16 . . . . .2F 107
Grimsby St. E2 . . . . .4K 9 (4F 85)
Grim's Dyke Golf Course 5A 26
Grimsdyke Rd. HA5: Hat E 1D 40
Grimsel Path SE5 . . . . .7B 102
Grimshaw Cl. N6 . . . . .7E 46
Grimston Rd. SW6 . . . . .2H 117
Grimthorpe Ho. EC1 . . . . .3A 8
Grimwade Av. CR0: C'don 3G 169
Grimwade Cl. SE15 . . . . .3J 121
Grimwood Rd. TW1: Twick 7K 113
Grindall Cl. CR0: Wadd 4B 168
Grindall Ho. E1 . . . . .4H 85
   (off Darling Row)
Grindal St. SE1 . . . . .7J 13 (2A 102)
Grindleford Av. N11 . . . . .2K 31
Grindley Gdns. CR0: C'don 6F 157
Grindley Ho. E3 . . . . .5B 86
   (off Leopold St.)
Grinling Pl. SE8 . . . . .6C 104
Grinstead Rd. SE8 . . . . .5A 104
Grisedale NW1 .1A 6
   (off Cumberland Mkt.)
Grittleton Av. HA9: Wemb 6H 61
Grittleton Rd. W9 . . . . .4J 81
Grizedale Ter. SE23 . . . . .2H 139
Grocer's Hall Ct. EC2 . . . . . .1E 14 (6D 84)
Grocer's Hall Gdns. EC2 . . . . .1E 14
Grogan Cl. TW12: Hamp 6D 130
Groombridge Cl. DA16: Well 5B 126
Groombridge Ho. SE17 . . . . .5E 102
   (off Upnor Way)
Groombridge Rd. E9 . . . . .7K 67
Groom Cl. BR2: Brom 4K 159
Groom Cres. SW18 . . . . .7B 118
Groome Ho. SE11 . . . . .4H 19 (4K 101)
Groomfield Cl. SW17 . . . . .4E 136
Groom Pl. SW1 . . . . .1H 17 (3E 100)
Grooms Dr. HA5: Eastc 5J 39
Groomsend Rd. SE18 . . . . .5K 107
Grosse Way SW15 . . . . .6D 116
Grosvenor Av. HA2: Harr 6F 41
N5 . . . . .5C 66
SM5: Cars 5D 166
SW14 . . . . .3A 116
TW10: Rich 5E 114
UB4: Hayes 2H 75
Grosvenor Cotts. SW1 . . . . . .3G 17 (4E 100)
Grosvenor Ct. E10 . . . . .1D 68
E14 . . . . .6B 86
   (off Wharf La.)
N14 . . . . .7B 22
NW6 . . . . .1F 81
NW7 . . . . .5E 28
   (off Hale La.)
SE5 . . . . .6C 102
SM2: Sutt .6K 165

Grosvenor Ct. SM4: Mord 4J 153
TW11: Tedd 6A 132
W3 . . . . .1G 97
W5 . . . . .7E 78
   (off The Grove)
W14 . . . . .3F 99
   (off Irving Rd.)
Grosvenor Ct. Mans. W2 . . . . .1E 10
   (off Edgware Rd.)
Grosvenor Cres. NW9 . . . . .4G 43
SW1 . . . . .7H 11 (2E 100)
UB10: Ick 7D 56
Grosvenor Cres. M. SW1 . . . .7G 11 (2E 100)
Grosvenor Est. SW1 . . . . . . .3D 18 (4H 101)
Grosvenor Gdns. E6 . . . . .3B 88
IG8: Wfd G .6D 36
KT2: King T 6D 132
N10 . . . . .3G 47
N14 . . . . .4C 22
NW2 . . . . .6E 62
NW11 . . . . .6H 45
SM6: Wall .7G 167
SW1 . . . . .1J 17 (3F 101)
SW14 . . . . .3A 116
Grosvenor Gdns. M. E. SW1 . . . . .1K 17
Grosvenor Gdns. M. Nth. SW1 . . . . . . .2J 17
Grosvenor Gdns. M. Sth. SW1 . . . . . . .2K 17
Grosvenor Ga. W1 . . . . .3G 11 (7E 82)
Grosvenor Hill SW19 . . . . .6G 135
W1 . . . . .2J 11 (7F 83)
Grosvenor Hill Ct. W1 . . . . .2J 11
   (off Bourdon St.)
Grosvenor Ho. SM1: Sutt 5K 165
   (off West St.)
Grosvenor Pde. W5 . . . . .1G 97
   (off Uxbridge Rd.)
Grosvenor Pk. SE5 . . . . .7C 102
Grosvenor Pk. Rd. E17 . . . . .5C 50
Grosvenor Pl. SW1 . . . . .7H 11 (2E 100)
Grosvenor Ri. E. E17 . . . . .5D 50
Grosvenor Rd.
BR4: W W'ck 1D 170
BR5: St M Cry 6J 161
DA6: Bex 5D 126
DA17: Belv 6G 109
E6 . . . . .1B 88
E7 . . . . .6K 69
E10 . . . . .1E 68
E11 . . . . .5K 51
IG1: Ilf 3G 71
N3 . . . . .7C 30
N9 . . . . .1C 34
N10 . . . . .1F 47
RM7: Rush G 7K 55
RM8: Dag 1F 73
SE25 . . . . .4F 157
SM6: Wall .6F 167
SW1 . . . . .7J 17 (6F 101)
TW1: Twick 1A 132
TW3: Houn 3D 112
TW8: Bford .6D 96
TW10: Rich 5E 114
UB2: S'hall .3D 94
W4 . . . . .5H 97
W7 . . . . .1A 96
Grosvenor Sq. W1 . . . . .2H 11 (7E 82)
Grosvenor St. W1 . . . . .2J 11 (7F 83)
Grosvenor Studios SW1 . . . . .3G 17
   (off Eaton Ter.)
Grosvenor Ter. SE5 . . . . .7C 102
Grosvenor Va. HA4: Ruis 2H 57
Grosvenor Way E5 . . . . .2J 67
SW17 . . . . .3B 136
Grosvenor Wharf Rd. E14 . . . . .4F 105
Grotes Bldgs. SE3 . . . . .2G 123
Grote's Pl. SE3 . . . . .2G 123
Groton Rd. SW18 . . . . .2K 135
Grotto Ct. SE1 . . . . .6B 14 (2B 102)
Grotto Pas. W1 . . . . .5H 5 (5E 82)
Grotto Rd. TW1: Twick 2K 131
GROVE, THE .1G 139

Grove, The
BR4: W W'ck 3D 170
DA6: Bex 4D 126
DA14: Sidc 5E 144
E15 . . . . .6G 69
EN2: Enf 2F 23
HA1: Harr 7J 41
HA7: Stan 2F 27
HA8: Edg 4C 28
KT12: Walt T 7K 147
N3 . . . . .1J 45
N4 . . . . .7K 47
N6 . . . . .1E 64
N8 . . . . .5H 47
N13 . . . . .4F 33
   (not continuous)
N14 . . . . .5B 22
NW9 . . . . .5K 43
NW11 . . . . .7G 45
TW1: Twick 6B 114
TW7: Isle 1J 113
TW11: Tedd 4A 132
UB6: G'frd 6G 77
UB10: Ick 5C 56
W5 . . . . .1D 96
Grove Av. HA5: Pinn 4C 40
N3 . . . . .7D 30
N10 . . . . .2G 47
SM1: Sutt .6J 165
TW1: Twick 1K 131
W7 . . . . .7J 77
Grovebury Cl. DA8: Erith 6K 109
Grovebury Ct. DA6: Bex 5H 127
N14 . . . . .7C 22
Grovebury Rd. SE2 . . . . .2B 108
Grove Cl. BR2: Hayes 2J 171
KT1: King T 4F 151
N14 . . . . .7B 22
SE23 . . . . .1A 140
TW13: Hanw 4C 130
UB10: Ick 5C 56
Grove Cotts. SW3 . . . . .7D 16
W4 . . . . .6A 98
Grove Ct. EN5: Barn 3C 20
   (off Hadley Ridge)
KT1: King T 3E 150
   (off Grove Cres.)
KT8: E Mos 5H 149
NW8 . . . . .1A 4
SE15 . . . . .7E 102
   (off Peckham Rd.)
SW10 . . . . .6A 16
   (off Drayton Gdns.)
TW3: Houn 4E 112
W5 . . . . .1E 96
Grove Cres. E18 . . . . .2H 51
KT1: King T 3E 150
KT12: Walt T 7K 147
NW9 . . . . .4J 43
TW13: Hanw 4C 130
Grove Cres. Rd. E15 . . . . .6F 69
Grovedale Rd. N19 . . . . .2H 65
Grove Dwellings E1 . . . . .5J 85
Grove End E18 . . . . .2H 51
NW5 . . . . .4F 65
Grove End Gdns. NW8 . . . . .2B 82
Grove End Ho. NW8 . . . . .2A 4
Grove End La. KT10: Esh 7H 149
Grove End Rd. NW8 . . . . .1A 4 (2B 82)
Grove Farm Retail Pk.
RM6: Chad H 7C 54
Grovefield N11 . . . . .4A 32
   (off Coppies Gro.)
Grove Footpath KT5: Surb 4E 150
Grove Gdns. EN3: Enf W 1E 24
NW4 . . . . .5C 44
NW8 . . . . .2D 4 (3C 82)
RM10: Dag .3J 73
TW10: Rich 6F 115
TW11: Tedd 4A 132
Grove Grn. Rd. E11 . . . . .3E 68

Grove Hall Ct. E3 . . . . .2C 86
   (off Jebb St.)
NW8 . . . . .1A 4 (3A 82)
Grove Hill E18 .2H 51
HA1: Harr 7J 41
Grovehill Ct. BR1: Brom 6H 141
Grove Hill Rd. HA1: Harr 7K 41
SE5 . . . . .3E 120
Grove Ho. N3 . . . . .3F 45
SW3 . . . . .7D 16
   (off Chelsea Mnr. St.)
Grove Ho. Rd. N8 . . . . .4J 47
Groveland Av. SW16 . . . . .7K 137
Groveland Ct. EC4 . . . . .1D 14
Groveland Rd. BR3: Beck 3B 158
Grovelands KT1: King T 4D 150
   (off Palace Rd.)
KT8: W Mole 4E 148
Grovelands Cl. HA2: Harr 3F 59
SE5 . . . . .2E 120
Grovelands Ct. N14 . . . . .7C 22
Grovelands Rd. BR5: St P 7A 144
N13 . . . . .4E 32
N15 . . . . .6G 49
Groveland Way KT3: N Mald 5J 151
Grove La. KT1: King T 4E 150
SE5 . . . . .1D 120
UB8: Hil 5B 74
Grove La. Ter. SE5 . . . . .2D 120
Groveley Rd. TW13: Felt 5G 129
TW16: Sun 5G 129
Grove Mans. W6 . . . . .2E 98
   (off Hammersmith Gro.)
Grove Mkt. Pl. SE9 . . . . .6D 124
Grove M. W6 . . . . .3E 98
Grove Mill Pl. SM5: Cars 3E 166
Grove Nature Reserve, The 4B 74
GROVE PARK .3K 141
   . . . . .1J 115
Grove Pk. E11 .6K 51
NW9 . . . . .4J 43
SE5 . . . . .2E 120
Grove Pk. Av. E4 . . . . .7J 35
Grove Pk. Bri. W4 . . . . .7J 97
Grove Pk. Gdns. W4 . . . . .7J 97
Grove Pk. Ind. Est. NW9 . . . . .3K 43
Grove Pk. M. W4 . . . . .7J 97
Grove Pk. Rd. N15 . . . . .4E 48
SE9 . . . . .3A 142
W4 . . . . .7H 97
Grove Pk. Ter. W4 . . . . .7H 97
Grove Pas. E2 .2H 85
Grove Pl. IG11: Bark 7G 71
NW3 . . . . .3B 64
SW12 . . . . .7F 119
W3 . . . . .1J 97
Grover Ct. SE13 . . . . .2D 122
Grover Ho. SE11 . . . . .6H 19 (5K 101)
Grove Ho. CR4: Mitc 3E 154
   (not continuous)
CR7: Thor H 4A 156
DA7: Bex 4J 127
DA17: Belv .6F 109
E3 . . . . .1K 85
E4 . . . . .4K 35
E11 . . . . .7H 51
E17 . . . . .6D 50
E18 . . . . .2H 51
EN4: Cockf .3H 21
HA5: Pinn 5D 40
HA8: Edg 6B 28
KT6: Surb .5D 150
KT8: E Mos 4H 149
N11 . . . . .5A 32
N12 . . . . .5G 31
N15 . . . . .5E 48
NW2 . . . . .6E 62
RM6: Chad H 7B 54
SM1: Sutt .6J 165
SW13 . . . . .2B 116

Grove Rd. SW19 . . . . .7A **136**
TW2: Twick 3H **131**
TW3: Houn 4E **112**
TW7: Isle 1J **113**
TW8: Bford 5C **96**
TW10: Rich 6F **115**
TW17: Shep 6E **146**
UB8: Uxb 7A **56**
W3 .1J **97**
W5 .7D **78**
Groveside Cl. SM5: Cars 2C **166**
W3 .5G **79**
Groveside Ct. SW11 . . . . .2B **118**
Groveside Rd. E4 . . . . .2B **36**
Grovestile Waye TW14: Bedf . . .7F **111**
Grove St. N18 . . . . .5A **34**
SE8 .4B **104**
Grove Ter. NW5 . . . . .3F **65**
TW11: Tedd 4A **132**
UB1: S'hall 7E **76**
Grove Ter. M. NW5 . . . . .3F **65**
Grove Va. BR7: Chst 6E **142**
SE22 . . . . .4F **121**
Grove Vs. E14 . . . . .7D **86**
Grove Way HA9: Wemb 5H **61**
KT10: Esh 7G **149**
UB8: Uxb 7A **56**
Groveway RM8: Dag 3D **72**
SW9 . . . . .1K **119**
Grovewood TW9: Kew 1G **115**
Grove Wood Cl. BR1: Brom 3E **160**
Grovewood Pl. IG8: Wfd G 6J **37**
Grummant Rd. SE15 . . . . .1F **121**
Grundy St. E14 . . . . .6D **86**
Gruneisen Rd. N3 . . . . .7E **30**
Grunwick Cl. NW2 . . . . .5C **62**
Gtec Ho. E15 . . . . .2F **87**
(off Canning Rd.)
Guardian Ct. SE12 . . . . .5G **123**
Guards Memorial 5D 12 (1H **101**)
Guards' Museum, The 7B 12 (2G **101**)
Gubyon Av. SE24 . . . . .5B **120**
Guerin Sq. E3 . . . . .3B **86**
Guernsey Cl. TW5: Hest 7E **94**
Guernsey Gro. SE24 . . . . .7C **120**
Guernsey Ho. EN3: Enf W 1E **24**
(off Eastfield Rd.)
N1 . . . . .6C **66**
(off Channel Island Est.)
Guernsey Rd. E11 . . . . .1F **69**
Guibal Rd. SE12 . . . . .7K **123**
Guildable Mnr. Wlk. SE1 . . . . . . .4F **15**
(off London Bri. St.)
Guildersfield Rd. SW16 . . . . . . .7J **137**
Guildford Av. TW13: Felt 2H **129**
Guildford Ct. SW8 . . . . .7J **101**
(off Guildford Rd.)
Guildford Gro. SE10 . . . . .1D **122**
Guildford Rd.
CR0: C'don 6D **156**
E6 . . . . .6D **88**
E17 .1E **50**
IG3: Ilf 2J **71**
SW8 . . . . .1J **119**
Guildford Way SM6: Wall 5J **167**
Guildhall
City 7E **8**
Guildhall Art Gallery 7E **8**
(off Aldermanbury)
Guildhall Bldgs. EC2 . . . . .7E **8**
Guildhall Library 7D **8**
Guildhall Offices EC2 . . . . .7D **8**
Guildhall Yd. EC2 . . . . . . .7D 8 (6C **84**)
Guildhouse St. SW1 . . . . .3A 18 (4G **101**)
Guildown Av. N12 . . . . .4E **30**
Guild Rd. SE7 . . . . .6B **106**
Guildsway E17 . . . . .1B **50**
Guilford Av. KT5: Surb 5F **151**
Guilford Pl. WC1 . . . . . . .4G 7 (4K **83**)
Guilford St. WC1 . . . . . . .4E 6 (4J **83**)
Guilfoyle NW9 . . . . .2B **44**

Guillemot Ct. SE8 . . . . .6B **104**
(off Alexandra Cl.)
Guillemot Pl. N22 . . . . .2K **47**
Guinea Ct. E1 . . . . .7G **85**
(off Royal Mint St.)
Guinea Point E14 . . . . .6A **86**
(off Repton St.)
Guinness Cl. E9 . . . . .7A **68**
UB3: Harl 3F **93**
Guinness Ct. CR0: C'don 2F **169**
E1 . . . . .1J **15**
EC1 .2D **8**
SE1 .6G **15**
SW3 . . . . .4E 16 (4D **100**)
Guinness Sq. SE1 . . . . .4E **102**
Guinness Trust SW3 . . . . .4E **16**
(off Cadogan St.)
Guinness Trust Bldgs. SE11 . . . .5B **102**
W6 . . . . .5F **99**
(off Fulham Pal. Rd.)
Guinness Trust Estate, The N16 . . .1E **66**
Guion Rd. SW6 . . . . .2H **117**
Gulland Wlk. N1 . . . . .6C **66**
(off Church Rd.)
Gullane Ho. E3 . . . . .2B **86**
(off Shetland Rd.)
Gulliver Cl. UB5: N'olt 1D **76**
Gulliver Rd. DA15: Sidc 2H **143**
Gulliver's Ho. EC1 . . . . .4C **8**
Gulliver St. SE16 . . . . .3A **104**
Gulston Wlk. SW3 . . . . .4F **17**
Gumleigh Rd. W5 . . . . .4C **96**
Gumley Gdns. TW7: Isle 3A **114**
Gumping Rd. BR5: Farnb 2G **173**
Gundulph Rd. BR2: Brom 3A **160**
Gun Ho. E1 . . . . .1H **103**
(off Wapping High St.)
Gunmakers La. E3 . . . . .1A **86**
Gunnell Cl. CR0: C'don 6G **157**
SE25 . . . . .6G **157**
(off Beckley Gdns.)
SE26 . . . . .4G **139**
Gunner La. SE18 . . . . .5E **106**
GUNNERSBURY 5H **97**
Gunnersbury Av.
W3 . . . . .1F **97**
W4 . . . . .1F **97**
W5 . . . . .1F **97**
Gunnersbury Cl. W4 . . . . .5H **97**
Gunnersbury Ct. W3 . . . . .2H **97**
Gunnersbury Cres. W3 . . . . .2G **97**
Gunnersbury Dr. W5 . . . . .2F **97**
Gunnersbury Gdns. W3 . . . . .2G **97**
Gunnersbury La. W3 . . . . .3G **97**
Gunnersbury Mnr. W5 . . . . .1F **97**
Gunnersbury M. W4 . . . . .5H **97**
GUNNERSBURY PARK 3G **97**
Gunnersbury Park Mus. 3G **97**
Gunnersbury Triangle Nature Reserve
. . . . .4J **97**
Gunners Gro. E4 . . . . .3K **35**
Gunners Rd. SW18 . . . . .2B **136**
Gunnery Ter. SE18 . . . . .3G **107**
Gunning St. SE18 . . . . .4J **107**
Gunpowder Sq. EC4 . . . . .7K **7**
(off E. Harding St., not continuous)
Gunstor Rd. N16 . . . . .4E **66**
Gun St. E1 . . . . .6J 9 (5F **85**)
Gunter Gro. HA8: Edg 1K **43**
SW10 . . . . .6A **100**
Gunter Hall Studios SW10 . . . . . .6A **100**
(off Gunter Gro.)
Gunterstone Rd. W14 . . . . .4G **99**
Gunthorpe St. E1 . . . . . . .6K 9 (5F **85**)
Gunton Rd. SE13 . . . . .5F **123**
Gunton Rd. E5 . . . . .3H **67**
SW17 . . . . .6E **136**
Gunwhale Cl. SE16 . . . . .1K **103**
Gun Wharf E1 . . . . .1J **103**
(off Wapping High St.)
Gunyard M. SE18 . . . . .7C **106**

Gurdon Ho. E14 . . . . .6C **86**
(off Dod St.)
Gurdon Rd. SE7 . . . . .5J **105**
Gurnard Cl. UB7: Yiew 7A **74**
Gurnell Gro. W13 . . . . .4K **77**
Gurnell Leisure Cen. 3K **77**
Gurney Cl. E15 . . . . .5G **69**
E17 .1K **49**
IG11: Bark 6F **71**
Gurney Cres. CR0: C'don 1K **167**
Gurney Dr. N2 . . . . .4A **46**
Gurney Ho. E2 . . . . .2G **85**
(off Goldsmiths Row)
UB3: Harl 5G **93**
Gurney Rd. E15 . . . . .5G **69**
SM5: Cars 4E **166**
SW6 . . . . .3A **118**
UB5: N'olt 3K **75**
Gutenberg Ct. SE1 . . . . .3F **103**
(off Grange Rd.)
Guthrie Cl. SE1 . . . . .7K **13**
Guthrie St. SW3 . . . . . . .5C 16 (5B **100**)
Gutter La. EC2 . . . . .7C 8 (6C **84**)
Guyatt Gdns. CR4: Mitc 2E **154**
Guy Barnett Gro. SE3 . . . . .3J **123**
Guy Rd. SM6: Bedd 3H **167**
Guyscliff Rd. SE13 . . . . .5E **122**
Guy St. SE1 . . . . .6F 15 (2D **102**)
Gwalior Ho. N14 . . . . .6B **22**
Gwalior Rd. SW15 . . . . .4F **117**
Gwendolen Av. SW15 . . . . .4F **117**
Gwendolen Cl. SW15 . . . . .5F **117**
Gwendolen Ho. TW19: Stanw . . .1A **128**
(off Yeoman Dr.)
Gwendoline Av. E13 . . . . .1K **87**
Gwendwr Rd. W14 . . . . .5G **99**
Gweneth Cotts. HA8: Edg 6B **28**
Gwen Morris Ho. SE5 . . . . .7C **102**
Gwent Cl. SE16 . . . . .1K **103**
(off Rotherhithe St.)
Gwillim Cl. DA15: Sidc 5A **126**
Gwilym Maries Ho. E2 . . . . .3H **85**
(off Blythe St.)
Gwydor Rd. BR3: Beck 3K **157**
Gwydyr Rd. BR2: Brom 3H **159**
Gwyn Cl. SW6 . . . . .7A **100**
Gwynne Av. CR0: C'don 7K **157**
Gwynne Cl. W4 . . . . .6B **98**
Gwynne Ho. E1 . . . . .5H **85**
(off Turner St.)
SW1 . . . . .5G **17**
(off Lwr. Sloane St.)
WC1 . . . . .2J **7**
(off Lloyd Baker St.)
Gwynne Pk. Av. IG8: Wfd G 6J **37**
Gwynne Pl. WC1 . . . . .2H 7 (3K **83**)
Gwynne Rd. SW11 . . . . .2B **118**
Gylcote Cl. SE5 . . . . .4D **120**
Gyles Pk. HA7: Stan 1C **42**
Gyllyngdune Gdns. IG3: Ilf 2K **71**
Gym, The
Hounslow 3F **113**
Gymnasium, The N1 . . . . .2J **83**
GYPSY CORNER 5K **79**

H

Haarlem Rd. W14 . . . . .3F **99**
Haberdasher Est. N1 . . . . .1F 9 (3D **84**)
Haberdasher Pl. N1 . . . . . .1F 9 (3D **84**)
Haberdashers Ct. SE14 . . . . .3K **121**
Haberdasher St. N1 . . . . . .1F 9 (3D **84**)
Habitat Cl. SE15 . . . . .2H **121**
Habitat Sq. SE10 . . . . .3H **105**
(off Teal St.)
Haccombe Rd. SW19 . . . . .6A **136**
HACKBRIDGE 1E **166**
Hackbridge Pk. Gdns. SM5: Cars . .2D **166**
Hackbridge Rd. SM6: Wall 2E **166**

Hackford Rd. SW9 . . . . .1K **119**
Hackford Wlk. SW9 . . . . .1K **119**
Hackington Cres. BR3: Beck 6C **140**
HACKNEY 6H **67**
Hackney City Farm 2G **85**
Hackney Empire Theatre 6H **67**
Hackney Gro. E8 . . . . .6H **67**
Hackney Mus. 6H **67**
Hackney Picturehouse 6H **67**
(off Mare St.)
Hackney Rd. E2 . . . . . . .2J **9** (3F **85**)
HACKNEY WICK 6B **68**
HACKNEY WICK 6A **68**
Hackworth Point E3 . . . . .3D **86**
(off Rainhill Way)
Hacon Sq. E8 . . . . .7H **67**
(off Mare St.)
Hadar Cl. N20 . . . . .1D **30**
Hadden Rd. SE28 . . . . .3J **107**
Hadden Way UB6: G'frd 6H **59**
Haddington Rd. BR1: Brom 3F **141**
Haddo Ho. SE10 . . . . .6D **104**
(off Haddo St.)
Haddon Cl. EN1: Enf 6B **24**
KT3: N Mald 5B **152**
Haddon Ct. NW4 . . . . .3E **44**
W3 . . . . .7B **80**
Haddonfield SE8 . . . . .4K **103**
Haddon Gro. DA15: Sidc 7K **125**
Haddon Hall St. SE1 . . . . .3D **102**
(off Rephidim St.)
Haddon Rd. SM1: Sutt 4K **165**
(not continuous)
Haddo St. SE10 . . . . .6D **104**
Haden Ct. N4 . . . . .2A **66**
Haden La. N11 . . . . .4B **32**
Hadfield Cl. UB1: S'hall 3D **76**
Hadfield Ho. E1 . . . . .6G **85**
(off Ellen St.)
Hadleigh Cl. E1 . . . . .4J **85**
HA2: Harr 4E **58**
SW20 . . . . .2H **153**
Hadleigh Ct. E4 . . . . .1B **36**
NW2 .6E **62**
Hadleigh Ho. E1 . . . . .4J **85**
(off Hadleigh Cl.)
Hadleigh Lodge IG8: Wfd G 6D **36**
(off Snakes La. W.)
Hadleigh Rd. N9 . . . . .7C **24**
Hadleigh St. E2 . . . . .3J **85**
Hadleigh Wlk. E6 . . . . .6C **88**
HADLEY .3C **20**
Hadley Cl. N21 . . . . .6F **23**
Hadley Comn. EN5: Barn, New Bar . .2D **20**
Hadley Ct. EN5: New Bar 3E **20**
N16 .1G **67**
SL3: Poyle 4A **174**
(off Coleridge Cres.)
Hadley Gdns. UB2: S'hall 5D **94**
W4 . . . . .5K **97**
Hadley Grn. EN5: Barn 2C **20**
Hadley Grn. Rd. EN5: Barn 2C **20**
Hadley Grn. W. EN5: Barn 2C **20**
Hadley Gro. EN5: Barn 2B **20**
Hadley Highstone EN5: Barn 1C **20**
Hadley M. EN5: Barn 3C **20**
Hadley Pde. EN5: Barn 3B **20**
(off High St.)
Hadley Ridge EN5: Barn 3C **20**
Hadley Rd. CR4: Mitc 4H **155**
DA17: Belv 4F **109**
EN2: Enf 1A **22**
EN4: Had W 1K **21**
EN5: New Bar 2E **20**
Hadley St. NW1 . . . . .6F **65**
(not continuous)
Hadley Way N21 . . . . .6F **23**
HADLEY WOOD 1F **21**
Hadley Wood Golf Course 1H **21**
Hadley Wood Lawn Tennis Club . . .1F **21**
Hadley Wood Nature Reserve 2F **21**

Hadley Wood Rd.—Hambridge Way

Hadley Wood Rd. EN4: Cockf 2F 21
EN5: Cockf, New Bar 2F 21
Hadlow Ho. *SE17* *5E 102*
(off Kinglake Est.)
Hadlow Pl. SE19 7G 139
Hadlow Rd. DA14: Sidc 4A 144
DA16: Well 7C 108
Hadrian Cl. *E3* *1C 86*
(off Garrison Rd.)
TW19: Stanw 7A 110
Hadrian Ct. SM2: Sutt 7K 165
Hadrian Est. E2 2G 85
Hadrian M. CR4: Mitc 3F 155
N7 7K 65
Hadrians Ride EN1: Enf 5A 24
Hadrian St. SE10 5G 105
Hadrian Way TW19: Stanw 7A 110
(not continuous)
Hadstock Ho. *NW1* *1D 6*
(off Ossulston St.)
Hadyn Pk. Ct. *W12* *2C 98*
(off Curwen Rd.)
Hadyn Pk. Rd. W12 2C 98
Hafer Rd. SW11 4D 118
Hafton Rd. SE6 1G 141
Haggard Rd. TW1: Twick 7B 114
Hagger Ct. E17 3F 51
HAGGERSTON 7F 67
Haggerston Rd. E8 7F 67
Haggerston Studios *E8* *1F 85*
(off Kingsland Rd.)
Hague St. E2 3G 85
Ha Ha Rd. SE18 6D 106
Haig Ho. *E2* *1K 9*
(off Shipton St.)
Haig Pl. SM4: Mord 6J 153
Haig Rd. HA7: Stan 5H 27
UB8: Hil 5D 74
Haig Rd. E. E13 3A 88
Haig Rd. W. E13 3A 88
Haigville Gdns. IG6: Ilf 4F 53
Hailes Cl. CR0: Bedd 2H 167
SW19 6A 136
Haileybury Av. EN1: Enf 6A 24
Hailey Rd. DA18: Erith 2G 109
Hailey Rd. Bus. Pk. DA18: Erith 2G 109
Hailing M. *BR2: Brom* *3K 159*
(off Wendover Rd.)
Hailsham Av. SW2 2K 137
Hailsham Cl. KT6: Surb 7D 150
Hailsham Dr. HA1: Harr 3H 41
Hailsham Ho. *NW8* *4C 4*
(off Salisbury St.)
Hailsham Rd. SW17 6E 136
Hailsham Ter. N18 5J 33
Haimo Rd. SE9 5B 124
Hainault Bri. Pde. *IG1: Ilf* *2F 71*
(off Hainault St.)
Hainault Ct. *E17* *4F 51*
(off Forest Ri.)
Hainault Gore RM6: Chad H 5E 54
Hainault Rd. E11 1E 68
RM5: Col R, Rom 2J 55
RM6: Chad H 1B 54
(Forest Rd.)
RM6: Chad H 6F 55
(Sylvan Av.)
Hainault St. IG1: Ilf 2G 71
SE9 1F 143
Haines Cl. N1 7E 66
Haines St. SW8 7G 101
Haines Wlk. SM4: Mord 7K 153
Hainford Cl. SE4 4K 121
Haining Cl. W4 5G 97
Hainthorpe Rd. SE27 3B 138
Hainton Cl. E1 6H 85
Halberd M. E5 2H 67
Halbutt Gdns. RM9: Dag 3F 73
Halbutt St. RM9: Dag 4F 73
Halcomb St. N1 1E 84
Halcot Av. DA6: Bex 5H 127
Halcrow St. E1 5H 85
Halcyon *EN1: Enf* *5K 23*
(off Private Rd.)
Halcyon Cl. SW13 3C 116
Halcyon Wharf *E1* *1G 103*
(off Hermitage Wall)
Haldane Cl. N10 7A 32
Haldane Pl. SW18 1K 135
Haldane Rd. E6 3B 88
SE28 7D 90
SW6 7H 99
UB1: S'hall 7G 77
Haldan Rd. E4 6K 35
Haldon Rd. SW18 6H 117
HALE, THE 5E 28
Hale, The E4 7A 36
N17 3G 49
Hale Cl. BR6: Farnb 4G 173
E4 3K 35
HA8: Edg 5D 28
Hale Ct. HA8: Edg 5D 28
Hale Dr. NW7 6D 28
HALE END 6B 36
Hale End Cl. HA4: Ruis 6J 39
Hale End Rd. E4 6A 36
E17 1E 50
IG8: Wfd G 7A 36
Halefield Rd. N17 1H 49
Hale Gdns. N17 4G 49
W3 1G 97
Hale Gro. Gdns. NW7 5F 29
Hale Ho. *SW1* *5D 18*
(off Lindsay Sq.)
Hale La. HA8: Edg 5C 28
NW7 5E 28
Hale Path SE27 4B 138
Hale Rd. E6 4C 88
N17 3G 49
Halesowen Rd. SM4: Mord 7K 153
Hales Prior *N1* *1G 7*
(off Calshot St.)
Hales St. SE8 7C 104
Hale St. E14 7D 86
Halesworth Cl. E5 2J 67
Halesworth Rd. SE13 3D 122
Hale Wlk. W7 5J 77
Haley Rd. NW4 6E 44
Half Acre HA7: Stan 5H 27
TW8: Bford 6D 96
Half Acre Rd. W7 1J 95
Half Moon Ct. CR0: C'don 7B 156
EC1 6C 8
Half Moon Cres. N1 2K 83
(not continuous)
Half Moon La. SE24 6C 120
Half Moon Pas. E1 1K 15 (6F 85)
(not continuous)
Half Moon St. W1 4K 11 (1F 101)
Halford Cl. HA8: Edg 2H 43
Halford Rd. E10 5F 51
SW6 6J 99
TW10: Rich 5E 114
UB10: Ick 4C 56
Halfway St. DA15: Sidc 7H 125
Haliburton Rd. TW1: Twick 5A 114
Haliday Ho. *N1* *6D 66*
(off Mildmay St.)
Haliday Wlk. N1 6D 66
Halidon Cl. E9 5J 67
Halifax NW9 2B 44
Halifax Cl. TW11: Tedd 6J 131
Halifax Rd. EN2: Enf 2H 23
UB6: G'frd 1F 77
Halifax St. SE26 3H 139
Halifield Dr. DA17: Belv 3E 108
Haling Down Pas. CR8: Purl 7C 168
(not continuous)
Haling Gro. CR2: S Croy 7C 168
Haling Pk. Gdns. CR2: S Croy 6B 168
Haling Pk. Rd. CR2: S Croy 5B 168
Haling Rd. CR2: S Croy 6D 168
Haliwell Ho. *NW6* *1K 81*
(off Mortimer Cres.)
Halkett Ho. *E2* *1J 85*
(off Waterloo Gdns.)
Halkin Arc. SW1 1F 17 (3D 100)
Halkin M. SW1 1G 17 (3E 100)
Halkin Pl. SW1 1G 17 (3E 100)
Halkin St. SW1 7H 11 (2E 100)
Hall, The SE3 3J 123
Hallam Cl. BR7: Chst 5D 142
Hallam Ct. *W1* *5K 5*
(off Hallam St.)
Hallam Gdns. HA5: Hat E 1C 40
Hallam Ho. *SW1* *6B 18*
(off Churchill Gdns.)
Hallam M. W1 5K 5 (5F 83)
Hallam Rd. N15 4B 48
SW13 3D 116
Hallam St. W1 4K 5 (5F 83)
Hallane Ho. SE27 5C 138
Hall Apartments *E3* *5B 86*
(off Geoff Cade Way)
Hall Cl. W5 5E 78
Hall Ct. TW11: Tedd 5K 131
Hall Dr. SE26 5J 139
W7 6J 77
Halley Gdns. SE13 4F 123
Halley Ho. *E2* *2G 85*
(off Pritchards Rd.)
SE10 *5H 105*
(off Armitage Rd.)
Halley Rd. E7 6A 70
E12 6A 70
Halley St. E14 5A 86
Hall Farm Cl. HA7: Stan 4G 27
Hall Farm Dr. TW2: Whitt 7H 113
Hallfield Est. W2 6A 82
(not continuous)
Hall Gdns. E4 4G 35
Hall Ga. NW8 1A 4 (3B 82)
Halliards, The KT12: Walt T 6J 147
Halliday Ho. *E1* *6G 85*
(off Christian St.)
Halliday Sq. UB2: S'hall 1H 95
Halliford Cl. TW17: Shep 4F 147
Halliford Rd. TW16: Sun 5G 147
TW17: Shep 5G 147
Halliford St. N1 7C 66
Hallingbury Ct. E17 3D 50
Halling Ho. *SE1* *7F 15*
(off Long La.)
Hallings Wharf Studios E15 1F 87
Halliwell Ct. SE22 5G 121
Halliwell Rd. SW2 6K 119
Halliwick Ct. Pde. *N12* *6J 31*
(off Woodhouse Rd.)
Halliwick Rd. N10 1E 46
HALL LANE 5E 34
Hall La. E4 5F 35
NW4 1C 44
UB3: Harl 7F 93
Hallmark Ho. *E14* *5C 86*
(off Ursula Gould Way)
Hallmark Trad. Est. HA9: Wemb 4J 61
Hallmead Rd. SM1: Sutt 3K 165
Hall Oak Wlk. NW6 6H 63
Hallowell Av. CR0: Bedd 4J 167
Hallowell Cl. CR4: Mitc 3E 154
Hallowell Gdns. CR7: Thor H 2C 156
Hallowell Rd. HA6: Nwood 1G 39
Hallowfield Way CR4: Mitc 3B 154
Hallows Gro. TW16: Sun 5H 129
Hall Pl. W2 4A 4 (4B 82)
(not continuous)
Hall Place & Gardens 6J 127
Hall Pl. Cres. DA5: Bexl 5J 127
Hall Place Sports Pavilion 6J 127
Hall Rd. E6 1D 88
E15 4F 69
NW8 1A 4 (3A 82)
RM6: Chad H 6C 54
Hall Rd. SM6: Wall 7F 167
TW7: Isle 5H 113
Hallside Rd. EN1: Enf 1A 24
Halls Ter. UB10: Hil 4D 74
Hall St. EC1 1B 8 (3B 84)
N12 5F 31
Hallsville Rd. E16 6H 87
Hallswelle Pde. NW11 5H 45
Hallswelle Rd. NW11 5H 45
Hall Twr. W2 5B 4
Hall Vw. SE9 2B 142
Hallywell Cres. E6 5D 88
Halo E15 1E 86
Halons Rd. SE9 7E 124
Halpin Pl. SE17 4D 102
Halsbrook Rd. SE3 3A 124
Halsbury Cl. HA7: Stan 4G 27
Halsbury Ct. HA7: Stan 5G 27
Halsbury Ho. *N7* *4K 65*
(off Biddestone Rd.)
Halsbury Rd. W12 1D 98
Halsbury Rd. E. UB5: N'olt 4G 59
Halsbury Rd. W. UB5: N'olt 5F 59
Halsend UB3: Hayes 1K 93
Halsey Ho. *WC1* *6G 7*
(off Red Lion Sq.)
Halsey M. SW3 3E 16 (4D 100)
Halsey St. SW3 3E 16 (4D 100)
Halsham Cres. IG11: Bark 5K 71
Halsmere Rd. SE5 1B 120
Halstead Cl. CR0: C'don 3C 168
Halstead Ct. E17 7B 50
N1 *1F 9*
(off Murray Gro.)
Halstead Gdns. N21 1J 33
Halstead Rd. E11 5J 51
EN1: Enf 4K 23
N21 1H 33
Halston Cl. SW11 6D 118
Halstow Rd. NW10 3F 81
SE10 5J 105
Halsway UB3: Hayes 1J 93
Halton Cl. N11 6J 31
Halton Ct. SE3 3K 123
Halton Cross St. N1 1B 84
Halton Ho. *N1* *7B 66*
(off Halton Rd.)
Halton Mans. N1 7B 66
Halton Pl. N1 1C 84
Halton Rd. N1 7B 66
Halt Robin La. DA17: Belv 4H 109
Halt Robin Rd. DA17: Belv 4G 109
(not continuous)
Halyard Ho. *E14* *3E 104*
(off Manchester Rd.)
Halyard St. RM9: Dag 4E 90
HAM 3C 132
Ham, The TW8: Bford 7C 96
Hamara Ghar E13 1A 88
Hambalt Rd. SW4 5G 119
Hamble Cl. HA4: Ruis 2G 57
Hambledon *SE17* *6D 102*
(off Villa St.)
Hambledon Cl. UB8: Hil 4D 74
Hambledon Ct. SE22 4E 120
W5 7E 78
Hambledon Gdns. SE25 3F 157
Hambledon Pl. SE21 1E 138
Hambledon Rd. SW18 7H 117
Hambledown Rd. DA15: Sidc 7H 125
Hamble Dr. UB3: Hayes 7H 75
Hamblehyrst BR3: Beck 2D 158
Hamble St. SW6 3K 117
Hambleton Cl. KT4: Wor Pk 2E 164
Hamble Wlk. *UB5: N'olt* *2E 76*
(off Brabazon Rd.)
Hambley Ho. *SE16* *4H 103*
(off Camilla Rd.)
Hamblin Ho. *UB1: S'hall* *7C 76*
(off The Broadway)
Hambridge Way SW2 7A 120

Hambro Av. BR2: Hayes 1J 171
Hambrook Rd. SE25 . . . . .3H 157
Hambro Rd. SW16 . . . . .6H 137
Hambrough Ho. UB4: Yead 5A 76
Hambrough Rd. UB1: S'hall 1C 94
Ham Cl. TW10: Ham 3C 132
   (not continuous)
Ham Comn. TW10: Ham 3D 132
Ham Common (Nature Reserve) 4E 132
Ham Ct. NW9 . . . . .2A 44
Ham Ct. Cl. TW13: Felt 3J 129
Hamden Cres.
   RM10: Dag 3H 73
Hamel Cl. HA3: Kenton 4D 42
Hamella Ho. E9 . . . . .5A 68
   (off Sadler Pl.)
Hameway E6 . . . . .3E 88
Ham Farm Rd. TW10: Ham 4D 132
Ham Flds. TW10: Ham 3B 132
Hamfrith Rd. E15 . . . . .6H 69
Ham Ga. Av. TW10: Ham 3D 132
Ham House & Garden 1C 132
Hamilton Av. IG6: Ilf 4F 53
   KT6: Surb 2G 163
   N9 . . . . .7B 24
   RM1: Rom 2K 55
   SM3: Cheam 2G 165
Hamilton Cl. EN4: Cockf 4H 21
   HA7: Stan 2D 26
   N17 . . . . .3F 49
   NW8 . . . . .2A 4 (3B 82)
   SE16 . . . . .2A 104
   TW11: Tedd 6B 132
   TW13: Felt 5H 129
Hamilton Ct. CRO: C'don 1G 169
   SE6 .1H 141
   SW15 . . . . .3G 117
   TW3: Houn 4F 113
   (off Hanworth Rd.)
   W5 . . . . .7E 78
   W9 . . . . .3A 82
   (off Maida Vale)
Hamilton Cres. HA2: Harr 3D 58
   N13 . . . . .4F 33
   TW3: Houn 5F 113
Hamilton Gdns. NW8 . . . .1A 4 (3A 82)
Hamilton Hall NW8 . . . . .2A 82
   (off Hamilton Ter.)
Hamilton Ho. E3 . . . . .3B 86
   (off British St.)
   E14 .5D 104
   (off St Davids Sq., St Davids Sq.)
   E14 .7B 86
   (off Victory Pl., Victory Pl.)
   NW8 .1A 4
   W4 . . . . .6A 98
   W8 . . . . .2K 99
   (off Vicarage Ga.)
Hamilton La. N5 . . . . .4B 66
Hamilton Lodge E1 . . . . .4J 85
   (off Cleveland Gro.)
Hamilton M. SW18 . . . . .1J 135
   SW19 . . . . .7J 135
   W1 . . . . .6J 11 (2F 101)
Hamilton Pde. TW13: Felt 4H 129
Hamilton Pk. N5 . . . . .4B 66
Hamilton Pk. W. N5 . . . . .4B 66
Hamilton Pl. N19 . . . . .3H 65
   TW16: Sun 7K 129
   W1 . . . . .5H 11 (1E 100)
Hamilton Rd. CR7: Thor H 3D 156
   DA7: Bex 2E 126
   DA15: Sidc 4A 144
   E15 . . . . .3G 87
   E17 . . . . .2A 50
   EN4: Cockf 4H 21
   HA1: Harr 5J 41
   IG1: Ilf 4F 71
   N2 . . . . .3A 46
   N9 . . . . .7B 24
   NW10 . . . . .5C 62

Hamilton Rd. NW11 . . . . .7F 45
   SE27 . . . . .4D 138
   SW19 . . . . .7K 135
   TW2: Twick 1J 131
   TW8: Bford 6D 96
   TW13: Felt 4H 129
   UB1: S'hall 1D 94
   UB3: Hayes 7K 75
   W4 . . . . .2A 98
   W5 . . . . .7E 78
Hamilton Rd. Ind. Est. SE27 . . . . . .4D 138
Hamilton Rd. M. SW19 . . . . .7K 135
Hamilton Sq. N12 . . . . .6G 31
   SE1 . . . . .6F 15 (2D 102)
Hamilton St. SE8 . . . . .6C 104
Hamilton Ter. NW8 . . . . .2A 4 (2K 81)
Hamilton Way N3 . . . . .6D 30
   N13 . . . . .4G 33
   SM6: Wall 7H 167
Ham Lands Nature Reserve 2A 132
Hamlea Cl. SE12 . . . . .5J 123
Hamlet, The SE5 . . . . .3D 120
Hamlet Cl. RM5: Col R 1G 55
   SE13 . . . . .4G 123
Hamlet Ct. E3 . . . . .3C 86
   (off Tomlin's Gro.)
   EN1: Enf 5K 23
   SE11 . . . . .5B 102
   (off Opal St.)
   W6 . . . . .4C 98
Hamlet Gdns. W6 . . . . .4C 98
Hamlet Ind. Est. E9 . . . . .7C 68
Hamlet Ind. Est. E9 . . . . .7C 68
Hamlet Intl. Ind. Est. DA8: Erith . . .5K 109
Hamlet Lodge UB10: Hil 6D 56
Hamlet M. SE21 . . . . .1D 138
Hamleton Ter. RM9: Dag 7C 72
   (off Flamstead Rd.)
Hamlet Rd. RM5: Col R 1G 55
   SE19 . . . . .7F 139
Hamlet Sq. NW2 . . . . .3G 63
Hamlets Way E3 . . . . .4B 86
Hamlet Way SE1 . . . . . .6F 15 (2D 102)
Hamlin Cres. HA5: Eastc 5A 40
Hamlyn Cl. HA8: Edg 3K 27
Hamlyn Gdns. SE19 . . . . .7E 138
Hamlyn Ho. TW13: Felt 1K 129
Hammelton Ct. BR1: Brom 1H 159
   (off London Rd.)
Hammelton Rd. BR1: Brom 1H 159
Hammerfield Ho. SW3 . . . . .5D 16
   (off Cale St.)
Hammers La. NW7 . . . . .5H 29
Hammersley Ho. SE14 . . . . .7J 103
   (off Pomeroy St.)
Hammersmith Rd. E16 . . . . .5J 87
HAMMERSMITH 4E 98
Hammersmith Apollo 5E 98
Hammersmith Bri. SW13 . . . . .6D 98
Hammersmith Bri. Rd. W6 . . . . .5E 98
HAMMERSMITH BROADWAY 4E 98
Hammersmith B'way. W6 . . . . .4E 98
Hammersmith Emb. W6 . . . . .6E 98
Hammersmith Fitness & Squash Cen.
   . . . . .4F 99
   (off Chalk Hill Rd.)
HAMMERSMITH FLYOVER 5E 98
Hammersmith Flyover W6 . . . . .5E 98
Hammersmith Gro. W6 . . . . .2E 98
Hammersmith Rd. W6 . . . . .4F 99
   W14 .4F 99
Hammersmith Ter. W6 . . . . .5C 98
Hammet Cl. UB4: Yead 5B 76
Hammett St. EC3 . . . . . .2J 15 (7F 85)
Hammond Av. CR4: Mitc 2F 155
Hammond Cl. EN5: Barn 5B 20
   TW12: Hamp 1E 148
   UB6: G'frd 5H 59
Hammond Ct. E10 . . . . .2D 68
   (off Leyton Grange Est.)
   E17 . . . . .5A 50
   (off Maude Rd.)

Hammond Ct. SE11 . . . . .5J 19
   (off Hotspur St.)
Hammond Ho. E14 . . . . .3C 104
   (off Tiller Rd.)
   SE14 . . . . .7J 103
   (off Lubbock St.)
Hammond Lodge W9 . . . . .5J 81
   (off Admiral Wlk.)
Hammond Rd. EN1: Enf 2C 24
   UB2: S'hall 3C 94
Hammonds Cl. RM8: Dag 3C 72
Hammond St. NW5 . . . . .6G 65
Hammond Way SE28 . . . . .7B 90
Hamond Cl. CR2: S Croy 7B 168
Hamond Cl. HA8: Edg 2C 28
Hamond Sq. N1 . . . . .2E 84
Ham Pk. Rd. E7 . . . . .7H 69
   E15 . . . . .7H 69
Hampden Av. BR3: Beck 2A 158
Hampden Cl. NW1 . . . . .2H 83
Hampden Ct. N10 . . . . .7K 31
Hampden Gurney St. W1 . . .1E 10 (6D 82)
Hampden Ho. SW9 . . . . .2A 120
   (off Overton Rd.)
Hampden La. N17 . . . . .1F 49
Hampden Rd. BR3: Beck 2A 158
   HA3: Hrw W 1G 41
   KT1: King T 3G 151
   N8 . . . . .4A 48
   N10 . . . . .7K 31
   N17 . . . . .1G 49
   N19 . . . . .2H 65
   RM5: Col R 1H 55
Hampden Sq. N14 . . . . .1A 32
Hampden Way N14 . . . . .1A 32
Hampshire Cl. N18 . . . . .5C 34
Hampshire Hog La. W6 . . . . .5D 98
Hampshire Rd. N22 . . . . .7E 32
Hampshire St. NW5 . . . . .6H 65
Hampson Way SW8 . . . . .1K 119
HAMPSTEAD 4B 64
Hampstead Av. IG8: Wfd G 7K 37
Hampstead Cl. SE28 . . . . .1B 108
Hampstead Gdns. NW11 . . . . .6J 45
   RM6: Chad H 5B 54
HAMPSTEAD GARDEN SUBURB 5A 46
Hampstead Ga. NW3 . . . . .5A 64
Hampstead Golf Course 7B 46
Hampstead Grn. NW3 . . . . .5C 64
Hampstead Gro. NW3 . . . . .3A 64
Hampstead Heath 2B 64
Hampstead Hgts. N2 . . . . .3A 46
Hampstead High St. NW3 . . . . .4B 64
Hampstead Hill Gdns. NW3 . . . . . . .4B 64
Hampstead Ho. NW1 . . . . .2A 6
   (off William Rd.)
Hampstead La. N6 . . . . .1B 64
   NW3 .1B 64
Hampstead Lodge NW1 . . . . .5C 4
   (off Bell St.)
Hampstead M. BR3: Beck 4D 158
Hampstead Mus. 4B 64
   (off New End Sq.)
Hampstead Rd. NW1 . . . .1A 6 (2G 83)
Hampstead Sq. NW3 . . . . .3A 64
Hampstead Theatre 7B 64
Hampstead Wlk. E3 . . . . .1B 86
Hampstead Way NW11 . . . . .5H 45
Hampstead W. NW6 . . . . .6J 63
HAMPTON 1F 149
Hampton & Richmond Borough FC . .1F 149
Hampton Bus. Pk. TW13: Hanw 3C 130
Hampton Cl. N11 . . . . .5A 32
   NW6 .3J 81
   SW20 . . . . .7E 134
HAMPTON COURT 4J 149
HAMPTON COURT 3J 149
Hampton Ct. N1 . . . . .6B 66
   N22 . . . . .1G 47
   SE14 . . . . .7A 104
   (off Batavia Rd.)

Hampton Ct. SE16 . . . . .7K 85
   (off King & Queen Wharf)
Hampton Ct. Av. KT8: E Mos 6H 149
Hampton Ct. Bri. KT8: E Mos 4J 149
Hampton Ct. Cres. KT8: E Mos 3H 149
Hampton Ct. Est. KT7: T Ditt 4J 149
Hampton Ct. M. KT8: E Mos 4J 149
   (off Feltham Av.)
Hampton Court Palace 4K 149
Hampton Court Palace Golf Course
   . . . . .5C 150
Hampton Ct. Pde. KT8: E Mos 4J 149
Hampton Ct. Rd. KT1: Hamp W 3K 149
   KT8: E Mos 3K 149
   TW12: E Mos, Hamp 2G 149
Hampton Ct. Way KT7: T Ditt 7J 149
   KT8: E Mos 7J 149
Hampton Golf Course 3E 130
HAMPTON HILL 5G 131
   TW12: Hamp H 5G 131
   (off High St.)
Hampton Hill Bus. Pk.
   TW12: Hamp H 5G 131
Hampton Hill Playhouse Theatre . . .5G 131
Hampton Ho. DA7: Bex 2H 127
   (off Erith Rd.)
   SW8 .7G 101
   (off Ascalon St.)
Hampton La. TW13: Hanw 4C 130
Hampton M. EN3: Enf H 3D 24
   NW10 . . . . .3K 79
   WD23: B Hea 1B 26
Hampton Open Air Pool 7G 131
Hampton Ri. HA3: Kenton 6E 42
Hampton Rd. CR0: C'don 6C 156
   E4 . . . . .5G 35
   E7 . . . . .5K 69
   E11 . . . . .1F 69
   HA7: Stan 3D 26
   IG1: Ilf 4G 71
   KT4: Wor Pk 2C 164
   TW2: Twick 3H 131
   TW11: Tedd 5H 131
   TW12: Hamp H 5H 131
Hampton Rd. E. TW13: Hanw 4D 130
Hampton Rd. Ind. Pk. CR0: C'don . . .6C 156
Hampton Rd. W. TW13: Hanw 3C 130
Hampton Sports & Fitness Cen. 5E 130
Hampton St. SE1 . . . . .4C 102
   SE17 . . . . .4B 102
HAMPTON WICK 1C 150
Hampton Youth Project (Sports Hall)
   . . . . .6D 130
Ham Ridings TW10: Ham 5F 133
Hamshades Cl. DA15: Sidc 3K 143
Hamston Ho. W8 . . . . .3K 99
   (off Kensington Ct. Pl.)
Ham St. TW10: Ham 1B 132
Ham Vw. CR0: C'don 6A 158
Ham Yd. W1 . . . . .2C 12 (7H 83)
Hanah Ct. SW19 . . . . .7F 135
Hanameel St. E16 . . . . .1K 105
Hana M. E5 . . . . .4H 67
Hanbury Cl. NW4 . . . . .3E 44
Hanbury Ct. HA1: Harr 6K 41
Hanbury Dr. E11 . . . . .7H 51
   N21 . . . . .5E 22
Hanbury Ho. E1 . . . . .5G 85
   (off Hanbury St.)
   SW8 .7J 101
   (off Regent's Bri. Gdns.)
Hanbury M. N1 . . . . .1C 84
Hanbury Rd. N17 . . . . .2H 49
   W3 . . . . .2H 97
Hanbury St. E1 . . . . .5K 9 (5F 85)
Hanbury Wlk. DA5: Bexl 3K 145
Hancock Nunn Ho. NW3 . . . . .6D 64
   (off Fellows Rd.)
Hancock Rd. E3 . . . . .3E 86
   SE19 . . . . .6D 138
Handa Wlk. N1 . . . . .6D 66
Hand Ct. WC1 . . . . .6H 7 (5K 83)

Handcroft Rd.—Harewood Pl.

Handcroft Rd. CR0: C'don 7B 156
Handel Bus. Cen. SW8 7E 18 (6J 101)
Handel Cl. HA8: Edg 6A 28
Handel House Mus. 2J 11
(off Brook St.)
Handel Mans. SW13 7E 98
WC1 3F 7
(off Handel St.)
Handel Pde. HA8: Edg 7B 28
(off Whitchurch La.)
Handel Pl. NW10 6K 61
Handel St. WC1 3E 6 (4J 83)
Handel Way HA8: Edg 7B 28
Handen Rd. SE12 5G 123
Handforth Rd. IG1: Ilf 3F 71
SW9 7A 102
Handley Dr. SE3 3K 123
Handley Gro. NW2 3F 63
Handley Page Rd. SM6: Wall 7K 167
Handley Rd. E9 7J 67
Handowe Cl. NW4 4C 44
Handside Cl. KT4: Wor Pk 1F 165
Hands Wlk. E16 6J 87
Handsworth Av. E4 6A 36
Handsworth Rd. N17 3D 48
Handtrough Way IG11: Bark 2F 89
Handyside St. N1 1J 83
Hanford Cl. SW18 1J 135
Hanford Row SW19 6E 134
Hanger Ct. W5 4F 79
Hanger Grn. W5 4G 79
HANGER HILL 4F 79
HANGER LANE 3E 78
Hanger La. W5 2E 78
Hanger Va. La. W5 6F 79
(not continuous)
Hanger Vw. Way W3 6G 79
Hanging Sword All. EC4 1K 13
Hankey Ho. SE1 7F 15
(off Hankey Pl.)
Hankey Pl. SE1 7F 15 (2D 102)
Hankins La. NW7 2F 29
Hanley Gdns. N4 1K 65
Hanley Pl. BR3: Beck 7C 140
Hanley Rd. N4 1J 65
Hanmer Wlk. N7 2K 65
Hannaford Wlk. E3 4D 86
Hannah Barlow Ho. SW8 1K 119
Hannah Bldg. E1 6H 85
(off Watney St.)
Hannah Cl. BR3: Beck 3E 158
NW10 4J 61
Hannah Ct. E15 2H 87
Hannah Mary Way SE1 4G 103
Hannah M. SM6: Wall 7G 167
Hannay Ho. SW15 6G 117
Hannay La. N8 7H 47
Hannay Wlk. SW16 2H 137
Hannell Rd. SW6 7G 99
Hannen Rd. SE27 3B 138
Hannibal Rd. E1 5J 85
TW19: Stanw 7A 110
Hannibal Way CR0: Wadd 5K 167
Hannington Rd. SW4 3F 119
Hanno Cl. SM6: Wall 7H 167
Hanover Av. E16 1J 105
TW13: Felt 1J 129
Hanover Circ. UB3: Hayes 6E 74
Hanover Cl. SM3: Cheam 4G 165
TW9: Kew 7G 97
TW15: Ashf 4A 128
Hanover Ct. E8 1F 85
(off Stean St.)
HA4: Ruis 3J 57
NW9 3A 44
SE19 7G 139
(off Anerley Rd.)
SW15 4B 116
W12 1C 98
(off Uxbridge Rd.)
Hanover Dr. BR7: Chst 4G 143
Hanover Flats W1 2H 11
(off Binney St.)
Hanover Gdns. IG6: Ilf 1G 53
SE11 6A 102
Hanover Ga. NW1 2D 4 (3C 82)
Hanover Ga. Mans. NW1 3D 4 (4C 82)
Hanover Ho. E14 1B 104
(off Westferry Cir.)
NW8 2C 82
(off St John's Wood High St.)
SE16 2K 103
(off Dominion Dr.)
SW9 3A 120
Hanover Mans. SW2 5A 120
(off Barnwell Rd.)
Hanover Mead NW11 5G 45
Hanover Pk. SE15 1G 121
Hanover Pl. E3 3B 86
WC2 1F 13 (6J 83)
Hanover Rd. N15 4F 49
NW10 7E 62
SW19 7A 136
Hanover Sq. W1 1K 11 (6F 83)
Hanover Steps W2 1D 10
Hanover St. CR0: C'don 3B 168
W1 1K 11 (6F 83)
Hanover Ter. NW1 2E 4 (3D 82)
TW7: Isle 1A 114
Hanover Ter. M. NW1 2D 4 (3C 82)
Hanover Trad. Est. N7 5J 65
Hanover Way DA6: Bex 3D 126
Hanover W. Ind. Est. NW10 3K 79
Hanover Yd. N1 2C 84
(off Noel Rd.)
Hansa Cl. UB2: S'hall 3A 94
Hansard M. W14 2F 99
Hansart Way EN2: Enf 1F 23
Hanscomb M. SW4 4G 119
Hans Ct. SW3 1E 16
Hans Cres. SW1 1E 16 (3D 100)
Hanseatic Wlk. EC4 3E 14
Hanselin Cl. HA7: Stan 5E 26
Hansel Rd. NW6 3J 81
Hansen Dr. N21 5E 22
Hanshaw Dr. HA8: Edg 1K 43
Hansler Ct. SW19 1G 135
(off Princes Way)
Hansler Gro. KT8: E Mos 4H 149
Hansler Rd. SE22 5F 121
Hansol Rd. DA6: Bex 5E 126
Hansom M. SE11 5H 19 (5K 101)
Hansom Ter. BR1: Brom 1K 159
(off Freelands Gro.)
Hanson Cl. BR3: Beck 6D 140
SW12 7F 119
SW14 3J 115
UB7: W Dray 3B 92
Hanson Ct. E17 6D 50
Hanson Gdns. UB1: S'hall 2C 94
Hanson Ho. E1 7G 85
(off Pinchin St.)
Hanson St. W1 5A 6 (5G 83)
Hans Pl. SW1 1F 17 (3D 100)
Hans Rd. SW3 1E 16 (3D 100)
Hans St. SW1 2F 17 (3D 100)
Hanway Pl. W1 7C 6 (6H 83)
Hanway Rd. W7 6H 77
Hanway St. W1 7C 6 (6H 83)
HANWELL 1K 95
Hanwell Ho. W2 5J 81
(off Gt. Western Rd.)
HANWORTH 4B 130
Hanworth Air Pk. Leisure Cen. 2B 130
Hanworth Ho. SE5 7B 102
Hanworth Rd. TW3: Houn 1C 130
TW4: Houn 1C 130
TW12: Hamp 4D 130
TW13: Felt 1K 129
TW16: Sun 7J 129
(not continuous)
Hanworth Ter. TW3: Houn 4F 113
Hanworth Trad. Est. TW13: Hanw 3C 130
Hapgood Cl. UB6: G'frd 5H 59
Harad's Pl. E1 7G 85
Harbans Ct. SL3: Poyle 4A 174
Harben Pde. NW3 7A 64
(off Finchley Rd.)
Harben Rd. NW6 7A 64
Harberson Rd. E15 1H 87
SW12 1F 137
Harberton Rd. N19 1G 65
Harbet Rd. E4 5F 35
N18 5F 35
W2 6B 4 (5B 82)
Harbex Cl. DA5: Bexl 7H 127
Harbinger Rd. E14 4D 104
Harbledown Ho. SE1 7E 14
(off Manciple St.)
Harbledown Rd. SW6 1J 117
Harbord Cl. SE5 2D 120
Harbord Ho. SE16 4K 103
(off Cope St.)
Harbord St. SW6 1F 117
Harborough Av. DA15: Sidc 7J 125
Harborough Ho. UB5: N'olt 3D 76
(off Taywood Rd.)
Harborough Rd. SW16 4K 137
Harbour Av. SW10 1A 118
Harbour Cl. CR4: Mitc 1E 154
Harbour Club, The
Chelsea 2A 118
Harbour Club Notting Hill 5J 81
Harbour Exchange Sq. E14 2D 104
Harbour Quay E14 1E 104
Harbour Reach SW6 1A 118
Harbour Rd. SE5 3C 120
Harbour Yd. SW10 1A 118
Harbridge Av. SW15 7B 116
Harbury Rd. SM5: Cars 7C 166
Harbut Rd. SW11 4B 118
Harcombe Rd. N16 3E 66
Harcourt Av. DA15: Sidc 6C 126
E12 4D 70
HA8: Edg 3D 28
SM6: Wall 4F 167
Harcourt Bldgs. EC4 2J 13
Harcourt Cl. TW7: Isle 3A 114
Harcourt Fld. SM6: Wall 4F 167
Harcourt Ho. W1 7J 5
Harcourt Lodge SM6: Wall 4F 167
Harcourt Rd. CR7: Thor H 6K 155
DA6: Bex 4E 126
E15 2H 87
N22 1H 47
SE4 3B 122
SM6: Wall 4F 167
SW19 7J 135
Harcourt St. W1 6D 4 (5C 82)
Harcourt Ter. SW10 5K 99
Hardcastle Cl. CR0: C'don 6G 157
Hardcastle Ho. SE14 1A 122
(off Loring Rd.)
Hardcourts Cl. BR4: W W'ck 3D 170
Hardel Ri. SW2 1B 138
Hardel Wlk. SW2 7A 120
Harden Ct. SE7 4C 106
Harden Ho. SE5 2E 120
Harden's Manorway SE7 3B 106
(not continuous)
Harders Rd. SE15 2H 121
Hardess St. SE24 3C 120
Hardie Cl. NW10 5K 61
Hardie Rd. RM10: Dag 3J 73
Harding Cl. CR0: C'don 3F 169
SE17 6C 102
Harding Dr. RM8: Dag 1E 72
Hardinge Cl. UB8: Hil 5D 74
Hardinge Cres. SE18 3G 107
Hardinge La. E1 6J 85
(not continuous)
Hardinge Rd. N18 6K 33
NW10 1D 80
Hardinge St. E1 7J 85
(Johnson St.)
E1 6J 85
(Steel's La.)
Harding Ho. SW13 6D 98
(off Wyatt Dr.)
UB3: Hayes 6K 75
Harding Rd. DA7: Bex 2F 127
Harding's Cl. KT2: King T 1F 151
Hardings La. SE20 6K 139
Hardington NW1 7E 64
(off Belmont St.)
Hardman Rd. KT2: King T 2E 150
SE7 5K 105
Hardwick Cl. HA7: Stan 5H 27
Hardwick Ct. DA8: Erith 6K 109
Hardwicke Av. TW5: Hest 1E 112
Hardwicke M. WC1 2H 7
Hardwicke Rd. N13 6D 32
TW10: Ham 4C 132
W4 4K 97
Hardwicke St. IG11: Bark 1G 89
Hardwick Grn. W13 5B 78
Hardwick Ho. NW8 3D 4
(off Lilestone St.)
Hardwick Pl. SW16 7G 137
Hardwicks Sq. SW18 5J 117
Hardwick St. EC1 2K 7 (3A 84)
Hardwidge St. SE1 6G 15 (2E 102)
Hardy Av. E16 1J 105
HA4: Ruis 5K 57
Hardy Cl. EN5: Barn 6B 20
HA5: Pinn 7B 40
SE16 2K 103
Hardy Cotts. SE10 6F 105
Hardy Ct. SW17 3B 136
(off Grosvenor Way)
W3 3J 97
(off Bollo Bri. Rd.)
Hardy Ho. SW4 7G 119
SW18 7K 117
Hardying Ho. E17 4A 50
Hardy Pas. N22 1K 47
Hardy Rd. E4 6G 35
SE3 7H 105
SW19 7K 135
Hardy's M. KT8: E Mos 4J 149
Hardy Way EN2: Enf 1F 23
Hare & Billet Rd. SE3 1F 123
Harebell Dr. E6 5E 88
Harecastle Cl. UB4: Yead 4C 76
Hare Ct. EC4 1J 13
Harecourt Rd. N1 6C 66
Harecroft La. UB10: Ick 3E 56
Haredale Ho. SE16 2G 103
(off East La.)
Haredale Rd. SE24 4C 120
Haredon Cl. SE23 7K 121
HAREFIELD 1A 38
Harefield Cl. EN2: Enf 1F 23
Harefield Grn. NW7 6K 29
Harefield M. SE4 3B 122
Harefield Rd. DA14: Sidc 3D 144
N8 5H 47
SE4 3B 122
SW16 7K 137
UB8: Uxb 5A 56
Hare Marsh E2 4G 85
Harepit Cl. CR2: S Croy 7B 168
Hare Pl. EC4 1K 13
(off Fleet St.)
Hare Row E2 2H 85
Haresfield Rd. RM10: Dag 6G 73
Hare St. SE18 3E 106
Hare Wlk. N1 2E 84
(not continuous)
Harewood Av. NW1 4D 4 (4C 82)
UB5: N'olt 7D 58
Harewood Cl. UB5: N'olt 7D 58
Harewood Dr. IG5: Ilf 2D 52
Harewood Pl. W1 1K 11 (6F 83)

Harewood Rd.—Harrow Rd.

Harewood Rd. CR2: S Croy . . . 6E 168
SW19 . . . 6C 136
TW7: Isle . . . 7K 95
Harewood Row NW1 . . . 5D 4 (5C 82)
Harewood Ter. UB2: S'hall . . . 4D 94
Harfield Gdns. SE5 . . . 3E 120
Harfield Rd. TW16: Sun . . . 2B 148
Harfleur Ct. *SE11* . . . *4B 102*
(off Opal St.)
Harford Cl. E4 . . . 7J 25
Harford Ho. *SE5* . . . *6C 102*
(off Bethwin Rd.)
W11 . . . 5H 81
Harford M. N19 . . . 3H 65
Harford Rd. E4 . . . 7J 25
Harford St. E1 . . . 4A 86
Harford Wlk. N2 . . . 4B 46
Harfst Way BR8: Swan . . . 7J 145
Hargood Cl. HA3: Kenton . . . 6E 42
Hargood Rd. SE3 . . . 1A 124
Hargrave Mans. N19 . . . 2H 65
Hargrave Pk. N19 . . . 2G 65
Hargrave Pl. N7 . . . 5H 65
Hargrave Rd. N19 . . . 2G 65
Hargraves Ho. *W12* . . . *7D 80*
(off White City Est.)
Hargwyne St. SW9 . . . 3K 119
Hari Cl. UB5: N'olt . . . 5F 59
Haringey Independent Cinema . . . 4C 48
Haringey Pk. N8 . . . 6J 47
Haringey Pas. N8 . . . 4A 48
Haringey Rd. N8 . . . 4J 47
Harington Ter.
N9 . . . 3J 33
N18 . . . 3J 33
Harkett Cl. HA3: W'stone . . . 2K 41
Harkett Ct. HA3: W'stone . . . 2K 41
Harkness Ct. *SM1: Sutt* . . . *1K 165*
(off Cleeve Way)
Harkness Ho. *E1* . . . *6G 85*
(off Christian St.)
Harland Av. CR0: C'don . . . 3F 169
DA15: Sidc . . . 3H 143
Harland Cl. SW19 . . . 3K 153
Harland Rd. SE12 . . . 7J 123
Harlands Gro. BR6: Farnb . . . 4F 173
Harlech Gdns. HA5: Pinn . . . 7B 40
TW5: Hest . . . 6A 94
Harlech Rd. N14 . . . 3D 32
Harlech Twr. W3 . . . 2J 97
Harlequin Av. TW8: Bford . . . 6A 96
Harlequin Cl. IG11: Bark . . . 4A 90
TW7: Isle . . . 5J 113
UB4: Yead . . . 5B 76
Harlequin Ct. *E1* . . . *7G 85*
(off Thomas More St.)
NW10 . . . *6K 61*
(off Mitchellbrook Way)
W5 . . . 7C 78
Harlequin Ho. *DA18: Erith* . . . *3E 108*
(off Kale Rd.)
Harlequin Rd. TW11: Tedd . . . 7B 132
Harlequins RUFC . . . 7J 113
Harlescott Rd. SE15 . . . 4K 121
HARLESDEN . . . 2B 80
Harlesden Gdns. NW10 . . . 1B 80
Harlesden La. NW10 . . . 1C 80
Harlesden Plaza NW10 . . . 2B 80
Harlesden Rd. NW10 . . . 1C 80
Harleston Cl. E5 . . . 2J 67
Harley Cl. HA0: Wemb . . . 6D 60
Harley Ct. E11 . . . 7J 51
HA1: Harr . . . 4H 41
N20 . . . 3F 31
Harley Cres. HA1: Harr . . . 4H 41
Harleyford BR1: Brom . . . 1K 159
Harleyford Ct. SE11 . . . 7G 19
Harleyford Mnr. *W3* . . . *1J 97*
(off Edgecote Cl.)
Harleyford Rd. SE11 . . . 7G 19 (6K 101)
Harleyford St. SE11 . . . 7J 19 (6A 102)
Harley Gdns. BR6: Orp . . . 4J 173
SW10 . . . 5A 100
Harley Gro. E3 . . . 3B 86
Harley Ho. E11 . . . 7F 51
E14 . . . *6B 86*
(off Frances Wharf)
NW1 . . . 4H 5
Harley Pl. W1 . . . 6J 5 (5F 83)
Harley Rd. HA1: Harr . . . 4H 41
NW3 . . . 7B 64
NW10 . . . 2A 80
Harley St. W1 . . . 4J 5 (4F 83)
Harley Vs. NW10 . . . 2A 80
Harling Ct. SW11 . . . 2D 118
Harlinger St. SE18 . . . 3C 106
HARLINGTON . . . 6F 93
Harlington Cl. UB3: Harl . . . 7E 92
HARLINGTON CORNER . . . 1F 111
Harlington Rd. DA7: Bex . . . 3E 126
UB8: Hil . . . 3C 74
Harlington Rd. E. TW13: Felt . . . 7K 111
TW14: Felt . . . 7K 111
Harlington Rd. W. TW14: Felt . . . 6K 111
Harlington Sports Centre, The . . . *4F 93*
(off Pinkwell La.)
Harlow Mans. *IG11: Bark* . . . *7F 71*
(off Whiting Av.)
Harlow Rd. N13 . . . 3J 33
Harlyn Dr. HA5: Eastc . . . 3K 39
Harlynwood *SE5* . . . *7C 102*
(off Wyndham Rd.)
Harman Av. IG8: Wfd G . . . 6C 36
Harman Cl. E4 . . . 4A 36
NW2 . . . 3G 63
SE1 . . . 5G 103
Harman Dr. DA15: Sidc . . . 6K 125
NW2 . . . 3G 63
Harman Ri. IG3: Ilf . . . 4J 71
Harman Rd. EN1: Enf . . . 5A 24
HARMONDSWORTH . . . 2E 174
Harmondsworth La. UB7: Harm, Sip . . . 6A 92
Harmondsworth Moor Waterside . . . 2C 174
Harmondsworth Moor Waterside Vis. Cen. . . . 2C 174
Harmondsworth Rd. UB7: W Dray . . . 5A 92
Harmon Ho. SE8 . . . 4B 104
Harmont Ho. *W1* . . . *6J 5*
(off Harley St.)
Harmony Cl. NW11 . . . 5G 45
(not continuous)
SM6: Wall . . . 7J 167
Harmony Pl. SE1 . . . 5F 103
SE8 . . . *6D 104*
(off Dancers Way)
Harmony Ter. HA2: Harr . . . 1F 59
Harmony Way BR1: Brom . . . 2J 159
NW4 . . . 4E 44
Harmood Gro. NW1 . . . 7F 65
Harmood Ho. *NW1* . . . *7F 65*
(off Harmood St.)
Harmood Pl. NW1 . . . 7F 65
Harmood St. NW1 . . . 6F 65
Harmsworth M. SE11 . . . 2K 19 (3A 102)
Harmsworth St. SE17 . . . 6K 19 (5B 102)
Harmsworth Way N20 . . . 1C 30
Harold Av. DA17: Belv . . . 5F 109
UB3: Hayes . . . 3H 93
Harold Ct. *SE16* . . . *2K 103*
(off Christopher Cl.)
Harold Est. SE1 . . . 3E 102
Harold Gibbons Ct. SE7 . . . 6A 106
Harold Ho. *E2* . . . *2K 85*
(off Mace St.)
Harold Laski Ho. *EC1* . . . *2B 8*
(off Percival St.)
Harold Maddison Ho. *SE17* . . . *5B 102*
(off Penton Pl.)
Harold Mugford Ter. *E6* . . . *6E 88*
(off Pearl Cl.)
Harold Pinter Theatre . . . *3C 12*
(off Panton St.)
Harold Pl. SE11 . . . 6J 19 (5A 102)
Harold Rd. E4 . . . 4K 35
E11 . . . 1G 69
E13 . . . 1K 87
IG8: Wfd G . . . 1J 51
N8 . . . 5K 47
N15 . . . 5F 49
NW10 . . . 3K 79
SE19 . . . 7D 138
SM1: Sutt . . . 4B 166
Haroldstone Rd. E17 . . . 5K 49
Harold Wilson Ho. SE28 . . . 1B 108
SW6 . . . *6H 99*
(off Clem Attlee Ct.)
Harp All. EC4 . . . 7A 8 (6B 84)
Harp Bus. Centre, The NW2 . . . 2C 62
Harpenden Rd. E12 . . . 2A 70
SE27 . . . 3B 138
Harpenmead Point NW2 . . . 2H 63
Harper Cl. N14 . . . 5B 22
Harper Ho. SW9 . . . 3B 120
Harper M. SW17 . . . 3A 136
Harper Rd. E6 . . . 6D 88
SE1 . . . 7C 14 (3C 102)
Harpers Yd. N17 . . . 1F 49
TW7: Isle . . . *2J 113*
(off Rennels Way)
Harp Island Cl. NW10 . . . 2K 61
Harp La. EC3 . . . 3G 15 (7E 84)
Harpley Sq. E1 . . . 4K 85
Harpour Rd. IG11: Bark . . . 6G 71
Harp Rd. W7 . . . 4K 77
Harpsden St. SW11 . . . 1E 118
Harpur M. WC1 . . . 5G 7 (5K 83)
Harpur St. WC1 . . . 5G 7 (5K 83)
Harraden Rd. SE3 . . . 1A 124
Harrier Av. E11 . . . 6K 51
Harrier Centre, The . . . 6K 163
Harrier Ct. TW4: Houn . . . 3C 112
Harrier M. SE28 . . . 2H 107
Harrier Rd. NW9 . . . 2A 44
Harriers Cl. W5 . . . 7E 78
Harrier Way E6 . . . 5D 88
Harries Rd. UB4: Yead . . . 4A 76
Harriet Cl. E8 . . . 1G 85
Harriet Gdns. CR0: C'don . . . 2G 169
Harriet Ho. *SW6* . . . *7K 99*
(off Wandon Rd.)
Harriet M. DA16: Well . . . 2B 126
Harriet St. SW1 . . . 7F 11 (2D 100)
Harriet Tubman Cl. SW2 . . . 7K 119
Harriet Wlk. SW1 . . . 7F 11 (2D 100)
Harriet Way WD23: Bush . . . 1C 26
HARRINGAY . . . 5B 48
Harringay Gdns. N8 . . . 4B 48
Harringay Rd. N15 . . . 5B 48
(not continuous)
Harrington Cl. CR0: Bedd . . . 2J 167
NW10 . . . 3K 61
Harrington Ct.
CR0: C'don . . . 2D 168
SW7 . . . *3B 16*
(off Harrington Rd.)
W10 . . . 3H 81
Harrington Gdns. SW7 . . . 4K 99
Harrington Hill E5 . . . 1H 67
Harrington Ho. *NW1* . . . *1A 6*
(off Harrington St.)
UB10: Ick . . . 4D 56
Harrington Rd. E11 . . . 1G 69
SE25 . . . 4G 157
SW7 . . . 3A 16 (4B 100)
Harrington Sq. NW1 . . . 2G 83
Harrington St. NW1 . . . 1A 6 (2G 83)
(not continuous)
Harrington Way SE18 . . . 3B 106
Harriott Cl. SE10 . . . 4H 105
Harriott Ho. *E1* . . . *5J 85*
(off Jamaica St.)
Harris Bldgs. *E1* . . . *6G 85*
(off Burslem St.)
Harris Cl. EN2: Enf . . . 1G 23
TW3: Houn . . . 1E 112
Harris Ct. HA9: Wemb . . . 3F 61
Harris Ho. *E3* . . . *3C 86*
(off Alfred St.)
E11 . . . 1G 69
SW9 . . . *3A 120*
(off St James's Cres.)
Harris Lodge SE6 . . . 1E 140
Harrison Cl. N20 . . . 1H 31
RM7: Mawney . . . 3G 55
Harrison Ct. *E18* . . . *1J 51*
(off Queen Mary Av.)
Harrison Dr. BR1: Brom . . . 4E 160
Harrison Ho. E1 . . . 6H 85
SE17 . . . *5D 102*
(off Brandon St.)
Harrison Rd. NW10 . . . 1K 79
RM10: Dag . . . 6H 73
Harrisons Ct. *SE14* . . . *6K 103*
(off Myers La.)
Harrison's Ri. CR0: Wadd . . . 3B 168
Harrison St. WC1 . . . 2F 7 (3J 83)
Harrison Way TW17: Shep . . . 5D 146
Harris Rd. DA7: Bex . . . 1E 126
RM9: Dag . . . 5F 73
Harris Sports Cen. . . . 5J 121
Harris St. E17 . . . 7B 50
SE5 . . . 7D 102
Harris Way TW16: Sun . . . 1G 147
Harrod Ct. NW9 . . . 4J 43
Harrods . . . 1E 16 (3D 100)
Harrogate Ct. N11 . . . 6K 31
SE12 . . . 7J 123
SE26 . . . *3G 139*
(off Droitwich Cl.)
Harrold Ho. NW3 . . . 7B 64
Harrold Rd. RM8: Dag . . . 5B 72
Harrovian Bus. Village HA1: Harr . . . 7J 41
HARROW . . . 6J 41
Harrow Arts Cen. . . . 7A 26
Harrow Av. EN1: Enf . . . 6A 24
Harroway Rd. SW11 . . . 2B 118
Harrow Borough FC . . . 4D 58
Harrowby Ho. *W1* . . . *7E 4*
(off Harrowby St.)
Harrowby St. W1 . . . 7D 4 (6C 82)
Harrow Cl. KT9: Chess . . . 7D 162
Harrow Club W10 . . . 7F 81
Harrowdene Cl. HA0: Wemb . . . 4D 60
Harrowdene Gdns. TW11: Tedd . . . 6A 132
Harrowdene Rd. HA0: Wemb . . . 3D 60
Harrow Dr. N9 . . . 1A 34
Harrowes Meade HA8: Edg . . . 3B 28
Harrow Flds. Gdns. HA1: Harr . . . 3J 59
Harrow Gdns. KT8: E Mos . . . 3H 149
Harrowgate Ho. E9 . . . 6K 67
Harrowgate Rd. E9 . . . 6A 68
Harrow Grn. E11 . . . 3G 69
Harrow Hill Golf Course . . . 7K 41
Harrow La. E14 . . . 7D 86
Harrow Leisure Cen. . . . 3K 41
Harrow Lodge *NW8* . . . *3A 4*
(off Northwick Ter.)
Harrow Mnr. Way SE2 . . . 1C 108
SE28 . . . 7C 90
Harrow Mus. . . . 3G 41
HARROW ON THE HILL . . . 1J 59
Harrow Pk. HA1: Harr . . . 2J 59
Harrow Pl. E1 . . . 7H 9 (6E 84)
HARROW ROAD . . . 7H 61
Harrow Rd.
E6 . . . 1C 88
E11 . . . 3G 69
HA0: Wemb . . . 4K 59
HA9: Wemb . . . 5G 61
IG1: Ilf . . . 4G 71
IG11: Bark . . . 1J 89
NW10 . . . 3D 80
SM5: Cars . . . 6C 166
TW14: Bedf . . . 2C 128

Harrow Rd. W2 . . . . .6A 4 (5A 82)
(not continuous)
W9 . . . . .4F 81
W10 . . . . .4G 81
Harrow Rd. Bri. W2 . . . . .5A 82
Harrow Safari Cinema 5K 41
Harrow School Golf Course 2K 59
Harrow Sports Hall 7A 42
Harrow St. NW1 . . . . .5D 4
Harrow Vw. HA1: Harr 2G 41
HA2: Harr 2G 41
UB3: Hayes 6J 75
UB10: Hil 3E 74
Harrow Vw. Rd. W5 . . . . .4B 78
Harrow Way TW17: Shep 2E 146
HARROW WEALD 1J 41
Harrow Weald Lawn Tennis Club 1J 41
Harrow Weald Pk. HA3: Hrw W 6C 26
Harry Cl. CRO: C'don 6C 156
Harry Day M. SE27 . . . . .3C 138
Harry Hinkins Ho. SE17 . . . . .5C 102
(off Bronti Cl.)
Harry Lambourn Ho. SE15 . . . . .7H 103
(off Gervase St.)
Harry Zeital Way E5 . . . . .2J 67
Harston Wlk. E3 . . . . .4D 86
Hartcliff Cl. W7 . . . . .2K 95
Hart Cl. CRO: C'don 3B 168
Hart Ct. E6 . . . . .7E 70
Harte Rd. TW3: Houn 2D 112
Hartfield Av. UB5: N'olt 2K 75
Hartfield Cres. BR4: W W'ck 3J 171
SW19 . . . . .7H 135
Hartfield Gro. SE20 . . . . .1J 157
Hartfield Ho. UB5: N'olt 2K 75
(off Hartfield Av.)
Hartfield Rd. BR4: W W'ck 4J 171
KT9: Chess 5D 162
SW19 . . . . .7H 135
Hartfield Ter. E3 . . . . .2C 86
Hartford Av. HA3: Kenton 3A 42
Hartford Rd. DA5: Bexl 6G 127
KT19: Ewe 6H 163
Hart Gro. UB1: S'hall 5E 76
W5 .1G 97
Hart Gro. Ct. W5 . . . . .1G 97
Hartham Cl. N7 . . . . .5J 65
TW7: Isle 1A 114
Hartham Rd. N7 . . . . .5J 65
N17 . . . . .2F 49
TW7: Isle 1K 113
Harting Rd. SE9 . . . . .3C 142
Hartington Cl. BR6: Farnb 5G 173
HA1: Harr 4J 59
Hartington Cl. SW8 . . . . .1J 119
W4 .7H 97
Hartington Ho. SW1 . . . . .5D 18
(off Drummond Ga.)
Hartington Rd. E16 . . . . .6K 87
E6 .6A 50
SW8 . . . . .1J 119
TW1: Twick 7B 114
UB2: S'hall 3C 94
W4 .7H 97
W13 . . . . .7B 78
Hartismere Rd. SW6 . . . . .7H 99
Hartlake Rd. E9 . . . . .6K 67
Hartland NW1 .1G 83
(off Royal College St.)
Hartland Cl. HA8: Edg 2B 28
N21 . . . . .6H 23
Hartland Ct. N11 . . . . .5J 31
(off Hartland Rd.)
Hartland Dr. HA4: Ruis 3K 57
HA8: Edg 2B 28
Hartland Rd.
E15 . . . . .7H 69
N11 . . . . .5J 31
NW1 . . . . .7F 65
NW6 . . . . .2H 81
SM4: Mord 7J 153

Hartland Rd. TW7: Isle 3A 114
TW12: Hamp H 4F 131
Hartlands, The TW5: Cran 6K 93
Hartlands Cl. DA5: Bexl 6F 127
Hartland Way CRO: C'don 3A 170
SM4: Mord 7H 153
Hartlepool Ct. E16 . . . . .1F 107
Hartley Av. E6 . . . . .1C 88
NW7 . . . . .5G 29
Hartley Cl. BR1: Brom 2D 160
NW7 . . . . .5G 29
Hartley Ho. SE1 . . . . .4F 103
(off Longfield Est.)
Hartley Rd. CRO: C'don 7C 156
DA16: Well 7C 108
E11 . . . . .1H 69
Hartley St. E2 .3J 85
(not continuous)
Hart Lodge EN5: Barn 3B 20
Hartmann Rd. E16 . . . . .1B 106
Hartnoll St. N7 . . . . .5K 65
Harton Cl. BR1: Brom 1B 160
Harton Lodge SE8 . . . . .1C 122
(off Harton St.)
Harton Rd. N9 .2C 34
Harton St. SE8 . . . . .1C 122
Hartop Point SW6 . . . . .7G 99
(off Pellant Rd.)
Hartsbourne Av. WD23: B Hea 2B 26
Hartsbourne Cl. WD23: B Hea 2C 26
Hartsbourne Country Club & Golf Course
. . . . .2B 26
Hartsbourne Rd. UB1: S'hall 6G 77
(off Fleming Rd.)
Hartsbourne Pl. WD23: B Hea 2D 26
Hartsbourne Rd. WD23: B Hea 2C 26
Harts Gro. IG8: Wfd G 5D 36
Hartshill Cl. UB10: Hil 7D 56
Hartshorn All. EC3 . . . . .1H 15
Hartshorn Gdns. E6 . . . . .4E 88
Harts La. IG11: Bark 6F 71
SE14 . . . . .1A 122
Hartslock Dr. SE2 . . . . .2D 108
Hartsmead Rd. SE9 . . . . .2D 142
Hart Sq. SM4: Mord 6J 153
Hart St. EC3 . . . . .2H 15 (7E 84)
Hartsway EN3: Pond E 4D 24
Hartswood Gdns. W12 . . . . .3B 98
Hartswood Grn. WD23: B Hea 2C 26
Hartswood Rd. W12 . . . . .2B 98
Hartsworth Cl. E13 . . . . .2H 87
Hartville Rd. SE18 . . . . .4J 107
Hartwell Cl. SW2 . . . . .1K 137
Hartwell Dr. E4 . . . . .6K 35
Hartwell Ho. SE7 . . . . .5K 105
(off Troughton Rd.)
Hartwell St. E8 . . . . .6F 67
Harvard Ct. NW6 . . . . .5K 63
Harvard Hill W4 . . . . .6H 97
Harvard Ho. SE17 . . . . .6B 102
(off Doddington Gro.)
Harvard La. W4 . . . . .5J 97
Harvard Rd. SE13 . . . . .5E 122
TW7: Isle 1J 113
W4 . . . . .5H 97
Harvel Cl. BR5: St P 3K 161
Harvel Cres. SE2 . . . . .5D 108
Harvest Bank Rd. BR4: W W'ck 3H 171
Harvest Ct. RM13: Rain 2K 91
(off Broadis Way)
TW17: Shep 4C 146
Harvesters Cl. TW7: Isle 5H 113
Harvest La. KT7: T Ditt 6A 150
Harvest Rd. TW13: Felt 4J 129
Harvey Cl. NW9 . . . . .2A 44
Harvey Ct. E17 . . . . .5C 50
(off Brookscroft Rd.)
TW17: Shep 4C 146
Harvey Dr. TW12: Hamp 1F 149
Harvey Gdns. E11 . . . . .1H 69
SE7 . . . . .5A 106
Harvey Ho. E1 .4H 85
(off Brady St.)

Harvey Ho. N1 . . . . .1D 84
(off Colville Est.)
RM6: Chad H 4D 54
SW1 . . . . .6D 18
(off Aylesford St.)
TW8: Bford 5E 96
Harvey Lodge W9 . . . . .5J 81
(off Admiral Wlk.)
Harvey M. N8 .5K 47
(off Harvey Rd.)
Harvey Rd. E11 . . . . .1G 69
IG1: Ilf 5F 71
KT12: Walt T 7H 147
N8 .5K 47
SE5 . . . . .1D 120
(not continuous)
TW4: Houn 7D 112
UB5: N'olt 7A 58
UB10: Hil 2C 74
Harvey's Bldgs. WC2 . . . . . .3F 13 (7J 83)
Harveys La. RM7: Rush G 2K 73
Harvey St. N1 . . . . .1D 84
Harvil Ct. NW9 . . . . .3A 44
(off Mornington Cl.)
Harvill Rd. DA14: Sidc 5E 144
Harvil Rd. UB9: Hare 6A 38
UB10: Ick 6A 38
Harvington Wlk. E8 . . . . .7G 67
Harvist Est. N7 . . . . .4A 66
Harvist Rd. NW6 . . . . .2F 81
Harwell Cl. HA4: Ruis 1F 57
Harwell Pas. N2 . . . . .4D 46
Harwicke Ho. E3 . . . . .3D 86
(off Bow Rd.)
Harwood Av. BR1: Brom 2K 159
CR4: Mitc 3C 154
Harwood Cl. HA0: Wemb 4D 60
N12 . . . . .6H 31
Harwood Ct. N1 . . . . .1D 84
(off Colville Est.)
SW15 . . . . .4E 116
Harwood Dr. UB10: Hil 1B 74
Harwood M. SW6 . . . . .7J 99
Harwood Point SE16 . . . . .2B 104
Harwood Rd. SW6 . . . . .7J 99
Harwoods Yd. N21 . . . . .7F 23
Harwood Ter. SW6 . . . . .1K 117
Hascombe Ter. SE5 . . . . .2D 120
(off Love Wlk.)
Haselbury Rd. N9 . . . . .4K 33
N18 . . . . .4K 33
Haseley End SE23 . . . . .7J 121
Haselrigge Rd. SW4 . . . . .4H 119
Haseltine Rd. SE26 . . . . .4B 140
Haselwood Dr. EN2: Enf 4G 23
Haskard Rd. RM9: Dag 4D 72
Hasker St. SW3 . . . . .3D 16 (4C 100)
Haslam Av. SM3: Sutt 1G 165
Haslam Cl. N1 .7A 66
UB10: Ick 2E 56
Haslam Ct. N11 . . . . .4A 32
Haslam Ho. N1 . . . . .7C 66
(off Canonbury Rd.)
Haslam St. SE15 . . . . .7F 103
Haslemere Av. CR4: Mitc 2B 154
EN4: E Barn 1J 31
NW4 . . . . .6F 45
SW18 . . . . .2K 135
TW5: Cran 2A 112
W7 . . . . .3A 96
W13 . . . . .3A 96
Haslemere Bus. Cen. EN1: Enf 4C 24
Haslemere Cl. SM6: Wall 5J 167
TW12: Hamp 5D 130
Haslemere Gdns. N3 . . . . .3H 45
Haslemere Heathrow Estate, The
. . . . .2K 111
TW4: Cran 2K 111
Haslemere Ind. Est. SW18 . . . . .2K 135
Haslemere Rd. CR7: Thor H 5B 156
DA7: Bex 2F 127
IG3: Ilf 2K 71

Haslemere Rd. N8 . . . . .7H 47
N21 . . . . .2G 33
Hasler Cl. SE28 . . . . .7B 90
Haslers Wharf E3 . . . . .1A 86
(off Old Ford Rd.)
Haslett Rd. TW17: Shep 2G 147
Hasluck Gdns. EN5: New Bar 6E 20
Hassard St. E2 . . . . .1K 9 (2F 85)
Hassendean Rd. SE3 . . . . .7K 105
Hassett Rd. E9 . . . . .6K 67
Hassocks Cl. SE26 . . . . .3H 139
Hassocks Rd. SW16 . . . . .1H 155
Hassock Wood BR2: Kes 4B 172
Hassop Rd. NW2 . . . . .4F 63
Hassop Wlk. SE9 . . . . .4C 142
Hasted Rd. SE7 . . . . .5B 106
Haste Hill Golf Course 2G 39
Hastings Cl. EN5: New Bar 4F 21
HA0: Wemb 4C 60
SE15 . . . . .7G 103
Hastings Dr. TW11: Tedd 5H 131
Hastings Dr. KT6: Surb 6C 150
Hastings Ho. EN3: Enf H 2D 24
SE18 . . . . .4D 106
(off Mulgrave Rd.)
W12 . . . . .7D 80
(off White City Est.)
W13 . . . . .7B 78
WC1 . . . . .2E 6
(off Hastings St.)
Hastings Pl. CRO: C'don 1F 169
(off Hastings Rd.)
Hastings Rd. BR2: Brom 1C 172
CRO: C'don 1F 169
E16 . . . . .5J 87
N11 . . . . .5B 32
N17 . . . . .3D 48
W13 . . . . .7B 78
Hastings St. SE18 . . . . .3G 107
WC1 . . . . .2E 6 (3J 83)
Hastingwood Ct. E17 . . . . .5D 50
Hastingwood Trad. Est. N18 . . . . .6E 34
Hastoe Cl. UB4: Yead 4C 76
Hasty Cl. CR4: Mitc 1F 155
Hat & Mitre Ct. EC1 . . . . .4B 8
Hatch, The EN3: Enf H 1E 24
Hatcham Mews Bus. Cen. SE14 . . . . . . .1K 121
(off Hatcham Pk. Rd.)
Hatcham Pk. M. SE14 . . . . .1K 121
Hatcham Pk. Rd. SE14 . . . . .1K 121
Hatchard Rd. N19 . . . . .2H 65
Hatchcroft NW4 . . . . .3D 44
HATCH END 7A 26
Hatch End Lawn Tennis Club 6A 26
Hatch End Swimming Pool 7A 26
Hatchers M. SE1 . . . . .7H 15
Hatchett Rd. TW14: Bedf 1E 128
Hatchfield Ho. N15 . . . . .6E 48
(off Albert Rd.)
Hatch Gro. RM6: Chad H 4E 54
Hatch La. E4 . . . . .4A 36
UB7: Harm 3E 174
Hatch Pl. KT2: King T 5F 133
Hatch Rd. SW16 . . . . .2J 155
Hatch Side IG7: Chig 5K 37
Hatchwood Cl. IG8: Wfd G 4C 36
Hatcliffe Almshouses SE10 . . . . .5G 105
(off Tuskar St.)
Hatcliffe Cl. SE3 . . . . .3H 123
Hatcliffe St. SE10 . . . . .5H 105
Hatfield Cl. CR4: Mitc 4B 154
Hatfield Mead SM4: Mord 5J 153
Hatfield Cl. IG6: Ilf 3F 53
SE14 . . . . .7K 103
Hatfield Ct. SE3 . . . . .7J 105
UB5: N'olt 3A 76
(off Canberra Dr.)
Hatfield Ho. EC1 . . . . .4C 8
SE10 . . . . .7D 104

Hatfield M. RM9: Dag . . . 7E 72
Hatfield Rd. E15 . . . 5G 69
  RM9: Dag . . . 6E 72
  W4 . . . 2K 97
  HA1 . . . 1A 96
Hatfields SE1 . . . 4K 13 (1A 102)
Hathaway Cl. BR2: Brom . . . 1D 172
  HA4: Ruis . . . 4H 57
  HA7: Stan . . . 5F 27
Hathaway Cres. E12 . . . 6D 70
Hathaway Gdns. RM6: Chad H . . . 5D 54
  W13 . . . 5K 77
Hathaway Ho. N1 . . . 1G 9 (2E 84)
Hathaway Rd. CR0: C'don . . . 7B 156
Hatherleigh Cl. KT9: Chess . . . 5D 162
  NW7 . . . 6A 30
  SM4: Mord . . . 4J 153
Hatherleigh Rd. HA4: Ruis . . . 2J 57
Hatherley Ct. W2 . . . 6K 81
   (off Hatherley Gro.)
Hatherley Cres. DA14: Sidc . . . 2A 144
Hatherley Gdns. E6 . . . 3B 88
  N8 . . . 6J 47
Hatherley Gro. W2 . . . 6K 81
Hatherley Ho. E17 . . . 4C 50
Hatherley M. E17 . . . 4C 50
Hatherley Rd. DA14: Sidc . . . 4A 144
  E17 . . . 4B 50
  TW9: Kew . . . 1F 115
Hatherley St. SW1 . . . 4B 18 (4G 101)
Hathern Gdns. SE9 . . . 4E 142
Hatherop Rd. TW12: Hamp . . . 7D 130
Hathersage Ct. N1 . . . 5D 66
Hathorne Cl. SE15 . . . 2H 121
Hathway St. SE14 . . . 2K 121
Hathway Ter. SE14 . . . 2K 121
   (off Hathway St.)
Hatley Av. IG6: Ilf . . . 4G 53
Hatley Cl. N11 . . . 5J 31
Hatley Rd. N4 . . . 2K 65
Hatteraick St. SE16 . . . 2J 103
Hattersfield Cl. DA17: Belv . . . 4H 109
HATTON . . . 4H 111
Hatton Cl. SE18 . . . 7H 107
HATTON CROSS . . . 4H 111
Hatton Cross Cen. TW6: H'row A . . . 3H 111
Hatton Gdn. EC1 . . . 5K 7 (5A 84)
Hatton Gdns. CR4: Mitc . . . 5D 154
Hatton Grn. TW14: Felt . . . 4J 111
Hatton Gro. UB7: W Dray . . . 2A 92
Hatton Ho. E1 . . . 7G 85
   (off Hindmarsh Cl.)
  KT1: King T . . . 2F 151
   (off Victoria Rd.)
Hatton Pl. EC1 . . . 5K 7 (5A 84)
Hatton Rd. CR0: C'don . . . 1A 168
  TW14: Bedf, Felt . . . 7E 110
Hatton Rd. Sth. TW14: Felt . . . 4H 111
Hatton Row NW8 . . . 4B 4
Hatton St. NW8 . . . 4B 4 (4B 82)
Hatton Wlk. EN2: Enf . . . 5J 23
   (off London Rd.)
Hatton Wall EC1 . . . 5K 7 (5A 84)
Haughmond N12 . . . 4E 30
Haunch of Venison Yd. W1 . . . 1J 11 (6F 83)
Hauteville Ct. Gdns. W6 . . . 3B 98
   (off South Side)
Havana Rd. SW19 . . . 2J 135
Havanna Dr. NW11 . . . 5G 45
Havannah St. E14 . . . 2C 104
Havant Rd. E17 . . . 3E 50
Havelock Cl. W12 . . . 7D 80
   (off Havelock Pl.)
Havelock Ho. SE1 . . . 4F 103
   (off Fort Rd.)
  SE23 . . . 1J 139
Havelock Pl. HA1: Harr . . . 6J 41
Havelock Rd. BR2: Brom . . . 4A 160
  CR0: C'don . . . 2F 169
  DA17: Belv . . . 4F 109

Havelock Rd. HA3: W'stone . . . 3J 41
  N17 . . . 2G 49
  SW19 . . . 5A 136
  UB2: S'hall . . . 3C 94
Havelock St. IG1: Ilf . . . 2F 71
  N1 . . . 1J 83
Havelock Ter. SW8 . . . 1F 119
Havelock Ter. Arches SW8 . . . 1F 119
   (off Havelock Ter.)
Havelock Wlk. SE23 . . . 1J 139
Haven, The TW9: Rich . . . 3G 115
  TW16: Sun . . . 7J 129
Haven Cl. DA14: Sidc . . . 6C 144
  SE9 . . . 3D 142
  SW19 . . . 3F 135
  UB4: Hayes . . . 4G 75
Haven Ct. BR3: Beck . . . 2E 158
  KT5: Surb . . . 6F 151
Haven Grn. W5 . . . 6D 78
Haven Grn. Ct. W5 . . . 6D 78
Havenhurst Ri. EN2: Enf . . . 2F 23
Haven La. W5 . . . 6E 78
Haven Lodge EN1: Enf . . . 6K 23
   (off Village Rd.)
  SE18 . . . 4F 107
   (off Vincent Rd.)
Haven M. E3 . . . 5B 86
  N1 . . . 7A 66
Haven Pl. W5 . . . 7D 78
Havenpool NW8 . . . 1K 81
   (off Abbey Rd.)
Haven Rd. TW15: Ashf . . . 4D 128
Haven St. NW1 . . . 7F 65
Haven Way SE1 . . . 3F 103
Havenwood HA9: Wemb . . . 3H 61
Haverfield Gdns. TW9: Kew . . . 7G 97
Haverfield Rd. E3 . . . 3A 86
Haverford Way HA8: Edg . . . 1F 43
Haverhill Rd. E4 . . . 1K 35
  SW12 . . . 1G 137
Havering NW1 . . . 7F 65
   (off Castlehaven Rd.)
Havering Dr. RM1: Rom . . . 4K 55
Havering Gdns. RM6: Chad H . . . 5C 54
Havering Mus. . . . 5K 55
Havering Rd. RM1: Rom . . . 3K 55
Havering St. E1 . . . 6K 85
Havering Way IG11: Bark . . . 3B 90
Haversham Cl. TW1: Twick . . . 6D 114
Haversham Ct. UB6: G'frd . . . 6K 59
Haversham Pl. N6 . . . 2D 64
Haverstock Ct. HA1: Harr . . . 7G 41
Haverstock Hill NW3 . . . 5C 64
Haverstock Pl. N1 . . . 1B 8
   (off Haverstock St.)
Haverstock Rd. NW5 . . . 5E 64
Haverstock St. N1 . . . 1B 8 (2B 84)
Haverthwaite Rd. BR6: Orp . . . 2H 173
Havil St. SE5 . . . 7E 102
Havisham Apartments E15 . . . 6F 69
   (off Grove Cres. Rd.)
Havisham Ho. SE16 . . . 2G 103
Havisham Pl. SE19 . . . 7B 138
Hawarden Gro. SE24 . . . 7C 120
Hawarden Hill NW2 . . . 3C 62
Hawarden Rd. E17 . . . 4K 49
Hawbridge Rd. E11 . . . 1F 69
Hawbush Ct. RM6: Ilf . . . 4B 54
Hawes Ho. E17 . . . 4K 49
Hawes La. BR4: W W'ck . . . 1E 170
Hawes Rd. BR1: Brom . . . 1K 159
   (not continuous)
  N18 . . . 6C 34
Hawes St. N1 . . . 7B 66
Haweswater Ho. TW7: Isle . . . 5K 113
Hawfinch Ho. NW9 . . . 7B 44
Hawgood St. E3 . . . 5C 86
Hawkdene E4 . . . 6J 25
Hawke Ct. UB4: Yead . . . 4A 76

Hawke Ho. E1 . . . 4K 85
   (off Ernest St.)
Hawke Pk. Rd. N22 . . . 3B 48
Hawke Pl. SE16 . . . 2K 103
Hawker NW9 . . . 1B 44
   (off Everglade Strand)
Hawker Ct. KT1: King T . . . 2F 151
   (off Church Rd.)
Hawke Rd. SE19 . . . 6D 138
Hawker Pl. E17 . . . 2E 50
Hawker Rd. CR0: Wadd . . . 6A 168
Hawkesbury Rd. SW15 . . . 5D 116
Hawkesfield Rd. SE23 . . . 2A 140
Hawkesley Cl. TW1: Twick . . . 4A 132
Hawkes Rd. CR4: Mitc . . . 1D 154
  TW14: Felt . . . 7J 111
Hawkesworth Cl. HA6: Nwood . . . 1G 39
Hawkes Yd. KT7: T Ditt . . . 6K 149
Hawke Twr. SE14 . . . 6A 104
Hawkewood Rd. TW16: Sun . . . 3J 147
Hawkfield Ct. TW7: Isle . . . 2J 113
Hawkhurst Gdns. KT9: Chess . . . 4E 162
Hawkhurst Rd. SW16 . . . 1H 155
Hawkhurst Way BR4: W W'ck . . . 2D 170
  KT3: N Mald . . . 5K 151
Hawkinge N17 . . . 2D 48
   (off Gloucester Rd.)
Hawkins Cl. HA1: Harr . . . 7H 41
  NW7 . . . 5E 28
Hawkins Ct. SE18 . . . 4C 106
Hawkins Ho. SE8 . . . 6C 104
   (off New King St.)
  SW1 . . . 7B 18
   (off Dolphin Sq.)
Hawkins Rd. NW10 . . . 7A 62
  TW11: Tedd . . . 6B 132
Hawkins Ter. SE7 . . . 5C 106
Hawksby Way SE6 . . . 5C 140
Hawksley Gdns. SE27 . . . 2B 138
Hawkridge Cl. RM6: Chad H . . . 6C 54
Hawksbrook La. BR3: Beck . . . 6D 158
Hawkshaw Cl. SW2 . . . 7J 119
Hawkshead NW1 . . . 1A 6
Hawkshead Cl. BR1: Brom . . . 7G 141
Hawkshead Rd. NW10 . . . 7B 62
  W4 . . . 2A 98
Hawkslade Rd. SE15 . . . 5K 121
Hawksley Rd. N16 . . . 3E 66
Hawks M. SE10 . . . 7E 104
Hawksmoor Cl. E6 . . . 6C 88
  SE18 . . . 5J 107
Hawksmoor Gro.
  BR2: Brom . . . 6B 160
Hawksmoor M. E1 . . . 7H 85
Hawksmoor Pl. E2 . . . 3K 9
   (off Cheshire St.)
Hawksmoor St. W6 . . . 6F 99
Hawksmouth E4 . . . 7K 25
Hawks Pas. KT1: King T . . . 2F 151
   (off Minerva Rd.)
Hawks Rd. KT1: King T . . . 2F 151
Hawkstone Rd. SE16 . . . 4J 103
Hawksworth Ho. BR1: Brom . . . 2J 159
Hawkwell Ct. E4 . . . 3K 35
Hawkwell Ho. RM8: Dag . . . 1G 73
Hawkwell Wlk. N1 . . . 1C 84
   (off Maldon Cl.)
Hawkwood Cres. E4 . . . 6J 25
Hawkwood La. BR7: Chst . . . 1G 161
Hawkwood Mt. E5 . . . 1H 67
Hawlands Dr. HA5: Pinn . . . 7C 40
Hawley Cl. TW12: Hamp . . . 6D 130
Hawley Cres. NW1 . . . 7F 65
Hawley M. NW1 . . . 7F 65
Hawley Rd. N18 . . . 5E 34
  NW1 . . . 7F 65
   (not continuous)
Hawley St. NW1 . . . 7F 65
Hawley Way TW15: Ashf . . . 5C 128
Hawstead Rd. SE6 . . . 6D 122
Hawsted IG9: Buck H . . . 1E 36

Hawthorn Av. CR7: Thor H . . . 1B 156
  E3 . . . 1B 86
  N13 . . . 5D 32
Hawthorn Centre, The HA1: Harr . . . 5K 41
Hawthorn Cl. BR5: Pet W . . . 6H 161
  TW5: Cran . . . 7K 93
  TW12: Hamp . . . 5E 130
Hawthorn Cotts. DA16: Well . . . 3A 126
   (off Hook La.)
Hawthorn Ct. HA5: Pinn . . . 2A 40
   (off Rickmansworth Rd.)
  TW9: Kew . . . 1H 115
  TW15: Ashf . . . 7E 128
Hawthorn Cres. SW17 . . . 5E 136
Hawthornden Cl. N12 . . . 6H 31
Hawthorndene Cl. BR2: Hayes . . . 2H 171
Hawthorndene Rd. BR2: Hayes . . . 2H 171
Hawthorn Dr. BR4: W W'ck . . . 4G 171
  HA2: Harr . . . 6E 40
Hawthorne Av. CR4: Mitc . . . 2B 154
  HA3: Kenton . . . 6A 42
  HA4: Ruis . . . 6K 39
  SM5: Cars . . . 7E 166
Hawthorne Cl. BR1: Brom . . . 3D 160
  N1 . . . 6E 66
  SM1: Sutt . . . 2A 166
Hawthorne Ct. HA6: Nwood . . . 2J 39
  W5 . . . 1E 96
Hawthorne Cres. SE10 . . . 5H 105
  UB7: W Dray . . . 2B 92
Hawthorne Gro. NW9 . . . 7J 43
Hawthorne Ho. N15 . . . 5G 49
  SW1 . . . 6B 18
   (off Churchill Gdns.)
Hawthorne M. UB6: G'frd . . . 6G 77
Hawthorne Pl. UB3: Hayes . . . 7H 75
Hawthorne Rd. BR1: Brom . . . 3C 160
  E17 . . . 3C 50
Hawthorne Way N9 . . . 2A 34
Hawthorn Farm Av. UB5: N'olt . . . 1C 76
Hawthorn Gdns. W5 . . . 3D 96
Hawthorn Gro. EN2: Enf . . . 1J 23
  SE20 . . . 7H 139
Hawthorn Hatch TW8: Bford . . . 7B 96
Hawthorn M. NW7 . . . 1G 45
Hawthorn Pl. DA8: Erith . . . 5J 109
Hawthorn Rd. DA6: Bex . . . 4F 127
  IG9: Buck H . . . 4G 37
  N8 . . . 3H 47
  N18 . . . 6A 34
  NW10 . . . 7C 62
  SM1: Sutt . . . 6C 166
  SM6: Wall . . . 7F 167
  TW8: Bford . . . 7B 96
  TW13: Felt . . . 1J 129
Hawthorns CR2: S Croy . . . 4C 168
   (off Bramley Hill)
  IG8: Wfd G . . . 3D 36
Hawthorns, The KT17: Ewe . . . 7B 164
  SL3: Poyle . . . 4A 174
Hawthorn Ter. DA15: Sidc . . . 5K 125
  N19 . . . 1H 65
   (off Calverley Gro.)
Hawthorn Wlk. W10 . . . 4G 81
Hawthorn Way TW17: Shep . . . 4F 147
Hawtrey Av. UB5: N'olt . . . 2B 76
Hawtrey Dr. HA4: Ruis . . . 7J 39
Hawtrey Rd. NW3 . . . 7C 64
Haxted Rd. BR1: Brom . . . 1K 159
Hay Cl. E15 . . . 7G 69
Haycroft Gdns. NW10 . . . 1C 80
Haycroft Rd. KT6: Surb . . . 2D 162
  SW2 . . . 5J 119
Hay Currie St. E14 . . . 6D 86
Hayday Rd. E16 . . . 5J 87
   (not continuous)
Hayden Ct. TW13: Felt . . . 4G 129
Hayden Piper Ho. SW3 . . . 7E 16
   (off Caversham St.)
Haydens M. W3 . . . 6J 79
Hayden's Pl. W11 . . . 6H 81

Hayden Way RM5: Col R 2J 55
Haydock Av. UB5: N'olt 6E 58
Haydock Grn. UB5: N'olt 6E 58
Haydock Grn. Flats UB5: N'olt 6E 58
               (off Haydock Grn.)
Haydon Cl. EN1: Enf 6K 23
  NW9 . . . . .4J 43
Haydon Cl. NW9 . . . . .4J 43
Haydon Dr. HA5: Eastc 4J 39
Haydon Pk. Rd. SW19 . . . . .5J 135
Haydon Rd. RM8: Dag 2C 72
Haydons Rd. SW19 . . . . .5K 135
Haydon St. E1 . . . . .6F 85
  EC3 . . . . .2J 15 (7F 85)
Haydon Wlk. E1 . . . . .1K 15 (6F 85)
Haydon Way SW11 . . . . .4B 118
Hay Dr. CR4: Mitc 2C 154
HAYES
  BR2 . . . . .1J 171
  UB3 . . . . .6G 75
Hayes & Yeading United FC 1A 94
Hayes Bri. Retail Pk. UB4: Yead . .7A 76
Hayes Chase BR4: W W'ck 6F 159
Hayes Cl. BR2: Hayes 2J 171
Hayes Ct. HA0: Wemb 1E 78
  SE5 . . . . .7C 102
         (off Camberwell New Rd.)
  SW2 . . . . .1J 137
Hayes Cres. NW11 . . . . .5H 45
  SM3: Cheam 4F 165
HAYES END 4F 75
Hayes End Cl. UB4: Hayes 4F 75
Hayes End Dr. UB4: Hayes 4F 75
Hayes End Rd. UB4: Hayes 4F 75
Hayesens Ho. SW17 . . . . .4A 136
Hayesford Pk. Dr. BR2: Brom 5H 159
Hayes Gdn. BR2: Hayes 1J 171
Hayes Gro. SE22 . . . . .3F 121
Hayes Hill BR2: Hayes 1G 171
Hayes Hill Rd. BR2: Hayes 1H 171
Hayes La. BR2: Brom, Hayes 5K 159
  BR3: Beck 3E 158
Hayes Mead Rd. BR2: Hayes 1G 171
Hayes Metro Cen. UB3: Yead 7A 76
Hayes Pk. Lodge UB4: Hayes 4F 75
Hayes Pl. NW1 . . . . .4D 4 (4C 82)
Hayes Rd. BR2: Brom 4J 159
  UB2: S'hall 4K 93
Hayes St. BR2: Hayes 1K 171
Hayes Swimming Pool 1H 93
HAYES TOWN 2H 93
Hayes Way BR3: Beck 4E 158
Hayes Wood Av. BR2: Hayes 1K 171
Hayfield Pas. E1 . . . . .4J 85
Hayfield Yd. E1 . . . . .4J 85
Haygarth Pl. SW19 . . . . .5F 135
Haygreen Cl. KT2: King T 6H 133
Hay Hill W1 . . . . .3K 11 (7F 83)
Hayhurst Ct. N1 . . . . .1B 84
             (off Dibden St.)
Hayland Cl. NW9 . . . . .4K 43
Hay La. NW9 . . . . .4J 43
Hayles Bldgs. SE11 . . . . .4B 102
             (off Elliotts Row)
Hayles St. SE11 . . . . .4B 102
Haylett Gdns. KT1: King T 4D 150
Hayling Av. TW13: Felt 3J 129
Hayling Cl. N16 . . . . .5E 66
Hayling Ct. SM3: Cheam 4E 164
Haymaker Cl. UB10: Uxb 7B 56
Hayman Cres. UB4: Hayes 2F 75
Haymans Point SE11 . . . .5G 19 (4K 101)
Hayman St. N1 . . . . .7B 66
Haymarket SW1 . . . . .3C 12 (7H 83)
Haymarket Arc. SW1 . . . . .3C 12
Haymarket Ct. E8 . . . . .7F 67
         (off Jacaranda Gro.)
Haymarket Theatre Royal 3D 12
Haymer Gdns. KT4: Wor Pk 3C 164
Haymerle Ho. SE15 . . . . .6G 103
           (off Haymerle Rd.)

Haymerle Rd. SE15 . . . . .6G 103
Hay M. NW3 . . . . .6D 64
Haymill Cl. UB6: G'frd 3K 77
Hayne Ho. W11 . . . . .1G 99
         (off Penzance Pl.)
Hayne Rd. BR3: Beck 2B 158
Haynes Cl. N11 . . . . .3K 31
  N17 . . . . .7C 34
  SE3 . . . . .3G 123
Haynes Dr. N9 . . . . .3C 34
Haynes La. SE19 . . . . .6E 138
Haynes Rd. HA0: Wemb 7E 60
Hayne St. EC1 . . . . .5B 8 (5B 84)
Haynt Wlk. SW20 . . . . .3G 153
Hayre Dr. UB2: S'hall 5C 94
Hay's Ct. SE16 . . . . .2J 103
         (off Rotherhithe St.)
Hay's Galleria SE1 . . . . . .4G 15 (1E 102)
Hays La. SE1 . . . . .4G 15 (1E 102)
Haysleigh Gdns. SE20 . . . . .2G 157
Hay's M. W1 . . . . .4J 11 (1F 101)
Haysoms Cl. RM1: Rom 4K 55
Haystall Cl. UB4: Hayes 2G 75
Hay St. E2 .1G 85
Hayter Cl. E11 . . . . .2K 69
Hayter Rd. SW2 . . . . .5J 119
Hayton Cl. E8 . . . . .6F 67
Hayward Cl. DA1: Cray 5K 127
  SW19 . . . . .7K 135
Hayward Ct. SW9 . . . . .2J 119
         (off Studley Rd.)
Hayward Gallery 5H 13 (1K 101)
Hayward Gdns. SW15 . . . . .6E 116
Hayward Ho. N1 . . . . .2A 84
         (off Penton St.)
Hayward M. SE4 . . . . .5B 122
Hayward Rd. KT7: T Ditt 7K 149
  N20 . . . . .2F 31
Haywards Cl. RM6: Chad H 5B 54
Hayward's Pl. EC1 . . . . . . .3A 8 (4B 84)
Haywood Cl. HA5: Pinn 2B 40
Haywood Lodge N11 . . . . .6D 32
         (off York Rd.)
Haywood Ri. BR6: Orp 5J 173
Haywood Rd.
  BR2: Brom 4B 160
Hazel Av. UB7: W Dray 3C 92
Hazel Bank SE25 . . . . .2E 156
Hazelbank KT5: Surb 1J 163
Hazelbank Rd. SE6 . . . . .2F 141
Hazelbourne Rd. SW12 . . . . .6F 119
Hazelbury Cl. SW19 . . . . .2J 153
Hazelbury Grn. N9 . . . . .3K 33
Hazelbury La. N9 . . . . .3K 33
Hazel Cl. CR0: C'don 7K 157
  CR4: Mitc 4H 155
  N13 . . . . .3J 33
  N19 . . . . .2G 65
  NW9 . . . . .2A 44
  SE15 . . . . .2G 121
        (off Bournemouth Cl.)
  TW2: Whitt 7G 113
  TW8: Bford 7B 96
Hazel Ct. W5 . . . . .7E 78
Hazelcroft HA5: Hat E 6A 26
Hazelcroft Cl. UB10: Hil 7B 56
Hazeldean Rd. NW10 . . . . .7K 61
Hazeldene Dr. HA5: Pinn 3A 40
Hazeldene Gdns. UB10: Hil 1E 74
Hazeldene Rd. DA16: Well 2C 126
  IG3: Ilf .2B 72
Hazeldon Rd. SE4 . . . . .5A 122
Hazeleigh Gdns. IG8: Wfd G 5H 37
Hazel Gdns. HA8: Edg 4C 28
Hazel Gro. EN1: Enf 1G 33
Hazel Gro. BR6: Farnb 2F 173
  EN1: Enf 6B 24
  HA0: Wemb 1E 78
  RM6: Chad H 3E 54
  SE26 . . . . .4K 139
  TW13: Felt 1J 129

Hazel Ho. E3 . . . . .1B 86
         (off Barge La.)
Hazelhurst BR3: Beck 1F 159
Hazelhurst Ct. SE6 . . . . .5E 140
        (off Beckenham Hill Rd.)
Hazelhurst Rd. SW17 . . . . .4A 136
Hazel La. IG6: Ilf 6K 37
  SE10 . . . . .5H 105
  TW10: Ham 2E 132
Hazell Cres. RM5: Col R 1H 55
Hazellville Rd. N19 . . . . .7H 47
Hazelmere Cl. TW14: Felt 6G 111
  UB5: N'olt 2D 76
Hazelmere Dr. SW2 . . . . .1K 137
Hazelmere Rd. BR5: Pet W 4G 161
  NW6 . . . . .1H 81
  UB5: N'olt 2D 76
Hazelmere Wlk. UB5: N'olt 2D 76
          (not continuous)
Hazelmere Way BR2: Hayes 6J 159
Hazel M. N22 . . . . .3A 48
         (off High Rd.)
Hazel Rd. E15 . . . . .5G 69
  NW10 . . . . .3D 80
         (not continuous)
Hazeltree La. UB5: N'olt 3C 76
Hazel Wlk. BR2: Brom 6E 160
Hazel Way E4 . . . . .6G 35
  SE1 . . . . .4F 103
Hazelwood Av. SM4: Mord 4K 153
Hazelwood Cl. HA2: Harr 4F 41
  W5 . . . . .2E 96
Hazelwood Ct. KT6: Surb 6E 150
  N13 . . . . .4F 33
         (off Hazelwood La.)
  NW10 . . . . .3A 62
Hazelwood Cres. N13 . . . . .4F 33
Hazelwood Ho. BR2: Brom 3G 159
Hazelwood La. N13 . . . . .4F 33
Hazelwood Rd. E17 . . . . .5A 50
  EN1: Enf 6A 24
Hazelwood Sports Club 7H 23
Hazlebury Rd. SW6 . . . . .2K 117
Hazledean Rd. CR0: C'don 2D 168
Hazledene Rd. W4 . . . . .6J 97
Hazlemere Gdns. KT4: Wor Pk 1C 164
Hazlewell Rd. SW15 . . . . .5E 116
Hazlewood Cl. E5 . . . . .3A 68
Hazlewood Cres. W10 . . . . .4G 81
Hazlewood M. SW9 . . . . .3J 119
Hazlewood Twr. W10 . . . . .4G 81
        (off Golborne Gdns.)
Hazlitt Cl. TW13: Hanw 4C 130
Hazlitt M. W14 . . . . .3G 99
Hazlitt Rd. W14 . . . . .3G 99
Heacham Av. UB10: Ick 3E 56
Headbourne Ho. E17 . . . . .3A 50
         (off Sutherland Rd.)
Headcorn Pl. CR7: Thor H 4K 155
Headcorn Rd. BR1: Brom 5H 141
  CR7: Thor H 4K 155
  N17 . . . . .7A 34
Headfort Pl. SW1 . . . . . . .7H 11 (2E 100)
Headingley Dr. BR3: Beck 6C 140
Headington Ct. CR0: C'don 4C 168
         (off Tanfield Rd.)
Headington Rd. SW18 . . . . .2A 136
Headlam Rd. SW4 . . . . .6H 119
         (not continuous)
Headlam St. E1 . . . . .4H 85
Headley App. IG2: Ilf 5F 53
Headley Av. SM6: Wall 5K 167
Headley Cl. KT19: Ewe 6G 163
Headley Ct. SE26 . . . . .5J 139
Headley Dr. CR0: New Ad 7D 170
  IG2: Ilf .6F 53

Head's M. W11 . . . . .6J 81
HEADSTONE 4G 41
Headstone Dr. HA1: Harr 3H 41
  HA3: W'stone 3H 41
Headstone Gdns. HA2: Harr 4G 41
Headstone La. HA2: Harr 1E 40
  HA3: Hrw W 7A 26
Headstone Manor 3G 41
Headstone Pde. HA1: Harr 4H 41
Headstone Rd. HA1: Harr 5J 41
Head St. E1 . . . . .6K 85
         (not continuous)
Headway Cl. TW10: Ham 4C 132
Headway Gdns. E17 . . . . .1C 50
Heald St. SE14 . . . . .1C 122
Healey Ho. E3 . . . . .4C 86
         (off Wellington Way)
  SW9 . . . . .7A 102
Healey St. NW1 . . . . .6F 65
Healy Cl. EN5: Barn 6A 20
Healy Dr. BR6: Orp 4K 173
Hearne Rd. W4 . . . . .6G 97
Hearn Ri. UB5: N'olt 1B 76
Hearn's Bldgs. SE17 . . . . .4D 102
Hearnshaw St. E14 . . . . .6A 86
Hearn St. EC2 . . . . .4H 9 (4E 84)
Hearnville Rd. SW12 . . . . .1E 136
Heart, The KT12: Walt T 7J 147
Heath, The W7 . . . . .1J 95
Heatham Pk. TW2: Twick 7K 113
Heath Av. DA7: Bex 6D 108
Heathbourne Rd. HA7: Stan 2D 26
  WD23: B Hea 1D 26
Heath Brow NW3 . . . . .3A 64
Heath Bus. Cen. TW3: Houn 4G 113
Heath Cl. CR2: S Croy 6B 168
  NW11 . . . . .7K 45
  UB3: Harl 7F 93
  W5 . . . . .4F 79
Heathcock Ct. WC2 . . . . .3F 13
         (off Exchange Ct.)
Heathcote Av. IG5: Ilf 2D 52
Heathcote Ct. IG5: Ilf 1D 52
         (not continuous)
Heathcote Gro. E4 . . . . .3K 35
Heathcote Rd. TW1: Twick 6B 114
Heathcote St. WC1 . . . . . .3G 7 (4K 83)
Heath Ct. CR0: C'don 4D 168
         (off Heathfield Rd.)
  SE9 . . . . .1G 143
  TW4: Houn 4D 112
  UB8: Uxb 7A 56
Heath Cft. NW11 . . . . .1K 63
Heathcroft W5 . . . . .4F 79
Heathcroft Av. TW16: Sun 7H 129
Heathcroft Gdns. E17 . . . . .1F 51
Heathdale Av. TW4: Houn 3C 112
Heathdene Dr. DA17: Belv 4H 109
Heathdene Rd. SM6: Wall 7F 167
  SW16 . . . . .7K 137
Heath Dr. NW3 . . . . .4K 63
  SM2: Sutt 7A 166
  SW20 . . . . .4E 152
Heathedge SE26 . . . . .2H 139
Heath End Rd. DA5: Bexl 1K 145
Heather Av. RM1: Rom 2K 55
Heatherbank BR7: Chst 2E 160
  SE9 . . . . .2D 124
Heather Cl. E6 . . . . .6D 88
  N7 . . . . .3K 65
  RM1: Rom 1K 55
  SE13 . . . . .7F 123
  SW8 . . . . .3F 119
  TW7: Isle 5H 113
  TW12: Hamp 1D 148
  UB8: Hil 5B 74
Heather Ct. DA14: Sidc 6D 144
Heatherdale Cl. KT2: King T 6G 133
Heatherdene Cl.
  CR4: Mitc 4B 154
  N12 . . . . .7F 31

Heather Dr.—Hemmings Cl.

Heather Dr. EN2: Enf 2G **23**
RM1: Rom 2K **55**
Heatherfold Way HA5: Eastc 3H **39**
Heather Gdns. NW11 6G **45**
RM1: Rom 2K **55**
SM2: Sutt 6J **165**
Heather Glen RM1: Rom 2K **55**
Heather Ho. *E14* *6E 86*
(off Dee St.)
Heatherlands TW16: Sun 6J **129**
Heather La. UB7: Yiew 6A **74**
Heatherlea Gro. KT4: Wor Pk 1D **164**
Heatherley Ct. E5 3G **67**
Heatherley Dr. IG5: Ilf 3C **52**
Heather Pk. Dr. HA0: Wemb 7G **61**
Heather Pk. Pde. *HA0: Wemb* *7F 61*
(off Heather Pk. Dr.)
Heather Rd. E4 6G **35**
NW2 2B **62**
SE12 2J **141**
Heathers, The TW19: Stanw 7B **110**
Heatherset Gdns. SW16 7K **137**
Heatherside Rd. DA14: Sidc 3C **144**
KT19: Ewe 7K **163**
Heatherton Ter. N3 2K **45**
Heather Wlk. HA8: Edg 5C **28**
TW2: Whitt *7E 112*
(off Stephenson Rd.)
W10 4G **81**
Heather Way CR2: Sels 7K **169**
HA7: Stan 6E **26**
RM1: Rom 2K **55**
Heatherwood Cl. E12 2A **70**
Heatherwood Dr. UB4: Hayes 2F **75**
Heathfield BR7: Chst 6G **143**
E4 3K **35**
HA1: Harr 7K **41**
Heathfield Av. SW18 7B **118**
Heathfield Cl. BR2: Kes 5A **172**
E16 5B **88**
Heathfield Ct. *E3* *2C 86*
(off Tredegar Rd.)
SE14 7J **103**
SE20 7J **139**
TW15: Ashf 3A **128**
W4 5K **97**
Heathfield Dr. CR4: Mitc 1C **154**
Heathfield Gdns. CR0: C'don 4D **168**
NW11 6F **45**
SE3 *2G 123*
(off Baizdon Rd.)
SW18 6B **118**
W4 5J **97**
Heathfield Ho. SE3 2G **123**
Heathfield La. BR7: Chst 6G **143**
Heathfield Nth. TW2: Twick 7J **113**
Heathfield Pk. NW2 6E **62**
Heathfield Pk. Dr. RM6: Chad H 5B **54**
Heathfield Ri. HA4: Ruis 7E **38**
Heathfield Rd. BR1: Brom 7H **141**
BR2: Kes 5A **172**
CR0: C'don 4D **168**
DA6: Bex 4F **127**
SW18 6A **118**
W3 2H **97**
Heathfields Ct. TW4: Houn 5C **112**
Heathfield Sth. TW2: Twick 7K **113**
Heathfield Sq. SW18 7B **118**
Heathfield Ter.
SE18 6J **107**
W4 5J **97**
Heathfield Va. CR2: Sels 7K **169**
Heath Gdns. TW1: Twick 1K **131**
Heathgate NW11 6K **45**
Heathgate Pl. NW3 5D **64**
Heath Gro. SE20 7J **139**
TW16: Sun 7H **129**
Heath Ho. DA15: Sidc 4K **143**
Heath Hurst Rd. NW3 4C **64**
Heathhurst Rd. CR2: Sande 7E **168**
Heathland Rd. N16 1E **66**
Heathlands Cl. TW1: Twick 2K **131**
TW16: Sun 2J **147**
Heathlands Way TW4: Houn 5C **112**
Heath La. SE3 2F **123**
(not continuous)
Heathlee Rd. SE3 4H **123**
Heathley End BR7: Chst 6G **143**
Heath Lodge WD23: B Hea 1D **26**
Heathmans Rd. SW6 1H **117**
Heath Mead SW19 3F **135**
Heath Pk. Dr. BR1: Brom 3C **160**
Heathpark Golf Course 3C **92**
Heath Pas. NW3 2K **63**
Heathpool Ct. E1 4H **85**
Heath Ri. BR2: Hayes 6H **159**
SW15 6F **117**
Heath Rd. CR7: Thor H 3C **156**
DA5: Bexl 1J **145**
HA1: Harr 7G **41**
RM6: Chad H 7D **54**
SW8 2F **119**
TW1: Twick 1K **131**
TW2: Twick 1K **131**
TW3: Houn, Isle 4F **113**
TW7: Isle 4F **113**
UB10: Hil 4E **74**
Heathrow Academy 1E **110**
HEATHROW AIRPORT
TERMINAL 4 5D **110**
TERMINAL 5 6D **174**
TERMINALS 1, 2, 3 3C **110**
Heathrow Blvd. UB7: Sip 7B **92**
(not continuous)
Heathrow Causeway Cen.
TW4: Houn 3K **111**
Heathrow Cl. UB7: Lford 4C **174**
Heathrow Gateway TW4: Houn 7C **112**
Heathrow Interchange UB4: Yead 1A **94**
Heathrow Intl. Trad. Est. TW4: Houn 3K **111**
Heathrow Prologis Pk. UB3: Harl 3D **92**
Heath Royal SW15 6F **117**
Heaths Cl. EN1: Enf 2K **23**
Heath Side BR5: Pet W 1G **173**
NW3 4B **64**
Heathside NW11 1J **63**
SE13 2E **122**
TW4: Houn 7D **112**
Heathside Av. DA7: Bex 1E **126**
Heathside Cl. IG2: Ilf 5H **53**
Heathstan Rd. W12 6C **80**
Heath St. NW3 3A **64**
Heath Ter. RM6: Chad H 7D **54**
Heath Vw. N2 4A **46**
Heathview NW5 4E **64**
Heath Vw. Cl. N2 4A **46**
Heathview Dr. SE2 6D **108**
Heathview Gdns. SW15 7E **116**
Heathview Rd. CR7: Thor H 4A **156**
Heath Vs. NW3 3B **64**
SE18 5K **107**
Heathville Rd. N19 7J **47**
Heathwall St. SW11 3D **118**
HEATHWAY 1G **91**
Heath Way DA8: Erith 1J **127**
Heathway CR0: C'don 3B **170**
IG8: Wfd G 5F **37**
RM9: Dag 3F **73**
RM10: Dag 3F **73**
SE3 7J **105**
UB2: S'hall 4B **94**
Heathway Ct. NW3 2J **63**
Heathway Ind. Est. RM10: Dag 4H **73**
Heathwood Gdns. SE7 4C **106**
Heathwood Point SE23 3K **139**
Heathwood Wlk. DA5: Bexl 1K **145**
Heaton Cl. E4 3K **35**
Heaton Ho. *SW10* *6A 100*
(off Fulham Rd.)
Heaton Rd. CR4: Mitc 7E **136**
SE15 2H **121**
Heaven Tree Cl. N1 6C **66**
Heaver Rd. SW11 3B **118**
Heavitree Cl. SE18 5H **107**
Heavitree Rd. SE18 5H **107**
(not continuous)
Hebden Ter. N17 6K **33**
Hebdon Rd. SW17 3C **136**
Heber Mans. *W14* *6G 99*
(off Queen's Club Gdns.)
Heber Rd. NW2 5F **63**
SE22 6F **121**
Hebrides Ct. *E1* *5A 86*
(off Ocean Est.)
Hebron Rd. W6 3E **98**
Hecham Cl. E17 2A **50**
Heckfield Pl. SW6 7J **99**
Heckford Ho. *E14* *6D 86*
(off Grundy St.)
Heckford St. E1 7K **85**
Heckford St. Bus. Cen. *E1* *7K 85*
(off Heckford St.)
Hector *NW9* *1B 44*
(off Five Acre)
Hector Cl. N9 2B **34**
Hector Ct. *SW9* *7A 102*
(off Caldwell St.)
Hector Ho. *E2* *2H 85*
(off Old Bethnal Grn. Rd.)
Hector St. SE18 4J **107**
Heddington Gro. N7 5K **65**
Heddon Cl. TW7: Isle 4A **114**
Heddon Ct. Av. EN4: Cockf 5J **21**
Heddon Ct. Pde. EN4: Cockf 5K **21**
Heddon Rd. EN4: Cockf 5J **21**
Heddon St. W1 2A **12** (7G **83**)
Hedera Pl. TW4: Houn 4D **112**
Hedgegate Ct. *W11* *6H 81*
(off Powis Ter.)
Hedge Hill EN2: Enf 1G **23**
Hedge La. N13 3G **33**
Hedgeley IG4: Ilf 4D **52**
Hedgemans Rd. RM9: Dag 7D **72**
Hedgemans Way RM9: Dag 6E **72**
Hedgerley Gdns. UB6: G'frd 2G **77**
Hedgerow Ct. *E6* *1D 88*
(off Nelson St.)
Hedgers Gro. E9 6A **68**
Hedger St. SE11 4B **102**
Hedges Cl. TW14: Felt 6K **111**
Hedge Wlk. SE6 5D **140**
Hedgewood Gdns. IG5: Ilf 5E **52**
Hedgley M. SE12 5H **123**
Hedgley St. SE12 5H **123**
Hedingham Cl. N1 7C **66**
Hedingham Ho. *KT2: King T* *1E 150*
(off Royal Quarter)
Hedingham Rd. RM8: Dag 5B **72**
Hedley Cl. RM1: Rom 5K **55**
Hedley Ho. *E14* *3E 104*
(off Stewart St.)
Hedley Rd. TW2: Whitt 7E **112**
Hedley Row N5 5D **66**
Hedsor Ho. *E2* *3J 9*
(off Ligonier St.)
Heenan Cl. IG11: Bark 6G **71**
Heene Rd. EN2: Enf 1J **23**
Heer M. *E2* *2G 85*
(off Hackney Rd.)
Hega Ho. *E14* *5E 86*
(off Ullin St.)
Heidegger Cres. SW13 7D **98**
Heigham Rd. E6 7C **70**
Heighton Gdns. CR0: Wadd 5B **168**
Heights, The BR3: Beck 7E **140**
(not continuous)
SE7 5A **106**
UB5: N'olt 5D **58**
Heights Cl. SW20 7D **134**
Heiron St. SE17 6B **102**
Helby Rd. SW4 6H **119**
Heldar Ct. SE1 7F **15** (2D **102**)
Helder Gro. SE12 7H **123**
Helder St. CR2: S Croy 6D **168**
Heldmann Cl. TW3: Houn 4H **113**
Helegan Cl. BR6: Chels 4K **173**
Helena Ct. *NW6* *7K 63*
(off Compayne Gdns.)
W5 5D **78**
Helena Pl. E9 1H **85**
Helena Rd. E13 2H **87**
E17 5C **50**
NW10 5D **62**
W5 5D **78**
Helena Sq. *SE16* *7A 86*
(off Sovereign Cres.)
Helen Av. TW14: Felt 7K **111**
Helen Cl. KT8: W Mole 4F **149**
N2 3A **46**
Helen Gladstone Ho. *SE1* *6A 14*
(off Surrey Row)
Helen Ho. *E2* *2H 85*
(off Old Bethnal Grn. Rd.)
Helen Mackay Ho. *E14* *6F 87*
(off Blair St.)
Helen Peele Cotts. *SE16* *3J 103*
(off Lower Rd.)
Helenslea Av. NW11 1J **63**
Helen's Pl. E2 3J **85**
Helen St. SE18 4F **107**
Helen Taylor Ho. *SE16* *3G 103*
(off Evelyn Lowe Est.)
Helford Cl. HA4: Ruis 2G **57**
Helgiford Gdns. TW16: Sun 7G **129**
Heligan Ho. *SE16* *2K 103*
(off Water Gdns. Sq.)
Helios Rd. SM6: Wall 1E **166**
Heliport Ind. Est. SW11 2B **118**
Helix Ct. *W11* *1F 99*
(off Swanscombe Rd.)
Helix Gdns. SW2 6K **119**
Helix Rd. SW2 6K **119**
Helix Ter. SW19 2F **135**
Hellings St. E1 1G **103**
Helm, The E16 7F **89**
Helme Cl. SW19 5H **135**
Helmet Row EC1 2D **8** (4C **84**)
Helmore Rd. IG11: Bark 7K **71**
Helmsdale Cl. UB4: Yead 4C **76**
Helmsdale Ho. *NW6* *2K 81*
(off Carlton Vale)
Helmsdale Rd. SW16 1H **155**
Helmsley Pl. E8 7H **67**
Helmsley St. E8 7H **67**
Helperby Rd. NW10 7A **62**
Helsby Ct. *NW8* *3A 4*
(off Pollitt Dr.)
Helsinki Sq. SE16 3A **104**
Helston *NW1* *1G 83*
(off Camden St.)
Helston Cl. HA5: Hat E 1D **40**
Helston Ct. *N15* *5E 48*
(off Culvert Rd.)
Helston Ho. *SE11* *5K 19*
(off Kennings Way)
Helvetia St. SE6 2B **140**
Helwys Ct. E4 6J **35**
Hemans St. SW8 7H **101**
Hemans St. Est. SW8 7J **101**
Hemberton Rd. SW9 3J **119**
Hemery Rd. UB6: G'frd 5H **59**
Hemingford Cl. N12 5G **31**
Hemingford Rd. N1 1K **83**
SM3: Cheam 4E **164**
Heming Rd. HA8: Edg 7C **28**
Hemington Av. N11 5J **31**
Hemingway Cl. NW5 4E **64**
Hemlock Cl. SW16 2G **155**
Hemlock Rd. W12 7B **80**
(not continuous)
Hemmen La. UB3: Hayes 6H **75**
Hemming Cl.
TW12: Hamp 1E **148**
Hemmings Cl. DA14: Sidc 2B **144**

Hemmings Mead—Hermitage La.

Hemmings Mead KT19: Ewe 6J **163**
Hemming St. E1 4G **85**
Hempstead Cl. IG9: Buck H 2D **36**
Hempstead Rd. E17 3F **51**
Hemp Wlk. SE17 4D **102**
Hemsby Rd. KT9: Chess 6F **163**
Hemstal Rd. NW6 7J **63**
Hemsted Rd. DA8: Erith 7K **109**
Hemswell Dr. NW9 1A **44**
Hemsworth Ct. N1 2E **84**
Hemsworth St. N1 2E **84**
Hemus Pl. SW3 6D **16** (5C **100**)
Hen & Chicken Ct. *EC4* *1J* ***13***
(off Fleet St.)
Hen & Chickens Theatre *6B* ***66***
(off St Paul's Rd.)
Henchman St. W12 6B **80**
Hendale Av. NW4 3D **44**
Henderson Cl. NW10 6J **61**
Henderson Ct. N12 4E **30**
NW3 *5B* ***64***
(off Fitzjohn's Av.)
SE14 *6K* ***103***
(off Myers La.)
Henderson Dr. NW8 3A **4** (4B **82**)
Henderson Ho. *RM10: Dag* *3G* ***73***
(off Kershaw Rd.)
Henderson Rd. CR0: C'don 6D **156**
E7 6A **70**
N9 1C **34**
SW18 7C **118**
UB4: Yead 3J **75**
Hendfield Ct. SM6: Wall 6F **167**
Hendham Rd. SW17 2C **136**
HENDON 4E **44**
Hendon Av. N3 1G **45**
Hendon Crematorium NW7 1F **45**
Hendon FC 4B **60**
Hendon Golf Course 7K **29**
Hendon Hall Ct. NW4 3F **45**
Hendon Ho. NW4 5F **45**
Hendon La. N3 3G **45**
Hendon Leisure Cen. 7F **45**
Hendon Lodge NW4 3D **44**
Hendon Pk. Mans. NW4 5E **44**
Hendon Pk. Row NW11 6H **45**
Hendon Rd. N9 2B **34**
Hendon Ter. TW15: Ashf 6F **129**
Hendon Way NW2 7F **45**
NW4 6D **44**
Hendon Wood La. NW7 1G **29**
Hendre Ho. *SE1* *4E* ***102***
(off Hendre Rd.)
Hendren Cl. UB6: G'frd 5H **59**
Hendre Rd. SE1 4E **102**
Hendrick Av. SW12 7D **118**
Heneage La. EC3 1H **15** (6E **84**)
Heneage Pl. EC3 1H **15** (6E **84**)
Heneage St. E1 5K **9** (5F **85**)
Henera's Ct. *BR1: Brom* *3E* ***160***
(off Brady Dr.)
Henfield Cl. DA5: Bexl 6G **127**
N19 1G **65**
Henfield Rd. SW19 1H **153**
Hengelo Gdns. CR4: Mitc 4B **154**
Hengest Av. KT10: Surb 3A **162**
Hengist Rd. DA8: Erith 7H **109**
SE12 7K **123**
Hengist Way BR2: Brom 4G **159**
SM6: Wall 7H **167**
Hengrave Rd. SE23 6J **121**
Hengrove Ct. DA5: Bexl 1E **144**
Hengrove Cres. TW15: Ashf 3A **128**
Henham Ct. RM5: Col R 1J **55**
Henley Av. SM3: Cheam 3G **165**
Henley Cl. *SE16* *2J* ***103***
(off St Marychurch St.)
TW7: Isle 1K **113**
UB6: G'frd 2G **77**
Henley Ct. N14 7B **22**
NW2 6F **63**
Henley Dr. KT2: King T 7B **134**
SE1 4F **103**
Henley Gdns. HA5: Eastc 3K **39**
RM6: Chad H 5E **54**
Henley Ho. *E2* *3K* ***9***
(off Swanfield St.)
Henley Prior *N1* *1G* ***7***
(off Affleck St.)
Henley Rd. E16 2D **106**
IG1: Ilf 4G **71**
N18 4K **33**
NW10 1E **80**
Henley St. SW11 2E **118**
Henley Way TW13: Hanw 5B **130**
Henlow Pl. TW10: Ham 2D **132**
HENLYS CORNER **4H 45**
HENLYS RDBT. **2A 112**
Hennel Cl. SE23 3J **139**
Hennessy Ct. E10 6E **50**
Hennessy Rd. N9 2D **34**
Henniker Gdns. E6 3B **88**
Henniker M. SW3 7A **16** (6B **100**)
Henniker Point *E15* *5G* ***69***
(off Leytonstone Rd.)
Henniker Rd. E15 5F **69**
Henningham Rd. N17 1D **48**
Henning St. SW11 1C **118**
Henrietta Barnet Wlk. NW11 6J **45**
Henrietta Cl. SE8 6C **104**
Henrietta Ct. *TW1: Twick* *7C* ***114***
(off Richmond Rd.)
Henrietta Gdns. N21 1F **33**
Henrietta Ho. *N15* *6E* ***48***
(off St Ann's Rd.)
W6 *5E* ***98***
(off Queen Caroline St.)
Henrietta M. WC1 3F **7** (4J **83**)
Henrietta Pl. W1 1J **11** (6F **83**)
Henrietta St. WC2 2F **13** (7J **83**)
Henriques St. E1 6G **85**
Henry Addlington Cl. E6 5F **89**
Henry Cl. EN2: Enf 1K **23**
Henry Cooper Way SE9 3B **142**
Henry Ct. HA7: Stan 7J **27**
Henry Dent Cl. SE5 3D **120**
Henry Dickens Ct. W11 7F **81**
Henry Doulton Dr. SW17 4E **136**
Henry Hatch Ct. SM2: Sutt 7A **166**
Henry Ho. SE1 5J **13** (1A **102**)
SW8 *7J* ***101***
(off Wyvil Rd.)
Henry Jackson Rd. SW15 3F **117**
Henry Macaulay Av. KT2: King T 1D **150**
Henry Moore Ct. SW3 6C **16** (5C **100**)
Henry Peters Dr. *TW11: Tedd* *5J* ***131***
(off Somerset Gdns.)
Henry Purcell Ho. *E16* *1K* ***105***
(off Evelyn Rd.)
Henry Rd. E6 2C **88**
EN4: E Barn 5G **21**
N4 1C **66**
SW9 1A **120**
Henrys Av. IG8: Wfd G 5C **36**
Henryson Rd. SE4 5C **122**
Henry St. BR1: Brom 1K **159**
Henry's Wlk. IG6: Ilf 1H **53**
Henry Tate M. SW16 5K **137**
Henry Tudor Ct. SE9 7G **125**
Henry Wise Ho. *SW1* *4B* ***18***
(off Vauxhall Bri. Rd.)
Hensford Gdns. SE26 4H **139**
Henshall Point *E3* *3D* ***86***
(off Bromley High St.)
Henshall St. N1 6D **66**
Henshawe Rd. RM8: Dag 3D **72**
Henshaw St. SE17 4D **102**
Henslowe Rd. SE22 5G **121**
Henslow Ho. *SE15* *7G* ***103***
(off Peckham Pk. Rd.)
Henson Av. NW2 5E **62**
Henson Cl. BR6: Farnb 2F **173**
Henson Path HA3: Kenton 3D **42**
Henson Pl. UB5: N'olt 1A **76**
Henstridge Pl. NW8 1C **82**
Henty Cl. SW11 7C **100**
Henty Wlk. SW15 5D **116**
Henville Rd. BR1: Brom 1K **159**
Henwick Rd. SE9 3B **124**
Henwood Side IG8: Wfd G 6J **37**
Hepburn Gdns. BR2: Hayes 1G **171**
Hepburn M. SW11 5D **118**
Hepburn Pl. W3 7H **79**
Hepdon M. SW17 5B **136**
Hepple Cl. TW7: Isle 2B **114**
Hepplestone Cl. SW15 6D **116**
Hepscott Rd. E9 6C **68**
Hepworth Ct. *N1* *1B* ***84***
(off Gaskin St.)
NW3 5C **64**
SM3: Sutt 1J **165**
SW1 6J **17** (5F **101**)
Hepworth Gdns. IG11: Bark 5A **72**
Hepworth Rd. SW16 7J **137**
Hepworth Way KT12: Walt T 7H **147**
Heracles *NW9* *1B* ***44***
(off Five Acre)
Hera Ct. *E14* *4C* ***104***
(off Homer Dr.)
Herald Gdns. SM6: Wall 2F **167**
Herald's Pl. SE11 3K **19** (4B **102**)
Herald St. E2 4H **85**
Herbal Hill EC1 4K **7** (4A **84**)
Herbal Hill Gdns. *EC1* *4K* ***7***
(off Herbal Hill)
Herbal Pl. EC1 4K **7**
Herbert Cres. SW1 1F **17** (3D **100**)
Herbert Gdns. NW10 2D **80**
RM6: Chad H 7D **54**
W4 6H **97**
Herbert Ho. *E1* *7J* ***9***
(off Old Castle St.)
Herbert M. SW2 6A **120**
Herbert Morrison Ho. *SW6* *6H* ***99***
(off Clem Attlee Ct.)
Herbert Pl. SE18 6F **107**
TW7: Isle 2H **113**
Herbert Rd. BR2: Brom 5B **160**
DA7: Bex 2E **126**
E12 4C **70**
E17 7B **50**
IG3: Ilf 2J **71**
KT1: King T 3F **151**
N11 7D **32**
N15 5F **49**
NW9 6C **44**
SE18 7E **106**
(not continuous)
SW19 7H **135**
(not continuous)
UB1: S'hall 1D **94**
Herbert St. E13 2J **87**
NW5 6E **64**
Herbrand Est. WC1 3E **6** (4J **83**)
Herbrand St. WC1 3E **6** (4J **83**)
Hercies Rd. UB10: Hil 7B **56**
Hercules Ct. SE14 6A **104**
Hercules Pl. N7 3J **65**
(not continuous)
Hercules Rd. SE1 2H **19** (3K **101**)
Hercules St. N7 3J **65**
Hercules Wharf *E14* *7G* ***87***
(off Orchard Pl.)
Hercules Yd. N7 3J **65**
Hereford Av. EN4: E Barn 1J **31**
Hereford Bldgs. *SW3* *7B* ***16***
(off Old Church St.)
Hereford Ct. HA1: Harr 4J **41**
SM2: Sutt 7J **165**
W7 *5K* ***77***
(off Copley Cl.)
Hereford Gdns. HA5: Pinn 5C **40**
IG1: Ilf 7C **52**
Hereford Gdns. SE13 5G **123**
TW2: Twick 1G **131**
Hereford Ho. *N18* *5C* ***34***
(off Cameron Cl.)
NW6 *2J* ***81***
(off Carlton Vale)
SW3 *1D* ***16***
(off Ovington Gdns.)
SW10 *7K* ***99***
(off Fulham Rd.)
Hereford Mans. *W2* *6J* ***81***
(off Hereford Rd.)
Hereford M. W2 6J **81**
Hereford Pl. SE14 7B **104**
Hereford Retreat SE15 7G **103**
Hereford Rd. E3 2B **86**
E11 5K **51**
TW13: Felt 1A **130**
W2 6J **81**
W3 7H **79**
W5 3C **96**
Hereford Sq. SW7 4A **100**
Hereford St. E2 4G **85**
Hereford Way KT9: Chess 5C **162**
Herent Dr. IG5: Ilf 4C **52**
Herent Gdns. IG5: Ilf 4D **52**
Hereward Gdns. N13 5F **33**
Hereward Rd. SW17 4D **136**
Herga Ct. HA1: Harr 3J **59**
Herga Rd. HA3: W'stone 4K **41**
Heriot Av. E4 2H **35**
Heriot Rd. NW4 5E **44**
Heriots Cl. HA7: Stan 4F **27**
Heritage Av. NW9 3B **44**
Heritage Cl. SW9 3B **120**
TW16: Sun 1J **147**
Heritage Ct. SE8 5K **103**
Heritage Hill BR2: Kes 5A **172**
Heritage Pl. SW18 1A **136**
Heritage Vw. HA1: Harr 3K **59**
Herlwyn Av. HA4: Ruis 2G **57**
Herlwyn Gdns. SW17 4D **136**
Her Majesty's Theatre *4C* ***12***
(off Haymarket)
Herm Cl. TW7: Isle 7G **95**
Hermes Cl. W9 4J **81**
Hermes Ct. SW2 6K **119**
SW9 *1A* ***120***
(off Southey Rd.)
Hermes St. N1 1J **7** (2A **84**)
Hermes Wlk. UB5: N'olt 2E **76**
Herm Ho. EN3: Enf W 1E **24**
N1 *6C* ***66***
(off Clifton Rd.)
Hermiston Av. N8 5J **47**
Hermitage, The KT1: King T 4D **150**
SE13 2E **122**
SE23 1J **139**
SW13 1B **116**
TW10: Rich 5E **114**
TW13: Felt 3H **129**
UB8: Uxb 6A **56**
Hermitage Cl. E18 4H **51**
EN2: Enf 2G **23**
KT10: Clay 6A **162**
SE2 3C **108**
TW17: Shep 4C **146**
Hermitage Ct. *E1* *1G* ***103***
(off Knighten St.)
E18 4J **51**
NW2 3J **63**
Hermitage Gdns. NW2 3J **63**
SE19 7C **138**
Hermitage Grn. SW16 1J **155**
Hermitage Ho. *N1* *2B* ***84***
(off Gerrard Rd.)
Hermitage La. CR0: C'don 7G **157**
N18 5J **33**
NW2 3J **63**
SE25 6G **157**
SW16 7K **137**

Hermitage Moorings E1 . . . . .1G 103
Hermitage Path SW16 . . . . .1J 155
Hermitage Rd. N4 . . . . .7B 48
N15 . . . . .7B 48
SE19 .7C 138
Hermitage Row E8 . . . . .5G 67
Hermitage St. W2 . . . . . . .6A 4 (5B 82)
Hermitage Vs. SW6 . . . . .6J 99
(off Lillie Rd.)
Hermitage Wlk. E18 . . . . .4H 51
Hermitage Wall E1 . . . . .1G 103
Hermitage Waterside E1 . . . . .1G 103
(off Thomas More St.)
Hermitage Way HA7: Stan 1A 42
Hermit Pl. NW6 . . . . .1K 81
Hermit Rd. E16 . . . . .5H 87
Hermit St. EC1 . . . . .1A 8 (3B 84)
Hermon Gro. UB3: Hayes 1J 93
Hermon Hill E11 . . . . .5J 51
E18 . . . . .5J 51
Herndon Rd. SW18 . . . . .5A 118
Herne Cl. NW10 . . . . .5K 61
UB3: Hayes 6H 75
Herne Ct. WD23: Bush 1B 26
HERNE HILL 5C 120
Herne Hill SE24 . . . . .6C 120
Herne Hill Ho. SE24 . . . . .6B 120
(off Railton Rd.)
Herne Hill Rd. SE24 . . . . .3C 120
Herne Hill Stadium 6D 120
Herne M. N18 . . . . .4B 34
Herne Pl. SE24 . . . . .5B 120
Herne Rd. KT6: Surb 2D 162
Heron Cl. E17 . . . . .2B 50
IG9: Buck H 1D 36
NW10 .6A 62
SM1: Sutt 5H 165
Heron Ct. BR2: Brom 4A 160
E14 . . . . .3E 104
(off New Union Cl.)
HA4: Ruis 2F 57
KT1: King T 3E 150
NW9 . . . . .2A 44
TW19: Stanw 1A 128
Heron Cres. DA14: Sidc 3J 143
Herondale Av. SW18 . . . . .1B 136
Heron Dr. N4 . . . . .2C 66
Herongate Rd. E12 . . . . .2A 70
Heron Hill DA17: Belv 5F 109
Heron Ho. DA14: Sidc 3B 144
E3 . . . . .1B 86
(off Sycamore Av.)
E6 . . . . .7C 70
NW8 . . . . .1C 4
(off Newcourt St.)
SW11 . . . . .7C 100
(off Searles Cl.)
W13 . . . . .4A 78
Heron Mead EN3: Enf L 1H 25
Heron M. IG1: Ilf 2F 71
Heron Pl. E16 . . . . .1A 106
(off Bramwell Way)
SE16 . . . . .1A 104
W1 . . . . .7H 5
(off Thayer St.)
Heron Quay E14 . . . . .1C 104
Heron Rd. CR0: C'don 2E 168
SE24 .4C 120
TW1: Twick 4A 114
Herons, The E11 . . . . .6H 51
Heronsforde W13 . . . . .6C 78
Heronsgate HA8: Edg 5B 28
Heron's Lea N6 . . . . .6D 46
Heronslea Dr. HA7: Stan 5K 27
Heron's Pl. TW7: Isle 3B 114
Heron Sq. TW9: Rich 5D 114
Herons Ri. EN4: E Barn 4H 21
Heron Tower 7H 9
Heron Trad. Est. W3 . . . . .5H 79

Heron Vw. TW8: Bford 7C 96
(off Commerce Rd.)
Heron Way SM6: Wall 7H 167
TW14: Felt 4J 111
Heronway IG8: Wfd G 4F 37
Herrick Ct. W3 . . . . .3J 97
(off Bollo Bri. Rd.)
Herrick Ho. N16 . . . . .4D 66
(off Howard Rd.)
SE5 . . . . .7D 102
(off Elmington St.)
Herrick Rd. N5 . . . . .3C 66
Herries St. W10 . . . . .2G 81
Herringham Rd. SE7 . . . . .3A 106
Herron Ct. BR2: Brom 4H 159
Herrongate Cl. EN1: Enf 2A 24
Hersant Cl. NW10 . . . . .1C 80
Herschell M. SE5 . . . . .3C 120
Herschell Rd. SE23 . . . . .7A 122
Hersham Cl. SW15 . . . . .7C 116
Hershell Ct. SW14 . . . . .4H 115
Hertford Av. SW14 . . . . .5K 115
Hertford Ct. EN4: Cockf 3G 21
Hertford Ct. E6 . . . . .3D 88
N13 . . . . .3F 33
Hertford Ho. UB5: N'olt 4D 76
Hertford Lock Ho. E3 . . . . .1B 86
(off Parnell Rd.)
Hertford Pl. W1 . . . . .4B 6 (4G 83)
Hertford Rd. EN3: Enf H, Enf W . . .3D 24
EN4: Cockf 3F 21
IG2: Ilf 6J 53
IG11: Bark 7E 70
N1 . . . . .1E 84
(not continuous)
N2 . . . . .3C 46
N9 . . . . .2C 34
Hertford St. W1 . . . . . . .5J 11 (1F 101)
Hertford Wlk. DA17: Belv 5G 109
Hertford Way CR4: Mitc 4J 155
Hertford Wharf N1 . . . . .1E 84
(off Hertford Rd.)
Hertslet Rd. N7 . . . . .3K 65
Hertsmere Ho. E14 . . . . .7C 86
(off Hertsmere Rd.)
Hertsmere Rd. E14 . . . . .1C 104
Hervey Cl. N3 . . . . .1J 45
Hervey Pk. Rd. E17 . . . . .4A 50
Hervey Rd. SE3 . . . . .1K 123
Hervey Way N3 . . . . .1J 45
Hesa Rd. UB3: Hayes 6J 75
Hesewall Cl. SW4 . . . . .2G 119
Hesketh Pl. W11 . . . . .7G 81
Hesketh Rd. E7 . . . . .3J 69
Heslop Rd. SW12 . . . . .1D 136
Hesper M. SW5 . . . . .4K 99
Hesperus Cres. E14 . . . . .4D 104
Hessel Rd. W13 . . . . .2A 96
Hessel St. E1 . . . . .6H 85
Hestercombe Av. SW6 . . . . .2G 117
Hesterman Way CR0: Wadd 1K 167
Hester Rd. N18 . . . . .5B 34
SW11 .7C 100
Hester Ter. TW9: Rich 3G 115
Hestia Ho. SE1 . . . . .7G 15
HESTON 7E 94
Heston Av. TW5: Hest 6C 94
Heston Centre, The TW5: Cran 5A 94
Heston Community Sports Hall 7E 94
Heston Grange TW5: Hest 6D 94
Heston Grange La. TW5: Hest 6D 94
Heston Ho. SE8 . . . . .1C 122
Heston Ind. Mall TW5: Hest 7D 94
Heston Phoenix Distribution Pk.
TW5: Hest 6A 94
Heston Pool 6D 94
Heston Rd. TW5: Hest 6C 94
HESTON SERVICE AREA 6B 94
Heston St. SE14 . . . . .1C 122

Hetherington Rd. SW4 . . . . .4J 119
TW17: Shep 2E 146
Hetherington Way UB10: Ick 4A 56
Hethpool Ho. W2 . . . . .4A 4
Hetley Gdns. SE19 . . . . .7F 139
Hetley Rd. W12 . . . . .1D 98
Heton Gdns. NW4 . . . . .4D 44
Hevelius Cl. SE10 . . . . .5H 105
Hever Ct. SE9 . . . . .4E 142
Hever Gdns. BR1: Brom 2E 160
Heverham Rd. SE18 . . . . .4J 107
Hever Ho. SE15 . . . . .6K 103
(off Lovelinch Cl.)
Hever Pl. KT8: E Mos 3G 149
Heversham Ho. SE15 . . . . .6J 103
Heversham Rd. DA7: Bex 2G 127
Hevingham Dr. RM6: Chad H 5C 54
Hewens Rd. UB4: Hil 4E 74
UB10: Hil 4E 74
Hewer St. W10 . . . . .5F 81
Hewett Cl. HA7: Stan 4G 27
Hewett Rd. RM8: Dag 5D 72
Hewetts Quay IG11: Bark 1F 89
Hewett St. EC2 . . . . .4H 9 (4E 84)
Hewish Rd. N18 . . . . .4K 33
Hewison St. E3 . . . . .2B 86
Hewitt Av. N22 . . . . .2B 48
Hewitt Cl. CR0: C'don 3C 170
Hewitt Rd. N8 . . . . .5A 48
Hewlett Ho. SW8 . . . . .7F 101
(off Havelock Ter.)
Hewlett Rd. E3 . . . . .2A 86
Hexagon, The N6 . . . . .1D 64
Hexagon Bus. Cen. UB4: Yead 7A 76
Hexal Rd. SE6 . . . . .3G 141
Hexham Gdns. TW7: Isle 7A 96
UB5: N'olt 5D 58
Hexham Rd. EN5: New Bar 4E 20
SE27 .2C 138
SM4: Mord 1K 165
Heybourne Cres. NW9 . . . . .1A 44
Heybourne Rd. N17 . . . . .7C 34
Heybridge NW1 . . . . .6F 65
(off Lewis St.)
Heybridge Av. SW16 . . . . .7J 137
Heybridge Dr. IG6: Ilf 2H 53
Heybridge Way E10 . . . . .7A 50
Heydon Cl. BR4: W W'ck 2G 171
(off Deer Pk. Way)
Heydon Ho. SE14 . . . . .1J 121
(off Kender St.)
Heyford Av. SW8 . . . . .7J 101
SW20 . . . . .3H 153
Heyford Rd. CR4: Mitc 2C 154
Heyford Ter. SW8 . . . . .7J 101
Heygate St. SE17 . . . . .4C 102
Heylyn Sq. E3 . . . . .3B 86
Heynes Rd. RM8: Dag 4C 72
Heysham La. NW3 . . . . .3K 63
Heysham Rd. N15 . . . . .6D 48
Heythorp St. SW18 . . . . .1H 135
Heythorp Dr. UB10: Ick 4B 56
Heywood Av. NW9 . . . . .1A 44
Heywood Ct. HA7: Stan 5H 27
Heywood Ho. SE14 . . . . .6K 103
(off Myers La.)
Heyworth Rd. E5 . . . . .4H 67
E15 . . . . .5H 69
Hibbert Ho. E14 . . . . .3C 104
(off Tiller Rd.)
Hibbert Rd. E17 . . . . .7B 50
HA3: W'stone 2K 41
Hibbert St. SW11 . . . . .3B 118
Hibernia Gdns. TW3: Houn 4E 112
Hibernia Point SE2 . . . . .2D 108
(off Wolvercote Rd.)
Hibernia Rd. TW3: Houn 4E 112
Hibiscus Cl. HA8: Edg 4D 28
Hibiscus Ho.
E17 . . . . .3D 50
TW13: Felt 1J 129

Hibiscus Lodge E15 . . . . .7G 69
(off Glenavon Rd.)
Hichisson Rd. SE15 . . . . .5J 121
Hicken Rd. SW2 . . . . .5K 119
Hickes Ho. NW6 . . . . .7B 64
Hickey's Almshouses TW9: Rich . . .4F 115
Hickin Cl. SE7 . . . . .4B 106
Hickin St. E14 . . . . .3E 104
Hickleton NW1 . . . . .1G 83
(off Camden St.)
Hickling Ho. SE16 . . . . .3H 103
(off Slippers Pl.)
Hickling Rd. IG1: Ilf 5F 71
Hickman Av. E4 . . . . .6K 35
Hickman Cl. E16 . . . . .5B 88
Hickman Rd. RM6: Chad H 7C 54
Hickmore Wlk. SW4 . . . . .3H 119
Hickory Cl. N9 . . . . .7B 24
Hicks Av. UB6: G'frd 3H 77
Hicks Bolton Ho. NW6 . . . . .2H 81
(off Denmark Rd.)
Hicks Cl. SW11 . . . . .3C 118
Hicks Ct. RM10: Dag 3H 73
Hicks Gallery 5J 135
Hicks Ho. SE16 . . . . .3G 103
(off Spa Rd.)
Hicks St. SE8 . . . . .5A 104
Hidcote Apartments SW11 . . . . . . .4C 118
(off Danvers Av.)
Hidcote Gdns. SW20 . . . . .3D 152
Hidden Cl. KT8: W Mole 4G 149
Hide E6 . . . . .6E 88
Hide Pl. SW1 . . . . .4C 18 (4H 101)
Hider Cl. SE3 . . . . .7A 106
Hide Rd. HA1: Harr 4G 41
Hides St. N7 . . . . .6K 65
Hide Twr. SW1 . . . . .4C 18
(off Regency St.)
Hierro Ct. E1 . . . . .5A 86
(off Ocean Est.)
Higgins Ho. N1 . . . . .1E 84
(off Colville Est.)
Higginson Ho. NW3 . . . . .7D 64
(off Fellows Rd.)
Higgins Wlk. TW12: Hamp 6C 130
(off Abbott Cl.)
Higgs Ind. Est. SE24 . . . . .3B 120
High Acres EN2: Enf 3G 23
HIGHAM HILL 2A 50
Higham Hill Rd. E17 . . . . .1A 50
Higham M. UB5: N'olt 4D 76
Higham Path E17 . . . . .3A 50
Higham Pl. E17 . . . . .3A 50
Higham Rd. IG8: Wfd G 6D 36
N17 . . . . .3D 48
Highams, The E17 . . . . .1E 50
Highams Ct. E4 . . . . .3K 35
Highams Lodge Bus. Cen. E17 . . . .3K 49
HIGHAMS PARK 6A 36
Higham Sta. Av. E4 . . . . .6H 35
Higham St. E17 . . . . .3A 50
High Ashton KT2: King T 7H 133
Highbanks Cl. DA16: Well 7B 108
Highbanks Rd. HA5: Hat E 6A 26
Highbank Way N8 . . . . .6A 48
HIGH BARNET 2A 20
Highbarrow Rd. CR0: C'don 1G 169
High Beech CR2: S Croy 7E 168
N21 . . . . .6E 22
High Beeches DA14: Sidc 5E 144
High Birch Ct. EN4: E Barn 4H 21
(off Park Rd.)
High Bri. SE10 . . . . .5F 105
Highbridge Ct. SE14 . . . . .7J 103
(off Farrow La.)
Highbridge Rd. IG11: Bark 1F 89
High Bri. Wharf SE10 . . . . .5F 105
(off High Bri.)
Highbrook Rd. SE3 . . . . .3B 124
High Broom Cres. BR4: W W'ck . . .7D 158
HIGHBURY .4B 66

Highbury Av. CR7: Thor H 2A 156
Highbury Cl. BR4: W W'ck 2D 170
KT3: N Mald 4J 151
HIGHBURY CORNER 6B 66
Highbury Cres. N5 ....5B 66
Highbury Est. N5 ....5C 66
Highbury Gdns. IG3: IIf 2J 71
N7 ....5A 66
Highbury Grange N5 ....4C 66
Highbury Gro. N5 ....5B 66
Highbury Gro. Ct. N5 ....6C 66
Highbury Hill N5 ....3A 66
Highbury Mans. N1 ....7B 66
(off Upper St.)
Highbury New Pk. N5 ....5C 66
Highbury Pk. N5 ....3B 66
Highbury Pk. M. N5 ....4C 66
Highbury Pl. N5 ....6B 66
Highbury Pool 6B 66
Highbury Quad. N5 ....3C 66
Highbury Rd. SW19 ....5G 135
Highbury Sq. N14 ....1B 32
Highbury Stadium Sq. N5 ....3B 66
Highbury Sta. Rd. N1 ....6A 66
Highbury Ter. N5 ....5B 66
Highbury Ter. M. N5 ....5B 66
High Cedar Dr. SW20 ....7E 134
Highclere Rd. KT3: N Mald 3K 151
Highclere St. SE26 ....4A 140
Highcliffe W13 ....5B 78
(off Clivedon Ct.)
Highcliffe Dr. SW15 ....6B 116
Highcliffe Gdns. IG4: IIf 5C 52
Highcombe SE7 ....6K 105
Highcombe Cl. SE9 ....1B 142
High Coombe Pl. KT2: King T 6K 133
Highcroft NW9 ....5A 44
Highcroft Av. HA0: Wemb 7G 61
Highcroft Est. N19 ....7J 47
Highcroft Gdns. NW11 ....6H 45
Highcroft Rd. N19 ....7J 47
High Cross Centre, The N15 ....4G 49
High Cross Rd. N17 ....3G 49
Highcross Way SW15 ....1C 134
Highdaun Dr. SW16 ....4K 155
Highdown KT4: Wor Pk 2A 164
Highdown Rd. SW15 ....6D 116
High Dr. KT3: N Mald 1J 151
High Elms IG8: Wfd G 5D 36
High Elms Country Pk.
(Local Nature Reserve) 7H 173
High Elms Golf Course 7G 173
High Elms Rd. BR6: Downe 7G 173
Highfield WD23: B Hea 2D 26
Highfield Av. BR6: Chels 5K 173
DA8: Erith 6H 109
HA5: Pinn 5D 40
HA9: Wemb 3F 61
NW9 ....5J 43
NW11 ....7F 45
UB6: G'frd 5J 59
Highfield Cl. HA6: Nwood 1G 39
KT6: Surb 1C 162
N22 ....1A 48
NW9 ....5J 43
SE13 ....6F 123
Highfield Ct. N14 ....6B 22
NW11 ....6G 45
Highfield Cres. HA6: Nwood 1G 39
Highfield Dr. BR2: Brom 4G 159
BR4: W W'ck 2D 170
KT19: Ewe 6B 164
UB10: Ick 4A 56
Highfield Gdns. NW11 ....6G 45
Highfield Hill SE19 ....7D 138
Highfield M. NW6 ....7K 63
(off Compayne Gdns.)
Highfield Rd. BR1: Brom 4D 160
BR7: Chst 3K 161
DA6: Bex 5F 127
HA6: Nwood 1G 39

Highfield Rd. IG8: Wfd G 7H 37
KT5: Surb 7J 151
KT12: Walt T 7J 147
N21 ....2G 33
NW11 ....6G 45
SM1: Sutt 5C 166
TW7: Isle 1K 113
TW13: Felt 2J 129
TW16: Sun 5H 147
W3 ....5H 79
Highfields SM1: Sutt 2J 165
Highfields Gro. N6 ....1D 64
High Foleys KT10: Clay 7B 162
High Gables BR2: Brom 2G 159
HIGHGATE 6E 46
Highgate Av. N6 ....7F 47
Highgate Cemetery N6 ....1E 64
Highgate Cl. N6 ....7E 46
Highgate Edge N2 ....5C 46
Highgate Golf Course 6C 46
Highgate Hgts. N6 ....6G 47
Highgate High St. N6 ....1E 64
Highgate Hill N6 ....1F 65
N19 ....1F 65
Highgate Ho. SE26 ....3G 139
Highgate Rd. NW5 ....3E 64
Highgate Spinney N8 ....6H 47
Highgate Wlk. SE23 ....2J 139
Highgate West Hill N6 ....1E 64
Highgate Wood School Sports Cen. 5G 47
High Gro. BR1: Brom 1B 160
SE18 ....7H 107
Highgrove Cl. BR7: Chst 1C 160
N11 ....5K 31
Highgrove Ct. BR3: Beck 7C 140
SM1: Sutt 6J 165
Highgrove Ho. HA4: Ruis 6J 39
Highgrove M. SM5: Cars 3D 166
Highgrove Rd. RM8: Dag 5C 72
Highgrove Swimming Pool 6J 39
Highgrove Ter. E4 ....2A 36
Highgrove Way HA4: Ruis 6J 39
High Hill Est. E5 ....1H 67
High Hill Ferry E5 ....1H 67
High Holborn WC1 ....7E 6 (6J 83)
Highland Av. RM10: Dag 3J 73
W7 ....6J 77
Highland Cotts. SM6: Wall 4G 167
Highland Ct. BR1: Brom 1H 159
E18 ....1K 51
Highland Cft. BR3: Beck 5D 140
Highland Dr. WD23: Bush 1A 26
Highland Pk. TW13: Felt 4H 129
Highland Rd. BR1: Brom 1H 159
BR2: Brom 5G 127
DA6: Bex 4H 127
HA6: Nwood 2H 39
SE19 ....6E 138
Highlands N20 ....2G 31
Highlands, The
EN5: New Bar 4D 20
HA8: Edg 2H 43
Highlands Av. N21 ....5E 22
W3 ....7J 79
Highlands Cl. N4 ....7J 47
TW3: Houn 1F 113
Highlands Ct. SE19 ....6E 138
Highlands Gdns. IG1: IIf 1D 70
Highlands Heath SW15 ....7E 116
Highlands Rd.
EN5: New Bar 5D 20
HIGHLANDS VILLAGE 5E 22
Highland Ter. SE13 ....3D 122
(off Algernon Rd.)
Highland Vw. Pk. Homes
UB7: W Dray 1D 174
High La. W7 ....5H 77
Highlawn Hall HA1: Harr 3J 59
Highlea Cl. NW9 ....7F 29
High Level Dr. SE26 ....4G 139
Highlever Rd. W10 ....5E 80

High Mead BR4: W W'ck 2F 171
HA1: Harr 5J 41
Highmead N18 ....5B 34
(off Fore St.)
SE18 ....7K 107
Highmead Cres. HA0: Wemb 7F 61
High Mdw. Cl. HA5: Eastc 4A 40
Highmeadow Cres. NW9 ....5K 43
High Meads Rd. E16 ....6B 88
Highmore Rd. SE3 ....7G 105
High Mt. NW4 ....6C 44
High Oaks EN2: Enf 1E 22
High Parade, The SW16 ....3J 137
High Pk. Av. TW9: Kew 1G 115
High Pk. Rd. TW9: Kew 1G 115
High Path SW19 ....1K 153
High Point N10 ....7E 46
SE9 ....3F 143
High Ridge N10 ....1F 47
Highridge Pl. EN2: Enf 1E 22
(off Oak Av.)
High Rd. E18 ....1J 51
HA0: Wemb 5D 60
HA3: Hrw W 7D 26
HA5: Eastc 6J 39
HA9: Wemb 5D 60
IG1: IIf 3F 71
(not continuous)
IG3: IIf 1K 71
IG7: Chig 5K 37
IG9: Buck H 2E 36
N11 ....5A 32
N15 ....4F 49
N17 ....2F 49
N22 ....7E 32
NW10 ....6A 62
RM6: Chad H 7D 54
UB4: Hayes 5G 75
UB10: Ick 3D 56
WD23: B Hea 1C 26
High Rd. E. Finchley N2 ....1B 46
High Rd. Leyton E10 ....6D 50
E15 ....2D 68
High Rd. Leytonstone E11 ....4G 69
E15 ....4G 69
High Rd. Nth. Finchley N12 ....3F 31
(not continuous)
High Rd. Whetstone N20 ....7F 21
High Rd. Woodford Grn. E18 ....1J 51
IG8: Wfd G 6C 36
High Sheldon N6 ....6D 46
Highshore Rd. SE15 ....2F 121
(not continuous)
Highstead Cres. DA8: Erith 1K 127
Highstone Av. E11 ....6J 51
Highstone Ct. E11 ....6H 51
(off New Wanstead)
Highstone Mans. NW1 ....7G 65
(off Camden Rd.)
High St. BR1: Brom 2J 159
(not continuous)
BR3: Beck 2C 158
BR4: W W'ck 1D 170
BR6: Chels 7K 173
BR6: Farnb 5F 173
BR6: Orp 2K 173
BR7: Chst 6F 143
CR0: C'don 3C 168
CR7: Thor H 4C 156
E11 ....5J 51
E13 ....2J 87
E15 ....2F 87
E17 ....5A 50
EN3: Pond E 6D 24
EN5: Barn 3B 20
HA1: Harr 1J 59
HA3: Hrw W, W'stone 2J 41
HA4: Ruis 7G 39
HA5: Pinn 3C 40
HA6: Nwood 1H 39
HA8: Edg 6B 28

High St. HA9: Wemb 4F 61
IG6: IIf 3G 53
KT1: Hamp W 1C 150
KT1: King T 3D 150
KT3: N Mald 4A 152
KT7: T Ditt 6A 150
KT8: W Mole 4E 148
KT12: Walt T 7J 147
KT17: Ewe 7B 164
N8 ....4J 47
N14 ....1C 32
NW7 ....5J 29
RM1: Rom 5K 55
SE20 ....6J 139
SE25 ....4F 157
SM1: Sutt 4K 165
SM3: Cheam 6G 165
SM5: Cars 5E 166
SW19 ....5F 135
TW2: Whitt 7G 113
TW3: Houn 3F 113
TW5: Cran 1J 111
TW8: Bford 7C 96
TW11: Tedd 5K 131
TW12: Hamp, Hamp H 1G 149
TW13: Felt 3H 129
TW17: Shep 6D 146
TW19: Stanw 6A 110
UB1: S'hall 1D 94
UB3: Harl 6F 93
UB7: Harm 2E 174
UB7: View 7A 74
UB8: Uxb 1A 74
W3 ....1H 97
W5 ....1D 96
High St. Colliers Wood SW19 ....7B 136
High St. Harlesden NW10 ....2B 80
High St. Mews SW19 ....5G 135
High St. Nth. E6 ....5C 70
E12 ....5C 70
High St. Sth. E6 ....2D 88
High Timber St. EC4 ....2C 14 (7C 84)
High Tor Cl. BR1: Brom 7K 141
High Tor Vw. SE28 ....1J 107
High Trees CR0: C'don 1A 170
EN4: E Barn 5H 21
N20 ....3F 31
SW2 ....1A 138
Hightrees Ct. W7 ....7J 77
Hightrees Ho. SW12 ....6E 118
Highview HA5: Pinn 4A 40
NW6 ....6G 47
NW7 ....3E 28
UB5: N'olt 3C 76
Highview Av. HA8: Edg 4D 28
SM6: Wall 5K 167
High Vw. Cl. SE19 ....2F 157
High Vw. Cl. HA3: Hrw W 7D 26
Highview Gdns. HA8: Edg 4D 28
N3 ....3G 45
N11 ....5B 32
Highview Ho. RM6: Chad H 4E 54
Highview Lodge EN2: Enf 3G 23
(off The Ridgeway)
High Vw. Pde. IG4: IIf 5D 52
High Vw. Rd. E18 ....2H 51
SE19 ....6D 138
Highview Rd. DA14: Sidc 4B 144
W13 ....5A 78
Highway, The E1 ....7G 85
HA7: Stan 1K 41
SM2: Sutt 7A 166
Highway Bus. Park, The E1 ....7K 85
(off Heckford St.)
Highway Trad. Centre, The E1 ....7K 85
(off Heckford St.)
Highwood BR2: Brom 3F 159
Highwood Av. N12 ....4F 31
Highwood Cl.
BR6: Farnb 2G 173
SE22 ....1G 139

Highwood Ct. EN5: New Bar 5D **20**
   N12 .3F **31**
Highwood Dr. BR6: Farnb 2G **173**
Highwood Gdns. IG5: Ilf 5D **52**
Highwood Gro. NW7 . . . . .5E **28**
HIGHWOOD HILL 3G **29**
Highwood Hill NW7 . . . . .2G **29**
Highwood Rd. N19 . . . . .3J **65**
Highworth Rd. N11 . . . . .6C **32**
Highworth St. NW1 . . . . .5D **4**
Hi-Gloss Cen. SE8 . . . . .5A **104**
Hilary Av. CR4: Mitc 3E **154**
Hilary Cl. DA8: Erith 1H **127**
   SW6 . . . . .7K **99**
Hilary Dennis Ct. E11 . . . . .4J **51**
Hilary Rd. W12 . . . . .6B **80**
   (not continuous)
Hilberry Ct. WD23: Bush 1A **26**
Hilbert Rd. SM3: Cheam 3F **165**
Hilborough Ct. E8 . . . . .7F **67**
Hilborough Way BR6: Farnb 5H **173**
Hilda Ct. KT6: Surb 7D **150**
Hilda Lockert Wlk. SW9 . . . . .2B **120**
   (off Loughborough Rd.)
Hilda Rd. E6 . . . . .7B **70**
   E16 . . . . .4G **87**
Hilda Ter. SW9 . . . . .2A **120**
Hilda Va. Cl. BR6: Farnb 4F **173**
Hilda Va. Rd. BR6: Farnb 4E **172**
Hildenborough Gdns.
   BR1: Brom 6G **141**
Hildenborough Ho. BR3: Beck 7B **140**
   (off Bethersden Cl.)
Hildenlea Pl. BR2: Brom 2F **159**
Hilderley Ho. KT1: King T 3F **151**
   (off Winery La.)
Hildreth St. SW12 . . . . .1F **137**
Hildreth St. M. SW12 . . . . .1F **137**
Hildyard Rd. SW6 . . . . .6J **99**
Hiley Rd. NW10 . . . . .3E **80**
Hilgrove Rd. NW6 . . . . .7A **64**
Hiliary Gdns. HA7: Stan 2C **42**
Hillary N8 . . . . .3J **47**
   (off Boyton Cl.)
Hillary Ct. TW19: Stanw 1A **128**
   (off Explorer Av.)
   W12 . . . . .2E **98**
   (off Titmuss St.)
Hillary Cres. KT12: Walt T 7A **148**
Hillary Dr. TW7: Isle 5K **113**
Hillary M. E14 . . . . .5D **86**
Hillary Ri. EN5: New Bar 4D **20**
Hillary Rd. UB2: S'hall 3E **94**
Hillbeck Cl. SE15 . . . . .7J **103**
   (not continuous)
Hillbeck Way UB6: G'frd 1H **77**
Hillborne Cl. UB3: Harl 5J **93**
Hillboro Ct. E11 . . . . .7F **51**
Hillborough Cl. SW19 . . . . .7A **136**
Hillbrook Rd. SW17 . . . . .3D **136**
Hill Brow BR1: Brom 1B **160**
Hillbrow KT3: N Mald 3B **152**
Hillbrow Cl. DA5: Bexl 4K **145**
Hillbrow Rd. BR1: Brom 7G **141**
Hillbury Av. HA3: Kenton 5B **42**
Hillbury Rd. SW17 . . . . .3F **137**
Hill Cl. BR7: Chst 5F **143**
   HA1: Harr 3J **59**
   HA7: Stan 4G **27**
   NW2 . . . . .3D **62**
   NW11 . . . . .6J **45**
Hillcote Av. SW16 . . . . .7A **138**
Hill Ct. EN4: E Barn 4H **21**
   UB5: N'olt 5E **58**
   W5 . . . . .4F **79**
Hillcourt Av. N12 . . . . .6E **30**
Hillcourt Est. N16 . . . . .1D **66**
Hillcourt Rd. SE22 . . . . .6H **121**
Hill Cres. DA5: Bexl 1J **145**
   HA1: Harr 5A **42**

Hill Cres. KT4: Wor Pk 2E **164**
   KT5: Surb 5F **151**
   N20 . . . . .2E **30**
Hill Crest DA15: Sidc 7A **126**
   KT6: Surb 5F **151**
Hillcrest N6 .7E **46**
   N21 . . . . .7F **23**
   SE24 .4D **120**
   W11 . . . . .7H **81**
   (off St John's Gdns.)
Hillcrest Av. HA5: Pinn 4B **40**
   HA8: Edg 4C **28**
   NW11 . . . . .5H **45**
Hillcrest Cl. BR3: Beck 6B **158**
   SE26 .4G **139**
Hillcrest Ct. RM5: Col R 1K **55**
   SM2: Sutt 6B **166**
   (off Eaton Rd.)
Hillcrest Gdns. KT10: Hin W 3A **162**
   N3 . . . . .4G **45**
   NW2 . . . . .3C **62**
Hillcrest Rd. BR1: Brom 5J **141**
   BR6: Chels 2K **173**
   E17 . . . . .2F **51**
   E18 . . . . .2H **51**
   W3 . . . . .1H **97**
   W5 . . . . .5E **78**
Hillcrest Vw. BR3: Beck 6B **158**
Hillcroft Av. HA5: Pinn 6D **40**
Hillcroft Cres. HA4: Ruis 3B **58**
   HA9: Wemb 4F **61**
   W5 . . . . .6D **78**
Hillcroft Rd. E6 . . . . .5F **89**
Hillcroome Rd. SM2: Sutt 6B **166**
Hillcross Av. SM4: Mord 6F **153**
Hilldale Rd. SM1: Sutt 4H **165**
Hilldown Ct. SW16 . . . . .7J **137**
Hilldown Rd. BR2: Hayes 1G **171**
   SW16 .7J **137**
Hill Dr. NW9 . . . . .1J **61**
   SW16 .3K **155**
Hilldrop Cres. N7 . . . . .5H **65**
Hilldrop Est. N7 . . . . .5H **65**
   (not continuous)
Hilldrop La. N7 . . . . .5H **65**
Hilldrop Rd. BR1: Brom 6K **141**
   N7 . . . . .5H **65**
Hill End BR6: Orp 2K **173**
Hillend SE18 . . . . .1F **123**
Hillersden Ho. SW1 . . . . .5J **17**
   (off Ebury Bri. Rd.)
Hillersdon Av. HA8: Edg 5A **28**
   SW13 .2C **116**
Hillery Cl. SE17 . . . . .4D **102**
Hill Farm Cotts. HA4: Ruis 7E **38**
Hill Farm Rd. UB10: Ick 4F **57**
   W10 . . . . .5F **80**
Hillfield Av. HA0: Wemb 7E **60**
   N8 . . . . .5J **47**
   NW9 . . . . .5A **44**
   SM4: Mord 6C **154**
Hillfield Cl. HA2: Harr 4G **41**
Hillfield Ct. NW3 . . . . .5C **64**
Hillfield Ho. N5 . . . . .5C **66**
Hillfield M. N8 . . . . .4K **47**
Hillfield Pk. N10 . . . . .4F **47**
   N21 . . . . .2F **33**
Hillfield Pk. M. N10 . . . . .4F **47**
Hill Fld. Rd. TW12: Hamp 7D **130**
Hillfield Rd. NW6 . . . . .5H **63**
Hillfoot Av. RM5: Col R 1J **55**
Hillfoot Rd. RM5: Col R 1J **55**
Hillgate Pl. SW12 . . . . .7F **119**
   W8 . . . . .1J **99**
Hillgate St. W8 . . . . .1J **99**
Hill Ga. Wlk. N6 . . . . .6G **47**
Hill Gro. RM1: Rom 3K **55**
   TW13: Hanw 2D **130**
Hill Ho. BR2: Brom 2H **159**
   E5 . . . . .1H **67**
   (off Harrington Hill)

Hill Ho. SE28 . . . . .1H **107**
Hill Ho. Apartments N1 . . . . .1H **7**
   (off Pentonville Rd.)
Hill Ho. Av. HA7: Stan 7E **26**
Hill Ho. Cl. N21 . . . . .7F **23**
Hill Ho. Dr. TW12: Hamp 1E **148**
Hill Ho. M. BR2: Brom 2H **159**
Hill Ho. Rd. SW16 . . . . .5K **137**
Hilliard Ho. E1 . . . . .1H **103**
   (off Prusom St.)
Hilliard Rd. HA6: Nwood 1H **39**
Hilliards Ct. E1 . . . . .1J **103**
Hillier Cl. EN5: New Bar 6E **20**
Hillier Gdns. CR0: Wadd 5A **168**
Hillier Ho. NW1 . . . . .7H **65**
   (off Camden Sq.)
Hillier Lodge TW11: Tedd 5H **131**
Hillier Pl. KT9: Chess 6D **162**
Hillier Rd. SW11 . . . . .6D **118**
Hilliers Av. UB8: Hil 3C **74**
Hilliers La. CR0: Bedd 3J **167**
HILLINGDON 3C **74**
Hillingdon Athletic Club 5F **39**
Hillingdon Athletics Stadium 6A **56**
Hillingdon Av. TW19: Stanw 1A **128**
HILLINGDON CIRCUS 6D **56**
Hillingdon Cl. HA3: Kenton 4D **42**
Hillingdon Cycling Circuit 1A **94**
Hillingdon Golf Course 2B **74**
HILLINGDON HEATH 4D **74**
Hillingdon Hill UB10: Hil 2A **74**
Hillingdon Pde. UB10: Hil 4D **74**
   (off Uxbridge Rd.)
Hillingdon Rd. DA7: Bex 2J **127**
   UB8: Uxb 1A **74**
   UB10: Uxb 1A **74**
Hillingdon Sports & Leisure Complex
    . . . . .6A **56**
Hillingdon St. SE17 . . . . .6B **102**
Hillingdon Gdns. IG8: Wfd G 2B **52**
Hill La. HA4: Ruis 1E **56**
Hillman Cl. UB8: Uxb 5A **56**
Hillman Dr. W10 . . . . .4E **80**
Hillman St. E8 . . . . .6H **67**
Hillmarton Rd. N7 . . . . .5J **65**
Hillmarton Ter. N7 . . . . .5J **65**
   (off Hillmarton Rd.)
Hillmead Dr. SW9 . . . . .4B **120**
Hillmore Cl. SE13 . . . . .3F **123**
   (off Belmont Hill)
Hillmore Gro. SE26 . . . . .5A **140**
Hill Path SW16 . . . . .5K **137**
Hillreach SE18 . . . . .5D **106**
Hill Ri. HA4: Ruis 1E **56**
   KT10: Hin W 2B **162**
   N9 . . . . .6C **24**
   NW11 . . . . .4K **45**
   SE23 . . . . .1H **139**
   TW10: Rich 5D **114**
   UB6: G'frd 7G **59**
Hillrise KT12: Walt T 7H **147**
Hillrise Mans. N19 . . . . .7J **47**
   (off Warltersville Rd.)
Hillrise Rd. N19 . . . . .7J **47**
Hill Rd. CR4: Mitc 1F **155**
   HA0: Wemb 3B **60**
   HA1: Harr 5A **42**
   HA5: Pinn 5C **40**
   N10 . . . . .1D **46**
   NW8 . . . . .2A **82**
   SM1: Sutt 5K **165**
   SM5: Cars 6C **166**
Hillsboro' Rd. SE22 . . . . .5E **120**
Hillsborough Ct. NW6 . . . . .1K **81**
   (off Mortimer Cres.)
Hillsgrove Cl. DA16: Well 7C **108**
HILLSIDE 4J **109**
Hillside DA8: Erith 4J **109**
   EN5: New Bar 5F **21**
   N8 . . . . .6H **47**
   NW5 . . . . .3E **64**

Hillside NW9 . . . . .4K **43**
   NW10 . . . . .7J **61**
   SE10 .7F **105**
   (off Croom's Hill)
   SW19 .6F **135**
Hillside Av. HA9: Wemb 4F **61**
   IG8: Wfd G 6F **37**
   N11 . . . . .6J **31**
Hillside Cl. IG8: Wfd G 5F **37**
   NW8 . . . . .2K **81**
   SM4: Mord 4G **153**
Hillside Cres. HA2: Harr 1G **59**
   HA6: Nwood 1J **39**
Hillside Dr. HA8: Edg 6B **28**
Hillside Gdns. E17 . . . . .3F **51**
   EN5: Barn 4B **20**
   HA3: Kenton 7E **42**
   HA6: Nwood 1J **39**
   HA8: Edg 4A **28**
   N6 . . . . .6F **47**
   N11 . . . . .6B **32**
   SM6: Wall 7G **167**
   SW2 . . . . .2A **138**
Hillside Gro. N14 . . . . .7C **22**
   NW7 . . . . .7H **29**
Hillside Ho. CR0: Wadd 4B **168**
   (off Duppas Av.)
Hillside La. BR2: Hayes 2H **171**
   (not continuous)
Hillside Mans. EN5: Barn 4C **20**
Hillside Pas. SW16 . . . . .2K **137**
Hillside Ri. HA6: Nwood 1J **39**
Hillside Rd. BR2: Brom 3H **159**
   CR0: Wadd 5B **168**
   HA5: Pinn 1K **39**
   HA6: Nwood 1J **39**
   KT5: Surb 4F **151**
   N15 . . . . .7E **48**
   SM2: Sutt 7H **165**
   SW2 . . . . .2K **137**
   UB1: S'hall 4E **76**
   W5 . . . . .5E **78**
Hills La. HA6: Nwood 1G **39**
Hillsleigh Rd. W8 . . . . .1H **99**
Hills M. W5 .7E **78**
Hills Pl. W1 . . . . .1A **12** (6G **83**)
Hills Rd. IG9: Buck H 1E **36**
Hillstone Ct. E3 . . . . .4D **86**
   (off Empson St.)
Hillstowe St. E5 . . . . .3J **67**
Hill St. TW9: Rich 5D **114**
   W1 . . . . .4H **11** (1E **100**)
Hill Top NW11 . . . . .4K **45**
   SM3: Sutt 7H **153**
   SM4: Mord 6J **153**
Hilltop E17 .3D **50**
Hilltop Av. NW10 . . . . .7J **61**
   (not continuous)
Hill Top Ct. IG8: Wfd G 6J **37**
Hilltop Ct. NW8 . . . . .7A **64**
   (off Alexandra Rd.)
Hilltop Gdns. BR6: Orp 2J **173**
   NW4 . . . . .2D **44**
Hilltop Ho. N6 . . . . .7H **47**
Hilltop Rd. NW6 . . . . .7J **63**
Hill Top Vw. IG8: Wfd G 6J **37**
Hilltop Way HA7: Stan 3F **27**
Hill Vw. NW3 . . . . .1D **82**
   (off Ainger Rd.)
Hillview SW20 . . . . .7D **134**
Hillview Av. HA3: Kenton 5E **42**
Hillview Cl. HA9: Wemb 2F **61**
Hillview Cres. IG1: Ilf 6D **52**
Hillview Cres. BR6: Orp 1J **173**
Hill Vw. Dr. DA16: Well 2J **125**
   SE28 . . . . .1J **107**
Hill Vw. Gdns. NW9 . . . . .5K **43**
Hillview Gdns. HA2: Harr 3E **40**
   NW4 . . . . .4F **45**
Hill Vw. Rd. KT10: Clay 7A **162**
   TW1: Twick 6A **114**

Hillview Rd. BR6: Orp 1K **173**
BR7: Chst 5E **142**
HA5: Hat E 1D **40**
NW7 . . . . .4A **30**
SM1: Sutt 3A **166**
Hillway N6 . . . . .2E **64**
NW9 . . . . .1A **62**
Hill-Wood Ho. NW1 . . . .*18 6*
(off Polygon Rd.)
Hillworth BR3: Beck 2D **158**
Hillworth Rd. SW2 . . . . .7A **120**
Hillyard Ho. SW9 . . . . .1A **120**
Hillyard Rd. W7 . . . . .5J **77**
Hillyard St. SW9 . . . . .1A **120**
Hillyfield E17 . . . . .2A **50**
Hillyfield Cl. E9 . . . . .5A **68**
Hilly Flds. Cres. SE4 . . . . .3C **122**
SE13 . . . . .3C **122**
Hilsea Point SW15 . . . . .1D **134**
Hilsea St. E5 . . . . .4J **67**
Hilton W13 . . . . .6C **78**
Hilton Av. N12 . . . . .5G **31**
Hilton Ho. SE4 . . . . .4K **121**
Hilton's Wharf SE10 . . . . .6D **104**
(off Norman Rd.)
Hilversum Cres. SE22 . . . . .5E **120**
Himalaya Palace Cinema 1D **94**
Hinchinbrook Ho. NW6 . . . . .1K **81**
(off Mortimer Cres.)
Hinchley Cl. KT10: Hin W 4A **162**
Hinchley Dr. KT10: Hin W 3A **162**
Hinchley Mnr. KT10: Hin W 3A **162**
Hinchley Way KT10: Hin W 3A **162**
HINCHLEY WOOD 3A **162**
Hinckley Rd. SE15 . . . . .4G **121**
Hind Cl. EC4 . . . . .1K **13** (6A **84**)
Hind Cres. DA8: Erith 6K **109**
Hinde Ho. W1 . . . . .7H **5**
(off Hinde St.)
Hinde M. W1 . . . . .7H **5**
Hindes Rd. HA1: Harr 5H **41**
Hinde St. W1 . . . . .7H **5** (6E **82**)
Hind Gro. E14 . . . . .6C **86**
Hindhead Cl. N16 . . . . .1E **66**
UB8: Hil 5D **74**
Hindhead Gdns. UB5: N'olt 1C **76**
Hindhead Point SW15 . . . . . . .1D **134**
Hindhead Way SM6: Wall 5J **167**
Hind Ho. N7 . . . . .4A **66**
SE14 . . . . .6C **103**
(off Myers La.)
Hindle Ho. E8 . . . . .5F **67**
Hindlip Ho. SW8 . . . . .1H **119**
Hindmans Rd. SE22 . . . . .5G **121**
Hindmans Way RM9: Dag 4F **91**
Hindmarsh Cl. E1 . . . . .7G **85**
Hindon Cl. SW1 . . . . .3A **18**
Hindrey Rd. E5 . . . . .5H **67**
Hindsley's Pl. SE23 . . . . .2J **139**
Hinkler Rd. HA3: Kenton 3D **42**
Hinksey Path SE2 . . . . .2D **108**
Hinstock NW6 . . . . .1K **81**
(off Belsize Rd.)
Hinstock Rd. SE18 . . . . .6G **107**
Hinton Av. TW4: Houn 4B **112**
Hinton Cl. SE9 . . . . .1C **142**
Hinton Ct. E10 . . . . .2D **68**
(off Leyton Grange Est.)
Hinton Rd. N18 . . . . .4K **33**
SE24 . . . . .3C **120**
SM6: Wall 6G **167**
SW9 . . . . .3B **120**
Hippisley Ct. TW7: Isle 3K **113**
Hippodrome M. W11 . . . . .7G **81**
Hippodrome Pl. W11 . . . . .7G **81**
Hiroshima Prom. SE7 . . . . .3A **106**
Hirst Ct. SW1 . . . . .7J **17** (6F **101**)
Hirst Cres. HA9: Wemb 3E **60**
Hitcham Rd. E17 . . . . .7B **50**
Hitchcock Cl. TW17: Shep 3B **146**

Hitchcock La. E20 . . . . .6E **68**
Hitchin La. HA7: Stan 7J **27**
Hitchin Rd. HA7: Stan 7K **27**
Hitchin Sq. E3 . . . . .2A **86**
Hithe Gro. SE16 . . . . .3J **103**
Hitherbroom Rd. UB3: Hayes . . .1J **93**
Hither Farm Rd. SE3 . . . . .3A **124**
Hitherfield Rd. RM8: Dag 2E **72**
SW16 . . . . .2K **137**
HITHER GREEN 6F **123**
Hither Grn. La. SE13 . . . . .5E **122**
Hithermoor Rd. TW19: Stanw M . .7B **174**
Hitherwell Dr. HA3: Hrw W 1H **41**
Hitherwood Dr. SE19 . . . . .4F **139**
Hittard Ct. SE17 . . . . .6D **102**
(off Red Lion Row)
The Hive 1E **42**
Hive Cl. WD23: B Hea 2C **26**
Hive Football & Fitness Centre, The
. . . . .1E **42**
Hive Rd. WD23: B Hea 2C **26**
HMP Belmarsh SE28 . . . . .2J **107**
HMP Brixton SW2 . . . . .6J **119**
HMP Holloway N7 . . . . .4J **65**
HMP Pentonville N7 . . . . .6K **65**
HMP Wandsworth SW18 . . . . . . .7B **118**
HMP Wormwood Scrubs W12 . . .6C **80**
HMS Belfast 4H **15** (1E **102**)
HMYOI Feltham TW13: Felt 3F **129**
Hoadly Ho. SE1 . . . . .5C **14**
(off Union St.)
Hoadly Rd. SW16 . . . . .3H **137**
Hobart Cl. N20 . . . . .2H **31**
UB4: Yead 4B **76**
Hobart Ct. CR2: S Croy 5D **168**
(off South Pk. Hill Rd.)
IG8: Wfd G 4C **36**
Hobart Dr. UB4: Yead 4B **76**
Hobart Gdns. CR7: Thor H 3D **156**
Hobart La. UB4: Yead 4B **76**
Hobart Pl. SW1 . . . . . .1J **17** (3F **101**)
TW10: Rich 7F **115**
Hobart Rd. IG6: Ilf 2G **53**
KT4: Wor Pk 3D **164**
RM9: Dag 4D **72**
UB4: Yead 4B **76**
Hobbayne Rd. W7 . . . . .6H **77**
Hobbes Wlk. SW15 . . . . .5D **116**
Hobbs Cl. SE1 . . . . .6K **15**
(off Mill St.)
Hobbs Grn. N2 . . . . .3A **46**
Hobbs M. IG3: Ilf 2K **71**
Hobbs Pl. N1 . . . . .1E **84**
Hobbs Pl. Est. N1 . . . . .2E **84**
(off Hobbs Pl.)
Hobbs Rd. SE27 . . . . .4C **138**
Hobby Ho. SE1 . . . . .4H **103**
Hobby St. EN3: Pond E 5E **24**
Hobday St. E14 . . . . .6D **86**
Hobhouse Ct. SW1 . . . . .3D **12**
(off Suffolk St.)
Hobill Wlk. KT5: Surb 6F **151**
Hoblands End BR7: Chst 6J **143**
Hobson's Pl. E1 . . . . .5G **85**
Hobury St. SW10 . . . . .7A **16** (6A **100**)
Hocker St. E2 . . . . . . .2J **9** (3F **85**)
Hockett Cl. SE8 . . . . .4A **104**
Hockington Ct. EN5: New Bar 4E **20**
Hockley Av. E6 . . . . .2C **88**
Hockley Cl. E18 . . . . .1J **51**
Hockley M. IG11: Bark 3J **89**
Hockliffe Ho. W10 . . . . .5E **80**
(off Sutton Way)
Hockney Cl. SE16 . . . . .5H **103**
(off Rossetti Rd.)
Hocroft Av. NW2 . . . . .3H **63**
Hocroft Ct. NW2 . . . . .3H **63**
Hocroft Rd. NW2 . . . . .4H **63**
Hocroft Wlk. NW2 . . . . .3H **63**
Hodder Dr. UB6: G'frd 2K **77**

Hoddesdon Rd. DA17: Belv 5G **109**
Hodes Row NW3 . . . . .4E **64**
Hodford Rd. NW11 . . . . .1H **63**
Hodgkin Cl. SE28 . . . . .7D **90**
Hodgkins M. HA7: Stan 5G **27**
Hodister Cl. SE5 . . . . .7C **102**
Hodnet Gro. SE16 . . . . .4K **103**
Hodson Cl. HA2: Harr 3D **58**
Hoecroft Cl. EN3: Enf W 1D **24**
(off Hoe La.)
Hoe La. EN1: Enf 1B **24**
EN3: Enf W 1C **24**
Hoe St. E17 . . . . .4C **50**
Hoever Ho. SE6 . . . . .4E **140**
Hoffmann Gdns. CR2: Sels 7H **169**
Hoffman Sq. N1 . . . . .1F **9**
Hofland Rd. W14 . . . . .3G **99**
Hogan M. W2 . . . . .5A **4** (5A **82**)
Hogan Way E5 . . . . .2G **67**
Hogarth Av. TW15: Ashf 6E **128**
Hogarth Bus. Pk. W4 . . . . .6A **98**
Hogarth Cl. E16 . . . . .5B **88**
W5 . . . . .5E **78**
Hogarth Ct. E1 . . . . .6G **85**
(off Batty St.)
EC3 . . . . .2H **15** (6E **84**)
NW1 . . . . .7G **65**
(off St Pancras Way)
SE19 . . . . .4F **139**
TW5: Hest 7C **94**
Hogarth Cres. CR0: C'don 7C **156**
SW19 . . . . .1B **154**
Hogarth Gdns. TW5: Hest 7E **94**
Hogarth Health Club, The 4B **98**
Hogarth Hill NW11 . . . . .4H **45**
Hogarth Ho. SW1 . . . . .4D **18**
(off Erasmus St.)
UB5: N'olt 2B **76**
(off Gallery Gdns.)
Hogarth Ind. Est. NW10 . . . . . . .4C **80**
Hogarth La. W4 . . . . .6A **98**
Hogarth Pl. SW5 . . . . .4K **99**
(off Hogarth Rd.)
Hogarth Rd. HA8: Edg 2G **43**
RM8: Dag 5B **72**
SW5 . . . . .4K **99**
HOGARTH RDBT. 6A **98**
Hogarth's House 6A **98**
(off Hogarth La.)
Hogarth Ter. W4 . . . . .6A **98**
Hogarth Way TW12: Hamp 1G **149**
Hog Hill Rd. RM5: Col R 1F **55**
Hogshead Pas. E1 . . . . .7H **85**
(off Tobacco Dock)
Hogsmill Ho. KT1: King T 3F **151**
(off Vineyard Cl.)
Hogsmill La. KT1: King T 3F **151**
Hogsmill Local Nature Reserve . .5H **163**
Hogsmill Wlk. KT1: King T 3E **150**
(off Penrhyn Rd.)
Hogsmill Way KT19: Ewe 5J **163**
Holbeach Cl. NW9 . . . . .1A **44**
Holbeach Gdns. DA15: Sidc 6J **125**
Holbeach M. SW12 . . . . .1F **137**
Holbeach Rd. SE6 . . . . .7C **122**
Holbeck Row SE15 . . . . .7G **103**
Holbein Ho. SW1 . . . . .5G **17**
(off Holbein M.)
Holbein M. SW1 . . . . . .5G **17** (5E **100**)
Holbein Pl. SW1 . . . . . .4G **17** (4E **100**)
Holbein Ter. RM8: Dag 4C **72**
(off Marlborough Rd.)
Holberton Gdns. NW10 . . . . .3D **80**
HOLBORN 7F **7** (6J **83**)
Holborn EC1 . . . . .6J **7** (5A **84**)
Holborn Bars EC1 . . . . .6J **7**
(off Holborn)
Holborn Cir. EC1 . . . . . .6K **7** (5A **84**)
Holborn Cl. NW7 . . . . .4G **29**
Holborn Ho. W12 . . . . .6D **80**
Holborn Pl. WC1 . . . . . .6G **7** (5K **83**)

Holborn Rd. E13 . . . . .4K **87**
Holborn Viaduct EC1 . . . . . .6K **7** (5B **84**)
Holborn Way CR4: Mitc 2D **154**
Holbrook Cl. EN1: Enf 1A **24**
N19 . . . . .1F **65**
Holbrook Ct. N7 . . . . .4J **65**
Holbrooke Pl. TW10: Rich 5D **114**
Holbrook Ho. BR7: Chst 1H **161**
Holbrook La. BR7: Chst 7H **143**
Holbrook Rd. E15 . . . . .2H **87**
Holbrook Way BR2: Brom 6D **160**
Holburne Cl. SE3 . . . . .1A **124**
Holburne Gdns. SE3 . . . . .1B **124**
Holburne Rd. SE3 . . . . .1A **124**
Holcombe Hill NW7 . . . . .3H **29**
Holcombe Ho. SW9 . . . . .3J **119**
(off Landor Rd.)
Holcombe Pl. SE4 . . . . .3A **122**
(off St Asaph Rd.)
Holcombe Rd. IG1: Ilf 7E **52**
N17 . . . . .3F **49**
Holcombe St. W6 . . . . .4D **98**
Holcote Cl. DA17: Belv 3E **108**
Holcroft Ct. W1 . . . . .5A **6**
Holcroft Ho. SW11 . . . . .3B **118**
Holcroft Rd. E9 . . . . .7J **67**
Holden Av. N12 . . . . .5E **30**
NW9 . . . . .1J **61**
Holdenby Rd. SE4 . . . . .5A **122**
Holden Cl. RM8: Dag 3B **72**
Holden Ho. N1 . . . . .1C **84**
(off Prebend St.)
SE8 . . . . .7C **104**
Holdenhurst Av. N12 . . . . .7F **31**
Holden Point E15 . . . . .6F **69**
(off Waddington St.)
Holden Rd. N12 . . . . .5E **30**
Holden St. SW11 . . . . .2E **118**
Holder Cl. N3 . . . . .7E **30**
Holdernesse Cl. TW7: Isle 1A **114**
Holdernesse Rd. SW17 . . . . .3D **136**
Holderness Ho. SE5 . . . . .3E **120**
Holderness Way SE27 . . . . .5B **138**
HOLDERS HILL 2F **45**
Holder's Hill Av. NW4 . . . . .2F **45**
Holders Hill Cir. NW7 . . . . .7B **30**
Holders Hill Cres. NW4 . . . . .2F **45**
Holders Hill Dr. NW4 . . . . .3F **45**
Holder's Hill Gdns. NW4 . . . . . . .2G **45**
Holders Hill Pde. NW7 . . . . .1G **45**
Holders Hill Rd. NW4 . . . . .2F **45**
NW7 . . . . .2F **45**
Holford Ho. SE16 . . . . .4H **103**
(off Camilla Rd.)
WC1 . . . . .1H **7**
(off Gt. Percy St.)
Holford M. WC1 . . . . .1J **7**
Holford Pl. WC1 . . . . . .1H **7** (3K **83**)
Holford Rd. NW3 . . . . .3A **64**
Holford St. WC1 . . . . . .1J **7** (3K **83**)
Holford Way SW15 . . . . .6C **116**
Holford Yd. WC1 . . . . .1J **7**
(off Cruikshank St.)
Holgate Av. SW11 . . . . .3B **118**
Holgate Gdns. RM10: Dag 6G **73**
Holgate Rd. RM10: Dag 5G **73**
Holgate St. SE7 . . . . .3B **106**
Holinser Ter. W5 . . . . .1D **96**
Hollam Ho. N8 . . . . .4K **47**
Holland Av. SM2: Sutt 7J **165**
SW20 . . . . .1B **152**
Holland Cl.
BR2: Hayes 2H **171**
EN5: New Bar 7G **21**
HA7: Stan 5G **27**
RM7: Rom 5J **55**
Holland Ct. E17 . . . . .4E **50**
(off Evelyn Rd.)
KT6: Surb 7D **150**
NW7 . . . . .6H **29**
Holland Dr. SE23 . . . . .3A **140**

Holland Dwellings WC2 . . . . .7F 7
(off Newton St.)
Holland Gdns. TW8: Bford 6F 97
W14 . . . . .3G 99
Holland Gro. SW9 . . . . .7A 102
Holland Ho. E4 . . . . .4K 35
NW10 . . . . .2D 80
(off Holland Rd.)
HOLLAND PARK 1H 99
Holland Park 2H 99
Holland Pk. W11 . . . . .1G 99
Holland Pk. Av.
IG3: IIf 6J 53
W11 . . . . .2G 99
Holland Pk. Ct. W14 . . . . .2G 99
(off Holland Pk. Gdns.)
Holland Pk. Gdns. W14 . . . . .2G 99
Holland Pk. Mans. W14 . . . . .1G 99
(off Holland Pk. Gdns.)
Holland Pk. M. W11 . . . . .1G 99
Holland Pk. Rd. W14 . . . . .3H 99
HOLLAND PARK RDBT. 2F 99
Holland Pk. Ter. W11 . . . . .1G 99
(off Portland Rd.)
Holland Park Theatre (Open Air) 2H 99
Holland Pas. N1 . . . . .1C 84
(off Basire St.)
Holland Pl. W8 . . . . .2K 99
(off Kensington Chu. St.)
Holland Pl. Chambers W8 . . . . .2K 99
(off Holland Pl.)
Holland Ri. Ho. SW9 . . . . .7K 101
(off Clapham Rd.)
Holland Rd. E6 . . . . .1D 88
E15 . . . . .3G 87
HA0: Wemb 6D 60
NW10 . . . . .1C 80
SE25 . . . . .5G 157
W14 . . . . .2F 99
Hollands, The KT4: Wor Pk 1B 164
TW13: Hanw 4B 130
Holland St. SE1 . . . . .4B 14 (1B 102)
W8 . . . . .2J 99
Holland Vs. Rd. W14 . . . . .2G 99
Holland Wlk. HA7: Stan 5F 27
N19 . . . . .1H 65
W8 . . . . .1H 99
Holland Way BR2: Hayes 2H 171
Hollar Rd. N16 . . . . .3F 67
Hollen St. W1 . . . . .7C 6 (6H 83)
Holles Cl. TW12: Hamp 6E 130
Holles Ho. SW9 . . . . .2A 120
Holles St. W1 . . . . .7K 5 (6F 83)
Holley Rd. W3 . . . . .2A 98
Hollickwood Av. N12 . . . . .6J 31
Holliday Sq. SW11 . . . . .3B 118
(off Fowler Cl.)
Hollidge Way RM10: Dag 7H 73
Hollies, The E11 . . . . .5J 51
(off New Wanstead)
HA3: W'stone 4A 42
N20 . . . . .1G 31
Hollies Av. DA15: Sidc 2K 143
Hollies Cl. SW16 . . . . .6A 138
TW1: Twick 2K 131
Hollies End NW7 . . . . .5J 29
Hollies Rd. W5 . . . . .4C 96
Hollies Way SW12 . . . . .7E 118
Holligrave Rd. BR1: Brom 1J 159
Hollingbourne Av. DA7: Bex 1F 127
Hollingbourne Gdns. W13 . . . . .5B 78
Hollingbourne Rd. SE24 . . . . .5C 120
Hollingsworth Ct. KT6: Surb 7D 150
Hollingsworth Rd. CR0: C'don 6H 169
Hollington Ct. BR7: Chst 6F 143
Hollington Cres. KT3: N Mald 6B 152
Hollington Rd. E6 . . . . .3D 88
N17 . . . . .2G 49
Hollingworth Cl. KT8: W Mole 4D 148
Hollingworth Rd. BR5: Pet W 6F 161
Hollins Ho. N7 . . . . .4J 65

Hollisfield WC1 . . . . .2F 7
(off Cromer St.)
Hollister Ho. NW6 . . . . .3J 81
(off Kilburn Pk. Rd.)
Hollman Gdns. SW16 . . . . .6B 138
Hollow, The IG8: Wfd G 4C 36
HOLLOWAY .3J 65
Holloway Cl. UB7: Harm 5A 92
Holloway Ho. NW2 . . . . .3E 62
(off Stoll Cl.)
Holloway La. UB7: Harm, W Dray 2E 174
Holloway Rd. E6 . . . . .3D 88
E11 . . . . .3F 69
N7 . . . . .4K 65
N19 . . . . .2H 65
Holloway St. TW3: Houn 3F 113
Hollowfield Wlk. UB5: N'olt 6C 58
Hollows, The TW8: Bford 6F 97
Holly Av. HA7: Stan 2E 42
KT12: Walt T 7B 148
Hollybank Cl. TW12: Hamp 5E 130
Hollyberry La. NW3 . . . . .4A 64
Hollybrake Cl. BR7: Chst 7H 143
Hollybush Cl. E11 . . . . .5J 51
HA3: Hrw W 1J 41
Hollybush Gdns. E2 . . . . .3H 85
Holly Bush Hill NW3 . . . . .4A 64
Hollybush Hill E11 . . . . .6H 51
Hollybush Ho. E2 . . . . .3H 85
Holly Bush La. TW12: Hamp 7D 130
Hollybush Pl. E2 . . . . .3H 85
Hollybush Rd. KT2: King T 5E 132
Holly Bush Steps NW3 . . . . .4A 64
(off Holly Mt.)
Hollybush St. E13 . . . . .3K 87
Holly Bush Va. NW3 . . . . .4A 64
Hollybush Wlk. SW9 . . . . .4B 120
Holly Cl. BR3: Beck 4E 158
IG9: Buck H 3G 37
KT19: Eps 7K 163
SM6: Wall 7F 167
TW13: Hanw 5C 130
TW16: Sun 3K 147
Holly Cott. M. UB8: Hil 5C 74
Holly Ct. DA14: Sidc 4B 144
(off Sidcup Hill)
N15 . . . . .4E 48
SE10 .3H 105
SM2: Sutt 7J 165
Holly Cres. BR3: Beck 5B 158
IG8: Wfd G 7A 36
Hollycroft Av. HA9: Wemb 2F 61
NW3 . . . . .3J 63
Hollycroft Cl. CR2: S Croy 5E 168
UB7: Sip 6C 92
Hollycroft Gdns. UB7: Sip 6C 92
Hollydale Cl. UB5: N'olt 4F 59
Hollydale Dr. BR2: Brom 3D 172
Hollydale Rd. SE15 . . . . .1J 121
Hollydene BR2: Brom 1H 159
(off Beckenham La.)
SE13 .6F 123
SE15 . . . . .1H 121
Hollydown Way E11 . . . . .3F 69
Holly Dr. E4 .7J 25
Holly Farm Rd. UB2: S'hall 5C 94
Hollyfield Av. N11 . . . . .5J 31
Hollyfield Rd. KT5: Surb 7F 151
Holly Gdns. DA7: Bex 4J 127
UB7: W Dray 2B 92
Holly Gro. HA5: Pinn 1C 40
NW9 . . . . .7J 43
SE15 .2F 121
Hollygrove WD23: Bush 1C 26
Hollygrove Cl. TW3: Houn 4D 112
Holly Hedge Ter. SE13 . . . . .5F 123
Holly Hill N21 . . . . .6E 22
NW3 . . . . .4A 64
Holly Hill Rd.
DA8: Erith 5H 109
DA17: Belv, Erith 5H 109

Holly Ho. TW8: Bford 6C 96
W10 . . . . .4G 81
(off Hawthorn Wlk.)
Holly Lodge HA1: Harr 5H 41
W8 . . . . .2J 99
(off Thornwood Gdns.)
Holly Lodge Gdns. N6 . . . . .2E 64
Holly Lodge Mans. N6 . . . . .2E 64
Hollymead SM5: Cars 3D 166
Holly M. SW10 . . . . .6A 16 (5A 100)
Holly Mt. NW3 . . . . .4A 64
Hollymount Cl. SE10 . . . . .1E 122
Holly Pde. TW13: Felt 3H 129
(off High St.)
Holly Pk. N3 .3H 45
N4 . . . . .7J 47
(not continuous)
Holly Pk. Est. N4 . . . . .7K 47
Holly Pk. Gdns. N3 . . . . .3J 45
Holly Pk. Rd. N11 . . . . .5K 31
W7 . . . . .1K 95
Holly Pl. NW3 . . . . .4A 64
(off Holly Berry La.)
Holly Rd. E11 . . . . .7H 51
TW1: Twick 1K 131
TW3: Houn 4F 113
TW12: Hamp H 6G 131
W4 . . . . .4K 97
Holly St. E8 .7F 67
Holly Ter. N6 .1E 64
N20 . . . . .2F 31
Holly Tree Cl. SW19 . . . . .1F 135
Holly Tree Ho. SE4 . . . . .3B 122
(off Brockley Rd.)
Hollytree Pde. DA14: Sidc 6C 144
(off Sidcup Hill)
Hollyview Cl. NW4 . . . . .6C 44
Holly Village N6 . . . . .2F 65
Holly Vs. W6 .3D 98
(off Wellesley Av.)
Holly Wlk. EN2: Enf 3H 23
NW3 . . . . .4A 64
Holly Way CR4: Mitc 4H 155
Hollywood Bowl
Finchley 7G 31
Surrey Quays 3K 103
Tolworth 2H 163
Hollywood Ct. SW10 . . . . .6A 100
(off Hollywood Rd.)
W5 . . . . .7F 79
Hollywood Gdns. UB4: Yead 6K 75
Hollywood M. SW10 . . . . .6A 100
Hollywood Rd. E4 . . . . .5F 35
SW10 .6A 100
Hollywood Way IG8: Wfd G 7A 36
Holman Ct. KT17: Ewe 7C 164
Holman Ho. E2 . . . . .3K 85
(off Roman Rd.)
Holman Hunt Ho. W6 . . . . .5G 99
(off Field Rd.)
Holman Rd. KT19: Ewe 5A 163
SW11 .2B 118
Holmanch Rd. TW17: Shep 4G 147
Holmbridge Gdns. EN3: Pond E 4E 24
Holmbrook NW1 . . . . .2G 83
(off Eversholt St.)
Holmbrook Dr. NW4 . . . . .5F 45
Holmbury Ct. CR2: S Croy 5C 168
SW17 .3D 136
SW19 .7C 136
Holmbury Gdns. UB3: Hayes 1H 93
Holmbury Gro. CR0: Sels 7B 170
Holmbury Ho. SE24 . . . . .5B 120
Holmbury Mnr. DA14: Sidc 4A 144
Holmbury Pk. BR1: Brom 7C 142
Holmbury Vw. E5 . . . . .1H 67
Holmbush Rd. SW15 . . . . .6G 117
Holmcote Gdns. N5 . . . . .5C 66
Holmcroft Ct. SE12 . . . . .3K 141
Holmcroft Ho. E17 . . . . .4D 50
Holmcroft Way BR2: Brom 5D 160

Holmdale Gdns. NW4 . . . . .5F 45
Holmdale Rd. BR7: Chst 5G 143
NW6 . . . . .5J 63
Holmdale Ter. N15 . . . . .7E 48
Holmdene N12 . . . . .5E 30
Holmdene Av. HA2: Harr 3F 41
NW7 . . . . .6H 29
SE24 .5C 120
Holmdene Cl. BR3: Beck 2E 158
Holmdene Ct. BR1: Brom 3C 160
Holmead Rd. SW6 . . . . .7K 99
Holmebury Ct. WD23: B Hea 2D 26
Holme Ct. TW7: Isle 3A 114
Holmefield Ho. W10 . . . . .4G 81
(off Hazlewood Cres.)
Holme Ho. SE15 . . . . .7H 103
(off Studholme St.)
Holme Lacey Rd. SE12 . . . . .6H 123
Holmeoak Av. RM13: Rain 2K 91
Holme Rd. E6 . . . . .1C 88
Holmes Av. E17 . . . . .3B 50
Holmes Cl. SE22 . . . . .4G 121
Holmesdale Av. SW14 . . . . .3H 115
Holmesdale Cl. SE25 . . . . .3F 157
Holmesdale Ho. NW6 . . . . .1J 81
(off Kilburn Vale)
Holmesdale Rd. CR0: C'don 5D 156
DA7: Bex 2D 126
N6 . . . . .7F 47
SE25 .5D 156
TW9: Kew 1F 115
TW11: Tedd 7C 132
Holmesley Rd. SE23 . . . . .6A 122
Holmes Pl. SW10 . . . . .6A 100
Holmes Rd. NW5 . . . . .5F 65
SW19 .7A 136
TW1: Twick 2K 131
Holmes Ter. SE1 . . . . .6J 13
Holmesville Ct. N22 . . . . .2A 48
Holme Way HA7: Stan 6E 26
Holmewood Gdns. SW2 . . . . .7K 119
Holmewood Rd. SE25 . . . . .3E 156
SW2 . . . . .7K 119
Holmfield Av. NW4 . . . . .5F 45
Holmfield Ct. NW3 . . . . .5C 64
Holm Gro. UB10: Hil 7C 56
Holmhurst SE13 . . . . .6F 123
Holmhurst Rd. DA17: Belv 5H 109
Holmlea Ct. CR0: C'don 4D 168
(off Chatsworth Rd.)
Holmleigh Ct. EN3: Pond E 4D 24
Holmleigh Rd. N16 . . . . .1E 66
Holmleigh Rd. Est. N16 . . . . .1E 66
Holm Oak Cl. SW15 . . . . .6H 117
Holm Oak M. SW4 . . . . .5J 119
Holmoaks Ho. BR3: Beck 2E 158
Holmsdale Ho. E14 . . . . .7D 86
(off Poplar High St.)
N11 . . . . .4A 32
(off Coppies Gro.)
Holmshaw Cl. SE26 . . . . .4A 140
Holmside Rd. SW12 . . . . .6E 118
Holmsley Cl. KT3: N Mald 6B 152
Holmsley Ho. SW15 . . . . .7B 116
(off Tangley Gro.)
Holmstall Av. HA8: Edg 3J 43
Holmstall Pde. HA8: Edg 2J 43
Holmstead Ct. CR2: S Croy 5D 168
Holm Wlk. SE3 . . . . .2J 123
Holmwood
HA2: Harr 3G 41
SM2: Cheam 7F 165
UB5: N'olt 6F 59
Holmwood Gdns. N3 . . . . .2J 45
SM6: Wall 6F 167
Holmwood Gro. NW7 . . . . .5E 28
Holmwood Rd. IG3: IIf 2J 71
KT9: Chess 5D 162
SM2: Cheam 7E 164
Holmwood Vs. SE7 . . . . .5J 105

Holne Chase N2 . . . 6A 46
  SM4: Mord . . . 6H 153
Holness Rd. E15 . . . 4K 69
Holocaust Memorial . . . 2D 100
Holocaust Memorial Garden, The . . . 6F 11
Holroyd Rd. KT10: Clay . . . 7A 162
  SW15 . . . 4E 116
Holsgrove Ho. W3 . . . 1A 98
Holst Ct. SE1 . . . 1J 19
  (off Kennington Rd.)
Holstein Way DA18: Erith . . . 3D 108
Holst Ho. W12 . . . 6D 80
  (off Du Cane Rd.)
Holst Mans. SW13 . . . 6E 98
Holstock Rd. IG1: Ilf . . . 2G 71
Holsworthy Ho. HA2: Harr . . . 5G 41
Holsworthy Ho. E3 . . . 3D 86
  (off Talwin St.)
Holsworthy Sq. WC1 . . . 4H 7
Holsworthy Way KT9: Chess . . . 5C 162
Holt, The SM4: Mord . . . 4J 153
  SM6: Wall . . . 4G 167
Holt Cl. BR7: Chst . . . 5D 142
  DA14: Sidc . . . 4E 144
  N10 . . . 4E 46
  SE28 . . . 7B 90
Holt Ct. SE10 . . . 6E 104
  (off Horseferry Pl.)
Holt Ho. SW2 . . . 6A 120
Holton St. E1 . . . 4K 85
Holt Rd. E16 . . . 1C 106
  HA0: Wemb . . . 3B 60
Holtwhite Av. EN2: Enf . . . 2H 23
Holtwhite's Hill EN2: Enf . . . 1G 23
Holwell Pl. HA5: Pinn . . . 4C 40
Holwood Est. BR2: Kes . . . 6C 172
Holwood Pk. Av. BR6: Farnb . . . 4D 172
Holwood Pl. SW4 . . . 4H 119
Holybourne Av. SW15 . . . 7C 116
Holycross Cl. SM4: Mord . . . 7J 153
Holyhead Cl. E6 . . . 5D 88
Holyhead Ct. KT1: King T . . . 4D 150
  (off Anglesea Rd.)
Holyoake Ct. SE16 . . . 2B 104
Holyoake Ho. W5 . . . 4C 78
Holyoake Wlk. N2 . . . 3A 46
  W5 . . . 4C 78
Holyoak Rd. SE11 . . . 4B 102
Holyport Rd. SW6 . . . 7F 99
Holyrood Av. HA2: Harr . . . 4C 58
Holyrood Ct. NW1 . . . 1F 83
  (off Gloucester Av.)
Holyrood Gdns. HA8: Edg . . . 3H 43
Holyrood M. E16 . . . 1J 105
Holyrood Rd. EN5: New Bar . . . 6F 21
Holyrood St. SE1 . . . 5G 15 (1E 102)
Holywell Cl. BR6: Chels . . . 4K 173
  SE3 . . . 6J 105
  SE16 . . . 5H 103
  TW19: Stanw . . . 1A 128
Holywell La. EC2 . . . 3H 9 (4E 84)
Holywell Row EC2 . . . 4G 9 (4E 84)
Holywell Way TW19: Stanw . . . 1A 128
Homan Ct. N12 . . . 4G 31
Homebush Ho. E4 . . . 7J 25
Homecedars Ho. WD23: B Hea . . . 1C 26
Home Cl. SM5: Cars . . . 2D 166
  UB5: N'olt . . . 3D 76
Home Ct. KT6: Surb . . . 5D 150
Homecroft Rd. N22 . . . 1C 48
  SE26 . . . 5J 139
Home Farm Cl. KT7: T Ditt . . . 7K 149
  TW17: Shep . . . 4G 147
Homefarm Rd. W7 . . . 6J 77
Home Fld. EN5: Barn . . . 5C 20
Homefield SM4: Mord . . . 4J 153
Homefield Av. IG2: Ilf . . . 5J 53
Homefield Cl. NW10 . . . 6J 61
  UB4: Yead . . . 4B 76
Homefield Gdns. CR4: Mitc . . . 2A 154
  N2 . . . 3B 46

Homefield Ho. SE23 . . . 3J 139
Homefield M. BR3: Beck . . . 1C 158
Homefield Pk. SM1: Sutt . . . 6K 165
Homefield Pl. CR0: C'don . . . 2F 169
Homefield Rd. BR1: Brom . . . 1A 160
  HA0: Wemb . . . 4A 60
  HA8: Edg . . . 6E 28
  KT12: Walt T . . . 7C 148
  SW19 . . . 6F 135
  W4 . . . 5B 98
Homefield St. N1 . . . 1G 9 (2E 84)
Homefirs Ho. HA9: Wemb . . . 3F 61
Home Gdns. RM10: Dag . . . 3J 73
Homeheather Ho. IG4: Ilf . . . 5D 52
Homeland Dr. SM2: Sutt . . . 7K 165
Homelands Dr. SE19 . . . 7E 138
Home Lea BR6: Chels . . . 5K 173
Homeleigh Ct. SW16 . . . 3J 137
Homeleigh Rd. SE15 . . . 5K 121
Home Mead HA7: Stan . . . 1C 42
Home Mdw. M. SE22 . . . 5G 121
Homemead Rd. BR2: Brom . . . 5D 160
  CR0: C'don . . . 6G 155
Home Pk. Ct. KT1: King T . . . 4D 150
  (off Palace Rd.)
Home Pk. Pde. KT1: Hamp W . . . 2D 150
  (off High St.)
Home Pk. Rd. SW19 . . . 4H 135
Home Pk. Ter. KT1: Hamp W . . . 2D 150
  (off Hampton Ct. Rd.)
Home Pk. Wlk. KT1: King T . . . 4D 150
Homer Cl. DA7: Bex . . . 1J 127
Homer Dr. E14 . . . 4C 104
Homer Rd. CR0: C'don . . . 6K 157
  E9 . . . 6A 68
Homer Row W1 . . . 6D 4 (5C 82)
Homersham Rd. KT1: King T . . . 2G 151
Homer St. W1 . . . 6D 4 (5C 82)
HOMERTON . . . 5K 67
Homerton Gro. E9 . . . 5K 67
Homerton High St. E9 . . . 5K 67
Homerton Rd. E9 . . . 5A 68
Homerton Row E9 . . . 5J 67
Homerton Ter. E9 . . . 6J 67
  (not continuous)
Homesdale Cl. E11 . . . 5J 51
Homesdale Rd. BR1: Brom . . . 4A 160
  BR2: Brom . . . 4A 160
  BR5: Pet W . . . 7J 161
Homesfield NW11 . . . 5J 45
Homestall Rd. SE22 . . . 5J 121
Homestead Ct. EN5: New Bar . . . 5D 20
Homestead Paddock N14 . . . 5A 22
Homestead Pk. NW2 . . . 3B 62
Homestead Rd. RM8: Dag . . . 2F 73
  SW6 . . . 7H 99
Homesteads, The N11 . . . 4A 32
Homevale Ct. BR2: Hayes . . . 7H 159
Homewalk Ho. SE26 . . . 4H 139
Homewaters Av. TW16: Sun . . . 1H 147
Homewillow Cl. N21 . . . 6G 23
Homewood Cl. TW12: Hamp . . . 6D 130
Homewood Cres. BR7: Chst . . . 6J 143
Homewoods SW12 . . . 7G 119
Homildon Ho. SE26 . . . 3G 139
Honduras St. EC1 . . . 3C 8 (4C 84)
Honeybourne Rd. NW6 . . . 5K 63
Honeybourne Way BR5: Pet W . . . 1H 173
Honeybrook Rd. SW12 . . . 7G 119
Honey Cl. RM10: Dag . . . 6H 73
Honeycroft Hill UB10: Uxb . . . 7A 56
Honeyden Rd. DA14: Sidc . . . 6E 144
Honeyfield M. SE23 . . . 3K 139
Honey Hill UB10: Uxb . . . 7B 56
Honey La. EC2 . . . 1D 14
Honey La. Ho. SW10 . . . 6K 99
  (off Finborough Rd.)
Honeyman Cl. NW6 . . . 7F 63
Honeymead N8 . . . 3J 47
  (off Campsfield Rd.)

Honey M. RM7: Rom . . . 5J 55
  SE27 . . . 4C 138
  (off Norwood High St.)
Honeypot Bus. Cen. HA7: Stan . . . 1E 42
Honeypot Cl. NW9 . . . 4F 43
Honeypot La. HA7: Stan . . . 7J 27
  NW9 . . . 1D 42
Honeysett Rd. N17 . . . 2F 49
Honeysuckle Cl. UB1: S'hall . . . 7C 76
Honeysuckle Cl. IG1: Ilf . . . 6F 71
  IG9: Buck H . . . 3G 37
Honeysuckle Gdns. CR0: C'don . . . 7K 157
Honeysuckle La. N22 . . . 2C 48
Honeywell Rd. SW11 . . . 6D 118
Honeywood Ho. SE15 . . . 1G 121
  (off Goldsmith Rd.)
Honeywood Mus. . . . 5D 166
Honeywood Rd. NW10 . . . 2B 80
  TW7: Isle . . . 4A 114
Honeywood Wlk. SM5: Cars . . . 4D 166
Honister Cl. HA7: Stan . . . 1B 42
Honister Gdns. HA7: Stan . . . 7G 27
Honister Pl. HA7: Stan . . . 1B 42
Honiton Gdns. NW7 . . . 7A 30
  SE15 . . . 2J 121
  (off Gibbon Rd.)
Honiton Ho. EN3: Pond E . . . 3E 24
Honiton Rd. DA16: Well . . . 2K 125
  NW6 . . . 2H 81
  RM7: Rom . . . 6K 55
Honley Rd. SE6 . . . 7D 122
Honnor Gdns. TW7: Isle . . . 2H 113
HONOR OAK . . . 6J 121
Honor Oak Crematorium SE23 . . . 5K 121
HONOR OAK PARK . . . 7A 122
Honor Oak Pk. SE23 . . . 6J 121
Honor Oak Ri. SE23 . . . 6J 121
Honor Oak Rd. SE23 . . . 1J 139
Honour Gdns. RM8: Dag . . . 4A 72
Honour Lea Av. E20 . . . 5D 68
Hood Av. N14 . . . 6A 22
  SW14 . . . 5J 115
Hood Cl. CR0: C'don . . . 1B 168
Hoodcote Gdns. N21 . . . 7G 23
Hood Ct. EC4 . . . 1K 13
Hood Ho. SE5 . . . 7D 102
  (off Elmington Est.)
  SW1 . . . 6C 18
  (off Dolphin Sq.)
Hood Point SE16 . . . 2B 104
  (off Rotherhithe St.)
Hood Rd. SW20 . . . 7B 134
Hood Wlk. RM7: Mawney . . . 1H 55
HOOK . . . 4D 162
Hook, The EN5: New Bar . . . 6G 21
Hooke Ct. SE10 . . . 1E 122
  (off Winforton St.)
Hooke Ho. E3 . . . 2A 86
  (off Gernon Rd.)
Hookers Rd. E17 . . . 3K 49
Hook Farm Rd. BR2: Brom . . . 5B 160
Hookham Ct. SW8 . . . 1H 119
Hooking Grn. HA2: Harr . . . 5F 41
HOOK JUNC. . . . 3E 162
Hook La. DA16: Well . . . 4K 125
Hook Rise Nth. KT6: Surb . . . 3E 162
Hook Rise Sth. KT6: Surb . . . 3E 162
Hook Rise Sth. Ind. Pk.
  KT6: Surb . . . 3F 163
Hook Rd. KT6: Surb . . . 2E 162
  KT9: Chess . . . 5D 162
  KT19: Eps, Ewe . . . 7J 163
Hooks Cl. SE15 . . . 1H 121
Hooks Hall Dr. RM10: Dag . . . 3J 73
Hookstone Way IG8: Wfd G . . . 7G 37
Hook Wlk. HA8: Edg . . . 6D 28
Hool Cl. NW9 . . . 5J 43
Hooper Dr. UB8: Hil . . . 5D 74
Hooper Ho. TW15: Ashf . . . 3A 128
Hooper Rd. E16 . . . 6J 87
Hooper's Ct. SW3 . . . 7E 10 (2D 100)

Hoopers M. W3 . . . 1J 97
  WD23: Bush . . . 1A 26
Hooper Sq. E1 . . . 6G 85
  (off Hooper St.)
Hooper St. E1 . . . 6G 85
Hoopers Yd. E1 . . . 6G 85
  (off Hooper St.)
  NW6 . . . 1H 81
  (off Kimberley Rd.)
Hop La. NW11 . . . 7H 45
Hop Ct. HA0: Wemb . . . 5A 60
  (off Brewery Cl.)
Hope Cl. IG8: Wfd G . . . 6F 37
  N1 . . . 6C 66
  RM6: Chad H . . . 4D 54
  SE12 . . . 3K 141
  SM1: Sutt . . . 5A 166
  TW8: Bford . . . 5E 96
Hope Ct. NW10 . . . 3F 81
  (off Chamberlayne Rd.)
  SE1 . . . 5G 103
  (off Avocet Cl.)
Hopedale Rd. SE7 . . . 6K 105
Hopefield Av. NW6 . . . 2G 81
Hope Gdns. W3 . . . 2H 97
Hope Ho. CR0: C'don . . . 4E 168
  (off Steep Hill)
Hope La. SE9 . . . 2F 143
Hope Pk. BR1: Brom . . . 7H 141
Hopes Cl. TW5: Hest . . . 6E 94
Hope Sq. EC2 . . . 6G 9
Hope St. SW11 . . . 3B 118
Hopetown St. E1 . . . 6K 9 (5F 85)
Hopewell St. SE5 . . . 7D 102
Hopewell Yd. SE5 . . . 7D 102
  (off Hopewell St.)
Hope Wharf SE16 . . . 2J 103
Hop Gdns. WC2 . . . 3E 12 (7J 83)
Hopground Ho. E20 . . . 6E 68
  (off De Coubertin St.)
Hopkins Cl. N10 . . . 7K 31
Hopkins Ho. E14 . . . 6C 86
  (off Canton St.)
Hopkins M. E15 . . . 1H 87
Hopkinsons Pl. NW1 . . . 1E 82
Hopkins Rd. E10 . . . 7D 50
Hopkins St. W1 . . . 1B 12 (6G 83)
Hoppers Rd. N13 . . . 2F 33
  N21 . . . 2F 33
Hoppett Rd. E4 . . . 2B 36
Hopping La. N1 . . . 6B 66
Hoppingwood Av.
  KT3: N Mald . . . 3A 152
Hoppner Rd. UB4: Hayes . . . 2F 75
Hop St. SE10 . . . 4H 105
Hopton Ct. BR2: Hayes . . . 1K 171
Hopton Gdns. KT3: N Mald . . . 6C 152
Hopton Rd. SE18 . . . 3F 107
  SW16 . . . 5J 137
Hopton's Gdns. SE1 . . . 4B 14
Hopton St. SE1 . . . 3A 14 (7B 84)
Hoptree Cl. N12 . . . 5E 30
Hopwood Cl. SW17 . . . 3A 136
Hopwood Rd. SE17 . . . 6D 102
Hopwood St. W12 . . . 1E 98
Hopwood Wlk. E8 . . . 7G 67
Horace Av. RM7: Rush G . . . 1J 73
Horace Bldg. SW8 . . . 7F 101
Horace Rd. E7 . . . 4K 69
  IG6: Ilf . . . 3G 53
  KT1: King T . . . 3F 151
Horatio Ct. SE16 . . . 1J 103
  (off Rotherhithe St.)
Horatio Ho. E2 . . . 2F 85
  (off Horatio St.)
  W6 . . . 5F 99
  (off Fulham Pal. Rd.)
Horatio Pl. E14 . . . 1E 104
  (off Managers St.)
  SW19 . . . 1J 153
Horatio St. E2 . . . 2F 85

Horatius Way CRO: Wadd 5K 167
Horbury Cres. W11 . . . . .7J 81
Horbury M. W11 .7H 81
Horder Rd. SW6 .1G 117
Hordle Prom. E. SE15 . . . . .7F 103
Hordle Prom. Sth. SE15 . . . . .7F 103
　　　　　　　　　　　　　(off Quarley Way)
Horizon Bldg. E14 . . . . .7C 86
　　　　　　　　　　　　　(off Hertsmere Rd.)
Horizon Bus. Cen. N9 . . . . .2E 34
　　　　　　　　　　　　　(off Goodwin Rd.)
Horizon Ct. SM2: Cheam 7G 165
　　　　　　　　　　　　　(off Up. Mulgrave Rd.)
Horizon Ho. SW18 . . . . .3A 118
　　　　　　　　　　　　　(off Juniper Dr.)
Horizon Ind. Est. SE15 . . . . .6G 103
Horizon Way SE7 . . . . .4K 105
Horle Wlk. SE5 . . . . .2B 120
Horley Cl. DA6: Bex 5G 127
Horley Rd. SE9 . . . . .4C 142
Hormead Rd. W9 . . . . .4H 81
Hornbeam Cl. IG1: Ilf 5H 71
　　IG9: Buck H 3G 37
　　IG11: Bark 3A 90
　　NW7 . . . . .3G 29
　　SE11 . . . . .3J 19 (4A 102)
　　UB5: N'olt 5D 58
Hornbeam Cres. TW8: Bford 7B 96
Hornbeam Gdns. KT3: N Mald 6C 152
Hornbeam Gro. E4 . . . . .3B 36
Hornbeam Ho. IG9: Buck H 3H 37
Hornbeam La. DA7: Bex 2J 127
Hornbeam Rd. IG9: Buck H 3G 37
　　UB4: Yead 5A 76
Hornbeam Sq. E3 . . . . .1B 86
Hornbeams Ri. N11 . . . . .6K 31
Hornbeam Ter. SM5: Cars 1C 166
Hornbeam Wlk. TW10: Rich 2F 133
Hornbeam Way BR2: Brom 6E 160
Hornbean Ho. E15 . . . . .3G 87
　　　　　　　　　　　　　(off Manor Rd.)
Hornblower Cl. SE16 . . . . .3A 104
Hornbuckle Cl. HA2: Harr 2H 59
Hornby Cl. NW3 .7B 64
Hornby Ct. NW10 . . . . .6B 62
Hornby Ho. SE11 . . . . .7J 19
Horncastle Cl. SE12 . . . . .7J 123
Horncastle Rd. SE12 . . . . .7J 123
Hornchurch N17 .2D 48
　　　　　　　　　　　　　(off Gloucester Rd.)
Hornchurch Cl. KT2: King T 4D 132
Horndean Cl. SW15 . . . . .1C 134
Horndon Cl. RM5: Col R 1J 55
Horndon Grn. RM5: Col R 1J 55
Horndon Rd. RM5: Col R 1J 55
Horner Ho. N1 . . . . .1E 84
　　　　　　　　　　　　　(off Nuttall St.)
Horner La. CR4: Mitc 2B 154
Horne Rd. TW17: Shep 4C 146
Horner Sq. E1 . . . . .5J 9
　　　　　　　　(within Old Spitalfields Market)
Hornet Way E6 . . . . .5H 89
Horne Way SW15 . . . . .2E 116
Hornfair Rd. SE7 .6A 106
Horniman Dr. SE23 . . . . .1H 139
Horniman Mus. 1H 139
Horning Cl. SE9 .4C 142
Horn La. IG8: Wfd G 6D 36
　　SE10 . . . . .5J 105
　　　　　　　　　　　　　(not continuous)
　　W3 . . . . .7J 79
　　　　　　　　　　　　　(not continuous)
Horn Link Way SE10 . . . . .4J 105
HORN PARK 5K 123
Horn Pk. Cl. SE12 . . . . .5K 123
Horn Pk. La. SE12 . . . . .5K 123
Hornscroft Cl. IG11: Bark 7J 71
Horns End Pl. HA5: Eastc 4A 40
HORNSEY 4J 47
Hornsey N8 . . . . .4J 47
Hornsey Cricket Club 5H 47

Hornsey La. N6 . . . . .1F 65
Hornsey La. Est. N19 . . . . .7H 47
Hornsey La. Gdns. N6 . . . . .7G 47
Hornsey Pk. Rd. N8 . . . . .3K 47
Hornsey Ri. N19 .7H 47
Hornsey Ri. Gdns. N19 . . . . .7H 47
Hornsey Rd. N7 . . . . .1J 65
　　N19 . . . . .1J 65
Hornsey St. N7 . . . . .5K 65
HORNSEY VALE .5K 47
Hornshay St. SE15 . . . . .6J 103
Horns Rd. IG2: Ilf .5G 53
　　IG6: Ilf 4H 53
Hornton Ct. W8 . . . . .2J 99
　　　　　　　　　　　(off Kensington High St.)
Hornton Pl. W8 . . . . .2K 99
Hornton St. W8 . . . . .2J 99
Horsa Rd. DA8: Erith 7H 109
　　SE12 . . . . .7A 124
Horse & Dolphin Yd. W1 . . . . .2D 12
Horsebridges Cl. RM9: Dag 1E 90
Horsecroft Rd. HA8: Edg 7E 28
Horse Fair KT1: King T 2D 150
Horseferry Pl. SE10 . . . . .6E 104
Horseferry Rd. E14 . . . . .7A 86
　　SW1 . . . . .2C 18 (3H 101)
Horseferry Rd. Est. SW1 . . . . .2C 18
Horse Guards Av. SW1 . . . . . .5E 12 (1H 101)
Horse Guards Parade 5E 12 (1H 101)
Horse Guards Rd. SW1 . . . . . .5D 12 (1H 101)
Horse Leaze E6 . . . . .6E 88
Horseley Cl. E1 . . . . .5A 86
Horsell Rd. BR5: St P 7B 144
　　N5 . . . . .5A 66
　　　　　　　　　　　　　(not continuous)
Horselydown La. SE1 . . . . .6J 15 (2F 103)
Horselydown Mans. SE1 . . . . .6J 15
　　　　　　　　　　　　　(off Lafone St.)
Horsemongers M. SE1 . . . . .7D 14
Horsenden Av. UB6: G'frd 5K 59
Horsenden Cres. UB6: G'frd 5K 59
Horsenden Hill Golf Course 7A 60
Horsenden La. Nth.
　　UB6: G'frd 6J 59
Horsenden La. Sth.
　　UB6: G'frd 1A 78
Horse Ride SW1 . . . . .5C 12 (1G 101)
Horseshoe Cl. E14 . . . . .5E 104
　　NW2 . . . . .2D 62
Horseshoe Ct. EC1 . . . . .3B 8
　　　　　　　　　　　　　(off Brewhouse Yd.)
Horse Shoe Cres. UB5: N'olt 2E 76
Horseshoe Dr. UB8: Hil 6C 74
Horse Shoe Grn. SM1: Sutt 2K 165
Horseshoe La. EN2: Enf 3H 23
　　N20 . . . . .1A 30
Horseshoe M. SW2 . . . . .4J 119
Horseshoe Wharf SE1 . . . . .4E 14
　　　　　　　　　　　　　(off Clink St.)
Horse Yd. N1 . . . . .1B 84
　　　　　　　　　　　　　(off Essex Rd.)
Horsfeld Gdns. SE9 . . . . .5C 124
Horsfeld Rd. SE9 .5B 124
Horsfield Ho. N1 .7C 66
　　　　　　　　　　　　　(off Northampton St.)
Horsford Rd. SW2 . . . . .5K 119
Horsham Av. N12 . . . . .5H 31
Horsham Ct. N17 .1G 49
　　　　　　　　　　　　　(off Lansdowne Rd.)
Horsham Rd. DA6: Bex 5G 127
　　TW14: Bedf 6E 110
Horsley Cl. SW1 .4D 18
　　　　　　　　　　　　　(off Vincent St.)
Horsley Dr. CRO: New Ad 7E 170
　　KT2: King T 5D 132
Horsley Rd. BR1: Brom 1K 159
　　E4 . . . . .2K 35
Horsley St. SE17 .6D 102
Horsman Ho. SE5 . . . . .6C 102
　　　　　　　　　　　　　(off Bethwin Rd.)
Horsman St. SE5 .6C 102

Horsmonden Cl. BR6: Orp 7K 161
Horsmonden Rd. SE4 . . . . .5B 122
Hortensia Ho. SW10 . . . . .7A 100
　　　　　　　　　　　　　(off Gunter Gro.)
Hortensia Rd. SW10 . . . . .7A 100
Horticultural Pl. W4 . . . . .5K 97
Horton Av. NW2 .4G 63
Horton Bri. Rd. UB7: Yew 1B 92
Horton Cl. UB7: Yew 1C 92
Horton Country Pk. Local Nature Reserve
　　. . . . . .7G 163
Horton Halls SW17 . . . . .3B 136
Horton Ho. SE15 .6J 103
　　SW8 . . . . .7K 101
　　W6 . . . . .5G 99
　　　　　　　　　　　　　(off Field Rd.)
Horton Ind. Pk. UB7: Yew 1B 92
Horton La. KT19: Eps 7H 163
Horton Pde. UB7: Yew 1A 92
Horton Pk. Golf Course 7J 163
Horton Rd. E8 . . . . .6H 67
　　SL3: Poyle 6A 174
　　TW19: Stanw M 7A 174
　　UB7: Yew 1A 92
　　UB11: Stock P .1A 92
Horton Rd. Ind. Est. UB7: Yew 1B 92
Horton Way CRO: C'don 5K 157
Hortus Rd. E4 . . . . .2K 35
　　UB2: S'hall 2D 94
Horwood Ho. E2 .3H 85
　　　　　　　　　　　　　(off Pott St.)
　　NW8 . . . . .3D 4
　　　　　　　　　　　　　(off Paveley St.)
Hosack Rd. SW17 . . . . .2E 136
Hoser Av. SE12 . . . . .2J 141
Hosier La. EC1 . . . . .6A 8 (5B 84)
Hoskins Cl. E16 . . . . .6A 88
　　UB3: Harl 5H 93
Hoskins St. SE10 . . . . .5F 105
HOSPITAL BRIDGE RDBT. 7F 131
Hospital Bri. Rd. TW2: Twick, Whitt 7F 113
Hospital Rd. E9 . . . . .5K 67
　　E11 . . . . .5F 51
　　TW3: Houn 3E 112
Hospital Way SE13 . . . . .7F 123
Hotham Cl. KT8: W Mole 3E 148
Hotham Rd. SW15 . . . . .3E 116
　　SW19 . . . . .7A 136
Hotham Rd. M. SW19 . . . . .7A 136
Hotham St. E15 . . . . .1G 87
Hothfield Pl. SE16 . . . . .3J 103
Hotspur Ind. Est. N17 . . . . .6C 34
Hotspur Rd. UB5: N'olt 2E 76
Hotspur St. SE11 . . . . .5J 19 (4A 102)
Houblon Rd. TW10: Rich 5E 114
Houghton Cl. E8 . . . . .6F 67
　　TW12: Hamp 6C 130
Houghton Ct. EC1 . . . . .4C 8
　　　　　　　　　　　　　(off Glasshouse Yd.)
Houghton Rd. N15 . . . . .4F 49
Houghton Sq. SW9 . . . . .2J 119
Houghton St. WC2 . . . . .1H 13 (6K 83)
　　　　　　　　　　　　　(not continuous)
Houlder Cres. CRO: Wadd 6B 168
Houlton Ho. SW3 .5E 16
　　　　　　　　　　　　　(off Walpole St.)
Houlton Pl. E3 . . . . .4B 86
　　　　　　　　　　　　　(off Hamlets Way)
Hounsden Rd. N21 . . . . .6E 22
Houndsditch EC3 . . . . .7H 9 (6E 84)
Houndsfield Rd. N9 . . . . .7C 24
HOUNSLOW 3F 113
Hounslow and District Indoor Bowls Club
　　. . . . . .2D 112
Hounslow Av. TW3: Houn 5F 113
Hounslow Bus. Pk. TW3: Houn 4E 112
Hounslow Cen. TW3: Houn 3F 113
Hounslow Gdns. TW3: Houn 5F 113
Hounslow Heath Golf Course 5A 112
Hounslow Heath Nature Reserve 6C 112

Hounslow Rd. TW2: Whitt 6F 113
　　TW13: Hanw 4B 130
　　TW14: Felt 1K 129
Hounslow Urban Farm 5J 111
HOUNSLOW WEST 3C 112
Household Cavalry Museum, The
　　Whitehall 5D 12 (1H 101)
Houseman Way SE5 . . . . .7D 102
House Mill, The 3E 86
Houses of Parliament 1F 19 (3J 101)
Houston Bus. Pk. UB4: Yead 1A 94
Houston Pl. KT10: Esh 7J 149
Houston Rd. KT6: Surb 6B 150
　　SE23 . . . . .2A 140
Houstoun Ct. TW5: Hest 7D 94
Hove Av. E17 . . . . .5B 50
Hoveden Rd. NW2 . . . . .5G 63
Hove Gdns. SM1: Sutt 1K 165
Hove St. SE15 . . . . .7J 103
　　　　　　　　　　　　　(off Culmore Rd.)
Hoveton Rd. SE28 . . . . .6C 90
Hoveton Way IG6: Ilf 1F 53
Howard Av. DA5: Bexl 1C 144
Howard Bldg. SW8 . . . . .7J 17 (6F 101)
Howard Cl. N11 . . . . .2K 31
　　NW2 . . . . .4G 63
　　TW12: Hamp 7G 131
　　TW16: Sun 6H 129
　　W3 . . . . .6H 79
　　WD23: B Hea 1D 26
Howard Ct. IG11: Bark 1H 89
Howard Ho. E16 . . . . .1K 105
　　　　　　　　　　　　　(off Wesley Av.)
　　SE8 . . . . .6B 104
　　　　　　　　　　　　　(off Evelyn St.)
　　SW1 . . . . .6B 18
　　　　　　　　　　　　　(off Dolphin Sq.)
　　SW9 . . . . .3B 120
　　　　　　　　　　　　　(off Barrington Rd.)
　　W1 . . . . .4K 5
　　　　　　　　　　　　　(off Cleveland St.)
Howard M. N5 . . . . .4B 66
Howard Rd. BR1: Brom 7J 141
　　E6 . . . . .2D 88
　　E11 . . . . .3G 69
　　E17 . . . . .3C 50
　　HA7: Stan 1D 42
　　IG1: Ilf 4F 71
　　IG11: Bark 1H 89
　　KT3: N Mald 3A 152
　　KT5: Surb 6F 151
　　N15 . . . . .6E 48
　　N16 . . . . .4D 66
　　NW2 . . . . .4F 63
　　SE20 . . . . .1J 157
　　SE25 . . . . .5G 157
　　TW7: Isle 3K 113
　　UB1: S'hall 6F 77
Howards Cl. HA5: Pinn 2K 39
Howards Crest Cl. BR3: Beck 2E 158
Howard's La. SW15 . . . . .4D 116
Howards Rd. E13 .3J 87
Howard Wlk. N2 . . . . .4A 46
Howard Rd. SE2 .5A 108
Howberry Cl. HA8: Edg 6J 27
Howberry Rd. CR7: Thor H 1D 156
　　HA7: Stan 6J 27
　　HA8: Edg 6J 27
Howbury Rd. SE15 . . . . .3J 121
Howcroft Cres. N3 . . . . .7D 30
Howcroft Ho. E3 . . . . .3B 86
　　　　　　　　　　　　　(off Benworth St.)
Howcroft La. UB6: G'frd 3H 77
Howden Cl. SE28 .7C 90
Howden Rd. SE25 . . . . .2F 157
Howden St. SE15 . . . . .3G 121
Howe Cl. RM7: Mawney 1G 55
Howell Cl. RM6: Chad H 5D 54
Howell Ct. E10 . . . . .7D 50

Howell Wlk.—Hurst Ho.

Howell Wlk. SE1 4B 102
Howerd Way SE18 1C 124
(not continuous)
Howes Cl. N3 3J 45
Howeth Ct. *N11* *6J 31*
(off Ribblesdale Av.)
Howfield Pl. N17 3F 49
Howgate Rd. SW14 3K 115
Howick Pl. SW1 2B 18 (3G 101)
Howie St. SW11 7C 100
Howitt Cl. N16 4E 66
NW3 6C 64
Howitt Rd. NW3 6C 64
Howland Est. SE16 3J 103
Howland Ho. SW16 3J 137
Howland Mews E. W1 5B 6 (5G 83)
Howland St. W1 5A 6 (5G 83)
Howland Way SE16 2A 104
Howletts La. HA4: Ruis 5E 38
Howlett's Rd. SE24 6C 120
Howley Pl. W2 5A 4 (5A 82)
Howley Rd. CR0: C'don 3B 168
Howsman Rd. SW13 6C 98
Howson Rd. SE4 4A 122
Howson Ter. TW10: Rich 6E 114
How's St. E2 2F 85
Howton Pl. WD23: B Hea 1C 26
HOXTON 2E 84
Hoxton Hall Theatre *2E 84*
(off Hoxton St.)
Hoxton Mkt. N1 2G 9
Hoxton Sq. N1 2G 9 (3E 84)
Hoxton St. N1 2H 9 (1E 84)
Hoylake Cres. UB10: Ick 2C 56
Hoylake Gdns. CR4: Mitc 3G 155
HA4: Ruis 1K 57
Hoylake Rd. W3 6A 80
Hoyland Cl. SE15 7H 103
Hoyle Rd. SW17 5C 136
Hoy St. E16 6H 87
HQS Wellington 3J 13
Hub, The
Westminster 1F 5 (2D 82)
Hubbard Ct. IG10: Lough 1H 37
Hubbard Dr. KT9: Chess 6D 162
Hubbard Ho. *SW10* *7B 100*
(off World's End Pas.)
Hubbard Rd. SE27 4C 138
Hubbards Cl. UB8: Hil 6D 74
Hubbard St. E15 1G 87
Hubbinet Ind. Est.
RM7: Mawney 3J 55
Huberd Ho. *SE1* *7F 15*
(off Manciple St.)
Hubert Gro. SW9 3J 119
Hubert Ho. *NW8* *4C 4*
(off Ashbridge St.)
Hubert Rd. E6 3B 88
Hucknall Ct. *NW8* *3A 4*
(off Cunningham Pl.)
Huddart St. E3 5B 86
(not continuous)
Huddleston Cl. E2 2J 85
Huddlestone Rd. E7 4H 69
NW2 6D 62
Huddleston Rd. N7 3G 65
Hudson *NW9* *1B 44*
(off Five Acre)
Hudson Apartments N8 3K 47
Hudson Bldg. *E1* *6K 9*
(off Chicksand St.)
Hudson Cl. E15 1J 87
W12 7D 80
Hudson Ct. *E14* *5C 104*
(off Maritime Quay)
Hudson Gdns. BR6: Chels 6K 173
Hudson Ho. *SW10* *7A 100*
(off Hortensia Rd.)
W11 *6G 81*
(off Ladbroke Gro.)
Hudson Pl. SE18 5G 107
Hudson Rd. DA7: Bex 2F 127
UB3: Harl 6F 93
Hudson's Pl. SW1 3A 18 (4F 101)
Hudson Way N9 3D 34
NW2 3F 63
Huggin Ct. EC4 2D 14
Huggin Hill EC4 2C 14 (7C 84)
Huggins Ho. *E3* *3C 86*
(off Alfred St.)
Huggins Pl. SW2 1K 137
Hughan Rd. E15 5F 69
Hugh Astor Ct. *SE1* *7B 14*
(off Keyworth St.)
Hugh Clark Ho. *W13* *1A 96*
(off Singapore Rd.)
Hugh Cubitt Ho. *N1* *2K 83*
(off Collier St.)
Hugh Dalton Av. SW6 6H 99
Hughenden Av. HA3: Kenton 5B 42
Hughenden Gdns. UB5: N'olt 3A 76
(not continuous)
Hughenden Ho. NW8 3C 4
Hughenden Rd. KT4: Wor Pk 7C 152
Hughendon EN5: New Bar 4E 20
Hughendon Ct. *UB3: Hayes* *7H 75*
(off Chamberlain Cl.)
Hughendon Ter. E15 4E 68
Hughes Cl. N12 5F 31
Hughes Ct. N7 5H 65
Hughes Ho. *E2* *3J 85*
(off Sceptre Ho.)
E3 *3C 86*
(off Trevithick Way)
SE5 *1C 120*
(off Flodden Rd.)
SE8 *6C 104*
(off Benbow St.)
SE17 *4B 102*
(off Peacock St.)
Hughes Mans. E1 4G 85
Hughes Rd. TW15: Ashf 7E 128
UB3: Hayes 7K 75
Hughes Ter. *SW9* *3B 120*
(off Styles Gdns.)
Hughes Wlk. CR0: C'don 7C 156
Hugh Gaitskell Cl. SW6 6H 99
Hugh Gaitskell Ho. N16 2F 67
Hugh Herland Ho. KT1: King T 3E 150
Hugh M. SW1 4K 17 (4F 101)
Hugh Platt Ho. *E2* *2H 85*
(off Patriot Sq.)
Hugh St. SW1 4K 17 (4F 101)
Hugo Ho. *SW1* *1F 17*
(off Sloane St.)
Hugon Rd. SW6 3K 117
Hugo Rd. N19 4G 65
Huguenot Pl. E1 5K 9 (5F 85)
SW18 5A 118
Huguenot Sq. SE15 3H 121
Hullbridge M. N1 1D 84
Hull Cl. SE16 2K 103
Hull Pl. E16 1G 107
Hull St. EC1 2C 8 (3C 84)
Hulme Pl. SE1 7D 14 (2C 102)
Hulse Av. IG11: Bark 6H 71
RM7: Mawney 1H 55
Hulverston Cl. SM2: Sutt 7K 165
Humber Cl. UB7: W Dray 1A 92
Humber Ct. *W7* *6H 77*
(off Hobbayne Rd.)
Humber Dr. W10 4F 81
Humber Rd. NW2 2D 62
SE3 6H 105
Humberstone Rd. E13 3A 88
Humberton Cl. E9 5A 68
Humber Trad. Est. NW2 2D 62
Humbolt Rd. W6 6G 99
Hume Ct. *N1* *7B 66*
(off Hawes St.)
Hume Ho. *W11* *1F 99*
(off Queensdale Cres.)
Humes Av. W7 3J 95
Hume Ter. E16 5K 87
Hume Way HA4: Ruis 6J 39
Humphrey Cl. IG5: Ilf 1D 52
Humphrey St. SE1 5F 103
Humphries Cl. RM9: Dag 4F 73
Hundred Acre NW9 2B 44
Hungerdown E4 1K 35
Hungerford Ho. *SW1* *7B 18*
(off Churchill Gdns.)
Hungerford La. WC2 4F 13
(not continuous)
Hungerford Rd. N7 6H 65
Hungerford St. E1 6H 85
Hunsdon Cl. RM9: Dag 6E 72
Hunsdon Rd. SE14 7K 103
Hunslett St. E2 3J 85
Hunstanton Ho. *NW1* *5D 4*
(off Cosway St.)
Hunston Rd. SM4: Mord 1K 165
Hunt Cl. W11 1F 99
Hunt Ct. N14 7A 22
RM7: Rush G *6K 55*
(off Union Rd.)
UB5: N'olt *2B 76*
(off Gallery Gdns.)
Hunter Cl. SE1 3D 102
SM6: Wall 7J 167
SW12 1E 136
Hunter Ho. *SE1* *7B 14*
(off King James St.)
SW5 *5J 99*
(off Old Brompton Rd.)
SW8 *7H 101*
(off Fount St.)
TW13: Felt *1J 129*
(off Hazel Gro.)
WC1 *3F 7*
(off Hunter St.)
Hunterian Museum, The *7H 7*
(off Portugal St.)
Hunter Lodge *W9* *5J 81*
(off Admiral Wlk.)
Hunter Rd. CR7: Thor H 3D 156
IG1: Ilf 5F 71
SW20 1E 152
Hunters Cl. DA5: Bexl 3K 145
Hunters Ct. TW9: Rich 5D 114
Hunters Gro. BR6: Farnb 4G 173
HA3: Kenton 4C 42
UB3: Hayes 1J 93
Hunters Hall Rd. RM10: Dag 4G 73
Hunters Hill HA4: Ruis 3A 58
Hunters Mdw. SE19 4E 138
Hunter's Rd. KT9: Chess 3E 162
Hunters Sq. RM10: Dag 4G 73
Hunter St. WC1 3F 7 (4J 83)
Hunters Way CR0: C'don 4E 168
EN2: Enf 1F 23
Hunter Wlk. E13 2J 87
Huntingdon Cl. CR4: Mitc 3J 155
UB5: N'olt 6E 58
Huntingdon Gdns.
KT4: Wor Pk 3E 164
W4 7J 97
Huntingdon Rd. N2 3C 46
N9 2D 34
Huntingdon St. E16 6H 87
N1 7K 65
Huntingfield CR0: Sels 7B 170
Huntingfield Rd. SW15 4C 116
Hunting Ga. Cl. EN2: Enf 3F 23
Hunting Ga. Dr. KT9: Chess 7E 162
Hunting Ga. M. SM1: Sutt 3K 165
TW2: Twick 1J 131
Huntings Farm IG1: Ilf 2J 71
Huntings Rd. RM10: Dag 6G 73
Huntington Cl. DA5: Bexl 1H 145
Huntley Cl. TW19: Stanw 7A 110
Huntley St. WC1 4B 6 (4G 83)
Huntley Way SW20 2C 152
Huntloe Ho. *SE14* *1J 121*
(off Kender St.)
Huntly Dr. N3 6D 30
Huntly Rd. SE25 4E 156
Hunton St. E1 4K 9 (5G 85)
Hunt Rd. UB2: S'hall 3E 94
Hunt's Cl. SE3 2J 123
Hunt's Ct. WC2 3D 12 (7H 83)
Huntshaw Ho. *E3* *3D 86*
(off Devons Rd.)
Hunts La. E15 2E 86
Huntsmans Cl. TW13: Felt 4K 129
Huntsman St. SE17 4E 102
Hunts Mead EN3: Enf H 3E 24
Hunts Mead Cl. BR7: Chst 7D 142
Huntsmoor Rd. KT19: Ewe 5K 163
Huntspill St. SW17 3A 136
Hunts Slip Rd. SE21 3E 138
Huntsworth M. NW1 3E 4 (4D 82)
Hurdwick Ho. *NW1* *2G 83*
(off Harrington Sq.)
Hurdwick Pl. *NW1* *2G 83*
(off Hampstead Rd.)
Hurleston Ho. SE8 5B 104
Hurley Ct. *SW17* *6E 136*
(off Mitcham Rd.)
W5 6C 78
Hurley Cres. SE16 2K 103
Hurley Ho. SE11 4K 19 (4B 102)
UB7: W Dray *2B 92*
(off Park Lodge Av.)
Hurley Rd. UB6: G'frd 6F 77
HURLINGHAM 3K 117
Hurlingham Bus. Pk. SW6 3J 117
Hurlingham Club, The 3J 117
Hurlingham Ct. SW6 3H 117
Hurlingham Gdns. SW6 3H 117
Hurlingham Pk. 2H 117
Hurlingham Retail Pk. SW6 3K 117
Hurlingham Rd. DA7: Bex 7F 109
SW6 2H 117
Hurlingham Sq. SW6 3J 117
Hurlingham Yacht Club 3G 117
Hurlock St. N5 3B 66
Hurlstone Rd. SE25 5E 156
Hurn Ct. TW4: Houn 2B 112
Hurn Ct. Rd. TW4: Houn 2B 112
Huron Cl. BR6: Chels 6J 173
Huron Rd. SW17 2E 136
Hurren Cl. SE3 3G 123
Hurricane Rd. SM6: Wall 7J 167
Hurricane Trad. Cen. NW9 1C 44
Hurry Cl. E15 7G 69
Hurst Av. E4 4H 35
N6 6G 47
Hurstbourne KT10: Clay 6A 162
Hurstbourne Gdns. IG11: Bark 6J 71
Hurstbourne Ho. *SW15* *6B 116*
(off Tangley Gro.)
Hurstbourne Rd. SE23 1A 140
Hurst Cl.
BR2: Hayes 1H 171
E4 3H 35
KT9: Chess 5G 163
NW11 6K 45
UB5: N'olt 6D 58
Hurstcombe IG9: Buck H 2D 36
Hurst Ct. DA15: Sidc 2A 144
E6 *5B 88*
(off Tollgate Rd.)
IG8: Wfd G *6E 36*
(off Snakes La. W.)
Hurstcourt Rd. SM1: Sutt 2K 165
Hurstdene Av. BR2: Hayes 1H 171
Hurstdene Gdns. N15 7E 48
Hurstfield BR2: Brom 5J 159
Hurstfield Cres. UB4: Hayes 4G 75
Hurstfield Rd. KT8: W Mole 3E 148
Hurst Gro. KT12: Walt T 7H 147
Hurst Ho. *WC1* *1H 7*
(off Penton Ri.)

Hurst La. KT8: E Mos 4G 149
  SE2 . . . . .5D 108
Hurst La. Est. SE2 . . . . .5D 108
Hurstleigh Gdns. IG5: Ilf 1D 52
Hurstmead Ct. HA8: Edg 4C 28
HURST PARK 2G 149
Hurst Pl. HA6: Nwood 1D 38
Hurst Pool 3F 149
Hurst Ri. EN5: New Bar 3D 20
Hurst Rd. CR0: C'don 5D 168
  DA5: Bexl 1D 144
  DA8: Erith 1J 127
  DA15: Bexl, Sidc 2A 144
  E17 . . . . .3D 50
  IG9: Buck H 1G 37
  KT8: W Mole, E Mos 3F 149
  KT12: Walt T 5A 148
  N21 . . . . .1F 33
Hurst Springs DA5: Bexl 1E 144
Hurst St. SE24 . . . . .6B 120
Hurstview Grange CR2: S Croy 7B 168
Hurst Vw. Rd. CR2: S Croy 7E 168
Hurst Way CR2: S Croy 6E 168
Hurstway Rd. W11 . . . . .7F 81
  (off Hurstway Wlk.)
Hurstway Wlk. W11 . . . . .7F 81
Hurstwood Av. DA5: Bexl 1E 144
  E18 . . . . .4K 51
Hurstwood Ct. N12 . . . . .6H 31
  NW11 .4H 45
  (off Finchley Rd.)
Hurstwood Dr. BR1: Brom 3D 160
Hurstwood Rd. NW11 . . . . .4G 45
Hurtwood Rd. KT12: Walt T 7D 148
Husborne Ho. SE8 . . . . .4A 104
  (off Chilton Gro.)
Huson Cl. NW3 . . . . .7C 64
Hussain Cl. HA1: Harr 4K 59
Hussars Cl. TW4: Houn 3C 112
Husseywell Cres. BR2: Hayes 1J 171
Hutchings St. E14 . . . . .2C 104
Hutchings Wlk. NW11 . . . . .4K 45
Hutchings Wharf E14 . . . . .2C 104
  (off Hutchings St.)
Hutchins Cl. E15 . . . . .7E 68
Hutchinson Ct. RM6: Chad H 4D 54
Hutchinson Ho. NW3 . . . . .7D 64
  SE14 .7J 103
Hutchinson Ter. HA9: Wemb 3D 60
Hutchins Rd. SE28 . . . . .7A 90
Hutton Cl. IG8: Wfd G 6E 36
  UB6: G'frd 5H 59
Hutton Ct. N4 . . . . .1K 65
  (off Victoria Rd.)
  N9 . . . . .7D 24
  (off Tramway Av.)
  W5 . . . . .5B 78
Hutton Gdns. HA3: Hrw W 7B 26
Hutton Gro. N12 . . . . .5E 30
Hutton La. HA3: Hrw W 7B 26
Hutton M. SW15 . . . . .5D 116
Hutton Row HA8: Edg 7D 28
Hutton St. EC4 . . . . .2K 13 (6B 84)
Hutton Wlk. HA3: Hrw W 7B 26
Huxbear St. SE4 . . . . .5B 122
Huxley Cl. UB5: N'olt 2C 76
  UB8: Cowl 4A 74
Huxley Dr. RM6: Chad H 7B 54
Huxley Gdns. NW10 . . . . .3F 79
Huxley Ho. NW8 . . . . .4B 4
  (off Fisherton St.)
Huxley Pde. N18 . . . . .5J 33
Huxley Pl. N13 . . . . .3G 33
Huxley Rd. DA16: Well 3K 125
  E10 . . . . .2E 68
  N18 . . . . .4J 33
Huxley Sayze N18 . . . . .5J 33
Huxley Sth. N18 . . . . .5J 33
Huxley St. W10 . . . . .3G 81
Hyacinth Cl. IG1: Ilf 6F 71
  TW12: Hamp 6E 130

Hyacinth Dr. UB10: Uxb 7A 56
Hyacinth Ho. E17 . . . . .3D 50
  (off Vine St.)
Hyacinth Rd. SW15 . . . . .1C 134
Hybrid Ho. W3 . . . . .1B 98
HYDE, THE .5B 44
Hyde, The NW9 . . . . .4A 44
  (not continuous)
Hyde Cl. E13 . . . . .2J 87
  EN5: Barn 3C 20
  TW15: Ashf 6G 129
Hyde Ct. N20 . . . . .3G 31
Hyde Cres. NW9 . . . . .5A 44
Hyde Est. Rd. NW9 . . . . .5B 44
Hyde Farm M. SW12 . . . . .1H 137
Hydefield Cl. N21 . . . . .1J 33
Hydefield Ct. N9 . . . . .2K 33
Hyde Ho. E3 . . . . .5C 86
  (off Furze St.)
  TW3: Houn 3G 113
  UB8: Uxb 6A 56
  W13 . . . . .1A 96
  (off Singapore Rd.)
Hyde Ind. Estate, The NW9 . . . . .5B 44
Hyde La. SW11 . . . . .1C 118
Hyde Park 4D 10 (1D 100)
Hyde Pk. Av. N21 . . . . .2H 33
Hyde Pk. Cnr. W1 . . . . .6H 11 (2E 100)
Hyde Pk. Cres. W2 . . . . .1C 10 (6C 82)
Hyde Pk. Gdns. N21 . . . . .1H 33
  W2 . . . . .2B 10 (7B 82)
  (not continuous)
Hyde Pk. Gdns. M. W2 . . .2B 10 (7B 82)
Hyde Pk. Ga. SW7 . . . . .2A 100
  (not continuous)
Hyde Pk. Ga. M. SW7 . . . . .2A 100
Hyde Pk. Mans. NW1 . . . . .6C 4
  (off Cabbell St., not continuous)
Hyde Pk. Pl. W2 . . . . .2D 10 (7C 82)
Hyde Pk. Sq. W2 . . . . .1C 10 (6C 82)
Hyde Pk. Sq. M. W2 . . . . .1C 10
Hyde Pk. St. W2 . . . . .1C 10 (6C 82)
Hyde Pk. Towers W2 . . . . .7A 82
Hyderabad Way E15 . . . . .7G 69
Hyde Rd. DA7: Bex 2F 127
  N1 . . . . .1E 84
  TW10: Rich 5F 115
Hydeside Gdns. N9 . . . . .2A 34
Hyde's Pl. N1 . . . . .7B 66
Hyde St. SE8 . . . . .6C 104
Hyde Ter. TW15: Ashf 6G 129
Hydethorpe Av. N9 . . . . .2A 34
Hydethorpe Rd. SW12 . . . . .1G 137
Hyde Va. SE10 . . . . .7E 104
Hyde Wlk. SM4: Mord 7J 153
Hyde Way N9 . . . . .2A 34
  UB3: Harl 4H 93
Hydon Ct. N11 . . . . .5J 31
Hylands Rd. E17 . . . . .2E 51
Hylton St. SE18 . . . . .4K 107
Hyndewood SE23 . . . . .3K 139
Hyndman Ho. RM10: Dag 3G 73
  (off Kershaw Rd.)
Hyndman St. SE15 . . . . .6H 103
Hynton Rd. RM8: Dag 2C 72
Hyperion Ct. E16 . . . . .5J 87
  (off Robertson Rd.)
Hyperion Ho. E3 . . . . .2A 86
  (off Arbery Rd.)
  SW2 . . . . .6K 119
Hyrstdene
  CR2: S Croy 4B 168
Hyson Rd. SE16 . . . . .5H 103
Hythe Av. DA7: Bex 7E 108
Hythe Cl. N18 . . . . .4B 34
Hythe Ho. SE16 . . . . .2J 103
  (off Swan Rd.)
  W6 . . . . .4E 98
  (off Shepherd's Bush Rd.)

Hythe Rd. CR7: Thor H 2D 156
  NW10 .3B 80
Hythe Rd. Ind. Est. NW10 . . . . .3C 80

I

Ian Bowater Ct. N1 . . . . .1F 9
  (off East Rd.)
Ian Ct. SE23 . . . . .2J 139
Ian Sq. EN3: Enf H 1E 24
Ibberton Ho. SW8 . . . . .7K 101
  (off Meadow Rd.)
  W14 . . . . .3G 99
  (off Russell Rd.)
Ibbotson Av. E16 . . . . .6H 87
Ibbott St. E1 . . . . .4J 85
Iberia Ho. N19 . . . . .7H 47
Iberian Av. SM6: Bedd 4H 167
Ibex Ho. E15 . . . . .5G 69
  (off Forest La.)
Ibis Ct. BR3: Beck 1F 159
  (off Albemarle Rd.)
  SE8 . . . . .6B 104
  (off Edward Pl.)
Ibis La. W4 .1J 115
Ibis Way UB4: Yead 6B 76
Ibrox Ct. IG9: Buck H 2F 37
Ibscott Cl. RM10: Dag 6J 73
Ibsley Gdns. SW15 . . . . .1C 134
Ibsley Way EN4: Cockf 5H 21
ICA Cinema 4D 12
  (off Carlton Ho. Ter.)
Icarus Ho. E3 . . . . .3B 86
  (off British St.)
ICA Theatre 4D 12
  (off Carlton Ho. Ter.)
Iceland Rd. E3 . . . . .1C 86
Iceland Wharf SE16 . . . . .4A 104
Iceni Ct. E3 . . . . .1B 86
  (off Parnell Rd.)
  IG9: Buck H 1E 36
Ice Wharf N1 . . . . .2J 83
Ice Wharf Marina N1 . . . . .2J 83
  (off New Wharf Rd.)
Ice Works, The NW1 . . . . .7F 65
  (off Jamestown Rd.)
Ickburgh Est. E5 . . . . .2H 67
Ickburgh Rd. E5 . . . . .3H 67
ICKENHAM .3D 56
Ickenham Cl. HA4: Ruis 2F 57
Ickenham Grn. UB10: Ick 1D 56
Ickenham Rd. HA4: Ruis 2E 56
Ickleton Rd. SE9 . . . . .4C 142
Icklield Dr. IG2: Ilf 5F 53
Icknield Ho. SW3 . . . . .5D 16
  (off Cale St.)
Ickworth Pk. Rd. E17 . . . . .4A 50
Icon Apartments SE1 . . . . .7G 15
  (off Cluny Pl.)
Icona Point E15 . . . . .1E 86
  (off Warton Rd.)
Iconia Ho. BR2: Brom 4A 160
Idaho Bldg. SE13 . . . . .1D 122
  (off Deal's Gateway)
Ida Rd. N15 .4D 48
Ida St. E14 .6E 86
  (not continuous)
Ide Mans. E1 . . . . .7K 85
  (off Cable St.)
Iden Cl. BR2: Brom 3G 159
Idlecombe Rd. SW17 . . . . .6E 136
Idmiston Rd.
  E15 . . . . .4H 69
  KT4: Wor Pk 7B 152
  SE27 .3C 138
Idmiston Sq. KT4: Wor Pk 7B 152
Idol La. EC3 . . . . .3G 15 (7E 84)
Idonia St. SE8 . . . . .7C 104
Iffley Cl. UB8: Uxb 7A 56
Iffley Rd. W6 . . . . .3D 98

Ifield Ho. SE17 . . . . .5E 102
  (off Madron St.)
Ifield Rd. SW10 . . . . .6K 99
Ifor Evans Pl. E1 . . . . .4K 85
Ightham Ho. BR3: Beck 7B 140
  (off Bethersden Cl.)
  SE17 . . . . .4E 102
  (off Beckway St.)
Ightham Rd. DA8: Erith 7G 109
Ikon Ho. E1 .7J 85
  (off Devonport St.)
Ilbert St. W10 . . . . .3F 81
Ilchester Gdns. W2 . . . . .7K 81
Ilchester Mans. W8 . . . . .3J 99
  (off Abingdon Rd.)
Ilchester Pl. W14 . . . . .3H 99
Ilchester Rd. RM8: Dag 5B 72
Ildersly Gro. SE21 . . . . .2D 138
Ilderton Rd. SE15 . . . . .5J 103
  SE16 .5J 103
Ilderton Wharf SE15 . . . . .6J 103
  (off Rollins St.)
Ilex Cl. TW16: Sun 2A 148
Ilex Ho. N4 . . . . .6B 48
Ilex Rd. NW10 . . . . .6B 62
Ilex Way SW16 . . . . .5A 138
ILFORD 3F 71
Ilford Bldg. IG1: Ilf 3E 70
Ilford Golf Course 1D 70
Ilford Hill IG1: Ilf 3E 70
Ilford Ho. N1 . . . . .6D 66
  (off Dove Rd.)
Ilford La. IG1: Ilf 3F 71
Ilford Sports Club 2J 71
Ilfracombe Flats SE1 . . . . .6D 14
  (off Marshalsea Rd.)
Ilfracombe Gdns. RM6: Chad H 7B 54
Ilfracombe Rd. BR1: Brom 3H 141
Iliffe St. SE17 . . . . .5B 102
Iliffe Yd. SE17 . . . . .5B 102
  (off Crampton St.)
Ilkeston Ct. E5 . . . . .4K 67
  (off Overbury St.)
Ilkley Cl. SE19 . . . . .6D 138
Ilkley Rd. E16 . . . . .5A 88
Illingworth Cl. CR4: Mitc 3B 154
Illingworth Way EN1: Enf 5K 23
Illumina Ho. SW18 . . . . .5J 117
  (off Broomhill Rd.)
Ilmington Rd. HA3: Kenton 6D 42
Ilminster Gdns. SW11 . . . . .4C 118
Ilsley Ct. SW8 . . . . .2G 119
Images IG2: Ilf 6E 52
Imani Mans. SW11 . . . . .2B 118
IMAX (BFI) 5J 13 (1A 102)
Imber Ct. N14 . . . . .7B 22
Imber Court 7H 149
Imber Ct. Trad. Est. KT8: E Mos 6H 149
Imber Cross KT7: T Ditt 6K 149
Imber Gro. KT10: Esh 7H 149
Imber Pk. Rd. KT10: Esh 7H 149
Imber St. N1 .1D 84
Impact Bus. Pk. UB6: G'frd 2B 78
Impact Ct. SE20 . . . . .2H 157
Imperial Av. N16 . . . . .4E 66
Imperial Cl. HA2: Harr 6E 40
  NW2 . . . . .5D 62
Imperial College London
    Chelsea & Westminster Campus
  . . . . .6A 100
  (within Chelsea & Westminster Hospital)
    Royal Brompton Campus 6C 16
    St Mary's 6B 82
  (off Norfolk Pl.)
    Sth. Kensington Campus
  . . . . .1A 16 (3B 100)
Imperial Coll. Rd. SW7 . . . .2A 16 (3B 100)
Imperial Ct. HA2: Harr 7E 40
  N6 . . . . .6G 47
  N20 . . . . .3F 31
  NW8 . . . . .2C 82
  (off Prince Albert Rd.)

Imperial Ct. SE11 . . . . .6J **19** (5A **102**)
Imperial Cres. SW6 . . . . .2A **118**
Imperial Dr. HA2: Harr 7E **40**
Imperial Gdns. CR4: Mitc 3F **155**
Imperial Gro. EN4: Had W 1E **20**
Imperial Hgts. E18 . . . . .1J **51**
        (off Queen Mary Av.)
Imperial Ho. E3 . . . . .3A **86**
        (off Grove Rd.)
  E14 . . . . .7B **86**
        (off Victory Pl.)
Imperial M. E6 . . . . .2B **88**
  SW9 . . . . .4K **119**
        (off Brighton Ter.)
Imperial Pl. BR7: Chst 1F **160**
Imperial Rd. N22 . . . . .7D **32**
  SW6 . . . . .1K **117**
  TW14: Felt 7G **111**
Imperial Sq. SW6 . . . . .1K **117**
Imperial St. E3 . . . . .3E **86**
Imperial War Mus.
  All Saints Annexe 3K **19**
        (off Austral St.)
  Lambeth Rd. 2K **19** (3A **102**)
Imperial Way BR7: Chst 3G **143**
  CR0: Wadd 6K **167**
  HA3: Kenton 6E **42**
Imperial Wharf E2 . . . . .2H **85**
        (off Darwen Pl.)
  SW6 . . . . .2A **118**
Imperium Ho. E1 . . . . .6H **85**
        (off Cannon St. Rd.)
Imre Cl. W12 .1D **98**
Inca Dr. SE9 .7F **125**
Inca Ter. N15 .3B **48**
Inchmery Rd. SE6 . . . . .2D **140**
Inchwood BR4: Addtn 4D **170**
Independence Ho. SW19 . . . . .1B **154**
        (off Chapter Way)
Independent Ind. Est. UB7: Yiew 1A **92**
Independent Pl. E8 . . . . .5F **67**
Independents Rd. SE3 . . . . .3H **123**
Inderwick Rd. N8 . . . . .5K **47**
Indescon Ct. E14 . . . . .2D **104**
Indescon Sq. E14 . . . . .2C **104**
India Gdns. UB5: N'olt 7A **58**
India Ho. WC2 . . . . .1F **13**
        (off Aldwych)
Indiana Bldg. SE13 . . . . .1C **122**
        (off Deal's Gateway)
India Rd. WC2 . . . . .2G **13**
India St. EC3 . . . . .1J **15** (6F **85**)
India Way SW15 . . . . .6C **116**
  W12 . . . . .7D **80**
IndigO2 . . . . .1G **105**
Indigo Ho. E14 . . . . .7E **86**
  N16 . . . . .3D **66**
Indigo Wlk. N6 . . . . .4D **46**
Indus Ct. SE15 . . . . .7F **103**
        (off Amstel Ct.)
Indus Rd. SE7 . . . . .7A **106**
Infirmary Ct. SW3 . . . . .7F **17**
Inforum M. SE15 . . . . .7G **103**
Ingal Rd. E13 .4J **87**
Ingate Pl. SW8 . . . . .1F **119**
Ingatestone Rd. E12 . . . . .1A **70**
  IG8: Wfd G 7E **36**
  SE25 . . . . .4H **157**
Ingelow Ho. W8 . . . . .2K **99**
        (off Holland St.)
Ingelow Rd. SW8 . . . . .2F **119**
Ingersoll Rd. EN3: Enf W 1D **24**
  W12 . . . . .1D **98**
Ingestre Pl. W1 . . . . .1B **12** (6G **83**)
Ingestre Rd. E7 . . . . .4J **69**
  NW5 . . . . .4F **65**
Ingham Cl. CR2: Sels 7K **169**
Ingham Rd. CR2: Sels 7J **169**
  NW6 . . . . .4J **63**
Inglebert St. EC1 . . . . .1J **7** (3A **84**)
Ingleborough St. SW9 . . . . .2A **120**

Ingleby Dr. HA1: Harr 3H **59**
Ingleby Rd. IG1: Ilf 1F **71**
  N7 . . . . .3J **65**
  RM10: Dag 6H **73**
Ingleby Way BR7: Chst 5E **142**
  SM6: Wall 7H **167**
Ingle Cl. HA5: Pinn 3C **40**
Ingledew Rd. SE18 . . . . .5H **107**
Inglefield Sq. E1 . . . . .1H **103**
        (off Prusom St.)
Inglehurst Gdns. IG4: Ilf 5D **52**
Inglemere Rd. CR4: Mitc 7D **136**
  SE23 . . . . .3K **139**
Ingle M. EC1 . . . . .1J **7** (3A **84**)
Inglesham Wlk. E9 . . . . .6B **68**
Ingleside SL3: Poyle 4A **174**
Ingleside Cl. BR3: Beck 7C **140**
Ingleside Gro. SE3 . . . . .6H **105**
Inglethorpe St. SW6 . . . . .1F **117**
Ingleton Av. DA16: Well 5A **126**
Ingleton Rd. N18 . . . . .6B **34**
  SM5: Cars 7C **166**
Ingleton St. SW9 . . . . .2A **120**
Ingleway N12 .6G **31**
Inglewood BR7: Chst 6H **143**
  CR0: Sels 7A **170**
Inglewood Cl. E14 . . . . .4C **104**
  Inglewood Copse BR1: Brom 2C **160**
Inglewood Ct. BR1: Brom 7G **141**
Inglewood M. KT6: Surb 1G **163**
  SE27 . . . . .5C **138**
        (off Elder Rd.)
Inglewood Rd. DA7: Bex 4K **127**
  NW6 . . . . .5J **63**
Inglis Barracks NW7 . . . . .6A **30**
Inglis Rd. CR0: C'don 1F **169**
  W5 . . . . .7F **79**
Inglis St. SE5 . . . . .1B **120**
Inglis Way NW7 . . . . .6A **30**
Ingoldisthorpe Gro. SE15 . . . . .6F **103**
Ingot Ter. E14 . . . . .5C **86**
        (off Ursula Gould Way)
Ingram Av. NW11 . . . . .7A **46**
Ingram Cl. HA7: Stan 5H **27**
  SE11 . . . . .3H **19** (4K **101**)
Ingram Ct. CR0: C'don 1B **168**
Ingram Ho. E3 . . . . .1A **86**
Ingram Rd. CR7: Thor H 1C **156**
  N2 . . . . .4C **46**
Ingram Way UB6: G'frd 1H **77**
Ingrave Rd. RM1: Rom 4K **55**
Ingrave St. SW11 . . . . .3B **118**
Ingrebourne Ct. E4 . . . . .3J **35**
Ingrebourne Ho. BR1: Brom 5F **141**
        (off Brangbourne Rd.)
  NW8 . . . . .5B **4**
        (off Broadley St.)
Ingress St. W4 . . . . .5A **98**
Inigo Jones Rd. SE7 . . . . .7C **106**
Inigo Pl. WC2 .2E **12**
Ink Bldg. W10 .5F **81**
Inkerman Rd. NW5 . . . . .6F **65**
Inkerman Ter. W8 . . . . .3J **99**
        (off Allen St.)
Inks Grn. E4 . . . . .5K **35**
Inkster Ho. SW11 . . . . .3C **118**
Inkwell Cl. N12 . . . . .3F **31**
Ink Works Ct. SE1 . . . . .2E **102**
        (off Bell Yd. M.)
Inman Rd. NW10 . . . . .1A **80**
  SW18 . . . . .7A **118**
Inmans Row IG8: Wfd G 4D **36**
Inner Circ. NW1 . . . . .2G **5** (3E **82**)
Inner Ct. SW3 . . . . .7C **16** (6C **100**)
Innerd Ct. CR0: C'don 6C **156**
        (off Harry Cl.)
Inner London Family Proceedings Court
  Magistrates' Court 7A **6** (5G **83**)
Inner Pk. Rd. SW19 . . . . .1F **135**
Inner Ring E. TW6: H'row A 3D **110**
Inner Ring W. TW6: H'row A 3C **110**

Inner Temple La. EC4 . . . . .1J **13**
Innes Cl. SW20 . . . . .2G **153**
Innes Gdns. SW15 . . . . .6D **116**
Innes St. SE15 . . . . .7E **102**
Innes Yd. CR0: C'don 3C **168**
Innis Ho. SE17 . . . . .5E **102**
        (off East St.)
Inniskilling Rd. E13 . . . . .2A **88**
Innova Ct. CR0: C'don 1E **168**
Innova Pas. E1 . . . . .3J **9**
        (off Sclater St.)
Innovation Centre, The E14 . . . . .2E **104**
        (off Marsh Wall)
Innovation Cl. HA0: Wemb 1E **78**
Inns of Court & City Yeomanry Mus.
  . . . . .6H **7** (5K **83**)
Inskip Cl. E10 .2D **68**
Inskip Rd. RM8: Dag 1D **72**
Insley Ho. E3 .3D **86**
        (off Bow Rd.)
Institute of Archaeology Collections . .4H **83**
Institute of Contemporary Arts 4D **12**
Institute Pl. E8 . . . . .5H **67**
Instone Cl. SM6: Wall 7J **167**
Integer Gdns. E11 . . . . .7F **51**
Interchange, The NW1 . . . . .7F **65**
        (off Camden Lock Pl.)
Interface Ho. TW3: Houn 3E **112**
        (off Staines Rd.)
International Av. TW5: Cran 5A **94**
International Bus. Pk. E15 . . . . .1F **87**
International Ho. E1 . . . . .3K **15**
        (off St Katharine's Way)
  TW8: Bford 5E **96**
        (off Gt. West Rd.)
International Sq. E20 . . . . .6E **68**
  (within Westfield Stratford City Shop. Cen.)
International Trad. Est. UB2: S'hall 3K **93**
International Way E20 . . . . .6E **68**
  TW16: Sun 1G **147**
INTU Shop. Cen. BR1: Brom 2J **159**
Inveary Rd. SE18 . . . . .6H **107**
Inver Cl. E5 . . . . .2J **67**
Inverclyde Gdns. RM6: Chad H 4C **54**
        (not continuous)
Inver Ct. W2 . . . . .6K **81**
  W6 . . . . .3C **98**
Inveresk Gdns. KT4: Wor Pk 3C **164**
Inverforth Cl. NW3 . . . . .2A **64**
Inverforth Rd. N11 . . . . .5A **32**
Invergarry Ho. NW6 . . . . .2K **81**
        (off Carlton Vale)
Inverine Rd. SE7 . . . . .5K **105**
Invermead Cl. W6 . . . . .3C **98**
Invermore Pl. SE18 . . . . .4G **107**
Inverness Av. EN1: Enf 1K **23**
Inverness Ct. SE6 . . . . .1H **141**
Inverness Gdns. W8 . . . . .1K **99**
Inverness M. E16 . . . . .1G **107**
  W2 . . . . .7K **81**
Inverness Pl. W2 . . . . .7K **81**
Inverness Rd. KT4: Wor Pk 1F **165**
  N18 . . . . .5C **34**
  TW3: Houn 4D **112**
  UB2: S'hall 4C **94**
Inverness St. NW1 . . . . .1F **83**
Inverness Ter. W2 . . . . .6K **81**
Inverton Rd. SE15 . . . . .4K **121**
Invicta Centre, The IG11: Bark 1A **90**
Invicta Cl. BR7: Chst 5E **142**
  E3 . . . . .5C **86**
  TW14: Felt 1H **129**
Invicta Gro. UB5: N'olt 3D **76**
Invicta Pde. DA14: Sidc 4B **144**
Invicta Plaza SE1 . . . . .4A **14** (1B **102**)
Invicta Rd. SE3 . . . . .7J **105**
Inville Rd. SE17 . . . . .5D **102**
        (not continuous)
Inville Wlk. SE17 . . . . .5D **102**
Invito IG2: Ilf 6E **52**
Inwen Ct. SE8 . . . . .5A **104**
        (not continuous)

Inwood Av. TW3: Houn 3G **113**
Inwood Bus. Pk. TW3: Houn 4F **113**
Inwood Cl. CR0: C'don 2A **170**
Inwood Ct. NW1 . . . . .7G **65**
        (off Rochester Sq.)
Inwood Ho. N1 . . . . .1B **84**
        (off Elliott's Pl.)
Inwood Rd. TW3: Houn 4F **113**
Inworth St. SW11 . . . . .2C **118**
Inworth Wlk. N1 . . . . .1C **84**
        (off Popham St.)
IO Centre SE18 . . . . .3G **107**
        (not continuous)
Iona Cl. SE6 .7C **122**
  SM4: Mord 7K **153**
Ion Ct. E2 . . . . .2G **85**
Ionian Bldg. E14 . . . . .7A **86**
        (off Narrow St.)
Ionian Ho. E1 .4K **85**
        (off Duckett St.)
Ion Sq. E2 . . . . .2G **85**
IO Trade Cen. CR0: Bedd 4K **167**
Ipsden Bldgs. SE1 . . . . .5K **13**
Ipswich Ho. SE4 . . . . .5B **122**
Ipswich Rd. SW17 . . . . .6E **136**
Ira Ct. SE27 .2B **138**
Ireland Cl. E6 .5D **88**
Ireland Pl. N22 . . . . .7D **32**
Ireland Yd. EC4 . . . . .1B **14** (6B **84**)
Irene M. W7 . . . . .1K **95**
        (off Uxbridge Rd.)
Irene Rd. BR6: Orp 7K **161**
  SW6 . . . . .1J **117**
Ireton Cl. N10 .7K **31**
Ireton Ho. SW15 . . . . .5G **117**
        (off Stamford Sq.)
Ireton St. E3 . . . . .4C **86**
Iris Av. DA5: Bexl 5E **126**
Iris Cl. CR0: C'don 1K **169**
  E6 . . . . .5C **88**
  KT6: Surb 7F **151**
  N14 . . . . .7C **22**
Iris Ct. SE14 .1J **121**
        (off Briant St.)
Iris Cres. DA7: Bex 6F **109**
Iris M. TW4: Houn 6E **112**
Iris Rd. KT19: Ewe 5H **163**
Iris Wlk. HA8: Edg 4D **28**
Iris Way E4 . . . . .6G **35**
Irkdale Av. EN1: Enf 1A **24**
Iron Bri. Cl. NW10 . . . . .5A **62**
Ironbridge Cl. UB2: S'hall 1G **95**
Iron Bri. Ho. NW1 . . . . .7D **64**
Iron Bri. Rd. Nth. UB11: Stock P 2C **92**
Iron Bri. Rd. Sth. UB7: W Dray 2C **92**
Iron Mill Pl. SW18 . . . . .6K **117**
Iron Mill Rd. SW18 . . . . .6K **117**
Ironmonger La. EC2 . . . . . . .1D **14** (6C **84**)
Ironmonger Pas. EC1 . . . . .2D **8**
        (off Ironmonger Row)
Ironmonger Row EC1 . . . . . . .2D **8** (3C **84**)
Ironmonger Row Baths 2C **8**
Ironmongers Pl. E14 . . . . .4C **104**
Ironside Cl. SE16 . . . . .2K **103**
Ironside Ct. TW11: Hamp W 1C **150**
Ironside Ho. E9 . . . . .4A **68**
Irons Way RM5: Col R 1J **55**
Iron Works E3 .1C **86**
Ironworks, The N1 . . . . .2J **83**
        (off Albion Wlk.)
Irvine Av. HA3: Kenton 3A **42**
Irvine Cl. E14 .5D **86**
  N20 . . . . .2H **31**
Irvine Ct. W1 . . . . .4B **6**
        (off Whitfield St.)
Irvine Ho. N7 .6K **65**
        (off Caledonian Rd.)
Irvine Way BR6: Orp 7K **161**
Irving Av. UB5: N'olt 1B **76**
Irving Gro. SW9 . . . . .2K **119**
Irving Ho. SE17 . . . . .5B **102**
        (off Doddington Gro.)

Irving Mans. *W14* *6G 99*
  (off Queen's Club Gdns.)
Irving M. N1 . . . .*6C 66*
Irving Rd. W14 . . . .*3F 99*
Irving St. WC2 . . . . .3D 12 (7H 83)
Irving Way NW9 . . . .*5C 44*
Irwell Ct. *W7* *6H 77*
  (off Hobbayne Rd.)
Irwell Est. SE16 . . . .*3J 103*
Irwin Av. SE18 . . . .*7J 107*
Irwin Cl. UB10: Ick *3C 56*
Irwin Gdns. NW10 . . . .*1D 80*
Isaac Way *SE1* *6D 14*
  (off Sanctuary St.)
Isabel Hill Cl. TW12: Hamp 1F 149
Isabella Cl. N14 . . . . .7B 22
Isabella Cl. *TW10: Rich* *6F 115*
  (off Kingsmead)
Isabella Dr. BR6: Farnb 4G 173
Isabella Ho. SE11 . . . . .5K 19
  W6 . . . .*5E 98*
  (off Queen Caroline St.)
Isabella Pl. KT2: King T 5F 133
Isabella Plantation Garden 3H 133
Isabella Rd. E9 .5J 67
Isabella St. SE1 . . . . .5A 14 (1B 102)
Isambard M. E14 . . . . .3E 104
Isambard Pl. SE16 . . . . .1J 103
Isard Ho. BR2: Hayes 1K 171
Isel Way SE22 . . . . .5E 120
Isham Rd. SW16 . . . . .2J 155
Isis Cl. HA4: Ruis 6E 38
  SW15 . . . . .4E 116
Isis Ct. W4 . . . . .7H 97
Isis Ho. N18 . . . . .6A 34
  NW8 . . . . .4B 4
  (off Church St. Est.)
  SE20 . . . . .7G 139
Isis St. SW18 .2A 136
Island, The KT7: T Ditt 6A 150
  UB7: Lford 3D 174
Island Apartments N1 . . . . .1C 84
Island Barn Reservoir Sailing Club
  . . . . .6F 149
Island Farm Av. KT8: W Mole 5D 148
Island Farm Rd. KT8: W Mole 5D 148
Island Ho. E3 . . . . .3E 86
Island Rd. CR4: Mitc 7D 136
  SE16 . . . . .4K 103
Island Row E14 . . . . .6B 86
Isla Rd. SE18 . . . . .6G 107
Islay Gdns. TW4: Houn 5B 112
Islay Wlk. *N1* *6C 66*
  (off Douglas Rd. Sth.)
Isleden Ho. *N1* *1C 84*
  (off Prebend St.)
Isledon Rd. N7 .3A 66
ISLEDON VILLAGE 3A 66
Islehurst Cl. BR7: Chst 1E 160
ISLE OF DOGS 2D 104
ISLEWORTH 3A 114
Isleworth Ait Nature Reserve 3B 114
Isleworth Bus. Complex TW7: Isle . . .2K 113
Isleworth Prom. TW1: Twick 4B 114
Isleworth Recreation Cen. 4K 113
Isley Ct. SW8 .2G 119
ISLINGTON 7B 66
Islington Bus. Cen. *N1* *1C 84*
  (off Coleman Flds.)
Islington Crematorium N2 . . . . .1D 46
Islington Ecology Centre, The 3A 66
Islington Grn. N1 . . . . .1B 84
  (not continuous)
Islington High St. N1 . . . . .2A 84
  (not continuous)
Islington Mus. 2A 8 (3B 84)
Islington Pk. M. N1 . . . . .7B 66
Islington Pk. St. N1 . . . . .7A 66
Islington Rd. N1 . . . . .1A 84
Islington Sq. N1 . . . . .1B 84

Islington Tennis Cen. 6J 65
Islip Gdns. HA8: Edg 7E 28
  UB5: N'olt 7C 58
Islip Mnr. Rd. UB5: N'olt 7C 58
Islip St. NW5 . . . . .5G 65
Ismailia Rd. E7 .7K 69
Isobel Ho. HA1: Harr 5K 41
Isola Ct. *N1* *1C 84*
  (off Popham Rd.)
Isom Cl. E13 . . . . .3K 87
Issa Rd. TW3: Houn 4D 112
Issigonis Ho. *W3* *1B 98*
  (off Cowley Rd.)
Istra Ho. E20 . . . .*5E 68*
  (off Logan Cl.)
Italia Conti Academy of Theatre Arts
  Avondale *3J 119*
  (off Landor Rd.)
Itaska Cotts. WD23: B Hea 1D 26
Ithell Ct. HA0: Wemb 5D 60
Ivanhoe Cl. UB8: Cowl 5A 74
Ivanhoe Dr. HA3: Kenton 3A 42
Ivanhoe Ho. *E3* *2A 86*
  (off Grove Rd.)
Ivanhoe Rd. SE5 . . . . .3F 121
  TW4: Houn 3B 112
Ivatt Pl. W14 . . . . .5H 99
Ivatt Way N17 .3B 48
Iveagh Av. NW10 . . . . .2G 79
Iveagh Cl. E9 . . . . .1K 85
  HA6: Nwood 1D 38
  NW10 . . . . .2G 79
Iveagh Ct. BR3: Beck 3E 158
  E1 . . . . .1J 15
Iveagh Ho. SW9 . . . . .2B 120
  SW10 . . . .*7A 100*
  (off King's Rd.)
Iveagh Ter. *NW10* *2G 79*
  (off Iveagh Av.)
Ivedon Rd. DA16: Well 2C 126
Ive Farm Cl. E10 . . . . .2C 68
Ive Farm La. E10 . . . . .2C 68
Iveley Rd. SW4 . . . . .2G 119
Ivere Dr. EN5: New Bar 6E 20
Iver Ho. *N1* *1E 84*
  (off Halcomb St.)
Iverhurst Cl. DA6: Bex 5D 126
Iverna Ct. W8 . . . . .3J 99
Iverna Gdns. TW14: Felt 5F 111
  W8 . . . . .3J 99
Iverson Rd. NW6 . . . . .6H 63
Ivers Way CR0: New Ad 7D 170
Ives Rd. E16 . . . . .5G 87
Ives St. SW3 . . . . .3D 16 (4C 100)
Ivestor Ter. SE23 . . . . .7J 121
Ivimey St. E2 . . . . .3G 85
Ivinghoe Cl. EN1: Enf 1K 23
Ivinghoe Ho. N7 . . . . .5H 65
Ivinghoe Rd. RM8: Dag 5B 72
Ivo Pl. N19 . . . . .3H 65
Ivor Ct. N8 . . . . .6J 47
  NW1 . . . . .3E 4
  (off Gloucester Pl.)
Ivor Gro. SE9 .1F 143
Ivories, The *N1* *7C 66*
  (off Northampton St.)
Ivor Pl. NW1 . . . . .4E 4 (4D 82)
Ivor St. NW1 . . . . .7G 65
Ivory Ct. E18 . . . . .1J 51
  TW13: Felt 1J 129
Ivorydown BR1: Brom 4J 141
Ivory Ho. E1 . . . . .3K 15 (1F 103)
Ivory Pl. *W11* *7G 81*
  (off Treadgold St.)
Ivory Sq. SW11 . . . . .3A 118
Ivybridge Cl. TW1: Twick 7A 114
  UB8: Uxb 3A 74
Ivybridge Ct. *BR7: Chst* *1E 160*
  (off Old Hill)
  NW1 . . . .*7F 65*
  (off Lewis St.)

Ivybridge La. WC2 . . . . .3F 13 (7J 83)
Ivy Bri. Retail Pk. TW7: Isle 5K 113
Ivychurch Cl. SE20 . . . . .7J 139
Ivychurch La. SE17 . . . . .5F 103
Ivy Cl. HA2: Harr 4D 58
  HA5: Eastc 7A 40
  TW16: Sun 2A 148
Ivy Cotts. E14 .7E 86
  UB10: Hil 3C 74
  . . . .*5G 103*
  (off Argyle Way)
Ivy Cres. W4 . . . . .4J 97
Ivydale Rd. SE15 . . . . .3K 121
  SM5: Cars 2D 166
Ivyday Gro. SW16 . . . . .3K 137
Ivydene KT8: W Mole 5E 148
Ivydene Cl. SM1: Sutt 4A 166
Ivydene Ct. *IG9: Buck H* *2F 37*
  (off Queen's Rd.)
Ivy Gdns. CR4: Mitc 3H 155
  N8 . . . . .6J 47
Ivy Ho. Rd. UB10: Ick 3D 56
Ivyhouse Rd. RM9: Dag 6D 72
Ivy La. TW4: Houn 4D 112
Ivy Lodge *W11* *1J 99*
  (off Notting Hill Ga.)
Ivymount Rd. SE27 . . . . .3A 138
Ivy Rd. E16 . . . . .6J 87
  E17 . . . . .6C 50
  KT6: Surb 1G 163
  N14 . . . . .7B 22
  NW2 . . . . .4E 62
  SE4 . . . . .4B 122
  SW17 . . . . .5C 136
  TW3: Houn 4F 113
Ivy St. N1 . . . . .2E 84
Ivy Wlk. HA6: Nwood 1G 39
  RM9: Dag 6E 72
Ixworth Pl. SW3 . . . . .5C 16 (5C 100)
Izane Rd. DA6: Bex 4F 127

J

Jacana Ct. *E1* *3K 15*
  (off Star Pl.)
Jacaranda Cl. KT3: N Mald 3A 152
Jacaranda Gro. E8 . . . . .7F 67
Jackass La. BR2: Kes 5K 171
Jack Barnett Way N22 . . . . .2K 47
Jack Clow Rd. E15 . . . . .2G 87
Jack Cook Ho. IG11: Bark 7F 71
Jack Cornwell St. E12 . . . . .4E 70
Jack Dash Way E6 . . . . .4C 88
Jack Dimmer Cl. SW16 . . . . .2G 155
Jackets La. HA6: Nwood 1D 38
Jack Goodchild Way KT1: King T 3H 151
Jack Jones Way RM9: Dag 1F 91
Jacklin Grn. IG8: Wfd G 4D 36
Jackman Ho. *E1* *1H 103*
  (off Watts St.)
Jackman M. NW2 . . . . .3A 62
Jackman St. E8 . . . . .1H 85
Jacks Farm Way E4 . . . . .6K 35
Jackson & Joseph Bldg. *E1* *5K 9*
  (off Princelet St.)
Jackson Cl. E9 .7J 67
  UB10: Uxb 4A 56
Jackson Ct. E7 .6K 69
  N11 . . . . .5B 32
Jackson Rd. BR2: Brom 2D 172
  EN4: E Barn 6H 21
  IG11: Bark 1H 89
  N7 . . . . .4K 65
  UB10: Uxb 4A 56
Jacksons La. N6 . . . . .7E 46
Jacksons Lane Theatre 6F 47
  (off Archway Rd.)
Jacksons Pl. CR0: C'don 1D 168
Jackson St. SE18 . . . . .6E 106
Jackson's Way CR0: C'don 3C 170

Jackson Way UB2: S'hall 2F 95
Jacks Pl. *E1* *5J 9*
  (off Corbet Pl.)
Jack Walker Ct. N5 . . . . .4B 66
Jacob Ho. *DA18: Erith* *2D 108*
  (off Kale Rd.)
Jacobin Lodge N7 . . . . .5J 65
Jacob Mans. *E1* *6H 85*
  (off Commercial Rd.)
Jacob M. HA7: Stan 2F 27
Jacobs Cl. RM10: Dag 4H 73
Jacobs Ct. *E1* *6G 85*
  (off Plumber's Row)
Jacobs Ho. E13 . . . . .3A 88
  (off New City Rd.)
Jacobs Island Ho. *SE16* *3F 103*
  (off Spa Rd.)
Jacobs Island Pier SE16 . . . . .2G 103
  (off Bermondsey Wall W.)
Jacob St. SE1 . . . . .6K 15 (2G 103)
Jacob's Well M. W1 . . . . .6H 5 (5E 82)
Jacotts Ho. *W10* *4E 80*
  (off Sutton Way)
Jacqueline Cl. UB5: N'olt 1C 76
Jacqueline Creft Ter. *N6* *6E 46*
  (off Grange Rd.)
Jacqueline Ho. *NW1* *1D 82*
  (off Regent's Pk. Rd.)
Jacqueline Vs. *E17* *5E 50*
  (off Shernhall St.)
Jade Cl. E16 . . . . .6B 88
  NW2 . . . . .7F 45
  RM8: Dag 1C 72
Jade Ter. NW6 .7A 64
Jaffray Rd. IG1: Ilf 1H 71
Jaffray Pl. SE27 . . . . .4B 138
Jaffray Rd. BR2: Brom 4B 160
Jaggard Way SW12 . . . . .7D 118
Jagger Ho. *SW11* *1D 118*
  (off Rosenau Rd.)
Jago Cl. SE18 .6G 107
Jago Wlk. SE5 .7D 102
Jake Russell Wlk. E16 . . . . .7A 88
Jamaica Rd. CR7: Thor H 6B 156
  SE1 . . . . .7K 15 (2F 103)
  SE16 . . . . .7K 15 (2F 103)
Jamaica St. E1 .6J 85
James Allens School Swimming Pool
  . . . . .5E 120
James Anderson Ct. *E2* *2E 84*
  (off Kingsland Rd.)
James Av. NW2 .5E 62
  RM8: Dag 1F 73
James Bedford Cl. HA5: Pinn 2A 40
James Boswell Cl. SW16 . . . . .4K 137
James Brine Ho. *E2* *1K 9*
  (off Ravenscroft St.)
James Campbell Ho. *E2* *2J 85*
  (off Old Ford Rd.)
James Clavell Sq. *SE18* *3F 107*
  (off No 1 St.)
James Cl. E13 . . . . .2J 87
  NW11 . . . . .6G 45
James Collins Cl. W9 . . . . .4H 81
James Ct. HA6: Nwood 1H 39
  N1 . . . . .1C 84
  (off Raynor Pl.)
  NW9 . . . . .2A 44
  UB5: N'olt 2C 76
  (off Church Rd.)
James Docherty Ho. *E2* *2H 85*
  (off Patriot Sq.)
James Dudson Ct. NW10 . . . . .7J 61
James Est. CR4: Mitc 2D 154
James Gdns. N22 . . . . .7G 33
James Hammett Ho. *E2* *1K 9*
  (off Ravenscroft St.)
James Hill Ho. *W10* *4G 81*
  (off Kensal Rd.)
James Ho. *E1* *4A 86*
  (off Solebay St.)

James Ho. *SE16* 2K *103*
(off Wolfe Cres.)
SW8 . . . . .7J *101*
(off Wyvil Rd.)
W10 .4G 81
James Joyce Wlk. *SE24* 4B 120
James La. E10 . . . . .7E 50
E11 . . . . .7F 51
James Leal Cen.
Woodford 5G 37
James Lighthill Ho. *WC1* 1H 7
(off Penton Ri.)
James Lind Ho. *SE8* 4B *104*
(off Grove St.)
James Middleton Ho. *E2* 3H 85
(off Middleton St.)
James Morgan M. N1 . . . . .1C 84
James Newman Ct. SE9 . . . . .3E *142*
Jameson Cl. W3 . . . . .2J 97
Jameson Ct. *E2* 2J 85
(off Russia La.)
Jameson Ho. *SE11* 4K 19
(off Glasshouse Wlk.)
Jameson Lodge N6 . . . . .6G 47
Jameson St. W8 . . . . .1J 99
James Pl. N17 . . . . .1F 49
James Riley Point E15 . . . . .1E 86
(off Carpenters Rd.)
James's Cotts. TW9: Kew 7G 97
James Stewart Ho.
NW6 . . . . .7H 63
James St.
EN1: Enf 5A 24
IG11: Bark 7G 71
TW3: Houn 3H 113
W1 . . . . .1H 11 (6E 82)
WC2 . . . . .1F 13 (7J 83)
James Stroud Ho. *SE17* 5C *102*
(off Walworth Pl.)
James Ter. *SW14* 3K *115*
(off Church Path)
Jameston Lodge HA4: Ruis 1H 57
Jamestown Rd. NW1 . . . . .1F 83
Jamestown Way E14 . . . . .7F 87
James Voller Way E1 . . . . .6J 85
James Yd. E4 . . . . .6A 36
Jam Factory, The *SE1* 3E *102*
(off Green Wlk.)
Jamieson Ho. TW4: Houn 6D 112
Jamilah Ho. *E16* 7E 88
(off University Way)
Jamuna Cl. E14 . . . . .5A 86
Jane Austen Hall E16 . . . . .1K 105
(off Wesley Av.)
Jane Austen Ho. *SW1* 6A 18
(off Churchill Gdns.)
Jane Seymour Ct. SE9 . . . . .7H 125
Janet St. E14 . . . . .3C 104
Janeway Pl. SE16 . . . . .2H 103
Janeway St. SE16 . . . . .2G 103
Janice M. IG1: Ilf 2F 71
Jansen Wlk. SW11 . . . . .3B 118
Janson Cl. E15 . . . . .5G 69
NW10 . . . . .3A 62
Janson Rd. E15 . . . . .5G 69
Jansons Rd. N15 . . . . .3E 48
Japan Cres. N4 . . . . .7K 47
Japan Rd. RM6: Chad H 6D 54
Jaquard Cl. *E2* 2J 85
(off Bishop's Way)
Jardine Rd. E1 . . . . .7K 85
Jarman Ho. *E1* 5J 85
(off Jubilee St.)
SE16 . . . . .4K *103*
(off Hawkstone Rd.)
Jarret Ho. *E3* 3C 86
(off Bow Rd.)
Jarrett Cl. SW2 . . . . .1B 138
Jarrow Cl. SM4: Mord 5K 153

Jarrow Rd. N17 . . . . .4H 49
RM6: Chad H 6C 54
SE16 . . . . .4J 103
Jarrow Way E9 . . . . .4B 68
Jarvis Cl. EN5: Barn 5A 20
IG11: Bark 1H 89
Jarvis Ho. *SE15* 1G *121*
(off Goldsmith Rd.)
Jarvis Rd. CR2: S Croy 6D 168
SE22 . . . . .4E 120
Jashoda Ho. *SE18* 5E *106*
(off Connaught M.)
Jasmin Cl. HA6: Nwood 1H 39
Jasmin Ct. SE12 . . . . .6J 123
Jasmine Cl. BR6: Farnb 2F *173*
IG1: Ilf 5F 71
UB1: S'hall 7C 76
Jasmine Gdns. CR0: C'don 3D 170
HA2: Harr 2E 58
Jasmine Gro. SE20 . . . . .1H 157
Jasmine Ho. SW18 . . . . .3A 118
Jasmine Rd. RM7: Rush G 2K 73
Jasmine Sq. *E3* 1B 86
(off Hawthorn Av.)
Jasmine Ter. UB7: W Dray 2C 92
Jasmine Way KT8: E Mos 4J 149
Jasmin Lodge *SE16* 5H *103*
(off Sherwood Gdns.)
Jason Rd. KT19: Ewe 5H 163
Jason Ct. *SW9* 1A *120*
(off Southey Rd.)
W1 . . . . .7H 5
Jason Wlk. SE9 . . . . .4E *142*
Jasper Av. W7 . . . . .2K 95
Jasper Cl. EN3: Enf W 1D 24
Jasper Pas. SE19 . . . . .6F 139
Jasper Rd. E16 . . . . .6B 88
SE19 . . . . .5F 139
Jasper Wlk. N1 . . . . .3D 84
Java Wharf *SE1* 6K 15
(off Shad Thames)
Javelin Cl. *HA7: Stan* 5G 27
(off William Dr.)
Javelin Way UB5: N'olt 3B 76
Jaycroft EN2: Enf 1F 23
Jay Gdns. BR7: Chst 4D 142
Jay Ho. *E3* 1B 86
(off Hawthorn Av.)
Jay M. SW7 . . . . .7A 10 (2A 100)
Jays St. N1 . . . . .1K 83
Jazzfern Ter. HA0: Wemb 5A 60
Jean Batten Cl. SM6: Wall 7K 167
Jean Brown Indoor Arena, The 1H 53
Jean Darling Ho. *SW10* 6B *100*
(off Milman's St.)
Jean Ho. SW17 . . . . .5C 136
Jean Pardies Ho. *E1* 5J 85
(off Jubilee St.)
Jebb Av. SW2 . . . . .6J 119
(not continuous)
Jebb St. E3 . . . . .2C 86
Jedburgh Rd. E13 . . . . .3A 88
Jedburgh St. SW11 . . . . .4E 118
Jeddo M. W12 . . . . .2B 98
Jeddo Rd. W12 . . . . .2B 98
Jeeyas Apartments E16 . . . . .5H 87
Jefferson Bldg. E14 . . . . .2C 104
Jefferson Cl. IG2: Ilf 5F 53
W13 . . . . .3B 96
Jefferson Ho. *UB7: W Dray* 2B 92
(off Park Lodge Av.)
Jefferson Pl. BR2: Brom 6B 160
Jefferson Plaza *E3* 4E 86
(off Hannaford Wlk.)
Jefferson Wlk. SE18 . . . . .6E 106
Jeffrey Row SE12 . . . . .5K 123
Jeffrey's Pl. NW1 . . . . .7G 65
Jeffreys Rd. EN3: Brim 4F 25
SW4 . . . . .2J 119
Jeffrey's St. NW1 . . . . .7G 65

Jeffreys Wlk. SW4 . . . . .2J 119
Jeffs Cl. TW12: Hamp 6F 131
Jeffs Rd. SM1: Sutt 4H 165
Jeger Av. E2 . . . . .1F 85
Jeken Rd. SE9 . . . . .4A 124
Jelf Rd. SW2 . . . . .5A 120
Jelico Point *SE16* 2B *104*
(off Rotherhithe St.)
Jellicoe Gdns. HA7: Stan 6E 26
Jellicoe Ho. *E2* 2G 85
(off Ropley St.)
Jellicoe Rd. E13 . . . . .4J 87
N17 . . . . .7J 33
Jemma Knowles Cl. SW2 . . . . . . .1A *138*
(off Tulse Hill)
Jemmett Cl. KT2: King T 1H 151
Jemotts Ct. *SE14* 6K *103*
(off Myers La.)
Jem Paterson Ct. HA1: Harr 4J 59
Jengar Cl. SM1: Sutt 4K 165
Jenkins La. IG11: Bark 2G 89
Jenkinson Ho. *E2* 3K 85
(off Usk St.)
Jenkins Rd. E13 . . . . .4K 87
Jenner Av. W3 . . . . .5K 79
Jenner Cl. DA14: Sidc 4A 144
Jenner Ct. N21 . . . . .5D 22
(off Pennington Dr.)
Jenner Ho. *WC1* 3F 7
(off Hunter St.)
Jenner Pl. SW13 . . . . .6D 98
Jenner Rd. N16 . . . . .3F 67
Jennett Rd. CR0: Wadd 3A 168
Jennifer Ho. E14 . . . . .6E 86
SE11 . . . . .4K 19
(off Reedworth St.)
Jennifer Rd. BR1: Brom 3H 141
Jenningsbury Ho. SW3 . . . . .5D 16
(off Cale St.)
Jennings Cl. KT6: Surb 7C 150
RM8: Dag 1E 72
Jennings Ho. SE10 . . . . .5F 105
(off Old Woolwich Rd.)
Jennings Rd. SE22 . . . . .6F 121
Jennings Way EN5: Barn 3A 20
Jenningtree Way DA17: Belv 2J 109
Jenny Hammond Cl. E11 . . . . .3K 69
Jensen Ho. *E3* 4C 86
(off Wellington Way)
Jenson Way SE19 . . . . .7F 139
Jenton Av. DA7: Bex 1E 126
Jephson Cl. SW4 . . . . .2J 119
Jephson Ho. *SE17* 6B *102*
(off Doddington Gro.)
Jephson Rd. E7 . . . . .7A 70
Jephson St. SE5 . . . . .1D 120
Jephtha Rd. SW18 . . . . .6J 117
Jeppos La.
CR4: Mitc 4D 154
Jepson Ho. *SW6* 1K 117
(off Pearscroft Rd.)
Jerdan Ho. SW6 . . . . .7J 99
(off North End Rd.)
Jerdan Pl. SW6 . . . . .7J 99
Jeremiah St. E14 . . . . .6D 86
Jeremy Bentham Ho. *E2* 3G 85
(off Mansford St.)
Jeremy's Grn. N18 . . . . .4C 34
Jermyn St. SW1 . . . . .4A 12 (1G 101)
Jermyn Street Theatre 3C 12
(off Jermyn St.)
Jerningham Av. IG5: Ilf 2F 53
Jerningham Ct. SE14 . . . . .1A 122
Jerningham Rd. SE14 . . . . .2A 122
Jerome Cres. NW8 . . . . . .3C 4 (4C 82)
Jerome Ho. KT1: Hamp W 2D *150*
(off Old Bridge St.)
NW1 . . . . .5B 4
(off Lisson Gro.)
SW7 . . . . .3A 16
(off Glendower Pl.)

Jerome Pl. *KT1: King T* 2D *150*
(off Wadbrook St.)
Jerome St. E1 . . . . .5J 9 (4F 85)
Jerome Twr. W3 . . . . .2H 97
Jerrard St. SE13 . . . . .3D 122
Jerrold St. N1 . . . . .1H 9 (2E 84)
Jersey Av. HA7: Stan 2B 42
Jersey Dr. BR5: Pet W 6H 161
Jersey Ho. *EN3: Enf W* 1E 24
(off Eastfield Rd.)
N1 .6C 66
(off Jersey Rd.)
Jersey Rd. E11 . . . . .1F 69
E16 . . . . .6A 88
IG1: Ilf 4F 71
N1 .6C 66
SW17 . . . . .6F 137
TW3: Houn 1F 113
TW5: Hest, Isle 1F 113
TW7: Isle 7H 95
W7 .2A 96
Jersey St. E2 . . . . .3H 85
Jerusalem Pas. EC1 . . . . .4A 8 (4B 84)
Jervis Bay Ho. E14 . . . . .6F 87
(off Blair St.)
Jervis Ct. RM10: Dag 6H 73
SE10 . . . . .1E 122
(off Blissett St.)
W1 .1K 11
Jervis Rd. SW6 . . . . .6H 99
Jerviston Gdns. SW16 . . . . .6A 138
Jerwood Space Art Gallery 6C 14
Jesmond Av. HA9: Wemb 6F 61
Jesmond Cl. CR4: Mitc 3F 155
Jesmond Rd. CR0: C'don 7F 157
Jesmond Way HA7: Stan 5K 27
Jessam Av. E5 . . . . .1H 67
Jessamine Rd. W7 . . . . .1K 95
Jessel Ho. *SW1* 3D 18
(off Page St.)
WC1 . . . . .2E 6
(off Judd St.)
Jessel Mans. *W14* 6G 99
(off Queen's Club Gdns.)
Jesse Rd. E10 . . . . .1E 68
Jessett Cl. DA8: Erith 4K 109
Jessica Rd. SW18 . . . . .6A 118
Jessie Blythe La. N19 . . . . .7J 47
Jessie Duffett Ho. *SE5* 7C *102*
(off Pitman St.)
Jessie Wood Ct. *SW9* 7A *102*
(off Caldwell St.)
Jessiman Ter. TW17: Shep 5C 146
Jesson Ho. *SE17* 4D *102*
(off Orb St.)
Jessop Av. UB2: S'hall 4D 94
Jessop Ct. N1 . . . . .2B 84
Jessop Ho. W4 . . . . .4K 97
(off Kirton Cl.)
Jessop Pl. W7 . . . . .3J 95
Jessop Rd. SE24 . . . . .4B 120
Jessop Sq. E14 . . . . .1C 104
Jessops Way CR0: Bedd, Mitc 6G 155
Jessup Cl. SE18 . . . . .4G 107
Jetstar Way UB5: N'olt 3C 76
Jevington Way SE12 . . . . .1K 141
Jevons Ho. NW8 . . . . .7B 64
(off Hilgrove Rd.)
Jewel Rd. E17 . . . . .3C 50
Jewel Tower 1E 18
(off College M.)
Jewish Military Mus. 4E 44
(off Harmony Way)
Jewish Mus.
Camden Town 1F 83
Jewry St. EC3 . . . . .1J 15 (6F 85)
Jew's Row SW18 . . . . .4K 117
Jews' Wlk. SE26 . . . . .4H 139
Jeymer Av. NW2 . . . . .5D 62
Jeymer Dr. UB6: G'frd 1F 77
(not continuous)

Jeypore Rd. SW18 . . . . .7A 118
Jeypore Rd. Pas. SW18 . . . . .6A 118
Jigger Mast Ho. SE18 . . . . .3E 106
Jillian Cl. TW12: Hamp 7E 130
Jim Bradley Cl. SE18 . . . . .4E 105
Jim Griffiths Ho. SW6 . . . . .6H 99
(off Clem Attlee Ct.)
Jim Veal Dr. N7 . . . . .6J 65
Joan Cres. SE9 . . . . .7B 124
Joan Gdns. RM8: Dag 2E 72
Joanna Ho. W6 . . . . .5E 98
(off Queen Caroline St.)
Joan Rd. RM8: Dag 2E 72
Joan St. SE1 . . . . .5A 14 (1B 102)
Job Drain Pl. IG11: Bark 2A 90
Jocelin Ho. N1 . . . . .1K 83
(off Barnsbury Est.)
Jocelyn Rd. TW9: Rich 3E 114
Jocelyn St. SE15 . . . . .1G 121
Jockey's Flds. WC1 . . . . .5H 7 (5K 83)
Jodane St. SE8 . . . . .4B 104
Jodrell Cl. TW7: Isle 1A 114
Jodrell Rd. E3 . . . . .1B 86
Joe Hunte Ct. SE27 . . . . .5B 138
Joel St. HA5: Eastc 3J 39
HA6: Nwood 2J 39
Johanna St. SE1 . . . . . . .7J 13 (2A 102)
John Adams Ct. N9 . . . . .2A 34
John Adam St. WC2 . . . . . . .3F 13 (7J 83)
John Aird Ct. W2 . . . . .5A 4
(not continuous)
John Archer Way SW18 . . . . .6B 118
John Ashby Cl. SW2 . . . . .6J 119
John Austin Cl. KT2: King T 1F 151
John Baird Ct. SE26 . . . . .4J 139
John Barker Ct. NW6 . . . . .7G 63
John Barnes Wlk. E15 . . . . .6H 69
John Bell Twr. E. E3 . . . . .2C 86
(off Pancras Way)
John Bell Twr. W. E3 . . . . .2C 86
(off Pancras Way)
John Betts' Ho. W12 . . . . .3B 98
John Bond Ho. E3 . . . . .2B 86
(off Wright's Rd.)
John Bowles Ct. E1 . . . . .7K 85
(off Schoolhouse La.)
John Bradshaw Rd. N14 . . . . .1C 32
John Brent Ho. SE8 . . . . .4K 103
(off Haddonfield)
John Buck Ho. NW10 . . . . .1B 80
John Burns Dr. IG11: Bark 7J 71
John Campbell Rd. N16 . . . . .5E 66
John Carpenter St. EC4 . . . .2A 14 (7B 84)
John Cartwright Ho. E2 . . . . .3H 85
(off Old Bethnal Grn. Rd.)
John Crane St. SE17 . . . . .6D 102
John Drinkwater Cl. E11 . . . . .7H 51
John Fearon Wlk. W10 . . . . .3G 81
(off Dart St.)
John Felton Rd. SE16 . . . . .2G 103
John Fielden Ho. E2 . . . . .3H 85
(off Canrobert St.)
John Fisher St. E1 . . . . . . .2K 15 (7G 85)
John Goddard Way TW13: Felt 2K 129
John Gooch Dr. EN2: Enf 1G 23
John Harrison Way SE10 . . . . .3H 105
John Horner M. N1 . . . . .2C 84
John Islip St. SW1 . . . . . . .5D 18 (4H 101)
John Kaye Ct. TW17: Shep 5C 146
John Keats Ho. N22 . . . . .7E 32
John Keats Lodge EN2: Enf 1J 23
John Kennedy Ct. N1 . . . . .6D 66
(off Newington Grn. Rd.)
John Kennedy Ho. SE16 . . . . .4K 103
(off Rotherhithe Old Rd.)
John Kirk Ho. E6 . . . . .4G 87
(off Pearl Cl.)
John Knight Lodge SW6 . . . . .7J 99
John Lamb Ct. HA3: W'stone 1J 41
John McDonald Ho. E14 . . . . .3E 104
(off Glengall Gro.)

John McKenna Wlk. SE16 . . . . .3G 103
John Masefield Ho. N15 . . . . .6D 48
(off Fladbury Rd.)
John Maurice Cl. SE17 . . . . .4D 102
John Milton Pas. EC4 . . . . .1D 14
(off Bow La.)
John Nash M. E14 . . . . .6A 86
(off Commercial Rd.)
John Newton Ct. DA16: Well 3B 126
Johnny Andrews Ho. E1 . . . . .6K 85
(off Boulcott St.)
John Orwell Sports Cen. 1H 103
John Parker Cl. RM10: Dag 7H 73
John Parker Sq. SW11 . . . . .3B 118
John Parry Ct. N1 . . . . .2E 84
(off Hare Wlk.)
John Penn Ho. SE14 . . . . .7B 104
(off Amersham Va.)
John Penn St. SE13 . . . . .1D 122
John Penry Ho. SE1 . . . . .5G 103
(off Marlborough Gro.)
John Perrin Pl. HA3: Kenton 7E 42
John Prince's St. W1 . . . . . .7K 5 (6F 83)
John Pritchard Ho. E1 . . . . .4G 85
(off Buxton St.)
John Ratcliffe Ho. NW6 . . . . .3J 81
(off Chippenham Gdns.)
John Rennie Wlk. E1 . . . . .7H 85
John Riley Ho. E3 . . . . .5B 86
(off Geoffrey Chaucer Way)
John Roll Way SE16 . . . . .3G 103
John Ruskin St. SE5 . . . . .7B 102
John's Av. NW4 . . . . .4E 44
John Sayer Cl. IG11: Bark 3K 89
John's Cl. TW15: Ashf 4E 128
John Scurr Ho. E14 . . . . .6A 86
(off Ratcliffe La.)
John Silkin La. SE8 . . . . .5K 103
John's La. SM4: Mord 5A 154
John's M. WC1 . . . . .4H 7 (4K 83)
John Smith Av. SW6 . . . . .7H 99
John Smith M. E14 . . . . .7F 87
Johnson Cl. E8 . . . . .1G 85
Johnson Cl. SE9 . . . . .4A 124
Johnson Ho. E2 . . . . .2H 85
(off Roberta St.)
NW1 . . . . .2G 83
(off Cranleigh St.)
NW3 . . . . .7D 64
(off Adelaide Rd.)
SW1 . . . . .4H 17
(off Cundy St.)
SW8 . . . . .7H 101
(off Wandsworth Rd.)
W8 . . . . .2J 99
(off Campden Hill)
Johnson Lock Ct. E1 . . . . .5A 86
Johnson Lodge W9 . . . . .5J 81
(off Admiral Wlk.)
Johnson Mans. W14 . . . . .6G 99
(off Queen's Club Gdns.)
Johnson Rd. BR2: Brom 5B 160
CR0: C'don 7D 156
NW10 .1K 79
TW5: Hest 7A 94
Johnsons Cl. SM5: Cars 2D 166
Johnson's Ct. EC4 . . . . .6A 84
Johnsons Dr. TW12: Hamp 1G 149
Johnsons Ind. Est.
UB3: Hayes 2H 93
Johnson's Pl. SW1 . . . . . . .6A 18 (5G 101)
Johnson St. E1 . . . . .7J 85
UB2: S'hall 3A 94
Johnsons Way NW10 . . . . .4H 79
John Spencer Sq. N1 . . . . .6B 66
John's Pl. E1 . . . . .6H 85
John's Ter. CR0: C'don 1E 168
Johnston Cl. SW9 . . . . .1K 119
Johnston Ct. E10 . . . . .3D 68
Johnstone Ho. SE13 . . . . .3F 123
(off Belmont Hill)

Johnstone Rd. E6 . . . . .3D 88
Johnston Rd. IG8: Wfd G 6D 36
Johnston Ter. NW2 . . . . .3F 63
John Strachey Ho. SW6 . . . . .6H 99
(off Clem Attlee Ct.)
John St. E15 . . . . .1H 87
EN1: Enf 5A 24
SE25 . . . . .4G 157
TW3: Houn 2C 112
WC1 . . . . .4H 7 (4K 83)
John Strype Ct. E10 . . . . .1D 68
John Trundle Ct. EC2 . . . . .5C 8
John Trundle Highwalk EC2 . . . . .5C 8
(off Aldersgate St.)
John Tucker Ho. E14 . . . . .3C 104
(off Mellish St.)
John Watkin Cl. KT19: Eps 7H 163
John Wesley Cl. E6 . . . . .3D 88
John Wesley Ct.
TW1: Twick 1A 132
John Wesley Highwalk EC2 . . . . .6C 8
(off Aldersgate St.)
John Wetherby Ct. E15 . . . . .2D 86
(off High St.)
John Wetherby Ct. E. E15 . . . . .2D 86
(off High St.)
John Wetherby Ct. W. E15 . . . . .2D 86
(off High St.)
John Wheatley Ho. SW6 . . . . .6H 99
(off Clem Attlee Ct.)
John Williams Cl. KT2: King T 1D 150
SE14 . . . . .6K 103
John Wilson St. SE18 . . . . .3E 106
John Woolley Cl. SE13 . . . . .4G 123
Joiners Arms Yd. SE5 . . . . .1D 120
Joiners Pl. N5 . . . . .4D 66
Joiner St. SE1 . . . . .5F 15 (1D 102)
Joiners Yd. N1 . . . . .1F 7
(off Caledonia St.)
Joiles Ho. E3 . . . . .3D 86
(off Bromley High St.)
Jolly M. SW16: Mitc 2G 155
Jollys La. HA2: Harr 1H 59
UB4: Yead 5B 76
Jonathan St. SE11 . . . . . . .5G 19 (5K 101)
Jones Ho. E14 . . . . .6F 87
(off Blair St.)
Jones M. SW15 . . . . .4G 117
Jones Rd. E13 . . . . .4K 87
Jones St. W1 . . . . .3J 11 (7F 83)
Jones Wlk. TW10: Rich 6F 115
Jonquil Gdns. TW12: Hamp 6E 130
Jonson Cl. CR4: Mitc 4F 155
UB4: Hayes 5J 75
Jonson Ho. SE1 . . . . .3D 102
(off Burbage Cl.)
Jonzen Wlk. E14 . . . . .6C 86
Jordan Cl. HA2: Harr 3D 58
Jordan Cl. SW15 . . . . .4F 117
Jordan Ho. N1 . . . . .1D 84
(off Colville Est.)
SE4 . . . . .4K 121
(off St Norbert Rd.)
Jordan Rd. UB6: G'frd 1B 78
Jordans Cl. RM10: Dag 4H 73
TW7: Isle 1J 113
Jordans Ho. NW8 . . . . .3C 4
(off Capland St.)
Jordans M. TW2: Twick 2J 131
Joscoyne Ho. E1 . . . . .6H 85
(off Philpot St.)
Joseph Av. W3 . . . . .6K 79
Joseph Cl. N4 . . . . .2B 66
Joseph Conrad Ho. SW1 . . . . .4B 18
(off Tachbrook St.)
Joseph Ct. N16 . . . . .6E 48
(off Amhurst Pk.)
Joseph Hardcastle Cl. SE14 . . . . .7K 103
Josephine Av. SW2 . . . . .5K 119
Joseph Irwin Ho. E14 . . . . .7B 86
(off Gill St.)

Joseph Lister Ct. E7 . . . . .7J 69
Joseph M. N7 . . . . .6A 66
(off Westbourne Rd.)
SE15 . . . . .5K 121
Joseph Powell Cl. SW12 . . . . .6G 119
Joseph Priestley Ho. E2 . . . . .3H 85
(off Canrobert St.)
Joseph Ray Rd. E11 . . . . .2G 69
Joseph St. E3 . . . . .4B 86
Joseph Trotter Cl. EC1 . . . . .2K 7
Joshua Cl. CR2: S Croy 7B 168
N10 . . . . .7A 32
Joshua Pedley M. E3 . . . . .2C 86
(off Douro St.)
Joshua St. E14 . . . . .6E 86
Joslin Av. NW9 . . . . .3A 44
Joslings Cl. W12 . . . . .7C 80
Joslyn Cl. EN3: Enf L 1H 25
Jossiline Ct. E3 . . . . .2A 86
(off Ford St.)
Joubert Mans. SW3 . . . . .5D 16
(off Jubilee Pl.)
Joubert St. SW11 . . . . .2D 118
Jowett St. SE15 . . . . .7F 103
Jowitt Ho. E2 . . . . .3K 85
(off Morpeth St.)
Joyce Av. N18 . . . . .5A 34
Joyce Butler Ho. N22 . . . . .1K 47
Joyce Dawson Way SE28 . . . . .7A 90
Joyce Latimore Ct. N9 . . . . .3C 34
(off Colthurst Dr.)
Joyce Page Cl. SE7 . . . . .6B 106
Joyce Wlk. SW2 . . . . .6A 120
JOYDENS WOOD 4K 145
Joydens Wood 4H 145
Joydens Wood Rd. DA5: Bexl 4K 145
Joydon Dr. RM6: Chad H 6B 54
Joyners Cl. RM9: Dag 4F 73
Joy of Life Fountain 1D 100
Joystone Ct. EN4: E Barn 4H 21
(off Park Rd.)
Jubb Powell Ho. N15 . . . . .6E 48
Jubilee, The SE10 . . . . .7D 104
Jubilee Av. E4 . . . . .6K 35
RM7: Rom 5H 55
TW2: Whitt 1G 131
Jubilee Bldgs. NW8 . . . . .1B 82
Jubilee Cl. HA5: Pinn 2A 40
KT1: Hamp W 1C 150
NW9 . . . . .6K 43
NW10 .2A 80
RM7: Rom 5H 55
Jubilee Country Pk. 4F 161
Jubilee Country Pk. Local Nature Reserve
. . . . .5E 160
Jubilee Ct. BR4: W W'ck 1E 170
E16 . . . . .5H 87
(off Rathbone St.)
E18 . . . . .1J 51
HA3: Kenton 7E 42
N10 . . . . .3E 46
SE10 . . . . .6D 104
(off Dowells St.)
TW3: Houn 3F 113
(off Bristow Rd.)
Jubilee Cres. E14 . . . . .3E 104
N9 . . . . .1B 34
Jubilee Dr. HA4: Ruis 4B 58
Jubilee Gdns. UB1: S'hall 5E 76
Jubilee Hall Gym 2F 13
(off The Piazza)
Jubilee Hgts. SE10 . . . . .1E 122
(off Parkside Av.)
Jubilee Ho. HA7: Stan 5J 27
SE11 . . . . .4K 19
(off Reedworth St.)
WC1 . . . . .3G 7
Jubilee La. W5 . . . . .6E 78
Jubilee Mans. E1 . . . . .6J 85
(off Jubilee St.)

Jubilee Mkt. IG8: Wfd G 6F **37**
  WC2 . . . . .2F **13**
Jubilee Pde. IG8: Wfd G 6F **37**
Jubilee Pl. SW3 . . . . .5D **16** (5C **100**)
Jubilee Pl. Shop. Mall E14 . . . . .1D **104**
  (off Bank St.)
Jubilee Rd. SM3: Cheam 7F **165**
  UB6: G'frd .1B **78**
Jubilee Sports Cen.
  London 3G **81**
Jubilee St. E1 . . . . .6J **85**
Jubilee Vs. KT10: Esh 1H **162**
Jubilee Walkway SE1 . . . . .3B **14** (7B **84**)
Jubilee Way DA14: Sidc 2A **144**
  KT9: Chess 4G **163**
  SW19 . . . . .1K **153**
  TW14: Felt .1J **129**
Judd Apartments N8 . . . . .3K **47**
  (off Gt. Amwell La.)
Judd St. WC1 . . . . .2E **6** (3J **83**)
Jude St. E16 . . . . .6H **87**
Judge Heath La. UB3: Hayes 6E **74**
  UB8: Hil 6E **74**
Judges Wlk. NW3 . . . . .3A **64**
Juer St. SW11 . . . . .7C **100**
Jules Thorn Av. EN1: Enf 4B **24**
Julia Ct. E17 . . . . .5D **50**
Julia Gdns. IG11: Bark 2D **90**
Julia Garfield M. E16 . . . . .1K **105**
  (not continuous)
Juliana Cl. N2 . . . . .2A **46**
Julian Av. W3 . . . . .7H **79**
Julian Cl. EN5: New Bar 3E **20**
Julian Ct. NW1 . . . . .7G **65**
  (off Rochester Sq.)
Julian Hill HA1: Harr 2J **59**
Julian Ho. SE21 . . . . .4E **138**
Julian Pl. E14 . . . . .5D **104**
Julian Taylor Path SE23 . . . . .2H **139**
Julia St. NW5 . . . . .4E **64**
Julian Rd. W5 . . . . .3C **96**
Juliet Ho. N1 . . . . .2E **84**
  (off Arden Est.)
Juliette Rd. E13 . . . . .2J **87**
Julius Caesar Way HA7: Stan 3J **27**
Julius Ho. E14 . . . . .6F **87**
  (off E. India Dock Rd.)
Julius Nyerere Cl. N1 . . . . .1K **83**
  (off Copenhagen St.)
Junction App. SE13 . . . . .3E **122**
  SW11 . . . . .3C **118**
Junction M. W2 . . . . .7C **4** (6C **82**)
Junction Pl. W2 . . . . .7B **4**
Junction Rd. CR2: S Croy 5D **168**
  E13 . . . . .2K **87**
  HA1: Harr 6H **41**
  (not continuous)
  N9 . . . . .1B **34**
  N17 . . . . .3G **49**
  N19 . . . . .4G **65**
  TW8: Bford 4C **96**
  TW15: Ashf 5E **128**
  W5 . . . . .4C **96**
Junction Rd. E. RM6: Chad H 7E **54**
Junction Rd. W. RM6: Chad H 7E **54**
Junction Shop. Centre, The SW11 . . .4C **118**
Juniper Cl. EN5: Barn 5A **20**
  HA2: Harr 2F **59**
  HA9: Wemb 5G **61**
  KT9: Chess 5F **163**
  TW13: Felt 3K **129**
Juniper Ct. HA3: Hrw W 1K **41**
  HA6: Nwood 1J **39**
  KT8: W Mole 4F **149**
  RM6: Chad H 6G **54**
  TW3: Houn 4F **113**
  (off Grove Rd.)
  W8 . . . . .3K **99**
  (off St Mary's Pl.)

Juniper Cres. NW1 . . . . .7E **64**
Juniper Dr. SW18 . . . . .4A **118**
Juniper Gdns. SW16 . . . . .1G **155**
  TW16: Sun 6H **129**
Juniper Ho. SE14 . . . . .7J **103**
  TW9: Kew .1H **115**
  W10 . . . . .4G **81**
  (off Fourth Av.)
Juniper La. E6 . . . . .5C **88**
Juniper Rd. IG1: Ilf 3E **70**
Juniper St. E1 . . . . .7J **85**
Juniper Way UB3: Hayes 7F **75**
Juno Ct. SW9 . . . . .7A **102**
  (off Caldwell St.)
Juno Ho. E3 .1C **86**
  (off Garrison Rd.)
Juno Way SE14 . . . . .6K **103**
Juno Way Ind. Est. SE14 . . . . .6K **103**
Jupiter Ct. SW9 . . . . .2C **86**
  (off Four Seasons Cl.)
  SW9 . . . . .7A **102**
  (off Caldwell St.)
  UB5: N'olt 3B **76**
  (off Seasprite Cl.)
Jupiter Hgts. UB10: Uxb 1B **74**
Jupiter Ho. E14 . . . . .5D **104**
  (off St Davids Sq.)
  E16 . . . . .6H **87**
  (off Turner St.)
  HA2: Harr 1E **58**
Jupiter Way N7 . . . . .6K **65**
Jupp Rd. E15 . . . . .7F **69**
Jupp Rd. W. E15 . . . . .1F **87**
Jura Ho. SE16 . . . . .4K **103**
  (off Plough Way)
Jurassic Encounter 3C **152**
Jurston Ct. SE1 . . . . .7K **13**
Justice Apartments E1 . . . . .6K **85**
  (off Aylward St.)
Justice Wlk. SW3 . . . . .7C **16** (6C **100**)
Justin Cl. TW8: Bford 7D **96**
Justines Pl. E2 . . . . .3K **85**
Justin Pl. N22 . . . . .7E **32**
Justin Plaza CR4: Mitc 4C **154**
Justin Rd. E4 . . . . .6G **35**
Jute La. EN3: Brim 2F **25**
Jutland Cl. N19 . . . . .1J **65**
Jutland Ho. SE5 . . . . .2C **120**
  SE18 . . . . .4C **106**
  (off Prospect Va.)
Jutland Rd. E13 . . . . .4J **87**
  SE6 . . . . .7E **122**
Jutsums Av. RM7: Rom 6H **55**
Jutsums Cl. RM7: Rom 6H **55**
Jutsums La. RM7: Rom, Rush G 6H **55**
Juxon Cl. HA3: Hrw W 1F **41**
Juxon Ho. EC4 . . . . .1B **14**
  (off St Paul's Chyd.)
Juxon St. SE11 . . . . .3H **19** (4K **101**)
JVC Bus. Pk. NW2 . . . . .1C **62**

K

Kaduna Cl. HA5: Eastc 5J **39**
Kaine Pl. CR0: C'don 7A **158**
Kaleidoscope Ho. E20 . . . . .5E **68**
  (off Mirabelle Gdns.)
Kale Rd. DA18: Erith 2D **108**
Kambala Rd. SW11 . . . . .3B **118**
Kamen Ho. SE1 . . . . .5G **15**
  (off Magdalen St.)
Kamrans Pl. HA8: Edg 2F **43**
Kangley Bri. Rd. SE26 . . . . .6B **140**
Kangley Bus. Cen. SE26 . . . . .5B **140**
Kaplan Dr. N21 . . . . .5E **22**
Kapuvar Cl. SE15 . . . . .2G **121**
Karachi Ho. E15 . . . . .6G **69**
  (off Well St.)
Karanja Ct. NW2 . . . . .6E **62**

Kara Way NW2 . . . . .4F **63**
Karen Ct. BR1: Brom 1H **159**
Karen Ter. E11 . . . . .2H **69**
Karenza Ct. HA9: Wemb 7C **42**
Kariba Cl. N9 . . . . .3D **34**
Karim M. E17 . . . . .4A **50**
Karma Way HA2: Harr 1E **58**
Karner Ho. E20 . . . . .5D **68**
  (off Logan Cl.)
Karoline Gdns. UB6: G'frd 2H **77**
Kashgar Rd. SE18 . . . . .4K **107**
Kashmir Rd. SE7 . . . . .7B **106**
Kassala Rd. SW11 . . . . .1D **118**
Katella Trad. Est. IG11: Bark 3J **89**
Katharine Ho. CR0: C'don 3C **168**
  (off Katharine St.)
Katharine St. CR0: C'don 3C **168**
Katherine Bell Twr. E3 . . . . .2C **86**
  (off Pancras Way)
Katherine Cl. N4 . . . . .7C **48**
  NW7 . . . . .7K **29**
  SE16 . . . . .1K **103**
Katherine Ct. SE23 . . . . .1H **139**
Katherine Gdns. SE9 . . . . .4B **124**
Katherine Ho. W10 . . . . .4G **81**
  (off Portobello Rd.)
Katherine Rd. E6 . . . . .5A **70**
  E7 . . . . .5A **70**
  TW1: Twick 1A **132**
Katherine Sq. W11 . . . . .1G **99**
Kathleen Av.
  HA0: Wemb 7E **60**
  W3 . . . . .5J **79**
Kathleen Godfree Ct. SW19 . . . . . . .6J **135**
Kathleen Rd. SW11 . . . . .3D **118**
Kavan Gdns. TW5: Cran 7J **93**
Kavsan Pl. TW5: Cran 7J **93**
Kayani Av. N4 . . . . .1C **66**
Kayani Ho. E16 . . . . .6K **87**
  (off Burrard Rd.)
Kayemoor Rd. SM2: Sutt 6B **166**
Kay Rd. SW9 . . . . .2J **119**
Kays Ter. E18 . . . . .1H **51**
Kay St. DA16: Well 1B **126**
  E2 . . . . .2G **85**
  E15 . . . . .7F **69**
  (off New Mount St.)
Kean Cres. RM8: Dag 1E **72**
Kean Ho. SE17 . . . . .6B **102**
  TW1: Twick 6D **114**
  (off Arosa Rd.)
Kean St. WC2 . . . . .1G **13** (6K **83**)
Keatley Grn. E4 . . . . .6G **35**
Keats CR0: C'don 1C **168**
  (off Saffron Central Sq.)
Keats Apartments E3 . . . . .4B **86**
  (off Wraxall Rd.)
Keats Av. E16 . . . . .1K **105**
Keats Cl.
  E11 . . . . .5K **51**
  EN3: Pond E 5E **24**
  NW3 . . . . .4C **64**
  SE1 . . . . .4F **103**
  SE7 . . . . .7A **106**
  SW19 . . . . .6B **136**
  UB4: Hayes 5J **75**
Keats Est. N16 . . . . .2F **67**
Keats Gro. NW3 . . . . .4C **64**
Keats House .4C **64**
Keats Ho. E2 .3J **85**
  (off Roman Rd.)
  HA2: Harr 2J **59**
  SE5 . . . . .7C **102**
  (off Elmington Est.)
  SW1 . . . . .7B **18**
  (off Churchill Gdns.)
Keats Pde. N9 . . . . .2B **34**
  (off Church St.)
Keats Pl. EC2 . . . . .6E **8**
  (off Moorfields)

Keats Rd. DA16: Well 1J **125**
  DA17: Belv 3J **109**
  E10 . . . . .7D **50**
Keats Way CR0: C'don 6J **157**
  UB6: G'frd .5F **77**
  UB7: W Dray 4B **92**
Kebbell Ter. E7 . . . . .5J **69**
  (off Claremont Rd.)
Keble Cl. KT4: Wor Pk 1B **164**
  UB5: N'olt 5G **59**
Keble Pl. SW13 . . . . .6D **98**
Keble St. SW17 . . . . .4A **136**
Kebony Cl. UB7: W Dray 2C **92**
Kechill Gdns.
  BR2: Hayes 7J **159**
Kedeston Cl. SM1: Sutt 1K **165**
Kedge Ho. E14 . . . . .3C **104**
  (off Tiller Rd.)
Kedleston Dr. BR5: St M Cry 5K **161**
Kedleston Wlk. E2 . . . . .3H **85**
Kedyngton Ho. HA8: Edg 2J **43**
  (off Burnt Oak B'way.)
Keeble Cl. SE18 . . . . .6F **107**
Keedonwood Rd. BR1: Brom 5G **141**
Keel Cl. IG11: Bark 2C **90**
  N18 . . . . .6K **33**
  SE16 . . . . .1K **103**
Keel Ct. E14 .7F **87**
  (off Newport Av.)
Keele Ho. RM8: Dag 4A **72**
Keeley Rd. CR0: C'don 2C **168**
Keeley St. WC2 . . . . .1G **13** (6K **83**)
Keeling Ho. E2 . . . . .2H **85**
  (off Claredale St.)
Keeling Rd. SE9 . . . . .5B **124**
Keelson Ho. E14 . . . . .3C **104**
  (off Mellish St.)
Keely Cl. EN4: E Barn 5H **21**
Keemor Cl. SE18 . . . . .7E **106**
Keens Cl. SW16 . . . . .5H **137**
Keens Rd. CR0: C'don 4C **168**
Keen's Yd. N1 . . . . .6B **66**
Keep, The KT2: King T 6F **133**
  SE3 . . . . .2J **123**
Keepers Cl. CR2: S Croy 5C **168**
  (off Warham Rd.)
Keepers M. TW11: Tedd 6C **132**
Keepier Wharf E14 . . . . .7K **85**
  (off Narrow St.)
Keeton's Rd. SE16 . . . . .3H **103**
  (not continuous)
Keevil Dr. SW19 . . . . .7F **117**
Keighley Cl. N7 . . . . .5J **65**
Keighley Dr. SE9 . . . . .1G **143**
Keilder Cl. UB10: Hil 2C **74**
Keildon Rd. SW11 . . . . .4D **118**
Keiller Ho. E14 . . . . .1D **106**
  (off Kennard St.)
Keir, The SW19 . . . . .5E **134**
Keir Hardie Est. E5 . . . . .1H **67**
Keir Hardie Ho. N19 . . . . .7H **47**
  NW10 . . . . .7B **62**
  W6 . . . . .6F **99**
  (off Fulham Pal. Rd.)
Keir Hardie Way IG11: Bark 7A **72**
  UB4: Yead .3J **75**
Keith Connor Cl. SW8 . . . . .3F **119**
Keith Gro. W12 . . . . .2C **98**
Keith Ho. NW6 . . . . .2K **81**
  (off Carlton Vale)
  SW8 . . . . .7J **101**
  (off Wheatsheaf La.)
Keith Pk. Rd. UB10: Uxb 7B **56**
Keith Rd. E17 . . . . .1B **50**
  IG11: Bark .2H **89**
  UB3: Hayes 3G **93**
Kelbrook Rd. SE3 . . . . .2C **124**
Kelby Ho. N7 .6K **65**
  (off Sutterton St.)
Kelby Path SE9 . . . . .3F **143**
Kelceda Cl. NW2 . . . . .2C **62**

Kelday Hgts.—Kennistoun Ho.

Kelday Hgts. *E1* ... *6H* **85**
(off Spencer Way)
Kelf Gro. UB3: Hayes ... 6H **75**
Kelfield Ct. W10 ... 6F **81**
Kelfield Gdns. W10 ... 6E **80**
Kelfield M. W10 ... 6F **81**
Kelland Cl. N8 ... 5H **47**
Kelland Rd. E13 ... 4J **87**
Kellaway Rd. SE3 ... 2B **124**
Keller Cres. E12 ... 4B **70**
Kellerton Rd. SE13 ... 5G **123**
Kellet Ho's. *WC1* ... *2F* **7**
(off Tankerton St.)
Kellett Ho. *N1* ... *1E* **84**
(off Colville Est.)
Kellett Rd. SW2 ... 4A **120**
Kelling Gdns. CR0: C'don ... 7B **156**
Kellino St. SW17 ... 4D **136**
Kellner Rd. SE28 ... 3K **107**
Kellogg Twr. UB6: G'frd ... 5J **59**
Kellow Ho. *SE1* ... *6E* **14**
(off Tennis St.)
Kell St. SE1 ... 7B **14** (3B **102**)
Kelly Av. SE15 ... 7F **103**
Kelly Cl. NW10 ... 3K **61**
TW17: Shep ... 2G **147**
Kelly Ct. *E14* ... *7C* **86**
(off Garford St.)
Kelly M. W9 ... 4H **81**
Kelly St. NW1 ... 6F **65**
Kelly Ter. E17 ... 4C **50**
Kelly Way RM6: Chad H ... 5E **54**
Kelman Cl. SW4 ... 2H **119**
Kelmore Gro. SE22 ... 4G **121**
Kelmscott Cl. E17 ... 1B **50**
Kelmscott Gdns. W12 ... 3C **98**
Kelmscott House ... 5D **98**
Kelmscott Leisure Cen. ... 6B **50**
Kelmscott Rd. SW11 ... 5C **118**
Kelross Pas. N5 ... 4C **66**
Kelross Rd. N5 ... 4C **66**
Kelsall Cl. SE3 ... 2K **123**
Kelsall M. TW9: Kew ... 1H **115**
Kelsey Cl. KT9: Chess ... 7D **162**
Kelsey Ga. BR3: Beck ... 2D **158**
Kelsey La. BR3: Beck ... 2C **158**
Kelsey Pk. Av. BR3: Beck ... 2D **158**
Kelsey Pk. Rd. BR3: Beck ... 2C **158**
Kelsey Sq. BR3: Beck ... 2C **158**
Kelsey St. E2 ... 4G **85**
Kelsey Way BR3: Beck ... 3C **158**
Kelson Ho. E14 ... 3E **104**
Kelso Pl. W8 ... 3K **99**
Kelso Rd. SM5: Cars ... 7A **154**
Kelston Rd. IG6: Ilf ... 2F **53**
Kelvedon Cl. KT2: King T ... 6G **133**
Kelvedon Ho. SW8 ... 1J **119**
Kelvedon Rd. SW6 ... 7H **99**
Kelvedon Way IG8: Wfd G ... 6J **37**
Kelvin Av. N13 ... 6E **32**
TW11: Tedd ... 6J **131**
Kelvinbrook KT8: W Mole ... 3F **149**
Kelvin Cl. KT19: Ewe ... 6G **163**
Kelvin Ct. SE20 ... 1H **157**
TW7: Isle ... 2J **113**
W11 ... *7J* **81**
(off Kensington Pk. Rd.)
Kelvin Cres. HA3: Hrw W ... 7D **26**
Kelvin Dr. TW1: Twick ... 6B **114**
Kelvin Gdns. CR0: Wadd ... 7J **155**
UB1: S'hall ... 6E **76**
Kelvin Gro. KT9: Chess ... 3D **162**
SE26 ... 3H **139**
Kelvington Cl. CR0: C'don ... 7A **158**
Kelvington Rd. SE15 ... 5K **121**
Kelvin Ind. Est. UB6: G'frd ... 7F **59**
Kelvin Pde. BR6: Orp ... 1J **173**
Kelvin Rd. DA16: Well ... 3A **126**
N5 ... 4C **66**
Kelway Ho. W14 ... 5H **99**
Kember St. N1 ... 7K **65**
Kemble Dr. BR2: Brom ... 3C **172**
Kemble Ho. *SW9* ... *3B* **120**
(off Barrington Rd.)
Kemble Rd. CR0: Wadd ... 3B **168**
N17 ... 1G **49**
SE23 ... 1K **139**
Kemble St. WC2 ... 1G **13** (6K **83**)
Kemerton Rd. BR3: Beck ... 2D **158**
CR0: C'don ... 7F **157**
SE5 ... 3C **120**
Kemey's St. E9 ... 5A **68**
Kemmel Rd. RM9: Dag ... 1B **90**
Kemnal Rd. BR7: Chst ... 4H **143**
Kemp *NW9* ... *1B* **44**
(off Quakers Course)
Kemp Ct. *SW8* ... *7J* **101**
(off Hartington Rd.)
Kempe Ho. *SE1* ... *3D* **102**
(off Burbage Cl.)
Kempe Rd. NW6 ... 2F **81**
Kemp Gdns. CR0: C'don ... 6C **156**
Kemp Ho. *E2* ... *2K* **85**
(off Sewardstone Rd.)
E6 ... 6E **70**
W1 ... *2C* **12**
(off Berwick St.)
Kempis Way SE22 ... 5E **120**
Kemplay Rd. NW3 ... 4B **64**
Kemp Rd. RM8: Dag ... 1D **72**
Kemps Ct. *W1* ... *1B* **12**
(off Hopkins St.)
Kemps Dr. E14 ... 7C **86**
HA6: Nwood ... 1H **39**
Kempsford Gdns. SW5 ... 5J **99**
Kempsford Rd. SE11 ... 4K **19** (4B **102**)
(not continuous)
Kemps Gdns. SE13 ... 5E **122**
Kempshott Rd. SW16 ... 7H **137**
Kempson Rd. SW6 ... 1J **117**
Kempthorne Rd. SE8 ... 4B **104**
Kempton Av. TW16: Sun ... 1K **147**
UB5: N'olt ... 6E **58**
Kempton Cl. DA8: Erith ... 6J **109**
UB10: Ick ... 4E **56**
Kempton Ct. E1 ... 5H **85**
TW16: Sun ... 1K **147**
Kempton Ga. TW12: Hamp ... 1D **148**
Kempton Ho. *N1* ... *1E* **84**
(off Hoxton St.)
Kempton Nature Reserve ... 6B **130**
Kempton Park Racecourse ... 7K **129**
Kempton Rd. E6 ... 1D **88**
Kemptons, The
TW15: Ashf ... 2C **128**
Kempton Wlk. CR0: C'don ... 6A **158**
Kempt St. SE18 ... 6E **106**
Kemsing Cl. BR2: Hayes ... 2H **171**
CR7: Thor H ... 4C **156**
DA5: Bexl ... 7E **126**
Kemsing Ho. *SE1* ... *7F* **15**
(off Long La.)
Kemsing Rd. SE10 ... 5J **105**
Kemsley SE13 ... 5D **122**
Kemsley Ct. W13 ... 1C **96**
Kenbrook Ho. NW5 ... 5G **65**
W14 ... 3H **99**
Kenbury Cl. UB10: Ick ... 3C **56**
Kenbury Gdns. SE5 ... 2C **120**
Kenbury Mans. *SE5* ... *2C* **120**
(off Kenbury St.)
Kenbury St. SE5 ... 2C **120**
Kenchester Cl. SW8 ... 7J **101**
Kencot Way DA18: Erith ... 2F **109**
Kendal *NW1* ... *1K* **5**
(off Augustus St.)
Kendal Av. IG11: Bark ... 1J **89**
N18 ... 4J **33**
W3 ... 4G **79**
Kendal Cl. IG8: Wfd G ... 2C **36**
N20 ... 2H **31**
SW9 ... 7B **102**
Kendal Cl. TW14: Felt ... 1H **129**
UB4: Hayes ... 2G **75**
Kendal Ct. W3 ... 5G **79**
Kendale Rd. BR1: Brom ... 5G **141**
Kendal Gdns. N18 ... 4J **33**
SM1: Sutt ... 2A **166**
Kendal Ho. E9 ... 1J **85**
N1 ... *2K* **83**
(off Priory Grn. Est.)
SE20 ... *2G* **157**
(off Derwent Rd.)
Kendall Av. BR3: Beck ... 2A **158**
CR2: Sande ... 7D **168**
Kendall Ct. DA15: Sidc ... 3A **144**
SW19 ... 6B **136**
Kendall Lodge *BR1: Brom* ... *1K* **159**
(off Willow Tree Wlk.)
Kendall Mnr. HA6: Nwood ... 1D **38**
Kendall Pl. W1 ... 6G **5** (5E **82**)
Kendall Rd. BR3: Beck ... 2A **158**
SE18 ... 1C **124**
TW7: Isle ... 2A **114**
Kendalmere Cl. N10 ... 1F **47**
Kendal Pde. N18 ... 4J **33**
Kendal Pl. SW15 ... 5H **117**
Kendal Rd. NW10 ... 4C **62**
Kendal Steps W2 ... 1D **10**
Kendal St. W2 ... 1D **10** (6C **82**)
Kender Est. *SE14* ... *1J* **121**
(off Queen's Rd.)
Kender St. SE14 ... 7J **103**
Kendoa Rd. SW4 ... 4H **119**
Kendon Cl. E11 ... 5K **51**
Kendon Ho. *E15* ... *7F* **69**
(off Bryant St.)
Kendra Hall Rd. CR2: S Croy ... 7B **168**
Kendrey Gdns. TW2: Whitt ... 7J **113**
Kendrick Ct. *SE15* ... *1H* **121**
(off Colmore M.)
Kendrick M. SW7 ... 3A **16** (4B **100**)
Kendrick Pl. SW7 ... 4A **16** (4B **100**)
Kenelm Cl. HA1: Harr ... 3A **60**
Kenerne Dr. EN5: Barn ... 5B **20**
Ken Friar Bri. N7 ... 4A **66**
Kenilford Rd. SW12 ... 7F **119**
Kenilworth Av. E17 ... 2C **50**
HA2: Harr ... 4D **58**
SW19 ... 5J **135**
Kenilworth Ct. *SW15* ... *3G* **117**
(off Lwr. Richmond Rd.)
Kenilworth Cres. EN1: Enf ... 1K **23**
Kenilworth Gdns. IG3: Ilf ... 2K **71**
SE18 ... 2F **125**
UB1: S'hall ... 3D **76**
UB4: Hayes ... 5H **75**
Kenilworth Rd. BR5: Pet W ... 6G **161**
E3 ... 2A **86**
HA8: Edg ... 3D **28**
KT17: Ewe ... 5C **164**
NW6 ... 1H **81**
SE20 ... 1K **157**
TW15: Ashf ... 3A **128**
W5 ... 1E **96**
Kenley *N17* ... *2D* **48**
(off Gloucester Rd.)
Kenley Av. NW9 ... 1A **44**
Kenley Cl. BR7: Chst ... 3J **161**
DA5: Bexl ... 7G **127**
EN4: E Barn ... 4H **21**
Kenley Gdns. CR7: Thor H ... 4B **156**
Kenley Rd. KT1: King T ... 2H **151**
SW19 ... 2J **153**
TW1: Twick ... 6B **114**
Kenley Wlk. SM3: Cheam ... 4F **165**
W11 ... 7G **81**
Kenlor Rd. SW17 ... 5B **136**
Kenmare Cl. UB10: Ick ... 2F **57**
Kenmare Dr. CR4: Mitc ... 7D **136**
N17 ... 2F **49**
Kenmare Gdns. N13 ... 4H **33**
Kenmare Rd. CR7: Thor H ... 6A **156**
Kenmere Gdns. HA0: Wemb ... 1G **79**
Kenmere Rd. DA16: Well ... 2C **126**
Kenmont Gdns. NW10 ... 3D **80**
(not continuous)
Kenmore Av. HA3: Kenton, W'stone ... 4A **42**
Kenmore Cl. TW9: Kew ... 7G **97**
Kenmore Ct. *NW6* ... *7K* **63**
(off Acol Rd.)
Kenmore Cres. UB4: Hayes ... 3H **75**
Kenmore Gdns. HA8: Edg ... 2H **43**
Kenmore Rd. HA3: Kenton ... 3D **42**
Kenmure Rd. E8 ... 5H **67**
Kenmure Yd. E8 ... 5H **67**
Kennacraig Cl. E16 ... 1J **105**
Kennard Ho. SW11 ... 2E **118**
Kennard Rd. E15 ... 7F **69**
N11 ... 5J **31**
Kennard St. E16 ... 1D **106**
SW11 ... 1E **118**
Kennedy Av. EN3: Pond E ... 6D **24**
Kennedy Cl. BR5: Pet W ... 1H **173**
CR4: Mitc ... 1E **154**
E13 ... 2J **87**
Kennedy Ct. TW15: Ashf ... 5E **128**
WD23: B Hea ... 2C **26**
Kennedy Cox Ho. *E16* ... *5H* **87**
(off Burke St.)
Kennedy Ho. *SE11* ... *5G* **19**
(off Vauxhall Wlk.)
Kennedy Path W7 ... 4K **77**
Kennedy Rd. IG11: Bark ... 1J **89**
W7 ... 5J **77**
Kennedy Wlk. *SE17* ... *4D* **102**
(off Elsted St.)
Kennet Cl. SW11 ... 4B **118**
Kennet Ct. *W9* ... *5J* **81**
(off Elmfield Way)
Kenneth Av. IG1: Ilf ... 4F **71**
Kenneth Campbell Ho. *NW8* ... *3B* **4**
(off Orchardson St.)
Kenneth Chambers Ct. IG8: Wfd G ... 6H **37**
Kenneth Ct. SE11 ... 3K **19** (4A **102**)
Kenneth Cres. NW2 ... 5D **62**
Kenneth Gdns. HA7: Stan ... 6F **27**
Kenneth Moore Rd. IG1: Ilf ... 3F **71**
Kenneth More Theatre ... 3F **71**
Kennet Ho. *NW8* ... *4B* **4**
(off Church St. Est.)
SW18 ... *4J* **117**
(off Enterprise Way)
Kenneth Rd. RM6: Chad H ... 7D **54**
Kenneth Robbins Ho. N17 ... 7C **34**
Kenneth Younger Ho. *SW6* ... *6H* **99**
(off Clem Attlee Ct.)
Kennet Rd. TW7: Isle ... 3K **113**
W9 ... 4H **81**
Kennet Sq. CR4: Mitc ... 1C **154**
Kennet St. E1 ... 1G **103**
Kennett Ct. W4 ... 7H **97**
Kennett Dr. UB4: Yead ... 5C **76**
Kennett Wharf La. EC4 ... 3D **14** (7C **84**)
KENNINGHALL ... **5D 34**
Kenninghall Rd. E5 ... 3G **67**
N18 ... 5D **34**
Kenning Ho. *N1* ... *1E* **84**
(off Colville Est.)
Kenning St. SE16 ... 2J **103**
Kennings Way SE11 ... 5K **19** (5A **102**)
KENNINGTON ... 7K **19** (6A **102**)
Kennington Grn. SE11 ... 6J **19** (5A **102**)
Kennington La. SE11 ... 6G **19** (5K **101**)
KENNINGTON OVAL ... **6A 102**
Kennington Oval SE11 ... 7H **19** (6K **101**)
Kennington Pal. Ct. SE11 ... 5J **19**
Kennington Pk. Gdns. SE11 ... 7K **19** (6B **102**)
Kennington Pk. Ho. SE11 ... 6K **19**
Kennington Pk. Pl. SE11 ... 7K **19** (6A **102**)
Kennington Pk. Rd. SE11 ... 7K **19** (6A **102**)
Kennington Rd. SE1 ... 1J **19** (3A **102**)
SE11 ... 1J **19** (3A **102**)
Kennistoun Ho. NW5 ... 5G **65**

Kennoldes *SE21* 2D *138*
(off Croxted Rd.)
Kenny Dr. SM5: Cars 7E *166*
Kennyland Ct. *NW4* 6D *44*
(off Hendon Way)
Kenrick Pl. W1 . . . . .6G **5** (5E **82**)
KENSAL GREEN 3E *80*
Kensal Ho. *W10* 4F *81*
(off Ladbroke Gro.)
Kensal Rd. W10 . . . . .4G *81*
KENSAL TOWN 4G *81*
Kensal Wharf W10 . . . . .4F *81*
KENSINGTON 3J *99*
Kensington Arc. *W8* 2K *99*
(off Kensington High St.)
Kensington Av. CR7: Thor H 1A *156*
E12 . . . . .6C *70*
Kensington Cen. W14 . . . . .4G *99*
(not continuous)
Kensington Chu. Ct. W8 . . . . .2K *99*
Kensington Chu. St. W8 . . . . .1J *99*
Kensington Chu. Wlk. W8 . . . . .2K *99*
(not continuous)
Kensington Cl. N11 . . . . .6K *31*
Kensington Ct. *SE16* 1K *103*
(off King & Queen Wharf)
W8 . . . . .2K *99*
Kensington Ct. Gdns. *W8* 3K *99*
(off Kensington Ct. Pl.)
Kensington Ct. Mans. *W8* 2K *99*
(off Kensington Ct. Pl.)
Kensington Ct. M. *W8* 3K *99*
(off Kensington Ct. Pl.)
Kensington Ct. Pl. W8 . . . . .3K *99*
Kensington Dr. IG8: Wfd G 2B *52*
Kensington Gdns. 4A *10* (1A *100*)
Kensington Gdns. IG1: Ilf 1D *70*
KT1: King T 3D *150*
Kensington Gdns. Sq. W2 . . . . .6K *81*
Kensington Ga. W8 . . . . .3A *100*
Kensington Gore SW7 . . . .7A *10* (2A *100*)
Kensington Hall Gdns.
W14 .5H *99*
Kensington Hgts. HA1: Harr 6K *41*
(off Sheepcote Rd.)
W8 . . . . .1J *99*
Kensington High St. W8 . . . . .3H *99*
W14 .3H *99*
Kensington Ho. IG8: Wfd G 7K *37*
UB7: W Dray 2B *92*
(off Park Lodge Av.)
W8 . . . . .2K *99*
(off Kensington Ct.)
W14 .2F *99*
Kensington Leisure Cen. 7G *81*
Kensington Mall W8 . . . . .1J *99*
Kensington Mans. SW5 . . . . .5J *99*
(off Trebovir Rd., not continuous)
Kensington Palace 1K *99*
Kensington Pal. Gdns. W8 . . . . .1K *99*
Kensington Pk. Gdns. W11 . . . . .7H *81*
Kensington Pk. M. W11 . . . . .6H *81*
Kensington Pk. Rd. W11 . . . . .6H *81*
Kensington Path *E10* 2D *68*
(off Osborne Rd.)
Kensington Pl. W8 . . . . .1J *99*
Kensington Rd. RM7: Rom 6J *55*
SW7 .2B *100*
UB5: N'olt 3E *76*
W8 . . . . .2K *99*
Kensington Sq. W8 . . . . .3K *99*
Kensington Ter.
CR2: S Croy 7D *168*
Kensington Village W14 . . . . .4H *99*
Kensington W. W14 . . . . .4G *99*
Kensworth Ho. *EC1* 2F **9**
(off Cranwood St.)
Kent Av. DA16: Well 5K *125*
RM9: Dag 4G *91*
W13 .5B *78*

Kent Cl. BR6: Chels 6J *173*
CR4: Mitc 4J *155*
Kent Ct. E2 .2F *85*
NW9 .2A *44*
Kent Dr. EN4: Cockf 4K *21*
TW11: Tedd 5J *131*
Kentford Way UB5: N'olt 1C *76*
Kent Gdns. HA4: Ruis 6J *39*
W13 .5B *78*
Kent Ga. Way CR0: Addtn 6B *170*
Kent Ho. SE1 . . . . .5F *103*
SW1 .5C *18*
(off Aylesford St.)
W4 . . . . .5A *98*
(off Devonshire St.)
Kent Ho. W8 . . . . .2K *99*
(off Kensington Ct.)
W11 .1H *99*
(off Boyne Ter. M.)
Kent Ho. App. Rd. BR3: Beck 1A *158*
Kent Ho. La. BR3: Beck 6A *140*
Kent Ho. Rd. BR3: Beck 1K *157*
SE26 .5A *140*
Kentish Bldgs. SE1 . . . . . .5E *14* (2D *102*)
Kentish Pl. SE2 . . . . .3A *108*
Kentish Rd. DA17: Belv 4G *109*
KENTISH TOWN 5F *65*
Kentish Town Forum 5F *65*
Kentish Town Ind. Est. NW5 . . . . . . .5F *65*
Kentish Town Rd. NW1 . . . . .7F *65*
NW5 .7F *65*
Kentish Town Sports Cen. 6F *65*
Kentish Way BR1: Brom 2K *159*
BR2: Brom 2K *159*
Kentlea Rd. SE28 . . . . .2J *107*
Kentmere Ho. SE15 . . . . .6J *103*
Kentmere Mans. W5 . . . . .4B *78*
Kentmere Rd. SE18 . . . . .4J *107*
KENTON 5C *42*
Kenton Av. HA1: Harr 7K *41*
TW16: Sun 2B *148*
UB1: S'hall 7E *76*
Kenton Ct. HA3: Kenton 6B *42*
SE26 .4A *140*
(off Adamsrill Rd.)
TW1: Twick 6D *114*
W14 .3G *99*
Kentone Ct. SE25 . . . . .4H *157*
Kenton Gdns. HA3: Kenton 5C *42*
Kenton Ho. *E1* 4J *85*
(off Mantus Cl.)
Kentonian Cl. HA3: Kenton 5B *42*
Kenton La.
HA3: Hrw W, Kenton, W'stone . . .6E *26*
Kenton Pk. Av. HA3: Kenton 5D *42*
Kenton Pk. Cl. HA3: Kenton 4C *42*
Kenton Pk. Cres. HA3: Kenton 4D *42*
Kenton Pk. Mans. *HA3: Kenton* 5C *42*
(off Kenton Rd.)
Kenton Pk. Pde. HA3: Kenton 5C *42*
Kenton Pk. Rd. HA3: Kenton 4C *42*
Kenton Rd. E9 . . . . .6K *67*
HA1: Harr 7K *41*
HA3: Kenton 6A *42*
Kenton St. WC1 . . . . .3E **6** (4J **83**)
Kenton Way UB4: Hayes 3G *75*
Kent Pk. Ind. Est. SE15 . . . . .6H *103*
Kent Pas. NW1 . . . . .3E **4** (4D **82**)
Kent Rd. BR4: W W'ck 1D *170*
KT1: King T 3D *150*
KT8: E Mos 4G *149*
N21 .1J *33*
RM10: Dag 5H *73*
TW9: Kew 7G *97*
W4 . . . . .3J *97*
Kent's Pas. TW12: Hamp 1D *148*
Kent St. E2 .2F *85*
E13 . . . . .3A *88*
Kent Ter. NW1 . . . . .2D **4** (3C **82**)
Kent Vw. Gdns. IG3: Ilf 2J *71*
Kent Wlk. SW9 . . . . .4B *120*

Kent Way KT6: Surb 3E *162*
Kentwell Cl. SE4 . . . . .4A *122*
Kent Wharf *SE8* 7D *104*
(off Creekside)
Kentwode Grn. SW13 . . . . .7C *98*
Kent Yd. SW7 . . . . .7D *10* (2C *100*)
Kenver Av. N12 . . . . .6G *31*
Kenward Rd. SE9 . . . . .5A *124*
Kenward Way SW11 . . . . .2E *118*
Ken Way HA9: Wemb 3J *61*
Kenway RM5: Col R 2J *55*
Kenway Rd. SW5 . . . . .4K *99*
Ken Wilson Ho. *E2* 2G *85*
(off Pritchards Rd.)
Kenwood Av. N14 . . . . .5C *22*
Kenwood Cl. NW3 . . . . .1B *64*
UB7: Sip 6C *92*
Kenwood Ct. NW9 . . . . .4J *43*
(off Elmwood Cres.)
Kenwood Dr. BR3: Beck 3E *158*
Kenwood Gdns. E18 . . . . .3K *51*
IG2: Ilf 5E *52*
IG5: Ilf 4E *52*
Kenwood House 1C *64*
Kenwood Ho. SW9 . . . . .4B *120*
Kenwood Pl. N6 . . . . .1D *64*
Kenwood Rd. N6 . . . . .6D *46*
N9 . . . . .1B *34*
Kenworthy Rd. E9 . . . . .5A *68*
Kenwrick Ho. *N1* 1K *83*
(off Barnsbury Est.)
Kenwyn Dr. NW2 . . . . .2A *62*
Kenwyn Lodge N2 . . . . .4D *46*
Kenwyn Rd. SW4 . . . . .4H *119*
SW20 . . . . .1E *152*
Kenya Rd. SE7 . . . . .7B *106*
Kenyngton Ct. TW16: Sun 5J *129*
Kenyngton Dr. TW16: Sun 5J *129*
Kenyngton Pl. HA3: Kenton 5C *42*
Kenyon Ho. *SE5* 7C *102*
(off Camberwell Rd.)
Kenyon Mans. *W14* 6G *99*
(off Queen's Club Gdns.)
Kenyon St. SW6 . . . . .1F *117*
Keogh Rd. E15 . . . . .6G *69*
Kepler Ho. *SE10* 5H *105*
(off Armitage Rd.)
Kepler Rd. SW4 . . . . .4J *119*
Keppel Ho. SE8 . . . . .5B *104*
SW3 .4C *16*
(off Elystan St.)
Keppel Rd. E6 . . . . .7D *70*
RM9: Dag 4E *72*
Keppel Row SE1 . . . . .5C *14* (1C *102*)
Keppel St. WC1 . . . . .5D **6** (5H **83**)
Kepplestone M. BR3: Beck 2D *158*
Kerbela St. E2 . . . . .3K **9** (4G **85**)
Kerbey St. E14 . . . . .6D *86*
Kerfield Cres. SE5 . . . . .1D *120*
Kerfield Pl. SE5 . . . . .1D *120*
Kerlin Vw. SW16: Mitc 2G *155*
Kerr Cl. CR2: Sels 7A *170*
Kerridge Ct. *N1* 1E *66*
(off Balls Pond Rd.)
Kerrier Ho. *SW10* 7A *100*
(off Stadium St.)
Kerrington Ct. *W10* 4G *81*
(off Wornington Rd.)
W12 .2E *98*
(off Uxbridge Rd.)
Kerris Ho. *SE11* 5K *19*
(off Tavy Cl.)
Kerrison Pl. W5 . . . . .1D *96*
Kerrison Rd. E15 . . . . .1F *87*
SW11 . . . . .3C *118*
W5 . . . . .1D *96*
Kerrison Vs. W5 . . . . .1D *96*
Kerry Av. HA7: Stan 4H *27*
Kerry Cl. E16 . . . . .6K *87*
N13 . . . . .2E *32*
Kerry Ct. HA7: Stan 4J *27*

Kerry Ho. *E1* 6J *85*
(off Sidney St.)
Kerry Path SE14 . . . . .6B *104*
Kerry Rd. SE14 . . . . .6B *104*
Kerscott Ho. *E3* 3D *86*
(off Rainhill Way)
Kersey Gdns. SE9 . . . . .4C *142*
Kersfield Ho. SW15 . . . . .6F *117*
Kersfield Rd. SW15 . . . . .6F *117*
Kershaw Cl. SW18 . . . . .6B *118*
Kershaw Rd. RM10: Dag 3G *73*
Kersley M. SW11 . . . . .1D *118*
Kersley Rd. N16 . . . . .2E *66*
Kersley St. SW11 . . . . .2D *118*
Kerstin Cl. UB3: Hayes 7H *75*
Kerswell Cl. N15 . . . . .5E *48*
Kerwick Cl. N7 . . . . .7J *65*
Keslake Mans. *NW10* 2F *81*
(off Station Ter.)
Keslake Rd. NW6 . . . . .2F *81*
Kessock Cl. N17 . . . . .5H *49*
Kestlake Rd. DA5: Bexl 6C *126*
KESTON 5A *172*
Keston Av. BR2: Kes 5A *172*
Keston Cl. DA16: Well 7C *108*
N18 . . . . .3J *33*
Keston Ct. DA5: Bexl 7F *127*
KT5: Surb 5F *151*
(off Cranes Pk.)
Keston Gdns. BR2: Kes 4A *172*
Keston Ho. *SE17* 5E *102*
(off Kinglake Est.)
KESTON MARK 4C *172*
KESTON MARK 3C *172*
Keston Pk. Cl. BR2: Kes 3D *172*
Keston Rd. CR7: Thor H 6A *156*
N17 . . . . .3D *48*
SE15 .3G *121*
Kestrel Av. E6 . . . . .5C *88*
SE24 .5B *120*
Kestrel Cl. KT2: King T 4D *132*
NW9 .2A *44*
NW10 . . . . .5K *61*
Kestrel Ct. CR2: S Croy 6C *168*
E3 . . . . .2C *86*
(off Four Seasons Cl.)
E17 . . . . .2K *49*
HA4: Ruis 2G *57*
SM6: Wall 5G *167*
Kestrel Ho. *EC1* 1C **8**
(off Pickard St.)
EN3: Pond E 5F *25*
SE10 .1E *122*
(off Parkside Av.)
Kestrel Pl. SE14 . . . . .6A *104*
Kestrel Way CR0: New Ad 7F *171*
UB3: Hayes 2F *93*
Keswick Av. SW15 . . . . .5A *134*
SW19 . . . . .2J *153*
TW17: Shep 3G *147*
Keswick B'way. SW15 . . . . .5H *117*
(off Up. Richmond Rd.)
Keswick Cl. SM1: Sutt 4A *166*
Keswick Ct. BR2: Brom 4H *159*
SE6 . . . . .1H *141*
SE13 .5D *122*
Keswick Gdns. HA4: Ruis 6F *39*
HA9: Wemb 4E *60*
IG4: Ilf 4C *52*
Keswick Ho. SE5 . . . . .2C *120*
Keswick M. W5 . . . . .1E *96*
Keswick Rd.
BR4: W W'ck 2G *171*
BR6: Orp 1K *173*
DA7: Bex 1G *127*
SW15 . . . . .5G *117*
TW2: Whitt 6G *113*
Kettering Ct. CR7: Thor H 4C *156*
Kettering St. SW16 . . . . .6G *137*
Kett Gdns. SW2 . . . . .5K *119*
Kettlebaston Rd. E10 . . . . .1B *68*

Kettleby Ho. *SW9* *3B* **120**
(off Barrington Rd.)
Kettlewell Cl. N11 . . . . .6K **31**
Ketton Ho. *W10* 4E **80**
(off Sutton Way)
Kevan Ct. E17 . . . . .4C **50**
Kevan Ho. SE5 . . . . .7C **102**
Kevelioc Rd. N17 . . . . .1C **48**
Kevin Cl. TW4: Houn 2B **112**
Kevington Cl. BR5: St P 4K **161**
Kevington Dr. BR5: St P 4K **161**
BR7: Chst 4K **161**
KEW 1G **115**
KEW BRIDGE 5F **97**
Kew Bri. TW8: Bford 6G **97**
Kew Bri. Arches TW9: Kew 6G **97**
Kew Bri. Ct. W4 . . . . .5G **97**
Kew Bri. Distribution Cen.
TW8: Bford 5F **97**
Kew Bri. Rd. TW8: Bford 6F **97**
Kew Bridge Steam Mus. 5F **97**
Kew Ct. KT2: King T 1E **150**
Kew Cres. SM3: Cheam 3G **165**
Kew Foot Rd. TW9: Rich 4E **114**
Kew Gardens 7E **96**
Kew Gdns. Rd. TW9: Kew 7F **97**
KEW GREEN 7G **97**
Kew Grn. TW9: Kew 6F **97**
Kew Mdw. Path TW9: Kew 2J **115**
(Clifford Av.)
TW9: Kew 1H **115**
(Magnolia Ct.)
Kew Retail Pk. TW9: Kew 1H **115**
Kew Riverside Pk. TW9: Kew 7H **97**
Kew Rd. TW9: Kew, Rich 6G **97**
Keybridge Ho. SW8 . . . . .7F **19**
(off Miles St.)
Key Cl. E1 . . . . .4J **85**
Keyes Ho. *SW1* 6C **18**
(off Dolphin Sq.)
Keyes Rd. NW2 . . . . .5F **63**
Keyham Ho. *W2* 5J **81**
(off Westbourne Pk. Rd.)
Key Ho. SE11 . . . . .7K **19** (6A **102**)
Keymer Rd. SW2 . . . . .2K **137**
Keynell Cl. N2 . . . . .4D **46**
Keynes Ct. SE28 . . . . .7B **90**
(off Attlee Rd.)
Keynsham Av. IG8: Wfd G 4B **36**
Keynsham Gdns. SE9 . . . . .5C **124**
Keynsham Rd. SE9 . . . . .5B **124**
SM4: Mord 1K **165**
Keynsham Wlk. SM4: Mord 1K **165**
Keys Ct. CR0: C'don 3D **168**
(off Beech Ho. Rd.)
Keyse Rd. SE1 . . . . .3F **103**
Keysham Av. TW5: Cran 1J **111**
Keystone Cres. N1 . . . . . .1F **7** (2J **83**)
Keywood Dr. TW16: Sun 6J **129**
Keyworth Cl. E5 . . . . .4A **68**
Keyworth Pl. SE1 . . . . .7B **14**
Keyworth St. SE1 . . . . . . .7B **14** (3B **102**)
Kezia M. SE8 . . . . .5A **104**
Kezia St. SE8 . . . . .5A **104**
Khalsa Ct. N22 . . . . .1B **48**
Khama Rd. SW17 . . . . .4C **136**
Khartoum Rd. E13 . . . . .3K **87**
IG1: Ilf 5F **71**
SW17 . . . . .4B **136**
Khyber Rd. SW11 . . . . .2C **118**
Kia Oval 7H **19** (6K **101**)
Kibble Cl. RM6: Chad H 7C **54**
Kibworth St. SW8 . . . . .7K **101**
KIDBROOKE 2K **123**
Kidbrooke Est. SE3 . . . . .3A **124**
Kidbrooke Gdns. SE3 . . . . .2J **123**
Kidbrooke Green Nature Reserve . . .3A **124**
Kidbrooke Gro. SE3 . . . . .1J **123**
Kidbrooke La. SE9 . . . . .4C **124**
Kidbrooke Pk. Cl. SE3 . . . . .1K **123**
Kidbrooke Pk. Rd. SE3 . . . . .1K **123**

Kidbrooke Way SE3 . . . . .2K **123**
Kidderminster Pl. CR0: C'don . . .1B **168**
Kidderminster Rd. CR0: C'don . . .1B **168**
Kidderpore Av. NW3 . . . . .4J **63**
Kidderpore Gdns. NW3 . . . . .4J **63**
Kidd Pl. SE7 . . . . .5C **106**
Kidspace
Croydon 6A **168**
Kierbeck Bus. Complex E16 . . . . .2K **105**
(not continuous)
Kiffen St. EC2 . . . . .3F **9** (4D **84**)
Kilberry Cl. TW7: Isle 1H **113**
Kilbrennan Ho. *E14* 6E **86**
(off Findhorn St.)
KILBURN 2H **81**
Kilburn Bri. NW6 . . . . .1J **81**
Kilburn Ga. NW6 . . . . .2K **81**
Kilburn High Rd. NW6 . . . . .7H **63**
Kilburn Ho. *W9* 2H **81**
(off Malvern Pl.)
Kilburn La. W9 . . . . .3F **81**
W10 . . . . .3F **81**
Kilburn Pk. Rd. NW6 . . . . .3J **81**
Kilburn Pl. NW6 . . . . .1J **81**
Kilburn Priory NW6 . . . . .1K **81**
Kilburn Sq. NW6 . . . . .1J **81**
Kilburn Va. NW6 . . . . .1K **81**
Kilburn Va. Est. NW6 . . . . .1K **81**
(off Kilburn Vale)
Kilby Ct. SE10 . . . . .3H **105**
(off Greenroof Way)
Kildare Cl. HA4: Ruis 1A **58**
Kildare Ct. W2 . . . . .6J **81**
(off Kildare Ter.)
Kildare Gdns. W2 . . . . .6J **81**
Kildare Rd. E16 . . . . .5J **87**
Kildare Ter. W2 . . . . .6J **81**
Kildare Wlk. E14 . . . . .6C **86**
Kildoran Rd. SW2 . . . . .5J **119**
Kildowan Rd. IG3: Ilf 1A **72**
Kilgour Rd. SE23 . . . . .6A **122**
Kilkie St. SW6 . . . . .2A **118**
Killarney Rd. SW18 . . . . .6A **118**
Killburns Mill Cl. SM6: Wall 2F **167**
Killearn Rd. SE6 . . . . .1F **141**
Killester Gdns. KT4: Wor Pk 4D **164**
Killick Ho. SM1: Sutt 4K **165**
Killick St. N1 . . . . .1G **7** (2K **83**)
Killick Way E1 . . . . .5K **85**
Killieser Av. SW2 . . . . .2J **137**
Killigarth Ct. DA14: Sidc 4A **144**
Killigrew Ho. TW16: Sun 7G **129**
Killip Cl. E16 . . . . .6H **87**
Killoran Ho. *E14* 3E **104**
(off Galbraith St.)
Killowen Av. UB5: N'olt 5G **59**
Killowen Rd. E9 . . . . .6K **67**
Killyon Rd. SW8 . . . . .2G **119**
Killyon Ter. SW8 . . . . .2G **119**
Kilmaine Rd. SW6 . . . . .7G **99**
Kilmarnock Gdns. RM8: Dag 3C **72**
Kilmarsh Rd. W6 . . . . .4E **98**
Kilmartin Av. SW16 . . . . .3A **156**
Kilmartin Rd. IG3: Ilf 2A **72**
Kilmington Rd. SW13 . . . . .6C **98**
Kilmiston Av. TW17: Shep 6E **146**
Kilmiston Ho. TW17: Shep 6E **146**
Kilmore Ho. *E14* 6D **86**
(off Vesey Path)
Kilmorey Gdns. TW1: Twick 5B **114**
Kilmorey Rd. TW1: Twick 4B **114**
Kilmorie Rd. SE23 . . . . .1A **140**
Kilmuir Ho. *SW1* 4H **17**
(off Bury St.)
Kiln Cl. UB3: Harl 6F **93**
Kiln Ct. E14 . . . . .7B **86**
(off Newell St.)
Kilner Ho. E16 . . . . .4H **87**
(off Freemasons Rd.)
SE11 . . . . .7J **19**

Kilner St. E14 . . . . .5C **86**
Kiln Ho. *E1* 5K **85**
(off Duckett St.)
Kiln M. SW17 . . . . .5B **136**
Kiln Pl. NW5 . . . . .5E **64**
Kilnside KT10: Clay 7A **162**
Kilpatrick Way UB4: Yead 5C **76**
Kilravock St. W10 . . . . .3G **81**
Kilronan W3 . . . . .6K **79**
Kilross Rd. TW14: Bedf 1F **129**
Kilsby Wlk. RM9: Dag 6B **72**
Kilsha Rd. KT12: Walt T 6A **148**
Kimball Gdns. SW6 . . . . .1G **117**
Kimbell Pl. SE3 . . . . .4A **124**
Kimber Ct. SE1 . . . . .7G **15**
(off Long La.)
Kimberley Av. E6 . . . . .2C **88**
IG2: Ilf 7H **53**
RM7: Rom 6J **55**
SE15 . . . . .2H **121**
Kimberley Ct. NW6 . . . . .1H **81**
(off Kimberley Rd.)
Kimberley Dr. DA14: Sidc 2D **144**
Kimberley Gdns. EN1: Enf 3A **24**
N4 . . . . .5B **48**
Kimberley Ga. BR1: Brom 7G **141**
Kimberley Ho. *E14* 3E **104**
(off Galbraith St.)
Kimberley Rd. BR3: Beck 2K **157**
CR0: C'don 6B **156**
E4 . . . . .1B **36**
E11 . . . . .2F **69**
E16 . . . . .4H **87**
E17 . . . . .1A **50**
N17 . . . . .2G **49**
N18 . . . . .6C **34**
NW6 . . . . .1G **81**
SW9 . . . . .2J **119**
Kimberley Wlk. KT12: Walt T 7K **147**
Kimberley Way E4 . . . . .1B **36**
Kimber Pl. TW4: Houn 7D **112**
(Conway Rd.)
TW4: Houn 4D **112**
(Marryat Cl.)
Kimber Rd. SW18 . . . . .7J **117**
Kimble Cres. WD23: Bush 1B **26**
Kimble Ho. NW8 . . . . .3D **4**
Kimble Rd. SW19 . . . . .6B **136**
Kimbolton Cl. SE12 . . . . .6H **123**
Kimbolton Ct. SW3 . . . . .4C **16**
(off Fulham Rd.)
Kimbolton Row SW3 . . . . .4C **16**
(off Fulham Rd.)
Kimmeridge Gdns. SE9 . . . . .4C **142**
Kimmeridge Rd. SE9 . . . . .4C **142**
Kimmins Ct. SE16 . . . . .7K **15**
(off Old Jamaica Rd.)
Kimpton Ho. SW15 . . . . .7C **116**
Kimpton Ind. Est. SM3: Sutt 2H **165**
Kimpton Link Bus. Cen.
SM3: Sutt 2H **165**
Kimpton Pk. Way SM1: Sutt 2G **165**
SM3: Sutt 2G **165**
Kimpton Rd. SE5 . . . . .1D **120**
SM3: Sutt 2H **165**
Kimpton Trade & Business Cen.
SM3: Sutt 2H **165**
Kinburn St. SE16 . . . . .2K **103**
Kincaid Rd. SE15 . . . . .7H **103**
Kincardine Gdns. W9 . . . . .4J **81**
(off Harrow Rd.)
Kincha Lodge KT2: King T 1F **151**
(off Elm Rd.)
Kinch Gro. HA9: Wemb 7F **43**
Kinder Cl. SE28 . . . . .7D **90**
Kinder Ho. N1 . . . . .2D **84**
(off Cranston Est.)
Kindersley Ho. *E1* 6G **85**
(off Pinchin St.)
Kinder St. E1 . . . . .6H **85**
Kinderton Cl. N14 . . . . .1B **32**

Kinefold Ho. N7 . . . . .6J **65**
(off York Way Est.)
Kinfauns Rd. IG3: Ilf 1A **72**
SW2 . . . . .2A **138**
King Alfred Av. SE6 . . . . .4C **140**
(not continuous)
King & Queen Cl. SE9 . . . . .4C **142**
King & Queen St. SE17 . . . . .5C **102**
King & Queen Wharf SE16 . . . . . .7K **85**
King Arthur Cl. SE15 . . . . .7J **103**
KING CHARLES I ISLAND 4E **12**
King Charles Ct. SE17 . . . . .6B **102**
(off Royal Rd.)
King Charles Cres. KT5: Surb 7F **151**
King Charles Ho. SW6 . . . . .7K **99**
(off Wandon Rd.)
King Charles Rd. KT5: Surb 5F **151**
King Charles's Ct. SE10 . . . . .6E **104**
(off Park Row)
King Charles St. SW1 . . . .6D **12** (2H **101**)
King Charles Ter. *E1* 7H **85**
(off Sovereign Cl.)
King Charles Wlk. SW19 . . . . . . .1G **135**
King Ct. E10 . . . . .7D **50**
Kingcup Cl. CR0: C'don 7K **157**
King David La. E1 . . . . .7J **85**
Kingdom St. W2 . . . . .5A **82**
Kingdon Ho. *E14* 3E **104**
(off Galbraith St.)
Kingdon Rd. NW6 . . . . .6J **63**
King Edward III M. SE16 . . . . .2H **103**
King Edward Bldg. *EC1* 7B **8**
(off King Edward St.)
King Edward Ct. HA9: Wemb 5E **60**
(off Elm Rd.)
King Edward Dr. KT9: Chess 3E **162**
King Edward Mans. E8 . . . . .1H **85**
(off Mare St.)
King Edward M. SW13 . . . . .1C **116**
King Edward Rd. E10 . . . . .1E **68**
E17 . . . . .3A **50**
EN5: New Bar 4D **20**
King Edward's Gdns. W3 . . . . . . .1G **97**
King Edwards Gro. TW11: Tedd . . .6B **132**
King Edwards Mans. SW6 . . . . . . .7J **99**
(off Fulham Rd.)
King Edward's Pl. W3 . . . . .1G **97**
King Edwards Rd. E9 . . . . .1H **85**
EN3: Pond E 4E **24**
HA4: Ruis 1F **57**
IG11: Bark 1H **89**
N9 . . . . .7C **24**
King Edward St. EC1 . . . . .7C **8** (6C **84**)
King Edward Wlk. SE1 . . . .1K **19** (3A **102**)
Kingfield Rd. W5 . . . . .4C **78**
Kingfield St. E14 . . . . .4E **104**
Kingfisher Av. E11 . . . . .6K **51**
Kingfisher Cl. HA3: Hrw W 7E **26**
HA6: Nwood 1D **38**
SE28 . . . . .7C **90**
Kingfisher Ct. CR0: C'don 3C **168**
(off Wandle Rd.)
E14 . . . . .2E **104**
(off River Barge Cl.)
EN2: Enf 1E **22**
KT8: E Mos 4J **149**
SE1 . . . . .7D **14**
(off Swan St.)
SM1: Sutt 5H **165**
SW19 . . . . .2F **135**
TW3: Houn 5F **113**
Kingfisher Dr. TW10: Ham 4B **132**
Kingfisher Hgts. E16 . . . . .1A **106**
(off Bramwell Way)
Kingfisher Ho. SW18 . . . . .3A **118**
W14 . . . . .3H **99**
(off Melbury Rd.)
Kingfisher Leisure Cen.
Kingston upon Thames 2E **150**
Kingfisher M. SE13 . . . . .4C **122**

Kingfisher Pl. N22 . . . . .2K **47**
Kingfisher Sq. SE8 . . . . .6B **104**
    (off Clyde St.)
Kingfisher St. E6 . . . . .5C **88**
Kingfisher Wlk. NW9 . . . . .2A **44**
Kingfisher Way
  BR3: Beck 5K **157**
  NW10 . . . . .6K **61**
King Frederick IX Twr. SE16 . . . . .3B **104**
King Gdns. CR0: Wadd 5B **168**
King George IV Ct. SE17 . . . . .5D **102**
    (off Dawes St.)
King George VI Av. CR4: Mitc 4D **154**
King George VI Memorial 5C **12**
King George Av. E16 . . . . .6A **88**
  IG2: Ilf 5H **53**
King George Cl. RM7: Mawney 3J **55**
  TW16: Sun .5G **129**
King George Cres. HA0: Wemb 5D **60**
King George M. SW17 . . . . .5D **136**
King George Sq. TW10: Rich 6F **115**
King George's Dr. UB1: S'hall 5D **76**
King George's Sailing Club 6H **25**
King George's Trad. Est.
  KT9: Chess .4G **163**
King George St. SE10 . . . . .7E **104**
King George Way E1 . . . . .4J **25**
Kingham Cl. SW18 . . . . .7A **118**
  W11 . . . . .2G **99**
King Harolds Way
  DA7: Belv, Bex 7D **108**
  DA17: Belv .7D **108**
King Henry Lodge E4 . . . . .4H **35**
King Henry M. BR6: Chels 5K **173**
  HA2: Harr 1J **59**
King Henry's Dr. CR0: New Ad 7D **170**
King Henry's Reach W6 . . . . .6E **98**
King Henry's Rd. KT1: King T 3H **151**
  NW3 . . . . .7C **64**
King Henry's Stairs E1 . . . . .1H **103**
King Henry St. N16 . . . . .5E **66**
King Henry's Wlk. N1 . . . . .6E **66**
King Henry Ter. E1 . . . . .7H **85**
    (off Sovereign Cl.)
Kinghorn St. EC1 . . . . .6C **8** (5C **84**)
King Ho. W12 . . . . .6D **80**
Kingisholt Ct. NW10 . . . . .3F **81**
    (off Wellington Rd.)
King James Ct. SE1 . . . . .7B **14**
King James St. SE1 . . . . .7B **14** (2B **102**)
King John Ct. EC2 . . . . .3H **9** (4E **84**)
King John St. E1 . . . . .5K **85**
King John's Wlk. SE9 . . . . .7C **124**
Kinglake Est. SE17 . . . . .5E **102**
Kinglake St. SE17 . . . . .5E **102**
    (not continuous)
Kinglet Cl. E7 . . . . .6J **69**
Kingly Ct. W1 . . . . .2B **12**
Kingly St. W1 . . . . .1A **12** (6G **83**)
Kingsand Rd. SE12 . . . . .2J **141**
Kings Arbour UB2: S'hall 5C **94**
King's Arms All. TW8: Bford 6D **96**
Kings Arms Ct. E1 . . . . .5G **85**
Kings Arms Yd. EC2 . . . . .7E **8** (6D **84**)
  SW18 . . . . .5K **117**
Kingsash Dr. UB4: Yead 4C **76**
Kings Av. BR1: Brom 6H **141**
  IG8: Wfd G .6E **36**
  IG9: Buck H .2G **37**
    (Langfords)
  IG9: Buck H .6E **36**
    (The Broadway)
  KT3: N Mald 4A **152**
  N10 . . . . .3E **46**
  N21 . . . . .1G **33**
  RM6: Chad H 6F **55**
  SM5: Cars .7C **166**
  SW4 . . . . .1H **137**
  SW12 . . . . .1H **137**
  TW3: Houn .1F **113**
  TW16: Sun .5H **129**

Kings Av. UB6: G'frd 5F **77**
  W5 . . . . .6D **78**
King's Bench St. SE1 . . . . .6B **14** (2B **102**)
King's Bench Wlk. EC4 . . . . .1K **13** (6A **84**)
King's Blvd. N1 .2J **83**
Kingsbridge Av. W3 . . . . .2F **97**
Kingsbridge Ct. E14 . . . . .3C **104**
    (off Dockers Tanner Rd.)
  NW1 . . . . .7F **65**
    (off Castlehaven Rd.)
Kingsbridge Cres. UB1: S'hall 5D **76**
Kingsbridge Dr. NW7 . . . . .7A **30**
Kingsbridge Rd. IG11: Bark 2H **89**
  KT12: Walt T 7K **147**
  SM4: Mord .6F **153**
  UB2: S'hall .4D **94**
  W10 . . . . .6E **80**
Kingsbridge Way UB4: Hayes 3G **75**
Kingsbridge Wharf IG11: Bark 3J **89**
KINGSBURY 5H **43**
Kingsbury Circ. NW9 . . . . .5G **43**
KINGSBURY GREEN 6K **43**
Kingsbury Rd. N1 . . . . .6E **66**
  NW9 . . . . .5G **43**
Kingsbury Ter. N1 . . . . .6E **66**
Kingsbury Trad. Est. NW9 . . . . .6K **43**
Kings Chase KT8: E Mos 3G **149**
Kings Chase Vw. EN2: Enf 2F **23**
Kingsclere Cl. SW15 . . . . .7C **116**
Kingsclere Ct. N12 . . . . .5H **31**
Kingsclere Pl. EN2: Enf 2H **23**
Kingscliffe Gdns. SW19 . . . . .1H **135**
Kings Cl. DA1: Cray 4K **127**
  E10 . . . . .7D **50**
  KT7: T Ditt .6A **150**
  KT12: Walt T 7K **147**
  NW4 . . . . .4F **45**
  TW18: Staines 7A **128**
King's Club, The 6E **134**
Kings Coll. Ct. NW3 . . . . .7C **64**
King's College London
  Denmark Hill Campus 2D **120**
  Guy's Campus 1D **102**
  St Thomas' Campus - Lambeth Pal. Rd.
    . . . . .2F **19**
  St Thomas' Campus -
    St Thomas' House 1G **19**
  Strand Campus 2H **13** (7K **83**)
  Waterloo Campus 5J **13** (1A **102**)
Kings Coll. Rd. HA4: Ruis 6H **39**
  NW3 . . . . .7C **64**
King's College School of
  Medicine & Dentistry 2C **120**
Kingscote Rd. CR0: C'don 7H **157**
  KT3: N Mald 3K **151**
  W4 . . . . .3K **97**
Kingscote St. EC4 . . . . .2A **14** (7B **84**)
Kings Ct. E13 . . . . .1K **87**
  HA9: Wemb 2H **61**
  IG9: Buck H .2G **37**
  N7 . . . . .7K **65**
    (off Caledonian Rd.)
  NW8 . . . . .1D **82**
    (off Prince Albert Rd.)
  SE1 . . . . .6B **14** (2B **102**)
  W6 . . . . .4C **98**
Kings Ct. Mans. SW6 . . . . .1H **117**
    (off Fulham Rd.)
Kings Ct. M. KT8: E Mos 5H **149**
Kingscourt Rd. SW16 . . . . .3H **137**
Kings Ct. Sth. SW3 . . . . .6C **16**
Kings Cres. N4 .3C **66**
Kings Cres. Est. N4 . . . . .2C **66**
Kingscroft SW4 . . . . .6J **119**
Kingscroft Rd. NW2 . . . . .6H **63**
KING'S CROSS 2J **83**
King's Cross Bri. N1 . . . . .1F **7**
King's Cross Rd. WC1 . . . . .1G **7** (3K **83**)
King's Cross Sq. N1 . . . . .3J **83**
    (off Euston Rd.)

Kingsdale Gdns. W11 . . . . .1F **99**
Kingsdale Rd. SE18 . . . . .7K **107**
  SE20 . . . . .7K **139**
Kingsdown Av. CR2: S Croy 7C **168**
  W3 . . . . .7A **80**
  W13 . . . . .2B **96**
Kingsdown Cl. SE16 . . . . .5H **103**
    (off Masters Dr.)
  W10 . . . . .6F **81**
Kingsdowne Rd. KT6: Surb 7E **150**
Kingsdown Ho. E8 . . . . .5G **67**
Kingsdown Point SW2 . . . . .2A **138**
Kingsdown Rd. E11 . . . . .3G **69**
  N19 . . . . .2J **65**
  SM3: Cheam 5G **165**
Kingsdown Way BR2: Hayes 7J **159**
Kings Dr. HA8: Edg 4A **28**
  HA9: Wemb 2H **61**
  KT5: Surb 7G **151**
  KT7: T Ditt .7B **150**
  TW11: Tedd 5H **131**
Kingsend HA4: Ruis 1F **57**
Kingsend Cl. HA4: Ruis 1G **57**
Kings Farm E17 . . . . .1D **50**
Kings Farm Av. TW10: Rich 4G **115**
Kingsfield Av. HA2: Harr 4F **41**
Kingsfield Ho. SE9 . . . . .3B **142**
Kingsfield Rd. HA1: Harr 7H **41**
Kingsfield Ter. HA1: Harr 1H **59**
Kingsford St. NW5 . . . . .5D **64**
Kingsford Way E6 . . . . .5D **88**
Kings Gdns. IG1: Ilf 1H **71**
  KT12: Walt T 7K **147**
  NW6 . . . . .7J **63**
Kings Gth. M. SE23 . . . . .2J **139**
Kingsgate NW9 : Wemb 3J **61**
Kingsgate Av. N3 . . . . .3J **45**
Kingsgate Bus. Cen. KT2: King T 1E **150**
    (off Kingsgate Rd.)
Kingsgate Cl. DA7: Bex 1E **126**
  KT2: King T 1E **150**
Kingsgate Est. N1 . . . . .6E **66**
Kingsgate Ho. SW9 . . . . .1A **120**
Kingsgate Mans. WC1 . . . . .6G **7**
    (off Red Lion Sq.)
Kingsgate Pde. SW1 . . . . .2B **18**
Kingsgate Pl. NW6 . . . . .7J **63**
Kingsgate Rd. KT1: King T 1E **150**
  KT2: King T 1E **150**
  NW6 . . . . .7J **63**
Kings Grange HA4: Ruis 1H **57**
Kingsground SE9 . . . . .7B **124**
King's Gro. SE15 . . . . .7H **103**
    (not continuous)
Kings Hall Leisure Cen. 5J **67**
Kings Hall M. SE13 . . . . .3E **122**
Kings Hall Rd. BR3: Beck 7A **140**
Kings Head Hill E4 . . . . .7J **25**
Kingshead Ho. NW7 . . . . .4J **29**
Kings Head Pas. SW4 . . . . .4H **119**
    (off Clapham Pk. Rd.)
Kings Head Theatre 1B **84**
King's Head Yd. SE1 . . . . .5E **14** (1D **102**)
King's Highway SE18 . . . . .6J **107**
Kingshill Av. HA3: Kenton 4B **42**
  KT4: Wor Pk 7C **152**
  UB4: Hayes, Yead 3G **75**
  UB5: N'olt 3G **75**
Kingshill Cl. UB4: Hayes 3J **75**
Kingshill Ct. EN5: Barn 4B **20**
Kingshill Dr. HA3: Kenton 2B **42**
Kingshold Rd. E9 . . . . .7J **67**
Kingsholm Gdns. SE9 . . . . .4B **124**
Kings Ho. SW8 .7J **101**
    (off Sth. Lambeth Rd.)
  SW10 . . . . .7A **16**
    (off King's Rd.)
King's Ho. Studios SW10 . . . . .7A **16**
    (off Lamont Rd. Pas.)

Kingshurst Rd. SE12 . . . . .7J **123**
Kingside SE18 .3C **106**
Kings Keep BR2: Brom 2G **159**
  KT1: King T 4E **150**
  SW15 . . . . .5F **117**
KINGSLAND 6E **66**
Kingsland NW8 .1C **82**
Kingsland Grn. E8 . . . . .6E **66**
Kingsland High St. E8 . . . . .6F **67**
Kingsland Pas. E8 . . . . .6E **66**
Kingsland Rd. E2 . . . . .2H **9** (3E **84**)
  E8 . . . . .3E **84**
  E13 . . . . .3A **88**
Kingsland Shop. Cen. E8 . . . . .6F **67**
Kingslawn Cl. SW15 . . . . .5D **116**
Kingslee Ct. SM2: Sutt 7K **165**
Kingsleigh Cl. TW8: Bford 6D **96**
Kingsleigh Pl. CR4: Mitc 3D **154**
Kingsleigh Wlk. BR2: Brom 4H **159**
Kingsley Av. SM1: Sutt 4B **166**
  TW3: Houn .2G **113**
  UB1: S'hall .7E **76**
  W13 . . . . .5A **78**
Kingsley Cl. N2 .5A **46**
  RM10: Dag .4H **73**
Kingsley Ct. DA6: Bex 4G **127**
  HA8: Edg 3C **28**
  KT4: Wor Pk 2B **164**
    (off The Avenue)
  NW2 . . . . .6D **62**
Kingsley Dr. KT4: Wor Pk 2B **164**
Kingsley Flats SE1 . . . . .4E **102**
    (off Old Kent Rd.)
Kingsley Gdns. E4 . . . . .5H **35**
Kingsley Ho. SW3 . . . . .6D **16**
    (off Beaufort St.)
  W14 . . . . .4G **99**
    (off Avonmore Pl.)
Kingsley Mans. W14 . . . . .6G **99**
    (off Greyhound Rd.)
Kingsley M. BR7: Chst 6F **143**
  E1 . . . . .7H **85**
  W8 . . . . .3K **99**
Kingsley Pl. N6 .7E **46**
Kingsley Rd. BR6: Chels 7K **173**
  CR0: C'don 1A **168**
  E7 . . . . .7J **69**
  E17 . . . . .2E **50**
  HA2: Harr 4G **59**
  HA5: Pinn 4D **40**
  IG6: Ilf 1G **53**
  N13 . . . . .4F **33**
  NW6 . . . . .1H **81**
  SW19 . . . . .5K **135**
  TW3: Houn .1F **113**
Kingsley St. SW11 . . . . .3D **118**
Kingsley Way N2 . . . . .5A **46**
Kingsley Wood Dr. SE9 . . . . .3D **142**
Kings Lodge HA4: Ruis 1G **57**
    (off Pembroke Rd.)
  N12 . . . . .6F **31**
Kingslyn Cres. SE19 . . . . .1E **156**
Kings Mall W6 . . . . .4E **98**
Kingsman Pde. SE18 . . . . .3D **106**
Kings Mans. SW3 . . . . .7C **16**
    (off Lawrence St.)
Kingsman St. SE18 . . . . .3D **106**
Kingsmead EN5: New Bar 4D **20**
  TW10: Rich .6F **115**
Kingsmead Av. CR4: Mitc 3G **155**
  KT4: Wor Pk 2D **164**
  KT6: Surb 2G **163**
  N9 . . . . .1C **34**
  NW9 . . . . .7K **43**
  TW16: Sun .2A **148**
Kingsmead Cl. DA15: Sidc 2A **144**
  KT19: Ewe .7K **163**
  TW11: Tedd 6B **132**
Kingsmead Cotts. BR2: Brom 1C **172**
Kingsmead Ct. N6 . . . . .7H **47**

Kingsmead Dr. UB5: N'olt 7D 58
Kingsmead Ho. E9 . . . . .4A 68
Kingsmead Lodge SM2: Sutt 6B 166
Kingsmeadow .3G 151
Kingsmeadow Athletics Cen. 3G 151
Kingsmead Rd. SW2 . . . . .2A 138
Kingsmead Way E9 . . . . .4A 68
Kingsmere Cl. SW15 . . . . .3F 117
Kingsmere Pk. NW9 . . . . .1H 61
Kingsmere Pl. N16 . . . . .1D 66
Kingsmere Rd. SW19 . . . . .2F 135
King's M. SW4 .5J 119
  WC1 . . . . .4H 7 (4K 83)
Kingsmill NW8 .2B 82
  (off Kingsmill Ter.)
Kingsmill Bus. Pk. KT1: King T 3F 151
Kingsmill Gdns. RM9: Dag 5F 73
Kingsmill Ho. SW3 . . . . .5D 16
  (off Cale St.)
Kingsmill Rd. RM9: Dag 5F 73
Kingsmill Ter. NW8 . . . . .2B 82
Kingsnorth Ho. W10 . . . . .6F 81
Kingsnympton Pk. KT2: King T 7H 133
Kings Oak RM7: Mawney 3G 55
King's Orchard SE9 . . . . .6C 124
King's Paddock TW12: Hamp 1G 149
Kings Pde. HA8: Edg 5B 28
  (off Edgwarebury La.)
  N17 . . . . .3F 49
  NW10 .1E 80
  SM5: Cars 3D 166
  (off Wrythe La.)
  W12 . . . . .3C 98
Kingspark Bus. Cen. KT3: N Mald 4J 151
Kingspark Ct. E18 . . . . .3J 51
Kings Pas. E11 . . . . .7G 51
  KT1: King T 2D 150
  KT2: King T 1D 150
Kings Place 2J 83
Kings Pl. IG9: Buck H 2F 37
  SE1 . . . . .7C 14
  W4 . . . . .5J 97
King Sq. EC1 . . . . .2C 8 (3C 84)
Kings Quarter Apartments N1 . . . . .1K 83
  (off Copenhagen St.)
King's Quay SW10 . . . . .1A 118
  (off Chelsea Harbour Dr.)
Kings Reach Twr. SE1 . . . . .4A 14
Kings Ride Ga. TW10: Rich 4G 115
Kingsridge SW19 . . . . .2G 135
Kings Rd. BR6: Orp 4K 173
  CR4: Mitc 3E 154
  E4 . . . . .1A 36
  E6 . . . . .1A 88
  E11 . . . . .7G 51
  EN5: Barn 3A 20
  HA2: Harr 2D 58
  IG11: Bark 7G 71
  KT2: King T 7E 132
  KT6: Surb 1C 162
  KT12: Walt T 7K 147
  N17 . . . . .1F 49
  N18 . . . . .5B 34
  N22 . . . . .1K 47
  NW10 . . . . .7D 62
  SE25 . . . . .3G 157
  SW3 . . . . .6D 16 (2J 117)
  SW6 .7K 99
  SW10 . . . . .7A 16 (7K 99)
  SW14 . . . . .3K 115
  SW19 . . . . .6J 135
  TW1: Twick 6B 114
  TW10: Rich 6F 115
  TW11: Tedd 5H 131
  TW13: Felt 1A 130
  UB7: W Dray 2B 92
  W5 . . . . .5D 78
King's Scholars' Pas. SW1 . . . . .2A 18
King Stairs Cl. SE16 . . . . .2H 103
King's Ter. NW1 . . . . .1G 83
  TW7: Isle 4A 114

Kingsthorpe Rd. SE26 . . . . .4K 139
Kingston Av. SM3: Cheam 3G 165
  TW14: Felt 6G 111
  UB7: Yiew 7B 74
  (Ash Gro.)
  UB7: Yiew 1B 92
  (Whitethorn Av.)
Kingston Bri. KT1: King T 2D 150
Kingston Bus. Cen. KT9: Chess 3E 162
Kingston By-Pass KT3: N Mald 5A 152
  KT6: Surb 3D 162
  SW15 . . . . .4A 134
  SW20 . . . . .2C 152
Kingston By-Pass Rd. KT6: Surb 3B 162
  KT10: Hin W, Surb 3A 162
Kingston Cl. RM6: Chad H 3E 54
  (not continuous)
  TW11: Tedd 6B 132
  UB5: N'olt 1D 76
Kingston Crematorium KT1: King T . . .3G 151
Kingston Cres. BR3: Beck 1B 158
Kingston Gdns. CR0: Bedd 3J 167
Kingston Hall Rd. KT1: King T 3D 150
Kingston Hill KT2: King T 1G 151
Kingston Hill Av. RM6: Chad H 3E 54
Kingston Hill Pl. KT2: King T 4J 133
Kingston Ho. KT1: King T 4D 150
  (off Surbiton Rd.)
  NW1 .1G 83
  (off Camden St.)
  NW6 .7G 63
Kingston Ho. E. SW7 . . . . .7C 10
  (off Prince's Ga.)
Kingston Ho. Est. KT6: Surb 6B 150
Kingston Ho. Nth. SW7 . . . . .7C 10
  (off Prince's Ga.)
Kingston Ho. Sth. SW7 . . . . .7C 10
  (off Ennismore Gdns.)
Kingstonian FC 3G 151
Kingston La. TW11: Tedd 5A 132
  UB7: W Dray 2B 92
  UB8: Hil 3A 74
Kingston Lodge KT3: N Mald 4A 152
Kingston Mans. SW9 . . . . .1K 119
  (off Clapham Rd.)
Kingston Pl. HA3: Hrw W 7E 26
Kingston Rd. EN4: E Barn 5G 21
  IG1: Ilf 4F 71
  KT1: King T 3H 151
  KT3: N Mald 3H 151
  KT4: Wor Pk 2H 163
  KT5: Surb 2H 163
  KT17: Ewe 7B 164
  KT19: Ewe 2H 163
  N9 . . . . .2B 34
  SW15 . . . . .2C 134
  SW19 . . . . .2C 134
  (Norstead Pk.)
  SW19 . . . . .2H 153
  (Rothesay Av.)
  SW20 . . . . .2F 153
  TW11: Tedd 5B 132
  TW15: Ashf 6A 128
  UB2: S'hall 2D 94
Kingston Sq. SE19 . . . . .5D 138
Kingston University
  Kingston Hill Campus 5K 133
  Knights Park Campus 3E 150
  Penrhyn Road Campus 4E 150
  Roehampton Vale Cen. 3B 134
KINGSTON UPON THAMES 2D 150
Kingston upon Thames Art Gallery
  & Museum 2E 150
KINGSTON VALE 4A 134
Kingston Va. SW15 . . . . .4K 133
Kingstown St. NW1 . . . . .1E 82
  (not continuous)
King St. E13 . . . . .4J 87
  EC2 . . . . .1D 14 (6C 84)
  N2 . . . . .3B 46
  N17 . . . . .1F 49

King St. SW1 . . . . .5B 12 (1G 101)
  TW1: Twick 1A 132
  TW9: Rich 5D 114
  UB2: S'hall 3C 94
  W3 . . . . .1J 97
  W6 . . . . .4C 98
  WC2 . . . . .2E 12 (7J 83)
King St. Cloisters W6 . . . . .4D 98
  (off King St.)
King St. M. N2 .3B 46
King St. Pde. TW1: Twick 1A 132
  (off King St.)
Kings Wlk. Shop. Cen.
  SW3 . . . . .5E 16 (5D 100)
Kingswater Pl. SW11 . . . . .7C 100
Kings Way CR0: Wadd 5K 167
  HA1: Harr 4J 41
Kingsway BR4: W W'ck 3G 171
  BR5: Pet W 5H 161
  EN3: Pond E 5C 24
  HA9: Wemb 4E 60
  IG8: Wfd G 5F 37
  KT3: N Mald 4E 152
  N12 . . . . .6F 31
  SW14 . . . . .3H 115
  TW19: Stanw 1A 128
  UB3: Hayes 5E 74
  WC2 . . . . .7G 7 (6K 83)
Kingsway Bus. Pk. TW12: Hamp 1D 148
Kingsway Cres. HA2: Harr 4G 41
Kingsway Est. N18 . . . . .6E 34
Kingsway Mans. WC1 . . . . .5G 7
  (off Red Lion Sq.)
Kingsway Pde. N16 . . . . .3D 66
  (off Albion Rd.)
Kingsway Pl. EC1 . . . . .3K 7
  (off Sans Wlk.)
Kingsway Rd. SM3: Cheam 7G 165
Kingswear Rd. HA4: Ruis 2J 57
  NW5 .3F 65
Kings Wharf E8 . . . . .1E 84
  (off Kingsland Rd.)
  SE10 . . . . .6D 104
  (off Wood Wharf)
Kingswood E2 .2J 85
  (off Cyprus St.)
Kingswood Av. BR2: Brom 3G 159
  CR7: Thor H 5A 156
  DA17: Belv 4F 109
  NW6 .1G 81
  TW3: Houn 1D 112
  TW12: Hamp 6F 131
Kingswood Cl. BR6: Orp 7J 161
  EN1: Enf 5K 23
  KT3: N Mald 6B 152
  KT6: Surb 7E 150
  N20 . . . . .7F 21
  SW8 .7J 101
  TW15: Ashf 5F 129
Kings Wood Ct. TW10: Rich 5F 115
Kingswood Ct. E4 . . . . .5H 35
  NW6 .7J 63
  (off West End La.)
  SE13 . . . . .6F 123
Kingswood Dr. SE19 . . . . .4E 138
  SM2: Sutt 7K 165
  SM5: Cars 1D 166
Kingswood Est. SE21 . . . . .4E 138
Kingswood Hgts. E18 . . . . .1J 51
  (off Queen Mary Av.)
Kingswood M. N15 . . . . .4B 48
Kingswood Pk. N3 . . . . .2H 45
Kingswood Pl. SE13 . . . . .4G 123
Kingswood Rd. BR2: Brom 4F 159
  E11 . . . . .7G 51
  HA9: Wemb 3G 61
  IG3: Ilf 1A 72
  SE20 . . . . .6J 139
  SW2 .6J 119
  SW19 . . . . .7H 135
  W4 . . . . .3J 97

Kingswood Ter. W4 . . . . .3J 97
Kingswood Way SM6: Wall 5J 167
Kingsworth Cl. BR3: Beck 5A 158
Kingsworthy Cl. KT1: King T 3F 151
Kings Yd. SW15 . . . . .3E 116
  (off Lwr. Richmond Rd.)
Kingthorpe Rd. NW10 . . . . .7K 61
Kingthorpe Ter. NW10 . . . . .6K 61
Kington Ho. NW6 . . . . .1K 81
  (off Mortimer Cres.)
Kingward Ho. E1 . . . . .5G 85
  (off Hanbury St.)
King Wardrobe Apartments EC4 . . . . .1B 14
  (off Carter La.)
Kingweston Cl. NW2 . . . . .3G 63
King William IV Gdns. SE20 . . . . .6J 139
King William La. SE10 . . . . .5G 105
King William's Ct. SE10 . . . . .6F 105
  (off Park Row)
King William St. EC4 . . . . . . .1F 15 (6D 84)
King William Wlk. SE10 . . . . .6E 104
  (not continuous)
Kingwood Gdns. E1 . . . . .1K 15
  (off Piazza Wlk.)
Kingwood Rd. SW6 . . . . .1G 117
Kinlet Rd. SE18 . . . . .1G 125
Kinloch Dr. NW9 . . . . .7K 43
Kinloch St. N7 .3K 65
Kinloss Ct. N3 . . . . .4H 45
Kinloss Gdns. N3 . . . . .3H 45
Kinloss Rd. SM5: Cars 7A 154
Kinnaird Av. BR1: Brom 6H 141
  W4 . . . . .7J 97
Kinnaird Cl. BR1: Brom 6H 141
Kinnaird Ho. SE17 . . . . .4D 102
Kinnaird Way IG8: Wfd G 6J 37
Kinnear Apartments N8 . . . . .3K 47
Kinnear Rd. W12 . . . . .2B 98
Kinnerton Pl. Nth. SW1 . . . . .7F 11
Kinnerton Pl. Sth. SW1 . . . . .7F 11
Kinnerton St. SW1 . . . . .7G 11 (2E 100)
Kinnerton Yd. SW1 . . . . .7G 11
Kinnoul Rd. W6 . . . . .6G 99
Kinross Av. KT4: Wor Pk 2C 164
Kinross Cl. HA3: Kenton 5F 43
  HA8: Edg 2C 28
  TW16: Sun 5H 129
Kinross Ct. BR1: Brom 1H 159
  (off Highland Rd.)
  SE6 .1H 141
Kinross Dr. TW16: Sun 5H 129
Kinross Ho. N1 . . . . .1K 83
  (off Bemerton Est.)
Kinross Ter. E17 . . . . .2B 50
Kinsale Rd. SE15 . . . . .3G 121
Kinsella Gdns. SW19 . . . . .5D 134
Kinsham Ho. E2 . . . . .4G 85
  (off Ramsey St.)
Kintore Way SE1 . . . . .4F 103
Kintyre Cl. SW16 . . . . .2K 155
Kintyre Ct. SW2 . . . . .7J 119
Kintyre Ho. E14 . . . . .1E 104
  (off Coldharbour)
Kinveachy Gdns. SE7 . . . . .5C 106
Kinver Ho. N19 . . . . .2H 65
Kinver Rd. SE26 . . . . .4J 139
Kipling Cl. W7 .7K 77
Kipling Ct. SW19 . . . . .6B 136
Kipling Est. SE1 . . . . .7F 15 (2D 102)
Kipling Ho. N19 .1J 65
  (off Charles St.)
  SE5 .7D 102
  (off Elmington Est.)
Kipling Pl. HA7: Stan 6E 26
Kipling Rd. DA7: Bex 1E 126
Kipling St. SE1 . . . . .7F 15 (2D 102)
Kipling Ter. N9 .3J 33
Kipling Twr. W3 . . . . .3J 97
  (off Palmerston Rd.)
Kippington Dr. SE9 . . . . .1B 142
Kira Bldg. E3 . . . . .3B 86

iran Apartments E1 . . . . .6K 9
Irby Cl. KT19: Ewe 5B 164
Irby Est. SE16 . . . . .3H 103
　UB7: Yiew 7A 74
Irby Gro. SE1 . . . . .6G 15 (2E 102)
Irby St. EC1 . . . . .5K 7 (5A 84)
Irby Way KT12: Walt T 6A 148
　UB8: Hil 4B 74
Irchen Rd. W13 . . . . .7B 78
Irkby Apartments E3 . . . . .5B 86
　　　　　　　　　　(off St Paul's Way)
Irkby Cl. N11 . . . . .6K 31
Irkdale SE26 . . . . .2H 139
Irkdale Cnr. SE26 . . . . .4J 139
Irkdale Rd. E11 . . . . .1G 69
Irkeby Ho. EC1 . . . . .5J 7
　　　　　　　　　　(off Leather La.)
Irkfield Cl. W13 . . . . .1B 96
Irkham Apartments IG11: Bark 7G 71
　　　　　　　　　　(off Linton Rd.)
Irkham Rd. E6 . . . . .6C 88
Irkham St. SE18 . . . . .6J 107
Irk Ho. HA9: Wemb 3E 60
Irkland Av. IG5: Ilf 2E 52
Irkland Cl. DA15: Sidc 6J 125
Irkland Dr. EN2: Enf 1H 23
Irkland Ho. E14 . . . . .5D 104
　　　　　　　(off St Davids Sq., St Davids Sq.)
　E14 . . . . .5D 104
　　　　　　　(off Westferry Rd., Westferry Rd.)
Irkland Ter. BR3: Beck 6C 140
Irkland Wlk. E8 . . . . .6F 67
Irk La. SE18 . . . . .6G 107
Irkleas Rd. KT6: Surb 1E 162
Irklees Rd. CR7: Thor H 5A 156
　RM8: Dag 2H 73
Irkley Rd. SW19 . . . . .1J 153
Irkman Pl. W1 . . . . .6C 6
Irkmichael Rd. E14 . . . . .6E 86
Irk Ri. SM1: Sutt 3K 165
Irk Rd. E17 . . . . .6B 50
Irkside Rd. SE3 . . . . .6J 105
Irk's Place 5B 86
Irkstall Av. N17 . . . . .4D 48
Irkstall Gdns. SW2 . . . . .1J 137
Irkstall Ho. SW1 . . . . .5J 17
　　　　　　　　　　(part of Abbots Mnr.)
Irkstall Rd. SW2 . . . . .1H 137
Irkstead Ct. E5 . . . . .4K 67
Irkstead Rd. SM4: Mord 1K 165
Irkstone Rd. 1A 6
　　　　　　　　　　(off Harrington St.)
Irkstone Way BR1: Brom 7G 141
Irk St. WC1 . . . . .4G 7
Irkton Rd. N15 . . . . .4E 48
Irkwall Pl. E2 . . . . .3J 85
Irkwood Pl. NW1 . . . . .7E 64
Irkwood Rd. SE15 . . . . .2H 121
Irn Rd. W13 . . . . .7B 78
Irrane Cl. KT3: N Mald 5B 152
Irtley Ho. SW8 . . . . .1G 119
Irtley Rd. SE26 . . . . .4A 140
Irtling St. SW8 . . . . .7G 101
Irton Cl. W4 . . . . .4K 97
Irton Gdns. E2 . . . . .2K 9 (3F 85)
　　　　　　　　　　(not continuous)
Irton Lodge SW18 . . . . .6K 117
Irton Rd. E13 . . . . .2A 88
Irton Wlk. HA8: Edg 7D 28
Irwyn Way SE5 . . . . .7B 102
itcat Ter. E3 . . . . .3C 86
itchen Cl. E10 . . . . .2D 68
itchener Ho. SE18 . . . . .7E 106
itchener Rd.
　CR7: Thor H 3D 156
　E7 . . . . .6K 69
　E17 . . . . .1D 50
　N2 . . . . .3C 46
　N17 . . . . .3E 48
　RM10: Dag 6H 73

Kite Ho. SE1 . . . . .4H 103
　SE3 . . . . .4K 123
Kite Pl. E2 . . . . .3G 85
　　　　　　　　　　(off Warner Pl.)
Kite Yd. SW11 . . . . .1D 118
　　　　　　　　　　(off Cambridge Rd.)
Kitley Gdns. SE19 . . . . .1F 157
Kitson Rd. SE5 . . . . .7D 102
　SW13 . . . . .1C 116
Kittiwake Ct. SE1 . . . . .7D 14
　　　　　　　　　　(off Gt. Dover St.)
　SE8 . . . . .6B 104
　　　　　　　　　　(off Abinger Gro.)
Kittiwake Pl. SM1: Sutt 5H 165
Kittiwake Rd. UB5: N'olt 3B 76
Kittiwake Way UB4: Yead 5B 76
Kitto Rd. SE14 . . . . .2K 121
Kitts End Rd. EN5: Barn 1C 20
Kiver Rd. N19 . . . . .2H 65
Klea Av. SW4 . . . . .6G 119
Kleine Wharf N1 . . . . .1E 84
Klein's Wharf E14 . . . . .3C 104
　　　　　　　　　　(off Westferry Rd.)
Knapdale Cl. SE23 . . . . .2H 139
Knapmill Rd. SE6 . . . . .2C 140
Knapmill Way SE6 . . . . .2D 140
Knapp Cl. NW10 . . . . .6A 62
Knapp Rd. E3 . . . . .4C 86
　TW15: Ashf 4B 128
Knapton M. SW17 . . . . .6E 136
Knaresborough Dr. SW18 . . . . . . .1K 135
Knaresborough Pl. SW5 . . . . .4K 99
Knatchbull Rd. NW10 . . . . .1K 79
　SE5 .2B 120
Knebworth Av. E17 . . . . .1C 50
Knebworth Cl. EN5: New Bar 4E 20
Knebworth Ho. SW8 . . . . .2H 119
Knebworth Rd. N16 . . . . .4E 66
Knee Hill SE2 . . . . .4C 108
Knee Hill Cres. SE2 . . . . .4C 108
Kneller Gdns. TW7: Isle 6H 113
Kneller Ho. UB5: N'olt 2B 76
　　　　　　　　　　(off Academy Gdns.)
Kneller Rd. KT3: N Mald 7A 152
　SE4 .4A 122
　TW2: Whitt 6G 113
Knevett Ter. TW3: Houn 4E 112
Knight Cl. RM8: Dag 2C 72
Knight Ct. E4 . . . . .1K 35
　　　　　　　　　　(off The Ridgeway)
　N15 . . . . .5E 48
Knighten St. E1 . . . . .1H 103
Knighthead Point E14 . . . . .2C 104
Knight Ho. SE17 . . . . .4E 102
　　　　　　　　　　(off Tatum St.)
Knightland Rd. E5 . . . . .2H 67
Knightleas Ct. NW2 . . . . .6E 62
Knightleys Ct. E10 . . . . .1A 68
　　　　　　　　　　(off Wellington Rd.)
Knightley Wlk. SW18 . . . . .4J 117
Knighton Cl. CR2: S Croy 7B 168
　IG8: Wfd G 4E 36
　RM7: Rom 6K 55
Knighton Dr. IG8: Wfd G 4E 36
Knighton Grn. IG9: Buck H 2E 36
Knighton La. IG9: Buck H 2E 36
Knighton Pk. Rd. SE26 . . . . .5K 139
Knighton Pl. IG9: Buck H 2E 36
　　　　　　　　　　(off Knighton La.)
Knighton Rd. E7 . . . . .3J 69
　RM7: Rom 6J 55
Knightrider Ct. EC4 . . . . .2B 14
Knightrider St. EC4 . . . . . .2B 14 (6B 84)
Knights Arc. SW1 . . . . .7E 10
Knights Av. W5 . . . . .2E 96
KNIGHTSBRIDGE 7D 10 (2C 100)
Knightsbridge SW1 . . . . . . .7D 10 (2D 100)
　SW7 . . . . .7D 10 (2D 100)
Knightsbridge Apartments, The
　SW7 . . . . .7E 10
　　　　　　　　　　(off Knightsbridge)

Knightsbridge Ct. BR2: Brom 6C 160
　　　　　　　　　　(off Wells Vw. Dr.)
　SW1 . . . . .7F 11
Knightsbridge Gdns. RM7: Rom 5K 55
Knightsbridge Grn. SW1 . . .7E 10 (2D 100)
　　　　　　　　　　(not continuous)
Knights Cl. E9 . . . . .5D 67
　KT8: W Mole 5D 148
Knightscote Cl. UB9: Hare 2A 38
Knights Ct. BR1: Brom 3H 141
　KT1: King T 3E 150
　RM6: Chad H 6E 54
　　　　　　　　　　(off High Rd.)
　WD23: B Hea 1C 26
Knights Hill SE27 . . . . .5B 138
Knight's Hill Sq. SE27 . . . . .4B 138
Knights Ho. SW8 . . . . .7J 101
　　　　　　　　　　(off Sth. Lambeth Rd.)
　SW10 . . . . .7A 100
　　　　　　　　　　(off Hortensia Rd.)
　W14 . . . . .5H 99
　　　　　　　　　　(off Baron's Ct. Rd.)
Knight's Pk. KT1: King T 3E 150
Knight's Pl. TW2: Twick 1J 131
Knights Rd. E16 . . . . .2J 105
　HA7: Stan 4H 27
Knights Twr. SE8 . . . . .5C 104
Knight's Wlk. SE11 . . . . . .4K 19 (4B 102)
　　　　　　　　　　(not continuous)
Knightswood Cl. HA8: Edg 2D 28
Knightswood Ct. N6 . . . . .7H 47
Knightswood Ho. N12 . . . . .6F 31
Knightwood Cres. KT3: N Mald 6A 152
Knivet Rd. SW6 . . . . .6J 99
Knockholt Rd. SE9 . . . . .5B 124
Knole, The SE9 . . . . .4E 142
Knole Cl. CR0: C'don 6J 157
Knole Ct. UB5: N'olt 3A 76
　　　　　　　　　　(off Broomcroft Av.)
Knole Ga. DA15: Sidc 3J 143
Knoll, The BR2: Hayes 2J 171
　BR3: Beck 1D 158
　HA1: Harr 1K 59
　W13 . . . . .5C 78
Knoll Ct. SE19 . . . . .5F 139
　　　　　　　　　　(off Farquhar Rd.)
Knoll Cres. HA6: Nwood 2G 39
　　　　　　　　　　(not continuous)
Knoll Dr. N14 . . . . .7K 21
Knoll Ho. NW8 . . . . .2A 82
　　　　　　　　　　(off Carlton Hill)
Knollmead KT5: Surb 1J 163
Knoll Ri. BR6: Orp 1K 173
Knoll Rd. DA5: Bexl 7G 127
　DA14: Sidc 5B 144
　SW18 . . . . .5A 118
Knolls Cl. KT4: Wor Pk 3D 164
Knollys Cl. SW16 . . . . .3A 138
Knolly's Ho. WC1 . . . . .3E 6
　　　　　　　　　　(off Tavistock Pl.)
Knollys Rd. SW16 . . . . .3K 137
Knot Ho. SE1 . . . . .5J 15
　　　　　　　　　　(off Brewery Sq.)
Knotley Way BR4: W W'ck 2D 170
Knottisford St. E2 . . . . .3J 85
Knotts Grn. M. E10 . . . . .6D 50
Knotts Grn. Rd. E10 . . . . .6D 50
Knowlden Ho. E1 . . . . .7J 85
　　　　　　　　　　(off Cable St.)
Knowle Av. DA7: Bex 7E 108
Knowle Cl. SW9 . . . . .3A 120
Knowledge St. SW16 . . . . .3K 155
Knowle Rd.
　BR2: Brom 2D 172
　TW2: Twick 1J 131
Knowles Cl. UB7: Yiew 1A 92
Knowles Ct. HA1: Harr 6K 41
Knowles Hill Cres. SE13 . . . . .5F 123
Knowles Ho. SW18 . . . . .6K 117
　　　　　　　　　　(off Neville Gill Cl.)
Knowles Wlk. SW4 . . . . .3G 119

Knowles Wharf NW1 . . . . .1G 83
　　　　　　　　　　(off St Pancras Way)
Knowlton Grn. BR2: Brom 5H 159
Knowlton Ho. SW9 . . . . .1A 120
　　　　　　　　　　(off Cowley Rd.)
Knowl Wood La. BR6: Farnb 2E 172
Knowsley Av. UB1: S'hall 1F 95
Knowsley Rd. SW11 . . . . .2D 118
Knox Ct. SW4 . . . . .2J 119
Knox Rd. E7 . . . . .6H 69
Knox St. W1 . . . . .5E 4 (5D 82)
Knoyle Ho. W14 . . . . .3G 99
　　　　　　　　　　(off Russell Rd.)
Knoyle St. SE14 . . . . .6A 104
Koblenz Ho. N8 . . . . .3J 47
　　　　　　　　　　(off Newland Rd.)
Kohat Rd. SW19 . . . . .5K 135
Korda Cl. TW17: Shep 3B 146
Kossuth St. SE10 . . . . .5G 105
Kotata Ho. E20 . . . . .6E 68
　　　　　　　　　　(off Ravens Wlk.)
Kotree Way SE1 . . . . .4G 103
Kramer M. SW5 . . . . .5J 99
Kreedman Wlk. E8 . . . . .5G 67
Kreisel Wlk. TW9: Kew 6F 97
Kristina Ct. SM2: Sutt 6J 165
　　　　　　　　　　(off Overton Rd.)
Krithia Rd. RM9: Dag 1B 90
Krupnik Pl. EC2 . . . . .3H 9
　　　　　　　　　(shown as Curtain Pl.)
Kuala Gdns. SW16 . . . . .1K 155
Kubrick Bus. Est. E7 . . . . .4K 69
　　　　　　　　　　(off Station App.)
Kuhn Way E7 . . . . .5J 69
Kurdish Mus. 4C 98
Kwame Ho. E16 . . . . .7F 89
　　　　　　　　　　(off University Way)
Kwesi M. SE27 . . . . .5A 138
Kydbrook Cl. BR5: Pet W 7G 161
Kyle Ho. NW6 . . . . .1J 81
Kylemore Cl. E6 . . . . .2B 88
Kylemore Rd. NW6 . . . . .7J 63
Kylestrome Ho. SW1 . . . . .4H 17
　　　　　　　　　　(off Cundy St.)
Kymberley Rd. HA1: Harr 6J 41
Kymes Ct. HA2: Harr 2H 59
Kynance Gdns. HA7: Stan 1C 42
Kynance M. SW7 . . . . .3K 99
Kynance Pl. SW7 . . . . .3A 100
Kynaston Av. CR7: Thor H 5C 156
　N16 . . . . .3F 67
Kynaston Cl. HA3: Hrw W 7C 26
Kynaston Cres. CR7: Thor H 5C 156
Kynaston Rd. BR1: Brom 5J 141
　CR7: Thor H 5C 156
　EN2: Enf 1J 23
　N16 . . . . .3E 66
Kynaston Wood HA3: Hrw W 7C 26
Kynersley Cl. SM5: Cars 3D 166
Kynoch Rd. N18 . . . . .4D 34
Kyrle Rd. SW11 . . . . .6E 118
Kyverdale Rd. N16 . . . . .7F 49

L

Laban Cen. 6D 104
Laban Wlk. SE8 . . . . .6D 104
　　　　　　　　　　(off Copperas St.)
Laboratory Spa and Health Club, The
　. . . . . .3G 47
Labrun Sq. SE3 . . . . .3K 123
Laburnham Ct. EN5: Barn 3C 20
Laburnum Av. N9 . . . . .2A 34
　N17 . . . . .7J 33
　SM1: Sutt 3C 166
　UB7: Yiew 7B 74
Laburnum Cl. E4 . . . . .6G 35
　HA0: Wemb 1G 79
　N11 . . . . .6K 31
　SE15 .7J 103

Laburnum Ct.—Lambrook Ho.

Laburnum Ct. E2 . . . . 1F 85
HA1: Harr 5F 41
HA7: Stan 4H 27
SE16 . . . . 2J 103
(off Albion St.)
Laburnum Cres. TW16: Sun 1K 147
Laburnum Gdns. CR0: C'don 7K 157
N21 . . . . 2H 33
Laburnum Gro. HA4: Ruis 6F 39
KT3: N Mald 2K 151
N21 . . . . 2H 33
NW9 . . . . 7J 43
TW3: Houn 4D 112
UB1: S'hall 4D 76
Laburnum Ho. BR2: Brom 1F 159
RM10: Dag 2G 73
Laburnum Lodge N3 . . . . 2H 45
Laburnum Pl. SE9 . . . . 5E 124
Laburnum Rd. CR4: Mitc 2E 154
SW19 . . . . 7A 136
UB3: Harl 4H 93
Laburnums, The E6 . . . . 4C 88
Laburnum St. E2 . . . . 1F 85
Laburnum Way BR2: Brom 7E 160
TW19: Stanw 1B 128
Labyrinth Twr. *E8 . . . . 6F 67*
(off Dalston Sq.)
Lacebark Cl. DA15: Sidc 7K 125
Lace Ct. *E1 . . . . 5K 85*
(off Master's St.)
Lacewing Cl. E13 . . . . 3J 87
Lacey Cl. N9 . . . . 2B 34
Lacey Dr. HA8: Edg 4K 27
RM8: Dag 3C 72
TW12: Hamp 1D 148
Lacey M. E3 . . . . 2C 86
Lacine Ct. *SE16 . . . . 2K 103*
(off Christopher Cl.)
Lackington St. EC2 . . . . 5F 9 (5D 84)
Lackland Ho. *SE1 . . . . 5F 103*
(off Rowcross St.)
Lacland Ho. *SW10 . . . . 7B 100*
(off Worlds End Est.)
Lacock Cl. SW19 . . . . 6A 136
Lacock Ct. W13 . . . . 1A 96
Lacon Ho. *WC1 . . . . 5G 7*
(off Theobald's Rd.)
Lacon Rd. SE22 . . . . 4G 121
Lacrosse Way SW16 . . . . 1H 155
Lacy Rd. SW15 . . . . 4F 117
Ladas Rd. SE27 . . . . 4C 138
Ladbroke Ct. E1 . . . . 6F 85
Ladbroke Cres. W11 . . . . 6G 81
Ladbroke Gdns. W11 . . . . 7H 81
Ladbroke Gro. W10 . . . . 4F 81
W11 . . . . 4F 81
Ladbroke Gro. Ho. *W11 . . . . 7H 81*
(off Ladbroke Gro.)
Ladbroke Grove Memorial *4F 81*
(off Canal Way)
Ladbroke M. W11 . . . . 1G 99
Ladbroke Rd. EN1: Enf 6A 24
W11 . . . . 1H 99
Ladbroke Sq. W11 . . . . 7H 81
Ladbroke Ter. W11 . . . . 7H 81
Ladbroke Wlk. W11 . . . . 1H 99
Ladbrook Cl. BR1: Brom 6G 141
HA5: Pinn 5D 40
Ladbrooke Cres. DA14: Sidc 3D 144
Ladbrook Rd. SE25 . . . . 4D 156
Ladderstile Ride KT2: King T 5H 133
Ladderswood Way N11 . . . . 5B 32
Ladlands SE22 . . . . 7G 121
Lady Anne Ct. *E18 . . . . 1J 51*
(off Queen Mary Av.)
Lady Aylesford Av. HA7: Stan 5F 27
Lady Booth Rd. KT1: King T 2E 150
Lady Craig Ct. UB8: Hil 5D 74
Ladycroft Gdns. BR6: Farnb 5G 173
Ladycroft Rd. SE13 . . . . 3D 122
Ladycroft Wlk. HA7: Stan 1D 42
Ladycroft Way BR6: Farnb 5G 173
Lady Dock Path SE16 . . . . 2A 104
Lady Elizabeth Ho. SW14 . . . . 3J 115
Ladyfern Ho. *E3 . . . . 5C 86*
(off Gail St.)
Lady Florence Courtyard *SE8 . . . . 7C 104*
(off Reginald Sq.)
Lady Forsdyke Way KT19: Eps 7G 163
Ladygate La. HA4: Ruis 6D 38
Lady Harewood Way KT19: Eps 7G 163
Lady Hay KT4: Wor Pk 2B 164
Lady Jane Ct. *KT2: King T 2F 151*
(off Cambridge Rd.)
Lady Margaret Ho. *SE17 . . . . 6D 102*
(off Queen's Row)
Lady Margaret Rd. N19 . . . . 5G 65
NW5 . . . . 5G 65
UB1: S'hall 7D 76
Lady May Ho. *SE5 . . . . 7C 102*
(off Pitman St.)
Lady Micos Almshouses *E1 . . . . 6J 85*
(off Aylward St.)
Lady Sarah Cohen Ho. *N11 . . . . 6J 31*
(off Asher Loftus Way)
Lady Shaw Ct. N13 . . . . 2E 32
Ladyship Ter. SE22 . . . . 7G 121
Ladysmith Av. E6 . . . . 2C 88
IG2: Ilf 7J 53
Ladysmith Cl. NW7 . . . . 7H 29
Ladysmith Rd. E16 . . . . 3H 87
EN1: Enf 3K 23
(not continuous)
HA3: W'stone 2J 41
N17 . . . . 2G 49
N18 . . . . 5C 34
SE9 . . . . 6E 124
Lady Somerset Rd. NW5 . . . . 4F 65
LADYWELL 5D 122
Ladywell Arena (Running Track) 6C 122
Ladywell Cl. SE4 . . . . 5C 122
Ladywell Hgts. SE4 . . . . 6B 122
Ladywell Rd. SE13 . . . . 5C 122
Ladywell St. E15 . . . . 1H 87
Ladywood Av. BR5: Pet W 5J 161
Ladywood Rd. KT6: Surb 2G 163
LA Fitness
Bayswater 7K 81
(off Moscow Pl.)
Bloomsbury 5G 7
(off Theobald's Rd.)
Croydon 7A 168
Edgware 6B 28
Epsom 4K 163
Finchley 3K 45
Golders Green 7H 45
Gospel Oak 4F 65
Isleworth 3B 114
(off Swan St.)
Leadenhall 1H 15
(off Leadenhall St.)
London Wall 6E 8
Marylebone, Balcombe St.
. . . . 5E 4 (5D 82)
Marylebone, Hallam St. 5K 5
(off Hallam St.)
Muswell Hill 4F 47
(off Hillfield Pk.)
New Barnet 4G 21
Northolt 1E 76
Northwood 2H 39
Novello 2G 13
Orpington 7D 144
Piccadilly 3C 12
(off Regent St.)
St Pauls 6C 8
(off Little Britain)
South Kensington 3C 16 (4C 100)
Southgate 1C 32
Sydenham 4J 139
West India Quay 7C 86
Lafone Av. TW13: Felt 2A 130
Lafone St. SE1 . . . . 6J 15 (2F 103)
Lagado M. SE16 . . . . 1K 103
Lagare Apartments *SE1 . . . . 6B 14*
(off Surrey Row)
Lagonda Ho. *E3 . . . . 4C 86*
(off Tidworth Rd.)
Lagonier Ho. *EC1 . . . . 2D 8*
(off Ironmonger Row)
Laidlaw Dr. N21 . . . . 5E 22
Laing Dean UB5: N'olt 1A 76
Laing Ho. SE5 . . . . 7C 102
Laings Av. CR4: Mitc 2D 154
Lainlock Pl. TW3: Houn 1F 113
Lainson St. SW18 . . . . 7J 117
Lairdale Cl. SE21 . . . . 1C 138
Laird Ho. *SE5 . . . . 7C 102*
(off Redcar St.)
Lairs Cl. N7 . . . . 5J 65
Lait Ho. BR3: Beck 1D 158
Laitwood Rd. SW12 . . . . 1F 137
Lakanal *SE5 . . . . 1E 120*
(off Sceaux Gdns.)
Lake, The WD23: B Hea 1C 26
Lake Av. BR1: Brom 6J 141
Lake Bus. Cen. N17 . . . . 7B 34
Lake Cl. RM8: Dag 3D 72
SW19 . . . . 5H 135
Lakedale Ct. IG11: Bark 4B 90
Lakedale Rd. SE18 . . . . 6J 107
Lake Dr. WD23: B Hea 2C 26
Lake Farm Country Pk. 1G 93
Lakefield Cl. SE20 . . . . 7H 139
Lakefield Rd. N22 . . . . 2B 48
Lake Gdns. RM10: Dag 5G 73
SM6: Wall 3F 167
TW10: Ham 2B 132
Lakehall Gdns. CR7: Thor H 5B 156
Lakehall Rd. CR7: Thor H 5B 156
Lake Ho. *SE1 . . . . 7C 14*
(off Southwark Bri. Rd.)
Lake Ho. Rd. E11 . . . . 3J 69
Lakehurst Rd. KT19: Ewe 5A 164
Lakeland Cl. HA3: Hrw W 6C 26
Lakenham Pl. E3 . . . . 4B 86
Lakenheath N14 . . . . 5B 22
Laker Ct. SW4 . . . . 1J 119
Laker Ind. Est. BR3: Beck 5A 140
Lake Rd. CR0: C'don 2B 170
E10 . . . . 7D 50
RM6: Chad H 4D 54
RM9: Dag 3H 91
SW19 . . . . 5H 135
Laker Pl. SW15 . . . . 6G 117
Lakeside BR3: Beck 3D 158
EN2: Enf 4C 22
KT2: King T 7H 133
KT19: Ewe 6A 164
N3 . . . . 2K 45
SM6: Wall 4F 167
W13 . . . . 6C 78
Lakeside Av. IG4: Ilf 4B 52
SE28 . . . . 1A 108
Lakeside Cl. DA15: Sidc 5C 126
HA4: Ruis 4F 39
SE25 . . . . 2G 157
Lakeside Ct. N4 . . . . 2C 66
Lakeside Cres. EN4: E Barn 5J 21
Lakeside Dr. BR2: Brom 3C 172
NW10 . . . . 3F 79
Lakeside Ind. Est. SL3: Coln 2B 174
Lakeside Rd. N13 . . . . 4E 32
SL0: Rich P 3A 174
SL3: Coln, Rich P 3A 174
W14 . . . . 3F 99
Lakeside Ter. EC2 . . . . 5D 8
Lakeside Way HA9: Wemb 4G 61
Lakes Rd. BR2: Kes 5A 172
Lakeswood Rd. BR5: Pet W 6F 161
Lake Vw. HA8: Edg 5A 28
Lake Vw. Ct. *SW1 . . . . 1K 17*
(off Bressenden Pl.)
Lakeview Ct. SE28 . . . . 7B
Lake Vw. Est. E3 . . . . 2A
Lakeview Rd. DA16: Well 4B 1
SE27 . . . . 5A 1
Lake Vw. Ter. *N18 . . . . 4A*
(off Sweet Briar Wl
Lakin Cl. SM5: Cars 4E 1
Lakis Cl. NW3 . . . . 4A
Laleham Av. NW7 . . . . 3E
Laleham Ct. SM1: Sutt 5A 1
Laleham Ho. *E2 . . . . 3J*
(off Camlet S
Laleham Rd. SE6 . . . . 7E 1
TW17: Shep 4B 1
Lalor St. SW6 . . . . 2G 1
Lambarde Av. SE9 . . . . 4E 1
Lambard Ho. *SE10 . . . . 7E 1*
(off Langdale R
Lamb Cl. UB5: N'olt 3C
Lamb Ct. *E14 . . . . 7A*
(off Narrow S
Lamberhurst Ho. SE15 . . . . 6J 1
Lamberhurst Rd. RM8: Dag 1F
SE27 . . . . 4A 1
Lambert Av. TW9: Rich 3G 1
Lambert Ct. *DA8: Erith 6J 1*
(off Park Cres
Lambert Jones M. EC2 . . . . 5C
Lambert Lodge *TW8: Bford 5D*
(off Layton R
Lambert Rd. E16 . . . . 6K
N12 . . . . 5G 3
SW2 . . . . 5J 1
Lambert's Pl. CR0: C'don 1D 1
Lamberts Rd. KT5: Surb 5E 1
Lambert St. N1 . . . . 7A
Lambert Wlk. HA9: Wemb 3E
Lambert Way N12 . . . . 5F
LAMBETH 3G 19 (3K 10
Lambeth Bri. SW1 . . . . 3F 19 (4J 10
Lambeth Crematorium SW17 . . . . 4A 1
Lambeth High St. SE1 . . . . 4G 19 (4K 10
Lambeth Hill EC4 . . . . 2C 14 (7C 8
Lambeth Palace 2G 19 (3K 10
Lambeth Pal. Rd. SE1 . . . . 2G 19 (3K 10
Lambeth Rd. CR0: C'don 7A 1
SE1 . . . . 3G 19 (4K 10
SE11 . . . . 3G 19 (3A 10
Lambeth Towers SE11 . . . . 2J
Lambeth Wlk. SE11 . . . . 4H 19 (4K 10
(not continuou
Lambfold Ho. *N7 . . . . 6J*
(off North R
Lamb Ho. *SE5 . . . . 7C 1*
(off Elmington Es
SE10 . . . . 6E 1
(off Haddo S
Lambkins M. E17 . . . . 4E 5
Lamb La. E8 . . . . 7H
Lamble St. NW5 . . . . 5E
Lambley Rd. RM9: Dag 6B
Lambolle Pl. NW3 . . . . 6C
Lambolle Rd. NW3 . . . . 6C 6
Lambourn Cl. CR2: S Croy 7B 16
NW5 . . . . 4G 6
W7 . . . . 2K 9
Lambourne Av. SW19 . . . . 4H 13
Lambourne Ct. IG8: Wfd G 7F 3
Lambourne Gdns. E4 . . . . 2H 3
EN1: Enf 2A 2
IG11: Bark 7K
Lambourne Gro. SE16 . . . . 5K 10
Lambourne Ho. *NW8 . . . . 5B*
(off Broadley St
Lambourne Pl. SE3 . . . . 1K 12
Lambourne Rd. E11 . . . . 7E 5
IG3: Ilf 2J 7
IG11: Bark 7J 7
Lambourn Gro. KT1: King T 2H 15
Lambourn Rd. SW4 . . . . 3F 11
Lambrook Ho. SE15 . . . . 1G 12

316 A-Z London

Lambrook Ter. SW6 ....1G 117
Lamb's Bldgs. EC1 ....4E 8 (4D 84)
Lamb's Cl. N9 ....2B 34
Lamb's Conduit Pas. WC1 .....5G 7 (5K 83)
Lamb's Conduit St. WC1 ......4G 7 (4K 83)
(not continuous)
Lambscroft Av. SE9 ....3A 142
Lambs Mdw. IG8: Wfd G 2B 52
Lamb's M. N1 ....1B 84
Lambs Pas. EC1 ....5E 8 (4D 84)
Lambs Ter. N9 ....2J 33
Lamb St. E1 ....5J 9 (5F 85)
Lamb's Wlk. EN2: Enf 2H 23
Lambton M. N19 ....1J 65
(off Lambton Rd.)
Lambton Pl. W11 ....7H 81
Lambton Rd. N19 ....1J 65
SW20 ....1E 152
Lamb Wlk. SE1 ....7G 15 (2E 102)
LAMDA 5F 99
Lamerock Rd.
BR1: Brom 4H 141
Lamerton Rd. IG6: Ilf 2F 53
Lamerton St. SE8 ....6C 104
Lamford Cl. N17 ....7J 33
Lamington St. W6 ....4D 98
Lamlash St. SE11 ....4B 102
Lamley Ho. SE10 ....7D 104
(off Ashburnham Pl.)
Lammas Av. CR4: Mitc 2E 154
Lammas Grn. SE26 ....3H 139
Lammas Pk. Gdns. W5 ....1C 96
Lammas Pk. Rd. W5 ....2D 96
Lammas Rd. E9 ....7K 67
E10 ....2A 68
TW10: Ham 4C 132
Lammermoor Rd. SW12 ....7F 119
Lamont Rd. SW10 ....7A 16 (6B 100)
Lamont Rd. Pas. SW10 ....7A 16
LAMORBEY 1K 143
Lamorbey Cl. DA15: Sidc 1K 143
Lamorna Cl. BR6: Orp 7K 161
E17 ....2E 50
Lamorna Gro. HA7: Stan 1D 42
Lampard Gro. N16 ....1F 67
Lampern Sq. E2 ....3G 85
Lampeter Cl. NW9 ....6A 44
Lampeter Sq. W6 ....6G 99
Lamplighter Cl. E1 ....4J 85
Lampmead Rd. SE12 ....5H 123
Lamp Office Ct. WC1 ....4G 7
Lampton Ct. SE18 ....4D 106
LAMPTON 1F 113
Lampton Av. TW3: Houn 1F 113
Lampton Ct. TW3: Houn 1F 113
Lampton Ho. Cl. SW19 ....4F 135
Lampton Pk. Rd. TW3: Houn 2F 113
Lampton Rd. TW3: Houn 2F 113
Lampton Sports Cen. 2E 112
Lamwaren Cl. TW7: Isle 2K 113
Lanacre Av. NW9 ....1K 43
Lanadron Cl. TW7: Isle 2K 113
Lanain Ct. SE12 ....7H 123
Lanark Cl. W5 ....5C 78
Lanark Ct. UB5: N'olt 5E 58
(off Newmarket Av.)
Lanark Ho. SE1 ....5G 103
(off Old Kent Rd.)
Lanark Mans. W9 ....4A 82
(off Lanark Rd.)
W12 ....2E 98
(off Pennard Rd.)
Lanark M. W9 ....3A 82
Lanark Pl. W9 ....3A 4 (4A 82)
Lanark Rd. W9 ....3K 81
Lanark Sq. E14 ....3D 104
Lanata Wlk. UB4: Yead 4B 76
(off Alba Cl.)
Lanbury Rd. SE15 ....4K 121
Lancashire Ct. W1 ....2K 11 (7F 83)
Lancaster Av. CR4: Mitc 5J 155
E18 ....4K 51

Lancaster Av. EN4: Had W 1F 21
IG11: Bark 7J 71
SE27 ....2B 138
SW19 ....5F 135
Lancaster Cl. BR2: Brom 4H 159
KT2: King T 5D 132
N1 ....7E 66
N17 ....7B 34
NW9 ....7G 29
TW15: Ashf 4A 128
TW19: Stanw 6A 110
W2 ....7K 81
(off St Petersburgh Pl.)
Lancaster Cotts. TW10: Rich 6E 114
Lancaster Ct. KT12: Walt T 7J 147
SE27 ....2B 138
SM2: Sutt 7J 165
(off Mulgrave Rd.)
SW6 ....7H 99
TW19: Stanw 1A 128
W2 ....2A 10
(off Lancaster Ga.)
Lancaster Dr. E14 ....1E 104
NW3 ....6C 64
Lancaster Gdns. BR1: Brom 5C 160
KT2: King T 5D 132
SW19 ....5G 135
W13 ....2B 96
Lancaster Ga. W2 ....2A 10 (7A 82)
Lancaster Gro. NW3 ....6B 64
Lancaster Hall E16 ....1J 105
(off Wesley Av.)
Lancaster House 6A 12
Lancaster Ho. E11 ....2H 69
EN2: Enf 1J 23
RM8: Dag 4B 72
TW7: Isle 7K 95
Lancaster Lodge W11 ....6G 81
(off Lancaster Rd.)
Lancaster M. SW18 ....5K 117
TW10: Rich 6E 114
W2 ....2A 10 (7A 82)
Lancaster Pk. TW10: Rich 5E 114
Lancaster Pl. IG1: Ilf 5G 71
SW19 ....5F 135
TW1: Twick 6A 114
TW4: Houn 2A 112
WC2 ....2J 13 (7K 83)
Lancaster Rd. E7 ....7J 69
E11 ....2G 69
E17 ....2K 49
EN2: Enf 1J 23
EN4: E Barn 5G 21
HA2: Harr 5E 40
N4 ....7K 47
N11 ....6C 32
N18 ....5A 34
NW10 ....5C 62
SE25 ....2F 157
SW19 ....5F 135
UB1: S'hall 7C 76
UB5: N'olt 6G 59
W11 ....6G 81
Lancaster Rd. Ind. Est. EN4: E Barn ...5G 21
Lancaster Stables NW3 ....6C 64
Lancaster St. SE1 ....7A 14 (2B 102)
Lancaster Ter. W2 ....2A 10 (7B 82)
Lancaster Wlk. UB3: Hayes 6E 74
W2 ....3A 10 (1A 100)
Lancaster Way KT4: Wor Pk 7D 152
Lancastrian Rd. SM6: Wall 7J 167
Lancefield Ho. SE15 ....4H 121
Lancefield St. W10 ....3H 81
Lancell St. N16 ....2F 67
Lancelot Av. HA0: Wemb 4D 60
Lancelot Cres. HA0: Wemb 4D 60
Lancelot Gdns. EN4: E Barn 7K 21
Lancelot Pl. SW7 ....7E 10 (2D 100)
Lancelot Rd. DA16: Well 4A 126
HA0: Wemb 4D 60
Lance Rd. HA1: Harr 7G 41

Lancer Sq. W8 ....2K 99
(off Kensington Chu. St.)
Lancey Cl. SE7 ....4C 106
Lanchester Ct. W2 ....1E 10
(off Seymour St.)
Lanchester Rd. N6 ....5D 46
Lanchester Way SE14 ....1J 121
Lancing Ho. CRO: C'don 4D 168
(off Coombe Rd.)
Lancing Rd. CRO: C'don 7K 155
IG2: Ilf 6H 53
TW13: Felt 2H 129
W13 ....7B 78
Lancing St. NW1 ....2C 6 (3H 83)
Lancresse Ct. N1 ....1E 84
(off De Beauvoir Est.)
Landale Ho. SE16 ....3J 103
(off Lower Rd.)
Landau Ct. CR2: S Croy 5C 168
(off Warham Rd.)
Landcroft Rd. SE22 ....5F 121
Landells Rd. SE22 ....6F 121
Landford Rd. SW15 ....3E 116
Landgrove Rd. SW19 ....5J 135
Landin Ho. E14 ....6C 86
(off Thomas Rd.)
Landleys Fld. N7 ....5H 65
(off Long Mdw.)
Landmann Ho. SE16 ....4H 103
(off Rennie Est.)
Landmann Way SE14 ....5K 103
Landmark Arts Cen. 5B 132
Landmark Commercial Cen. N18 ...6K 33
Landmark East Twr. E14 ....2C 104
(off Marsh Wall)
Landmark Hgts. E5 ....4A 68
Landmark Ho. W6 ....5E 98
(off Hammersmith Bri. Rd.)
Landmark Sq. E14 ....2C 104
Landmark West Twr. E14 ....2C 104
(off Marsh Wall)
Landon Pl. SW1 ....1E 16 (3D 100)
Landon's Cl. E14 ....1E 104
Landon Wlk. E14 ....7D 86
Landon Way TW15: Ashf 6D 128
Landor Ho. SE5 ....7D 102
(off Elmington Est.)
W2 ....5J 81
(off Westbourne Pk. Rd.)
Landor Rd. SW9 ....3J 119
Landor Theatre 3J 119
Landor Wlk. W12 ....2C 98
Landra Gdns. N21 ....6G 23
Landrake NW1 ....1G 83
(off Plender St.)
Landridge Dr. EN1: Enf 1C 24
Landridge Rd. SW6 ....2H 117
Landrock Rd. N8 ....6J 47
Landscape Rd. IG8: Wfd G 7E 36
Landsdown Cl.
EN5: New Bar 4F 21
Landsdowne Ct. N19 ....1J 65
(off Fairbridge Rd.)
Landseer Av. E12 ....5E 70
Landseer Cl. HA8: Edg 2G 43
SW19 ....1A 154
Landseer Ct. UB4: Hayes 2F 75
Landseer Ho. NW8 ....3B 4
(off Frampton St.)
SW1 ....4D 18
(off Herrick St.)
SW11 ....1E 118
UB5: N'olt 2B 76
(off Parkfield Dr.)
Landseer Rd. EN1: Enf 5B 24
KT3: N Mald 7K 151
N19 ....3J 65
(not continuous)
SM1: Sutt 6J 165
Landstead Rd. SE18 ....7H 107

Landulph Ho. SE11 ....5K 19
(off Kennings Way)
Landward Ct. W1 ....7D 4
(off Harrowby St.)
Lane, The NW8 ....2A 82
SE3 ....3J 123
Lane Cl. NW2 ....3D 62
Lane End DA7: Bex 3H 127
SW15 ....6F 117
Lane Gdns. WD23: B Hea 1D 26
Lane M. E12 ....3D 70
Lanercost Cl. SW2 ....2A 138
Lanercost Gdns. N14 ....7D 22
Lanercost Rd. SW2 ....2A 138
Lanesborough Ct. N1 ....1G 9
(off Fanshaw St.)
Lanesborough Pl. SW1 ....6H 11
Lanesborough Way SW17 ....3B 136
Laneside DA7: Chst 5F 143
HA8: Edg 5D 28
Laneside Av. RM8: Dag 7F 55
Laneway SW15 ....5D 116
Laney Ho. EC1 ....5J 7
(off Leather La.)
Lanfranc Cl. HA1: Harr 3K 59
Lanfranc Rd. E3 ....2A 86
Lanfrey Pl. W14 ....5H 99
Langbourne Av. N6 ....2E 64
Langbourne Ct. E17 ....6A 50
Langbourne Mans. N6 ....2E 64
Langbourne Pl. E14 ....5D 104
Langbourne Way KT10: Clay 6A 162
Langbrook Rd. SE3 ....3B 124
Langcroft Cl. SM5: Cars 3D 166
Langdale NW1 ....1A 6
(off Stanhope St.)
Langdale Av. CR4: Mitc 3D 154
Langdale Cl. BR6: Farnb 3F 173
RM8: Dag 1C 72
SE17 ....6C 102
SW14 ....4H 115
Langdale Cres. DA7: Bex 7G 109
Langdale Dr. UB4: Hayes 2G 75
Langdale Gdns. UB6: G'frd 3B 78
Langdale Ho. SW1 ....6A 18
(off Churchill Gdns.)
Langdale Pde. CR4: Mitc 3D 154
Langdale Rd. CR7: Thor H 4A 156
SE10 ....7E 104
Langdale St. E1 ....6H 85
Langdon Ct. EC1 ....1B 8
(off City Rd.)
NW10 ....1A 80
Langdon Cres. E6 ....2E 88
Langdon Dr. NW9 ....1J 61
Langdon Ho. E14 ....6E 86
(off Ida St.)
Langdon Pk. TW11: Tedd 7C 132
Langdon Pk. Rd. N6 ....7G 47
Langdon Pl. SW14 ....3J 115
Langdon Rd. BR2: Brom 3K 159
E6 ....1E 88
SM4: Mord 5A 154
Langdons Ct. UB2: S'hall 3E 94
Langdon Shaw
DA14: Sidc 5K 143
Langdon Wlk. SM4: Mord 5A 154
Langdon Way SE1 ....4G 103
Langford Cl. E8 ....5G 67
NW8 ....2A 82
W3 ....2H 97
Langford Ct. NW8 ....2A 82
(off Abbey Rd.)
Langford Cres. EN4: Cockf 4J 21
Langford Grn. SE5 ....3E 120
Langford Ho. SE8 ....6C 104
Langford M. N1 ....7A 66
SW11 ....2B 118
(off St John's Hill)
Langford Pl. DA14: Sidc 3A 144
NW8 ....2A 82

Langford Rd.—Lascelles Ho.

Langford Rd. EN4: Cockf 4J 21
IG8: Wfd G 6F 37
SW6 2K 117
Langfords IG9: Buck H 2G 37
Langham Cl. BR2: Brom 2C 172
N15 *3B 48*
(off Langham Rd.)
Langham Ct. HA4: Ruis 5K 57
NW4 5F 45
SW20 2E 152
Langham Dr. RM6: Chad H 6B 54
Langham Gdns. HA0: Wemb 2C 60
HA8: Edg 7D 28
N21 5F 23
TW10: Ham 4C 132
W13 7B 78
Langham Ho. Cl. TW10: Ham 4D 132
Langham Mans. *SW5* *5K 99*
(off Earl's Ct. Sq.)
Langham Pk. Pl. BR2: Brom 4H 159
Langham Pl. N15 3B 48
W1 6K 5 (5F 83)
W4 6A 98
Langham Rd. HA8: Edg 6D 28
N15 3B 48
SW20 1E 152
TW11: Tedd 5B 132
Langham St. W1 6K 5 (5F 83)
Langhedge Cl. N18 6A 34
Langhedge La. N18 6A 34
Langhedge La. Ind. Est. N18 6A 34
Langholm Cl. SW12 7H 119
Langholme WD23: Bush 1B 26
Langhorn Dr. TW2: Twick 7J 113
Langhorne Ct. *NW8* *7B 64*
(off Dorman Way)
Langhorne Rd. RM10: Dag 7G 73
Langhorne St. SE18 7D 106
Lang Ho. *SW8* *7J 101*
(off Hartington Rd.)
TW19: Stanw 1A 128
Langland Cres. HA7: Stan 2D 42
Langland Dr. HA5: Pinn 1C 40
Langland Gdns. CR0: C'don 2B 170
NW3 5K 63
Langland Ho. *SE5* *7D 102*
(off Edmund St.)
Langler Rd. NW10 2E 80
Langley Av. HA4: Ruis 2K 57
KT4: Wor Pk 1F 165
KT6: Surb 1D 162
Langley Ct. WC2 2E 12 (7J 83)
Langley Cres. E11 7A 52
HA8: Edg 3D 28
RM9: Dag 7C 72
UB3: Harl 7H 93
Langley Dr. E11 7K 51
W3 2H 97
Langley Gdns. BR2: Brom 4A 160
BR5: Pet W 6F 161
RM9: Dag 7D 72
Langley Gro. KT3: N Mald 2A 152
Langley Ho. *W2* *5J 81*
(off Alfred Rd.)
Langley La. SW8 7F 19 (6K 101)
Langley Mans. SW8 7F 19
Langley M. RM9: Dag 7D 72
Langley Pk. NW7 6F 29
Langley Pk. Golf Course 6F 159
Langley Pk. Rd. SM1: Sutt 5A 166
SM2: Sutt 5A 166
Langley Pk. Sports Cen. 6E 158
Langley Rd. BR3: Beck 4A 158
DA16: Well 6C 108
KT6: Surb 7E 150
SW19 1H 153
TW7: Isle 2K 113
Langley Row EN5: Barn 1C 20
Langley St. WC2 1E 12 (6J 83)
Langley Way BR4: W W'ck 1F 171
Langmead Dr. WD23: B Hea 1D 26
Langmead Ho. *E3* *3D 86*
(off Bruce Rd.)
Langmead St. SE27 4B 138
Langmore Ct. DA6: Bex 3D 126
Langmore Ho. *E1* *6G 85*
(off Stutfield St.)
Langport Ct. KT12: Walt T 7A 148
Langport Ho. SW9 2B 120
Langridge M. TW12: Hamp 6D 130
Langroyd Rd. SW17 2D 136
Langside Av. SW15 4C 116
Langside Cres. N14 3C 32
Langstone Way NW7 7A 30
Langston Hughes Cl. SE24 4B 120
Lang St. E1 4J 85
Langthorn Ct. EC2 7E 8 (6D 84)
Langthorne Ho. *E3* *3B 86*
(off Merchant St.)
UB3: Harl 4G 93
Langthorne Rd. E11 3E 68
(not continuous)
Langthorne St. SW6 7F 99
Langton Av. E6 3E 88
N20 7F 21
Langton Cl. WC1 3H 7 (4K 83)
Langton Ho. SE11 3H 19
Langton Pl. SW18 1J 135
Langton Ri. SE23 7H 121
Langton Rd. HA3: Hrw W 7B 26
KT8: W Mole 4G 149
NW2 3E 62
SW9 7B 102
Langton St. SW10 6A 100
Langton Way CR0: C'don 3E 168
SE3 1H 123
Langtry Ct. TW7: Isle 2K 113
Langtry Ho. *KT2: King T* *1G 151*
(off London Rd.)
Langtry Pl. SW6 6J 99
Langtry Rd. NW8 1K 81
UB5: N'olt 2B 76
Langtry Wlk. NW8 1K 81
Langwood Chase
TW11: Tedd 6C 132
Langworth Dr. UB4: Yead 6K 75
Lanhill Rd. W9 4J 81
Lanier Rd. SE13 6F 123
Lanigan Dr. TW3: Houn 5F 113
Lankaster Gdns. N2 1B 46
Lankers Dr. HA2: Harr 6D 40
Lankton Cl. BR3: Beck 1E 158
Lannock Rd. UB3: Hayes 1H 93
Lannoy Point *SW6* *7G 99*
(off Pellant Rd.)
Lannoy Rd. SE9 1G 143
Lanrick Rd. E14 6F 87
Lanridge Rd. SE2 3D 108
Lansbury Av. IG11: Bark 7A 72
N18 5J 33
RM6: Chad H 5E 54
TW14: Felt 6K 111
Lansbury Cl. NW10 5J 61
Lansbury Ct. *SE28* *7B 90*
(off Saunders Way)
Lansbury Dr. UB4: Hayes 2G 75
Lansbury Est. E14 6D 86
Lansbury Gdns. E14 6F 87
Lansbury Rd. EN3: Enf H 1E 24
Lansbury Way N18 5K 33
Lanscombe Wlk. SW8 1J 119
Lansdell Ho. SW2 6A 120
Lansdell Rd. CR4: Mitc 2E 154
Lansdowne Av. BR6: Farnb 1F 173
DA7: Bex 7D 108
Lansdowne Cl. KT6: Surb 2H 163
SW20 7F 135
TW1: Twick 1K 131
Lansdowne Ct. IG5: Ilf 3C 52
KT4: Wor Pk 2C 164
W11 *7G 81*
(off Lansdowne Ri.)
Lansdowne Cres. W11 7G 81
Lansdowne Dr. E8 6G 67
Lansdowne Gdns. SW8 1J 119
Lansdowne Grn. SW8 1J 119
Lansdowne Gro. NW10 4A 62
Lansdowne Hill SE27 3B 138
Lansdowne Ho. *W11* *1H 99*
(off Ladbroke Rd.)
Lansdowne La. SE7 6B 106
Lansdowne M. SE7 5B 106
W11 1H 99
Lansdowne Pl. SE1 3D 102
SE19 7F 139
Lansdowne Ri. W11 7G 81
Lansdowne Rd. BR1: Brom 7J 141
CR0: C'don 2D 168
E4 2H 35
E11 2H 69
E17 6C 50
E18 3J 51
HA1: Harr 7J 41
HA7: Stan 6H 27
IG3: Ilf 1K 71
KT19: Ewe 7J 163
N3 7D 30
N10 2G 47
N17 1F 49
SW20 7E 134
TW3: Houn 3F 113
UB8: Hil 6E 74
W11 7G 81
Lansdowne Row W1 4K 11 (1F 101)
Lansdowne Ter. WC1 4F 7 (4J 83)
Lansdowne Wlk. W11 1H 99
Lansdowne Way SW8 1H 119
Lansdowne Wood Cl. SE27 3B 138
Lansdowne Workshops SE7 5A 106
Lansdown Rd. DA14: Sidc 3B 144
E7 7A 70
Lansfield Av. N18 4B 34
Lanson Apartments SW8 7F 101
Lantern *SE1* *6C 14*
(off Lant St.)
Lantern Cl. BR6: Farnb 4F 173
HA0: Wemb 5D 60
SW15 4C 116
Lantern Ho. *UB3: Harl* *3E 92*
(off Nine Acres Cl.)
Lanterns Way E14 2C 104
Lantern Way UB7: W Dray 2A 92
Lant Ho. *SE1* *7C 14*
(off Toulmin St.)
Lantry Ct. W3 1H 97
Lant St. SE1 6C 14 (2C 102)
Lanvanor Rd. SE15 2J 121
Lanyard Ho. SE8 4B 104
Lapford Cl. W9 4H 81
Lapis Cl. NW10 3G 79
Lapis M. E15 1E 86
Lapponum Wlk. UB4: Yead 4B 76
Lapse Wood Wlk. SE23 1H 139
Lapstone Gdns. HA3: Kenton 6C 42
Lapwing Ct. KT6: Surb 3G 163
SE1 *7D 14*
(off Swan St.)
Lapwing Ter. E7 5B 70
Lapwing Twr. *SE8* *6B 104*
(off Taylor Cl.)
Lapwing Way UB4: Yead 6B 76
Lapworth *N11* *4A 32*
(off Coppies Gro.)
Lapworth Ct. *W2* *5K 81*
(off Delamere Ter.)
Lara Cl. KT9: Chess 7E 162
SE13 6E 122
Larbert Rd. SW16 7G 137
Larch Av. W3 1A 98
Larch Cl.
E13 4K 87
N11 7K 31
N19 2G 65
Larch Cl. SE8 6B 10
SW12 2F 13
Larch Ct. *SE1* *7G 1*
(off Royal Oak Yd
W9 *5J 8*
(off Admiral Wlk.
Larch Cres. KT19: Ewe 6H 16
UB4: Yead 4A 7
Larch Dene BR6: Farnb 2E 17
Larch Dr. W4 5G 9
Larches, The N13 3H 3
UB10: Hil 3D 7
Larches Av. SW14 4K 11
Larch Grn. NW9 1A 4
Larch Gro. DA15: Sidc 1K 14
Larch Ho. BR2: Brom 1G 15
SE16 *2J 10*
(off Ainsty Est.
UB4: Yead 5A 7
W10 *4G 8*
(off Rowan Wlk.
Larch Rd. E10 2C 6
NW2 4E 6
Larch Tree Way CR0: C'don 3C 17
Larchvale Ct. SM2: Sutt 7K 16
Larch Way BR2: Brom 7E 16
Larchwood Ho. *UB7: W Dray* *2B 9*
(off Park Lodge Av
Larchwood Rd. SE9 2F 14
Larcombe Cl. CR0: C'don 4F 16
Larcombe Ct. *SM2: Sutt* *7K 16*
(off Worcester Ro
Larcom St. SE17 4C 10
Larden Rd. W3 1A 9
Largewood Av. KT6: Surb 2G 16
Larissa St. SE17 5D 10
Larkbere Rd. SE26 4A 14
Lark Ct. *NW9* *1A 4*
(off Lanacre Av
Larken Cl. WD23: Bush 1B 2
Larken Dr. WD23: Bush 1B 2
Larkfield Av. HA3: Kenton 3B 4
Larkfield Cl. BR2: Hayes 2H 17
Larkfield Rd. DA14: Sidc 3K 14
TW9: Rich 4E 11
Larkhall La. SW4 2H 11
Larkhall Ri. SW4 3G 11
(not continuous
Larkham Cl. TW13: Felt 3G 12
Lark Hill Ter. *SE18* *7E 10*
(off Prince Imperial Ro
Lark Row E2 1J 8
Larksfield Gro. EN1: Enf 1C 2
Larks Gro. IG11: Bark 7J 7
Larkshall Ct. RM7: Mawney 2J 5
Larkshall Cres. E4 4K 3
Larkshall Rd. E4 5K 3
Larkspur Cl. E6 5C 8
HA4: Ruis 7E 3
N17 7J 3
NW9 5H 4
Larkspur Gro. HA8: Edg 4D 2
Larkspur Lodge DA14: Sidc 3B 14
Larkspur Way KT19: Ewe 5J 16
Larkswood Ct. E4 5A 3
Larkswood Leisure Cen. 4K 3
Larkswood Ri. HA5: Eastc 4A 4
Larkswood Rd. E4 4H 3
Lark Way SM5: Cars 7C 15
Larkway Cl. NW9 4K 4
Larnach Rd. W6 6F 9
Larne Rd. HA4: Ruis 7H 3
Larpent Av. SW15 5E 11
Larson Wlk. E14 3C 10
Larwood Cl. UB6: G'frd 5H 5
Lascar Cl. TW3: Houn 3D 11
Lascar Wharf Bldg. *E14* *6A 8*
(off Parnham St
Lascelles Av. HA1: Harr 7H 4
Lascelles Cl. E11 2F 6
Lascelles Ho. NW1 4D

318 A-Z London

Lascotts Rd. N22 . . . . .6E **32**
Laseron Ho. N15 . . . . .4F **49**
    (off Tottenham Grn. E.)
Laserquest
    Sutton .5K **165**
Las Palmas Est. TW17: Shep 7E **146**
Lassa Rd. SE9 . . . . .5C **124**
Lassell St. SE10 . . . . .5F **105**
Lasseter Pl. SE3 . . . . .6H **105**
Latchett Rd. E18 . . . . .1K **51**
Latchingdon Ct. E17 . . . . .4K **49**
Latchingdon Gdns. IG8: Wfd G 6H **37**
Latchmere Cl. TW10: Ham 5E **132**
Latchmere La. KT2: King T 6F **133**
    TW10: Ham 6F **133**
Latchmere Leisure Cen. 2D **118**
Latchmere Pas. SW11 . . . . .2C **118**
Latchmere Pl. TW15: Ashf 2A **128**
Latchmere Rd. KT2: King T 7E **132**
    SW11 . . . . .2D **118**
Latchmere St. SW11 . . . . .2D **118**
Lateward Rd. TW8: Bford 6D **96**
Latham Cl. E6 . . . . .5C **88**
    TW1: Twick 7A **114**
Latham Cl. N11 . . . . .6D **32**
    (off Brownlow Rd.)
    SW5 . . . . .4J **99**
    (off W. Cromwell Rd.)
    UB5: N'olt 3B **76**
    (off Delta Gro.)
Latham Ho. E1 . . . . .6K **85**
    (off Chudleigh St.)
Latham Rd. DA6: Bex 5G **127**
    TW1: Twick 7K **113**
Latham's Way CRO: Wadd 1K **167**
Lathkill Cl. EN1: Enf 7B **24**
Lathkill Ct. BR3: Beck 1B **158**
Lathom Rd. E6 . . . . .7C **70**
Latimer Av. E6 . . . . .1D **88**
Latimer Cl. HA5: Pinn 1A **40**
    KT4: Wor Pk 4D **164**
Latimer Ct. BR2: Brom 4H **159**
    (off Durham Rd.)
Latimer Gdns. HA5: Pinn 1A **40**
Latimer Ho. E9 . . . . .6K **67**
    W11 . . . . .7H **81**
    (off Kensington Pk. Rd.)
Latimer Ind. Est. W10 . . . . .6E **80**
Latimer Pl. W10 . . . . .6E **80**
Latimer Rd. CRO: C'don 3B **168**
    E7 . . . . .4K **69**
    EN5: New Bar 3E **20**
    N15 . . . . .6E **48**
    SW19 . . . . .6K **135**
    TW11: Tedd 5K **131**
    W10 . . . . .5E **80**
    (not continuous)
Latitude Apartments CRO: C'don 3D **168**
    (off Fairfield Rd.)
Latitude Ct. E16 . . . . .7G **89**
Latitude Ho. NW1 . . . . .1F **83**
    (off Oval Rd.)
Latona Ct. SW9 . . . . .7A **102**
    (off Caldwell St.)
Latona Rd. SE15 . . . . .6G **103**
La Tourne Gdns. BR6: Farnb 3G **173**
Lattimer Pl. W4 . . . . .7A **98**
Latton Cl. KT12: Walt T 7C **148**
Latvia Ct. SE17 . . . . .5C **102**
    (off Macleod St.)
Latymer Ct. W6 . . . . .4F **99**
Latymer Gdns. N3 . . . . .2G **45**
Latymer Rd. N9 . . . . .1A **34**
Latymer Way N9 . . . . .2K **33**
Laubin Cl. TW1: Twick 4B **114**
Lauder Cl. UB5: N'olt 2B **76**
Lauder Ct. N14 . . . . .7D **22**
Lauderdale Dr. TW10: Ham 3D **132**
Lauderdale House 1F **65**
Lauderdale Ho. SW9 . . . . .1A **120**
    (off Gosling Way)

Lauderdale House Community Arts Cen.
    . . . . .1F **65**
Lauderdale Mans. W9 . . . . .3K **81**
    (off Lauderdale Rd.)
Lauderdale Pde. W9 . . . . .4K **81**
Lauderdale Pl. EC2 . . . . .5C **8**
    (off Beech St.)
Lauderdale Rd. W9 . . . . .3K **81**
Lauderdale Twr. EC2 . . . . .5C **8**
Laud St. CRO: C'don 3C **168**
    SE11 . . . . .5G **19** (5K **101**)
Laugan Wlk. SE17 . . . . .5C **102**
Laughton Rd. UB5: N'olt 1B **76**
Launcelot Rd. BR1: Brom 4J **141**
Launcelot St. SE1 . . . . . . .7J **13** (2A **102**)
Launceston Gdns. UB6: G'frd 1C **78**
Launceston Pl. W8 . . . . .3A **100**
Launceston Rd. UB6: G'frd 1C **78**
Launch St. E14 . . . . .3E **104**
Launders Ga. W3 . . . . .2H **97**
Laundress La. N16 . . . . .3G **67**
Laundry La. N1 . . . . .1C **84**
Laundry M. SE23 . . . . .7A **122**
Laundry Rd. W6 . . . . .6G **99**
Launton Dr. DA6: Bex 4D **126**
Laura Cl. E11 . . . . .5A **52**
    EN1: Enf 5K **23**
Lauradale Rd. N2 . . . . .4D **46**
Laura Pl. E5 . . . . .4J **67**
Laura Ter. N4 . . . . .2B **66**
Laurel Apartments SE17 . . . . . . .4E **102**
    (off Townsend St.)
Laurel Av. TW1: Twick 1K **131**
Laurel Bank N12 . . . . .4F **31**
Laurel Bank Gdns. SW6 . . . . .2H **117**
Laurel Bank Rd. EN2: Enf 1H **23**
Laurel Bank Vs. W7 . . . . .2J **95**
    (off Lwr. Boston Rd.)
Laurel Cl. DA14: Sidc 3A **144**
    N19 . . . . .2G **65**
    SW17 .5C **136**
Laurel Ct. CR2: S Croy 4E **168**
    (off South Pk. Hill Rd.)
    HA0: Wemb 2E **78**
    SE1 . . . . .3D **102**
    (off Garland Cl.)
Laurel Cres. CRO: C'don 3C **170**
    RM7: Rush G 1K **73**
Laurel Dr. N21 . . . . .7F **23**
Laurel Gdns. BR1: Brom 4C **160**
    E4 . . . . .7J **25**
    NW7 . . . . .3E **28**
    TW4: Houn 4C **112**
    TW15: Ashf 5E **128**
    W7 . . . . .1J **95**
Laurel Gro. SE20 . . . . .7J **139**
    SE26 .4K **139**
Laurel Ho. BR2: Brom 1G **159**
    E3 . . . . .1B **86**
    (off Hornbeam Sq.)
    SE8 . . . . .6B **104**
Laurel La. UB7: W Dray 4A **92**
Laurel Mnr. SM2: Sutt 7A **166**
Laurel M. SE5 . . . . .3C **120**
    (off Harbour Rd.)
Laurel Pk. HA3: Hrw W 7E **26**
Laurel Rd. SW13 . . . . .2C **116**
    SW20 . . . . .1D **152**
    TW12: Hamp H 5H **131**
Laurels, The BR1: Brom 1K **159**
    BR2: Brom 4J **159**
    IG9: Buck H 1F **37**
    NW10 . . . . .1D **80**
    SW9 .7B **102**
    (off Langton Rd.)
    WD23: B Hea 2D **26**
Laurel St. E8 . . . . .6F **67**
Laurel Vw. N12 . . . . .3E **30**
Laurel Way E18 . . . . .4H **51**
    N20 . . . . .3D **30**
Laurence Calvert Cl. IG11: Bark 2J **89**

Laurence Ct. E10 . . . . .7D **50**
    W11 . . . . .7G **81**
    (off Lansdowne Rd.)
Laurence M. W12 . . . . .2C **98**
Laurence Pountney Hill
    EC4 . . . . .2E **14** (7D **84**)
Laurence Pountney La. EC4 . . .2E **14** (7D **84**)
Laurence Rd. TW3: Houn 3G **113**
Laurie Gro. SE14 . . . . .1A **122**
Laurie Ho. SE1 . . . . .3B **102**
    (off St George's Rd.)
    W8 . . . . .1J **99**
    (off Airlie Gdns.)
Laurie Rd. W7 . . . . .5J **77**
Laurier Rd. CRO: C'don 7F **157**
    NW5 . . . . .3F **65**
Laurimel Cl. HA7: Stan 6G **27**
Laurino Pl. WD23: B Hea 2B **26**
Lauriston Ho. E9 . . . . .7J **67**
    (off Lauriston Rd.)
Lauriston Rd. E9 . . . . .7J **67**
    SW19 . . . . .6F **135**
Lausanne Rd. N8 . . . . .4A **48**
    SE15 .1J **121**
Laval Ho. TW8: Bford 5E **96**
    (off Ealing Rd.)
Lavell St. N16 . . . . .4D **66**
Lavender Av. CR4: Mitc 1C **154**
    KT4: Wor Pk 3E **164**
    NW9 . . . . .1J **61**
Lavender Cl. BR2: Brom 6C **160**
    E4 . . . . .4H **35**
    SM5: Cars 4F **167**
    SW3 . . . . .7B **16** (6B **100**)
Lavender Ct. KT8: W Mole 3F **149**
    SM2: Sutt 7A **166**
    TW14: Felt 6K **111**
Lavender Gdns. EN2: Enf 1G **23**
    HA3: Hrw W 6D **26**
    SW11 . . . . .4D **118**
Lavender Gro. CR4: Mitc 1C **154**
    E8 . . . . .7G **67**
Lavender Hill EN2: Enf 1F **23**
    SW11 . . . . .4C **118**
Lavender Ho. SE16 . . . . .1K **103**
    (off Rotherhithe St.)
    TW9: Kew 1H **115**
Lavender Pl. IG1: Ilf 5F **71**
Lavender Pond Nature Pk. 1A **104**
Lavender Ri. UB7: W Dray 2C **92**
Lavender Rd. CRO: C'don 6K **155**
    EN2: Enf 1J **23**
    KT19: Ewe 5H **163**
    SE16 .1A **104**
    SM1: Sutt 4B **166**
    SM5: Cars 4E **166**
    SW11 . . . . .3B **118**
    UB8: Hil 5B **74**
Lavender Sq. SW9 . . . . .1K **119**
    (off Printers Rd.)
Lavender St. E15 . . . . .6G **69**
Lavender Sweep SW11 . . . . .4D **118**
Lavender Ter. SW11 . . . . .3C **118**
Lavender Va. SM6: Wall 6H **167**
Lavender Wlk. CR4: Mitc 3E **154**
    SW11 . . . . .4D **118**
Lavender Way CRO: C'don 6K **157**
Lavendon Ho. NW8 . . . . .3D **4**
    (off Paveley St.)
Lavengro Rd. SE27 . . . . .2C **138**
Lavenham Rd. SW18 . . . . .2H **135**
Lavernock Rd. DA7: Bex 2G **127**
Lavers Rd. N16 . . . . .3E **66**
Laverstoke Gdns. SW15 . . . . .7B **116**
Laverton M. SW5 . . . . .4K **99**
Laverton Pl. SW5 . . . . .4K **99**
Lavette Ho. E3 . . . . .3C **86**
    (off Rainhill Way)
Lavidge Rd. SE9 . . . . .2C **142**
Lavina Gro. N1 . . . . .2K **83**
Lavington Cl. E9 . . . . .6B **68**

Lavington Rd. CRO: Bedd 3K **167**
    W13 . . . . .1B **96**
Lavington St. SE1 . . . . .5B **14** (1B **102**)
Lavisham Ho. BR1: Brom 5K **141**
Lawdons Gdns. CRO: Wadd 4B **168**
Lawes Ho. W10 . . . . .3H **81**
    (off Lancefield St.)
Lawes Way IG11: Bark 3K **89**
Lawford Rd. N1 . . . . .7E **66**
    NW5 . . . . .6G **65**
    W4 . . . . .7J **97**
Lawfords Wharf NW1 . . . . .7G **65**
    (off Lyme St.)
Law Ho. IG11: Bark 2A **90**
Lawless Ho. E14 . . . . .7E **86**
    (off Bazely St.)
Lawless St. E14 . . . . .7D **86**
Lawley Ho. TW1: Twick 6D **114**
Lawley Rd. N14 . . . . .7A **22**
Lawley St. E5 . . . . .4J **67**
Lawn, The UB2: S'hall 5E **94**
Lawn Cl. BR1: Brom 6K **141**
    HA4: Ruis 3H **57**
    KT3: N Mald 2A **152**
    N9 . . . . .7A **24**
Lawn Cres. TW9: Kew 2G **115**
Lawn Farm Gro. RM6: Chad H 4E **54**
Lawnfield Ct. NW6 . . . . .7F **63**
    (off Coverdale Rd.)
Lawn Gdns. W7 . . . . .1J **95**
Lawn Ho. Cl. E14 . . . . .2E **104**
Lawn La. SW8 . . . . .7F **19** (6K **101**)
Lawn Rd. BR3: Beck 7B **140**
    NW3 . . . . .5D **64**
Lawns, The DA14: Sidc 4B **144**
    E4 . . . . .5H **35**
    HA5: Hat E 7A **26**
    SE3 . . . . .3H **123**
    SE19 .1D **156**
    SM2: Cheam 7G **165**
    SW19 . . . . .5H **135**
Lawns Cl. HA9: Wemb 2F **61**
Lawnside SE3 . . . . .4H **123**
Lawns Way RM5: Col R 1J **55**
Lawnswood EN5: Barn 5B **20**
Lawn Ter. SE3 . . . . .3G **123**
Lawn Va. HA5: Pinn 2C **40**
Lawrence Av. E12 . . . . .4E **70**
    E17 . . . . .1K **49**
    KT3: N Mald 6K **151**
    N13 . . . . .4G **33**
    NW7 . . . . .4F **29**
    NW10 . . . . .1K **79**
Lawrence Bldgs. N16 . . . . .3F **67**
Lawrence Campe Cl. N20 . . . . .3G **31**
Lawrence Cl. E3 . . . . .3C **86**
    N15 . . . . .4E **48**
    W12 . . . . .7D **80**
Lawrence Cl. N10 . . . . .3G **47**
    N16 . . . . .3F **67**
    (off Smalley Rd. Est.)
    NW7 . . . . .5F **29**
    W3 . . . . .3J **97**
    (off Stanley Rd.)
Lawrence Cres. HA8: Edg 2G **43**
    RM10: Dag 3H **73**
Lawrence Dr. UB10: Ick 4E **56**
Lawrence Est.
    TW4: Houn 4A **112**
Lawrence Gdns. NW7 . . . . .3G **29**
Lawrence Hill E4 . . . . .2H **35**
Lawrence Ho. NW1 . . . . .7F **65**
    (off Hawley Cres.)
    SW1 . . . . .4D **18**
    (off Cureton St.)
Lawrence La. EC2 . . . . .7D **8** (6C **84**)
Lawrence Mans. SW3 . . . . .7C **16**
    (off Lordship Pl.)
Lawrence M. SW15 . . . . .4E **116**
Lawrence Pde. TW7: Isle 3B **114**
    (off Lower Sq.)

Lawrence Pl. N1 .....1J 83
(off Brydon Wlk.)
Lawrence Rd. BR4: W W'ck 4J 171
 DA8: Erith 7H 109
 E6 .....1C 88
 E13 .....1K 87
 HA5: Pinn 6B 40
 N15 .....4E 48
 N18 .....4C 34
 (not continuous)
 SE25 .....4F 157
 TW4: Houn 4A 112
 TW10: Ham 4C 132
 TW12: Hamp 7D 130
 UB4: Hayes 2E 74
 W5 .....4D 96
Lawrence St. E16 .....5H 87
 NW7 .....5G 29
 SW3 .....7C 16 (6D 100)
Lawrence Trad. Est. SE10 .....4G 105
Lawrence Way NW10 .....3J 61
Lawrence Weaver Cl. SM4: Mord 6J 153
Lawrence Yd. N15 .....4E 48
Lawrie Ho. SW19 .....5K 135
(off Durnsford Rd.)
Lawrie Pk. Av. SE26 .....5H 139
Lawrie Pk. Cres. SE26 .....5H 139
Lawrie Pk. Gdns. SE26 .....4H 139
Lawrie Pk. Rd. SE26 .....6H 139
Laws Cl. SE25 .....4D 156
Lawson Cl. E16 .....5A 88
 IG1: Ilf 5H 71
 SW19 .....3F 135
Lawson Ct. KT6: Surb 7D 150
 N4 .....4C 66
 (off Lorne Rd.)
 N11 .....6B 32
 (off Ring Way)
Lawson Gdns. HA5: Eastc 3K 39
Lawson Ho. SE18 .....6E 106
(off Nightingale Pl.)
 W12 .....7D 80
 (off White City Est.)
Lawson Rd. EN3: Enf H 1D 24
 UB1: S'hall 4E 76
Lawson Ter. SE15 .....4J 121
Law St. SE1 .....3D 102
Lawton Rd. E3 .....3A 86
 (not continuous)
 E10 .....1E 68
 EN4: Cockf 3G 21
Laxcon Cl. NW10 .....5K 61
Laxey Rd. BR6: Chels 6K 173
Laxfield Ct. E8 .....1G 85
(off Pownall Rd.)
Laxford Ho. SW1 .....4H 17
(off Cundy St.)
Laxley Cl. SE5 .....7B 102
Laxton Cl. CR7: Thor H 4C 156
Laxton Pl. NW1 .....3K 5 (4F 83)
Layard Rd. CR7: Thor H 2D 156
 EN1: Enf 1A 24
 SE16 .....4H 103
Layard Sq. SE16 .....4H 103
Laybourne Ho. E14 .....2C 104
(off Admirals Way)
Laybrook Lodge E18 .....4H 51
Laycock St. N1 .....6A 66
Layer Gdns. W3 .....7G 79
Layfield Cl. NW4 .....7D 44
Layfield Cres. NW4 .....7D 44
Layfield Ho. SE10 .....5J 105
(off Kemsing Rd.)
Layfield Rd. NW4 .....7D 44
Layhams Rd. BR2: Kes 4G 171
 BR4: W W'ck 4G 171
Laymarsh Cl. DA17: Belv 3F 109
Laymead Cl. UB5: N'olt 6C 58
Laystall Ct. WC1 .....4J 7
(off Mt. Pleasant)
Laystall St. EC1 .....4J 7 (4A 84)

Layton Ct. TW8: Bford 5D 96
Layton Cres. CR0: Wadd 5A 168
Layton Pl. TW9: Kew 1G 115
Layton Rd. TW3: Houn 4F 113
 TW8: Bford 5D 96
Layton's La. TW16: Sun 2H 147
Layzell Wlk. SE9 .....1B 142
Lazar Wlk. N7 .....2K 65
Lazenby Ct. WC2 .....2E 12
Leabank Cl. HA1: Harr 3J 59
Leabank Sq. E9 .....6C 68
Leabank Vw. N15 .....6G 49
Lea Bon Ct. E15 .....1H 87
(off Plaistow Gro.)
Leabourne Rd. N16 .....7G 49
LEA BRIDGE 3K 67
Lea Bri. Ind. Cen. E10 .....1A 68
Lea Bri. Rd. E5 .....3J 67
 E10 .....3J 67
 E17 .....5F 51
Lea Cl. TW2: Whitt 7D 112
Lea Ct. E4 .....2K 35
 E13 .....3J 87
 N15 .....4G 49
Lea Cres. HA4: Ruis 4H 57
Leacroft Av. SW12 .....7D 118
Leacroft Cl. N21 .....2G 33
 UB7: Yiew 6A 74
Leadale Av. E4 .....2H 35
Leadale Rd. N15 .....6G 49
 N16 .....6G 49
Leadbeaters Cl. N11 .....5J 31
Leadbetter Ct. NW10 .....7K 61
(off Melville Rd.)
Leadenhall Mkt. EC3 .....1G 15 (6E 84)
Leadenhall Pl. EC3 .....1G 15 (6E 84)
Leadenhall St. EC3 .....1G 15 (6E 84)
Leadenham Ct. E3 .....4C 86
Leader Av. E12 .....5E 70
Leadings, The HA9: Wemb 3J 61
Leadmill La. E20 .....4D 68
Leaf Cl. HA6: Nwood 1F 39
 KT7: T Ditt 5J 149
Leaf Gro. SE27 .....5A 138
Leaf Ho. HA1: Harr 5K 41
(off Catherine Pl.)
Leafield Cl. SW16 .....6B 138
Leafield La. DA14: Sidc 3F 145
Leafield Rd. SM1: Sutt 2J 165
 SW20 .....3H 153
Leafy Gro. BR2: Kes 5A 172
Leafy Oak Rd. SE12 .....4A 142
Leafy Way CR0: C'don 2F 169
Lea Gdns. HA9: Wemb 4F 61
Leagrave St. E5 .....3J 67
Lea Hall Gdns. E10 .....1C 68
Lea Hall Rd. E10 .....1C 68
Leaholme Way HA4: Ruis 6E 38
Lea Ho. NW8 .....4C 4
(off Salisbury St.)
Leahurst Rd. SE13 .....5F 123
LEA INTERCHANGE 5C 68
Leake Ct. SE1 .....7H 13 (2K 101)
Leake St. SE1 .....6H 13 (2K 101)
(not continuous)
Lealand Rd. N15 .....6F 49
Leamington Av. BR1: Brom 5A 142
 BR6: Orp 4J 173
 E17 .....5C 50
 SM4: Mord 4G 153
Leamington Cl. BR1: Brom 4A 142
 E12 .....5C 70
 TW3: Houn 5G 113
Leamington Ct. SE3 .....6G 105
Leamington Cres. HA2: Harr 3C 58
Leamington Gdns. IG3: Ilf 2K 71
Leamington Ho. HA8: Edg 5A 28
 W11 .....5H 81
 (off Tavistock Rd.)
Leamington Pk. W3 .....5K 79
Leamington Pl. UB4: Hayes 4H 75

Leamington Rd. UB2: S'hall 4B 94
Leamington Rd. Vs. W11 .....5H 81
Leamore Ct. E2 .....3K 85
Leamore St. W6 .....4E 98
LEAMOUTH 7G 87
Leamouth Rd. E6 .....5C 88
 E14 .....6F 87
Leander Ct. E9 .....7K 67
(off Lauriston Rd.)
 KT6: Surb 7D 150
 NW9 .....1A 44
 SE8 .....1C 122
Leander Rd. CR7: Thor H 4K 155
 SW2 .....6K 119
 UB5: N'olt 2E 76
Lea Pk. Trad. Est. E10 .....7B 50
Learner Dr. HA2: Harr 2E 58
Lea Rd. BR3: Beck 2C 158
 EN2: Enf 1J 23
 UB2: S'hall 4C 94
Learoyd Gdns. E6 .....7E 88
Leary Ho. SE11 .....5K 101
Leas Cl. KT9: Chess 7F 163
Leas Dale SE9 .....3E 142
Leas Grn. BR7: Chst 6H 143
Leaside Av. N10 .....3E 46
Leaside Bus. Cen. EN3: Brim 2G 25
Leaside Ct. UB10: Hil 3D 74
Leaside Mans. N10 .....3E 46
(off Fortis Grn.)
Leaside Rd. E5 .....1J 67
Leasowes Rd. E10 .....1C 68
Lea Sq. E3 .....1B 86
Leatherbottle Grn. DA18: Erith 3F 109
Leather Bottle La. DA17: Belv 4E 108
Leather Cl. CR4: Mitc 2E 154
Leatherdale St. E1 .....3K 85
Leather Gdns. E15 .....1G 87
Leatherhead Cl. N16 .....1F 67
Leatherhead Rd. KT9: Chess 7D 162
Leather La. EC1 .....5J 7 (5A 84)
(not continuous)
Leathermarket, The SE1 .....7G 15
Leathermarket Ct. SE1 .....7G 15 (2E 102)
Leathermarket St. SE1 .....7G 15 (2E 102)
Leather Rd. SE16 .....4K 103
Leathersellers Cl. EN5: Barn 3B 20
(off The Avenue)
Leather St. E1 .....7K 85
Leathsail Rd. HA2: Harr 3F 59
Leathwaite Rd. SW11 .....4D 118
Leathwell Rd. SE8 .....2D 122
Lea Va. DA1: Cray 4K 127
Lea Valley Bus. Pk. E10 .....2A 68
Lea Valley Rd. E4 .....5F 25
 EN3: Pond E 5F 25
Lea Valley Trad. Est. N18 .....6E 34
Lea Valley Viaduct E4 .....5E 34
 N18 .....5E 34
Leaveland Cl. BR3: Beck 4C 158
Leaver Gdns. UB6: G'frd 2H 77
Leavesden Rd. HA7: Stan 6F 27
Leaves Grn. Rd. BR2: Kes 7B 172
Lea Vw. Ho. E5 .....1H 67
Leaway E10 .....1K 67
Lebanon Av. TW13: Hanw 5B 130
Lebanon Ct. TW1: Twick 7B 114
Lebanon Gdns. SW18 .....6J 117
Lebanon Pk. TW1: Twick 7B 114
Lebanon Rd. CR0: C'don 1E 168
 SW18 .....5J 117
Lebus Ho. NW8 .....1C 4
(off Cochrane St.)
Lebus St. N17 .....3H 49
Le Chateau CR0: C'don 3D 168
(off Chatsworth Rd.)
Lechmere App. IG8: Wfd G 2A 52
Lechmere Av. IG8: Wfd G 2B 52
Lechmere Rd. NW2 .....6D 62
Leckford Rd. SW18 .....2A 136
Leckhampton Pl. SW2 .....7A 120

Leckwith Av. DA7: Bex 6E 108
Lecky St. SW7 .....5A 16 (5B 100)
L'École Internationale Franco-Anglaise
 .....5K 5
(in Portland Pl.)
Leconfield Av. SW13 .....3B 116
Leconfield Ho. SE5 .....4E 120
Leconfield Rd. N5 .....4D 66
Le Cordon
Bleu London Culinary Arts Institute
 .....6H 5
(off Marylebone La.)
Le Cordon Bleu
London 5J 83
(off Bloomsbury Sq.)
Leda Av. EN3: Enf W 1E 24
Leda Ct. SW9 .....7A 102
(off Caldwell St.)
Ledam Ho. EC1 .....5J 7
(off Bourne Est.)
Leda Rd. SE18 .....3D 106
Ledbury Ho. SE22 .....3E 120
 W11 .....6H 81
 (off Colville Rd.)
Ledbury M. Nth. W11 .....7J 81
Ledbury M. W11 .....7J 81
Ledbury Pl. CR0: C'don 4C 168
Ledbury Rd. CR0: C'don 4D 168
 W11 .....6H 81
Ledbury St. SE15 .....7G 103
Ledrington Rd. SE19 .....6G 139
Ledway Dr. HA9: Wemb 7F 43
LEE 6J 123
Lee Av. RM6: Chad H 6E 54
Lee Bri. SE13 .....3E 122
Leechcroft Av. DA15: Sidc 5K 125
Leechcroft Rd. SM6: Wall 3E 166
Lee Chu. St. SE13 .....4G 123
Lee Cl. E17 .....1K 49
 EN5: New Bar 4F 21
Lee Conservancy Rd. E9 .....5B 68
Lee Ct. SE13 .....4F 123
(off Lee High Rd.)
Leecroft Rd. EN5: Barn 5B 20
Leeds Ct. EC1 .....3A 8
(off St John St.)
Leeds Pl. N4 .....1K 65
Leeds Rd. IG1: Ilf 1H 71
Leeds St. N18 .....5B 34
Leefern Rd. W12 .....2C 98
Leegate SE12 .....5H 123
LEE GREEN 5H 123
Lee Gro. IG7: Chig 2K 37
Lee High Rd. SE12 .....3E 122
 SE13 .....3E 122
Leeke St. WC1 .....1G 7 (3K 83)
Leeland Rd. W13 .....1A 96
Leeland Ter. W13 .....1A 96
Leeland Way NW10 .....4B 62
Lee M. BR3: Beck 3A 158
Leemount Ho. NW4 .....4F 45
Lee Pk. SE3 .....4H 123
Lee Pk. Way N9 .....4E 34
 N18 .....4E 34
Leerdam Dr. E14 .....3E 104
Lee Rd. EN1: Enf 6B 24
 NW7 .....7A 30
 SE3 .....3H 123
 SW19 .....1K 153
 UB6: G'frd 1C 78
Lees, The CR0: C'don 2B 170
Lees Av. HA6: Nwood 1H 39
Lees Ct. W1 .....2G 11
(off Lees Pl.)
Lees Ho. SE17 .....5D 102
(off Inville Rd.)
Leeside EN5: Barn 5B 20
Leeside Ct. SE16 .....1K 103
(off Rotherhithe St.)
Leeside Cres. NW11 .....6G 45
Leeside Ind. Est. N17 .....7D 34

Leeside Rd. N17 ...6C 34
Leeside Works N17 ...7D 34
Leeson Ho. TW1: Twick ...7B 114
Leeson Rd. SE24 ...4A 120
Leesons Hill BR5: St P ...3J 161
  BR7: Chst ...3J 161
Leeson's Way BR5: St P ...2K 161
Lees Pde. UB10: Hil ...4D 74
Lees Pl. W1 ...2G 11 (7E 82)
Lees Rd. UB8: Hil ...4D 74
Lee St. E8 ...1F 85
Lee Ter. SE3 ...3G 123
  SE13 ...3G 123
Lee Valley Athletics Cen. ...1E 34
Lee Valley Golf Course ...7F 25
Lee Valley Hockey & Tennis Cen. ...4D 68
Lee Valley Ice Cen. ...2K 67
Lee Valley Park ...7E 34
Lee Valley Technopark N17 ...3G 49
Lee Valley VeloPark ...5D 68
Leeve Ho. W10 ...3H 81
  (off Lancefield St.)
Lee Vw. EN2: Enf ...1G 23
Leeward Cl. E1 ...7G 85
  SE8 ...4A 104
  (off Yeoman St.)
Leeward Gdns. SW19 ...5G 135
Leeward Ho. N1 ...1E 84
  (off Halcomb St.)
Leeway SE8 ...5B 104
Leeway Cl. HA5: Hat E ...1D 40
Leeways, The SM3: Cheam ...6G 165
Leewood Cl. SE12 ...6J 123
Lefa Bus. & Ind. Pk. DA14: Sidc ...6D 144
Lefevre Wlk. E3 ...2C 86
Leff Ho. NW6 ...1G 81
Lefroy Ho. SE1 ...7C 14
  (off Southwark Bri. Rd.)
Lefroy Rd. W12 ...2B 98
Left Side N14 ...1C 32
  (off Statione Pde.)
Legard Rd. N5 ...3B 66
Legatt Rd. SE9 ...5B 124
Leggatt Rd. E15 ...2E 86
Legge St. SE13 ...5E 122
Leghorn Rd. NW10 ...2B 80
  SE18 ...5H 107
Legion Cl. N1 ...7A 66
Legion Ct. SM4: Mord ...6J 153
Legion Rd. UB6: G'frd ...1G 77
Legion Ter. E3 ...1B 86
Legion Way N12 ...7H 31
Leg O'Mutton Local Nature Reserve
...7B 98
Legon Av. RM7: Rush G ...1J 73
Legrace Av. TW4: Houn ...2B 112
Leicester Av. CR4: Mitc ...4J 155
Leicester Cl. KT4: Wor Pk ...4E 164
Leicester Ct. TW1: Twick ...6D 114
  (off Clevedon Rd.)
  W9 ...3B 120
  (off Elmfield Way)
  WC2 ...2D 12
Leicester Flds. WC2 ...3D 12
Leicester Gdns. IG3: Ilf ...7J 53
Leicester Ho. N18 ...5C 34
  (off Cavendish Cl.)
  SW9 ...3B 120
  (off Loughborough Rd.)
Leicester M. N2 ...3C 46
Leicester Pl. WC2 ...2D 12 (7H 83)
Leicester Rd. CR0: C'don ...7E 156
  E11 ...5K 51
  EN5: New Bar ...5E 20
  N2 ...3C 46
  NW10 ...7K 61
Leicester Sq. WC2 ...3D 12 (7H 83)
Leicester Square Theatre ...7H 83
  (off Leicester Pl.)
Leicester St. WC2 ...2D 12 (7H 83)
Leigh, The KT2: King T ...7A 134

Leigham Av. SW16 ...3J 137
Leigham Cl. SW16 ...3K 137
Leigham Ct. SM6: Wall ...6G 167
Leigham Ct. Rd. SW16 ...2J 137
Leigham Dr. TW7: Isle ...7J 95
Leigham Hall Pde. SW16 ...3J 137
  (off Streatham High Rd.)
Leigham Va. SW2 ...3K 137
  SW16 ...3K 137
Leigh Av. IG4: Ilf ...4B 52
Leigh Cl. KT3: N Mald ...4J 151
Leigh Cl. Ind. Est. KT3: N Mald ...4K 151
Leigh Ct. HA2: Harr ...1J 59
  W14 ...4H 99
  (off Avonmore Pl.)
Leigh Cres. CR0: New Ad ...7D 170
Leigh Gdns. NW10 ...2E 80
Leigh Hunt Dr. N14 ...1C 32
Leigh Orchard Cl. SW16 ...3K 137
Leigh Pl. DA16: Well ...2A 126
  EC1 ...5J 7 (5A 84)
  TW13: Felt ...1A 130
Leigh Rd. E6 ...6E 70
  E10 ...7E 50
  N5 ...4B 66
  TW3: Houn ...4H 113
Leigh St. WC1 ...2E 6 (3J 83)
Leighton Av. E12 ...5E 70
  HA5: Pinn ...3C 40
Leighton Cl. HA8: Edg ...2G 43
Leighton Cres. NW5 ...5G 65
Leighton Gdns. CR0: C'don ...1B 168
  NW10 ...2D 80
Leighton Gro. NW5 ...5G 65
Leighton Ho. SW1 ...4D 18
  (off Herrick St.)
Leighton House Mus. ...3H 99
Leighton Mans. W14 ...6G 99
  (off Greyhound Rd.)
Leighton Pl. NW5 ...5G 65
Leighton Rd. EN1: Enf ...5A 24
  HA3: Hrw W ...2H 41
  NW5 ...5G 65
  W13 ...2A 96
Leighton St. CR0: C'don ...1B 168
Leila Parnell Pl. SE7 ...6A 106
Leinster Av. SW14 ...3J 115
Leinster Gdns. W2 ...6A 82
Leinster M. EN5: Barn ...3B 20
  W2 ...7A 82
Leinster Pl. W2 ...6A 82
Leinster Rd. N10 ...4F 47
Leinster Sq. W2 ...6J 81
  (not continuous)
Leinster Ter. W2 ...7A 82
Leirum St. N1 ...1K 83
Leisure Way N12 ...7G 31
Leisure West TW13: Felt ...2K 129
Leitch Ho. NW8 ...7B 64
  (off Hilgrove Rd.)
Leith Cl. NW9 ...1K 61
Leithcote Gdns. SW16 ...4K 137
Leithcote Path SW16 ...3K 137
Leith Hill BR5: St P ...1K 161
Leith Hill Grn. BR5: St P ...1K 161
Leith Mans. W9 ...3K 81
  (off Grantully Rd.)
Leith Rd. N22 ...1B 48
Leith Towers SM2: Sutt ...7K 165
Leith Yd. NW6 ...1J 81
  (off Quex Rd.)
Lela Av. TW4: Houn ...2A 112
Lelitia Cl. E8 ...1G 85
Lely Ho. UB5: N'olt ...2B 76
  (off Academy Gdns.)
Leman Pas. E1 ...6G 85
  (off Leman St.)
Leman St. E1 ...7K 9 (6F 85)
Lemark Cl. HA7: Stan ...6H 27
Le May Av. SE12 ...3K 141
Lemmon Rd. SE10 ...6G 105

Lemna Rd. E11 ...7H 51
Le Moal Ho. E1 ...5J 85
  (off Stepney Way)
Lemonade Bldg. IG11: Bark ...7G 71
  (off Ripple Rd.)
Lemon Gro. TW13: Felt ...1J 129
Lemon Tree Ho. E3 ...3B 86
  (off Bow Rd.)
Lemonwell Dr. SE9 ...5G 125
Lemsford Cl. N15 ...6G 49
Lemsford Ct. N4 ...2C 66
Lemuel St. SW18 ...6A 118
Lena Cres. N9 ...2D 34
Lena Gdns. W6 ...3E 98
Lena Kennedy Cl. E4 ...6K 35
Lenanton Steps E14 ...2C 104
  (off Manilla St.)
Len Bishop Ct. E1 ...7K 85
  (off Schoolhouse La.)
Len Clifton Ho. SE18 ...4D 106
  (off Cambridge Barracks Rd.)
Lendal Ter. SW4 ...3H 119
Lendy Pl. TW16: Sun ...4J 147
Lenelby Rd. KT6: Surb ...1G 163
Len Freeman Pl. SW6 ...6H 99
  W6 ...4B 98
  (off Goldhawk Rd.)
Lenham Ho. SE1 ...7F 15
  (off Staple St.)
Lenham Rd. CR7: Thor H ...2D 156
  DA7: Bex ...6F 109
  SE12 ...4H 123
  SM1: Sutt ...4K 165
Lennard Av. BR4: W W'ck ...2G 171
Lennard Cl. BR4: W W'ck ...2G 171
Lennard Rd. BR2: Brom ...1D 172
  BR3: Beck ...6K 139
  CR0: C'don ...1C 168
  SE20 ...6K 139
Lennon Rd. NW2 ...5E 62
Lennox Gdns. CR0: Wadd ...4B 168
  IG1: Ilf ...1D 70
  NW10 ...4B 62
  SW1 ...2E 16 (3D 100)
Lennox Gdns. M. SW1 ...2E 16 (3D 100)
Lennox Ho. DA17: Belv ...3G 109
  (off Ambrooke Rd.)
  TW1: Twick ...6D 114
  (off Clevedon Rd.)
Lennox Rd. E17 ...6B 50
  N4 ...2K 65
  SW9 ...1B 120
Lenor Cl. DA6: Bex ...4E 126
Lensbury Av. SW6 ...2A 118
Lensbury Way SE2 ...3C 108
Lens Rd. E7 ...7A 70
Lenthall Av. IG5: Ilf ...3E 52
  SW17 ...4D 136
Lenthall Ho. SW1 ...6B 18
  (off Churchill Gdns.)
Lenthall Rd. E8 ...7G 67
Lenthorp Rd. SE10 ...4H 105
Lentmead Rd. BR1: Brom ...3H 141
Lenton Path SE18 ...6H 107
Lenton Ri. TW9: Rich ...3E 114
Lenton St. SE18 ...4H 107
Lenton Ter. N4 ...2A 66
Len Williams Ct. NW6 ...2J 81
Leo Cl. TW8: Bford ...7D 96
Leof Cres. SE6 ...5D 140
Leominster Rd. SM4: Mord ...6A 154
Leominster Wlk.
  SM4: Mord ...6A 154
Leonard Av. RM7: Rush G ...1K 73
  SM4: Mord ...5A 154
Leonard Ct. HA3: Hrw W ...1J 41
  W8 ...3J 99
  WC1 ...3D 6 (4H 83)
Leonard Pl. N16 ...4E 66
Leonard Rd. E4 ...6H 35
  E7 ...4J 69
  N9 ...3A 34

Leonard Rd. SW16 ...1G 155
  UB2: S'hall ...3B 94
Leonard Robbins Path SE28 ...7B 90
  (off Tawney Rd.)
Leonard St. E16 ...1C 106
  EC2 ...3F 9 (4D 84)
Leonora Ho. W9 ...4A 82
  (off Lanark Rd.)
Leonora Tyson M. SE21 ...2D 138
Leontine Cl. SE15 ...7G 103
Leopards Ct. EC1 ...5J 7
Leopold Av. SW19 ...5H 135
Leopold Bldgs. E2 ...1J 9
  (off Columbia Rd.)
Leopold M. E9 ...1J 85
Leopold Rd. E17 ...5C 50
  N2 ...3B 46
  N18 ...5C 34
  NW10 ...7A 62
  SW19 ...4H 135
  W5 ...1F 97
Leopold St. E3 ...5B 86
Leopold Ter. SW19 ...5H 135
Leopold Wlk. SE11 ...6G 19
  (off Tyers St.)
Leo St. SE15 ...7H 103
Leo Yd. EC1 ...4B 8
Leppoc Rd. SW4 ...5H 119
Leroy St. SE1 ...4E 102
Lerry Cl. W14 ...6H 99
Lerwick Ct. EN1: Enf ...5K 23
Lescombe Cl. SE23 ...3A 140
Lescombe Rd. SE23 ...3A 140
Lescot Pl. BR2: Brom ...6C 160
Lesley Cl. DA5: Bexl ...7H 127
Lesley Ct. SW1 ...2C 18
  (off Strutton Ground)
Leslie Foster Cl. IG11: Bark ...2K 89
Leslie Gdns. SM2: Sutt ...6J 165
Leslie Gro. CR0: C'don ...1E 168
Leslie Gro. Pl. CR0: C'don ...1E 168
Leslie Ho. SW8 ...7J 101
  (off Wheatsheaf La.)
Leslie Pk. Rd. CR0: C'don ...1E 168
Leslie Prince Ct. SE5 ...7D 102
Leslie Rd. E11 ...4E 68
  E16 ...6K 87
  N2 ...3B 46
Leslie Smith Sq. SE18 ...6E 106
Lesnes Abbey ...4D 108
Lesnes Abbey Woods (Nature Reserve)
...4D 108
Lesney Farm Est. DA8: Erith ...7K 109
Lesney Pk. DA8: Erith ...6K 109
Lesney Pk. Rd. DA8: Erith ...6K 109
Lessar Av. SW4 ...6G 119
Lessingham Av. IG5: Ilf ...3E 52
  SW17 ...4D 136
Lessing St. SE23 ...7A 122
Lessington Av. RM7: Rom ...6J 55
Lessness Av. DA7: Bex ...7D 108
LESSNESS HEATH ...5G 109
Lessness Pk. DA17: Belv ...5F 109
Lessness Rd. DA17: Belv ...6G 109
  SM4: Mord ...6A 154
Lester Av. E15 ...4G 87
Lester Cl. E3 ...3D 86
  (off Bruce Rd.)
Leston Cl. SE25 ...3G 157
  (off Manor Rd.)
Leswin Pl. N16 ...3F 67
Leswin Rd. N16 ...3F 67
Letchford Gdns. NW10 ...3C 80
Letchford Ho. E3 ...2C 86
  (off Thomas Fyre Dr.)
Letchford M. NW10 ...3C 80
Letchford Ter. HA3: Hrw W ...1F 41
Letchmore Ho. W10 ...4E 80
  (off Sutton Way)
Letchworth Av. TW14: Felt ...7H 111
Letchworth Cl. BR2: Brom ...5J 159

Letchworth Dr. BR2: Brom 5J 159
Letchworth Rd. HA7: Stan 7K 27
Letchworth St. SW17 . . . . .4D 136
Lethbridge Cl. SE13 . . . . .1E 122
Letterstone Rd. SW6 . . . . .7H 99
Lettice St. SW6 . . . . .1H 117
Lett Rd. E15 . . . . .7F 69
SW9 . . . . .1K 119
Lettsom St. SE5 . . . . .2E 120
Lettsom Wlk. E13 . . . . .2J 87
Leucha Rd. E17 . . . . .5A 50
Levana Cl. SW19 . . . . .1G 135
Levant Ho. E1 . . . . .4K 85
(off Ernest St.)
Levehurst Ho. SE27 . . . . .5C 138
Levendale Rd. SE23 . . . . .2A 140
Levenhurst Way SW4 . . . . .2J 119
Leven Rd. E14 . . . . .5E 86
Leven Way UB3: Hayes 6G 75
Leverett St. SW3 . . . . . . .3D 16 (4C 100)
Leverholme Gdns. SE9 . . . . .4E 142
Leverington Pl. N1 . . . . .2F 9 (3D 84)
Leverson St. SW16 . . . . .6G 137
Leverstock Ho. SW3 . . . . .5D 16
(off Cale St.)
Lever St. EC1 . . . . .2B 8 (3B 84)
Leverton Cl. N22 . . . . .1K 47
Leverton Pl. NW5 . . . . .5G 65
Leverton St. NW5 . . . . .5G 65
Levett Gdns. IG3: Ilf 4K 71
Levett Rd. IG11: Bark 6J 71
Levine Gdns.
IG11: Bark 2D 90
Levison Way N19 . . . . .1H 65
Levita Ho. NW1 . . . . .1D 6
(not continuous)
Levyne Ct. EC1 . . . . .3J 7
(off Pine St.)
Lewen Cl. CR0: C'don 1D 168
Lewes Cl. UB5: N'olt 6E 58
Lewes Ct. CR4: Mitc 3D 154
(off Chatsworth Pl.)
Lewesdon Cl. SW19 . . . . .1F 135
Lewes Ho. SE1 . . . . .6H 15
(off Druid St.)
SE15 . . . . .6G 103
(off Friary Est.)
Lewes Rd. BR1: Brom 2B 160
N12 . . . . .5H 31
Leweston Pl. N16 . . . . .7F 49
Lew Evans Ho. SE22 . . . . .5G 121
Lewey Ho. E3 . . . . .4B 86
(off Joseph St.)
Lewgars Av. NW9 . . . . .6J 43
Lewing Cl. BR6: Orp 1J 173
Lewington Apartments SE16 . . . . . . .4J 103
(off Alpine Rd.)
Lewington Cen. SE16 . . . . .4J 103
(off Alpine Rd.)
Lewin Rd. DA6: Bex 4E 126
SW14 . . . . .3K 115
SW16 . . . . .6H 137
Lewin Ter. TW14: Bedf 7F 111
Lewis Av. E17 . . . . .1C 50
Lewis Cl. N14 . . . . .7B 22
Lewis Ct. SE16 . . . . .5H 103
(off Stubbs Dr.)
Lewis Cres. NW10 . . . . .5K 61
Lewis Gdns. N2 . . . . .2B 46
N16 . . . . .6F 49
Lewis Gro. SE13 . . . . .3E 122
LEWISHAM .3E 122
Lewisham Cen. SE13 . . . . .4E 122
Lewisham Hgts. SE23 . . . . .1J 139
Lewisham High St. SE13 . . . . .6D 122
(not continuous)
Lewisham Hill SE13 . . . . .2E 122
Lewisham Indoor Bowls Cen. 5B 140
Lewisham Lions Cen. 5J 103
Lewisham Model Mkt. SE13 . . . . . . .4E 122
(off Lewisham High St.)

Lewisham Pk. SE13 . . . . .5E 122
Lewisham Rd. SE13 . . . . .1D 122
Lewisham St. SW1 . . . . . .7D 12 (2H 101)
Lewisham Way SE4 . . . . .1B 122
SE14 . . . . .1B 122
Lewis Ho. E14 . . . . .1E 104
(off Coldharbour)
N1 . . . . .6B 66
(off Canonbury La.)
Lewis M. BR7: Chst 5D 142
Lewis Pl. E8 .5G 67
Lewis Rd. CR4: Mitc 2B 154
DA14: Sidc 3C 144
DA16: Well 3C 126
SM1: Sutt 4K 165
TW10: Rich 5D 114
UB1: S'hall 2C 94
Lewis Silkin Ho. SE15 . . . . .6J 103
(off Lovelinch Cl.)
Lewis Sports and Leisure Cen. 1F 157
Lewis St. NW1 . . . . .6F 65
(not continuous)
Lewiston Cl. KT4: Wor Pk 7D 152
Lewis Way RM10: Dag 6B 73
Lexden Dr. RM6: Chad H 6B 54
Lexden Rd. CR4: Mitc 4H 155
W3 . . . . .7H 79
Lexham Gdns. W8 . . . . .4J 99
Lexham Gdns. M. W8 . . . . .3K 99
Lexham Ho. W8 . . . . .4K 99
(off Lexham Gdns.)
Lexham M. W8 . . . . .4J 99
Lexham Wlk. W8 . . . . .3K 99
Lexington Apartments EC1 . . . .3F 9 (4D 84)
Lexington Bldg. E3 . . . . .2C 86
Lexington Ho. UB7: W Dray 2B 92
(off Park Lodge Av.)
Lexington Pl. KT1: Hamp W 7D 132
Lexington St. W1 . . . . .2B 12 (7G 83)
Lexington Way EN5: Barn 4A 20
Lexton Gdns. SW12 . . . . .1H 137
Leyborne Av. W13 . . . . .2B 96
Leyborne Pk. TW9: Kew 1G 115
Leybourne Cl. BR2: Brom 6J 159
Leybourne Ho. E14 . . . . .6B 86
(off Dod St.)
SE15 . . . . .6J 103
Leybourne Rd. E11 . . . . .1H 69
NW1 .7F 65
NW9 .5G 43
UB10: Hil 1E 74
Leybourne St. NW1 . . . . .7F 65
Leybridge Ct. SE12 . . . . .5J 123
Leyburn Cl. E17 . . . . .4D 50
Leyburn Gdns. CR0: C'don 2E 168
Leyburn Gro. N18 . . . . .6B 34
Leyburn Rd. N18 . . . . .6B 34
Leydenhatch La. BR8: Swan 7J 145
Leyden Mans. N19 . . . . .7J 47
Leyden St. E1 . . . . .6J 9 (5F 85)
Leydon Cl. SE16 . . . . .1K 103
Leyes Rd. E16 . . . . .6B 88
Leyfield KT4: Wor Pk 1A 164
Ley Ho. SE1 .7C 14
(off Scovell Rd.)
Leyland Av. EN3: Enf H 2F 25
Leyland Gdns. IG8: Wfd G 5F 37
Leyland Ho. E14 . . . . .7D 86
(off Hale St.)
Leyland Rd. SE12 . . . . .5J 123
Leylands SW18 . . . . .6H 117
Leylands La. TW19: Stanw M 7A 174
(not continuous)
Leylang Rd. SE14 . . . . .7K 103
Leys, The HA3: Kenton 6F 43
N2 . . . . .4A 46
Leys Av. RM10: Dag 1J 91
Leys Cl. HA1: Harr 5H 41
RM10: Dag 7J 73
Leys Ct. SW9 . . . . .2A 120
Leysdown Av. DA7: Bex 4J 127

Leysdown Ho. SE17 . . . . .5E 102
(off Madron St.)
Leysdown Rd. SE9 . . . . .2C 142
Leysfield Rd. W12 . . . . .3C 98
Leys Gdns. EN4: Cockf 5K 21
Leyspring Rd. E11 . . . . .1H 69
Leys Rd. E. EN3: Enf H 1F 25
Leys Rd. W. EN3: Enf H 1F 25
Leys Sq. N3 .1K 45
Ley St. IG1: Ilf 2F 71
IG2: Ilf 2G 71
Leyswood Dr. IG2: Ilf 5J 53
Leythe Rd. W3 . . . . .2J 97
LEYTON 2E 68
Leyton Bus. Cen. E10 . . . . .2C 68
Leyton Ct. SE23 . . . . .1J 139
Leyton Grange E10 . . . . .1C 68
Leyton Grn. Rd. E10 . . . . .6E 50
Leyton Grn. Twr. E10 . . . . .6E 50
(off Leyton Grn. Rd.)
Leyton Ho. E2 . . . . .2J 9
(off Calvert Av.)
Leyton Ind. Village E10 . . . . .7K 49
Leyton Leisure Lagoon 7E 50
Leyton Link Est. E10 . . . . .7A 50
Leyton Mills E10 . . . . .3E 68
Leyton Orient FC
Brisbane Road Stadium 3D 68
Leyton Pk. Rd. E10 . . . . .3E 68
Leyton Rd. E15 . . . . .5E 68
SW19 . . . . .7A 136
LEYTONSTONE 1G 69
Leytonstone Ho. E11 . . . . .7H 51
(off Hanbury Dr.)
Leytonstone Rd. E15 . . . . .6G 69
Leyton Way E11 . . . . .7G 51
Leywick St. E15 . . . . .2G 87
Lezayre Rd. BR6: Chels 6K 173
Lianne Gro. SE9 . . . . .3A 142
Liardet St. SE14 . . . . .6A 104
Libari Mans. E20 . . . . .5E 68
(off Victory Pde.)
Liberia Rd. N5 . . . . .6B 66
Liberty Av. SW19 . . . . .1B 154
Liberty Bri. Rd. E15 . . . . .5E 68
E20 . . . . .5E 68
Liberty Cen. HA0: Wemb 1F 79
Liberty Cl.
KT4: Wor Pk 1E 164
N18 . . . . .4A 34
Liberty Ct. BR1: Brom 3B 160
IG11: Bark 2B 90
Liberty Ho. CR7: Thor H 5A 156
(off Thornton Rd.)
E1 . . . . .7G 85
(off Ensign St.)
E13 . . . . .2J 87
Liberty M. N22 . . . . .1B 48
SW12 . . . . .6F 119
Liberty Point CR0: C'don 7G 157
(off Blackhorse La.)
Liberty St. SW9 . . . . .1K 119
Libra Mans. E3 . . . . .2B 86
(off Libra Rd.)
Libra Rd. E3 .1B 86
E13 . . . . .2J 87
Library Ct. N17 . . . . .3F 49
Library Mans. W12 . . . . .2E 98
(off Pennard Rd.)
Library M. TW12: Hamp H 6G 131
Library Pde. NW10 . . . . .1A 80
(off Craven Pk. Rd.)
Library Pl. E1 . . . . .7H 85
Library Sq. E1 . . . . .4A 86
Library St. SE1 . . . . .7A 14 (2B 102)
Library Way TW2: Whitt 7G 113
Lib'ry Bldg. E3 . . . . .4H 35
Lichfield Cl. EN4: Cockf 3J 21
Lichfield Ct. KT6: Surb 5E 150
(off Claremont Rd.)
TW9: Rich 5E 114

Lichfield Gdns. TW9: Rich 4E 114
Lichfield Gro. N3 . . . . .1J 45
Lichfield La. TW2: Whitt 1G 131
Lichfield Rd. E3 . . . . .3A 86
E6 . . . . .3B 88
HA6: Nwood 3J 39
IG8: Wfd G 4B 36
N9 . . . . .2B 34
NW2 . . . . .4G 63
RM8: Dag 4B 72
TW4: Houn 3A 112
TW9: Kew 1F 115
Lichfield Ter. TW9: Rich 5E 114
(off Sheen Rd.)
Lichlade Cl. BR6: Orp 4K 173
Lickey Ho. W14 . . . . .6H 99
(off North End Rd.)
Lidcote Gdns. SW9 . . . . .2K 119
Liddall Way UB7: Yiew 1B 92
Liddell Cl. HA3: Kenton 3D 42
Liddell Gdns. NW10 . . . . .2E 80
Liddell Rd. NW6 . . . . .6J 63
Liddiard Ho. W11 . . . . .7G 81
(off Lansdowne Rd.)
Lidding Rd. HA3: Kenton 5D 42
Liddington Rd. E15 . . . . .1H 87
Liddon Rd. BR1: Brom 3A 160
E13 . . . . .3K 87
Liden Cl. E17 . . . . .7B 50
Lidfield Rd. N16 . . . . .4D 66
Lidgate Rd. SE15 . . . . .7F 103
Lidgould Gro. HA4: Ruis 6J 39
Lidiard Rd. SW18 . . . . .2A 136
Lidlington Pl. NW1 . . . . .2G 83
Lido Sq. N17 . . . . .2D 48
Lidyard Rd. N19 . . . . .1G 65
Liffler Rd. SE18 . . . . .5J 107
Lifford Pl. SW13 . . . . .2B 116
Lifford St. SW15 . . . . .4F 117
Lightcliffe Rd. N13 . . . . .4F 33
Lighterage Ct. TW8: Bford 6E 96
Lighter Cl. SE16 . . . . .4A 104
Lighterman Ho. E14 . . . . .7E 86
Lighterman M. E1 . . . . .6K 85
Lightermans Rd. E14 . . . . .2C 104
Lightermans Wlk. SW18 . . . . .4J 117
Lightfoot Rd. N8 . . . . .5J 47
Lightfoot Vs. N1 . . . . .7A 66
(off Augustas La.)
Light Horse Ct. SW3 . . . . .6G 17
Lighthouse Apartments E1 . . . . .6J 85
(off Commercial Rd.)
Lightley Cl. HA0: Wemb 1E 78
Ligonier St. E2 . . . . .3J 9 (4F 85)
Lilac Cl. E4 . . . . .6G 35
Lilac Ct. E13 .1A 88
TW11: Tedd 4K 131
Lilac Gdns. CR0: C'don 3C 170
RM7: Rush G 1K 73
UB3: Hayes 6G 75
W5 . . . . .3D 96
Lilac Ho. SE4 . . . . .3C 122
Lilac M. N22 .3A 48
(off High Rd.)
Lilac Pl. SE11 . . . . .4G 19 (4K 101)
UB7: Yiew 7B 74
Lilac St. W12 . . . . .7C 80
Lilah M. BR2: Brom 2H 159
Liliburne Gdns. SE9 . . . . .5C 124
Lilburne Rd. SE9 . . . . .5C 124
Lilburne Wlk. NW10 . . . . .6J 61
Lile Cres. W7 .5J 77
Lilestone Ho. NW8 . . . . .3B 4
(off Frampton St.)
Lilestone St. NW8 . . . . .3C 4 (4C 82)
Lilford Ho. SE5 . . . . .2C 120
Lilford Rd. SE5 . . . . .2B 120
Lilian Barker Cl. SE12 . . . . .5J 123
Lilian Board Way UB6: G'frd 5H 59
Lilian Cl. N16 .3E 66
Lilian Gdns. IG8: Wfd G 1K 51

Lilian Knowles Ho. E1 . . . . .6J 9
(off Crispin St.)
Lilian Rd. SW16 . . . . .1G 155
Lilium M. E10 . . . . .7C 50
Lillechurch Rd. RM8: Dag 6B 72
Lilleshall Rd. SM4: Mord 6B 154
Lilley Cl. E1 . . . . .1G 103
Lilley La. NW3 . . . . .5E 28
Lillian Av. W3 . . . . .2G 97
Lillian Rd. SW13 . . . . .6C 98
Lillie Bri. Dpt. W14 . . . . .5H 99
Lillie Mans. SW6 . . . . .6G 99
(off Lillie Rd.)
Lillie Rd. SW6 . . . . .6G 99
Lillie Road Fitness Cen. 7F 99
Lillieshall Rd. SW4 . . . . .3F 119
Lillie Sq. SW6 . . . . .6J 99
Lillie Yd. SW6 . . . . .6J 99
Lillingston Ho. N7 . . . . .4A 66
Lilliput Av. UB5: N'olt 1C 76
Lilliput Ct. SE12 . . . . .5K 123
Lilliput Rd. RM7: Rush G 7K 55
Lily Cl. HA5: Pinn 2A 40
W14 . . . . .4F 99
Lily Gdns. HA0: Wemb 2C 78
Lily Nichols Ho. E16 . . . . .1B 106
(off Connaught Rd.)
Lily Pl. EC1 . . . . .5K 7 (5A 84)
Lily Rd. E17 . . . . .6C 50
Lilyville Rd. SW6 . . . . .1H 117
Limasol St. SE1 . . . . .3F 103
Limborough Ho. E14 . . . . .5C 86
(off Thomas Rd.)
Limbourne Av. RM8: Dag 7F 55
Limburg Rd. SW11 . . . . .4C 118
Lime Av. UB7: Yiew 7B 74
Limeburner La. EC4 . . . . .1A 14 (6B 84)
Lime Cl. BR1: Brom 4C 160
E1 . . . . .1G 103
HA3: W'stone 2A 42
HA5: Eastc 3H 39
IG9: Buck H 2G 37
RM7: Rom .4J 55
SM5: Cars 2D 166
Lime Ct. CR4: Mitc 2B 154
E11 . . . . .2G 69
(off Trinity Cl.)
E17 . . . . .5E 50
HA1: Harr .6K 41
(off Gayton Rd.)
HA4: Ruis .7K 39
SE9 . . . . .2F 143
Lime Cres. TW16: Sun 2A 148
Limecroft Cl. KT19: Ewe 7K 163
Limedene Cl. HA5: Pinn 1B 40
Lime Gro. BR6: Farnb 2F 173
DA15: Sidc 6K 125
E4 . . . . .6G 35
HA4: Ruis .6K 39
KT3: N Mald 3K 151
N20 . . . . .1C 30
TW1: Twick 6K 113
UB3: Hayes 7F 75
W12 . . . . .2E 98
Limeharbour E14 . . . . .3D 104
LIMEHOUSE 6B 86
Lime Ho. TW9: Kew 1H 115
Limehouse C'way. E14 . . . . .7B 86
Lime Ho. Ct. E14 . . . . .6C 86
(off Wharf La.)
Limehouse Cut E14 . . . . .5D 86
(off Morris Rd.)
Limehouse Flds. Est. E14 . . . . .5A 86
Limehouse Link E14 . . . . .6A 86
Limehouse Lodge E5 . . . . .2J 67
(off Harry Zeital Way)
Lime Kiln Dr. SE7 . . . . .6K 105
Limekiln Pl. SE19 . . . . .7F 139
Limekiln Wharf E14 . . . . .7B 86

Limelight Ho. SE11 . . . . .4B 102
(off Dugard Way)
Lime Lodge TW16: Sun 7H 129
(off Forest Dr.)
Lime Quay E14 .4E 86
Limerick Cl. SW12 . . . . .7G 119
Limerick M. N2 .3C 46
Lime Rd. TW9: Rich 4F 115
Lime Row DA18: Erith 3F 109
Limerston St. SW10 . . . . .7A 16 (6A 100)
Limes, The BR2: Brom 2C 172
KT8: W Mole 4F 149
SW18 . . . . .6J 117
W2 . . . . .7J 81
Limes Av. CR0: Wadd 3A 168
E11 . . . . .4K 51
N12 . . . . .4F 31
NW7 . . . . .6F 29
NW11 . . . . .7G 45
SE20 . . . . .7H 139
SW13 . . . . .2B 116
Limes Avenue, The N11 . . . . .5A 32
Limes Cl. N11 . . . . .5B 32
TW15: Ashf 5C 128
Limes Ct. BR3: Beck 2D 158
NW6 . . . . .7G 63
(off Brondesbury Pk.)
Limesdale Gdns. HA8: Edg 2J 43
Limes Fld. Rd. SW13 . . . . .3A 116
Limesford Rd. SE15 . . . . .4K 121
Limes Gdns. SW18 . . . . .6J 117
Limes Gro. SE13 . . . . .4E 122
Limes Pl. CR0: C'don 7D 156
Limes Rd. BR3: Beck 2D 158
CR0: C'don 7D 156
Limes Row BR6: Farnb 5F 173
Limestone Wlk. DA18: Erith 2D 108
Lime St. E17 . . . . .4A 50
EC3 . . . . .2G 15 (7E 84)
Lime St. Pas. EC3 . . . . .1G 15 (6E 84)
Limes Wlk. SE15 . . . . .4J 121
W5 . . . . .2D 96
Lime Ter. W7 . . . . .7J 77
Lime Tree Av. KT7: T Ditt 7H 149
KT10: Esh .7H 149
Lime Tree Cl. E18 . . . . .4A 52
Limetree Cl. SW2 . . . . .1K 137
Lime Tree Ct. CR2: S Croy 6C 168
E3 . . . . .5C 86
(off Whitehorn St.)
SE17 . . . . .5C 102
(off Walworth Rd.)
Lime Tree Gro. CR0: C'don 3B 170
Lime Tree Pl. CR4: Mitc 1F 155
Lime Tree Rd. TW5: Hest 1F 113
Lime Trees Pk. Golf Course 1A 76
Limetree Ter. DA16: Well 3A 126
SE6 . . . . .1B 140
Lime Tree Wlk. BR4: W W'ck 4H 171
EN2: Enf 1H 23
WD23: B Hea 1D 26
Limetree Wlk. SW17 . . . . .5E 136
Lime View Apartments E14 . . . . .6A 86
(off Commerical Rd.)
Lime Wlk. E15 .1G 87
KT8: E Mos 4K 149
Limewood Cl. BR3: Beck 5E 158
E17 . . . . .4B 50
W13 . . . . .6B 78
Limewood Ct. IG4: Ilf 5D 52
Limewood M. SE20 . . . . .7G 139
(off Lullington Rd.)
Limewood Rd. DA8: Erith 7J 109
Limpsfield Av. CR7: Thor H 5K 155
SW19 . . . . .2F 135
Limscott Ho. E3 . . . . .3D 86
(off Bruce Rd.)
Linacre Cl. SE15 . . . . .3H 121
Linacre Ct. W6 .5F 99
Linacre Rd. NW2 . . . . .6D 62

Linale Ho. N1 . . . . .1E 8
Linberry Wlk. SE8 . . . . .4B 104
Linchmere Rd. SE12 . . . . .7H 123
Lincoln Av. N14 .3B 32
RM7: Rush G 2K 73
SW19 . . . . .3F 135
TW2: Twick 2G 131
Lincoln Cl. HA2: Harr 5D 40
SE25 . . . . .6G 157
IG6: G'frd .1G 77
Lincoln Ct. CR2: S Croy 5C 168
(off Warham Rd.)
IG2: Ilf 6G 53
N16 . . . . .7D 48
SE12 . . . . .3K 141
Lincoln Cres. EN1: Enf 5K 23
Lincoln Gdns. IG1: Ilf 7C 52
Lincoln Grn. Rd. BR5: St M Cry 5K 161
Lincoln Ho. SE5 . . . . .7A 102
SW3 . . . . .2D 100
TW8: Bford 5D 96
(off Ealing Rd.)
Lincoln M. N15 .4C 48
NW6 . . . . .1H 81
SE21 . . . . .2D 138
Lincoln Pde. HA9: Wemb 1E 60
N2 . . . . .3C 46
(off Lincoln Rd.)
Lincoln Plaza E14 . . . . .2D 104
(off Lightermans Rd.)
Lincoln Rd. CR4: Mitc 5J 155
DA14: Sidc 5B 144
E7 . . . . .6B 70
E13 . . . . .4K 87
E18 . . . . .1J 51
EN1: Enf 4K 23
EN3: Pond E 5B 24
HA0: Wemb 6D 60
HA2: Harr .5D 40
HA6: Nwood 3H 39
KT3: N Mald 3J 151
KT4: Wor Pk 1D 164
N2 . . . . .3C 46
SE25 . . . . .3H 157
TW13: Hanw 3D 130
Lincolns, The NW7 . . . . .3G 29
Lincoln's Inn Flds. WC2 . . . . . .7G 7 (6K 83)
Lincoln's Inn Hall 7H 7 (6K 83)
Lincoln St. E11 .2G 69
SW3 . . . . .4E 16 (4D 100)
Lincoln Way EN1: Enf 5C 24
TW16: Sun 1G 147
Lincombe Rd. BR1: Brom 3H 141
Lindal Ct. E18 . . . . .1H 51
Lindal Cres. EN2: Enf 4D 22
Lindale Cl. IG4: Ilf 5D 52
Lindales, The N17 . . . . .6B 34
(off Grasmere Rd.)
Lindal Rd. SE4 .5B 122
Lindbergh Rd. SM6: Wall 7J 167
Linden Av. CR7: Thor H 4B 156
EN1: Enf 1B 24
HA4: Ruis .1H 57
HA9: Wemb 5F 61
NW10 . . . . .2F 81
TW3: Houn 5F 113
Linden Cl. HA4: Ruis 1J 57
HA7: Stan .5G 27
KT7: T Ditt 7K 149
N14 . . . . .6B 22
Linden Ct. DA14: Sidc 4J 143
SE20 . . . . .7H 139
(off Anerley Pk.)
W12 . . . . .1E 98
Linden Cres. IG8: Wfd G 6E 36
KT1: King T 2F 151
UB6: G'frd .6K 59
Lindenfield BR7: Chst 2F 161
Linden Gdns. EN1: Enf 1B 24
W2 . . . . .7J 81
W4 . . . . .5A 98

Linden Gro. KT3: N Mald 3A 152
SE15 . . . . .3H 121
SE26 . . . . .6J 139
TW11: Tedd 5K 131
Linden Ho. SE8 . . . . .6B 104
(off Abinger Gro.)
TW12: Hamp 6E 130
Linden Lawns HA9: Wemb 4F 61
Linden Lea N2 . . . . .5A 46
Linden Leas BR4: W W'ck 2F 171
Linden Mans. N6 . . . . .1F 65
(off Hornsey La.)
Linden M. N1 . . . . .5D 66
W2 . . . . .7J 81
Linden Pl. CR4: Mitc 4C 154
Linden Rd. N10 .4F 47
N11 . . . . .2J 31
N15 . . . . .4C 48
TW12: Hamp 7E 130
Lindens, The CR0: New Ad 6E 170
E17 . . . . .4D 50
(off Prospect Hill)
N12 . . . . .5G 31
W4 . . . . .1J 115
Linden St. RM7: Rom 4K 55
Linden Wlk. N19 . . . . .2G 65
Linden Way N14 . . . . .6B 22
TW17: Shep 5E 146
Linder's Field Local Nature Reserve
. . . . .1G 37
Lindeth Cl. HA7: Stan 6G 27
Lindfield Gdns. NW3 . . . . .5K 63
Lindfield Rd. CR0: C'don 6F 157
W5 . . . . .4C 78
Lindfield St. E14 . . . . .6C 86
Lindhill Cl. EN3: Enf H 2E 24
Lindholme Ct. NW9 . . . . .1A 44
(off Pageant Av.)
Lindie Gdns. UB8: Uxb 7A 56
Lindisfarne Ct. HA8: Edg 4A 28
Lindisfarne Rd. RM8: Dag 3C 72
SW20 . . . . .7C 134
Lindisfarne Way E9 . . . . .4A 68
Lindley Ct. KT1: Hamp W 1C 150
Lindley Est. SE15 . . . . .7G 103
Lindley Ho. E1 . . . . .5J 85
(off Lindley St.)
SE15 . . . . .7G 103
(off Peckham Pk. Rd.)
Lindley Pl. TW9: Kew 1G 115
Lindley Rd. E10 .2E 68
Lindley St. E1 . . . . .5J 85
Lindop Ho. E1 . . . . .4A 86
(off Mile End Rd.)
Lindore Rd. SW11 . . . . .4D 118
Lindores Rd. SM5: Cars 7A 154
Lind St. SE15 .2J 121
Lind Rd. SM1: Sutt 5A 166
Lindrop St. SW6 . . . . .2A 118
Lindsay Cl. KT9: Chess 7E 162
TW19: Stanw 5A 110
Lindsay Ct. CR0: C'don 4D 168
(off Eden Rd.)
SE13 . . . . .3D 122
(off Loampit Va.)
SW11 . . . . .1B 118
(off Battersea High St.)
Lindsay Dr. HA3: Kenton 6E 42
TW17: Shep 6F 147
Lindsay Ho. SW7 . . . . .3A 100
(off Gloucester Rd.)
Lindsay Rd. KT4: Wor Pk 2D 164
TW12: Hamp H 4F 131
Lindsay Sq. SW1 . . . . .5D 18 (5H 101)
Lindsell St. SE10 . . . . .1E 122
Lindsey Cl. BR1: Brom 3B 160
CR4: Mitc .4J 155
Lindsey Ct. N13 .3F 33
(off Green Lanes)
Lindsey Gdns. TW14: Bedf 7F 111
Lindsey Ho. W5 .4D 96

Lindsey M. N1 .7C 66
Lindsey Rd. RM8: Dag 4C 72
Lindsey St. EC1 . . . . .5B 8 (5B 84)
Lind St. SE8 . . . . .2C 122
Lindum Rd. TW11: Tedd 7C 132
Lindway SE27 .5B 138
Lindwood Cl. E6 . . . . .6D 88
Linen House, The W10 . . . . .2G 81
Linfield WC1 . . . . .7E 7
                              (off Sidmouth St.)
Linfield Cl. NW4 . . . . .3E 44
Linford Christie Stadium 5C 80
Linford Rd. E2 .1G 85
                              (off Whiston Rd.)
E16 . . . . .5J 87
                              (off Hammersley Rd.)
Linford Rd. E17 . . . . .3E 50
Linford St. SW8 . . . . .1G 119
Linford St. Bus. Est. SW8 . . . . .1G 119
                              (off Linford St.)
Lingard Av. NW9 . . . . .3A 44
Lingard Ho. E14 . . . . .3E 104
                              (off Marshfield St.)
Lingards Rd. SE13 . . . . .4E 122
Lingey Cl. DA15: Sidc 2K 143
Lingfield Apartments E4 . . . . .7J 35
Lingfield Av. KT1: King T 4E 150
Lingfield Cl. EN1: Enf 6K 23
HA6: Nwood 1G 39
Lingfield Ct. UB5: N'olt 2E 76
Lingfield Cres. SE9 . . . . .4H 125
Lingfield Gdns. N9 . . . . .7C 24
Lingfield Ho. SE1 . . . . .7B 14
Lingfield Rd. KT4: Wor Pk 3E 164
SW19 . . . . .5F 135
Lingham Ct. SW9 . . . . .2J 119
Lingham St. SW9 . . . . .2J 119
Lingholm Way EN5: Barn 5A 20
Ling Rd. DA8: Erith 6J 109
E16 . . . . .5J 87
Lingrove Gdns. IG9: Buck H 2E 36
Lings Coppice SE21 . . . . .2D 138
Lingwell Rd. SW17 . . . . .3C 136
Lingwood DA7: Bex 2H 127
Lingwood Cl. N2 . . . . .3C 46
                              (off Norfolk Cl.)
Lingwood Gdns. TW7: Isle 7J 95
Lingwood Rd. E5 . . . . .7G 49
Linhope St. NW1 . . . . .3E 4 (4D 82)
Link, The EN3: Enf H 1F 25
HA0: Wemb 1C 60
HA5: Eastc 7A 40
NW2 . . . . .1C 62
SE9 . . . . .3E 142
                              (off William Barefoot Dr.)
UB5: N'olt 5D 58
W3 . . . . .6H 79
Linkenholt Mans. W6 . . . . .4B 98
                              (off Stamford Brook Av.)
Linkfield BR2: Hayes 6J 159
KT8: W Mole 3F 149
Linkfield Rd. TW7: Isle 2K 113
Link Ho. E3 . . . . .2D 86
W10 . . . . .6F 81
                              (off Kingsdown Cl.)
Link La. SM6: Wall 6H 167
Linklea Cl. NW9 . . . . .7F 29
Link Rd. E1 . . . . .2K 15 (7G 85)
N11 . . . . .4K 31
RM9: Dag 2H 91
SM6: Wall 1E 166
TW14: Felt 7H 111
Links, The E17 . . . . .4A 50
Links Av. SM4: Mord 4J 153
Linkscroft Av. TW15: Ashf 6D 128
Links Dr. N20 . . . . .1D 30
Links Gdns. SW16 . . . . .7A 138
Linkside KT3: N Mald 2A 152
N12 . . . . .6D 30
Linkside Cl. EN2: Enf 3E 22
Linkside Gdns. EN2: Enf 3E 22

Links Rd. BR4: W W'ck 1E 170
IG8: Wfd G 5D 36
NW2 . . . . .2B 62
SW17 . . . . .6E 136
TW15: Ashf 5A 128
W3 . . . . .6G 79
Links Side EN2: Enf 3E 22
Link St. E9 . . . . .6J 67
Links Vw. N3 . . . . .7C 30
Linksview N2 . . . . .5D 46
                              (off Great Nth. Rd.)
Links Vw. Cl. HA7: Stan 7F 27
Linksview Ct. TW12: Hamp H 4H 131
Links Vw. Rd. CR0: C'don 3C 170
TW12: Hamp H 5G 131
Links Way BR3: Beck 6C 158
Linksway HA6: Nwood 1E 38
NW4 . . . . .2F 45
Links Yd. E1 . . . . .5K 9
Link Way BR2: Brom 7C 160
HA5: Pinn 1B 40
Linkway N4 . . . . .2C 48
RM8: Dag 4C 72
SW20 . . . . .3D 152
TW10: Ham 2B 132
Linkway, The EN5: Barn 6E 20
Linkwood Wlk. NW1 . . . . .7H 65
Linley Cl. SM1: Sutt 4A 166
Linley Cres. RM7: Mawney 3H 55
Linley Rd. N17 .2E 48
Linnell Cl. NW11 . . . . .6K 45
Linnell Dr. NW11 . . . . .6K 45
Linnell Ho. E1 . . . . .5J 9
                              (off Folgate St.)
NW8 . . . . .1A 82
                              (off Ainsworth Way)
Linnell Rd. N18 . . . . .5B 34
SE5 . . . . .2E 120
Linnet Cl. N9 . . . . .1E 34
SE28 . . . . .7C 90
WD23: Bush 1B 26
Linnet M. SW12 . . . . .7E 118
Linnett Cl. E4 . . . . .4K 35
Linom Rd. SW4 . . . . .4J 119
Linscott Rd. E5 . . . . .4J 67
Linsdell Rd. IG11: Bark 1G 89
Linsey Ct. E10 . . . . .1C 68
                              (off Grange Rd.)
Linsey St. SE16 . . . . .4G 103
                              (not continuous)
Linslade Cl. HA5: Eastc 4K 39
TW4: Houn 5C 112
Linslade Ho. E2 . . . . .1G 85
NW8 . . . . .3D 4
                              (off Paveley St.)
Linslade Rd. BR6: Chels 6K 173
Linstead St. NW6 . . . . .7J 63
Linstead Way SW18 . . . . .7G 117
Linsted Ct. SE9 . . . . .6J 125
Linthorpe Av. HA0: Wemb 6C 60
Linthorpe Rd. EN4: Cockf 3H 21
N16 . . . . .7E 48
Linton Cl. CR4: Mitc 7D 154
DA16: Well 1B 126
SE7 . . . . .5A 106
Linton Ct. NW1 . . . . .7G 65
                              (off Agar Gro.)
RM1: Rom 2A 55
Linton Gdns. E6 . . . . .6C 88
Linton Gro. SE27 . . . . .5B 138
Linton Ho. E3 . . . . .5C 86
                              (off St Paul's Way)
Linton Rd. IG11: Bark 7G 71
Linton St. N1 . . . . .1C 84
                              (not continuous)
Lintott Ct. TW19: Stanw 6J 111
Linver Rd. SW6 . . . . .2J 117
Linwood Cl. SE5 . . . . .2F 121
Linwood Cres. EN1: Enf 1B 24
Linzee Rd. N8 . . . . .4J 47

Lion Apartments SE16 . . . . .5H 103
                              (off Rotherhithe New Rd.)
Lion Av. TW1: Twick 1K 131
Lion Cl. SE4 . . . . .6C 122
TW17: Shep 3A 146
Lion Ct. E1 . . . . .7K 85
                              (off The Highway)
N1 . . . . .1K 83
                              (off Copenhagen St.)
Lion Ct. SE1 . . . . .5G 15
                              (off Magdalen St.)
Lionel Gdns. SE9 . . . . .5B 124
Lionel Ho. W10 . . . . .5G 81
                              (off Portobello Rd.)
Lionel Mans. W14 . . . . .3F 99
                              (off Haarlem Rd.)
Lionel M. W10 .5G 81
Lionel Rd. SE9 . . . . .5B 124
Lionel Rd. Nth. TW8: Bford 3E 96
Lionel Rd. Sth. TW8: Bford 5F 97
Liongate Ent. Pk. CR4: Mitc 4B 154
Lion Ga. Gdns. TW9: Rich 3F 115
Lion Ga. M. SW18 . . . . .7J 117
Liongate M. KT8: E Mos 3K 149
Lion Head Ct. CR0: C'don 4C 168
                              (off St Andrew's Rd.)
Lions Cl. SE9 .3A 142
Lion Way TW8: Bford 7D 96
Lion Pk. Av. KT9: Chess 4G 163
Lion Rd. CR0: C'don 5C 156
DA6: Bex 4E 126
E6 . . . . .5D 88
N9 . . . . .2B 34
TW1: Twick 1K 131
Lion Wharf Rd. TW7: Isle 3B 114
Lion Yd. SW4 .4H 119
Liphook Cres. SE23 . . . . .7J 121
Lipton Cl. SE28 . . . . .7C 90
Lipton Rd. E1 . . . . .6K 85
Lisbon Av. TW2: Twick 2G 131
Lisbon Cl. E17 .2B 50
Lisburne Rd. NW3 . . . . .4D 64
Lisford St. SE15 . . . . .1F 121
Lisgar Ter. W14 . . . . .4H 99
Liskeard Cl. BR7: Chst 6G 143
Liskeard Gdns. SE3 . . . . .1J 123
Liskeard Ho. SE11 . . . . .5K 19
                              (off Kennings Way)
Lisle Cl. SW17 . . . . .4F 137
Lisle Cl. NW2 . . . . .3G 63
Lisle St. WC2 . . . . .2D 12 (7H 83)
Lismore SW19 . . . . .5H 135
                              (off Woodside)
Lismore Cir. NW5 . . . . .5E 64
Lismore Cl. TW7: Isle 2A 114
Lismore Rd. CR2: S Croy 6E 168
N17 . . . . .3D 48
Lismore Wlk. N1 . . . . .6C 66
                              (off Clephane Rd. Nth.)
Lissant Cl. KT6: Surb 7D 150
Lisselton Ho. NW4 . . . . .4F 45
                              (off Belle Vue Est.)
Lissenden Gdns. NW5 . . . . .4E 64
                              (not continuous)
Lissenden Mans. NW5 . . . . .4E 64
Lisson Grn. Est. NW8 . . . . .3C 4
                              (off Tresham Cres.)
LISSON GROVE 5B 4 (5B 82)
Lisson Gro. NW1 . . . . .3B 4 (4B 82)
NW8 . . . . .3B 4 (4B 82)
Lisson Ho. NW1 .5C 4
                              (off Lisson St.)
Lisson St. NW1 . . . . .5C 4 (5C 82)
Lister Cl. CR4: Mitc 1C 154
W3 . . . . .5K 79
Lister Ct. HA1: Harr 7B 42
N16 . . . . .2E 66
NW9 . . . . .2A 44
Lister Gdns. N18 . . . . .5H 33
Listergate Ct. SW15 . . . . .4E 116

Lister Ho. E1 . . . . .5G 85
                              (off Lomas St.)
HA9: Wemb 3J 61
                              (off Barnhill Rd.)
UB3: Harl 4G 93
Lister Lodge W9 . . . . .5J 81
                              (off Admiral Wlk.)
Lister Rd. E11 .1G 69
Lister Wlk. SE28 . . . . .7D 90
Liston Rd. N17 . . . . .1G 49
SW4 . . . . .3G 119
Liston Way IG8: Wfd G 7F 37
Listowel Cl. SW9 . . . . .7A 102
Listowel Rd. RM10: Dag 3G 73
Listria Pk. N16 .2E 66
Litcham Ho. E1 .3K 85
                              (off Longnor Rd.)
Litchfield Av. E15 . . . . .6G 69
SM4: Mord 7H 153
Litchfield Ct. E17 . . . . .6C 50
Litchfield Gdns. NW10 . . . . .6C 62
Litchfield Rd. SM1: Sutt 4A 166
Litchfield St. WC2 . . . . .2D 12 (7H 83)
Lithgow's Rd. TW6: H'row A 4G 111
Lithos Rd. NW3 . . . . .6K 63
Litten Nature Reserve 3G 77
Little Acre BR3: Beck 3C 158
Lit. Albany St. NW1 . . . . .3K 5
Little Angel Theatre 1B 84
                              (off Dagmar Ter.)
Lit. Argyll St. W1 . . . . .1A 12 (6G 83)
Little Benty UB7: W Dray 1E 174
Little Birches DA15: Sidc 2J 143
Lit. Boltons, The SW5 . . . . .5K 99
SW10 . . . . .5K 99
Little Bornes SE21 . . . . .4E 138
Littlebourne SE13 . . . . .7G 123
Littlebourne Ho. SE17 . . . . .5E 102
                              (off Upnor Way)
Lit. Brights Rd. DA17: Belv 2H 109
Little Britain EC1 . . . . .6B 8 (5B 84)
Littlebrook Cl. CR0: C'don 6K 157
Little Brownings SE23 . . . . .2H 139
Littlebury Rd. SW4 . . . . .3H 119
Lit. Bury St. N9 .1J 33
Lit. Bushey La. WD23: Bush 1C 26
Little Cedars N12 . . . . .4F 31
Lit. Chelsea Ho. SW10 . . . . .6A 100
                              (off Edith Gro.)
Little Chester St. SW1 . . . . . . .1J 17 (3F 101)
Lit. Cloisters SW1 . . . . .1E 18 (3J 101)
Lit. College La. EC4 . . . . .2E 14
                              (off College St.)
Lit. College St. SW1 . . . . . . .1E 18 (3J 101)
Littlecombe SE7 . . . . .6K 105
Littlecombe Cl. SW15 . . . . .6F 117
Little Comn. HA7: Stan 3F 27
Littlecote Cl. SW19 . . . . .7G 117
Littlecote Pl. HA5: Hat E 1C 40
Lit. Cottage Pl. SE10 . . . . .7D 104
Little Ct. BR4: W W'ck 2G 171
Littlecroft SE9 .3E 124
Littledale SE2 .6A 108
Lit. Dean's Yd. SW1 . . . . .1E 18
Little Dimocks SW12 . . . . .2F 137
Lit. Dorrit Ct. SE1 . . . . .6D 14 (2C 102)
LITTLE EALING .3D 96
Lit. Ealing La. W5 . . . . .4C 96
Lit. Edward St. NW1 . . . . .1K 5 (3F 83)
Little Elms UB3: Harl 7F 93
Lit. Essex St. WC2 . . . . .2J 13
Lit. Ferry Rd. TW1: Twick 1B 132
Littlefield Cl. KT1: King T 2E 150
N19 . . . . .4G 65
Littlefield Ho. KT1: King T 2E 150
                              (off Littlefield Cl.)
Littlefield Rd. HA8: Edg 7D 28
Lit. Friday Rd. E4 . . . . .2B 36
Little Gearies IG6: Ilf 4F 53
Lit. George St. SW1 . . . . .7E 12 (2J 101)

Little Grange UB6: G'frd 3A **78**
Little Green TW9: Rich 4D **114**
Lit. Green St. NW5 . . . . .4F **65**
Littlegrove EN4: E Barn 6H **21**
Little Halliards KT12: Walt T 6J **147**
LITTLE HEATH 5B **54**
Little Heath RM6: Chad H 4B **54**
SE7 . . . . .6C **106**
Lit. Heath Rd. DA7: Bex 1F **127**
Littleheath Rd. CR2: Sels 7H **169**
Little Holland House 7D **166**
Little Holt E11 . . . . .5J **51**
LITTLE ILFORD 5D **70**
Lit. Ilford La. E12 . . . . .4D **70**
Littlejohn Rd. W7 . . . . .6K **77**
Little Larkins EN5: Barn 6B **20**
Lit. London Cl. UB8: Hil 5D **74**
Lit. London Ct. SE1 . . . . .7K **15**
(off Wolseley St.)
Lit. Marlborough St. W1 . . . . .1A **12**
Littlemede SE9 . . . . .3D **142**
Littlemoor Rd. IG1: Ilf 3H **71**
Littlemore Rd. SE2 . . . . .2A **108**
Lit. Moss La. HA5: Pinn 2C **40**
Lit. Newport St. WC2 . . . . .2D **12** (7H **83**)
Little New St. EC4 . . . . .7K **7** (6A **84**)
Lit. Oaks Cl. TW17: Shep 4B **146**
Lit. Orchard Cl. HA5: Pinn 2C **40**
Lit. Park Dr. TW13: Felt 2C **130**
Lit. Park Gdns. EN2: Enf 2H **23**
Lit. Pluckett's Way IG9: Buck H 1G **37**
Lit. Portland St. W1 . . . . . . .7K **5** (6G **83**)
Little Potters WD23: Bush 1C **26**
Lit. Queen's Rd. TW11: Tedd 6K **131**
Little Redlands BR1: Brom 2C **160**
Little Rd. UB3: Hayes 2H **93**
Littlers CI. SW19 . . . . .1B **154**
Lit. Russell St. WC1 . . . . . . .6E **6** (5J **83**)
Little St James's St. SW1 . . .5A **12** (1G **101**)
Little St Leonard's SW14 . . . . .3J **115**
Little Sanctuary SW1 . . . . .7D **12** (2H **101**)
Lit. Smith St. SW1 . . . . . . .1D **18** (3H **101**)
Lit. Somerset St. E1 . . . . . .1J **15** (6F **85**)
Lit. South St. SE5 . . . . .1E **120**
LITTLE STANMORE 7A **28**
Littlestone CI. BR3: Beck 6C **140**
Little Strand NW9 . . . . .2B **44**
Lit. Thames Wlk. SE8 . . . . .6D **104**
(off Dancers Way)
Little Thrift BR5: Pet W 4G **161**
Lit. Titchfield St. W1 . . . . . .6A **6** (5G **83**)
LITTLETON .3C **146**
Littleton Av. E4 . . . . .1C **36**
LITTLETON COMMON 7E **128**
Littleton Cres. HA1: Harr 2K **59**
Littleton Ho. SW1 . . . . .6J **18**
(off Lupus St.)
Littleton La. TW17: Shep 7A **146**
Littleton Rd. HA1: Harr 2K **59**
TW15: Ashf 7E **128**
Littleton St. SW18 . . . . .2A **136**
Lit. Trinity La. EC4 . . . . . . .2D **14** (7C **84**)
Little Turnstile WC1 . . . . . . .6G **7** (5K **83**)
Little Venice 5A **82**
(off Maida Av.)
Little Venice Sports Cen. 5A **4** (5A **82**)
Littlewood SE13 . . . . .6E **122**
Littlewood Cl. W13 . . . . .3B **96**
Lit. Wood St. KT1: King T 2D **150**
Livermere Ct. E8 . . . . .1G **85**
(off Queensbridge Rd.)
Livermere Rd. E8 . . . . .1F **85**
Liverpool Gro. SE17 . . . . .5C **102**
Liverpool Rd. CR7: Thor H 3C **156**
E10 . . . . .6E **50**
E16 . . . . .5G **87**
KT2: King T 7G **133**
N1 . . . . .5A **66**
N7 . . . . .5A **66**
W5 . . . . .2D **96**
Liverpool St. EC2 . . . . .6G **9** (5E **84**)

Livesey CI. KT1: King T 3F **151**
SE28 . . . . .3G **107**
Livesey PI. SE15 . . . . .6G **103**
Livingstone CI. E10 . . . . .6E **50**
EN5: Barn 2B **20**
(off Church La.)
HA3: W'stone 3K **41**
TW19: Stanw 1A **128**
(off Explorer Av.)
Livingstone Ho. NW10 . . . . .7K **61**
SE5 . . . . .7C **102**
(off Wyndham Rd.)
Livingstone Lodge W9 . . . . .5J **81**
(off Admiral Wlk.)
Livingstone Mans. W14 . . . . .6G **99**
(off Queen's Club Gdns.)
Livingstone Pl. E14 . . . . .5E **104**
Livingstone Rd. CR7: Thor H 2C **156**
E17 . . . . .6D **50**
N13 . . . . .6D **32**
SW11 . . . . .3B **118**
TW3: Houn 4G **113**
UB1: S'hall 7B **76**
LivingWell Health Club
London Heathrow Hilton 6E **110**
Wembley 4G **61**
Livonia St. W1 . . . . .1B **12** (6G **83**)
Lizard St. EC1 . . . . .2D **8** (3C **84**)
Lizban St. SE3 . . . . .7K **105**
Lizmans Ter. W8 . . . . .3J **99**
(off Earl's Ct. Rd.)
Llandovery Ho. E14 . . . . .2E **104**
(off Chipka St.)
Llanelly Rd. NW2 . . . . .2H **63**
Llanover Rd. HA9: Wemb 3D **60**
SE18 . . . . .6E **106**
Llanthony Rd. SM4: Mord 5B **154**
Llanvanor Rd. NW2 . . . . .2H **63**
Llewellyn Ct. SE20 . . . . .1J **157**
Llewellyn Mans. W14 . . . . .4G **99**
(off Hammersmith Rd.)
Llewellyn St. SE16 . . . . .2G **103**
Lloyd Av. SW16 . . . . .1J **155**
(not continuous)
Lloyd Baker St. WC1 . . . . . .2H **7** (3K **83**)
Lloyd Ct. HA5: Pinn 5B **40**
Lloyd Ho. BR3: Beck 6D **140**
CR0: C'don 1D **168**
(off Tavistock Rd.)
Lloyd M. EN3: Enf L 1H **25**
Lloyd Pk. Av. CR0: C'don 4F **169**
Lloyd Pk. Ho. E17 . . . . .3C **50**
Lloyd Rd. E6 . . . . .1D **88**
E17 . . . . .4K **49**
KT4: Wor Pk 3E **164**
RM9: Dag 7F **73**
Lloyd's Av. EC3 . . . . .1H **15** (6E **84**)
Lloyd's Building 1G **15** (6E **84**)
Lloyds Lanes Raynes Pk. 3F **153**
Lloyd's PI. SE3 . . . . .2G **123**
Lloyd Sq. WC1 . . . . .1J **7** (3A **84**)
Lloyd's Row EC1 . . . . .2K **7** (3A **84**)
Lloyd St. WC1 . . . . .1J **7** (3A **84**)
Lloyds Way BR3: Beck 5A **158**
Lloyds Wharf SE1 . . . . .6K **15**
Lloyd Thomas Ct. N22 . . . . .7E **32**
Lloyd Vs. E6 . . . . .4C **88**
SE4 . . . . .2C **122**
Loampit Hill SE13 . . . . .2C **122**
LOAMPIT VALE 3E **122**
Loampit Va. SE13 . . . . .3D **122**
Loanda CI. E8 . . . . .1F **85**
Loats Rd. SW2 . . . . .6J **119**
Lobelia CI. E6 . . . . .5C **88**
Locarno Ct. SW16 . . . . .5G **137**
Locarno Rd. UB6: G'frd 4H **77**
W3 . . . . .1J **97**
Lochaber Rd. SE13 . . . . .4G **123**
Lochaline St. W6 . . . . .6E **98**
Lochan Cl. UB4: Yead 4C **76**
Loch Cres. HA8: Edg 4A **28**

Lochinvar St. SW12 . . . . .7F **119**
Lochleven Ho. N2 . . . . .2B **46**
(off The Grange)
Lochmere Cl. DA8: Erith 6H **109**
Lochmore Ho. SW1 . . . . .4H **17**
(off Cundy St.)
Lochnagar St. E14 . . . . .5E **86**
Lockbridge Ct. W9 . . . . .5J **81**
(off Woodfield Rd.)
Lock Building, The E15 . . . . .2E **86**
Lock Chase SE3 . . . . .3G **123**
Lock Cl. UB2: S'hall 2G **95**
Lock Cotts. UB1: S'hall 2H **95**
Lock Ct. E5 . . . . .2K **67**
Locke Ho. SW8 . . . . .1G **119**
(off Wadhurst Rd.)
Lockesfield Pl. E14 . . . . .5D **104**
Lockesley Dr. BR5: St M Cry 6K **161**
Lockesley Sq. KT6: Surb 6D **150**
Locket Rd. HA3: W'stone 3J **41**
Locket Rd. M. HA3: W'stone 2J **41**
Lockfield Av. EN3: Brim 2F **25**
Lockgate Cl. E9 . . . . .5B **68**
Lockhart Cl. EN3: Pond E 5C **24**
N7 . . . . .6K **65**
Lockhart St. E3 . . . . .4B **86**
Lockhouse, The NW1 . . . . .1E **82**
Lockhurst St. E5 . . . . .4K **67**
Lockie Pl. SE25 . . . . .3G **157**
Lockier Wlk. HA9: Wemb 3D **60**
Lockington Rd. SW8 . . . . .1F **119**
Lock Keepers Hgts. SE16 . . . . .3K **103**
(off Brunswick Quay)
Lockmead Rd. N15 . . . . .6G **49**
SE13 . . . . .3E **122**
Lock M. NW1 . . . . .6H **65**
(off Northpoint Sq.)
Lock Rd. TW10: Ham 4C **132**
LOCKSBOTTOM 3E **172**
Locksfields SE17 . . . . .4D **102**
(off Catesby St.)
Lockside E14 . . . . .7A **86**
(off Narrow St.)
Locks La. CR4: Mitc 1E **154**
Locksley Est. E14 . . . . .6B **86**
Locksley St. E14 . . . . .5B **86**
Locksmeade Rd. TW10: Ham 4C **132**
Locksons Cl. E14 . . . . .5D **86**
Lockswood Cl. EN4: Cockf 4J **21**
Lockton St. W10 . . . . .7F **81**
(off Bramley Rd.)
Lock Vw. Ct. E14 . . . . .7A **86**
(off Narrow St.)
Lockwell Rd. RM10: Dag 3G **73**
Lockwood Cl. SE26 . . . . .4K **139**
Lockwood Ho. E5 . . . . .2J **67**
SE11 . . . . .7J **19** (6A **102**)
Lockwood Ind. Pk. N17 . . . . .3H **49**
Lockwood Pl. E4 . . . . .6H **35**
Lockwood Sq. SE16 . . . . .3H **103**
Lockwood Way E17 . . . . .2K **49**
KT9: Chess 5G **163**
Lockyer Est. SE1 . . . . .7F **15**
(not continuous)
Lockyer Ho. SE10 . . . . .5H **105**
(off Armitage Rd.)
SW8 . . . . .7H **101**
(off Wandsworth Rd.)
SW15 . . . . .3F **117**
Lockyer M. EN3: Enf L 1J **25**
Lockyer St. SE1 . . . . .7F **15** (2D **102**)
Locomotive Dr.
TW14: Felt 1J **129**
Locton Grn. E3 . . . . .1B **86**
Loddiges Ho. E9 . . . . .7J **67**
Loddiges Rd. E9 . . . . .7J **67**
Loddon Ho. NW8 . . . . .4B **4**
(off Church St. Est.)
Loder St. SE15 . . . . .7J **103**
Lodge, The W12 . . . . .2F **99**
(off Richmond Way)

Lodge Av. CR0: Wadd 3A **168**
HA3: Kenton 4E **42**
RM8: Dag 6B **72**
RM9: Dag 1A **90**
SW14 . . . . .3A **116**
LODGE AVENUE FLYOVER JUNC. 1A **90**
Lodge Cl. HA8: Edg 6A **28**
N18 . . . . .5H **33**
SM6: Wall 1E **166**
TW7: Isle .1B **114**
Lodge Ct. HA0: Wemb 5E **60**
(off Station Gro.)
Lodge Dr. N13 . . . . .4F **33**
Lodge Gdns. BR3: Beck 5B **158**
Lodge Hill DA16: Well 7B **108**
IG4: Ilf 4C **52**
SE2 . . . . .7B **108**
Lodgehill Pk. Cl. HA2: Harr 2F **59**
Lodge La.
CR0: New Ad 6C **170**
DA5: Bexl 6E **126**
N12 . . . . .5F **31**
RM5: Col R 1G **55**
Lodge Pl. SM1: Sutt 5K **165**
Lodge Rd. BR1: Brom 7A **142**
CR0: C'don 6B **156**
NW4 . . . . .4E **44**
NW8 . . . . .2B **4** (3B **82**)
SM6: Wall 5F **167**
Lodge Vs. IG8: Wfd G 6C **36**
Lodore Gdns. NW9 . . . . .5A **44**
Lodore Grn. UB10: Ick 3A **56**
Lodore St. E14 . . . . .6E **86**
Loft, The W12 . . . . .1F **99**
Loft Ho. E1 .7J **9**
(off Middlesex St.)
Lofthouse Pl. KT9: Chess 6C **162**
Loftie St. SE16 . . . . .2G **103**
Lofting Ho. N1 . . . . .7A **66**
(off Liverpool Rd.)
Lofting Rd. N1 . . . . .7K **65**
Lofts on the Park E9 . . . . .6K **67**
(off Cassland Rd.)
Loftus Road 1D **98**
Loftus Rd. IG11: Bark 1J **89**
W12 . . . . .1D **98**
Loftus Vs. W12 . . . . .1D **98**
(off Loftus Rd.)
Logan Cl. E20 . . . . .5D **68**
EN3: Enf H 1E **24**
TW4: Houn 3D **112**
Logan M. RM1: Rom 5K **55**
W8 . . . . .4J **99**
Logan Pl. W8 . . . . .4J **99**
Logan Rd. HA9: Wemb 2D **60**
N9 . . . . .2C **34**
Loggetts SE21 . . . . .2E **138**
Logs Hill BR1: Brom 7C **142**
BR7: Chst 7C **142**
Logs Hill Cl. BR7: Chst 1C **160**
Lohmann Ho. SE11 . . . . .7J **19**
Lois Dr. TW17: Shep 5D **146**
Lolesworth Cl. E1 . . . . .6J **9** (5F **85**)
Lolland Ho. SE7 . . . . .4C **106**
Lollard St. SE11 . . . . .3H **19** (4K **101**)
(not continuous)
Loman St. SE1 . . . . .6B **14** (2B **102**)
Lomas Cl. CR0: New Ad 7E **170**
Lomas Dr. E8 . . . . .7F **67**
Lomas St. E1 . . . . .5G **85**
Lombard Av. EN3: Enf H 1D **24**
IG3: Ilf 1J **71**
Lombard Bus. Pk.
CR0: C'don 7K **155**
SW19 . . . . .2K **153**
Lombard Ct. EC3 . . . . .2F **15** (7D **84**)
RM7: Rom 4J **55**
W3 . . . . .1H **97**
Lombard La. EC4 . . . . .1K **13** (6A **84**)

Lombard Rd. N11 . . . . .5A 32
   SW11 . . . . .2B 118
   SW19 . . . . .2K 153
LOMBARD RDBT. 7K 155
Lombard St. EC3 . . . . .1F 15 (6D 84)
Lombard Trad. Est. SE7 . . . . .4K 105
Lombard Wall SE7 . . . . .3K 105
Lombarby Cl. IG6: Ilf 7K 37
Lombarby Pl. W2 . . . . .7K 81
Lombardy Retail Pk. UB3: Hayes . . .7K 75
Lomond Cl. HA0: Wemb 7F 61
   N15 . . . . .5E 48
Lomond Gdns. CR2: Sels 7A 170
Lomond Gro. SE5 . . . . .7D 102
Lomond Ho. SE5 . . . . .7D 102
Loncroft Rd. SE5 . . . . .6F 103
Londesborough Rd. N16 . . . . .4E 66
Londinium Twr. E1 . . . . .2K 15
(off W. Tenter St.)
London Ambulance Service Mus. . . .5K 53
London Bri. SE1 . . . . .4F 15 (1D 102)
London Bridge Experience 4F 15
(off Tooley St.)
London Bri. St. SE1 . . . . .5F 15 (1D 102)
London Bri. Wlk. SE1 . . . . .4F 15
(off Duke St. Hill)
London Broncos RLFC 1E 42
London Business School . . .3E 4 (4D 82)
London Canal Mus. 2J 83
LONDON CITY AIRPORT 1C 106
London City College 5J 13
(off Waterloo Rd.)
London Coliseum 3E 12
(off St Martin's La.)
London College of Fashion, The
   Hackney 7J 67
Londonderry Pde. DA8: Erith 7K 109
London Designer Outlet
   HA9: Wemb 4G 61
London Dungeon 6G 13 (2K 101)
London Eye 6G 13 (2K 101)
London Flds. East Side E8 . . . . . . .7H 67
London Fields Lido 7H 67
London Flds. West Side E8 . . . . . . .7G 67
London Film Mus. 2F 13
London Fire Brigade Mus. . .6C 14 (2C 102)
London Fruit Exchange E1 . . . . .6J 9
(off Brushfield St.)
LONDON GATEWAY SERVICE AREA . . .1D 28
London Group Bus. Pk. NW2 . . . . . .1B 62
LONDON HEATHROW AIRPORT
   TERMINAL 4 . . . . .5D 110
   TERMINAL 5 . . . . .6D 174
   TERMINALS 1, 2, 3 . . . . .3C 110
London Heliport, The 2A 118
London Ho. EC1 . . . . .6C 8
(off Aldersgate St.)
   NW8 . . . . .2C 82
(off Avenue Rd.)
   WC1 . . . . .3G 7 (4K 83)
London Ind. Park, The E6 . . . . .5F 89
(not continuous)
London La. BR1: Brom 7H 141
   E8 . . . . .7H 67
London Master Bakers Almshouses
   E10 . . . . .6D 50
London Metropolitan Archives 3K 7
London Metropolitan University
   London City Campus, Calcutta House
     & Goulston St. 7K 9 (6F 85)
   London City Campus, Central House
   . . . . .7K 9
   London City Campus, Commercial Rd.
   . . . . .6G 85
   London City Campus, Jewry St.
   . . . . .1J 15
(off Jewry St.)
   London City Campus, Moorgate
   . . . . .6E 8
   London City Campus, Tower Hill
   . . . . .2J 15

London Metropolitan University
   North London Campus, Eden Grove
   . . . . .5K 65
   North London Campus,
     Stapleton House 5K 65
   North London Campus, Tower Bldg.
     & Graduate Cen. 5A 66
London M. W2 . . . . .7B 4 (6B 82)
London Mill Apartments E2 . . . . . . .1F 85
(off Whiston Rd.)
London Motorcycle Mus.
   (Ravenor Farm) 3G 77
London Motor Mus. 3H 93
London Palladium 1A 12
(off Argyll St.)
London Pavilion 3C 12
(off Shaftesbury Av.)
London Plane Ho. E15 . . . . .3G 87
(off Teasel Way)
London Regatta Cen. 7B 88
London Rd. BR1: Brom 7H 141
   CR0: C'don 7B 156
   CR4: Mitc 5C 154
(Brookfields Av.)
   CR4: Mitc 7E 154
(Mill Grn. Rd.)
   CR7: Thor H 1K 155
   DA1: Bexl, Cray 5K 127
   E13 . . . . .2J 87
   EN2: Enf 3J 23
   HA1: Harr 2J 59
   HA7: Stan 5H 27
   HA9: Wemb 5E 60
   IG11: Bark 7F 71
   KT2: King T 2F 151
   KT17: Ewe 7B 164
   RM6: Chad H 6G 55
   RM7: Chad H, Rom 6G 55
   SE1 . . . . .7A 14 (3B 102)
   SE23 . . . . .1H 139
   SM3: Cheam 3F 165
   SM4: Mord 5J 153
   SM6: Wall 4F 167
   SW16 . . . . .1K 155
   SW17 . . . . .7D 136
   TW1: Twick 7A 114
   TW3: Houn 3G 113
   TW7: Bford, Isle 2K 113
   TW7: Isle, Twick 5A 114
   TW8: Bford 2K 113
   TW14: Bedf 2A 128
   TW15: Ashf 2A 128
LONDON ROAD RDBT. 6A 114
London School of Economics &
   Political Science, The
   . . . . .1G 13 (6K 83)
London Scottish & Richmond
   Rugby Football Ground . .3D 114
London Scottish Golf Course 3D 134
London's Death Trap 7G 13
London Shootfighters Gym 4G 79
London Soccerdome 2H 105
London South Bank University
   Keyworth St. 7B 14 (3B 102)
   London Rd. 7A 14
   Southwark Campus . .7B 14 (3B 102)
London South Bank University Sports Cen.
   . . . . .7B 14
(off London Rd.)
London South Bank University Technopark
   . . . . .3B 102
(off London Rd.)
London's Roman Amphitheatre 7E 8
(off Aldermanbury)
London Stile W4 . . . . .5G 97
London Stock Exchange 7C 8
London St. EC3 . . . . . . .2H 15 (7E 84)
   W2 . . . . .7A 4 (6B 82)
London Telecom Tower, The 5A 6
London Television Centre, The
   . . . . .4J 13 (7A 84)

London Ter. E2 . . . . .2G 85
London Transport Mus. 2F 13 (7J 83)
London Transport Mus. Depot 2G 97
London Trocadero 2C 12 (7H 83)
London Underwriting Cen. 2H 15
London Wall EC2 . . . . .6D 8 (5C 84)
London Wall Bldgs. EC2 . . . . .6F 9
London Wall Pl. EC2 . . . . .6E 8
(off Fore St.)
London Wetland Cen. 1D 116
London Wetland Cen. Vis. Cen. 1D 116
London Wharf E2 . . . . .1H 85
(off Wharf Pl.)
London Zoo 2E 82
LONESOME 1G 155
Lonesome Caravan Site SW16 . . . . .1F 155
Lonesome Way SW16 . . . . .1F 155
Long Acre WC2 . . . . .2E 12 (7J 83)
Long Acre Ct. W13 . . . . .5A 78
Longacre Pl. SM5: Cars 6E 166
Longacre Rd. E17 . . . . .1F 51
Longbeach Rd. SW11 . . . . .3D 118
Longbenrys NE9 . . . . .3H 63
Longboat Row UB1: S'hall 6D 76
Longbow Ho. EC1 . . . . .5E 8
(off Chiswell St.)
Longbridge Ho. E16 . . . . .7F 89
(off University Way)
   RM8: Dag 4B 72
(off Longbridge Rd.)
Longbridge Rd. IG11: Bark 6H 71
   RM8: Dag 6H 71
Longbridge Way SE13 . . . . .5E 122
Longcourt M. E11 . . . . .4A 52
Longcroft SE9 . . . . .3D 142
Longcrofte Rd. HA8: Edg 7J 27
Long Deacon Rd. E4 . . . . .1B 36
LONG DITTON 1C 162
Longdon Wood BR2: Kes 3C 172
Longdown Rd. SE6 . . . . .4C 140
Long Dr. HA4: Ruis 5A 58
   UB6: G'frd 1F 77
   UB7: W Dray 2A 92
   W3 . . . . .6A 80
Long Elmes HA3: Hrw W 1F 41
Longfellow Rd. E17 . . . . .6B 50
   KT4: Wor Pk 2C 164
Longfellow Way SE1 . . . . .4F 103
Long Fld. NW9 . . . . .7F 29
Longfield BR1: Brom 1H 159
Longfield Av. E17 . . . . .4A 50
   HA9: Wemb 1E 60
   NW7 . . . . .7H 29
   SM6: Wall 1E 166
   W5 . . . . .7C 78
Longfield Cres. SE26 . . . . .3J 139
Longfield Dr. CR4: Mitc 1C 154
   SW14 . . . . .5H 115
Longfield Est. SE1 . . . . .4F 103
Longfield Ho. E17 . . . . .5B 50
   W5 . . . . .7C 78
Longfield Rd. W5 . . . . .6C 78
Longfield St. SW18 . . . . .7J 117
Longfield Wlk. W5 . . . . .6C 78
LONGFORD 4C 174
Longford Av. TW14: Felt 6G 111
   TW19: Stanw 1A 128
   UB1: S'hall 7F 77
Longford Cir. UB7: Lford 4C 174
Longford Cl. TW12: Hamp H 4E 130
   TW13: Hanw 3C 130
   UB4: Yead 7B 76
Longford Ct. E5 . . . . .4K 67
(off Pedro St.)
   KT19: Ewe 4J 163
   NW4 . . . . .4F 45
   TW12: Hamp H 6F 131
   UB1: S'hall 1E 94
(off Uxbridge St.)
Longford Gdns. SM1: Sutt 3A 166
   UB4: Yead 7B 76

Longford Ho. BR1: Brom 5F 141
(off Brangbourne Rd.)
   E1 . . . . .6J 85
(off Jubilee St.)
   TW12: Hamp H 4E 130
Longford Ind. Est. TW12: Hamp 6F 131
LONGFORDMOOR 4B 174
Longford Rd. TW2: Whitt 1E 130
Longford St. NW1 . . . . . .3K 5 (4F 83)
Longford Wlk. SW2 . . . . .7A 120
Longhayes Av. RM6: Chad H 4D 54
Longhayes Ct. RM6: Chad H 4D 54
Longheath Gdns. CR0: C'don 5J 157
Longhedge Ho. SE26 . . . . .4G 139
(off High Level Dr.)
Long Hedges TW3: Houn 2E 112
Longhedge St. SW11 . . . . .2E 118
Longhill Rd. SE6 . . . . .2F 141
Longhook Gdns. UB5: N'olt 2J 75
Longhope Cl. SE15 . . . . .6E 102
Longhurst Ho. W10 . . . . .3H 81
(off Lancefield St.)
Longhurst Rd. CR0: C'don 6H 157
   SE13 . . . . .5F 123
Longitude Apartments CR0: C'don . .2D 168
(off Addiscombe Gro.)
Longland Ct. E9 . . . . .5A 68
(off Mabley St.)
   SE1 . . . . .5G 103
Longland Dr. N20 . . . . .3E 30
LONGLANDS 3G 143
Longlands Cl. CR4: Mitc 1E 154
   DA15: Sidc 2K 143
   W11 . . . . .7H 81
Longlands Pk. Cres. DA15: Sidc 3J 143
Longlands Rd. DA15: Sidc 3J 143
Long La. CR0: C'don 6J 157
   DA7: Bex 7D 108
   EC1 . . . . .6B 8 (5B 84)
   N2 . . . . .7E 30
   N3 . . . . .7E 30
   SE1 . . . . .7E 14 (2D 102)
   TW19: Stanw 2B 128
   UB10: Hil, Ick 3C 74
Longleat Ho. SW1 . . . . .5C 18
(off Rampayne St.)
Longleat Rd. EN1: Enf 5K 23
Longleat Way TW14: Bedf 7F 111
Longleigh Ho. SE5 . . . . .1E 120
(off Peckham Rd.)
Longleigh La. DA7: Bex 6C 108
   SE2 . . . . .6C 108
Long Lents Ho. NW10 . . . . .1K 79
(off Shrewsbury Rd.)
Longley Av. HA0: Wemb 1F 79
Longley Ct. SW8 . . . . .1J 119
Longley Rd. CR0: C'don 7B 156
   HA1: Harr 5G 41
   SW17 . . . . .6C 136
Long Leys E4 . . . . .6J 35
Longley St. SE1 . . . . .4G 103
Longley Way NW2 . . . . .3E 62
Longman Ho. E2 . . . . .2K 85
(off Mace St.)
   E8 . . . . .1F 85
(off Haggerston Rd.)
Long Mark Rd. E16 . . . . .5B 88
Longmarsh La. SE28 . . . . .1J 107
Long Mead NW9 . . . . .1B 44
Longmead BR7: Chst 2E 160
Longmead Dr. DA14: Sidc 2D 144
Longmead Ho. SE27 . . . . .5C 138
Long Mdw. NW5 . . . . .5H 65
Long Meadow Cl. BR4: W W'ck 7E 158
Longmeadow Rd. DA15: Sidc 1J 143
Longmead Rd. KT7: T Ditt 7J 149
   SW17 . . . . .5D 136
   UB3: Hayes 7H 75
Long Mill SE10 . . . . .1D 122
(off Greenwich High Rd.)

Longmoore St. SW1 . . . . .4A **18** (4G **101**)
Longmoor Point SW15 . . . . .1D **134**
(off Norley Va.)
Longmore Av. EN4: E Barn 6F **21**
EN5: New Bar 6F **21**
Longmore Gdns. Est. SW1 . . . . .4B **18**
Longnor Est. E1 . . . . .3K **85**
Longnor Rd. E1 . . . . .3K **85**
Long Pond Rd. SE3 . . . . .1G **123**
Longreach Ct. IG11: Bark 2H **89**
Long Reach Rd. IG11: Bark 4K **89**
Longridge Ho. SE1 . . . . .3C **102**
Longridge La. UB1: S'hall 6F **77**
Longridge Rd. IG11: Bark 7G **71**
SW5 . . . . .4J **99**
Long Ridges N2 . . . . .3E **46**
(off Fortis Grn.)
Long Rd. SW4 . . . . .4F **119**
Longs Ct. TW9: Rich 4F **115**
WC2 . . . . .3D **12**
Longshaw Rd. E4 . . . . .3A **36**
Longshore SE8 . . . . .4B **104**
Longshott Ct. SW5 . . . . .7E **14**
(off W. Cromwell Rd.)
Longstaff Cres. SW18 . . . . .6J **117**
Longstaff Rd. SW18 . . . . .6J **117**
Longstone Av. NW10 . . . . .7B **62**
Longstone Ct. SE1 . . . . .7E **14**
(off Gt. Dover St.)
Longstone Rd. SW17 . . . . .5F **137**
Long St. E2 . . . . .1J **9** (3F **85**)
Longthornton Rd. SW16 . . . . .2G **155**
Longthorpe Ct. W6 . . . . .4C **98**
Longton Av. SE26 . . . . .4G **139**
Longton Gro. SE26 . . . . .4H **139**
Longview Vs. RM5: Col R 1F **55**
Longview Way RM5: Col R 1K **55**
Longville Rd. SE11 . . . . .4B **102**
Long Wlk. KT3: N Mald 3J **151**
SE1 . . . . .3E **102**
SE18 . . . . .6F **107**
SW13 .2A **116**
Longwalk Rd. UB11: Stock P 1D **92**
Long Wall E15 . . . . .3F **87**
Longwater Ho. KT1: King T 3D **150**
(off Portsmouth Rd.)
Longwood Bus. Pk. TW16: Sun 5H **147**
Longwood Dr. SW15 . . . . .6C **116**
Longwood Gdns. IG5: Ilf 4D **52**
IG6: Ilf .4D **52**
Longworth Cl. SE28 . . . . .6D **90**
Long Yd. WC1 . . . . .4G **7** (4K **83**)
Loning, The NW9 . . . . .4A **44**
Lonsdale Av. E6 . . . . .4B **88**
HA9: Wemb 5E **60**
RM7: Rom 6J **55**
Lonsdale Cl. E6 . . . . .4C **88**
HA5: Hat E 1C **40**
HA8: Edg 3B **28**
SE9 . . . . .3B **142**
UB8: Hill 5B **74**
Lonsdale Ct. KT6: Surb 7D **150**
Lonsdale Cres. IG2: Ilf 6F **53**
Lonsdale Dr. EN2: Enf 4C **22**
Lonsdale Dr. Nth. EN2: Enf 5D **22**
Lonsdale Gdns. CR7: Thor H 4K **155**
Lonsdale Ho. W11 . . . . .6H **81**
(off Lonsdale Rd.)
Lonsdale M. TW9: Kew 1G **115**
W11 . . . . .6H **81**
(off Colville M.)
Lonsdale Pl. N1 . . . . .7A **66**
Lonsdale Rd. DA7: Bex 2F **127**
E11 . . . . .6H **51**
NW6 . . . . .2H **81**
SE25 . . . . .4H **157**
SW13 .1B **116**
UB2: S'hall 3B **94**
W4 . . . . .4A **98**
W11 . . . . .6H **81**
Lonsdale Sq. N1 . . . . .7A **66**

Lonsdale Yd. W11 . . . . .7J **81**
Loobert Rd. N15 . . . . .3E **48**
Looe Gdns. IG6: Ilf 3F **53**
Lookout Education Centre, The
. . . . .4E **10** (1D **100**)
Loop Rd. BR7: Chst 6G **143**
Lopen Rd. N18 . . . . .4K **33**
Lopez Ho. SW9 . . . . .3J **119**
Lorac Ct. SM2: Sutt 7J **165**
Loraine Cl. EN3: Pond E 5D **24**
Loraine Cotts. N7 . . . . .4K **65**
Loraine Ct. BR7: Chst 5F **143**
Loraine Ho. SM6: Wall 4F **167**
Loraine Rd. N7 . . . . .4K **65**
W4 . . . . .6H **97**
Lord Admiral's Vw. SE18 . . . . .4D **106**
(off Frances St.)
Lord Amory Way E14 . . . . .2E **104**
Lord Av. IG5: Ilf 4D **52**
Lord Chancellor Wlk. KT2: King T 1J **151**
Lord Cl. IG5: Ilf 4D **52**
Lordell Pl. SW19 . . . . .6E **134**
Lorden Wlk. E2 . . . . .2K **9** (3G **85**)
Lord Gdns. IG5: Ilf 4D **52**
Lord Hills Bri. W2 . . . . .5K **81**
Lord Hills Rd. W2 . . . . .5K **81**
Lord Holland La. SW9 . . . . .2A **120**
Lord Knyvetts Ct. TW19: Stanw 6A **110**
Lord Napier Pl. W6 . . . . .5C **98**
Lord Nth. St. SW1 . . . . . . .2E **18** (3J **101**)
Lord Roberts M. SW6 . . . . .7K **99**
Lord Robert's Ter. SE18 . . . . .5E **106**
Lord's 2B **4** (3B **82**)
Lords Cl. SE21 . . . . .2C **138**
TW13: Hanw 2C **130**
Lordship Gro. N16 . . . . .2D **66**
Lordship La. N17 . . . . .1D **48**
N22 . . . . .2A **48**
SE22 . . . . .4F **121**
Lordship La. Est. SE21 . . . . .7G **121**
Lordship Pk. N16 . . . . .2C **66**
Lordship Pk. M. N16 . . . . .2C **66**
Lordship Pl. SW3 . . . . .7C **16** (6C **100**)
Lordship Rd. N16 . . . . .1D **66**
UB5: N'olt 7C **58**
Lordship Ter. N16 . . . . .2D **66**
Lordsmead Rd. N17 . . . . .1E **48**
Lord St. E16 . . . . .1C **106**
Lords Vw. NW8 . . . . .2C **4** (3B **82**)
(not continuous)
Lordswood Cl. DA6: Bex 5E **126**
Lord Warwick St. SE18 . . . . .3D **106**
Loreburn Ho. N7 . . . . .4K **65**
Lorenzo Ho. IG3: Ilf 6A **54**
Lorenzo St. WC1 . . . . .1G **7** (3K **83**)
Loretto Gdns. HA3: Kenton 4E **42**
Lorian Cl. N12 . . . . .4E **30**
Lorimer Row BR2: Brom 6B **160**
Loring Rd. N20 . . . . .2H **31**
SE14 . . . . .1A **122**
TW7: Isle 2K **113**
Loris Rd. W6 . . . . .3E **98**
Lorn Ct. SW9 . . . . .2A **120**
Lorne Av. CR0: C'don 7K **157**
Lorne Cl. NW8 . . . . .2D **4** (3C **82**)
Lorne Gdns. CR0: C'don 7K **157**
E11 . . . . .4A **52**
W11 . . . . .2F **99**
Lorne Ho. E1 . . . . .5A **86**
(off Ben Jonson Rd.)
Lorne Rd. E7 . . . . .4K **69**
E17 . . . . .5C **50**
HA3: W'stone 2K **41**
N4 . . . . .1K **65**
TW10: Rich 5F **115**
Lorne Ter. N3 . . . . .2H **45**
Lorn Rd. SW9 . . . . .2K **119**
Lorraine Ct. NW1 . . . . .7F **65**
Lorraine Pk. HA3: Hrw W 7D **26**
Lorrimore Rd. SE17 . . . . .6B **102**
Lorrimore Sq. SE17 . . . . .6B **102**

Lorton Rd. NW6 . . . . .1J **81**
(off Kilburn Vale)
Lost Theatre 1H **119**
Lothair Rd. W5 . . . . .2D **96**
Lothair Rd. Nth. N4 . . . . .6B **48**
Lothair Rd. Sth. N4 . . . . .7A **48**
Lothian St. SW11 . . . . .3C **118**
Lothbury EC2 . . . . .7E **8** (6D **84**)
Lothian Av. UB4: Yead 5K **75**
Lothian Rd. HA0: Wemb 3A **60**
Lothian Rd. SW9 . . . . .1B **120**
Lothrop St. W10 . . . . .3G **81**
Lots Rd. SW10 . . . . .7A **100**
Lotus Cl. SE21 . . . . .2D **138**
Lotus M. N19 . . . . .2J **65**
Loubet St. SW17 . . . . .6D **136**
Loudoun Av. IG6: Ilf 5F **53**
Loudoun Rd. NW8 . . . . .1A **82**
Loudwater Cl. TW16: Sun 4J **147**
Loudwater Rd. TW16: Sun 4J **147**
Loughborough Est. SW9 . . . . .3B **120**
Loughborough Ho. RM8: Dag 4A **72**
(off Academy Way)
Loughborough Pk. SW9 . . . . .4B **120**
Loughborough Rd. SW9 . . . . .2A **120**
Loughborough St. SE11 . . . . .5H **19** (5K **101**)
Lough Rd. N7 . . . . .5K **65**
Loughton Way IG9: Buck H 1G **37**
Louisa Cl. E9 . . . . .1K **85**
Louisa Ct. TW2: Twick 2J **131**
Louisa Gdns. E1 . . . . .4K **85**
Louisa Ho. IG3: Ilf 6A **54**
Louisa Oakes Cl. E4 . . . . .4G **35**
Louisa St. E1 . . . . .4K **85**
Louise Aumonier Wlk. N19 . . . . .7J **47**
(off Jessie Blythe La.)
Louise Bennett Cl. SE24 . . . . .4B **120**
Louise Cl. E11 . . . . .5K **51**
N22 . . . . .1A **48**
Louise De Marillac Ho. E1 . . . . .5J **85**
(off Smithy St.)
Louise Rd. E15 . . . . .6G **69**
Louise White Ho. N19 . . . . .1H **65**
Louis Gdns. BR7: Chst 4D **142**
Louis M. N10 . . . . .1F **47**
Louisville Rd. SW17 . . . . .3E **136**
Lousada Lodge N14 . . . . .6B **22**
(off Avenue Rd.)
Louvaine Rd. SW11 . . . . .4B **118**
Lovage App. E6 . . . . .5C **88**
Lovat Cl. E14 . . . . .6B **86**
NW2 . . . . .3B **62**
Lovat La. EC3 . . . . .2G **15** (7E **84**)
Lovatt Cl. HA8: Edg 6C **28**
Lovatt Ct. SW12 . . . . .1F **137**
Lovatt Dr. HA4: Ruis 5J **39**
Lovat Wlk. TW5: Hest 7C **94**
Loveday Rd. W13 . . . . .2B **96**
Lovegrove St. SE1 . . . . .5G **103**
Lovegrove Wlk. E14 . . . . .1E **104**
Lovekyn Cl. KT2: King T 2E **150**
Lovelace Av. BR2: Brom 6E **160**
Lovelace Gdns. IG11: Bark 4A **72**
KT6: Surb 7D **150**
Lovelace Grn. SE9 . . . . .3D **124**
Lovelace Ho. W13 . . . . .7B **78**
Lovelace Rd. EN4: E Barn 7H **21**
KT6: Surb 7C **150**
SE21 . . . . .2C **138**
Lovelace St. E8 . . . . .1F **85**
Lovelace Vs. KT7: T Ditt 7B **150**
(off Portsmouth Rd.)
Loveland Ct. SE1 . . . . .7K **15**
(off Jamaica Rd.)
Loveland Mans. IG11: Bark 7K **71**
(off Upney La.)
Love La. BR1: Brom 3K **159**
CR4: Mitc 3C **154**
(not continuous)
DA5: Bexl 6G **127**
EC2 . . . . .7D **8** (6C **84**)

Love La. HA5: Pinn 2B **40**
IG8: Wfd G 6J **37**
KT6: Surb 2C **162**
N17 . . . . .7A **34**
SE18 . . . . .4F **107**
SE25 . . . . .3H **157**
SM1: Sutt 6H **165**
SM3: Cheam, Sutt 6G **165**
SM4: Mord 7J **153**
Lovel Av. DA16: Well 2A **126**
Lovelinch Cl. SE15 . . . . .6J **103**
Lovell Ho. E8 . . . . .1G **85**
(off Shrubland Rd.)
Lovell Pl. SE16 . . . . .3A **104**
Lovell Rd. TW10: Ham 3C **132**
UB1: S'hall 6F **77**
Loveridge M. NW6 . . . . .6H **63**
Loveridge Rd. NW6 . . . . .6H **63**
Lovers Wlk. N3 . . . . .7D **30**
(not continuous)
NW7 . . . . .6C **30**
SE10 . . . . .6F **105**
W1 . . . . .4G **11** (1E **100**)
Lovett Dr. SM5: Cars 7A **154**
Lovett's Pl. SW18 . . . . .4K **117**
Lovett Way NW10 . . . . .5J **61**
Love Wlk. SE5 . . . . .2D **120**
Lovibonds Av. BR6: Farnb 4F **173**
UB7: Yiew 6B **74**
Lowbrook Rd. IG1: Ilf 5F **71**
Low Cross Wood La. SE21 . . . . .3F **139**
Lowdell Cl. UB7: Yiew 6A **74**
Lowden Rd. N9 . . . . .1C **34**
SE24 . . . . .4B **120**
UB1: S'hall 7C **76**
Lowder Ho. E1 . . . . .1H **103**
(off Wapping La.)
Lowe Av. E16 . . . . .5J **87**
Lowell Ho. SE5 . . . . .7C **102**
(off Wyndham Est.)
Lowell St. E14 . . . . .6A **86**
Lowen Rd. RM13: Rain 2K **91**
Lwr. Addiscombe Rd. CR0: C'don 1E **168**
Lwr. Addison Gdns. W14 . . . . .2G **99**
Lwr. Ash Est. TW17: Shep 6H **147**
Lwr. Belgrave St. SW1 . . . . .2J **17** (3F **101**)
Lwr. Boston Rd. W7 . . . . .1J **95**
Lwr. Broad St. RM10: Dag 1G **91**
Lwr. Camden BR7: Chst 7D **142**
Lwr. Church St. CR0: C'don 2B **168**
LOWER CLAPTON 4H **67**
Lwr. Clapton Rd. E5 . . . . .3H **67**
Lwr. Clarendon Wlk. W11 . . . . .6G **81**
(off Clarendon Rd.)
Lwr. Common Sth. SW15 . . . . .3D **116**
Lwr. Coombe St. CR0: C'don 4C **168**
Lwr. Downs Rd. SW20 . . . . .1F **153**
Lwr. Drayton Pl. CR0: C'don 2B **168**
LOWER EDMONTON 2B **34**
LOWER FELTHAM 3J **129**
Lower Fosters NW4 . . . . .5E **44**
(off New Brent St.)
Lwr. George St. TW9: Rich 5D **114**
Lwr. Gravel Rd. BR2: Brom 1C **172**
Lower Grn. Gdns. KT4: Wor Pk 1C **164**
Lwr. Grn. W. CR4: Mitc 3C **154**
Lwr. Grosvenor Pl. SW1 . . . . .1K **17** (3F **101**)
Lower Gro. Rd. TW10: Rich 6E **114**
LOWER HALLIFORD 7F **147**
Lwr. Hall La. E4 . . . . .5F **35**
(not continuous)
Lwr. Hampton Rd. TW16: Sun 3A **148**
Lwr. Ham Rd. KT2: King T 5D **132**
LOWER HOLLOWAY 5K **65**
Lwr. Hook Bus. Pk. BR6: Downe 7D **172**
Lwr. James St. W1 . . . . . . .2B **12** (7G **83**)
Lwr. John St. W1 . . . . .2B **12** (7G **83**)
Lwr. Kenwood Av. EN2: Enf 5D **22**
Lwr. King's Rd. KT2: King T 1E **150**
Lwr. Lea Crossing E14 . . . . .7G **87**
E16 . . . . .7G **87**

Lwr. Maidstone Rd.—Lyceum Theatre

Lwr. Maidstone Rd. N11 . . . 6B **32**
Lower Mall W6 . . . 5D **98**
Lwr. Mardyke Av. RM13: Rain . . . 2J **91**
Lower Marsh SE1 . . . 7J **13** (2A **102**)
Lwr. Marsh La. KT1: King T . . . 4F **151**
Lwr. Merton Ri. NW3 . . . 7C **64**
Lower Mill KT17: Ewe . . . 7B **164**
Lwr. Morden La. SM4: Mord . . . 6E **152**
Lwr. Mortlake Rd. TW9: Rich . . . 4E **114**
Lwr. New Change Pas. *EC4* . . . *1D **14***
(off One New Change)
Lwr. Park Rd. DA17: Belv . . . 4G **109**
N11 . . . 5B **32**
Lwr. Park Trad. Est. NW10 . . . 4J **79**
LOWER PLACE . . . 2J **79**
Lower Pl. Bus. Cen. *NW10* . . . *2K **79***
(off Steele Rd.)
Lwr. Queen's Rd. IG9: Buck H . . . 2G **37**
Lwr. Richmond Rd. SW14 . . . 3G **115**
SW15 . . . 3D **116**
TW9: Rich . . . 3G **115**
Lower Rd. DA8: Erith . . . 3H **109**
DA17: Belv . . . 3H **109**
HA2: Harr . . . 1H **59**
SE1 . . . 6J **13** (2A **102**)
SE8 . . . 4K **103**
SE16 . . . 2J **103**
(not continuous)
SM1: Sutt . . . 4A **166**
Lwr. Robert St. *WC2* . . . *3F **13***
(off Robert St.)
Lwr. Sand Hills KT6: Surb . . . 7C **150**
Lwr. Sloane St. SW1 . . . 4G **17** (4E **100**)
Lower Sq. TW7: Isle . . . 3B **114**
Lower Square, The *SM1: Sutt* . . . *5K **165***
(off St Nicholas Way)
Lower Strand NW9 . . . 2B **44**
Lwr. Sunbury Rd. TW12: Hamp . . . 2D **148**
LOWER SYDENHAM . . . 4K **139**
Lwr. Sydenham Ind. Est. SE26 . . . 5B **140**
Lwr. Teddington Rd. KT1: Hamp W . . . 1D **150**
Lower Ter. NW3 . . . 3A **64**
SE27 . . . *5B **138***
(off Woodcote Pl.)
Lwr. Thames St. EC3 . . . 3F **15** (7D **84**)
Lowerwood Ct. *W11* . . . *6G **81***
(off Westbourne Pk. Rd.)
Lwr. Wood Rd. KT10: Clay . . . 6B **162**
Lowestoft Cl. *E5* . . . *2J **67***
(off Theydon Rd.)
Lowestoft M. E16 . . . 2F **107**
Loweswater Cl. HA9: Wemb . . . 2D **60**
Loweswater Ho. E3 . . . 4B **86**
Lowfield Rd. NW6 . . . 7J **63**
W3 . . . 6H **79**
Low Hall Cl. E4 . . . 7J **25**
Low Hall La. E17 . . . 6A **50**
Low Hall Mnr. Bus. Cen. E17 . . . 6A **50**
Lowick Rd. HA1: Harr . . . 4J **41**
Lowlands Gdns. RM7: Rom . . . 6H **55**
Lowlands Rd. HA1: Harr . . . 6J **41**
HA5: Eastc . . . 7A **40**
Lowman Rd. N7 . . . 4K **65**
Lownde M. SW16 . . . 2J **137**
Lowndes Cl. SW1 . . . 2H **17** (3E **100**)
Lowndes Ct. SW1 . . . 1F **17** (3D **100**)
W1 . . . *1A **12***
(off Carnaby St.)
Lowndes Lodge *SW1* . . . *1F **17***
(off Cadogan Pl.)
Lowndes M. SW16 . . . 2J **137**
Lowndes Pl. SW1 . . . 2G **17** (3E **100**)
Lowndes Sq. SW1 . . . 7F **11** (2D **100**)
Lowndes St. SW1 . . . 1F **17** (3E **100**)
Lownds Ct. BR1: Brom . . . 2J **159**
Lowood Ct. *SE19* . . . *5F **139***
(off Farquhar Rd.)
Lowood Ho. *E1* . . . *7J **85***
(off Bewley St.)
Lowood St. E1 . . . 7H **85**
Lowry Cl. DA8: Erith . . . 4K **109**
Lowry Ct. *SE16* . . . *5H **103***
(off Stubbs Dr.)
Lowry Cres. CR4: Mitc . . . 2C **154**
Lowry Ho. *E14* . . . *2C **104***
(off Cassilis Rd.)
N17 . . . *1F **49***
(off Pembury Rd.)
W3 . . . *3J **97***
(off Palmerston Rd.)
Lowry Rd. RM8: Dag . . . 5B **72**
Lowshoe La. RM5: Col R . . . 1G **55**
Lowswood Cl. HA6: Nwood . . . 1E **38**
Lowther Dr. EN2: Enf . . . 4D **22**
Lowther Hill SE23 . . . 7A **122**
Lowther Ho. *SW1* . . . *6B **18***
(off Churchill Gdns.)
Lowther Rd. E17 . . . 2A **50**
HA7: Stan . . . 3F **43**
KT2: King T . . . 1F **151**
N7 . . . 5A **66**
SW13 . . . 1B **116**
Lowth Rd. SE5 . . . 1C **120**
LOXFORD . . . 5G **71**
Loxford Av. E6 . . . 2B **88**
Loxford Gdns. N5 . . . 4B **66**
Loxford La. IG1: Ilf . . . 5G **71**
IG3: Ilf . . . 5G **71**
Loxford Rd. IG11: Bark . . . 6F **71**
Loxford Ter. IG11: Bark . . . 6G **71**
Loxham Rd. E4 . . . 7J **35**
Loxham St. WC1 . . . 2F **7** (3J **83**)
Loxley Cl. SE26 . . . 5K **139**
Loxley Ho. HA9: Wemb . . . 3E **60**
Loxley Rd. SW18 . . . 1B **136**
TW12: Hamp . . . 4D **130**
Loxton Rd. SE23 . . . 1K **139**
Loxwood Cl. TW14: Bedf . . . 1F **129**
Loxwood Rd. N17 . . . 3E **48**
LSO St Lukes . . . *3D **8***
(off Old St.)
Lubbock Ho. *E14* . . . *7D **86***
(off Poplar High St.)
Lubbock Rd. BR7: Chst . . . 7D **142**
Lubbock St. SE14 . . . 7J **103**
Lucan Ho. *N1* . . . *1D **84***
(off Colville Est.)
Lucan Pl. SW3 . . . 4C **16** (4C **100**)
Lucan Rd. EN5: Barn . . . 3B **20**
Lucas Av. E13 . . . 1K **87**
HA2: Harr . . . 2E **58**
Lucas Cl. NW10 . . . 7C **62**
Lucas Ct. SE26 . . . 5A **140**
SW11 . . . 1E **118**
Lucas Gdns. N2 . . . 2A **46**
Lucas Ho. *SW10* . . . *7K **99***
(off Coleridge Gdns.)
WC1 . . . *3J **83***
(off Argyle Wlk.)
Lucas Rd. SE20 . . . 6J **139**
Lucas Sq. NW11 . . . 6J **45**
Lucas St. SE8 . . . 1C **122**
Lucent Ho. *SW18* . . . *5J **117***
(off Hardwicks Sq.)
Lucerne Cl. N13 . . . 3D **32**
Lucerne Ct. DA18: Erith . . . 3E **108**
Lucerne Gro. E17 . . . 4F **51**
Lucerne M. W8 . . . 1J **99**
Lucerne Rd. BR6: Orp . . . 1K **173**
CR7: Thor H . . . 5B **156**
N5 . . . 4B **66**
Lucey Rd. SE16 . . . 3G **103**
Lucey Way SE16 . . . 3G **103**
Lucia Hgts. *E20* . . . *5E **68***
(off Logan Cl.)
Lucie Av. TW15: Ashf . . . 6D **128**
Lucien Rd. SW17 . . . 4E **136**
SW19 . . . 2K **135**
Lucinda Ct. E17 . . . 2K **49**
EN1: Enf . . . 4K **23**
Lucknow St. SE18 . . . 7J **107**
Lucorn Cl. SE12 . . . 6H **123**
Luctons Av. IG9: Buck H . . . 1F **37**
Lucy Brown Ho. SE1 . . . 5D **14**
Lucy Cres. W3 . . . 5J **79**
Lucy Gdns. RM8: Dag . . . 3F **73**
Luddesdon Rd. DA8: Erith . . . 7G **109**
Ludford Cl. CR0: Wadd . . . 3B **168**
Ludgate B'way. EC4 . . . 1A **14** (6B **84**)
Ludgate Cir. EC4 . . . 1A **14** (6B **84**)
Ludgate Hill EC4 . . . 1A **14** (6B **84**)
Ludgate Sq. EC4 . . . 1B **14** (6B **84**)
Ludham NW5 . . . 5D **64**
Ludham Cl. IG6: Ilf . . . 1G **53**
SE28 . . . 6C **90**
Ludlow Cl. BR2: Brom . . . 3J **159**
HA2: Harr . . . 4D **58**
Ludlow Ct. W3 . . . 2J **97**
Ludlow Rd. TW13: Felt . . . 4J **129**
W5 . . . 4C **78**
Ludlow St. EC1 . . . 3C **8** (4C **84**)
Ludlow Way N2 . . . 4A **46**
Ludovick Wlk. SW15 . . . 4A **116**
Ludwell Ho. *W14* . . . *3G **99***
(off Russell Rd.)
Ludwick M. SE14 . . . 7A **104**
Luffield Rd. SE2 . . . 3B **108**
Luffman Rd. SE12 . . . 3K **141**
Lugard Ho. *W12* . . . *1D **98***
(off Bloemfontein Rd.)
Lugard Rd. SE15 . . . 2H **121**
Lugg App. E12 . . . 3E **70**
Luke Allsopp Sq. RM10: Dag . . . 3H **73**
Luke Ho. *E1* . . . *6H **85***
(off Tillman St.)
Luke St. EC2 . . . 3G **9** (4E **84**)
Lukin Cres. E4 . . . 3A **36**
Lukin St. E1 . . . 6J **85**
Luli Ct. SE14 . . . 6B **104**
Lullingstone Cl. BR5: St P . . . 7B **144**
Lullingstone Cres. BR5: St P . . . 7A **144**
Lullingstone Ho. *SE15* . . . *6J **103***
(off Lovelinch Cl.)
Lullingstone La. SE13 . . . 6F **123**
Lullingstone Rd. DA17: Belv . . . 6F **109**
Lullington Gth. BR1: Brom . . . 7G **141**
N12 . . . 5C **30**
Lullington Rd. RM9: Dag . . . 7E **72**
SE20 . . . 7G **139**
Lulot Gdns. N19 . . . 2F **65**
Lulsgate M. E3 . . . 4B **86**
Lulworth *NW1* . . . *7H **65***
(off Wrotham Rd.)
SE17 . . . *5D **102***
(off Portland St.)
Lulworth Av. HA9: Wemb . . . 7C **42**
TW5: Hest . . . 1F **113**
Lulworth Cl. HA2: Harr . . . 3D **58**
Lulworth Ct. *N1* . . . *7E **66***
(off St Peter's Way)
Lulworth Cres. CR4: Mitc . . . 2C **154**
Lulworth Dr. HA5: Pinn . . . 6B **40**
Lulworth Gdns. HA2: Harr . . . 2C **58**
Lulworth Ho. SW8 . . . 7K **101**
Lulworth Rd.
DA16: Well . . . 2K **125**
SE9 . . . 2C **142**
SE15 . . . 2H **121**
Lulworth Waye UB4: Yead . . . 6K **75**
Lumen Rd. HA9: Wemb . . . 2D **60**
Lumiere Apartments SW11 . . . 4B **118**
Lumiere Building, The *E7* . . . *5B **70***
(off Romford Rd.)
Lumiere Ct. SW17 . . . 2E **136**
Lumina Bldgs. *E14* . . . *1E **104***
(off Prestons Rd.)
Lumina Bus. Pk. EN1: Enf . . . 5B **24**
Lumina Loft Apartments *SE1* . . . *7H **15***
(off Tower Bri. Rd.)
Lumina Way EN1: Enf . . . 5B **24**
Luminosity Ct. W13 . . . 7B **78**
Lumley Cl. DA17: Belv . . . 5G **109**
Lumley Ct. WC2 . . . 3F **13** (7J **83**)
Lumley Flats *SW1* . . . *5G **17***
(off Holbein Pl.)
Lumley Gdns. SM3: Cheam . . . 5G **165**
Lumley Rd. SM3: Cheam . . . 5G **165**
Lumley St. W1 . . . 1H **11** (6E **82**)
Lumsdon *NW8* . . . *1K **81***
(off Abbey Rd.)
Luna Ho. SE16 . . . 2G **103**
Lunan Ho. *E3* . . . *2B **86***
(off Shetland Rd.)
Lunaria Ho. *E20* . . . *5E **68***
(off Elis Way)
Luna Rd. CR7: Thor H . . . 3C **156**
Lund Point E15 . . . 1E **86**
Lundy Dr. UB3: Harl . . . 4G **93**
Lundy Wlk. N1 . . . 6C **66**
Lunham Rd. SE19 . . . 6E **138**
Luntley Pl. *E1* . . . *6K **9***
(off Chicksand St.)
Lupin Cl. CR0: C'don . . . 1K **169**
RM7: Rush G . . . 2K **73**
SW2 . . . 2B **138**
UB7: W Dray . . . 1E **174**
Lupin Cres. IG1: Ilf . . . 6F **71**
Lupino Ct. SE11 . . . 3H **19** (4K **101**)
Lupin Point SE1 . . . 7K **15**
Lupton Cl. SE12 . . . 3K **141**
Lupton St. NW5 . . . 4G **65**
(not continuous)
Lupus St. SW1 . . . 6K **17** (5F **101**)
Luralda Wharf E14 . . . 5F **105**
Lurgan Av. W6 . . . 6F **99**
Lurline Gdns. SW11 . . . 1E **118**
Luscombe Ct. BR2: Brom . . . 2G **159**
Luscombe Way SW8 . . . 7J **101**
Lushington Ho.
KT12: Walt T . . . 6A **148**
Lushington Rd. NW10 . . . 2D **80**
SE6 . . . 4D **140**
Lushington Ter. E8 . . . 5G **67**
Lutea Ho. *SM2: Sutt* . . . *7A **166***
(off Walnut M.)
Luther Cl. HA8: Edg . . . 2D **28**
Luther King Cl. E17 . . . 6B **50**
Luther M. TW11: Tedd . . . 5K **131**
Luther Rd. TW11: Tedd . . . 5K **131**
Luton Ho. *E13* . . . *4J **87***
(off Luton Rd.)
Luton Pl. SE10 . . . 7E **104**
Luton Rd. DA14: Sidc . . . 3C **144**
E13 . . . 4J **87**
E17 . . . 3B **50**
Luton St. NW8 . . . 4B **4** (4B **82**)
Lutton Ter. *NW3* . . . *4A **64***
(off Lakis Cl.)
Luttrell Av. SW15 . . . 5D **116**
Lutwyche M. SE6 . . . 2B **140**
Lutwyche Rd. SE6 . . . 2B **140**
Lutyens Ho. *SW1* . . . *6A **18***
(off Churchill Gdns.)
Lux Apartments *SW18* . . . *5J **117***
(off Broomhill Rd.)
Luxborough Ho. *W1* . . . *5G **5***
(off Luxborough St.)
Luxborough La. IG7: Chig . . . 3H **37**
Luxborough St. W1 . . . 5G **5** (5E **82**)
Luxborough Twr. W1 . . . 5G **5**
Luxembourg M. E15 . . . 5G **69**
Luxemburg Gdns. W6 . . . 4F **99**
Luxfield Rd. SE9 . . . 1C **142**
Luxford St. SE16 . . . 4K **103**
Luxmore St. SE4 . . . 1B **122**
Luxor St. SE5 . . . 3C **120**
Lyall Av. SE21 . . . 4E **138**
Lyall M. SW1 . . . 2G **17** (3E **100**)
Lyall M. W. SW1 . . . 2G **17** (3E **100**)
Lyall St. SW1 . . . 2G **17** (3E **100**)
Lyal Rd. E3 . . . 2A **86**
Lycett Pl. W12 . . . 2C **98**
Lyceum Theatre
Covent Garden . . . 2G **13**

Lychgate Mnr. HA1: Harr 7J 41
Lych Ga. Wlk. UB3: Hayes 7H 75
    (not continuous)
Lyconby Gdns. CR0: C'don 7A 158
Lydd Cl. DA14: Sidc 3J 143
Lydden Cl. SE9 . . . . .6J 125
Lydden Gro. SW18 . . . . .7K 117
Lydden Rd. SW18 . . . . .7K 117
Lydd Rd. DA7: Bex 7F 109
Lydeard Rd. E6 . . . . .7D 70
Lydford NW1 . . . . .1G 83
    (off Royal College St.)
Lydford Cl. N16 . . . . .5E 66
    (off Pellerin Rd.)
Lydford Rd. N15 . . . . .5D 48
    NW2 . . . . .6E 62
    W9 .4H 81
Lydhurst Av. SW2 . . . . .2K 137
Lydia Cl. KT1: King T 3E 150
    (off Grove Cres.)
    N12 . . . . .6F 31
Lydney Cl. SW19 . . . . .2G 135
Lydon Rd. SW4 . . . . .3G 119
Lydstep Rd. BR7: Chst 4E 142
Lyford Rd. SW18 . . . . .7B 118
Lyford St. SE7 . . . . .4C 106
Lygon Ho. E2 . . . . .1K 9
    (off Gosset St.)
    SW6 . . . . .1G 117
    (off Fulham Pal. Rd.)
Lygon Pl. SW1 . . . . .2J 17 (3F 101)
Lyham Cl. SW2 . . . . .6J 119
Lyham Rd. SW2 . . . . .5J 119
Lyle Cl. CR4: Mitc 7E 154
Lyle Cl. SM4: Mord 6B 154
Lyly Ho. SE1 . . . . .3D 102
    (off Burbage Cl.)
Lyme Farm Rd. SE12 . . . . .4J 123
Lyme Gro. E9 . . . . .7J 67
Lyme Gro. Ho. E9 . . . . .7J 67
    (off Lyme Gro.)
Lymer Av. SE19 . . . . .5F 139
Lyme Rd. DA16: Well 1B 126
Lymescote Gdns.
    SM1: Sutt 2J 165
Lyme St. NW1 . . . . .7G 65
Lyme Ter. NW1 . . . . .7G 65
Lyminge Cl. DA14: Sidc 4K 143
Lyminge Gdns. SW18 . . . . .1C 136
Lymington Av. N22 . . . . .2A 48
Lymington Cl. E6 . . . . .5D 88
    SW16 . . . . .2H 155
Lymington Cl. SM1: Sutt 3K 165
Lymington Dr. HA4: Ruis 2F 57
Lymington Gdns.
    KT19: Ewe 5B 164
Lymington Lodge E14 . . . . .3F 105
    (off Schooner Cl.)
Lymington Rd. NW6 . . . . .6K 63
    RM8: Dag 1D 72
Lyminster Cl. UB4: Yead 5C 76
Lympne N17 . . . . .2D 48
    (off Gloucester Rd.)
Lympstone Gdns. SE15 . . . . .7G 103
Lynbridge Gdns. N13 . . . . .4G 33
Lynbrook Cl. IG43: Rain 2K 91
Lynbrook Gro. SE15 . . . . .7E 102
Lynch Cl. SE3 . . . . .2H 123
Lynchen Cl. TW5: Cran 1K 111
Lynch Wlk. SE8 . . . . .6B 104
    (off Prince St.)
Lyncott Cres. SW4 . . . . .4F 119
Lyncourt SE3 . . . . .2F 123
Lyncroft Av. HA5: Pinn 5C 40
Lyncroft Gdns. NW6 . . . . .5J 63
    TW3: Houn 5G 113
    W13 . . . . .2C 96
Lyncroft Mans. NW6 . . . . .5J 63
Lyndale NW2 . . . . .4H 63
Lyndale Av. NW2 . . . . .3H 63

Lyndale Cl. SE3 . . . . .6H 105
Lyndean Ind. Est. SE2 . . . . .3C 108
Lynde Ho. KT12: Walt T 6A 148
    SW4 . . . . .3H 119
Lynden Ho. E1 . . . . .3K 85
    (off Westfield Way)
Lynden Hyrst CRO: C'don 2F 169
Lyndhurst Av. HA5: Pinn 1K 39
    KT5: Surb 1H 163
    N12 . . . . .6J 31
    NW7 . . . . .6F 29
    SW16 . . . . .2H 155
    TW2: Whitt 1D 130
    TW16: Sun 3J 147
    UB1: S'hall 1F 95
Lyndhurst Cl. BR6: Farnb 4F 173
    CRO: C'don 3F 169
    DA7: Bex 3H 127
    NW10 . . . . .3K 61
Lyndhurst Ct. E18 . . . . .1J 51
    NW8 . . . . .1B 82
    (off Finchley Rd.)
    SM2: Sutt 7J 165
    (off Grange Rd.)
Lyndhurst Dr. E10 . . . . .7E 50
    KT3: N Mald 7A 152
Lyndhurst Gdns. EN1: Enf 4K 23
    HA5: Pinn 1K 39
    IG2: Ilf 6H 53
    IG11: Bark 6J 71
    N3 .1G 45
    NW3 . . . . .5B 64
Lyndhurst Gro. SE15 . . . . .2E 120
Lyndhurst Lodge E14 . . . . .4F 105
    (off Millennium Dr.)
Lyndhurst Ri. IG7: Chig 4K 37
Lyndhurst Rd. CR7: Thor H 4A 156
    DA7: Bex 3H 127
    E4 .7K 35
    N18 . . . . .4B 34
    N22 . . . . .6F 33
    NW3 . . . . .5B 64
    UB6: G'frd 4F 77
Lyndhurst Sq. SE15 . . . . .1F 121
Lyndhurst Ter. NW3 . . . . .5B 64
Lyndhurst Way SE15 . . . . .1F 121
    SM2: Sutt 7J 165
Lyndon Av. DA15: Sidc 5K 125
    SM6: Wall 3E 166
Lyndon Ho. E18 . . . . .1J 51
    (off Queen Mary Av.)
Lyndon Rd. DA17: Belv 4G 109
Lyndon Yd. SW17 . . . . .4A 136
Lyne Cres. E17 . . . . .1B 50
Lynegrove Av. TW15: Ashf 5E 128
Lyneham Dr. NW9 . . . . .1A 44
Lyneham Wlk. E5 . . . . .5A 68
    HA5: Eastc 3H 39
Lynette Av. SW4 . . . . .6F 119
Lynford Cl. HA8: Edg 1J 43
Lynford Ct. CR2: S Croy 4E 168
    (off Coombe Rd.)
Lynford French Ho. SE17 . . . . .5C 102
    (off Thrush St.)
Lynford Gdns. HA8: Edg 3C 28
    IG3: Ilf 2K 71
Lynford Ter. N9 . . . . .1A 34
Lynhurst Cres. UB10: Hil 7E 56
Lynhurst Rd. UB10: Hil 7E 56
Lynmere Rd. DA16: Well 2B 126
Lyn M. E3 . . . . .3B 86
    N16 . . . . .4E 66
Lynmouth Av. EN1: Enf 6A 24
    SM4: Mord 6F 153
Lynmouth Dr. HA4: Ruis 2K 57
Lynmouth Gdns. TW5: Hest 7B 94
    UB6: G'frd 1B 78
Lynmouth Rd. E17 . . . . .6A 50
    N2 .3D 46
    N16 . . . . .1F 67
    UB6: G'frd 1B 78

Lynn Cl. HA3: Hrw W 2H 41
    TW15: Ashf 5F 129
Lynne Cl. BR6: Chels 6K 173
    SE23 . . . . .7B 122
Lynne Ct. CR2: S Croy 4E 168
    (off Birdhurst Rd.)
    NW6 . . . . .7K 63
    (off Priory Rd.)
Lynnett Ct. E9 . . . . .6A 68
    (off Annis Rd.)
Lynnett Rd. RM8: Dag 2D 72
Lynne Way UB5: N'olt 2B 76
Lynn Ho. SE15 . . . . .6H 103
    (off Friary Est.)
Lynn M. E11 . . . . .2G 69
Lynn Rd. E11 . . . . .2G 69
    IG2: Ilf 7H 53
    SW12 . . . . .7F 119
Lynn St. EN2: Enf 1J 23
Lynscott Way CR2: S Croy 7B 168
Lynstead Ct. BR3: Beck 2A 158
Lynsted Cl. BR1: Brom 2A 160
    DA6: Bex 5H 127
Lynsted Gdns. SE9 . . . . .4B 124
Lynton Av. N12 . . . . .4G 31
    NW9 . . . . .4B 44
    RM7: Mawney 1G 55
    W13 . . . . .6A 78
Lynton Cl. KT9: Chess 4E 162
    NW10 . . . . .5A 62
    TW7: Isle 4K 113
Lynton Cres. IG2: Ilf 6F 53
Lynton Est. SE1 . . . . .4G 103
Lynton Gdns. EN1: Enf 7K 23
    N11 . . . . .6C 32
Lynton Grange N2 . . . . .3D 46
Lynton Ho. IG1: Ilf 2G 71
    (off High Rd.)
    W2 .6A 82
    (off Hallfield Est.)
Lynton Mans. SE1 . . . . .1J 19
    (off Westminster Bri. Rd.)
Lynton Mead N20 . . . . .3D 30
Lynton Rd. CR0: C'don 6A 156
    E4 .5J 35
    HA2: Harr 2C 58
    KT3: N Mald 5K 151
    N8 .5H 47
    (not continuous)
    NW6 . . . . .2H 81
    SE1 . . . . .4F 103
    W3 .7G 79
Lynton Ter. W3 . . . . .6J 79
Lynton Wlk. UB4: Hayes 3G 75
Lynwood Cl. E18 . . . . .1A 52
    HA2: Harr 3C 58
Lynwood Ct. KT1: King T 2H 151
Lynwood Dr.
    HA6: Nwood 1H 39
    KT4: Wor Pk 2C 164
Lynwood Gdns. CR0: Wadd 4K 167
    UB1: S'hall 6D 76
Lynwood Gro. BR6: Orp 7J 161
    N21 . . . . .1F 33
Lynwood Rd. KT7: T Ditt 2A 162
    SW17 . . . . .3D 136
    W5 .3D 78
Lynx Way E16 . . . . .7B 88
Lyon Bus. Pk. IG11: Bark 2J 89
Lyon Cl. HA4: Ruis 1H 57
Lyon Ho. NW8 . . . . .4C 4
    (off Broadley St.)
Lyon Ind. Est. NW2 . . . . .2D 62
Lyon Meade HA7: Stan 1C 42
Lyon Pk. Av. HA0: Wemb 6E 60
    (not continuous)
Lyon Rd. HA1: Harr 6K 41
    SW19 . . . . .1A 154
LYONSDOWN 5F 21
Lyonsdown Av. EN5: New Bar 6F 21
Lyonsdown Rd. EN5: New Bar 6F 21

Lyons Pl. HA7: Stan 3D 26
    NW8 . . . . .4A 4 (4B 82)
Lyon St. N1 . . . . .7K 65
Lyons Wlk. W14 . . . . .4G 99
Lyon Way UB6: G'frd 1J 77
Lyoth Rd. BR5: Farnb 2G 173
Lyric Cl. E8 . . . . .7F 67
    (off Holly St.)
Lyric Dr. UB6: G'frd 4F 77
Lyric M. SE26 . . . . .4J 139
Lyric Rd. SW13 . . . . .1B 116
Lyric Sq. W6 . . . . .4E 98
    (off King St.)
Lyric Theatre
    Hammersmith 4E 98
    Westminster 2C 12
    (off Shaftesbury Av.)
Lysander NW9 . . . . .1B 44
Lysander Cl. KT6: Surb 6F 151
Lysander Gdns. N19 . . . . .1H 65
Lysander Ho. E2 . . . . .2H 85
    (off Temple St.)
Lysander M. N19 . . . . .1G 65
Lysander Rd. CR0: Wadd 6K 167
    HA4: Ruis 2F 57
Lysander Way BR6: Farnb 3G 173
Lysia Cl. SW6 . . . . .7F 99
    (off Lysia St.)
Lysias Rd. SW12 . . . . .6F 119
Lysia St. SW6 . . . . .7F 99
Lysons Wlk. SW15 . . . . .4C 116
Lytchet Rd. BR1: Brom 7J 141
Lytchet Way EN3: Enf H 1D 24
Lytchgate Cl. CR2: S Croy 7E 168
Lytcott Dr. KT8: W Mole 3D 148
Lytcott Gro. SE22 . . . . .5E 120
Lytham Cl. SE28 . . . . .6E 90
Lytham Ct. UB1: S'hall 6F 77
    (off Whitecote Rd.)
Lytham Gro. W5 . . . . .3F 79
Lytham St. SE17 . . . . .5D 102
Lyttelton Cl. NW3 . . . . .7C 64
Lyttelton Cl. N2 . . . . .5A 46
Lyttelton Ho. E9 . . . . .7J 67
    (off Well St.)
Lyttelton Rd. E10 . . . . .3D 68
    N2 .5A 46
Lyttelton Theatre 4H 13
    (within National Theatre)
Lyttleton Ct. UB4: Yead 4A 76
    (off Dunedin Way)
Lyttleton Rd. N8 . . . . .3A 48
Lytton Av. EN3: Enf L 1F 25
    N13 . . . . .2F 33
Lytton Cl. N2 . . . . .6B 46
    UB5: N'olt 7D 58
Lytton Ct. WC1 . . . . .6F 7
    (off Barter St.)
Lytton Gdns. SM6: Bedd 4H 167
Lytton Gro. SW15 . . . . .5F 117
Lytton Rd. E11 . . . . .7G 51
    EN5: New Bar 4F 21
    HA5: Pinn 1C 40
Lytton Strachey Path SE28 . . . . . . .7B 90
Lytton Ter. E12 . . . . .6D 70
Lyveden Rd. SE3 . . . . .7K 105
    SW17 . . . . .6D 136

M

Mabbett Ho. SE18 . . . . .6E 106
    (off Nightingale Pl.)
Mabel Evetts Ct. UB3: Hayes 7K 75
Maberley Cres. SE19 . . . . .7G 139
Maberley Rd.
    BR3: Beck 3K 157
    SE19 . . . . .1F 157
Mabledon Pl. WC1 . . . . .2D 6 (3H 83)
Mablethorpe Rd. SW6 . . . . .7G 99
Mabley St. E9 . . . . .5A 68

Mablin Lodge—Maguire St.

Mablin Lodge IG9: Buck H . . . 1F 37
McAdam Dr. EN2: Enf . . . 2G 23
McAllister Gro. IG11: Bark . . . 3A 90
Macaret Cl. N20 . . . 7E 20
Macarthur Cl. DA8: Erith . . . 5K 109
E7 . . . 6J 69
HA9: Wemb . . . 6H 61
Macarthur Ter. SE7 . . . 6B 106
Macartney Ho. SE10 . . . 7F 105
(off Chesterfield Wlk.)
SW9 . . . 1A 120
(off Gosling Way)
Macaulay Ct. SW4 . . . 3F 119
Macaulay Rd. E6 . . . 2B 88
SW4 . . . 3F 119
Macaulay Sq. SW4 . . . 4F 119
Macaulay Wlk. SW9 . . . 1K 119
(off Lett Rd.)
Macaulay Way SE28 . . . 1B 108
McAuley Cl. SE1 . . . 1J 19 (3A 102)
SE9 . . . 5F 125
Macauley Ho. W10 . . . 5G 81
(off Portobello Rd.)
Macauley M. SE13 . . . 2E 122
McAusland Ho. E3 . . . 2B 86
(off Wright's Rd.)
Macbean St. SE18 . . . 3F 107
Macbeth Ho. N1 . . . 2E 84
Macbeth St. W6 . . . 5D 98
McBride Ho. E3 . . . 2B 86
(off Libra Rd.)
McCabe Ct. E16 . . . 5H 87
(off Barking Rd.)
McCall Cl. SW4 . . . 2J 119
McCall Cres. SE7 . . . 5C 106
McCall Ho. N7 . . . 4J 65
McCarthy Rd. TW13: Hanw . . . 5B 130
Macclesfield Apartments N1 . . . 1D 84
(off Branch Pl.)
Macclesfield Ho. EC1 . . . 2C 8
(off Central St.)
Macclesfield Rd. EC1 . . . 1C 8 (3C 84)
SE25 . . . 5J 157
Macclesfield St. W1 . . . 2D 12 (7H 83)
McCoid Way SE1 . . . 7C 14 (2C 102)
McCrone M. NW3 . . . 6B 64
McCullum Rd. E3 . . . 1B 86
McDermott Cl. SW11 . . . 3C 118
McDermott Rd. SE15 . . . 3G 121
Macdonald Av. RM10: Dag . . . 3H 73
Macdonald Ho. SW11 . . . 2E 118
(off Dagnall St.)
McDonald Ho. NW6 . . . 3J 81
(off Malvern Rd.)
Macdonald Rd. E7 . . . 4J 69
E17 . . . 2E 50
(not continuous)
N11 . . . 5J 31
N19 . . . 2G 65
McDonough Cl. KT9: Chess . . . 4E 162
McDougall Ct. TW9: Rich . . . 2G 115
McDowall Cl. E16 . . . 5H 87
McDowall Rd. SE5 . . . 1C 120
Macduff Rd. SW11 . . . 1E 118
Mace Cl. E1 . . . 1H 103
Mace Ho. TW7: Isle . . . 1B 114
McEntee Av. E17 . . . 1A 50
Mace St. E2 . . . 2K 85
McEwan Ho. E3 . . . 2B 86
(off Roman Rd.)
McEwen Way E15 . . . 1F 87
(off Rokeby St.)
Macey Ho. SW11 . . . 1C 118
Macey St. SE10 . . . 6E 104
(off Thames St.)
McFadden Ct. E10 . . . 3D 68
(off Buckingham Rd.)
Macfarland Gro. SE15 . . . 7E 102
Macfarlane La. TW7: Isle . . . 6K 95
Macfarlane Rd. W12 . . . 1E 98
Macfarren Pl. NW1 . . . 4H 5 (4E 82)
Macfarron Ho. W10 . . . 3G 81
(off Parry Rd.)
McGlashon Ho. E1 . . . 4K 9
(off Hunton St.)
McGrath Rd. E15 . . . 5H 69
McGregor Ct. N1 . . . 1H 9
Macgregor Rd. E16 . . . 5A 88
McGregor Rd. W11 . . . 6H 81
Machell Rd. SE15 . . . 3J 121
McIndoe Ct. N1 . . . 1D 84
(off Sherborne St.)
McIntosh Cl. RM1: Rom . . . 3K 55
SM6: Wall . . . 7J 167
Macintosh Ho. W1 . . . 5H 5
(off Beaumont St.)
McIntosh Ho. SE16 . . . 4J 103
(off Millender Wlk.)
McIntosh Rd. RM1: Rom . . . 3K 55
McIntyre Ct. SE18 . . . 4C 106
(off Prospect Va.)
Mackay Ho. W12 . . . 7D 80
(off White City Est.)
Mackay Rd. SW4 . . . 3F 119
McKay Rd. SW20 . . . 7D 134
McKeever Ho. E16 . . . 5J 87
(off Hammersley Rd.)
McKellar Cl. WD23: B Hea . . . 2B 26
McKenna Ho. E3 . . . 2B 86
(off Wright's Rd.)
Mackennal St. NW8 . . . 2C 82
Mackenzie Cl. W12 . . . 7D 80
Mackenzie Ho. N8 . . . 4J 47
(off Pembroke Rd.)
NW2 . . . 3C 62
Mackenzie Rd. BR3: Beck . . . 2J 157
N7 . . . 6K 65
Mackenzie Wlk. E14 . . . 1C 104
McKerrell Rd. SE15 . . . 1G 121
Mackeson Rd. NW3 . . . 4D 64
Mackie Rd. SW2 . . . 7A 120
McKillop Way DA14: Sidc . . . 7C 144
Mackintosh La. E9 . . . 5K 67
Mackintosh St. BR2: Brom . . . 6B 160
Macklin St. WC2 . . . 7F 7 (6J 83)
Mackonochie Ho. EC1 . . . 5J 7
(off Baldwins Gdns.)
Mackrow Wlk. E14 . . . 7E 86
Mack's Rd. SE16 . . . 4G 103
Mackworth Ho. NW1 . . . 1A 6
(off Augustus St.)
Mackworth St. NW1 . . . 1A 6 (3G 83)
McLaren Ho. SE1 . . . 7A 14
(off St Georges Cir.)
Maclaren M. SW15 . . . 4E 116
Maclean Rd. SE23 . . . 6A 122
McLeod Ct. SE22 . . . 1G 139
Macleod Rd. N21 . . . 5D 22
McLeod Rd. SE2 . . . 4B 108
McLeod's M. SW7 . . . 4K 99
Macleod St. SE17 . . . 5C 102
Maclise Ho. SW1 . . . 4E 18
(off Marsham St.)
Maclise Rd. W14 . . . 3G 99
Macmillan Ct. HA2: Harr . . . 1E 58
UB6: G'frd . . . 4H 77
Macmillan Ho. NW8 . . . 2D 4
(off Lorne Cl.)
McMillan Ho. SE4 . . . 3A 122
(off Arica Rd.)
SE14 . . . 1A 122
McMillan St. SE8 . . . 6C 104
McMillan Student Village SE8 . . . 6C 104
Macmillan Way SW17 . . . 4F 137
McNair Rd. UB2: S'hall . . . 3F 95
Macnamara Ho. SW10 . . . 7B 100
(off Worlds End Est.)
McNeil Rd. SE5 . . . 2E 120
McNicol Dr. NW10 . . . 2J 79
Macoma Rd. SE18 . . . 6H 107
Macoma Ter. SE18 . . . 6H 107
Maconochies Rd. E14 . . . 5D 104
MacOwan Theatre . . . 4J 99
(off Logan Pl.)
Macquarie Way E14 . . . 4D 104
McRae La. CR4: Mitc . . . 7D 154
Macready Ho. W1 . . . 6E 4
(off Crawford St.)
Macready Pl. N7 . . . 4J 65
(not continuous)
Macrea Ho. E3 . . . 3B 86
(off Bow Rd.)
Macroom Ho. W9 . . . 3H 81
(off Macroom Rd.)
Macroom Rd. W9 . . . 3H 81
Macs Ho. E17 . . . 3D 50
Mac's Pl. EC4 . . . 7J 7
Madame Tussaud's . . . 4G 5 (4E 82)
Mada Rd. BR6: Farnb . . . 3F 173
Maddams St. E3 . . . 4D 86
Madderfields Ct. N11 . . . 1H 47
Maddison Cl. N2 . . . 2A 46
TW11: Tedd . . . 6K 131
Maddison Ct. E16 . . . 5J 87
(off Hastings Rd.)
Maddocks Cl. DA14: Sidc . . . 5E 144
Maddocks Ho. E1 . . . 7H 85
(off Cornwall St.)
Maddock Way SE17 . . . 6B 102
Maddox St. W1 . . . 2K 11 (7F 83)
Madeira Av. BR1: Brom . . . 7G 141
Madeira Gro. IG8: Wfd G . . . 6F 37
Madeira Rd. CR4: Mitc . . . 4D 154
E11 . . . 1F 69
N13 . . . 4G 33
SW16 . . . 5J 137
Madeleine Cl. RM6: Chad H . . . 6C 54
Madeleine Ct. HA7: Stan . . . 7K 27
(off Letchworth Rd.)
Madeley Rd. W5 . . . 6D 78
Madeline Gro. IG1: Ilf . . . 5H 71
Madeline Rd. SE20 . . . 7G 139
Madge Gill Way E6 . . . 1C 88
(off High St. Nth.)
Madge Hill W7 . . . 7J 77
Madinah Rd. E8 . . . 6G 67
Madison, The SE1 . . . 6E 14
(off Long La.)
Madison Bldg. SE10 . . . 1D 122
(off Blackheath Rd.)
Madison Cl. SM2: Sutt . . . 7B 166
Madison Ct. RM10: Dag . . . 6H 73
Madison Cres. DA7: Bex . . . 7C 108
Madison Gdns. BR2: Brom . . . 3H 159
DA7: Bex . . . 7C 108
Madison Ho. E14 . . . 7B 86
(off Victory Pl.)
Madoc Cl. NW2 . . . 2J 63
Madras Pl. N7 . . . 6A 66
Madras Rd. IG1: Ilf . . . 4F 71
Madrid Rd. SW13 . . . 1C 116
Madrigal La. SE5 . . . 7B 102
Madron St. SE17 . . . 5E 102
Mafeking Av. E6 . . . 2C 88
IG2: Ilf . . . 7H 53
TW8: Bford . . . 6E 96
Mafeking Rd. E16 . . . 4H 87
EN1: Enf . . . 3A 24
N17 . . . 2G 49
Magazine Ga. W2 . . . 4D 10 (1C 100)
Magdala Av. N19 . . . 2G 65
Magdala Rd. CR2: S Croy . . . 7D 168
TW7: Isle . . . 3A 114
Magdalene Cl. SE15 . . . 2H 121
Magdalene Gdns. E6 . . . 4E 88
N20 . . . 1J 31
Magdalene Rd. TW17: Shep . . . 4B 146
Magdalen Ho. E16 . . . 1K 105
(off Keats Av.)
Magdalen M. NW3 . . . 6A 64
(off Frognal)
Magdalen Pas. E1 . . . 2K 15 (7F 85)
Magdalen Rd. SW18 . . . 1A 136
Magdalen St. SE1 . . . 5G 15 (1E 102)
Magee St. SE11 . . . 7J 19 (6A 102)
Magellan Blvd. E16 . . . 7G 89
Magellan Ct. NW10 . . . 7K 61
(off Brentfield Rd.)
Magellan Ho. E1 . . . 4K 85
(off Ernest St.)
Magellan Pl. E14 . . . 4C 104
Magistrates' Court
Barkingside . . . 3G 53
Belmarsh . . . 2J 107
Bexley . . . 4G 127
Bromley . . . 1H 159
Camberwell Green . . . 1D 120
City of London . . . 1E 14
Croydon . . . 3D 168
Ealing . . . 1A 96
(off Green Man La.)
Feltham . . . 1K 129
Greenwich . . . 1D 122
Hammersmith . . . 5F 99
Hendon . . . 6B 44
Highbury Corner . . . 6A 66
Inner London Family Proceedings Court . . . 7A 6 (5G 83)
Lavender Hill . . . 3D 118
Richmond-upon-Thames . . . 4D 114
Stratford . . . 7F 69
Thames . . . 3C 86
Tottenham . . . 1F 49
Waltham Forest . . . 3D 50
Westminster . . . 5D 4 (5C 82)
Willesden . . . 6B 62
Wimbledon . . . 6J 135
Magna Sq. SW14 . . . 3J 115
(off Moore Cl.)
Magnaville Rd. WD23: B Hea . . . 1D 26
Magnet Rd. HA9: Wemb . . . 2D 60
Magnin Cl. E8 . . . 1G 85
Magnolia Cl. E10 . . . 2C 68
KT2: King T . . . 6H 133
Magnolia Ct. HA3: Kenton . . . 7F 43
SM2: Sutt . . . 7J 165
(off Grange Rd.)
SM6: Wall . . . 5F 167
TW9: Kew . . . 1H 115
TW13: Felt . . . 1J 129
(off Plum Cl.)
UB5: N'olt . . . 4C 76
UB10: Hil . . . 6D 56
Magnolia Gdns. E10 . . . 2C 68
HA8: Edg . . . 4D 28
Magnolia Ho. SE8 . . . 6B 104
(off Evelyn St.)
TW16: Sun . . . 7H 129
Magnolia Lodge E4 . . . 3J 35
W8 . . . 3K 99
(off St Mary's Ga.)
Magnolia Pl. HA2: Harr . . . 2H 41
SW4 . . . 5J 119
W5 . . . 5D 78
Magnolia Rd. W4 . . . 6H 97
Magnolia St. UB7: W Dray . . . 4A 92
Magnolia Way KT19: Ewe . . . 5J 163
Magnolia Wharf W4 . . . 6G 97
Magpie All. EC4 . . . 1K 13 (6A 84)
Magpie Cl.
E7 . . . 5H 69
EN1: Enf . . . 1B 24
NW9 . . . 2A 44
Magpie Hall Cl. BR2: Brom . . . 6C 160
Magpie Hall La. BR2: Brom . . . 5D 160
Magpie Hall Rd. WD23: B Hea . . . 2D 26
Magpie Ho. E3 . . . 1B 86
(off Sycamore Av.)
Magpie Pl. SE14 . . . 6A 104
Magri Wlk. E1 . . . 5J 85
Maguire Apartments E3 . . . 5B 86
(off Geoff Cade Way)
Maguire Dr. TW10: Ham . . . 4C 132
Maguire St. SE1 . . . 6K 15 (2F 103)

330 A-Z London

Maha Bldg. *E3* *3C 86*
    (off Merchant St.)
Mahatma Gandhi Ind. Est. SE24 . . . . .4B **120**
Mahlon Av. HA4: Ruis 5K **57**
    (not continuous)
Mahogany Cl. SE16 . . . . .1A **104**
Mahon Cl. EN1: Enf 1A **24**
Mahoney Ho. *SE14* *1B 122*
    (off Heald St.)
Maibeth Gdns. BR3: Beck 4A **158**
Maida Av. E4 . . . . .7J **25**
    W2 . . . . .4A **4** (5A **82**)
MAIDA HILL .4H **81**
Maida Rd. DA17: Belv 3G **109**
MAIDA VALE 4K **81**
Maida Vale W9 . . . . .3A **4** (2K **81**)
Maida Way E4 . . . . .7J **25**
Maiden Erlegh Av. DA5: Bexl 1E **144**
Maiden La. NW1 . . . . .7H **65**
    SE1 . . . . .5D **14** (1C **102**)
    WC2 . . . . .2F **13** (7J **83**)
Maiden Pl. NW5 . . . . .3G **65**
Maiden Rd. E15 . . . . .7G **69**
Maidenstone Hill SE10 . . . . .1E **122**
Maids of Honour Row TW9: Rich 5D **114**
Maidstone Av. RM5: Col R 2J **55**
Maidstone Bldgs. M. SE1 . . . .5D **14** (1C **102**)
Maidstone Ho. *E14* *6D 86*
    (off Carmen St.)
Maidstone Rd. DA14: Sidc, Swan 6D **144**
    N11 . . . . .6B **32**
Mailcoach Yd. E2 . . . . .1H **9** (3E **84**)
Main Av. EN1: Enf 5A **24**
Main Dr. HA9: Wemb 3D **60**
Main Mill *SE10* *7D 104*
    (off Greenwich High St.)
Mainridge Rd. BR7: Chst 4E **142**
Main Rd. DA14: Sidc 3H **143**
Main St. TW13: Hanw 5B **130**
Mainwaring Ct. CR4: Mitc 2E **154**
Mais Ho. SE26 . . . . .2H **139**
Maismore St. SE15 . . . . .6G **103**
Maisonettes, The SM1: Sutt 5H **165**
Maitland Cl. SE10 . . . . .7D **104**
    TW4: Houn 3D **112**
Maitland Ct. *W2* *2A 10*
    (off Lancaster Ter.)
Maitland Ho. *E2* *2J 85*
    (off Waterloo Gdns.)
    SW1 . . . .*7A 18*
    (off Churchill Gdns.)
Maitland Pk. Est. NW3 . . . . .6D **64**
Maitland Pk. Rd. NW3 . . . . .6D **64**
Maitland Pk. Vs. NW3 . . . . .6D **64**
Maitland Pl. E5 . . . . .4H **67**
Maitland Rd. E15 . . . . .6H **69**
    SE26 . . . . .6K **139**
Maitland Yd. W13 . . . . .1A **96**
Maize Row E14 . . . . .7B **86**
Majendie Rd. SE18 . . . . .5H **107**
Majestic Way CR4: Mitc 2D **154**
Major Cl. SW9 . . . . .3B **120**
Major Draper St. SE18 . . . . .3F **107**
Major Rd. E15 . . . . .5F **69**
    SE16 . . . . .3G **103**
Makepeace Av. N6 . . . . .2E **64**
Makepeace Mans. N6 . . . . .2E **64**
Makepeace Rd. E11 . . . . .4J **51**
    UB5: N'olt 2C **76**
Makinen Ho. IG9: Buck H 1F **37**
Makins St. SW3 . . . . . . .4D **16** (4C **100**)
Malabar Ct. *W12* *7D 80*
    (off India Way)
Malabar St. E14 . . . . .2C **104**
Malam Ct. SE11 . . . . . .4J **19** (4A **102**)
Malam Gdns. E14 . . . . .7D **86**
Malbrook Rd. SW15 . . . . .4D **116**
Malcolm Cl. SE20 . . . . .7J **139**
Malcolm Ct. E7 . . . . .6H **69**
    HA7: Stan 5H **27**
    NW4 .6C **44**

Malcolm Cres. NW4 . . . . .6C **44**
Malcolm Dr. KT6: Surb 1E **162**
Malcolm Ho. *N1* *2E 84*
    (off Arden Est.)
Malcolm Pl. E2 . . . . .4J **85**
Malcolm Rd. E1 . . . . .4J **85**
    SE20 . . . . .7J **139**
    SE25 . . . . .6G **157**
    SW19 . . . . .6G **135**
    UB10: Ick 4B **56**
Malcolm Sargent Ho. *E16* *1K 105*
    (off Evelyn Rd.)
Malcolmson Ho. *SW1* *6C 18*
    (off Aylesford St.)
Malcoms Way N14 . . . . .5B **22**
Malcolm Way E11 . . . . .5J **51**
Malden Av. SE25 . . . . .4H **157**
    UB6: G'frd 5J **59**
Malden Cl. KT3: N Mald 3D **152**
    N4 . . . . .6C **48**
Malden Cres. NW1 . . . . .6E **64**
Malden Golf Course 2A **152**
MALDEN GREEN 1C **164**
Malden Grn. Av. KT4: Wor Pk 1B **164**
Malden Grn. M. KT4: Wor Pk 1C **164**
Malden Hill KT3: N Mald 3B **152**
Malden Hill Gdns. KT3: N Mald 3B **152**
MALDEN JUNC. 5B **152**
Malden Pk. KT3: N Mald 6B **152**
Malden Pl. NW5 . . . . .5E **64**
Malden Rd. KT3: N Mald 5A **152**
    KT4: Wor Pk 5A **152**
    NW5 .5D **64**
    SM3: Cheam 4F **165**
Malden Way KT3: N Mald 6K **151**
Maldon Cl. E15 . . . . .5G **69**
    N1 . . . . .1C **84**
    SE5 .3E **120**
Maldon Ct. E6 . . . . .1E **88**
    SM6: Wall 5G **167**
Maldon Pk. KT3: N Mald 6B **152**
Maldon Pl. NW5 . . . . .5E **64**
Maldon Rd. N9 . . . . .3A **34**
    RM7: Rush G 7J **55**
    SM6: Wall 5F **167**
    W3 . . . . .7J **79**
Maldon Wlk. IG8: Wfd G 6F **37**
Malet Pl. WC1 . . . . .4C **6** (4H **83**)
Malet St. WC1 . . . . .4C **6** (4H **83**)
Maley Av. SE27 . . . . .2B **138**
Malford Cl. E18 . . . . .2J **51**
Malford Gro. E18 . . . . .4H **51**
Malford Rd. SE5 . . . . .3E **120**
Malham Cl. N11 . . . . .6K **31**
Malham Rd. SE23 . . . . .1K **139**
Malham Rd. Ind. Est. SE23 . . . . .1K **139**
Malham Ter. N18 . . . . .5C **34**
Malibu Cl. SE26 . . . . .3H **139**
Mall, The BR1: Brom 3J **159**
    CR0: C'don 2C **168**
    DA6: Bex 4G **127**
    E15 . . . . .7F **69**
    HA3: Kenton 6F **43**
    KT6: Surb 5D **150**
    N14 . . . . .3D **32**
    RM10: Dag 6G **73**
    SW1 . . . . .6B **12** (2G **101**)
    SW14 . . . . .5J **115**
    TW8: Bford 6D **96**
    W5 . . . . .7E **78**
Mallams M. SW9 . . . . .3B **120**
Mallard Cl. E9 . . . . .6B **68**
    EN5: New Bar 6G **21**
    NW6 .2J **81**
    TW2: Whitt 7E **112**
    W7 . . . . .2J **95**
Mallard Ct. E17 . . . . .3F **51**
Mallard Ho. *NW8* *2C 82*
    (off Bridgeman St.)
    SW6 . . . .*1A 118*
    (off Station Ct.)

Mallard Path SE28 . . . . .3H **107**
Mallard Pl. N22 . . . . .2K **47**
    TW1: Twick 3A **132**
Mallard Point *E3* *3D 86*
    (off Rainhill Way)
Mallards E11 . . . . .7J **51**
    (off Blake Hall Rd.)
Mallards Rd. IG8: Wfd G 7E **36**
    IG11: Bark 4A **90**
Mallard Wlk. BR3: Beck 5K **157**
    DA14: Sidc 6C **144**
Mallard Way NW9 . . . . .7J **43**
    SM6: Wall 7G **167**
Mall Chambers *W8* *1J 99*
    (off Kensington Mall)
Mallet Dr. UB5: N'olt 5D **58**
Mallet Rd. SE13 . . . . .6F **123**
Mall Galleries 4D **12**
Malling SE13 . . . . .5D **122**
Malling Cl. CR0: C'don 6J **157**
Malling Gdns. SM4: Mord 6A **154**
Malling Way BR2: Hayes 7H **159**
Mallinson Rd. CR0: Bedd 3H **167**
    SW11 . . . . .5C **118**
Mallinson Sports Cen. 7D **46**
Mallon Gdns. *E1* *7K 9*
    (off Commercial St.)
Mallord St. SW3 . . . . . .7B **16** (6B **100**)
Mallory Bldgs. *EC1* *4A 8*
    (off St John St.)
Mallory Cl. E14 . . . . .5D **86**
    SE4 .4A **122**
Mallory Ct. SE12 . . . . .7K **123**
Mallory Gdns. EN4: E Barn 7K **21**
Mallory St. NW8 . . . . .3D **4** (4C **82**)
Mallory Way SE3 . . . . .4K **123**
Mallow Cl. CR0: C'don 1K **169**
Mallow Mead NW7 . . . . .7B **30**
Mallows, The UB10: Ick 3D **56**
Mallow St. EC1 . . . . .3E **8** (4D **84**)
Mall Rd. W6 . . . . .5D **98**
Mall Vs. *W6* *5D 98*
    (off Mall Rd.)
Malmains Cl. BR3: Beck 4F **159**
Malmains Way BR3: Beck 4E **158**
Malmesbury *E2* *2J 85*
    (off Cyprus St.)
Malmesbury Cl. HA5: Eastc 4H **39**
Malmesbury Rd. E3 . . . . .3B **86**
    E16 . . . . .5G **87**
    E18 . . . . .1H **51**
    SM4: Mord 7A **154**
Malmesbury Ter. E16 . . . . .5H **87**
Malmsey Ho. SE11 . . . . . .5H **19** (5K **101**)
Malmsmead Ho. E9 . . . . .5B **68**
    (off Homerton Rd.)
Malory Cl. BR3: Beck 2A **158**
Malpas Dr. HA5: Pinn 5B **40**
Malpas Rd. E8 . . . . .5H **67**
    RM9: Dag 6D **72**
    SE4 .2B **122**
Malswick Ct. SE15 . . . . .7E **102**
    (off Tower Mill Rd.)
Malta Rd. E10 . . . . .1C **68**
Malta St. EC1 . . . . .3A **8** (4B **84**)
Maltby Cl. BR6: Orp 1K **173**
Maltby Dr. EN1: Enf 1C **24**
Maltby Ho. *SE1* *7J 15*
    (off Maltby St.)
    SE3 .4A **124**
Maltby Rd. KT9: Chess 6G **163**
Maltby St. SE1 . . . . .7J **15** (2F **103**)
Malthouse Cl. TW8: Bford 6E **96**
    (off High St.)
Malthouse Dr. TW13: Hanw 5B **130**
    W4 . . . . .6B **98**
Malthouse Pas. *SW13* *2B 116*
    (off Clevelands Gdns.)
Malthus Path SE28 . . . . .1C **108**
Malting Ho. *E14* *7B 86*
    (off Oak La.)

Maltings, The BR6: Orp 1K **173**
    W4 . . . .*5G 97*
    (off Spring Gro.)
Maltings Cl. E3 . . . . .3E **86**
    SW13 . . . . .2B **116**
Maltings Lodge *W4* *6A 98*
    (off Corney Reach Way)
Maltings M. DA15: Sidc 3A **144**
Maltings Pl. SE1 . . . . .7H **15**
    SW6 .1K **117**
Malting Way TW7: Isle 3K **113**
Malton M. SE18 . . . . .6J **107**
    W10 .6G **81**
Malton Rd. W10 . . . . .6G **81**
Malton St. SE18 . . . . .6J **107**
Maltravers St. WC2 . . . .2H **13** (7K **83**)
Malt St. SE1 . . . . .6G **103**
Malva Cl. SW18 . . . . .5K **117**
Malvern Av. DA7: Bex 7E **108**
    E4 . . . . .7A **36**
    HA2: Harr 3C **58**
Malvern Cl.
    CR4: Mitc 3G **155**
    KT6: Surb 1E **162**
    SE20 . . . . .2G **157**
    UB10: Ick 2C **56**
    W10 .5H **81**
Malvern Ct. SM2: Sutt 7J **165**
    SW7 .3B **16**
    W12 . . . .*2C 98*
    (off Hadyn Pk. Rd.)
Malvern Dr. IG3: Bark, Ilf 4K **71**
    IG8: Wfd G 5F **37**
    TW13: Hanw 5B **130**
Malvern Gdns. HA3: Kenton 4E **42**
    NW2 .2G **63**
Malvern Ho. N16 . . . . .1F **67**
    SE17 . . . .*5C 102*
    (off Liverpool Gro.)
Malvern M. NW6 . . . . .3J **81**
Malvern Pl. NW6 . . . . .3H **81**
Malvern Rd. CR7: Thor H 4A **156**
    E6 . . . . .1C **88**
    E8 . . . . .7G **67**
    E11 . . . . .2G **69**
    KT6: Surb 2E **162**
    N8 . . . . .3K **47**
    N17 . . . . .3G **49**
    NW6 .2H **81**
    (not continuous)
    TW12: Hamp 7E **130**
    UB3: Harl 7G **93**
Malvern Ter. N1 . . . . .1A **84**
    N9 . . . . .1A **34**
Malvern Way W13 . . . . .5B **78**
Malwood Rd. SW12 . . . . .6F **119**
Malyons, The TW17: Shep 6F **147**
Malyons Rd. SE13 . . . . .6D **122**
Malyons Ter. SE13 . . . . .5D **122**
Managers St. E14 . . . . .1E **104**
Manatee Pl. SM6: Bedd 3H **167**
Manaton Cl. SE15 . . . . .3H **121**
Manaton Cres. UB1: S'hall 6E **76**
Manbey Gro. E15 . . . . .6G **69**
Manbey Pk. Rd. E15 . . . . .6G **69**
Manbey Rd. E15 . . . . .6G **69**
Manbey St. E15 . . . . .6G **69**
Manbre Rd. W6 . . . . .6E **98**
Manbrough Av. E6 . . . . .3D **88**
Manchester Ct. *E16* *6K 87*
    (off Garvary Rd.)
Manchester Dr. W10 . . . . .4G **81**
Manchester Gro. E14 . . . . .5E **104**
Manchester Ho. *SE17* *5C 102*
    (off East St.)
Manchester M. W1 . . . . .6G **5**
Manchester Rd. CR7: Thor H 3C **156**
    E14 . . . . .5E **104**
    N15 . . . . .6D **48**
Manchester Sq. W1 . . . . . . .7G **5** (6E **82**)
Manchester St. W1 . . . . . . .6G **5** (5E **82**)

Manchester Way—Mansfield Ct.

Manchester Way RM10: Dag 4H 73
Manchuria Rd. SW11 ....6E 118
Manciple St. SE1 ....7E 14 (2D 102)
Mancroft Ct. NW8 ....1B 82
(off St John's Wood Pk.)
Mandalay Rd. SW4 ....5G 119
Mandarin Ct. NW10 ....6K 61
(off Mitchellbrook Way)
SE8 ....6B 104
Mandarin St. E14 ....7C 86
Mandarin Way UB4: Yead 6B 76
Mandarin Wharf N1 ....1E 84
(off De Beauvoir Cres.)
Mandela Cl. NW10 ....7J 61
W12 ....7D 80
Mandela Ho. E2 ....2J 9
(off Virginia Rd.)
SE5 ....2B 120
Mandela Rd. E16 ....6J 87
Mandela St. NW1 ....1G 83
SW9 ....7A 102
(not continuous)
Mandela Way SE1 ....4E 102
Mandel Ho. SW18 ....4J 117
Manderley W14 ....3H 99
(off Oakwood La.)
Mandeville Cl. SE3 ....7H 105
SW20 ....7G 135
Mandeville Ct. E4 ....5F 35
Mandeville Dr. KT6: Surb 1D 162
Mandeville Ho. SE1 ....5F 103
(off Rolls Rd.)
SW4 ....5G 119
Mandeville M. SW4 ....4J 119
Mandeville Pl. W1 ....7H 5 (6E 82)
Mandeville Rd. N14 ....2A 32
TW7: Isle 2A 114
TW17: Shep 5C 146
UB5: N'olt 7E 58
Mandeville St. E5 ....3A 68
Mandrake Rd. SW17 ....3D 136
Mandrake Way E15 ....7G 69
Mandrell Rd. SW2 ....5J 119
Manesty Ct. N14 ....7C 22
(off Ivy Rd.)
Manette St. W1 ....1D 12 (6H 83)
Manfred Rd. SW15 ....5H 117
Manger Rd. N7 ....6J 65
Mangold Way DA18: Erith 3D 108
Manhattan Bldg. E3 ....2C 86
Manhattan Bus. Pk. W5 ....3E 78
Manhattan Loft Gdns. E20 ....6E 68
Manilla Ct. RM6: Chad H 6B 54
(off Quarles Pk. Rd.)
Manilla St. E14 ....2C 104
Manister Rd. SE2 ....3A 108
Manitoba Ct. SE16 ....2J 103
(off Canada Est.)
Manitoba Gdns. BR6: Chels 6K 173
Manley Ct. N16 ....3F 67
Manley Ho. SE11 ....5J 19 (4A 102)
Manley St. NW1 ....1E 82
Manna Ho. E20 ....6E 68
(off Glade Wlk.)
Mannan Ho. E3 ....2B 86
(off Roman Rd.)
Mann Cl. CR0: C'don 3C 168
Manneby Prior N1 ....1H 7
(off Cumming St.)
Manning Ct. SE28 ....1B 108
(off Titmuss Av.)
Manningford Cl. EC1 ....1A 8 (3B 84)
Manning Gdns. CR0: C'don 7H 157
HA3: Kenton 7D 42
Manning Ho. W11 ....6G 81
(off Westbourne Pk. Rd.)
Manning Pl. TW10: Rich 6F 115
Manning Rd. E17 ....5A 50
RM10: Dag 6G 73
Manningtree Cl. SW19 ....1G 135
Manningtree Rd. HA4: Ruis 4K 57
Manningtree St. E1 ....6G 85
Mannin Rd. RM6: Chad H 7B 54
Mannock Cl. NW9 ....3K 43
Mannock M. E18 ....1A 52
Mannock Rd. N22 ....3B 48
Mann's Cl. TW7: Isle 5K 113
Manns Rd. HA8: Edg 6B 28
Manns Ter. SE27 ....3C 138
Manny Shinwell Ho. SW6 ....6H 99
(off Clem Attlee Ct.)
Manoel Rd. TW2: Twick 2G 131
Manor, The IG8: Wfd G 7K 37
Manor Av. SE4 ....2B 122
TW4: Houn 3B 112
UB5: N'olt 7D 58
Manorbrook SE3 ....4J 123
MANOR CIRCUS 3G 115
Manor Cl. DA1: Cray 4K 127
E17 ....1A 50
EN5: Barn 4B 20
HA4: Ruis 1H 57
KT4: Wor Pk 1A 164
NW7 ....5E 28
NW9 ....5H 43
RM10: Dag 6K 73
SE28 ....7C 90
Manor Cotts. HA6: Nwood 1H 39
N2 ....2A 46
(off Manor Cotts. App.)
Manor Cotts. App. N2 ....2A 46
Manor Ct. BR4: W W'ck 1D 170
DA7: Bex 4H 127
E4 ....1B 36
E10 ....1D 68
HA1: Harr 6K 41
HA9: Wemb 5E 60
IG11: Bark 7K 71
KT2: King T 1G 151
KT8: W Mole 4E 148
N2 ....5D 46
N14 ....2C 32
N20 ....3J 31
(off York Way)
SM5: Cars 3E 166
SW2 ....5K 119
SW3 ....6D 16
(off Hemus Pl.)
SW6 ....1K 117
SW16 ....3J 137
TW2: Twick 2G 131
W3 ....4G 97
Manor Ct. Rd. W7 ....7J 77
Manor Cres. KT5: Surb 6G 151
Manor Dene SE28 ....6C 90
Manordene Cl. KT7: T Ditt 1A 162
Manordene Rd. SE28 ....6C 90
Manor Dr. HA9: Wemb 4F 61
KT5: Surb 6F 151
KT10: Hin W 2A 162
KT19: Ewe 6A 164
N14 ....1A 32
N20 ....4J 31
NW7 ....5E 28
TW13: Hanw 5B 130
TW16: Sun 2J 147
Manor Drive, The KT4: Wor Pk 1A 164
Manor Dr. Nth. KT3: N Mald 7K 151
KT4: Wor Pk 1A 164
Manor Est. SE16 ....4H 103
Manor Farm
Ruislip 7G 39
Mnr. Farm Av. TW17: Shep 6D 146
Mnr. Farm Cl. KT4: Wor Pk 1A 164
Mnr. Farm Ct. E6 ....3D 88
Mnr. Farm Dr. E4 ....3B 36
Mnr. Farm Rd. HA0: Wemb 2D 78
SW16 ....2A 156
Manorfield Cl. N19 ....4G 65
(off Fulbrook M.)
Manor Flds. SW15 ....6F 117
Manorfields Cl. BR7: Chst 3K 161
Manor Gdns. CR2: S Croy 6F 169
HA4: Ruis 5A 58
N7 ....3J 65
SW4 ....2G 119
(off Larkhall Ri.)
SW20 ....2H 153
TW9: Rich 4F 115
TW12: Hamp 7F 131
TW16: Sun 1J 147
W3 ....4G 97
W4 ....5A 98
Manor Ga. UB5: N'olt 7C 58
Manorgate Rd. KT2: King T 1G 151
Manor Gro. BR3: Beck 2D 158
SE15 ....6J 103
TW9: Rich 4G 115
Manor Hall Av. NW4 ....2F 45
Manor Hall Dr. NW4 ....2F 45
Manorhall Gdns. E10 ....1C 68
MANOR HOUSE 7D 48
MANOR HOUSE 7C 48
Manor Ho. NW1 ....5D 4
(off Lisson Gro.)
UB2: S'hall 3C 94
Manor Ho. Ct. TW17: Shep 7D 146
W9 ....4A 82
(off Warrington Gdns.)
Manor Ho. Dr. HA6: Nwood 1D 38
NW6 ....7F 63
Manor Ho. Est. HA7: Stan 6G 27
Manor Ho. Gdn. E11 ....6K 51
Manor Ho. Way TW7: Isle 3B 114
Manor La. SE12 ....5G 123
SE13 ....5G 123
SM1: Sutt 5A 166
TW13: Felt 2J 129
TW16: Sun 2J 147
UB3: Harl 6F 93
Manor La. Ter. SE13 ....4G 123
Manor Lodge NW6 ....7F 63
(off Willesden La.)
Manor M. NW6 ....2J 81
(off Cambridge Av.)
SE4 ....2B 122
Manor Mt. SE23 ....1J 139
Manor Pde. HA1: Harr 6K 41
N16 ....2F 67
NW10 ....2B 80
(off High St. Harlesden)
MANOR PARK 4B 70
Manor Pk. BR7: Chst 2H 161
SE13 ....4F 123
TW9: Rich 4F 115
TW13: Felt 2J 129
Manor Pk. Cl. BR4: W W'ck 1D 170
Manor Pk. Crematorium E7 ....4A 70
Manor Pk. Cres. HA8: Edg 6B 28
Manor Pk. Dr. HA2: Harr 3F 41
Manor Pk. Gdns. HA8: Edg 5B 28
Manor Pk. Pde. SE13 ....4F 123
(off Lee High Rd.)
Manor Pk. Rd. BR4: W W'ck 1D 170
BR7: Chst 1G 161
E12 ....4B 70
(not continuous)
N2 ....3A 46
NW10 ....1B 80
SM1: Sutt 5A 166
Manor Pl. BR1: Brom 1C 160
BR7: Chst 2H 161
CR4: Mitc 3G 155
KT12: Walt T 7H 147
(not continuous)
SE17 ....5B 102
SM1: Sutt 4K 165
TW14: Felt 1J 129
Manor Rd. BR3: Beck 2D 158
BR4: W W'ck 2D 170
CR4: Mitc 4G 155
DA1: Cray 4K 127
DA5: Bexl 1H 145
Manor Rd. DA15: Sidc 3K 143
E10 ....7C 50
E15 ....2G 87
E16 ....2G 87
E17 ....2A 50
EN2: Enf 2H 23
EN5: Barn 4B 20
HA1: Harr 6A 42
HA4: Ruis 1F 57
IG7: Chig 6J 37
IG8: Wfd G 6J 37
IG11: Bark 6K 71
KT8: E Mos 4H 149
KT12: Walt T 7H 147
N16 ....2D 66
N17 ....1G 49
N22 ....6D 32
RM6: Chad H 6D 54
RM10: Dag 6J 73
SE25 ....4G 157
SM2: Cheam 7H 165
SM6: Wall 4F 167
SW20 ....2H 153
TW2: Twick 2G 131
TW9: Rich 4G 115
TW11: Tedd 5A 132
(not continuous)
TW15: Ashf 5B 128
UB3: Hayes 6J 75
W13 ....7A 78
Manor Rd. Ho. HA1: Harr 6A 42
Manor Rd. Nth. KT7: T Ditt 3A 162
KT10: Hin W, T Ditt 3A 162
SM6: Wall 4F 167
Manorside EN5: Barn 4B 20
Manorside Cl. SE2 ....4C 108
Manor Sq. RM8: Dag 2C 72
Manor Va. TW8: Bford 5C 96
Manor Vw. N3 ....2K 45
Manor Way BR2: Brom 6C 160
BR3: Beck 2C 158
BR5: Pet W 4G 161
CR2: S Croy 6E 168
CR4: Mitc 3G 155
DA5: Bexl 1G 145
DA7: Bex 3K 127
E4 ....4A 36
HA2: Harr 4F 41
HA4: Ruis 7G 39
KT4: Wor Pk 1A 164
NW9 ....4A 44
RM13: Rain 4K 91
SE3 ....4H 123
SE23 ....7J 121
UB2: S'hall 4B 94
Manor Way, The SM6: Wall 4F 167
Manorway EN1: Enf 7K 23
IG8: Wfd G 5F 37
Manor Way Bus. Cen. RM13: Rain 5K 91
Manor Waye UB8: Uxb 1A 74
Manpreet Ct. E12 ....5D 70
Manresa Rd. SW3 ....6C 16 (5C 100)
Mansard Beeches SW17 ....5E 136
Mansard Cl. HA5: Pinn 3B 40
Manse Cl. UB3: Harl 6F 93
Mansel Gro. E17 ....1C 50
Mansell Rd. UB6: G'frd 5F 77
W3 ....2K 97
Mansell St. E1 ....1K 15 (6F 85)
EC3 ....7F 85
Mansel Rd. SW19 ....6G 135
Manser Ct. RM13: Rain 3K 91
Mansergh Cl. SE18 ....7C 106
Manse Rd. N16 ....3F 67
Manser Rd. RM13: Rain 3K 91
Mansfield Av. EN4: E Barn 6J 21
HA4: Ruis 1K 57
N15 ....4D 48
Mansfield Cl. N9 ....6B 24
Mansfield Ct. E2 ....1F 85
(off Whiston Rd.)

Mansfield Ct. *SE15* 7F **103**
(off Sumner Rd.)
Mansfield Dr. UB4: Hayes 4G **75**
Mansfield Hgts. N2 . . . . .5C **46**
Mansfield Hill E4 . . . . .7J **25**
Mansfield Ho. *N1* 1E **84**
(off Halcomb St.)
Mansfield M. W1 . . . . .6J **5** (5F **83**)
Mansfield Pl. CR2: S Croy 6D **168**
NW3 . . . . .4A **64**
Mansfield Rd. CR2: S Croy 6D **168**
E11 . . . . .6K **51**
E17 . . . . .4B **50**
IG1: Ilf .2E **70**
KT9: Chess 5C **162**
NW3 . . . . .5D **64**
W3 . . . . .4H **79**
Mansfield St. W1 . . . . .6J **5** (5F **83**)
Mansford St. E2 . . . . .2G **85**
Manship Rd. CR4: Mitc 7E **136**
Mansion Cl. SW9 . . . . .1A **120**
(not continuous)
Mansion Gdns. NW3 . . . . .3K **63**
Mansion House 1E **14** (6D **84**)
Mansion Ho. Dr. HA7: Stan 2D **26**
Mansion Ho. Pl. EC4 . . . . .1E **14** (6D **84**)
Mansion Ho. St. EC4 . . . . .1E **14**
Mansion Lock Ho. *NW1* 7F **65**
(off Hawley Cres.)
Mansions, The SW5 . . . . .5K **99**
(Earl's Ct. Rd.)
SW5 . . . . .5K **99**
(off Old Brompton Rd., Old Brompton Rd.)
Mansion Vw. *E15* 1B **87**
(off High St.)
Manson Ho. *N1* 7A **66**
(off Drummond Way)
Manson M. SW7 . . . . .4A **16** (4B **100**)
Manson Pl. SW7 . . . . .4A **16** (4B **100**)
Mansted Gdns. RM6: Chad H 7C **54**
Manston *N17* 2D **48**
(off Adams Rd.)
NW1 . . . . .7G **65**
(off Agar Gro.)
Manston Av. UB2: S'hall 4E **94**
Manston Cl. SE20 . . . . .1J **157**
Manstone Ct. E17 . . . . .1B **50**
Manston Rd. NW2 . . . . .5G **63**
Manston Gro. KT2: King T 5D **132**
Manston Ho. *W14* 3G **99**
(off Russell Rd.)
Manthorp Rd. SE18 . . . . .5G **107**
Mantilla Rd. SW17 . . . . .4E **136**
Mantle Ct. *SW18* 6K **117**
(off Mapleton Rd.)
Mantle Rd. SE4 . . . . .3A **122**
Mantlet Cl. SW16 . . . . .7G **137**
Mantle Way E15 . . . . .7G **69**
Manton Av. W7 . . . . .2K **95**
Manton Cl. UB3: Hayes 7G **75**
Manton Rd. EN3: Enf L 1H **25**
SE2 . . . . .4A **108**
Manton Way EN3: Enf L 1J **25**
Mantua St. SW11 . . . . .3B **118**
Mantus Cl. E1 . . . . .4J **85**
Mantus Rd. E1 . . . . .4J **85**
Manuka Cl. W7 . . . . .1A **96**
Manuka Hgts. *E20* 5E **68**
(off Napa Cl.)
Manus Way N20 . . . . .2F **31**
Manville Gdns. SW17 . . . . .3F **137**
Manville Rd. SW17 . . . . .2E **136**
Manwood Rd. SE4 . . . . .5B **122**
Manwood St. E16 . . . . .1D **106**
Manygate La. TW17: Shep 7E **146**
Manygate Pk. *TW17: Shep* 6F **147**
(off Mitre Cl.)
Manygates SW12 . . . . .2F **137**
Mapesbury Ct. NW2 . . . . .5G **63**
Mapesbury M. NW4 . . . . .6C **44**
Mapesbury Rd. NW2 . . . . .7G **63**

Mapeshill Pl. NW2 . . . . .6E **62**
Mapes Ho. NW6 . . . . .7G **63**
Mape St. E2 . . . . .4H **85**
(not continuous)
Maple Av. E4 . . . . .5G **35**
HA2: Harr 2F **59**
UB7: Yiew 7A **74**
W3 . . . . .1A **98**
Maple Cl. BR5: Pet W 5H **161**
CR4: Mitc 1F **155**
HA4: Ruis 6K **39**
IG9: Buck H 3G **37**
N3 . . . . .6D **30**
N16 . . . . .6G **49**
SW4 . . . . .6H **119**
TW12: Hamp 6D **130**
UB4: Yead 3B **76**
Maple Ct. CR0: C'don 4C **168**
(off Lwr. Coombe St., Lwr. Coombe St.)
CR0: C'don 4C **168**
(off The Waldrons, The Waldrons)
E3 . . . . .2C **86**
(off Four Seasons Cl.)
E6 . . . . .5E **88**
KT3: N Mald 3K **151**
SE6 . . . . .1D **140**
TW15: Ashf 7F **129**
Maple Cres. DA15: Sidc 6A **126**
Maplecroft Cl. E6 . . . . .6B **88**
Mapledale Av. CR0: C'don 2G **169**
Mapledene BR7: Chst 6G **143**
Mapledene Est. E8 . . . . .7G **67**
Mapledene Rd. E8 . . . . .7F **67**
Maple Gdns. HA8: Edg 7F **29**
TW19: Stanw 2A **128**
Maple Gro. NW9 . . . . .7J **43**
TW8: Bford 7B **96**
UB1: S'hall 5D **76**
W5 . . . . .3D **96**
Maple Gro. Bus. Cen. TW4: Houn . .4A **112**
Maple Ho. E17 . . . . .3D **50**
KT1: King T 5E **150**
(off Maple Rd.)
N19 . . . . .3G **65**
SE8 . . . . .7B **104**
(off Idonia St.)
TW9: Kew 1H **115**
Maplehurst BR2: Brom 2G **159**
Maplehurst Cl. KT1: King T 4E **150**
Maple Ind. Est. TW13: Felt 3J **129**
Maple Leaf Dr. DA15: Sidc 1K **143**
Mapleleafe Gdns. IG6: Ilf 3F **53**
Maple Leaf Sq. SE16 . . . . .2K **103**
Maple Lodge *W8* 3K **99**
(off Abbots Wlk.)
Maple M. NW6 . . . . .2K **81**
SE16 . . . . .2K **103**
SW16 . . . . .5K **137**
Maple Pl. N17 . . . . .7B **34**
UB7: Yiew 1A **92**
W1 . . . . .5B **6** (4G **83**)
Maple Rd. E11 . . . . .6G **51**
KT6: Surb 6D **150**
SE20 . . . . .1H **157**
UB4: Yead 3A **76**
Maples, The KT1: Hamp W 7C **132**
KT10: Clay 7A **162**
Maples Pl. E1 . . . . .5H **85**
Maplestead Rd. RM9: Dag 1B **90**
Maple St. E2 . . . . .7K **119**
RM7: Rom 4J **55**
W1 . . . . .5A **6** (5G **83**)
Maplethorpe Rd. CR7: Thor H 4A **156**
Mapleton Cl. BR2: Brom 6J **159**
Mapleton Cres. EN3: Enf W 1D **24**
SW18 . . . . .6K **117**
Mapleton Rd. E4 . . . . .3K **35**
EN1: Enf 2C **24**
SW18 . . . . .6J **117**
(not continuous)

Maple Tree Pl. SE3 . . . . .1C **124**
Maple Wlk. W10 . . . . .3F **81**
Maple Way TW13: Felt 3J **129**
Maplewood Apartments *N4* 7C **48**
(off Katherine Cl.)
Maplewood Ct. TW15: Ashf 4A **128**
Maplin Cl. N21 . . . . .6E **22**
Maplin Ho. *SE2* 2D **108**
(off Wolvercote Rd.)
Maplin Rd. E16 . . . . .6J **87**
Maplin St. E3 . . . . .3B **86**
Mapperley Cl. E11 . . . . .6H **51**
Mapperley Dr. IG8: Wfd G 7B **36**
Marabou Cl. E12 . . . . .5C **70**
Mara Ho. *E20* 5D **68**
(off Victory Pde.)
Maran Way DA18: Erith 2D **108**
Maraschino Apartment CR0: C'don . .1D **168**
(off Cherry Orchard Rd.)
Marathon Ho. *NW1* 5E **4**
(off Marylebone Rd.)
Marathon Way SE28 . . . . .2K **107**
Marbaix Gdns. TW7: Isle 1H **113**
Marban Rd. W9 . . . . .3H **81**
Marble Arch 2F **11**
MARBLE ARCH 7D **82**
Marble Arch W1 . . . . . .2E **10** (7D **82**)
Marble Arch Apartments *W1* 7E **4**
(off Harrowby St.)
Marble Cl. W3 . . . . .1H **97**
Marble Dr. NW2 . . . . .1F **63**
Marble Hill Cl. TW1: Twick 7B **114**
Marble Hill Gdns. TW1: Twick 7B **114**
Marble Hill House 7C **114**
Marble Ho. SE18 . . . . .5K **107**
W9 . . . . .4H **81**
Marble Quay E1 . . . . . .4K **15** (1G **103**)
Marbles Ho. *SE5* 6C **102**
(off Grosvenor Ter.)
Marbrook Ct. SE12 . . . . .3A **142**
Marcella Rd. SW9 . . . . .2A **120**
Marcellina Way BR6: Orp 3J **173**
March *NW9* .1B **44**
(off Long Mead)
Marchant Cl. NW7 . . . . .6F **29**
Marchant Ho. *N1* 1E **84**
(off Halcomb St.)
Marchant Rd. E11 . . . . .2F **69**
Marchant St. SE14 . . . . .6A **104**
Marchbank Rd. W14 . . . . .6H **99**
March Ct. SW15 . . . . .4D **116**
Marchmont Gdns. TW10: Rich 5F **115**
Marchmont Rd. SM6: Wall 7G **167**
TW10: Rich 5F **115**
Marchmont St. WC1 . . . . .3E **6** (4J **83**)
March Rd. TW1: Twick 7A **114**
Marchside Cl. TW5: Hest 1B **112**
Marchwood Cl. SE5 . . . . .7E **102**
Marchwood Cres. W5 . . . . .6C **78**
Marcia Cl. *SE1* 4E **102**
(off Marcia Rd.)
Marcia Rd. SE1 . . . . .4E **102**
Marcilly Rd. SW18 . . . . .5B **118**
Marco Dr. HA5: Hat E 1D **40**
Marcon Ct. *E8* 5H **67**
(off Amhurst Rd.)
Marconi Pl. N11 . . . . .4A **32**
Marconi Rd. E10 . . . . .1C **68**
Marconi Way UB1: S'hall 6F **77**
Marcon Pl. E8 . . . . .5H **67**
Marco Rd. W6 . . . . .3E **98**
Marcourt Lawns W5 . . . . .4E **78**
Marcus Ct. E15 . . . . .1G **87**
Marcus Garvey M. SE22 . . . . .6H **121**
Marcus Garvey Way SE24 . . . . .4A **120**
Marcus St. E15 . . . . .1H **87**
SW18 . . . . .6K **117**
Marcus Ter. SW18 . . . . .6K **117**
Mardale Cl. NW7 . . . . .7H **29**
Mardale Dr. NW9 . . . . .5K **43**
Mardell Rd. CR0: C'don 5K **157**

Marden Av. BR2: Hayes 6J **159**
Marden Cres. CR0: C'don 6K **155**
DA5: Bexl 5J **127**
Marden Ho. E8 . . . . .5H **67**
Marden Rd. CR0: C'don 6K **155**
N17 . . . . .2E **48**
Marden Sq. SE16 . . . . .3H **103**
Marder Rd. W13 . . . . .2A **96**
Mardyke Cl. RM13: Rain 2J **91**
Mardyke Ho. *SE17* 4D **102**
(off Mason St.)
Marechal Niel Av. DA15: Sidc 3H **143**
Marechal Niel Pde. *DA14: Sidc* 3H **143**
(off Main Rd.)
Maresby Ho. E4 . . . . .2J **35**
Maresfield CR0: C'don 3E **168**
Maresfield Gdns. NW3 . . . . .5A **64**
Mare St. E8 .5H **67**
Marlfeet Cl. SM5: Cars 2C **166**
Margaret Av. E4 . . . . .6J **25**
Margaret Bondfield Av. IG11: Bark . .7A **72**
Margaret Bondfield Ho. *E3* 2A **86**
(off Driffield Rd.)
Margaret Cl. E11 . . . . .6G **51**
Margaret Ct. EN4: E Barn 4G **21**
W1 . . . . .7A **6**
Margaret Gardner Dr. SE9 . . . . .2D **142**
Margaret Herbison Ho. *SW6* 6H **99**
(off Clem Attlee Ct.)
Margaret Ho. *W6* 5E **98**
(off Queen Caroline St.)
Margaret Ingram Cl. SW6 . . . . .6H **99**
Margaret Lockwood Cl. KT1: King T . .4F **151**
Margaret McMillan Ho. E16 . . . . . . .6A **88**
Margaret Rd. DA5: Bexl 6D **126**
EN4: E Barn 4G **21**
N16 . . . . .1F **67**
Margaret Rutherford Pl. SW12 . . . . .1G **137**
Margaret St. W1 . . . . . . .7K **5** (6F **83**)
Margaretta Ter. SW3 . . . .7C **16** (6C **100**)
Margaretting Rd. E12 . . . . .1A **70**
Margaret Way IG4: Ilf 6C **52**
Margaret White Ho. *NW1* 1D **6**
(off Chalton St.)
Margate Rd. SW2 . . . . .5J **119**
Margery Fry Ct. N7 . . . . .3J **65**
Margery Pk. Rd. E7 . . . . .6J **69**
Margery Rd. RM8: Dag 3D **72**
Margery St. WC1 . . . . . . .2J **7** (3A **84**)
Margery Ter. *E7* 6J **69**
(off Margery Pk. Rd.)
Margin Dr. SW19 . . . . .5F **135**
Margravine Gdns. W6 . . . . .5F **99**
Margravine Rd. W6 . . . . .5F **99**
Marham Dr. NW9 . . . . .1A **44**
Marham Gdns. SM4: Mord 6A **154**
SW18 . . . . .1C **136**
Mar Ho. NW9 . . . . .3K **43**
Maria Cl. SE1 . . . . .4H **103**
Maria Ct. SE25 . . . . .2E **156**
Marian Cl. UB4: Yead 4B **76**
Marian Ct. E9 . . . . .5J **67**
SM1: Sutt 5K **165**
Marian Gdns. BR1: Brom 7A **142**
Marianne Cl. SE5 . . . . .1E **120**
Marian Pl. E2 . . . . .2H **85**
Marian Rd. SW16 . . . . .1G **155**
Marian St. E2 . . . . .2H **85**
Marian Way NW10 . . . . .7B **62**
Maria Ter. E1 . . . . .5K **85**
Maria Theresa Cl. KT3: N Mald 5K **151**
Maribor *SE10* 7E **104**
(off Burney St.)
Maricas Av. HA3: Hrw W 1H **41**
Marie Curie SE5 . . . . .1F **121**
Marie Lloyd Gdns. N19 . . . . .7J **47**
Marie Lloyd Ho. *N1* 1E **8**
(off Murray Gro.)
Marie Lloyd Wlk. E8 . . . . .6F **67**
Marien Cl. E4 . . . . .5A **36**
Mariette Way SM6: Wall 7J **167**

Marigold All. SE1 .....3A 14 (7B 84)
Marigold Cl. UB1: S'hall 7C 76
Marigold Rd. N17 .....7D 34
Marigold St. SE16 .....2H 103
Marigold Way CRO: C'don 1K 169
Marina App. UB4: Yead 5C 76
Marina Av. KT3: N Mald 5D 152
Marina Cl. BR2: Brom 3J 159
Marina Ct. E3 .....3B 86
(off Alfred St.)
SW6 .....2A 118
Marina Dr. DA16: Well 2J 125
Marina Gdns. RM7: Rom 5J 55
Marina One N1 .....2J 83
(off New Wharf Rd.)
Marina Pl. KT1: Hamp W 1D 150
Marina Point E14 .....3D 104
(off Lanark Sq.)
Marina Way TW11: Tedd 7D 132
Marine Ct. E11 .....2G 69
Marine Dr. IG11: Bark 4A 90
SE18 .....4D 106
Marinefield Rd. SW6 .....2K 117
Marinel Ho. SE5 .....7C 102
Mariner Bus. Cen. CRO: Wadd 5A 168
Mariner Gdns. TW10: Ham 3C 132
Marine Rd. RM9: Dag 1B 90
Mariner Rd. E12 .....4E 70
Mariners Cl. EN4: E Barn 5G 21
Mariners M. E14 .....4F 105
Marine St. SE16 .....7K 15 (3G 103)
Marine Twr. SE8 .....6B 104
(off Abinger Gro.)
Marion Av. TW17: Shep 5D 146
Marion Gro. IG8: Wfd G 5B 36
Marion Ho. NW1 .....1D 82
(off Regent's Pk. Rd.)
Marion M. SE21 .....3D 138
Marion Rd. CR7: Thor H 5C 156
NW7 .....5H 29
Marischal Rd. SE13 .....3F 123
Maritime Ho. SE18 .....4F 107
Maritime Ind. Est. SE7 .....4K 105
Maritime Quay E14 .....5C 104
Maritime St. E3 .....4B 86
Marius Mans. SW17 .....2E 136
Marius Rd. SW17 .....2E 136
Marjorie Gro. SW11 .....4D 118
Marjorie M. E1 .....6K 85
Mark Av. E4 .....6J 25
Mark Cl. DA7: Bex 1E 126
UB1: S'hall 7F 77
Marke, The SM1: Sutt 1A 166
SM5: Cars 1A 166
Market App. W12 .....2E 98
Market Chambers EN2: Enf 3J 23
(off Church St.)
Market Ct. W1 .....7A 6
Market Dr. W4 .....7A 98
Market Entrance SW8 .....7G 101
Market Est. N7 .....6J 65
Market Hall N22 .....2A 48
Market Hill SE18 .....3E 106
Market La. HA8: Edg 1J 43
W12 .....2E 98
Market Link RM1: Rom 4K 55
Market M. W1 .....5J 11 (1F 101)
Market Pde. BR1: Brom 1J 159
(off East St.)
DA14: Sidc 4B 144
E10 .....6E 50
(off High Rd. Leyton)
E17 .....3B 50
(off Higham Hill Rd.)
N9 .....2B 34
(off Winchester Rd.)
N16 .....1G 67
(off Oldhill St.)
SE25 .....4G 157
TW13: Hanw 3C 130

Market Pav. E10 .....3C 68
Market Pl. DA6: Bex 4G 127
EN2: Enf 3J 23
KT1: King T 2D 150
N2 .....3B 46
SE16 .....4G 103
(not continuous)
TW8: Bford 7C 96
UB1: S'hall 1D 94
W1 .....7A 6 (6G 83)
W3 .....1J 97
Market Place, The NW11 .....4A 46
Market Rd. N7 .....6J 65
TW9: Rich 3G 115
Market Row SW9 .....4A 120
Market Sq. BR1: Brom 2J 159
(not continuous)
E14 .....6D 86
KT1: King T 2D 150
(off Market Pl.)
Market Square, The N9 .....2C 34
(within Edmonton Grn. Shop. Cen.)
Market St. E1 .....5J 9 (5F 85)
E6 .....2D 88
SE18 .....4E 106
Market Ter. TW8: Bford 6E 96
(off Albany Rd.)
Market Trad. Est. UB2: S'hall 4K 93
Market Way E14 .....6D 86
HA0: Wemb 5C 60
Market Yd. SE8 .....7C 104
Market Yd. M. SE1 .....7G 15 (2E 102)
Markfield Beam Engine & Museum 5G 49
Markfield Gdns. E4 .....7J 25
Markfield Rd. N15 .....4G 49
Markham Ho. RM10: Dag 3G 73
(off Uvedale Rd.)
Markham Pl. SW3 .....5E 16 (5D 100)
Markham Sq. SW3 .....5E 16 (5D 100)
Markham St. SW3 .....5D 16 (5C 100)
Markhole Cl. TW12: Hamp 7D 130
Mark Ho. E2 .....2H 85
(off Sewardstone Rd.)
Markhouse Av. E17 .....6A 50
Markhouse Pas. E17 .....6B 50
(off Downsfield Rd.)
Markhouse Rd. E17 .....6B 50
Markland Ho. W10 .....7F 81
(off Darfield Way)
Mark La. EC3 .....2H 15 (7E 84)
Mark Lodge EN4: Cockf 4H 21
(off Edgeworth Rd.)
Markmanor Av. E17 .....7A 50
Mark Rd. N22 .....2B 48
Marksbury Av. TW9: Rich 3G 115
MARKS GATE 1E 54
Mark Sq. EC2 .....3G 9 (4E 84)
Marks Rd. RM7: Rom 5J 55
(not continuous)
Markstone Ho. SE1 .....7A 14
(off Lancaster St.)
Mark St. E15 .....7G 69
EC2 .....3G 9 (4E 84)
Mark Wade Cl. E12 .....1B 70
Markway TW16: Sun 2A 148
Markwell Cl. SE26 .....4H 139
Markyate Ho. W10 .....4E 80
(off Sutton Way)
Markyate Rd. RM8: Dag 5B 72
Marland Ho. SW1 .....1F 17
(off Sloane St.)
Marlands Rd. IG5: Ilf 3C 52
Marlborough SW19 .....1F 135
(off Inner Pk. Rd.)
W9 .....3A 82
(off Maida Vale)
Marlborough Av. E8 .....1G 85
(not continuous)
HA4: Ruis 6E 38
HA8: Edg 3C 28
N14 .....3B 32

Marlborough Cl. BR6: Orp 6K 161
N20 .....3J 31
SE17 .....4C 102
SW19 .....6C 136
Marlborough Ct. CR2: S Croy 4C 168
(off Birdhurst Rd.)
EN1: Enf 5K 23
HA1: Harr 4H 41
HA6: Nwood 1H 39
IG9: Buck H 2F 37
N17 .....1G 49
(off Kemble Rd.)
SM6: Wall 7G 167
W1 .....2A 12
(off Carnaby St.)
W8 .....4J 99
(off Pembroke Rd.)
Marlborough Cres. UB3: Harl 7F 93
W4 .....3K 97
Marlborough Dr. IG5: Ilf 3C 52
Marlborough Flats SW3 .....3D 16
Marlborough Gdns. KT6: Surb 7D 150
N20 .....3J 31
Marlborough Ga. Ho. W2 .....2A 10
(off Elms M.)
Marlborough Gro. SE1 .....5G 103
Marlborough Hill HA1: Harr 4H 41
NW8 .....1A 82
Marlborough House 5B 12 (1G 101)
Marlborough Ho. E16 .....1J 105
(off Hardy Av.)
UB7: W Dray 2B 92
Marlborough La. SE7 .....6A 106
Marlborough Lodge NW8 .....2A 82
(off Hamilton Ter.)
Marlborough Mans. NW6 .....5K 63
(off Canon Hill)
Marlborough M. SW2 .....4K 119
Marlborough Pde. HA8: Edg 3C 28
(off Marlborough Av.)
UB10: Hil 4D 74
Marlborough Pk. Av. DA15: Sidc 7A 126
Marlborough Pl. NW8 .....2A 82
Marlborough Rd.
BR2: Brom 4A 160
CR2: S Croy 7C 168
DA7: Bex 3D 126
E4 .....6J 35
E7 .....7A 70
E15 .....4G 69
E18 .....2H 65
N9 .....1B 34
N19 .....2H 65
N22 .....7D 32
RM7: Mawney 4G 55
RM8: Dag 4B 72
SE18 .....3F 107
SE28 .....3G 107
SM1: Sutt 3J 165
SW1 .....5B 12 (1G 101)
SW19 .....6C 136
TW7: Isle 1B 114
TW10: Rich 6F 115
TW12: Hamp 6E 130
TW13: Felt 2B 130
TW15: Ashf 5A 128
UB2: S'hall 3A 94
UB10: Hil 4D 74
W4 .....5J 97
W5 .....2D 96
Marlborough St. SW3 .....4C 16 (4C 100)
Marlborough Yd. N19 .....2H 65
Marlbury NW8 .....1K 81
(off Abbey Rd.)
Marler Rd. SE23 .....1A 140
Marley Av. DA7: Bex 6D 108
Marley Cl. N15 .....4B 48
UB6: G'frd 3E 76
Marley Ho. E16 .....7F 89
(off University Way)

Marley Ho. W11 .....7F 81
(off St Ann's Rd.)
Marley St. SE16 .....4K 103
Marley Wlk. NW2 .....5E 62
Marl Fld. Cl. KT4: Wor Pk 1C 164
Marlin Cl. TW16: Sun 6G 129
Marling Cl. TW12: Hamp 6D 130
Marlingdene Cl. TW12: Hamp 6E 130
MARLING PARK 7D 130
Marlings Cl. BR7: Chst 4J 161
Marlings Pk. Av. BR7: Chst 4J 161
Marlin Pk. TW14: Felt 5K 111
Marlins Cl. SM1: Sutt 5A 166
Marloes Cl. HA0: Wemb 4D 60
Marloes Rd. W8 .....3K 99
Marlow Cl. SE20 .....3H 157
Marlow Ct. N14 .....7B 22
NW6 .....7F 63
NW9 .....3B 44
Marlow Cres. TW1: Twick 6K 113
Marlow Dr. SM3: Cheam 2F 165
Marlowe Bus. Cen. SE14 .....7A 104
(off Batavia Rd.)
Marlowe Cl. BR7: Chst 6H 143
IG6: Ilf 1G 53
Marlowe Ct. SE19 .....5F 139
SW3 .....4D 16
(off Petyward)
Marlowe Gdns. SE9 .....6E 124
Marlowe Ho. IG8: Wfd G 7K 37
KT1: King T 4D 150
(off Portsmouth St.)
Marlowe Path SE8 .....6C 104
Marlowe Rd. E17 .....4E 50
Marlowes, The DA1: Cray 4K 127
NW8 .....1B 82
Marlowe Sq. CR4: Mitc 4G 155
Marlowe Way CR0: Bedd 2J 167
Marlow Gdns. UB3: Harl 3F 93
Marlow Ho. E2 .....2J 9
(off Calvert Av.)
KT5: Surb 5E 150
(off Cranes Pk.)
SE1 .....7J 15
(off Abbey St.)
TW11: Tedd 4A 132
W2 .....6K 81
(off Hallfield Est.)
Marlow Rd. E6 .....3D 88
SE20 .....3H 157
UB2: S'hall 3D 94
Marlow Way SE16 .....2K 103
Marlow Workshops E2 .....2J 9
(off Virginia Rd.)
Marl Rd. SW18 .....4A 118
Marlston NW1 .....2K 5
Marlton St. SE10 .....5H 105
Marlu Ct. SE14 .....1K 121
(off Hatcham Pk. M.)
Marlu Ho. SE14 .....1K 121
(off Hatcham Pk. M.)
Marlwood Cl. DA15: Sidc 2J 143
Marmadon Rd. SE18 .....4K 107
Marmara Apartments E16 .....7J 87
(off Western Gateway)
Marmion App. E4 .....4H 35
Marmion Av. E4 .....4G 35
Marmion Cl. E4 .....4G 35
Marmion M. SW11 .....3E 118
Marmion Rd. SW11 .....4E 118
Marmont Rd. SE15 .....1G 121
Marmora Rd. SE22 .....6J 121
Marmot Rd. TW4: Houn 3B 112
Marne Av. DA16: Well 3A 126
N11 .....4A 32
Marnell Way TW4: Houn 3B 112
Marner Point E3 .....4E 86
Marne St. W10 .....3G 81
Marney Rd. SW11 .....4E 118
Marnfield Cres. SW2 .....1A 138
Marnham Av. NW2 .....4G 63

Marnham Ct.—Masefield Av.

Marnham Ct. HA0: Wemb 5C 60
Marnham Cres. UB6: G'frd 3F 77
Marnock Ho. *SE17* *5D 102*
(off Brandon St.)
Marnock Rd. SE4 5B 122
Maroon St. E14 5A 86
Maroons Way SE6 5C 140
Marqueen Ct. *W8* *2K 99*
(off Kensington Chu. St.)
Marqueen Towers SW16 7K 137
Marquess Hgts. E18 1K 51
Marquess Rd. N1 6D 66
Marquis Cl. HA0: Wemb 7F 61
Marquis Ct. IG11: Bark 5J 71
KT1: King T *4D 150*
(off Anglesea Rd.)
N4 *1K 65*
(off Marquis Rd.)
TW19: Stanw 1A 128
Marquis Rd. N4 1K 65
N22 6E 32
NW1 6H 65
Marrabon Cl. DA15: Sidc 1A 144
Marrick Cl. SW15 4C 116
Marrick Ho. *NW6* *1K 81*
(off Mortimer Cres.)
Marriett Ho. SE6 4E 140
Marrilyne Av. EN3: Enf L 1G 25
Marriner Ct. *UB3: Hayes* *7G 75*
(off Barra Hall Rd.)
Marriott Cl. TW14: Felt 6F 111
Marriott Rd. E15 1G 87
EN5: Barn 3A 20
N4 1K 65
N10 1D 46
Marriotts Cl. NW9 6B 44
Marryat Cl. TW4: Houn 4D 112
Marryat Ho. *SW1* *6A 18*
(off Churchill Gdns.)
Marryat Pl. SW19 4G 135
Marryat Rd. SW19 5F 135
Marryat Sq. SW6 1G 117
Marsala Rd. SE13 4D 122
Marsalis Ho. *E3* *3C 86*
(off Rainhill Way)
Marsden Rd. N9 2C 34
SE15 3F 121
Marsden St. NW5 6E 64
Marsden Way BR6: Orp 4K 173
Marshall Bldg. *W2* *6A 4*
(off Hermitage St.)
Marshall Cl. HA1: Harr 7H 41
SW18 6A 118
TW4: Houn 5D 112
Marshall Ct. *NW6* *7F 63*
(off Coverdale Rd.)
SE20 *7H 139*
(off Anerley Pk.)
Marshall Dr. UB4: Hayes 5H 75
Marshall Est. NW7 4H 29
Marshall Ho. *N1* *2D 84*
(off Cranston Est.)
SE1 *3E 102*
(off Page's Wlk.)
SE17 *5D 102*
(off East St.)
Marshall Path SE28 7B 90
Marshall Rd. E10 3D 68
N17 1D 48
Marshalls Cl. N11 4A 32
Marshalls Dr. RM1: Rom 3K 55
Marshalls Gro. SE18 4C 106
Marshall's Pl. SE16 3F 103
Marshalls Rd. RM7: Rom 4K 55
SM1: Sutt 4K 165
Marshall St. NW10 7K 61
W1 1B 12 (6G 83)
Marshall Street Leisure Cen. 1B 12 (6G 83)
Marshalsea Rd. SE1 6D 14 (2C 102)
Marsham Cl. BR7: Chst 5F 143
Marsham Ct. SW1 3D 18 (4H 101)
Marsham St. SW1 2D 18 (3H 101)
Marsh Av. CR4: Mitc 2D 154
Marshbrook Cl. SE3 3B 124
Marsh Centre, The *E1* *7K 9*
(off Whitechapel High St.)
Marsh Cl. NW7 3G 29
Marsh Ct. E8 6G 67
SW19 1A 154
Marsh Dr. NW9 6B 44
Marsh Farm Rd. TW2: Twick 1K 131
Marshfield St. E14 3E 104
Marshgate E20 7C 68
Marshgate La. E15 1D 86
E20 7C 68
Marshgate Path SE28 3G 107
Marsh Grn. Rd. RM10: Dag 1G 91
Marsh Hall HA9: Wemb 3F 61
Marsh Hill E9 5A 68
Marsh Ho. *SW1* *6D 18*
(off Aylesford St.)
SW8 1G 119
Marsh La. E10 2B 68
HA7: Stan 5H 27
N17 7C 34
NW7 3F 29
Marsh Rd. HA0: Wemb 3D 78
HA5: Pinn 4C 40
Marshside Cl. N9 1D 34
Marsh St. E14 4D 104
Marsh Wall E14 1C 104
Marsh Way RM13: Rain 3K 91
Marshwood Ho. *NW6* *1J 81*
(off Kilburn Vale)
Marsland Cl. SE17 5B 102
Marsom Ho. *N1* *1E 8*
(off Provost St.)
Marston Av. KT9: Chess 6E 162
RM10: Dag 2G 73
Marston Cl. NW6 7A 64
RM10: Dag 3G 73
Marston Ho. SW9 2A 120
Marston Rd. IG5: Ilf 1C 52
TW11: Tedd 5B 132
Marston Way SE19 7B 138
Marsworth Av. HA5: Pinn 1B 40
Marsworth Cl. UB4: Yead 5C 76
Marsworth Ho. *E2* *1G 85*
(off Whiston Rd.)
Martaban Rd. N16 2F 67
Martara M. SE17 5C 102
Marta Rose Ct. *SE20* *2H 157*
(off Wadhurst Cl.)
Martello St. E8 7H 67
Martello Ter. E8 7H 67
Martell Rd. SE21 3D 138
Martel Pl. E8 6F 67
Marten Rd. E17 2C 50
Martens Av. DA7: Bex 4H 127
Martens Cl. DA7: Bex 4J 127
Martham Cl. IG6: Ilf 1F 53
SE28 7D 90
Martha Rd. E15 6G 69
Martha's Bldgs. EC1 3E 8 (4D 84)
Martha St. E1 6J 85
Marthorne Cres. HA3: Hrw W 2H 41
Martin Bowes Rd. SE9 3D 124
Martinbridge Trad. Est. EN1: Enf 5B 24
Martin Cl. N9 1E 34
UB10: Uxb 2A 74
Martin Ct. *CR2: S Croy* *5E 168*
(off Birdhurst Rd.)
E14 *2E 104*
(off River Barge Cl.)
Martin Cres. CR0: C'don 1A 168
Martindale SW14 5J 115
Martindale Av. BR6: Chels 5K 173
E16 7J 87
Martindale Ho. *E14* *7D 86*
(off Poplar High St.)
Martin Dale Ind. Est. EN1: Enf 3C 24
Martindale Rd. SW12 7F 119
TW4: Houn 3C 112
Martin Dene DA6: Bex 5F 127
Martin Dr. UB5: N'olt 5D 58
Martineau Dr. TW1: Twick 4B 114
Martineau Est. E1 7J 85
Martineau Ho. *SW1* *6A 18*
(off Churchill Gdns.)
Martineau M. N5 4B 66
Martineau Rd. N5 4B 66
Martineau Sq. E1 7G 85
Martingale Cl. TW16: Sun 4J 147
Martingale Ho. *E1* *1H 103*
(off Raine St.)
Martingales Cl. TW10: Ham 3D 132
Martin Gdns. RM8: Dag 4C 72
Martin Gro. SM4: Mord 3J 153
Martin Ho. *E3* *1B 86*
(off Old Ford Rd.)
SE1 3C 102
SW8 *7J 101*
(off Wyvil Rd.)
Martin Kinggett Gdns. RM9: Dag 1E 90
Martin La. EC4 2F 15 (7D 84)
(not continuous)
Martin Ri. DA6: Bex 5F 127
Martin Rd. RM8: Dag 4C 72
Martins, The HA9: Wemb 3F 61
SE26 5H 139
Martins Cl. BR4: W W'ck 1F 171
Martin's Mt. EN5: New Bar 4D 20
Martins Pl. SE28 1J 107
Martin's Rd. BR2: Brom 2G 159
Martin St. SE28 1J 107
Martins Wlk. N10 1E 46
N22 3A 48
SE28 1J 107
Martin Way SM4: Mord 2F 153
SW20 2F 153
Martlesham *N17* *2E 48*
(off Adams Rd.)
Martlesham Wlk. NW9 2A 44
Martlet Gro. UB5: N'olt 3B 76
Martlett Ct. WC2 1F 13 (6J 83)
Martley Dr. IG2: Ilf 5F 53
Martock Cl. HA3: W'stone 4A 42
Martock Gdns. N11 5J 31
Marton Cl. SE6 3C 140
Marton Rd. N16 2E 66
Martynside NW9 1B 44
Martys Yd. NW3 4B 64
Marvell Av. UB4: Hayes 5J 75
Marvell Ct. *RM6: Chad H* *6B 54*
(off Quarles Pk. Rd.)
Marvell Ho. *SE5* *7D 102*
(off Camberwell Rd.)
Marvels Cl. SE12 2K 141
Marvels La. SE12 2K 141
Marville Rd. SW6 7H 99
Marvin St. E8 6H 67
Marwell Cl. BR4: W W'ck 2H 171
Marwood Cl. DA16: Well 3B 126
Marwood Dr. NW7 7A 30
Mary Adelaide Cl. SW15 4A 134
Mary Ann Gdns. SE8 6C 104
Maryatt Av. HA2: Harr 2F 59
Marybank SE18 4D 106
Mary Bayly Ho. *W11* *1G 99*
(off Wilsham St.)
Mary Boast Wlk. SE5 2D 120
Mary Cl. HA7: Stan 4F 43
Mary Datchelor Cl. SE5 1D 120
Mary Datchelor Ho. *SE5* *1D 120*
(off Grove La.)
Maryfield Cl. DA5: Bexl 3K 145
Mary Flux Ct. *SW5* *5K 99*
(off Bramham Gdns.)
Mary Grn. NW8 1K 81
Mary Holben Ho. SW16 5G 137
Mary Ho. *W6* *5E 98*
(off Queen Caroline St.)
Mary Jones Ct. *E14* *7C 86*
(off Garford St.)
Maryland Ind. Est. E15 5G 69
Maryland Pk. E15 5G 69
(not continuous)
Maryland Point *E15* *6G 69*
(off The Grove)
Maryland Rd. CR7: Thor H 1B 156
E15 5F 69
N22 6E 32
Maryland Sq. E15 5G 69
Marylands Rd. W9 4J 81
(not continuous)
Maryland St. E15 5F 69
Maryland Wlk. *N1* *1C 84*
(off Popham St.)
Maryland Way TW16: Sun 2J 147
Mary Lawrenson Pl. SE3 7J 105
MARYLEBONE 5H 5 (5E 82)
Marylebone Cricket Club 2B 4
MARYLEBONE FLYOVER 5C 82
Marylebone Fly-Over NW1 5B 82
W2 6B 4 (5B 82)
Marylebone Gdns. TW9: Rich 4G 115
Marylebone High St. W1 5H 5 (5E 82)
Marylebone La. W1 6H 5 (5E 82)
Marylebone M. W1 6J 5 (5F 83)
Marylebone Pas. W1 7B 6 (6G 83)
Marylebone Rd. NW1 5D 4 (5C 82)
Marylebone St. W1 6H 5 (5E 82)
Marylee Way SE11 4H 19 (4K 101)
Mary Macarthur Ho. *E2* *3K 85*
(off Warley St.)
RM10: Dag *3G 73*
(off Wythenshawe Rd.)
W6 6G 99
Mary Neuner Rd. N8 3K 47
N22 3K 47
Maryon Gro. SE7 4C 106
Maryon Ho. *NW6* *7A 64*
(off Goldhurst Ter.)
Maryon M. NW3 4C 64
Maryon Rd. SE7 4C 106
SE18 4C 106
Mary Peters Dr. UB6: G'frd 5H 59
Mary Pl. W11 7G 81
Mary Rose Cl. TW12: Hamp 1E 148
Mary Rose Mall E6 5D 88
Mary Rose Sq. *SE8* *4A 104*
(off Cary Av.)
Maryrose Way N20 1G 31
Marys Ct. NW1 3D 4
Mary Seacole Cl. E8 1F 85
Mary Seacole Ho. *W6* *3C 98*
(off Invermead Cl.)
Mary Smith Ct. *SW5* *4J 99*
(off Trebovir Rd.)
Marysmith Ho. *SW1* *5D 18*
(off Cureton St.)
Mary's Ter. TW1: Twick 7A 114
Mary St. E16 5H 87
N1 1C 84
Mary Ter. NW1 1F 83
Maryville DA16: Well 2K 125
Mary Wallace Theatre
Twickenham 1A 132
Mary Wharrie Ho. *NW3* *7D 64*
(off Fellows Rd.)
Marzell Ho. *W14* *5H 99*
(off North End Rd.)
Marzena Ct. TW3: Houn 6G 113
Masault Ct. *TW9: Rich* *4E 114*
(off Kew Foot Rd.)
Masbro' Rd. W14 3F 99
Mascalls Ct. SE7 6A 106
Mascalls Rd. SE7 6A 106
Mascotte Rd. SW15 4F 117
Mascotts Cl. NW2 3D 62
Masefield Av.
HA7: Stan 5E 26
UB1: S'hall 7E 76

Masefield Ct.—Mayfield Ho.

Masefield Ct. EN5: New Bar 4F 21
KT6: Surb 7D 150
Masefield Cres. N14 5B 22
Masefield Gdns. E6 4E 88
Masefield Ho. NW6 3J 81
(off Stafford Rd.)
Masefield La. UB4: Yead 4K 75
Masefield Rd. TW12: Hamp 4D 130
Masefield Vw. BR6: Farnb 3G 173
Masefield Way TW19: Stanw 1B 128
Masey M. SW2 5A 120
Masham Ho. DA18: Erith 2D 108
(off Kale Rd.)
Mashie Rd. W3 6A 80
Mashiters Hill RM1: Rom 1K 55
Maskall Cl. SW2 1A 138
Maskani Wlk. SW16 7G 137
Maskell Rd. SW17 3A 136
Maskelyne Cl. SW11 1C 118
Mason Cl. DA7: Bex 3H 127
E16 7J 87
SE16 5G 103
SW20 1F 153
TW12: Hamp 1D 148
Mason Ho. E9 7J 67
(off Frampton Pk. Rd.)
SE1 4G 103
(off Simms Rd.)
Mason Rd. IG8: Wfd G 4B 36
SM1: Sutt 5K 165
Masonry Ho. SE14 1K 121
(off Fishers Ct.)
Mason's Arms M. W1 1K 11 (6F 83)
Masons Av. CR0: C'don 3C 168
EC2 7E 8 (6D 84)
HA3: W'stone 4K 41
Masons Grn. La. W3 4G 79
W5 4G 79
Masons Hill BR1: Brom 3J 159
BR2: Brom 3K 159
SE18 4F 107
Masons Pl. CR4: Mitc 1D 154
EC1 1B 8 (3C 84)
Mason St. SE17 4D 102
Masons Yd. EC1 1B 8 (3B 84)
SW1 4B 12 (1G 101)
SW19 5F 135
Massey Cl. N11 5A 32
Massey Ct. E6 1A 88
(off Florence Rd.)
Massie Rd. E8 6G 67
Massingberd Way SW17 4F 137
Massinger St. SE17 4E 102
Massingham St. E1 4K 85
Masson Av. HA4: Ruis 6A 58
Mast, The E16 7G 89
Mast Ct. SE16 4A 104
(off Boat Lifter Way)
Master Gunner Pl. SE18 7C 106
Masterman Ho. SE5 7D 102
(off Elmington Est.)
Masterman Rd. E6 3C 88
Masters Cl. SW16 6G 137
Masters Dr. SE16 5H 103
Masters Lodge E1 6J 85
(off Johnson St.)
Masters St. E1 5K 85
Mast Ho. Ter. E14 4C 104
(not continuous)
Mastmaker Ct. E14 2C 104
Mastmaker Rd. E14 2C 104
Mast Quay SE18 3D 106
MASWELL PARK 5G 113
Maswell Pk. Cres.
TW3: Houn 5G 113
Maswell Pk. Rd. TW3: Houn 5F 113
Matcham Ct. TW1: Twick 6D 114
(off Clevedon Rd.)
Matcham Rd. E11 3G 69
Match Ct. E3 2C 86
(off Blondin St.)
Matching Ct. E3 3B 86
(off Merchant St.)
Matchless Dr. SE18 7E 106
Matfield Cl. BR2: Brom 5J 159
Matfield Rd. DA17: Belv 6G 109
Matham Gro. SE22 4F 121
Matham Rd. KT8: E Mos 5H 149
Matheson Lang Ho. SE1 7J 13
Matheson Rd. W14 4H 99
Mathews Av. E6 2E 88
Mathews Pk. Av. E15 6H 69
Mathews Yd. WC2 1E 12 (6J 83)
Mathieson Ct. SE1 7B 14
(off King James St.)
Mathison Ho. SW10 7A 100
(off Coleridge Gdns.)
Matilda Cl. SE19 7D 138
Matilda Gdns. E3 2C 86
Matilda Ho. E1 1G 103
(off St Katherine's Way)
Matilda St. N1 1K 83
Matisse Ct. EC1 3E 8
Matisse Rd. TW3: Houn 3F 113
Matlock Cl. EN5: Barn 5A 20
SE24 4C 120
Matlock Ct. NW8 2A 82
(off Abbey Rd.)
SE5 4D 120
W11 7J 81
(off Kensington Pk. Rd.)
Matlock Cres. SM3: Cheam 4G 165
Matlock Gdns. SM3: Cheam 4G 165
Matlock Pl. SM3: Cheam 4G 165
Matlock Rd. E10 6E 50
Matlock St. E14 6A 86
Matlock Way KT3: N Mald 1K 151
Maton Ho. SW6 7H 99
(off Estcourt Rd.)
Matrimony Pl. SW8 2G 119
Matson Ct. IG8: Wfd G 7B 36
Matson Ho. SE16 3H 103
Matthew Cl. W10 4F 81
Matthew Ct. CR4: Mitc 5H 155
E17 3E 50
Matthew Parker St. SW1 7D 12 (2H 101)
Matthews Ct. E17 1C 50
(off Chingford Rd.)
Matthews Ho. E14 5C 86
(off Burgess St.)
Matthews Rd. UB6: G'frd 5H 59
Matthews St. SW11 2D 118
Matthews Yd. CR0: C'don 3C 168
(off Surrey St.)
Matthias Apartments N1 7D 66
(off Northchurch Rd.)
Matthias Ct. TW10: Rich 5E 114
Matthias Rd. N16 5E 66
Mattison Rd. N4 6A 48
Mattock La. W5 1B 96
W13 1B 96
Maud Cashmore Way SE18 3D 106
Maud Chadburn Pl. SW4 6F 119
Maude Ho. E2 2G 85
(off Ropley St.)
Maude Rd. E17 5A 50
SE5 1E 120
Maude Ter. E17 5A 50
Maud Gdns. E13 1H 87
IG11: Bark 2K 89
Maudlins Grn. E1 4K 15 (1G 103)
Maud Rd. E10 3E 68
E13 2H 87
Maudslay Rd. SE9 3D 124
Maudsley Ho. TW8: Bford 5E 96
Maud St. E16 5H 87
Maudsville Cotts. W7 1J 95
Maud Wilkes Cl. NW5 5G 65
Maugham Way W3 3J 97
Mauleverer Rd. SW2 5J 119
Maundeby Wlk. NW10 6A 62
Maunder Rd. W7 1K 95
Maunsel St. SW1 3C 18 (4H 101)
Maureen Campbell Ct.
TW17: Shep 5D 146
(off Harrison Way)
Maureen Ct. BR3: Beck 2J 157
Maurer Ct. SE10 3H 105
Mauretania Bldg. E1 7K 85
(off Jardine Rd.)
Maurice Av. N22 2B 48
Maurice Browne Av. NW7 6B 30
Maurice Ct. E1 3K 85
N22 1K 47
TW8: Bford 7D 96
Maurice Drummond Ho. SE10 1D 122
(off Catherine Gro.)
Maurice St. W12 6D 80
Maurice Wlk. NW11 4A 46
Maurier Cl. UB5: N'olt 1A 76
Mauritius Rd. SE10 4G 105
Maury Rd. N16 2G 67
Mauveine Gdns. TW3: Houn 4E 112
Mavelstone Cl. BR1: Brom 1C 160
Mavelstone Rd. BR1: Brom 1B 160
Maverton Rd. E3 1C 86
Mavery Ct. BR1: Brom 7H 141
(off Bromley Av.)
Mavis Av. KT19: Ewe 5A 164
Mavis Cl. KT19: Ewe 5A 164
Mavis Wlk. E6 5C 88
(off Greenwich Cres.)
Mavor Ho. N1 1K 83
(off Barnsbury Est.)
Mawbey Ho. SE1 5G 103
Mawbey Pl. SE1 5F 103
Mawbey Rd. SE1 5F 103
Mawbey St. SW8 7J 101
Mawdley Ho. SE1 7A 14
MAWNEY 3H 55
Mawney Cl. RM7: Mawney 2H 55
Mawney Rd. RM7: Mawney, Rom 2H 55
Mawson Cl. SW20 2G 153
Mawson Ct. N1 1D 84
(off Gopsall St.)
Mawson Ho. EC1 5J 7
(off Baldwins Gdns.)
Mawson La. W4 6B 98
Maxden Ct. SE15 3F 121
Maxey Gdns. RM9: Dag 4E 72
Maxey Rd. RM9: Dag 4E 72
SE18 4G 107
Maxfield Cl. N20 7F 21
Maxilla Wlk. W10 6F 81
Maxim Apartments BR2: Brom 4K 159
(off Tiger La.)
Maximfeldt Rd. DA8: Erith 5K 109
Maxim Rd. DA8: Erith 4K 109
N21 6F 23
Maxted Pk. HA1: Harr 7J 41
Maxted Rd. SE15 3F 121
Maxwell Cl. CR0: Wadd 1J 167
UB3: Hayes 7J 75
Maxwell Ct. SE22 1G 139
SW4 5H 119
Maxwell Gdns. BR6: Orp 3K 173
Maxwell Rd.
DA16: Well 3K 125
HA6: Nwood 1F 39
RM7: Rush G 6K 55
SW6 7K 99
TW15: Ashf 6E 128
UB7: W Dray 4B 92
Maxwelton Av. NW7 5E 28
Maxwelton Cl. NW7 5E 28
Maya Angelou Ct. E4 4K 35
Maya Apartments E20 5E 68
(off Victory Pde.)
Maya Cl. SE15 2H 121
Mayall Cl. EN3: Enf L 1H 25
Mayall Rd. SE24 5B 120
Maya Pl. N11 7C 32
Maya Rd. N2 4A 46
Maybank Av. E18 2K 51
HA0: Wemb 5K 59
Maybank Gdns. HA5: Eastc 5J 39
Maybank Rd. E18 1K 51
May Bate Av. KT2: King T 1D 150
Maybells Commercial Est.
IG11: Bark 2D 90
Mayberry Ct. BR3: Beck 7B 140
(off Copers Cope Rd.)
Mayberry Pl. KT5: Surb 7F 151
Maybourne Cl. SE26 6H 139
Maybury Cl. BR5: Pet W 5F 161
EN1: Enf 1C 24
Maybury Ct. CR2: S Croy 5B 168
(off Haling Pk. Rd.)
HA1: Harr 6H 41
W1 6H 5
(off Marylebone St.)
Maybury Gdns. NW10 6D 62
Maybury M. N6 7G 47
Maybury Rd. E13 4A 88
IG11: Bark 2K 89
Maybury St. SW17 5C 136
Maychurch Cl. HA7: Stan 7J 27
May Cl. KT9: Chess 6F 163
May Ct. SW19 1A 154
(off Pincott Rd.)
Maycroft HA5: Pinn 2K 39
Maycross Av. SM4: Mord 4H 153
Mayday Gdns. SE3 2C 124
Mayday Rd. CR7: Thor H 6B 156
Maydeb Ct. RM6: Chad H 6F 55
Maydew Ho. SE16 4J 103
(off Abbeyfield Est.)
Maydwell Ho. E14 5C 86
(off Thomas Rd.)
Mayerne Rd. SE9 5B 124
Mayesbrook Park Arena 5A 72
Mayesbrook Rd. IG3: Ilf 3A 72
IG11: Bark 1K 89
RM8: Dag 3A 72
Mayes Cl. CR0: New Ad 7F 171
Mayesford Rd. RM6: Chad H 7C 54
Mayes Rd. N22 2K 47
Mayeswood Rd. SE12 4A 142
MAYFAIR 3J 11 (7F 83)
Mayfair Av. DA7: Bex 1D 126
IG1: Ilf 2D 70
KT4: Wor Pk 1C 164
RM6: Chad H 6D 54
TW2: Whitt 7G 113
Mayfair Cl. BR3: Beck 1D 158
KT6: Surb 1E 162
Mayfair Ct. HA8: Edg 5A 28
Mayfair Gdns. IG8: Wfd G 7D 36
N17 6H 33
Mayfair M. NW1 7D 64
(off Regents Pk. Rd.)
Mayfair Pl. W1 4K 11 (1F 101)
Mayfair Ter. N14 7C 22
Mayfield DA7: Bex 3F 127
Mayfield Av. BR6: Orp 1K 173
HA3: Kenton 5B 42
IG8: Wfd G 6D 36
N12 4F 31
N14 2C 32
W4 4A 98
W13 3B 96
Mayfield Cl. E8 6F 67
KT7: T Ditt 1B 162
SE20 1H 157
SW4 5H 119
TW15: Ashf 6D 128
UB10: Hil 3D 74
Mayfield Cres. CR7: Thor H 4K 155
N9 6C 24
Mayfield Dr. HA5: Pinn 4D 40
Mayfield Gdns. NW4 6F 45
W7 6H 77
Mayfield Ho. E2 2H 85
(off Cambridge Heath Rd.)

Mayfield Mans. SW15 . . . . .5H 117
Mayfield Rd. BR1: Brom 5C 160
   CR2: Sande 7D 168
   CR7: Thor H 4K 155
   DA17: Belv 4J 109
   E4 . . . . .2K 35
   E8 . . . . .7F 67
   E13 . . . . .4H 87
   E17 . . . . .2A 50
   EN3: Enf H 2E 24
   N8 . . . . .5K 47
   RM8: Dag .1C 72
   SM2: Sutt 6B 166
   SW19 . . . . .1H 153
   W3 . . . . .1J 79
   W12 . . . . .2A 98
Mayfield Rd. Flats N8 . . . . .6K 47
Mayfields HA9: Wemb 2G 61
Mayfields CI. HA9: Wemb 2G 61
Mayfield Vs. DA14: Sidc 6C 144
Mayflower CI. HA4: Ruis 6E 38
   SE16 . . . . .4K 103
Mayflower Ho. E14 . . . . .2C 104
     (off Westferry Rd.)
   IG11: Bark 1H 89
     (off Westbury Rd.)
Mayflower Rd. SW9 . . . . .3J 119
Mayflower St. SE16 . . . . .2J 103
Mayfly CI. HA5: Eastc 7A 40
Mayfly Gdns. UB5: N'olt 3B 76
Mayford NW1 .2G 83
     (not continuous)
Mayford CI. BR3: Beck 3K 157
   SW12 . . . . .7D 118
Mayford Rd. SW12 . . . . .7D 118
May Gdns. HA0: Wemb 3C 78
Maygood Ho. N1 . . . . .2K 83
     (off Maygood St.)
Maygood St. N1 . . . . .2A 84
Maygrove Rd. NW6 . . . . .6H 63
Mayhew CI. E4 . . . . .3H 35
Mayhew CI. SE10 . . . . .4D 120
Mayhill CI. SE15 . . . . .7E 102
     (off Tower Mill Rd.)
Mayhill Rd. EN5: Barn 6B 20
   SE7 . . . . .6K 105
May Ho. E3 . . . . .2C 86
     (off Thomas Fyre Dr.)
Mayland Mans. IG11: Bark 7F 71
     (off Whiting Av.)
Maylands Dr. DA14: Sidc 3D 144
   UB8: Uxb 6A 56
Maylands Ho. SW3 . . . . .4D 16
     (off Cale St.)
May La. HA3: Kenton 7F 43
Maylie Ho. SE16 . . . . .2H 103
     (off Marigold St.)
Maynard CI. N15 . . . . .5E 48
   SW6 . . . . .7K 99
Maynard Path E17 . . . . .5E 50
Maynard Rd. E17 . . . . .5E 50
Maynards Quay E1 . . . . .7J 85
Mayne CI. SE26 . . . . .5H 139
Maynooth Gdns. SM5: Cars 7D 154
Mayo CI. W13 .3B 96
Mayo Ho. E1 . . . . .5J 85
     (off Lindley St.)
Mayola Rd. E5 .4J 67
Mayo Rd. CR0: C'don 5D 156
   KT12: Walt T 7J 147
   NW10 . . . . .6A 62
Mayor's & City of London Court, The . . .7E 8
Mayow Rd. SE23 . . . . .4K 139
   SE26 . . . . .4K 139
Mayplace CI. DA7: Bex 3H 127
Mayplace La. SE18 . . . . .6F 107
     (not continuous)
Mayplace Rd. E. DA1: Cray 3J 127
   DA7: Bex .3H 127
Mayplace Rd. W. DA7: Bex 4G 127
MAYPOLE 1K 145

Maypole Ct. UB2: S'hall 2D 94
     (off Merrick Rd.)
May Rd. E4 . . . . .6H 35
   E13 . . . . .2J 87
   TW2: Twick 1J 131
Mayroyd Av. KT6: Surb 2G 163
May's Bldgs. M. SE10 . . . . .7E 104
Mays Ct. SE10 . . . . .7F 105
   WC2 . . . . .3E 12 (7J 83)
Mays Hill Rd. BR2: Brom 2G 159
Mays La. EN5: Ark, Barn . . . . .6A 20 & 1H 29
Maysoule Rd. SW11 . . . . .4B 118
Mays Rd. TW11: Tedd 5H 131
Mayston M. SE10 . . . . .5J 105
     (off Ormiston Rd.)
May St. W14 . . . . .5H 99
     (Kelway Ho.)
   W14 . . . . .5H 99
     (Orchard Sq.)
Maysswood Gdns. RM10: Dag 6J 73
Maythorne Cotts. SE13 . . . . .5F 123
Mayton St. N7 . . . . .3K 65
Maytree CI. HA8: Edg 3D 28
Maytree Ct. CR4: Mitc 3E 154
   UB5: N'olt .3C 76
Maytree Gdns. W5 . . . . .2D 96
May Tree Ho. SE4 . . . . .3B 122
     (off Wickham Rd.)
Maytree La. HA7: Stan 7F 27
Maytree Wlk. SW2 . . . . .2A 138
Mayville Est. N16 . . . . .5E 66
Mayville Rd. E11 . . . . .2G 69
     (not continuous)
   IG1: Ilf 5F 71
May Wlk. E13 .2K 87
Mayward Ho. SE5 . . . . .1E 120
     (off Peckham Rd.)
Maywood CI. BR3: Beck 7D 140
May Wynne Ho. E16 . . . . .7K 87
     (off Murray Sq.)
Maze Hill SE3 . . . . .7H 105
   SE10 . . . . .6G 105
Maze Hill Lodge SE10 . . . . .6F 105
     (off Park Vista)
Mazenod Av. NW6 . . . . .7J 63
Maze Rd. TW9: Kew 7G 97
MCC Cricket Museum & Tours
    . . . . .1A 4 (3B 82)
Mead, The BR3: Beck 1E 158
   BR4: W W'ck 1F 171
   N2 . . . . .2A 46
   SM6: Wall 6H 167
   UB10: Ick .2C 56
   W13 . . . . .5B 78
Meadbank Studios SW11 . . . . .7C 100
     (off Parkgate Rd.)
Mead CI. HA3: Hrw W 1H 41
   NW1 . . . . .6E 64
Mead Ct. NW9 . . . . .5J 43
Mead Cres. E4 . . . . .4K 35
   SM1: Sutt 3C 166
Meadcroft Rd. SE11 . . . . . .7K 19 (6B 102)
     (not continuous)
   SE17 . . . . .6B 102
Meade CI. W4 .6G 97
Meade M. SW1 . . . . .5D 18
Meader Ct. SE14 . . . . .7K 103
Mead Fld. HA2: Harr 3D 58
Meadfield HA8: Edg 2C 28
     (not continuous)
Meadfield Grn. HA8: Edg 2C 28
Meadfoot Rd. SW16 . . . . .7G 137
Meadgate Av. IG8: Wfd G 5H 37
Mead Gro. RM6: Chad H 3D 54
Mead Ho. W11 . . . . .1H 99
     (off Ladbroke Rd.)
Mead Ho. La. UB4: Hayes 4F 75
Meadhurst Club 5H 129
Meadhurst Pk. TW16: Sun 6G 129
Meadlands Dr. TW10: Ham 2D 132
Mead Lodge W4 . . . . .2K 97

Meadow, The BR7: Chst 6G 143
   N10 . . . . .3E 46
Meadow Av. CR0: C'don 6K 157
Meadow Bank N21 . . . . .6E 22
Meadowbank KT5: Surb 6F 151
   NW3 . . . . .7D 64
   SE3 . . . . .3H 123
Meadowbank CI. SW6 . . . . .7E 98
   TW7: Isle 1J 113
Meadowbank Rd. NW9 . . . . .7K 43
Meadowbridge Ct. CR0: C'don 5D 156
     (off Princess Rd.)
Meadowbrook CI. SL3: Poyle 4A 174
Meadowbrook Ct. TW7: Isle 3J 113
Meadow CI.
   BR7: Chst 5F 143
   DA6: Bex .5F 127
   E4 . . . . .1J 35
   E9 . . . . .6B 68
   EN3: Enf H 1F 25
   EN5: Barn .6H 39
   HA4: Ruis .6H 39
   IG11: Bark 7A 72
   KT10: Hin W 3A 162
   SE6 . . . . .5C 140
   SM1: Sutt 2A 166
   SW20 . . . . .4E 152
   TW4: Houn 6E 112
   TW10: Ham 1E 132
   UB5: N'olt .2E 76
Meadow Ct. E16 . . . . .1A 106
     (off Booth Rd.)
   N1 . . . . .2E 84
   TW10: Ham 6F 113
Meadowcourt Rd. SE3 . . . . .4H 123
Meadowcroft BR1: Brom 3D 160
   W4 . . . . .5G 97
     (off Brooks Rd.)
Meadowcroft CI. E10 . . . . .7D 50
   N13 . . . . .2F 33
     (off Cable St.)
   SE6 . . . . .6D 122
Meadowcroft M. E1 . . . . .7G 85
     (off Cable St.)
   SE6 . . . . .6D 122
Meadowcroft Rd. N13 . . . . .2F 33
Meadow Dr. N10 . . . . .3F 47
   NW4 . . . . .2E 44
Meadowford CI. SE28 . . . . .7A 90
Meadow Gdns. HA8: Edg 6C 28
Meadow Gth. NW10 . . . . .6J 61
Meadowgate CI. NW7 . . . . .5G 29
Meadow Hill KT3: N Mald 6A 152
Meadowlark Ho. NW9 . . . . .7B 44
Meadowlea CI. UB7: Harm 2E 174
Meadow M. SW8 . . . . .6K 101
Meadow PI. SW8 . . . . .7J 101
   W4 . . . . .7A 98
Meadow Rd. BR2: Brom 2G 159
   HA5: Pinn .4B 40
   IG11: Bark 7K 71
   RM7: Rush G 1J 73
   RM9: Dag .6F 73
   SM1: Sutt 4C 166
   SW8 . . . . .7H 19 (7K 101)
   SW19 . . . . .7A 136
   TW13: Felt 2C 130
   TW15: Ashf 5F 129
   UB1: S'hall 7D 76
Meadow Row SE1 . . . . .3C 102
Meadows, The E4 . . . . .4A 36
Meadows CI. E10 . . . . .2C 68
Meadows Ct. DA14: Sidc 6B 144
Meadows End TW16: Sun 1J 147
Meadowside SE3 . . . . .4A 124
   SE9 . . . . .4A 124
   TW1: Twick 7D 114
Meadow Stile CR0: C'don 3C 168
Meadowsweet CI. E16 . . . . .5B 88
   SW20 . . . . .4E 152

Meadow Vw. DA15: Sidc 7B 126
   HA1: Harr .1J 59
Meadowview Rd. TW9: Stanw M 7A 174
Meadow Vw. Rd. CR7: Thor H 5B 156
   SW20 . . . . .4E 152
   UB4: Hayes 4F 75
Meadowview Rd. DA5: Bexl 6E 126
   KT19: Ewe 7A 164
   SE6 . . . . .5B 140
Meadow Wlk. E18 . . . . .4J 51
   KT17: Ewe 6A 164
   KT19: Ewe 6A 164
   RM9: Dag .6F 73
   SM6: Wall 3F 167
Meadow Walks EN5: New Bar 6E 20
Meadow Way BR6: Farnb 3E 172
   HA4: Ruis .6X 39
   HA9: Wemb 4D 60
   KT9: Chess 5E 162
   NW9 . . . . .5K 43
Meadow Way, The HA3: Hrw W 1J 41
Meadow Waye TW5: Hest 6C 94
Mead Path SW17 . . . . .4A 136
Mead PI. CR0: C'don 1C 168
   E9 . . . . .6J 67
Mead Plat NW10 . . . . .6J 61
Mead Rd. BR7: Chst 6G 143
   HA8: Edg .6B 28
   TW10: Ham 3C 132
Mead Row SE1 . . . . .1J 19 (3A 102)
Meads, The HA8: Edg 6E 28
   SM3: Cheam 3G 165
   SM4: Mord 5C 154
   UB8: Cowl 4A 74
Meads Ct. E15 . . . . .6H 69
Meadside CI. BR3: Beck 1A 158
Meads La. IG3: Ilf 7J 53
Meads Rd. EN3: Enf H 1F 25
   N22 . . . . .2B 48
Meadvale Rd. CR0: C'don 7F 157
   W5 . . . . .4B 78
Mead Way BR2: Hayes 6H 159
   CR0: C'don 2A 170
   HA4: Ruis .6F 39
Meadway BR3: Beck 1E 158
   EN5: Barn, New Bar 4D 20
   IG3: Bark, Ilf 4J 71
   IG8: Wfd G 5F 37
   KT5: Surb 1J 163
   N14 . . . . .2C 32
   NW11 . . . . .6J 45
   SW20 . . . . .4E 152
   TW2: Twick 1H 131
   TW15: Ashf 4C 128
Meadway, The
   IG9: Buck H 1G 37
   SE3 . . . . .2F 123
Meadway CI. EN5: Barn 4D 20
   HA5: Hat E 6A 26
   NW11 . . . . .6K 45
Meadway Ct. RM8: Dag 2F 73
   TW11: Tedd 5C 132
   W5 . . . . .4F 79
Meadway Gdns. HA4: Ruis 6F 39
Meadway Ga. NW11 . . . . .6J 45
Meaford Way SE20 . . . . .7H 139
Meakin Est. SE1 . . . . .3E 102
Meander Ho. E20 . . . . .5D 68
     (off Logan CI.)
Meanley Rd. E12 . . . . .4C 70
Meard St. W1 . . . . .1C 12 (6H 83)
     (not continuous)
Mears CI. E1 . . . . .5G 85
     (off Settles St.)
Meath Cres. E2 . . . . .3K 85
Meath Ho. SE24 . . . . .6B 120
     (off Dulwich Rd.)
Meath Rd. E15 . . . . .2H 87
   IG1: Ilf 3G 71
Meath St. SW11 . . . . .1F 119

Mecca Bingo
Burnt Oak 2J 43
Camden 1F 83
        (off Arlington Rd.)
Catford 7D 122
Chadwell Heath 7D 54
Croydon 2C 168
Dagenham 1E 90
Hackney 1K 9
Hayes 5K 75
Morden 7A 154
Wandsworth 1K 135
Wood Green 2A 48
Mecklenburgh Pl. WC1 . . . . . .3G 7 (4K 83)
Mecklenburgh Sq. WC1 . . . . . .3G 7 (4K 83)
Mecklenburgh St. WC1 . . . . . .3G 7 (4K 83)
Medals Way E20 . . . . .5E 68
Medburn St. NW1 . . . . .2H 83
Medcroft Gdns. SW14 . . . . .4J 115
Mede Ho. BR1: Brom 5K 141
        (off Pike Cl.)
Medesenge Way N13 . . . . .6G 33
Medfield St. SW15 . . . . .7C 116
Medhurst Cl. E3 . . . . .2A 86
        (not continuous)
Medhurst Dr. BR1: Brom 5G 141
Median Rd. E5 . . . . .5J 67
Medici Cl. IG3: Ilf 6A 54
        (not continuous)
Medina Gro. N7 . . . . .3A 66
Medina Rd. N7 . . . . .3A 66
Medland Cl. SM6: Wall 1E 166
Medland Ho. E14 . . . . .7A 86
Medlar Cl. UB5: N'olt 2B 76
Medlar Ho. DA15: Sidc 3A 144
Medlar St. SE5 . . . . .1C 120
Medley Rd. NW6 . . . . .6J 63
Medora Ho. RM7: Rom 4K 55
SW2 . . . . .7K 119
Medusa Rd. SE6 . . . . .6D 122
Medway Bldgs. E3 . . . . .2A 86
        (off Medway Rd.)
Medway Cl. CR0: C'don 6J 157
IG1: Ilf 5G 71
Medway Ct. NW11 . . . . .6K 45
WC1 . . . . .2E 6
        (off Judd St.)
Medway Dr. UB6: G'frd 2K 77
Medway Gdns. HA0: Wemb 4A 60
Medway Ho. KT2: King T 1D 150
NW8 . . . . .4C 4
        (off Penfold St.)
SE1 .7F 15
        (off Hankey Pl.)
Medway M. E3 . . . . .2A 86
Medway Pde. UB6: G'frd 2K 77
Medway Rd. E3 . . . . .2A 86
Medway St. SW1 . . . . . .2D 18 (3H 101)
Medwin St. SW4 . . . . .4K 119
Meerbrook Rd. SE3 . . . . .3A 124
Meeson Rd. E15 . . . . .7H 69
Meeson St. E5 . . . . .4A 68
Meeson's Wharf E15 . . . . .2E 86
Meeting Fld. Path E9 . . . . .6J 67
Meeting Ho. All. E1 . . . . .1H 103
Meeting Ho. La. SE15 . . . . .1H 121
Megelish M. UB1: S'hall 3E 76
Mehetabel Rd. E9 . . . . .5J 67
Meister Cl. IG1: Ilf 1H 71
Melancholy Wlk. TW10: Ham 2C 132
Melanda Cl. BR7: Chst 5D 142
Melanie Cl. DA7: Bex 1E 126
Melba Way SE13 . . . . .1D 122
Melbourne Av. HA5: Pinn 3F 41
N13 . . . . .6E 32
W13 . . . . .1A 96
Melbourne Cl.
BR6: Orp 7J 161
SE20 . . . . .7G 139

Melbourne Cl. SM6: Wall 5G 167
UB10: Ick 4C 56
Melbourne Ct. E5 . . . . .4A 68
        (off Daubeney Rd.)
N10 . . . . .7A 32
W9 .4A 82
        (off Randolph Av.)
Melbourne Gdns. RM6: Chad H . . .5E 54
Melbourne Gro. SE22 . . . . .4E 120
Melbourne Ho. UB4: Yead 4A 76
W8 .1J 99
        (off Kensington Pl.)
Melbourne Mans. W14 . . . . .6G 99
        (off Musard Rd.)
Melbourne M. SE6 . . . . .7E 122
SW9 . . . . .1A 120
Melbourne Pl. WC2 . . . . . .1H 13 (6K 83)
Melbourne Rd. E6 . . . . .2D 88
E10 . . . . .7D 50
E17 . . . . .4A 50
IG1: Ilf 1F 71
SM6: Wall 5F 167
SW19 . . . . .1J 153
TW11: Tedd 6C 132
Melbourne Sq. SW9 . . . . .1A 120
Melbourne Ter. SW6 . . . . .7K 99
        (off Moore Pk. Rd.)
Melbourne Way EN1: Enf 6A 24
Melbourne Yd. SE19 . . . . .6E 138
Melbray M. SW6 . . . . .2H 117
Melbreak Ho. SE22 . . . . .3E 120
Melbury Av. UB2: S'hall 3F 95
Melbury Cl. BR7: Chst 6C 142
KT10: Clay 6B 162
Melbury Ct. W8 . . . . .3H 99
Melbury Dr. SE5 . . . . .7E 102
Melbury Gdns. SW20 . . . . .1D 152
Melbury Ho. SW8 . . . . .7K 101
        (off Richborne Ter.)
Melbury Rd. HA3: Kenton 5F 43
W14 . . . . .3H 99
Melchester W11 . . . . .6H 81
        (off Ledbury Rd.)
Melchester Ho. N19 . . . . .3H 65
        (off Wedmore St.)
Melcombe Ct. NW1 . . . . .5E 4
        (off Melcombe Pl.)
Melcombe Gdns. HA3: Kenton . . .6F 43
Melcombe Ho. SW8 . . . . .7K 101
        (off Dorset Rd.)
Melcombe Pl. NW1 . . . . . .5E 4 (5D 82)
Melcombe Regis Ct. W1 . . . . .6H 5
        (off Weymouth St.)
Melcombe St. NW1 . . . . . .4F 5 (4D 82)
Meldex Cl. NW7 . . . . .6K 29
Meldon Cl. SW6 . . . . .1K 117
Meldone Cl. KT5: Surb 7H 151
Meldrum Rd. IG3: Ilf 2A 72
Melfield Gdns. SE6 . . . . .4E 140
Melford Av. IG11: Bark 6J 71
Melford Cl. KT9: Chess 5F 163
Melford Ct. SE1 . . . . .3E 102
        (off Fendall St.)
SE22 . . . . .1G 139
        (not continuous)
Melford Pas. SE22 . . . . .7G 121
Melford Rd. E6 . . . . .4D 88
E11 . . . . .2G 69
E17 . . . . .4A 50
IG1: Ilf 2H 71
SE22 . . . . .7G 121
Melfort Av. CR7: Thor H 3B 156
Melfort Rd. CR7: Thor H 3B 156
Melgund Rd. N5 . . . . .5A 66
Melia Cl. UB3: Hayes 5F 75
Melina Cl. NW8 . . . . .2A 4
SW15 . . . . .3C 116
Melina Pl. NW8 . . . . .2A 4 (3B 82)
Melina Rd. W12 . . . . .2D 98
Melior Cl. N6 . . . . .6G 47
Melior Pl. SE1 . . . . .6G 15 (2E 102)

Melior St. SE1 . . . . .6G 15 (2E 102)
Meliot Rd. SE6 . . . . .2F 141
Meller Cl. CR0: Bedd 3J 167
Meller Ho. E20 . . . . .6E 68
        (off Champions Wlk.)
Mellifont Cl. SM5: Cars 7B 154
Melling Dr. EN1: Enf 1B 24
Melling St. SE18 . . . . .6J 107
Mellish Cl. IG11: Bark 1K 89
Mellish Flats E10 . . . . .7C 50
Mellish Gdns. IG8: Wfd G 5D 36
Mellish Ho. E1 . . . . .6H 85
        (off Varden St.)
Mellish Ind. Est. SE18 . . . . .3B 106
Mellish St. E14 . . . . .3C 104
Mellison Rd. SW17 . . . . .5C 136
Mellitus St. W12 . . . . .5B 80
Mellor Cl. KT12: Walt T 7K 147
Mellow La. E. UB4: Hayes 3E 74
Mellow La. W. UB10: Hil 3E 74
Mellows Rd. IG5: Ilf 3D 52
SM6: Wall 5H 167
Mells Cres. SE9 . . . . .4D 142
Mell St. SE10 . . . . .5G 105
Melody La. N5 . . . . .5C 66
Melody Rd. SW18 . . . . .5A 118
Melon Pl. W8 . . . . .2J 99
Melon Rd. E11 . . . . .3G 69
SE15 . . . . .1G 121
Melrose Av. CR4: Mitc 7F 137
DA1: Cray 7K 127
N22 . . . . .1B 48
NW2 . . . . .5D 62
SW16 . . . . .3K 155
SW19 . . . . .2H 135
TW2: Whitt 7F 113
UB6: G'frd 2F 77
Melrose Cl. SE12 . . . . .1J 141
UB4: Hayes 5J 75
UB6: G'frd 2F 77
Melrose Ct. W13 . . . . .1A 96
        (off Williams Rd.)
Melrose Cres. BR6: Orp 4H 173
Melrose Dr. UB1: S'hall 1E 94
Melrose Gdns. HA8: Edg 3H 43
KT3: N Mald 3K 151
W6 .3E 98
Melrose Ho. NW6 . . . . .3J 81
        (off Carlton Vale)
SW1 . . . . .5J 17
        (part of Abbots Mnr.)
Melrose Rd. HA5: Pinn 4D 40
SW13 . . . . .2B 116
SW18 . . . . .6H 117
SW19 . . . . .2J 153
W3 .3J 97
Melrose Ter. W6 . . . . .3E 98
Melrose Tudor SM6: Wall 5J 167
        (off Plough La.)
Melsa Rd. SM4: Mord 6A 154
Melthorne Dr. HA4: Ruis 3A 58
Melthorpe Gdns. SE3 . . . . .1C 124
Melton Cl. HA4: Ruis 1A 58
Melton Ct. SM2: Sutt 7A 166
SW7 . . . . .4B 16 (4B 100)
Melton St. NW1 . . . . . . .2B 6 (3G 83)
Melville Av. CR2: S Croy 5F 169
SW20 . . . . .7C 134
UB6: G'frd 5K 59
Melville Cl. UB10: Ick 2F 57
Melville Ct. SE8 . . . . .4A 104
W4 .6A 98
        (off Haining Cl.)
W12 . . . . .3D 98
        (off Goldhawk Rd.)
Melville Gdns. N13 . . . . .5G 33
Melville Ho. EN5: New Bar 5G 21
SE10 . . . . .1E 122
        (off Sparta St.)
Melville Pl. N1 . . . . .7C 66

Melville Rd. DA14: Sidc 2C 144
E17 . . . . .3B 50
NW10 . . . . .7K 61
RM5: Col R 1H 55
SW13 . . . . .1C 116
Melville Vs. Rd. W3 . . . . .1J 97
Melville Rd. SE20 . . . . .1J 157
Melwood Ho. E1 . . . . .6H 85
        (off Watney Mkt.)
Melyn Cl. N7 . . . . .4G 65
Memel Ct. EC1 . . . . .4C 8
Memel St. EC1 . . . . .4C 8 (4C 84)
Memess Path SE18 . . . . .6E 106
Memorial Av. E15 . . . . .3G 87
Memorial Cl. TW5: Hest 6D 94
Memorial Hgts. IG2: Ilf 6H 53
Menai Pl. E3 . . . . .2C 86
        (off Blondin St.)
Menard Ct. EC1 . . . . .2D 8
        (off Galway St.)
Mendez Way SW15 . . . . .6C 116
Mendham Ho. SE1 . . . . .7G 15
        (off Cluny Pl.)
Mendip Cl. KT4: Wor Pk 1E 164
SE26 . . . . .4J 139
UB3: Harl 7F 93
Mendip Ct. SE14 . . . . .6J 103
        (off Avonley Rd.)
SW11 . . . . .3A 118
Mendip Dr. NW2 . . . . .2G 63
Mendip Ho. N9 . . . . .2B 34
  (within Edmonton Grn. Shop. Cen.)
Mendip Ho's. E2 . . . . .3J 85
        (off Welwyn St.)
Mendip Rd. DA7: Bex 1K 127
IG2: Ilf 5J 53
SW11 . . . . .3A 118
Mendora Rd. SW6 . . . . .7G 99
Menelik Rd. NW2 . . . . .4G 63
Menier Chocolate Factory
  (Theatre and Art Gallery) 5D 14
        (off Southwark St.)
Menlo Gdns. SE19 . . . . .7D 138
Menlo Lodge N13 . . . . .3E 32
        (off Crothall Cl.)
Menon Dr. N9 . . . . .3C 34
Menotti St. E2 . . . . .4G 85
Menteath Ho. E14 . . . . .6C 86
        (off Dod St.)
Mentmore Cl. HA3: Kenton 6C 42
Mentmore Ter. E8 . . . . .7H 67
Mentone Mans. SW10 . . . . .7K 99
        (off Fulham Rd.)
Meon Ct. TW7: Isle 2J 113
Meon Rd. W3 . . . . .2J 97
Meopham Rd. CR4: Mitc 1G 155
Mepham Cres. HA3: Hrw W 7B 26
Mepham Gdns. HA3: Hrw W 7B 26
Mepham St. SE1 . . . . . . .5H 13 (1A 102)
Mera Dr. DA7: Bex 4G 127
Meranti Ho. E1 . . . . .7K 9
        (off Goodman's Stile)
Merantun Way SW19 . . . . .1K 153
Merbury Cl. SE13 . . . . .5E 122
SE28 . . . . .1H 107
Merbury Rd. SE28 . . . . .2H 107
Mercator Pl. E14 . . . . .5C 104
Mercator Rd. SE13 . . . . .4F 123
Mercer Bldg. EC2 . . . . .3H 9
        (off New Inn Yd.)
Mercer Cl. KT7: T Ditt 7K 149
Mercer Ct. E1 . . . . .5A 86
Mercer Ho. SW1 . . . . .5J 17
        (off Ebury Bri. Rd.)
Merceron Ho's. E2 . . . . .3J 85
        (off Globe Rd.)
Merceron St. E1 . . . . .4H 85
Mercer Pl. HA5: Pinn 2A 40
Mercers Cl. SE10 . . . . .4H 105
Mercer's Cotts. E1 . . . . .6A 86
        (off White Horse Rd.)

Mercers M. N19 . . . . .3H 65
Mercers Pl. W6 . . . . .4F 99
Mercers Rd. N19 . . . . .3H 65
 (not continuous)
Mercer St. WC2 . . . . .1E 12 (6J 83)
Merchant Ct. KT19: Ewe 5K 163
Merchant Ct. E1 . . . . .1J 103
 (off Wapping Wall)
Merchant Ho. E14 . . . . .3D 104
 (off Selsdon Way)
Merchant Ind. Ter. NW10 . . . . .4J 79
Merchants Cl. SE25 . . . . .4G 157
Merchants Ho. SE10 . . . . .5F 105
 (off Collington St.)
Merchants Lodge E17 . . . . .4C 50
 (off Westbury Rd.)
Merchants Row SE10 . . . . .5F 105
 (off Hoskins St.)
Merchant St. E3 . . . . .3B 86
Merchiston Rd. SE6 . . . . .2F 141
Merchland Rd. SE9 . . . . .1G 143
Mercia Ho. SE5 . . . . .2C 120
 (off Denmark Rd.)
 TW15: Ashf 1E 146
Mercier Rd. SW15 . . . . .5G 117
Mercury NW9 . . . . .1B 44
 (off Quakers Course)
Mercury Cen. TW14: Felt 5J 111
Mercury Ct. E14 . . . . .4C 104
 (off Homer Dr.)
 SW9 . . . . .1A 120
 (off Southey Rd.)
Mercury Ho. E3 . . . . .1C 86
 (off Garrison Rd.)
 E16 . . . . .6H 87
 (off Jude St.)
 TW8: Bford 6C 96
 (off Glenhurst Rd.)
 W5 . . . . .4F 79
Mercury Way SE14 . . . . .6K 103
Mercy Ter. SE13 . . . . .5D 122
Merebank La. CR0: Wadd 5K 167
Mere Cl. BR6: Farnb 2E 172
 SW15 .7F 117
Meredith Av. NW2 . . . . .5E 62
Meredith Cl. HA5: Pinn 1B 40
Meredith Ho. N16 . . . . .5E 66
Meredith M. SE4 . . . . .4B 122
Meredith St. E13 . . . . .3J 87
 EC1 . . . . .2A 8 (3B 84)
Meredith Twr. W3 . . . . .3H 97
 (off Hanbury Rd.)
Meredyth Rd. SW13 . . . . .2C 116
Mere End CR0: C'don 7K 157
 TW17: Shep 6D 146
Mere Rd. SE2 . . . . .2D 108
Mereside BR6: Farnb 2E 172
Mereside Pk. TW15: Ashf 4E 128
Meretone Cl. SE4 . . . . .4A 122
Mereton Mans. SE8 . . . . .1C 122
 (off Brookmill Rd.)
Merevale Cres. SM4: Mord 6A 154
Mereway Rd. TW2: Twick 1H 131
Merewood Cl. BR1: Brom 2E 160
Merewood Gdns. CR0: C'don 7K 157
Merewood Rd. DA7: Bex 2J 127
Mereworth Cl. BR2: Brom 5H 159
Mereworth Dr. SE18 . . . . .7F 107
Mereworth Ho. SE15 . . . . .6J 103
Merganser Ct. E1 . . . . .3K 15
 (off Star Pl.)
 SE8 . . . . .6B 104
 (off Edward St.)
Merganser Gdns. SE28 . . . . .3H 107
Meriden Cl.
 BR1: Brom 7B 142
 IG6: Ilf .1G 53
Meriden Ct. SW3 . . . . .6C 16

Meriden Ho. N1 . . . . .1E 84
 (off Wilmer Gdns.)
Meridene N21 . . . . .6G 23
Meridia Ct. KT1: King T 2F 151
Meridia Cl. E15 . . . . .1E 86
 (off Biggerstaff Rd.)
Meridian Bus. Pk. EN3: Pond E 6F 25
Meridian Cl. NW7 . . . . .4E 28
Meridian Cl. SE15 . . . . .7H 103
 (off Gervase St.)
 SE16 . . . . .2G 103
 (off East La.)
 UB4: Yead 4A 76
Meridian Ga. E14 . . . . .2D 104
Meridian Ho. NW1 . . . . .7G 65
 (off Baynes St.)
 SE10 . . . . .4G 105
 (off Azof St., Azof St.)
 SE10 . . . . .7E 104
 (off Royal Hill, Royal Hill)
Meridian Pl. E14 . . . . .2D 104
Meridian Point SE18 . . . . .6D 104
Meridian Rd. SE7 . . . . .7B 106
Meridian Sq. E15 . . . . .7F 69
Meridian Trad. Est. SE7 . . . . .4K 105
Meridian Wlk. N17 . . . . .6K 33
Meridian Way EN3: Pond E 4D 34
 N9 . . . . .4D 34
 N18 . . . . .5D 34
Merifield Rd. SE9 . . . . .4A 124
Merino Cl. E11 . . . . .4A 52
Merino Pl. EC1 . . . . .2D 8
 (off Lever St.)
Merino Pl. DA15: Sidc 6A 126
Merioneth Cl. W7 . . . . .5K 77
 (off Copley Cl.)
Merita Ho. E1 . . . . .1G 103
 (off Nesham St.)
Merivale Rd. HA1: Harr 7G 41
 SW15 .4G 117
Merle Mans. E20 . . . . .6E 68
 (off Glade Wlk.)
Merlewood Dr. BR7: Chst 1D 160
Merley Ct. NW9 . . . . .1J 61
Merlin NW9 .1B 44
 (off Near Acre)
Merlin Cl. CR0: C'don 4E 168
 CR4: Mitc 3C 154
 SM6: Wall 6K 167
 UB5: N'olt 3A 76
Merlin Ct. BR2: Brom 3H 159
 HA4: Ruis 2F 57
 HA7: Stan 5G 27
 (off William Dr.)
 SE3 . . . . .4K 123
Merlin Cres. HA8: Edg 1F 43
Merlin Gdns. BR1: Brom 3J 141
Merling Cl. KT9: Chess 5C 162
Merlin Gro. BR3: Beck 4B 158
Merlin Hgts. N17 . . . . .3H 49
 (off Daneland Wlk.)
Merlin Ho. EN3: Pond E 5E 24
Merlin Rd. DA16: Well 4A 126
 E12 . . . . .2B 70
Merlin Rd. Nth. DA16: Well 4A 126
Merlins Av. HA2: Harr 3D 58
Merlins Ct. WC1 . . . . .2J 7
 (off Margery St.)
Merlin St. WC1 . . . . .2J 7 (3A 84)
Mermaid Ct. E8 . . . . .7F 67
 (off Celandine Dr.)
 SE1 . . . . .6E 14 (2D 102)
 SE16 . . . . .1B 104
Mermaid Ho. E14 . . . . .7E 86
 (off Bazely St.)
Mermaid Twr. SE8 . . . . .6B 104
 (off Abinger Gro.)
Meroe Ct. N16 . . . . .2E 66
Merredene St. SW2 . . . . .6K 119
Merriam Av. E9 . . . . .6B 68
Merriam Cl. E4 . . . . .5K 35
Merrick Rd. UB2: S'hall 2D 94

Merrick Sq. SE1 . . . . .7E 14 (3D 102)
Merridene N21 . . . . .6G 23
Merrielands Cres. RM9: Dag 2F 91
Merrielands Retail Pk. RM9: Dag 1F 91
Merrilands Rd. KT4: Wor Pk 1E 164
Merrilees Rd. DA15: Sidc 7J 125
Merrilyn Cl. KT10: Clay 6A 162
Merriman Rd. SE3 . . . . .1A 124
Merrington Rd. SW6 . . . . .6J 99
Merrion Av. HA7: Stan 5J 27
Merrion Ct. HA4: Ruis 1H 57
 (off Pembroke Rd.)
Merritt Gdns. KT9: Chess 6C 162
Merritt Rd. SE4 . . . . .5B 122
Merrivale N14 . . . . .6C 22
 NW1 . . . . .1G 83
 (off Camden St.)
Merrivale Av. IG4: Ilf 4B 52
Merrow Bldgs. SE1 . . . . .6B 14
 (off Rushworth St.)
Merrow Ct. CR4: Mitc 2B 154
Merrow Rd. SM2: Cheam 7F 165
Merrow St. SE17 . . . . .5D 102
Merrow St. SE17 . . . . .5D 102
Merrow Way CR0: New Ad 6E 170
Merrydown Way BR7: Chst 1C 160
Merryfield SE3 . . . . .2H 123
Merryfield Gdns. HA7: Stan 5H 27
Merryfield Ho. SE9 . . . . .3A 142
 (off Grove Pk. Rd.)
Merryfields UB8: Uxb 2A 74
Merryfields Way SE6 . . . . .7D 122
MERRY HILL 1A 26
Merryhill Cl. E4 . . . . .7J 25
Merry Hill Mt. WD23: Bush 1A 26
Merry Hill Rd. WD23: Bush 1A 26
Merryhills Ct. N14 . . . . .5B 22
Merryhills Dr. EN2: Enf 4C 22
Merryweather Ct. KT3: N Mald 5A 152
 N19 . . . . .3G 65
Merryweather Pl. SE10 . . . . .7D 104
Mersea Ho. IG11: Bark 6F 71
Mersey Ct. KT2: King T 1D 150
 (off Samuel Gray Gdns.)
Mersey Rd. E17 . . . . .3B 50
Mersey Wlk. UB5: N'olt 2E 76
Mersham Dr. NW9 . . . . .5G 43
Mersham Pl. CR7: Thor H 2D 156
 (off Livingstone Rd.)
 SE20 . . . . .1H 157
Mersham Rd. CR7: Thor H 3D 156
Merten Rd. RM6: Chad H 7E 54
Merthyr Ter. SW13 . . . . .6D 98
MERTON 7A 136
Merton Abbey Mills SW19 . . . . .1A 154
Merton Av. UB5: N'olt 5G 59
 UB10: Hil 7D 56
 W4 . . . . .4B 98
Merton Ct. DA16: Well 2B 126
 IG1: Ilf 6C 52
Merton Gdns. BR5: Pet W 5F 161
Merton Hall Gdns. SW20 . . . . .1G 153
Merton Hall Rd. SW19 . . . . .7G 135
Merton High St. SW19 . . . . .7K 135
Merton Ind. Pk. SW19 . . . . .1K 153
Merton La. N6 . . . . .2D 64
Merton Lodge EN5: New Bar 5F 21
Merton Mans. SW20 . . . . .2F 153
MERTON PARK 2J 153
Merton Pk. Pde. SW19 . . . . .1H 153
Merton Pl. SW19 . . . . .1A 154
 (off Nelson Gro. Rd.)
Merton Ri. NW3 . . . . .7C 64
Merton Rd. E17 . . . . .5E 50
 EN2: Enf 1J 23
 HA2: Harr 1G 59
 IG3: Ilf .7K 53
 IG11: Bark 7K 71
 SE25 . . . . .5F 157
 SW18 . . . . .6J 117
 SW19 .7K 135

Merton's Intergenerational Cen. 2F 155
Merton Way KT8: W Mole 4F 149
 UB10: Hil 7D 56
Merloun Ter. W1 . . . . .7E 4
 (off Seymour Pl.)
Mertlins Rd. SE15 . . . . .5K 121
Meru Cl. NW5 . . . . .4E 64
Mervan Rd. SW2 . . . . .4A 120
Mervyn Av. SE9 . . . . .3G 143
Mervyn Rd. TW17: Shep 7E 146
 W13 . . . . .3A 96
Messaline Av. W3 . . . . .6J 79
Messenger Cl. SE16 . . . . .3G 103
 (off Spa Rd.)
Messent Rd. SE9 . . . . .5A 124
Messeter Pl. SE9 . . . . .6E 124
Messina Av. NW6 . . . . .7J 63
Messiter Ho. N1 . . . . .1K 83
 (off Barnsbury Est.)
Metcalfe Ct. SE10 . . . . .3H 105
Metcalf Rd. TW15: Ashf 5D 128
Metcalf Wlk. TW13: Hanw 4C 130
Meteor St. SW11 . . . . .4E 118
Meteor Way SM6: Wall 7J 167
Methley St. SE11 . . . . .6K 19 (5A 102)
Methuen Cl. HA8: Edg 7B 28
Methuen Pk. N10 . . . . .3F 47
Methuen Rd. DA6: Bex 4F 127
 DA17: Belv 4H 109
 HA8: Edg 7B 28
Methwold Ho. N9 . . . . .3B 34
 (off The Broadway)
Methwold Rd. W10 . . . . .5F 81
Metro Bus. Cen. SE26 . . . . .6B 140
Metro Central Hgts. SE1 . . . . .3C 102
 (off Newington C'way.)
Metro Golf Cen. 7K 29
Metro Ind. Cen. TW7: Isle 2J 113
Metropolis SE11 . . . . .3B 102
 (off Oswin St.)
Metropolitan Bus. Cen. N1 . . . . .7E 66
 (off Enfield Rd.)
Metropolitan Centre, The UB6: G'frd . .1F 77
Metropolitan Cl. E14 . . . . .5C 86
Metropolitan Police FC 6H 149
Metropolitan Sta. Bldgs. W6 . . . . .4E 98
 (off Beadon Rd.)
Metropolitan Wharf E1 . . . . .1J 103
Metro Trad. Est. HA9: Wemb 4H 61
Mews, The DA14: Sidc 4A 144
 IG4: Ilf 5B 52
 N1 . . . . .1C 84
 N8 . . . . .3A 48
 RM1: Rom 4K 55
 TW1: Twick 6B 114
 TW2: Hamp H 6G 131
Mews Pl. IG8: Wfd G 4D 36
Mews St. E1 . . . . .4K 15 (1G 103)
Mexborough NW1 . . . . .1G 83
Mexfield Rd. SW15 . . . . .5H 117
Meyer Grn. EN1: Enf 1B 24
Meyer Rd. DA8: Erith 6K 109
Meymott St. SE1 . . . . .5A 14 (1B 102)
Meyneli Cres. E9 . . . . .7K 67
Meyneli Gdns. E9 . . . . .7K 67
Meyneli Rd. E9 . . . . .7K 67
Meyrick Ho. E14 . . . . .5C 86
 (off Burgess St.)
Meyrick Rd. NW10 . . . . .6C 62
 SW11 . . . . .3B 118
Miah Ter. E1 . . . . .1G 103
Miall Wlk. SE26 . . . . .4A 140
Mica Ho. N1 .7A 66
Micawber Av. UB8: Hil 4C 74
Micawber Ct. N1 . . . . .1D 8
 (off Windsor Ter.)
Micawber Ho. SE16 . . . . .2G 103
 (off Llewellyn St.)
Micawber St. N1 . . . . .1D 8 (3C 84)
Michael Cliffe Ho. EC1 . . . . .2A 8
Michael Cl. E3 . . . . .4B 86

Michael Edwards Studio Theatre, The
. . . . .6E 104
(within Cutty Sark)
Michael Faraday Ho. SE17 . . . . .5E 102
(off Beaconsfield Rd.)
Michael Gaynor Cl. W7 . . . . .1K 95
Michael Haines Ho. SW9 . . . . .7A 102
(off Sth. Island Pl.)
Michael Manley Ind. Est. SW8 . . . . . .1G 119
Michaelmas Cl. SW20 . . . . .3E 152
Michael Rd. E11 . . . . .1G 69
SE25 .3E 156
SW6 .1K 117
Michaels Cl. SE13 . . . . .4G 123
Michael Stewart Ho. SW6 . . . . .6H 99
(off Clem Attlee Ct.)
Michelangelo Ct. SE16 . . . . .5H 103
(off Stubbs Dr.)
Micheldever Rd. SE12 . . . . .6G 123
Michelham Gdns. TW1: Twick 3K 131
Michelle Ct. BR1: Brom 1H 159
(off Blyth Rd.)
N12 . . . . .5F 31
W3 . . . . .7K 79
Michelsdale Dr. TW9: Rich 4E 114
Michelson Ho. SE11 . . . . .4H 19
Michel's Row TW9: Rich 4E 114
(off Michelsdale Dr.)
Michel Wlk. SE18 . . . . .5F 107
Michigan Av. E12 . . . . .4D 70
Michigan Bldg. E14 . . . . .1F 105
(off Biscayne Av.)
Michigan Ho. E14 . . . . .3C 104
Michleham Down N12 . . . . .4C 30
Mickledore NW1 . . . . .1B 6
(off Ampthill Est.)
Mickleham Cl. BR5: St P 2K 161
Mickleham Gdns. SM3: Cheam 6G 165
Mickleham Rd. BR5: St P 1K 161
Mickleham Way CR0: New Ad 7F 171
Micklethwaite Rd. SW6 . . . . .6J 99
Mickleton Ho. W2 . . . . .5J 81
(off Westbourne Pk. Rd.)
Midas Bus. Cen. RM10: Dag 4H 73
Midas Metropolitan Ind. Est.
SM4: Mord 7E 152
MID BECKTON 5D 88
Midcroft HA4: Ruis 1G 57
Middle Dartrey Wlk. SW10 . . . . .7A 100
(off Dartrey Wlk.)
Middle Dene NW7 . . . . .3E 28
Middlefield NW8 . . . . .1B 82
Middlefielde W13 . . . . .5B 78
Middlefield Gdns. IG2: Ilf 6F 53
Middle Grn. Cl. KT5: Surb 6F 151
Middleham Gdns. N18 . . . . .6B 34
Middleham Rd. N18 . . . . .6B 34
Middle La. N8 . . . . .5J 47
TW11: Tedd 6K 131
Middle La. M. N8 . . . . .5J 47
Middle Mall Halls of Residence
KT1: King T 3F 151
Middle New St. EC4 . . . . .7K 7
(off Pemberton Row)
Middle Pk. Av. SE9 . . . . .6B 124
Middle Path HA2: Harr 1H 59
Middle Rd. E13 . . . . .2J 87
EN4: E Barn 6H 21
HA2: Harr 2H 59
SW16 . . . . .2H 155
Middle Row W10 . . . . .4G 81
Middlesborough Rd. N18 . . . . .6B 34
Middlesex Building, The E1 . . . . .5K 9
(off Artillery La.)
Middlesex Bus. Cen. UB2: S'hall 2E 94
Middlesex CCC 1B 4 (3B 82)
Middlesex Cl. UB1: S'hall 4F 77
Middlesex Ct. HA1: Harr 5K 41
TW8: Bford 5C 96
(off Glenhurst Rd.)
W4 . . . . .4B 98

Middlesex Filter Beds Nature Reserve
. . . . .3K 67
Middlesex Guildhall 7E 12
(off Lit. George St.)
Middlesex Ho. HA0: Wemb 1D 78
Middlesex Pas. EC1 . . . . .6B 8
Middlesex Pl. E9 . . . . .6J 67
(off Elsdale St.)
Middlesex Rd. CR4: Mitc 5J 155
Middlesex St. E1 . . . . .6H 9 (5E 84)
Middlesex University
Hendon Campus 4D 44
The Archway Campus 1G 65
Middlesex Wharf E5 . . . . .2J 67
Middle St. CR0: C'don 2C 168
(not continuous)
EC1 . . . . .5C 8 (5C 84)
Middle Temple La. EC4 . . . .1J 13 (6A 84)
Middleton Av. DA14: Sidc 6G 143
E4 . . . . .4G 35
UB6: G'frd 2H 77
Middleton Cl. E4 . . . . .3G 35
Middleton Dr. HA5: Eastc 3J 39
SE16 . . . . .2K 103
Middleton Gdns. IG2: Ilf 6F 53
Middleton Gro. IG11: Bark 3A 90
N7 . . . . .5J 65
Middleton Ho. E8 . . . . .7G 67
SE1 . . . . .3D 102
(off Burbage Cl.)
SW1 .4D 18
(off Causton St.)
Middleton M. N7 . . . . .5J 65
Middleton Pl. W1 . . . . .6A 6
Middleton Rd. E8 . . . . .7F 67
NW11 . . . . .7J 45
SM4: Mord 6K 153
SM5: Cars 6A 154
UB3: Hayes 5F 75
Middleton St. E2 . . . . .3H 85
Middleton Way SE13 . . . . .4F 123
Middle Way
DA18: Erith 3E 108
SW16 . . . . .2H 155
UB4: Yead 4A 76
Middle Way, The HA3: W'stone 2K 41
Middleway NW11 . . . . .5K 45
Middle Yd. SE1 . . . . .4G 15 (1E 102)
Midfield Av. DA7: Bex 3J 127
Midfield Pde. DA7: Bex 3J 127
Midfield Way BR5: St P 7A 144
Midford Ho. NW4 . . . . .4E 44
(off Belle Vue Est.)
Midford Pl. W1 . . . . .4B 6 (4G 83)
Midholm HA9: Wemb 1G 61
NW11 . . . . .4K 45
Midholm Cl. NW11 . . . . .4K 45
Midholm Rd. CR0: C'don 2A 170
Midhope St. WC1 . . . . .2F 7 (3J 83)
Midhurst SE26 . . . . .6J 139
Midhurst Av. CR0: C'don 7A 156
N10 . . . . .3E 46
Midhurst Gdns. UB10: Hil 1E 74
Midhurst Hill DA6: Bex 6G 127
Midhurst Ho. E14 . . . . .6B 86
(off Salmon La.)
Midhurst Pde. N10 . . . . .3E 46
(off Fortis Grn.)
Midhurst Rd. W13 . . . . .2A 96
Midhurst Way E5 . . . . .4G 67
Midland Goods Shed N1 . . . . .1J 83
(off Handyside St.)
Midland Pde. NW6 . . . . .6K 63
Midland Pl. E14 . . . . .5E 104
Midland Rd. E10 . . . . .7E 50
NW1 . . . . .1D 6 (2H 83)
Midland Ter. NW2 . . . . .3F 63
NW10 . . . . .4A 80
Midleton Rd. KT3: N Mald 3J 151

Midlothian Rd. E3 . . . . .4B 86
(off Burdett Rd.)
Midmoor Rd. SW12 . . . . .1G 137
SW19 . . . . .1F 153
Midnight Av. SE5 . . . . .7B 102
Midship Cl. SE16 . . . . .1K 103
Midship Point E14 . . . . .2C 104
(off The Quarterdeck)
Midstrath Rd. NW10 . . . . .4A 62
Midsummer Av. TW4: Houn 4D 112
Midway SM3: Sutt 7H 153
Midway Ho. EC1 . . . . .1A 8
Midwinter Cl.
DA16: Well 3A 126
Midwood Cl. NW2 . . . . .3D 62
Miers Cl. E6 . . . . .1E 88
Mighell Av. IG4: Ilf 5B 52
Mikardo Ct. E14 . . . . .7E 86
(off Poplar High St.)
Milan Cl. N11 . . . . .1H 47
Milan Rd. UB1: S'hall 2D 94
Milborne Gro. SW10 . . . . . . .6A 16 (5A 100)
Milborne St. E9 . . . . .6J 67
Milborough Cres. SE12 . . . . .6G 123
Milbourne Ho. KT1: King T 1G 151
(off Coombe Rd.)
Milbourne Pl. KT19: Ewe 4K 163
Milburn Dr. UB7: Yiew 7A 74
Milcote St. SE1 . . . . .7A 14 (2B 102)
Mildenhall Rd. E5 . . . . .4J 67
N14 .6D 66
Mildmay Av. N1 . . . . .5D 66
Mildmay Gro. Nth. N1 . . . . .5D 66
Mildmay Gro. Sth. N1 . . . . .5D 66
Mildmay Pk. N1 . . . . .5D 66
Mildmay Pl. N16 . . . . .5E 66
Mildmay Rd. IG1: Ilf 3F 71
N1 . . . . .5D 66
RM7: Rom 5J 55
N16 .6D 66
Mildred Av. UB3: Harl 4F 93
UB5: N'olt 5F 59
Mildred Rd. CR0: C'don 1G 169
Mildred Rd. DA8: Erith 5K 109
Mildrose Ct. NW6 . . . . .3J 81
(off Malvern M.)
Mildura Ct. N8 . . . . .4K 47
MILE END 4B 86
Mile End, The E17 . . . . .1K 49
Mile End Climbing Wall 3A 86
Mile End Park 2A 86
Mile End Park Leisure Cen. 5A 86
Mile End Pl. E1 . . . . .4K 85
Mile End Rd. E1 . . . . .5J 85
E3 . . . . .5J 85
Mile End Stadium 5B 86
Mile Rd. SM6: Bedd, Wall 1F 167
(not continuous)
Miles Bldgs. NW1 . . . . .5C 4
(off Penfold Pl., not continuous)
Miles Cl. SE28 . . . . .1H 107
Miles Ct. CR0: C'don 2B 168
(off Cuthbert St.)
E1 . . . . .6H 85
(off Tillman St.)
Miles Dr. SE28 . . . . .1J 107
Miles Ho. SE10 . . . . .5G 105
(off Tuskar St.)
Miles Lodge E15 . . . . .5F 69
(off Colegrave Rd.)
HA1: Harr 5H 41
Milespit Hill NW7 . . . . .5J 29
Miles Pl. KT5: Surb 4F 151
NW8 .5B 4
Miles Rd. CR4: Mitc 3D 154
N8 . . . . .3J 47
Miles St. SW8 . . . . .7E 18 (6J 101)
(not continuous)
Milestone Cl. N9 . . . . .2B 34
SM2: Sutt 6B 166
Milestone Ct. E10 . . . . .7D 50
MILESTONE GREEN 4J 115

Milestone Ho. KT1: King T 3D 150
(off Surbiton Rd.)
Milestone Rd. SE19 . . . . .6F 139
Miles Way N20 . . . . .2H 31
Milfoil St. W12 . . . . .7C 80
Milford Cl. SE2 . . . . .6E 108
Milford Ct. UB1: S'hall 1E 94
Milford Gdns. CR0: C'don 5J 157
HA0: Wemb 4D 60
HA8: Edg 7B 28
Milford Gro. SM1: Sutt 4A 166
Milford La. WC2 . . . . .2H 13 (7A 84)
Milford M. SW16 . . . . .3K 137
Milford Rd. UB1: S'hall 7E 76
W13 .1B 96
Milford Towers SE6 . . . . .7D 122
Milk St. BR1: Brom 6K 141
E16 . . . . .1F 107
EC2 . . . . .7D 8 (6C 84)
Milkwell Gdns. IG8: Wfd G 7E 36
Milkwell Yd. SE5 . . . . .1C 120
Milkwood Rd. SE24 . . . . .5B 120
Milk Yd. E1 .7J 85
Millais Av. E12 . . . . .5E 70
Millais Ct. UB5: N'olt 2B 76
(off Academy Gdns.)
Millais Cres. KT19: Ewe 5A 164
Millais Gdns. HA8: Edg 2G 43
Millais Ho. SW1 . . . . .4E 18
(off Marsham St.)
Millais Rd. E11 . . . . .4E 68
EN1: Enf 5A 24
KT3: N Mald 7A 152
Millais Way KT19: Ewe 4J 163
Millard Cl. N16 . . . . .5E 66
Millard Rd. SE8 . . . . .5B 104
Millard Ter. RM10: Dag 6G 73
Millbank SM6: Wall 5H 167
SW1 . . . . .2E 18 (3J 101)
Millbank Ct. SW1 . . . . .3E 18
Millbank Twr. SW1 . . . . .4E 18 (4J 101)
Millbank Way SE12 . . . . .5J 123
Millbourne Rd. TW13: Hanw 4C 130
Mill Bri. EN5: Barn 6C 20
Millbrooke Cl. UB8: Wfd G 6B 36
Millbrook Av. DA16: Well 4H 125
Millbrooke Ct. SW15 . . . . .5G 117
(off Keswick Rd.)
Millbrook Gdns. RM6: Chad H 6F 55
Millbrook Ho. SE15 . . . . .6G 103
(off Peckham Pk. Rd.)
Millbrook Pas. SW9 . . . . .3B 120
Millbrook Pl. NW1 . . . . .2G 83
(off Hampstead Rd.)
Millbrook Rd. N9 . . . . .1C 34
SW9 .3B 120
SM5: Cars 2E 166
Mill Cl. SM5: Cars 2E 166
Mill Ct. E5 . . . . .2J 67
E10 . . . . .3E 68
SE28 . . . . .7B 90
(off Titmuss Av.)
Millcroft Ho. SE6 . . . . .4E 140
(off Melfield Gdns.)
Mill Dr. HA4: Ruis 7F 39
Millender Wlk. SE16 . . . . .4J 103
(off New Rotherhithe Rd.)
Millennium Arena 7E 100
Millennium Bridge 3B 14 (7B 84)
(off Up. Thames St.)
Millennium Bri. Ho. EC4 . . . . .2C 14
(off Up. Thames St.)
Millennium Bus. Cen. NW2 . . . . .2D 62
Millennium Centre, The
Dagenham 4K 73
Millennium Cl. E16 . . . . .6K 87
Millennium Dr. E14 . . . . .4F 105
Millennium Ho. E17 . . . . .5K 49
SW15 . . . . .5G 117
(off Plaza Gdns.)
Millennium Pl. E2 . . . . .2H 85
Millennium Sq. SE1 . . . . .6K 15 (2F 103)

Millennium Way SE10 . . . . .2G 105
Miller Av. EN3: Enf L 1H 25
Miller Cl. BR1: Brom 5K 141
  CR4: Mitc 7D 154
  HA5: Pinn 2A 40
  RM5: Col R 1G 55
Miller Ct. DA7: Bex 3J 127
Miller Ho. E1 . . . . .5K 85
    (off Shandy St.)
  W10 . . . . .4H 81
    (off Harrow Rd.)
Miller Rd. CR0: C'don 1K 167
  SW19 .6B 136
Miller's Av. E8 . . . . .5F 67
Millers Cl. NW7 . . . . .4H 29
Millers Ct. HA0: Wemb 2E 78
    (off Vicars Bri. Cl.)
Millers Grn. Cl. EN2: Enf 3G 23
Millers Mdw. Cl. SE3 . . . . .4H 123
Miller's Ter. E8 . . . . .5F 67
Miller St. NW1 . . . . .2G 83
    (not continuous)
Millers Way W6 . . . . .2E 98
Millers Wharf Ho. E1 . . . . .5K 15
    (off St Katherine's Way)
Millers Yd. N3 . . . . .1K 45
Miller Wlk. SE1 . . . . . . .5K 13 (1A 102)
Milles Sq. SW9 . . . . .4A 120
Millet Rd. UB6: G'frd 2F 77
Mill Farm Av. TW16: Sun 7G 129
Mill Farm Bus. Pk. TW4: Houn 7C 112
Mill Farm Cl. HA5: Pinn 2A 40
Mill Farm Cres. TW4: Houn 1C 130
Millfield KT1: King T 3F 151
  N4 . . . . .2A 66
  TW16: Sun 1F 147
Millfield Av. E17 . . . . .1A 50
Millfield La. N6 . . . . .1C 64
Millfield Pl. N6 . . . . .2E 64
Millfield Rd. HA8: Edg 2J 43
  TW4: Houn 1C 130
Millfields Rd. E5 . . . . .4J 67
Millfield Theatre 4J 33
Mill Gdns. SE26 . . . . .3H 139
Mill Grn. CR4: Mitc 7E 154
Mill Grn. Bus. Pk. CR4: Mitc 7E 154
Mill Grn. Rd. CR4: Mitc 7D 154
Millgrove St. SW11 . . . . .1E 118
Millharbour E14 . . . . .2D 104
Millhaven Cl. RM6: Chad H 6B 54
MILL HILL .5F 29
Mill Hill SW13 . . . . .2C 116
MILL HILL CIRCUS 5G 29
Mill Hill Cir. NW7 . . . . .5G 29
Mill Hill Golf Course 2F 29
Mill Hill Gro. W3 . . . . .1J 97
Mill Hill Ind. Est. NW7 . . . . .6G 29
Mill Hill Old Railway Nature Reserve
  . . . . .6D 28
Mill Hill Rd. SW13 . . . . .2C 116
  W3 . . . . .2H 97
Mill Hill School Sports Cen. 4H 29
Mill Hill Ter. W3 . . . . .1H 97
Mill Ho. IG8: Wfd G 5C 36
Millhouse Pl. SE27 . . . . .4B 138
Millicent Fawcett Ct. N17 . . . . .1F 49
Millicent Gro. N13 . . . . .5G 33
Millicent Preston Ho. IG11: Bark 1H 89
    (off Ripple Rd.)
Millicent Rd. E10 . . . . .1B 68
Milligan St. E14 . . . . .7B 86
Milliner Ho. SW10 . . . . .7A 100
    (off Hortensia Rd.)
Milliners Ho. SE1 . . . . .7H 15
    (off Bermondsey St.)
  SW18 .4J 117
Milling Rd. HA8: Edg 7E 28
Millington Ho. N16 . . . . .3D 66
Millington Rd. UB3: Harl 3G 93
Mill La. CR0: Wadd 3K 167
  E4 . . . . .3J 25

Mill La. IG8: Wfd G 5C 36
  KT17: Ewe 7B 164
  NW6 . . . . .5H 63
  RM6: Chad H 6E 54
  SE18 . . . . .5E 106
  SM5: Cars 4D 166
Mill La. Trad. Est. CR0: Wadd 3K 167
Millman Ct. WC1 . . . . .4G 7
    (off Millman St.)
Millman M. WC1 . . . . .4G 7 (4K 83)
Millman Pl. WC1 . . . . .4G 7
    (off Millman St.)
Millman Rd. E16 . . . . .7D 88
Millman St. WC1 . . . . .4G 7 (4K 83)
Millmark Gro. SE14 . . . . .2A 122
Millmarsh La. EN3: Brim 2F 25
Millmead Ind. Cen. N17 . . . . .2H 49
Mill Mead Rd. N17 . . . . .3H 49
MILL MEADS 2F 87
Mill Pl. BR7: Chst 1E 160
  E14 . . . . .6A 86
  KT1: King T 3F 151
Mill Plat TW7: Isle 2A 114
    (not continuous)
Mill Plat Av. TW7: Isle 2A 114
Mill Pond Cl. SW8 . . . . .7H 101
Millpond Est. SE16 . . . . .2H 103
Millpond Pl. SM5: Cars 3E 166
Mill Ridge HA8: Edg 5A 28
Mill River Trad. Est. EN3: Pond E . . .3F 25
Mill Rd. DA8: Erith 7J 109
  E16 . . . . .1K 105
  IG1: Ilf 3E 70
  SW19 .7A 136
  TW2: Twick 2G 131
Mill Row DA5: Bexl 1H 145
  N1 . . . . .1E 84
Mills Ct. UB10: Hil 2C 74
Mills Ct. EC2 . . . . .3G 9
Mills Gro. E14 . . . . .6E 86
  NW4 . . . . .3F 45
Millshott Cl. SW6 . . . . .1E 116
Mills Ho. SW8 . . . . .1G 119
    (off Thessaly Rd.)
Millside SM5: Cars 2D 166
Millside Pl. TW7: Isle 2B 114
Millson Cl. N20 . . . . .2G 31
Mills Row W4 . . . . .4K 97
Millstone Cl. E15 . . . . .6F 69
Millstream Cl. N13 . . . . .5F 33
Millstream Ho. SE16 . . . . .2H 103
    (off Jamaica Rd.)
Millstream Rd. SE1 . . . . .7J 15 (2F 103)
Mill St. KT1: King T 3E 150
  SE1 . . . . .7K 15 (2F 103)
  W1 . . . . .2A 12 (7F 83)
Mills Yd. SW6 . . . . .3K 117
Mill Trad. Estate, The NW10 . . . . . . .3J 79
Mill Va. BR2: Brom 2H 159
Mill Vw. Cl. KT17: Ewe 7B 164
Mill Vw. Gdns. CR0: C'don 3K 169
MILLWALL .4D 104
Millwall Dock Rd. E14 . . . . .3C 104
Millwall FC .5J 103
Millwall Park 4E 104
Mill Way TW14: Felt 5K 111
Millway NW7 . . . . .4F 29
Millway Gdns. UB5: N'olt 6D 58
Millwood Rd. TW3: Houn 5G 113
Millwood St. W10 . . . . .5G 81
Mill Yd. E1 . . . . .7G 85
Mill Yd. Ind. Est. HA8: Edg 1H 43
Milman Cl. HA5: Pinn 3B 40
Milman Rd. NW6 . . . . .2F 81
Milman's Ho. SW10 . . . . .6B 100
    (off Milman's St.)
Milman's St. SW10 . . . . .6B 100
Milne Ct. E18 . . . . .1J 51
Milne Gdns. SE9 . . . . .5C 124
Milne Ho. SE18 . . . . .4D 106
    (off Ogilby St.)

Milner Ct. SE15 . . . . .7F 103
    (off Colegrove Rd.)
Milner Dr. TW2: Whitt 7H 113
Milner Pl. N1 . . . . .1A 84
  SM5: Cars 4E 166
Milner Rd. CR7: Thor H 3D 156
  E15 . . . . .3G 87
  KT1: King T 3D 150
  RM8: Dag 2C 72
  SM4: Mord 5B 154
  SW19 .1K 153
Milner Sq. N1 . . . . .7B 66
Milner St. SW3 . . . . .3E 16 (4D 100)
Milner Wlk. SE9 . . . . .2H 143
Milnthorpe Rd. W4 . . . . .6K 97
Milo Gdns. SE22 . . . . .6F 121
Milo Rd. SE22 . . . . .6F 121
Milroad Ho. E1 . . . . .5K 85
    (off Stepney Grn.)
Milroy Wlk. SE1 . . . . .4A 14 (1B 102)
Milson Rd. W14 . . . . .3F 99
Milstead Ho. E5 . . . . .5H 67
Milton Av. CR0: C'don 7D 156
  E6 . . . . .7B 70
  EN5: Barn 5C 20
  N6 . . . . .7G 47
  NW9 . . . . .3J 43
  NW10 . . . . .1J 79
  SM1: Sutt 3B 166
Milton Cl. N2 . . . . .5A 46
  SE1 . . . . .4F 103
  SM1: Sutt 3B 166
  UB4: Hayes 6J 75
Milton Ct. E17 . . . . .4C 50
  EC2 . . . . .5E 8 (5D 84)
  RM6: Chad H 7C 54
  SE14 . . . . .6B 104
    (not continuous)
  SW18 . . . . .5J 117
  TW2: Twick 3J 131
  UB10: Ick 3D 56
Milton Court Concert Hall 5D 84
    (off Milton Ct.)
Milton Ct. Rd. SE14 . . . . .6A 104
Milton Cres. IG2: Ilf 7F 53
Milton Dr. TW17: Shep 4A 146
Milton Gdn. Est. N16 . . . . .4D 66
Milton Gdns.
  TW19: Stanw 1B 128
Milton Gro. N11 . . . . .5B 32
  N16 . . . . .4D 66
Milton Ho. E2 . . . . .3J 85
    (off Roman Rd.)
  E17 . . . . .4C 50
  SE5 . . . . .7D 102
    (off Elmington Est.)
  SM1: Sutt 3J 165
Milton Lodge DA14: Sidc 4K 144
  TW1: Twick 7K 113
Milton Mans. W14 . . . . .6G 99
    (off Queen's Club Gdns.)
Milton Pk. N6 . . . . .7G 47
Milton Pl. N7 . . . . .5A 66
    (off Eastwood Cl.)
Milton Rd. CR0: C'don 7D 156
  CR4: Mitc 7E 136
  DA16: Well 1K 125
  DA17: Belv 4G 109
  E17 . . . . .4C 50
  HA1: Harr 4J 41
  N6 . . . . .7G 47
  N15 . . . . .4B 48
  NW7 . . . . .5G 29
  NW9 . . . . .7C 44
  SE24 . . . . .5B 120
  SM1: Sutt 3J 165
  SM6: Wall 6G 167
  SW14 . . . . .3K 115
  SW19 . . . . .6A 136
  TW12: Hamp 7E 130
  UB10: Ick 4D 56

Milton Rd. W3 . . . . .1K 97
  W7 . . . . .7K 77
Milton St. EC2 . . . . .5E 8 (5D 84)
Milton Way UB7: W Dray 4B 92
Milverton Dr. UB10: Ick 4E 56
Milverton Gdns. IG3: Ilf 2K 71
Milverton Ho. SE6 . . . . .3A 140
Milverton Rd. BR1: Brom 5A 142
Milverton Rd. NW6 . . . . .7E 62
Milverton St. SE11 . . . . . .6K 19 (5A 102)
Milverton Way SE9 . . . . .4E 142
Milward St. E1 . . . . .5H 85
Milward Wlk. SE18 . . . . .6E 106
Mimosa Ho. E20 . . . . .5E 68
    (off Liberty Bri. Rd.)
  UB4: Yead 5A 76
Mimosa Lodge NW10 . . . . .5B 62
Mimosa Rd. UB4: Yead 5A 76
Mimosa St. SW6 . . . . .1H 117
Minard Rd. SE6 . . . . .7G 123
Mina Rd. SE17 . . . . .5E 102
  SW19 . . . . .1J 153
Minchenden Cl. N14 . . . . .2C 32
Minchenden Cres. N14 . . . . .3B 32
Minchin Ho. E14 . . . . .6C 86
    (off Dod St.)
Mincing La. EC3 . . . . .2G 15 (7E 84)
Minden Gdns. IG11: Bark 3B 90
Minden Rd. SE20 . . . . .1H 157
  SM3: Sutt 2G 165
Minehead Rd. HA2: Harr 3E 58
  SW16 . . . . .5K 137
Mineral Cl. EN5: Barn 6A 20
Mineral St. SE18 . . . . .4J 107
Minera M. SW1 . . . . .3G 17 (4E 100)
Minerva Cl. DA14: Sidc 3J 143
  SW9 . . . . .7A 102
  TW19: Stanw M 7B 174
Minerva Ct. EC1 . . . . .4K 7
    (off Bowling Grn. La.)
Minerva Lodge N7 . . . . .6K 65
Minerva Rd. E4 . . . . .7J 35
  KT1: King T 2F 151
  NW10 . . . . .4J 79
Minerva St. E2 . . . . .2H 85
Minerva Wlk. EC1 . . . . . . .7B 8 (6B 84)
Minet Av. NW10 . . . . .2A 80
Minet Country Pk. 2A 94
Minet Dr. UB3: Hayes 1J 93
Minet Gdns. NW10 . . . . .2A 80
  UB3: Hayes 1K 93
Minet Rd. SW9 . . . . .2B 120
Minford Gdns. W14 . . . . .2F 99
Minford Ho. W14 . . . . .2F 99
    (off Minford Gdns.)
Mingard Wlk. N7 . . . . .2K 65
Ming St. E14 . . . . .7C 86
Minima St. TW14: Felt 6J 111
Minima Yacht Club 3D 150
    (off High St.)
Ministry Way SE9 . . . . .2D 142
Miniver Pl. EC4 . . . . .2D 14
Minniedale KT5: Surb 5F 151
Minnow St. SE17 . . . . .4E 102
Minnow Wlk. SE17 . . . . .4E 102
Minories EC3 . . . . .1J 15 (6F 85)
Minshaw Ct. DA14: Sidc 4K 143
Minshill St. SW8 . . . . .1H 119
Minshull Pl. BR3: Beck 7C 140
Minson Rd. E9 . . . . .1K 85
Minstead Gdns. SW15 . . . . .7B 116
Minstead Way KT3: N Mald 6A 152
Minster Av. SM1: Sutt 2J 165
Minster Ct. EC3 . . . . .2H 15
  W5 . . . . .4E 78
Minster Dr. CR0: C'don 4E 168
Minster Gdns. KT8: W Mole 4D 148
Minsterley Av. TW17: Shep 4G 147
Minster Pavement EC3 . . . . .2H 15
    (off Mincing La.)

Minster Rd.—Mono La.

Minster Rd. BR1: Brom 7K 141
NW2 5G 63
Minster Wlk. N8 4J 47
Minstrel Gdns. KT5: Surb 4F 151
Mint Bus. Pk. E16 5K 87
Mint Cl. UB10: Hil 3D 74
Mintern Cl. N13 3G 33
Minterne Av. UB2: S'hall 4E 94
Minterne Rd. HA3: Kenton 5F 43
Minterne Waye UB4: Yead 6A 76
Mintern St. N1 2D 84
Minter Rd. IG11: Bark 4A 90
Minton Ho. SE11 3J 19
Minton M. NW6 6K 63
Mint Rd. SM6: Wall 4F 167
Mint St. *E2* *4H 85*
(off Three Colts La.)
SE1 6C 14 (2C 102)
Mint Wlk. CR0: C'don 3C 168
Mirabelle Gdns. E20 5E 68
Mirabel Rd. SW6 7H 99
Mira Ho. *E20* *5E 68*
(off Prize Wlk.)
Miranda Cl. E1 5J 85
Miranda Ct. W3 6F 79
Miranda Ho. *N1* *1G 9*
(off Crondall St.)
Miranda Rd. N19 1G 65
Mirfield St. SE7 4B 106
Miriam Rd. SE18 5J 107
Mirravale Trad. Est. RM8: Dag 7E 54
Mirren Cl. HA2: Harr 4D 58
Mirror Path SE9 3A 142
Misbourne Rd. UB10: Hil 1C 74
Missenden *SE17* *5D 102*
(off Roland Way)
Missenden Cl. TW14: Felt 1H 129
Missenden Gdns. SM4: Mord 6A 154
Missenden Ho. NW8 3C 4
Mission, The *E14* *6B 86*
(off Commercial Rd.)
Mission Gro. E17 5A 50
Mission Pl. SE15 1G 121
Mission Sq. TW8: Bford 6E 96
Missouri Ct. HA5: Eastc 6A 40
Mistletoe Cl. CR0: C'don 1K 169
Mistral SE5 1E 120
Misty's Fld. KT12: Walt T 7A 148
Mitali Pas. E1 6G 85
MITCHAM 3D 154
Mitcham Gdn. Village CR4: Mitc 5E 154
Mitcham Golf Course 5E 154
Mitcham Ho. SE5 1C 120
Mitcham Ind. Est. CR4: Mitc 1E 154
Mitcham La. SW16 6G 137
Mitcham Pk. CR4: Mitc 4C 154
Mitcham Rd. CR0: C'don 6J 155
E6 3C 88
IG3: Ilf 7K 53
SW17 5D 136
Mitchell *NW9* *1B 44*
(off Quakers Course)
Mitchellbrook Way NW10 6K 61
Mitchell Cl. DA17: Belv 3J 109
SE2 4C 108
Mitchell Ho. *N1* *7B 66*
(off College Cross)
W12 *7D 80*
(off White City Est.)
Mitchell Rd. BR6: Orp 4K 173
N13 5H 33
Mitchell's Pl. *SE21* *6E 120*
(off Aysgarth Rd.)
Mitchell St. EC1 3C 8 (4C 84)
(not continuous)
Mitchell Wlk. *E6* *5C 88*
(off Allhallows Rd., Allhallows Rd.)
E6 5D 88
(Elmley Cl.)
Mitchell Way BR1: Brom 1J 159
NW10 6J 61
Mitchison Ct. *TW16: Sun* *1J 147*
(off Downside)
Mitchison Rd. N1 6D 66
Mitchley Rd. N17 3G 49
Mitford Bldgs. *SW6* *7J 99*
(off Dawes Rd.)
Mitford Cl. KT9: Chess 6C 162
Mitford Rd. N19 2J 65
Mitre, The E14 7B 86
Mitre Av. E17 3C 50
Mitre Bri. Ind. Pk. W10 4D 80
(not continuous)
Mitre Cl. BR2: Brom 2H 159
SM2: Sutt 7A 166
TW17: Shep 6F 147
Mitre Ho. *SW3* *5E 16*
(off King's Rd.)
Mitre Pas. *EC3* *1H 15*
(off Mitre Sq.)
SE10 2G 105
Mitre Rd. E15 2G 87
SE1 6K 13 (2A 102)
Mitre Sq. EC3 1H 15 (6E 84)
Mitre St. EC3 1H 15 (6E 84)
Mitre Way W10 4D 80
Mitre Yd. SW3 3D 16 (4C 100)
Mizen Ct. *E14* *2C 104*
(off Alpha Gro.)
Mizzen Mast Ho. SE18 3D 106
Moat, The KT3: N Mald 1A 152
Moat Cl. BR6: Chels 6K 173
Moat Ct. DA15: Sidc 3K 143
SE9 6D 124
Moat Cres. N3 3K 45
Moat Cft. DA16: Well 3C 126
Moat Dr. E13 2A 88
HA1: Harr 4G 41
HA4: Ruis 7G 39
Moat Farm Rd. UB5: N'olt 6D 58
Moatfield NW6 7G 63
Moatlands Ho. *WC1* *2F 7*
(off Cromer St.)
Moat La. KT8: E Mos 3K 149
Moat Lodge, The HA2: Harr 2J 59
Moat Pl. SW9 3K 119
W3 6H 79
Moat Side EN3: Pond E 4E 24
TW13: Hanw 4A 130
Moberly Rd. SW4 7H 119
Moberly Sports & Education Cen. 3F 81
(off Chamberlayne Rd.)
Mobil Ct. *WC2* *1H 13*
(off Clement's Inn)
MOBY DICK 4E 54
Mocatta Ho. *E1* *4H 85*
(off Brady St.)
Mocha Ct. *E3* *2D 86*
(off Taylor Pl.)
MODA
Museum of Domestic Design
& Architecture 2B 44
Modbury Gdns. NW5 6E 64
Modder Pl. SW15 4F 117
Model Cotts. SW14 4J 115
W13 2B 96
Model Farm Cl. SE9 3C 142
Modern Ct. EC4 7A 8
Modling Ho. *E2* *2K 85*
(off Mace St.)
Moelwyn N7 5H 65
Moelyn M. HA1: Harr 5A 42
Moffat Ct. SW19 5J 135
Moffat Ho. SE5 7C 102
Moffat Rd. CR7: Thor H 2C 156
N13 6D 32
SW17 4D 136
Mogden La. TW7: Isle 5K 113
Mohammedi Pk. UB5: N'olt 1E 76
Mohawk Ho. *E3* *2A 86*
(off Gernon Rd.)
Mohmmad Khan Rd. E11 1H 69
Moineau *NW9* *1B 44*
(off Long Mead)
Moira Cl. N17 2E 48
Moira Ho. *SW9* *1A 120*
(off Gosling Way)
Moira Rd. SE9 4D 124
Mokswell Ct. N10 1E 46
Molasses Ho. *SW11* *3A 118*
(off Clove Hitch Quay)
Molasses Row SW11 3A 118
Mole Abbey Gdns. KT8: W Mole 3F 149
Mole Ct. KT19: Ewe 4J 163
Mole Ho. *NW8* *4B 4*
(off Church St. Est.)
Molember Ct. KT8: E Mos 4J 149
Molember Rd. KT8: E Mos 5J 149
Mole Pl. KT8: W Mole 4F 149
Molescroft SE9 3G 143
Molesey Av. KT8: W Mole 5D 148
Molesey Dr. SM3: Cheam 2G 165
Molesey Heath Local Nature Reserve
6E 148
Molesey Pk. Av. KT8: W Mole 5F 149
Molesey Pk. Cl. KT8: E Mos 5G 149
Molesey Pk. Rd.
KT8: W Mole, E Mos 5F 149
Molesey Rd. KT8: W Mole 5C 148
KT12: Walt T 7C 148
Molesford Rd. SW6 1J 117
Molesham Cl. KT8: W Mole 3F 149
Molesham Way KT8: W Mole 3F 149
Molesworth Ho. *SE17* *6B 102*
(off Brandon Est.)
Molesworth St. SE13 4E 122
Moliner Ct. BR3: Beck 7C 140
Mollis Ho. *E3* *5C 86*
(off Gale St.)
Mollison Av.
EN3: Brim, Enf L, Enf W, Pond E
4F 25
Mollison Dr. SM6: Wall 7H 167
Mollison Sq. *SM6: Wall* *7H 167*
(off Mollison Dr.)
Mollison Way HA8: Edg 2F 43
Molly Huggins Cl. SW12 7G 119
Molton Ho. *N1* *1K 83*
(off Barnsbury Est.)
Molyneux Dr. SW17 4F 137
Molyneux St. W1 6D 4 (5C 82)
Monarch Cl. BR4: W W'ck 4H 171
TW14: Felt 7G 111
Monarch Ct. *HA7: Stan* *7J 27*
(off Howard Rd.)
N2 5B 46
Monarch Dr. E16 5B 88
UB3: Hayes 7H 75
Monarch Ho. *W8* *3J 99*
(off Kensington High St.)
Monarch M. E17 6D 50
SW16 5A 138
Monarch Pde. CR4: Mitc 2D 154
Monarch Pl. IG9: Buck H 2F 37
Monarch Point SW6 2A 118
Monarch Rd. DA17: Belv 3G 109
Monarch Sq. SW11 4C 118
Monarchs Way HA4: Ruis 1F 57
Monarch Way IG2: Ilf 6H 53
Mona Rd. SE15 2J 121
Monastery Gdns. EN2: Enf 2J 23
Mona St. E16 5H 87
Monaveen Gdns. KT8: W Mole 3F 149
Monck Ho. *SE1* *7D 14*
(off Cole St.)
Moncks Row SW18 6H 117
Monck St. SW1 2D 18 (3H 101)
Monckton Ct. *W14* *3H 99*
(off Strangways Ter.)
Monclar Rd. SE5 4D 120
Moncorvo Cl. SW7 7C 10 (2C 100)
Moncrieff Cl. E6 6C 88
Moncrieff Pl. SE15 2G 121
Moncrieff St. SE15 2G 121
Monday All. *N16* *2F 67*
(off High St.)
Mondial Way UB3: Harl 7E 92
Mondragon Ho. *SW8* *1J 119*
(off Guildford Rd.)
Monega Rd. E7 6A 70
E12 6A 70
Monet Ct. *SE16* *5H 103*
(off Stubbs Dr.)
Moneyer Ho. *N1* *1E 8*
(off Provost St.)
Money La. UB7: W Dray 3A 92
Mongers Almshouses *E9* *7K 67*
(off Church Cres.)
Monica Ct. EN1: Enf 5K 23
Monica James Ho. DA14: Sidc 3A 144
Monica Shaw Ct. *NW1* *1D 6*
(off Purchese St., not continuous)
Monier Rd. E3 7C 68
Monivea Rd. BR3: Beck 7B 140
Monk Ct. W12 1C 98
Monk Dr. E16 7J 87
MONKEN HADLEY 2C 20
Monkfrith Av. N14 6A 22
Monkfrith Cl. N14 7A 22
Monkfrith Way N14 7K 21
Monkham's Av. IG8: Wfd G 5E 36
Monkham's Dr. IG8: Wfd G 5E 36
Monkham's La. IG8: Wfd G 5D 36
IG9: Buck H 3E 36
Monkleigh Rd. SM4: Mord 3G 153
Monk Pas. *E16* *7J 87*
(off Monk Dr.)
Monks Av. EN5: New Bar 6F 21
KT8: W Mole 5D 148
Monks Cl. EN2: Enf 2H 23
HA2: Harr 2F 59
HA4: Ruis 4B 58
SE2 4D 108
Monks Cres. KT12: Walt T 7K 147
Monksdene Gdns. SM1: Sutt 3K 165
Monks Dr. W3 5G 79
MONKS ORCHARD 7A 158
Monks Orchard Rd. BR3: Beck 1C 170
Monks Pk. HA9: Wemb 6H 61
Monks Pk. Gdns. HA9: Wemb 7H 61
Monks Rd. EN2: Enf 2G 23
Monk St. SE18 4E 106
Monks Way BR3: Beck 6C 158
BR5: Farnb 1G 173
NW11 4H 45
UB7: Harm 6A 92
Monkswood Gdns. IG5: Ilf 3E 52
Monkton Ho. E5 5H 67
SE16 *2K 103*
(off Wolfe Cres.)
Monkton Rd. DA16: Well 2K 125
Monkton St. SE11 3K 19 (4A 102)
Monkville Av. NW11 4H 45
Monkville Pde. NW11 4H 45
Monkwell Sq. EC2 6D 8 (5C 84)
Monmouth Av. E18 3K 51
KT1: Hamp W 7C 132
Monmouth Cl. CR4: Mitc 4J 155
DA16: Well 4A 126
W4 3J 97
Monmouth Ct. *W7* *5K 77*
(off Copley Cl.)
Monmouth Gro. TW8: Bford 4E 96
Monmouth Pl. *W2* *6K 81*
(off Monmouth Rd.)
Monmouth Rd. E6 3D 88
N9 2C 34
RM9: Dag 5F 73
UB3: Harl 4G 93
W2 6J 81
Monmouth St. WC2 1E 12 (6J 83)
Monnery Rd. N19 3G 65
Monnow Rd. SE1 5G 103
Mono La. TW13: Felt 2K 129

Monoux Almshouses E17 . . . . .4D 50
Monoux Gro. E17 . . . . .1C 50
Monro Ct. E16 . . . . .4H 87
Monroe Cres. EN1: Enf 1C 24
Monroe Dr. SW14 . . . . .5H 115
Monroe Ho. NW8 . . . . .2D 4
(off Lorne Cl.)
Monro Gdns. HA3: Hrw W 7D 26
Monro Way E5 . . . . .4G 67
Monsell Ct. N4 . . . . .3B 66
Monsell Rd. N4 . . . . .3A 66
Monson Rd. NW10 . . . . .2C 80
SE14 .7K 103
Mons Way BR2: Brom 6C 160
Montacute Rd.
CR0: New Ad 7E 170
SE6 . . . . .7B 122
SM4: Mord 6B 154
WD23: B Hea 1E 26
Montagu Ct. W1 . . . . .6F 5
(off Montagu Pl.)
Montagu Cres. N18 . . . . .4C 34
Montague Av. SE4 . . . . .4B 122
W7 . . . . .1K 95
Montague Cl. EN5: Barn 4C 20
KT12: Walt T 7K 147
SE1 . . . . .4E 14 (1D 102)
Montague Ct. DA15: Sidc 3A 144
N7 . . . . .7A 66
(off St Clements Cl.)
Montague Gdns. W3 . . . . .7G 79
Montague Ho. E16 . . . . .1K 105
(off Wesley Av.)
IG3: Ilf 1A 72
N1 . . . . .1E 84
(off Halcomb St.)
Montague M. E3 . . . . .3B 86
(off Tredegar Ter.)
SE20 . . . . .6J 139
Montague Pas. UB8: Uxb 7A 56
Montague Pl. WC1 . . . . .5D 6 (5H 83)
Montague Rd. CR0: C'don 1B 168
E8 . . . . .5G 67
E11 . . . . .2H 69
N8 . . . . .5K 47
N15 .4G 49
SW19 . . . . .7K 135
TW3: Houn 3F 113
TW10: Rich 6E 114
UB2: S'hall 4C 94
UB8: Uxb 7A 56
W7 . . . . .1K 95
W13 .6B 78
Montague Sq. SE15 . . . . .7J 103
Montague St. EC1 . . . . .6C 8 (5C 84)
WC1 . . . . .5E 6 (5J 83)
Montague Ter. BR2: Brom 4H 159
Montague Walks HA0: Wemb 1F 79
Montague Waye UB2: S'hall 3C 94
Montagu Gdns. N18 . . . . .4C 34
SM6: Wall 4G 167
Montagu Ind. Est. N18 . . . . .4D 34
Montagu Mans. W1 . . . . .5F 5 (5D 82)
Montagu M. Nth. W1 . . . . .6F 5 (5D 82)
Montagu M. Sth. W1 . . . . .7F 5 (6D 82)
Montagu M. W. W1 . . . . .7F 5 (6D 82)
Montagu Pl. W1 . . . . .6E 4 (5D 82)
Montagu Rd. N9 . . . . .4C 34
N18 .5C 34
NW4 .6C 44
Montagu Row W1 . . . . .6F 5 (5D 82)
Montagu Sq. W1 . . . . .6F 5 (5D 82)
Montagu St. W1 . . . . .7F 5 (6D 82)
Montaigne Cl. SW1 . . . . . . .4D 18 (4H 101)
Montalt Rd. IG8: Wfd G 4C 36
Montana Bldg. SE13 . . . . .1D 122
(off Deal's Gateway)
Montana Gdns. SE26 . . . . .5B 140
SM1: Sutt 5A 166
Montana Rd. SW17 . . . . .3E 136
SW20 . . . . .1E 152

Montanaro Ct. N1 . . . . .1C 84
(off Coleman Flds.)
Montbelle Rd. SE9 . . . . .3F 143
Montcalm Cl. BR2: Hayes 6J 159
UB4: Yead 3K 75
Montcalm Ho. E14 . . . . .4B 104
Montcalm Rd. SE7 . . . . .7B 106
Montclare St. E2 . . . . .3J 9 (4F 85)
Monteagle Av. IG11: Bark 6G 71
Monteagle Ct. N1 . . . . .2E 84
Monteagle Way E5 . . . . .3G 67
SE15 . . . . .3H 121
Montefiore Ct. N16 . . . . .1F 67
Montefiore St. SW8 . . . . .2F 119
Montego Cl. SE24 . . . . .4A 120
Montem Rd. KT3: N Mald 4A 152
SE23 . . . . .7B 122
Montem St. N4 . . . . .1K 65
Montenotte Rd. N8 . . . . .5G 47
Monterey Apartments N15 . . . . .5D 48
NW7 .5F 29
(off The Broadway)
UB10: Hil 7C 56
Monterey Studios W10 . . . . .2G 81
Montesole Ct. HA5: Pinn 2A 40
Montevetro SW11 . . . . .1B 118
Montfichet Rd. E20 . . . . .7E 68
Montford Pl. SE11 . . . . .6J 19 (5A 102)
Montford Rd. TW16: Sun 4J 147
Montfort Ho. E2 . . . . .2J 85
(off Victoria Pk. Sq.)
E14 .3E 104
(off Galbraith St.)
Montfort Pl. SW19 . . . . .1F 135
Montgolfier Wlk. UB5: N'olt 3C 76
Montgomerie M. SE23 . . . . .7J 121
Montgomery Cl. CR4: Mitc 4J 155
DA15: Sidc 6K 125
Montgomery Ct. CR2: S Croy 5E 168
(off Birdhurst Rd.)
W4 . . . . .7J 97
Montgomery Gdns. SM2: Sutt 7B 166
Montgomery Ho. UB5: N'olt 3D 76
(off Taywood Rd.)
W2 . . . . .6A 4
(off Harrow Rd.)
Montgomery Lodge E1 . . . . .4J 85
(off Cleveland Gro.)
Montgomery Rd. HA8: Edg 6A 28
W4 . . . . .4J 97
Montgomery Sq. E14 . . . . .1D 104
Montgomery St. E14 . . . . .1D 104
Montholme Rd. SW11 . . . . .6D 118
Monthope Rd. E1 . . . . .6K 9 (5G 85)
Montolieu Gdns. SW15 . . . . .5D 116
Montpelier Av. DA5: Bexl 7D 126
W5 . . . . .5C 78
Montpelier Cl. UB10: Hil 1C 74
Montpelier Ct. BR2: Brom 4H 159
(off Westmoreland Rd.)
W5 . . . . .5D 78
Montpelier Gdns. E6 . . . . .3B 88
RM6: Chad H 7C 54
Montpelier Gro. NW5 . . . . .5G 65
Montpelier M. SW7 . . . . . . .1D 16 (3C 100)
Montpelier Pl. E1 . . . . .6J 85
SW7 . . . . .1D 16 (3C 100)
Montpelier Ri. HA9: Wemb 1D 60
NW11 . . . . .7G 45
Montpelier Rd. N3 . . . . .1A 46
SE15 . . . . .1H 121
SM1: Sutt 4A 166
W5 . . . . .5D 78
Montpelier Row SE3 . . . . .2H 123
TW1: Twick 7C 114
Montpelier Sq. SW7 . . . . . . .7D 10 (2C 100)
Montpelier St. SW7 . . . . . . .1D 16 (3C 100)
Montpelier Ter. SW7 . . . . . . .7D 10 (2C 100)
Montpelier Va. SE3 . . . . .2H 123
Montpelier Wlk. SW7 . . . . . .1D 16 (3C 100)

Montpelier Way NW11 . . . . .7G 45
Montpellier Ct. KT12: Walt T 6J 147
Montrave Rd. SE20 . . . . .6J 139
Montreal Ho. SE16 . . . . .2K 103
(off Maple M.)
UB4: Yead 3K 75
(off Ayles Rd.)
Montreal Pl. WC2 . . . . .2G 13 (7K 83)
Montreal Rd. IG1: Ilf 7G 53
Montrell Rd. SW2 . . . . .1J 137
Montrose Av. DA15: Sidc 7A 126
DA16: Well 3H 125
HA8: Edg 2J 43
NW6 .2G 81
TW2: Whitt 7F 113
Montrose Cl. DA16: Well 3K 125
IG8: Wfd G 4D 36
TW15: Ashf 6E 128
Montrose Ct. HA1: Harr 5F 41
NW9 .2J 43
NW11 . . . . .4H 45
SE6 .2H 141
SW7 . . . . .7B 10 (2B 100)
Montrose Cres. HA0: Wemb 6E 60
N12 .6F 31
Montrose Gdns. CR4: Mitc 2D 154
SM1: Sutt 2K 165
Montrose Ho. E14 . . . . .3C 104
SW1 .7H 11
(off Montrose Pl.)
Montrose Pl. SW1 . . . . .7H 11 (2E 100)
Montrose Rd. HA3: W'stone 2J 41
TW14: Bedf 6F 111
Montrose Wlk. HA7: Stan 6G 27
Montserrat Av. IG8: Wfd G 7A 36
Montserrat Cl. SE19 . . . . .5D 138
Montserrat Rd. SW15 . . . . .4G 117
Monument, The 3F 15
Monument Gdns. SE13 . . . . .5E 122
Monument St. EC3 . . . . .2F 15 (7D 84)
Monument Way N17 . . . . .3F 49
Monza St. E1 . . . . .7J 85
Moodkee St. SE16 . . . . .3J 103
Moody Rd. SE15 . . . . .1F 121
Moody St. E1 . . . . .3K 85
Moon Ct. SE12 . . . . .4J 123
Moon Ho. HA1: Harr 4J 41
Moon La. EN5: Barn 3C 20
Moonraker Point SE1 . . . . .6B 14
(off Pocock St.)
Moon St. N1 .1B 84
Moorcroft HA8: Edg 1H 43
Moorcroft Gdns. BR2: Brom 5C 160
Moorcroft La. UB8: Hil 5C 74
Moorcroft Rd. SW16 . . . . .3J 137
Moorcroft Way HA5: Pinn 5C 40
Moordown SE18 . . . . .7F 107
Moore Cl. CR4: Mitc 2F 155
SW14 . . . . .3J 115
Moore Ct. HA0: Wemb 6E 60
HA7: Stan 1D 42
N1 . . . . .1B 84
(off Gaskin St.)
Moore Cres. RM9: Dag 1B 90
Moorefield Rd. N17 . . . . .2F 49
Moore Ho. E1 . . . . .7J 85
(off Cable St.)
E2 . . . . .3J 85
(off Roman Rd.)
E14 .2C 104
N8 . . . . .4J 47
(off Pembroke Rd.)
SE10 . . . . .5H 105
(off Armitage Rd.)
SW1 .6J 17
Mooreland Rd. BR1: Brom 7H 141
Moore Pk. Rd. SW6 . . . . .7J 99
Moore Rd. SE19 . . . . .6C 138
Moore St. SW3 . . . . .3E 16 (4D 100)
Moore Wlk. E7 . . . . .4J 69

Moore Way SM2: Sutt 7J 165
Moorey Cl. E15 . . . . .1H 87
Moorfield Av. W5 . . . . .4D 78
Moorfield Rd. EN3: Enf H 1D 24
KT9: Chess 5E 162
UB8: Cowl 6A 74
Moorfields EC2 . . . . .6E 8 (5D 84)
Moorfields Highwalk EC2 . . . . .6E 8
(off New Union St., not continuous)
Moorgate EC2 . . . . .7E 8 (6D 84)
Moorgate Pl. EC2 . . . . .7E 8
Moorgreen Ho. EC1 . . . . .1A 8
Moorhead Way SE3 . . . . .3J 123
Moorhen Dr. NW9 . . . . .6B 44
Moorhen Ho. E3 . . . . .1B 86
(off Old Ford Rd.)
Moorhouse NW9 . . . . .1B 44
Moorhouse Rd. HA3: Kenton 3D 42
W2 . . . . .6J 81
Moorings, The E16 . . . . .5A 88
(off Prince Regent La.)
Moorings Ho. TW8: Bford 7C 96
MOOR JUNC. 3C 174
Moorland Cl. RM5: Col R 1H 55
TW2: Whitt 7E 112
Moorland Rd. SW9 . . . . .4B 120
UB7: Harm 2D 174
Moorlands UB5: N'olt 1C 76
Moorlands Av. NW7 . . . . .6J 29
Moor La. EC2 . . . . .6E 8 (5D 84)
(not continuous)
KT9: Chess 4E 162
UB7: Harm 2D 174
Moormead Dr. KT19: Ewe 5A 164
Moor Mead Rd. TW1: Twick 6A 114
Moor Pk. Gdns. KT2: King T 7A 134
Moor Pl. EC2 . . . . .6E 8 (5D 84)
Moorside Rd. BR1: Brom 3G 141
Moor St. W1 . . . . .1D 12 (6H 83)
Moot Ct. NW9 . . . . .5G 43
Moran Ho. E1 . . . . .1H 103
(off Wapping La.)
Morant Pl. N22 . . . . .1K 47
Morant St. E14 . . . . .7C 86
Mora Rd. NW2 . . . . .4E 62
Mora St. EC1 . . . . .2D 8 (3C 84)
Morat St. SW9 . . . . .1K 119
Moravian Cl. SW10 . . . . .7A 16 (6B 100)
Moravian Pl. SW10 . . . . .6B 100
Moravian St. E2 . . . . .2J 85
Moray Av. UB3: Hayes 1H 93
Moray Cl. HA8: Edg 2C 28
RM1: Rom 1K 55
Moray Ct. CR2: S Croy 5D 168
(off Warham Rd.)
Moray Ho. E1 . . . . .4A 86
(off Harford St.)
Moray M. N7 . . . . .2K 65
Moray Rd. N4 . . . . .2K 65
Moray Way RM1: Rom 1K 55
Mordaunt Gdns. RM9: Dag 7E 72
Mordaunt Ho. NW10 . . . . .1K 79
(off Stracey Rd.)
Mordaunt Rd. NW10 . . . . .1K 79
Mordaunt St. SW9 . . . . .3K 119
MORDEN 3K 153
Morden Ct. SM4: Mord 4K 153
Morden Ct. Pde. SM4: Mord 4K 153
Morden Gdns. CR4: Mitc 4B 154
UB6: G'frd 5K 59
Morden Hall Pk. 3A 154
Morden Hall Rd.
SM4: Mord 3K 153
Morden Hill SE13 . . . . .2E 122
Morden Ho. SM4: Mord 4J 153
Morden La. SE13 . . . . .2E 122
MORDEN PARK 6G 153
Morden Park Pools 6H 153
Morden Rd. CR4: Mitc 4A 154
RM6: Chad H 7E 54
SE3 .2J 123

Morden Rd.—Moss Gdns.

Morden Rd. SM4: Mord . . . 4A **154**
SW19 . . . 1K **153**
Morden Rd. M. SE3 . . . 2J **123**
Morden St. SE13 . . . 1D **122**
Morden Way SM3: Sutt . . . 7J **153**
Morden Wharf *SE10* . . . *3G* ***105***
(off Morden Wharf Rd.)
Morden Wharf Rd. SE10 . . . 3G **105**
Mordern Ho. NW1 . . . 3D **4**
Mordon Rd. IG3: Ilf . . . 7K **53**
Mordred Rd. SE6 . . . 2G **141**
Morea M. N5 . . . 5C **66**
Morecambe Cl. E1 . . . 5K **85**
Morecambe Gdns. HA7: Stan . . . 4J **27**
Morecambe St. SE17 . . . 4C **102**
More Cl. E16 . . . 6H **87**
W14 . . . 4F **99**
Morecoombe Cl. KT2: King T . . . 7H **133**
More Copper Ho. *SE1* . . . *5G* ***15***
(off Magdalen St.)
Moree Way N18 . . . 4B **34**
Moreland Cotts. *E3* . . . *2C* ***86***
(off Fairfield Rd.)
Moreland Ct. NW2 . . . 3J **63**
Moreland St. EC1 . . . 1B **8** (3B **84**)
Moreland Way E4 . . . 3J **35**
Morella Rd. SW12 . . . 7D **118**
Morell Cl. EN5: New Bar . . . 3F **21**
Morello Av. UB8: Hil . . . 5D **74**
Morel Mews RM8: Dag . . . 1D **72**
More London Pl. SE1 . . . 5G **15** (1E **102**)
(not continuous)
More London Riverside
SE1 . . . 5H **15** (1E **102**)
(not continuous)
Moremead Rd. SE6 . . . 4B **140**
Morena St. SE6 . . . 7D **122**
Moresby Av. KT5: Surb . . . 7H **151**
Moresby Rd. E5 . . . 1H **67**
Moresby Wlk. SW8 . . . 2G **119**
More's Gdn. *SW3* . . . *6B* ***100***
(off Cheyne Wlk.)
Moreton Av. TW7: Isle . . . 1J **113**
Moreton Cl. E5 . . . 2H **67**
N15 . . . 6D **48**
NW7 . . . 6K **29**
SW1 . . . 5B **18**
Moreton Gdns. IG8: Wfd G . . . 5H **37**
Moreton Ho. SE16 . . . 3H **103**
Moreton Pl. SW1 . . . 5B **18** (5G **101**)
Moreton Rd. CR2: S Croy . . . 5D **168**
KT4: Wor Pk . . . 2C **164**
N15 . . . 6D **48**
Moretons HA1: Harr . . . 1J **59**
Moreton St. SW1 . . . 5B **18** (5G **101**)
Moreton Ter. SW1 . . . 5B **18** (5G **101**)
Moreton Ter. M. Nth. SW1 . . . 5B **18** (5G **101**)
Moreton Ter. M. Sth. SW1 . . . 5B **18** (5G **101**)
Moreton Twr. W3 . . . 1H **97**
Morford Cl. HA4: Ruis . . . 7K **39**
Morford Way HA4: Ruis . . . 7K **39**
Morgan Av. E17 . . . 4F **51**
Morgan Cl. RM10: Dag . . . 7G **73**
Morgan Ct. SM5: Cars . . . 4D **166**
TW15: Ashf . . . 5D **128**
Morgan Ho. *SW1* . . . *4B* ***18***
(off Vauxhall Bri. Rd.)
SW8 . . . *1G* ***119***
(off Wadhurst Rd.)
Morgan Mans. *N7* . . . *5A* ***66***
(off Morgan Rd.)
Morgan Rd. BR1: Brom . . . 7J **141**
N7 . . . 5A **66**
W10 . . . 5H **81**
Morgans La. *SE1* . . . *5G* ***15***
(off Tooley St.)
UB3: Hayes . . . 5F **75**
Morgan St. E3 . . . 3A **86**
(not continuous)
E16 . . . 5H **87**
Morgan Wlk. BR3: Beck . . . 4D **158**
Morgan Way IG8: Wfd G . . . 6H **37**
Moriarty Cl. BR1: Brom . . . 4E **160**
Moriatry Cl. N7 . . . 4J **65**
Morie St. SW18 . . . 5K **117**
Morieux Rd. E10 . . . 1B **68**
Moring Rd. SW17 . . . 4E **136**
Morkyns Wlk. SE21 . . . 3E **138**
Morland Av. CR0: C'don . . . 1E **168**
Morland Cl. CR4: Mitc . . . 3C **154**
NW11 . . . 1K **63**
TW12: Hamp . . . 5D **130**
Morland Ct. *W12* . . . *2D* ***98***
(off Coningham Rd.)
Morland Est. E8 . . . 7G **67**
Morland Gdns. NW10 . . . 7K **61**
UB1: S'hall . . . 1F **95**
Morland Ho. *NW1* . . . *1B* ***6***
(off Werrington St.)
NW6 . . . 1J **81**
SW1 . . . *3E* ***18***
(off Marsham St.)
W11 . . . *6G* ***81***
(off Lancaster Rd.)
Morland M. N1 . . . 7A **66**
Morland Pl. N15 . . . 4E **48**
Morland Rd.
CR0: C'don . . . 1E **168**
E17 . . . 5K **49**
HA3: Kenton . . . 5E **42**
IG1: Ilf . . . 2F **71**
RM10: Dag . . . 7G **73**
SE20 . . . 6K **139**
SM1: Sutt . . . 5A **166**
Morley Av. E4 . . . 7A **36**
N18 . . . 4B **34**
N22 . . . 2A **48**
Morley Cl. BR6: Farnb . . . 2F **173**
Morley Ct. BR2: Brom . . . 4H **159**
E4 . . . 5G **35**
Morley Cres. HA4: Ruis . . . 2A **58**
HA8: Edg . . . 2D **28**
Morley Cres. E. HA7: Stan . . . 2C **42**
Morley Cres. W. HA7: Stan . . . 3C **42**
Morley Hill EN2: Enf . . . 1J **23**
Morley Ho. *SE15* . . . *7F* ***103***
(off Commercial Way)
Morley Rd. BR7: Chst . . . 1G **161**
E10 . . . 1E **68**
E15 . . . 2H **87**
IG11: Bark . . . 1H **89**
RM6: Chad H . . . 5E **54**
SE13 . . . 4E **122**
SM3: Sutt . . . 1H **165**
TW1: Twick . . . 6D **114**
Morley St. SE1 . . . 1K **19** (3A **102**)
Morna Rd. SE5 . . . 2C **120**
Morning La. E9 . . . 6J **67**
Morningside Rd. KT4: Wor Pk . . . 2E **164**
Mornington Av. BR1: Brom . . . 3A **160**
IG1: Ilf . . . 7E **52**
W14 . . . 4H **99**
Mornington Av. Mans. *W14* . . . *4H* ***99***
(off Mornington Av.)
Mornington Cl. IG8: Wfd G . . . 4D **36**
NW9 . . . 3A **44**
Mornington Ct. DA5: Bexl . . . 1K **145**
NW1 . . . *2G* ***83***
(off Mornington Cres.)
Mornington Cres. NW1 . . . 2G **83**
TW5: Cran . . . 1K **111**
Mornington Gro. E3 . . . 3C **86**
Mornington M. SE5 . . . 1C **120**
Mornington Pl. NW1 . . . 2G **83**
SE8 . . . *7B* ***104***
(off Mornington Rd.)
Mornington Rd. E4 . . . 7K **25** & 1A **36**
E11 . . . 7H **51**
IG8: Wfd G . . . 4C **36**
SE8 . . . 7B **104**
TW15: Ashf . . . 5E **128**
UB6: G'frd . . . 5F **77**
Mornington Sports & Leisure Cen. . . . *1F* ***83***
(off Arlington Rd.)
Mornington St. NW1 . . . 2F **83**
Mornington Ter. NW1 . . . 1F **83**
Mornington Wlk. TW10: Ham . . . 4C **132**
Moro Apartments *E14* . . . *6C* ***86***
(off New Festival Av.)
Morocco St. SE1 . . . 7G **15** (2E **102**)
Morocco Wharf *E1* . . . *1H* ***103***
(off Wapping High St.)
Morpeth Gro. E9 . . . 1K **85**
Morpeth Mans. *SW1* . . . *2A* ***18***
(off Morpeth Ter.)
Morpeth Rd. E9 . . . 1K **85**
Morpeth St. E2 . . . 3J **85**
Morpeth Ter. SW1 . . . 2A **18** (3G **101**)
Morpeth Wlk. N17 . . . 7C **34**
Morphou Rd. NW7 . . . 6B **30**
Morrab Gdns. IG3: Ilf . . . 3K **71**
Morrel Ct. *E2* . . . *2G* ***85***
(off Goldsmiths Row)
Morrells Yd. *SE11* . . . *5K* ***19***
(off Cleaver St.)
Morris Av. E12 . . . 5D **70**
UB8: Uxb . . . 6A **56**
Morris Blitz Ct. N16 . . . 4F **67**
Morris Cl. BR6: Orp . . . 3J **173**
CR0: C'don . . . 5A **158**
Morris Ct. E4 . . . 3J **35**
Morris Gdns. SW18 . . . 7J **117**
Morris Ho. *E2* . . . *3J* ***85***
(off Roman Rd.)
NW8 . . . *4C* ***4***
(off Salisbury St.)
W3 . . . 2B **98**
Morrish Rd. SW2 . . . 7J **119**
Morrison Av. E4 . . . 6H **35**
N17 . . . 3E **48**
Morrison Bldgs. Nth. *E1* . . . *6G* ***85***
(off Commercial Rd.)
Morrison Ct. *EN5: Barn* . . . *4B* ***20***
(off Manor Way)
N12 . . . 7H **31**
SW1 . . . *3H* ***101***
(off Gt. Smith St.)
Morrison Ho. *SW2* . . . *1A* ***138***
(off Tulse Hill)
Morrison Rd. IG11: Bark . . . 2E **90**
RM9: Bark, Dag . . . 2E **90**
SW9 . . . 2A **120**
UB4: Yead . . . 3K **75**
Morrison St. SW11 . . . 3E **118**
Morris Pl. N4 . . . 2A **66**
Morris Rd. E14 . . . 5D **86**
E15 . . . 4G **69**
RM8: Dag . . . 2F **73**
TW7: Isle . . . 3K **113**
Morriss Ho. *SE16* . . . *2H* ***103***
(off Cherry Gdn. St.)
Morris St. E1 . . . 6H **85**
Morritt Ho. *HA0: Wemb* . . . *5D* ***60***
(off Talbot Rd.)
Morse Cl. E13 . . . 3J **87**
Morshead Mans. *W9* . . . *3J* ***81***
(off Morshead Rd.)
Morshead Rd. W9 . . . 3J **81**
Morson Rd. EN3: Pond E . . . 6F **25**
Morston Gdns. SE9 . . . 4D **142**
Mortain Ho. *SE16* . . . *4H* ***103***
(off Roseberry St.)
Morten Cl. SW4 . . . 6H **119**
Morteyne Rd. N17 . . . 1D **48**
Mortgramit Sq. SE18 . . . 3E **106**
Mortham St. E15 . . . 1G **87**
Mortimer Cl. NW2 . . . 2H **63**
SW16 . . . 2H **137**
Mortimer Ct. *NW8* . . . *1A* ***4***
(off Abbey Rd.)
Mortimer Cres. KT4: Wor Pk . . . 3K **163**
NW6 . . . 1K **81**
Mortimer Dr. EN1: Enf . . . 5K **23**
Mortimer Est. *NW6* . . . *1K* ***81***
(off Mortimer Pl.)
Mortimer Ho. W11 . . . 1F **99**
W14 . . . *4G* ***99***
(off North End Rd.)
Mortimer Mkt. WC1 . . . 4B **6** (4G **83**)
Mortimer Pl. NW6 . . . 1K **81**
Mortimer Rd. CR4: Mitc . . . 1D **154**
DA8: Erith . . . 6K **109**
E6 . . . 3D **88**
N1 . . . 7E **66**
(not continuous)
NW10 . . . 3E **80**
W13 . . . 6C **78**
Mortimer Sq. W11 . . . 7F **81**
Mortimer St. W1 . . . 7K **5** (6G **83**)
Mortimer Ter. NW5 . . . 4F **65**
MORTLAKE . . . 3K **115**
Mortlake Cl. CR0: Bedd . . . 3J **167**
Mortlake Crematorium TW9: Kew . . . 2H **115**
Mortlake Dr. CR4: Mitc . . . 1C **154**
Mortlake High St. SW14 . . . 3K **115**
Mortlake Rd. E16 . . . 6K **87**
IG1: Ilf . . . 4G **71**
TW9: Kew, Rich . . . 7G **97**
Mortlake Ter. *TW9: Kew* . . . *7G* ***97***
(off Mortlake Rd.)
Mortlock Cl. SE15 . . . 1H **121**
Mortlock Ct. E7 . . . 4B **70**
Morton Cl. E1 . . . 6J **85**
SM6: Wall . . . 7K **167**
UB8: Hil . . . 4B **74**
Morton Ct. UB5: N'olt . . . 5G **59**
Morton Cres. N14 . . . 4C **32**
Morton Gdns. SM6: Wall . . . 5G **167**
Morton Ho. SE17 . . . 6B **102**
Morton M. SW5 . . . 4K **99**
Morton Pl. SE1 . . . 2J **19** (3A **102**)
Morton Rd. E15 . . . 7H **69**
N1 . . . 7C **66**
SM4: Mord . . . 5B **154**
Morton Way N14 . . . 3B **32**
Morvale Cl. DA17: Belv . . . 4F **109**
Morval Rd. SW2 . . . 5A **120**
Morven Rd. SW17 . . . 3D **136**
Morville Ho. *SW18* . . . *6B* ***118***
(off Fitzhugh Gro.)
Morville St. E3 . . . 2C **86**
Morwell St. WC1 . . . 6C **6** (5H **83**)
Moscow Mans. *SW5* . . . *4J* ***99***
(off Cromwell Rd.)
Moscow Pl. W2 . . . 7K **81**
Moscow Rd. W2 . . . 7J **81**
Mosedale *NW1* . . . *2K* ***5***
(off Cumberland Mkt.)
Moseley Row SE10 . . . 4H **105**
Moselle Av. N22 . . . 2A **48**
Moselle Cl. N8 . . . 3K **47**
Moselle Ho. *N17* . . . *7A* ***34***
(off William St.)
Moselle Pl. N17 . . . 7A **34**
Moselle St. N17 . . . 7A **34**
Mosque Ter. *E1* . . . *5G* ***85***
(off Whitechapel Rd.)
Mosque Twr. *E1* . . . *5G* ***85***
(off Fieldgate St.)
E3 . . . *2A* ***86***
(off Ford St.)
Mosquito Cl. SM6: Wall . . . 7J **167**
Mossborough Cl. N12 . . . 6E **30**
Mossbury Rd. SW11 . . . 3C **118**
Moss Cl. E1 . . . 5G **85**
HA5: Pinn . . . 2D **40**
N9 . . . 1B **34**
Mossdown Cl. DA17: Belv . . . 4G **109**
Mossford Ct. IG6: Ilf . . . 3F **53**
Mossford Grn. IG6: Ilf . . . 3F **53**
Mossford La. IG6: Ilf . . . 2F **53**
Mossford St. E3 . . . 4B **86**
Moss Gdns. CR2: Sels . . . 7K **169**
TW13: Felt . . . 2J **129**

344 A-Z London

Moss Hall Ct.—Mulholland Cl.

Moss Hall Ct. N12 6E 30
Moss Hall Cres. N12 6E 30
Moss Hall Gro. N12 6E 30
Mossington Gdns. SE16 4J 103
Moss La. HA5: Pinn 1C 40
Mosslea Rd. BR2: Brom 5B 160
BR6: Farnb 3G 173
SE20 6J 139
(not continuous)
Mossop St. SW3 3D 16 (4C 100)
Moss Rd. RM10: Dag 7G 73
Mossville Gdns. SM4: Mord 3H 153
Mosswell Ho. N10 1E 46
Moston Cl. UB3: Harl 5H 93
Mostyn Av. HA9: Wemb 5F 61
Mostyn Gdns. NW10 3F 81
Mostyn Gro. E3 2C 86
Mostyn Rd.
HA8: Edg 7F 29
SW9 1A 120
SW19 1H 153
Mosul Way BR2: Brom 6C 160
Motcomb St. SW1 1G 17 (3E 100)
Moth Cl. SM6: Wall 7J 167
Mothers Sq. E5 4H 67
Motley Av. EC2 4G 9
MOTSPUR PARK 6C 152
Motspur Pk. KT3: N Mald 6B 152
MOTTINGHAM 2C 142
Mottingham Gdns. SE9 1B 142
Mottingham La. SE9 1A 142
SE12 1A 142
Mottingham Rd. N9 6E 24
SE9 2C 142
Mottisfont Rd. SE2 3A 108
Mottistone Gro. SM2: Sutt 7K 165
Motts La. RM8: Dag 2F 73
Mott St. E4 1K 25
Moules Ct. SE5 7C 102
Moulins Rd. E9 7J 67
Moulsford Ho. N7 5H 65
W2 *5J 81*
(off Westbourne Pk. Rd.)
Moulton Av. TW3: Houn 2C 112
Mound, The SE9 3E 142
Moundfield Rd. N16 6G 49
Mounsey Ho. *W10* *3G 81*
(off Third Av.)
Mount, The BR1: Brom 1C 160
CR2: S Croy *5C 168*
(off Warham Rd.)
DA6: Bex 5H 127
E5 2H 67
(not continuous)
HA9: Wemb 2H 61
KT3: N Mald 3B 152
KT4: Wor Pk 4D 164
N20 2F 31
NW3 3A 64
UB5: N'olt 5F 59
W3 1J 97
W8 *1J 99*
(off Bedford Gdns.)
Mountacre Cl. SE26 4F 139
Mt. Adon Pk. SE22 7G 121
Mountague Pl. E14 7E 86
Mountain Ho. SE11 4H 19 (4K 101)
Mt. Angelus Rd. SW15 7B 116
Mt. Ararat Rd. TW10: Rich 5E 114
Mt. Arlington *BR2: Brom* *2G 159*
(off Park Hill Rd.)
Mt. Ash Rd. SE26 3H 139
Mount Av. E4 3H 35
UB1: S'hall 6E 76
W5 5C 78
Mountbatten Cl. SE18 6J 107
SE19 5E 138
Mountbatten Ct. IG9: Buck H 2G 37
SE16 *1J 103*
(off Rotherhithe St.)
Mountbatten Gdns. BR3: Beck 4A 158
Mountbatten Ho. *N6* *7E 46*
(off Hillcrest)
Mountbatten M. SW18 7A 118
Mountbel Rd. HA7: Stan 1A 42
Mt. Carmel Chambers *W8* *2J 99*
(off Dukes La.)
Mount Cl. BR1: Brom 1C 160
EN4: Cockf 4K 21
SM5: Cars 7E 166
W5 5C 78
Mountcombe Cl. KT6: Surb 7E 150
Mount Ct. BR4: W W'ck 2G 171
SW15 3G 117
Mt. Culver Av. DA14: Sidc 6D 144
Mount Dr. DA6: Bex 5E 126
HA2: Harr 5D 40
HA9: Wemb 2J 61
Mountearl Gdns. SW16 3K 137
Mt. Eaton Ct. *W5* *5C 78*
(off Mount Av.)
Mt. Echo Av. E4 2J 35
Mt. Echo Dr. E4 1J 35
Mt. Ephraim La. SW16 3H 137
Mt. Ephraim Rd. SW16 3H 137
Mount Felix KT12: Walt T 7H 147
Mountfield Cl. SE6 7F 123
Mountfield Rd. E6 2E 88
N3 3H 45
W5 6D 78
Mountfield Ter. SE6 7F 123
Mountford Mans. *SW11* *1E 118*
(off Battersea Pk. Rd.)
Mountfort Cres. N1 7A 66
Mountfort Ho. *N1* *7A 66*
(off Barnsbury Sq.)
Mountfort Ter. N1 7A 66
Mount Gdns. SE26 3H 139
Mount Gro. HA8: Edg 3D 28
Mountgrove Rd. N5 3B 66
Mount Holme KT7: T Ditt 7B 150
Mounthurst Rd. BR2: Hayes 7H 159
Mountington Pk. Cl. HA3: Kenton 6D 42
Mountjoy Cl. *EC2* *6D 8*
(off Monkwell Sq.)
SE2 2B 108
Mountjoy Ho. EC2 6C 8
Mount Lodge N6 6G 47
Mount Mews TW12: Hamp 1F 149
Mount Mills EC1 2B 8 (3B 84)
Mt. Nod Rd. SW16 3K 137
Mt. Olive Ct. W7 2J 95
Mount Pde. EN4: Cockf 4H 21
Mount Pk. SM5: Cars 7E 166
Mount Pk. Av. CR2: S Croy 7B 168
HA1: Harr 2H 59
Mount Pk. Cres. W5 6D 78
Mount Pk. Rd. HA1: Harr 3H 59
HA5: Eastc 5J 39
W5 5D 78
Mount Pl. W3 1H 97
Mt. Pleasant EN4: Cockf 4H 21
HA0: Wemb 1E 78
HA4: Ruis 2A 58
IG1: Ilf 5G 71
SE27 4C 138
WC1 4J 7 (4A 84)
Mt. Pleasant Cotts. *N14* *7C 22*
(off The Wells)
Mt. Pleasant Cres. N4 1K 65
Mt. Pleasant Hill E5 2H 67
Mt. Pleasant La. E5 1H 67
Mt. Pleasant M. *N4* *1K 65*
(off Mt. Pleasant Cres.)
Mt. Pleasant Pl. SE18 4H 107
Mt. Pleasant Rd. E17 2A 50
KT3: N Mald 3J 151
N17 2E 48
NW10 7E 62
SE13 6D 122
W5 4C 78
Mt. Pleasant Vs. N4 7K 47
Mt. Pleasant Wlk. DA5: Bexl 5J 127
Mount Rd. CR4: Mitc 2B 154
DA6: Bex 5D 126
EN4: E Barn 5H 21
KT3: N Mald 3K 151
KT9: Chess 5F 163
NW2 3D 62
NW4 6C 44
RM8: Dag 1F 73
SE19 6D 138
SW19 2J 135
TW13: Hanw 3C 130
UB3: Hayes 2J 93
Mount Row W1 3J 11 (7F 83)
Mountsfield Ct. SE13 6F 123
Mountsfield Ho. *SE10* *1E 122*
(off Primrose Way)
Mountside HA7: Stan 1A 42
Mounts Pond Rd. SE3 2F 123
(not continuous)
Mount Square, The NW3 3A 64
Mt. Stewart Av. HA3: Kenton 7D 42
Mount St. W1 3G 11 (7E 82)
Mount St. M. W1 3J 11 (7F 83)
Mountstuart Ct. TW11: Hamp W 1B 150
Mount Ter. E1 5H 85
Mount Vernon NW3 4A 64
Mount Vw. EN2: Enf 1E 22
NW7 3E 28
UB2: S'hall 4B 94
W5 4D 78
Mountview Academy of Theatre Arts *2K 47*
(off Clarendon Rd.)
Mountview Cl. NW11 1K 63
Mountview Ct. N8 4B 48
Mount Vw. Rd. E4 7K 25 & 1A 36
KT10: Clay 7B 162
N4 7J 47
NW9 5K 43
Mountview Rd. BR6: Orp, St M Cry 7K 161
(not continuous)
Mount Vs. SE27 3B 138
Mount Way SM5: Cars 7E 166
Mountwood KT8: W Mole 3F 149
MOVERS LANE 2J 89
Movers La. IG11: Bark 1H 89
Mowat Ct. *KT4: Wor Pk* *2B 164*
(off The Avenue)
Mowatt Cl. N19 1H 65
Mowbray Ct. N22 1A 48
SE19 7F 139
Mowbray Gdns. UB5: N'olt 1E 76
Mowbray Ho. *N2* *2B 46*
(off The Grange)
Mowbray Pde. HA8: Edg 4B 28
Mowbray Rd. EN5: New Bar 5F 21
HA8: Edg 4B 28
NW6 7G 63
SE19 1F 157
TW10: Ham 3C 132
Mowbrays Cl. RM5: Col R 1J 55
Mowbrays Rd. RM5: Col R 2J 55
Mowlem St. E2 2H 85
Mowlem Trad. Est. N17 7D 34
Mowll St. SW9 7A 102
Moxon Cl. E13 2H 87
Moxon Pl. UB10: Uxb 1B 74
Moxon St. EN5: Barn 3C 20
W1 6G 5 (5E 82)
Moye Cl. E2 2G 85
Moyers Rd. E10 7E 50
Moylan Rd. W6 6G 99
Moyle Ho. DA17: Belv 2H 109
SW1 *6B 18*
(off Churchill Gdns.)
Moyne Ho. SW9 5B 120
Moyne Pl. NW10 2G 79
Moynihan Dr. N21 5D 22
Moys Cl. CR0: C'don 6J 155
Moyser Rd. SW16 5F 137
Mozart St. W10 3H 81
Mozart Ter. SW1 4H 17 (4E 100)
MTV Europe 7F 65
Muchelney Rd. SM4: Mord 6A 154
Mudchute Farm 4E 104
Mudlarks Blvd. SE10 3H 105
Mudlarks Way SE10 3J 105
Muffin La. E2 2G 85
Muggeridge Cl. CR2: S Croy 5D 168
Muggeridge Rd. RM10: Dag 4H 73
Muirdown Av. SW14 4K 115
Muir Dr. SW18 6C 118
Muirfield W3 6A 80
Muirfield Cl. SE16 5H 103
Muirfield Cres. E14 3D 104
Muirhead Quay IG11: Bark 2G 89
Muirkirk Rd. SE6 1E 140
Muir Rd. E5 3G 67
Muir St. E16 1C 106
(not continuous)
Mulberry Av. TW19: Stanw 1A 128
Mulberry Cl. E4 2H 35
EN4: E Barn 4G 21
N8 5J 47
NW3 4B 64
NW4 3E 44
SE7 6B 106
SE22 5G 121
SW3 7B 16
SW16 4G 137
TW13: Felt 3K 129
UB5: N'olt 2C 76
Mulberry Ct. DA1: Cray 5K 127
E11 *4F 69*
(off Langthorne Rd.)
EC1 *2B 8*
(off Tompion St.)
IG11: Bark 6K 71
KT6: Surb 7D 150
N2 *3C 46*
(off Bedford Rd.)
SW3 7B 16 (6B 100)
(not continuous)
TW1: Twick 3K 131
W9 *3H 81*
(off Ashmore Rd.)
Mulberry Cres. TW8: Bford 7B 96
UB7: W Dray 2C 92
Mulberry Ho. BR2: Brom 1G 159
E2 *3J 85*
(off Victoria Pk. Sq.)
SE8 6B 104
Mulberry Housing Co-operative
SE1 4K 13
Mulberry La. CR0: C'don 1F 169
Mulberry M. SE14 1B 122
SM6: Wall 6G 167
Mulberry Pde. UB7: W Dray 3C 92
Mulberry Pl. *E14* *7E 86*
(off Clove Cres.)
HA2: Harr 2H 41
SE9 4B 124
W6 5C 98
Mulberry Rd. E8 7F 67
Mulberry St. E1 6G 85
Mulberry Tree M. W4 2J 97
Mulberry Trees TW17: Shep 7F 147
Mulberry Wlk. SW3 7B 16 (6B 100)
Mulberry Way DA17: Belv 2J 109
E18 2K 51
IG6: Ilf 4G 53
Mulgrave Ct. *SM2: Sutt* *6K 165*
(off Mulgrave Rd.)
Mulgrave Rd. CR0: C'don 3D 168
HA1: Harr 2A 60
NW10 4B 62
SE18 4D 106
SM2: Sutt 7H 165
SW6 6H 99
W5 3D 78
Mulholland Cl. CR4: Mitc 2F 155

Mulkern Rd.—Narborough Cl.

Mulkern Rd. N19 1H **65** (not continuous)
Mullards Cl. CR4: Mitc 1D **166**
Mullen Twr. *WC1* *4J 7* *(off Mt. Pleasant)*
Muller Ho. SE18 5E **106**
Muller Rd. SW4 6H **119**
Mullet Gdns. E2 3G **85**
Mulletsfield *WC1* *2F 7* *(off Cromer St.)*
Mull Ho. *E3* *2B 86* *(off Stafford Rd.)*
Mulligans Apartments *NW6* *7J 63* *(off Kilburn High Rd.)*
Mullins Path SW14 3K **115**
Mullins Pl. SW4 7J **119**
Mullion Cl. HA3: Hrw W 1F **41**
Mull Wlk. *N1* *6C 66* *(off Clephane Rd.)*
Mulready Ho. *SW1* *4E 18* *(off Marsham St.)*
Mulready St. NW8 4C **4** (4C **82**)
Multi Way W3 2A **98**
Multon Ho. E9 7J **67**
Multon Rd. SW18 7B **118**
Mulvaney Way SE1 7F **15** (2D **102**) (not continuous)
Mumford Mills *SE10* *1D 122* *(off Greenwich High Rd.)*
Mumford Rd. SE24 5B **120**
Muncaster Cl. TW15: Ashf 4C **128**
Muncaster Rd. SW11 5D **118**
TW15: Ashf 5D **128**
Muncies M. SE6 2E **140**
Mundania Ct. SE22 6H **121**
Mundania Rd. SE22 6H **121**
Munday Ho. *SE1* *3D 102* *(off Burbage Cl.)*
Munday Rd. E16 7J **87**
Munden Ho. *E3* *3D 86* *(off Bromley High St.)*
Munden St. W14 4G **99**
Mundford Rd. E5 2J **67**
Mundon Gdns. IG1: Ilf 1H **71**
Mund St. W14 5H **99**
Mundy Ho. *W10* *3G 81* *(off Dart St.)*
Mundy St. N1 1G **9** (3E **84**)
Mungo Pk. Cl. WD23: B Hea 2B **26**
Munkenbeck Bldg. *W2* *6A 4* *(off Hermitage St.)*
Munnery Way BR6: Farnb 3E **172**
Munnings Gdns. TW7: Isle 5H **113**
Munnings Ho. *E16* *1K 105* *(off Portsmouth M.)*
Munro Dr. N11 6B **32**
Munro Ho. SE1 7J **13** (2A **102**)
Munro M. W10 5G **81** (not continuous)
Munro Ter. SW10 7B **100**
Munslow Gdns. SM1: Sutt 4B **166**
Munster Av. TW4: Houn 5C **112**
Munster Ct. SW6 2H **117**
TW11: Tedd 6C **132**
Munster Gdns. N13 4G **33**
Munster M. SW6 7G **99**
Munster Rd. SW6 7G **99**
TW11: Tedd 6B **132**
Munster Sq. NW1 2K **5** (3F **83**)
Munton Rd. SE17 4C **102**
Muratori Ho. *WC1* *2J 7* *(off Margery St.)*
Murchison Av. DA5: Bexl 1D **144**
Murchison Ho. *W10* *5G 81* *(off Ladbroke Gro.)*
Murchison Rd. E10 2E **68**
Murdoch Ho. *SE16* *3J 103* *(off Moodkee St.)*
Murdock Cl. E16 6H **87**
Murdock St. SE15 6H **103**
Murfett Cl. SW19 2G **135**
Muriel St. N1 2K **83** (not continuous)
Murillo Rd. SE13 4F **123**
Muro Ct. *SE1* *7B 14* *(off Milcote St.)*
Murphy Ho. *SE1* *7B 14* *(off Borough Rd.)*
Murphy St. SE1 7J **13** (2A **102**)
Murray Av. BR1: Brom 3K **159**
TW3: Houn 5F **113**
Murray Cl. SE28 1J **107**
Murray Ct. *E3* *5B 86* *(off Geoff Cade Way)*
HA1: Harr 6K **41**
TW2: Twick 2H **131**
W7 2J **95**
Murray Cres. HA5: Pinn 1B **40**
Murray Gro. N1 1D **8** (2C **84**)
Murray Ho. *SE18* *4D 106* *(off Rideout St.)*
Murray M. NW1 7H **65**
Murray Rd. HA6: Nwood 1G **39**
SW19 6F **135**
TW10: Ham 2B **132**
W5 4C **96**
Murray Sq. E16 6J **87**
Murray St. NW1 7G **65**
Murrays Yd. SE18 4F **107**
Murray Ter. NW3 4A **64**
W5 4D **96**
Mursell Est. SW8 1K **119**
Musard Rd. W6 6G **99**
W14 6G **99**
Musbury St. E1 6J **85**
Muscal *W6* *6G 99* *(off Field Rd.)*
Muscatel Pl. SE5 1E **120**
Muschamp Rd. SE15 3F **121**
SM5: Cars 2C **166**
Muscott Ho. *E2* *1G 85* *(off Whiston Rd.)*
Muscovy Ho. *DA18: Erith* *2E 108* *(off Kale Rd.)*
Muscovy St. EC3 2H **15** (7E **84**)
Museum Chambers *WC1* *6E 6* *(off Bury Pl.)*
Museum Ho. *E2* *3J 85* *(off Burnham St.)*
Museum La. SW7 2B **16** (3B **100**)
Museum Mans. *WC1* *6E 6* *(off Gt. Russell St.)*
Museum of Brands, Packaging and Advertising *6H 81* *(off Colville M.)*
Museum of Childhood Bethnal Green 3J 85
Museum of Croydon *3C 168* *(off High St.)*
Museum of Domestic Design & Architecture MODA 2B 44
Museum of Freemasonry *7F 7* *(off Gt. Queen St.)*
Museum of London 6C 8 (5C 84)
Museum of London Docklands 7C 86
Museum of Richmond 5D 114
Museum of The Order of St John *4A 8* *(off St John's La.)*
Museum Pas. E2 3J **85**
Museum St. WC1 6E **6** (5J **83**)
Museum Way W3 2G **97**
Musgrave Cl. EN4: Had W 1F **21**
Musgrave Ct. SW11 1C **118**
Musgrave Cres. SW6 7J **99**
Musgrave Rd. TW7: Isle 1K **113**
Musgrove Rd. SE14 1K **121**
Musical Museum, The 6F 97
Musjid Rd. SW11 2B **118**
Musket Cl. EN4: E Barn 6G **21**
Musquash Way TW4: Houn 2A **112**
Mustang Ho. *N1* *6B 66* *(off Canonbury Rd.)*
Muston Rd. E5 2H **67**
Mustow Pl. SW6 2H **117**
Muswell Av. N10 1F **47**
MUSWELL HILL 3F 47
Muswell Hill N10 3F **47**
Muswell Hill B'way. N10 3F **47**
Muswell Hill Golf Course 1G 47
Muswell Hill Pl. N10 4F **47**
Muswell Hill Rd. N6 6E **46**
N10 6E **46**
Muswell M. N10 3F **47**
Muswell Rd. N10 3F **47**
Mutrix Rd. NW6 1J **81**
Mutton Pl. NW1 6E **64**
Muybridge Rd. KT3: N Mald 2J **151**
Muybridge Yd. KT5: Surb 7F **151**
Myatt Rd. SW9 1B **120**
Myatts Fld. Sth. SW9 2A **120**
Mycenae Rd. SE3 7J **105**
Myddelton Av. EN1: Enf 1K **23**
Myddelton Cl. EN1: Enf 1A **24**
Myddelton Gdns. N21 7H **23**
Myddelton Pk. N20 3G **31**
Myddelton Pas. EC1 1K **7** (3A **84**)
Myddelton Rd. N8 4J **47** (not continuous)
Myddelton Sq. EC1 1K **7** (3A **84**)
Myddelton St. EC1 2K **7** (3A **84**)
Myddleton Av. N4 2C **66**
Myddleton Cl. HA7: Stan 2F **27**
Myddleton Ho. N1 1J **7**
Myddleton M. N22 7D **32**
Myddleton Rd. N22 7D **32**
Myers Ho. *SE5* *7C 102* *(off Bethwin Rd.)*
Myers La. SE14 6K **103**
Myles Ct. *SE16* *3J 103* *(off Neptune St.)*
Mylis Cl. SE26 4H **139**
Mylius Cl. SE14 7J **103**
Mylne Cl. W6 5C **98**
Mylne St. EC1 1J **7** (2A **84**)
Myra St. SE2 4A **108**
Myrdle Ct. *E1* *6G 85* *(off Myrdle St.)*
Myrdle St. E1 5G **85**
Myrna Cl. SW19 7C **136**
Myron Pl. SE13 3E **122**
Myrtle Av. HA4: Ruis 7J **39**
TW14: Felt 5G **111**
Myrtleberry Cl. *E8* *6F 67* *(off Beechwood Rd.)*
Myrtle Cl. EN4: E Barn 1J **31**
UB7: W Dray 3B **92**
UB8: Hil 5B **74**
Myrtledene Rd. SE2 5A **108**
Myrtle Gdns. W7 1J **95**
Myrtle Gro. EN2: Enf 1J **23**
KT3: N Mald 2J **151**
Myrtle Rd. CR0: C'don 3C **170**
E6 1D **88**
E17 6A **50**
IG1: Ilf 2F **71**
N13 3H **33**
SM1: Sutt 5A **166**
TW3: Houn 2G **113**
TW12: Hamp H 6G **131**
W3 1J **97**
Myrtle Wlk. N1 1G **9** (2E **84**)
Mysore Rd. SW11 3D **118**
Myton Rd. SE21 3D **138**
Mytton Ho. *SW8* *7K 101* *(off St Stephens Ter.)*

N

N1 Shop. Cen. N1 2A **84**
Nacton Ct. *RM6: Chad H* *5C 54* *(off Hevingham Dr.)*
Nadine Ct. SM6: Wall 7G **167**
Nadine St. SE7 5A **106**
Nagasaki Wlk. SE7 3K **105**
Nagle Cl. E17 2F **51**
NAG'S HEAD 3J **65**
Nags Head Ct. EC1 4D **8**
Nags Head La. DA16: Well 3B **126**
Nags Head Rd. EN3: Pond E 4D **24**
Nags Head Shop. Cen. N7 4K **65**
Nainby Ho. SE11 4J **19**
Nairne Gro. SE24 5D **120**
Nairn Rd. HA4: Ruis 6A **58**
Nairn St. E14 5E **86**
Naldera Gdns. SE3 6J **105**
Nallhead Rd. TW13: Hanw 5A **130**
Nalton Ho. *NW6* *7A 64* *(off Belsize Rd.)*
Namba Roy Cl. SW16 4K **137**
Namco Funscape Romford 6K 55
Namton Dr. CR7: Thor H 4K **155**
Nan Clark's La. NW7 2F **29**
Nankin St. E14 6C **86**
Nansen Ho. *NW10* *7K 61* *(off Stonebridge Pk.)*
Nansen Rd. SW11 3E **118**
Nansen Village N12 4E **30**
Nant Ct. NW2 2H **63**
Nantes Cl. SW18 4A **118**
Nantes Pas. E1 5J **9** (5F **85**)
Nant Rd. NW2 2H **63**
Nant St. E2 3H **85**
Naoroji St. WC1 2J **7** (3A **84**)
Napa Cl. E20 5E **68**
Napier NW9 1B **44**
Napier Av. E14 5C **104**
SW6 3H **117**
Napier Cl. SE8 7B **104**
UB7: W Dray 3B **92**
W14 3G **99**
Napier Ct. *BR2: Brom* *4K 159* *(off Napier Rd.)*
N1 *2D 84* *(off Cropley St.)*
SE12 3K **141**
SW6 *3H 117* *(off Ranelagh Gdns.)*
UB4: Yead *4A 76* *(off Dunedin Way)*
Napier Gro. N1 2C **84**
Napier Ho. *E3* *3C 86* *(off Campbell Rd.)*
SE17 *6B 102* *(off Cooks Rd.)*
W3 1B **98**
Napier Lodge TW15: Ashf 6F **129**
Napier Pl. W14 3H **99**
Napier Rd. BR2: Brom 4K **159**
CR2: S Croy 7D **168**
DA17: Belv 4F **109**
E6 1E **88**
E11 4G **69**
E15 2G **87** (not continuous)
EN3: Pond E 5E **24**
HA0: Wemb 6D **60**
N17 3E **48**
NW10 3D **80**
SE25 4H **157**
TW7: Isle 4A **114**
TW15: Ashf 7F **129**
W14 3H **99**
Napier St. *SE8* *7B 104* *(off Napier Cl.)*
Napier Ter. N1 7B **66**
Napier Wlk. TW15: Ashf 7F **129**
Napoleon Rd. E5 3H **67**
TW1: Twick 7B **114**
Napton Cl. UB4: Yead 4C **76**
Nara SE13 2D **122**
Narbonne Av. SW4 5G **119**
Narborough Cl. UB10: Ick 2E **56**

Narborough St. SW6 ....2K 117
Narcissus Rd. NW6 ....5J 63
Nardini NW9 ....1B 44
(off Long Mead)
Naresby Fold HA7: Stan 1K 7
Nares Cl. TW19: Stanw 1A 128
Narford Rd. E5 ....3G 67
Narrow Boat Cl. SE28 ....2H 107
Narrow St. E14 ....7A 86
W3 ....1H 97
Narrow Way BR2: Brom 6C 160
Narvic Ho. SE5 ....2C 120
Narwhal Inuit Art Gallery 4K 97
Nascot St. W12 ....6E 80
Naseby Cl. NW6 ....7A 64
TW7: Isle 1J 113
Naseby Ct. DA14: Sidc 4K 143
Naseby Rd. IG5: Ilf 1D 52
RM10: Dag 3G 73
SE19 ....6D 138
NASH 6J 171
Nash Cl. SM1: Sutt 3B 166
Nash Cl. HA3: Kenton 6B 42
Nashe Ho. SE1 ....3D 102
(off Burbage Cl.)
Nash Grn. BR1: Brom 6J 141
Nash Ho. E14 ....2C 104
(off Alpha Gro.)
E17 ....3D 50
NW1 ....2F 83
(off Park Village E.)
SW1 ....6K 17
(off Lupus St.)
Nash La. BR2: Kes 7J 171
Nash Pl. E14 ....1D 104
Nash Rd. N9 ....2D 34
RM6: Chad H 4D 54
SE4 ....4A 122
Nash St. NW1 ....1K 5 (3F 83)
Nash Way HA3: Kenton 6B 42
Nasmyth St. W6 ....3D 98
Nassau Path SE28 ....1C 108
Nassau Rd. SW13 ....1B 116
Nassau St. W1 ....6A 6 (5G 83)
Nassington Rd. NW3 ....4D 64
Natalie Cl. TW14: Bedf 7F 111
Natalie M. N22 ....6D 32
TW2: Twick 3H 131
Natal Rd. CR7: Thor H 3D 156
IG1: Ilf 4F 71
N11 ....6D 32
SW16 ....6H 137
Natasha M. SE15 ....4J 121
Nathan Ct. N9 ....7D 24
(off Causeware Rd.)
Nathan Ho. SE11 ....4K 19
(off Reedworth St.)
Nathaniel Cl. E1 ....6K 9 (5F 85)
Nathaniel Ct. E17 ....7A 50
Nathans Rd. HA0: Wemb 1C 60
Nathan Way SE28 ....4J 107
National Archives, The 7H 97
National Army Mus. 7F 17 (6D 100)
National Gallery 3D 12 (7H 83)
National Maritime Mus. 6F 105
National Portrait Gallery 3D 12
National Tennis Cen. 5A 116
National Ter. SE16 ....2H 103
(off Bermondsey Wall E.)
National Theatre 4H 13 (1A 102)
National Works TW4: Houn 3D 112
Nation Way E4 ....1K 35
Natural History Mus.
Knightsbridge 2A 16 (3B 100)
Nautilus Building, The EC1 ....1K 7
(off Myddelton Pas.)
Naval Ho. E14 ....4E 87
(off Quixley St.)
Naval Row E14 ....7E 86
Naval Wlk. BR1: Brom 2J 159
(off Mitre Cl.)

Navarino Gro. E8 ....6G 67
Navarino Mans. E8 ....6G 67
Navarino Rd. E8 ....6G 67
Navarre Rd. E6 ....2C 88
Navarre St. E2 ....3J 9 (4F 85)
SW9 ....1B 120
Navarre St. E2 ....3J 9 (4F 85)
Navenby Wlk. E3 ....4C 86
Navestock Cl. E4 ....3K 35
Navestock Cres. IG8: Wfd G 7F 37
Navigation Ct. E16 ....7G 89
Navigation Dr. EN3: Enf L 1H 25
Navigation Ho. SE8 ....4A 104
(off Grand Canal Av.)
Navigator Dr. UB2: S'hall 2G 95
Navigator Pk. UB2: S'hall 4A 94
Navy St. SW4 ....3H 119
Naxos Bldg. E14 ....2B 104
Nayim Pl. E8 ....5H 67
Nayland Ho. SE6 ....4E 140
Naylor Bldg. E. E1 ....6G 85
(off Assam St.)
Naylor Bldg. W. E1 ....6G 85
(off Adler St.)
Naylor Gro. EN3: Pond E 5E 24
Naylor Ho. SE17 ....4D 102
(off Flint St.)
W10 ....3G 81
(off Dart St.)
Naylor Rd. N20 ....2F 31
SE15 ....7H 103
Nazareth Gdns. SE15 ....2H 121
Nazrul St. E2 ....1J 9 (3F 85)
NCR Bus. Cen. NW10 ....5A 62
Neagle Ho. NW2 ....3E 62
(off Stoll Cl.)
Neal Av. UB1: S'hall 4D 76
Neal Cl. HA6: Nwood 1J 39
Nealden St. SW9 ....3K 119
Neale Cl. N2 ....3A 46
Neal Ct. RM9: Dag 6B 72
Neal St. WC2 ....1E 12 (6J 83)
Neal's Yd. WC2 ....1E 12 (6J 83)
Near Acre NW9 ....1B 44
NEASDEN 3A 62
Neasden Cl. NW10 ....5A 62
NEASDEN JUNC. 4A 62
Neasden La. NW10 ....3A 62
Neasden La. Nth. NW10 ....3K 61
Neasham Rd. RM8: Dag 5B 72
Neate Ho. SW1 ....6B 18
(off Lupus St.)
Neate St. SE5 ....6E 102
Neath Gdns. SM4: Mord 6A 154
Neathouse Pl. SW1 ....3A 18 (4G 101)
Neats Acre HA4: Ruis 7F 39
Neatscourt Rd. E6 ....5B 88
Nebraska Bldg. SE13 ....1D 122
(off Deal's Gateway)
Nebraska St. SE1 ....7E 14 (2D 102)
Nebula SW11 ....2D 118
Nebula Ct. E13 ....2J 87
(off Umbriel Pl.)
Neckinger SE16 ....7K 15 (3F 103)
Neckinger Est. SE16 ....3F 103
Neckinger St. SE1 ....7K 15 (2F 103)
Nectarine Way SE13 ....2D 122
Needham Ho. SE11 ....4J 19
Needham Rd. W11 ....6J 81
Needham Ter. NW2 ....3F 63
Needleman Cl. NW9 ....2A 44
Needleman St. SE16 ....2K 103
Needwood Ho. N4 ....1C 66
Neela Cl. UB10: Ick 4D 56
Neeld Cres. HA9: Wemb 5G 61
NW4 ....5D 44
Neeld Pde. HA9: Wemb 5F 61
Neil Cl. TW15: Ashf 5E 128
Neil Wates Cres. SW2 ....1A 138
Nelgarde Rd. SE6 ....7C 122
Nella Rd. W6 ....6F 99
Nelldale Rd. SE16 ....4J 103

Neilgrove Rd. UB10: Hil 4D 74
Nell Gwynn Av. TW17: Shep 6F 147
Nell Gwynn Ho. SW3 ......4D 16 (4C 100)
Nello James Gdns. SE27 ....4D 138
Nelson Cl. CR0: C'don 1B 168
KT12: Walt T 7K 147
NW6 ....3J 81
Nelson Cl. RM7: Mawney 1H 55
TW14: Felt 1H 129
UB10: Hil 3D 74
SE16 ....1J 103
(off Brunel Rd.)
Nelson Gdns. E2 ....3G 85
TW3: Houn 6E 112
Nelson Gro. Rd. SW19 ....1K 153
Nelson Ho. SW1 ....7B 18
(off Dolphin Sq.)
Nelson La. UB10: Hil 3D 74
Nelson Mandela Cl. N10 ....2E 46
Nelson Mandela Ho. N16 ....2G 67
Nelson Mandela Rd. SE3 ....3A 124
Nelson Pas. EC1 ....1D 8 (3C 84)
Nelson Pl. DA14: Sidc 4A 144
N1 ....1B 8 (2B 84)
Nelson Rd. BR2: Brom 4A 160
DA14: Sidc 4A 144
DA17: Belv 5F 109
E4 ....6J 35
E11 ....4J 51
EN3: Pond E 6E 24
HA1: Harr 1H 59
HA7: Stan 6H 27
KT3: N Mald 5K 151
N8 ....5K 47
N9 ....2C 34
N15 ....4E 48
SE10 ....6E 104
SW19 ....7K 135
TW2: Whitt 7F 113
TW3: Houn 6E 112
TW6: H'row A 1B 110
TW15: Ashf 5A 128
UB10: Hil 3D 74
Nelson Rd. M. SW19 ....7K 135
(off Nelson Rd.)
Nelson's Column 4D 12 (1H 101)
Nelson Sq. SE1 ....6A 14 (2B 102)
Nelson's Row SW4 ....4H 119
Nelson St. E1 ....6H 85
E6 ....2D 88
(not continuous)
E16 ....6H 87
Nelsons Yd. NW1 ....2G 83
(off Mornington Cres.)
Nelson Ter. N1 ....1B 8 (2B 84)
Nelson Trad. Est. SW19 ....1K 153
Nelson Wlk. E3 ....4D 86
KT19: Eps 7G 163
SE16 ....1A 104
Nemoure Rd. W3 ....7J 79
Nemus Apartments SE8 ....4K 103
Nene Gdns. TW13: Hanw 3D 130
Nene Rd. TW6: H'row A 1D 110
NENE ROAD RDBT. 1D 110
Nepaul Rd. SW11 ....2C 118
Nepean St. SW15 ....6C 116
Neptune Ct. E14 ....4C 104
(off Homer Dr.)
E16 ....5J 87
(off Hammersley Rd.)
Neptune Ho. E3 ....1C 86
(off Garrison Rd.)
SE16 ....3J 103
(off Moodkee St.)
Neptune Rd. HA1: Harr 6H 41
TW6: H'row A 1F 111
Neptune St. SE16 ....3J 103
Neptune Wlk. DA8: Erith 4K 109
Nero Ct. TW8: Bford 7D 96
Nero Ho. E20 ....6E 68
(off Anthems Way)

Nesbit Cl. SE17 ....6B 102
(off Cook's Rd.)
Nesbit Rd. SE9 ....4B 124
Nesbitt Cl. SE3 ....3G 123
Nesbitts All. EN5: Barn 3C 20
Nesbitt Sq. SE19 ....7E 138
Nesham Ho. N1 ....1E 84
(off Hoxton St.)
Nesham St. E1 ....7G 85
Ness St. SE16 ....3G 103
Nesta Rd. IG8: Wfd G 6B 36
Nestles Av. UB3: Hayes 3H 93
Nestor Av. N21 ....6G 23
Nestor Ho. E2 ....2H 85
(off Old Bethnal Grn. Rd.)
Netheravon Rd. W4 ....4B 98
W7 ....1K 95
Netheravon Rd. Sth. W4 ....5B 98
Netherbury Rd. W5 ....3D 96
Netherby Gdns. EN2: Enf 4D 22
Netherby Rd. SE23 ....7J 121
Nether Cl. N3 ....7D 30
Nethercott Ho. E3 ....3D 86
(off Bruce Rd.)
Nethercourt Av. N3 ....6D 30
Netherfield Gdns. IG11: Bark 6H 71
Netherfield Rd. N12 ....5E 30
SW17 ....3E 136
Netherford Rd. SW4 ....2G 119
Netherhall Gdns. NW3 ....6A 64
Netherhall Way NW3 ....5A 64
Netherheyes Dr. CR2: S Croy 7B 168
Netherlands Rd. EN5: New Bar ...6G 21
Netherleigh Cl. N6 ....1F 65
Nether St. N3 ....7D 30
N12 ....7D 30
(not continuous)
Netherton Gro. SW10 ....6A 100
Netherton Rd. N15 ....6D 48
TW1: Twick 5A 114
Netherwood N2 ....2B 46
Netherwood Pl. W14 ....3F 99
(off Netherwood Rd.)
Netherwood Rd. W14 ....3F 99
Netherwood St. NW6 ....7H 63
Nethewode Ct. DA17: Belv 3H 109
(off Lower Pk. Rd.)
Netley SE5 ....1E 120
(off Redbridge Gdns.)
Netley Cl. CR0: New Ad 7E 170
SM3: Cheam 5F 165
Netley Dr. KT12: Walt T 7D 148
Netley Gdns. SM4: Mord 7A 154
Netley Rd. E17 ....5B 50
IG2: Ilf 5H 53
SM4: Mord 7A 154
TW8: Bford 6E 96
Netley St. NW1 ....2A 6 (3G 83)
Nettlecombe NW1 ....7H 65
(off Agar Gro.)
Nettleden Av. HA9: Wemb 6G 61
Nettleden Ho. SW3 ....4D 16
(off Cale St.)
Nettlefold Pl. SE27 ....3B 138
TW16: Sun 5J 147
Nettlefold Wlk. KT12: Walt T 7H 147
Nettlestead Cl. BR3: Beck 7B 140
Nettleton Ct. EC2 ....6C 8
(off London Wall)
Nettleton Rd. E14 ....1K 121
TW6: H'row A 1D 110
UB10: Ick 4B 56
Nettlewood Rd. SW16 ....7H 137
Neuchatel Rd. SE6 ....2B 140
Neutron Twr. E14 ....7F 87
Nevada Bldg. SE10 ....1D 122
(off Blackheath Rd.)
Nevada Cl. KT3: N Mald 4J 151
Nevada St. SE10 ....6E 104
Nevern Mans. SW5 ....5J 99
(off Warwick Rd.)

Nevern Pl. SW5 . . . . .4J **99**
Nevern Rd. SW5 . . . . .4J **99**
Nevern Sq. SW5 . . . . .4J **99**
Nevil Ho. SW9 . . . . .2B **120**
 (off Loughborough Est.)
Nevill Ct. SW10 . . . . .7A **100**
 (off Edith Ter.)
Neville Av. KT3: N Mald 1K **151**
Neville Cl. DA15: Sidc 4K **143**
 E11 . . . . .3H **69**
 NW1 . . . . .2H **83**
 NW6 . . . . .2H **81**
 SE15 .1G **121**
 TW3: Houn 2F **113**
 W3 . . . . .2J **97**
Neville Cl. NW8 . . . . .1A **4**
Neville Dr. N2 . . . . .6A **46**
Neville Gdns. RM8: Dag 3D **72**
Neville Gill Cl. SW18 . . . . .6J **117**
Neville Ho. N11 . . . . .4K **31**
 N22 . . . . .1K **47**
 (off Neville Pl.)
 NW6 . . . . .2H **81**
 (off Denmark Rd.)
Neville Ho. Yd. KT1: King T 2E **150**
Neville Pl. N22 . . . . .1K **47**
Neville Rd. CR0: C'don 7D **156**
 E7 . . . . .7J **69**
 IG6: Ilf .1G **53**
 KT1: King T 2G **151**
 NW6 . . . . .2H **81**
 RM8: Dag 3D **72**
 TW10: Ham 3C **132**
 W5 . . . . .4D **78**
Nevilles Ct. NW2 . . . . .3C **62**
Neville St. SW7 . . . . .5A **16** (5B **100**)
Neville Ter. SW7 . . . . .5A **16** (5B **100**)
Neville Wlk. SM5: Cars 7C **154**
Nevill La. EC4 . . . . .7K **7**
Nevill Rd. N16 . . . . .4E **66**
Nevin Dr. E4 . . . . .1J **35**
Nevin Ho. UB3: Harl 3E **92**
Nevinson Cl. SW18 . . . . .6B **118**
Nevis Cl. E13 . . . . .2K **87**
Nevis Rd. SW17 . . . . .2E **136**
Nevitt Ho. N1 . . . . .2D **84**
 (off Cranston Est.)
New Acres Rd. SE28 . . . . .2J **107**
NEW ADDINGTON 7F **171**
Newall Ho. SE1 . . . . .3C **102**
 (off Bath Ter.)
Newall Rd. TW6: H'row A 1E **110**
Newark Cres. NW10 . . . . .3K **79**
Newark Ho. SW9 . . . . .2B **120**
Newark Knok E6 . . . . .6E **88**
Newark Rd. CR2: S Croy 6D **168**
Newark St. E1 . . . . .5H **85**
 (not continuous)
New Ash Cl. N2 . . . . .3B **46**
New Atlas Wharf E14 . . . . .3C **104**
 (off Arnhem Pl.)
New Baltic Wharf SE8 . . . . .5A **104**
 (off Evelyn St.)
New Barn Cl. SM6: Wall 6K **167**
NEW BARNET 4G **21**
New Barn Rd. BR8: Swan 7K **145**
New Barns Av. CR4: Mitc 4H **155**
New Barn St. E13 . . . . .4J **87**
New Barns Way IG7: Chig 3K **37**
NEW BECKENHAM 6B **140**
New Bell Yd. EC4 . . . . .1B **14**
 (off Knightrider St.)
New Bentham Ct. N1 . . . . .7C **66**
 (off Ecclesbourne Rd.)
Newbery Ho. N1 . . . . .7C **66**
 (off Northampton St.)
Newbold Cotts. E1 . . . . .6J **85**
Newbolt Av. SM3: Cheam 5E **164**
Newbolt Ho. SE17 . . . . .5D **102**
 (off Brandon St.)

Newbolt Rd. HA7: Stan 5E **26**
New Bond St. W1 . . . . .1J **11** (6F **83**)
Newborough Grn. KT3: N Mald 4K **151**
New Brent St. NW4 . . . . .5E **44**
Newbridge Point SE23 . . . . .3K **139**
 (off Windrush La.)
New Bridge St. EC4 . . . . . . .1A **14** (6B **84**)
New Broad St. EC2 . . . . .6G **9** (5E **84**)
New Broadway
 TW12: Hamp H 5H **131**
 UB10: Hil 3D **74**
 W5 . . . . .7D **78**
New Broadway Bldgs. W5 . . . . .7D **78**
Newburgh Rd. W3 . . . . .1J **97**
Newburgh St. W1 . . . . .1B **12** (6G **83**)
New Burlington M. W1 . . . . .2A **12** (7G **83**)
New Burlington Pl. W1 . . . . .2A **12** (7G **83**)
New Burlington St. W1 . . . . .2A **12** (7G **83**)
Newburn Ho. SE11 . . . . .5H **19**
 (off Newburn St.)
Newburn St. SE11 . . . . .5H **19** (5K **101**)
Newbury Cl. UB5: N'olt 6D **58**
Newbury Ct. DA14: Sidc 4K **143**
 E5 . . . . .5A **68**
 (off Daubeney Rd.)
Newbury Gdns. KT19: Ewe 4B **164**
Newbury Ho. N22 . . . . .1J **47**
 SW9 .2B **120**
 W2 . . . . .6K **81**
 (off Hallfield Est.)
Newbury M. NW5 . . . . .6E **64**
NEWBURY PARK 5H **53**
Newbury Rd. BR2: Brom 3J **159**
 E4 . . . . .6K **35**
 IG2: Ilf .6J **53**
 TW6: H'row A 1B **110**
Newbury St. EC1 . . . . .6C **8** (5C **84**)
Newbury Way UB5: N'olt 6C **58**
New Bus. Centre, The NW10 . . . . . .3B **80**
New Butt La. SE8 . . . . .7C **104**
New Butt La. Nth. SE8 . . . . .7C **104**
 (off Hales St.)
Newby NW1 .2A **6**
 (off Robert St.)
Newby Cl. EN1: Enf 2K **23**
Newby Ho. E14 . . . . .7E **86**
 (off Newby Pl.)
Newby Pl. E14 . . . . .7E **86**
Newby St. SW8 . . . . .3F **119**
New Caledonian Mkt. SE1 . . . . . . .7H **15**
 (off Bermondsey Sq.)
New Caledonian Wharf SE16 . . . . .3B **104**
Newcastle Cl. EC4 . . . . .7A **8** (6B **84**)
Newcastle Ct. EC4 . . . . .2D **14**
 (off College Hill)
Newcastle Ho. W1 . . . . .5G **5**
 (off Luxborough St.)
Newcastle Pl. W2 . . . . .5B **4** (5B **82**)
Newcastle Row EC1 . . . . . . .4K **7** (4A **84**)
New Cavendish St. W1 . . . . .6H **5** (5E **82**)
New Century Ho. E16 . . . . .6H **87**
 (off Jude St.)
New Change EC4 . . . . .1C **14** (6C **84**)
New Change Pas. EC4 . . . . .1C **14**
 (off New Change)
New Chapel Sq. TW13: Felt 1K **129**
New Charles St. EC1 . . . . . . .1B **8** (3B **84**)
NEW CHARLTON 4A **106**
New Chiswick Pool 7A **98**
New Church Rd. SE5 . . . . .7C **102**
 (not continuous)
New City Rd. E13 . . . . .3A **88**
New Claremont Apartments SE1 . . .4F **103**
 (off Setchell Rd.)
New Clock Twr. Pl. N7 . . . . .6J **65**
New Cl. SW19 . . . . .3A **154**
 TW13: Hanw 5C **130**
New Colebrooke Ct. SM5: Cars . . .7D **166**
New College Ct. NW3 . . . . .6A **64**
 (off College Cres.)
New College M. N1 . . . . .7A **66**

New College Pde. NW3 . . . . .6B **64**
 (off Finchley Rd.)
Newcombe Gdns. SW16 . . . . .4J **137**
 TW4: Houn 4D **112**
Newcombe Ho. E5 . . . . .3H **67**
Newcombe Pk. HA0: Wemb 1F **79**
 NW7 . . . . .5F **29**
Newcombe Ri. UB7: View 6A **74**
Newcombe St. W8 . . . . .1J **99**
Newcomen Rd. E11 . . . . .3H **69**
 SW11 . . . . .3B **118**
Newcomen St. SE1 . . . . . . .6E **14** (2D **102**)
New Compton St. WC2 . . . .1D **12** (6H **83**)
New Concordia Wharf SE1 . . .6K **15** (2G **103**)
New Ct. EC4 . . . . .2J **13**
 UB5: N'olt 5F **59**
Newcourt Ho. E2 . . . . .3H **85**
 (off Pott St.)
Newcourt St. NW8 . . . . .1C **4** (2C **82**)
New Covent Garden Market
 .7D **18** (7H **101**)
New Crane Pl. E1 . . . . .1J **103**
New Crane Wharf E1 . . . . .1J **103**
 (off New Crane Pl.)
New Cres. Yd. NW10 . . . . .2B **80**
Newcroft Cl. UB8: Hil 5B **74**
Newcroft Ho. CR0: C'don 2F **169**
 (off Homefield Pl.)
NEW CROSS 7B **104**
NEW CROSS 1B **122**
NEW CROSS GATE 1K **121**
NEW CROSS GATE 1K **121**
New Cross Rd. SE14 . . . . .7J **103**
Newdales Cl. N9 . . . . .2B **34**
Newdene Av. UB5: N'olt 2B **76**
Newdigate Ho. E14 . . . . .6B **86**
 (off Norbiton Rd.)
New Diorama Theatre 4F **83**
Newell St. E14 . . . . .6B **86**
NEW ELTHAM 2G **143**
New End NW3 . . . . .3A **64**
New End Sq. NW3 . . . . .4B **64**
New England Ind. Est. IG11: Bark . . .2G **89**
Newent Cl. SE15 . . . . .7E **102**
 SM5: Cars 1D **166**
New Era Est. N1 . . . . .1E **84**
 (off Halcomb St.)
New Era Ho. N1 . . . . .1E **84**
 (off Halcomb St.)
New Farm Av. BR2: Brom 4J **159**
New Farm La. HA6: Nwood 1G **39**
New Festival Av. E14 . . . . .6C **86**
New Fetter La. EC4 . . . . .7K **7** (6A **84**)
Newfield Cl. TW12: Hamp 1E **148**
Newfield Ri. NW2 . . . . .3C **62**
New Forest La. IG7: Chig 6K **37**
Newgale Gdns. HA8: Edg 1F **43**
New Gdn. Dr. UB7: W Dray 2A **92**
Newgate CR0: C'don 1C **168**
Newgate Cl. TW13: Hanw 2C **130**
Newgate St. E4 . . . . .3B **36**
 (not continuous)
 EC1 . . . . .7B **8** (6B **84**)
New Globe Wlk. SE1 . . . . . .4C **14** (1C **102**)
New Goulston St. E1 . . . . . . .7J **9** (6F **85**)
New Grn. Pl. SE19 . . . . .6E **138**
New Gun Wharf E3 . . . . .1A **86**
 (off Gunmaker's La.)
Newhall Ct. N1 . . . . .1C **84**
 (off Popham Rd.)
Newham City Farm 6B **88**
Newham Dockside E16 . . . . .7C **88**
Newham Leisure Cen. 4A **88**
Newham's Row SE1 . . . . . . .7H **15** (3E **102**)
Newham Way E6 . . . . .5A **88**
 E16 . . . . .5H **87**
Newhaven Cl. UB3: Harl 4H **93**
Newhaven Cres. TW15: Ashf 5F **129**
Newhaven Gdns. SE9 . . . . .4B **124**
Newhaven La. E16 . . . . .4H **87**
Newhaven Rd. SE25 . . . . .5D **156**

New Heston Rd. TW5: Hest 7D **9**
New Hope Cl. NW10 . . . . .3D **8**
New Horizons Ct. TW8: Bford 6A **9**
Newhouse Av. RM6: Chad H 3D **5**
Newhouse Cl. KT3: N Mald 7A **15**
Newhouse Wlk. SM4: Mord 7A **15**
Newick Cl. DA5: Bexl 6H **12**
Newick Rd. E5 . . . . .4H **6**
Newing Grn. BR1: Brom 7B **14**
NEWINGTON 3C **10**
Newington Barrow Way N7 . . . . .3K **6**
Newington Butts SE1 . . . . .4B **10**
 SE11 .4B **10**
Newington C'way. SE1 . . . .7C **14** (3B **102**)
Newington Ct. N16 . . . . .4C **6**
 (off Green Lanes)
Newington Ct. Bus. Cen. SE1 . . . . . .7C **1**
Newington Grn. N1 . . . . .5D **6**
 N16 . . . . .5D **6**
Newington Grn. Community Gdns.
 N16 . . . . .5D **6**
 (off Newington Grn.)
Newington Grn. Mans. N16 . . . . .5D **6**
Newington Grn. Rd. N1 . . . . .6D **6**
Newington Ind. Est. SE17 . . . . .4B **10**
New In B'way. EC2 . . . . .3H **9** (4E **84**)
New Inn Pas. WC2 . . . . .1H **1**
New Inn Sq. EC2 . . . . .3H **9**
New Inn St. EC2 . . . . .3H **9** (4E **84**)
New Inn Yd. EC2 . . . . .3H **9** (4E **84**)
New Jubilee Ct. IG8: Wfd G 7D **3**
New Jubilee Wharf E1 . . . . .1J **10**
 (off Wapping Wa)
New Kelvin Av. TW11: Tedd 6J **13**
New Kent Rd. SE1 . . . . .3C **10**
New Kings Rd. SW6 . . . . .2H **11**
New King St. SE8 . . . . .6C **10**
Newland Apartments E16 . . . . .5J **8**
 (off Fords Pk. Ro)
Newland Ct. EC1 . . . . .2E **8**
 HA9: Wemb 2G **6**
Newland Dr. EN1: Enf 1C **2**
Newland Gdns. W13 . . . . .2A **9**
Newland Ho. N8 . . . . .3J **4**
 (off Newland Ro)
 SE14 . . . . .6K **10**
 (off John Williams C)
Newland Rd. N8 . . . . .3J **4**
NEWLANDS .3K **2**
Newlands HA1: Harr 1J **5**
 NW1 . . . . .1A **6**
 (off Harrington St)
Newlands, The KT7: T Ditt 7J **14**
 SM6: Wall 7G **16**
Newlands Av. KT7: T Ditt 7J **14**
Newlands Cl. HA0: Wemb 6C **6**
 HA8: Edg 3K **2**
 UB2: S'hall 5C **9**
Newlands Ct. SE9 . . . . .6E **12**
Newlands Dr. SL3: Poyle 6A **17**
Newlands Pk. SE26 . . . . .6J **13**
Newlands Pl. EN5: Barn 5A **2**
Newlands Quay E1 . . . . .7J **8**
Newlands Rd. IG8: Wfd G 2C **3**
 SW16 .2J **15**
Newland St. E16 . . . . .1C **10**
Newlands Way KT9: Chess 5C **16**
Newlands Woods CR0: Sels 7B **17**
Newling Cl. E6 . . . . .6D **8**
New London Performing Arts Cen. 4F **4**
New London St. EC3 . . . . .2H **1**
New London Theatre . . . . .7F **
 (off Parker St)
New Lydenburg Commercial Est.
 SE7 . . . . .3A **10**
New Lydenburg St. SE7 . . . . .3A **10**
Newlyn NW1 .1G **8**
 (off Plender St)
Newlyn Cl. BR6: Chels 4K **17**
 UB8: Hil 5C **7**

Newlyn Gdns. HA2: Harr 7D **40**
Newlyn Ho. HA5: Hat E 1D **40**
Newlyn Rd. DA16: Well 2K **125**
   EN5: Barn 4C **20**
   N17 . . . . .1F **49**
NEW MALDEN 4A **152**
Newman Cl. SE26 . . . . .4J **139**
Newman Ct. BR1: Brom 1J **159**
                   (off North St.)
   TW15: Ashf 6D **128**
Newman Ho. SE1 . . . . .3B **102**
Newman Pas. W1 . . . . .6B **6** (5G **83**)
Newman Rd. BR1: Brom 1J **159**
   CR0: C'don 1K **167**
   E13 . . . . .3K **87**
   E17 . . . . .5K **49**
   UB3: Hayes 7K **75**
Newman Rd. Ind. Est. CR0: C'don . .7K **155**
Newman's Ct. EC3 . . . . .1F **15**
Newmans La. KT6: Surb 6D **150**
Newman's Row WC2 . . . . . .6H **7** (5K **83**)
Newman St. W1 . . . . .6B **6** (5G **83**)
Newman's Way EN4: Had W 1F **21**
Newmarket Av. UB5: N'olt 5E **58**
Newmarket Grn. SE9 . . . . .7B **124**
Newmarsh Rd. SE28 . . . . .1K **107**
Newmill Ho. E3 . . . . .4E **86**
New Mill Way SW8 . . . . .6H **101**
Newminster Rd. SM4: Mord 6A **154**
New Mossford Way IG6: Ilf 4G **53**
New Mount St. E15 . . . . .7F **69**
Newnes Path SW15 . . . . .4D **116**
Newnham Av. HA4: Ruis 1A **58**
Newnham Cl. CR7: Thor H 2C **156**
   UB5: N'olt 6G **59**
Newnham Gdns. UB5: N'olt 6G **59**
Newnham Grn. N22 . . . . .1A **48**
                (off Highfield Cl.)
Newnham Lodge DA17: Belv 5G **109**
                 (off Erith Rd.)
Newnham M. N22 . . . . .7F **33**
Newnham Rd. N22 . . . . .1K **47**
Newnhams Cl. BR1: Brom 3D **160**
Newnham Ter. SE1 . . . . .1J **19** (3A **102**)
Newnham Way HA3: Kenton 5E **42**
New North Pl. EC2 . . . . . .2G **9** (4E **84**)
New North Rd. IG6: Ilf 1G **53**
   N1 . . . . .1F **9** (1C **84**)
New North St. WC1 . . . . . .5G **7** (5K **83**)
New Oak Rd. N2 . . . . .2A **46**
New Orleans Wlk. N19 . . . . .7H **47**
New Oxford St. WC1 . . . . . .7D **6** (6H **83**)
New Pde. TW15: Ashf 4B **128**
   UB7: Yiew 1A **92**
New Pk. Av. N13 . . . . .3H **33**
New Pk. Cl. UB5: N'olt 6C **58**
New Pk. Est. N18 . . . . .5D **34**
New Park Ho. N13 . . . . .4E **32**
New Pk. Pde. SW2 . . . . .7J **119**
               (off New Pk. Rd.)
New Pk. Rd. SW2 . . . . .1H **137**
   TW15: Ashf 5E **128**
New Pl. CR0: Addtn 6C **170**
New Pl. Sq. SE16 . . . . .3H **103**
New Plaistow Rd. E15 . . . . .1G **87**
New Pond Pde. HA4: Ruis 3J **57**
Newport Av. E13 . . . . .4K **87**
   E14 .7E **87**
Newport Ct. WC2 . . . . . . .2D **12** (7H **83**)
Newport Ho. E3 . . . . .3A **86**
               (off Strahan Rd.)
Newport Lodge EN1: Enf 5K **23**
               (off Village Rd.)
Newport Pl. WC2 . . . . . . .2D **12** (7H **83**)
Newport Rd. E10 . . . . .2E **68**
   E17 . . . . .4A **50**
   SW13 . . . . .1C **116**
   TW6: H'row A 1C **110**
   UB4: Hayes 5F **75**
   W3 . . . . .2J **97**

Newport St. SE11 . . . . .4G **19** (4K **101**)
New Priory Ct. NW6 . . . . .7J **63**
             (off Mazenod Av.)
New Providence Wharf E14 . . . . . .1F **105**
Newquay Cres. HA2: Harr 2C **58**
Newquay Ho. SE11 . . . . . . .5J **19** (5A **102**)
Newquay Rd. SE6 . . . . .2D **140**
New Quebec St. W1 . . . . . .1F **11** (6D **82**)
New Ride SW1 . . . . .2C **100**
   SW7 . . . . .6C **10** (2C **100**)
New River Av. N8 . . . . .3K **47**
New River Ct. N5 . . . . .4C **66**
New River Cres. N13 . . . . .4G **33**
New River Head EC1 . . . . .1K **7** (3A **84**)
New River Wlk. N1 . . . . .6C **66**
              (not continuous)
New River Way N4 . . . . .7D **48**
New Rd. CR4: Mitc 1D **166**
   DA16: Well 2B **126**
   E1 . . . . .5H **85**
   E4 . . . . .4J **35**
   HA1: Harr 4K **59**
   IG3: Ilf 2J **71**
   KT2: King T 7G **133**
   KT8: W Mole 4E **148**
   N8 . . . . .5J **47**
   N9 . . . . .2C **34**
   N17 . . . . .1F **49**
   N22 . . . . .1C **48**
   NW7 .7B **30**
   RM8: Dag 2G **91**
   RM10: Dag 2G **91**
   RM13: Rain 2G **91**
   SE2 .4D **108**
   TW3: Houn 4F **113**
   TW8: Bford 6D **96**
   TW10: Ham 4C **132**
   TW14: Harw 5C **130**
   TW14: Bedf 6F **111**
   TW14: Felt 1K **129**
   TW17: Shep 3C **146**
   UB3: Harl 7E **92**
   UB8: Hil 4E **74**
New Rd. Hill BR2: Kes 7C **172**
   BR6: Downe 7C **172**
New Rochford St. NW5 . . . . .5D **64**
New Row NW2 . . . . .3E **62**
   WC2 . . . . .2E **12** (7J **83**)
Newry Rd. TW1: Twick 5A **114**
Newsam Av. N15 . . . . .5D **48**
Newsholme Dr. N21 . . . . .5E **22**
NEW SOUTHGATE 5A **32**
New Southgate Crematorium
   N11 . . . . .3A **32**
New Southgate Ind. Est. N11 . . . . . .5B **32**
New Spitalfields Mkt. E10 . . . . .3C **68**
New Spring Gdns. Wlk.
   SE11 . . . . .6F **19** (5J **101**)
New Sq. TW14: Bedf 1E **128**
   WC2 . . . . .7J **7** (6A **84**)
New Sq. Pk. TW14: Bedf 1E **128**
New Sq. Pas. WC2 . . . . .7J **7**
Newstead Av. BR6: Orp 3H **173**
Newstead Cl. N12 . . . . .6H **31**
Newstead Ct. UB5: N'olt 3C **76**
Newstead Ho. N1 . . . . .2A **84**
              (off Tolpuddle St.)
Newstead Rd. SE12 . . . . .7H **123**
Newstead Wlk. SM5: Cars 7A **154**
Newstead Way SW19 . . . . .4F **135**
New St. EC2 . . . . .6H **9** (5E **84**)
New St. Hill BR1: Brom 5K **141**
New St. Sq. EC4 . . . . .7K **7** (6A **84**)
             (not continuous)
Newton Av. N10 . . . . .1E **46**
   W3 . . . . .2J **97**
Newton Cl. E17 . . . . .6A **50**
   HA2: Harr 2E **58**
Newton Ct. E3 . . . . .5C **86**
   NW6 .7A **64**
              (off Fairfax Rd.)

Newton Ct. SW17 . . . . .3B **136**
            (off Grosvenor Way)
   W8 . . . . .2J **99**
           (off Kensington Chu. St.)
Newton Gro. W4 . . . . .4A **98**
Newton Ho. E1 . . . . .7H **85**
              (off Cornwall St.)
   E17 . . . . .3D **50**
              (off Prospect Hill)
   EN3: Enf H 3E **24**
   NW8 .1K **81**
              (off Abbey Rd.)
   SE20 . . . . .7K **139**
Newton Ind. Est. RM6: Chad H 4D **54**
Newton Pl. E14 . . . . .4C **104**
Newton Rd. DA16: Well 3A **126**
   E15 . . . . .5F **69**
   HA0: Wemb 7F **61**
   HA3: H'row W 2J **41**
   N15 . . . . .5G **49**
   NW2 .4E **62**
   SW19 . . . . .7G **135**
   TW7: Isle 2K **113**
   W2 . . . . .6K **81**
Newton St. WC2 . . . . .7F **7** (6J **83**)
Newton's Yd. SW18 . . . . .5J **117**
Newton Ter. BR2: Brom 6B **160**
Newton Wlk. HA8: Edg 1H **43**
Newton Way N18 . . . . .5H **33**
New Tower Bldgs. E1 . . . . .1H **103**
Newtown St. SW11 . . . . .1F **119**
New Trinity Rd. N2 . . . . .3B **46**
New Turnstile WC1 . . . . .6G **7**
New Union Cl. E14 . . . . .3E **104**
New Union Sq. SW8 . . . . .6H **101**
New Union St. EC2 . . . . .6E **8** (5D **84**)
New Wanstead E11 . . . . .6H **51**
New Way Rd. NW9 . . . . .4A **44**
New Wharf Rd. N1 . . . . .2J **83**
New Willow Ho. E13 . . . . .2J **87**
             (off Plaistow Rd.)
NEWYEARS GREEN 7B **38**
New Years Grn. La. UB9: Hare 6A **38**
New Zealand Av. KT12: Walt T 7H **147**
New Zealand War Memorial 2E **100**
             (off Hyde Pk. Cnr.)
New Zealand Way W12 . . . . .7D **80**
Nexus Cl. TW14: Felt 5J **111**
Nexus Ct. E11 . . . . .1G **69**
   NW6 .3J **81**
Niagara Av. W5 . . . . .4C **96**
Niagara Cl. N1 . . . . .2C **84**
Niagra Ct. SE16 . . . . .3J **103**
              (off Canada Est.)
Nibthwaite Rd. HA1: Harr 5J **41**
Nice Bus. Pk. SE15 . . . . .6H **103**
Nicholas Cl. UB6: G'frd 2F **77**
Nicholas Cl. E13 . . . . .3K **87**
   N7 . . . . .5K **65**
   SE12 . . . . .1J **141**
            (off Corney Reach Way)
Nicholas Gdns. W5 . . . . .2D **96**
Nicholas La. EC4 . . . . .2F **15** (7D **84**)
             (not continuous)
Nicholas M. W4 . . . . .6A **98**
Nicholas Pas. EC4 . . . . .2F **15**
Nicholas Rd. CR0: Bedd 4J **167**
   E1 . . . . .4J **85**
   RM8: Dag 2F **73**
   W11 .7F **81**
Nicholas Stacey Ho. SE7 . . . . .5K **105**
            (off Frank Burton Cl.)
Nicholas Way HA6: Nwood 1E **38**
Nicholay Rd. N19 . . . . .1H **65**
             (not continuous)

Nichol Cl. N14 . . . . .1C **32**
Nicholes Rd. TW3: Houn 4E **112**
Nichol La. BR1: Brom 7J **141**
Nicholl Ho. N4 . . . . .1C **66**
Nicholls Av. UB8: Hil 4C **74**
Nicholsfield Wlk. N7 . . . . .5K **65**
Nicholls M. SW16 . . . . .4J **137**
Nicholls Point E15 . . . . .1J **87**
             (off Park Gro.)
Nicholl St. E2 . . . . .1G **85**
Nichols Cl. KT9: Chess 6C **162**
   N4 . . . . .1C **66**
             (off Osborne Rd.)
Nichols Ct. E2 . . . . .2F **85**
Nichols Grn. W5 . . . . .5E **78**
Nicholson Ct. E17 . . . . .4K **49**
   N17 . . . . .3F **49**
Nicholson Ho. SE17 . . . . .5D **102**
Nicholson M. KT1: King T 4E **150**
Nicholson Rd. CR0: C'don 1F **169**
Nicholson St. SE1 . . . .5A **14** (1B **102**)
Nickelby Apartments E15 . . . . .6F **69**
             (off Grove Cres. Rd.)
Nickelby Cl. SE28 . . . . .6C **90**
Nicklebv Cl. UB8: Hil 6D **74**
Nickleby Ho. SE16 . . . . .2K **103**
             (off Parkers Row)
   W11 .1F **99**
             (off St Ann's Rd.)
Nickols Wlk. SW18 . . . . .4K **117**
Nicola Cl. CR2: S Croy 6C **168**
   HA3: H'row W 2H **41**
Nicola Ter. DA7: Bex 1E **126**
Nicol Cl. TW1: Twick 6B **114**
Nicoll Cl. N10 . . . . .7A **32**
   NW10 . . . . .1A **80**
Nicoll Pl. NW4 . . . . .6D **44**
Nicoll Rd. NW10 . . . . .1A **80**
Nicolson NW9 . . . . .1A **44**
Nicolson Dr. WD23: B Hea 1B **26**
Nicosia Rd. SW18 . . . . .7C **118**
Niederwald Rd. SE26 . . . . .4A **140**
Nield Rd. UB3: Hayes 2H **93**
Nigel Cl. UB5: N'olt 1C **76**
Nigel Cl. N3 . . . . .7E **30**
Nigel Fisher Way KT9: Chess 7C **162**
Nigel Ho. EC1 . . . . .5J **7**
             (off Portpool La.)
Nigel M. IG1: Ilf 4F **71**
Nigel Playfair Av. W6 . . . . .4D **98**
Nigel Rd. E7 . . . . .5A **70**
   SE15 . . . . .3G **121**
Nigeria Rd. SE7 . . . . .7A **106**
Nighthawk NW9 . . . . .1B **44**
Nightingale Av. E4 . . . . .5B **36**
   HA1: Harr 7B **42**
Nightingale Cl. E4 . . . . .4A **36**
   HA5: Eastc 5A **40**
   SM5: Cars 2E **166**
   W4 . . . . .6J **97**
Nightingale Cl.
   BR2: Brom 2G **159**
   E14 .2E **104**
              (off Ovex Cl.)
   HA1: Harr 6K **41**
   N4 . . . . .2K **65**
             (off Tollington Pk.)
   SM1: Sutt 5A **166**
   SW6 .1K **117**
             (off Maltings Pl.)
Nightingale Dr. KT19: Ewe 6H **163**
Nightingale Gro. SE13 . . . . .5F **123**
Nightingale Hgts. SE18 . . . . .6F **107**
Nightingale Ho. E1 . . . . .1G **103**
            (off Thomas More St.)
   E2 . . . . .1E **84**
             (off Kingsland Rd.)
   NW8 .4C **4**
             (off Samford St.)
   SE18 . . . . .5E **106**
             (off Connaught M.)

Nightingale Ho. UB7: W Dray 2B 92
  W12 ....6E 80
  (off Du Cane Rd.)
Nightingale La. BR1: Brom 2A 160
  E11 ....4K 51
  N8 ....4J 47
  SW4 ....7D 118
  SW12 ....7D 118
  TW10: Rich 7E 114
Nightingale Lodge W9 ....5J 81
  (off Admiral Wlk.)
Nightingale M. E3 ....2K 85
  E11 ....5J 51
  KT1: King T 3D 150
  (off South La.)
  SE11 ....3K 19 (4B 102)
Nightingale Pl. SE18 ....6E 106
  SW10 ....7A 16 (6A 100)
Nightingale Rd. BR5: Pet W 6G 161
  E5 ....3H 67
  KT8: W Mole 5F 149
  KT12: Walt T 7A 148
  N1 ....6C 66
  N9 ....6D 24
  N22 ....1J 47
  NW10 ....2B 80
  SM5: Cars 3D 166
  TW12: Hamp 5E 130
  W7 ....1K 95
Nightingales, The TW19: Stanw 1B 128
Nightingale Sq. SW12 ....7E 118
Nightingale Va. SE18 ....6E 106
Nightingale Wlk. N1 ....6C 66
  SW4 ....6F 119
Nightingale Way E6 ....5C 88
Nile Cl. N16 ....3F 67
Nile Dr. N9 ....2D 34
Nile Ho. N1 ....1E 8
  (off Nile St.)
Nile Path SE18 ....6E 106
Nile Rd. E13 ....2A 88
Nile St. N1 ....1D 8 (3C 84)
Nile Ter. SE15 ....5F 103
Nimegen Way SE22 ....5E 120
Nimmo Dr. WD23: B Hea 1C 26
Nimrod NW9 ....1A 44
Nimrod Cl. UB5: N'olt 3B 76
Nimrod Ho. E16 ....5K 87
  (off Vanguard Cl.)
Nimrod Pas. N1 ....6E 66
Nimrod Rd. SW16 ....6F 137
Nina Mackay Cl. E15 ....1G 87
Nine Acres Cl. E12 ....5C 70
  UB3: Harl 3E 92
NINE ELMS 7G 101
Nine Elms Cl. TW14: Felt 1H 129
Nine Elms La. SW8 ....7C 18 (7G 101)
Nineteenth Rd. CR4: Mitc 4J 155
Ninhams Wood BR6: Farnb 4E 172
Ninth Av. UB3: Hayes 7J 75
Nipper All. KT1: King T 2E 150
  (off Clarence St.)
Nipponzan Myohoji Peace Pagoda ...6D 100
Nisbet Ho. E9 ....5K 67
Nisbett Wlk. DA14: Sidc 4A 144
  (off Sidcup High St.)
Nita Ct. SE12 ....1J 141
Nithdale Rd. SE18 ....7F 107
Nithsdale Gro. UB10: Ick 3E 56
Niton Cl. EN5: Barn 6A 20
Niton Rd. TW9: Rich 3G 115
Niton St. SW6 ....7F 99
Niveda Cl. N12 ....2C 98
No 1 St. SE18 ....3F 107
Noah Cl. EN3: Enf W 1D 24
Nobel Dr. UB3: Harl 1F 111
Nobel Ho. SE5 ....2C 120
Nobel Rd. N18 ....4D 34
Noble Cnr. TW5: Hest 1E 112
Noble Ct. CR4: Mitc 2B 154
  E1 ....7H 85

Noblefield Hgts. N2 ....5C 46
Noble M. N16 ....3D 66
  (off Albion Rd.)
Noble St. EC2 ....7C 8 (6C 84)
Noble Yd. N1 ....1B 84
  (off Camden Pas.)
Nocavia Ho. SW6 ....2A 118
  (off Townmead Rd.)
Noel NW9 ....1A 44
Noel Cl. CR0: C'don 7D 156
  TW4: Houn 3D 112
Noel Coward Ho. SW1 ....4B 18
  (off Vauxhall Bri. Rd.)
Noel Coward Theatre 2E 12
  (off St Martin's La.)
Noel Ho. NW6 ....7B 64
  (off Harben Rd.)
NOEL PARK 2B 48
Noel Pk. Rd. N22 ....2A 48
Noel Rd. E6 ....4C 88
  N1 ....2B 84
  W3 ....7G 79
Noel Sq. RM8: Dag 4C 72
Noel St. W1 ....1B 12 (6G 83)
Noel Ter. DA14: Sidc 4B 144
  SE23 ....2J 139
Noko W10 ....3F 81
Nolands Cl. RM5: Col R 2J 55
Nolan Way E5 ....4G 67
Noll Ho. N7 ....2K 65
  (off Tomlins Wlk.)
Nolton Pl. HA8: Edg 1F 43
Nonsuch Ho. SW19 ....1B 154
  (off Chapter Way)
Nonsuch Pl. SM3: Cheam 1G 165
  (off Ewell Rd.)
Nonsuch Wlk. SM2: Cheam 7F 165
  (not continuous)
Nook Apartments E1 ....1K 15
  (off Scarborough St.)
Nora Gdns. NW4 ....4F 45
Nora Leverton Ct. NW1 ....7G 65
  (off Randolph St.)
NORBITON 2G 151
Norbiton Av. KT1: King T 1G 151
Norbiton Comn. Rd. KT1: King T ..3H 151
Norbiton Hall KT2: King T 2F 151
Norbiton Ho. NW1 ....1G 83
  (off Camden St.)
Norbiton Rd. E14 ....6B 86
Norbreck Gdns. NW10 ....3F 79
Norbreck Pde. NW10 ....3E 78
Norbroke St. W12 ....7B 80
Norburn St. W10 ....5G 81
NORBURY 1K 155
Norbury Av. CR7: Thor H 1K 155
  SW16 ....1K 155
  TW3: Houn 4H 113
Norbury Cl. SW16 ....1A 156
Norbury Ct. Rd. SW16 ....3J 155
Norbury Cres. SW16 ....1K 155
Norbury Cross SW16 ....3J 155
Norbury Gdns. RM6: Chad H 5D 54
Norbury Gro. NW7 ....3F 29
Norbury Hill SW16 ....7A 138
Norbury Ri. SW16 ....3J 155
Norbury Rd. CR7: Thor H 2C 156
  E4 ....5A 35
  TW13: Felt 3H 129
Norbury Trad. Est. SW16 ....2K 155
Norcombe Gdns. HA3: Kenton 6C 42
Norcombe Ho. N19 ....3H 65
  (off Wedmore St.)
Norcott Cl. UB4: Yead 4A 76
Norcott Rd. N16 ....2G 67
Norcroft Gdns. SE22 ....7G 121
Norcutt Rd. TW2: Twick 1J 131
Nordenfeldt Rd.
  DA8: Erith 5K 109
Norden Ho. E2 ....3H 85
  (off Pott St.)

Norfold Rd. DA2: Wilm 4J 145
Norfolk Apartments E4 ....7J 35
Norfolk Av. N13 ....6G 33
  N15 ....6F 49
Norfolk Cl. EN4: Cockf 4K 21
  N2 ....3C 46
  N13 ....6G 33
  TW1: Twick 6B 114
Norfolk Ct. EN5: Barn 4B 20
  RM6: Chad H 5B 54
  (off Norwich Cres.)
Norfolk Cres. DA15: Sidc 7J 125
  W2 ....7C 4 (6C 82)
Norfolk Gdns. DA7: Bex 1F 127
Norfolk Ho. BR2: Brom 4H 159
  (off Westmoreland Rd.)
  EC4 ....2C 14
  SE8 ....1C 122
  (off Brookmill Rd.)
  SE20 ....1J 157
  SW1 ....3D 18
  (off Page St.)
Norfolk Ho. Rd. SW16 ....3H 137
Norfolk Mans. SW11 ....1D 118
  (off Prince of Wales Dr.)
Norfolk M. W10 ....5G 81
  (off Blagrove Rd.)
Norfolk Pl. DA16: Well 2A 126
  W2 ....7B 4 (6B 82)
  (not continuous)
Norfolk Rd. CR7: Thor H 3C 156
  E6 ....1D 88
  E17 ....2K 49
  EN3: Pond E 6C 24
  EN5: New Bar 3D 20
  HA1: Harr 5F 41
  IG3: Ilf 1J 71
  IG11: Bark 7J 71
  NW8 ....1B 82
  NW10 ....7A 62
  RM7: Rom 6J 55
  RM10: Dag 5H 73
  SW19 ....7C 136
  TW13: Felt 1A 130
  UB8: Uxb 6A 56
Norfolk Row SE1 ....3G 19 (4K 101)
Norfolk Sq. W2 ....1B 10 (6B 82)
Norfolk Sq. M. W2 ....1B 10
Norfolk St. E7 ....5J 69
Norfolk Ter. W6 ....5G 99
Norgrove St. SW12 ....7E 118
Norhyrst Av. SE25 ....3F 157
Norland Ho. W11 ....1F 99
  (off Queensdale Cres.)
Norland Pl. W11 ....1G 99
Norland Pl. School W11 ....1F 99
Norlands Cres.
  BR7: Chst 1F 161
Norlands Ga. BR7: Chst 1F 161
Norland Sq. W11 ....1G 99
Norland Sq. Mans. W11 ....1G 99
  (off Norland Sq.)
Norley Va. SW15 ....1C 134
Norlington Rd. E10 ....1E 68
  E11 ....1E 68
Norman Av. N22 ....1B 48
  TW1: Twick 7C 114
  TW13: Hanw 2C 130
  UB1: S'hall 7C 76
Norman Butler Ho. W10 ....4G 81
  (off Ladbroke Gro.)
Normanby Cl. SW15 ....5H 117
Normanby Rd. NW10 ....4B 62
Norman Cl. BR6: Farnb 3G 173
  N22 ....1C 48
  RM5: Col R 1H 55
Norman Ct. IG2: Ilf 7H 53
  N3 ....1J 45
  (off Nether St.)
  N4 ....7A 48
  NW10 ....7C 62

Norman Ct. W13 ....1B 96
  (off Kirkfield Cl.)
Norman Cres. HA5: Pinn 1A 40
  TW5: Hest 7B 94
Normand Gdns. W14 ....6G 99
  (off Greyhound Rd.)
Normand Mans. W14 ....6G 99
  (off Normand M.)
Norman M. W14 ....6G 99
Normand Rd. W14 ....6H 99
Normandy Av. EN5: Barn 5C 20
Normandy Cl. SE26 ....3A 140
Normandy Dr. UB3: Hayes 7F 75
Normandy Ho. E14 ....2E 104
  (off Plevna St.)
  EN2: Enf 1H 23
Normandy Pl. W12 ....1F 99
Normandy Rd. SW9 ....1A 120
Normandy Ter. E16 ....6K 87
Normandy Way DA8: Erith 1K 127
Norman Gro. E3 ....2A 86
Norman Hay Trad. Estate, The
  UB7: Sip 7B 92
Norman Ho. SE1 ....7H 15
  (off Riley Rd.)
  SW8 ....7J 101
  (off Wyvil Rd.)
  TW13: Hanw 2C 130
  (off Watermill Way)
Normanhurst TW15: Ashf 5C 128
Normanhurst Av. DA7: Bex 1D 126
Normanhurst Dr. TW1: Twick 5A 114
Normanhurst Rd. SW2 ....2K 137
Norman Leddy Memorial Gdns. 6H 71
Norman Pde. DA14: Sidc 2D 144
Norman Park Athletics Track 6K 159
Norman Rd. CR7: Thor H 5B 156
  DA17: Belv 3H 109
  (not continuous)
  E6 ....4D 88
  E11 ....2F 69
  IG1: Ilf 5F 71
  N15 ....5F 49
  SE10 ....7D 104
  SM1: Sutt 5J 165
  SW19 ....7A 136
  TW15: Ashf 6F 129
Normans Cl. NW10 ....6K 61
  UB8: Hill 5B 74
Normansfield Av. TW11: Tedd 7C 132
Normanshire Dr. E4 ....4H 35
Norman's Mead NW10 ....6K 61
Norman St. EC1 ....2D 8 (3C 84)
Norman Ter. NW6 ....5H 63
Normanton Av. SW19 ....2J 135
Normanton Cl. CR2: S Croy 5E 168
  (off Croham Rd.)
Normanton Pk. E4 ....2B 36
Normanton Rd. CR2: S Croy 5E 168
Normanton St. SE23 ....2K 139
Norman Way N14 ....2D 32
  W3 ....5H 79
Normington Cl. SW16 ....5A 138
Norrice Lea N2 ....5B 46
Norris NW9 ....1B 44
  (off Withers Mead)
Norris Ho. E9 ....1J 85
  (off Handley Rd.)
  N1 ....1E 84
  (off Colville St.)
  SE8 ....5B 104
  (off Grove St.)
  TW7: Isle 2A 114
Norris St. SW1 ....3C 12 (7H 83)
Norroy Rd. SW15 ....4F 117
Norry's Cl. EN4: Cockf 4J 21
Norry's Rd. EN4: Cockf 4J 21
Norseman Cl. IG3: Ilf 1B 72
Norseman Way UB6: G'frd 1F 77
Norstead Pl. SW15 ....2C 134
Nth. Access Rd. E17 ....6K 49

North Acre—Nth. Tenter St.

North Acre NW9 1A 44
NORTH ACTON 4K 79
Nth. Acton Bus. Pk. W3 5K 79
Nth. Acton Rd. NW10 2K 79
Northall Rd. DA7: Bex 2J 127
Northampton Gro. N1 5D 66
Northampton Pk. N1 6C 66
Northampton Rd. CR0: C'don 2G 169
EC1 3K 7 (4A 84)
EN3: Pond E 4F 25
Northampton Row EC1 3K 7
Northampton Sq. EC1 2A 8 (3B 84)
Northampton St. N1 7C 66
Northanger Rd. SW16 6J 137
Nth. Audley St. W1 1G 11 (7E 82)
North Av. HA2: Harr 6F 41
N18 4B 34
SM5: Cars 7E 166
TW9: Kew 1G 115
UB1: S'hall 7D 76
UB3: Hayes 7J 75
W13 5B 78
Northaw Ho. W10 4E 80
(off Sutton Way)
North Bank NW8 2C 4 (3C 82)
Northbank Rd. E17 2E 50
NORTH BECKTON 5D 88
Nth. Birkbeck Rd. E11 3F 69
North Block SE1 6H 13
(off Chicheley St.)
Northborough Rd. SW16 3H 155
Northbourne BR2: Hayes 7J 159
Northbourne Rd. SW4 5H 119
Northbrook Dr. HA6: Nwood 1G 39
Northbrook Rd. CR0: C'don 5D 156
EN5: Barn 6B 20
IG1: Ilf 2E 70
N22 7D 32
SE13 5G 123
Northburgh St. EC1 4B 8 (4B 84)
Northbury Cl. IG11: Bark 7G 71
Nth. Carriage Dr. W2 2C 10
NORTH CHEAM 3E 164
Northchurch SE17 5D 102
(not continuous)
Northchurch Ho. E2 1G 85
(off Whiston Rd.)
Northchurch Rd. HA9: Wemb 6G 61
N1 7D 66
(not continuous)
Northchurch Ter. N1 7E 66
Nth. Circular Rd. E4 6G 35
E12 3E 70
E18 2H 51
IG1: Ilf 4E 70
IG11: Bark 4E 70
N3 4H 45
N12 4H 45
N13 5F 33
NW2 3A 62
NW4 7E 44
NW10 2F 79
NW11 7E 44
Northcliffe Cl. KT4: Wor Pk 3A 164
Northcliffe Dr. N20 1C 30
North Cl. DA6: Bex 4D 126
RM10: Dag 1G 91
SM4: Mord 4G 153
TW14: Bedf 6F 111
Nth. Colonnade, The E14 1C 104
(not continuous)
North Comn. Rd. UB8: Uxb 5A 56
W5 7E 78
Northcote HA5: Pinn 2A 40
Northcote Av. KT5: Surb 7H 151
TW7: Isle 5A 114
UB1: S'hall 7C 76
W5 7E 78
Northcote Rd. CR0: C'don 6D 156
DA14: Sidc 4J 143
E17 4A 50
Northcote Rd. KT3: N Mald 3J 151
NW10 7A 62
SW11 5C 118
TW1: Twick 5A 114
Northcott Av. N22 1J 47
Nth. Countess Rd. E17 2B 50
North Ct. BR1: Brom 1K 159
(off Palace Gro.)
SE24 3B 120
SW1 2E 18
(off Gt. Peter St.)
W1 5B 6 (5G 83)
NORTH CRAY 5E 144
Nth. Cray Rd. DA5: Bexl 1H 145
DA14: Sidc 6E 144
North Cray Woods 4D 144
North Cres. E16 4F 87
N3 2H 45
WC1 5C 6 (5H 83)
Northcroft Ct. W12 2C 98
Northcroft Rd. KT19: Ewe 7A 164
W13 2B 96
North Crofts SE23 1H 139
Northcroft Ter. W13 2B 96
Nth. Cross Rd. IG6: Ilf 4G 53
SE22 5F 121
Northdale Ct. SE25 3F 157
North Dene NW7 3E 28
TW3: Houn 1F 113
Northdene Gdns. N15 6F 49
Northdown Cl. HA4: Ruis 3H 57
Northdown Gdns. IG2: Ilf 5J 53
Northdown Rd. DA16: Well 2B 126
Northdown St. N1 1G 7 (2J 83)
North Dr. BR3: Beck 4D 158
BR6: Orp 4J 173
HA4: Ruis 7G 39
SW16 4G 137
TW3: Houn 2G 113
North E. Surrey Crematorium
SM4: Mord 6E 152
NORTH END 2A 64
North End CR0: C'don 2C 168
IG9: Buck H 1F 37
NW3 2A 64
North End Av. NW3 2A 64
North End Cres. W14 4H 99
North End Ho. W14 4G 99
North End La. BR6: Downe 7F 173
North End Pde. W14 4G 99
(off North End Rd.)
North End Rd. HA9: Wemb 3G 61
NW11 1J 63
SW6 4G 99
W14 4G 99
North End Way NW3 2A 64
Northern Av. N9 2K 33
Northernhay Wlk. SM4: Mord 4G 153
Northern Hgts. N8 7H 47
(off Crescent Rd.)
Northern La. E2 2G 85
(off Kay St.)
Northern Perimeter Rd.
TW6: H'row A 1D 110
Northern Perimeter Rd. (West)
TW6: H'row A 4E 174
Northern Rd. E13 2K 87
Northesk Ho. E1 4H 85
(off Tent St.)
Nth. Eyot Gdns. W6 5B 98
Northey St. E14 7A 86
NORTH FELTHAM 6K 111
Nth. Feltham Trad. Est. TW14: Felt 5K 111
Northfield Av. HA5: Pinn 4B 40
W5 1B 96
W13 1B 96
Northfield Cl. BR1: Brom 1C 160
UB3: Harl 3H 93
Northfield Cres. SM3: Cheam 4G 165
Northfield Gdns. RM9: Dag 4F 73
Northfield Ho. SE15 6G 103
Northfield Pde. UB3: Harl 3G 93
Northfield Pk. UB3: Harl 3H 93
Northfield Path RM9: Dag 4F 73
Northfield Rd. E6 7D 70
EN3: Pond E 5C 24
EN4: Cockf 3H 21
N16 7E 48
RM9: Dag 4F 73
TW5: Hest 6B 94
W13 2B 96
NORTHFIELDS 3B 96
Northfields SW18 4J 117
Northfields Ind. Est. HA0: Wemb 1G 79
Northfields Prospect Bus. Cen.
SW18 4J 117
Northfields Rd. W3 5H 79
NORTH FINCHLEY 5F 31
Northfleet Ho. SE1 6E 14
(off Tennis St.)
Northflock St. SE16 2G 103
Nth. Flower Wlk. W2 3A 10
North Gdn. E14 1B 104
North Gdns. SW19 7B 136
North Gate NW8 1C 4
Northgate HA6: Nwood 1E 38
Northgate Bus. Cen. EN1: Enf 3C 24
Northgate Ct. SW9 3A 120
Northgate Dr. NW9 6A 44
Northgate Ho. E14 7C 86
(off E. India Dock Rd.)
Northgate Ind. Pk. RM5: Col R 1F 55
North Gates N12 1A 46
(off Bow La.)
Nth. Glade, The DA5: Bexl 7F 127
Nth. Gower St. NW1 2B 6 (3G 83)
North Grn. NW9 7F 29
North Gro. N6 7E 46
N15 5D 48
NORTH HARROW 5F 41
Nth. Hatton Rd. TW6: H'row A 1F 111
North Hill N6 6D 46
North Hill Av. N6 6E 46
NORTH HILLINGDON 7E 56
North Ho. SE8 5B 104
Nth. Hyde Gdns. UB3: Harl, Hayes 4J 93
Nth. Hyde La. TW5: Hest 5C 94
UB2: S'hall 5B 94
Nth. Hyde Rd. UB3: Harl, Hayes 3G 93
Northiam N12 4D 30
(not continuous)
WC1 2F 7
(off Cromer St.)
Northiam St. E9 1H 85
Northington St. WC1 4H 7 (4K 83)
NORTH KENSINGTON 5E 80
North Kent Indoor Bowls Club 3H 109
Northlands Av. BR6: Orp 4J 173
Northlands St. SE5 2C 120
North La. TW11: Tedd 6K 131
Northleigh Ho. E3 3D 86
(off Powis Rd.)
North Lodge E16 1K 105
(off Wesley Av.)
EN5: New Bar 5F 21
Nth. Lodge Cl. SW15 5F 117
Nth. London Bus. Pk. N11 2K 31
North Mall N9 2C 34
(within Edmonton Grn. Shop. Cen.)
SW18 5K 117
(off Southside Shop. Cen.)
North M. WC1 4H 7 (4K 83)
North Middlesex Golf Course 3G 31
North Mill Apartments E8 1F 85
(off Lovelace St.)
North Mt. N20 2F 31
(off High Rd.)
Northolm HA8: Edg 4E 28
Northolme Gdns. HA8: Edg 1G 43
Northolme Ri. BR6: Orp 2J 173
Northolme Rd. N5 4C 66
NORTHOLT 7E 58
Northolt N17 2E 48
(off Griffin Rd.)
Northolt Av. HA4: Ruis 5K 57
Northolt Gdns. UB6: G'frd 5K 59
Northolt Golf Course 2C 76
Northolt Leisure Cen. 6E 58
Northolt Rd. HA2: Harr 4F 59
TW6: H'row A 1A 110
(not continuous)
Northolt Trad. Est. UB5: N'olt 7F 59
Northover BR1: Brom 3H 141
North Pde. HA8: Edg 2G 43
KT9: Chess 5F 163
UB1: S'hall 6E 76
(off North Rd.)
North Pk. SE9 6D 124
North Pas. SW18 5J 117
North Pl. CR4: Mitc 7D 136
TW11: Tedd 6K 131
North Point N8 5K 47
Northpoint Cl. SM1: Sutt 3A 166
Northpoint Ho. N1 6D 66
(off Essex Rd.)
Northpoint Sq. NW1 6H 65
Nth. Pole La. BR2: Kes 6H 171
Nth. Pole Rd. W10 5E 80
Northport St. N1 1D 84
North Quay Pl. E14 7D 86
North Ride W2 3C 10 (7C 82)
North Ri. W2 1D 10 (6C 82)
North Rd. BR1: Brom 1K 159
BR4: W W'ck 1D 170
DA17: Belv 3H 109
HA1: Harr 7A 42
HA8: Edg 1H 43
IG3: Ilf 2J 71
KT6: Surb 6D 150
N6 7E 46
N7 6J 65
N9 1C 34
RM6: Chad H 5E 54
SE18 4J 107
SW19 6A 136
TW5: Hest 6A 94
TW8: Bford 6E 96
TW9: Kew, Rich 3G 115
TW14: Bedf 6F 111
UB1: S'hall 6E 76
UB3: Hayes 5F 75
UB7: W Dray 3B 92
W5 3D 96
Northrop Rd. TW6: H'row A 1G 111
North Row W1 2F 11 (7D 82)
Nth. Row Bldgs. W1 2G 11
(off North Row)
North Several SE3 2F 123
NORTH SHEEN 3G 115
Northside Rd. BR1: Brom 1J 159
Northside Studios E8 1H 85
(off Andrew's Rd.)
Nth. Side Wandsworth Comn.
SW18 5B 118
Northspur Rd. SM1: Sutt 3J 165
North Sq. N9 2C 34
(off New Rd.)
NW11 5J 45
North Stand N5 3B 66
Northstead Rd. SW2 2A 138
North St. BR1: Brom 1J 159
DA7: Bex 4G 127
E13 2K 87
IG11: Bark 6F 71
NW4 5E 44
RM1: Rom 3K 55
(not continuous)
RM5: Rom 3K 55
SM5: Cars 3D 166
SW4 3G 119
TW7: Isle 3A 114
North St. Pas. E13 2K 87
Nth. Tenter St. E1 1K 15 (6F 85)

A-Z London 351

North Ter. SW3 . . . . .2C 16 (3C 100)
  WC2 . . . . 4E 12
Northumberland All. EC3 . . . . .1H 15 (6E 84)
  (not continuous)
Northumberland Av. DA16: Well 4H 125
  E12 . . . . .1A 70
  EN1: Enf 1C 24
  TW7: Isle 1K 113
  WC2 . . . . .4E 12 (1J 101)
Northumberland Cl. DA8: Erith 7J 109
  TW19: Stanw 6A 110
Northumberland Cres. TW14: Felt 6G 111
Northumberland Gdns. BR1: Brom 4E 160
  CR4: Mitc 5H 155
  N9 . . . . .3A 34
  TW7: Isle 7A 96
Northumberland Gro. N17 . . . . .7C 34
NORTHUMBERLAND HEATH 7J 109
Northumberland Ho. IG8: Wfd G 7K 37
  SW1 . . . . .4E 12
  (off Northumberland Av.)
Northumberland Pk. DA8: Erith 7J 109
  N17 . . . . .7A 34
Northumberland Pk. Ind. Est. N17 . . . .7C 34
Northumberland Pk. School Sports Cen.
  . . . . .7B 34
Northumberland Pl. TW10: Rich 5D 114
  W2 . . . . .6J 81
Northumberland Rd. E6 . . . . .6C 88
  E17 . . . . .7C 50
  EN5: New Bar 6F 21
  HA2: Harr 5D 40
Northumberland St. WC2 . . . . .4E 12 (1J 101)
Northumberland Way DA8: Erith 1J 127
Northumbria St. E14 . . . . .6C 86
Nth. Verbena Gdns. W6 . . . . .5C 98
North Vw. HA5: Eastc 7A 40
  SW19 . . . . .5E 134
  W5 . . . . .4C 78
North Vw. Caravan Site IG6: Ilf 1A 54
Northview Cres. NW10 . . . . .4B 62
North Vw. Dr. IG8: Wfd G 2B 52
Northview Pde. N7 . . . . .3J 65
North Vw. Rd. N8 . . . . .2H 47
North Vs. NW1 .6H 65
North Wlk. CR0: New Ad 6D 170
  (not continuous)
  W2 . . . . .7K 81
  W8 . . . . .7K 81
  (off The Broad Wlk.)
Northwall Rd. E20 . . . . .5C 68
North Way HA5: Pinn 4B 40
  N9 . . . . .2E 34
  N11 . . . . .6B 32
  NW9 . . . . .3H 43
  UB10: Uxb 7A 56
Northway NW11 . . . . .5K 45
  SM4: Mord 3G 153
  SM6: Wall 4G 167
Northway Cir. NW7 . . . . .4E 28
Northway Ct. NW7 . . . . .4F 29
Northway Cres. NW7 . . . . .4E 28
Northway Gdns. NW11 . . . . .5K 45
Northway Rd. CR0: C'don 6F 157
  SE5 . . . . .3C 120
Northways NW3 . . . . .7B 64
  (off College Cres.)
Northways Pde. NW3 . . . . .7B 64
  (off College Cres., not continuous)
Northweald La. KT2: King T 5D 132
NORTH WEMBLEY 3D 60
Northwest Pl. N1 . . . . .2A 84
North Wharf E14 . . . . .1E 104
  (off Coldharbour)
Nth. Wharf Rd. W2 . . . . .6A 4 (5B 82)
Northwick Av. HA3: Kenton 6A 42
Northwick Circ. HA3: Kenton 6C 42
Northwick Cl. HA1: Harr 1B 60
  NW8 . . . . .3A 4 (4B 82)
Northwick Ho. NW8 . . . . .3A 4
Northwick Pk. Playgolf 1A 60

Northwick Pk. Rd. HA1: Harr 6K 41
NORTHWICK PARK RDBT. 7A 42
Northwick Rd. HA0: Wemb 1D 78
Northwick Ter. NW8 . . . . .3A 4 (4B 82)
Northwick Wlk. HA1: Harr 7K 41
Northwold Dr. HA5: Pinn 2A 40
Northwold Rd. E5 . . . . .2F 67
  N16 . . . . .2F 67
NORTHWOOD 1H 39
Nth. Wood Ct. SE25 . . . . .3G 157
Northwood Est. E5 . . . . .2G 67
Northwood Gdns. IG5: Ilf 4E 52
  N12 . . . . .5G 31
  UB6: G'frd 5K 59
Northwood Golf Course 1F 39
Northwood Hall N6 . . . . .7G 47
NORTHWOOD HILLS 2J 39
Northwood Hills Cir. HA6: Nwood 1J 39
Northwood Ho. KT2: King T 2G 151
  (off Coombe Rd.)
  SE27 . . . . .4D 138
Northwood Pl. DA18: Erith 3F 109
Northwood Rd. CR7: Thor H 2B 156
  N6 . . . . .7F 47
  SE23 . . . . .1B 140
  SM5: Cars 6E 166
  TW6: H'row A 4E 174
  UB9: Hare 1A 38
Northwood Way HA6: Nwood 1J 39
  SE19 . . . . .6D 138
  UB9: Hare 1A 38
NORTH WOOLWICH 2E 106
Nth. Woolwich Rd. E16 . . . . .1H 105
Nth. Worple Way SW14 . . . . .3K 115
Norton Av. KT5: Surb 7H 151
Norton Cl. E4 . . . . .5H 35
  EN1: Enf 2C 24
Norton Ct. BR3: Beck 1B 158
Norton Folgate E1 . . . . .5H 9 (5E 84)
Norton Folgate Ho. E1 . . . . .5J 9
  (off Puma Ct.)
Norton Gdns. SW16 . . . . .2J 155
Norton Ho. E1 . . . . .6H 85
  (off Bigland St.)
  E2 . . . . .2K 85
  (off Mace St.)
  SW1 . . . . .2D 18
  (off Arneway St.)
  SW9 . . . . .2K 119
  (off Aytoun Rd.)
Norton Rd. E10 .1B 68
  HA0: Wemb 6D 60
  RM10: Dag 6K 73
Norval Rd. HA0: Wemb 2B 60
Norway Ga. SE16 . . . . .3A 104
Norway Ho. N1 .1E 84
  (off Hertford Rd.)
Norway Pl. E14 .6B 86
Norway St. SE10 . . . . .6D 104
Norway Wharf E14 . . . . .6B 86
Norwegian War Memorial 1C 100
Norwich Cres. RM6: Chad H 5B 54
Norwich Ho. E14 . . . . .6D 86
  (off Cordelia St.)
Norwich M. IG3: Ilf 1A 72
Norwich Pl. DA6: Bex 4G 127
Norwich Rd. CR7: Thor H 3C 156
  E7 . . . . .5J 69
  HA6: Nwood 3H 39
  RM9: Dag 2G 91
  UB6: G'frd 1F 77
Norwich St. EC4 . . . . .7J 7 (6A 84)
Norwich Wlk. HA8: Edg 7D 28
NORWOOD 6E 138
Norwood Av. HA0: Wemb 1F 79
  RM7: Rush G 7K 55
Norwood Cl.
  NW2 . . . . .3G 63
  TW2: Twick 2H 131
  UB2: S'hall 4E 94
Norwood Dr. HA2: Harr 6D 40

Norwood Gdns. UB2: S'hall 4D 94
  UB4: Yead 4A 76
NORWOOD GREEN 4D 94
Norwood Grn. Rd.
  UB2: S'hall 4E 94
Norwood High St. SE27 . . . . .3B 138
Norwood Ho. E14 . . . . .7D 86
  (off Poplar High St.)
NORWOOD NEW TOWN 6C 138
Norwood Pk. Rd. SE27 . . . . .5C 138
Norwood Rd. SE24 . . . . .1B 138
  SE27 . . . . .2B 138
  UB2: S'hall 3C 94
Norwood Ter. UB2: S'hall 4F 95
Nota M. N3 . . . . .1J 45
Notley Pl. SW4 . . . . .7J 119
Notley St. SE5 .7D 102
Nolson Rd. SE25 . . . . .4H 157
Notting Barn Rd. W10 . . . . .4F 81
Nottingdale Sq. W11 . . . . .1G 99
Nottingham Av. E16 . . . . .5A 88
Nottingham Ct. WC2 . . . . . .1E 12 (6J 83)
Nottingham Ho. WC2 . . . . .1E 12
  (off Shorts Gdns.)
Nottingham Pl. W1 . . . . .4G 5 (5E 82)
Nottingham Rd. CR2: S Croy 4C 168
  E10 . . . . .6E 50
  SW17 . . . . .1D 136
  TW7: Isle 2K 113
Nottingham St. W1 . . . . .5G 5 (5E 82)
Nottingham Ter. NW1 . . . . .4G 5
NOTTING HILL 7H 81
Notting Hill Ga. W11 . . . . .1J 99
Nottingwood Ho. W11 . . . . .7G 81
  (off Clarendon Rd.)
Nova Bldg. E14 . . . . .4C 104
Nova Ct. E. E14 . . . . .1E 104
  (off Yabsley St.)
Nova Ct. W. E14 . . . . .1E 104
  (off Yabsley St.)
Nova M. SM3: Sutt 1G 165
Novar Cl. BR6: Orp 7K 161
Novar Rd. CR0: C'don 1B 168
Novar Rd. SE9 .1G 143
Novello Cl. N1 . . . . .1C 84
  (off Dibden St.)
Novello St. SW6 . . . . .1J 117
Novello Theatre
  Covent Garden 7K 83
  (off Aldwych)
Novem Ho. E1 . . . . .6K 9
  (off Chicksand St.)
Nowell Rd. SW13 . . . . .6C 98
Nower Ct. HA5: Pinn 4D 40
Nower Hill HA5: Pinn 4D 40
Noyna Rd. SW17 . . . . .3D 136
Nubia Way BR1: Brom 3G 141
Nuding Cl. SE13 . . . . .3C 122
Nuffield Ct. TW5: Hest 7D 94
Nuffield Health
  Battersea 2D 118
  (within Latchmere Leisure Cen.)
  Bloomsbury 3G 7
  (off Mecklenburgh Pl.)
  Bromley 5K 159
  Cannon Street 3E 14
  Cheam 7G 165
  Covent Garden 1F 13
  (off Endell St.)
  Croydon 6A 168
  Fulham 1F 117
  Norbury 2K 155
  Paddington 5A 82
  Surbiton 6C 150
  Twickenham .7J 113
  Wandsworth .7K 117
  Willesden Green 7E 62
  Wimbledon 6H 135
Nuffield Lodge N6 . . . . .6G 47
  W9 . . . . .5J 81
  (off Admiral Wlk.)

Nugent Rd. N19 .1J 65
  SE25 . . . . .3F 157
Nugents Ct. HA5: Pinn 1C 40
Nugent's Pk. HA5: Hat E 1C 40
Nugent Ter. NW8 . . . . .2A 82
Numa Ct. TW8: Bford 7D 96
Number One EC1 . . . . .4D 8 (4C 84)
Nun Cl. EC2 . . . . .7E 8
Nuneaton Rd. RM9: Dag 7E 72
NUNHEAD 3H 121
Nunhead Cemetery Nature Reserve
  . . . . .4J 121
Nunhead Cres. SE15 . . . . .3H 121
Nunhead Est. SE15 . . . . .4H 121
Nunhead Grn. SE15 . . . . .3H 121
Nunhead Gro. SE15 . . . . .3H 121
Nunhead La. SE15 . . . . .3H 121
Nunhead Pas. SE15 . . . . .3G 121
Nunnington Cl. SE9 . . . . .3C 142
Nunns Rd. EN2: Enf 2H 23
Nupton Dr. EN5: Barn 6A 20
Nurse Cl. HA8: Edg 1J 43
Nursery App. N12 . . . . .6H 31
Nursery Av. CR0: C'don 2K 169
  DA7: Bex 3F 127
  N3 . . . . .2A 46
Nursery Cl. BR6: Orp 7K 161
  CR0: C'don 2K 169
  EN3: Enf H 1E 24
  IG8: Wfd G 5E 36
  RM6: Chad H 6D 54
  SE4 . . . . .2B 122
  SW15 . . . . .4F 117
  TW14: Felt 7K 111
  (not continuous)
Nursery Ct. N17 . . . . .7A 34
  W13 . . . . .5A 78
Nursery Gdns. BR7: Chst 6F 143
  EN3: Enf H 1E 24
  TW4: Houn 5D 112
  TW12: Hamp 4D 130
  TW16: Sun 2H 147
Nursery La. E2 . . . . .1F 85
  E7 . . . . .6J 69
  UB8: Cowl 4A 74
  W10 . . . . .5E 80
Nurserymans Rd. N11 . . . . .2K 31
Nursery Rd. CR4: Mitc 3D 154
  CR7: Thor H 4D 156
  E9 . . . . .6J 67
  HA5: Pinn 3A 40
  N2 . . . . .1B 46
  N14 . . . . .7B 22
  SM1: Sutt 4A 166
  SW9 . . . . .4K 119
  SW19 . . . . .7G 135
  (Elm Gro.)
  SW19 . . . . .2K 153
  (Parkleigh Rd.)
  TW16: Sun 2G 147
Nursery Row EN5: Barn 3B 20
  SE17 . . . . .4D 102
Nursery St. N17 .7A 34
Nursery Wlk. NW4 . . . . .3E 44
  RM7: Rush G 7K 55
Nursery Waye UB8: Uxb 1A 74
Nurstead Rd. DA8: Erith 7G 109
Nutbourne St. W10 . . . . .3G 81
Nutbrook St. SE15 . . . . .3G 121
Nutbrowne Rd. RM9: Dag 1F 91
Nutcroft Rd. SE15 . . . . .7H 103
Nutfield Cl. N18 .6B 34
  SM5: Cars 3C 166
Nutfield Ct. BR1: Brom 3J 159
Nutfield Gdns.
  IG3: Ilf 2K 71
  UB5: N'olt 2A 76
Nutfield Pas. CR7: Thor H 4B 156
  (off Nutfield Rd.)
Nutfield Rd. CR7: Thor H 4B 156
  E15 . . . . .4E 68

Nutfield Rd. NW2 . . . . .3C **62**
      SE22 . . . . .4F **121**
Nutfield Way BR6: Farnb 2F **173**
Nutford Pl. W1 . . . . .7D **4** (6D **82**)
Nuthatch Cl. TW19: Stanw 1B **128**
Nuthatch Gdns. SE28 . . . . .2H **107**
            (not continuous)
Nuthatch Row KT10: Clay 6A **162**
Nuthurst Av. SW2 . . . . .2K **137**
Nutkin Wlk. UB8: Uxb 7A **56**
Nutley Ter. NW3 . . . . .6A **64**
Nutmeg Cl. DA5: Bexl 1J **145**
Nutmeg Cl. E16 . . . . .4G **87**
Nutmeg La. E14 . . . . .6F **87**
Nuttall St. N1 . . . . .2E **84**
Nutter La. E11 .6A **52**
Nutt Gro. HA8: Edg 2J **27**
Nutt St. SE15 . . . . .7F **103**
Nutty La. TW17: Shep 3E **146**
Nutwell St. SW17 . . . . .5C **136**
Nuxley Rd. DA17: Belv 6F **109**
Nyanza St. SE18 . . . . .6H **107**
Nye Bevan Est. E5 . . . . .3K **67**
Nye Bevan Ho. SW6 . . . . .7H **99**
         (off St Thomas's Way)
Nylands Av. TW9: Kew 1G **115**
Nymans Gdns. SW20 . . . . .3D **152**
Nynehead St. SE14 . . . . .7A **104**
Nyon Gro. SE6 .2B **140**
Nyssa Cl. IG8: Wfd G 6J **37**
Nyton Cl. N19 . . . . .1J **65**

O

O2, The 1G **105**
O2 Brixton Academy 3A **120**
O2 Centre NW3 . . . . .6A **64**
O2 Shepherd's Bush Empire Theatre
         . . . . .2E **98**
Oak Apple Ct. SE12 . . . . .1J **141**
Oak Av. CR0: C'don 1C **170**
      EN2: Enf .1E **22**
      N8 . . . . .4J **47**
      N10 . . . . .7A **32**
      N17 . . . . .7J **33**
      TW5: Hest .7B **94**
      TW12: Hamp 5C **130**
      UB7: W Dray 3C **92**
      UB10: Ick 2D **56**
Oak Avenue Local Nature Reserve 5C **130**
Oak Bank CR0: New Ad 6E **170**
Oakbank Av. KT12: Walt T 7D **148**
Oakbank Gro. SE24 . . . . .4C **120**
Oakbark Ho. TW8: Bford 7C **96**
             (off High St.)
Oakbrook Cl. BR1: Brom 4K **141**
Oakbury Rd. SW6 . . . . .2K **117**
Oak Cl. N14 . . . . .7A **22**
      SM1: Sutt 2A **166**
Oakcombe Cl. KT3: N Mald 1A **152**
Oak Cott. Cl. SE6 . . . . .1H **141**
Oak Cotts. W7 . . . . .2J **95**
Oak Ct. SE15 . . . . .7F **103**
           (off Sumner Rd.)
Oak Cres. E16 . . . . .5G **87**
Oakcroft Bus. Cen. KT9: Chess 4F **163**
Oakcroft Cl. HA5: Pinn 2K **39**
Oakcroft Rd. KT9: Chess 4F **163**
      SE13 . . . . .2F **123**
Oakcroft Vs. KT9: Chess 4F **163**
Oakdale N14 . . . . .1A **32**
Oakdale Av. HA3: Kenton 5E **42**
      HA6: Nwood 2J **39**
Oakdale Cl. E4 .5K **35**
Oakdale Gdns. E4 . . . . .5K **35**
Oakdale Rd. E7 . . . . .7K **69**
      E11 . . . . .2F **69**
      E18 . . . . .2K **51**
      KT19: Ewe 7K **163**
      N4 . . . . .6C **48**

Oakdale Rd. SE15 . . . . .3J **121**
      SW16 . . . . .5J **137**
Oakdale Way CR4: Mitc 7E **154**
Oak Dene W13 .5B **78**
Oakdene SE15 .1H **121**
Oakdene Av. BR7: Chst 5E **142**
      DA8: Erith 6J **109**
      KT7: T Ditt 1A **162**
Oakdene Cl. HA5: Hat E 1D **40**
Oakdene Dr. KT5: Surb 7J **151**
Oakdene M. SM3: Sutt 1H **165**
Oakdene Pk. N3 . . . . .7C **30**
Oakdene Rd. BR5: St M Cry 5K **161**
      UB10: Hil .2D **74**
Oakden St. SE11 . . . . .3K **19** (4A **102**)
Oake Cl. SW15 .5G **117**
Oakeford Ho. W14 . . . . .3G **99**
            (off Russell Rd.)
Oakenholt Ho. SE2 . . . . .1D **108**
Oakenshaw Cl. KT6: Surb 7E **150**
Oakes Cl. E6 . . . . .6D **88**
Oakeshott Av. N6 . . . . .2E **64**
Oakes M. E14 . . . . .5E **86**
            (off Nairn St.)
Oakey La. SE1 . . . . .1J **19** (3A **102**)
Oakfield E4 . . . . .5J **35**
Oakfield Av. HA3: Kenton 3B **42**
Oakfield Cen. SE20 . . . . .7H **139**
Oakfield Cl. HA4: Ruis 6H **39**
      KT3: N Mald 5B **152**
Oakfield Ct. N8 .7J **47**
      NW2 . . . . .7F **45**
Oakfield Gdns. BR3: Beck 5D **158**
      N18 . . . . .4K **33**
      SE19 . . . . .5E **138**
             (not continuous)
      SM5: Cars 1C **166**
      UB6: G'frd .4H **77**
Oakfield Ho. E3 .5C **86**
            (off Gale St.)
Oakfield La. BR2: Kes 4A **172**
Oakfield Lodge IG1: Ilf 3F **71**
            (off Albert Rd.)
Oakfield Rd. CR0: C'don 1C **168**
      E6 . . . . .1C **88**
      E17 . . . . .2A **50**
      IG1: Ilf 3F **71**
      N3 . . . . .1K **45**
      N4 . . . . .6A **48**
      N14 . . . . .2D **32**
      SE20 . . . . .7H **139**
      SW19 . . . . .3F **135**
      TW15: Ashf 5D **128**
Oakfield Rd. Ind. Est. SE20 . . . . .7H **139**
Oakfields Rd. NW11 . . . . .6G **45**
Oakfield St. SW10 . . . . .6A **100**
Oakford Rd. NW5 . . . . .4G **65**
Oak Gdns. CR0: C'don 2C **170**
      HA8: Edg .2J **43**
Oak Glade HA6: Nwood 1D **38**
Oak Gro. BR4: W W'ck 1E **170**
      HA4: Ruis .7K **39**
      NW2 . . . . .4G **63**
      TW16: Sun 7K **129**
Oak Gro. Rd. SE20 . . . . .1J **157**
Oakhall Ct. E11 . . . . .6K **51**
      TW16: Sun 5H **129**
Oakhall Dr. TW16: Sun 5H **129**
Oak Hall Rd. E11 . . . . .6K **51**
Oakham Cl. EN4: Cockf 3J **21**
      SE6 . . . . .2B **140**
Oakham Dr. BR2: Brom 4H **159**
Oakham Ho. W10 . . . . .4E **80**
           (off Sutton Way)
Oakhampton Rd. NW7 . . . . .7A **30**
Oak Hill IG8: Wfd G 7A **36**
      KT6: Surb .7E **150**
Oakhill KT10: Clay 6A **162**
Oakhill Av. HA5: Pinn 2C **40**
      NW3 . . . . .4K **63**
Oak Hill Cl. IG8: Wfd G 7A **36**

Oak Hill Ct. IG8: Wfd G 7A **36**
Oakhill Ct. SE23 . . . . .6J **121**
      SW19 . . . . .7F **135**
Oak Hill Cres. IG8: Wfd G 7A **36**
      KT6: Surb .7E **150**
Oakhill Dr. KT6: Surb 7E **150**
Oak Hill Gdns. IG8: Wfd G 1G **51**
Oak Hill Gro. KT6: Surb 6E **150**
Oak Hill Pk. M. NW3 . . . . .4K **63**
Oak Hill Pk. M. NW3 . . . . .4A **64**
Oak Hill Path KT6: Surb 6E **150**
Oakhill Pl. SW15 . . . . .5J **117**
Oak Hill Rd. KT6: Surb 6E **150**
Oakhill Rd. BR3: Beck 2E **158**
      BR6: Orp 1K **173**
      SM1: Sutt 3K **165**
      SW15 . . . . .5H **117**
      SW16 . . . . .1K **155**
Oak Hill Way NW3 . . . . .4K **63**
            (not continuous)
Oak Hill Woods Nature Reserve 6J **21**
Oak Ho. E14 . . . . .2E **104**
            (off Stewart St.)
      N2 . . . . .2B **46**
      RM7: Rom 5K **55**
      TW9: Kew .1H **115**
      W10 . . . . .4G **81**
            (off Sycamore Wlk.)
Oakhouse Rd. DA6: Bex 5G **127**
Oakhurst Av. DA7: Bex 7E **108**
      EN4: E Barn 7H **21**
Oakhurst Cl. BR7: Chst 1D **160**
      E17 . . . . .4G **51**
      IG6: Ilf 1G **53**
      KT2: King T 6F **133**
      TW11: Tedd 5J **131**
Oakhurst Ct. E17 . . . . .4G **51**
           (off Woodford New Rd.)
Oakhurst Gdns. DA7: Bex 7E **108**
      E4 . . . . .1C **36**
      E17 . . . . .4G **51**
Oakhurst Gro. SE22 . . . . .4G **121**
Oakhurst Rd. KT19: Ewe 6J **163**
Oakington Av. HA2: Harr 7E **40**
      HA9: Wemb 3F **61**
      UB3: Harl .4F **93**
Oakington Cl. TW16: Sun 2A **148**
Oakington Ct. EN2: Enf 2G **23**
Oakington Dr. TW16: Sun 2A **148**
Oakington Mnr. Dr. HA9: Wemb 5G **61**
Oakington Rd. W9 . . . . .4J **81**
Oakington Way N8 . . . . .7J **47**
Oakland Pl. IG9: Buck H 2D **36**
Oakland Quay E14 . . . . .3D **104**
Oakland Rd. E15 . . . . .4F **69**
Oaklands BR3: Beck 1D **158**
      N21 . . . . .2E **32**
      W13 . . . . .5A **78**
Oaklands Av. BR4: W W'ck 3D **170**
      CR7: Thor H 4A **156**
      DA15: Sidc 7K **125**
      KT10: Esh .7H **149**
      N9 . . . . .6C **24**
      TW7: Isle .6K **95**
Oaklands Cl. BR5: Pet W 6J **161**
      DA6: Bex .5F **127**
      HA0: Wemb 5D **60**
      KT9: Chess 4C **162**
Oaklands Ct. HA0: Wemb 5D **60**
      NW10 . . . . .1A **80**
            (off Nicoll Rd.)
      SE20 . . . . .7J **139**
           (off Chestnut Gro.)
Oaklands Dr. TW2: Whitt 7G **113**
Oaklands Est. SW4 . . . . .6G **119**
Oaklands Gro. W12 . . . . .1C **98**
Oaklands M. NW2 . . . . .4F **63**
           (off Oaklands Rd.)
Oaklands Pk. Av. IG1: Ilf 2G **71**
Oaklands Pas. NW2 . . . . .4F **63**
           (off Oaklands Rd.)

Oaklands Pl. SW4 . . . . .4G **119**
Oaklands Rd. BR1: Brom 7G **141**
      DA6: Bex .4F **127**
      N20 . . . . .7C **20**
      NW2 . . . . .4F **63**
      SW14 . . . . .3K **115**
      W7 . . . . .2K **95**
           (not continuous)
                 . . . . .1A **96**
Oaklands Way SM6: Wall 7H **167**
Oakland Way KT19: Ewe 6A **164**
Oak La. E14 . . . . .7B **86**
      IG8: Wfd G 4C **36**
      N2 . . . . .2B **46**
      N11 . . . . .6C **32**
      TW1: Twick 7A **114**
      TW7: Isle .4J **113**
Oakleafe Gdns. IG6: Ilf 3F **53**
Oaklea Lodge IG3: Ilf 3A **72**
Oaklea Pas. KT1: King T 3D **150**
Oakleigh Av. HA8: Edg 2H **43**
      KT6: Surb .1G **163**
      N20 . . . . .2G **31**
Oakleigh Cl. N20 . . . . .3J **31**
Oakleigh Ct. EN4: S Barn 6H **21**
      HA8: Edg .2J **43**
      N1 . . . . .1E **8**
      UB1: S'hall 1D **94**
Oakleigh Cres. N20 . . . . .2H **31**
Oakleigh Gdns. BR6: Orp 4J **173**
      HA8: Edg .5A **28**
      N20 . . . . .1F **31**
Oakleigh M. N20 . . . . .1F **31**
OAKLEIGH PARK 1F **31**
Oakleigh Pk. Av. BR7: Chst 1E **160**
Oakleigh Pk. Nth. N20 . . . . .1G **31**
Oakleigh Pk. Sth. N20 . . . . .7H **21**
Oakleigh Rd. UB10: Hil 1F **56**
Oakleigh Rd. Nth. N20 . . . . .2G **31**
Oakleigh Rd. Sth. N11 . . . . .3K **31**
Oakleigh Way CR4: Mitc 1F **155**
      KT6: Surb .1G **163**
Oakley Av. CR0: Bedd 4K **167**
      IG11: Bark 7K **71**
      W5 . . . . .7G **79**
Oakley Cl. E4 . . . . .3K **35**
      E6 . . . . .6C **88**
      TW7: Isle .1H **113**
      W7 . . . . .7J **77**
Oakley Ct. CR4: Mitc 7E **154**
Oakley Cres. EC1 . . . . .2B **84**
Oakley Dr. BR2: Brom 3C **172**
      SE9 . . . . .1H **143**
      SE13 . . . . .6F **123**
Oakley Gdns. N8 . . . . .5K **47**
      SW3 . . . . .7D **16** (6C **100**)
Oakley Grange HA1: Harr 2H **59**
Oakley Ho. SE11 . . . . .4J **19**
            (off Hotspur St.)
      SW1 . . . . .2F **17** (4D **100**)
      W5 . . . . .7G **79**
Oakley Pk. DA5: Bexl 7C **126**
Oakley Pl. SE1 .5F **103**
Oakley Rd. BR2: Brom 3C **172**
      HA1: Harr .6J **41**
      N1 . . . . .7D **66**
      SE25 . . . . .5H **157**
Oakley Sq. NW1 . . . . .2G **83**
Oakley St. SW3 . . . . .7C **16** (6C **100**)
Oakley Studios SW3 . . . . .7C **16**
           (off Up. Cheyne Row)
Oakley Wlk. W6 .6F **99**
Oakley Yd. E2 . . . . .3K **9** (4F **85**)
Oak Lock M. W4 . . . . .5A **98**
Oak Lodge E11 .6J **51**
      SM1: Sutt 4A **166**
      TW16: Sun 7H **129**
           (off Forest Dr.)
      W8 . . . . .3K **99**
           (off Chantry Sq.)
Oak Lodge Cl. HA7: Stan 5H **27**

Oak Lodge Dr. BR4: W W'ck 7D 158
Oaklodge Way NW7 ....5G 29
Oakman Ho. SW19 ....1F 135
Oakmead Av. BR2: Hayes 6J 159
Oakmead Cl. HA7: Stan 4H 27
Oakmeade HA5: Hat E 6A 26
Oakmead Gdns. Felt 4E 28
Oakmead Pl. CR4: Mitc 1C 154
Oakmead Rd. CR0: C'don 6H 155
　SW12 ....1E 136
Oakmede EN5: Barn 4A 20
Oakmere Rd. SE2 ....6A 108
Oakmont Pl. BR6: Orp 1H 173
Oak Pk. Gdns. SW19 ....1F 135
Oak Pk. M. N16 ....3F 67
Oak Pl. SW18 ....5K 117
Oakridge Dr. N2 ....3B 46
Oakridge La. BR1: Brom 5F 141
Oakridge Rd. BR1: Brom 4F 141
Oak Ri. IG9: Buck H 3G 37
Oak Rd. BR6: Chels 7K 173
　DA8: Erith 7J 109
　KT3: N Mald 2K 151
　W5 ....7D 78
Oak Row SW16 ....2G 155
Oaks, The BR2: Brom 6E 160
　EN2: Enf 3G 23
　HA4: Ruis 7F 39
　IG8: Wfd G 6B 36
　N12 ....4E 30
　NW6 ....7F 63
　(off Brondesbury Pk.)
　NW10 ....7D 62
　SE18 ....5G 107
　SM4: Mord 4G 153
　TW13: Felt 2B 130
　UB4: Hayes 2E 74
Oaks Av. KT4: Wor Pk 3D 164
　RM5: Col R 2J 55
　SE19 ....5E 138
　TW13: Felt 2C 130
Oaks Caravan Park, The KT9: Chess ...3C 162
Oaksford Av. SE26 ....3H 139
Oaks Gro. E4 ....2B 36
Oakshade Rd. BR1: Brom 4F 141
Oakshaw Rd. SW18 ....7K 117
Oakshott Ct. NW1 ....1C 6 (2H 83)
　(not continuous)
Oakside Cl. IG6: Ilf 2H 53
Oaks La. CR0: C'don 3H 169
　IG2: Ilf 5J 53
Oaks Pavilion M. SE19 ....5E 138
Oak Sq. SW9 ....2K 119
Oaks Rd. CR0: C'don 5H 169
　TW19: Stanw 5A 110
Oaks Shop. Centre, The W3 ....1J 97
Oak St. RM7: Rom 5J 55
Oaks Way KT6: Surb 1D 162
　SM5: Cars 7D 166
Oakthorpe Ct. N13 ....5H 33
Oakthorpe Est. N13 ....5H 33
Oakthorpe Rd. N13 ....5F 33
Oaktree Av. N13 ....3G 33
Oak Tree Cl. HA7: Stan 7H 27
　KT19: Ewe 6H 163
　W5 ....6C 78
Oak Tree Ct. UB5: N'olt 2A 76
　W3 ....7H 79
Oak Tree Dell NW9 ....5J 43
Oak Tree Dr. N20 ....1E 30
Oak Tree Gdns. BR1: Brom 5K 141
Oaktree Gro. IG1: Ilf 5H 71
Oak Tree Ho. W9 ....4J 81
　(off Shirland Rd.)
Oak Tree M. NW2 ....6C 62
Oak Tree Rd. NW8 ....2B 4 (3C 82)
Oakview Apartments SM1: Sutt 4B 166
Oakview Gdns. N2 ....4B 46
Oakview Gro. CR0: C'don 1A 170
Oakview Lodge NW11 ....7H 45
　(off Beechcroft Av.)

Oakview Rd. SE6 ....5D 140
Oak Village NW5 ....4E 64
Oak Vs. NW11 ....6H 45
　(off Hendon Pk. Row)
Oakville Ho. SE16 ....2K 103
　(off Dominion Dr.)
Oak Wlk. SM6: Wall 1E 166
　(off Helios Rd.)
Oak Way CR0: C'don 6K 157
　N14 ....7A 22
　TW14: Felt 1G 129
　W3 ....1A 98
Oakway Br2: Brom 2F 159
　SW20 ....4E 152
Oakway Cl. DA5: Bexl 6E 126
Oakways SE9 ....6F 125
OAKWOOD 4C 22
Oakwood SM6: Wall 7F 167
Oakwood Av. BR2: Brom 3K 159
　BR3: Beck 2E 158
　CR4: Mitc 2B 154
　N14 ....7C 22
　UB1: S'hall 7E 76
Oakwood Bus. Pk. NW10 ....4K 79
Oakwood Cl. BR7: Chst 6D 142
　IG8: Wfd G 6H 37
　N14 ....6B 22
　SE13 ....6F 123
Oakwood Ct. E6 ....1C 88
　HA1: Harr 6H 41
　W14 ....3H 99
Oakwood Cres. N21 ....6D 22
　UB6: G'frd 6A 60
Oakwood Dr. DA7: Bex 4J 127
　HA8: Edg 6D 28
　SE19 ....6D 138
Oakwood Gdns. BR6: Farnb 2G 173
　IG3: Ilf 2K 71
　SM1: Sutt 2J 165
Oakwood Ho. E9 ....6J 67
　(off Frampton Pk. Rd.)
Oakwood La. W14 ....3H 99
Oakwood Lodge N14 ....6B 22
　(off Avenue Rd.)
Oakwood Mans. W14 ....3H 99
　(off Oakwood Ct.)
Oakwood Pde. N14 ....5H 22
Oakwood Pk. Rd. N14 ....7C 22
Oakwood Pl. CR0: C'don 6A 156
Oakwood Rd.
　BR6: Farnb 2G 173
　CR0: C'don 6A 156
　HA5: Pinn 2K 39
　NW11 ....4J 45
　SW20 ....1C 152
Oakwood Vw. N14 ....6C 22
Oakworth Rd. W10 ....5E 80
Oarsman Pl. KT8: E Mos 4J 149
Oast Cl. E14 ....7B 86
　(off Newell St.)
Oast Lodge W4 ....7A 98
　(off Corney Reach Way)
Oates Cl. BR2: Brom 3F 159
Oatfield Ho. N15 ....6E 48
　(off Perry Ct.)
Oatfield Rd. BR6: Orp 1K 173
Oatland Ri. E17 ....2A 50
Oatlands Ct. KT13: Weyb 7G 147
Oatlands Rd. EN3: Enf H 1D 24
Oat La. EC2 ....7C 8 (6C 84)
Oatwell Ho. SW3 ....4D 16
　(off Cale St.)
Oban Cl. E13 ....4A 88
Oban Ho. E14 ....6F 87
　(off Oban St.)
　IG11: Bark 2H 89
　SE25 ....4D 156

Oban St. E14 ....6F 87
Oberon Cl. E6 ....7B 70
Oberon Ho. N1 ....2E 84
　(off Arden Est.)
Oberon Way TW17: Shep 3A 146
Oberstein Rd. SW11 ....4B 118
Oborne Cl. SE24 ....5B 120
O'Brien Ho. E2 ....3K 85
　(off Roman Rd.)
Observatory Gdns. W8 ....2J 99
Observatory M. E14 ....4F 105
Observatory Rd. SW7 ....2A 16 (3B 100)
　SW14 ....4J 115
Occupation La.
　SE18 ....1F 125
　W5 ....4D 96
Occupation Rd. KT19: Ewe 7K 163
　SE17 ....5C 102
　W13 ....2B 96
Ocean Est. E1 ....5A 86
　(Ben Jonson Rd.)
　E1 ....4K 85
　(Ernest St.)
Oceanis Apartments E16 ....7J 87
　(off Seagull La.)
Ocean St. E1 ....5K 85
Ocean Wharf E14 ....2B 104
Ockbrook E1 ....5J 85
　(off Hannibal Rd.)
Ockenden M. N1 ....6D 66
Ockendon Rd. N1 ....6D 66
Ockham Dr. BR5: St P 7A 144
　UB6: G'frd 7G 59
Ockley Ct. DA14: Sidc 3J 143
　SM1: Sutt 4A 166
Ockley Rd. CR0: C'don 7K 155
　SW16 ....4J 137
Octagon, The SW10 ....7K 99
　(off Coleridge Gdns.)
Octagon Arc. EC2 ....6G 9 (5E 84)
Octagon Ct. SE16 ....1K 103
　(off Rotherhithe St.)
Octavia Cl. CR4: Mitc 5C 154
Octavia Ho. SW1 ....2C 18
　(off Medway St.)
　W10 ....4G 81
Octavia M. W9 ....4H 81
Octavia Rd. TW7: Isle 3J 113
Octavia St. SW11 ....1C 118
Octavia Way SE28 ....7B 90
Octavius St. SE8 ....7C 104
October Pl. NW4 ....3F 45
Odard Rd. KT8: W Mole 4E 148
Oddmark Ho. IG11: Bark 2H 89
Odelia Ct. E15 ....1E 86
　(off Biggerstaff Rd.)
Odell Cl. IG11: Bark 7K 71
Odell Ho. E14 ....6C 86
　(off New Festival Av.)
Odeon, The IG11: Bark 7H 71
Odeon Cinema
　Barnet 5D 20
　Beckenham 2C 158
　Camden Town 1F 83
　(off Parkway)
　Covent Garden 6H 83
　(off Shaftesbury Av.)
　Edmonton 7E 24
　Eltham 4D 124
　(off Well Hall Rd.)
　Greenwich 4H 105
　Holloway 3J 65
　IMAX (BFI) 5J 13 (1A 102)
　Kensington 3J 99
　Kingston upon Thames 2E 150
　(within The Rotunda Cen.)
　Leicester Square 3D 12
　(off Leicester Sq.)
　Marble Arch 6D 82
　(off Marble Arch)

Odeon Cinema
　Muswell Hill 4F 47
　Panton Street 3D 12
　(off Panton St.)
　Putney 3G 117
　Richmond upon Thames, Hill Street 5D 114
　Richmond upon Thames,
　Red Lion Street 5D 114
　South Woodford 2J 51
　Streatham 3J 137
　Surrey Quays 3K 103
　Swiss Cottage 7B 64
　Tottenham Court Road 5H 83
　(off Tottenham Ct. Rd.)
　West End 3D 12
　(off Leicester Sq.)
　Whiteleys 6K 81
　Wimbledon 6H 135
Odeon Ct. E16 ....5J 87
　NW10 ....1A 80
　(off St Albans Rd.)
Odeon Pde. SE9 ....4C 124
　(off Well Hall Rd.)
　UB6: G'frd 6B 60
　(off Allendale Rd.)
　W3 ....2G 97
　(off Allendale Rd.)
Odessa Rd. E7 ....3H 69
　NW10 ....2C 80
Odessa St. SE16 ....2B 104
Odessa Wharf SE16 ....3B 104
　(off Odessa St.)
Odette Duval Ho. E1 ....5J 85
　(off Stepney Way)
Odger St. SW11 ....2D 118
Odhams Wlk. WC2 ....1F 13 (6J 83)
Odin Ho. SE5 ....2C 120
O'Donnell Ct. WC1 ....3F 7 (4J 83)
O'Driscoll Ho. W12 ....6D 80
Odyssey Bus. Pk. HA4: Ruis 5K 57
Offa's Mead E9 ....4B 68
Offenbach Ho. E2 ....2K 85
　(off Mace St.)
Offenham Rd. SE9 ....4D 142
　SW9 ....1A 120
Offers Ct. KT1: King T 3F 151
Offerton Rd. SW4 ....3G 119
Offham Ho. SE17 ....4E 102
　(off Beckway St.)
Offham Slope N12 ....5C 30
Offley Pl. TW7: Isle 2H 113
Offley Rd. SW9 ....7A 102
Offord Cl. N17 ....6B 34
Offord Rd. N1 ....7K 65
Offord St. N1 ....7K 65
Ogden Ho. TW13: Hanw 3C 130
Ogilby St. SE18 ....4D 106
Ogilvie Ho. E1 ....6K 85
　(off Stepney C'way.)
Oglander Rd. SE15 ....4F 121
Ogle St. W1 ....5A 6 (5G 83)
Oglethorpe Rd. RM10: Dag 3F 73
O'Gorman Ho. SW10 ....7A 100
　(off King's Rd.)
O'Grady Ho. E17 ....3D 50
Ohio Bldg. SE13 ....1D 122
　(off Deal's Gateway)
Ohio Rd. E13 ....4H 87
Oil Mill La. W6 ....5C 98
Okeburn Rd. SW17 ....5E 136
Okehampton Cl. N12 ....5G 31
Okehampton Cres.
　DA16: Well 1B 126
Okehampton Rd. NW10 ....1E 80
Olaf Ct. W8 ....2J 99
　(off Kensington Chu. St.)
Olaf St. W11 ....7F 81
Oldacre M. SW12 ....7E 118
Old Aeroworks, The NW8 ....4B 4
　(off Hatton St.)

Old Bailey
   Central Criminal Court 7B 8 (6B 84)
Old Bailey EC4 . . . . .1B 14 (6B 84)
Old Barge Ho. All. SE1 . . . . .3K 13
Old Barn Cl. SM2: Cheam 7G 165
Old Barn Way DA7: Bex 3K 127
Old Barracks W8 . . . . .2K 99
Old Barrack Yd. SW1 . . . . . .7G 11 (2E 100)
   (not continuous)
Old Barrowfield E15 . . . . .1G 87
Old Bellgate Pl. E14 . . . . .3C 104
Oldberry Rd. HA8: Edg 6E 28
Old Bethnal Grn. Rd. E2 . . . . .3G 85
OLD BEXLEY 7H 127
Old Bexley Bus. Pk. DA5: Bexl 7H 127
Old Bexley La. DA5: Bexl, Dart 2K 145
Old Billingsgate Mkt. EC3 . . . . .3F 15
Old Billingsgate Wlk. EC3 . . .3G 15 (7E 84)
Old Bond St. W1 . . . . .3A 12 (7G 83)
Oldborough Rd. HA0: Wemb 3C 60
OLD BRENTFORD 7D 96
Old Brewer's Yd. WC2 . . . . . . .1E 12 (6J 83)
Old Brewery M. NW3 . . . . .4B 64
Old Bridge Cl. UB5: N'olt 2E 76
Old Bridge St. KT1: Hamp W 2D 150
Old Broad St. EC2 . . . . .7F 9 (6D 84)
Old Bromley Rd. BR1: Brom 5F 141
Old Brompton Rd. SW5 . . . . .5J 99
   SW7 . . . . .4A 16 (5J 99)
Old Buildings WC2 . . . . .7J 7
Old Burlington St. W1 . . . . .2A 12 (7G 83)
Oldbury Ct. E9 . . . . .5A 68
   (off Mabley St.)
Oldbury Ho. W2 .5K 81
   (off Harrow Rd.)
Oldbury Pl. W1 . . . . .5H 5 (5E 82)
Oldbury Rd. EN1: Enf 2B 24
Old Canal M. SE15 . . . . .5F 103
   (off Trafalgar Av.)
Old Castle St. E1 . . . . .7J 9 (6F 85)
Old Cavendish St. W1 . . . . .7J 5 (6F 83)
Old Change Ct. EC4 . . . . .1C 14
Old Chapel Pl. SW9 . . . . .2A 120
Old Charlton Rd. TW17: Shep 5E 146
Old Chelsea M. SW3 . . . . .7C 16 (6C 100)
Old Chiswick Yd. W4 . . . . .6A 98
   (off Pumping Sta. Rd.)
Old Church Ct. N11 . . . . .5A 32
Oldchurch Gdns. RM7: Rush G 7K 55
Old Church La. HA7: Stan 5G 27
   NW9 . . . . .2K 61
   UB6: G'frd 3A 78
Oldchurch Ri. RM7: Rush G 7K 55
Old Church Rd. E1 . . . . .6K 85
   E4 . . . . .4H 35
Oldchurch Rd. RM7: Rush G 7K 55
Old Church St. SW3 . . . . . . .6B 16 (5B 100)
Old Claygate La. KT10: Clay 6A 162
Olden Cres. SE18 . . . . .6E 106
   (off Woolwich Comn.)
Old Coal Yd. SE28 . . . . .4H 107
Old College La. DA17: Belv 5H 109
Old Compton St. W1 . . . . .2C 12 (7H 83)
Old Cople La. SE19 . . . . .5F 139
Old Cote Dr. TW5: Hest 6E 94
Old Court Ho. W8 . . . . .2K 99
   (off Old Court Pl.)
Old Court Pl. W8 . . . . .2K 99
Old Courtyard, The BR1: Brom 1K 159
Old Curiosity Shop 7G 7
   (off Portsmouth St.)
Old Dairy N15 . . . . .6E 48
Old Dairy M. NW5 . . . . .6F 65
   SW4 . . . . .4J 119
   (off Tintern St.)
   SW12 . . . . .1E 136
Old Dairy Sq. N21 . . . . .7F 23
   (off Wade Hill)
Old Deer Pk. 2C 114
Old Deer Pk. Gdns. TW9: Rich 3E 114
Old Devonshire Rd. SW12 . . . . .7F 119

Old Dock Cl. TW9: Kew 6G 97
Old Dover Rd. SE3 . . . . .7J 105
Oldegate Ho. E6 . . . . .7B 70
Old Farm Av. DA15: Sidc 1H 143
   N14 . . . . .7B 22
Old Farm Cl. SW17 . . . . .2C 136
   TW4: Houn 4D 112
Old Farm La. SW19 . . . . .5K 135
Old Farm Pas. TW12: Hamp 1G 149
Old Farm Rd. N2 .1B 46
   TW12: Hamp 6D 130
   UB7: W Dray 2A 92
Old Farm Rd. E. DA15: Sidc 2A 144
Old Farm Rd. W. DA15: Sidc 2K 143
Oldfield Cl. BR1: Brom 4D 160
   HA7: Stan 5F 27
   UB6: G'frd 5J 59
Oldfield Ct. KT5: Surb 4F 151
   (off Cranes Pk. Cres.)
Oldfield Farm Gdns. UB6: G'frd 1H 77
Oldfield Gro. SE16 . . . . .4K 103
Oldfield Ho. W4 .5A 98
   (off Devonshire Rd.)
Oldfield La. Nth. UB6: G'frd 2H 77
Oldfield La. Sth. UB6: G'frd 4G 77
Oldfield M. N6 . . . . .7G 47
Oldfield Rd. BR1: Brom 4D 160
   DA7: Bex 2E 126
   N16 . . . . .3E 66
   NW10 . . . . .7B 62
   SW19 . . . . .6G 135
   TW12: Hamp 1D 148
   W3 . . . . .2B 98
Oldfields Cir. UB5: N'olt 6G 59
Oldfields Rd. SM1: Sutt 3H 165
Old Fire Station, The SE18 . . . . .7F 107
Old Fish St. Hill EC4 . . . . .2C 14
   (off Queen Victoria St.)
Old Fleet La. EC4 . . . . .7A 8 (6B 84)
Old Fold Cl. EN5: Barn 1C 20
Old Fold La. EN5: Barn 1C 20
Old Fold Manor Golf Course 1B 20
Old Fold Vw. EN5: Barn 3A 20
OLD FORD 1B 86
OLD FORD 1C 86
Old Ford Rd. E2 . . . . .3J 85
   E3 . . . . .2A 86
Old Ford Trading Cen. E3 . . . . .1C 86
   (off Maverton Rd.)
Old Forge Cl. HA7: Stan 4F 27
Old Forge Cres. TW17: Shep 6D 146
Old Forge M. W12 . . . . .2D 98
Old Forge Rd. EN1: Enf 1A 24
   N19 . . . . .2H 65
Old Forge Way DA14: Sidc 4B 144
Old Gloucester St. WC1 . . . . . .5F 7 (5J 83)
Old Goods Yard, The W2 . . . . .5A 82
Old Hall Cl. HA5: Pinn 1C 40
Old Hall Dr. HA5: Pinn 1C 40
Oldham Ter. W3 . . . . .1J 97
   (not continuous)
Old Hatch Mnr. HA4: Ruis 7H 39
Old Hill BR6: Downe 6H 173
   BR7: Chst 1E 160
Oldhill St. N16 . . . . .1G 67
Old Homestead Rd. BR2: Brom 4A 160
Old Hospital Cl. SW12 . . . . .1D 136
Old House Cl. SW19 . . . . .5G 135
Old House Gdns. TW1: Twick 6C 114
Old Howlett's La. HA4: Ruis 6F 39
OLD ISLEWORTH 3B 114
Old Jamaica Bus. Est. SE16 . . .7K 15 (3F 103)
Old Jamaica Rd. SE16 . . . . . .7K 15 (3G 103)
Old James St. SE15 . . . . .3H 121
Old Jewry EC2 . . . . .1E 14 (6D 84)
Old Kenton La. NW9 . . . . .5H 43
Old Kent Rd. SE1 . . . . .4E 102
   SE15 . . . . .4E 102
Old Kingston Rd. KT4: Wor Pk 2J 163
Old Laundry, The BR7: Chst 1G 161
Old Library Ct. HA4: Ruis 2J 57

Old Library Ho. E3 . . . . .2A 86
   (off Roman Rd.)
Old Lodge Pl. TW1: Twick 6B 114
Old Lodge Way HA7: Stan 5F 27
Old London Rd. DA14: Sidc, Swan . . .7G 145
   KT2: King T .2E 150
Old Lyonian Sports Club 5G 41
Old Maidstone Rd. DA14: Sidc 7F 145
Old Malden La. KT4: Wor Pk 2K 163
OLD MALDEN 1A 164
Old Manor Ct. NW8 . . . . .2A 82
Old Manor Dr. TW7: Isle 6G 113
Old Manor Ho. M. TW17: Shep 3C 146
Old Manor Rd. UB2: S'hall 4B 94
Old Manor Way BR7: Chst 5D 142
   DA7: Bex 2K 127
Old Manor Yd. SW5 . . . . .4K 99
Old Market Sq. SM1: Sutt 4K 165
Old Market Sq. E2 . . . . .1J 9 (3F 85)
Old Marylebone Rd. NW1 . . .6D 4 (5C 82)
Oldmead Ho. RM10: Dag 6H 73
Old Mews HA1: Harr 5J 41
Old Mill Ct. E18 . . . . .3A 52
Old Mill Pl. RM7: Rom 6K 55
Old Mill Rd. SE18 . . . . .6H 107
Old Mitre Ct. EC4 . . . . .1K 13 (6A 84)
Old Montague St. E1 . . . . .6K 9 (5G 85)
Old Nichol St. E2 . . . . .3J 9 (4F 85)
Old North St. WC1 . . . . .5G 7
Old Nursery Ct. E2 . . . . .2F 85
   (off Dawson St.)
Old Nursery Pl. TW15: Ashf 5D 128
Old Oak Cl. KT9: Chess 4F 163
OLD OAK COMMON 5A 80
Old Oak Comn. La. NW10 . . . . .5A 80
   W3 . . . . .5A 80
Old Oak La. NW10 . . . . .3A 80
Old Oak Rd. W3 .7B 80
Old Operating Theatre Museum
   & Herb Garret .5F 15
Old Orchard TW16: Sun 2A 148
Old Orchard, The NW3 . . . . .4D 64
Old Orchard Cl. EN4: Had W 1G 21
   UB8: Hil 6C 74
Old Palace La. TW9: Rich 5C 114
Old Palace Rd. CRO: C'don 3B 168
Old Palace Ter. TW9: Rich 5D 114
Old Palace Yd. SW1 . . . . . .1E 18 (3J 101)
   TW9: Rich 5D 114
Old Paradise St. SE11 . . . . .3G 19 (4K 101)
Old Park Av. EN2: Enf 4H 23
   SW12 . . . . .6E 118
Old Park Gro. EN2: Enf 4H 23
Old Park La. W1 . . . . .5J 11 (1F 101)
Old Park M. TW5: Hest 7D 94
Old Park Ridings N21 . . . . .6G 23
Old Pk. Rd. EN2: Enf 3G 23
   N13 . . . . .4E 32
   SE2 . . . . .5A 108
Old Pk. Rd. Sth. EN2: Enf 4G 23
Old Park Vw. EN2: Enf 3F 23
Old Pearson St. SE10 . . . . .7D 104
Old Perry St. BR7: Chst 6J 143
Old Police Station, The SW17 . . . . . . .2D 136
Old Post Office La. SE3 . . . . .3K 123
Old Post Office Wlk. KT6: Surb 6D 150
   (off Victoria Rd.)
Old Pound Cl. TW7: Isle 1A 114
Old Priory UB9: Hare 7D 38
Old Pye St. SW1 . . . . .1C 18 (3H 101)
Old Pye St. Est. SW1 . . . . .2C 18
   (off Old Pye St.)
Old Quebec St. W1 . . . . .1F 11 (6D 82)
   (not continuous)
Old Queen St. SW1 . . . . .7D 12 (2H 101)
Old Railway Wlk. SE16 . . . . .2J 103
   (off Brunel Rd.)
Old Rectory Gdns. HA8: Edg 6B 28
Old Redding HA3: Hrw W 5A 26
Old Red Lion Theatre 1K 7
   (off St John St.)

Oldridge Rd. SW12 . . . . .7E 118
Old Rd. DA1: Cray 5K 127
   EN3: Enf H 1D 24
   SE13 . . . . .4G 123
Old Rope Wlk. TW16: Sun 3K 147
Old Royal Free Pl. N1 . . . . .1A 84
Old Royal Free Sq. N1 . . . . .1A 84
Old Royal Naval College 5F 105
Old Ruislip Rd. UB5: N'olt 2A 76
Old School, The WC1 . . . . .5H 7
   (off Princeton St.)
Old School Cl. BR3: Beck 2K 157
   SE10 . . . . .3G 105
   SW19 . . . . .2J 153
Old School Ct. N17 . . . . .3F 49
Old School Cres. E7 . . . . .6J 69
Old School Pl. CRO: Wadd 4A 168
Old School Rd. UB8: Hil 4B 74
Old Schools La. KT17: Ewe 7B 164
Old School Sq. E14 . . . . .6C 86
   (off Pelling St.)
   KT7: T Ditt 6K 149
Old School Ter. SM3: Cheam 7F 165
Old Seacoal La. EC4 . . . . .7A 8 (6B 84)
Old Slade La. SL0: Rich P 1A 174
   SL3: Coln 1A 174
Old South Cl. HA5: Pinn 1B 40
Old Sth. Lambeth Rd. SW8 . . . . .7J 101
Old Speech Room Gallery 1J 59
Old Spitalfields Market 5J 9 (5F 85)
Old Square WC2 . . . . .7J 7 (6K 83)
Old Stable M. N5 .3C 66
Old Stables Ct. SE5 . . . . .1C 120
   (off Camberwell New Rd.)
Old Station Gdns. TW11: Tedd 6A 132
   (off Victoria Rd.)
Old Station Ho. SE17 . . . . .5C 102
Old Station Pas. TW9: Rich 4D 114
   (off Little Green)
Old Station Rd. UB3: Harl 3H 93
Old Station Way SW9 . . . . .3H 119
   (off Voltaire Rd.)
Old Station Yd., The E17 . . . . .4E 50
Oldstead Rd. BR1: Brom 4E 140
Old Stockley Rd. UB7: W Dray 2D 92
OLD STREET 4D 84
Old St. E13 . . . . .2K 87
   EC1 .3C 8 (4C 84)
Old Studio Cl. CRO: C'don 7D 156
Old Sungate Cotts. RM5: Col R 1F 55
Old Sun Wharf E14 . . . . .7A 86
   (off Narrow St.)
Old Swan Wharf SW11 . . . . .1B 118
Old Swan Yd. SM5: Cars 4D 166
Old Theatre Ct. SE1 . . . . .4D 14
Old Town CRO: C'don 3B 168
   SW4 . . . . .3G 119
Old Town Hall Apartments SE16 . . . . .3F 103
Old Tramyard SE18 . . . . .4J 107
Old Twelve Cl. W7 . . . . .4J 77
Old Vic Theatre, The 6K 13
Old Watermen's Walk EC3 . . . . .3F 15
   (off Lower Thames St.)
Old Woolwich Rd. SE10 . . . . .6E 105
Old York Rd. SW18 . . . . .5K 117
Oleander Cl. BR6: Farnb 5H 173
Oleander Ho. SE15 . . . . .5F 103
O'Leary Sq. E1 . . . . .5J 85
Olga St. E3 . . . . .2A 86
Olinda Rd. N16 . . . . .6F 49
Oliphant St. W10 .3F 81
Olive Blythe Ho. W10 . . . . .4G 81
   (off Ladbroke Gro.)
Olive Ct. E5 . . . . .2J 67
   (off Woodmill Rd.)
   N1 . . . . .1A 84
   (off Liverpool Rd.)
Olive Gro. N15 . . . . .4C 48
Olive Haines Lodge SW15 . . . . .5H 117
Olive Ho. EC1 . . . . .3K 7
   (off Bowling Grn. La.)

Oliver Av. SE25 . . . . .3F **157**
Oliver Bus. Pk. NW10 . . . . .2J **79**
Oliver Cl. W4 . . . . .6H **97**
Oliver Ct. SE18 . . . . .4G **107**
Oliver Gdns. E6 . . . . .5C **88**
Oliver Goldsmith Est. SE15 . . . . . . .1G **121**
Oliver Gro. SE25 . . . . .4F **157**
Oliver Ho. SE14 . . . . .7B **104**
(off New Cross Rd.)
SE16 . . . . .2G **103**
(off George Row)
SW8 . . . . .1B **4**
(off Wyvil Rd.)
Oliver M. SE15 . . . . .2G **121**
Olive Rd. E13 . . . . .3A **88**
NW2 . . . . .4D **62**
SW19 .7A **136**
W5 . . . . .3D **96**
Oliver Rd. E10 . . . . .2D **68**
E17 . . . . .5E **50**
KT3: N Mald 2J **151**
NW10 .2J **79**
SM1: Sutt 4B **166**
Olivers Wharf E1 . . . . .1H **103**
(off Wapping High St.)
Olivers Yd. EC1 . . . . .3F 9 (4D **84**)
Olive St. RM7: Rom 5K **55**
Olive Tree Ho. SE15 . . . . .6J **103**
(off Sharratt St.)
Olivette St. SW15 . . . . .3F **117**
Olive Waite Ho. NW6 . . . . .7J **63**
(off Whitehorse Rd.)
Olivia Ct. CRO: C'don 7C **156**
(off Chase Side)
EN2: Enf 1H **23**
Olivia M. HA3: Hrw W 7D **26**
Olivier Theatre 4H **13**
(within National Theatre)
Ollerton Grn. E3 . . . . .1B **86**
Ollerton Rd. N11 . . . . .5C **32**
Olley Cl. SM6: Wall 7J **167**
Oligar Cl. W12 . . . . .1B **98**
Olliffe St. E14 . . . . .3E **104**
Olmar St. SE1 . . . . .6G **103**
Olney Ho. NW8 . . . . .3D **4**
(off Tresham Cres.)
Olney Rd. SE17 . . . . .6B **102**
(not continuous)
Olron Cres. DA6: Bex 5D **126**
Olven Rd. SE18 . . . . .6G **107**
Olveston Wlk. SM5: Cars 6B **154**
Olwen Ho. HA5: Pinn 2B **40**
Olyffe Av. DA16: Well 1A **126**
Olyffe Dr. BR3: Beck 1E **158**
Olympia 3G **99**
Olympia Ind. Est. N22 . . . . .3K **47**
Olympia Sq. C5 . . . . .3G **67**
Olympia M. W2 . . . . .7K **81**
Olympian Ct. E3 . . . . .2C **86**
(off Wick La.)
E14 .4C **104**
(off Homer Dr.)
Olympia Way W14 . . . . .3G **99**
Olympic Ho. N16 . . . . .4F **67**
Olympic M. SW18 . . . . .5A **118**
Olympic Pk. Av. E20 . . . . .5D **68**
Olympic Sq. HA9: Wemb 3G **61**
Olympic Way HA9: Wemb 3G **61**
UB6: G'frd 1G **77**
Olympus Gro. N22 . . . . .1A **48**
Olympus Sq. E5 . . . . .3G **67**
O'Mahoney St. SW17 . . . . .3A **136**
Oman Av. NW2 . . . . .6J **62**
O'Meara St. SE1 . . . . . . .5D 14 (1C **102**)
Omega Cl. E14 . . . . .3D **104**
Omega Ct. RM7: Rom 5K **55**
Omega Ho. SW10 . . . . .7A **100**
(off King's Rd.)
Omega Pl. N1 . . . . .1F **7**
Omega St. SE14 . . . . .1C **122**
Omega Works E3 . . . . .7C **68**
Ommaney Rd. SE14 . . . . .1K **121**

Omnibus Ho. N22 . . . . .2A **48**
(off Lordship La.)
Omnibus Way E17 . . . . .2C **50**
Omnium Ct. WC1 . . . . .5G **7**
(off Princeton St.)
Ondine Rd. SE15 . . . . .4F **121**
Onedin Ct. E1 . . . . .7G **85**
(off Ensign St.)
Onega Ga. SE16 . . . . .3A **104**
One Hyde Pk. SW1 . . . . . .7E 10 (2D **100**)
O'Neill Ho. NW8 . . . . .1B **4**
(off Cochrane St.)
O'Neill Path SE18 . . . . .6E **106**
One New Change EC4 . . . .1C 14 (6C **84**)
One Owen St. EC1 . . . . .1A **8**
(off Goswell St.)
One The Elephant SE1 . . . . .4B **102**
(off Brook Dr.)
One Tree Cl. SE23 . . . . .6J **121**
One Tree Hill Local Nature Reserve
. . . . .6J **121**
Ongar Cl. RM6: Chad H 5C **54**
Ongar Rd. SW6 . . . . .6J **99**
Onra Rd. E17 . . . . .7C **50**
Onslow Av. TW10: Rich 5E **114**
Onslow Cl. E4 . . . . .2K **35**
KT7: T Ditt 7J **149**
W10 .3H **81**
Onslow Ct. SW10 . . . . .6A **16**
Onslow Cres. BR7: Chst 1F **161**
SW7 . . . . .4B 16 (4B **100**)
Onslow Dr. DA14: Sidc 2D **144**
Onslow Gdns. E18 . . . . .3K **51**
KT7: T Ditt 7J **149**
N10 . . . . .5F **47**
N21 . . . . .5F **23**
SM6: Wall 6G **167**
SW7 . . . . .4A 16 (4B **100**)
Onslow Ho. KT2: King T 1F **151**
(off Acre Rd.)
Onslow M. E. SW7 . . . . . . .4A 16 (4B **100**)
Onslow M. W. SW7 . . . . . . .4A 16 (4B **100**)
Onslow Pde. N14 . . . . .1A **32**
Onslow Rd. CRO: C'don 7K **155**
KT3: N Mald 4C **152**
TW10: Rich 5E **114**
Onslow Sq. SW7 . . . . .3B 16 (4B **100**)
Onslow St. EC1 . . . . .4K 7 (4A **84**)
Onslow Way KT7: T Ditt 7J **149**
Ontario Point SE16 . . . . .2J **103**
(off Surrey Quays Rd.)
Ontario St. SE1 . . . . .3B **102**
Ontario Twr. E14 . . . . .7E **87**
Ontario Way E14 . . . . .7C **86**
(not continuous)
Onyx M. E15 . . . . .6H **69**
Opal Apartments W2 . . . . .6J **81**
(off Hereford Rd.)
Opal Cl. E16 . . . . .6B **88**
Opal Ct. E15 . . . . .1E **86**
Opal M. IG1: Ilf 2F **71**
NW6 .1H **81**
Opal St. SE11 . . . . .5K 19 (5B **102**)
Openshaw Rd. SE2 . . . . .4B **108**
Openview SW18 . . . . .1A **136**
Opera Ct. N19 . . . . .3H **65**
(off Wedmore St.)
Ophelia Gdns. NW2 . . . . .3G **63**
Ophelia Ho. W6 . . . . .5F **99**
(off Fulham Pal. Rd.)
Ophir Ter. SE15 . . . . .1G **121**
Opie Ho. NW8 . . . . .2C **82**
(off Townshend Est.)
Opossum Way TW4: Houn 3A **112**
Oppenheim Rd. SE13 . . . . .2E **122**
Oppidan Apartments NW6 . . . . .7J **63**
(off Netherwood St.)
Opulens Ho. NW3 . . . . .7D **64**
Opulens Pl. HA6: N'wood 1E **38**
Orange Ct. La. BR6: Downe 7E **172**

Orange Gro. E11 . . . . .3G **69**
Orange Hill Rd. HA8: Edg 7D **28**
Orange Pl. SE16 . . . . .3J **103**
Orangery, The TW10: Ham 2C **132**
Orangery Gallery, The 2H **99**
Orangery La. SE9 . . . . .5D **124**
Orange St. WC2 . . . . .3D 12 (7H **83**)
Orange Tree Ct. SE5 . . . . .7E **102**
(off Havil St.)
Orange Tree Theatre 4E **114**
Orange Yd. W1 . . . . .1D **12**
Oransay Rd. N1 . . . . .6C **66**
Oratory La. SW3 . . . . . . .5B 16 (5B **100**)
Orbain Rd. SW6 . . . . .7G **99**
Orbis Wharf SW11 . . . . .3B **118**
Orbel St. SW11 . . . . .1C **118**
Orbit, The 7D **68**
Orbital Centre IG8: Wfd G 2B **52**
Orb St. SE17 . . . . .4D **102**
Orchard, The KT17: Ewe 7B **164**
N14 . . . . .5A **22**
N20 . . . . .1E **30**
N21 . . . . .6J **23**
NW11 .5J **45**
SE3 . . . . .2F **123**
TW3: Houn 2G **113**
W4 . . . . .4K **97**
W5 . . . . .5D **78**
(off Montpelier Rd.)
Orchard Av. CRO: C'don 2A **170**
CR4: Mitc 1E **166**
DA17: Belv 6E **108**
KT3: N Mald 2A **152**
KT7: T Ditt 1A **162**
N3 . . . . .3J **45**
N14 . . . . .6B **22**
N20 . . . . .2G **31**
TW5: Hest 7C **94**
TW14: Felt 5F **111**
TW15: Ashf 6E **128**
UB1: S'hall 1D **94**
Orchard Bus. Cen. SE26 . . . . .5B **140**
Orchard Cl. DA7: Bex 1E **126**
E4 . . . . .4H **35**
E11 . . . . .4K **51**
HA0: Wemb 1E **78**
HA4: Ruis 7E **38**
HA8: Edg 6K **27**
KT6: Surb 1B **162**
KT12: Walt T 7K **147**
KT19: Ewe 6H **163**
N1 . . . . .7C **66**
NW2 .3C **62**
SE23 . . . . .6J **121**
SW20 . . . . .4E **152**
TW15: Ashf 6E **128**
UB5: N'olt 6G **59**
W10 .5H **81**
WD23: B Hea 1C **26**
Orchard Cotts. KT2: King T 1F **151**
UB3: Hayes 2G **93**
Orchard Ct. E10 . . . . .1D **68**
EN5: New Bar 3E **20**
HA8: Edg 5A **28**
KT4: Wor Pk 1C **164**
KT12: Walt T 7H **147**
(off Bridge St.)
N14 . . . . .6B **22**
SM6: Wall 5F **167**
TW2: Twick 2H **131**
TW7: Isle 1H **113**
UB7: Lford 3D **174**
UB8: Uxb 2A **74**
(off The Greenway)
W1 . . . . .7G **5**
(off Fitzhardinge St.)
Orchard Cres. EN1: Enf 1A **24**
HA8: Edg 5D **28**
Orchard Dr. HA8: Edg 5A **28**
SE3 . . . . .2F **123**
TW17: Shep 3G **147**

Orchard Gdns. KT9: Chess 4E **162**
SM1: Sutt 5J **165**
Orchard Ga. KT10: Esh 7H **149**
NW9 .4A **44**
UB6: G'frd 6B **60**
Orchard Grn. BR6: Orp 2J **173**
Orchard Gro. BR6: Orp 2K **173**
CRO: C'don 7A **158**
HA3: Kenton 5F **43**
HA8: Edg 1G **43**
SE20 . . . . .7G **139**
Orchard Hill DA1: Cray 5K **127**
SE13 . . . . .2D **122**
SM5: Cars 5D **166**
Orchard Ho. SE5 . . . . .1C **120**
(off County Gro.)
SE16 . . . . .3J **103**
SW6 .7H **99**
(off Varna Rd.)
W12 .1C **98**
Orchard La. IG8: Wfd G 4F **37**
KT8: E Mos 6H **149**
SW20 . . . . .1D **152**
Orchardleigh Av. EN3: Enf H 2D **24**
Orchard Mead Ho. NW2 . . . . .2J **63**
Orchardmede N21 . . . . .6J **23**
Orchard M. N1 . . . . .7D **66**
N6 . . . . .7F **47**
SW17 . . . . .3A **136**
Orchard Pl. BR2: Kes 7A **172**
E5 . . . . .5H **67**
E14 . . . . .7G **87**
(not continuous)
N17 . . . . .7A **34**
W4 . . . . .4A **98**
Orchard Ri. CRO: C'don 1A **170**
HA5: Eastc 3H **39**
KT2: King T 1J **151**
TW10: Rich 4H **115**
Orchard Ri. E. DA15: Sidc 5K **125**
Orchard Ri. W. DA15: Sidc 5J **125**
Orchard Rd. BR1: Brom 1A **160**
BR6: Farnb 5F **173**
CR4: Mitc 1E **166**
DA14: Sidc 4J **143**
DA16: Well 3B **126**
DA17: Belv 4G **109**
EN3: Pond E 5D **24**
EN5: Barn 4C **20**
KT1: King T 2E **150**
KT9: Chess 4E **162**
N6 . . . . .7F **47**
RM7: Mawney 1H **55**
RM10: Dag 1G **91**
SE3 . . . . .2G **123**
SE18 . . . . .4H **107**
SM1: Sutt 5J **165**
TW1: Twick 5A **114**
TW4: Houn 6C **96**
TW8: Bford 6C **96**
TW9: Rich 3G **115**
TW12: Hamp 7D **130**
TW13: Felt 1J **129**
TW16: Sun 7K **129**
UB3: Hayes 7J **75**
Orchardson Ho. NW8 . . . . .4A **4**
Orchardson St. NW8 . . . . . .4A 4 (4B **82**)
Orchard Sq. W14 . . . . .5H **99**
Orchard St. E17 . . . . .4A **50**
W1 . . . . .1G 11 (6E **82**)
Orchard Studios W6 . . . . .4F **99**
(off Brook Grn.)
Orchard Ter. EN1: Enf 6B **24**
NW10 .4B **62**
Orchard Vs. DA14: Sidc 6C **144**
Orchard Wlk. KT2: King T 1G **151**
(off Gordon Rd.)
Orchard Way BR3: Beck 7C **158**
(Monks Orchard Rd.)
BR3: Beck 1A **170**
(Orchard Av.)

Orchard Way CR0: C'don 1A **170**
  EN1: Enf .3K **23**
  SM1: Sutt 4B **166**
  TW15: Ashf 2B **128**
Orchard Waye UB8: Uxb 2A **74**
Orchard Wharf E14 . . . . .7G **87**
                   (off Orchard Pl.)
Orchestra Ct. HA8: Edg 7C **28**
Orchid Cl. E6 . . . . .5C **88**
  KT9: Chess 7C **162**
  SE13 . . . . .5F **123**
  UB1: S'hall 7C **76**
Orchid Ct. HA9: Wemb 2E **60**
Orchid Gdns. TW3: Houn 4D **112**
Orchid Grange N14 . . . . .7B **22**
Orchid Rd. N14 . . . . .7B **22**
Orchid St. W12 . . . . .7C **80**
Orde NW9 . . . . .1B **44**
Orde Hall St. WC1 . . . . .4G **7** (4K **83**)
Ordell Ct. E3 . . . . .2B **86**
                 (off Ordell Rd.)
Ordell Rd. E3 . . . . .2B **86**
Ordnance Cl. TW13: Felt 2J **129**
Ordnance Cres. SE10 . . . . .2G **105**
Ordnance Dock Pl. UB2: S'hall 4B **94**
Ordnance Hill NW8 . . . . .1B **82**
Ordnance M. NW8 . . . . .2B **82**
Ordnance Rd. E16 . . . . .5H **87**
  SE18 . . . . .6E **106**
Oregano Cl. UB7: Yiew 6A **74**
Oregano Dr. E14 . . . . .6F **87**
Oregon Av. E12 . . . . .4D **70**
Oregon Bldg. SE13 . . . . .1D **122**
              (off Deal's Gateway)
Oregon Cl. KT3: N Mald 4J **151**
Oregon Sq. BR6: Orp 1H **173**
Orestes M. NW6 . . . . .5J **63**
Orford Ct. HA7: Stan 6H **27**
  SE27 . . . . .2B **138**
Orford Gdns. TW1: Twick 2K **131**
Orford Rd. E17 . . . . .5C **50**
  E18 . . . . .3K **51**
  SE6 . . . . .3D **140**
ORGAN CROSSROADS 7C **164**
Organ La. E4 . . . . .2K **35**
Oriana Ho. E10 . . . . .2D **68**
             (off Grange Pk. Rd.)
  E14 . . . . .7B **86**
                  (off Victory Pl.)
Oriel Cl. CR4: Mitc 4H **155**
Oriel Ct. CR0: C'don 1D **168**
  NW3 . . . . .4A **64**
Oriel Dr. SW13 . . . . .6E **98**
Oriel Gdns. IG5: Ilf 3D **52**
Oriel Ho. NW6 . . . . .1J **81**
                (off Priory Pk. Rd.)
  RM7: Rom 6K **55**
Oriel M. E18 . . . . .2J **51**
Oriel Pl. NW3 . . . . .4A **64**
                  (off Heath St.)
Oriel Rd. E9 .6K **67**
Oriel Way UB5: N'olt 7F **59**
Oriens M. E20 . . . . .5E **68**
Oriental Rd. E16 . . . . .1B **106**
Oriental St. E14 . . . . .7C **86**
                (off Pennyfields)
Orient Ho. SW6 . . . . .1A **118**
                (off Station Ct.)
Orient Ind. Pk. E10 . . . . .2C **68**
Orient St. SE11 . . . . .4B **102**
Orient Way E5 . . . . .3K **67**
  E10 . . . . .1A **68**
Orient Wharf E1 . . . . .1H **103**
            (off Wapping High St.)
Oriole Way SE28 . . . . .7B **90**
Orion E14 . . . . .4C **104**
                (off Crews St.)
Orion Bus. Cen. SE14 . . . . .5K **103**
Orion Centre, The CR0: Bedd 2J **167**
Orion Ho. E1 .4H **85**
               (off Coventry Rd.)

Orion M. SM4: Mord 4J **153**
Orion Rd. N11 . . . . .7K **31**
Orissa Rd. SE18 . . . . .5J **107**
Orkney Ct. E1 . . . . .5A **86**
                (off Ocean Est.)
Orkney Ho. N1 . . . . .1K **83**
             (off Bemerton Est.)
Orkney St. SW11 . . . . .2E **118**
Orlando Rd. SW4 . . . . .3G **119**
Orleans Ct. TW1: Twick 7B **114**
Orleans House Gallery 1B **132**
Orleans Pk. School Sports Cen. . . .7B **114**
Orleans Rd. SE19 . . . . .6D **138**
  TW1: Twick 7B **114**
Orleston M. N7 . . . . .6A **66**
Orleston Rd. N7 . . . . .6A **66**
Orley Ct. HA1: Harr 4K **59**
Orley Farm Rd. HA1: Harr 3J **59**
Orlop St. SE10 . . . . .5G **105**
Ormanton Rd. SE26 . . . . .4G **139**
Orme Ct. W2 .7K **81**
Orme Ct. M. W2 . . . . .7K **81**
                 (off Orme La.)
Orme Ho. E8 .1F **85**
Orme La. W2 .7K **81**
Ormeley Rd. SW12 . . . . .1F **137**
Orme Rd. KT1: King T 2H **151**
  SM1: Sutt 6K **165**
Ormerod Gdns. CR4: Mitc 2E **154**
Ormesby Cl. SE28 . . . . .7D **90**
Ormesby Way HA3: Kenton 6F **43**
Orme Sq. W2 . . . . .7K **81**
Ormiston Gro. W12 . . . . .1D **98**
Ormiston Rd. SE10 . . . . .5J **105**
Ormond Av. TW10: Rich 5D **114**
  TW12: Hamp 1F **149**
Ormond Cl. WC1 . . . . .5F **7** (5J **83**)
Ormond Cres. TW12: Hamp 1F **149**
Ormond Dr. TW12: Hamp 7F **131**
Ormonde Av. BR6: Farnb 2G **173**
Ormonde Ct. NW8 . . . . .1D **82**
           (off St Edmund's Cl.)
  SW15 . . . . .4E **116**
Ormonde Ga. SW3 . . . . . . .6F **17** (5D **100**)
                (not continuous)
Ormonde Mans. WC1 . . . . .5F **7**
           (off Southampton Row)
Ormonde Pl. SW1 . . . . . . .4G **17** (4E **100**)
Ormonde Ri. IG9: Buck H 1F **37**
Ormonde Rd. SW14 . . . . .3J **115**
Ormonde Ter. NW8 . . . . .1D **82**
Ormond Ho. N16 . . . . .2D **66**
Ormond M. WC1 . . . . .4F **7** (4J **83**)
Ormond Rd. N19 . . . . .1J **65**
  TW10: Rich 5D **114**
Ormond Yd. SW1 . . . . . .4B **12** (1G **101**)
Ormrod Ct. W11 . . . . .6G **81**
            (off Westbourne Pk. Rd.)
Ormsby SM2: Sutt 7K **165**
Ormsby Gdns. UB6: G'frd 2G **77**
Ormsby Lodge W4 . . . . .3A **98**
Ormsby Pl. N16 . . . . .3F **67**
Ormsby Point SE18 . . . . .4F **107**
               (off Vincent Rd.)
Ormsby St. E2 . . . . .2F **85**
Ormside St. SE15 . . . . .6J **103**
Ornan Rd. NW3 . . . . .5C **64**
Orpen Ho. SW5 . . . . .4J **99**
                (off Trebovir Rd.)
Orpen Wlk. N16 . . . . .3E **66**
Orpheus Ho. W10 . . . . .4H **81**
                (off Harrow Rd.)
Orpheus St. SE5 . . . . .1D **120**
ORPINGTON 1K **173**
Orpington Gdns. N18 . . . . .3K **33**
Orpington Mans. N21 . . . . .1G **33**
Orpington Rd. BR7: Chst 3J **161**
  N21 . . . . .1G **33**
Orpwood Cl. TW12: Hamp 6D **130**
Orsett M. W2 . . . . .6K **81**
                (not continuous)

Orsett St. SE11 . . . . .5H **19** (5K **101**)
Orsett Ter. IG8: Wfd G 7F **37**
  W2 . . . . .6K **81**
Orsman Rd. N1 . . . . .1E **84**
Orton Gro. EN1: Enf 1B **24**
Orton St. E1 . . . . .1G **103**
Orville Rd. SW11 . . . . .2B **118**
Orwell Cl. RM13: Rain 5K **91**
  UB3: Hayes 7G **75**
Orwell Ct. E8 . . . . .1G **85**
                (off Pownall Rd.)
  N5 . . . . .4C **66**
  SE13 . . . . .3D **122**
  SW17 . . . . .3B **136**
              (off Grosvenor Way)
Orwell Rd. E13 . . . . .2A **88**
Osbaldeston Rd. N16 . . . . .2G **67**
Osberton Rd. SE12 . . . . .5J **123**
Osbert St. SW1 . . . . .4C **18** (4H **101**)
Osborn Cl. E8 . . . . .1G **85**
Osborne Av. TW19: Stanw 1A **128**
Osborne Cl. BR3: Beck 4A **158**
  EN4: Cockf 3J **21**
  TW13: Hanw 5B **130**
Osborne Ct. E10 . . . . .7D **50**
  W5 . . . . .5E **78**
Osborne Gdns. CR7: Thor H 2C **156**
Osborne Gro. E17 . . . . .4B **50**
Osborne Ho. E16 . . . . .1J **105**
                (off Wesley Av.)
Osborne M. E17 . . . . .4B **50**
Osborne Pl. SM1: Sutt 5B **166**
Osborne Rd. CR7: Thor H 2C **156**
  DA17: Belv 5F **109**
  E7 . . . . .5K **69**
  E9 . . . . .6B **68**
  E10 . . . . .2D **68**
  EN3: Enf H 2F **25**
  IG9: Buck H 1E **36**
  KT2: King T 7E **132**
  KT12: Walt T 7J **147**
  N4 . . . . .1A **66**
  N13 . . . . .3F **33**
  NW2 . . . . .6D **62**
  RM9: Dag 5F **73**
  TW3: Houn 3D **112**
  UB1: S'hall 6G **77**
  W3 . . . . .3H **97**
Osborne Sq. RM9: Dag 4F **73**
Osborne Ter. SW17 . . . . .5D **136**
                (off Church La.)
Osborne Way KT9: Chess 5F **163**
Osborn Gdns. NW7 . . . . .7A **30**
Osborn La. SE23 . . . . .7A **122**
Osborn St. E1 . . . . .6K **9** (5F **85**)
Osborn Ter. SE3 . . . . .4H **123**
Osbourne Ct. HA2: Harr 4F **41**
Osbourne Ho. IG8: Wfd G 7K **37**
  TW2: Twick 2G **131**
Oscar Ct. SE16 . . . . .2A **104**
Oscar Faber Pl. N1 . . . . .7E **66**
Oscar St. SE8 . . . . .2C **122**
                (not continuous)
Oseney Cres. NW5 . . . . .5G **65**
Osgood Av. BR6: Chels 5K **173**
Osgood Gdns. BR6: Chels 5K **173**
OSIDGE 1A **32**
Osidge La. N14 . . . . .1K **31**
Osier Cl. E1 .4K **85**
                 (off Osier St.)
  RM7: Rom 6K **55**
  TW8: Bford 6E **96**
                (off Ealing Rd.)
Osier Cres. N10 . . . . .1D **46**
Osier La. SE10 . . . . .3H **105**
Osier M. W4 .6A **98**
Osiers Ct. KT1: King T 1D **150**
              (off Steadfast Rd.)
Osiers Rd. SW18 . . . . .4J **117**
Osiers Twr. SW18 . . . . .4J **117**
             (off Enterprise Way)

Osier St. E1 .4J **85**
Osier Way CR4: Mitc 5D **154**
  E10 . . . . .3D **68**
Oslac Rd. SE6 . . . . .5D **140**
Oslo Ct. NW8 . . . . .2C **82**
             (off Prince Albert Rd.)
Oslo Ho. E9 .6B **68**
                (off Felstead St.)
  SE5 . . . . .2C **120**
                (off Carew St.)
Oslo Sq. SE16 . . . . .3A **104**
Osman Cl. N15 . . . . .6D **48**
Osmani Youth Cen. 5G **85**
Osman Rd. N9 . . . . .3B **34**
  W6 . . . . .3E **98**
Osmington Ho. SW8 . . . . .7K **101**
                (off Dorset Rd.)
Osmond Cl. HA2: Harr 2G **59**
Osmond Gdns. SM6: Wall 5G **167**
Osmunda Ct. E1 . . . . .6G **85**
                (off Myrtle St.)
Osmund St. W12 . . . . .5B **80**
Osnaburgh St. NW1 . . . . . . .4K **5** (4F **83**)
                (Euston Rd.)
  NW1 . . . . .2K **5**
                (Robert St.)
Osnaburgh Ter. NW1 . . . . . .3K **5** (4F **83**)
Osney Ho. SE2 . . . . .2D **108**
Osney Wlk. SM5: Cars 6B **154**
Osprey NW9 . . . . .1B **44**
Osprey Cl. BR2: Brom 1C **172**
  E6 . . . . .5C **88**
  E11 . . . . .4J **51**
  E17 . . . . .7F **35**
  SM1: Sutt 5H **165**
  UB7: W Dray 2A **92**
Osprey Ct. BR3: Beck 7C **140**
  CR0: C'don 3C **168**
                 (off Innes Yd.)
  E1 . . . . .3K **15**
                  (off Star Pl.)
Osprey Est. SE16 . . . . .4K **103**
Osprey Ho. E14 . . . . .7A **86**
                (off Victory Pl.)
  SE1 . . . . .5H **103**
                (off Lynton Rd.)
Osprey La. HA2: Harr 2F **59**
Osprey M. EN3: Pond E 5D **24**
Ospringe Cl. SE20 . . . . .7J **139**
Ospringe Ct. SE9 . . . . .6H **125**
Ospringe Ho. SE1 . . . . .6K **13**
                (off Wootton St.)
Ospringe Rd. NW5 . . . . .4G **65**
Osram Ct. W6 . . . . .3D **98**
Osram Rd. HA9: Wemb 3D **60**
Osric Path N1 . . . . .2E **84**
Ossian M. N4 . . . . .7K **47**
Ossian Rd. N4 . . . . .7K **47**
OSSIE GARVIN RDBT. 7K **75**
Ossington Bldgs. W1 . . . . . .5G **5** (5E **82**)
Ossington Cl. W2 . . . . .7J **81**
Ossington St. W2 . . . . .7J **81**
Ossory Rd. SE1 . . . . .6G **103**
Ossulston St. NW1 . . . . .1D **6** (2H **83**)
Ossulton Pl. N2 . . . . .3A **46**
Ossulton Way N2 . . . . .4A **46**
Ostade Rd. SW2 . . . . .7K **119**
Ostell Cres. EN3: Enf L 1H **25**
Ostend Pl. SE1 . . . . .4C **102**
Osten M. SW7 . . . . .3K **99**
OSTERLEY 7H **95**
Osterley Av. TW7: Isle 7H **95**
Osterley Cl. BR5: St P 1K **161**
Osterley Ct. TW7: Isle 1H **113**
  UB5: N'olt 2A **76**
              (off Canberra Dr.)
Osterley Cres. TW7: Isle 1J **113**
Osterley Gdns. CR7: Thor H 2C **156**
  UB2: S'hall 2G **95**
Osterley Ho. E14 . . . . .6D **86**
                (off Giraud St.)

Osterley La. TW7: Isle 4G 95
   UB2: S'hall 5E 94
Osterley Lodge TW7: Isle 7J 95
   (off Church Rd.)
Osterley Pk. 6G 95
Osterley Pk. House 6G 95
Osterley Pk. Rd. UB2: S'hall 3D 94
Osterley Pk. Vw. Rd. W7 . . . . .2G 97
Osterley Rd. N16 . . . . .4E 66
   TW7: Isle 7J 95
Osterley Sports & Athletics Cen. 7J 95
Osterley Sports Club 3G 95
Osterley Views UB2: S'hall 2H 95
Oster Ter. E17 . . . . .5K 49
Ostlers Dr. TW15: Ashf 5E 128
Ostliffe Rd. N13 . . . . .5H 33
Oswald Bldg. SW8 . . . . .6F 101
Oswald Rd. UB1: S'hall 1C 94
Oswald's Mead E9 . . . . .4A 68
Oswald St. E5 . . . . .3K 67
Oswald Ter. NW2 . . . . .3E 62
Osward CRO: Sels 7B 170
   (not continuous)
Osward Pl. N9 . . . . .2C 34
Osward Rd. SW17 . . . . .2D 136
Oswell Ho. E1 . . . . .1H 103
   (off Farthing Flds.)
Oswin St. SE11 . . . . .4B 102
Oswyth Rd. SE5 . . . . .2E 120
Otford Cl. BR1: Brom 3E 160
   DA5: Bexl 6H 127
   SE20 . . . . .1J 157
Otford Cres. SE4 . . . . .6B 122
Otford Ho. SE1 . . . . .7F 15
   (off Staple St.)
   SE15 . . . . .6J 103
   (off Lovelinch Cl.)
Othello Cl. SE11 . . . . . . .5K 19 (5B 102)
Otho Ct. TW8: Bford 7D 96
Otis St. E3 . . . . .3E 86
Otley App. IG2: Ilf 6F 53
Otley Dr. IG2: Ilf 5F 53
Otley Ho. N5 .3A 66
Otley Rd. E16 . . . . .6A 88
Otley Ter. E5 . . . . .3K 67
Ottawa Gdns.
   RM10: Dag 7K 73
Ottawa Ho. SE16 . . . . .2J 103
   (off Province Dr.)
   UB4: Yead 3K 75
   (off Ayles Rd.)
Ottaway St. E5 . . . . .3G 67
Otterbourne Rd.
   CRO: C'don 2C 168
   E4 . . . . .3A 36
Otterburn Gdns. TW7: Isle 7A 96
Otterburn Ho. SE5 . . . . .7C 102
   (off Sultan St.)
Otterburn St. SW17 . . . . .6D 136
Otter Cl. E15 .1E 86
Otterden St. BR6: Orp 3J 173
Otterden St. SE6 . . . . .4C 140
Otterden Ter. SE1 . . . . .4F 103
   (off Lynton Rd.)
Otter Rd. SM5: Cars 1D 166
Otterfield Rd. UB7: Yiew 7A 74
Otter Rd. UB6: G'frd 4G 77
Ottley Dr. SE3 . . . . .4A 124
Otto Cl. SE26 . . . . .3H 139
Otto St. SE17 . . . . .6B 102
Ott's Yard N19 . . . . .4G 65
   (off Southcote Rd.)
Otway Gdns. WD23: Bush 1D 26
Oulton Cl. E5 .2J 67
   SE28 . . . . .6C 90
Oulton Cres. IG11: Bark 5K 71
Oulton Rd. N15 . . . . .5D 48
Ouseley Rd. SW12 . . . . .1D 136
Outer Circ. NW1 . . . . .1D 4 (2C 82) & 1J 5
Outgate Rd. NW10 . . . . .7B 62
Outram Pl. N1 . . . . .1J 83

Outram Rd. CRO: C'don 2F 169
   E6 . . . . .1C 88
   N22 . . . . .1H 47
Outwich St. EC3 . . . . .7H 9
Outwood Ho. SW2 . . . . .7K 119
   (off Deepdene Gdns.)
Oval, The 7H 19 (6K 101)
Oval, The DA15: Sidc 7A 126
   E2 . . . . .2H 85
Oval Ct. HA8: Edg 7D 28
Oval Ho. CRO: C'don 1E 168
   (off Oval Rd.)
Oval Mans. SE11 . . . . . .7H 19 (6K 101)
Oval Pl. SW8 . . . . .7K 101
Oval Rd. CRO: C'don 2D 168
   NW1 . . . . .1F 83
Oval Rd. Nth. RM10: Dag 1H 91
Oval Rd. Sth. RM10: Dag 2H 91
Ovanna M. N1 . . . . .6E 66
Overbrae BR3: Beck 6C 140
Overbrook Wlk. HA8: Edg 7B 28
   (not continuous)
Overbury Av. BR3: Beck 3D 158
Overbury Rd. N15 . . . . .6D 48
Overbury St. E5 . . . . .4K 67
Overcliff Rd. SE13 . . . . .3C 122
Overcourt Cl. DA15: Sidc 6B 126
Overdale Av. KT3: N Mald 2J 151
Overdale Rd. W5 . . . . .3C 96
Overdown Rd. SE6 . . . . .4C 140
Overhill Rd. SE22 . . . . .7G 121
Overhill Way BR3: Beck 5F 159
Overlea Rd. E5 . . . . .7G 49
Overmead DA15: Sidc 7H 125
Oversley Ho. W2 . . . . .5J 81
   (off Alfred Rd.)
Overstand Cl. BR3: Beck 5C 158
Overstone Gdns. CRO: C'don 7B 158
Overstone Ho. E14 . . . . .6C 86
   (off E. India Dock Rd.)
Overstone Rd. W6 . . . . .3E 98
Overstrand Mans. SW11 . . . . .1D 118
Overton Cl. NW10 . . . . .6J 61
   TW7: Isle 1K 113
Overton Cl. E11 . . . . .7J 51
   SM2: Sutt 7J 165
Overton Dr. E11 . . . . .7J 51
   RM6: Chad H 7C 54
Overton Ho. SW15 . . . . .7B 116
   (off Tangley Gro.)
Overton Rd. E10 . . . . .1A 68
   N14 . . . . .5D 22
   SE2 . . . . .3C 108
   SM2: Sutt 6J 165
   SW9 . . . . .2A 120
Overton Rd. E. SE2 . . . . .3D 108
Overton's Yd. CRO: C'don 3C 168
Overy Ho. SE1 . . . . .7A 14 (2B 102)
Ovesdon Av. HA2: Harr 1D 58
Ovett Cl. SE19 . . . . .6E 138
Ovex Cl. E14 .2E 104
Ovington Ct. SW3 . . . . .2D 16
Ovington Gdns. SW3 . . .2D 16 (3C 100)
Ovington M. SW3 . . . . .2D 16
Ovington Sq. SW3 . . . . .2D 16 (3C 100)
Ovington St. SW3 . . . . . .3D 16 (4C 100)
Owen Cl.
   CRO: C'don 6D 156
   SE28 . . . . .1C 108
   TW16: Sun 1G 147
   UB5: N'olt 6C 58
   (Arnold Rd.)
   UB5: N'olt 3K 75
   (Attlee Rd.)
Owen Gdns. IG8: Wfd G 6H 37
Owen Ho. TW1: Twick 7B 114
   TW14: Felt 7J 111
Owenite St. SE2 . . . . .4B 108

Owen Mans. W14 . . . . .6G 99
   (off Queen's Club Gdns.)
Owen Rd. N13 . . . . .5H 33
   UB4: Yead 3K 75
Owens M. E11 . . . . .2G 69
Owen St. EC1 . . . . .1A 8 (3B 84)
Owen's Row EC1 . . . . .1A 8 (2B 84)
Owens Way SE23 . . . . .7A 122
Owen Wlk. SE20 . . . . .1G 157
Owen Way NW10 . . . . .6J 61
Owgan Cl. SE5 . . . . .7D 102
Owgan Av. SW6 . . . . .2G 117
Oxberry Av. SW6 . . . . .2G 117
Oxborough Ho. SW18 . . . . .4A 118
   (off Eltringham St.)
Oxendon St. SW1 . . . . . .3C 12 (7H 83)
Oxenford St. SE15 . . . . .3F 121
Oxenham Ho. SE8 . . . . .6C 104
   (off Benbow St.)
Oxenholme NW1 . . . . .1A 6
   (off Hampstead Rd.)
Oxenpark Av. HA9: Wemb 5E 42
Oxestall's Rd. SE8 . . . . .5A 104
Oxford & Cambridge Mans. NW1 . . .6D 4
   (off Old Marylebone Rd.)
Oxford Av. N14 . . . . .1B 32
   SW20 .2G 153
   TW5: Hest 5E 94
   UB3: Harl 7H 93
Oxford Cir. W1 . . . . .1A 12
Oxford Cir. Av. W1 . . . . . . .1A 12 (6G 83)
Oxford Cl. CR4: Mitc 3G 155
   N9 . . . . .2C 34
   TW15: Ashf 7E 128
Oxford Ct. EC4 . . . . .2E 14
   KT6: Surb 7D 150
   (off Avenue Elmers)
   TW13: Hanw 4B 130
   W3 . . . . .6G 79
   W4 . . . . .5H 97
   W7 . . . . .5H 97
   (off Copley Cl.)
   W9 . . . . .5J 81
   (off Elmfield Way)
Oxford Cres. KT3: N Mald 6K 151
Oxford Dr. HA4: Ruis 2A 58
   SE1 . . . . .5G 15 (1E 102)
Oxford Gdns. N20 . . . . .1G 31
   N21 . . . . .7H 23
   W4 . . . . .5G 97
   W10 . . . . .6E 80
Oxford Ga. W6 . . . . .4F 99
Oxford Ho. BR2: Brom 8B 160
   (off Wells Vw. Dr.)
   E3 . . . . .5B 86
   (off William Whiffin Sq.)
   NW6 . . . . .2J 81
   (off Oxford Rd.)
   RM8: Dag 4A 72
Oxford M. DA5: Bexl 7G 127
Oxford Pl. NW10 . . . . .3K 61
   (off Press Rd.)
Oxford Rd. DA14: Sidc 5B 144
   E15 . . . . .6F 69
   (not continuous)
   EN3: Pond E 5C 24
   HA1: Harr 6G 41
   HA3: W'stone 3K 41
   IG1: Ilf .5G 71
   IG8: Wfd G 5G 37
   N4 . . . . .1A 66
   N9 . . . . .2C 34
   NW6 . . . . .2J 81
   SE19 . . . . .6D 138
   SM5: Cars 6C 166
   SM6: Wall 5G 167
   SW15 .4G 117
   TW11: Tedd 5H 131
   W5 . . . . .7D 78
Oxford Rd. Nth. W4 . . . . .5H 97
Oxford Rd. Sth. W4 . . . . .5G 97
Oxford Row TW16: Sun 3A 148

Oxford Sq. W2 . . . . .1D 10 (6C 82)
Oxford St. W1 . . . . .1G 11 (6E 82)
Oxford Ter. NW6 . . . . .2K 81
   (off Oxford Rd.)
Oxford Wlk. UB1: S'hall 1D 94
Oxford Way TW13: Hanw 4B 130
Oxgate Cen. NW2 . . . . .2D 62
Oxgate Ct. NW2 . . . . .2C 62
Oxgate Ct. Pde. NW2 . . . . .2C 62
Oxgate Gdns. NW2 . . . . .3D 62
Oxgate La. NW2 . . . . .2D 62
Oxgate Pde. NW2 . . . . .2C 62
Oxhawth Cres. BR2: Brom 5E 160
Oxhey La. HA3: Hrw W 5A 26
   HA5: Hat E 5A 26
Oxleas E6 . . . . .6F 89
Oxleas Cl. DA16: Well 2H 125
Oxleay Rd. HA2: Harr 1E 58
Oxleigh Cl. KT3: N Mald 5A 152
Oxley Cl. SE1 . . . . .5F 103
Oxley Sq. E3 .4D 86
   (off Truman Wlk.)
Oxleys Rd. NW2 . . . . .3D 62
Oxlip Cl. CRO: C'don 1K 169
Oxlow La. RM9: Dag 4F 73
   RM10: Dag 4F 73
Oxonian St. SE22 . . . . .4F 121
Oxo Tower Wharf SE1 . . . .3K 13 (7A 84)
Oxted Cl. CR4: Mitc 3B 154
Oxtoby Way SW16 . . . . .1H 155
Oxygen, The E16 . . . . .7J 87
OYO Business Units DA17: Belv 2J 109
Oyo Bus. Units RM9: Dag 4F 91
Oystercatcher Cl. E16 . . . . .6K 87
Oyster Ct. SE17 . . . . .4C 102
   (off Crampton St.)
Oystergate Wlk. EC4 . . . . .3E 14
Oyster Row E1 . . . . .6J 85
Oyster Wharf SW11 . . . . .2B 118
Ozolins Way E16 . . . . .6J 87

P

Pablo Neruda Cl. SE24 . . . . .4B 120
Pace Pl. E1 . . . . .6H 85
Pacific Cl. TW14: Felt 1H 129
Pacific Ct. E1 . . . . .5J 85
Pacific Ho. E1 . . . . .4K 85
   (off Ernest St.)
Pacific M. SW9 . . . . .4A 120
Pacific Rd. E16 . . . . .6J 87
Pacific Wharf SE16 . . . . .1K 103
Packenham Ho. E2 . . . . .1K 9
   (off Wellington Row)
Packham Ct. KT4: Wor Pk 3E 164
Packington Rd. W3 . . . . .3J 97
Packington Sq. N1 . . . . .1C 84
   (not continuous)
Packington St. N1 . . . . .1B 84
Packmores Rd. SE9 . . . . .5H 125
Padbury SE17 . . . . .5E 102
   (off Bagshot St.)
Padbury Cl. TW14: Bedf 1F 129
Padbury Ct. E2 . . . . .2K 9 (3K 85)
Padbury Ho. NW8 . . . . .3D 4
   (off Tresham Cres.)
Padbury Oaks UB7: Lford 4C 174
Padcroft Rd.
   UB7: Yiew 1A 92
Paddenswick Rd. W6 . . . . .3C 98
PADDINGTON 7A 4 (6B 82)
Paddington Cl. UB4: Yead 4B 76
Paddington Ct. W7 . . . . .5K 77
   (off Copley Cl.)
Paddington Grn. W2 . . . . . .5A 4 (5B 82)
Paddington Sports Club 4K 81
Paddington St. W1 . . . . . . .5G 5 (5E 82)
Paddock, The N10 . . . . .3E 46
   NW9 . . . . .5G 43
   UB10: Ick 4D 56

Paddock Cl.—Panmure Ct.

Paddock Cl. BR6: Farnb 4F 173
KT4: Wor Pk 1A 164
SE3 2J 123
SE26 4K 139
UB5: N'olt 2E 76
Paddock Gdns. SE19 6E 138
Paddock Lodge EN1: Enf 5K 23
(off Village Rd.)
Paddock Mobile Home Pk. BR2: Kes 7C 172
Paddock Pas. SE19 6E 138
(off Paddock Gdns.)
Paddock Rd. DA6: Bex 4E 126
HA4: Ruis 3B 58
NW2 3C 62
Paddocks, The CR0: Addtn 6C 170
EN4: Cockf 3J 21
HA9: Wemb 2H 61
W5 3D 96
(off Popes La.)
Paddocks Cl. HA2: Harr 4F 59
Paddocks Grn. NW9 1H 61
Paddock Way BR7: Chst 7H 143
SW15 7E 116
Padelford La. HA7: Stan 2F 27
Padfield Ct. HA9: Wemb 3F 61
Padfield Rd. SE5 3C 120
Padley Cl. KT9: Chess 5F 163
Padnall Ct. RM6: Chad H 3D 54
Padnall Rd. RM6: Chad H 3D 54
Padstone Ho. E3 3D 86
(off Talwin St.)
Padstow Cl. BR6: Chels 4K 173
Padstow Ho. E14 7B 86
(off Three Colt St.)
Padstow Rd. EN2: Enf 1G 23
Padstow Wlk. TW14: Felt 1H 129
Padua Rd. SE20 1J 157
Pagden St. SW8 1F 119
Pageant Av. NW9 1K 43
Pageant Cres. SE16 1A 104
Pageantmaster Ct. EC4 1A 14
Pageant Wlk. CR0: C'don 3E 168
Page Av. HA9: Wemb 3J 61
Page Cl. HA3: Kenton 6F 43
RM9: Dag 5E 72
TW12: Hamp 6C 130
Page Ct. NW7 7J 29
Page Cres. CR0: Wadd 5B 168
Page Grn. Rd. N15 5G 49
Page Grn. Ter. N15 5F 49
Page Heath La.
BR1: Brom 3B 160
Page Heath Vs. BR1: Brom 3B 160
Page High N22 2A 48
(off Lymington Av.)
Page Ho. SE10 6E 104
(off Welland St.)
Pagehurst Rd. CR0: C'don 7H 157
Page Mdw. NW7 7J 29
Page M. SW11 2E 118
Page Rd. TW14: Bedf 6F 111
Pages Hill N10 2E 46
Pages La. N10 2E 46
Page St. NW7 1C 44
SW1 3D 18 (4H 101)
Page's Wlk. SE1 4E 102
Pages Yd. W4 6B 98
Paget Av. SM1: Sutt 3B 166
Paget Cl. TW12: Hamp H 4H 131
Paget Gdns. BR7: Chst 1F 161
Paget Ho. E2 2J 85
(off Bishop's Way)
Paget La. TW7: Isle 3H 113
Paget Pl. KT2: King T 6J 133
KT7: T Ditt 1A 162
Paget Ri. SE18 6E 106
Paget Rd. IG1: Ilf 4F 71
N16 1D 66
UB10: Hil 4E 74
Paget St. EC1 1A 8 (3B 84)
Paget Ter. SE18 6F 107
Pagham Ho. W10 4E 80
(off Sutton Way)
Pagin Ho. N15 5E 48
(off Braemar Rd.)
Pagitts Gro. EN4: Had W 1E 20
Pagnell St. SE14 7B 104
Pagoda Av. TW9: Rich 3F 115
Pagoda Gdns. SE3 2F 123
Pagoda Gro. SE27 2C 138
Paignton Rd. HA4: Ruis 3J 57
N15 6E 48
Paines Cl. HA5: Pinn 3C 40
Paines La. HA5: Pinn 1C 40
Pain's Cl. CR4: Mitc 2F 155
Painsthorpe Rd. N16 3E 66
Painted Hall
Greenwich 6F 105
Painters M. SE16 4G 103
Painters Rd. IG2: Ilf 3K 53
Paisley Rd. N22 1B 48
SM5: Cars 1B 166
Paisley Ter. SM5: Cars 7B 154
Pakeman Ho. SE1 6B 14
(off Surrey Row)
Pakeman St. N7 3K 65
Pakenham Cl. SW12 1E 136
Pakenham St. WC1 2H 7 (3K 83)
Pakington Ho. SW9 2J 119
(off Stockwell Gdns. Est.)
Palace Av. W8 2K 99
Palace Bingo Club 4C 102
(within Elephant & Castle Shop. Cen.)
Palace Cl. E9 6B 68
Palace Ct. BR1: Brom 1K 159
(off Palace Gro.)
HA3: Kenton 6E 42
NW3 5K 63
W2 7K 81
(not continuous)
Palace Ct. Gdns. N10 3G 47
Palace Exchange EN2: Enf 4J 23
Palace Gdns. IG9: Buck H 1G 37
Palace Gdns. M. W8 1K 99
Palace Gdns. Shop. Cen.
EN2: Enf 4J 23
Palace Gdns. Ter. W8 1J 99
Palace Ga. W8 2A 100
Palace Gates M. N8 4J 47
(off The Campsbourne)
Palace Gates Rd. N22 1H 47
Palace Grn. CR0: Sels 7B 170
W8 1K 99
Palace Gro.
BR1: Brom 1K 159
SE19 7F 139
Palace Ice Rink, The 2H 47
Palace Mans. KT1: King T 4D 150
(off Palace Rd.)
W14 4G 99
(off Hammersmith Rd.)
Palace M. E17 4B 50
EN2: Enf 3J 23
SW1 4H 17
SW6 7H 99
Palace Pde. E17 4B 50
Palace Pl. SW1 1A 18 (3G 101)
Palace Pl. Mans. W8 2K 99
(off Kensington Ct.)
Palace Rd. BR1: Brom 1K 159
HA4: Ruis 4C 58
KT1: King T 4D 150
KT8: E Mos 3G 149
N8 5H 47
(not continuous)
N11 7D 32
SE19 7F 139
SW2 1K 137
Palace Sq. SE19 7F 139
Palace St. SW1 1A 18 (3G 101)
Palace Superbowl 4C 102
(within Elephant & Castle Shop. Cen.)
Palace Theatre
Soho 1D 12
(off Shaftesbury Av.)
Palace Vw. BR1: Brom 3K 159
(not continuous)
CR0: C'don 4B 170
SE12 2J 141
Palace Vw. Rd. E4 5J 35
Palace Wharf W6 7E 98
(off Rainville Rd.)
Palamos Rd. E10 1C 68
Palatine Av. N16 4E 66
Palatine Rd. N16 4E 66
Palazzo Apartments N1 7E 66
(off Ardleigh Rd.)
Palemead Cl. SW6 1F 117
Palermo Rd. NW10 2C 80
Palestine Gro. SW19 1B 154
Palestra Ho. SE1 5A 14
(off Blackfriars Rd.)
Palewell Comn. Dr. SW14 5K 115
Palewell Pk. SW14 5K 115
Palfrey Pl. SW8 7K 101
Palgrave Av. UB1: S'hall 7E 76
Palgrave Ct. TW11: Hamp W 7C 132
Palgrave Gdns. NW1 3D 4 (4C 82)
Palgrave Ho. SE5 7C 102
(off Wyndham Est.)
TW2: Whitt 7G 113
Palgrave Rd. W12 3B 98
Palissy St. E2 2J 9 (3F 85)
(not continuous)
Palladino Ho. SW17 5C 136
(off Laurel Cl.)
Palladio Ct. SW18 6K 117
(off Mapleton Cres.)
Palladium Ct. E8 7F 67
(off Queensbridge Rd.)
Pallant Ho. SE1 3D 102
(off Tabard St.)
Pallant Way BR6: Farnb 3E 172
Pallet Way SE18 1C 124
Palliser Ct. W14 5G 99
(off Palliser Rd.)
Palliser Ho. E1 4K 85
(off Ernest St.)
SE10 6F 105
(off Trafalgar Rd.)
Palliser Rd. W14 5G 99
Pallister Ter. SW15 3B 134
Pall Mall SW1 5B 12 (1G 101)
Pall Mall E. SW1 4D 12 (1H 101)
Pall Mall Pl. SW1 5B 12
Palmar Cres. DA7: Bex 3G 127
Palmar Rd. DA7: Bex 2G 127
Palm Av. DA14: Sidc 6D 144
Palm Cl. E10 3D 68
Palm Ct. SE15 7F 103
(off Garnies Cl.)
Palmeira Rd. DA7: Bex 3D 126
Palmer Av. SM3: Cheam 4E 164
Palmer Cl. BR4: W W'ck 3F 171
TW5: Hest 1E 112
UB5: N'olt 6C 58
Palmer Cres. KT1: King T 3E 150
Palmer Dr. BR1: Brom 4F 161
Palmer Gdns. EN5: Barn 5A 20
Palmer Ho. SE14 7K 103
(off Lubbock St.)
Palmer Pl. N7 5A 66
Palmer Rd. E13 4K 87
RM8: Dag 1D 72
Palmer's Ct. N11 5B 32
(off Palmer's Rd.)
PALMERS GREEN 3F 33
Palmers Gro.
KT8: W Mole 4E 148
Palmers La. EN1: Enf 1C 24
EN3: Enf H 1C 24
Palmers Pas. SW14 3J 115
(off Little St Leonard's)
Palmers Rd. E2 2K 85
N11 5B 32
SW14 3J 115
SW16 2K 155
Palmerston Cen. HA3: W'stone 3K 41
Palmerston Ct. E3 2K 85
(off Old Ford Rd.)
IG9: Buck H 1F 37
KT6: Surb 7D 150
Palmerston Cres. N13 5E 32
SE18 6G 107
Palmerston Gro. SW19 7J 135
Palmerston Ho. SE1 7J 13
(off Westminster Bri. Rd.)
W8 1J 99
(off Kensington Pl.)
Palmerston Mans. W14 6G 99
(off Queen's Club Gdns.)
Palmerston Rd. BR6: Farnb 4G 173
CR0: C'don 5D 156
E7 6K 69
E17 3B 50
HA3: W'stone 3J 41
IG9: Buck H 2E 36
N22 7E 32
NW6 7H 63
(not continuous)
SM1: Sutt 5A 166
SM5: Cars 4D 166
SW14 4J 115
SW19 7J 135
TW2: Twick 6J 113
TW3: Houn 1G 113
W3 3J 97
Palmerston Way SW8 7F 101
Palmer St. SW1 1C 18 (3H 101)
(not continuous)
Palmers Wharf KT1: King T 2D 150
(off Emms Pas.)
Palm Gro. W5 3E 96
Palm Rd. RM7: Rom 5J 55
Palyn Ho. EC1 2D 8
(off Radnor St.)
Pamela Ct. N12 6E 30
Pamela Gdns. HA5: Eastc 5K 39
Pamela St. E8 1F 85
Pamela Wlk. E8 1G 85
(off Marlborough Av.)
Pampisford Rd. CR8: Purl 7B 168
Pams Way KT19: Ewe 5K 163
Panama Ho. E1 5K 85
(off Beaumont Sq.)
Pancras La. EC4 1E 14 (6C 84)
Pancras Rd. N1 1E 6 (2J 83)
NW1 2H 83
Pancras Sq. N1 2J 83
Pancras Way E3 2C 86
Pandangle Ho. E8 1F 85
(off Kingsland Rd.)
Pandian Way NW1 6H 65
Pandora Ct. E16 5J 87
(off Robertson Rd.)
Pandora M. E1 4J 9
Pandora Rd. NW6 6J 63
Panfield M. IG2: Ilf 6E 52
Panfield Rd. SE2 3A 108
Pangbourne NW1 2A 6
(off Stanhope St.)
Pangbourne Av. W10 5E 80
Pangbourne Dr. HA7: Stan 5J 27
Panhard Pl. UB1: S'hall 7F 77
Pank Av. EN5: New Bar 5F 21
Pankhurst Av. E16 1K 105
Pankhurst Cl. SE14 7K 103
TW7: Isle 3K 113
Pankhurst Ho. W12 6D 80
Pankhurst Rd. KT12: Walt T 7A 148
Panmuir Rd. SW20 1D 152
Panmure Cl. N5 4B 66
Panmure Ct. UB1: S'hall 6G 77
(off Osborne Rd.)

Panmure Rd. SE26 . . . . .3H **139**
Pannells Ct. TW5: Hest 6E **94**
Panorama Ct. N6 . . . . .6G **47**
Panoramic Twr. E14 . . . . .6D **86**
(off Burcham St.)
Pan Peninsula Sq. E14 . . . . .2D **104**
Pansy Gdns. W12 . . . . .7C **80**
Panther Dr. NW10 . . . . .5K **61**
Pantiles, The BR1: Brom 3C **160**
DA7: Bex 7F **109**
NW11 . . . . .4H **45**
WD23: B Hea 1C **26**
Pantiles Cl. N13 . . . . .5G **33**
Panton Cl. CR0: C'don 1B **168**
Panton St. SW1 . . . . .3C **12** (7H **83**)
Panyer All. EC1 . . . . .7C **8**
(off Newgate St.)
Panyers Gdns. RM10: Dag 3H **73**
Paper Bldgs. EC4 . . . . .2K **13**
Papermill Cl. SM5: Cars 4E **166**
Papermill Pl. E17 . . . . .2A **50**
Paper Mill Wharf E14 . . . . .7A **86**
Papillons Wlk. SE3 . . . . .2J **123**
Papworth Gdns. N7 . . . . .5K **65**
Papworth Way SW2 . . . . .7A **120**
Papyrus Ho. N1 . . . . .1C **8**
Parabola Ct. KT8: E Mos 4G **149**
Parade, The CR0: C'don 6J **155**
KT2: King T 2E **150**
(off London Rd.)
KT4: Wor Pk 4B **164**
N4 . . . . .1A **66**
SE4 .2B **122**
(off Up. Brockley Rd.)
SE26 . . . . .3H **139**
(off Wells Pk. Rd.)
SM1: Sutt 3H **165**
SM5: Cars 5D **166**
(off Beynon Rd.)
SW11 . . . . .7D **100**
TW12: Hamp H 5H **131**
TW16: Sun 7H **129**
UB6: G'frd 5B **60**
Parade Gdns. E4 . . . . .7J **35**
Parade Ground Path SE18 . . . . .7D **106**
Parade Mans. NW4 . . . . .5D **44**
Parade M. SE27 . . . . .2B **138**
Paradise Pas. N7 . . . . .5A **66**
Paradise Path SE28 . . . . .1A **108**
Paradise Pl. SE18 . . . . .4C **106**
Paradise Rd. SW4 . . . . .2J **119**
TW9: Rich 5D **114**
Paradise Row E2 . . . . .3H **85**
Paradise St. SE16 . . . . .2H **103**
Paradise Wlk. SW3 . . . . . .7F **17** (6D **100**)
Paragon TW8: Bford 5E **96**
(off Boston Pk. Rd.)
Paragon, The SE3 . . . . .2H **123**
Paragon Cl. E16 . . . . .6J **87**
Paragon Gro. KT5: Surb 6F **151**
Paragon M. SE1 . . . . .4D **102**
Paragon Pl. KT5: Surb 6F **151**
SE3 .2H **123**
Paragon Rd. E9 . . . . .6J **67**
Paramount Bldg. EC1 . . . . .3A **8**
(off St John St.)
Paramount Ct. WC1 . . . . .4B **6**
Parbury Ri. KT9: Chess 6E **162**
Parbury Rd. SE23 . . . . .6A **122**
Parchmore Rd. CR7: Thor H 2B **156**
Parchmore Way CR7: Thor H 2B **156**
Pardoe Rd. E10 . . . . .7D **50**
Pardoner Ho. SE1 . . . . .3D **102**
(off Pardoner St.)
Pardoner St. SE1 . . . . . . .7F **15** (3D **102**)
(not continuous)
Pardon St. EC1 . . . . .3B **8** (4B **84**)
Parent Shop. Mall E18 . . . . .2J **51**
(off Marlborough Rd.)
Parfett St. E1 . . . . .5G **85**
(not continuous)

Parfitt Cl. NW3 . . . . .1A **64**
Parfrey St. W6 . . . . .6E **98**
Pargraves Ct. HA9: Wemb 2G **61**
Parham Dr. IG2: Ilf 6F **53**
Parham Way N10 . . . . .2G **47**
Paris Corte SE13 . . . . .3D **122**
(off Loampit Va.)
Paris Gdn. SE1 . . . . .4A **14** (1B **102**)
Parish Ct. KT6: Surb 5E **150**
Parish Ga. Dr. DA15: Sidc 6J **125**
Parish La. SE20 . . . . .6K **139**
Parish M. SE20 . . . . .7K **139**
Paris Ho. E2 . . . . .2H **85**
(off Old Bethnal Grn. Rd.)
Parison Cl. TW9: Rich 3G **115**
Park, The DA14: Sidc 5A **144**
HA1: Harr 1J **59**
N6 . . . . .6E **46**
NW11 . . . . .1K **63**
SE23 . . . . .1J **139**
SM5: Cars 5D **166**
W5 . . . . .1D **96**
Park App. DA16: Well 4B **126**
SE16 . . . . .3H **103**
Park Av. BR1: Brom 6H **141**
BR4: W W'ck 2E **170**
BR6: Chels 2K **173**
BR6: Farnb 3D **172**
CR4: Mitc 7F **137**
E6 . . . . .1E **88**
E15 .6G **69**
EN1: Enf 5J **23**
HA4: Ruis 6F **39**
IG1: Ilf 1E **70**
IG8: Wfd G 5E **36**
IG11: Bark 6G **71**
N3 . . . . .1K **45**
N13 .3F **33**
N18 .4B **34**
N22 .2J **47**
NW2 . . . . .5D **62**
NW10 . . . . .2F **79**
(Brent Cres., not continuous)
NW10 . . . . .5D **62**
(Park Av. Nth.)
NW11 . . . . .1K **63**
SM5: Cars 6E **166**
SW14 . . . . .4K **115**
TW3: Houn 6F **113**
TW17: Shep 3G **147**
UB1: S'hall 2D **94**
Park Av. E. KT17: Ewe 6C **164**
Park Av. M. CR4: Mitc 7F **137**
Park Av. Nth. N8 . . . . .3H **47**
NW10 . . . . .5D **62**
Park Av. Rd. N17 . . . . .7C **34**
Park Av. Sth. N8 . . . . .4H **47**
Park Av. W. KT17: Ewe 6C **164**
Park Chase HA9: Wemb 4F **61**
Park Cl. E9 . . . . .1J **85**
HA3: Hrw W 1J **41**
KT2: King T 1G **151**
N12 .3G **31**
NW2 . . . . .3D **62**
NW10 . . . . .3F **79**
SM5: Cars 6D **166**
SW1 . . . . .7E **10** (2D **100**)
TW3: Houn 5G **113**
TW12: Hamp 1G **149**
W4 . . . . .6K **97**
W14 .3H **99**
Park Club, The
Acton 2A **118**
Park Ct. CR2: S Croy 5C **168**
(off Warham Rd.)
E4 . . . . .2K **35**
E17 .5D **50**
HA3: Kenton 7E **42**
HA9: Wemb 5E **60**

Park Ct. KT1: Hamp W 1C **150**
KT3: N Mald 4K **151**
N11 .7C **32**
N17 .7B **34**
SE21 . . . . .3C **138**
SE26 . . . . .6H **139**
SM6: Wall 5H **167**
SW11 . . . . .1F **119**
UB8: Uxb 1A **74**
W6 . . . . .4D **98**
Park Cres. DA8: Erith 6J **109**
EN2: Enf 4J **23**
HA3: Hrw W 1J **41**
N3 . . . . .7F **31**
TW2: Twick 1H **131**
W1 . . . . .4J **5** (4F **83**)
Park Cres. M. E. W1 . . . . . .4K **5** (4F **83**)
Park Cres. M. W. W1 . . . . . .4J **5** (4F **83**)
Park Cres. Rd. DA8: Erith 6K **109**
Park Cft. HA8: Edg 1J **43**
Parkcroft Rd. SE12 . . . . .7H **123**
Parkdale N11 . . . . .6C **32**
Parkdale Cres. KT4: Wor Pk 3K **163**
Parkdale Rd. SE18 . . . . .5J **107**
Park Dr. HA2: Harr 7E **40**
HA3: Hrw W 6C **26**
N21 .6H **23**
NW11 . . . . .1K **63**
RM1: Rom 4K **55**
RM10: Dag 3J **73**
SE7 .6C **106**
SW14 . . . . .5K **115**
W3 . . . . .3G **97**
Park Dwellings NW3 . . . . .5D **64**
Park East Bldg. E3 . . . . .2C **86**
(off Fairfield Rd.)
Park End BR1: Brom 1H **159**
NW3 . . . . .4C **64**
Parker Bldg. SE16 . . . . .7K **15**
(off Old Jamaica Rd.)
Parker Cl. E16 . . . . .1C **106**
SM5: Cars 6D **166**
Parker Ct. N1 . . . . .1C **84**
(off Basire St.)
Parker Ho. E14 . . . . .2C **104**
(off Admirals Way)
Parker M. WC2 . . . . .7F **7** (6J **83**)
Parke Rd. SW13 . . . . .1C **116**
TW16: Sun 4J **147**
Parker Rd. CR0: C'don 4C **168**
Parkers Row SE1 . . . . . . .7K **15** (2G **103**)
Parker St. E16 . . . . .1C **106**
WC2 . . . . .7F **7** (6J **83**)
Park Farm Cl. HA5: Eastc 5K **39**
N2 . . . . .3A **46**
Park Farm Ct. UB3: Hayes 7G **75**
Park Farm Rd. BR1: Brom 1B **160**
KT2: King T 7E **132**
Parkfield Av. HA2: Harr 2G **41**
SW14 . . . . .4A **116**
TW13: Felt 3J **129**
UB5: N'olt 2B **76**
UB10: Hil 3D **74**
Parkfield Cl. HA8: Edg 6C **28**
UB5: N'olt 2C **76**
Parkfield Ct. SE14 . . . . .1B **122**
(off Parkfield Rd.)
Parkfield Cres. HA2: Harr 2G **41**
HA4: Ruis 2C **58**
TW13: Felt 3J **129**
Parkfield Dr. UB5: N'olt 2B **76**
Parkfield Gdns. HA2: Harr 3F **41**
Parkfield Ho. HA2: Harr 1F **41**
Parkfield Ind. Est. SW11 . . . . .2E **118**
Parkfield Pde. TW13: Felt 3J **129**
Parkfield Rd. HA2: Harr 3G **59**
NW10 . . . . .7D **62**
SE14 . . . . .1B **122**
SW4 . . . . .6H **119**
(not continuous)

Parkfield Rd. TW13: Felt 3J **129**
UB5: N'olt 2C **76**
UB10: Ick 1D **56**
Parkfields CR0: C'don 1B **170**
SW15 . . . . .4E **116**
Parkfields Av. NW9 . . . . .1K **61**
SW20 . . . . .1D **152**
Parkfields Cl. SM5: Cars 4E **166**
Parkfields Rd. KT2: King T 5F **133**
Parkfield St. N1 . . . . .2A **84**
Parkfield Way BR2: Brom 6D **160**
Park Gdns. DA8: Erith 4K **109**
E10 .1C **68**
KT2: King T 5F **133**
NW9 . . . . .3H **43**
Park Ga. N2 . . . . .3B **46**
N21 .7E **22**
W5 . . . . .5D **78**
Parkgate N1 . . . . .1D **84**
(off Southgate Rd.)
SE3 .3H **123**
Parkgate Av. EN4: Had W 1F **21**
Parkgate Cl. KT2: King T 6H **133**
Park Ga. Ct. TW12: Hamp H 6G **131**
Parkgate Cres. EN4: Had W 1F **21**
Parkgate Gdns. SW14 . . . . .5K **115**
Parkgate M. N6 . . . . .7G **47**
Parkgate Rd. SM6: Wall 5E **166**
SW11 . . . . .7C **100**
Park Gates HA2: Harr 4E **58**
Park Gro. BR1: Brom 1K **159**
DA7: Bex 3J **127**
E15 .1J **87**
HA8: Edg 5A **28**
N11 .7C **32**
Park Gro. Rd. E11 . . . . .2G **69**
Park Hall SE10 . . . . .7F **105**
(off Croom's Hill)
Park Hall Rd. N2 . . . . .4C **46**
SE21 . . . . .3C **138**
Park Hall Trad. Est. SE21 . . . . .3C **138**
Parkham Ct. BR2: Brom 2G **159**
Parkham St. SW11 . . . . .1C **118**
Park Hgts. Ct. E14 . . . . .6B **86**
(off Wharf La.)
Park Hill BR1: Brom 4C **160**
SE23 . . . . .2H **139**
SM5: Cars 6C **166**
SW4 . . . . .5H **119**
TW10: Rich 6F **115**
W5 . . . . .5D **78**
Park Hill Cl. SM5: Cars 5C **166**
Park Hill Ct. SW17 . . . . .3D **136**
Park Hill M. CR2: S Croy 5D **168**
Park Hill Ri. CR0: C'don 2E **168**
Park Hill Rd. BR2: Brom 2G **159**
CR0: C'don 2E **168**
SM6: Wall 7F **167**
Parkhill Rd. DA5: Bexl 7F **127**
DA14: Sidc 3H **143**
DA15: Sidc 3H **143**
E4 . . . . .1K **35**
NW3 . . . . .5D **64**
Parkhill Wlk. NW3 . . . . .5D **64**
Parkholme Rd. E8 . . . . .6G **67**
Park Ho. E9 . . . . .7J **67**
(off Shore Rd.)
N21 .7E **22**
SE5 .1D **120**
(off Camberwell Grn.)
W1 . . . . .1G **11**
Park Ho. Gdns. TW1: Twick 5C **114**
Park Ho. Pas. N6 . . . . .7E **46**
Parkhouse St. SE5 . . . . .7D **102**
Parkhurst Ct. N7 . . . . .4J **65**
Parkhurst Gdns. DA5: Bexl 7G **127**
Parkhurst Rd. DA5: Bexl 7G **127**
E12 .4E **70**
E17 .4A **50**
N7 . . . . .4J **65**
N11 .5K **31**

Parkhurst Rd. N17 .....2G **49**
  N22 .....6E **32**
  SM1: Sutt 4B **166**
Parkinson Ct. N1 .....2F **9**
(off Charles Sq. Est.)
Parkinson Ho. E9 .....7J **67**
(off Frampton Pk. Rd.)
  SW1 .....5C **18**
(off Tachbrook St.)
Parkland Ct. E15 .....5G **69**
(off Maryland Rd.)
  W14 .....2G **99**
(off Holland Pk. Av.)
Parkland Gdns. SW19 .....1F **135**
Parkland Gro. TW15: Ashf 3C **128**
Parkland Mead BR1: Brom 3F **161**
(not continuous)
Parkland M. BR7: Chst 7H **143**
Parkland Rd. IG8: Wfd G 7E **36**
  N22 .....2K **47**
  TW15: Ashf 4C **128**
Parklands KT5: Surb 5F **151**
  N6 .....7F **47**
Parklands Cl. EN4: Had W 1G **21**
  IG2: Ilf 7G **53**
  SW14 .....5J **115**
Parklands Ct. TW5: Hest 2B **112**
Parklands Dr. N3 .....3G **45**
Parklands Gro. TW7: Isle 1K **113**
Parklands Pde. TW5: Hest 2B **112**
(off Parklands Ct.)
Parklands Rd. SW16 .....5F **137**
Parklands Way KT4: Wor Pk 2A **164**
Parkland Walk Local Nature Reserve
.....7J **47**
Park La. CR0: C'don 3D **168**
  E15 .....1F **87**
  HA2: Harr 3F **59**
  HA7: Stan 3F **27**
  HA9: Wemb 5E **60**
  N9 .....3K **33**
(not continuous)
  N17 .....7A **34**
(not continuous)
  RM6: Chad H 6D **54**
  SM3: Cheam 6G **165**
  SM5: Cars 4E **166**
  SM6: Wall 5E **166**
  TW5: Cran 7J **93**
  TW9: Rich 4D **114**
  TW11: Tedd 6K **131**
  UB4: Hayes 7B **76**
  W1 .....2F **11** (7D **82**)
Park La. Cl. N17 .....7B **34**
Park La. Mans. CR0: C'don 3D **168**
(off Park La.)
PARK LANGLEY 4E **158**
Parklangley Club, The 4E **158**
Parklea Cl. NW9 .....1A **44**
Park Lee Ct. N16 .....7E **48**
Parkleigh Rd. SW19 .....2K **153**
Parkleys TW10: Ham 4D **132**
Parkleys Pde. TW10: Ham 4D **132**
Park Lodge NW8 .....7B **64**
  W14 .....3H **99**
(off Melbury Rd.)
Park Lodge Av. UB7: W Dray 2B **92**
Park Lofts SW2 .....5J **119**
(off Lyham Rd.)
Park Lorne NW8 .....2D **4**
(off Park Rd.)
Park Mnr. SM2: Sutt 7A **166**
(off Christchurch Pk.)
Park Mans. NW4 .....5D **44**
  NW8 .....2C **82**
(off Allitsen Rd.)
  SW1 .....7E **10**
(off Knightsbridge)
  SW8 .....7F **19** (6J **101**)
  SW11 .....1D **118**
(off Prince of Wales Dr.)

Park Mead DA15: Sidc 5B **126**
  HA2: Harr 3F **59**
Parkmead SW15 .....6D **116**
Parkmead Cl. CR0: C'don 6K **157**
Parkmead Gdns. NW7 .....6G **29**
Park M. BR7: Chst 6F **143**
  N8 .....6J **47**
  SE10 .....5H **105**
  SE24 .....7C **120**
  TW19: Stanw 7B **110**
  W10 .....2G **81**
Parkmore Cl. IG8: Wfd G 4D **36**
Park Pde. NW10 .....2B **80**
  UB3: Hayes 6G **75**
  W3 .....3G **97**
Park Piazza SE13 .....6F **123**
Park Pl. BR1: Brom 1K **159**
(off Park Rd.)
  E14 .....1C **104**
  HA9: Wemb 4F **61**
  N1 .....7D **66**
(off Downham Rd.)
  SW1 .....5A **12** (1G **101**)
  TW12: Hamp H 6G **131**
  W3 .....4G **97**
  W5 .....1D **96**
Park Pl. Dr. W3 .....3G **97**
Park Pl. Vs. W2 .....5A **4** (5A **82**)
Park Ridings N8 .....3A **48**
Park Ri. HA3: Hrw W 1J **41**
  SE23 .....1A **140**
Park Ri. Rd. SE23 .....1A **140**
Park Rd.
  BR1: Brom 1K **159**
  BR3: Beck 7B **140**
  BR7: Chst 6F **143**
  E6 .....1A **88**
  E10 .....1C **68**
  E12 .....1K **69**
  E15 .....1J **87**
  E17 .....5B **50**
  EN4: E Barn 4G **21**
  EN5: Barn 4C **20**
  HA0: Wemb 6E **60**
  IG1: Ilf 3H **71**
  KT1: Hamp W 1C **150**
  KT2: King T 5F **133**
  KT3: N Mald 4K **151**
  KT5: Surb 6F **151**
  KT8: E Mos 4G **149**
  N2 .....3B **46**
  N8 .....4G **47**
  N11 .....7C **32**
  N14 .....1C **32**
  N15 .....4B **48**
  N18 .....4B **34**
  NW1 .....2D **4** (3C **82**)
  NW4 .....7C **44**
  NW8 .....2D **4** (3C **82**)
  NW9 .....7K **43**
  NW10 .....1A **80**
  SE25 .....4E **156**
  SM3: Cheam 6G **165**
  SM6: Wall 5F **167**
(Clifton Rd.)
  SM6: Wall 5F **167**
(Elmwood Cl.)
  SW19 .....6B **136**
  TW1: Twick 6C **114**
  TW3: Houn 5F **113**
  TW7: Isle 1B **114**
  TW10: Rich 6F **115**
  TW11: Tedd 6K **131**
  TW12: Hamp H 4F **131**
  TW13: Hanw 4B **130**
  TW15: Ashf 5D **128**
  TW16: Sun 7K **129**
  UB4: Hayes 5G **75**
  UB8: Uxb 1A **74**
  W4 .....7J **97**
  W7 .....7K **77**

Park Rd. E. UB10: Uxb 2A **74**
  W3 .....2H **97**
Park Rd. Ho. KT2: King T 7G **133**
Park Road Leisure Cen. 5H **47**
Park Rd. Nth. W3 .....2H **97**
  W4 .....5K **97**
Park Row SE10 .....6F **105**
  SW2 .....6A **120**
PARK ROYAL 3H **79**
Park Royal NW10 .....3G **79**
PARK ROYAL JUNC. 1G **79**
Park Royal Metro Cen. NW10 .....4H **79**
Park Royal Rd. NW10 .....3J **79**
  W3 .....3J **79**
Park St James NW8 .....1D **82**
(off St James's Ter. M.)
Parkshot TW9: Rich 4D **114**
Park Side NW2 .....3C **62**
Parkside DA14: Sidc 2B **144**
  IG9: Buck H 2E **36**
  N3 .....1K **45**
  NW7 .....6H **29**
  SE3 .....7H **105**
  SM3: Cheam 6G **165**
  SW1 .....6F **11**
  SW3 .....3F **135**
  TW12: Hamp H 5H **131**
  UB3: Hayes 7G **75**
  W3 .....1A **98**
  W5 .....7E **78**
Parkside Av. BR1: Brom 4C **160**
  DA7: Bex 2K **127**
  RM1: Rom 3K **55**
  SE10 .....1E **122**
  SW19 .....5F **135**
Parkside Bus. Est. SE8 .....6A **104**
Parkside Cl. SE20 .....7J **139**
Parkside Ct. E11 .....6J **51**
(off Wanstead Pl.)
  E16 .....2A **106**
(off Booth Rd.)
  N22 .....6E **32**
Parkside Cres. KT5: Surb 6J **151**
  N7 .....3A **66**
Parkside Cross DA7: Bex 2K **127**
Parkside Dr. HA8: Edg 3B **28**
Parkside Est. E9 .....1J **85**
(not continuous)
Parkside Gdns. EN4: E Barn 1J **31**
  SW19 .....4F **135**
Parkside Ho. RM10: Dag 3J **73**
Parkside Lodge DA17: Belv 5J **109**
Parkside Rd. DA17: Belv 4H **109**
  SW11 .....1E **118**
  TW3: Houn 5F **113**
Parkside Sq. SE10 .....1E **122**
Parkside Ter. BR6: Farnb 3F **173**
(off Willow Wlk.)
  N18 .....4J **33**
Parkside Way HA2: Harr 4F **41**
Parks Info. Cen. 4D **10** (1C **100**)
Park Sth. SW11 .....1E **118**
(off Austin Rd.)
Park Sq. E. NW1 .....3J **5** (4F **83**)
Park Sq. M. NW1 .....4J **5** (4F **83**)
Park Sq. W. NW1 .....3J **5** (4F **83**)
Parkstead Rd. SW15 .....5C **116**
Park Steps W2 .....2D **10**
Parkstone Av. N18 .....6A **34**
Parkstone Rd. E17 .....3E **50**
  SE15 .....2G **121**
Park St. CR0: C'don 2C **168**
  SE1 .....4C **14** (1C **102**)
  SW6 .....1A **118**
  TW11: Tedd 6A **132**
  W1 .....2G **11** (7E **82**)
Park Ter. EN3: Enf H 1F **25**
  KT4: Wor Pk 1C **164**
  SM5: Cars 3C **166**
Park Theatre 2A **66**
Parkthorne Cl. HA2: Harr 6F **41**

Parkthorne Dr. HA2: Harr 6E **40**
Parkthorne Rd. SW12 .....7H **119**
Park Towers W1 .....5J **11**
(off Brick St.)
Park Vw. HA5: Hat E 1D **40**
  HA9: Wemb 5H **61**
  KT3: N Mald 3B **152**
  N5 .....4C **66**
  N21 .....7E **22**
  RM6: Chad H 6D **54**
  SE8 .....5K **103**
(off Trundleys Rd.)
  UB7: Yiew 7A **74**
  W3 .....5J **79**
Parkview DA18: Erith 3D **108**
  UB6: G'frd 3A **78**
(off Perivale La.)
Park View Academy Sports Cen. 4C **48**
Park Vw. Apartments SE16 .....3H **103**
(off Banyard Rd.)
Parkview Apartments E14 .....6D **86**
(off Chrisp St.)
Park Vw. Cl. E3 .....5C **86**
  N12 .....4H **31**
  SE12 .....3A **142**
  SE20 .....1H **157**
Parkview Cl. HA3: Hrw W 7D **26**
  IG2: Ilf 6J **53**
  SW6 .....2G **117**
  SW18 .....6J **117**
Park Vw. Cres. N11 .....4A **32**
Parkview Cres. KT4: Wor Pk 7E **152**
Park Vw. Dr. CR4: Mitc 2B **154**
Park Vw. Est. E2 .....2K **85**
Park Vw. Gdns. IG4: Ilf 4D **52**
  N22 .....1A **48**
  NW4 .....5E **44**
Park Vw. Ho. E4 .....5H **35**
  SE24 .....6B **120**
(off Hurst St.)
Parkview Ho. N9 .....7C **24**
Park Vw. Mans. N4 .....6B **48**
Park Vw. M. SW9 .....2K **119**
Park View Road 3C **126**
Park Vw. Rd. DA16: Well 3C **126**
  N3 .....1K **45**
  N17 .....3G **49**
  NW10 .....4B **62**
  UB1: S'hall 1E **94**
  UB8: Hil 6B **74**
  W5 .....5E **78**
Parkview Rd. CR0: C'don 1G **169**
  SE9 .....1E **143**
Park Village E. NW1 .....1K **5** (2F **83**)
Park Village W. NW1 .....2F **83**
Park Vs. RM6: Chad H 6D **54**
Parkville Rd. SW6 .....7H **99**
Park Vista SE10 .....6F **105**
Park Wlk.
  EN4: Cockf 3G **21**
  IG1: Ilf 2F **71**
(within The Exchange)
  N6 .....7E **46**
  SE10 .....7F **105**
  SW10 .....7A **16** (6A **100**)
Park Way EN2: Enf 2F **23**
  HA4: Ruis 1J **57**
  HA8: Edg 1H **43**
  KT8: W Mole 3F **149**
  N20 .....4J **31**
  NW11 .....5G **45**
  TW14: Felt 7K **111**
  W3 .....3G **97**
Parkway DA18: Erith 3E **108**
  IG3: Ilf 3K **71**
  IG8: Wfd G 5F **37**
  N14 .....2D **32**
  NW1 .....1F **83**
  SW20 .....4F **153**
  UB10: Hil 7C **56**

Parkway, The TW4: Cran 2K 111
   TW5: Cran 5J 93
   UB2: S'hall .5J 93
   UB3: Hayes 3K 93
   UB4: Yead .3K 93
   UB5: N'olt 3B 76
Park Way Cl. HA4: Ruis 1H 57
Parkway Cres. E15 . . . . .5E 68
Parkway Trad. Est. TW5: Hest 6A 94
Park West W2 .7D 4
Park West Bldg. E3 . . . . .2C 86
Park West Pl. W2 . . . . . .7D 4 (6C 82)
Park Wharf SE8 . . . . .5A 104
            (off Evelyn St.)
Parkwood BR3: Beck 7C 140
  N20 . . . . .3K 31
  NW8 . . . . .1D 82
      (off St Edmund's Ter.)
Parkwood Av. KT10: Esh 7G 149
Park Wood Cl. HA4: Ruis 4E 38
Parkwood Flats N20 . . . . .3J 31
Parkwood Gro. TW16: Sun 3J 147
Parkwood M. N6 . . . . .6F 47
Parkwood Rd. DA5: Bexl 7F 127
  SW19 . . . . .5H 135
  TW7: Isle 1K 113
Parliament Cl. E1 . . . . .6H 9
Parliament Hill 3D 64
Parliament Hill NW3 . . . . .4C 64
Parliament Hill Fields 3E 64
Parliament Hill Lido 3E 64
Parliament Hill Mans.
  NW5 . . . . .4E 64
Parliament M. SW14 . . . . .2J 115
Parliament Sq. SW1 . . . . .7E 12 (2J 101)
Parliament St. SW1 . . . . .6E 12 (2J 101)
Parliament Vw. SE1 . . . . .3G 19 (4K 101)
Parma Cres. SW11 . . . . .4D 118
Parmiter St. E2 . . . . .2H 85
Parmoor Cl. EC1 . . . . .3C 8
Parndon Ho. IG10: Lough 1H 37
Parnell Cl. HA8: Edg 4C 28
  W12 . . . . .3D 98
Parnell Ho. WC1 . . . . .6D 6 (5H 83)
Parnelli Ho. N1 . . . . .6B 66
      (off Canonbury Rd.)
Parnell Rd. E3 . . . . .1B 86
Parnell Way HA3: Stan 1B 42
Parnham Cl. BR1: Brom 3F 161
Parnham St. E14 . . . . .6A 86
      (not continuous)
Parolles Rd. N19 . . . . .1G 65
Paroma Rd. DA17: Belv 4G 109
Parr Cl. N9 . . . . .4C 34
  N18 . . . . .4C 34
Parr Ct. N1 . . . . .2D 84
      (off New North Rd.)
  TW13: Hanw 4A 130
Parr Ho. E16 . . . . .1K 105
      (off Beaulieu Av.)
Parrington Ho. SW4 . . . . .6H 119
Parr Rd. E6 . . . . .1B 88
  HA7: Stan 1D 42
Parrs Cl. CR2: Sande 7D 168
Parrs Pl. TW12: Hamp 7E 130
Parr St. N1 . . . . .2D 84
Parrs Way W6 . . . . .6E 98
Parry Av. E6 .6D 88
Parry Cl. KT17: Ewe 7D 164
Parry Ho. E1 . . . . .1H 103
      (off Green Bank)
Parry Pl. SE18 . . . . .4F 107
Parry Rd. SE25 . . . . .3E 156
  W10 . . . . .3G 81
Parry St. SW8 . . . . .7F 19 (6J 101)
Parsifal Rd. NW6 . . . . .5J 63
Parsley Gdns. CR0: C'don 1K 169
Parsloes Av. RM9: Dag 4D 72
Parsonage Cl. UB3: Hayes 6H 75
Parsonage Gdns.
  EN2: Enf .2H 23

Parsonage La. DA14: Sidc 4F 145
  EN1: Enf .2H 23
  EN2: Enf .2H 23
Parsonage Manorway DA17: Belv . . .6G 109
Parsonage St. E14 . . . . .4E 104
Parsons Cl. SM1: Sutt 3K 165
Parson's Cres. HA8: Edg 3B 28
Parsons Ga. M. SW6 . . . . .2J 117
PARSONS GREEN 2H 117
Parson's Grn. SW6 . . . . .1J 117
Parson's Grn. La. SW6 . . . . .1J 117
Parson's Gro. HA8: Edg 3B 28
Parsons Hill SE18 . . . . .3E 106
      (off Powis St.)
Parsons Ho. W2 . . . . .4A 4
Parsons Lodge NW6 . . . . .7K 63
      (off Priory Rd.)
Parsons Mead CR0: C'don 1B 168
  KT8: E Mos 3G 149
Parsons M. SW18 . . . . .5A 118
Parson's Rd. E13 . . . . .2A 88
Parson St. NW4 . . . . .4E 44
Parthenia Dr. TW7: Isle 3A 114
Parthenia Rd. SW6 . . . . .1J 117
Partingdale La. NW7 . . . . .5A 30
Partington Cl. N19 . . . . .1H 65
Partridge Cl. E16 . . . . .5B 88
  EN5: Barn 6A 20
  HA7: Stan 4K 27
  WD23: Bush 1B 26
Partridge Ct. EC1 . . . . .3A 8
Partridge Dr. BR6: Farnb 3G 173
Partridge Grn. SE9 . . . . .3E 142
Partridge Ho. E3 . . . . .2B 86
      (off Stafford Rd.)
Partridge Rd. DA14: Sidc 3J 143
  TW12: Hamp 6D 130
Partridge Sq. E6 . . . . .5C 88
Partridge Way N22 . . . . .1J 47
Pasadena Cl. UB3: Hayes 2J 93
Pasadena Cl. Trad. Est. UB3: Hayes . .2K 93
Pascall Ho. SE17 . . . . .6C 102
      (off Draco St.)
Pascal M. SE19 . . . . .7G 139
Pascal St. SW8 . . . . .7H 101
Pascoe Rd. SE13 . . . . .5F 123
Pasley Cl. SE17 . . . . .5B 102
Pasquier Rd. E17 . . . . .3A 50
Passage, The TW9: Rich 5E 114
Passey Pl. SE9 . . . . .6D 124
Passfield Dr. E14 . . . . .5D 86
Passfield Hall WC1 . . . . .3D 6
      (off Endsleigh Pl.)
Passfield Path SE28 . . . . .7B 90
Passfields SE6 . . . . .3D 140
  W14 . . . . .5H 99
      (off Star Rd.)
Passing All. EC1 . . . . .4B 8
Passingham Ho. TW5: Hest 6E 94
Passmore Ct. E14 . . . . .6C 86
      (off New Festival Av.)
Passmore Edwards Ho. N11 . . . . .6C 32
Passmore Gdns. N11 . . . . .6C 32
Passmore Ho. E2 . . . . .1F 85
      (off Kingsland Rd.)
Passmore St. SW1 . . . . . .5G 17 (5E 100)
Pastel Ct. E1 .5K 85
      (off Shandy St.)
Pasteur Cl. NW9 . . . . .2A 44
Pasteur Ct. HA1: Harr 1B 60
Pasteur Gdns. N18 . . . . .5G 33
Paston Cl. E5 . . . . .3K 67
  SM6: Wall 3G 167
Paston Cres. SE12 . . . . .7K 123
Paston Ct. N6 . . . . .6G 47
Pastor St. SE11 . . . . .4B 102
Pasture Cl. HA0: Wemb 3B 60
Pasture Rd. HA0: Wemb 2B 60
  RM9: Dag 5F 73
  SE6 . . . . .1H 141
Pastures, The N20 . . . . .1C 30

Pastures Mead UB10: Hil 6C 56
Pastures Path E11 . . . . .1H 69
Patch Cl. UB10: Uxb 1B 74
Patching Way UB4: Yead 5C 76
Patent Ho. E14 . . . . .5D 86
      (off Morris Rd.)
Paternoster La. EC4 . . . . . . .1B 14 (6B 84)
Paternoster Row EC4 . . . . . .1C 14 (6C 84)
Paternoster Sq. EC4 . . . . . . .1B 14 (6B 84)
Paterson Cl. E1 . . . . .2E 8
Pater St. W8 .3J 99
Path, The SW19 . . . . .1K 153
Pathfield Rd. SW16 . . . . .6H 137
Patience Rd. SW11 . . . . .2C 118
Patina Mans. E20 . . . . .5E 68
      (off Mirabelle Gdns.)
Patio Cl. SW4 . . . . .6H 119
Patmore Est. SW8 . . . . .1G 119
Patmore Ho. N16 . . . . .5E 66
Patmore St. SW8 . . . . .1G 119
Patmos Lodge SW9 . . . . .1B 120
      (off Elliott Rd.)
Patmos Rd. SW9 . . . . .7B 102
Paton Cl. E3 . . . . .3C 86
Paton Ho. SW9 . . . . .2K 119
      (off Stockwell Rd.)
Paton St. EC1 . . . . .2C 8 (3C 84)
Patricia Cl. BR7: Chst 1H 161
  DA16: Well 7B 108
Patrick Coman Ho. EC1 . . . . .2A 8
      (off St John St.)
Patrick Connolly Gdns. E3 . . . . .3D 86
Patrick Ct. SE1 . . . . .7B 14
      (off Webber St.)
Patrick Pas. SW11 . . . . .2C 118
Patrick Rd. E13 . . . . .3A 88
Patriot Sq. E2 . . . . .2H 85
Patrol Pl. SE6 . . . . .6D 122
Patroni Ct. E15 . . . . .3G 87
      (off Durban Rd.)
Pat Shaw Ho. E1 . . . . .4K 85
      (off Globe Rd.)
Patshull Pl. NW5 . . . . .6G 65
Patshull Rd. NW5 . . . . .6G 65
Patten All. TW10: Rich 5D 114
Pattenden Rd. SE6 . . . . .1B 140
Patten Ho. N4 . . . . .1C 66
Patten Rd. SW18 . . . . .7C 118
Patterdale NW1 . . . . .2K 5
      (off Osnaburgh St.)
Patterdale Cl. BR1: Brom 6H 141
Patterdale Rd. SE15 . . . . .7J 103
Pattern Ho. EC1 . . . . .3A 8 (4B 84)
Patterson Cl. SE19 . . . . .7F 139
Patterson Rd. SE19 . . . . .6F 139
Pattina Wlk. SE16 . . . . .1A 104
      (off Silver Wlk.)
Pattison Ho. E1 . . . . .6K 85
      (off Wellesley St.)
  SE1 . . . . .6D 14
      (off Redcross Way)
Pattison Rd. NW2 . . . . .3J 63
Pattison Wlk. SE18 . . . . .5G 107
Paul Cl. E15 .1G 87
Paul Cl. N18 .4B 34
      (off Fairfield Rd.)
  RM7: Rom 5J 55
Paul Daisley Ct. NW6 . . . . .7G 63
      (off Christchurch Av.)
Paulet Rd. SE5 . . . . .2B 120
Paulet Way NW10 . . . . .7A 62
Paul Gdns. CR0: C'don 2F 169
Paulhan Rd.
  HA3: Kenton 4D 42
Paul Ho. W10 . . . . .4G 81
      (off Ladbroke Gro.)
Paulin Dr. N21 . . . . .7F 23
Pauline Cres. TW2: Whitt 1G 131

Pauline Ho. E1 . . . . .5G 85
      (off Old Montague St.)
Paul Julius Cl. E14 . . . . .7F 87
Paul Robeson Cl. E6 . . . . .3E 88
Paul Robeson Ho. WC1 . . . . .1H 7
      (off Penton Ri.)
Paul Robeson Theatre, The 3F 113
Paul St. E15 .1G 87
  EC2 . . . . .4F 9 (4D 84)
Paul's Wlk. EC4 . . . . .2B 14 (7C 84)
Paultons Ho. SW3 . . . . .7B 16
      (off Paultons Sq.)
Paultons Sq. SW3 . . . . .7B 16 (6B 100)
Paultons St. SW3 . . . . .6B 100
Pauntley St. N19 . . . . .1G 65
Pavan Ct. E2 .3J 85
      (off Sceptre Rd.)
Paved Ct. TW9: Rich 5D 114
Paveley Ct. NW7 . . . . .7A 30
      (off Langstone Way)
Paveley Dr. SW11 . . . . .7C 100
Paveley Ho. N1 . . . . .2K 83
      (off Priory Grn. Est.)
Paveley St. NW8 . . . . .2C 4 (3C 82)
Pavement, The E11 . . . . .1E 68
      (off Hainault Rd.)
  SW4 . . . . .4G 119
  TW7: Isle 3A 114
      (off South St.)
  TW11: Tedd 7B 132
  W5 . . . . .3E 96
Pavement M. RM6: Chad H 7D 54
Pavement Sq. CR0: C'don 1G 169
Pavet Cl. RM10: Dag 6H 73
Pavilion, The SW8 . . . . .7H 101
Pavilion Apartments NW8 . .2B 4 (3B 82)
Pavilion Ct. NW6 . . . . .3J 81
      (off Stafford Rd.)
Pavilion La. BR3: Beck 6B 140
Pavilion Leisure Cen. 2J 159
Pavilion Lodge HA2: Harr 1H 59
Pavilion M. N3 . . . . .3J 45
Pavilion Pde. W12 . . . . .6E 80
      (off Wood La.)
Pavilion Rd. IG1: Ilf 7D 52
  SW1 . . . . .7F 11 (3D 100)
  SW3 . . . . .4D 100
Pavilion Sports & Fitness Club, The
  . . . . .3G 149
Pavilion Sq. SW17 . . . . .3D 136
Pavilion St. E13 . . . . .2A 88
  SW1 . . . . .2F 17 (3D 100)
Pavilion Ter. IG2: Ilf 5J 53
  W12 . . . . .6E 80
      (off Wood La.)
Pavilion Way HA4: Ruis 2A 58
  HA8: Edg 7C 28
  SE10 . . . . .2G 105
Pavillion Ho. SE16 . . . . .2K 103
      (off Water Gdns. Sq.)
Pavillion M. N4 . . . . .2K 65
      (off Tollington Pl.)
Pawleyne Cl. SE20 . . . . .7J 139
Pawsey Cl. E13 . . . . .1K 87
Pawsons Rd. CR0: C'don 6C 156
Paxfold HA7: Stan 5J 27
Paxford Rd. HA0: Wemb 2B 60
Paxton Cl. KT12: Walt T 7A 148
  TW9: Kew 2F 115
Paxton Ct. CR4: Mitc 2D 154
      (off Armfield Cres.)
  N7 . . . . .6A 66
      (off Westbourne Rd.)
  SE12 . . . . .3A 142
  SE26 . . . . .4A 140
      (off Adamsrill Rd.)
Paxton Ho. SE17 . . . . .5D 102
      (off Morecambe St.)
Paxton M. SE19 . . . . .7E 138
      (off Westow St.)
Paxton Pl. SE27 . . . . .4E 138

Paxton Point. SE10 . . . . .7D **104**
Paxton Rd. BR1: Brom 7J **141**
  N17 . . . . .7A **34**
  SE23 . . . . .3A **140**
Paxton Ter. SW1 . . . . .7K **17** (6F **101**)
Paymal Ho. E1 . . . . .5J **85**
           (off Stepney Way)
Payne Cl. IG11: Bark 7J **71**
Payne Ho. N1 . . . . .1K **83**
          (off Barnsbury Est.)
Paynell Ct. SE3 . . . . .3G **123**
Payne Rd. E3 . . . . .2D **86**
Paynesfield Av. SW14 . . . . .3K **115**
Paynesfield Rd. WD23: B Hea 1E **26**
Payne St. SE8 . . . . .7B **104**
Paynes Wlk. W6 . . . . .6G **99**
Payzes Gdns. IG8: Wfd G 6C **36**
Peaberry Cl. NW4 . . . . .3C **44**
Peabody Av. SW1 . . . . . .5J **17** (5F **101**)
Peabody Bldgs. E1 . . . . .2K **15**
  EC1 . . . . .4D **8**
            (off Banner St.)
  SW3 . . . . .7C **16**
Peabody Cl. CR0: C'don 1J **169**
  SE10 . . . . .3G **105**
  SW1 . . . . .7K **17** (5F **101**)
Peabody Cotts. N17 . . . . .1E **48**
Peabody Ct. EC1 . . . . .4D **8**
           (off Roscoe St.)
  SE5 . . . . .1D **120**
        (off Kimpton Rd.)
Peabody Est. E1 . . . . .7K **85**
        (off Brodlove La.)
  E2 . . . . .2H **85**
          (off Minerva St.)
  EC1 . . . . .4D **8**
     (off Dufferin St., not continuous)
  EC1 . . . . .4K **7**
        (off Farringdon La.)
  N1 . . . . .1C **84**
  SE1 . . . . .5K **13** (1A **102**)
            (Duchy St.)
  SE1 . . . . .6D **14**
        (Marshalsea Rd.)
  SE1 . . . . .5C **14** (1C **102**)
        (Southwark St.)
  SE5 . . . . .1D **120**
       (off Camberwell Grn.)
  SE24 . . . . .7B **120**
  SW1 . . . . .3B **18**
  SW3 . . . . .7D **16** (6C **100**)
  SW6 . . . . .6J **99**
           (off Lillie Rd.)
  SW11 . . . . .4C **118**
  W6 . . . . .5E **98**
  W10 . . . . .5E **80**
Peabody Hill SE21 . . . . .1B **138**
Peabody Ho. N1 . . . . .1C **84**
       (off Greenman St.)
Peabody Sq. SE1 . . . . . . .7A **14** (2B **102**)
        (not continuous)
Peabody Ter. EC1 . . . . .4K **7**
        (off Farringdon La.)
Peabody Twr. EC1 . . . . .4D **8**
         (off Golden La.)
Peabody Trust SE17 . . . . .4D **102**
Peabody Yd. N1 . . . . .1C **84**
Peace Cl. N14 . . . . .5A **22**
  SE25 . . . . .4E **156**
  UB6: G'frd 1H **77**
Peace Ct. SE1 . . . . .5G **103**
        (off Harmony Pl.)
Peace Gro. HA9: Wemb 3H **61**
Peace St. SE18 . . . . .6E **106**
Peaches Cl. SM2: Cheam 7G **165**
Peachey Ho. SW18 . . . . .4A **118**
       (off Eltringham St.)
Peachey La. UB8: Cowl 5A **74**
Peach Gro. E11 . . . . .3F **69**

Peach Rd. TW13: Felt 1J **129**
  W10 . . . . .3F **81**
Peach Tree Av. UB7: Yiew 6B **74**
Peachum Rd. SE3 . . . . .6H **105**
Peachwalk M. E3 . . . . .2K **85**
Peachy Cl. HA8: Edg 6B **28**
Peacock Av. TW14: Bedf 1F **129**
Peacock Cl. E4 . . . . .7G **35**
  NW7 . . . . .5B **30**
  RM8: Dag 1C **72**
Peacock Ho. SE5 . . . . .1E **120**
        (off St Giles Rd.)
Peacock Ind. Est. N17 . . . . .7A **34**
Peacock Pl. N1 . . . . .6A **66**
Peacock St. SE17 . . . . .4B **102**
Peacock Theatre 1G **13**
        (off Portugal St.)
Peacock Wlk. E16 . . . . .6K **87**
        (off Mortlake Rd.)
  N6 . . . . .7F **47**
Peacock Yd. SE17 . . . . .5B **102**
          (off Iliffe St.)
Peak, The SE26 . . . . .3J **139**
Peaketon Av. IG4: Ilf 4B **52**
Peak Hill SE26 . . . . .4J **139**
Peak Hill Av. SE26 . . . . .4J **139**
Peak Hill Gdns. SE26 . . . . .4J **139**
Peak Ho. N4 . . . . .1C **66**
     (off Woodberry Down Est.)
Peal Gdns. W13 . . . . .4A **78**
Peall Rd. CR0: C'don 6K **155**
Peall Rd. Ind. Est. CR0: C'don 6K **155**
Pearce Cl. CR4: Mitc 2E **154**
Pearcefield Av. SE23 . . . . .1J **139**
Pearce Ho. SW1 . . . . .4D **18**
        (off Causton St.)
Pear Cl. NW9 . . . . .4K **43**
  SE14 . . . . .7A **104**
Pear Ct. SE15 . . . . .7F **103**
        (off Thruxton Way)
Pearcroft Rd. E11 . . . . .2F **69**
Peardon St. SW8 . . . . .2F **119**
Peareswood Gdns. HA7: Stan 1D **42**
Pearfield Rd. SE23 . . . . .3A **140**
Pearing Cl. KT4: Wor Pk 2F **165**
Pearl Cl. E6 . . . . .6E **88**
  NW2 . . . . .7F **45**
Pearl Rd. E17 . . . . .3C **50**
Pearl St. E1 . . . . .1H **103**
Pearmain Cl. TW17: Shep 5D **146**
Pearman St. SE1 . . . . . . .1K **19** (3A **102**)
Pear Pl. SE1 . . . . .6J **13** (2A **102**)
Pear Rd. E11 . . . . .3F **69**
Pears Av. TW17: Shep 3G **147**
Pearscroft Ct. SW6 . . . . .1K **117**
Pearscroft Rd. SW6 . . . . .1K **117**
Pearse St. SE15 . . . . .6E **102**
Pearson Cl. EN5: New Bar 3E **20**
  SE5 . . . . .1C **120**
     (off Camberwell New Rd.)
Pearson M. SW4 . . . . .3H **119**
        (off Edgeley Rd.)
Pearson's Av. SE14 . . . . .1C **122**
Pearson St. E2 . . . . .2F **85**
Pearson Way CR4: Mitc 1E **154**
Pears Rd. TW3: Houn 3G **113**
Peartree SE26 . . . . .5A **140**
Peartree Av. UB7: Yiew 6B **74**
Pear Tree Av. SW17 . . . . .3A **136**
Pear Tree Cl. BR2: Brom 5B **160**
  CR4: Mitc 2C **154**
  E2 . . . . .1F **85**
  KT9: Chess 5G **163**
  KT19: Eps 7K **163**
Pear Tree Cl. DA8: Erith 1K **127**
Pear Tree Ct. E18 . . . . .1K **51**
  EC1 . . . . .4K **7** (4A **84**)
Peartree Gdns. RM7: Mawney 2H **55**
  RM8: Dag 4B **72**
Pear Tree Ho. SE4 . . . . .3B **122**
Peartree La. E1 . . . . .7J **85**

Pear Tree Rd. TW15: Ashf 5E **128**
Peartree Rd. EN1: Enf 3K **23**
Peartrees UB7: Yiew 7A **74**
Pear Tree St. EC1 . . . . .3B **8** (4C **84**)
Peartree Way SE10 . . . . .4J **105**
Peary Ho. NW10 . . . . .7K **61**
Peary Pl. E2 . . . . .3J **85**
Peasmead Ter. E4 . . . . .4K **35**
Peatfield Cl. DA15: Sidc 3J **143**
Pebble Way W3 . . . . .1H **97**
        (off Steyne Rd.)
Pebworth Rd. HA1: Harr 2A **60**
Peckarmans Wood SE26 . . . . .3G **139**
Peckett Sq. N5 . . . . .4C **66**
Peckford Pl. SW9 . . . . .2A **120**
PECKHAM 1G **121**
Peckham Gro. SE15 . . . . .7E **102**
Peckham High St. SE15 . . . . .1G **121**
Peckham Hill St. SE15 . . . . .7G **103**
Peckham Pk. Rd. SE15 . . . . .7G **103**
Peckham Pulse Health & Leisure Cen.
  . . . . .1G **121**
Peckham Rd. SE5 . . . . .1E **120**
  SE15 . . . . .1E **120**
Peckham Rye SE15 . . . . .3G **121**
  SE22 . . . . .4G **121**
Peckham Sq. SE15 . . . . .1G **121**
Pecks Yd. E1 . . . . .5J **9**
        (off Hanbury St.)
Peckwater St. NW5 . . . . .5G **65**
Pedlar's Wlk. N7 . . . . .5K **65**
Pedley Rd. RM8: Dag 1C **72**
Pedley St. E1 . . . . .4G **85**
Pedro St. E5 . . . . .3K **67**
Pedworth Gdns. SE16 . . . . .4J **103**
Peebles Ct. UB1: S'hall 6G **77**
        (off Haldane Rd.)
Peebles Ho. NW6 . . . . .2K **81**
        (off Carlton Vale)
Peek Cres. SW19 . . . . .5F **135**
Peel Cl. E4 .2J **35**
  N9 . . . . .3B **34**
Peel Dr. IG5: Ilf 3C **52**
  NW9 . . . . .3B **44**
Peel Gro. E2 . . . . .2J **85**
Peel Pas. W8 . . . . .1J **99**
Peel Pl. IG5: Ilf 2C **52**
  SE18 . . . . .1D **124**
Peel Pct. NW6 . . . . .2J **81**
Peel Rd. BR6: Farnb 5G **173**
  E18 . . . . .1H **51**
  HA3: W'stone 3K **41**
  HA9: Wemb 3D **60**
Peel St. W8 . . . . .1J **99**
Peel Way UB8: Hil 5A **74**
Peerglow Est. EN3: Pond E 5C **24**
Peerless St. EC1 . . . . . . .2E **8** (3D **84**)
Pegamoid Rd. N18 . . . . .3D **34**
Pegasus Cl. N16 . . . . .4D **66**
Pegasus Ct. KT1: King T 3D **150**
  N21 . . . . .7H **23**
  NW10 . . . . .3D **80**
        (off Trenmar Gdns.)
  TW8: Bford 5F **97**
  W3 . . . . .6J **79**
         (off Horn La.)
Pegasus Ho. E1 . . . . .4K **85**
       (off Beaumont Sq.)
  E13 . . . . .3K **87**
Pegasus Pl. SE11 . . . . . . .7J **19** (6A **102**)
  SW6 . . . . .1J **117**
Pegasus Rd. CR0: Wadd 6A **168**
Pegasus Way N11 . . . . .6A **32**
Peggotty Way UB8: Hil 6D **74**
Pegg Rd. TW5: Hest 7B **94**
Pegley Gdns. SE12 . . . . .2J **141**
Pegswood Cl. E1 . . . . .7G **85**
        (off Cable St.)
Pegwell St. SE18 . . . . .7J **107**
Pekin Cl. E14 . . . . .6C **86**
          (off Pekin St.)

Pekin St. E14 . . . . .6C **86**
Pelabon Ho. TW1: Twick 6D **114**
       (off Clevedon Rd.)
Peldon Ct. TW9: Rich 4F **115**
Peldon Pas. TW10: Rich 4F **115**
Peldon Wlk. N1 . . . . .1B **84**
        (off Popham St.)
Pelham Av. IG11: Bark 1K **89**
Pelham Cl. SE5 . . . . .3E **120**
Pelham Cotts. DA5: Bexl 1H **145**
Pelham Ct. DA14: Sidc 3A **144**
  SW3 . . . . .4D **16**
        (off Fulham Rd.)
Pelham Cres. SW7 . . . . . . .4C **16** (4C **100**)
Pelham Ho. SW1 . . . . .2D **18**
       (off Gt. Peter St.)
  W14 . . . . .4H **99**
       (off Mornington Av.)
Pelham Pl. SW7 . . . . .4C **16** (4C **100**)
  W13 . . . . .4K **77**
Pelham Rd. BR3: Beck 2J **157**
  DA7: Bex 3G **127**
  E18 . . . . .3K **51**
  IG1: Ilf 2H **71**
  N15 . . . . .4F **49**
  N22 . . . . .2A **48**
  SW19 . . . . .7J **135**
Pelham St. SW7 . . . . .3B **16** (4B **100**)
Pelican Dr. HA2: Harr 2F **59**
Pelican Est. SE15 . . . . .1F **121**
Pelican Ho. SE5 . . . . .1F **121**
  SE8 . . . . .4B **104**
Pelican Pas. E1 . . . . .4J **85**
Pelican Wlk. SW9 . . . . .4B **120**
Pelican Wharf E1 . . . . .1J **103**
       (off Wapping Wall)
Pelier St. SE17 . . . . .6C **102**
Pelinore Rd. SE6 . . . . .2G **141**
Pella Ho. SE11 . . . . .5H **19** (5K **101**)
Pellant Rd. SW6 . . . . .7G **99**
Pellatt Gro. N22 . . . . .1A **48**
Pellatt Rd. HA9: Wemb 2D **60**
  SE22 . . . . .5F **121**
Pellerin Rd. N16 . . . . .5E **66**
Pelling Ho. E1 . . . . .4H **85**
       (off Somerford St.)
Pellings Cl. BR2: Brom 3G **159**
Pelling St. E14 . . . . .6C **86**
Pellipar Cl. N13 . . . . .3F **33**
Pellipar Gdns. SE18 . . . . .5D **106**
Pellipar Rd. SE18 . . . . .5D **106**
Pellow Cl. EN5: Barn 6C **20**
Pelly Rd. E13 . . . . .1J **87**
        (not continuous)
Pelter St. E2 . . . . .1J **9** (3F **85**)
Pelton Rd. SE10 . . . . .5G **105**
Pembar Av. E17 . . . . .3A **50**
Pemberley Chase KT19: Ewe 5H **163**
Pemberley Cl. KT19: Ewe 5H **163**
Pemberley Ho. KT19: Ewe 5H **163**
       (off Pemberley Chase)
Pember Rd. NW10 . . . . .3F **81**
Pemberton Cl. TW19: Stanw 1A **128**
Pemberton Ct. E1 . . . . .3K **85**
        (off Portelet Rd.)
  EN1: Enf 3K **23**
Pemberton Gdns. N19 . . . . .3G **65**
  RM6: Chad H 5E **54**
Pemberton Ho. SE26 . . . . .4G **139**
       (off High Level Dr.)
Pemberton Pl. E8 . . . . .7H **67**
Pemberton Rd. KT8: E Mos 4G **149**
  N4 . . . . .5A **48**
Pemberton Row EC4 . . . . . .7K **7** (6A **84**)
Pemberton Ter. N19 . . . . .3G **65**
Pembridge Av. TW2: Whitt 1D **130**
Pembridge Cres. W11 . . . . .7J **81**
Pembridge Gdns. W2 . . . . .7J **81**
Pembridge M. W11 . . . . .7J **81**
Pembridge Pl. SW15 . . . . .5J **117**
  W2 . . . . .7J **81**

Pembridge Rd. W11 . . . . .7J 81
Pembridge Sq. W2 . . . . .7J 81
Pembridge Studios W11 . . . . .7J 81
                (off Pembridge Vs.)
Pembridge Vs. W2 . . . . .7J 81
  W11 . . . . .7J 81
Pembroke W14 . . . . .4H 99
          (off Kensington Village)
Pembroke Av. EN1: Enf 1C 24
  HA3: Kenton 3A 42
  HA5: Pinn .1B 58
  KT5: Surb 5H 151
  N1 . . . . .1J 83
Pembroke Bldgs. NW10 . . . . .3C 80
Pembroke Bus. Cen. BR8: Swan 7K 145
Pembroke Centre, The HA4: Ruis 1H 57
Pembroke Cl. SW1 . . . . . .7H 11 (2E 100)
Pembroke Cotts. W8 . . . . .3J 99
                (off Pembroke Sq.)
Pembroke Ct. W7 . . . . .6K 77
                   (off Copley Cl.)
  W8 . . . . .3J 99
         (off Sth. Edwardes Sq.)
Pembroke Gdns. HA4: Ruis 1H 57
  RM10: Dag 3H 73
  W8 . . . . .4H 99
Pembroke Gdns. Cl. W8 . . . . .3J 99
Pembroke Hall NW4 . . . . .3E 44
                 (off Mulberry Cl.)
Pembroke Ho. RM8: Dag 5A 72
  SW1 . . . . .2G 17
               (off Chesham St.)
  W2 . . . . .6K 81
              (off Hallfield Est.)
  W3 . . . . .2J 97
            (off Park Rd. E.)
Pembroke Lodge HA7: Stan 6J 27
Pembroke Mans. NW6 . . . . .6A 64
              (off Canfield Gdns.)
Pembroke M. E3 . . . . .3A 86
  N10 . . . . .1E 46
  W8 . . . . .3J 99
Pembroke Pde. DA8: Erith 5J 109
Pembroke Pl. HA8: Edg 7B 28
  TW7: Isle .2J 113
  W8 . . . . .3J 99
Pembroke Rd. BR1: Brom 2A 160
  CR4: Mitc .2E 154
  DA8: Erith 5J 109
  E6 . . . . .5D 88
  E17 . . . . .5D 50
  HA4: Ruis .1G 57
  HA9: Wemb 3D 60
  IG3: Ilf 1K 71
  N8 . . . . .4J 47
  N10 . . . . .1E 46
  N13 . . . . .3H 33
  N15 . . . . .5F 49
  SE25 . . . . .4E 156
  UB6: G'frd .4F 77
  W8 . . . . .4H 99
Pembroke Sq. W8 . . . . .3J 99
Pembroke St. N1 . . . . .7J 65
             (not continuous)
Pembroke Studios W8 . . . . .3H 99
Pembroke Ter. NW8 . . . . .1B 82
             (off Queen's Ter.)
Pembroke Vs. TW9: Rich 4D 114
  W8 . . . . .4J 99
Pembroke Wlk. W8 . . . . .4J 99
Pembroke Way UB3: Harl 3E 92
Pembrook M. SW11 . . . . .4B 118
Pembry Cl. SW9 . . . . .1A 120
Pembury Av. KT4: Wor Pk 1C 164
Pembury Cl. BR2: Hayes 7H 159
  E5 . . . . .5H 67
Pembury Cl. UB3: Harl 6F 93
Pembury Cres. DA14: Sidc 2E 144
Pembury Pl. E5 . . . . .5H 67
Pembury Rd. DA7: Bex 7E 108
  E5 . . . . .5H 67

Pembury Rd. N17 . . . . .1F 49
  SE25 . . . . .4G 157
Pemdevon Rd. CR0: C'don 7A 156
Pemell Cl. E1 .4J 85
Pemell Ho. E1 . . . . .4J 85
                  (off Pemell Cl.)
Pemerich Cl. UB3: Harl 5H 93
Pempath Pl. HA9: Wemb 2D 60
Penally Pl. N1 . . . . .1D 84
Penang Ho. E1 . . . . .1H 103
                 (off Prusom St.)
Penang St. E1 . . . . .1H 103
Penard Rd. UB2: S'hall 3F 95
Penarth Cl. SM2: Sutt 7A 166
Penarth Cen. SE15 . . . . .6J 103
Penarth St. SE15 . . . . .6J 103
Penberth Rd. SE6 . . . . .2E 140
Penbury Rd. UB2: S'hall 4D 94
Pencombe M. W11 . . . . .7H 81
Pencraig Way SE15 . . . . .6H 103
Pendall Cl. EN4: E Barn 4H 21
Penda Rd. DA8: Erith 7H 109
Pendarves Rd. SW20 . . . . .1E 152
Penda's Mead E9 . . . . .4A 68
Pendell Av. UB3: Harl 7H 93
Pendennis Ho. SE8 . . . . .4A 104
Pendennis Rd. N17 . . . . .3D 48
  SW16 . . . . .4J 137
Penderel Rd. TW3: Houn 5E 112
Penderry Ri. SE6 . . . . .2F 141
Penderyn Way N7 . . . . .4H 65
Pendlebury Ct. KT5: Surb 4E 150
              (off Cranes Pk.)
Pendle Ct. UB10: Hil 1D 74
Pendle Ho. SE26 . . . . .3G 139
Pendle Rd. SW16 . . . . .6F 137
Pendlestone Rd. E17 . . . . .5D 50
Pendlewood Cl. W5 . . . . .5C 78
Pendley Ho. E2 . . . . .1G 85
                 (off Whiston Rd.)
Pendolino Way NW10 . . . . .7G 61
Pendragon Rd. BR1: Brom 3H 141
Pendragon Wlk. NW9 . . . . .6A 44
Pendrell Ho. WC2 . . . . .1D 12
          (off New Compton St.)
Pendrell Rd. SE4 . . . . .2A 122
Pendrell St. SE18 . . . . .6H 107
Pendulum Dr. UB4: Yead 4B 76
Pendulum M. E8 . . . . .5F 67
Penerley Rd. SE6 . . . . .1D 140
Penfield Lodge W9 . . . . .5J 81
               (off Admiral Wlk.)
Penfields Ho. N7 . . . . .6J 65
              (off York Way Est.)
Penfold Cl. CR0: Wadd 3A 168
Penfold La. DA5: Bexl 2D 144
              (not continuous)
Penfold Pl. NW1 . . . . .5C 4 (5C 82)
Penfold Rd. N9 . . . . .1E 34
Penfold St. NW1 . . . . .4B 4 (4B 82)
  NW8 . . . . .4B 4 (4B 82)
Penford Gdns. SE9 . . . . .3B 124
Penford St. SE5 . . . . .2B 120
Pengarth Rd.
  DA5: Bexl 5D 126
PENGE 7J 139
Penge Ho. SW11 . . . . .3B 118
Penge La. SE20 . . . . .7J 139
Pengelly Apartments E14 . . . . .5D 104
                (off Bartlett M.)
Penge Rd. E13 . . . . .1A 88
  SE20 . . . . .3G 157
  SE25 . . . . .3G 157
Penhale Cl. BR6: Chels 4K 173
Penhall Rd. SE7 . . . . .4B 106
Penhill Rd. DA5: Bexl 6C 126
Penhurst Mans. SW6 . . . . .1H 117
             (off Rostrevor Rd.)
Penhurst Pl. SE1 . . . . .1H 19
Penhurst Rd. IG6: Ilf 1F 53
Penifather La. UB6: G'frd 3H 77

Peninsula Apartments N1 . . . . .1C 84
                 (off Basire St.)
  W2 . . . . .6C 4
                 (off Praed St.)
Peninsula Ct. E14 . . . . .3D 104
              (off E. Ferry Rd.)
  N1 . . . . .1C 84
                 (off Basire St.)
Peninsula Hgts. SE1 . . . .5F 19 (5J 101)
Peninsular Ct. E14 . . . . .6F 111
Peninsular Pk. SE7 . . . . .4J 105
Peninsular Pk. Rd. SE7 . . . . .4J 105
Peninsula Sq. SE10 . . . . .2G 105
Penistone Rd. SW16 . . . . .7J 137
Penketh Dr. HA1: Harr 3H 59
Penley Ct. WC2 . . . . .2H 13 (7K 83)
Penmayne Ho. SE11 . . . . .5K 19
              (off Kennings Way)
Penmon Rd. SE2 . . . . .3A 108
Pennack Rd. SE15 . . . . .6F 103
Penn Almshouses SE10 . . . . .1E 122
         (off Greenwich Sth. St.)
Pennant M. W8 . . . . .4K 99
Pennant Ter. E17 . . . . .2B 50
Pennard Mans. W12 . . . . .2E 98
             (off Goldhawk Rd.)
Pennard Rd. W12 . . . . .2E 98
Pennards, The TW16: Sun 3A 148
Penn Cl. HA3: Kenton 4C 42
  UB6: G'frd .2F 77
Penn Cl. NW9 . . . . .3K 43
Penner Cl. SW19 . . . . .2G 135
Penners Gdns. KT6: Surb 7E 150
Pennethorne Cl. E9 . . . . .1J 85
Pennethorne Ho. SW11 . . . . .3B 118
Pennethorne Rd. SE15 . . . . .7H 103
Penn Gdns. BR7: Chst 2F 161
  RM5: Col R 1G 55
Penn Ho. NW8 . . . . .4C 4
                 (off Mallory St.)
Pennine Dr. NW2 . . . . .2F 63
Pennine Ho. N9 . . . . .3B 34
               (off Plevna Rd.)
Pennine La. NW2 . . . . .2G 63
Pennine Pde. NW2 . . . . .2G 63
Pennine Way DA7: Bex 1K 127
  UB3: Harl .7F 93
Pennington Cl. SE27 . . . . .4D 138
Pennington Ct. SE16 . . . . .1A 104
Pennington Dr. N21 . . . . .5D 22
Pennington Lodge KT5: Surb 5E 150
              (off Cranes Dr.)
Pennington St. E1 . . . . .7H 85
Pennington Way SE12 . . . . .2K 141
Penniston Cl. N17 . . . . .2C 48
Penniwell Cl. HA8: Edg 4A 28
Penn La. DA5: Bexl 5D 126
Penn Rd. N7 .5J 65
Penn St. N1 . . . . .1D 84
Penny Brookes St. E15 . . . . .6F 69
  E20 . . . . .6E 68
Penny Cl. E4 .3B 36
Pennycroft CR0: Sels 7A 170
Pennyfather La. EN2: Enf 3H 23
Pennyfields E14 . . . . .7C 86
              (not continuous)
Pennyford Ct. NW8 . . . . .3A 4
          (off St John's Wood Rd.)
Penny La. TW17: Shep 7G 147
Penny M. SW12 . . . . .7F 119
Pennymoor Wlk. W9 . . . . .4H 81
              (off Fernhead Rd.)
Penny Rd. NW10 . . . . .3H 79
Penny Royal SM6: Wall 6H 167
Pennyroyal Av. E6 . . . . .6E 88
Pennyroyal Dr. UB7: W Dray 2B 92
Penpoll Rd. E8 . . . . .6H 67
Penpool La. DA16: Well 3B 126
Penrhyn Av. E17 . . . . .1B 50
Penrhyn Cres. E17 . . . . .1C 50
  SW14 . . . . .4J 115

Penrhyn Gdns. KT1: King T 4D 150
Penrhyn Rd. KT1: King T 4E 150
Penrith Cl. BR3: Beck 1D 158
  SW15 . . . . .5G 117
  UB8: Uxb 7A 56
Penrith Pl. SE27 . . . . .2B 138
Penrith Rd. CR7: Thor H 2C 156
  KT3: N Mald 4K 151
  N15 . . . . .5D 48
Penrith St. SW16 . . . . .6G 137
Penrose Gro. SE17 . . . . .5C 102
Penrose Ho. N21 . . . . .5E 22
  SE17 . . . . .5C 102
Penrose Way SE10 . . . . .1G 105
Penryn Gro. E17 . . . . .1C 50
Penryn Ho. SE11 . . . . .5B 102
               (off Seaton Cl.)
Penryn St. NW1 . . . . .2H 83
Penry St. SE1 . . . . .4E 102
Pensbury Pl. SW8 . . . . .2G 119
Pensbury St. SW8 . . . . .2G 119
Pensford Av. TW9: Kew 2G 115
Penshurst NW5 . . . . .6E 64
Penshurst Av. DA15: Sidc 6A 126
Penshurst Gdns. HA8: Edg 5C 28
Penshurst Grn. BR2: Brom 5H 159
Penshurst Ho. SE15 . . . . .6J 103
            (off Lovelinch Cl.)
Penshurst Rd. CR7: Thor H 5B 156
  DA7: Bex .1F 127
  E9 . . . . .7K 67
  N17 . . . . .7A 34
Penshurst Wlk. BR2: Brom 5H 159
Penshurst Way SM2: Sutt 7J 165
Pensilver Cl. EN4: E Barn 4H 21
Penstemon Cl. N3 . . . . .6D 30
Penstock Footpath N8 . . . . .3K 47
  N22 . . . . .3K 47
Pentagram Yd. W11 . . . . .6J 81
              (off Needham Rd.)
Pentavia Retail Pk. NW7 . . . . .7G 29
Pentelow Gdns. TW14: Felt 6J 111
Pentire Rd. E17 . . . . .1F 51
Pentland Av. HA8: Edg 2C 28
  TW17: Shep 5C 146
Pentland Cl. N9 . . . . .2D 34
  NW11 . . . . .2G 63
Pentland Gdns. SW18 . . . . .6A 118
Pentland Pl. UB5: N'olt 1C 76
Pentland Rd. NW6 . . . . .3J 81
Pentlands Cl. CR4: Mitc 3F 155
Pentlands Cl. SW18 . . . . .6A 118
Pentland Way UB10: Ick 3E 56
Pentlow St. SW15 . . . . .3E 116
Pentlow Way IG9: Buck H 1H 37
Pentney Rd. E4 . . . . .1A 36
  SW12 . . . . .1G 137
  SW19 . . . . .1G 153
Penton Gro. N1 . . . . .2A 84
Penton Ho. N1 . . . . .1J 7
            (off Pentonville Rd.)
  SE2 . . . . .1D 108
Penton Pl. SE17 . . . . .5B 102
Penton Ri. WC1 . . . . .1H 7 (3K 83)
Penton St. N1 . . . . .2A 84
PENTONVILLE 2K 83
Pentonville Rd. N1 . . . . . . .1F 7 (2J 83)
Pentrich Av. EN1: Enf 1B 24
Pentridge St. SE15 . . . . .7F 103
Pentyre Av. N18 . . . . .5J 33
Penwerris Av. TW7: Isle 7G 95
Penwerris Ct. TW5: Hest 7G 95
Penwith Rd. SW18 . . . . .2J 135
Penwood Ct. HA5: Pinn 4D 40
Penwood Ho. SW15 . . . . .6B 116
Penwortham Ct. N22 . . . . .2A 48
               (off Mayes Rd.)
Penwortham Rd. SW16 . . . . .6F 137
Penylan Pl. HA8: Edg 7B 28
Penywern Rd. SW5 . . . . .5J 99

Penzance Pl. W11 . . . . .1G **99**
Penzance St. W11 . . . . .1G **99**
Peony Ct. IG8: Wfd G 7B **36**
  SW10 . . . . .7A **16** (6A **100**)
Peony Gdns. W12 . . . . .7C **80**
Peperfield WC1 . . . . .2G **7**
  (off Cromer St.)
Pepler Ho. W10 . . . . .4G **81**
  (off Wornington Rd.)
Pepler M. SE5 .5F **103**
Peploe Rd. NW6 . . . . .2F **81**
Peplow Cl. UB7: Yiew 1A **92**
Pepper Cl. E6 . . . . .5D **88**
Peppercorn Cl. CR7: Thor H 2D **156**
Peppermead Sq. SE13 . . . . .5C **122**
Peppermint Cl. CR0: C'don 7J **155**
Peppermint Pl. E11 . . . . .3G **69**
Pepper St. E14 . . . . .3D **104**
  SE1 . . . . .6C **14** (2C **102**)
Peppie Cl. N16 . . . . .2E **66**
Pepys Cl. UB10: Ick 4D **56**
Pepys Cres. E16 . . . . .1J **105**
  EN5: Barn 5A **20**
Pepys Ho. E2 . . . . .3J **85**
  (off Kirkwall Pl.)
Pepys Ri. BR6: Orp 1K **173**
Pepys Rd. SE14 . . . . .1K **121**
  SW20 .1E **152**
Pepys St. EC3 . . . . .2H **15** (7E **84**)
Perceval Av. NW3 . . . . .5C **64**
Perceval Ct. UB5: N'olt 5E **58**
Perceval Ho. W5 . . . . .7C **78**
Percheron Cl. TW7: Isle 3K **113**
Perch St. E8 . . . . .4F **67**
Percival Cl. N17 . . . . .7A **34**
Percival Gdns. RM6: Chad H 6C **54**
Percival Rd. BR6: Farnb 2F **173**
  EN1: Enf 4A **24**
  SW14 .4J **115**
  TW13: Felt 2A **129**
Percival St. EC1 . . . . .3A **8** (4B **84**)
Percival Way KT19: Ewe 4K **163**
Percy Av. TW15: Ashf 5C **128**
Percy Bilton Ct. TW5: Hest 1F **113**
  (off Skinners La.)
Percy Bryant Rd. TW16: Sun 7G **129**
Percy Bush Rd. UB7: W Dray 3B **92**
Percy Cir. WC1 . . . . .1H **7** (3K **83**)
Percy Gdns. EN3: Pond E 5E **24**
  KT4: Wor Pk 1K **163**
  TW7: Isle 3B **114**
  UB4: Hayes 3G **75**
Percy Laurie Ho. SW15 . . . . .4F **117**
  (off Nursery Cl.)
Percy M. W1 . . . . .6C **6**
Percy Pas. W1 .6C **6**
Percy Rd. CR4: Mitc 7E **154**
  DA7: Bex 2E **126**
  E11 . . . . .7G **51**
  E16 . . . . .5G **87**
  IG3: Ilf .7A **54**
  N12 . . . . .5F **31**
  N21 . . . . .7H **23**
  RM7: Mawney 3H **55**
  SE20 .1K **157**
  SE25 .5G **157**
  TW2: Whitt 1F **131**
  TW7: Isle 4A **114**
  TW12: Hamp 7E **130**
  W12 . . . . .2C **98**
Percy St. W1 . . . . .6C **6** (5H **83**)
Percy Ter. BR1: Brom 3F **161**
Percy Way TW2: Whitt 1G **131**
Percy Yd. WC1 . . . . .1H **7** (3K **83**)
Peregrine Cl. NW10 . . . . .5K **61**
Peregrine Ct. DA16: Well 1K **125**
  SE8 . . . . .6B **104**
  (off Edward St.)
  SW16 .4K **137**
Peregrine Gdns. CR0: C'don 2A **170**
Peregrine Ho. EC1 . . . . .1B **8**

Peregrine Rd. N17 . . . . .7H **33**
  TW16: Sun 2H **147**
Peregrine Way SW19 . . . . .7E **134**
Perendale Dr. TW17: Shep 1E **146**
Perham Rd. W14 . . . . .5G **99**
Peridot Cl. E2 . . . . .2J **9**
  (off Virginia Rd.)
Peridot St. E6 . . . . .5C **88**
Perifield SE21 . . . . .1C **138**
Perimeade Rd. UB6: G'frd 2C **78**
Periton Rd. SE9 . . . . .4B **124**
PERIVALE 1C **78**
Perivale Gdns. W13 . . . . .4B **78**
Perivale Grange UB6: G'frd 3A **78**
Perivale La. UB6: G'frd 3A **78**
Perivale Lodge UB6: G'frd 3A **78**
  (off Perivale La.)
Perivale New Bus. Cen. UB6: G'frd 2C **78**
Perivale Pk. UB6: G'frd 2B **78**
Perivale Pk. Athletics Track 3J **77**
Perivale Pk. Golf Course 3J **77**
Perivale Wood Local Nature Reserve
  . . . . .1K **77**
Periwood Cres. UB6: G'frd 1A **78**
Perkin Cl. HA0: Wemb 5B **60**
  TW3: Houn 4E **112**
Perkins Ct. TW15: Ashf 5B **128**
Perkins Gdns. UB10: Ick 2E **56**
Perkins Ho. E14 . . . . .5B **86**
  (off Wallwood St.)
Perkin's Rents SW1 . . . . . .2C **18** (3H **101**)
Perkins Rd. IG2: Ilf 5H **53**
Perkins Sq. SE1 . . . . . . .4D **14** (1C **102**)
Perks Cl. SE3 .3G **123**
Perkyn Sq. N17 . . . . .3H **49**
Perley Ho. E3 . . . . .5B **86**
  (off Weatherley Cl.)
Perpins Rd. SE9 . . . . .6J **125**
Perran Rd. SW2 . . . . .1B **138**
Perran Wlk. TW8: Bford 5E **96**
Perren St. NW5 . . . . .6F **65**
Perrers Rd. W6 . . . . .4D **98**
Perrin Cl. TW15: Ashf 5B **128**
Perrin Ct. TW15: Ashf 4C **128**
Perring Est. E3 .5C **86**
  (off Gale St.)
Perrin Ho. NW6 . . . . .3J **81**
Perrin Rd. HA0: Wemb 4B **60**
Perrin's Ct. NW3 . . . . .4A **64**
Perrin's La. NW3 . . . . .4A **64**
Perrin's Wlk. NW3 . . . . .4A **64**
Perronet Ho. SE1 . . . . .3B **102**
  (off Princess St.)
Perrott St. SE18 . . . . .4G **107**
Perry Av. W3 . . . . .6K **79**
Perry Cl. IG2: Ilf 6H **53**
  UB8: Hil 6D **74**
Perry Ct. E14 . . . . .5C **104**
  (off Maritime Quay)
  KT1: King T 2E **150**
  (off Old London Rd.)
  N15 . . . . .6E **48**
Perryfield Way NW9 . . . . .6B **44**
  TW10: Ham 3B **132**
Perry Gdns. N9 . . . . .3J **33**
Perry Gth. UB5: N'olt 1A **76**
Perry Hall Rd. BR6: St M Cry 6K **161**
Perry Hill SE6 . . . . .3B **140**
Perry How KT4: Wor Pk 1B **164**
Perry Lodge E12 . . . . .1B **70**
Perryman Ho. IG11: Bark 1G **89**
  (off The Shaftesburys)
Perrymans Farm Rd. IG2: Ilf 6H **53**
Perry Mead EN2: Enf 2G **23**
Perrymead St. SW6 . . . . .1J **117**
Perryn Ct. TW1: Twick 6A **114**
Perryn Ho. W3 .7A **80**
Perryn Rd. SE16 . . . . .3H **103**
  W3 . . . . .1K **97**
Perry Ri. SE23 . . . . .3A **140**
Perry Rd. RM9: Dag 5F **91**

Perry's Pl. W1 . . . . .7C **6** (6H **83**)
Perry St. BR7: Chst 6H **143**
  DA1: Cray 4K **127**
Perry St. Gdns. BR7: Chst 6J **143**
Perry St. Shaw BR7: Chst 7J **143**
Perry Va. SE23 . . . . .2J **139**
Persant Rd. SE6 . . . . .2G **141**
Perseverance Pl. SW9 . . . . .7A **102**
  TW9: Rich 4E **114**
Perseverance Works E2 . . . . .1H **9**
  (off Kingsland Rd.)
Pershore Cl. IG2: Ilf 5F **53**
Pershore Gro. SM5: Cars 6B **154**
Pershore Ho. W13 . . . . .1A **96**
  (off Singapore Rd.)
Pert Cl. N10 . . . . .7A **32**
Perth Av. NW9 .7K **43**
  UB4: Yead 4A **76**
Perth Cl. SE5 .4D **120**
  SW20 .2B **152**
  UB5: N'olt 5E **58**
Perth Ho. N1 . . . . .7K **65**
  (off Bemerton Est.)
Perth Rd. BR3: Beck 2E **158**
  E10 . . . . .1A **68**
  E13 . . . . .2K **87**
  IG2: Ilf .6E **52**
  IG11: Bark 2H **89**
  N4 . . . . .1A **66**
  N22 . . . . .1B **48**
Perth Ter. IG2: Ilf 7G **53**
Perwell Av. HA2: Harr 1D **58**
Perystreete SE23 . . . . .2J **139**
Petavel Rd. TW11: Tedd 6J **131**
Peter Av. NW10 . . . . .7D **62**
  (off Nelson St.)
Peter Best Ho. E1 . . . . .6H **85**
  (off Nelson St.)
Peterboat Cl. SE10 . . . . .4G **105**
Peterborough Ct. EC4 . . . . . .1K **13** (6A **84**)
Peterborough Gdns. IG1: Ilf 7C **52**
Peterborough M. SW6 . . . . .2J **117**
Peterborough Rd. E10 . . . . .5E **50**
  HA1: Harr 1J **59**
  SM5: Cars 6C **154**
  SW6 . . . . .2J **117**
Peterborough Vs. SW6 . . . . .1K **117**
Peter Butler Ho. SE1 . . . . .7F **85**
  (off Wolseley St.)
Peterchurch Ho. SE15 . . . . .6H **103**
  (off Commercial Way)
Petergate SW11 . . . . .4A **118**
Peter Harrison Planetarium 7F **105**
Peterhead Ct. UB1: S'hall 6G **77**
  (off Osborne Rd.)
Peter Heathfield Ho. E15 . . . . .1F **87**
  (off Wise Rd.)
Peter Hills Ho. SE16 . . . . .4G **103**
  (off Alexis St.)
Peter Ho. SW8 . . . . .7J **101**
  (off Luscombe Way)
Peter James Bus. Cen. UB3: Hayes . . .2J **93**
Peter James Ent. Cen. NW10 . . . . . .3J **79**
Peter Kennedy Ct. CR0: C'don 6B **158**
Peterley Bus. Cen. E2 . . . . .2H **85**
Peter Lyell Ct. HA4: Ruis 2K **57**
Peter May Sports Cen. 7K **35**
Peter Pan Statue 4A **10** (1B **100**)
Peters Cl. DA16: Well 2J **125**
  HA7: Stan 6J **27**
  RM8: Dag 1D **72**
Peters Ct. W2 . . . . .6K **81**
  (off Porchester Rd.)
Petersfield Cl. N18 . . . . .5H **33**
Petersfield Ri. SW15 . . . . .1D **134**
Petersfield Rd. W3 . . . . .2J **97**
Petersgate KT2: King T 6J **133**
  (off Warren Rd.)
PETERSHAM 1E **132**
Petersham Cl. SM1: Sutt 5J **165**
  TW10: Ham 2D **132**
Petersham Dr. BR5: St P 2K **161**

Petersham Gdns. BR5: St P 2K **161**
Petersham Ho. SW7 . . . . .3A **16**
  (off Kendrick M.)
Petersham La. SW7 . . . . .3A **100**
Petersham M. SW7 . . . . .3A **100**
Petersham Pl. SW7 . . . . .3A **100**
Petersham Rd. TW10: Rich, Ham . . .6D **114**
Petersham Ter. CR0: Bedd 3J **167**
  (off Richmond Grn.)
Peter's Hill EC4 . . . . .2C **14** (7C **84**)
  (off Beaumont Sq.)
Peter Shore Ct. E1 . . . . .5K **85**
  (off Beaumont Sq.)
Peter's La. EC1 . . . . .5B **8** (5B **84**)
  (not continuous)
Peter's Path SE26 . . . . .4H **139**
Peterstone Rd. SE2 . . . . .2B **108**
Peterstow Cl. SW19 . . . . .2G **135**
Peter St. W1 . . . . .2C **12** (7H **83**)
Peterwood Pk. CR0: Wadd 2K **167**
Peterwood Way CR0: Wadd 2K **167**
Petherton Ct. HA1: Harr 6K **41**
  (off Gayton Rd.)
  NW10 . . . . .1F **81**
  (off Tiverton Rd.)
Petherton Ho. N4 . . . . .1C **66**
  (off Woodberry Down Est.)
Petherton Rd. N5 . . . . .5C **66**
Petiver Cl. E9 . . . . .7J **67**
Petley Rd. W6 . . . . .6F **99**
Peto Pl. NW1 . . . . .3K **5** (4F **83**)
Peto St. Nth. E16 . . . . .6H **87**
Petrie Cl. NW2 .6G **63**
Petrie Ho. SE18 . . . . .6E **106**
  (off Woolwich Comn.)
Petrie Museum of Egyptian Archaeology
  .4C **6** (4H **83**)
Petros Gdns. NW3 . . . . .6A **64**
Pettacre Cl. SE28 . . . . .3G **107**
Petticoat La. E1 . . . . .6J **9** (5E **84**)
Petticoat Lane Market
  . . . . .7J **9**
  (off Middlesex St.)
Petticoat Sq. E1 . . . . .7J **9** (6F **85**)
Petticoat Twr. E1 . . . . .7J **9**
Pettits Cl. RM1: Rom 2K **55**
Pettits La. Nth. RM1: Rom 1K **55**
Pettits Pl. RM10: Dag 5G **73**
Pettits Rd. RM10: Dag 5G **73**
Pettiward Cl. SW15 . . . . .4E **116**
Pettley Gdns. RM7: Rom 5K **55**
Pettman Cres. SE28 . . . . .3H **107**
Pettsgrove Av. HA0: Wemb 5C **60**
Pett's Hill UB5: N'olt 5F **59**
Petts La. TW17: Shep 4C **146**
Pett St. SE18 .4C **106**
PETTS WOOD 5H **161**
Petts Wood Rd.
  BR5: Pet W 5G **161**
Petty France SW1 . . . . .1B **18** (3G **101**)
Petty Wales EC3 . . . . .3H **15** (7E **84**)
Petworth Cl. UB5: N'olt 7D **58**
Petworth Gdns. SW20 . . . . .3D **152**
  UB10: Hil 1E **74**
Petworth Rd. DA6: Bex 5G **127**
  N12 . . . . .5H **31**
Petworth St. SW11 . . . . .1C **118**
Petyt Pl. SW3 .6C **100**
Petyward SW3 . . . . .4D **16** (4C **100**)
Pevensey Av. EN1: Enf 2K **23**
  N11 . . . . .5C **32**
Pevensey Cl. TW7: Isle 7G **95**
Pevensey Ct. SW16 . . . . .3A **138**
  W3 . . . . .2H **97**
Pevensey Ho. E1 . . . . .5K **85**
  (off Ben Jonson Rd.)
Pevensey Rd. E7 . . . . .4H **69**
  SW17 .4B **136**
  TW13: Felt 1C **130**
Peverel E6 . . . . .6E **88**
Peverel Ho. RM10: Dag 2G **73**
Peverel Cl. N11 . . . . .5A **32**
Peveril Dr. TW11: Tedd 5H **131**

Peveril Ho. *SE1* *3D 102*
   (off Rephidim St.)
Pewsey Cl. E4 . . . . .5H **35**
Peyton Pl. SE10 . . . . .7E **104**
Pharamond NW2 . . . . .6F **63**
Pharaoh Cl. CR4: Mitc 7D **154**
Pheasant Cl. E16 . . . . .6K **87**
Pheasantry Ho. *SW3* 5D **16**
   (off Jubilee Pl.)
Pheasantry Welcome Centre, The . .1K **149**
Phelps Lodge N1 . . . . .1K **83**
Phelp St. SE17 . . . . .6D **102**
Phelps Way UB3: Harl 4H **93**
Phene St. SW3 . . . . .7D 16 (6C **100**)
Philadelphia Ct. *SW10* 7A **100**
   (off Uverdale Rd.)
Philbeach Gdns. SW5 . . . . .5J **99**
Phil Brown Pl. *SW8* 3F **119**
   (off Daley Thompson Way)
Philchurch Pl. E1 . . . . .6G **85**
Philia Ho. *NW1* 7G **65**
   (off Farrier St.)
Philimore Ct. SE18 . . . . .5J **107**
Philip Av. RM7: Rush G 1K **73**
Philip Cl. RM7: Rush G 1K **73**
Philip Cl. *W2* 5A **4**
   (off Hall Pl.)
Philip Gdns. CR0: C'don 2B **170**
Philip Ho. *NW6* 1K **81**
   (off Mortimer Pl.)
Philip Jones Ct. N4 . . . . .1K **65**
Philip La. N15 . . . . .4D **48**
Philip Mole Ho. W9 . . . . .4J **81**
   (off Chippenham Rd.)
Philpot Path SE9 . . . . .6D **124**
Philippa Gdns. SE9 . . . . .5B **124**
Philip Rd. N15 . . . . .4D **48**
   TW18: Staines 6A **128**
Philips Cl. SM5: Cars 1E **166**
Philip Sq. SW8 . . . . .2F **119**
Philip St. E13 . . . . .4J **87**
Philip Wlk. SE15 . . . . .3G **121**
   (not continuous)
Phillimore Ct. *W8* 2J **99**
   (off Kensington High St.)
Phillimore Gdns. NW10 . . . . .1E **80**
   W3 .1G **97**
   W8 . . . . .2J **99**
Phillimore Gdns. Cl. W8 . . . . .3J **99**
Phillimore Pl. W8 . . . . .2J **99**
Phillimore Ter. *W8* 3J **99**
   (off Allen St.)
Phillimore Wlk. W8 . . . . .3J **99**
Phillip Ho. *E1* 6K **9**
   (off Heneage St.)
Phillipp St. N1 . . . . .1E **84**
Phillips Ct. HA8: Edg 6B **28**
Philpot La. EC3 . . . . .2G **15** (7E **84**)
Philpot Path IG1: Ilf 3G **71**
Philpots Cl. UB7: Yiew 7A **74**
Philpot Sq. SW6 . . . . .3K **117**
Philpot St. E1 . . . . .6H **85**
Phineas Pett Rd. SE9 . . . . .3C **124**
Phipps Bri. Rd. CR4: Mitc 3B **154**
   SW19 . . . . .2A **154**
Phipps Hatch La. EN2: Enf 1H **23**
Phipps Ho. *SE7* 5K **105**
   (off Woolwich Rd.)
   W12 . . . . .7D **80**
   (off White City Est.)
Phipp's M. *SW1* 3F **101**
   (off Buckingham Palace Rd.)
Phipp St. EC2 . . . . .3G **9** (4E **84**)
Phoebeth Rd. SE4 . . . . .5C **122**
Phoebe Wik. E16 . . . . .6K **87**
Phoenix Av. SE10 . . . . .2G **105**
Phoenix Cen. 7J **167**
Phoenix Cinema
   East Finchley 4C **46**
Phoenix Cl. BR4: W W'ck 2F **171**
   CR4: Mitc 3B **154**

Phoenix Cl. E8 . . . . .1F **85**
   E17 .2B **50**
   W12 . . . . .7D **80**
Phoenix Ct. CR2: S Croy 5F **169**
   E1 . . . . .5F **85**
   (off Buckhurst St.)
   E4 . . . . .3J **35**
   E14 . . . . .4C **104**
   KT3: N Mald 3B **152**
   NW1 . . . . .1D **6**
   (off Purchese St.)
   SE14 . . . . .6A **104**
   (off Chipley St.)
   TW3: Houn 3E **112**
   TW4: Houn 5B **112**
   TW8: Bford 5E **96**
   TW13: Felt 4G **129**
Phoenix Dr. BR2: Kes 4B **172**
Phoenix Hgts. E. *E14* 2C **104**
   (off Byng St.)
Phoenix Hgts. W. *E14* 2C **104**
   (off Mastmaker Ct.)
Phoenix Ho. SM1: Sutt 4K **165**
Phoenix Ind. Est. HA1: Harr 4K **41**
Phoenix Lodge Mans. *W6* 4F **99**
   (off Brook Grn.)
Phoenix Pk. NW2 . . . . .2C **62**
Phoenix Pl. WC1 . . . . . . .3H **7** (4K **83**)
Phoenix Point SE28 . . . . .1C **108**
Phoenix Rd. NW1 . . . . . . .1C **6** (2H **83**)
   SE20 . . . . .6J **139**
Phoenix Sports Cen.
   Hammersmith 7C **80**
Phoenix St. WC2 . . . . . . .1D **12** (6H **83**)
Phoenix Theatre 1D **12**
   (off Charing Cross Rd.)
Phoenix Trad. Est. UB6: G'frd 1C **78**
Phoenix Trad. Pk. TW8: Bford 5D **96**
Phoenix Way E16 . . . . .5H **87**
   (off Barking Rd.)
   SW18 . . . . .5A **118**
   TW5: Hest 6B **94**
Phoenix Wharf *E1* 1H **103**
   (off Wapping High St.)
Phoenix Wharf Rd. SE1 . . . . .7K **15**
Phoenix Yd. WC1 . . . . .2H **7**
Photographers Gallery 1A **12**
   (off Ramillies St.)
Phyllis Av. KT3: N Mald 5D **152**
Phyllis Hodges Ho. *NW1* 1C **6**
   (off Aldenham St.)
Phyllis Ho. *CR0: Wadd* 4B **168**
   (off Ashley La.)
Physical Energy Statue . .5A 10 (1A **100**)
Physic Pl. SW3 . . . . .7E **16** (6D **100**)
Piano La. N16 . . . . .3D **66**
Piano Works *IG11: Bark* 7G **71**
   (off Ripple Rd.)
Piazza, The UB8: Uxb 7A **56**
   WC2 . . . . .2F **13**
   (not continuous)
Piazza Wlk. E1 . . . . .6G **85**
Picardy Ho. EN2: Enf 1H **23**
Picardy Manorway
   DA17: Belv 3H **109**
Picardy Rd. DA17: Belv 5G **109**
Picardy St. DA17: Belv 3G **109**
Piccadilly W1 . . . . .5K 11 (1F **101**)
Piccadilly Circus 3C 12 (7H **83**)
Piccadilly Cir. W1 . . . . .3C **12** (7H **83**)
Piccadilly Ct. N7 . . . . .6K **65**
   (off Caledonian Rd.)
Piccadilly Pl. W1 . . . . .3B **12**
Piccadilly Theatre 2B **12**
   (off Denman St.)
Pickard Cl. N14 . . . . .1C **32**
Pickard Gdns. E3 . . . . .5B **86**
Pickard St. EC1 . . . . .1B **8** (3B **84**)
Pickering Av. E6 . . . . .2E **88**
Pickering Cl. E9 . . . . .7K **67**

Pickering Gdns. CR0: C'don 6F **157**
   N11 .6K **31**
Pickering Ho. *W2* 6A **82**
   (off Hallfield Est.)
   W5 .4C **96**
   (off Windmill Rd.)
Pickering La. BR5: Farnb 1H **173**
Pickering M. W2 . . . . .6K **81**
Pickering Pl. SW1 . . . . .5B **12**
Pickering Rd. IG11: Bark 6G **71**
Pickering St. N1 . . . . .1B **84**
Picketts Cl. WD23: B Hea 1C **26**
Picketts St. SW12 . . . . .7F **119**
Pickett Cft. HA7: Stan 1D **42**
Picketts Lock La. N9 . . . . .2D **34**
Picketts Lock La. Ind. Est. N9 . . . .2F **35**
Picketts Ter. SE22 . . . . .5G **121**
Pickford Cl. DA7: Bex 2E **126**
Pickford La. DA7: Bex 2E **126**
Pickford Rd. DA7: Bex 3E **126**
Pickfords Wharf N1 . . . . .2C **84**
   SE1 . . . . .4E **14** (1D **102**)
Pickhurst Grn. BR2: Hayes 7H **159**
Pickhurst La. BR2: Hayes 5G **159**
   BR4: W W'ck 5G **159**
Pickhurst Mead BR2: Hayes 7H **159**
Pickhurst Pk. BR2: Brom 5G **159**
Pickhurst Ri. BR4: W W'ck 7E **158**
Pickhurst Cl. TW4: Houn 5C **112**
Pickwick Ct. SE9 . . . . .1C **142**
Pickwick Ho. *SE16* 2G **103**
   (off George Row)
   W11 . . . . .1F **99**
   (off St Ann's Rd.)
Pickwick M. N18 . . . . .4K **33**
Pickwick Pl. HA1: Harr 7J **41**
Pickwick Rd. SE21 . . . . .7D **120**
Pickwick St. SE1 . . . . . . .7C **14** (2C **102**)
Pickwick Way BR7: Chst 6G **143**
Pickworth Cl. SW8 . . . . .7J **101**
Picton Pl. KT6: Surb 1G **163**
   W1 . . . . .1H **11** (6E **82**)
Picton St. SE5 . . . . .7D **102**
Picture Ho. SW16 . . . . .2J **137**
Pied Bull Ct. *WC1* 6E **6**
   (off Bury Pl.)
Pied Bull Yd. *N1* 1B **84**
   (off Theberton St.)
   WC1 .6E **6**
Piedmont Rd. SE18 . . . . .5H **107**
   (not continuous)
PIELD HEATH 4B **74**
Pield Heath Av. UB8: Hil 4C **74**
Pield Heath Rd.
   UB8: Cowl, Hil 4A **74**
Pierce Campion Cl. E17 . . . . .3B **50**
Pier Head E1 . . . . .1H **103**
   (not continuous)
Pierhead Wharf *E1* 1H **103**
   (off Wapping High St.)
Pier Ho. SW3 . . . . .7D **16** (6C **100**)
Pieris Ho. *TW13: Felt* 2J **129**
Piermont Grn. SE22 . . . . .5H **121**
Piermont Pl. BR1: Brom 2C **160**
Piermont Rd. SE22 . . . . .5H **121**
Pier Pde. E16 . . . . .1E **106**
   (off Pier Rd.)
Pierpoint Bldg. E14 . . . . .2B **104**
Pierrepoint Rd. W3 . . . . .7H **79**
Pierrepont Arc. *N1* 2B **84**
   (off Islington High St.)
Pierrepont Row *N1* 2B **84**
   (off Camden Pas.)
Pier Rd. E16 . . . . .1E **106**
   TW14: Felt 5K **111**
Pier St. E14 . . . . .4E **104**
   (not continuous)
Pier Ter. SW18 . . . . .4K **117**
Pier Wlk. SE10 . . . . .2G **105**
Pier Way SE28 . . . . .2G **107**

Pietra Lara Bldg. *EC1* 3C **8**
   (off Pear Tree St.)
Pigeon La. TW12: Hamp 4E **130**
Piggott Ho. *E2* 2K **85**
   (off Sewardstone Rd.)
Pigott St. E14 . . . . .6C **86**
Pike Cl. BR1: Brom 5K **141**
   UB10: Uxb 1B **74**
Pikemans Ct. *SW5* 4J **99**
   (off W. Cromwell Rd.)
Pike Rd. NW7 . . . . .4E **28**
Pike's End HA5: Eastc 4K **39**
Pikestone Cl. UB4: Yead 4C **76**
Pikethorne SE23 . . . . .2K **139**
Pilgrimage St. SE1 . . . . . .7E **14** (2D **102**)
Pilgrim Cl. SM4: Mord 7K **153**
Pilgrim Hill SE27 . . . . .4C **138**
Pilgrim Ho. *SE1* 3D **102**
   (off Tabard St.)
   SE16 . . . . .2J **103**
   (off Brunel Rd.)
Pilgrims Cloisters *SE5* 7E **102**
   (off Sedgmoor Pl.)
Pilgrims Cl. N13 . . . . .4E **32**
   UB5: N'olt 5G **59**
Pilgrims Cnr. *NW6* 2J **81**
   (off Chichester Rd.)
Pilgrims Ct. EN1: Enf 2J **23**
Pilgrim's La. NW3 . . . . .4B **64**
Pilgrims M. E14 . . . . .7G **87**
Pilgrim's Pl. NW3 . . . . .4B **64**
Pilgrims Ri. EN4: E Barn 5H **21**
Pilgrim St. EC4 . . . . .1A 14 (6B **84**)
Pilgrims Way CR2: S Croy 6F **169**
   E6 . . . . .1C **88**
   HA9: Wemb 1H **61**
   N19 .1H **65**
Pilkington Rd. BR6: Farnb 3G **173**
   SE15 . . . . .2H **121**
Pill Box Studios *E2* 4H **85**
   (off Coventry Rd.)
Pillfold Ho. *SE11* 3G **19**
   (off Old Paradise St.)
Pillions La. UB4: Hayes 4F **75**
Pilot Cl. SE8 . . . . .6B **104**
Pilot Ind. Cen. NW10 . . . . .4K **79**
Pilsdon Cl. SW19 . . . . .1F **135**
Pilton Estate, The CR0: C'don 2B **168**
Pilton Pl. SE17 . . . . .5C **102**
Pimento Ct. W5 . . . . .3D **96**
PIMLICO 6B 18 (5G **101**)
Pimlico Ho. *SW1* 5J **17**
   (off Ebury Bri. Rd.)
Pimlico Rd. SW1 . . . . .5G 17 (5E **100**)
Pimlico Wlk. N1 . . . . .1G **9**
Pimp Hall Nature Reserve 2A **36**
Pinchbeck Rd. BR6: Chels 6K **173**
Pinchin & Johnsons Yd. *E1* 7G **85**
   (off Pinchin St.)
Pinchin St. E1 . . . . .7G **85**
Pincombe Ho. *SE17* 5D **102**
   (off Orb St.)
Pincott Pl. SE4 . . . . .3K **121**
Pincott Rd. DA6: Bex 5G **127**
   SW19 . . . . .7A **136**
Pindar St. EC2 . . . . .5G **9** (5E **84**)
Pindock M. W9 . . . . .4K **81**
Pindoria M. *E1* 4F **85**
   (off Quaker St.)
Pineapple Cl. SW1 . . . . .1B **18**
Pine Av. BR4: W W'ck 1D **170**
   E15 . . . . .5F **69**
Pine Cl. E10 . . . . .2D **68**
   HA7: Stan 4G **27**
   N14 .7B **22**
   N19 .2G **65**
   SE20 . . . . .1J **157**
Pine Coombe CR0: C'don 4K **169**
Pine Ct. N21 . . . . .5E **22**
   UB5: N'olt 4C **76**
Pinecrest Gdns. BR6: Farnb 4F **173**

Pinecroft Ct. DA16: Well 7A 108
Pinecroft Cres. EN5: Barn 4B 20
Pinedene SE15 . . . . .1H 121
Pinefield Cl. E14 . . . . .7C 86
Pine Gdns. HA4: Ruis 1K 57
 KT5: Surb .6G 151
Pine Glade BR6: Farnb 4D 172
Pine Gro. N4 . . . . .2J 65
 N20 . . . . .1C 30
 SW19 . . . . .5H 135
Pine Ho. E3 . . . . .1A 86
 (off Barge La.)
 SE16 . . . . .2J 103
 (off Ainsty Est.)
 W10 . . . . .4G 81
 (off Droop St.)
Pinehurst Ct. W11 . . . . .6H 81
 (off Colville Gdns.)
Pinehurst Wlk. BR6: Orp 1H 173
Pinemartin Cl. NW2 . . . . .3E 62
Pine M. NW10 .2F 81
 (off Clifford Gdns.)
Pine Pl. UB4: Hayes 4H 75
Pine Ridge SM5: Cars 7E 166
Pineridge Ct. EN5: Barn 4A 20
Pine Rd. N11 .2K 31
 NW2 . . . . .4E 62
Pines, The IG8: Wfd G 3C 36
 KT9: Chess 3E 162
 N14 . . . . .5B 22
 SE19 . . . . .6B 138
 TW16: Sun .3J 147
Pines Rd. BR1: Brom 2C 160
Pine St. EC1 . . . . .3K 7 (4A 84)
Pine Tree Cl. TW5: Cran 1K 111
Pine Tree Lodge BR2: Brom 4H 159
Pine Trees Dr. UB10: Ick 4A 56
Pine Tree Way SE13 . . . . .3D 122
Pineview Ct. E4 . . . . .1K 35
Pine Wlk. KT5: Surb 6G 151
Pine Wood TW16: Sun 1J 147
Pinewood Av. DA15: Sidc 1J 143
 HA5: Hat E .6A 26
 UB8: Hil 6B 74
Pinewood Cl. BR6: Orp 1H 173
 CR0: C'don 3A 170
 HA5: Hat E .6A 26
Pinewood Ct. EN2: Enf 3G 23
 SW4 . . . . .6H 119
Pinewood Dr. BR6: Orp 5J 173
Pinewood Gro. W5 . . . . .6C 78
Pinewood Lodge WD23: B Hea 1C 26
Pinewood Pl. DA2: Wilm 2K 145
 (not continuous)
 KT19: Ewe .4K 163
Pinewood Rd. BR2: Brom 4J 159
 SE2 . . . . .6D 108
 TW13: Felt .3K 129
Pinfold Rd. SW16 . . . . .4J 137
Pinglestone Cl. UB7: Harm 7A 92
Pinkcoat Cl. TW13: Felt 3K 129
Pinkerton Pl. SW16 . . . . .4H 137
Pinkham Mans. W4 . . . . .5G 97
Pinkham Way N11 . . . . .7K 31
Pinkwell Av. UB3: Harl 4F 93
Pinkwell La. UB3: Harl 4E 92
Pinley Gdns. RM9: Dag 1B 90
Pinnace Ho. E14 . . . . .3E 104
 (off Manchester Rd.)
Pinnacle, The EC2 . . . . .1G 15
 (off Bishopsgate)
Pinnacle Apartments CR0: C'don 1C 168
 (off Saffron Central Sq.)
Pinnacle Hill DA7: Bex 4H 127
Pinnacle Hill Nth. DA7: Bex 4H 127
Pinnacle Ho. EN1: Enf 3K 23
 (off Colman Pde.)
 NW9 . . . . .2B 44
 (off Heritage Av.)
 SW18 . . . . .4A 118
Pinnacle Pl. HA7: Stan 4G 27

Pinnacle Way E14 . . . . .6A 86
 (off Commercial Rd.)
Pinnata Cl. EN2: Enf 1H 23
Pinnell Rd. SE9 . . . . .4B 124
PINNER 4C 40
Pinner Ct. HA5: Pinn 4E 40
 NW8 . . . . .3A 4
PINNER GREEN 2A 40
Pinner Grn. HA5: Pinn 2A 40
Pinner Gro. HA5: Pinn 4C 40
Pinner Hill Farm HA5: Pinn 1K 39
Pinner Hill Golf Course 1A 40
Pinner Hill Rd. HA5: Pinn 1K 39
Pinner Park 1E 40
Pinner Pk. HA5: Pinn 2E 40
Pinner Pk. Av. HA2: Harr 3F 41
Pinner Pk. Gdns. HA2: Harr 2G 41
Pinner Rd. HA1: Harr 4E 40
 HA2: Harr 4E 40
 HA5: Pinn .4D 40
 HA6: Nwood, Pinn 1H 39
 HA6: Pinn .1H 39
Pinners Cl. SM5: Cars 2C 166
Pinners Pas. EC2 . . . . .7F 9
 (off Old Broad St.)
Pinner Vw. HA1: Harr 4G 41
 HA2: Harr 3G 41
PINNERWOOD PARK 1A 40
Pinn Way HA4: Ruis 7F 39
Pintail Cl. E6 . . . . .5C 88
Pintail Ct. SE8 . . . . .6B 104
 (off Pilot Cl.)
Pintail Rd. IG8: Wfd G 7E 36
Pintail Way UB4: Yead 5B 76
Pinter Ho. SW9 . . . . .2J 119
 (off Grantham Rd.)
Pinto Way SE3 . . . . .4K 123
Pioneer Centre, The SE15 . . . . .1J 121
Pioneer Cl. E14 . . . . .5D 86
Pioneer Ct. E16 . . . . .5J 87
 (off Hammersley Rd.)
Pioneer Ho. WC1 . . . . .1G 7
 (off Britannia St.)
Pioneer Pl. CR0: Sels 7C 170
Pioneer Point IG1: Ilf 3F 71
Pioneers Ind. Pk. CR0: Bedd 1J 167
Pioneer St. SE15 . . . . .1G 121
Pioneer Way W12 . . . . .6D 80
Piper Building, The SW6 . . . . .3K 117
Piper Cl. N7 . . . . .6K 65
Piper Rd. KT1: King T 3G 151
Piper's Gdns. CR0: C'don 7A 158
Pipers Grn. La. HA8: Edg 3K 27
 (not continuous)
Pipers Ho. SE10 . . . . .5F 105
 (off Collington St.)
Piper Way IG1: Ilf 1H 71
Pipewell Rd. SM5: Cars 6C 154
Pippenhall SE9 . . . . .6F 125
Pippin Cl. CR0: C'don 1B 170
 NW2 . . . . .3C 62
 TW13: Hanw 3D 130
Pippin Ct. SW8 . . . . .7G 19
 (off Vauxhall Gro.)
Pippin Ho. W10 . . . . .7F 81
 (off Freston Rd.)
Pippin Mans. E20 . . . . .5E 68
 (off Mirabelle Gdns.)
Pippins Cl. UB7: W Dray 3A 92
Pippins Ct. TW15: Ashf 6D 128
Pique M. E1 . . . . .7K 85
 (off Glasshouse Flds.)
Piquet Rd. SE20 . . . . .2J 157
Pirbright Cres. CR0: New Ad 6E 170
Pirbright Rd. SW18 . . . . .1H 135
Pirie Cl. SE5 . . . . .3D 120
Pirie St. E16 . . . . .1K 105
Pirin Cl. E4 . . . . .4H 35
Pissaro Ho. N1 .7A 66
 (off Augustas La.)

Pitcairn Cl. RM7: Mawney 4G 55
Pitcairn Ho. E9 .7J 67
Pitcairn Rd. CR4: Mitc 7D 136
Pitcairn's Path HA2: Harr 3G 59
Pitchford St. E15 . . . . .7F 69
Pitfield Cres. SE28 . . . . .1A 108
Pitfield Est. N1 . . . . .1G 9 (3E 84)
Pitfield St. N1 . . . . .1G 9 (3E 84)
Pitfield Way EN3: Enf H 1D 24
 NW10 . . . . .6J 61
Pitfold Cl. SE12 . . . . .6K 123
Pitfold Rd. SE12 . . . . .6J 123
Pitlake CR0: C'don 2B 168
Pitlochry Ho. SE27 . . . . .2B 138
 (off Elmcourt Rd.)
Pitman Bldg. SE16 . . . . .7K 15
 (off Old Jamaica Rd.)
Pitman Ho. SE8 . . . . .1C 122
Pitman St. SE5 . . . . .7C 102
Pitmaston Ho. SE13 . . . . .2E 122
 (off Lewisham Rd.)
Pitmaston Rd. SE13 . . . . .2E 122
Pitsea Pl. E1 . . . . .6K 85
Pitsea St. E1 . . . . .6K 85
Pitshanger La. W5 . . . . .4B 78
Pitt Cres. SW19 . . . . .4K 135
Pittman Gdns. IG1: Ilf 5G 71
Pitt Rd. BR6: Farnb 4G 173
 CR0: C'don 5C 156
 CR7: Thor H 5C 156
 HA2: Harr 2G 59
Pitt's Head M. W1 . . . . .5H 11 (1E 100)
Pittsmead Av. BR2: Hayes 7J 159
Pitt St. W8 . . . . .2J 99
Pittville Gdns. SE25 . . . . .3G 157
Pitwell M. E8 . . . . .6G 67
Pixfield Ct. BR2: Brom 2H 159
 (off Beckenham La.)
Pixley St. E14 . . . . .6B 86
Pixton Way CR0: Sels 7A 170
Place, The 3H 83
Place, The SE1 . . . . .5F 15 (1D 102)
Place Farm Av. BR6: Orp 1H 173
Plaisterers Highwalk EC2 . . . . .6C 8
 (off London Wall)
PLAISTOW
 BR1 . . . . .7J 141
 E13 . . . . .2J 87
Plaistow Gro. BR1: Brom 7K 141
 E15 . . . . .1H 87
Plaistow La. BR1: Brom 7J 141
Plaistow Pk. Rd. E13 . . . . .2K 87
 (not continuous)
Plaistow Rd. E13 . . . . .1H 87
 E15 . . . . .1H 87
Plaistow Wharf E16 . . . . .2J 105
Plane Ho. BR2: Brom 2G 159
Plane St. SE26 . . . . .3H 139
Planetree Ct. W6 . . . . .4F 99
 (off Brook Grn.)
Plane Tree Cres. TW13: Felt 3K 129
Plane Tree Ho. SE8 . . . . .6A 104
 (off Etta St.)
 W8 . . . . .2H 99
 (off Duchess of Bedford's Wlk.)
Plane Tree Wlk. N2 . . . . .3C 46
 SE19 . . . . .6E 138
Plantagenet Cl. KT4: Wor Pk 4K 163
Plantagenet Gdns.
 RM6: Chad H 7D 54
Plantagenet Ho. SE18 . . . . .3D 106
 (off Leda Rd.)
Plantagenet Pl. RM6: Chad H 7D 54
Plantagenet Rd. EN5: New Bar 4F 21
Plantain Gdns. E11 . . . . .3F 69
 (off Hollydown Way)
Plantain Pl. SE1 . . . . .6E 14 (2D 102)
Plantation, The SE3 . . . . .2J 123
Plantation Cl. SW4 . . . . .5J 119
Plantation La. EC3 . . . . .2G 15
Plantation Pl. EC3 . . . . .2G 15

Plantation Wharf SW11 . . . . .3A 118
Plantree Path E17 . . . . .4C 50
 (off Selborne Rd.)
Plasel Ct. E13 .1K 87
 (off Pawsey Cl.)
PLASHET 6C 70
Plashet Gro. E6 . . . . .1A 88
Plashet Rd. E13 . . . . .1J 87
Plassy Rd. SE6 . . . . .7D 122
Plate Ho. E14 .5D 104
 (off Burrells Wharf Sq.)
Platform Theatre 1J 83
Platina St. EC2 . . . . .3F 9
Platinum Ct. E1 .4J 85
 (off Cephas Av.)
 RM7: Mawney 3H 55
Platinum M. N15 . . . . .5F 49
Plato Rd. SW2 . . . . .4J 119
Platt, The SW15 . . . . .3F 117
Platt Halls NW9 . . . . .2B 44
Platt's Eyot TW12: Hamp 2E 148
Platt's La. NW3 . . . . .4J 63
Platts Rd. EN3: Enf H 1D 24
Platt St. NW1 .2H 83
Plawsfield Rd. BR3: Beck 1K 157
Plaxdale Ho. SE17 . . . . .4E 102
 (off Congreve St.)
Plaxtol Cl. BR1: Brom 1A 160
Plaxtol Rd. DA8: Erith 7G 109
Plaxton Ct. E11 . . . . .3H 69
Playfair Ho. E14 . . . . .6C 86
 (off Saracen St.)
Playfair Mans. W14 . . . . .6G 99
 (off Queen's Club Gdns.)
Playfair St. W6 .5E 98
Playfield Av. RM5: Col R 1J 55
Playfield Cres. SE22 . . . . .5F 121
Playfield Rd. HA8: Edg 2J 43
Playford Rd. N4 . . . . .2K 65
 (not continuous)
Playgreen Way SE6 . . . . .3C 140
Playground Cl. BR3: Beck 2A 158
Playhouse Ct. SE1 . . . . .6C 14
 (off Southwark Bri. Rd.)
Playhouse Theatre 4F 13
 (off Northumberland Av.)
Playhouse Yd. EC4 . . . . .1A 14 (6B 84)
Plaza Bus. Cen. EN3: Brim 2G 25
Plaza Gdns. SW15 . . . . .5G 117
Plaza Hgts. E10 . . . . .3E 68
Plaza Pde. HA0: Wemb 6E 60
 (off Ealing Rd.)
 NW6 . . . . .2K 81
Plaza Shop. Cen. The W1 . . . .7B 6 (6G 83)
Plaza Wlk. NW9 . . . . .3J 43
Pleasance, The SW15 . . . . .4D 116
Pleasance Rd. SW15 . . . . .5D 116
Pleasance Theatre
 London 6J 65
 (off Carpenters M.)
Pleasant Gro. CR0: C'don 3B 170
Pleasant Pl. N1 . . . . .7B 66
Pleasant Row NW1 . . . . .1F 83
Pleasant Vw. Pl.
 BR6: Farnb .5F 173
Pleasant Way HA0: Wemb 2C 78
Pleasaunce Mans. SE10 . . . . .5J 105
 (off Halstow Rd.)
Plender Ct. NW1 . . . . .1G 83
 (off College Pl.)
Plender St. NW1 . . . . .1G 83
Pleshey Rd. N7 . . . . .4H 65
Plesman Way SM6: Wall 7J 167
Plessey Bldg. E14 . . . . .6C 86
 (off Dod St.)
Plevna Cres. N15 . . . . .6E 48
Plevna Rd. N9 .3B 34
 TW12: Hamp 1F 149
Plevna St. E14 . . . . .3E 104
Pleydell Av. SE19 . . . . .7F 139
 W6 . . . . .4B 98

Pleydell Ct. *EC4* *1K 13*
(off Pleydell St.)
Pleydell Est. EC1 . . . . .2D 8
Pleydell Gdns. *SE19* 6F *139*
(off Anerley Hill)
Pleydell Ho. *EC4* 6A *84*
(off Pleydell St.)
Pleydell St. EC4 . . . . .1K 13
Plimley Pl. *W12* 2F *99*
(off Shepherd's Bush Pl.)
Plimsoll Cl. E14 . . . . .6D 86
Plimsoll Rd. N4 . . . . .3A 66
Plough Cl. NW10 . . . . .3D 80
Plough Ct. EC3 . . . . .2F 15 (7D 84)
RM13: Rain 2K *91*
(off Broadis Way)
Plough Farm Cl. HA4: Ruis 6F 39
SE22 . . . . .6F 121
SM6: Bedd, Wall 4J 167
SW17 . . . . .5K 135
SW19 . . . . .5K 135
TW11: Tedd 5A 132
Plough La. Cl. SM6: Bedd 5J 167
Ploughmans Cl. NW1 . . . . .1H 83
Ploughmans End TW7: Isle 5H 113
Ploughmans Wlk. *SE17* 2A *46*
(off Long La.)
Plough M. SW11 . . . . .4B 118
Plough Pl. EC4 . . . . .7K 7 (6A *84*)
Plough Rd. KT19: Ewe 7K 163
SW11 . . . . .3B 118
Plough St. E1 .7K 9
Plough Ter. SW11 . . . . .4B 118
Plough Way SE16 . . . . .4K 103
Plough Yd. EC2 . . . . .4H 9 (4E 84)
Plover Ho. *SW9* 7A *102*
(off Brixton Rd.)
Plover Way SE16 . . . . .3A 104
UB4: Yead 6B 76
Plowden Bldgs. EC4 . . . . .2J 13
Plowman Cl. N18 . . . . .5J 33
Plowman Way RM8: Dag 1C 72
Plumber's Row E1 . . . . .5G 85
Plumbridge St. SE10 . . . . .1E 122
Plum Cl. TW13: Felt 1J 129
Plume Ho. *SE10* 6D *104*
(off Creek Rd.)
Plum Gth. TW8: Bford 4D 96
Plum La. RM13: Rain 2K *91*
SE18 . . . . .7F 107
Plummer La. CR4: Mitc 2D 154
Plummer Rd. SW4 . . . . .7H 119
Plumpton Cl. UB5: N'olt 6E 58
Plumpton Way SM5: Cars 3C 166
PLUMSTEAD .4J 107
PLUMSTEAD COMMON 6F 107
Plumstead Comn. Rd. SE18 . . . . .6F 107
Plumstead High St. SE18 . . . . .4H 107
Plumstead Rd. SE18 . . . . .4F 107
(not continuous)
Plumtree Cl. RM10: Dag 6H 73
SM6: Wall 7H 167
Plumtree Ct. EC4 . . . . .7A 8 (6B *84*)
Plymen Ho. KT8: W Mole 5E 148
Plymouth Ct. *KT5: Surb* 4E *150*
(off Cranes Pk. Av.)
Plymouth Ho. *IG11: Bark* 7A *72*
(off Margaret Bondfield Av.)
SE10 . . . . .1D *122*
(off Devonshire Dr.)
Plymouth Rd. BR1: Brom 1K 159
E16 . . . . .5J 87
Plymouth Ter. *NW2* 6E *62*
(off Sidmouth Rd.)
Plymouth Wharf E14 . . . . .4F 105
Plympton Av. NW6 . . . . .7H 63
Plympton Cl. DA17: Belv 3E 108
Plympton Pl. NW8 . . . . .4C 4 (4C 82)
Plympton Rd. NW6 . . . . .7H 63
Plympton St. NW8 . . . . .4C 4 (4C 82)

Plymstock Rd. DA16: Well 7C 108
PM Gallery & House 1D 96
Pocklington Ct. NW9 . . . . .2A 44
W12 . . . . .3C 98
(off Ashchurch Pk. Vs.)
Pocklington Ct. SW15 . . . . .1C 134
Pocklington Lodge W12 . . . . .3C 98
Pocock Av. UB7: W Dray 3B 92
Pocock St. SE1 . . . . .6A 14 (2B 102)
Podmore Rd. SW18 . . . . .4A 118
Poet Cl. *E1* .5K *85*
(off Shandy St.)
Poets Cl. SE25 . . . . .4G 157
W3 . . . . .1J 97
Poet's Rd. N5 . . . . .5D 66
Poets Way HA1: Harr 4J 41
Point, The *E17* 4C *50*
(off Tower M.)
HA4: Ruis 4J 57
W2 . . . . .6A 4
Pointalls Cl. N3 . . . . .2A 46
Point Cl. SE10 . . . . .1E 122
Pointer Cl. SE28 . . . . .6D 90
Pointers Cl. E14 . . . . .5D 104
Pointers Cotts. TW10: Ham 2C 132
Point Hill SE10 . . . . .7E 104
Point Pl. HA9: Wemb 7H 61
Point Pleasant SW18 . . . . .4J 117
Point Ter. *E7* 5K *69*
(off Claremont Rd.)
Point West SW7 . . . . .4K 99
Point Wharf TW8: Bford 7E 96
Point Wharf La. TW8: Bford 7D 96
Poland St. W1 . . . . .1B 12 (6G 83)
Polar Pk. UB7: Harm 7B 92
Polebrook Rd. SE3 . . . . .3A 124
Pole Cat All. BR2: Hayes 2H 171
Polecroft La. SE6 . . . . .2E 140
Polehamptons, The TW12: Hamp 7G 131
Pole Hill Rd. E4 . . . . .7K 25
UB4: Hayes 4D 74
UB10: Hil .4D 74
Polesden Gdns. SW20 . . . . .2D 152
Polesworth Ho. *W2* 5J *81*
(off Alfred Rd.)
Polesworth Rd. RM9: Dag 7D 72
Police Sta. La. WD23: Bush 1A 26
POLISH WAR MEMORIAL 7A 58
Polka Theatre for Children 6K 135
Pollard Cl. E16 . . . . .7J 87
N7 . . . . .4K 65
Pollard Ho. KT4: Wor Pk 4E 164
N1 . . . . .1G 7
(off Northdown St.)
SE16 . . . . .3F *103*
(off Spa Rd.)
Pollard Rd. N20 . . . . .2H 31
SM4: Mord 5B 154
Pollard Row E2 . . . . .3G 85
Pollards Cres. SW16 . . . . .3J 155
Pollards Hill E. SW16 . . . . .3K 155
Pollards Hill Nth. SW16 . . . . .3J 155
Pollards Hill Sth. SW16 . . . . .3J 155
Pollards Hill W. SW16 . . . . .3K 155
Pollard St. E2 . . . . .3G 85
Pollards Wood Rd. SW16 . . . . .3J 155
Pollard Wlk. DA14: Sidc 6C 144
Pollen St. W1 . . . . .1A 12 (6G 83)
Pollitt Dr. NW8 . . . . .3B 4 (4B 82)
Pollock Ho. *W10* 4G *81*
(off Kensal Rd.)
Pollock's Toy Mus. 5B 6 (5G 83)
Polperro Cl. BR6: St M Cry 6K 161
Polperro Ho. *W2* 5J *81*
(off Westbourne Pk. Rd.)
Polperro M. SE11 . . . . . . .3K 19 (4B 102)
Polsted Rd. SE6 . . . . .7B 122
Polthorne Est. *SE18* 4H *107*
(off Polthorne Gro.)
Polthorne Gro. SE18 . . . . .4G 107

Polworth Rd. SW16 . . . . .5J 137
Polychrome Ct. *SE1* 7A *14*
(off Waterloo Rd.)
Polydamas Cl. E3 . . . . .2C 86
Polygon, The *NW8* 1B *82*
(off Avenue Rd.)
SW4 . . . . .4G 119
Polygon Bus. Cen. SL3: Poyle 5A 174
Polygon Rd. NW1 . . . . .1C 6 (2H 83)
(not continuous)
Polytechnic St. SE18 . . . . .4E 106
Pomell Way E1 . . . . .7K 9 (6F 85)
Pomeroy Cl. TW1: Twick 4B 114
Pomeroy Ho. *E2* 2K *85*
(off St James's Av.)
W11 . . . . .6G *81*
(off Lancaster Rd.)
Pomeroy St. SE14 . . . . .7J 103
Pomfret Rd. SE5 . . . . .3B 120
Pomoja La. N19 . . . . .2J 65
Pomona Ho. *SE8* 4A *104*
(off Evelyn St.)
Pompadour Av. IG11: Bark 2B 90
Pond Cl. N12 .6H 31
SE3 . . . . .2J 123
Pond Cott. La. BR4: W W'ck 1C 170
Pond Cotts. SE21 . . . . .1E 138
PONDERS END 5D 24
Pond Grn. HA4: Ruis 2G 57
Pond Hill Gdns. SM3: Cheam 6G 165
Pond Ho. HA7: Stan 6G 27
SW3 . . . . .4C 16 (4C 100)
Pond Lees Cl. RM10: Dag 7K 73
Pond Mead SE21 . . . . .6D 120
Pond Path BR7: Chst 6F 143
Pond Pl. SW3 . . . . .4C 16 (4C 100)
Pond Rd. E15 . . . . .2G 87
SE3 . . . . .2H 123
Pondside Av. KT4: Wor Pk 1E 164
Pondside Cl. UB3: Harl 6F 93
Pond Sq. N6 .1E 64
Pond St. NW3 . . . . .5C 64
Pond Way TW11: Tedd 6C 132
Pondwood Ri. BR6: Orp 7J 161
Ponler St. E1 .6H 85
Ponsard Rd. NW10 . . . . .3D 80
Ponsford St. E9 . . . . .6J 67
Ponsonby Ho. *E2* 2J *85*
(off Bishop's Way, not continuous)
Ponsonby Pl. SW1 . . . . .5D 18 (5H 101)
Ponsonby Rd. SW15 . . . . .7D 116
Ponsonby Ter. SW1 . . . . .5D 18 (5H 101)
Ponsonby Vs. *E2* 2J *85*
(off Lark Row)
Pontefract Ct. *UB5: N'olt* 5F *59*
(off Newmarket Av.)
Pontefract Rd. BR1: Brom 5H 141
Pontes Av. TW3: Houn 4D 112
Pontifex Apartments *SE1* 4E *14*
(off Stoney St.)
Ponton Way SW8 . . . . .7C 18 (6H 101)
Pontoon Rd. E16 . . . . .1K 105
Pont St. SW1 . . . . .2E 16 (3D 100)
Pont St. M. SW1 . . . . .2E 16 (3D 100)
Pontypool Pl. SE1 . . . . . . .6A 14 (2B 102)
Pooja Ct. *NW1* 7G *65*
(off Agar Gro.)
Pool Cl. BR3: Beck 5C 140
KT8: W Mole 5D 148
Pool Ct. SE6 . . . . .2C 140
Poole Cl. HA4: Ruis 2G 57
Poole Ct. *N1* .7E *66*
(off St Peter's Way)
TW4: Houn 2C 112

Poole Ct. Rd. TW4: Houn 2C 112
Poole Ho. SE11 . . . . .2H 19
POOL END 5C 146
Pool End Cl. TW17: Shep 5C 146
Poole Rd. E9 .6K 67
KT19: Ewe 6K 163
Pooles Bldgs. WC1 . . . . .4J 7
Pooles Cotts. TW10: Ham 2D 132
Pooles La. RM9: Dag 2E 90
SW10 . . . . .7A 100
Pooles Pk. N4 . . . . .2A 66
Poole St. N1 .1D 84
Poole Way UB4: Hayes 3G 75
Pooley Dr. SW14 . . . . .3J 115
Pooley Ho. E1 . . . . .3K 85
E18 . . . . .1J 51
Pool Ho. *NW8* 5C *4*
(off Penfold St.)
Poolmans St. SE16 . . . . .2K 103
Pool Rd. HA1: Harr 7H 41
KT8: W Mole 5D 148
Poolsford Rd. NW9 . . . . .4A 44
Poolside Manor 1H 45
Pools on the Park 4D 114
Pool St. E20 .7E 68
Poonah St. E1 . . . . .6J 85
Pope Cl. SW19 . . . . .6B 136
TW14: Felt 1H 129
Pope Ho. *SE5* 7D *102*
(off Elmington Est.)
SE16 . . . . .4H *103*
(off Manor Est.)
Pope Rd. BR2: Brom 5B 160
Popes Av. TW2: Twick 2J 131
Popes Ct. TW2: Twick 2J 131
Popes Dr. N3 .1J 45
Popes Gro. CR0: C'don 3B 170
TW1: Twick 2K 131
TW2: Twick 2K 131
Pope's Head All. EC3 . . . . .1F 15 (6D *84*)
Popes La. W5 . . . . .3D 96
Pope's Rd. SW9 . . . . .3A 120
Pope St. SE1 . . . . .7H 15 (2E 102)
Popham Cl. TW13: Hanw 3D 130
Popham Gdns. TW9: Rich 3G 115
Popham Rd. N1 . . . . .1C 84
Popham St. N1 . . . . .1B 84
(not continuous)
Pop in Commercial Cen.
HA9: Wemb 5H 61
Popinjays Row *SM3: Cheam* 5F *165*
(off Netley Cl.)
POPLAR 7D 86
Poplar Av. BR6: Farnb 2F 173
CR4: Mitc 1D 154
UB2: S'hall 3F 95
UB7: View 7B 74
Poplar Bath St. E14 . . . . .6D 86
Poplar Bus. Pk. E14 . . . . .7E 86
Poplar Cl. E9 .5B 68
HA5: Pinn 1B 40
SL3: Poyle 4A 174
Poplar Ct. SW19 . . . . .5J 135
TW1: Twick 6C 114
UB5: N'olt 2A 76
Poplar Cres. KT19: Ewe 6J 163
Poplar Farm Cl. KT19: Ewe 6J 163
Poplar Gdns. KT3: N Mald 2K 151
SE28 . . . . .7C 90
Poplar Gro. HA9: Wemb 3J 61
KT3: N Mald 2K 151
N11 . . . . .6K 31
W6 . . . . .2E 98
Poplar High St. E14 . . . . .7D 86
Poplar Ho. *SE4* 4B *122*
(off Wickham Rd.)
SE16 . . . . .2K *103*
(off Woodland Cres.)
Poplar Leisure Cen. 7D 86
Poplar M. W12 . . . . .1E 98
Poplar Mt. DA17: Belv 4H 109

Poplar Pl. SE28 . . . . .7C 90
  UB3: Hayes 7J 75
  W2 . . . . .7K 81
Poplar Rd. KT10: Surb 3B 162
  SE24 .4C 120
  SM3: Sutt 1H 165
  SW19 .2J 153
  TW15: Ashf 5E 128
Poplar Rd. Sth. SW19 . . . . .3J 153
Poplars, The N14 . . . . .5A 22
Poplars Av. NW2 . . . . .6E 62
Poplars Cl. HA4: Ruis 1G 57
Poplars Rd. E17 . . . . .6D 50
Poplar St. RM7: Rom 4J 55
Poplar Vw. HA9: Wemb 2D 60
Poplar Wlk. CRO: C'don 2C 168
  SE24 .3C 120
            (not continuous)
Poplar Way IG6: Ilf 4G 53
  TW13: Felt 3J 129
Poppins Ct. EC4 . . . . .1A 14 (6B 84)
Poppleton Rd. E11 . . . . .6G 51
Poppy Cl. DA17: Belv 3H 109
  EN5: New Bar 6F 21
  SM6: Wall 1E 166
  UB5: N'olt 6D 58
Poppy Dr. EN3: Pond E 4C 24
Poppy La. CRO: C'don 7J 157
Poppy M. SE22 . . . . .5G 121
Porchester Cl. SE5 . . . . .4C 120
Porchester Ct. W2 . . . . .7K 81
         (off Porchester Gdns.)
Porchester Gdns. W2 . . . . .7K 81
Porchester Gdns. M. W2 . . . . .6K 81
Porchester Ga. W2 . . . . .7K 81
    (off Bayswater Rd., not continuous)
Porchester Ho. E1 . . . . .6H 85
             (off Philpot St.)
Porchester Leisure Cen. 6K 81
Porchester Mead BR3: Beck 6D 140
Porchester Pl. W2 . . . . . .1D 10 (6C 82)
  W2 . . . . .6K 81
Porchester Rd. KT1: King T 2H 151
  W2 . . . . .6K 81
Porchester Sq. W2 . . . . .6K 81
Porchester Sq. M. W2 . . . . .6K 81
Porchester Ter. W2 . . . . .7A 82
Porchester Ter. Nth. W2 . . . . .6K 81
Porchester Wlk. W2 . . . . .6K 81
        (off Porchester Ter. Nth.)
Porch Way N20 . . . . .3J 31
Porcupine Cl. SE9 . . . . .2C 142
Porden Rd. SW2 . . . . .4K 119
Porlock Av. HA2: Harr 1G 59
Porlock Ho. SE26 . . . . .3G 139
Porlock Rd. EN1: Enf 7A 24
Porlock St. SE1 . . . . .6F 15 (2D 102)
Porrington Cl. BR7: Chst 1D 160
Portal Cl. HA4: Ruis 4J 57
  SE27 .3A 138
  UB10: Uxb 7A 56
Portal Way W3 . . . . .5K 79
Portbury Cl. SE15 . . . . .1G 121
Port Cres. E13 . . . . .4K 87
Portcullis Ho. SW1 . . . . .7E 12
Portcullis Lodge Rd. EN1: Enf 3J 23
Port East Apartments E14 . . . . .7C 86
          (off Hertsmere Rd.)
Portelet Ct. N1 . . . . .1E 84
         (off De Beauvoir Est.)
Portelet Rd. E1 . . . . .3K 85
Porten Ho's. W14 . . . . .3G 99
            (off Porten Rd.)
Porten Rd. W14 . . . . .3G 99
Porter Rd. E6 . . . . .6D 88
Porters & Walters Almshouses N22 . . .7E 32
         (off Nightingale Rd.)
Porters Av. RM8: Dag 6B 72
  RM9: Dag 6B 72
Porters Lodge, The SW10 . . . . .7A 100
          (off Coleridge Gdns.)
Porter Sq. N19 . . . . .1J 65

Porter St. SE1 . . . . .4D 14 (1C 102)
  W1 . . . . .5F 5 (5D 82)
Porters Wlk. E1 . . . . .7H 85
          (off Tobacco Dock)
Porters Way N12 . . . . .6H 31
  UB7: W Dray 3B 92
Porteus Rd. W2 . . . . .3G 119
Porteus Rd. SW4 . . . . .5A 4 (5A 82)
Portfleet Pl. N1 . . . . .1E 84
        (off De Beauvoir Rd.)
Portgate Cl. W9 . . . . .4H 81
Porthallow Cl. BR6: Chels 4K 173
Porthcawe Rd. SE26 . . . . .4A 140
Porthkerry Av. DA16: Well 4A 126
Port Ho. E14 . . . . .5D 104
        (off Burrells Wharf Sq.)
Portia Cl. IG11: Bark 7A 72
  SE11 .5B 102
            (off Opal St.)
Portia Way E3 . . . . .4B 86
Porticos, The SW3 . . . . .7A 16
Portinscale Rd. SW15 . . . . .5G 117
Portishead Ho. W2 . . . . .5J 81
      (off Westbourne Pk. Rd.)
Portland Av. DA15: Sidc 6A 126
  KT3: N Mald 7B 152
  N16 . . . . .7F 49
Portland Cl. KT4: Wor Pk 7D 152
  RM6: Chad H 5E 54
Portland Commercial Est.
  IG11: Bark 2C 90
Portland Cotts. CRO: Bedd 7H 155
Portland Ct. N1 . . . . .7E 66
        (off St Peter's Way)
  SE1 . . . . .7E 14
          (off Gt. Dover St.)
  SE14 .6A 104
           (off Whitcher Cl.)
Portland Cres. HA7: Stan 2D 42
  SE9 . . . . .2C 142
  TW13: Felt 4F 129
  UB6: G'frd 4F 77
Portland Dr. EN2: Enf 1K 23
Portland Gdns. N4 . . . . .6B 48
  RM6: Chad H 5D 54
Portland Gro. SW8 . . . . .1K 119
Portland Ho. SW1 . . . . .1A 18
  SW15 .5F 117
Portland Mans. W14 . . . . .4H 99
        (off Addison Bri. Pl.)
Portland M. W1 . . . . .1B 12 (6G 83)
Portland Pl. SE25 . . . . .4G 157
       (off Sth. Norwood Hill)
  W1 . . . . .4J 5 (5B 82)
Portland Ri. N4 . . . . .1B 66
          (not continuous)
Portland Rd. BR1: Brom 4A 142
  CR4: Mitc 2C 154
  KT1: King T 3E 150
  N15 . . . . .4F 49
  SE9 . . . . .2C 142
  SE25 .4G 157
  TW15: Ashf 3A 128
  UB2: S'hall 3D 94
  UB4: Hayes 3G 75
  W11 . . . . .7G 81
Portland Sq. E1 . . . . .1H 103
Portland St. SE17 . . . . .5D 102
Portland Ter. HA8: Edg 7B 28
  TW9: Rich 4D 114
Portland Wlk. SE17 . . . . .6D 102
Portman Av. SW14 . . . . .3K 115
Portman Cl. DA5: Bexl 1K 145
  DA7: Bex 3E 126
  W1 . . . . .7F 5 (6D 82)
Portman Dr. IG8: Wfd G 2B 52
Portman Gdns. NW9 . . . . .2K 43
  UB10: Hil 7C 56
Portman Ga. NW1 . . . . . . .4D 4 (4C 82)
Portman Mans. W1 . . . . .5F 5
           (off Chiltern St.)

Portman M. Sth. W1 . . . . . . .1G 11 (6E 82)
Portman Pl. E2 . . . . .3J 85
Portman Rd. KT1: King T 2F 151
Portman Sq. W1 . . . . .7G 5 (6E 82)
Portman St. W1 . . . . .1G 11 (6E 82)
Portman Towers W1 . . . . .7F 5 (6D 82)
Portmeadow Wlk. SE2 . . . . .2D 108
Portmeers Cl. E17 . . . . .6B 50
Portnall Ho. W9 . . . . .3H 81
          (off Portnall Rd.)
Portnall Rd. W9 . . . . .2H 81
Portnoi Cl. RM1: Rom 2K 55
Portobello Ct. W11 . . . . .6H 81
Portobello Grn. W10 . . . . .5G 81
         (off Portobello Rd.)
Portobello Ho. BR2: Brom 6B 160
Portobello Lofts W10 . . . . .4G 81
          (off Kensal Rd.)
Portobello M. W11 . . . . .7J 81
Portobello Rd. W10 . . . . .5G 81
  W11 . . . . .6H 81
Portobello Road Market 7H 81
         (off Portobello Rd.)
Porton Ct. KT6: Surb 6C 150
Portpool La. EC1 . . . . .5J 7 (5A 84)
Portree Cl. N22 . . . . .7E 32
Portree St. E14 . . . . .6F 87
Portrush Ct. UB1: S'hall 6G 77
         (off Whitecote Rd.)
Portsdown HA8: Edg 5B 28
Portsdown Av. NW11 . . . . .6H 45
Portsdown M. NW11 . . . . .6H 45
Portsea Hall W2 . . . . .1D 10
           (off Portsea Pl.)
Portsea M. W2 . . . . .1D 10
Portsea Pl. W2 . . . . .1D 10 (6C 82)
Portslade Rd. SW8 . . . . .2G 119
Portsmouth Av. KT7: T Ditt 7A 150
Portsmouth M. E16 . . . . .1K 105
Portsmouth Rd.
  KT1: King T 7A 150
  KT6: Surb 7A 150
  KT7: T Ditt 7A 150
  KT10: Esh 1A 162
  SW15 .7D 116
Portsmouth St. WC2 . . . . . .1G 13 (6K 83)
Portsoken St. E1 . . . . .2J 15 (7F 85)
Portswood Pl. SW15 . . . . .6B 116
Portugal Gdns. TW2: Twick 2G 131
Portugal St. WC2 . . . . .1G 13 (6K 83)
Portway E15 . . . . .1H 87
Portway Gdns. SE18 . . . . .7B 106
Pory Ho. SE11 . . . . .4H 19 (4K 101)
Poseidon Ct. E14 . . . . .4C 104
           (off Homer Dr.)
POSK 4C 98
           (off King St.)
Postern, The EC2 . . . . .6D 8
Postern Grn. EN2: Enf 2F 23
Post La. TW2: Twick 1H 131
Postmasters Lodge HA5: Pinn 7C 40
Postmill Cl. CRO: C'don 3J 169
Post Office All. W4 . . . . .6H 97
          (off Thames Rd.)
Post Office App. E7 . . . . .5K 69
Post Office Ct. EC3 . . . . .1F 15
        (off King William St.)
Post Office Way SW8 . . . . .7H 101
Post Rd. UB2: S'hall 3F 95
Postway M. IG1: Ilf 3F 71
          (not continuous)
Potier St. SE1 . . . . .3D 102
Potter Cl. CR4: Mitc 2F 155
  SE15 .7E 102
Potter Ho. E1 . . . . .5K 79
         (off Beaufort Gdns.)
Potteries, The EN5: Barn 5D 20
Potterne Cl. SW19 . . . . .7F 117
Potters Cl. CRO: C'don 1A 170
Potters Ct. SM1: Sutt 6H 165
         (off Rosebery Rd.)

Potters Fld. EN1: Enf 4K 23
          (off Lincoln Rd.)
Potters Flds. SE1 . . . . .5H 15 (1E 102)
Potters Gro. KT3: N Mald 4J 151
Potters Hgts. Cl. HA5: Pinn 1K 39
Potters La. EN5: New Bar 4D 20
  SW16 .6H 137
Potters Lodge E14 . . . . .5E 104
           (off Ferry St.)
Potters Rd. EN5: New Bar 4E 20
  SW6 . . . . .2A 118
Potter St. HA5: Pinn 1K 39
  HA6: N'wood 1J 39
Potter St. Hill HA5: Pinn 1K 39
Pottery Cl. SE25 . . . . .3G 157
Pottery Ga. N11 . . . . .6C 32
Pottery La. W11 . . . . .1G 99
Pottery Rd. DA5: Bexl 2J 145
  TW8: Bford 6E 96
Pottery St. SE16 . . . . .2H 103
Pott St. E2 .3H 85
Poulett Gdns. TW1: Twick 1A 132
Poulett Rd. E6 . . . . .2D 88
Poulter Park 6C 154
Poulters Wood BR2: Kes 5B 172
Poulton Av. SM1: Sutt 3B 166
Poulton Cl. E8 . . . . .6H 67
Poulton Ho. W3 . . . . .5K 79
          (off Victoria Rd.)
Poultry EC2 . . . . .1E 14 (6D 84)
Pound Cl. BR6: Orp 2H 173
  KT6: Surb 1C 162
Pound Ct. Dr. BR6: Orp 2H 173
Pound Farm Cl. KT10: Esh 7G 149
Pound Grn. DA5: Bexl 7G 127
Pound La. NW10 . . . . .6C 62
Pound Pk. Rd. SE7 . . . . .4B 106
Pound Pl. SE9 . . . . .6E 124
Pound St. SM5: Cars 5D 166
Pound Way BR7: Chst 7G 143
Pountney Rd. SW11 . . . . .3E 118
POVEREST 4K 161
Poverest Rd. BR5: St M Cry 5K 161
Povey Ho. SE17 . . . . .4E 102
         (off Beckway St.)
Powder Mill La. TW2: Whitt 7D 112
Powell Cl.
  HA8: Edg 6A 28
  KT9: Chess 5D 162
  SM6: Wall 4B 168
         (off Bramley Hill)
Powell Ct. E17 . . . . .3D 50
Powell Dr. E4 . . . . .4J 25
Powell Gdns. RM10: Dag 4G 73
Powell Ho. EN1: Enf 4K 23
         (off Dunstan M.)
  W2 . . . . .2A 10
         (off Gloucester Ter.)
Powell Rd. E5 . . . . .3H 67
  IG9: Buck H 1F 37
Powell's Wlk. W4 . . . . .6A 98
Powergate Bus. Pk. NW10 . . . . .3K 79
Powerhouse, The 2G 93
Powerleague
  Barking 3G 89
  Colney Hatch 7K 31
  Croydon 6K 167
  Ilford 1K 53
  Mill Hill 7J 29
  Tottenham 6C 34
Power Rd. W4 . . . . .4G 97
Powers Ct. TW1: Twick 7D 114
Powerscroft Rd. DA14: Sidc 6C 144
         (not continuous)
  E5 . . . . .4J 67
Powis Cl. W11 . . . . .6H 81
          (off Powis Gdns.)
  WD23: B Hea 1C 26
       (off Rutherford Way)
Powis Gdns. NW11 . . . . .7H 45
  W11 . . . . .6H 81

Powis Ho. *WC2* 7F **7**
(off Macklin St.)
Powis M. *W11* .6H **81**
Powis Pl. *WC1* 4F 7 (4J **83**)
Powis Rd. *E3* .3D **86**
Powis Sq. *W11* 6H **81**
(not continuous)
Powis St. *SE18* 3E **106**
Powis Ter. *W11* 6H **81**
Powlesland Ct. *E1* 5F **85**
(off White Horse Rd.)
Powlett Ho. *NW1* 6F **65**
(off Powlett Pl.)
Powlett Pl. *NW1* 7E **64**
Pownall Gdns. *TW3: Houn* 4F **113**
Pownall Rd. *E8* 1F **85**
TW3: Houn 4F **113**
Pownsett Ter. *IG1: Ilf* 5G **71**
Powster Rd. *BR1: Brom* 5J **141**
Powys Cl. *DA7: Bex* 6D **108**
Powys Ct. *N11* 5D **32**
Powys La. *N13* 4D **32**
N14 . . . . .4D **32**
POYLE 4A **174**
Poyle Ind. Est. *SL3: Poyle* 6A **174**
Poyle New Cotts. *SL3: Poyle* 5A **174**
Poyle Technical Cen.
SL3: Poyle 5A **174**
Poyle Trad. Est. *SL3: Poyle* 6A **174**
Poynders Ct. *SW4* 6G **119**
Poynders Gdns. *SW4* 7G **119**
Poynders Rd. *SW4* 6G **119**
Poynings, The *SL0: Rich P* 1A **174**
Poynings Rd. *N19* 3G **65**
Poynings Way *N12* 5D **30**
Poyntell Cres. *BR7: Chst* 1H **161**
Poynter Ct. *UB5: N'olt* 2B **76**
(off Gallery Gdns.)
Poynter Ho. *NW8* 3A **4**
(off Fisherton St.)
W11 . . . . .1F **99**
(off Queensdale Cres.)
Poynter Rd. *EN1: Enf* 5B **24**
Poynton Rd. *N17* 2G **49**
Poyntz Rd. *SW11* 2D **118**
Poyser St. *E2* .2H **85**
Prado Path *TW1: Twick* 1K **131**
(off Laurel Av.)
Praed M. *W2* 7B 4 (6B **82**)
Praed St. *W2* 1A 10 (6B **82**)
Pragel St. *E13* 2A **88**
Pragnell Rd. *SE12* 2K **141**
Prague Pl. *SW2* 5J **119**
Prah Rd. *N4* 2A **66**
Prairie St. *SW8* 2E **118**
Praline Ct. *E3* 2D **86**
(off Taylor Pl.)
Pratt M. *NW1* 1G **83**
Pratts Pas. *KT1: King T* 2E **150**
Pratt St. *NW1* 1G **83**
Pratt Wlk. *SE11* 3H 19 (4K **101**)
Prayle Gro. *NW2* 1F **63**
Preachers Ct. *EC1* 5B **8**
(off Charterhouse Sq.)
Prebend Gdns. *W4* 4B **98**
W6 . . . . .4B **98**
(not continuous)
Prebend Mans. *W4* 4B **98**
(off Chiswick High Rd.)
Prebend St. *N1* 1C **84**
Precinct, The *N1* 1C **84**
(not continuous)
Precinct Rd. *UB3: Hayes* 7J **75**
Precincts, The *SM4: Mord* 6J **153**
Premier Cinema
Peckham 2G **121**
Premier Cnr. *W9* 2H **81**
Premier Ct. *EN3: Enf W* 1D **24**
Premiere Pl. *E14* 7C **86**
Premier Ho. *N1* 7B **66**
(off Waterloo Ter.)

Premier Pk. *NW10* 1H **79**
(not continuous)
Premier Pk. Rd. *NW10* 2H **79**
Premier Pl. *SW15* 4G **117**
Prendergast Rd. *SE3* 3G **123**
Prentice Cl. *SW19* 5H **135**
Prentis Rd. *SW16* 4H **137**
Prentiss Ct. *SE7* 4B **106**
Presburg Rd. *KT3: N Mald* 5A **152**
Presburg St. *E5* 3K **67**
Prescelly Pl. *HA8: Edg* 1F **43**
Prescot St. *E1* 2K 15 (7F **85**)
Prescott Av. *BR5: Pet W* 6F **161**
Prescott Cl. *SW16* 7J **137**
Prescott Ho. *SE17* 6B **102**
(off Hillingdon St.)
Prescott Pl. *SW4* 3H **119**
Presentation M. *SW2* 2K **137**
Preshaw Cres. *CR4: Mitc* 3C **154**
President Dr. *E1* 1H **103**
President Ho. *EC1* 2B 8 (3B **84**)
President Quay *E1* 4K **15**
President St. *EC1* 1C **8**
Prespa Cl. *N9* 2D **34**
Press Ct. *SE1* 5G **103**
Press Ho. *E1* .5K **85**
(off Trafalgar Gdns.)
Press Rd. *NW10* 3K **61**
Prestage Way *E14* 7E **86**
Prestbury Rd. *E7* 7A **70**
Prestbury Sq. *SE9* 4D **142**
Prested Rd. *SW11* 4C **118**
Prestige Way *NW4* 5E **44**
PRESTON 1E **60**
Preston Av. *E4* 6A **36**
Preston Cl. *SE1* 4E **102**
TW2: Twick 3J **131**
Preston Ct. *DA14: Sidc* 4K **143**
(off The Crescent)
EN5: New Bar 4F **21**
Preston Dr. *DA7: Bex* 1D **126**
E11 . . . . .5A **52**
KT19: Ewe 6A **164**
Preston Gdns. *IG1: Ilf* 6C **52**
NW10 .6B **62**
Preston Hill *HA3: Kenton* 7E **42**
Preston Ho. *RM10: Dag* 3G **73**
(off Uvedale Rd.)
SE1 . . . . .4E **102**
(off Preston Cl., Preston Cl.)
SE1 . . . . .7J **15**
(off St Saviour's Est., St Saviour's Est.)
Preston Pl. *NW2* 6C **62**
TW10: Rich 5E **114**
Preston Rd. *E11* 6G **51**
HA3: Kenton 1E **60**
HA9: Wemb 1E **60**
SE19 . . . . .6B **138**
SW20 . . . . .7B **134**
TW17: Shep 5C **146**
Prestons Rd. *BR2: Hayes* 3J **171**
E14 . . . . .7E **86**
Preston St. *E2* 2K **85**
Preston Waye *HA3: Kenton* 1E **60**
Prestwich Ter. *SW4* 5G **119**
Prestwick Cl. *UB2: S'hall* 5C **94**
Prestwick Ct. *UB1: S'hall* 7D **77**
(off Baird Av.)
Prestwood Av. *HA3: Kenton* 4B **42**
Prestwood Cl. *HA3: Kenton* 4B **42**
SE18 . . . . .6A **108**
Prestwood Gdns. *CR0: C'don* 7C **156**
Prestwood Ho. *SE16* 3H **103**
(off Drummond Rd.)
Prestwood St. *N1* 1D 8 (2C **84**)
Pretoria Av. *E17* 4A **50**
Pretoria Cres. *E4* 1K **35**
Pretoria Rd. *E4* 1K **35**
E11 . . . . .1F **69**
E16 . . . . .4H **87**

Pretoria Rd. *IG1: Ilf* 5F **71**
N17 . . . . .7A **34**
RM7: Rom 4J **55**
SW16 . . . . .6F **137**
Pretoria Rd. Nth. *N18* 6A **34**
Prevost Rd. *N11* 2K **31**
Priam Ho. *E2* .2H **85**
(off Old Bethnal Grn. Rd.)
Price Cl. *SW17* 3D **136**
Price Ho. *N1* 1C **84**
(off Britannia Row)
Price Rd. *CR0: Wadd* 5B **168**
Price's Cl. *SW11* 3B **118**
Price's M. *N1* .1K **83**
Price's St. *SE1* 5B 14 (1B **102**)
Price Way *TW12: Hamp* 6C **130**
Prichard Cl. *N7* 5K **65**
Prichard Ho. *SE11* 4J **19**
(off Kennington Rd.)
Pricklers Hill *EN5: New Bar* 6E **20**
Prickley Wood *BR2: Hayes* 1H **171**
Priddy's Yd. *CR0: C'don* 2C **168**
Prideaux Ho. *WC1* 1H **7**
(off Prideaux Pl.)
Prideaux Pl. *W3* 7K **79**
WC1 . . . . .1H 7 (3K **83**)
Prideaux Rd. *SW9* 3J **119**
Pridham Rd. *CR7: Thor H* 4D **156**
Priest Cl. *TW12: Hamp* 4E **130**
Priestfield Rd. *SE23* 3A **140**
Priestlands Pk. Rd. *DA15: Sidc* 3K **143**
Priestley Cl. *N16* 7E **49**
Priestley Gdns. *RM6: Chad H* 6B **54**
Priestley Ho. *EC1* 3D **8**
(off Old St.)
HA9: Wemb 3J **61**
(off Barnhill Rd.)
Priestley Rd. *CR4: Mitc* 2E **154**
Priestley Way *E17* 3K **49**
NW2 .1C **62**
Priestman Point *E3* 3D **86**
(off Rainhill Way)
Priest Pk. Av. *HA2: Harr* 2E **58**
Priests Av. *RM1: Rom* 2K **55**
Priests Bri. *SW14* 3A **116**
SW15 . . . . .3A **116**
Priest's Ct. *EC2* 7C **8**
Prima Rd. *SW9* 7A **102**
Prime Meridian Line 7F **105**
Prime Meridian Wlk. *E14* 7F **87**
Primeplace M. *CR7: Thor H* 2C **156**
Primrose Av. *EN2: Enf* 1J **23**
RM6: Chad H 7B **54**
Primrose Cl. *E3* 2C **86**
HA2: Harr 3D **58**
N3 . . . . .2K **45**
SE6 .5E **140**
SM6: Wall 7F **155**
Primrose Ct. *NW8* 2D **82**
(off Prince Albert Rd.)
SW12 . . . . .7H **119**
Primrose Gdns. *HA4: Ruis* 5A **58**
NW3 .6C **64**
WD23: Bush 1A **26**
PRIMROSE HILL 1E **82**
Primrose Hill *EC4* 1K 13 (6A **84**)
Primrose Hill Cl. *NW3* 7D **64**
Primrose Hill Rd. *NW3* 7D **64**
Primrose Hill Studios *NW1* 1E **82**
Primrose Ho. *SE15* 1G **121**
(off Peckham Hill St.)
Primrose La. *CR0: C'don* 1J **169**
Primrose Mans. *SW11* 1E **118**
Primrose M. *NW1* 7D **64**
(off Sharpleshall St.)
SE3 . . . . .7J **105**
Primrose Pl. *TW7: Isle* 2K **113**
Primrose Rd. *E10* 1D **68**
E18 . . . . .2K **51**
Primrose Sq. *E9* 7J **67**

Primrose St. *EC2* 5G 9 (5E **84**)
Primrose Wlk. *KT17: Ewe* 7B **164**
SE14 . . . . .7A **104**
Primrose Way *HA0: Wemb* 2D **78**
SE10 . . . . .1E **122**
Primula St. *W12* 6C **80**
Prince Albert Ct. *NW8* 1D **82**
(off Prince Albert Rd.)
TW16: Sun 7H **129**
Prince Albert Rd. *NW1* 1C 4 (3C **82**)
NW8 . . . . .1C 4 (3C **82**)
Prince Arthur M. *NW3* 4A **64**
Prince Arthur Rd. *NW3* 5A **64**
Prince Charles Cinema 2D **12**
(off Leicester Pl.)
Prince Charles Dr. *NW4* 7E **44**
Prince Charles Rd. *SE3* 2H **123**
Prince Charles Way *SM6: Wall* 3F **167**
Prince Consort Dr. *BR7: Chst* 1H **161**
Prince Consort Rd. *SW7* 1A **16** (3A **100**)
Princedale Rd. *W11* 1G **99**
Prince Edward Mans. *W2* 7J **81**
(off Moscow Rd.)
Prince Edward Rd. *E9* 6B **68**
Prince Edward Theatre 1D **12**
(off Old Compton St.)
Prince George Av. *N14* 5C **22**
Prince George Rd. *N16* 4E **66**
Prince George's Av. *SW20* 2E **152**
Prince George's Rd. *SW19* 1B **154**
Prince Henry Rd. *SE7* 7B **106**
Prince Imperial Rd. *BR7: Chst* 1F **161**
SE18 . . . . .1D **124**
Prince John Rd. *SE9* 5C **124**
Princelet St. *E1* 5K 9 (5F **85**)
Prince of Orange Ct. *SE16* 3J **103**
(off Lower Rd.)
Prince of Orange La. *SE10* 7E **104**
Prince of Wales Cl. *NW4* 4D **44**
Prince of Wales Dr. *SW8* 7F **101**
SW11 . . . . .1C **118**
Prince of Wales Mans. *SW11* 1E **118**
Prince of Wales Pas. *NW1* 2A **6**
Prince of Wales Rd. *E16* 6A **88**
NW5 .6E **64**
SE3 .2H **123**
SM1: Sutt 2B **166**
Prince of Wales Ter. *W4* 5A **98**
W8 . . . . .2K **99**
Prince of Wales Theatre 3C **12**
(off Coventry St.)
Prince Regent Ct. *NW8* 2C **82**
(off Avenue Rd.)
SE16 . . . . .7A **86**
(off Edward Sq.)
Prince Regent La. *E13* 3K **87**
E16 . . . . .3K **87**
Prince Regent M. *NW1* 2A **6**
Prince Regent Rd. *TW3: Houn* 3F **113**
Prince Rd. *SE25* 5E **156**
Prince Rupert Rd. *SE9* 4D **124**
Princes Arc. *SW1* 4B **12**
Princes Av. *BR5: Pet W* 5J **161**
IG8: Wfd G 4E **36**
KT6: Surb 1G **163**
N3 . . . . .1J **45**
N10 . . . . .3F **47**
N13 . . . . .5F **33**
N22 . . . . .1H **47**
NW9 .4G **43**
SM5: Cars 7D **166**
UB6: G'frd 6F **77**
W3 . . . . .3G **97**
Princes Cir. *WC2* 7E 6 (6J **83**)
Princes Cl.
DA14: Sidc 3D **144**
HA8: Edg 5B **28**
N4 . . . . .1B **66**
NW9 .4G **43**
SW4 .3G **119**
TW11: Tedd 4H **131**

Princes Ct. HA9: Wemb 5E **60**
SE16 . . . . .3B **104**
SW3 . . . .*1E* **16**
(off Brompton Rd.)
Princes Ct. Bus. Cen. E1 . . . . .7H **85**
Princes Dr. HA1: Harr 3J **41**
Prince's Ga. SW7 . . . . . .1B **16** (3B **100**)
W3 . . . . .5G **79**
W5 . . . . .4C **78**
Prince's Ga. Ct. SW7 . . . . . .7B **10** (2B **100**)
(not continuous)
Prince's Ga. Ct. SW7 . . . . . .7B **10** (2B **100**)
Prince's Ga. M. SW7 . . . . .1B **16** (3B **100**)
Princes Ho. W11 . . . . .7H **81**
Princes La. HA4: Ruis 1G **57**
N10 .3F **47**
Princes M. TW3: Houn 4E **112**
W2 . . . . .7K **81**
W6 . . . .*5D* **98**
(off Down Pl.)
Princes Pde. NW11 . . . . .6G **45**
(off Golders Grn. Rd.)
Princes Pk. Av. NW11 . . . . .6G **45**
UB3: Hayes 7F **75**
Princes Pk. Circ. UB3: Hayes 7F **75**
Princes Pk. Cl. UB3: Hayes 7F **75**
Princes Pk. La. UB3: Hayes 7F **75**
Princes Pk. Pde. UB3: Hayes 7F **75**
Princes Pl. SW1 . . . . .4B **12**
W11 .1G **99**
Prince's Plain BR2: Brom 7C **160**
Prince's Ri. SE13 . . . . .2E **122**
Princes Riverside Rd. SE16 . . . . . .1K **103**
Princes Rd. IG6: Ilf 4H **53**
IG9: Buck H 2F **37**
KT2: King T 7G **133**
N18 .4D **34**
SE20 . . . . .6K **139**
SW14 . . . . .3K **115**
SW19 . . . . .6J **135**
TW9: Kew 1F **115**
TW10: Rich 5F **115**
TW11: Tedd 4H **131**
TW13: Felt 2H **129**
TW15: Ashf 5B **128**
W13 .1B **96**
Princessa Ct. EN2: Enf 5J **23**
Princess Alice Ho. W10 . . . . .4E **80**
Princess Alice Way SE28 . . . . .2H **107**
Princess Av. HA9: Wemb 2E **60**
Princess Av. E. HA9: Wemb 2E **60**
Princess Cl. SE28 . . . . .6D **90**
Princess Ct. KT1: King T 3F **151**
(off Horace Rd.)
N6 . . . . .7G **47**
NW6 .6K **63**
(off Compayne Gdns.)
W1 . . . .*6E* **4**
(off Bryanston Pl.)
W2 . . . .*7K* **81**
(off Queensway)
Princess Cres. N4 . . . . .2B **66**
Princess Louise Bldg. *SE8* *7C* **104**
(off Hales St.)
Princess Louise Cl. W2 . . . .5B **4** (5B **82**)
Princess Mary Ho. *SW1* *3D* **18**
(off Vincent St.)
Princess May Rd. N16 . . . . .4E **66**
Princess M. KT1: King T 3F **151**
NW3 .5B **64**
Princess of Wales Memorial Fountain
. . . . .6B **10** (2B **100**)
Princess Pde. BR6: Farnb 3E **172**
RM10: Dag 2G **91**
Princess Pk. Mnr. N11 . . . . .5K **31**
Princes Sq. W2 . . . . .7K **81**
(not continuous)
Princess Rd. CR0: C'don 6C **156**
NW1 .1E **82**
NW6 .2J **81**
Princess St. SE1 . . . . .3B **102**

Princes St. DA7: Bex 3F **127**
EC2 . . . . .1E **14** (6D **84**)
N17 .6K **33**
SM1: Sutt 4B **166**
TW9: Rich 4E **114**
W1 . . . . .1K **11** (6F **83**)
Princes Ter. E13 . . . . .1K **87**
Prince's Twr. *SE16* *2J* **103**
(off Elephant La.)
Prince St. SE8 . . . . .6B **104**
Princes Way BR4: W W'ck 4H **171**
CR0: Wadd 5K **167**
HA4: Ruis 4C **58**
IG9: Buck H 2F **37**
SW19 . . . . .7F **117**
W3 . . . . .3G **97**
Prince's Yd. W11 . . . . .1G **99**
Princethorpe Ho. *W2* *5K* **81**
(off Woodchester Sq.)
Princethorpe Rd. SE26 . . . . .4K **139**
Princeton Cl. SW15 . . . . .3F **117**
Princeton M. KT2: King T 1G **151**
Princeton St. WC1 . . . . .6G **7** (5K **83**)
Prince William Ct. *TW15: Ashf* *5B* **128**
(off Clarendon Rd.)
Principal Cl. N14 . . . . .1B **32**
Principal Pl. EC2 . . . . .4H **9**
Principal Sq. E9 . . . . .5K **67**
Pringle Gdns. SW16 . . . . .4G **137**
(not continuous)
Printers Inn Ct. EC4 . . . . .6A **84**
Printers M. E3 . . . . .1A **86**
Printers Rd. SW9 . . . . .1K **119**
Printer St. EC4 . . . . .7K **7** (6A **84**)
Printing Ho. La.
UB3: Hayes 2G **93**
Printing Ho. Yd. *E2* 1H **9** (3E **84**)
Printon Ho. *E14* *5B* **86**
(off Wallwood St.)
Print Room, The 6J **81**
(off Hereford Rd.)
Print Village SE15 . . . . .2F **121**
Printwork Apartments *SE1* *7G* **15**
(off Long La.)
SE2 .2C **120**
(off Coldharbour La.)
Priolo Rd. SE7 . . . . .5A **106**
Prior Av. SM2: Sutt 7C **166**
Prior Bolton St. N1 . . . . .6B **66**
Prior Ct. KT8: W Mole 5D **148**
Prioress Ho. *E3* *3D* **86**
(off Bromley High St.)
Prioress Rd. SE27 . . . . .3B **138**
Prioress St. SE1 . . . . .3E **102**
Prior Rd. IG1: Ilf 3E **70**
Priors, The NW3 . . . . .3B **64**
Priors Ct. E17 . . . . .2A **50**
Priors Farm La. UB5: N'olt 6C **58**
Priors Fld. UB5: N'olt 6C **58**
Priors Gdns. HA4: Ruis 5A **58**
Priors Mead EN1: Enf 1K **23**
Prior St. SE10 . . . . .7E **104**
Priors Wood KT10: Hin W 2A **162**
Priory, The CR0: Wadd 4A **168**
N8 . . . . .4H **47**
SE3 .3H **123**
Priory Apartments, The SE6 . . . . . .1D **140**
Priory Av. BR5: Pet W 6H **161**
E4 . . . . .3G **35**
E17 .5C **50**
HA0: Wemb 4K **59**
N8 . . . . .4H **47**
SM3: Cheam 4F **165**
W4 . . . . .4A **98**
Priory Cl. BR3: Beck 3A **158**
BR7: Chst 1D **160**
E4 . . . . .3G **35**
E18 .1J **51**
HA0: Wemb 4K **59**
HA4: Ruis 1H **57**
HA7: Stan 3E **26**

Priory Cl. N3 . . . . .1H **45**
N14 .5A **22**
N20 .1C **30**
SW19 . . . . .1K **153**
TW12: Hamp 1D **148**
TW16: Sun 7J **129**
UB3: Hayes 7K **75**
Priory Ct. E6 . . . . .1A **88**
E9 . . . . .5K **67**
E17 .2B **50**
EC4 . . . .*1B* **14**
(off Pilgrim St.)
HA0: Wemb 2E **78**
KT1: King T *3E* **150**
(off Denmark Rd.)
KT17: Ewe 7B **164**
SM3: Cheam 4G **165**
SW8 . . . . .1H **119**
TW3: Houn 3F **113**
WD23: Bush *1B* **26**
(off Sparrows Herne)
Priory Cres. HA0: Wemb 3A **60**
SE19 . . . . .7C **138**
SM3: Cheam 4F **165**
Priory Dr. HA7: Stan 3E **26**
SE2 . . . . .5D **108**
Priory Fld. Dr. HA8: Edg 4C **28**
Priory Gdns. HA0: Wemb 4A **60**
N6 . . . . .6F **47**
NW10 . . . . .3E **78**
SE25 . . . . .4F **157**
SW13 . . . . .3B **116**
TW12: Hamp 7D **130**
TW15: Ashf 5F **129**
W4 . . . . .4A **98**
W5 . . . . .3E **78**
Priory Grange *N2* *3D* **46**
(off Fortis Grn.)
Priory Grn. N1 . . . . .2K **83**
Priory Grn. Est. N1 . . . . .2K **83**
Priory Gro. EN5: Barn 5D **20**
SW8 . . . . .1J **119**
Priory Hgts. *N1* *2K* **83**
(off Wynford Rd.)
Priory Hill HA0: Wemb 4A **60**
Priory Ho. *E1* *5J* **9**
(off Folgate St.)
EC1 . . . .*3A* **8**
(off Sans Wlk.)
SW1 . . . .*5C* **18**
(off Rampayne St.)
Priory La. KT8: W Mole 4F **149**
SW15 . . . . .6A **116**
Priory Leas SE9 . . . . .1C **142**
Priory Lodge *W4* *5G* **97**
(off Kew Bri. Ct.)
Priory Mans. SW10 . . . . .5A **100**
(off Drayton Gdns.)
Priory M. SW8 . . . . .1J **119**
Priory Pk. SE3 . . . . .3H **123**
Priory Pk. Rd.
HA0: Wemb 4A **60**
NW6 .1H **81**
Priory Retail Pk. SW19 . . . . .7B **136**
Priory Rd. CR0: C'don 7A **156**
E6 . . . . .1B **88**
IG11: Bark 7H **71**
KT9: Chess 3E **162**
N8 . . . . .4G **47**
NW6 .1K **81**
SM3: Cheam 4F **165**
SW19 . . . . .7B **136**
TW3: Houn 5G **113**
TW9: Kew 6G **97**
TW12: Hamp 7D **130**
W4 . . . . .3K **97**
Priory St. E3 . . . . .3D **86**
Priory Ter. NW6 . . . . .1K **81**
TW16: Sun 7J **129**
Priory Vw. WD23: B Hea 1D **26**

Priory Vs. *N11* *6J* **31**
(off Colney Hatch La.)
Priory Wlk. SW10 . . . . .5A **100**
TW16: Sun 7J **129**
Priory Way HA2: Harr 4F **41**
UB2: S'hall 3B **94**
UB7: Harm 6A **92**
Priscilla Cl. N15 . . . . .5C **48**
Pritchard Ho. *E2* *2H* **85**
(off Ada Pl.)
Pritchard's Rd. E2 . . . . .1G **85**
Priter Rd. SE16 . . . . .3G **103**
Priter Rd. Hostel *SE16* *3G* **103**
(off Dockley Rd.)
Priter Way SE16 . . . . .3G **103**
Private Rd. EN1: Enf 5J **23**
Prize Wlk. E20 . . . . .5E **68**
Probert Rd. SW2 . . . . .5A **120**
Probyn Ho. *SW1* *3D* **18**
(off Page St.)
Probyn Rd. SW2 . . . . .2B **138**
Procter Ho. *SE1* *5G* **103**
(off Avondale Sq.)
SE5 . . . .*7D* **102**
(off Picton St.)
Procter St. WC1 . . . . .6G **7** (5K **83**)
Proctor Cl. CR4: Mitc 1E **154**
Proctors Cl. TW14: Felt 1J **129**
Progress Bus. Pk. CR0: Wadd 2K **167**
Progress Centre, The EN3: Pond E . .3E **24**
Progress Way CR0: Wadd 2K **167**
EN1: Enf 5B **24**
N22 .1A **48**
Project Pk. E16 . . . . .4F **87**
Prologis Pk. CR0: Bedd 7H **155**
E3 . . . . .4E **86**
TW4: Houn 4A **112**
Promenade, The HA8: Edg 5B **28**
W4 . . . . .2A **116**
Promenade App. Rd. W4 . . . . .7A **98**
Pronto Trad. Est.
UB3: Hayes 5G **75**
Propeller Cres. CR0: Wadd 5A **168**
Propeller Way NW9 . . . . .3C **44**
Prospect Cl. DA17: Belv 4G **109**
HA4: Ruis 7B **40**
SE26 . . . . .4H **139**
TW3: Houn 1D **112**
Prospect Cotts. SW18 . . . . .4J **117**
Prospect Cres. TW2: Whitt 6G **113**
Prospect Hill E17 . . . . .4D **50**
Prospect Ho. *E3* *3C* **86**
(off Campbell Rd.)
E17 . . . .*3E* **50**
(off Prospect Hill)
N1 . . . .*2A* **84**
(off Donegal St.)
SE1 . . . .*3B* **102**
(off Gaywood St.)
SE16 . . . .*3G* **103**
(off Frean St.)
SW19 . . . .*1B* **154**
(off Chapter Way)
W10 . . . .*6F* **81**
(off Bridge Cl.)
Prospect Pl. BR2: Brom 3K **159**
CR2: S Croy 6C **168**
E1 . . . . .1J **103**
(not continuous)
N2 . . . . .4B **46**
N7 . . . . .4J **65**
N17 .7K **33**
NW2 .3H **63**
NW3 .4A **64**
RM5: Col R 2J **55**
SE8 . . . .*6B* **104**
(off Evelyn St.)
SW20 . . . . .7D **134**
W4 . . . . .5K **97**
Prospect Quay *SW18* *4J* **117**
(off Lightermans Wlk.)

Prospect Ring N2 . . . . .3B 46
Prospect Rd.
  EN5: New Bar 4D 20
  IG8: Wfd G 6F 37
  KT6: Surb 6C 150
  NW2 .3H 63
Prospect St. SE16 . . . . .3H 103
Prospect Va. SE18 . . . . .4C 106
Prospect Wharf E1 . . . . .7J 85
Prospero Ho. E1 . . . . .2J 15
          (off Portsoken St.)
Prospero Rd. N19 . . . . .1H 65
Protea Cl. E16 . . . . .4H 87
Protea Pl. E9 . . . . .7J 67
          (off Lyme Gro.)
Protheroe Ho. N17 . . . . .3F 49
Prothero Gdns. NW4 . . . . .5D 44
Prothero Ho. NW10 . . . . .7K 61
          (off Fawood Av.)
Prothero Rd. SW6 . . . . .7G 99
Proton Twr. E14 . . . . .7F 87
Proud Ho. E1 . . . . .6H 85
          (off Amazon St.)
Prout Gro. NW10 . . . . .4A 62
Prout Rd. E5 . . . . .3H 67
Provence St. N1 . . . . .2C 84
Providence Av. HA2: Harr 1E 58
Providence Cl. E9 . . . . .1K 85
Providence Ct. W1 . . . . . .2H 11 (7E 82)
Providence Ho. E14 . . . . .6B 86
          (off Three Colt St.)
Providence La. UB3: Harl 7F 93
Providence Pl. N1 . . . . .1B 84
  RM5: Col R 1F 55
Providence Rd. UB7: View 1A 92
Providence Row N1 . . . . .2K 83
          (off Pentonville Rd.)
Providence Row Cl. E2 . . . . .3H 85
Providence Sq. SE1 . . . . . .6K 15 (2G 103)
Providence Twr. E14 . . . . .7F 87
          (off Fairmont Av.)
  SE16 . . . . .2G 103
          (off Bermondsey Wall E.)
Providence Yd. E2 . . . . .1K 9
          (off Ezra St.)
Provident Ind. Est. UB3: Hayes 2J 93
Province Dr. SE16 . . . . .2J 103
Province Sq. E14 . . . . .1E 104
          (off Blackwall Way)
Provincial Ter. SE20 . . . . .7K 139
Provost Ct. NW3 . . . . .6D 64
          (off Eton Rd.)
Provost Est. N1 . . . . .1E 8
Provost Rd. NW3 . . . . .7D 64
Provost St. N1 . . . . .1E 8 (2D 84)
Prowse Av. WD23: B Hea 1B 26
Prowse Pl. NW1 . . . . .7G 65
Proyers Path HA1: Harr 7B 42
Prudence La. BR6: Farnb 4E 172
Pruden Cl. N14 . . . . .2B 32
Prudent Pas. EC2 . . . . .7D 8
Prusom's Island E1 . . . . .1J 103
          (off Wapping High St.)
Prusom St. E1 . . . . .1H 103
Pryce Ho. E3 . . . . .3C 86
          (off Campbell Rd.)
Puccinia Ct. TW19: Stanw 1A 128
          (off Yeoman Dr.)
Pucknells Cl. BR8: Swan 7J 145
Pudding La. EC3 . . . . . . .3F 15 (7D 84)
Pudding Mill La. E15 . . . . .1D 86
Puddle Dock EC4 . . . . . . .2A 14 (7B 84)
          (not continuous)
Puffin Cl. BR3: Beck 5K 157
  IG11: Bark 3B 90
Pugin Ct. N1 . . . . .7A 66
          (off Liverpool Rd.)
Pulborough Rd. SW18 . . . . .7H 117
Pulborough Way TW4: Houn 4A 112
Pulford Rd. N15 . . . . .6D 48
Pulham Av. N2 . . . . .4A 46

Pulham Ho. SW8 . . . . .7K 101
          (off Dorset Rd.)
Pullen's Bldgs. SE17 . . . . .5B 102
          (off Iliffe St.)
Puller Rd. EN5: Barn 2B 20
Pulleyns Av. E6 . . . . .3C 88
Pullman Ct. SW2 . . . . .1J 137
Pullman Gdns. SW15 . . . . .6E 116
Pullman M. SE12 . . . . .3K 141
Pullman Pl. SE9 . . . . .5C 124
Pulross Rd. SW9 . . . . .3K 119
Pulse Apartments NW6 . . . . .5K 63
          (off Lymington Rd.)
Pulse Ct. RM7: Rush G 6K 55
Pulteney Cl. E3 . . . . .1B 86
  TW7: Isle 3A 114
Pulteney Gdns. E18 . . . . .3J 51
Pulteney Rd. E18 . . . . .3K 51
Pulteney Ter. N1 . . . . .1K 83
          (not continuous)
Pulton Ho. SE4 . . . . .4A 122
          (off Turnham Rd.)
Pulton Pl. SW6 . . . . .7J 99
Puma Ct. E1 . . . . .5J 9 (5F 85)
Pump All. TW8: Bford 7D 96
Pump Cl. UB5: N'olt 2E 76
Pump Ct. EC4 . . . . .1J 13 (6A 84)
          (off Oak La.)
Pumphandle Path N2 . . . . .2B 46
          (off Oak La.)
Pumphouse, The 4K 47
Pump Ho. Cl. BR2: Brom 2G 159
  SE16 . . . . .2J 103
Pumphouse Educational Museum, The
          . . . . .1A 104
Pump House Gallery 7E 100
Pump Ho. M. E1 . . . . .7G 85
          (off Hooper St.)
Pump House Steam & Transport Mus. . . .6A 50
Pumping Ho. E14 . . . . .7F 87
          (off Naval Row)
Pumping Sta. Rd. W4 . . . . .7A 98
Pump La. SE14 . . . . .7J 103
  UB3: Hayes 2J 93
Pump Pail Nth. CR0: C'don 3C 168
Pump Pail Sth. CR0: C'don 3C 168
Punchard Cres. EN3: Enf L 1J 25
Punderson's Gdns. E2 . . . . .3H 85
Purbeck Av. KT3: N Mald 6B 152
Purbeck Dr. NW2 . . . . .2F 63
Purbeck Ho. SW8 . . . . .7K 101
          (off Bolney St.)
Purbrook Est. SE1 . . . . . .7H 15 (2E 102)
Purbrook St. SE1 . . . . . . .7H 15 (3E 102)
Purcell Cres. SW6 . . . . .7F 99
Purcell Ho. EN1: Enf 1B 24
  SW10 . . . . .6B 100
          (off Milman's St.)
Purcell Mans. W14 . . . . .6G 99
          (off Queen's Club Gdns.)
Purcell M. NW10 . . . . .7A 62
Purcell Rd. UB6: G'frd 5F 77
Purcell Room 4H 13
          (off Belvedere Rd.)
Purcells Av. HA8: Edg 5B 28
Purcell St. N1 . . . . .2E 84
Purchese St. NW1 . . . . . . .1D 6 (2H 83)
Purday Ho. W10 . . . . .3G 81
          (off Bruckner St.)
Purdon Ho. SE15 . . . . .1G 121
          (off Oliver Goldsmith Est.)
Purdy Ho. KT4: Wor Pk 2C 164
Purdy St. E3 . . . . .4D 86
Purelake M. SE13 . . . . .3F 123
          (off Marischal Rd.)
Purkis Cl. UB8: Hil 7E 74
Purland Cl. RM8: Dag 1F 73
Purland Rd. SE28 . . . . .2K 107
          (not continuous)
Purleigh Av. IG8: Wfd G 6H 37
Purley Av. NW2 . . . . .2G 63

Purley Cl. IG5: Ilf 2E 52
Purley Pl. N1 . . . . .7B 66
Purley Rd. CR2: S Croy 7D 168
  N9 . . . . .3K 33
Purley Vw. Ter. CR2: S Croy 7D 168
          (off Sanderstead Rd.)
Purley Way CR0: C'don, Wadd 7K 155
Purley Way Centre, The CR0: Wadd . .2A 168
Purley Way Cres. CR0: C'don 7K 155
Purneys Rd. SE9 . . . . .4B 124
Purrett Rd. SE18 . . . . .5K 107
Purser Ho. SW2 . . . . .6A 120
Pursers Cross Rd. SW6 . . . . .1H 117
Pursewardens Cl. W13 . . . . .1C 96
Pursley Rd. NW7 . . . . .7J 29
Purves Rd. NW10 . . . . .3D 80
Purvis Ho. CR0: C'don 7D 156
Pusey Ho. E14 . . . . .6C 86
          (off Saracen St.)
Puteaux Ho. E2 . . . . .2K 85
          (off Mace St.)
PUTNEY 4F 117
Putney Arts Theatre 4F 117
Putney Bri. SW15 . . . . .3G 117
Putney Bri. App. SW6 . . . . .3G 117
Putney Bri. Rd. SW15 . . . . .4G 117
  SW18 . . . . .4G 117
Putney Comn. SW15 . . . . .3E 116
Putney Exchange (Shop. Cen.)
          SW15 . . . . .4F 117
Putney Gdns. RM6: Chad H 5B 54
PUTNEY HEATH 6E 116
Putney Heath SW15 . . . . .7D 116
Putney Heath La. SW15 . . . . .6F 117
Putney High St. SW15 . . . . .4F 117
Putney Hill SW15 . . . . .7F 117
          (not continuous)
Putney Leisure Cen. 4E 116
Putney Pk. Av. SW15 . . . . .4C 116
Putney Pk. La. SW15 . . . . .4D 116
          (not continuous)
PUTNEY VALE 3C 134
Putney Va. Crematorium SW19 . . . . .2D 134
Putney Wharf SW15 . . . . .3G 117
Putt in the Park 4H 117
Pycroft Way N9 . . . . .4A 34
Pycombe Cnr. N12 . . . . .4C 30
Pylbrook Rd. SM1: Sutt 3J 165
Pylon Way CR0: Bedd 1J 167
Pym Cl. EN4: E Barn 5G 21
Pymers Mead SE21 . . . . .1C 138
Pymmes Brook Dr. EN4: E Barn 4H 21
Pymmes Brook Ho. N10 . . . . .7K 31
Pymmes Cl. N13 . . . . .5E 32
  N17 . . . . .1H 49
Pymmes Gdns. Nth. N9 . . . . .3A 34
Pymmes Gdns. Sth. N9 . . . . .3A 34
Pymmes Grn. Rd. N11 . . . . .4A 32
Pymmes Rd. N13 . . . . .6D 32
Pyne Rd. KT6: Surb 1G 163
Pynfolds SE16 . . . . .2H 103
Pynham Cl. SE2 . . . . .3B 108
Pynnacles Cl. HA7: Stan 5G 27
Pynnersmead SE24 . . . . .5C 120
Pyramid Ct. KT1: King T 2E 150
          (off Cambridge Rd.)
Pyramid Ho. TW4: Houn 2C 112
Pyrford Ho. SW9 . . . . .4B 120
Pyrland Rd. N5 . . . . .5D 66
  TW10: Rich 6F 115
Pyrmont Gro. SE27 . . . . .3B 138
Pyrmont Rd. W4 . . . . .6G 97
Pytchley Cres. SE19 . . . . .6C 138
Pytchley Rd. SE22 . . . . .3E 120

Q

Q Building, The E15 . . . . .6G 69
          (off The Grove)

Quad Ct. SE1 . . . . .3E 102
          (off Grigg's Pl.)
Quadrangle, The E15 . . . . .6G 69
  SE24 . . . . .5C 120
  SW6 .7G 99
  SW10 . . . . .1A 118
  W2 . . . . .7C 4 (6C 82)
Quadrangle Cl. SE1 . . . . .4E 102
Quadrangle M. HA7: Stan 7H 27
Quadrant, The HA7: Bex 7D 108
  HA2: Harr 3H 41
  HA8: Edg 6B 28
          (off Manor Pk. Cres.)
  NW4 .4E 44
  SM2: Sutt 6A 166
  SW20 . . . . .1G 153
  TW9: Rich 4D 114
  W10 .3F 81
Quadrant Arc. W1 . . . . .3B 12
Quadrant Bus. Cen. NW6 . . . . .1G 81
Quadrant Cl. NW4 . . . . .5D 44
Quadrant Gro. NW5 . . . . .5G 64
Quadrant Ho. E1 . . . . .7G 85
          (off Nesham St.)
  E15 . . . . .3G 87
          (off Durban Rd.)
  SE1 . . . . .4A 14
Quadrant Rd. CR7: Thor H 4B 156
  TW9: Rich 4D 114
Quadrant Wlk. E14 . . . . .30 104
          (off Lanterns Way)
Quaggy Ho. HA9: Wemb 3D 60
Quaggy Wlk. SE3 . . . . .4J 123
Quain Mans. W14 . . . . .6G 99
          (off Queen's Club Gdns.)
Quainton St. NW10 . . . . .3K 61
Quaker Ct. E1 . . . . .4J 9
          (off Quaker St.)
  EC1 . . . . .3E 8
Quaker La. UB2: S'hall 3E 94
Quakers Course NW9 . . . . .1B 44
Quakers La. TW7: Isle 7A 96
Quakers Pl. E7 . . . . .5B 70
Quaker St. E1 . . . . .4J 9 (4F 85)
Quality Ct. WC2 . . . . .7J 7
Quant Bldg. E17 . . . . .4C 50
Quantock Cl. UB3: Harl 7F 93
Quantock Dr. KT4: Wor Pk 2E 164
Quantock Gdns. NW2 . . . . .2F 63
Quantock Ho. N16 . . . . .1F 67
Quantock M. SE15 . . . . .2G 121
Quarles Pk. Rd.
  RM6: Chad H 6B 54
Quarrendon St. SW6 . . . . .2J 117
Quarr Rd. SM5: Cars 6B 154
Quarry Pk. Rd. SM1: Sutt 6H 165
Quarry Ri. SM1: Sutt 6H 165
Quarry Rd. SW18 . . . . .6A 118
Quarterdeck, The E14 . . . . .2C 104
Quarter Ho. SW18 . . . . .4A 118
Quartz Ho. HA2: Harr 1E 58
Quastel Ho. SE1 . . . . .7E 14
          (off Long La.)
Quatre Ports E4 . . . . .5A 36
Quay Ho. E14 . . . . .2C 104
          (off Admirals Way)
Quayside Cotts. E1 . . . . .4K 15
          (off Mews St.)
Quayside Ct. SE16 . . . . .1K 103
          (off Abbotshade Rd.)
Quayside Ho. E14 . . . . .1B 104
  E16 . . . . .6H 87
          (off Tarling Rd.)
  W10 . . . . .4G 81
Quayside Wlk. KT1: King T 2D 150
          (off Wadbrook St.)
Quay Vw. Apartments E14 . . . . .3C 104
          (off Arden Cres.)
Quebec M. W1 . . . . .1F 11 (6D 82)

Quebec Rd. IG1: Ilf 7F **53**
   IG2: Ilf 7F **53**
   UB4: Yead 6A **76**
Quebec Way SE16 . . . . . . .2K **103**
Quebec Way Ind. Est. SE16 . . . . . .2A **104**
   (not continuous)
Quebec Wharf E8 . . . . .1E **84**
   (off Kingsland Rd.)
   E14 . . . . .6C **86**
Quedgeley Ct. SE15 . . . . .6F **103**
   (off Ebley Cl.)
Queen Adelaide Ct. SE20 . . . . . .6J **139**
Queen Adelaide Rd. SE20 . . . . . .6J **139**
Queen Alexandra Mans. WC1 . . . . . . .2E **6**
   (off Bidborough St.)
Queen Alexandra's Ct. SW19 . . . . .5H **135**
Queen Anne Alcove 3A **10**
Queen Anne Av. BR2: Brom 3H **159**
Queen Anne Ho. E16 . . . . .1J **105**
   (off Hardy Av.)
Queen Anne M. W1 . . . . . . .6K **5** (5F **83**)
Queen Anne Rd. E9 . . . . .6K **67**
Queen Anne's Cl. TW2: Twick 3H **131**
Queen Anne's Ct. SE10 . . . . .5F **105**
   (off Park Row)
Queen Anne's Gdns. CR4: Mitc 3D **154**
   EN1: Enf 6K **23**
   W4 . . . . .3A **98**
   W5 . . . . .2C **96**
Queen Anne's Ga. DA7: Bex 3D **126**
   SW1 . . . . .7C **12** (2H **101**)
Queen Anne's Gro. EN1: Enf 7J **23**
   W4 . . . . .3A **98**
   W5 . . . . .2C **96**
Queen Anne's Pl. EN1: Enf 6K **23**
Queen Annes Sq. SE1 . . . . .4G **103**
   (off Monnow Rd.)
Queen Anne St. W1 . . . . . .7J **5** (6F **83**)
Queen Anne's Wlk. WC1 . . . . .4F **7**
Queen Anne Ter. E1 . . . . .7H **85**
   (off Sovereign Cl.)
Queenborough Gdns. BR7: Chst 6H **143**
   IG2: Ilf 4E **52**
Queen Caroline St. W6 . . . . .5E **98**
Queen Catherine Ho. SW6 . . . . .7K **99**
   (off Wandon Rd.)
Queen Ct. WC1 . . . . .4F **7**
   (off Queen Sq.)
Queen Elizabeth II Stadium 2A **24**
Queen Elizabeth Bldgs. EC4 . . . . . .2J **13**
Queen Elizabeth Ct. EN5: Barn 3D **20**
Queen Elizabeth Gdns.
   SM4: Mord 4J **153**
Queen Elizabeth Hall 4H **13** (1K **101**)
Queen Elizabeth Ho. SW12 . . . . . . .7E **118**
Queen Elizabeth II Conference Cen.
   . . . . .7D **12** (2H **101**)
Queen Elizabeth Olympic Pk. 7D **68**
Queen Elizabeth Rd. E17 . . . . .3A **50**
   KT2: King T 2F **151**
Queen Elizabeth's Cl. N16 . . . . . . .2D **66**
Queen Elizabeth's Coll. SE10 . . . . .7E **104**
Queen Elizabeth's Dr.
   CR0: New Ad 7F **171**
   N14 . . . . .1D **32**
Queen Elizabeth's Hunting Lodge 1C **36**
Queen Elizabeth Sports Cen. 4C **20**
Queen Elizabeth St. SE1 . . . .6J **15** (2E **102**)
Queen Elizabeth Wlk.
   N16 . . . . .1D **66**
   SM6: Bedd 4H **167**
Queen Elizabeth Wlk. SW13 . . . . . .1C **116**
Queenhithe EC4 . . . . .2D **14** (7C **84**)
Queen Isabella Way EC1 . . . . .7B **8**
Queen Margaret Flats SE1 . . . . . . .8B **82**
   (off St Jude's Rd.)
Queen Margaret's Gro. N1 . . . . . . .5E **66**
Queen Mary Av. E18 . . . . .1J **51**
   SM4: Mord 5F **153**
Queen Mary Cl. KT6: Surb 3G **163**
Queen Mary Ct. TW19: Stanw 1A **128**

Queen Mary Ho. E16 . . . . .1K **105**
   (off Wesley Av.)
   E18 . . . . .1K **51**
Queen Mary Rd. SE19 . . . . .6B **138**
   TW17: Shep 2E **146**
Queen Mary's Av. SM5: Cars 7D **166**
Queen Marys Bldgs. SW1 . . . . .3B **18**
   (off Stillington St.)
Queen Mary's Ct. SE10 . . . . .6F **105**
   (off Park Row)
Queen Mary's Ho. SW15 . . . . .6C **116**
Queen Mary University of London
   Charterhouse Square 4B **8** (4B **84**)
   Lincoln's Inn Fields Campus 7G **7**
   (off Remnant St.)
   Mile End Campus 4A **86**
   West Smithfield Campus 6B **8**
Queen Mother Memorial 1H **101**
Queen Mother Sports Centre, The . . .3A **18**
Queen of Denmark Ct. SE16 . . . . . .3B **104**
Queens Acre SM3: Cheam 7F **165**
Queens Av. HA7: Stan 3C **42**
   IG8: Wfd G 5E **36**
   N3 . . . . .7F **31**
   N10 . . . . .3E **46**
   N20 . . . . .2G **31**
   N21 . . . . .1G **33**
   TW13: Hanw 4A **130**
   UB6: G'frd 6F **77**
Queens Ho. TW9: Rich 5C **114**
Queensberry Mews W.
   SW7 . . . . .3A **16** (4B **100**)
Queensberry Pl. E12 . . . . .5B **70**
   SW7 . . . . .3A **16** (4B **100**)
   TW9: Rich 5D **114**
   (off Friars La.)
Queensberry Way SW7 . .3A **16** (4B **100**)
Queensborough Ct. N3 . . . . .4H **45**
   (off Tillingbourne Gdns.)
Queensborough M. W2 . . . . .7A **82**
   (off Queensborough M.)
Queensborough Pas. W2 . . . . .7A **82**
   (off Queensborough M.)
Queensborough Studios W2 . . . . . . .7A **82**
   (off Queensborough M.)
Queensborough Ter. W2 . . . . .7K **81**
Queensbridge Cl. E2 . . . . .1F **85**
   (off Queensbridge Rd.)
Queensbridge Pk. TW7: Isle 5J **113**
Queensbridge Rd. E2 . . . . .6F **67**
   E8 . . . . .6F **67**
Queensbridge Sports & Community Cen.
   .7F **67**
QUEENSBURY 3E **42**
Queensbury Circ. Pde.
   HA3: Kenton 3E **42**
   HA7: Kenton 3E **42**
Queensbury Rd. HA0: Wemb 2F **79**
   NW9 . . . . .7K **43**
Queensbury Sta. Pde. HA8: Edg 3F **43**
Queensbury St. N1 . . . . .7C **66**
Queen's Cir. SW8 . . . . .7F **101**
Queens Cl. HA8: Edg 5B **28**
   SM6: Wall 5F **167**
Queen's Club Gdns. W14 . . . . .6G **99**
Queen's Club, The (Tennis Courts) . . .5G **99**
Queens Club Ter. W14 . . . . .6H **99**
   (off Normand Rd.)
Queens Ct. CR2: S Croy 5C **168**
   (off Warham Rd.)
   CR7: Thor H 5A **156**
   E11 . . . . .7G **51**
   HA3: Kenton 2B **42**
   IG9: Buck H 2G **37**
   NW6 . . . . .5K **63**
   NW8 . . . . .2B **82**
   (off Queen's Ter.)
   NW11 . . . . .5H **45**
   SE23 . . . . .2J **139**
   TW10: Rich 6F **115**
   W2 . . . . .7K **81**
   (off Queensway)

Queenscourt HA9: Wemb 4E **60**
Queen's Cres. NW5 . . . . .6E **64**
   TW10: Rich 5F **115**
Queenscroft Rd. SE9 . . . . .5B **124**
Queensdale Cres. W11 . . . . .1F **99**
   (not continuous)
Queensdale Pl. W11 . . . . .1G **99**
Queensdale Rd. W11 . . . . .1F **99**
Queensdale Wlk. W11 . . . . .1G **99**
Queensdown Rd. E5 . . . . .4H **67**
Queens Dr. E10 . . . . .7C **50**
   KT5: Surb 7G **151**
   KT7: T Ditt 6A **150**
   N4 . . . . .2B **66**
   W3 . . . . .6F **79**
   W5 . . . . .6F **79**
Queen's Elm Pde. SW3 . . . . .5B **16**
   (off Old Church St.)
Queen's Elm Sq. SW3 . . . .6B **16** (5B **100**)
Queensferry Wlk. N17 . . . . .4H **49**
Queensfield Ct. SM3: Cheam 4E **164**
Queen's Gallery 7K **11** (2F **101**)
Queen's Gdns. NW4 . . . . .5E **44**
   RM13: Rain 2K **91**
   TW5: Hest 1C **112**
   W2 . . . . .7A **82**
   W5 . . . . .4C **78**
Queen's Ga. SW7 . . . . . .7A **10** (2A **100**)
Queensgate Cl. N12 . . . . .5E **30**
Queens Ga. Gdns. BR7: Chst 1H **161**
   SW7 . . . . .3A **100**
   SW15 . . . . .4D **116**
Queensgate Ho. E3 . . . . .2B **86**
   (off Hereford Rd.)
Queen's Ga. M. SW7 . . . . .3A **100**
Queensgate M. BR3: Beck 1A **158**
Queen's Ga. Pl. SW7 . . . . .3A **100**
Queensgate Pl. NW6 . . . . .7J **63**
Queen's Ga. Pl. M. SW7 . .2A **16** (3A **100**)
Queen's Ga. Ter. SW7 . . . .1A **16** (3A **100**)
Queens Ga. Vs. E9 . . . . .7A **68**
Queen's Gro. NW8 . . . . .1B **82**
Queen's Gro. Rd. E4 . . . . .1A **36**
Queen's Gro. Studios NW8 . . . . . . .1B **82**
Queen's Head Pas. EC4 . . . . .7C **8** (6C **84**)
Queen's Head St. N1 . . . . .1B **84**
Queen's Head Yd. SE1 . . . . .5E **14**
Queen's House, The 6F **105**
   (within National Maritime Mus.)
Queens Ho. SE17 . . . . .6D **102**
   (off Merrow St.)
   SW8 . . . . .7J **101**
   (off Sth. Lambeth Rd.)
   TW11: Tedd 6K **131**
   W2 . . . . .7K **81**
   (off Queensway)
Queen's Ice & Bowl 7K **81**
Queen's Keep TW1: Twick 6C **114**
Queensland Av. N18 . . . . .6H **33**
   SW19 . . . . .1K **153**
Queensland Cl. E17 . . . . .2B **50**
Queensland Ho. E16 . . . . .1E **106**
   (off Rymill St.)
Queensland Rd. N7 . . . . .4A **66**
Queens La. N10 . . . . .3F **47**
Queen's Mans. W6 . . . . .4F **99**
   (off Brook Grn.)
Queen's Mkt. E13 . . . . .1A **88**
Queens Mead HA8: Edg 6A **28**
Queensmead NW8 . . . . .1B **82**
Queens Mead Rd.
   BR2: Brom 2H **159**
Queensmead Sports Cen. 4B **58**
Queensmere Cl. SW19 . . . . .2F **135**
Queensmere Ct. SW13 . . . . .7B **98**
Queensmere Rd. SW19 . . . . .2F **135**
Queen's M. W2 . . . . .7K **81**
Queensmill Rd. SW6 . . . . .7G **99**
Queens Pde. N8 . . . . .4B **48**
   N11 . . . . .5J **31**
   (off Friern Barnet Rd.)

Queens Pde. NW2 . . . . .6E **62**
   (off Willesden La.)
   NW4 . . . . .5E **44**
   (off Queens Rd.)
   W5 . . . . .6F **79**
Queen's Pde. Cl. N11 . . . . .5J **31**
QUEENS PARK 2G **81**
Queen's Pk. Cl. W10 . . . . .3F **81**
Queen's Pk. Gdns. TW13: Felt 3H **129**
Queen's Park Rangers FC 1D **98**
Queens Pas. BR7: Chst 6F **143**
Queens Pl. SM4: Mord 4J **153**
Queen's Prom.
   KT1: King T, Surb 4D **150**
Queen Sq. WC1 . . . . .4F **7** (4J **83**)
Queen Sq. Pl. WC1 . . . . .4F **7**
Queen's Quay EC4 . . . . .2C **14**
   (off Up. Thames St.)
Queens Reach KT1: King T 2D **150**
   KT8: E Mos 4J **149**
Queens Ride SW13 . . . . .3C **116**
   SW15 . . . . .3C **116**
Queens Ri. TW10: Rich 6F **115**
Queens Rd. BR1: Brom 2J **159**
   BR3: Beck 2A **158**
   BR7: Chst 6F **143**
   CR0: C'don 6B **156**
   CR4: Mitc 3B **154**
   DA16: Well 2B **126**
   E11 . . . . .7F **51**
   E13 . . . . .1K **87**
   E17 . . . . .6B **50**
   EN1: Enf 4K **23**
   EN5: Barn 3A **20**
   IG9: Buck H 2E **36**
   IG11: Bark 6G **71**
   KT2: King T 7G **133**
   KT3: N Mald 4B **152**
   KT7: T Ditt 5K **149**
   N3 . . . . .1A **46**
   N9 . . . . .3C **34**
   N11 . . . . .7D **32**
   NW4 . . . . .5E **44**
   SE14 . . . . .1H **121**
   SE15 . . . . .1H **121**
   SM4: Mord 4J **153**
   SM6: Wall 5F **167**
   SW14 . . . . .3K **115**
   SW19 . . . . .6H **135**
   TW1: Twick 1A **132**
   TW3: Houn 3F **113**
   TW10: Rich 7F **115**
   TW11: Tedd 6K **131**
   TW12: Hamp H 4F **131**
   TW13: Felt 1K **129**
   UB2: S'hall 2B **94**
   UB3: Hayes 6G **75**
   UB7: W Dray 2B **92**
   W5 . . . . .6E **78**
Queens Rd. Est.
   EN5: Barn 3A **20**
Queens Rd. W. E13 . . . . .2J **87**
Queen's Row SE17 . . . . .6D **102**
Queens St. TW15: Ashf 4B **128**
Queens Ter. E1 . . . . .4J **85**
   (off Cephas St.)
   E13 . . . . .1K **87**
   KT7: T Ditt 6A **150**
   (off Queens Dr.)
   NW8 . . . . .1B **82**
   TW7: Isle 4A **114**
Queen's Ter. Cotts. W7 . . . . .2J **95**
Queen's Theatre
   Westminster 2C **12**
   (off Shaftesbury Av.)
Queensthorpe M. SE26 . . . . .4K **139**
Queensthorpe Rd. SE26 . . . . .4K **139**
Queens Tower 3B **100**
   (within Imperial College London)
Queenstown M. SW8 . . . . .2F **119**
Queenstown Rd. SW8 . . . . . .7J **17** (6F **101**)

Queen St. CR0: C'don 4C 168
 DA7: Bex 3F 127
 EC4 . . . . .2D 14 (7C 84)
 (not continuous)
 N17 . . . . .6K 33
 RM7: Rom 6K 55
 W1 . . . . .4J 11 (1F 101)
Queen St. Pl. EC4 . . . . . .2D 14 (7C 84)
Queensville Rd. SW12 . . . . . . .7H 119
Queens Wlk. E4 . . . . .1A 36
 HA1: Harr 4J 41
 HA4: Ruis 2A 58
 N5 . . . . .5B 66
 NW9 . . . . .2J 61
 SW1 . . . . .5A 12 (1G 101)
 TW15: Ashf 4A 128
 W5 . . . . .4C 78
Queen's Walk, The SE1 . . . .3K 13 (7A 84)
 (Oxo Tower Wharf)
 SE1 . . . . .4F 15 (1E 102)
 (Tooley St.)
 SE1 . . . . .4H 13 (1K 101)
 (Waterloo Rd.)
Queens Wlk. Ter. HA4: Ruis 3A 58
Queens Way NW4 . . . . .5E 44
 TW13: Hanw 4A 130
Queensway BR4: W W'ck 3G 171
 BR5: Pet W 5G 161
 CR0: Wadd 6K 167
 EN3: Pond E 4C 24
 TW16: Sun 2K 147
 W2 .6K 81
Queensway Bus. Cen. EN3: Pond E . . .4C 24
Queensway Ind. Est. EN3: Pond E 4D 24
Queensway M. BR1: Brom 4E 140
Queenswell Av. N20 . . . . .3H 31
Queens Wharf W6 . . . . .5E 98
Queenswood Av. CR7: Thor H 5A 156
 E17 . . . . .1E 50
 SM6: Bedd 4H 167
 TW3: Houn 2D 112
 TW12: Hamp 6F 131
Queenswood Ct. KT2: King T 1G 151
 SE27 . . . . .4D 138
 SW4 . . . . .5J 119
Queenswood Gdns. E11 . . . . .1K 69
Queenswood Pk. N3 . . . . .2G 45
Queens Wood Rd. N10 . . . . .6F 47
Queenswood Rd. DA15: Sidc 5K 125
 SE23 . . . . .3K 139
Queens Yd. E9 . . . . .6C 68
 WC1 . . . . .4B 6 (5G 83)
QUEEN VICTORIA 4F 165
Queen Victoria Av. HA0: Wemb 7D 60
Queen Victoria Memorial 7A 12 (2G 101)
Queen Victoria Seaman's Rest
 E14 . . . . .6D 86
 (off E. India Dock Rd.)
Queen Victoria Statue 1K 99
Queen Victoria St. EC4 . . . . .2A 14 (7B 84)
Queen Victoria Ter. E1 . . . . .7H 85
 (off Sovereign Cl.)
Quemerford Rd. N7 . . . . .5K 65
Quendon Ho. W10 . . . . .4E 80
 (off Sutton Way)
Quenington Ct. SE15 . . . . .6F 103
Quentin Ho. SE1 . . . . .6A 14
 (off Chaplin Cl., not continuous)
Quentin Pl. SE13 . . . . .3G 123
Quentin Rd. SE13 . . . . .3G 123
Quermore Cl. BR1: Brom 6J 141
Quermore Rd. BR1: Brom 6J 141
 N4 . . . . .6A 48
Querrin St. SW6 . . . . .2A 118
Quest, The W11 . . . . .7G 81
 (off Clarendon Rd.)
Quested Ct. E8 . . . . .5H 67
 (off Brett Rd.)
Questors Theatre, The 7C 78
Quex Ct. NW6 . . . . .1K 81
 (off West End La.)

Quex M. NW6 . . . . .1J 81
Quex Rd. NW6 . . . . .1J 81
Quiberon Ct. TW16: Sun 3J 147
Quick Rd. W4 . . . . .5A 98
Quicks Rd. SW19 . . . . .7K 135
Quick St. N1 . . . . .2B 84
Quick St. M. N1 . . . . .2B 84
Quickswood NW3 . . . . .7C 64
Quiet Nook BR2: Hayes 3B 172
Quill Ho. E2 . . . . .3K 9
 (off Cheshire St.)
Quill La. SW15 . . . . .4F 117
Quill St. N4 . . . . .3A 66
 W5 . . . . .3E 78
Quilp St. SE1 . . . . .6C 14 (2C 102)
 (not continuous)
Quilters Pl. SE9 . . . . .1G 143
Quilter St. E2 . . . . .1K 9 (3G 85)
 SE18 . . . . .5K 107
Quilting Ct. SE16 . . . . .2K 103
 (off Garter Way)
Quince Ho. SE13 . . . . .2D 122
 (off Quince Rd.)
Quince Rd. SE13 . . . . .2D 122
Quinion Cl. E2 . . . . .2J 85
Quinnell Cl. SE18 . . . . .5K 107
Quinta Dr. EN5: Barn 5A 20
Quinta Ho. KT1: King T 2D 150
 (off Wood St.)
Quintain Ho. KT12: Walt T 7J 147
Quintin Av. SW20 . . . . .1H 153
Quintin Cl. HA5: Eastc 4K 39
Quinton Cl. BR3: Beck 3E 158
 SM6: Wall 4F 167
 TW5: Cran 7K 93
Quinton Ho. SW8 . . . . .7J 101
 (off Wyvil Rd.)
Quinton Rd. KT7: T Ditt 1A 162
Quinton St. SW18 . . . . .2A 136
Quixley St. E14 . . . . .7F 87
Quorn Rd. SE22 . . . . .4E 120

R

Rabbit Row W8 . . . . .1J 99
Rabbits Rd. E12 . . . . .4C 70
Rabournmead Dr.
 UB5: N'olt 5C 58
Raby Rd. KT3: N Mald 4K 151
Raby St. E14 . . . . .6A 86
Raccoon Way TW4: Houn 2A 112
Rachel Cl. IG6: Ilf 3H 53
Racine SE5 . . . . .1E 120
 (off Sceaux Gdns.)
Rackham Cl. DA16: Well 2B 126
Rackham M. SW16 . . . . .6G 137
Rackstraw Ho. NW3 . . . . .7D 64
Racton Rd. SW6 . . . . .6J 99
RADA
 Chenies St. 5C 6
 Gower St. 5H 83
 (off Gower St.)
RADA Studios 5H 83
 (off Chenies St.)
Radbourne Av. W5 . . . . .4C 96
Radbourne Cl. E5 . . . . .4K 67
Radbourne Ct.
 HA3: Kenton 6B 42
Radbourne Cres. E17 . . . . .2F 51
Radbourne Rd. SW12 . . . . .7G 119
Radcliff Ct. E3 . . . . .4B 86
 (off Jospeh St.)
Radcliffe Av. EN2: Enf 1H 23
 NW10 . . . . .2C 80
Radcliffe Gdns. SM5: Cars 7C 166
Radcliffe Ho. SE16 . . . . .4H 103
 (off Anchor St.)
 SE20 . . . . .1G 157
Radcliffe M. TW12: Hamp H 5G 131
Radcliffe Path SW8 . . . . .2F 119

Radcliffe Rd.
 CR0: C'don 2F 169
 HA3: W'stone 2A 42
 N21 .1G 33
 SE1 .3E 102
Radcliffe Sq. SW15 . . . . .6F 117
Radcliffe Way UB5: N'olt 3B 76
Radcot Point SE23 . . . . .3K 139
Radcot St. SE11 . . . . .6K 19 (5A 102)
Raddington Rd. W10 . . . . .5G 81
Raddon Twr. E8 . . . . .6F 67
 (off Dalston Sq.)
Radfield Way DA15: Sidc 7H 125
Radford Ct. SE15 . . . . .7H 103
 (off Old Kent Rd.)
Radford Est. NW10 . . . . .3A 80
Radford Ho. E14 . . . . .5D 86
 (off St Leonard's Rd.)
 N7 . . . . .5K 65
Radford Rd. SE13 . . . . .6E 122
Radford Way IG11: Bark 3K 89
Radipole Rd. SW6 . . . . .1H 117
Radisson Ct. SE1 . . . . .7G 15
 (off Long La.)
Radius Apartments N1 . . . . .1G 7
 (off Omega Pl.)
Radius Pk. TW14: Felt 4H 111
Radland Rd. E16 . . . . .6H 87
Radleigh Pl. BR3: Beck 6C 140
Radlet Av. SE26 . . . . .3H 139
Radlett Cl. E7 . . . . .6H 69
Radlett Pl. NW8 . . . . .1C 82
Radley Av. IG3: Bark, Ilf 4A 72
Radley Cl. TW14: Felt 1H 129
Radley Ct. SE16 . . . . .2K 103
Radley Gdns. HA3: Kenton 4E 42
Radley Ho. NW1 . . . . .3E 4
 (off Gloucester Pl.)
 SE2 . . . . .2D 108
 (off Wolvercote Rd.)
Radley M. W8 . . . . .3J 99
Radley Rd. N17 . . . . .2E 48
Radley's La. E18 . . . . .2J 51
Radleys Mead
 RM10: Dag 6H 73
Radley Sq. E5 . . . . .2J 67
Radley Ter. E16 . . . . .5H 87
 (off Hermit Rd.)
Radlix Rd. E10 . . . . .1C 68
Radnor Av. DA16: Well 5B 126
 HA1: Harr 5J 41
Radnor Cl. BR7: Chst 6J 143
 CR4: Mitc 4J 155
Radnor Ct. HA3: Hrw W 1K 41
 W7 . . . . .6K 77
 (off Copley Cl.)
Radnor Cres. IG4: Ilf 5D 52
 SE18 . . . . .7A 108
Radnor Gdns. EN1: Enf 1K 23
 TW1: Twick 2K 131
Radnor Ho. EC1 . . . . .2D 8
 (off Radnor St.)
 SW16 . . . . .1B 10
 (off Radnor St.)
Radnor Lodge W2 . . . . .1B 10
 (off Sussex Pl.)
Radnor M. W2 . . . . .1B 10 (6B 82)
Radnor Pl. W2 . . . . .1C 10 (6C 82)
Radnor Rd.
 HA1: Harr 5J 41
 NW6 .1G 81
 SE15 . . . . .7G 103
 TW1: Twick 1K 131
Radnor St. EC1 . . . . .2D 8 (3C 84)
Radnor Ter. SM2: Sutt 7J 165
 W14 .4H 99
Radnor Wlk. CR0: C'don 6A 158
 E14 .4C 104
 (off Barnsdale Av.)
 SW3 . . . . .6D 16 (5C 100)
Radnor Way NW10 . . . . .4H 79

Radstock Av. HA3: Kenton 3A 42
Radstock Cl. N11 . . . . .6K 31
Radstock St. SW11 . . . . .7C 100
 (not continuous)
Radway Ho. W2 . . . . .5J 81
 (off Alfred Rd.)
Raeburn Av. KT5: Surb 1H 163
Raeburn Cl. KT1: Hamp W 7D 132
 NW11 . . . . .6A 46
Raeburn Ho. UB5: N'olt 2B 76
 (off Academy Gdns.)
Raeburn Rd. DA15: Sidc 6J 125
 HA8: Edg 1G 43
 UB4: Hayes 2F 75
Raeburn St. SW2 . . . . .4J 119
RAF Bomber Command Memorial
 . . . . .6J 11 (2F 101)
Raffles Ho. NW4 . . . . .4D 44
Rafford Way BR1: Brom 2K 159
RAF Museum London 2C 44
RAF Northolt Aerodrome 6H 57
RAF Uxbridge, Battle of Britain Bunker
 . . . . .1B 74
Ragged School Mus. 5A 86
Raggleswood BR7: Chst 1E 160
Raglan Cl. TW4: Houn 5D 112
Raglan Ct. CR2: S Croy 5B 168
 E17 .5E 50
 HA9: Wemb 4F 61
 SE12 . . . . .5J 123
Raglan Rd. BR2: Brom 4A 160
 DA17: Belv 4F 109
 E17 .5E 50
 EN1: Enf 7A 24
 SE18 . . . . .5G 107
Raglan St. NW5 . . . . .6F 65
Raglan Ter. HA2: Harr 4F 59
Raglan Way UB5: N'olt 6G 59
Ragley Cl. W3 . . . . .2J 97
Ragwort Cl. SE26 . . . . .5H 139
Rahere Ct. E1 . . . . .4A 86
 (off Toby La.)
Raider Cl. RM7: Mawney 1G 55
Railey M. NW5 . . . . .5F 65
Railshead Rd. TW1: Isle 4B 114
 TW7: Isle 4B 114
Railton Rd. SE24 . . . . .4A 120
Railway App. HA1: Harr 4K 41
 HA3: Harr 4K 41
 N4 . . . . .6A 48
 RM7: Rush G 6K 55
 SM6: Wall 5F 167
 TW1: Twick 7A 114
Railway Arches E1 . . . . .6K 85
 (off Barnardo St., Barnardo St.)
 E1 . . . . .7H 85
 (off Chapman St., Chapman St.)
 E2 . . . . .1J 9
 (off Cremer St., Cremer St.)
 E2 . . . . .2F 85
 (off Geffrye St., Geffrye St.)
 E2 . . . . .1F 85
 (off Laburnum St., Laburnum St.)
 E3 . . . . .4B 86
 (off Cantrell Rd.)
 E7 . . . . .4J 69
 (off Winchelsea Rd.)
 E8 . . . . .7H 67
 (off Mentmore Ter.)
 E10 .1E 68
 E11 .1F 69
 (off Grove Grn. Rd.)
 E16 .1J 105
 W6 .3E 98
 W12 .2E 98
 (off Shepherd's Bush Mkt.)
Railway Av. SE16 . . . . .2J 103
 (not continuous)
Railway Children Wlk.
 BR1: Brom 2J 141
 SE12 . . . . .2J 141

Railway Cotts. *E15* 2G **87**
  (off Baker's Row)
  SW19 . . . . .4K **135**
  W6 . . . . .2E **98**
  (off Sulgrave Rd.)
Railway Fields Local Nature Reserve
  . . . . .6B **48**
Railway Gro. SE14 . . . . .7B **104**
Railway M. W10 . . . . .6G **81**
Railway Pas. TW11: Tedd 6A **132**
Railway Pl. DA17: Belv 3G **109**
Railway Ri. SE22 . . . . .4E **120**
Railway Rd. TW11: Tedd 4J **131**
Railway Side SW13 . . . . .3A **116**
Railway Sidings Rd.
  SE16 . . . . .3G **103**
Railway St. N1 . . . . .2J **83**
  RM6: Chad H 7C **54**
Railway Ter. E17 . . . . .1E **50**
  SE13 . . . . .5D **122**
  TW13: Felt 1J **129**
Railway Wharf *KT1: King T* 1D **150**
  (off Thames Side)
Rainborough Cl. NW10 . . . . .6J **61**
Rainbow Av. E14 . . . . .5D **104**
Rainbow Ct. *SE14* 6A **104**
  (off Chipley St.)
Rainbow Ind. Est. SW20 . . . . .2D **152**
  UB7: View 7A **74**
Rainbow Quay SE16 . . . . .3A **104**
  (not continuous)
Rainbow St. SE5 . . . . .7E **102**
Raine Gdns. IG8: Wfd G 4D **36**
Rainer Apartment *CRO: C'don* 1D **168**
  (off Cherry Orchard Rd.)
Raines Est. Ct. N16 . . . . .2F **67**
Raine St. E1 . . . . .1H **103**
Rainham Cl. SE9 . . . . .6J **125**
  SW11 .6C **118**
Rainham Ho. *NW1* 1G **83**
  (off Bayham Pl.)
Rainham Rd. NW10 . . . . .3E **80**
Rainham Rd. Nth. RM10: Dag 2G **73**
Rainham Rd. Sth. RM10: Dag 4H **73**
Rainhill Way E3 . . . . .3C **86**
  (not continuous)
Rainsborough Av. SE8 . . . . .4A **104**
Rainsborough Ho. *SW15* 5G **117**
  (off Stamford Sq.)
Rainsford Cl. HA7: Stan 5H **27**
Rainsford Rd. NW10 . . . . .3G **79**
Rainton Rd. SE7 . . . . .7C **4** (6C **82**)
Rainville Rd. W6 . . . . .6E **98**
Raisins Hill
  HA5: Eastc 3A **40**
Raith Av. N14 . . . . .3C **32**
Rajsee Apartments *E2* 3G **85**
  (off Bethnal Grn. Rd.)
Raleana Rd. E14 . . . . .1E **104**
Raleigh Av.
  SM6: Bedd 4H **167**
  UB4: Yead 5K **75**
Raleigh Cl. HA4: Ruis 2H **57**
  HA5: Pinn 7B **40**
  NW4 . . . . .5E **44**
Raleigh Ct.
  BR3: Beck 1D **158**
  SE8 . . . . .5A **104**
  (off Evelyn St.)
  SE16 .1K **103**
  (off Clarence M.)
  SM6: Wall 6F **167**
  W12 . . . . .2E **98**
  (off Scott's Rd.)
  W13 . . . . .5B **78**
Raleigh Dr. KT5: Surb 1J **163**
  N20 . . . . .3H **31**
Raleigh Gdns. CR4: Mitc 3D **154**
  (not continuous)
  SW2 . . . . .6K **119**

Raleigh Ho. *BR1: Brom* 1J **159**
  (off Hammelton Rd.)
  E14 . . . . .2D **104**
  (off Admirals Way)
  SW1 . . . . .7C **18**
  (off Dolphin Sq.)
Raleigh M. BR6: Chels 5K **173**
  N1 . . . . .1B **84**
  (off Packington St.)
Raleigh Rd. EN2: Enf 4J **23**
  N8 . . . . .4A **48**
  SE20 .7K **139**
  TW9: Rich 3F **115**
  TW13: Felt 3H **129**
  UB2: S'hall 5C **94**
Raleigh St. N1 . . . . .1B **84**
Raleigh Way N14 . . . . .1C **32**
  TW13: Hanw 5A **130**
Rale La. E4 .1A **36**
Ralph Bayer Ct. *E3* 5C **86**
  (off Geoff Cade Way)
Ralph Brook Ct. *N1* 1F **9**
  (off Chart St.)
Ralph Ct. *W2* 6K **81**
  (off Queensway)
Ralph Perring Ct. BR3: Beck 4C **158**
Ralston St. SW3 . . . . . . .6E **16** (5D **100**)
Ramac Ind. Est. SE7 . . . . .4K **105**
Rama Cl. SW16 . . . . .7J **137**
Rama Ct. HA1: Harr 2J **59**
Ramac Way SE7 . . . . .4K **105**
Rama La. SE19 . . . . .7F **139**
Ramar Ho. *E1* 5G **85**
  (off Hanbury St.)
Rambler Cl. SW16 . . . . .4G **137**
Rame Cl. SW17 . . . . .5E **136**
Ramilles Cl. SW2 . . . . .6J **119**
Ramillies Pl. W1 . . . . . . .1A **12** (6G **83**)
Ramillies Rd. DA15: Sidc 6B **126**
  NW7 . . . . .2F **29**
  W4 . . . . .4K **97**
Ramillies St. W1 . . . . . . .1A **12** (6G **83**)
Ramones Ter. CR4: Mitc 4J **155**
  (off Yorkshire Rd.)
Rampart St. E1 . . . . .6H **85**
Ram Pas. KT1: King T 2D **150**
Rampayne St. SW1 . . . . . .5C **18** (5H **101**)
Ram Pl. E9 .6J **67**
Rampton Cl. E4 . . . . .3H **35**
Ramsay Ho. *NW8* 2C **82**
  (off Townshend Est.)
Ramsay M. SW3 . . . . . . .7C **16** (6C **100**)
Ramsay Rd. E7 . . . . .4G **69**
  W3 . . . . .3J **97**
Ramscroft Cl. N9 . . . . .7K **23**
Ramsdale Rd. SW17 . . . . .5E **136**
Ramsden Dr. RM5: Col R 1G **55**
Ramsden Rd. DA8: Erith 7K **109**
  N11 . . . . .5J **31**
  SW12 .6E **118**
Ramsey Cl. NW9 . . . . .6B **44**
  UB6: G'frd 5H **59**
Ramsey Ct. *CRO: C'don* 2B **168**
  (off Church St.)
Ramsey Ho. SW9 . . . . .7A **102**
Ramsey Rd. CR7: Thor H 6K **155**
Ramsey St. E2 . . . . .4G **85**
Ramsey Wlk. N1 . . . . .6D **66**
Ramsey Way N14 . . . . .7B **22**
Ramsfort Ho. *SE16* 4H **103**
  (off Camilla Rd.)
Ramsgate Cl. E16 . . . . .1K **105**
Ramsgate St. E8 . . . . .6F **67**
Ramsgill App. IG2: Ilf 4K **53**
Ramsgill Dr. IG2: Ilf 5K **53**
Rams Gro. RM6: Chad H 4E **54**
Ram St. SW18 . . . . .5K **117**
Ram Twr. SW18 . . . . .5K **117**
Ramulis Dr. UB4: Yead 4B **76**
Ramuswood Av. BR6: Chels 5J **173**
Rancliffe Gdns. SE9 . . . . .4C **124**

Rancliffe Rd. E6 . . . . .2C **88**
Randall Av. NW2 . . . . .2A **62**
Randall Cl. DA8: Erith 6J **109**
  SW11 .1C **118**
Randall Ct. NW7 . . . . .7H **29**
Randall Pl. SE10 . . . . .7E **104**
Randall Rd. SE11 . . . . . . .4G **19** (5K **101**)
Randall Row SE11 . . . . . . .4G **19** (4K **101**)
Randalls Rents *SE16* 3B **104**
  (off Gulliver St.)
Randell's Rd. N1 . . . . .1J **83**
Randisbourne Gdns. SE6 . . . . .3D **140**
Randle Rd. TW10: Ham 4C **132**
Randlesdown Rd. SE6 . . . . .4C **140**
  (not continuous)
Randolph App. E16 . . . . .6A **88**
Randolph Av. W9 . . . . .4A **4** (2K **81**)
Randolph Cl. DA7: Bex 3J **127**
  KT2: King T 5J **133**
Randolph Ct. NW8 . . . . .1A **82**
Randolph Cres. W9 . . . . .4A **82**
Randolph Gdns. NW6 . . . . .2K **81**
Randolph Gro. RM6: Chad H 5C **54**
Randolph M. W9 . . . . .4A **82**
Randolph Rd. BR2: Brom 1D **172**
  E17 . . . . .5D **50**
  UB1: S'hall 2D **94**
  W9 . . . . .4A **82**
Randolph St. NW1 . . . . .7G **65**
Randon Cl. HA2: Harr 2F **41**
Ranelagh Av. SW6 . . . . .3H **117**
  SW13 .2C **116**
Ranelagh Bri. *W2* 5K **81**
Ranelagh Cl. HA8: Edg 4B **28**
Ranelagh Cotts. *SW1* 5J **17**
  (off Ebury Bri. Rd.)
Ranelagh Dr. HA8: Edg 4B **28**
  TW1: Twick 4B **114**
Ranelagh Gdns. E11 . . . . .5A **52**
  IG1: Ilf .1D **70**
  SW6 . . . . .3G **117**
  (not continuous)
  W4 . . . . .7J **97**
  W6 . . . . .4B **98**
Ranelagh Gdns. Mans. *SW6* 3G **117**
  (off Ranelagh Gdns.)
Ranelagh Gro. SW1 . . . . . .5H **17** (5E **100**)
Ranelagh Ho. *SW3* 5E **16**
  (off Elystan Pl.)
Ranelagh M. W5 . . . . .2D **96**
Ranelagh Pl. KT3: N Mald 5A **152**
Ranelagh Rd. E6 . . . . .1E **88**
  E11 . . . . .4G **69**
  E15 . . . . .2G **87**
  HA0: Wemb 6D **60**
  N17 . . . . .3E **48**
  N22 . . . . .1K **47**
  NW10 .2B **80**
  SW1 . . . . .6B **18** (5G **101**)
  UB1: S'hall 1B **94**
  W5 . . . . .2D **96**
Ranfurly Rd. SM1: Sutt 2J **165**
Rangbourne Ho. N7 . . . . .5J **65**
Rangefield Rd. BR1: Brom 5G **141**
Rangemoor Rd. N15 . . . . .5F **49**
Ranger's House 1F **123**
Ranger's Rd. E4 . . . . .1B **36**
Rangers Sq. SE10 . . . . .1F **123**
Range Way TW17: Shep 7C **146**
Rangeworth Pl. DA15: Sidc 3K **143**
Rangoon St. EC3 . . . . .1J **15**
Rankin Cl. NW9 . . . . .3A **44**
Rankine Ho. *SE1* 3C **102**
  (off Bath Ter.)
Ranleigh Gdns. DA7: Bex 7F **109**
Ranmere St. SW12 . . . . .1F **137**
Ranmoor Cl. HA1: Harr 4H **41**
Ranmoor Gdns. HA1: Harr 4H **41**
Ranmore Av. CRO: C'don 3F **169**
Ranmore Cl. KT6: Surb 5D **150**
Ranmore Path BR5: St M Cry 4K **161**

Ranmore Rd. SM2: Cheam 7F **165**
Rannoch Cl. HA8: Edg 2C **28**
Rannoch Rd. W6 . . . . .6E **98**
Rannock Av. NW9 . . . . .7K **43**
Ransome's Dock Bus. Cen. SW11 . . .7C **100**
Ransom Rd. SE7 . . . . .4A **106**
Ranston St. NW1 . . . . .5C **4** (5C **82**)
Ranulf Rd. NW2 . . . . .4H **63**
Ranwell Cl. E3 . . . . .1B **86**
Ranwell Ho. *E3* 1B **86**
  (off Ranwell Cl.)
Ranworth Rd. N9 . . . . .2D **34**
Ranyard Cl. KT9: Chess 3F **163**
Raphael Cl. KT1: King T 4D **150**
Raphael Ct. *SE16* 5H **103**
  (off Stubbs Dr.)
Raphael Dr. KT7: T Ditt 7K **149**
Raphael St. SW7 . . . . . . .7E **10** (2D **100**)
Raphen Apartments *E3* 2A **86**
  (off Medway Rd.)
Rapley Ho. *E2* 2K **9**
  (off Turin St.)
Raquel Ct. *SE1* 6G **15**
  (off Snowfields)
Rashleigh Ct. SW8 . . . . .2F **119**
Rashleigh Ho. *WC1* 2E **6**
  (off Thanet St.)
Rashleigh St. SW8 . . . . .2F **119**
  (off Peardon St.)
Rasper Rd. N20 . . . . .2F **31**
Rastell Av. SW2 . . . . .2H **137**
RATCLIFF 5A **86**
Ratcliffe Cl. SE12 . . . . .7J **123**
Ratcliffe Ct. *SE1* 7D **14**
  (off Gt. Dover St.)
Ratcliffe Cross St. E1 . . . . .6K **85**
Ratcliffe Ho. *E14* 6A **86**
  (off Barnes St.)
Ratcliffe La. E14 . . . . .6A **86**
Ratcliffe Orchard E1 . . . . .7K **85**
Ratcliff Rd. E7 . . . . .5A **70**
Rathbone Ho. *E16* 6H **87**
  (off Rathbone St.)
  NW6 . . . . .1J **81**
Rathbone Mkt. E16 . . . . .5H **87**
Rathbone Pl. W1 . . . . .6C **6** (5H **83**)
Rathbone Sq. CR0: C'don 4C **168**
Rathbone St. E16 . . . . .6H **87**
  W1 . . . . .6B **6** (5G **83**)
Rathcoole Av. N8 . . . . .5K **47**
Rathcoole Gdns. N8 . . . . .5K **47**
Rathfern Rd. SE6 . . . . .1B **140**
Rathgar Av. W13 . . . . .1B **96**
Rathgar Cl. N3 . . . . .2H **45**
Rathgar Rd. SW9 . . . . .3B **120**
Rathmell Dr. SW4 . . . . .6H **119**
Rathmore Rd. SE7 . . . . .5K **105**
Rathnew Ct. *E2* 3K **85**
  (off Meath Cres.)
Rathore Cl. RM6: Chad H 5D **54**
Rattray Ct. SE6 . . . . .2H **141**
Rattray Rd. SW2 . . . . .4A **120**
Raul Rd. SE15 . . . . .2G **121**
Raveley St. NW5 . . . . .4G **65**
  (not continuous)
Raven Cl. NW9 . . . . .2A **44**
  RM7: Rush G 7G **55**
Ravendale Rd. TW16: Sun 2H **147**
Ravenet St. SW8 . . . . .1F **119**
  SW11 .1F **119**
  (not continuous)
Ravenfield Rd. SW17 . . . . .3D **136**
Ravenhill Rd. E13 . . . . .2A **88**
Raven Ho. *SE16* 4K **103**
  (off Tawny Way)
Ravenings Pde. IG3: Ilf 1A **72**
Ravenna Rd. SW15 . . . . .5F **117**
Ravenor Ct. UB6: G'frd 4F **77**
Ravenor Pk. Rd. UB6: G'frd 3F **77**
Raven Rd. E18 . . . . .2A **52**
Raven Row E1 . . . . .5H **85**

Raven Row Contemporary Art Cen. . . .5F 85
Raven's Ait 5D 150
Ravensbourne Av. BR2: Brom 7F 141
　BR3: Beck .7F 141
　TW19: Stanw 1A 128
Ravensbourne Ct. SE6 . . . . .7C 122
Ravensbourne Gdns. IG5: Ilf 1E 52
　W13 . . . . .5B 78
Ravensbourne Ho. BR1: Brom 5F 141
　NW8 . . . . .5C 4
　　　　　　　　　　　　(off Broadley St.)
Ravensbourne Mans. SE8 . . . . .6C 104
　　　　　　　　　　　　(off Berthon St.)
Ravensbourne Pk. SE6 . . . . .7C 122
Ravensbourne Pk. Cres. SE6 . . . . . . .7B 122
Ravensbourne Pl. SE8 . . . . .1C 122
　SE13 . . . . .2D 122
Ravensbourne Rd. BR1: Brom 3J 159
　SE6 . . . . .7B 122
　TW1: Twick .6C 114
Ravensbourne Ter. TW19: Stanw 1A 128
Ravensbury Av. SM4: Mord 5A 154
Ravensbury Ct. CR4: Mitc 4B 154
　　　　　　　　　　　(off Ravensbury Gro.)
Ravensbury Gro. CR4: Mitc 4B 154
Ravensbury La. CR4: Mitc 4B 154
Ravensbury Path CR4: Mitc 4B 154
Ravensbury Rd. BR5: St P 3K 161
　SW18 . . . . .2K 135
Ravensbury Ter. SW18 . . . . .2K 135
Ravenscar NW1 . . . . .1G 83
　　　　　　　　　　　　(off Bayham St.)
Ravenscar Rd. BR1: Brom 4G 141
　KT6: Surb .2F 163
Ravens Cl. BR2: Brom 2H 159
　EN1: Enf 2K 23
　KT6: Surb .6D 150
Ravens Ct. KT1: King T 5D 150
　　　　　　　　　　　　(off Uxbridge Rd.)
Ravenscourt TW16: Sun 1H 147
Ravenscourt Av. W6 . . . . .4C 98
Ravenscourt Cl. HA4: Ruis 7E 38
Ravenscourt Gdns. W6 . . . . .4C 98
Ravenscourt Pk. EN5: Barn 4A 20
　W6 . . . . .3C 98
Ravenscourt Pk. Mans. W6 . . . . .3D 98
　　　　　　　　　　　(off Paddenswick Rd.)
Ravenscourt Pl. W6 . . . . .4D 98
Ravenscourt Rd. W6 . . . . .4D 98
Ravenscourt Sq. W6 . . . . .3C 98
Ravenscraig Rd. N11 . . . . .4B 32
Ravenscroft Av. HA9: Wemb 1E 60
　NW11 . . . . .7H 45
　　　　　　　　　　　　(not continuous)
Ravenscroft Cl. E16 . . . . .5J 87
Ravenscroft Cotts. EN5: New Bar 4D 20
Ravenscroft Cres. SE9 . . . . .3D 142
Ravenscroft Pk. E2 . . . . .3F 85
　　　　　　　　　　　　(off Baroness Rd.)
　EN5: Barn 3A 20
Ravenscroft Rd. BR3: Beck 2J 157
　E16 . . . . .5J 87
　W4 . . . . .4J 97
Ravenscroft St. E2 . . . . .1K 9 (2F 85)
Ravensdale Av. N12 . . . . .4F 31
Ravensdale Gdns. SE19 . . . . .7D 138
　TW4: Houn .3C 112
Ravensdale Ind. Est. N16 . . . . .6G 49
Ravensdale Mans. N8 . . . . .6J 47
　　　　　　　　　　　　(off Haringey Pk.)
Ravensdale Rd. N16 . . . . .7F 49
　TW4: Houn .3C 112
Ravens Dene BR7: Chst 5D 142
Ravensdon St. SE11 . . . . . . .6K 19 (5A 102)
Ravensfield Cl. RM9: Dag 4D 72
Ravensfield Gdns.
　KT19: Ewe .5A 164
Ravens Ga. M. BR2: Brom 2G 159
Ravenshaw St. NW6 . . . . .5H 63
Ravenshill BR7: Chst 1F 161
Ravenshurst Av. NW4 . . . . .4E 44

Ravenside KT1: King T 5D 150
　　　　　　　　　　　(off Portsmouth Rd.)
Ravenside Cl. N18 . . . . .5E 34
Ravenside Retail Pk. N18 . . . . .5E 34
Ravenslea Rd. SW12 . . . . .7D 118
Ravensleigh Gdns. BR1: Brom 5K 141
Ravensmead Rd. BR2: Brom 7F 141
Ravensmede Way W4 . . . . .4B 98
Ravens M. SE12 . . . . .5J 123
Ravenstone SE17 . . . . .5E 102
Ravenstone Rd. N8 . . . . .3A 48
　NW9 . . . . .6B 44
Ravenstone St. SW12 . . . . .1E 136
Ravens Wlk. E20 . . . . .6D 68
Ravens Way SE12 . . . . .5J 123
Ravenswood DA5: Bexl 1E 144
Ravenswood Av. BR4: W W'ck 1E 170
　KT6: Surb .2F 163
Ravenswood Ct. KT2: King T 6H 133
Ravenswood Cres. BR4: W W'ck 1E 170
　HA2: Harr 2D 58
Ravenswood Gdns. TW7: Isle 1J 113
Ravenswood Ind. Est. E17 . . . . .4E 50
Ravenswood Rd. CR0: Wadd 3B 168
　E17 . . . . .4E 50
　SW12 . . . . .7F 119
Ravensworth Ct. SW6 . . . . .7J 99
　　　　　　　　　　　　(off Fulham Rd.)
Ravensworth Rd. NW10 . . . . .3D 80
　SE9 . . . . .3D 142
Raven Wharf SE1 . . . . .6J 15
　　　　　　　　　　　　(off Lafone St.)
Ravey St. EC2 . . . . .3G 9 (4E 84)
Ravine Gro. SE18 . . . . .6J 107
Raw Pinter Cl. N16 . . . . .7E 48
Rawchester Cl. SW18 . . . . .1H 135
Rawlings Cl. BR3: Beck 5E 158
　BR6: Chels .5K 173
Rawlings Cres. HA9: Wemb 3H 61
Rawlings St. SW3 . . . . .3E 16 (4D 100)
Rawlins Cl. CR2: Sels 7B 170
　N3 . . . . .3G 45
Rawlinson Ct. NW2 . . . . .7E 44
Rawlinson Ho. SE13 . . . . .4F 123
　　　　　　　　　　　　(off Mercator Rd.)
Rawnsley Av. CR4: Mitc 5B 154
Rawreth Wlk. N1 . . . . .1C 84
　　　　　　　　　　　　(off Basire St.)
Rawson St. SW11 . . . . .1E 118
　　　　　　　　　　　　(not continuous)
Rawsthorne Cl. E16 . . . . .1D 106
Rawthorne Ct. TW4: Houn 4D 112
Rawstone Wlk. E13 . . . . .2J 87
Rawstorne Pl. EC1 . . . . .1A 8 (3B 84)
Rawstorne St. EC1 . . . . .1A 8 (3B 84)
　　　　　　　　　　　　(not continuous)
Raybell Ct. TW7: Isle 2K 113
Rayburne Ct. IG9: Buck H 1F 37
　W14 . . . . .3G 99
Ray Cl. KT9: Chess 6C 162
Raydean Rd.
　EN5: New Bar 5E 20
Raydons Gdns. RM9: Dag 5E 72
Raydons Rd. RM9: Dag 5E 72
Raydon St. N19 . . . . .2F 65
Rayfield Cl. BR2: Brom 6C 160
Rayford Av. SE12 . . . . .7H 123
Ray Gdns. HA7: Stan 5G 27
　IG11: Bark 2A 90
Ray Gunter Ho. SE17 . . . . .5B 102
　　　　　　　　　　　　(off Marsland Cl.)
Ray Ho. N1 . . . . .1C 84
　　　　　　　　　　　　(off Colville Est.)
　W10 . . . . .6F 81
　　　　　　　　　　　　(off Cambridge Gdns.)
Rayleas Cl. SE18 . . . . .1F 125
Rayleigh Av. TW11: Tedd 6J 131
Rayleigh Cl. N13 . . . . .3J 33
Rayleigh Ct. KT1: King T 2G 151
　N22 . . . . .1C 48
Rayleigh Ri. CR2: S Croy 6E 168

Rayleigh Rd. E16 . . . . .1K 105
　IG8: Wfd G .6F 37
　N13 . . . . .3H 33
　SW19 . . . . .1H 153
Ray Lodge Rd. IG8: Wfd G 6F 37
Ray Massey Way E6 . . . . .1C 88
　　　　　　　　　　　　(off High St. Nth.)
Raymead Av. CR7: Thor H 5A 156
Raymead Pas. CR7: Thor H 5A 156
　　　　　　　　　　　　(off Raymead Av.)
Raymede Towers W10 . . . . .5F 81
　　　　　　　　　　　　(off Treverton St.)
Raymere Gdns. SE18 . . . . .7H 107
Raymond Av. E18 . . . . .3H 51
　W13 . . . . .3A 96
Raymond Bldgs. WC1 . . . . . .5H 7 (5K 83)
Raymond Chadburn Ho. E7 . . . . .4K 69
Raymond Cl. SE26 . . . . .5J 139
　SL3: Poyle .4A 174
Raymond Ct. N10 . . . . .7A 32
Raymond Postgate Ct. SE28 . . . . . . .7B 90
Raymond Rd. BR3: Beck 4A 158
　E13 . . . . .1A 88
　IG2: Ilf 7H 53
　SW19 . . . . .6G 135
Raymond Way KT10: Clay 6A 162
Raymouth Rd. SE16 . . . . .4H 103
Raynald Ho. SW16 . . . . .3J 137
Rayne Ct. E18 .4H 51
Rayne Ho. SW12 . . . . .6E 118
　W9 . . . . .4K 81
　　　　　　　　　　　　(off Delaware Rd.)
Rayner Ct. W12 . . . . .2E 98
　　　　　　　　　　　(off Bamborough Gdns.)
Rayners Cl. HA0: Wemb 5D 60
Rayners Cres. UB5: N'olt 3K 75
Rayners Gdns. UB5: N'olt 2K 75
RAYNERS LANE 1D 58
Rayners La. HA2: Harr 1E 58
　HA5: Pinn 5D 40
Rayners Rd. SW15 . . . . .5G 117
Rayners Ter. E14 . . . . .5D 86
　　　　　　　　　　　　(off Carr St.)
Rayner Towers E10 . . . . .7C 50
　　　　　　　　　　　　(off Albany Rd.)
Raynes Av. E11 . . . . .7A 52
RAYNES PARK 4E 152
Raynes Pk. Bri. SW20 . . . . .2E 152
Raynes Park School Sports Cen. . . .3D 152
Raynham W2 . . . . .7D 4
　　　　　　　　　　　　(off Norfolk Cres.)
Raynham Av. N18 . . . . .6B 34
Raynham Ho. E1 . . . . .4K 85
　　　　　　　　　　　　(off Harpley Sq.)
Raynham Rd. N18 . . . . .5B 34
　W6 . . . . .4D 98
Raynham Ter. N18 . . . . .5B 34
Raynor Cl. UB1: S'hall 1D 94
Raynor Pl. N1 .7C 66
Raynton Cl. HA2: Harr 1C 58
　UB4: Hayes 4H 75
Raynton Dr. UB4: Hayes 4H 75
Ray Rd. KT8: W Mole 5F 149
Rays Av. N18 .4D 34
Rays Rd. BR4: W W'ck 7E 158
　N18 . . . . .4D 34
Ray St. EC1 . . . . .4K 7 (4A 84)
Ray St. Bri. EC1 . . . . .4K 7
Ray Wlk. N7 . . . . .2K 65
Raymouth Cl. UB3: Harl 7E 92
Raywood Mans. E20 . . . . .6E 68
　　　　　　　　　　　　(off West Pk. Wlk.)
Razia M. E12 . . . . .5C 70
Reachview Cl. NW1 . . . . .7G 65
Read Cl. KT7: T Ditt 7A 150
Read Ct. E17 .6C 50
Reade Ct. W3 . . . . .3J 97
　　　　　　　　　　　　(off Stanley Rd.)
Reader Ho. SE5 . . . . .1C 120
　　　　　　　　　　　　(off Badsworth Rd.)
Read Ho. SE11 . . . . .7J 19

Reading Cl. SE22 . . . . .6G 121
Reading Ho. SE15 . . . . .6G 103
　　　　　　　　　　　　(off Friary Est.)
　W2 . . . . .6A 82
　　　　　　　　　　　　(off Hallfield Est.)
Reading La. E8 . . . . .6H 67
Reading Rd. SM1: Sutt 5A 166
　UB5: N'olt 5D 58
Readman Ct. SE20 . . . . .1H 157
Reads Cl. IG1: Ilf 3F 71
Ream Apartments SE23 . . . . .2J 139
　　　　　　　　　　　　(off Clyde Ter.)
Reapers Cl. NW1 . . . . .1H 83
Reapers Way TW7: Isle 5H 113
Reardon Ct. N21 . . . . .2G 33
Reardon Ho. E1 . . . . .1H 103
　　　　　　　　　　　　(off Reardon St.)
Reardon Path E1 . . . . .1H 103
　　　　　　　　　　　　(not continuous)
Reardon St. E1 . . . . .1H 103
Reaston St. SE14 . . . . .7K 103
Rebecca Cl. DA14: Sidc 4B 144
Rebecca Ho. E3 . . . . .4B 86
　　　　　　　　　　　　(off Brokesley St.)
　N12 . . . . .4E 30
　　　　　　　　　　　(off Woodside Pk. Rd.)
Reckitt Rd. W4 . . . . .5A 98
Record St. SE15 . . . . .6J 103
Recovery St. SW17 . . . . .5C 136
Recreation Av. RM7: Rom 5J 55
Recreation Rd. BR2: Brom 2H 159
　DA15: Sidc .3J 143
　SE26 . . . . .4K 139
　UB2: S'hall .4C 94
Recreation Way CR4: Mitc 3H 155
Rector St. N1 . . . . .1C 84
Rectory Bus. Cen. DA14: Sidc 4B 144
Rectory Chambers SW3 . . . . .7C 16
　　　　　　　　　　　　(off Old Church St.)
Rectory Cl. DA14: Sidc 4B 144
　E4 . . . . .3H 35
　HA7: Stan 5G 27
　KT6: Surb 1C 162
　N3 . . . . .1H 45
　SW20 . . . . .3E 152
　TW17: Shep 3C 146
Rectory Ct. E18 . . . . .1H 51
　SM6: Wall 4G 167
　TW13: Felt .4A 130
Rectory Cres. E11 . . . . .6A 52
　　　　　　　　　　　　(not continuous)
Rectory Farm Rd. EN2: Enf 1E 22
　　　　　　　　　　　　(not continuous)
Rectory Field .7K 105
Rectory Fld. Cres. SE7 . . . . .7A 106
Rectory Gdns. BR3: Beck 1C 158
　　　　　　　　　　　　(off Rectory Rd.)
　N8 . . . . .4J 47
　SW4 . . . . .3G 119
　UB5: N'olt 1D 76
Rectory Grn. BR3: Beck 1B 158
Rectory Gro. CR0: C'don 2B 168
　SW4 . . . . .3G 119
　TW12: Hamp 4D 130
Rectory La. DA14: Sidc 4B 144
　HA7: Stan 5G 27
　HA8: Edg 6B 28
　KT6: Surb 1B 162
　SM6: Wall 4G 167
　SW17 . . . . .6E 136
Rectory Orchard SW19 . . . . .4G 135
Rectory Pk. Av. UB5: N'olt 3D 76
Rectory Pl. SE18 . . . . .4E 106
Rectory Rd. BR2: Kes 7B 172
　BR3: Beck 1C 158
　E12 . . . . .5D 70
　E17 . . . . .4D 50
　N16 . . . . .2F 67
　RM10: Dag .6H 73
　SM1: Sutt 3J 165
　SW13 . . . . .2C 116

Rectory Rd.
TW4: Cran 2A 112
UB2: S'hall 3D 94
UB3: Hayes 6J 75
W3 . . . . .1H 97
Rectory Sq. E1 . . . . .5K 85
Rectory Way UB10: Ick 2D 56
Reculver Ho. SE15 . . . . .6J 103
(off Lovelinch Cl.)
Reculver M. N18 . . . . .4B 34
Reculver Rd. SE16 . . . . .5K 103
Red Anchor Cl. SW3 . . . . .6B 100
Redan Pl. W2 . . . . .6K 81
Redan St. W14 . . . . .3F 99
Redan Ter. SE5 . . . . .2B 120
Red Barracks Rd. SE18 . . . . .4D 106
Redberry Gro. SE26 . . . . .3J 139
Redbourne Av. N3 . . . . .1J 45
Redbourne Dr. SE28 . . . . .6D 90
(not continuous)
Redbourne Ho. E14 . . . . .6B 86
(off Norbiton Rd.)
Redbourn Ho. W10 . . . . .4E 80
(off Sutton Way)
REDBRIDGE 6C 52
Redbridge Ent. Cen. IG1: Ilf 2G 71
Redbridge Foyer IG1: Ilf 2G 71
(off Hainault St.)
Redbridge Gdns. SE5 . . . . .7E 102
Redbridge Ho. E16 . . . . .7F 89
(off University Way)
Redbridge La. E. IG4: Ilf 6B 52
Redbridge La. W. E11 . . . . .6K 51
REDBRIDGE RDBT. 6B 52
Redbridge Sports & Leisure Cen. . . .1H 53
Redburn Ind. Est. EN3: Pond E 6E 24
Redburn St. SW3 . . . . . .7E 16 (6D 100)
Redcar Cl. UB5: N'olt 5F 59
Redcar St. SE5 . . . . .7C 102
Redcastle Cl. E1 . . . . .7J 85
Red Cedars Rd. BR6: Orp 7J 161
Redchurch St. E2 . . . . .3J 9 (4F 85)
Redcliffe Cl. SW5 . . . . .5K 99
(off Old Brompton Rd.)
Redcliffe Ct. E5 . . . . .3H 67
(off Napoleon Rd.)
Redcliffe Gdns. IG1: Ilf 1E 70
SW10 . . . . .5K 99
W4 . . . . .7H 97
Redcliffe M. SW10 . . . . .5K 99
Redcliffe Pl. SW10 . . . . .6A 100
Redcliffe Rd. SW10 . . . . .5A 100
Redcliffe Sq. SW10 . . . . .5K 99
Redcliffe St. SW10 . . . . .6K 99
Redclose Av. SM4: Mord 5J 153
Redclyfe Rd. E6 . . . . .1A 88
Redclyf Ho. E1 . . . . .4J 85
(off Cephas St.)
Redcourt CR0: C'don 3E 168
Red Cow La. EC1 . . . . .3C 8 (4C 84)
Redcroft Rd. UB1: S'hall 7G 77
Red Cross Cotts. SE1 . . . . .6D 14
(off Ayres St.)
Redcross Way SE1 . . . . . .6D 14 (2C 102)
Redding Ho. SE18 . . . . .3C 106
Reddings, The NW7 . . . . .3G 29
Reddings Cl. NW7 . . . . .4G 29
Reddins Rd. SE15 . . . . .6G 103
Reddons Rd. BR3: Beck 7A 140
Redenham Ho. SW15 . . . . .7C 116
(off Ellisfield Dr.)
Rede Pl. W2 . . . . .6J 81
Redesdale Gdns. TW7: Isle 7A 96
Redesdale St. SW3 . . . . . .7D 16 (6C 100)
Redfern Av. TW4: Houn 7E 112
Redfern Ho. E13 . . . . .1H 87
(off Redriffe Rd.)
NW8 .1B 82
(off Dorman Way)
Redfern Rd. NW10 . . . . .7A 62
SE6 . . . . .7E 122

Redfield La. SW5 . . . . .4J 99
Redfield M. SW5 . . . . .4K 99
Redford Av. CR7: Thor H 4K 155
SM6: Wall 6J 167
Redford Cl. TW13: Felt 2H 129
Redford Wlk. N1 . . . . .1C 84
(off Popham St.)
Redgate Dr. BR2: Hayes 2K 171
Redgate Ter. SW15 . . . . .6F 117
Redgrave Cl. CR0: C'don 6F 157
Redgrave Rd. SW15 . . . . .3F 117
Redgrave Ter. E2 . . . . .3G 85
(off Derbyshire St.)
Red Hill BR7: Chst 5F 143
Redhill Cl. SW2 . . . . .2A 138
Redhill Dr. HA8: Edg 2H 43
Redhill St. NW1 . . . . .1K 5 (2F 83)
Red House 4E 126
Red Ho. SE20 . . . . .7H 139
(off Anerley Pk.)
Red Ho. La. DA6: Bex 4D 126
Redhouse Rd. CR0: C'don 6H 155
Red Ho. Sq. N1 . . . . .7C 66
Redif Ho. RM10: Dag 4H 73
Redington Gdns. NW3 . . . . .4K 63
Redington Ho. N1 . . . . .2K 83
(off Priory Grn. Est.)
Redington Rd. NW3 . . . . .3K 63
Redknap Ho. TW10: Ham 3C 132
Redland Gdns. KT8: W Mole 4D 148
Redlands N15 . . . . .4D 48
TW11: Tedd 6A 132
Redlands, The BR3: Beck 2D 158
Redlands Ct. BR1: Brom 7H 141
Redlands Rd. EN3: Enf H 1F 25
Redlands Way SW2 . . . . .7K 119
Red La. KT10: Clay 6A 162
Redleaf Cl. DA17: Belv 6G 109
Redleaves Av. TW15: Ashf 6D 128
Redlees Cl. TW7: Isle 4A 114
Red Leys UB8: Uxb 7A 56
Red Lion Bus. Pk. KT6: Surb 3F 163
Red Lion Ct. SE17 . . . . .6D 102
(off Red Lion Row)
Red Lion Ct. EC4 . . . . . . .1K 13 (6A 84)
SE1 . . . . .4D 14 (1C 102)
TW3: Houn 3F 113
(off Alexandra St.)
Red Lion Hill N2 . . . . .2B 46
(not continuous)
Red Lion La. SE18 . . . . .7E 106
Red Lion Pde. HA5: Pinn 3C 40
Red Lion Pl. SE18 . . . . .1E 124
Red Lion Rd. KT6: Surb 2F 163
Red Lion Row SE17 . . . . .6C 102
Red Lion Sq. SW18 . . . . .5J 117
WC1 . . . . .6G 7 (5K 83)
Red Lion St. TW9: Rich 5D 114
WC1 . . . . .5G 7 (5K 83)
Red Lion Wlk. TW3: Houn 3F 113
(off High St.)
Red Lion Yd. W1 . . . . .4H 11
Red Lodge BR4: W W'ck 1E 170
Red Lodge Cres. DA5: Bexl 3K 145
Red Lodge Rd. BR4: W W'ck 1E 170
DA5: Bexl 3K 145
Redlynch Ct. W14 . . . . .2G 99
(off Addison Cres.)
Redlynch Ho. SW9 . . . . .1A 120
(off Gosling Way)
Redman Cl. UB5: N'olt 2A 76
Redman Ho. EC1 . . . . .5J 7
(off Bourne Est.)
SE1 .7D 14
(off Borough High St.)
Redman's Rd. E1 . . . . .5J 85
Redmead La. E1 . . . . .1G 103
Redmead Rd. UB3: Harl 4G 93
Redmill Ho. E1 . . . . .4H 85
(off Headlam St.)

Redmond Ho. N1 . . . . .1K 83
(off Barnsbury Est.)
Redmore Rd. W6 . . . . .4D 98
Red Oak Cl. BR6: Farnb 3F 173
CR0: C'don 2C 170
Redo Ho. E12 . . . . .5E 70
(off Dore Av.)
Red Path E9 . . . . .6A 68
Redpath Way SE10 . . . . .2G 105
Red Pl. W1 . . . . .2G 11 (7E 82)
Redpoll Way DA18: Erith 3D 108
Red Post Hill SE21 . . . . .4D 120
SE24 . . . . .4D 120
Red Post Ho. E6 . . . . .7B 70
Redriffe Rd. E13 . . . . .1H 87
Redriff Est. SE16 . . . . .3B 104
Redriff Rd. RM7: Mawney 2H 55
SE16 . . . . .4K 103
Redroofs Cl. BR3: Beck 1D 158
Redrose Trad. Cen. EN4: E Barn . . .5G 21
RED ROVER 4C 116
Redrup Ho. SE14 . . . . .6K 103
(off John Williams Cl.)
Redruth Cl. N22 . . . . .7E 32
Redruth Gdns. KT10: Clay 7A 162
Redruth Ho. SM2: Sutt 7K 165
Redruth Rd. E9 . . . . .1J 85
Redsan Cl. CR2: S Croy 7D 168
Redshank Ho. SE1 . . . . .5F 103
(off Avocet Cl.)
Red Sq. N16 . . . . .3D 66
Redstart Cl. E6 . . . . .5C 88
SE14 . . . . .7A 104
Redstart Mans. IG1: Ilf 3E 70
(off Mill Rd.)
Redston Rd. N8 . . . . .4H 47
Redvers Rd. N22 . . . . .2A 48
Redvers St. N1 . . . . .1H 9 (3E 84)
Redwald Rd. E5 . . . . .4K 67
Redway Dr. TW2: Whitt 7G 113
Redwing Cl. SE1 . . . . .7D 14
(off Swan St.)
Redwing M. SE5 . . . . .2D 120
Redwing Path SE28 . . . . .2H 107
Redwing Rd. SM6: Wall 7J 167
Redwood Cl. DA15: Sidc 1A 144
E3 . . . . .2C 86
N14 . . . . .7C 22
SE16 . . . . .1A 104
UB10: Hil 2D 74
Redwood Ct. KT6: Surb 7D 150
N19 .7H 47
NW6 .7G 63
UB5: N'olt 3C 76
Redwood Est. TW5: Cran 6K 93
Redwood Gdns. E4 . . . . .6J 25
Redwood Gro. W5 . . . . .3B 96
Redwood Mans. W8 . . . . .3K 99
(off Chantry Sq.)
Redwood M. SW4 . . . . .3F 119
TW15: Ashf 7F 129
(off Staines Rd. W.)
Redwoods SW15 . . . . .1C 134
Redwoods Cl. IG9: Buck H 2E 36
Redwood Wlk. KT6: Surb 1D 162
Redwood Way EN5: Barn 5A 20
Reece M. SW7 . . . . .3A 16 (4B 100)
Reed Av. BR6: Orp 3J 173
Reed Cl. E16 . . . . .5J 87
SE12 . . . . .5J 123
Reede Gdns. RM10: Dag 5H 73
Reede Rd. RM10: Dag 6G 73
Reede Way RM10: Dag 6H 73
Reedham Cl. N17 . . . . .4H 49
Reedham St. SE15 . . . . .2G 121
Reedholm Vs. N16 . . . . .4D 66
Reed Ho. SW19 . . . . .4K 135
Reed Pl. SW4 . . . . .4H 119
Reed Rd. N17 . . . . .2F 49
Reedsfield Cl. TW15: Ashf 3D 128
Reedsfield Rd. TW15: Ashf 4D 128

Reed's Pl. NW1 . . . . .7G 65
Reedworth St. SE11 . . . . . .4K 19 (4A 102)
Reef Ho. E14 . . . . .3E 104
(off Manchester St.)
Reenglass Rd. HA7: Stan 4J 27
Rees Dr. HA7: Stan 4K 27
Rees Gdns. CR0: C'don 6F 157
Reesland Cl. E12 . . . . .6E 70
Rees St. N1 . . . . .1C 84
Reets Farm Cl. NW9 . . . . .6A 44
Reeves Av. NW9 . . . . .7K 43
Reeves Cnr. CR0: C'don 2B 168
Reeves Ho. SE1 . . . . .7J 13
(off Baylis Rd.)
Reeves M. W1 . . . . .3G 11 (7E 82)
Reeves Rd. E3 . . . . .4D 86
SE18 . . . . .6F 107
Reflection, The E16 . . . . .2F 107
(off Woolwich Mnr. Way)
Reflection Ho. E2 . . . . .4G 85
(off Cheshire St.)
Reflex Apartments BR2: Brom 4K 159
(off Wheeler Pl.)
Reform Row N17 . . . . .2F 49
Reform St. SW11 . . . . .2D 118
Regal Bldg. W10 . . . . .3F 81
Regal Cl. E1 . . . . .5G 85
W5 . . . . .5D 78
Regal Ct. CR4: Mitc 3D 154
N18 .5A 34
NW6 .2H 81
(off Malvern Rd.)
SW6 .7J 99
(off Dawes Rd.)
Regal Cres. SM6: Wall 3F 167
Regal Dr. N11 . . . . .5A 32
Regal Ho. IG2: Ilf 6H 53
Regal House, The SW6 . . . . .2A 118
Regal La. NW1 . . . . .1E 82
Regal Pl. E3 . . . . .3B 86
SW6 .7K 99
Regal Row SE15 . . . . .1J 121
Regal Way HA3: Kenton 6E 42
Regal Wharf Apartments N1 . . . . . .1E 84
(off De Beauvoir Cr.)
Regan Ho. N18 . . . . .6A 34
Regan Way N1 . . . . .1G 9 (2E 84)
Regatta Ho. TW11: Tedd 4A 132
Regatta La. W6 . . . . .6E 98
Regatta Point E14 . . . . .2C 104
(off Westferry Rd.)
TW8: Bford 6F 97
Regenct Ct. HA7: Stan 7J 27
(off Unwin Way)
Regency Cl. TW12: Hamp 5D 130
W5 . . . . .6E 78
Regency Ct. BR2: Brom 6B 160
E3 . . . . .2B 86
(off Norman Gro.)
E9 . . . . .1J 85
(off Park Cl.)
E18 .2J 51
EN1: Enf 5J 23
SE8 .7B 104
(off Glenville Gro.)
SM1: Sutt 4A 166
TW11: Tedd 6B 132
Regency Cres. NW4 . . . . .2F 45
Regency Dr. HA4: Ruis 1G 57
Regency Gdns. KT12: Walt T 7A 148
Regency Ho. E16 . . . . .1J 105
(off Pepys Cres.)
N3 . . . . .2H 45
SW1 .3D 18
(off Regency St.)
SW6 .1A 118
(off The Boulevard)
Regency Lawn NW5 . . . . .3F 65
Regency Lodge IG9: Buck H 2G 37
NW3 .7B 64
(off Adelaide Rd.)

Regency M. BR3: Beck 1E **158**
   NW10 . . . . .6C **62**
   SW9 . . . . .7B **102**
   TW7: Isle 5J **113**
Regency Pde. NW3 . . . . .7B **64**
   (off Finchley Rd.)
Regency Pl. SW1 . . . . . . .3D **18** (4H **101**)
Regency St. NW10 . . . . .4A **80**
   SW1 . . . . .3D **18** (4H **101**)
Regency Ter. SW7 . . . . .5A **16**
Regency Wlk. CRO: C'don 6B **158**
   TW10: Rich 5E **114**
   (off The Vineyard)
Regency Way DA6: Bex 3D **126**
Regeneration House 1J **83**
Regeneration Rd. SE16 . . . . .4K **103**
Regent Av. UB10: Hil 7D **56**
Regent Bus. Cen.
   UB3: Hayes .2K **93**
Regent Cl. HA3: Kenton 6E **42**
   N12 . . . . .5F **31**
   TW4: Cran 1K **111**
Regent Ct. N3 . . . . .7E **30**
   N20 . . . . .2G **31**
   NW6 . . . . .7H **63**
   (off Cavendish Rd.)
   NW8 . . . . .2C **4**
   W8 . . . . .3K **99**
   (off Wright's La.)
Regent Gdns. IG3: Ilf 7A **54**
Regent Ho. W14 .4G **99**
   (off Windsor Way)
Regent Pde. SM2: Sutt 6A **166**
Regent Pl. CRO: C'don 1F **169**
   SW19 . . . . .5A **136**
   W1 . . . . .2B **12** (7G **83**)
Regent Rd. KT5: Surb 5F **151**
   SE24 . . . . .6B **120**
Regents Av. N13 .5F **33**
Regent's Bri. Gdns. SW8 . . . . .7J **101**
Regents Canal Ho. E14 . . . . .6A **86**
   (off Commercial Rd.)
Regents Cl. CR2: S Croy 6E **168**
   HA8: Edg 4K **27**
   UB4: Hayes 5H **75**
Regents Ct. BR1: Brom 7H **141**
   E8 . . . . .1G **85**
   HA5: Pinn 2B **40**
   KT2: King T 1E **150**
   (off Sopwith Way)
Regents Dr. BR2: Kes 5B **172**
   IG8: Wfd G .6K **37**
Regents Ga. Ho. E14 . . . . .7A **86**
   (off Horseferry Rd.)
Regents Ho. E3 .5C **86**
   (off Bow Common La.)
Regents M. NW8 . . . . .2A **82**
REGENT'S PARK 2K 5 (3F **83**)
Regent's Park 1F 5 (2D 82)
Regent's Park Barracks 1K 5
Regents Pk. Est. NW1 . . . . .1A 6
Regent's Pk. Gdns. M.
   NW1 . . . . .1D **82**
Regent's Pk. Ho. NW8 . . . . .2D **4**
   (off Park Rd.)
Regent's Park Open Air Theatre
   . . . . .2G 5 (3E 82)
Regents Pk. Rd. N3 . . . . .3H **45**
   NW1 . . . . .7D **64**
   (not continuous)
Regent's Pk. Ter. NW1 . . . . .1F **83**
Regents Pl. NW1 . . . . .3A 6 (4G **83**)
   SE3 . . . . .2J **123**
Regent's Pl. Plaza NW1 . . . . .4G **83**
Regents Plaza NW6 . . . . .2K **81**
   (off Kilburn High Rd.)
Regent Sq. DA17: Belv 4H **109**
   E3 . . . . .3D **86**
   WC1 . . . . .2F 7 (3J **83**)
Regent's Row E8 . . . . .1G **85**
Regents Studios E8 . . . . .1H **85**

Regent St. NW10 . . . . .3F **81**
   SW1 . . . . .3C **12** (7H **83**)
   W1 . . . . .7K 5 (6F **83**)
   W4 . . . . .5G **97**
Regent's University London . . .3F 5 (4D 82)
Regents Wharf E2 . . . . .1H **85**
   (off Wharf Pl.)
   N1 . . . . .2K **83**
Regent Ter. SW8 . . . . .6J **101**
Regina Cl. EN5: Barn 3A **20**
Regina Ho. SE20 . . . . .1K **157**
Reginald Ellingworth St.
   RM9: Dag .1B **90**
Reginald Pl. SE8 . . . . .7C **104**
   (off Deptford High St.)
Reginald Rd. E7 . . . . .7J **69**
   HA6: Nwood 1H **39**
   SE8 . . . . .7C **104**
Reginald Sorenson Ho.
   E11 . . . . .7F **51**
Reginald Sq. SE8 . . . . .7C **104**
Regina Point SE16 . . . . .3J **103**
   (off Canada Est.)
Regina Rd. N4 .1K **65**
   SE25 . . . . .3G **157**
   UB2: S'hall 4C **94**
   W13 . . . . .1A **96**
Regina Ter. W13 . . . . .1B **96**
Regis Ct. CR4: Mitc 1C **154**
   N8 . . . . .4K **47**
   NW1 . . . . .5E **4**
   (off Melcombe Pl.)
Regis Ho. W1 . . . . .5H **5**
   (off Beaumont St.)
Regis Pl. SW2 .4K **119**
Regis Rd. NW5 .5F **65**
Regnart Bldgs. NW1 . . . . .3B **6**
Regnas Ho. E15 . . . . .6H **69**
   (off Carnarvon Rd.)
Regnolruf Ct. KT12: Walt T 7J **147**
Regnum Apartments E1 . . . . .4J **9**
   (off Wheler St.)
Reid Bldg. E3 . . . . .4B **86**
   (off Eric St.)
Reid Cl. HA5: Eastc 4J **39**
   UB3: Hayes 6G **75**
Reidhaven Rd. SE18 . . . . .4J **107**
Reigate Av. SM1: Sutt 1J **165**
Reigate Rd. BR1: Brom 3H **141**
   IG3: Ilf 2K **71**
Reigate Way SM6: Wall 5J **167**
Reighton Rd. E5 . . . . .3G **67**
Reindeer Cl. E13 . . . . .1J **87**
Reinickendorf Av. SE9 . . . . .6G **125**
Reis Pl. N15 . . . . .4F **49**
   (off Blenheim Ri.)
Reizel Cl. N16 . . . . .1F **67**
Relay Rd. W12 . . . . .1E **98**
Relf Rd. SE15 .3G **121**
Reliance Arc. SW9 . . . . .4A **120**
Reliance Sq. EC2 . . . . .3H 9 (4E **84**)
Reliance Wharf N1 . . . . .1E **84**
Relko Gdns. SM1: Sutt 5B **166**
Relton M. SW7 . . . . .1D **16** (3D **100**)
Rembrandt Cl. E14 . . . . .3F **105**
   SW1 . . . . .4G **17**
Rembrandt Ct. KT19: Ewe 6B **164**
   SE16 . . . . .5H **103**
   (off Stubbs Dr.)
Rembrandt Rd. HA8: Edg 2G **43**
   SE13 . . . . .4G **123**
Reminder La. SE10 . . . . .3H **105**
Remington Rd. E6 . . . . .6C **88**
   N15 . . . . .6D **48**
Remington St. N1 . . . . .1B 8 (2B **84**)
Remnant St. WC2 . . . . .7G 7 (6K **83**)
Remsted Ho. NW6 . . . . .1K **81**
   (off Mortimer Cres.)
Remus Building, The EC1 . . . . .2K **7**
   (off Hardwick St.)
Remus Rd. E3 . . . . .7C **68**

Renaissance Ct. SM1: Sutt 1A **166**
   TW3: Houn 3G **113**
   (off Prince Regent Rd.)
Renaissance Wlk. SE10 . . . . .3H **105**
   (off Teal St.)
Renbold Ho. SE10 . . . . .1E **122**
   (off Blissett St.)
Rendalls HA1: Harr 1J **59**
   (off Grove Hill)
Rendle Cl. CRO: C'don 5F **157**
Rendle Ho. W10 . . . . .4G **81**
   (off Wornington Rd.)
Rendlesham Rd. E5 . . . . .4G **67**
   EN2: Enf 1G **23**
Renforth St. SE16 . . . . .3J **103**
Renfrew Cl. E6 . . . . .7E **88**
Renfrew Ct. TW4: Houn 2C **112**
Renfrew Ho. E17 . . . . .2B **50**
   NW6 . . . . .2K **81**
   (off Carlton Vale)
Renfrew Rd. KT2: King T 7H **133**
   SE11 . . . . .3K **19** (4B **102**)
   TW4: Houn 2B **112**
Renmuir St. SW17 . . . . .6D **136**
Rennell St. SE13 . . . . .3E **122**
Rennels Way TW7: Isle 2J **113**
Renness Rd. E17 . . . . .3A **50**
Rennets Cl. SE9 . . . . .5J **125**
Rennets Wood Rd. SE9 . . . . .5H **125**
Rennie Cotts. E1 . . . . .4J **85**
   (off Pemell Cl.)
Rennie Ct. EN3: Enf L 1H **25**
   SE1 . . . . .4A **14**
Rennie Est. SE16 . . . . .4H **103**
Rennie Ho. SE1 . . . . .3C **102**
   (off Bath Ter.)
Rennie St. SE1 . . . . .4A **14** (1B **102**)
   (not continuous)
Renoir Cinema
   Brunswick Square 4J **83**
Renoir Ct. SE16 . . . . .1H **103**
   (off Stubbs Dr.)
Renovation, The E16 . . . . .2F **107**
   (off Woolwich Mnr. Way)
Renown Cl. CRO: C'don 1B **168**
   RM7: Mawney 1G **55**
Rensburg Rd. E17 . . . . .5K **49**
Renshaw Cl. DA17: Belv 6F **109**
   SE6 . . . . .7C **122**
Renters Av. NW4 . . . . .6E **44**
Renton Cl. SW2 . . . . .6K **119**
Renwick Dr. BR2: Brom 6B **160**
Renwick Ind. Est. IG11: Bark 2B **90**
Renwick Rd. IG11: Bark 4B **90**
Repens Way UB4: Yead 4B **76**
Rephidim St. SE1 . . . . .3E **102**
Replingham Rd. SW18 . . . . .1H **135**
Reporton Rd. SW6 . . . . .7G **99**
Repository Rd. SE18 . . . . .6D **106**
Repton Av. HA0: Wemb 4C **60**
   UB3: Harl 4F **93**
Repton Cl. SM5: Cars 5C **166**
Repton Ct. BR3: Beck 1D **158**
   IG5: Ilf 1D **52**
Repton Gro. IG5: Ilf 1D **52**
Repton Ho. E4 .6K **35**
   SW1 . . . . .4B **18**
   (off Charlwood St.)
REPTON PARK .7K **37**
Repton Rd. BR6: Chels 3K **173**
   HA3: Kenton 4F **43**
Repton St. E14 .6A **86**
Repulse Cl. RM5: Col R 1G **55**
Reservoir Cl. CR7: Thor H 3D **156**
Reservoir Rd. HA4: Ruis 4E **38**
   N14 . . . . .5B **22**
   SE4 . . . . .2A **122**
Reservoir Studios E1 . . . . .6K **85**
   (off Cable St.)
Resham Cl. UB2: S'hall 3A **94**

Residence Twr. N4 . . . . .7C **48**
   (off Goodchild Rd.)
Resolution Plaza E1 . . . . .7K **9**
Resolution Wlk. SE18 . . . . .3D **106**
Resolution Way SE8 . . . . .7C **104**
   (off Deptford High St.)
Restell Cl. SE3 .6G **105**
Restmor Way SM6: Wall 2E **166**
Reston Pl. SW7 . . . . .2A **100**
Restons Cres. SE9 . . . . .6H **125**
Restoration Sq. SW11 . . . . .1B **118**
Restormel Cl. TW3: Houn 5E **112**
Restormel Ho. SE11 . . . . .4J **19**
Retcar Pl. N19 . . . . .2F **65**
Retford St. N1 . . . . .1H **9** (2E **84**)
Retingham Way E4 . . . . .2J **35**
Retlas Ct. HA1: Harr 7J **41**
Retreat, The CR7: Thor H 4D **156**
   HA2: Harr 7E **40**
   KT4: Wor Pk 2D **164**
   KT5: Surb .6F **151**
   NW9 . . . . .5K **43**
   SW14 . . . . .3A **116**
Retreat Cl. HA3: Kenton 5C **42**
Retreat Ho. E9 . . . . .6J **67**
Retreat Mobile Home Park, The
   IG9: Buck H 2D **36**
Retreat Pl. E9 . . . . .6J **67**
Retreat Rd. TW9: Rich 5D **114**
Reubens Ct. W4 . . . . .5H **97**
   (off Chaseley Dr.)
Reunion Row E1 . . . . .7H **85**
Reuters Plaza E14 . . . . .1D **104**
   (off The South Colonnade)
Reveley Sq. SE16 . . . . .2A **104**
Revell Ri. SE18 . . . . .6K **107**
Revell Rd. KT1: King T 2H **151**
   SM1: Sutt .6H **165**
Revelon Rd. SE4 . . . . .4A **122**
Revelstoke Rd. SW18 . . . . .2H **135**
Reventlow Rd. SE9 . . . . .1G **143**
Reverdy Rd. SE1 . . . . .4G **103**
Reverend Cl. HA2: Harr 3F **59**
Revesby Rd. SM5: Cars 6B **154**
Review Lodge RM10: Dag 1H **91**
Review Rd. NW2 . . . . .2B **62**
   RM10: Dag 1H **91**
Rewell St. SW6 . . . . .7A **100**
Rewley Rd. SM5: Cars 6B **154**
Rex Av. TW15: Ashf 6C **128**
Rex Cl. RM5: Col R 1H **55**
Rex Pl. W1 . . . . .3H **11** (7E **82**)
Reydon Av. E11 .5A **52**
Reynard Bus. Pk. TW8: Bford 5C **96**
Reynard Cl. BR1: Brom 3E **160**
   SE4 . . . . .3A **122**
Reynard Dr. SE19 . . . . .7F **139**
Reynard Pl. SE14 . . . . .6A **104**
Reynardson Rd. N17 . . . . .7H **33**
Reynolah Gdns. SE7 . . . . .5K **105**
Reynolds Av. E12 . . . . .5E **70**
   KT9: Chess 7E **162**
   RM6: Chad H 7C **54**
Reynolds Cl. NW11 . . . . .7K **45**
   SM5: Cars 1D **166**
   SW19 . . . . .1B **154**
Reynolds Ct. RM6: Chad H 3D **54**
Reynolds Dr. HA8: Edg 3F **43**
Reynolds Ho. E2 . . . . .2J **85**
   (off Approach Rd.)
   NW8 . . . . .2B **82**
   (off Wellington Rd.)
   SW1 . . . . .4D **18**
   (off Erasmus St.)
Reynolds Pl. SE3 . . . . .7K **105**
   TW10: Rich 6F **115**
Reynolds Rd. KT3: N Mald 7K **151**
   SE15 . . . . .4J **121**
   UB4: Yead .4A **76**
   W4 . . . . .3J **97**
Reynolds Sports Cen. 1G **97**

Reynolds Way CRO: C'don 4E **168**
Rheidol M. N1 .2C **84**
Rheidol Ter. N1 . . . . .1C **84**
Rheingold Way SM6: Wall 7J **167**
Rhein Ho. N8 . . . . .3J **47**
    (off Campsfield Rd.)
Rheola Cl. N17 . . . . .1F **49**
Rhoda St. E2 . . . . .3K **9** (4F **85**)
Rhodes Av. N22 . . . . .1G **47**
Rhodes Ho. N1 . . . . .1E **8**
    (off Provost St.)
Rhodesia Rd. E11 . . . . .2J **69**
    SW9 . . . . .2J **119**
Rhodes Moorhouse Ct.
    SM4: Mord 6J **153**
Rhodes St. N7 . . . . .5K **65**
Rhodeswell Rd. E14 . . . . .5A **86**
    (not continuous)
Rhodium Ct. E14 . . . . .5C **86**
    (off Thomas Rd.)
Rhodrons Av. KT9: Chess 5E **162**
Rhondda Gro. E3 . . . . .3A **86**
Rhyl Rd. UB6: G'frd 2K **77**
Rhyl St. NW5 . . . . .6E **64**
Rhys Av. N11 .7C **32**
Rialto Rd. CR4: Mitc 2E **154**
Ribble Cl. IG8: Wfd G 6F **37**
Ribblesdale Av. N11 . . . . .6K **31**
    UB5: N'olt 6F **59**
Ribblesdale Ho. NW6 . . . . .1J **81**
    (off Kilburn Vale)
Ribblesdale Rd. N8 . . . . .4K **47**
    SW16 . . . . .6F **137**
Ribbon Dance M. SE5 . . . . .1D **120**
Ribbons Wlk. E20 . . . . .5E **68**
Ribchester Av. UB6: G'frd 3K **77**
Ribston Cl. BR2: Brom 1D **172**
Ricardo Path SE28 . . . . .1C **108**
Ricardo St. E14 . . . . .6D **86**
Ricards Rd. SW19 . . . . .5H **135**
Riccall Ct. NW9 . . . . .1A **44**
    (off Pageant Av.)
Rice Pde. BR5: Pet W 5H **161**
Riceyman Ho. WC1 . . . . .2J **7**
    (off Lloyd Baker St.)
Richard Anderson Ct. SE14 . . . . . . .7K **103**
    (off Monson Rd.)
Richard Burbidge Mans. SW13 . . . . .6E **98**
    (off Brasenose Dr.)
Richard Burton Ct. IG9: Buck H 2F **37**
    (off Palmerston Rd.)
Richard Challoner Sports Cen. 7K **151**
Richard Cl. SE18 . . . . .4C **106**
Richard Fell Ho. E12 . . . . .4E **70**
    (off Walton Rd.)
Richard Fielden Ho. E1 . . . . .3A **86**
Richard Ho. SE16 . . . . .4J **103**
    (off Silwood St.)
Richard Ho. Dr. E16 . . . . .6B **88**
    (off Cornwall St.)
Richard Neale Ho. E1 . . . . .7H **85**
    (off Plumstead High St.)
Richard Neve Ho. SE18 . . . . .4J **107**
    (off Salway Rd.)
Richard Robert Residence, The E15 . .6F **69**
    (off Salway Rd.)
Richard Ryan Pl. RM9: Dag 1E **90**
Richards Av. RM7: Rom 6J **55**
Richards Cl. HA1: Harr 5A **42**
    UB3: Harl 6F **93**
    UB10: Hil 1C **74**
    WD23: Bush 1C **26**
Richards Fld. KT19: Ewe 7K **163**
Richard Sharples Ct. SM2: Sutt 7A **166**
Richardson Cl. E8 . . . . .1F **85**
Richardson Ct. SW4 . . . . .2J **119**
    (off Studley Rd.)
Richardson Gdns. RM10: Dag 6H **73**
Richardson Rd. E15 . . . . .2G **87**
Richardson's M. W1 . . . . .4A **6**
Richards Pl. E17 . . . . .3C **50**
    SW3 . . . . .3D **16** (4C **100**)

Richard St. E1 . . . . .6H **85**
Richbell WC1 .5F **7**
    (off Boswell St.)
Richbell Pl. WC1 . . . . .5G **7** (5K **83**)
Richborne Ter. SW8 . . . . .7K **101**
Richborough Ho. SE15 . . . . .6J **103**
    (off Sharratt St.)
Richborough Rd. NW2 . . . . .4G **63**
Richbourne Ct. W1 . . . . .7D **4**
    (off Harrowby St.)
Richens Cl. TW3: Houn 2H **113**
Riches Rd. IG1: Ilf 2G **71**
Richfield Rd.
    WD23: Bush 1B **26**
Richford Ga. W6 . . . . .3E **98**
Richford Rd. E15 . . . . .1H **87**
Richford St. W6 . . . . .2E **98**
Rich Ind. Est. SE1 . . . . .3E **102**
    SE15 . . . . .6H **103**
Richland Ho. SE15 . . . . .1G **121**
    (off Goldsmith Rd.)
Richlands Av. KT17: Ewe 4C **164**
Rich La. SW5 .5K **99**
Richman Ho. SE8 . . . . .5B **104**
    (off Grove St.)
Richmix Sq. E1 . . . . .3K **9**
    (off Bethnal Grn. Rd.)
RICHMOND .5D **114**
**Richmond, The American International
    University in London
    Kensington Campus, Ansdell Street**
    . . . . .3K **99**
    (off Ansdell St.)
    Kensington Campus, St Albans Grove
    . . . . .3K **99**
    Kensington Campus, Young Street
    . . . . .2K **99**
    Richmond Hill Campus 7E **114**
Richmond & London Scottish RUFC
    . . . . .3D **114**
Richmond Athletic Ground 3D **114**
Richmond Av. E4 . . . . .5A **36**
    N1 . . . . .1K **83**
    NW10 . . . . .6E **62**
    SW20 .1G **153**
    TW14: Felt 6G **111**
    UB10: Hil 6D **56**
Richmond Bri. TW1: Twick 6D **114**
Richmond Bldgs. W1 . . . . . .1C **12** (6H **83**)
RICHMOND CIRCUS 4E **114**
Richmond Cl. E17 . . . . .6B **50**
Richmond Cotts. W14 . . . . .4G **99**
    (off Hammersmith Rd.)
Richmond Ct. CR4: Mitc 3B **154**
    E8 . . . . .7H **67**
    (off Mare St.)
    HA9: Wemb 3F **61**
    N11 . . . . .6K **31**
    (off Pickering Gdns.)
    NW6 . . . . .7F **63**
    (off Willesden La.)
    SW1 . . . . .7F **11**
    (off Sloane St.)
    W14 . . . . .4G **99**
    (off Hammersmith Rd.)
Richmond Cres. E4 . . . . .5A **36**
    N1 . . . . .1K **83**
    N9 . . . . .1B **34**
Richmond Cricket Ground 3E **114**
Richmond Dr. IG8: Wfd G 7K **37**
    TW17: Shep 6F **147**
Richmond Gdns. HA3: Hrw W 7E **26**
    NW4 . . . . .5C **44**
Richmond Golf Course 2E **132**
Richmond Grn. CRO: Bedd 3J **167**
Richmond Gro. KT5: Surb 6F **151**
    N1 . . . . .7B **66**
    (not continuous)
Richmond Hill TW10: Rich 6E **114**
Richmond Hill Ct.
    TW10: Rich 6E **114**

Richmond Ho. E3 . . . . .5C **86**
    (off Bow Common La.)
    NW1 . . . . .1K **5**
    (off Park Village E.)
    SE17 . . . . .5D **102**
    (off Portland St.)
Richmond Mans. SW5 . . . . .5K **99**
    (off Old Brompton Rd.)
    TW1: Twick 6D **114**
Richmond M. TW11: Tedd 5K **131**
    W1 . . . . .1C **12** (6H **83**)
Richmond Pde. TW1: Twick 6C **114**
    (off Richmond Rd.)
Richmond Pk. Golf Course 7A **116**
Richmond Pk. (National Nature Reserve)
    . . . . .1G **133**
Richmond Pk. Rd. KT2: King T 1E **150**
    SW14 . . . . .5J **115**
Richmond Pl. SE18 . . . . .4G **107**
Richmond Rd. CRO: Bedd 3J **167**
    CR7: Thor H 3B **156**
    E4 . . . . .1A **36**
    E7 . . . . .5K **69**
    E8 . . . . .7F **67**
    E11 . . . . .2F **69**
    EN5: New Bar 5E **20**
    IG1: Ilf 3G **71**
    KT2: King T 5D **132**
    N2 . . . . .2A **46**
    N11 . . . . .6D **32**
    N15 . . . . .6E **48**
    SW20 . . . . .1D **152**
    TW1: Twick 7B **114**
    TW7: Isle 3A **114**
    W5 . . . . .2E **96**
Richmond St. E13 . . . . .2J **87**
Richmond Ter. SW1 . . . . . .6E **12** (2J **101**)
Richmond Theatre 4D **114**
Richmond Way E11 . . . . .2J **69**
    W12 . . . . .2F **99**
    W14 . . . . .2F **99**
Richmount Gdns. SE3 . . . . .3J **123**
Rich St. E14 .7B **86**
Rickard Cl. NW4 . . . . .4D **44**
    SW2 . . . . .1A **138**
Rickards Cl. KT6: Surb 2E **162**
Rickett St. SW6 . . . . .6J **99**
Rickman Ho. E1 . . . . .3J **85**
    (off Rickman St.)
Rickman St. E1 . . . . .4J **85**
Rickmansworth Rd. HA5: Pinn 2K **39**
    HA6: Nwood 1F **39**
Rick Roberts Way E15 . . . . .1E **86**
Rickthorne Rd. N19 . . . . .2J **65**
Rickyard Path SE9 . . . . .4C **124**
Riddell Ct. SE5 . . . . .5F **103**
    (off Albany Rd.)
Ridding La. UB6: G'frd 5K **59**
Riddons Rd. SE12 . . . . .3A **142**
Ride, The EN3: Pond E 3D **24**
    TW8: Bford 5B **96**
Rideout St. SE18 . . . . .4D **106**
Rider Cl. DA15: Sidc 6J **125**
Rideway Dr. W3 . . . . .3G **97**
Ridgdale St. E3 . . . . .2D **86**
Ridge, The BR6: Orp 2H **173**
    DA5: Bexl 7F **127**
    EN5: Barn 5C **20**
    KT5: Surb 5G **151**
    TW2: Whitt 7H **113**
Ridge Av. N21 . . . . .7H **23**
Ridgebrook Rd. SE3 . . . . .3B **124**
Ridge Cl. NW4 . . . . .2F **45**
    NW9 . . . . .4K **43**
    SE28 . . . . .2H **107**
Ridge Ct. SE22 . . . . .7G **121**
Ridge Crest EN2: Enf 1E **22**
Ridgecroft Cl. DA5: Bexl 1J **145**
Ridge Hill NW11 . . . . .1G **63**
Ridgemead Cl. N14 . . . . .2D **32**
Ridgemont Gdns. HA8: Edg 4D **28**

Ridgeburn Av. CRO: C'don 1K **169**
Ridgemount Cl. SE20 . . . . .7H **139**
Ridgemount Gdns. EN2: Enf 3G **23**
Ridge Rd. CR4: Mitc 7F **137**
    N8 . . . . .6K **47**
    N21 . . . . .1H **33**
    NW2 . . . . .3H **63**
    SM3: Sutt 1G **165**
    (not continuous)
Ridges Yd. CRO: C'don 3B **168**
Ridgeview Cl. EN5: Barn 6A **20**
Ridgeview Rd. N20 . . . . .3E **30**
Ridge Way SE19 . . . . .6E **138**
    TW13: Hanw 3C **130**
Ridgeway BR2: Hayes 2J **171**
    IG8: Wfd G 4F **37**
Ridgeway, The CRO: Wadd 3K **167**
    E4 . . . . .2J **35**
    EN2: Enf .1E **22**
    HA2: Harr 5D **40**
    (not continuous)
    HA3: Kenton 6C **42**
    HA4: Ruis 7J **39**
    HA7: Stan 6H **27**
    KT12: Walt T 7H **147**
    N3 . . . . .7E **30**
    N11 . . . . .4J **31**
    N14 . . . . .2D **32**
    NW7 . . . . .3H **29**
    NW9 . . . . .4K **43**
    NW11 . . . . .7G **45**
    W3 . . . . .3G **97**
Ridgeway Av. EN4: E Barn 6J **21**
Ridgeway Cres. BR6: Orp 3J **173**
Ridgeway Cres. Gdns. BR6: Orp 2J **173**
Ridgeway Dr. BR1: Brom 4K **141**
Ridgeway E. DA15: Sidc 5K **125**
Ridgeway Gdns. IG4: Ilf 5C **52**
    N6 . . . . .7G **47**
Ridgeway Rd. TW7: Isle 7J **95**
Ridgeway Rd. Nth. TW7: Isle 6J **95**
Ridgeway Wlk. UB5: N'olt 6C **58**
    (off Cowings Mead)
Ridgeway W. DA15: Sidc 5J **125**
Ridgewell Cl. N1 . . . . .1C **84**
    RM10: Dag 1H **91**
    SE26 . . . . .4B **140**
Ridgmount Gdns. WC1 . . . . . .5C **6** (5H **83**)
Ridgmount Pl. WC1 . . . . .5C **6** (5H **83**)
Ridgmount Rd. SW18 . . . . .5K **117**
Ridgmount St. WC1 . . . . .5C **6** (5H **83**)
Ridgway SW19 . . . . .7E **134**
    TW10: Rich 6E **114**
Ridgway, The SM2: Sutt 7B **166**
Ridgway Cl. SW19 . . . . .6F **135**
Ridgway Gdns. SW19 . . . . .7F **135**
Ridgway Pl. SW19 . . . . .6G **135**
Ridgway Rd. SW9 . . . . .3B **120**
Ridgwell Rd. E16 . . . . .5A **88**
Ridings Av. N21 . . . . .4G **23**
Ridings Cl. N6 . . . . .7G **47**
Ridler Rd. EN1: Enf 1K **23**
Ridley Av. W13 . . . . .3B **96**
Ridley Cl. IG11: Bark 7K **71**
Ridley Ct. SW16 . . . . .6J **137**
Ridley Ho. SW1 . . . . .2D **18**
    (off Monck St.)
Ridley Rd. BR2: Brom 3H **159**
    DA16: Well 1B **126**
    E7 . . . . .4A **70**
    E8 . . . . .5F **67**
    NW10 . . . . .2C **80**
    SW19 . . . . .7K **135**

Ridsdale Rd. SE20 . . . . .7H **139**
Riefield Rd. SE9 . . . . .4G **125**
Riesco Dr. CR0: C'don 6J **169**
Riffel Rd. NW2 . . . . .5E **62**
Rifle Ct. SE11 . . . . .7K **19** (6A **102**)
Rifle St. E14 . . . . .5D **86**
Riga M. E1 . . . . .7K **9**
Rigault Rd. SW6 . . . . .2G **117**
Rigby Cl. CR0: Wadd 3A **168**
Rigby La. UB3: Hayes 2E **92**
Rigby M. IG1: Ilf 2E **70**
Rigden St. E14 . . . . .6D **86**
Rigeley Rd. NW10 . . . . .3C **80**
Rigg App. E10 . . . . .1K **67**
Rigge Pl. SW4 . . . . .4H **119**
Riley Ho. E3 . . . . .4C **86**
                         (off Ireton St.)
   SW10 . . . . .7B **100**
                         (off Riley St.)
Riley Rd. EN3: Enf W 1D **24**
   SE1 . . . . .7H **15** (3F **103**)
Riley St. SW10 . . . . .6B **100**
Rill Ct. IG11: Bark 2G **89**
                       (off Spring Pl.)
Rill Ho. SE5 . . . . .7D **102**
                       (off Harris St.)
Rima Ho. SW3 . . . . .7A **16**
                      (off Callow St.)
Rinaldo Rd. SW12 . . . . .7F **119**
Ring, The SW7 . . . . . . .7B **10** (2B **100**)
   W2 . . . . .2C **10** (7B **82**)
Ring Cl. BR1: Brom 7K **141**
Ring Cl. SE1 . . . . .2B **102**
                        (off The Cut)
Ringcroft St. N7 . . . . .5A **66**
Ringers Ct. BR1: Brom 3J **159**
                     (off Ringers Rd.)
Ringers Rd. BR1: Brom 3J **159**
Ringford Rd. SW18 . . . . .5H **117**
Ring Ho. E1 . . . . .7J **85**
                       (off Sage St.)
Ringles Ct. E6 . . . . .1D **88**
Ringlet Cl. E16 . . . . .5K **87**
Ringlewell Cl. EN1: Enf 2C **24**
Ringmer Av. SW6 . . . . .1G **117**
Ringmer Gdns. N19 . . . . .2J **65**
Ringmer Pl. N21 . . . . .5J **23**
Ringmer Way BR1: Brom 5C **160**
Ringmore Ri. SE23 . . . . .7H **121**
Ringmore Vw. SE23 . . . . .7H **121**
Ring Rd. W12 . . . . .1E **98**
                 (not continuous)
Ringsfield Ho. SE17 . . . . .5C **102**
                      (off Bronti Cl.)
Ringside Ct. SE28 . . . . .1C **108**
Ringslade Rd. N22 . . . . .2K **47**
Ringstead Rd. SE6 . . . . .7D **122**
   SM1: Sutt 4B **166**
Ring Way N11 . . . . .6B **32**
Ringway UB2: S'hall 5B **94**
Ringwold Cl. BR3: Beck 7A **140**
Ringwood Av. CR0: C'don 7J **155**
   N2 . . . . .2D **46**
Ringwood Cl. HA5: Pinn 3A **40**
Ringwood Gdns. E14 . . . . .4C **104**
   SW15 . . . . .1C **134**
Ringwood Rd. E17 . . . . .6B **50**
Ringwood Way N21 . . . . .1G **33**
   TW12: Hamp H 4E **130**
Rio Cinema
   Dalston 5E **66**
             (off Kingsland High St.)
Ripley Bldgs. SE1 . . . . .6B **14**
                   (off Rushworth St.)
Ripley Cl. BR1: Brom 5D **160**
   CR0: New Ad 6E **170**
Ripley Ct. CR4: Mitc 2B **154**
Ripley Gdns. SM1: Sutt 4A **166**
                   (not continuous)
   SW14 . . . . .3K **115**

Ripley Ho. SW1 . . . . .7A **18**
                   (off Churchill Gdns.)
Ripley M. E11 . . . . .6G **51**
Ripley Rd. DA17: Belv 4G **109**
   E16 . . . . .6A **88**
   EN2: Enf 1H **23**
   IG3: Ilf 2K **71**
   TW12: Hamp 7E **130**
Ripley's Believe It or Not 3C **12**
               (within London Pavilion)
Ripley Vs. W5 . . . . .6C **78**
Ripon Cl. UB5: N'olt 5E **58**
Ripon Ct. N11 . . . . .6K **31**
                   (off Ribblesdale Av.)
Ripon Gdns. IG1: Ilf 6C **52**
   KT9: Chess 5D **162**
Ripon Rd. N9 . . . . .7C **24**
   N17 . . . . .3D **48**
   SE18 . . . . .6F **107**
Rippersley Rd. DA16: Well 1A **126**
Ripple Nature Reserve, The 3B **90**
Ripple Rd. IG11: Bark, Dag 7G **71**
   RM9: Dag 1B **90**
RIPPLESIDE 1B **90**
Rippleside Commercial Est.
   IG11: Bark 2C **90**
Ripplevale Gro. N1 . . . . .7K **65**
Rippolson Rd. SE18 . . . . .5K **107**
Ripston Rd. TW15: Ashf 5F **129**
Risborough Cl. N10 . . . . .3F **47**
Risborough Dr. KT4: Wor Pk 7C **152**
Risborough Ho. NW8 . . . . .3D **4**
                      (off Mallory St.)
Risborough St. SE1 . . . . .6B **14** (2B **102**)
Risdon Ho. SE16 . . . . .2J **103**
                      (off Risdon St.)
Risdon St. SE16 . . . . .3J **103**
Rise, The DA5: Bexl 7C **126**
   E11 . . . . .5J **51**
   HA0: Wemb 5A **60**
   HA8: Edg 5C **28**
   IG9: Buck H 1G **37**
   N13 . . . . .4F **33**
   NW7 . . . . .6G **29**
   NW10 . . . . .4K **61**
   UB6: G'frd 5A **60**
   UB10: Hil 2B **74**
Risedale Rd. DA7: Bex 3J **127**
Riseholme Ct. E9 . . . . .6B **68**
Riseldine Rd. SE23 . . . . .6A **122**
RISE PARK 2K **55**
Rise Pk. Pde. RM1: Rom 2K **55**
Risinghill St. N1 . . . . .2K **83**
Risingholme Cl. HA3: Hrw W 1J **41**
   WD23: Bush 1A **26**
Risingholme Rd. HA3: Hrw W . . .2J **41**
Risings, The E17 . . . . .4F **51**
Rising Sun Ct. EC1 . . . . .5B **8**
Risley Av. N17 . . . . .1C **48**
Rita Rd. SW8 . . . . .6J **101**
Ritches Rd. N15 . . . . .5C **48**
Ritchie Ho. E14 . . . . .6F **87**
                       (off Blair St.)
   N19 . . . . .1H **65**
   SE16 . . . . .3J **103**
                    (off Howland Est.)
Ritchie Rd. CR0: C'don 6H **157**
Ritchie St. N1 . . . . .2A **84**
Ritchings Av. E17 . . . . .4A **50**
Ritherdon Rd. SW17 . . . . .2E **136**
Ritson Ho. N1 . . . . .1K **83**
                      (off Barnsbury Est.)
Ritson Rd. E8 . . . . .6G **67**
Ritter St. SE18 . . . . .6E **106**
Ritz Pde. W5 . . . . .4F **79**
Ritzy Picturehouse 4A **120**
                 (off Coldharbour La.)
Riva Building, The SE13 . . . . . . .4F **123**
Rivaz Pl. E9 . . . . .6J **67**
                       (not continuous)
Riven Ct. W2 . . . . .6K **81**
                      (off Inverness Ter.)

Rivenhall Gdns. E18 . . . . .4H **51**
River App. HA8: Edg 1J **43**
RIVER ASH ESTATE 7H **147**
River Av. KT7: T Ditt 7A **150**
   N13 . . . . .3G **33**
River Av. Ind. Est. N13 . . . . .5F **33**
River Bank KT7: T Ditt 5K **149**
   KT8: E Mos 3J **149**
   N21 . . . . .7H **23**
   TW12: Hamp 2G **149**
Riverbank Rd. BR1: Brom 3J **141**
Riverbank Way TW8: Bford 6C **96**
River Barge Cl. E14 . . . . .2E **104**
River Brent Bus. Pk. W7 . . . . . . .3J **95**
River Cl. E11 . . . . .6A **52**
   HA4: Ruis 6H **39**
   UB2: S'hall 2G **95**
River Ct. KT6: Surb 5D **150**
                    (off Portsmouth Rd.)
   SE1 . . . . .3A **14** (7B **84**)
   TW17: Shep 7E **146**
Rivercourt Rd. W6 . . . . .4D **98**
River Crane Way TW13: Hanw . . .2D **130**
                   (off Watermill Way)
Riverdale SE13 . . . . .4E **122**
Riverdale Cl. IG11: Bark 4B **90**
Riverdale Ct. N21 . . . . .5J **23**
Riverdale Dr. SW18 . . . . .1K **135**
Riverdale Gdns. TW1: Twick 6C **114**
Riverdale Rd. DA5: Bexl 7F **127**
   DA8: Erith 5H **109**
   SE18 . . . . .5K **107**
   TW1: Twick 6A **114**
   TW13: Hanw 4C **130**
Riverdale Shop. Cen. SE13 . . . . .3E **122**
Riverdene HA8: Edg 3D **28**
Riverdene Rd. IG1: Ilf 3E **70**
Riverfleet WC1 . . . . .1F **7**
                     (off Birkenhead St.)
Riverford Ho. W2 . . . . .5J **81**
                (off Westbourne Pk. Rd.)
River Front EN1: Enf 3K **23**
River Gdns. SM5: Cars 2E **166**
   TW14: Felt 5K **111**
River Gdns. Bus. Cen. TW14: Felt . .5K **111**
River Gro. Pk. BR3: Beck 1B **158**
Riverhead Cl. E17 . . . . .2K **49**
River Hgts. E15 . . . . .1E **86**
   N17 . . . . .1F **49**
Riverhill KT4: Wor Pk 2K **163**
Riverhill M. KT4: Wor Pk 3K **163**
Riverhill Mobile Home Pl.
   KT4: Wor Pk 2K **163**
Riverholme Dr. KT19: Ewe 7K **163**
Riverhope Mans. SE18 . . . . .3C **106**
River Ho. SE26 . . . . .3H **139**
Riverhouse Barn 7H **147**
River La. TW10: Ham 7D **114**
Riverleigh Ct. E4 . . . . .5G **35**
Riverlight Quay SW8 . . . . .6G **101**
River Lodge SW1 . . . . .7B **18**
                       (off Grosvenor Rd.)
Rivermead KT1: King T 5D **150**
   KT8: E Mos 3G **149**
Rivermead Cl. TW11: Tedd 5B **132**
Rivermead Ct. SW6 . . . . .3H **117**
Rivermead Ho. E9 . . . . .5A **68**
   TW16: Sun 3A **148**
                       (off Thames St.)
Rivermead Rd. N18 . . . . .6E **34**
River Meads Av. TW2: Twick 3E **130**
River Mt. KT12: Walt T 7H **147**
Rivernook Cl. KT12: Walt T 5A **148**
River Pk. Gdns. BR2: Brom 7F **141**
River Pk. Rd. N22 . . . . .2K **47**
River Pl. N1 . . . . .7C **66**
River Reach TW11: Tedd 5C **132**
River Rd. IG9: Buck H 1H **37**
   IG11: Bark 2J **89**
River Rd. Bus. Pk. IG11: Bark . . .3K **89**
Riverside Gdns. N22 . . . . .1A **48**

Riversdale Rd. KT7: T Ditt 5A **150**
   N5 . . . . .3B **66**
   RM5: Col R 1H **55**
Riversfield Rd. EN1: Enf 3K **23**
Rivers Ho. TW7: Isle 4B **114**
                      (off Richmond Rd.)
   TW8: Bford 5G **97**
                       (off Aitman Dr.)
Riverside E3 . . . . .1C **86**
   NW4 . . . . .7D **44**
   SE7 . . . . .3K **105**
   SW11 . . . . .7C **100**
   TW1: Twick 1B **132**
   TW9: Rich 5D **114**
   TW10: Rich 5D **114**
   TW16: Sun 2B **148**
   TW17: Shep 7G **147**
   W6 . . . . .6E **98**
   WC1 . . . . .1F **7**
                       (off Birkenhead St.)
Riverside, The KT8: E Mos 3H **149**
Riverside Apartments N4 . . . . . . .7D **48**
                       (off Goodchild Rd.)
   N13 . . . . .5E **32**
Riverside Arts Cen. 3A **148**
Riverside Av. KT8: E Mos 5H **149**
Riverside Bus. Cen. SW18 . . . . .1K **135**
Riverside Bus. Pk. SW19 . . . . . .1A **154**
Riverside Cl. E5 . . . . .1J **67**
   KT1: King T 4D **150**
   RM1: Rom 4K **55**
   SM6: Wall 3F **167**
   W7 . . . . .4J **77**
Riverside Cotts. IG11: Bark 2H **89**
Riverside Ct. E4 . . . . .6H **25**
   SE3 . . . . .4H **123**
   SW8 . . . . .7D **18** (6H **101**)
   TW7: Isle 3A **114**
                      (off Woodlands Rd.)
   TW14: Felt 7G **111**
Riverside Dr. CR4: Mitc 5C **154**
   NW11 . . . . .6G **45**
   TW10: Ham 3B **132**
   W4 . . . . .7K **97**
Riverside Gdns. EN2: Enf 2H **23**
   HA0: Wemb 2E **78**
   N3 . . . . .3G **45**
   W6 . . . . .5D **98**
Riverside Ho. N1 . . . . .7C **66**
                      (off Canonbury St.)
Riverside Ind. Est. EN3: Pond E . .6F **25**
   IG11: Bark 3A **90**
Riverside Mans. E1 . . . . .1J **103**
                       (off Milk Yd.)
Riverside M. CR0: Bedd 3J **167**
Riverside Pl. N11 . . . . .3B **32**
   TW19: Stanw 6A **110**
Riverside Rd. DA14: Sidc 3E **144**
   E15 . . . . .2E **86**
   N15 . . . . .6G **49**
   SW17 . . . . .4K **135**
   TW19: Stanw 5A **110**
Riverside Studios 5E **98**
Riverside Twr. SW6 . . . . .2A **118**
                     (off The Boulevard)
Riverside Vs. KT6: Surb 6C **150**
Riverside Wlk. BR4: W W'ck 1D **170**
   EN5: Barn 6A **20**
                       (not continuous)
   KT1: King T 3D **150**
   N12 . . . . .6D **30**
                       (not continuous)
   N20 . . . . .3E **30**
   SE10 . . . . .3G **105**
                    (Morden Wharf Rd.)
   SE10 . . . . .2F **105**
                       (Tunnel Av.)
   SW6 . . . . .3G **117**
   TW7: Isle 3J **113**
   W4 . . . . .6B **98**
                      (off Chiswick Wharf)

Riverside Wharf E3 . . . . .1C 86
Riverside Works
  IG11: Bark 7F 71
Riverside Yd. SW17 . . . . .4A 136
Riverstone Cl. HA2: Harr 1H 59
Riverstone Ct. KT2: King T 1F 151
River St. EC1 . . . . .1J 7 (3A 84)
River St. M. EC1 . . . . .1J 7
River Ter. W6 . . . . .5E 98
  WC2 . . . . .3G 13
Riverton Cl. W9 . . . . .3H 81
River Vw. EN2: Enf 3H 23
River Vw. Ct. E14 . . . . .3B 104
River Vw. Gdns.
  TW1: Twick 2K 131
Riverview Gdns. SW13 . . . . .6D 98
Riverview Gro. W4 . . . . .6H 97
River Vw. Hgts. SE16 . . . . .2G 103
     (off Bermondsey Wall W.)
Riverview Pk. SE6 . . . . .2C 140
Riverview Rd. KT19: Ewe 4J 163
  W4 . . . . .7H 97
Riverview Wlk. SE6 . . . . .3B 140
River Wlk. E4 . . . . .7K 35
  KT12: Walt T 6J 147
  SW6 .2A 118
  W6 . . . . .7E 98
Riverwalk SW1 . . . . .5J 101
Riverwalk Bus. Pk. EN3: Brim 4G 25
River Wlk. Rd. EN3: Brim 4G 25
River Way BR3: Beck 1C 170
  KT19: Ewe 5K 163
  SE10 .3H 105
  TW2: Twick 2F 131
Riverway N13 . . . . .5F 33
River Wharf Bus. Pk. DA17: Belv . .1K 109
Rixsen Rd. E12 . . . . .5C 70
Rixon Ho. SE18 . . . . .6F 107
Rixon St. N7 . . . . .3A 66
Roach Rd. E3 . . . . .7C 68
Roads Pl. N19 . . . . .2J 65
Roan Gdns. CR4: Mitc 1D 154
Roan St. SE10 . . . . .6E 104
Robarts Cl. HA5: Eastc 5K 39
Robbins Hall EN3: Pond E 6E 24
Robb Rd. HA7: Stan 6F 27
Robert Adam St. W1 . . . .7G 5 (6E 82)
Roberta St. E2 . . . . .3G 85
Robert Bell Ho. SE16 . . . . .4G 103
     (off Rouel Rd.)
Robert Burns Ho. N17 . . . . .7C 34
     (off Northumberland Pk.)
Robert Burns M. SE24 . . . . .5B 120
Robert Clack Leisure Cen. 1G 73
Robert Cl. W9 . . . . .4A 4 (4A 82)
Robert Ct. SE15 . . . . .2G 121
Robert Dashwood Way
  SE17 .4C 102
Robert Gentry Ho. W14 . . . . .5G 99
     (off Gledstanes Rd.)
Robert Jones Ho. SE16 . . . . .4G 103
     (off Rouel Rd.)
Robert Keen Cl. SE15 . . . . .1G 121
Robert Lowe Cl. SE14 . . . . .7K 103
Robert Morton Ho. NW8 . . . . .7A 64
Roberton Dr. BR1: Brom 1A 160

Robert Owen Ho. E2 . . . . .1K 9
     (off Baroness Rd.)
  N22 . . . . .1A 48
     (off Progress Way)
  SW6 .1F 117
Robert Runcie Ct. SW2 . . . . .4K 119
Roberts All. W5 . . . . .2D 96
Robertsbridge Rd. SM5: Cars 1A 166
Roberts Cl. CR7: Thor H 3D 156
  IG11: Bark 6G 71
     (off Tanner St.)
  SE9 . . . . .1H 143
  SE16 .2K 103
  SM3: Cheam 7F 165
  UB7: Yiew 1A 92
Roberts Ct. KT9: Chess 5D 162
  N1 . . . . .1B 84
     (off Essex Rd.)
  NW10 .6A 62
  SE20 . . . . .1J 157
     (off Maple Rd.)
Roberts Gro. SW17 . . . . .5C 136
Robertson Rd. E16 . . . . .5J 87
Robertson St. SW8 . . . . .3F 119
Roberts Pl. EC1 . . . . .3K 7 (4A 84)
  RM10: Dag 6G 73
Roberts Rd. DA17: Belv 5G 109
  E17 . . . . .1D 50
Robert St. CRO: C'don 3C 168
  E16 . . . . .1F 107
  NW1 . . . . .2K 5 (3F 83)
  SE18 .5H 107
     (not continuous)
  WC2 . . . . .3F 13 (7J 83)
Robert Sutton Ho. E1 . . . . .6J 85
     (off Tarling St.)
Robeson St. E3 . . . . .5B 86
Robina Cl. DA6: Bex 4D 126
  HA6: Nwood 1H 39
Robin Cl. NW7 . . . . .3F 29
  RM5: Col R 1K 55
  TW12: Hamp 5C 130
Robin Ct. E14 . . . . .2E 104
  SE16 .4G 103
  SM6: Wall 5G 167
Robin Cres. E6 . . . . .5B 88
Robin Gro. HA3: Kenton 6F 43
  N6 . . . . .2E 64
  TW8: Bford 6C 96
Robin Hill Dr. BR7: Chst 6C 142
ROBIN HOOD 3A 134
Robinhood Cl. CR4: Mitc 3G 155
Robin Hood Ct. EC4 . . . . .7K 7
     (off Shoe La.)
Robin Hood Dr. HA3: Hrw W 7E 26
Robin Hood Gdns. E14 . . . . .7E 86
     (off Woolmore St., not continuous)
Robin Hood Grn. BR5: St M Cry . . .5K 161
Robin Hood La. DA6: Bex 5E 126
  E14 . . . . .7E 86
  SM1: Sutt 5J 165
  SW15 .3A 134
Robinhood La. CR4: Mitc 3G 155
Robin Hood Rd. SW19 . . . . .5C 134
Robin Hood Way SW15 . . . . .3A 134
  SW20 .3A 134
  UB6: G'frd 6K 59
Robin Ho. NW8 . . . . .2C 82
     (off Newcourt St.)
Robin Howard Dance Theatre 2D 6
     (off Duke's Rd.)
Robinia Cl. SE20 . . . . .1G 157
     (off Sycamore Gro.)
Robinia Cres. E10 . . . . .2D 68
Robin La. NW4 . . . . .3F 45
Robins Cl. BR3: Beck 2F 159
  CR2: S Croy 4E 168
     (off Birdhurst Rd.)
  SE12 .3A 142

Robinscroft M. SE10 . . . . .1E 122
Robins Gro. BR4: W W'ck 3J 171
Robinson Cl. E11 . . . . .3G 69
  EN2: Enf 3H 23
Robinson Ct. CR7: Thor H 6B 156
  N1 . . . . .1B 84
     (off St Mary's Path)
  TW9: Rich 4F 115
Robinson Cres. WD23: B Hea 1B 26
Robinson Ho. E14 . . . . .5C 86
     (off Selsey St.)
  W10 . . . . .6F 81
     (off Bramley Rd.)
Robinson Rd. E2 . . . . .2J 85
  RM10: Dag 4G 73
  SW17 .6C 136
Robinson's Cl. W13 . . . . .5A 78
Robinson St. SW3 . . . . . . .7E 16 (6D 100)
Robinswood Gdns. E17 . . . . .1B 50
Robinswood Rd. N5 . . . . .5B 66
Robinwood Gro. UB8: Hil 4B 74
Robinwood Pl. SW15 . . . . .4K 133
Rob Pasco La. RM9: Dag 4E 90
Robsart St. SW9 . . . . .2K 119
Robson Av. NW10 . . . . .7C 62
Robson Cl. E6 . . . . .6C 88
  EN2: Enf 2G 23
Robson Rd. SE27 . . . . .3C 138
Roby Ho. EC1 . . . . .3C 8
     (off Mitchell St.)
Roca Ct. E11 . . . . .5J 51
Rocastle Rd. SE4 . . . . .5A 122
Roch Av. HA8: Edg 2F 43
Rochdale Rd. E17 . . . . .7C 50
  SE2 . . . . .5B 108
Rochdale Way SE8 . . . . .7C 104
     (not continuous)
Roche Ho. E14 . . . . .7B 86
     (off Beccles St.)
Rochelle Cl. SW11 . . . . .4B 118
Rochelle St. E2 . . . . .2J 9 (3F 85)
     (not continuous)
Rochemont Wlk. E8 . . . . .1G 85
     (off Pownall Rd.)
Roche Rd. SW16 . . . . .1K 155
Rochester Av. BR1: Brom 2K 159
  E13 . . . . .1A 88
  TW13: Felt 2H 129
Rochester Cl. DA15: Sidc 6B 126
  EN1: Enf 1K 23
  SW16 .7J 137
Rochester Ct. E2 . . . . .4H 85
     (off Wilmot St.)
  NW1 . . . . .7G 65
     (off Rochester Sq.)
Rochester Dr. DA5: Bexl 6F 127
  HA5: Pinn 5B 40
Rochester Gdns. CRO: C'don 3E 168
  IG1: Ilf .7D 52
Rochester Ho. SE1 . . . . .7F 15
     (off Manciple St.)
  SE15 . . . . .6J 103
     (off Sharratt St.)
Rochester M. NW1 . . . . .7G 65
  W5 . . . . .4C 96
Rochester Pde. TW13: Felt 2J 129
Rochester Pl. NW1 . . . . .6G 65
Rochester Rd. HA6: Nwood 3H 39
  NW1 . . . . .6G 65
  SM5: Cars 4D 166
Rochester Row SW1 . . . . .3B 18 (4G 101)
Rochester Sq. NW1 . . . . .7G 65
Rochester St. SW1 . . . . . . .2C 18 (3H 101)
Rochester Ter. NW1 . . . . .6G 65
Rochester Wlk. SE1 . . . . . .4E 14 (1D 102)
Rochester Way DA1: Dart 7K 127
  SE3 . . . . .1K 123
  SE9 . . . . .2A 124
Rochester Way Relief Rd. SE3 . . . .1K 123
  SE9 . . . . .4A 124
Roche Wlk. SM5: Cars 6B 154

Rochford N17 . . . . .2E 48
     (off Griffin Rd.)
Rochford Av. RM6: Chad H 5C 54
Rochford Cl. E6 . . . . .2B 88
Rochford Wlk. E8 . . . . .7G 67
Rochford Way CRO: C'don 6J 155
Rochfort Ho. SE8 . . . . .5B 104
Rock Av. SW14 . . . . .3K 115
Rockbourne M. SE23 . . . . .1K 139
Rockbourne Rd. SE23 . . . . .1K 139
Rock Cl. CR4: Mitc 2B 154
Rockell's Pl. SE22 . . . . .6H 121
Rockfield Ho. NW4 . . . . .4F 45
     (off Belle Vue Est.)
  SE10 .6E 104
     (off Welland St.)
Rockford Av. UB6: G'frd 2A 78
Rock Gdns. RM10: Dag 5H 73
Rock Gro. Way SE16 . . . . .4G 103
     (not continuous)
Rockhall Rd. NW2 . . . . .4F 63
Rockhall Way NW2 . . . . .3F 63
Rockhampton Cl. SE27 . . . . .4A 138
Rockhampton Rd. CR2: S Croy 5E 168
  SE27 .4A 138
Rock Hill SE26 . . . . .4F 139
Rockingham Cl. SW15 . . . . .4B 116
Rockingham St. SE1 . . . . .3C 102
Rockland Rd. SW15 . . . . .4G 117
Rocklands Dr. CR2: S Croy 6D 168
  HA7: Stan 2B 42
Rockley Ct. W14 . . . . .2F 99
     (off Rockley Rd.)
Rockley Rd. W14 . . . . .2F 99
Rockmount Rd. SE18 . . . . .5K 107
  SE19 .6D 138
Rocks La. SW13 . . . . .1C 116
Rock St. N4 . . . . .2A 66
Rockware Av. UB6: G'frd 1H 77
Rockware Av. Bus. Cen. UB6: G'frd . .1H 77
Rockwell Gdns. SE19 . . . . .5E 138
Rockwell Rd. RM10: Dag 5H 73
Rockwood Pl. W12 . . . . .2E 98
Rocliffe St. N1 . . . . .2B 84
Rocombe Cres. SE23 . . . . .7J 121
Rocque Ho. SW6 . . . . .7H 99
     (off Estcourt Rd.)
Rocque La. SE3 . . . . .3H 123
Rodale Mans. SW18 . . . . .6K 117
Rodborough Ct. W9 . . . . .4J 81
     (off Hermes Cl.)
Rodborough Rd. NW11 . . . . .1J 63
Rodd Est. TW17: Shep 5E 146
Roden Cl. N6 . . . . .7H 47
Roden Gdns. CRO: C'don 6A 158
Rodenhurst Rd. SW4 . . . . .6G 119
Roden St. IG1: Ilf 3E 70
  N7 . . . . .3K 65
Roden Way IG1: Ilf 3E 70
     (off Roden St.)
Roderick Ho. SE16 . . . . .4J 103
     (off Raymouth Rd.)
Roderick Rd. NW3 . . . . .4D 64
Rodgers Ho. SW4 . . . . .7H 119
     (off Clapham Pk. Est.)
Rodin Ct. N1 . . . . .1B 84
     (off Essex Rd.)
Roding Av. IG8: Wfd G 6F 37
Roding Ho. N1 . . . . .1A 84
     (off Barnsbury Est.)
Roding La. IG7: Chig 2K 37
  IG9: Buck H 1F 37
Roding La. Nth. IG8: Wfd G 6H 37
Roding La. Sth. IG4: Ilf, Wfd G 4B 52
     (not continuous)
  IG8: Wfd G 4B 52
Roding M. E1 . . . . .1G 103
Roding Rd. E5 . . . . .4K 67
  E6 . . . . .7E 88
Rodings, The IG8: Wfd G 6F 37

Rodings Row EN5: Barn 4B 20
    (off Leecroft Rd.)
Roding Trad. Est. IG11: Bark 7F 71
Roding Valley Meadows Nature Reserve
. . . . .1K 37
Roding Vw. IG9: Buck H 1G 37
Rodmarton St. W1 . . . . .6F 5 (5D 82)
Rodmell WC1 . . . . .2F 7
    (off Regent Sq.)
Rodmell Cl. UB4: Yead 4C 76
Rodmell Slope N12 . . . . .5C 30
Rodmere St. SE10 . . . . .5G 105
Rodmill La. SW2 . . . . .7J 119
Rodney Cl. CRO: C'don 1B 168
    HA5: Pinn 7C 40
    KT3: N Mald 5A 152
Rodney Ct. EN5: Barn 3C 20
    W9 . . . . .3A 4 (4A 82)
Rodney Gdns. BR4: W W'ck 4J 171
    HA5: Eastc 5K 39
Rodney Ho. E14 . . . . .4D 104
    (off Cahir St.)
    N1 . . . . .2K 83
    (off Donegal St.)
    SW1 . . . . .6B 18
    (off Dolphin Sq.)
    W11 . . . . .7J 81
    (off Pembridge Cres.)
Rodney Pl. E17 . . . . .2A 50
    SE17 .4C 102
    SW19 . . . . .1A 154
Rodney Point SE16 . . . . .2B 104
    (off Rotherhithe St.)
Rodney Rd. CR4: Mitc 3C 154
    E11 . . . . .4K 51
    KT3: N Mald 5A 152
    SE17 .4C 102
    (not continuous)
    TW2: Whitt 6E 112
Rodney St. N1 . . . . .1H 7 (2K 83)
Rodney Way RM7: Mawney 1H 55
    SL3: Poyle 4A 174
Rodway Rd. BR1: Brom 1K 159
    SW15 . . . . .7C 116
Rodwell Cl. HA4: Ruis 1A 58
Rodwell Pl. HA8: Edg 6B 28
Rodwell Rd. SE22 . . . . .6F 121
Roe NW9 . . . . .7G 29
Roebourne Way E16 . . . . .1E 106
Roebuck Cl. N17 . . . . .6A 34
    TW13: Felt 4K 129
Roebuck Hgts. IG9: Buck H 1F 37
Roebuck La. IG9: Buck H 1F 37
Roebuck Rd. KT9: Chess 5G 163
Roedean Av. EN3: Enf H 1D 24
Roedean Cl. EN3: Enf H 1D 24
Roedean Cres. SW15 . . . . .6A 116
Roe End NW9 . . . . .4J 43
ROE GREEN .4J 43
Roe Grn. NW9 . . . . .5J 43
ROEHAMPTON 7C 116
Roehampton Cl. SW15 . . . . .4C 116
Roehampton Dr. BR7: Chst 6G 143
Roehampton Ga. SW15 . . . . .6A 116
Roehampton Golf Course 4B 116
Roehampton High St. SW15 . . . . . . .7C 116
Roehampton Ho. RM8: Dag 5A 72
ROEHAMPTON LANE 1D 134
Roehampton La. SW15 . . . . .4C 116
Roehampton Sport & Fitness Cen.
. . . . .7C 116
Roehampton University 6B 116
Roehampton Va. SW15 . . . . .3B 134
Roe La. NW9 .4H 43
Roesel Pl. BR5: Pet W 5F 161
Roe Way SM6: Wall 6J 167
Rofley St. E14 . . . . .2E 104
Rogate Ho. E5 . . . . .3G 67
Roger Dowley Ct. E2 . . . . .2J 85
Roger Harriss Almshouses E15 . . . . . .1H 87
    (off Gift La.)

Roger Reede's Almshouses
    RM1: Rom 4K 55
Rogers Cl. E14 . . . . .7C 86
    (off Premiere Pl.)
Rogers Est. E2 . . . . .3J 85
    (not continuous)
Rogers Gdns. RM10: Dag 5G 73
Rogers Ho. RM10: Dag 3G 73
    SW1 . . . . .3D 18
    (off Page St.)
Rogers Rd. E16 . . . . .6H 87
    RM10: Dag 5G 73
    SW17 . . . . .4B 136
Rogers Ruff HA6: Nwood 1E 38
Roger St. WC1 . . . . .4H 7 (4K 83)
Rogers Wlk. N12 . . . . .3E 30
Rohere Ho. EC1 . . . . .1C 8 (3C 84)
Rojack Rd. SE23 . . . . .1K 139
Rokeby Gdns. IG8: Wfd G 1J 51
Rokeby Ho. SW12 . . . . .7F 119
    (off Lochinvar St.)
    WC1 . . . . .4G 7
    (off Lamb's Conduit St.)
Rokeby Pl. SW20 . . . . .7D 134
Rokeby Rd. HA1: Harr 3H 41
    SE4 . . . . .2B 122
Rokeby St. E15 . . . . .1F 87
Rokell Ho. BR3: Beck 5D 140
    (off Beckenham Hill Rd.)
Roker Pk. Av. UB10: Ick 4A 56
Rokesby Cl. DA16: Well 2H 125
Rokesby Pl. HA0: Wemb 5D 60
Rokesly Av. N8 . . . . .5J 47
Rokewood Apartments BR3: Beck . . .1C 158
Roland Gdns. SW7 . . . . .5A 16 (5A 100)
Roland Ho. SW7 . . . . .5A 16
    (off Old Brompton Rd.)
Roland Mans. SW7 . . . . .5A 100
    (off Old Brompton Rd.)
Roland M. E1 .5K 85
Roland Rd. E17 . . . . .4F 51
Roland Way KT4: Wor Pk 2B 164
    SE17 .5D 102
    SW7 . . . . .5A 16 (5A 100)
Roles Gro. RM6: Chad H 4D 54
Rolfe Cl. EN4: E Barn 4H 21
Rolinsden Way BR2: Kes 5B 172
Rolland Ho. W7 . . . . .5J 77
Rollesby Rd. KT9: Chess 6G 163
Rollesby Way SE28 . . . . .6C 90
Rolleston Av. BR5: Pet W 6F 161
Rolleston Cl. BR5: Pet W 7F 161
Rolleston Rd. CR2: S Croy 7D 168
Roll Gdns. IG2: Ilf 5E 52
Rollins Ho. SE15 . . . . .6J 103
    (off Rollins St.)
Rollins St. SE15 . . . . .6J 103
Rollit Cres. TW3: Houn 5E 112
Rollit St. N7 . . . . .5A 66
Rolls Bldgs. EC4 . . . . .7J 7 (6A 84)
Rollscourt Av. SE24 . . . . .5C 120
Rolls Pk. Av. E4 . . . . .5H 35
Rolls Pk. Rd. E4 . . . . .5J 35
Rolls Pas. EC4 .7J 7
Rolls Rd. SE1 . . . . .5F 103
Rolls Royce Cl. SM6: Wall 7J 167
Rolt St. SE8 . . . . .6A 104
    (not continuous)
Rolvenden Gdns. BR1: Brom 7B 142
Rolvenden Pl. N17 . . . . .1G 49
Roma Corte SE13 . . . . .3D 122
    (off Elmira St.)
Roman Apartments E8 . . . . .7H 67
    (off Silesia Bldgs.)
Roman Cl. RM13: Rain 2K 91
    TW14: Felt 5A 112
    W3 . . . . .2H 97
Roman Ct. N7 .6K 65
Romanfield Rd. SW2 . . . . .7K 119
Roman Ho. EC2 . . . . .6D 8
    RM13: Rain 2K 91

Romanhurst Av. BR2: Brom 4G 159
Romanhurst Gdns.
    BR2: Brom 4G 159
Roman Ind. Est.
    CR0: C'don 7E 156
Roman Ri. SE19 . . . . .6D 138
Roman Rd. E2 . . . . .3J 85
    E3 . . . . .2A 86
    E6 . . . . .4B 88
    IG1: Ilf .6F 71
    N10 . . . . .7A 32
    NW2 . . . . .3E 62
    W4 . . . . .4A 98
Roman Sq. SE28 . . . . .1A 108
Roman Way CR0: C'don 2B 168
    EN1: Enf 5A 24
    N7 . . . . .6K 65
    SE15 .7J 103
Roman Way Ind. Est. N7 . . . . .7K 65
    (off Roman Way)
Romany Gdns. E17 . . . . .1A 50
    SM3: Sutt 7J 153
Romany Ri. BR5: Farnb 1G 173
Roma Read Cl. SW15 . . . . .7D 116
Roma Rd. E17 . . . . .3A 50
Romayne Ho. SW4 . . . . .3H 119
Romberg Rd. SW17 . . . . .3E 136
Romborough Gdns. SE13 . . . . .5E 122
Romborough Way SE13 . . . . .5E 122
Romero Cl. SW9 . . . . .3K 119
Romero Sq. SW16 . . . . .3K 137
ROMFORD 5K 55
Romford Rd. E7 . . . . .6G 69
    E12 . . . . .5A 70
    E15 . . . . .6G 69
    RM5: Col R 1E 54
Romford Stadium (Greyhound) 6J 55
Romford St. E1 . . . . .5G 85
Romilly Ho. W11 . . . . .7G 81
    (off Wilsham St.)
Romilly Rd. N4 . . . . .2B 66
Romilly St. W1 . . . . .2D 12 (7H 83)
Romily Ct. SW6 . . . . .2H 117
Rommany Rd. SE27 . . . . .4D 138
    (not continuous)
Romney Cl. HA2: Harr 7E 40
    KT9: Chess 4E 162
    N17 . . . . .1H 49
    NW11 .1A 64
    SE14 .7J 103
    TW15: Ashf 5E 128
Romney Ct. NW3 . . . . .6C 64
    W12 . . . . .2F 99
    (off Shepherd's Bush Grn.)
Romney Dr. BR1: Brom 7B 142
    HA2: Harr 7E 40
Romney Gdns. DA7: Bex 1F 127
Romney Ho. SW1 . . . . .2D 18
    (off Marsham St.)
Romney M. W1 . . . . .5G 5 (5E 82)
Romney Pde. UB4: Hayes 2F 75
Romney Rd.
    KT3: N Mald 6K 151
    SE10 .6F 105
    UB4: Hayes 2F 75
Romney Row NW2 . . . . .2F 63
    (off Brent Ter.)
Romney St. SW1 . . . . .2E 18 (3J 101)
Romola Rd. SE24 . . . . .1B 138
Romsey Cl. BR6: Farnb 4F 173
Romsey Gdns. RM9: Dag 1D 90
Romsey Rd. RM9: Dag 1D 90
    W13 . . . . .7A 78
Ronald Buckingham Ct. SE16 . . . . . . .2J 103
    (off Kenning St.)
Ronald Cl. BR3: Beck 4B 158
Ronald Ct. EN5: New Bar 3E 20
Ronaldshay N4 . . . . .7A 48

Ronalds Rd. BR1: Brom 1J 15
    N5 . . . . .5A 6
    (not continuous)
Ronaldstone Rd. DA15: Sidc 6J 12
Ronald St. E1 .6J 8
Rona Rd. NW3 . . . . .4E 6
Ronart St. HA3: W'stone 3K 4
Rona Wlk. N1 .6D 6
Rondel Ct. DA5: Bexl 6E 12
Rondu Rd. NW2 . . . . .5G 6
Ronelean Rd. KT6: Surb 2F 16
Ron Grn. Ct. DA8: Erith 6K 10
Ron Leighton Way E6 . . . . .1C 8
Ronnie La. E12 . . . . .4E 7
Ron Todd Cl. RM10: Dag 1G 9
Ronver Rd. SE12 . . . . .7H 12
Roof La. EC3 . . . . .2G 15 (7E 84)
Roof Ter. Apartments, The EC1 . . . . . . .4B
    (off Gt. Sutton St)
Rookby Ct. N21 . . . . .2G 3
Rook Cl. HA9: Wemb 3H 6
Rookeries Cl. TW13: Felt 3K 12
Rookery Cl. NW9 . . . . .5B 4
Rookery Cres. RM10: Dag 7H 7
Rookery Dr. BR7: Chst 1E 16
Rookery La. BR2: Brom 6B 16
Rookery Rd. SW4 . . . . .4G 11
Rookery Way NW9 . . . . .5B 4
Rooke Way SE10 . . . . .5H 10
Rookfield Av. N10 . . . . .4G 4
Rookfield Cl. N10 . . . . .4G 4
Rooksmead Rd. TW16: Sun 2H 14
Rooks Ter. UB7: W Dray 2A 9
Rookstone Rd. SW17 . . . . .5D 13
Rook Wlk. E6 .6B 8
Rookwood Av. KT3: N Mald 4C 15
    SM6: Bedd 4H 16
Rookwood Gdns. E4 . . . . .2C 3
Rookwood Ho. IG11: Bark 2H 8
Rookwood Rd. N16 . . . . .7D 4
Roosevelt Memorial 2H 11 (7E 82)
Roosevelt Way RM10: Dag 6K 7
Rootes Dr. W10 . . . . .5F 8
Ropemaker Rd. SE16 . . . . .2A 10
Ropemaker's Flds. E14 . . . . .7B 8
Ropemaker St. EC2 . . . . .5E 8 (5D 84)
Roper La. SE1 . . . . .7H 15 (2E 102)
Ropers Av. E4 .5J 3
Ropers Orchard SW3 . . . . .6C 10
    (off Danvers St)
Roper St. SE9 . . . . .5D 12
Ropers Wlk. SW2 . . . . .7A 12
Roper Way CR4: Mitc 2E 15
Ropery Bus. Pk. SE7 . . . . .4A 10
Ropery St. E3 .4B 8
Rope St. SE16 . . . . .3A 10
Rope Wlk. TW16: Sun 3A 14
Rope Wlk. Gdns. E1 . . . . .6G 8
Ropewalk M. E8 . . . . .7G 6
Ropeworks, The IG11: Bark 1G 8
Rope Yd. Rails SE18 . . . . .3F 10
Ropley St. E2 .2G 8
Rosa Alba M. N5 . . . . .4C 6
Rosa Av. TW15: Ashf 4C 12
Rosalind Ct. IG11: Bark 7A 7
    (off Meadow Rd
Rosalind Ho. N1 . . . . .2E 8
    (off Arden Est
Rosaline Rd. SW6 . . . . .7G 9
Rosaline Ter. SW6 . . . . .7G 9
    (off Rosaline Rd.
Rosa M. E17 . . . . .3B 5
Rosamond St. SE26 . . . . .3H 13
Rosamund Cl. CR2: S Croy 4D 16
Rosamun St. UB2: S'hall 4C 9
Rosa Parks Ho. SE17 . . . . .4C 10
    (off Munton Rd.
Rosary Cl. TW3: Houn 2C 11
Rosary Gdns. SW7 . . . . .4A 10
    TW15: Ashf 4D 12
Rosaville Rd. SW6 . . . . .7H 9

Roscoe St. EC1 . . . . .4D **8** (4C **84**)
(not continuous)
Roscoe St. Est. EC1 . . . . .4D **8** (4C **84**)
Roscoff Cl. HA8: Edg 1J **43**
Rosea Apartments SW11 . . . . .4C **118**
(off Danvers Av.)
Roseacre Cl. SM1: Sutt 2A **166**
TW17: Shep 5C **146**
W13 .5B **78**
Rose All. EC2 . . . . .6H **9**
(off Bishopsgate)
SE1 . . . . .4D **14** (1C **102**)
Rose & Crown Ct. EC2 . . . . .7D **8**
Rose & Crown Yd. SW1 . . . .4B **12** (1G **101**)
Rose Apartments SE11 . . . . .7K **19**
Rosebank Cl. UB7: W Dray 4A **92**
Rose Av. CR4: Mitc 1D **154**
E18 .2K **51**
SM4: Mord 5A **154**
Rosebank SE20 . . . . .7H **139**
SW6 .7E **98**
W3 . . . . .6K **79**
Rosebank Av. HA0: Wemb 4K **59**
Rosebank Cl. N12 . . . . .5H **31**
TW11: Tedd 6A **132**
Rosebank Gdns. E3 . . . . .2B **86**
W3 . . . . .6K **79**
Rosebank Gro. E17 . . . . .3B **50**
Rosebank Rd. E17 . . . . .6D **50**
W7 . . . . .2J **95**
Rosebank Vs. E17 . . . . .4C **50**
Rosebank Wlk. NW1 . . . . .7H **65**
SE18 . . . . .4C **106**
Rosebank Way W3 . . . . .6K **79**
Rose Bates Dr. NW9 . . . . .4G **43**
Rosebay Dr. N17 . . . . .2F **49**
Rosebay Ho. E3 . . . . .3C **86**
(off Hawgood St.)
Roseberry Dr. HA8: Edg 2C **28**
Roseberry Gdns. BR6: Orp 3J **173**
N4 . . . . .6B **48**
Roseberry Mans. N1 . . . . .1J **83**
(off Tapper Wlk.)
Roseberry M. SW2 . . . . .6J **119**
Roseberry Pl. E8 . . . . .6F **67**
Roseberry St. SE16 . . . . .4H **103**
Roseberry Av. CR7: Thor H 2C **156**
DA15: Sidc 7J **125**
E12 .6C **70**
EC1 . . . . .4J **7** (4A **84**)
HA2: Harr 4C **58**
KT3: N Mald 2B **152**
N17 .2G **49**
Roseberry Cl. SM4: Mord 6F **153**
Roseberry Ct. EC1 . . . . .3J **7**
(off Rosebery Av.)
W1 . . . . .4J **11**
(off Charles St.)
Roseberry Gdns. N8 . . . . .5J **47**
SM1: Sutt 4K **165**
W13 .6A **78**
Roseberry Ho. E2 . . . . .2J **85**
(off Sewardstone Rd.)
Roseberry Ind. Pk. N17 . . . . .2H **49**
Roseberry M. N10 . . . . .2G **47**
Roseberry Rd.
KT1: King T 2H **151**
N10 .2G **47**
SM1: Sutt 6H **165**
SW2 .6J **119**
TW3: Houn 5G **113**
WD23: Bush 1A **26**
Roseberry Sq. EC1 . . . . .4J **7**
KT1: King T 2H **151**
Rosebine Av. TW2: Twick 7H **113**
Rosebury Rd. SW6 . . . . .2K **117**
Rosebury Sq.
IG8: Wfd G 7K **37**
Rosebury Va. HA4: Ruis 2J **57**
Rose Bush Ct. NW3 . . . . .5D **64**

Rose Ct. E1 .6K **9**
E8 . . . . .7F **67**
(off Richmond Rd.)
HA0: Wemb 2E **78**
(off Vicars Bri. Cl.)
HA2: Harr 2G **59**
N1 . . . . .1B **84**
(off Collin's Yd.)
SE8 . . . . .4K **103**
Rosecourt Rd. CR0: C'don 6K **155**
Rosecroft N14 . . . . .2D **32**
Rosecroft Av. NW3 . . . . .3J **63**
Rosecroft Gdns. NW2 . . . . .3C **62**
TW2: Twick 1H **131**
Rosecroft Rd. UB1: S'hall 4E **76**
Rosecroft Wlk. HA0: Wemb 5D **60**
HA5: Pinn 5B **40**
Rose Dale BR6: Farnb 2F **173**
Rosedale Av. UB3: Hayes 5F **75**
Rosedale Cl. HA7: Stan 6G **27**
SE2 . . . . .3B **108**
W7 . . . . .2K **95**
Rosedale Ct. HA1: Harr 4K **59**
N5 . . . . .4B **66**
Rosedale Dr. RM9: Dag 7B **72**
Rosedale Gdns. RM9: Dag 7B **72**
Rosedale Ho. N16 . . . . .1D **66**
Rosedale Pl. CR0: C'don 7K **157**
Rosedale Rd. E7 . . . . .5A **70**
KT17: Ewe 5C **164**
RM1: Rom 2J **55**
RM9: Dag 7B **72**
TW9: Rich 3E **114**
Rosedale Ter. W6 . . . . .3D **98**
(off Dalling Rd.)
Rosedene NW6 . . . . .1F **81**
Rosedene Av. CR0: C'don 7J **155**
SM4: Mord 5J **153**
SW16 . . . . .3K **137**
UB6: G'frd 3E **76**
Rosedene Ct. HA4: Ruis 1G **57**
Rosedene Gdns. IG2: Ilf 4E **52**
Rosedene Ter. E10 . . . . .2D **68**
Rosedew Rd. W6 . . . . .6F **99**
Rose End KT4: Wor Pk 1F **165**
Rose Gdn. Cl. HA8: Edg 6K **27**
Rose Gdns. TW13: Felt 2J **129**
UB1: S'hall 4E **76**
W5 .3D **96**
Rosegate Ho. E3 . . . . .2B **86**
(off Hereford Rd.)
Rose Glen NW9 . . . . .4K **43**
RM7: Rush G 1K **73**
Rosehart M. W11 . . . . .6J **81**
Rose Hatch Av. RM6: Chad H 3D **54**
Roseheath Rd. TW4: Houn 5D **112**
ROSEHILL 7A **154**
Rose Hill SM1: Sutt 2K **165**
KT10: Clay 6A **162**
TW12: Hamp 1E **148**
Rosehill Av. SM1: Sutt 1A **166**
Rosehill Ct. SM4: Mord 7A **154**
(off St Helier Av.)
Rosehill Ct. Pde. SM4: Mord 7A **154**
(off St Helier Av.)
Rosehill Gdns. SM1: Sutt 2K **165**
UB6: G'frd 5K **59**
Rose Hill Pk. W. SM1: Sutt 1A **166**
Rosehill Rd. SW18 . . . . .6A **118**
ROSE HILL RDBT. 7A **154**
Rose Joan M. NW6 . . . . .4J **63**
Rosekey Ct. SE8 . . . . .7B **104**
(off Baildon St.)
Roseland Cl. N17 . . . . .7J **33**
Rose La. RM6: Chad H 3D **54**
Rose Lawn WD23: B Hea 1B **26**
Roseleigh Av. N5 . . . . .4B **66**

Roseleigh Cl. TW1: Twick 6D **114**
Rosemary Av. EN2: Enf 1K **23**
KT8: W Mole 3E **148**
N3 . . . . .2K **45**
N9 . . . . .1C **34**
TW4: Houn 2B **112**
Rosemary Branch Theatre 1D **84**
(off Rosemary St.)
Rosemary Cl. CR0: C'don 6J **155**
UB8: Hil 5C **74**
Rosemary Ct. SE8 . . . . .6B **104**
(off Dorking Cl.)
Rosemary Dr. E14 . . . . .6F **87**
IG4: Ilf 5B **52**
Rosemary Gdns. KT9: Chess 4E **162**
RM8: Dag 1F **73**
SW14 . . . . .3J **115**
Rosemary Ho. N1 . . . . .1D **84**
(off Colville Est.)
NW10 . . . . .1D **80**
(off Uffington Rd.)
Rosemary La. SW14 . . . . .3J **115**
Rosemary Rd. DA16: Well 1K **125**
SE15 . . . . .7F **103**
SW17 . . . . .3A **136**
Rosemary St. N1 . . . . .1D **84**
Rosemary Works N1 . . . . .1D **84**
(off Branch Pl.)
Rosemead Av. CR4: Mitc 3G **155**
HA9: Wemb 5E **60**
TW13: Felt 2H **129**
Rosemead Cl. KT6: Surb 1G **163**
Rosemere Pl. BR2: Brom 4G **159**
Rose M. N18 .4C **34**
Rosemont Av. N12 . . . . .6F **31**
Rosemont Cl. W3 . . . . .1H **97**
(off Rosemont Rd.)
Rosemont Rd. HA0: Wemb 1E **78**
KT3: N Mald 3J **151**
NW3 . . . . .6A **64**
TW10: Rich 6E **114**
W3 . . . . .7H **79**
Rosemoor Ho. W13 . . . . .1A **96**
(off Broadway)
Rosemoor St. SW3 . . . . .4E **16** (4D **100**)
Rosemount SM6: Wall 6G **167**
(off Clarendon Rd.)
Rosemount Cl. IG8: Wfd G 6J **37**
Rosemount Dr. BR1: Brom 4D **160**
Rosemount Point SE23 . . . . .3K **139**
Rosemount Rd. W13 . . . . .6A **78**
Rosenau Cres. SW11 . . . . .1D **118**
Rosenau Rd. SW11 . . . . .1C **118**
Rosendale Rd. SE21 . . . . .7C **120**
SE24 . . . . .7C **120**
Roseneath Av. N21 . . . . .1G **33**
Roseneath Pl. SW16 . . . . .4K **137**
(off Curtis Fld. Rd.)
Roseneath Rd. SW11 . . . . .6E **118**
Roseneath Wlk. EN1: Enf 4K **23**
Rosen's Wlk. HA8: Edg 3C **28**
Rosenthal Rd. SE6 . . . . .6D **122**
Rosenthorpe Rd. SE15 . . . . .5K **121**
Rose Pk. Cl. UB4: Yead 5A **76**
Rosepark Ct. IG5: Ilf 2D **52**
Rose Pl. N8 . . . . .6J **47**
Roserton St. E14 . . . . .2E **104**
Rosery, The CR0: C'don 6K **157**
Roses, The IG8: Wfd G 7C **36**
Rose Sq. SW3 . . . . .5B **16** (5B **100**)
Rose Stapleton Ter. SE1 . . . . .3E **102**
(off Page's Wlk.)
Rose St. EC4 . . . . .7B **8** (6B **84**)
WC2 . . . . .2E **12** (7J **83**)
(not continuous)
Rose Theatre
Sidcup 1B **144**
Rose Theatre, The 4D **14**
(off Park St.)
Rose Theatre Kingston 2D **150**

Rosethorn Cl. SW12 . . . . .7H **119**
Rose Tree M. IG8: Wfd G 6H **37**
Rosetree Pl. TW12: Hamp 7E **130**
Rosetta Cl. SW8 . . . . .7J **101**
(off Kenchester Cl.)
Rosetta Ct. SE19 . . . . .7E **138**
Rosetti Ter. RM8: Dag 4B **72**
(off Marlborough Rd.)
Roseveare Rd. SE12 . . . . .4A **142**
Roseville N21 . . . . .1E **33**
(off The Green)
Roseville Av. TW3: Houn 5E **112**
Roseville Rd. UB3: Harl 5J **93**
Roseville Sq. SW20 . . . . .1E **152**
Rose Wlk. BR4: W W'ck 2E **170**
KT5: Surb 5H **151**
Rose Way HA8: Edg 4D **28**
SE12 . . . . .5J **123**
Roseway SE21 . . . . .6D **120**
Rosewell Cl. SE20 . . . . .7H **139**
Rosewood KT7: T Ditt 2A **162**
Rosewood Av. UB6: G'frd 5A **60**
Rosewood Cl. DA14: Sidc 3C **144**
Rosewood Ct. BR1: Brom 1A **160**
E11 .4F **69**
KT2: King T 7G **133**
RM6: Chad H 5C **54**
Rosewood Dr. TW17: Shep 5B **146**
Rosewood Gdns. SE13 . . . . .2E **122**
Rosewood Gro. SM1: Sutt 2A **166**
Rosewood Ho. SW8 . . . . . . .7G **19** (6K **101**)
Rosewood Sq. W12 . . . . .6C **80**
Rosher Cl. E15 . . . . .7F **69**
Roshni Ho. SW17 . . . . .6C **136**
Rosina St. E9 .6K **67**
Rosing Apartments BR2: Brom 4A **160**
(off Homesdale Rd.)
Roskeen Cl. SW20 . . . . .7E **134**
Roskell Rd. SW15 . . . . .3F **117**
Rosler Bldg. SE1 . . . . .5C **14**
(off Ewer St.)
Roslin Ho. E1 .7K **85**
(off Brodlove La.)
Roslin Rd. W3 . . . . .3H **97**
Roslin Way BR1: Brom 5J **141**
Roslyn Cl. CR4: Mitc 2B **154**
Roslyn Rd. N15 . . . . .5E **48**
Rosmead Rd. W11 . . . . .7G **81**
Rosoman Pl. EC1 . . . . .3K **7** (4A **84**)
Rosoman St. EC1 . . . . .2K **7** (3A **84**)
Rossall Cres. NW10 . . . . .3F **79**
Ross Apartments E16 . . . . .7J **87**
(off Seagull La.)
Ross Av. RM8: Dag 1F **73**
Ross Cl. HA3: Hrw W 7B **26**
UB3: Harl 4F **93**
UB5: N'olt 4H **59**
Ross Ct. E5 . . . . .4H **67**
(off Napoleon Rd.)
NW9 . . . . .3A **44**
SW15 . . . . .7F **117**
W13 .5B **78**
(off Cleveland Rd.)
Rosscourt Mans. SW1 . . . . .1A **18**
(off Buckingham Pal. Rd.)
Rossdale SM1: Sutt 5C **166**
Rossdale Dr. N9 . . . . .6D **24**
NW9 . . . . .1J **61**
Rossdale Rd. SW15 . . . . .4E **116**
Rosse Gdns. SE13 . . . . .6E **123**
Rosse M. SE3 . . . . .1K **123**
Rossendale St. E5 . . . . .2H **67**
Rossendale Way NW1 . . . . .7G **65**
Rossetti CR0: C'don 1C **168**
(off Saffron Central Sq.)
Rossetti Ct. WC1 . . . . .5C **6**
(off Ridgmount Pl.)
Rossetti Gdn. Mans. SW3 . . . . .5E **16**
Rossetti Ho. SW1 . . . . .4D **18**
(off Erasmus St.)
Rossetti M. NW8 . . . . .1B **82**

Rossetti Rd. SE16 . . . . .5H 103
Rossetti Studios SW3 . . . . .7D 16
 (off Flood St.)
Ross Haven Pl. HA6: Nwood 1H 39
Ross Ho. E1 . . . . .1H 103
 (off Prusom St.)
Rossignol Gdns. SM5: Cars 2E 166
Rossindel Rd. TW3: Houn 5E 112
Rossington Cl. EN1: Enf 1C 24
Rossington St. E5 . . . . .2G 67
Rossiter Cl. SE19 . . . . .7C 138
Rossiter Flds. EN5: Barn 6B 20
Rossiter Gro. SW9 . . . . .3A 120
Rossiter Rd. SW12 . . . . .1F 137
Rossland Cl. DA6: Bex 5H 127
Rosslyn Av. E4 . . . . .2C 36
 EN4: E Barn 6H 21
 RM8: Dag 7F 55
 SW13 .3A 116
 TW14: Felt 6J 111
Rosslyn Cl. BR4: W W'ck 3H 171
 TW16: Sun 6G 129
 UB3: Hayes 5F 75
Rosslyn Cres. HA1: Harr 4K 41
 HA9: Wemb 4E 60
Rosslyn Gdns. HA9: Wemb 3E 60
Rosslyn Hill NW3 . . . . .4B 64
Rosslyn Mans. NW6 . . . . .7A 64
 (off Goldhurst Ter.)
Rosslyn M. NW3 . . . . .4B 64
Rosslyn Pk. M. NW3 . . . . .5B 64
Rosslyn Rd. E17 . . . . .4E 50
 IG11: Bark 7H 71
 TW1: Twick 6C 114
Rossmore Cl. EN3: Pond E 4E 24
 NW1 . . . . .4D 4
 (off Rossmore Rd.)
Rossmore Ct. NW1 . . . . . .3E 4 (4D 82)
Rossmore Rd. NW1 . . . . . .4D 4 (4C 82)
Ross Pde. SM6: Wall 6F 167
Ross Rd. SE25 . . . . .3D 156
 SM6: Wall 5G 167
 TW2: Whitt 1F 131
Ross Wlk. SE27 . . . . .3D 138
Ross Way E14 . . . . .6A 86
 SE9 . . . . .3C 124
Rosswood Gdns. SM6: Wall 6G 167
Rostella Rd. SW17 . . . . .4B 136
Rostrevor Av. N15 . . . . .6F 49
Rostrevor Gdns. UB2: S'hall 5C 94
 UB3: Hayes 1G 93
Rostrevor Mans. SW6 . . . . .1H 117
 (off Rostrevor Rd.)
Rostrevor M. SW6 . . . . .1H 117
Rostrevor Rd. SW6 . . . . .1H 117
 SW19 .5J 135
Roswell Apartments E3 . . . . .5B 86
 (off Joseph St.)
Rotary St. SE1 . . . . .7A 14 (3B 102)
Rothay NW1 . . . . .1K 5
 (off Albany St.)
Rothbury Cotts. SE10 . . . . .4G 105
 (off Maritius Rd.)
Rothbury Gdns. TW7: Isle 7A 96
Rothbury Rd. E9 . . . . .7B 68
Rothbury Wlk. N17 . . . . .7B 34
Rotheley Ho. E9 . . . . .7J 67
 (off Balcorne St.)
Rotherfield Ct. N1 . . . . .7D 66
 (off Rotherfield St., not continuous)
Rotherfield Rd. SM5: Cars 4E 166
Rotherfield St. N1 . . . . .7C 66
Rotherham Wlk. SE1 . . . . .5A 14
Rotherhill Av. SW16 . . . . .6H 137
ROTHERHITHE 2J 103
Rotherhithe Bus. Est. SE16 . . . . . . .4H 103
Rotherhithe New Rd. SE16 . . . . . . .5H 103
Rotherhithe Old Rd. SE16 . . . . .4K 103
Rotherhithe St. SE16 . . . . .2J 103
Rotherhithe Tunnel SE16 . . . . .1K 103
Rother Ho. SE15 . . . . .4H 121

Rotherwick Hill W5 . . . . .4F 79
Rotherwick Ho. E1 . . . . .7G 85
 (off Thomas More St.)
Rotherwick Rd. NW11 . . . . .7J 45
Rotherwood Cl. SW20 . . . . .1G 153
Rotherwood Rd. SW15 . . . . .3F 117
Rothery St. N1 . . . . .1B 84
 (off St Marys Path)
Rothery Ter. SW9 . . . . .7B 102
 (off Foxley Rd.)
Rothesay Av. SW20 . . . . .2G 153
 TW10: Rich 4H 115
 UB6: G'frd 6G 59
 (not continuous)
Rothesay Ct. SE6 . . . . .2H 141
 (off Cumberland Pl.)
 SE11 . . . . .7J 19
 SE12 . . . . .3K 141
Rothesay Rd. SE25 . . . . .4D 156
Rothley Ct. NW8 . . . . .3A 4
 (off St John's Wood Rd.)
Rothsay Rd. E7 . . . . .7A 70
Rothsay St. SE1 . . . . .3E 102
Rothsay Wlk. E14 . . . . .4C 104
 (off Charnwood Gdns.)
Rothschild Rd. W4 . . . . .4J 97
Rothschild St. SE27 . . . . .4B 138
Roth Wlk. N7 . . . . .2K 65
Rothwell Ct. HA1: Harr 5K 41
Rothwell Gdns. RM9: Dag 7C 72
Rothwell Ho. TW5: Hest 6E 94
Rothwell Rd. RM9: Dag 1C 90
Rothwell St. NW1 . . . . .1D 82
Rotten Row NW3 . . . . .1A 64
 SW1 . . . . .6B 10 (2B 100)
 SW7 . . . . .6B 10 (2B 100)
Rotterdam Dr. E14 . . . . .3E 104
Rotunda, The RM7: Rom 5K 55
 (off Yew Tree Gdns.)
Rotunda Centre, The 2E 150
Rotunda Ct. BR1: Brom 5K 141
 (off Burnt Ash La.)
Rouel Rd. SE16 . . . . .3G 103
 (Dockley Rd.)
 SE16 . . . . .4G 103
 (Southwark Pk. Rd.)
Rougemont Av. SM4: Mord 6J 153
Roundabout Ho. HA6: Nwood 1J 39
Roundacre SW19 . . . . .2F 135
Roundaway Rd. IG5: Ilf 1D 52
Roundel Cl. SE4 . . . . .4B 122
Round Gro. CRO: C'don 7K 157
Roundhay Cl. SE23 . . . . .2K 139
Roundhedge Way EN2: Enf 1E 22
Round Hill SE26 . . . . .2J 139
 (not continuous)
Roundhill Dr. EN2: Enf 4E 22
Roundhouse, The 7E 64
Roundhouse, La. E20 . . . . .6E 68
 (off International Way)
ROUNDSHAW 7J 167
Roundshaw Downs Local Nature Reserve
 . . . . .7K 167
Roundtable Rd. BR1: Brom 3H 141
Roundtree Rd. HA0: Wemb 5B 60
Roundway, The KT10: Clay 6A 162
 N17 . . . . .1C 48
Roundways HA4: Ruis 3A 57
Roundwood BR7: Chst 2F 161
Roundwood Av. UB11: Stock P 1E 92
Roundwood Ct. HA4: Ruis 7F 39
Roundwood Ct. E2 . . . . .3K 85
Roundwood Rd. NW10 . . . . .6B 62
Rounton Rd. E3 . . . . .4C 86
Roupell Ho. KT2: King T 7F 133
 (off Florence St.)
Roupell Rd. SW2 . . . . .1K 137
Roupell St. SE1 . . . . .5K 13 (1A 102)
Rousden St. NW1 . . . . .7G 65
Rouse Gdns. SE21 . . . . .4E 138
Rous Rd. IG9: Buck H 1H 37

Routemaster Cl. E13 . . . . .3K 87
Routh Ct. TW14: Bedf 1F 129
Routh Ho. SW18 . . . . .7C 118
Routh St. E6 . . . . .5D 88
Rover Ho. N1 . . . . .1E 84
 (off Whitmore Est.)
Rowallan Rd. SW6 . . . . .7G 99
Rowallen Pde. RM8: Dag 1C 72
Rowan N10 . . . . .2F 47
Rowan Av. E4 . . . . .6G 35
Rowan Cl. HA0: Wemb 3A 60
 HA7: Stan 6E 26
 IG1: Ilf 5H 71
 KT3: N Mald 2A 152
 SW16 .1G 155
 W5 . . . . .2E 96
Rowan Ct. E13 . . . . .3K 87
 (off High St.)
 SE15 . . . . .7C 103
 (off Garnies Cl.)
 SW11 .6D 118
Rowan Cres. SW16 . . . . .1G 155
Rowan Dr. NW9 . . . . .3C 44
Rowan Gdns. CRO: C'don 3F 169
Rowan Ho. BR2: Brom 2G 159
 DA14: Sidc 3K 143
 E3 . . . . .1B 86
 (off Hornbeam Sq.)
 IG1: Ilf 5H 71
 SE16 . . . . .2K 103
 (off Woodland Cres.)
Rowan Lodge W8 . . . . .3K 99
 (off Chantry Sq.)
Rowan Pl. UB3: Hayes 7H 75
Rowan Rd. DA7: Bex 3E 126
 SW16 .2G 155
 TW8: Bford 7B 96
 UB7: W Dray 4A 92
 W6 . . . . .4F 99
Rowans, The N13 . . . . .3G 33
 TW16: Sun 5H 129
Rowans Complex 2A 66
Rowan Ter. W6 . . . . .4F 99
Rowantree Cl. N21 . . . . .1J 33
Rowantree Rd. EN2: Enf 2G 23
 N21 . . . . .1J 33
Rowan Wlk. BR2: Brom 3D 172
 EN5: New Bar 5E 20
 N2 . . . . .5A 46
 N19 . . . . .2G 65
 W10 . . . . .4G 81
Rowan Way RM6: Chad H 3C 54
Rowanwood Av. DA15: Sidc 1A 144
Rowanwood M. EN2: Enf 2G 23
Rowben Cl. N20 . . . . .1E 30
Rowberry Cl. SW6 . . . . .7E 98
Rowcross St. SE1 . . . . .5F 103
Rowdell Rd. UB5: N'olt 1E 76
Rowden Pde. E4 . . . . .6A 36
 (off Chingford Rd.)
Rowden Pk. Gdns. E4 . . . . .7H 35
Rowden Rd. BR3: Beck 1A 158
 E4 . . . . .6J 35
 KT19: Ewe 4H 163
Rowditch La. SW11 . . . . .2E 118
Rowdon Av. NW10 . . . . .7D 62
Rowdown Cres.
 CRO: New Ad 7F 171
Rowdowns Rd. RM9: Dag 1F 91
Rowe Gdns. IG11: Bark 2K 89
Rowe Ho. E9 . . . . .6J 67
Rowe La. E9 . . . . .5J 67
Rowena Cres. SW11 . . . . .2C 118
Rowenhurst Mans. NW6 . . . . .6A 64
 (off Canfield Gdns.)
Rowe Wlk. HA2: Harr 3E 58
Rowfant Rd. SW17 . . . . .1E 136
Rowhill Rd. E5 . . . . .4H 67
Rowington Cl. W2 . . . . .5K 81
Rowland Av. HA3: Kenton 3C 42
Rowland Ct. E16 . . . . .4H 87

Rowland Gro. SE26 . . . . .3H 139
 (not continuous)
Rowland Hill Almshouses
 TW15: Ashf 5C 128
 (off Feltham Hill Rd.)
Rowland Hill Av. N17 . . . . .7H 33
Rowland Hill Ho. SE1 . . . . . .6A 14 (2B 102)
Rowland Hill St. NW3 . . . . .5C 64
Rowlands Av. HA5: Hat E 5A 26
Rowlands Cl. N6 . . . . .6E 46
 NW7 . . . . .7H 29
Rowlands Rd. RM8: Dag 2F 73
Rowland Way SW19 . . . . .1K 153
 TW15: Ashf 7F 129
Rowley Av. DA15: Sidc 7B 126
Rowley Cl. HA0: Wemb 7F 61
Rowley Ct. EN1: Enf 5K 23
 (off Wellington Rd.)
Rowley Gdns. N4 . . . . .7C 48
Rowley Ho. SE8 . . . . .5C 104
 (off Watergate St.)
Rowley Ind. Pk. W3 . . . . .3A 98
Rowley Rd. N15 . . . . .5C 48
Rowley Way NW8 . . . . .1K 81
Rowlheys Pl. UB7: W Dray 3A 92
Rowlls Rd. KT1: King T 3F 151
Rowney Gdns. RM9: Dag 6C 72
Rowney Rd. RM9: Dag 6B 72
Rowntree Clifford Cl. E13 . . . . .4J 87
Rowntree Cl. NW6 . . . . .6J 63
Rowntree M. E17 . . . . .1B 50
Rowntree Path SE28 . . . . .1B 108
Rowntree Rd.
 TW2: Twick 1J 131
Rowse Cl. E15 . . . . .1E 86
Rowsley Av. NW4 . . . . .3E 44
Rowstock Gdns. N7 . . . . .5H 65
Rowton Rd. SE18 . . . . .7G 107
Roxborough Av. HA1: Harr 7H 41
 TW7: Isle 7K 95
Roxborough Hgts. HA1: Harr 6J 41
 (off College Rd.)
Roxborough Pk. HA1: Harr 7J 41
Roxborough Rd. HA1: Harr 5H 41
Roxbourne Cl. UB5: N'olt 6B 58
Roxbourne Pk. Miniature Railway . . .2B 58
Roxburghe Mans. W8 . . . . .2K 99
 (off Kensington Ct.)
Roxburgh Pl. BR1: Brom 1C 160
Roxburgh Rd. SE27 . . . . .5B 138
Roxburn Way HA4: Ruis 3H 57
ROXETH .2H 59
Roxeth Ct. TW15: Ashf 5C 128
Roxeth Grn. Av. HA2: Harr 3F 59
 UB5: N'olt 5E 58
Roxeth Gro. HA2: Harr 4F 59
Roxeth Hill HA2: Harr 2H 59
Roxford Cl. TW17: Shep 5G 147
Roxford Ho. E3 . . . . .4D 86
 (off Devas St.)
Roxley Rd. SE13 . . . . .6D 122
Roxton Gdns. CRO: Addtn 5C 170
Roxwell NW1 . . . . .6F 65
 (off Hartland Rd.)
Roxwell Rd. IG11: Bark 2A 90
 W12 . . . . .2C 98
Roxwell Trad. Pk. E10 . . . . .7A 50
Roxwell Way IG8: Wfd G 7F 37
Roxy Av. RM6: Chad H 7C 54
Royal Academy of Arts (Burlington House
 . . . . .3A 12 (7G 83)
Royal Academy of Music Mus. 4H 5
Royal Air Force Memorial 1J 101
Royal Albert Hall 7A 10 (2B 100)
ROYAL ALBERT RDBT. 7C 88
 (OFF ROYAL ALBERT WAY)
Royal Albert Way E16 . . . . .7B 88
Royal Arc. W1 . . . . .3A 12
Royal Archer SE14 . . . . .7K 103
 (off Egmont St.)
ROYAL ARSENAL WEST 3F 107

Royal Av.—Rupert Av.

Royal Av. KT4: Wor Pk 2A **164**
SW3 5E **16** (5D **100**)
Royal Av. Ho. *SW3* *5E* ***16***
(off Royal Av.)
Royal Ballet School *1F 13*
(in Floral St.)
Royal Belgrave Ho. *SW1* *4K* ***17***
(off Hugh St.)
Royal Blackheath Golf Course 7D 124
Royal Botanic Gdns.
Kew 1E 114
Royal Brass Foundry 3F 107
Royal Carriage M. SE18 3F **107**
Royal Cir. SE27 3A **138**
Royal Cl. BR6: Farnb 4F **173**
IG3: Ilf 7A **54**
KT4: Wor Pk 2A **164**
N16 1E **66**
SE8 6B **104**
SW19 3F **135**
UB8: Hil 6B **74**
Royal College of Art 7A 10 (2B 100)
Royal College of Music 1A 16 (3B 100)
Royal College of Obstetricians
& Gynaecologists 3E 4 (4D 82)
Royal College of Physicians 3J 5
Royal College of Physicians Mus. *3K 5*
(off Albany St.)
Royal College of Surgeons 7H 7
Royal Coll. St. NW1 7G **65**
Royal Connaught Apartments *E16* *1B* ***106***
(off Connaught Rd.)
Royal Ct. *EC3* *1F* ***15***
(off Cornhill)
EN1: Enf 6K **23**
HA4: Ruis 6J **39**
SE9 1D **142**
SE16 3B **104**
Royal Courts of Justice 1H 13
Royal Court Theatre *4G 17*
(off Sloane Sq.)
Royal Cres. HA4: Ruis 4C **58**
IG2: Ilf 6H **53**
W11 1F **99**
Royal Cres. M. W11 1F **99**
Royal Docks Rd. E6 6F **89**
IG11: Bark 6F **89**
Royal Dr. N11 5K **31**
(not continuous)
Royal Duchess M. SW12 7F **119**
Royale Leisure Pk. W3 4G **79**
Royal Engineers Way
NW7 6B **30**
Royal Epping Forest & Chingford Golf Course
6K 25
Royal Exchange 1F 15 (6D 84)
Royal Exchange Av. EC3 1F **15**
Royal Exchange Bldgs. EC3 1F **15**
Royal Festival Hall 5H 13 (1K 101)
Royal Fusiliers Mus. 7F 85
Royal Gdns. W7 3A **96**
Royal Geographical Society 7A 10
Royal George M. SE5 4D **120**
Royal Herbert Pavilions
SE18 1D **124**
Royal Hill SE10 7E **104**
Royal Hill Ct. *SE10* *7E* ***104***
(off Greenwich High St.)
Royal Holloway (University of London)
Gower Street 5D 6
Royal Hospital Chelsea Mus.
6G 17 (5E 100)
Royal Hospital Rd. SW3 7E **16** (6D **100**)
Royal Institution Mus. 3A 12 (7G 83)
Royal La. UB7: Yiew 5B **74**
UB8: Hil 5B **74**
Royal Langford Apartments *NW6* *2K* ***81***
(off Greville Rd.)
Royal London Bldgs. *SE15* *6H* ***103***
(off Old Kent Rd.)
Royal London Estate, The N17 6C **34**
Royal London Hospital Archives & Museum
5H 85
(off Newark St.)
Royal London Ind. Est. NW10 2K **79**
Royal Mews, The 1K 17 (2F 101)
Royal M. KT8: E Mos 3J **149**
SW1 1K **17** (3F **101**)
Royal Mid-Surrey Golf Course 3D 114
Royal Mint Ct. EC3 3K **15** (7F **85**)
Royal Mint Pl. E1 2K **15** (7G **85**)
Royal Mint St. E1 2K **15** (7G **85**)
Royal Naval Pl. SE14 7B **104**
Royal Oak Ct. *N1* *1G* ***9***
(off Pitfield St.)
Royal Oak M. TW11: Tedd 5A **132**
Royal Oak Pl. SE22 6H **121**
Royal Oak Rd. DA6: Bex 5F **127**
(not continuous)
E8 6H **67**
Royal Oak Yd. SE1 7G **15** (2E **102**)
Royal Observatory Greenwich 7G 105
Royal Opera Arc. SW1 4C **12** (1H **101**)
Royal Opera House 1F 13 (6J 83)
Royal Orchard Cl. SW18 7G **117**
Royal Pde. BR7: Chst 7G **143**
RM10: Dag 6H **73**
SE3 2H **123**
SW6 7G **99**
TW9: Kew *1G* ***115***
(off Station App.)
W5 3E **78**
Royal Pde. M. *BR7: Chst* *7G* ***143***
(off Royal Pde.)
SE3 *2H* ***123***
(off Royal Pde.)
Royal Pl. SE10 7E **104**
Royal Quarter KT2: King T 1E **150**
Royal Quay Rd. E16 7F **89**
Royal Rd. DA14: Sidc 3D **144**
E16 6B **88**
SE17 6B **102**
TW11: Tedd 5H **131**
Royal Route HA9: Wemb 4F **61**
Royal St. SE1 1H **19** (3K **101**)
Royal Twr. Lodge *E1* *3K* ***15***
(off Cartwright St.)
Royalty Mans. *W1* *1C* ***12***
(off Meard St.)
Royalty M. W1 1C **12** (6H **83**)
Royalty Studios *W11* *6G* ***81***
(off Lancaster Rd.)
Royal Veterinary College
Camden Town 1H 83
Royal Victoria Docks Watersports Cen.
7J 87
Royal Victoria Gdns. *SE8* *4A* ***104***
(off Whiting Way)
Royal Victoria Patriotic Bldg.
SW18 6B **118**
Royal Victoria Pl. E16 1K **105**
Royal Victoria Sq. E16 7K **87**
Royal Victor Pl. E3 2K **85**
Royal Wlk. SM6: Wall 2F **167**
Royal Westminster Lodge *SW1* *3C* ***18***
(off Elverton St.)
Royal Wimbledon Golf Course 5D 134
Roycraft Av. IG11: Bark 2K **89**
Roycroft Av. IG11: Bark 2K **89**
Roycroft Cl. E18 1K **51**
SW2 1A **138**
Roydene Rd. SE18 6J **107**
Roydon Cl. IG10: Lough 1H **37**
SW11 *2D* ***118***
(off Battersea Pk. Rd.)
Roy Gdns. IG2: Ilf 4J **53**
Roy Gro. TW12: Hamp 6F **131**
Royle Bldg. *N1* *2C* ***84***
(off Wenlock Rd.)
Royle Cres. W13 4A **78**
Royley Ho. *EC1* *3D* ***8***
(off Old St.)
Roymount Ct. TW2: Twick 3J **131**
Roy Rd. HA6: Nwood 1H **39**
Roy Sq. E14 7A **86**
Royston Av. E4 5H **35**
SM1: Sutt 3B **166**
SM6: Bedd 4H **167**
Royston Cl. KT12: Walt T 7J **147**
TW5: Cran 1K **111**
Royston Ct. *E13* *1J* ***87***
(off Stopford Rd.)
SE24 6C **120**
TW9: Kew 1F **115**
W8 *1J* ***99***
(off Kensington Chu. St.)
Royston Gdns. IG1: Ilf 6B **52**
Royston Ho. N11 4J **31**
SE15 *6H* ***103***
(off Friary Est.)
Royston Pde. IG1: Ilf 6B **52**
Royston Pk. Rd. HA5: Hat E 5A **26**
Royston Rd. SE20 1K **157**
TW10: Rich 5E **114**
Roystons, The KT5: Surb 5H **151**
Royston St. E2 2J **85**
Rozel Ct. N1 1E **84**
Rozel Rd. SW4 3G **119**
Rozel Ter. *CR0: C'don* *3C* ***168***
(off Church Rd.)
RQ33 SW18 4J **117**
Rubastic Rd. UB2: S'hall 3A **94**
Rubens Gdns. *SE22* *7G* ***121***
(off Lordship La.)
Rubens Pl. SW4 4J **119**
Rubens Rd. UB5: N'olt 2A **76**
Rubens St. SE6 2B **140**
Rubicon Ct. N1 1J **83**
Ruby Cl. E5 3K **67**
Ruby Ct. *E15* *1E* ***86***
(off Warton Rd.)
RM8: Dag *1G* ***73***
(off Emerald Gdns.)
Ruby Rd. E17 3C **50**
Ruby St. NW10 7J **61**
SE15 6H **103**
Ruby Triangle SE15 6H **103**
Ruby Way NW9 1B **44**
Ruckholt Cl. E10 3D **68**
Ruckholt Rd. E10 4C **68**
Rucklidge Av. NW10 2B **80**
Rucklidge Pas. *NW10* *2B* ***80***
(off Rucklidge Av.)
Rudall Cres. NW3 4B **64**
Rudbeck Ho. *SE15* *7G* ***103***
(off Peckham Pk. Rd.)
Ruddington Cl. E5 4A **68**
Ruddock Cl. HA8: Edg 7D **28**
Ruddstreet Cl. SE18 4F **107**
Ruddy Way NW7 6G **29**
Rudge Ho. *SE16* *3G* ***103***
(off Jamaica Rd.)
Rudgwick Ct. *SE18* *4C* ***106***
(off Woodville St.)
Rudgwick Ter. NW8 1C **82**
Rudland Rd. DA7: Bex 3H **127**
Rudloe Rd. SW12 7G **119**
Rudolf Pl. SW8 7F **19** (6J **101**)
Rudolph Rd. E13 2H **87**
NW6 2J **81**
Rudstone Ho. *E3* *3D* ***86***
(off Bromley High St.)
Rudyard Ct. *SE1* *7F* ***15***
(off Long La.)
Rudyard Gro. NW7 6D **28**
Ruegg Ho. *SE18* *6E* ***106***
(off Woolwich Comn.)
Ruffetts, The CR2: Sels 7H **169**
Ruffetts Cl. CR2: Sels 7H **169**
Ruffle Cl. UB7: W Dray 2A **92**
Rufford Cl. HA3: Kenton 6A **42**
Rufford St. N1 1J **83**
Rufford St. M. N1 7J **65**
Rufford Twr. W3 1H **97**
Rufforth Ct. *NW9* *1A* ***44***
(off Pageant Av.)
Rufus Bus. Cen. SW18 2K **135**
Rufus Cl. HA4: Ruis 3C **58**
Rufus Ho. *SE1* *7K* ***15***
(off St Saviour's Est.)
Rufus St. N1 2G **9** (3E **84**)
Rugby Av. HA0: Wemb 5B **60**
N9 1A **34**
UB6: G'frd 6H **59**
Rugby Cl. HA1: Harr 4J **41**
Rugby Gdns. RM9: Dag 6C **72**
Rugby Mans. *W14* *4G* ***99***
(off Bishop King's Rd.)
Rugby Rd. NW9 4H **43**
RM9: Dag 7B **72**
TW1: Twick 5J **113**
W4 2A **98**
Rugby St. WC1 4G **7** (4K **83**)
Rugg St. E14 7C **86**
Rugless Ho. *E14* *2E* ***104***
(off E. Ferry Rd.)
Rugmere *NW1* *7E* ***64***
(off Ferdinand St.)
RUISLIP 1G 57
Ruislip Cl. UB6: G'frd 4F **77**
RUISLIP COMMON 4E 38
Ruislip Ct. HA4: Ruis 2H **57**
RUISLIP GARDENS 3J 57
Ruislip Golf Course 2E 56
Ruislip Lido 4F 39
Ruislip Lido Railway 4F 39
Ruislip Lido Woodlands Cen. 4F 39
RUISLIP MANOR 2J 57
Ruislip Rd. UB5: N'olt 1A **76**
UB6: G'frd 3E **76**
Ruislip Rd. E. UB6: G'frd 4H **77**
W7 4J **77**
W13 4H **77**
Ruislip St. SW17 4D **136**
Ruislip Woods (National Nature Reserve)
3E 38
Rumball Ho. *SE5* *7E* ***102***
(off Harris St.)
Rumbold Rd. SW6 7K **99**
Rum Cl. E1 7J **85**
Rumford Ho. *SE1* *3C* ***102***
(off Tiverton St.)
Rumney Ct. *UB5: N'olt* *2B* ***76***
(off Parkfield Dr.)
Rumsey Cl. TW12: Hamp 6D **130**
Rumsey M. N4 3B **66**
Rumsey Rd. SW9 3K **119**
Runacres Ct. SE17 5C **102**
Runbury Circ. NW9 2K **61**
Runcie Ct. IG6: Ilf 4H **53**
Runcorn Cl. N17 4H **49**
Runcorn Pl. W11 7G **81**
Rundell Cres. NW4 5D **44**
Rundell Twr. SW8 1K **119**
Runes Cl. CR4: Mitc 4B **154**
Runnel Ct. *IG11: Bark* *2G* ***89***
(off Spring Pl.)
Runnelfield HA1: Harr 3J **59**
Running Horse Yd.
TW8: Bford 6E **96**
Runnymede SW19 1A **154**
Runnymede Cl. TW2: Whitt 6F **113**
Runnymede Ct. SM6: Wall 6F **167**
SW15 1C **134**
Runnymede Cres. SW16 1H **155**
Runnymede Gdns.
TW2: Whitt 6F **113**
UB6: G'frd 2J **77**
Runnymede Ho. E9 4A **68**
Runnymede Rd. TW2: Whitt 6F **113**
Runway, The HA4: Ruis 5K **57**
Runway Cl. NW9 2B **44**
Rupack St. SE16 2J **103**
Rupert Av. HA9: Wemb 5E **60**

A-Z London 385

Rupert Ct. *KT8: W Mole* 4E **148**
    (off St Peter's Rd.)
  W1 .2C **12** (7H **83**)
Rupert Gdns. SW9 . . . . .2B **120**
Rupert Ho. SE11 . . . . .4K **19** (4A **102**)
  SW5 . . . . .4J **99**
    (off Nevern Sq.)
Rupert Rd. N19 .3H **65**
    (not continuous)
  NW6 . . . . .2H **81**
  W4 . . . . .3A **98**
Rupert St. W1 . . . . .2C **12** (7H **83**)
Rural Way SW16 . . . . .7F **137**
Rusbridge Cl. E8 . . . . .5G **67**
Ruscoe Rd. E16 . . . . .6H **87**
Ruscombe *NW1* 1F **83**
    (off Delancey St.)
Ruscombe Way TW14: Felt 7H **111**
Ruscus Rd. E17 . . . . .1C **50**
Rush, The *SW19* 1H **153**
    (off Watery La.)
Rusham Rd. SW12 . . . . .6D **118**
Rushbridge Cl. CR0: C'don 6C **156**
Rushbrook Cres. E17 . . . . .1B **50**
Rushbrook Rd. SE9 . . . . .2G **143**
Rushbury Ct. TW12: Hamp 1E **148**
Rushcroft Rd. E4 . . . . .7J **35**
  SW2 . . . . .4A **120**
Rushcutters Ct. *SE16* 4A **104**
    (off Boat Lifter Way)
Rushden Cl. SE19 . . . . .7D **138**
Rushdene SE2 . . . . .3D **108**
    (not continuous)
Rushdene Av. EN4: E Barn 7H **21**
Rushdene Cl. UB5: N'olt 2A **76**
Rushdene Cres. UB5: N'olt 2K **75**
Rushdene Rd. HA5: Eastc 6B **40**
Rushden Gdns. IG5: Ilf 2E **52**
  NW7 . . . . .6K **29**
Rushen Wlk. SM5: Cars 1B **166**
Rushett Cl. KT7: T Ditt 1B **162**
Rushett Rd. KT7: T Ditt 7B **150**
Rushey Cl. KT3: N Mald 4K **151**
Rushey Grn. SE6 . . . . .7D **122**
Rushey Hill EN2: Enf 4E **22**
Rushey Mead SE4 . . . . .5C **122**
Rushford Rd. SE4 . . . . .6B **122**
RUSH GREEN 1K **73**
Rush Grn. Gdns. RM7: Rush G 1J **73**
Rush Grn. Rd. RM7: Rush G 1H **73**
Rushgrove Av. NW9 . . . . .5A **44**
Rushgrove Ct. NW9 . . . . .5A **44**
Rushgrove Pde. NW9 . . . . .5A **44**
Rushgrove St. SE18 . . . . .4D **106**
Rush Hill M. *SW11* 3E **118**
    (off Rush Hill Rd.)
Rush Hill Rd. SW11 . . . . .3E **118**
Rushley Cl. BR2: Kes 4B **172**
Rushmead E2 . . . . .3H **85**
  TW10: Ham 3B **132**
Rushmead Cl. CR0: C'don 4F **169**
  HA8: Edg 2C **28**
Rushmere Ct. KT4: Wor Pk 2C **164**
Rushmere Pl. SW19 . . . . .5F **135**
Rushmon Pl. SM3: Cheam 6G **165**
Rushmon Vs. KT3: N Mald 4B **152**
Rushmoor Cl. HA5: Eastc 4K **39**
Rushmore Cl. BR1: Brom 3C **160**
Rushmore Cres. E5 . . . . .4K **67**
Rushmore Ho. SW15 . . . . .7C **116**
  W14 . . . . .3G **99**
    (off Russell Rd.)
Rushmore Rd. E5 . . . . .4J **67**
    (not continuous)
Rusholme Av. RM10: Dag 3G **73**
Rusholme Gro. SE19 . . . . .5E **138**
Rusholme Rd. SW15 . . . . .6F **117**
Rushout Av. HA3: Kenton 6B **42**
Rushton Ho. SW8 . . . . .2H **119**
Rushton St. N1 . . . . .2D **84**

Rushton Wlk. E3 . . . . .4B **86**
    (off Hamlets Way)
Rushworth St. SE1 . . . . .6B **14** (2B **102**)
Rushy Mdw. La. SM5: Cars 2C **166**
Ruskin Av. DA16: Well 2A **126**
  E12 . . . . .6C **70**
  TW9: Kew 7G **97**
  TW14: Felt .6H **111**
Ruskin Cl. NW11 . . . . .6K **45**
Ruskin Ct. N21 . . . . .7E **22**
  SE5 . . . . .3D **120**
    (off Champion Hill)
Ruskin Dr. BR6: Orp 3J **173**
  DA16: Well .3A **126**
  KT4: Wor Pk 2D **164**
Ruskin Gdns. HA3: Kenton 5F **43**
  W5 . . . . .4D **78**
Ruskin Gro. DA16: Well 2A **126**
Ruskin Ho. CR2: S Croy 5D **168**
    (off Selsdon Rd.)
  SW1 . . . . .5D **168**
    (off Herrick St.)
Ruskin Mans. *W14* 6G **99**
    (off Queen's Club Gdns.)
Ruskin Pde. CR2: S Croy 5D **168**
    (off Selsdon Rd.)
Ruskin Pk. Ho. SE5 . . . . .3D **120**
Ruskin Rd. CR0: C'don 2B **168**
  DA17: Belv 4G **109**
  N17 . . . . .1F **49**
  SM5: Cars 5D **166**
  TW7: Isle 3K **113**
  UB1: S'hall .7C **76**
Ruskin Wlk. BR2: Brom 6D **160**
  N9 . . . . .2B **34**
  SE24 . . . . .5C **120**
Ruskin Way SW19 . . . . .1B **154**
Rusland Av. BR6: Orp 3H **173**
Rusland Hgts. HA1: Harr 4J **41**
Rusland Pk. Rd. HA1: Harr 4J **41**
Rusper Cl. HA7: Stan 4H **27**
  NW2 . . . . .3E **62**
Rusper Ct. *SW9* 2J **119**
    (off Clapham Rd.)
Rusper Rd. N17 . . . . .3C **48**
  N22 . . . . .2B **48**
  RM9: Dag 6C **72**
Russell Av. N22 . . . . .2A **48**
Russell Chambers *WC1* 6F **7**
    (off Bury Pl.)
Russell Cl. BR3: Beck 3E **158**
  DA7: Bex 4G **127**
  HA4: Ruis 2A **58**
  NW10 . . . . .7J **61**
  SE7 . . . . .7A **106**
  W4 . . . . .6B **98**
Russell Ct. E10 . . . . .7D **50**
  EN5: New Bar 4F **21**
  N14 . . . . .6C **22**
  SE15 . . . . .2H **121**
    (off Heaton Rd.)
  SM6: Wall .5G **167**
    (off Ross Rd.)
  SW1 . . . . .5B **12**
  SW16 . . . . .5K **137**
  WC1 . . . . .4E **6**
Russell Flint Ho. *E16* 1K **105**
    (off Pankhurst Av.)
Russell Gdns. IG2: Ilf 7H **53**
  N20 . . . . .2G **31**
  NW11 . . . . .6G **45**
  TW10: Ham 2C **132**
  UB7: Sip 5C **92**
  W14 . . . . .3G **99**
Russell Gdns. M. W14 . . . . .2G **99**
Russell Gro. NW7 . . . . .5F **29**
  SW9 . . . . .7A **102**
Russell Ho. BR2: Brom 6C **160**
    (off Wells Vw. Dr.)
  E14 . . . . .6C **86**
    (off Saracen St.)

Russell Ho. SW1 . . . . .5A **18**
    (off Cambridge St.)
Russell Kerr Cl. W4 . . . . .7J **97**
Russell La. N20 . . . . .2H **31**
Russell Lodge E4 . . . . .2K **35**
  SE1 . . . . .3D **102**
    (off Spurgeon St.)
Russell Mans. *WC1* 5F **7**
    (off Southampton Row)
Russell Mead HA3: Hrw W 1K **41**
Russell Pde. *NW11* 6G **45**
    (off Golders Grn. Rd.)
Russell Pl. NW3 . . . . .5C **64**
  SE16 . . . . .3A **104**
  SM2: Sutt .7K **165**
Russell Rd. CR4: Mitc 3C **154**
  E4 . . . . .4G **35**
  E10 . . . . .6D **50**
  E16 . . . . .6J **87**
  E17 . . . . .3B **50**
  EN1: Enf 1A **24**
  IG9: Buck H 1E **36**
  KT12: Walt T 6J **147**
  N8 . . . . .6H **47**
  N13 . . . . .6E **32**
  N15 . . . . .5E **48**
  N20 . . . . .2H **31**
  NW9 . . . . .6A **44**
  SW19 . . . . .7J **135**
  TW2: Twick 6K **113**
  TW17: Shep 7E **146**
  UB5: N'olt .5G **59**
  W14 . . . . .3G **99**
Russell's Footpath SW16 . . . . .5J **137**
Russell Sq. WC1 . . . . .4E **6** (5J **83**)
Russell Sq. Mans. *WC1* 5F **7**
    (off Southampton Row)
Russell St. WC2 . . . . .2F **13** (7J **83**)
Russell's Wharf Flats W10 . . . . .4H **81**
Russell Wlk. TW10: Rich 6F **115**
Russell Way SM1: Sutt 5K **165**
Russell Yd. SW15 . . . . .4G **117**
Russet Av. TW17: Shep 3G **147**
Russet Cl. UB10: Hil 4E **74**
Russet Cres. N7 . . . . .5K **65**
Russet Dr. CR0: C'don 1A **170**
Russets Cl. E4 . . . . .4A **36**
Russett Way SE13 . . . . .2D **122**
Russia Dock Rd. SE16 . . . . .1A **104**
Russia La. E2 .2J **85**
Russia Row EC2 . . . . .1D **14** (6C **84**)
Russia Wlk. SE16 . . . . .2A **104**
Russington Rd. TW17: Shep 6F **147**
Rusthall Av. W4 . . . . .4K **97**
Rusthall Cl. CR0: C'don 6J **157**
Rusthall Pl. SW16 . . . . .7F **137**
Rustic Av. SW16 . . . . .7F **137**
Rustic Pl. HA0: Wemb 4D **60**
Rustic Wlk. *E16* 6K **87**
    (off Lambert Rd.)
Rustington Wlk. SM4: Mord 7H **153**
Ruston Av. KT5: Surb 7H **151**
Ruston Gdns. N14 . . . . .6K **21**
Ruston M. W11 . . . . .6G **81**
Ruston Rd. SE18 . . . . .3D **106**
Ruston St. E3 .1B **86**
Rust Sq. SE5 . . . . .7D **102**
Rutford Rd. SW16 . . . . .5J **137**
Ruth Cl. HA7: Stan 4F **43**
Ruth Ct. E3 . . . . .2A **86**
Rutherford Cl. SM2: Sutt 6B **166**
  UB8: Hil 4B **74**
Rutherford Ho. *E1* 4H **85**
    (off Brady St.)
  HA9: Wemb .3J **61**
    (off Barnhill Rd.)
  SW11 . . . . .2D **118**
    (off Battersea Pk. Rd.)
Rutherford St. SW1 . . . . . . .3C **18** (4H **101**)
Rutherford Twr. UB1: S'hall 6F **77**
Rutherford Way HA9: Wemb 4G **61**
  WD23: B Hea 1C **26**

Rutherglen Rd. SE2 . . . . .6A **108**
Rutherwyke Cl. KT17: Ewe 6C **164**
Ruth Ho. *W10* .4G **81**
    (off Kensal Rd.)
Ruthin Cl. NW9 . . . . .6A **44**
Ruthin Rd. SE3 . . . . .6J **105**
Ruthven St. E9 . . . . .1K **85**
Rutland Av. DA15: Sidc 7A **126**
Rutland Cl. DA5: Bexl 2D **144**
  KT9: Chess 6F **163**
  SW14 . . . . .3H **115**
  SW19 . . . . .7C **136**
Rutland Ct. BR7: Chst 1E **160**
  EN3: Pond E 5C **24**
  KT1: King T 4D **150**
    (off Palace Rd.)
  SE5 . . . . .4D **120**
  SE9 . . . . .2G **143**
  SW7 . . . . .7D **10**
  W3 . . . . .6G **79**
Rutland Dr. SM4: Mord 6H **153**
  TW10: Ham 1D **132**
Rutland Gdns. CR0: C'don 4E **168**
  N4 . . . . .6B **48**
  RM8: Dag 5C **72**
  SW7 . . . . .7D **10** (2C **100**)
  W13 . . . . .5A **78**
Rutland Gdns. M. SW7 . . . . . .7D **10** (2C **100**)
Rutland Ga. BR2: Brom 4H **159**
  DA17: Belv 5H **109**
  SW7 . . . . .7D **10** (2C **100**)
Rutland Ga. M. SW7 . . . . .7C **10**
Rutland Gro. W6 . . . . .5D **98**
Rutland Ho. UB5: N'olt 6E **58**
    (off The Farmlands)
  W8 . . . . .3K **99**
    (off Marloes Rd.)
Rutland M. NW8 . . . . .1K **81**
Rutland M. E. SW7 . . . . .1C **16**
Rutland M. Sth. SW7 . . . . .1C **16**
Rutland M. W. SW7 . . . . .1C **16**
Rutland Pk. NW2 . . . . .6E **62**
  SE6 . . . . .2B **140**
Rutland Pk. Gdns. NW2 . . . . .6E **62**
    (off Rutland Pk.)
Rutland Pk. Mans. NW2 . . . . .6E **62**
Rutland Pl. EC1 . . . . .5B **8** (4B **84**)
  WD23: B Hea 1D **26**
Rutland Rd. E7 . . . . .7B **70**
  E9 . . . . .1K **85**
  E11 . . . . .5K **51**
  E17 . . . . .6C **50**
  HA1: Harr 6G **41**
  IG1: Ilf 3F **71**
  SW19 . . . . .7C **136**
  TW2: Twick 2H **131**
  UB1: S'hall .5E **76**
  UB3: Harl 4F **93**
Rutland St. SW7 . . . . .1D **16** (3C **100**)
Rutland Wlk. SE6 . . . . .2B **140**
Rutley Cl. SE17 . . . . .6B **102**
Rutlish Rd. SW19 . . . . .1J **153**
Rutter Gdns. CR4: Mitc 4A **154**
Rutters Cl. UB7: W Dray 2C **92**
Rutt's Ter. SE14 . . . . .1K **121**
Ruvigny Gdns. SW15 . . . . .3F **117**
Ruxbury Ct. TW15: Ashf 3A **128**
RUXLEY 7D **144**
Ruxley Cl. DA14: Sidc 6D **144**
  KT19: Ewe 5H **163**
Ruxley Cnr. Ind. Est. DA14: Sidc 6D **144**
Ruxley Cl. KT19: Ewe 5J **163**
Ruxley Cres. KT10: Clay 6B **162**
Ruxley Gdns. TW17: Shep 5E **146**
Ruxley La. KT19: Ewe 6H **163**
Ruxley M. KT19: Ewe 5H **163**
Ruxley Park Golf Course 7D **144**
Ruxley Ridge KT10: Clay 7A **162**
Ruxley Towers KT10: Clay 7A **162**
Ryalls Ct. N20 .3J **31**

Ryan Cl. HA4: Ruis 1K 57
  SE3 ....4A 124
Ryan Ct. RM7: Rom 6J 55
  SW16 ....7J 137
Ryan Dr. TW8: Bford 6A 96
Ryarsh Cres. BR6: Orp 4J 173
Rycott Path SE22 ....7G 121
Rycroft Way N17 ....3F 49
Ryculff Sq. SE3 ....2H 123
Rydal Cl. NW4 ....1G 45
Rydal Cl. HA8: Edg 5A 28
  HA9: Wemb 7F 43
Rydal Cres. UB6: G'frd 3B 78
Rydal Dr. BR4: W W'ck 2G 171
  DA7: Bex 1G 127
Rydal Gdns. HA9: Wemb 1C 60
  NW9 ....5A 44
  SW15 ....5A 134
  TW3: Houn 6F 113
Rydal Mt. BR2: Brom 4H 159
Rydal Rd. SW16 ....4H 137
Rydal Water NW1 ....2A 6 (3G 83)
Rydal Way EN3: Pond E 6D 24
  HA4: Ruis 4A 58
Ryde Ho. NW6 ....1J 81
   (off Priory Pk. Rd.)
Rydens Ho. SE9 ....3A 142
Rydens Rd. KT12: Walt T 7C 148
Ryde Pl. TW1: Twick 6D 114
Ryder Av. E10 ....7D 50
Ryder Cl. BR1: Brom 5K 141
Ryder Ct. E10 ....2D 68
  SW1 ....4B 12
Ryder Dr. SE16 ....5H 103
Ryder Ho. E1 ....5J 85
   (off Colbert Av.)
Ryder M. E9 ....5J 67
Ryder's Ter. NW8 ....2A 82
Ryder St. SW1 ....4B 12 (1G 101)
Ryder Yd. SW1 ....4B 12 (1G 101)
Ryde Va. Rd. SW12 ....2G 137
Rye, The N14 ....7C 22
Rye Cl. DA5: Bexl 6H 127
Ryecotes Mead SE21 ....1E 138
Ryecroft Av. IG5: Ilf 2F 53
  TW2: Whitt 7F 113
Ryecroft Rd. BR5: Pet W 6H 161
  SE13 ....5E 122
  SW16 ....6A 138
Ryecroft St. SW6 ....1K 117
Ryedale SE22 ....6H 121
Ryefield Av. UB10: Hil 7D 56
Ryefield Cl. HA6: Nwood 2J 39
Ryefield Cres. HA6: Nwood 2J 39
Ryefield Pde. HA6: Nwood 2J 39
   (off Joel St.)
Ryefield Path SW15 ....1C 134
Ryefield Rd. SE19 ....6C 138
Ryegates SE15 ....2H 121
   (off Caulfield Rd.)
Rye Hill Pk. SE15 ....4J 121
Rye Ho. SE16 ....2J 103
   (off Swan Rd.)
  SW1 ....5J 17
   (off Ebury Bri. Rd.)
Ryeland Cl. UB7: Yiew 6A 74
Ryelands Cres. SE12 ....6A 124
Rye La. SE15 ....1G 121
Rye Mans. E20 ....5E 68
   (off Napa Cl.)
Rye Pas. SE15 ....3G 121
Rye Rd. SE15 ....4K 121
Rye Wlk. SW15 ....5F 117
Rye Way HA8: Edg 6A 28
Ryfold Rd. SW19 ....3J 135
Ryhope Rd. N11 ....4A 32
Ryland Cl. TW13: Felt 4H 129

Rylandes Rd. NW2 ....3C 62
Ryland Rd. NW5 ....6F 65
Rylett Cres. W12 ....2B 98
Rylett Rd. W12 ....2B 98
Rylston Rd. N13 ....3J 33
  SW6 ....6H 99
Rymer Rd. CR0: C'don 7E 156
Rymer St. SE24 ....6B 120
Rymill St. E16 ....1E 106
Rysbrack St. SW3 ....1E 16 (3D 100)
Rythe Bank Cl. KT7: T Ditt 7B 150
Rythe Cl. KT9: Chess 7C 162
Rythe Ct. KT7: T Ditt 7A 150

S

Saatchi Gallery 5F 17 (5D 100)
Sabah Ct. TW15: Ashf 4C 128
Sabella Ct. E3 ....2B 86
Sabine Rd. SW11 ....3D 118
Sable Cl. TW4: Houn 3A 112
Sable Ho. E20 ....5D 68
   (off Scarlet Cl.)
Sable St. N1 ....7B 66
Sach Rd. E5 ....2H 67
Sackville Av. BR2: Hayes 1J 171
Sackville Cl. HA2: Harr 3H 59
Sackville Gdns. IG1: Ilf 1D 70
Sackville Ho. SW16 ....3J 137
Sackville Rd. SM2: Sutt 7J 165
Sackville St. W1 ....3B 12 (7G 83)
Saddleback La. W7 ....3J 95
Saddlebrook Pk. TW16: Sun 7G 129
Saddle M. CR0: C'don 7C 156
Saddlers Cl. HA5: Hat E 6A 26
Saddlers Ho. E20 ....5E 68
   (off Ribbons Wlk.)
Saddlers M. HA0: Wemb 4K 59
  KT1: Hamp W 1C 150
  SW8 ....1J 119
Saddlescombe Way N12 ....5D 30
Saddle Yd. W1 ....4J 11 (1F 101)
Sadler Cl. CR4: Mitc 2D 154
Sadler Ho. E3 ....3D 86
   (off Bromley High St.)
  EC1 ....1K 7
   (off Spa Grn. Est.)
Sadler Pl. E9 ....5A 68
Sadlers Cl. SE1 ....7G 15
Sadlers Ga. M. SW15 ....3E 116
Sadlers Ride KT8: W Mole 2G 149
Sadler's Wells Theatre 1K 7 (3A 84)
Safara Ho. SE5 ....1E 120
   (off Dalwood St.)
Saffron Av. E14 ....7F 87
Saffron Cen. Sq. CR0: C'don 1C 168
Saffron Cl. CR0: C'don 6J 155
  NW11 ....6H 45
Saffron Ct. E15 ....5G 69
   (off Maryland Pk.)
  TW14: Bedf 7E 110
Saffron Hill EC1 ....5K 7 (5A 84)
Saffron Ho. SM2: Sutt 7K 165
  TW9: Kew 1H 115
Saffron M. SW19 ....7G 135
Saffron Rd. RM5: Col R 2K 55
Saffron St. EC1 ....5K 7 (5A 84)
Saffron Way KT6: Surb 1D 162
Saffron Wharf SE1 ....6K 15
   (off Shad Thames)
Sage Cl. E6 ....5D 88
Sage M. SE22 ....5F 121
Sage St. E1 ....7J 85
Sage Way WC1 ....2G 7
Sage Yd. KT6: Surb 1F 163
Sahara Ct. UB1: S'hall 7C 76
Saigasso Cl. E16 ....6B 88
Sailacre Ho. SE10 ....5H 105
Sail Ct. E14 ....7F 87
   (off Newport Av.)

Sailmakers Ct. SW6 ....3A 118
Sail St. SE11 ....3H 19 (4K 101)
Saimet NW9 ....7G 29
   (off Wiggins Mead)
Sainfoin Rd. SW17 ....2E 136
Sainsbury Rd. SE19 ....5E 138
Sainsbury Wing 3D 12
   (within National Gallery)
St Agatha's Dr. KT2: King T 6F 133
St Agatha's Gro. SM5: Cars 1D 166
St Agnes Cl. E9 ....1J 85
St Agnes Ho. E3 ....2C 86
   (off Ordell Rd.)
St Agnes Pl. SE11 ....7K 19 (6A 102)
St Agnes Well EC1 ....3F 9
St Aidans Cl. IG11: Bark 2B 90
St Aidan's Rd. SE22 ....6H 121
  W13 ....2B 96
St Albans Av. E6 ....3D 88
  TW13: Hanw 5B 130
  W4 ....4K 97
St Albans Cl. NW11 ....1J 63
St Alban's Cres. IG8: Wfd G 7D 36
  N22 ....1A 48
St Albans Farm TW14: Houn 5A 112
St Alban's Gdns. TW11: Tedd 5A 132
St Albans Gro. SM5: Cars 7C 154
  W8 ....3K 99
St Alban's La. NW11 ....1J 63
St Albans Mans. W8 ....3K 99
   (off Kensington Ct. Pl.)
St Albans Pl. N1 ....1B 84
St Alban's Rd. EN5: Barn 1A 20
  IG3: Ilf 1K 71
  IG8: Wfd G 7D 36
  KT2: King T 6E 132
  NW5 ....3E 64
  NW10 ....1A 80
  SM1: Sutt 4H 165
St Alban's St. SW1 ....3C 12 (7H 83)
St Albans Studios W8 ....3K 99
   (off St Albans Gro.)
St Albans Ter. W6 ....6G 99
St Albans Vs. NW5 ....3E 64
St Alfege Pas. SE10 ....6E 104
St Alfege Rd. SE7 ....6B 106
St Alphage Ct. NW9 ....3K 43
St Alphage Gdn. EC2 ....6D 8 (5C 84)
St Alphage Highwalk EC2 ....6D 8
St Alphage Wlk. HA8: Edg 2J 43
St Alphege Rd. N9 ....7D 24
St Alphonsus Rd. SW4 ....4G 119
St Amunds Cl. SE6 ....4C 140
St Andrew's Av. HA0: Wemb 4A 60
St Andrews Chambers W1 ....6B 6
   (off Wells St.)
St Andrews Cl. HA4: Ruis 2B 58
  HA7: Stan 2C 42
  KT7: T Ditt 1B 162
  N12 ....4F 31
  NW2 ....3D 62
  SE16 ....5H 103
  SE28 ....6D 90
  SW19 ....6K 135
  TW7: Isle 1J 113
  TW17: Shep 4F 147
St Andrews Dr. HA7: Stan 1C 42
St Andrew's Gro. N16 ....1D 66
St Andrew's Hill EC4 ....2B 14 (6B 84)
   (not continuous)
St Andrews Ho. RM8: Dag 4A 72
  SE16 ....3H 103
   (off Southwark Pk. Rd.)
St Andrews Mans. W1 ....6G 5
   (off Dorset St.)
  W14 ....6G 99
   (off St Andrew's Rd.)

St Andrews M. N16 ....1E 66
  SE3 ....7J 105
  SW12 ....1H 137
St Andrew's Pl. NW1 ....3K 5 (4F 83)
St Andrew's Rd. CR0: C'don 4C 168
  DA14: Sidc 3D 144
  E11 ....6G 51
  E13 ....3K 87
  E17 ....2K 49
  EN1: Enf 3J 23
  IG1: Ilf 7D 52
  KT6: Surb 6D 150
  N9 ....7D 24
  NW9 ....1A 62
  NW10 ....6D 62
  NW11 ....6H 45
  RM7: Rom 6K 55
  SM5: Cars 3C 166
  UB10: Uxb 1A 74
  W3 ....7A 80
  W7 ....2J 95
  W14 ....6G 99
St Andrews Sq. KT6: Surb 6D 150
  W11 ....6G 81
St Andrew's Twr. UB1: S'hall 7G 77
St Andrew St. EC4 ....6K 7 (5A 84)
St Andrews Way E3 ....4D 86
St Andrew's Wharf SE1 ....2F 103
St Anna Rd. EN5: Barn 5A 20
St Anne's Cl. N6 ....3E 64
St Anne's Ct. BR4: W W'ck 4G 171
  NW6 ....1G 81
  W1 ....1C 12 (6H 83)
St Anne's Flats NW1 ....1C 6
   (off Doric Way)
St Annes Gdns. NW10 ....3F 79
St Annes M. SW20 ....7F 135
St Anne's Pas. E14 ....6B 86
St Anne's Rd. E11 ....2F 69
  HA0: Wemb 5D 60
St Anne's Row E14 ....6B 86
St Anne's Trad. Est. E14 ....6B 86
   (off St Anne's Row)
St Anne St. E14 ....6B 86
St Ann's IG11: Bark 1G 89
St Ann's Cl. NW4 ....3D 44
St Ann's Cres. SW18 ....6K 117
St Ann's Gdns. NW5 ....6E 64
St Ann's Hill SW18 ....5K 117
St Ann's Ho. WC1 ....2J 7
   (off Margery St.)
St Ann's La. SW1 ....2D 18 (3H 101)
St Ann's Pk. Rd. SW18 ....6A 118
St Ann's Pas. SW13 ....3A 116
St Ann's Rd. HA1: Harr 6J 41
  IG11: Bark 1G 89
  N9 ....2A 34
  N15 ....5B 48
  SW13 ....2B 116
  W11 ....7F 81
St Ann's Shop. Cen. HA1: Harr 6J 41
St Ann's St. SW1 ....1D 18 (3H 101)
St Ann's Ter. NW8 ....2B 82
St Ann's Vs. W11 ....1F 99
St Ann's Way CR2: S Croy 6B 168
St Anselms Ct. SW16 ....5J 137
St Anselm's Pl. W1 ....2J 11 (7F 83)
St Anselm's Rd. UB3: Hayes 2H 93
St Anthony's Av. IG8: Wfd G 6F 37
St Anthony's Cl. E1 ....1G 103
  E9 ....6B 68
   (off Wallis Rd.)
  SW17 ....2C 136
St Anthony's Ct. BR6: Farnb 2F 173
  SW17 ....2E 136
St Anthony's Flats NW1 ....2H 83
   (off Aldenham St.)
St Anthony's Way TW14: Felt 4H 111
St Antony's Rd. E7 ....7K 69
St Arvan's Cl. CR0: C'don 3E 168

St Asaph Rd. SE4 . . . . .3K 121
St Aubins Cl. N1 . . . . .1D 84
St Aubyn's Av. SW19 . . . . .5H 135
  TW3: Houn 5E 112
St Aubyn's Cl. BR6: Orp 3K 173
St Aubyn's Gdns. BR6: Orp 2K 173
St Aubyn's Rd. SE19 . . . . .6F 139
St Audrey Av. DA7: Bex 2G 127
St Augustine's Av. BR2: Brom 5C 160
  CR2: S Croy 2D 168
  HA9: Wemb 3E 60
  W5 .2E 78
St Augustine's Ct. SE1 . . . . .5H 103
    (off Lynton Rd.)
St Augustine's Ho. NW1 . . . . .1C 6
    (off Werrington St.)
St Augustine's Mans. SW1 . . . . . . .4B 18
    (off Bloomburg St.)
St Augustine's Path N5 . . . . .4C 66
St Augustine's Rd. DA17: Belv 4F 109
  NW1 . . . . .7H 65
St Augustine's Sports Cen. 2J 81
St Austell Cl. HA8: Edg 2F 43
St Austell Rd. SE13 . . . . .2E 122
St Awdry's Rd. IG11: Bark 7H 71
St Awdry's Wlk. IG11: Bark 7G 71
St Barnabas Cl. BR3: Beck 2E 158
  SE22 . . . . .5E 120
St Barnabas Ct. HA3: Hrw W 1G 41
St Barnabas Gdns. KT8: W Mole . . .5H 148
St Barnabas M. SW1 . . . . .5H 17
St Barnabas Rd. CR4: Mitc 7E 136
  E17 .6C 50
  IG8: Wfd G 1K 51
  SM1: Sutt 5B 166
St Barnabas St. SW1 . . . . . .5H 17 (5E 100)
St Barnabas Ter. E9 . . . . .5K 67
St Barnabas Vs. SW8 . . . . .1J 119
St Bartholomew's Cl. SE26 . . . . . .4J 139
St Bartholomew's Ct. E6 . . . . .2C 88
    (off St Bartholomew's Rd.)
St Bartholomew's Hospital Mus. 6B 8
St Bartholomew's Rd. E6 . . . . .2D 88
St Benedict's Cl. SW17 . . . . .5E 136
St Benet's Gro. SM5: Cars 7A 154
St Benet's Pl. EC3 . . . . . . .2F 15 (7D 84)
St Bernards CR0: C'don 3E 168
St Bernard's Cl. SE27 . . . . .4D 138
St Bernards Ho. E14 . . . . .3E 104
    (off Galbraith St.)
St Bernard's Rd. E6 . . . . .1B 88
St Blaise Av. BR1: Brom 2K 159
St Botolph Row EC3 . . . . . .1J 15 (6F 85)
St Botolphs E1 . . . . .7J 9
    (off St Botolph St.)
St Botolph St. EC3 . . . . .7J 9 (6F 85)
St Brelades Cl. N1 . . . . .1E 84
St Bride's Av. EC4 . . . . .1A 14
  HA8: Edg 1F 43
St Brides Cl. DA18: Erith 2D 108
St Bride's Crypt Mus. 1A 14
    (within St Bride's, off Fleet St.)
St Bride's Ho. E3 . . . . .2C 86
    (off Ordell Rd.)
St Bride's Pas. EC4 . . . . .1A 14
St Bride St. EC4 . . . . .7A 8 (6B 84)
St Catherine's Apartments E3 . . . . .3D 86
    (off Bow Rd.)
St Catherines Cl. KT9: Chess 6D 162
  SW17 . . . . .2C 136
  SW20 . . . . .4E 152
St Catherines Ct. TW13: Felt 1J 129
  W4 . . . . .3A 98
St Catherine's Dr. SE14 . . . . .2K 121
St Catherine's Farm Ct. HA4: Ruis . .6E 38
St Catherines M. SW3 . . . .3E 16 (4D 100)
St Catherine's Rd. E4 . . . . .2H 35
  HA4: Ruis 6F 39
St Cecelia's Pl. SE3 . . . . .5J 105
St Cecilia's Cl. SM3: Sutt 1G 165

St Chads Cl. KT6: Surb 7C 150
St Chad's Gdns. RM6: Chad H 7E 54
St Chad's Pl. WC1 . . . . .1F 7 (3J 83)
St Chad's Rd. RM6: Chad H 7E 54
St Chad's St. WC1 . . . . .1F 7 (3J 83)
    (not continuous)
St Charles Pl. W10 . . . . .5G 81
St Charles Sq. W10 . . . . .5F 81
St Chloe's Ho. E3 . . . . .2C 86
    (off Ordell Rd.)
St Christopher Rd. UB8: Cowl 6A 74
St Christophers Cl. TW7: Isle 1J 113
St Christophers Dr. UB3: Hayes 7K 75
St Christopher's Gdns.
  CR7: Thor H 3A 156
St Christopher's Ho. NW1 . . . . .2G 83
    (off Bridgeway St.)
St Christopher's M. SM6: Wall 5G 167
St Christopher's Pl. W1 . . . . .7H 5 (6E 82)
St Clair Cl. IG5: Ilf 2D 52
St Clair Dr. KT4: Wor Pk 3D 164
St Clair Ho. E3 . . . . .3B 86
    (off British St.)
St Clair Rd. E13 . . . . .2K 87
St Clair's Rd. CR0: C'don 2E 168
St Clare Bus. Pk.
  TW12: Hamp H 6G 131
St Clare St. EC3 . . . . .1J 15 (6F 85)
St Clements Ct. EC4 . . . . .2F 15
  N7 . . . . .6A 66
  SE14 . . . . .6K 103
    (off Myers La.)
  W11 .7F 81
    (off Stoneleigh St.)
St Clement's Development E3 . . . . .3B 86
St Clements Hgts. SE26 . . . . .3G 139
St Clements Ho. E1 . . . . .6J 9
    (off Leyden St.)
St Clement's La. WC2 . . . . .1G 13 (6K 83)
St Clements Mans. SW6 . . . . .6F 99
    (off Lillie Rd.)
St Clements St. N7 . . . . .6A 66
St Clements Yd. SE22 . . . . .4F 121
St Cloud Rd. SE27 . . . . .4C 138
St Columba's Cl. E15 . . . . .4G 69
    (off Janson Rd.)
St Columbas Ho. E17 . . . . .4D 50
St Columb's Ho. W10 . . . . .5G 81
    (off Blagrove Rd.)
St Crispin's Cl. NW3 . . . . .4C 64
  UB1: S'hall 6D 76
St Cross St. EC1 . . . . .5K 7 (5A 84)
St Cuthberts Rd. N13 . . . . .6F 33
  NW2 .6H 63
St Cyprian's St. SW17 . . . . .4D 136
St Daniel Ct. BR3: Beck 7C 140
    (off Brackley Rd.)
St Davids Cl. BR4: W W'ck 7D 158
  HA9: Wemb 3J 61
  SE16 . . . . .5H 103
    (off Masters Dr.)
St Davids Ct. BR1: Brom 3F 161
  E17 .3E 50
  TW15: Ashf 2B 128
St David's Dr. HA8: Edg 1F 43
St Davids M. E3 . . . . .3A 86
    (off Morgan St.)
  E18 .1J 51
St David's Pl. NW4 . . . . .7D 44
St Davids Sq. E14 . . . . .5D 104
St Denis Rd. SE27 . . . . .4D 138
St Dionis Rd. SW6 . . . . .2H 117
St Domingo Ho. SE18 . . . . .3D 106
    (off Leda Rd.)
St Donatt's Rd. SE14 . . . . .1B 122
ST DUNSTAN'S 6H 165
St Dunstans All. EC3 . . . . .2G 15
St Dunstans Av. W3 . . . . .7K 79
St Dunstan's Cl. UB3: Harl 5H 93
St Dunstan's Ct. EC4 . . . . . .1K 13 (6A 84)
St Dunstan's Gdns. W3 . . . . .7K 79

St Dunstans Hill EC3 . . . . . .3G 15 (7E 84)
  SM1: Sutt 5G 165
St Dunstan's Ho. WC2 . . . . .1J 13
    (off Chancery La.)
St Dunstan's La. BR3: Beck 6E 158
  EC3 . . . . .3G 15 (7E 84)
St Dunstans M. E1 . . . . .5A 86
    (off White Horse Rd.)
St Dunstan's Rd. E7 . . . . .6K 69
  SE25 . . . . .4F 157
  TW4: Cran 2K 111
    (not continuous)
  TW13: Felt 3H 129
  W6 . . . . .5F 99
  W7 . . . . .2J 95
St Edmund's Av. HA4: Ruis 6F 39
St Edmunds Cl. DA18: Erith 2D 108
  NW8 .1D 82
  SW17 . . . . .2C 136
St Edmund's Ct. NW8 . . . . .1D 82
    (off St Edmund's Ter.)
St Edmund's Dr. HA7: Stan 1A 42
St Edmund's La. TW2: Whitt 7F 113
St Edmund's Rd. IG1: Ilf 6D 52
  N9 . . . . .7B 24
St Edmunds Sq. SW13 . . . . .6E 98
St Edmund's Ter. NW8 . . . . .1C 82
St Edward's Cl. NW11 . . . . .6J 45
St Edwards Ct. NW11 . . . . .6J 45
St Edwards Way
  RM1: Rom 5K 55
St Egberts Way E4 . . . . .1K 35
St Elmo Rd. W12 . . . . .1B 98
St Elmos Rd. SE16 . . . . .2A 104
St Erkenwald M. IG11: Bark 1H 89
St Erkenwald Rd.
  IG11: Bark 1H 89
St Ermin's Hill SW1 . . . . .1C 18
St Ervan's Rd. W10 . . . . .5H 81
St Eugene Ct. NW6 . . . . .1G 81
    (off Salusbury Rd.)
St Faith's Cl. EN2: Enf 1H 23
St Faith's Rd. SE21 . . . . .1B 138
St Fidelis Rd. DA8: Erith 4K 109
St Fillans Rd. SE6 . . . . .1E 140
St Francis Cl. BR5: Pet W 6J 161
St Francis' Ho. NW1 . . . . .2H 83
    (off Bridgeway St.)
St Francis Rd. SW12 . . . . .6F 119
St Francis Rd. DA8: Erith 4K 109
  SE22 . . . . .4E 120
St Francis Way IG1: Ilf 4H 71
St Frideswide's M. E14 . . . . .6E 86
St Gabriel's Cl. E11 . . . . .2K 69
  E14 .5D 86
St Gabriels Ct. N11 . . . . .7C 32
St Gabriels Mnr. SE5 . . . . .1B 120
    (off Cormont Rd.)
St Gabriels Rd. NW2 . . . . .5F 63
St George's Av. E7 . . . . .7K 69
  N7 . . . . .4H 65
  NW9 .4K 43
  UB1: S'hall 7D 76
  W5 . . . . .2D 96
St George's Bldgs. SE1 . . . . .3B 102
    (off St George's Rd.)
St George's Cathedral 1K 5
St George's Cir. SE1 . . . . . .7A 14 (3B 102)
St George's Cl. HA0: Wemb 3A 60
  NW11 . . . . .6H 45
  SE28 . . . . .6D 90
  SW8 . . . . .1G 119
St Georges Ct. E6 . . . . .4D 88
  E17 .5F 51
  EC4 . . . . .7A 8 (6B 84)
  HA3: Kenton 6A 42
    (off Kenton Rd.)
  SE1 .3B 102
    (off Garden Row)
  SW1 .5A 18
    (off St George's Dr.)

St Georges Ct. SW3 . . . . .3C 16
    (off Brompton Rd.)
  SW7 .3A 100
  SW15 . . . . .4H 117
St George's Dr. SW1 . . . . . .4K 17 (4F 101)
  UB10: Ick 3B 56
ST GEORGE'S FIELD 7C 82
St George's Flds. W2 . . . . . .1D 10 (6C 82)
St George's Gdns.
  KT6: Surb 2H 163
St George's Gro. SW17 . . . . .3B 136
St George's Ho. NW1 . . . . .2H 83
    (off Bridgeway St.)
  SW11 . . . . .1E 118
    (off Charlotte Despard Av.)
St George's Ind. Est. KT2: King T . . .5D 132
  N22 .7G 33
St George's La. EC3 . . . . .2F 15
St George's Leisure Cen. 7H 85
St George's Mans. SW1 . . . . .5D 18
    (off Causton St.)
St George's M. NW1 . . . . .7D 64
  SE1 .1K 19
  SE8 .4B 104
St Georges Pde. SE6 . . . . .2B 140
    (off Perry Hill)
St George's Path SE4 . . . . .4C 122
    (off Adelaide Av.)
St George's Pl. TW1: Twick 1A 132
St George's RC Cathedral . . .1K 19 (3A 102)
St Georges Rd. BR1: Brom 2D 160
  BR3: Beck 1D 158
  BR5: Pet W 6H 161
  CR4: Mitc 3F 155
  DA14: Sidc 6D 144
  E7 . . . . .7K 69
  E10 .3E 68
  EN1: Enf 1A 24
  IG1: Ilf 7D 52
  KT2: King T 7G 133
  N13 .3E 32
  NW11 . . . . .6H 45
  RM9: Dag 5E 72
  SE1 . . . . .1K 19 (3A 102)
  SM6: Wall 5F 167
  SW19 . . . . .7H 135
    (not continuous)
  TW1: Twick 5B 114
  TW9: Rich 3F 115
  TW13: Hanw 4B 130
  W4 . . . . .2K 97
  W7 . . . . .1K 95
St George's Rd. W.
  BR1: Brom 1C 160
St George's Shop. & Leisure Cen.
  HA1: Harr 6J 41
St Georges Sq. E7 . . . . .7K 69
  E14 .7A 86
  KT3: N Mald 3A 152
  SE8 .4B 104
    (not continuous)
  SW1 . . . . .5C 18 (5H 101)
St George's Sq. M.
  SW1 . . . . .6C 18 (5H 101)
St George's Stadium 2H 57
St George's Ter. E6 . . . . .3C 88
    (off Masterman Rd.)
  NW1 .7D 64
  SE15 . . . . .7G 103
    (off Peckham Hill St.)
St George's St. W1 . . . . . . .1K 11 (7F 83)
St George's Wlk. CR0: C'don 3C 168
St George's Way SE15 . . . . .6E 102
St George's Wharf SE1 . . . . .6K 15
    (off Shad Thames)
St George Wharf SW8 . . . . . .7E 18 (6J 101)
St Gerards Cl. SW4 . . . . .5G 119
St German's Pl. SE3 . . . . .1J 123
St German's Rd. SE23 . . . . .1A 140
St Giles Av. RM10: Dag 7H 73
  UB10: Ick 4E 56

St Giles Cir.—St Leonard's Ri.

St Giles Cir. W1 . . . 6H 83
St Giles Cl. BR6: Farnb . . . 5H 173
RM10: Dag . . . 7H 73
TW5: Hest . . . 7C 94
St Giles High St. WC2 . . . 7D 6 (6H 83)
St Giles Ho. EN5: New Bar . . . 4F 21
SE5 . . . 1E 120
St Giles Pas. WC2 . . . 1D 12
St Giles Rd. SE5 . . . 7E 102
St Giles Ter. EC2 . . . 6D 8
(off Wood St.)
St Giles Twr. SE5 . . . 1E 120
(off Gables Cl.)
St Gilles Ho. E2 . . . 2K 85
(off Mace St.)
St Gothard Rd. SE27 . . . 4D 138
(not continuous)
St Gregory Cl. HA4: Ruis . . . 4A 58
St Helena Ho. WC1 . . . 2J 7
(off Margery St.)
St Helena Rd. SE16 . . . 4K 103
St Helena St. WC1 . . . 2J 7 (3A 84)
St Helena Ter. TW9: Rich . . . 5D 114
St Helens KT7: T Ditt . . . 7K 149
St Helens Cl.
KT4: Wor Pk . . . 1C 164
UB8: Cowl . . . 5A 74
St Helen's Cres. SW16 . . . 1K 155
St Helen's Gdns. W10 . . . 5F 81
St Helens Pl. E10 . . . 7A 50
EC3 . . . 7G 9 (6E 84)
St Helen's Rd. DA18: Erith . . . 2D 108
IG1: Ilf . . . 6D 52
SW16 . . . 1K 155
W13 . . . 1B 96
ST HELIER . . . 7C 154
St Helier Av. SM4: Mord . . . 7A 154
St Helier Ct. N1 . . . 1E 84
(off De Beauvoir Est.)
SE16 . . . 2K 103
(off Poolmans St.)
St Helier's Av. TW3: Houn . . . 5E 112
St Helier's Rd. E10 . . . 6E 50
St Hilary's Ct. BR1: Brom . . . 3F 161
St Hilda's Av. TW15: Ashf . . . 5A 128
St Hilda's Cl. NW6 . . . 7F 63
SW17 . . . 2C 136
St Hilda's Rd. SW13 . . . 6D 98
St Hilda's Wharf E1 . . . 1J 103
(off Wapping High St.)
St Hubert's Ho. E14 . . . 3C 104
(off Janet St.)
St Hughes Cl. SW17 . . . 2C 136
St Hugh's Rd. SE20 . . . 1H 157
St Ivian Ct. N10 . . . 2E 46
St James SE14 . . . 1A 122
St James Apartments E17 . . . 5A 50
(off Pretoria Av.)
St James Av. N20 . . . 3H 31
SM1: Sutt . . . 5J 165
W13 . . . 1A 96
St James Cl.
EN4: E Barn . . . 4G 21
HA4: Ruis . . . 2A 58
KT3: N Mald . . . 5B 152
N20 . . . 3H 31
SE18 . . . 5G 107
St James Ct. CR0: C'don . . . 7B 156
E2 . . . 3G 85
(off Bethnal Grn. Rd.)
E12 . . . 2A 70
SE3 . . . 1K 123
SW1 . . . 1B 18 (3G 101)
St James Gdns.
HA0: Wemb . . . 7D 60
RM6: Chad H . . . 4B 54
St James Ga. IG9: Buck H . . . 1F 37
St James Gro. SW11 . . . 2D 118
St James Hall N1 . . . 1C 84
(off Prebend St.)
St James Ind. M. SE1 . . . 5G 103
St James Mans. NW6 . . . 7J 63
(off West End La.)
SE1 . . . 1J 19
(off McAuley Cl.)
St James M. E14 . . . 3E 104
E17 . . . 5A 50
(off St James's St.)
St James Path E17 . . . 5A 50
St James Residences W1 . . . 2C 12
(off Brewer St.)
St James Rd. CR4: Mitc . . . 7E 136
E15 . . . 5H 69
KT6: Surb . . . 6D 150
N9 . . . 2C 34
SM1: Sutt . . . 5J 165
SM5: Cars . . . 3C 166
ST JAMES'S . . . 4B 12 (1H 101)
St James's App. EC2 . . . 4G 9 (4E 84)
St James's Av. BR3: Beck . . . 3A 158
E2 . . . 2J 85
TW12: Hamp H . . . 5G 131
St James's Chambers SW1 . . . 4B 12
(off Jermyn St.)
St James's Cl. NW8 . . . 1D 82
(off St James's Ter. M.)
SW17 . . . 2D 136
St James's Cotts. TW9: Rich . . . 5D 114
St James's Ct. HA1: Harr . . . 6A 42
KT1: King T . . . 3E 150
N18 . . . 5B 34
(off Fore St.)
St James's Cres. SW9 . . . 3A 120
St James's Dr. SW12 . . . 1D 136
SW17 . . . 1D 136
St James's Gdns. W11 . . . 1G 99
(not continuous)
St James's Ho. SE1 . . . 4G 103
(off Strathnairn St.)
St James's La. N10 . . . 4F 47
St James's Mkt. SW1 . . . 3C 12 (7H 83)
St James's Palace . . . 6B 12 (2G 101)
St James's Park . . . 6C 12 (2H 101)
St James's Pk.
CR0: C'don . . . 7C 156
St James's Pas. EC3 . . . 1H 15
St James's Pl. SW1 . . . 5A 12 (1G 101)
St James's Rd.
CR0: C'don . . . 7B 156
KT1: King T . . . 2D 150
SE1 . . . 6G 103
SE16 . . . 3G 103
TW12: Hamp H . . . 5F 131
St James's Sq. SW1 . . . 4B 12 (1G 101)
St James's St. E17 . . . 5A 50
SW1 . . . 4A 12 (1G 101)
St James's Ter. NW8 . . . 1D 82
(off Prince Albert Rd.)
St James's Ter. M. NW8 . . . 1D 82
St James St. W6 . . . 5E 98
St James's Wlk. EC1 . . . 3A 8 (4B 84)
St James Ter. SW12 . . . 1E 136
St James Theatre . . . 3G 101
(off Palace St.)
St James Way DA14: Sidc . . . 5E 144
St Jeromes Gro. UB3: Hayes . . . 6E 74
St Joan's Ho. NW1 . . . 1C 6
(off Phoenix Rd.)
St Joan's Rd. N9 . . . 2A 34
St John Fisher Rd. DA18: Erith . . . 3D 108
ST JOHNS . . . 2C 122
St John's Av. N11 . . . 5J 31
NW10 . . . 1B 80
SW15 . . . 5F 117
St Johns Chu. Rd. E9 . . . 5J 67
St Johns Cl. HA9: Wemb . . . 5E 60
N14 . . . 6B 22
N20 . . . 3F 31
(off Rasper Rd.)
SW6 . . . 7J 99
St John's Concert Hall . . . 2E 18
St John's Cotts. SE20 . . . 7J 139
St Johns Ct. DA8: Erith . . . 4K 109
E1 . . . 1H 103
(off Scandrett St.)
HA1: Harr . . . 6K 41
HA6: Nwood . . . 1G 39
(off Murray Rd.)
IG9: Buck H . . . 1E 36
KT1: King T . . . 4E 150
(off Beaufort Rd.)
N4 . . . 2B 66
SE13 . . . 2E 122
SW10 . . . 7A 100
(off Ashburnham Rd.)
TW7: Isle . . . 2K 113
W6 . . . 4D 98
(off Glenthorne Rd.)
St John's Cres. SW9 . . . 3A 120
St Johns Dr. SW18 . . . 1K 135
St John's Est. N1 . . . 2D 84
SE1 . . . 6J 15
St John's Gdns. W11 . . . 7G 81
St John's Gate . . . 4A 8
St John's Gro. N19 . . . 2G 65
SW13 . . . 2B 116
TW9: Rich . . . 4E 114
St John's Hill SW11 . . . 5B 118
St John's Hill Gro. SW11 . . . 4B 118
St Johns Ho. E14 . . . 4E 104
(off Pier St.)
SE17 . . . 6D 102
(off Lytham St.)
St John's La. EC1 . . . 4A 8 (4B 84)
St John's Lodge NW3 . . . 7C 64
(off King Henry's Rd.)
St John's Mans. EC1 . . . 1A 8
(off St John St.)
St John's M. KT1: Hamp W . . . 2C 150
W11 . . . 6J 81
St Johns Pde. DA14: Sidc . . . 4A 144
(off Sidcup High St.)
W13 . . . 1B 96
St John's Pk. SE3 . . . 7H 105
St John's Pk. Mans. N19 . . . 3G 65
St John's Pas. SW19 . . . 6G 135
St John's Path EC1 . . . 4A 8
St Johns Pathway SE23 . . . 1J 139
St John's Pl. EC1 . . . 4A 8 (4B 84)
St John's Rd. BR5: Pet W . . . 6H 161
CR0: C'don . . . 3B 168
DA8: Erith . . . 5K 109
DA14: Sidc . . . 4B 144
(not continuous)
DA16: Well . . . 3B 126
E4 . . . 4J 35
E6 . . . 1C 88
E16 . . . 6J 87
E17 . . . 2D 50
HA1: Harr . . . 6K 41
HA9: Wemb . . . 4D 60
IG2: Ilf . . . 7H 53
IG11: Bark . . . 1J 89
KT1: Hamp W . . . 2C 150
KT3: N Mald . . . 3J 151
KT8: E Mos . . . 4H 149
N15 . . . 6E 48
NW11 . . . 6H 45
SE20 . . . 6J 139
SM1: Sutt . . . 2K 165
SM5: Cars . . . 3C 166
SW11 . . . 4C 118
SW19 . . . 7G 135
TW7: Isle . . . 2K 113
TW9: Rich . . . 4E 114
TW13: Hanw . . . 4C 130
UB2: S'hall . . . 3C 94
St John's Sq. EC1 . . . 4A 8 (4B 84)
St John's Ter. E7 . . . 6K 69
SE18 . . . 6G 107
SW15 . . . 3A 134
(off Kingston Va.)
W10 . . . 4F 81
St John St. EC1 . . . 1K 7 (2A 84)
St John's Va. SE8 . . . 2C 122
St John's Vs. N11 . . . 5J 31
(off Friern Barnet Rd.)
N19 . . . 2H 65
W8 . . . 3K 99
(off St Mary's Pl.)
St John's Way N19 . . . 2G 65
ST JOHN'S WOOD . . . 1A 4 (2B 82)
St John's Wood Ct. NW8 . . . 2B 4
St John's Wood High St.
NW8 . . . 1C 4 (2B 82)
St John's Wood Pk. NW8 . . . 1B 82
St John's Wood Rd. NW8 . . . 3A 4 (4B 82)
St John's Wood Ter. NW8 . . . 2B 82
St John's Yd. N17 . . . 7A 34
St Josephs Almshouses W6 . . . 4F 99
(off Brook Grn.)
St Joseph's Cl. BR6: Orp . . . 4K 173
W10 . . . 5G 81
St Joseph's College Sports Cen. . . . 6B 138
St Joseph's Cotts. SW3 . . . 4E 16
(off Cadagon St.)
St Josephs Ct. SE2 . . . 6D 108
SE7 . . . 6K 105
St Joseph's Dr. UB1: S'hall . . . 1C 94
St Joseph's Flats NW1 . . . 1C 6
(off Drummond Cres.)
St Joseph's Gro. NW4 . . . 4D 44
St Joseph's Ho. W6 . . . 4F 99
(off Brook Grn.)
St Joseph's Rd. N9 . . . 7C 24
St Joseph's St. SW8 . . . 1F 119
St Joseph's Va. SE3 . . . 3F 123
St Judes Ct. IG8: Wfd G . . . 7H 37
St Jude's Rd. E2 . . . 2H 85
St Jude St. N16 . . . 5E 66
St Julian's Cl. SW16 . . . 4A 138
St Julian's Farm Rd. SE27 . . . 4A 138
St Julian's Rd. NW6 . . . 1J 81
St Katharine Docks . . . 3K 15
St Katharine's Pier . . . 1F 103
St Katharine's Pct. NW1 . . . 2F 83
St Katharine's Way E1 . . . 4K 15 (1F 103)
(not continuous)
St Katharine's Yacht Haven . . . 1F 103
(off St Katharine's Way)
St Katherine's Rd. DA18: Erith . . . 2D 108
St Katherine's Row EC3 . . . 2H 15
St Katherines Wlk. W11 . . . 1F 99
(off St Ann's Rd.)
St Keverne Rd. SE9 . . . 4C 142
St Kilda Rd. BR6: Orp . . . 1K 173
W13 . . . 1A 96
St Kilda's Rd. HA1: Harr . . . 6J 41
N16 . . . 1D 66
St Kitts Ter. SE19 . . . 5E 138
St Laurence Cl. NW6 . . . 1F 81
St Lawrence Bus. Cen. TW13: Felt . . . 2K 129
St Lawrence Cl. HA8: Edg . . . 7A 28
St Lawrence Cotts. E14 . . . 1E 104
(off St Lawrence St.)
St Lawrence Ct. N1 . . . 7D 66
St Lawrence Dr. HA5: Eastc . . . 5K 39
St Lawrence Ho. SE1 . . . 7H 15
(off Purbrook St.)
St Lawrence St. E14 . . . 1E 104
St Lawrence Ter. W10 . . . 5G 81
St Lawrence Way SW9 . . . 1A 120
St Leger Ct. NW6 . . . 7F 63
(off Coverdale Rd.)
St Leonard M. N1 . . . 2E 84
(off Hoxton St.)
St Leonard's Av. E4 . . . 6A 36
HA3: Kenton . . . 5C 42
St Leonard's Cl. DA16: Well . . . 3A 126
St Leonards Ct. N1 . . . 1F 9
SW14 . . . 3J 115
St Leonard's Gdns. IG1: Ilf . . . 5G 71
TW5: Hest . . . 7C 94
St Leonard's Ri. BR6: Orp . . . 4J 173

St Leonard's Rd. CR0: Wadd 3B **168**
  E14 . . . . .5D **86**
  (not continuous)
  KT6: Surb 5D **150**
  KT7: T Ditt 6A **150**
  KT10: Clay 6A **162**
  NW10 . . . . .4K **79**
  SW14 .3H **115**
  W13 . . . . .7C **78**
St Leonards Sq. KT6: Surb 5D **150**
  NW5 . . . . .6E **64**
St Leonard's St. E3 . . . . .3D **86**
St Leonard's Studios SW3 . . . . . . .6E **16**
  (off Smith St.)
St Leonard's Ter. SW3 . . . . .6E **16** (5D **100**)
St Leonard's Wlk. SW16 . . . . .7K **137**
St Loo Av. SW3 . . . . .7D **16** (6C **100**)
St Loo Ct. SW3 . . . . .7D **16**
  (off St Loo Av.)
St Louis Rd. SE27 . . . . .4D **138**
St Loy's Rd. N17 . . . . .2E **48**
St Lucia Dr. E15 . . . . .1H **87**
St Lucia Cl. UB8: Cowl 6A **74**
ST LUKE'S 3D **8** (4C **84**)
St Luke's Av. EN2: Enf 1J **23**
  IG1: Ilf 5F **71**
  SW4 . . . . .4H **119**
St Luke's Cl. EC1 . . . . .3D **8** (4C **84**)
  SE25 . . . . .6H **157**
St Lukes Ct. E10 . . . . .7D **50**
  (off Capworth St.)
  W11 . . . . .6H **81**
  (off St Luke's Rd.)
St Luke's Est. EC1 . . . . .2E **8** (3D **84**)
St Lukes M. E14 . . . . .2C **104**
  (off Strafford St.)
  W11 . . . . .6H **81**
St Luke's Pas. KT2: King T 1F **151**
St Luke's Path IG1: Ilf 5F **71**
St Luke's Rd. UB10: Uxb 1A **74**
  W11 . . . . .5H **81**
St Luke's Sq. E16 . . . . .6H **87**
St Luke's St. SW3 . . . . .5D **16** (5C **100**)
St Luke's Yd. W9 . . . . .2H **81**
  (not continuous)
St Malo Av. N9 . . . . .3D **34**
ST MARGARETS 6B **114**
St Margarets IG11: Bark 1H **89**
  KT2: King T 5J **133**
St Margarets Av. DA15: Sidc 3H **143**
  HA2: Harr 3G **59**
  N15 . . . . .4B **48**
  N20 . . . . .1F **31**
  SM3: Cheam 3G **165**
  TW15: Ashf 5D **128**
  UB8: Hil 4C **74**
St Margarets Bus. Cen.
  TW1: Twick 6B **114**
St Margarets Cl. EC2 . . . . .6D **84**
St Margarets Ct. HA8: Edg 5C **28**
  N11 . . . . .4K **31**
  SE1 . . . . .5D **14** (1C **102**)
  SW15 .4D **116**
St Margaret's Cres. SW15 . . . . . . .5D **116**
St Margaret's Dr. TW1: Twick 5B **114**
St Margaret's Gro. E11 . . . . .3H **69**
  SE18 . . . . .6G **107**
  TW1: Twick 6A **114**
St Margaret's Ho. NW1 . . . . .2E **12**
  (off Polygon Rd.)
St Margaret's La. W8 . . . . .3K **99**
St Margaret's M. KT2: King T 5J **133**
St Margaret's Pas. SE13 . . . . .3G **123**
  (not continuous)
St Margarets Path SE18 . . . . .5G **107**
St Margarets Rd. E12 . . . . .2A **70**
  HA4: Ruis 6F **39**
  HA8: Edg 5C **28**
  N17 . . . . .3E **48**
  NW10 . . . . .3E **80**

St Margarets Rd. SE4 . . . . .4B **122**
  (not continuous)
  TW1: Twick 6B **114**
  TW7: Isle, Twick 4B **114**
  W7 . . . . .2J **95**
ST MARGARETS RDBT. 6B **114**
St Margaret's Sports Cen. 1A **26**
St Margaret's Ter. SE18 . . . . .5G **107**
St Margaret St. SW1 . . . . .7E **12** (2J **101**)
St Marks Cl. EN5: New Bar 3E **20**
  HA1: Harr 7B **42**
  SE10 . . . . .7E **104**
  SW6 . . . . .1J **117**
  W11 . . . . .6G **81**
St Marks Ct. NW8 . . . . .2A **82**
  (off Abercorn Pl.)
  W7 . . . . .2J **95**
  (off Lwr. Boston Rd.)
St Mark's Cres. NW1 . . . . .1E **82**
St Mark's Ga. E9 . . . . .7B **68**
St Mark's Gro. SW10 . . . . .7K **99**
St Marks Hill KT6: Surb 6E **150**
St Marks Ho. SE17 . . . . .6D **102**
  (off Lytham St.)
St Marks Ind. Est. E16 . . . . .1B **106**
St Mark's Pl. RM10: Dag 6G **73**
  SW19 .6H **135**
  W11 . . . . .6G **81**
St Mark's Ri. E8 . . . . .5F **67**
St Marks Rd. BR2: Brom 3J **159**
  CR4: Mitc 2D **154**
  EN1: Enf 6A **24**
  SE25 . . . . .4G **157**
  TW11: Tedd 7B **132**
  W5 . . . . .1E **96**
  W7 . . . . .2J **95**
  W10 . . . . .5F **81**
  W11 . . . . .6G **81**
St Mark's Sq. NW1 . . . . .1E **82**
St Mark St. E1 . . . . .1K **15** (6F **85**)
St Mark's Vs. N4 . . . . .2K **65**
  (off Moray Rd.)
St Martin Cl. UB8: Cowl 6A **74**
St Martin-in-the-Fields Church . . .3E **12**
  (off St Martin's Pl.)
St Martin's Almshouses NW1 . . . . .1G **83**
St Martin's App. HA4: Ruis 7G **39**
St Martin's Av. E6 . . . . .2B **88**
St Martin's Cl. DA18: Erith 2D **108**
  EN1: Enf 1C **24**
  NW1 . . . . .1G **83**
St Martins Ct. EC4 . . . . .7C **8**
  (off Newgate St.)
  N1 . . . . .1E **84**
  (off De Beauvoir Est.)
  WC2 . . . . .2E **12** (7J **83**)
St Martin's Courtyard WC2 . . . . . . .2E **12**
  (off Up. St Martin's La.)
St Martins Est. SW2 . . . . .1A **138**
St Martin's Ho. NW1 . . . . .1C **6**
  (off Polygon Rd.)
St Martin's La. BR3: Beck 5D **158**
  WC2 . . . . .2E **12** (7J **83**)
St Martin's Le-Grand EC1 . . . .7C **8** (6C **84**)
St Martin's Pl. WC2 . . . . . . .3E **12** (7J **83**)
St Martin's Rd. N9 . . . . .2C **34**
  SW9 . . . . .2K **119**
St Martin's St. WC2 . . . . . . .3D **12** (7H **83**)
  (not continuous)
St Martin's Theatre 2E **12**
  (off West St.)
St Martins Way SW17 . . . . .3A **136**
St Mary Abbot's Ct. W14 . . . . .3H **99**
  (off Warwick Gdns.)
St Mary Abbot's Pl. W8 . . . . .3H **99**
St Mary Abbot's Ter. W14 . . . . .3H **99**
St Mary at Hill EC3 . . . . . . .3G **15** (7E **84**)
St Mary Av. SM6: Wall 3E **166**
St Mary Axe EC3 . . . . .1G **15** (6E **84**)
St Marychurch St. SE16 . . . . .2J **103**
St Mary Graces Ct. E1 . . . . . .3K **15** (7F **85**)

St Marylebone Cl. NW10 . . . . .1A **80**
St Marylebone Crematorium N2 . . .3K **45**
St Mary le-Park Ct. SW11 . . . . .7C **100**
  (off Parkgate Rd.)
St Mary Newington Cl. SE17 . . . . . .5E **102**
  (off Surrey Sq.)
St Mary Rd. E17 . . . . .4C **50**
St Mary's IG11: Bark 1H **89**
St Mary's App. E12 . . . . .5D **70**
St Mary's Av. BR2: Brom 3G **159**
  E11 . . . . .7K **51**
  N3 . . . . .2G **45**
  TW11: Tedd 6K **131**
St Mary's Av. Central UB2: S'hall . . .4F **95**
St Mary's Av. Nth. UB2: S'hall 4F **95**
St Mary's Av. Sth. UB2: S'hall 4F **95**
St Mary's Cl. KT9: Chess 7F **163**
  KT17: Ewe 7B **164**
  N17 . . . . .1G **49**
  TW16: Sun 4J **147**
St Mary's Copse KT4: Wor Pk 2A **164**
St Mary's Ct. E3 . . . . .3D **86**
  (off Bow Rd.)
  E6 . . . . .4D **88**
  KT3: N Mald 3A **152**
  SE7 . . . . .7A **106**
  SM6: Wall 4G **167**
  W5 . . . . .2D **96**
  W6 . . . . .3B **98**
St Mary's Cres. NW4 . . . . .3D **44**
  TW7: Isle 7H **95**
  UB3: Hayes 7H **75**
St Mary's Dr. TW14: Bedf 7E **110**
St Mary's Est. SE16 . . . . .2J **103**
  (off Elephant La.)
St Mary's Flats NW1 . . . . .1C **6**
  (off Drummond Cres.)
St Mary's Gdns. SE11 . . . .3K **19** (4A **102**)
St Mary's Ga. W8 . . . . .3K **99**
St Mary's Grn. N2 . . . . .2A **46**
St Mary's Gro. N1 . . . . .6B **66**
  SW13 .3D **116**
  TW9: Rich 4F **115**
  W4 . . . . .6H **97**
St Mary's Ho. N1 . . . . .1B **84**
  (off St Mary's Path)
St Mary's Mans. W2 . . . . . .5A **4** (5B **82**)
St Marys M. NW6 . . . . .7K **63**
  TW10: Ham 2C **132**
St Mary's Path E1 . . . . .6G **85**
  (off White Church La.)
  N1 . . . . .1B **84**
St Mary's Pl. SE9 . . . . .6D **124**
  W5 . . . . .2D **96**
  W8 . . . . .3K **99**
St Marys Rd. DA5: Bexl 1J **145**
  E10 . . . . .3E **68**
  E13 . . . . .2K **87**
  EN4: E Barn 7J **21**
  IG1: Ilf 2G **71**
  KT4: Wor Pk 2A **164**
  KT6: Surb 7C **150**
    (St Chads Cl.)
  KT6: Surb 6D **150**
    (Victoria Rd.)
  KT8: E Mos 5H **149**
  N8 . . . . .4J **47**
  N9 . . . . .1C **34**
  (not continuous)
  NW10 . . . . .1A **80**
  NW11 . . . . .7G **45**
  SE15 . . . . .1J **121**
  SE25 . . . . .3E **156**
  SW19 .5G **135**
  UB3: Hayes 7H **75**
  W5 . . . . .2D **96**
St Mary's Sq. W2 . . . . .5A **4** (5B **82**)
  W5 . . . . .2D **96**
St Mary's Ter. W2 . . . . .5A **4** (5B **82**)
St Mary's Twr. EC1 . . . . .4D **8**
  (off Fortune St.)

St Mary St. SE18 . . . . .4D **106**
St Mary's University College 3K **131**
St Mary's University College Sports Cen.
  . . . . .4K **131**
St Mary's Vw. HA3: Kenton 5C **42**
St Mary's Wlk. SE11 . . . . .3K **19** (4A **102**)
  UB3: Hayes 7H **75**
St Mary's Way IG7: Chig 5K **37**
St Matthew Cl. UB8: Cowl 6A **74**
St Matthew's Av. KT6: Surb 1E **162**
St Matthews Ct. E10 . . . . .7D **50**
  N10 . . . . .2E **46**
  SE1 . . . . .3C **102**
  (off Meadow Row)
  TW15: Ashf 4C **128**
  (off Feltham Rd.)
St Matthew's Dr. BR1: Brom 3D **160**
St Matthews Ho. SE17 . . . . .6D **102**
  (off Phelp St.)
St Matthew's Lodge NW1 . . . . .2G **83**
  (off Oakley Sq.)
St Matthew's Rd. SW2 . . . . .4K **119**
  W5 . . . . .1E **96**
St Matthew's Row E2 . . . . .3G **85**
St Matthew St. SW1 . . . . . .2C **18** (3H **101**)
St Matthias Cl. NW9 . . . . .5B **44**
St Maur Rd. SW6 . . . . .1H **117**
St Mellion Cl. SE28 . . . . .6D **90**
St Merryn Cl. SE18 . . . . .7H **107**
St Merryn Ct. BR3: Beck 7C **140**
St Michael's All. EC3 . . . .1F **15** (6D **84**)
St Michael's Av. HA9: Wemb 6G **61**
  N9 . . . . .7D **24**
St Michaels Cl. BR1: Brom 3C **160**
  DA18: Erith 2D **108**
  E16 . . . . .5B **88**
  KT4: Wor Pk 2B **164**
  N3 . . . . .2H **45**
  N12 . . . . .5H **31**
St Michaels Ct. CR0: C'don 1C **168**
  (off Poplar Wlk.)
  E14 . . . . .5E **86**
  (off St Leonard's Rd.)
  SE1 . . . . .7D **14**
  (off Trinity St.)
St Michael's Cres. HA5: Pinn 6C **40**
St Michael's Flats NW1 . . . . .1C **6**
  (off Aldenham St.)
St Michael's Gdns. W10 . . . . .5G **81**
St Michael's M. SW1 . . . . . .4G **17** (4E **100**)
St Michael's Ri. DA16: Well 1B **126**
St Michael's Rd. CR0: C'don 1C **168**
  DA16: Well 3B **126**
  NW2 . . . . .4E **62**
  SM6: Wall 6G **167**
  SW9 . . . . .2K **119**
  TW15: Ashf 5C **128**
St Michael's St. W2 . . . . . . .7B **4** (6B **82**)
St Michaels Ter. N6 . . . . .1E **64**
  (off South Gro.)
  N22 . . . . .1J **47**
St Mildred's Ct. EC2 . . . . . .1E **14** (6D **84**)
St Mildreds Rd. SE6 . . . . .7G **123**
  SE12 . . . . .7G **123**
St Mirren Ct. EN5: New Bar 5F **21**
St Nicholas Cen. SM1: Sutt 5K **165**
St Nicholas Cl. UB8: Cowl 6A **74**
St Nicholas Ct. KT1: King T 4E **150**
  (off Surbiton Rd.)
St Nicholas Dr. TW17: Shep 7C **146**
St Nicholas' Flats NW1 . . . . .1C **6**
  (off Werrington St.)
St Nicholas Glebe SW17 . . . . .5E **136**
St Nicholas Ho. SE8 . . . . .6C **104**
  (off Deptford Grn.)
St Nicholas M. KT7: T Ditt 6K **149**
St Nicholas Rd. KT7: T Ditt 6K **149**
  SE18 . . . . .5K **107**
  SM1: Sutt 5K **165**
St Nicholas St. SE8 . . . . .1B **122**
St Nicholas Way SM1: Sutt 4K **165**

St Nicolas La. BR7: Chst 1C 160
St Ninian's Ct. N20 . . . . .3J 31
St Norbert Grn. SE4 . . . . .4A 122
St Norbert Rd. SE4 . . . . .5K 121
St Olaf Ho. SE1 . . . . .4F 15
St Olaf's Rd. SW6 . . . . .7G 99
St Olaf Stairs SE1 . . . . .4F 15
St Olave's Cl. EC2 . . . . .1E 14 (6D 84)
St Olave's Est. SE1 . . . . .6H 15 (2E 102)
St Olave's Gdns. SE11 . . . . .3J 19 (4A 102)
St Olaves Ho. SE11 . . . . .3J 19
(off Walnut Tree Wlk.)
St Olave's Mans. SE11 . . . . .3J 19
St Olave's Rd. E6 . . . . .1E 88
St Olaves Wlk. SW16 . . . . .2G 155
St Olav's Sq. SE16 . . . . .2J 103
St Onge Pde. EN1: Enf 3J 23
(off Southbury Rd.)
St Oswald's Pl. SE11 . . . . . .6G 19 (5K 101)
St Oswald's Rd. SW16 . . . . .1B 156
St Oswalds Studios SW6 . . . . .6J 99
(off Sedlescombe Rd.)
St Oswulf St. SW1 . . . . .4D 18 (4H 101)
St Owen Ho. SE1 . . . . .3E 102
(off St Saviour's Est.)
ST PANCRAS 2F 7 (3J 83)
St Pancras Commercial Cen. NW1 . . .1G 83
(off Pratt St.)
St Pancras Cl. N2 . . . . .2B 46
St Pancras Way NW1 . . . . .7G 65
St Patrick's Cl. IG8: Wfd G 7B 36
St Paul Cl. UB8: Cowl 5A 74
St Paulinus Ct. DA1: Cray 4K 127
(off Manor Rd.)
St Paul's All. EC4 . . . . .1B 14
(off St Paul's Chyd.)
St Paul's Av. HA3: Kenton 4F 43
NW2 . . . . .6E 62
SE16 . . . . .1K 103
St Paul's Bldgs. EC1 . . . . .3B 8
(off Dallington St.)
St Paul's Cathedral
London 1B 14 (6C 84)
St Paul's Chyd. EC4 . . . . . .1B 14 (6B 84)
St Pauls Cl. KT9: Chess 4D 162
SE7 . . . . .5B 106
SM5: Cars 1C 166
TW3: Houn 2C 112
TW15: Ashf 5E 128
UB3: Harl 5F 93
W5 . . . . .2F 97
St Pauls Ct. SW4 . . . . .5H 119
TW4: Houn 3C 112
St Pauls Courtyard SE8 . . . . .7C 104
(off Crossfield St.)
ST PAUL'S CRAY 2K 161
St Paul's Cray Rd. BR7: Chst 1H 161
St Paul's Cres. NW1 . . . . .7H 65
(not continuous)
St Paul's Dr. E15 . . . . .5F 69
St Pauls Ho. SE8 . . . . .7C 104
(off Market Yd.)
St Paul's M. NW1 . . . . .7H 65
St Paul's Pl. N1 . . . . .6D 66
St Paul's Ri. N13 . . . . .6G 33
St Paul's Rd. CR7: Thor H 3C 156
DA8: Erith 7J 109
IG11: Bark 1G 89
N1 . . . . .6D 66
N17 . . . . .7B 34
TW8: Bford 6D 96
TW9: Rich 3F 115
St Paul's Shrubbery N1 . . . . .6D 66
St Paul's Sq. BR2: Brom 2H 159
St Paul's Studios W14 . . . . .5G 99
(off Talgarth Rd.)
St Pauls Ter. SE17 . . . . .6B 102
St Paul St. N1 . . . . .1C 84
(not continuous)
St Pauls Vw. Apartments EC1 . . . . . .2J 7
(off Amwell St.)

St Paul's Wlk. KT2: King T 7G 133
St Paul's Way E3 . . . . .5B 86
N3 . . . . .7E 30
St Paul's Wood Hill BR5: St P 2J 161
St Peter Claver Ct. BR3: Beck 1D 158
(off Albemarle Rd.)
St Peter's All. EC3 . . . . .1F 15
(off Gracechurch St.)
St Peter's Av. E2 . . . . .2G 85
E17 . . . . .4G 51
N18 . . . . .4B 34
St Petersburgh M. W2 . . . . .7K 81
St Petersburgh Pl. W2 . . . . .7K 81
St Peter's Cen. E1 . . . . .1H 103
(off Reardon St.)
St Peter's Chu. Ct. N1 . . . . .1B 84
(off St Peter's St.)
St Peters Cl. BR7: Chst 7H 143
E2 . . . . .2G 85
HA4: Ruis 2B 58
IG2: Ilf .4J 53
SW17 . . . . .2C 136
WD23: B Hea 1C 26
St Peters Cl. E1 . . . . .4J 85
(off Cephas St.)
KT8: W Mole 4E 148
NW4 . . . . .5E 44
SE12 .5H 123
WC1 . . . . .2F 7
(off Seaford St.)
St Peter's Gdns. SE27 . . . . .3A 138
St Peter's Gro. W6 . . . . .4C 98
St Peters Ho. SE17 . . . . .6D 102
WC1 . . . . .2F 7
(off Regent Sq.)
St Peters M. N4 . . . . .5B 48
N8 . . . . .5A 48
St Peter's Path E17 . . . . .3G 51
St Peters Pl. W9 . . . . .4K 81
St Peters Rd. CR0: C'don 4D 168
KT1: King T 2G 151
KT8: W Mole 4E 148
N9 . . . . .1C 34
TW1: Twick 5B 114
UB1: S'hall 5E 76
UB8: Cowl 5A 74
W6 . . . . .5C 98
St Peter's Sq. E2 . . . . .2G 85
W6 . . . . .4B 98
St Peter's St. CR2: S Croy 5D 168
N1 . . . . .1B 84
(off St Peters St.)
St Peter's Ter. SW6 . . . . .7H 99
St Peter's Vs. W6 . . . . .4C 98
St Peters Way N1 . . . . .7E 66
UB3: Harl 5F 93
W5 . . . . .5D 78
St Peter's Wharf W4 . . . . .5C 98
St Philip Ho. WC1 . . . . .2J 7
(off Lloyd Baker St.)
St Philip's Av. KT4: Wor Pk 2D 164
St Philip's Ga. KT4: Wor Pk 2D 164
St Philip Sq. SW8 . . . . .2F 119
St Philips Rd. E8 . . . . .6G 67
KT6: Surb 6D 150
St Philip's Way N1 . . . . .1C 84
St Quentin Ho. SW18 . . . . .6B 118
St Quentin Rd. DA16: Well 3K 125
St Quintin Av. W10 . . . . .5E 80
St Quintin Gdns. W10 . . . . .5E 80
St Quintin Rd. E13 . . . . .3K 87
St Quintin Vw. W10 . . . . .5E 80
St Raphael's Way NW10 . . . . .5J 61
St Regis Cl. N10 . . . . .2F 47
St Regis Hgts. NW3 . . . . .3K 63
St Richard's Ho. NW1 . . . . .1C 6
(off Eversholt St.)
St Ronan's Cl. EN4: Had W 1G 21
St Ronan's Cres. IG8: Wfd G 7D 36

St Rule St. SW8 . . . . .2G 119
St Saviours Ct. HA1: Harr 5J 41
N22 . . . . .2H 47
St Saviour's Est. SE1 . . . . . . .7J 15 (2F 103)
St Saviour's Rd. CR0: C'don 6B 156
SW2 . . . . .5K 119
St Saviour's Wharf SE1 . . . . .6K 15
(off Mill St., Mill St.)
SE1 . . . . .6K 15
(off Shad Thames, Shad Thames)
Saints Cl. SE27 . . . . .4B 138
Saints Dr. E7 . . . . .5B 70
St Silas Pl. NW5 . . . . .6E 64
St Simon's Av. SW15 . . . . .5E 116
Saints M. CR4: Mitc 3C 154
St Stephen's Av. E17 . . . . .5E 50
W12 . . . . .1D 98
(not continuous)
W13 . . . . .6B 78
St Stephens Cl. E17 . . . . .5D 50
NW5 . . . . .5D 64
(off Malden Rd.)
NW8 . . . . .1C 82
UB1: S'hall 5E 76
St Stephens Cr. EN1: Enf 6K 23
(off Park Av.)
N8 . . . . .6K 47
W2 . . . . .6B 78
St Stephen's Cres. CR7: Thor H 3A 156
W2 . . . . .6J 81
St Stephen's Gdns. SW15 . . . . .5H 117
TW1: Twick 6C 114
W2 . . . . .6J 81
(not continuous)
St Stephens Gro. SE13 . . . . .3E 122
St Stephens Ho. SE17 . . . . .6D 102
(off Lytham St.)
St Stephen's M. W2 . . . . .5J 81
St Stephens Pde. E7 . . . . .7A 70
St Stephen's Pas. TW1: Twick 6C 114
St Stephen's Rd. E3 . . . . .1A 86
E6 . . . . .7A 70
E17 . . . . .5D 50
EN5: Barn 5A 20
TW3: Houn 6E 112
UB7: Yiew 1A 92
W13 . . . . .6B 78
St Stephen's Row EC4 . . . . .1E 14
St Stephen's Ter. SW8 . . . . .7K 101
St Stephen's Wlk. SW7 . . . . .4A 100
(off Southwell Gdns.)
St Swithins La. EC4 . . . . . . .2E 14 (7D 84)
St Swithun's Rd. SE13 . . . . .6F 123
St Theresa's Cl. E9 . . . . .4C 68
St Theresa's Rd. TW14: Felt 4H 111
St Thomas Cl. KT6: Surb 1F 163
St Thomas Ct. DA5: Bexl 7G 127
E10 . . . . .7D 50
(off Lake Rd.)
HA5: Pinn 1C 40
NW1 . . . . .7G 65
(off Wrotham Rd.)
St Thomas Dr. BR5: Farnb 1G 173
HA5: Pinn 1C 40
St Thomas Gdns. IG1: Ilf 6G 71
St Thomas Ho. E1 . . . . .6K 85
(off W. Arbour St.)
St Thomas M. SW18 . . . . .5J 117
St Thomas Rd. DA17: Belv 2J 109
E16 . . . . .6J 87
N14 . . . . .7C 22
W4 . . . . .6J 97
St Thomas's Gdns. NW5 . . . . .6E 64
St Thomas's Pl. E9 . . . . .7J 67
St Thomas's Rd. N4 . . . . .2A 66
NW10 .1A 80
St Thomas's Sq. E9 . . . . .7J 67
St Thomas St. SE1 . . . . .5F 15 (1D 102)
St Thomas's Way SW6 . . . . .7H 99
St Timothys M. BR1: Brom 1K 159
St Ursula Gro. HA5: Pinn 5B 40

St Ursula Rd. UB1: S'hall 6E 76
St Vincent Cl. SE27 . . . . .5B 138
St Vincent De Paul Ho. E1 . . . . .5J 85
(off Jubilee St.)
St Vincent Ho. SE1 . . . . .3F 103
(off St Saviour's Est.)
St Vincent Rd. TW2: Whitt 6G 113
St Vincent's La. NW7 . . . . .4K 29
St Vincent St. W1 . . . . .6H 5 (5E 82)
St Wilfrid's Cl. EN4: E Barn 5H 21
St Wilfrid's Rd. EN4: E Barn 5G 21
St Williams Ct. N1 . . . . .7J 65
St Winefride's Av. E12 . . . . .5D 70
St Winifred's Rd. TW11: Tedd 6B 132
Sakura Dr. N22 . . . . .1H 47
Salamanca Pl. IG11: Bark 2B 90
SE1 . . . . .4G 19 (4K 101)
Salamanca Sq. SE1 . . . . .4G 19
(off Salamanca Pl.)
Salamanca St. SE1 . . . . .4G 19 (4K 101)
SE11 . . . . .4G 19 (4K 101)
Salamander Cl. KT2: King T 5C 132
Salamander Quay KT1: Hamp W 1D 150
Salcombe Dr. RM6: Chad H 6F 55
SM4: Mord 1F 165
Salcombe Gdns. NW7 . . . . .6K 29
Salcombe Rd. E17 . . . . .7B 50
N16 . . . . .5E 66
TW15: Ashf 3A 128
Salcombe Vs. TW10: Rich 5E 114
Salcombe Way HA4: Ruis 2J 57
UB4: Hayes 3F 75
Salcott Rd. CR0: Bedd 3J 167
SW11 .5C 118
Salehurst Cl. HA3: Kenton 5E 42
Salehurst Rd. SE4 . . . . .6B 122
Salem Pl. CR0: C'don 3C 168
Salem Rd. W2 . . . . .7K 81
Salento Cl. N3 . . . . .7D 30
Sale Pl. W2 . . . . .6C 4 (5C 82)
Sale St. E2 .4G 85
Salford Ho. E14 . . . . .4E 104
(off Seyssel St.)
Salford Rd. SW2 . . . . .1H 137
Salhouse Cl. SE28 . . . . .6C 90
Salisbury Av. IG11: Bark 7H 71
N3 . . . . .3H 45
SM1: Sutt 6H 165
Salisbury Cl. KT4: Wor Pk 3B 164
SE17 .4D 102
Salisbury Ct. E9 . . . . .5A 68
(off Mabley St.)
EC4 . . . . .1A 14 (6B 84)
EN2: Enf 4J 23
(off London Rd.)
SE16 . . . . .3G 103
(off Stork's Rd.)
SM5: Cars 5D 166
UB5: N'olt 5F 59
(off Newmarket Av.)
Salisbury Gdns. IG9: Buck H 2G 37
SW19 .7G 135
Salisbury Hall Gdns. E4 . . . . .6H 35
Salisbury Ho. E14 . . . . .6D 86
(off Hobday St.)
EC2 . . . . .6F 9
(off London Wall)
HA7: Stan 6F 27
N1 . . . . .1B 84
(off St Mary's Path)
SM6: Wall 5F 167
SW1 . . . . .5D 18
(off Drummond Ga.)
SW9 . . . . .7A 102
(off Cranmer Rd.)
Salisbury Mans. N15 . . . . .5B 48
Salisbury M. SW6 . . . . .7H 99
Salisbury Pas. SW6 . . . . .7H 99
(off Dawes Rd.)
Salisbury Pavement SW6 . . . . .7H 99
(off Dawes Rd.)

Salisbury Pl. SW9 . . . . .7B **102**
  W1 . . . . .5E **4** (5D **82**)
Salisbury Prom. N8 . . . . .5B **48**
Salisbury Rd. BR2: Brom 5C **160**
  DA5: Bexl 1G **145**
  E4 . . . . .3H **35**
  E7 . . . . .6J **69**
  E10 .2E **68**
  E12 .5B **70**
  E17 .5E **50**
  EN5: Barn 3B **20**
  HA1: Harr 5H **41**
  HA5: Eastc 4J **39**
  IG3: Ilf 2J **71**
  KT3: N Mald 3K **151**
  KT4: Wor Pk 4K **163**
  N4 . . . . .5B **48**
  N22 .1B **48**
  RM10: Dag 6H **73**
  SE25 . . . . .6G **157**
  SM5: Cars 6D **166**
  SW19 . . . . .7G **135**
  TW4: Houn 3A **112**
  TW6: H'row A 6E **110**
    (not continuous)
  TW9: Rich 4E **114**
  TW13: Felt 1A **130**
  UB2: S'hall 4C **94**
  W13 .2B **96**
Salisbury Sq. EC4 . . . . .1K **13** (6A **84**)
Salisbury St. NW8 . . . . .4C **4** (4C **82**)
  W3 . . . . .2J **97**
Salisbury Ter. SE15 . . . . .3J **121**
Salisbury Wlk. N19 . . . . .2G **65**
Salix Cl. TW16: Sun 7K **129**
Salix Ct. N3 . . . . .6D **30**
Salix La. IG8: Wfd G 1C **52**
Salk Cl. NW9 . . . . .2A **44**
Salliesfield TW2: Whitt 6H **113**
Sally Murray Cl. E12 . . . . .4E **70**
Salmen Rd. E13 . . . . .2H **87**
Salmond Cl. HA7: Stan 6F **27**
Salmon La. E14 . . . . .6A **86**
Salmon M. NW6 . . . . .5J **63**
Salmon Rd. DA17: Belv 5G **109**
  N9 . . . . .1B **34**
Salmon St. E14 . . . . .6B **86**
  NW9 .1H **61**
Salomons Rd. E13 . . . . .5A **88**
Salop Rd. E17 . . . . .6K **49**
Saltash Cl. SM1: Sutt 4H **165**
Saltash Rd. DA16: Well 1C **126**
  IG6: Ilf 1H **53**
Saltcoats Rd. W4 . . . . .2A **98**
Saltcroft Cl. HA9: Wemb 1H **61**
Saltdene N4 . . . . .1K **65**
Salter Cl. HA2: Harr 4D **58**
Salterford Rd. SW17 . . . . .6E **136**
Saltern Ct. IG11: Bark 3B **90**
    (off Galleons Dr.)
Salter Rd. SE16 . . . . .1K **103**
Salters Ct. EC4 . . . . .1D **14**
Salter's Hall Ct. EC4 . . . . .2E **14**
Salter's Hill SE19 . . . . .5D **138**
Salters Rd. E17 . . . . .4F **51**
  W10 .4F **81**
Salters Row N1 . . . . .6D **66**
    (off Tilney Gdns.)
Salter St. E14 . . . . .7B **86**
  NW10 . . . . .3C **80**
Salterton Rd. N7 . . . . .3K **65**
Salt Hill Cl. UB8: Uxb 5A **56**
Saltley Cl. E6 . . . . .6C **88**
Salton Cl. N3 . . . . .2J **45**
Salton Sq. E14 . . . . .6B **86**
Saltoun Rd. SW2 . . . . .4A **120**
Saltram Cl. N15 . . . . .4F **49**
Saltram Cres. W9 . . . . .3H **81**
Saltwell St. E14 . . . . .7C **86**
Saltwood Gro. SE17 . . . . .5D **102**

Saltwood Ho. SE15 . . . . .6J **103**
    (off Lovelinch Cl.)
Salusbury Rd. NW6 . . . . .1G **81**
Salus Ct. CRO: C'don 4C **168**
    (off Parker Rd.)
  CRO: C'don 4C **168**
    (off Parker Rd.)
Salutation Rd. SE10 . . . . .4G **105**
Salvador SW17 . . . . .5D **136**
Salvia Gdns. UB6: G'frd 2A **78**
Salvin Rd. SW15 . . . . .3F **117**
Salway Cl. IG8: Wfd G 7D **36**
Salway Pl. E15 . . . . .6F **69**
Salway Rd. E15 . . . . .6F **69**
Samantha Cl. E17 . . . . .7B **50**
Samaras Mans. E20 . . . . .5E **68**
    (off Liberty Bri. Rd.)
Sam Bartram Cl. SE7 . . . . .5A **106**
Sambourne Family Home, The
  18 Stafford Terrace 3J **99**
    (off Stafford Ter.)
Sambrook Ho. E1 . . . . .5J **85**
    (off Jubilee St.)
  SE11 . . . . .4J **19**
Sambruck M. SE6 . . . . .1D **140**
Samels Cl. W6 . . . . .5C **98**
Samford Ho. N1 . . . . .1A **84**
    (off Barnsbury Est.)
Samford St. NW8 . . . . .4C **4** (4B **82**)
Samira Cl. E17 . . . . .6C **50**
Sam Manners Ho. SE10 . . . . .5G **105**
    (off Tuskar St.)
Sam March Ho. E14 . . . . .6F **87**
    (off Blair St.)
Sammi Cl. CR7: Thor H 4C **156**
Samos Rd. SE20 . . . . .2H **157**
Samphire Hgts. E20 . . . . .5E **68**
    (off Napa Cl.)
Sampson Av. EN5: Barn 5A **20**
Sampson Cl. DA17: Belv 3D **108**
Sampson Ct. TW17: Shep 5E **146**
Sampson Ho. SE1 . . . . . .4A **14** (1B **102**)
Sampson St. E1 . . . . .1G **103**
Samsbrooke Ct. EN1: Enf 6K **23**
Samsuda Est. E14 . . . . .2A **88**
Samual Ferguson Pl. IG11: Bark . . .2K **89**
Samuda Est. E14 . . . . .3K **15**
Samuel Cl. E8 . . . . .1F **85**
  HA7: Stan 2F **27**
  SE14 . . . . .6K **103**
  SE18 . . . . .4C **106**
Samuel Ct. N1 . . . . .2G **9**
    (off Pitfield St.)
Samuel Gray Gdns. KT2: King T . . .1D **150**
Samuel Ho. E8 . . . . .1F **85**
    (off Clarissa St.)
Samuel Johnson Cl. SW16 . . . . . . .4K **137**
Samuel Jones Ct. SE15 . . . . .7E **102**
Samuel Lewis Bldgs. N1 . . . . .6A **66**
Samuel Lewis Trust Dwellings E8 . .5G **67**
    (off Amhurst Rd.)
  N16 .6E **48**
  SW3 . . . . .4C **16** (4C **100**)
  SW6 .7J **99**
    (off Vanston Pl.)
  W14 .4H **99**
    (off Lisgar Ter.)
Samuel Lewis Trust Est. SE5 . . . . .1C **120**
    (off Warner Rd.)
Samuel Richardson Ho. W14 . . . . . .4H **99**
    (off North End Cres.)
Samuel's Cl. W6 . . . . .4E **98**
Samuel St. SE15 . . . . .7F **103**
  SE18 . . . . .4D **106**
Samuel Wallis Lodge SE3 . . . . . . .3H **123**
    (off Banning St.)
  SE10 . . . . .4G **105**
    (off Banning St.)
Sanchia Ct. E2 . . . . .3G **85**
    (off Wellington Row)
Sancroft Ho. NW2 . . . . .3D **62**

Sancroft Ho. SE11 . . . . .5H **19**
Sancroft Rd. HA3: W'stone 2K **41**
Sancroft St. SE11 . . . . .5H **19** (5K **101**)
Sanctuary, The
  DA5: Bexl 6D **126**
  SM4: Mord 6J **153**
  SW1 .1D **18**
Sanctuary M. E8 . . . . .6F **67**
Sanctuary Rd. TW6: H'row A 6C **110**
Sanctuary St. SE1 . . . . . .6D **14** (2C **102**)
Sandale Cl. N16 . . . . .3D **66**
Sandall Cl. W5 . . . . .4E **78**
Sandall Rd. E3 . . . . .2A **86**
  NW5 .6G **65**
  W5 . . . . .4E **78**
Sandal Rd. KT3: N Mald 5K **151**
  N18 .5B **34**
Sandal St. E15 . . . . .1G **87**
Sandalwood Cl. E1 . . . . .4A **86**
Sandalwood Dr. HA4: Ruis 7E **38**
Sandalwood Ho.
  DA15: Sidc 2K **143**
Sandalwood Mans. W8 . . . . .3K **99**
    (off Stone Hall Gdns.)
Sandalwood Rd. TW13: Felt 3K **129**
Sandbach Pl. SE18 . . . . .4G **107**
Sandbanks TW14: Felt 1G **129**
Sandbourne NW8 . . . . .1K **81**
    (off Abbey Rd.)
  W11 .6J **81**
    (off Dartmouth Cl.)
Sandbourne Av. SW19 . . . . .2K **153**
Sandbourne Rd. SE4 . . . . .2A **122**
Sandbrook Cl. NW7 . . . . .6E **28**
Sandbrook Rd. N16 . . . . .3E **66**
Sandby Ho. NW10 . . . . .3D **80**
    (off Plough Cl.)
Sandby Grn. SE9 . . . . .3C **124**
Sandby Ho. NW6 . . . . .1J **81**
Sandcliff Rd. DA8: Erith 4K **109**
Sandcroft Cl. N13 . . . . .6G **33**
Sandell's Av. TW15: Ashf 4E **128**
Sandell St. SE1 . . . . .6J **13** (2A **102**)
Sanderling Cl. SE8 . . . . .6B **104**
    (off Abinger Gro.)
  SE28 . . . . .7C **90**
Sanderling Lodge E1 . . . . .3K **15**
    (off Star Pl.)
Sanders Cl. TW12: Hamp H 5G **131**
Sanders Ho. WC1 . . . . .1J **7**
    (off Gt. Percy St.)
Sanders La. NW7 . . . . .7A **30**
    (Bittacy Ri.)
  NW7 .7A **30**
    (Grants Cl.)
  TW4: Houn 5D **112**
Sanderson Ho. E16 . . . . .5J **87**
    (off Hammersley Rd.)
  SE8 .5B **104**
    (off Grove St.)
Sandersons La. W4 . . . . .5K **97**
    (off Chiswick High Rd.)
Sanderson Sq. BR1: Brom 3E **160**
Sanderstead Av. NW2 . . . . .2G **63**
Sanderstead Cl. SW12 . . . . .7G **119**
Sanderstead Rd.
  CR2: Sande, S Croy 7D **168**
  E10 .1A **68**
Sanders Way N19 . . . . .1H **65**
Sandes Ct. CR7: Thor H 3C **156**
Sandfield WC1 . . . . .2F **7**
    (off Cromer St.)
Sandfield Gdns. CR7: Thor H 3B **156**
Sandfield Pas. CR7: Thor H 3C **156**
Sandfield Pl. CR7: Thor H 3C **156**
Sandfield Rd. CR7: Thor H 3B **156**
Sandford Av. N22 . . . . .1C **48**
Sandford Cl. E6 . . . . .4D **88**
Sandford Ct. EN5: New Bar 3E **20**
  N16 .1E **66**

Sandford Rd. BR2: Brom 3J **159**
  DA7: Bex 4E **126**
  E6 . . . . .3C **88**
Sandford St. SW6 . . . . .7K **99**
Sandgate Cl. RM7: Rush G 7J **55**
Sandgate Ho. E5 . . . . .5H **67**
  W5 . . . . .5C **78**
Sandgate La. SW18 . . . . .1C **136**
Sandgate Rd. DA16: Well 7C **108**
Sandgate St. SE15 . . . . .6H **103**
Sandgate Trad. Est. SE15 . . . . .6H **103**
    (off Sandgate St.)
Sandham Ct. SW4 . . . . .1J **119**
Sandham Point SE18 . . . . .4F **107**
    (off Vincent Rd.)
Sandhills SM6: Bedd 4H **167**
Sandhills, The SW10 . . . . .7A **16**
    (off Limerston St.)
Sandhills Mdw. TW17: Shep 7E **146**
Sandhurst Av. HA2: Harr 6F **41**
  KT5: Surb 7H **151**
Sandhurst Cl. CR2: Sande 7E **168**
  NW9 .3G **43**
Sandhurst Ct. SW2 . . . . .4J **119**
Sandhurst Dr. IG3: Bark, Ilf 4K **71**
Sandhurst Ho. E1 . . . . .5J **85**
    (off Wolsey St.)
  E17 .1B **50**
    (off Robinswood Gdns.)
Sandhurst Mkt. SE6 . . . . .1E **140**
    (off Sandhurst Rd.)
Sandhurst Rd. BR6: Chels 3K **173**
  DA5: Bexl 5D **126**
  DA15: Sidc 3K **143**
  N9 . . . . .6D **24**
  NW9 .3G **43**
  SE6 .1F **141**
Sandhurst Way CR2: Sande 7E **168**
Sandifer Dr. NW2 . . . . .3F **63**
Sandiford Rd. SM3: Sutt 2H **165**
Sandiland Cres. BR2: Hayes 2H **171**
Sandilands CRO: C'don 2G **169**
Sandilands Rd. SW6 . . . . .1K **117**
Sandison St. SE15 . . . . .3G **121**
Sandland St. WC1 . . . . .6H **7** (5K **83**)
Sandling Ri. SE9 . . . . .3E **142**
Sandlings, The N22 . . . . .2A **48**
Sandlings Cl. SE15 . . . . .2H **121**
Sandmartin Way SM6: Wall 1E **166**
Sandmere Rd. SW4 . . . . .4J **119**
Sandon Cl. KT10: Esh 7H **149**
Sandover Ho. SE16 . . . . .3G **103**
    (off Spa Rd.)
Sandow Cres. UB3: Hayes 3H **93**
Sandown Av. RM10: Dag 6J **73**
Sandown Ct. TW5: Cran 1J **111**
Sandown Ct. HA7: Stan 5H **27**
  RM10: Dag 6J **73**
    (off Sandown Av.)
  SE26 . . . . .3H **139**
  SM2: Sutt 7K **165**
Sandown Dr. SM5: Cars 7E **166**
Sandown Rd. SE25 . . . . .5H **157**
Sandown Way UB5: N'olt 6C **58**
Sandpiper Cl. E17 . . . . .7E **34**
  SE16 . . . . .2B **104**
Sandpiper Ct. E1 . . . . .7G **85**
    (off Thomas More St.)
  E14 .3E **104**
    (off New Union Cl.)
  SE8 .6C **104**
    (off Edward Pl.)
Sandpiper Rd. SM1: Sutt 5H **165**
Sandpiper Ter. IG5: Ilf 3F **53**
Sandpit Pl. SE7 . . . . .5C **106**
Sandpit Rd. BR1: Brom 5G **141**
Sandpits Rd. CRO: C'don 4K **169**
  TW10: Ham 2D **132**
Sandra Cl. N22 . . . . .1C **48**
  TW3: Houn 5F **113**
Sandra Ct. CR4: Mitc 6D **136**

Sandra Ho. KT8: E Mos 5H 149
Sandridge Cl. HA1: Harr 4J 41
Sandridge St. N19 . . . . .2G 65
Sandringham Av. SW20 . . . . .1G 153
Sandringham Bldgs. SE17 . . . . . . .4D 102
(off Balfour St.)
Sandringham Cl. EN1: Enf 2K 23
IG6: Ilf 3G 53
SW19 . . . . .1F 135
Sandringham Ct. DA15: Sidc 6K 125
KT2: King T 1E 150
(off Skerne Way)
SE16 . . . . .1K 103
(off King & Queen Wharf)
UB10: Hil 4E 74
W1 . . . . .1B 12
(off Dufour's Pl.)
W9 . . . . .3A 82
(off Maida Vale)
Sandringham Cres. HA2: Harr 2E 58
Sandringham Dr. DA2: Wilm 2K 145
DA16: Well 2J 125
TW15: Ashf 4A 128
Sandringham Flats WC2 . . . . .2D 12
(off Charing Cross Rd.)
Sandringham Gdns. IG6: Ilf 3G 53
KT8: W Mole 4E 148
N8 . . . . .6J 47
N12 . . . . .6G 31
TW5: Cran 1J 111
Sandringham Ho. W14 . . . . .4G 99
(off Windsor Way)
Sandringham M. TW12: Hamp 1D 148
W5 . . . . .7D 78
Sandringham Rd. BR1: Brom 5J 141
CR7: Thor H 5C 156
E7 . . . . .5A 70
E8 . . . . .5F 67
E10 . . . . .6F 51
IG11: Bark 5K 71
KT4: Wor Pk 3C 164
N22 . . . . .3C 48
NW2 . . . . .6D 62
NW11 . . . . .7G 45
TW6: H'row A 5A 110
UB5: N'olt 7E 58
Sandrock Pl. CRO: C'don 4K 169
Sandrock Rd. SE13 . . . . .3C 122
SANDS END 1A 118
Sand's End La. SW6 . . . . .1K 117
Sandstone La. E16 . . . . .7K 87
Sandstone Pl. N19 . . . . .2F 65
Sandstone Rd. SE12 . . . . .2K 141
Sands Way Wfd G 6J 37
Sandtoft Rd. SE7 . . . . .6K 105
Sandwell Cres. NW6 . . . . .6J 63
Sandwich Ho. SE16 . . . . .2J 103
(off Swan Rd.)
WC1 . . . . .2E 6
(off Sandwich St.)
Sandwich St. WC1 . . . . . .2E 6 (3J 83)
Sandwick Cl. NW7 . . . . .7H 29
Sandy Bury BR6: Orp 3H 173
Sandycombe Rd.
TW9: Kew, Rich 3F 115
TW14: Felt 1J 129
Sandycoombe Rd. TW1: Twick 6C 114
Sandycroft SE2 . . . . .6A 108
Sandy Dr. TW14: Felt 1G 129
Sandy Hill Av. SE18 . . . . .5F 107
Sandy Hill Rd. SE18 . . . . .5F 107
SM6: Wall 7G 167
Sandyhill Rd. IG1: Ilf 4F 71
Sandy La. BR5: St P 7D 144
BR6: Orp 7K 161
CR4: Mitc 1E 154
DA14: Sidc 7D 144
HA3: Kenton 6F 43
KT1: Hamp W 7A 132
KT12: Walt T 6K 147
SM2: Cheam 7G 165

Sandy La.
SM6: Wall 6H 167
TW10: Ham 2C 132
TW11: Hamp W, Tedd 7A 132
Sandy La. Nth. SM6: Wall 6H 167
Sandy La. Sth. SM6: Wall 7G 167
Sandymount Av. HA7: Stan 5H 27
Sandy Ridge BR7: Chst 6E 142
Sandy Rd. NW3 . . . . .2K 63
NW11 . . . . .2K 63
Sandys Row E1 . . . . .6H 9 (5E 84)
Sandy Way CRO: C'don 3B 170
KT12: Walt T 7H 147
Sanford La. N16 . . . . .3F 67
Sanford St. SE14 . . . . .6A 104
Sanford Ter. N16 . . . . .3F 67
Sanford Wlk. N16 . . . . .2F 67
SE14 . . . . .6A 104
Sangam Cl. UB2: S'hall 3C 94
Sanger Av. KT9: Chess 5E 162
Sangley Rd. SE6 . . . . .7D 122
SE25 . . . . .4E 156
Sangora Rd. SW11 . . . . .4B 118
Sankey Ho. E2 . . . . .2J 85
(off St James's Av.)
Sansom Rd. E11 . . . . .2H 69
Sansom St. SE5 . . . . .1D 120
Sans Wlk. EC1 . . . . .3K 7 (4A 84)
Santa Maria Cl. E1 . . . . .5A 86
(off Ocean Est.)
Sant Ho. SE17 . . . . .4C 102
(off Browning St.)
Santiago Ct. E1 . . . . .5A 86
(off Ocean Est.)
Santina Apartment CRO: C'don 1D 168
(off Cherry Orchard Rd.)
Santley Ho. SE1 . . . . .7K 13 (2A 102)
Santley St. SW4 . . . . .4K 119
Santos Rd. SW18 . . . . .5J 117
Santway, The HA7: Stan 5D 26
Sapcote Trad. Cen. NW10 . . . . .6B 62
Saperton Wlk. SE11 . . . . .3H 19
Saphire Ct. E15 . . . . .1E 86
(off Warton Rd.)
Saphora Cl. BR6: Farnb 5H 173
Sapperton Ct. EC1 . . . . .3C 8
Sapperton Ho. W2 . . . . .5J 81
(off Westbourne Pk. Rd.)
Sapphire Cl. E6 . . . . .6E 88
RM8: Dag 1C 72
Sapphire Ct. E1 . . . . .7G 85
(off Cable St.)
Sapphire Rd. NW10 . . . . .7J 61
SE8 . . . . .4A 104
Saracen Cl. CRO: C'don 6D 156
Saracens Head Yd.
EC3 . . . . .1J 15
Saracens RUFC 7K 29
Saracen St. E14 . . . . .6C 86
Sarah Ct. UB5: N'olt 1D 76
Sarah Ho. E1 . . . . .6H 85
(off Commercial Rd.)
Sarah Swift Ho. SE1 . . . . .6F 15
(off Kipling St.)
Sara La. Ct. N1 . . . . .2E 84
(off Stanway St.)
Saratoga Rd. E5 . . . . .4J 67
Sara Turnbull Ho. SE18 . . . . .4D 106
Saravia Ct. SE13 . . . . .6G 123
Sardinia St. WC2 . . . . .1G 13 (6K 83)
Sarita Cl. HA3: Hrw W 2H 41
Sarjant Path SW19 . . . . .2F 135
(off Blincoe Cl.)
Sarjeant Ct. BR4: W W'ck 2F 171
(off Bencurtis Pk.)
Sark Cl. TW5: Hest 7E 94
Sark Ho. EN3: Enf W 1E 24
Sark Twr. SE28 . . . . .2G 107
Sark Wlk. E16 . . . . .6K 87
Sarnes Ct. N11 . . . . .4A 32
(off Oakleigh Rd. Sth.)

Sarnesfield Ho. SE15 . . . . .6H 103
(off Pencraig Way)
Sarnesfield Rd. EN2: Enf 4J 23
Sarratt Ho. W10 . . . . .5E 80
(off Sutton Way)
Sarre Rd. NW2 . . . . .5H 63
Sarsen Av. TW3: Houn 2E 112
Sarsfeld Rd. SW12 . . . . .2D 136
Sarsfield Rd. UB6: G'frd 2B 78
Sartor Rd. SE15 . . . . .4K 121
Sarum Ho. W11 . . . . .7H 81
(off Portobello Rd.)
Sarum Ter. E3 . . . . .4B 86
Sassoon NW9 . . . . .1B 44
Satanita Cl. E16 . . . . .6B 88
Satchell Mead NW9 . . . . .1B 44
Satchell Rd. E2 . . . . .2K 9 (3G 85)
Satchwell St. E2 . . . . .2K 9 (3G 85)
Satin Ho. E1 . . . . .1K 15
Sattar M. N16 . . . . .3D 66
Saturn Ho. E3 . . . . .1F 87
(off Garrison Rd.)
E15 . . . . .1F 87
(off High St.)
Sauls Grn. E11 . . . . .3G 69
Saundby La. SE3 . . . . .4K 123
Saunders Apartments E3 . . . . .3C 86
(off Marchant St.)
Saunders Cl. E14 . . . . .7B 86
(off Limehouse C'way.)
IG1: Ilf 1H 71
Saunders Ho. SE16 . . . . .2K 103
(off Quebec Way)
Saunders Ness Rd. E14 . . . . .5E 104
Saunders Rd. SE18 . . . . .5K 107
UB10: Uxb 7B 56
Saunders St. SE11 . . . . . . .3J 19 (4A 102)
Saunders Way SE28 . . . . .7B 90
Saunderton Rd. HA0: Wemb 5B 60
Saunton Av. UB3: Harl 7H 93
Saunton Ct. UB1: S'hall 7G 77
(off Haldane Rd.)
Savage Gdns. E6 . . . . .6D 88
EC3 . . . . .2H 15 (7E 84)
(not continuous)
Savannah Cl. SE15 . . . . .7F 103
Savera Cl. UB2: S'hall 3A 94
Savernake Rd. HA7: Stan 6G 27
Savernake Ho. N4 . . . . .7C 48
Savernake Rd. N9 . . . . .6B 24
NW3 . . . . .4D 64
Savery Dr. KT6: Surb 7B 150
Savile Cl. KT3: N Mald 5A 152
KT7: T Ditt 7K 149
Savile Gdns. CRO: C'don 2F 169
Saville Row W1 . . . . .2A 12 (7G 83)
Saville Cres. TW15: Ashf 6F 129
Saville Rd. E16 . . . . .1C 106
RM6: Chad H 6F 55
TW1: Twick 1K 131
W4 . . . . .3K 97
Saville Row BR2: Hayes 1H 171
EN3: Enf H 2E 24
Savill Gdns. SW20 . . . . .3C 152
Savill Ho. E16 . . . . .1F 107
(off Robert St.)
SW4 . . . . .6H 119
Savill Row Wfd G 6C 36
Savin Lodge SM2: Sutt 7A 166
(off Walnut M.)
Savona Cl. SW19 . . . . .7F 135
Savona Ho. SW8 . . . . .7G 101
(off Savona St.)
Savona St. SW8 . . . . .7G 101
Savoy Av. UB3: Harl 5G 93
Savoy Bldgs. WC2 . . . . .3G 13
Savoy Chapel 3G 13
(off Savoy Hill)
SAVOY CIRCUS 7B 80
Savoy Cl. E15 . . . . .1G 87
HA8: Edg 5B 28

Savoy Ct. HA2: Harr 5F 41
NW3 . . . . .3A 64
SW5 . . . . .4J 99
(off Cromwell Rd.)
WC2 . . . . .3F 13 (7K 83)
Savoy Hill WC2 . . . . .3G 13 (7K 83)
Savoy M. SW9 . . . . .3J 119
Savoy Pde. EN1: Enf 3K 23
Savoy Pl. W12 . . . . .1F 99
WC2 . . . . .3F 13 (7J 83)
Savoy Row WC2 . . . . .2G 13
Savoy Steps WC2 . . . . .3G 13
Savoy St. WC2 . . . . .3G 13 (7K 83)
Savoy Theatre 3F 13
(off Strand)
Savoy Way WC2 . . . . .3G 13
Sawbill Cl. UB4: Yead 5B 76
Sawkins Cl. SW19 . . . . .2G 135
Sawley Rd. W12 . . . . .1C 98
Saw Mill Way N16 . . . . .6G 49
Sawmill Yd. E3 . . . . .1A 86
Sawtry Cl. SM5: Cars 7C 154
Sawyer Cl. N9 . . . . .2B 34
Sawyer Ct. NW10 . . . . .7K 61
Sawyers Cl. RM10: Dag 6J 73
Sawyer's Hill TW10: Rich 7F 115
Sawyers Lawn W13 . . . . .6A 78
Sawyer St. SE1 . . . . .6C 14 (2C 102)
Saxby Rd. SW2 . . . . .7J 119
Saxham Rd. IG11: Bark 2J 89
Saxlingham Rd. E4 . . . . .3A 36
Saxon Av. TW13: Hanw 2C 130
Saxonbury Av. TW16: Sun 3K 147
Saxonbury Cl. CR4: Mitc 3B 154
Saxonbury Ct. N7 . . . . .5J 65
Saxonbury Gdns. KT6: Surb 1C 162
Saxon Bus. Cen. SW19 . . . . .2A 154
Saxon Chase N8 . . . . .6K 47
Saxon Cl. E17 . . . . .7C 50
KT6: Surb 6D 150
UB8: Hil 5B 74
Saxon Dr. W3 . . . . .6G 79
Saxonfield Cl. SW2 . . . . .7K 119
Saxon Gdns. UB1: S'hall 7C 76
Saxon Hall W2 . . . . .7K 81
(off Palace Ct.)
Saxon Ho. E1 . . . . .6K 9
(off Thrawl St.)
KT1: King T 4F 151
SM6: Wall 1E 166
(off London Rd.)
TW13: Hanw 2D 130
Saxon Lea Ct. E3 . . . . .2B 86
(off Saxon Rd.)
Saxon Lodge CRO: C'don 1C 168
(off Tavistock Rd.)
Saxon Rd. BR1: Brom 7H 141
E3 . . . . .2B 86
E6 . . . . .4D 88
HA9: Wemb 3J 61
IG1: Ilf 6F 71
KT2: King T 1E 150
N22 . . . . .1B 48
SE25 . . . . .5D 156
TW15: Ashf 6F 129
UB1: S'hall 7C 76
Saxon Ter. SE6 . . . . .2B 140
Saxon Wlk. DA14: Sidc 6C 144
Saxon Way N14 . . . . .6C 22
UB7: Harm 2D 174
Saxon Way Ind. Est. UB7: Harm 2D 174
Saxony Pde. UB3: Hayes 5E 74
Saxton Cl. SE13 . . . . .3F 123
Sayer Ct. SW5 . . . . .2D 96
Sayers Ho. N2 . . . . .2B 46
(off The Grange)
Sayer's Wlk. TW10: Rich 7F 115
Sayesbury La. N18 . . . . .5B 34
Sayes Ct. SE8 . . . . .6B 104
Sayes Ct. St. SE8 . . . . .6B 104

Scadbury Park (Nature Reserve) 7K 143
Scads Hill Cl. BR6: Pet W 6K 161
Scafell NW1 . . . . .1A 6
    (off Stanhope St.)
Scala 1F 7
Scala St. W1 . . . . .5B 6 (5G 83)
Scales Rd. N17 . . . . .3F 49
Scalpel, The 1G 15
Scampston M. W10 . . . . .6F 81
Scandrett St. E1 . . . . .1H 103
Scarab Cl. E16 . . . . .7H 87
Scarba Wlk. N1 . . . . .6D 66
    (off Essex Rd.)
Scarborough Rd. E11 . . . . .1F 69
    N4 . . . . .7A 48
    N9 . . . . .7D 24
    TW6: H'row A 6E 110
Scarborough St. E1 . . . . . .1K 15 (6F 85)
Scarbrook Rd. CR0: C'don 3C 168
Scarle Rd. HA0: Wemb 6D 60
Scarlet Cl. E20 . . . . .5D 68
Scarlet Rd. SE6 . . . . .3G 141
Scarlette Mnr. Way SW2 . . . . .7A 120
Scarlet Wlk.
    EN3: Pond E 5E 24
Scarsbrook Rd. SE3 . . . . .3B 124
Scarsdale Pl. W8 . . . . .3K 99
Scarsdale Rd. HA2: Harr 3G 59
Scarsdale Studios W8 . . . . .3J 99
    (off Stratford Rd.)
Scarsdale Vs. W8 . . . . .3J 99
Scarth Rd. SW13 . . . . .3B 116
Scawen Cl. SM5: Cars 4E 166
Scawen Rd. SE8 . . . . .5A 104
Scawfell St. E2 . . . . .2F 85
Sceaux Gdns. SE5 . . . . .1E 120
Sceptre Ct. EC3 . . . . .3K 15
    (off Tower Hill)
Sceptre Ho. E1 . . . . .4J 85
    (off Malcolm Rd.)
Sceptre Rd. E2 . . . . .3J 85
Sceynes Link N12 . . . . .4D 30
Schafer Ho. NW1 . . . . .2A 6 (3G 83)
Schofield Wlk. SE3 . . . . .7J 105
Scholars Cl. EN5: Barn 4B 20
Scholars Ho. NW6 . . . . .1J 81
    (off Glengall Rd.)
Scholars Pl. N16 . . . . .3E 66
Scholars Rd. E4 . . . . .1A 36
    SW12 . . . . .1G 137
Scholars Way RM8: Dag 4A 72
Scholefield Rd. N19 . . . . .2H 65
Scholey Ho. SW11 . . . . .3C 118
Schomberg Ho. SW1 . . . . .3D 18
    (off Page St.)
Schonfeld Sq. N16 . . . . .2D 66
School All. TW1: Twick 1A 132
School App. E2 . . . . .1H 9
    UB4: Hayes 4H 75
Schoolbank Rd. SE10 . . . . .3H 105
Schoolbell M. E3 . . . . .2A 86
Schoolgate Dr. SM4: Mord 5K 153
School Ho. SE1 . . . . .4E 102
    (off Page's Wlk.)
School Ho. La. NW7 . . . . .6B 30
    TW11: Tedd 7B 132
Schoolhouse La. E1 . . . . .7K 85
Schoolhouse Yd. SE18 . . . . .5F 107
School La.
    DA16: Well 3B 126
    HA5: Pinn .4C 40
    KT1: Hamp W 1C 150
    KT6: Surb .1F 163
    SE23 . . . . .2H 139
    TW17: Shep 6D 146
    WD23: Bush 1A 26
School M. E1 .7H 85
    (off Hawksmoor M.)
School Nook E5 . . . . .2K 67
School Pas. KT1: King T 2F 151
    UB1: S'hall .7D 76

School Rd. BR7: Chst 1G 161
    E12 . . . . .4D 70
    KT1: Hamp W 1C 150
    KT8: E Mos 4H 149
    NW10 . . . . .4K 79
    RM10: Dag .1G 91
    TW3: Houn 3G 113
    TW12: Hamp H 6G 131
    TW15: Ashf 6D 128
    UB7: Harm 2E 174
School Rd. Av. TW12: Hamp H 6G 131
SCHOOL ROAD JUNC. 7D 128
School Sq. SE10 . . . . .3H 105
School Wlk. TW16: Sun 4H 147
School Way N12 . . . . .6G 31
    RM8: Dag 3C 72
Schooner Cl. E14 . . . . .3F 105
    IG11: Bark .3B 90
    SE16 . . . . .2K 103
Schubert Rd. SW15 . . . . .5H 117
Schurlock Pl. TW2: Twick 2J 131
Schwartz Wharf E9 . . . . .7C 68
Science Mus.
    Knightsbridge 2B 16 (3B 100)
Sclater St. E1 . . . . .3J 9 (4F 85)
Scoble Pl. N16 . . . . .4F 67
Scoles Cres. SW2 . . . . .1B 138
Scoop, The 5H 15 (1E 102)
Scope Way KT1: King T 4E 150
Score Complex, The
    Leyton 3D 68
Scoresby St. SE1 . . . . .5A 14 (1B 102)
Scorton Av. UB6: G'frd 2A 78
Scorton Ho. N1 . . . . .2E 84
    (off Whitmore Est.)
Scotch Comn. W13 . . . . .5A 78
SCOTCH HOUSE 2D 100
Scoter Cl. IG8: Wfd G 7E 36
Scoter Ct. SE8 . . . . .6B 104
    (off Abinger Gro.)
Scot Gro. HA5: Pinn 1B 40
Scotia Bldg. E1 . . . . .7K 85
    (off Jardine Rd.)
Scotia Ct. SE16 . . . . .2J 103
    (off Canada Est.)
Scotia Rd. SW2 . . . . .7A 120
Scotland Grn. N17 . . . . .2F 49
Scotland Grn. Rd.
    EN3: Pond E 5E 24
Scotland Grn. Rd. Nth.
    EN3: Pond E 4E 24
Scotland Pl. SW1 . . . . .5E 12 (1J 101)
Scotland Rd. IG9: Buck H 1F 37
Scotland Yard 6E 12
Scotney Cl. BR6: Farnb 4E 172
Scotney Ho. E9 . . . . .6J 67
Scots Cl. TW19: Stanw 1A 128
Scotsdale Cl.
    BR5: Pet W 4J 161
    SM3: Cheam 7G 165
Scotsdale Rd. SE12 . . . . .5K 123
Scotson Ho. SE11 . . . . .4J 19
Scotswood St. EC1 . . . . .3K 7 (4A 84)
Scotswood Wlk. N17 . . . . .7B 34
Scott Av. SW15 . . . . .6G 117
Scott Cl. KT19: Ewe 5J 163
    SW16 . . . . .1K 155
    UB7: W Dray 4B 92
Scott Ct. W3 . . . . .2K 97
Scott Cres. HA2: Harr 1F 59
Scott Ellis Gdns. NW8 . . . . . .2A 4 (3B 82)
Scottes La. RM8: Dag 1D 72
Scott Farm Cl. KT7: T Ditt 1B 162
Scott Gdns. TW5: Hest 7B 94
Scott Ho. DA17: Belv 5F 109
    E13 . . . . .2J 87
    (off Queens Rd.)
    E14 . . . . .2C 104
    (off Admirals Way)
    N7 . . . . .6K 65
    (off Caledonian Rd.)

Scott Ho. N18 .5B 34
    (off Woolmer Rd.)
    NW8 . . . . .4C 4
    (off Broadley St.)
    NW10 . . . . .7K 61
    (off Stonebridge Pk.)
    SE8 . . . . .5B 104
    (off Grove St.)
Scott Lidgett Cres. SE16 . . . . .2G 103
Scott Rd. HA8: Edg 2H 43
Scott Russell Pl. E14 . . . . .5D 104
Scotts Av. BR2: Brom 2F 159
    TW16: Sun 7G 129
Scotts Cl. SE12 . . . . .2E 98
    (off Scott's Rd.)
Scotts Dr. TW12: Hamp 7F 131
Scotts Farm Rd. KT19: Ewe 6J 163
Scott's La. BR2: Brom 3F 159
Scotts Pas. SE18 . . . . .4F 107
Scotts Rd. BR1: Brom 7J 141
    E10 . . . . .1E 68
    UB2: S'hall .3A 94
    W12 . . . . .2D 98
Scott's Sufferance Wharf SE1 . . . . . .7K 15
Scotts Ter. SE9 . . . . .2C 142
Scott St. E1 . . . . .4H 85
Scotts Way TW16: Sun 7G 129
Scott's Yd. EC4 . . . . .2E 14 (7D 84)
Scott Trimmer Way TW3: Houn 2C 112
Scottwell Dr. NW9 . . . . .5B 44
Scoulding Ho. E14 . . . . .3C 104
    (off Mellish St.)
Scoulding Rd. E16 . . . . .6J 87
Scouler St. E14 . . . . .7E 86
Scout App. NW10 . . . . .4A 62
Scout La. SW4 . . . . .3G 119
Scout Pk. 7C 32
Scout Way NW7 . . . . .4E 28
Scovell Cres. SE1 . . . . .7C 14
Scovell Rd. SE1 . . . . .7C 14 (2C 102)
Scrattons Farm Eco-Park 2E 90
Scrattons Ter. IG11: Bark 2D 90
Screen on the Green Cinema 1B 84
    (off Upper St.)
Screenworks N5 . . . . .5C 66
Scriven Ct. E8 .1F 85
Scriven St. E8 .1F 85
Scrooby St. SE6 . . . . .6D 122
Scrope Ho. EC1 . . . . .5J 7
    (off Bourne Est.)
Scrubs La. NW10 . . . . .3C 80
    W10 . . . . .3C 80
Scrutton Cl. SW12 . . . . .7H 119
Scrutton St. EC2 . . . . .4G 9 (4E 84)
Scudamore La. NW9 . . . . .4J 43
Sculpture Ho. E1 . . . . .5K 85
    (off Duckett St.)
Scutari Rd. SE22 . . . . .5J 121
Scylla Cres. TW6: H'row A 7D 110
    (not continuous)
Scylla Rd. SE15 . . . . .3G 121
    (not continuous)
    TW6: H'row A 6D 110
Seaborne Wharf E3 . . . . .5C 86
    (off Invicta Cl.)
Seabright St. E2 . . . . .3H 85
Seabrook Dr. BR4: W W'ck 2G 171
Seabrook Gdns. RM7: Rush G 7G 55
Seabrook Rd. RM8: Dag 3D 72
Seaburn Cl. RM13: Rain 2K 91
Seacole Cl. W3 . . . . .6K 79
Seacole Ct. N21 . . . . .5F 22
    (off Pennington Dr.)
Sea Containers Ho. SE1 . . . . .3K 13
Seacon Twr. E14 . . . . .2B 104
Seacourt Rd. SE2 . . . . .2D 108
Seafarer Way SE8 . . . . .4A 104
Seafield Rd. N11 . . . . .4C 32
Seaford Cl. HA4: Ruis 1F 57
Seaford Ho. SE16 . . . . .2J 103
    (off Swan Rd.)

Seaford Rd. E17 . . . . .3D 50
    EN1: Enf 4K 23
    N15 . . . . .5D 48
    TW6: H'row A 5A 110
    W13 . . . . .1B 96
Seaford St. WC1 . . . . .2E 7 (3J 83)
Seaforth Av. KT3: N Mald 5D 152
Seaforth Cres. N5 . . . . .5C 66
Seaforth Gdns. IG8: Wfd G 5F 37
    KT19: Ewe .4B 164
    N21 . . . . .7E 22
Seaforth Pl. SW1 . . . . .1B 18
Seager Pl. SE8 . . . . .1C 122
    (off Deptford Bri.)
Seagrave Cl. E1 . . . . .5K 85
Seagrave Lodge SW6 . . . . .6J 99
    (off Seagrave Rd.)
Seagrave Rd. SW6 . . . . .6J 99
Seagry Rd. E11 . . . . .7J 51
Seagull Cl. IG11: Bark 3A 90
Seagull La. E16 . . . . .7J 87
Seahorse Sailing Club 2K 61
Sealand Rd. TW6: H'row A 6C 110
Sealand Wlk. UB5: N'olt 3B 76
Seal Ho. SE1 . . . . .7F 15
    (off Weston St.)
Sea Life London Aquarium
    . . . . .6G 13 (2K 101)
Seal St. E8 . . . . .4F 67
Searle Ho. NW8 . . . . .1C 82
    (off Cecil Gro.)
    SW11 . . . . .1E 118
    (off Macduff Rd.)
Searle Pl. N4 . . . . .1K 65
Searles Cl. SW11 . . . . .7C 100
Searles Dr. E6 .5F 89
Searles Rd. SE1 . . . . .4D 102
Searson Ho. SE17 . . . . .4B 102
    (off Canterbury Pl.)
Sears St. SE5 . . . . .7D 102
Seasalter Ho. SW9 . . . . .1A 120
    (off Gosling Way)
Seasons Cl. W7 . . . . .1K 95
Seasons Ho. E20 . . . . .6E 68
    (off Mirabelle Gdns.)
Seasprite Cl. UB5: N'olt 3B 76
Seaton Av. IG3: Ilf 5K 71
Seaton Cl. E13 .4J 87
    SE11 . . . . .5K 19 (5A 102)
    SW15 . . . . .1D 134
    TW2: Whitt .6H 113
Seaton Dr. TW15: Ashf 2A 128
Seaton Gdns. HA4: Ruis 3H 57
Seaton Point E5 . . . . .4G 67
Seaton Rd. CR4: Mitc 2C 154
    DA16: Well 7C 108
    HA0: Wemb 2E 78
    TW2: Whitt 6G 113
    UB3: Harl 4F 93
Seaton Sq. NW7 . . . . .7A 30
Seaton St. N18 . . . . .5B 34
Seawall Ct. IG11: Bark 2G 89
    (off Dock Rd.)
Sebastian Cl. IG11: Bark 1K 89
Sebastian Ho. N1 . . . . .1G 9
    (off Hoxton St.)
Sebastian St. EC1 . . . . .2B 8 (3B 84)
Sebastopol Rd. N9 . . . . .4B 34
Sebbon St. N1 .7B 66
Sebergham Gro. NW7 . . . . .7H 29
Sebert Rd. E7 .5K 69
Sebright Ho. E2 . . . . .2G 85
    (off Coate St.)
Sebright Pas. E2 . . . . .2G 85
Sebright Rd. EN5: Barn 2A 20
Secker Cres. HA3: Hrw W 1G 41
Secker Ho. SW9 . . . . .2B 120
    (off Loughborough Est.)
Secker St. SE1 . . . . .5J 13 (1A 102)
Secombe Theatre
    Sutton 5K 165

Second Av. E12 ....4C **70**
E13 ....3J **87**
E17 ....5C **50**
EN1: Enf 5A **24**
HA9: Wemb 2D **60**
KT12: Walt T 6K **147**
N18 ....4D **34**
NW4 ....4F **45**
RM6: Chad H 5C **54**
RM10: Dag 2H **91**
SW14 ....3A **116**
UB3: Hayes 1H **93**
W3 ....1B **98**
W10 ....4G **81**
Second Cl. KT8: W Mole 4G **149**
Second Cross Rd. TW2: Twick 2J **131**
Second Way HA9: Wemb 4H **61**
Sedan Way SE17 ....5E **102**
Sedcombe Cl. DA14: Sidc 4B **144**
Sedcote Rd. EN3: Pond E 5D **24**
Sedding St. SW1 ....3G **17** (4E **100**)
Sedding Studios SW1 ....3G **17**
(off Sedding St.)
Seddon Highwalk EC2 ....5C **8**
(off Aldersgate St.)
Seddon Rd. EC2 ....5C **8**
Seddon Rd. SM4: Mord 5B **154**
Seddon St. WC1 ....2H **7** (3K **83**)
Sedgebrook Rd. SE3 ....2B **124**
Sedgecombe Av. HA3: Kenton 5C **42**
Sedgefield Cl. UB5: N'olt 5F **59**
(off Newmarket Av.)
Sedgeford Rd. W12 ....1B **98**
Sedge Gdns. IG11: Bark 3A **90**
Sedgehill Rd. SE6 ....4C **140**
Sedgemere Av. N2 ....3A **46**
Sedgemere Rd. SE2 ....3C **108**
Sedgemoor Dr. RM10: Dag 4G **73**
Sedge Rd. N17 ....7D **34**
Sedgeway SE6 ....1H **141**
Sedgewood Cl. BR2: Hayes 7H **159**
Sedgmoor Pl. SE5 ....7E **102**
Sedgwick Av. UB10: Hil 7D **56**
Sedgwick Ho. E3 ....5C **86**
(off Gale St.)
Sedgwick Rd. E10 ....2E **68**
Sedgwick St. E9 ....5K **67**
Sedleigh Rd. SW18 ....6H **117**
Sedlescombe Rd. SW6 ....6J **99**
Sedley Cl. EN1: Enf 1C **24**
Sedley Ct. SE26 ....2H **139**
Sedley Ho. SE11 ....5H **19**
(off Newburn St.)
Sedley Pl. W1 ....1J **11** (6F **83**)
Sedona Ho. E20 ....6D **68**
(off Victory Pde.)
Sedum Cl. NW9 ....5H **43**
Seeley Dr. SE21 ....4E **138**
Seelig Av. NW9 ....7C **44**
Seely Rd. SW17 ....6E **136**
Seetha Ho. IG1: Ilf 2H **71**
(off High Rd.)
Seething La. EC3 ....2H **15** (7E **84**)
SEETHING WELLS 6C **150**
Seething Wells La. KT6: Surb 6C **150**
Sefton Av. HA3: Hrw W 2H **41**
NW7 ....5E **28**
Sefton Cl. BR5: St M Cry 4K **161**
Sefton Ct. EN2: Enf 2G **23**
TW3: Houn 1F **113**
Sefton Rd. BR5: St M Cry 4K **161**
CRO: C'don 1G **169**
Sefton St. SW15 ....3E **116**
Segal Cl. SE23 ....7A **122**
Sekforde St. EC1 ....4A **8** (4B **84**)
Sekhon Ter. TW13: Hanw 3E **130**
Selah Dr. BR8: Swan 7J **145**
Selan Gdns. UB4: Yead 5K **75**
Selbie Av. NW10 ....5B **62**
Selborne Av. DA5: Bexl 1E **144**
E12 ....4E **70**

Selborne Gdns. NW4 ....4C **44**
UB6: G'frd 2A **78**
Selborne Rd. CRO: C'don 3E **168**
DA14: Sidc 4B **144**
E17 ....5B **50**
IG1: Ilf 2E **70**
KT3: N Mald 2A **152**
N14 ....3D **32**
N22 ....1K **47**
SE5 ....2D **120**
Selborne Wlk. E17 ....5B **50**
Selborne Wlk. Shop. Cen. E17 ....4B **50**
Selbourne Av. KT6: Surb 2F **163**
E17 ....7E **14**
Selby Cl. BR7: Chst 6E **142**
E6 ....5C **88**
KT9: Chess 7E **162**
Selby Gdns. UB1: S'hall 4E **76**
Selby Grn. SM5: Cars 7C **154**
Selby Rd. E11 ....3G **69**
E13 ....5K **87**
N17 ....7K **33**
SE20 ....2G **157**
SM5: Cars 7C **154**
TW15: Ashf 6E **128**
W5 ....4B **78**
Selby St. W10 ....3G **81**
(off Dowland St.)
Selby St. E1 ....4G **85**
Selcroft Ho. SE10 ....5H **105**
(off Glenister Rd.)
Selden Ho. SE15 ....2J **121**
(off Selden Rd.)
Selden Rd. SE15 ....2J **121**
Selden Wlk. N7 ....2K **65**
Seldon Ho. SW1 ....6A **18**
(off Churchill Gdns.)
SW8 ....7G **101**
(off Stewart's Rd.)
Seltridges 1G **11**
SELHURST 6E **156**
Selhurst Cl. SW19 ....1F **135**
Selhurst New Rd. SE25 ....6E **156**
Selhurst Pk. 4E **156**
Selhurst Pl. SE25 ....6E **156**
Selhurst Rd. N9 ....3J **33**
SE25 ....6E **156**
Selig Cl. NW11 ....7G **45**
Selina Ho. NW8 ....3B **4**
(off Frampton St.)
Selinas La. RM8: Dag 7E **54**
Selkirk Ho. N1 ....1K **83**
(off Bingfield St.)
SW17 ....4C **136**
Selkirk Rd. SW17 ....4C **136**
TW2: Twick 2G **131**
Sellers Hall Cl. N3 ....7D **30**
Sellincourt Rd. SW17 ....5C **136**
Sellindge Cl. BR3: Beck 7B **140**
Sellons Av. NW10 ....1B **80**
Sellwood Dr. EN5: Barn 5A **20**
Selman Ho. E9 ....6A **68**
SELSDON 7J **169**
Selsdon Av. CR2: S Croy 6D **168**
Selsdon Cl. KT6: Surb 5E **150**
RM5: Col R 1J **55**
Selsdon Pk. Rd. CRO: Sels 7K **169**
CR2: Sels 7K **169**
Selsdon Rd. CR2: S Croy 5D **168**
E11 ....7J **51**
E13 ....1A **88**
NW2 ....2B **62**
SE27 ....3A **138**
Selsdon Way E14 ....3D **104**
Selsea Pl. N16 ....5E **66**
Selsey WC1 ....2F **7**
(off Tavistock Pl.)
Selsey Cres. DA16: Well 1D **126**
Selsey St. E14 ....5C **86**
Selvage La. NW7 ....5E **28**

Selway Cl. HA5: Eastc 4K **39**
Selway Ho. SW8 ....1J **119**
(off Sth. Lambeth Rd.)
Selwood Pl. SW7 ....5A **16** (5B **100**)
Selwood Rd. CRO: C'don 2H **169**
KT9: Chess 4D **162**
SM3: Sutt 1H **165**
Selwoods SW2 ....7A **120**
Selwood Ter. SW7 ....5A **16** (5B **100**)
Selworthy Cl. E11 ....5J **51**
Selworthy Ho. SW11 ....1B **118**
(off Battersea Church Rd.)
Selworthy Rd. SE6 ....3B **140**
Selwyn Av. E4 ....6K **35**
IG3: Ilf 6K **53**
TW9: Rich 3E **114**
Selwyn Cl. TW4: Houn 4C **112**
Selwyn Ct. E17 ....5C **50**
(off Yunus Khan Cl.)
HA8: Edg 7C **28**
HA9: Wemb 3J **61**
SE3 ....3H **123**
TW10: Rich 5F **115**
(off Church Rd.)
Selwyn Cres. DA16: Well 3B **126**
Selwyn Rd. E3 ....2B **86**
E13 ....1K **87**
KT3: N Mald 5K **151**
NW10 ....7A **62**
Semley Ga. E9 ....6B **68**
(not continuous)
Semley Ho. SW1 ....4J **17**
(off Semley Pl.)
Semley Pl. SW1 ....4H **17** (4E **100**)
Semley Rd. SW16 ....2J **155**
Senate St. SE15 ....2J **121**
Senators Lodge E3 ....2A **86**
(off Roman Rd.)
Senator Wlk. SE28 ....3H **107**
Sendall Cl. SW11 ....3B **118**
(off Winstanley Rd.)
Seneca Rd. CR7: Thor H 4C **156**
Sener Ct. CR2: S Croy 6C **168**
Senga Rd. SM6: Wall 1E **166**
Senhouse Rd. SM3: Cheam 3F **165**
Senior St. W2 ....5K **81**
Senlac Rd. SE12 ....1K **141**
Sennen Rd. EN1: Enf 7A **24**
Sennen Wlk. SE9 ....3C **142**
Senrab St. E1 ....6K **85**
Sentamu Cl. SE24 ....1B **138**
Sentinel Cl. UB5: N'olt 4C **76**
Sentinel Sq. NW4 ....4E **44**
September Ct. UB1: S'hall 1F **95**
(off Dormer's Wells La.)
UB8: Uxb 2A **74**
September Way HA7: Stan 6G **27**
Septimus Pl. EN1: Enf 5B **24**
Sequoia Cl. WD23: B Hea 1C **26**
Sequoia Gdns. BR6: Orp 7K **161**
Sequoia Pk. HA5: Hat E 6A **26**
Seraph Ct. EC1 ....1C **8**
(off Moreland St.)
Serbin Cl. E10 ....7E **50**
Serenaders Rd. SW9 ....2A **120**
Serenity Apartments E17 ....5D **50**
SW11 ....4C **118**
(off Monarch Sq.)
Serenity Cl. HA2: Harr 2F **59**
Seren Pk. Gdns. SE3 ....6G **105**
Sergeant Ind. Est. SW18 ....6K **117**
Serica Ct. SE10 ....7E **104**
Serjeants Inn EC4 ....1K **13** (6A **84**)
Seriby Cl. W14 ....3H **99**
(off Somerset Sq.)
Serle St. WC2 ....7H **7** (6K **83**)
Sermon La. EC4 ....1C **14**
Serpentine, The 5D **10** (1C **100**)
Serpentine Cl. RM6: Chad H 7C **54**
Serpentine Ct. SE16 ....2K **103**
(off Christopher Cl.)

Serpentine Gallery 6A **10** (2B **100**)
Serpentine Rd. W2 ....5C **10** (1C **100**)
Serpentine Sackler Gallery
.....................4B **10** (1B **100**)
Serviden Dr. BR1: Brom 1B **160**
Servite Ho. BR3: Beck 1B **158**
KT4: Wor Pk 2B **164**
(off The Avenue)
N14 ....5A **22**
(off Bramley Rd.)
Servius Ct. TW8: Bford 7D **96**
Setchell Rd. SE1 ....4F **103**
Setchell Way SE1 ....4F **103**
Seth St. SE16 ....2J **103**
Seton Gdns. RM9: Dag 7C **72**
Settle Point E13 ....2J **87**
Settlers Ct. E14 ....7F **87**
Settles St. E1 ....5G **85**
Settrington Rd. SW6 ....2K **117**
Seven Acres SM5: Cars 2C **166**
Seven Dials WC2 ....1E **12** (6J **83**)
Seven Dials Ct. WC2 ....1E **12**
(off Shorts Gdns.)
Sevenex Pde. HA9: Wemb 5E **60**
Seven Islands Leisure Cen. 3J **103**
SEVEN KINGS 1K **71**
Seven Kings Rd. IG3: Ilf 1J **71**
Seven Kings Way KT2: King T 1E **150**
Sevenoaks Cl. DA7: Bex 4H **127**
Sevenoaks Ho. SE25 ....3F **157**
Sevenoaks Rd. BR6: Chels, Orp 5K **173**
BR6: Prat B 7K **173**
SE4 ....6A **122**
Sevenoaks Way BR5: St P 7C **144**
DA14: Sidc 7C **144**
Seven Sea Gdns. E3 ....5D **86**
Sevenseas Rd. TW6: H'row A 6E **110**
SEVEN SISTERS 5F **49**
Seven Sisters Rd. N4 ....2A **66**
N7 ....3K **65**
N15 ....7C **48**
Seven Stars Cnr. W12 ....3C **98**
Seven Stars Yd. E1 ....5K **9**
Seventh Av. E12 ....4D **70**
UB3: Hayes 1J **93**
Seven Ways Pde. IG2: Ilf 5E **52**
Severnake Cl. E14 ....4C **104**
Severn Av. W10 ....3G **81**
Severn Cl. KT2: King T 1D **150**
(off John Williams Cl.)
Severn Dr. KT10: Hin W 2A **162**
Severn Ho. SW18 ....4J **117**
(off Enterprise Way)
Severn Way NW10 ....5B **62**
Severus Ho. UB3: Hayes 6F **75**
Severus Rd. SW11 ....4C **118**
Seville Ho. E1 ....1G **103**
(off Wapping High St.)
Seville M. N1 ....7E **66**
Seville St. SW1 ....7F **11** (2D **100**)
Sevington Rd. NW4 ....6D **44**
Sevington St. W9 ....4K **81**
Seward Rd. BR3: Beck 2K **157**
W7 ....2A **96**
SEWARDSTONE 1K **25**
Sewardstone Cl. E4 ....1K **25**
Sewardstone Gdns. E4 ....5J **25**
Sewardstone Rd. E2 ....2J **85**
E4 ....7J **25**
Seward St. EC1 ....3B **8** (3B **84**)
Sewdley St. E5 ....3K **67**
Sewell Rd. SE2 ....3A **108**
Sewell St. E13 ....3J **87**
Sextant Av. E14 ....4F **105**
Sexton Ct. E14 ....7F **87**
(off Newport Av.)
Sextons Ho. SE10 ....6E **104**
(off Bardsley La.)
Seymer Rd. RM1: Rom 3K **55**
Seymore M. SE14 ....7B **104**
(off New Cross Rd.)

Seymour Av. KT17: Ewe 7E **164**
   N17 . . . . .2G **49**
   SM4: Mord .7F **153**
Seymour Cl. HA5: Hat E 1D **40**
   KT8: E Mos 5G **149**
Seymour Ct. E4 . . . . .2C **36**
   KT1: Hamp W 1D **150**
   N10 . . . . .2E **46**
   N21 . . . . .6E **22**
   NW2 . . . . .2D **62**
Seymour Dr. BR2: Brom 1D **172**
Seymour Gdns. HA4: Ruis 1B **58**
   IG1: Ilf 1D **70**
   KT5: Surb 5F **151**
   SE4 . . . . .3A **122**
   TW1: Twick 7B **114**
   TW13: Hanw 4A **130**
Seymour Ho. E16 . . . . .1J **105**
               (off De Quincey M.)
   NW1 . . . . .1D **6**
                (off Churchway)
   SM2: Sutt .6K **165**
             (off Mulgrave Rd.)
   WC1 . . . . .3E **6**
             (off Tavistock Pl.)
Seymour Leisure Cen. 6E **4** (5D **82**)
Seymour M. W1 . . . . .7G **5** (6E **82**)
Seymour Pl. SE25 . . . . .4H **157**
   W1 . . . . .6E **4** (5D **82**)
Seymour Rd. CR4: Mitc 7E **154**
   E4 . . . . .1J **35**
   E6 . . . . .2B **88**
   E10 . . . . .1B **68**
   KT1: Hamp W 1D **150**
   KT8: W Mole, E Mos 5G **149**
   N3 . . . . .7E **30**
   N8 . . . . .5A **48**
   N9 . . . . .2C **34**
   SM5: Cars .5E **166**
   SW18 . . . . .7H **117**
   SW19 . . . . .3F **135**
   TW12: Hamp H 5G **131**
   W4 . . . . .4J **97**
Seymour St. SE18 . . . . .3G **107**
   W1 . . . . .1E **10** (6D **82**)
   W2 . . . . .1E **10** (6D **82**)
Seymour Ter. SE20 . . . . .1H **157**
Seymour Vs. SE20 . . . . .1H **157**
Seymour Wlk. SW10 . . . . .6A **100**
Seymour Way TW16: Sun 7H **129**
Seyssel St. E14 . . . . .4E **104**
Shaa Rd. W3 . . . . .7K **79**
Shabana Rd. W12 . . . . .1D **98**
Shacklegate La. TW11: Tedd 4J **131**
Shackleton Cl. SE23 . . . . .2H **139**
Shackleton Ct. E14 . . . . .5C **104**
             (off Maritime Quay)
   TW19: Stanw 6A **110**
              (off Whitley Cl.)
   W12 . . . . .2D **98**
              (off Scott's Rd.)
Shackleton Ho. E1 . . . . .1J **103**
             (off Prusom St.)
   NW10 . . . . .7K **61**
Shackleton Rd. UB1: S'hall 7D **76**
SHACKLEWELL 4F **67**
Shacklewell Grn. E8 . . . . .4F **67**
Shacklewell Ho. E8 . . . . .4F **67**
Shacklewell La. E8 . . . . .5F **67**
   N16 . . . . .4F **67**
Shacklewell Rd. N16 . . . . .4F **67**
Shacklewell Row E8 . . . . .4F **67**
Shacklewell St. E2 . . . . .2K **9** (3F **85**)
Shadbolt Av. E4 . . . . .5F **35**
Shadbolt Cl. KT4: Wor Pk 2B **164**
Shad Thames SE1 . . . . .5J **15** (1F **103**)
          (Anchor Brewhouse)
   SE1 . . . . .2F **103**
              (Jamaica Rd.)
SHADWELL 7H **85**
Shadwell Cl. UB5: N'olt 2D **76**

Shadwell Dr. UB5: N'olt 3D **76**
Shadwell Gdns. E1 . . . . .7J **85**
Shadwell Pierhead E1 . . . . .7J **85**
Shadwell Pl. E1 . . . . .7J **85**
              (off Sutton Cl.)
Shady Bush Cl. WD23: Bush 1B **26**
Shaef Way TW11: Tedd 7A **132**
Shafter Rd. RM10: Dag 6J **73**
Shaftesbury Av. EN3: Enf H 2E **24**
   EN5: New Bar 4F **21**
   HA2: Harr 1F **59**
   HA3: Kenton 5D **42**
   TW14: Felt 6J **111**
   UB2: S'hall .4E **94**
   W1 . . . . .3C **12** (7H **83**)
   WC1 . . . . .7E **6** (6J **83**)
   WC2 . . . . .7E **6** (6J **83**)
Shaftesbury Cen. W10 . . . . .4F **81**
              (off Barlby Rd.)
Shaftesbury Circ. HA2: Harr 1G **59**
Shaftesbury Ct. E6 . . . . .6E **88**
             (off Sapphire Cl.)
   N1 . . . . .2D **84**
           (off Shaftesbury St.)
   SE1 . . . . .3D **102**
             (off Alderney M.)
   SE5 . . . . .4D **120**
   SW6 . . . . .1K **117**
             (off Maltings Pl.)
   SW16 . . . . .3H **137**
Shaftesbury Cres. TW18: Staines 7A **128**
Shaftesbury Gdns. NW10 . . . . .4A **80**
Shaftesbury Lodge E14 . . . . .6D **86**
            (off Upper Nth. St.)
Shaftesbury M. SW4 . . . . .5G **119**
   W8 . . . . .3J **99**
Shaftesbury Pde. HA2: Harr 1G **59**
Shaftesbury Pl. EC2 . . . . .6C **8**
             (off London Wall)
   W14 . . . . .4H **99**
             (off Warwick Rd.)
Shaftesbury Point E13 . . . . .2J **87**
               (off High St.)
Shaftesbury Rd. BR3: Beck 2B **158**
   E4 . . . . .1A **36**
   E7 . . . . .7A **70**
   E10 . . . . .1C **68**
   E17 . . . . .6D **50**
   N18 . . . . .6K **33**
   N19 . . . . .1J **65**
   SM5: Cars .7B **154**
   TW9: Rich .3E **114**
Shaftesbury Row SE8 . . . . .7C **104**
             (off Speedwell St.)
Shaftesburys, The IG11: Bark 2G **89**
Shaftesbury St. N1 . . . . .2C **84**
              (not continuous)
Shaftesbury Theatre 7E **6**
           (off Shaftesbury Av.)
Shaftesbury Vs. W8 . . . . .3J **99**
              (off Allen St.)
Shaftesbury Way TW2: Twick 3H **131**
Shaftesbury Waye UB4: Yead 5A **76**
Shafto M. SW1 . . . . .2F **17** (3D **100**)
Shafton M. E9 . . . . .1K **85**
Shafton Rd. E9 .1K **85**
Shafts Ct. EC3 . . . . .1G **15** (6E **84**)
Shaftswood Cl. SW17 . . . . .3D **136**
             (off Lynwood Rd.)
Shahjalal Ho. E2 . . . . .2G **85**
           (off Pritchards Rd.)
Shakespeare Av. N11 . . . . .5B **32**
   NW10 . . . . .1A **80**
   TW14: Felt 6J **111**
   UB4: Hayes, Yead 6J **75**
              (not continuous)
Shakespeare Cl. HA3: Kenton 7G **43**
Shakespeare Ct. EN5: New Bar 3E **20**
   HA3: Kenton 6F **43**
   NW6 . . . . .7A **64**
              (off Fairfax Rd.)

Shakespeare Cres. E12 . . . . .6D **70**
Shakespeare Dr. HA3: Kenton 6F **43**
Shakespeare Gdns. N2 . . . . .4D **46**
Shakespeare Ho. E9 . . . . .7J **67**
              (off Lyme Gro.)
   N14 . . . . .2C **32**
Shakespeare Rd. DA7: Bex 1E **126**
   E17 . . . . .2K **49**
   N3 . . . . .1J **45**
   NW7 . . . . .4G **29**
   NW10 . . . . .1K **79**
   SE24 . . . . .5B **120**
   W3 . . . . .1J **97**
   W7 . . . . .7K **77**
Shakespeare's Globe & Exhibition
   . . . . .4C **14** (1C **102**)
Shakespeare Twr. EC2 . . . . .5D **8**
Shakespeare Way TW13: Hanw 4A **130**
Shakspeare M. N16 . . . . .4E **66**
Shakspeare Wlk. N16 . . . . .4E **66**
Shalbourne Sq. E9 . . . . .6B **68**
Shalcomb St. SW10 . . . . .6A **100**
Shalden Ho. SW15 . . . . .6B **116**
Shaldon Dr. HA4: Ruis 3A **58**
   SM4: Mord 5G **153**
Shaldon Rd. HA8: Edg 2F **43**
Shalfleet Dr. W10 . . . . .7F **81**
Shalford Cl. BR6: Farnb 4G **173**
Shalford Ct. N1 .2B **84**
Shalford Ho. SE1 . . . . .3D **102**
Shalimar Gdns. W3 . . . . .7J **79**
Shalimar Rd. W3 . . . . .7J **79**
Shallons Rd. SE9 . . . . .4F **143**
Shalstone Rd. SW14 . . . . .3H **115**
Shalston Vs. KT6: Surb 6F **151**
Shamrock Ho. SE26 . . . . .4G **139**
             (off Talisman Sq.)
Shamrock Rd. CR0: C'don 6K **155**
Shamrock St. SW4 . . . . .3H **119**
Shamrock Way N14 . . . . .1A **32**
Shandon Rd. SW4 . . . . .6G **119**
Shand St. SE1 . . . . .6H **15** (2E **102**)
Shandy St. E1 . . . . .5K **85**
Shan Ho. WC1 . . . . .4G **7**
              (off Millman St.)
Shanklin Ho. E17 . . . . .2B **50**
Shanklin Rd. N8 . . . . .5H **47**
   N15 . . . . .4G **49**
Shannon Cl. NW2 . . . . .3F **63**
   UB2: S'hall .5B **94**
Shannon Commercial Cen.
   KT3: N Mald 4C **152**
SHANNON CORNER 4C **152**
Shannon Cnr. Retail Pk.
   KT3: N Mald 4C **152**
Shannon Ct. CR0: C'don 1C **168**
            (off Tavistock Rd.)
   N16 . . . . .3E **66**
   SE15 . . . . .7F **103**
             (off Garnies Cl.)
Shannon Gro. SW9 . . . . .4K **119**
Shannon M. SE3 . . . . .4H **123**
Shannon Pl. NW8 . . . . .2C **82**
Shannon Way BR3: Beck 6D **140**
Shanti Ct. SW18 . . . . .1J **135**
Shap Cres. SM5: Cars 1D **166**
Shapland Way N13 . . . . .5E **32**
Shapwick Cl. N11 . . . . .5J **31**
Shard, The 5F **15** (1D **102**)
Shardcroft Av. SE24 . . . . .5B **120**
Shardeloes Rd. SE4 . . . . .3B **122**
   SE14 . . . . .2B **122**
Shard's Sq. SE15 . . . . .6G **103**
Sharland Cl. CR7: Thor H 6A **156**
Sharman Ct. DA14: Sidc 4A **144**
Sharnbrooke Cl. DA16: Well 3C **126**
Sharnbrook Ho. W14 . . . . .6J **99**
Sharon Cl. KT6: Surb 1C **162**
Sharon Ct. CR2: S Croy 5C **168**
             (off Warham Rd.)
Sharon Gdns. E9 . . . . .1J **85**

Sharon Rd. EN3: Enf H 2F **25**
   W4 . . . . .5K **97**
Sharpe Cl. W7 . . . . .5K **77**
Sharp Ho. SW8 . . . . .3F **119**
   TW1: Twick 6D **114**
Sharpleshall St. NW1 . . . . .7D **64**
Sharpley Ct. SE1 . . . . .6A **14**
             (off Pocock St.)
Sharpness Cl. UB4: Yead 5C **76**
Sharp's La. HA4: Ruis 7F **39**
Sharratt St. SE15 . . . . .6J **103**
Sharsted St. SE17 . . . . .5B **102**
Sharvel La. UB5: N'olt 1J **75**
Sharwood WC1 . . . . .1H **7**
             (off Penton Ri.)
Shaver's Pl. SW1 . . . . .3C **12**
Shaw, The BR7: Chst 7G **143**
Shaw Av. IG11: Bark 2E **90**
Shawbrooke Rd. SE9 . . . . .5A **124**
Shawbury Cl. NW9 . . . . .1A **44**
Shawbury Rd. SE22 . . . . .5F **121**
Shaw Cl. SE28 .1B **108**
   TW19: Stanw 1A **128**
   WD23: B Hea 2D **26**
Shaw Ct. SM4: Mord 7A **154**
   W3 . . . . .3J **97**
             (off All Saints Rd.)
Shaw Cres. E14 .5A **86**
Shaw Dr. KT12: Walt T 7A **148**
Shawfield Ct. UB7: W Dray 3A **92**
Shawfield Pk. BR1: Brom 2B **160**
Shawfield St. SW3 . . . . . . .6D **16** (5C **100**)
Shawford Ct. SW15 . . . . .7C **116**
Shawford Rd. KT19: Ewe 6K **163**
Shaw Gdns. IG11: Bark 2E **90**
Shaw Ho. DA17: Belv 5F **109**
   E16 . . . . .1E **106**
            (off Claremont St.)
Shaw Path BR1: Brom 3H **141**
Shaw Pl. N2 . . . . .3E **46**
Shaw Rd. BR1: Brom 3H **141**
   EN3: Enf H .1E **24**
   SE22 . . . . .4E **120**
Shaws Cotts. SE23 . . . . .3A **140**
Shaws Path KT1: Hamp W 1C **150**
             (off Bennett Cl.)
Shaw Sq. E17 . . . . .1A **50**
Shaw Theatre 2D **6** (3H **83**)
Shaw Way SM6: Wall 7J **167**
Shead Ct. E1 . . . . .6H **85**
          (off James Voller Way)
Shearing Dr. SM5: Cars 7A **154**
Shearling Way N7 . . . . .6J **65**
Shearman Rd. SE3 . . . . .4H **123**
SHEARS, THE .7G **129**
Shears Ct. TW16: Sun 7G **129**
Shears La. SW16 . . . . .7J **137**
Shearsmith Ho. E1 . . . . .7G **85**
            (off Hindmarsh Cl.)
Shears Way TW16: Sun 1G **147**
Shearwater Cl. IG11: Bark 3A **90**
Shearwater Ct. E1 . . . . .3K **15**
              (off Star Pl.)
   SE8 . . . . .6B **104**
             (off Abinger Gro.)
Shearwater Dr. NW9 . . . . .7C **44**
Shearwater Rd. SM1: Sutt 5H **165**
Shearwater Way UB4: Yead 6B **76**
Sheath Cotts. KT7: T Ditt 6B **150**
              (off Ferry Rd.)
Sheaveshill Av. NW9 . . . . .4K **43**
Sheaveshill Ct. NW9 . . . . .4K **43**
Sheaveshill Pde. NW9 . . . . .4A **44**
           (off Sheaveshill Av.)
Sheba Cl. N17 . . . . .6B **34**
              (off Altair Cl.)
Sheba Pl. E1 . . . . .4K **9** (4F **85**)
Sheen Comn. Dr. TW10: Rich 4G **115**
Sheen Ct. TW10: Rich 4G **115**
Sheen Ct. Rd. TW10: Rich 4G **115**
Sheendale Rd. TW9: Rich 4F **115**

Sheeenewood SE26 . . . . .4H 139
Sheen Ga. Gdns. SW14 . . . . .4J 115
Sheengate Mans. SW14 . . . . .4K 115
Sheen Gro. N1 . . . . .1A 84
Sheen La. SW14 . . . . .5J 115
Sheen Pk. TW9: Rich 4F 115
Sheen Rd. BR5: St M Cry 4K 161
TW9: Rich 5E 114
TW10: Rich 5E 114
Sheen Way SW6: Wall 5K 167
Sheen Wood SW14 . . . . .5J 115
Sheepcote La. SW11 . . . . .2D 118
Sheepcote Rd. HA1: Harr 6K 41
Sheepcotes Rd. RM6: Chad H 4E 54
Sheephouse Way KT3: N Mald 1K 163
Sheep La. E8 . . . . .1H 85
Sheep Wlk. TW17: Shep 7B 146
Sheep Wlk. M. SW19 . . . . .6F 135
Sheerness M. E16 . . . . .2F 107
Sheerwater Rd. E16 . . . . .5B 88
Sheffield Dr. TW6: H'row A 6E 110
Sheffield Sq. E3 . . . . .3B 86
Sheffield St. WC2 . . . . .1G 13 (6K 83)
Sheffield Ter. W8 . . . . .1J 99
Sheffield Way TW6: H'row A 5F 111
Shelbourne Cl. HA5: Pinn 3D 40
Shelbourne Pl. BR3: Beck 7B 140
Shelbourne Rd. N17 . . . . .2H 49
Shelburne Dr. TW4: Houn 6E 112
Shelburne Rd. N7 . . . . .4K 65
Shelbury Cl. DA14: Sidc 3A 144
Shelbury Rd. SE22 . . . . .5H 121
Sheldon Av. IG5: Ilf 2F 53
N6 . . . . .7C 46
Sheldon Cl. SE12 . . . . .5K 123
SE20 . . . . .1H 157
Sheldon Cl. EN5: New Bar 4E 20
RM7: Rush G 6K 55
(off Union Rd.)
SW8 . . . . .7J 101
(off Lansdowne Grn.)
Sheldon Ho. N1 . . . . .1E 84
(off Kingsland Rd.)
Sheldon Pl. E2 . . . . .2G 85
(not continuous)
Sheldon Rd. DA7: Bex 1F 127
N18 . . . . .4K 33
NW2 . . . . .4F 63
RM9: Dag 7E 72
Sheldon Sq. W2 . . . . .6A 4 (5A 82)
Sheldon St.
CR0: C'don 3C 168
Sheldrake Cl. E16 . . . . .1D 106
Sheldrake Cl. E6 . . . . .2C 88
(off St Bartholomew's Rd.)
Sheldrake Ho. SE16 . . . . .4K 103
(off Tawny Way)
Sheldrake Pl. W8 . . . . .2J 99
Sheldrick Cl. SW19 . . . . .2B 154
Shelduck Cl. E15 . . . . .5H 69
Shelduck Ct. SE8 . . . . .6B 104
(off Pilot Cl.)
Sheldwich Ter. BR2: Brom 6C 160
Shelford KT1: King T 2G 151
Shelford Pl. N16 . . . . .3D 66
Shelford Ri. SE19 . . . . .7F 139
Shelford Rd. EN5: Barn 6A 20
Shelgate Rd. SW11 . . . . .5C 118
Shell Cen. SE1 . . . . .5H 13 (1K 101)
Shell Cl. BR2: Brom 6C 160
Shellduck Cl. NW9 . . . . .2A 44
Shelley N8 . . . . .3J 47
(off Boyton Rd.)
Shelley Av. E12 . . . . .6C 70
UB6: G'frd 3H 77
Shelley Cl. BR6: Orp 3J 173
HA8: Edg 4B 28
SE15 . . . . .2H 121
UB4: Hayes 5J 75
UB6: G'frd 3H 77

Shelley Ct. E10 . . . . .7D 50
(off Skelton's La.)
E11 . . . . .4K 51
(off Makepeace Rd.)
N19 . . . . .1K 65
SW3 . . . . .7F 17
(off Tite St.)
Shelley Cres. TW5: Hest 1B 112
UB1: S'hall 6D 76
Shelley Dr. DA16: Well 1J 125
Shelley Gdns. HA0: Wemb 2C 60
Shelley Ho. E2 . . . . .3J 85
(off Cornwall Av.)
N16 . . . . .4E 66
SE17 . . . . .5C 102
(off Browning St.)
SW1 . . . . .7B 18
(off Churchill Gdns.)
Shelley Lodge EN2: Enf 1J 23
Shelley Rd. NW10 . . . . .1K 79
Shelley Way SW19 . . . . .5B 136
Shellness Rd. E5 . . . . .5H 67
Shell Rd. SE13 . . . . .3D 122
Shellwood Rd. SW11 . . . . .2D 118
Shelmerdine Cl. E3 . . . . .5C 86
Shelson Av. TW13: Felt 3H 129
Shelson Pde. TW13: Felt 3H 129
Shelton Rd. SW19 . . . . .1J 153
Shelton St. WC2 . . . . .1E 12 (6J 83)
(not continuous)
Shene Ho. EC1 . . . . .5J 7
(off Bourne Est.)
Shene Sports & Fitness Cen. 4A 116
Shenfield Ho. SE18 . . . . .1B 124
(off Portway Gdns.)
Shenfield Rd. IG8: Wfd G 7E 36
Shenfield St. N1 . . . . .1H 9 (2E 84)
(not continuous)
Shenley Av. HA4: Ruis 2H 57
Shenley Rd. SE5 . . . . .1E 120
TW5: Hest 1C 112
Shenstone W13 . . . . .1C 96
Shenstone Cl. DA1: Cray 4K 127
Shenstone Ho. SW16 . . . . .5G 137
Shepherd Cl.
TW13: Hanw 4C 130
Shepherdess Pl. N1 . . . . . .1D 8 (3C 84)
Shepherdess Wlk. N1 . . . . .1D 8 (2C 84)
Shepherd Ho. E14 . . . . .6D 86
(off Annabel Cl.)
E16 . . . . .7F 89
(off University Way)
Shepherd Mkt. W1 . . . . . . .4J 11 (1F 101)
SHEPHERD'S BUSH 2E 98
Shepherd's Bush Empire Theatre 2E 98
Shepherd's Bush Grn. W12 . . . . .2E 98
Shepherd's Bush Mkt. W12 . . . . .2E 98
(not continuous)
Shepherd's Bush Pl. W12 . . . . .2F 99
Shepherd's Bush Rd. W6 . . . . .4E 98
Shepherds Cl. BR6: Orp 3K 173
HA7: Stan 5F 27
(not continuous)
N6 . . . . .6F 47
RM6: Chad H 5D 54
TW17: Shep 6D 146
W1 . . . . .2G 11
(off Lees Pl.)
Shepherds Ct. W12 . . . . .2F 99
(off Shepherd's Bush Grn.)
Shepherds Grn. BR7: Chst 7H 143
Shepherd's Hill N6 . . . . .6F 47
Shepherds La. E9 . . . . .6K 67
SE28 . . . . .1J 107
Shepherds Leas SE9 . . . . .4G 125
Shepherds Path NW3 . . . . .5B 64
(off Lyndhurst Rd.)
UB5: N'olt 6C 58
(off Arnold Rd.)
Shepherds Pl. W1 . . . . . . .2G 11 (7E 82)
Shepherd St. W1 . . . . .5J 11 (1F 101)

Shepherds Wlk. NW2 . . . . .2C 62
NW3 .5B 64
WD23: B Hea 2C 26
Shepherds Way CR2: Sels 7K 169
Shepiston La. UB3: Harl 4D 92
Shepley Cl. SM5: Cars 3E 166
Shepperd Cl. EN1: Enf 1C 24
KT1: King T 4E 150
Sheppard Dr. SE16 . . . . .5H 103
Sheppard Ho. E2 . . . . .2G 85
(off Warner Pl.)
SW2 .1A 138
Sheppards Coll. BR1: Brom 1J 159
(off London Rd.)
Sheppard St. E16 . . . . .4H 87
SHEPPERTON 6D 146
Shepperton Bus. Pk. TW17: Shep . . .5E 146
Shepperton Ct. TW17: Shep 5D 146
Shepperton Film Studios 3B 146
SHEPPERTON GREEN 4C 146
Shepperton Marina TW17: Shep 6G 147
Shepperton Rd. BR5: Pet W 6G 161
N1 . . . . .1C 84
TW18: Lale, Shep 4A 146
Sheppey Gdns. RM9: Dag 7C 72
Sheppey Rd. RM9: Dag 7B 72
Shepton Ho's. E2 . . . . .3J 85
(off Welwyn St.)
Sherard Ct. N7 . . . . .3J 65
Sherard Ho. E9 . . . . .7J 67
(off Frampton Pk. Rd.)
Sherard Rd. SE9 . . . . .5C 124
Sheraton Bus. Cen. UB6: G'frd 2B 78
Sheraton Ho. SW1 . . . . .7K 17
(off Churchill Gdns.)
Sheraton St. W1 . . . . .1C 12 (6H 83)
Sherborne NW1 . . . . .7H 65
(off Agar Gro.)
Sherborne Av. EN3: Enf H 2D 24
UB2: S'hall 4E 94
Sherborne Cl. SL3: Poyle 4A 174
UB4: Yead 6A 76
Sherborne Cres. SM5: Cars 7C 154
Sherborne Gdns. NW9 . . . . .3G 43
W13 .5B 78
Sherborne Ho. SW1 . . . . .5K 17
(part of Abbots Mnr.)
SW8 .7K 101
(off Bolney St.)
Sherborne La. EC4 . . . . . . .2E 14 (7D 84)
Sherborne Rd. BR5: St M Cry 4K 161
KT9: Chess 5E 162
SM3: Sutt 2J 165
TW14: Bedf 1F 129
(not continuous)
Sherborne St. N1 . . . . .1D 84
Sherboro Rd. N15 . . . . .6F 49
Sherbourne Ct. SM2: Sutt 6A 166
SW5 .4K 99
(off Cromwell Rd.)
Sherbourne Gdns. TW17: Shep 7G 147
Sherbourne Pl. HA7: Stan 6F 27
Sherbrooke Ho. DA6: Bex 4G 127
Sherbrooke Ho. E2 . . . . .2J 85
(off Bonner Rd.)
SW1 .2D 18
(off Monck St.)
Sherbrooke Rd. SW6 . . . . .7G 99
Sherbrooke Ter. SW6 . . . . .7G 99
(off Sherbrooke Rd.)
Sherbrooke Way KT4: Wor Pk 7D 152
Sherbrook Gdns. N21 . . . . .7G 23
Sherbrook Ho. SE16 . . . . .2J 103
(off Albatross Way)
Shere Cl. KT9: Chess 5D 162
Sheredan Rd. E4 . . . . .5A 36
Shere Ho. SE1 . . . . .7E 14
Shere Rd. IG2: Ilf 5E 52
Sherfield Cl. KT3: N Mald 4H 151
Sherfield Gdns. SW15 . . . . .6B 116

Sherfield M. UB3: Hayes 6G 75
Sheridan Bldgs. WC2 . . . . .1F 13
(off Martlett Ct.)
Sheridan Cl. UB10: Hil 4E 74
Sheridan Ct. CR0: C'don 4E 168
(off Coombe Rd.)
HA1: Harr 6H 41
NW6 . . . . .7A 64
(off Belsize Rd.)
SW5 .4K 99
(off Barkston Gdns.)
TW4: Houn 5C 112
UB5: N'olt 5F 59
W7 . . . . .7K 77
(off Milton Rd.)
Sheridan Cres. BR7: Chst 2F 161
Sheridan Gdns. HA3: Kenton 6D 42
Sheridan Hgts. E1 . . . . .6H 85
(off Watney St.)
Sheridan Ho. SE11 . . . . .4K 19
(off Wincott St.)
Sheridan Lodge BR2: Brom 4A 160
(off Homesdale Rd.)
Sheridan M. E11 . . . . .6K 51
Sheridan Pl. BR1: Brom 2B 160
SW13 . . . . .3B 116
TW12: Hamp 1F 149
Sheridan Rd. DA7: Bex 3E 126
DA17: Belv 4G 109
E7 . . . . .3H 69
E12 . . . . .5C 70
SW19 . . . . .1H 153
TW10: Ham 3C 132
Sheridan Ter. UB5: N'olt 5F 59
Sheridan Wlk. NW11 . . . . .6J 45
SM5: Cars 5D 166
Sheridan Way BR3: Beck 1B 158
Sheriden Pl. HA1: Harr 7J 41
Sheringham NW8 . . . . .1B 82
Sheringham Av. E12 . . . . .4D 70
N14 . . . . .5C 22
RM7: Rom 6J 55
TW2: Whitt 1D 130
TW13: Felt 3J 129
Sheringham Ct. TW13: Felt 3J 129
(off Sheringham Av.)
UB3: Hayes 2H 93
Sheringham Ho. NW1 . . . . .5C 4
Sheringham Rd. N7 . . . . .6K 65
SE20 . . . . .3J 157
Sheringham Twr. UB1: S'hall 7F 77
Sherington Av. HA5: Hat E 7A 26
Sherington Rd. SE7 . . . . .6K 105
Sherland Rd. TW1: Twick 1K 131
Sherleys Cl. HA4: Ruis 2G 57
Sherlies Av. BR6: Orp 2J 173
Sherlock Cl. SW16 . . . . .2K 155
Sherlock Ct. NW8 . . . . .1B 82
(off Dorman Way)
Sherlock Holmes Mus. 4F 5
Sherlock M. W1 . . . . .5G 5 (5E 82)
Sherman Gdns. RM6: Chad H 6C 54
Sherman Ho. E14 . . . . .6E 86
(off Dee St.)
UB3: Harl 3E 92
(off Nine Acres Cl.)
Sherman Rd. BR1: Brom 1J 159
Shernhall St. E17 . . . . .3E 50
Sherrard Rd. E7 . . . . .6A 70
E12 . . . . .6A 70
Sherrards Way EN5: Barn 5D 20
Sherren Ho. E1 . . . . .4J 85
Sherrick Grn. Rd. NW10 . . . . .5D 62
Sherriff Ct. NW6 . . . . .6J 63
(off Sherriff Rd.)
Sherriff Rd. NW6 . . . . .6J 63
Sherringham Av. N17 . . . . .2G 49
Sherrington Ct. E16 . . . . .5H 87
(off Rathbone St.)
Sherrin Rd. E10 . . . . .4D 68

Sherrock Gdns. NW4 . . . . .4D **44**
Sherry M. IG11: Bark 7H **71**
Sherston Cl. SE1 . . . . .4B **102**
    (off Newington Butts)
  WC1 . . . . .2J **7**
Sherwin Ho. SE11 . . . . .7J **19**
Sherwin Rd. SE14 . . . . .1K **121**
Sherwood KT6: Surb 2D **162**
  NW6 .7G **63**
Sherwood Av. E18 . . . . .3K **51**
  HA4: Ruis 6G **39**
  SW16 . . . . .7H **137**
  UB4: Yead 4K **75**
  UB6: S'hall 6J **59**
Sherwood Cl. DA5: Bexl 6C **126**
  E17 . . . . .2B **50**
  SW13 . . . . .3D **116**
  W13 . . . . .1B **96**
Sherwood Ct. CR2: S Croy 5C **168**
    (off Nottingham Rd.)
  HA2: Harr 2F **59**
  SW11 . . . . .3A **118**
  W1 . . . . .6E **4**
    (off Bryanston Pl.)
Sherwood Gdns. E14 . . . . .4C **104**
  IG11: Bark 7H **71**
  SE16 . . . . .5G **103**
Sherwood Pk. Av. DA15: Sidc 7A **126**
Sherwood Pk. Rd. CR4: Mitc 4G **155**
  SM1: Sutt 5J **165**
Sherwood Rd. CR0: C'don 7H **157**
  DA16: Well 2J **125**
  HA2: Harr 2G **59**
  IG6: Ilf .4H **53**
  NW4 . . . . .3E **44**
  SW19 . . . . .7H **135**
  TW12: Hamp H 5G **131**
Sherwood St. N20 . . . . .3G **31**
  W1 . . . . .2B **12** (7G **83**)
Sherwood Ter. E16 . . . . .6A **88**
    (off Bingley Rd.)
  N20 . . . . .3G **31**
Sherwood Way BR4: W W'ck 2E **170**
Shetland Ho. DA17: Belv 2H **109**
Shetland Rd. E3 . . . . .2B **86**
  TW6: H'row A 6E **110**
Shield Dr. TW8: Bford 6A **96**
Shieldhall St. SE2 . . . . .4C **108**
Shield Rd. TW15: Ashf 4E **128**
Shifford Path SE23 . . . . .3K **139**
Shillaker Ct. W3 . . . . .1B **98**
Shillibeer Pl. W1 . . . . .6D **4**
Shillingford Cl. NW7 . . . . .7A **30**
Shillingford Ho. E3 . . . . .3D **86**
    (off Talwin St.)
Shillingford St. N1 . . . . .7B **66**
Shilling Pl. W7 . . . . .2A **96**
Shillingshaw Lodge E16 . . . . .6J **87**
    (off Butchers Rd.)
Shillingstone Ho. W14 . . . . .3G **99**
    (off Russell Rd.)
Shinfield St. W12 . . . . .6E **80**
Shinglewell Rd. DA8: Erith 7G **109**
Shingly Pl. E4 . . . . .1K **35**
Shinners Cl. SE25 . . . . .5G **157**
Ship All. W4 . . . . .6G **97**
Ship & Mermaid Row SE1 . .6F **15** (2D **102**)
Shipka Rd. SW12 . . . . .1F **137**
Shiplake Ho. E2 . . . . .2J **9**
    (off Arnold Cir.)
Ship La. SW14 . . . . .3J **115**
Shipman Rd. E16 . . . . .6K **87**
  SE23 . . . . .2K **139**
Ship St. SE8 . . . . .1C **122**
Ship Tavern Pas. EC3 . . . . .2G **15** (7E **84**)
Shipton Cl. RM8: Dag 3D **72**
Shipton Ho. E2 . . . . .1K **9**
    (off Shipton St.)
Shipton Rd. UB10: Ick 4B **56**
Shipton St. E2 . . . . .1K **9** (2F **85**)
Shipwright Rd. SE16 . . . . .2A **104**

Shipwright Yd. SE1 . . . . . .5G **15** (1E **102**)
Ship Yd. E14 . . . . .5D **104**
Shirburn Cl. SE23 . . . . .7J **121**
Shirebrook Rd. SE3 . . . . .3B **124**
Shire Ct. DA18: Erith 3D **108**
  KT17: Ewe 7B **164**
Shirehall Cl. NW4 . . . . .6F **45**
Shirehall Gdns. NW4 . . . . .6F **45**
Shirehall La. NW4 . . . . .6F **45**
Shirehall Pk. NW4 . . . . .5F **45**
Shire Horse Way TW7: Isle 3K **113**
Shire Ho. E3 . . . . .3D **86**
    (off Talwin St.)
  EC1 . . . . .4E **8**
    (off Lambs Pas.)
Shire La. BR2: Kes 7C **172**
  BR6: Chels, Downe 7F **173**
    (not continuous)
Shire London Golf Course, The 1A **20**
Shire M. TW2: Whitt 6G **113**
Shire Pl. SW18 . . . . .7A **118**
  TW8: Bford 7D **96**
Shirland M. W9 . . . . .3H **81**
Shirland Rd. W9 . . . . .3H **81**
Shirlbutt St. E14 . . . . .7D **86**
SHIRLEY 2K **169**
Shirley Av. CR0: C'don 1J **169**
  DA5: Bexl 7D **126**
  SM1: Sutt 4B **166**
Shirley Chu. Rd. CR0: C'don 3K **169**
Shirley Cl. E17 . . . . .5D **50**
  TW3: Houn 5G **113**
Shirley Cres. BR3: Beck 4A **158**
Shirley Dr. TW3: Houn 5G **113**
Shirley Gdns. IG11: Bark 6J **71**
  W7 . . . . .1K **95**
Shirley Ho. N9 . . . . .7D **24**
  SW11 . . . . .3E **118**
Shirley Hgts. SM6: Wall 7G **167**
Shirley Hills Rd. CR0: C'don 5J **169**
Shirley Ho. Dr. SE7 . . . . .7A **106**
    (off Picton St.)
SHIRLEY OAKS 1K **169**
Shirley Oaks Rd.
  CR0: C'don 1K **169**
Shirley Pk. CR0: C'don 2J **169**
Shirley Pk. Golf Course 2H **169**
Shirley Pk. Rd. CR0: C'don 1H **169**
Shirley Rd. CR0: C'don 7H **157**
  DA15: Sidc 3J **143**
  E15 . . . . .7G **69**
  EN2: Enf 3H **23**
  SM6: Wall 7G **167**
  W4 . . . . .2K **97**
Shirley St. E16 . . . . .6H **87**
Shirley Way CR0: C'don 3A **170**
Shirley Windmill 3J **169**
Shirlock Rd. NW3 . . . . .4D **64**
Shirwell Cl. NW7 . . . . .7A **30**
Shobden Rd. N17 . . . . .1D **48**
Shobroke Cl. NW2 . . . . .3E **62**
Shoebury Rd. E6 . . . . .7D **70**
Shoelands Cl. NW9 . . . . .3K **43**
Shoe La. EC4 . . . . .7K **7** (6A **84**)
Sholto Rd. TW6: H'row A 5B **110**
Shona Ho. E13 . . . . .5A **88**
Shooters Av. HA3: Kenton 4C **42**
SHOOTERS HILL 1E **124**
Shooters Hill DA16: Well 1D **124**
  SE18 . . . . .1D **124**
Shooters Hill Golf Course 1G **125**
Shooters Hill Rd. SE3 . . . . .1F **123**
  SE10 . . . . .1F **123**
  SE18 . . . . .1F **123**
Shooters Rd. EN2: Enf 1G **23**
Shoot Up Hill NW2 . . . . .5G **63**
Shopping Hall, The E6 . . . . .1C **88**
Shore Bus. Cen. E9 . . . . .7J **67**

Shore Cl. TW12: Hamp 6C **130**
  TW14: Felt 7J **111**
Shorediche Cl. UB10: Ick 3B **56**
SHOREDITCH 1G **9** (3E **84**)
Shoreditch Ct. E8 . . . . .7F **67**
    (off Queensbridge Rd.)
Shoreditch High St. E1 . . . . .4H **9** (4E **84**)
Shoreditch Ho. BR2: Brom 6C **160**
  N1 . . . . .2F **9**
Shore Gro. TW13: Hanw 2E **130**
Shoreham Cl. CR0: C'don 6J **157**
  DA5: Bexl 1D **144**
  SW18 . . . . .5K **117**
Shoreham Rd. E. TW6: H'row A . . .5A **110**
Shoreham Rd. W. TW6: H'row A . . .5A **110**
Shoreham Way BR2: Hayes 6J **159**
Shore Pl. E9 . . . . .7J **67**
    (off Shore Rd.)
Shore Point IG9: Buck H 2E **36**
Shore Rd. E9 . . . . .7J **67**
Shore Way SW9 . . . . .2A **120**
    (off Crowhurst Cl.)
Shorncliffe Rd. SE1 . . . . .5F **103**
Shorndean St. SE6 . . . . .1E **140**
Shorne Cl. DA15: Sidc 6B **126**
Shornefield Cl. BR1: Brom 3E **160**
Shornells Way SE2 . . . . .4C **108**
Shorrold's Rd. SW6 . . . . .7H **99**
Short Blue Pl. IG11: Bark 7G **71**
Shortcroft Rd. KT17: Ewe 7B **164**
Shortcrofts Rd. RM9: Dag 6F **73**
Shorter St. E1 . . . . .2J **15** (7F **85**)
Shortgate N12 . . . . .4C **30**
Short Hedges TW3: Houn 1E **112**
Short Hill HA1: Harr 1J **59**
SHORTLANDS 2G **159**
Shortlands UB3: Harl 6F **93**
  W6 . . . . .4F **99**
Shortlands Cl. DA17: Belv 3F **109**
  N18 . . . . .3J **33**
Shortlands Gdns. BR2: Brom 2G **159**
Shortlands Golf Course 1G **159**
Shortlands Gro. BR2: Brom 3F **159**
Shortlands Rd. BR2: Brom 3F **159**
  E10 . . . . .7D **50**
  KT2: King T 7F **133**
Short La. TW19: Stanw 7B **110**
Short Path SE18 . . . . .6F **107**
Short Rd. E11 . . . . .2G **69**
  TW6: H'row A 6A **110**
  W4 . . . . .6A **98**
Shorts Cft. NW9 . . . . .4H **43**
Shorts Gdns. WC2 . . . . . . .1E **12** (6J **83**)
Shorts Rd. SM5: Cars 4C **166**
Short St. NW4 . . . . .4E **44**
    (off Foster St.)
  SE1 . . . . .6K **13** (2A **102**)
Short Wall E15 . . . . .3E **86**
Shortwave Cinema 3E **102**
    (off Bermondsey Sq.)
Short Way N12 . . . . .6H **31**
  SE9 . . . . .3C **124**
  TW2: Whitt 7G **113**
Shotfield SM6: Wall 6F **167**
Shott Cl. SM1: Sutt 5A **166**
Shottendane Rd. SW6 . . . . .1J **117**
Shottery Cl. SE9 . . . . .3C **142**
Shottfield Av. SW14 . . . . .4A **116**
Shottsford W2 . . . . .6J **81**
    (off Talbot Rd.)
Shoulder of Mutton All. E14 . . . . . .7A **86**
Shouldham St. W1 . . . . . . .6D **4** (5C **82**)
Showcase Cinema
  Barking 3H **89**
Showers Way UB3: Hayes 1J **93**
Shrapnel Cl. SE18 . . . . .7C **106**
Shrapnel Rd. SE9 . . . . .3D **124**
Shrewsbury Av. HA3: Kenton 4E **42**
  SW14 . . . . .4J **115**

Shrewsbury Cl. KT6: Surb 2E **162**
Shrewsbury Ct. EC1 . . . . .4D **8**
Shrewsbury Ho. SW3 . . . . .7C **16**
  SW8 . . . . .7H **19**
Shrewsbury La. SE18 . . . . .1F **125**
Shrewsbury M. W2 . . . . .5J **81**
    (off Chepstow Rd.)
Shrewsbury Rd. BR3: Beck 3A **158**
  E7 . . . . .5B **70**
  N11 . . . . .6B **32**
  NW10 . . . . .1K **79**
  SM5: Cars 6C **154**
  TW6: H'row A 6E **110**
    (not continuous)
  W2 . . . . .6J **81**
Shrewsbury St. W10 . . . . .4E **80**
Shrewsbury Wlk. TW7: Isle 3A **114**
    (off Magdala Rd.)
Shrewton Rd. SW17 . . . . .7D **136**
Shri Swaminarayan Mandir
  London .6K **61**
Shroffold Rd. BR1: Brom 4G **141**
Shropshire Cl. CR4: Mitc 4J **155**
Shropshire Ct. W7 . . . . .6K **77**
    (off Copley Cl.)
Shropshire Ho. N18 . . . . .5C **34**
    (off Cavendish Cl.)
Shropshire Pl. WC1 . . . . . . .4C **6** (4G **83**)
Shropshire Rd. N22 . . . . .7E **32**
Shroton St. NW1 . . . . .5D **4** (5C **82**)
Shrubberies, The E18 . . . . .2J **51**
Shrubbery, The E11 . . . . .5K **51**
  KT6: Surb 1E **162**
Shrubbery Cl. N1 . . . . .1C **84**
Shrubbery Gdns. N21 . . . . .7G **23**
Shrubbery Rd. N9 . . . . .3B **34**
  SW16 . . . . .4J **137**
  UB1: S'hall 1D **94**
Shrubland Gro. KT4: Wor Pk 3E **164**
Shrubland Rd. E8 . . . . .1F **85**
  E10 . . . . .7C **50**
  E17 . . . . .5C **50**
Shrublands Av. CR0: C'don 3C **170**
Shrublands Cl. N20 . . . . .1G **31**
  SE26 . . . . .3J **139**
Shrubsall Cl. SE9 . . . . .1C **142**
Shuna Wlk. N1 . . . . .6D **66**
Shurland Av. EN4: E Barn 6G **21**
Shurland Gdns. SE15 . . . . .7F **103**
Shurlock Dr. BR6: Farnb 4G **173**
Shushan Cl. N16 . . . . .7E **48**
Shuters Sq. W14 . . . . .5H **99**
Shuttle Cl. DA15: Sidc 7K **125**
Shuttlemead DA5: Bexl 7F **127**
Shuttle St. E1 . . . . .4G **85**
Shuttleworth Rd. SW11 . . . . .2C **118**
Siamese M. N3 . . . . .1J **45**
Siani M. N8 . . . . .4B **48**
Sibella Rd. SW4 . . . . .2H **119**
Sibley Cl. BR1: Brom 5C **160**
  DA6: Bex 5E **126**
Sibley Ct. BR2: Brom 2F **159**
  UB8: Hil 5E **74**
Sibley Gro. E12 . . . . .7C **70**
Sibthorpe Rd. SE12 . . . . .6K **123**
Sibthorp Rd. CR4: Mitc 2D **154**
Sibton Rd. SM5: Cars 7C **154**
Sicilian Av. WC1 . . . . .6F **7**
Sickle Cnr. RM9: Dag 4H **91**
Sidbury St. SW6 . . . . .1G **117**
SIDCUP .4A **144**
Sidcup By-Pass BR5: Sidc, St P . . .6A **144**
  BR7: Chst, Sidc 3H **143**
  DA14: Sidc 6A **144**
Sidcup Golf Course 1B **144**
Sidcup High St. DA14: Sidc 4A **144**
Sidcup Hill DA14: Sidc 4B **144**
Sidcup Hill Gdns. DA14: Sidc 5C **144**
Sidcup Leisure Cen. 2A **144**
Sidcup Place 5A **144**
Sidcup Pl. DA14: Sidc 5A **144**

Sidcup Rd. SE9 . . . . .1D 142
  SE12 . . . . .6A 124
Sidcup Technology Cen. DA14: Sidc . .5D 144
Siddeley Dr. TW4: Houn 3C 112
Siddeley Rd. E17 . . . . .2E 50
Siddons La. NW1 . . . . .4F 5 (4D 82)
Siddons Rd. CR0: Wadd 3A 168
  N17 . . . . .1G 49
  SE23 . . . . .2A 140
Side Rd. E17 .5B 50
Sidewood Rd. SE9 . . . . .1H 143
Sidford Ho. SE1 . . . . .2H 19
Sidford Pl. SE1 . . . . .2H 19 (3A 102)
Sidgwick Ho. SW9 . . . . .2K 119
  (off Stockwell Rd.)
Sidi Cl. N15 .3B 48
Sidings, The E11 . . . . .1E 68
Sidings Apartments, The E16 . . . . . . .2E 106
Sidings M. N7 . . . . .3A 66
Siding St. E20 . . . . .1D 86
Sidlaw Ho. N16 . . . . .1F 67
Sidmouth Av. TW7: Isle 2J 113
Sidmouth Dr. HA4: Ruis 3J 57
Sidmouth Ho. SE15 . . . . .7G 103
  (off Lindsey Est.)
  W1 . . . . .7D 4
  (off Cato St.)
Sidmouth M. WC1 . . . . .2G 7 (3K 83)
Sidmouth Pde. NW2 . . . . .7E 62
Sidmouth Rd. DA16: Well 7C 108
  E10 . . . . .3E 68
  NW2 . . . . .7E 62
Sidmouth St. WC1 . . . . .2F 7 (3K 83)
Sidney Av. N13 . . . . .5E 32
Sidney Boyd Ct. NW6 . . . . .7J 63
Sidney Elson Way E6 . . . . .2E 88
Sidney Est. E1 . . . . .6J 85
  (Bromhead St.)
  E1 . . . . .5J 85
  (Lindley St.)
Sidney Gdns. TW8: Bford 6D 96
Sidney Godley (VC) Ho. E2 . . . . .3J 85
  (off Digby St.)
Sidney Gro. EC1 . . . . .1A 8 (2B 84)
Sidney Ho. E2 . . . . .2K 85
  (off Old Ford Rd.)
Sidney Miller Ct. W3 . . . . .1H 97
  (off Crown St.)
Sidney Rd. BR3: Beck 2A 158
  E7 . . . . .3J 69
  HA2: Harr 3G 41
  KT12: Walt T 7J 147
  N22 . . . . .7E 32
  SE25 . . . . .5G 157
  SW9 . . . . .2K 119
  TW1: Twick 6A 114
Sidney Sq. E1 . . . . .5J 85
Sidney St. E1 . . . . .5H 85
  (not continuous)
Sidney Webb Ho. SE1 . . . . .3D 102
  (off Tabard St.)
Sidonie Apartments SW11 . . . . .4C 118
  (off Danvers Av.)
Sidworth St. E8 . . . . .7H 67
Siebert Rd. SE3 . . . . .6J 105
Siege Ho. E1 .6H 85
  (off Sidney St.)
Siemens Brothers Way E16 . . . . .7J 87
Siemens Rd. SE18 . . . . .3B 106
Sienna SE28 . . . . .3A 108
Sienna Alto SE13 . . . . .3E 122
  (off Cornmill La.)
Sienna Cl. KT9: Chess 6D 162
Sienna Ho. E20 . . . . .6D 68
  (off Victory Pde.)
Sienna Ter. NW2 . . . . .2C 62
Sierra Dr. RM9: Dag 2H 91
Sigdon Pas. E8 . . . . .5G 67
Sigdon Rd. E8 . . . . .5G 67
Sigers, The HA5: Eastc 6K 39
Sigmund Freud Statue 6B 64

Signal Ho. E8 . . . . .7H 67
  (off Martello Ter.)
  SE1 . . . . .7C 14
  (off Gt. Suffolk St.)
Signal Wlk. E4 . . . . .6K 35
Signmakers Yd. NW1 . . . . .1F 83
  (off Delancey St.)
Sigrist Sq. KT2: King T 1E 150
Sikorski Mus. 7B 10 (2B 100)
Silbury Av. CR4: Mitc 1C 154
Silbury Ho. SE26 . . . . .3G 139
Silbury St. N1 . . . . .1E 8 (3D 84)
Silchester Ct. CR7: Thor H 4A 156
  TW15: Ashf 2A 128
Silchester Rd. W10 . . . . .6F 81
Silecroft Rd. DA7: Bex 1G 127
Silesia Bldgs. E8 . . . . .7H 67
Silex St. SE1 . . . . .7B 14 (2B 102)
Silicon Bus. Cen. UB6: G'frd 2C 78
Silicon Way N1 . . . . .2F 9
Silk Cl. SE12 . . . . .5J 123
Silk Ct. E2 . . . . .3G 85
  (off Squirries St.)
Silkfield Rd. NW9 . . . . .5A 44
Silk Ho. E1 . . . . .1K 15
  E2 . . . . .2F 85
  (off How's St.)
  NW9 . . . . .3K 43
Silkin M. SE15 . . . . .7G 103
Silkin M. SE11 . . . . .5K 19
Silk Mills Ct. SE13 . . . . .2D 122
Silk Mills Path SE13 . . . . .2E 122
Silk Mills Sq. E9 . . . . .6B 68
Silkstream Pde. HA8: Edg 1J 43
Silkstream Rd. HA8: Edg 1J 43
Silk St. EC2 . . . . .5D 8 (5C 84)
Silk Weaver Way E2 . . . . .2H 85
Sillitoe Ho. N1 . . . . .1D 84
  (off Colville Est.)
Silsoe Ho. NW1 . . . . .2F 83
Silsoe Rd. N22 . . . . .2K 47
Silverbeck Way TW19: Stanw M 7B 174
Silver Birch Av. E4 . . . . .5G 35
Silver Birch Cl. DA2: Wilm 4K 145
  N11 . . . . .6K 31
  SE6 . . . . .3B 140
  UB10: Ick 4A 56
Silver Birch Gdns. E6 . . . . .4D 88
Silverbirch Wlk. NW5 . . . . .6E 64
Silverburn Ho. SW9 . . . . .1B 120
  (off Lothian Rd.)
Silvercliffe Gdns. EN4: E Barn 4H 21
Silver Cl. HA3: Hrw W 7C 26
  SE14 . . . . .7A 104
Silver Cres. W4 . . . . .4H 97
Silverdale EN2: Enf 4D 22
  NW1 . . . . .1A 6
  (off Harrington St.)
  SE26 . . . . .4J 139
Silverdale Av. IG2: Ilf 5J 53
Silverdale Centre, The HA0: Wemb 1F 79
Silverdale Ct. SM1: Sutt 4H 165
  UB5: N'olt 5D 58
  W7 . . . . .1J 95
Silverdale Dr. SE9 . . . . .2C 142
  TW16: Sun 2K 147
Silverdale Gdns. UB3: Hayes 2J 93
Silverdale Ind. Est. UB3: Hayes 2J 93
Silverdale Rd. BR5: Pet W 4G 161
  DA7: Bex 2H 127
  E4 . . . . .6A 36
  UB3: Hayes 2H 93
Silverdene N12 . . . . .6E 30
  (off Thyra Gro.)
Silvergate KT19: Ewe 5J 163
Silverhall St. TW7: Isle 3A 114

Silverholme Cl. HA3: Kenton 7E 42
Silver Jubilee Way TW4: Cran 2K 111
Silverland St. E16 . . . . .1D 106
Silver La. BR4: W W'ck 2F 171
Silverleigh Rd. CR7: Thor H 4K 155
Silver Mead E18 . . . . .1J 51
Silvermere Dr. N18 . . . . .6E 34
Silvermere Rd. SE6 . . . . .7D 122
Silver Pl. W1 . . . . .2B 12 (6G 83)
Silver Rd. SE13 . . . . .3D 122
  W12 . . . . .7F 81
Silvers IG9: Buck H 1F 37
  (off Palmerston Rd.)
Silver Spring Cl. DA8: Erith 6H 109
Silverston Way HA7: Stan 6H 27
Silver St. EN1: Enf 3J 23
  N18 . . . . .4J 33
Silverthorn NW8 . . . . .1K 81
  (off Abbey Rd.)
Silverthorne Loft Apartments SE5 . . . .6D 102
  (off Albany Rd.)
Silverthorne Rd. SW8 . . . . .2F 119
Silverthorn Gdns. E4 . . . . .2H 35
Silverton Rd. W6 . . . . .6F 99
SILVERTOWN 1A 106
Silvertown Sq. E16 . . . . .5H 87
Silvertown Viaduct E16 . . . . .6H 87
Silvertown Way E16 . . . . .6G 87
  (Clarkson Rd.)
  E16 . . . . .1J 105
  (Hanover Av.)
Silvertree La. UB6: G'frd 3H 77
Silver Wlk. SE16 . . . . .1A 104
Silver Way RM7: Mawney 3H 55
  UB10: Hil 2D 74
Silver Wing Ind. Est. CR0: Wadd 6K 167
Silverwood Ct. BR3: Beck 7C 140
  CR0: Sels .7B 170
  HA6: Nwood 1E 38
Silvester Ho. E1 . . . . .6K 85
  (off Varden St.)
  E2 . . . . .3J 85
  (off Sceptre Rd.)
  W11 . . . . .6H 81
  (off Basing St.)
Silvester Rd. SE22 . . . . .5F 121
Silvester St. SE1 . . . . .7E 14 (2D 102)
Silvocea Way E14 . . . . .6F 87
Silwood Est. SE16 . . . . .4J 103
Silwood St. SE16 . . . . .4J 103
  (off Rotherhithe New Rd.)
Simkins Cl. SW2 . . . . .4J 119
Simla Cl. N7 .7J 65
  (off Brewery Rd.)
Simla Ho. SE1 . . . . .7F 15
  (off Kipling Est.)
Simmonds Ct. SW5 . . . . .4K 99
  (off Earl's Ct. Gdns.)
Simmonds Ho. TW8: Bford 5E 96
  (off Clayponds La.)
Simmons Cl. KT9: Chess 6C 162
  N20 . . . . .2H 31
Simmons Dr. RM8: Dag 3E 72
Simmons La. E4 . . . . .2A 36
Simmons Rd. SE18 . . . . .5F 107
Simmons Way N20 . . . . .2H 31
Sims Cl. SM5: Cars 2C 166
Sims Gdns. N2 . . . . .2A 46
Sims Rd. SE1 . . . . .4G 103
Simnel Rd. SE12 . . . . .7K 123
Simon Cl. W11 . . . . .7H 81
Simon Ct. W9 .3J 81
  (off Saltram Cres.)
Simonds Rd. E10 . . . . .2C 68
Simone Cl. BR1: Brom 1B 160
Simone Ct. SE26 . . . . .3J 139
Simons Ct. N16 . . . . .2F 67
Simons Wlk. E15 . . . . .5F 69
Simpson Cl. CR0: C'don 5C 156
  N21 . . . . .5D 22
Simpson Dr. W3 . . . . .6K 79

Simpson Ho. NW8 . . . . . . .2D 4 (4C 82)
  SE11 . . . . .6G 19 (5K 101)
Simpson Rd. TW4: Houn 6D 112
  TW10: Ham 4C 132
Simpson's Rd. E14 . . . . .7D 86
Simpson St. SW11 . . . . .2C 118
Simpson Way KT6: Surb 6C 150
Simrose Ct. SW18 . . . . .5J 117
Sims Wlk. SE3 . . . . .4H 123
Sinclair Ct. CR0: C'don 2E 168
Sinclair Dr. SM2: Sutt 7K 165
Sinclair Gdns. W14 . . . . .2F 99
Sinclair Gro. NW11 . . . . .6F 45
Sinclair Ho. WC1 . . . . .2E 6
  (off Sandwich St.)
Sinclair Mans. W12 . . . . .2F 99
  (off Richmond Way)
Sinclair Pl. SE4 . . . . .6C 122
Sinclair Rd. E4 . . . . .5G 35
  W14 . . . . .2F 99
Sinclairs Ho. E3 . . . . .2B 86
  (off St Stephen's Rd.)
Sinclare Cl. EN1: Enf 1A 24
Singapore Rd. W13 . . . . .1A 96
Singer M. SW4 . . . . .2J 119
  (off Union Rd.)
Singer St. EC2 . . . . .2F 9 (3D 84)
Singleton Cl. CR0: C'don 7C 156
  SW17 . . . . .7D 136
Singleton Rd. RM9: Dag 5F 73
Singleton Scarp N12 . . . . .5D 30
Sinnott Rd. E17 . . . . .1K 49
Siobhan Davis Dance Studios 3B 102
  (off St George's Rd.)
Sion Cl. TW1: Twick 1B 132
Sion Rd. TW1: Twick 1B 132
Sippets Ct. IG1: Ilf 1H 71
SIPSON 6C 92
Sipson Cl. UB7: Sip 6C 92
Sipson La. UB3: Harl 6C 92
  UB7: Sip 6C 92
Sipson Rd. UB7: Sip, W Dray 3B 92
  (not continuous)
Sipson Way UB7: Sip 7C 92
Sir Abraham Dawes Cotts. SW15 . . . .4G 117
Sir Alexander Rd. W3 . . . . .1B 98
Sir Christopher France Ho. E1 . . . . . . .3A 86
Sir Cyril Black Way SW19 . . . . .7J 135
Sirdar Rd. CR4: Mitc 6E 136
  N22 . . . . .3B 48
  W11 . . . . .7F 81
Sir Francis Drake Ct. SE10 . . . . .5F 105
Sirinham Point SW8 . . . . .7H 19
Sirius SW11 .2D 118
Sirius Bldg. E1 . . . . .7K 85
  (off Jardine Rd.)
Sirius Ho. SE8 . . . . .4A 104
  (off Seafarer Way)
Sirius Ho. SE5 . . . . .2D 120
  (off Coldharbour La.)
Sir James Black Ho. SE5 . . . . .7C 102
Sir John Kirk Cl. SE5 . . . . .7C 102
Sir John Lyon Ho. EC4 . . . . .2C 14
  (off High Timber St.)
Sir John Morden Wlk. SE3 . . . . .2J 123
Sir John Soane's Mus. 7G 7 (6K 83)
Sir Nicholas Garrow Ho. W10 . . . . .4G 81
  (off Kensal Rd.)
Sir Oswald Stoll Foundation, The
  SW6 . . . . .7K 99
  (off Fulham Rd.)
Sir Oswald Stoll Mans. SW6 . . . . .7K 99
  (off Fulham Rd.)
Sir Walter Raleigh Ct. SE10 . . . . .5G 105
Sir William Powell's Almshouses
  SW6 . . . . .2G 117
Sise La. EC4 . . . . .1E 14 (6D 84)
Siskin Ho. SE16 . . . . .4K 103
  (off Tawny Way)
Sisley Rd. IG11: Bark 1J 89
Sispara Gdns. SW18 . . . . .6H 117
Sissinghurst Cl. BR1: Brom 5G 141

Sissinghurst Ho. *SE15* 6J *103*
(off Sharratt St.)
Sissinghurst Rd. CR0: C'don 7G *157*
Sissulu Cl. E6 . . . . .1A *88*
Sister Mabel's Way SE15 . . . . . . .7G *103*
Sisters Av. SW11 . . . . .3D *118*
Sistova Rd. SW12 . . . . .1F *137*
Sisulu Pl. SW9 . . . . .3A *120*
Sitarey Ct. W12 . . . . .1D *98*
Sittingbourne Av. EN1: Enf 6J *23*
Sitwell Gro. HA7: Stan 5E *26*
Siverst Cl. UB5: N'olt 6F *59*
Sivill Ho. *E2* .1K *9*
(off Columbia Rd.)
Siviter Way RM10: Dag 7H *73*
Siward Rd. BR2: Brom 3K *159*
    N17 . . . . .1D *48*
    SW17 . . . . .3A *136*
Six Acres Est. N4 . . . . .2K *65*
Six Bridges Ind. Est. SE1 . . . . .5G *103*
(not continuous)
Sixpenny Ct. IG11: Bark 6G *71*
Sixth Av. E12 . . . . .4D *70*
    UB3: Hayes 1H *93*
    W10 . . . . .3G *81*
Sixth Cross Rd. TW2: Twick 3G *131*
Skardu Rd. NW2 . . . . .5G *63*
Skeena Hill SW18 . . . . .7G *117*
Skeffington Rd. E6 . . . . .1D *88*
Skeffington St. SE18 . . . . .3E *107*
Skeggs Ho. *E14* 3E *104*
(off Glengall St.)
Skegness Ho. *N7* 7K *65*
(off Sutterton St.)
Skelbrook St. SW18 . . . . .2A *136*
Skelgill Rd. SW15 . . . . .4H *117*
Skelley Rd. E15 . . . . .7H *69*
Skelton Cl. E8 . . . . .6F *67*
Skelton Rd. E7 . . . . .6J *69*
Skelton's La. E10 . . . . .7D *50*
Skelwith Rd. W6 . . . . .6E *98*
Skenfrith Ho. *SE15* 6H *103*
(off Commercial Way)
Skerne Rd. KT2: King T 1D *150*
Skerne Wlk. KT2: King T 1D *150*
Sketch Apartments *E1* 5K *85*
(off Shandy St.)
Sketchley Gdns. SE16 . . . . .5K *103*
Sketty Rd. EN1: Enf 3A *24*
Skiers St. E15 . . . . .1G *87*
Skiffington Cl. SW2 . . . . .1A *138*
Skillen Lodge HA5: Pinn 1B *40*
Skinner Pl. SW1 . . . . .4G *17*
Skinners Cl. N13 . . . . .3F *33*
Skinners La. EC4 . . . . . . .2D *14* (7C *84*)
    TW5: Hest 1F *113*
Skinner's Row SE10 . . . . .1D *122*
Skinner St. EC1 . . . . .2K *7* (3A *84*)
Skip La. UB9: Hare 1A *56*
Skipper Ct. IG11: Bark 1G *89*
Skipsea Ho. SW18 . . . . .6C *118*
Skipsey Av. E6 . . . . .3D *88*
Skipton Cl. N11 . . . . .6K *31*
Skipton Dr. UB3: Harl 3E *92*
Skipton Ho. SE4 . . . . .4A *122*
Skipwith Ho. *EC1* 5J *7*
(off Bourne Est.)
Skipworth Rd. E9 . . . . .1J *85*
Skua Ct. *SE8* 6B *104*
(off Dorking Cl.)
Skye La. HA8: Edg 4A *28*
Sky Garden Wlk. *EC3* 2G *15*
(off Philpot La.)
Skylark Ct. RM13: Rain 2K *91*
    SE1 . . . . .7D *14*
(off Swan St.)
Skyline Ct. CR0: C'don 3D *168*
(off Park La.)
    SE1 . . . . .3F *103*
Skyline Plaza Bldg. *E1* 6G *85*
(off Commercial Rd.)

Skylines E14 . . . . .2E *104*
Skylines Village E14 . . . . .2E *104*
Sky Peals Rd. IG8: Wfd G 7A *36*
Skyport Dr. UB7: Harm 3E *174*
Sky Studios E16 . . . . .2E *106*
Skyvan Cl. TW6: H'row A 5E *110*
Skyview Apartments CR0: C'don . . .2C *168*
(off Park St.)
Skyway 14 SL3: Poyle 6A *174*
Slade, The SE18 . . . . .6J *107*
Sladebrook Rd. SE3 . . . . .3B *124*
Slade Ct. EN5: New Bar 3E *20*
Sladedale Rd. SE18 . . . . .5J *107*
Slade Ho. TW4: Houn 6D *112*
Sladen Pl. E5 . . . . .4H *67*
Slades Cl. EN2: Enf 3F *23*
Slades Dr. BR7: Chst 3G *143*
Slades Gdns. EN2: Enf 2F *23*
Slades Hill EN2: Enf 3F *23*
Slades Ri. EN2: Enf 3F *23*
Slade Twr. *E10* 2C *68*
(off Leyton Grange Est.)
Slade Wlk. SE17 . . . . .6B *102*
Slade Way CR4: Mitc 1E *154*
Slagrove Pl. SE13 . . . . .5C *122*
Slaidburn St. SW10 . . . . .6A *100*
Slaithwaite Rd. SE13 . . . . .4E *122*
Slaney Cl. NW10 . . . . .7E *62*
Slaney Pl. N7 . . . . .5A *66*
Slater Cl. SE18 . . . . .5E *106*
Slater M. SW4 . . . . .3G *119*
(off Grafton Sq.)
Slatter NW9 . . . . .7G *29*
Slattery Rd. TW13: Felt 1B *130*
Sleaford Ho. *E3* 4C *86*
(off Fern St.)
Sleaford Ind. Est. SW8 . . . . .7G *101*
Sleaford St. SW8 . . . . .7G *101*
Sleat Ho. *E3* 2B *86*
(off Saxon Rd.)
Sledmere Ct. TW14: Bedf 1G *129*
Sleigh Ho. *E2* 3J *85*
(off Bacton St.)
Slievemore Cl. SW4 . . . . .3H *119*
Sligo Ho. *E1* 4K *85*
(off Beaumont Gro.)
Slindon Ct. N16 . . . . .3F *67*
Slingsby Pl. WC2 . . . . .2E *12* (7J *83*)
Slippers Pl. SE16 . . . . .3H *103*
Slipway Ho. *E14* 5D *104*
(off Burrells Wharf Sq.)
Sloane Av. SW3 . . . . .4D *16* (4C *100*)
Sloane Av. Mans. SW3 . . . .4E *16* (4D *100*)
Sloane Cl. TW7: Isle 1J *113*
Sloane Ct. E. SW3 . . . . .5G *17* (5A *100*)
Sloane Ct. W. SW3 . . . . . . .5G *17* (5A *100*)
Sloane Gdns. BR6: Farnb 3G *173*
    SW1 . . . . .4G *17* (4E *100*)
Sloane Ga. Mans. SW1 . . . . .3G *17*
(off D'Oyley St.)
Sloane Ho. *E9* 7J *67*
(off Loddiges Rd.)
Sloane M. N8 . . . . .5J *47*
Sloane Sq. SW1 . . . . .4G *17* (4E *100*)
Sloane St. SW1 . . . . .7E *11* (2D *100*)
Sloane Ter. SW1 . . . . .3G *17* (4E *100*)
Sloane Ter. Mans. SW1 . . . . .3G *17*
(off Sloane Ter.)
Sloane Wlk. CR0: C'don 6B *158*
Slocum Cl. SE28 . . . . .7C *90*
Slough La. NW9 . . . . .5J *43*
Sly St. E1 . . . . .6H *85*
Smaldon Cl. UB7: W Dray 3C *92*
Smallberry Av. TW7: Isle 2K *113*
Smallbrook M. W2 . . . . .1A *10* (6B *82*)
Smalley Cl. N16 . . . . .3F *67*
Smalley Rd. Est. *N16* 3F *67*
(off Smalley Cl.)
Smallwood Rd. SW17 . . . . .4B *136*
Smarden Cl. DA17: Belv 5G *109*
Smarden Gro. SE9 . . . . .4D *142*

Smart's Pl. N18 . . . . .5B *34*
    WC2 . . . . .7F *7* (6J *83*)
Smart St. E2 . . . . .3K *85*
Smead Way SE13 . . . . .3D *122*
Smeaton Cl. KT9: Chess 6D *162*
Smeaton Ct. SE1 . . . . .3C *102*
Smeaton Rd. IG8: Wfd G 5J *37*
    SW18 . . . . .7J *117*
Smeaton St. E1 . . . . .1H *103*
Smedley St. SW4 . . . . .2H *119*
    SW8 . . . . .2H *119*
Smeed Rd. E3 . . . . .7C *68*
Smikle Ct. *SE14* 1K *121*
(off Hatcham Pk. M.)
Smiles Pl. SE13 . . . . .2E *122*
Smith Cl. SE16 . . . . .1K *103*
Smithfield (Central Markets) 6A *8*
Smithfield Ct. *E1* 7G *85*
(off Cable St.)
Smithfield St. EC1 . . . . .6A *8* (5B *84*)
Smith Hill TW8: Bford 6E *96*
Smithies Rd. SE2 . . . . .4B *108*
Smith's Ct. W1 . . . . .2B *12*
Smithson Rd. N17 . . . . .1D *48*
Smiths Point *E13* 1J *87*
(off Brooks Rd.)
Smith Sq. SW1 . . . . .2E *18* (3J *101*)
Smith St. KT5: Surb 6F *151*
    SW3 . . . . .5E *16* (5D *100*)
Smiths Yd. CR0: C'don 3C *168*
(off St George's Wlk.)
    SW18 . . . . .2A *136*
Smith Ter. SW3 . . . . .6E *16* (5D *100*)
Smithwood Cl. SW19 . . . . .1G *135*
Smithy La. TW3: Houn 3F *113*
Smithy St. E1 . . . . .5J *85*
Smock Wlk. CR0: C'don 6C *156*
Smokehouse Yd. *EC1* 5B *8*
(off St John St.)
Smoothfield Ct. TW3: Houn 4E *112*
Smugglers Way SW18 . . . . .4K *117*
Smyrk's Rd. SE17 . . . . .5E *102*
Smyrna Mans. *NW6* 7J *63*
(off Smyrna Rd.)
Smyrna Rd. NW6 . . . . .7J *63*
Smythe Cl. N9 . . . . .3B *34*
Smythe St. E14 . . . . .7D *86*
Snag La. BR6: Prat B 7K *173*
Snakes La. N14 . . . . .3A *22*
Snakes La. E. IG8: Buck H, Wfd G . . .6F *37*
Snakes La. W. IG8: Wfd G 5D *36*
Snakey La. TW13: Felt 4J *129*
SNARESBROOK 5J *51*
Snaresbrook Dr. HA7: Stan 4J *27*
Snaresbrook Hall E18 . . . . .4J *51*
Snaresbrook Ho. E18 . . . . .4H *51*
Snaresbrook Rd. E11 . . . . .4G *51*
Snarsgate St. W10 . . . . .5E *80*
Sneath Av. NW11 . . . . .7H *45*
Snells Pk. N18 . . . . .6A *34*
Sneyd Rd. NW2 . . . . .4E *62*
Snowberry Cl. E15 . . . . .4F *69*
    EN5: Barn 3C *20*
Snowbury Rd. SW6 . . . . .2K *117*
Snowden Av. UB10: Hil 2D *74*
Snowden St. EC2 . . . . .4G *9* (4E *84*)
Snowdon Aviary 1D *82*
(in London Zoo)
Snowdon Cres. UB3: Harl 3E *92*
Snowdon Dr. NW9 . . . . .6A *44*
Snowdon Rd. TW6: H'row A 6E *110*
Snowdown Cl. SE20 . . . . .1K *157*
Snowdrop Cl. TW12: Hamp 6E *130*
Snowdrop Ct. RM13: Rain 2J *91*
Snow Hill EC1 . . . . .6A *8* (5B *84*)
Snow Hill Ct. EC1 . . . . .7B *8* (6B *84*)
Snowman Ho. NW6 . . . . .1K *81*
Snowsfields SE1 . . . . .6F *15* (2D *102*)
Snowshill Rd. E12 . . . . .5C *70*
Snowy Fielder Waye TW7: Isle 2B *114*
Soames Pl. EN4: Had W 2E *20*

Soames St. SE15 . . . . .3F *121*
Soames Wlk. KT3: N Mald 1A *152*
Soane Cl. W5 . . . . .2D *96*
Soane Ct. NW1 . . . . .7G *65*
(off St Pancras Way)
Soane Ho. *SE17* 5D *102*
(off Roland Way)
Soane Sq. HA7: Stan 3D *26*
Soap Ho. La. TW8: Bford 7E *96*
Sobell Leisure Cen. 3K *65*
Sobraon Ho. *KT2: King T* 7F *133*
(off Elm Rd.)
Socket La. BR2: Hayes 6K *159*
Soda Studios *E8* 1F *85*
(off Kingsland Rd.)
SOHO 1C *12* (6G *83*)
Soho Sq. W1 . . . . .7C *6* (6H *83*)
Soho St. W1 . . . . .7C *6* (6H *83*)
Soho Theatre & Writers Cen. 1C *12*
(off Dean St.)
Sojourner Truth Cl. E8 . . . . .6H *67*
Sola Ct. CR0: C'don 1D *168*
(off Sydenham Rd.)
Solander Gdns. *E1* 7H *85*
(off Cable St., Cable St.)
    E1 . . . . .7J *85*
(The Highway)
Solar Ct. N3 . . . . .7E *30*
    SE16 . . . . .2G *103*
(off Chambers St.)
Solar Ho. E6 . . . . .5E *88*
    E15 . . . . .6G *69*
(off Romford Rd.)
Solarium Ct. *SE1* 4F *103*
(off Alscot Rd.)
Soldene Ct. N7 . . . . .6K *65*
Solebay St. E1 . . . . .4A *86*
Solent Cl. SW16 . . . . .2K *155*
Solent Ho. *E1* 5A *86*
(off Ben Jonson Rd.)
Solent Ri. E13 . . . . .3J *87*
Solent Rd. NW6 . . . . .5J *63*
Soley M. WC1 . . . . .1J *7* (3A *84*)
Solna Av. SW15 . . . . .5E *116*
Solna Rd. N21 . . . . .1J *33*
Solomon Av. N9 . . . . .4B *34*
Solomons Ct. N12 . . . . .7F *31*
Solomon's Pas. SE15 . . . . .4H *121*
Solon New Rd. SW4 . . . . .4J *119*
Solon New Rd. Est. SW4 . . . . .4J *119*
Solon Rd. SW2 . . . . .4J *119*
Solway Cl. E8 . . . . .6F *67*
(off Queensbridge Rd.)
    TW4: Houn 3C *112*
Solway Ho. *E1* 4K *85*
(off Ernest St.)
Solway Rd. N22 . . . . .1B *48*
    SE22 . . . . .4G *121*
Somaford Gro. EN4: E Barn 6G *21*
Somali Rd. NW2 . . . . .5H *63*
Sombourne Ho. SW15 . . . . .7C *116*
(off Fontley Way)
Somerby Rd. IG11: Bark 7H *71*
Somercoates Cl. EN4: Cockf 3H *21*
Somer Ct. SW6 . . . . .6J *99*
(off Anselm Rd.)
Somerden Rd. N4 . . . . .2B *66*
(not continuous)
Somerfield St. SE16 . . . . .5K *103*
Somerford Cl. HA5: Eastc 4J *39*
Somerford Gro. N16 . . . . .4F *67*
    N17 . . . . .7B *34*
(not continuous)
Somerford Gro. Est. N16 . . . . .4F *67*
Somerford St. E1 . . . . .4H *85*
Somerford Way SE16 . . . . .2A *104*
Somerhill Av. DA15: Sidc 7B *126*
Somerhill Rd. DA16: Well 2B *126*
Someritton Pas. SW9 . . . . .4B *120*
Somerleyton Rd. SW9 . . . . .4A *120*
Somersby Gdns. IG4: Ilf 5D *52*

Somers Cl. NW1 . . . . .2H 83
Somers Cres. W2 . . . . .1C 10 (6C 82)
Somerset Av. DA16: Well 5K 125
KT9: Chess 4D 162
SW20 . . . . .2D 152
Somerset Cl. IG8: Wfd G 1J 51
KT3: N Mald 6A 152
N17 . . . . .2D 48
SM3: Wor Pk 4E 164
Somerset Ct. IG9: Buck H 2F 37
NW1 . . . . .1C 6 (2H 83)
TW11: Tedd 5J 131
W7 . . . . .6K 77
(off Copley Cl.)
Somerset Est. SW11 . . . . .1B 118
Somerset Gdns. HA0: Wemb 5C 60
N6 . . . . .7E 46
N17 .7K 33
SE13 . . . . .2D 122
SW16 . . . . .3K 155
TW11: Tedd 5J 131
Somerset Hall N17 . . . . .7K 33
Somerset House 2G 13 (7K 83)
Somerset Ho. SW19 . . . . .3F 135
Somerset Lodge TW8: Bford 6D 96
Somerset Rd. E17 . . . . .5C 50
EN5: New Bar 5E 20
HA1: Harr 5G 41
KT1: King T 2F 151
N17 .3F 49
N18 .5A 34
NW4 .4E 44
SW19 . . . . .3F 135
TW8: Bford 6D 96
TW11: Tedd 5J 131
UB1: S'hall 5D 76
W4 . . . . .3K 97
W13 .1B 96
Somerset Sq. W14 . . . . .2G 99
Somerset Waye TW5: Hest 6C 94
Somersham Rd. DA7: Bex 2E 126
Somers Pl. SW2 . . . . .7K 119
Somers Rd. E17 . . . . .4B 50
SW2 .6K 119
Somerston Ho. NW1 . . . . .1G 83
(off St Pancras Way)
SOMERS TOWN 1C 6 (2H 83)
Somers Town Community Sports Cen.
. . . . .2H 83
Somerton Av. TW9: Rich 3H 115
Somerton Ho. WC1 . . . . .2D 6
Somerton Rd. NW2 . . . . .3F 63
SE15 . . . . .4H 121
Somertrees Av. SE12 . . . . .2K 141
Somervell Rd. HA2: Harr 5D 58
Somerville Av. SW13 . . . . .6D 98
Somerville Cl. SW9 . . . . .1K 119
Somerville Point SE16 . . . . .2B 104
Somerville Rd. RM6: Chad H 6C 54
SE20 . . . . .7K 139
Sonderburg Rd. N7 . . . . .2K 65
Sondes St. SE17 . . . . .6D 102
Sonesta Apartments SE15 . . . . .1H 121
Songhurst Cl. CR0: C'don 6K 155
Sonia Cl. HA1: Harr 6K 41
HA8: Edg 7A 28
Sonia Gdns. N12 . . . . .4F 31
NW10 .4B 62
TW5: Hest 7E 94
Sonning Ct.
TW12: Hamp 6C 130
Sonning Ho. E2 . . . . .2J 9
(off Swanfield St.)
Sonning Rd. SE25 . . . . .6G 157
Sontan Ct. TW2: Twick 1H 131
Soper Cl. E4 . . . . .5G 35
SE23 . . . . .1K 139
Soper M. EN3: Enf L 1H 25
Sophia Cl. N7 . . . . .6K 65
Sophia Ho. W6 . . . . .5E 98
(off Queen Caroline St.)

Sophia Rd. E10 . . . . .1D 68
E16 .6K 87
Sophia Sq. SE16 . . . . .7A 86
(off Sovereign Cres.)
Sophora Ho. SW8 . . . . .7F 101
Soprano Ct. E15 . . . . .1H 87
(off Plaistow Rd.)
Soprano Way KT10: Surb 3B 162
Sopwith NW9 . . . . .7G 29
Sopwith Av. KT9: Chess 5E 162
Sopwith Cl. KT2: King T 5F 133
Sopwith Rd. TW5: Hest 7A 94
Sopwith Way KT2: King T 1E 150
SW8 . . . . .7J 17 (7F 101)
Sorbus Ct. EN2: Enf 2G 23
Sorensen Ct. E10 . . . . .2D 68
(off Leyton Grange Est.)
Sorrel Cl. SE28 . . . . .1A 108
Sorrel Gdns. E6 . . . . .5C 88
Sorrel La. E14 . . . . .6F 87
Sorrell Cl. SE14 . . . . .7A 104
SW9 .2A 120
Sorrel Mead NW9 . . . . .7C 44
Sorrento Rd. SM1: Sutt 3K 165
Sotheby Rd. N5 . . . . .3B 66
Sotheran Cl. E8 . . . . .1G 85
Sotherby Lodge E2 . . . . .2J 85
(off Sewardstone Rd.)
Sotheron Pl. SW6 . . . . .7K 99
Soudan Rd. SW11 . . . . .1D 118
Souldern Rd. W14 . . . . .3F 99
Sounding All. E3 . . . . .1C 86
Sth. Access Rd. E17 . . . . .7A 50
Southacre W2 . . . . .1C 10
(off Hyde Pk. Cres.)
Southacre Way HA5: Pinn 1A 40
SOUTH ACTON 2J 97
Sth. Africa Rd. W12 . . . . .1D 98
SOUTHALL .1D 94
Southall Cl. UB1: S'hall 7D 76
Southall Ent. Cen. UB2: S'hall 2E 94
SOUTHALL GREEN 3C 94
Southall La. TW5: Cran 6K 93
UB2: S'hall 6K 93
Southall Pl. SE1 . . . . .7E 14 (2D 102)
Southam Ho. W10 . . . . .4G 81
(off Southam St.)
Southampton Bldgs. WC2 . . . . . .6J 7 (5A 84)
Southampton Gdns. CR4: Mitc 5J 155
Southampton M. E16 . . . . .1K 105
Southampton Pl. WC1 . . . . . . .6F 7 (5J 83)
Southampton Rd. E. TW6: H'row A . . .6B 110
Southampton Rd. W.
TW6: H'row A 6A 110
Southampton Row WC1 . . . . . . .5F 7 (5J 83)
Southampton St. WC2 . . . . . .2F 13 (7J 83)
Southampton Way SE5 . . . . .7D 102
Southam St. W10 . . . . .4G 81
Sth. Audley St. W1 . . . . .3H 11 (7E 82)
South Av. E4 . . . . .7J 25
SM5: Cars 7E 166
TW9: Kew 2G 115
UB1: S'hall 7D 76
South Av. Gdns. UB1: S'hall 7D 76
South Bank KT6: Surb 6E 150
Southbank KT7: T Ditt 7B 150
Southbank Bus. Cen. SW11 . . . . . . .1D 118
Southbank Cen. 4H 13 (1K 101)
Sth. Bank Ter. KT6: Surb 6E 150
SOUTH BARNET 1K 31
SOUTH BEDDINGTON 6H 167
Sth. Birkbeck Rd. E11 . . . . .3F 69
Sth. Black Lion La. W6 . . . . .5C 98
South Block SE1 . . . . .7G 13
(off Belvedere Rd.)
Southborough 5D 160
. . . . .1E 162
Southborough Cl. KT6: Surb 1D 162

Southborough Ho. SE17 . . . . .5E 102
(off Kinglake Est.)
Southborough La. BR2: Brom 5C 160
Southborough Rd. BR1: Brom 3C 160
E9 . . . . .1K 85
KT6: Surb 1E 162
Southbourne BR2: Hayes 7J 159
Southbourne Av. NW9 . . . . .2J 43
Southbourne Cl. HA5: Pinn 7C 40
Southbourne Ct. NW9 . . . . .2J 43
Southbourne Cres. NW4 . . . . .4G 45
Southbourne Gdns.
HA4: Ruis 1K 57
IG1: Ilf 5G 71
SE12 . . . . .5K 123
Southbridge Pl. CR0: C'don 4C 168
Southbridge Rd. CR0: C'don 4C 168
Southbridge Way UB2: S'hall 2C 94
SOUTH BROMLEY 7E 86
Southbrook M. SE12 . . . . .6H 123
Southbrook Rd. SE12 . . . . .6H 123
SW16 . . . . .1J 155
Southbury NW8 . . . . .1A 82
(off Loudoun Rd.)
Southbury Av. EN1: Enf 4B 24
Southbury Leisure Cen. 3B 24
Southbury Rd. EN1: Enf 3K 23
EN3: Pond E 3K 23
Sth. Carriage Dr. SW1 . . . .7B 10 (2B 100)
SW7 . . . . .7B 10 (2B 100)
SOUTH CHINGFORD 5G 35
Southchurch Ct. E6 . . . . .2D 88
(off High St. Sth.)
Southchurch Rd. E6 . . . . .2D 88
South City Cl. SE15 . . . . .7E 102
South Cl. DA6: Bex 4D 126
EN5: Barn 3C 20
HA5: Pinn 7D 40
N6 . . . . .6F 47
RM10: Dag 1G 91
SM4: Mord 6J 153
TW2: Twick 3C 130
UB7: W Dray 3B 92
Sth. Colonnade, The E14 . . . . .1C 104
(not continuous)
Southcombe St. W14 . . . . .4G 99
South Comn. Rd. UB8: Uxb 6A 56
Southcote Av. KT5: Surb 7H 151
TW13: Felt 2H 129
Southcote Ri. HA4: Ruis 7F 39
Southcote Rd. E17 . . . . .5K 49
N19 .4G 65
SE25 . . . . .5H 157
Southcott Ho. E3 . . . . .3D 86
(off Devons Rd.)
W9 . . . . .4A 82
(off Clifton Gdns.)
Southcott M. NW8 . . . . .2C 82
Southcott Rd. TW11: Hamp W 1C 150
Sth. Countess Rd. E17 . . . . .3B 50
South Cres. E16 . . . . .4H 87
WC1 . . . . .6C 6 (5H 83)
Sth. Crescent M. WC1 . . . . .4J 83
Southcroft Av. BR4: W W'ck 2E 170
DA16: Well 3J 125
Southcroft Rd. BR6: Orp 3J 173
SW16 . . . . .6E 136
SW17 . . . . .6E 136
Sth. Cross Rd. IG6: Ilf 5G 53
Sth. Croxted Rd. SE21 . . . . .3D 138
SOUTH CROYDON 5D 168
South Croydon Sports Club 5E 168
Southdean Gdns. SW19 . . . . .2H 135
South Dene NW7 . . . . .3E 28
Southdene Ct. N11 . . . . .3A 32
Southdown Av. W7 . . . . .3A 96
Southdown Cres. HA2: Harr 1G 59
IG2: Ilf 5J 53
Sth. Down Dr. SW20 . . . . .7F 135
Southdown Rd. SM5: Cars 7E 166
SW20 . . . . .1F 153

South Dr. BR6: Orp 5J 173
HA4: Ruis 1G 57
Sth. Ealing Rd. W5 . . . . .2D 96
Sth. Eastern Av. N9 . . . . .3A 34
Sth. Eaton Pl. SW1 . . . . .3H 17 (4E 100)
Sth. Eden Pk. Rd. BR3: Beck 6D 158
Sth. Edwardes Sq. W8 . . . . .3H 99
SOUTHEND .4F 141
South End CR0: C'don 4C 168
CR2: S Croy 4C 168
W8 . . . . .3K 99
Southend Cl. SE9 . . . . .6C 124
Southend Cres. SE9 . . . . .6F 125
Southend Grn. NW3 . . . . .4C 64
Southend La. SE6 . . . . .4B 140
SE26 . . . . .4B 140
Southend Rd. NW3 . . . . .4C 64
BR3: Beck 1C 158
E4 . . . . .5F 35
E6 . . . . .7D 70
E17 .1D 50
E18 .1J 51
IG8: Wfd G 2A 52
South End Row W8 . . . . .3K 99
Southern Av. SE25 . . . . .3F 157
TW14: Felt 1J 129
Southern Cotts. TW19: Stanw M 7B 174
Southerngate Way SE14 . . . . .7A 104
Southern Gro. E3 . . . . .3B 86
Southern Perimeter Rd.
TW6: H'row A, Stanw 5A 110
TW6: H'row A, Stanw 7C 174
(not continuous)
Southern Pl. HA1: Harr 4K 59
Southern Rd. E13 . . . . .2K 87
N2 . . . . .4D 46
Southern Row W10 . . . . .4G 81
Southern St. N1 . . . . .2K 83
Southern Ter. W12 . . . . .1E 98
Southern Way RM7: Rom 6G 55
SE10 . . . . .4H 105
Southernwood Retail Pk. SE1 . . . . . .5F 103
Southerton Rd. W6 . . . . .4E 98
South Esk Rd. E7 . . . . .6A 70
Southey Ho. SE17 . . . . .5C 102
(off Browning St.)
Southey M. E16 . . . . .1J 105
Southey Rd. N15 . . . . .5E 48
SW9 .1A 120
SW19 . . . . .7J 135
Southey St. SE20 . . . . .7K 139
Southfield EN5: Barn 6A 20
Southfield Cl. UB8: Hil 4C 74
Southfield Cotts. TW7: Isle 2K 95
Southfield Ct. E11 . . . . .3H 69
Southfield Gdns. TW1: Twick 4K 131
Southfield Pk. HA2: Harr 4F 41
Southfield Rd. BR7: Chst 3K 161
EN3: Pond E 6C 24
N17 .2E 48
W4 . . . . .2K 97
SOUTHFIELDS 1H 135
Southfields KT8: E Mos 6J 149
NW4 .3D 44
Southfields Av. TW15: Ashf 6D 128
Southfields Ct. SM1: Sutt 2J 165
SW18 . . . . .6J 117
Southfields Pas. SW18 . . . . .6J 117
Southfields Rd. SW18 . . . . .6J 117
Southfleet NW5 . . . . .6E 64
Southfleet Rd. BR6: Orp 3J 173
Sth. Gdns. HA9: Wemb 2G 61
SW19 . . . . .7B 136
SOUTHGATE 1C 32
Southgate Av. TW13: Felt 4F 129
Southgate Cir. N14 . . . . .1C 32
Southgate Ct. N1 . . . . .7D 66
(off Downham Rd.)
Southgate Gro. N1 . . . . .7D 66
Southgate Hockey Cen. 3A 22

Southgate Leisure Cen. 7C 22
Southgate Rd. N1 . . . . .1D 84
Sth. Gipsy Rd. DA16: Well 3D 126
Sth. Glade, The DA5: Bexl 1F 145
South Grn. NW9 . . . . .1A 44
           (off Parklea Cl.)
South Gro. E17 . . . . .5B 50
  N6 . . . . .1E 64
  N15 . . . . .5D 48
South Gro. Ho. N6 . . . . .1E 64
SOUTH HACKNEY 1K 85
SOUTH HAMPSTEAD 7A 64
SOUTH HARROW 3G 59
Sth. Harrow Ind. Est. HA2: Harr . . .2G 59
South Herts Golf Course 1D 30
South Hill BR7: Chst 6D 142
  HA6: Nwood 1G 39
South Hill Av. HA1: Harr 3G 59
  HA2: Harr 3G 59
South Hill Gro. HA1: Harr 4J 59
South Hill Pk. NW3 . . . . .4C 64
South Hill Pk. Gdns. NW3 . . . . .3C 64
South Hill Rd. BR2: Brom 3G 159
Southholme Cl. SE19 . . . . .1E 156
SOUTH HORNCHURCH 2K 91
Southill Ct. BR2: Brom 5H 159
Southill La. HA5: Eastc 4K 39
Southill Rd. BR7: Chst 7C 142
Southill St. E14 . . . . .6D 86
Sth. Island Pl. SW9 . . . . .7K 101
SOUTH KENSINGTON 4B 100
Sth. Kensington Sta. Arc. SW7 . . . .3B 16
          (off Pelham St.)
SOUTH LAMBETH 7J 101
Sth. Lambeth Pl. SW8 . . . . . .7F 19 (6J 101)
Sth. Lambeth Rd. SW8 . . . . . .7F 19 (6J 101)
Southland Rd. SE18 . . . . .7K 107
Southlands Av. BR6: Orp 4H 173
Southlands Dr. SW19 . . . . .2F 135
Southlands Gro. BR1: Brom 3C 160
Southlands Rd. BR1: Brom 5A 160
  BR2: Brom 5A 160
Southland Way TW3: Houn 5H 113
South La. KT1: King T 3D 150
  KT3: N Mald 4K 151
South La. W. KT3: N Mald 4K 151
South Lodge E16 . . . . .1K 105
          (off Audley Dr.)
  NW8 . . . . .1A 4 (2B 82)
  SW7 . . . . .7D 10
          (off Knightsbridge)
  TW2: Whitt 6G 113
Sth. Lodge Av. CR4: Mitc 4J 155
Sth. Lodge Cres. EN2: Enf 4C 22
        (not continuous)
Sth. Lodge Dr. N14 . . . . .4C 22
Sth. London Crematorium
  CR4: Mitc 2G 155
South London Gallery 1E 120
South London Theatre 3B 138
       (off Norwood High St.)
South Mall N9 . . . . .3B 34
       (off Plevna Rd.)
  SW18 . . . . .6K 117
South Mead KT19: Ewe 7B 164
  NW9 . . . . .1B 44
Southmead Gdns. TW11: Tedd 6A 132
Southmead Rd. SW19 . . . . .1G 135
Southmere Boating Cen. 2C 108
Southmere Dr. SE2 . . . . .3B 108
Sth. Molton La. W1 . . . . . . .1J 11 (6F 83)
Sth. Molton Rd. E16 . . . . .6J 87
Sth. Molton St. W1 . . . . . . .1J 11 (6F 83)
Southmoor Way E9 . . . . .6B 68
South Mt. N20 . . . . .2F 31
       (off High Rd.)
SOUTH NORWOOD 4F 157
South Norwood Country Pk. 4J 157
South Norwood Country Pk. Vis. Cen.
  . . . . .4H 157
Sth. Norwood Hill SE25 . . . . .1E 156

South Norwood Leisure Cen. 5H 157
South Oak Rd. SW16 . . . . .4K 137
Southold Ri. SE9 . . . . .3D 142
Southolm St. SW11 . . . . .1F 119
Southover BR1: Brom 5J 141
  N12 . . . . .3D 30
South Pde. HA8: Edg 2G 43
  SM6: Wall 6G 167
  SW3 . . . . .5B 16 (5B 100)
  W4 . . . . .4K 97
South Pk. Ct. BR3: Beck 7C 140
South Pk. Cres. IG1: Ilf 3H 71
  SE6 . . . . .1G 141
South Pk. Dr. IG3: Ilf 2J 71
  IG11: Bark 5J 71
South Pk. Gro. KT3: N Mald 4J 151
South Pk. Hill Rd.
  CR2: S Croy 5D 168
South Pk. M. SW6 . . . . .3K 117
South Pk. Rd. IG1: Ilf 3H 71
  SW19 . . . . .6J 135
South Pk. Ter. IG1: Ilf 3J 71
South Pk. Vs. IG3: Ilf 4J 71
South Pk. Way HA4: Ruis 6A 58
South Pl. EC2 . . . . .5F 9 (5D 84)
  EN3: Pond E 5D 24
  KT5: Surb 7F 151
South Pl. M. EC2 . . . . .6F 9 (5D 84)
Southport Rd. SE18 . . . . .4H 107
Sth. Quay Plaza E14 . . . . .2D 104
Sth. Quay Sq. E14 . . . . .2D 104
Southridge Pl. SW20 . . . . .7F 135
South Ri. SM5: Cars 7C 166
  W2 . . . . .2D 10
South Ri. Way SE18 . . . . .5H 107
South Rd. HA1: Harr 1A 60
  HA8: Edg 1H 43
  N9 . . . . .1B 34
  RM6: Chad H 5C 54
        (Dunmow Cl.)
  RM6: Chad H 6E 54
          (Mill La.)
  SE23 . . . . .2K 139
  SW19 . . . . .6A 136
  TW2: Twick 3H 131
  TW5: Hest 6A 94
  TW12: Hamp 6C 130
  TW13: Hanw 5B 130
  UB1: S'hall 2D 94
  UB7: W Dray 3C 92
  W5 . . . . .4D 96
South Row SE3 . . . . .2H 123
SOUTH RUISLIP 4A 58
Southsea Rd. KT1: King T 4E 150
South Sea St. SE16 . . . . .3B 104
South Side N15 . . . . .4F 49
  W6 . . . . .3B 98
Southside Comn. SW19 . . . . .6E 134
Southside Halls SW7 . . . . .1B 16
       (off Prince's Gdns.)
Southside House 6E 134
Southside Ind. Est. SW8 . . . . .1G 119
       (off Havelock Ter.)
Southside Shop. Cen. SW18 . . . . . . .6K 117
Southspring DA15: Sidc 7H 125
South Sq. NW11 . . . . .6K 45
  WC1 . . . . .6J 7 (5A 84)
South Stand N5 . . . . .4B 66
South St. BR1: Brom 2J 159
  EN3: Pond E 5D 24
  RM1: Rom 5K 55
  RM13: Rain 2J 91
  TW7: Isle .3A 114
  W1 . . . . .4H 11 (1E 100)
Sth. Tenter St. E1 . . . . . . .2K 15 (7F 85)
South Ter. KT6: Surb 6E 150
  SW7 . . . . .3C 16 (4C 100)
SOUTH TOTTENHAM 5F 49
South Vale HA1: Harr 4J 59
  SE19 . . . . .6E 138

Southvale Rd. SE3 . . . . .2G 123
South Vw. BR1: Brom 2A 160
  SW19 . . . . .6F 135
Southview Av. NW10 . . . . .5B 62
South Vw. Cl. DA5: Bexl 6F 127
Southview Cl. SW17 . . . . .5E 136
South Vw. Ct. SE19 . . . . .7C 138
Southview Cres. IG2: Ilf 6F 53
South Vw. Dr. E18 . . . . .3K 51
Southview Gdns. SM6: Wall 7G 167
Southview Pde. RM13: Rain 3K 91
South Vw. Rd. HA5: Pinn 1K 39
  N8 . . . . .3H 47
South Vs. NW1 . . . . .6H 65
Southville SW8 . . . . .1H 119
Southville Cl. KT19: Ewe 7K 163
  TW14: Bedf, Felt 1E 129
       (not continuous)
Southville Cres. TW14: Felt 1E 129
Southville Rd. KT7: T Ditt 7A 150
  TW14: Felt 1E 129
South Wlk. BR4: W W'ck 3G 171
  UB3: Hayes 5F 75
SOUTHWARK 5A 14 (1B 102)
Southwark Bri. SE1 . . . . .3D 14 (7C 84)
Southwark Bri. Bus. Cen. SE1 . . . . . .5D 14
       (off Southwark Bri. Rd.)
Southwark Bri. Rd. SE1 . . . . .3B 102
Southwark Cathedral 4E 14 (1D 102)
Southwark Park 3H 103
Southwark Pk. Est. SE16 . . . . .4H 103
       (off Southwark Pk. Rd.)
Southwark Pk. Rd. SE16 . . . . .4F 103
Southwark Pk. Sports Cen. 4J 103
Southwark Pk. Sports Complex 4J 103
Southwark Pl. BR1: Brom 3D 160
Southwark Playhouse 3C 102
       (off Newington C'way)
Southwark St. SE1 . . . . .4A 14 (1B 102)
Southwater Cl. BR3: Beck 7D 140
  E14 . . . . .6B 86
South Way CR0: C'don 3A 170
  HA2: Harr .4E 40
  HA9: Wemb 5G 61
  N9 . . . . .2D 34
  N11 . . . . .6B 32
Southway
  BR2: Hayes 7J 159
  N20 . . . . .2G 30
  NW11 . . . . .6K 45
  SM6: Wall 4G 167
  SW20 . . . . .5E 152
Southwell Av. UB5: N'olt 6E 58
Southwell Gdns. SW7 . . . . .4A 100
Southwell Gro. Rd. E11 . . . . .2G 69
Southwell Ho. SE16 . . . . .4H 103
       (off Anchor St.)
Southwell Rd. CR0: C'don 6A 156
  HA3: Kenton 6D 42
  SE5 . . . . .3C 120
Sth. Western Rd. TW1: Twick 6A 114
South W. India Dock Entrance
  E14 . . . . .2E 104
South West Middlesex Crematorium
  TW13: Felt 1C 130
Southwest Rd. E11 . . . . .1F 69
Sth. Wharf Rd. W2 . . . . . . .7A 4 (6B 82)
Southwick M. W2 . . . . .7B 4 (6B 82)
Southwick Pl. W2 . . . . . . .1C 10 (6C 82)
Southwick St. W2 . . . . . . .7C 4 (6C 82)
Southwick Yd. W2 . . . . . . .1C 10 (6C 82)
SOUTH WIMBLEDON 6K 135
Southwold Dr. IG11: Bark 5A 72
Southwold Mans. W9 . . . . .3J 81
       (off Widley Rd.)
Southwold Rd. DA5: Bexl 6H 127
  E5 . . . . .2H 67
Southwood Av. KT2: King T 1J 151
  N6 . . . . .7F 47

Southwood Cl. BR1: Brom 4D 160
  KT4: Wor Pk 1F 165
Southwood Ct. EC1 . . . . .2A 8
       (off Wynyatt St.)
  NW11 . . . . .5K 45
Southwood Dr. KT5: Surb 7J 151
SOUTH WOODFORD 2J 51
South Woodford to Barking Relief Rd.
  E11 . . . . .5B 52
  E12 . . . . .4E 70
  IG1: Ilf 5B 52
  IG4: Ilf 5B 52
Southwood Gdns. IG2: Ilf 4F 53
  KT10: Hin W 3A 162
Southwood Hall N6 . . . . .6F 47
Southwood Hgts. N6 . . . . .7F 47
Southwood Ho. W11 . . . . .7G 81
       (off Avondale Pk. Rd.)
Southwood La. N6 . . . . .7E 46
Southwood Lawn Rd. N6 . . . . .7E 46
Southwood Mans. N6 . . . . .6E 46
       (off Southwood La.)
Southwood Pk. N6 . . . . .7E 46
Southwood Rd. SE9 . . . . .2F 143
  SE28 . . . . .1B 108
Southwood Smith Ho. E2 . . . . .3H 85
       (off Florida St.)
Southwood Smith St. N1 . . . . .1B 84
Sth. Worple Av. SW14 . . . . .3A 116
Sth. Worple Way SW14 . . . . .3K 115
Southwyck Ho. SW9 . . . . .4B 120
Soval Ct. HA6: Nwood 1F 39
Sovereign Bus. Cen. EN3: Brim 3G 25
Sovereign Cl. E1 . . . . .7H 85
  HA4: Ruis .1G 57
  W5 . . . . .5C 78
Sovereign Ct. CR2: S Croy 5C 168
       (off Warham Rd.)
  HA6: Nwood 1J 39
  HA7: Stan 7J 27
  KT8: W Mole 4D 148
  TW3: Houn 3E 112
  W8 . . . . .3K 99
       (off Wright's La.)
Sovereign Cres. SE16 . . . . .7A 86
Sovereign Gro. HA0: Wemb 3D 60
Sovereign Ho. E1 . . . . .4H 85
       (off Cambridge Heath Rd.)
  SE18 . . . . .3D 106
       (off Leda Rd.)
  TW15: Ashf 4A 128
Sovereign M. E2 . . . . .2F 85
  EN4: Cockf 3J 21
Sovereign Pk. NW10 . . . . .4H 79
Sovereign Pk. Trad. Est. NW10 . . . .4H 79
Sovereign Pl. HA1: Harr 5K 41
Sovereign Rd. IG11: Bark 3C 90
Sowerby Cl. SE9 . . . . .5D 124
Spa at Beckenham, The 1B 158
Space Arts Centre, The 4C 104
       (off Westferry Rd.)
Space Bus. Pk. NW10 . . . . .3H 79
Spaces Bus. Cen. SW8 . . . . .1G 119
Space Waye TW14: Felt 5J 111
Spa Cl. SE25 . . . . .1E 156
Spa Ct. SE16 . . . . .3G 103
  SW16 . . . . .4K 137
Spafield St. EC1 . . . . .3J 7 (4A 84)
Spa Grn. Est. EC1 . . . . .1K 7 (3B 84)
Spa Hill SE19 . . . . .1D 156
Spalding Cl. HA8: Edg 7F 29
Spalding Ho. SE4 . . . . .4A 122
Spalding Rd. NW4 . . . . .7E 44
  SW17 . . . . .5F 137
Spanby Rd. E3 . . . . .4C 86
Spaniards Cl. NW11 . . . . .1B 64
Spaniards End NW3 . . . . .1A 64
Spaniards Rd. NW3 . . . . .2A 64
Spanish Pl. W1 . . . . .7H 5 (6E 82)
Spanish Rd. SW18 . . . . .5A 118
Spanswick Lodge N15 . . . . .4B 48

Sparkbridge Rd. HA1: Harr 4J **41**
Sparkes Cl. BR2: Brom 4K **159**
Sparkes Cotts. SW1 . . . . 4G **17**
Sparkford Gdns. N11 . . . . 5K **31**
Sparkford Ho. SW11 . . . .*1B 118*
          (off Battersea Church Rd.)
Sparks Cl. RM8: Dag 2D **72**
  TW12: Hamp 6C **130**
  W3 . . . . 6K **79**
Spa Rd. SE16 . . . . 3F **103**
Sparrick's Row SE1 . . . . . . .6F **15** (2D **102**)
Sparrow Cl. TW12: Hamp 6C **130**
Sparrow Dr. BR5: Farnb 1G **173**
Sparrow Farm Dr. TW14: Felt 7A **112**
Sparrow Farm Rd. KT17: Ewe 4C **164**
Sparrow Grn. RM10: Dag 3H **73**
Sparrow Ho. E1 . . . .*4J **85***
          (off Cephas Av.)
Sparrow's Farm Leisure Cen. 7G **125**
Sparrows Herne WD23: Bush 1A **26**
Sparrows La. SE9 . . . . 7G **125**
Sparrows Way WD23: Bush 1B **26**
Sparsholt Cl. IG11: Bark *1J **89***
          (off St John's Rd.)
Sparsholt Rd. IG11: Bark 1J **89**
  N19 . . . . 1K **65**
Spartan Cl. SM6: Wall 7J **167**
Sparta St. SE10 . . . . 1E **122**
Speakers' Corner 2F **11** (7D **82**)
Speakers Ct. CRO: C'don 1D **168**
Speakman Ho. SE4 . . . .*3A **122***
          (off Arica Rd.)
Spearman Ho. E14 . . . .*6C **86***
          (off Upper Nth. St.)
Spearman St. SE18 . . . . 6E **106**
Spearpoint Gdns. IG2: Ilf 5K **53**
Spears Rd. N19 . . . . 1J **65**
Speart La. TW5: Hest 7C **94**
Spectacle Works E13 . . . . 3A **88**
Spectrum Bldg., The N1 . . . .*3D **84***
          (off East Rd.)
Spectrum Pl. SE17 . . . .*6D **102***
          (off Lytham St.)
Spectrum Twr. IG1: Ilf 2G **71**
          (off Hainault St.)
Spectrum Way SW18 . . . . 5J **117**
Spedan Cl. NW3 . . . . 3A **64**
Speechly Ho. E8 . . . . 5F **67**
Speedbird Way UB7: Harm 3C **174**
Speed Highwalk EC2 . . . .*5D **8***
          (off Silk St.)
Speed Ho. EC2 . . . . .5D **8**
Speedway Ind. Est.
  UB3: Hayes 2F **93**
Speedwell Ho. N12 . . . . .4E **30**
Speedwell St. SE8 . . . . 7C **104**
Speedy Pl. WC1 . . . . .2E **6**
Speer Rd. KT7: T Ditt 6K **149**
Speirs Cl. KT3: N Mald 6B **152**
Spekehill SE9 . . . . 3D **142**
Speke Rd. CR7: Thor H 2D **156**
Speke's Monument 4A **10** (1A **100**)
Speldhurst Cl. BR2: Brom 5H **159**
Speldhurst Rd. E9 . . . . .7K **67**
  W4 . . . . 3K **97**
Spellbrook Wlk. N1 . . . . 1C **84**
Spelman Ho. E1 . . . .*6K **9***
          (off Spelman St.)
Spelman St. E1 . . . . .5K **9** (5G **85**)
          (not continuous)
Spelthorne Gro. TW16: Sun 7H **129**
Spelthorne La. TW15: Ashf 1E **146**
Spence Cl. SE16 . . . . 2B **104**
Spencer Av. N13 . . . . 6E **32**
  UB4: Hayes 5J **75**
Spencer Cl.
  BR6: Orp 2J **173**
  IG8: Wfd G 5F **37**
  N3 . . . . 2J **45**
  NW10 . . . . 3F **79**

Spencer Ct. BR6: Farnb 5G **173**
  NW8 . . . . 2A **82**
          (off Marlborough Pl.)
  SW20 . . . . 1D **152**
Spencer Courtyard N3 . . . .*2H **45***
          (off Regents Pk. Rd.)
Spencer Dr. N2 . . . . 6A **46**
Spencer Gdns. SE9 . . . . 5D **124**
  SW14 . . . . 5J **115**
Spencer Hill SW19 . . . . 6G **135**
Spencer Hill Rd. SW19 . . . . .7G **135**
Spencer House 5A **12**
Spencer Mans. W14 . . . .*6G **99***
          (off Queen's Club Gdns.)
Spencer M. SW8 . . . .*1K **119***
          (off Lansdowne Way)
  W6 . . . . 6G **99**
SPENCER PARK 5B **118**
Spencer Pk. KT8: E Mos 5G **149**
  SW18 . . . . 5B **118**
Spencer Pl. CRO: C'don 7D **156**
  N1 . . . . 7B **66**
Spencer Ri. NW5 . . . . 4F **65**
Spencer Rd. BR1: Brom 7H **141**
  CR2: S Croy 5E **168**
  CR4: Mitc 3E **154**
          (Commonside E.)
  CR4: Mitc 7E **154**
          (Wood St.)
  E6 . . . . 1B **88**
  E17 . . . . 2E **50**
  HA0: Wemb 2C **60**
  HA3: W'stone 2J **41**
  IG3: Ilf 1K **71**
  KT8: E Mos 4G **149**
  N8 . . . . 5K **47**
          (not continuous)
  N11 . . . . 4A **32**
  N17 . . . . 1G **49**
  RM13: Rain 3K **91**
  SW18 . . . . 4B **118**
  SW20 . . . . 1D **152**
  TW2: Twick 3J **131**
  TW7: Isle 1G **113**
  W3 . . . . 1J **97**
  W4 . . . . 7J **97**
Spencer St. EC1 . . . . .2A **8** (3B **84**)
  UB2: S'hall 2B **94**
Spencer Wlk. NW3 . . . . 4B **64**
  SW15 . . . . 4F **117**
Spencer Way E1 . . . . 6H **85**
Spencer Yd. SE3 . . . .*2H **123***
          (off Tranquil Va.)
Spenlow Ho. SE16 . . . .*3G **103***
          (off Jamaica Rd.)
Spenser Gro. N16 . . . . 5E **66**
Spenser M. SE21 . . . . 2D **138**
Spenser Rd. SE24 . . . . 5B **120**
Spenser St. SW1 . . . . .1B **18** (3G **101**)
Spens Ho. WC1 . . . .*4G **7***
          (off Lamb's Conduit St.)
Spensley Wlk. N16 . . . . 3D **66**
Speranza St. SE18 . . . . 5K **107**
Sperling Rd. N17 . . . . 2E **48**
Spert St. E14 . . . . 7A **86**
Speyside N14 . . . . 6B **22**
Spey St. E14 . . . . 5E **86**
Spey Way RM1: Rom 1K **55**
Spezia Rd. NW10 . . . . 2C **80**
Sphere, The E16 . . . .*6H **87***
          (off Hallsville Rd.)
Spice Cl. E1 . . . . 7G **85**
Spice Quay Hgts. SE1 . . . . . . .5K **15** (1F **103**)
Spicer Cl. KT12: Walt T 6A **148**
Spicer Ct. EN1: Enf 3K **23**
Spicer St. SW3. CRO: C'don 4C **168**
Spigurnell Rd. N17 . . . . 1D **48**
Spikes Bri. Moorings
  UB1: S'hall 7C **76**
Spikes Bri. Rd. UB1: S'hall 6C **76**

Spindle Cl. SE18 . . . . 3C **106**
Spindlewood Gdns. CRO: C'don 4E **168**
Spindrift Av. E14 . . . . .4C **104**
Spinel Cl. SE18 .5K **107**
Spinnaker Cl. IG11: Bark 3B **90**
Spinnaker Ct. KT1: Hamp W 1D **150**
          (off Becketts Pl.)
Spinnaker Ho. E14 . . . .*2C **104***
          (off Byng St.)
  SW18 . . . .*4A **118***
          (off Juniper Dr.)
Spinnells Rd. HA2: Harr 1D **58**
Spinner Ho. E8 . . . .*1F **85***
          (off Lovelace St.)
Spinney, The DA14: Sidc 5E **144**
  EN5: New Bar 2E **20**
  HA0: Wemb 3A **60**
  HA7: Stan 4K **27**
  N21 . . . . 7F **23**
  SM3: Cheam 4E **164**
  SW13 . . . . 7D **98**
  SW16 . . . . 3G **137**
  TW16: Sun 1J **147**
Spinney Cl. BR3: Beck 4D **158**
  KT3: N Mald 5A **152**
  KT4: Wor Pk 2B **164**
  UB7: Yiew 7A **74**
Spinney Dr. TW14: Bedf 7E **110**
Spinney Gdns. RM9: Dag 5E **72**
  SE19 . . . . 5F **139**
Spinney Oak BR1: Brom 2C **160**
Spinneys, The BR1: Brom 2D **160**
Spire Ct. BR3: Beck *2D **158***
          (off Crescent Rd.)
Spire Ho. W2 . . . .*7A **82***
          (off Lancaster Ga.)
Spires Shop. Centre, The
  EN5: Barn 3B **20**
Spirit Quay E1 . . . . 1G **103**
SPITALFIELDS 5J **9** (5F **85**)
Spitalfields City Farm 4G **85**
Spital Sq. E1 . . . . .5H **9** (5E **84**)
Spital St. E1 . . . . .5K **9** (5G **85**)
Spital Yd. E1 . . . . .5H **9** (5E **84**)
Spitfire Bldg. N1 . . . .*2K **83***
          (off Collier St.)
Spitfire Bus. Pk. CRO: Wadd 6A **168**
Spitfire Estate, The TW5: Cran 5A **94**
Spitfire Rd. SM6: Wall 7J **167**
  TW6: H'row A 6E **110**
Spitfire Way TW5: Cran 5A **94**
Splendour Wlk. SE16 . . . . .5J **103**
          (off Verney Rd.)
Spode Ho. SE11 . . . . 2J **19**
Spode Wlk. NW6 . . . . 5K **63**
Spondon Rd. N15 . . . . 4G **49**
Spoonbill Way UB4: Yead 5B **76**
Spooner Ho. TW5: Hest 6E **94**
Spooners M. W3 . . . . 1K **97**
Spooner Wlk. SM6: Wall 5J **167**
Sporle Rd. Ct. SW11 . . . . 3B **118**
Sportsbank St. SE6 . . . . 7E **122**
SportsDock 7F **89**
Sportsman Pl. E2 . . . . 1G **85**
Spottiswood Ct. CRO: C'don 6C **156**
          (off Harry Cl.)
Spottons Gro. N17 . . . . 1C **48**
Spout Hill CRO: Addtn 5C **170**
Spout La. TW19: Stanw M 7B **174**
Spout La. Nth.
  TW19: Stanw M 7C **174**
Spratt Hall Rd. E11 . . . . .6J **51**
Spray La. TW2: Whitt 6J **113**
Spray St. SE18 .4F **107**
Spreighton Rd. KT8: W Mole 4F **149**
Spriggs Ho. N1 . . . .*7B **66***
          (off Canonbury Rd.)
Sprimont Pl. SW3 . . . . .5E **16** (5D **100**)
Springall St. SE15 . . . . .7H **103**
Springalls Wharf SE16 . . . .*2G **103***
          (off Bermondsey Wall W.)

Spring Apartments CRO: C'don 2D **168**
          (off Addiscombe Gro.)
Springbank N21 . . . . 6E **22**
Springbank Rd. SE13 . . . . 6F **123**
Springbank Wlk. NW1 . . . . 7H **65**
Springbourne Ct. BR3: Beck 1E **158**
Spring Bri. M. W5 . . . . 7D **78**
Spring Bri. Rd. W5 . . . . 7D **78**
Spring Cl.
  EN5: Barn 5A **20**
  RM8: Dag 1D **72**
Spring Cnr. TW13: Felt 3J **129**
Spring Cotts. KT6: Surb 5D **150**
Spring Ct. KT17: Ewe 7B **164**
  NW6 . . . . 6H **63**
  W7 . . . . 7H **77**
Spring Ct. Rd. EN2: Enf 1F **23**
Springcroft Av. N2 . . . . 4D **46**
Springdale M. N16 . . . . 4D **66**
Springdale Rd. N16 . . . . 4D **66**
Spring Dr. HA5: Eastc 6J **39**
Springett Ho. SW2 . . . .*5A **120***
          (off St Matthews Rd.)
Springfield E5 . . . . 1H **67**
  SE25 . . . . 3G **157**
  WD23: B Hea 1C **26**
Springfield Av. N10 . . . . 3G **47**
  SW20 . . . . 3H **153**
  TW12: Hamp 6F **131**
Springfield Cl. HA7: Stan 3F **27**
  N12 . . . . 5E **30**
Springfield Ct. IG1: Ilf 5F **71**
  KT1: King T .3E **150**
          (off Springfield Rd.)
  NW3 . . . . 7C **64**
          (off Eton Av.)
  SM6: Wall 5F **167**
Springfield Dr. IG2: Ilf 5G **53**
Springfield Gdns. BR1: Brom 4D **160**
  BR4: W W'ck 2D **170**
  E5 . . . . 1H **67**
  HA4: Ruis 1K **57**
  IG8: Wfd G 7F **37**
  NW9 . . . . 5K **43**
Springfield Gro.
  SE7 . . . . 6A **106**
  TW16: Sun 1H **147**
Springfield La. NW6 . . . . 1K **81**
Springfield Mt. NW9 . . . . 5A **44**
Springfield Pde. M. N13 . . . . 4F **33**
Springfield Pl.
  KT3: N Mald 4J **151**
Springfield Ri. SE26 . . . . 3H **139**
Springfield Rd.
  BR1: Brom .4D **160**
  CR7: Thor H 1C **156**
  DA7: Bex 4H **127**
  DA16: Well 3B **126**
  E4 . . . . 1B **36**
  E6 . . . . 7D **70**
  E15 . . . . 3G **87**
  E17 . . . . 6B **50**
  HA1: Harr 6J **41**
  KT1: King T .3E **150**
  N11 . . . . 5A **32**
  N15 . . . . 4G **49**
  NW8 . . . . 1A **82**
  SE26 . . . . 5H **139**
  SM6: Wall 5F **167**
  SW19 . . . . 5H **135**
  TW11: Tedd 1E **130**
  TW11: Tedd 5A **132**
  TW15: Ashf 5B **128**
  UB4: Yead 1A **94**
  W7 . . . . 1J **95**
Springfields EN5: New Bar 5E **20**
          (off Somerset Rd.)
Springfield Wlk. BR6: Orp 1H **173**
          (off Place Farm Av.)
  NW6 . . . . 1K **81**

Spring Gdns. IG8: Wfd G 7F **37**
  KT8: W Mole 5F **149**
  N5 .5C **66**
  RM7: Rom 5J **55**
  SM6: Wall 5G **167**
  SW1 . . . . .4D **12** (1H **101**)
    (not continuous)
Spring Gdns. Bus. Pk. RM7: Rom . . .6J **55**
SPRING GROVE 1J **113**
Spring Gro. CR4: Mitc 1E **154**
  SE19 . . . . .7F **139**
  TW12: Hamp 1F **149**
  W4 .5G **97**
  W7 . . . . .7J **77**
Spring Gro. Cres. TW3: Houn 1G **113**
Spring Gro. Rd. TW3: Houn, Isle . . .1F **113**
  TW7: Isle 1F **113**
  TW10: Rich 5F **115**
SpringHealth Leisure Club
  Richmond 4D **114**
   (within Pools on the Park)
Spring Hill E5 . . . . .7G **49**
  SE26 . . . . .4J **139**
Springhill Cl. SE5 . . . . .3D **120**
Spring Ho. E17 . . . . .2E **50**
    (off Fulbourne Rd.)
  WC1 .2J **7**
Springhurst Cl. CR0: C'don 4B **170**
Spring Lake HA7: Stan 4G **27**
Spring La. E5 . . . . .7H **49**
  N10 .3E **46**
  SE25 . . . . .6H **157**
Spring M. KT17: Ewe 7B **164**
  TW9: Rich 4E **114**
    (off Rosedale Rd.)
  W1 . . . . .5F **5** (5D **82**)
SPRING PARK 3C **170**
Spring Pk. Av. CR0: C'don 2K **169**
Spring Pk. Dr. N4 . . . . .1C **66**
Springpark Dr. BR3: Beck 3E **158**
Spring Pk. Rd. CR0: C'don 2K **169**
Spring Pas. SW15 . . . . .3F **117**
Spring Path NW3 . . . . .5B **64**
Spring Pl. IG11: Bark 2G **89**
  N3 . . . . .3J **45**
  NW5 . . . . .5F **65**
Springpond Rd. RM9: Dag 5E **72**
Spring Prom. UB7: W Dray 2B **92**
Spring Promenade UB7: W Dray . . .2B **92**
Springrice Rd. SE13 . . . . .6F **123**
Spring Rd. TW13: Felt 3H **129**
Springs Cl. TW19: Stanw 1A **128**
Spring Shaw Rd. BR5: St P 7A **144**
Spring St. W2 . . . . . . .1A **10** (6B **82**)
Spring Ter. TW9: Rich 5E **114**
Spring Tide Cl. SE15 . . . . .1H **121**
Spring Vale DA7: Bex 4H **127**
Springvale Av. TW8: Bford 5D **96**
Springvale Ter. W14 . . . . .3F **99**
Spring Villa Pk. HA8: Edg 7B **28**
Spring Villa Rd. HA8: Edg 7B **28**
Spring Wlk. E1 . . . . .5G **85**
Springwater WC1 . . . . .5C **7**
Springwater Cl. SE18 . . . . .1E **124**
Springway HA1: Harr 7H **41**
Springwell Av. NW10 . . . . .1B **80**
Springwell Cl. SW16 . . . . .4K **137**
Springwell Rd. SW16 . . . . .4A **138**
  TW4: Houn 2B **112**
  TW5: Hest 2B **112**
Springwood Cl. E3 . . . . .2C **86**
Springwood Ct. CR2: S Croy 4E **168**
    (off Birdhurst Rd.)
Springwood Cres. HA8: Edg 2C **28**
Sproggit Ind. Est.
  TW19: Stanw 6B **110**
Sprowston M. E7 . . . . .6J **69**
Sprowston Rd. E7 . . . . .5J **69**
Spruce Cl. W5 . . . . .3E **96**
Sprucedale Gdns. CR0: C'don 4K **169**
Spruce Hills Rd. E17 . . . . .2E **50**

Spruce Ho. SE16 . . . . .2K **103**
    (off Woodland Cres.)
Spruce Pk. BR2: Brom 4H **159**
Sprules Rd. SE4 . . . . .2A **122**
Spurfield KT8: W Mole 3F **149**
Spurgeon Av. SE19 . . . . .1D **156**
Spurgeon Rd. SE19 . . . . .1D **156**
Spurgeon St. SE1 . . . . .3D **102**
Spurling Rd. RM9: Dag 6F **73**
  SE22 . . . . .4F **121**
Spurrell Av. DA5: Bexl 4K **145**
Spur Rd. BR6: Orp 2K **173**
  HA8: Edg 4K **27**
  N15 .4D **48**
  SE1 . . . . .6J **13** (2A **102**)
  SW1 . . . . .7A **12** (2G **101**)
  TW7: Isle 7B **96**
  TW14: Felt 4K **111**
Spurstowe Rd. E8 . . . . .6H **67**
Spurstowe Ter. E8 . . . . .5G **67**
Spurway Pde. IG2: Ilf 5D **52**
    (off Woodford Av.)
Square, The E10 . . . . .3E **68**
  IG1: Ilf 7E **52**
  IG8: Wfd G 5D **36**
  SM5: Cars 5E **166**
  TW9: Rich 5D **114**
  UB7: Lford 4C **174**
  UB11: Stock P 1F **93**
  W6 .5E **98**
Square of Fame 4G **61**
    (off Arena Sq.)
Square Rigger Row SW11 . . . . .3A **118**
Squarey St. SW17 . . . . .3A **136**
Squire Gdns. NW8 . . . . .2A **4**
    (off Grove End Rd.)
Squires, The RM7: Rom 6J **55**
Squire's Bri. Rd. TW17: Shep 4B **146**
Squires Ct. SW4 . . . . .1J **119**
  SW19 . . . . .4J **135**
Squires La. N3 . . . . .2K **45**
Squires Mt. NW3 . . . . .3B **64**
Squire's Rd. TW17: Shep 4C **146**
Squires Wlk. TW15: Ashf 7F **129**
    (not continuous)
Squires Way DA2: Wilm 4K **145**
Squires Wood Dr. BR7: Chst 7C **142**
Squirrel Cl. TW4: Houn 3A **112**
Squirrel M. W13 . . . . .7K **77**
Squirrels, The HA5: Pinn 3D **40**
  SE13 . . . . .3F **123**
Squirrels Cl. BR6: Orp 1J **173**
  N12 .4F **31**
  UB10: Hil 7C **56**
Squirrels Drey BR2: Brom 2G **159**
    (off Park Hill Rd.)
Squirrels Grn. KT4: Wor Pk 2B **164**
Squirrel's La. IG9: Buck H 3G **37**
Squirrels Trad. Estate UB3: Hayes . . .3H **93**
Squirries St. E2 . . . . .3G **85**
  SS Robin 7C **86**
Stable Cl. KT2: King T 6F **133**
  UB5: N'olt 2E **76**
Stable Ct. EC1 . . . . .4B **8**
    (off Clerkenwell Rd.)
  SM6: Wall 3E **166**
Stable M. NW5 . . . . .6F **65**
  SE6 . . . . .1G **141**
  TW1: Twick 1K **131**
Stables, The IG9: Buck H 1F **37**
Stables End BR6: Farnb 3G **173**
Stables Gallery & Arts Cen. 3C **62**
Stables Lodge E8 . . . . .7H **67**
    (off Mare St.)
Stables Market, The NW1 . . . . .7F **65**
Stables M. SE27 . . . . .5C **138**
Stables St. N1 . . . . .1J **83**
Stables Way SE11 . . . . .5J **19** (5A **102**)
Stables Yd. SW18 . . . . .6J **117**

Stable Wlk. N2 . . . . .1B **46**
Stable Way W10 . . . . .6E **80**
Stable Yd. SW1 . . . . .6A **12**
  SW15 . . . . .3E **116**
Stableyard, The SW9 . . . . .2K **119**
Stableyard M. TW11: Tedd 6K **131**
Stable Yd. Rd. SW1 . . .6B **12** (2G **101**)
    (not continuous)
Staburn Cl. HA8: Edg 2J **43**
Stacey Av. N18 . . . . .4D **34**
Stacey Cl. E10 . . . . .5F **51**
Stacey St. N7 . . . . .3A **66**
  WC2 . . . . .1D **12** (6H **83**)
Stack Ho. SW1 . . . . .4H **17**
    (off Cundy St.)
Stackhouse St. SW3 . . . . .1E **16**
Stacy Path SE5 . . . . .7E **102**
Staddon Cl. BR3: Beck 4A **158**
Stadium, The
  Bromley FC 5K **159**
  Queen Elizabeth Olympic Pk.
  . . . . .7D **68**
Stadium Bus. Cen. HA9: Wemb 3H **61**
Stadium M. N5 . . . . .3A **66**
Stadium Retail Pk. HA9: Wemb 3G **61**
Stadium Rd. SE18 . . . . .7C **106**
Stadium Rd. E. NW4 . . . . .7D **44**
Stadium St. SW10 . . . . .7A **100**
Stadium Way HA9: Wemb 4F **61**
Staffa Rd. E10 . . . . .1A **68**
Stafford Cl. E17 . . . . .6B **50**
    (not continuous)
  N14 .5B **22**
  NW6 .3J **81**
  SM3: Cheam 6G **165**
Stafford Ct. DA5: Bexl 7F **127**
  SW8 .7J **101**
  W7 . . . . .6K **77**
    (off Copley Cl.)
  W8 . . . . .3J **99**
Stafford Cripps Ho. E2 . . . . .3J **85**
    (off Globe Rd.)
  SW6 . . . . .6H **99**
    (off Clem Attlee Cl.)
Stafford Cross Bus. Pk. CR0: Wadd . .5K **167**
Stafford Gdns. CR0: Wadd 5K **167**
Stafford Ho. SE1 . . . . .5F **103**
    (off Cooper's Rd.)
Stafford Mans. SW1 . . . . .1A **18**
    (off Stafford Pl.)
  SW4 . . . . .4J **119**
  SW11 . . . . .7D **100**
    (off Albert Bri. Rd.)
  W14 .3F **99**
    (off Haarlem Rd.)
Stafford Pl. SW1 . . . . . .1A **18** (3G **101**)
  TW10: Rich 7F **115**
Stafford Rd. CR0: Wadd 4A **168**
  DA14: Sidc 4J **143**
  E3 . . . . .2B **86**
  E7 . . . . .7A **70**
  HA3: Hrw W 7B **26**
  HA4: Ruis 4H **57**
  KT3: N Mald 3J **151**
  NW6 .3J **81**
  SM6: Wall 6G **167**
Staffordshire St. SE15 . . . . .1G **121**
Stafford St. W1 . . . . . . .4A **12** (1G **101**)
Stafford Ter. W8 . . . . .3J **99**
Staff St. EC1 . . . . .2F **9** (3D **84**)
Stag Cl. HA8: Edg 2H **43**
Stag Ct. KT2: King T 1G **151**
    (off Coombe Rd.)
STAG LANE 2B **134**
Stag La. HA8: Edg 2H **43**
  IG9: Buck H 2E **36**
  NW9 .2H **43**
  SW15 . . . . .3B **134**
Stags Way TW7: Isle 6K **95**
Stainbank Rd. CR4: Mitc 3F **155**
Stainby Cl. UB7: W Dray 3A **92**

Stainby Rd. N15 . . . . .4F **49**
Stainer St. SE1 . . . . . . .5F **15** (1D **102**)
Staines Av. SM3: Cheam 2F **165**
Staines By-Pass TW15: Ashf 5A **128**
Staines Rd. IG1: Ilf 5G **71**
  TW2: Twick 3E **130**
  TW3: Houn 7F **111**
  TW4: Houn 7F **111**
  TW14: Bedf, Felt 1C **128**
Staines Rd. E. TW16: Sun 7J **129**
Staines Rd. W. TW15: Ashf 6D **128**
  TW16: Sun 6D **128**
Staines Wlk. DA14: Sidc 6C **144**
Stainford Cl. TW15: Ashf 5F **129**
Stainforth Rd. E17 . . . . .4C **50**
  IG2: Ilf 7H **53**
Staining La. EC2 . . . . . . .7D **8** (6C **84**)
Stainmore Cl. BR7: Chst 1H **161**
Stainsbury St. E2 . . . . .2J **85**
Stainsby Rd. E14 . . . . .6C **86**
Stainton Rd. EN3: Enf H 1D **24**
  SE6 . . . . .6F **123**
Stalbridge Flats W1 . . . . .1H **11**
    (off Lumley St.)
Stalbridge Ho. NW1 . . . . .1A **6**
    (off Hampstead Rd.)
Stalbridge St. NW1 . . . . .5D **4** (5C **82**)
Stalham St. SE16 . . . . .3H **103**
Stalham Way IG6: Ilf 1F **53**
Stambourne Way BR4: W W'ck 2E **170**
  SE19 . . . . .7E **138**
Stambourne Woodland Wlk. SE19 . . .7E **138**
Stamford Bridge 7K **99**
Stamford Bri. Studios SW6 . . . . . . .7K **99**
    (off Wandon Rd.)
Stamford Brook Arches W6 . . . . . . .4C **98**
Stamford Brook Av. W6 . . . . .3B **98**
Stamford Brook Gdns. W6 . . . . .3B **98**
Stamford Brook Mans. W6 . . . . .4B **98**
    (off Goldhawk Rd.)
Stamford Brook Rd. W6 . . . . .3B **98**
Stamford Bldgs. SW8 . . . . .7J **101**
    (off Meadow Pl.)
Stamford Cl. HA3: Hrw W 7D **26**
  N15 .4G **49**
  NW3 .3A **64**
    (off Heath St.)
  UB1: S'hall 7E **76**
Stamford Cotts. SW10 . . . . .7K **99**
    (off Billing St.)
Stamford Ct. W6 . . . . .4C **98**
Stamford Dr. BR2: Brom 4H **159**
Stamford Gdns. RM9: Dag 7C **72**
Stamford Ga. SW6 . . . . .7K **99**
Stamford Gro. E. N16 . . . . .1G **67**
Stamford Gro. W. N16 . . . . .1G **67**
STAMFORD HILL 1F **67**
Stamford Hill N16 . . . . .2F **67**
Stamford Lodge N16 . . . . .7F **49**
Stamford Rd. E6 . . . . .1C **88**
  N1 . . . . .7E **66**
  N15 .5G **49**
  RM9: Dag 1B **90**
Stamford Sq. SW15 . . . . .5G **117**
Stamford St. SE1 . . . . . .5J **13** (1A **102**)
Stamp Pl. E2 . . . . .1J **9** (2F **85**)
Stanard Cl. N16 . . . . .7E **48**
Stanborough Cl. TW12: Hamp 6D **130**
Stanborough Ho. E3 . . . . .4D **86**
    (off Empson St.)
Stanborough Pas. E8 . . . . .6F **67**
Stanborough Rd. TW3: Houn 3H **113**
Stanbridge Pl. N21 . . . . .2G **33**
Stanbridge Rd. SW15 . . . . .3E **116**
Stanbrook Rd. SE2 . . . . .2B **108**
Stanbury Cl. NW3 . . . . .6D **64**
Stanbury Rd. SE15 . . . . .2H **121**
    (not continuous)
Stancroft NW9 . . . . .5A **44**
Standale Gro. HA4: Ruis 5E **38**
Standard Ind. Est. E16 . . . . .2D **106**

Standard Pl.—State Pde.

Standard Pl. EC2 2H **9**
Standard Rd. DA6: Bex 4E **126**
DA17: Belv 5G **109**
NW10 4J **79**
TW4: Houn 3C **112**
Standen Rd. SW18 7H **117**
Standfield Gdns. RM10: Dag 6G **73**
Standfield Rd. RM10: Dag 5G **73**
Standish Ho. *W6* *4C* ***98***
(off St Peter's Gro.)
Standish Rd. W6 4C **98**
Standlake Point SE23 3K **139**
Stane Cl. SW19 7K **135**
Stane Gro. SW9 2J **119**
Stanesgate Ho. *SE15* *7G* ***103***
(off Friary Est.)
Stane Way SE18 7B **106**
Stanfield Ho. *NW8* *3B* ***4***
(off Frampton St.)
UB5: N'olt *2B* ***76***
(off Academy Gdns.)
Stanfield Rd. E3 2A **86**
Stanford Cl. HA4: Ruis 6E **38**
IG8: Wfd G 5H **37**
RM7: Rom 6H **55**
TW12: Hamp 6D **130**
Stanford Ct. SW6 1K **117**
W8 *3K* ***99***
(off Cornwall Gdns.)
Stanford M. E8 5G **67**
Stanford Pl. SE17 4E **102**
Stanford Rd. N11 5J **31**
SW16 2H **155**
W8 3K **99**
Stanford St. SW1 4C **18** (4H **101**)
Stanford Way SW16 2H **155**
Stangate SE1 1H **19**
Stangate Gdns. HA7: Stan 4G **27**
Stangate Lodge N21 6E **22**
Stanger Rd. SE25 4G **157**
Stanhill Cotts. DA2: Wilm 7K **145**
Stanhope Av. BR2: Hayes 1H **171**
HA3: Hrw W 1H **41**
N3 3H **45**
Stanhope Cl. SE16 2K **103**
Stanhope Gdns. IG1: Ilf 1D **70**
N4 6B **48**
N6 6F **47**
NW7 5G **29**
RM8: Dag 3F **73**
SW7 3A **16** (4A **100**)
Stanhope Ga. W1 5H **11** (1E **100**)
Stanhope Gro. BR3: Beck 5B **158**
Stanhope Ho. *N11* *4A* ***32***
(off Coppies Gro.)
SE8 *7B* ***104***
(off Adolphus St.)
Stanhope M. E. SW7 3A **16** (4A **100**)
Stanhope M. Sth. SW7 4A **100**
Stanhope M. W. SW7 4A **100**
Stanhope Pde. NW1 1A **6** (3G **83**)
Stanhope Pk. Rd. UB6: G'frd 4G **77**
Stanhope Pl. W2 1E **10** (7D **82**)
Stanhope Rd. CR0: C'don 3E **168**
DA7: Bex 2E **126**
DA15: Sidc 4A **144**
E17 5D **50**
EN5: Barn 6A **20**
N6 6G **47**
N12 5F **31**
RM8: Dag 2F **73**
SM5: Cars 7E **166**
UB6: G'frd 5G **77**
Stanhope Row W1 5J **11** (1F **101**)
Stanhope St. NW1 1A **6** (2G **83**)
Stanhope Ter. TW2: Twick 7K **113**
W2 2B **10** (7B **82**)
Stanier Cl. W14 5H **99**
Stanier Ho. *SW6* *1A* ***118***
(off Station Ct.)
Stanlake M. W12 1E **98**
Stanlake Rd. W12 1E **98**
Stanlake Vs. W12 1E **98**
Stanley Av. BR3: Beck 2E **158**
HA0: Wemb 7E **60**
IG11: Bark 2K **89**
KT3: N Mald 5C **152**
RM8: Dag 1F **73**
UB6: G'frd 1G **77**
Stanley Bri. Studios *SW6* *7K* ***99***
(off King's Rd.)
Stanley Cl. HA0: Wemb 7E **60**
SE9 1G **143**
SW8 6K **101**
Stanley Cohen Ho. *EC1* *4C* ***8***
(off Golden La.)
Stanley Ct. SM2: Sutt 7K **165**
SM5: Cars 7E **166**
W5 5C **78**
Stanley Cres. W11 7H **81**
Stanleycroft Cl. TW7: Isle 1J **113**
Stanley Gdns.
CR4: Mitc 6E **136**
NW2 5E **62**
SM6: Wall 6G **167**
W3 2A **98**
W11 7H **81**
Stanley Gdns. M. *W11* *7H* ***81***
(off Kensington Pk. Rd.)
Stanley Gdns. Rd. TW11: Tedd 5J **131**
Stanley Gro. CR0: C'don 6A **156**
SW8 2E **118**
Stanley Holloway Ct. *E16* *6J* ***87***
(off Coolfin Rd.)
Stanley Ho. *E14* *6C* ***86***
(off Saracen St.)
SW10 *7A* ***100***
(off Coleridge Gdns.)
Stanley Mans. *SW10* *7A* ***16***
(off Park Wlk.)
Stanley M. *SW10* *7A* ***100***
(off Coleridge Gdns.)
Stanley Pk. Dr. HA0: Wemb 1F **79**
Stanley Pk. Rd. SM5: Cars 7C **166**
SM6: Wall 6F **167**
Stanley Picker Gallery *3E* ***150***
(off Springfield Rd.)
Stanley Rd. BR2: Brom 4K **159**
BR6: Orp 1K **173**
CR0: C'don 7A **156**
CR4: Mitc 7E **136**
DA14: Sidc 3A **144**
E4 1A **36**
E10 6D **50**
E12 5C **70**
E18 1H **51**
EN1: Enf 3K **23**
HA2: Harr 2G **59**
HA6: Nwood 1J **39**
HA9: Wemb 6F **61**
IG1: Ilf 2H **71**
N2 3B **46**
N9 1A **34**
N10 7A **32**
N11 6C **32**
N15 4B **48**
NW9 7C **44**
SM2: Sutt 6K **165**
SM4: Mord 4J **153**
SM5: Cars 7E **166**
SW14 4H **115**
SW19 6J **135**
TW2: Twick 3H **131**
TW3: Houn 4G **113**
TW11: Tedd 4J **131**
TW15: Ashf 5A **128**
UB1: S'hall 7C **76**
W3 3J **97**
Stanley Sq. SM5: Cars 7D **166**
Stanley St. SE8 7B **104**
Stanley Studios *SW10* *7A* ***16***
(off Park Wlk.)
Stanley Ter. DA6: Bex 4G **127**
N19 2J **65**
Stanliff Ho. E14 3C **104**
Stanmer St. SW11 1C **118**
STANMORE 5G **27**
Stanmore & Edgware Golf Cen. 3J **27**
Stanmore Common Local Nature Reserve 2E **26**
Stanmore Country Park (Local Nature Reserve) 3H **27**
Stanmore Gdns. SM1: Sutt 3A **166**
TW9: Rich 3F **115**
Stanmore Golf Course 7G **27**
Stanmore Hill HA7: Stan 3F **27**
Stanmore Lodge HA7: Stan 4G **27**
Stanmore Pl. NW1 1F **83**
Stanmore Rd. DA17: Belv 4J **109**
E11 1H **69**
N15 4B **48**
TW9: Rich 3F **115**
Stanmore St. N1 1K **83**
Stanmore Ter. BR3: Beck 2C **158**
Stannard Cotts. *E1* *4J* ***85***
(off Fox Cl.)
Stannard Ct. SE6 1D **140**
Stannard Ho. SW19 4A **136**
Stannard M. *E8* *6G* ***67***
(off Stannard Rd.)
Stannard Rd. E8 6G **67**
Stannary Pl. SE11 6K **19** (5A **102**)
Stannary St. SE11 7K **19** (6A **102**)
Stannet Way SM6: Wall 4G **167**
Stansborough Ho. *E3* *4D* ***86***
(off Empson St.)
Stansbury Sq. W10 3G **81**
Stansfeld Ho. *SE1* *4F* ***103***
(off Longfield Est.)
Stansfeld Rd. E6 5B **88**
E16 5B **88**
Stansfield Rd. SW9 3K **119**
TW4: Cran 2K **111**
Stansgate Rd. RM10: Dag 2G **73**
Stanstead *WC1* *2F* ***7***
(off Tavistock Pl.)
Stanstead Cl. BR2: Brom 5H **159**
Stanstead Gro. SE6 1B **140**
Stanstead Ho. *E3* *4E* ***86***
(off Devas St.)
Stanstead Mnr. SM1: Sutt 6J **165**
Stanstead Rd. E11 5K **51**
SE6 1A **140**
SE23 1K **139**
Stansted Cres. DA5: Bexl 1D **144**
Stansted Rd.
TW6: H'row A 6B **110**
Stanswood Gdns. SE5 7E **102**
Stanthorpe Cl. SW16 5J **137**
Stanthorpe Rd. SW16 5J **137**
Stanton Av. TW11: Tedd 6J **131**
Stanton Cl. KT4: Wor Pk 1F **165**
KT19: Ewe 5H **163**
Stanton Ct. *CR2: S Croy* *5E* ***168***
(off Birdhurst Ri.)
Stanton Ho. *SE10* *6E* ***104***
(off Thames St.)
SE16 *2B* ***104***
(off Rotherhithe St.)
Stanton Rd. CR0: C'don 7C **156**
SE26 4B **140**
SW13 2B **116**
SW20 1F **153**
Stanton Sq. SE26 4B **140**
Stanton Way SE26 4B **140**
Stanway Ct. N1 2E **84**
(not continuous)
Stanway Gdns. HA8: Edg 5D **28**
W3 1G **97**
Stanway St. N1 2E **84**
STANWELL 6A **110**
Stanwell Cl. TW19: Stanw 6A **110**
STANWELL MOOR 7B **174**
Stanwell Moor Rd.
TW19: Staines, Stanw M 7C **174**
UB7: Lford 7C **174**
Stanwell Rd. TW14: Bedf 7D **110**
TW15: Ashf 2A **128**
Stanwick Rd. W14 4H **99**
Stanworth Ct. TW5: Hest 7D **94**
Stanworth St. SE1 7J **15** (3F **103**)
Stanyhurst SE23 1A **140**
Stapenhill Rd. HA0: Wemb 3B **60**
Staple Cl. DA5: Bexl 3K **145**
Staplefield Cl. SW2 1J **137**
Stapleford *N17* *2E* ***48***
(off Willan Rd.)
Stapleford Av. IG2: Ilf 5J **53**
Stapleford Cl. E4 3K **35**
KT1: King T 2G **151**
SW19 7G **117**
Stapleford Rd. HA0: Wemb 7D **60**
Staplehurst Rd. SE13 5F **123**
SM5: Cars 7C **166**
Staple Inn WC1 6J **7**
Staple Inn Bldgs. WC1 6J **7** (5A **84**)
Staples Cl. SE16 1A **104**
STAPLES CORNER 1D **62**
Staples Cnr. Bus. Pk. NW2 1D **62**
Staples Cnr. Retail Pk.
NW2 1D **62**
Staples Ho. *E6* *6E* ***88***
(off Savage Gdns.)
Staple St. SE1 7F **15** (2D **102**)
Stapleton Gdns. CR0: Wadd 5A **168**
Stapleton Hall Rd. N4 1K **65**
Stapleton Ho. *E2* *3H* ***85***
(off Ellsworth St.)
Stapleton Rd. BR6: Orp 4K **173**
DA7: Bex 7F **109**
SW17 3E **136**
Stapleton Vs. *N16* *4E* ***66***
(off Wordsworth Rd.)
Stapley Rd. DA17: Belv 5G **109**
Stapylton Rd. EN5: Barn 3B **20**
Star All. EC3 2H **15**
Star & Garter Hill TW10: Rich 1E **132**
Starboard Way E14 3C **104**
Starbuck Cl. SE9 7E **124**
Star Bus. Cen. RM13: Rain 5K **91**
Starch Ho. La. IG6: Ilf 2H **53**
Star Cl. EN3: Pond E 6D **24**
Starcross St. NW1 2B **6** (3G **83**)
Starfield Rd. W12 2C **98**
Star Hill DA1: Cray 5K **127**
Star La. E16 4G **87**
Starley Cl. E17 1F **51**
Starlight Way TW6: H'row A 5E **110**
Starling Cl. CR0: C'don 6A **158**
HA5: Pinn 3A **40**
IG9: Buck H 1D **36**
Starling Ho. *NW8* *2C* ***82***
(off Charlbert St.)
Starling Wlk. TW12: Hamp 5C **130**
Starmans Cl. RM9: Dag 1E **90**
Star Path *UB5: N'olt* *2E* ***76***
(off Brabazon Rd.)
Star Pl. E1 3K **15** (7F **85**)
Star Rd. TW7: Isle 2H **113**
UB10: Hil 4E **74**
W14 6H **99**
Star St. W2 7B **4** (6C **82**)
Starts Cl. BR6: Farnb 3E **172**
Starts Hill Av. BR6: Farnb 4F **173**
Starts Hill Rd. BR6: Farnb 3E **172**
Starveall Cl. UB7: W Dray 3B **92**
Star Wharf *NW1* *1G* ***83***
(off St Pancras Way)
Star Yd. WC2 7J **7** (6A **84**)
State Farm Av. BR6: Farnb 4F **173**
Staten Bldg. *E3* *2C* ***86***
(off Fairfield Rd.)
Staten Gdns. TW1: Twick 1K **131**
State Pde. IG6: Ilf 2G **53**

Statham Gro. N16 . . . .4D 66
  N18 . . . .5K 33
Statham Ho. SW8 . . . .1G 119
  (off Wadhurst Rd.)
Station App.
  BR1: Brom 3J 159
  (off High St.)
  BR2: Hayes 1J 171
  BR3: Beck 1C 158
  BR4: W W'ck 7E 158
  BR6: Orp 2K 173
  BR7: Chst 6C 142
  (Bennetts Copse)
  BR7: Chst 1E 160
  (Vale Rd.)
  CR0: C'don 2D 168
  (off Dingwall Rd.)
  CR2: Sande 7D 168
  DA5: Bexl 1G 145
  DA7: Bex 2J 127
  (Barnehurst Rd.)
  DA7: Bex 2E 126
  (Percy Rd.)
  DA16: Well 2A 126
  E4 . . . .6A 36
  E7 . . . .4K 69
  E11 . . . .5J 51
  E17 . . . .5C 50
  E18 . . . .2K 51
  EN5: New Bar 4F 21
  HA0: Wemb 6B 60
  HA1: Harr 7J 41
  HA4: Ruis 5K 57
  (Mahlon Av.)
  HA4: Ruis 1G 57
  (Pembroke Rd.)
  HA5: Pinn 3C 40
  IG8: Wfd G 6E 36
  IG9: Buck H 4G 37
  KT1: King T 1G 151
  KT4: Wor Pk 1C 164
  KT17: Ewe 7B 164
  KT19: Ewe 5C 164
  N11 . . . .5A 32
  N12 . . . .4E 30
  N16 . . . .2F 67
  (off Stamford Hill)
  NW1 . . . .4F 5 (4D 82)
  NW10 . . . .3B 80
  NW11 . . . .7F 45
  SE1 . . . .4F 15 (1D 102)
  SE3 . . . .3K 123
  SE9 . . . .2G 143
  (Bercta Rd.)
  SE9 . . . .1D 142
  (Crossmead)
  SE12 . . . .6J 123
  (off Burnt Ash Hill)
  SE26 . . . .4J 139
  SM2: Cheam 7G 165
  SM5: Cars 4D 166
  SW6 . . . .3G 117
  SW14 . . . .3J 115
  SW16 . . . .6H 137
  (Estreham Rd.)
  SW16 . . . .5H 137
  (Gleneagle Rd.)
  SW20 . . . .2D 152
  TW8: Bford 6C 96
  (off Sidney Gdns.)
  TW9: Kew 1G 115
  TW12: Hamp 1E 148
  TW15: Ashf 4B 128
  TW16: Sun 1J 147
  TW17: Shep 5E 146
  UB3: Hayes 3H 93
  UB6: G'frd 7G 59
  UB7: Yiew 1A 92
  W7 . . . .1J 95
Station App. Nth.
  DA15: Sidc 2A 144

Station App. Rd. SE1 . . . .7H 13 (2A 102)
  W4 . . . .7J 97
Station App. Sth. DA15: Sidc 2A 144
  (off Jubilee Way)
Station Arc. W1 . . . .4K 5
  (off Gt. Portland St.)
Station Av.
  KT3: N Mald 3A 152
  KT19: Ewe 7A 164
  SW9 . . . .3B 120
  TW9: Kew 1G 115
Station Bldgs. KT1: King T 2E 150
  (off Fife Rd.)
Station Chambers E6 . . . .7C 70
  (off High St. Nth.)
Station Cl. N3 . . . .1J 45
  N12 . . . .4E 30
  TW12: Hamp 1F 149
Station Cotts. BR6: Orp 2K 173
Station Ct. N15 . . . .5F 49
  SW6 . . . .1A 118
Station Cres.
  HA0: Wemb 6B 60
  N15 . . . .4D 48
  SE3 . . . .5J 105
  TW15: Ashf 4A 128
Stationer's Hall Ct. EC4 . . . .1B 14 (6B 84)
Station Est.
  BR3: Beck 3K 157
  E18 . . . .2K 51
Station Est. Rd.
  TW14: Felt 1K 129
Station Garage M. SW16 . . . .6H 137
Station Gdns. W4 . . . .7J 97
Station Gro.
  HA0: Wemb 6E 60
Station Hill BR2: Hayes 2J 171
Station Ho. SE8 . . . .7C 104
  (off Carriage Way)
Station Ho. M. N9 . . . .4B 34
Station Pde.
  BR1: Brom 3J 159
  (off Tweedy Rd.)
  DA7: Bex 2E 126
  (off Pickford La.)
  DA15: Sidc 2A 144
  E6 . . . .7C 70
  E11 . . . .5J 51
  E13 . . . .1A 88
  (off Green St.)
  EN4: Cockf 4K 21
  HA2: Harr 4F 59
  HA3: Kenton 2A 42
  HA4: Ruis 2F 57
  HA8: Edg 7K 27
  IG9: Buck H 4G 37
  IG11: Bark 7G 71
  N14 . . . .1C 32
  NW2 . . . .6E 62
  RM9: Dag 6G 73
  SM2: Sutt 6A 166
  (off High St.)
  SW12 . . . .1E 136
  TW9: Kew 1G 115
  TW14: Felt 1K 129
  TW15: Ashf 4B 128
  UB5: N'olt 4F 59
  (Accock Gro.)
  UB5: N'olt 7E 58
  (Court Farm Rd.)
  W3 . . . .6G 79
  W4 . . . .7J 97
  W5 . . . .1F 97
Station Pas. E18 . . . .2K 51
  E20 . . . .6E 68
  SE15 . . . .1J 121
Station Path E8 . . . .6H 67
  (off Graham Rd.)
  SW6 . . . .3H 117
Station Pl. N4 . . . .2A 66
Station Ri. SE27 . . . .2B 138

Station Rd. BR1: Brom 1J 159
  BR2: Brom 2G 159
  BR4: W W'ck 1E 170
  BR6: Orp 2K 173
  CR0: C'don 1C 168
  DA7: Bex 3E 126
  DA15: Sidc 2A 144
  DA17: Belv 3G 109
  E4 . . . .1A 36
  E7 . . . .4J 69
  E12 . . . .4C 70
  E17 . . . .6A 50
  EN5: New Bar 5E 20
  HA1: Harr 4K 41
  HA2: Harr 5F 41
  HA8: Edg 6B 28
  IG1: Ilf 3F 71
  IG6: Ilf 3H 53
  KT1: Hamp W 1C 150
  KT2: King T 1G 151
  KT3: N Mald 5D 152
  KT7: T Ditt 7K 149
  KT9: Chess 5E 162
  N3 . . . .1J 45
  N11 . . . .5A 32
  N17 . . . .3G 49
  N19 . . . .3G 65
  N21 . . . .1G 33
  N22 . . . .2J 47
  (not continuous)
  NW4 . . . .6C 44
  NW7 . . . .6F 29
  NW10 . . . .2B 80
  RM6: Chad H, Dag 7D 54
  SE13 . . . .3E 122
  SE20 . . . .6J 139
  SE25 . . . .4F 157
  SM5: Cars 4D 166
  SW13 . . . .2B 116
  SW19 . . . .1A 154
  TW1: Twick 1K 131
  TW3: Houn 4F 113
  TW11: Tedd 6A 132
  TW12: Hamp 1E 148
  TW15: Ashf 4B 128
  TW16: Sun 7J 129
  TW17: Shep 5E 146
  UB3: Harl, Hayes 4G 93
  (not continuous)
  UB7: W Dray 2A 92
  W5 . . . .6F 79
  W7 . . . .1J 95
Station Rd. Nth. DA17: Belv 3H 109
Station Sq. BR5: Pet W 5G 161
Station St. E15 . . . .7F 69
  E16 . . . .1F 107
Station Ter. NW10 . . . .2F 81
  SE5 . . . .1C 120
Station Ter. M. SE3 . . . .5J 105
Station Vw. UB6: G'frd 1H 77
Station Wlk. IG1: Ilf 2F 71
  (within The Exchange)
Station Way IG9: Buck H 4F 37
  SE15 . . . .2G 121
  SM3: Cheam 6G 165
Station Yd. HA4: Ruis 2E 56
  TW1: Twick 7A 114
Staton Ct. E10 . . . .7D 50
  (off Kings Cl.)
Staunton Ho. SE17 . . . .4E 102
  (off Wansey St.)
Staunton Rd. KT2: King T 6E 132
Staunton St. SE8 . . . .6B 104
Stave Hill Ecological Pk. 2A 104
Staveley NW1 . . . .1A 6
  (off Varndell St.)
Staveley Cl. E9 . . . .5J 67
  N7 . . . .4J 65
  SE15 . . . .1H 121
Staveley Cl. E11 . . . .5J 51
Staveley Gdns. W4 . . . .1K 115

Staveley Rd. TW15: Ashf 6F 129
  W4 . . . .6J 97
Stavers Ho. E3 . . . .2B 86
  (off Tredegar Rd.)
Staverton Rd. NW2 . . . .7E 62
Stave Yd. Rd. SE16 . . . .1A 104
Stavordale Lodge W14 . . . .3H 99
  (off Melbury Rd.)
Stavordale Rd. N5 . . . .4B 66
  SM5: Cars 7A 154
Stayner's Rd. E1 . . . .4K 85
Stayton Rd. SM1: Sutt 3J 165
Stead Cl. BR7: Chst 5E 142
Steadfast Rd. KT1: King T 1D 150
Steadman Ct. EC1 . . . .3D 8
  (off Old St.)
Steadman Ho. RM10: Dag 3G 73
  (off Uvedale Rd.)
Stead St. SE17 . . . .4D 102
Steam Farm La. TW14: Felt 4H 111
Stean St. E8 . . . .1F 85
Stebbing Ho. W11 . . . .1F 99
  (off Queensdale Cres.)
Stebbing Way IG11: Bark 2A 90
Stebondale St. E14 . . . .4E 104
Stedham Pl. WC1 . . . .7E 6
Stedman Cl. DA5: Bexl 3K 145
  UB10: Ick 3C 56
Steedman St. SE17 . . . .4C 102
Steeds Rd. N10 . . . .1D 46
Steele Ct. TW11: Tedd 7C 132
Steele Ho. E15 . . . .2G 87
  (off Eve Rd.)
Steele Rd. E11 . . . .4G 69
  N17 . . . .3E 48
  NW10 . . . .2J 79
  TW7: Isle 4A 114
  W4 . . . .3J 97
Steele's M. Nth. NW3 . . . .6D 64
Steele's M. Sth. NW3 . . . .6D 64
Steele's Rd. NW3 . . . .6D 64
Steele's Studios NW3 . . . .6D 64
Steel's La. E1 . . . .6J 85
Steelyard Pas. EC4 . . . .3E 14
Steen Way SE22 . . . .5E 120
Steep Cl. BR6: Chels 6K 173
Steep Hill CR0: C'don 4K 168
  SW16 . . . .3H 137
Steeple Cl. SW6 . . . .2G 117
  SW19 . . . .5G 135
Steeple Cl. E1 . . . .4H 85
Steeplestone Cl. N18 . . . .5H 33
Steeple Wlk. N1 . . . .1C 84
  (off New Nth. Rd.)
Steerforth St. SW18 . . . .2A 136
Steering Cl. N9 . . . .1D 34
Steers Mead CR4: Mitc 1D 154
Steers Way SE16 . . . .2A 104
Stelfox Ho. WC1 . . . .1H 7
  (off Penton Ri.)
Stella Cl. UB8: Hil 5D 74
Stella Ho. N17 . . . .6A 34
Stella Rd. SW17 . . . .6D 136
Stelling Rd. DA8: Erith 7K 109
Stellman Cl. E5 . . . .3G 67
Stembridge Rd. SE20 . . . .2H 157
Stephan Cl. E8 . . . .1G 85
Stephen Cl. BR6: Orp 3J 173
Stephendale Rd. SW6 . . . .3K 117
Stephen Fox Ho. W4 . . . .5A 98
  (off Chiswick La.)
Stephen M. W1 . . . .6C 6 (5H 83)
Stephen Pl. SW4 . . . .3G 119
Stephen Rd. DA7: Bex 3J 127
Stephens Ct. E16 . . . .4H 87
  SE4 . . . .3A 122
Stephens Lodge N12 . . . .3F 31
  (off Woodside La.)
Stephenson Cl. DA16: Well 2A 126
  E3 . . . .3D 86

Stephenson Ct. SM2: Cheam 7G 165
   (off Station App.)
Stephenson Ho. SE1 . . . . 3C 102
Stephenson Rd. E17 . . . . 5A 50
   TW2: Whitt 7E 112
   W7 . . . . 6K 77
Stephenson St. E16 . . . . 4G 87
   NW10 . . . . 3A 80
Stephenson Way NW1 . . . . . 3B 6 (4G 83)
Stephen's Rd. E15 . . . . 1E 87
Stephen St. W1 . . . . 6C 6 (5H 83)
STEPNEY 5K 85
Stepney C'way. E1 . . . . 6K 85
Stepney City Apartments E1 . . . . .5J 85
Stepney Cl. CR4: Mitc 1E 154
Stepney Grn. E1 . . . . .5J 85
Stepney Grn. Ct. E1 . . . . .5K 85
   (off Stepney Grn.)
Stepney High St. E1 . . . . .5K 85
Stepney Way E1 . . . . .5H 85
Stepping City Farm 5K 85
Sterling Av. HA8: Edg 4A 28
Sterling Cl. NW10 . . . . 7C 62
Sterling Gdns. SE14 . . . . .6A 104
Sterling Ind. Est. RM10: Dag 4H 73
Sterling Pl. W5 . . . . 4E 96
Sterling Rd. EN2: Enf 1J 23
Sterling St. SW7 . . . . .1D 16 (3C 100)
   N18 . . . . .4J 33
Sterling Way DA7: Bex 4H 127
Sternberg Centre, The 3J 45
Stern Cl. IG11: Bark 2C 90
Sterndale Rd. W14 . . . . .3F 99
Sterne St. W12 . . . . .2F 99
Sternhall La. SE15 . . . . .3G 121
Sternhold Av. SW2 . . . . .2H 137
Sterry Cres. RM10: Dag 5G 73
Sterry Dr. KT7: T Ditt 6J 149
   KT19: Ewe 4A 164
Sterry Gdns. RM10: Dag 6G 73
Sterry Rd. IG11: Bark 1K 89
   RM10: Dag 4G 73
Sterry St. SE1 . . . . 7E 14 (2D 102)
Steucers La. SE23 . . . . 1A 140
Stevannie Ct. DA17: Belv 5F 109
Steve Biko Ct. W10 . . . . 4F 81
   (off St John's Ter.)
Steve Biko La. SE6 . . . . 4C 140
Steve Biko Lodge E13 . . . . 2J 87
   (off London Rd.)
Steve Biko Rd. N7 . . . . 3A 66
Steve Biko Way TW3: Houn 3E 112
Stevedale Rd. DA16: Well 2C 126
Stevedore St. E1 . . . . 1H 103
Stevenage Rd. E6 . . . . 6E 70
   SW6 . . . . .7F 99
Stevens Av. E9 . . . . 6J 67
Stevens Cl. BR3: Beck 6C 140
   DA5: Bexl .4K 145
   HA5: Eastc 5A 40
   TW12: Hamp 6D 130
Stevens Grn. WD23: B Hea 1B 26
Stevens La. KT10: Clay 7A 162
Stevenson Cl. EN5: New Bar 7G 21
Stevenson Ct. CR4: Mitc 3C 154
   SE6 . . . . 2H 141
Stevenson Cres. SE16 . . . . 5G 103
Stevenson Ho. NW8 . . . . 1A 82
   (off Boundary Rd.)
Stevens Rd. RM8: Dag 2C 72
Stevens St. SE1 . . . . .7H 15 (3E 102)
Steventon Rd. W12 . . . . .7B 80
Steward Ho. E3 . . . . 3C 86
   (off Trevithick Way)
Stewards Holte Wlk. N11 . . . . 4A 32
Steward St. E1 . . . . 6H 9 (5E 84)
Stewart Av. TW17: Shep 4C 146
Stewart Cl. BR7: Chst 5F 143
   NW9 . . . . 6J 43
   TW12: Hamp 6C 130
Stewart Ho. KT1: King T 3F 151

Stewart Quay UB3: Hayes 2G 93
Stewart Rainbird Ho. E12 . . . . 5E 70
   (off Parkhurst Rd.)
Stewart Rd. E15 . . . . 4F 69
Stewartsby Cl. N18 . . . . .5H 33
Stewart's Gro. SW3 . . . . .5B 16 (5B 100)
Stewart's Pl. SW2 . . . . 6K 119
Stewart's Rd. SW8 . . . . 7G 101
Stewart St. E14 . . . . 2E 104
Stew La. EC4 . . . . 2C 14 (7C 84)
Steyne Horn La. W3 . . . . 1J 97
Steyne Ho. W3 . . . . 1J 97
   (off Narrow St.)
Steyne Rd. W3 . . . . 1H 97
Steyning Gro. SE9 . . . . .4D 142
Steynings Way N12 . . . . .5D 30
Steyning Way TW4: Houn 4A 112
Steynton Av. DA5: Bexl 2D 144
Stibbington Ho. NW1 . . . . 2G 83
   (off Cranleigh St.)
Stickland Rd. DA17: Belv 4G 109
Stickleton Cl. UB6: G'frd 3F 77
Stifford Ho. E1 . . . . 5J 85
   (off Stepney Way)
Stilecroft Gdns. HA0: Wemb 3B 60
Stile Hall Gdns. W4 . . . . 5G 97
Stile Hall Mans. W4 . . . . 5G 97
   (off Wellesley Rd.)
Stile Hall Pde. W4 . . . . 5G 97
Stileman Ho. E3 . . . . 5B 86
   (off Ackroyd Dr.)
Stile Path TW16: Sun 3J 147
Stiles Cl. BR2: Brom 6D 160
   DA8: Erith 5H 109
Stillingfleet Rd. SW13 . . . . .6C 98
Stillington St. SW1 . . . . .3B 18 (4G 101)
Stillness Rd. SE23 . . . . .6A 122
Stilwell Dr. UB8: Hil 4B 74
STILWELL RDBT. 7C 74
Stipularis Dr. UB4: Yead 4B 76
Stirling Av. HA5: Pinn 1B 58
   SM6: Wall .7J 167
   TW17: Shep 3G 147
Stirling Cl. DA14: Sidc 4J 143
   SW16 . . . . 1H 155
Stirling Cl. EC1 . . . . 3A 8
   (off St John St.)
   W13 . . . . .7B 78
Stirling Gro. TW3: Houn 2G 113
Stirling Ho. SE18 . . . . 5F 107
Stirling Rd. E13 . . . . .2K 87
   E17 . . . . .3A 50
   HA3: W'stone 3K 41
   N17 . . . . .1G 49
   N22 . . . . .1B 48
   SW9 . . . . 2J 119
   TW2: Whitt 7E 112
   TW6: H'row A 6B 110
   UB3: Hayes 7K 75
   W3 . . . . .3H 97
Stirling Rd. Path E17 . . . . .3A 50
Stirling Wlk. KT5: Surb 6H 151
Stirling Way CR0: Bedd 7J 155
Stiven Cres. HA2: Harr 3D 58
Stockbeck NW1 . . . . 1B 6
   (off Ampthill Est.)
Stockbridge Ho. SW18 . . . . .4A 118
   (off Eltringham St.)
Stockbury Rd. CR0: C'don 6J 157
Stockdale Rd. RM8: Dag 2F 73
Stockdove Way UB6: G'frd 3K 77
Stocker Gdns. RM9: Dag 7G 72
Stockfield Rd. SW16 . . . . .3K 137
Stockford Av. NW7 . . . . .7A 30
Stockholm Apartments NW1 . . . . 7E 64
   (off Chalk Farm Rd.)
Stockholm Ho. E1 . . . . .7G 85
   (off Swedenborg Gdns.)
Stockholm Rd. SE16 . . . . 5J 103
Stockholm Way E1 . . . . 1G 103
Stockhurst Cl. SW15 . . . . 2E 116

Stockingswater La. EN3: Brim 2G 25
Stockland Rd. RM7: Rom 6K 55
Stockleigh Hall NW8 . . . . 2C 82
   (off Prince Albert Rd.)
Stockley Cl. UB7: W Dray 2D 92
Stockley Country Pk. 7C 74
Stockley Farm Rd. UB7: W Dray 3D 92
STOCKLEY PARK 1D 92
Stockley Pk. Golf Course 7E 74
Stockley Rd. UB7: W Dray 4D 92
   UB8: Hil 6C 74
   UB11: Stock P 6C 74
Stock Orchard Cres. N7 . . . . 5K 65
Stock Orchard St. N7 . . . . 5K 65
Stockport Rd. SW16 . . . . .1H 155
Stocksfield Rd. E17 . . . . 3E 50
Stocks Pl. E14 . . . . 7B 86
   UB10: Hil 1C 74
Stock St. E13 .2J 87
Stockton Cl. EN5: New Bar 4F 21
Stockton Ct. SW1 . . . . 2C 18
   (off Greycoat St.)
Stockton Gdns. N17 . . . . .7H 33
   NW7 . . . . .3F 29
Stockton Ho. E2 . . . . 3H 85
   (off Ellsworth St.)
   HA2: Harr .1E 58
Stockton Rd. N17 . . . . .7H 33
   N18 . . . . .6B 34
STOCKWELL .2K 119
Stockwell Av. SW9 . . . . .3K 119
Stockwell Cl. BR1: Brom 2K 159
   HA8: Edg 2J 43
Stockwell Gdns. SW9 . . . . .1K 119
Stockwell Gdns. Est. SW9 . . . . 2J 119
Stockwell Grn. SW9 . . . . .2K 119
Stockwell Grn. Ct. SW9 . . . . .2K 119
Stockwell La. SW9 . . . . .2K 119
Stockwell Pk. Cres. SW9 . . . . .2K 119
Stockwell Pk. Est. SW9 . . . . .2K 119
Stockwell Pk. Rd. SW9 . . . . 1K 119
Stockwell Pk. Wlk. SW9 . . . . .3A 120
Stockwell Rd. SW9 . . . . .2K 119
Stockwell St. SE10 . . . . .6E 104
Stockwell Ter. SW9 . . . . 1K 119
Stodart Rd. SE20 . . . . 1J 157
Stoddart Ho. SW8 . . . . 7H 19 (6K 101)
Stodmarsh Ho. SW9 . . . . .1A 120
   (off Cowley Rd.)
Stofield Gdns. SE9 . . . . .3B 142
Stoford Cl. SW19 . . . . 7G 117
Stokenchurch St. SW6 . . . . .1K 117
STOKE NEWINGTON 3F 67
Stoke Newington Chu. St. N16 . . . . 3D 66
Stoke Newington Comn. N16 . . . . 3F 67
Stoke Newington High St. N16 . . . . .3F 67
Stoke Newington Rd. N16 . . . . 5F 67
Stoke Pl. NW10 . . . . 3B 80
Stoke Rd. KT2: King T 7J 133
Stokesby Rd. KT9: Chess 6F 163
Stokes Cotts. IG6: Ilf 1G 53
Stokes Ct. N2 . . . . 4C 46
Stokes Field (Local Nature Reserve)
. . . . .2B 162
Stokesley St. W12 . . . . .6B 80
Stokes M. TW11: Tedd 5A 132
Stokes Rd. CR0: C'don 6K 157
   E6 . . . . .4C 88
Stokley Ct. N8 . . . . 4J 47
Stoll Cl. NW2 . . . . 3E 62
Stoms Path SE6 . . . . 5C 140
   (off Maroons Way)
Stonard Rd. N13 . . . . 3F 33
   RM8: Dag 5B 72
Stondon Pk. SE23 . . . . .6A 122
Stondon Wlk. E6 . . . . 2B 88
Stonebanks KT12: Walt T 7J 147
STONEBRIDGE 1K 79
Stonebridge Cen. N15 . . . . 5F 49
Stonebridge M. SE19 . . . . .7D 138

Stonebridge Pk. NW10 . . . . .7K 61
Stonebridge Rd. N15 . . . . .5F 49
Stonebridge Way HA9: Wemb 6H 61
Stone Bldgs. WC2 . . . . 6H 7
Stonechat Sq. E6 . . . . 5C 88
Stone Cl. RM8: Dag 2F 73
   SW4 . . . . .2G 119
   UB7: Yiew .1B 92
Stonecot Cl. SM3: Sutt 1G 165
Stonecot Hill SM3: Sutt 1G 165
Stone Cres. TW14: Felt 7H 111
Stonecroft Rd. DA8: Erith 7J 109
Stonecroft Way CR0: C'don 7J 155
Stonecrop Cl. NW9 . . . . .3K 43
Stonecutter St. EC4 . . . . .7A 8 (6B 84)
Stonefield N4 .2K 65
Stonefield Cl. DA7: Bex 3G 127
   HA4: Ruis 5C 58
Stonefield Mans. N1 . . . . 1A 84
   (off Cloudesley St.)
Stonefield St. N1 . . . . 1A 84
Stonefield Way HA4: Ruis 4C 58
   SE7 . . . . 7B 106
STONEGROVE 4A 28
Stonegrove HA8: Edg 4K 27
Stone Gro. Ct. HA8: Edg 5A 28
Stonegrove Gdns. HA8: Edg 5K 27
Stone Hall W8 . . . . 3K 99
   (off Stone Hall Gdns.)
Stonehall Av. IG1: Ilf 6C 52
Stone Hall Gdns. W8 . . . . .3K 99
Stone Hall Pl. W8 . . . . .3K 99
Stoneham Rd. N11 . . . . .7E 22
Stoneharm Rd. N11 . . . . .5B 32
Stonehill Bus. Pk. N18 . . . . 6F 35
Stonehill Cl. SW14 . . . . .5K 115
Stonehill Ct. E4 . . . . .7J 25
STONEHILL GREEN 7J 145
Stonehill Rd. SW14 . . . . 5J 115
   W4 . . . . 5G 97
Stonehills Ct. SE21 . . . . 3E 138
Stonehill Woods Pk. DA14: Sidc 6H 145
Stonehorse Rd. EN3: Pond E 5D 24
Stonehouse NW1 . . . . 1G 83
   (off Plender St.)
Stone Ho. Ct. EC3 . . . . 6H 9
Stonehouse Ho. W2 . . . . 5J 81
   (off Westbourne Pk. Rd.)
Stone Lake Ind. Pk. SE7 . . . . 4A 106
Stone Lake Retail Pk. SE7 . . . . 4A 106
STONELEIGH 5C 164
Stoneleigh Av. EN1: Enf 1C 24
   KT4: Wor Pk 4C 164
Stoneleigh Cl. IG5: Ilf 3C 52
Stoneleigh Cres. KT19: Ewe 5B 164
Stoneleigh M. E3 . . . . 2A 86
Stoneleigh Pk. Av. CR0: C'don 6K 157
Stoneleigh Pk. Rd. KT4: Wor Pk 4C 164
   KT19: Ewe 6B 164
Stoneleigh Pl. W11 . . . . .7F 81
Stoneleigh Rd. BR1: Brom 3F 161
   IG5: Ilf 3C 52
   N17 . . . . .3F 49
   SM5: Cars .7C 154
Stoneleigh St. W11 . . . . .7F 81
Stoneleigh Ter. N19 . . . . .2F 65
Stonell's Rd. SW11 . . . . 6D 118
Stonemason Ct. SE1 . . . . 7C 14
   (off Borough Rd.)
Stonemasons Cl. N15 . . . . .4D 48
Stonemasons Ho. SE14 . . . . .1K 121
   (off Fishers Ct.)
Stonemasons Yd. SW18 . . . . .7B 118
Stonenest St. N4 . . . . .1K 65
Stone Pk. Av. BR3: Beck 4C 158
Stone Pl. KT4: Wor Pk 2C 164
Stone Rd. BR2: Brom 5J 159
Stones End St. SE1 . . . . .7C 14 (2C 102)
Stonewall E6 . . . . .5E 88
Stonewell Rd. TW19: Stanw 1A 128

Stonewold Ct. W5 . . . . .6D 78
Stoney All. SE18 . . . . .2E 124
Stoneyard La. E14 . . . . .7D 86
Stoneycroft Cl. SE12 . . . . .7H 123
Stoneycroft Rd.
    IG8: Wfd G 6H 37
Stoneydeep TW11: Tedd 4A 132
Stoneydown E17 . . . . .4A 50
Stoneydown Av. E17 . . . . .4A 50
Stoneydown Ho. E17 . . . . .4A 50
                            (off Stoneydown)
Stoneyfields Gdns. HA8: Edg 4E 28
Stoneyfields La. HA8: Edg 5D 28
Stoney La. E1 . . . . .7H 9 (6F 85)
    SE19 .6F 139
Stoney St. SE1 . . . . .4E 14 (1D 102)
Stonhouse St. SW4 . . . . .4H 119
Stonor Rd. W14 . . . . .4H 99
Stonycroft Cl. EN3: Enf H 2F 25
Stopes St. SE15 . . . . .7F 103
Stopford Rd. E13 . . . . .1J 87
    SE17 .5B 102
Stopher Ho. SE1 . . . . .7B 14
                            (off Webber St.)
Storehouse M. E14 . . . . .7C 86
Store Rd. E16 . . . . .2E 106
Storers Quay E14 . . . . .4F 105
Store St. E15 . . . . .5F 69
    WC1 . . . . .6C 6 (5H 83)
Storey Cl. UB10: Ick 3E 56
Storey Ct. NW8 . . . . .2A 4
Storey Ho. E14 . . . . .7D 86
                            (off Cottage St.)
Storey Rd. E17 . . . . .4B 50
    N6 . . . . .6D 46
Storey's Ga. SW1 . . . . . . .7D 12 (2H 101)
Storey St. E16 . . . . .1E 106
Stories M. SE5 . . . . .2E 120
Stories Rd. SE5 . . . . .3E 120
Stork Rd. E7 . . . . .6H 69
Storksmead Rd. HA8: Edg 7F 29
Stork's Rd. SE16 . . . . .3G 103
Stormont Lawn Tennis & Squash Club
                            . . . . .5D 46
Stormont Rd. N6 . . . . .7D 46
    SW11 .3E 118
Stormont Way KT9: Chess 5C 162
Stormount Dr. UB3: Harl 2E 92
Storrington WC1 . . . . .2F 7
                            (off Regent Sq.)
Storrington Rd. CR0: C'don 1F 169
Storth Oaks Mead BR7: Chst 5D 142
Story St. N1 . . . . .7K 65
Stothard Ho. E1 . . . . .4J 85
                            (off Amiel St.)
Stothard Pl. E1 . . . . .5H 9 (5E 84)
Stott Cl. SW18 . . . . .6B 118
Stoughton Av. SM3: Cheam 5F 165
Stoughton Cl. SE11 . . . . . . .4H 19 (4K 101)
    SW15 .1C 134
Stour Av. UB2: S'hall 3E 94
Stourcliffe Cl. W1 . . . . .1E 10 (6D 82)
Stourcliffe St. W1 . . . . .1E 10 (6D 82)
Stour Cl. BR2: Kes 4A 172
Stourhead Cl. SW19 . . . . .7F 117
Stourhead Gdns. SW20 . . . . .3C 152
Stourhead Ho. SW1 . . . . .5C 18
                            (off Tachbrook St.)
Stour Rd. E3 . . . . .7C 68
    RM10: Dag 2G 73
Stourton Av. TW13: Hanw 4D 130
Stowage SE8 . . . . .6C 104
Stow Cres. E17 . . . . .7F 35
Stowe Cres. HA4: Ruis 6D 38
Stowe Gdns. N9 . . . . .1A 34
Stowe Ho. NW11 . . . . .6A 46
Stowell Ho. N8 . . . . .4J 47
                            (off Pembroke Rd.)
Stowe Pl. N15 . . . . .3E 48
Stowe Rd. W12 . . . . .2D 98

Stowting Rd. BR6: Orp 4J 173
Stox Mead HA3: Hrw W 1H 41
Stracey Rd. E7 . . . . .4J 69
    NW10 .1K 79
Strachan Pl. SW19 . . . . .6E 134
Stradbroke Dr. IG7: Chig 6K 37
Stradbroke Gro. IG5: Ilf 3C 52
    IG9: Buck H 1G 37
Stradbroke Pk. IG7: Chig 6K 37
Stradbroke Rd. N5 . . . . .4C 66
Stradbrook Cl. HA2: Harr 3D 58
Stradella Rd. SE24 . . . . .6C 120
Strafford Av. IG5: Ilf 2E 52
Strafford Ho. SE8 . . . . .5B 104
                            (off Grove St.)
Strafford Rd. EN5: Barn 3B 20
    TW1: Twick 7A 114
    TW3: Houn 3D 112
    W3 . . . . .2J 97
Strafford St. E14 . . . . .2C 104
Strahan Rd. E3 . . . . .3A 86
Straight, The UB1: S'hall 2B 94
Strait Rd. E6 . . . . .7C 88
Strakers Rd. SE15 . . . . .4H 121
Strale Ho. N1 . . . . .1E 84
                            (off Whitmore Est.)
Strand WC2 . . . . .3F 13 (7J 83)
Strand Ct. SE18 . . . . .5K 107
Strand Dr. TW9: Kew 7H 97
Strandfield Cl. SE18 . . . . .5J 107
Strand Ho. BR2: Brom 6B 160
                            (off Wells Vw. Dr.)
    SE28 .1H 107
Strand La. WC2 . . . . .2H 13 (7K 83)
STRAND ON THE GREEN 6G 97
Strand on the Green W4 . . . . .6G 97
Strand Pl. N18 . . . . .4K 33
Strand School App. W4 . . . . .6G 97
Strang Ho. N1 . . . . .1C 84
Strangways Ter. W14 . . . . .3H 99
Stranraer Way N1 . . . . .7J 65
    TW6: H'row A 6A 110
Strasburg Rd. SW11 . . . . .1E 118
Strata SE1 .4C 102
                            (off Walworth Rd.)
Strata Cl. KT12: Walt T 7H 147
Stratfield Pk. Cl. N21 . . . . .7G 23
STRATFORD 7F 69
Stratford Av. UB10: Hil 2B 74
Stratford Centre, The E15 . . . . .7F 69
Stratford Circus (Performing Arts Cen.)
                            . . . . .6F 69
Stratford Cl. IG11: Bark 7A 72
    RM10: Dag 7J 73
Stratford Ct. KT3: N Mald 4K 151
Stratford Eye E15 . . . . .6F 69
Stratford Gro. SW15 . . . . .4F 117
Stratford Ho. Av.
    BR1: Brom 3C 160
STRATFORD NEW TOWN 6F 69
Stratford Office Village, The E15 . . . .7G 69
                            (off Romford Rd.)
Stratford Picture House
    London 6F 69
                (within Westfield Stratford City Shop. Cen.)
    W1 . . . . .1J 11 (6F 83)
Stratford Pl. E20 . . . . .6E 68
Stratford Rd. CR7: Thor H 4A 156
    E13 . . . . .1H 87
                            (not continuous)
    NW4 . . . . .4F 45
    TW6: H'row A 6D 110
    UB2: S'hall 4C 94
    UB4: Yead 4K 75
    W8 . . . . .3J 99
Stratford Studios W8 . . . . .3J 99
Stratford Theatre Royal 7F 69
Stratford Vs. NW1 . . . . .7G 65
Stratford Workshops E15 . . . . .1F 87
                            (off Burford Rd.)

Stratham Ct. N19 . . . . .3J 65
                            (off Alexander Rd.)
Strathan Cl. SW18 . . . . .6G 117
Strathaven Rd. SE12 . . . . .6K 123
Strathblaine Rd. SW11 . . . . .5B 118
Strathbrook Rd. SW16 . . . . .7K 137
Strathcona Rd.
    HA9: Wemb 2D 60
Strathdale SW16 . . . . .5K 137
Strathdon Dr. SW17 . . . . .3B 136
Strathearn Av. TW2: Whitt 1F 131
    UB3: Harl 7H 93
Strathearn Ho. W2 . . . . .2C 10
                            (off Strathearn Pl.)
Strathearn Pl. W2 . . . . .1C 10 (6C 82)
Strathearn Rd. SM1: Sutt 5J 165
    SW19 .5J 135
Stratheden Pde. SE3 . . . . .7J 105
Stratheden Rd. SE3 . . . . .1J 123
Strathfield Gdns. IG11: Bark 6H 71
Strathleven Rd. SW2 . . . . .5J 119
Strathmore Ct. NW8 . . . . .1C 4
                            (off Park Rd.)
Strathmore Gdns. HA8: Edg 2H 43
    N3 . . . . .1K 45
    W8 . . . . .1J 99
Strathmore Rd. CR0: C'don 7D 156
    SW19 .3J 135
    TW11: Tedd 4J 131
Strathnairn St. SE1 . . . . .4G 103
                            (not continuous)
Strathray Gdns. NW3 . . . . .6C 64
Strath Ter. SW11 . . . . .4C 118
Strathville Rd. SW18 . . . . .2J 135
                            (not continuous)
Strathyre Av. SW16 . . . . .3A 156
Stratosphere Twr. E15 . . . . .7F 69
                            (off Gt. Eastern Rd.)
Stratton Cl. DA7: Bex 3E 126
    HA8: Edg 6A 28
    SW19 .2J 153
    TW3: Houn 1E 112
Stratton Ct. HA5: Hat E 1D 40
                            (off Devonshire Rd.)
    N1 . . . . .7E 66
                            (off Hertford Rd.)
Strattondale St. E14 . . . . .3E 104
Stratton Dr. IG11: Bark 5J 71
Stratton Gdns. UB1: S'hall 6D 76
Stratton Rd. DA7: Bex 3E 126
    SW19 .2J 153
    TW16: Sun 2H 147
Stratton St. W1 . . . . .4K 11 (1F 101)
Strauss Rd. W4 . . . . .2K 97
Strawberry Flds. BR6: Farnb 5F 173
STRAWBERRY HILL 3K 131
Strawberry Hill 3K 131
Strawberry Hill KT9: Chess 6D 162
    TW1: Twick 3K 131
Strawberry Hill Cl. TW1: Twick 3K 131
Strawberry Hill Golf Course 3J 131
Strawberry Hill Rd. TW1: Twick 3K 131
Strawberry La. SM5: Cars 3E 166
Strawberry Ter. N10 . . . . .1D 46
Strawberry Va. N2 . . . . .1B 46
    TW1: Twick 3A 132
                            (not continuous)
Streakes Fld. Rd. NW2 . . . . .2C 62
Streamdale SE2 . . . . .6B 108
Stream La. HA8: Edg 5C 28
Streamline Ct. SE22 . . . . .1G 139
                            (off Streamline M.)
Streamline M. SE22 . . . . .1G 139
Streamside Cl. BR2: Brom 4J 159
    N9 . . . . .1A 34
Streamway DA17: Belv 6G 109
Streatfeild Av. E6 . . . . .1D 88
Streatfield Rd. HA3: Kenton 3C 42
STREATHAM 3J 137
Streatham Cl. SW16 . . . . .2J 137
STREATHAM COMMON 6H 137

Streatham Comn. Nth. SW16 . . . . .5J 137
Streatham Comn. Sth. SW16 . . . . .6J 137
Streatham Ct. SW16 . . . . .3J 137
Streatham High Rd. SW16 . . . . .4J 137
STREATHAM HILL 2J 137
Streatham Hill SW2 . . . . .2J 137
Streatham Hub 5H 137
STREATHAM PARK 5G 137
Streatham Pl. SW2 . . . . .7J 119
Streatham Rd. CR4: Mitc 1E 154
    SW16 .1E 154
Streatham St. WC1 . . . . . . .7E 6 (6J 83)
STREATHAM VALE 7G 137
Streatham Va. SW16 . . . . .1G 155
Strathbourne Rd. SW17 . . . . .2E 136
Streatley Pl. NW3 . . . . .4A 64
Streatley Rd. NW6 . . . . .7H 63
Street, The E20 . . . . .6E 68
            (within Westfield Stratford City Shop. Cen.)
Streeters La. SM6: Bedd 3H 167
Streetfield M. SE3 . . . . .3J 123
Streimer Rd. E15 . . . . .2E 86
Strelley Way W3 . . . . .7A 80
Stretton Mans. SE8 . . . . .5C 104
Stretton Rd. CR0: C'don 7E 156
    TW10: Ham 2C 132
Strickland Ct. SE15 . . . . .3G 121
Strickland Ho. E2 . . . . .2K 9
                            (off Chambord St.)
Strickland Row SW18 . . . . .7B 118
Strickland St. SE8 . . . . .2C 122
Strickland Way BR6: Orp 4K 173
Stride Rd. E13 . . . . .2H 87
Strimon Cl. N9 . . . . .2D 34
Stringer Ho. N1 . . . . .1E 84
                            (off Whitmore Est.)
Strode Cl. N10 . . . . .7K 31
Strode Rd. E7 . . . . .4J 69
    N17 . . . . .2E 48
    NW10 .6C 62
    SW6 . . . . .7G 99
Strome Ho. NW6 . . . . .2K 81
                            (off Carlton Vale)
Strone Rd. E7 . . . . .6A 70
    E12 . . . . .6A 70
Strone Way UB4: Yead 4C 76
Strongbow Cres. SE9 . . . . .5D 124
Strongbow Rd. SE9 . . . . .5D 124
Strongbridge Cl. HA2: Harr 1E 58
Stronsa Rd. W12 . . . . .2B 98
Stroud Av. RM7: Rush G 1K 73
Stroud Ho. SE1 . . . . .7F 15
                            (off Staple St.)
Stroud Cres. SW15 . . . . .3C 134
Stroudes Cl. KT4: Wor Pk 7A 152
Stroud Fld. UB5: N'olt 6C 58
Stroud Ga. HA2: Harr 4F 59
STROUD GREEN 7K 47
Stroud Grn. Gdns. CR0: C'don 7J 157
Stroud Grn. Rd. N4 . . . . .1K 65
Stroud Grn. Way CR0: C'don 7H 157
Stroudley Ho. SW8 . . . . .1G 119
Stroudley Wlk. E3 . . . . .3D 86
Stroud Rd. SE25 . . . . .6G 157
    SW19 .3J 135
Stroud's Cl. RM6: Chad H 5B 54
Stroud Way TW15: Ashf 6D 128
Strouts Pl. E2 . . . . .2J 9 (3F 85)
Strudwick Ct. SW4 . . . . .1J 119
                            (off Binfield Rd.)
Strutton Cl. SW1 . . . . .2C 18
                            (off Gt. Peter St.)
Strutton Ground SW1 . . . . . .1C 18 (3H 101)
Strype St. E1 . . . . .6J 9 (5F 85)
Stuart Av.
    BR2: Hayes 1K 171
    HA2: Harr 3D 58
    KT12: Walt T 7K 147
    NW9 . . . . .7C 44
    W5 . . . . .2F 97
Stuart Cl. UB10: Hil 6C 56

Stuart Ct. CR0: C'don 3B 168
   (off St John's Rd.)
Stuart Cres. CR0: C'don 3B 170
N22 . . . . .1K 47
UB3: Hayes 6E 74
Stuart Evans Cl. DA16: Well 3C 126
Stuart Gro. TW11: Tedd 5J 131
Stuart Ho. E9 . . . . .6K 67
   (off Queen Anne Rd.)
E16 . . . . .1K 105
   (off Beaulieu Av.)
W14 . . . . .4G 99
   (off Windsor Way)
Stuart Mantle Way DA8: Erith 7K 109
   (not continuous)
Stuart Mill Ho. N1 . . . . .1D 7
   (off Killick St.)
Stuart Pl. CR4: Mitc 1D 154
Stuart Rd. CR7: Thor H 4C 156
DA16: Well 1B 126
EN4: E Barn 7H 21
HA3: W'stone 3K 41
IG11: Bark 7K 71
NW6 . . . . .3J 81
SE15 . . . . .4J 121
SW19 .3J 135
TW10: Ham 2B 132
W3 . . . . .1J 97
Stuart Twr. W9 . . . . .3A 82
   (off Maida Vale)
Stubbs Cl. NW9 . . . . .5J 43
Stubbs Ct. W4 . . . . .5H 97
   (off Chaseley Dr.)
Stubbs Dr. SE16 . . . . .5H 103
Stubbs Ho. E2 . . . . .3K 85
   (off Bonner St.)
SW1 . . . . .4D 18
   (off Erasmus St.)
Stubbs M. RM8: Dag 4B 72
   (off Marlborough Rd.)
Stubbs Point E13 . . . . .4J 87
Stubbs Way SW19 . . . . .1B 154
Stucley Pl. NW1 . . . . .7F 65
Stucley Rd. TW5: Hest 7G 95
Studdridge St. SW6 . . . . .2J 117
Studd St. N1 . . . . .1B 84
Studholme Ct. NW3 . . . . .4J 63
Studholme St. SE15 . . . . .7H 103
Studio Ct. N15 . . . . .4E 48
Studio La. W5 . . . . .1D 96
Studio M. NW4 . . . . .4E 44
Studio Pl. SW1 . . . . .7F 11
Studio Plaza KT12: Walt T 7J 147
Studios, The SW4 . . . . .4G 119
   (off Crescent La.)
SW4 . . . .
   (off Edge St.)
Studios Rd. TW17: Shep 3B 146
Studio Theatre
  Carshalton 4E 166
Studland SE17 . . . . .5D 102
   (off Portland Pl.)
Studland Cl. DA15: Sidc 3K 143
Studland Ho. E14 . . . . .6A 86
   (off Aston St.)
Studland Rd. KT2: King T 6E 132
SE26 . . . . .5K 139
W7 . . . . .6H 77
Studland St. W6 . . . . .4D 98
Studley Av. E4 . . . . .7A 36
Studley Cl. E5 . . . . .5A 68
Studley Ct. DA14: Sidc 5B 144
E14 . . . . .7F 87
   (off Jamestown Way)
Studley Dr. IG4: Ilf 6B 52
Studley Est. SW4 . . . . .1J 119
Studley Grange Rd. W7 . . . . .2J 95
Studley Rd. E7 . . . . .6K 69
RM9: Dag 7D 72
SW4 . . . . .1J 119
Stukeley Rd. E7 . . . . .7K 69

Stukeley St. WC2 . . . . .7F 7 (6J 83)
Stumps Hill La. BR3: Beck 6C 140
Stunell Ho. SE14 . . . . .6K 103
   (off John Williams Cl.)
Sturdee Ho. E2 . . . . .2G 85
   (off Horatio St.)
Sturdy Ho. E3 . . . . .2A 86
   (off Gernon Rd.)
Sturdy Rd. SE15 . . . . .2H 121
Sturge Av. E17 . . . . .2D 50
Sturgeon Rd. SE17 . . . . .5C 102
Sturges Fld. BR7: Chst 6H 143
Sturgess Av. NW4 . . . . .7D 44
Sturge St. SE1 . . . . .6C 14 (2C 102)
Sturmer Way N7 . . . . .5K 65
Sturminster NW1 . . . . .7H 65
   (off Agar Gro.)
Sturminster Cl. UB4: Yead 6A 76
Sturminster Ho. SW8 . . . . .7K 101
   (off Dorset Rd.)
Sturrock Cl. N15 . . . . .4D 48
Sturry St. E14 . . . . .6D 86
Sturts Apartments N1 . . . . .1D 84
   (off Branch Pl.)
Sturt St. N1 . . . . .1D 8 (2C 84)
Stutfield St. E1 . . . . .6G 85
Stuttle Ho. E1 . . . . .4K 9
   (off Buxton St.)
Styles Gdns. SW9 . . . . .3B 120
Styles Ho. SE1 . . . . .6A 14
Styles Way BR3: Beck 4E 158
Stylus Ho. E1 . . . . .6J 85
Success Ho. SE1 . . . . .5F 103
   (off Cooper's Rd.)
Sudbourne Rd. SW2 . . . . .5J 119
Sudbrooke Rd. SW12 . . . . .6D 118
Sudbrook Gdns. TW10: Ham 3D 132
Sudbrook La. TW10: Ham 1E 132
SUDBURY 5B 60
Sudbury E6 . . . . .5E 88
Sudbury Av. HA0: Wemb 3C 60
Sudbury Ct. RM6: Chad H 5B 54
Sudbury Ct. E3 . . . . .1H 119
   (off Allen Edwards Dr.)
Sudbury Ct. Dr. HA1: Harr 3K 59
Sudbury Ct. Rd. HA1: Harr 3K 59
Sudbury Cres. BR1: Brom 6J 141
HA0: Wemb 5B 60
Sudbury Cft. HA0: Wemb 4K 59
Sudbury Gdns. CR0: C'don 4E 168
Sudbury Golf Course 7C 60
Sudbury Hgts. Av. UB6: G'frd 5K 59
Sudbury Hill HA1: Harr 2J 59
Sudbury Hill Cl.
  HA0: Wemb 4K 59
Sudbury Ho. SW18 . . . . .5K 117
Sudbury Rd. IG11: Bark 5K 71
Sudeley Cl. E17 . . . . .1B 50
   (off Broughton Pl.)
Sudeley St. N1 . . . . .2B 84
Sudlow Rd. SW18 . . . . .5J 117
Sudrey St. SE1 . . . . .7C 14 (2C 102)
Suez Av. UB6: G'frd 2K 77
Suez Rd. EN3: Brim 4F 25
SUFFIELD HATCH 4K 35
Suffield Ho. SE17 . . . . .5B 102
   (off Berryfield Rd.)
Suffield Rd. E4 . . . . .3J 35
N15 . . . . .5F 49
SE20 . . . . .2J 157
Suffolk Cl. E10 . . . . .7C 50
IG3: Ilf 6J 53
RM6: Chad H 6C 54
Suffolk Ho. CR0: C'don 2D 168
   (off George St.)
SE20 . . . . .1K 157
   (off Croydon Rd.)
Suffolk La. EC4 . . . . .2E 14 (7D 84)
Suffolk Pk. Rd. E17 . . . . .4A 50
Suffolk Pl. SE2 . . . . .5C 108
SW1 . . . . .4D 12 (1H 101)

Suffolk Rd. DA14: Sidc 6C 144
E13 . . . . .3J 87
EN3: Pond E 5C 24
HA2: Harr 6D 40
IG3: Ilf 6J 53
IG11: Bark 7H 71
KT4: Wor Pk 2B 164
N15 . . . . .5D 48
NW10 . . . . .7A 62
RM10: Dag 5J 73
SE25 . . . . .4F 157
SW13 . . . . .7B 98
Suffolk St. E7 . . . . .4J 69
SW1 . . . . .3D 12 (7H 83)
Sugar Bakers Ct. EC3 . . . . .1H 15
Sugar Ho. E1 . . . . .1K 15
   (off Leman St.)
Sugar Ho. La. E15 . . . . .2E 86
Sugar Loaf Wlk. E2 . . . . .3J 85
Sugar Quay EC3 . . . . .3H 15
Sugar Quay Wlk. EC3 . . . . . .3H 15 (7E 84)
Sugden Rd. KT7: T Ditt 1B 162
SW11 . . . . .3E 118
Sugden Way IG11: Bark 2K 89
Sulby Ho. SE4 . . . . .4A 122
   (off Turnham Rd.)
Sulgrave Gdns. W6 . . . . .2E 98
Sulgrave Rd. W6 . . . . .3E 98
Sulina Rd. SW2 . . . . .7J 119
Sulivan Cl. SW6 . . . . .2J 117
Sulivan Ent. Cen. SW6 . . . . .3K 117
Sulivan Rd. SW6 . . . . .3J 117
Sulkin Ho. E2 . . . . .3K 85
   (off Knottisford St.)
Sullivan Av. E16 . . . . .5B 88
Sullivan Cl. KT8: W Mole 3F 149
SW11 . . . . .3C 118
UB4: Yead 5A 76
Sullivan Ct. E3 . . . . .4B 86
   (off Eric St.)
N16 . . . . .7F 49
SW5 . . . . .4J 99
   (off Earls Ct. Rd.)
Sullivan Cres. UB9: Hare 2A 38
Sullivan Ho. SE11 . . . . .4H 19
   (off Vauxhall St.)
SW1 . . . . .7K 17
   (off Churchill Gdns.)
Sullivan Rd. SE11 . . . . .3K 19 (4A 102)
Sullivan Row BR2: Brom 6B 160
Sullivans Reach KT12: Walt T 7H 147
Sultan Ho. SE1 . . . . .5G 103
   (off St James's Rd.)
Sultan Rd. E11 . . . . .4K 51
Sultan St. BR3: Beck 2K 157
SE5 . . . . .7C 102
Sultan Ter. N22 . . . . .2A 48
Sumatra Rd. NW6 . . . . .5J 63
Sumburgh Rd. SW12 . . . . .6E 118
Sumeria Ct. SE16 . . . . .4J 103
   (off Rotherhithe New Rd.)
Summer Av. KT8: E Mos 5J 149
Summerbee Ho. SW18 . . . . .4A 118
   (off Eltringham St.)
Summercourt Rd. E1 . . . . .6J 85
Summer Crossing KT7: T Ditt 5J 149
Summer Dr. UB7: W Dray 2C 92
Summerene Cl. SW16 . . . . .7G 137
Summerfield BR1: Brom 1K 159
   (off Freelands Rd.)
Summerfield Av. NW6 . . . . .2G 81
Summerfield La. KT6: Surb 2D 162
Summerfield Rd. W5 . . . . .4B 78
Summerfields Av. N12 . . . . .6H 31
Summerfield St. SE12 . . . . .7H 123
Summer Gdns. KT8: E Mos 5J 149
  UB10: Ick 2E 56
Summer Gro. BR4: W W'ck 2G 171
Summer Hill BR7: Chst 2E 160
Summerhill Cl. BR6: Orp 3J 173
Summerhill Gro. EN1: Enf 6K 23

Summerhill Rd. N15 . . . . .4D 48
Summerhill Vs. BR7: Chst 1E 160
   (off Susan Wood)
Summerhill Way CR4: Mitc 1E 154
Summerhouse Av. TW5: Hest 1C 112
Summerhouse Dr. DA2: Wilm 4K 145
  DA5: Bexl, Dart 4K 145
Summerhouse La. UB7: Harm 2E 174
Summerhouse Rd. N16 . . . . .2E 66
Summerland Gdns. N10 . . . . .3F 47
Summerland Grange N10 . . . . .3F 47
Summerlands Av. W3 . . . . .7J 79
Summerlands Lodge BR6: Farnb 4E 172
Summer La. N2 . . . . .4D 46
Summerlee Av. N2 . . . . .4D 46
Summerlee Gdns. N2 . . . . .4D 46
Summerley St. SW18 . . . . .2K 135
Summer Rd. KT7: T Ditt 5J 149
KT8: E Mos 5H 149
   (not continuous)
Summersby Rd. N6 . . . . .6F 47
Summers Cl. HA9: Wemb 1H 61
SM2: Sutt 7J 165
Summerskill Cl. SE15 . . . . .3H 121
Summerskille Cl. N9 . . . . .2C 34
Summers La. N12 . . . . .7G 31
Summers Row N12 . . . . .6H 31
Summers St. EC1 . . . . .4J 7 (4A 84)
SUMMERSTOWN 3A 136
Summerstown SW17 . . . . .3A 136
Summerton Way SE28 . . . . .6D 90
Summer Trees TW16: Sun 1K 147
Summerville Gdns. SM1: Sutt 6H 165
Summerwood Rd. TW7: Isle 5K 113
Summit Av. NW9 . . . . .5K 43
Summit Bus. Pk. TW16: Sun 7J 129
Summit Cl. HA8: Edg 7B 28
N14 . . . . .2B 32
NW9 . . . . .4K 43
Summit Ct. NW2 . . . . .5G 63
Summit Dr. IG8: Wfd G 2B 52
Summit Est. N16 . . . . .7G 49
Summit Rd. E17 . . . . .4D 50
UB5: N'olt 7F 58
Summit Way N14 . . . . .2A 32
SE19 . . . . .7E 138
Sumner Av. SE15 . . . . .1F 121
Sumner Bldgs. SE1 . . . . .4C 14
Sumner Cl. BR6: Farnb 4G 173
Sumner Ct. SW8 . . . . .7J 101
Sumner Est. SE15 . . . . .7F 103
Sumner Gdns. CR0: C'don 1A 168
Sumner Ho. E3 . . . . .5D 86
   (off Watts Gro.)
Sumner Pl. SW7 . . . . .4B 16 (4B 100)
Sumner Pl. M. SW7 . . . . .4B 16 (4B 100)
Sumner Rd. CR0: C'don 1A 168
HA1: Harr 7G 41
SE15 . . . . .6F 103
Sumner Rd. Sth. CR0: C'don 1A 168
Sumner St. SE1 . . . . .4B 14 (1B 102)
Sumpter Cl. NW3 . . . . .6A 64
Sun All. TW9: Rich 4E 114
Sunbeam Cres. W10 . . . . .4E 80
Sunbeam Rd. NW10 . . . . .4J 79
Sunbeam Way NW10 . . . . .4K 79
SUNBURY 3A 148
Sunbury Av. NW7 . . . . .5E 28
SW14 . . . . .4K 115
Sunbury Av. Pas. SW14 . . . . .4A 116
Sunbury Bus. Cen. TW16: Sun 1H 147
Sunbury Ct. KT12: Walt T 6J 147
SUNBURY COMMON 7H 129
Sunbury Ct. EN5: Barn 4B 20
Sunbury Ct. Island TW16: Sun 3B 148
Sunbury Ct. M. TW16: Sun 2B 148
Sunbury Ct. Rd. TW16: Sun 2A 148
Sunbury Cres. TW13: Felt 4H 129
SUNBURY CROSS 7J 129
Sunbury Cross Cen. TW16: Sun 7J 129
Sunbury Embroidery Gallery, The . . .3K 147
Sunbury Gdns. NW7 . . . . .5E 28

Sunbury Golf Course 4F 147
Sunbury Ho. E2 . . . . .2J 9
(off Swanfield St.)
SE14 . . . . .6K 103
(off Myers La.)
TW16: Sun 1G 147
(off Brooklands Cl.)
Sunbury La. KT12: Walt T 6J 147
SW11 . . . . .1B 118
(not continuous)
Sunbury Leisure Cen. 1H 147
Sunburylock Ait
KT12: Walt T 4K 147
Sunbury Pk. Walled Garden 3K 147
Sunbury Rd. SM3: Cheam 3F 165
TW13: Felt 3H 129
Sunbury St. SE18 . . . . .3D 106
Sunbury Way TW13: Hanw 5A 130
Sunbury Workshops E2 . . . . .2J 9
(off Swanfield St.)
Sun Ct. EC3 .1F 15
Suncroft Pl. SE26 . . . . .3J 139
Sundeala Cl. TW16: Sun 7J 129
(off Hanworth Rd.)
Sunderland Ct. SE22 . . . . .7G 121
TW19: Stanw 6A 110
(off Whitley Cl.)
Sunderland Ho. W2 . . . . .5J 81
(off Westbourne Pk. Rd.)
Sunderland Mt. SE23 . . . . .2K 139
Sunderland Point E16 . . . . .1G 107
Sunderland Rd. SE23 . . . . .1K 139
W5 . . . . .3D 96
Sunderland Ter. W2 . . . . .6K 81
Sunderland Way E12 . . . . .2B 70
Sundew Av. W12 . . . . .7C 80
Sundew Cl. W12 . . . . .7C 80
Sundew Ct. HA0: Wemb 2E 78
(off Elmore Cl.)
Sundial Av. SE25 . . . . .3F 157
Sundial Ct. EC1 . . . . .5E 8
(off Chiswell St.)
Sundorne Rd. SE7 . . . . .5A 106
Sundown Rd. TW15: Ashf 5E 128
Sundra Wlk. E1 . . . . .4K 85
SUNDRIDGE 6K 141
Sundridge Av.
BR1: Brom 1B 160
BR7: Chst 1B 160
DA16: Well 2H 125
Sundridge Ho. E9 . . . . .7K 67
(off Church Cres.)
Sundridge Pde. BR1: Brom 7K 141
SUNDRIDGE PARK 7K 141
Sundridge Pk. Golf Course 6K 141
Sundridge Pl. CR0: C'don 1G 169
Sundridge Rd. CR0: C'don 7F 157
Sunfields Pl. SE3 . . . . .7K 105
Sunflower Cl. NW2 . . . . .2H 63
RM13: Rain 2J 91
Sungate Cotts. RM5: Col R 1F 55
Sun Ga. Ho. KT3: N Mald 4B 152
Sunguard Ct. SE1 . . . . . . .4A 14 (1B 102)
SUN-IN-THE-SANDS 7K 105
Sunken Rd. CR0: C'don 5J 169
Sunkist Way SM6: Wall 7J 167
Sunland Av. DA6: Bex 4E 126
Sun La. SE3 . . . . .7K 105
Sunleigh Rd. HA0: Wemb 1E 78
Sunley Gdns. UB6: G'frd 1A 78
Sun Life Trad. Est.
TW14: Felt 3J 111
Sunlight Cl. SW19 . . . . .6A 136
Sunlight Sq. E2 . . . . .3H 85
Sunmead Rd. TW16: Sun 3J 147
Sunna Gdns. TW16: Sun 2K 147
Sunniholme Ct. CR2: S Croy 5C 168
(off Warham Rd.)
Sunningdale N14 . . . . .5C 32
W13 . . . . .5B 78
(off Hardwick Grn.)

Sunningdale Av. HA4: Ruis 1A 58
IG11: Bark 1H 89
TW13: Hanw 2C 130
W3 . . . . .7A 80
Sunningdale Cl. E6 . . . . .3D 88
HA7: Stan 6F 27
KT6: Surb 2E 162
SE16 . . . . .5H 103
SE28 . . . . .6E 90
Sunningdale Ct. TW7: Isle 6H 113
(off Whitton Dene)
UB1: S'hall 6G 77
(off Fleming Rd.)
Sunningdale Gdns. NW9 . . . . .5J 43
W8 . . . . .3J 99
(off Stratford Rd.)
Sunningdale Lodge HA8: Edg 5A 28
(off Stonegrove)
Sunningdale Rd. BR1: Brom 4C 160
SM1: Sutt 3H 165
Sunningfields Cres. NW4 . . . . .2D 44
Sunningfields Rd. NW4 . . . . .2C 44
Sunninghill Cl. W3 . . . . .2J 97
Sunninghill Rd. SE13 . . . . .2D 122
Sunny Bank SE25 . . . . .3G 157
Sunny Cres. NW10 . . . . .7J 61
Sunnycroft Rd. SE25 . . . . .3G 157
TW3: Houn 2F 113
UB1: S'hall 5E 76
Sunnydale BR6: Farnb 2E 172
Sunnydale Gdns. NW7 . . . . .6E 28
Sunnydale Rd. SE12 . . . . .5K 123
Sunnydene Av. E4 . . . . .5A 36
HA4: Ruis 1J 57
Sunnydene Gdns. HA0: Wemb 6G 60
Sunnydene St. SE26 . . . . .4A 140
Sunnyfield NW7 . . . . .4G 29
Sunnyfield Rd. BR7: Chst 3K 161
Sunny Gdns. Pde. NW4 . . . . .2D 44
Sunny Gdns. Rd. NW4 . . . . .2D 44
Sunny Hill NW4 . . . . .3D 44
Sunnyhill Cl. E5 . . . . .4A 68
Sunnyhill Rd. SW16 . . . . .4J 137
Sunnyhurst Cl. SM1: Sutt 3J 165
Sunnymead Av. CR4: Mitc 3H 155
Sunnymead Rd. NW9 . . . . .7K 43
SW15 . . . . .5D 116
Sunnymede Av. KT19: Ewe 7A 164
Sunnymede Dr. IG2: Ilf 5F 53
IG6: Ilf 5F 53
Sunny M. NW1 . . . . .7E 64
Sunny Nook Gdns.
CR2: S Croy 6D 168
Sunny Pl. NW4 . . . . .4E 44
Sunny Road, The EN3: Enf H 1E 24
Sunnyside KT12: Walt T 5A 148
NW2 . . . . .3H 63
SE6 . . . . .7B 122
(off Blythe Hill)
SW19 . . . . .6G 135
Sunnyside Dr. E4 . . . . .7K 25
Sunnyside Ho's. NW2 . . . . .3H 63
(off Sunnyside)
Sunnyside Pas. SW19 . . . . .6G 135
Sunnyside Pl. SW19 . . . . .6G 135
Sunnyside Rd. E10 . . . . .1C 68
IG1: Ilf 3G 71
N19 . . . . .7H 47
TW11: Tedd 4H 131
W5 . . . . .1D 96
Sunnyside Rd. E. N9 . . . . .3B 34
Sunnyside Rd. Nth. N9 . . . . .3A 34
Sunnyside Rd. Sth. N9 . . . . .3A 34
Sunnyside Ter. NW9 . . . . .3K 43
Sunny Vw. NW9 . . . . .5K 43
Sunny Way N12 . . . . .7H 31
Sun Pas. SE16 . . . . .3G 103
(off Old Jamaica Rd.)
Sunray Av. BR2: Brom 6C 160
KT5: Surb 2H 163
SE24 . . . . .4D 120

Sunrise Cl. E20 . . . . .5E 68
TW13: Hanw 3D 130
Sunrise Vw. NW7 . . . . .6G 29
Sun Rd. W14 . . . . .5H 99
Sunset Av. E4 . . . . .1J 35
IG8: Wfd G 4C 36
Sunset Ct. IG8: Wfd G 7F 37
Sunset Gdns. SE25 . . . . .2F 157
Sunset Lodge NW10 . . . . .7E 62
(off Hanover Rd.)
Sunset Rd. SE5 . . . . .4C 120
SE28 . . . . .1A 108
SW19 . . . . .5D 134
Sunshine Way CR4: Mitc 2D 154
Sun St. EC2 . . . . .5F 9 (5D 84)
(Finsbury Sq.)
EC2 . . . . .5G 9 (5E 84)
(Primrose St.)
Sun St. Pas. EC2 . . . . .6G 9 (5E 84)
Sun Wlk. E1 . . . . .3K 15 (7F 85)
Sunwell Cl. SE15 . . . . .1H 121
Sun Wharf SE8 . . . . .7D 104
(off Creekside)
Superbowl
Sutton .5K 165
Superior Dr. BR6: Chels 6K 173
Supreme Court
Westminster 2J 101
Supreme Point E16 . . . . .5J 87
(off Butchers Rd.)
SURBITON 6D 150
Surbiton Ct. KT6: Surb 6C 150
Surbiton Cres. KT1: King T 4E 150
Surbiton Golf Course 4B 162
Surbiton Hall Cl.
KT1: King T 4E 150
Surbiton Hill Pk. KT5: Surb 5F 151
Surbiton Hill Rd. KT6: Surb 4E 150
Surbiton Pde. KT6: Surb 6E 150
Surbiton Raceway 3K 163
Surbiton Rd. KT1: King T 4D 150
Surlingham Cl. SE28 . . . . .7D 90
Surma Cl. E1 . . . . .4H 85
Surmans Cl. RM9: Dag 1C 90
Surrendale Pl. W9 . . . . .4J 81
Surrey Canal Rd. SE14 . . . . .6J 103
SE15 . . . . .6J 103
Surrey Cl. N3 . . . . .3G 45
Surrey County Cricket Club
. . . . .7H 19 (6K 101)
Surrey Cres. W4 . . . . .5G 97
Surrey Docks Farm 2B 104
Surrey Docks Watersports Cen. 3A 104
Surrey Gdns. N4 . . . . .6C 48
Surrey Gro. SE17 . . . . .5E 102
SM1: Sutt 3B 166
Surrey Health & Racquets Club, The
. . . . .6K 167
Surrey Ho. SE16 . . . . .1K 103
(off Rotherhithe St.)
Surrey La. SW11 . . . . .1C 118
Surrey La. Est. SW11 . . . . .1C 118
Surrey M. SE27 . . . . .4E 138
Surrey Mt. SE23 . . . . .1H 139
Surrey Quays Rd. SE16 . . . . .3J 103
Surrey Quays Shop. Cen.
SE16 . . . . .3K 103
Surrey Rd. BR4: W W'ck 1D 170
HA1: Harr 5G 41
IG11: Bark 7J 71
RM10: Dag 5H 73
SE15 . . . . .5K 121
Surrey Row SE1 . . . . .6A 14 (2B 102)
Surrey Sq. SE17 . . . . .5E 102
Surrey Steps WC2 . . . . .2H 13
(off Surrey St.)
Surrey St. CR0: C'don 2C 168
E13 . . . . .3K 87
WC2 . . . . .2H 13 (7K 83)
Surrey Ter. SE17 . . . . .5E 102

Surrey Water Rd.
SE16 . . . . .1K 103
Surridge Cl. SW9 . . . . .2J 119
(off Clapham Rd.)
Surridge Gdns. SE19 . . . . .6D 138
Surr St. N7 . . . . .5J 65
Sury Basin KT2: King T 1E 150
Susan Cl. RM7: Mawney 3J 55
Susan Constant Ct. E14 . . . . .7F 87
(off Newport Av.)
Susan Lawrence Ho. E3 . . . . .2A 86
(off Zealand Rd.)
E12 . . . . .4E 70
(off Walton Rd.)
Susannah St. E14 . . . . .6D 86
Susan Rd. SE3 . . . . .2K 123
Susan Wood BR7: Chst 1E 160
Sussex Av. TW7: Isle 3J 113
Sussex Cl. IG4: Ilf 5D 52
KT3: N Mald 4A 152
N19 . . . . .2J 65
TW1: Twick 6B 114
SE10 . . . . .6E 104
(off Roan St.)
W2 . . . . .1A 10
(off Spring St.)
Sussex Cres. UB5: N'olt 6E 58
Sussex Gdns. KT9: Chess 6D 162
N4 . . . . .5C 48
N6 . . . . .5D 46
W2 . . . . .2A 10 (7B 82)
Sussex Ga. N6 . . . . .5D 46
Sussex Ho. NW1 . . . . .2H 83
(off Chalton St.)
Sussex Lodge W2 . . . . .1B 10
(off Sussex Pl.)
Sussex Mans. NW7 . . . . .4A 16
SW7 . . . . .4A 16
WC2 . . . . .2F 13
(off Maiden La.)
Sussex M. SE6 . . . . .7C 122
Sussex M. E. W2 . . . . .1B 10
Sussex M. W. W2 . . . . .2B 10 (7B 82)
Sussex Pl. KT3: N Mald 4A 152
NW1 . . . . .3E 4 (4D 82)
W2 . . . . .1B 10 (6B 82)
W6 . . . . .5E 98
Sussex Ring N12 . . . . .5D 30
Sussex Rd.
BR4: W W'ck 1D 170
CR2: S Croy 6D 168
CR4: Mitc 5J 155
DA8: Erith 7H 109
DA14: Sidc 5B 144
E6 . . . . .1E 88
HA1: Harr 5G 41
KT3: N Mald 4A 152
SM5: Cars 6D 166
UB2: S'hall 3B 94
UB10: Ick 4E 56
Sussex Sq. W2 . . . . .2B 10 (7B 82)
Sussex St. E13 . . . . .3K 87
SW1 . . . . .6K 17 (5F 101)
Sussex Ter. SE20 . . . . .7J 139
(off Graveney Gro.)
Sussex Way EN4: Cockf 5K 21
N7 . . . . .2J 65
N19 . . . . .1H 65
(not continuous)
Sutcliffe Cl. NW11 . . . . .5K 45
Sutcliffe Ho. UB3: Hayes 6J 75
Sutcliffe Pk. Athletics Track 5A 124
Sutcliffe Rd. DA16: Well 2C 126
SE18 . . . . .6J 107
Sutherland Av.
BR5: St M Cry 6K 161
DA16: Well 4J 125
TW16: Sun 2H 147
UB3: Hayes 4J 93
W9 . . . . .4J 81
W13 . . . . .6B 78
Sutherland Cl. EN5: Barn 4B 20

Sutherland Ct.—Sycamore Cl.

Sutherland Ct. N16 . . . 3D 66
NW9 . . . 5H 43
W9 . . . 4J 81
(off Marylands Rd.)
Sutherland Dr. SW19 . . . 1B 154
Sutherland Gdns. KT4: Wor Pk . . . 1D 164
SW14 . . . 3A 116
TW16: Sun . . . 2H 147
Sutherland Gro. SW18 . . . 6G 117
TW11: Tedd . . . 5J 131
Sutherland Ho. IG8: Wfd G . . . 7K 37
W8 . . . 3K 99
Sutherland Pl. W2 . . . 6J 81
Sutherland Rd. CR0: C'don . . . 7A 156
DA17: Belv . . . 3G 109
E3 . . . 2B 86
E17 . . . 2K 49
EN3: Pond E . . . 6E 24
N9 . . . 1C 34
N17 . . . 7B 34
UB1: S'hall . . . 6D 76
W4 . . . 6A 98
W13 . . . 6A 78
Sutherland Rd. Path E17 . . . 3K 49
Sutherland Row SW1 . . . 5K 17 (5F 101)
Sutherland Sq. SE17 . . . 5C 102
Sutherland St. SW1 . . . 5J 17 (5F 101)
Sutherland Wlk. SE17 . . . 5C 102
Sutlej Rd. SE7 . . . 7A 106
Sutterton St. N7 . . . 6K 65
SUTTON . . . 5K 165
Sutton Arena Leisure Cen. . . . 7A 154
Sutton Cl. BR3: Beck . . . 1D 158
HA5: Eastc . . . 5J 39
IG10: Lough . . . 1H 37
W4 . . . 6J 97
(off Sutton La. Sth.)
Sutton Comn. Rd. SM1: Sutt . . . 7H 153
SM3: Sutt . . . 7H 153
Sutton Ct. KT8: W Mole . . . 5D 148
SE19 . . . 7F 139
SM2: Sutt . . . 6A 166
W4 . . . 6J 97
W5 . . . 1E 96
Sutton Ct. Rd. E13 . . . 3A 88
SM1: Sutt . . . 6A 166
UB10: Hil . . . 1D 74
W4 . . . 7J 97
Sutton Cres. EN5: Barn . . . 5A 20
Sutton Dene TW3: Houn . . . 1F 113
Sutton Ecology Cen. . . . 4D 166
Sutton Est. EC1 . . . 2F 9
SW3 . . . 5D 16 (5C 100)
W10 . . . 5E 80
Sutton Estate, The N1 . . . 7B 66
Sutton Gdns.
CR0: C'don . . . 5F 157
IG11: Bark . . . 1J 89
Sutton Grn. IG11: Bark . . . 1J 89
(off Sutton Rd.)
Sutton Gro. SM1: Sutt . . . 4B 166
Sutton Hall Rd.
TW5: Hest . . . 7E 94
Sutton Hgts. SM2: Sutt . . . 7B 166
Sutton La. EC1 . . . 4B 8
(off Gt. Sutton St.)
TW3: Houn . . . 3D 112
Sutton La. Nth. W4 . . . 5J 97
Sutton La. Sth. W4 . . . 6J 97
Sutton Pde. NW4 . . . 4E 44
(off Church Rd.)
Sutton Pk. Rd. SM1: Sutt . . . 6K 165
Sutton Pl. E9 . . . 5J 67
Sutton Rd. E13 . . . 4H 87
E17 . . . 1K 49
IG11: Bark . . . 2J 89
N10 . . . 1E 46
TW5: Hest . . . 1E 112
Sutton Row W1 . . . 7D 6 (6H 83)
Suttons Bus. Pk.
RM13: Rain . . . 3K 91
Sutton Sq. E9 . . . 5J 67
TW5: Hest . . . 1D 112
Sutton St. E1 . . . 7J 85
Sutton's Way EC1 . . . 4D 8
Suttons Wharf E2 . . . 3K 85
Sutton Tennis Academy . . . 1K 165
Sutton United FC . . . 4J 165
Sutton Wlk. SE1 . . . 5H 13 (1K 101)
Sutton Way
TW5: Hest . . . 1D 112
W10 . . . 4E 80
SW1 Gallery . . . 1A 18 (3G 101)
Swaby Rd. SW18 . . . 1A 136
Swaffam Ct.
RM6: Chad H . . . 6C 54
Swaffham Way N22 . . . 7G 33
Swaffield Rd. SW18 . . . 7K 117
Swain Cl. SW16 . . . 6F 137
Swain Rd. CR7: Thor H . . . 5C 156
Swains Cl.
UB7: W Dray . . . 2A 92
Swain's La. N6 . . . 1E 64
Swainson Rd. W3 . . . 2B 98
Swains Rd. SW17 . . . 7D 136
Swain St. NW8 . . . 3C 4 (4C 82)
Swakeleys Dr. UB10: Ick . . . 4C 56
Swakeleys Rd. UB10: Ick . . . 4A 56
SWAKELEYS RDBT. . . . 4A 56
Swalecliffe Rd.
DA17: Belv . . . 5H 109
Swaledale Cl. N11 . . . 6K 31
Swallands Rd. SE6 . . . 3C 140
(not continuous)
Swallow Cl. DA8: Erith . . . 1K 127
SE14 . . . 1K 121
WD23: Bush . . . 1B 26
Swallow Ct. HA4: Ruis . . . 1A 58
IG2: Ilf . . . 5F 53
SE1 . . . 7D 14
(off Swan St.)
SE12 . . . 7J 123
W9 . . . 5J 81
(off Admiral Wlk.)
Swallow Dr. NW10 . . . 6K 61
UB5: N'olt . . . 2E 76
Swallowfield NW1 . . . 2K 5
(off Munster Sq.)
Swallowfield Rd. SE7 . . . 5K 105
Swallowfield Way
UB3: Hayes . . . 2F 93
Swallow Gdns. SW16 . . . 5H 137
Swallow Ho. NW8 . . . 2C 82
(off Allitsen Rd.)
Swallow Pk. KT6: Surb . . . 3F 163
Swallow Pk. Cl.
KT6: Surb . . . 3F 163
Swallow Pas. W1 . . . 1K 11
(off Swallow Pl.)
Swallow Pl. E14 . . . 6B 86
(off Newell St.)
W1 . . . 1K 11 (6F 83)
Swallow St. E6 . . . 5C 88
W1 . . . 3B 12 (7G 83)
Swallowtail Ho. E20 . . . 5E 68
(off Sunrise Cl.)
SWAN, THE . . . 2E 170
Swanage Ct. N1 . . . 7E 66
(off Hertford Rd.)
Swanage Ho. SW8 . . . 7K 101
(off Dorset Rd.)
Swanage Rd. E4 . . . 7K 35
SW18 . . . 6A 118
Swanage Waye
UB4: Yead . . . 6A 76
Swan & Pike Rd. EN3: Enf L . . . 1H 25
Swan App. E6 . . . 5C 88
Swanbourne Ho. NW8 . . . 3C 4
(off Capland St.)
Swanbridge Rd. DA7: Bex . . . 1G 127
Swan Centre, The
SW17 . . . 3K 135
Swan Cl. CR0: C'don . . . 7E 156
E17 . . . 1A 50
TW13: Hanw . . . 4C 130
Swan Ct. E1 . . . 3K 15
(off Star Pl.)
E14 . . . 6B 86
(off Agnes St.)
HA4: Ruis . . . 7F 39
SW3 . . . 6D 16 (5C 100)
SW6 . . . 7J 99
(off Fulham Rd.)
TW7: Isle . . . 3B 114
(off Swan St.)
Swandon Way SW18 . . . 4K 117
Swan Dr. NW9 . . . 2A 44
Swanfield St. E2 . . . 2J 9 (3F 85)
Swan Ho. E15 . . . 7G 69
(off Broadway)
EN3: Pond E . . . 5D 24
N1 . . . 7D 66
(off Oakley Rd.)
Swan Island TW1: Twick . . . 3A 132
Swan La. EC4 . . . 3F 15 (7D 84)
N20 . . . 3F 31
Swanley Ho. SE17 . . . 5E 102
(off Kinglake Est.)
Swanley Rd. DA16: Well . . . 1C 126
Swan Mead SE1 . . . 3E 102
Swan M. CR4: Mitc . . . 1D 154
RM7: Mawney . . . 4H 55
SW6 . . . 1H 117
SW9 . . . 2K 119
Swann Ct. TW7: Isle . . . 3A 114
(off South St.)
Swanne Ho. SE10 . . . 7E 104
(off Gloucester Cir.)
Swan Pas. E1 . . . 3K 15
Swan Path KT1: King T . . . 3F 151
Swan Pl. SW13 . . . 2B 116
Swan Rd. SE16 . . . 2J 103
SE18 . . . 3B 106
TW13: Hanw . . . 5C 130
UB1: S'hall . . . 6F 77
UB7: W Dray . . . 2A 92
Swan Sanctuary, The . . . 6G 147
Swanscombe Ho. W11 . . . 1F 99
(off St Ann's Rd.)
Swanscombe Rd. W4 . . . 5A 98
W11 . . . 1F 99
Swansea Ct. E16 . . . 1F 107
(off Fishguard Way)
Swansea Rd. EN3: Pond E . . . 4D 24
TW14: Felt . . . 6E 110
Swansland Gdns. E17 . . . 1A 50
Swansmere Cl. KT12: Walt T . . . 7A 148
Swan St.
SE1 . . . 7D 14 (3C 102)
TW7: Isle . . . 3B 114
Swanton Ct. SE13 . . . 3D 122
Swanton Gdns. SW19 . . . 1F 135
Swanton Rd. DA8: Erith . . . 7G 109
Swan Wlk. SW3 . . . 7E 16 (6D 100)
TW17: Shep . . . 7G 147
Swan Way EN3: Enf H . . . 2E 24
Swanwick Cl. SW15 . . . 7B 116
Swan Yd. N1 . . . 6B 66
Sward Rd. BR5: St M Cry . . . 6K 161
Swathling Ho. SW15 . . . 6B 116
(off Tunworth Cres.)
Swaton Rd. E3 . . . 4C 86
Swaylands Rd.
DA17: Belv . . . 6G 109
Swaythling Cl. N18 . . . 4C 34
Swedeland Ct. E1 . . . 6H 9
Swedenborg Gdns. E1 . . . 7H 85
Sweden Ga. SE16 . . . 3A 104
Swedish Quays SE16 . . . 3A 104
(not continuous)
Sweeney Cres. SE1 . . . 7K 15 (2F 103)
Sweetbriar Av.
SM5: Cars . . . 1D 166
Sweet Briar Grn. N9 . . . 3A 34
Sweet Briar Gro. N9 . . . 3A 34
Sweet Briar Wlk. N18 . . . 4A 34
Sweetcroft La. UB10: Hil . . . 7B 56
Sweetland Ct. RM8: Dag . . . 6B 72
Sweetmans Av. HA5: Pinn . . . 3B 40
Sweets Way N20 . . . 2G 31
Swell Ct. E17 . . . 6C 50
Swetenham Wlk. SE18 . . . 5G 107
Swete St. E13 . . . 2J 87
Sweyn Pl. SE3 . . . 2J 123
Swift Cen. CR0: Wadd . . . 7K 167
Swift Cl. E17 . . . 7F 35
HA2: Harr . . . 2F 59
SE28 . . . 7B 90
UB3: Hayes . . . 6H 75
Swift Ct. SM2: Sutt . . . 7K 165
Swift Ho. E3 . . . 1B 86
(off Old Ford Rd.)
NW6 . . . 2H 81
(off Albert Rd.)
Swift Lodge W9 . . . 5J 81
(off Admiral Wlk.)
Swift Rd. TW13: Hanw . . . 3C 130
UB2: S'hall . . . 3E 94
Swiftsden Way BR1: Brom . . . 6G 141
Swift St. SW6 . . . 1H 117
Swinbrook Rd. W10 . . . 5G 81
Swinburne Ct. SE5 . . . 4D 120
(off Basingdon Way)
Swinburne Cres. CR0: C'don . . . 6J 157
Swinburne Ho. E2 . . . 3J 85
(off Roman Rd.)
Swinburne Rd. SW15 . . . 4C 116
Swinderby Rd. HA0: Wemb . . . 6E 60
Swindon Cl. IG3: Ilf . . . 2J 71
Swindon Rd.
TW6: H'row A . . . 5E 110
Swindon St. W12 . . . 1D 98
Swinfield Cl. TW13: Hanw . . . 3C 130
Swinford Gdns. SW9 . . . 3B 120
Swingate La. SE18 . . . 6J 107
Swingfield Ho. E9 . . . 1J 85
(off Templecombe Rd.)
Swinley Ho. NW1 . . . 1K 5
(off Redhill St.)
Swinnerton St. E9 . . . 5A 68
Swinson Ho. N11 . . . 5B 32
Swinton Cl. HA9: Wemb . . . 1H 61
Swinton Pl. WC1 . . . 1G 7 (3K 83)
Swinton St. WC1 . . . 1G 7 (3K 83)
Swires Shaw BR2: Kes . . . 4B 172
SWISS COTTAGE . . . 7B 64
Swiss Cottage Sports Cen. . . . 7B 64
Swiss Ct. W1 . . . 3D 12
Swiss Ter. NW6 . . . 7B 64
Switch Ho. E14 . . . 7F 87
Swithland Gdns. SE9 . . . 4E 142
Swyncombe Av. W5 . . . 4B 96
Swynford Gdns. NW4 . . . 4C 44
Sybil M. N4 . . . 6B 48
Sybil Phoenix Cl. SE8 . . . 5K 103
Sybil Thorndike Casson Ho. SW5 . . . 5J 99
(off Kramer M.)
Sybourn St. E17 . . . 7B 50
Sycamore Av. DA15: Sidc . . . 6K 125
E3 . . . 1B 86
UB3: Hayes . . . 7G 75
W5 . . . 3D 96
Sycamore Cl.
CR2: S Croy . . . 5E 168
E16 . . . 4G 87
EN4: E Barn . . . 6G 21
HA8: Edg . . . 4D 28
N9 . . . 4B 34
SE9 . . . 2C 142
SM5: Cars . . . 4D 166
TW13: Felt . . . 3J 129
UB5: N'olt . . . 1C 76
UB7: Yiew . . . 7B 74
W3 . . . 1A 98

Sycamore Ct. *DA8: Erith* 5K **109**
(off Sandcliff Rd.)
   E7 . . . . .6J **69**
   KT3: N Mald 3A **152**
   NW6 . . . . .1J **81**
(off Bransdale Cl.)
   SE1 . . . . .7G **15**
(off Royal Oak Yd.)
   TW4: Houn 4C **112**
Sycamore Gdns.
   CR4: Mitc 2B **154**
   N15 . . . . .4F **49**
   W6 . . . . .2D **98**
Sycamore Gro.
   KT3: N Mald 3K **151**
   NW9 . . . . .7J **43**
   SE6 . . . . .6E **122**
   SE20 . . . . .1G **157**
Sycamore Hill N11 . . . . .6K **31**
Sycamore Ho. BR2: Brom 2G **159**
   IG9: Buck H 2G **37**
   N2 . . . . .2B **46**
(off The Grange)
   SE16 . . . . .2K **103**
(off Woodland Cres.)
   W6 . . . . .2D **98**
Sycamore Lodge BR6: Orp 2K **173**
   TW16: Sun 7H **129**
   W8 . . . . .3K **99**
(off Stone Hall Pl.)
Sycamore M. *DA8: Erith* 5K **109**
(off St John's Rd.)
   SW4 . . . . .3G **119**
Sycamore Path E17 . . . . .6D **50**
(off Poplars Rd.)
Sycamore Pl. BR1: Brom 3E **160**
Sycamore Rd. SW19 . . . . .6E **134**
Sycamore St. EC1 . . . . . .4C **8** (4D **84**)
Sycamore Wlk. IG6: Ilf 4G **53**
   W10 . . . . .4G **81**
Sycamore Way
   CR7: Thor H 5A **156**
   TW11: Tedd 6C **132**
Sydcote SE21 . . . . .1C **138**
SYDENHAM 4J **139**
Sydenham Av. N21 . . . . .5E **22**
   SE26 . . . . .5H **139**
Sydenham Cotts. SE12 . . . . .2A **142**
Sydenham Ct. CR0: C'don 1D **168**
(off Sydenham Rd.)
Sydenham Hill S
   E23 . . . . .1H **139**
   SE26 . . . . .4F **139**
Sydenham Hill Local Nature Reserve
   . . . . .2G **139**
Sydenham Pk. SE26 . . . . .3J **139**
Sydenham Pk. Mans. SE26 . . . . .3J **139**
(off Sydenham Pk.)
Sydenham Pk. Rd. SE26 . . . . . . .3J **139**
Sydenham Pl. SE27 . . . . .3B **138**
Sydenham Ri. SE23 . . . . .2H **139**
Sydenham Rd.
   CR0: C'don 1C **168**
   SE26 . . . . .4J **139**
Sydmons Ct. SE23 . . . . .7J **121**
Sydner M. N16 . . . . .4F **67**
Sydner Rd. N16 . . . . .4F **67**
Sydney Chapman Way
   EN5: Barn 2C **20**
Sydney Cl. SW3 . . . . . . .4B **16** (4B **100**)
Sydney Ct. UB4: Yead 4A **76**
Sydney Cres.
   TW15: Ashf 6D **128**
Sydney Gro. NW4 . . . . .5E **44**
Sydney M. SW3 . . . . . . .4B **16** (4B **100**)
Sydney Pl. SW7 . . . . . . .4B **16** (4B **100**)
Sydney Rd. DA6: Bex 4D **126**
   DA14: Sidc 4J **143**
   E11 . . . . .6K **51**
   EN2: Enf 4J **23**
   IG6: Ilf 2G **53**

Sydney Rd.
   IG8: Wfd G 4D **36**
   N8 . . . . .4A **48**
   N10 . . . . .1E **46**
   SE2 . . . . .3C **108**
   SM1: Sutt 4J **165**
   SW20 . . . . .2F **153**
   TW9: Rich 4E **114**
   TW11: Tedd 5K **131**
   TW14: Felt 1J **129**
   W13 . . . . .1A **96**
Sydney Russell Leisure Cen. . . .5E **72**
Sydney St. SW3 . . . . . .5C **16** (5C **100**)
Sylvana Cl. UB10: Hil 1B **74**
Sylvan Av. N3 . . . . .2J **45**
   N22 . . . . .7E **32**
   NW7 . . . . .6F **29**
   RM6: Chad H 6F **55**
Sylvan Cl. N12 . . . . .3E **30**
   NW6 . . . . .1K **81**
(off Abbey Rd.)
Sylvan Est. SE19 . . . . .1F **157**
Sylvan Gdns. KT6: Surb 7D **150**
Sylvan Gro. NW2 . . . . .4F **63**
   SE15 . . . . .6H **103**
Sylvan Hill SE19 . . . . .1E **156**
Sylvan Rd. E7 . . . . .6K **69**
   E11 . . . . .5J **51**
   E17 . . . . .5C **50**
   IG1: Ilf 2G **71**
   SE19 . . . . .1F **157**
Sylvan Ter. SE15 . . . . .6H **103**
(off Sylvan Gro.)
Sylvan Wlk. BR1: Brom 3D **160**
Sylvan Way
   BR4: W W'ck 4G **171**
   RM8: Dag 4B **72**
Sylverdale Rd. CR0: C'don 3B **168**
Sylvester Av. BR7: Chst 6D **142**
Sylvester Path E8 . . . . .6H **67**
Sylvester Rd. E8 . . . . .6H **67**
   E17 . . . . .7B **50**
   HA0: Wemb 5C **60**
   N2 . . . . .2A **46**
Sylvestrian Leisure Cen. 4G **51**
Sylvestrus Cl. KT1: King T 1G **151**
Sylvia Cl. HA9: Wemb 7H **43**
   N1 . . . . .2D **84**
(off Wenlock St.)
Sylvia Gdns. HA9: Wemb 7H **61**
Sylvia Pankhurst Ho. RM10: Dag 3G **73**
(off Wythenshawe Rd.)
Symes M. NW1 . . . . .2G **83**
Symington Ho. SE1 . . . . .3D **102**
(off Deverell St.)
Symington M. E9 . . . . .5K **67**
Symister M. N1 . . . . .2G **9**
Symons Cl. SE15 . . . . .2J **121**
Symons St. SW3 . . . . . .4F **17** (4D **100**)
Syon Cl. E11 . . . . .5K **51**
Syon Ga. Way TW8: Bford 7A **96**
Syon La. TW7: Isle 6J **95**
Syon Lodge SE12 . . . . .7J **123**
Syon Park 1C **114**
Syon Pk. Gdns. TW7: Isle 7K **95**
Syringa Ho. SE4 . . . . .3B **122**

T

Tabard Ct. E14 . . . . .6E **86**
(off Lodore St.)
Tabard Gdn. Est. SE1 . . . . . . .7E **14** (3D **102**)
Tabard Ho. SE1 . . . . .7F **15**
(off Manciple St.)
Tabard St. SE1 . . . . .6D **14** (2D **102**)
Tabard Theatre 4A **98**
Tabernacle, The 6H **81**
(off Powis Sq.)

Tabernacle Av. E13 . . . . .4J **87**
Tabernacle Gdns. E2 . . . . .3F **85**
(off Hackney Rd.)
Tabernacle St. EC2 . . . . . .4F **9** (4D **84**)
Tableer Av. SW4 . . . . .5G **119**
Tabley Rd. N7 . . . . .4J **65**
Tabor Cl.
   SM3: Cheam 6G **165**
Tabor Gdns.
   SM3: Cheam 6H **165**
Tabor Gro. SW19 . . . . .7H **135**
Tabor Rd. W6 . . . . .3D **98**
Tachbrook Est.
   SW1 . . . . .6C **18** (5H **101**)
Tachbrook M. SW1 . . . . .3A **18** (4G **101**)
Tachbrook Rd.
   TW14: Felt 7H **111**
   UB2: S'hall 4B **94**
   UB7: W Dray 1A **92**
Tachbrook St. SW1 . . . .4B **18** (4G **101**)
Tack M. SE4 . . . . .3C **122**
Tadema Ho. NW8 . . . . .4B **4**
Tadema Rd. SW10 . . . . .7A **100**
Tadlow KT1: King T 3G **151**
(off Washington Rd.)
Tadmor Cl. TW16: Sun 4H **147**
Tadmor St. W12 . . . . .1F **99**
Tadworth Av.
   KT3: N Mald 4B **152**
Tadworth Ho. SE1 . . . . .7A **14**
Tadworth Rd. NW2 . . . . .2C **62**
Taeping St. E14 . . . . .4D **104**
Taffeta Ho. E20 . . . . .5E **68**
(off De Coubertin St.)
Taff Ho. KT2: King T 1D **150**
(off Henry Macaulay Av.)
Taffrail Ho. E14 . . . . .5D **104**
(off Burrells Wharf Sq.)
Taffy's How CR4: Mitc 3C **154**
Taft Way E3 . . . . .3D **86**
Taggs Ho. KT1: King T 2D **150**
(off Market Sq.)
Taggs Island TW12: Hamp 2H **149**
Tagore Cl. HA3: W'stone 3K **41**
Tagwright Ho. N1 . . . . .2E **8**
(off Westland Pl.)
Tailor Ho. WC1 . . . . .4F **7**
(off Colonnade)
Tailworth St. E1 . . . . .6K **9**
(off Chicksand St.)
Tait Cl. E3 . . . . .1B **86**
(off St Stephen's Rd.)
   SW8 . . . . .1J **119**
(off Lansdowne Grn.)
Tait Ho. SE1 . . . . .5K **13**
(off Greet St.)
Tait Rd. CR0: C'don 7E **156**
Tait Rd. Ind. Est. CR0: C'don 7E **156**
(off Tait Rd.)
Tait St. E1 . . . . .6H **85**
Taj Apartments E1 . . . . .5K **9**
(off Brick La.)
Takeley Cl. RM5: Col R 2K **55**
Takhar M. SW11 . . . . .2C **118**
Talacre Community Sports Cen. . . .6E **64**
Talacre Rd. NW5 . . . . .6E **64**
Talbot Av. N2 . . . . .3B **46**
Talbot Cl.
   CR4: Mitc 4G **155**
   N15 . . . . .4F **49**
Talbot Ct. EC3 . . . . .2F **15**
   NW9 . . . . .3K **61**
Talbot Cres. NW4 . . . . .5C **44**
Talbot Gdns.
   IG3: Ilf 2A **72**
Talbot Gro. Ho. W11 . . . . .6G **81**
(off Lancaster Rd.)
Talbot Ho. E14 . . . . .6D **86**
(off Giraud St.)
   N7 . . . . .3A **66**
Talbot Pl. SE3 . . . . .2G **123**

Talbot Rd. CR7: Thor H 4D **156**
   E6 . . . . .2E **88**
   E7 . . . . .4J **69**
   HA0: Wemb 6D **60**
   HA3: W'stone 2K **41**
   N6 . . . . .6E **46**
   N15 . . . . .4F **49**
   N22 . . . . .2G **47**
   RM9: Dag 6F **73**
   SE22 . . . . .4E **120**
   SM5: Cars 5E **166**
   TW2: Twick 1J **131**
   TW7: Isle 4A **114**
   TW15: Ashf 5A **128**
   UB2: S'hall 4C **94**
   W2 . . . . .6H **81**
   W11 . . . . .6H **81**
(not continuous)
   W13 . . . . .1A **96**
Talbot Sq. W2 . . . . .1B **10** (6B **82**)
Talbot Wlk. NW10 . . . . .6A **62**
   W11 . . . . .6G **81**
(off St Mark's Rd.)
Talbot Yd. SE1 . . . . .5E **14** (1D **102**)
Talcott Path SW2 . . . . .1A **138**
Talehangers Cl. DA6: Bex 4D **126**
Talfourd Pl. SE15 . . . . .1F **121**
Talfourd Rd. SE15 . . . . .1F **121**
Talgarth Mans. W14 . . . . .5G **99**
(off Talgarth Rd.)
Talgarth Rd. W6 . . . . .5F **99**
   W14 . . . . .5F **99**
Talgarth Wlk. NW9 . . . . .5A **44**
Talia Ho. E14 . . . . .3E **104**
(off Manchester Rd.)
Talina Cen. SW6 . . . . .1A **118**
Talisman Cl. IG3: Ilf 1B **72**
Talisman Sq. SE26 . . . . .4G **139**
Talisman Way HA9: Wemb 3F **61**
Tallack Cl. HA3: Hrw W 7D **26**
Tallack Rd. E10 . . . . .1B **68**
Tall Elms Cl. BR2: Brom 5H **159**
Talleyrand Ho. SE5 . . . . .2C **120**
(off Lilford Rd.)
Tallis Cl. E16 . . . . .6K **87**
Tallis Gro. SE7 . . . . .6K **105**
Tallis St. EC4 . . . . .2K **13** (7A **84**)
Tallis Vw. NW10 . . . . .6A **61**
Tallow Cl. RM9: Dag 7D **72**
Tallow Rd. TW8: Bford 6C **96**
Tall Trees SW16 . . . . .3K **155**
Talma Gdns. TW2: Twick 6J **113**
Talmage Cl. SE23 . . . . .7J **121**
Talman Gro. HA7: Stan 6J **27**
Talma Rd. SW2 . . . . .4A **120**
Talwin St. E3 . . . . .3D **86**
Tamar Cl. E3 . . . . .1B **86**
Tamar Ho. E14 . . . . .2E **104**
(off Plevna St.)
   SE11 . . . . .5K **19**
(off Kennington La.)
Tamarind Ct. SE1 . . . . .6K **15**
   W8 . . . . .3K **99**
(off Stone Hall Gdns.)
Tamarind Ho. SE15 . . . . .7G **103**
(off Reddins Rd.)
Tamarind Yd. E1 . . . . .1G **103**
(off Kennet St.)
Tamarisk Sq. W12 . . . . .7B **80**
Tamar Sq. IG8: Wfd G 6E **36**
Tamar St. SE7 . . . . .3C **106**
Tamar Way N17 . . . . .3F **49**
Tamesis Gdns. KT4: Wor Pk 2A **164**
Tamian Ind. Est. TW4: Houn 4A **112**
Tamian Way TW4: Houn 4A **112**
Tamworth Av. IG8: Wfd G 6B **36**
Tamworth La. CR4: Mitc 2F **155**
Tamworth Pk. CR4: Mitc 4F **155**
Tamworth Pl. CR0: C'don 2C **168**
Tamworth Rd. CR0: C'don 2B **168**
Tamworth St. SW6 . . . . .6J **99**

Tamworth Vs. CR4: Mitc 4F 155
Tancred Rd. N4 . . . .6B 48
Tandem Cen. SW19 . . . .1B 154
Tandem Way SW19 . . . .1B 154
Tandridge Dr. BR6: Orp 1H 173
Tandridge Pl. BR6: Orp 1H 173
Tanfield Av. NW2 . . . .4B 62
Tanfield Rd. CR0: C'don 4C 168
Tangerine Ho. SE1 . . . .7F 15
(off Long La.)
Tangier Rd. TW10: Rich 4G 115
Tangleberry Cl. BR1: Brom 4D 160
Tangle Tree Cl. N3 . . . .2K 45
Tanglewood Cl. CR0: C'don 3J 169
HA7: Stan 2D 26
UB10: Hil 4C 74
Tanglewood Way TW13: Felt 3K 129
Tangley Gro. SW15 . . . .6B 116
Tangley Pk. Rd.
TW12: Hamp 6D 130
Tanglyn Av. TW17: Shep 5D 146
Tangmere N17 . . . .2D 48
(off Willan Rd.)
WC1 . . . .2G 7
(off Sidmouth St.)
Tangmere Gdns. UB5: N'olt 2A 76
Tangmere Gro. KT2: King T 5D 132
Tangmere Way NW9 . . . .2A 44
Tan Ho. E9 . . . .5A 68
(off Sadler Pl.)
Tanhouse Fld. NW5 . . . .5H 65
(off Torriano Av.)
Tanhurst Ho. SW2 . . . .7K 119
(off Redlands Way)
Tanhurst Wlk. SE2 . . . .3D 108
(off Alsike Rd.)
Tankerton Ho's. WC1 . . . .2F 7
(off Tankerton St.)
Tankerton Rd. KT6: Surb 2F 163
Tankerton St. WC1 . . . .2F 7 (3J 83)
Tankerton Ter. CR0: C'don 6K 155
Tankerville Cl. TW3: Houn 3G 113
Tankerville Rd. SW16 . . . .7H 137
Tankridge Rd. NW2 . . . .2D 62
Tanner Ho. E1 . . . .5K 85
(off White Horse La.)
SE1 . . . .7H 15
(off Tanner St.)
Tanneries, The E1 . . . .4J 85
(off Cephas Av.)
Tanner Point E13 . . . .1J 87
(off Pelly Rd.)
Tanners Cl. KT12: Walt T 6K 147
Tanners End La. N18 . . . .4K 33
Tanner's Hill SE8 . . . .1B 122
Tanners La. IG6: Ilf 3G 53
Tanners M. SE8 . . . .1B 122
(off Tanner's Hill)
Tanner St. IG11: Bark 6G 71
SE1 . . . .7H 15 (2E 102)
Tanners Yd. E2 . . . .2H 85
(off Treadway St.)
Tannery, The SE1 . . . .2E 102
(off Black Swan Yd.)
Tannery Cl. BR3: Beck 5K 157
RM10: Dag 3H 73
Tannery Ho. E1 . . . .5G 85
(off Deal St.)
Tannington Ter. N5 . . . .3B 66
Tannsy Sq. SE27 . . . .4D 138
Tannsfeld Rd. SE26 . . . .5K 139
Tansley Cl. N7 . . . .5H 65
Tanswell St. SE1 . . . .7J 13 (2A 102)
Tansy Cl. E6 . . . .6E 88
Tantallon Rd. SW12 . . . .1E 136
Tant Av. E16 . . . .6H 87
Tantony Gro. RM6: Chad H 3D 54
Tanworth Gdns. HA5: Pinn 2K 39
Tanyard Ho. TW8: Bford 7C 96
(off High St.)
Tanyard La. DA5: Bexl 7G 127

Tanza Rd. NW3 . . . .4D 64
Tapestry Bldg. EC2 . . . .6H 9
(off New St.)
Tapestry Cl. SM2: Sutt 7K 165
Tapley Cl. E1 . . . .6E 86
Tapley Ho. SE1 . . . .7K 15
(off Wolseley St.)
Taplow NW3 . . . .7B 64
SE17 . . . .5D 102
(off Thurlow St.)
Taplow Ct. CR4: Mitc 4C 154
Taplow Ho. E2 . . . .2G 9
(off Palissy St.)
Taplow Rd. N13 . . . .4H 33
Taplow St. N1 . . . .1D 8 (2C 84)
Tapper Wlk. N1 . . . .1J 83
Tappesfield Rd. SE15 . . . .3J 121
Tapping Cl. KT2: King T 7G 133
Tapp St. E1 . . . .4H 85
Tapster St. EN5: Barn 3C 20
Tara Arts Cen. 1A 136
Tara Ct. BR3: Beck 2D 158
Tara Ho. E14 . . . .4C 104
(off Deptford Ferry Rd.)
Tara M. N8 . . . .6J 47
Taransay Wlk. N1 . . . .6D 66
Tarbert M. N15 . . . .5E 48
Tarbert Rd. SE22 . . . .5E 120
Tarbert Wlk. E1 . . . .7J 85
Target Cl. TW14: Felt 6G 111
Target Ho. W13 . . . .1B 96
(off Sherwood Cl.)
TARGET RDBT. 1D 76
Tariff Cres. SE8 . . . .4B 104
Tariff Rd. N17 . . . .6B 34
Tarleton Ct. N22 . . . .2A 48
Tarleton Gdns. SE23 . . . .2H 139
Tarling Cl. DA14: Sidc 3B 144
Tarling Rd. E16 . . . .6H 87
N2 . . . .2A 46
Tarling St. E1 . . . .6H 85
Tarling St. Est. E1 . . . .6J 85
Tarmac Way UB7: Harm 3C 174
Tarnbank EN2: Enf 5D 22
Tarnbrook Ct. SW1 . . . .4G 17
(off Holbein Pl.)
Tarns, The NW1 . . . .1A 6
(off Varndell St.)
Tarn St. SE1 . . . .3C 102
Tarnwood Pk. SE9 . . . .7D 124
Tarplett Ho. SE14 . . . .6K 103
(off John Williams Cl.)
Tarquin Ho. SE26 . . . .4G 139
(off High Level Dr.)
Tarragon Cl. SE14 . . . .7A 104
Tarragon Cl. IG1: Ilf 2J 71
Tarragon Gro. SE26 . . . .6K 139
Tarranbrae NW6 . . . .7G 63
Tarrant Ho. E2 . . . .3J 85
(off Roman Rd.)
W14 . . . .3G 99
(off Russell Rd.)
Tarrant Pl. W1 . . . .6E 4 (5D 82)
Tarrington Cl. SW16 . . . .3H 137
Tartan Ho. E14 . . . .6E 86
(off Dee St.)
Tarver Rd. SE17 . . . .5B 102
Tarves Way SE10 . . . .7D 104
(Lit. Cottage Pl.)
SE10 . . . .7D 104
(Norman Rd.)
Taryn Gro. BR1: Brom 3D 160
Tash Pl. N11 . . . .5A 32
Tasker Cl.
UB3: Harl 7E 92
Tasker Ho. E14 . . . .5B 86
(off Wallwood St.)
IG11: Bark 2H 89
Tasker Lodge W8 . . . .2J 99
(off Campden Hill)
Tasker Rd. NW3 . . . .5D 64

Tasman Ct. E14 . . . .4D 104
(off Westferry Rd.)
TW16: Sun 7G 129
Tasman Ho. E1 . . . .1H 103
(off Clegg St.)
Tasmania Ter. N18 . . . .6H 33
Tasman Rd. SW9 . . . .3J 119
Tasman Wlk. E16 . . . .6B 88
Tasso Rd. W6 . . . .6G 99
Tasso Yd. W6 . . . .6G 99
(off Tasso Rd.)
Tatam Rd. NW10 . . . .7K 61
Tatchbury Ho. SW15 . . . .6B 116
(off Tunworth Cres.)
Tate Apartments E1 . . . .6H 85
(off Sly St.)
Tate Britain 4E 18 (4J 101)
Tate Ho. E2 . . . .2K 85
(off Mace St.)
Tate Modern 4B 14 (1B 102)
Tate Rd. E16 . . . .1D 106
(not continuous)
SM1: Sutt 5J 165
Tatham Pl. NW8 . . . .2B 82
Tatnell Rd. SE23 . . . .6A 122
Tatsfield Ho. SE1 . . . .7F 15
(off Pardoner St.)
Tattersall Cl. SE9 . . . .5C 124
Tatton Cl. SM5: Wall 1E 166
Tatton Cres. N16 . . . .7F 49
Tatum St. SE17 . . . .4D 102
Tauheed Cl. N4 . . . .2C 66
Taunton Av. SW20 . . . .2D 152
TW3: Houn 2G 113
Taunton Cl. DA7: Bex 2K 127
SM3: Sutt 1J 165
Taunton Dr. EN2: Enf 3F 23
N2 . . . .2A 46
Taunton Ho. W2 . . . .6A 82
(off Hallfield Est.)
Taunton M. NW1 . . . .4E 4 (4D 82)
Taunton Pl. NW1 . . . .3E 4 (4D 82)
Taunton Rd.
SE12 . . . .5G 123
UB6: G'frd 1F 77
Taunton Way
HA7: Stan 2E 42
Tavern Cl. SM5: Cars 7C 154
Tavern Ct. SE1 . . . .3C 102
(off New Kent Rd.)
Taverners Cl. W11 . . . .1G 99
Taverners Ct. E3 . . . .3A 86
(off Grove Rd.)
Taverner Sq. N5 . . . .4C 66
Taverners Way E4 . . . .1B 36
Tavern La. SW9 . . . .2A 120
Tavern Quay SE16 . . . .4A 104
Tavistock Av. E17 . . . .3K 49
NW7 . . . .7A 30
UB6: G'frd 2A 78
Tavistock Cl. N16 . . . .5E 66
TW18: Staines 7A 128
Tavistock Ct. CR0: C'don 1D 168
(off Tavistock Rd.)
WC1 . . . .3D 6
(off Tavistock Sq.)
WC2 . . . .2F 13
(off Tavistock St.)
Tavistock Cres. CR4: Mitc 4J 155
W11 . . . .5H 81
(not continuous)
Tavistock Gdns. IG3: Ilf 4J 71
Tavistock Ga. CR0: C'don 1D 168
Tavistock Gro. CR0: C'don 7D 156
Tavistock Ho. IG8: Wfd G 6D 36
WC1 . . . .3D 6 (4H 83)
(off Tavistock Sq.)
Tavistock M. N19 . . . .3J 65
(off Tavistock Ter.)
W11 . . . .6H 81
Tavistock Pl. N14 . . . .6A 22
WC1 . . . .3E 6 (4J 83)

Tavistock Rd. BR2: Brom 4H 159
CR0: C'don 1D 168
DA16: Well 1C 126
E7 . . . .4H 69
E15 . . . .6F 69
E18 . . . .3J 51
HA8: Edg 1G 43
N4 . . . .6D 48
NW10 . . . .2B 80
SM5: Cars 1B 166
UB7: Yiew 1A 92
UB10: Ick 5F 57
W11 . . . .6H 81
Tavistock Sq. WC1 . . . .3D 6 (4H 83)
Tavistock St. WC2 . . . .2F 13 (7J 83)
Tavistock Ter. N19 . . . .3H 65
Tavistock Twr. SE16 . . . .3A 104
Tavistock Wlk. SM5: Cars 1B 166
Taviton St. WC1 . . . .3C 6 (4H 83)
Tavy Bri. SE2 . . . .2C 108
Tavy Cl. SE11 . . . .5K 19
Tawney Rd. SE28 . . . .7B 90
Tawny Cl. TW13: Felt 3J 129
W13 . . . .1B 96
Tawny Way SE16 . . . .4K 103
Tayben Av. TW2: Twick 6J 113
Tayberry Ho. E20 . . . .6D 68
(off Ravens Wlk.)
Taybridge Rd. SW11 . . . .3E 118
Tay Bldgs. SE1 . . . .7G 15
Tayburn Cl. E14 . . . .6E 86
Tay Ct. E2 . . . .3K 85
(off Meath Cres.)
SE1 . . . .7G 15
(off Decima St.)
Tayfield Cl. UB10: Ick 3F 57
Tay Ho. E3 . . . .2B 86
(off St Stephen's Rd.)
Tayler Cl. NW8 . . . .1B 82
Taylor Av. TW9: Kew 2H 115
Taylor Cl. BR6: Orp 4K 173
N17 . . . .7B 34
SE8 . . . .6B 104
TW3: Houn 1G 113
TW12: Hamp H 5G 131
Taylor Ct. SE20 . . . .2J 157
(off Elmers End Rd.)
Taylor Ho. E14 . . . .7C 86
(off Storehouse M.)
Taylor Pl. E3 . . . .2D 86
Taylor Rd. CR4: Mitc 7C 136
SM6: Wall 5F 167
Taylors Bldgs. SE18 . . . .4F 107
Taylors Cl. DA14: Sidc 3K 143
Taylors Ct. TW13: Felt 2J 129
Taylors Grn. W3 . . . .6A 80
Taylors La. EN5: Barn 1C 20
NW10 . . . .6A 62
SE26 . . . .4H 139
Taylors Mead NW7 . . . .5H 29
Taylors Yd. E1 . . . .4K 9
(off Brick La.)
Taymount Grange SE23 . . . .2J 139
Taymount Ri. SE23 . . . .2J 139
Tayport Cl. N1 . . . .7J 65
Tayside Cl. SE5 . . . .4D 120
Tayside Dr. HA8: Edg 3C 28
Taywood Rd. UB5: N'olt 4D 76
Tazzeta Ho. E20 . . . .5E 68
(off Victory Pde.)
Teak Cl. SE16 . . . .1A 104
Tealby Ct. N7 . . . .6K 65
Teal Cl. E16 . . . .5B 88
Teal Ct. E1 . . . .1K 15
(off Star Pl.)
NW10 . . . .6K 61
SE8 . . . .6B 104
(off Taylor Cl.)
SM6: Wall 5G 167
Teal Dr. HA6: Nwood 1E 38

Teale St. E2 . . . . 2G 85
Tealing Dr. KT19: Ewe 4K 163
Teal Pl. SM1: Sutt 5H 165
Teal St. SE10 . . . . 3H 105
Teamsport Karting
Edmonton 4E 34
Teasel Cl. CR0: C'don 1K 169
Teasel Cres. SE28 . . . . 1J 107
Teasel Way E15 . . . . 3G 87
Tea Trade Wharf SE1 . . . . 6K 15
(off Shad Thames)
Tea Tree Cl. TW15: Ashf 5E 128
Tebworth Rd. N17 . . . . 7A 34
Technology Park, The NW9 . . . . 3A 44
Teck Cl. TW7: Isle 2A 114
Tedder Cl. HA4: Ruis 5J 57
KT9: Chess 5C 162
UB10: Uxb 7B 56
Tedder Rd. CR2: Sels 7J 169
TEDDINGTON 5A 132
Teddington Bus. Pk. TW11: Tedd . . . 6K 131
(off Station Rd.)
Teddington Lock 4B 132
Teddington Pk. TW11: Tedd 5K 131
Teddington Pk. Rd.
TW11: Tedd 4K 131
Teddington Pool & Fitness Cen. 5A 132
Teddington Sports Cen. 6D 132
Teddy Bear Collection 6K 135
(within Polka Theatre for Children)
Ted Hennem Ho. RM10: Dag 3H 73
Ted Roberts Ho. E2 . . . . 2H 85
(off Parmiter St.)
Tedworth Gdns. SW3 . . . . . 6E 16 (5D 100)
Tedworth Sq. SW3 . . . . 6E 16 (5D 100)
Tee, The W3 . . . . 6A 80
Tees Av. UB6: G'frd 2J 77
Tees Cl. W7 . . . . 6H 77
(off Hanway Rd.)
Teesdale Av. TW7: Isle 1A 114
Teesdale Cl. E2 . . . . 2G 85
Teesdale Gdns. SE25 . . . . 2E 156
TW7: Isle 1A 114
Teesdale Rd. E11 . . . . 6H 51
Teesdale St. E2 . . . . 2H 85
Teesdale Yd. E2 . . . . 2H 85
(off Teesdale St.)
Teeswater Ct. DA18: Erith 3D 108
Teevan Cl. CR0: C'don 7G 157
Teevan Rd. CR0: C'don 1G 169
Tegan Cl. SM2: Sutt 7J 165
Teign M. SE9 . . . . 2C 142
Teignmouth Cl. HA8: Edg 2F 43
SW4 . . . . 4H 119
Teignmouth Gdns. UB6: G'frd 2A 78
Teignmouth Pde. UB6: G'frd 2A 78
Teignmouth Rd. DA16: Well 2C 126
NW2 . . . . 5F 63
Telcote Way HA4: Ruis 7A 40
Telegraph Hill NW3 . . . . 3K 63
Telegraph La. KT10: Clay 4A 162
Telegraph M. IG3: Ilf 1A 72
Telegraph Pas. SW2 . . . . 7J 119
(off New Pk. Rd.)
Telegraph Path BR7: Chst 5F 143
Telegraph Pl. E14 . . . . 4D 104
Telegraph Rd. SW15 . . . . 7D 116
Telegraph St. EC2 . . . . 7E 8 (6D 84)
Telemann Sq. SE3 . . . . 4K 123
Telephone Pl. SW6 . . . . 6H 99
Telfer Cl. W3 . . . . 2J 97
Telfer Ho. EC1 . . . . 2B 8
Telferscot Rd. SW12 . . . . 1H 137
Telford Av. SW2 . . . . 1H 137
Telford Cl. E17 . . . . 7A 50
SE19 . . . . 6F 139
Telford Dr. KT12: Walt T 7A 148
Telford Ho. SE1 . . . . 3C 102
(off Tiverton St.)
W10 . . . . 5G 81
(off Portobello Rd.)

Telford Rd. N11 . . . . 5B 32
NW9 . . . . 6C 44
SE9 . . . . 2H 143
TW2: Whitt 7E 112
UB1: S'hall 7F 77
W10 . . . . 5G 81
Telfords Yd. E1 . . . . 7G 85
Telford Ter. SW1 . . . . 7A 18 (6G 101)
Telford Way UB4: Yead 5C 76
W3 . . . . 5A 80
Telham Rd. E6 . . . . 2E 88
Tell Gro. SE22 . . . . 4F 121
Tellson Av. SE18 . . . . 1B 124
Telscombe Cl. BR6: Orp 2J 173
Temair Ho. SE10 . . . . 7D 104
(off Tarves Way)
Temeraire Pl. TW8: Bford 5E 96
Temeraire St. SE16 . . . . 2J 103
Tempelhof Av. NW2 . . . . 7E 44
NW4 . . . . 7E 44
Temperley Rd. SW12 . . . . 7E 118
Templar Ct. NW8 . . . . 2A 4
RM7: Mawney 4H 55
Templar Dr. SE28 . . . . 6D 90
Templar Ho. HA2: Harr 2G 59
NW2 . . . . 6H 63
Templar Pl. TW12: Hamp 7E 130
Templars Av. NW11 . . . . 6H 45
Templars Cres. N3 . . . . 2J 45
Templars Dr. HA3: Hrw W 6C 26
Templars Ho. E16 . . . . 7F 89
(off University Way)
Templar St. SE5 . . . . 2B 120
Temple Av. CR0: C'don 2B 170
EC4 . . . . 2K 13 (7A 84)
N20 . . . . 7G 21
RM8: Dag 1G 73
Temple Bar 1J 13
Temple Bar Gate 1B 14
(off Paternoster Sq.)
Temple Chambers EC4 . . . . 2K 13
Temple Cl. E11 . . . . 7G 51
N3 . . . . 2J 45
SE28 . . . . 3G 107
Templecombe Rd. E9 . . . . 1J 85
Templecombe Way
SM4: Mord 5G 153
Temple Ct. E1 . . . . 5K 85
(off Rectory Sq.)
SW8 . . . . 7J 101
(off Thorncroft St.)
Templecroft TW15: Ashf 6F 129
Temple Dwellings E2 . . . . 2H 85
(off Temple St.)
TEMPLE FORTUNE 5H 45
Temple Fortune Hill NW11 . . . . 5J 45
Temple Fortune La. NW11 . . . . 6H 45
Temple Fortune Pde. NW11 . . . . 5H 45
Temple Gdns. EC4 . . . . 2J 13
N21 . . . . 2G 33
NW11 . . . . 6H 45
RM8: Dag 3D 72
Temple Gro. EN2: Enf 2G 23
NW11 . . . . 6J 45
Temple Hall Ct. E4 . . . . 2A 36
Temple La. EC4 . . . . 1K 13 (6A 84)
Templeman Rd. W7 . . . . 5K 77
Temple Mead Cl.
HA7: Stan 6G 27
Templemead Cl. W3 . . . . 6A 80
Templemead Ho. E9 . . . . 4A 68
TEMPLE MILLS 4D 68
Temple Mills La. E10 . . . . 4D 68
E15 . . . . 5E 68
E20 . . . . 5E 68
Temple of Mithras (remains) 1E 14
(off Queen Victoria St.)
Temple Pde. EN5: New Bar 7G 21
(off Netherlands Rd.)
Temple Pk. UB8: Hil 3C 74
Temple Pl. WC2 . . . . 2H 13 (7K 83)

Temple Rd. CR0: C'don 4D 168
E6 . . . . 1C 88
N8 . . . . 4K 47
NW2 . . . . 4E 62
TW3: Houn 4F 113
TW9: Rich 2F 115
W4 . . . . 3J 97
W5 . . . . 3D 96
Temple Sheen SW14 . . . . 4J 115
Temple Sheen Rd. SW14 . . . . 4H 115
Temple St. E2 . . . . 2H 85
Temple Ter. N22 . . . . 2A 48
(off Vincent Rd.)
Templeton Av. E4 . . . . 4H 35
Templeton Cl. N15 . . . . 6D 48
N16 . . . . 5E 66
SE19 . . . . 1D 156
Templeton Ct. EN3: Enf W 1D 24
Templeton Pl. SW5 . . . . 4J 99
Templeton Rd. N15 . . . . 6D 48
Temple Way SM1: Sutt 3B 166
Temple West M. SE11 . . . . 3B 102
Templewood W13 . . . . 5B 78
Templewood Av. NW3 . . . . 3K 63
Templewood Gdns. NW3 . . . . 3K 63
Templewood Point NW2 . . . . 2H 63
(off Granville Rd.)
Temple Yd. E2 . . . . 2H 85
(off Temple St.)
Tempo Ho. UB5: N'olt 3B 76
Tempsford Cl. EN2: Enf 4H 23
Tempsford Ct. HA1: Harr 6K 41
Tempus Apartments EC1 . . . . 1A 8
(off Goswell Rd.)
Tempus Ct. E18 . . . . 1J 51
Tempus Wharf SE16 . . . . 2G 103
(off Bermondsey Wall W.)
Temsford Cl. HA2: Harr 2G 41
Tenbury Cl. E7 . . . . 5B 70
Tenbury Ct. SW2 . . . . 1H 137
Tenby Av. HA3: Kenton 2B 42
Tenby Cl. N15 . . . . 4F 49
RM6: Chad H 6E 54
Tenby Ct. E17 . . . . 5A 50
Tenby Gdns. UB5: N'olt 6E 58
Tenby Ho. UB3: Harl 3E 92
W2 . . . . 6A 82
(off Hallfield Est.)
Tenby Mans. W1 . . . . 5H 5
(off Nottingham St.)
Tenby Rd. DA16: Well 1D 126
E17 . . . . 5A 50
EN3: Pond E 4D 24
HA8: Edg 1F 43
RM6: Chad H 6E 54
Tench St. E1 . . . . 1H 103
Tenda Rd. SE16 . . . . 4H 103
Tendring Way RM6: Chad H 5C 54
Tenham Av. SW2 . . . . 1H 137
Tenison Ct. W1 . . . . 2A 12 (7G 83)
Tenison Way SE1 . . . . 5J 13
Tenniel Cl. W2 . . . . 7A 82
Tennis Cl. La. KT8: E Mos 3K 149
Tennison Rd. SE25 . . . . 4F 157
Tennis St. SE1 . . . . 6E 14 (2D 102)
Tenniswood Rd. EN1: Enf 1K 23
Tennyson CR0: C'don 1C 168
N8 . . . . 3J 47
(off Boyton Cl.)
Tennyson Av. E11 . . . . 7J 51
E12 . . . . 7C 70
KT3: N Mald 5D 152
NW9 . . . . 3J 43
TW1: Twick 1K 131
Tennyson Cl. DA16: Well 1J 125
EN3: Pond E 5E 24
TW14: Felt 6H 111
Tennyson Ct. NW1 . . . . 4E 4
(off Dorset Sq.)
SW6 . . . . 1A 118
(off Imperial Rd.)

Tennyson Ho. DA17: Belv 5F 109
SE17 . . . . 5C 102
(off Browning St.)
Tennyson Mans. SW3 . . . . 7C 16
(off Lordship Pl.)
W14 . . . . 6H 99
(off Queen's Club Gdns.)
Tennyson Rd. E10 . . . . 1D 68
E15 . . . . 7G 69
E17 . . . . 6B 50
NW6 . . . . 1H 81
NW7 . . . . 5H 29
SE20 . . . . 7K 139
SW19 . . . . 6A 136
TW3: Houn 2G 113
TW15: Ashf 5A 128
W7 . . . . 7K 77
Tennyson St. SW8 . . . . 2F 119
Tenpin
Acton 4G 79
Bexleyheath 4F 127
Croydon 2K 167
Feltham 2K 129
Kingston upon Thames 2E 150
(within The Rotunda Cen.)
Tensing Ct. TW19: Stanw 1A 128
Tensing Rd. UB2: S'hall 3E 94
Tentelow La. UB2: S'hall 5E 94
Tenterden Cl. NW4 . . . . 3F 45
SE9 . . . . 4D 142
Tenterden Dr. NW4 . . . . 3F 45
Tenterden Gdns. CR0: C'don 7G 157
NW4 . . . . 3F 45
Tenterden Gro. NW4 . . . . 3F 45
Tenterden Ho. SE17 . . . . 5E 102
(off Surrey Gro.)
Tenterden Rd. CR0: C'don 7G 157
N17 . . . . 7A 34
RM8: Dag 2F 73
Tenterden St. W1 . . . . 1K 11 (6F 83)
Tenter Ground E1 . . . . 6J 9 (5F 85)
Tenter Pas. E1 . . . . 1K 15
(off Nth. Tenter St.)
Tent Peg La. BR5: Pet W 5G 161
Tent St. E1 . . . . 4H 85
Tenzing Ct. E14 . . . . 5D 86
(off Hillary M.)
Tequila Wharf E14 . . . . 6A 86
Tera 40 UB6: G'frd 7G 59
Terborch Way SE22 . . . . 5E 120
Teredo St. SE16 . . . . 3K 103
Terence Ct. DA17: Belv 6F 109
(off Nuxley Rd.)
Terence McMillan Stadium 4A 88
Terence Messenger Twr. E10 . . . . . . 2D 68
(off Alpine Rd.)
Teresa M. E17 . . . . 4C 50
Teresa Wlk. N10 . . . . 5F 47
Terling Cl. E11 . . . . 3H 69
Terling Ho. W10 . . . . 5E 80
(off Sutton Way)
Terling Rd. RM8: Dag 2G 73
Terling Wlk. N1 . . . . 1C 84
(off Popham St.)
TERMINAL 4 RDBT. 6E 110
TERMINAL 5 RDBT. 5C 174
Terminal Ho. HA7: Stan 5J 27
Terminus Pl. SW1 . . . . 2K 17 (3F 101)
Terrace, The E2 . . . . 3J 85
(off Old Ford Rd.)
E4 . . . . 3B 36
(off Newgate St.)
EC4 . . . . 1K 13
IG8: Wfd G 6D 36
N3 . . . . 2H 45
NW6 . . . . 1J 81
SE8 . . . . 4B 104
(off Longshore,
SE23 . . . . 2A 140
SW13 . . . . 2A 116
Terrace Apartments N5 . . . . 5A 66

Terrace Gdns. SW13 . . . . .2B 116
Terrace Hill CRO: C'don 3B 168
   (off Hanover St.)
Terrace La. TW10: Rich 6E 114
Terrace Rd. E9 . . . . .7J 67
  E13 . . . . .2J 87
  KT12: Walt T 7J 147
Terraces, The E2 . . . . .2G 85
   (off Garner St.)
  NW8 . . . . .2A 4
   (off Queen's Ter.)
Terrace Wlk. RM9: Dag 5E 72
  SW11 . . . . .7H 17 (7D 100)
Terrano Ho. TW9: Kew 7H 97
Terrapin Rd. SW17 . . . . .3F 137
Terretts Pl. N1 . . . . .7B 66
   (off Upper St.)
Terrick Rd. N22 . . . . .1J 47
Terrick St. W12 . . . . .6D 80
Terrilands HA5: Pinn 3D 40
Territorial Ho. SE11 . . . . .4K 19
Terront Rd. N15 . . . . .4C 48
Terry Spinks Pl. E16 . . . . .5G 87
   (off Barking Rd.)
Tersha St. TW9: Rich 4F 115
Tesla Ct. W3 . . . . .2A 98
Tessa Sanderson Pl. SW8 . . . . .3F 119
   (off Daley Thompson Way)
Tessa Sanderson Way UB6: G'frd 5H 59
Testerton Rd. W11 . . . . .7F 81
   (off Hurstway Wlk.)
Testerton Wlk. W11 . . . . .7F 81
Testwood Ct. W7 . . . . .7J 77
Tetbury Pl. N1 . . . . .1B 84
Tetcott Rd. SW10 . . . . .7A 100
   (not continuous)
Tetherdown N10 . . . . .3E 46
Tetty Way BR1: Brom 2J 159
Tevatree Ho. SE1 . . . . .5G 103
   (off Old Kent Rd.)
Teversham La. SW8 . . . . .1J 119
Teviot Cl. DA16: Well 1B 126
Teviot Est. E14 . . . . .5D 86
Teviot St. E14 . . . . .5E 86
Tewkesbury Av. HA5: Pinn 5C 40
  SE23 . . . . .1H 139
Tewkesbury Cl. EN4: E Barn 4G 21
  N15 . . . . .6D 48
Tewkesbury Gdns. NW9 . . . . .3H 43
Tewkesbury Rd. N15 . . . . .6D 48
  SM5: Cars 1B 166
  W13 . . . . .1A 96
Tewkesbury Ter. N11 . . . . .6B 32
Tewson Rd. SE18 . . . . .5J 107
   (off Southgate Rd.)
Textile Ho. E1 . . . . .5K 85
   (off Duckett St.)
Teynham Av. EN1: Enf 6J 23
Teynham Ct. BR3: Beck 3D 158
Teynham Grn. BR2: Brom 5J 159
Teynton Ter. N17 . . . . .1C 48
Thackeray Av. N17 . . . . .2G 49
Thackeray Cl. SW19 . . . . .7F 135
  TW7: Isle 2A 114
  UB8: Hil .6D 74
Thackeray Ct. NW6 . . . . .7A 64
   (off Fairfax Rd.)
  SW3 . . . . .5E 16
   (off Elystan Pl.)
  W5 . . . . .6F 79
   (off Hanger Va. La.)
  W14 . . . . .4G 99
   (off Blythe Rd.)
Thackeray Dr. RM6: Chad H 7A 54
Thackeray Ho. WC1 . . . . .3E 6
Thackeray Lodge
  TW14: Bedf 6F 111
Thackeray M. E8 . . . . .6G 67
Thackeray Rd. E6 . . . . .2B 88
  SW8 . . . . .2F 119

Thackeray St. W8 . . . . .3K 99
Thackery Ct. EC1 . . . . .5A 8
   (off Turnmill St.)
Thackrah Cl. N2 . . . . .2A 46
   (off Simms Gdns.)
Thakeham Cl. SE26 . . . . .4H 139
Thalia Cl. SE10 . . . . .6F 105
Thalia Ct. E8 . . . . .7F 67
   (off Albion Dr.)
Thame Rd. SE16 . . . . .2K 103
Thames Av. KT4: Wor Pk 1E 164
  RM9: Dag, Rain 4H 91
  SW10 .1A 118
  UB6: G'frd 2K 77
Thames Bank SW14 . . . . .2J 115
Thamesbank Pl. SE28 . . . . .6C 90
Thames Barrier 2B 106
Thames Barrier Ind. Area SE18 . . . . .3B 106
   (off Faraday Way)
Thames Barrier Pk. 2A 106
Thames Barrier Vis. Cen. 3B 106
Thamesbrook SW3 . . . . .6C 16
Thames Circ. E14 . . . . .4C 104
Thames Cl. TW12: Hamp 2F 149
Thames Cotts. KT7: T Ditt 6B 150
Thames Ct. KT8: W Mole 2F 149
  NW6 . . . . .2H 81
   (off Albert Rd.)
  SE15 . . . . .7F 103
   (off Daniel Gdns.)
  W7 . . . . .6J 77
   (off Hanway Rd.)
Thames Cres. W4 . . . . .7A 98
THAMES DITTON 6A 150
Thames Dr. HA4: Ruis 6E 38
Thames Exchange Bldg. EC4 . . . . . . .3D 14
Thames Eyot TW1: Twick 1A 132
Thamesfield Ct. TW17: Shep 7E 146
Thamesfield M. TW17: Shep 7E 146
Thamesgate Cl. TW10: Ham 4B 132
Thames Gateway RM9: Dag 2F 91
  RM13: Rain 2F 91
Thames Gateway Pk.
  RM9: Dag 3F 91
Thames Haven KT6: Surb 5D 150
Thames Hgts. SE1 . . . . .6J 15
   (off Gainsford St.)
Thameshill Av. RM5: Col R 2J 55
Thames Ho. EC4 . . . . .2D 14
   (off Queen St. Pl.)
  KT1: King T 4D 150
   (off Surbiton Rd.)
  SW1 . . . . .3E 18
   (off Millbank)
Thameside KT8: W Mole 3F 149
  TW11: Tedd 7D 132
Thameside Cen. TW8: Bford 6F 97
Thameside Ind. Est. E16 . . . . .2B 106
Thameside Pl. KT1: Hamp W 1D 150
Thameside Wlk. SE28 . . . . .6A 90
Thames Innovation Cen.
  DA18: Erith 2F 109
Thames Lock KT12: Walt T 3A 148
THAMESMEAD 1B 108
Thamesmead KT12: Walt T 6J 147
THAMESMEAD CENTRAL 1A 108
THAMESMEAD EAST 2F 109
THAMESMEAD NORTH 6D 90
Thames Mdw. KT8: W Mole 2E 148
  TW17: Shep 7F 147
THAMESMEAD SOUTH 2D 108
THAMESMEAD SOUTH WEST 2K 107
THAMESMEAD WEST 3G 107
Thamesmere Dr. SE28 . . . . .7A 90
Thamesmere Leisure Cen. 7A 90
Thames Path SE7 . . . . .3J 105
  SE10 . . . . .1G 105
Thames Pl. SW15 . . . . .3F 117
Thames Point SW6 . . . . .2A 118
Thamespoint
  TW11: Tedd 7D 132

Thames Quay E14 . . . . .2D 104
  SW10 .1A 118
   (off Chelsea Harbour)
Thames Reach KT1: Hamp W 1D 150
  SE28 . . . . .2J 107
  W6 . . . . .6E 98
   (off Rainville Rd.)
Thames Rd. E16 . . . . .1B 106
  IG11: Bark 3K 89
  W4 . . . . .6G 97
Thames Rd. Ind. Est. E16 . . . . .1B 106
Thames Side KT1: King T 1D 150
  KT7: T Ditt 6B 150
Thames St. KT1: King T 2D 150
  KT12: Walt T 7H 147
  SE10 . . . . .6D 104
  TW12: Hamp 1F 149
  TW16: Sun 4J 147
Thames Tunnel Mills SE16 . . . . .2J 103
Thamesvale Ct. TW3: Houn 3E 112
Thames Vw. IG1: Ilf 2G 71
   (off Axon Pl.)
Thamesview Bus. Cen.
  RM13: Rain 5K 91
Thamesview Golf Course 6E 90
Thamesview Ho's.
  KT12: Walt T 6J 147
Thames Vw. Lodge IG11: Bark 3J 89
Thames Village W4 . . . . .1J 115
Thames Wlk. KT12: Walt T 7J 147
   (off Manor Rd.)
  SW11 .7C 100
Thames Wharf Studios W6 . . . . .6E 98
   (off Rainville Rd.)
Thanescroft Gdns. CRO: C'don 3E 168
Thanet Cl. W3 . . . . .6G 79
Thanet Dr. BR2: Kes 3B 172
Thanet Ho. CRO: C'don 2E 6
   (off Coombe Rd.)
  WC1 . . . . .2E 6
   (off Thanet St.)
Thanet Lodge NW2 . . . . .6G 63
   (off Mapesbury Rd.)
Thanet Pl. CRO: C'don 4C 168
Thanet Rd. DA5: Bexl 7G 127
Thanet St. WC1 . . . . .2E 6 (3J 83)
Thanet Wharf SE8 . . . . .6D 104
   (off Copperas St.)
Thane Vs. N7 . . . . .3K 65
Thane Works N7 . . . . .3K 65
Thanington Ct. SE9 . . . . .6J 125
Thant Cl. E10 . . . . .3D 68
Tharp Rd. SM6: Wall 5H 167
Thatcham Ct. N20 . . . . .7F 21
Thatcham Gdns. N20 . . . . .7F 21
Thatcher Cl. UB7: W Dray 2A 92
Thatchers Way TW7: Isle 5H 113
Thatches Gro. RM6: Chad H 4E 54
Thavie's Inn EC4 . . . . .7K 7 (6A 84)
Thaxted Ct. N1 . . . . .1E 8
   (off Murray Gro.)
Thaxted Ho. RM10: Dag 7H 73
  SE16 . . . . .4J 103
   (off Abbeyfield Est.)
Thaxted Pl. SW20 . . . . .7F 135
Thaxted Rd. IG9: Buck H 1H 37
  SE9 . . . . .3G 143
Thaxton Pl. E4 . . . . .1A 36
Thaxton Rd. W14 . . . . .6H 99
Thayers Farm Rd.
  BR3: Beck 1A 158
Thayer St. W1 . . . . .6H 5 (6E 82)
The . . . .
   Names prefixed with 'The'
   for example 'The Acacias'
   are indexed under the main
   name such as 'Acacias, The'
Theatre Bldg. E3 . . . . .3C 86
   (off Paton Cl.)
Theatre Pl. SE8 . . . . .7C 104
   (off Speedwell St.)

Theatre-Rites 2B 102
   (off Blackfriars Rd.)
Theatre Royal
  Drury Lane 2G 13
   (off Catherine St.)
  Haymarket 3D 12
   (off Haymarket)
  Stratford 7F 69
Theatre Sq. E15 . . . . .6F 69
Theatre St. SW11 . . . . .3D 118
Theatre Vw. Apartments SE1 . . . . . . .6K 13
   (off Short St.)
Theatro Technis 1G 83
   (off Crowndale Rd.)
Theatro Twr. SE8 . . . . .6C 104
Theberton St. N1 . . . . .1A 84
Theed St. SE1 . . . . .5K 13 (1A 102)
Thelbridge Ho. E3 . . . . .3D 86
   (off Bruce Rd.)
Thelma Gdns. SE3 . . . . .1B 124
Thelma Gro. TW11: Tedd 6A 132
Theobald Cres. HA3: Hrw W 1G 41
Theobald Rd. CRO: C'don 2B 168
  E17 . . . . .7B 50
Theobalds Av. N12 . . . . .4F 31
Theobalds Ct. N4 . . . . .3C 66
Theobald's Rd. WC1 . . . . . . .5G 7 (5K 83)
Theobald St. SE1 . . . . .3D 102
Theodora Way HA5: Eastc 3H 39
Theodore Ct. SE13 . . . . .6F 123
Theodore Rd. SE13 . . . . .6F 123
Therapia La. CRO: Bedd 7H 155
  CRO: C'don 6J 155
Therapia Rd. SE22 . . . . .6J 121
Theresa Rd. W6 . . . . .4C 98
Therfield Ct. N4 . . . . .2C 66
Thermopylae Ga. E14 . . . . .4D 104
Theseus Wlk. N1 . . . . .1B 8
Thesiger Rd. SE20 . . . . .7K 139
Thessaly Ho. SW8 . . . . .7G 101
   (off Thessaly Rd.)
Thessaly Rd. SW8 . . . . .7G 101
   (not continuous)
Thesus Ho. E14 . . . . .6E 86
   (off Blair St.)
Thetford Cl. N13 . . . . .6G 33
Thetford Gdns. RM9: Dag 7E 72
Thetford Ho. SE1 . . . . .7J 15
   (off St Saviour's Est.)
Thetford Rd. KT3: N Mald 6K 151
  RM9: Dag 7D 72
  TW15: Ashf 4A 128
Thetis Ter. TW9: Kew 6G 97
Theven St. E1 . . . . .4J 85
Theydon Gro. IG8: Wfd G 6F 37
Theydon Rd. E5 . . . . .2J 67
Theydon St. E17 . . . . .7B 50
Thicket, The UB7: Yiew 6A 74
Thicket Cres. SM1: Sutt 4A 166
Thicket Gro. RM9: Dag 6C 72
  SE20 . . . . .7G 139
Thicket Rd. SE20 . . . . .7G 139
  SM1: Sutt 4A 166
Third Av. E12 . . . . .4C 70
  E13 . . . . .3J 87
  E17 . . . . .5C 50
  EN1: Enf 5A 24
  HA9: Wemb 2D 60
  RM6: Chad H 6C 54
  RM10: Dag 1H 91
  UB3: Hayes 1H 93
  W3 . . . . .1B 98
  W10 . . . . .3G 81
Third Cl. KT8: W Mole 4G 149
Third Cross Rd.
  TW2: Twick 2H 131
Third Way HA9: Wemb 4H 61
Thirleby Rd. HA8: Edg 1K 43
  NW7 . . . . .5B 30
  SW1 . . . . .2B 18 (3G 101)
Thirlestane Ct. N10 . . . . .2E 46

Thirlmere NW1 .1K **5**
    (off Cumberland Mkt.)
Thirlmere Av. UB6: G'frd 3C **78**
Thirlmere Gdns. HA9: Wemb 1C **60**
Thirlmere Ho. N16 . . . . .4D **66**
    (off Howard Rd.)
  TW7: Isle 5K **113**
Thirlmere Ri. BR1: Brom 6H **141**
Thirlmere Rd. DA7: Bex 1J **127**
  N10 . . . . .1F **47**
  SW16 . . . . .4H **137**
Thirsk Cl. UB5: N'olt 6E **58**
Thirsk Rd. CR4: Mitc 7E **136**
  SE25 . . . . .4D **156**
  SW11 . . . . .3E **118**
Thirza Ho. E1 .6J **85**
    (off Devonport St.)
Thistlebrook SE2 . . . . .3C **108**
Thistlebrook Ind. Est. SE2 . . . . .3C **108**
Thistle Ct. SE12 . . . . .2J **141**
Thistlecroft Gdns. HA7: Stan 1D **42**
Thistledene KT7: T Ditt 6J **149**
Thistledene Av. HA2: Harr 3C **58**
Thistlefield Cl. DA5: Bexl 1F **145**
Thistle Gro. SW10 . . . . .6A **16** (5A **100**)
Thistle Ho. E14 . . . . .6E **86**
    (off Dee St.)
Thistlemead BR7: Chst 2F **161**
Thistlewaite Rd. E5 . . . . .3H **67**
Thistlewood Cl. N7 . . . . .2K **65**
Thistleworth Cl. TW7: Isle 7H **95**
Thistleworth Marina TW7: Isle 4B **114**
    (off Railshead Rd.)
Thistley Cl. N12 . . . . .6H **31**
Thistley Ct. SE8 . . . . .6D **104**
Thomas A Beckett Cl. HA0: Wemb . . .4K **59**
Thomas Baines Rd. SW11 . . . . .3B **118**
Thomas Burt Ho. E2 . . . . .3H **85**
    (off Canrobert St.)
Thomas Ct. IG6: Ilf 4G **53**
Thomas Cribb M. E6 . . . . .6E **88**
Thomas Darby Ct. W11 . . . . .6G **81**
    (off Lancaster Rd.)
Thomas Dean Rd. SE26 . . . . .4B **140**
Thomas Dinwiddy Rd.
  SE12 . . . . .2K **141**
Thomas Doyle St. SE1 . . . . .7A **14** (3B **102**)
Thomas Dr. UB8: Uxb 6A **56**
Thomas England Ho. RM7: Rom 6K **55**
    (off Waterloo Gdns.)
Thomas Frye Ct. E15 . . . . .2D **86**
    (off High St.)
Thomas Fyre Dr. E3 . . . . .2C **86**
Thomas Hardy Ho. N22 . . . . .7E **32**
Thomas Hewlett Ho.
  HA1: Harr 4J **59**
Thomas Hollywood Ho. E2 . . . . .2J **85**
    (off Approach Rd.)
Thomas Ho. SM2: Sutt 7K **165**
Thomas Jacomb Pl. E17 . . . . .4B **50**
Thomas Joseph Ho. SE4 . . . . .5K **121**
    (off St Norbert Rd.)
Thomas La. E6 . . . . .7C **122**
Thomas Lodge E17 . . . . .5D **50**
Thomas More Highwalk EC2 . . . . .6C **8**
    (off Aldersgate St.)
Thomas More Ho. EC2 . . . . .6C **8**
  HA4: Ruis 1G **57**
Thomas More Sq. E1 . . . . .7G **85**
Thomas More St. E1 . . . . .7G **85**
Thomas More Way N2 . . . . .3A **46**
Thomas Neal's Cen. WC2 . . . .1E **12** (6J **83**)
Thomas Pl. W8 . . . . .3K **99**
Thomas Rd. E14 . . . . .6B **86**
Thomas Rd. Ind. Est. E14 . . . . .5C **86**
    (not continuous)
Thomas Spencer Hall of Residence
  SE18 . . . . .4E **106**
    (off Grand Depot Rd.)
Thomas St. SE18 . . . . .4F **107**
Thomas Tallis Sports Cen. 3K **123**

Thomas Twr. E8 . . . . .6F **67**
    (off Dalston Sq.)
Thomas Turner Path CR0: C'don 2C **168**
    (off George St.)
Thomas Wall Cl. SM1: Sutt 5K **165**
Thomas Watson Cott. Homes
  EN5: Barn 4B **20**
    (off Leecroft Rd.)
Thompson Av. TW9: Rich 3G **115**
Thompson Cl. IG1: Ilf 2G **71**
  SM3: Sutt 1J **165**
Thompson Ho. SE14 . . . . .6G **103**
    (off John Williams Cl.)
  W10 . . . . .4G **81**
    (off Wornington Rd.)
Thompson Rd. RM9: Dag 3F **73**
  SE22 . . . . .6F **121**
  TW3: Houn 4F **113**
  UB10: Uxb 7A **56**
Thompson's Av. SE5 . . . . .7C **102**
Thomson Cres. CR0: C'don 1A **168**
Thomson Ho. E14 . . . . .6C **86**
    (off Saracen St.)
  SE17 . . . . .4E **102**
    (off Tatum St.)
  SW1 . . . . .6D **18**
  UB1: S'hall 7C **76**
    (off The Broadway)
Thomson Rd. HA3: W'stone 3J **41**
Thorburn Ho. SW1 . . . . .7F **11**
    (off Kinnerton St.)
Thorburn Sq. SE1 . . . . .4G **103**
Thorburn Way SW19 . . . . .1B **154**
Thoresby St. N1 . . . . .1D **8** (3C **84**)
Thorkhill Gdns. KT7: T Ditt 1A **162**
Thorkhill Rd. KT7: T Ditt 1A **162**
Thornaby Gdns. N18 . . . . .6B **34**
Thornby Ho. E2 . . . . .3H **85**
    (off Canrobert St.)
Thorn Apartments E3 . . . . .5C **86**
    (off St Paul's Way)
Thorn Av. WD23: B Hea 1B **26**
Thornbill Ho. SE15 . . . . .7G **103**
    (off Bird in Bush Rd.)
Thornbury NW4 . . . . .4D **44**
    (off Prince of Wales Cl.)
Thornbury Av. TW7: Isle 7H **95**
Thornbury Cl. N16 . . . . .5E **66**
  NW7 . . . . .7A **30**
Thornbury Ct. CR2: S Croy 5D **168**
    (off Blunt Rd.)
  TW7: Isle 7J **95**
  W11 . . . . .7J **81**
    (off Chepstow Vs.)
Thornbury Lodge EN2: Enf 3G **23**
Thornbury Rd. SW2 . . . . .6J **119**
  TW7: Isle 7H **95**
Thornbury Sq. N6 . . . . .1G **65**
Thornbury Way E17 . . . . .1B **50**
Thornby Rd. E5 . . . . .3J **67**
Thorncliffe Rd. SW2 . . . . .6J **119**
  UB2: S'hall 5D **94**
Thorn Cl. BR2: Brom 6E **160**
  UB5: N'olt 3D **76**
Thorncombe Rd. SE22 . . . . .5E **120**
Thorncroft Rd.
  SM1: Sutt 5K **165**
Thorncroft St. SW8 . . . . .7J **101**
Thorndean St. SW18 . . . . .2A **136**
Thorndene SE28 . . . . .1B **108**
Thorndene Av. N11 . . . . .1K **31**
Thorndike Av. UB5: N'olt 1B **76**
Thorndike Cl. SW10 . . . . .7A **100**
Thorndike Ho. SW1 . . . . .5C **18**
    (off Vauxhall Bri. Rd.)
Thorndike Rd. N1 . . . . .6D **66**
Thorndike St. SW1 . . . . .4C **18** (4H **101**)
Thorndon Cl. BR5: St P 2K **161**
Thorndon Gdns.
  KT19: Ewe 5A **164**
Thorndon Rd. BR5: St P 2K **161**

Thorne Cl. DA8: Erith 6H **109**
  E11 . . . . .4F **69**
  E16 . . . . .6J **87**
  KT10: Clay 7A **162**
  TW15: Ashf 7E **128**
Thorne Ho. E2 . . . . .3J **85**
    (off Roman Rd.)
  E14 . . . . .3E **104**
    (off Launch St.)
Thorneloe Gdns. CR0: Wadd 5A **168**
Thorne Pas. SW13 . . . . .2A **116**
Thorne Rd. SW8 . . . . .7J **101**
Thornes Cl. BR3: Beck 3E **158**
Thorne St. SW13 . . . . .3A **116**
Thornet Wood Rd. BR1: Brom 3E **160**
Thornewill Ho. E1 . . . . .7J **85**
    (off Cable St.)
Thorney Ct. W8 . . . . .2A **100**
    (off Palace Ga.)
Thorney Cres. SW11 . . . . .7B **100**
Thorneycroft Cl. KT12: Walt T 6A **148**
Thorney Hedge Rd. W4 . . . . .4H **97**
Thorney St. SW1 . . . . .3E **18** (4J **101**)
Thornfield Av. NW7 . . . . .1G **45**
Thornfield Ct. NW7 . . . . .1G **45**
Thornfield Ho. E14 . . . . .7C **86**
    (off Rosefield Gdns.)
Thornfield Pde. NW7 . . . . .7B **30**
    (off Holders Hill Rd.)
Thornfield Rd. W12 . . . . .2D **98**
    (not continuous)
Thornford Rd. SE13 . . . . .5E **122**
Thorngate Rd. W9 . . . . .4J **81**
Thorngrove Rd. E13 . . . . .1K **87**
Thornham Gro. E15 . . . . .5F **69**
Thornham Ind. Est. E15 . . . . .5F **69**
Thornham St. SE10 . . . . .6D **104**
Thornhaugh M. WC1 . . . . .4D **6** (4H **83**)
Thornhaugh St. WC1 . . . . .4D **6** (4H **83**)
Thornhill Av. KT6: Surb 2E **162**
  SE18 . . . . .7J **107**
Thornhill Bri. N1 . . . . .1K **83**
    (off Caledonian Rd.)
Thornhill Bri. Wharf N1 . . . . .1K **83**
Thornhill Cres. N1 . . . . .7K **65**
Thornhill Gdns. E10 . . . . .2D **68**
  IG11: Bark 7J **71**
Thornhill Gro. N1 . . . . .7K **65**
Thornhill Ho. W4 . . . . .5A **98**
    (off Wood St.)
Thornhill Ho's. N1 . . . . .7A **66**
    (off Thornhill Rd.)
Thornhill M. SW15 . . . . .4H **117**
Thornhill Rd. CR0: C'don 7C **156**
  E10 . . . . .2D **68**
  KT6: Surb 2E **162**
  N1 . . . . .7A **66**
  UB10: Ick 4B **56**
Thornhill Sq. N1 . . . . .7K **65**
Thornhill Way TW17: Shep 5C **146**
Thornicroft Ho. SW9 . . . . .2K **119**
    (off Stockwell Rd.)
Thornlaw Rd. SE27 . . . . .4A **138**
Thornley Cl. N17 . . . . .7B **34**
Thornley Dr. HA2: Harr 2F **59**
Thornley Pl. SE10 . . . . .5G **105**
Thornsbeach Rd. SE6 . . . . .1E **140**
Thornsett Pl. SE20 . . . . .2H **157**
Thornsett Rd. SE20 . . . . .2H **157**
  SW18 . . . . .1K **135**
Thornsett Ter. SE20 . . . . .2H **157**
    (off Croydon Rd.)
Thorn Ter. SE15 . . . . .3H **121**
Thornton Av. CR0: C'don 6K **155**
  SW2 . . . . .1H **137**
  UB7: W Dray 3B **92**
  W4 . . . . .4A **98**
Thornton Cl. UB7: W Dray 3B **92**
Thornton Dene BR3: Beck 2C **158**
Thornton Gdns. SW12 . . . . .1H **137**
THORNTON HEATH 4C **156**

Thornton Heath Leisure Cen. 4C **156**
THORNTON HEATH POND 5A **156**
Thornton Hill SW19 . . . . .7G **135**
Thornton Ho. SE17 . . . . .4E **102**
    (off Townsend St.)
Thornton Pl. W1 . . . . .5F **5** (5D **82**)
Thornton Rd. BR1: Brom 5J **141**
  CR0: C'don 7K **155**
  CR7: Thor H 7K **155**
  DA17: Belv 4H **109**
  E11 . . . . .2F **69**
  EN5: Barn 3B **20**
  IG1: Ilf 4F **71**
  N18 . . . . .3D **34**
  SM5: Cars 1B **166**
  SW12 . . . . .7H **119**
  SW14 . . . . .4K **115**
  SW19 . . . . .6F **135**
Thornton Rd. E. SW19 . . . . .6F **135**
Thornton Rd. Ind. Est. CR0: C'don . . .6K **155**
Thornton Row CR7: Thor H 5A **156**
Thornton's Farm Av. RM7: Rush G . . .1J **73**
Thornton St. E20 . . . . .7D **68**
  SW9 . . . . .2A **120**
Thornton Way NW11 . . . . .5K **45**
Thorntree Cl. W5 . . . . .5E **78**
Thorntree Rd. SE7 . . . . .5B **106**
Thornville Gro. CR4: Mitc 2B **154**
Thornville St. SE8 . . . . .1C **122**
Thornwell Ct. W7 . . . . .2J **95**
    (off Lwr. Boston Rd.)
Thornwood Cl. E18 . . . . .2K **51**
Thornwood Gdns. W8 . . . . .2J **99**
Thornwood Ho. IG9: Buck H 1H **37**
Thornwood Lodge W8 . . . . .2J **99**
    (off Thornwood Gdns.)
Thornwood Rd. SE13 . . . . .5G **123**
Thornycroft Ho. W4 . . . . .5A **98**
    (off Fraser St.)
Thorogood Gdns. E15 . . . . .5G **69**
Thorogood Way RM13: Rain 1K **91**
Thorold Ho. SE1 . . . . .6C **14**
    (off Pepper St.)
Thorold Rd. IG1: Ilf 2F **71**
  N22 . . . . .7D **32**
Thorparch Rd. SW8 . . . . .1H **119**
Thorpebank Rd. W12 . . . . .1C **98**
Thorpe Cl. BR6: Orp 2J **173**
  SE26 . . . . .4K **139**
  W10 . . . . .6G **81**
Thorpe Ct. EN2: Enf 3G **23**
Thorpe Cres. E17 . . . . .2B **50**
Thorpedale Gdns. IG2: Ilf 4E **52**
  IG6: Ilf 4E **52**
Thorpedale Rd. N4 . . . . .2J **65**
Thorpe Hall Rd. E17 . . . . .1E **50**
Thorpe Ho. N1 . . . . .1K **83**
    (off Barnsbury Est.)
Thorpe Rd. E6 . . . . .1D **88**
  E7 . . . . .4H **69**
  E17 . . . . .2E **50**
  IG11: Bark 7H **71**
  KT2: King T 7E **132**
  N15 . . . . .6E **48**
Thorpewood Av. SE26 . . . . .2H **139**
Thorpland Av. UB10: Ick 3E **56**
Thorsden Way SE19 . . . . .5E **138**
Thorverton Rd. NW2 . . . . .3G **63**
Thoydon Rd. E3 . . . . .2A **86**
Thrale Rd. SW16 . . . . .4G **137**
Thrale St. SE1 . . . . .5D **14** (1C **102**)
Thrasher Cl. E8 . . . . .1F **85**
Thrawl St. E1 . . . . .6K **9** (5F **85**)
Thrayle Ho. SW9 . . . . .3K **119**
    (off Benedict Rd.)
Threadgold Ho. N1 . . . . .6D **66**
    (off Dovercourt Est.)
Threadneedle St. EC2 . . . . . .1F **15** (6D **84**)
Threadneedle Wlk. EC2 . . . . .1F **15**
Three Barrels Wlk. EC4 . . . . .3D **14**
    (off Queenhithe)

Three Bridges Bus. Cen. UB2: S'hall ...2G **95**
Three Bridges Path KT1: King T 3E **150**
   (off Bellvue Rd.)
Three Colt Cnr. E2 ....3K **9**
Three Colts La. E2 ....4H **85**
Three Colt St. E14 ....6B **86**
Three Corners DA7: Bex 2H **127**
Three Cranes Wlk. EC4 ....3D **14**
Three Cups Yd. WC1 ....6H **7**
Three Kings Yd. W1 ....2J **11** (7F **83**)
Three Meadows M. HA3: Hrw W 1K **41**
Three Mill La. E3 ....3E **86**
Three Mills Studios E3 ....3E **86**
Three Nun Ct. EC2 ....7D **8**
   (off Aldermanbury)
Three Oak La. SE1 ....6J **15** (2F **103**)
Three Oaks Cl. UB10: Ick 3B **56**
Three Quays EC3 ....3H **15**
Three Quays Wlk. EC3 ......3H **15** (7E **84**)
Threshers Pl. W11 ....7G **81**
Thriftwood SE26 ....3J **139**
Thrigby Rd. KT9: Chess 6F **163**
Thring Ho. SW9 ....2K **119**
   (off Stockwell Rd.)
Throckmorton Rd. E16 ....6K **87**
Throgmorton Av. EC2 ....7F **9** (6D **84**)
   (not continuous)
Throgmorton St. EC2 ....7F **9** (6D **84**)
Throwley Cl. SE2 ....3C **108**
   (not continuous)
Throwley Rd. SM1: Sutt 5K **165**
Throwley Way SM1: Sutt 4K **165**
Thrupp Cl. CR4: Mitc 2F **155**
Thrush Grn. HA2: Harr 4E **40**
Thrush St. SE17 ....5C **102**
Thurbarn Rd. SE6 ....5D **140**
Thurland Ho. SE16 ....4H **103**
   (off Camilla Rd.)
Thurland Rd. SE16 ....3G **103**
Thurlby Cl. HA1: Harr 6A **42**
  IG8: Wfd G 5J **37**
Thurlby Cft. NW4 ....3E **44**
   (off Mulberry Cl.)
Thurlby Rd. HA0: Wemb 6D **60**
  SE27 ....4A **138**
Thurleigh Av. SW12 ....6E **118**
Thurleigh Ct. SW12 ....6E **118**
Thurleigh Rd. SW12 ....7D **118**
Thurleston Av. SM4: Mord 5G **153**
Thurlestone Av. IG3: Bark, Ilf 4K **71**
  N12 ....6J **31**
Thurlestone Cl. TW17: Shep 6E **146**
Thurlestone Yd. UB1: S'hall 6F **77**
   (off Howard Rd.)
Thurlestone Pde. TW17: Shep 6E **146**
   (off High St.)
Thurlestone Rd. SE27 ....3A **138**
Thurloe Cl. SW7 ....3C **16** (4C **100**)
Thurloe Cl. SW3 ....4C **16**
   (off Fulham Rd.)
Thurloe Pl. SW7 ....3B **16** (4B **100**)
Thurloe Pl. M. SW7 ....3B **16**
Thurloe Sq. SW7 ....3C **16** (4C **100**)
Thurloe St. SW7 ....3B **16** (4B **100**)
Thurlow Cl. E4 ....6K **35**
Thurlow Gdns. HA0: Wemb 5D **60**
Thurlow Hill SE21 ....1C **138**
Thurlow Ho. SW16 ....3J **137**
Thurlow Pk. Rd. SE21 ....2B **138**
Thurlow Rd. NW3 ....5B **64**
  W7 ....2A **96**
Thurlow St. SE17 ....5D **102**
   (not continuous)
Thurlow Ter. NW5 ....5E **64**
Thurlow Wlk. SE17 ....5E **102**
   (not continuous)
Thurlstone Rd. HA4: Ruis 3J **57**
Thurnby Ct. TW2: Twick 3J **131**
Thurnscoe NW1 ....1G **83**
   (off Pratt St.)
Thursland Rd. DA14: Sidc 5E **144**

Thursley Cres. CR0: New Ad 7E **170**
Thursley Gdns. SW19 ....2F **135**
Thursley Ho. SW2 ....7K **119**
   (off Holmewood Gdns.)
Thursley Rd. SE9 ....3D **142**
Thurso Ho. NW6 ....2K **81**
Thurso St. SW17 ....4B **136**
Thurstan Dwellings WC2 ....7F **7**
   (off Newton St.)
Thurstan Rd. SW20 ....7D **134**
Thurston Ho. BR3: Beck 6D **140**
  N1 ....1K **83**
   (off Barnsbury Est.)
Thurston Rd. SE13 ....2D **122**
  UB1: S'hall 6D **76**
Thurtle Rd. E2 ....1F **85**
Thwaite Cl. DA8: Erith 6J **109**
Thyer Cl. BR6: Farnb 4G **173**
Thyme Cl. SE3 ....3A **124**
Thyme Ct. NW7 ....1G **45**
Thyra Gro. N12 ....6E **30**
Tibbatt's Rd. E3 ....4D **86**
Tibbenham Pl. SE6 ....2C **140**
Tibbenham Wlk. E13 ....2H **87**
Tibberton Sq. N1 ....1C **84**
Tibbet's Cl. SW19 ....1F **135**
TIBBET'S CORNER 7F **117**
Tibbet's Ride SW15 ....7F **117**
Tiber Cl. E3 ....1C **86**
Tiber Gdns. N1 ....1J **83**
Ticehurst Cl. BR5: St P 7A **144**
Ticehurst Rd. SE23 ....2A **140**
Tickford Cl. SE2 ....2C **108**
Tickford Ho. NW8 ....2C **4** (3C **82**)
Tidal Basin Rd. E16 ....7H **87**
   (not continuous)
Tidbury Ct. SW8 ....7G **101**
   (off Stewart's Rd.)
Tide Cl. CR4: Mitc 1E **154**
Tideham Ho. SE28 ....1H **107**
Tidelea Twr. SE28 ....2G **107**
Tidemill Way SE8 ....7C **104**
Tidenham Gdns. CR0: C'don 3E **168**
Tideside Ct. SE18 ....3C **106**
Tideslea Path SE28 ....1H **107**
Tideswell Rd. CR0: C'don 3C **170**
  SW15 ....4E **116**
Tideway Cl. TW10: Ham 4B **132**
Tideway Ct. SE16 ....1K **103**
Tideway Ho. E14 ....2C **104**
   (off Strafford St.)
Tideway Ind. Est. SW8 ....6G **101**
Tideway Wlk. SW8 ....7B **18** (6G **101**)
Tidey St. E3 ....5C **86**
Tidford Rd. DA16: Well 2K **125**
Tidlock Ho. SE28 ....2H **107**
Tidworth Rd. E3 ....4C **86**
Tiepigs La. BR2: Hayes 2G **171**
  BR4: W W'ck 2G **171**
Tierney Ct. CR0: C'don 2E **168**
Tierney Rd. SW2 ....1J **137**
Tiffany Hgts. SW18 ....7J **117**
Tiffin Girls Community Sports Cen.
  ....6E **132**
Tiffin Sports Cen. 2F **151**
Tiger Cl. IG11: Bark 2B **90**
Tiger Ho. WC1 ....2D **6**
   (off Burton St.)
Tiger La. BR2: Brom 4K **159**
Tiger Way E5 ....4H **67**
Tigris Cl. N9 ....2D **34**
Tilbrook Rd. SE3 ....3A **124**
Tilbury Cl.
  HA5: Hat E 1D **40**
  SE15 ....7F **103**
Tilbury Ho. SE14 ....6K **103**
   (off Myers La.)
Tilbury Rd. E6 ....2D **88**
  E10 ....7E **50**
Tildesley Rd. SW15 ....6E **116**
Tile Farm Rd. BR6: Orp 3H **173**

Tile Ho. N1 ....1J **83**
   (off Beaconsfield St.)
Tilehurst NW1 ....2K **5**
   (off Lit. Albany St.)
Tilehurst Point SE2 ....2C **108**
   (not continuous)
Tilehurst Rd. SM3: Cheam 5G **165**
  SW18 ....1B **136**
Tile Kiln La. DA5: Bexl 3J **145**
  N6 ....1F **65**
  N13 ....5H **33**
  N17 ....7D **38**
Tile Kiln Studios N6 ....7G **47**
Tileyard Rd. N7 ....7J **65**
Tilford Av. CR0: New Ad 7E **170**
Tilford Gdns. SW19 ....1F **135**
Tilford Ho. SW2 ....7K **119**
   (off Holmewood Gdns.)
Tilia Cl. SM1: Sutt 5H **165**
Tilia Rd. E5 ....4H **67**
Tilia Wlk. SW9 ....4B **120**
Tiller Ho. N1 ....1E **84**
   (off Whitmore Est.)
Tiller Leisure Cen. 3C **104**
Tiller Rd. E14 ....3C **104**
Tillett Cl. NW10 ....6J **61**
Tillett Sq. SE16 ....2A **104**
Tillet Way E2 ....3G **85**
Tilley Rd. TW13: Felt 1J **129**
Tillingbourne Gdns. N3 ....3H **45**
Tillingbourne Grn.
  BR5: St M Cry ......4K **161** & 5K **161**
Tillingbourne Way N3 ....4H **45**
Tillingham Way N12 ....4D **30**
Tilling Rd. NW2 ....1E **62**
Tillings Cl. SE5 ....1C **120**
Tilling Way HA9: Wemb 2D **60**
Tillman St. E1 ....6H **85**
Tilloch St. N1 ....7K **65**
Tillotson Ct. SW8 ....7H **101**
   (off Wandsworth Rd.)
Tillotson Rd. HA3: Hrw W 7A **26**
  IG1: Ilf 7E **52**
  N9 ....2A **34**
Tilney Ct. EC1 ....3D **8** (4C **84**)
  IG9: Buck H 2D **36**
Tilney Dr. IG9: Buck H 2D **36**
Tilney Gdns. N1 ....6D **66**
Tilney Rd.
  RM9: Dag 6F **73**
  UB2: S'hall 4A **94**
Tilney St. W1 ....4H **11** (1E **100**)
Tilson Cl. SE5 ....7E **102**
Tilson Gdns. SW2 ....7J **119**
Tilson Ho. SW2 ....7J **119**
Tilson Rd. N17 ....1G **49**
Tilston Cl. E11 ....3H **69**
Tiltman Pl. N7 ....3K **65**
Tilton St. SW6 ....6G **99**
Tiltwood, The W3 ....7J **79**
Tilt Yd. App. SE9 ....6D **124**
Timber Cl. BR7: Chst 2E **160**
Timbercroft KT19: Ewe 4A **164**
Timbercroft La. SE18 ....6J **107**
Timberdene NW4 ....2F **45**
Timberdene Av. IG6: Ilf 1G **53**
Timberland Cl. SE15 ....7G **103**
Timberland Rd. E1 ....6H **85**
Timberley Ct. DA14: Sidc 5K **143**
Timber Mill Way SW4 ....3H **119**
Timber Pond Rd. SE16 ....1K **103**
Timbers, The SM3: Cheam 6G **165**
Timberslip Dr. SM6: Wall 7H **167**
Timber St. EC1 ....3C **8** (4C **84**)
Timberwharf Rd. E2 ....1F **85**
Timberwharf Rd. N16 ....6G **49**
Timber Wharves Est. E14 ....4C **104**
   (off Copeland Dr.)
Timber Yard, The N1 ....2H **9**
   (off Drysdale St.)
Timbrell Pl. SE16 ....1B **104**

Time Sq. E8 ....5F **67**
Times Sq. E1 ....6G **85**
  SM1: Sutt 5K **165**
Timmins Apartments E2 ....3K **85**
Timms Cl. BR1: Brom 4D **160**
Timor Ho. E1 ....4A **86**
   (off Duckett St.)
Timothy Cl. DA6: Bex 5E **126**
  SW4 ....5G **119**
Timothy Ho. DA18: Erith 2E **108**
   (off Kale Rd.)
Timothy Pl. KT8: W Mole 5D **148**
Timperley Ct. SW19 ....1G **135**
Timsbury Wlk. SW15 ....1C **134**
Tina Cl. SE6 ....7B **122**
Tindal St. SW9 ....1B **120**
Tinderbox All. SW14 ....3K **115**
Tinderbox Ho. SE8 ....7C **104**
   (off Octavius St.)
Tinniswood Cl. N5 ....5A **66**
Tinsley Cl. SE25 ....3H **157**
Tinsley Rd. E1 ....5J **85**
Tintagel Ct. EC1 ....3A **8**
   (off St John St.)
Tintagel Cres. SE22 ....4F **121**
Tintagel Dr. HA7: Stan 4J **27**
Tintagel Gdns. SE22 ....4F **121**
Tintern Av. NW9 ....3H **43**
Tintern Cl. SW15 ....5G **117**
  SW19 ....6A **136**
Tintern Ct. W13 ....7A **78**
Tintern Gdns. N14 ....7D **22**
Tintern Ho. NW1 ....1K **5**
   (off Augustus St.)
  SW1 ....4J **17**
   (part of Abbots Mnr.)
Tintern Path NW9 ....6A **44**
   (off Fryent Gro.)
Tintern Rd. N22 ....1C **48**
  SM5: Cars 1B **166**
Tintern St. SW4 ....4J **119**
Tintern Way HA2: Harr 1F **59**
Tinto Rd. E16 ....4J **87**
Tinworth Ct. SE17 ....6B **102**
   (off Royal Rd.)
Tinworth St. SE11 ....5F **19** (5J **101**)
Tippett Ct. E6 ....2D **88**
Tippetts Cl. EN2: Enf 1H **23**
Tipthorpe Rd. SW11 ....3E **118**
Tipton Dr. CR0: C'don 4E **168**
Tiptree NW1 ....7F **65**
   (off Castlehaven Rd.)
Tiptree Cl. E4 ....3K **35**
Tiptree Cres. IG5: Ilf 3E **52**
Tiptree Dr. EN2: Enf 4J **23**
Tiptree Rd. HA4: Ruis 4K **57**
Tirlemont Rd. CR2: S Croy 7C **168**
Tirrell Rd. CR0: C'don 6C **156**
Tisbury Ct. W1 ....2C **12**
Tisbury Rd. SW16 ....2J **155**
Tisdall Ho. SE17 ....4D **102**
   (off Barlow St.)
Tisdall Pl. SE17 ....4D **102**
Tissington Ct. SE16 ....4J **103**
Titan Bus. Est. SE8 ....7C **104**
   (off Ffinch St.)
Titan Ct. TW8: Bford 5F **97**
Titan Ho. E20 ....5E **68**
   (off Napa Cl.)
Titchborne Row W2 ....1D **10** (6C **82**)
Titchfield Rd. NW8 ....1C **82**
  SM5: Cars 1B **166**
Titchfield Wlk. SM5: Cars 7B **154**
Titchwell Rd. SW18 ....1B **136**
Tite St. SW3 ....6E **16** (5D **100**)
Tithe Barn Cl. KT2: King T 1F **151**
Tithe Barn Way UB5: N'olt 2K **75**
Tithe Cl. KT12: Walt T 6K **147**
  NW7 ....1C **44**
  UB4: Hayes 6H **75**
Tithe Farm Av. HA2: Harr 3E **58**

Tithe Farm Cl. HA2: Harr 3E 58
Tithe Wlk. NW7 . . . .1C 44
Titian Av. WD23: B Hea 1D 26
Titian Hgts. E20 . . . .5D 68
(off Scarlet Cl.)
Titley Cl. E4 . . . .5H 35
Titmus Cl. UB8: Hil 6E 74
Titmuss Av. SE28 . . . .7B 90
Titmuss St. W12 . . . .2E 98
Tivendale N8 . . . .3J 47
Tiverton Av. IG5: Ilf 3E 52
Tiverton Cl. CR0: C'don 7F 157
Tiverton Dr. SE9 . . . .1G 143
Tiverton Ho. EN3: Enf H 3E 24
Tiverton Rd. HA0: Wemb 2E 78
HA4: Ruis 3J 57
HA8: Edg 2F 43
N15 . . . .6D 48
N18 . . . .5K 33
NW10 . . . .1F 81
TW3: Houn 2G 113
Tiverton St. SE1 . . . .3C 102
Tiverton Way KT9: Chess 5D 162
NW7 . . . .7A 30
Tivoli Ct. SE16 . . . .1B 104
Tivoli Gdns. SE18 . . . .4C 106
(not continuous)
Tivoli M. E14 . . . .6B 86
Tivoli Rd. N8 . . . .5H 47
SE27 . . . .5C 138
TW4: Houn 4C 112
Tivoli Way E14 . . . .6B 86
Tizzard Gro. SE3 . . . .4K 123
Toad La. TW4: Houn 4D 112
Tobacco Dock E1 . . . .7H 85
Tobacco Quay E1 . . . .7H 85
Tobago St. E14 . . . .2C 104
Tobin Cl. NW3 . . . .7C 64
Toby Ct. N9 . . . .7D 24
(off Tramway Av.)
Toby La. E1 . . . .4A 86
Toby Way KT5: Surb 2H 163
Todber Ho. W14 . . . .3G 99
(off Russell Rd.)
Todd Ho. N2 . . . .2B 46
(off The Grange)
Todds Wlk. N7 . . . .2K 65
Todhunter Ter.
EN5: New Bar 4D 20
Token Ho. CR0: C'don 3C 168
(off Robert St.)
Tokenhouse Yd. EC2 . . . .7E 8 (6D 84)
Token Yd. SW15 . . . .4G 117
TOKYNGTON 6H 61
Tokyngton Av. HA9: Wemb 6G 61
Toland Sq. SW15 . . . .5C 116
Tolcairn Dr. DA17: Belv 5G 109
Tolcarne Dr. HA5: Eastc 2J 39
Tolchurch W11 . . . .6H 81
(off Dartmouth Cl.)
Toley Av. HA9: Wemb 7E 42
Tolhurst Dr. W10 . . . .3G 81
Tollard Ho. W14 . . . .3H 99
(off Kensington High St.)
Toll Bar Ct. SM2: Sutt 7K 165
Tollbridge Cl. W10 . . . .4G 81
Tollesbury Gdns. IG6: Ilf 3H 53
Tollet St. E1 . . . .4K 85
Tollgate Ct. CR2: S Croy 5D 168
Tollgate Dr. SE21 . . . .2E 138
UB4: Yead 7B 76
Tollgate Ho. NW6 . . . .2K 81
(off Tollgate Gdns.)
Tollgate Lodge BR7: Chst 1E 160
(off Caveside Cl.)
Tollgate Rd. E6 . . . .5A 88
E16 . . . .5A 88
Tollgate Sq. E6 . . . .5D 88
Tollhouse Way N19 . . . .2G 65
Tollington Pk. N4 . . . .2K 65
Tollington Pl. N4 . . . .2K 65

Tollington Rd. N7 . . . .4K 65
Tollington Way N7 . . . .3J 65
Tolmers Sq. NW1 . . . .3B 6 (4G 83)
(not continuous)
Tolpaide Ho. SE11 . . . .4J 19
Tolpuddle Av. E13 . . . .1A 88
Tolpuddle St. N1 . . . .2A 84
Tolsford Rd. E5 . . . .5H 67
Tolson Rd. TW7: Isle 3A 114
Tolverne Rd. SW20 . . . .1E 152
TOLWORTH 2H 163
Tolworth B'way. KT6: Surb 1H 163
Tolworth Cl. KT6: Surb 1H 163
Tolworth Gdns. RM6: Chad H 5D 54
TOLWORTH JUNC. (TOBY JUG) 2H 163
Tolworth Pde. RM6: Chad H 5E 54
Tolworth Recreation Cen. 3F 163
Tolworth Ri. Nth. KT5: Surb 1H 163
Tolworth Ri. Sth. KT5: Surb 1H 163
Tolworth Rd. KT6: Surb 2E 162
Tolworth Twr. KT6: Surb 2H 163
Tomahawk Gdns. UB5: N'olt 3B 76
Tomblin M. SW16 . . . .2G 155
Tom Coombs Cl. SE9 . . . .4C 124
Tom Cribb Rd. SE28 . . . .3G 107
Tom Groves Cl. E15 . . . .5F 69
Tom Hood Cl. E15 . . . .5F 69
Tom Jenkinson Rd. E16 . . . .1J 105
Tomkyns Ho. SE11 . . . .3J 19
Tomline Ho. SE1 . . . .5C 14
(off Union St.)
Tomlins All. TW1: Twick 1A 132
Tomlin's Gro. E3 . . . .3C 86
Tomlinson Cl. E2 . . . .2K 9 (3F 85)
W4 . . . .5H 97
Tomlins Orchard IG11: Bark 1G 89
Tomlins Ter. E14 . . . .6A 86
Tomlins Wlk. N7 . . . .2K 65
Tom Mann Cl. IG11: Bark 1J 89
Tom Nolan Cl. E15 . . . .2G 87
Tompion Ho. EC1 . . . .3B 8
(off Percival St.)
Tompion St. EC1 . . . .2A 8 (3B 84)
(not continuous)
Tom Smith Cl. SE10 . . . .6G 105
Tomson Ho. SE1 . . . .7J 15
(off St Saviour's Est.)
Tomswood Ct. IG6: Ilf 1G 53
Tomswood Hill IG6: Ilf . . . .6K 37 & 1F 53
Tomswood Rd. IG7: Chig 6K 37
Tom Williams Ho. SW6 . . . .6H 99
(off Clem Attlee Ct.)
Tonbridge Cres. HA3: Kenton 4E 42
Tonbridge Ho's. WC1 . . . .2E 6
(off Tonbridge St., not continuous)
Tonbridge Rd. KT8: W Mole 4D 148
Tonbridge St. WC1 . . . .1E 6 (3J 83)
Tonbridge Wlk. WC1 . . . .1E 6
(off Abbey Rd.)
Tonborough NW8 . . . .1K 81
Tonfield Rd. SM3: Sutt 1H 165
Tonge Cl. BR3: Beck 5C 158
Tonsley Hill SW18 . . . .5K 117
Tonsley Pl. SW18 . . . .5K 117
Tonsley Rd. SW18 . . . .5K 117
Tonsley St. SW18 . . . .5K 117
Tonstall Rd. CR4: Mitc 2E 154
Tony Cannell M. E3 . . . .3B 86
Tony Law Ho. SE20 . . . .1H 157
Tony Rawson Way
RM10: Dag 4H 73
Tooke Cl. HA5: Pinn 1C 40
Tookey Cl. HA3: Kenton 7F 43
Took's Ct. EC4 . . . .7J 7 (6A 84)
Tooley St. SE1 . . . .4F 15 (1D 102)
Toomy Cen. E16 . . . .1K 105
(off Evelyn Rd.)
Toorack Rd. HA3: Hrw W 2H 41
TOOTING 5C 136
TOOTING BEC 3D 136

Tooting Bec Gdns. SW16 . . . .4H 137
(not continuous)
Tooting Bec Lido 4G 137
Tooting Bec Rd. SW16 . . . .3E 136
SW17 . . . .3E 136
Tooting B'way. SW17 . . . .5C 136
TOOTING GRAVENEY 6D 136
Tooting Gro. SW17 . . . .5C 136
Tooting High St. SW17 . . . .6C 136
Tooting Leisure Cen. 4B 136
Tooting Mkt. SW17 . . . .4D 136
Tootswood Rd. BR2: Brom 5G 159
Topaz Cl. E11 . . . .1G 69
Topaz Ho. NW2 . . . .7F 45
Topcliffe Dr. BR6: Farnb 4H 173
Topham Ho. SE10 . . . .7E 104
(off Prior St.)
Topham Sq. N17 . . . .1C 48
Topham St. EC1 . . . .3J 7 (4A 84)
Top Ho. Ri. E4 . . . .7K 25
Topiary Sq. TW9: Rich 3F 115
Topley St. SE9 . . . .4A 124
Topmast Point E14 . . . .2C 104
Top Pk. BR3: Beck 5G 159
Topp Wlk. NW2 . . . .2E 62
Topsfield Cl. N8 . . . .5H 47
Topsfield Pde. N8 . . . .5J 47
(off Tottenham La.)
Topsfield Rd. N8 . . . .5J 47
Topsham Rd. SW17 . . . .3D 136
Tora Ct. IG9: Buck H 2F 37
Torbay Ct. NW1 . . . .7F 65
Torbay Mans. NW6 . . . .1H 81
(off Willesden La.)
Torbay Rd. HA2: Harr 2C 58
NW6 . . . .7H 63
Torbay St. NW1 . . . .7F 65
Torbitt Way IG2: Ilf 5K 53
Torbridge Cl. HA8: Edg 7K 27
Torbrook Cl. DA5: Bexl 6E 126
Tor Ct. W8 . . . .2J 99
Torcross Dr. SE23 . . . .2J 139
Torcross Rd. HA4: Ruis 3K 57
Toreno Mansion E20 . . . .5D 68
(off Olympic Pk. Av.)
Tor Gdns. W8 . . . .2J 99
Tor Gro. SE28 . . . .1J 107
Tor Ho. N6 . . . .6F 47
Tormead Cl. SM1: Sutt 6J 165
Tormount Rd. SE18 . . . .6J 107
Tornay Ho. E9 . . . .7J 67
N1 . . . .2K 83
(off Priory Grn. Est.)
Toronto Av. E12 . . . .4D 70
Toronto Ho. SE16 . . . .2K 103
Toronto Rd. IG1: Ilf 1F 71
E11 . . . .2A 84
Torquay Gdns. IG4: Ilf 4B 52
Torquay St. W2 . . . .5K 81
Torrance Cl. SE7 . . . .6B 106
Torrens Cl. SE5 . . . .3D 120
Torrens Rd. E15 . . . .6H 69
SW2 . . . .5K 119
Torrens Sq. E15 . . . .6H 69
Torrens St. EC1 . . . .2A 84
Torrent Lodge SE10 . . . .7D 104
(off Merryweather Pl.)
Torres Sq. E14 . . . .5C 104
Torre Vista SE13 . . . .3E 122
(off Loampit Va.)
Torriano Av. NW5 . . . .5H 65
Torriano Cotts. NW5 . . . .5G 65
Torriano M. NW5 . . . .5G 65
Torridge Gdns. SE15 . . . .4J 121
Torridge Rd. CR7: Thor H 5B 156
Torridon Ho. NW6 . . . .2K 81
(off Randolph Gdns.)
Torridon Rd. SE6 . . . .7F 123
SE13 . . . .7F 123
Torrington Av. N12 . . . .5G 31

Torrington Cl. N12 . . . .4G 31
Torrington Ct. SE26 . . . .5G 139
(off Crystal Palace Pk. Rd.)
Torrington Dr. HA2: Harr 4F 59
Torrington Gdns. N11 . . . .6B 32
UB6: G'frd 1C 78
Torrington Gro. N12 . . . .5H 31
Torrington Pk. N12 . . . .5F 31
Torrington Pl. E1 . . . .1G 103
WC1 . . . .5C 6 (5H 83)
Torrington Rd. E18 . . . .3J 51
HA4: Ruis 3H 57
RM8: Dag 1F 73
UB6: G'frd 1C 78
Torrington Sq. CR0: C'don 7D 156
WC1 . . . .4D 6 (4H 83)
Torrington Way SM4: Mord 6J 153
Tor Rd. DA16: Well 1C 126
Tor St. SE20 . . . .7K 139
Torrian Rd. SE15 . . . .7G 103
(off Friary Est.)
Torver Rd. HA1: Harr 4J 41
Torver Way BR6: Orp 3H 173
Torwood Rd. SW15 . . . .5C 116
Tothill Ho. SW1 . . . .3D 18
(off Page St.)
Tothill St. SW1 . . . .7D 12 (2H 101)
Totnes Rd. DA16: Well 7B 108
Totnes Vs. N11 . . . .5B 32
(off Telford Rd.)
Totnes Wlk. N2 . . . .4B 46
Tottan Ter. E1 . . . .6K 85
Tottenhall NW1 . . . .7E 64
(off Ferdinand St.)
Tottenhall Rd. N13 . . . .6F 33
TOTTENHAM 2F 49
Tottenham Community Sports Cen. 1F 49
Tottenham Ct. Rd. W1 . . . .4B 6 (4G 83)
Tottenham Ent. Cen. N17 . . . .2F 49
Tottenham Grn. E. N15 . . . .4F 49
(not continuous)
Tottenham Green Leisure Cen. 4F 49
TOTTENHAM HALE 2G 49
TOTTENHAM HALE GYRATORY 4G 49
Tottenham Hale Retail Pk. N15 . . . .4G 49
Tottenham Hotspur FC 7B 34
Tottenham La. N8 . . . .6J 47
Tottenham M. W1 . . . .5B 6 (5G 83)
Tottenham Rd. N1 . . . .6B 66
Tottenham St. W1 . . . .6B 6 (5G 83)
Totterdown St. SW17 . . . .4D 136
TOTTERIDGE 1C 30
Totteridge Comn. N20 . . . .2H 29
Totteridge Fields Local Nature Reserve 1H 29
Totteridge Grn. N20 . . . .2D 30
Totteridge Ho. SW11 . . . .2B 118
(off Yelverton Rd.)
Totteridge La. N20 . . . .2D 30
Totteridge Village N20 . . . .1B 30
Totternhoe Cl. HA3: Kenton 5C 42
Totters Cl. SE17 . . . .6D 102
(off Westmorland Rd.)
Totton Rd. CR7: Thor H 3A 156
Toucan Cl. NW10 . . . .3G 79
Touchard Ho. N1 . . . .2F 9
Toulmin St. SE1 . . . .7C 14 (2C 102)
Toulon St. SE5 . . . .7C 102
Toulouse Ct. SE16 . . . .5H 103
(off Rossetti Rd.)
Tounson Ct. SW1 . . . .4D 18
(off Montaigne Cl.)
Tourist Info. Cen.
Bexleyheath 4F 127
City of London 1C 14 (6C 84)
Enfield 4J 23
Greenwich 6E 104
Heathrow Central 3D 110
Kingston upon Thames 2D 150
Leicester Square 3D 12
Lewisham 4E 122

Tournay Rd. SW6 ....7H 99
Tours Pas. SW11 ....4A 118
Toussaint Wlk. SE16 ....3G 103
Tovil Cl. SE20 ....2H 157
Tovy Ho. E1 ....5G 103
  (off Avondale Sq.)
Towcester Rd. E3 ....4D 86
Tower, The SW8 ....6J 101
  TW8: Bford 5D 96
  (off Ealing Rd.)
Tower 42 ....7G 9 (6E 84)
Tower Bri. SE1 ....5J 15 (1F 103)
Tower Bri. App. E1 ....4J 15 (1F 103)
Tower Bri. Bus. Complex
  SE16 ....3G 103
Tower Bri. Bus. Sq. SE16 ....4H 103
Tower Bridge Exhibition 4J 15
Tower Bri. M. HA1: Harr 4K 59
Tower Bri. Plaza SE1 ....5J 15 (1F 103)
Tower Bri. Rd. SE1 ....7H 15 (3E 102)
Tower Bri. Sq. SE1 ....6J 15
Tower Bri. Wharf E1 ....5K 15 (1G 103)
Tower Bldgs. E1 ....1H 103
  (off Brewhouse La.)
Tower Cl. BR6: Orp 2K 173
  NW3 ....5B 64
  SE20 ....7H 139
Tower Ct. E5 ....7F 49
  N1 ....7C 66
  (off Canonbury St.)
  NW8 ....2C 82
  (off Mackennal St.)
  WC2 ....1E 12
Tower Gdns. KT10: Clay 7A 162
Tower Gdns. Rd. N17 ....1C 48
Towergate SE1 ....4E 102
  (off Page's Wlk.)
Towergate Cl. UB8: Uxb 5A 56
Towergate Ho. E3 ....2B 86
  (off Ordell Rd.)
Tower Hamlets Rd. E7 ....4H 69
  E17 ....3C 50
TOWER HILL 7F 85
Tower Hill EC3 ....3H 15 (7E 84)
Tower Hill Ter. EC3 ....3H 15
Tower Ho. E1 ....5G 85
  (off Fieldgate St.)
Tower La. HA9: Wemb 3D 60
Tower Mans. SE1 ....3F 103
  (off Grange Rd.)
Tower M. E5 ....4A 68
  E17 ....4C 50
Tower Mill Rd. SE15 ....7E 102
Tower of London, The 3H 15 (7F 85)
Tower of London Welcome Cen.
  ....3H 15 (7E 84)
Tower Pl. EC3 ....3H 15 (7E 84)
Tower Pl. E. EC3 ....3H 15
Tower Pl. W. EC3 ....3H 15
  (off Lwr. Thames St.)
Tower Rd.
  BR6: Orp 2K 173
  DA7: Bex 4G 127
  DA17: Belv 4J 109
  NW10 ....7C 62
  TW1: Twick 3K 131
Tower Royal EC4 ....2E 14 (7D 84)
Towers Av. UB10: Hil 3E 74
Towers Bus. Pk. HA9: Wemb 4J 61
  (off Carey Way)
Towers Ct. UB10: Hil 3E 74
Towers Pl. TW9: Rich 5E 114
Towers Rd. HA5: Pinn 1C 40
  UB1: S'hall 4E 76
Tower St. WC2 ....1E 12 (6J 83)
Tower Ter. N22 ....2K 47
Tower Vw. CR0: C'don 7A 158
  WD23: B Hea 1D 26

Tower Wlk. SE1 ....4E 102
  (off Leroy St.)
Tower Wharf SE1 ....6J 15
  (off Tooley St.)
Tower Workshops SE1 ....7J 15
Tower Yd. TW10: Rich 5F 115
Towfield Ct. TW13: Hanw 2D 130
Towfield Rd. TW13: Hanw 2D 130
Town, The EN2: Enf 3J 23
Towncourt Cres. BR5: Pet W 5G 161
Towncourt La. BR5: Pet W 6H 161
Town Ct. Path N4 ....1C 66
Townend Ct. BR1: Brom 1H 159
Town End Pde. KT1: King T 3D 150
  (off High St.)
Towney Mead UB5: N'olt 2D 76
Towney Mead Ct. UB5: N'olt 2D 76
Townfield Rd. UB3: Hayes 1H 93
Townfield Sq. UB3: Hayes 7H 75
Town Fld. Way TW7: Isle 2A 114
Town Hall App. N16 ....4D 66
  (off Albion Rd.)
Town Hall App. Rd. N15 ....4F 49
Town Hall Av. W4 ....5K 97
Town Hall Rd. SW11 ....3D 118
Townholm Cres. W7 ....3K 95
Town La. TW19: Stanw 1A 128
  (not continuous)
Townley Ct. E15 ....6H 69
Townley Rd. DA6: Bex 5F 127
  SE22 ....5E 120
Townley St. SE17 ....5D 102
  (not continuous)
Townmead Bus. Cen. SW6 ....3A 118
Town Mdw. TW8: Bford 6D 96
Town Mdw. Rd. TW8: Bford 7D 96
Townmead Rd. SW6 ....3K 117
  TW9: Kew 2H 115
Town Quay IG11: Bark 1F 89
Town Quay Wharf IG11: Bark 1F 89
Town Rd. N9 ....2C 34
Townsend Av. N14 ....4C 32
Townsend Ho. SE1 ....4G 103
  (off Strathnairn St.)
Townsend Ind. Est. NW10 ....2J 79
Townsend La. NW9 ....7K 43
Townsend M. SW18 ....2A 136
Townsend N. N15 ....5F 49
  TW15: Ashf 5A 128
  UB1: S'hall 1C 94
Townsend St. SE17 ....4E 102
Townsend Way HA6: Nwood 1H 39
Townsend Yd. N6 ....1F 65
Townshend Cl. DA14: Sidc 6B 144
Townshend Ct. NW8 ....2C 82
  (off Townshend Rd.)
Townshend Est. NW8 ....2C 82
Townshend Rd. BR7: Chst 5F 143
  NW8 ....1C 82
  (not continuous)
  TW9: Rich 4F 115
Townshend Ter. TW9: Rich 4F 115
Towns Ho. SW4 ....3H 119
Townson Av. UB5: N'olt 2J 75
Townson Way UB5: N'olt 2J 75
Town Sq. IG11: Bark 1G 89
  (off Clockhouse Av.)
  TW7: Isle 3B 114
  (off Swan St.)
Town Tree Rd. TW15: Ashf 5C 128
Town Wharf TW7: Isle 3B 114
Towpath KT12: Walt T 5J 147
Towpath TW17: Shep 7B 146
Towpath, The SW10 ....1B 118
Towpath Rd. N18 ....6E 34
Towpath Wlk. E9 ....5B 68
Towpath Way CR0: C'don 6F 157
Towton N. N11 ....6C 32
Towton Rd. SE27 ....2C 138
Toynbec Cl. BR7: Chst 4F 143
Toynbee Rd. SW20 ....1G 153

Toynbee St. E1 ....6J 9 (5F 85)
Toynbee Studios 7K 9
Toyne Way N6 ....6D 46
Tracey Av. NW2 ....5E 62
Tracy Ct. HA7: Stan 7H 27
Tracy Ho. E3 ....3B 86
  (off Mile End Rd.)
Trade City Bus. Pk. TW16: Sun 1G 147
Trade Cl. N13 ....4F 33
Trader Rd. E6 ....6F 89
Tradescant Ho. E9 ....7J 67
  (off Frampton Pk. Rd.)
Tradescant Rd. SW8 ....7J 101
Tradewind Hgts. SE16 ....1K 103
  (off Rotherhithe St.)
Tradewinds Cl. E1 ....7G 85
Trading Est. Rd. NW10 ....4J 79
Trafalgar Av. KT4: Wor Pk 1F 165
  N17 ....6K 33
  SE15 ....5F 103
Trafalgar Bus. Cen. IG11: Bark 4K 89
Trafalgar Chambers SW3 ....5B 16
  (off South Pde.)
Trafalgar Cl. SE16 ....3A 104
Trafalgar Ct. E1 ....1J 103
  (off Wapping Wall)
Trafalgar Gdns. E1 ....5K 85
  W8 ....3K 99
Trafalgar Gro. SE10 ....6F 105
Trafalgar Ho. SE17 ....5C 102
  (off Bronti Cl.)
  SW18 ....4A 118
Trafalgar M. E9 ....6B 68
Trafalgar Pl. E11 ....4J 51
  N18 ....5B 34
Trafalgar Point N1 ....7D 66
  (off Downham Rd.)
Trafalgar Quarters SE10 ....6F 105
  (off Park Row)
Trafalgar Rd. SE10 ....6F 105
  SW19 ....7K 135
  TW2: Twick 2H 131
Trafalgar Square 4D 12 (1H 101)
Trafalgar Sq. SW1 ....1H 101
  WC2 ....4D 12 (1H 101)
Trafalgar St. SE17 ....5D 102
Trafalgar Studios 4E 12
  (off Whitehall)
Trafalgar Ter. HA1: Harr 1J 59
Trafalgar Trad. Est. EN3: Brim 4F 25
  E14 ....1E 104
Trafford Ho. N1 ....2D 84
  (off Cranston Est.)
Trafford Rd. CR7: Thor H 5K 155
Trafford Way BR3: Beck 6C 140
Traherne Lodge TW11: Tedd 5K 131
Trahorn Cl. E1 ....4H 85
Traitors' Gate 4J 15
Tralee Ct. SE16 ....5H 103
  (off Masters Dr.)
Tram Cl. SE24 ....3B 120
  (off Milkwood Rd.)
Tramlink, The SW19 ....2A 154
Tramsheds, The CR0: Bedd 7H 155
Tramway Av. E15 ....7G 69
  N9 ....7C 24
Tramway Cl. SE20 ....1J 157
Tramway Ct. E1 ....5A 86
Tramway Path CR4: Mitc 4C 154
  (not continuous)
Tramway M. E9 ....5K 67
  (off Brooksby's Wlk.)
Tranley M. NW3 ....4C 64
  (off Fleet Rd.)
Tranmere Ct. SM2: Sutt 7A 166
Tranmere Rd.
  N9 ....7A 24
  SW18 ....2A 136
  TW2: Whitt 7G 113
Tranquil La. HA2: Harr 1F 59

Tranquil Pas. SE3 ....2H 123
  (off Montpelier Va.)
Tranquil Va. SE3 ....2G 123
Transenna Works N1 ....6B 66
  (off Laycock St.)
Transept St. NW1 ....6D 4 (5C 82)
Transmere Cl. BR5: Pet W 6G 161
Transmere Rd. BR5: Pet W 6G 161
Transom Cl. SE16 ....4A 104
Transom Sq. E14 ....5D 104
Transport Av. TW8: Bford 5A 96
Tranton Rd. SE16 ....3G 103
Trappes Ho. SE16 ....4H 103
  (off Camilla Rd.)
Traps La. KT3: N Mald 1A 152
Traq Motor Racing 6G 155
Travellers Way
  TW4: Cran 2A 112
Travers Cl. E17 ....1K 49
Travers Ho. SE10 ....6F 105
  (off Trafalgar Gro.)
Travers Rd. N7 ....3A 66
Travis Ho. SE10 ....1E 122
Treacy Cl. WD23: B Hea 2B 26
Treadgold Ho. W11 ....7F 81
  (off Bomore Rd.)
Treadgold St. W11 ....7F 81
Treadway St. E2 ....2H 85
Treasury Cl. SM6: Wall 5H 167
Treasury M. DA5: Bexl 7H 127
Treasury Pas. SE1 ....6E 12
Treaty Cen. TW3: Houn 3F 113
Treaty St. N1 ....1K 83
Trebeck St. W1 ....4J 11 (1F 101)
Trebovir Rd. SW5 ....5J 99
Treby St. E3 ....4B 86
Trecastle Way N7 ....4H 65
Tredegar Ho. E3 ....3C 86
  (off Bow Rd.)
Tredegar M. E3 ....3B 86
Tredegar Rd. E3 ....2B 86
  N11 ....7C 32
Tredegar Sq. E3 ....3B 86
Tredegar Ter. E3 ....3B 86
Trederwen Rd. E8 ....1G 85
Tredown Rd. SE26 ....5J 139
Tredwell Cl. BR2: Brom 4C 160
  SW2 ....2K 137
Tredwell Rd. SE27 ....4B 138
Tree Cl. TW10: Ham 1D 132
Tree Av. SW13 ....3B 116
Tree Rd. E16 ....6A 88
Treeside Cl. UB7: W Dray 4A 92
Treeside Pl. N10 ....1F 47
Treetop Cl. CR7: Thor H 5C 156
Tree Top M. RM10: Dag 6K 73
Treetop M. NW6 ....7G 63
Treetops Cl. SE2 ....5E 108
Tree Vw. Cl. SE19 ....1E 156
Treewall Gdns. BR1: Brom 4K 141
Trefgarne Rd. RM10: Dag 2G 73
Trefil Wlk. N7 ....4J 65
Trefoil Ho. DA18: Erith 2E 108
  (off Kale Rd.)
Trefoil Rd. SW18 ....5A 118
Trefusis Ct. TW5: Cran 1K 111
Tregaron Av. N8 ....6J 47
Tregaron Gdns. KT3: N Mald 4A 152
Tregarvon Rd. SW11 ....4E 118
Tregenna Av. HA2: Harr 4E 58
Tregenna Cl. N14 ....5B 22
Tregenna Ct. HA2: Harr 4E 58
Tregony Rd. BR6: Chels 4K 173
Trego Rd. E9 ....7C 68
Tregothnan Rd. SW9 ....3J 119
Tregunter Rd. SW10 ....6K 99
Treheam Rd. IG6: Ilf 1H 53
Treherne Ct. SW17 ....4E 136
Trehern Rd. SW14 ....3K 115
Trehurst St. E5 ....5A 68
Trelawney Est. E9 ....6J 67

Trelawney Ho. *SE1* 5C 14
   (off Union St.)
Trelawney Rd. IG6: Ilf 1H 53
Trelawn Rd. E10 . . . . .3E 68
  SW2 . . . . .5A 120
Trelawny Cl. E17 . . . . .4D 50
Trellick Twr. *W10* 4H 81
   (off Golborne Rd.)
Trellis Ho. SW19 . . . . .7A 136
Trellis Sq. E3 . . . . .3B 86
Treloar Gdns. SE19 . . . . .6D 138
Tremadoc Rd. SW4 . . . . .4H 119
Tremaine Cl. SE4 . . . . .2C 122
Tremaine Rd. SE20 . . . . .2H 157
Trematon Bldg. *N1* 2J 83
   (off Trematon Wlk.)
Trematon Ho. *SE11* 5K 19
   (off Kennings Way)
Trematon M. N1 . . . . .2J 83
Trematon Pl. TW11: Tedd 7C 132
Trematon Wlk. *N1* 2J 83
   (off Trematon M.)
Tremelo Grn. RM8: Dag 1E 72
Tremlett Gro. N19 . . . . .3G 65
Trenance Gdns. IG3: Ilf 3A 72
Trenchard Av. HA4: Ruis 4K 57
Trenchard Cl. HA7: Stan 6F 27
  NW9 . . . . .1A 44
Trenchard Ct. NW4 . . . . .5C 44
  SM4: Mord 6J 153
Trenchard St. SE10 . . . . .5F 105
Trendell Ho. *E14* 6C 86
   (off Dod St.)
Trenear Cl. BR6: Chels 4K 173
Trenholme Cl. SE20 . . . . .7H 139
Trenholme Rd. SE20 . . . . .7H 139
Trenholme Ter. SE20 . . . . .7H 139
Trenmar Gdns. NW10 . . . . .3D 80
Trent Av. W5 .3C 96
Trent Ct. *CR2: S Croy* 5C 168
   (off Nottingham Rd.)
Trent Gdns. N14 . . . . .6A 22
Trentham Ho. W3 . . . . .5K 79
Trentham St. SW18 . . . . .1J 135
Trent Ho. KT2: King T 1D 150
  SE15 . . . . .4J 121
TRENT PARK 2A 22
Trent Park (Country Park) 1K 21
Trent Park Golf Course 4B 22
Trent Rd. IG9: Buck H 1E 36
  SW2 . . . . .5K 119
Trent Way KT4: Wor Pk 3E 164
  UB4: Hayes 2G 75
Trentwood Side EN2: Enf 3E 22
Treport St. SW18 . . . . .7K 117
Tresco Cl. BR1: Brom 6G 141
Trescoe Gdns. HA2: Harr 7C 40
Tresco Gdns. IG3: Ilf 2A 72
Tresco Rd. SE15 . . . . .4H 121
Tresham Cres. NW8 . . . . .3D 4 (4C 82)
Tresham Ho. *WC1* 5G 7
   (off Red Lion Sq.)
Tresham Rd. IG11: Bark 7K 71
Tresham Wlk. E9 . . . . .5J 67
Tresidder Ho. SW4 . . . . .7H 119
Tresilian Av. N21 . . . . .5E 22
Tressell Cl. N1 . . . . .7B 66
Tressillian Cres. SE4 . . . . .3C 122
Tressillian Rd. SE4 . . . . .4B 122
Tress Pl. SE1 .4A 14
Trestis Cl. UB4: Yead 5B 76
Treswell Rd. RM9: Dag 1E 90
Tretawn Gdns. NW7 . . . . .4F 29
Tretawn Pk. NW7 . . . . .4F 29
Trevanion Rd. W14 . . . . .4G 99
Treve Av. HA1: Harr 7H 41
Trevelyan Av. E12 . . . . .4D 70
Trevelyan Cl. KT3: N Mald 7A 152
Trevelyan Cres. HA3: Kenton 7D 42

Trevelyan Gdns. NW10 . . . . .1E 80
Trevelyan Ho. *E2* 3K 85
   (off Morpeth St.)
  SE5 . . . . .7B 102
   (off John Ruskin St.)
Trevelyan Rd. E15 . . . . .4H 69
  SW17 . . . . .5C 136
Trevenna Ho. *SE23* 3K 139
   (off Dacres Rd.)
Trevera Ct. EN3: Pond E 4F 25
Treveris St. SE1 . . . . .5B 14 (1B 102)
Treversh Ct. BR1: Brom 1G 159
Treverton St. W10 . . . . .4F 81
Treverton Towers *W10* 5F 81
   (off Treverton St.)
Treves Cl. N21 . . . . .5E 22
Treves Ho. *E1* 4G 85
   (off Vallance Rd.)
Treville St. SW15 . . . . .7D 116
Treviso Rd. SE23 . . . . .2K 139
Trevithick Cl. TW14: Felt 1H 129
Trevithick Ho. *SE16* 4H 103
   (off Rennie Est.)
  SE8 . . . . .6C 104
Trevithick Way E3 . . . . .3C 86
Trevithick St. SE8 . . . . .6C 104
Trevone Gdns. HA5: Pinn 6C 40
Trevor Cl. BR2: Hayes 7H 159
  EN4: E Barn 6G 21
  HA3: Hrw W 7E 26
  TW7: Isle .5K 113
  UB5: N'olt .2A 76
Trevor Cres. HA4: Ruis 4H 57
Trevor Gdns. HA4: Ruis 4J 57
  HA8: Edg .1K 43
  UB5: N'olt .2A 76
Trevor Pl. SW7 . . . . .7D 10 (2C 100)
Trevor Rd. HA8: Edg 1K 43
  IG8: Wfd G 7D 36
  SW19 . . . . .7G 135
  UB3: Hayes 2G 93
Trevor Sq. SW7 . . . . .7E 10 (2D 100)
Trevor St. SW7 . . . . .7D 10 (2C 100)
Trevor Wlk. *SW7* 7E 10
   (off Lancelot Pl., not continuous)
Trevose Ho. *SE11* 5H 19
   (off Orsett St.)
Trevose Rd. E17 . . . . .1F 51
Trewenna Dr. KT9: Chess 5D 162
Trewince Rd. SW20 . . . . .1E 152
Trewint St. SW18 . . . . .2A 136
Trewsbury Ho. SE2 . . . . .1D 108
Trewsbury Rd. SE26 . . . . .5K 139
Tria Apartments *E2* 3G 85
   (off Durant St.)
Triandra Way UB4: Yead 5B 76
Triangle, The *DA15: Sidc* 7A 126
   (off Burnt Oak La.)
  E8 . . . . .1H 85
  EC1 . . . . .3B 8
  IG11: Bark 6G 71
  KT1: King T 2H 151
  N13 . . . . .4E 32
Triangle Bus. Centre, The
  NW10 . . . . .3B 80
Triangle Cen. UB1: S'hall 1H 95
Triangle Ct. E16 . . . . .5B 88
  SE1 . . . . .5D 14
   (off Redcross Way)
Triangle Est. *SE11* 6J 19
   (off Kennington La.)
  SE11 . . . . .5A 102
   (off Kennington Rd.)
Triangle Ho. *SE1* 6J 15
   (off Three Oak La.)
Triangle Pas. EN4: E Barn 4F 21
Triangle Pl. SW4 . . . . .4H 119
Triangle Rd. E8 . . . . .1H 85
Triangle Way W3 . . . . .3G 97
Tribeca Apartments *E1* 6K 9
   (off Heneage St.)
Trickett Ho. SM2: Sutt 7K 165

Trico Ho. *TW8: Bford* 5D 96
   (off Ealing Rd.)
Tricorn Ho. SE28 . . . . .1J 107
Tricycle Cinema, The 7H 63
Tricycle Theatre, The 7H 63
Trident Bus. Cen. SW17 . . . . .5D 136
Trident Gdns. UB5: N'olt 3B 76
Trident Ho. *E14* 6E 86
   (off Blair St.)
  SE28 . . . . .1H 107
  TW19: Stanw 7A 110
   (off Clare Rd.)
Trident Pl. *SW3* 7B 16
   (off Old Church St.)
Trident St. SE16 . . . . .4K 103
Trident Way UB2: S'hall 3K 93
Trig La. EC4 . . . . .2C 14 (7C 84)
Trigon Rd. SW8 . . . . .7K 101
Trilby Rd. SE23 . . . . .2K 139
Trillo Ct. IG2: Ilf 7J 53
Trimdon NW1 .1G 83
Trimmer Wlk. TW8: Bford 6E 96
Trim St. SE14 . . . . .6B 104
Trinder Gdns. N19 . . . . .1J 65
Trinder M. SW12 . . . . .1E 136
  TW11: Tedd 5A 132
Trinder Rd. EN5: Barn 5A 20
  N19 . . . . .1J 65
Tring Av. HA9: Wemb 6G 61
  UB1: S'hall 6D 76
  W5 . . . . .1F 97
Tring Cl. IG2: Ilf 5H 53
Tring Ct. TW1: Twick 4A 132
Trinidad Gdns. RM10: Dag 7K 73
Trinidad Ho. *E14* 7B 86
   (off Gill St.)
Trinidad St. E14 . . . . .7B 86
Trinity Av. EN1: Enf 6A 24
  N2 . . . . .3B 46
Trinity Buoy Wharf *E14* 7G 87
   (off Orchard Pl.)
Trinity Chu. Pas. SW13 . . . . .6D 98
Trinity Chu. Rd. SW13 . . . . .6D 98
Trinity Chu. Sq. SE1 . . . . . . .7D 14 (3C 102)
Trinity Cl. BR2: Brom 1C 172
  CR2: Sande 7E 168
  E8 . . . . .6F 67
  E11 . . . . .2G 69
  NW3 . . . . .4B 64
  SE13 . . . . .4F 123
  SW4 . . . . .4G 119
  TW4: Houn 4C 112
Trinity College of Music 6E 104
Trinity Cotts. TW9: Rich 3F 115
Trinity Ct. *BR1: Brom* 1H 159
   (off Highland Rd.)
  CR0: C'don 2C 168
  EN2: Enf 2H 23
  N1 . . . . .1E 84
   (off Downham Rd.)
  N18 . . . . .6A 34
  NW2 . . . . .5E 62
  SE7 . . . . .4B 106
  SE8 . . . . .5A 104
   (off Evelyn St.)
  SE25 . . . . .6E 156
  SE26 . . . . .3J 139
  SW9 . . . . .3K 119
  W2 . . . . .6A 82
   (off Gloucester Ter.)
  W9 . . . . .3H 81
   (off Croxley Rd.)
  WC1 . . . . .3G 7
Trinity Cres. SW17 . . . . .2D 136
Trinity Dr. UB8: Hil 5E 74
Trinity Gdns. E16 . . . . .5H 87
   (not continuous)
  SW9 . . . . .4K 119
Trinity Grn. E1 .4J 85
Trinity Gro. SE10 . . . . .1E 122

Trinity Hospital (Almshouses)
  SE10 . . . . .5F 105
Trinity Ho. EC3 . . . . .2J 15
  RM8: Dag 5B 72
  SE1 . . . . .3C 102
   (off Bath Ter.)
  W14 . . . . .4H 99
Trinity M. *E1* .5J 85
   (off Redman's Rd.)
  SE20 . . . . .1H 157
  W10 . . . . .6F 81
Trinity Pk. E4 .6G 35
Trinity Path SE23 . . . . .3J 139
  SE26 . . . . .3J 139
Trinity Pl. DA6: Bex 4F 127
  EC3 . . . . .2J 15 (7F 85)
Trinity Ri. SW2 . . . . .1A 138
Trinity Rd. IG6: Ilf 3G 53
  N2 . . . . .3B 46
  N22 . . . . .7D 32
   (not continuous)
  SW17 . . . . .4A 118
  SW18 . . . . .4A 118
  SW19 . . . . .6J 135
  TW9: Rich 3F 115
  UB1: S'hall 1C 94
Trinity Sq. EC3 . . . . .3H 15 (7E 84)
Trinity St. E16 .5H 87
  EN2: Enf 2H 23
  SE1 . . . . .7D 14 (2C 102)
   (not continuous)
Trinity Ter. IG9: Lough 1E 36
Trinity Twr. *E1* 7G 85
   (off Vaughan Way)
  E14 . . . . .3D 104
Trinity Wlk. NW3 . . . . .6A 64
Trinity Way E4 . . . . .6G 35
  W3 . . . . .7A 80
Trio Pl. SE1 . . . . .7D 14 (2C 102)
Triscott Ho. UB3: Hayes 1J 93
Tristan Ct. *SE8* 6B 104
   (off Dorking Cl.)
Tristan Sq. SE3 . . . . .3G 123
Tristram Cl. E17 . . . . .3F 51
Tristram Dr. N9 . . . . .3B 34
Tristram Rd. BR1: Brom 4H 141
Triton Ct. E16 .5J 87
   (off Robertson Rd.)
Triton Ho. *E14* 4D 104
   (off Cahir St.)
Triton Sq. NW1 . . . . .3A 6 (4G 83)
Triton St. NW1 . . . . .3K 5 (4F 83)
Tritton Av. CR0: Bedd 4J 167
Tritton Rd. SE21 . . . . .3D 138
Triumph Cl. UB3: Harl 1E 110
Triumph Ho. IG11: Bark 3A 90
Triumph Rd. E6 . . . . .6D 88
Triumph Trad. Est. N17 . . . . .6B 34
Trocette Mans. *SE1* 3E 102
   (off Bermondsey St.)
Trojan Ct. NW6 . . . . .7G 63
Trojan Ind. Est. NW10 . . . . .6B 62
Trojan M. SW19 . . . . .7J 135
Trojan Way CR0: Wadd 3K 167
Troon Cl. SE16 . . . . .5H 103
  SE28 . . . . .6D 90
Troon Ho. *E1* .6A 86
   (off White Horse Rd.)
Troon St. E1 . . . . .6A 86
Tropical Ct. *W10* 3F 81
   (off Kilburn La.)
Trosley Rd. DA17: Belv 6G 109
Trossachs Rd. SE22 . . . . .5E 120
Trothy Rd. SE1 . . . . .4G 103
Trotman Ho. *SE14* 1J 121
   (off Pomeroy St.)
Trott Rd. N10 .7J 31
Trott St. SW11 . . . . .1C 118
Trotwood Ho. *SE16* 2H 103
   (off Wilson Gro.)
Troughton Rd. SE7 . . . . .5K 105

Troutbeck NW1 . . . . .2K **5**
Troutbeck Rd. SE14 . . . . .1A **122**
Trout Rd.
  UB7: Yiew 7A **74**
Trouville Rd. SW4 . . . . .6G **119**
Trowbridge Est. E9 . . . . .6B **68**
            (off Osborne Rd.)
Trowbridge Ho. E9 . . . . .6B **68**
            (off Felstead St.)
Trowbridge Rd. E9 . . . . .6B **68**
Trowlock Av. TW11: Tedd 6C **132**
Trowlock Island
  TW11: Tedd 6D **132**
Trowlock Way TW11: Tedd 6D **132**
Troy Ct.
  SE18 . . . . .4F **107**
  W8 . . . . .3J **99**
       (off Kensington High St.)
Troy Ind. Est. HA1: Harr 5K **41**
Troy Rd. SE19 . . . . .6D **138**
Troy Town SE15 . . . . .3G **121**
Trubshaw Rd. UB2: S'hall 3F **95**
True Lovers Ct.
  HA6: Nwood 1F **39**
Trueman Cl.
  HA8: Edg 7C **28**
Truesdale Rd. E6 . . . . .6D **88**
Truesdales UB10: Ick 2E **56**
truGym
  Bromley 1J **159**
              (off East St.)
  Crouch End 6J **47**
Trulock Ct. N17 . . . . .7B **34**
Trulock Rd. N17 . . . . .7B **34**
Trumans Rd. N16 . . . . .5F **67**
Truman Wlk. E3 . . . . .4D **86**
Trumble Gdns.
  CR7: Thor H 4C **156**
Trumpers Way W7 . . . . .3J **95**
Trumpington Rd. E7 . . . . .4H **69**
Trump St. EC2 . . . . . . .1D **14** (6C **84**)
Trundle Ho. SE1 . . . . .6C **14**
           (off Trundle St.)
Trundlers Way WD23: B Hea 1D **26**
Trundle St. SE1 . . . . . . .6C **14** (2C **102**)
Trundleys Rd. SE8 . . . . .5K **103**
Trundley's Ter. SE8 . . . . .4K **103**
Truro Gdns. IG1: Ilf 7C **52**
Truro Ho. HA5: Hat E 1D **40**
  W2 . . . . .5J **81**
        (off Westbourne Pk. Rd.)
Truro Rd. E17 .4B **50**
  N22 . . . . .7D **32**
Truro St. NW5 . . . . .6E **64**
Truro Way UB4: Hayes 3G **75**
Truslove Rd. SE27 . . . . .5A **138**
Trussley Rd. W6 . . . . .3E **98**
Trust Wlk. SE21 . . . . .1B **138**
Tryfan Cl. IG4: Ilf 5B **52**
Tryon Cres. E9 . . . . .1J **85**
Tryon St. SW3 . . . . . .5E **16** (5D **100**)
Trystings Cl.
  KT10: Clay 6A **162**
Tuam Rd. SE18 . . . . .6H **107**
Tubbenden Cl.
  BR6: Orp .3J **173**
Tubbenden Dr.
  BR6: Orp 4H **173**
Tubbenden La. BR6: Orp 4H **173**
Tubbenden La. Sth.
  BR6: Farnb 5H **173**
Tubbs Rd. NW10 . . . . .2B **80**
Tucana Cl. E1 . . . . .3K **9**
           (off Cygnet St.)
Tucana Hgts. E20 . . . . .5E **68**
         (off Cheering La.)
Tucklow Wlk. SW15 . . . . .7B **116**
Tudo Pl. IG9: Buck H 2H **37**
Tudor Av.
  KT4: Wor Pk 3D **164**
  TW12: Hamp 7E **130**

Tudor Cl. BR7: Chst 1D **160**
  HA5: Eastc 5J **39**
  IG7: Chig 4K **37**
  IG8: Wfd G 5E **36**
  KT9: Chess 5E **162**
  N6 . . . . .7G **47**
  NW3 . . . . .5C **64**
  NW7 . . . . .6H **29**
  NW9 . . . . .2J **61**
  SM3: Cheam 5F **165**
  SM6: Wall 7G **167**
  SW2 . . . . .6K **119**
  TW12: Hamp H 5G **131**
  TW15: Ashf 4A **128**
       (off Princes Riverside Rd.)
Tudor Ct. DA14: Sidc 3A **144**
  E17 . . . . .7B **50**
  N1 . . . . .6E **66**
  N22 . . . . .7D **32**
  SE9 . . . . .4C **124**
  SE16 . . . . .1K **103**
       (off Princes Riverside Rd.)
  TW11: Tedd 6K **131**
  TW13: Hanw 4A **130**
  TW19: Stanw 6A **110**
  W3 . . . . .2G **97**
Tudor Ct. Nth. HA9: Wemb 5G **61**
Tudor Ct. Sth. HA9: Wemb 5G **61**
Tudor Cres. EN2: Enf 1H **23**
Tudor Dr. KT2: King T 5D **132**
  SM4: Mord 6F **153**
Tudor Ent. Pk. HA1: Harr 3K **59**
  HA3: W'stone 3H **41**
Tudor Est. NW10 . . . . .2H **79**
Tudor Gdns. BR4: W W'ck 3E **170**
  HA3: Hrw W 2H **41**
  NW9 . . . . .2J **61**
  SW13 . . . . .3A **116**
  TW1: Twick 1K **131**
  W3 . . . . .5G **79**
Tudor Gro. E9 . . . . .7J **67**
Tudor Ho. E9 .7J **67**
  E16 . . . . .1K **105**
           (off Wesley Av.)
  HA5: Pinn 2A **40**
         (off Pinner Hill Rd.)
  W14 . . . . .4F **99**
          (off Windsor Way)
Tudor M. E17 .4B **50**
Tudor Pde. RM6: Chad H 7D **54**
  SE9 . . . . .4C **124**
Tudor Pl. CR4: Mitc 7C **136**
  SE19 . . . . .7F **139**
Tudor Rd. BR3: Beck 3E **158**
  E4 . . . . .6J **35**
  E6 . . . . .1A **88**
  E9 . . . . .1H **85**
  EN5: New Bar 3D **20**
  HA3: Hrw W, W'stone 2H **41**
  HA5: Pinn 2A **40**
  IG11: Bark 1K **89**
  KT2: King T 7G **133**
  N9 . . . . .7C **24**
  SE19 . . . . .7F **139**
  SE25 . . . . .5H **157**
  TW3: Houn 4H **113**
  TW12: Hamp 7E **130**
  TW15: Ashf 6F **129**
  UB1: S'hall 7C **76**
  UB3: Hayes 6F **75**
Tudor Sq. UB3: Hayes 5F **75**
Tudor Stacks SE24 . . . . .4C **120**
Tudor St. EC4 . . . . . . .2K **13** (7A **84**)
Tudor Wlk. DA5: Bexl 6E **126**
Tudor Way
  BR5: Pet W 6H **161**
  N14 . . . . .1C **32**
  UB10: Hil .6C **56**
  W3 . . . . .2G **97**
Tudor Well Cl. HA7: Stan 5G **27**
Tudor Works UB4: Yead 1A **94**
Tudway Rd. SE3 . . . . .3K **123**

Tufnell Ct. E3 . . . . .1B **86**
         (off Old Ford Rd.)
TUFNELL PARK 4G **65**
Tufnell Pk. Rd. N7 . . . . .4G **65**
  N19 . . . . .4G **65**
Tufton Cl. SW1 . . . . .2E **18**
           (off Tufton St.)
Tufton Gdns. KT8: W Mole 2F **149**
Tufton Rd. E4 . . . . .4H **35**
Tufton St. SW1 . . . . . . .1E **18** (3J **101**)
Tugboat St. SE28 . . . . .2J **107**
Tugela Rd. CR0: C'don 6D **156**
Tugela St. SE6 . . . . .2B **140**
Tugmutton Cl. BR6: Farnb 4F **173**
Tulip Cl. CR0: C'don 1K **169**
  E6 . . . . .5D **88**
  TW12: Hamp 6D **130**
  UB2: S'hall 2G **95**
Tulip Gdns. E4 . . . . .3A **36**
  IG1: Ilf 6F **71**
Tullis Ho. E9 .7J **67**
        (off Frampton Pk. Rd.)
Tull St. CR4: Mitc 7D **154**
Tulse Cl. BR3: Beck 3E **158**
TULSE HILL .1B **138**
Tulse Hill SW2 . . . . .6A **120**
Tulse Hill Est. SW2 . . . . .6A **120**
Tulse Ho. SW2 . . . . .6A **120**
Tulsemere Rd. SE27 . . . . .2C **138**
Tumbling Bay KT12: Walt T 6J **147**
Tummons Gdns. SE25 . . . . .2E **156**
Tump Ho. SE28 . . . . .1J **107**
Tunbridge Ho. EC1 . . . . .1K **7**
Tuncombe Rd. N18 . . . . .4K **33**
Tunis Rd. W12 . . . . .1E **98**
Tunley Grn. E14 . . . . .5B **86**
Tunley Rd. NW10 . . . . .1A **80**
  SW17 . . . . .1E **136**
Tunmarsh La. E13 . . . . .3K **87**
Tunnan Leys E6 . . . . .6E **88**
Tunnel App. E14 . . . . .7A **86**
  SE10 . . . . .2G **105**
  SE16 . . . . .2J **103**
Tunnel Av. SE10 . . . . .2F **105**
         (not continuous)
Tunnel Av. Trad. Est. SE10 . . . . .2F **105**
Tunnel Gdns. N11 . . . . .7B **32**
Tunnel Link Rd. TW6: H'row A 6C **110**
Tunnel Rd. SE16 . . . . .2J **103**
Tunnel Rd. E. TW6: H'row A 1D **110**
Tunnel Rd. W. TW6: H'row A 1C **110**
Tunstall Cl. BR6: Orp 4J **173**
Tunstall Rd. CR0: C'don 1E **168**
  SW9 . . . . .4K **119**
Tunstall Wlk. TW8: Bford 6E **96**
Tunstock Way DA17: Belv 3E **108**
Tunworth Cl. NW9 . . . . .6J **43**
Tunworth Cres. SW15 . . . . .6B **116**
Tun Yd. SW8 . . . . .2F **119**
          (off Peardon St.)
Tupelo Rd. E10 . . . . .2D **68**
Tupman Ho. SE16 . . . . .2G **103**
       (off Scott Lidgett Cres.)
Tuppy St. SE28 . . . . .3G **107**
Turenne Cl. SW18 . . . . .4A **118**
Turin Rd. N9 .7D **24**
Turin St. E2 . . . . .2K **9** (3G **85**)
Turkey Oak Cl. SE19 . . . . .1E **156**
Turks Boatyard KT1: King T 1D **150**
Turks Cl. UB8: Hil 3C **74**
Turk's Head Yd. EC1 . . . . . .5A **8** (5B **84**)
Turk's Row SW3 . . . . . .5F **17** (5D **100**)
Turle Rd. N4 . . . . .2K **65**
  SW16 . . . . .2J **155**
Turlewray Cl. N4 . . . . .1K **65**
Turley Cl. E15 . . . . .1G **87**
Turnagain La. EC4 . . . . .7A **8**
Turnage Rd. RM8: Dag 1E **72**
Turnant Rd. N17 . . . . .1C **48**
Turnberry Cl. NW4 . . . . .2F **45**
  SE16 . . . . .5H **103**

Turnberry Quay E14 . . . . .3D **104**
Turnberry Way BR6: Orp 1H **173**
Turnbull Ho. N1 . . . . .1B **84**
Turnbury Cl. SE28 . . . . .6D **90**
Turnchapel M. SW4 . . . . .3F **119**
Turner Av. CR4: Mitc 1D **154**
  N15 . . . . .4E **48**
  TW2: Twick 3G **131**
Turner Cl. HA0: Wemb 6D **60**
  NW11 . . . . .6K **45**
  SW9 . . . . .7B **102**
  UB4: Hayes 2E **74**
Turner Ct. SE16 . . . . .2J **103**
          (off Albion St.)
Turner Cres. CR0: C'don 6C **156**
Turner Dr. NW11 . . . . .6K **45**
Turner Ho. E14 . . . . .2C **104**
         (off Cassilis Rd.)
  NW6 . . . . .5A **64**
         (off Dresden Cl.)
  NW8 . . . . .2C **82**
        (off Townshend Est.)
  SW1 . . . . .4D **18**
         (off Herrick St.)
  TW1: Twick 6D **114**
         (off Clevedon Rd.)
Turner M. SM2: Sutt 7K **165**
Turner Pde. N1 . . . . .7A **66**
         (off Barnsbury Pk.)
Turner Pl. SW11 . . . . .5C **118**
Turner Rd. E17 . . . . .3E **50**
  HA8: Edg .2E **42**
  KT3: N Mald 7K **151**
Turners Cl. N20 . . . . .3J **31**
Turners Ct. E15 . . . . .4E **68**
         (off Drapers Rd.)
  N15 . . . . .5D **48**
Turners Mdw. Way BR3: Beck 1B **158**
Turners Rd. E3 . . . . .5B **86**
Turner St.
  E1 . . . . .5H **85**
  E16 . . . . .6H **87**
Turners Way CR0: Wadd 2A **168**
Turners Wood NW11 . . . . .7A **46**
Turneville Rd. W14 . . . . .6H **99**
Turney Rd. SE21 . . . . .7C **120**
TURNHAM GREEN 4A **98**
Turnham Grn. Ter. W4 . . . . .4A **98**
Turnham Grn. Ter. M. W4 . . . . .4A **98**
Turnham Rd. SE4 . . . . .5A **122**
Turnmill St. EC1 . . . . . . .4A **8** (4B **84**)
Turnour Ho. E1 . . . . .6H **85**
         (off Walburgh St.)
Turnpike Cl. DA16: Well 3A **126**
  SE8 . . . . .7B **104**
Turnpike Ct. DA6: Bex 4D **126**
Turnpike Ho. EC1 . . . . . . .2B **8** (3B **84**)
Turnpike La. N8 . . . . .4K **47**
  SM1: Sutt 5A **166**
  UB10: Uxb 3A **74**
Turnpike M. N8 . . . . .3A **48**
         (off Turnpike La.)
Turnpike Pde. N15 . . . . .3B **48**
         (off Green Lanes)
Turnpike Way TW7: Isle 1A **114**
Turnpin La. SE10 . . . . .6E **104**
Turnstone Cl. E13 . . . . .3J **87**
  NW9 . . . . .2A **44**
  UB10: Ick .5D **56**
Turnstone Ho. E1 . . . . .3K **15**
           (off Star Pl.)
Turpentine La. SW1 . . . . . .5K **17** (5F **101**)
Turpin Cl. E1 .7K **85**
Turpington Cl. BR2: Brom 7C **160**
Turpington La. BR2: Brom 7C **160**
Turpin Ho. SW11 . . . . .1F **119**
Turpin Rd. TW14: Felt 6H **111**
Turpin's La. IG8: Wfd G 5J **37**
Turpins Yd. NW2 . . . . .5F **63**
  SE10 . . . . .7E **104**

Turpin Way N19 . . . . .2H 65
SM6: Wall 7F 167
Turquand St. SE17 . . . . .4C 102
Turret Gro. SW4 . . . . .3G 119
Turton Rd. HA0: Wemb 5E 60
Turville Ho. NW8 . . . . .3C 4
(off Grendon St.)
Turville St. E2 . . . . .3J 9 (4F 85)
Tuscan Ho. E2 . . . . .3J 85
(off Knottisford St.)
Tuscan Rd. SE18 . . . . .5H 107
Tuscany Corte SE13 . . . . .3D 122
(off Loampit Va.)
Tuscany Ho. E17 . . . . .2B 50
IG3: Ilf 6A 54
Tuskar St. SE10 . . . . .6G 105

Tussah Ho. E2 . . . . .2J 85
(off Russia La.)
Tustin Est. SE15 . . . . .6J 103
Tuttlebee La. IG9: Buck H 2D 36
Tuttle Ho. SW1 . . . . .6C 18
(off Aylesford St.)
Tweed Ct. W7 .6J 77
(off Hanway Rd.)
Tweeddale Gro. UB10: Ick 3E 56
Tweeddale Rd. SM5: Cars 1B 166
Tweed Glen RM1: Rom 1K 55
Tweed Grn. RM1: Rom 1K 55
Tweedmouth Rd. E13 . . . . .2K 87
Tweed Way RM1: Rom 1K 55
Tweedy Cl. EN1: Enf 5A 24
Tweedy Rd. BR1: Brom 1J 159
Tweezer's All. WC2 . . . . .2J 13
Twelve Acre Ho. E12 . . . . .3E 70
(off Grantham Rd.)
Twelvetrees Bus. Pk. E3 . . . . .4F 87
Twelvetrees Cres. E3 . . . . .4E 86
(not continuous)
E16 . . . . .4E 86
Twentyman Cl. IG8: Wfd G 5D 36
TWICKENHAM 1A 132
Twickenham Bri. TW1: Twick 5C 114
Twickenham Cl. CR0: Bedd 3K 167
Twickenham Gdns. HA3: Hrw W 7D 26
UB6: G'frd 5A 60
Twickenham Mus. 1A 132
(off The Embankment)
Twickenham Rd. E11 . . . . .2E 68
TW7: Isle 5A 114
TW9: Rich 4C 114
TW11: Tedd 4A 132
(not continuous)
TW13: Hanw 3D 130
Twickenham Stadium 6J 113
Twickenham Stoop 7J 113
Twickenham Trad. Est.
TW1: Twick 6K 113
Twig Folly Cl. E2 . . . . .2K 85
Twigg Cl. DA8: Erith 7K 109
Twilley St. SW18 . . . . .7K 117
Twin Bridges Bus. Pk.
CR2: S Croy 6D 168
Twine Cl. IG11: Bark 3B 90
Twine Ct. E1 .7J 85
Twineham Grn. N12 . . . . .4D 30
Twine Ter. E3 . . . . .4B 86
(off Ropery St.)
Twining Av. TW2: Twick 3G 131
Twin Tumps Way SE28 . . . . .7A 90
Twisden Rd. NW5 . . . . .4F 65
Twist Ho. SE1 . . . . .3E 102
Twitten Gro. BR1: Brom 3D 160
Twycross M. SE10 . . . . .5G 105
Twyford Abbey Rd. NW10 . . . . .3F 79
Twyford Av. N2 . . . . .3D 46
W3 . . . . .7G 79
Twyford Ct. HA0: Wemb 2E 78
(off Vicars Bri. Cl.)
N10 .3E 46

Twyford Cres. W3 . . . . .1G 97
Twyford Ho. N5 . . . . .3B 66
N15 .6E 48
(off Chisley Rd.)
Twyford Pl. WC2 . . . . .7G 7 (6K 83)
Twyford Rd. HA2: Harr 1F 59
IG1: Ilf 5G 71
SM5: Cars 1B 166
Twyford Sports Cen. 1H 97
Twyford St. N1 . . . . .1K 83
Twynholm Mans. SW6 . . . . .7G 99
(off Lillie Rd.)
Tyas Rd. E16 .4H 87
Tybenham Rd. SW19 . . . . .3J 153
Tyberry Rd. EN3: Enf H 3C 24
Tyburn Ho. NW8 . . . . .3B 4
(off Fisherton St.)
Tyburn La. HA1: Harr 7K 41
Tyburn Tree (site of) 1F 11
Tyburn Way W1 . . . . .2F 11 (7D 82)
Tye La. BR6: Farnb 5G 173
Tyers Est. SE1 . . . . .6G 15
Tyer's Ga. SE1 . . . . .7G 15 (2E 102)
Tyers St. SE11 . . . . .6G 19 (5K 101)
Tyers Ter. SE11 . . . . .6G 19 (5K 101)
Tyeshurst Cl. SE2 . . . . .5E 108
Tygan Ho. SM3: Cheam 6G 165
(off The Broadway)
Tylecroft Rd. SW16 . . . . .2J 155
Tylehurst Gdns.
IG1: Ilf 5G 71
Tyler Cl. DA8: Erith 7H 109
E2 . . . . .2F 85
Tyler Rd. UB2: S'hall 3F 95
Tylers Ct. E17 . . . . .4C 50
(off Westbury Rd.)
HA0: Wemb 2E 78
W1 .1C 12
Tylers Ga. HA3: Kenton 6E 42
Tylers Path SM5: Cars 4D 166
Tyler St. SE10 . . . . .5G 105
(not continuous)
Tylney Av. SE19 . . . . .5F 139
(not continuous)
Tylney Ho. E1 . . . . .6H 85
(off Nelson St.)
Tylney Rd. BR1: Brom 2B 160
E7 . . . . .4A 70
Tynamara KT1: King T 4D 150
(off Portsmouth Rd.)
Tynan Cl. TW14: Felt 1J 129
Tyndale Ct. E9 . . . . .6A 68
(off Brookfield Rd.)
E14 .5D 104
(off Transom Sq.)
Tyndale Ho. N1 . . . . .7B 66
(off Tyndale La.)
Tyndale La. N1 . . . . .7B 66
Tyndale Mans. N1 . . . . .7B 66
(off Upper St.)
Tyndale Ter. N1 . . . . .7B 66
Tyndall Gdns. E10 . . . . .2E 68
Tyndall Rd. DA16: Well 3K 125
E10 .2E 68
Tyne Ct. W7 .6J 77
(off Hanway Rd.)
Tyneham Cl. SW11 . . . . .3E 118
Tyneham Rd. SW11 . . . . .2E 118
Tyne Ho. KT2: King T 1D 150
Tynemouth Cl. E6 . . . . .6F 89
Tynemouth Dr. EN1: Enf 1B 24
Tynemouth Rd. CR4: Mitc 7E 136
N15 .4F 49
SE18 . . . . .5J 107
Tynemouth St. SW6 . . . . .2A 118
Tyne St. E1 . . . . .7K 9 (6F 85)
Tynsdale Rd. NW10 . . . . .7A 62
Tynte Ct. E9 .5A 68
(off Mabley St.)
Tynwald Ho. SE26 . . . . .3G 139
Type St. E2 . . . . .2K 85

Typhoon Way SM6: Wall 7J 167
Tyrawley Rd. SW6 . . . . .1K 117
Tyre La. NW9 .4A 44
Tyrell Cl. HA1: Harr 4J 59
Tyrell Ct. SM5: Cars 4D 166
Tyrell Ho. BR3: Beck 5D 140
(off Beckenham Hill Rd.)
Tyrian Pl. E1 .5G 85
Tyrols Rd. SE23 . . . . .1K 139
Tyrone Rd. E6 . . . . .2D 88
Tyron Way DA14: Sidc 4J 143
Tyrrell Av. DA16: Well 5A 126
Tyrrell Ho. SW1 . . . . .7B 18
(off Churchill Gdns.)
Tyrrell Rd. SE22 . . . . .4G 121
Tyrrell Sq. CR4: Mitc 1C 154
Tyrrel Way NW9 . . . . .7C 44
Tyrwhitt Rd. SE4 . . . . .3C 122
Tysoe St. EC1 . . . . .2K 7 (3A 84)
Tyson Gdns. SE23 . . . . .7J 121
Tyson Rd. SE23 . . . . .7J 121
Tyssen Pas. E8 . . . . .6F 67
Tyssen Rd. N16 . . . . .3F 67
Tyssen St. E8 . . . . .6F 67
N1 . . . . .2E 84
Tytherton E2 .2J 85
(off Cyprus St.)
Tytherton Rd. N19 . . . . .3H 65

U

Uamvar St. E14 . . . . .5D 86
Uber E17 . . . .
4B 50
Uckfield Gro. CR4: Mitc 7E 136
Udall St. SW1 . . . . .4B 18 (4G 101)
Udimore Ho. W10 . . . . .5E 80
(off Sutton Way)
Udney Pk. Rd. TW11: Tedd 6A 132
Uffington Rd. NW10 . . . . .1C 80
SE27 . . . . .4A 138
Ufford Cl. HA3: Hrw W 7A 26
Ufford Rd. HA3: Hrw W 7A 26
Ufford St. SE1 . . . . .6K 13 (2A 102)
Ufton Ct. UB5: N'olt 3B 76
Ufton Gro. N1 . . . . .7D 66
Ufton Rd. N1 .7D 66
(not continuous)
Uhura Sq. N16 . . . . .3E 66
Ujima Ct. SW16 . . . . .4J 137
Ullathorne Rd. SW16 . . . . .4G 137
Ulleswater Rd. N14 . . . . .3D 32
Ullin St. E14 .5E 86
Ullswater E18 . . . . .2J 51
Ullswater Cl. BR1: Brom 7G 141
SW15 . . . . .4K 133
UB4: Hayes 2G 75
Ullswater Cres. SW15 . . . . .4K 133
Ullswater Ho. SE15 . . . . .6J 103
(off Hillbeck Cl.)
Ullswater Rd. SE27 . . . . .2B 138
SW13 . . . . .7C 98
Ulster Gdns. N13 . . . . .4H 33
Ulster Pl. NW1 . . . . .4J 5 (4F 83)
Ulster Ter. NW1 . . . . .3H 5 (4F 83)
Ulundi Rd. SE3 . . . . .6G 105
Ulva Rd. SW15 . . . . .5F 117
Ulverscroft Rd. SE22 . . . . .5F 121
Ulverstone Rd. SE27 . . . . .2B 138
Ulverston Rd. E17 . . . . .2F 51
Ulysses Rd. NW6 . . . . .5H 63
Umberston St. E1 . . . . .6G 85
Umbria St. SW15 . . . . .6C 116
Umbriel Pl. E13 . . . . .2J 87
Umfreville Rd. N4 . . . . .6B 48
Undercliff Rd. SE13 . . . . .3C 122
UNDERHILL 5D 20
Underhill EN5: Barn 5D 20
Underhill Ct. EN5: Barn 5D 20

Underhill Ho. E14 . . . . .5C 86
(off Burgess St.)
Underhill Pas. NW1 . . . . .1F 83
(off Camden High St.)
Underhill Rd. SE22 . . . . .5G 121
Underhill St. NW1 . . . . .1F 83
Underne Av. N14 . . . . .2A 32
Undershaft EC3 . . . . .1G 15 (6E 84)
Undershaw Rd.
BR1: Brom 3H 141
Underwood CR0: New Ad 5E 170
Underwood, The SE9 . . . . .2D 142
Underwood Ct. E10 . . . . .1D 68
(off Leyton Grange Est.)
Underwood Ho. KT8: W Mole 5E 148
(off Approach Rd.)
W6 . . . . .3D 98
(off Sycamore Gdns.)
Underwood Rd. E1 . . . . .4G 85
E4 . . . . .5J 35
IG8: Wfd G 7F 37
Underwood Row N1 . . . . . . .1D 8 (3C 84)
Underwood St. N1 . . . . .1D 8 (3C 84)
Undine Rd. E14 . . . . .4D 104
Undine St. SW17 . . . . .5D 136
Uneeda Dr. UB6: G'frd 1H 77
Unex Twr. E15 . . . . .7F 69
(off Station St.)
Unicorn Bldg. E1 . . . . .7K 85
(off Jardine Rd.)
Unicorn Theatre
London 1E 102
Unicorn Works N17 . . . . .7D 34
Union Cl. E11 . . . . .4F 69
Union Cotts. E15 . . . . .7G 69
Union Ct. EC2 .7G 9
SW4 .2J 119
TW9: Rich 5E 114
W9 . . . . .5J 81
(off Elmfield Way)
Union Dr. E1 .4A 86
Union Gro. SW8 . . . . .2H 119
Union Ho. CR0: C'don 7C 156
Union La. TW7: Isle 2A 114
Union M. SW4 . . . . .2J 119
Union Pk. SE10 . . . . .5H 105
Union Rd. BR2: Brom 5B 160
CR0: C'don 7C 156
HA0: Wemb 6E 60
N11 .6C 32
RM7: Rush G 6K 55
SW4 .2H 119
SW8 .2H 119
UB5: N'olt 2E 76
Union Sq. N1 . . . . .1C 84
Union St. EN5: Barn 3B 20
KT1: King T 2D 150
SE1 . . . . .5A 14 (1B 102)
Union Theatre 5B 14
Union Wlk. E2 . . . . .1H 9 (3E 84)
Union Wharf N1 . . . . .1C 84
(Arlington Av.)
N1 . . . . .2C 84
(off Wenlock Rd., Wenlock Rd.)
UB7: View 1A 92
(off Bentinck Rd.)
Union Yd. W1 . . . . .1K 11 (6F 83)
Unitair Cen. TW14: Bedf 6E 110
United Ho. SE16 . . . . .2J 103
(off Brunel Rd.)
Unit Workshops E1 . . . . .6G 85
(off Adler St.)
Unity Cl. CR0: New Ad 7D 170
NW10 . . . . .6C 62
SE19 . . . . .5C 138
Unity Ct. SE1 . . . . .5F 103
(off Fortune Pl.)
Unity M. NW1 . . . . .2H 83
Unity Pl. E17 .3A 50
Unity Ter. HA2: Harr 1F 59
Unity Trad. Est. IG8: Wfd G 2B 52

Unity Way SE18 . . . . .3B **106**
Unity Wharf *SE1* 6K **15**
  (off Mill St.)
Universal Ho. UB1: S'hall 7C **76**
University Cl. NW7 . . . . .7G **29**
University College London
  Art Museum 3C **6**
    (off Gower St.)
  Bloomsbury Campus . . 3C 6 (4H **83**)
  Department of Geological Collections
    . . . . .4C **6**
    (off Gower St.)
  Institute of Neurology 4F **7**
    (off Queen Sq.)
  Slade School of Fine Art 3C **6**
    (off Gower Ct.)
University Gdns. DA5: Bexl 7F **127**
University of East Anglia
  London 6J **9**
University of East London
  Docklands Campus 7E **88**
  Duncan House 1F **87**
  Stratford Campus 6G **69**
University of Greenwich
  Avery Hill Campus 6G **125**
  Greenwich Campus,
  King William Wlk. 6F **105**
  Maritime Greenwich Campus
    . . . . .6E **104**
University of London
  Birkbeck College 5D 6 (5H **83**)
  Heythrop College 3K **99**
    (off Kensington Sq.)
  School of Hygiene
    & Tropical Medicine 5D **6**
  School of Oriental & African Studies
    . . . . .4D **6**
  Senate House 5D 6 (5H **83**)
  Warburg Institute 4D 6 (4H **83**)
University of London Institute of Education &
  Institute of Advanced Legal Studies
    . . . . .4D 6 (4H **83**)
University of London Observatory . . .6G **29**
University of North London
  Hornsey Rd. 4A **66**
  Ladbrooke House 5C **66**
  North London Campus, Spring House
    . . . . .6A **66**
University of the Arts London
  Camberwell College of Arts,
  Peckham Rd. 1E **120**
  Camberwell College of Arts,
  Wilson Rd. 1E **120**
  Chelsea College of Art & Design
    . . . . .5D 18 (5H **101**)
  London College of Fashion -
  Golden La. 4C **8**
  London College of Fashion - Mare St.
    . . . . .6G **67**
  Wimbledon College of Art . . .1G **153**
University of West London
  Brentford Campus 5C **96**
    . . . . .1D **96**
  Ealing Campus, Grove House
    . . . . .1D **96**
  Ealing Campus, Spesom House
    . . . . .7C **78**
  Ealing Campus St Marys Road
    . . . . .1D **96**
  Ealing Campus, Vestry Hall . . .2D **96**
  Ealing Campus, Walpole House
    . . . . .7D **78**
University of Westminster
  Cavendish Campus, Hanson St.
    . . . . .5A 6 (5G **83**)
  Cavendish Campus, Lit. Titchfield St.
    . . . . .6A **6**
  Harrow Campus 7A **42**
  Marylebone Campus . .5G 5 (5E **82**)
  Regent Campus, Regent St. . . .7K **5**
  Regent Campus, Wells St. 7B **6**
University Pl. DA8: Erith 7J **109**

University Rd. SW19 . . . . .6B **136**
University St. WC1 . . . . .4B 6 (4G **83**)
University Way E16 . . . . .7E **88**
Unwin Av. TW14: Felt 5F **111**
Unwin Cl. SE15 . . . . .6G **103**
Unwin Ct. N2 . . . . .4C **46**
Unwin Mans. *W14* 6H **99**
  (off Queen's Club Gdns.)
Unwin Rd. SW7 . . . . . . .1A 16 (3B **100**)
  TW7: Isle 3J **113**
Unwin Way HA7: Stan 7J **27**
Up at The O2 . . . . .1G **105**
Upbrook M. W2 . . . . . . .1A 10 (6A **82**)
Upcerne Rd. SW10 . . . . .7A **100**
Upchurch Cl. SE20 . . . . .7H **139**
Upcott Ho. *E3* 3D **86**
  (off Bruce Rd.)
  E9 .7J **67**
  (off Frampton Pk. Rd.)
Upcroft Av. HA8: Edg 5D **28**
Updale Rd. DA14: Sidc 4K **143**
Upfield CRO: C'don 3H **169**
Upfield Rd. W7 . . . . .5K **77**
Upgrove Mnr. Way SW2 . . . . .7A **120**
Uphall Rd. IG1: Ilf 5F **71**
Upham Pk. Rd. W4 . . . . .4A **98**
Uphill *BR2*: Brom 4H **159**
  (off Westmoreland Rd.)
Uphill Dr. NW7 . . . . .5F **29**
  NW9 . . . . .5J **43**
Uphill Gro. NW7 . . . . .4F **29**
Uphill Rd. NW7 . . . . .4F **29**
Upland M. SE22 . . . . .5G **121**
Upland Rd. CR2: S Croy 5D **168**
  DA7: Bex 3F **127**
  E13 .4J **87**
  SE22 . . . . .5G **121**
  (not continuous)
  SM2: Sutt 7B **166**
Uplands BR3: Beck 2C **158**
Uplands, The HA4: Ruis 1J **57**
Uplands Av. E17 . . . . .2K **49**
Uplands Bus. Pk. E17 . . . . .3K **49**
Uplands Cl. SE18 . . . . .5F **107**
  SW14 . . . . .5H **115**
Uplands Ct. *N21* 7F **23**
  (off The Green)
Uplands End IG8: Wfd G 7H **37**
Uplands Pk. Rd. EN2: Enf 2F **23**
Uplands Rd. EN4: E Barn 1K **31**
  IG8: Wfd G 7H **37**
  N8 . . . . .5K **47**
  RM6: Chad H 3D **54**
Uplands Way N21 . . . . .5F **23**
Upnall Ho. SE15 . . . . .6J **103**
Upney La. IG11: Bark 6J **71**
Upnor Way SE17 . . . . .5E **102**
Uppark Dr. IG2: Ilf 6G **53**
Up. Abbey Rd. DA17: Belv 4F **109**
Up. Addison Gdns. W14 . . . . .2G **99**
Up. Bank St. E14 . . . . .1D **104**
  (not continuous)
Up. Bardsey Wlk. *N1* 6C **66**
  (off Douglas Rd. Nth.)
Up. Belgrave St. SW1 . . . . . .1H 17 (3E **100**)
Up. Berenger Wlk. *SW10* 7B **100**
  (off Berenger Wlk.)
Up. Berkeley St. W1 . . . . . .1E 10 (6D **82**)
Up. Beulah Hill SE19 . . . . .1E **156**
Up. Blantyre Wlk. *SW10* 7B **100**
  (off Blantyre Wlk.)
Up. Brighton Rd. KT6: Surb 6D **150**
Up. Brockley Rd. SE4 . . . . .1B **122**
  (not continuous)
Up. Brook St. W1 . . . . . .2A 12 (7E **82**)
Upper Butts TW8: Bford 6C **96**
Up. Caldy Wlk. *N1* 6C **66**
  (off Caldy Wlk.)
Up. Camelford Wlk. *W11* 6G **81**
  (off St Mark's Rd.)
Up. Cavendish Av. N3 . . . . .3J **45**

Up. Cheapside Pas. EC2 . . . . .1C **14**
  (off Cheapside)
Up. Cheyne Row SW3 . . . .7C 16 (6D **100**)
UPPER CLAPTON 2H **67**
Up. Clapton Rd. E5 . . . . .1H **67**
Up. Clarendon Wlk. *W11* 6G **81**
  (off Clarendon Rd.)
Up. Dartrey Wlk. *SW10* 7A **100**
  (off Whistler Wlk.)
Up. Dengie Wlk. *N1* 1C **84**
  (off Baddow Wlk.)
UPPER EDMONTON 5B **34**
UPPER ELMERS END 5B **158**
Up. Elmers End Rd. BR3: Beck 4A **158**
Up. Farm Rd. KT8: W Mole 4D **148**
Upper Feilde *W1* 2G **11**
  (off Park St.)
Up. Green E. CR4: Mitc 3D **154**
Up. Green W. CR4: Mitc 2D **154**
  (not continuous)
Up. Grosvenor St. W1 . . . . . .3G 11 (7E **82**)
Up. Grotto Rd. TW1: Twick 2K **131**
Upper Ground SE1 . . . . . .4J 13 (1A **102**)
Upper Gro. SE25 . . . . .4E **156**
Up. Grove Rd. DA17: Belv 6F **109**
Up. Gulland Wlk. *N1* 6C **66**
  (off Church Rd.)
UPPER HALLIFORD 4G **147**
Up. Halliford By-Pass TW17: Shep . .5G **147**
Up. Halliford Grn. TW17: Shep 4G **147**
Up. Halliford Rd. TW17: Shep 3G **147**
  (not continuous)
Up. Hampstead Wlk. NW3 . . . . . . .4A **64**
Up. Ham Rd. KT2: King T 4D **132**
  TW10: Ham 4D **132**
Up. Handa Wlk. *N1* 6D **66**
  (off Handa Wlk.)
Up. Hawkwell Wlk. *N1* 1C **84**
  (off Maldon Cl.)
UPPER HOLLOWAY 4G **147**
Up. Holly Hill Rd. DA17: Belv 5H **109**
Up. James St. W1 . . . . . .2B 12 (7G **83**)
Up. John St. W1 . . . . . . .2B 12 (7G **83**)
Up. Lismore Wlk. *N1* 6C **66**
  (off Clephane Rd.)
Upper Lodge *W8* 1K **99**
  (off Palace Grn.)
Up. Lodge M. TW12: Hamp H 6H **131**
Upper Mall W6 . . . . .5C **98**
  (not continuous)
Upper Marsh SE1 . . . . . . .1H 19 (3K **101**)
Up. Montagu St. W1 . . . . . .5E 4 (5D **82**)
Up. Mulgrave Rd. SM2: Cheam 7G **165**
Upper Nth. St. E14 . . . . .5C **86**
UPPER NORWOOD 1E **156**
Up. Park Rd. BR1: Brom 1K **159**
  DA17: Belv 4H **109**
  KT2: King T 6G **133**
  N11 .5A **32**
  NW3 . . . . .5D **64**
Up. Phillimore Gdns. W8 . . . . .2J **99**
Up. Ramsey Wlk. *N1* 6D **66**
  (off Ramsey Wlk.)
Up. Rawreth Wlk. *N1* 1C **84**
  (off Basire St.)
Up. Richmond Rd. SW15 . . . . .4B **116**
Up. Richmond Rd. W. SW14 . . . . . .4G **115**
  TW10: Rich 4G **115**
Upper Rd. E13 . . . . .3J **87**
  SM6: Wall 5H **167**
UPPER RUXLEY 7G **145**
Up. St Martin's La. WC2 . . . .2E 12 (7J **83**)
Up. Selsdon Rd. CR2: Sande, Sels . .7F **169**
Up. Sheridan Rd. DA17: Belv 4G **109**
UPPER SHIRLEY 4K **169**
Up. Shirley Rd. CR0: C'don 2J **169**
Upper Sq. TW7: Isle 3A **114**
Upper St. N1 . . . . .2A **84**
Up. Sunbury Rd. TW12: Hamp 1C **148**

Up. Sutton La. TW5: Hest 7E **94**
UPPER SYDENHAM 3H **139**
Up. Talbot Wlk. SW1 . . . .3B 18 (4G **101**)
Up. Talbot Wlk. *W11* 6G **81**
  (off Talbot Wlk.)
Up. Teddington Rd. KT1: Hamp W . . .7C **132**
Upper Ter. NW3 . . . . .3A **64**
Up. Thames St. EC4 . . . . . .2B 14 (7B **84**)
Up. Tollington Pk. N4 . . . . .1A **66**
  (not continuous)
Upperton Rd. DA14: Sidc 5K **143**
Upperton Rd. E. E13 . . . . .3A **88**
Upperton Rd. W. E13 . . . . .3A **88**
UPPER TOOTING 4D **136**
Up. Tooting Pk. SW17 . . . . .2D **136**
Up. Tooting Rd. SW17 . . . . .4D **136**
Up. Town Rd. UB6: G'frd 4F **77**
Up. Tulse Hill SW2 . . . . .7K **119**
Up. Vernon Rd. SM1: Sutt 5B **166**
UPPER WALTHAMSTOW 4F **51**
Up. Walthamstow Rd. E17 . . . . . . .4E **50**
Up. Whistler Wlk. *SW10* 7A **100**
  (off Worlds End Est.)
Up. Wickham La. DA16: Well 7B **108**
Up. Wimpole St. W1 . . . . .5H 5 (5E **82**)
Up. Woburn Pl. WC1 . . . . . . .2D 6 (3H **83**)
Uppingham Av. HA7: Stan 1B **42**
Upsdell Av. N13 . . . . .6F **33**
Upshire Ho. E17 . . . . .2B **50**
Upstall St. SE5 . . . . .1B **120**
UPTON
  DA6 .5D **126**
  E7 . . . . .7J **69**
Upton Av. E7 . . . . .7J **69**
Upton Cl. DA5: Bexl 6F **127**
  NW2 . . . . .3G **63**
Upton Ct. *SE20* 7J **139**
  (off Blean Gro.)
Upton Dene SM2: Sutt 7K **165**
Upton Gdns. HA3: Kenton 5B **42**
Upton Hgts. E7 . . . . .7J **69**
Upton Ho. *E9* 5A **68**
  (off Ward La.)
Upton La. E7 . . . . .7J **69**
Upton Lodge E7 . . . . .6J **69**
Upton Lodge Cl. WD23: Bush 1B **26**
UPTON PARK 1B **88**
Upton Park Boleyn Cinema 2B **88**
Upton Park/Boleyn Ground 2A **88**
Upton Pk. Rd. E7 . . . . .7K **69**
Upton Rd. CR7: Thor H 2D **156**
  DA5: Bexl 4E **126**
  DA6: Bexl 4E **126**
  N18 .5B **34**
  SE18 . . . . .6G **107**
  TW3: Houn 3E **112**
Upton Rd. Sth. DA5: Bexl 6F **127**
Upton Vs. DA6: Bex 4E **126**
Upway N12 . . . . .6H **31**
Upwey Ho. N1 . . . . .1E **84**
Upwood Rd. SE12 . . . . .6J **123**
  SW16 . . . . .1J **155**
Urban M. N4 . . . . .6B **48**
Urdang, The 2K **7**
  (off Rosebery Av.)
Urlwin St. SE5 . . . . .6C **102**
Urlwin Wlk. SW9 . . . . .1A **120**
Urmston Dr. SW19 . . . . .1G **135**
Urmston Ho. *E14* 4E **104**
  (off Seyssel St.)
Urquhart Ct. BR3: Beck 7B **140**
Ursa Mans. *E20* 5E **68**
  (off Cheering La.)
Ursula Gould Way E14 . . . . .5C **86**
Ursula Lodges DA14: Sidc 5B **144**
Ursula M. N4 . . . . .1C **66**
Ursula St. SW11 . . . . .1C **118**
Urswick Gdns. RM9: Dag 7E **72**
Urswick Rd. E9 . . . . .5J **67**
  RM9: Dag 7D **72**
Usborne M. SW8 . . . . .7K **101**

Usher Hall NW4 ....4D 44
  (off The Burroughs)
Usher Rd. E3 ....1B 86
  (not continuous)
Usk Rd. SW11 ....4A 118
Usk St. E2 ....3K 85
Utah Bldg. SE13 ....1D 122
  (off Deal's Gateway)
Utopia Village NW1 ....7E 64
Uvedale Rd. EN2: Enf 5J 23
  RM10: Dag 3G 73
Uverdale Rd. SW10 ....7A 100
UXBRIDGE 1A 74
Uxbridge Rd. KT1: King T 5D 150
  (off Uxbridge Rd.)
Uxbridge Golf Course 2A 56
Uxbridge Lido 6A 56
Uxbridge Rd. HA3: Hrw W 7A 26
  HA5: Hat E, Pinn 2A 40
  HA7: Stan 7A 26
  KT1: King T 4D 150
  TW12: Hamp, Hamp H 4E 130
  TW13: Felt 2A 130
  UB1: S'hall 1E 94
  UB4: Hayes, Yead 5G 75
  UB10: Hil 3C 74
  W3 ....7E 78
  W5 ....7E 78
  W7 ....1K 95
  W12 ....1C 98
  W13 ....1B 96
Uxbridge Rd. Retail Pk. UB4: Yead 7A 76
Uxbridge St. W8 ....1J 99
Uxendon Cres. HA9: Wemb 1E 60
Uxendon Hill HA9: Wemb 1F 61

V

Vaine Ho. E9 ....6A 68
Vaizeys Wharf SE7 ....3K 105
Valance Av. E4 ....1B 36
Valan Leas BR2: Brom 3G 159
Vale, The CR0: C'don 2K 169
  HA4: Ruis 4A 58
  IG8: Wfd G 7D 36
  N10 ....1E 46
  N14 ....7C 22
  NW11 ....3F 63
  SW3 ....7A 16 (6B 100)
  TW5: Hest 6C 94
  TW14: Felt 6K 111
  TW16: Sun 6J 129
  W3 ....1K 97
Vale Cl. BR6: Farnb 4E 172
  N2 ....3D 46
  TW1: Twick 3A 132
  W9 ....3A 82
Vale Cotts. SW15 ....3A 134
Vale Ct. EN5: New Bar 4E 20
  W3 ....1B 98
  W9 ....3A 82
Vale Cres. SW15 ....4A 134
Vale Cft. HA5: Pinn 5C 40
Vale Dr. EN5: Barn 4C 20
Vale End SE22 ....4F 121
Vale Estate, The W3 ....1A 98
Vale Farm 4B 60
Vale Farm Sports Cen. 4B 60
Vale Gro. N4 ....7C 48
  W3 ....2K 97
Vale La. W3 ....5G 79
Vale Lodge SE23 ....2J 139
Valence Av. RM8: Dag 1D 72
Valence Cir. RM8: Dag 3D 72
Valence House Mus. 3E 72
Valence Rd. DA8: Erith 7K 109
Valence Wood Rd. RM8: Dag 3D 72
Valencia Rd. HA7: Stan 4H 27
Valentia Pl. SW9 ....4A 120
Valentine Av. DA5: Bexl 2E 144

Valentine Ct. SE23 ....2K 139
  (not continuous)
Valentine Ho. E3 ....1B 86
  (off Garrison Rd.)
Valentine Pl. SE1 ....6A 14 (2B 102)
Valentine Rd. E9 ....6K 67
  HA2: Harr 3F 59
Valentine Row SE1 ....7A 14 (2B 102)
Valentines Mansion & Gardens 7E 52
Valentines Rd. IG1: Ilf 1F 71
Valentine's Way RM7: Rush G 2K 73
VALE OF HEALTH 3A 64
Vale of Health NW3 ....3B 64
Vale Pde. SW15 ....3A 134
Valerian Wlk. N11 ....2K 31
Valerian Way E15 ....3G 87
Valerie Ct. SM2: Sutt 7K 165
  WD23: Bush 1B 26
Valerio M. N1 ....6D 66
Vale Ri. NW11 ....1H 63
Vale Rd. BR1: Brom 1E 160
  CR4: Mitc 3H 155
  E7 ....6K 69
  KT4: Wor Pk 3B 164
  KT19: Ewe 4B 164
  N4 ....7C 48
  SM1: Sutt 4K 165
Vale Rd. Nth. KT6: Surb 2E 162
Vale Rd. Sth. KT6: Surb 2E 162
Vale Row N5 ....3B 66
Vale Royal N7 ....7J 65
Vale Royal Ho. WC2 ....2D 12
  (off Charing Cross Rd.)
Valery Pl. TW12: Hamp 7E 130
Valeside Ct. EN5: New Bar 4E 20
Vale St. SE27 ....3D 138
Valeswood Rd. BR1: Brom 5H 141
Vale Ter. N4 ....6C 48
Valetta Gro. E13 ....2J 87
Valetta Rd. W3 ....2A 98
Valette Ct. N10 ....4F 47
  (off St James's La.)
Valette Ho. E9 ....6J 67
Valette St. E9 ....6J 67
Valiant Cl. RM7: Mawney 2H 55
  UB5: N'olt 3B 76
Valiant Ho. E14 ....2E 104
  (off Plevna St.)
  SE7 ....5A 106
Valiant Path NW9 ....7F 29
Valiant Way E6 ....5D 88
Vallance Rd. E1 ....3G 85
  E2 ....3G 85
  N22 ....2G 47
Vallentin Rd. E17 ....4E 50
Valley, The 5A 106
Valley Av. N12 ....4G 31
Valley Cl. HA5: Pinn 2K 39
Valley Dr. NW9 ....6G 43
Valleyfield Rd. SW16 ....5K 137
Valley Flds. Cres. EN2: Enf 2F 23
Valley Gdns. HA0: Wemb 7F 61
  SW19 ....7B 136
Valley Gro. SE7 ....5A 106
Valley Leisure Pk. CR0: Wadd 1J 167
Valleylink Est. EN3: Pond E 6F 25
Valley M. TW1: Twick 2K 131
Valley Point Ind. Est. CR0: Bedd 1J 155
Valley Rd. BR2: Brom 2G 159
  BR5: St P 7B 144
  DA8: Erith 4J 109
  DA17: Belv 4H 109
  SW16 ....5K 137
  UB10: Uxb 2A 74
Valley Side E4 ....2H 35
  SE7 ....5B 106
Valley Side Pde. E4 ....2H 35
Valley Vw. EN5: Barn 6B 20
Valley Wlk. CR0: C'don 2J 169
Valliers Wood Rd. DA15: Sidc 1J 143

Vallings Pl. KT6: Surb 7B 150
Vallis Way KT9: Chess 4D 162
  W13 ....5A 78
Val McKenzie Av. N7 ....3A 66
Valmar Rd. SE5 ....1C 120
Valmar Trad. Est. SE5 ....1C 120
Valnay St. SW17 ....5D 136
Valognes Av. E17 ....1A 50
Valois Ho. SE1 ....3F 103
  (off St Saviour's Est.)
Valonia Gdns. SW18 ....6H 117
Vambery Rd. SE18 ....6G 107
V&A Museum of Childhood 3J 85
Vanbrough Cres. UB5: N'olt 1A 76
Vanbrugh Castle SE10 ......6G 105
  (off Maze Hill)
Vanbrugh Cl. E16 ....5B 88
Vanbrugh Ct. SE11 ....4K 19
Vanbrugh Dr. KT12: Walt T 7A 148
Vanbrugh Flds. SE3 ....6H 105
Vanbrugh Hill SE3 ....5H 105
  SE10 ....5H 105
Vanbrugh Ho. E9 ....7J 67
  (off Loddiges Rd.)
Vanbrugh M. KT12: Walt T 7A 148
Vanbrugh Pk. SE3 ....7H 105
Vanbrugh Pk. Rd. SE3 ....7H 105
Vanbrugh Pk. Rd. W. SE3 .....7H 105
Vanbrugh Rd. W4 ....3K 97
Vanbrugh Ter. SE3 ....1H 123
Vanburgh Cl. BR6: Orp 1J 173
Vanburgh Ho. E1 ....5J 9
  (off Folgate St.)
Vancouver Cl. BR6: Chels 4K 173
Vancouver Ho. E1 ....1H 103
  (off Reardon Path)
  SE16 ....2K 103
  (off Needleman St.)
Vancouver Mans. HA8: Edg 1H 43
Vancouver Rd. HA8: Edg 1H 43
  SE23 ....2A 140
  TW10: Ham 4C 132
  UB4: Yead 4K 75
Vanderbilt Rd. SW18 ....1K 135
Vanderbilt Vs. W12 ....2F 99
  (off Sterne St.)
Vandervell Ct. W3 ....2A 98
  (off Amber Way)
Vanderville Gdns. N2 ....2B 46
Vandome Cl. E16 ....6K 87
Vandon Ct. SW1 ....1B 18
  (off Petty France)
Vandon Pas. SW1 ....1B 18 (3G 101)
Vandon St. SW1 .....1B 18 (3G 101)
Van Dyck Av. KT3: N Mald 7K 151
Vandyke Cl. SW15 ....7F 117
Vandyke Cross SE9 ....5C 124
Vandy St. EC2 ....4G 9 (4E 84)
Vane Cl. HA3: Kenton 6F 43
  NW3 ....5B 64
Vanessa Cl. DA17: Belv 5G 109
Vanessa Way DA5: Bexl 3K 145
Vane St. SW1 ....3B 18 (4G 101)
Vange Ho. W10 ....5E 80
  (off Sutton Way)
Van Gogh Cl. TW7: Isle 3A 114
Van Gogh Ct. E14 ....3F 105
Vanguard NW9 ....7F 29
Vanguard Bldg. E14 ....2B 104
Vanguard Cl. CR0: C'don 1K 169
  E16 ....5J 87
  RM7: Mawney 2G 55
Vanguard Ct. SE5 ....1E 120
Vanguard Ho. E8 ....7H 67
Vanguard St. SE8 ....1C 122
Vanguard Way SM6: Wall 7J 167
  TW6: H'row A 2G 111
Vanilla & Sesame Ct. SE1 .....6K 15
  (off Curlew St.)
Vanneck Sq. SW15 ....5C 116
Vanoc Gdns. BR1: Brom 4J 141

Vanquish Cl. TW2: Whitt 7E 112
Vansittart Rd. E7 ....4H 69
Vansittart St. SE14 ....7A 104
Vanstone Ct. N7 ....6A 66
  (off Blackthorn Av.)
Vanston Pl. SW6 ....7J 99
Vantage Bldg. UB3: Hayes 3H 93
  (off Station App.)
Vantage Ct. UB3: Harl 7G 93
Vantage M. E14 ....1E 104
  (off Coldharbour)
Vantage Pl. TW14: Felt 6J 111
  W8 ....3J 99
Vantage Point BR3: Beck 1F 159
  (off Albemarle Rd.)
  EN5: Barn 4C 20
  (off Victors Way)
Vantage W. TW8: Bford 4F 97
Vantrey Ho. SE11 ....4J 19
Vant Rd. SW17 ....5D 136
Varcoe Gdns. UB3: Hayes 6F 75
Varcoe Rd. SE16 ....5H 103
Vardens Rd. SW11 ....4B 118
Varden St. E1 ....6H 85
Vardon Cl. W3 ....6K 79
Vardon Ho. SE10 ....1E 122
Varley Dr. TW1: Isle 4B 114
Varley Ho. NW6 ....1J 81
  SE1 ....3C 102
  (off County St.)
Varley Pde. NW9 ....4A 44
Varley Rd. E16 ....6K 87
Varley Way CR4: Mitc 2B 154
Varna Rd. SW6 ....7G 99
  TW12: Hamp 1F 149
Varndell St. NW1 ......1A 6 (3G 83)
Varnishers Yd. N1 ....1F 7
  (off York Way)
Varsity Dr. TW1: Twick 5J 113
Varsity Row SW14 ....2J 115
Vartry Rd. N15 ....6D 48
Vascroft Est. NW10 ....4H 79
Vassall Ho. E3 ....3A 86
  (off Antill Rd.)
Vassall Rd. SW9 ....7A 102
Vat Ho. SW8 ....7J 101
  (off Rita Rd.)
Vauban Est. SE16 ....3F 103
Vauban St. SE16 ....3F 103
Vaudeville Theatre 3F 13
  (off Strand)
Vaughan Almshouses TW15: Ashf 5D 128
  (off Feltham Hill Rd.)
Vaughan Av. NW4 ....5C 44
  W6 ....4B 98
Vaughan Cl. TW12: Hamp 6C 130
Vaughan Est. E2 ....1J 9
Vaughan Gdns. IG1: Ilf 7D 52
Vaughan Ho. SE1 ....6A 14
  (off Blackfriars Rd.)
  SW4 ....7G 119
Vaughan Rd. DA16: Well 2K 125
  E15 ....6H 69
  HA1: Harr 6G 41
  KT7: T Ditt 7B 150
  SE5 ....2C 120
Vaughan St. SE16 ....2B 104
Vaughan Way E1 ....7G 85
Vaughan Williams Cl. SE8 .....7C 104
VAUXHALL 5H 19 (5J 101)
Vauxhall Bri. SW1 .....6E 18 (5J 101)
Vauxhall Bri. Rd. SW1 .....2A 18 (3G 101)
Vauxhall City Farm 6G 19
Vauxhall Climbing Cen. 7F 19
  (off Sth. Lambeth Rd.)
VAUXHALL CROSS 5J 101
Vauxhall Gdns.
  CR2: S Croy 6C 168
Vauxhall Gro. SW8 .....7G 19 (6K 101)
Vauxhall St. SE11 .....5H 19 (5K 101)
Vauxhall Wlk. SE11 .....5G 19 (5K 101)

Vawdrey Cl. E1 .4J 85
Veals Mead CR4: Mitc 1C 154
Vectis Gdns. SW17 . . . . .6F 137
Vectis Rd. SW17 . . . . .6F 137
Veda Rd. SE13 . . . . .4C 122
Vega Ho. E20 . . . . .5E 68
(off Prize Wlk.)
Vega Rd. WD23: Bush 1B 26
Veitch Cl. TW14: Felt 7H 111
Veldene Way HA2: Harr 3D 58
Velde Way SE22 . . . . .5E 120
Velletri Ho. E2 .2K 85
(off Mace St.)
Vellum Ct. E17 .2A 50
Vellum Dr. SM5: Cars 3E 166
Velodrome
Queen Elizabeth Olympic Pk.
. . . . .5D 68
Velo Pl. E20 . . . . .5D 68
Velvet Ho. E2 . . . . .2F 85
(off Whiston Rd.)
Venables Cl. RM10: Dag 4H 73
Venables St. NW8 . . . . .5B 4 (4B 82)
Vencourt Pl. W6 . . . . .4C 98
Veneer Building, The UB3: Hayes . . .2G 93
Venerable Ho. E3 . . . . .4B 86
(off Portia Way)
Venetian Ho. E20 . . . . .6D 68
(off Victory Pde.)
Venetian Rd. SE5 . . . . .2C 120
Venetia Rd. N4 .6B 48
W5 . . . . .2D 96
Venice Corte SE13 . . . . .3E 122
(off Elmira St.)
Venice Ct. SE5 . . . . .7C 102
(off Bowyer St.)
Venice Wlk. W2 . . . . .5A 82
Venner Rd. SE26 . . . . .6J 139
(not continuous)
Venners Cl. DA7: Bex 2K 127
Venn Ho. N1 . . . . .1K 83
(off Barnsbury Est.)
Venn St. SW4 .4G 119
Ventnor Av. HA7: Stan 1B 42
Ventnor Dr. N20 . . . . .3E 30
Ventnor Gdns. IG11: Bark 6J 71
Ventnor Rd. SE14 . . . . .7K 103
SM2: Sutt 7K 165
Venture Cl. DA5: Bexl 7E 126
Venture Ct. SE1 . . . . .7H 15
(off Market Yd. M.)
SE12 . . . . .7J 123
Venture Ho. W10 . . . . .6F 81
(off Bridge Cl.)
Venue St. E14 .5C 86
Venus Ho. E3 . . . . .1C 86
(off Garrison Rd.)
E14 . . . . .4C 104
(off Westferry Rd.)
Venus M. CR4: Mitc 3C 154
Venus Rd. SE18 . . . . .3D 106
Vera Av. N21 . . . . .5F 23
Vera Ct. E3 . . . . .3B 86
(off Grace Pl.)
Vera Lynn Cl. E7 . . . . .4J 69
Vera Rd. SW6 .1G 117
Verbena Cl. E16 . . . . .4H 87
UB7: W Dray 1E 174
Verbena Gdns. W6 . . . . .5C 98
Verdant Ct. SE6 . . . . .7C 123
(off Verdant La.)
Verdant La. SE6 . . . . .7G 123
Verdayne Av. CR0: C'don 2K 169
Verdi Cres. W10 . . . . .2G 81
Verdon Roe Ct. E4 . . . . .3J 35
Verdun Rd. SE18 . . . . .6A 108
SW13 . . . . .6C 98
Vere Ct. W2 . . . . .6K 81
(off Westbourne Gdns.)
Vereker Dr. TW16: Sun 3J 147
Vereker Rd. W14 . . . . .5G 99

Vere St. W1 . . . . .1J 11 (6F 83)
Veridion Way DA18: Erith 2F 109
Veritas Ho. DA14: Sidc 2A 144
(off Jubilee Way)
Verity Cl. W11 .7G 81
Verity Ho. E3 . . . . .3B 86
(off Merchant St.)
Vermeer Ct. E14 . . . . .3F 105
Vermeer Gdns. SE15 . . . . .4J 121
Vermilion Apartments E3 . . . . .1A 86
(off Gunmaker's La.)
Vermont Cl. EN2: Enf 4G 23
Vermont Ho. E17 . . . . .2B 50
Vermont Rd. SE19 . . . . .6D 138
SM1: Sutt 3K 165
SW18 . . . . .6K 117
Verna Ho. E20 .5E 68
(off Sunrise Cl.)
Verne Ct. W3 . . . . .3J 97
(off Vincent Rd.)
Verney Gdns. RM9: Dag 4E 72
Verney Ho. NW8 . . . . .3B 4
Verney Rd. RM9: Dag 4E 72
(not continuous)
SE16 . . . . .6G 103
Verney St. NW10 . . . . .3K 61
Verney Way SE16 . . . . .5H 103
Vernham Rd. SE18 . . . . .6G 107
Vernon Av. E12 . . . . .4D 70
IG8: Wfd G .7E 36
SW20 . . . . .2F 153
Vernon Cl. KT19: Ewe 6J 163
TW19: Stanw 1A 128
Vernon Ct. HA7: Stan 1B 42
NW2 . . . . .3H 63
W5 . . . . .7C 78
Vernon Cres. EN4: E Barn 6K 21
Vernon Dr. HA7: Stan 1A 42
Vernon Ho. SE11 . . . . .6H 19
WC1 . . . . .6F 7
(off Vernon Pl.)
Vernon Mans. W14 . . . . .6H 99
(off Queen's Club Gdns.)
Vernon M. E17 . . . . .5B 50
W14 . . . . .4G 99
Vernon Pl. WC1 . . . . .6F 7 (5J 83)
Vernon Ri.
UB6: G'frd .5H 59
WC1 . . . . .1H 7 (3K 83)
Vernon Rd.
E3 . . . . .2B 86
E11 . . . . .1G 69
E15 . . . . .7G 69
E17 . . . . .5B 50
IG3: Ilf 1K 71
N8 . . . . .3A 48
SM1: Sutt 5A 166
SW14 . . . . .3K 115
TW13: Felt 2H 129
Vernon Sq. WC1 . . . . .1H 7 (3K 83)
Vernon St. W14 . . . . .4G 99
Vernon Yd. W11 . . . . .7H 81
Verona Dr. DA7: Bex 2E 126
Verona Ct. SE14 . . . . .6K 103
(off Myers La.)
TW15: Ashf 4D 128
W4 . . . . .5A 98
Verona Dr. KT6: Surb 2E 162
Verona Ho. CR4: Mitc 3F 155
(off Aventine Av.)
Verona Rd. E7 .7J 69
Veronica Gdns. SW16 . . . . .1G 155
Veronica Ho. E3 . . . . .3D 86
(off Talwin St.)
SE4 . . . . .3B 122
Veronica Rd. SW17 . . . . .2F 137
Veronique Gdns. IG6: Ilf 5G 53
Verran Rd. SW12 . . . . .7F 119
Versailles Rd. SE20 . . . . .7G 139
Verulam Av. E17 . . . . .6B 50
Verulam Bldgs. WC1 . . . . .5H 7

Verulam Ct. NW9 . . . . .7C 44
UB1: S'hall .6G 77
(off Haldane Rd.)
Verulam Ho. W6 . . . . .2E 98
(off Hammersmith Gro.)
Verulam Rd. UB6: G'frd 4E 76
Verulam St. WC1 . . . . .5J 7 (5A 84)
Vervian Ho. SE15 . . . . .7G 103
(off Reddins Rd.)
Verwood Dr. EN4: Cockf 3J 21
Verwood Ho. SW8 . . . . .7K 101
(off Cobbett St.)
Verwood Lodge E14 . . . . .3F 105
(off Manchester Rd.)
Verwood Rd. HA2: Harr 2G 41
Veryan Cl. N8 . . . . .5H 47
Vesage Ct. EC1 .6K 7
Vesey Path E14 . . . . .6D 86
Vespan Rd. W12 . . . . .2C 98
Vesta Ct. SE1 . . . . .7G 15
Vesta Ho. E3 . . . . .1C 86
(off Garrison Rd.)
E20 . . . . .5E 68
(off Liberty Bri. Rd.)
Vesta Rd. SE4 .2A 122
Vestris Rd. SE23 . . . . .2K 139
Vestry Rd. RM7: Rush G 6K 55
SW1 . . . . .2D 18
(off Monck St.)
Vestry House Mus. 4D 50
Vestry M. SE5 .1E 120
SW18 . . . . .5B 118
Vestry Rd. E17 . . . . .4D 50
SE5 . . . . .1E 120
Vestry St. N1 . . . . .1E 8 (3D 84)
Vesuvius Apartments E3 . . . . .2B 86
(off Centurion La.)
Vevey St. SE6 .2B 140
Veysey Gdns. RM10: Dag 3G 73
Viaduct, The E18 . . . . .2J 51
HA0: Wemb 1E 78
N10 . . . . .4F 47
Viaduct Bldgs. EC1 . . . . .6K 7 (5A 84)
Viaduct Pl. E2 . . . . .3H 85
Viaduct Rd. N2 .2B 46
Viaduct St. E2 . . . . .3H 85
Vian St. SE13 .3D 122
Viant Ho. NW10 . . . . .7K 61
(off Fawood Av.)
Vibart Gdns. SW2 . . . . .7K 119
Vibart Wlk. N1 .1J 83
(off Outram Pl.)
Vibeca Apartments E1 . . . . .6K 9
(off Chicksand St.)
Vibia Cl. TW19: Stanw 7A 110
Vicarage Av. SE3 . . . . .7J 105
Vicarage Cl.
DA8: Erith .6J 109
HA4: Ruis 7F 39
KT4: Wor Pk 1A 164
UB5: N'olt 7D 58
Vicarage Ct. BR3: Beck 3A 158
IG1: Ilf 5F 71
TW14: Bedf 7E 110
W8 . . . . .2K 99
Vicarage Cres. SW11 . . . . .1B 118
Vicarage Dr.
BR3: Beck .1C 158
IG11: Bark .7G 71
SW14 . . . . .5K 115
Vicarage Farm Ct. TW5: Hest 7D 94
Vicarage Farm Rd.
TW3: Houn 2C 112
TW5: Hest .1C 112
Vicarage Flds. KT12: Walt T 6A 148
Vicarage Fld. Shop. Cen.
IG11: Bark .7G 71
Vicarage Gdns.
CR4: Mitc .3C 154
SW14 . . . . .5J 115
W8 . . . . .1J 99

Vicarage Ga. W8 . . . . .1K 99
Vicarage Gro. SE5 . . . . .1D 120
Vicarage Ho. KT1: King T 2F 151
(off Cambridge Rd.)
Vicarage La. E6 . . . . .3D 88
E15 . . . . .7G 69
IG1: Ilf 1H 71
KT17: Ewe .7C 164
(not continuous)
Vicarage M. NW9 . . . . .2K 61
Vicarage Pde.
N15 . . . . .4C 48
Vicarage Path N8 . . . . .7J 47
Vicarage Rd.
CR0: Wadd 3A 168
DA5: Bexl .1H 145
E10 . . . . .7C 50
E15 . . . . .7H 69
IG8: Wfd G .7H 37
KT1: Hamp W 1C 150
KT1: King T 2D 150
N17 . . . . .1G 49
NW4 . . . . .6C 44
RM10: Dag .7H 73
SE18 . . . . .5G 107
(not continuous)
SM1: Sutt 3K 165
SW14 . . . . .5J 115
TW2: Twick 2J 131
TW2: Whitt 6G 113
TW11: Tedd 5A 132
TW16: Sun .5H 129
Vicarage Wlk.
KT12: Walt T 7J 147
SW11 . . . . .1B 118
Vicarage Way
HA2: Harr 7E 40
NW10 . . . . .3K 61
Vicars Bri. Cl.
HA0: Wemb 2E 78
Vicars Cl. E9 . . . . .1J 85
E15 . . . . .1J 87
EN1: Enf 2K 23
Vicar's Hill SE13 . . . . .4D 122
Vicars Moor La. N21 . . . . .7F 23
Vicars Oak Rd. SE19 . . . . .6E 138
Vicar's Rd. NW5 . . . . .5E 64
Vicars Wlks.
RM8: Dag 3B 72
Vicentia Ct. SW11 . . . . .3A 118
Viceroy Cl. N2 .4C 46
(off East End Rd.)
Viceroy Ct. CR0: C'don 1D 168
NW8 . . . . .2C 82
(off Prince Albert Rd.)
Viceroy Pde. N2 . . . . .4C 46
(off High Rd.)
Viceroy Rd. SW8 . . . . .1J 119
Vicinity Ho. E14 . . . . .7C 86
(off Storehouse M.)
Vic Johnson Ho. E3 . . . . .1B 86
(off Armagh Rd.)
Vickers Cl. SM6: Wall 7K 167
Vickers Ct. N17 . . . . .3H 49
SE20 . . . . .7K 139
TW19: Stanw 6A 110
(off Whitley Cl.)
Vickers Rd. DA8: Erith 5K 109
Vickers Way
TW4: Houn 5C 112
Vickery Ct. EC1 .3D 8
(off Mitchell St.)
Vickery's Wharf E14 . . . . .6C 86
Victor Cazalet Ho. N1 . . . . .1B 84
(off Gaskin St.)
Victor Gro. HA0: Wemb 7E 60
Victor Ho. SE7 .6A 106
Victoria & Albert Mus. 2B 16 (3B 100)
Victoria Arc. SW1 . . . . .2K 17
(off Victoria St.)

Victoria Av. E6 . . . . .1B **88**
  EC2 . . . . .6H **9** (5E **84**)
  EN4: E Barn 4G **21**
  HA9: Wemb 6H **61**
  KT6: Surb 6D **150**
  KT8: W Mole 3F **149**
  N3 . . . . .1H **45**
  SM6: Wall 3E **166**
  TW3: Houn 5E **112**
  UB10: Hil 6D **56**
Victoria Bldgs. E8 . . . . .1H **85**
  (off Mare St.)
Victoria Chambers EC2 . . . . .3G **9**
  (off Paul St.)
Victoria Cl.
  EN4: E Barn 4G **21**
  HA1: Harr 6K **41**
  KT8: W Mole 3E **148**
  SE22 . . . . .5G **121**
  UB3: Hayes 6F **75**
Victoria Colonnade WC1 . . . . .6F **7**
  (off Southampton Row)
Victoria Cotts. E1 . . . . .5G **85**
  (off Deal St.)
  N10 . . . . .2E **46**
  TW9: Kew 1F **115**
Victoria Ct. E18 . . . . .3K **51**
  HA7: Stan 7J **27**
  (off Howard Rd.)
  HA9: Wemb 6G **61**
  SE1 . . . . .4E **102**
  (off Hendre Rd.)
  SE26 . . . . .6J **139**
  W3 . . . . .2G **97**
Victoria Cres. N15 . . . . .5E **48**
  SE19 . . . . .6E **138**
  SW19 . . . . .7H **135**
Victoria Dock Rd. E16 . . . . .7H **87**
Victoria Dr. SW19 . . . . .7F **117**
Victoria Emb. EC4 . . . .6F **13** (7K **83**)
  SW1 . . . . .6F **13** (2J **101**)
  WC2 . . . . .6F **13** (2J **101**)
Victoria Gdns. TW5: Hest 1C **112**
  W11 . . . . .1J **99**
Victoria Gro. N12 . . . . .5G **31**
  W8 . . . . .3A **100**
Victoria Gro. M.
  W2 . . . . .7J **81**
Victoria Hall E16 . . . . .1J **105**
  (off Wesley Av., not continuous)
Victoria Ho. E6 . . . . .6E **88**
  HA8: Edg 6C **28**
  SE16 . . . . .2J **103**
  (off Surrey Quays Rd.)
  SW1 . . . . .5J **17**
  (off Ebury Bri. Rd., Ebury Bri. Rd.)
  SW1 . . . . .3B **18**
  (off Francis St., Francis St.)
  SW8 . . . . .7J **101**
  (off Sth. Lambeth Rd.)
Victoria Ind. Est. W3 . . . . .5A **80**
Victoria La.
  EN5: Barn 4C **20**
  UB3: Harl 5F **93**
Victoria Mans. NW10 . . . . .7D **62**
  SW8 . . . . .7J **101**
  (off Sth. Lambeth Rd.)
  W14 . . . . .6H **99**
  (off Queen's Club Gdns.)
Victoria M. E8 . . . . .6G **67**
  NW6 . . . . .1J **81**
  SW4 . . . . .4F **119**
  SW18 . . . . .1A **136**
Victoria Mills Studios E15 . . . . . . .1F **87**
  (off Burford Rd.)
Victorian Gro. N16 . . . . .4E **66**
Victorian Hgts. SW8 . . . . .2F **119**
  (off Thackeray Rd.)
Victorian Rd. N16 . . . . .3E **66**
Victoria Palace Theatre 2A **18**
  (off Victoria St.)

Victoria Pde. SE10 . . . . .6D **104**
  TW9: Kew 1G **115**
  (off Sandycombe Rd.)
Victoria Park
  Hackney .1K **85**
Victoria Pk. Ct. E9 . . . . .7J **67**
  (off Well St.)
Victoria Pk. Ind. Cen. E9 . . . . .7C **68**
  (off Rothbury Rd.)
Victoria Pk. Rd. E9 . . . . .1J **85**
Victoria Pk. Sq. E2 . . . . .3J **85**
Victoria Pk. Studios E9 . . . . .6J **67**
  (off Milborne St.)
Victoria Pas. NW8 . . . . .3B **4**
Victoria Pl. TW9: Rich 5D **114**
Victoria Pl. Shop. Cen.
  SW1 . . . . .3K **17**
Victoria Point E13 . . . . .2J **87**
  (off Victoria Rd.)
Victoria Retail Pk. HA4: Ruis 5B **58**
Victoria Ri. NW6 . . . . .7A **64**
  (off Hilgrove Rd.)
  SW4 . . . . .3F **119**
Victoria Road 5H **73**
Victoria Rd. BR2: Brom 5B **160**
  BR7: Chst 5E **142**
  CR4: Mitc 7C **136**
  DA6: Bex 4G **127**
  DA8: Erith 6K **109**
  DA15: Sidc 3K **143**
  E4 . . . . .1B **36**
  E11 . . . . .4G **69**
  E13 . . . . .2J **87**
  E17 . . . . .2E **50**
  E18 . . . . .2K **51**
  EN4: E Barn 4G **21**
  HA4: Ruis 1J **57**
  IG9: Buck H 2E **37**
  IG11: Bark 6F **71**
  KT1: King T 2F **151**
  KT6: Surb 6D **150**
  N4 . . . . .7K **47**
  N9 . . . . .4A **34**
  N15 . . . . .4G **49**
  N18 . . . . .4A **34**
  N22 . . . . .1G **47**
  NW4 . . . . .4E **44**
  NW6 . . . . .2H **81**
  NW7 . . . . .5G **29**
  NW10 . . . . .5K **79**
  RM10: Dag 5H **73**
  SM1: Sutt 5B **166**
  SW14 . . . . .3K **115**
  TW1: Twick 7B **114**
  TW11: Tedd 6A **132**
  TW13: Felt 1K **129**
  UB2: S'hall 3D **94**
  W3 . . . . .5K **79**
  W5 . . . . .5B **78**
  W8 . . . . .3A **100**
  WD23: Bush 1A **26**
Victoria Sq. SW1 . . . . . . .1K **17** (3F **101**)
Victoria St.
  DA17: Belv 5F **109**
  E15 . . . . .7G **69**
  SW1 . . . . .2K **17** (3G **101**)
Victoria Ter.
  HA1: Harr 1J **59**
  N4 . . . . .1A **66**
  NW10 . . . . .4B **80**
  W5 . . . . .1D **96**
Victoria Vs. TW9: Rich 3F **115**
Victoria Way HA4: Ruis 1A **123**
  SE7 . . . . .5K **105**
Victoria Wharf E2 . . . . .2K **85**
  (off Palmers Rd.)
  E14 . . . . .7A **86**
  SE8 . . . . .5B **104**
  (off Dragoon Rd.)
Victoria Works NW2 . . . . .2D **62**
Victoria Yd. E1 . . . . .6G **85**

Victor Rd. HA2: Harr 3G **41**
  NW10 . . . . .3D **80**
  SE20 . . . . .7K **139**
  TW11: Tedd 4J **131**
Victors Dr. TW12: Hamp 6C **130**
Victors Way EN5: Barn 3C **20**
Victor Ter. NW10 . . . . .4A **80**
Victor Vs. N9 . . . . .3J **33**
Victor Wlk. NW9 . . . . .2A **44**
Victor Wharf SE1 . . . . .4E **14**
  (off Clink St.)
Victory Av. SM4: Mord 5A **154**
Victory Bus. Cen. TW7: Isle 4K **113**
Victory Cl. TW19: Stanw 1A **128**
  TW19: Stanw 1A **128**
Victory Ct. IG11: Bark 4B **90**
  W9 . . . . .4J **81**
  (off Hermes Cl.)
Victory M. UB2: S'hall 3C **94**
Victory Pde. E20 . . . . .6D **68**
Victory Pk. HA9: Wemb 3D **60**
Victory Pl. E14 . . . . .7A **86**
  SE17 . . . . .4D **102**
  SE19 . . . . .7E **138**
Victory Rd. E11 . . . . .4J **51**
  SW19 . . . . .7A **136**
Victory Rd. M. SW19 . . . . .7A **136**
  (off Victory Rd.)
Victory Wlk. SE8 . . . . .1C **122**
Victory Way RM7: Mawney 2H **55**
  SE16 . . . . .2A **104**
  TW5: Cran 5A **94**
Vida Ho. SE8 . . . . .5K **103**
Video Cl. N4 . . . . .7K **47**
Vidler Cl. KT9: Chess 6C **162**
Vienna Cl. IG5: Ilf 2B **52**
View, The SE2 . . . . .5E **108**
View Cl. HA1: Harr 4H **41**
  N6 . . . . .7D **46**
View Cres. N8 . . . . .5H **47**
Viewfield Cl. HA3: Kenton 7E **42**
Viewfield Rd. DA5: Bexl 1C **144**
  SW18 . . . . .6H **117**
Viewland Rd. SE18 . . . . .5K **107**
View Rd. N6 . . . . .7D **46**
Viga Rd. N21 . . . . .6F **23**
Vigers Ct. NW10 . . . . .3D **80**
  (off Harrow Rd.)
Vigilant Cl. SE26 . . . . .4G **139**
Vignoles Rd. RM7: Rush G 7G **55**
Vigo St. W1 . . . . .3A **12** (7G **83**)
Viking Bus. Cen.
  RM7: Rush G 7J **55**
Viking Cl. E3 . . . . .2A **86**
Viking Ct. SW6 . . . . .6J **99**
Viking Gdns. E6 . . . . .4C **88**
Viking Ho. SE5 . . . . .2C **120**
  (off Denmark Rd.)
  SE18 . . . . .4C **106**
  (off Pett St.)
Viking Pl. E10 . . . . .1B **68**
Viking Rd. UB1: S'hall 7C **76**
Viking Way DA8: Erith 3J **109**
Villacourt Rd. SE18 . . . . .7A **108**
Village, The NW3 . . . . .2A **64**
  SE7 . . . . .6A **106**
  W12 . . . . .1F **99**
Village Arc. E4 . . . . .1A **36**
Village Cl. E4 . . . . .5K **35**
  NW3 . . . . .5B **64**
  (off Belsize La.)
Village Ct. E17 . . . . .5D **50**
  (off Eden Rd.)
  SE3 . . . . .3G **123**
  (off Hurren Cl.)
Village Ga. TW17: Shep 5D **146**
Village Hgts. IG8: Wfd G 5C **36**
Village M. NW9 . . . . .2K **61**
  SW18 . . . . .1H **135**
  (off Elsenham St.)
Village Mt. NW3 . . . . .4A **64**
  (off Perrins Ct.)

Village Pk. Cl. EN1: Enf 6K **23**
Village Rd. EN1: Enf 5K **23**
  N3 . . . . .2G **45**
Village Row SM2: Sutt 7J **165**
Village Way
  BR3: Beck 2C **158**
  HA5: Pinn 7C **40**
  IG6: Ilf 3G **53**
  NW10 . . . . .4K **61**
  SE21 . . . . .6D **120**
  TW15: Ashf 4B **128**
Village Way E. HA2: Harr 7E **40**
Villa Rd. SW9 . . . . .3A **120**
Villas on the Heath
  NW3 . . . . .3A **64**
Villas Rd. SE18 . . . . .5G **107**
Villa St. SE17 . . . . .5D **102**
Villa Wlk SE17 . . . . .5D **102**
  (off Villa St.)
Villiers Av. KT5: Surb 5F **151**
  TW2: Whitt 1D **130**
Villiers Cl. E10 . . . . .2C **68**
  KT5: Surb 4F **151**
Villiers Ct. SW11 . . . . .1C **118**
  (off Battersea Bri. Rd.)
Villiers Gro. SM2: Cheam 7F **165**
Villiers Path KT6: Surb 5E **150**
Villiers Rd. BR3: Beck 2K **157**
  KT1: King T 4F **151**
  NW2 . . . . .6C **62**
  TW7: Isle 2J **113**
  UB1: S'hall 1D **94**
Villiers St. WC2 . . . . .3E **12** (1J **101**)
Vimy Cl. TW4: Houn 5D **112**
Vincam Cl. TW2: Whitt 7E **112**
Vince Ct. N1 . . . . .2F **9** (3D **84**)
Vincennes Est. SE27 . . . . .4D **138**
Vincent Av. KT5: Surb 2J **163**
Vincent Cl. BR2: Brom 4K **159**
  DA15: Sidc 1J **143**
  EN5: New Bar 3E **20**
  SE16 . . . . .2A **104**
  UB7: Sip .6C **92**
Vincent Ct. HA6: Nwood 1H **39**
  N4 . . . . .1J **65**
  NW4 . . . . .4F **45**
  SW9 . . . . .1K **119**
  W1 . . . . .7E **4**
  (off Seymour Pl.)
Vincent Dr. TW17: Shep 3G **147**
  UB10: Uxb 1B **74**
Vincent Gdns. NW2 . . . . .3B **62**
Vincent Ho. SW1 . . . . .3D **18**
  (off Regency St., Regency St.)
  SW1 . . . . .4C **18**
  (off Vincent Sq., Vincent Sq.)
Vincent M. E3 . . . . .2C **86**
Vincent Rd.
  CR0: C'don 7E **156**
  E4 . . . . .6A **36**
  HA0: Wemb 7F **61**
  KT1: King T 3G **151**
  N15 . . . . .4C **48**
  N22 . . . . .2A **48**
  RM9: Dag 7E **72**
  SE18 . . . . .4F **107**
  TW4: Houn 2B **112**
  TW7: Isle 1H **113**
  W3 . . . . .3J **97**
Vincent Row
  TW12: Hamp H 6G **131**
Vincents Path UB5: N'olt 6C **58**
  (off Arnold Rd.)
Vincent Sq. N22 . . . . .2A **48**
  SW1 . . . . .3C **18** (4H **101**)
Vincent Sq. Mans. SW1 . . . . .3B **18**
  (off Walcott St.)
Vincent St. E16 . . . . .5H **87**
  SW1 . . . . .3C **18** (4H **101**)
Vincent Ter. N1 . . . . .2B **84**

Vince St. EC1 . . . . .2F **9** (3D **84**)
Vine Cl. E5 . . . . .4G **67**
   KT5: Surb 6F **151**
   SM1: Sutt 3A **166**
   TW19: Stanw M 7B **174**
   UB7: W Dray 4C **92**
Vine Cotts. E1 .6J **85**
              (off Sidney Sq.)
   W7 . . . . .1J **95**
Vine Ct. E1 . . . . .5G **85**
   HA3: Kenton 6E **42**
Vinegar All. E17 . . . . .4D **50**
Vine Gdns. IG1: Ilf 5G **71**
Vinegar St. E1 . . . . .1H **103**
Vinegar Yd. SE1 . . . . .6G **15** (2E **102**)
Vine Gro. UB10: Hil 7C **56**
Vine Hill EC1 . . . . .4J **7** (4A **84**)
Vine La. SE1 . . . . .5H **15** (1E **102**)
   UB10: Hil .1B **74**
Vine Pl. TW3: Houn 4F **113**
   W5 . . . . .1E **96**
             (off St Mark's Rd.)
Viner Cl. KT12: Walt T 6A **148**
Vineries, The EN1: Enf 3K **23**
   N14 . . . . .6B **22**
   SE6 . . . . .1C **140**
Vineries Bank NW7 . . . . .5J **29**
Vineries Cl. RM9: Dag 6F **73**
   UB7: Sip .6C **92**
Vine Rd. BR6: Chels 6K **173**
   E15 . . . . .7H **69**
   KT8: E Mos 4G **149**
   SW13 . . . . .3B **116**
Vinery, The SW8 . . . . .7J **101**
            (off Regent's Bri. Gdns.)
Vinery Row W6 . . . . .3D **98**
Vines Av. N3 .1K **45**
Vine Sq. W14 .5H **99**
             (off Star Rd.)
Vine St. E17 . . . . .4D **50**
   EC3 . . . . .1J **15** (6F **85**)
   RM7: Rom 4J **55**
   W1 . . . . .3B **12** (7G **83**)
Vine St. Bri. EC1 . . . . .4K **7** (4A **84**)
Vine Yd. SE1 .6D **14**
Vineyard, The
   TW10: Rich 5E **114**
Vineyard Av. NW7 . . . . .7B **30**
Vineyard Cl.
   KT1: King T 3F **151**
   SE6 . . . . .1C **140**
Vineyard Gro. N3 . . . . .1K **45**
Vineyard Hill Rd. SW19 . . . . .4H **135**
Vineyard Pas. TW10: Rich 5E **114**
Vineyard Path SW14 . . . . .3K **115**
Vineyard Rd. TW13: Felt 3J **129**
Vineyard Row
   KT1: Hamp W 1C **150**
Vineyards, The TW13: Felt 3J **129**
             (off High St.)
   TW16: Sun 3J **147**
Vineyard Wlk. EC1 . . . . .3J **7** (4A **84**)
Viney Bank CR0: Sels 7B **170**
Viney Rd. SE13 . . . . .3D **122**
Vining St. SW9 . . . . .4A **120**
Vinlake Av. UB10: Ick 3B **56**
Vinopolis 4D **14** (1C **102**)
Vinson Cl. BR6: Orp 1K **173**
Vinson Ho. N1 .2D **9**
             (off Cranston Est.)
Vintage Ho. E4 . . . . .4H **35**
Vinter Ct. TW17: Shep 5C **146**
Vintner's Ct. EC4 . . . . .3D **14** (7C **84**)
Vintner's Pl. EC4 . . . . .3D **14** (7C **84**)
Vintry Ct. SE1 .7F **15**
             (off Porlock St.)
Vintry M. E17 .4C **50**
Viola Av. SE7 . . . . .4B **108**
   TW14: Felt 6A **112**
   TW19: Stanw 1A **128**

Viola Sq. W12 . . . . .7B **80**
Violet Av. EN2: Enf 1J **23**
   UB8: Hil 5B **74**
Violet Cl.
   E16 . . . . .4G **87**
   SE8 . . . . .6B **104**
   SM3: Sutt 1G **165**
   SM6: Wall 1E **166**
Violet Ct. E15 .7G **69**
             (off Victoria St.)
   NW9 . . . . .1A **44**
Violet Gdns. CR0: Wadd 5B **168**
Violet Hill NW8 . . . . .2A **82**
Violet Hill Ho. NW8 . . . . .2A **82**
             (off Violet Hill)
Violet La. CR0: Wadd 6B **168**
Violet Rd. E3 .4D **86**
   E17 . . . . .6C **50**
   E18 . . . . .2K **51**
Violet St. E2 . . . . .4H **85**
Violet Ter. UB8: Hil 5C **74**
VIP Trading Est. SE7 . . . . .4A **106**
Virgil Pl. W1 . . . . .6E **4** (5D **82**)
Virgil St. SE1 . . . . .1H **19** (3K **101**)
Virgin Active
   Aldersgate 6C **8**
             (in Aldersgate)
   Barbican 5C **8**
             (off Aldersgate St.)
   Bromley 4B **160**
   Chislehurst 5J **143**
   Chiswick 1A **116**
   Chiswick Park 4H **97**
   City 5C **84**
             (off Aldersgate St.)
   Cricklewood 3G **63**
   Crouch End 5J **47**
             (off Tottenham La.)
   Croydon 3C **168**
             (off Surrey St.)
   Ealing 7D **78**
            (within Ealing Broadway Cen.)
   Enfield 4J **23**
   Friern Barnet 5K **31**
   Fulham .6G **99**
            (within Fulham Pools)
   Hammersmith 4F **99**
            (off Hammersmith Rd.)
   Hendon .5E **44**
   Ilford 3F **71**
            (off Clements Rd.)
   Islington, Essex Road 1B **84**
   Islington, Goswell Road 1A **8**
            (off Goswell Rd.)
   Kensington 2K **99**
            (off Old Court Rd.)
   Kingston upon Thames, Richmond Rd.
    . . . . .1E **150**
   Kingston upon Thames,
   The Bentall Cen. 2D **150**
            (within The Bentall Cen.)
   Mayfair 2F **11** (6E **82**)
   Merton .1B **154**
            (off Watermill Way)
   Mill Hill East 7B **30**
   Moorgate 4E **8** (4D **84**)
   Notting Hill 6G **81**
   Putney .4G **117**
   Repton Park 7K **37**
   Romford .5K **55**
   Stockley Park 7E **74**
   Strand 7J **83**
   Streatham 3J **137**
   Sunbury 1J **147**
   Swiss Cottage 6A **64**
            (within O2 Centre)
   The Surrey Health & Racquets Club
    . . . . .6K **167**
   The Twickenham Club 6J **113**
   Wandsworth, Smugglers Way
    . . . . .4K **117**

Virgin Active
   Wandsworth, Southside Shop. Cen.
    . . . . .5J **117**
   West London 1A **98**
   Wimbledon, North Rd. 6A **136**
   Wimbledon, Worple Rd. 6H **135**
Virginia Cl. BR2: Brom 3G **159**
   KT3: N Mald 4J **151**
   RM5: Col R 1J **55**
Virginia Ct. SE16 . . . . .2K **103**
            (off Eleanor Cl.)
   WC1 . . . . .3D **6**
            (off Burton St.)
Virginia Gdns. IG6: Ilf 2G **53**
Virginia Ho. E14 . . . . .7E **86**
            (off Newby Pl.)
   TW11: Tedd 5B **132**
Virginia Rd. CR7: Thor H 1B **156**
   E2 . . . . .2J **9** (3F **85**)
Virginia St. E1 . . . . .1G **85**
Virginia Wlk. SW2 . . . . .6K **119**
Viridian Apartments SW8 . . . . .7G **101**
Visage NW3 . . . . .7B **64**
            (off Winchester Rd.)
Viscount Cl. N11 . . . . .6A **32**
Viscount Ct. W2 . . . . .6J **81**
            (off Pembridge Vs.)
Viscount Dr. E6 . . . . .5D **88**
Viscount Rd. TW19: Stanw 1A **128**
Viscount Gro. UB5: N'olt 3B **76**
Viscount St. EC1 . . . . .4C **8** (4C **84**)
Viscount Way
   TW6: H'row A 4G **111**
Vision 20 IG1: Ilf 2G **71**
Vision Ind. Pk. W3 . . . . .5H **79**
Vista, The DA14: Sidc 5K **143**
   SE9 . . . . .6B **124**
Vista Av. EN3: Enf H 2E **24**
Vista Bldg. E3 .3B **86**
            (off Bow Rd.)
   SE18 . . . . .4E **106**
Vista Ct. E1 . . . . .5A **86**
            (off Ocean Est.)
Vista Dr. IG4: Ilf 5B **52**
Vista Ho. N4 .2A **66**
   SW19 . . . . .1B **154**
            (off Chapter Way)
Vista Way HA3: Kenton 6E **42**
Vitae Apartments W6 . . . . .3C **98**
Vitali Cl. SW15 . . . . .6C **116**
Vittoria Ho. N1 . . . . .1K **83**
            (off High Rd.)
Viveash Cl. UB3: Hayes 3H **93**
Vivian Av. HA9: Wemb 5G **61**
   NW4 . . . . .5D **44**
Vivian Comma Cl. N4 . . . . .3B **66**
Vivian Ct. N12 . . . . .5E **30**
   W9 . . . . .2K **81**
Vivian Gdns. HA9: Wemb 5G **61**
Vivian Mans. NW4 . . . . .5D **44**
            (off Vivian Av.)
Vivian Rd. E3 .2A **86**
Vivian Sq. SE15 . . . . .3H **121**
Vivian Way N2 . . . . .5B **46**
Vivien Cl. KT9: Chess 7E **162**
Vivienne Cl. TW1: Twick 6D **114**
Vixen M. E8 . . . . .7F **67**
            (off Haggerston Rd.)
Voce Rd. SE18 . . . . .7H **107**
Voewood Cl. KT3: N Mald 6B **152**
Vogans Mill SE1 . . . . .6K **15** (2F **103**)
Vogler Ho. E1 .7J **85**
            (off Cable St.)
Vogue Cl. BR1: Brom 1K **159**
Vollasky Ho. E1 . . . . .5K **9**
            (off Daplyn St.)
Volta Cl. N9 . . . . .3D **34**
Voltaire Rd. SW4 . . . . .3H **119**
Voltaire Way UB3: Hayes 7G **75**
Volt Av. NW10 . . . . .3K **79**
Volta Way CR0: Wadd 1K **167**

Voluntary Pl. E11 . . . . .6J **51**
Vorley Rd. N19 . . . . .2G **65**
Voss Cl. SW16 . . . . .6J **137**
Voss St. E2 . . . . .3G **85**
Voyager Bus. Est. SE16 . . . . .3G **103**
            (off Spa Rd.)
Voyager Ct. E16 . . . . .5J **87**
            (off Hammersley Rd.)
Voyagers Cl. SE28 . . . . .6C **90**
Voysey Cl. N3 . . . . .3G **45**
Voysey Sq. E3 . . . . .5D **86**
Vue Cinema
   Acton 4G **79**
   Apollo 3C **12**
            (off Regent St.)
   Bromley .3J **159**
   Croydon, High St. 3C **168**
   Croydon, Purley Way 1K **167**
   Dagenham 1E **90**
   Fallow Corner 7G **31**
   Finchley Rd. 6A **64**
            (within O2 Centre)
   Fulham Broadway 7J **99**
   Harrow 6J **41**
      (within St George's Shop. & Leisure Cen.)
   Hayes 2G **93**
   Islington .2A **84**
   Leicester Square 2D **12**
            (off Cranbourn St.)
   Romford .6K **55**
   Shepherds Bush 2F **99**
   Westfield .1E **98**
   Wood Green 2A **48**
Vulcan Cl. E6 .6E **88**
Vulcan Ga.
   EN2: Enf .2F **23**
Vulcan Rd. SE4 . . . . .2B **122**
Vulcan Sq. E14 . . . . .4D **104**
Vulcan Ter. SE4 . . . . .2B **122**
Vulcan Way N7 . . . . .6K **65**
   SM6: Wall 7J **167**
Vulcan Wharf E15 . . . . .2D **86**
            (off Cook's Rd.)
Vyne, The DA7: Bex 3H **127**
Vyner Rd. W3 .7K **79**
Vyner St. E2 .1H **85**
Vyners Way UB10: Ick 5C **56**

W

Wadbrook St. KT1: King T 2D **150**
Wadding St. SE17 . . . . .4D **102**
Waddington Cl. EN1: Enf 4K **23**
Waddington Rd. E15 . . . . .5F **69**
Waddington St. E15 . . . . .6F **69**
Waddington Way SE19 . . . . .7C **138**
WADDON 3A **168**
Waddon Cl. CR0: Wadd 3A **168**
Waddon Ct. Rd. CR0: Wadd 3A **168**
Waddon Leisure Cen. 5A **168**
Waddon Marsh Way
   CR0: Wadd 1K **167**
Waddon New Rd. CR0: C'don 3B **168**
Waddon Pk. Av. CR0: Wadd 4A **168**
Waddon Rd. CR0: C'don, Wadd 3A **168**
Waddon Way CR0: Wadd 6A **168**
Wade Ct. N10 . . . . .7A **32**
Wade Ho. EN1: Enf 5J **23**
   SE1 . . . . .7K **15**
            (off Parkers Row)
Wades Gro. N21 . . . . .7F **23**
Wades Hill N21 . . . . .6F **23**
Wades La. TW11: Tedd 5A **132**
Wades M. N21 . . . . .7F **23**
Wadeson St. E2 . . . . .2H **85**
Wade's Pl. E14 . . . . .7D **86**
Wadeville Av.
   RM6: Chad H 6E **54**
Wadeville Cl. DA17: Belv 5G **109**
Wadham Av. E17 . . . . .7J **35**

Wadham Cl. TW17: Shep 7E **146**
Wadham Gdns. NW3 . . . . .1C **82**
  UB6: G'frd .6H **59**
Wadham Ho. N18 . . . . .5A **34**
Wadham M. SW14 . . . . .2J **115**
Wadham Rd. E17 . . . . .7J **35**
  SW15 . . . . .4G **117**
Wadhurst Cl. SE20 . . . . .2H **157**
Wadhurst Rd. SW8 . . . . .1G **119**
  W4 . . . . .3K **97**
Wadley Rd. E11 . . . . .7G **51**
Wadsworth Bus. Cen. UB6: G'frd 2C **78**
Wadsworth Cl. SE15: Pond E 5E **24**
  UB6: G'frd .2C **78**
Wadsworth Rd. UB6: G'frd 2B **78**
Wager St. E3 . . . . .4B **86**
WAGGONERS RDBT. 1K **111**
Waggon La. N17 . . . . .6B **34**
Waggon M. N14 . . . . .1B **32**
Waghorn Rd. E13 . . . . .1A **88**
  HA3: Kenton 3D **42**
Waghorn St. SE15 . . . . .3G **121**
Wagner M. KT6: Surb 5E **150**
  (off Avenue Elmers)
Wagner St. SE15 . . . . .7J **103**
Wagstaff Gdns. RM9: Dag 7C **72**
Wagtail Cl. EN1: Enf 1C **24**
  NW9 . . . . .2A **44**
Wagtail Rd. TW6: H'row A 5C **174**
Wagtail Wlk. BR3: Beck 5E **158**
Waight's Ct. KT2: King T 1E **150**
Wainfleet Av. RM5: Col R 2J **55**
Wainford Cl. SW19 . . . . .1F **135**
Wainwright Gro. TW7: Isle 4H **113**
Wainwright Ho. E1 . . . . .1J **103**
  (off Garnet St.)
Waite Davies Rd. SE12 . . . . .7H **123**
Waite Ho. W3 . . . . .1B **98**
Waite St. SE15 . . . . .6F **103**
Waithman St. EC4 . . . . .1A **14**
  (off Black Friars La.)
Wakefield Ct. SE26 . . . . .6J **139**
Wakefield Gdns. IG1: Ilf 6C **52**
  SE19 . . . . .7E **138**
Wakefield Ho. SE15 . . . . .1G **121**
Wakefield M. WC1 . . . . .2F **7** (3J **83**)
Wakefield Rd. N11 . . . . .5C **32**
  N15 . . . . .5F **49**
  TW10: Rich 5D **114**
Wakefield St. E6 . . . . .1B **88**
  N18 . . . . .5B **34**
  WC1 . . . . .2F **7** (3J **83**)
Wakeford Cl. DA5: Bexl 1D **144**
  SW4 . . . . .5G **119**
Wakehams Hill HA5: Pinn 3D **40**
Wakeham St. N1 . . . . .6D **66**
Wakehurst Rd. SW11 . . . . .5C **118**
Wakeling La. HA0: Wemb 3B **60**
Wakeling Rd. W7 . . . . .5K **77**
Wakeling St. E14 . . . . .6A **86**
Wakelin Ho. N1 . . . . .7B **66**
  (off Sebbon St.)
Wakelin Rd. E15 . . . . .2G **87**
Wakeman Ho. NW10 . . . . .3F **81**
  (off Wakeman Rd.)
Wakeman Rd. NW10 . . . . .3E **80**
Wakemans Hill Av. NW9 . . . . .5K **43**
Wakering Rd. IG11: Bark 6G **71**
  (not continuous)
Wakerley Cl. E6 . . . . .6D **88**
Wakley St. EC1 . . . . .1A **8** (3B **84**)
Walberswick St. SW8 . . . . .7J **101**
Walbrook EC4 . . . . .2E **14** (7D **84**)
  (not continuous)
Walbrook Ct. N1 . . . . .2E **84**
  (off Hemsworth St.)
Walbrook Ho. N9 . . . . .2D **34**
  (off Huntingdon Rd.)
Walbrook Wharf EC4 . . . . .3D **14**
  (off Cousin La.)
Walburgh St. E1 . . . . .6H **85**

Walcorde Av. SE17 . . . . .4C **102**
Walcot Gdns. SE11 . . . . .3J **19**
Walcot Rd. EN3: Brim 2G **25**
Walcot Sq. SE11 . . . . .3K **19** (4A **102**)
Walcott St. SW1 . . . . .3B **18** (4G **101**)
Waldair Cl. E16 . . . . .2F **107**
Waldeck Gro. SE27 . . . . .3B **138**
Waldeck Rd. N15 . . . . .4B **48**
  SW14 . . . . .3J **115**
  W4 . . . . .6G **97**
  W13 . . . . .6B **78**
Waldeck Ter. SW14 . . . . .3J **115**
  (off Waldeck Rd.)
Waldegrave Ct. IG11: Bark 1H **89**
Waldegrave Gdns.
  TW1: Twick 2K **131**
Waldegrave Pk. TW1: Twick 4K **131**
Waldegrave Rd. BR1: Brom 4C **160**
  N8 . . . . .3A **48**
  RM8: Dag .2C **72**
  SE19 . . . . .7E **139**
  TW1: Twick 4K **131**
  TW11: Tedd 4K **131**
  W5 . . . . .7F **79**
Waldegrove CR0: C'don 3F **169**
Waldemar Av. SW6 . . . . .1G **117**
  W13 . . . . .1C **96**
Waldemar Rd. SW19 . . . . .5J **135**
Walden Av. BR7: Chst 4D **142**
  N13 . . . . .4H **33**
  RM13: Rain 2K **91**
Walden Cl. DA17: Belv 5F **109**
Walden Ct. SW8 . . . . .1H **119**
Walden Gdns. CR7: Thor H 3K **155**
Walden Ho. SW1 . . . . .4H **17**
  (off Pimlico Rd.)
  SW11 . . . . .1E **118**
  (off Dagnall St.)
Walden Pde. BR7: Chst 6D **142**
  (not continuous)
Walden Rd. BR7: Chst 6D **142**
  N17 . . . . .1D **48**
Waldenshaw Rd. SE23 . . . . .1J **139**
Walden St. E1 . . . . .6H **85**
  (not continuous)
Walden Way NW7 . . . . .6A **30**
Waldo Cl. SW4 . . . . .5G **119**
Waldo Ho. NW10 . . . . .3D **80**
  (off Waldo Rd.)
Waldo Ind. Est. BR1: Brom 3B **160**
Waldo Pl. CR4: Mitc 7C **136**
Waldorf Cl. CR2: S Croy 7B **168**
Waldo Rd. BR1: Brom 3B **160**
  NW10 . . . . .3C **80**
Waldram Cres. SE23 . . . . .1J **139**
Waldram Pk. Rd. SE23 . . . . .1K **139**
Waldram Pl. SE23 . . . . .1J **139**
Waldrist Way DA18: Erith 3F **109**
Waldron Gdns. BR2: Brom 3F **159**
Waldron Ho. SW3 . . . . .7B **16** (6B **100**)
Waldron Rd. HA1: Harr 1J **59**
  HA2: Harr .1J **59**
  SW18 . . . . .3A **136**
Waldrons, The CR0: C'don 4B **168**
Waldron's Path CR2: S Croy 4C **168**
Waldrons Yd. HA2: Harr 2H **59**
Waldstock Rd. SE28 . . . . .7A **90**
Waleran Cl. HA7: Stan 5E **26**
Walerand Rd. SE13 . . . . .2E **122**
Waleran Flats SE1 . . . . .4E **102**
Wales Av. SM5: Cars 5C **166**
Wales Cl. SE15 . . . . .6H **103**
Wales Farm Rd. W3 . . . . .5K **79**
Waleton Acres SM6: Wall 6G **167**
Waley St. E1 . . . . .5A **86**
Walfield Av. N20 . . . . .7E **20**
Walford Ho. E1 . . . . .6H **85**
Walford Rd. N16 . . . . .4E **66**
Walfrey Gdns. RM9: Dag 7F **73**
WALHAM GREEN 1J **117**

Walham Grn. Ct. SW6 . . . . .7K **99**
  (off Waterford Rd.)
Walham Gro. SW6 . . . . .7J **99**
Walham Ri. SW19 . . . . .6G **135**
Walham Yd. SW6 . . . . .7J **99**
Walk, The N13 . . . . .3F **33**
  (off Fox La.)
Walkato Lodge IG9: Buck H 1F **37**
Walkden Rd. BR7: Chst 5E **142**
Walker Cl. CR0: New Ad 7E **170**
  N11 . . . . .4B **32**
  SE18 . . . . .4G **107**
  TW12: Hamp 6D **130**
  TW14: Felt .7H **111**
  W7 . . . . .1J **95**
Walker Ho. NW1 . . . . .1C **6** (2H **83**)
  SE16 . . . . .3B **104**
  (off Redriff Est.)
Walker M. SW2 . . . . .5A **120**
Walker's Ct. W1 . . . . .2C **12**
Walkerscroft Mead SE21 . . . . .1C **138**
Walkers Lodge E14 . . . . .2E **104**
  (off Manchester Rd.)
Walkers Pl. SW15 . . . . .4G **117**
Walkie-Talkie, The 2G **15**
Walkinshaw Ct. N1 . . . . .7C **66**
  (off Rotherfield St.)
Walks, The N2 . . . . .3B **46**
Walkynscroft SE15 . . . . .2H **121**
  (off Caulfield Rd.)
Wallace Bldg. NW8 . . . . .4B **4**
  (off Penfold St.)
Wallace Cl. SE28 . . . . .7D **90**
  TW17: Shep 4F **147**
  UB10: Uxb 2A **74**
Wallace Collection 7H **5** (6E **82**)
Wallace Ct. NW1 . . . . .6D **4**
  (off Old Marylebone Rd.)
  SE3 . . . . .4K **123**
Wallace Cres. SM5: Cars 5D **166**
Wallace Ho. N7 . . . . .6K **65**
  (off Caledonian Rd.)
Wallace Rd. N1 . . . . .6C **66**
Wallace Way N19 . . . . .2H **65**
  (off St John's Way)
  RM1: Rom .1K **55**
Wallasey Cres. UB10: Ick 2C **56**
Wallbrook Bus. Cen.
  TW4: Houn 3K **111**
Waliburton Rd. SE4 . . . . .2A **122**
Wallcote Av. NW2 . . . . .1F **63**
Wall Ct. N4 .1K **65**
  (off Stroud Grn. Rd.)
Walled Garden Cl. BR3: Beck 4D **158**
Walled Garden Cl. HA7: Stan 3D **26**
WALLEND 1E **88**
Wall End Cl. E6 . . . . .1E **88**
  (off Wall End Rd.)
Wall End Rd. E6 . . . . .7E **70**
Waller Dr. HA6: Nwood 2J **39**
Waller Rd. SE14 . . . . .1K **121**
Wallers Cl.
  IG8: Wfd G 6J **37**
  RM9: Dag .1E **90**
Waller Way SE10 . . . . .7D **104**
Wallflower St. W12 . . . . .7B **80**
Wallgrave Rd. SW5 . . . . .4K **99**
Wallingford Av. W10 . . . . .5F **81**
WALLINGTON 6F **167**
Wallington Cl. HA4: Ruis 6E **38**
Wallington Cnr. SM6: Wall 4F **167**
  (off Manor Rd. Nth.)
Wallington Ct. SM6: Wall 6F **167**
  (off Stanley Pk. Rd.)
WALLINGTON GREEN 4F **167**
Wallington Rd. IG3: Ilf 7K **53**
Wallington Sq.
  SM6: Wall .6F **167**
Wallis All. SE1 . . . . .6D **14**
Wallis Cl. SW11 . . . . .3B **118**

Wallis Ho. HA4: Ruis 1F **57**
  SE14 . . . . .1A **122**
  TW8: Bford 5E **96**
Wallis M. N8 . . . . .3A **48**
  (off Courcy Rd.)
Wallis Rd. E9 . . . . .6B **68**
  TW6: H'row A 5C **174**
  UB1: S'hall 6F **77**
Wallis's Cotts. SW2 . . . . .7J **119**
Wallman Pl. N22 . . . . .1K **47**
Wallorton Gdns. SW14 . . . . .4K **115**
Wallpaper Apartments, The N1 . . . . .7A **66**
  (off Offord Rd.)
Wallside EC2 .6D **8**
Wall St. N1 .6D **66**
Wallwood Rd. E11 . . . . .7F **51**
Wallwood St. E14 . . . . .5B **86**
Walmar Cl. EN4: Had W 1G **21**
Walmer Cl. BR6: Farnb 4H **173**
  E4 . . . . .2J **35**
  RM7: Mawney 2H **55**
Walmer Ct. KT5: Surb 5E **150**
  (off Cranes Pk.)
Walmer Gdns. W13 . . . . .2A **96**
Walmer Ho. W10 . . . . .6F **81**
  (off Bramley Rd.)
Walmer Pl. W1 . . . . .5E **4**
Walmer Rd. W10 . . . . .6E **80**
  W11 . . . . .7G **81**
Walmer St. W1 . . . . .5E **4** (5D **82**)
Walmer Ter. SE18 . . . . .4G **107**
Walmgate Rd. UB6: G'frd 1B **78**
Walmington Fold N12 . . . . .6D **30**
Walm La. NW2 . . . . .6E **62**
Walney Wlk. N1 . . . . .6C **66**
Walnut Av. UB7: W Dray 3C **92**
Walnut Cl. IG6: Ilf 4G **53**
  SE8 . . . . .6B **104**
  SM5: Cars .5D **166**
  UB3: Hayes 7G **75**
Walnut Ct. E17 . . . . .4E **50**
  W5 . . . . .2E **96**
  W8 . . . . .3K **99**
  (off St Mary's Ga.)
Walnut Flds. KT17: Ewe 7B **164**
Walnut Gdns. E15 . . . . .5G **69**
Walnut Gro. EN1: Enf 5J **23**
Walnut Ho. E3 . . . . .1B **86**
  (off Barge La.)
Walnut M. N22 . . . . .3A **48**
  (off High Rd.)
  SM2: Sutt .7A **166**
Walnut Rd. E10 . . . . .2C **68**
Walnut Tree Av. CR4: Mitc 3C **154**
  (off De'Arn Gdns.)
Walnut Tree Cl. BR7: Chst 1H **161**
  SW13 . . . . .1B **116**
  TW17: Shep 3E **146**
  UB10: Ick .4A **56**
Walnut Tree Cotts. SW19 . . . . .5G **135**
Walnut Tree Ho. SW10 . . . . .6K **99**
  (off Tregunter Rd.)
Walnut Tree Rd. RM8: Dag 2E **72**
  SE10 . . . . .5G **105**
  (not continuous)
  TW5: Hest .6D **94**
  TW8: Bford 6E **96**
  TW17: Shep 2E **146**
Walnut Tree Wlk.
  SE11 . . . . .3J **19** (4A **102**)
Walnut Way
  HA4: Ruis .6A **58**
  IG9: Buck H 3G **37**
Walpole Av. TW9: Kew 2F **115**
Walpole Cl. W13 . . . . .2C **96**
Walpole Ct. NW6 . . . . .7A **64**
  (off Fairfax Rd.)
  TW2: Twick 2J **131**
  W14 . . . . .3F **99**
  (off Blythe Rd.)
Walpole Cres. TW11: Tedd 5K **131**

Walpole Gdns.
TW2: Twick 2J **131**
W4 . . . . .5J **97**
Walpole Ho. KT8: W Mole 5E **148**
(off Approach Rd.)
SE1 .7J **13**
(off Westminster Bri. Rd.)
SW15 . . . . .5G **117**
(off Plaza Gdns.)
Walpole Lodge W13 . . . . .1C **96**
Walpole M. NW8 . . . . .1B **82**
SW19 .6B **136**
Walpole Pl. SE18 . . . . .4F **107**
TW11: Tedd 5K **131**
Walpole Rd. BR2: Brom 5B **160**
CRO: C'don 2D **168**
E6 . . . . .7A **70**
E17 . . . . .4A **50**
E18 . . . . .1H **51**
KT6: Surb 7E **150**
N17 . . . . .3G **49**
(not continuous)
SW19 .6B **136**
TW2: Twick 2J **131**
TW11: Tedd 5K **131**
Walpole St. SW3 . . . . . .5E **16** (5D **100**)
Walrond Av. HA9: Wemb 5E **60**
Walsham Cl. N16 . . . . .1G **67**
SE28 .7D **90**
Walsham Ho. SE14 . . . . .2K **121**
SE17 . . . . .5D **102**
(off Blackwood St.)
Walsham Rd. SE14 . . . . .2K **121**
TW14: Felt 7K **111**
Walsingham NW8 . . . . .1B **82**
Walsingham Gdns. KT19: Ewe 4A **164**
Walsingham Lodge SW13 . . . . .1C **116**
Walsingham Mans. SW6 . . . . .7K **99**
(off Fulham Rd.)
Walsingham Pk. BR7: Chst 2H **161**
Walsingham Pl. SW4 . . . . .6E **118**
Walsingham Rd. CR4: Mitc 5D **154**
E5 . . . . .3G **67**
EN2: Enf 4J **23**
W13 .1A **96**
Walsingham Wlk. DA17: Belv 6G **109**
Walston Ho. SW1 . . . . .5C **18**
(off Aylesford St.)
Walter Besant Ho. E1 . . . . .3K **85**
(off Bancroft Rd.)
Walter Ct. W3 . . . . .6J **79**
(off Lynton Ter.)
Walter Grn. Ho. SE15 . . . . .1J **121**
(off Lausanne Rd.)
Walter Ho. SW10 . . . . .7B **100**
(off Riley St.)
Walter Hurford Pde. E12 . . . . .4E **70**
(off Grantham Rd.)
Walter Langley Ct. SE16 . . . . .2J **103**
(off Brunel Rd.)
Walter Rodney Cl. E6 . . . . .6D **70**
Walter Savil Twr. E17 . . . . .6C **50**
(off Colchester Rd.)
Walters Cl. SE17 . . . . .4D **102**
(off Brandon St.)
UB3: Hayes 2H **93**
Walters Ho. N1 . . . . .1B **84**
(off Essex Rd.)
SE17 . . . . .6B **102**
(off Otto St.)
Walter Sickert Hall N1 . . . . .1C **8**
(off Graham St.)
Walters Rd. EN3: Pond E 4D **24**
SE25 .4E **156**
Walter St. E2 . . . . .3K **85**
KT2: King T 1E **150**
Walters Way SE23 . . . . .6K **121**
Walters Yd.
BR1: Brom 2J **159**
Walter Ter. E1 . . . . .6K **85**
Walterton Rd. W9 . . . . .4H **81**

Walter Wlk. HA8: Edg 6D **28**
Waltham Av.
NW9 .6G **43**
UB3: Harl 3E **92**
Waltham Dr. HA8: Edg 2G **43**
Waltham Ho. NW8 . . . . .1A **82**
Waltham Pk. Way E17 . . . . .1C **50**
Waltham Rd.
IG8: Wfd G 6H **37**
SM5: Cars 7B **154**
UB2: S'hall 3C **94**
WALTHAMSTOW 3C **50**
Walthamstow Av. E4 . . . . .6G **35**
Walthamstow Bus. Cen. E17 . . . . . .2E **50**
Walthamstow Marsh Nature Reserve
. . . . .7H **49**
Waltham Way E4 . . . . .3G **35**
Waltheof Av. N17 . . . . .1D **48**
Waltheof Gdns. N17 . . . . .1D **48**
Walton Av.
HA2: Harr 5D **58**
HA9: Wemb 3H **61**
KT3: N Mald 4B **152**
SM3: Cheam 3H **165**
Walton Bri. KT12: Walt T 7G **147**
TW17: Shep 7G **147**
Walton Bri. Rd. TW17: Shep 7G **147**
Walton Cl. E4 . . . . .5H **35**
E5 . . . . .3K **67**
(off Orient Way)
HA1: Harr 4H **41**
NW2 .2D **62**
SW8 . . . . .7J **101**
Walton Ct. CR2: S Croy 5C **168**
(off Warham Rd.)
EN5: New Bar 5F **21**
NW6 .7A **64**
(off Fairfax Rd.)
Walton Dr. HA1: Harr 4J **59**
Walton Dr. HA1: Harr 4H **41**
NW10 . . . . .6K **61**
Walton Gdns. HA9: Wemb 2E **60**
TW13: Felt 4H **129**
W3 . . . . .5H **79**
Walton Grn. CR0: New Ad 7D **170**
Walton Ho. E2 . . . . .3K **9**
(off Montclare St.)
E17 . . . . .3D **50**
NW1 . . . . .3K **5**
(off Longford St.)
SW3 .2E **16**
(off Walton St.)
Walton La. KT13: Weyb . . . .7F **147** & 7G **147**
TW17: Shep 7F **147**
WALTON-ON-THAMES 7J **147**
Walton on Thames Camping & Caravan Site
KT12: Walt T 7E **148**
Walton Pl. SW3 . . . . . . .1E **16** (3D **100**)
Walton Rd. DA14: Sidc 2C **144**
E12 . . . . .4E **70**
(not continuous)
E13 . . . . .2A **88**
HA1: Harr 4H **41**
KT8: W Mole, E Mos 4D **148**
KT12: Walt T 5A **148**
N15 . . . . .4F **49**
RM5: Col R 1F **55**
Walton St. EN2: Enf 1J **23**
SW3 . . . . .3D **16** (4C **100**)
Walton Vs. N1 . . . . .7E **66**
(off Downham Rd.)
Walton Way CR4: Mitc 4G **155**
W3 . . . . .5H **79**
Walt Whitman Cl. SE24 . . . . .4B **120**
WALWORTH 5C **102**
Walworth Pl. SE17 . . . . .5C **102**
Walworth Rd.
SE1 . . . . .4C **102**
SE17 . . . . .4C **102**
Walwyn Av. BR1: Brom 3B **160**

Wanborough Dr. SW15 . . . . .1D **134**
Wanderer Dr. IG11: Bark 3C **90**
Wandle Bank CR0: Bedd 3J **167**
SW19 .7B **136**
Wandle Ct. CR0: Bedd 3J **167**
KT19: Ewe 4J **163**
Wandle Ct. Gdns.
CR0: Bedd 3J **167**
Wandle Ho. BR1: Brom 5F **141**
NW8 . . . . .5B **4**
(off Penfold St.)
Wandle Industrial Mus. 3D **154**
Wandle Meadow Nature Pk. 5A **136**
Wandle Pk. 2B **168**
Wandle Pk. Trad. Estate, The
CR0: C'don 1B **168**
Wandle Recreation Cen. 6K **117**
Wandle Rd. CR0: Bedd 3J **167**
CR0: C'don 3C **168**
SM4: Mord 4A **154**
SM6: Wall 3F **167**
SW17 .2C **136**
Wandle Side CR0: Wadd 3K **167**
SM6: Wall 3F **167**
Wandle Technology Pk.
CR4: Mitc 7D **154**
Wandle Trad. Est. CR4: Mitc 7D **154**
Wandle Way CR4: Mitc 5A **154**
SW18 .1K **135**
Wandon Rd. SW6 . . . . .7K **99**
WANDSWORTH 5K **117**
Wandsworth Bri. SW6 . . . . .3K **117**
Wandsworth Bri. Rd. SW6 . . . . .1K **117**
WANDSWORTH COMMON 1D **136**
Wandsworth Comn. West Side
SW18 .5A **118**
WANDSWORTH GYRATORY 5K **117**
Wandsworth High St. SW18 . . . . . . .5J **117**
Wandsworth Mus. 5J **117**
Wandsworth Plain SW18 . . . . .5K **117**
Wandsworth Rd. SW8 . . . . .7E **18** (3F **119**)
Wangey Rd. RM6: Chad H 7D **54**
Wangford Ho. SW9 . . . . .4B **120**
(off Loughborough Pk.)
Wanless Rd. SE24 . . . . .3C **120**
Wanley Rd. SE5 . . . . .4D **120**
Wanlip Rd. E13 . . . . .4K **87**
Wannock Gdns. IG6: Ilf 1F **53**
Wansbeck Ct. EN2: Enf 3G **23**
(off Waverley Rd.)
Wansbeck Rd. E9 . . . . .7B **68**
Wansdown Pl. SW6 . . . . .7K **99**
Wansey St. SE17 . . . . .4C **102**
WANSTEAD 6K **51**
Wanstead Cl. BR1: Brom 2A **160**
Wanstead Gdns. IG4: Ilf 6B **52**
Wanstead Golf Course 7A **52**
Wanstead La. IG1: Ilf 6B **52**
Wanstead Leisure Cen. 6A **52**
Wanstead Pk. Av. E12 . . . . .1B **70**
Wanstead Pk. Rd. IG1: Ilf 6B **52**
Wanstead Pl. E11 . . . . .6J **51**
Wanstead Rd. BR1: Brom 2A **160**
Wansunt Rd. DA5: Bexl 1J **145**
Wantage Rd. SE12 . . . . .5H **123**
Wantz Rd. RM10: Dag 4H **73**
WAPPING 1H **103**
Wapping Dock St. E1 . . . . .1H **103**
Wapping High St. E1 . . . . .1G **103**
Wapping La. E1 . . . . .7H **85**
Wapping Wall E1 . . . . .1J **103**
Waratah Dr. BR7: Chst 5D **142**
Warbank La. KT2: King T 7B **134**
Warbeck Rd. W12 . . . . .2D **98**
Warberry Rd. N22 . . . . .1K **47**
Warboys App. KT2: King T 6H **133**
Warboys Cres. E4 . . . . .5K **35**
Warboys Rd. KT2: King T 6H **133**
Warburg Ct. NW9 . . . . .3A **44**
(off Mornington Cl.)

Warburton Cl. HA3: Hrw W 6C **26**
N1 . . . . .6E **66**
(off Culford Rd.)
Warburton Ct. HA4: Ruis 2J **57**
Warburton Ho. E8 . . . . .1H **85**
(off Warburton St.)
Warburton Rd. E8 . . . . .1H **85**
TW2: Whitt 1F **131**
Warburton St. E8 . . . . .1H **85**
Warburton Ter. E17 . . . . .2D **50**
Wardalls Gro. SE14 . . . . .7J **103**
Wardalls Ho. SE8 . . . . .6B **104**
(off Staunton St.)
Ward Cl. CR2: S Croy 6E **168**
DA8: Erith 6K **109**
Wardell Cl. NW7 . . . . .7F **29**
Wardell Fld. NW9 . . . . .1A **44**
Wardell Ho. SE10 . . . . .6E **104**
(off Welland St.)
Wardell M. SW4 . . . . .3F **119**
Warden Av. HA2: Harr 1D **58**
Warden Rd. NW5 . . . . .6E **64**
Wardens Fld. Cl. BR6: Chels 6J **173**
Wardens Gro. SE1 . . . . . . .5C **14** (1C **102**)
Ward La. E9 . . . . .5A **68**
Wardle St. E9 . . . . .5K **67**
Wardley St. SW18 . . . . .7K **117**
Wardo Av. SW6 . . . . .1G **117**
Wardour M. W1 . . . . .1B **12**
Wardour St. W1 . . . . .7B **6** (6G **83**)
Ward Point SE11 . . . . . . .4J **19** (4A **102**)
Ward Rd. E15 . . . . .1F **87**
N19 . . . . .3G **65**
SW19 .1A **154**
Wardrobe, The TW9: Rich 5D **114**
(off Old Palace Yd.)
Wardrobe Pl. EC4 . . . . .1B **14**
Wardrobe Ter. EC4 . . . . .2B **14**
Wardroper Ho. SE1 . . . . .3B **102**
(off St George's Rd.)
Wards Rd. IG2: Ilf 7H **53**
Wards Wharf App. E16 . . . . .1B **106**
Ware Ct. SM1: Sutt 4H **165**
Wareham Cl. TW3: Houn 4F **113**
Wareham Ct. N1 . . . . .7E **66**
(off Hertford Rd.)
Wareham Ho. SW8 . . . . .7K **101**
Warehome M. E13 . . . . .4K **87**
(off Jutland Rd.)
Warehouse Ct. SE18 . . . . .3F **107**
Warehouse Sports &
Performing Arts Centre, The . . .5K **107**
Warehouse Way E16 . . . . .7K **87**
Waremead Rd. IG2: Ilf 5F **53**
Warepoint Dr. SE28 . . . . .2H **107**
Warfield Rd. NW10 . . . . .3F **81**
TW12: Hamp 1F **149**
TW14: Felt 7G **111**
Warfield Yd. NW10 . . . . .3F **81**
(off Warfield Rd.)
Wargrave Av. N15 . . . . .6F **49**
Wargrave Ho. E2 . . . . .2J **9**
(off Navarre St.)
Wargrave Rd. HA2: Harr 3G **59**
Warham Rd.
CR2: S Croy 5B **168**
HA3: W'stone 2K **41**
N4 . . . . .5A **48**
Warham St. SE5 . . . . .7B **102**
Waring & Gillow Est. W3 . . . . .4G **79**
Waring Cl. BR6: Chels 6K **173**
Waring Dr. BR6: Chels 6K **173**
Waring Rd. DA14: Sidc 6C **144**
Waring St. SE27 . . . . .4C **138**
Warkworth Gdns.
TW7: Isle 7A **96**
Warkworth Rd. N17 . . . . .7J **33**
Warland Rd. SE18 . . . . .7H **107**
Warley Av. RM8: Dag 7F **55**
UB4: Hayes 6J **75**
Warley Cl. E10 . . . . .1B **68**

Warley Rd. IG5: Ilf 1E **52**
  IG8: Wfd G 7E **36**
  N9 . . . . .2D **34**
  UB4: Hayes 6J **75**
Warley St. E2 . . . . .3K **85**
Warlingham Ct. SE13 . . . . .6E **122**
Warlingham Rd. CR7: Thor H 4B **156**
Warlock Rd. W9 . . . . .4H **81**
Warlters Cl. N7 . . . . .4J **65**
Warlters Rd. N7 . . . . .4J **65**
Warltersville Mans. N19 . . . . .7J **47**
Warltersville Rd. N19 . . . . .7J **47**
War Memorial Sports Ground 4C **166**
Warmington Cl. E5 . . . . .3K **67**
Warmington Rd. SE24 . . . . .6C **120**
Warminster Gdns. SE25 . . . . .2G **157**
Warminster Rd. SE25 . . . . .2F **157**
Warminster Sq. SE25 . . . . .2G **157**
Warminster Way CR4: Mitc 1F **155**
Warmsworth NW1 . . . . .1G **83**
         (off Pratt St.)
Warmwell Av. NW9 . . . . .1A **44**
Warndon St. SE16 . . . . .4K **103**
Warneford Rd. HA3: Kenton 3D **42**
  TW6: H'row A 5C **174**
Warneford St. E9 . . . . .1H **85**
Warne Pl. DA15: Sidc 6B **126**
Warner Av. SM3: Cheam 2G **165**
Warner Cl. E15 . . . . .5G **69**
  NW9 .7B **44**
  TW12: Hamp 5D **130**
  UB3: Harl 7F **93**
Warner Ho. BR3: Beck 6D **140**
  NW8 .3A **82**
  SE13 .2D **122**
         (off Russett Way)
Warner Pl. E2 . . . . .2G **85**
Warner Rd. BR1: Brom 7H **141**
  E17 . . . . .4A **50**
  N8 . . . . .4H **47**
  SE5 . . . . .1C **120**
Warners Cl. IG8: Wfd G 5D **36**
Warners La. KT2: King T 4D **132**
Warners Path IG8: Wfd G 5D **36**
Warner St. EC1 . . . . .4J **7** (4A **84**)
Warner Ter. E14 . . . . .5D **86**
         (off Broomfield St.)
Warner Yd. EC1 . . . . .4J **7**
Warnford Ct. EC2 . . . . .7F **9**
         (off Throgmorton Av.)
Warnford Ho. SW15 . . . . .6A **116**
         (off Tunworth Cres.)
Warnford Ind. Est. UB3: Hayes 2G **93**
Warnford Rd. BR6: Chels 5K **173**
Warnham WC1 . . . . .2G **7**
         (off Sidmouth St.)
Warnham Ct. Rd. SM5: Cars 7D **166**
Warnham Ho. SW2 . . . . .7K **119**
         (off Up. Tulse Hill)
Warnham Rd. N12 . . . . .5H **31**
Warple M. W3 . . . . .2A **98**
Warple Way W3 . . . . .2A **98**
Warren, The 2A **94**
Warren, The E12 . . . . .4C **70**
  KT4: Wor Pk 4K **163**
  SE7 . . . . .6A **106**
  TW5: Hest 7D **94**
  UB4: Hayes 6J **75**
Warren Av.
  BR1: Brom 7G **141**
  BR6: Chels 5K **173**
  CR2: Sels 7K **169**
  E10 . . . . .3E **68**
  TW10: Rich 4H **115**
Warren Cl.
  DA6: Bex 5G **127**
  HA9: Wemb 2D **60**
  N9 . . . . .7E **24**
  SE21 .7C **120**
  UB4: Yead 5A **76**

Warren Ct. BR3: Beck 7C **140**
  CR0: C'don 1E **168**
  N17 . . . . .3G **49**
         (off High Cross Rd.)
  NW1 . . . . .3B **6**
         (off Warren St.)
  W5 . . . . .5C **78**
Warren Cres. N9 . . . . .7A **24**
Warren Cutting KT2: King T 7K **133**
Warrender Rd. N19 . . . . .3G **65**
Warrender Way HA4: Ruis 7J **39**
Warren Dr. HA4: Ruis 2A **58**
  UB6: G'frd 4F **77**
Warren Drive, The E11 . . . . .7A **52**
Warren Dr. Nth. KT5: Surb 1H **163**
Warren Dr. Sth. KT5: Surb 1J **163**
Warren Farm Cotts. RM6: Chad H . . .4F **55**
Warren Farm Sports Cen. 3H **95**
Warren Flds. HA7: Stan 4H **27**
Warren Footpath TW1: Twick 1C **132**
Warren Gdns. BR6: Chels 5K **173**
  E15 . . . . .5F **69**
Warren Ho. E3 . . . . .3D **86**
         (off Bromley High St.)
  N17 . . . . .3G **49**
         (off High Cross Rd.)
  W14 . . . . .4H **99**
Warren La. HA7: Stan 2F **27**
  SE18 .3F **107**
Warren La. Ga. SE18 . . . . .3F **107**
Warren M. W1 . . . . .4A **6** (4G **83**)
Warren Pk. KT2: King T 6J **133**
Warren Pk. Rd. SM1: Sutt 6B **166**
Warren Pl. E1 . . . . .6K **85**
         (off Pitsea St.)
Warren Pond Rd. E4 . . . . .1C **36**
Warren Ri. KT3: N Mald 1K **151**
Warren Rd.
  BR2: Hayes 2J **171**
  BR6: Chels 5K **173**
         (not continuous)
  CR0: C'don 1E **168**
  DA6: Bex 5G **127**
  DA14: Sidc 3C **144**
  E4 . . . . .2K **35**
  E10 . . . . .3E **68**
  E11 . . . . .6A **52**
  IG6: Ilf .5H **53**
  KT2: King T 6J **133**
  NW2 .2B **62**
  SW19 . . . . .6C **136**
  TW2: Whitt 6G **113**
  TW15: Ashf 7G **129**
  UB10: Ick 4A **56**
  WD23: B Hea 1B **26**
Warren Sports Cen. 5F **55**
Warrens Shawe La. HA8: Edg 2C **28**
Warren St. W1 . . . . .4A **6** (4G **83**)
Warren Ter. RM6: Chad H 4D **54**
Warren Wlk. SE7 . . . . .6A **106**
Warren Way HA8: Edg 2H **43**
Warren Wood Cl. BR2: Hayes 2H **171**
Warriner Dr. N9 . . . . .3B **34**
Warriner Gdns. SW11 . . . . .1D **118**
Warrington Ct. CR0: Wadd 3B **168**
         (off Warrington Rd.)
Warrington Cres. W9 . . . . .4A **82**
Warrington Gdns. W9 . . . . .4A **82**
         (not continuous)
Warrington Rd. CR0: Wadd 3B **168**
  HA1: Harr 5J **41**
  RM8: Dag 2D **72**
  TW10: Rich 5D **114**
Warrington Sq. RM8: Dag 2D **72**
Warrior Cl. SE28 . . . . .1H **107**
Warrior Ct. SW9 . . . . .3B **120**
         (off Coldharbour Rd.)
Warrior Sq. E12 . . . . .4E **70**
Warsaw Cl. HA4: Ruis 6K **57**
Warspite Ho. E14 . . . . .4D **104**
         (off Cahir St.)

Warspite Rd. SE18 . . . . .3C **106**
Warton Ct. E1 . . . . .7K **85**
         (off Cable St.)
  W3 . . . . .3J **97**
         (off All Saints Rd.)
Warton Ho. E15 . . . . .1E **86**
         (off High St.)
Warton Rd. E15 . . . . .1E **86**
Warwall E6 . . . . .6F **89**
Warwick Ct. KT6: Surb 2E **162**
Warwick W14 . . . . .4H **99**
         (off Kensington Village)
Warwick Av. HA2: Harr 4D **58**
  HA8: Edg 3C **28**
  W2 . . . . .4A **82**
  W9 . . . . .4K **81**
Warwick Bldg. SW8 . . . . .6F **101**
Warwick Chambers W8 . . . . .3J **99**
         (off Pater St.)
Warwick Cl. DA5: Bexl 7F **127**
  EN4: E Barn 5G **21**
  TW12: Hamp 7G **131**
  W8 . . . . .3H **99**
         (off Kensington High St.)
  WD23: B Hea 1D **26**
  BR2: Brom 2G **159**
  EC4 . . . . .1B **14**
         (off Warwick La.)
  EN5: New Bar 5E **20**
         (off Station Rd.)
  HA1: Harr 3J **41**
  N11 . . . . .6C **32**
  UB5: N'olt 5E **58**
         (off Newmarket Av.)
Warwick Ct.
  W7 . . . . .6K **77**
         (off Copley Cl.)
  WC1 . . . . .6H **7** (5K **83**)
Warwick Cres. UB4: Hayes 4H **75**
  W2 . . . . .5A **82**
Warwick Dene W5 . . . . .1E **96**
Warwick Dr. SW15 . . . . .3D **116**
Warwick Est. W2 . . . . .5K **81**
Warwick Gdns. CR7: Thor H 3A **156**
  EN5: Barn 1C **20**
  IG1: Ilf .1F **71**
  KT7: T Ditt 5K **149**
  N4 . . . . .5C **48**
  W14 . . . . .3H **99**
Warwick Gro. E5 . . . . .1H **67**
  KT5: Surb 7F **151**
Warwick Ho. E16 . . . . .1J **105**
         (off Wesley Av.)
  KT2: King T 1E **150**
         (off Acre Rd.)
  SW9 .2A **120**
Warwick Ho. St. SW1 . . . . .4D **12** (1H **101**)
Warwick La. EC4 . . . . .7B **8** (6B **84**)
Warwick Lodge TW2: Twick 3F **131**
Warwick Mans. SW5 . . . . .4J **99**
         (off Cromwell Cres.)
Warwick Pde. HA3: Kenton 2B **42**
Warwick Pas. EC4 . . . . .7B **8**
         (off Old Bailey)
Warwick Pl. KT7: T Ditt 6A **150**
  W5 . . . . .2D **96**
  W9 . . . . .5A **82**
Warwick Pl. Nth. SW1 . . . . .4A **18** (4G **101**)
Warwick Rd. CR7: Thor H 3A **156**
  DA14: Sidc 5B **144**
  DA16: Well 3C **126**
  E4 . . . . .5H **35**
  E11 . . . . .5K **51**
  E12 . . . . .5C **70**
  E15 . . . . .6H **69**
  E17 . . . . .1B **50**
  EN5: New Bar 4E **20**
  KT1: Hamp W 1C **150**
  KT3: N Mald 3J **151**
  KT7: T Ditt 5K **149**
  N11 . . . . .6C **32**

Warwick Rd. N18 . . . . .4K **33**
  SE20 .3H **157**
  SM1: Sutt 4A **166**
  SW5 .4H **99**
  TW2: Twick 1J **131**
  TW4: Houn 3K **111**
  TW15: Ashf 5A **128**
  UB2: S'hall 3D **94**
  UB7: W Dray 2A **92**
  W5 . . . . .2D **96**
  W14 . . . . .4H **99**
Warwick Row SW1 . . . . . . .1K **17** (3G **101**)
Warwickshire Path
  SE8 . . . . .7B **104**
Warwickshire Rd. N16 . . . . .4E **66**
Warwick Sq. EC4 . . . . .7B **8** (6B **84**)
  SW1 . . . . .5A **18** (5G **101**)
         (not continuous)
Warwick Sq. M. SW1 . . . . . .4A **18** (4G **101**)
Warwick St. W1 . . . . .2B **12** (7G **83**)
Warwick Ter. E17 . . . . .5F **51**
         (off Lea Bri. Rd.)
  SE18 .6H **107**
Warwick Way SW1 . . . . .5J **17** (5F **101**)
Warwick Yd. EC1 . . . . .4D **8** (4C **84**)
Wasdale NW1 . . . . .3F **83**
         (off Cumberland Mkt.)
Washbourne Ct. N9 . . . . .2B **34**
         (off Acton Cl.)
Washbourne Rd. NW10 . . . . .1K **79**
Washington Av. E12 . . . . .4D **70**
Washington Bldg. SE13 . . . . .1D **122**
         (off Deal's Gateway)
Washington Cl. E3 . . . . .3D **86**
Washington Ho. E17 . . . . .2B **50**
  SW3 . . . . .7E **10**
         (off Basil St.)
Washington Rd. E6 . . . . .7A **70**
  E18 . . . . .2H **51**
  KT1: King T 2G **151**
  KT4: Wor Pk 2D **164**
  SW13 . . . . .7C **98**
  TW6: H'row A 6D **174**
Wasp Rd. TW6: H'row A 5C **174**
         (off Welland Rd.)
Wastdale Rd. SE23 . . . . .1K **139**
Watch, The N12 . . . . .4F **31**
Watchfield Ct. W4 . . . . .5J **97**
Watcombe Cotts. TW9: Kew 6G **97**
Watcombe Pl. SE25 . . . . .5H **157**
Watcombe Rd. SE25 . . . . .5H **157**
Waterbank Rd. SE6 . . . . .3D **140**
Waterbeach Rd.
  RM9: Dag 6C **72**
Water Brook La. NW4 . . . . .5E **44**
Watercress Pl. N1 . . . . .7E **66**
Waterdale Rd. SE2 . . . . .6A **108**
Waterden Cl. W11 . . . . .1G **99**
Waterden Rd. E20 . . . . .5C **68**
Waterer Ho. SE6 . . . . .4E **140**
Waterer Ri. SM6: Wall 6H **167**
Waterfall Cl. N14 . . . . .3B **32**
Waterfall Cotts. SW19 . . . . .6B **136**
Waterfall Rd. N11 . . . . .4A **32**
  N14 . . . . .4A **32**
  SW19 . . . . .6B **136**
Waterfall Ter. SW17 . . . . .6C **136**
Waterfall Wlk. N14 . . . . .1A **32**
Waterfield Cl. DA17: Belv 3G **109**
  SE28 .1B **108**
Waterfield Gdns. SE25 . . . . .4D **156**
Waterford Ho. W11 . . . . .7H **81**
         (off Kensington Pk. Rd.)
Waterford Rd. SW6 . . . . .7K **99**
Waterford Way NW10 . . . . .5D **62**
Waterfront W6 . . . . .6E **98**
Waterfront Ho. E5 . . . . .2J **67**
         (off Harry Zeital Way)
Waterfront Leisure Cen.
  Woolwich 3E **106**
Waterfront M. N1 . . . . .2C **84**

Waterfront Studios Bus. Cen. E16 ....1H **105**
                 (off Dock Rd.)
Water Gdns. HA7: Stan 6G **27**
Water Gardens, The W2 ....7D 4 (6C **82**)
Watergardens, The KT2: King T 6J **133**
Water Gdns. Sq. SE16 ....2K **103**
Watergate EC4 ....2A 14 (7B **84**)
Watergate St. SE8 ....6C **104**
Watergate Wlk. WC2 ....4F **13** (1J **101**)
Waterhall Av. E4 ....4B **36**
Waterhall Cl. E17 ....1K **49**
Waterhead NW1 ....1A **6**
                 (off Varndell St.)
Waterhouse CRO: C'don 1C **168**
           (off Saffron Central Sq.)
Waterhouse Cl. E16 ....5B **88**
  NW3 ....5B **64**
  W6 ....4F **99**
Waterhouse Sq. EC1 ....6J 7 (5A **84**)
Wateridge Cl. E14 ....3C **104**
Water La. DA14: Sidc 2F **145**
  E15 ....6G **69**
  EC3 ....3H **15** (7E **84**)
  IG3: Ilf 3J **71**
  KT1: King T 1D **150**
  N9 ....1C **34**
  NW1 ....7F **65**
  SE14 ....7J **103**
  TW1: Twick 1A **132**
  TW9: Rich 5D **114**
Water Lily Cl. UB2: S'hall 2G **95**
Waterline Ho. W2 ....6B **4**
Waterloo Bri. WC2 ....3G **13** (7K **83**)
Waterloo Cl. E9 ....5J **67**
  TW14: Felt 1H **129**
Waterloo East Theatre 1A **102**
                 (off Brad St.)
Waterloo Gdns. E2 ....2J **85**
  N1 ....7B **66**
  RM7: Rom 6K **55**
Waterloo Pas. NW6 ....7H **63**
Waterloo Pl. SM5: Cars 4H **165**
               (off Wrythe Grn.)
  SW1 ....4C **12** (1H **101**)
  TW9: Rich 4E **114**
Waterloo Rd. E6 ....4A **70**
  E7 ....5H **69**
  E10 ....7C **50**
  IG6: Ilf 2G **53**
  NW2 ....1C **62**
  RM7: Rom, Rush G 5K **55**
  SE1 ....4H **13** (1K **101**)
  SM1: Sutt 5B **166**
Waterloo Ter. N1 ....7B **66**
Waterlow Ct. NW11 ....7K **45**
Waterlow Park Cen. 1F **65**
Waterlow Rd. N19 ....1G **65**
Waterman Bldg. E14 ....2B **104**
Watermans Art Centre, Cinema & Theatre
                              .6E **96**
Watermans Cl. KT2: King T 7E **132**
Watermans Ct. TW8: Bford 6D **96**
                 (off High St.)
Watermans M. W5 ....7E **78**
Waterman's Quay SW6 ....2A **118**
Waterman St. SW15 ....3F **117**
Watermans Wlk. SE16 ....2A **104**
Waterman Way E1 ....1H **103**
Watermark Ct. RM6: Chad H 6B **54**
               (off Quarles Pk. Rd.)
Watermead TW14: Felt 1G **129**
Watermead Ho. E9 ....5A **68**
Watermead La. SM5: Cars 7D **154**
Watermead Lodge SE16 ....1K **103**
            (off Princes Riverside Rd.)
Watermeadow La. SW6 ....2A **118**
Watermead Rd. SE6 ....4E **140**
Watermead Way N17 ....3H **49**
Watermen's Sq. SE20 ....7J **139**
Water M. SE15 ....4J **121**
Watermill Bus. Cen. EN3: Brim 2G **25**

Watermill Cl. TW10: Ham 3C **132**
Water Mill Ho. TW13: Hanw 2E **130**
Watermill La. N18 ....5K **33**
Watermill Way SW19 ....1A **154**
  TW13: Hanw 2D **130**
Water Rd. HAO: Wemb 1F **79**
Water's Edge SW6 ....1E **116**
               (off Palemead Cl.)
Watersedge KT19: Ewe 4J **163**
Watersfield Way HA8: Edg 7J **27**
Waters Gdns. RM10: Dag 5G **73**
Waterside BR3: Beck 1B **158**
  E17 ....6J **49**
  N1 ....2C **84**
  UB7: Harm 3D **174**
  W2 ....6A **4**
Waterside Apartments N4 ....1C **66**
               (off Goodchild Rd.)
Waterside Av. BR3: Beck 5E **158**
              (off Adamson Way)
Waterside Bus. Cen. TW7: Isle 4B **114**
Waterside Cl. E3 ....1B **86**
  HA9: Wemb 3J **61**
  IG11: Bark 4A **72**
  KT6: Surb 2E **162**
  SE16 ....2G **103**
  SE28 ....1K **107**
  TW17: Shep 1E **146**
  UB5: N'olt 3D **76**
Waterside Ct. SM5: Cars 3E **166**
                (off Millpond Pl.)
Waterside Dr. KT12: Walt T 5J **147**
Waterside Hgts. E16 ....2A **106**
                 (off Booth Rd.)
Waterside Pl. NW1 ....1E **82**
Waterside Point SW11 ....7C **100**
Waterside Trad. Cen. W7 ....3J **95**
Waterside Way N17 ....3H **49**
  SW17 ....4A **136**
Watersmeet Way SE28 ....6C **90**
Waterson St. E2 ....1H 9 (3E **84**)
Waters Pl. SW15 ....2E **116**
Watersplash Cl. KT1: King T 3E **150**
Watersplash La. TW5: Cran 5K **93**
  UB3: Harl 4J **93**
Watersplash Rd. TW17: Shep 5C **146**
Waters Rd. KT1: King T 2H **151**
  SE6 ....3G **141**
Waters Sq. KT1: King T 3H **151**
Water St. WC2 ....2J **13**
Water Twr. Cl. UB8: Uxb 5A **56**
Water Twr. Hill CRO: C'don 4D **168**
Waterview Cl. DA6: Bex 5D **126**
Waterview Ho. E14 ....5A **86**
                  (off Carr St.)
Waterway Av. SE13 ....3D **122**
Waterway Pk. UB3: Hayes 2E **92**
Waterways Bus. Cen.
  EN3: Enf L 1G **25**
WATERWORKS CORNER 1G **51**
Waterworks Golf Course (Nature Reserve)
                              .2A **68**
Waterworks La. E5 ....2K **67**
Waterworks Rd. SW2 ....6K **119**
Waterworks Vis. Cen. 2A **68**
Waterworks Yd. CRO: C'don 3C **168**
                 (off Charles St.)
Watery La. DA14: Sidc 6B **144**
  SW19 ....1H **153**
  SW20 ....2H **153**
  UB3: Harl 5F **93**
  UB5: N'olt 2A **76**
Wates Way CR4: Mitc 6D **154**
Wateville Rd. N17 ....1C **48**

Watford By-Pass HA8: Edg 1G **27**
Watford Cl. SW11 ....1C **118**
Watford Rd. E16 ....5J **87**
  HAO: Wemb 2A **60**
  HA1: Harr 7A **42**
Watford Way NW4 ....4C **44**
  NW7 ....4F **29**
Watkin Rd. HA9: Wemb 3H **61**
Watkins Cl. HA6: Nwood 1H **39**
Watkins Ho. E14 ....2E **104**
               (off Manchester Rd.)
Watkinson Rd. N7 ....6K **65**
Watkins Way
  RM8: Dag 1E **72**
WATLING 7E **28**
Watling Av. HA8: Edg 1J **43**
Watling Ct. EC4 ....1D **14**
Watling Farm Cl. HA7: Stan 1H **27**
Watling Gdns. NW2 ....6G **63**
Watling Ga. NW9 ....4A **44**
Watling Ho. SE1 ....4C **102**
                (off New Kent Rd.)
Watlings Cl. CRO: C'don 6A **158**
Watling St. DA1: Cray 5K **127**
  DA6: Bex 4H **127**
  EC4 ....1D **14** (6C **84**)
  SE15 ....6E **102**
Watlington Gro. SE26 ....5A **140**
Watney Cotts. SW14 ....3J **115**
Watney Mkt. E1 ....6H **85**
Watney Rd. SW14 ....3J **115**
Watney's Rd. CR4: Mitc 5H **155**
Watney St. E1 ....6H **85**
Watson Av. E6 ....7E **70**
  SM3: Cheam 2G **165**
Watson Cl. N16 ....5D **66**
  SW19 ....6C **136**
Watson Ct. E3 ....3C **86**
               (off Campbell Rd.)
Watson Pl. SE25 ....5F **157**
Watsons Ho. N1 ....1E **84**
               (off Nuttall St.)
Watson's M. W1 ....6D **4** (5C **82**)
Watsons Rd. N22 ....1K **47**
Watsons St. SE8 ....7C **104**
Watt Cl. W3 ....2A **98**
Wattisfield Rd. E5 ....3J **67**
Watts Cl. N15 ....5E **48**
Wattsdown Cl. E13 ....1J **87**
Watts Ho. W10 ....5G **81**
                (off Wornington Rd.)
Watts La. BR7: Chst 1F **161**
  TW11: Tedd 5A **132**
Watts Point E13 ....1J **87**
                (off Brooks Rd.)
Watts Rd. KT7: T Ditt 7A **150**
Watts St. E1 ....1H **103**
  SE15 ....1F **121**
Wat Tyler Ho. N8 ....3J **47**
               (off Boyton Rd.)
Wat Tyler Rd. SE3 ....2E **122**
  SE10 ....2E **122**
Wauthier Cl. N13 ....5G **33**
Wave Ct. RM7: Rush G 6K **55**
Wavel Ct. CRO: C'don 5D **168**
                 (off Hurst Rd.)
  E1 ....1J **103**
                 (off Garnet St.)
Wavelengths Leisure Cen. 7C **104**
Wavell Dr. DA15: Sidc 6J **125**
Wavell Ho. N6 ....6E **46**
                 (off Hillcrest)
Wavel M. N8 ....4H **47**
  NW6 ....7K **63**
Wavendon Av. W4 ....5K **97**
Waveney Av. SE15 ....4H **121**
Waveney Cl. E1 ....1G **103**
Waveney Ho. SE15 ....4H **121**

Waverley Av. E4 ....4G **35**
  E17 ....3F **51**
  HA9: Wemb 5F **61**
  KT5: Surb 6H **151**
  SM1: Sutt 2K **165**
  TW2: Whitt 1D **130**
Waverley Cl. BR2: Brom 5B **160**
  E18 ....1A **52**
  KT8: W Mole 5E **148**
  UB3: Harl 4F **93**
Waverley Ct. EN2: Enf 3G **23**
  NW3 ....6D **64**
  NW6 ....7G **63**
  SE26 ....5J **139**
Waverley Cres. SE18 ....5H **107**
Waverley Gdns. E6 ....5C **88**
  HA6: Nwood 1J **39**
  IG6: Ilf 2G **53**
  IG11: Bark 2J **89**
  NW10 ....2F **79**
Waverley Gro. N3 ....3F **45**
Waverley Ind. Est. HA1: Harr 3H **41**
Waverley Lodge E15 ....6G **69**
                (off Litchfield Rd.)
Waverley Pl. N4 ....2B **66**
  NW8 ....2B **82**
Waverley Rd. E17 ....3E **50**
  E18 ....1A **52**
  EN2: Enf 3G **23**
  HA2: Harr 2C **58**
  KT17: Ewe 6D **164**
  N8 ....6J **47**
  N17 ....7C **34**
  SE18 ....5G **107**
  SE25 ....4H **157**
  UB1: S'hall 7E **76**
Waverley Vs. N17 ....2F **49**
Waverley Way SM5: Cars 6C **166**
Waverton Ho. E3 ....1B **86**
Waverton Rd. SW18 ....7A **118**
Waverton St. W1 ....4J **11** (1E **100**)
Wavertree Ct. SW2 ....1J **137**
Wavertree Rd. E18 ....2J **51**
  SW2 ....1K **137**
Waxham NW3 ....5D **64**
Waxlow Cres. UB1: S'hall 6E **76**
Waxlow Ho. UB4: Yead 5B **76**
Waxlow Rd. NW10 ....2J **79**
Waxlow Way UB5: N'olt 4D **76**
Waxwell Cl. HA5: Pinn 2B **40**
Waxwell Farm Ho. HA5: Pinn 2B **40**
Waxwell La. HA5: Pinn 2B **40**
Wayborne Gro. HA4: Ruis 6E **38**
Way Av. TW5: Cran 1J **111**
Wayfarer Rd.
  TW6: H'row A 5C **174**
  UB5: N'olt 3B **76**
Wayfield Link SE9 ....6H **125**
Wayford St. SW11 ....2C **118**
Wayland Av. E8 ....5G **67**
Wayland Ho. SW9 ....2A **120**
                (off Robsart St.)
Waylands UB3: Hayes 5F **75**
Waylands Mead
  BR3: Beck 1D **158**
Waylett Ho. SE11 ....6J **19**
Waylett Pl. HAO: Wemb 4D **60**
  SE27 ....3B **138**
Wayman Ct. E8 ....6H **67**
Wayne Cl. BR6: Orp 3K **173**
Wayne Kirkum Way NW6 ....5H **63**
Waynflete Av. CRO: Wadd 3B **168**
Waynflete Ho. SE1 ....5C **14**
                 (off Union St.)
Waynflete Sq. W10 ....7F **81**
              (not continuous)
Waynflete St. SW18 ....2A **136**
Wayside CRO: New Ad 6D **170**
  NW11 ....1G **63**
  SW14 ....5J **115**
Wayside Cl. N14 ....6B **22**

Wayside Commercial Est.
IG11: Bark 1K **89**
Wayside Ct. HA9: Wemb 3G **61**
TW1: Twick 6C **114**
Wayside Gdns. RM10: Dag 5G **73**
Wayside M. IG2: Ilf 5E **52**
Weald, The BR7: Chst 6D **142**
Weald Cl. BR2: Brom 2C **172**
SE16 . . . . .5H **103**
Wealden Ho. E3 . . . . .3D **86**
(off Talwin St.)
Weald La. HA3: Hrw W 2H **41**
Weald Ri. HA3: Hrw W 7E **26**
Weald Rd. UB10: Hil 2C **74**
Weald Sq. E5 . . . . .2G **67**
WEALDSTONE 3J **41**
Wealdstone Centre, The 3J **41**
(off High St.)
Wealdstone FC 2H **57**
Wealdstone Rd. SM3: Sutt 2H **165**
Weald Way RM7: Rom 6H **55**
UB4: Hayes 3G **75**
Wealdwood Gdns. HA5: Hat E . . .6A **26**
Weale Rd. E4 . . . . .3A **36**
Weall Ct. HA5: Pinn 4C **40**
Weardale Gdns. EN2: Enf 1J **23**
Weardale Rd. SE13 . . . . .4F **123**
Wearmouth Ho. E3 . . . . .4B **86**
(off Joseph St.)
Wear Pl. E2 . . . . .3H **85**
(not continuous)
Wearside Rd. SE13 . . . . .4D **122**
Weatherbury W2 . . . . .6J **81**
(off Talbot Rd.)
Weatherbury Ho. N19 . . . . .3H **65**
(off Wedmore St.)
Weatherley Cl. E3 . . . . .5B **86**
Weaver Cl. CRO: C'don 4F **169**
E6 . . . . .7F **89**
Weaver Ho. E1 . . . . .4G **85**
(off Pedley St.)
Weavers Almshouses E11 . . . . . .6H **51**
(off Cambridge Rd.)
Weavers Cl. TW7: Isle 4J **113**
Weavers Ho. E11 . . . . .6J **51**
(off Micklethwaite Rd.)
Weaver St. E1 . . . . .4G **85**
(not continuous)
Weavers Ter. SW6 . . . . .6J **99**
(off Micklethwaite Rd.)
Weavers Way NW1 . . . . .1H **83**
Weaver Wlk. SE27 . . . . .4C **138**
Webb Cl. W10 . . . . .4E **80**
Webb Ct. SE28 . . . . .7B **90**
(off Attlee Rd.)
Webber Ho. IG11: Bark 7G **71**
(off North St.)
Webber Row SE1 . . . . .2B **102**
Webber St. SE1 . . . . . .6K **13** (2A **102**)
Webb Est. E5 . . . . .7G **49**
Webb Gdns. E13 . . . . .4J **87**
Webb Ho. E3 . . . . .3C **86**
(off Trevithick Way)
RM10: Dag 3G **73**
(off Kershaw Rd.)
SW8 . . . . .7H **101**
TW13: Hanw 3C **130**
Webb Pl. NW10 . . . . .3B **80**
Webb Rd. SE3 . . . . .6H **105**
Webbscroft Rd.
RM10: Dag 4H **73**
Webbs Rd. SW11 . . . . .4D **118**
UB4: Yead 3K **75**
Webb St. SE1 . . . . .3E **102**
Webheath NW6 . . . . .7H **63**
(not continuous)
Webster Gdns. W5 . . . . .1D **96**
Webster Rd. E11 . . . . .3E **68**
SE16 . . . . .3G **103**

Weddell Ho. E1 . . . . .4K **85**
(off Duckett St.)
Wedderburn Ho. SW1 . . . . .5G **17**
(off Lwr. Sloane St.)
Wedderburn Rd. IG11: Bark 1J **89**
NW3 . . . . .5B **64**
Wedgewood Ct. BR2: Brom 3H **159**
(off Cumberland Rd.)
DA5: Bexl 7G **127**
Wedgewood Ho. SW1 . . . . .6K **17**
(off Churchill Gdns.)
SE11 . . . . .2J **19**
Wedgewood M. W1 . . . .1D **12** (6H **83**)
Wedgwood Wlk. NW6 . . . . .5K **63**
(off Dresden Cl.)
Wedgwood Way SE19 . . . . .7C **138**
Wedlake St. W10 . . . . .4G **81**
Wedmore Av. IG5: Ilf 1E **52**
Wedmore Gdns. N19 . . . . .2H **65**
Wedmore M. N19 . . . . .3H **65**
Wedmore Rd. UB6: G'frd 3H **77**
Wedmore St. N19 . . . . .3H **65**
Weech Rd. NW6 . . . . .4J **63**
Weedington Rd. NW5 . . . . .5E **64**
Weedon Ho. W12 . . . . .6C **80**
Weekley Sq. SW11 . . . . .3B **118**
Weigall Rd. SE12 . . . . .5J **123**
Weighhouse St. W1 . . . .1H **11** (6E **82**)
Weightman Ho. SE16 . . . . .3G **103**
Weighton M. SE20 . . . . .2H **157**
Weighton Rd. HA3: Hrw W 1H **41**
SE20 . . . . .2H **157**
Weihurst Ct. SM1: Sutt 5C **166**
Weihurst Gdns. SM1: Sutt 5B **166**
Weimar St. SW15 . . . . .3G **117**
Weirdale Av. N20 . . . . .2J **31**
Weir Hall Av. N18 . . . . .6J **33**
Weir Hall Gdns. N18 . . . . .5J **33**
Weir Hall Rd. N17 . . . . .5J **33**
N18 . . . . .5J **33**
Weir Rd. DA5: Bexl 7H **127**
KT12: Walt T 6J **147**
SW12 . . . . .7G **119**
SW19 . . . . .3K **135**
Weir's Pas. NW1 . . . . . .1D **6** (3H **83**)
Weiss Rd. SW15 . . . . .3F **117**
Welbeck Av. BR1: Brom 4J **141**
DA15: Sidc 1A **144**
UB4: Yead 4K **75**
Welbeck Cl. KT3: N Mald 5B **152**
KT17: Ewe 7C **164**
N12 . . . . .5G **31**
Welbeck Ct. UB4: Yead 4K **75**
W14 . . . . .4H **99**
(off Addison Bri. Pl.)
Welbeck Ho. W1 . . . . .7J **5**
(off Welbeck St.)
Welbeck Rd. E6 . . . . .3B **88**
EN4: E Barn 6H **21**
HA2: Harr 1F **59**
SM1: Sutt 2B **166**
SM5: Cars 2B **166**
Welbeck St. W1 . . . . . . .6H **5** (5E **82**)
Welbeck Vs. N21 . . . . .2H **33**
Welbeck Wlk. SM5: Cars 1B **166**
Welbeck Way W1 . . . . . .7J **5** (6F **83**)
Welbury Ct. E8 . . . . .7E **66**
(off Kingsland Rd.)
Welby Ho. N19 . . . . .7H **47**
Welby St. SE5 . . . . .1B **120**
Welch Pl. HA5: Pinn 1A **40**
Welcome Ct. E17 . . . . .7C **50**
(off Saxon Cl.)
Weldin M. SW18 . . . . .5J **117**
(off Lebanon Rd.)
Weldon Cl. HA4: Ruis 6K **57**
Weldon Ct. N21 . . . . .5G **23**
Weldon Dr. KT8: W Mole 4D **148**

Weld Pl. N11 . . . . .5A **32**
(not continuous)
Weld Works M. SW2 . . . . .6K **119**
Welfare Rd. E15 . . . . .7G **69**
Welford Cl. E5 . . . . .3K **67**
Welford Ct. NW1 . . . . .7F **65**
(off Castlehaven Rd.)
SW8 . . . . .2G **119**
W9 . . . . .5J **81**
(off Elmfield Way)
Welford Ho. UB5: N'olt 4D **76**
(off Waxlow Way)
Welford Pl. SW19 . . . . .4G **135**
Welham Rd. SW16 . . . . .5E **136**
SW17 . . . . .5E **136**
Welhouse Rd. SM5: Cars 1C **166**
Wellacre Rd. HA3: Kenton 6B **42**
Wellan Cl. DA15: Sidc 5B **126**
Welland Cl. SE6 . . . . .2B **140**
(off Oakham Cl.)
Welland Gdns. UB6: G'frd 2K **77**
Welland Ho. SE15 . . . . .4J **121**
Welland M. E1 . . . . .1G **103**
Welland Rd. TW6: H'row A 5C **174**
Wellands Cl. BR1: Brom 2D **160**
Welland St. SE10 . . . . .6E **104**
Well App. EN5: Barn 5A **20**
Wellbrook Rd. BR6: Farnb 4E **172**
Wellby Cl. N9 . . . . .1B **34**
Wellby Ct. E13 . . . . .1A **88**
Well Cl. HA4: Ruis 3C **58**
SW16 . . . . .4K **137**
Wellclose Sq. E1 . . . . .7G **85**
(not continuous)
Wellclose St. E1 . . . . .7G **85**
Wellcome Collection 3C **6**
Wellcome Museum, The 7H **7**
(within Royal College of Surgeons)
Well Cott. Cl. E11 . . . . .6A **52**
Well Ct. EC4 . . . . .1D **14** (6C **84**)
(not continuous)
Wellday Ho. E9 . . . . .6A **68**
(off Hedger's Gro.)
Welldon Ct. HA1: Harr 5J **41**
Welldon Cres. HA1: Harr 5J **41**
Weller Ct. W11 . . . . .1H **99**
(off Ladbroke Rd.)
Weller Ho. SE16 . . . . .2G **103**
(off George Row)
Weller M. BR2: Brom 4K **159**
EN2: Enf 1F **23**
Weller St. SE1 . . . . . . .6C **14** (2C **102**)
Welles Ct. E14 . . . . .7C **86**
(off Premiere Pl.)
Wellesley Av. W6 . . . . .3D **98**
Wellesley Cl. SE7 . . . . .5A **106**
Wellesley Ct. NW2 . . . . .2C **62**
SE1 . . . . .3C **102**
(off Rockingham St.)
SM3: Sutt 1G **165**
W9 . . . . .3A **82**
Wellesley Ct. Rd. CRO: C'don 2D **168**
Wellesley Cres. TW2: Twick 2J **131**
Wellesley Pas. CRO: C'don 2C **168**
Wellesley Ho. NW1 . . . . .2D **6**
(off Wellesley Pl.)
SW1 . . . . .5J **17**
(off Ebury Bri. Rd.)
Wellesley Mans. W14 . . . . .5H **99**
(off Edith Vs.)
Wellesley Pde. TW2: Twick 3J **131**
Wellesley Pk. M. EN2: Enf 2G **23**
Wellesley Pas. CRO: C'don 2C **168**
Wellesley Pl. NW1 . . . . . .2C **6** (3H **83**)
NW5 . . . . .5E **64**
Wellesley Rd. CRO: C'don 1C **168**
E11 . . . . .5J **51**
E17 . . . . .6C **50**
HA1: Harr 5J **41**
IG1: Ilf 2F **71**
N22 . . . . .2A **48**

Wellesley Rd. NW5 . . . . .5E **64**
SE18 . . . . .7E **106**
SM2: Sutt 6A **166**
(not continuous)
TW2: Twick 3H **131**
W4 . . . . .5G **97**
Wellesley St. E1 . . . . .5K **85**
Wellesley Ter. N1 . . . . . .1D **8** (3C **84**)
Wellfield Av. N10 . . . . .3F **47**
Wellfield Rd. SW16 . . . . .4J **137**
Wellfield Wlk. SW16 . . . . .4K **137**
Wellfit St. SE24 . . . . .3B **120**
Wellgarth UB6: G'frd 6B **60**
Wellgarth Rd. NW11 . . . . .1K **63**
Well Gro. N20 . . . . .1F **31**
Well Hall Pde. SE9 . . . . .4D **124**
Well Hall Rd. SE9 . . . . .3C **124**
WELL HALL RDBT. 4C **124**
Wellhouse La. EN5: Barn 4A **20**
Wellhouse Rd.
BR3: Beck 4C **158**
Wellhurst Cl. BR6: Chels 7K **173**
WELLING 3B **126**
Welling High St.
DA16: Well 3B **126**
Wellings Ho. UB3: Hayes 1K **93**
Wellington N8 . . . . .4J **47**
(not continuous)
Wellington Arch 6H **11**
Wellington Av. DA15: Sidc 6A **126**
E4 . . . . .2H **35**
HA5: Hat E 1D **40**
KT4: Wor Pk 3E **164**
N9 . . . . .3C **34**
N15 . . . . .5E **49**
TW3: Houn 5E **112**
Wellington Bldgs. E3 . . . . .3C **86**
(off Wellington Way)
SW1 . . . . .6H **17** (5E **100**)
Wellington Cl. KT12: Walt T 7H **147**
RM10: Dag 7J **73**
SE14 . . . . .1K **121**
W11 . . . . .6J **81**
Wellington Ct. NW8 . . . . .2B **82**
(off Wellington Rd.)
SW1 . . . . .7E **10**
(off Knightsbridge)
SW6 . . . . .1K **117**
(off Maltings Pl.)
TW12: Hamp H 5H **131**
TW15: Ashf 5A **128**
TW19: Stanw 7A **110**
Wellington Cres. KT3: N Mald 3J **151**
Wellington Dr. RM10: Dag 7J **73**
Wellington Gdns. SE7 . . . . .6A **106**
TW2: Twick 4H **131**
Wellington Gro. SE10 . . . . .7F **105**
Wellington Ho. E16 . . . . .1J **105**
(off Pepys Cres.)
NW3 . . . . .6D **64**
(off Eton Rd.)
SE17 . . . . .6C **102**
(off Arnside St.)
UB5: N'olt 7E **58**
(off The Farmlands)
W5 . . . . .3E **78**
Wellington Lodge SE1 . . . . .7A **14**
(off Waterloo Rd.)
Wellington Mans. E10 . . . . .1C **68**
SE7 . . . . .5A **106**
(off Wellington Gdns.)
W14 . . . . .6H **99**
(off Queen's Club Gdns.)
Wellington M. N7 . . . . .6K **65**
(off Roman Way)
SE7 . . . . .6A **106**
SE22 . . . . .4G **121**
SW16 . . . . .3H **137**
Wellington Monument 6H **11**
Wellington Pde. DA15: Sidc 5A **126**
Wellington Pk. Est. NW2 . . . . . . .2C **62**

Wellington Pas. E11 . . . . .5J 51
Wellington Pl. N2 . . . . .5C 46
NW8 . . . . .1B 4 (3B 82)
Wellington Rd. BR2: Brom 4A 160
CR0: C'don 7B 156
DA5: Bexl 5D 126
DA17: Belv 5F 109
E6 .1D 88
E7 .4H 69
E10 . . . . .1A 68
E11 . . . . .5J 51
E17 . . . . .4A 50
EN1: Enf 5K 23
HA3: W'stone 3J 41
HA5: Hat E 1D 40
NW8 . . . . .1B 4 (2B 82)
NW10 . . . . .3F 81
SW19 . . . . .2J 135
TW2: Twick 5H 131
TW6: H'row A 6D 174
(off Whittle Rd.)
TW12: Hamp H 5H 131
TW14: Felt 5G 111
TW15: Ashf 5A 128
W5 . . . . .3C 96
Wellington Rd. Nth. TW4: Houn . . .3D 112
Wellington Rd. Sth. TW4: Houn . . .4D 112
Wellington Row E2 . . . . . . .1K 9 (3F 85)
Wellington Sq. N1 . . . . .1J 83
SW3 . . . . .5E 16 (5D 100)
Wellington St. IG11: Bark 1G 89
SE18 . . . . .4E 106
WC2 . . . . .2G 13 (7K 83)
Wellington Ter. E1 . . . . .1H 103
HA1: Harr 1H 59
N8 .3A 48
(off Turnpike La.)
W2 .7J 81
Wellington Way E3 . . . . .3C 86
Welling United FC 3C 126
Welling Way DA16: Well 3G 125
SE9 . . . . .3G 125
Well La. SW14 . . . . .5J 115
Wellmeadow Rd. SE6 . . . . .7G 123
SE13 . . . . .6G 123
(not continuous)
W7 .4A 96
Wellow Wlk. SM5: Cars 1B 166
Well Pl. NW3 . . . . .3B 64
Well Rd. EN5: Barn 5A 20
NW3 . . . . .3B 64
Wells, The N14 . . . . .7C 22
Wells Cl. CR2: S Croy 5E 168
UB5: N'olt 3A 76
Wells Ct. BR2: Brom 2F 159
NW6 . . . . .2J 81
(off Cambridge Av.)
Wells Dr. NW9 . . . . .1K 61
Wells Gdns. IG1: Ilf 7C 52
RM10: Dag 5H 73
Wells Ga. Cl. IG8: W'fd G 4D 36
Wells Ho. BR1: Brom 5K 141
(off Pike Cl.)
EC1 . . . . .1K 7
(off Spa Grn. Est.)
IG11: Bark 7A 72
(off Margaret Bondfield Av.)
SE16 . . . . .3J 103
(off Howland Est.)
W5 . . . . .7D 78
(off Grove Rd.)
W10 . . . . .4G 81
(off Wornington Rd.)
Wells Ho. Rd. NW10 . . . . .5A 80
Wellside Cl. EN5: Barn 4A 20
Wellside Gdns. SW14 . . . . .4J 115
Wells La. TW3: Houn 3F 113
Wells M. W1 . . . . .6B 6 (5G 83)
Wellsmoor Gdns. BR1: Brom 3E 160
Wells Pk. Rd. SE26 . . . . .3G 139
Wells Path UB4: Hayes 3G 75

Wells Pl. SW18 . . . . .7A 118
Wellspring Cl. E14 . . . . .5E 86
Wellspring Cres. HA9: Wemb 3H 61
Wellspring M. SE26 . . . . .3H 139
Wells Ri. NW8 . . . . .1D 82
Wells Rd. BR1: Brom 2D 160
W12 . . . . .2E 98
Wells Sq. WC1 . . . . .2G 7 (3K 83)
Wells St. W1 . . . . .6A 6 (5G 83)
Wellstead Av. N9 . . . . .7E 24
Wellstead Rd. E6 . . . . .2E 88
Wells Ter. N4 . . . . .2A 66
Well St. E9 . . . . .7J 67
E15 . . . . .6G 69
Wells Vw. Dr. BR2: Brom 6C 160
Wells Way SE5 . . . . .6D 102
SW7 . . . . .1A 16 (3B 100)
Wells Yd. N7 . . . . .5A 66
Well Wlk. NW3 . . . . .4B 64
Wellwood Rd. IG3: Ilf 1A 72
Welmar M. SW4 . . . . .5H 119
(off Clapham Pk. Rd.)
Welsby Ct. W5 . . . . .5C 78
Welstead St. SE1 . . . . .4G 103
(not continuous)
Welsh Cl. E13 . . . . .3J 87
Welsh Harp (Brent Reservoir)
Nature Reserve 1B 62
Welsh Ho. E1 . . . . .1H 103
(off Wapping La.)
Welshpool Ho. E8 . . . . .1G 85
(off Welshpool St.)
Welshpool St. E8 . . . . .1G 85
(not continuous)
Welshside NW9 . . . . .6A 44
(off Ruthin Cl.)
Welshside Wlk. NW9 . . . . .6A 44
Welstead Ho. E1 . . . . .6H 85
(off Cannon St. Rd.)
Welstead Way W4 . . . . .4B 98
Weltje Rd. W6 . . . . .4C 98
Welton Cl. SE5 . . . . .1E 120
Welton Ho. E1 . . . . .5K 85
(off Stepney Way)
Welton Rd. SE18 . . . . .7J 107
Welwyn Av. TW14: Felt 6H 111
Welwyn St. E2 . . . . .3J 85
Welwyn Way UB4: Hayes 4G 75
WEMBLEY 5E 60
Wembley & Sudbury Tennis & Squash Club
. . . . .5D 60
Wembley Arena 4G 61
Wembley Commercial Cen.
. . . . .2D 60
Wembley Hill Rd. HA9: Wemb 3F 61
(East La.)
HA9: Wemb 5F 61
(South Way)
WEMBLEY PARK 4G 61
Wembley Pk. Blvd. HA9: Wemb 4G 61
Wembley Pk. Bus. Cen. HA9: Wemb .4H 61
Wembley Pk. Dr. HA9: Wemb 4F 61
Wembley Retail Pk. HA9: Wemb 4H 61
Wembley Rd. TW12: Hamp 1E 148
Wembley Sailing Club 2K 61
Wembley Stadium 4G 61
Wembley Stadium Ind. Est.
. . . . .4H 61
Wembley Way HA9: Wemb 6H 61
Wemborough Rd. HA7: Stan 1B 42
Wembury M. N6 . . . . .7G 47
Wemyss Rd. SE3 . . . . .2H 123
Wendela Ct. HA1: Harr 2J 59
Wendell Rd. W12 . . . . .3B 98
Wenderholme CR2: S Croy 5D 168
(off South Pk. Hill Rd.)
Wendle Ct. SW8 . . . . .7E 18 (6J 101)
Wendle Sq. SW11 . . . . .1C 118
Wendling NW5 . . . . .5D 64
Wendling Rd. SM1: Sutt 1B 166

Wendon St. E3 . . . . .1B 86
Wendover SE17 . . . . .5E 102
(not continuous)
Wendover Cl. UB4: Yead 4C 76
Wendover Ct. BR2: Brom 3K 159
(off Wendover Rd.)
NW2 . . . . .3J 63
NW10 . . . . .4H 79
W1 .6G 5
(off Chiltern St.)
Wendover Ho. W1 . . . . .6G 5
(off Chiltern St.)
Wendover Rd. BR2: Brom 4K 159
NW10 . . . . .2B 80
SE9 . . . . .3B 124
Wendover Way DA16: Well 5A 126
Wendy Cl. EN1: Enf 6A 24
Wendy Way HA0: Wemb 1E 78
Wenham Ho. SW8 . . . . .7G 101
Wenlake Ho. EC1 . . . . .3C 8
(off Old St.)
Wenlock Barn Est. N1 . . . . .2D 84
(off Wenlock St.)
Wenlock Ct. N1 . . . . .1F 9 (2D 84)
Wenlock Gdns. NW4 . . . . .4D 44
Wenlock M. E10 . . . . .7C 50
Wenlock Rd. HA8: Edg 7C 28
N1 . . . . .1D 8 (2C 84)
Wenlock St. N1 . . . . .1D 8 (2C 84)
Wennington Rd. E3 . . . . .2K 85
Wensdale Ho. E5 . . . . .2G 67
Wensley Av. IG8: W'fd G 7C 36
Wensley Cl. N11 . . . . .6K 31
SE9 . . . . .6D 124
Wensleydale Av. IG5: Ilf 2C 52
Wensleydale Gdns. TW12: Hamp . . .7F 131
Wensleydale Pas. TW12: Hamp 1E 148
Wensleydale Rd. TW12: Hamp 6E 130
Wensley Rd. N18 . . . . .6C 34
Wentland Cl. SE6 . . . . .2F 141
Wentland Rd. SE6 . . . . .2F 141
Wentway Ct. W13 . . . . .4K 77
(off Ruislip Rd. E.)
Wentworth Av. N3 . . . . .7D 30
Wentworth Cl. BR2: Hayes 2J 171
BR6: Farnb 5J 173
KT6: Surb 2D 162
N3 .7E 30
SE28 . . . . .6D 90
SM4: Mord 7J 153
TW15: Ashf 4D 128
Wentworth Ct. SW1 . . . . . .6J 17 (5F 101)
SW18 . . . . .6K 117
(off Garratt La.)
TW2: Twick 3J 131
W6 .6G 99
(off Paynes Wlk.)
Wentworth Cres. SE15 . . . . .7G 103
UB3: Harl 3F 93
Wentworth Dr. HA5: Eastc 5J 39
TW6: H'row A 5C 174
Wentworth Dwellings E1 . . . . .7J 9
(off Wentworth St.)
Wentworth Flds. UB4: Hayes 2F 75
Wentworth Gdns. N13 . . . . .3G 33
Wentworth Hill HA9: Wemb 1F 61
Wentworth Ho. IG8: W'fd G 7K 37
Wentworth M. E3 . . . . .4A 86
W3 .6A 80
Wentworth Pk. N3 . . . . .7D 30
Wentworth Pl. HA7: Stan 6G 27
Wentworth Rd. CR0: C'don 7A 156
E12 . . . . .4B 70
EN5: Barn 3A 20
NW11 . . . . .6H 45
UB2: S'hall 4A 94
Wentworth St. E1 . . . . .7J 9 (6F 85)
Wentworth Way HA5: Pinn 4C 40
Wenvoe Av. DA7: Bex 2H 127
Wepham Cl. UB4: Yead 5B 76

Wernbrook St. SE18 . . . . .6G 107
Werndee Rd. SE25 . . . . .4G 157
Werneth Hall Rd. IG5: Ilf 3E 52
Werrington St. NW1 . . . . . .1B 6 (2G 83)
Werter Rd. SW15 . . . . .4G 117
Wesleyan Pl. NW5 . . . . .4F 65
Wesley Apartments SW8 . . . . .1H 119
Wesley Av. E16 . . . . .1J 105
NW10 . . . . .3K 79
TW3: Houn 2C 112
Wesley Cl. HA2: Harr 2G 59
KT19: Ewe 5J 163
N7 .2K 65
SE17 . . . . .4B 102
Wesley Ct. SE16 . . . . .3H 103
Wesley Rd. E10 . . . . .7E 50
NW10 . . . . .1J 79
UB3: Hayes 7J 75
Wesley's Chapel & Museum of Methodism
. . . . .3F 9 (4D 84)
Wesley's House 3F 9 (4D 84)
Wesley Sq. W11 . . . . .6G 81
Wesley St. W1 . . . . .6H 5 (5E 82)
Wessex Av. SW19 . . . . .3J 153
Wessex Cl. IG3: Ilf 6J 53
KT1: King T 1H 151
Wessex Ct. BR3: Beck 1A 158
EN5: Barn 4A 20
HA9: Wemb 2F 61
TW19: Stanw 6A 110
Wessex Dr. HA5: Hat E 1C 40
Wessex Gdns. NW11 . . . . .1G 63
Wessex Ho. SE1 . . . . .5F 103
Wessex La. UB6: G'frd 3H 77
Wessex St. E2 . . . . .3J 85
Wessex Wlk. DA2: Wilm 2K 145
Wessex Way NW11 . . . . .1G 63
Wesson Mead SE5 . . . . .7C 102
(off Camberwell Rd.)
West 12 Shop. Cen. W12 . . . . .2F 99
Westacott UB4: Hayes 5G 75
Westacott Cl. N19 . . . . .1H 65
West Acre HA2: Harr 2J 59
WEST ACTON 6G 79
West App. BR5: Pet W 5G 161
W. Arbour St. E1 . . . . .6K 85
West Av. E17 . . . . .4D 50
HA5: Pinn 6D 40
N3 .6D 30
NW4 . . . . .5F 45
SM6: Wall 5J 167
UB1: S'hall 7D 76
UB3: Hayes 7H 75
West Av. Rd. E17 . . . . .4C 50
West Bank EN2: Enf 2H 23
IG11: Bark 1F 89
N16 . . . . .7E 48
Westbank Rd. TW12: Hamp H 6G 131
WEST BARNES 5D 152
W. Barnes La. KT3: N Mald 3D 152
SW20 . . . . .3D 152
WEST BECKTON 6B 88
WEST BEDFONT 6B 110
Westbeech Rd. N22 . . . . .3A 48
Westbere Dr. HA7: Stan 5J 27
Westbere Rd. NW2 . . . . .4G 63
West Block SE1 . . . . .7H 13
(off York Rd.)
Westbourne Av. SM3: Cheam 2G 165
W3 .6K 79
Westbourne Bri. W2 . . . . .5A 82
Westbourne Cl. UB4: Yead 4A 76
Westbourne Ct. W2 . . . . .5A 82
Westbourne Cres. W2 . . . . . .2A 10 (7B 82)
Westbourne Cres. M. W2 . . . . .2A 10
Westbourne Dr. SE23 . . . . .2K 139
Westbourne Gdns. W2 . . . . .6K 81
WESTBOURNE GREEN 5J 81
Westbourne Gro. W2 . . . . .6J 81
W11 . . . . .6J 81
Westbourne Gro. M. W11 . . . . .6J 81

Westbourne Gro. Ter. W2 . . . . .6K 81
Westbourne Ho. SW1 . . . . .5J 17
   (off Ebury Bri. Rd.)
  TW5: Hest 6E 94
Westbourne Pde. UB10: Hil 4D 74
Westbourne Pk. Pas. W2 . . . . .5J 81
   (off Harrow Rd.)
Westbourne Pk. Rd. W2 . . . . .5J 81
  W11 . . . . .6G 81
Westbourne Pk. Vs. W2 . . . . .5J 81
Westbourne Pl. N9 . . . . .3C 34
Westbourne Rd.
  CR0: C'don 6F 157
  DA7: Bex 7D 108
  N7 . . . . .6K 65
  SE26 . . . . .6K 139
  TW13: Felt 3H 129
  UB8: Hil 4D 74
Westbourne St. W2 . . . . .2A 10 (7B 82)
Westbourne Ter. SE23 . . . . .2K 139
   (off Westbourne Dr.)
  W2 . . . . .1A 10 (6A 82)
Westbourne Ter. M. W2 . . . . .6A 82
Westbourne Ter. Rd. W2 . . . . .5K 81
Westbourne Ter. Rd. Bri. W2 . . . . .5A 82
   (off Westbourne Ter. Rd.)
Westbridge Cl. W12 . . . . .2C 98
Westbridge Ho. SW11 . . . . .1C 118
   (off Westbridge Rd.)
Westbridge Rd. SW11 . . . . .1B 118
WEST BROMPTON 6A 100
Westbrook Av. TW12: Hamp 7D 130
Westbrook Cl. EN4: Cockf 3G 21
Westbrook Cres. EN4: Cockf 3G 21
Westbrooke Cres.
  DA16: Well 3C 126
Westbrooke Rd.
  DA15: Sidc 2H 143
  DA16: Well 3B 126
Westbrook Ho. E2 . . . . .3J 85
   (off Victoria Pk. Sq.)
Westbrook Rd. CR7: Thor H 1D 156
  SE3 .1K 123
  TW5: Hest 7D 94
Westbrook Sq. EN4: Cockf 3G 21
Westbury Av. HA0: Wemb 7E 60
  N22 . . . . .3B 48
  UB1: S'hall 4E 76
Westbury Cl. HA4: Ruis 7J 39
  TW17: Shep 6D 146
Westbury Ct. IG11: Bark 1H 89
   (off Ripple Rd.)
Westbury Gro. N12 . . . . .6D 30
Westbury Ho. E17 . . . . .4B 50
  W11 . . . . .5J 81
   (off Aldridge Rd. Vs.)
Westbury La. IG9: Buck H 2E 36
Westbury Lodge Cl. HA5: Pinn 3B 40
Westbury Pde. SW12 . . . . .6F 119
   (off Balham Hill)
Westbury Pl. TW8: Bford 6D 96
Westbury Rd. BR1: Brom 1B 160
  BR3: Beck 3A 158
  CR0: C'don 6D 156
  E7 . . . . .6K 69
  E17 . . . . .4B 50
  HA0: Wemb 7E 60
  IG1: Ilf 2E 70
  IG9: Buck H 2F 37
  IG11: Bark 1H 89
  KT3: N Mald 4K 151
  N11 . . . . .6D 32
  N12 . . . . .6D 30
  SE20 . . . . .1K 157
  TW13: Felt 1B 130
  W5 . . . . .6E 78
Westbury Ter. E7 . . . . .6K 69
Westbush Ct. W12 . . . . .2D 98
   (off Goldhawk M.)
W. Cadet Apartments SE18 . . . . .7E 106
   (off Langhorne St.)

W. Carriage Dr. W2 . . . . .3C 10 (7C 82)
   (North Ride)
  W2 . . . . .2B 100
   (Rotten Row)
W. Carriage Ho. SE18 . . . . .3F 107
W. Central St. WC1 . . . . .7E 6 (6J 83)
West Chantry HA3: Hrw W 1F 41
Westchester Dr. NW4 . . . . .3F 45
Westcliffe Apartments W2 . . . .6B 4 (5B 82)
West Cl. EN4: Cockf 4K 21
  HA9: Wemb 1F 61
  N9 . . . . .3A 34
  TW12: Hamp 6C 130
  TW15: Ashf 4A 128
  UB6: G'frd 2G 77
Westcombe Av. CR0: C'don 7J 155
Westcombe Ct. SE3 . . . . .7H 105
Westcombe Dr. EN5: Barn 5D 20
Westcombe Hill SE3 . . . . .7J 105
  SE10 . . . . .5J 105
Westcombe Lodge Dr. UB4: Hayes . . .5G 75
Westcombe Pk. Rd. SE3 . . . . .6G 105
West Comn. Rd. BR2: Hayes, Kes . . .1J 171
  UB8: Uxb 5A 56
Westcombe Av. SW20 . . . . .1B 152
Westcote Ri. HA4: Ruis 7E 38
Westcote Rd. SW16 . . . . .5G 137
West Cotts. NW6 . . . . .5J 63
Westcott Cl. BR1: Brom 5D 160
  CR0: New Ad 7D 170
  N15 . . . . .6F 49
Westcott Cres. W7 . . . . .6J 77
Westcott Ho. E14 . . . . .7C 86
Westcott Rd. SE17 . . . . .6B 102
West Ct. E17 . . . . .4G 50
  HA0: Wemb 2C 60
  TW5: Isle 7G 95
Westcroft Cl. EN3: Enf W 1D 24
  NW2 .4G 63
Westcroft Est. NW2 . . . . .4G 63
Westcroft Gdns. SM4: Mord 3H 153
Westcroft Leisure Cen. 4E 166
Westcroft Rd. SM5: Cars 4E 166
  SM6: Wall 4E 166
Westcroft Sq. W6 . . . . .4C 98
Westcroft Way NW2 . . . . .4G 63
W. Cromwell Rd. SW5 . . . . .5H 99
  W14 . . . . .5H 99
W. Cross Cen. TW8: Bford 6A 96
W. Cross Route W10 . . . . .7F 81
  W11 . . . . .7F 81
  W12 . . . . .7F 81
W. Cross Way TW8: Bford 6B 96
Westdale Pas. SE18 . . . . .6F 107
Westdale Rd. SE18 . . . . .6F 107
Westdean Av. SE12 . . . . .1K 141
Westdean Cl. SW18 . . . . .6K 117
West Dene SM3: Cheam 6G 165
Westdene CR0: C'don 4D 168
   (off Chatsworth Rd.)
Westdown Rd. E15 . . . . .4E 68
  SE6 .7C 122
WEST DRAYTON 2A 92
W. Drayton Pk. Av. UB7: W Dray 3A 92
W. Drayton Rd. UB8: Hil 6D 74
West Dr. HA3: Hrw W 6C 26
  SM2: Cheam 7F 165
  SW16 . . . . .4G 137
West Dr. Gdns. HA3: Hrw W 6C 26
WEST DULWICH 2D 138
WEST EALING 1B 96
W. Ealing Bus. Cen. W13 . . . . .7A 78
W. Eaton Pl. SW1 . . . . .3G 17 (4E 100)
W. Eaton Pl. M. SW1 . . . . .2G 17
W. Ella Rd. NW10 . . . . .7A 62
WEST END 2B 76
West End Av. E10 . . . . .5F 51
  HA5: Pinn 4B 40
West End Cl. NW10 . . . . .7J 61
West End Ct. HA5: Pinn 4B 40
  NW6 . . . . .7K 63

West End Gdns. UB5: N'olt 2A 76
West End La. EN5: Barn 4A 20
  HA5: Pinn 3B 40
  NW6 . . . . .5J 63
   (not continuous)
  UB3: Harl 7E 92
West End Quay W2 . . . . .6B 4
West End Rd. HA4: Ruis 2G 57
  UB1: S'hall 1C 94
  UB5: N'olt 7A 58
Westerdale Rd. SE10 . . . . .5J 105
Westerfield Rd. N15 . . . . .5F 49
Westergate W5 . . . . .5E 78
Westergate Ho. KT1: King T 4D 150
   (off Portsmouth Rd.)
Westergate Rd. SE2 . . . . .6E 108
Westerham Av. N9 . . . . .3J 33
Westerham Dr. DA15: Sidc 6B 126
Westerham Ho. SE1 . . . . .3D 102
   (off Law St.)
Westerham Lodge BR3: Beck 7C 140
   (off Park Rd.)
Westerham Rd. BR2: Kes 6B 172
  E10 . . . . .7D 50
Westerley Cres. SE26 . . . . .5B 140
Westerley Ware TW9: Kew 6G 97
   (off Kew Gm.)
Western Av. HA4: Ruis 6D 56
  NW11 .6F 45
  RM10: Dag 6J 73
  UB5: N'olt 7A 58
  UB6: G'frd 7A 58
  UB10: Hil, Uxb 4A 56
  W3 . . . . .4F 79
  W5 . . . . .4F 79
Western Av. Bus. Pk. W3 . . . . .4H 79
Western Beach Apartments E16 . . . . .7J 87
Western Ct. N3 . . . . .6D 30
  NW6 . . . . .2H 81
  W3 . . . . .6K 79
Western Courtyard EC2 . . . . .7H 9
   (off Cutlers Gdns.)
Western Dr. TW17: Shep 6F 147
Western Gdns. W5 . . . . .7G 79
Western Gateway E16 . . . . .7J 87
Western Intl. Mkt. UB2: S'hall 4K 93
Western La. SW12 . . . . .7E 118
Western Mans. EN5: New Bar 5E 20
   (off Great Nth. Rd.)
Western M. W9 . . . . .4H 81
Western Pde. EN5: New Bar 5D 20
Western Perimeter Rd.
  TW6: H'row A, Lford 5C 174
Western Pl. SE16 . . . . .2J 103
Western Rd. CR4: Mitc 1B 154
  E13 . . . . .2A 88
  E17 . . . . .5E 50
  N2 . . . . .4D 46
  N22 . . . . .2K 47
  NW10 .4J 79
  SM1: Sutt 5J 165
  SW9 .3A 120
  SW19 . . . . .1B 154
  UB2: S'hall 4A 94
  W5 . . . . .7D 78
Western Ter. W6 . . . . .5C 98
Western Transit Shed N1 . . . . .1J 83
Western Vw. UB3: Hayes 2H 93
Westerville Gdns. IG2: Ilf 7G 53
Western Way EN5: Barn 6D 20
  SE28 . . . . .3H 107
WEST EWELL 7K 163
Westferry Cir. E14 . . . . .1B 104
Westferry Rd. E14 . . . . .7B 86
Westfield Av. E20 . . . . .6D 68
Westfield Cl. EN3: Enf H 3F 25
  NW9 . . . . .3J 43
  SM1: Sutt 4H 165
  SW10 . . . . .7A 100

Westfield Ct. KT6: Surb 5D 150
   (off Portsmouth Rd.)
  NW10 . . . . .3F 81
   (off Chamberlayne Rd.)
Westfield Dr. HA3: Kenton 4D 42
Westfield Gdns. HA3: Kenton 4D 42
  RM6: Chad H 6C 54
Westfield Ho. SE16 . . . . .4K 103
   (off Rotherhithe New Rd.)
  SW10 . . . . .7B 100
   (off Cremorne Est.)
  SW18 . . . . .1K 135
Westfield La. HA3: Kenton 5D 42
Westfield Pk. HA5: Hat E 1D 40
Westfield Pk. Dr. IG8: Wfd G 6H 37
Westfield Rd. BR3: Beck 2B 158
  CR0: C'don 2B 168
  CR4: Mitc 2C 154
  DA7: Bex 3J 127
  KT6: Surb 5D 150
  KT12: Walt T 7C 148
  NW7 . . . . .3E 28
  RM9: Dag 4E 72
  SM1: Sutt 4H 165
  W13 . . . . .1A 96
Westfields SW13 . . . . .3B 116
Westfields Av. SW13 . . . . .3A 116
Westfield Shop. Cen. E20 . . . . .6E 68
  W12 . . . . .1E 98
Westfields Rd. W3 . . . . .5H 79
Westfield St. SE18 . . . . .3B 106
Westfield Way E1 . . . . .3A 86
  HA4: Ruis 3G 57
West Gdn. Pl. W2 . . . . .1D 10 (6C 82)
West Gdns. E1 . . . . .7H 85
  SW17 . . . . .6C 136
Westgate W5 .3E 78
Westgate Apartments E16 . . . . .7J 87
   (off Western Gateway)
Westgate Centre, The E8 . . . . .1H 85
   (off Bocking St.)
Westgate Ct. SE12 . . . . .1J 141
   (off Burnt Ash Hill)
  SW9 .3A 120
   (off Canterbury Cres.)
Westgate Est. TW14: Bedf 1D 128
Westgate Ho. TW7: Isle 2H 113
  TW8: Bford 5D 96
   (off Ealing Rd.)
Westgate M. W10 . . . . .4G 81
   (off West Row)
Westgate Rd. BR3: Beck 1E 158
  SE25 . . . . .4H 157
Westgate St. E8 . . . . .1H 85
Westgate Ter. SW10 . . . . .6K 99
Westglade Ct. HA3: Kenton 5D 42
WEST GREEN 4B 48
West Green Pl. UB6: G'frd 1H 77
West Green Rd. N15 . . . . .4B 48
West Gro. IG8: Wfd G 6F 37
  SE10 . . . . .1E 122
Westgrove La. SE10 . . . . .1E 122
W. Halkin St. SW1 . . . . .1G 17 (3E 100)
West Hallowes SE9 . . . . .1B 142
West Hall Rd. TW9: Kew 1H 115
WEST HAM 1H 87
West Ham La. E15 . . . . .7F 69
WEST HAMPSTEAD 6K 63
W. Hampstead M. NW6 . . . . .6K 63
West Ham United FC 2A 88
W. Handyside Canopy N1 . . . . .1J 83
W. Harding St. EC4 . . . . .7K 7 (6A 84)
WEST HARROW 7G 41
W. Hatch Mnr. HA4: Ruis 1H 57
Westhay Gdns. SW14 . . . . .5H 115
WEST HEATH 6D 108
W. Heath Av. NW11 . . . . .1J 63
W. Heath Cl. NW3 . . . . .3J 63
W. Heath Ct. NW11 . . . . .1J 63
W. Heath Dr. NW11 . . . . .1J 63
W. Heath Gdns. NW3 . . . . .2J 63

W. Heath Rd. NW3 . . . . .2J 63
   SE2 . . . . .6C 108
WEST HENDON 7C 44
W. Hendon B'way. NW9 . . . . .6B 44
WEST HILL .6H 117
West Hill CR2: Sande 7E 168
   HA2: Harr 2J 59
   HA9: Wemb 1F 61
   SW15 .7F 117
   SW18 .7F 117
West Hill Ct. N6 . . . . .3E 64
Westhill Cl. W11 . . . . .7H 81
           (off Denbigh Rd.)
West Hill Pk. N6 . . . . .3E 64
           (not continuous)
West Hill Rd. SW18 . . . . .6H 117
West Hill Way N20 . . . . .1E 30
Westholm NW11 . . . . .4K 45
West Holme DA8: Erith 1J 127
Westholme BR6: Orp 7J 161
Westholme Gdns.
   HA4: Ruis 1J 57
Westhope Ho. E2 . . . . .4G 85
          (off Derbyshire St.)
Westhorne Av. SE9 . . . . .7J 123
   SE12 .7J 123
Westhorpe Gdns. NW4 . . . . .3E 44
Westhorpe Rd. SW15 . . . . .3E 116
West House IG11: Bark 6F 71
West Ho. Cl. SW19 . . . . .1G 135
West Ho. Cotts. HA5: Pinn 4B 40
Westhurst Dr. BR7: Chst 5F 143
W. India Av. E14 . . . . .1C 104
W. India Dock Rd. E14 . . . . .7B 86
W. India Ho. E14 . . . . .7C 86
       (off W. India Dock Rd.)
WEST KENSINGTON 4G 99
W. Kensington Ct. W14 . . . . .5H 99
           (off Edith Vs.)
W. Kensington Mans. W14 . . . . .5H 99
       (off Beaumont Cres.)
WEST KILBURN 3H 81
Westlake SE16 . . . . .4J 103
      (off Rotherhithe New Rd.)
Westlake Cl. N13 . . . . .3F 33
   UB4: Yead 4C 76
Westlake Rd. HA9: Wemb 2D 60
Westland Cl. TW19: Stanw 6A 110
Westland Ct. UB5: N'olt 3B 76
        (off Seasprite Cl.)
Westland Dr. BR2: Hayes 2H 171
Westland Ho. E16 . . . . .1E 106
          (off Rymill St.)
Westland Pl. N1 . . . . .1E 8 (3D 84)
Westlands Cl. UB3: Harl 4J 93
Westlands Ct. KT8: E Mos 4H 149
Westlands Est. UB3: Harl 3G 93
Westlands Ter. SW12 . . . . .6G 119
West La. SE16 . . . . .2H 103
Westlea Rd. W7 . . . . .3A 96
Westleigh Av. SW15 . . . . .5D 116
Westleigh Ct. CR2: S Croy 4E 168
         (off Birdhurst Rd.)
   E11 . . . . .5J 51
Westleigh Dr. BR1: Brom 1C 160
Westleigh Gdns. HA8: Edg 1G 43
West Links HA0: Wemb 3D 78
Westlinton Cl. NW7 . . . . .6B 30
West Lodge E16 . . . . .1J 105
         (off Britannia Ga.)
W. Lodge Av. W3 . . . . .1G 97
W. Lodge Ct. W3 . . . . .1G 97
W. London Crematorium NW10 . . . . .4D 80
W. London Studios SW6 . . . . .7K 99
         (off Fulham Rd.)
Westmacott Dr. TW14: Felt 1H 129
Westmacott Ho. NW8 . . . . .4B 4
         (off Hatton St.)
West Mall N9 . . . . .3B 34
   W8 . . . . .1J 99
       (off Kensington Mall)

Westmark Point SW15 . . . . .1D 134
         (off Norley Va.)
West Mead HA4: Ruis 4A 58
   KT19: Ewe 6A 164
Westmead SW15 . . . . .6D 116
Westmead Cnr. SM5: Cars 4C 166
Westmead Ho. SM1: Sutt 4B 166
Westmead Rd. SM1: Sutt 4B 166
W. Mersea Cl. E16 . . . . .1K 105
West M. N17 . . . . .7C 34
   SW1 . . . . .4A 18
West Middlesex Golf Course 7G 77
WESTMINSTER 7E 12 (2J 101)
Westminster Abbey 7E 12 (3H 101)
Westminster Abbey Chapter House . .1E 18
    (within Westminster Abbey)
Westminster Abbey Mus. 1E 18
    (within Westminster Abbey)
Westminster Abbey Pyx Chamber . . .1E 18
    (within Westminster Abbey)
Westminster Av. CR7: Thor H 2B 156
Westminster Boating Base & Pier
   . . . . .7C 18 (6H 101)
Westminster Bri. SW1 . . .7F 13 (2J 101)
Westminster Bri. Ho. SE1 . . . . .7A 14
         (off Lambeth Rd.)
Westminster Bri. Rd. SE1 . .7G 13 (2K 101)
Westminster Bus. Sq. SE11 . . . . . . .7H 19
Westminster Cl. IG6: Ilf 2H 53
   TW11: Tedd 5A 132
   TW14: Felt 1J 129
Westminster Ct. E11 . . . . .6K 51
        (off Cambridge Pk.)
   NW8 . . . . .4A 4
         (off Aberdeen Pl.)
   SE16 .1K 103
      (off King & Queen Wharf)
Westminster Dr. N13 . . . . .5D 32
Westminster Gdns. E4 . . . . .1B 36
   IG6: Ilf .2G 53
   IG11: Bark 2J 89
   SW1 . . . . .3E 18
         (off Vincent St.)
Westminster Hall 7E 12
Westminster Ind. Est. SE18 . . . . . . .3B 106
Westminster Mans. SW1 . . . . .2D 18
        (off Gt. Smith St.)
Westminster Pal. Gdns. SW1 . . . . . .2C 18
Westminster RC Cathedral
   . . . . .2A 18 (3G 101)
Westminster Rd. N9 . . . . .1C 34
   SM1: Sutt 2B 166
   W7 . . . . .1J 95
Westmoat Cl. BR3: Beck 7E 140
WEST MOLESEY 4E 148
Westmoor Gdns. EN3: Enf H 2E 24
Westmoor Rd. EN3: Enf H 2E 24
Westmoor St. SE7 . . . . .3A 106
Westmore Ct. SW15 . . . . .5G 117
Westmoreland Av. DA16: Well 3J 125
Westmoreland Dr. SM2: Sutt 7K 165
Westmoreland Ho. E16 . . . . .1J 105
        (off Gatcombe Rd.)
Westmoreland Pl. BR1: Brom 3J 159
   SW1 . . . . .6K 17 (5F 101)
   W5 . . . . .5D 78
Westmoreland Rd. BR1: Brom 5G 159
   BR2: Brom 5G 159
   NW9 . . . . .3F 43
   SE17 .6D 102
         (not continuous)
   SW13 .1B 116
Westmoreland St. W1 . . . .6H 5 (5E 82)
Westmoreland Ter. SE20 . . . . .7H 139
   SW1 . . . . .6K 17 (5F 101)
Westmoreland Wlk. SE17 . . . . .6D 102
         (not continuous)
Westmorland Cl. E12 . . . . .2B 70
   TW1: Twick 6B 114
Westmorland Ct. KT6: Surb 7D 150

Westmorland Rd. E17 . . . . .6C 50
   HA1: Harr 5F 41
Westmorland Sq. CR4: Mitc 5J 155
Westmorland Way CR4: Mitc 4H 155
Westmount Cen. UB4: Yead 7B 76
Westmount Cl. KT4: Wor Pk 1E 164
Westmount Rd. SE9 . . . . .6F 79
Westmount Rd. SE9 . . . . .2D 124
WEST NORWOOD 4C 138
West Norwood Crematorium
   SE27 .3C 138
West Oak BR3: Beck 1F 159
Westoe Rd. N9 . . . . .2C 34
W. Officers Apartments SE18 . . . . . .7E 106
Weston Av. KT7: T Ditt 7J 149
   KT8: W Mole 3C 148
Westonbirt Ct. SE15 . . . . .6F 103
         (off Ebley Cl.)
Weston Ct. KT1: King T 3E 150
        (off Grove Cres.)
   N4 . . . . .3C 66
   N20 . . . . .7F 21
        (off Farnham Cl.)
Weston Dr. HA7: Stan 1B 42
West One Ho. W1 . . . . .6A 6
         (off Wells St.)
Westone Mans. IG11: Bark 7K 71
         (off Upney La.)
West One Shop. Cen. W1 . . . . .1H 11
Weston Gdns. TW7: Isle 1J 113
WESTON GREEN 7J 149
Weston Grn. KT7: T Ditt 7J 149
   RM9: Dag 4F 73
Weston Grn. Rd. KT7: T Ditt 7J 149
   KT10: Esh 7J 149
Weston Gro. BR1: Brom 1H 159
Weston Ho. E9 . . . . .1J 85
       (off King Edward's Rd.)
   NW6 . . . . .7G 63
Weston Pk. KT1: King T 2E 150
   KT7: T Ditt 7J 149
   N8 . . . . .6J 47
Weston Ri. WC1 . . . . .1H 7 (3K 83)
Weston Rd. BR1: Brom 7H 141
   EN2: Enf 2J 23
   RM9: Dag 4E 72
   W4 . . . . .3J 97
Weston St. SE1 . . . . . .7F 15 (2E 102)
         (not continuous)
Weston Wlk. E8 . . . . .7H 67
Westover Hill NW3 . . . . .2J 63
Westover Rd. SW18 . . . . .7A 118
Westow Hill SE19 . . . . .6E 138
Westow St. SE19 . . . . .6E 138
West Pk. SE9 . . . . .2C 142
Westpark W5 . . . . .6D 78
West Pk. Av. TW9: Kew 1G 115
West Pk. Cl. RM6: Chad H 5D 54
   TW5: Hest 6D 94
West Pk. Rd. TW9: Kew 1G 115
   UB2: S'hall 1G 95
West Parkside SE10 . . . . .2G 105
West Pk. Wlk. E20 . . . . .6E 68
West Pl. SW19 . . . . .5E 134
West Plaza TW15: Ashf 2A 128
West Point E14 . . . . .7B 86
         (off Grenade St.)
   SE1 . . . . .5G 103
Westpoint Apartments N8 . . . . .3K 47
W. Point Cl. TW4: Houn 3D 112
       (off Grosvenor Rd.)
Westpoint Trad. Est. W3 . . . . .5H 79
Westpole Av. EN4: Cockf 4K 21
Westport Cl. UB4: Yead 4A 76
Westport Rd. E13 . . . . .4K 87
Westport St. E1 . . . . .6K 85
W. Poultry Av. EC1 . . . . . .6A 8 (5B 84)
West Quarters W12 . . . . .6C 80
West Quay SW10 . . . . .1A 118
West Quay Dr. UB4: Yead 5C 76
West Quay Wlk. E14 . . . . .3D 104

West Ramp TW6: H'row A 1C 110
West Reservoir Cen. 1C 66
W. Ridge Gdns. UB6: G'frd 2G 77
West Ri. W2 . . . . .2D 10
West Rd. E15 . . . . .1K 87
   EN4: E Barn 1K 31
   KT2: King T 1J 151
   N17 . . . . .6C 34
   RM6: Chad H 6D 54
   RM7: Rush G 7K 55
   SE1 . . . . .6H 13 (2K 101)
   SW3 . . . . .6F 17 (5D 100)
   SW4 . . . . .5H 119
   TW14: Bedf 6F 111
   UB7: W Dray 3B 92
   W5 . . . . .5E 78
Westrovia Ct. SW1 . . . . .4C 18
        (off Moreton St.)
West Row W10 . . . . .4G 81
Westrow SW15 . . . . .6E 116
Westrow Dr. IG11: Bark 5A 72
Westrow Gdns. IG3: Ilf 2K 71
WEST RUISLIP 2E 56
W. Ruislip Ct. HA4: Ruis 2F 57
       (off Ickenham Rd.)
W. Sheen Va. TW9: Rich 4F 115
Westside N2 . . . . .3D 46
   NW4 . . . . .2D 44
Westside Apartments IG1: Ilf 3E 70
         (off Roden St.)
West Side Comn. SW19 . . . . .5E 134
West Side Ct. TW16: Sun 7G 129
        (off Scotts Av.)
Westside Ct. W9 . . . . .4J 81
         (off Elgin Av.)
West Smithfield EC1 . . . . . .6A 8 (5B 84)
West Sq. E10 . . . . .7D 50
   SE11 . . . . .2K 19 (3B 102)
West Stand N5 . . . . .4B 66
West St. BR1: Brom 1J 159
   CR0: C'don 4C 168
   DA7: Bex 3F 127
   DA8: Erith 4K 109
   E2 . . . . .2H 85
   E11 . . . . .3G 69
   E17 . . . . .5D 50
   HA1: Harr 1H 59
   SM1: Sutt 5K 165
   SM5: Cars 3D 166
   TW8: Bford 6C 96
   WC2 . . . . .1D 12 (6H 83)
West St. La. SM5: Cars 4D 166
West St. Pl. CR0: C'don 4C 168
         (off West St.)
W. Temple Sheen SW14 . . . . .5H 115
W. Tenter St. E1 . . . . .1K 15 (6F 85)
West Ter. DA15: Sidc 1J 143
W. Thamesmead Bus. Pk. SE28 . . . .3J 107
         (not continuous)
West Twr. E14 . . . . .2D 104
       (off Pan Peninsula Sq.)
West Towers HA5: Pinn 5B 40
Westvale M. W3 . . . . .2A 98
West Vw. NW4 . . . . .4E 44
   TW14: Bedf 7E 110
West View W7 . . . . .6J 77
W. View Apartments N7 . . . . .7J 65
         (off York Way)
Westview Cl. NW10 . . . . .5B 62
   W10 . . . . .6E 80
Westview Ct. N20 . . . . .1F 31
Westview Cres. N9 . . . . .7K 23
Westview Dr. IG8: Wfd G 2B 52
Westville Rd. KT7: T Ditt 1A 162
   W12 . . . . .2C 98
West Wlk. EN4: E Barn 7K 21
   UB3: Hayes 1J 93
   W5 . . . . .5E 78
Westward Rd. E4 . . . . .5G 35
         (not continuous)
Westward Way HA3: Kenton 6E 42

W. Warwick Pl. SW1 . . . . . . .4A 18 (4G 101)
West Way BR4: W W'ck 6F 159
 BR5: Pet W 5H 161
 CRO: C'don 2A 170
 HA4: Ruis 1H 57
 HA5: Pinn 4B 40
 HA8: Edg 6C 28
 N18 . . . . .4J 33
 NW10 .3K 61
 TW5: Hest 1D 112
 TW17: Shep 6F 147
Westway SW20 . . . . .3D 152
 UB6: G'frd 1J 77
 W2 . . . . .6A 4 (5H 81)
 W9 . . . . .5H 81
 W10 . . . . .5H 81
 W12 . . . . .7B 80
Westway Cl. SW20 . . . . .3D 152
Westway Cl. UB5: N'olt 1E 76
Westway Est. W3 . . . . .5A 80
West Way Gdns. CRO: C'don 2K 169
Westway Lodge W9 . . . . .5J 81
                                    (off Amberley Rd.)
West Ways HA6: Nwood 2J 39
Westways KT19: Ewe 4B 164
Westway Sports Cen. 6F 81
Westway Travellers Site W12 . . . . . .7F 81
                                     (off Stable Way)
Westwell M. SW16 . . . . .6J 137
Westwell Rd. SW16 . . . . .6J 137
Westwell Rd. App. SW16 . . . . .6J 137
Westwick KT1: King T 2G 151
                                (off Chesterton Ter.)
Westwick Gdns. TW4: Cran 2K 111
 W14 . . . . .2F 99
WEST WICKHAM 1E 170
West Wickham Leisure Cen. 1E 170
West Wintergarden 1D 104
                                       (off Bank St.)
Westwood Av. HA2: Harr 4F 59
 SE19 .1C 156
Westwood Bus. Cen. NW10 . . . . . .4A 80
Westwood Cl. BR1: Brom 2B 160
 HA4: Ruis 6D 38
Westwood Ct. EN1: Enf 6K 23
                                      (off Village Rd.)
 HA0: Wemb 4B 60
 UB6: G'frd 5H 59
Westwood Gdns. SW13 . . . . .3B 116
Westwood Hill SE26 . . . . .5G 139
Westwood Ho. W12 . . . . .1E 98
                                      (off Wood La.)
Westwood La. DA15: Sidc 5A 126
 DA16: Well 3K 125
Westwood M. E3 . . . . .3C 86
                                (off Addington Rd.)
Westwood Pk. SE23 . . . . .7H 121
Westwood Pk. Trad. Est. W3 . . . . .5H 79
Westwood Pl. SE26 . . . . .4G 139
Westwood Rd. E16 . . . . .1K 105
 IG3: IIf .1K 71
 SW13 .3B 116
West Woodside DA5: Bexl 7E 126
Wetheral Dr. HA7: Stan 1B 42
Wetherby Cl. UB5: N'olt 6F 59
Wetherby Gdns. SW5 . . . . .4A 100
Wetherby Mans. SW5 . . . . .5K 99
                                     (off Earls Ct. Sq.)
Wetherby M. SW5 . . . . .5K 99
Wetherby Pl. SW7 . . . . .4A 100
Wetherby Rd. EN2: Enf 1H 23
Wetherby Way KT9: Chess 7E 162
Wetherden St. E17 . . . . .7B 50
Wetherell Rd. E9 . . . . .1K 85
Wetherill Rd. N10 . . . . .1E 46
Wevco Wharf SE15 . . . . .6H 103
Wexford Ho. E1 . . . . .5J 85
                                     (off Sidney St.)
Wexford Rd. SW12 . . . . .7D 118
Wexner Bldg. E1 . . . . .5J 85
                                     (off Strype St.)

Weybourne St. SW18 . . . . .2A 136
Weybridge Ct. SE16 . . . . .5H 103
Weybridge Point SW11 . . . . .2D 118
Weybridge Rd. CR7: Thor H 4A 156
Wey Ct. KT19: Ewe 4J 163
Weydown Cl. SW19 . . . . .1G 135
Weyhill Rd. E1 . . . . .6G 85
Wey Ho. NW8 . . . . .4B 4
                                  (off Church St. Est.)
 UB5: N'olt 4D 76
                                  (off Taywood Rd.)
Weylands Cl. KT12: Walt T 7D 148
Weylond Rd. RM8: Dag 3F 73
Weyman Rd. SE3 . . . . .1A 124
Weymarks, The N17 . . . . .6J 33
Weymouth Av. NW7 . . . . .5F 29
 W5 . . . . .3C 96
Weymouth Cl. E6 . . . . .6F 89
Weymouth Ct. E2 . . . . .2F 85
 SM2: Sutt 7J 165
Weymouth Ho. BR2: Brom 2H 159
                                      (off Hill Ho. M.)
 SW8 . . . . .7K 101
                                      (off Bolney St.)
Weymouth M. W1 . . . . .5J 5 (5F 83)
Weymouth Pl. SE2 . . . . .3A 108
Weymouth Rd. UB4: Hayes 3G 75
Weymouth St. W1 . . . . .6H 5 (5E 82)
Weymouth Ter. E2 . . . . .1K 9 (2F 85)
Weymouth Vs. N4 . . . . .2K 65
                                     (off Moray Rd.)
Whadcoat St. N4 . . . . .2A 66
Whaddon Ho. SE22 . . . . .3E 120
Whalebone Av. RM6: Chad H 6F 55
Whalebone Ct. EC2 . . . . .7E 8
Whalebone Gro.
 RM6: Chad H 6F 55
Whalebone La. E15 . . . . .7G 69
Whalebone La. Nth.
 RM6: Chad H, Col R 1E 54
Whalebone La. Sth.
 RM6: Chad H, Dag 7F 55
 RM8: Dag 7F 55
Whales Yd. E15 . . . . .7G 69
                                   (off West Ham La.)
Wharf, The EC3 . . . . .4H 15 (1F 103)
Wharfdale Cl. N11 . . . . .6K 31
Wharfdale Rd. N1 . . . . .2J 83
Wharfedale Cl. E5 . . . . .4K 67
Wharfedale Gdns.
 CR7: Thor H 4K 155
Wharfedale Ho. NW6 . . . . .1K 81
                                  (off Kilburn Vale)
Wharfedale St. SW10 . . . . .5K 99
Wharfedale Yd. N1 . . . . .2J 83
                                  (off Wharfedale Rd.)
Wharf La. E14 . . . . .6B 86
 TW1: Twick 1A 132
Wharf Pl. E2 . . . . .1H 85
Wharf Rd. E16 . . . . .1A 106
 EN3: Pond E 6F 25
 N1 . . . . .1C 8 (2C 84)
                                     (Baldwin Ter.)
 N1 . . . . .1J 83
                                        (York Way)
Wharf Rd. Ind. Est. EN3: Pond E 6F 25
Wharfside Point Nth. E14 . . . . .7F 86
                                  (off Poplar High St.)
Wharfside Point Sth. E14 . . . . .7E 86
Wharfside Rd. E16 . . . . .5G 87
Wharf St. E16 . . . . .5G 87
 SE8 . . . . .5C 104
Wharf Vw. Ct. E14 . . . . .6E 86
                                      (off Blair St.)
Wharncliffe Dr. UB1: S'hall 1H 95
Wharncliffe Gdns. SE25 . . . . .2E 156
Wharncliffe Rd. SE25 . . . . .2E 156
Wharnecliffe M. SW4 . . . . .6H 119
Wharton Cl. NW10 . . . . .6A 62
Wharton Cotts. WC1 . . . . .2J 7 (3A 84)

Wharton Ho. E2 . . . . .3K 85
 SE1 . . . . .7J 15
                                  (off St Saviour's Est.)
Wharton Rd. BR1: Brom 1K 159
Wharton St. WC1 . . . . .2H 7 (3K 83)
Whatcott's Yd. N16 . . . . .4E 66
Whateley Rd. SE20 . . . . .7K 139
 SE22 .5F 121
Whatley Av. SW20 . . . . .3F 153
Whatman Ho. E14 . . . . .6B 86
                                  (off Wallwood St.)
Whatman Rd. SE23 . . . . .7K 121
Wheatcroft Ct. SM1: Sutt 1K 165
                                  (off Cleeve Way)
Wheatfield Ho. NW6 . . . . .3J 81
                                  (off Kilburn Pk. Rd.)
Wheatfields E6 . . . . .6F 89
 EN3: Enf H 1F 25
Wheatfield Way KT1: King T 2E 150
Wheathill Ho. SE20 . . . . .2H 157
                                      (off Penge Rd.)
Wheathill Rd. SE20 . . . . .3H 157
Wheatland Ho. SE22 . . . . .3E 120
Wheatlands TW5: Hest 6E 94
Wheatlands Rd. SW17 . . . . .3E 136
Wheatley Cl. NW4 . . . . .2C 44
Wheatley Ct. E3 . . . . .3D 86
                                      (off Bruce Rd.)
Wheatley Cres. UB3: Hayes 7J 75
Wheatley Gdns. N9 . . . . .2K 33
Wheatley Ho. SW15 . . . . .7C 116
                                  (off Ellisfield Dr.)
Wheatley Mans. IG11: Bark 7A 72
                                  (off Lansbury Av.)
Wheatley M. KT8: E Mos 4H 149
Wheatley Rd. TW7: Isle 3K 113
Wheatley's Eyot
 TW16: Sun 5J 147
Wheatley St. W1 . . . . .6H 5 (5E 82)
Wheat Sheaf Cl. E14 . . . . .4D 104
Wheatsheaf Cl. UB5: N'olt 5C 58
Wheatsheaf La. SW6 . . . . .7E 98
 SW8 . . . . .7J 101
Wheatsheaf Ter. SW6 . . . . .7H 99
Wheatstone Cl. CR4: Mitc 1C 154
Wheatstone Ho. SE1 . . . . .3C 102
                                      (off County St.)
 W10 . . . . .5G 81
                                      (off Telford Rd.)
Wheatstone Rd. DA8: Erith 5K 109
 W10 . . . . .5G 81
Wheeler Cl. IG8: Wfd G 6J 37
Wheeler Gdns. N1 . . . . .1J 83
                                  (off Outram Pl.)
Wheeler Pl. BR2: Brom 4K 159
Wheelers Cross IG11: Bark 2H 89
Wheelers Dr. HA4: Ruis 6E 38
Wheel Farm Dr. RM10: Dag 3J 73
Wheel Ho. E14 . . . . .5D 104
                                  (off Burrells Wharf Sq.)
Wheelock Cl. DA8: Erith 7H 109
Wheelwright St. N7 . . . . .7K 65
Whelan Way SM6: Bedd 3H 167
Wheler Ho. E1 . . . . .4J 9
                                  (off Quaker St.)
Wheler St. E1 . . . . .4J 9 (4F 85)
Whellock Rd. W4 . . . . .3A 98
Whenman Av. DA5: Bexl 2J 145
Whernside Cl. SE28 . . . . .7C 90
WHETSTONE 2F 31
Whetstone Cl. N20 . . . . .2G 31
Whetstone Pk. WC2 . . . . .7G 7 (6K 83)
Whetstone Rd. SE3 . . . . .2A 124
Whewell Rd. N19 . . . . .2J 65
Whidborne Bldgs. WC1 . . . . .2F 7
                                  (off Whidborne St.)
Whidborne Cl. SE8 . . . . .2C 122
Whidborne St. WC1 . . . . .2F 7 (3J 83)
                                     (not continuous)
Whidbourne St. SW8 . . . . .1H 119
Whimbrel Cl. SE28 . . . . .7C 90

Whimbrel Way UB4: Yead 6B 76
Whinchat Rd. SE28 . . . . .3H 107
Whinfell Cl. SW16 . . . . .5H 137
Whinyates Rd. SE9 . . . . .3C 124
Whippendell Way BR5: St P 7B 144
Whippingham Ho. E3 . . . . .3B 86
                                  (off Merchant St.)
Whipps Cross E17 . . . . .5F 51
Whipps Cross Ho. E17 . . . . .7B 51
                                      (off Wood St.)
Whipps Cross Rd. E11 . . . . .5F 51
                                     (not continuous)
Whiskin St. EC1 . . . . .2A 8 (3B 84)
Whisperwood Cl.
 HA3: Hrw W 1J 41
Whistler Gdns. HA8: Edg 2F 43
Whistler M. RM8: Dag 5B 72
                                  (off Fitzstephen Rd.)
 SE15 .7F 103
Whistlers Av. SW11 . . . . .7B 100
Whistlers Gro. DA15: Sidc 7J 125
Whistler St. N5 . . . . .5B 66
Whistler Twr. SW10 . . . . .7A 100
                                  (off Worlds End Est.)
Whistler Wlk. SW10 . . . . .7B 100
Whiston Ho. N1 . . . . .7B 66
                                  (off Richmond Gro.)
Whiston Rd. E2 . . . . .2F 85
Whitacre M. SE11 . . . . .6K 19 (5A 102)
Whitakers Lodge EN2: Enf 1J 23
Whitbread Cl. N17 . . . . .1G 49
Whitbread Rd. SE4 . . . . .4A 122
Whitburn Rd. SE13 . . . . .4D 122
Whitby Av. NW10 . . . . .3H 79
Whitby Cl. N7 . . . . .4J 65
Whitby Gdns. NW9 . . . . .3G 43
 SM1: Sutt 2B 166
Whitby Ho. NW8 . . . . .1A 82
                                  (off Boundary Rd.)
Whitby Pde. HA4: Ruis 2A 58
Whitby Rd. HA2: Harr 3G 59
 HA4: Ruis 3K 57
 SE18 .4D 106
 SM1: Sutt 2B 166
Whitby St. E1 . . . . .3J 9 (4F 85)
                                     (not continuous)
Whitcher Cl. SE14 . . . . .6A 104
Whitcher Pl. NW1 . . . . .6G 65
Whitchurch Av. HA8: Edg 7A 28
Whitchurch Cl. HA8: Edg 6A 28
Whitchurch Gdns. HA8: Edg 6A 28
Whitchurch Ho. W10 . . . . .6F 81
                                  (off Kingsdown Cl.)
Whitchurch La. HA8: Edg 7J 27
Whitchurch Pde.
 HA8: Edg 7B 28
Whitchurch Rd. W11 . . . . .7F 81
Whitcomb Ct. WC2 . . . . .3D 12
Whitcomb St. WC2 . . . . .3D 12 (7H 83)
Whitcome M. TW9: Kew 1H 115
Whitcomb St. WC2 . . . . .3D 12 (7H 83)
Whiteadder Way E14 . . . . .4D 104
Whitear Wlk. E15 . . . . .6F 69
Whitebarn La. RM10: Dag 1G 91
Whitebeam Av. BR2: Brom 7E 160
Whitebeam Cl. SW9 . . . . .7K 101
Whitebeam Ho. E15 . . . . .3G 87
                                  (off Teasel Way)
White Bear Pl. NW3 . . . . .4B 64
White Bear Yd. EC1 . . . . .4J 7
                                  (off Clerkenwell Rd.)
White Bri. Av. CR4: Mitc 3B 154
Whitebridge Cl.
 TW14: Felt 6H 111
White Butts Rd. HA4: Ruis 3B 58
WHITECHAPEL 5G 85
Whitechapel Art Gallery 7K 9 (6F 85)
Whitechapel High St. E1 . . . . .7K 9 (6F 85)
Whitechapel Rd. E1 . . . . .7K 9 (5G 85)
Whitechapel Sports Cen. 5H 85
White Church La. E1 . . . . .7K 9 (6G 85)

White Church Pas.—Wickham St.

White Church Pas. E1 7K 9
(off White Church La.)
WHITE CITY 7D 80
WHITE CITY 6E 80
White City Cl. W12 7E 80
White City Est. W12 7D 80
White City Rd. W12 7E 80
White Conduit St. N1 2A 84
Whitecote Rd. UB1: S'hall 6G 77
Whitecroft Cl. BR3: Beck 4F 159
Whitecroft Way BR3: Beck 5E 158
Whitecross Pl. EC2 5F 9 (5D 84)
Whitecross St. EC1 3D 8 (4C 84)
Whitefield Av. NW2 1E 62
Whitefield Cl. SW15 6G 117
Whitefoot La. BR1: Brom 4E 140
(not continuous)
Whitefoot Ter. BR1: Brom 3H 141
Whitefriars Av. HA3: W'stone 2J 41
Whitefriars Ct. N12 5G 31
Whitefriars Dr. HA3: Hrw W 2H 41
Whitefriars St. EC4 1K 13 (6A 84)
Whitefriars Trad. Est.
HA3: W'stone 3H 41
White Gables Ct. CR2: S Croy 5E 168
White Gdns. RM10: Dag 6G 73
Whitegate Gdns. HA3: Hrw W 7E 26
White Gates KT7: T Ditt 7A 150
Whitehall 6G 165
Whitehall SW1 5E 12 (1J 101)
Whitehall Ct. SW1 5F 13 (1J 101)
(not continuous)
Whitehall Cres. KT9: Chess 5D 162
Whitehall Gdns. E4 1B 36
SW1 5E 12
W3 1G 97
W4 6H 97
Whitehall La. IG9: Buck H 2D 36
Whitehall Lodge N10 2E 46
Whitehall Pk. N19 1G 65
Whitehall Pk. Rd. W4 6H 97
Whitehall Pl. E7 5J 69
SM6: Wall 4F 167
SW1 5E 12 (1J 101)
Whitehall Rd. BR2: Brom 5B 160
CR7: Thor H 5A 156
E4 2B 36
HA1: Harr 7J 41
IG8: Wfd G 2B 36
W7 2A 96
Whitehall St. N17 7A 34
White Hart Av. SE18 4K 107
SE28 4K 107
White Hart Cl. UB3: Harl 6F 93
White Hart Ct. EC2 6G 9
White Hart Lane 7B 34
White Hart La. N17 7H 33
N22 1K 47
NW10 6B 62
RM7: Col R, Mawney 1G 55
SW13 2A 116
White Hart Lane Community Sports Cen.
7G 33
White Hart Rd. SE18 4J 107
WHITE HART RDBT. 2B 76
White Hart Slip BR1: Brom 2J 159
White Hart St. EC4 7B 8 (6B 84)
SE11 5K 19 (5A 102)
White Hart Triangle SE28 2K 107
White Hart Triangle Bus. Pk.
SE28 2A 108
White Hart Yd. SE1 5E 14 (1D 102)
Whitehaven Cl. BR2: Brom 4J 159
Whitehaven St. NW8 4C 4 (4C 82)
Whitehead Cl. N18 5J 33
SW18 7A 118
Whiteheads Gro. SW3 4D 16 (4C 100)
White Heart Av. UB8: Hil 5E 74
Whiteheath Av. HA4: Ruis 7E 38
White Heather Ho. WC1 2F 7
(off Cromer St.)
White Heron M. TW11: Tedd 6K 131
White Horse All. EC1 5A 8
White Horse Hill BR7: Chst 4E 142
White Horse La. E1 5K 85
Whitehorse La. SE25 4D 156
White Horse M. EN3: Enf H 2E 24
Whitehorse M. SE1 1K 19 (3A 102)
White Horse Rd. E1 6A 86
(not continuous)
E6 3D 88
Whitehorse Rd. CR0: C'don 7C 156
CR7: Thor H 7C 156
White Horse St. W1 5K 11 (1F 101)
White Horse Yd. EC2 7E 8 (6D 84)
White Ho. CR0: C'don 4D 168
(off Coombe Rd.)
SW4 7H 119
(off Clapham Pk. Est.)
SW11 1B 118
White House, The NW1 3K 5
Whitehouse E10 6E 50
(off Leyton Grn. Rd.)
Whitehouse Apartments SE1 1K 101
White Ho. Ct. N14 2D 32
White Ho. Dr. HA7: Stan 4H 27
IG8: Wfd G 6C 36
White Ho. La. EN2: Enf 1H 23
White Ho. M. E10 6E 50
Whitehouse Way N14 2A 32
Whitehurst Dr. N18 5E 34
White Kennett St. E1 7H 9 (6F 85)
Whitelands Cres. SW18 7G 117
Whitelands Ho. SW3 5F 17
(off Cheltenham Ter.)
Whiteledges W13 6C 78
Whitelegg Rd. E13 2H 87
Whiteley Rd. SE19 5D 138
Whiteleys Cen. (Shop. Cen.)
W2 6K 81
Whiteleys Pde. UB10: Hil 4D 74
Whiteley's Way TW13: Hanw 3E 130
White Lion Ct. EC3 1G 15
SE15 6J 103
TW7: Isle 3B 114
White Lion Hill EC4 2B 14 (7B 84)
White Lion St. N1 2A 84
White Lodge SE19 7B 138
W5 5C 78
White Lodge Cl. N2 6B 46
SM2: Sutt 7A 166
TW7: Isle 2A 114
White Lodge Ct. TW16: Sun 1A 148
White Lodge Mus. 1K 133
White Lyon Ct. EC2 5C 8
Whiteoak Ct. BR7: Chst 6E 142
White Oak Dr. BR3: Beck 2E 158
White Oak Gdns. DA15: Sidc 7K 125
Whiteoaks La. UB6: G'frd 3H 77
White Orchards HA7: Stan 5F 27
N20 1C 30
White Post La. E9 7B 68
White Post St. SE15 7J 103
White Rd. E15 7G 69
Whiterose Trad. Est. EN4: E Barn 5G 21
(off Margaret Rd.)
Whites Av. IG2: Ilf 6J 53
Whites Grounds SE1 7H 15 (2E 102)
White's Grounds Est. SE1 6H 15
White's Mdw. BR1: Brom 4E 160
White's Row E1 6J 9 (5F 85)
Whites Sq. SW4 4H 119
Whitestile Rd. TW8: Bford 5C 96
Whitestone Cl. EN4: Had W 1H 21
Whitestone La. NW3 3A 64
Whitestone Wlk. NW3 3A 64
Whitestone Way CR0: Wadd 2A 168
White St. UB1: S'hall 2B 94
White Swan M. W4 5A 98
Whitethorn Av. UB7: Yiew 7A 74
Whitethorn Gdns. CR0: C'don 2H 169
EN2: Enf 5J 23
Whitethorn Ho. E1 1J 103
(off Prusom St.)
Whitethorn Pas. E3 4C 86
(off Whitethorn St.)
Whitethorn Pl. UB7: Yiew 1B 92
Whitethorn St. E3 5C 86
White Twr. Way E1 5A 86
Whitewebbs Way BR5: St P 1K 161
Whitfield Ct. IG1: Ilf 7D 52
Whitfield Ho. NW8 4C 4
(off Salisbury St.)
Whitfield Pl. W1 4A 6
Whitfield Rd. DA7: Bex 7F 109
E6 7A 70
Whitfield St. W1 4A 6 (4G 83)
Whitford Gdns. CR4: Mitc 3D 154
Whitgift Av. CR2: S Croy 5B 168
Whitgift Cen. CR0: C'don 2C 168
Whitgift Ct. CR2: S Croy 5C 168
(off Nottingham Rd.)
Whitgift Ho. SE11 3G 19 (4K 101)
SW11 1C 118
Whitgift Sq. CR0: C'don 2C 168
Whitgift St. CR0: C'don 3C 168
SE11 3G 19 (4K 101)
Whiting Av. IG11: Bark 7F 71
Whitings IG2: Ilf 5J 53
Whitings Rd. EN5: Barn 5A 20
Whitings Way E6 5E 88
Whiting Way SE8 4A 104
Whitland Rd. SM5: Cars 1B 166
Whitley Cl. TW19: Stanw 6A 110
Whitley Ho. SW1 7B 18
(off Churchill Gdns.)
Whitley Rd. N17 2E 48
Whitlock Dr. SW19 7G 117
Whitman Ho. E2 3J 85
(off Cornwall Av.)
Whitman Rd. E3 4A 86
Whitmead Cl. CR2: S Croy 6E 168
Whitmore Cl. N11 5A 32
Whitmore Est. N1 1E 84
Whitmore Gdns. NW10 2E 80
Whitmore Ho. N1 1E 84
(off Whitmore Est.)
Whitmore Rd. BR3: Beck 3B 158
HA1: Harr 7G 41
N1 1E 84
Whitmore Sports Cen. 1G 59
Whitnell Way SW15 5E 116
(not continuous)
Whitney Av. IG4: Ilf 4B 52
Whitney Rd. E10 7D 50
Whitney Wlk. DA14: Sidc 6E 144
Whitstable Cl. BR3: Beck 1B 158
HA4: Ruis 2G 57
Whitstable Ho. W10 6F 81
(off Silchester Rd.)
Whitstable Pl. CR0: C'don 4C 168
Whitstone La. BR3: Beck 5D 158
Whittaker Av. TW9: Rich 5D 114
Whittaker Pl. TW9: Rich 5D 114
(off Whittaker Av.)
Whittaker Rd. E6 7A 70
SM3: Sutt 3H 165
Whittaker St. SW1 4G 17 (4E 100)
Whittaker Way SE1 4G 103
Whitta Rd. E12 4B 70
Whittell Gdns. SE26 3J 139
Whittingham N17 7C 34
Whittingham Ct. W4 7A 98
Whittingstall Rd. SW6 1H 117
Whittington Apartments E1 6K 85
(off E. Arbour St.)
Whittington Av. EC3 1G 15 (6E 84)
UB4: Hayes 5H 75
Whittington Ct. N2 5D 46
Whittington Ho. N19 2H 65
(off Holloway Rd.)
Whittington M. N12 4F 31
Whittington Rd. N22 7D 32
Whittington Way HA5: Pinn 5C 40
Whittlebury Cl. SM5: Cars 7D 166
Whittle Cl. E17 6A 50
UB1: S'hall 6F 77
Whittle Rd. TW5: Hest 7A 94
TW6: H'row A 6C 174
UB2: S'hall 2F 95
Whittlesea Cl. HA3: Hrw W 7B 26
Whittlesea Path HA3: Hrw W 1G 41
Whittlesea Rd. HA3: Hrw W 7B 26
Whittlesey St. SE1 5J 13 (1A 102)
WHITTON 7G 113
Whitton NW3 7D 64
Whitton Av. E. UB6: G'frd 5J 59
Whitton Av. W. UB5: N'olt 5F 59
UB6: G'frd 5F 59
Whitton Cl. UB6: G'frd 6B 60
Whitton Dene TW3: Houn, Isle 5G 113
TW7: Isle 6H 113
Whitton Dr. UB6: G'frd 6A 60
Whitton Mnr. Rd. TW7: Isle 6G 113
Whitton Rd. TW1: Twick 6K 113
TW2: Twick 6J 113
TW3: Houn 4F 113
WHITTON ROAD RDBT. 6K 113
Whitton Sports & Fitness Cen. 2F 131
Whitton Wlk. E3 3C 86
(not continuous)
Whitton Waye TW3: Houn 6E 112
Whitwell Rd. E13 3J 87
Whitworth Ho. SE1 3C 102
Whitworth Rd. SE18 7E 106
SE25 3E 156
Whitworth St. SE10 5G 105
Whorlton Rd. SE15 3H 121
Whychcote Point NW2 1E 62
(off Whitefield Av.)
Whymark Av. N22 3A 48
Whytecroft TW5: Hest 7B 94
Whyte M. SM3: Cheam 7G 165
Whyteville Rd. E7 6K 69
Whytlaw Ho. E3 5B 86
(off Baythorne St.)
Wickersley Rd. SW11 2E 118
Wickers Oake SE19 4F 139
Wicker St. E1 6H 85
Wicket, The CR0: Addtn 5C 170
Wicket Rd. UB6: G'frd 3A 78
Wickets, The TW15: Ashf 4A 128
Wickfield Apartments E15 6F 69
(off Grove Cres. Rd.)
Wickfield Ho. SE16 2H 103
(off Wilson Gro.)
Wickford Ho. E1 4J 85
(off Wickford St.)
Wickford St. E1 4J 85
Wickford Way E17 4K 49
Wickham Av. CR0: C'don 2A 170
SM3: Cheam 5E 164
Wickham Chase BR4: W W'ck 1F 171
Wickham Cl. E1 5J 85
EN3: Enf H 3C 24
KT3: N Mald 6B 152
Wickham Ct. KT5: Surb 5F 151
(off Cranes Pk.)
Wickham Ct. Rd. BR4: W W'ck 2E 170
Wickham Cres. BR4: W W'ck 2E 170
Wickham Gdns. SE4 3B 122
Wickham Ho. N1 1E 84
(off Halcomb St.)
Wickham La. DA16: Well 5A 108
SE2 5A 108
Wickham M. SE4 2B 122
Wickham Noakes Ct. BR3: Beck 1D 158
Wickham Rd. BR3: Beck 2D 158
CR0: C'don 2K 169
E4 7K 35
HA3: Hrw W 2H 41
SE4 4B 122
Wickham St. DA16: Well 2J 125
SE11 5G 19 (5K 101)

Wickham Theatre Cen. 2F 171
Wickham Way BR3: Beck 4E 158
Wick Ho. KT1: Hamp W 1D 150
(off Station Rd.)
Wick La. E3 . . . . .1C 86
Wickliffe Av. N3 . . . . .2G 45
Wickliffe Gdns. HA9: Wemb . . .2H 61
Wicklow Ho. N16 . . . . .1F 67
Wicklow St. WC1 . . . . .1G 7 (3K 83)
Wick Rd. E9 . . . . .6K 67
  TW11: Tedd 7B 132
Wicks Cl. SE9 . . . . .4B 142
Wicksteed Cl. DA5: Bexl 3K 145
Wicksteed Ho. SE1 . . . . . . .3C 102
  TW8: Bford 5F 97
Wickway Ct. SE15 . . . . .6F 103
(off Cator St.)
Wickwood St. SE5 . . . . .2B 120
Widdecombe Av. HA2: Harr . . .2C 58
Widdenham Rd. N7 . . . . . . .4K 65
Widdin St. E15 . . . . .7G 69
Widecombe Gdns. IG4: Ilf 4C 52
Widecombe Rd. SE9 . . . . . . .3C 142
Widecombe Way N2 . . . . . . .5B 46
Widegate St. E1 . . . . . .6H 9 (5E 84)
Widenham Cl. HA5: Eastc 5A 40
Wide Way CR4: Mitc 3H 155
Widewing Cl. TW11: Tedd 7B 132
Widford NW1 . . . . .6F 65
(off Lewis St.)
Widford Ho. N1 . . . . .2B 84
(off Colebrooke Rd.)
Widgeon Cl. E16 . . . . .6K 87
Widgeon Rd. TW6: H'row A . . .5C 174
Widley Rd. W9 . . . . .3J 81
Widmer Ct. TW3: Houn 2C 112
WIDMORE 3A 160
WIDMORE GREEN 2B 160
Widmore Lodge Rd. BR1: Brom . .2B 160
Widmore Rd. BR1: Brom 2J 159
  UB8: Hil 4D 74
Wigan Ho. E5 . . . . .1H 67
Wigeon Path SE28 . . . . .3H 107
Wigeon Way UB4: Yead 6B 76
Wiggins La. TW10: Ham 2C 132
Wiggins Mead NW9 . . . . . . .7G 29
Wigginton Av. HA9: Wemb 6H 61
Wight Ho. KT1: King T 3D 150
(off Portsmouth Rd.)
Wightman Rd. N4 . . . . .4A 48
  N8 . . . . .4A 48
Wighton M. TW7: Isle 2J 113
Wigley Rd. TW13: Felt 2B 130
Wigmore Hall 7J 5
Wigmore Pl. E17 . . . . .3A 50
  W1 . . . . .7J 5 (6F 83)
Wigmore Rd. SM5: Cars 2B 166
Wigmore St. W1 . . . . . . .7H 5 (6E 82)
Wigmore Wlk. SM5: Cars 2B 166
Wigram Ho. E14 . . . . .7D 86
(off Wade's Pl.)
Wigram Rd. E11 . . . . .6A 52
Wigram Sq. E17 . . . . .3E 50
Wigston Cl. N18 . . . . .5K 33
Wigston Rd. E13 . . . . .4K 87
Wigton Gdns. HA7: Stan 1E 42
Wigton Pl. SE11 . . . . . .6K 19 (5A 102)
Wigton Rd. E17 . . . . .1B 50
Wilberforce Ct. BR2: Kes 7B 172
  HA8: Edg 4A 28
(off King's Dr.)
Wilberforce M. SW4 . . . . .4H 119
Wilberforce Rd. N4 . . . . .2B 66
  NW9 . . . . .6C 44
Wilberforce Wlk. E15 . . . . . . .5G 69
Wilberforce Way SE25 . . . . . .4F 157
  SW19 . . . . .6F 135
Wilbraham Ho. SW8 . . . . . . .7J 101
(off Wandsworth Rd.)
Wilbraham Mans. SW1 . . . . . .3G 17
(off Wilbraham Pl.)

Wilbraham Pl. SW1 . . . . .3F 17 (4D 100)
Wilbrahams Almshouses
  EN5: Barn 2C 20
Wilbrooke Pl. SE3 . . . . .1K 123
Wilbury Way N18 . . . . .5J 33
Wilby M. W11 . . . . .1H 99
Wilcox Cl. SW8 . . . . .7J 101
(not continuous)
Wilcox Gdns. TW17: Shep 3A 146
Wilcox Ho. E3 . . . . .5B 86
(off Ackroyd Dr.)
Wilcox Pl. SW1 . . . . . . .2B 18 (3G 101)
Wilcox Rd. SM1: Sutt 4K 165
  SW8 . . . . .7J 101
  TW11: Tedd 4H 131
Wildberry Cl. W7 . . . . .4A 96
Wildbore Ho. N1 . . . . .7A 66
(off Liverpool Rd.)
Wildcat Rd. TW6: H'row A 6C 174
(off Wayfarer Rd.)
Wild Ct. WC2 . . . . .1G 13 (6K 83)
Wildcroft Gdns. HA8: Edg 6J 27
Wildcroft Mnr. SW15 . . . . . . .7E 116
Wildcroft Rd. SW15 . . . . .7E 116
Wilde Cl. E8 . . . . .1G 85
Wilde Ho. W2 . . . . .2A 10
(off Gloucester Ter.)
Wilde Pl. N13 . . . . .6G 33
  SW18 . . . . .7B 118
Wilder Cl. HA4: Ruis 1K 57
Wilderness, The
  KT8: W Mole, E Mos 5G 149
  TW12: Hamp H 4F 131
Wilderness Island Nature Reserve
  . . . . .4E 166
Wilderness M. SW4 . . . . .4G 119
Wilderness Rd. BR7: Chst 7F 143
Wilde Rd. DA8: Erith 7H 109
Wilderton Rd. N16 . . . . .7E 48
Wilder Wlk. W1 . . . . .3B 12
(off Glasshouse St.)
Wildfell Rd. SE6 . . . . .7D 122
Wild Goose Dr. SE14 . . . . . . .1J 121
Wild Hatch NW11 . . . . .6J 45
Wild's Rents SE1 . . . . . .7G 15 (3E 102)
Wild St. WC2 . . . . .1F 13 (6J 83)
Wildwood Cl. SE12 . . . . .7H 123
Wildwood Gro. NW3 . . . . . . .1A 64
Wildwood Ri. NW11 . . . . .1A 64
Wildwood Rd. NW11 . . . . . . .6K 45
Wildwood Ter. NW3 . . . . .1A 64
Wilford Cl. EN2: Enf 3J 23
Wilford Rd. CR0: C'don 6C 156
Wilfred Cl. N15 . . . . .5D 48
(off South Gro.)
Wilfred Owen Cl. SW19 . . . . . .6A 136
Wilfred St. SW1 . . . . . .1A 18 (3G 101)
Wilfred Wood Ct. W6 . . . . . . .4E 98
(off Samuel's Cl)
Wilkes Rd. TW8: Bford 6E 96
Wilkes St. E1 . . . . .5K 9 (5F 85)
Wilkie Ho. SW1 . . . . .5D 18
(off Cureton St.)
Wilkins Cl. CR4: Mitc 1C 154
  UB3: Harl 5H 93
Wilkins Ho. SW1 . . . . .7A 18
(off Churchill Gdns.)
Wilkinson Cl. UB10: Hil 1D 74
Wilkinson Cl. SW17 . . . . .4B 136
Wilkinson Gdns. SE25 . . . . . .1E 156
Wilkinson Ho. N1 . . . . .2D 84
(off Cranston Est.)
Wilkinson Rd. E16 . . . . .6A 88
Wilkinson St. SW8 . . . . .7K 101
Wilkinson Way W4 . . . . .2K 97
Wilkin St. NW5 . . . . .6E 64
Wilkin St. M. NW5 . . . . .6F 65
Wilks Gdns. CR0: C'don 1A 170
Wilks Pl. N1 . . . . .2E 84
Willan Rd. N17 . . . . .2D 48

Willard St. SW8 . . . . .3F 119
Willcocks Cl. KT9: Chess 3E 162
Willcott Rd. W3 . . . . .1H 97
Will Crooks Gdns. SE9 . . . . . .4A 124
Willen Fld. Rd. NW10 . . . . . . .2J 79
Willenhall Av. EN5: New Bar . . .6F 21
Willenhall Ct. EN5: New Bar . . .6F 21
Willenhall Dr. UB3: Hayes 7G 75
Willenhall Rd. SE18 . . . . .5F 107
Willersley Av. BR6: Orp 3H 173
  DA15: Sidc 1K 143
Willersley Cl. DA15: Sidc 1K 143
WILLESDEN 6C 62
Willesden Belle Vue Cinema . . .6D 62
(off High Rd.)
WILLESDEN GREEN 6E 62
Willesden La. NW2 . . . . .6E 62
  NW6 . . . . .6E 62
Willesden Section Ho. NW6 . . . .7F 63
(off Willesden La.)
Willesden Sports Cen. 1D 80
Willesden Sports Stadium 1D 80
Willes Rd. NW5 . . . . .6F 65
Willett Cl. BR5: Pet W 6J 161
  UB5: N'olt 3A 76
Willett Ho. E13 . . . . .2K 87
(off Queens Rd. W.)
Willett Pl. CR7: Thor H 5A 156
Willett Rd. CR7: Thor H 5A 156
Willett Way BR5: Pet W 5H 161
William IV St. WC2 . . . . .3E 12 (7J 83)
William Allen Ho. HA8: Edg 7A 28
William Ash Cl. RM9: Dag 6B 72
William Banfield Ho. SW6 . . . . .2H 117
(off Munster Rd.)
William Barefoot Dr. SE9 . . . . .4E 142
William Blake Ho. SW11 . . . . . .1C 118
William Bonney Est. SW4 . . . . .4H 119
William Booth Ho. E14 . . . . . . .6C 86
(off Hind Gro.)
William Booth Rd. SE20 . . . . .1G 157
William Carey Way HA1: Harr . . .6J 41
William Caslon Ho. E2 . . . . . . .2H 85
(off Patriot Sq.)
William Channing Ho. E2 . . . . .3H 85
(off Canrobert St.)
William Cl. N2 . . . . .2B 46
  RM5: Col R 1J 55
  SE13 . . . . .3E 122
  UB2: S'hall 2G 95
William Cobbett Ho. W8 . . . . . .3K 99
(off Scarsdale Pl.)
William Congreve M. N1 . . . . . .1C 84
William Cotton Ct. E14 . . . . . . .5C 86
(off Selsey St.)
William Ct. NW8 . . . . .3A 82
  SE10 . . . . .1D 122
(off Greenwich High Rd.)
  SE25 . . . . .3F 157
(off Chalfont Rd.)
  SW16 . . . . .7K 137
(off Streatham High Rd.)
  W5 . . . . .5C 78
William Covell Cl. EN2: Enf 1E 22
William Dr. HA7: Stan 6F 27
William Dromey Ct.
  NW6 . . . . .7H 63
William Dunbar Ho. NW6 . . . . .2H 81
(off Albert Rd.)
William Dyce M. SW16 . . . . . .4H 137
William Ellis Way SE16 . . . . . .3G 103
(off St James's Rd.)
William Evans Ho. SE8 . . . . . .4K 103
(off Haddonfield)
William Farm La. SW15 . . . . . .3D 116
William Fenn Ho. E2 . . . . .1K 9
(off Shipton Rd.)
William Foster La. DA16: Well . . .2A 126
William Fry Ho. E1 . . . . .6K 85
(off W. Arbour St.)
William Gdns. SW15 . . . . .5D 116

William Gibbs Ct. SW1 . . . . . .2C 18
(off Old Pye St.)
William Gunn Ho. NW3 . . . . . .5C 64
William Guy Gdns. E3 . . . . . . .3D 86
William Harvey Ho. SW19 . . . . .1G 135
(off Whitlock Dr.)
William Henry Wlk. SW8 . . . .7C 18 (6H 101)
William Hope Cl.
  IG11: Bark 2J 89
William Ho. BR1: Brom 3J 159
William Hunt Mans. SW13 . . . . .6E 98
William Margrie Cl. SE15 . . . . .2G 121
William Marshall Cl. E17 . . . . . .6A 50
William M. N1 . . . . .7E 66
  SW1 . . . . .7F 11 (2D 100)
William Morley Cl. E6 . . . . .1B 88
William Morris Cl. E17 . . . . . . .3B 50
William Morris Gallery 3C 50
William Morris Ho. W6 . . . . . . .6F 99
William Morris Way SW6 . . . . . .3A 118
William Owston Ct. E16 . . . . . .1C 106
(off Connaught Rd.)
William Perkin Ct. UB6: G'frd . . .6J 59
William Pike Ho. RM7: Rom 6K 55
(off Waterloo Gdns.)
William Pl. E3 . . . . .2B 86
William Rathbone Ho. E2 . . . . . .3H 85
(off Florida St.)
William Rd. NW1 . . . . . .2A 6 (3G 83)
  SM1: Sutt 5A 166
  SW19 . . . . .7G 135
William Rushbrooke Ho. SE16 . . .4G 103
(off Rouel Rd.)
Williams Av. E17 . . . . .1B 50
William Saville Ho. NW6 . . . . . .2H 81
(off Denmark Rd.)
William's Bldgs. E2 . . . . .4J 85
Williams Cl. N8 . . . . .6H 47
  SW6 . . . . .7G 99
Williams Dr. TW3: Houn 4E 112
Williams Gro. KT6: Surb 6C 150
  N22 . . . . .1A 48
Williams Ho. E3 . . . . .3C 86
(off Alfred St.)
  E9 . . . . .1H 85
(off King Edward's St.)
  NW2 . . . . .3E 62
(off Stoll Cl.)
  SW1 . . . . .4D 18
(off Montaigne Cl.)
Williams La. SM4: Mord 5A 154
  SW14 . . . . .3J 115
William Smith Ho. DA17: Belv . . .3G 109
(off Ambrooke Rd.)
  E3 . . . . .3C 86
(off Ireton St.)
Williamson Cl. SE10 . . . . .5H 105
Williamson Ct. SE17 . . . . .5C 102
Williamson Rd. N4 . . . . .6B 48
Williamson St. N7 . . . . .4J 65
William Sq. SE16 . . . . .7B 86
(off Sovereign Cres.)
Williams Ter. CR0: Wadd 6A 168
William St. E10 . . . . .6D 50
  IG11: Bark 7G 71
  N17 . . . . .7A 34
  SM5: Cars 3C 166
  SW1 . . . . .7F 11 (2D 100)
Williams Way DA2: Wilm 2K 145
  HA0: Wemb 5B 60
William Whiffin Sq. E3 . . . . . . .4B 86
William White Ct. E13 . . . . .1A 88
(off Green St.)
William Wood Ho. SE26 . . . . . .3J 139
(off Shrublands Cl.)
Willifield Way NW11 . . . . .4H 45
Willingale Cl. IG8: Wfd G 6F 37
Willingdon Rd. N22 . . . . .2B 48
Willingham Cl. NW5 . . . . .5G 65

Willingham Ter. NW5 . . . . .5G 65
Willingham Way
  KT1: King T 3G 151
Willington Cl. E5 . . . . .3A 68
Willington Rd. SW9 . . . . .3J 119
Willis Av. SM2: Sutt 6C 166
Willis Cl. BR4: W W'ck 2F 171
  CR7: Thor H 6A 156
Willis Ho. E14 .7D 86
                  (off Hale St.)
Willis Rd. CR0: C'don 7C 156
  DA8: Erith .4J 109
  E15 . . . . .2H 87
Willis St. E14 . . . . .6D 86
Willis Yd. N14 .7C 22
Will Miles Ct. SW19 . . . . .7A 136
Willmore End SW19 . . . . .1K 153
Willoughby Av. CR0: Bedd 4K 167
Willoughby Dr. RM13: Rain 7K 73
Willoughby Gro. N17 . . . . .7C 34
Willoughby Highwalk EC2 . . . . .6D 8
                  (off Moor La.)
Willoughby Ho. E1 . . . . .1H 103

              (off Reardon Path)
  EC2 . . . . .5E 8
Willoughby La. BR1: Brom 7K 141
  N17 . . . . .6C 34
  SW4 . . . . .4F 119
                (off Cedars M.)
Willoughby M. N17 . . . . .7C 34
Willoughby Pas. E14 . . . . .1C 104
              (off W. India Av.)
Willoughby Rd. KT2: King T 1F 151
  N8 . . . . .3A 48
  NW3 . . . . .4B 64
  TW1: Twick 5C 114
             (not continuous)
Willoughbys, The SW14 . . . . .3A 116
Willoughby St. WC1 . . . . .6E 6
Willoughby Way SE7 . . . . .4K 105
Willow Av. DA15: Sidc 6A 126
  SW13 . . . . .2B 116
  UB7: Yiew .7B 74
Willow Bank SW6 . . . . .3G 117
  TW10: Ham 3B 132
Willowbank KT7: T Ditt 1A 162
Willowbay Cl. EN5: Barn 6A 20
Willow Bri. Rd. N1 . . . . .6C 66
             (not continuous)
Willowbrook TW12: Hamp H 5F 131
Willowbrook Est. SE15 . . . . .7G 103
Willow Brook Rd. SE15 . . . . .7F 103
Willowbrook Rd.
  TW19: Stanw 2A 128
  UB2: S'hall 3E 94
Willow Bus. Pk. SE26 . . . . .3J 139
Willow Cl. BR2: Brom 5D 160
  DA5: Bexl 6F 127
  IG9: Buck H 3G 37
  SE6 . . . . .1H 141
  TW8: Bford 6C 96
Willow Cotts. TW9: Kew 6G 97
  TW13: Hanw 3C 130
Willow Ct. E11 . . . . .2G 69
              (off Trinity Cl.)
  EC2 . . . . .3G 9 (4E 84)
  HA3: Hrw W 1K 41
  HA8: Edg 4K 27
  N12 . . . . .4E 30
  NW6 . . . . .7G 63
  SM6: Wall .7F 167
              (off Willow Rd.)
  TW16: Sun 7G 129
           (off Staines Rd. W.)
  W4 . . . . .7A 98
          (off Corney Reach Way)
  W9 . . . . .5J 81
             (off Admiral Wlk.)
Willowcourt Av. HA3: Kenton 5B 42

Willow Dene HA5: Pinn 2B 40
  WD23: B Hea 1D 26
Willowdene N6 .7D 46
  SE15 . . . . .7H 103
Willowdene Cl.
  TW2: Whitt 7G 113
Willowdene Ct. N20 . . . . .7F 21
         (off High Rd. Whetstone)
Willow Dr. EN5: Barn 4B 20
Willow End KT6: Surb 1E 162
  N20 . . . . .2D 30
Willowfields Cl. SE18 . . . . .5J 107
Willow Gdns.
  HA4: Ruis .2H 57
  TW3: Houn 1E 112
Willow Grange
  DA14: Sidc 3B 144
Willow Grn. NW9 . . . . .1A 44
Willow Gro. BR7: Chst 6E 142
  E13 . . . . .2J 87
  HA4: Ruis .2H 57
Willowhayne Cl. KT12: Walt T 7K 147
           (off Willowhayne Dr.)
Willowhayne Dr. KT12: Walt T 7K 147
Willowhayne Gdns.
  KT4: Wor Pk 3E 164
Willow Ho. BR2: Brom 2G 159
  SE1 . . . . .4F 103
             (off Curtis St.)
  SE4 . . . . .3A 122
           (off Dragonfly Pl.)
  W10 . . . . .4F 81
            (off Maple Wlk.)
Willow La. CR4: Mitc 5D 154
  SE18 . . . . .4D 106
Willow La. Bus. Pk.
  CR4: Mitc .6D 154
Willow La. Ind. Est.
  CR4: Mitc .6D 154
Willow Lodge RM7: Rom 5K 55
  SW6 . . . . .1F 117
  TW16: Sun 7H 129
          (off Grangewood Dr.)
Willowmead Cl. W5 . . . . .4D 78
Willow Mt. CR0: C'don 3E 168
Willow Pl. SW1 . . . . .3B 18 (4G 101)
Willow Rd. EN1: Enf 3K 23
  KT3: N Mald 4J 151
  NW3 . . . . .4B 64
  RM6: Chad H 6E 54
  SL3: Poyle 5A 174
  SM6: Wall .7F 167
  W5 . . . . .2E 96
Willows, The BR3: Beck 1C 158
  E6 . . . . .7D 70
  SE1 . . . . .4E 102
Willows Av. SM4: Mord 5K 153
Willows Cl. HA5: Pinn 2A 40
Willowside Cl. EN2: Enf 3G 23
Willows Ter. NW10 . . . . .2B 80
           (off Rucklidge Av.)
Willow St. E4 .1A 36
  EC2 . . . . .3G 9 (4E 84)
  RM7: Rom .4J 55
Willow Tree Cen. 5D 38
Willow Tree Cl. E3 . . . . .1B 86
  SW18 . . . . .1K 135
  UB4: Yead .4A 76
  UB5: N'olt .6D 58
Willowtree Cl. UB10: Ick 3E 56
Willow Tree Ct. DA14: Sidc 5A 144
  HA0: Wemb 5D 60
Willow Tree La. UB4: Yead 4A 76
WILLOW TREE RDBT. 5B 76
Willow Tree Wlk.
  BR1: Brom 1K 159
Willowtree Way
  CR7: Thor H 1A 156
Willow Va. BR7: Chst 6F 143
  W12 . . . . .1C 98
Willow Vw. SW19 . . . . .1B 154

Willow Wlk.
  BR6: Farnb 3F 173
  E17 . . . . .5B 50
  IG1: Ilf 2F 71
  N1 . . . . .2B 84
  N2 . . . . .2B 46
  N15 . . . . .4B 48
  N21 . . . . .6E 22
  SE1 . . . . .3E 102
  SM3: Sutt .3H 165
Willow Way HA0: Wemb 3A 60
  KT19: Ewe 6K 163
  N3 . . . . .7E 30
  SE26 . . . . .3J 139
  TW2: Twick 2F 131
  TW16: Sun 4J 147
  W11 . . . . .7F 81
Willow Wood Cres. SE25 . . . . .6E 156
Willow Wren Wharf UB2: S'hall 4K 93
Willrose Cres. SE2 . . . . .5B 108
Willsbridge Ct. SE15 . . . . .6F 103
Wills Cres. TW3: Houn 6F 113
Wills Gro. NW7 . . . . .5H 29
Will Wyatt Ct. N1 . . . . .2E 84
              (off Pitfield St.)
Wilman Gro. E8 . . . . .7G 67
Wilmar Cl. UB4: Hayes 4F 75
Wilmar Gdns. BR4: W W'ck 1D 170
Wilmcote Ho. W2 . . . . .5K 81
          (off Woodchester Sq.)
Wilment Ct. NW2 . . . . .3E 62
Wilmer Cl. KT2: King T 5F 133
Wilmer Cres. KT2: King T 5F 133
Wilmer Gdns. N1 . . . . .1E 84
             (not continuous)
Wilmer Ho. E3 . . . . .2A 86
             (off Daling Way)
Wilmer Lea Cl. E15 . . . . .7F 69
Wilmer Pl. N16 . . . . .2F 67
Wilmers Ct. NW10 . . . . .1K 79
            (off Lawrence Av.)
Wilmer Way N14 . . . . .5C 32
Wilmington Av. W4 . . . . .7K 97
Wilmington Ct. SW16 . . . . .7J 137
Wilmington Gdns. IG11: Bark 6H 71
Wilmington Sq. WC1 . . . . .2J 7 (3A 84)
             (not continuous)
Wilmington St. WC1 . . . . .2J 7 (3A 84)
Wilmington Ter. SE16 . . . . .4H 103
             (off Camilla Rd.)
Wilmot Cl. N2 . . . . .2A 46
  SE15 . . . . .7G 103
Wilmot Ho. SE11 . . . . .4B 102
          (off George Mathers Rd.)
Wilmot Pl. NW1 . . . . .7G 65
             (not continuous)
  W7 . . . . .1J 95
Wilmot Rd. E10 . . . . .2D 68
  N17 . . . . .3D 48
  SM5: Cars 5D 166
Wilmot St. E2 .4H 85
Wilmount St. SE18 . . . . .4F 107
Wilna Rd. SW18 . . . . .7A 118
Wilsham St. W11 . . . . .1F 99
Wilshaw Cl. NW4 . . . . .3C 44
Wilshaw Ho. SE8 . . . . .7C 104
Wilshaw St. SE14 . . . . .1C 122
Wilsmere Dr. HA3: Hrw W 7D 26
  UB5: N'olt .6C 58
Wilson Av. CR4: Mitc 7C 136
Wilson Cl. CR2: S Croy 5D 168
  HA9: Wemb 7F 43
Wilson Cl. NW9 . . . . .2K 43
  RM7: Rush G 6K 55
              (off Union Rd.)
  SE28 . . . . .3G 107
Wilson Dr. HA9: Wemb 7F 43
Wilson Gdns. HA1: Harr 7G 41
Wilson Gro. SE16 . . . . .2H 103
Wilson Ho. NW6 . . . . .7A 64
            (off Goldhurst Ter.)

Wilson Rd. E6 .3B 88
  IG1: Ilf 7D 52
  KT9: Chess 6F 163
  SE5 . . . . .1E 120
Wilson's Av. N17 . . . . .2F 49
Wilson's Rd. W6 . . . . .5F 99
Wilson St. E17 .5B 50
  EC2 . . . . .5F 9 (5D 84)
  N21 . . . . .7F 23
Wilson Wlk. W4 . . . . .4B 98
            (off Prebend Gdns.)
Wilstone Cl. UB4: Yead 4C 76
Wiltern Ct. NW2 . . . . .6G 63
Wilthorne Gdns. RM10: Dag 7H 73
Wilton Av. W4 .5A 98
Wilton Cl. UB7: Harm 2E 174
Wilton Cl. E1 . . . . .6H 85
              (off Cavell St.)
Wilton Cres. SW1 . . . . .7G 11 (2E 100)
  SW19 . . . . .1H 153
Wilton Dr. RM5: Col R 1J 55
Wilton Est. E8 .6G 67
Wilton Gdns.
  KT8: W Mole 3E 148
Wilton Gro. KT3: N Mald 6B 152
  SW19 . . . . .1H 153
Wilton Ho. CR2: S Croy 5C 168
          (off Nottingham Rd.)
Wilton M. E8 . . . . .6H 67
  SW1 . . . . .1H 17 (3E 100)
Wilton Pde. TW13: Felt 2J 129
Wilton Pl. E4 . . . . .6A 36
  HA1: Harr 6K 41
  SW1 . . . . .7G 11 (2E 100)
Wilton Plaza SW1 . . . . .3A 18
             (off Wilton Rd.)
Wilton Rd. EN4: Cockf 4J 21
  N10 . . . . .2E 46
  SE2 . . . . .4C 108
  SW1 . . . . .2K 17 (3F 101)
  SW19 . . . . .7C 136
  TW4: Houn 3B 112
Wilton Row SW1 . . . . .7G 11 (2E 100)
Wiltons Music Hall 7G 85
             (off Graces All.)
Wilton Sq. N1 .1D 84
Wilton St. SW1 . . . . .1J 17 (3F 101)
Wilton Ter. SW1 . . . . .1G 17 (3E 100)
Wilton Vs. N1 . . . . .1D 84
             (off Wilton Sq.)
Wilton Way E8 .6G 67
Wiltshire Cl. NW7 . . . . .5G 29
  SW3 . . . . .3E 16 (4D 100)
Wiltshire Ct. CR2: S Croy 5C 168
  IG1: Ilf 6G 71
  N4 . . . . .1B 66
            (off Marquis Rd.)
Wiltshire Gdns. N4 . . . . .6C 48
  TW2: Twick 1G 131
Wiltshire La. HA5: Eastc 3H 39
Wiltshire Rd. BR6: Orp 7K 161
  CR7: Thor H 3A 156
  SW9 . . . . .3A 120
Wiltshire Row N1 . . . . .1D 84
Wilverley Cres. KT3: N Mald 6A 152
Wimbart Rd. SW2 . . . . .7K 119
WIMBLEDON .6G 135
Wimbledon All England Lawn Tennis
    & Croquet Club 4G 135
Wimbledon Bri. SW19 . . . . .6H 135
Wimbledon Cl. SW20 . . . . .7F 135
Wimbledon Common 4C 134
Wimbledon Common Golf Course 5D 134
Wimbledon Hill Rd. SW19 . . . . .6G 135
Wimbledon Lawn Tennis Mus. 3G 135
Wimbledon Leisure Cen. 6K 135
Wimbledon Museum of Local History

                             .6G 135
WIMBLEDON PARK 3J 135
Wimbledon Pk. Athletics Track 2K 135
Wimbledon Pk. Ct. SW19 . . . . .1H 135

Wimbledon Pk. Golf Course 3H 135
Wimbledon Pk. Rd. SW18 . . . . .2G **135**
         SW19 . . . . .2G **135**
Wimbledon Pk. Side SW19 . . . . .3F **135**
Wimbledon Pk. Watersports Cen. . . .2H 135
Wimbledon Pk. Women's Fitness Suite
Wimbledon Rd. SW17 . . . . .4A 136
Wimbledon Stadium Bus. Cen.
         SW17 . . . . .3K **135**
Wimbledon Stadium (Greyhound) . . .4A 136
Wimbledon Theatre 7J 135
Wimbledon Windmill Mus. 2D 134
Wimbolt St. E2 . . . . .3G 85
Wimborne Av. BR5: St P 4K **161**
         BR7: Chst 4K **161**
         UB2: S'hall 4E 94
         UB4: Yead 6K 75
Wimborne Cl. IG9: Buck H 2E 36
         KT4: Wor Pk 1E **164**
         SE12 . . . . .5H **123**
Wimborne Ct. SW12 . . . . .3G **137**
         UB5: N'olt 6E 58
Wimborne Dr. HA5: Pinn 7B 40
         NW9 . . . . .3G 43
Wimborne Gdns. W13 . . . . .5B 78
Wimborne Ho. E16 . . . . .7H 87
         (off Victoria Dock Rd.)
         NW1 . . . . .4D **4**
         (off Harewood Av.)
         SW8 . . . . .7K **101**
         (off Dorset Rd.)
         SW12 . . . . .3G **137**
Wimborne Rd. N9 . . . . .2B 34
         N17 . . . . .2E 48
Wimborne Way BR3: Beck 3K 157
Wimbourne Ct. N1 . . . . .2D **84**
         (off Wimbourne St.)
Wimbourne St. N1 . . . . .2D 84
Wimpole Cl. BR2: Brom 4A 160
         KT1: King T 2F 151
Wimpole M. W1 . . . . .5J 5 (5F **83**)
Wimpole Rd. UB7: Yiew 1A 92
Wimpole St. W1 . . . . . . .6J 5 (5F **83**)
Wimshurst Cl. CR0: Wadd 1J 167
Winans Wlk. SW9 . . . . .2A 120
Winant Ho. E14 . . . . .7D **86**
         (off Simpson's Rd.)
Wincanton Ct. N11 . . . . .6K **31**
         (off Martock Gdns.)
Wincanton Cres. UB5: N'olt 5E 58
Wincanton Gdns. IG6: Ilf 3F 53
Wincanton Rd. SW18 . . . . .7H 117
Winchcombe Rd.
         SM5: Cars 7B 154
Winchcomb Gdns. SE9 . . . . .3B 124
Winchelsea Av. DA7: Bex 7F 109
Winchelsea Cl. SW15 . . . . .5F 117
Winchelsea Ho. SE16 . . . . .2J **103**
         (off Swan Rd.)
Winchelsea Rd. E7 . . . . .3J 69
         N17 . . . . .3E 48
         NW10 . . . . .1K 79
Winchelsey Ri.
         CR2: S Croy 6F 169
Winchendon Rd. SW6 . . . . .1H 117
         TW11: Tedd 4H 131
Winchester Av. NW6 . . . . .1G 81
         NW9 . . . . .3G 43
         TW5: Hest 6D 94
Winchester Bldgs. SE1 . . . . .6C **14**
         (off Copperfield St.)
Winchester Cl. BR2: Brom 3H 159
         E6 . . . . .6D 88
         EN1: Enf 5K 23
         KT2: King T 7H 133
         SE17 . . . . .4B 102
         SL3: Poyle 4A 174
Winchester Ct. W8 . . . . .2J **99**
         (off Vicarage Ga.)
Winchester Dr. HA5: Pinn 5B 40

Winchester Ho. E3 . . . . .3B **86**
         (off Hamlets Way)
         E14 . . . . .6C **86**
         (off New Festival Av.)
         IG11: Bark 7A **72**
         (off Margaret Bondfield Av.)
         SE18 . . . . .7B **106**
         (off Portway Gdns.)
         SW3 . . . . .7B 16
         SW9 . . . . .7A 102
         W2 . . . . .6A **82**
         (off Hallfield Est.)
Winchester M. KT4: Wor Pk 2F 165
         NW3 . . . . .7B **64**
         (off Winchester Rd.)
Winchester Palace 4E 14
         (off Stoney St.)
Winchester Pk. BR2: Brom 3H 159
Winchester Pl. E8 . . . . .5F 67
         N6 . . . . .1F 65
Winchester Rd. BR2: Brom 3H 159
         DA7: Bex 2D 126
         E4 . . . . .7K 35
         HA3: Kenton 4E 42
         HA6: Nwood 2H 39
         IG1: Ilf 3H 71
         KT12: Walt T 7J 147
         N6 . . . . .7F 47
         N9 . . . . .1A 34
         NW3 . . . . .7B 64
         TW1: Twick 6B 114
         TW13: Hanw 3D 130
         UB3: Harl 7G 93
Winchester Sq. SE1 . . . . .4E 14
Winchester St. SW1 . . . . .5K 17 (5F **101**)
         W3 . . . . .1J 97
Winchester Wlk. SE1 . . . .4E 14 (1D **102**)
         SW15 . . . . .5H **117**
         (off Up. Richmond Rd.)
Winchester Wharf SE1 . . . . .4E **14**
         (off Clink St.)
Winchet Wlk. CR0: C'don 6J 157
Winchfield Cl. HA3: Kenton 6C 42
Winchfield Ho. SW15 . . . . .6B 116
Winchfield Rd. SE26 . . . . .5A 140
Winch Ho. E14 . . . . .3D **104**
         (off Tiller Rd.)
         SW10 . . . . .7A **100**
         (off King's Rd.)
Winchilsea Cres. KT8: W Mole 2G 149
Winchilsea Ho. NW8 . . . . .2B **4**
         (off St John's Wood Rd.)
WINCHMORE HILL 7F 23
Winchmore Hill Rd. N14 . . . . .1C 32
         N21 . . . . .1C 32
Winchmore Vs. N21 . . . . .7E **22**
         (off Winchmore Hill Rd.)
Winchstone Cl. TW17: Shep 4B 146
Winckley Cl. HA3: Kenton 5F 43
Winckworth Ct. N1 . . . . .2F **9**
         (off Charles Sq. Est.)
Wincott Pde. SE11 . . . . .3K **19**
         (off Wincott St.)
Wincott St. SE11 . . . . . .4K 19 (4A **102**)
Wincrofts Dr. SE9 . . . . .4H 125
Windall Cl. SE19 . . . . .1G 157
Windborough Rd. SM5: Cars 7E 166
Windermere NW1 . . . . .2K **5**
         (off Albany St.)
Windermere Av. HA4: Ruis 7A 40
         HA9: Kenton, Wemb 7C 42
         N3 . . . . .3J 45
         NW6 . . . . .1G 81
         SW19 . . . . .3K 153
Windermere Cl. BR6: Farnb 3F 173
         TW14: Felt 1H 129
         TW19: Stanw 1A 128
Windermere Ct. HA9: Wemb 7C 42
         SM5: Cars 3E 166
         SW13 . . . . .6B 98
Windermere Gdns. IG4: Ilf 5C 52

Windermere Gro. HA9: Wemb 1C 60
Windermere Hall HA8: Edg 5A 28
Windermere Ho. E3 . . . . .4B 86
         EN5: New Bar 4E 20
         TW7: Isle 5K 113
Windermere Point SE15 . . . . .7J **103**
         (off Old Kent Rd.)
Windermere Rd. BR4: W W'ck 2G 171
         CR0: C'don 1F 169
         DA7: Bex 2J 127
         N10 . . . . .1F 47
         N19 . . . . .2G 65
         SW15 . . . . .4A 134
         SW16 . . . . .1G 155
         UB1: S'hall 5D 76
         W5 . . . . .3C 96
Windermere Way UB7: Yiew 1A 92
Winders Rd. SW11 . . . . .2C 118
         (not continuous)
Windfield Cl. SE26 . . . . .4K 139
Windham Rd. TW9: Rich 3F 115
Winding Way RM8: Dag 3C 72
Windlass Pl. SE8 . . . . .4A 104
Windlesham Gro. SW19 . . . . .1F 135
Windlesham M.
         TW12: Hamp H 6G 131
Windley Cl. SE23 . . . . .2J 139
Windmill WC1 . . . . .5G **7**
         (off New North St.)
Windmill Av. UB2: S'hall 1G 95
Windmill Bri. Ho. CR0: C'don 1E **168**
         (off Freemasons Rd.)
Windmill Bus. Village
         TW16: Sun 1G 147
Windmill Cl. KT6: Surb 1C 162
         SE1 . . . . .4G **103**
         (off Beatrice Rd.)
         SE13 . . . . .2E 122
         TW16: Sun 7G 129
Windmill Ct. E4 . . . . .2B 36
         HA4: Ruis 1J 57
         NW2 . . . . .6G 63
         W5 . . . . .4C **96**
         (off Windmill Rd.)
Windmill Dr. BR2: Kes 4A 172
         NW2 . . . . .3G 63
         SW4 . . . . .5F 119
Windmill Gdns. EN2: Enf 3F 23
Windmill Grn. TW17: Shep 7G 147
Windmill Gro. CR0: C'don 6C 156
Windmill Hill EN2: Enf 3G 23
         HA4: Ruis 7H 39
         NW3 . . . . .3A 64
Windmill Ho. E14 . . . . .4C 104
         SE1 . . . . .5K **13**
         (off Windmill Wlk.)
Windmill La. E15 . . . . .6F 69
         KT6: Surb 6B 150
         TW7: Isle 3G 95
         UB2: S'hall 1G 95
         UB6: G'frd 6G 77
         WD23: B Hea 1D 26
Windmill M. W4 . . . . .4A 98
Windmill Pas. W4 . . . . .4A 98
Windmill Pl. UB2: S'hall 1G 95
Windmill Ri. KT2: King T 7H 133
Windmill Rd. CR0: C'don 7C 156
         CR4: Mitc 5G 155
         N18 . . . . .4J 33
         SW18 . . . . .6B 118
         SW19 . . . . .2D 134
         TW8: Bford 4C 96
         TW12: Hamp H 5F 131
         TW16: Sun 1G 147
         W4 . . . . .4A 98
         W5 . . . . .4C 96
Windmill Rd. W. TW16: Sun 1G 147
Windmill Row SE11 . . . . .6J 19 (5A **102**)
Windmill St. W1 . . . . . . .6C 6 (5H **83**)
         (not continuous)
         WD23: B Hea 1D 26

Windmill Ter. TW17: Shep 7G 147
Windmill Wlk. SE1 . . . . .5K 13 (1A **102**)
Windmore Cl. HA0: Wemb 5A 60
Windover Way HA4: Ruis 1H 57
Windrose Cl. SE16 . . . . .2K 103
Windrush KT3: N Mald 4H 151
         SE28 . . . . .1B 108
Windrush Cl. E8 . . . . .7G 67
         N17 . . . . .1E 48
         SW11 . . . . .4B 118
         UB10: Ick 4B 56
         W4 . . . . .1J 115
Windrush Ho. NW8 . . . . .5B **4**
         (off Church St.)
Windrush La. SE23 . . . . .3K 139
Windrush Rd. NW10 . . . . .1K 79
Windrush Sq. SW2 . . . . .4A 120
Windsock Cl. SE16 . . . . .4B 104
Windsock Way TW6: H'row A 5C 174
Windsor Av. E17 . . . . .2A 50
         HA8: Edg 4C 28
         KT3: N Mald 5J 151
         KT8: W Mole 3E 148
         SM3: Cheam 3G 165
         SW19 . . . . .1A 154
         UB10: Hil 1D 74
Windsor Centre, The N1 . . . . .1B **84**
         (off Windsor St.)
Windsor Cl. BR7: Chst 5F 143
         HA2: Harr 3E 58
         HA6: Nwood 2J 39
         N3 . . . . .2G 45
         SE27 . . . . .4C 138
         TW6: H'row A 6D **174**
         (off Whittle Rd.)
         TW8: Bford 6B 96
Windsor Cotts. SE14 . . . . .7B **104**
         (off Amersham Gro.)
Windsor Ct. E3 . . . . .2C **86**
         (off Mostyn Gro.)
         HA5: Pinn 3B 40
         KT1: King T 4D **150**
         (off Palace Rd.)
         N11 . . . . .5J 31
         N14 . . . . .7B 22
         NW3 . . . . .4J 63
         NW11 . . . . .6G **45**
         (off Golders Grn. Rd.)
         SE16 . . . . .7K **85**
         (off King & Queen Wharf)
         SW3 . . . . .5D **16**
         (off Jubilee Pl.)
         SW11 . . . . .2B 118
         TW16: Sun 7J 129
         W2 . . . . .7K **81**
         (off Moscow Rd.)
         W10 . . . . .6F **81**
         (off Bramley Rd.)
         WD23: Bush 1B **26**
         (off Catsey La.)
Windsor Cres. HA2: Harr 3E 58
         HA9: Wemb 3H 61
Windsor Dr. BR6: Chels 6K 173
         EN4: E Barn 6J 21
Windsor Gdns. CR0: Bedd 3J 167
         UB3: Harl 3F 93
         W9 . . . . .5J 81
Windsor Gro. SE27 . . . . .4C 138
Windsor Hall E16 . . . . .1K **105**
         (off Wesley Av.)
Windsor Ho. E2 . . . . .3K **85**
         (off Knottisford St.)
         N1 . . . . .2C 84
         NW1 . . . . .1K 5
         NW2 . . . . .6G **63**
         (off Chatsworth Rd.)
         UB5: N'olt 6E **58**
         (off The Farmlands)
Windsor M. SE6 . . . . .1E 140
         SE23 . . . . .1A 140
Windsor Pk. Rd. UB3: Harl 7H 93

Windsor Pl. SW1 ....3B 18 (3G 101)
Windsor Rd. CR7: Thor H 2B 156
  DA6: Bex 4E 126
  E4 ....4J 35
  E7 ....5K 69
  E10 ....2D 68
  E11 ....1J 69
  EN5: Barn 6A 20
  HA3: Hrw W 1G 41
  IG1: Ilf 4F 71
  KT2: King T 7E 132
  KT4: Wor Pk 2C 164
  N3 ....2G 45
  N7 ....3J 65
  N13 ....3F 33
  N17 ....2G 49
  NW2 ....6D 62
  RM8: Dag 3E 72
  TW4: Cran 2K 111
  TW9: Kew 2F 115
  TW11: Tedd 5H 131
  TW16: Sun 6J 129
  UB2: S'hall 3D 94
  W5 ....7E 78
  (not continuous)
Windsors, The IG9: Buck H 2H 37
Windsor St. N1 ....1B 84
Windsor Ter. N1 ....1D 8 (3C 84)
Windsor Wlk. SE5 ....2D 120
Windsor Way W14 ....4F 99
Windsor Wharf E9 ....5B 68
Windspoint Dr. SE15 ....6H 103
Windus Rd. N16 ....1F 67
Windus Wlk. N16 ....1F 67
Windward Ct. E16 ....7F 89
  (off Gallions Rd.)
Windy Ridge BR1: Brom 1C 160
Windy Ridge Cl. SW19 ....5F 135
Wine Cl. E1 ....1J 103
  (not continuous)
Wine Office Ct. EC4 ....7K 7 (6A 84)
Winery La. KT1: King T 3F 151
Winey Cl. KT9: Chess 7C 162
Winford Ct. SE15 ....1H 121
Winford Ho. E3 ....7B 68
Winford Pde. UB1: S'hall 6F 77
  (off Marconi Way)
Winforton St. SE10 ....1E 122
Winfrith Rd. SW18 ....7A 118
Wingate & Finchley FC
  Harry Abrahams Stadium ...7G 31
Wingate Cres. CR0: C'don 6J 155
Wingate Ho. E3 ....3D 86
  (off Bruce Rd.)
Wingate Rd. DA14: Sidc 6C 144
  IG1: Ilf 5F 71
  W6 ....3D 98
Wingate Sq. SW4 ....3G 119
Wingfield Ct. DA15: Sidc 2K 143
  E14 ....7F 87
  (off Newport Av.)
Wingfield Ho. E2 ....2J 9
  (off Virginia Rd.)
Wingfield M. SE15 ....3G 121
Wingfield Rd. E15 ....4G 69
  E17 ....5D 50
  KT2: King T 6F 133
Wingfield St. SE15 ....3G 121
Wingfield Way
  HA4: Ruis 5K 57
Wingford Rd. SW2 ....6J 119
Wingmore Rd. SE24 ....3C 120
Wingrad Ho. E1 ....5J 85
  (off Jubilee St.)
Wingrave Rd. W6 ....6E 98
Wingreen NW8 ....1K 81
  (off Abbey Rd.)
Wingrove E4 ....7H 25
Wingrove Ct. RM7: Rom 5J 55
Wingrove Rd. SE6 ....2G 141
Wings Cl. SM1: Sutt 4J 165

Wings Rd. TW6: H'row A 6C 174
  (off Whittle Rd.)
Wing Yip Bus. Cen. NW2 ....2D 62
Winicotte Ho. W2 ....5B 4
  (off Paddington Grn.)
Winifred Pl. N12 ....5F 31
Winifred Rd. DA8: Erith 5K 109
  RM8: Dag 2E 72
  SW19 ....1J 153
  TW12: Hamp H 4E 130
Winifred St. E16 ....1D 106
Winifred Ter. EN1: Enf 7A 24
Winkfield Rd. E13 ....2K 87
  N22 ....1A 48
Winkley Ct. HA2: Harr 3E 58
  N10 ....4F 47
  (off St James's La.)
Winkley St. E2 ....2H 85
Winkworth Cotts. E1 ....4J 85
  (off Cephas St.)
Winlaton Rd. BR1: Brom 4F 141
Winmill Rd. RM8: Dag 3F 73
Winnepeg Ho. SE16 ....2J 103
  (off Province Dr.)
Winnett St. W1 ....2C 12 (7H 83)
Winningales Ct. IG5: Ilf 2C 52
Winnings Wlk. UB5: N'olt 6C 58
Winnington Cl. N2 ....6B 46
Winnington Ho. SE5 ....7C 102
  (off Wyndham Est.)
  W10 ....4G 81
  (off Southern Row)
Winnington Rd. N2 ....6B 46
Winnipeg Dr. BR6: Chels 6K 173
Winnock Rd. UB7: View 1A 92
Winn Rd. SE12 ....1J 141
Winns Av. E17 ....3B 50
Winns Comn. Rd. SE18 ....6J 107
Winns M. N15 ....4E 48
Winns Ter. E17 ....3C 50
Winsbeach E17 ....2F 51
Winscombe Cres. W5 ....4D 78
Winscombe St. N19 ....2F 65
Winscombe Way HA7: Stan 5F 27
Winsford Rd. SE6 ....3B 140
Winsford Ter. N18 ....5J 33
Winsham Gro. SW11 ....5E 118
Winsham Ho. NW1 ....1D 6
  (off Churchway)
Winslade Rd. SW2 ....5J 119
Winslade Way SE6 ....7D 122
Winsland M. W2 ....7A 4 (6B 82)
Winsland St. W2 ....7A 4 (6B 82)
Winsley St. W1 ....7B 6 (6G 83)
Winslow SE17 ....5E 102
Winslow Cl. HA5: Eastc 6K 39
  NW10 ....3A 62
Winslow Gro. E4 ....2B 36
Winslow Rd. W6 ....6E 98
Winslow Way TW13: Hanw 3B 130
Winsmoor Ct. EN2: Enf 3G 23
WINSOR PARK 5F 89
Winsor Ter. E6 ....5E 88
Winstanley Est. SW11 ....3B 118
Winstanley Rd. SW11 ....3B 118
  (not continuous)
Winstead Gdns. RM10: Dag 5J 73
Winston Av. NW9 ....7A 44
Winston Cl. HA3: Hrw W 6E 26
  RM7: Mawney 4H 55
Winston Ct. BR1: Brom 1K 159
  (off Widmore Rd.)
  HA3: Hrw W 7A 26
Winston Ho. W13 ....2A 96
  (off Balfour Rd.)
  WC1 ....3D 6
Winston Rd. N16 ....4D 66
Winston Wlk. W4 ....3K 97
Winston Way IG1: Ilf 3F 71
Winter Av. E6 ....1C 88
Winterborne Av. BR6: Orp 3H 173

Winterbourne Ho. W11 ....7G 81
  (off Portland Rd.)
Winterbourne Rd. CR7: Thor H 4A 156
  RM8: Dag 2C 72
  SE6 ....1B 140
Winter Box Wlk. TW10: Rich 5F 115
Winterbrook Rd. SE24 ....6C 120
Winterburn Cl. N11 ....6K 31
Winterfold Cl. SW19 ....2G 135
Winter Gdns. TW11: Tedd 4A 132
Wintergreen Blvd. UB7: W Dray 2B 92
Wintergreen Cl. E6 ....5C 88
Winterleys NW6 ....2H 81
  (off Denmark Rd.)
Winter Lodge SE16 ....5G 103
  (off Fern Wlk.)
Winter's Ct. E4 ....3J 35
Winterslow Ho. SE5 ....2C 120
  (off Flaxman Rd.)
Winterstoke Rd. SW9 ....1B 120
Winterstoke Gdns. NW7 ....5H 29
Winterstoke Rd. SE6 ....1B 140
Winterton Cl. KT1: Hamp W 1D 150
  (off Lwr. Teddington Rd.)
  SE20 ....2G 157
Winterton Ho. E1 ....6J 85
  (off Deancross St.)
Winterton Pl. SW10 ....7A 16 (6A 100)
Winterwell Rd. SW2 ....5J 119
Winthorpe Rd. SW15 ....4G 117
Winthrop Ho. W12 ....7D 80
  (off White City Est.)
Winthrop St. E1 ....5H 85
Winthrop Wlk. HA9: Wemb 3E 60
  (off Everard Way)
Winton Av. N11 ....7B 32
Winton Cl. N9 ....7E 24
Winton Cl. N1 ....2K 83
  (off Calshot St.)
Winton Gdns. HA8: Edg 7A 28
Winton Rd. BR6: Farnb 4F 173
Winton Way SW16 ....5A 138
Wireworks Ct. SE1 ....7C 14
  (off Gt. Suffolk St.)
Wirrall Ho. SE26 ....3G 139
Wirral Wood Cl. BR7: Chst 6E 142
Wirra Rd. TW6: H'row A 5C 174
  (off Wayfarer Rd.)
Wisbeach Rd. CR0: C'don 5D 156
Wisbech N4 ....1K 65
  (off Lorne Rd.)
Wisborough Rd. CR2: Sande 7F 169
Wisden Ho. SW8 ....7H 19 (6K 101)
Wisdom Ct. TW7: Isle 3A 114
  (off South St.)
Wisdons Cl. RM10: Dag 1H 73
Wise La. NW7 ....5H 29
  UB7: W Dray 4A 92
Wiseman Rd. E10 ....2C 68
Wise Rd. E15 ....1F 87
Wiseton Rd. SW17 ....1C 136
Wishart Rd. SE3 ....2B 124
Wishaw Wlk. N13 ....6D 32
Wisley Ho. SW1 ....5C 18
  (off Rampayne St.)
Wisley Rd. BR5: St P 7A 144
  SW11 ....5E 118
Wistaria Cl. BR6: Farnb 2F 173
Wisteria Apartments E9 ....6J 67
  (off Chatham Pl.)
Wisteria Cl. IG1: Ilf 5F 71
  NW7 ....6G 29
Wisteria Gdns. IG8: Wfd G 5D 36
Wisteria Rd. SE13 ....4F 123
Wistow Ho. E2 ....1G 85
  (off Whiston Rd.)
Witanhurst La. N6 ....1E 64
Witan St. E2 ....3H 85
Witchwood Ho. SW9 ....3A 120
  (off Gresham Rd.)

Witham Ct. E10 ....3D 68
  SW17 ....3D 136
Witham Rd. RM10: Dag 5G 73
  SE20 ....3J 157
  TW7: Isle 1H 113
  W13 ....1A 96
Witherby Cl. CR0: C'don 5E 168
Witherington Rd. N5 ....5A 66
Withers Cl. KT9: Chess 6C 162
Withers Mead NW9 ....1B 44
Withers Pl. EC1 ....3D 8 (4C 84)
Witherston Way SE9 ....2E 142
Withycombe Rd. SW19 ....7F 117
Withy Ho. E1 ....4K 85
  (off Globe Rd.)
Withy La. HA4: Ruis 5E 38
Withy Mead E4 ....3A 36
Witley Ct. WC1 ....4E 6
Witley Cres. CR0: New Ad 6E 170
Witley Gdns. UB2: S'hall 4D 94
Witley Ho. SW2 ....7J 119
Witley Ind. Est. UB2: S'hall 4D 94
Witley Point SW15 ....1D 134
  (off Wanborough Dr.)
Witley Rd. N19 ....2G 65
Witney Cl. UB10: Ick 6B 56
Witney Path SE23 ....3K 139
Wittenham Way E4 ....3A 36
Wittering Cl. KT2: King T 5D 132
Wittersham Rd.
  BR1: Brom 5H 141
Witts Ho. KT1: King T 3F 151
  (off Winery La.)
Wivenhoe Cl. SE15 ....3H 121
Wivenhoe Ct. TW3: Houn 4D 112
Wivenhoe Rd. IG11: Bark 2A 90
Wiverton Rd. SE26 ....6J 139
Wix Rd. RM9: Dag 1D 90
Wix's La. SW4 ....3F 119
WLA Community Sports Cen. 1C 76
Woburn W13 ....5B 78
  (off Clivedon Ct.)
Woburn Cl. SE28 ....6D 90
  SW19 ....6A 136
Woburn Ct. CR0: C'don 1C 168
  E18 ....2J 51
  SE16 ....5H 103
  (off Masters Dr.)
  WC1 ....4E 6
  (off Bernard St.)
Woburn Mans. WC1 ....5C 6
  (off Torrington Pl.)
Woburn M. WC1 ....4D 6 (4H 83)
Woburn Pl. WC1 ....4E 6 (4J 83)
Woburn Rd. CR0: C'don 1C 168
  SM5: Cars 1C 166
Woburn Sq. WC1 ....4D 6 (4H 83)
  (not continuous)
Woburn Twr. UB5: N'olt 3B 76
  (off Broomcroft Av.)
Woburn Wlk. WC1 ....2D 6 (3H 83)
Wodeham Gdns. E1 ....5G 85
Wodehouse Av. SE5 ....1F 121
Wodehouse Ct. W3 ....3J 97
  (off Vincent Rd.)
Woffington Cl. KT1: Hamp W ...1C 150
Woking Cl. SW15 ....4B 116
Wolcot Ho. NW1 ....1B 6
  (off Aldenham St.)
Woldham Pl. BR2: Brom 4A 160
Woldham Rd. BR2: Brom 4A 160
Wolds Dr. BR6: Farnb 4E 172
Wolfe Cl. BR2: Hayes 6J 159
  UB4: Yead 3K 75
Wolfe Cres. SE7 ....5B 106
  SE16 ....2K 103
Wolfe Ho. W12 ....7D 80
  (off White City Est.)
  W14 ....4H 99
Wolferton Rd. E12 ....4D 70
Wolffe Gdns. E15 ....6H 69

Wolfington Rd. SE27 . . . . .4B 138
Wolfram Cl. SE13 . . . . .5G 123
Wolftencroft Cl. SW11 . . . . .3C 118
Wollaston Cl. SE1 . . . . .4C 102
Wollaton Ho. *N1* *2A 84*
(off Batchelor St.)
Wollett Ct. NW1 . . . . .7G 65
(off St Pancras Way)
Wolmer Cl. HA8: Edg 4B 28
Wolmer Gdns. HA8: Edg 3B 28
Wolseley Av. SW19 . . . . .2J 135
Wolseley Gdns. W4 . . . . .6H 97
Wolseley Rd. CR4: Mitc 7E 154
E7 . . . . .7K 69
HA3: W'stone 3J 41
N8 . . . . .6H 47
N22 .1K 47
RM7: Rush G 7K 55
W4 . . . . .4J 97
Wolseley St. SE1 . . . . . .7K 15 (2G 103)
Wolsey Av. E6 . . . . .3E 88
E17 .3B 50
KT7: T Ditt 5K 149
Wolsey Cl. KT2: King T 1H 151
KT4: Wor Pk 4C 164
SE2 .2C 108
SW20 . . . . .7D 134
TW3: Houn 4G 113
UB2: S'hall 3G 95
Wolsey Ct. NW6 . . . . .7A 64
SW11 . . . . .1C 118
(off Westbridge Rd.)
Wolsey Cres. CR0: New Ad 7E 170
SM4: Mord 7G 153
Wolsey Dr. KT2: King T 5E 132
KT12: Walt T 7B 148
Wolsey Gro. HA8: Edg 7E 28
Wolsey M. BR6: Chels 5K 173
NW5 . . . . .6G 65
Wolsey Rd. EN1: Enf 2C 24
KT8: E Mos 4H 149
N1 . . . . .5D 66
TW12: Hamp H 6F 131
TW15: Ashf 4A 128
TW16: Sun 7H 129
Wolsey St. E1 . . . . .5J 85
Wolsey Way KT9: Chess 5G 163
Wolstenholme HA7: Stan 5G 27
Wolstonbury N12 . . . . .5D 30
Wolvercote Rd. SE2 . . . . .2D 108
Wolverley St. E2 . . . . .3H 85
Wolverton SE17 . . . . .5E 102
(not continuous)
Wolverton Av. KT2: King T 1G 151
Wolverton Gdns. W5 . . . . .7F 79
W6 .4F 99
Wolverton Rd. HA7: Stan 6G 27
Wolverton Way N14 . . . . .5B 22
Wolves La. N13 . . . . .7F 33
N22 .7F 33
Womersley Rd. N8 . . . . .6K 47
Wonersh Way SM2: Cheam 7F 165
Wonford Cl. KT2: King T 1A 152
Wontner Cl. N1 . . . . .7C 66
Wontner Rd. SW17 . . . . .2D 136
Wooburn Cl. UB8: Hil 4D 74
Woodall Av. EN3: Pond E 6E 24
Woodall Cl. E14 . . . . .7D 86
KT9: Chess 7C 162
Woodall Rd. EN3: Pond E 6E 24
Woodbank Rd. BR1: Brom 3H 141
Woodbastwick Rd. SE26 . . . . . . .5K 139
Woodberry Av. HA2: Harr 4F 41
N21 .2F 33
Woodberry Cl. NW7 . . . . .7A 30
TW16: Sun 6J 129
Woodberry Cres. N10 . . . . .3F 47
Woodberry Down N4 . . . . .7C 48
Woodberry Down Est. N4 . . . . . . .7C 48
(not continuous)
Woodberry Gdns. N12 . . . . .6F 31

Woodberry Gro. DA5: Bexl 3K 145
N4 . . . . .7C 48
N12 .6F 31
Woodberry Way E4 . . . . .7K 25
N12 .6F 31
Woodbine Cl. TW2: Twick 2H 131
Woodbine Gro. EN2: Enf 1J 23
SE20 . . . . .7H 139
Woodbine La. KT4: Wor Pk 3D 164
Woodbine Pl. E11 . . . . .6J 51
Woodbine Rd. DA15: Sidc 1J 143
Woodbines Av. KT1: King T 3D 150
Woodbine Ter. E9 . . . . .6J 67
Woodborough Rd. SW15 . . . . . . .4D 116
Woodbourne Av. SW16 . . . . .3H 137
Woodbourne Cl. SW16 . . . . .3J 137
Woodbourne Gdns. SM6: Wall . . .7F 167
Woodbridge Cl. N7 . . . . .2K 65
NW2 . . . . .3C 62
Woodbridge Ct. IG8: Wfd G 7H 37
Woodbridge Ho. E11 . . . . .1H 69
Woodbridge Rd. IG11: Bark 5K 71
Woodbridge St. EC1 . . . . .3A 8 (4B 84)
(not continuous)
Woodbridge Ter. RM6: Chad H . . .6B 54
Woodbrook Rd. SE2 . . . . .6A 108
Woodburn Cl. NW4 . . . . .5F 45
Woodbury Cl. CR0: C'don 2F 169
E11 .4K 51
Woodbury Gdns. SE12 . . . . .3K 141
Woodbury Ho. SE26 . . . . .3G 139
Woodbury Pk. Rd. W13 . . . . .4B 78
Woodbury Rd. E17 . . . . .4D 50
Woodbury St. SW17 . . . . .5C 136
Woodchester Ho. E14 . . . . .3D 104
(off Selsdon Way)
Woodchester Sq. W2 . . . . .5K 81
Woodchurch Cl. DA14: Sidc 3H 143
Woodchurch Dr. BR1: Brom 7B 142
Woodchurch Rd. NW6 . . . . .7J 63
Wood Cl. E2 . . . . .4G 85
HA1: Harr 7H 41
NW9 . . . . .7K 43
Woodclyffe Dr. BR7: Chst 2E 160
Woodcock Cl. TW6: H'row A 7C 174
Woodcock Ct. HA3: Kenton 7E 42
Woodcock Dell Av.
HA3: Kenton 7D 42
Woodcock Hill HA3: Kenton 5C 42
Woodcock Ho. E14 . . . . .5C 86
(off Burgess St.)
Woodcocks E16 . . . . .5A 88
Woodcombe Cres. SE23 . . . . .1J 139
Woodcote Av. CR7: Thor H 4B 156
NW7 . . . . .6K 29
SM6: Wall 7F 167
Woodcote Cl. EN3: Pond E 6D 24
KT2: King T 5F 133
Woodcote Dr. BR6: Orp 1H 173
Woodcote Grn. SM6: Wall 7G 167
Woodcote Ho. SE8 . . . . .6B 104
(off Prince St.)
Woodcote M. SM6: Wall 6F 167
Woodcote Pl. SE27 . . . . .5B 138
Woodcote Rd. E11 . . . . .7J 51
SM6: Wall 6F 167
Woodcote Vs. SE27 . . . . .5C 138
(off Woodcote Pl.)
Wood Ct. DA8: Erith 7K 109
Wood Crest SM2: Sutt 7A 166
(off Christchurch Pk.)
Woodcroft N21 . . . . .1F 33
SE9 .3E 142
UB6: G'frd 6A 60
Woodcroft Av. HA7: Stan 1A 42
NW7 . . . . .6F 29
Woodcroft Cl. SE9 . . . . .6E 124
Woodcroft Cres. UB10: Hil 1D 74
Woodcroft M. SE8 . . . . .4A 104
Woodcroft Rd. CR7: Thor H 5B 156
Wood Dr. BR7: Chst 6C 142

Woodedge Cl. E4 . . . . .1C 36
WOOD END 6F 37
UB4 .5H 75
UB5 .5G 59
Wood End UB3: Hayes 6G 75
Wood End, The SM6: Wall 7F 167
Woodend SE19 . . . . .6C 138
SM1: Sutt 2A 166
Wood End Av. HA2: Harr 4F 59
UB5: N'olt 4F 59
Wood End Cl. UB5: N'olt 5H 59
Wood End Gdns. UB5: N'olt 5G 59
Woodend Gdns. EN2: Enf 4D 22
Wood End La. UB5: N'olt 6F 59
Wood End Rd. HA1: Harr 4H 59
Woodend Rd. E17 . . . . .2E 50
Wood End Way UB5: N'olt 5G 59
Wooder Gdns. E7 . . . . .4J 69
Wooderson Cl. SE25 . . . . .4E 156
Woodfall Av. EN5: Barn 5C 20
Woodfall Rd. N4 . . . . .2A 66
Woodfall St. SW3 . . . . .6E 16 (5D 100)
Woodfarrs SE5 . . . . .4D 120
Wood Fld. NW3 . . . . .5D 64
Woodfield Av. HA0: Wemb 3C 60
NW9 . . . . .4A 44
SM5: Cars 6E 166
SW16 . . . . .3H 137
W5 . . . . .4C 78
Woodfield Cl. EN1: Enf 4K 23
SE19 . . . . .7C 138
Woodfield Cres. W5 . . . . .4C 78
Woodfield Dr. EN4: E Barn 1K 31
Woodfield Gdns. KT3: N Mald 5B 152
Woodfield Gro. SW16 . . . . .3H 137
Woodfield Ho. SE23 . . . . .3K 139
(off Dacres Rd.)
Woodfield La. SW16 . . . . .3H 137
Woodfield Pl. W9 . . . . .4H 81
Woodfield Ri. WD23: Bush 1C 26
Woodfield Rd. TW4: Cran 2A 111
W5 . . . . .4C 78
W9 . . . . .5H 81
Woodfield Way N11 . . . . .7C 32
WOODFORD 6F 37
Woodford Av. IG2: Ilf 5D 52
IG4: Ilf, Wfd G 3B 52
WOODFORD BRIDGE 6H 37
Woodford Bri. Rd. IG4: Ilf 3B 52
Woodford Ct. W12 . . . . .2F 99
(off Shepherd's Bush Grn.)
Woodford Cres. HA5: Pinn 2K 39
Woodforde Ct. UB3: Harl 5F 93
Woodford Golf Course 5D 36
WOODFORD GREEN 6D 36
Woodford Green Athletics Club . . .6H 37
Woodford Hall Path E18 . . . . .1H 51
Woodford Ho. E18 . . . . .4J 51
Woodford New Rd. E17 . . . . .4G 51
E18 .1G 51
IG8: Wfd G 1G 51
Woodford Pl. HA9: Wemb 1E 60
Woodford Rd. E7 . . . . .3K 69
E18 .4J 51
WOODFORD SIDE 5C 36
Woodford Trad. Est. IG8: Wfd G . .2B 52
WOODFORD WELLS 3E 36
Woodgate Av. KT9: Chess 5D 162
Woodgate Dr. SW16 . . . . .7H 137
Woodger Rd. W12 . . . . .2E 98
Woodget Cl. E6 . . . . .6C 88
Woodgrange Av. EN1: Enf 6B 24
HA3: Kenton 5C 42
N12 .6G 31
W5 . . . . .1G 97
Woodgrange Cl. HA3: Kenton 5D 42
Woodgrange Gdns. EN1: Enf 6B 24
Woodgrange Ho. W5 . . . . .1F 97
(off Woodgrange Av.)

Woodgrange Mans. HA3: Kenton . .5D 42
Woodgrange Rd. E7 . . . . .5K 69
Woodgrange Ter. EN1: Enf 6B 24
WOOD GREEN 2K 47
Wood Grn. Hall N22 . . . . .2K 47
(off Station Rd.)
Wood Grn. Shop. City N22 . . . . . .2A 48
Woodhall NW1 . . . . .2A 6
(off Robert St.)
Woodhall Av. HA5: Pinn 1C 40
SE21 . . . . .3F 139
Woodhall Cl. UB8: Uxb 5A 56
Woodhall Dr. HA5: Pinn 1B 40
SE21 . . . . .3F 139
Woodhall Ga. HA5: Pinn 1B 40
Woodhall Ho. SW18 . . . . .6B 118
Woodham Ct. E18 . . . . .4H 51
Woodham Rd. SE6 . . . . .3E 140
Woodhatch Cl. E6 . . . . .5C 88
Woodhaven Gdns. IG6: Ilf 4G 53
Woodhayes Rd. SW19 . . . . .7E 134
Woodhead Dr. BR6: Orp 3J 173
Woodheyes Rd. NW10 . . . . .5K 61
Woodhill SE18 . . . . .4C 106
Woodhill Cres. HA3: Kenton 6D 42
Wood Ho. NW6 . . . . .2H 81
(off Albert Rd.)
Woodhouse Av. UB6: G'frd 2K 77
Woodhouse Cl. SE22 . . . . .4G 121
UB3: Harl 3G 93
UB6: G'frd 1K 77
Woodhouse Gro. E12 . . . . .6C 70
Woodhouse Rd. E11 . . . . .3H 69
N12 .6G 31
Woodhurst Av. BR5: Pet W 6G 161
Woodhurst Rd. SE2 . . . . .5A 108
W3 . . . . .7J 79
Woodies La. KT3: N Mald 6K 151
Woodington Cl. SE9 . . . . .6E 124
Woodknoll Dr. BR7: Chst 1D 160
Woodland App. UB6: G'frd 6A 60
Woodland Cl. IG8: Wfd G 3E 36
KT19: Ewe 6A 164
NW9 . . . . .6J 43
SE19 . . . . .6E 138
UB10: Ick 2D 56
Woodland Ct. E11 . . . . .6J 51
(off New Wanstead)
N7 . . . . .6J 65
Woodland Cres. SE10 . . . . .6G 105
SE16 . . . . .2K 103
Woodland Gdns. N10 . . . . .5F 47
TW7: Isle 3J 113
Woodland Gro. SE10 . . . . .5G 105
Woodland Hill SE19 . . . . .6E 138
Woodland M. SW16 . . . . .3J 137
Woodland Ri. N10 . . . . .4F 47
UB6: G'frd 6A 60
Woodland Rd.
CR7: Thor H 4A 156
E4 . . . . .1K 35
N11 .5A 32
SE19 . . . . .5E 138
WOODLANDS 3J 113
Woodlands BR2: Brom 4H 159
DA6: Bex 5H 127
HA2: Harr 4E 40
NW11 . . . . .5G 45
SW20 . . . . .4E 152
Woodlands, The
HA1: Harr 2J 59
HA7: Stan 5G 27
N5 . . . . .4C 66
N12 .6F 31
N14 .1A 32
SE13 . . . . .7F 123
SE19 . . . . .7C 138
SM6: Wall 7F 167
SW9 . . . . .7B 102
(off Langton Rd.)
TW7: Isle 2K 113

Woodlands Av. DA15: Sidc 1J **143**
    E11 . . . . .1K **69**
    HA4: Ruis .7A **40**
    KT3: N Mald 1J **151**
    KT4: Wor Pk 2B **164**
    N3 . . . . .7F **31**
    RM6: Chad H 7E **54**
    W3 . . . . .1H **97**
Woodlands Cl. BR1: Brom 2D **160**
    KT10: Clay 7A **162**
    NW11 . . . . .5G **45**
Woodlands Ct. BR1: Brom 1H **159**
    HA1: Harr .5K **41**
    KT12: Walt T 7K **147**
    NW10 . . . .*1F 81*
          (off Wrentham Av.)
    SE23 . . . . .7H **121**
Woodlands Dr. HA7: Stan 6E **26**
    TW16: Sun 2A **148**
Woodlands Gdns. E17 . . . . .4G **51**
Woodlands Ga. *SW15* *5H 117*
          (off Woodlands Way)
Woodlands Gro. TW7: Isle 2J **113**
    W5 . . . .*6H 105*
          (off Vanburgh Hill)
Woodlands Hgts. *SE3* *6H 105*
          (off Vanburgh Hill)
Woodlands Pde.
    TW15: Ashf 6E **128**
Woodlands Pk. DA5: Bexl 4K **145**
Woodlands Pk. Rd. N15 . . . . .5B **48**
    SE10 . . . . .6G **105**
          (not continuous)
Woodlands Rd.
    BR1: Brom 2C **160**
    BR6: Chels 6K **173**
    DA7: Bex .3E **126**
    E11 . . . . .2G **69**
    E17 . . . . .3E **50**
    EN2: Enf .1J **23**
    HA1: Harr .5K **41**
    IG1: Ilf 3G **71**
    KT6: Surb 7D **150**
    N9 . . . . .1D **34**
    SW13 . . . . .3B **116**
    TW7: Isle 3H **113**
    UB1: S'hall 1B **94**
Woodlands St. SE13 . . . . .7F **123**
Woodland St. E8 . . . . .5F **67**
Woodlands Way SW15 . . . . .5H **117**
Woodland Ter. SE7 . . . . .4C **106**
Woodland Wlk. BR1: Brom 4F **141**
          (not continuous)
    KT19: Ewe 6G **163**
    NW3 . . . . .5C **64**
    SE10 . . . . .5G **105**
Woodland Way
    BR4: W W'ck 4D **170**
    BR5: Pet W 4G **161**
    CR0: C'don 1A **170**
    CR4: Mitc 7E **136**
    IG8: Wfd G 3E **36**
    KT5: Surb 2H **163**
    N21 . . . . .2F **33**
    NW7 . . . . .6G **29**
    SE2 . . . . .4D **108**
    SM4: Mord 4H **153**
Wood La. HA4: Ruis 1F **57**
    HA7: Stan .3F **27**
    IG8: Wfd G 4C **36**
    N6 . . . . .6F **47**
    NW9 . . . . .7K **43**
    RM8: Dag 4D **72**
    RM9: Dag 4D **72**
    RM10: Dag 2G **73**
    TW7: Isle 6J **95**
    W12 . . . . .6E **80**
Wood La. Studios *W12* *6E 80*
Woodlark Ct. KT10: Clay 6A **162**
Woodlawn Cl. SW15 . . . . .5H **117**
Woodlawn Cres. TW2: Whitt 2F **131**
Woodlawn Dr. TW13: Felt 2B **130**
Woodlawn Rd. SW6 . . . . .7F **99**

Woodlawns KT19: Ewe 7K **163**
Woodlea Dr. BR2: Brom 5G **159**
Woodlea Rd. N16 . . . . .3E **66**
Woodleigh E18 . . . . .1J **51**
Woodleigh Av. N12 . . . . .6H **31**
Woodleigh Gdns. SW16 . . . . .3J **137**
Woodley Cl. SW17 . . . . .7D **136**
Woodley La. SM5: Cars 3C **166**
Wood Lodge Gdns.
    BR1: Brom 7C **142**
Wood Lodge La.
    BR4: W W'ck 3E **170**
Woodman M. TW9: Kew 1H **115**
Woodman Pde. *E16* *1E 106*
          (off Woodman St.)
Woodmans Gro. NW10 . . . . .5B **62**
Woodman's M. *W12* 5D **80**
Woodmansterne Rd. SM5: Cars 7C **166**
    SW16 . . . . .7G **137**
Woodman St. E16 . . . . .1E **106**
Wood Martyn Ct. *BR6: Orp* *2K 173*
          (off Orchard Gro.)
Wood Mead N17 . . . . .6B **34**
Woodmere SE9 . . . . .1D **142**
Woodmere Av. CR0: C'don 7J **157**
Woodmere Cl. CR0: C'don 7K **157**
    SW11 . . . . .3E **118**
Woodmere Ct. N14 . . . . .7A **22**
Woodmere Gdns. CR0: C'don 7K **157**
Woodmere Way BR3: Beck 5F **159**
Woodmill Cl. SW15 . . . . .6C **116**
Woodmill Rd. E5 . . . . .2J **67**
Woodmill St. SE1 . . . . .3F **103**
Woodnook Rd. SW16 . . . . .5F **137**
Woodpecker Cl. HA3: Hrw W 1K **41**
    N9 . . . . .6C **24**
    WD23: Bush 1B **26**
Woodpecker M. *SE13* *4F 123*
          (off Freshfield Cl.)
Woodpecker Mt. CR0: Sels 7A **170**
Woodpecker Rd. SE14 . . . . .6A **104**
    SE28 . . . . .7C **90**
Woodquest Av. SE24 . . . . .5C **120**
Wood Retreat SE18 . . . . .7H **107**
Wood Ride BR5: Pet W 4H **161**
    EN4: Had W 1G **21**
Woodridge Cl. EN2: Enf 1F **23**
Woodridings Av. HA5: Hat E 1D **40**
Woodridings Cl. HA5: Hat E 1C **40**
Woodridings Ct. N22 . . . . .1H **47**
Woodriffe Rd. E11 . . . . .7F **51**
Wood Ri. HA5: Eastc 5J **39**
Wood Rd. NW10 . . . . .7J **61**
    TW17: Shep 4C **146**
Woodrow SE18 . . . . .4D **106**
Woodrow Av. UB4: Hayes 5H **75**
Woodrow Cl. UB6: G'frd 7B **60**
Woodrow Cl. N17 . . . . .7C **34**
Woodrush Cl. SE14 . . . . .7A **104**
Woodrush Way
    RM6: Chad H 4D **54**
Woods, The UB10: Ick 4D **56**
Wood's Bldgs. *E1* *5H 85*
          (off Winthrop St.)
Woods Cl. *TW3: Houn* *3F 113*
          (off High St.)
Woodseer St. E1 . . . . .5K **9** (5F **85**)
Woodsford *SE17* *5D 102*
          (off Portland St.)
Woodsford Sq. W14 . . . . .2G **99**
Woodshire Rd.
    RM10: Dag 3H **73**
Woods Ho. SW1 . . . . .6J **17** (5F **101**)
    SW8 . . . .*1G 119*
          (off Wadhurst Rd.)
WOODSIDE 6G **157**
Woodside
    IG9: Buck H 2F **37**
    N10 . . . . .3E **46**
    NW11 . . . . .5J **45**
    SW19 . . . . .6H **135**

Woodside Av. BR7: Chst 5G **143**
    HA0: Wemb 1E **78**
    KT10: Esh 7J **149**
    N6 . . . . .5D **46**
    N10 . . . . .5D **46**
    N12 . . . . .4E **30**
    SE25 . . . . .6H **157**
Woodside Cl. DA7: Bex 4K **127**
    HA0: Wemb 1E **78**
    HA4: Ruis .6F **39**
    HA7: Stan 5G **27**
    KT5: Surb 7J **151**
Woodside Ct. E12 . . . . .1A **70**
    N12 . . . . .4E **30**
    RM7: Mawney 4G **55**
    W5 . . . . .1E **96**
Woodside Ct. Rd. CR0: C'don 7G **157**
Woodside Cres. DA15: Sidc 3J **143**
Woodside Dr. DA2: Wilm 4K **145**
Woodside End HA0: Wemb 1E **78**
Woodside Gdns. E4 . . . . .6J **35**
    N17 . . . . .2E **48**
Woodside Grange Rd. N12 . . . . .4E **30**
Woodside Grn. SE25 . . . . .6G **157**
Woodside Gro. N12 . . . . .3F **31**
Woodside Ho. SW19 . . . . .6H **135**
Woodside La. DA5: Bexl 6D **126**
    N12 . . . . .3F **31**
Woodside M. SE22 . . . . .5F **121**
Woodside Pde. DA15: Sidc 3J **143**
WOODSIDE PARK 4D **30**
Woodside Pk. SE25 . . . . .6H **157**
Woodside Pk. Av. E17 . . . . .4F **51**
Woodside Pk. Rd. N12 . . . . .4E **30**
Woodside Pl.
    HA0: Wemb 1E **78**
Woodside Rd.
    BR1: Brom 5C **160**
    DA7: Bex .4K **127**
    DA15: Sidc 3J **143**
    E13 . . . . .4A **88**
    IG8: Wfd G 4D **36**
    KT2: King T 7E **132**
    KT3: N Mald 2K **151**
    N22 . . . . .7E **32**
    SE25 . . . . .6H **157**
    SM1: Sutt 3A **166**
Woodside Way
    CR0: C'don 6J **157**
    CR4: Mitc 1F **155**
Woods M. W1 . . . . .2G **11** (7E **82**)
Woodsome Rd. NW5 . . . . .3E **64**
Woods Pl. SE1 . . . . .3E **102**
Woodspring Rd. SW19 . . . . .2G **135**
Woods Rd. SE15 . . . . .1H **121**
Woodstar Ho. *SE15* *7G 103*
          (off Reddins Rd.)
Woodstead Gro. HA8: Edg 6K **27**
WOODSTOCK, THE 7H **153**
Woodstock Av. NW11 . . . . .7G **45**
    SM3: Sutt 7H **153**
    TW7: Isle 5A **114**
    UB1: S'hall 3D **76**
    W13 . . . . .3A **96**
Woodstock Cl. DA5: Bexl 7F **127**
    HA7: Stan 2E **42**
Woodstock Ct. SE11 . . . . . .5H **19** (5K **101**)
    SE12 . . . . .6J **123**
Woodstock Cres. N9 . . . . .6C **24**
Woodstock Dr. UB10: Ick 4A **56**
Woodstock Gdns. BR3: Beck 1D **158**
    IG3: Ilf 1J **72**
    UB4: Hayes 5H **75**
Woodstock Grange W5 . . . . .1E **96**
Woodstock Gro. W12 . . . . .2F **99**
Woodstock La. KT9: Chess 4B **162**
Woodstock La. Nth. KT6: Surb 2C **162**
Woodstock La. Sth.
    KT9: Chess 5B **162**
    KT10: Clay 5B **162**
Woodstock M. W1 . . . . .6H **5**

Woodstock Ri. SM3: Sutt 7H **153**
Woodstock Rd. CR0: C'don 3D **168**
    E7 . . . . .7A **70**
    E17 . . . . .2F **51**
    HA0: Wemb 1F **79**
    N4 . . . . .1A **66**
    N11 . . . . .7H **45**
    SM5: Cars 5E **166**
    W4 . . . . .4A **98**
Woodstock St. W1 . . . . .1J **11** (6F **83**)
Woodstock Studios *W12* *2F 99*
          (off Woodstock Gro.)
Woodstock Ter. E14 . . . . .7D **86**
Woodstock Way CR4: Mitc 2F **155**
Woodstone Av. KT17: Ewe 5C **164**
WOOD STREET 3E **50**
Wood St. CR4: Mitc 7E **154**
    E17 . . . . .3E **50**
    EC2 . . . . .7D **8** (6C **84**)
          (not continuous)
    EN5: Barn .4A **20**
    KT1: King T 2D **150**
    W4 . . . . .5A **98**
Woodsyre SE26 . . . . .4F **139**
Wood Ter. NW2 . . . . .3D **62**
Woodthorpe Rd. SW15 . . . . .4D **116**
    TW15: Ashf 5A **128**
Woodtree Cl. NW4 . . . . .2F **45**
Wood Va. N10 .5G **47**
    SE23 . . . . .1H **139**
Woodvale Av. SE25 . . . . .3F **157**
Wood Va. Est. SE23 . . . . .7J **121**
Woodvale Ct. *BR1: Brom* *1K 159*
          (off Widmore Rd.)
Woodvale Wlk. SE27 . . . . .5C **138**
Woodvale Way NW11 . . . . .3F **63**
Woodview Av. E4 . . . . .4K **35**
Woodview Cl. BR6: Farnb 2G **173**
    N4 . . . . .7B **48**
    SW15 . . . . .4K **133**
Wood Vw. M. RM1: Rom 1K **55**
Woodville Av. SE19 . . . . .1E **156**
Woodville, The *W5* *6D 78*
          (off Woodville Rd.)
Woodville Cl. SE3 . . . . .1K **123**
    SE12 . . . . .5J **123**
    TW11: Tedd 4A **132**
Woodville Ct. N14 . . . . .5B **22**
    SE10 . . . .*1E 122*
          (off Blissett St.)
    SE19 . . . . .1F **157**
Woodville Gdns. HA4: Ruis 7E **38**
    IG6: Ilf 3F **53**
    KT6: Surb 7D **150**
    NW11 . . . . .7F **45**
    W5 . . . . .6E **78**
Woodville Gro. DA16: Well 3A **126**
Woodville Ho. *SE1* *3F 103*
          (off St Saviour's Est.)
Woodville Rd. CR7: Thor H 4C **156**
    E11 . . . . .1H **69**
    E17 . . . . .4B **50**
    E18 . . . . .2K **51**
    EN5: New Bar 3E **20**
    N16 . . . . .5E **66**
    NW6 . . . . .2H **81**
    NW11 . . . . .7F **45**
    SM4: Mord 4J **153**
    TW10: Ham 3B **132**
    W5 . . . . .6D **78**
Woodville St. SE18 . . . . .4C **106**
Woodward Av. NW4 . . . . .5C **44**
Woodward Cl. KT10: Clay 6A **162**
Woodwarde Rd. SE22 . . . . .6E **120**
Woodward Gdns. HA7: Stan 7E **26**
    RM9: Dag 7C **72**
Woodward Rd. RM9: Dag 7B **72**
Woodward's Footpath TW2: Whitt 6G **113**
Wood Way BR6: Farnb 2E **172**
Woodway Cres. HA1: Harr 6A **42**
Woodwell St. SW18 . . . . .5A **118**

Wood Wharf SE10 . . . . .6D 104
Wood Wharf Bus. Pk. E14 . . . . .1D 104
Woodyard Cl. NW5 . . . . .5E 64
Woodyard La. SE21 . . . . .7E 120
Woodyates Rd. SE12 . . . . .6J 123
Woolacombe Rd. SE3 . . . . .1A 124
Woolacombe Way UB3: Harl 4G 93
Woolcombes Ct. SE16 . . . . .1K 103
(off Princes Riverside Rd.)
Wooldridge Cl. TW14: Bedf 1E 128
Wooler St. SE17 . . . . .5D 102
Woolf Cl. SE28 . . . . .1B 108
Woolf Ct. W3 .3J 97
(off Vincent Rd.)
Woolf M. WC1 . . . . .3D 6
(off Burton Pl.)
Woolford Ct. SE5 . . . . .2C 120
(off Coldharbour La.)
Woolgar M. N16 . . . . .5E 66
(off Gillett St.)
Woollaston Rd. N4 . . . . .6B 48
Woolley Ho. SW9 . . . . .3B 120
(off Loughborough Rd.)
Woollon Ho. E1 . . . . .6J 85
(off Clark St.)
Woolmead Av. NW9 . . . . .7C 44
Woolmer Gdns. N18 . . . . .6B 34
Woolmer Rd. N18 . . . . .5B 34
Woolmore St. E14 . . . . .7E 86
Woolneigh St. SW6 . . . . .3K 117
Woolridge Way E9 . . . . .7J 67
Wool Rd. SW20 . . . . .6D 134
Woolstaplers Way SE16 . . . . .3G 103
Woolston Cl. E17 . . . . .2K 49
Woolstone Ho. E2 . . . . .1G 85
(off Whiston Rd.)
Woolstone Rd. SE23 . . . . .2A 140
WOOLWICH .3D 106
Woolwich Centre, The SE18 . . . . .4E 106
(off Wellington St.)
Woolwich Chu. St. SE18 . . . . .3C 106
Woolwich Comn. SE18 . . . . .6E 106
Woolwich Dockyard Ind. Est.
SE18 . . . . .3C 106
Woolwich High St. SE18 . . . . .3E 106
Woolwich Ho. UB3: Harl 3E 92
(off Nine Acres Cl.)
Woolwich Mnr. Way E6 . . . . .4D 88
E16 . . . . .2F 107
Woolwich New Rd. SE18 . . . . .5E 106
Woolwich Rd. DA6: Bex 3G 127
DA7: Bex 3G 127
DA17: Belv 5F 109
SE2 . . . . .6D 108
SE7 . . . . .5H 105
SE10 .5H 105
Woolwich Trade Pk. SE28 . . . . .3H 107
Wooster Gdns. E14 . . . . .6F 87
Wooster M. HA2: Harr 3G 41
Wooster Pl. SE1 . . . . .4D 102
(off Searles Rd.)
Wootton Gro. N3 . . . . .1J 45
Wootton St. SE1 . . . . .5K 13 (1A 102)
Worbeck Rd. SE20 . . . . .2H 157
Worcester Av. N17 . . . . .7B 34
Worcester Cl.
CR0: C'don 2C 170
CR4: Mitc 2E 154
NW2 . . . . .3D 62
SE20 .1G 157
Worcester Ct. HA1: Harr 3J 41
KT4: Wor Pk 3A 164
N12 . . . . .5E 30
W7 . . . . .6K 77
(off Copley Cl.)
W9 . . . . .5J 81
(off Elmfield Way)
Worcester Cres. IG8: Wfd G 5E 36
NW7 . . . . .3F 29
Worcester Dr. TW15: Ashf 5D 128
W4 . . . . .2A 98

Worcester Gdns. IG1: Ilf 7C 52
KT4: Wor Pk 3A 164
SW11 .5D 118
(off Grandison Rd.)
UB6: G'frd 6H 59
Worcester Ho. SE11 . . . . .2J 19
(off Kennington Rd.)
SW9 . . . . .7A 102
(off Cranmer Rd.)
W2 . . . . .6A 82
(off Hallfield Est.)
Worcester M. NW6 . . . . .6K 63
WORCESTER PARK 1C 164
Worcester Pk. Rd. KT4: Wor Pk 3K 163
Worcester Point EC1 . . . . .3C 84
Worcester Rd. E12 . . . . .4D 70
E17 . . . . .2K 49
SM2: Sutt 7J 165
SW19 .5H 135
Worcesters Av. EN1: Enf 1B 24
Wordsworth Av. E12 . . . . .7C 70
E18 . . . . .3H 51
UB6: G'frd 3H 77
Wordsworth Ct. HA1: Harr 7J 41
Wordsworth Dr. SM3: Cheam 4E 164
Wordsworth Ho. NW6 . . . . .3J 81
(off Stafford Rd.)
SE18 . . . . .6E 106
(off Woolwich Comn.)
Wordsworth Mans. W14 . . . . .6H 99
(off Queens Club Gdns.)
Wordsworth Pde. N8 . . . . .4B 48
Wordsworth Pl. NW5 . . . . .5D 64
Wordsworth Rd. DA16: Well 1J 125
N16 . . . . .4E 66
SE1 . . . . .4F 103
SE20 .7K 139
SM6: Wall 6G 167
TW12: Hamp 4D 130
Wordsworth Wlk. NW11 . . . . .4J 45
Wordsworth Way UB7: W Dray 4A 92
Worfield St. SW11 . . . . .7C 100
Worgan St. SE11 . . . . . . .5G 19 (5K 101)
SE16 .4K 103
Worland Rd. E15 . . . . .7G 69
World Bus. Cen. TW6: H'row A 1E 110
World of Golf Cen.
Croydon 5J 157
New Malden 3C 152
Sidcup 3G 143
World Rugby Mus. 6J 113
WORLD'S END 3E 22
Worlds End Est. SW10 . . . . .7B 100
Worlds End La. BR6: Chels 6K 173
EN2: Enf 5E 22
N21 . . . . .5E 22
World's End Pas. SW10 . . . . .7B 100
(off Worlds End Est.)
World's End Pl. SW10 . . . . .7B 100
(off Worlds End Est.)
Worleys Dr. BR6: Orp 4H 173
Worlidge St. W6 . . . . .5E 98
Worlingham Rd. SE22 . . . . .4F 121
Wormholt Rd. W12 . . . . .7C 80
Wormwood Scrubs Pk.
(Local Nature Reserve) 5B 80
Wormwood St. EC2 . . . . .7G 9 (6E 84)
Wornington Rd. W10 . . . . .4G 81
(not continuous)
Woronzow Rd. NW8 . . . . .1B 82
Worple Av. SW19 . . . . .7F 135
TW7: Isle 5A 114
Worple Cl. HA2: Harr 1D 58
Worple Rd. SW19 . . . . .2E 152
SW20 .2E 152
TW7: Isle 4A 114
Worple Rd. M. SW19 . . . . .6H 135
Worple St. SW14 . . . . .3K 115
Worple Way HA2: Harr 1D 58
TW10: Rich 5E 114
Worrall La. UB8: Uxb 7A 56

Worship St. EC2 . . . . .4F 9 (4D 84)
(not continuous)
Worslade Rd. SW17 . . . . .4B 136
Worsley Bri. Rd.
BR3: Beck 7C 140
SE26 .4B 140
Worsley Grange BR7: Chst 6G 143
Worsley Gro. E5 . . . . .4G 67
Worsley Ho. SE23 . . . . .2J 139
Worsley Rd. E11 . . . . .4G 69
Worsopp Dr. SW4 . . . . .5G 119
Worth Cl. BR6: Orp 4J 173
Worthfield Cl. KT19: Ewe 7K 163
Worth Gro. SE17 . . . . .5D 102
Worthing Cl. E15 . . . . .1G 87
Worthing Rd. TW5: Hest 6D 94
Worthington Cl.
CR4: Mitc 4F 155
Worthington Ho. EC1 . . . . .1K 7
(off Myddelton Pas.)
Wortham Rd. KT6: Surb 1F 163
Wortley Rd. CR0: C'don 7A 156
E6 . . . . .7B 70
Worton Ct. TW7: Isle 4J 113
Worton Gdns. TW7: Isle 2H 113
Worton Hall Ind. Est.
TW7: Isle 4J 113
Worton Rd. TW7: Isle 4H 113
Worton Way
TW3: Houn 2H 113
TW7: Houn 2H 113
Wotton Ct. E14 . . . . .7F 87
(off Jamestown Way)
Wotton Rd. NW2 . . . . .3E 62
SE8 . . . . .6B 104
Wouldham Rd. E16 . . . . .6H 87
Wragby Rd. E11 . . . . .3G 69
Wrampling Pl. N9 . . . . .1B 34
Wrangthorn Wlk.
CR0: Wadd 4A 168
Wraxall Rd. E3 . . . . .4B 86
(off Hamlets Way)
Wray Av. IG5: Ilf 3E 52
Wrayburn Ho. SE16 . . . . .2G 103
(off Llewellyn St.)
Wray Cres. N4 . . . . .2J 65
Wrayfield Rd. SM3: Cheam 3F 165
Wray Rd. SM2: Cheam 7H 165
Wraysbury Cl.
TW4: Houn 5C 112
Wrays Way UB4: Hayes 4G 75
Wrekin Rd. SE18 . . . . .7G 107
Wren Av. NW2 . . . . .4E 62
UB2: S'hall 4D 94
UB10: Uxb 1B 74
Wren Cl. E16 .6H 87
N9 . . . . .1E 34
TW6: H'row A 6C 174
Wren Ct. CR0: C'don 4D 168
(off Coombe Rd.)
Wren Cres. WD23: Bush 1B 26
Wren Gdns. RM9: Dag 5D 72
Wren Ho. E3 .2A 86
(off Gernon Rd.)
KT1: Hamp W 2D 150
(off High St.)
SW1 . . . . .6C 18
(off Aylesford St.)
Wren Landing E14 . . . . .1C 104
Wren La. HA4: Ruis 6K 39
Wren M. SE13 . . . . .4G 123
Wrenn Ho. SW13 . . . . .6E 98
Wren Path SE28 . . . . .3H 107
Wren Rd. DA14: Sidc 4C 144
RM9: Dag 5D 72
SE5 . . . . .1D 120
Wren's Av. TW15: Ashf 4E 128
Wren's Pk. Ho. E5 . . . . .2H 67
Wren St. WC1 . . . . .3H 7 (4K 83)
Wrentham Av. NW10 . . . . .2F 81
Wrenthorpe Rd. BR1: Brom 4G 141

Wren Vw. N6 .7G 47
Wrenwood Way
HA5: Eastc 4K 39
Wrestlers Ct. EC3 . . . . .7G 9
Wrexham Rd. E3 . . . . .2C 86
Wricklemarsh Rd. SE3 . . . . .2K 123
(not continuous)
Wrigglesworth St. SE14 . . . . .7K 103
Wright Cl. SE13 . . . . .4F 123
Wright Gdns.
TW17: Shep 5C 146
Wright Rd. TW5: Hest 7A 94
Wrights All. SW19 . . . . .6E 134
Wrights Cl. RM10: Dag 4H 73
Wrights Grn. SW4 . . . . .4H 119
Wright's La. W8 . . . . .3K 99
Wrights Pl. NW10 . . . . .6J 61
Wrights Rd. E3 . . . . .2B 86
(not continuous)
SE25 . . . . .3E 156
Wrights Row SM6: Wall 4F 167
Wrights Wlk. SW14 . . . . .3K 115
Wright Way TW6: H'row A 5C 174
Wrigley Cl. E4 .5A 36
Writtle Ho. NW9 . . . . .2B 44
Wrotham Ho. BR3: Beck 7B 140
(off Sellindge Cl.)
SE1 . . . . .3D 102
(off Law St.)
Wrotham Rd. DA16: Well 1C 126
EN5: Barn 2B 20
NW1 . . . . .7G 65
W13 . . . . .1C 96
Wrottesley Rd. NW10 . . . . .2C 80
SE18 .6G 107
Wroughton Rd. SW11 . . . . .5D 118
Wroughton Ter. NW4 . . . . .4D 44
Wroxall Rd. RM9: Dag 6C 72
Wroxham Gdns. N11 . . . . .7C 32
Wroxham Rd. SE28 . . . . .7D 90
Wroxham Way IG6: Ilf 1F 53
Wroxton Rd. SE15 . . . . .2J 121
WRYTHE, THE 3D 166
Wrythe Grn. SM5: Cars 3D 166
Wrythe Grn. Rd.
SM5: Cars 3D 166
Wrythe La. SM5: Cars 1A 166
Wulfstan St. W12 . . . . .5B 80
Wyatt Cl. SE16 . . . . .2B 104
TW13: Felt 1B 130
UB4: Hayes 5J 75
WD23: Bush 1C 26
Wyatt Ct. HA0: Wemb 7E 60
W3 . . . . .3J 97
(off All Saints Rd.)
Wyatt Dr. SW13 . . . . .6D 98
Wyatt Ho. NW8 . . . . .4B 4
(off Frampton St.)
SE3 . . . . .2H 123
TW1: Twick 6D 114
Wyatt Pk. Rd. SW2 . . . . .2J 137
Wyatt Point SE28 . . . . .2G 107
Wyatt Rd. E7 .6J 69
N5 . . . . .3C 66
Wyatts La. E17 . . . . .3E 50
Wybert St. NW1 . . . . .3A 6 (4G 83)
Wyborne Ho. NW10 . . . . .7J 61
Wyborne Way NW10 . . . . .7J 61
Wyburn Av. EN5: Barn 3C 20
Wychcombe Studios NW3 . . . . .6D 64
Wyche Gro. CR2: S Croy 7D 168
Wych Elm Cl. KT2: King T 7F 133
Wych Elm Lodge
BR1: Brom 7H 141
Wych Elm Pas. KT2: King T 7F 133
Wycherley Cl. SE3 . . . . .7H 105
Wycherley Cres.
EN5: New Bar 6E 20
Wychwood Av.
CR7: Thor H 3C 156
HA8: Edg 6J 27

Wychwood Cl. HA8: Edg 6J **27**
TW16: Sun 6J **129**
Wychwood End N6 . . . . .7G **47**
Wychwood Gdns. IG5: Ilf 4D **52**
Wychwood Way SE19 . . . . .6D **138**
Wyclif Ct. EC1 . . . . .2A **8**
(off Wyclif St.)
Wycliffe Cl. DA16: Well 1K **125**
Wycliffe Rd. SW11 . . . . .2E **118**
SW19 . . . . .6K **135**
Wyclif St. EC1 . . . . .2A **8** (3B **84**)
Wycombe Gdns. NW11 . . . . .2J **63**
Wycombe Ho. NW8 . . . . .3C **4**
(off Grendon St.)
Wycombe Pl. SW18 . . . . .6A **118**
Wycombe Rd. HA0: Wemb 1G **79**
IG2: Ilf 5D **52**
N17 . . . . .1G **49**
Wycombe Sq. W8 . . . . .1H **99**
Wydehurst Rd. CR0: C'don 7G **157**
Wydell Cl. SM4: Mord 6F **153**
Wydeville Mnr. Rd. SE12 . . . . .4K **141**
Wye Cl. BR6: Orp 7K **161**
HA4: Ruis 6E **38**
TW15: Ashf 4D **128**
Wye Ct. W13 . . . . .5B **78**
(off Malvern Way)
Wyemead Cres. E4 . . . . .2B **36**
Wye St. SW11 . . . . .2B **118**
Wyevale Cl. HA5: Eastc 3J **39**
Wyfields IG5: Ilf 1F **53**
Wyfold Ho. SE2 . . . . .2D **108**
(off Wolvercote Rd.)
Wyfold Rd. SW6 . . . . .7G **99**
Wyhill Wlk. RM10: Dag 6J **73**
Wyke Cl. TW7: Isle 6K **95**
Wyke Gdns. W7 . . . . .3A **96**
Wyke Green Golf Course 6K **95**
Wykeham Av. RM9: Dag 6C **72**
Wykeham Cl. UB7: Sip 6C **92**
Wykeham Ct. NW4 . . . . .5E **44**
(off Wykeham Rd.)
Wykeham Grn. RM9: Dag 6C **72**
Wykeham Hill
HA9: Wemb 1F **61**
Wykeham Ho. SE1 . . . . .5C **14**
(off Union St.)
Wykeham Ri. N20 . . . . .1B **30**
Wykeham Rd.
HA3: Kenton 4B **42**
NW4 . . . . .4E **44**
Wyke Rd. E3 . . . . .7C **68**
SW20 . . . . .2E **152**
Wylchin Cl. HA5: Eastc 3H **39**
Wyldes Cl. NW11 . . . . .1A **64**
Wyldfield Gdns. N9 . . . . .2A **34**
Wyld Way HA9: Wemb 6H **61**
Wyleu St. SE23 . . . . .7A **122**
Wylie Rd. UB2: S'hall 3E **94**
Wyllen Cl. E1 . . . . .4J **85**
Wymering Mans. W9 . . . . .3J **81**
(off Wymering Rd.)
Wymering Rd. W9 . . . . .3J **81**
Wymondham Ct. NW8 . . . . .1B **82**
(off Queensmead)
Wymond St. SW15 . . . . .3E **116**
Wynan Rd. E14 . . . . .5D **104**
Wynash Gdns.
SM5: Cars 5C **166**
Wynaud Ct. N22 . . . . .6E **32**
Wyncham Av. DA15: Sidc 1J **143**
Wyncham Ho. DA15: Sidc 2A **144**
(off Longlands Rd.)
Wynchgate HA3: Hrw W 7D **26**
N14 . . . . .1C **32**
N21 . . . . .1C **32**
UB5: N'olt 5C **58**
Wyncroft Cl. BR1: Brom 3D **160**
Wyndale Av. NW9 . . . . .6G **43**
Wyndcliff Rd. SE7 . . . . .6K **105**
Wyndcroft Cl. EN2: Enf 3G **23**

Wyndham Cl.
BR6: Farnb 1G **173**
SM2: Sutt 7J **165**
Wyndham Ct. W7 . . . . .4A **96**
Wyndham Cres. N19 . . . . .3G **65**
TW4: Houn 6E **112**
Wyndham Deedes Ho. E2 . . . . .2G **85**
(off Hackney Rd.)
Wyndham Est. SE5 . . . . .7C **102**
Wyndham Ho. E14 . . . . .2D **104**
(off Marsh Wall)
SW1 . . . . .4G **17**
(off Sloane Sq.)
Wyndham M. W1 . . . . .6E **4** (5D **82**)
Wyndham Pl. W1 . . . . .6E **4** (5D **82**)
Wyndham Rd. E6 . . . . .7B **70**
EN4: E Barn 1J **31**
KT2: King T 7F **133**
SE5 . . . . .7C **102**
W13 . . . . .3B **96**
Wyndhams Ct. E8 . . . . .7F **67**
(off Celandine Dr.)
Wyndham's Theatre 2E **12**
(off Charing Cross Rd.)
Wyndham St. W1 . . . . .5E **4** (5D **82**)
Wyndham Yd. W1 . . . . .6E **4** (5D **82**)
Wyndhurst Cl. CR2: S Croy 7B **168**
Wyneham Rd. SE24 . . . . .5D **120**
Wynell Rd. SE23 . . . . .3K **139**
Wynford Pl. DA17: Belv 6G **109**
Wynford Rd. N1 . . . . .2K **83**
Wynford Way SE9 . . . . .3D **142**
Wynlie Gdns. HA5: Pinn 2K **39**
Wynn Bri. Cl. IG8: Wfd G 1B **52**
Wynndale Rd. E18 . . . . .1K **51**
Wynne Rd. SW9 . . . . .2A **120**
Wynn's Av. DA15: Sidc 5K **125**
Wynnstay Gdns. W8 . . . . .3J **99**
Wynter St. SW11 . . . . .4A **118**
Wynton Gdns. SE25 . . . . .5F **157**
Wynton Pl. W3 . . . . .6H **79**
Wynyard Ho. SE11 . . . . .5K **101**
(off Newburn St.)
Wynyard Ter. SE11 . . . . . .5H **19** (5K **101**)
Wynyatt St. EC1 . . . . .2A **8** (3B **84**)
Wyre Gro.
HA8: Edg 3C **28**
UB3: Harl 4J **93**
Wyresdale Cres.
UB6: G'frd 3K **77**
Wyteleaf Cl. HA4: Ruis 6E **38**
Wytham Ho. NW8 . . . . .4B **4**
(off Church St. Est.)
Wythburn Ct. W1 . . . . .7E **4**
(off Wythburn Pl.)
Wythburn Pl. W1 . . . . . . .1E **10** (6D **82**)
Wythenshawe Rd.
RM10: Dag 3G **73**
Wythens Wlk. SE9 . . . . .6F **125**
Wythes Cl. BR1: Brom 2D **160**
Wythes Rd. E16 . . . . .1C **106**
Wythfield Rd. SE9 . . . . .6D **124**
Wyvenhoe Rd. HA2: Harr 4G **59**
Wyvern Est. KT3: N Mald 4C **152**
Wyvil Rd. SW8 . . . . .7J **101**
Wyvis St. E14 . . . . .5D **86**

X

Xylon Ho. KT4: Wor Pk 2D **164**

Y

Yabsley St. E14 . . . . .1E **104**
Yaldham Ho. SE1 . . . . .4E **102**
(off Old Kent Rd.)
Yalding Rd. SE16 . . . . .3G **103**
Yale Cl. TW4: Houn 5D **112**
Yale Ct. NW6 . . . . .5K **63**

Yarborough Rd. SW19 . . . . .1B **154**
Yard, The N1 . . . . .1F **7**
(off Caledonia Rd.)
Yardley Cl. E4 . . . . .5J **25**
Yardley Ct. SM3: Cheam 4E **164**
Yardley La. E4 . . . . .5J **25**
Yardley St. WC1 . . . . .2J **7** (3A **84**)
(not continuous)
Yardmaster Ho. CR0: C'don 1D **168**
Yarlington Ct. N11 . . . . .5K **31**
(off Sparkford Gdns.)
Yarmouth Cres. N17 . . . . .5H **49**
Yarmouth Pl. W1 . . . . .5J **11** (1F **101**)
Yarnfield Sq. SE15 . . . . .1G **121**
Yarnton Way
DA18: Belv, Erith 3F **109**
SE2 . . . . .2C **108**
Yarrell Mans. W14 . . . . .6H **99**
(off Queen's Club Gdns.)
Yarrow Cres. E6 . . . . .5C **88**
Yarrow Ho. E14 . . . . .3E **104**
(off Stewart St.)
W10 . . . . .5E **80**
(off Sutton Way)
Yateley Cl. SE18 . . . . .3B **106**
Yatesbury Ct. E5 . . . . .5A **68**
(off Studley Cl.)
Yates Ct. NW2 . . . . .6F **63**
(off Willesden La.)
SE1 . . . . .7K **15**
(off Abbey St.)
Yates Ho. E2 . . . . .3G **85**
(off Roberta St.)
Yatton Ho. W10 . . . . .5E **80**
(off Sutton Way)
YEADING 4A **76**
Yeading Av. HA2: Harr 2C **58**
Yeading Brook Meadows Nature Reserve
. . . . .4J **75**
Yeading Ct. UB4: Yead 4A **76**
Yeading Fork UB4: Yead 5A **76**
Yeading Gdns. UB4: Yead 5K **75**
Yeading Ho. UB4: Yead 5B **76**
Yeading La.
UB4: Yead 6K **75**
UB5: N'olt 6K **75**
Yeading Wlk. HA2: Harr 5D **40**
Yeadon Ho. W10 . . . . .5E **80**
(off Sutton Way)
Yeames Cl. W13 . . . . .6A **78**
Yearby Ho. W10 . . . . .4E **80**
(off Sutton Way)
Yeate St. N1 . . . . .7D **66**
Yeatman Rd. N6 . . . . .6D **46**
Yeats Cl. NW10 . . . . .5A **62**
SE13 . . . . .2F **123**
W7 .7K **77**
Yeend Cl. KT8: W Mole 4E **148**
Yeldham Ho. W6 . . . . .5F **99**
(off Yeldham Rd.)
Yeldham Rd. W6 . . . . .5F **99**
Yeldham Vs. W6 . . . . .5F **99**
(off Yeldham Rd.)
Yellowhammer Ct. NW9 . . . . .2A **44**
(off Eagle Dr.)
Yelverton Lodge TW1: Twick 7C **114**
(off Richmond Rd.)
Yelverton Rd. SW11 . . . . .2B **118**
Ye Market CR2: S Croy 5D **168**
(off Selsdon Rd.)
Yenston Cl. SM4: Mord 6J **153**
Yeoman Cl. E6 . . . . .7F **89**
SE27 . . . . .3B **138**
Yeoman Ct. TW5: Hest 7D **94**
Yeoman Dr.
TW19: Stanw 1A **128**
Yeoman Rd. UB5: N'olt 7C **58**
Yeomans Acre HA4: Ruis 6J **39**
Yeomans M. TW7: Isle 6H **113**
Yeoman's Row SW3 . . . .2D **16** (3C **100**)
Yeoman St. SE8 . . . . .4A **104**

Yeomans Way
EN3: Enf H 2D **24**
Yeoman's Yd. E1 . . . . .2K **15**
Yeo St. E3 . . . . .5D **86**
Yeovil Cl. BR6: Orp 2J **173**
Yeovil Ho. W10 . . . . .4E **80**
(off Sutton Way)
Yeovilton Pl. KT2: King T 5C **132**
Yerbury Rd. N19 . . . . .3H **65**
(not continuous)
Yester Dr. BR7: Chst 7C **142**
Yester Pk. BR7: Chst 7D **142**
Yester Rd. BR7: Chst 7C **142**
Yetev Lev Ct. E5 . . . . .1G **67**
Yew Av. UB7: Yiew 7A **74**
Yew Cl. IG9: Buck H 2G **37**
Yewdale Cl.
BR1: Brom 6G **141**
Yewfield Rd. NW10 . . . . .6B **62**
Yew Gro. NW2 . . . . .4F **63**
Yew Ho. SE16 . . . . .2K **103**
(off Woodland Cres.)
Yews, The TW15: Ashf 4D **128**
Yew Tree Cl. DA16: Well 1A **126**
KT4: Wor Pk 1A **164**
N21 . . . . .7F **23**
SE13 . . . . .3E **122**
Yewtree Cl. HA2: Harr 4F **41**
N22 . . . . .1G **47**
Yew Tree Cl. NW11 . . . . .5H **45**
(off Bridge La.)
SM2: Sutt 7A **166**
(off Walnut M.)
Yew Tree Gdns. RM6: Chad H 5E **54**
RM7: Rom 5K **55**
Yew Tree Lodge
HA4: Ruis 6J **39**
RM7: Rom 5K **55**
(off Yew Tree Gdns.)
SW16 . . . . .4G **137**
Yew Tree Rd. BR3: Beck 3B **158**
UB10: Uxb 1B **74**
W12 . . . . .7B **80**
Yew Trees TW17: Shep 4B **146**
Yew Tree Wlk.
TW4: Houn 5D **112**
Yew Tree Way
CR0: Sels 7B **170**
Yew Wlk. HA1: Harr 1J **59**
YIEWSLEY .1A **92**
Yiewsley Ct.
UB7: Yiew 1A **92**
YMCA Hawker Cen. 5D **132**
Yoakley Rd. N16 . . . . .2E **66**
Yoga Way
KT4: Wor Pk 2C **164**
Yoke Cl. N7 .6J **65**
Yolande Gdns. SE9 . . . . .5C **124**
Yonge Pk. N4 . . . . .3A **66**
York Av.
DA15: Sidc 2J **143**
HA7: Stan 1B **42**
SE17 . . . . .5C **102**
SW14 . . . . .5J **115**
UB3: Hayes 5E **74**
W7 .1J **95**
York Bri. NW1 . . . . .3G **5** (4E **82**)
York Bldgs.
WC2 . . . . .3F **13** (7J **83**)
York Cl. E6 .6D **88**
SE5 . . . . .2C **120**
(off Lilford Rd.)
SM4: Mord 4K **153**
TW18: Staines 6A **128**
W7 .1J **95**
York Ct. N14 . . . . .3D **32**
York Ga. N14 . . . . .2D **32**
NW1 . . . . .4G **5** (4E **82**)
York Gro. SE15 . . . . .1J **121**
York Hall Leisure Cen. 2H **85**
York Hill SE27 . . . . .3B **138**

York Ho. *E16* 1J **105**
    (off De Quincey M.)
  EN2: Enf 1J **23**
  HA9: Wemb 4G **61**
  KT2: King T 7F **133**
    (off Elm Rd.)
  SE1 . . . . .2H **19** (3K **101**)
  SW3 . . . . .5F **17**
  W1 . . . . .5E **4**
    (off York St.)
  W8 . . . . .2K **99**
    (off York Ho. Pl.)
York Ho. Pl. *W8* 2K **99**
Yorkland Av.
  DA16: Well 3K **125**
Yorkley Ho. *W10* 4E **80**
    (off Sutton Way)
York Mans. *SE17* 5C **102**
    (off Browning St.)
  SW5 . . . . .5K **99**
    (off Earls Ct. Rd.)
  SW11 . . . . .1E **118**
    (off Prince of Wales Dr.)
  W1 . . . . .5G **5**
    (off Chiltern St.)
York M. IG1: Ilf 3E **70**
  NW5 . . . . .5F **65**
York Pde. *NW9* 6C **44**
    (off W. Hendon B'way.)
  TW8: Bford 5D **96**
York Pas. *W8* 2K **99**
    (off York Ho. Pl.)
York Pl. IG1: Ilf 2E **70**
  RM10: Dag 6J **73**
  SW11 . . . . .3B **118**
  WC2 . . . . .2F **13**
York Pl. Mans. *W1* 5F **5**
    (off Baker St.)
York Ri.
  BR6: Orp 2J **173**
  NW5 . . . . .3F **65**

York Rd. CR0: C'don 7A **156**
  E4 . . . . .4H **35**
  E7 . . . . .6J **69**
  E10 . . . . .3E **68**
  E17 . . . . .5K **49**
  EN5: New Bar 5F **21**
  HA6: Nwood 2J **39**
  IG1: Ilf 3E **70**
  KT2: King T 7F **133**
  N11 . . . . .6C **32**
  N18 . . . . .6C **34**
  N21 . . . . .7J **23**
  RM13: Rain 7K **73**
  SE1 . . . . .6H **13** (2K **101**)
  SM1: Sutt 6J **165**
  SM2: Sutt 6J **165**
  SW11 . . . . .4A **118**
  SW18 . . . . .4A **118**
  SW19 . . . . .6A **136**
  TW3: Houn 3F **113**
  TW8: Bford 5D **96**
  TW10: Rich 5F **115**
  TW11: Tedd 4J **131**
  W3 . . . . .6J **79**
  W5 . . . . .3C **96**
York Rd. Bus. Cen. SW11 . . . . .2B **118**
Yorkshire Cl. N16 . . . . .3E **66**
Yorkshire Gdns. N18 . . . . .5C **34**
YORKSHIRE GREY 5B **124**
Yorkshire Grey Pl. NW3 . . . . . . .4A **64**
Yorkshire Grey Yd. WC1 . . . . . . .6G **7**
Yorkshire Rd. CR4: Mitc 5J **155**
  E14 . . . . .6A **86**
York Sq. E14 . . . . .6A **86**
York St. CR4: Mitc 7E **154**
  TW1: Twick 1A **132**
  W1 . . . . .6E **4** (5D **82**)
York St. Chambers *W1* 6E **4**
    (off York St.)
York Ter. DA8: Erith 1J **127**
  EN2: Enf 1H **23**

York Ter. E. NW1 . . . . . . .4H **5** (4E **82**)
York Ter. W. NW1 . . . . . . .4G **5** (4E **82**)
Yorkton St. E2 . . . . .2G **85**
York Way KT9: Chess 7E **162**
  N1 . . . . .1F **7** (6J **65**)
  N7 . . . . .6H **65**
  N20 . . . . .3J **31**
  TW13: Hanw 3D **130**
    (not continuous)
York Way Ct. N1 . . . . .1J **83**
    (not continuous)
York Way Est. N7 . . . . .6J **65**
Youngmans Cl. EN2: Enf 1H **23**
Young Ct. NW6 . . . . .7G **63**
Young Rd. E16 . . . . .6A **88**
Youngs Bldgs. EC1 . . . . .3D **8**
Youngs Ct. SW11 . . . . .1E **118**
Youngs Rd. IG2: Ilf 5H **53**
Young St. W8 . . . . .2K **99**
Young Vic Theatre, The 6K **13**
Yoxall Ho. *W10* 4E **80**
    (off Sutton Way)
Yoxford Ct. RM6: Chad H 5B **54**
Yoxley App. IG2: Ilf 6G **53**
Yoxley Dr. IG2: Ilf 6G **53**
Yukon Rd. SW12 . . . . .7F **119**
Yunus Khan Cl. E17 . . . . .5C **50**
Yvon Ho. *SW11* 1E **118**
    (off Alexandra Av.)

Z

Zachary Ct. *SW1* 4D **18**
    (off Montaigne Cl.)
Zachary Ho. *SW9* 1K **119**
    (off Lett Rd.)
Zahra Ho. *NW10* 3E **80**
    (off Harrow Rd.)
Zambezi Dr. N9 . . . . .3D **34**
Zampa Rd. SE16 . . . . .5J **103**

Zander Ct. E2 . . . . .3G **85**
Zangwill Ho. *NW6* 2H **81**
    (off Carlton Vale)
Zangwill Rd. SE3 . . . . .1B **124**
Zapotec Ho. *SE8* 4K **103**
    (off Chilton Gro.)
Zealand Av. UB7: Harm 3E **174**
Zealand Ho. *SE5* 2C **120**
    (off Denmark Rd.)
  SE18 . . . . .4C **106**
Zealand Rd. E3 . . . . .2A **86**
Zeller Ho. *E20* 5D **68**
    (off Scarlet Cl.)
Zenith Cl. NW9 . . . . .3K **43**
Zenith Lodge N3 . . . . .7E **30**
Zennor Rd. SW12 . . . . .1G **137**
Zennor Rd. Ind. Est. SW12 . . . . . .1G **137**
Zenobia Mans. *W14* 6H **99**
    (off Queen's Club Gdns.)
Zenoria St. SE22 . . . . .4F **121**
Zermatt Rd. CR7: Thor H 4C **156**
Zetland Ho. *W8* 3K **99**
    (off Marloes Rd.)
Zetland St. E14 . . . . .5D **86**
Zeus Ct. UB7: Yiew 1A **92**
Zinc Building, The
  SE13 . . . . .4G **123**
Zinnia Mans. *E20* 6D **68**
    (off Olympic Pk. Av.)
Zion Ho. *E1* 6J **85**
    (off Jubilee St.)
Zion Pl. CR7: Thor H 4D **156**
Zion Rd. CR7: Thor H 4D **156**
Zoar St. SE1 . . . . .4C **14** (1C **102**)
Zodiac Ct. CR0: C'don 1B **168**
Zodiac Ho. *E3* 4C **86**
    (off Wellington Way)
Zoffany St. N19 . . . . .2H **65**
Zona Ct. *SE1* 3F **103**
    (off Grange Wlk.)
Zulu M. SW11 . . . . .2C **118**

HOSPITALS, HOSPICES and selected HEALTHCARE FACILITIES covered by this atlas.

N.B. Where it is not possible to name these facilities on the map, the reference given is for the road in which they are situated.

ASHFORD HOSPITAL 2A **128**
London Road
ASHFORD
TW15 3AA
Tel: 01784 884488

BARKING HOSPITAL 7K **71**
Upney Lane
BARKING
IG11 9LX
Tel: 020 3288 2300

BARNES HOSPITAL 3A **116**
South Worple Way
LONDON
SW14 8SU
Tel: 020 3513 3600

BARNET HOSPITAL 4A **20**
Wellhouse Lane
BARNET
EN5 3DJ
Tel: 0845 111 4000

BECKENHAM BEACON 2B **158**
379 Croydon Road
BECKENHAM
BR3 3QL
Tel: 01689 866667

BECKTON CYGNET HOSPITAL 6E **88**
23 Tunnan Leys
LONDON
E6 6ZB
Tel: 020 7511 2299

BELVEDERE PRIVATE HOSPITAL 5C **108**
Knee Hill
LONDON
SE2 0GD
Tel: 0800 917 2959

BETHLEM ROYAL HOSPITAL 7C **158**
Monks Orchard Road
BECKENHAM
BR3 3BX
Tel: 020 3228 6000

BLACKHEATH BMI HOSPITAL 3H **123**
40-42 Lee Terrace
LONDON
SE3 9UD
Tel: 020 8318 7722

**BLACKHEATH BMI HOSPITAL
(OUTPATIENT DEPARTMENT)** 3H **123**
Independents Road
LONDON
SE3 9LF
Tel: 020 8297 4500

BLACKHEATH CYGNET HOSPITAL 1E **122**
80 Blackheath Hill
LONDON
SE10 8AB
Tel: 020 8692 4007

BMI CITY MEDICAL 7G **9**
17 St Helen's Place
LONDON
EC3A 6DG
Tel: 0845 123 5380

BMI EMERGENCY CARE CENTRE 3K **59**
The Clementine Hospital
Sudbury Hill
HARROW
HA1 3RX
Tel: 020 8872 3999

BRENT OLDER PEOPLE DAY HOSPITAL 1C **80**
341 Harlesden Road
LONDON
NW10 3RX
Tel: 020 8459 3562

BUSHEY SPIRE HOSPITAL 1E **26**
Heathbourne Road
Bushey Heath
BUSHEY
WD23 1RD
Tel: 020 8901 5505

CAMDEN MEWS DAY HOSPITAL 7G **65**
1-5 Camden Mews
LONDON
NW1 9DB
Tel: 020 3317 4740

CASSEL HOSPITAL 4D **132**
1 Ham Common
RICHMOND
TW10 7JF
Tel: 020 8483 2900

CAVELL BMI HOSPITAL 2F **23**
Cavell Drive
ENFIELD
EN2 7PR
Tel: 020 8366 2122

CENTRAL MIDDLESEX HOSPITAL 3J **79**
Acton Lane
LONDON
NW10 7NS
Tel: 020 8965 5733

CHARING CROSS HOSPITAL 6F **99**
Fulham Palace Road
LONDON
W6 8RF
Tel: 020 3311 1234

CHASE FARM HOSPITAL 1F **23**
127 The Ridgeway
ENFIELD
EN2 8JL
Tel: 0845 111 4000

CHELSEA & WESTMINSTER HOSPITAL 6A **100**
369 Fulham Road
LONDON
SW10 9NH
Tel: 020 3315 8000

CHILDREN'S HOSPITAL, THE (LEWISHAM) 5D **122**
Lewisham University Hospital
Lewisham High Street
LONDON
SE13 6LH
Tel: 020 8333 3000

CHURCHILL CAMBIAN HOSPITAL 1K **19** (3A **102**)
Barkham Terrace
Lambeth Road
LONDON
SE1 7PW
Tel: 0800 138 1418

CITY AND HACKNEY CENTRE FOR MENTAL HEALTH ...5K **67**
Homerton Row
LONDON
E9 6SR
Tel: 020 8510 5000

CLAYPONDS HOSPITAL 4E **96**
Sterling Place
LONDON
W5 4RN
Tel: 020 8568 0064

CLEMENTINE CHURCHILL BMI HOSPITAL 3K **59**
Sudbury Hill
HARROW
HA1 3RX
Tel: 020 8872 3872

COBORN CENTRE FOR ADOLESCENT MENTAL HEALTH, THE
...........................4A **88**
Glen Road
LONDON
E13 8SP
Tel: 020 7540 6789

CROMWELL BUPA HOSPITAL 4K **99**
162-174 Cromwell Road
LONDON
SW5 0TU
Tel: 020 7460 2000

CROYDON UNIVERSITY HOSPITAL 6B **156**
530 London Road
THORNTON HEATH
CR7 7YE
Tel: 020 8401 3000

Hospitals, Hospices and selected Healthcare Facilities

DEMELZA HOSPICE CARE FOR CHILDREN 6D **124**
5 Wensley Close
LONDON
SE9 5AB
Tel: 020 8859 9800

DULWICH COMMUNITY HOSPITAL 4E **120**
East Dulwich Grove
LONDON
SE22 8PT
Tel: 020 3049 8800

EALING CYGNET HOSPITAL 5E **78**
22 Corfton Road
LONDON
W5 2HT
Tel: 020 8991 6699

EALING HOSPITAL 1H **95**
Uxbridge Road
SOUTHALL
UB1 3HW
Tel: 020 8967 5000

EAST HAM CARE CENTRE & DAY HOSPITAL 7B **70**
Shrewsbury Road
LONDON
E7 8QP
Tel: 020 8475 2001

EASTMAN DENTAL HOSPITAL & DENTAL INSTITUTE
.................................3G **7** (4K **83**)
256 Gray's Inn Road
LONDON
WC1X 8LD
Tel: 020 3456 7899

EDGWARE COMMUNITY HOSPITAL 7C **28**
Burnt Oak Broadway
EDGWARE
HA8 0AD
Tel: 020 8952 2381

EDRIDGE ROAD COMMUNITY HEALTH CENTRE 3C **168**
Impact House
Edridge Road
CROYDON
CR9 1PJ
Tel: 020 3040 0800

ELTHAM COMMUNITY HOSPITAL 6D **124**
Passey Place
LONDON
SE9 5DA

ERITH & DISTRICT HOSPITAL 6K **109**
Park Crescent
ERITH
DA8 3EE
Tel: 020 8308 3131

EVELINA CHILDREN'S HOSPITAL 1G **19** (3K **101**)
St Thomas' Hospital
Westminster Bridge Road
LONDON
SE1 7EH
Tel: 020 7188 7188

FINCHLEY MEMORIAL HOSPITAL 7F **31**
Granville Road
LONDON
N12 0JE
Tel: 020 8349 7500

FITZROY SQUARE BMI HOSPITAL 4A **6** (4G **83**)
14 Fitzroy Square
LONDON
W1T 6AH
Tel: 020 7388 4954

GARDEN BMI HOSPITAL 3E **44**
46-50 Sunny Gardens Road
LONDON
NW4 1RP
Tel: 020 8457 4500

GATEWAY SURGICAL CENTRE 4B **88**
Cherry Tree Way
Glen Road
LONDON
E13 8SL
Tel: 020 7476 4000

GENERAL MEDICAL WALK-IN CENTRE
(LIVERPOOL STREET) 5H **9** (5E **84**)
Exchange Arcade
Bishopsgate
LONDON
EC2M 3WA
Tel: 0845 437 0691

GOODMAYES HOSPITAL 5A **54**
Barley Lane
ILFORD
IG3 8XJ
Tel: 0844 600 1207

GORDON HOSPITAL 4C **18** (4H **101**)
Bloomburg Street
LONDON
SW1V 2RH
Tel: 020 8746 8733

GRAYS COURT COMMUNITY HOSPITAL 7H **73**
John Parker Close
DAGENHAM
RM10 9SR
Tel: 020 8724 1463

GREAT ORMOND STREET HOSPITAL FOR CHILDREN
.................................4G **7** (4J **83**)
Great Ormond Street
LONDON
WC1N 3JH
Tel: 020 7405 9200

GREENWICH & BEXLEY COMMUNITY HOSPICE 5C **108**
185 Bostall Hill
LONDON
SE2 0GB
Tel: 020 8312 2244

GUY'S HOSPITAL 5E **14** (2D **102**)
Great Maze Pond
LONDON
SE1 9RT
Tel: 020 7188 7188

GUY'S NUFFIELD HOUSE 6E **14**
Guy's Hospital
Newcomen Street
LONDON
SE1 1YR
Tel: 020 7188 5282

HAMMERSMITH HOSPITAL 6C **80**
Du Cane Road
LONDON
W12 0HS
Tel: 020 3313 1000

HARLEY STREET CLINIC 5J **5** (5F **83**)
35 Weymouth Street
LONDON
W1G 8BJ
Tel: 020 7935 7700

HARLINGTON HOSPICE 5F **93**
St Peters Way
HAYES
UB3 5AB
Tel: 020 8759 0453

HARRIS HOSPISCARE 4K **173**
Tregony Road
ORPINGTON
BR6 9XA
Tel: 01689 825755

HARROW CYGNET HARROW 2J **59**
London Road
HARROW
HA1 3JL
Tel: 020 8966 7000

HAVEN HOUSE CHILDREN'S HOSPICE 6C **36**
High Road
WOODFORD GREEN
IG8 9LB
Tel: 020 8505 9944

HAYES GROVE PRIORY HOSPITAL 2J **171**
Prestons Road
Hayes
BROMLEY
BR2 7AS
Tel: 020 8462 7722

HEART HOSPITAL 6J **5** (5E **82**)
16-18 Westmoreland Street
LONDON
W1G 8PH
Tel: 020 3456 7898

HIGHGATE HOSPITAL 6D **46**
17- 19 View Road
LONDON
N6 4DJ
Tel: 020 8341 4182

HIGHGATE MENTAL HEALTH CENTRE 2F **65**
Dartmouth Park Hill
LONDON
N19 5NX
Tel: 020 7561 4000

HILLINGDON HOSPITAL 5B **74**
Pield Heath Road
UXBRIDGE
UB8 3NN
Tel: 01895 238282

HOLLY HOUSE HOSPITAL 2E **36**
High Road
BUCKHURST HILL
IG9 5HX
Tel: 020 8505 3311

HOMERTON UNIVERSITY HOSPITAL 5K **67**
Homerton Row
LONDON
E9 6SR
Tel: 020 8510 5555

HOSPITAL FOR TROPICAL DISEASES 4B **6** (4G **83**)
Mortimer Market
Capper Street
LONDON
WC1E 6JB
Tel: 020 3456 7891

HOSPITAL OF ST JOHN & ST ELIZABETH 2B **82**
60 Grove End Road
LONDON
NW8 9NH
Tel: 020 7806 4000

JOHN HOWARD CENTRE 5A **68**
12 Kenworthy Road
LONDON
E9 5TD
Tel: 020 8510 2003

KING EDWARD VII'S HOSPITAL SISTER AGNES
....5H **5** (5E **82**)
5-10 Beaumont Street
LONDON
W1G 6AA
Tel: 020 7486 4411

KING GEORGE HOSPITAL 4A **54**
Barley Lane
ILFORD
IG3 8YB
Tel: 020 8983 8000

KING'S COLLEGE HOSPITAL 2D **120**
Denmark Hill
LONDON
SE5 9RS
Tel: 020 3299 9000

KING'S OAK BMI HOSPITAL 1F **23**
The Ridgeway
ENFIELD
EN2 8SD
Tel: 020 8370 9500

KINGSTON HOSPITAL 1H **151**
Galsworthy Road
KINGSTON UPON THAMES
KT2 7QB
Tel: 020 8546 7711

LAMBETH HOSPITAL 3K **119**
108 Landor Road
LONDON
SW9 9NU
Tel: 020 3228 6000

LISTER HOSPITAL 6J **17** (5F **101**)
Chelsea Bridge Road
LONDON
SW1W 8RH
Tel: 020 7730 3417

LONDON BRIDGE HOSPITAL 4F **15** (1D **102**)
27 Tooley Street
LONDON
SE1 2PR
Tel: 0845 602 7906

LONDON CHEST HOSPITAL 2J **85**
Bonner Road
LONDON
E9 9JX
Tel: 020 3146 5000

LONDON CLINIC 4H **5** (4E **82**)
20 Devonshire Place
LONDON
W1G 6BW
Tel: 020 7935 4444

LONDON EYE HOSPITAL 7J **5**
8-10 Harley Street
LONDON
W1G 9PF
Tel: 0800 612 2021

LONDON INDEPENDENT BMI HOSPITAL 5K **85**
1 Beaumont Square
LONDON
E1 4NL
Tel: 020 7780 2400

LONDON WELBECK HOSPITAL 6J **5** (5F **83**)
27 Welbeck Street
LONDON
W1G 8EN
Tel: 020 7224 2242

MARGARET CENTRE (HOSPICE) 6G **51**
Whipps Cross University Hospital
Whipps Cross Road
LONDON
E11 1NR
Tel: 020 8535 6604

MARIE CURIE HOSPICE, HAMPSTEAD 5B **64**
11 Lyndhurst Gardens
LONDON
NW3 5NS
Tel: 020 7853 3400

MAUDSLEY HOSPITAL 2D **120**
Denmark Hill
LONDON
SE5 8AZ
Tel: 020 3228 6000

MEADOW HOUSE HOSPICE 2H **95**
Uxbridge Road
SOUTHALL
UB1 3HW
Tel: 020 8967 5179

MEMORIAL HOSPITAL 2E **124**
Shooters Hill
LONDON
SE18 3RG
Tel: 020 8836 8500

MILDMAY HOSPITAL 2J **9** (3F **85**)
Tabernacle Gardens
LONDON
E2 7DZ
Tel: 020 7613 6300

MILE END HOSPITAL 4K **85**
Bancroft Road
LONDON
E1 4DG
Tel: 020 3416 5000

MINOR INJURIES UNIT (DAGENHAM) 7H **73**
Grays Court Community Hospital
John Parker Close
DAGENHAM
RM10 9SR
Tel: 202 8724 1463

**MINOR INJURIES UNIT
(NORTHUMBERLAND HEATH)** 6K **109**
Hind Crescent
Northumberland Heath
ERITH
DA8 3DB
Tel: 01322 336556

MINOR INJURIES UNIT (NORTH WOOLWICH) 1D **106**
Practice, The
76 Albert Road
LONDON
E16 2DY
Tel: 020 8104 2222

MINOR INJURIES UNIT (ROEHAMPTON) 6C **116**
Roehampton Lane
LONDON
SW15 5PN
Tel: 020 8487 6000

**MINOR INJURIES UNIT
(ST BARTHOLOMEW'S HOSPITAL)** 6B **8**
West Smithfield
LONDON
EC1A 7BE
Tel: 020 3465 6843

MINOR INJURIES UNIT (SILVERTOWN) 1K **105**
Practice Britannia Village, The
12a Wesley Avenue
LONDON
E16 1RZ
Tel: 020 3040 0100

MOLESEY HOSPITAL 5E **148**
High Street
WEST MOLESEY
KT8 2LU
Tel: 020 8941 4481

MOORFIELDS EYE HOSPITAL 2E **8** (3D **84**)
162 City Road
LONDON
EC1V 2PD
Tel: 020 7253 3411

NATIONAL HOSPITAL FOR NEUROLOGY & NEUROSURGERY
....4F **7** (4J **83**)
Queen Square
LONDON
WC1N 3BG
Tel: 020 3456 7890

NELSON HOSPITAL 2H **153**
Kingston Road
LONDON
SW20 8DB
Tel: 020 8296 3795

NEWHAM CENTRE FOR MENTAL HEALTH 4B **88**
Cherry Tree Way
Glen Road
LONDON
E13 8SP
Tel: 020 7540 4380

NEWHAM UNIVERSITY HOSPITAL 4A **88**
Glen Road
LONDON
E13 8SL
Tel: 020 7476 4000

NEW VICTORIA HOSPITAL 1A **152**
184 Coombe Lane West
KINGSTON UPON THAMES
KT2 7EG
Tel: 020 8949 9000

NHS WALK-IN CENTRE
(ANGEL MEDICAL PRACTICE) 2A **84**
Ritchie Street Group Practice
34 Ritchie Street
LONDON
N1 0DG
Tel: 020 7837 1663

NHS WALK-IN CENTRE (ASHFORD) 2A **128**
Ashford Hospital
London Road
ASHFORD
TW15 3FE
Tel: 01784 884000

NHS WALK-IN CENTRE (ASHFORD CLINIC) 3A **128**
66 Stanwell Road
ASHFORD
TW15 3DU
Tel: 01784 883700

NHS WALK-IN CENTRE (BARKING HOSPITAL) 7K **71**
Upney Lane
BARKING
IG11 9LX
Tel: 020 8924 6262

NHS WALK-IN CENTRE (BOW) 4D **86**
St. Andrew's Health Centre
2 Hannaford Walk
LONDON
E3 3FF

NHS WALK-IN CENTRE (CLAPHAM JUNCTION) 3C **118**
Junction Health Centre, The
Arch 5-8, Clapham Junction Station
Grant Road
LONDON
SW11 2NU
Tel: 020 3131 0532

NHS WALK-IN CENTRE
(CRICKLEWOOD HEALTH CENTRE) 4F **63**
Britannia Business Centre
Cricklewood Lane
NW2 1DZ
Tel: 03000 334335

NHS WALK-IN CENTRE (FINCHLEY) 7F **31**
Finchley Memorial Hospital
Granville Road
LONDON
N12 0JE
Tel: 020 8349 7470

NHS WALK-IN CENTRE (ISLE OF DOGS) 2C **104**
Barkantine Practice
121 Westferry Road
LONDON
E14 8JH
Tel: 020 7791 8080

NHS WALK-IN CENTRE (KENSAL TOWN) 4H **81**
427-429 Harrow Road
Paddington
LONDON
W10 4RE
Tel: 020 8962 8700

NHS WALK-IN CENTRE (LEYTON) 3D **68**
Oliver Road Medical Centre
75 Oliver Road
LONDON
E10 5LG
Tel: 020 8430 8282

NHS WALK-IN CENTRE (LISTER HEALTH CENTRE) 1F **121**
101 Peckham Road
LONDON
SE15 5LJ
Tel: 020 3049 8430

NHS WALK-IN CENTRE (LOXFORD, ILFORD) 5G **71**
Loxford Practice, The
417 Ilford Lane
ILFORD
IG1 2SN
Tel: 020 8822 3800

NHS WALK-IN CENTRE
(ORCHARD VILLAGE HEALTH CENTRE) 2K **91**
Roman Close
RAINHAM
RM13 8QB
Tel: 01708 793900

NHS WALK-IN CENTRE (PARSONS GREEN) 1J **117**
5-7 Parsons Green
LONDON
SW6 4UL
Tel: 020 8846 6758

NHS WALK-IN CENTRE (PINNER) 3C **40**
Pinn Medical Centre, The
37 Love Lane
PINNER
HA5 3EE
Tel: 020 8866 5766

NHS WALK-IN CENTRE (SOHO) 1C **12**
1 Frith Street
LONDON
W1D 3HZ
Tel: 020 7534 6575

NHS WALK-IN CENTRE (STREATHAM) 3J **137**
Gracefield Gardens Health Centre
Gracefield Gardens
LONDON
SW16 2ST
Tel: 020 3049 4040

NHS WALK-IN CENTRE (STREATHAM) 7G **69**
DMC Healthcare One
10 Vicarage Lane
Stratford
LONDON
E15 4ES
Tel: 020 8536 2277

NHS WALK-IN CENTRE (TEDDINGTON) 6J **131**
Teddington Memorial Hospital
Hampton Road
TEDDINGTON
TW11 0JL
Tel: 020 8714 4004

NHS WALK-IN CENTRE (THAMESMEAD) 2J **107**
Thamesmead Health Centre
4-5 Thames Reach
LONDON
SE28 0NY
Tel: 020 8319 5880

NHS WALK-IN CENTRE
(WALDRON HEALTH CENTRE) 7B **104**
Amersham Vale
New Cross
LONDON
SE14 6LD
Tel: 020 3049 2370

NHS WALK-IN CENTRE (WEMBLEY) 6D **60**
116 Chaplin Road
WEMBLEY
HA0 4UZ
Tel: 020 8900 6020

NHS WALK-IN CENTRE (WOOLWICH) 4F **107**
Clover Health Centre
General Gordon Place
Woolwich
LONDON
SE18 6AB
Tel: 020 8331 0567

NIGHTINGALE CAPIO HOSPITAL 5D **4** (5C **82**)
11-19 Lisson Grove
LONDON
NW1 6SH
Tel: 020 7535 7700

NOAH'S ARK CHILDREN'S HOSPICE 4C **20**
Beauchamp Court
10 Victors Way
BARNET
EN5 5TZ
Tel: 020 8449 8877

NORTH EAST LONDON NHS TREATMENT CENTRE 5A **54**
King George Hospital
Barley Lane
ILFORD
IG3 8YB
Tel: 0333 200 4069

NORTH LONDON CLINIC 2B **34**
15 Church Street
LONDON
N9 9DY
Tel: 020 8956 1234

NORTH LONDON HOSPICE (BARNET) 3F **31**
47 Woodside Avenue
LONDON
N12 8TT
Tel: 020 8343 8841

NORTH LONDON HOSPICE (ENFIELD) 3H **33**
110 Barrowell Green
ENFIELD
N21 3AY
Tel: 020 8343 8841

NORTH LONDON PRIORY HOSPITAL 1D **32**
The Bourne
LONDON
N14 6RA
Tel: 020 8882 8191

NORTH MIDDLESEX UNIVERSITY HOSPITAL 5K **33**
Sterling Way
LONDON
N18 1QX
Tel: 020 8887 2000

NORTHWICK PARK HOSPITAL 7A **42**
Watford Road
HARROW
HA1 3UJ
Tel: 020 8864 3232

OLD BROAD STREET PRIVATE MEDICAL CENTRE 7G **9**
31 Old Broad Street
LONDON
EC2N 1HT
Tel: 020 7496 3555

ORPINGTON HOSPITAL 4K **173**
Sevenoaks Road
ORPINGTON
BR6 9JU
Tel: 01689 863000

PARK ROYAL CENTRE (FOR MENTAL HEALTH) 2J **79**
Central Way
LONDON
NW10 7NS
Tel: 020 8955 4400

PARKSIDE HOSPITAL 3F **135**
53 Parkside
LONDON
SW19 5NX
Tel: 020 8971 8000

PEMBRIDGE PALLIATIVE CARE CENTRE 5F **81**
St Charles Hospital
Exmoor Street
LONDON
W10 6DZ
Tel: 020 8962 4410

PORTLAND HOSPITAL FOR WOMEN & CHILDREN
....4K **5** (4F **83**)
205-209 Great Portland Street
LONDON
W1W 5AH
Tel: 020 7580 4400

PRIMARY URGENT CARE CENTRE (HACKNEY) 5K **67**
Homerton University Hospital
Homerton Row
LONDON
E9 6SR
Tel: 020 8510 5793

PRINCESS GRACE HOSPITAL 5G **5** (4E **82**)
42-52 Nottingham Place
LONDON
W1M 3FD
Tel: 020 7486 1234

PRINCESS ROYAL UNIVERSITY HOSPITAL 3E **172**
Farnborough Common
ORPINGTON
BR6 8ND
Tel: 01689 863000

QUEEN CHARLOTTE'S & CHELSEA HOSPITAL 6C **80**
Du Cane Road
LONDON
W12 0HS
Tel: 020 3313 1111

QUEEN ELIZABETH HOSPITAL 7C **106**
Stadium Road
LONDON
SE18 4QH
Tel: 020 8836 6000

QUEEN MARY'S HOSPITAL FOR CHILDREN 1A **166**
Wrythe Lane
CARSHALTON
SM5 1AA
Tel: 020 8296 2000

QUEEN MARY'S HOSPITAL, ROEHAMPTON 6C **116**
Roehampton Lane
LONDON
SW15 5PN
Tel: 020 8725 3579

QUEEN MARY'S HOSPITAL, SIDCUP 5A **144**
Frognal Avenue
SIDCUP
DA14 6LT
Tel: 020 8302 2678

QUEEN MARY'S HOUSE 3A **64**
23 East Heath Road
LONDON
NW3 1DU
Tel: 020 3317 6584

QUEEN'S HOSPITAL 7K **55**
Rom Valley Way
ROMFORD
RM7 0AG
Tel: 01708 435000

RICHARD DESMOND CHILDREN'S EYE CENTRE 2E **8**
3 Peerless Street
LONDON
EC1V 9EZ
Tel: 020 7253 3411

RICHARD HOUSE CHILDREN'S HOSPICE 7B **88**
Richard House Drive
LONDON
E16 3RG
Tel: 020 7511 0222

RICHMOND ROYAL HOSPITAL 3E **114**
Kew Foot Road
RICHMOND
TW9 2TE
Tel: 020 3513 3238

RODING SPIRE HOSPITAL 3B **52**
Roding Lane South
ILFORD
IG4 5PZ
Tel: 020 8709 7817

ROEHAMPTON HUNTERCOMBE HOSPITAL 7C **116**
Holybourne Avenue
LONDON
SW15 4JD
Tel: 020 8780 6155

ROEHAMPTON PRIORY HOSPITAL 4B **116**
Priory Lane
LONDON
SW15 5JJ
Tel: 020 8876 8261

ROYAL BROMPTON HOSPITAL 5C **16** (5C **100**)
Sydney Street
LONDON
SW3 6NP
Tel: 020 7352 8121

ROYAL BROMPTON HOSPITAL (OUTPATIENTS)
....5B **16** (5B **100**)
Fulham Road
LONDON
SW3 6HP
Tel: 020 7351 8011

ROYAL FREE HOSPITAL 5C **64**
Pond Street
LONDON
NW3 2QG
Tel: 020 7794 0500

ROYAL HOSPITAL FOR NEURO-DISABILITY 6G **117**
West Hill
LONDON
SW15 3SW
Tel: 020 8780 4500

ROYAL LONDON HOSPITAL 5H **85**
Whitechapel Road
LONDON
E1 1BB
Tel: 020 3416 5000

ROYAL LONDON HOSPITAL FOR INTEGRATED MEDICINE
....5F **7** (5J **83**)
60 Great Ormond Street
LONDON
WC1N 3HR
Tel: 020 3456 7890

ROYAL MARSDEN HOSPITAL (FULHAM) 5B **16** (5B **100**)
Fulham Road
LONDON
SW3 6JJ
Tel: 020 7352 8171

ROYAL NATIONAL ORTHOPAEDIC HOSPITAL 2G **27**
Brockley Hill
STANMORE
HA7 4LP
Tel: 020 8954 2300

ROYAL NATIONAL ORTHOPAEDIC HOSPITAL
(CENTRAL LONDON OUTPATIENT DEPT.)
....4K **5** (4F **83**)
45-51 Bolsover Street
LONDON
W1W 5AQ
Tel: 020 8954 2300

ROYAL NATIONAL THROAT, NOSE & EAR HOSPITAL
....1G **7** (3K **83**)
330 Gray's Inn Road
LONDON
WC1X 8DA
Tel: 020 3456 7890

ST ANN'S HOSPITAL 5C **48**
St Ann's Road
LONDON
N15 3TH
Tel: 020 8442 6000

ST ANTHONY'S HOSPITAL 1F **165**
801 London Road
SUTTON
SM3 9DW
Tel: 020 8337 6691

ST BARTHOLOMEW'S HOSPITAL 6B **8** (5B **84**)
West Smithfield
LONDON
EC1A 7BE
Tel: 020 3416 5000

ST BERNARD'S HOSPITAL 2H **95**
Uxbridge Road
SOUTHALL
UB1 3EU
Tel: 020 8354 8354

ST CHARLES HOSPITAL 5F **81**
Exmoor Street
LONDON
W10 6DZ
Tel: 020 8206 7343

ST CHRISTOPHER'S HOSPICE 5J **139**
51-59 Lawrie Park Road
LONDON
SE26 6DZ
Tel: 020 8768 4500

ST EBBA'S 7J **163**
Hook Road
EPSOM
KT19 8QJ
Tel: 01883 388000

ST GEORGE'S HOSPITAL (TOOTING) 5B **136**
Blackshaw Road
LONDON
SW17 0QT
Tel: 020 8672 1255

ST HELIER HOSPITAL 1A **166**
Wrythe Lane
CARSHALTON
SM5 1AA
Tel: 020 8296 2000

ST JOHN'S HOSPICE 2B **82**
Hospital of St John & St Elizabeth
60 Grove End Road
LONDON
NW8 9NH
Tel: 020 7806 4050

ST JOSEPH'S HOSPICE 1H **85**
Mare Street
LONDON
E8 4SA
Tel: 020 8525 6047

**ST LUKE'S HEALTHCARE FOR THE CLERGY
(FITZROY SQUARE BMI HOSPITAL)** 4A **6** (4G **83**)
14 Fitzroy Square
LONDON
W1T 6AH
Tel: 020 7388 4954

ST LUKE'S HOSPICE 5D **42**
Kenton Road
HARROW
HA3 0YG
Tel: 020 8382 8000

ST MARK'S HOSPITAL 7B **42**
Watford Road
HARROW
HA1 3UJ
Tel: 020 8235 4000

ST MARY'S HOSPITAL 7B **4** (6B **82**)
Praed Street
LONDON
W2 1NY
Tel: 020 3312 6666

ST MICHAEL'S HOSPITAL 1J **23**
Gater Drive
ENFIELD
EN2 0JB
Tel: 020 8375 2941

ST PANCRAS HOSPITAL 1H **83**
4 St Pancras Way
LONDON
NW1 0PE
Tel: 020 7530 3500

ST RAPHAEL'S HOSPICE 2F **165**
London Road
SUTTON
SM3 9DX
Tel: 020 8335 4575

ST THOMAS' HOSPITAL 7G **13** (3K **101**)
Westminster Bridge Road
LONDON
SE1 7EH
Tel: 020 7188 7188

SHIRLEY OAKS BMI HOSPITAL 7J **157**
Poppy Lane
CROYDON
CR9 8AB
Tel: 020 8655 5500

SHOOTING STAR HOUSE, CHILDREN'S HOSPICE 6D **130**
The Avenue
HAMPTON
TW12 3RA
Tel: 020 8783 2000

SLOANE BMI HOSPITAL 1F **159**
125 Albemarle Road
BECKENHAM
BR3 5HS
Tel: 020 8466 4000

SPRINGFIELD UNIVERSITY HOSPITAL 2C **136**
61 Glenburnie Road
LONDON
SW17 7DJ
Tel: 020 3513 5000

TEDDINGTON MEMORIAL HOSPITAL 6J **131**
Hampton Road
TEDDINGTON
TW11 0JL
Tel: 020 8714 4000

THORPE COOMBE HOSPITAL 3E **50**
714 Forest Road
LONDON
E17 3HP
Tel: 0300 555 1239

TOLWORTH HOSPITAL 2G **163**
Red Lion Road
SURBITON
KT6 7QU
Tel: 020 8390 0102

TOWER HAMLETS CENTRE FOR MENTAL HEALTH 4K **85**
Bancroft Road
Mile End
LONDON
E1 4DG
Tel: 020 8121 5001

TRINITY HOSPICE 4F **119**
30 Clapham Common North Side
LONDON
SW4 0RN
Tel: 020 7787 1000

UCH MACMILLAN CANCER CENTRE 4B **6**
Huntley Street
LONDON
WC1E 6DH
Tel: 020 3456 7016

UNIVERSITY COLLEGE HOSPITAL 3B **6** (4G **83**)
235 Euston Road
LONDON
NW1 2BU
Tel: 020 3456 7890

UNIVERSITY HOSPITAL, LEWISHAM 5D **122**
Lewisham High Street
LONDON
SE13 6LH
Tel: 020 8333 3000

UPTON CENTRE 4E **126**
14 Upton Road
BEXLEYHEATH
DA6 8LQ
Tel: 020 8301 7911

URGENT CARE CENTRE (BARNET HOSPITAL) 4A **20**
Wellhouse Lane
BARNET
EN5 3DJ

URGENT CARE CENTRE (BECKENHAM BEACON) 2B **158**
379 Croydon Road
BECKENHAM
BR3 3QL
Tel: 01689 866037

URGENT CARE CENTRE (CARSHALTON) 1A **166**
St Helier Hospital
Wrythe Lane
CARSHALTON
SM5 1AA
Tel: 020 8296 2000

**URGENT CARE CENTRE
(CENTRAL MIDDLESEX HOSPITAL)** 3J **79**
Acton Lane
LONDON
NW10 7NS
Tel: 020 8965 5733

URGENT CARE CENTRE (CHASE FARM HOSPITAL) 1F **23**
The Ridgeway
ENFIELD
EN2 8JL
Tel: 020 8375 1010

**URGENT CARE CENTRE
(CHELSEA & WESTMINSTER HOSPITAL)** 6A **100**
369 Fulham Road
LONDON
SW10 9NH
Tel: 020 3315 8000

URGENT CARE CENTRE (EALING) 2H **95**
Ealing Hospital
Uxbridge Road
UB1 3HW
Tel: 0333 999 2577

URGENT CARE CENTRE (FULHAM) 5F **99**
Charing Cross Hospital
Fulham Palace Road
LONDON
W6 8RF
Tel: 020 8846 1005

URGENT CARE CENTRE
(GUY'S HOSPITAL) 6F **15** (2D **102**)
Great Maze Pond
LONDON
SE1 9RT
Tel: 020 3049 8970

URGENT CARE CENTRE
(HAMMERSMITH HOSPITAL) 6C **80**
Du Cane Road
LONDON
W12 0HS
Tel: 020 8383 4103

URGENT CARE CENTRE (HAMPSTEAD) 5C **64**
Royal Free Hospital
Pond Street
LONDON
NW3 2QG
Tel: 020 7794 0500

URGENT CARE CENTRE (HILLINGDON HOSPITAL) 5B **74**
Hillingdon Hospital
Pield Heath Road
UXBRIDGE
UB8 3NN
Tel: 01895 238282

URGENT CARE CENTRE
(HOMERTON UNIVERSITY HOSPITAL) 5K **67**
Homerton Row
LONDON
E9 6SR
Tel: 020 8510 5555

URGENT CARE CENTRE (KING GEORGE HOSPITAL) 5A **54**
Barley Lane
ILFORD
IG3 8YB
Tel: 020 8983 8000

URGENT CARE CENTRE (NEWHAM) 4A **88**
Newham University Hospital
Glen Road
LONDON
E13 8SL
Tel: 020 7476 4000

URGENT CARE CENTRE
(NORTH MIDDLESEX UNIVERSITY HOSPITAL)
.... 5K **33**
Sterling Way
LONDON
N18 1QX
Tel: 020 8887 2000

URGENT CARE CENTRE
(QUEEN ELIZABETH HOSPITAL) 6C **106**
Stadium Road
LONDON
SE18 4QH
Tel: 020 8836 6000

URGENT CARE CENTRE (QUEEN'S HOSPITAL) 7K **55**
Rom Valley Way
ROMFORD
RM7 0AG
Tel: 01708 435000

URGENT CARE CENTRE
(ST CHARLES CENTRE FOR WELL BEING) 5F **81**
Exmoor Street
LONDON
W10 6DZ
Tel: 020 8962 4262

URGENT CARE CENTRE
(ST MARY'S HOSPITAL) 7A **4** (6B **82**)
Praed Street
LONDON
W2 1NY
Tel: 020 3312 6666

URGENT CARE CENTRE (SIDCUP) 6A **144**
Queen Mary's Hospital
Frognal Avenue
SIDCUP
DA14 6LT
Tel: 020 8308 5611

URGENT CARE CENTRE (THORNTON HEATH) 6B **156**
Croydon University Hospital
530 London Road
THORNTON HEATH
CR7 7YE
Tel: 020 8401 3000

URGENT CARE CENTRE (TOOTING) 5C **136**
St George's Hospital
Blackshaw Road
LONDON
SW17 0QT
Tel: 020 8725 1255

URGENT CARE CENTRE
(UNIVERSITY COLLEGE HOSPITAL) 3B **6** (4G **83**)
235 Euston Road
LONDON
NW1 2BU

URGENT CARE CENTRE
(UNIVERSITY HOSPITAL LEWISHAM) 5D **122**
Lewisham High Street
LONDON
SE13 6LH
Tel: 020 8333 3000

URGENT CARE CENTRE
(WEST MIDDLESEX UNIVERSITY HOSPITAL)
.... 2A **114**
Twickenham Road
ISLEWORTH
TW7 6AF
Tel: 020 8560 2121

URGENT CARE CENTRE
(WHIPPS CROSS UNIVERSITY HOSPITAL) 6F **51**
Whipps Cross Road
LONDON
E11 1NR
Tel: 020 3416 5000

URGENT CARE CENTRE
(WHITTINGTON HOSPITAL) 2G **65**
Magdala Avenue
LONDON
N19 5NF
Tel: 020 7288 5216

WELLINGTON HOSPITAL 1B **4** (2B **82**)
8a Wellington Place
LONDON
NW8 9LE
Tel: 020 7483 5148

WESTERN EYE HOSPITAL 5E **4** (5D **82**)
171 Marylebone Road
LONDON
NW1 5QH
Tel: 020 3312 6666

WEST MIDDLESEX UNIVERSITY HOSPITAL 2A **114**
Twickenham Road
ISLEWORTH
TW7 6AF
Tel: 020 8560 2121

WEYMOUTH BMI HOSPITAL, THE 5H **5**
42-46 Weymouth Street
LONDON
W1G 6NP
Tel: 020 7935 1200

WHIPPS CROSS UNIVERSITY HOSPITAL 5F **51**
Whipps Cross Road
Leytonstone
LONDON
E11 1NR
Tel: 020 3416 5000

WHITTINGTON HOSPITAL 2G **65**
Magdala Avenue
LONDON
N19 5NF
Tel: 020 7272 3070

WILLESDEN CENTRE FOR HEALTH & CARE 7C **62**
Robson Avenue
LONDON
NW10 3RY
Tel: 020 8438 7006

WOODBURY UNIT 6G **51**
178 James Lane
LONDON
E11 1NR
Tel: 0300 555 1260

PUBLIC TRANSPORT
(RAIL, DLR, UNDERGROUND, OVERGROUND, TRAMLINK, RIVERBUS,
BUS STATIONS, CABLE CAR and PARK & RIDE)
with their map square reference

A

Abbey Road (DLR) 2G 87
Abbey Wood (Rail) 3C 108
Acton Central (Overground) 1K 97
Acton Main Line (Rail) 6J 79
Acton Town (Underground) 2G 97
Addington Bus 6C 170
Addington Village Stop (London Tramlink) 6C 170
Addiscombe Stop (London Tramlink) 1G 169
Albany Park (Rail) 2D 144
Aldgate Bus 1J 15 (6F 85)
Aldgate East (Underground) 7K 9 (6F 85)
Aldgate (Underground) 1J 15 (6F 85)
Alexandra Palace (Rail) 2J 47
All Saints (DLR) 7D 86
Alperton (Underground) 1D 78
Ampere Way Stop (London Tramlink) 1K 167
Anerley (Rail & Overground) 1H 157
Angel Road (Rail) 5D 34
Angel (Underground) 2A 84
Archway (Underground) 2G 65
Arena Stop (London Tramlink) 5J 157
Arnos Grove (Underground) 5B 32
Arsenal (Underground) 3A 66
Ashford (Rail) 4B 128
Avenue Road Stop (London Tramlink) 2K 157

B

Baker Street (Underground) 4F 5 (4D 82)
Balham (Rail & Underground) 1F 137
Bankside Pier (River Bus & Tours) 3C 14 (7C 84)
Bank (Underground & DLR) 1E 14 (6D 84)
Barbican (Underground) 5C 8 (5C 84)
Barkingside (Underground) 3H 53
Barking (Rail, Underground & Overground) 7G 71
Barnehurst (Rail) 2J 127
Barnes Bridge (Rail) 2B 116
Barnes (Rail) 3C 116
Barons Court (Underground) 5G 99
Battersea Park (Rail) 7F 101
Bayswater (Underground) 7K 81
Beckenham Hill (Rail) 5E 140
Beckenham Junction (Rail & London Tramlink) ...1C 158
Beckenham Road Stop (London Tramlink) 1A 158
Beckton Park (DLR) 7D 88
Beckton (DLR) 5E 88
Becontree (Underground) 6D 72
Beddington Lane Stop (London Tramlink) 6G 155
Belgrave Walk Stop (London Tramlink) 4B 154
Bellingham (Rail) 3D 140
Belsize Park (Underground) 5C 64
Belvedere (Rail) 3H 109
Bermondsey (Underground) 3G 103
Berrylands (Rail) 4H 151
Bethnal Green (Rail) 4H 85
Bethnal Green (Underground) 3J 85
Bexleyheath (Rail) 2E 126
Bexley (Rail) 1G 145
Bickley (Rail) 3C 160
Birkbeck (Rail & London Tramlink) 3J 157
Blackfriars Millennium Pier (River Bus) ...2A 14 (7B 84)
Blackfriars (Rail & Underground) 2A 14 (7B 84)
Blackheath (Rail) 3H 123
Blackhorse Lane Stop (London Tramlink) 7G 157
Blackhorse Road (Underground & Overground) 4K 49
Blackwall (DLR) 7E 86
Bond Street (Underground) 1J 11 (6E 82)
Borough (Underground) 7D 14 (2C 102)
Boston Manor (Underground) 4A 96
Bounds Green (Underground) 6C 32
Bow Church (DLR) 3C 86
Bowes Park (Rail) 7D 32

Bow Road (Underground) 3C 86
Brent Cross (Underground) 7F 45
Brentford (Rail) 6C 96
Brimsdown (Rail) 3F 25
Brixton (Rail & Underground) 4A 120
Brockley (Rail & Overground) 3A 122
Bromley-by-Bow (Underground) 3D 86
Bromley North (Rail) 1J 159
Bromley South (Rail) 3J 159
Brondesbury Park (Overground) 1G 81
Brondesbury (Overground) 7H 63
Bruce Grove (Rail) 2F 49
Buckhurst Hill (Underground) 2G 37
Burnt Oak (Underground) 1J 43
Bush Hill Park (Rail) 6A 24

C

Cable Car 2H 105
Cadogan Pier (River Bus) 6C 100
Caledonian Road & Barnsbury (Overground) 7K 65
Caledonian Road (Underground) 6K 65
Cambridge Heath (Rail) 2H 85
Camden Road (Overground) 7G 65
Camden Town (Underground) 1F 83
Canada Water Bus 2J 103
Canada Water (Underground & Overground) 2J 103
Canary Wharf Pier (River Bus) 1B 104
Canary Wharf (Underground & DLR) 1C 104
Canning Town (Underground & DLR) 6G 87
Cannon Street (Rail & Underground) 2E 14 (7D 84)
Canonbury (Overground) 5C 66
Canons Park (Underground) 7K 27
Carshalton Beeches (Rail) 6D 166
Carshalton (Rail) 4D 166
Castle Bar Park (Rail) 5K 77
Catford Bridge (Rail) 7C 122
Catford (Rail) 7C 122
Centrale Stop (London Tramlink) 2C 168
Chadwell Heath (Rail) 7D 54
Chalk Farm (Underground) 7E 64
Chancery Lane (Underground) 6J 7 (5A 84)
Charing Cross (Rail & Underground) 4E 12 (1J 101)
Charlton (Rail) 5A 106
Cheam (Rail) 7G 165
Chelsea Harbour Pier (River Bus) 1B 118
Chessington North (Rail) 5E 162
Chessington South (Rail) 7D 162
Chigwell (Underground) 3K 37
Chingford Bus 1B 36
Chingford (Rail) 1B 36
Chislehurst (Rail) 2E 160
Chiswick Park (Underground) 4J 97
Chiswick (Rail) 7J 97
Church Street Stop (London Tramlink) 2C 168
City Thameslink (Rail) 7A 8 (6B 84)
Clapham Common (Underground) 4G 119
Clapham High Street (Overground) 3H 119
Clapham Junction
.............(Rail & Overground) 3C 118
Clapham North (Underground) 3J 119
Clapham South (Underground) 6F 119
Clapton (Rail) 2H 67
Clock House (Rail) 1A 158
Cockfosters (Underground) 4K 21
Colindale (Underground) 3A 44
Colliers Wood (Underground) 7B 136
Coombe Lane Stop
.............(London Tramlink) 5J 169
Covent Garden (Underground) 2F 13 (7J 83)
Cricklewood (Rail) 4F 63
Crofton Park (Rail) 5B 122
Cromwell Road Bus 1E 150
Crossharbour (Underground & DLR) 3D 104
Crouch Hill (Rail) 7K 47

Crystal Palace (Rail & Overground) 6G 139
Custom House for ExCeL (DLR) 7K 87
Cutty Sark for Maritime Greenwich (DLR) 6E 104
Cyprus (DLR) 7E 88

D

Dagenham Dock (Rail) 2F 91
Dagenham East (Underground) 5J 73
Dagenham Heathway (Underground) 6F 73
Dalston Junction (Overground) 6F 67
Dalston Kingsland (Overground) 5E 66
Denmark Hill (Rail & Overground) 2D 120
Deptford Bridge (DLR) 1C 122
Deptford (Rail) 7C 104
Devons Road (DLR) 4D 86
Dollis Hill (Underground) 5C 62
Drayton Green (Rail) 6K 77
Drayton Park (Rail) 4A 66
Dundonald Road Stop (London Tramlink) 7H 135

E

Ealing Broadway (Rail & Underground) 7D 78
Ealing Common (Underground) 1F 97
Earl's Court (Underground) 4J 99
Earlsfield (Rail) 1A 136
East Acton (Underground) 6B 80
East Beckton Bus 6E 88
East Croydon (Rail & London Tramlink) 2D 168
East Dulwich (Rail) 4E 120
East Finchley (Underground) 4C 46
East Ham (Underground) 7C 70
East India (DLR) 7F 87
East Putney (Underground) 5G 117
Eden Park (Rail) 5C 158
Edgware Bus 6C 28
Edgware Road (Underground) 5C 4 (5C 82)
Edgware (Underground) 6C 28
Edmonton Bus 2C 34
Edmonton Green (Rail) 2B 34
Elephant & Castle (Rail & Underground) 4C 102
Elmers End (Rail & London Tramlink) 4K 157
Elmstead Woods (Rail) 6C 142
Eltham (Rail) 5D 124
Elverson Road (DLR) 2D 122
Embankment Pier (River Bus & Tours) ...4G 13 (1J 101)
Embankment (Underground) 4F 13 (1J 101)
Emirates Air Line (Cable Car)
...............Emirates Greenwich Peninsula 2H 105
........................Emirates Royal Docks 7J 87
Enfield Chase (Rail) 3H 23
Enfield Town (Rail) 3K 23
Erith (Rail) 5K 109
Essex Road (Rail) 7C 66
Euston Square (Underground) 3B 6 (4G 83)
Euston (Rail, Underground & Overground) ...2C 6 (3G 83)
Ewell West (Rail) 7A 164

F

Fairfield Road Bus 2E 150
Fairlop (Underground) 1H 53
Falconwood (Rail) 4H 125
Farringdon (Rail & Underground) 5A 8 (5B 84)
Feltham (Rail) 1K 129
Fenchurch Street (Rail) 2J 15 (7F 85)
Festival Pier (River Tours) 1K 101
Fieldway Stop (London Tramlink) 7D 170
Finchley Central (Underground) 1J 45
Finchley Road & Frognal (Overground) 5A 64
Finchley Road (Underground) 6A 64
Finsbury Park Interchange (Bus) 2A 66

Finsbury Park (Rail & Underground) 2A 66
Forest Gate (Rail) 5J 69
Forest Hill (Rail & Overground) 2J 139
Fulham Broadway (Underground) 7J 99
Fulwell (Rail) 4H 131

G

Gallions Reach (DLR) 7F 89
Gants Hill (Underground) .6E 52
George Street Stop (London Tramlink) 2C 168
Gipsy Hill (Rail) 5E 138
Gloucester Road (Underground) 4A 100
Golders Green (Underground) 1J 63
Goldhawk Road (Underground) 2E 98
Goodge Street (Underground) 5C 6 (5H 83)
Goodmayes (Rail) 1A 72
Gordon Hill (Rail) 1G 23
Gospel Oak (Overground) 4E 64
Grange Park (Rail) 5G 23
Gravel Hill Stop (London Tramlink) 6A 170
Great Portland Street (Underground) 4K 5 (4F 83)
Greenford (Rail & Underground) 1H 77
Greenland Pier (River Bus) 3B 104
Green Park (Underground) 4K 11 (1G 101)
Greenwich Pier (River Bus & Tours) 5E 104
Greenwich (Rail & DLR) .7D 104
Grove Park (Rail) 3K 141
Gunnersbury (Underground & Overground) 5H 97

H

Hackbridge (Rail) 2F 167
Hackney Central (Overground) 6H 67
Hackney Downs (Rail) 5H 67
Hackney Wick (Overground) 6C 68
Hadley Wood (Rail) 1F 21
Haggerston (Overground) .1F 85
Hammersmith Bus 4E 98
Hammersmith (Underground) 4E 98
Hampstead Heath (Overground) 4C 64
Hampstead (Underground) 4A 64
Hampton Court (Rail) 4J 149
Hampton (Rail) 1E 148
Hampton Wick (Rail) 1C 150
Hanger Lane (Underground) 3E 78
Hanwell (Rail) 7J 77
Harlesden (Underground & Overground) 2K 79
Harringay Green Lanes (Overground) 6B 48
Harringay (Rail) 6A 48
Harrington Road Stop (London Tramlink) 3J 157
Harrow Bus 6J 41
Harrow-on-the-Hill (Rail & Underground) 6J 41
Harrow & Wealdstone
  (Rail, Underground & Overground) 4J 41
Hatch End (Underground) 1E 40
Hatton Cross (Underground) 4H 111
Haydons Road (Rail) 5A 136
Hayes & Harlington (Rail) 3H 93
Hayes (Rail) 1J 171
Headstone Lane (Overground) 1F 41
Heathrow Central (Underground) 3C 110
Heathrow Terminal 5 (Rail & Underground) 6D 174
Heathrow Terminal 4 (Rail) 6E 110
Heathrow Terminal 4 (Underground) 5E 110
Heathrow Terminals 1, 2, 3 (Underground) 3D 110
Hendon Central (Underground) 5D 44
Hendon (Rail) 6C 44
Herne Hill (Rail) 6B 120
Heron Quays (DLR) 1C 104
Highams Park (Rail) 6A 36
High Barnet (Underground) 4D 20
Highbury & Islington
  (Rail, Underground & Overground) 6B 66
Highgate (Underground) 6F 47
High Street Kensington (Underground) 2K 99
Hillingdon (Underground) .5D 56
Hilton Docklands Pier (River Bus) 1B 104
Hither Green (Rail) 6G 123
Holborn (Underground) 6G 7 (6K 83)
Holland Park (Underground) 1H 99
Holloway Road (Underground) 5K 65
Homerton (Overground) 6K 67

Honor Oak Park (Rail & Overground) 6K 121
Hornsey (Rail) 4K 47
Hounslow Central (Underground) 3F 113
Hounslow East (Underground) 2G 113
Hounslow (Rail) 5F 113
Hounslow West (Underground) 2C 112
Hoxton (Overground) 2F 85
Hyde Park Corner (Underground) 6H 11 (2E 100)

I

Ickenham (Underground) .4E 56
Ilford (Rail) 3E 70
Imperial Wharf (Overground) 1A 118
Island Gardens (DLR) 5E 104
Isleworth (Rail) 2K 113

K

Kempton Park (Rail) 7K 129
Kennington (Underground) 5B 102
Kensal Green (Underground & Overground) 3E 80
Kensal Rise (Overground) .2F 81
Kensington Olympia
  (Rail, Underground & Overground) 3G 99
Kent House (Rail) 1A 158
Kentish Town (Rail & Underground) 5G 65
Kentish Town West (Overground) 6F 65
Kenton (Underground & Overground) 6B 42
Kew Bridge (Rail) 5F 97
Kew Gardens (Rail & Underground) 1G 115
Kidbrooke (Rail) 3K 123
King George V (DLR) 1E 106
Kingsbury (Underground) .5G 43
King's Cross (Rail & Underground) 1E 6 (2J 83)
King's Cross St Pancras (Underground) 1E 6 (3J 83)
Kingston (Rail) 1E 150
Kingston upon Thames (Park & Ride) 7C 162
Knightsbridge (Underground) 7F 11 (2D 100)

L

Ladbroke Grove (Underground) 6G 81
Ladywell (Rail) 5D 122
Lambeth North (Underground) 1J 19 (3A 102)
Lancaster Gate (Underground) 2A 10 (7B 82)
Langdon Park (DLR) 6D 86
Latimer Road (Underground) 7F 81
Lea Bridge (Rail) 1A 68
Lebanon Road Stop (London Tramlink) 2E 168
Lee (Rail) 6J 123
Leicester Square (Underground) 2D 12 (7J 83)
Lewisham (Rail & DLR) 3E 122
Leyton Midland Road (Overground) 7E 50
Leyton (Underground) 3E 68
Leytonstone High Road (Overground) 2G 69
Leytonstone (Underground) 1G 69
Limehouse (Rail & DLR) 6A 86
Liverpool Street (Rail & Underground) 6G 9 (5E 84)
Lloyd Park Stop (London Tramlink) 4F 169
London Bridge City Pier (River Bus) 4F 15 (1E 102)
London Bridge (Rail & Underground) 5F 15 (1D 102)
London City Airport (DLR) 1C 106
London Eye Millennium Pier
  (River Bus & Tours) 6G 13 (2K 101)
London Fields (Rail) 7H 67
Loughborough Junction (Rail) 3B 120
Lower Sydenham (Rail) 5B 140

M

Maida Vale (Underground) 3K 81
Malden Manor (Rail) 7A 152
Manor House (Underground) 7C 48
Manor Park (Rail) 4F 70
Mansion House (Underground) 2D 14 (7C 84)
Marble Arch (Underground) 1F 11 (6D 82)
Maryland (Rail) 6G 69
Marylebone (Rail & Underground) 4E 4 (4D 82)

Masthouse Terrace Pier (River Bus) 5C 104
Maze Hill (Rail) 6G 105
Merton Park Stop (London Tramlink) 1J 153
Mile End (Underground) 4B 86
Millbank Millennium Pier (River Bus) 4F 19 (4J 101)
Mill Hill Broadway Bus 6F 29
Mill Hill Broadway (Rail) 6F 29
Mill Hill East (Underground) 7B 30
Mitcham Eastfields (Rail) .2E 154
Mitcham Junction (Rail & London Tramlink) 5E 154
Mitcham Stop (London Tramlink) 4C 154
Monument (Underground) 2F 15 (7D 84)
Moorgate (Rail & Underground) 6E 8 (5D 84)
Morden Road Stop (London Tramlink) 2K 153
Morden South (Rail) 5J 153
Morden (Underground) 3K 153
Mornington Crescent (Underground) 2G 83
Mortlake (Rail) 3J 115
Motspur Park (Rail) 5D 152
Mottingham (Rail) 1D 142
Mudchute (DLR) 4D 104

N

Neasden (Underground) 5A 62
New Barnet (Rail) 5G 21
New Beckenham (Rail) 7B 140
Newbury Park (Underground) 6H 53
New Cross Gate (Rail & Overground) 7A 104
New Cross (Rail & Overground) 7B 104
New Eltham (Rail) 1F 143
New Malden (Rail) 3A 152
New Southgate (Rail) 5A 32
Norbiton (Rail) 1G 151
Norbury (Rail) 1K 155
North Acton (Underground) 5K 79
North Dulwich (Rail) 5D 120
North Ealing (Underground) 6F 79
Northfields (Underground) .3C 96
North Finchley Bus 5F 31
North Greenwich Pier (River Bus & Tours) 1H 105
North Greenwich (Underground) 2G 105
North Harrow (Underground) 5F 41
Northolt Park (Rail) 4F 59
Northolt (Underground) 6E 58
North Sheen (Rail) 4G 115
North Terminal (Riverbus) .2E 106
Northumberland Park (Rail) 7C 34
North Wembley (Underground & Overground) 3D 60
Northwick Park (Underground) 7B 42
Northwood Hills (Underground) 2J 39
Norwood Junction (Rail & Overground) 4G 157
Notting Hill Gate (Underground) 1J 99
Nunhead (Rail) 2J 121

O

Oakleigh Park (Rail) 7G 21
Oakwood (Underground) 5B 22
Old Street (Rail & Underground) 2F 9 (4D 84)
Orpington (Rail) 2J 173
Osterley (Underground) 7H 95
Oval (Underground) 6A 102
Oxford Circus (Underground) 1A 12 (6G 83)

P

Paddington (Rail & Underground) 7A 4 (6B 82)
Palmers Green (Rail) 4E 32
Park & Ride
  Kingston upon Thames 7C 162
Park Royal (Underground) .4G 79
Parsons Green (Underground) 1J 117
Peckham Bus 1G 121
Peckham Rye (Rail & Overground) 2G 121
Penge East (Rail) 6J 139
Penge West (Rail & Overground) 6H 139
Perivale (Underground) 2A 78
Petts Wood (Rail) 5G 161
Phipps Bridge Stop (London Tramlink) 3B 154
Piccadilly Circus (Underground) 3C 12 (7H 83)
Pimlico (Underground) 5C 18 (5H 101)

Pinner (Underground) .4C 40
Plaistow (Underground) 2H 87
Plantation Wharf Pier (River Bus) 3A 118
Plumstead (Rail) 4H 107
Ponders End (Rail) 5F 25
Pontoon Dock (DLR) 1A 106
Poplar (DLR) 7D 86
Preston Road (Underground) 1E 60
Prince Regent (DLR) 7A 88
Pudding Mill Lane (DLR) 1D 86
Putney Bridge (Underground) 3H 117
Putney Pier (River Bus) 3G 117
Putney (Rail) 4G 117

Q

Queensbury (Underground) 3F 43
Queen's Park (Underground & Overground) 2H 81
Queens Road, Peckham (Rail & Overground) . . .1J 121
Queenstown Road, Battersea (Rail) 1F 119
Queensway (Underground) 7K 81

R

Ravensbourne (Rail) 7F 141
Ravenscourt Park (Underground) 4D 98
Rayners Lane (Underground) 7D 40
Raynes Park (Rail) 2E 152
Rectory Road (Rail) 3F 67
Redbridge (Underground) 6B 52
Reeves Corner Stop (London Tramlink) 2B 168
Regent's Park (Underground) 4J 5 (4F 83)
Richmond (Rail, Underground & Overground) . . .4E 114
Roding Valley (Underground) 4G 37
Rotherhithe (Overground) 2J 103
Royal Albert (DLR) 7C 88
Royal Oak (Underground) 5K 81
Royal Victoria (DLR) 7J 87
Ruislip Gardens (Underground) 4J 57
Ruislip Manor (Underground) 1J 57
Ruislip (Underground) .1G 57
Russell Square (Underground) 4E 6 (4J 83)

S

Sanderstead (Rail) 7D 168
Sandilands Stop (London Tramlink) 2F 169
Selhurst (Rail) 5E 156
Seven Kings (Rail) 1J 71
Seven Sisters (Rail & Underground) 5E 48
Shadwell (Overground & DLR) 7H 85
Shepherd's Bush Market (Underground) 1E 98
Shepherd's Bush (Rail, Underground & Overground) . . .2F 99
Shepperton (Rail) 5E 146
Shoreditch High Street (Overground) 3J 9 (4F 85)
Shortlands (Rail) 2G 159
Sidcup (Rail) 2A 144
Silver Street (Rail) 4A 34
Sloane Square (Underground) 4G 17 (4E 100)
Snaresbrook (Underground) 5J 51
South Acton (Overground) 3J 97
Southall (Rail) 2D 94
South Bermondsey (Rail) 5J 103
Southbury (Rail) 4C 24
South Croydon (Rail) 5D 168
South Ealing (Underground) 3D 96
Southfields (Underground) 1H 135
Southgate (Underground) 1C 32
South Greenford (Rail) .3J 77
South Hampstead (Overground) 7A 64
South Harrow (Underground) 3G 59
South Kensington (Underground) 3B 16 (4B 100)
South Kenton (Underground & Overground) 1C 60
South Merton (Rail) 3H 153
South Quay (DLR) 2D 104
South Ruislip (Rail & Underground) 5A 58
South Terminal (River Bus) 3E 106
South Tottenham (Overground) 5F 49
Southwark (Underground) 5A 14 (1B 102)
South Wimbledon (Underground) 7K 135

South Woodford (Underground) 2K 51
Stamford Brook (Underground) 4B 98
Stamford Hill (Rail) 7E 48
Stanmore (Underground) 4J 27
Star Lane (DLR) 4G 87
Stepney Green (Underground) 4K 85
St George Wharf Pier (River Bus) 6E 18 (6J 101)
St Helier (Rail) 6J 153
St James's Park (Underground) 1C 18 (2H 101)
St James Street (Rail) .5A 50
St Johns (Rail) 2C 122
St John's Wood (Underground) 2B 82
St Katharine's Pier (River Tours) 1F 103
St Margarets (Rail) 6B 114
Stockwell (Underground) 1J 119
Stoke Newington (Rail) 2F 67
Stonebridge Park (Underground & Overground) . .7H 61
Stoneleigh (Rail) 5C 164
St Pancras International (Rail) 1E 6 (2J 83)
St Paul's (Underground) 7C 8 (6C 84)
Stratford Bus 7F 69
Stratford City Bus 6E 68
Stratford High Street (DLR) 1F 87
Stratford International (Rail & DLR) 6E 68
Stratford (Rail, Underground, Overground & DLR) . .7E 68
Strawberry Hill (Rail) 3K 131
Streatham Common (Rail) 6H 137
Streatham Hill (Rail) 2J 137
Streatham (Rail) 5H 137
Sudbury & Harrow Road (Rail) 5B 60
Sudbury Hill Harrow (Rail) 4J 59
Sudbury Hill (Underground) 4J 59
Sudbury Town (Underground) 6B 60
Sunbury (Rail) 1J 147
Sundridge Park (Rail) 7K 141
Surbiton (Rail) 6E 150
Surrey Quays (Overground) 4K 103
Sutton Common (Rail) .2K 165
Sutton (Rail) 6A 166
Swiss Cottage (Underground) 7B 64
Sydenham Hill (Rail) 3F 139
Sydenham (Rail & Overground) 4J 139
Syon Lane (Rail) 7A 96

T

Teddington (Rail) 6A 132
Temple (Underground) 2J 13 (7K 83)
Thames Ditton (Rail) 7K 149
Therapia Lane Stop (London Tramlink) 7J 155
Thornton Heath (Rail) .4C 156
Tolworth (Rail) 2H 163
Tooting Bec (Underground) 3E 136
Tooting Broadway (Underground) 5C 136
Tooting (Rail) 6D 136
Tottenham Court Road (Underground)
(Closed until December 2015) 7D 6 (6H 83)
Tottenham Hale Bus 3G 49
Tottenham Hale (Rail & Underground) 3H 49
Totteridge & Whetstone (Underground) 2F 31
Tower Gateway (DLR) 2J 15 (7F 85)
Tower Hill (Underground) 2J 15 (7F 85)
Tower Millennium Pier (River Bus & Tours) . .4H 15 (1E 102)
Tufnell Park (Underground) 4G 65
Tulse Hill (Rail) 2B 138
Turnham Green (Underground) 4A 98
Turnpike Lane (Underground) 3B 48
Twickenham (Rail) 7A 114

U

Upney (Underground) 7K 71
Upper Halliford (Rail) 2G 147
Upper Holloway (Overground) 2H 65
Upton Park (Underground) 1A 88

V

Vauxhall Bus 7E 18 (6J 101)
Vauxhall (Rail & Underground) 6F 19 (5J 101)

Victoria Bus 2K 17 (3F 101)
Victoria Coach .4J 17 (4F 101)
Victoria (Rail & Underground) 3K 17 (4F 101)

W

Waddon Marsh Stop (London Tramlink) 2A 168
Waddon (Rail) 4A 168
Wallington (Rail) 6F 167
Walthamstow Bus 4C 50
Walthamstow Central (Rail & Underground) 5C 50
Walthamstow Queens Road (Overground) 5C 50
Wandle Park Stop (London Tramlink) 2A 168
Wandsworth Common (Rail) 1D 136
Wandsworth Riverside Quarter Pier (River Bus) . .4J 117
Wandsworth Road (Overground) 2G 119
Wandsworth Town (Rail) 4K 117
Wanstead Park (Overground) 4K 69
Wanstead (Underground) 6K 51
Wapping (Overground) .1J 103
Warren Street (Underground) 3A 6 (4G 83)
Warwick Avenue (Underground) 4A 82
Waterloo East (Rail) 5K 13 (1A 102)
Waterloo (Rail & Underground) 6J 13 (2A 102)
Wellesley Road Stop (London Tramlink) 2D 168
Welling (Rail) 2A 126
Wembley Central
(Rail, Underground & Overground) 5E 60
Wembley Park (Underground) 3G 61
Wembley Stadium (Rail) 5F 61
West Acton (Underground) 6G 79
Westbourne Park (Underground) 5H 81
West Brompton (Underground & Overground) . . .6J 99
Westcombe Park (Rail) .5J 105
West Croydon Bus 1C 168
West Croydon
(Rail, Overground & London Tramlink) 1C 168
West Drayton (Rail) 1A 92
West Dulwich (Rail) 2D 138
West Ealing (Rail) 7B 78
Westferry (DLR) 7C 86
Westfield London Bus 1E 98
West Finchley (Underground) 6E 30
West Hampstead
(Underground & Overground) 6J 63
West Hampstead Thameslink (Rail) 6J 63
West Ham (DLR) 3G 87
West Ham (Rail & Underground) 3G 87
West Harrow (Underground) 6G 41
West India Quay (DLR) .7C 86
West Kensington (Underground) 5H 99
Westminster Millennium Pier (River Tours) 2J 101
Westminster (Underground) 7F 13 (2J 101)
West Norwood (Rail) 4B 138
West Ruislip (Rail & Underground) 2E 56
West Silvertown (DLR) .1J 105
West Sutton (Rail) 4J 165
West Wickham (Rail) 7E 158
Whitechapel (Underground & Overground) 5H 85
White City (Underground) 7E 80
White Hart Lane (Rail) .7A 34
Whitton (Rail) 7G 113
Willesden Green (Underground) 6E 62
Willesden Junction
(Underground & Overground) 3B 80
Wimbledon Chase (Rail) 2G 153
Wimbledon Park (Underground) 3J 135
Wimbledon
(Rail, Underground & London Tramlink) 6H 135
Winchmore Hill (Rail) 7G 23
Woodford (Underground) 6E 36
Woodgrange Park (Overground) 5B 70
Wood Green (Rail) 2A 48
Wood Lane (Underground) 7E 80
Woodside Park (Underground) 4E 30
Woodside Stop (London Tramlink) 6H 157
Wood Street Walthamstow (Rail) 4E 50
Woolwich Arsenal Pier (River Bus) 3F 107
Woolwich Arsenal (Rail & DLR) 4F 107
Woolwich Dockyard (Rail) 4D 106
Worcester Park (Rail) 1C 164

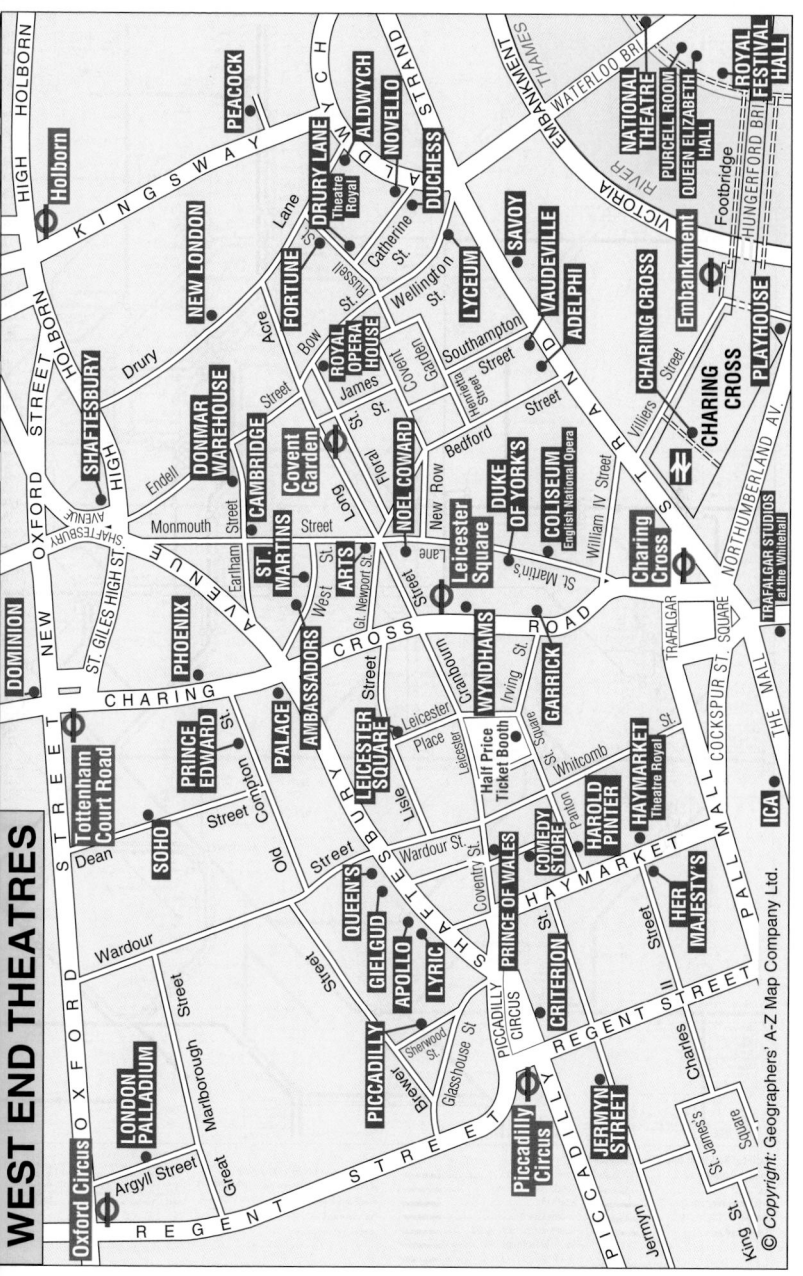

WEST END THEATRES

© Copyright: Geographers' A-Z Map Company Ltd.

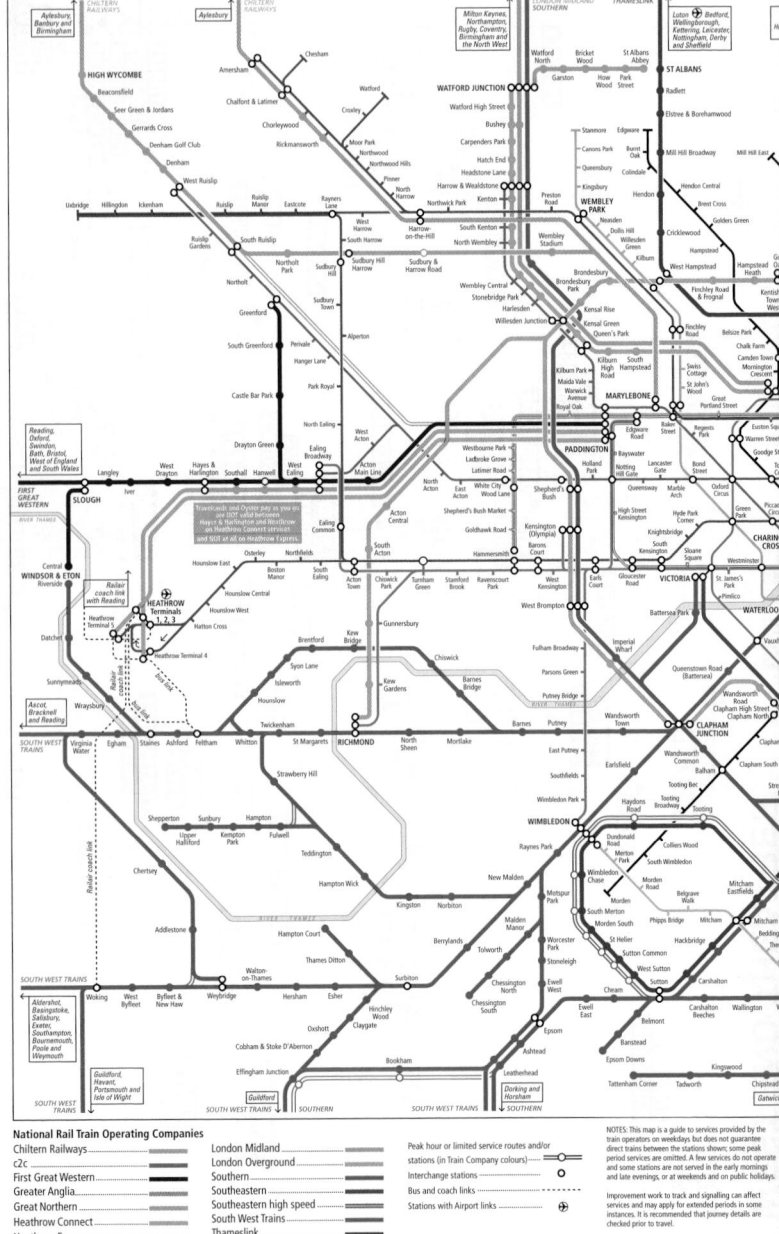

National Rail Train Operating Companies

Chiltern Railways
c2c
First Great Western
Greater Anglia
Great Northern
Heathrow Connect
Heathrow Express

London Midland
London Overground
Southern
Southeastern
Southeastern high speed
South West Trains
Thameslink

Peak hour or limited service routes and/or stations (in Train Company colours)
Interchange stations
Bus and coach links
Stations with Airport links

NOTES: This map is a guide to services provided by the train operators on weekdays but does not guarantee direct trains between the stations shown; some peak period services are omitted. A few services do not operate and some stations are not served in the early mornings and late evenings, or at weekends and on public holidays.

Improvement work to track and signalling can affect services and may apply for extended periods in some instances. It is recommended that journey details are checked prior to travel.

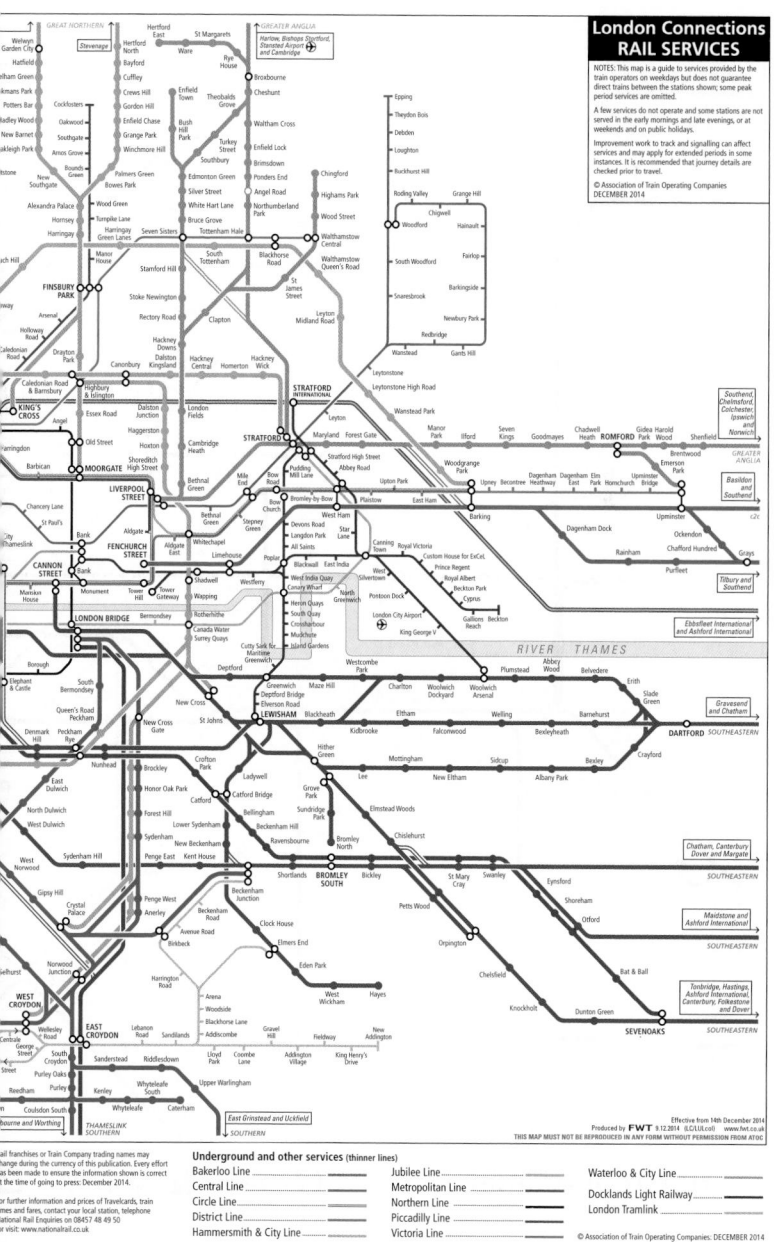

Effective from 14th December 2014
Produced by **FWT** 9.12.2014 (LC/LULcol) www.fwt.co.uk
THIS MAP MUST NOT BE REPRODUCED IN ANY FORM WITHOUT PERMISSION FROM ATOC

ail franchises or Train Company trading names may
hange during the currency of this publication. Every effort
as been made to ensure the information shown is correct
t the time of going to press: December 2014.

or further information and prices of Travelcards, train
mes and fares, contact your local station, telephone
ational Rail Enquiries on 0845 7 48 49 50
r visit: www.nationalrail.co.uk

Underground and other services (thinner lines)

Bakerloo Line	Jubilee Line
Central Line	Metropolitan Line
Circle Line	Northern Line
District Line	Piccadilly Line
Hammersmith & City Line	Victoria Line

Waterloo & City Line
Docklands Light Railway
London Tramlink

© Association of Train Operating Companies: DECEMBER 2014

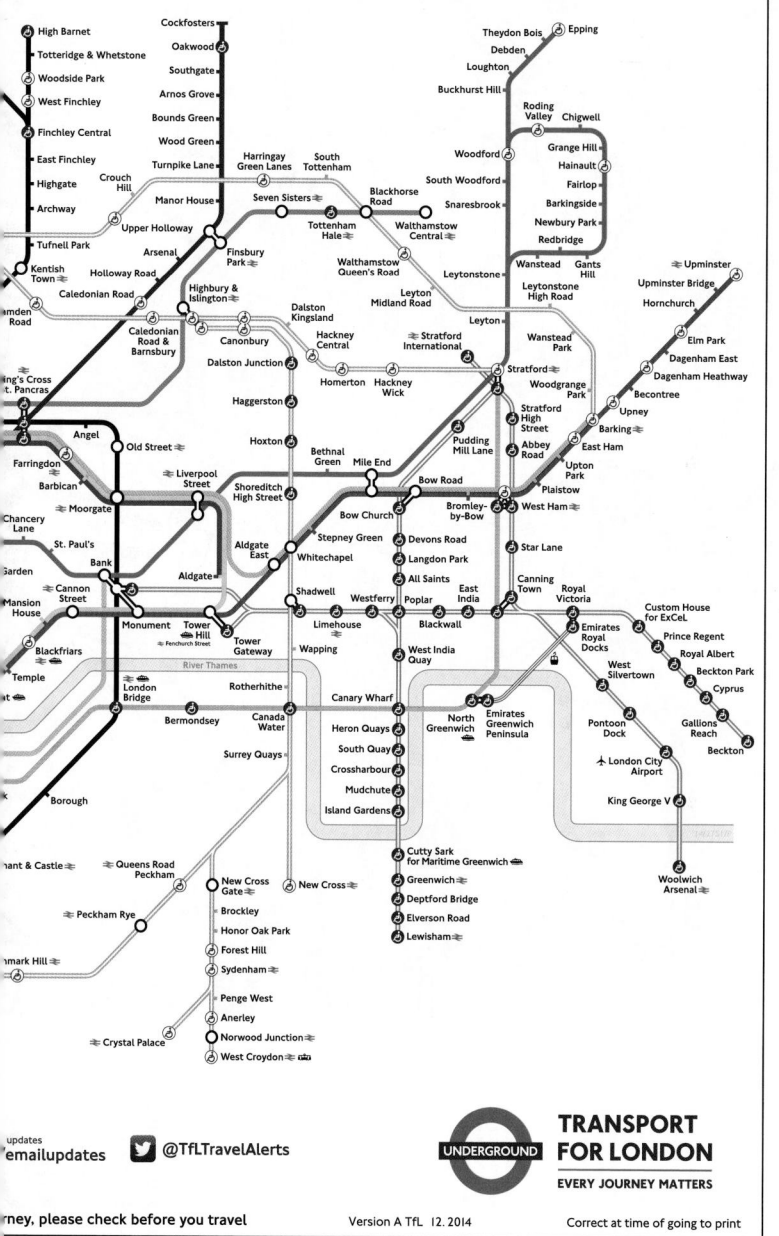

Congestion Charging Zone

- The daily charge applies Mon–Fri. 7·00am to 6·00pm excluding English bank and public holidays and designated non-charging days.

- Payment of the daily charge allows you to drive in, around, leave and re-enter the charging zone as many times as required.

- Payment must be made before or on the day of travel by midnight. Drivers who forget to pay the charge for the previous day's journey can pay a late payment charge the next day up until midnight by telephone or online and avoid a Penalty Charge.

- You can pay using Congestion Charging Auto Pay (registration required); online (www.cclondon.com); by telephone (0343 222 2222); by SMS text message (registration required) or by post (10 days in advance)

- Exemptions include motorcycles, mopeds and bicycles. Registration for discount schemes, including Congestion Charging Auto Pay, Fleet Auto Pay, Blue Badge holders, residents & Ultra Low Emission Vehicles, is available from Transport for London.

- Penalty charge for non-payment of the daily charge by midnight on the day after the day of travel.

This information is correct at the time of publication.

For further information www.tfl.gov.uk